THE *Virgin* ENCYCLOPEDIA OF

STAGE AND FILM MUSICALS

COLIN LARKIN

SENIOR CONTRIBUTOR: JOHN MARTLAND

Virgin

IN ASSOCIATION WITH MUZE UK LTD.

Dedicated To Lionel Bart & John Gorman

First published in Great Britain in 1999 by
VIRGIN BOOKS
an imprint of Virgin Publishing Ltd
Thames Wharf Studios, Rainville Road
London W6 9HT

A catalogue record for this book is available from the British Library

ISBN 0 7535 0375 1

Written, edited and produced by
MUZE UK Ltd
to whom all editorial enquiries should be sent
Iron Bridge House, 3 Bridge Approach, Chalk Farm, London NW1 8BD
e-mail: colin@muze.co.uk. http://www.muze.com
Editor In Chief: Colin Larkin
Production Editor: Susan Pipe
Research Assistant: Nic Oliver
Editorial Assistant: Jon Staines
Typographic Design Consultants: Roger Kohn & Aku
Special thanks to Trev Huxley, Tony Laudico, Paul Zullo
and all the Klugettes at Muze Inc.,
and to Rob Shreeve of Virgin Publishing.
Typeset by Gonks Go Beat Studios
Printed and bound in Great Britain by Butler & Tanner Ltd, Frome and London

INTRODUCTION

The Virgin Encyclopedia Of Stage And Film Musicals is one of the major series of books taken from the 8-volume Encyclopedia Of Popular Music. It was previously published as two books The Who's Who Of Stage Musicals and The Who's Who Of Film Musicals. This is a completely updated and greatly enlarged edition

Other titles already available in the series are:

The Virgin Encyclopedia Of Fifties Music
The Virgin Encyclopedia Of Sixties Music
The Virgin Encyclopedia Of Seventies Music
The Virgin Encyclopedia Of Eighties Music
The Virgin Encyclopedia Of Popular Music (Concise)
The Virgin Encyclopedia Of Indie & New Wave
The Virgin Encyclopedia Of The Blues
The Virgin Encyclopedia Of R&B And Soul
The Virgin Encyclopedia Of Reggae
The Virgin Encyclopedia Of Country Music
The Virgin Encyclopedia Of Dance Music
The Virgin Encyclopedia Of Heavy Rock
The Virgin Encyclopedia Of Jazz
The Virgin All-Time Top 1000 Albums

ENTRY STYLE

Albums, EPs (extended play 45s), newspapers, magazines, television programmes, films and stage musicals are referred to in italics. All song titles appear in single quotes. The further reading section at the end of each entry has been expanded to give the reader a much wider choice of available books. These are not necessarily recommended titles but we have attempted to leave out any publication that has little or no merit.

We have also started to add videos at the ends of the entries. Again, this is an area that is expanding more quickly than we can easily cope with, but there are many items in the videography and further items in the filmography, which is another new section we have decided to include. Release dates in keeping with albums attempt to show the release date in the country of origin. We have also tried to include both US and UK titles where applicable.

ALBUM RATING

Because of many requests from our readers, we have now decided to rate all albums. All new releases are reviewed either by me or by our team of contributors. We also take into consideration the review ratings of the leading music journals and critics' opinions.

Our system is slightly different to most 5 Star ratings in that we rate according to the artist in question's work.

Outstanding in every way. A classic and therefore strongly recommended. No comprehensive record collection should be without this album.

Excellent. A high standard album from this artist and therefore highly recommended.

Good. By the artist's usual standards and therefore recommended.

Disappointing. Flawed or lacking in some way.

Poor. An album to avoid unless you are a completist.

PLAGIARISM

In maintaining the largest text database of popular music in the world we are naturally protective of its content. We license to approved licensees only. It is both flattering and irritating to see our work reproduced without credit. Time and time again over the past few years I have read an obituary, when suddenly: hang on, I wrote that line. Secondly, it has come to our notice that other companies attempting to produce their own music encyclopedias use our material as a core. Flattering this might also be, but highly illegal. We have therefore dropped a few textual 'depth charges'. Be warned, the lawyers are waiting.

ACKNOWLEDGEMENTS

Our in-house editorial team is lean and efficient. The EPM Database is now a fully grown child and needs only regular food, attention and love. Thanks to the MUZEUK team for their continuing efficiency: Susan 'my train is on time' Pipe, Nic 'my train is late' Oliver and Jon 'my bike has a puncture' Staines with the steady timing of Roger Kohn's parrot, Acu. Our outside contributors are further reduced in number, as we now write and amend all our existing text. However, we could not function without the continuing efforts and dedication of Bruce Crowther.

This book however is really a labour of love for our film and stage expert John Martland. He has been with us almost from the very beginning, and we could not function properly without his wealth of knowledge and continuing enthusiasm for an area of popular music that is dear to his heart. I was able to let my editorial control slip and 'leave it to Martland'. He knows how much we appreciate him, yet he takes compliments with painful modesty.

Other past contributors' work may appear in this volume and I acknowledge with thanks once again the past work of Alex Ogg, Brian Hogg, Dave Laing, Spencer Leigh Johnny Rogan and Jeff Tamarkin. Please do not be offended if I have left out your name, it is a minefield to try to remember which entries John Martland did not do!

Thanks for the co-operation of our colleagues at Virgin Publishing under the guidance of Rob Shreeve, in particular to the diplomatic and thoughtful Roz Scott. To Terry Whitaker, I hope we got it right this time, if not I am sure you will let us know. To the continuing assistance of Terry Heard, Lisa Lobb and Nikki Goold, rarely a grumble, usually a smile. Thanks also to our software man Mike Kaye, problematical but ultimately worth it.

To the quite exceptional Pete Bassett, not to forget the delicious Bassettes: Emily Williams and Emma Morris. To our owners at Muze Inc., who continue to feed the smooth running of the UK operation and are the business partners I always knew I wanted but never knew where to find. Take a dip into the formidable MUZEstage and film database through their in-store kiosks, or search it out on the internet at www. MUZE.com. Thanks to all my colleagues and friends at the office on 304 Hudson Street in New York. In particular to the dynamic dancer Tony Laudico, Paul Zullo (the Fred Astaire of the 8th floor), Marc 'Tommy' Miller, Gary 'Ziegfeld Follies' Geller, Raisa 'Sunset Boulevard' Howe, Adam 'Sniffer' Silver, Stephen 'The Harder They Come' Hughes and the Belarusian minister for stage and film, Scott 'who wants to be a millionaire' Lehr.

Not To Ignore: Jim Allen, David Gil De Rubio (Down By The Schoolyard), Kim Osorio, Ric Hollander, Stephen Parker, Terry 'Grape' Vinyard, Deborah Freedman, Amanda 'High Sweedie' Denhoff, Jannett Diaz, Tracey Brandon, Ed 'Gentleman' Moore, Suzanne 'I Want Some Pie' Park, Solomon Sabel. The Impressive Yet Calm Phil Fletcher, Matt 'Violin Concerto' Puccini, Bill Schmitt, Michael Doustan, Thom Pappalardo, Duncan 'White Heather Club' Ledwith, Gail 'Cos I'm Worth It' Niovitch, Sandra 'Finally Got A Mention' Levanta, Paul Parreira, Bernadette Elliott, Myrtle Jones, Jo Amison, Silvia Kessel And All The Other Klugettes.

And to the long-running blockbuster, Trev 'The Sound Of Music' Huxley. Finally to my entertaining tin lids; Nancy, Dodger and Fagin.

Colin Larkin, March 1999

A DAY IN HOLLYWOOD, A NIGHT IN THE UKRAINE

This innovative revue started its life at the tiny New End Theatre in Hampstead, England, in January 1979, before moving to the larger Mayfair Theatre in March for a run of 168 performances. Dick Vosburgh, an expatriate American author and journalist, wrote the book and lyrics, and the music was composed by Frank Lazarus. In the first half of the piece, Lazarus and the cast, which consisted of Paddie O'Neil, Sheila Steafel, John Bay, Maureen Scott, Jon Glover and Alexandra Sebastian, ran through a series of sometimes hilarious sketches and songs culled from, and devoted to, the golden era of America's west coast film capital. After the interval, the action switched to the Chekhov play, *The Bear* - which Vosburgh had adapted in the fashion of a Marx Brothers film comedy. Not surprisingly, the London critics loved it. The show evidently came as welcome light relief after their recent 'glimpse of the future London musical' in the form of *Evita* at the Prince Edward Theatre. Ironically, it was *Evita* that triumphed over *A Day In Hollywood, A Night In The Ukraine* in several categories of the Tony Awards after Vosburgh's show had transferred to Broadway in 1980. However, the more intimate offering did win two of the Awards: featured actress (Priscilla Lopez) and outstanding choreography (Tommy Tune and Thommie Walsh). The New York production, with a revised book and three interpolated Jerry Herman songs, 'The Best In The World', 'Just Go The Movies', and 'Nelson' ('Eddy', not 'Horatio'), was extremely well received and ran for well over a year - a total of 588 performances.

AARONS, ALEX A.

b. 1891, Philadelphia, Pennsylvania, USA, d. 14 March 1943, Beverly Hills, California, USA. The son of producer and composer Alfred E. Aarons, Alex A. Aarons mounted a number of fondly remembered Broadway musicals during the 20s. Most of his success came in partnership with the actor-turned-producer Vinton Freedley (b. 5 November 1891, Philadelphia, Pennsylvania, USA, d. 5 June 1969, New York, USA). They came together in 1923, after Aarons had presented *La, La, Lucille* (1919), which contained George Gershwin's first complete Broadway score, and *For Goodness Sake* (1922). The latter show, in which Fred Astaire and his sister Adele introduced their famous 'runaround' routine, also had some Gershwin numbers (from this time forward, mostly with lyrics by Ira Gershwin), and was revised for London in 1923 where it ran for 418 performances under the title of *Stop Flirting!*

Vinton Freedley was in the Broadway cast of *For Goodness Sake*, and he and Aarons subsequently collaborated on seven shows with Gershwin scores: *Lady, Be Good!* (1924), *Tip-Toes* (1925), *Oh, Kay!* (1926), *Funny Face* (1927), *Treasure Girl* (1928), *Girl Crazy* (1930) and *Pardon My English* (1933). They were also responsible for staging *Here's Howe* (1928), in which Ben Bernie, Peggy Chamberlain and June O'Dea introduced Roger Wolfe Kahn, Joseph Meyer and Irving Caesar's lively 'Crazy Rhythm'; De Sylva, Brown And Henderson's prize-fighting musical, *Hold Everything!* (1928); and two shows with scores by Richard Rodgers and Lorenz Hart, *Spring Is Here* and *Heads Up!* (both 1929). Aarons produced another Gershwin show, *Tell Me More!* (1925), on his own account. At the peak of their careers, Aarons and Freedley built the Alvin Theatre in New York (titled by the initial letters of their first names, Alex and Vincent), which opened in November 1927. Several of their hit productions were staged there, but by 1933 and the flop *Pardon My English*, from which the British star, Jack Buchanan, made a speedy departure, the Alvin had been sold and the partners were in deep financial trouble. They split up, and Aarons was subsequently associated with a number of stage productions that never materialized, as well as working in various capacities in the film business. While Aarons failed to recover his previous prestigious position in the business, Freedley flourished through to the early 40s, producing four successful shows with music and lyrics by Cole Porter: *Anything Goes* (1934), *Red, Hot And Blue!* (1936), *Leave It To Me!* (1938) and *Let's Face It!* (1941), along with *Cabin In The Sky*, which contained a top-class Vernon Duke score. However, another of Duke's shows, *Jackpot* (1944), failed to hit, as did *Memphis Bound* (1945), with its Gilbert and Sullivan excerpts, and *Great To Be Alive!* (1950), which starred Vivienne Segal making her penultimate appearance in a Broadway musical.

ABBOTT, GEORGE

b. George Francis Abbott, 25 June 1887, Forestville, New York, USA, d. 31 January 1995, Miami Beach, Florida, USA. An important director, author, and producer, whose distinguished career in the American theatre spanned more than seven decades and gained him the title of 'Mr. Broadway'. Abbott wrote his first play, a comedy-farce entitled *Perfectly Harmless*, while studying at the University of Rochester in 1910. Three years later he made his Broadway debut playing a drunken college boy in *The Misleading Lady*. He continued to appear in productions such as *Lightnin'*, *Hell-Bent For Heaven* and *Holy Terror* until 1925. In the same year he launched his writing career with *The Fall Guy*, and in 1926, with *Love 'Em And Leave 'Em*, he began to direct. Shortly after that, he became a producer for the first time with *Bless You Sister*. Abbott subsequently served in some capacity in well over 100 Broadway productions, including a good many musicals. In the 30s and 40s there were shows such as *Jumbo* (1935), *On Your Toes*, *The Boys From Syracuse*, *Too Many Girls*, *Pal Joey*, *Best Foot Forward*, *Beat The Band*, *On The Town*, *Billion Dollar Baby*, *Barefoot Boy With Cheek*, *High Button Shoes*, *Look Ma, I'm Dancin'*, *Where's Charley?* and *Touch And Go* (1949). Although he produced the smash hit

Call Me Madam, *A Tree Grows In Brooklyn*, and a revival of *On Your Toes* in the early 50s, for the rest of the decade, and throughout the remainder of his career, Abbott gave up producing musicals in favour of directing, and writing librettos. Although it was a time when the number of new musicals on Broadway was beginning to decline, Abbott was involved with some of the most memorable - and one or two he would probably like to forget - including *Wonderful Town* (1953), *Me And Juliet*, *The Pajama Game*, *Damn Yankees*, *New Girl In Town*, *Once Upon A Mattress*, *Fiorello!*, *Tenderloin* (1960), *A Funny Thing Happened On The Way To The Forum*, *Fade Out-Fade In*, *Flora, The Red Menace*, *Anya*, *How Now, Dow Jones*, *The Education Of H*Y*M*A*N K*A*P*L*A*N*, *The Fig Leaves Are Falling* (1969), *The Pajama Game* (1973 revival), *Music Is*, *On Your Toes* (1983 revival), and *Damn Yankees* (1986 revival). George Abbott was 99 years old when he revised and directed the latter show, and Broadway celebrated in style during the following year when he became an extremely sprightly centenarian. He received a special Tony Award to add to his collection, which included six other Tonys (one presented in 1976 for lifetime achievement), the Society of Stage Directors and Choreographers Award of Merit (1965), and the 1959 Pulitzer Prize for Drama for *Fiorello!* Over the years, Abbott's contribution to the Broadway musical was immense. He introduced the fast-paced, tightly integrated style that influenced so many actors, dancers, singers, and particularly fellow-directors such as Jerome Robbins and Bob Fosse. Another disciple was Hal Prince, arguably the leading director of musicals during the 80s. At the age of 106, George Abbott advised director Jack O'Brien on revisions of his original book, for the 1994 Broadway revival of *Damn Yankees*, and in the same year, BBC Television devoted a fascinating *Omnibus* programme to his work. When he died early in 1995, all the lights on Broadway were dimmed in tribute to one of the district's legendary and much-loved figures.
● FURTHER READING: *Mister Abbott*, George Abbott.

ABRAHAMS, MAURICE

b. 18 March 1883, Russia, d. 13 April 1931, New York, USA. A composer and publisher, whose most effective numbers were written during the ragtime era, the first popular music 'craze' to sweep America and many other countries. Abrahams worked for several music publishers before setting up his own firm in 1923. During that time he was also writing songs such as 'Hitchy-Koo' (1912 with L. Wolfe Gilbert and Lewis F. Muir), which became the title of a series of Broadway shows some years later, and 'Ragtime Cowboy Joe' (1912, with Muir and Grant Clarke), a catchy item that was a hit at the time for baritone Bob Roberts. It endured over the years, and was successfully revived by Pinky Tomlin (1939), Eddy Howard (1947) and Jo Stafford (1949), and entered the Top 20 in both the UK and USA in 1959 in a version by David Seville and his cheeky Chipmunks. Another of Abrahams' appealing numbers, 'Get Out And Get Under' (full title 'He'd Have To Get Under - Get Out And Get Under - To Fix Up His Automobile', written with Clarke and Edgar Leslie), was interpolated into the New York Winter Garden revue, *The Pleasure Seekers*, in November 1913, where it was per-

formed by vaudeville star Bobby North, and was sung by Gerald Kirby later that year in the London revue *Hullo, Tango*. The song subsequently became popular for the legendary entertainer Billy Murray. Abrahams' other compositions included 'The Pullman Porters On Parade' (1913, with Ren G. May, said to be a *nom de plume* for Irving Berlin), 'The 20th Century Rag' (1914, Leslie-Clarke), 'Take Me To That Midnight Cakewalk Ball' (1916, Eddie Cox-Arthur Jackson), and 'High, High, High, Up In The Hills' (1926, Sam M. Lewis-Joe Young). Abrahams wrote the latter song - and many others - for his wife, the vaudeville headliner, singer and comedienne Belle Baker (b. c.1895, New York, USA, d. 28 April 1957, Los Angeles, California, USA). She had her first record hit in 1919 with 'Poor Little Butterfly Is A Fly Gal Now', which was followed by 'I've Got The Yes! We Have No Bananas Blues' (1923), 'Hard Hearted Hannah' (1924), 'My Man' (1929) and 'My Sin' (1929). Baker helped to popularize 'Mamma Goes Where Papa Goes' (1923, Milton Ager-Jack Yellen), 'Those Panama Mamas' (1924, Irving Bibo-Howard Johnson), '(Here I Am) Broken Hearted' (1927, De Sylva, Brown And Henderson, and introduced two all-time standards: Irving Berlin's 'Blue Skies' in the 1926 Broadway musical *Betsy*, and 'All Of Me' (1931, Gerald Marks-Seymour Simons), which she sang on radio and in her vaudeville act. She also appeared in two movie musicals, *The Song Of Love* (1929) and *Atlantic City* (1944).

ABSOLUTE BEGINNERS

Based on Colin MacInnes' 1958 cult novel, which foresaw the rise of the Mod movement and much of the youth explosion of the 60s, Julien Temple (*The Great Rock 'N' Roll Swindle*, 1979), once part of the Sex Pistols/Malcolm McLaren entourage, directed this stylized 1986 film adaptation. However, rather than focus on the novel's dramatic tension - part of the action revolves around the Notting Hill Race riots - he transformed the narrative into a gaudy musical. The result was not generally considered to be a success. In the screenplay, by Richard Burridge, Don Macpherson and Christopher Wicking, aspiring photographer Colin (Eddie O'Connell) and embryonic fashion designer Suzette (Patsy Kensit), are a definite item before haughty couturier Henley of Mayfair (James Fox) muscles in and slips a ring on the lady's engagement finger. Colin loses his cool, and embarks on a trip which brings him into contact with an assortment of low-lives who populate the 'arty' London area of Soho, such as pimps, hustlers, jazzers, and a promoter of young boy singers who bears a remarkable likeness to the infamous Larry Parnes. David Bowie plays advertising executive Vendice Partners, and also cast were Ray Davies, Mandy Rice-Davies, Eve Ferret, Lionel Blair, Tony Hippolyte, Graham Fletcher-Cook, Joe McKenna, Steven Berkoff, Sade, Bruce Payne, and Alan Freeman, portraying a character called Call-Me-Cobber. Sylvia Syms, who featured in a bona fide 50s screen musical, *Expresso Bongo*, was also on hand, along with future television *Cracker* star Robbie Coltrane. Musical highlights included Ray Davies' 'Quiet Life' and Slim Gaillard's 'Selling Out', as well as Bowie's own compositions 'Absolute Beginners' and 'That's Motivation'. With those on the soundtrack were 'Killer Blow' (Sade), 'Have You Ever

Had It Blue?' (Style Council), 'Ted Ain't Dead' (Tenpole Tudor), 'Rodrigo Bay' (Working Week), 'Having It All' (Eighth Wonder), 'Bongo Rock' (Jet Streams), 'Hey, Little Schoolgirl' (Paragons), 'So What' (Smiley Culture), 'Rock, Baby, Rock' (Bertice Reading), and 'Riot City' (Jerry Dammers). *Absolute Beginners*, filmed in Super Techniscope and Rank colour, was co-financed by leading UK company Goldcrest Films. They were involved in highly acclaimed movies such as *Chariots Of Fire*, *Gandhi*, and *Local Hero*, but *Absolute Beginners* prefaced a decline in fortunes that eventually resulted in them being acquired by Brent Walker in 1987. The *Absolute Beginners* tagline was 'Welcome to the world of your dreams' - more like a nightmare in many respects.

ACE OF CLUBS

A 'revue musical', with book, music and lyrics by Noël Coward, *Ace Of Clubs* opened at London's Cambridge Theatre on 7 July 1950. In contrast to Coward's previous sophisticated comedies, it was set mainly in a Soho night-club, and involved small-time gangsters and parcels of stolen jewels. The songs were still of the same high quality and Coward's score contained several amusing numbers such as 'Josephine', 'Three Juvenile Delinquents', the tongue-in-cheek 'I Like America' ('New Jersey dames go up in flames if someone mentions bed/In Chicago, Illinois, any girl who meets a boy, giggles, and shoots him dead'), and a late-night invitation from a female cat to her mate, entitled 'Chase Me, Charlie' ('I'd like to wander for miles and miles/Wreathed in smiles/Out on the tiles with you'). As usual with Coward, there were ballads of yearning and regret, such as 'Why Does Love Get In The Way?', 'I'd Never, Never Know', 'Nothing Can Last Forever' and 'Sail Away', which the composer used as the title song of one of his last shows in 1962. The main love interest was provided by Graham Payn, and Pat Kirkwood, who registered strongly with 'My Kind Of Man'. The cast also included Sylvia Cecil, Elwyn Brook-Jones, and future leading players such as June Whitfield, Vivien Merchant and Jean Carson. On the first night, a section of the audience continually booed the production, and, although Coward still retained a loyal theatrical following in London, *Ace Of Clubs* closed in January 1951, after a run of 211 performances. Several of the songs were subsequently featured regularly by Coward in his cabaret act.

ADAMS, LEE

b. 14 August 1924, Mansfield, Ohio, USA. A notable lyricist and librettist for the musical theatre, after studying at the Ohio State University and at Columbia University's Pulitzer School of Journalism in New York, Adams worked for a time in the newspaper and magazine business before meeting composer Charles Strouse in 1949. During the 50s the new team wrote material for a great many summer resort revues, and contributed to the New York production *Shoestring '57*. In 1960 they wrote the complete score for *Bye Bye Birdie* which ran for 607 performances and starred Dick Van Dyke and Chita Rivera. Two years later, their *All American* could only manage 80 performances, although it contained the lovely 'Once Upon A Time', which was introduced by Ray Bolger and Eileen Herlie. After collaborating with Jerry Herman on just one song - 'Before The Parade Passes By' - for his smash hit, *Hello, Dolly!* (1964), Adams and Strouse endured mixed fortunes during the next few years. *Golden Boy*, starring Sammy Davis Jnr. and Billy Daniels, ran for 569 performances, *It's A Bird, It's A Plane, It's Superman* could only manage 129, but *Applause* (1970), a vehicle for the Hollywood legend Lauren Bacall, gave the songwriters their second hit and stayed around for over two years. In the 70s and 80s, it was downhill all the way for Adams and Strouse, although the latter was more successful with other collaborators. *I And Albert* was dismissed by London audiences after only three months, *A Broadway Musical* gave just one performance at the Lunt-Fontanne Theatre in New York in 1978, and an attempt to cash in on a previous success with *Bring Back Birdie* was given the bird and folded after four nights. Adams turned to Mitch Leigh, the composer of *Man Of La Mancha*, a show that had run for well over 2,000 performances in the 60s, but their attempt to musicalize a biography of the legendary producer Mike Todd, which they called *Mike*, closed during its pre-Broadway try-out in 1988. Not to be outdone, five years later they managed to stage it in New York under the title of *Ain't Broadway Grand*, but it only ran for 25 performances. Lee Adams was inducted into the Songwriters Hall of Fame in 1989.

ADAMSON, HAROLD

b. 10 December 1906, Greenville, New Jersey, USA, d. 17 August 1980, Beverly Hills, California, USA. A successful lyricist from the late 20s through the 50s, Adamson began writing poetry for his school newspaper, and sketches for school shows. While studying at the University of Kansas, he wrote songs and worked with a professional company during vacations, before going on to Harvard, where he contributed to the famous Hasty Pudding shows, cradle of much Broadway talent. In the early 30s Adamson contributed to Broadway shows such as *Smiles*, which contained the enduring 'Time On My Hands' (lyric with Mack Gordon, music by Vincent Youmans), *Earl Carroll's Vanities* and *The Third Little Show*. Although he returned to Broadway in the 40s for *Banjo Eyes* and *As The Girls Go* ('I Got Lucky In The Rain', 'You Say the Nicest Things Baby', 'It's More Fun Than A Picnic', with Jimmy McHugh), for the remainder of his career Adamson concentrated on writing songs for movies with some of the most distinguished composers of the times. These included *Dancing Lady* (1933, 'Everything I Have Is Yours, 'Let's Go Bavarian', 'Heigh Ho, The Gang's All Here'), *Bottoms Up* ('Little Did I Dream', 'Turn On the Moon'), *Reckless* ('Everything's Been Done Before'), *Suzy* ('Did I Remember?'), *The Great Ziegfeld* ('You Never Looked So Beautiful', 'You', 'She's A Ziegfeld Follies Girl', 'You Gotta Pull Strings'), *Banjo On My Knee* ('Where The Lazy River Goes By', 'There's Something In The Air'), *Top Of The Town* ('Where Are You', 'That Foolish Feeling', 'Blame It On The Rhumba'), *Hitting A New High* ('This Never Happened Before', 'Let's Give Love A Chance'), *You're A Sweetheart* ('My Fine Feathered Friend', 'You're A Sweetheart'), *Merry-Go-Round Of 1938* ('You're My Dish'), *Mad About Music* ('I Love To Whistle', 'Serenade To The

Stars'), *That Certain Age* ('My Own', 'You're As Pretty As A Picture'), *Hold That Ghost* ('Aurora'), *Hit Parade Of 1943* ('Change Of Heart', 'Do These Old Eyes Deceive Me?'), *Four Jills In A Jeep* ('How Blue The Night'), *Higher And Higher* ('A Lovely Way To Spend An Evening', 'I Couldn't Sleep A Wink Last Night', 'The Music Stopped', 'I Saw You First'), *Something For The Boys* ('In The Middle Of Nowhere'), *Around The World* ('Candlelight And Wine', 'Don't Believe Everything You Dream'), *Hollywood Canteen* ('We're Having A Baby'), *Nob Hill* ('I Walked In', 'I Don't Care Who Knows It'), *Bring On The Girls* ('Uncle Sammy Hit Miami', 'How Would You Like To Take My Picture?', 'I'm Gonna Hate Myself In The Morning'), *Doll Face* ('Red Hot And Beautiful', 'Here Comes Heaven Again'), *Smash-Up* ('Hush-A-Bye Island', 'Life Can Be Beautiful'), *Calendar Girl* ('Lovely Night To Go Dancing'), *A Date With Judy* ('It's A Most Unusual Day'), *If You Knew Susie* ('My Brooklyn Love Song', 'My, How The Time Goes By'), and *Gentlemen Prefer Blondes* (1953). For the latter film, Adamson and Hoagy Carmichael added two amusing songs, 'When Love Goes Wrong' and 'Ain't There Anyone Here For Love', to Carmichael and Jule Styne's original score. In the 50s and 60s Adamson also contributed the title numbers to several popular, non-musical films, such as *Around The World In Eighty Days* (with music by Victor Young), *An Affair To Remember* (Harry Warren, Leo McCarey), *Separate Tables*, *The Seven Hills Of Rome* and *Satan Never Sleeps*. Among Adamson's other songs were 'Comin' In On A Wing And A Prayer' (McHugh), 'My Resistance Is Low' (Carmichael), 'Daybreak' (Ferde Grofé), 'Ferryboat Serenade' and 'The Woodpecker Song' (Eldo Di Lazzaro), '720 In The Books' (Jan Savitt), and 'It's A Wonderful World' (Savitt and Johnny Watson). His chief collaborator was Jimmy McHugh, but he worked with many others, including Vernon Duke, Duke Ellington, Walter Donaldson, Burton Lane, Louis Alter, Peter DeRose, Mario Lago and Roberto Roberti.

ADDINSELL, RICHARD

b. Richard Stewart Addinsell, 13 January 1904, Oxford, England, d. 14 November 1977, Chelsea, London, England. A leading composer for the theatre and feature films, Addinsell read law at Hertford College, Oxford, but was more interested in music and the theatre. He studied briefly at the Royal College of Music, and then in Berlin and Vienna. During the late 20s he began to contribute music to revues and shows such as *Little Miss Danger*, *R.S.V.P.*, *The Charlot Show* and *Adam's Opera*. In 1931 he supplied the music for the incidental songs in *The Good Companions* (from J.B. Priestley's novel), and, for some 30 years, continued to write for the theatre, often in collaboration with the entertainer Joyce Grenfell. He provided material for several shows in which she appeared, such as *Tuppence Coloured* (1947), *Penny Plain* (1951), *Joyce Grenfell Requests The Pleasure* (1954) and *Joyce Grenfell - A Miscellany* (1957). It was for his film work, however, that Addinsell is probably best remembered. From 1936 through to the early 60s, he wrote the music for some of the best British films, particularly those of the 'stiff upper lip' variety, so prevalent around the time of World War II. His scores included *The Amateur Gentleman* (1936), *Dark*

Journey, *Farewell Again*, *South Riding*, *Fire Over England*, *Vessel Of Wrath*, *Goodbye, Mr. Chips*, *The Lion Has Wings*, *Contraband*, *Men Of The Lightships*, *Gaslight*, *Dangerous Moonlight*, *Love On The Dole*, *The Siege Of Tobruk*, *Blithe Spirit*, *Diary For Timothy*, *The Passionate Friends*, *The Black Rose*, *Scrooge*, *Encore*, *Tom Brown's Schooldays*, *Sea Devils*, *Beau Brummell*, *The Prince And The Showgirl*, *The Admirable Crichton*, *A Tale Of Two Cities*, *Loss Of Innocence*, *The Greengage Summer*, *The Waltz Of The Toreadors*, *The Roman Spring Of Mrs. Stone* and *Life At The Top* (1965). The score of *Dangerous Moonlight* (1941) contained Addinsell's most well-known composition, 'The Warsaw Concerto', played on the soundtrack by pianist Louis Kentner with the London Symphony Orchestra. The piece became enormously popular, and was a hit for saxophonist Freddy Martin and his Orchestra in the USA. More than 10 years after his death, Addinsell's music was heard again at a London theatre when the revue *Re: Joyce* (1988), 'A celebration of the work of Joyce Grenfell' starring Maureen Lipman with Denis King, opened in the West End. It has since returned on two occasions, and a televised version was shown at Christmas 1991. In 1995 several of his attractive themes and melodies were released on CD, played by the BBC Concert Orchestra.
● COMPILATIONS: *British Light Music-Richard Addinsell* (Marco Polo 1994)★★★.

ADDISON, JOHN

b. John Mervin Addison, 16 March 1920, Cobham, Surrey, England, d. 7 December 1998. A composer for the theatre and films, Addison studied composition and several instruments, including the piano, oboe and clarinet, at the Royal College of Music shortly before and after World War II. He was Professor of Composition at the college from 1950-57; his own classical compositions included music for ballet, chamber orchestra and a trumpet concerto. For the theatre, in the 50s he collaborated with *avant garde* choreographer John Cranko on shows such as *Cranks* and *Keep Your Hair On*, and much later, in the early 70s, wrote the music to lyrics by David Heneker for *The Amazons* and *Popkiss*. He also contributed music to several plays, including *Luther*, *A Patriot For Me*, *Bloomsbury*, *The Entertainer* and *Antony And Cleopatra*. In the film world he was among the leading British composers, particularly during the 60s, with scores such as *Seven Days To Noon*, *The Man Between*, *Private's Progress*, *Reach For The Sky*, *Lucky Jim*, *I Was Monty's Double*, *Look Back In Anger*, *A French Mistress*, *The Entertainer*, *School For Scoundrels*, *A Taste Of Honey*, *The Girl In The Headlines*, *Girl With Green Eyes*, *The Loneliness Of The Long Distance Runner*, *Tom Jones* (for which Addison won an Academy Award), *Guns At Batasi*, *The Amorous Adventures Of Moll Flanders*, *The Loved Ones*, *Torn Curtain*, *A Fine Madness* (his first American film), *The Honey Pot*, *Smashing Time*, *The Charge Of The Light Brigade*, *Start The Revolution Without Me*, *Country Dance*, *Mr. Forbush And The Penguins*, *Sleuth* (nominated for an Academy Award), *Dead Cert*, *A Bridge Too Far*, *The Seven Per Cent Solution*, *The Pilot*, *Strange Invaders*, *The Ultimate Solution of Grace Quigley* and *Code Name: Emerald*. Addison also composed extensively for television programmes, including *Sambo And The Snow*

Mountain, *The Search For Ulysses*, *Grady* series (NBC), *Black Beauty*, *The Bastard*, *Centennial*, *Like Normal People*, *Love's Savage Fury*, *The French Atlantic Affair*, *Charles And Diana: A Royal Love Story*, *Eleanor-First Lady Of The World*, *Mistress Of Paradise*, *Mail Order Bride*, *Ellis Island*, *Murder She Wrote* (series), *Something In Common*, *Thirteen At Dinner*, *Deadman's Folly*, *Bigger Than A Breadbox*, *The Pumpkin Competition*, *Mr. Boogedy*, *Something In Common*, *Bridge Of Boogedy*, *Strange Voices*, *Beryl Markham*, *A Shadow Of The Sun* and *The Phantom Of The Opera*.

ADLER, LARRY

b. Lawrence Cecil Adler, 10 February 1914, Baltimore, Maryland, USA. Adler prefers to be described simply as a 'mouth-organist' - yet he is arguably the most accomplished and celebrated exponent of the instrument there has ever been. His orthodox Judaism gave him the opportunity to train in religious music, and he became a cantor at the age of 10. He sang, and learned to play the piano and mouth-organ by ear from listening to phonograph records, and could not actually read music until 1941. After being expelled from the Peabody Conservatory of Music, he won the Maryland Harmonica Championship in 1927. Shortly afterwards, he ran away to New York and joined one of the Paramount units, playing in movie theatres between features. He was also presented as a 'ragged urchin' ('just in from the street, folks!') in vaudeville, and in Lew Leslie's revue, *Clowns In Clover* (1928). He also served as Eddie Cantor's stooge for a time, and accompanied Fred Astaire in Florenz Ziegfeld's *Smiles*.

His lifelong admiration and appreciation of George Gershwin began when he was introduced to the composer by Paul Whiteman, and his interpretations of Gershwin's works, especially *Porgy And Bess* and 'Rhapsody In Blue' (on which Adler is sometimes accompanied by a piano-roll made by Gershwin himself), are definitive. (Many years later in 1981, Adler's haunting version of Gershwin's 'Summertime' played a significant role in the success of the enormously popular UK ice dancers Torvill and Dean.) In 1934, after further speciality roles on stage in *Flying Colors* and on film in Paramount's *Many Happy Returns* (the first of his five movies), in which he was backed by Duke Ellington's Orchestra, Adler was spotted at New York's Palace Theatre by the English producer Charles B. Cochran, who engaged him for the London revue *Streamline*. Shortly after the show opened, sales of mouth-organs in the UK increased by several thousand per cent, and fan clubs proliferated. Adler played the top nightclubs, and the 1937 revue *Tune Inn* was built around him. After marrying top model Eileen Walser, he toured South Africa and Australia before returning to the USA in 1939, where he gained national recognition in the classical field when he appeared as a soloist with the Chicago Women's Symphony Orchestra. During the 40s, Adler appeared at Carnegie Hall with the dancer Paul Draper, and toured with him extensively in the USA, Africa and the Middle East, entertaining troops, and insisting on a non-segregation policy between whites and blacks at concerts. Adler also entertained in the South Pacific with artists such Carol Landis, Martha Tilton and comedian Jack Benny, and worked consistently for the war effort

and the Allied forces. He was 'on duty' again in 1951 during the Korean conflict. By then, as a high-profile liberal, he had been included on McCarthy's 'communist' blacklist, and moved to live and work in England, only for the 'red spectre' to follow him even there. In 1954, he was forced by the Rank film organization to give up his billing rights on US prints of the classic comedy film *Genevieve*, for which he had written the gentle but highly distinctive score. The music was duly nominated for an Academy Award, and an embarrassed Rank could only offer orchestra conductor Muir Mathieson's name as composer. Fortunately for them it did not win the Oscar - voters preferred Dimitri Tiomkin's music for *The High And The Mighty* - and Adler had to wait until 1986 for the Academy's official recognition of his work. In 1952, Adler performed at a Royal Albert Hall Promenade Concert, when he was 'forced' to encore Ralph Vaughan Williams' 'Romance For Mouth-Organ, Piano And Strings', a piece that had been written especially for him. In the 50s, although domiciled in the UK, Adler made frequent, although often difficult, trips to the USA and worked in many other countries of the world with major symphony orchestras. In 1963 as a soloist at the Edinburgh Festival, Adler gave the first performance of 'Lullaby Time', a string quartet written by George Gershwin in 1921, and presented to Adler by Ira Gershwin. That piece, and several other unpublished works by composers such as Cole Porter, Harold Arlen and Richard Rodgers, were included on *Discovery*.

Adler's own most familiar composition is the music for *Genevieve*, but he has composed the music for other films, including *The Hellions*, *King And Country*, *High Wind In Jamaica* and *The Great Chase*. His work for television programmes and plays includes *Midnight Men*, along with concert pieces such as 'Theme And Variations'. Works have been specially written for him by Malcolm Arnold, Darius Milhaud, Arthur Benjamin, Gordon Jacobs, and others. In 1965 Adler was back at the Edinburgh Festival with his one-man show, *Hand To Mouth*, and in 1967 and 1973, gave his services to Israel in aid of those affected by the Six Day and Yom Kippur wars. In 1988, as busy as ever, he appeared at New York's Ballroom club with Harold Nicholas, one half of the legendary dance team the Nicholas Brothers. To many, the engagement brought back memories of Adler's tours in the 40s with his friend, tap-dancer Paul Draper. As usual on these occasions, Adler skilfully blended classical selections with a 'honky-tonk jazz' approach to numbers written by the great popular songwriters of the past. The following year he performed in concert at London's Royal Albert Hall, marking his 75th birthday, accompanied by pianist John Ogden, and the Wren Orchestra conducted by Stanley Black. During the early 90s he played regularly at the Pizza on the Park, sometimes accompanied by 'The Hot Club Of London', and recalled numbers forever associated with him, such as Ravel's 'Bolero'. After Adler guested on Sting's 1993 album, *Ten Summoner's Tales*, the rock singer returned the compliment and appeared on Adler's 80th birthday celebration, *The Glory Of Gershwin*. They were joined by other stars from the rock world such as Meat Loaf, Kate Bush, Peter Gabriel and Sinead O'Connor. The media interest generated by this project - the album just failed to reach the top of the UK album chart, although it gained Adler a place in *The Guinness Book Of Records* - led to him making sell-out appearances at venues such as the Jazz Café and the Café Royal. He also embarked on *A Living Legend-The Final Tour* late in 1994, and encored with appearances in Japan, Australia and New Zealand two years later. In 1998, he presented the BBC Radio 2 series *Larry Adler's Century*, which he laced with fascinating anecdotes. As a musician and journalist, Larry Adler seems to have met and worked with almost everyone who is (or has been) anyone in show business, politics, and many other walks of life. A tennis fanatic, he once played in a doubles match with Charlie Chaplin, Greta Garbo and Salvador Dali, and is always prepared to talk about it.

● ALBUMS: with Morton Gould *Discovery* (RCA 1969)★★★★, *Plays Gershwin, Porter, Kern, Rodgers, Arlen And Gould* (RCA 1985)★★★★, *Golden Age Of Larry Adler* (Golden Age 1986)★★★, *Works For Harmonica And Orchestra* (Accordion 1987)★★★, *The Mouth Organ Virtuoso* (EMI 1994)★★★, with others *The Glory Of Gershwin* (Mercury 1994)★★.

● FURTHER READING: All titles by Larry Adler *How I Play*, *Larry Adler's Own Arrangements. Jokes And How To Tell Them. It Ain't Necessarily So: His Autobiography. Me And My Big Mouth.*

● FILMS: *St Martin's Lane* (1938), *Music For Millions* (1944), *Genevieve* composer (1953), *The Hellions* composer (1961), *King And Country* composer (1963), *The Hook* composer (1963), *High Wind In Jamaica* composer (1964).

ADLER, RICHARD

b. 3 August 1921, New York, USA. This composer, lyricist and producer had two hit Broadway shows in the 50s, but has since been unable to produce another one. The son of a concert pianist, Adler was not attracted to classical music, and studied to be a writer at the University of North Carolina before spending three years in the US Navy. After his discharge he went into the advertising business, and occasionally composed songs in his spare time. In the early 50s he met Jerry Ross (b. Jerold Rosenberg, 9 March 1926, The Bronx, New York, USA, d. 11 November 1955, New York, USA), and they began to write songs together. In 1953, contracted to Frank Loesser's publishing company Frank Music, they had a hit with 'Rags To Riches', which became a US chart-topper for Tony Bennett. After contributing several numbers to the revue *John Murray Anderson's Almanac*, Adler and Ross wrote the complete score for *The Pajama Game*, which opened on Broadway in May 1954 and ran for 1,063 performances. Several of the songs became popular outside the show, including 'Hernando's Hideaway', 'Hey There' (a US number 1 for Rosemary Clooney) and 'Small Talk'. Almost exactly one year later they returned with the highly entertaining baseball musical *Damn Yankees*, which once again was full of lively and tuneful songs such as 'Heart', which became successful for Eddie Fisher and the Four Aces, and 'Whatever Lola Wants', a chart hit for Sarah Vaughan and Dinah Shore. The show was settling in for a run of 1,019 performances when Ross died of leukaemia in November 1955. Three years later, 'Everybody Loves A Lover', another Adler-Ross song, which does not appear to have been included in a show or film, became a hit for

Doris Day. After Ross's death Adler turned his hand to producing, but without success: *The Sin Of Pat Muldoon*, Richard Rodgers' *Rex*, and *Music Is* (for which Adler also wrote the music) were major disappointments. In the 60s he wrote both music and lyrics for *Kwamina* and *A Mother's Kisses*, but neither took off. His score for *Kwamina*, a show whose theme was a plea for racial tolerance in Africa and starred his then-wife Sally Ann Howes, was regarded as a fine piece of work, and can now be reassessed following the re-release of the Original Cast recording by Broadway Angel. Adler has also been actively writing for television commercials, and directing business conventions and political rallies.

● FURTHER READING: *You Gotta Have Heart*, Richard Adler with Lee Davis.

AFTER HOURS

A superb 27 minute-long jazz film which was a pilot for a US television series in 1961 that never was. The simple nightclub setting has a band led by Coleman Hawkins and Roy Eldridge with Johnny Guarnieri, Barry Galbraith, Milt Hinton and William 'Cozy' Cole. Among the songs featured are 'Lover Man' and a red-hot 'Sunday', during which Eldridge is so carried away he overruns his solo, to the obvious delight of a momentarily upstaged Hawkins.

AFTER THE BALL

One of Noël Coward's lesser-known efforts, *After The Ball* marked the first occasion on which he adapted an established work - Oscar Wilde's *Lady Windermere's Fan* - as the basis of one of his shows. The production opened at London's Globe Theatre on 10 June 1954, with a cast that included the delightful American actress Mary Ellis, Graham Payn, and Vanessa Lee and Peter Graves as Lord and Lady Windermere. A generally undistinguished score (for Coward) of some 20 songs had been truncated and revised prior to the West End opening, but it retained some exquisite moments, and included 'May I Have The Pleasure?', 'Mr Hopper's Chanty', 'I Knew That You Would Be My Love', 'I Feel So Terribly Alone', 'Sweet Day', 'Why Is It Always The Woman Who Pays?', 'Quartette', 'Something On A Tray' and 'Clear Bright Morning'. *After The Ball*, Coward's penultimate London show, closed in November 1954 after a run of 188 performances.

AHRENS, LYNN, AND STEPHEN FLAHERTY

Lyricist, librettist, and composer Lynn Ahrens (b. 1 October 1948, New York, USA) and composer Stephen Flaherty (b. 18 September 1960, Pittsburgh, Pennsylvania, USA) met in 1982 when they both attended the Broadcast Music Inc. (BMI) Musical Theatre Workshop. Ahrens was raised mostly in Neptune, New Jersey, and graduated with a degree in journalism from Syracuse University in 1970. After moving to New York, she worked in advertising, and then joined the creative team of *Schoolhouse Rock* (1973), a children's television series of animated educational shorts. In 1978, she formed her own production company, specializing in lively, informative programmes for youngsters, including the Emmy Award-winning *H.E.L.P.* Flaherty, on the other hand, had nursed ambitions to be a writer for the musical theatre since his early teens, and composed his first score at the age of 14. While he was studying at the Cincinnati College Conservatory, Flaherty was encouraged by Lehman Engel, the director of workshops for composers and lyricists at the BMI Workshop. Upon graduation, he enrolled in the workshop shortly after Engel's death in August 1982. Ahrens and Flaherty began working together on various projects during the following year, including a stage adaptation of the 1967 Peter Cook-Dudley Moore movie *Bedazzled*. However, it was 1988 before their first production, *Lucky Stiff* ('A Dead Funny Musical'), opened at Playwrights Horizons, off-Broadway. This musical farce, based on Michael Butterworth's novel, *The Man Who Broke The Bank At Monte Carlo*, had a book and lyrics by Ahrens, and music by Flaherty. It contained several witty and amusing numbers, including 'Nice', 'Welcome Back, Mr. Witherspoon', 'Fancy Meeting You Here', and 'Speaking French', and won Helen Hayes and Richard Rogers Awards, in spite of having only a brief run. The Caribbean-style *Once On This Island* (1990) fared much better, delighting Broadway audiences with its melodic charms for 469 performances. When it sailed for the West End in 1994, the Royalty Theatre was renamed the Island Theatre for the duration of the run, and *Once On This Island* won the 1995 Laurence Olivier Award for Best Musical. Not so sunny was the reception given to *My Favorite Year* (1992-3). It was said to be the first original musical produced by the Lincoln Center, but only stayed there for one month. Flaherty wanted to compose something indigenously American, so he and Ahrens grabbed at the opportunity to audition four songs for *Ragtime*, a musicalization of E.L. Doctorow's turn-of-the-century novel. Three of those four numbers, 'Till We Reach That Day', 'Gliding', and the splendidly syncopated title song, were in the score of the show that opened at New York's brand new Ford Center for the Performing Arts in January 1998. It became a smash hit, with Ahrens and Flaherty winning Tony Awards, as well as Drama Desk and Outer Critics Circle honours for best musical. Along the road to their mutual triumph, the duo have also worked separately. Ahrens wrote the book (with Mike Ockrent) and lyrics to Alan Menken's music for the immensely popular holiday-time entertainment, *A Christmas Carol*, which was launched at Madison Square Garden in 1994, and has since been continually revived. Flaherty composed the incidental music for Neil Simon's play *Proposals* (1997), and the concert pieces 'Ragtime Symphonic Suite' and 'Anastasia Suite' which were premiered by the Hollywood Bowl Orchestra. The *Anastasia* music stems from the 20th Century-Fox animated film of that name for which Ahrens and Flaherty wrote music and lyrics.

AIN'T BROADWAY GRAND

'No, it ain't,' said one reviewer. The subject of his disappointment had begun its life as *Mike*, five years before it was retitled *Ain't Broadway Grand* for the New York opening at the Lunt-Fontanne Theatre in New York on 18 April 1993. The 'Mike' in question was Mike Todd, the dynamic film producer, who even had a complete wide-screen process, Todd-AO, named after him. In this Broadway metamorphosis, set in 1948, Todd (Mike Burstyn) transforms an unsuccessful, high-brow musical satire of the US presidency called *Of The People*, into a smash-hit burlesque show. This considerable achievement requires the assistance of other famous names from the past, such as Joan Blondell (Maureen McNamara), Gypsy Rose Lee (Debbie Shapiro), and comedian Bobby Clark (Gerry Vichi). With a book by Broadway veterans Thomas Meehan (*Annie*) and Lee Adams (*Bye Bye Birdie*), and music and lyrics by Adams and Mitch Leigh (*Man Of La Mancha*), *Ain't Broadway Grand* attracted a barrage of criticism for a number of reasons, not least because of its 'indulging every Jewish stereotype', and a score that was so weak that the title number had to be reprised at least five times. The rest of the songs included 'The Theatre, The Theatre', 'Waiting In The Wings', 'Girls Ahoy!', 'A Big Job', 'The Man I Married', 'You're My Star', 'They'll Never Take Us Alive' and 'Time To Go'. That time came for *Ain't Broadway Grand* on 9 May, when it closed after just 25 performances.

AIN'T MISBEHAVIN'

This anthology celebrated the work of the great jazz pianist and entertainer, Thomas 'Fats' Waller, and included many of the songs he composed, and others that he recorded and with which he is indelibly associated. *Ain't Misbehavin'* started out as a series of cabaret performances at the Manhattan Theatre Club, New York, in February 1978, before moving to the Longacre Theatre in May of that year. Conceived by Murray Horwitz and Richard Maltby Jnr., who also staged the show, *Ain't Misbehavin'* immediately captured the imagination of critics and public alike, and settled in for a long run. The musical supervision, orchestrations and arrangements were by Luther Henderson, who also played the piano for a cast of five: Nell Carter, Andre De Shields, Armelia McQueen, Ken Page and Charlaine Woodard. During the show's spell on Broadway, Debbie Allen took over from Charlaine Woodard in a production that reeked of the Harlem joints of the 30s, and accurately captured the sheer exuberance of Waller's style and humour through a selection of some 30 songs, which included 'Your Feet's Too Big', 'I'm Gonna Sit Right Down And Write Myself A Letter', 'When The Nylons Bloom Again', 'Keepin' Out Of Mischief Now', 'Yacht Club Swing', 'Honeysuckle Rose', and 'The Jitterbug Waltz'. After a run of 1,604 performances, the show was revived on Broadway 10 years later complete with all five members of the original cast, and the fun started all over again. London audiences saw this 'Honky-Tonk, Knock-'Em Dead, Swing-Till-They-Drop Party' in 1979 and 1995.

ALADDIN

The third and most successful of Walt Disney Pictures' high-tech, computer-enhanced animated box-office sensations of the late 80s/early 90s. *Aladdin* was released late in 1992, and in hardly any time at all had generated US rentals in excess of over $50 million. Unlike its two predecessors, *The Little Mermaid* and *Beauty And The Beast*, the film was not welcomed with open arms worldwide. The seemingly harmless traditional story involved

Jasmine, the Sultan's daughter, who escapes from the royal castle and an arranged marriage, and falls for the pauper Aladdin. However, there were accusations of racism, and the Arab-American Anti-Discrimination Committee was unhappy about *Aladdin*'s depiction of their people 'as sleazy, nasty and mean'. They also objected to a section of the opening song in which an Arab trader sings: 'Oh, I come from a land/From a faraway place/Where the caravan camels roam/Where they cut off your ear/If they don't like your face/It's barbaric, but hey, it's home.' On foreign prints and the video release, the last three lines were amended to: 'Where it's flat and immense/And the heat is intense/It's barbaric, but hey, it's home', but, despite further protests, Disney refused to remove the word 'barbaric'. That song, 'Arabian Nights', and others such as 'Friend Like Me' and 'Prince Ali', had been written by Alan Menken and Howard Ashman before the latter died in 1991. Together with his new lyricist Tim Rice, Menken completed a hat-trick of Academy Awards with the song 'A Whole New World', and won another Oscar for the film's original score. 'A Whole New World' went to the top of the US chart in a version by Peabo Bryson and Regina Belle. The voices for the main characters were provided by Aladdin (Scott Weinger, Brad Kane singing), Jasmine (Linda Larkin, Lea Salonga singing), and Robin Williams as the Genie. Williams was sensational, metamorphosing into a variety of hilarious impersonations of actors such as Jack Nicholson, and various political and television personalities. *Aladdin* was directed by John Musker and Ron Clement, and, early in 1993, was being hailed by Disney as the highest-grossing release in the studio's 69-year history - then along came *The Lion King*. In 1994, the soundtrack recording of *Aladdin* attracted five Grammy awards.

ALBERT, EDDIE

b. Edward Albert Heimberger, 22 April 1908, Rock Island, Illinois, USA. A singer and actor in theatre and films, with a range that extends from 'amiable, best friend' parts, through to overbearing, thoroughly nasty character roles. Albert began his career as a singer, and worked in theatres and on radio with the Threesome, and then teamed with Grace Bradt to form the Honeymooners - Grace and Eddie. He made his Broadway debut at the Empire Theatre in the play *O Evening Star* (1935), which was followed by *Brother Rat* (1936) and *Room Service* (1937). A year later, he played Antipholus of Syracuse and introduced 'This Can't Be Love' in *The Boys From Syracuse*. During World War II, Albert served as a lieutenant in the US Navy, and it was 1949 before he returned to the Broadway musical theatre in *Miss Liberty* (1949), in which he sang the appealing 'Let's Take An Old-Fashioned Walk'. Nine years later he took over from David Wayne in *Say, Darling*, and then succeeded Robert Preston as Professor Harold Hill in *The Music Man*, in January 1960. In between, he continued to perform in serious plays on Broadway and in regional theatre. He also carved out an impressive career in films, which total more than 70 to date. These have included several musicals such as *On Your Toes* (1939), *Hit Parade Of 1947*, *Meet Me After The Show* (1951) and *The Girl Rush* (1955). In the 50s he had two particularly good roles, first-

ly in *Oklahoma!* (1955), in which he played pedlar-man Ali Hakim, and then in *The Joker Is Wild* (1957), where, as the accompanist of comedian Joe E. Lewis (played by Frank Sinatra), he was outstanding. Albert has been seen on the screen in dramatic roles in films such as *Brother Rat* (1938), *Four Wives* (1939), *Smash Up* (1947), *Carrie* (1952), *Roman Holiday* (1953), *I'll Cry Tomorrow* (1955), *Attack!* (1956), *The Teahouse Of The August Moon* (1956), *The Roots Of Heaven* (1958), *Orders To Kill* (1958), *The Longest Day* (1962), *Captain Newman MD* (1963), *The Heartbreak Kid* (1972) and *The Longest Yard* (1974), continuing into the 90s. His extensive television credits include many films and series, including *Leave It To Larry* (1952), *Green Acres* (1965-70), *Switch* (1975-76) and *The Chocolate Soldier* (1984). In the 50s Albert appeared in a television adaptation of *A Connecticut Yankee*, and had a sophisticated nightclub act with his wife Margo. Their son, Edward Albert, is a film and television actor.

● ALBUMS: *Eddie Albert* (Columbia 50s)★★★, *One God* (Kapp 1954)★★★, *Eddie Albert And Margo* (Kapp 1956)★★★★, *September Song* (Kapp 1957)★★★, Original Broadway Cast *Miss Liberty* (Columbia 50s)★★★.

ALBERY, DONALD

b. Donald Arthur Rolleston Albery, 19 June 1914, London, England, d. 14 September 1988, Monte Carlo. A producer and theatre-owner, Albery came from a family steeped in theatrical history - his paternal grandfather was the playwright James Albery, and his father was Sir Bronson Albery, who founded what became the Society of West End Theatres. Donald Albery was educated in Switzerland before serving as general manager of Sadlers Wells Ballet from 1941-45. He started out as a producer in 1953, and throughout the 50s and 60s presented or co-presented several notable plays, such as *The Living Room*, *Waiting For Godot*, *A Taste Of Honey* and *Who's Afraid Of Virginia Woolf?* His first musical production was *Grab Me A Gondola* in 1956, and this was followed by a mixture of smash hits and minor flops, which included *Zuleika* (1957), *Irma La Douce* (1958), *Make Me An Offer* (1959), *Fings Ain't Wot They Used T'Be* (1960), *Oliver!* (1960), *The Art Of Living* (1960), *Not To Worry* (1962), *Blitz!* (1962), *Fiorello!* (1962), *Oliver!* (New York 1963), *Instant Marriage* (1964), *Jorrocks* (1966), *Oliver!* (London revival 1967), *Man Of La Mancha* (1968), *Mandrake* (1970) and *Popkiss* (1972). Albery also enjoyed a long-runner with the revue *Beyond The Fringe* in 1961. In 1962 he took over the Wyndham Group of London theatres from his father, consisting of Wyndham's, the New (later re christened the Albery) and the Criterion; Albery later also acquired the Piccadilly Theatre. Albery was knighted in 1977, and sold his Group to Associated Newspapers a year later, when he retired. His son Ian took over as manager.

● FURTHER READING: *All On Stage: Charles Wyndham And The Alberys*, W. Trewin.

ALDA, ROBERT

b. Alphonso Giuseppe Giovanni Robert D'Abruzzo, 26 February 1914, New York, USA, d. 3 May 1986, Los Angeles, California, USA. An actor and singer who, although he enjoyed a long career in many areas of show business, is remembered mainly for his first film role, when he portrayed the composer George Gershwin in the 1945 Warner biopic *Rhapsody In Blue*. The son of a barber, Alda was educated at New York University, and worked as an architectural draughtsman before making his stage debut in vaudeville in 1933 with an act called Charlie Ahearn And His Millionaires. He subsequently worked on radio, toured in burlesque, and performed in summer stock in numerous straight plays, such as *Tobacco Road*, *The Postman Always Rings Twice*, *Room Service* and *The Time Of Your Life*. Alda made his Broadway debut in 1950, creating the role of gambler Sky Masterson in the Abe Burrows-Jo Swerling-Frank Loesser musical *Guys And Dolls*. He stayed with the show for nearly two years, and his performance gained him a Tony Award, as well as Donaldson and New York Drama Critics Poll honours. While touring Italy and Sicily in the mid-50s in *La Padrona Di Raggio Di Luna*, he received the Golden Wing Award for his performance as an Italian, and in the early 60s settled in Rome for some years. He continued to work occasionally in the USA, and in 1963 toured with *Can-Can*, before returning to Broadway in the following year, co-starring with Steve Lawrence and Sally Ann Howes in a musical spoof on Hollywood's Golden Age of the 30s, *What Makes Sammy Run?* Alda's own movie career never lived up to the promise of *Rhapsody In Blue*. He made only two more musicals, *Cinderella Jones* (1946) and *April Showers* (1948), along with some 20 or so other films, which included *The Beast With Five Fingers* (1947), *The Man I Love* (1947), *Tarzan And The Slave Girl* (1950), *Two Gals And A Guy* (1951), *Beautiful And Dangerous* (1958), *Imitation Of Life* (1959), *Cleopatra's Daughter* (1961), *The Girl Who Knew Too Much* (1968), *I Will, I Will, I Will ... For Now* (1976), *Bittersweet Love* (1976) and *The Squeeze* (1980). Alda also appeared frequently on US television, in programmes such as *By Popular Demand*, *The Milton Berle Show*, *The Kids From Fame*, *Police Story*, *Perfect Gentlemen*, *Days Of Our Lives*, *Supertrain* and *The Robert Alda Show*. He also starred on Italian radio and television, and played in cabaret throughout most of his career. In 1984, Alda suffered a stroke from which he never fully recovered. His son is the famous actor-director Alan Alda.

ALEXANDER'S RAGTIME BAND

Released in 1938, and one of the most entertaining musicals of the decade, this film celebrated the work of one of America's all-time great songwriters - Irving Berlin. The slight plot concerning the erratic domestic and professional arrangements of bandleader Alexander (Tyrone Power) and singer Stella Kirby (Alice Faye), was merely an occasional diversion compared to the continual flow of wonderful songs that effectively traced the evolution of popular song through a period of nearly 30 years. They included 'Alexander's Ragtime Band', 'Ragtime Violin', 'Everybody's Doing It', 'When The Midnight Choo-Choo Leaves For Alabam', 'That International Rag', 'For Your Country And My Country', 'Oh, How I Hate To Get Up In The Morning', 'I Can Always Find A Little Sunshine In The YMCA', 'A Pretty Girl Is Like A Melody', 'Say It With Music', 'Everybody Step', 'Pack Up Your Sins And Go To The Devil', 'All Alone', 'What'll I Do?', 'Remember', 'Easter

Parade' and 'Heat Wave'. Don Ameche introduced 'Now It Can Be Told', which Berlin wrote especially for the film. Also involved in Kathryn Scola and Lamar Trotti's screenplay were Ethel Merman, Jack Haley, Jean Hersholt, Dixie Dunbar, Chick Chandler, John Carradine, and a host of others. Photographed in black-and-white, produced by Darryl F. Zanuck and Harry Joe Brown, and directed by Henry King, *Alexander's Ragtime Band* was the first in a long and enjoyable series of lavish, all-star musicals produced by 20th Century-Fox.

ALEXANDER, VAN

b. Al Feldman, 2 May 1915, New York City, New York, USA. An accomplished arranger and composer, Alexander studied music at Columbia University. He achieved his first success while still in his early 20s when Ella Fitzgerald and the Chick Webb Orchestra had hits with his 'Gotta Pebble In My Shoe' and 'A-Tisket A-Tasket'. The latter was Alexander's adaptation of a 19th century children's song (with a new lyric by Fitzgerald). In 1938 he formed his own band which recorded for the Bluebird label (some tracks were issued in the UK by Regal-Zonophone), and then signed up with the Varsity label in the following year. In 1939 he had a hit with 'Hot Dog Joe' (vocal by Butch Stone). Although a commercial dance outfit, the band provided early experience for jazz musicians such as Si Zentner, Shelly Manne and Irving Cottler and also gave the leader further scope to develop his arranging skills in its few years of existence. Alexander later wrote for the bands of Larry Clinton, Kay Kyser, Abe Lyman and Tommy Tucker before giving up dance music to concentrate on studio work. He has scored several films, including *Andy Hardy Comes Home*, *Strait Jacket*, *Baby-Face Nelson* and *The Big Operator*, and also some television series, notably *Hazel*. He was musical director and/or arranger for Gordon MacRae, and his wife Sheila, and Art Lund, among others, and has written books on piano and arranging.
● ALBUMS: *The Home Of Happy Feet* (Capitol c.50s)★★★, with Jack Teagarden *Jack Teagarden With Van Alexander's Orchestra* (1956)★★★, *Let's Dance-Last Dance* (Capitol 1960)★★★, *Swing! Staged For Stereo* (Capitol 1961)★★★, *Savoy Stomp* (Capitol 1962)★★★.

ALICE'S RESTAURANT

Folk singer Arlo Guthrie avoided military service during the 60s owing to a conviction for illegally dumping garbage. He later immortalized the events surrounding this in a lengthy monologue, 'Alice's Restaurant Massacree', which was the lynchpin selection on his debut album. Arthur Penn, director of *Bonnie And Clyde*, took charge of this 1969 film, based on that particular song. Although humorous at intervals, the feature fails to match the wit Guthrie brought to his famed composition, despite his starring role. Instead, Penn concentrates on a picturesque view of hippies, accentuating a charming, but naïve, world view, rather than producing an incisive statement. Pete Seeger, friend and fellow activist of Arlo's father, Woody Guthrie, makes an appearance in this rather disappointing film that in some ways diluted the positive aspects of the song inspiring it.

ALL NIGHT LONG

Even in 1961, adapting William Shakespeare to outwardly incongruous settings was not a new departure for film-makers. Setting the Bard to a jazz background was. *All Night Long* was a jazz adaptation of *Othello* - with a good cast, including Richard Attenborough, Betsy Blair and Keith Michell supporting 'drummer' Patrick McGoohan, good direction from Basil Dearden, and an adequate script from Nel King and Peter Achilles, *All Night Long* had all the makings of success, but the end result was curiously dull. The soundtrack was the best aspect of the film, with the musicians who were heard (and occasionally seen) including Harry Beckett, Dave Brubeck, Keith Christie, Bert Courtley, John Dankworth, Allan Ganley (ghosting for McGoohan), Tubby Hayes, Cleo Laine, Charles Mingus and Kenny Napper. The film's musical director, Phillip Green, co-ordinated into the score works by Hayes, Mingus, Napper and Duke Ellington.

ALL THAT JAZZ

A musical 'This Is Your Life - Bob Fosse' was how the critics summarized this sometimes grim, but always brilliant, exposé of the agony and ecstasy (not much of the latter in this case) entailed in the creation of a Broadway musical. Bob Fosse's character, Joe Gideon - the obsessive, hard-drinking, womanizing, perfectionist choreographer-director - is played by Roy Scheider. Leland Palmer is Fosse's one-time wife, Gwen Verdon, with Ann Reinking as his mistress, and Erzsebet Foldi in the role of daughter Nicole. The spectre of Death (in the form of Jessica Lange) is never far away throughout a string of spectacular production numbers that culminate in an onstage recreation of Fosse's open-heart operation, during which Scheider lies connected to drips and monitors, surrounded by lightly clad showgirls waving feather boas: bizarre, to say the least. The main difference from reality was that, while Gideon dies, Fosse happily survived following his surgery, and continued to work for a number of years. Also taking part in this unpleasant (some said distasteful) look at the usually glamorous world of show business, were Ben Vereen, Cliff Gorman, John Lithgow and Keith Gordon. A marvellous opening sequence, based around 'On Broadway' (Mann-Weill-Leiber-Stoller), kicks off the proceedings in great style, and the remainder of a varied selection of musical numbers included 'Everything Old Is New Again' (Peter Allen-Carole Bayer Sager), 'There'll Be Some Changes Made' (W. Benton Overstreet-Billy Higgins), 'Bye Bye Love' (Felice and Boudleaux Bryant), 'Some Of These Days' (Shelton Brooks), 'After You've Gone' (Henry Creamer-Turner Layton), 'Who's Sorry Now?' (Bert Kalmar-Harry Ruby-Ted Snyder), and 'Going Home Now' (Ralph Burns). Bob Fosse's choreography was magnificent throughout, and he also directed and co-wrote the screenplay with Robert Alan Arthur, who produced the film for 20th Century-Fox and Columbia in 1979. It was photographed in Technicolor and Panavision by Giuseppe Rotunno. *All That Jazz* grossed over $20 million in the USA, ensuring it a place in the Top 10 musicals of the decade.

ALLEGRO

The third collaboration for the stage between Richard Rodgers and Oscar Hammerstein II, which opened at the Majestic Theatre in New York on 10 October 1947, was completely out of character, coming as it did between two of their blockbusters, *Carousel* and *South Pacific*. Instead of adapting an established work as the basis of the show, Hammerstein's original book dealt with the corruption of a young doctor by a large Chicago hospital, complete with its wealthy, not necessarily unhealthy, patients. Married to his childhood sweetheart who is intent on the good life regardless of her husband's happiness or ethics, Joseph Taylor Jnr. (John Battles), eventually becomes disillusioned with his meaningless life. He discovers his wife, Jennie Brinker (Roberta Jonay), is having an affair with one of the hospital's most important benefactors, turns down the offer of the hospital's top job, and goes back to his father's practice in the 'sticks', taking with him his new love (and a devoted admirer of his principles), Nurse Emily West (Lisa Kirk). Also cast were Annamary Dickey (Marjorie Taylor), William Ching (Dr. Joseph Taylor), John Conte (Charlie Townsend), and Muriel O'Malley (Grandma Taylor). A 'Greek chorus', which was placed at one side of the stage, spoke directly to the cast and to the audience, and provided a commentary on the proceedings. Rodgers and Hammerstein's score contrasted the romantically inclined 'A Fellow Needs A Girl', 'You Are Never Away', and 'So Far', with the affectionately reproachful 'The Gentleman Is A Dope', along with 'Allegro', 'Money Isn't Everything', 'I Know It Can Happen Again', 'One Foot, Other Foot', 'To Have And To Hold', 'Come Home', and 'Yatata, Yatata'. An ambitious, innovative work, with an unconventional set designed by Jo Mielziner, *Allegro* was directed and choreographed by Agnes De Mille, and ran for 315 performances on Broadway. Not many, when compared to some of the other Rodgers and Hammerstein productions, but it remains a show that is still regarded with affection and admiration. There was a revival at the Goodspeed Opera House, Connecticut, in 1968, and *Allegro* has also been seen in concert versions in both the UK *Lost Musicals* and US *City Center Encores* series.

ALLEN, FRED

b. John Florence Sullivan, 31 May 1894, Cambridge, Massachusetts, USA, d. 17 March 1956, New York, USA. A comedian, actor and singer, with a dry, gravelly voice, baggy eyes, and deadpan expression, all of which made him ideal for the kind of topical monologues that became his speciality. After studying at Boston University, he headlined in vaudeville before making his Broadway debut in the revue *The Passing Show* (1922). This was followed by *Vogues Of 1924*, and a good role as the wisecracking reporter Addie Stiles in the musical comedy *Polly* (1929), which folded after two weeks. Much more successful were the sophisticated hit revues *The Little Show* (1929) and *Three's A Crowd* (1930), in which Allen co-starred with Clifton Webb and Libby Holman. Allen went on to make several films, including the musicals *Thanks A Million* (1935), *Sally, Irene And Mary* (1938) and *Love Thy*

Neighbour (1940). The latter movie recreated the ongoing 'feud' with comedian Jack Benny that was a regular of Allen's top-rated network radio show. Allen's wife, Portland Hoffa, who had appeared with him in revue, was also a member of the cast of this immensely popular series, which ran throughout the 30s and 40s.
● FURTHER READING: *Much Ado About Me*, Fred Allen.

ALLYSON, JUNE

b. Ella Geisman, 7 October 1917, The Bronx, New York, USA. An attractive actress and singer with a distinctive husky voice, Allyson was often cast as the archetypal cute girl-next-door, and is probably best remembered for her portrayal of the bandleader's wife (opposite James Stewart) in *The Glenn Miller Story* (1954). Allyson was raised by her mother, who worked as a waitress to make ends meet. At the age of nine she was confined to a wheel-chair for a time after being injured by a falling tree, and took up dancing to strengthen her back. In the late 30s and early 40s she had small roles in the Broadway musicals *Sing Out The News*, *Very Warm For May*, *Higher And Higher* and *Panama Hattie*, and had a leading part in *Best Foot Forward* (1941). She recreated her role in the latter show for the 1943 film version, and in the same year appeared on screen in *Girl Crazy* and the multi-star extravaganza *Thousands Cheer*. From that point, she starred in a string of mostly MGM musicals, including *Meet The People*, *Two Girls And A Sailor*, *Music For Millions*, *Two Sisters From Boston*, *Till The Clouds Roll By*, *Good News*, *Words And Music*, *The Glenn Miller Story*, *You Can't Run Away From It* and *The Opposite Sex* (1956). In addition, she appeared in an equal number of straight, and rather sugary, films, such as the 1949 remake of *Little Women* and the dramatic and highly emotional *The Shrike* (1955), with Jose Ferrer. She and her husband, actor Dick Powell, were active on US television throughout the 50s and early 60s but after his death in 1963 Allyson withdrew from public life for a time. Later she continued to work in films, nightclubs, and on stage and television.
● FILMS: *All Girl Revue* (1937), *Swing For Sale* (1937), *Pixilated* (1937), *Dime A Dance* (1937), *Ups And Downs* (1937), *The Knight Is Young* (1938), *Dates And Nuts* (1938), *The Prisoner Of Swing* (1938), *Sing For Sweetie* (1938), *Rollin' In Rhythm* (1939), *Best Foot Forward* (1943), *Thousands Cheer* (1943), *Girl Crazy* (1943), *Meet The People* (1944), *Two Girls And A Sailor* (1944), *Her Highness And The Bellboy* (1945), *Music For Millions* (1945), *The Sailor Takes A Wife* (1946), *Till The Clouds Roll By* (1946), *Two Sisters From Boston* (1946), *The Secret Heart* (1946), *Good News* (1947), *High Barbaree* (1947), *The Bride Goes Wild* (1948), *Words And Music* (1948), *The Three Musketeers* (1948), *Little Women* (1949), *The Stratton Story* (1949), *Right Cross* (1950), *The Reformer And The Redhead* (1950), *Too Young To Kiss* (1951), *The Girl In White* (1952), *Battle Circus* (1953), *Remains To Be Seen* (1953), *Executive Suite* (1954), *Woman's World* (1954), *The Glenn MIller Story* (1954), *The McConnell Story* (1955), *The Strike* (1955), *Strategic Air Command* (1955), *The Opposite Sex* (1956), *You Can't Run Away From It* (1956), *My Man Godfrey* (1957), *Interlude* (1957), *The June Allyson Show (television series)* (1959), *Stranger In My Arms* (1959), *See The Man Run (television)* (1971), *They Only Kill Their Masters (television)* (1972), *Letters From Three Lovers (television)* (1973), *Curse Of The Black Widow (television)* (1977), *Blackout (television)* (1978), *Vega$ (television)* (1978), *Blackout* (1978), *Three On A Date (television)* (1979), *The Kid With The Broken Halo (television)* (1982), *That's Entertainment III* (1994).

ALMOST SUMMER

Released in 1977, *Almost Summer* starred unknowns Bruno Kirby, Lee Purcell, John Friedrich and Didi Conn. Its premise - combining high-school jinks, fraternity elections, love interest and pop music - invoked plotlines of 50s teen movies, but this particular feature lacked the knowing edge of the much superior *Grease*. Jazz saxophonist and flautist Charles Lloyd provided much of the score in partnership with Ron Altbach. The former enjoyed a professional relationship with the Beach Boys, inspired by a mutual interest in transcendental meditation, and he invited group members Mike Love, Al Jardine and Brian Wilson to contribute material. Love took lead vocals on the title song, together with 'Sad, Sad Summer', 'Lady Linda', 'Cruisin'' and 'Looking Good', the titles of which were as inspiring as the material itself. 'Fresh' and 'High Energy' added two more contemporary numbers.

ALTER, LOUIS

b. 18 June 1902, Haverhill, Massachusetts, USA, d. 3 November 1980, New York, USA. A composer, pianist and arranger, Alter studied at the New England Conservatory of Music. In his early teens, he played piano in silent-movie houses, and in the 20s served as accompanist for the flamboyant entertainer Nora Bayes, as well as Beatrice Lillie and Helen Morgan, among others. Later in the decade, he contributed songs to several Broadway musicals and revues, including *A La Carte* (1927), *Earl Carroll Vanities Of 1928*, *Americana Of 1928* ('My Kinda Love', lyric: Jo Trent), *Sweet And Low* (1930, 'Overnight', lyric: Billy Rose-Charlotte Kent), *Ballyhoo* (1931) and *Hold Your Horses* (1933). With the advent of talking pictures, Alter moved to Hollywood and wrote some scores and occasional numbers for movies such as *Lord Byron Of Broadway* (1929, 'Nothin' But The Blues', lyric: Joe Goodwin), *Hollywood Revue Of 1929* ('Gotta Feelin' For You', Jo Trent), *Take A Chance*, (1933, 'Come Up And See Me Sometime', Arthur Swanstrom), *Dizzy Dames* (1935, 'I Was Taken By Storm', *Edward Heyman*), *The Old Homestead* (1935, 'Moonlight In Heaven', Jack Scholl), *Sing, Baby, Sing* (1936, 'You Turned The Tables On Me', Sidney Mitchell), *Rainbow On The River* (1936, 'Rainbow On The River', 'You Only Live Once', 'A Thousand Dreams Of Love', Paul Francis Webster), *The Trail Of The Lonesome Pine* (1936, 'A Melody From The Sky' [Oscar nomination], 'Twilight On The Trail', Mitchell), *Make A Wish* (1937, 'Music In My Heart', 'My Campfire Dreams', 'Make A Wish', Webster-Oscar Straus; 'Old Man Rip', Webster-Alter) and *Vogues Of 1938* ('Turn On The Red Heat (Burn The Blues Away)', Webster; 'King Of Jam', Alter). During World War II Alter served as an Entertainments Officer for US Air Force bases, returning to compose the music for film songs such as 'Dolores' (Frank Loesser, Oscar nomination, *Las Vegas Nights*, 1941), 'Love Me As I Am' (*Caught In The Draft*, 1941), 'If I Had A Wishing Ring' (*Breakfast In Hollywood*, 1946) and 'The Blues Are Brewin'' and 'Do You Know What It Means

To Miss New Orleans?' (Eddie De Lange, *New Orleans*, 1947). One of his last movie projects was *Living In A Big Way* (1947), in which Gene Kelly, accompanied by small dog, did a charming dance to Alter and Heyman's 'Fido And Me'. Among Alter's other compositions were 'Au Revoir But Not Goodbye' (Raymond Klages), 'I've Got Sand In My Shoes' (1934), 'Manhattan Serenade' (1928, Harold Adamson, and revived by Harry James, Tommy Dorsey and Jimmy Dorsey in 1942), 'Circus' (Bob Russell), and 'Nina Never Knew' (1952, Milton Drake), an attractive ballad that received an excellent reading from Vic Damone. Alter also wrote several instrumental pieces, including 'Manhattan Masquerade', 'Manhattan Moonlight', 'American Serenade' and 'Side Street In Gotham'.

ALTON, ROBERT

b. Robert Alton Hart, 28 January 1897, Bennington, Vermont, USA, d. 12 June 1957, Hollywood, California, USA. A particularly innovative and stylish choreographer for the musical stage and Hollywood, Alton appeared on Broadway as a dancer in *Take It From Me* (1919) and *Greenwich Village Follies* (1924) before staging the dance scenes for comedian Joe Cook's last Broadway musical, *Hold Your Horses* (1933). Thereafter, during the rest of the 30s through to the early 50s, he choreographed a mixture of revues and musical comedies, among which were some of the biggest hits of the day. They included *Ziegfeld Follies* (1934), *Life Begins At 8:40* (1934), *Anything Goes* (1934), *Thumbs Up!* (1934), *Parade* (1935), *Ziegfeld Follies* (1936), *Hooray For What!* (1937), *Between The Devil* (1937), *You Never Know* (1938), *Leave It To Me!* (1938), *One For The Money* (1939), *The Streets Of Paris* (1939), *Too Many Girls* (1939), *Du Barry Was A Lady* (1939), *Two For The Show* (1940), *Panama Hattie* (1940), *Higher And Higher* (1940), *Pal Joey* (1940), *Sons O' Fun* (1941), *By Jupiter* (1942), *Count Me In* (1942), *Ziegfeld Follies* (1943), *Laffing Room Only* (1944), *Hazel Flagg* (1953) and *Me And Juliet* (1953). Alton also served as both choreographer and director on *Early To Bed* (1943), the 1952 Broadhurst Theatre revival of *Pal Joey* (with David Alexander), and *The Vamp* (1955).

In parallel with his stage work, Alton created some classic dance scenes in a number of highly successful and fondly remembered movie musicals, such as *You'll Never Get Rich* (1941, the 'Wedding Cake Walk' sequence), *The Harvey Girls* (1946, the Oscar-winning 'On The Atcheson, Topeka And The Santa Fe'), *Ziegfeld Follies* (1946, 'This Heart Of Mine'), *Good News* (1947, with Charles Walters, 'Varsity Drag'), *Easter Parade* (1948, 'The Girl On The Magazine Cover', 'Shaking The Blues Away', 'A Couple Of Swells'), *The Pirate* (1948, with Gene Kelly, 'Be A Clown'), *Annie Get Your Gun* (1950, 'I'm An Indian Too'), *Show Boat* (1951, 'I Might Fall Back On You', 'Life Upon The Wicked Stage'), and many more. His other film credits, mostly for MGM, included *Strike Me Pink* (1936), *Bathing Beauty* (1944, with Jack Donohue), *Till The Clouds Roll By* (1946), *Words And Music* (1948, with Kelly), *The Barkleys Of Broadway* (1949), *In The Good Old Summertime* (1949), *Pagan Love Song* (1950, also directed), *The Belle Of New York* (1952), *I Love Melvin* (1953), *Call Me Madam* (1953), *White Christmas* (1954), *There's No Business Like Show Business* (1955) and *The Girl Rush* (1955). In many cases, stars such as Gene

Kelly and Fred Astaire would stage one or more of the numbers in their own movies, and there were other occasions when additional choreographers were called in to work alongside Alton, such as on *There's No Business Like Show Business*, when all Marilyn Monroe's dance routines were created by Jack Cole. In a varied and distinguished career, Allen also directed *Merton Of The Movies* (1947), the second film remake of Harry Leon Wilson's endearing novel, which starred Red Skelton, Virginia O'Brien, Alan Mowbray, Gloria Grahame and Leon Ames.

ALWAYS

Originally workshopped by the Victorian Arts Center Trust, Melbourne, Australia, in August 1994, *Always* made its London debut at the Victoria Palace Theatre on 10 June 1997. Sub-titled 'The Ultimate Love Story', it was an attempt by William May and Jason Sprague (additional book by Frank Hauser) to construct a musical around the relationship between King Edward VIII (Clive Carter) and the American divorcée Wallis Simpson (Jan Hartley), which resulted in the King's Abdication in December 1936. The tumultuous events are remembered through the eyes of a black-veiled Mrs. Simpson at her husband's funeral in 1972, although the audience is only privy to her memories between 1931, and 1937 when they are both freed - he from the throne, she from her husband. This time scale, as critics were quick to point out, meant that 'a convenient veil could be drawn over the couple's hero worship of Hitler'. (In any case, that period of their lives was more than adequately covered in Snoo Wilson's play *HRH* at London's Playhouse in October 1997). So, the action in *Always* ranged from various British locations and events such as the Buckingham Palace Silver Jubilee Ball, where David and Wallis' eyes first meet across a crowded room, to the Cafe La Parisienne, South of France, and a powerhouse rendering of 'Love's Carousel' from Analise L'Avender (Sheila Ferguson, formerly of the Three Degrees vocal group). There is also a scene at a Welsh miners' village in which the men unite in the (as it turned out) over-optimistic 'Long May You Reign'. The remainder of the score included 'Someone Special', 'I Stand Before My Destiny', 'Why?', 'If Always Were A Place', 'This Time Around', 'It's The Party Of The Year', 'Hearts Have Their Reasons', 'The Reason For Life Is To Love', 'Invitation Is For Two', and 'Always'. Also prominent in the cast were Shani Wallis (Aunt Bessie), Chris Humphreys (Lord Mountbatten), David McAlister (Ernest Simpson), James Horne (Stanley Baldwin), and Ursula Smith (Queen Mary). The 'classy, minimalist' sets were by Hildegard Bechtler, and Tom Rand designed the 'elegant' costumes. It was directed by Frank Hauser and Tommy Tune protégé Thommie Walsh, and Walsh also handled the musical staging. Jan Hartley's acting and singing came out of it better than Clive Carter's, but, having despatched *The Goodbye Girl* and *Romance, Romance* earlier in the year, the critics were on a roll . . . 'syrupy rubbish . . . dire and uninspired' . . . and *Always* was withdrawn on 26 July. Shortly before that date the press advertisements read 'booking until November 1997', but if anyone did turn up at the Victoria Palace then, they would have seen a very different kind of musical - *Fame*.

Just a few months after the closure, another Edward and Mrs. Simpson musical, *It's Only A Kingdom*, premiered in the USA at the Mill Mountain Theatre in Roanoke, Virginia. Other royal romance plots for musical comedies have included *Merrie England* in 1902 (Good Queen Bess and Sir Walter Raleigh), *By Appointment* in 1934 (the Prince of Wales, future King George IV, and Mrs. Fitzherbert), and *I And Albert* in 1972 (Queen Victoria and Consort). There was also the *Edward & Mrs. Simpson* 1980 television mini-series, starring Edward Fox and Cynthia Harris, with former musical comedy actress Jessie Matthews as Aunt Bessie. It was not a musical, but it did have a very catchy title song.

AMECHE, DON

b. Dominic Felix Amici, 31 May 1908, Kenosha, Wisconsin, USA, d. 6 December 1993, Scottsdale, Arizona, USA. A suave, romantic leading man with an appealing style and mellifluous voice, Ameche was one of the most popular movie actors in Hollywood movies from the mid-30s through to the late 40s. After working in radio for a time, Ameche signed for 20th Century-Fox in 1936. He appeared in several straight roles before making a big impact in the musicals *One In A Million* (with Sonja Henie) and *Old Chicago* (1938) with Alice Faye and Tyrone Power. The trio reunited for *Alexander's Ragtime Band*, which was released in the same year. He proved a suitably dashing D'Artagnan in another musical, *The Three Musketeers*, and then came what is probably his best-remembered part in *The Story Of Alexander Graham Bell* (1939), which was so effective that it sparked off a popular joke that Ameche himself had invented the telephone. From then onwards, and throughout the 40s, he was smooth and splendid in numerous films, including musicals such as *Hollywood Cavalcade*, *Swanee River* (as composer Stephen Foster), *Lillian Russell*, *Down Argentine Way* and *Moon Over Miami* (both with Betty Grable), *Kiss The Boys Goodbye* (with Mary Martin), *Something To Shout About*, *Greenwich Village* and *Slightly French* (1949). Afterwards, the film roles dried up, and he moved to New York and began working in the relatively new medium of television, becoming involved in a long-running circus series in which he played a ringmaster. He also starred in three Broadway musicals, Cole Porter's *Silk Stockings* (1955) with Hildegarde Neff, *Goldilocks* (1958) with Elaine Stritch, and the short-lived *Thirteen Daughters* (1961). After a few minor movie roles in the 60s and 70s, he made his big comeback in the Eddie Murphy comedy *Trading Places* (1983), and then won the Oscar for Best Supporting Actor in *Cocoon* (1984). This was followed by the inevitable sequel, *Cocoon: The Return* (1988). He completed his role in *Corrina, Corrina* with Whoopi Goldberg a month before he died of prostate cancer at the age of 85.
● FILMS: *Beauty At The World's Fair* (1933), *Dante's Inferno* (1935), *Clive Of India* (1935), *Ladies In Love* (1936), *Ramona* (1936), *Sins Of Man* (1936), *Love Under Fire* (1937), *You Can't Have Everything* (1937), *One In A Million* (1937), *Love Is News* (1937), *Fifty Roads To Town* (1937), *Alexander's Ragtime Band* (1938), *Gateway* (1938), *Happy Landing* (1938), *Josette* (1938), *In Old Chicago* (1938), *Midnight* (1939), *Hollywood Cavalcade* (1939), *The Story Of Alexander Graham Bell* (1939), *The Three Musketeers* (1939), *Lillian Russell* (1940), *Swanee River* (1940), *Down Argentina Way* (1940), *Four Sons* (1940), *That Night In Rio* (1941), *The Feminine Touch* (1941), *Confirm Or Deny* (1941), *Kiss The Boys Goodbye* (1941), *Moon Over Miami* (1941), *Girl Trouble* (1942), *The Magnificent Dope* (1942), *Something To Shout About* (1943), *Happy Land* (1943), *Heaven Can Wait* (1943), *Greenwich Village* (1944), *Wing And A Prayer* (1944), *Guest Wife* (1945), *It's In The Bag* (1945), *So Goes My Love* (1946), *That's My Man* (1947), *Sleep My Love* (1948), *Slightly French* (1949), *Hollywood Night At 21 Club* (1952), *Phantom Caravan* (1954), *Fire One* (1955), *A Fever In The Blood* (1961), *Rings Around The World* (documentary) (1966), *Picture Mommy Dead* (1966), *Shadow Over Elveron* (television) (1968), *Suppose They Gave A War And Nobody Came* (1970), *The Boatniks* (1970), *Gidget Gets Married* (television) (1971), *Won Ton Ton - The Dog Who Saved Hollywood* (1975), *Trading Places* (1983), *Cocoon* (1985), *Pals* (television) (1986), *A Masterpiece Of Murder* (television) (1986), *Harry And The Hendersons* (1987), *Cocoon: The Return* (1988), *Things Change* (1988), *Coming To America* (1988), *Oddball Hall* (1990), *Oscar* (1991), *Sunstroke* (1992), *Folks!* (1992), *Homeward Bound: The Incredible Journey* (voice only) (1993), *Corrina, Corrina* (1994).

AMERICAN GRAFFITI

Released in 1973, written by George Lucas and produced by Francis Ford Coppola, *American Graffiti* was a haunting, affectionate paean to small-town America during the early 60s. The sense of innocence and loss it evoked was enhanced by an extensive soundtrack, the bulk of which featured songs drawn from the previous decade. The cast was thus already imbued with a sense of nostalgia, capturing to perfection the uncertainty of the post-Elvis Presley, pre-Beatles era. The accompanying album is a joy from beginning to end, collecting classic songs by Buddy Holly, Chuck Berry, the Beach Boys, Del Shannon and many more. It is highly satisfying in its own right, but takes on an extra resonance when combined with one of the finest 'rock' films of any era.

AMERICAN HOT WAX

Floyd Mutrix directed this superior 1977 film which starred Tim McIntyre as a character based on 50s disc jockey Alan Freed. The plot, in which 'Freed' stages a rock 'n' roll concert at New York's Brooklyn Theatre despite opposition from the 'moral majority', mirrored many of the era's exploitation features, notably *Rock Rock Rock* and *Go Johnny Go*. However, *American Hot Wax* possesses a certain poignancy, given the events surrounding Freed's career when, having helped to popularize black R&B, he fell from grace in the wake of a payola scandal. McIntyre excels in his role and the entire film captures the flavour of an exciting period in popular music. Kenny Vance, former mentor to Jay And The Americans, not only played the part of Professor La Piano, he also served as the film's musical director, assembling a stellar soundtrack that included the Coasters, the Spaniels, Jackie Wilson and Eddie Cochrane. Jerry Lee Lewis, Screaming Jay Hawkins and Chuck Berry are among the veterans who make appearances. The last-named, aware of the financial problems besetting the McIntyre character, agrees to waive his fee with the words 'this one's for the music', a surprising statement given his parsimonious attitude in real life. Exfolk-singer Hamilton Camp, Nils Lofgren and entrepreneur Artie Ripp are also among the cast, alongside future *Tonight* television show host, Jay Leno. Evocative and sympathetic, *American Hot Wax* pays tribute both to Freed and to the music he loved.

● FILMS: *American Hot Wax* (1976).

AMERICAN IN PARIS, AN

One of the most enchanting of all film musicals, *An American In Paris* was released in 1951 and became one of the top money-makers of the decade. It has endured simply because of the all-round high-class talent involved. Alan Jay Lerner's screenplay is set in Paris, where Jerry Mulligan (Gene Kelly) is gaining far more personal fulfilment as a painter than he did in his former occupation as a GI. Other areas of his life are not so satisfying: a wealthy American, the rather more mature Milo Richards (Nina Foch), seems more interested in him than in his canvasses; and the girl with whom he falls in love, Lise Bourvier (the delightful dancer Leslie Caron in her screen debut), is promised to another, Henri Baurel (Georges Guétary), who happens to be Jerry's best friend. Naturally, it all ends happily, with Jerry keeping his friend and getting the girl. In any case, the story was subservient to the songs - a great collection from George and Ira Gershwin that included 'By Strauss', 'I'll Build A Stairway To Paradise', 'Embraceable You', 'Love Is Here To Stay', 'Tra-La-La' and ''S Wonderful'. The film's climax was a spectacular 18 minute-long ballet, during which Kelly (who choreographed the complete film) found himself in various Parisian locations, each of which was presented in the style of a famous painter. Among the other highlights were Kelly's French lesson for an eager and engaging bunch of kids via 'I Got Rhythm', and a dream sequence during which Oscar Levant conducts part of the 'Piano Concerto In F', and every member of the orchestra appears to be him! A Technicolor production from Arthur Freed's MGM unit, *An American In Paris* was directed with supreme style and flair by Vincente Minnelli. It won Academy Awards for best picture, screenplay, musical arrangements (Saul Chaplin and Johnny Green), cinematography and art/set direction. At the same awards ceremony - in 1952 - Gene Kelly received a special Oscar for his versatility as an actor, singer, director, dancer - and especially - choreographer. In 1996 a double-CD was released containing extended and alternative versions of the musical sequences, along with several outtakes.

ANASTASIA

Having cleaned up at box offices worldwide with the blockbusters *Titanic* and *The Full Monty*, 1998 was a very good year for 20th Century-Fox, even before the release of *Anastasia* proved they had an animation department to rival that of Walt Disney Productions. It apparently took more than 300 animators three years to produce this $65 million sanitised, but highly enjoyable, account of the Russian Revolution. After fleeing the palace when the trouble begins, the young Romanov Princess Anastasia (voiced by Meg Ryan, singing voice Liz Callaway) loses her memory. Later, when she is 18, and called Anya, she meets up with ex-palace servant-turned conman Dmitri (John Cusak), who decides to try and pass her off as Princess Anastasia. Together with Dmitri's sidekick, Vladimir (Kelsey Grammer), they travel to Paris in order to present the teenager to her exiled grandmother, Dowager Empress Marie (Angela Lansbury), and collect a reward. After a hectic journey, involving incredibly animated shipboard adventures and a runaway train, Anya proves beyond doubt that she is the real Anastasia, and in spite of beyond-the-grave problems from Rasputin (aided by various creatures including a deadpan bat named Bartok (Hank Azaria), she and Dmitri go off together into the (obviously red) sunset. Vladimir and Dmitri's friend Sophie (Bernadette Peters) get on well too. Lynn Ahrens (lyrics) and Stephen Flaherty (music) wrote the delightful songs, 'Once Upon A December', 'A Rumour In St. Petersburg', 'Journey To The Past', 'In The Dark Of The Night', 'Learn To Do It', 'Paris Holds The Key (To Your Heart)', and 'At The Beginning', which were sung and reprised by various artists. Ironically, at Oscar time, Ahrens and Flaherty were beaten for Best Original Song by *Titanic*, and (with David Newman) for Original Musical or Comedy Score by *The Full Monty*. *Anastasia* was directed and produced by Don Bluth and Gary Goldman. The screenplay, written by Susan Gauthier, Bruce Graham, Bob Tzudiker, and Noni White, was based on the play by Marcelle Maurette as adapted by Guy Bolton, and Arthur Laurents's screenplay for the 1956 *Anastasia* movie. Ingrid Bergman won an Academy Award for her performance in that one.

ANCHORS AWEIGH

Considering Frank Sinatra's lifelong attraction to females the world over, it seems somewhat incongruous that in this, his first major film in 1945, he played a bashful sailor named Clarence Doolittle who seeks advice on 'how to handle a woman' from his shipmate, Joseph Brady (Gene Kelly) - 'the best wolf in the whole US Navy'. On leave in Hollywood, the pair become involved with a very small boy (Dean Stockwell) who is just leaving home to join the navy, and his singing guardian aunt (Kathryn Grayson), who yearns to audition for the Spanish pianist and conductor José Iturbi. After the usual complications, Kelly gets Grayson, Grayson passes the audition, and Sinatra finally conquers his shyness with a girl (Pamela Britton) from his own home-town of Brooklyn. The principal songs were by Sammy Cahn and Jule Styne and included three lovely ballads for Sinatra, 'What Makes The Sunset?', 'The Charm Of You' and 'I Fall In Love Too Easily', along with two amusing duets with Kelly, 'I Begged Her' and 'We Hate To Leave'. Among the songs by other composers were 'Cradle Song' (Sinatra), 'If You Knew Susie' (Kelly and Sinatra) and 'Jealousy' and 'My Heart Sings', which were sung by Grayson. She and Iturbi also performed several classical pieces. All that music stretched the film's running time to a marathon 140 minutes. It was photographed in Technicolor, directed by George Sidney, with a screenplay by Isobel Lennart. Gene Kelly choreographed, and also provided one of the film's highlights when he 'danced' with the animated mouse Jerry (of Tom and Jerry), while singing 'The Worry Song' by Ralph Freed and Sammy Fain. Sidney originally wanted Mickey Mouse for the sequence, but Walt Disney demurred - four full-length Disney animated features each took over $40 million in the US alone during the 40s; *Anchors Aweigh* earned about a tenth of that.

AND SO TO BED

A musical adaptation of J.B. Fagan's famous play about the English diarist Samuel Pepys, *And So To Bed* opened in London in October 1951, and was the somewhat surprising brainchild of Leslie Henson, one of England's most celebrated theatrical clowns; it proved to be his last West End musical. Vivian Ellis contributed an intriguing 17th century-style score, which contained a mixture of musical influences, such as madrigal, jig, sarabande and rigaudon, in a variety of numbers that included the charming 'Love Me Little, Love Me Long' and 'Gaze Not On The Swans', along with 'Amo, Amas', 'And So To Bed', 'Bartholemew Fair', 'Moppety Mo' and 'Beauty Retire'. Leslie Henson (complete with periwig) played Pepys, with Betty Paul as his wife. Paul had starred in one of Ellis' biggest successes, *Bless The Bride* (1947). The remainder of the cast included the American actress Jessie Royce Landis as Pepys' lover, Mistress Knight, and, fresh from his native Australia, Keith Michell as Charles II. Michell later went on to another celebrated regal role as the star of the television series and film of *Henry VIII And His Six Wives*, as well as starring in West End musicals. *And So To Bed* was a popular show, and ran in the West End for 323 performances, closing in July 1952. In the following year, Henson toured with a revised version in which Mistress Knight and the King were played by the popular husband-and-wife singing duo, Anne Ziegler and Webster Booth.

ANDERSON, JOHN MURRAY

b. 20 September 1886, St. John's, Newfoundland, d. 30 January 1954, New York, USA. An innovative director, producer, author and lyricist for the musical theatre, Anderson was educated in Glasgow, Scotland, and Lausanne, Switzerland, before serving with the American Bureau of Information during World War I. He made his initial impact as a director on Broadway with a series of lavish revues entitled *Greenwich Village Follies* (1919-24), for which he also served as lyricist and librettist. From then on, over the next 20 years, Anderson staged a mixture of revue and musical comedy for which he often wrote the sketches and books. His work for Broadway included *Jack And Jill* (1923), *Music Box Revue* (1924), *Dearest Enemy* (1925), *Hello, Daddy* (1928), *John Murray Anderson's Almanac* (1929, also producer), *Ziegfeld Follies* (1934), *Life Begins At 8:40* (1934), *Thumbs Up!* (1934), *Jumbo* (1935), *Ziegfeld Follies* (1936), *One For The Money* (1939), *Two For The Show* (1940), *Sunny River* (1941), *Ziegfeld Follies* (1943), *Laffing Room Only* (1944), *The Firebrand Of Florence* (1945), *Three To Make Ready* (1946), *Heaven On Earth* (1948), *New Faces Of 1952* (1952), *Two's Company* (1952) and *John Murray Anderson's Almanac* (1953), while London audiences saw *League Of Notions* (1921), *Bow Bells* (1932), *Fanfare* (1932), *Over The Page* and *Home And Beauty* (1937).

In addition to his association with the flamboyant Billy Rose on the extravagant circus musical *Jumbo*, Anderson

was the director of Rose's renowned Diamond Horseshoe nightspot in New York from 1938-50, and also worked for Ringling Brothers Circus and Radio City Music Hall. He spent hardly any time in Hollywood, apart from handling special projects such as the water ballet in *Bathing Beauty* (1944), starring Esther Williams, and the circus sequences in *The Greatest Show On Earth* (1942). He also devised and directed the spectacular 1930 movie musical *The King Of Jazz*, with its multi-star cast headed by another master showman, Paul Whiteman. As a lyricist, Anderson's best-known song is probably 'A Young Man's Fancy' (with Jack Yellen and Milton Ager), which was introduced by Rosalind Fuller in the 1920 revue *What's In A Name?*. The same trio was also responsible for various other items in the show, including the title number. Among Anderson's other compositions were 'The Last Waltz', 'The Valley Of Dreams', 'Marimba', 'The Girl In The Moon', 'Eileen', 'That Reminiscent Melody' and 'Come To Vienna'. His chief songwriting collaborators were A. Baldwin Sloane and Carey Morgan.

● FURTHER READING: *Out Without My Rubbers*, John Murray Anderson.

ANDERSON, LEROY

b. 29 June 1908, Cambridge, Massachusetts, USA, d. 18 May 1975, Woodbury, Connecticut, USA. A popular composer from the 30s through to the 50s, Anderson studied at the New England Conservatory of Music and at Harvard University, where he was organist and choirmaster from 1929-35. During most of this same period he was also orchestral director at the university. In 1935 he left the comparative security of academia to earn his living as a freelance musician. He composed and arranged music for the Boston 'Pops' Orchestra, then under the direction of Arthur Fiedler, and began to build a reputation as a composer of light orchestral works. One of his first successes, composed in 1939, was 'Jazz Pizzicato'. Anderson was in the US Army for four years from 1942, then returned to his career with a string of popular compositions, most of which he recorded with specially assembled orchestras. His best-known works include 'Fiddle-Faddle', 'Syncopated Clock', 'Sleigh Ride', 'Blue Tango', 'Belle Of The Ball', 'The Typewriter', 'Plink, Plank, Plunk', 'Serenata', 'Bugler's Holiday', 'Sandpaper Ballet', 'The Waltzing Cat', 'Song Of The Bells', 'Promenade', 'Phantom Regiment', and the tune that became his theme, 'Forgotten Dreams'. Anderson also composed the music for the 1958 Broadway musical *Goldilocks*, which starred Don Ameche and Elaine Stritch. Many of his loveliest melodies are available on *Frederick Fennell Conducts The Music Of Leroy Anderson*, which was released by Mercury in 1992.

● ALBUMS: conducting his own works *The Leroy Anderson Collection* (MCA 1988)★★★★, *Greatest Hits* (BMG 1993)★★★★.

ANDERSON, MAXWELL

b. 15 December 1888, Atlantic, Pennsylvania, USA, d. 28 February 1959, Stamford, Connecticut, USA. A distinguished author and librettist, Anderson studied at Stanford and North Dakota Universities before working on newspapers in the late teens/early 20s. As a playwright his works for the theatre include *What Price Glory?*, *Mary Of Scotland*, *Both Your Houses* (Pulitzer Prize for Drama 1933), *Winterset*, *The Wingless Victory* and *Key Largo*. He also wrote the book and lyrics for two Broadway musicals in collaboration with composer Kurt Weill. *Knickerbocker Holiday* (1938) contained the haunting 'September Song' and 'It Never Was You', and was filmed in 1944, while *Lost In the Stars* (1944) is perhaps best remembered for its title song, which is still being recorded in the 90s. Anderson also wrote for two films, *Never Steal Anything Small* ('It Takes Love To Make A Home' and the title song) and *Midnight Lace* ('What Does A Woman Do?').

● FURTHER READING: *Maxwell Anderson: The Man And His Plays*, B. Clark. *The Life Of Maxwell Anderson*, A.S. Shivers.

ANDREW LLOYD WEBBER: THE MUSICAL

This bizarre mix of spoof and satire, produced by the The Really Useless Company, was written and composed by cartoonist, musician, and author Nick Awde. He conceived it as a humorous attack on the general state of the London theatre. Lovingly structured on Mel Brooks's movie *The Producers*, it tells the story of Andrew Lloyb Webber, an aspiring composer of musicals, who meets up with an old friend, Tim Mandy-Rice Davies, in a south London pub. At the bar, Tim introduces Andrew to his friend Jesus, who believes he has a good idea for a musical. After a great deal of planning, in Act II they finally manage to put on *Jesús-María Christ Super Estar-A Rock Opera*. Wicked parodies of the Lloyd Webber canon, the songs drew from the composer's (reluctantly) acknowledged musical sources, and included such gems as 'Could I Love A Sailor?', 'Beat Me Whip Me', 'The Crucifixion Can-Can', 'Don't Cry For Me Clapham Common', and 'The Critics Will Eat You Alive'. In fact, the critics' reaction was mixed and fairly predictable (it often seems that some London scribes would rather give up drinking than risk Andrew Lloyd Webber's displeasure). Spontaneous audience participation was a regular feature of the shows which attracted a good deal of media attention. The performers at various stages of the musical's brief life (there were a reported six cast changes) included Tara Few/Francis Crampsie (ALW), Ben Stollery/Gary Melinor (TM-RD), Simon Finch/Jamie Cason (J), and Jeremy Suffell/Joanna Briggs (impresarios Cameron Dirty Mac/Nedine Sherry). There were also two non-speaking parts, Sarah Brightman and Julian Lloyd Webber. Despite cash, legal, and other difficulties, *Andrew Lloyd Webber: The Musical* managed to run for 36 performances during the summer of 1993 in small London venues such as the Canal Cafe and Bird's Nest theatres. By a curious coincidence, these all took place around the time ALW and his Really Useful Company were struggling to overcome a faulty hydraulics problems at the Adelphi Theatre which delayed the opening of *Sunset Boulevard*. Asked to comment, a spokesperson for the Company admitted that 'a couple of people from the music department have seen it, but we are not taking any action. Everyone is a bit tied up with *Sunset* at the moment'. It did not seem to bother ALW's former collaborator, Tim Rice, either. His PA said: 'He doesn't mind one way or the other.' Since then, more people have claimed to have seen the show than was physically possible, and in 1999 it began attracting new audiences in published form.

ANDREWS SISTERS

LaVerne (b. 6 July 1911, Mound, nr. Minneapolis, Minnesota, USA, d. 8 May 1967, Brentwood, California, USA), Maxene (b. 3 January 1916, Mound, nr. Minneapolis, Minnesota, USA, d. 21 October 1995, Boston, Massachusetts, USA) and Patti (b. 16 February 1918, Mound, nr. Minneapolis, Minnesota, USA), lead singer and soloist. In the early 30s the sisters appeared in vaudeville and toured with the Larry Rich band before joining Leon Belasco at New York's Hotel Edison in 1937. With their new manager Lou Levy (b. 3 December 1910, Brooklyn, New York, USA, d. October 1995), who later married Maxene, they signed for Decca Records and almost immediately had a massive hit in 1938 with 'Bei Mir Bist Du Schon', a Yiddish song from 1933, with a new lyric by Saul Chaplin and Sammy Cahn. This was followed by the novelty 'Hold Tight, Hold Tight', and 'Roll Out The Barrel', an Americanized version of the old Czechoslovakian melody, 'The Beer Barrel Polka', which became one of World War II's smash hits and helped them to become the most popular female vocal group of the war years. They went to Hollywood in 1940 to appear in the film *Argentine Nights* with the Ritz Brothers, and featured in several movies starring comedians Abbott and Costello, including *Buck Privates*, in which they sang 'Boogie Woogie Bugle Boy'. In *Hollywood Canteen*, Warner's 1944 star-studded morale booster, the sisters sang 'Don't Fence Me In', later a chart-topper with Bing Crosby. Their fruitful career-long collaboration with Crosby also included 'Pistol Packin' Mama', 'Is You Is, Or Is You Ain't My Baby?', 'Ac-Cent-Tchu-Ate The Positive', 'The Three Caballeros', 'Along The Navajo Trail', 'Jingle Bells' and 'Sparrow In The Tree Top'. They also recorded with several other artists such as Les Paul ('Rumours Are Flying'), Burl Ives ('Blue Tail Fly'), Danny Kaye ('Civilisation' and 'Woody Woodpecker'), Carmen Miranda ('Cuanto La Gusta'), Guy Lombardo ('Christmas Island') and country singer Ernest Tubbs ('I'm Bitin' My Fingernails And Thinking Of You'). Their own unaided hits, accompanied mainly by the Vic Schoen Orchestra, were a mixture of novelty, commercial boogie-woogie, calypso, jazzy numbers and heartfelt ballads. Following that first Yiddish hit in 1938, they were consistently in the charts with records such as 'Says My Heart', 'Say Si Si', 'Beat Me, Daddy, Eight To The Bar', 'I, Yi, Yi, Yi, Yi, (I Like You Very Much)', 'I'll Be With You In Apple Blossom Time', 'Three Little Sisters', 'Strip Polka', 'Straighten Up And Fly Right' and 'Underneath The Arches'/'You Call Everybody Darling', which was recorded in the UK and accompanied by the Billy Ternent Orchestra. In 1949 Patti Andrews topped the US chart with her solo record, 'I Can Dream, Can't I?'/'I Wanna Be Loved', and in 1953 she left the group to go solo. The sisters still worked together occasionally until LaVerne's death in 1967. At their peak for just over a decade, their immediately identifiable close harmony sound, coupled with a swinging, vigorous delivery, eventually gained them world record sales in excess of 60 million, making them perhaps the most successful and popular female group ever. Bette Midler's frenetic revival of 'Boogie Woogie Bugle Boy' in 1973 revived some interest in their records, and in 1974 Patti and Maxene were reunited for *Over Here*, a Broadway musical with a World War II setting that ran for over a year. In the early 80s Maxene underwent heart surgery, but in 1985 she was able to record her first solo album, *Maxene*, a mixture of new material and some of the group's old hits. In 1991, four years before her death, she made her 'in-person' debut as a solo artist, in aid of charity, at the Beaux Arts Ball in Brighton, England. Patti continues to work, touring the UK in 1990 on a wave of wartime nostalgia with the current Glenn Miller Orchestra.

● ALBUMS: *Merry Christmas* 10-inch album (Decca 1950)★★★, *Christmas Greetings* 10-inch album (Decca 1950)★★★, *Tropical Songs* 10-inch album (Decca 1950)★★★, *The Andrews Sisters* 10-inch album (Decca 1950)★★★★, *Club 15* 10-inch album (Decca 1950)★★★, *Berlin Songs* 10-inch album (Decca 1950)★★, *Christmas Cheer* 10-inch album (Decca 1950)★★★, *Mr Music* film soundtrack (Decca 1951)★★★, *I Love To Tell The Story* 10-inch album (Decca 1951)★★★, *Country Style* 10-inch album (Decca 1952)★★, *My Isle Of Golden Dreams* 10-inch album (Decca 1952)★★★, *Sing Sing Sing* 10-inch album (Decca 1953)★★★, *Curtain Call* (Decca 1956)★★★, *Jingle Bells* (Decca 1956)★★★, *By Popular Demand* (Decca 1957)★★★, *The Andrew Sisters In Hi-Fi* (Capitol 1957)★★★★, *Fresh And Fancy Free* (Capitol 1957)★★★★★, *Dancing Twenties* (Capitol 1958)★★★, *The Andrews Sisters Present* (1963)★★★, *Great Country Hits* (1964)★★, *The Andrews Sisters Go Hawaiian* (1965)★★.

Solo: Patti And Maxene Andrews *Over Here* stage cast (1974)★★★, Maxene Andrews *Maxene* (1985)★★★.

● COMPILATIONS: *The Best Of The Andrews Sisters* (MCA 1973)★★★★, *Boogie Woogie Bugle Girls* (1973)★★★★, *In The Mood* (1974)★★★★, *Beat Me Daddy Eight To The Bar* (MFP/EMI 1982)★★★★, *Jumpin' Jive* (MCA 1986)★★★★, *16 Golden Classics* (Timeless 1987)★★★★, *Hold Tight - It's The Andrews Sisters* (Dance Band Days/Prism 1987)★★★★, *Rarities* (MCA 1988)★★★, *Christmas With The Andrews Sisters* (Pickwick 1988)★★★, *Says My Heart* (Happy Days 1989)★★★, *Capitol Collectors Series* (Capitol 1991)★★★, with Bing Crosby *The Essential Collection* (Half Moon 1998)★★★.

● FILMS: *Argentine Nights* (1940), *Hold That Ghost* (1941), *Buck Privates In The Navy* (1941), *Private Buckaroo* (1942), *Give Out Sisters* (1942), *What's Cooking?* (1942), *How's About It?* (1943), *Always A Bridesmaid* (1943), *Swingtime Johnny* (1943), *Moonlight And Cactus* (1944), *Hollywood Canteen* (1944), *Follow The Boys* (1944), *Her Lucky Night* (1945), *Road To Rio* (1947), *The Phynx (Patti cameo)* (1970).

ANDREWS, JULIE

b. Julia Wells, 1 October 1935, Walton-On-Thames, Surrey, England. After singing lessons with Madam Lillian Stiles-Allan, which formed her precise vocal style and typically English delivery, Andrews made her professional debut in her parents' variety act at the age of 10. Two years later she performed at the London Hippodrome in the Pat Kirkwood musical, *Starlight Roof*, and the following year appeared in the Royal Command Performance. On BBC Radio, she was Archie Andrews' playmate in *Educating Archie*, while appearing on stage in the title role of *Humpty Dumpty* at the London Casino at the age of 13.

Her big break came in 1954 when she played Polly Brown in the Broadway production of Sandy Wilson's *The Boy Friend*. Having insisted on only a one-year contract for the latter show, she was available to star with Rex Harrison in one of Broadway's major musicals, Alan Jay Lerner and Frederick Loewe's *My Fair Lady*, later repeating her performance in London before returning to Broadway as Queen Guinevere, with Richard Burton as King Arthur, in *Camelot*. Although passed over in favour of Audrey Hepburn for the lead in the film of *My Fair Lady* in 1964, ironically, she won an Oscar for her performance as the 'flying nanny' in the title role of Walt Disney's *Mary Poppins* in the same year. Since then, her career in film musicals has taken her from the blockbuster heights of *The Sound Of Music* to the critical depths of the Gertrude Lawrence biopic *Star!*, with *Thoroughly Modern Millie* and a gender-bending role in *Victor/Victoria*, in-between. The latter film, and her straight roles in movies such as *10* and *S.O.B.*, which were directed by her second husband Blake Edwards, have sometimes seemed blatant attempts to counter her lifelong cosy, old-fashioned image. Nevertheless, she has been a major film star for over 25 years, and in 1989 was awarded BAFTA's Silver Mask in recognition of her outstanding contribution to the medium. She was less successful on the small screen with her 1992 ABC comedy series *Julie*, which was poorly received. It had been a different story back in the 60s when she and Carol Burnett starred in the multi-Emmy Award-winning television special, *Julie And Carol At Carnegie Hall*. The two actresses were paired in similar shows at the Lincoln center for the Performing Arts (1971) and at the Pantages Theatre in Los Angeles (1989). Also in 1992, Andrews sang the role of Anna in a CD recording of *The King And I*, amid general amazement that she had never played the part on stage; British actor Ben Kingsley was her regal partner in the studio. In 1993 audiences flocked to see her in the off-Broadway Stephen Sondheim revue *Putting It Together*, her first appearance on the New York stage since *Camelot* (1960). The critics were not so enthusiastic, and furthermore, they cared little for the stage version of *Victor/Victoria* that opened on Broadway in October 1995, although Andrews' name guaranteed nightly standing ovations until she finally bowed out, being replaced by Raquel Welch in June 1997. Andrews won Drama Desk and Outer Critics Circle Awards for her sterling performance, but controversially turned down the 1996 Tony Award nomination for leading actress in a musical because no one else connected with the show had been nominated. In 1996 she was also inducted into the Theatre Hall of Fame, and a year later released an album of songs by composers such as Kurt Weill, Frederick Loewe, Burton Lane and André Previn, all with lyrics by Alan Jay Lerner. After undergoing throat surgery in 1997, Andrews was warned to refrain from singing for some considerable time, or risk never again performing in public. By June 1998, she had recovered sufficiently to travel to London in order to record 700 lines of 'dialogue' for Polynesia, the robotic parrot, in the stage version of Leslie Bricusse's musical, *Doctor Dolittle*. During the same visit, she also compered the all-star gala tribute to Cameron Mackintosh, *Hey Mr. Producer!*.

● ALBUMS: *The Boy Friend* Broadway cast (RCA Victor 1954)★★★, *My Fair Lady* Broadway cast (Columbia 1956)★★★★, *Cinderella* film soundtrack (Columbia 1957)★★★, *The Lass With The Delicate Air* (RCA Victor 1957)★★★, *Julie Andrews Sings* (RCA Victor 1958)★★★, *Rose Marie* film soundtrack (RCA Victor 1958)★★★, *Camelot* Broadway cast (Columbia 1960)★★★, *Broadway's Fair Julie* (Columbia 1962)★★★, *Don't Go In The Lion's Cage Tonight* (Columbia 1962)★★★, with Carol Burnett *Julie And Carol At Carnegie Hall* (1962)★★★, *Mary Poppins* film soundtrack (RCA Victor 1964)★★★★, *The Sound Of Music* film soundtrack (RCA 1965)★★★★, *A Christmas Treasure* (1968)★★, *The Secret Of Christmas* (Embassy 1977)★★, *Victor/Victoria* film soundtrack (MGM 1982)★★★, *Love Me Tender* (Peach River 1983)★★, *Julie Andrews And Carol Burnett At The Lincoln Center* (Silva 1989)★★, *Love Julie* (Prestige 1989)★★★, *The King And I* studio cast (Philips 1992)★★, *Broadway: The Music Of Richard Rodgers* (Philips 1994)★★★, *Victor/Victoria* Broadway cast (Philips 1995), *Here I'll Stay* (Philips 1996)★★, *Julie Andrews Sings* (Philips 1997)★★★.
● COMPILATIONS: *The Best Of ...* (Rhino 1996)★★★.
● VIDEOS: *Julie Andrews Greatest Hits* (Castle Music Pictures 1990).
● FURTHER READING: *Life Story Of A Superstar*, John Cottrell. *Julie Andrews*, Robert Windeler. *Julie Andrews*, James Arntz and Thomas S. Wilson.
● FILMS: *Rose Of Baghdad* voice only (1952), *High Tor (television)* (1956), *Mary Poppins* (1964), *The Americanization Of Emily* (1964), *The Sound Of Music* (1965), *Torn Curtain* (1966), *Hawaii* (1966), *Thoroughly Modern Millie* (1967), *Star!* (1968), *Darling Lili* (1969), *The Tamarind Seed* (1974), *10* (1979), *Little Miss Marker* (1980), *S.O.B.* (1981), *Victor/Victoria* (1982), *The Man Who Loved Women* (1983), *Duet For One* (1986), *That's Life!* (1986), *Tchin-Tchin* (1991), *Our Sons (television)* (1991), *A Fine Romance* (1992).

ANIMAL CRACKERS

Before they came to worldwide fame via the Hollywood big screen, the Marx Brothers, Groucho, Chico, Harpo and Zeppo, honed their zany brand of comedy in Broadway musicals. Making their debut in 1924 with *I'll Say She Is*, they followed it a year later with *The Cocoanuts*, and then, into the 44th Street Theatre on 23 October 1928, came *Animal Crackers*. The book, by George S. Kaufman and Morrie Ryskind, has Groucho as the famous explorer Captain Spalding, searching for a stolen picture belonging to the wealthy Mrs. Rittenhouse, played by the Brothers' regular female foil, Margaret Dumont. In amongst the mayhem was a score by Bert Kalmar and Harry Ruby, a total of nine songs, of which the most famous remains 'Hooray For Captain Spalding/Hello, I Must Be Going'. Also present - and pleasant - were 'Who's Been Listening To My Heart?' and 'Long Island Low-Down'. The team's hilarious antics, which involved all manner of costume changes and highly imaginative gags, kept the show running for a creditable 191 performances. The film version, which was one of the highest-grossers of 1930, retained 'Hooray For Captain Spalding', dispensed with most of the rest, and introduced a few others, including 'Why Am I So Romantic?'. Since then, there have been US revivals of the show at Washington's Arena Stage (1982), Boston's Huntington Theater Company (1988) and Goodspeed Opera House, Connecticut (1992). The show also played in England at the Royal Exchange, Manchester, opening in December 1995. All of those productions amended the score in various ways, and interpolated other numbers from different sources.

ANNETTE

b. Annette Funicello, 22 October 1942, Utica, New York, USA. Initially billed as 'Annette', this singer/actress rose to fame under the aegis of the Walt Disney organization. A one-time Mouseketeer - the last of the original group who appeared on *The Mickey Mouse Club* - she enjoyed several hit singles between 1959 and 1961 which included two US Top 10 entries, 'Tall Paul' and 'O Dio Mio', as well as the enduring 'Pineapple Princess'. During the 60s Annette starred alongside Frankie Avalon in a series of 'quickie' beach films, including *Beach Party*, *Bikini Beach* (both 1964) and *How To Stuff A Wild Bikini* (1965), which combined slim plots, teenage themes and cameos from pop stars. *The Monkey's Uncle* (1964) drew its appeal from an appearance by the Beach Boys and musical contributions from their leader, Brian Wilson. The latter assisted songwriter/producer Gary Usher in creating material for *Muscle Beach Party*, Annette's strongest album, which also featured back-up from the all-female group the Honeys. She later appeared in the Monkees' cult film *Head* (1968), but subsequently devoted more time to her growing family, making occasional personal appearances, television commercials, and guest shots in series such as *Hondo*, *Love-American Style*, *Fantasy Island*, *The Love Boat*, *Full House*, and *Frasier*. In 1987 she and Avalon returned to the big screen in *Back To The Beach*, an amusing spoof of their earlier successes together. Five years later, after revealing that she had been fighting multiple sclerosis, the actress formed The Annette Funicello Teddy Bear Company and introduced the perfume 'Cello, by Annette'. A percentage of the profits from the latter line go to the Annette Funicello Research Fund for Neurological Diseases. The tribute programme, *A Dream Is A Wish Your Heart Makes: The Annette Funicello Story*, aired on US television in 1995.
● ALBUMS: *Annette* (Buena Vista 1959)★★, *Songs From Annette And Other Walt Disney Serials* (Mickey Mouse 1959)★, *Annette Sings Anka* (Buena Vista 1960)★, *Italianette* (Buena Vista 1960)★, *Hawaiiannette* (Buena Vista 1960)★, *Dance Annette* (Buena Vista 1961)★, *The Parent Trap* (Buena Vista 1961)★, *Babes In Toyland* (Buena Vista 1961)★, *The Story Of My Teens* (Buena Vista 1962)★, *Teen Street* (Buena Vista 1962)★, *Muscle Beach Party* (Buena Vista 1963)★★★, *Annette's Beach Party* (Buena Vista 1963)★★, *Annette On Campus* (Buena Vista 1964)★, *Annette At Bikini Beach* (Buena Vista 1964)★, *Pajama Party* (Buena Vista 1964)★, *Annette Sings Golden Surfin' Hits*, (Buena Vista 1964)★, *Something Borrowed, Something Blue* (Buena Vista 1964)★, *Walt Disney's Wonderful World Of Color* (Disneyland 1964)★, *The Beast Of Broadway* (Disneyland 1965)★, *Tubby The Tuba And Other Songs About Music* (Disneyland 1966)★, *State And College Songs* (Disneyland 1967)★, *Thunder Alley* (Sidewalk 1967)★, *Annette Funicello* (Buena Vista 1972)★, *Annette: A Musical Reunion With America's Girl Next Door* 2-CD set (Walt Disney 1993)★★★.
● FILMS: *Annette* (1958), *The Shaggy Dog* (1959), *Babes In Toyland* (1961), *Beach Party* (1963), *Pajama Party* (1964), *Muscle Beach Party* (1964), *Bikini Beach* (1964), *The Misadventures Of Merlin Jones* (1964), *How To Stuff A Wild Bikini* (1965), *Beach Blanket Bingo* (1965), *Ski Party* cameo (1965), *Dr. Goldfoot And The Bikini*

Machine guest (1965), *The Monkey's Uncle* (1965), *Fireball 500* (1966), *Thunder Alley* (1967), *Head* (1968), *Back To The Beach* (1987), *Troop Beverly Hills* as herself (1989).

ANNIE (FILM MUSICAL)

Adapted from the smash-hit Broadway musical which opened in 1977 and ran for over 2,000 performances, this screen version, which cost over $50 million to produce, differed in several respects from Thomas Meehan's Broadway libretto and its original source, Harold Gray's comic strip, 'Little Orphan Annie'. However, the screenplay by Carol Sobieski is still set in 1933 New York, when, after visiting his house, Annie (Aileen Quinn) is adopted by the millionaire industrialist Oliver 'Daddy' Warbucks (Albert Finney), aided by his secretary Grace Farrell (Anne Reinking). Unfortunately, Annie and her dog Sandy come up against the terrible trio of tipsy and callous orphanage manager Miss Hannigan (Carol Burnett), her scheming brother Rooster (Tim Curry), and Lily (Bernadette Peters), who have their own get-rich quick scheme. Also cast were Geoffrey Holder, Roger Minami, Toni Ann Gisondi, Rosanne Sorrentino, Lara Berk, April Lerman, Robin Ignico, Lucie Stewart, Edward Herrman as FDR. Several of the Charles Strouse and Martin Charnin songs from their original score were dropped, and new ones written. Among those retained were the show's big hit, 'Tomorrow', along with 'It's The Hard-Knock Life', 'Maybe', 'Easy Street', 'Little Girls', 'I Think I'm Gonna Like It Here', 'You're Never Fully Dressed Without A Smile', and 'I Don't Need Anything But You'. The choreographer was Arlene Phillips, and John Huston directed this Columbia picture which was photographed in Metrocolor and Panavision, and released in 1982. With $38 million in box office takings, it was second highest-grossing movie of the 80s in North America after *The Best Whorehouse In Town* (not counting Walt Disney animated features). Those figures put it ahead of *Dirty Dancing*, *Flashdance* or *Footloose*.

ANNIE (STAGE MUSICAL)

The events surrounding the chequered history of the making of *Annie*, the fourth biggest Broadway hit musical of the 70s, and its 90s sequel, *Annie Warbucks*, could probably form the basis of a dramatic production capable of winning a Pulitzer Prize. The lyricist and director Martin Charnin is credited with the idea of producing a musical show based on the famous US comic strip *Little Orphan Annie*. That was in 1971, but it was over five years later, on 21 April 1977, when *Annie* opened at the Alvin Theatre on Broadway. As his composer and librettist Charnin recruited Charles Strouse and Thomas Meehan. The basic concept of the show did not immediately appeal to producers or financiers, and so it was not until it was presented at the Goodspeed Opera House, Connecticut, in the summer of 1976 (at which point producer Mike Nicholls came on board) that the *Annie* bandwagon began to roll, and a Broadway opening became a feasible proposition. The story, set in 1933, concerns the orphan Annie (Andrea McCardle) and her dog Sandy. She is trying desperately to find her parents, so that she can escape the clutches of

Miss Hannigan (Dorothy Loudon), the orphanage's hard-hearted matron. In line with the show's 'greasepaint sentimentality' and 'unabashed corniness', Annie is eventually adopted by the millionaire industrialist Oliver 'Daddy' Warbucks (Reid Shelton), partly through the good offices of his friend, President Roosevelt (Raymond Thorne), whom Annie serenades with the perhaps over-optimistic 'Tomorrow', a song that apparently helps the President to work out his economic policy, and also ensures 'A New Deal For Christmas'. The other numbers, which contributed to an enormous Broadway hit, and a run of 2377 performances, included 'I Don't Need Anything But You', 'I Think I'm Gonna Like It Here', 'It's The Hard-Knock Life', 'Little Girls', 'You're Never Fully Dressed Without A Smile', 'Easy Street' and 'Maybe'. It all ended happily, if a little confusingly: Annie can finally be adopted because her parents are 'no longer with us', and the conniving Miss Hannigan is arrested for fraud. The show won several Tony Awards, including best score and best musical. In 1978, the prominent UK television actor Stratford Johns played Daddy Warbucks in a successful London production, and there was a West End revival in 1982. In the same year a film version of *Annie* was released, with Albert Finney as Warbucks and Aileen Quinn as Annie.

In January 1990, a sequel to *Annie*, entitled *Annie 2: Miss Hannigan's Revenge*, opened at the Kennedy Center Opera House in Washington, DC. During the next three years, with the constant and passionate co-operation of producer Karen Walter Goodwin, Charnin, Strouse and Meehan undertook extensive rewrites, and, with a revised title, *Annie Warbucks*, spent some time in Chicago, and toured theatres in Texas and west coast cities such as Los Angeles, Pasadena and San Diego. A Broadway opening was set for December 1992, postponed until March, and then April. Finally, with new producers on board, the show was slimmed down from a $5.5 million Broadway high-risk operation, to an adventurous $1 million production that opened - with its third Annie in three years - off-Broadway at the Variety Arts Theatre on 9 August 1993. (A weary Martin Charnin said: 'This is the ninth time I have put this mother into rehearsal.') Onstage, the time is Christmas morning, and the woman from the welfare, Commissioner Harriet Doyle (Arlene Robertson), is insisting that Daddy Warbucks (Harve Presnell) find a wife within 60 days or Annie (Kathryn Zaremba) has to return to the orphanage. The ideal candidate seems to be Daddy's Chinese secretary, Grace (Marguerite MacIntyre) ('That's The Kind Of Woman'), but he thinks that she is far too young, and favours the more mature Sheila Kelly (Donna McKechnie) ('A Younger Man'), who, we all know some time before the predictable ending, does not even stand a chance. The rest of the score included 'Annie Ain't Just Annie Any More', 'The Other Woman', 'Above The Law', 'I Got Me', 'Changes', 'Love', the jivey 'All Dolled Up', a touching tale of unrequited love, 'It Would Have Been Wonderful', and 'I Always Knew' (which was really 'Tomorrow' Mark II). The show will never be another *Annie*, but even so, as one critic pointed out, 'Charnin, Strouse, and Meehan can now get on with the rest of their lives.' It was not to be, and Charnin directed a 20th anniversary Broadway production of *Annie* in 1997. It starred Brittny Kissinger (Annie), Nell Carter (Miss Hannigan), Conrad John Schuck (Oliver Warbucks) and Colleen Dunn (Grace Farrell), and ran for nearly seven months before touring. He also helmed the 1998 West End revival, which had the popular television sitcom actress Lesley Joseph as Miss Hannigan, along with Kevin Colson (Warbucks), Kate Normington (Grace), and Charlene Barton/Sophie McShera (Annie). When Lesley Joseph went off to appear in Christmas pantomime, the role of Miss Hannigan was played by the popular Liverpudlian drag queen, Lily Savage. A rap version of one of the show's most popular numbers, 'It's The Hard-Knock Life' by Jay-Z went to number 2 in the UK chart.

ANNIE GET YOUR GUN (FILM MUSICAL)

Like many other films boasting Irving Berlin scores, *Annie Get Your Gun* is rarely seen nowadays, owing to the composer's original financial demands over any performance or broadcasting of his work. The film was released in 1950, five years after Ethel Merman's triumphant opening night in the original Broadway show. Unlike many other Broadway-to-Hollywood transfers, *Annie Get Your Gun*'s screen debut for MGM was generally regarded as being highly faithful to the stage show. Judy Garland was the first choice to play the lead, but a recurrence of the latter's personal problems gave Betty Hutton the best role of her career. She played sharpshooter Annie Oakley, who deliberately loses a shooting match with her rival, Frank Butler (Howard Keel), so that he will not consider her a threat to his masculinity, and they can be married. Naturally, this scenario took place long before the rise of feminism, in the days when men were men, and women were expected to be grateful. Although he had made a previous screen appearance in the UK while appearing in the West End in *Oklahoma!*, this was Keel's first Hollywood musical and he was in fine voice, giving an impressive performance. Among the rest of the cast were Louis Calhern (Buffalo Bill), J. Carrol Naish (Sitting Bull), Keenan Wynn, Edward Arnold and Benay Venuta. Berlin's superb stage score survived practically intact in its screen incarnation, the main casualty being the lovely ballad 'Moonshine Lullaby'. All the major hits were present, including 'Doin' What Comes Natur'lly', 'I Got The Sun In The Morning', 'You Can't Get A Man With A Gun', 'The Girl That I Marry', 'They Say It's Wonderful', 'My Defenses Are Down', 'Anything You Can Do', along with Hutton's highly amusing 'I'm An Indian, Too', and the rousing 'There's No Business Like Show Business'. *Annie Get Your Gun* was photographed in Technicolor and directed by George Sidney, with choreography by Robert Alton. It was the top musical money-spinner of 1950, and won Academy Awards for 'scoring of a musical picture' for Adolph Deutsch and Roger Edens.

ANNIE GET YOUR GUN (STAGE MUSICAL)

When *Annie Get Your Gun* opened at the Imperial Theatre in New York on 16 May 1946, it was to a changed Broadway. The old-fashioned style of musical comedy had been overtaken by the massive successes of *Oklahoma!* in 1943 and *Carousel* in 1945. Set in the 1880s, Herbert and Dorothy Fields's book, tells of the rivalry between sharpshooters Annie Oakley (Ethel Merman) and Frank Butler (Ray Middleton) - who kinda like each other - in the Wild West Show owned and operated by Buffalo Bill Cody (William O'Neal). Frank does not take it too well when a female (especially one that shoots like *that*) muscles in on the action. So he hightails it to another outfit, but that solves nothing. The reunion comes when wise old Chief Sitting Bull (Harry Bellaver) points out to Annie that if she is really clever she can still win the man by losing the head to head shooting match. Also involved in the action were Marty May (Charlie Davenport), Kenny Bowers (Tommy Keeler), Betty Anne Nyman (Winnie Tate), and Lea Penman (Dolly Tate). Merman, who was marvellous, had her share of Irving Berlin's magnificent score, including 'Doin' What Comes Natur'lly', 'You Can't Get A Man With A Gun', 'Who Do You Love, I Hope', I'm An Indian Too', 'Moonshine Lullaby', 'Lost In His Arms', 'I Got The Sun In The Morning', and, with Middleton, 'They Say It's Wonderful', and 'Anything You Can Do'. Middleton excelled with 'I'm A Bad, Bad Man', 'The Girl That I Marry', and 'My Defences Are Down'. The ensemble first act finalé, 'There's No Business Like Show Business', immediately achieved anthem status. The show was directed by Joshua Logan, and Helen Tamiris was the choreographer. Richard Rodgers and Oscar Hammerstein II produced it, and *Annie Get Your Gun* ran for 1,147 performances on Broadway. The 1947 London Coliseum production with Dolores Gray (Annie), Bill Johnson (Frank), Ellis Irving (Buffalo Bill), Wendy Toye (Winnie), and Irving Davies (Tommy), lasted even longer (1,304). Mary Martin and Earl Covert headed the 1947 US road tour. Merman reprised her original role for a 1966 Music Theatre of Lincoln Center production, along with Bruce Yarnell (Frank), Rufus Smith (Buffalo Bill), Jerry Orbach (Charlie), and the 1946 Chief Sitting Bull (Harry Bellaver). Berlin gave Annie and Frank a nice new song, 'Old Fashioned Wedding', and the show toured and called in briefly at the Broadway Theatre. Other sightings of *Annie ...* in the USA, have included one at the Paper Mill Playhouse (1987, Judy Kaye and Richard White), and a Houston Grand Opera presentation (1992, Cathy Rigby and Michael DeVries). West End audiences saw a Chichester Festival production in 1986, with glam rock singer Suzi Quatro as Annie, Eric Flynn (Frank), Edmund Hockridge (Buffalo Bill), and another created by the Theatre Royal, Plymouth (1992), Kim Criswell (Annie), John Diedrich (Frank), Brian Glover (Chief Sitting Bull), Norman Rossington (Charlie), Mel Cobb (Pawnee Bill), and Meg Johnson (Dolly). The Lincoln Center hosted the show again, at its Vivian Beamont Theatre, in March 1998 - but for one performance only. Patti LuPone and Peter Gallagher, were Annie and Frank, with Eli Wallach as Chief Sitting Bull. A potentially fascinating production of *Annie Get Your Gun* began its journey to Broadway late in 1998, with Bernadette Peters in the title role.

ANYONE CAN WHISTLE

A celebrated flop, all the more so because it was the second complete Broadway score to be written by Stephen Sondheim, following on from his smash-hit *A Funny Thing*

Happened On The Way To The Forum (1962). *Anyone Can Whistle* opened at the Majestic Theatre on 4 April 1964, and closed nine performances later. Subtitled 'A Wild New Musical', it had a book by Arthur Laurents, who also directed. Laurents had previously worked with Sondheim on the librettos of the enormously successful *West Side Story* and *Gypsy*. This time his story was not nearly so clear-cut - in fact, it was downright confused and eccentric. Cora (Angela Lansbury) is the mayoress of a small town whose corrupt council creates a phoney miracle - a non-stop flow of water from a rock - to attract tourists. However, a group of inmates from the Cookie Jar, the local mental institution, mix with the visiting tourists, so that nobody knows which is which. Nurse Fay Apple (Lee Remick) becomes romantically attached to Dr. Hapgood (Harry Guardino), who turns out to be another 'cookie'. When Sondheim's score was detached from the weird goings-on in the theatre, and heard on the Original Cast album, which was recorded on the day after the show closed, it proved to be one of his most appealing, and included songs such as 'A Parade In Town', 'Come Play Wiz Me', 'Everybody Says Don't', 'I've Got You To Lean On', 'See What It Gets You', 'With So Little To Be Sure Of' and 'Anyone Can Whistle'. The vinyl album became a highly priced cult item until the advent of the CD. A 1995 concert staging at Carnegie Hall, starring Angela Lansbury, Scott Bakula, Madeline Kahn, and Bernadette Peters, resulted in a companion recording being issued. Three years earlier, *Anyone Can Whistle* was mounted off-off-Broadway at the 47th Street Theatre, featuring Margery Beddow, Chris Innvar, Wendy Oliver, Mark Enis, Jim Fitzpatrick, and Joseph Gram. The show had what was claimed to be its British premiere in 1986 at the Everyman Theatre in Cheltenham (Pip Hinton as Cora, Marilyn Cutts as Fay). London audiences saw it for the first time, in a concert version, on 1 June 1997 at the Savoy Theatre, with Jenny Logan (Cora), Linzi Hately (Fay), Simon Green (Hapgood), and Stephanie Beecham (Narrator).

ANYTHING GOES (FILM MUSICAL)
In 1936, two years after the original show opened on Broadway, Paramount released this reasonably faithful screen version. Ethel Merman recreated her stage role as nightclub singer Reno Sweeney, whose friend, Billy Crocker (Bing Crosby), stows away on an ocean liner so that he can be close to his beloved Hope Harcourt (Ida Lupino). After the inevitable complications, which involve a Reverend (Charlie Ruggles) - who is really America's Public Enemy No. 13 - everyone is paired off satisfactorily, including Reno herself who bags a member of the English aristocracy. The majority of Cole Porter's songs from the stage production were axed, but fortunately three of the survivors, 'Anything Goes', 'I Get A Kick Out Of You', and 'You're The Top', were Merman specialities. The numbers that were added included 'Shanghai-Di-Ho', 'My Heart And I', 'Hopelessly In Love' (all written by Frederick Hollander and Leo Robin) and 'Sailor Beware' (Richard Whiting-Leo Robin), and the engaging 'Moonburn' by Hoagy Carmichael and Edward Heyman, which was smoothly delivered by Crosby. Howard

Lindsay, Russel Crouse and Guy Bolton adapted the screenplay from their original libretto, which was written in collaboration with P.G. Wodehouse, and the film was directed by Lewis Milestone. When *Anything Goes* was remade in Technicolor by Paramount 20 years later, Crosby was retained, and in Sidney Sheldon's new story, he and Donald O'Connor went on a talent-spotting cruise and came back with Mitzi Gaynor and Jeanmaire - which was not a bad result. The musical aspect was pretty satisfying too, with Sammy Cahn and Jimmy Van Heusen supplementing Porter's score with three numbers, 'You Can Bounce Right Back', 'You Gotta Give The People Hoke', and 'A Second-Hand Turban And A Crystal Ball'. Phil Harris, who is always worth seeing, was also in the cast, and the film was choreographed by Nick Castle and Roland Petit, and directed by Robert Lewis.

ANYTHING GOES (STAGE MUSICAL)
Regarded as the show that confirmed Ethel Merman as a Broadway star, *Anything Goes* was originally the brainchild of P.G. Wodehouse and Guy Bolton, but their book, which set the show around a shipwreck at sea, was hastily revised by Howard Lindsay and Russell Crouse prior to the show's Broadway opening on 21 November 1934, following the sinking of the *S.S. Morro Castle* a few weeks earlier. However, Wodehouse's influence is apparent in the 'goofy shipboard plot of intersecting romances', involving a hard-bitten nightclub singer, Reno Sweeney (Ethel Merman), and her friend, Billy Crocker (William Gaxton) who stows away on the liner so that he can be near his latest love, the debutante Hope Harcourt (Bettina Hall). Much of the comedy is provided by a 'toothy British milord', a 'bogus debutante', a 'boozy Manhattan tycoon', and the accident-prone Moonface Martin (Victor Moore), a small-time gangster masquerading as a minister of religion, who is intent on becoming America's Public Enemy No. 1, but cannot even make it into the Top 10. Cole Porter's outstanding score gave Merman four numbers that became forever associated with her: 'I Get A Kick Out Of You', 'Blow, Gabriel, Blow', one of Porter's wittiest 'catalogue' or 'list' songs, 'You're The Top' (a duet with Gaxton), and 'Anything Goes' ('If fast cars you like/If low bars you like/If old hymns you like/If bare limbs you like/If Mae West you like/Or me undressed you like/Why, nobody will oppose'). There was also a charming ballad, 'All Through The Night', which became a hit outside the show for Paul Whiteman. *Anything Goes* played 420 performances in New York, a substantial run for the 30s, and did well in London, too, where Reno Sweeney's name was changed to Reno Lagrange when she was played by the French actress Jeanne Aubert. In 1936, a film version starred Merman and Bing Crosby, and Crosby was present again, 20 years later, when Hollywood tried once more to capture the magic of the original show. Stage revivals abounded. The 1962 New York version was reasonably successful, while the 1969 London production, starring jazz singer Marian Montgomery, was a flop. The most satisfying revival was mounted in 1987 by the Lincoln Center Theatre, with a new book by Timothy Crouse and John Weidman, and a score that was augmented by several other classic Porter songs, such as 'It's

De-Lovely', 'Easy To Love' and 'Friendship'. Directed by Jerry Zaks and brilliantly choreographed by Michael Smuin, the new production starred Patti LuPone, who excelled in the role of Reno, with Howard McGillin as Billy Crocker. *Anything Goes* won three Tony Awards including 'best revival', and ran until September 1989, a total of nearly 800 performances. McGillin reprised his role when the Lincoln Center production transferred to London, with Elaine Paige as Reno, and the popular British actor Bernard Cribbins as Moonface. Paige, together with the lyricist Tim Rice, was instrumental in mounting the show in the West End. In the early 90s, over 50 years after Reno Sweeney changed her name and her nationality for the 1935 London production, a further (gender) change became necessary for Reno in the all-male, gay production of *Anything Goes*, which played several US venues before the performance rights were withdrawn.

APPLAUSE

Adapted by Betty Comden and Adolph Green from Mary Orr's short story *The Wisdom Of Eve*, and the highly acclaimed 1950 movie *All About Eve*, *Applause* marked the Broadway musical debut of the celebrated film star, Lauren Bacall. Her performance as Margo Channing, the ghastly, ageing stage actress, who somehow allows her life and her lover, Bill Sampson (Len Cariou), to be taken over by an adoring young fan, Eve Harrington (Penny Fuller), won Bacall a great deal of applause from the critics and public alike, following its opening at New York's Palace Theatre on 30 March 1970. The score, by Charles Strouse and Lee Adams, was not generally considered to be one of their best, and included 'Who's That Girl?', 'Fasten Your Seatbelts', 'Think How It's Gonna Be', 'But Alive', 'One Of A Kind', 'Welcome To The Theatre', 'Backstage Babble', 'She's No Longer A Gypsy', 'The Best Night Of My Life', 'Hurry Back', 'Inner Thoughts', 'Good Friends', 'One Hallow'een', 'Something Greater', and 'Applause', a rousing production number somewhat akin to 'There's No Business Like Show Business'. The show won Tony Awards for best musical, and for its director and choreographer, Ron Field, and ran for 896 performances. During the run, Lauren Bacall was succeeded by two other movie stars, Anne Baxter, who had played Eve Harrington in the movie, and Arlene Dahl. Bacall recreated her role in London in 1972, with Angela Richards (Eve) and Ken Walsh (Bill), where *Applause* ran for nearly a year. In 1996, a Broadway-bound Paper Mill Playhouse production of *Applause*, starring Stephanie Powers, closed on the road.

APPLE TREE, THE

An unconventional show, consisting of three one-act musical plays, *The Apple Tree* opened at the Shubert Theatre in New York on 18 October 1966. The cast included Barbara Harris, Larry Blyden, Carmen Alvarez, Robert Klein, Marc Jordan, and Alan Alda - several years before he made an enormous impact in the television series *M.A.S.H.* In Act I of *The Apple Tree*, Alda played the part of Adam in an adaptation of Mark Twain's *The Diary Of Adam And Eve*. In Act II, which was based on Frank R. Stockton's story *The Lady Or The Tiger*, he took the role of the brave Captain Sanjar, who, after being caught in an

ungentlemanly amorous situation with a Princess (Barbara Harris), is required to go through one of two doors - to greet the 'lady' or the 'tiger'. The third act was taken from Jules Feiffer's fantasy, *Passionella*, the tale of a poor little chimney sweep (Harris), who dreams she is a big movie star, and marries Flip (Alda), a hip-swivelling rock 'n' roll sensation, in a spectacular sequence directed by Mike Nicholls, making his Broadway musical debut. Jerry Bock and Sheldon Harnick wrote the score, and collaborated with Jerome Coopersmith on the book. The songs included 'The Apple Tree', 'Here In Eden', 'Eve', 'Lullaby (Go to Sleep, Whatever You Are)', 'Beautiful, Beautiful World', 'Oh, To Be A Movie Star', 'Which Door?', 'Gorgeous', 'Fish', 'What Makes Me Love Him?' and 'I've Got What You Want'. Barbara Harris won the 1967 Tony Award for best actress, and *The Apple Tree* ran for over a year, a total of 463 performances.

APPLESAUCE!

This (eventually) popular wartime George Black revue opened at the Holborn Empire, the home of variety, on 27 August 1940. A report at the time claimed that the show was only called a revue because one of its stars, Max Miller (b. 1895, d. 1963), was not allowed to appear in 'those gloriously clashing and bounderish colours' until the very end. In the meantime, Miller wore the uniform of the Home Guard and also dressed in evening clothes - which must have a been a sight to see. His co-stars, who included Doris Hare, Jack Stanford, Jean Carr, the Saucelets group, and the brand new 'forces sweetheart', Vera Lynn, combined in a fast-moving, bright and breezy show. Jean Carr later changed her name to Jean Kent, and went on to become one of Britain's favourite film stars. The music and lyrics were by Michael Carr and Jack Strachey *et al*, and among their appealing songs were 'Mademoiselle L'Amour' and 'Cheerio' (Carr-Westgarth-Kitchen). No doubt because Londoners were experiencing their first taste of the Blitz at the time, despite favourable reviews *Applesauce!* closed after only three weeks. It reopened on 5 March 1941 at the London Palladium, when the impressionist Florence Desmond (George Black's original choice for the female lead at the Holborn Empire) replaced Doris Hare, and the production ran for 10 months.

ARC DE TRIOMPHE

Ivor Novello and Mary Ellis, two of the West End's brightest stars of the 30s and 40s, were reunited in this show for the first time since *The Dancing Years* (1939). *Arc De Triomphe*, set in the early 1900s, opened at London's Phoenix Theatre on 9 November 1943. With Novello's book and music, and Christopher Hassall's lyrics, Ellis was cast as a French opera singer, Marie Forêt, whose progress through a tormented and dramatic plot, leading to her eventual elevation as a great prima donna, involved her in repelling the advances of the impresario, Adhémar Janze (Raymond Lovell), in favour of an on/off love affair with a struggling cabaret performer, Pierre Bachelet (Peter Graves), who was later killed in World War I. The climax of the piece was a one-act opera, *Joan Of Arc*, which gave Mary Ellis the opportunity to prove what a magnificent actress and singer she was. Elisabeth Welch, another favourite of Novello's, sang 'Dark Music', and the rest of the score, which was not considered by the critics to be out of Novello's top drawer, included 'Easy To Live With', 'The Shepherd's Song', 'Paris Reminds Me Of You', 'Waking Or Sleeping', 'Man Of My Heart' and 'France Will Rise Again', which received a rousing treatment from Ellis. Unable to secure the Adelphi Theatre because a smash-hit revival of *The Dancing Years*, in which he himself was appearing, was still in residence, Novello opted to present *Arc De Triomphe* at the Phoenix, where the stage was too small, and the production suffered. The show closed in May 1944 after a run of 222 performances.

ARCADIANS, THE

There has probably never been a more appropriate subtitle for a show than the one accorded *The Arcadians*: 'A Fantastic Musical Play' sums it up perfectly. One reason for its durability and continued popularity may well be that audiences are constantly returning in the hope of furthering their understanding of the extremely complicated plot. On the other hand, they may be luxuriating in the delightful and tuneful score, with music by Lionel Monkton and Howard Talbot, and lyrics by Arthur Wimperis. *The Arcadians* opened at the Shaftesbury Theatre in London on 28 April 1909, and the diabolical plot was the work of librettists Mark Ambient and Alexander M. Thompson. According to them, the peaceful community of Arcady, which has been forgotten by Old Father Time, is shattered when an aeroplane, which they think is a serpent, lands in their midst. The pilot, James Smith (Dan Rolyat), who thinks he is in the Garden of Eden, tells a lie (lying is not tolerated in Arcady), so he is dropped into the Well of Truth and emerges as the shepherd, Simplicitas. He and the lovely Sombra (Florence Smithson) travel to London where, since his transformation, he is no longer recognized, so he opens a restaurant with his former business partner's wife. And that is only a very small part of the story. In Act 2 there is a scene at the Askwood race track in which the fashionable spectators look through their binoculars at imaginary horses. A similar scene was created more than 40 years later by Alan Jay Lerner in *My Fair Lady*, although he did not arrange to bring the winning horse on stage, as producer Robert Courtneidge did for *The Arcadians*. The show had a truly memorable score, and was full of engaging songs such as 'The Pipes Of Pan', 'The Joy Of Life' and 'Arcadia Is Ever Young', all sung by Florence Smithson; 'The Girl With The Brogue' (Phyllis Dare), 'Charming Weather' and 'Half Past Two' (Phyllis Dare and Harry Welchman), 'Somewhere' (Dan Rolyat), and 'My Motter', which is sung in typically gloomy fashion by Alfred Lister. Another important song, 'All Down Piccadilly', was added at a later date, and became an accepted part of the score. *The Arcadians* became hugely popular in Edwardian London, and enjoyed an incredible run of 809 performances. Robert Courtneidge's daughter, Cicely Courtneidge, was in the cast for a time, and, some years later, starred with her husband, Jack Hulbert, in one of the many revivals of the show. An American production played at the Liberty Theatre in New York for 193 performances during the

early part of 1910, and a silent film version was released in 1927. In 1993, a CD containing a comprehensive recording of the complete score, first issued in 1968, was released in the UK, along with several tracks that were actually performed by members of the original cast.

ARE YOU LONESOME TONIGHT?

Alan Bleasdale's 'allegory-biography' of Elvis Presley, directed by Roger Lefévre, opened on 13 August 1985 at London's Phoenix Theatre, with the sight of the King's coffin being placed into the back of a hearse, closely attended in death (as in life) by his manager, Colonel Tom Parker (Roger Booth), who was clutching a Presley doll. This was seen by some as an attempt by Bleasdale to symbolize the singer as a working-class hero who was shamelessly exploited during his life, and to 'redress the balance' following the 'muck-raking biographies' that appeared following Presley's death in 1977. The stage set, designed by Voytek, and built on three levels, was dominated by an enormous floral guitar and foil-wrapped Cadillac radiators. Upstairs, the young Presley (Simon Bowman), gave an electric performance, and 'scaled the pelvic heights of "Jailhouse Rock" and "Hound Dog"', while disaffected roadies and other former aides dished the dirt to the gentlemen of the press. Downstairs, Martin Shaw, complete with purple jump-suit and protective shades, portrayed 'the bloated former idol, laden with obscene breakfasts', as a self-mocking, yet still sensually arrogant, wreck. The show's high spots were inevitably the spectacular set-pieces featuring Presley's imperishable hits, such as 'Blue Suede Shoes', 'All Shook Up', 'One Night With You', and many more. *Are You Lonesome Tonight?* was voted the best musical of 1985 in the Evening Standard Drama Awards, and ran until July 1986, a total of 354 performances.

ARLEN, HAROLD

b. Hyman Arluck, 15 February 1905, Buffalo, New York, USA, d. 23 April 1986, New York, USA. Acknowledged as one of the all-time great composers, Arlen was the son of a cantor and sang in his father's synagogue. However, he was soon playing ragtime piano in local bands and accompanying silent pictures. In the early 20s he played and arranged for the Buffalodians band, then in 1925 shook off small-town connections when he took a job in New York City, arranging for Fletcher Henderson, and working in radio and theatre as a rehearsal pianist. Indeed, one of his first compositions began as a rehearsal vamp, and was developed into 'Get Happy', with a lyric by Ted Koehler. Ruth Etting introduced it in the flop *9:15 Revue* in 1930. Arlen was soon composing songs regularly, and collaborated with Koehler on several Harlem Cotton Club revues, one of which included 'Stormy Weather'. Ethel Waters elevated that song into an American classic. Among Arlen and Koehler's other early 30s Cotton Club hits were 'Between The Devil And The Deep Blue Sea', sung by Aida Ward, 'I've Got The World On A String' and 'As Long As I Live', which was introduced by the 17-year-old Lena Horne with Avon Long. After contributing to Broadway shows such as *Earl Carroll's Vanities* ('I Gotta Right To Sing The Blues'), *You Said It*, *George White's Music Hall Varieties* and *Americana*, Arlen joined forces with E.Y. 'Yip'

Harburg and Ira Gershwin to write songs for the 1934 revue *Life Begins At 8:40*, which starred Ray Bolger, Bert Lahr, and Luella Gear. These included 'You're A Builder-Upper', 'Let's Take A Walk Around The Block', 'What Can You Say In A Love Song?' and 'Fun To Be Fooled'. Harburg was Arlen's lyricist in 1937 for the composer's first 'book' show, a vehicle for comedian Ed Wynn, entitled *Hooray For What!* ('Moanin' In The Mornin'', 'Down With Love', 'God's Country' and 'In the Shade Of The New Apple Tree'). After spending several years in Hollywood writing for films, Arlen returned to Broadway in 1944, and teamed with Harburg again for *Bloomer Girl*. Their splendid score included 'The Eagle And Me', 'I Got A Song', 'Right As Rain' and 'Evelina'. Two years later, Arlen worked again with Johnny Mercer on the all-black musical *St. Louis Woman*, which resulted in two enduring standards, 'Come Rain Or Come Shine' and 'Anyplace I Hang My Hat Is Home'. During the 50s, Arlen composed the music for three more Broadway musicals: *House Of Flowers* ('Two Ladies In De Shade Of De Banana Tree', 'A Sleepin' Bee'), for which he also co-wrote the lyrics with author Truman Capote; *Jamaica* (with Harburg, 'Take It Slow, Joe', 'Ain't It The Truth?', 'Push The Button', 'Incompatibility'); and the least successful of the trio, *Saratoga* (with Johnny Mercer, 'A Game Of Poker', 'Love Held Lightly', 'Dog Eat Dog' and 'Goose Never Be A Peacock'). In between, and in parallel with his work for Broadway, Arlen wrote prolifically for the screen. After composing 'Long Before You Came Along' (with Harburg) for *Rio Rita* in 1929, during the 30s he contributed complete scores or occasional songs to movies such as *Take A Chance* ('It's Only A Paper Moon'), *Let's Fall In Love* ('Love Is Love Anywhere', 'As Long As I Live', title song), *The Singing Kid* ('You're The Cure For What Ails Me'), *Stage Struck* ('Fancy Meeting You', 'In Your Own Quiet Way'), *Strike Me Pink* ('Shake It Off With Rhythm', 'The Lady Dances'), *Artists And Models* ('Public Melody Number One'), *Gold Diggers Of 1937* ('Let's Put Our Heads Together'), *The Marx Brothers At The Circus* ('Lydia, The Tattooed Lady'), *Love Affair* ('Sing, My Heart'), and *The Wizard Of Oz*. This film, which starred Judy Garland, is one of the most beloved in the history of the cinema, and Arlen and Harburg's memorable numbers included the immortal 'Over The Rainbow', 'Ding Dong, The Witch Is Dead' and 'We're Off To See The Wizard'. Arlen's songs continued to be featured throughout the 40s and into the early 50s in films such as *Blues In The Night* ('This Time The Dream's On Me' and the superb title number), *Star Spangled Rhythm* ('That Old Black Magic', 'Hit The Road To Dreamland'), *The Sky's The Limit* ('One For My Baby', 'My Shining Hour'), *Cabin In The Sky* ('Happiness Is Just A Thing Called Joe'), *Here Comes The Waves* ('Accent-Tchu-Ate The Positive', 'Let's Take The Long Way Home'), *Up In Arms* ('Tessa's Torch Song'), *Out Of This World* ('I'd Rather Be Me', title song), *Casbah* ('What's Good About Goodbye?', 'For Every Man There's A Woman', 'It Was Written In The Stars'), *My Blue Heaven* ('Don't Rock The Boat, Dear', 'The Friendly Islands'), *Mr. Imperium* ('Let Me Look At You') and *The Country Girl* ('Live And Learn'). In 1954, Arlen, with Ira Gershwin, was associated with another of the cinema's most treasured movies, and once again it starred Judy Garland. For the remake of *A Star Is Born*, the two men wrote what is considered to be the ultimate 'torch' song, 'The Man That Got Away', along with 'Gotta Have Me Go With You', 'It's A New World', and 'Someone At Last (Somewhere There's A Someone)'. It was a fitting climax to the Hollywood phase of Arlen's career, although he did provide songs such as 'Mewsette', 'Little Drops Of Rain' and 'Paris Is A Lonely Town' for the delightful 1962 cartoon, *Gay Purr-ee*. Many of the above songs, written with collaborators such as Lew Brown, Leo Robin, Dorothy Fields and Jack Yellen, as well as the other distinguished lyricists already mentioned, are among the most cherished in the history of American popular music. They have been consistently recorded by all the leading artists, and the composer also made the occasional record himself, playing the piano and singing with artists such as Duke Ellington and Barbra Streisand. He also had hits in the early 30s with his own 'Little Girl', 'Stormy Weather', 'Let's Fall In Love', 'Ill Wind' and 'You're A Builder-Upper'. Over the years, many tributes have been paid to him, and in 1993 a revue entitled *Sweet And Hot: The Songs Of Harold Arlen*, devised and directed by Julianne Boyd, was circulating in the USA.

● ALBUMS: *Harold Sings Arlen (With Friend)* (Vox Cum Lande 1966)★★, *Harold Arlen In Hollywood* (Monmouth 1979)★★, *Harold Sings Arlen* (CBS Cameo 1983)★★.

● FURTHER READING: *Harold Arlen-Happy With The Blues*, Edward Jablonski.

ARNDT, FELIX

b. 20 May 1889, New York, USA, d. 16 October 1918, Harmon-On-Hudson, New York, USA. A composer, pianist, and organist, Arndt attended the New York Conservatory before working for various music publishers and leading his own ensembles. He also made numerous piano rolls for the large Aeolian Company, which had several different labels. He was instrumental in encouraging other composers such as George Gershwin and Vincent Youmans to make rolls for the firm. Arndt's most famous composition, 'Nola' (1915, lyric: James F. Burns), was named after his singer-composer wife, and became the theme song of Vincent Lopez. His orchestra performed it in *The Big Broadcast* (1932), and the number was also featured on the screen in the Jack Oakie starrer *That's The Spirit* (1945). Among Arndt's other compositions were 'Soup To Nuts', 'Toots', 'Kakuda', 'Marionette', 'Love In June' and 'Operatic Nightmare'.

ARNOLD, MALCOLM

b. 21 October 1921, Northampton, England. A composer, conductor, arranger and trumpet player, Arnold became aware of music at the age of four, and taught himself to play trumpet - his inspiration was Louis Armstrong. He began his career in 1941 as an instrumentalist with the London Philharmonic Orchestra, and returned to the orchestra in 1946 after brief service in World War II, and a spell with the BBC Symphony Orchestra. During these times he was also composing; one of his best-known pieces, 'Sea Shanties', was written in 1943. He became a full-time composer in the early 50s, and soon won much critical acclaim as 'one of the great hopes of British music'. His work schedule was exhausting; from 1951-56 he is said to have written the music for over 70 films, as well as three operas, ballet music, concertos and other classical and light works. One of his more unusual compositions was the 'Grand Overture' for a Gerald Hoffnung concert, in which the more conventional instruments of the orchestra were augmented by three vacuum cleaners and an electric polisher. His film scores, many of which complemented classic British productions, include *The Sound Barrier* (1952), *The Holly And The Ivy*, *The Captain's Paradise*, *Hobson's Choice*, *Prize Of Gold*, *I Am A Camera*, *Trapeze*, *Tiger In The Smoke*, *The Deep Blue Sea*, *Island In The Sun*, *The Bridge On The River Kwai* (one of the film's six Oscars went to Arnold), *Blue Murder At St. Trinians*, *The Inn Of The Sixth Happiness* (the film theme won an Ivor Novello Award in 1959), *The Key*, *The Root Of Heaven*, *Dunkirk*, *Tunes Of Glory*, *The Angry Silence*, *No Love For Johnnie*, *The Inspector*, *Whistle Down The Wind*, *The Lion*, *Nine Hours To Rama*, *The Chalk Garden*, *The Heroes Of Telemark*, *The Thin Red Line*, *Sky West And Crooked*, and *The Reckoning* (1969). During the 60s Arnold was ignored, even reviled, by critics and sections of the concert and broadcasting establishment. He was dismissed as 'a clown', and his work was criticized as being 'out of phase' with contemporary trends in music. Arnold developed alcohol problems, suffered several nervous breakdowns, and attempted suicide more than once. He continued to write, when he was able, and was particularly interested in brass band music, but his work generally remained unappreciated. His ninth and final symphony, written in 1986, still had not received an official premiere by 1991, when low-key celebrations for his 70th birthday involved a concert at London's Queen Elizabeth Hall, which included his double violin concerto, commissioned by Yehudi Menuhin in 1962. In 1993 Malcolm Arnold received a knighthood in the Queen's New Year honours list.

● ALBUMS: *Malcolm Arnold Film Music* (Chandos 1992)★★★★, *Arnold Overtures* (Reference Recordings 1992)★★★★.
● FURTHER READING: *Malcolm Arnold: A Catalogue Of His Music*, A. Poulton.

ARNOLD, TOM

b. Thomas Charles Arnold, 19 August 1893, Richmond, Yorkshire, England, d. 2 February 1969, London, England. An important producer and manager of musicals and other lavish and spectacular events in London's West End and the provinces for many years. While still in his 20s, Arnold toured revues such as *The Showbox* and *The Vanity Box*, as well as a variety of other shows, including *Tom Arnold's Circus*, before presenting *Folies Bergere* at the London Palladium in 1925. From then on, until the late 30s, he continued to tour musicals, revues, and other kinds of productions at a phenomenal rate at home and in countries such as South Africa and Australia. These included Richard Rodgers and Lorenz Hart's *One Dam Thing After Another*, Charles B. Cochran and Noël Coward's *This Year Of Grace!*, Vivian Ellis and A.P. Herbert's *Streamline*, Cole Porter's *Anything Goes*, and Eric Maschwitz, George Posford, and Bernard Grun's hit, *Balalaika*. In 1938, Arnold presented *Henry V* at Drury Lane, with Ivor Novello as the King. This association flourished in the future, with the producer mounting Novello's

series of highly successful musicals, *The Dancing Years* (1939 in the West End, its regional tour, and the 1942 revival), *Arc De Triomphe* (1943), *Perchance To Dream* (1945), *King's Rhapsody* (1949), and *Gay's The Word* (1951) - the latter starring Cicely Courtneidge. Arnold had previously managed several of her earlier showcases, such as *Clowns In Clover*, *Full Swing*, *Something In The Air*, and *Under The Counter*. In keeping with his policy of working in many contrasting areas of showbusiness, in the early '50s Arnold presented Noël Coward's startlingly different 'revue-musical' *Ace Of Clubs*, as well as staging lavish spectacles such as *Rose Marie On Ice* at Harringay, *Dick Whittington On Ice* at Wembley, and the usual pantomimes. He had previously inaugurated *Tom Arnold's Harringay Circus Annual* at Christmas 1947 and *Latin Quarter* (1949) at the London Casino. During the rest of the 50s, Arnold mixed dramatic theatre with his other interests, which included the *Moscow State Circus*. In August 1960 he opened a revival of *Rose Marie* at the Victoria Palace, with singer David Whitfield, and then presented three brand new musicals: the conventional *Pickwick* (1963) and *Our Man Crichton* (1964), along with Lionel Bart and Alun Owen's dramatically different *Maggie May*. He also handled the West End transfer of the Broadway musical *Little Me*, which gave comedian Bruce Forsyth the opportunity to shine. After that, there were no major musical productions for Arnold, although he continued producing his annual spectaculars, and was awarded the OBE a few weeks before he died in 1969.

His son, Tom Arnold (b. Thomas Richard Arnold, 25 January 1947, London, England), also became a producing manager after being educated in Switzerland and at Pembroke College, Oxford. His projects included ice pantomimes at London's Wembley Arena, as well as West End presentations and regional tours of shows starring artists such as Danny La Rue, and plays and musicals including *The King And I*, *The Sunshine Boys*, and *Peter Pan*. He became a Conservative Member of Parliament in 1974, and was knighted in 1990.

ARTHUR, BEATRICE

b. Bernice Frankel, 13 May 1926, New York, USA. A stylish, droll, acid-tongued actress, comedienne and singer, with an attractive dark-brown voice, Bea Arthur came to prominence playing the role of Lucy Brown in Marc Blitzstein's adaptation of Kurt Weill and Bertolt Brecht's *The Threepenny Opera* - the second US version - which opened off-Broadway at the Theatre De Lys in March 1954, and ran for 2,706 performances. She then appeared in Ben Bagley's 1955 *Shoestring Revue*, and in the same year took the part of Mme. Suze in *Seventh Heaven*, a musicalized version of the Oscar-winning 1927 silent film classic, which starred Janice Gaynor and Charles Farrell. In 1960 Arthur was off-Broadway again, this time as Hortense in a brief revival of the 1932 Fred Astaire musical *Gay Divorce*. In direct contrast to that disappointment, Arthur's next appearance on Broadway in 1964 was in one of the best-loved musicals of all time, *Fiddler On The Roof*. She created the role of the village matchmaker, Yente, in a production that ran for 3,242 performances. Another blockbuster followed in 1966 when Arthur won a Tony

Award for her portrayal of the superbly bitchy Vera Charles in Jerry Herman's *Mame*. Her duet with star Angela Lansbury, 'Bosom Buddies' (Mame: 'I've been meaning to tell you for years, you should keep your hair natural like mine.' Vera: 'If I kept my hair natural like yours, I'd be bald.'), regularly brought the house down. Unfortunately, although the number was filmed as part of the 1974 film version of *Mame*, in which Arthur recreated her role opposite Lucille Ball, it was cut from most prints. In 1968, she led a cast that included Carl Ballantine and Bill Callaway in *A Mother's Kisses* (1968), with a score by Richard Adler, but it folded out of town. She was married to Gene Saks, the show's director, for some years. He also directed *Generation* (1965), *Half A Sixpence* (1965), *I Love My Wife* (1977) and *Rags* (1986), among others. Apart from *Mame*, Arthur made several more films, including *That Kind Of Woman* (1958), *Lovers And Other Strangers* (1969) and *History Of The World: Part One* (1981). She has also appeared extensively on television. Her telling performances in *All In The Family* led to *Maude*, her own series (1972-76), and eventually to the part of Dorothy in *The Golden Girls* situation comedy (1985), which was still being enjoyed by television audiences round the world in the 90s.

ARTHURS, GEORGE

b. 13 April 1875, Manchester, Lancashire, England, d. 14 March 1944, Harrow, Middlesex, England. A songwriter and author, Arthurs wrote several popular numbers for the stars of music hall before making his mark with material for the musical stage. He originally worked as an accountant in Manchester, but gave that up to write or co-write songs such as 'I Want To Sing In Opera', 'The Wriggley Rag', 'You've Got To Sing In Ragtime' and 'Chrysanthemums', which were sung by the comedian Wilkie Bard, 'Josh-u-a', a favourite for Clarice Mayne, 'The Caddie' (Neil Kenyon), 'A Different Girl Again' (Whit Cunliffe), and probably the most famous of all - 'A Little Of What You Fancy Does You Good', which is indelibly associated with the great Marie Lloyd. Among Arthurs' collaborators for these numbers were Bert Lee, Fred W. Leigh, and Worton David. Arthur also had lyrics interpolated into *The Belle Of Mayfair* (1906) and *Havana* (1908), before collaborating with composer Louis Hirsch on score for the 1913 revue *Hullo, Tango*. He followed this with the book and lyrics for *Honeymoon Express* (1914), and then contributed, often with others, to revues and musicals such as *The Whirl Of The Town* (1914), *The Million Dollar Girl* (1915), *Don't Tempt Me* (1915), *She's A Daisy* (1915), *We're All In It* (1916), *Seeing Life* (1917) and *Hanky Panky* (1917). Some of Arthurs' best work was in the musical comedies *Suzette* (1917, book with Austen Hurgon, score with Max Darewski), which starred Stanley Lupino, *Arlette* (1917, book and score with Hurgon, Jane Vieu, Guy Lefeuvre, Ivor Novello, Adrian Ross and Clifford Grey), another Lupino vehicle, *Yes, Uncle!* (1917, book with Hurgon, score with Nat D. Ayer, Clifford Grey, a 626-performance hit for Leslie Henson), and *The Girl For The Boy* (1919, book with Hurgon, score with Percy Greenbank, Howard Carr, Bernard Rolt and R. Penso). Among Arthurs' other productions, which mainly toured, were *Peri, The Slave Of*

Love (1921), *Many Happy Returns* (1922), *Archie* (1924), *Belles Of Britain* (1925), *Puzzles Of 1925*, *Pastimes* (1926), *Patsy From Paris* (1926), and *Wild Rose* (1930).

AS THE GIRLS GO

A vehicle for the ex-vaudeville headliner, 60-year-old Bobby Clark, who was making his last Broadway appearance in a musical, *As The Girls Go* opened at the Winter Garden Theatre on 13 November 1948. In William Roos's highly imaginative book, Waldo Wellington (Clark), is the husband of Lucille Thompson Wellington (Irene Rich), the first woman President of the United States. That makes Waldo the First Gentleman, which apparently gives him licence constantly to chase dozens of nearly naked girls while running through an extensive repertoire of pure hokum, with the accent on the clever manipulation of props, and other noisy, fast-moving pieces of business. Jimmy McHugh and Harold Adamson's score contained several good songs, such as 'You Say The Nicest Things, Baby' and 'I Got Lucky In The Rain', both of which proved to be appealing duets for Bill Callahan, who played the president's son, and his girlfriend, Kathy Robinson (Betty Jane Watson). Watson was replaced during the show's run by Fran Warren, a popular vocalist who had several US hits, including 'A Sunday Kind Of Love'. The show's other songs included 'As The Girls Go', 'Father's Day', 'It's More Fun Than A Picnic', 'There's No Getting Away From You', the brash and progressive 'Rock, Rock, Rock', and Clark's amusing 'It Takes A Woman To Take A Man'. Ostensibly, the choreographer was Hermes Pan, designer of the dances for several Fred Astaire movies, but Bobby Clark no doubt inserted much mayhem of his own during the production, which ran for 420 performances.

AS THOUSANDS CHEER

Appearing a year after their previous collaboration on *Face The Music*, this innovative revue, with some memorable music and lyrics by Irving Berlin and witty, satirical sketches by Moss Hart, opened on Broadway at the Music Box Theatre on 30 September 1933. The complete show was designed as a newspaper, with headlines and sections devoted to features, news stories, comic strips, social affairs, theatre, and so on. The weather section gave Berlin the opportunity to introduce 'Heatwave', which was sung by Ethel Waters, and the agony column was handled by Harry Stockwell, dispensing advice for the 'Lonely Heart'. Clifton Webb and Marilyn Miller (making her last Broadway appearance before her death three years later), emerged from an old photograph, singing 'Easter Parade' in the spectacular rotrogravure sequence ('The photographers will snap us/And you'll find that you're in the rotrogravure'), and some of the most prominent household names of the day flitted through the newspaper's pages: Marilyn Miller portrayed Barbara Hutton and Joan Crawford; Helen Broderick masqueraded as Aimee Semple MacPherson, Louise (Mrs Edgar) Hoover, Queen Mary - and the Statue of Liberty; Clifton Webb somehow became John D. Rockefeller, Douglas Fairbanks Jnr., and Mahatma Gandhi; and Ethel Waters was a superb Joséphine Baker. Waters was involved in the only deliberately serious news item in an otherwise light-hearted periodical when she sang 'Supper Time', which was preceded by the headline: 'UNKNOWN NEGRO LYNCHED BY FRENZIED MOB'. The show's other numbers included 'Harlem On My Mind' (Waters) and 'How's Chances?', in which Clifton Webb (Prince Alexis Mdivani) serenaded the Woolworth heiress, Barbara Hutton (Miller). The finale revealed one of Hart and Berlin's smartest ideas when the 'US Supreme Court' decreed that no musical show could finish with the conventional song reprises, thereby making way for a brand new number, 'Not For All The Rice In China'. *As Thousands Cheer* was a smash-hit - the Broadway show of the season that everyone wanted to see - and ran for 400 performances. In the summer of 1998, the Drama Dept., an off-Broadway theatre company with an impressive track record of reviving old, half-forgotten shows, presented *As Thousands Cheer* at the Greenwich House Theatre in New York. The illustrious cast included Judy Kuhn, Howard McGillin, B.D. Wong, Mary Beth Peil, Kevin Chamberlin, and Paula Newsome. It subsequently became the first production of this ground-breaking revue to be recorded - and released by Varése Sarabande.

AS YOU WERE

This 'Fantastic Revue', produced by Charles B. Cochran, which opened at the London Pavilion on 3 August 1918, had quite enough plot easily to have qualified as a musical comedy. Adapted from Rip's *Plus Ça Change*, Arthur Wimperis's scenario was set in the year 2018, and based itself on the rather contentious idea that wherever you go and in whatever age you live, you will find women drawing their cash from one man while they bestow their love on another. While Sir Bilyon Boost (John Humphries), the millionaire proprietor of Bilyon's Boiled Beans, pays the debts of Lady Boost (Alice Delysia) as she serenades him with the tender 'If You Could Care', the money is being passed on to the smirking Kiki (Leon Morton). Bursting with anger, Sir Bilyon swallows a series of pills which transport him through time to the courts of Louis XIV and Hunzollern at Potterdammerung, and various other locations such as the Trojan War (the revue at the local Hippodrome has been written by 'Arrystophanes'), and a primeval forest. Wherever he goes, there is a woman bearing a remarkable resemblance to Alice Delysia singing 'If You Could Care' while taking his cash and giving it to a Leon Morton lookalike. Also among the cast were Hayden Coffin, Clifford Morgan, Edward Sillward, and the up-and-coming Mona Vivian. Arthur Wimperis wrote the lyrics, and the music was composed by Herman Darewski and Edouard Mathe. The set of quite delightful songs included 'I Didn't 'Arf Larf', 'Live For All You're Worth', 'Watteau', 'With A Hey! And A Ho!', 'Fritz', 'Potsdam', 'Helen Of Troy', 'Old Man Adam', and, of course, 'If You Could Care'. The whole thing was a neat notion that paid off to the tune of an impressive 434 performances. However, American audiences were not so enthusiastic, and, even with a cast headed by Sam Bernard, Irene Bordoni, and Clifton Webb, the production that opened at the Central Theatre on 27 January 1920 stayed around for less than five months.

ASCHE, OSCAR

b. John Stanger Heiss, 26 June 1871, Geelong, Australia, d. 23 March 1936, Marlow, Buckinghamshire, England. An actor, author, director and producer who specialized in the spectacular, Asche was educated at Melbourne Grammar School, and studied for the stage at Christiania, before moving to England. Early in his career, he played extensively in Shakespearean productions managed by F.R. Benson and Sir Herbert Tree. Later, he appeared in similar productions under his own management, both in the UK and Australia. In 1915 he made his first appearance on the variety stage as Haaj, in a short play of that title, and a year later, on 31 August 1916, burst upon the musical scene at His Majesty's Theatre in London with the Arabian Nights fantasy *Chu Chin Chow* ('Any Time's Kissing Time', 'The Cobbler's Song', 'Robbers' Chorus'). Not only did he star in the piece with his wife, Lily Brayton, but he also wrote the book and lyrics (music: Frederick Norton), and directed it as well. *Chu Chin Chow* was one of the big hits of World War I, and ran until July 1921, a total of 2,238 performances. Ironically, *Chu Chin Chow*'s main rival for wartime popularity was *The Maid Of The Mountains* (1,352 performances), which Asche also directed. Meanwhile, Asche wrote and directed the short-lived *Eastward Ho!* (1919), in collaboration with Grace Torrens and John Ansell (music) and Dornford Yates (lyrics), and then appeared again at His Majesty's in *Cairo* (1921), a 'mosaic in music and mime' with an Eastern flavour, rather like *Chu Chin Chow*. Originally entitled *Mecca* when it was previously presented in New York, Asche was credited with the 'mime' (music: Percy Fletcher) and direction, and also played the part of Ali Shar. In the early 20s, Asche toured Australasia with *Chu Chin Chow* and *Cairo*, as well as dispensing his staple Shakespearean fare, before returning to the West End stage in 1925, at the Gaiety Theatre, in the 37-performance flop, *The Good Old Days* (music: Percy Fletcher), which he wrote, directed, and co-produced with his wife. Although he had enjoyed considerable success as a director with opulent productions such as *A Southern Maid* (1918), *Frasquita* (1925) and *Cleopatra* (1925), his later work, both as a performer and/or director was generally considered to be undistinguished. It included *Marjolaine* (1928), *The White Camelia* (1929) and *Eldorado* (1930). With the advent of talking pictures, Asche began to make films in 1933. These included *Don Quixote* (1933, with George Robey), *My Lucky Star* (1933, with Florence Desmond and Harry Tate), the musical *Two Hearts In Waltztime* (1934, with Carl Brisson, Frances Day, and the 17-year-old Valerie Hobson), *Scrooge* (1935, with Seymour Hicks), and *The Private Secretary* (1935, with Edward Everett Horton and Alastair Sim). He published his autobiography in 1929, and was also the author of *The Joss-Sticks Of Chung* (1930).

● FURTHER READING: *Oscar Asche: His Life, By Himself*, Oscar Asche.

ASHMAN, HOWARD

b. 1951, Baltimore, Maryland, USA, d. 14 March 1991, New York, USA. A lyricist, librettist, playwright and director. After studying at Boston University and Indiana University, where he gained a master's degree in 1974, Ashman moved to New York and worked for publishers Grosset & Dunlap, while starting to write plays. One of his earliest works, *Dreamstuff*, a musical version of *The Tempest*, was staged at the WPA Theatre, New York, where Ashman served as artistic director from 1977-82. In 1979 the WPA presented a musical version of Kurt Vonnegut's *God Bless You, Mr Rosewater*, written by Ashman in collaboration with composer Alan Menken (b. 22 July 1949, New Rochelle, New York, USA), which became a cult hit. In 1982, again at the WPA, they had even bigger success with *Little Shop Of Horrors*, an amusing musical about Audrey II, a man-eating plant. The show became the highest-grossing and third longest-running musical in off-Broadway history. It won the New York Drama Critics Award, Drama Desk Award, and Outer Critics Circle Award The London production won *Evening Standard* awards for 'Best Musical' and 'Best Score'. As well as writing the book and lyrics, Ashman also directed the show. One of the songs from the 1986 film version, 'Mean Green Mother From Outer Space', was nominated for an Academy Award. Disenchanted with Broadway following his flop show *Smile*, with music by Marvin Hamlisch, Ashman moved to Hollywood, and the animated features of Walt Disney. One of Ashman's own songs, with the ironic title, 'Once Upon A Time In New York', was sung by Huey Lewis in *Oliver & Company* (1988), and the following year he was back with Menken for *The Little Mermaid*. Two of their songs for this film, 'Kiss The Girl' and 'Under The Sea', were nominated for Academy Awards. The latter won, and Menken also received the Oscar for 'Best Score'. Two years later the duo did it again with their music and lyrics for *Beauty And The Beast* (1991) (one US theatre critic wrote: 'Disney's latest animated triumph boasts the most appealing musical comedy score in years, dammit'). Three songs from the film were nominated by the Academy, this time the title number emerged as the winner, along with the score. Menken received an unprecedented five BMI awards for this work on the film. In Ashman's case his Academy Award was posthumous - he died of AIDS on 14 March 1991, in New York, USA.

Menken signed a long-term contract with Disney, the first result of which was *Newsies* (1992; re-titled *The News Boys* in the UK), a turn-of-the-century live-action story, with lyrics by Jack Feldman. Before Ashman died he had been working with Menken on the songs for *Aladdin*, and one of them, 'Friend Like Me', was subsequently nominated for an Academy Award. Menken completed work on the film with British lyricist Tim Rice, and their tender ballad, 'A Whole New World', won an Oscar, as did Menken's score. 'A Whole New World' also won a Golden Globe award, and a version by Peabo Bryson and Regina Belle topped the US chart in 1993. Two years later, Menken worked with lyricist Stephen Schwartz on Disney's new movie, *Pocahontas*. The team won Oscars for 'Original Music or Comedy Score' and 'Original Song' ('Colours Of The Wind'), and reunited for *The Hunchback Of Notre Dame* (1996). Menken's other film work around this time included *Rocky V* ('The Measure Of A Man', 1990), *Home Alone 2: Lost In New York* ('My Christmas Tree', with Jack Feldman, 1992), *Life With Mikey* (aka *Give Me A Break*, 1993) and *Hercules* (1997). Early in the 90s, Menken returned to the stage, collaborating with David Spencer for the science-fiction musical, *Weird Romance* (1992), at the WPA, and with Lynn Ahrens for a new $10 million musical version of the Charles Dickens classic *A Christmas Carol* (1994) at Madison Square Garden in New York. In April of that year, a spectacular stage production of *Beauty And The Beast* opened in New York, and three years later, Menken (with Tim Rice as librettist-lyricist) was back on Broadway with a limited, nine-performance run of the 'concert event', *King David*.. Menken's other honours have included BMI, Golden Globe, and Grammy awards.

ASPECTS OF LOVE

It is an indication of Andrew Lloyd Webber's powerful influence on the British musical theatre during the 80s, that this show - his follow-up to the smash-hit *The Phantom Of The Opera* - ran for over three years, and yet was still considered to be a failure. Prior to its opening at the Prince of Wales Theatre on 17 April 1989, the show had a £2 million box office advance - and a widely publicized cast change. The film and television actor Roger Moore had been set to make his West End debut as the French aristocrat Charles Dillingham, but, after finding himself unable to cope with 'the technical side of the singing', he was replaced by the Australian actor Kevin Colson. Based on a novel by David Garnett, *Aspects Of Love* was another 'sung-through' opera-style show, with the book and music by Lloyd Webber, and lyrics by Don Black and Charles Hart. The tale of romantic entanglements involved the young hero, Alex Dillingham (Michael Ball), and a flighty French actress, Rose Vibert (Ann Crumb), whose lives are complicated by Alex's shady uncle, Charles (Kevin Colson), a bisexual Italian sculptress, Giulietta Trapani (Caron Skinns), and Jenny (Lottie Mayer), the teenage daughter of the French actress and the shady uncle. Colson and Mayer had one of the best numbers, the enchanting 'The First Man You Remember', but Michael Ball, the man with the 'stupendous tenor voice', sang the big hit, 'Love Changes Everything', which he took into the upper reaches of the UK chart. The show was a springboard to his own networked television show and concert tours. *Aspects Of Love*'s other musical selections included 'Parlez-Vous-Francais', 'Seeing Is Believing', 'A Memory Of Happy Moments', 'Everybody Loves A Hero', 'She'd Be Far Better Off With You', 'Other Pleasures', 'There Is More To Love', 'Falling' and 'Anything But Lonely'. The British critics reserved judgement on the show and it was ignored by the Laurence Olivier Awards committee, although it did receive the Ivor Novello Award for best musical. The US critics had no such reservations - they savaged it following the Broadway opening at the Broadhurst Theatre in April 1990, when Ball, Crumb and Colson reprised their London roles. 'Annoyingly shallow . . . an endless stream of clichés and predictable rhythms . . . grotesque and overproduced' were comments from one typical review. The show was nominated for six Tony Awards - did not win any - and folded after a run of 377 performances, losing several million dollars, and proving that even the Lloyd Webber name did not guarantee a stay of several years. However, *Aspects Of Love* did undertake road tours of the USA and several other countries around the world. The London production closed in June 1992 following 1,325 performances. During its time in the West End, the leading roles were taken by artists such as Michael Praed, Claire Burt, and Sarah Brightman, who played Rose for the last few weeks of the run. In 1992, a 'chamber version' of the show was presented in some parts of the USA, directed by Robin Phillips, whose concept differed widely from the original lavish staging by Trevor Nunn, and in 1993/4 the show returned to the West End for a limited run.

ASSASSINS

Stephen Sondheim's eagerly awaited first musical of the 90s opened for a limited engagement of two months, off-Broadway at the 139-seater Playwrights Horizons, on 27 January 1991, and, even for him, it was an extraordinary piece of work. Directed by Jerry Zaks, with a book by John Weidman, it told the stories of nine of the 13 people who have tried - four of them successfully - to kill the President of the United States. It was a cabaret-style show with a fairground setting complete with fairy lights, a shooting gallery, and a row of booths from which the assassins emerged to play out their individual dramas. Sondheim complemented their contrasting revelations and motives with a score that followed the opening 'Hail To The Chief' (intriguingly played on a calliope) with what amounted to a potted history of American popular music, with its collection of marches, Kentucky waltzes, folk songs, vaudeville - all manner of pastiche - and some wicked, mocking parodies. The assembled killers' agreement that 'Everybody's Got The Right' was followed by 'Ballad Of Booth' (John Wilkes Booth was the first successful assassin, killing Abraham Lincoln), 'How I Saved Roosevelt', 'Gun Song', 'The Ballad Of Czolgosz', 'Unworthy Of Your Love', 'The Ballad Of Guiteau' (a song-and-dance number on the steps of a scaffold), 'Another National Anthem', and a reprise of 'Everybody's Got The Right'. With an outstanding cast that included Terrence Mann (Leon Czolgosz), Greg Germann (John Hinckley), Jonathan Hadary (Charles Guiteau), Eddie Korbich (Guiseppe Zangara), Lee Wilkoff (Samuel Byck), Annie Golden (Lynette 'Squeaky' Fromme), Debra Monk (Sara Jane Moore), Victor Garber (John Wilkes Booth) and Jace Alexander (Lee Harvey Oswald), *Assassins* was described variously as 'an attack on the American Dream', 'Sondheim's angriest work since *Sweeney Todd*', 'a lethally brilliant musical', and 'an aimless project'. The New York run sold out immediately, as did the London production, which was mounted at the newly refurbished Donmar Warehouse in October 1992. For the West End version, which won the Critics' Circle London Drama Award for best new musical, Sondheim added a new number, 'Something Just Broke'. *Assassins* returned to London in a critically acclaimed staging at the New End Theatre, Hampstead, in 1997. Produced by 19-year-old David

Babani and directed by his 21-year-old Bristol University colleague Sam Buntrock, it starred ex-West End *'Tommy'* Paul Keating as the Balladeer, and Tom Rogers in the role of Lee Harvey Oswald.

ASTAIRE, FRED

b. Frederick Austerlitz, 10 May 1899, Omaha, Nebraska, USA, d. 22 June 1987, Los Angeles, California, USA. One of the greatest - with Gene Kelly - and best-loved dancers in the history of film, by the age of seven Astaire was dancing in vaudeville with his sister, Adele (b. 10 September 1898, Omaha, Nebraska, USA, d. 25 January 1981, Phoenix, Arizona, USA). The duo made their Broadway debut in 1917 and the following year were a huge success in *The Passing Show Of 1918*. During the 20s they continued to dance to great acclaim in New York and London, their shows including *Lady, Be Good!* (1924) and *Funny Face* (1927). They danced on into the 30s in *The Band Wagon* (1931), but their partnership came to an end with *Gay Divorce* (1932). Adele married Charles Cavendish, the younger son of the Duke of Devonshire, and retired from showbusiness. The Astaires had dabbled with motion pictures, perhaps as early as 1915 (although their role in a Mary Pickford feature from this year is barely supported by the flickering remains), but a screen test for a film version of *Funny Face* had resulted in an offhand summary of Adele as 'lively', and the now infamous dismissal of Astaire: 'Can't act. Can't sing. Balding. Can dance a little.' Despite this negative view of his screen potential, Astaire, now in need of a new direction for his career, again tried his luck in Hollywood. He had a small part in *Dancing Lady* (1933), and was then teamed with Ginger Rogers for a brief sequence in *Flying Down To Rio* (1933). Their dance duet atop seven white grand pianos to the tune of the 'Carioca' was a sensation, and soon thereafter they were back on the screen, this time as headliners in *The Gay Divorcee* (1934). A string of highly successful films followed, among them *Roberta* and *Top Hat* (both 1935), *Follow The Fleet* and *Swing Time* (both 1936), *Shall We Dance* (1937) and *The Story Of Vernon And Irene Castle* (1939). Astaire then made a succession of films with different dancing partners, including Paulette Goddard in *Second Chorus* (1940), Rita Hayworth in *You'll Never Get Rich* (1941) and *You Were Never Lovelier* (1942), and Lucille Bremer in *Yolanda And The Thief* (1945) and *Ziegfeld Follies* (1946). His singing co-leads included Bing Crosby in *Holiday Inn* (1942) and *Blue Skies* (1946) and Judy Garland in *Ziegfeld Follies* and *Easter Parade* (1948). He was reunited with Rogers in *The Barkleys Of Broadway* (1949), and danced with Vera-Ellen, Betty Hutton, Jane Powell, Cyd Charisse, Leslie Caron, Audrey Hepburn and others throughout the rest of the 40s and on through the 50s. By the late 50s he was more interested in acting than dancing and singing and began a new stage in his film career with a straight role in *On The Beach* (1959). A brief return to the musical screen came with *Finian's Rainbow* (1968), but apart from co-hosting celebrations of the golden age of MGM movie musicals, *That's Entertainment!* and *That's Entertainment, Part II*, he abandoned this side of his work. During the 50s, 60s and 70s he also appeared on US television, mostly in acting roles but occasionally, as with

An Evening With Fred Astaire (1958), *Another Evening With Fred Astaire* (1959) and *The Fred Astaire Show* (1968), to sing and dance (in the three cases cited, with Barrie Chase). By the early 80s, for all practical purposes he had retired. Off-screen Astaire led a happy and usually quiet life. His first marriage lasted from 1933 to 1954, when his wife died in her mid-40s; they had two children, Fred Jnr. and Phyllis Ava. He remarried in 1980, his second wife surviving his death on 22 June 1987.

Astaire made his recording debut in 1923, singing with Adele, and in 1926 the couple recorded a selection of tunes by George Gershwin with the composer at the piano. He recorded steadily but infrequently during the 30s and 40s, and in 1952 made his first long playing recordings for Norman Granz, *The Astaire Story*, on which he was accompanied by jazz pianist Oscar Peterson. He continued to make records into the mid-70s, usually of songs from his films or television shows, while soundtrack albums and compilations from many of his earlier film appearances continued to be issued. As a singer, Astaire presented songs with no artifice and never did anything to dispel the impression that he was merely an amateur with few natural gifts. Yet for all this, his interpretations of popular songs were frequently just what their composers and lyricists wanted, and many such writers commended him for the engaging manner in which he delivered their material. A key factor in their approval may well have derived from his decision, perhaps forced upon him by the limitations of his vocal range, to sing simply, directly and as written. Among the composers who rated him highly were masters of the Great American Popular Songbook such as Irving Berlin, Jerome Kern, Cole Porter, Gershwin, Harold Arlen, Johnny Mercer and Harry Warren.

As an actor, he was usually adequate and sometimes a little more so, but rarely immersed himself so completely in a role that he ceased to be himself and, indeed, did little to disprove the first part of his screen test summation. As a dancer, however, it is impossible to assess his contribution to stage, television and especially to musical films without superlatives. Like so many great artists, the ease with which Astaire danced made it seem as though anyone could do what he did. Indeed, this quality may well have been part of his popularity. He looked so ordinary that any male members of the audience, even those with two left feet, were convinced that, given the opportunity, they could do as well. In fact, the consummate ease of his screen dancing was the end result of countless hours of hard work, usually alone or with his long-time friend, colleague, co-choreographer and occasional stand-in, Hermes Pan. (Ginger Rogers, with whom Astaire had an uneasy off-screen relationship, recalled rehearsing one number until her feet bled.) For slow numbers he floated with an elegant grace and, when the tempo quickened, the elegance remained, as did the impression that he was forever dancing just a fraction above the ground. The sweatily energetic movements of many other screen dancers was, perhaps, more cinematic, but it was something that Astaire would not have considered even for a moment. Alone, he created an entirely original form of screen dance and after his first films, all previous perceptions of

dance were irrevocably altered. In the world of showbiz, where every artist is labelled 'great' and words like 'genius' have long ago ceased to have realistic currency, Fred Astaire truly was a great artist and a dancer of genius.

● ALBUMS: *The Fred Astaire Story* 4-LP set (Mercury/Clef 1953)★★★★, *Cavalcade Of Dance* (Coral 1955)★★★, *Nothing Thrilled Us Half As Much* (Epic 1955)★★★, *Mr. Top Hat* (Verve 1956)★★★★, *Easy To Dance With* (Verve 1958)★★★, *An Evening With Fred Astaire* (Chrysler 1958)★★★, *Another Evening With Fred Astaire* (Chrysler 1959)★★★, *Fred Astaire Now* (Kapp 1959)★★★, *Astaire Time* (Chrysler 1960)★★★, with Bing Crosby *A Couple Of Song And Dance Men* (United Artists 1975)★★★, *Fred Astaire At MGM* (Rhino/Turner 1997)★★★.

● COMPILATIONS: *The Best Of Fred Astaire* (Epic 1955)★★★, *Three Evenings With Fred Astaire* (Choreo 1960)★★★, *Crazy Feet* (Living Era 1983)★★★★, *Fred Astaire Collection* (Deja Vu 1985)★★★★, *An Evening With* (Nostalgia/Mainline 1987)★★★★, *Easy To Dance With* (MCA 1987)★★★★, *Starring Fred Astaire* (Avan-Guard 1987)★★★★, *Top Hat, White Tie And Tails* (Saville/Conifer 1987)★★★★, *Astairable Fred* (DRG 1988)★★★, *Cheek To Cheek* (Compact Selection 1988)★★★★, *Puttin' On The Ritz* (Nostalgia/Mainline 1988)★★★★, *The Fred Astaire And Ginger Rogers Story* (Deja Vu 1989)★★★★, *The Cream Of* (1993)★★★★, *Top Hat: Hits From Hollywood* (Sony 1994)★★★★, *Steppin' Out: Fred Astaire At MGM* (Sony 1994)★★★★, *The Best Of ... 18 Timeless Recordings* (Music Club 1995)★★★★.

● VIDEOS: *A.F.I. Salutes Fred Astaire* (Castle Vision 1991).

● FURTHER READING: *Steps In Time*, Fred Astaire. *Fred Astaire - A Bio-Bibliography*, Larry Billman.

● FILMS: *Flying Down To Rio* (1933), *Dancing Lady* (1933), *The Gay Divorcee* (1934), *Top Hat* (1935), *Roberta* (1935), *Swing Time* (1936), *Follow The Fleet* (1936), *A Damsel In Distress* (1937), *Shall We Dance* (1937), *Carefree* (1938), *The Story Of Vernon And Irene Castle* (1939), *Second Chorus* (1940), *Broadway Melody Of 1940* (1940), *You'll Never Get Rich* (1941), *You Were Never Lovelier* (1942), *Holiday Inn* (1942), *The Sky's The Limit* (1943), *Yolanda And The Thief* (1945), *Blue Skies* (1946), *Ziegfeld Follies* (1946), *Easter Parade* (1948), *The Barkleys Of Broadway* (1949), *Three Little Words* (1950), *Let's Dance* (1950), *Royal Wedding* (1951), *The Belle Of New York* (1952), *The Band Wagon* (1953), *Daddy Long Legs* (1955), *Funny Face* (1957), *Silk Stockings* (1957), *On The Beach* (1959), *The Pleasure Of His Company* (1961), *The Notorious Landlady* (1962), *Finian's Rainbow* (1968), *The Midas Run UK: A Run On Gold* (1969), *The Towering Inferno* (1974), *The Amazing Dobermans* (1976), *The Purple Taxi* (1977), *Ghost Story* (1981).

AT HOME ABROAD

Subtitled 'A Musical Holiday', this revue opened in New York at the Winter Garden Theatre on 19 September 1935. With music by Arthur Schwartz and lyrics by Howard Dietz, the setting was a world cruise, seen through the eyes of Otis and Henrietta Hatrick (Herb Williams and Vera Allen), which gave Beatrice Lillie, who played an alleged smuggler, the bride of an Alpine guide, and a ballet dancer, among other things, a good excuse to excel in 'Get Yourself A Geisha' ('Do you mind if we give you a tip on/The way you should really see a Nippon?') and 'Paree', along with a classic sketch set in a London department store in which she portrays a Mrs. Blogden-Blagg, attempting to order 'two dozen double damask dinner napkins'.

The other leading lady in the show was Ethel Waters, who adopted several roles, including a French lady, and a native of Harlem who lectured the natives in the Congo on her position as a 'Hottentot Potentate' ('The heathens live on a bed of roses now/And Cartier rings they're wearin' in their noses now'). Waters also sang 'Thief In The Night', 'Loadin' Time', and duetted on 'Got A Bran' New Suit' with tap-dancer Eleanor Powell, who was then on the brink of Hollywood stardom. In *At Home Abroad* Powell had three other numbers: 'That's Not Cricket', 'The Lady With The Tap', and 'What A Wonderful World', which she performed with Woods Miller, who also sang Schwartz and Dietz's most enduring song from the show, 'Love Is A Dancing Thing'. Comedians Eddie Foy Jnr. and Reginald Gardiner were in the cast, and the list of sketch writers included Dion Titheradge, who had written the amusing lyric to Ivor Novello's 'And Her Mother Came Too' more than 10 years previously. The show, which ran for 198 performances, was the first Broadway musical to be directed by Vincente Minnelli, one of the major influences in Hollywood musicals of the 50s.

AT LONG LAST LOVE

Released by 20th Century-Fox in 1975, this film was regarded as an attempt by writer-director Peter Bogdanovich to recapture the magic of the classic Fred Astaire-Ginger Rogers RKO musicals of the 30s. However, while the picture was lovely to look at, courtesy of the brilliant art deco sets and Laszlo Kovac's dazzling Technicolor photography, Burt Reynolds and Cybill Shepherd's song-and-dance talents were minimal, and the whole affair was a dreadful $6 million flop. It was a shame, because Bogdanovich's screenplay was endearingly scatty - just like the 30s originals - and the score contained some wonderful Cole Porter songs. Most of them, such as 'You're The Top', 'It's De-Lovely', 'Well, Did You Evah?', 'I Get A Kick Out Of You', 'Most Gentlemen Don't Like Love', 'Just One Of Those Things' and 'Friendship', were much-loved favourites, but other, less-familiar delights included 'But In The Morning, No', 'From Alpha To Omega' and 'Which'. Even with valiant support from Eileen Brennan, Madeline Kahn, Duilio del Prete, Mildred Natwick and John Hillerman, nothing worthwhile could be salvaged from the wreck. Cybill Shepherd claimed that they sang 'live' - the first time it had been done in films since the 30s.

AT THE DROP OF A HAT

(see Flanders And Swann)

ATTERIDGE, HAROLD

b. 9 July 1886, Lake Forest, Illinois, USA, d. 15 January 1938, Lynbrook, New York, USA. A librettist and lyricist for the legendary Shubert Brothers' production company, Atteridge was adept at adapting material from varied sources into lavish Broadway musical shows and revues. Educated at the University of Chicago, he worked in the local musical theatre before gaining his chance on Broadway with the Shuberts. One of his earliest projects was *Vera Violetta* (1911), in which Al Jolson confirmed the star quality he had displayed earlier in the year with *La*

Belle Paree. Atteridge also worked on several more Jolson vehicles: *The Whirl Of Society* (1912), *The Honeymoon Express* (1913), *Dancing Around* (1914), *Robinson Crusoe Jr.* (1916), *Sinbad* (1918), *Bombo* (1921) and *Big Boy* (1925). His other Broadway credits over a period of some 20 years included *Revue Of Revues* (1911), *Broadway To Paris* (1912), *Two Little Brides* (1912), *The Man With Three Wives* (1913), *The Belle Of Bond Street* (1914), *The Whirl Of The World* (1914), *Maid In America* (1915), *A World Of Pleasure* (1915), *The Peasant Girl* (1915), *Ruggles Of Red Gap* (1916), *The Show Of Wonders* (1916), *Over The Top* (1917), *Doing Our Bit* (1917), *Follow The Girl* (1918), *The Little Blue Devil* (1919), *Monte Cristo, Jr.* (1919), *Cinderella On Broadway* (1920), *The Last Waltz* (1921), *Midnight Rounders Of 1921*, *Make It Snappy* (1922), *The Rose Of Stamboul* (1922), *Artists And Models Of 1923*, *Topics Of 1923*, *The Dancing Girl* (1923), *The Dream Girl* (1924), *Innocent Eyes* (1924), *Marjorie* (1924), *Artists And Models Of 1925*, *Sky High* (1925), *Gay Paree* (1925), *Great Temptations* (1926), *A Night In Paris* (1926), *A Night In Spain* (1927), *Ziegfeld Follies Of 1927*, *Greenwich Village Follies Of 1928*, *Pleasure Bound* (1929), *Everybody's Welcome* (1931) and *Thumbs Up!* (1934). Atteridge also contributed to annual editions of *The Passing Show* in most years between 1912 and 1924. Many of his songs failed to register outside of the context of the shows in which they appeared, but he was partly responsible for some popular items, such as 'Bagdad' (1918, with Al Jolson, from *Sinbad*), 'Don't Send Your Wife To The Country' (1921, Buddy De Sylva-Con Conrad, from *Bombo*), and the immensely successful 'By The Beautiful Sea' (1914, with Harry Carroll), which was successful on record for the Heidelberg Quintet, Ada Jones with Billy Watkins, and Prince's Orchestra. The number was also interpolated into at least three films: *The Story Of Vernon And Irene Castle* (1939), *For Me And My Gal* (1942) and *Atlantic City* (1944). Atteridge himself adapted a number of properties for the screen, including the romantic musical *The Golden Calf* (1930). Among his composer collaborators were Sigmund Romberg, Al Goodman, Jean Schwartz and Louis Hirsch.

AURIC, GEORGES

b. 15 February 1899, Lodève, Hérault, France, d. 23 July 1983, Paris, France. A composer of many classical pieces including an opera and ballet, and choral and instrumental music. From 1930 up to the early 60s, he contributed the scores to French films such as *Quand J'étais*, *A Nous La Liberté*, *Orphée* and *Belles De Nuit*. He also wrote the music for numerous English-speaking films, including several classic Ealing comedies. His scores included *Dead Of Night* (1945), *Caesar And Cleopatra*, *Hue And Cry*, *It Always Rains On Sunday*, *Another Shore*, *Corridors Of Mirrors*, *Silent Dust*, *Passport To Pimlico*, *The Queen Of Spades*, *The Spider And The Fly*, *Cage Of Gold*, *The Galloping Major*, *The Lavender Hill Mob*, *Moulin Rouge*, *Roman Holiday*, *The Wages Of Fear*, *Father Brown*, *Rififi*, *The Witches Of Salem*, *Gervaise*, *The Picasso Mystery*, *Bonjour Tristesse*, *Heaven Knows Mr Allison*, *Heaven Fell That Night*, *The Innocents*, *The Mind Benders*, *Thomas The Impostor*, *Therese And Isabelle* and *The Christmas Tree* (1969). The haunting theme from *Moulin Rouge* (1952), with a lyric by Bill

Engvick ('Whenever we kiss, I worry and wonder/Your lips may be here, but where is your heart?'), became a hit in the USA for Percy Faith and his Orchestra, with the vocal by Felicia Sanders; and a record of the title music from *Bonjour Tristesse* (1957), with words added by the film's screenwriter, Arthur Laurents, was popular for Gogi Grant. Auric published his autobiography in 1974.

AUTRY, GENE

b. Orvin Gene Autry, 29 September 1907, near Tioga, Texas, USA, d. 2 October 1998, Studio City, California, USA. The eldest of four children of Delbert Autry, a poor tenant farmer, who moved his family many times over the years, before eventually arriving at Ravia, Oklahoma. His grandfather, a Baptist minister, taught him to sing when he was a child so that he could perform in his church choir and at other local events. Autry also learned to ride at an early age and worked the fields with his father. He grew up listening to cowboy songs and received his first guitar at the age of 12 (initially he studied the saxophone but chose the guitar so that he could sing as well). He graduated from school in 1924 and found work as a telegraph operator for the Frisco Railroad in Chelsea, Oklahoma. He used to take his guitar to work and one night his singing was heard by the famous entertainer Will Rogers, who stopped to send a telegram. He suggested that Autry should look for a job in radio. After trying unsuccessfully to find work in New York, he returned to Oklahoma and began to appear on KVOO Tulsa as The Oklahoma Yodeling Cowboy. After hearing recordings of Jimmie Rodgers, he became something of a Rodgers clone as he tried to further his career. In 1929, he made his first RCA Victor recordings, 'My Dreaming Of You' and 'My Alabama Home', on which he was accompanied by Jimmy Long (a fellow telegrapher) and Frankie and Johnny Marvin. Further recordings followed for ARC Records under the direction of Art Satherley, some being released on various labels for chain store sales. It was because of releases on Conqueror for Sears that Autry found himself given the opportunity to join WLS in Chicago. In 1931, he became a featured artist on *The National Barn Dance*, as well as having his own *Conqueror Record Time*. Before long, Gene Autry 'Roundup' guitars and songbooks were being sold by Sears. Interestingly, WLS portrayed him as a singing cowboy even though, at this time, few of his songs were of that genre. Between 1931 and 1934, he was a hillbilly singer, who still at times sounded like Rodgers. In fact, most experts later rated him the best of the Rodgers impersonators. He began to include his own songs and such numbers as 'The Gangster's Warning' and 'My Old Pal Of Yesterday' became very popular.

Late in 1931, he recorded 'That Silver Haired Daddy Of Mine' as a duet with Jimmy Long, with whom he had co-written the song. The song eventually became Autry's first million-selling record. By 1934, he was well known as a radio and recording personality. Having for some time been portrayed as a singing cowboy by the publicity departments of his record companies, he now took his first steps to make the publicity come true. He was given a small part in the Ken Maynard film *In Old Santa Fe*, and

soon afterwards starred in a strange 12-episode western/science fiction serial called *The Phantom Empire*. In 1935, Republic Pictures signed him to a contract and *Tumbling Tumbleweeds* became his first starring western film. His previous singing cowboy image was now reality. He sang eight songs in the film including the title track, 'That Silver Haired Daddy' and 'Ridin' Down The Canyon'. Further films followed in quick succession and by 1940 Autry ranked fourth among all Hollywood money-making stars at the box office. In January 1940, Gene Autry's *Melody Ranch* radio show, sponsored by the Wrigley Gum Company, first appeared on CBS and soon became a national institution, running until 1956. Helped out by such artists as Pat Buttram, Johnny Bond and the Cass County Boys, Autry regularly righted wrongs, sang his hits and as a result of the programme, built himself a new home in the San Fernando Valley called Melody Ranch.

Quite apart from the radio shows and films, he toured extensively with his stage show. It featured roping, Indian dancers, comedy, music, fancy riding from Autry, and smart horse tricks by Champion. By 1941, he was respected and famous all over the USA the little town of Berwyn, Oklahoma, even changed its name to Gene Autry, Oklahoma. His songs such as 'Be Honest With Me', 'Back In The Saddle Again' (which became his signature tune), 'You're The Only Star In My Blue Heaven', 'Goodbye, Little Darlin' Goodbye' (later recorded by Johnny Cash) and many more, became tremendously popular. In 1942, his income took a severe cut when he enlisted in the Air Force, being sworn in live on a *Melody Ranch* programme. He spent some time working on recruitment but then became a pilot in Air Ferry Command and saw service in the Far East, India and North Africa. During this period, he co-wrote with Fred Rose his classic song 'At Mail Call Today'. After his release from the services, he resumed his acting and recording career. Between 1944 and 1951, he registered 25 successive Top 10 country hits, including 'Here Comes Santa Claus' (later recorded by Elvis Presley), 'Rudolph, The Red-Nosed Reindeer', 'Peter Cottontail' and 'Frosty The Snow Man', each of which sold 1 million copies. He also had Top 20 US pop chart success with 'Buttons And Bows'. He left Republic in 1947 and formed his own Flying A Productions, which produced his later films for release by Columbia. When he made his last B-movie western, *Last Of The Pony Riders*, in 1953, he had 89 feature films to his credit. Contrary to prevailing belief, there never was a feud between Autry and his replacement at Republic, Roy Rogers - it was purely the invention of Republic's publicity department.

During the 50s, he became very successful in business and purchased many radio and television stations. Between 1950 and 1956, he produced 91 episodes of *The Gene Autry Show* for CBS-TV. His company also produced many other television series, including *The Range Rider*, *The Adventures Of Champion* and *Annie Oakley*. His business interest became even more involved during the 60s, when apart from owning various radio and television companies, he became the owner of the California Angels major league baseball team. *Melody Ranch* reappeared as a television programme in the 60s and ran for seven years on Autry's KTLA station. It was syndicated to stations across the country and although Autry did not appear as a regular, he did make guest appearances. In 1986, Nashville Network decided to screen his Republic and Columbia B-movie westerns under the title of *Melody Ranch Theatre* with Autry himself doing opening and closing announcements. During his long career, Autry had three horses to fill the role of Champion. The original died in 1947. Champion III, who appeared in the Gene Autry television series and also as the star of the *Adventures Of Champion* television series, died in 1991 at the age of 42. There was also a personal appearance Champion and a pony known as Little Champ. During his career he regularly sported a custom-made C.F. Martin guitar, with beautiful ornamental pearl inlay, together with his name. Autry was elected to the Country Music Hall Of Fame in 1969 for his songwriting abilities as well as his singing and acting. In 1980, he was inducted into the Cowboy Hall Of Fame Of Great Westerners. At the time of his induction, he was described as 'one of the most famous men, not only in America but in the world'. Autry sold the final 10 acres of his Melody Ranch film set in 1991. The ranch, in Placerita Canyon, California, which was used for the making of such classic westerns as *High Noon* and the television series *Gunsmoke*, is scheduled to become a historical feature. His last US country chart entry was 'Old Soldiers Never Die' in 1971.

● ALBUMS: *Stampede* 10-inch album (Columbia 1949)★★★, *Western Classics* 10-inch album (Columbia 1949)★★★, *Western Classics Volume 2* 10-inch album (Columbia 1949)★★★, *Easter Favorites* 10-inch album reissued as *Gene Autry Sings Peter Cottontail* (Columbia 1949)★★, *Champion* 10-inch album (Columbia 1950)★★★, *Merry Christmas With Gene Autry* 10-inch album (Columbia 1950)★★, *The Story Of The Nativity* 10-inch album (Columbia 1955)★★, *Little Johnny Pilgrim & Guffy The Goofy Gobbler* 10-inch album (Columbia 1955)★, *Rusty The Rocking Horse & Bucky, The Bucking Bronco* 10-inch album (Columbia 1955)★, *Gene Autry & Champion Western Adventures* (Columbia 1955)★★, *At The Rodeo* (Columbia 1958)★★★, *Christmas With Gene Autry* (Challenge 1958)★★, with Rosemary Clooney and Art Carney *Christmas Favorites* (Harmony 1964)★★★★, *Great Western Hits* (Harmony 1965)★★★, *Melody Ranch* (Melody Ranch 1965)★★★, with Clooney, Art Carney *Sings Peter Cottontail (First Easter Record For Children)* (Harmony 1965)★, *Back In The Saddle Again* (Harmony 1966)★★★, *Gene Autry Sings* (Harmony 1966)★★★, *Rudolph The Red-Nosed Reindeer* (Grand Prix 1968)★, *Live From Madison Square Garden* (Republic 1968)★★, *Christmas Time* (1974)★★★, *Melody Ranch - A Radio Adventure* (Radiola 1975)★★, *South Of The Border, All American Cowboy* (Republic 1976)★★, *Cowboy Hall Of Fame* (Republic 1976)★★★, *Murray Hill Record Theatre Presents Gene Autry's Melody Ranch* (1977)★★★, *50th Anniversary Album* (Republic 1978)★★★, *Songs Of Faith* (1978)★★, *Christmas Classics* (Starday 1978)★★, *Sounds Like Jimmie Rodgers* (1985)★★★.

● COMPILATIONS: *Gene Autry's Greatest Hits* (Columbia 1961)★★★, *Gene Autry's Golden Hits* (RCA Victor 1962)★★★★, *Country Music Hall Of Fame* (Columbia 1970)★★★, *Back In The Saddle Again* (Sony 1977)★★★, *22 All Time Favorites* (GRT 1977)★★★, *Columbia Historic Edition* (Columbia 1982)★★★, *Golden Hits* (Good Music 1985)★★★, *Christmas Favorites* (Columbia 1989)★★★, *Greatest Hits* (Sony 1992)★★★★, *The*

Essential 1933-46 (Columbia/Legacy 1992)★★★★, *South Of The Border* (Castle 1994)★★★, *Portrait Of An Artist* (Sound Exchange 1995)★★★★, *Blues Singer 1929-1931: Booger Rooger Saturday* (Columbia/Legacy 1996)★★★, *Sing, Cowboy, Sing! The Gene Autry Collection* 3-CD box set (Rhino 1997)★★★★, *The Singing Cowboy, Chapter One: Gene Autry With The Legendary Singing Groups Of The West* (Varese Sarabande 1997)★★★.

● FURTHER READING: *Back In The Saddle Again*, Gene Autry with Mickey Herskowitz. *The Gene Autry Book*, David Rothel.

AVALON, FRANKIE

b. Francis Avallone, 18 September 1939, Philadelphia, Pennsylvania, USA. The photogenic 50s teen-idol started as a trumpet-playing child prodigy. His first recordings in 1954 were the instrumentals 'Trumpet Sorrento' and 'Trumpet Tarantella' on X-Vik Records (an RCA Records subsidiary). In the mid-50s, he appeared on many television and radio shows including those of Paul Whiteman, Jackie Gleason and Ray Anthony. He joined Rocco & The Saints and was seen singing with them in the 1957 film *Jamboree* (*Disc Jockey Jamboree* in the UK). Avalon signed to Chancellor Records and in 1958 his third single for them, 'Dede Dinah', reached the US Top 10. It was the first of his 25 US chart entries, many of which were written by his hard-working manager, Bob Marucci. Despite the fact that he had a weak voice, he quickly became one of the top stars in the USA and managed two chart-toppers in 1959, 'Venus' and 'Why', which were his only UK Top 20 entries. He has had an astonishing 25 hits in the USA; astonishing because his musical talent was often in question. He had to wait until his 21st birthday in 1961 to receive the $100,000 he had earned to date, and by that time he had passed his peak as a singer and turned his attention to acting.

His acting career was also successful, with appearances in many films, including a string of beach movies alongside fellow 50s pop star Annette. He also appeared in the highly successful 1978 film *Grease*. He later recorded with little success on United Artists, Reprise, Metromedia, Regalia, Delite, Amos and Bobcat. Apart from his film and occasional television appearances, Avalon still performs on the supper-club circuit, and in 1986 toured in *Golden Boys Of Bandstand*. Alongside fellow Chancellor Records artist Fabian, he is often dismissed by rock critics, yet remains one of the American public's best-loved 50s teen-idols.

● ALBUMS: *Frankie Avalon* (Chancellor 1958)★★, *The Young Frankie Avalon* (Chancellor 1959)★★, *Swingin' On A Rainbow* (Chancellor 1959)★★, *Young And In Love* (Chancellor 1960)★★, *Summer Scene* (Chancellor 1960)★★, *And Now About Mr. Avalon* (Chancellor 1961)★★, *Italiano* (Chancellor 1962)★, *You Are Mine* (Chancellor 1962)★★, *Frankie Avalon's Christmas Album* (Chancellor 1962)★★, *Songs From Muscle Beach Party* film soundtrack (United Artists 1964)★★, *I'll Take Sweden* film soundtrack (United Artists 1965)★★, *I Want You Near Me* (1970)★, *Bobby Sox To Stockings* (Ace 1984)★★.

● COMPILATIONS: *A Whole Lotta Frankie* (Chancellor 1961)★★, *Frankie Avalon's 15 Greatest Hits* (United Artists 1964)★★★, *Best Of Frankie Avalon* (Creole 1984)★★★, *Frankie Avalon: Collection* (Castle 1990)★★, *The Fabulous Frankie Avalon* (Ace 1991)★★★, *Venus And Other Hits* (1993)★★★, *Venus: The Best Of Frankie*

Avalon (Varese Vintage 1995)★★★, *Greatest Hits* (Curb 1995)★★★.

● FILMS: (1957), *Jamboree a.k.a. Disc Jockey Jamboree* (1957), *Guns Of Timberland* (1960), *The Alamo* (1960), *Alakazam The Great (voice only)* (1961), *Voyage To The Bottom Of The Sea* (1961), *Sail A Crooked Ship* (1962), *Panic In The Year Zero!* (1962), *Operation Bikini* (1963), *Drums Of Africa* (1963), *The Castilion* (1963), *Beach Party* (1963), *Muscle Beach Party* (1964), *Bikini Beach* (1964), *Mr. Goldfoot And The Bikini Machine* (1965), *Sergeant Deadhead* (1965), *Ski Party* (1965), *Survival* (1965), *I'll Take Sweden* (1965), *How To Stuff A Wild Bikini* (1965), *Beach Blanket Bingo* (1965), *Fireball 500* (1966), *Sumura* (1967), *The Jet Set* (1967), *The Million Eyes Of Su-Muru* (1967), *Skidoo* (1968), *Ski Fever* (1969), *Horror House* (1970), *The Hunters (television)* (1974), *The Take* (1974), *Grease* (1978), *Back To The Beach* (1979), *Blood Song* (1982), *The Annette Funicello Story (television)* (1995), *Casino* (1995), *A Dream Is A Wish Your Heart Makes* (1995).

AYER, NAT D.

b. Nathaniel Davis, 30 September 1887, Boston, Massachusetts, USA, d. 19 September 1952, Bath, England. A composer, pianist, and performer, before moving to England where his career really took off, Ayer wrote one enduring standard, 'Oh, You Beautiful Doll' (1911), with A. Seymour Brown (b. 1885, d. 1952), and collaborated with Brown on several other numbers such as 'Moving Day In Jungle Town' (1909) (apparently a reference to Theodore Roosevelt's hunting trip to Africa) and 'If You Talk In Your Sleep, Don't Mention My Name' (1911). He also contributed to Broadway musical comedies and revues such as *Miss Innocence* (1908), *The Newlyweds And Their Baby* (1909), *The Echo* (1910), *A Winsome Widow* and *The Wall Street Girl* (1912). Ayer's first trip to England was as a member of the Ragtime Octet, at a time when American jazzy and ragtime music - particularly that of Irving Berlin - was beginning to sweep Europe. In 1916 Ayer teamed with lyricist Clifford Grey to write the score for one of the West End's biggest World War I hits, the revue *The Bing Boys Are Here*, which starred George Robey and Violet Loraine, and contained the immortal 'If You Were The Only Girl In The World', along with 'Another Little Drink Wouldn't Do Us Any Harm' and 'The Kipling Walk', among others. Ayer and Grey followed that with the music and lyrics for *The Bing Boys Are There* (1917, 'Let The Great Big World Keep Turning') and *The Bing Boys On Broadway* (1918), with its tender ballad, 'First Love, Last Love, Best Love', which was introduced by Robey and Clara Evelyn. As well as composing the music - and sometimes the lyrics - Ayer often appeared on stage himself, notably with Alice Delysia in the revue *Pell-Mell* (1916, Clifford Grey, Hugh E. Wright) and with Binnie Hale and Gertie Millar in the musical comedy *Houp-La!* (1916, Howard Talbot, Hugh E. Wright, Percy Greenbank). Among the many other London shows to which he contributed were *Hullo, Ragtime* (1912, 'You're My Baby' with A. Seymour Brown), *5064 Gerard* (1915, 'At The Foxtrot Ball' Dave Comer, Irving Berlin, Henry Marshall, Stanley Murphy, *et al.*), *Yes, Uncle!* (1917, Grey), *Baby Bunting* (1919, Grey), *Snap* (1922, Kenneth Duffield, Herman Hupfeld), 'Shufflin' Along' (with Ralph Stanley), *The Smith Family* (1922) and *Stop-Go!* (1935, Edgar Blatt).

BABES IN ARMS (FILM MUSICAL)

Adapted for the screen by Jack McGowan and Kay Van Riper from the 1937 Broadway musical of the same name, *Babes In Arms*, which was released by MGM two years later, retained only two of the songs - 'Babes In Arms' and 'Where Or When' - by Richard Rodgers and Lorenz Hart that had made the show so appealing. The story was much the same, however: a bunch of kids, whose vaudevillian parents are in a more or less permanent 'resting' situation, mount their own successful show and make the old folks proud. This theme of 'my uncle's got a barn, so we can do the show there', was used in many a future movie, and the idea was even worked into the title of a BBC radio quiz programme - *Let's Do The Show Right Here!* - more than 50 years later. After meeting for the first time in the minor musical *Thoroughbreds Don't Cry* (1937), two of the best-loved stars in movie history, Judy Garland and Mickey Rooney, came together again in *Babes In Arms*, and the magic was immediate: even at the age of 17, Garland's way with a song was awesome. There were some good numbers for her and the rest of the cast to work on, including four with lyrics by the film's producer, Arthur Freed, 'You Are My Lucky Star', 'Broadway Rhythm' and 'Good Morning' (all with Nacio Herb Brown), and 'I Cried For You' (with Abe Lyman and Gus Arnheim). The rest of the score included 'God's Country' (Harold Arlen-E.Y. 'Yip' Harburg), 'I'm Just Wild About Harry' (Eubie Blake-Noble Sissle), and 'Ja-Da' (Bob Carleton). *Babes In Arms* gave a boost to the already burgeoning career of director-choreographer Busby Berkeley, who collaborated with Garland, Rooney and Freed on three more movie milestones.

The first of these, *Strike Up The Band* (1940), borrowed George and Ira Gershwin's title song from the 1930 Broadway musical of that name, but nothing else. In the screenplay, by John Monks Jnr. and Fred Finklehoffe, Mickey Rooney assembles a school orchestra - with Judy Garland as the star vocalist - and, from his position on drums, drives them to the winning position in a nation-wide radio competition fronted by Paul Whiteman. The legendary bandleader and his orchestra were joined in the cast by June Preisser, William Tracy, Larry Nunn, Margaret Early, and Ann Shoemaker. Several of the songs were written by Freed's close musical associate, Roger Edens, including 'Do The La Conga', 'Nobody', 'Drummer Boy', 'Nell Of New Rochelle', and 'Our Love Affair' (lyric-Freed).

MGM's third vehicle for Garland and Rooney was *Babes On Broadway* (1941), and the formula worked yet again. This time, the show that just had to be put on was in aid of underprivileged children. The musical highlight was a delightful duet by Garland and Rooney on Ralph Freed and Burton Lane's 'How About You?', but there were lots of other good numbers, including 'Babes On Broadway' and 'Blackout Over Broadway' (both Ralph Freed-Lane), 'Hoe Down' (Ralph Freed-Roger Edens), 'Chin Up! Cheerio! Carry On! (Ralph Freed), and 'Anything Can Happen In New York (Lane-Harburg). Several older songs such as 'Mary Is A Grand Old Name', 'Yankee Doodle Boy', 'By The Light Of The Silvery Moon', 'Alabamy Bound' and 'Waiting For The Robert E. Lee' are used in a scene in which both of the young stars impersonate some legendary entertainers of the past and present: Rooney's uncanny (and hilarious) impression of Carmen Miranda (complete with tutti-frutti hat) still lingers in the memory. The final film in which Garland, Rooney, Arthur Freed and Busby Berkeley pooled their remarkable talents was *Girl Crazy* (1943). There had been an earlier film version - in 1932 - of the classic Broadway show with its outstanding score by George and Ira Gershwin, and for this remake most of the original storyline was retained, although a few locations were shifted around. Young philanderer Danny Churchill (Rooney), is chased out of town by his father and ends up in a males-only college out West. Not to be outdone, he falls for one of the dean's granddaughters (Judy Garland), who joins with Danny to get the college out of debt by . . . putting on a show. The film contained most of the Broadway score, plus another famous Gershwin song, 'Fascinating Rhythm'. 'Bidin' My Time', which had been sung in the original show by a cowboy quartet, now took on a new dimension when given the Garland treatment. The other numbers included 'Could You Use Me?', 'Treat Me Rough', 'Bronco Busters', 'Embraceable You', 'Cactus Time In Arizona' and 'But Not For Me'. Tommy Dorsey And His Orchestra were featured in several numbers including the rousing finale, 'I Got Rhythm', and Roger Edens contributed one new song, 'Happy Birthday, Ginger'. After *Girl Crazy*, Rooney went back to his Andy Hardy pictures, among other projects, and Judy Garland joined Gene Kelly in his first feature film, *For Me And My Gal*.

BABES IN ARMS (STAGE MUSICAL)

Richard Rodgers and Lorenz Hart were right at the peak of their form for this show, which opened at the Shubert Theatre in New York on 14 April 1937. Their libretto dealt with the familiar story of a future Broadway hit show that starts out with one of a group of kids shouting: 'Hey, let's put it on in my father's barn!'. In *Babes In Arms* the kids' parents are vaudevillians who are away, working in touring productions, and their offsprings have to produce an original show or be sent to a work farm. Nobody in the cast was that well-known - not then - but that did not seem to bother audiences who were enchanted by Rodgers and Hart's outstanding score, which contained some of the biggest hit songs in the history of American popular music, such as 'Where Or When', sung by the 16-year-old Mitzi Green and Ray Heatherton, 'The Lady Is A Tramp' (Green), 'Johnny One Note' (Wynn Murray), 'I Wish I Were In Love Again' (Grace McDonald and Rolly Pickert) and 'My Funny Valentine' (Green). Alfred Drake, who

later created the role of Curly in *Oklahoma!*, made his Broadway debut in *Babes In Arms*, singing the title song with Green and Heatherton, and Dan Dailey, destined to be one of Hollywood's favourite song-and-dance men, was in the chorus. Also featured were two more superior Hollywood hoofers, Harold and Fayard, the Nicholas Brothers. After transferring to the Majestic Theatre in October, the show continued for a run of 289 performances. The 1939 film version starred Judy Garland and Mickey Rooney.

BABES IN TOYLAND (STAGE MUSICAL)

Victor Herbert returned to the Broadway musical stage for *Babes In Toyland* following a sabbatical as the director of the Pittsburgh Symphony Orchestra between 1901 and 1903. The show opened at the Majestic Theatre in New York on 13 October 1903, with Herbert collaborating again with Glen MacDonough, the librettist and lyricist with whom he had worked on *The Gold Bug* (1896). MacDonough's story told of the 'Babes', Jane (Mabel Barrison) and Alan (William Norris), who find themselves in Toyland following a shipwreck that has been engineered by their evil Uncle Barnaby (George Denham). During their exciting journey to the magical city, they meet a host of nursery rhyme characters, such as Simple Simon, Bo Peep, Little Boy Blue, and many others, who help the Babes bring their wicked uncle to the Toyland court, where he gets his just deserts. The stage sets and special effects were spectacular, as was Herbert and MacDonough's beguiling score, which included the lively 'March Of The Toys', along with 'Song Of The Poet', 'Go To Sleep, Slumber Deep', 'I Can't Do The Sum', 'Toyland', 'Never Mind, Bo-Peep' and 'Barney O'Flynn'. *Babes In Toyland* ran for 192 performances - a creditable performance at a time when Broadway was seeing an average of over 20 new musicals each season. Since then there have been three film versions: the well-received 1934 production starring Laurel and Hardy; a 1961 Disney adaptation, with Ray Bolger, Tommy Sands, Jack Donahue, and Annette Funicello; and the 1986 version with Drew Barrymore, which dumped most of the songs in favour of a new Leslie Bricusse score.

BABES ON BROADWAY (FILM MUSICAL)

(see *Babes In Arms* (film musical))

BABY

Baby opened at the Ethel Barrymore Theatre in New York on 4 February 1983, and proved to be another of those musicals with a score that is considered outstanding, yet the show itself fails to achieve its potential, and loses a great deal of money. Sybille Pearson's book, based on a story by Susan Yankowitz, deals with three couples: a dean and his wife in their 40s with three children in college; an athletics coach and his wife in their 30s who are yearning for a child (Nick is 'shooting blanks', according to the doctor); and a pair of students who believe that becoming parents is 'a breeze'. As the show opens, all of the couples believe they are expecting babies. It transpires that Nick and his Pam are mistaken, and one of the highlights of the witty and sensitive score by lyricist Richard

Maltby Jnr. (who also directed) and composer David Shire, is 'Romance', the song that accompanies their efforts to reverse that fact, at 11 pm precisely on certain days of the month. There were several other emotional, amusing and pertinent numbers, such as 'And What If We Had Loved Like That?', 'Baby, Baby, Baby', 'What Could Be Better?', 'I Want It All', 'Fatherhood Blues', 'At Night She Comes Home To Me', and the ballad of affirmation, 'The Story Goes On'. One of the reasons for the failure of *Baby* to attract audiences in sufficient numbers to affray its costs, could well have been the word-of-mouth concerning a scene in which the progress of sperm and the development of a foetus was projected onto a large set of computer-operated curtains. Even in the enlightened 80s, many patrons of the musical theatre were not prepared for that. The cast of Liz Callaway, James Congdon, Catherine Cox, Beth Fowler, Todd Graff, and Martin Vidnoc, soldiered on for 241 performances in New York, and the show was premiered in the north of England in 1990, where it starred American song-and-dance man Tim Flavin, and the British actress Dilys Watling.

BACKBEAT

A high-profile tribute to one-time Beatles bass player Stuart Sutcliffe, who died aged 21 in April 1962, this 1994 film featured an all-star musical as well as acting cast. The film concerned itself with the origins of the Beatles and the time they spent in Hamburg, Germany, in that country's beat boom of the early 60s. Sutcliffe was played by Stephen Dorff, who was not even born when the Beatles enjoyed their heyday. His father had produced a record with Ringo Starr a year before he became involved in the project. Ian Hart stole the show with his portrayal of John Lennon, though it was not the first time he had tackled the 'role'. He had previously appeared in Christopher Munch's *The Hours And The Times*, a fictional account of a holiday trip with Lennon and Beatles manager Brian Epstein. Sheryl Lee, previously famous for playing Laura Palmer in *Twin Peaks*, took the part of Sutcliffe's photographer girlfriend, Astrid Kirchherr, who helped to define the Beatles' style in their embryonic days. Kirchherr herself helped Lee with the part. Meanwhile, a 90s supergroup was recruited to provide the soundtrack. Don Fleming (Gumball, etc.), Greg Dulli (Afghan Whigs), Mike Mills (R.E.M.) and Thurston Moore (Sonic Youth) were the principals behind the 'Backbeat Band'. Other key contributors included Dave Grohl (Nirvana) and Dave Pirner (Soul Asylum). This stellar cast was recruited by Don Was (Was (Not Was)) to provide *Backbeat* with a backbeat, and they released a promotional single, 'Money', as well as a soundtrack album.

BAD BOY JOHNNY AND THE PROPHETS OF DOOM

'The most blasphemous show in town - and it's being performed in a house of God', wrote one critic after this rock musical materialized on 27 January 1994 at the Union Chapel, a Congregational church in the London borough of Islington, following its successful run in Australia. Over the past several years, UK audiences have become accustomed to some extremely weird Antipodean goings-on via imported television soaps such as *Neighbours* and *Home And Away*, but even those programmes have so far stayed clear of storylines involving 'a foul-mouthed harmonica-playing pope in dark glasses who dies of heart failure while being seduced by a naked nun (there is also a Virgin Mary stripper and a priest who urinates into the Communion Cup)'. Daniel Abineri, a veteran of *The Rocky Horror Show*, conceived, wrote, and directed this highly controversial production, and chose Mark Shaw, the frontman of an appropriately titled band, Then Jerico, to play Big Bad Johnny, the first rock 'n' roll Pope. The permanently phlegmatic comedian Craig Ferguson was Father MacLean, the holy father's 'all-raping, all-pillaging' nemesis, and the lightly clad Desire was portrayed by Eve Barker. The show closed after only 10 performances following protests from nuns and others, including Father Kit Cunningham of St. Ethelreda's Church, Holborn, London, who said that the musical should be consigned to the dustbin. The author and critic Sheridan Morley commented: 'Suddenly there is a scary puritanism moving through. It's as if we've gone back to the 1950s.'

BADDELEY, HERMIONE

b. Hermione Clinton-Baddeley, 13 November 1906, Broseley, Shropshire, England, d. 19 August 1986, Los Angeles, California, USA. A distinguished actress and singer, Baddeley joined Margaret Morrison's School of Dancing when she was quite young, and then travelled with the Arts League of Service for three years. She had already established herself as a fine dramatic actress when she made her musical stage debut in May 1924 at London's Duke of York's Theatre in Archie de Bear's revue *Punch Bowl*. From then on, as well as continuing to appear in the straight theatre, she became one of the finest, and funniest, intimate revue artists ever seen in the West End. In September 1924 she joined the *Co-Optimists* at the Palace Theatre, and a few months later was in Noël Coward's *On With The Dance* (1925). This was followed by *Still Dancing* (1925), *Cochran's Revue* (1926), *Queen High* (a book show by Buddy De Sylva and Lawrence Schwab), *The Five O'Clock Girl* (1929, a Guy Bolton-Fred Thompson book show), *After Dinner* (1932), *Ballyhoo* (1932), and *Floodlight* (1937). She is thought to have reached her peak during the next few years in two supremely witty Herbert Farjeon revues, *Nine Sharp* (1938) and *The Little Revue* (1939), as well as *Rise Above It* (1941), in which she 'sparked off' another mistress of the genre, Hermione Gingold. After World War II, during which Baddeley spent long periods abroad entertaining the troops with ENSA, she returned to the London stage in *The Gaieties* (1945) with Leslie Henson, and then bade farewell to revue in great style with Alan Melville's *A La Carte* (1948) and *At The Lyric* (1953, later revised as *Going To Town*). In 1961 she went to America, and played on Broadway, toured with plays such as *Canterbury Tales* (1969), in which she played the Wife of Bath, and appeared in cabaret. She spent most of the rest of her life in the USA, returning occasionally to Britain, where she was in a revival of *The Threepenny Opera* (1972) as Mrs. Peachum. In America, Baddeley also starred frequently on television, and was particularly successful in *The Good Life* (1971) and *Maude* (1974-77). She also extended a film career that had begun with her taking the role of Calamity Kate in the comedy *A Daughter In Revolt* (1927), and eventually included the musicals *Expresso Bongo* (1959), *The Unsinkable Molly Brown* (1964), *Mary Poppins* (1964), *The Happiest Millionaire* (1967), and an Oscar nomination for Best Supporting Actress in 1959 for her role in *Room At The Top*. She was renowned for her portrayal of cheerful, yet somewhat eccentric, 'ordinary' women, who were able to rise above their problems.

One of her elder sisters was Angela Baddeley (b. 4 July 1904, d. 22 February 1976), who also had a long career as an actress, and is probably best remembered in both the UK and USA as housekeeper Mrs. Bridges in the 70s television series *Upstairs Downstairs*.

● FURTHER READING: *The Unsinkable Hermione Baddeley*, Hermione Baddeley.

● FILMS: *A Daughter In Revolt* (1927), *The Guns Of Loos* (1928), *Caste* (1930), *Love Life And Laughter* (1934), *Royal Cavalcade* (1935), *Kipps* (1941), *Brighton Rock* (1947), *It Always Rains On Sunday* (1947), *Quartet* (1948), *No Room At The Inn* (1948), *Passport To Pimlico* (1949), *Dear Mr. Prohack* (1949), *The Woman In Question* (1950), *Scrooge* (1951), *There Is Another Sun* (1951), *Hell Is Sold Out* (1951), *Tom Brown's Schooldays* (1951), *The Pickwick Papers* (1952), *Song Of Paris* (1952), *Time Gentlemen Please* (1952), *Counterspy* (1953), *Cosh Boy* (1953), *Women Without Men* (1954), *The Belles Of St. Trinian's* (1954), *Expresso Bongo* (1959), *Jetstorm* (1959), *Room At The Top* (1959), *Midnight Lace* (1960), *Let's Get Married* (1960), *Rag Doll* (1961), *Information Received* (1961), *The Unsinkable Molly Brown* (1964), *Mary Poppins* (1964), *Harlow* (1965), *Do Not Disturb* (1965), *Marriage On The Rocks* (1965), *Bullwhip Griffin* (1967), *The Happiest Millionaire* (1967), *Up The Front* (1972), *The Black Windmill* (1974), *C.H.O.M.P.S.* (1979), *There Goes The Bride* (1980), voice only *The Secret Of Nimh* (1982).

BAGLEY, BEN

b. 18 October 1933, Burlington, Vermont, USA, d. 21 March 1998, New York, USA. A record and theatre producer and director, Bagley is chiefly remembered by lovers of the musical theatre for his *Revisited* albums. These contain forgotten gems, songs composed by the leading stage and film composers of the century that were either cut from the productions for which they were intended, or swamped by more apparently attractive compositions. Ben Bagley came from a musical background: his maternal grandfather was the conductor of the Vermont Symphony Orchestra until it became a victim of the early 30s Depression, and his mother had been a concert pianist before she married Bagley's father. Both of his parents were fond of Broadway musicals, and Bagley was introduced to show tunes via the sheet music they would bring back from their trips to New York. He moved to New York himself at the age of 16, and worked for publishers McGraw Hill as an office boy. Five years later, backed by Marian and Judson Todd, millionaire owners of steamship yards, Bagley produced his first show, *The Shoestring Revue* (1955). This was followed a year later by *The Littlest Revue* (1956), and *Shoestring '57*. The latter opened with the overture to *My Fair Lady* - that is, until Alan Jay Lerner and Frederick Loewe learned of it. All three of these off-Broadway productions were well received by the

critics (although they were not long-runners), and featured sketches and songs by a group of young, talented writers, including Sheldon Harnick, Vernon Duke, Lee Adams, John Latouche, Tom Jones, Harvey Schmidt, Charles Strouse, Ogden Nash, and Arthur Siegel. Their material was performed by up-and-coming artists such as Beatrice Arthur, Dody Goodman, Chita Rivera, Nancy Walker, Joel Grey, Charles Strouse, Tammy Grimes, and Charlotte Rae. Arthur Siegel was an important element in the next phase in Bagley's career - the records. Reportedly, when Bagley was hospitalized with tuberculosis, Siegel sent tapes of himself singing rare show songs. They gave the patient the idea for a series of albums, the first of which, *Rodgers And Hart Revisited*, was released in 1960. Dorothy Loudon, Danny Meehan, Charlotte Rae and Cy Young sang the songs, which were beautifully arranged by Norman Paris. All the selections were fresh and exciting, but outstanding were Loudon's 'At The Roxy Music Hall', from *I Married An Angel* (1938), and Charlotte Rae's 'Everybody Loves You' (1937, cut from *I'd Rather Be Right* before its opening). The second album celebrated little-known numbers by Cole Porter, which led to Bagley's final, and longest-running, show, *The Decline And Fall Of The Entire World As Seen Through The Eyes Of Cole Porter* (1965). It starred Kaye Ballard, Harold Lang, William Hickey, and Carmen Alvarez, and proved to be the forerunner of a genre that would eventually include composer anthology shows such as *Side By Side By Sondheim*, *Smokey Joe's Café* (Leiber And Stoller), *And The World Goes 'Round* (John Kander and Fred Ebb), and *Sophisticated Ladies* (Duke Ellington). As for the *Revisited* albums, there were some 50 in all, mainly on Bagley's own Painted Smiles label, and dedicated to Arthur Schwartz, Noël Coward, Alan Jay Lerner, De Sylva, Brown And Henderson, Frank Loesser, Vernon Duke, Kurt Weill, Harold Arlen, Jerome Kern, Oscar Hammerstein II, *et al*. Some composers were revisited several times, and Bagley was an expert in persuading singers of the calibre of Bobby Short, Blossom Dearie, Barbara Cook, Margaret Whiting, Johnny Desmond, Tammy Grimes, Elaine Stritch, David Allyn, and Kaye Ballard to perform for hardly any money. Katharine Hepburn contributed her inimitable rendering of Porter's 'Thank You So Much, Mrs. Lowsborough-Goodby' for free, and she was only one of a number of more unlikely participants in Bagley's enterprise. Among the others not exactly renowned for their vocalizing were Rhonda Fleming, Laurence Harvey, Anthony Perkins, Joanne Woodward, and Gloria Swanson. During the last years of his life, Bagley spent much of his time supervising the transfer of his albums, complete with his own highly distinctive liner notes and a pictures of his beloved cat Emily, to CD. His most successful stage project, *The Decline And Fall Of The Entire World As Seen Through The Eyes Of Cole Porter*, was revived on the London Fringe in August 1998, a few months after his death.

BAGNERIS, VERNEL

b. 31 July 1949, New Orleans, Louisiana, USA. Bagneris was raised in an area of the city peopled by Creoles and rich with music. He studied at Xavier University, after which he briefly taught English in high school, but never lost hold of his attraction to and feeling for the music and the colourful culture of which he was to prove himself an important part. He abandoned teaching and after spending some time acting at the Mickery Theatre in Amsterdam, Bagneris began to direct his energies towards developing theatrical ventures in his home-town, forming the New Experience Players, an integrated company that presented straight drama. In 1978 he wrote a show that recreated the kind of vaudeville performance that had been immensely popular decades before his birth. The show, which was set on- and off-stage in a New Orleans theatre in 1926, was called *One Mo' Time*. After running for six months in the city, the show moved to New York, where it ran for three and a half years at the Village Gate, spawning numerous touring companies and playing overseas, including an 18-month spell in London's West End. Bagneris also pursued his acting career, appearing in the Hollywood version of Dennis Potter's *Pennies From Heaven* (1981) and in the Tom Waits vehicle, *Down By Law* (1986). He has also acted on television. In the theatre, Bagneris also wrote other shows, including a sequel to *One Mo' Time*, *Staggerlee*, which starred Ruth Brown, *Hoo-Dude*, *Further Mo'*, the New York run of which suffered from the advent of the Gulf War despite even better notices than *One Mo' Time*, and *Jelly Roll*, a two-man show in which Bagneris was accompanied by pianist Morten Gunnar Larsen. For *Jelly Roll*, a show based upon the racy life and timeless music of Jelly Roll Morton, Bagneris, Larsen and the show won high critical acclaim, including Obie Awards, the Outer Critics Circle Award, and the Lucille Lortel Award, the latter for Best Off-Broadway Musical. *Jelly Roll* was also performed in its entirety at the Oslo Jazz Festival, while in New York by the mid-90s it had moved into Manhattan's 47th Street Theatre. Bagneris has consistently proved himself to be a major figure of the American theatre and while he has always worked out of the great tradition of black music and culture, his approach, his skills and his integrity have been such that he has been able to attract and retain audiences of all races and cultural backgrounds.

● ALBUMS: *Jelly Roll* (GHB 1996)★★★★.

BAILEY, PEARL

b. 29 March 1918, Newport News, Virginia, USA, d. 17 August 1990, Philadelphia, Pennsylvania, USA. Pearlie Mae, as she was known, was an uninhibited performer, who mumbled her way through some songs and filled others with outrageous asides and sly innuendoes. She entered the world of entertainment as a dancer but later sang in vaudeville, graduating to the New York nightclub circuit in the early 40s. After working with the Noble Sissle Orchestra, she became band-vocalist with Cootie Williams, with whom she recorded 'Tessa's Torch Song', previously sung by Dinah Shore in the movie *Up In Arms*. Bailey received strong critical acclaim after substituting for Sister Rosetta Tharpe in a show, and was subsequently signed to star in the 1946 Harold Arlen/Johnny Mercer Broadway musical, *St. Louis Woman*. A year later her slurred version of 'Tired' was the highlight of the movie *Variety Girl*, and she gave several other outstanding per-

formances in films such as *Carmen Jones* (1954), *St. Louis Blues* (1958) and *Porgy And Bess* (1959). During her stay with Columbia Records (1945-50), Bailey recorded a series of duets with Frank Sinatra, trumpeter Oran 'Hot Lips' Page and comedienne Moms Mabley. She also recorded some solo tracks with outstanding arrangers/conductors, including Gil Evans and Tadd Dameron. Upon joining the Coral label in 1951, she employed Don Redman as her regular musical director, the association lasting for 10 years. In 1952, she had her biggest hit record, 'Takes Two To Tango'. In that same year she married drummer Louie Bellson and he took over from Redman as her musical director in 1961. Although few of her records sold in vast quantities, Bailey had always been a crowd-pulling live performer and, following her early stage triumph in *St. Louis Woman*, she was later cast in other shows including *The House Of Flowers*, *Bless You All*, *Arms And The Girl* and an all-black cast version of *Hello, Dolly!*. She also starred in several US television specials, playing down the double entendre that caused one of her albums, *For Adults Only*, to be 'restricted from air-play'. In 1991 Pearl Bailey was posthumously inducted into the New York Theater Hall Of Fame.

● ALBUMS: *Pearl Bailey Entertains* 10-inch album (Columbia 1950)★★★★, *Say Si Si* 10-inch album (Coral 1953)★★★, *I'm With You* 10-inch album (Coral 1953)★★★, *House Of Flowers* film soundtrack (Columbia 1954)★★★, *St. Louis Woman* film soundtrack (Capitol 1955)★★★, *The One And Only Pearl Bailey* (Mercury 1956)★★★★, *Birth Of The Blues* (Coral 1956)★★★★, *The One And Only Pearl Bailey Sings* (Mercury 1957)★★★, *Cultured Pearl* (Coral 1957)★★★, *The Intoxicating Pearl Bailey* (Mercury 1957)★★★★, *For Adults Only* (1958)★★★★, *Gems By Pearl Bailey* (Vocalion 1958)★★★★, *Pearl Bailey Sings!* (1959)★★★★, *St. Louis Blues* (1959)★★★★, *Porgy & Bess & Others* (Columbia 1959)★★★★, *More Songs For Adults* (1960)★★★, *Songs Of Bad Old Days* (1960)★★★, *Naughty But Nice* (1961)★★★, *Songs She Loves By Arlen* (1962)★★★★, *All About Good Little Girls And Bad Little Boys* (Roulette 1962)★★★, *Come On Let's Play With Pearlie Mae* (Roulette 1962)★★★, *Songs By Jimmy Van Heusen* (1964)★★★★, *Les Poupees De Paris* (RCA Victor 1964)★★★, *Hello, Dolly!* film soundtrack (RCA Victor 1964)★★★, *For Adult Listening* (60s)★★★, *C'est La Vie* (60s)★★★, *Risque World* (60s)★★★.

● COMPILATIONS: *The Definitive* (1965)★★★★, *The Best Of - The Roulette Years* (Roulette 1991)★★★★.

● FURTHER READING: *The Raw Pearl*, Pearl Bailey. *Talking To Myself*, Pearl Bailey.

● FILMS: *Variety Girl* (1947), *Isn't It Romantic* (1948), *Carmen Jones* (1954), *That Certain Feeling* (1955), *St. Louis Blues* (1957), *Porgy And Bess* (1959), *All The Fine Young Cannibals* (1960), *The Landlord* (1969).

BAKER STREET

Some three months after Lionel Bart's *Oliver!*, with its Victorian setting, ended a run of 774 performances on Broadway, New York audiences were transported to turn-of-the-century London with Alexander H. Cohen's presentation of this opulent musical comedy-drama. The show opened on 16 February 1965 at the Broadway Theatre, and, given its title, there were no prizes for guessing that the subject of the piece was Arthur Conan Doyle's supersleuth, Sherlock Holmes. Jerome Coopersmith's book was drawn from three of Holmes' cases: 'The Adventure Of The Empty House', 'A Scandal In Bohemia' and 'The Final Problem'. On this occasion, Holmes (Fritz Weaver) foils the sinister Professor Moriarty (Martin Gabel) in his attempt to steal Queen Victoria's jewels, thereby ruining the Diamond Jubilee celebrations. The action ranges over a wide area, before Moriarty finds himself (just like the 'bluebirds') over the white cliffs of Dover. Holmes himself is resolutely pursued throughout the length and breadth of Oliver Smith's sets by the beautiful actress Irene Adler (Inga Swenson). Along with all the melodrama, there was a spectacular Jubilee Parade scene involving the Bill Baird Marionettes, and some spirited dancing by the young Baker Street Irregulars led by Wiggins (Teddy Green), which was choreographed by Lee Becker Theodore. Also in the cast were Patrick Horgan (Captain Gregg), Paddy Edwards (Mrs Hudson), Daniel Keyes (Inspector Lestrade), Virginia Westoff (Daisy), Martin Wolfson (Baxter), Bert Michaels (Duckbellows), Sal Pernice (Nipper), George Lee (Perkins), Mark Jude Shell (Macipper), Jay Norman (Murillo), and Gwenn Lewis (Tavern Singer). One of the trio of 'Killers' was the future Broadway star and director, Tommy Tune. As always, the faithful Doctor Watson (Peter Sallis) was on hand, and sang the appealing 'A Married Man', one of the numbers composed by Marian Grudeff and Raymond Jessel. The two were responsible for most of what was generally regarded as a disappointing score, including Swenson's pleasant 'I'd Do It Again' and 'Letters', the Irregulars' 'Leave It To Us, Guv' and 'It's So Simple', 'Finding Words For Spring', 'What A Night This Is Going To Be', 'London Underworld', 'Roof Space', 'Pursuit', and 'Jewelry'. There were also two interpolations by Jerry Bock and Sheldon Harnick, 'I'm In London Again' and 'I Shall Miss You' (some sources say that an item called 'Cold, Clear World' was theirs, too). Harold Prince's imaginative staging was generally applauded, but even with producer Cohen's expert publicity, *Baker Street* came to the end of the road after 313 performances. There were Tony Award nominations for Swenson, Coopersmith, and costume designer, Motley. Oliver Smith won an award for *Baker Street* and other work; he also received a Special Tony Award.

A German Sherlock Holmes musical, *Ein Fall Für Sherlock Holmes*, conceived by Gerd Natschinski and Jürgen Degenhardt, was presented in 1982, and seven years later London audiences saw *Sherlock Holmes - The Musical*, which had a book, music, and lyrics by Leslie Bricusse, in 1989.

BAKER'S WIFE, THE

With a book by Joseph Stein based on the 1938 movie *La Femme De Boulanger*, by Marcel Pagnol and Jean Giono, and a score by Stephen Schwartz, *The Baker's Wife* was supposed to be the major musical attraction of the 1976/7 Broadway season, but it did not get as far as New York. After opening in Los Angeles at the Dorothy Chandler Pavilion on 11 May 1976, it then toured for six months before closing in Washington, DC. While the show was on the road the cast changed frequently, but Topol, the Israeli-born actor who had triumphed in *Fiddler On The Roof* more than 10 years earlier, stayed almost until the

end, and Patti LuPone, star of another famous film adaptation, the 1993 West End production of *Sunset Boulevard*, was the original leading lady. The simple plot involves a baker, who, after finding that a handsome chauffeur is driving his wife crazy, refuses to supply the town with any more bread until she comes to her senses and returns to him. Stephen Schwartz, whose run of hit shows had included *Godspell*, *Pippin* and *The Magic Show*, provided the music and lyrics for several delightful songs, including 'Gifts Of Love', 'If I Have To Live Alone', 'Merci, Madame', 'Chanson', 'Where Is The Warmth?', 'Endless Delights', 'The Luckiest Man In The World' and 'Serenade'. Ironically, the most enduring number has proved to be the intriguing ballad 'Meadowlark', which was sung by LuPone and which had been periodically withdrawn because, apparently, producer David Merrick disliked it intensely. Happily, it was included on the Original Cast album, and has since become a favourite of divas such as Betty Buckley. Such was the quality and accessibility of the score that *The Baker's Wife* became a favourite subject for provincial theatre groups. On 27 November 1989, a reworked production opened at the Phoenix Theatre in London. Directed by Trevor Nunn, whose 80s stage musical triumphs had included *Cats*, *Starlight Express* and *Les Misérables*, the show starred Nunn's then-wife, Sharon Lee Hill, and Alun Armstrong, who was to have great success four years later in a London 'chamber' version of Stephen Sondheim's *Sweeney Todd*. Schwartz wrote several new numbers, such as 'Buzz-A-Buzz', 'Plain And Simple' and 'If It Wasn't For You', for the London production, but *The Baker's Wife* folded after a disappointing run of only 56 performances.

BAKER, BELLE
(see Abrahams, Maurice)

BALALAIKA

A revised version of the 1933 musical play, *The Great Hussar*, with a book and lyrics by Eric Maschwitz, and music by George Posford and Bernard Grün, *Balalaika* opened at the Adelphi Theatre in London on 22 December 1936. The plot's initial locale is the exterior of the Balalaika Night Club in Montmartre just after World War I. An old man is singing a sad ballad ('Where Are The Snows?') that transports the audience to the singer's homeland, Russia in 1914, by way of the story of a lovely ballerina and singer, Lydia (Muriel Angelus), and her high-born lover, Peter (Roger Reville). With a series of lavish stage settings that rivalled even Ivor Novello's celebrated productions, the two young people survive the Revolution, foil an attempted assassination attempt on the Tsar, and finally melt into each other's arms while in exile in Paris. The happy couple's principal duet was the delightful 'If The World Were Mine', and other highlights of the romantic and dramatic score included 'Red, Red Rose', 'Be A Casanova', 'Ballerina, Sad And Lonely', 'Nitchevo', 'In the Moonlight'/'Two Guitars', 'Vodka'/'Red Shirt', 'The Devil In Red', and, of course, 'At The Balalaika', which was sung in the show by the aristocratic Peter; the song later achieved wider popularity, and was recorded by such artists as Richard Tauber and Greta

Keller. During its run *Balalaika* moved to different theatres within the West End, eventually closing in April 1938, after a run of 570 performances - a phenomenal performance for those days. Later in 1938 the show went on the road, and in the same year a Paris production was mounted with some additional songs by Robert Stolz. In 1939, *Balalaika* became the first British musical to be filmed in Hollywood, although, ironically, only the title song (with an amended lyric) survived from the original score. The rest of the songs were culled from various sources and composers. The film starred Nelson Eddy and the Hungarian soprano, Ilona Massey.

BALANCHINE, GEORGE

b. Georgi Melitonovitch Balanchivadze, 9 January 1904, St. Petersburg, Russia, d. 30 April 1983, New York, USA. One of the most celebrated and distinguished choreographers in the history of ballet, Balanchine also revolutionized the art of dance in the Broadway musical theatre. When he was nine, he passed an audition for the Imperial School of Ballet in St. Petersburg, and it was there that he made his first attempts at choreography. After graduating, he joined the Maryinski corps de ballet, and in 1924 defected to the west while on a tour of Europe with the Soviet State Dancers. Two years later, he sustained a knee injury that curtailed his dancing career. In 1925 he was named principal choreographer with the Ballet Russes, but when that folded Balanchine took a series of jobs, of which the most interesting and unusual was arranging the dances for a series of London revues: *Wake Up And Dream!* (1929) and *Cochran's Revue* (1930 and 1931). In 1933, Balanchine moved to the USA and founded the School of American Ballet, and later, the New York Ballet Company. When the former disbanded, he turned his attention to Broadway. In 1936, after collaborating with Robert Alton on the dance sequences for the *Ziegfeld Follies*, he caused quite a stir with his choreography for the Richard Rodgers and Lorenz Hart show *On Your Toes*. It was the first time that ballet had been utililized as a fundamental element in the story of a musical, and was particularly effective in the 'Slaughter On Tenth Avenue' sequence, which was danced by Tamara Geva and Ray Bolger. In the London production, Geva's part was taken by Vera Zorina, the second of Balanchine's four wives. Another revolutionary move in *On Your Toes* was Balanchine's abandonment of the traditional chorus line, giving the ensemble a far more important role. He continued to bring his innovative ideas to the musical theatre in shows such as *Babes In Arms* (1937), *I Married An Angel* (1938), *The Boys From Syracuse* (1938), *Keep Off The Grass* (1940), *Louisiana Purchase* (1940), *Cabin In The Sky* (1940, also co-directed with Albert Lewis), *The Lady Comes Across* (1942), *Rosalinda* (1942), *What's Up?* (1943, also directed), *Dream With Music* (1944), *Song Of Norway* (1944), *Mr. Strauss Goes To Boston* (1945), *The Chocolate Soldier* (1947 revival), *Where's Charley?* (1948), *Courtin' Time* (1951), and the 1954 revival of *On Your Toes*. Balanchine also worked in Hollywood on the films *The Goldwyn Follies* (1938), *On Your Toes* (1938), *I Was An Adventuress* (1940) and *Star Spangled Rhythm* (1943). During and after his Broadway period, he continued to create the most original ballets for the classical theatre, held a number of prestigious positions, and founded, with Lincoln Kirstein, the Ballet Society (1946), later renamed the New York City Ballet. He subsequently served as its Artistic Director and Director Emeritus. His honours included the Handel Medallion for Cultural Achievement, New York, 1970, and the Presidential Medal of Freedom, 1983.

● FURTHER READING: *Balanchine*, Bernard Taper. *Discovering Balanchine*, B.H. Haggin.

BALL OF FIRE

Hollywood has never been averse to squeezing the last drop of loot out of a good idea. This 1941 film broadly re-jigged *Snow White And The Seven Dwarfs* (1937) and obviously appealed to director Howard Hawks so much that seven years later he remade it as *A Song Is Born*. A group of professors have been cooped up writing an encyclopedia when a chance visitor from the outside makes them realize that, musically speaking, they are out of touch. One of their number, Gary Cooper, is sent forth to discover what is happening in the contemporary popular music business and meets band singer Barbara Stanwyck, with whom he becomes romantically involved. The Gene Krupa band, featuring the leader and Roy Eldridge, performs 'Drum Boogie' with Stanwyck, apparently ghosted by Martha Tilton (presumably because Irene Daye was in the process of leaving the band around this time). Good fun and all very professional, but not to be taken seriously by jazz fans.

BALL, LUCILLE

b. Lucille Désirée Ball, 6 August 1911, Celeron, near Jamestown, New York, USA, d. 26 April 1989, Los Angeles, California, USA. An actress and singer, with a trademark mop of red hair, Ball was one of the all-time great American comediennes. Her influence on US television, both as a performer and an executive, was immense. Her father was an electrician and her mother a concert pianist. Ball left high school at the age of 15 in order to join the John Murray Anderson-Robert Milton Dramatic School in New York, and subsequently worked in the chorus of several stage productions; she also featured on giant billboards as the Chesterfield Cigarette Girl, before becoming bed-ridden with rheumatoid arthritis for two years. In 1933, Ball secured the role of a Goldwyn Girl in the Eddie Cantor movie *Roman Scandals*, and she continued with Goldwyn until 1935, when she signed a seven-year contract with RKO. In addition to comedy and more serious assignments, Ball played numerous minor roles in movie musicals such as *Broadway Thru A Keyhole*, *Bottoms Up*, *Hold That Girl*, *Kid Millions*, *Broadway Bill*, *Roberta*, *Old Man Rhythm*, *Top Hat*, *I Dream Too Much* and *Follow The Fleet*, before taking more substantial, and then leading roles, in other musical features, including *Joy Of Living*, *Room Service*, *That's Right-You're Wrong*, *Dance Girl Dance*, *Seven Days Leave*, *Du Barry Was A Lady*, *Best Foot Forward*, *Meet The People* and *Ziegfeld Follies*. After she met the Cuban bandleader Desi Arnaz in 1940 on the set of *Too Many Girls*, in which she was top-billed for the first time, they were married in November of that year. During the 40s, as well as working consistently in movies for a variety of studios, Ball guested frequently on radio and gained her own network show, *My Favorite Husband*, in 1950. This concept transferred to television as *I Love Lucy* in 1951, with Arnaz playing the role of the fictional band-leader Ricky Ricardo to Ball's scatter-brained wife. As part of the deal, Arnaz and Ball's company Desilu Productions attained ownership of all 180 episodes of the series, which it sold back to CBS for $4.3 million in 1956. Playing an important part in the success of the show, which topped the ratings and won five Emmys, were William Frawley and Vivian Vance as the Ricardos' neighbours. It contin-ued to thrive in various formats during the next few years, but came to a halt in 1960 after Ball divorced Arnaz. Desilu, which had expanded rapidly, was split evenly between them. Two years later, Ball bought out Arnaz's holdings in Desilu, and in 1967 she sold the company, which was then producing several top-rated series such as *Star Trek* and *Mission: Impossible*, for $17 million to Gulf & Western. Shortly after her divorce, Ball appeared on Broadway in the Cy Coleman-Dorothy Fields musical *Wildcat* (1960), in which she introduced the exuberant 'Hey, Look Me Over'. During the show's run she met comedian Gary Morton and they were married in November 1961. Ball returned to television with *The Lucy Show* (1962-68), *Here's Lucy* (1968-73) and *Life With Lucy* (1986), without recreating the magic of that first series. She also co-starred with Robert Preston in the much-maligned film version of Jerry Herman's stage hit *Mame* (1973). As well as several Emmys, her many awards included membership of the Television Academy's Hall of Fame, the Academy's special citation as First Lady Of Television, and Kennedy Center Honours.

Ball's children, Desi Arnaz Jnr. (b. Desidario Arnaz, 19 January 1953, Los Angeles, California, USA) and Lucie Arnaz (b. Lucy Désirée Arnaz, 17 July 1951, Los Angeles, California, USA) are both television and feature film actors. Lucie is also a singer and cabaret performer. In 1979, she co-starred with Robert Klein in the Neil Simon-Marvin Hamlisch-Carole Bayer Sager Broadway musical *They're Playing Our Song*, and released her first solo album, *Just In Time*, in 1993. In the same year she and her husband, Laurence Luckinbill, were executive producers on the NBC television documentary film *Lucy And Desi: A Home Movie*. Desi Arnaz Jnr. played his father in the movie *The Mambo Kings* (1992).

● FURTHER READING: *The Lucille Ball Story*, J. Gregory. *Desilu: The Story Of Lucille Ball And Desi Arnaz*, Coyne Steven Sanders and Tom Gilbert.

● FILMS: *Stage Door* (1937), *Don't Tell The Wife* (1937), *Joy Of Living* (1938), *Go Chase Yourself* (1938), *Having Wonderful Time* (1938), *Affairs Of Annabel* (1938), *Room Service* (1938), *Annabel Takes A Tour* (1938), *The Next Time I Marry* (1938), *Beauty For The Asking* (1939), *Twelve Crowded Hours* (1939), *Panama Lady* (1939), *Five Came Back* (1939), *That's Right-You're Wrong* (1939), *The Marines Fly High* (1940), *Dance Girl Dance* (1940), *You Can't Fool Your Wife* (1940), *Too Many Girls* (1940), *A Girl, A Guy And A Gob* (1941), *Look Who's Laughing* (1941), *Valley Of The Sun* (1942), *The Big Street* (1942), *Seven Days Leave* (1943), *Du Barry Was A Lady* (1943), *Thousands Cheer* cameo (1943), *Best Foot Forward* as her-self (1943), *Meet The People* (1944), *Without Love* (1945), *Abbott And Costello In Hollywood* (1945), *Easy To Wed* (1946), *Ziegfeld Follies* (1946), *The Dark Corner* (1946), *Lover Come Back* (1946), *Two Smart People* (1946), *When Lovers Meet* (1946), *Personal Column* (1947), *Lured* (1947), *Her Husband's Affair* (1947), *Sorrowful Jones* (1949), *Interference* (1949), *Easy Living* (1949), *Miss Grant Takes Richmond* (1949), *The Fuller Brush Girl* (1950), *Fancy Pants* (1950), *The Magic Carpet* (1951), *The Long Trailer* (1954), *Forever Darling* (1956), *The Facts Of Life* (1960), *Critic's Choice* (1963), *Big Parade Of Comedy* (1964), *A Guide For The Married Man* cameo (1967), *Yours, Mine And Ours* (1968), *Diamond Jim Brady* (1969), *Mame* (1974).

BALL, MICHAEL

b. 27 July 1962, Stratford-Upon-Avon, England. After spending his early life in Plymouth, this popular actor and singer studied at the Guildford School of Drama in Surrey before embarking on what has been, even by modern standards, a meteoric rise to fame. His first professional job was in the chorus of *Godspell* on a tour of Wales, after which he auditioned for a Manchester production of *The Pirates Of Penzance* - again for the chorus. Much to his sur-prise, he was given a leading role alongside Paul Nicholas and Bonnie Langford. In 1985, Ball created the role of Marius in the smash-hit musical *Les Misérables* at the Palace Theatre in London, and introduced one of the show's oustanding numbers, 'Empty Chairs At Empty Tables'. He subsequently took over the role of Raoul, oppo-site Sarah Brightman, in *The Phantom Of The Opera*, and then toured with her in the concert presentation of *The Music Of Andrew Lloyd Webber*. In 1989 his career really took off when he played Alex, a role that called for him to age from 17 to 40, in the same composer's *Aspects Of Love*. He was also in the 1990 Broadway production. Ball took the show's hit ballad, 'Love Changes Everything', to num-ber 2 in the UK chart, and had modest success with one of the others, the poignant 'The First Man You Remember'. Further national recognition came his way when he was contracted (for a reported £100,000) to sing all six of Britain's entries for the 1992 Eurovision Song Contest on the top-rated *Wogan* television show. He came second with the chosen song, 'One Step Out Of Time', which just entered the UK Top 20. In the same year he embarked on an extensive tour of the UK, playing many top venues such as the London Palladium and the Apollo, Hammersmith. He surprised many people with his lively stage presence and a well-planned programme that catered for most tastes and included rock 'n' roll, Motown, standards such as 'Stormy Weather', 'You Made Me Love You', and 'New York, New York', and the inevitable show songs. The following year saw more concerts, the release of his version of the title song from *Sunset Boulevard* (he was tipped for the lead at one time), and his participation in a new studio recording of *West Side Story*, with Barbara Bonney, La Verne Williams, and the Royal Philharmonic Orchestra. However, the highlight of the year was his own six-part television series, which gave him the opportunity to sing with artists, including Cliff Richard, Dionne Warwick, Ray Charles, Monserrat Caballe and Tammy Wynette. A second television series followed in 1994, along with yet more touring, and on 8 October 1995 Ball recreated his original role of Marius for the 10th anniver-sary concert staging of *Les Misérables* at London's Royal

Albert Hall. In the following year he played Giorgio to Maria Friedman's Fosca in Stephen Sondheim and James Lapine's musical, *Passion*. In April 1998, he featured prominently in *Andrew Lloyd Webber - The Royal Albert Hall Celebration*, a concert held in London to mark the composer's 50th birthday, and a month or so later was on the Barbican stage in the all-star charity tribute, *Sondheim Tonight*. Ball gave his gender-bending version of 'Broadway Baby'. On record, he has enjoyed modest success with 'It's Still You', 'If I Can Dream (EP)', 'From Here To Eternity', 'The Lovers We Were', 'The Rose', and '(Something Inside) So Strong', while his first album topped the UK chart.

● ALBUMS: *Michael Ball* (Polydor 1992)★★★, *Always* (Polydor 1993)★★★, *West Side Story* (1993)★★★, *One Careful Owner* (Columbia 1994)★★★, *The Musicals* (PolyGram 1996)★★★, *First Love* (Columbia 1996)★★★, *The Movies* (PolyGram 1998)★★★.

● COMPILATIONS: *The Best Of ...* (PolyGram 1994)★★★.

● VIDEOS: *The Musicals And More* (BMG 1997).

● FILMS: *England My England* (1995).

BALLAD IN BLUE

Also known as *Blues For Lovers*, this 1964 British monochrome film starred Ray Charles (playing himself), who befriends an eight-year-old blind boy while on tour. Mary Peach and Tom Bell play the parts of the parents bickering over how to best deal with their offspring's handicap. Wholly sentimental, *Ballad In Blue* is saved from derision by Charles' musical contributions. Backed by his full band and vocalists the Raelettes, the singer storms through searing versions of his best-known material, including 'I Got A Woman', 'What'd I Say', 'Hallelujah, I Love Her So' and 'Let The Good Times Roll'. The setting may have been poor, but Charles's impassioned interludes, merging gospel, jazz and R&B, ensure continued interest.

BALLARD, KAYE

b. Catherine Gloria Balotta, 20 November 1926, Cleveland, Ohio, USA. An actress and singer with a long and distinguished career in the theatre and on television and film, Ballard came from Italian descent, and entered showbusiness when she was 14 years old, appearing in a US production of *Stage Door Canteen* in Cleveland. She began her professional career in vaudeville in 1943, and three years later was in the revue *Three To Make Ready* in New York. In the late 40s she toured in various stock productions including *Look Ma, I'm Dancin'* and *Annie Get Your Gun*, and was in the cast of the 1948 Harold Rome revue *That's The Ticket*, which closed out of town in the dreaded 'graveyard' for Broadway-bound shows, Philadelphia. In 1950 Ballard made her London debut at the Prince of Wales Theatre in the revue *Touch And Go*, and also starred in that year's *Royal Variety Performance*, before joining the US tour of *Top Banana*. In 1954, she was back on Broadway as Helen of Troy in *The Golden Apple* in which she introduced Jerome Moss and John Latouche's languorous 'Lazy Afternoon'. This was followed by *Reuben Reuben*, a Marc Blitzstein show that closed in Boston in 1955, and good roles in Broadway productions of *Carnival* (1961, Rosalie), the revue *The Beast In Me* (1963), and *Molly* (1973, Molly Goldberg). She also appeared in the

Ziegfeld Follies (1956, Canada), a revival of *Wonderful Town* at the New York City Center (1963), and the revue *The Decline And Fall Of The Entire World As Seen Through The Eyes Of Cole Porter Revisited* (1965, off-Broadway). In the 70s she was appearing in cabaret at prestige rooms such as Mr. Kelly's in Chicago, and the St. Regis and Hotel Plaza in New York. She made her only film musical, *The Girl Most Likely* (1958), with Jane Powell, Tommy Noonan, Cliff Robertson and Keith Andes, having entered television via *The Mel Tormé Show* some six years earlier. She was in the original television production of *Cinderella* (1957, starring Julie Andrews), and starred with Eve Arden in the fondly remembered series *The Mothers-In-Law* in the late 60s. Other frequent television work has included *The Love Boat*, *The Robber Bridegroom*, numerous guest appearances, and her own specials such as *Hello Kaye Ballard, Welcome To Las Vegas* (1980). In more recent times, she joined the Big Band Era 4 Girls 4 tour with Kay Starr, Margaret Whiting and Helen O'Connell, delighting audiences not only with her singing and comedy, but with added burlesque impressions and some sensitive flute playing. In the early 90s she was in the casts of the Long Beach Civic Light Opera production of *Chicago* with Juliet Prowse and Bebe Neuwirth, and the New York Festival's *Pirates Of Penzance*; at the Rainbow And Stars in New York with Jason Graae, Liz Callaway and Ron Raines in an Irving Berlin revue entitled *Say It With Music*; and with Jaye P. Morgan and Marcia Lewis in *Nunsense* in Florida. She also visited London in 1992 and presented her one-woman show at the Lyric Theatre. She has continued to record occasionally, and in 1958 made the album *The Fanny Brice Story In Song*, which she sent to producer Ray Stark suggesting that she star in a film of the entertainer's life. Stark rejected her offer, but eventually produced the biopic under the title of *Funny Girl*, starring Barbra Streisand. In 1997, Ballard headlined at the Paper Mill Playhouse in *No, No Nanette*, and returned to the same venue a year later to play Hattie ('Broadway Baby') in a revival of *Follies*.

● ALBUMS: *The Fanny Brice Story In Song* (MGM 1958)★★★★, *Kaye Ballard Swings* (United Artists 1959)★★★, *Kaye Ballard Live?* (United Artists 1960)★★★, *Ha-Ha Boo-Hoo* (United Artists 1960)★★★, *Kaye Ballard & Arthur Siegel* (1967)★★★, *Then And Again* (Original Cast Records 1994)★★★, with Jaye P. Morgan *Long-Time Friends* (Original Cast Records 1996)★★, with Arthur Siegel *The Ladies Who Wrote The Lyrics* reissue (1996)★★★.

● FILMS: *The Girl Most Likely* (1958), *A House Is Not A Home* (1964), *The Ritz* (1976), *Freaky Friday* (1977), *Falling In Love Again* (1980), *Tiger Warsaw* (1987), *Modern Love* (1990), *Fate* (1990), *Eternity* (1990), *Ava's Magical Adventure* (1994).

BALLROOM

This show brought the celebrated director/choreographer Michael Bennett back to Broadway for the first time since he contributed so much to *A Chorus Line* (1975), one of the biggest ever hits of the musical theatre. *Ballroom* opened at the Majestic Theatre in New York, on 14 December 1978. The book was adapted by Jerome Kass from his own television movie, *Queen Of The Stardust Ballroom*, which had a music score by composer Billy Goldenberg, and lyrics by Alan and Marilyn Bergman.

The trio remained on board for *Ballroom*, and added some new songs. Kass's story dealt with a lonely widow, Bea Asher (Dorothy Loudon), who meets and falls in love with Al Rossi (Vincent Gardenia) at the local dance hall, where middle-aged couples are still dancing 'in the old-fashioned way' (1978 was the year of *Saturday Night Fever*). As they become closer, Al reveals that he is (unhappily) married, and will never leave his wife, and Bea's decision to share him with someone else is spectacularly revealed in her show-stopping 'Fifty Percent'. Apart from that number and Loudon's 'A Terrific Band And A Real Nice Crowd', most of the songs, such as 'A Song for Dancin'', 'One By One', 'Dreams', 'Goodnight Is Not Goodbye' and 'More Of The Same', are performed by Nathan (Bernie Knee) and Marlene (Lynn Roberts), the vocalists at the Stardust Ballroom. Loudon and Roberts duet on 'Somebody Did All Right For Herself'/'Dreams', and Gardenia has only one chance to sing, in a duet with Loudon entitled 'I Love To Dance'. Bennett's dances ranged from foxtrots through waltzes to 'The Hustle', which was even then three years out of date. Bea ends the bittersweet story, following her elevation to the Queen of the Stardust Ballroom, with the heartfelt 'I Wish You A Waltz' (she died at the end of the television version), but 1978 Broadway audiences preferred the raunchy *The Best Little Whorehouse In Texas* and the nostalgic *Eubie* to the schmaltz of *Ballroom*, which ran for just over three months.

BAMBI

(see Disney, Walt)

BAMBOULA, THE

A comparatively undistinguished piece, considering the quality of the creative collaborators; the book was by H.M. Vernon and Guy Bolton (of the Bolton-Kern-Wodehouse team), and the lyrics were written by the humorist Douglas Furber and Irving Caesar, whose *No, No, Nanette* ('Tea For Two', 'I Want To Be Happy') made its debut on Broadway in the same year. With a music score composed by Albert Sirmay and Harry Rosenthal, *The Bamboula* opened at His Majesty's Theatre in London on 24 March 1925, complete with a somewhat complicated Ruritania-style plot concerning the Prince of Corona, played by the comedian W.H. Berry, who is mistaken for a youthful dance instructor, Jimmy Roberts (Harry Welchman), in his pursuit of the wealthy Donna Juanita da Costa (Dorothy Shale). The antics of all concerned bordered on farce, and the songs included 'Spring', 'Your Kiss Told Me', 'Sing A Song In The Rain', and 'After All These Years'. The West End run ended after 77 performances, but the show endured in subsequent provincial productions.

BAND WAGON, THE (FILM MUSICAL)

Taking the title from a highly successful 1931 Broadway revue that had a score by Arthur Schwartz and Howard Dietz, but no plot, Betty Comden and Adolph Green provided the screenplay for arguably the best and wittiest backstage film musical of them all. Released in 1953, the film's story dealt with an ageing, has-been hoofer, Tony Hunter (Fred Astaire), whose New York comeback is being masterminded and written by Lily and Lester

Marton (Oscar Levant and Nanette Fabray), two characters reputedly based on Comden and Green themselves. Ballerina Gabrielle Gerard (Cyd Charisse) reluctantly agrees to become Hunter's co-star, and Jeffrey Cordova (Jack Buchanan), the reigning theatrical virtuoso and super-egotist, is called in to direct, but his extravagant efforts result in something nearer *Faust* than *Funny Face*. However, all is not lost: after the cast have revamped the show (with the help of Cordova, who turns out to be a nice, modest - even insecure - guy underneath), it promises to run for years. Schwartz and Dietz's score was full of marvellous songs, including 'A Shine On Your Shoes', 'By Myself' (Astaire), 'I Guess I'll Have To Change My Plan' (Astaire-Buchanan), the ingenious 'Triplets' (Astaire-Buchanan-Fabray), 'New Sun In The Sky' (Charisse, dubbed by India Adams), and several others involving the principals and chorus, such as 'I Love Louisa', 'Louisiana Hayride', 'You And The Night And The Music', 'Dancing In The Dark' and 'Something To Remember Me By'. The one new number was 'That's Entertainment', which, along with Irving Berlin's 'There's No Business Like Show Business', attempts to explain why, despite Noël Coward's reservations, the show must always go on. Charisse and Astaire's dancing was a dream, especially in the ethereal 'Dancing In The Dark' sequence and the 'Girl Hunt' ballet. Much of the credit for the film's outstanding success was due to director Vincente Minnelli, choreographer Michael Kidd, and producer Arthur Freed, whose special musicals unit at MGM had created yet another winner.

BAND WAGON, THE (STAGE MUSICAL)

Arthur Schwartz and Howard Dietz's finest revue - some say the best that Broadway has ever seen. A Max Gordon production, *The Band Wagon* opened at the New Amsterdam Theatre in New York on 3 June 1931. Unlike most of the other revues of the time on which numerous writers and composers laboured, this show reduced the collaborators to three: the playwright, humorist and drama critic George S. Kaufman wrote the sketches with Howard Dietz, and Dietz (lyrics) and Schwartz (music) provided the songs. Heading the cast were Fred Astaire and his sister, Adele, who was making her final Broadway appearance before retiring to marry Lord Charles Cavendish. The critics were unanimous in their praise for a show in which 'each scene or episode serves to display a new angle of approach and craftsmanship'. Highlights included the opening 'It Had Better Be Good', 'New Sun In The Sky' (Astaire in white tie and tails, preening himself in front of a mirror), 'Hoops' (Fred and Adele as naughty Parisienne children), 'Where Can He Be?' (Helen Broderick), 'Dancing In The Dark' (sung by John Barker while ballerina Tilly Losch danced on an angled, illuminated mirrored floor), 'White Heat' and 'Sweet Music' (Fred and Adele Astaire), and the boisterous first act finale, 'I Love Louisa', in which the whole cast rode on a Bavarian-style merry-go-round mounted on the revolving stage. The show also featured the classic sketch 'The Pride Of The Claghorns', a highly satirical view of southern aristocratic values. Directed by Hassard Short, and choreographed by Albertina Rasch, *The Band Wagon* was one of those rare shows in which all the different elements -

authors, artists, songs, sketches, dances, innovative lighting, and the rest - combined to create the perfect whole. It ran for 260 performances on Broadway. For the 1953 film version, which teamed Fred Astaire with the top British song-and-dance man, Jack Buchanan, Schwartz and Dietz wrote 'That's Entertainment', and used several more songs taken from their other shows.

BAR MITZVAH BOY

Adapted by Jack Rosenthal from his original television play, *Bar Mitzvah Boy* opened at Her Majesty's Theatre in London on 31 October 1978. The story of a young Jewish boy (Barry Angel) who finds himself unable to face his Bar Mitzvah ceremony, with all its significance of grown-up times ahead, did not transfer satisfactorily to the musical stage. Critics felt that the down-to-earth credibility of the original had been compromised, and that some of the characters, particularly the boy's father (Harry Towb) and mother (Joyce Blair), had been made overly sweet and sentimental. The score, an Anglo-American affair by the veteran Broadway composer Jule Styne and the British lyricist Don Black, was not well received either, although there was some affection for a pretty item entitled 'You Wouldn't Be You', and an amusing list song, sung by the children, 'Thou Shalt Not'. The other numbers included 'Why', 'This Time Tomorrow', 'The Sun Shines Out Of Your Eyes', 'I've Just Begun' and 'Where Is The Music Coming From?'. The show closed in January 1979 after only 77 performances. In 1987, the American Jewish Theatre presented *Bar Mitzvah Boy* off-Broadway at the 92nd Street 'Y', but without much success.

BARER, MARSHALL

b. Marshall Louis Barer, 19 February 1923, Long Island City, New York, USA, d. 25 August 1998, Santa Fe, New Mexico. An author, songwriter and singer, Barer was an eccentric, witty, mercurial character. After attending Palm Beach High School and the Cavanagh School of Art, he worked in the advertising business as a designer and illustrator on magazines such as *Esquire* and *McCall's*. All this time, however, he was writing songs, and later special material for nightclub performers. In the early 50s he met Yale alumnus Dean Fuller, and they contributed words and music to the revues *Once Over Lightly* (1955, Zero Mostel, Jack Gilford, Sono Osato), *New Faces Of 1956* (Tiger Haynes, Inga Swenson, and future British stage star Maggie Smith), and the 1957 Golden Jubilee edition of the *Ziegfeld Follies*, starring Beatrice Lillie. Barer and Fuller, with Jay Thompson, were also credited with the book for the 1959 musical *Once Upon A Mattress* ('Shy', 'Song Of Love', 'Happily Ever After', 'Very Soft Shoes', 'Many Moons Ago', 'Yesterday I Loved You', 'In A Little While'). This expanded musical adaptation of the Hans Andersen comic fable *The Princess And The Pea*, which ran for a creditable 460 performances, also featured Barer's witty lyrics, beguiling music by Mary Rodgers, and introduced actress-comedienne Carol Burnett to Broadway. What is more, the show endured, and on its 25th anniversary in 1984, *Once Upon A Mattress* was reported to be the second most-produced musical in the USA - after *Oklahoma!*. It returned to Broadway briefly in 1996/97, with a cast headed by Sarah Jessica Parker. Thirty years earlier, in 1966, Barer had worked with Mary Rodgers again on *The Mad Show* (871 performances off-Broadway). In the same year he formed a lyrical partnership with Fred Tobias for *Pousse-Café* ('Someone To Care For', 'Thank You, Ma'am', 'Let's', 'My Heart Is A Stranger'). Jazz legend Duke Ellington composed the music for this adaptation of Heinrich Mann's novel, *Professor Unrath*, which starred Theodore Bikel, and folded after only three Broadway performances. It marked the end of Barer's association with Broadway, although he continued 'gleefully to mate his lyrics' (as his amusing *Playbill* biography puts it) to the melodies of Vernon Duke, David Shire, David Ross and David Raskin - along with William Roy, Michel Legrand, J. Fred Coots, and Leroy Anderson, among numerous others. He even opted for Offenbach at one stage, adapting that composer's *La Belle Helene* for the unstaged *La Belle*. More familiar are songs such as 'I'm Just A Country Boy', which he wrote with Fred Brooks, who, under the name of Fred Hellerman, was a founder-member of the Weavers US folk group. Notable recordings of the number included those by Harry Belafonte, Don Williams, and in Britain, Val Doonican. Another often-played number of his, 'Summer Is A-Comin' In', had music by Alec Wilder. From the 70s onwards Barer interpreted his own works, and parodied those by others, in cabaret, and that is the *milieu* in which his often acerbic but always entertaining songs still surface from time to time. One particularly appealing item, 'On Such A Night As This' (with Hugh Martin), was featured on *Andrea Marcovicci Sings Movies* (1988). He was active until just before his death, which occurred some two years after he received the 1996 ASCAP Richard Rodgers Award.
● ALBUMS: with Barbara Lea *Duke Ellington's Pousse-Café* (Audiophile 1992)★★★.

BARKLEYS OF BROADWAY, THE

After Judy Garland, his original co-star, withdrew through illness, Fred Astaire was reunited for the last time with his most famous dance partner, Ginger Rogers, for this 1949 production from Arthur Freed's MGM unit. Betty Comden and Adolph Green's screenplay cast the pair as husband and wife, Josh and Dinah Barkley, an enduring musical comedy couple whose comfortable and lucrative life is temporarily disturbed when Dinah gets an urge to become 'a great tragic actress'. Fortunately, she eventually comes to her senses, and the old Rogers/Astaire magic - not seen on the screen since they portrayed another famous dance team in *The Story Of Vernon And Irene Castle* in 1939 - was shining as bright as ever in Harry Warren and Ira Gershwin's numbers, such as 'Swing Trot', 'Bouncin' The Blues', 'You'd Be Hard To Replace', 'Weekend In The Country' and 'Manhattan Downbeat'. Two of the many highlights included Fred and Ginger kitted out with kilts and excruciating Scottish accents in 'My One And Only Highland Fling', and 'Shoes With Wings On', in which Fred dances while being 'bombarded' from all directions by flying pairs of shoes. This, and the other memorable and innovative routines, were choreographed by Robert Alton and Hermes Pan. There was a lovely poignant moment towards the end of the film when Fred and Ginger are reunited to the strains of George and Ira Gershwin's 'They Can't Take That Away From Me', a number that Fred introduced in the 1937 film *Shall We Dance?*. *The Barkleys Of Broadway* was photographed in Technicolor, and directed by Charles Walters. The cast also included Oscar Levant, Billie Burke, Gale Robbins, Jacques Francois, George Zucco, and Clinton Sundberg.

BARNUM

The larger-than-life career of Phineas Taylor Barnum, self-styled 'World's Greatest Showman', proved ideal source material for this spectacular musical which opened at the St. James Theatre in New York on 30 April 1980. Barnum composer Cy Coleman had noticed Jim Dale in the Old Vic's Broadway production of *Scapino* (1974-75), the Molière farce, in which he fell off the balcony, spun plates of spaghetti, and incorporated several other kinds of physical business. When it came to this show, Coleman required Dale to portray the spirit of the man - not the physical side (P.T. Barnum was over six feet tall and heavily built, so Dale could hardly do that). In order to prepare himself fully, he trained in juggling, tightrope walking, unicycle, trampoline, and a number of other skills, at the Big Apple Circus School in Manhattan. All the hard work paid off when Dale gave a bravura performance, ably supported by the future movie star Glenn Close as his wife Charity (Chairy) Barnum. In Mark Bramble's book, Marianne Tatum played Jenny Lind, the Swedish soprano Barnum imports when he decides to dump the freak shows, and move up-market - eventually returning to the circus world under the legendary Barnum and Bailey banner. Also cast were William C. Witter as the ringmaster, Leonard John Crofoot (Tom Thumb) and Terri White (Joice Heth). Coleman and Michael Stewart's score was full of entertaining numbers, such as 'There Is A Sucker Born Ev'ry Minute', 'Thank God I'm Old', 'The Colours Of My Life', 'One Brick At A Time', 'Museum Song', 'I Like Your Style', 'Bigger Isn't Better', 'Love Makes Such Fools Of Us All', 'Out There', 'Come Follow The Band', 'Black And White', 'The Prince Of Humbug', and 'Join The Circus'. Dale deservedly won the best actor in a musical Tony Award, and there were others for David Mitchell's wonderful sets, and, Theoni V. Aldredge's costumes. *Barnum* was directed and choreographed by Joe Layton, and ran on Broadway for 854 performances. Layton reprised his work for the 1981 London Palladium production (as did Ringmaster Witter). This lasted for 655 performances, and had another brilliant central performance from Michael Crawford, with Deborah Grant (Chairy) and Sarah Payne (Jenny Lind). In March 1985, after an 18-week run at the Manchester Opera House, Crawford brought the show back into town at the Victoria Palace for just over a year. A UK national touring production of *Barnum*, starring Paul Nicholas (Carol Duffy-Mrs. Barnum, Clara Miller-Jenny Lind) spent Christmas 1992 at London's Dominion Theatre. Three years later, a *Barnum* starring comedian Andrew O'Connor as the 'Prince of Humbug' (Kristin Blaikie as Chairy), circled warily in the regions without braving the West End.

BARRIS, HARRY

b. 24 November 1905, New York, USA, d. 13 December 1962, Burbank, California, USA. A songwriter, singer, pianist, author, and actor, Barris was raised in Denver and had his own band by the time he was 17. In 1926 he joined Bing Crosby and Al Rinker to form the Rhythm Boys vocal group, which was showcased regularly by Paul Whiteman And His Orchestra. Two of his early songs, 'Mississippi Mud' (1927, written with James Cavanaugh) and 'So The Bluebirds And The Blackbirds Got Together' (1929, Billy Moll), were featured in the film *King Of Jazz* (1930), and around the same time he also wrote 'From Monday On' (1928, Bing Crosby) which was a hit for the Rhythm Boys with the Whiteman band. His other compositions in the early 30s, some of which were immensely successful for Bing Crosby, included 'It Must Be True' (Gus Arnheim-Gordon Clifford), 'At Your Command' (Harry Tobias-Crosby), 'I Surrender, Dear' (Clifford), 'Lies' (George E. Springer), 'Wrap Your Troubles In Dreams' (Ted Koehler-Moll), 'It Was So Beautiful' (Arthur Freed), and 'Little Dutch Mill' (Ralph Freed). Among his other numbers were 'How Little I Knew', 'Thrilled' and 'Let's Spend An Evening At Home'. Several of his songs appeared over the years in films such as *Blondie Of The Follies* (1932), *The Big Broadcast* (1932), *Freshman Year* (1938), *I Surrender Dear* (1948), *Rainbow Round My Shoulder* (1952) and *The Eddie Duchin Story* (1957). After the Rhythm Boys left Whiteman they worked with Gus Arnheim's band for a time, before disbanding when Crosby began his long and distinguished solo career. Barris subsequently fronted a few bands, worked on radio, and took a number of modest roles in movies - some of which starred Crosby. During World War II, he toured abroad entertaining US troops, and was working in various capacities into the late 50s.

● FILMS: *King Of Jazz* (1930), *Hollywood Party* (1934), *Every Night At Eight* (1935), *Something To Sing About* (1937), *Double Or Nothing* (1937), *Birth Of The Blues* (1941), *Holiday Inn* (1942), *Priorities On Parade* (1942), *Here Come The Waves* (1944), *Penthouse Rhythm* (1945), *You Were Meant For Me* (1948).

BARRY, JOHN

b. Jonathan Barry Prendergast, 3 November 1933, York, Yorkshire, England. Renowned as one of the leading composers of film soundtrack music, Barry began his career leading the John Barry Seven. This rousing instrumental unit enjoyed several notable UK hits between 1960 and 1962, the best-known of which were 'Hit And Miss' and a version of the Ventures' Walk Don't Run' (both 1960). The former, which reached number 11 in the UK charts, was the theme to *Juke Box Jury*, BBC Television's long-running record release show. Barry made regular appearances on several early pop programmes, including *Oh Boy* and *Drumbeat* and also enjoyed concurrent fame as a writer and arranger, scoring the distinctive pizzicato strings on numerous Adam Faith hits including the number 1 'What Do You Want' (1959). He also composed the soundtrack to *Beat Girl*, the singer's film debut, and later took up a senior A&R post with the independent Ember label. In 1962 Barry had a UK Top 20 hit with the 'James Bond Theme', which was part of Monty Norman's score for the film *Dr. No*, the first in a highly successful series. He produced music for several subsequent Bond films, including *From Russia With Love*, *Goldfinger* and *You Only Live Twice*, the title songs from which provided hit singles for Matt Monro (1963), Shirley Bassey (1964) and Nancy Sinatra (1967). Such success led to a series of stylish soundtracks that encompassed contrasting moods and music, including *The Ipcress File*, *The Knack* (both 1965), *Born Free* (which won an Oscar in 1966), *Midnight Cowboy* (1969), and *Mary, Queen Of Scots* (1971). Although his theme songs have enjoyed a high commercial profile, it is Barry's imaginative incidental music that has assured his peerless reputation. By contrast, he pursued another lucrative direction, composing television commercials for disparate household items.

Barry's consistency remained intact throughout the 70s and 80s, although several attendant films, including *King Kong* (1976) and *Howard The Duck* (A second rate DC comic character)(1986), were highly criticized. 'Down Deep Inside', the theme from *The Deep* (1977), was a UK Top 5 hit for Donna Summer, and this disco-influenced composition emphasized the writer's versatility. *Out Of Africa* (1985) and *The Living Daylights* and *Hearts Of Fire* (both 1987) demonstrated his accustomed flair, while his music for *Dances With Wolves* (1990) earned him another Oscar. In the early 90s his scores included *Ruby Cairo*, *Indecent Proposal*, and Richard Attenborough's *Chaplin* (Oscar nomination), *My Life* (1993), and *The Specialist* (1994). His orchestrations combine elements of classical, jazz and popular themes and command the respect of enthusiastic aficionados. In April 1998 Barry conducted the 87-piece English Chamber Orchestra in a concert celebration of his own movie music at London's Royal Albert Hall, during which he previewed *The Beyondness Of Things*, a collection of 'string-driven musical poems'. Regarded as more subtle than his film scores, it was Barry's first non-soundtrack work for two decades.

● ALBUMS: (film soundtracks unless otherwise stated) *Beat Girl* (Columbia 1960)★★★, *Stringbeat* (Columbia 1961)★★★, *Dr. No* (United Artists 1962)★★★★, *It's All Happening* (1963)★★★, *A Handful Of Songs* (Ember 1963)★★★, *Zulu* (Ember 1963)★★★, *Elizabeth Taylor In London* television soundtrack (Colpix 1963)★★★, *From Russia With Love* (United Artists 1963)★★★, *Man In The Middle* (Stateside 1964)★★★, *Goldfinger* (United Artists 1964)★★★, *The Ipcress File* (Decca 1965)★★★, *Sophia Loren In Rome* (1965)★★★, *King Rat* (1965)★★★, *The Knack ... & How To Get It* (MCA 1965)★★★, *Four In The Morning* (1965)★★★, *Thunderball* (United Artists 1965)★★★, *Passion Flower Hotel* (1965)★★★, *The Wrong Box* (1966)★★★, *The Chase* (1966)★★★, *Born Free* (MGM 1966)★★★, *The Quiller Memorandum* (1966)★★★, *You Only Live Twice* (United Artists 1967)★★★, *Dutchman* (1967)★★★, *The Whisperers* (1967)★★★, *Deadfall* (1968)★★★, *Petulia* (1968)★★★, *Boom* (1968)★★★, *The Lion In Winter* (Columbia 1968)★★★★, *On Her Majesty's Secret Service* (United Artists 1969)★★★, *Midnight Cowboy* (United Artists 1969)★★★★, *The Last Valley* (Probe 1970)★★★, *Diamonds Are Forever* (United Artists 1971)★★★, *Follow Me* (1971)★★★, *Lolita My Love* (1971)★★★, *The Persuaders* (Columbia 1971)★★★, *Mary Queen Of Scots* (MCA 1971)★★★, *Alice's Adventures In Wonderland* (Warners 1972)★★★, *The John Barry Concert* (1972)★★★, *A Doll's*

House (1973)★★★, *Billy* (1974)★★★, *The Dove* (1974)★★★, *The Man With The Golden Gun* (United Artists 1974)★★★, *The Day Of The Locust* (1974)★★★, *Americans* (1975)★★★, *Robin And Marian* (1976)★★★, *King Kong* (Reprise 1976)★★★, *The Deep* (Casablanca 1977)★★★, *The Game Of Death* (1978)★★★, *Starcrash* (1978)★★★, *The Black Hole* (1979)★★★, *Moonraker* (United Artists 1979)★★★, *Inside Moves* (Warners 1980)★★★, *The Legend Of The Lone Ranger* (1981)★★★, *Frances* (1982)★★★, *High Road To China* (1983)★★★, *The Golden Seal* (1983)★★★, *Body Heat* (1983)★★★, *Until September* (1984)★★★, *Jagged Edge* (1985)★★★, *Out Of Africa* (MCA 1985)★★★, *A View To A Kill* (Capitol 1985)★★★, *Peggy Sue Got Married* (TER 1986)★★★, *Howard The Duck* (MCA 1986)★★★, *Golden Child* (Capitol 1986)★★★, *Somewhere In Time* (MCA 1986)★★★, *Living Daylights* (Warners 1987)★★★, *Dances With Wolves* (Epic 1990)★★★, *Moviola* (Epic 1992)★★★★, *My Life* (Epic 1994)★★★, *Moviola II - Action And Adventure* (Epic 1995)★★★, *The Beyondness Of Things* orchestral album (Decca 1998)★★★.

● COMPILATIONS: *Six-Five Special* (Parlophone 1957)★★★, *Oh Boy!* (Parlophone 1958)★★★, *Drumbeat* (Parlophone 1959)★★★, *Saturday Club* (Parlophone 1960)★★★, *Blackpool Nights* (Columbia 1960)★★★, *The Great Movie Sounds Of John Barry* (1966)★★★, *John Barry Conducts His Great Movie Hits* (1967)★★★, *Ready When You Are, John Barry* (1970)★★★, *John Barry Revisited* (1971)★★★, *Play It Again* (1974)★★★, *The Music Of John Barry* (1976)★★★, *The Very Best Of John Barry* (1977)★★★, *The John Barry Seven And Orchestra* (EMI 1979)★★★, *The Best Of John Barry* (Polydor 1981)★★★, *The Big Screen Hits Of John Barry* (Columbia 1981)★★★, *James Bond's Greatest Hits* (1982)★★★, *Music From The Big Screen* (Pickwick 1986)★★★, *Hit And Miss* (See For Miles 1988)★★★, *The Film Music Of John Barry* (1989)★★★, *John Barry Themes* (1989)★★★, *The Ember Years Volume 1* (Play It Again 1992)★★★, *The Ember Years Volume 2* (Play It Again 1992)★★★, *The Best Of EMI Years Volume 2* (EMI 1993)★★★, *The Ember Years Volume 3* (Play It Again 1996)★★★, *The John Barry Experience* (Carlton 1997)★★★, *Themeology: The Best Of . . .* (Columbia 1997)★★★★, *John Barry - The Hits And The Misses* (Play It Again 1998)★★★.

● FURTHER READING: *A Sixties Theme*, Eddi Fiegel.

● FILMS: *It's All Happening* (1963).

BART, LIONEL

b. Lionel Begleiter, 1 August 1930, London, England. The comparative inactivity of Bart for many years has tended to cloud the fact that he is one of the major songwriters of twentieth-century popular song. The former silk-screen printer was at the very hub of the rock 'n' roll and skiffle generation that came out of London's Soho in the mid-50s. As a member of the Cavemen with Tommy Steele he later became Steele's main source of non-American song material. In addition to writing the pioneering 'Rock With The Cavemen' he composed a series of glorious singalong numbers, including 'A Handful Of Songs', 'Water Water' and the trite but delightfully innocent 'Little White Bull'. Much of Bart's work was steeped in the English music-hall tradition, diffused with a strong working-class pride, and it was no surprise that he soon graduated into writing songs for full-length stage shows. *Lock Up Your Daughters* and *Fings Ain't Wot They Used T'Be* were two of his early successes, both appearing during 1959, the same year he wrote the classic 'Living Doll' for Cliff Richard. Bart was one of the first writers to introduce mild politics into his lyrics, beautifully transcribed with topical yet humorously ironic innocence, for example: 'They've changed our local Palais into a bowling alley and fings ain't wot they used to be.' As the 60s dawned Bart unconsciously embarked on a decade that saw him reach dizzy heights of success and made him one of the musical personalities of the decade. During the first quarter of the year he topped the charts with 'Do You Mind' for Anthony Newley, a brilliantly simple and catchy song complete with Bart's own finger-snapped accompaniment. The best was yet to come when that year he launched *Oliver!*, a musical based on Dickens' *Oliver Twist*. This became a phenomenal triumph, and remains one of the most successful musicals of all time. Bart's knack of simple melody, combined with unforgettable lyrics, produced many classics, including the pleading 'Who Will Buy', the rousing 'Food Glorious Food' and the poignant 'As Long As He Needs Me' (also a major hit for Shirley Bassey, although she reputedly never liked the song). Bart was a pivotal figure throughout the swinging London scene of the 60s, although he maintains that the party actually started in the 50s. Bart befriended Brian Epstein, the Beatles, the Rolling Stones, became an international star following *Oliver!*'s success as a film (winning six Oscars) and was romantically linked with Judy Garland and Alma Cogan. Following continued, although lesser, success with *Blitz!* and *Maggie May*, Bart was shaken into reality when the London critics damned his 1965 musical *Twang!!*, based upon the life of Robin Hood. Bart's philanthropic nature made him a prime target for business sharks and he lost much of his fortune as a result. By the end of the 60s the cracks were beginning to show; his dependence on drugs and alcohol increased and he watched many of his close friends die in tragic circumstances - Cogan with cancer, Garland through drink and drugs and Epstein's supposed suicide. In 1969, *La Strada* only had a short run in New York before Bart retreated into himself, and for many years maintained a relatively low profile, watching the 70s and 80s pass almost as a blur, only making contributions to *The Londoners* and *Costa Packet*. During this time the gutter press were eager for a kiss-and-tell story but Bart remained silent, a credible action considering the sums of money he was offered. During the late 80s Bart finally beat his battle with alcohol and ended the decade a saner, wiser and healthier man. His renaissance started in 1989 when he was commissioned by a UK building society to write a television jingle. The composition became part of an award-winning advertisement, featuring a number of angelic children singing with Bart, filmed in pristine monochrome. The song 'Happy Endings' was a justifiable exhumation of a man who remains an immensely talented figure and whose work ranks with some of the greatest of the American 'musical comedy' songwriters. In the early 90s his profile continued to be high, with revivals by the talented National Youth Theatre of *Oliver!*, *Maggie May* and *Blitz!* (the latter production commemorating the 50th anniversary of the real thing), and the inclusion of one of his early songs, 'Rock With The Caveman', in the blockbuster movie *The Flintstones*, in a version by Big Audio Dynamite. In December 1994 Lionel Bart's rehabilitation was complete when producer Cameron Mackintosh presented a major new production of *Oliver!* at the London Palladium, starring Jonathan Pryce. In a gesture rare in the cut-throat world of showbusiness, Mackintosh returned a portion of the show's rights to the composer (Bart had sold them during the bad old days), thereby assuring him an 'income for life'.

● FURTHER READING: *Bart!: The Unauthorized Life & Times, Ins & Outs, Ups & Downs Of Lionel Bart*, David Roper.

BATTLING BUTLER

A musical farce by Stanley Brightman and Austin Melford, *Battling Butler* opened at the New Oxford Theatre in London on 8 December 1922. Jack Buchanan starred as Alfred Butler, a man who likes a good time away from his wife now and then. He pretends that he is the renowned boxer, Battling Butler, who occasionally has to spend a few weeks in isolation preparing for a fight. This enables Alfred to make his own social arrangements. Complications arise when Mrs. Alfred Butler becomes suspicious, and Mrs. Battling Butler takes a fancy to Alfred, who almost, but not quite, has to engage in a real bout of fisticuffs in an effort to conceal his guilty secret. The score, by composer Philip Braham and lyricist Douglas Furber, contained several engaging songs, including Alfred's plaintive 'Why Can't I?' ('Jonah got away with it/Why can't I?'), 'It's A Far, Far Better Thing', his duet with Mrs. Battling Butler (Sylvia Leslie) entitled 'Dancing Honeymoon', and others, such as 'An Axe To Grind', 'Apples, Bananas And Pears', 'The Countryside', 'I Will Be Master', 'Mr Dumble' and 'Growing Up To Time'. The show, which marked Buchanan's first attempt at management, was a great success, and, after transferring to the Adelphi Theatre, it closed in June 1923 after a run of 238 performances. It did even better in New York, when a radically revised version, without Buchanan, but with several new numbers by other composers, opened at the Selwyn Theatre in October 1923, and retained audiences' affections for 312 performances.

BAYES, NORA

b. Dora Goldberg, 1880, Joliet, Illinois, USA, d. 19 March 1928, Brooklyn, New York, USA. An important actress and singer in vaudeville and on the musical stage, Bayes had an extravagant style and appealing contralto voice. Early on in her career she became known as 'The Wurzburger Girl', after having quite a hit with Vincent P. Bryan and Harry von Tilzer's drinking song, 'Down Where The Wurzburger Flows', which she introduced at the Orpheum Theatre, Brooklyn, in 1902. In the previous year she had made her Broadway debut in the vaudeville musical *The Rogers Brothers In Washington*, in which she impressed with her version of 'Watermelon Party'. After appearing in Florenz Ziegfeld's *Follies Of 1907* and the book musical *Nearly A Hero*, Bayes joined Jack Norworth, the second of her five husbands, in the *Follies Of 1908*. They also interpolated their own composition, 'Shine On Harvest Moon', into the show. Bayes would continue this practice throughout her career. The celebrated couple were together again in the *Follies Of 1909*, *The Jolly Bachelors* (1910, in which Bayes sang C.W. Murphy and William Letters' 'Has

Anybody Here Seen Kelly?', and she and Norworth 'Americanized' another British song, 'Come Along, My Mandy'), *Little Miss Fix-It* (1911, featuring another of their compositions, 'Turn Off Your Light, Mr. Moon-Man'), and *Roly Poly* (1912). In between the shows and revues, Bayes and Norworth headlined in vaudeville. In 1914 Bayes appeared in Fred Thompson's London revue *Merry-Go-Round*, before returning to Broadway with *Maid In America* (1915), *The Cohan Revue* (1917), *Ladies First* (1918), *Her Family Tree* (1920), *Snapshots Of 1921*, and *Queen O' Hearts* (1922). Her record successes from 1910-23 give a good indication of the kind of music that was popular at the time. They include 'Young America', 'Rosa Rosetta', 'That Lovin' Rag', 'The Good Ship Mary Ann', 'For Dixie And Uncle Sam', a few World War I songs: 'Over There', '(Goodbye, And Luck Be With You) Laddie Boy', 'Someday They're Coming Home Again', 'The Man Who Put The Germ In Germany', and 'Goodbye France', along with post-war numbers such as 'How Ya Gonna Keep 'Em Down On The Farm? (After They've Seen Paree)', 'You Can't Get Lovin' Where There Ain't No Love', 'Oh How I Laugh When I Think That I Cried Over You', 'The Argentines, The Portugese, And The Greeks', 'The Japanese Sandman', 'Broadway Blues', 'Why Worry?', 'Make Believe', 'Tea Leaves', 'Cherie', 'Saturday', 'All Over Nothing At All', 'Good Mornin' (It's Mighty Good To Be Home)', 'Homesick', 'Lovin' Sam (The Sheik Of Alabam)', 'Who Did You Fool, After All?', and 'Dearest, You're Nearest My Heart'. Apart from 'Shine On Harvest Moon', Bayes wrote numerous other songs with Norworth, including 'Fancy You Fancying Me', 'I'm Sorry', and 'Young America', and is said to have been the co-writer of several more numbers, such as 'Prohibition Blues' (with Ring Lardner) and 'Just Like A Gypsy' (with Seymour Simons). 'Shine On Harvest Moon', which was the first hit to come out of Ziegfeld's *Follies*, was also included in the last edition of the lavish revues to be mounted by the impresario himself in 1931, when it was sung by Ruth Etting. The number also featured in at least five movies over the years, and titled the entertaining 1944 biopic of Bayes and Norworth, who were portrayed on the screen by Ann Sheridan and Dennis Morgan.

Be Glad For The Song Has No Ending

Peter Neil directed this 1969 documentary about the Incredible String Band, one of the 60s' most beguiling acts. Founded as a folk/jug band, the group later evolved into a mystically inspired ensemble, adding exotic, Eastern instrumentation, Celtic fables and florid imagery to their early *métier*. *Be Glad For The Song Has No Ending* includes footage from their 1968 concert at London's Festival Hall, as well as portions of a subsequent mime-play, *The Pirate And The Crystal Ball*, filmed in Wales, where the String Band had established a commune. The featured songs include 'All Writ Down', 'Mercy, I Cry City' and 'The Iron Stone', but a resultant soundtrack album, released on Island Records, enshrines previously unreleased material. Released on video in 1994, *Be Glad For The Song Has No Ending* is a captivating work, a fitting tribute to a multi-talented troupe.

Beach Ball USA

Edd Byrnes, famed for his 'hip-cat' role of Kookie in television's *77 Sunset Strip*, starred in this 1964 feature. The Paramount company was responsible for a production clearly inspired by the American International Pictures' 'quickie' assembly line. Byrnes plays the manager of rock band the Wiggles, who is fearful that the group's instruments are about to be repossessed. He attempts to con a campus committee in order to stop this happening. Among the performers enlisted to enliven this flimsy premise are the Supremes, who sing the title songs and 'Surfer Boy', the Righteous Brothers who perform 'Baby What Do You Want Me To Do', and the Four Seasons, who offer their concurrent US Top 3 hit, 'Dawn'. The Walker Brothers, Jerry Lee Lewis and Nashville Teens also appear, but the only *bona fide* surf act to feature are the Hondells, who contribute the Gary Usher-penned 'My Buddy Seat' to this largely unremarkable film.

Beach Party

Former Walt Disney 'Mousketeer' Annette Funicello joined clean-cut pop singer Frankie Avalon in this 1963 feature, the first of a succession of 'beach' films from the American International Pictures group. Although inspired by California's surfing scene, *Beach Party* was more closely allied to 50s formula 'quickies', such as *Disneyland After Dark* and the *Gidet* series, in particular the notion of pitching teenagers against adults. Robert Cummings starred as a 'square' academic adopting farcical disguises in an attempt to observe the sexual antics of beach-orientated youths. Dorothy Provine and Morey Amsterdam (of the popular *Dick Van Dyke* television show) were cast alongside the winsome stars, while Peter Falk, later of *Colombo*, appeared as a member of a motorbike gang. Beach Boys leader Brian Wilson was briefly featured alongside sometime collaborators Gary Usher and Roger Christian, but the chief musical interest was provided by Dick Dale And His Del-Tones, founders of the instrumental 'surfing' sound. Dale's hard-edged guitar style, heard in a succession of stellar recordings, was not especially well served in this film. Indeed his pioneering technique was about to be eclipsed by a host of imitators and an increased interest in vocal harmony groups. Nevertheless, the power of his best work remains undiminished; maverick 90s director Quentin Tarantino employed Dale's music in his film *Pulp Fiction*.

Beauty And The Beast

After Walt Disney's tremendous success with *The Little Mermaid* in 1989, this blockbuster came along two years later and was immediately considered to be equal to the studio's animated gems of the distant past, including *Cinderella*, *Snow White And The Seven Dwarfs* and *Peter Pan*. The memory of earlier movie treatments of the classic French fairytale, such as Jean Cocteau's highly regarded 1946 version, were overwhelmed by the all-round brilliance of this triumph of animated storytelling, which was enhanced by spectacular extra computer graphics images by Jim Hillin. In Linda Woolverton's screenplay, Belle is portrayed as a modern, emancipated, well-read young lady who is kidnapped by the Beast and incarcerated in his castle, which, by a stroke of good fortune, houses a fine library. After overcoming her initial fear and revulsion, Belle forges a caring relationship with her captor when she becomes aware of his inner beauty and sensitivity. Belle's voice is provided by Paige O'Hara, and Robby Benson gives the Beast just the right mixture of terror and tenderness. There are also several well-known voices behind the supporting cast, which is mostly made up of objects from around the castle, such as Lumiere the candelabra (Jerry Orbach), Mrs. Potts the teapot (Angela Lansbury), her teacup son Chip (Bradley Michael Pierce), Cogsworth the mantel clock (David Ogden Stiers), Featherduster (Kimmy Robertson), Wardrobe (Jo Anne Worley), and Gaston (Richard White), Belle's determined but unrequited suitor. Composer Alan Menken and lyricist Howard Ashman excelled themselves with a bunch of witty and tuneful songs; even the *Variety* theatre critic wryly acknowledged that *Beauty And The Beast* 'boasted the most appealing musical comedy score in years, dammit'. For the second year in succession, Menken took the Academy Award for original score, and he and Ashman won another Oscar for the film's enchanting title song which was introduced by Mrs. Potts, and sung over the end titles by Celine Dion and Peabo Bryson; their version entered the US Top 10. Two other numbers, 'Belle' and the marvellous set piece, 'Be Our Guest', were also nominated for Oscars. *Beauty And The Beast* won five Grammys, three Golden Globe Awards, including best picture (musical or comedy), and was the first animated feature to be nominated for an Academy Award for best picture. No doubt real-live actors all over the world breathed a collective sigh of relief when the Academy's voting panel gave the Oscar to the grim and grisly *The Silence Of The Lambs*. Directed by Gary Trousdale and Kirk Wise, *Beauty And The Beast* was dedicated to lyricist and executive producer Howard Ashman, who died a few months before it was released.

'Human Again', one of Ashman and Menken's numbers that was dropped from the film, featured in the score of the stage version of *Beauty And The Beast*, which opened on 18 April 1994, at the Palace Theatre in New York. It marked the important debut of the Walt Disney Company in the theatrical arena. Menken's other new songs in the show, 'No Matter What', 'Me', 'Home', 'How Long Must This Go On?', 'Maison Des Lunes', 'Transformation', and the touching 'If I Can't Love Her', which complemented those in the original film, had lyrics by Tim Rice. Susan Egan (Belle) and Terrence Mann (Beast) headed a cast that also included Gary Beach (Lumiere), Tom Bosley (Maurice), Beth Fowler (Mrs Potts), Brian Press (Chip), Heath Lamberts (Cogsworth), Kenny Raskin (Lefou), Stacey Logan (Babette), Eleanor Glockner (Madame De La Grande Bouche), and Burke Moses as the villainous Gaston. Critics offered Linda Wolverton's overlong book, Stan Meyer's sets, Matt West's choreography, and Robert Jess Roth's often 'crude' staging as reasons why this stage production did not entirely capture the magic of the movie. Excepted from these misgivings was Ann Hould-Ward, who won a Tony Award for her costume design. Nevertheless, after breaking New York's record for single-

day legit ticket sales, *Beauty And The Beast* went on to become a smash hit on Broadway and in several other countries. It was the ninth production of the show that opened at London's Dominion Theatre on 13 May 1997. Heading the cast there were Julie Alanah Brighten (Belle), Alasdair Harvey (Beast), Derek Griffiths (Lumiere), Barry James (Cogsworth), Mary Millar (Potts), Norman Rossington (Maurice), Burke Moses (Gaston), Di Botcher (Madame), Richard Gauntlett (Lefou), Rebecca Thornhill (Babette), and Ben Butterfield/Dayle Hodge/Simon Kennedy (Chip). This 'most lavish, opulent, eye-popping show ever!' won the 1998 Laurence Olivier Award for Best New Musical.

Three years earlier, in November 1995, *Beauty And The Beast On Ice*, with music and lyrics by singer-actor David Essex, had its world premiere at London's Royal Albert Hall before touring the UK.

● FURTHER READING: *Beauty And The Beast: A Celebration Of The Broadway Musical*, Donald Frantz with Sue Heinemann.

BEAUTY PRIZE, THE

With a book and lyrics by George Grossmith and P.G. Wodehouse, and music by Jerome Kern, this show was a follow-up to the three collaborators' successful 1922 London musical, *The Cabaret Girl*. The Beauty Prize opened in the West End at the Winter Garden Theatre on 5 September 1923, but did not quite emulate the critical success of its predecessor, even though several artists who had appeared in *The Cabaret Girl*, including Dorothy Dickson, Heather Thatcher, and Grossmith himself, were in the cast. They were joined by the 'rubber-faced' comedian Leslie Henson, who portrayed a Mr. Odo Philpott - the first 'prize' in a beauty contest. The winner is Carol Stewart (Dorothy Dickson), and the duo's complicated escapades, which take them from Kensington to Florida, and several other places in-between, were eked out over three acts. The score included two amusing numbers, a duet for Grossmith and Dickson, 'You Can't Make Love By Wireless', and Henson's 'Non-stop Dancing Craze' ('Grandma's feet are getting tender/Father's burst his sock suspender'), along with others such 'It's A Long Long Day' (Grossmith), 'Honeymoon Isle' and 'Moon Love' (Dickson), 'Meet Me Down On Main Street' (Grossmith and Henson), and 'You'll Be Playing Mah-Jong', an allusion to one of the popular crazes of the day. The show had a reasonable run of 213 performances before its closure in March 1924.

BECAUSE THEY'RE YOUNG

By the end of the 50s, Dick Clark had taken over from Alan Freed as the leading US disc jockey. The payola scandal that had embroiled Freed had left Clark unscathed, and his daily television show, *American Bandstand*, was responsible for launching a new generation of 'clean-cut' acts, including Fabian and Bobby Rydell. Released in 1960, *Because They're Young* starred Clark as a schoolteacher, encountering problems as he becomes immersed in his students' 'outside' lives. The cast included James Darren, co-star of the previous year's *Gidget*, the antecedent of a string of surfing and 'beach' films. Darren's rendition of 'Because They're Young' did not chart in the USA, but the single gave the singer his first UK Top 30 entry. The aforementioned Rydell performed 'Swingin' School', a number 5 US hit, and guitarist Duane Eddy contributed the memorable 'Shazam'. His instrumental version of the title theme reached number 4 in the USA and number 2 in the UK. Although largely lightweight, *Because They're Young* is an interesting period piece, reflecting an era between the birth of rock 'n' roll and the arrival of the Beatles.

BEKKER, HENNIE

b. *c*.1932, Nkana, Zambia. Multi-instrumentalist and songwriter Hennie Bekker pursued a long and varied musical career before eventually realizing his potential in his mid-60s. By that time he had been based in Toronto, Canada, for over a decade. Bekker was raised in the small town of Mufulira, 10 miles south of the Congo/Zaire border. At the age of 15 he began playing piano in the Bulawayo, Zimbabwe-based Youth Marvels. His own jazz band, the Hennie Bekker Band, was formed in 1959. His apprenticeship as a session musician and arranger began in Johannesburg, South Africa, where he was forced to flee after his group's engagement at a Zairean nightclub was curtailed by the Katanga revolution. In Johannesburg he became a staff music director and producer for Gallo Records, and also worked periodically in England. He returned to South Africa to work as a highly successful composer of television and radio commercials, subsequently becoming a respected film composer. He then settled in Canada in 1987, forced there by racial tensions in Johannesburg. He worked for a time composing stock music for the John Parry library, before collaborating with Dan Gibson on combined wildlife/new age recordings. *Harmony* was the first in a series of 13 such albums recorded by the pair up to 1996. In the 90s Bekker began to release his own, new age-themed records. He quickly made up for lost time, issuing numerous records in two thematic series - the 'Kaleidoscope' cycle (*Summer Breeze, Spring Rain, Winter Reflections, Lullabies, Autumn Magic*) and the 'Tapestry' cycle (*Silk & Satin, Vivaldi, Temba*). In addition there has been a Christmas album, plus a television-marketed ambient music series of albums for Quality Music. Bekker is also part of a trio including Greg Kavanagh and DJ Chris Sheppard who record contemporary techno as BKS. Their albums, *For Those About To Rave ... We Salute You* (1992), *Dreamcatcher* (1993) and *Astroplane* (1996), have sold a combined 100,000 copies in Canada. Bekker continues to take great pleasure in shocking adolescent fans when they discover one of Canada's most successful techno groups is spearheaded by a man in his mid-60s. However, it is as one of the most successful and prolific new age composers on the North American continent that Bekker is best known.

● ALBUMS: with Dan Gibson *Harmony* (Holborne 1989)★★★, *Summer Breeze* (Holborne 1993)★★, *Spring Rain* (Holborne 1993)★★★, *Winter Reflections* (Holborne 1994)★★★, *Tranquillity Volume 1* (Quality Music 1994)★★★, *Awakenings* (Quality Music 1994)★★★, *Silk & Satin* (Holborne 1995)★★★★, *Vivaldi* (Holborne 1995)★★, *Temba* (Holborne 1995)★★★, *Classic Moods And Nature* (Quality Music 1995)★★★, *Christmas Spirit* (Holborne 1996)★★, *Christmas Noel* (Quality Music 1996)★★, *Transitions* (Quality Music 1996)★★★, *Classics By The Sea* (Holborne 1996)★★, *Lullabies* (Holborne 1997)★★, *Autumn Magic* (Holborne 1997)★★★, *Mirage* (Avalon 1997)★★★.

BELLE

One of the legendary flops of the London musical stage, *Belle* (or *The Ballad Of Doctor Crippen*) was adapted by the author Wolf Mankowitz from a play by Beverley Cross, and opened at the Strand Theatre, London, on 4 May 1961. It was more than 50 years earlier, in January 1910, that Dr. Hawley Harvey Crippen and his young mistress, Ethel le Neve, on the run from British police, were arrested on a ship off Canada after the captain had become suspicious and radioed Scotland Yard. The pair became known as the first criminal suspects to be 'caught by radio'. Back in London, the police found the remains of Crippen's wife, Cora Belle Elmore, buried under Crippen's cellar floor. She had once been a tawdry music-hall singer, and it was in a music hall, and as a melodrama, that Mankowitz and Cross set the story of *Belle*. Jerry Desmonde, who had made his name as a brilliant straight man for Sid Field and Norman Wisdom, played George Lasher, the compère and chairman, who linked the different items with snippets of 'The Ballad Of Doctor Crippen'. The show's main characters, Crippen (George Benson), Ethel (Virginia Vernon), and Belle (Rose Hill), were joined by the entertainers, Jenny Pearl (Nicolette Roeg), who bore more than a passing resemblance to the great Vesta Tilley, and Mighty Mick (Davy Kaye) whose role could only be a tribute to another music-hall legend, Little Tich. At the time Kaye was a noted comedy performer in London nightclubs. Monty Norman's score contained some 30 songs, including several entertaining pieces, mostly pastiche, such as 'Mister Lasher And The Mighty Mick', 'A Pint Of Wallop', 'Bird Of Paradise', 'Meet Me At The Strand', 'The Devil's Bandsmen', 'Waltzing With You' and 'Don't Ever Leave Me', but the show's hit number was 'The Dit-dit Song' ('His moniker was Marconi/He was such a clever sort of chap'), an amusing reference to the important role that radio played in the whole affair. The London critics savaged *Belle*, and the cartoonists had a field day. The show folded in June, after a run of only 44 performances.

BELLE OF MAYFAIR, THE

This musical comedy, which opened at the Vaudeville Theatre in London on 11 April 1906, was very similar in style and content to that of another Belle, *The Belle Of New York*, which was enormously popular at the turn of the century, and enjoyed several revivals in London through to the 40s. The two shows also had the same leading lady, the delightful Edna May, who was replaced during the run of *The Belle Of Mayfair* by Phyllis Dare. The rest of the cast included Farren Soutar, Murray Moncrieff, Louie Pounds and Arthur Williams. The music was composed by Leslie Stuart, probably best known for his work on the early London smash-hit *Floradora*, and the book and lyrics were by Charles H.E. Brookfield and Cosmo Hamilton. Their score contained several pleasant songs such as 'Where You Go, Will I Go', 'Montezuma' and 'Come To St. George's'. The show had an excellent London run of 416 performances, but could only manage 140 in New York, even though it had a first-rate American cast that included Irene Bentley, Christie MacDonald and Bessie Clayton. Also added to the score was the popular 'Why Do They Call Me A Gibson Girl' (lyric: Leslie Stiles), which was sung by Camille Clifford.

BELLE OF NEW YORK, THE

As the 20th century dawned, London audiences were all still singing the praises and the songs from this show, which had opened at the Casino Theatre in New York on 28 September 1897. It only lasted for 56 performances on Broadway, but when it arrived in London's West End in April of the following year, it immediately captured the imagination of the public, and surprised several important theatrical managers such as George Edwardes, who had turned it down. On Broadway, Edna May created the role of Violet Gray, a Salvation Army girl who becomes the heir to a fortune belonging to Ichabod Bronson (Dan Daly). She has been chosen as the recipient of this wind-fall because Ichabod, although not averse to squiring the odd chorus girl himself, is a firm believer in organizations such as the Young Men's Rescue League and the Anti-Cigarette Society, and has found out that his playboy son, Harry (Harry Davenport), intends to marry the actress Cora Angelique (Ada Dare). Violet, for her part, is intent on Harry getting the money - and her as well. Her saucy performance of 'At Ze Naughty Folies Bergére' does the trick - Ichabod cannot possibly leave his fortune to some-one who behaves like that, and Harry's name goes back in the will. That story was the product of the vivid imagina-tion of 'Hugh Morton' (Charles M.S. McLennen), who also wrote the lyrics for songs that had music by Gustave Kerker. These included 'They All Follow Me', 'Teach Me How To Kiss', 'The Purity Brigade', 'La Belle Parisienne', 'My Little Baby', 'On The Beach At Narragansett', and, of course, the lilting and lovely 'She Is The Belle Of New York', which was introduced by William Cameron in his somewhat bizarre role as Blinky Bill. Following the origi-nal 1898 West End production, in which the Broadway principals reprised their roles, *The Belle Of New York* was revived nine times in London between 1901 and 1942, in various revised versions. The 1942 production starred Billy Danvers, Evelyn Laye and Billy Tasker. The show proved to be extremely popular in Paris as well, and was presented there in 1903, 1916 and 1952. Broadway, too, enjoyed a retitled and revised version, *The Whirl Of New York*, in 1921, but only for 124 performances. The 1952 film version, with Fred Astaire and Vera-Ellen, replaced the original songs with a score by Johnny Mercer and Harry Warren.

BELLS ARE RINGING (FILM MUSICAL)

As Broadway-to-Hollywood transplants go, *Bells Are Ringing* was fairly satisfactory, mainly due to the presence of Judy Holliday. She recreated her stage role as Ella Peterson, the somewhat scatty telephone operator at Susanswerphone, who considers her clients 'family', and their problems her own. After sympathizing with her den-tist, who is more interested in music than molars, she turns her attention to Jeff Moss (Dean Martin), a play-

wright whose output is, as the Americans say, 'batting zero'. As they fall in love, he takes her to a smart party where, after she gets her 'Ethels' (Waters, Barrymore and Merman) mixed up with her 'Marys' (Pickford, Martin and Astor), the sophisticated theatre crowd explain that it is simply a question of being able to 'Drop That Name'. That neat number, and the rest of the score, was written by Jule Styne (music) and Betty Comden and Adolph Green (lyrics and screenplay). Most of the songs from the Broadway production survived, although the absence of 'Long Before I Knew You' was a pity. It was replaced by 'Better Than A Dream', and another newcomer, 'Do It Yourself', was slipped in alongside originals such as 'It's A Simple Life', 'It's A Perfect Relationship', 'I Met A Girl', 'It's A Simple Little System', 'The Midas Touch', and the popular duo, 'Just In Time' and 'The Party's Over'. Just before the film reaches its inevitable happy ending, Ella becomes tired of her complicated telephonic involvement in other people's lives, and yearns to return to her more simple existence in the delightful 'I'm Goin' Back' ('where I can be me/At the Bonjour Tristesse Brassiere Company)'. The rest of the fine cast, a few of whom were also in the Broadway show, included Fred Clark, Eddie Foy Jnr., Dort Clark, Jean Stapleton, Frank Gorshin, Bernie West, and Gerry Mulligan. The film, which was photographed in Metrocolor and released by MGM in 1960, was directed by Vincente Minnelli, choreographed by Charles O'Curran, and produced by Arthur Freed.

BELLS ARE RINGING (STAGE MUSICAL)

Lyricists and librettists Betty Comden and Adolph Green created this show for Judy Holliday, their former partner in a group called the Revuers, which used to play Greenwich Village nightclubs back in the 30s. It opened at the Shubert Theatre in New York on 29 November 1956, and Holliday was cast as Ella Peterson, the well-meaning answerphone girl with her cousin Sue's (Jean Stapleton) firm, Susanswerphone. Ella's ambition in life is to make all her clients happy, and to sort out their emotional prob-lems. One of her particular favourites, author Jeff Moss (Sydney Chaplin), has the impression that she is pretty mature (he calls her 'Mom'), so does not recognize her when she calls at his apartment in person to ensure he keeps an important appointment, and sort out his writers' block. Naturally (this is musical comedy), romance blos-soms. However, she still feels guilty about the deception, but comes to her senses 'Just In Time'. That elegantly sim-ple number was one of the highlights in a fine Jule Styne-Comden-Green score which also included 'The Party's Over' (another big hit), 'Long Before I Knew You', 'Drop That Name', Holliday's big solo number, 'I'm Goin' Back (to the Bonjour Tristesse brassiere company')', 'It's A Simple Little System', 'It's A Perfect Relationship', 'On My Own', 'Hello, Hello There!', 'I Met A Girl', 'Mu-Cha-Cha', and 'Is It A Crime?'. As well as the great songs, there were several hilarious sub-plots, one involving the dentist, Dr. Kitchell (Bernie West), who cannot stop writing songs, and another when the cops suspect Sue's place is a front for a vice ring, but her tenant, Sandor (Eddie Lawrence), is actually operating a bookmaking concern. However, it really was Holliday's show throughout. She won a Tony

Award for her delicious performance, and another went to Sydney Chaplin for 'best supporting or featured actor in a musical'. Also cast were Eddie Lawrence (Sandor), Dort Clark (Inspector Barnes), Frank Aletter (Blake Barton), George S. Irving (Larry Hastings), Peter Gennaro (Carl), Pat Wilkes (Gwynne Smith), Jack Weston (Francis). Jerome Robbins directed, and handled the choreography with Bob Fosse, and *Bells Are Ringing* ran for 924 performances on Broadway, and a further 292 at the London Coliseum in 1957 (Janet Blair and George Gaynes). A 1987 West End revival starred Lesley Mackie and Ray Lonnen, and the Goodspeed Opera House in Connecticut mounted a production in 1990 (Lynne Wintersteller and Anthony Cummings). In 1998, Faith Prince starred when *Bells Are Ringing* was one of a trio of overlooked musicals in the Kennedy Center's inaugural *Words & Music* series. The show also played at the Village Theatre, Issaquah, near Seattle, when two Asian-American actors, Lisa Estridge-Gray and Timothy McCuen Piggee, portrayed Ella and Jeff.

BENNETT, MICHAEL

b. Michael DiFiglia, 8 April 1943, Buffalo, New York, USA, d. 2 July 1987, Tucson, Arizona, USA. A director, choreographer and dancer, Bennett studied dance and choreography in his teens, and staged several shows at his local high school. After playing the role of Baby John in *West Side Story* on US and European tours, he began his Broadway career as a dancer in early 60s musicals such as *Subways Are For Sleeping*, *Here's Love* and *Bajour*. He made his debut as a choreographer in the 12-performance flop, *A Joyful Noise* (1966), which was followed a year later by another failure, *Henry And Sweet Henry*. His first hit came in 1968 with *Promises, Promises* when he created several original and lively dance sequences from Burt Bacharach and Hal David's highly contemporary score. During the next few years he choreographed the Katherine Hepburn vehicle *Coco* (1969), two Stephen Sondheim shows, *Company* (1970) and *Follies* (1971), along with *Seesaw* (1973), on which he was also the director and librettist. Then came *A Chorus Line*, which opened in July 1975 and closed nearly 15 years later in April 1990. In 1995 it was still the longest-running Broadway production, musical or otherwise. As its choreographer and director, Bennett devoted several years of his life to the show, auditioning, rehearsing, and directing productions throughout the world. He declined to spend any more time making a film version, and Richard Attenborough's 'uninspired' adaptation was released in 1985. Bennett's next musical was the short-lived *Ballroom* (1978), but he had one more major hit with *Dreamgirls* in 1981, which earned him his seventh and final Tony Award. In the early 80s he toyed with various projects including another musical, *Scandal*, but nothing materialized. In 1985 he signed as the director of *Chess*, but had to withdraw in January 1986 through illness. Later in the year he sold his New York property and moved to Tucson, Arizona, where he stayed until his death from AIDS in 1987.

● FURTHER READING: *A Chorus Line And The Musicals Of Michael Bennett*, Ken Mandelbaum.

BENNETT, RICHARD RODNEY

b. 29 March 1936, Broadstairs, Kent, England. A distinguished composer of classical and film music, who also appears as a cabaret performer, Bennett began taking piano lessons at the age of five, and had composed a number of highly proficient pieces by the time he was 15. Although seemingly destined for a career in classical music, from an early age he was also influenced by popular music and jazz. In 1955, while studying at the Royal Academy of Music, he met John Hollingsworth, a leading musical director for the British cinema, who invited him to compose the score for a short documentary film for an insurance company. This led to him writing the music for several late 50s films, primarily thrillers, including *Interpol* (1957, US: *Pickup Alley*), *Indiscreet* (1958), *The Man Inside* (1958), *A Face In The Night* (1958, US: *Menace In The Night*), *The Safecracker* (1958), *Blind Date* (1959), *The Angry Hills* (1959), *The Devil's Disciple* (1959), and *The Man Who Could Cheat Death* (1959). In 1957 Bennett received a grant from the French government that enabled him to study for two years in Paris with the *avant garde* superstar composer and conductor Pierre Boulez, although he still found time to further his non-classical interests by playing the piano in the city's thriving jazz clubs. In the early 60s, Bennett's name became associated with comedy films such as *Only Two Can Play* (1961), *The Wrong Arm Of The Law* (1963), *Billy Liar* (1963) and *Heavens Above* (1963), although he continued to score a variety of other movies, including *The Mark* (1961), *Satan Never Sleeps* (1962), *One Way Pendulum* (1964), *The Nanny* (1965), *The Witches* (1966, US: *The Devil's Own*), *Far From The Madding Crowd* (1967, Oscar nomination), *Billion Dollar Brain* (1967), and *Secret Ceremony* (1968). Since then, he has won further Academy Award nominations for his work on the historical epic *Nicholas And Alexandra* (1971), and the elegant Agatha Christie whodunnit, *Murder On The Orient Express* (1974), his most famous score, along with his other distinctive music which enhanced large and small screen projects such as *The Buttercup Chain* (1970), *Figures In A Landscape* (1971), *Lady Caroline Lamb* (1973), *Voices* (1973), *Of Jewels And Gold* (1973), *Permission To Kill* (1975), *Sherlock Holmes In New York* (1976, telefilm), *L'Iprecateur The Accuser* (1977), *Equus* (1977), *The Brink's Job* (1978), *Yanks* (1979), *Return Of The Soldier* (1982), *Agatha Christie's Murder With Mirrors* (1985, television), *Tender Is The Night* (1985, television mini-series), *The Ebony Tower* (1987, telefilm), *Poor Little Rich Girl: The Barbara Hutton Story* (1987, mini series), *The Attic: The Hiding Of Anne Frank* (1987, telefilm), *Enchanted April* (1991), and *Four Weddings And A Funeral* (1994). Bennett also collaborated with Neil Diamond on the song 'Amazed And Confused' which was sung by Diamond in *The Jazz Singer* (1980).

Bennett's prolific output of concert music includes operas, ballets, symphonies, concertos, sonatas, vocal works, and 'A Jazz Calendar' (1964), a chamber piece based on the nursery rhyme 'Monday's Child Is Fair Of Face', which served as the basis for a ballet. In 1995 he was appointed to the International Chair of Composition at the Royal Academy of Music. Bennett moved to live in New York in

1979, and around the same time began to sing and play in cabaret. Since then his urbane and sophisticated performances at venues such as J's, a jazz club on the Upper West Side of Manhattan, and London's Pizza On The Park, have incorporated an extensive repertoire of songs extending from the 20s through to the present day, as well as some of his own numbers, such as 'Let's Go And Live In The Country' and 'Words And Music', a send-up of people who talk incessantly at cabaret shows. Bennett is particularly fond of working with other classy artists in the popular-jazz field, including Cleo Laine, Marian Montgomery, Joyce Breach, and Mary Cleere Haran. His 'Concerto For Stan Getz', which Stan Getz never played, as he died in the year of its composition, was recorded by saxophonist John Harle in 1995. Bennett was created a CBE in 1977, and awarded a knighthood in the 1996 New Year Honours List for 'services to music'.

● ALBUMS: *I Got Rhythm* (HMV 1981)★★★, with Marian Montgomery *Surprise Surprise* (Cube 1981)★★★, *Harold Arlen's Songs* (Audiophile 1981)★★★, with Montgomery *Town And Country* (Cube 1982)★★★, *Little Jazz Bird* (1983)★★★, with Montgomery *Puttin' On The Ritz* (Cube 1984)★★★, *Take Love Easy* (Audiophile 1988)★★★, *I Never Went Away* (Delos 1990)★★★, with Montgomery *Nice And Easy* (Jazz House 1991)★★★, with Joyce Breach *Lovers After All* (ACD 1993)★★★, *Special Occasions* (DRG 1994)★★★.

● FURTHER READING: *Richard Rodney Bennett: A Bio-Bibliography*, Richard Rodney Bennett and Stewart R. Craggs (ed.).

BENNETT, ROBERT RUSSELL

b. 15 June 1894, Kansas City, Missouri, USA, d. 18 August 1981. A composer, arranger, conductor, and the leading orchestrator of Broadway musicals from the 20s through until 1960. At the age of 10 Bennett was giving piano recitals, and in his teens he studied harmony, counterpoint and composition, and also played in dancehalls and movie houses. While serving in the US Army during World War I, he conducted and scored the music for various bands, and on his release, secured a job with the music publishers T.B. Harms & Company. From then on, for more than 30 years, he orchestrated over 300 scores for Broadway's leading composers, including *Rose-Marie*, *Show Boat*, *Roberta*, *Very Warm For May*, *Of Thee I Sing*, *Girl Crazy*, *The Band Wagon*, *Porgy And Bess*, *Anything Goes*, *Carmen Jones*, *Bloomer Girl*, *Kiss Me, Kate*, *Finian's Rainbow*, *Lady In The Dark*, *Annie Get Your Gun*, *Bloomer Girl*, *Music In The Air*, *On A Clear Day You Can See Forever*, *Gay Divorce*, *Jumbo*, *Bells Are Ringing*, *Camelot*, *My Fair Lady*, and Richard Rodgers and Oscar Hammerstein II's blockbusters *Oklahoma!*, *Carousel*, *South Pacific* and *The Sound Of Music*. Bennett also worked on some 30 films, and won an Oscar for his scoring of *Oklahoma!* in 1955. Three years earlier he had orchestrated Richard Rodgers' music for *Victory At Sea*, a naval history of World War II presented on US television in 26 episodes. He also composed serious classical music, including several operas, symphonies, and many other orchestral, solo and chamber pieces, but it is for his work for Broadway that he will be best remembered. Although composers including Jerome Kern, Cole Porter, George Gershwin, Arthur Schwartz, Harold Arlen and Frederick Loewe wrote the music, the form in which it was heard in the theatre depended on Robert Russell Bennett, with his orchestral colourings, his empathy with lyrics and the book, and the inspired selection of *tempi* - particularly impressive in the overtures to *My Fair Lady* and *Oklahoma!*.

● FURTHER READING: *Instrumentally Speaking*, Robert Russell Bennett.

BENNY GOODMAN STORY, THE

Hollywood biopics almost always present the same paradox: if the subject is interesting enough to make a film of his/her life, why meddle with the facts? Goodman, portrayed by Steve Allen, but providing his own playing for the soundtrack, had a rags-to-riches life story that simultaneously fulfilled the American Dream and every screenwriter's wildest fantasy. Unfortunately, in real life, Goodman was a single-minded perfectionist who became a household name and a millionaire before he had reached 30. In other words, all he did was practise obsessively and perform, which did not make for good visual drama. Hence, the reality of his dedication was jettisoned in favour of a sloppy story about a home-loving boy who made good. In the course of the film, Goodman periodically whines to his Ma, 'Don't be that way'. This allows the introduction of the tune of that name as the dutiful son's grateful acknowledgement to his mother, thus overlooking the fact that Edgar Sampson wrote the song for another bandleader, Chick Webb. Goodman's not inconsiderable streak of ruthlessness was also overlooked. Nevertheless, the film has some nice musical moments from Allen/Goodman, Teddy Wilson, Lionel Hampton and Gene Krupa in the small group numbers. The specially assembled big band includes Buck Clayton, Stan Getz, Conrad Gozzo, Urbie Green, Manny Klein and Murray McEachern and plays very well, even though it does not sound much like the real Goodman band of the late 30s. Ben Pollack and Kid Ory also appear, as does Harry James (in a close-up solo feature but not in long-shot - contractual reasons were suggested, specifically, too little money). For all this 1955 film's flaws, among which is the famous 1938 Carnegie Hall concert attended by 'longhairs' - in real life the seats were packed with swing-era fans and jitterbugs - it remains one of the least embarrassing of the earlier jazz biopics.

BERGMAN, ALAN AND MARILYN

For over two decades, the Bergmans have been among the leading lyricists of songs for Hollywood films. Among the husband-and-wife partnership's earliest work for the screen was the theme for 'In The Heat Of The Night' (1967), co-written with Quincy Jones and sung by Ray Charles. The following year the Bergmans began one of their most important collaborations with a soundtrack composer when they wrote the Oscar-winning 'Windmills Of Your Mind' with Michel Legrand for *The Thomas Crown Affair*. Sung by Noel Harrison, it was an international hit in 1969. The Bergman-Legrand team were also responsible for 'What Are You Doing The Rest Of Your Life', which was featured in the 1969 movie *The Happy Ending*, 'How Do You Keep The Music Playing' for *Best Friends* (1982) and 'The Way He Makes Me Feel' for the Barbra Streisand film *Yentl* (1983). The trio won an Oscar for their original ssong score for the latter film. Streisand was the first to feature what is perhaps the Bergmans' most famous song (and another Oscar-winner), 'The Way We Were', in the 1973 film of the same name. The music for this yearning ballad was composed by Marvin Hamlisch and given an epic soul-tinged treatment by Gladys Knight. The same team wrote 'The Last Time I Felt Like This' for *Same Time, Next Year* (1978) and 'The Girl Who Used To Be Me' for *Shirley Valentine* (1990). Alan and Marilyn Bergman's other collaborators have included Billy Goldenberg, with whom they worked on the television movie *Queen Of The Stardust Ballroom*, and its subsequent stage adaptation, *Ballroom* (1978), Dave Grusin ('It Might Be You' for *Tootsie* in 1982), Henry Mancini ('Little Boys' for *The Man Who Loved Women* in 1983) and James Newton Howard, who provided the melody in 1991 for 'Places That Belong To You', performed by Barbra Streisand in *Prince Of Tides*. Streisand herself co-wrote 'Two People', the theme from *Nuts*, with the Bergmans. The couple have also provided themes for US television programmes such as *Alice* (1976), *Powers That Be* (1990), and *One Hour* (1991), where they again worked with Hamlisch. With a talent precisely tailored to providing cinema theme songs, among the few lyrics written by Alan and Marilyn Bergman for the recording studio was 'I Believe In Love', which became a minor hit for Kenny Loggins in 1977. In 1991, Alan Bergman, with singer Sandy Stewart, presented selections from the Bergman catalogue at the Russian Tea Room in New York, and in the following year he took over as the new president of the Academy Foundation, the educational and cultural arm of the Academy of Motion Picture Arts and Sciences.

BERKELEY, BUSBY

b. William Berkeley Enos, 29 November 1895, Los Angeles, California, USA, d. 1976. A legendary choreographer and director, renowned for his innovative work on the 'Depression Era' musical films of the 30s. Stories abound about him building a monorail along which the camera travelled at the most unusual angles, and his habit of cutting a hole in the studio roof just so that he could get that one special shot. Although Berkeley's mother was an actress and he appeared in a number of minor stage productions as a youngster, he had no formal theatrical training and attended the Mohegan Lake Military Academy near New York before working in a shoe factory for three years. After a brief spell in the US Army in 1917, Berkeley took small roles in a number of plays and musicals before taking up directing in the early 20s. For most of the decade he served primarily as a dance director on Broadway shows such as *Holka Polka*, *A Connecticut Yankee*, *Present Arms*, *Good Boy*, *Street Singer* and *The International Review* (1930). Samuel Goldwyn is credited with taking Berkeley to Hollywood in 1930 to stage the production numbers for the Eddie Cantor vehicle *Whoopee!*. His work on that film, which introduced his trademark 'top shots' and close-ups of the chorus girls, was further developed in the other United Artists films for which he staged the dances, *Palmy Days*, *The Kid From Spain*, and *Roman Scandals*. However, it was not until 1933

and *42nd Street*, the first of Berkeley's films for Warner Brothers, that the dance director's elaborate musical numbers, with the girls arranged in a series of complicated kaleidoscopic patterns that were continually moving in different directions, began to be fully appreciated. Dick Powell and Ruby Keeler were the stars of this slight backstage story, and they were in some of the other films to which he brought his highly individual flair and imagination. These included *Gold Diggers Of 1933*, *Footlight Parade*, *Dames*, *Go Into Your Dance*, *Gold Diggers Of 1937*, and *Gold Diggers In Paris* (1938). Berkeley left Warner Brothers in 1939 to continue to 'create and stage the dances and ensembles' for MGM and other studios for musicals such as *Broadway Serenade*, *Ziegfeld Girl*, *Lady Be Good*, *Born To Sing*, *Girl Crazy*, *Two Weeks With Love*, *Call Me Mister*, *Two Tickets To Broadway*, *Million Dollar Mermaid*, *Small Town Girl*, *Easy To Love*, and *Rose Marie* (1954). By then, he and his style of elaborate production numbers were out of fashion, but he returned in 1962 to stage the dance numbers for his last screen project, *Billy Rose's Jumbo*. From *Gold Diggers Of 1935* onwards, Berkeley was overall director of a number of films. The musicals among them included *Bright Lights* (1935), *Babes In Arms*, *Strike Up The Band*, *Babes On Broadway*, *For Me And My Gal*, *The Gang's All Here*, and *Take Me Out To The Ball Game* (1949). In the mid-60s Berkeley benefited from a general upsurge of interest in the films of the 30s, and there were several retrospective seasons of his work in the USA and other countries around the world. In 1971 he was the production supervisor for a Broadway revival of the musical *No, No, Nanette*, which starred Ruby Keeler and ran for 861 performances. Looking back on his career, he said: 'What I mostly remember is stress and strain and exhaustion.' His brilliant achievements were contrasted by a shambolic private life - he was married at least five times - and in 1946 he attempted suicide after his mother died It is also reported that in 1935 he was charged with second-degree murder after driving into another car, killing the three occupants. After two trials ended with hung juries, he was finally acquitted.

● FILMS: as choreographer *Whoopee* (1930), *Palmy Days* (1931), *Kiki* (1931), *Flying High* (1931), *Night World* (1932), *Bird Of Paradise* (1932), *The Kid From Spain* (1932), *Gold Diggers Of 1933* (1933), *42nd Street* (1933), *Footlight Parade* (1933), *Roman Scandals* (1933), *Wonder Bar* (1934), *Fashions Of 1934* (1934), *Dames* (1934), *Twenty Million Sweethearts* (1934), *Go Into Your Dance* (1935), *Stars Over Broadway* (1935), *In Caliente* (1935), *Gold Diggers Of 1937* (1937), *The Singing Marine* (1937), *Varsity Show* (1937), *Gold Diggers In Paris* (1938), *Broadway Serenade* (1939), *Lady Be Good* (1941), *Born To Sing* (1941), *Ziegfeld Girl* (1941), *Girl Crazy* (1943), *Romance On The High Seas* (1948), *Two Weeks With Love* (1950), *Call Me Mister* (1951), *Two Tickets To Broadway* (1951), *Million Dollar Mermaid* (1952), *Easy To Love* (1953), *Small Town Girl* (1953), *Rose Marie* (1954), *Billy Rose's Jumbo* (1962); as director *She Had To Say Yes* co-director (1933), *Gold Diggers Of 1935* (1935), *I Live For Love* (1935), *Bright Lights* (1935), *Stage Struck* (1936), *The Go-Getter* (1937), *Hollywood Hotel* (1937), *Comet Over Broadway* (1938), *Garden Of The Moon* (1938), *Men Are Such Fools* (1938), *They Made Me A Criminal* (1939), *Babes In Arms* (1939), *Fast And Furious* (1939), *Forty Little Mothers* (1940), *Strike Up The Band* (1940), *Blonde Inspiration* (1941), *Babes On Broadway* (1941), *For*

Me And My Gal (1942), *The Gang's All Here* (1943), *Cinderella Jones* (1946), *Take Me Out And To The Ball Game* (1949).

BERLIN, IRVING

b. Israel Baline, 11 May 1888, Temun, Siberia, Russia, d. 22 September 1989. Despite his foreign birth, Berlin became one of the greatest and most American of all songwriters. When he was four years old his family escaped a pogrom and travelled to the USA. His father was a cantor in his homeland, but in their new country he had to earn his living as a meat inspector in New York City, singing in the synagogue only when the regular cantor was unavailable. An indifferent student, Berlin was happier singing, but in 1896, following the death of his father, he was obliged to work. At the age of 14 he began singing in saloons and on street corners. It was while engaged in this latter activity that he was 'discovered' and recommended to songwriter and publisher Harry Von Tilzer, who hired him to sing songs from the balcony of a 14th Street theatre. By 1906 Berlin had not advanced far, working as a singing waiter in Pelham's, a Chinatown restaurant frequented by New York's upper set, but he had taught himself to play piano and had started to write his own material. His first published song (lyrics only, music by Michael Nicholson) was 'Marie From Sunny Italy', from which he earned 37 cents and, apparently through a misprint on the sheet music, acquired the name by which he was thereafter known.

During the next few years he continued to write words and music, but also hung onto his job as a singing waiter. Several of the songs he wrote in these years were in Yiddish, and were popular successes for artists such as Eddie Cantor and Fanny Brice. His first real songwriting success was 'My Wife's Gone To The Country' (1909, music by George Whiting), which was featured by Cantor. Like many other songwriters of the day, Berlin was fascinated by ragtime and tried his hand at several numbers, many of which had little to do with the reality of this musical form apart from their titles. In 1911, however, he had his first massive hit with 'Alexander's Ragtime Band', for which he wrote both words and music. It made him a household name, and Berlin capitalized upon the success of this song with others such as 'Everybody's Doing It' (1911) and 'The International Rag' (1913). A talented vaudeville performer, he performed many of these songs himself. As would be the case throughout his career, many of Berlin's early songs were introduced in stage shows and revues. From 1910-13, these included *The Jolly Bachelors, Up And Down Broadway, Temptations, Hanky-Panky*, and the *Ziegfeld Follies*. In 1914, he wrote his first complete score for *Watch Your Step* ('Play A Simple Melody'), which featured dancers Vernon And Irene Castle, and followed it a year later with *Stop! Look! Listen!* ('I Love A Piano', 'The Girl On The Magazine Cover'). Among his non-show songs around this time, were popular numbers such as 'Woodman, Spare That Tree', 'When The Midnight Choo-Choo Leaves For Alabama', 'Do It Again', 'Snooky Ookums', 'I Want To Go Back To Michigan', 'When I Lost You' (the first of his many exquisite ballads), and the sentimental 'When I Leave The World Behind' (1915). During World War I, Berlin was active in the theatre, and wrote several patriotic songs, such as 'I'm Gonna Pin A Medal On The Girl I Left Behind', 'When I Get Back To The USA', and 'For Your Country And My Country'. In 1918 he was drafted into the army and encouraged to write a show for the troops. For this hastily conceived all-soldier production, *Yip, Yip, Yaphank*, in which he also starred, he produced two memorable songs, 'Mandy' and 'Oh, How I Hate To Get Up In The Morning'. Berlin celebrated the end of the war with a satirical piece entitled 'I've Got My Captain Working For Me Now', and continued to write a steady stream of popular songs, mostly for Ziegfeld shows, including 'A Pretty Girl Is Like A Melody', 'You'd Be Surprised', 'I Want To See A Minstrel Show', 'The Girl Of My Dreams', 'I'll See You In C-U-B-A', and 'After You Get What You Want You Don't Want It' (1920). In 1919, he established the Irving Berlin Music Co., and two years later, the Music Box Theatre, which he built in association with the producer Sam M. Harris in order to showcase his own music. It opened with the first edition of the *Music Box Revue* ('Say It With Music', 'Everybody Step', 'They Call It Dancing'). In 1926, Berlin married the socialite Ellin Mackay against her father's wishes, and many of the poignant ballads he wrote during the 20s are said to reflect that event, and other areas of his private life. These included 'All By Myself', 'All Alone', 'What'll I Do?', 'Always', 'Marie', 'Russian Lullaby', 'Remember', 'The Song Is Ended' and 'How About Me'? More light-hearted pieces of the late 20s were 'Lazy', 'Shakin' The Blues Away', 'Blue Skies' (interpolated into the Richard Rodgers/Lorenz Hart score for *Betsy* (1927)), and songs such as 'Monkey Doodle Doo' and 'Lucky Boy' for the Marx Brothers' stage musical *Cocoanuts*. After contributing to some early talking pictures such as *Mammy* ('Let Me Sing And I'm Happy') and *Puttin' On The Ritz* (title song) in 1930, Berlin was inactive for a time during the early Depression years, but was soon back on top form again with the stage musicals *Face The Music* (1923, 'Soft Lights And Sweet Music', 'Let's Have Another Cup Of Coffee', 'On A Roof In Manhattan') and *As Thousands Cheer* (1933, 'Easter Parade', 'Heat Wave', 'Supper Time', 'Harlem On My Mind', 'Not For All The Rice In China'), as well as writing other memorable songs such as 'How Deep Is The Ocean?' and 'Say It Isn't So'. In the 30s, like so many other Broadway composers, Berlin turned to Hollywood, and wrote the scores for several immensely popular film musicals, including *Top Hat* (1935, 'Cheek To Cheek', 'No Strings', 'Top Hat, White Tie And Tails', 'Isn't This A Lovely Day?'), *Follow The Fleet* (1936, 'Let's Face The Music And Dance', 'I'm Putting All My Eggs In One Basket', 'Let Yourself Go'), *On The Avenue* (1937, 'This Year's Kisses', 'I've Got My Love To Keep Me Warm', 'The Girl On The Police Gazette', 'You're Laughing At Me'), *Carefree* (1938, 'Change Partners', 'I Used To Be Colour Blind'), and *Second Fiddle* (1939, 'I Poured My Heart In A Song', 'I'm Sorry For Myself'). He also contributed the lovely 'Now It Can Be Told', and 'My Walking Stick', along with a batch of his old numbers, to the highly entertaining *Alexander's Ragtime Band* (1938), which starred Alice Faye and Tyrone Power. With World War II on the horizon, Kate Smith introduced Berlin's 'God Bless America', which became a second US National Anthem, and raised thousands of dollars for the Boy Scouts and Girl Guides Of America. The catchy 'Any Bonds Today', also furthered Berlin's patriotic cause. However, in May 1940, a few months before the USA entered the war, he was back on Broadway with *Louisana Purchase* ('It's A Lovely Day Tomorrow', 'Outside Of That I Love You', 'You're Lonely And I'm Lonely'), which ran for over a year. In 1942, he donned World War I army uniform for *This Is The Army*, another all-soldier show, which he composed, produced and directed. In his small, high-pitched voice (Bing Crosby once said: 'You had to hug him to hear him'), Berlin reprised his 'Oh, How I Hate To get Up In The Morning', and also wrote 'This Is The Army, Mr. Jones', 'I Left My Heart At The Stage Door Canteen', and others, for the show, which toured the major US cities and American bases in Africa, Europe, and the South Pacific. In the same year, Berlin's score for the movie *Holiday Inn*, which starred Crosby and Fred Astaire, contained the Oscar-winning 'White Christmas', along with 'Count Your Blessings', 'Be Careful, It's My Heart', 'Let's Start The New Year Right', 'Happy Holiday', and 'I'll Capture Your Heart Singing', and several more new and old Berlin numbers. In 1946, Berlin's score for what is generally considered to be his masterpiece - *Annie Get Your Gun* - was full of hits, such as 'They Say It's Wonderful', 'Doin' What Comes Naturally', 'The Girl That I Marry', 'You Can't Get A Man With A Gun', 'Anything You Can Do', 'I Got The Sun In The Morning' and 'There's No Business Like Show Business', in addition to lesser-known gems like 'I Got Lost In His Arms'. In the same year, the movie *Blue Skies* introduced 'You Keep Coming Back Like A Song', 'A Couple Of Song And Dance Men' and 'Getting Nowhere'. In 1948, Fred Astaire was persuaded out of retirement to appear with Judy Garland in *Easter Parade*. Johnny Green and Roger Edens won Academy Awards for 'scoring of a motion picture', but the real stars were Berlin songs such as 'It Only Happens When I Dance With You', 'A Fella With An Umbrella', 'Steppin' Out With My Baby', 'Better Luck Next Time', and one of the most-played clips in the history of the cinema, 'A Couple Of Swells'. Berlin's last Broadway show of the 40s, *Miss Liberty* (1949, 'Let's Take An Old Fashioned Walk', 'A Man Chases A Girl (Until She Catches Him)', 'Just One Way To Say "I Love You"', 'Give Me Your Tired, Your Poor', 'You Can Have Him'), was considered to be a disappointment, but he began his fifth decade as a songwriter with the score for the smash hit Ethel Merman vehicle, *Call Me Madam* (1950, 'The Best Thing For You', 'You're Just In Love', 'It's A Lovely Day Today', 'The Hostess With The Mostes' On The Ball', 'Marrying For Love'). After writing several new songs, including 'Count Your Blessings Instead Of Sheep', 'Snow', 'Sisters', 'The Best Things Happen While You're Dancing' and 'Love, You Didn't Do Right By Me', for the movie *White Christmas*, and seeing many of his old numbers revived on screen in *There's No Business Like Show Business*, Irving Berlin retired until 1962, when he returned to Broadway with the score for the amusing political musical comedy *Mr. President* ('Let's Go Back To The Waltz', 'In Our Hideaway', 'Is He The Only Man In The World', 'Empty Pockets Filled With Love'). In spite of initial good notices, it only ran for eight months, and, apart from writing 'An Old Fashioned Wedding' for the 1966 Lincoln Center revival of *Annie Get Your Gun*, there were

no more comebacks for Berlin, especially when the movie *Say It With Music*, on which he had been working throughout the 60s, was finally abandoned in 1969.

Despite, or perhaps because of, his foreign birth, Berlin was intensely American, both in his personal patriotism and acute sense of what made American popular music distinctive. Five years after he wrote 'They Like Ike' for *Call Me Madam*, in 1955 Berlin received a gold medal from President Dwight D. Eisenhower, 'in recognition of his services in composing many patriotic songs including "God Bless America"'. His other honours included a medal of merit from the US Army for his work on *This Is The Army*, and a special Tony Award in 1963 for his 'distinguished contribution to the musical theatre these many years'. For the last 30 years of his long life, Berlin lived in semi-seclusion, ignoring media attempts to laud his achievements, even at such significant milestones as his 100th birthday. His unmatched contribution to the world of showbusiness is perhaps best summed up by the following quote, which is attributed to another great composer, Jerome Kern: 'Irving Berlin has no place in American music - he is American music.' In 1995, a musical conceived by George Faison and David Bishop, entitled *C'mon & Hear! Irving Berlin's America*, played some US provincial theatres, and Varèse Sarabande released *Unsung Irving Berlin*, consisting of '31 hidden treasures' heard for the first time, and performed by some of Broadway's brightest talent, such as Emily Loesser, Crista Moore, Laurie Beechman, Liz Callaway, and Davis Gaines. In the same year, Musica nel Chiostro, the summer opera festival organization based in Tuscany, presented a fund-raising gala performance of Berlin's first full-length show, *Watch Your Step*, at Her Majesty's Theatre in London. Two years later another production, *The Tin Pan Alley Rag*, featuring the music of Berlin and Scott Joplin, had its world premiere at the Pasadena Playhouse, California.

● FURTHER READING: *The Story Of Irving Berlin*, David Ewen. *Irving Berlin*, Michael Freedland. *Irving Berlin And Ragtime America*, I. Whitcomb. *As Thousands Cheer: The Life Of Irving Berlin*, L. Bergreen. *Irving Berlin: A Daughter's Memoir*, Mary Ellin Barrett.

BERNADETTE

One of the most bizarre and spectacular failures in London musical theatre history. The show, which opened at the 2,000-seat Dominion Theatre in London on 21 June 1990, was based on the story of Bernadette Soubrious, a young peasant girl who had visions of the Virgin Mary at Lourdes in 1858. It was the brainchild of a piano-tuner and his wife, Gwyn and Maureen Hughes, who wrote the book, music and lyrics, and whose only previous contact with the world of showbusiness had been when they wrote a song that was eliminated in a preliminary heat of the Eurovision Song Contest. From the start, *Bernadette* was dubbed 'The People's Musical'. Finance from conventional sources was scarce, and more than 2,500 readers of the *Daily Mirror* newspaper helped to raise the £1.25 million needed to stage it. The largest investor, however, was the show's producer, William Z. Fonfé, an ex-chauffeur, who remortgaged his house so that he could inject some £500,000 into a project that he predicted would be 'the greatest musical since *West Side Story*'. The cast was led by 16-year-old Natalie Wright, who had been spotted in Andrew Lloyd Webber's *Aspects Of Love*. With an advance of £250,000, the show received an ecstatic first-night reception, mainly because the audience consisted of hundreds of interested investors, who were easy to spot because they were dressed in anoraks, and sports - not dinner - jackets. The critics took a more jaundiced view: 'Pass the loaves and the fishes: they need a miracle', 'themeless songs to make laundry lists by', 'one-dimensional and confused', 'three thousand angels (investors), but not a prayer', were typical comments. To support their view, many of the reviewers quoted the song lyric: 'The seas may all run dry/but my love will never die.' In an effort to delay the inevitable, Natalie Wright released a record of the song 'Who Are You', the Pope blessed the cast and the composers, and the 'angels' received requests for more money - to which they responded. It was all to no avail: *Bernadette* closed on 14 July after a run of only three weeks, with losses 'approaching £1.25 million', having been dubbed 'a miraculous failure'. The 'miracle', if there ever was one, would seem to be twofold: that a director of Ernest Maxin's standing (*Black And White Minstrel Show*, *Morecambe And Wise Show*) ever became involved; and that a group of amateurs thought that they could mount a successful, large-scale West End musical at a time when professionals were constantly failing to do so.

BERNSTEIN, ELMER

b. 4 April 1922, New York, USA. An important and prolific arranger-conductor and composer of over 100 film scores. Bernstein was hailed as a 'musical genius' in the classical field at the age of 12. Despite being a talented actor, dancer and painter, he devoted himself to becoming a concert pianist and toured nationally while still in his teens. His education at New York University was interrupted when he joined the United States Air Force during World War II. Throughout his four years' service he composed and conducted music for propaganda programmes, and produced musical therapy projects for operationally fatigued personnel. After the war he attended the Juilliard School of Music and studied composition with the distinguished composer, Roger Sessions. Bernstein moved to Hollywood and started writing film scores in 1950, and two years later wrote the background music for *Sudden Fear*, a suspense thriller starring Joan Crawford and Jack Palance. Agent and producer Ingo Preminger, impressed by Bernstein's music, recommended him to his brother Otto for the latter's 1955 film project, *The Man With The Golden Arm*. A tense, controversial movie, its theme of drug addiction, accompanied by the Berstein modern jazz score, played by top instrumentalists such as Shelly Manne, Shorty Rogers, Pete Candoli and Milt Bernhart, caused distribution problems in some American states. The film won Oscar nominations for the star, Frank Sinatra, and for Bernstein's powerful, exciting music score. Bernstein made the US Top 20 with his record of the film's 'Main Title', and Billy May entered the UK Top 10 with his version. In 1956, Bernstein wrote the score for Cecil B. De Mille's epic *The Ten Commandments*. Thereafter, he provided the background music for an

impressive array of movies with varied styles and subjects, including *Fear Strikes Out* (1957), *Sweet Smell Of Success* (1957), *God's Little Acre* (1958), *Some Came Running* (1958), *The Rat Race* (1960), *The Birdman Of Alcatraz* (1962), *The Great Escape* (1963), *A Walk In The Spring Rain* (1970), *The Shootist* (1976), *National Lampoon's Animal House* (1978), *An American Werewolf In London* (1981), *Ghostbusters* (1984), *¡Three Amigos!* (1986), *Amazing Grace And Chuck* (1987), *Slipstream* (1988), *DA* (1988), *My Left Foot* (1989), *The Grifters* (1990), *The Field* (1990), *Rambling Rose* (1991), *Oscar* (1991), *A Rage In Harlem* (1991), *The Babe* (1992), *The Cemetery Club*, *Mad Dogs And Glory*, *The Good Son*, and *Neil Simon's Lost In Yonkers* (1993). In 1991, Bernstein was the musical director and arranger of Bernard Herrman's original score for the 1962 classic, *Cape Fear*. He has received Academy Award nominations for his work on *The Magnificent Seven* (1960); *Summer And Smoke* (1961), the title song for *Walk On The Wild Side* (1961), with a lyric by Mack David; *To Kill A Mockingbird* (1962), said to be Bernstein's favourite of his own scores; the scores for *Return Of The Seven* (1966), and *Hawaii* (1966) (and a song from *Hawaii*, 'Wishing Doll', lyric by Mack David); the title song from *True Grit* (1969) lyric by Don Black; a song from *Gold* (1974), 'Wherever Love Takes Me', lyric by Don Black; and *Trading Places* (1983). Bernstein won an Oscar for his original music score for the 20s spoof, *Thoroughly Modern Millie* (1967). Coincidentally, Bernstein was the musical arranger and conductor at the Academy Awards ceremony when his award was announced, and had to relinquish the baton before going on stage to receive his Oscar. Bernstein also worked extensively in television: in 1958 he signed for US Revue Productions to provide background music for television dramas. One of his most notable scores was for *Staccato* (1959) (later retitled *Johnny Staccato*), a series about a jazz musician turned private eye, starring John Cassavetes. The shows were extremely well received in the UK, where Bernstein's recording of 'Staccato's Theme' rose to Number 4 in the singles chart in 1959, and re-entered the following year. On a somewhat larger scale instrumentally, an 81-piece symphony orchestra was contracted to record Berstein's score for Martin Scorsese's 1993 film *Age Of Innocence*.

● ALBUMS: *What Is Jazz?* (1958)★★★, *Desire Under The Elms* (1959)★★★, *God's Little Acre* (1959)★★★, *King Go Forth* (1959)★★★, *Some Came Running* (1960)★★★★, *Walk On the Wild Side* (1962)★★★★, *To Kill A Mocking Bird* (1962)★★★, *Movie And TV Themes* (1963)★★, *The Great Escape* (1963)★★★, *The Carpetbaggers* (1964)★★★, *Hallelujah Trail* (1965)★★, *The Sons Of Katie Elder* (1965)★★★, *The Ten Commandments* (1966)★★★, *A Man And His Movies* (1992)★★★, *Elmer Bernstein By Elmer Bernstein* (Denon 1993)★★★, *Bernard Herrmann Film Scores* (Milan 1993)★★★.

BERNSTEIN, LEONARD

b. Louis Bernstein, 25 August 1918, Lawrence, Massachusetts, USA, d. 14 October 1990, New York, USA. Bernstein was a major and charismatic figure in modern classical music and the Broadway musical theatre. He was also a conductor, composer, pianist, author and lecturer. A son of immigrant Russian Jews, Bernstein started to play the piano at the age of 10. In his teens he showed an early interest in the theatre, organizing productions such as *The Mikado*, and an unconventional adaptation of *Carmen*, in which he played the title role. Determined to make a career in music, despite his father's insistence that 'music just keeps people awake at night', Bernstein eschewed the family beauty parlour business. He went on to study first with Walter Piston and Edward Burlingaunt Hill at Harvard, then with Fritz Reiner, Isabella Vengerova and Randall Thompson at the Curtis Institute in Philadelphia, and finally with Serge Koussevitzky at the Berkshire Music Institute at Tanglewood. Bernstein had entered Harvard regarding himself as a pianist, but became influenced by Dimitri Mitropoulos and Aaron Copland. They inspired him to write his first symphony, *Jeremiah*. In 1943 he was chosen by Artur Rodzinski to work as his assistant at the New York Philharmonic. On 14 November 1943, Bernstein deputized at the last minute for the ailing Bruno Walter, and conducted the New York Philharmonic in a concert that was broadcast live on network radio. The next day, he appeared on the front pages of the newspapers and became a celebrity overnight. In the same year he wrote the music for *Fancy Free*, a ballet, choreographed by Jerome Robbins, about three young sailors on 24 hours' shore leave in New York City. It was so successful that they expanded it into a Broadway musical, with libretto and lyrics by Betty Comden and Adolph Green. Retitled *On The Town* and directed by George Abbott, it opened in 1944, with a youthful, vibrant score which included the memorable anthem 'New York, New York', 'Lonely Town', 'I Get Carried Away' and 'Lucky To Be Me'. The 1949 film version, starring Frank Sinatra and Gene Kelly, and directed by Kelly and Stanley Donen, is often regarded as innovatory in its use of real New York locations, although Bernstein's score was somewhat truncated in the transfer. In 1950 Bernstein wrote both music and lyrics for a musical version of J. M. Barrie's *Peter Pan*, starring Jean Arthur and Boris Karloff. His next Broadway project, *Wonderful Town* (1953), adapted from the play *My Sister Eileen*, by Joseph Fields and Jerome Chodorov, again had lyrics by Comden and Green, and starred Rosalind Russell, returning to Broadway after a distinguished career in Hollywood. Bernstein's spirited, contemporary score, for which he won a Tony Award, included 'Conversation Piece', 'Conga', 'Swing', 'What A Waste', 'Ohio', 'A Quiet Girl' and 'A Little Bit Of Love'. The show had a successful revival in London in 1986, with Maureen Lipman in the starring role. *Candide* (1956) was one of Bernstein's most controversial works. Lillian Hellman's adaptation of the Voltaire classic, sometimes termed a 'comic operetta', ran for only 73 performances on Broadway. Bernstein's score was much admired, however, and one of the most attractive numbers, 'Glitter And Be Gay', was sung with great effect by Barbara Cook, one year before her Broadway triumph in Meredith Willson's *The Music Man*. *Candide* has been revived continually since 1956, at least twice by producer Hal Prince. It was his greatly revised production, which included additional lyrics by Stephen Sondheim and John Latouche (original lyrics by Richard Wilbur), that ran for 740 performances on Broadway in 1974. The Scottish Opera's production, directed by Jonathan Miller

in 1988, is said to have met with the composer's approval, and Bernstein conducted a concert version of the score at London's Barbican Theatre in 1989, which proved to be his last appearance in the UK.

Bernstein's greatest triumph in the popular field came with *West Side Story* in 1957. This brilliant musical adaptation of Shakespeare's *Romeo And Juliet* was set in the streets of New York, and highlighted the violence of the rival gangs, the Jets and the Sharks. With a book by Arthur Laurents, lyrics by Sondheim in his first Broadway production, and directed by Jerome Robbins, Bernstein created one of the most dynamic and exciting shows in the history of the musical theatre. The songs included 'Jet Song', 'Something's Coming', 'Maria', 'Tonight', 'America', 'Cool', 'I Feel Pretty', 'Somewhere' and 'Gee, Officer Krupke!'. In 1961, the film version gained 10 Academy Awards, including 'Best Picture'. Bernstein's music was not eligible for an award because it had not been written for the screen. In 1984, he conducted the complete score of *West Side Story* for the first time, in a recording for Deutsche Grammophon, with a cast of opera singers including Kiri Te Kanawa, José Carreras, Tatania Troyanos and Kurt Allman. Bernstein's last Broadway show, *1600 Pennsylvania Avenue* (1976), was an anticlimax. A story about American presidents, with book and lyrics by Alan Jay Lerner, it closed after only seven performances. Among Bernstein's many other works was the score for the Marlon Brando film, *On The Waterfront* (1954), for which he was nominated for an Oscar; a jazz piece, 'Prelude, Fugue and Riffs', premiered on US television by Benny Goodman in 1955; and 'My Twelve Tone Melody' written for Irving Berlin's 100th birthday in 1988. In his celebrated classical career, which ran parallel to his work in the popular field, he was highly accomplished and prolific, composing three symphonies, a full-length opera, and several choral works. He was musical director of the New York Philharmonic from 1958-69, conducted most of the world's premier orchestras, and recorded many of the major classical works. In the first week of October 1990, he announced his retirement from conducting because of ill-health, and expressed an intention to concentrate on composing. He died one week later on 14 October 1990. In 1993, BBC Radio marked the 75th anniversary of his birth by devoting a complete day to programmes about his varied and distinguished career. A year later, *The Leonard Bernstein Revue: A Helluva Town*, played the Rainbow & Stars in New York, and, on a rather larger scale, in June of that year the New York Philharmonic presented their own celebration entitled *Remembering Lenny*. Further contrasting interpretations of Bernstein's work were heard in 1994 when television coverage of the World Cup used his 1984 recording of 'America' as its theme, while the new pop band, Thunderballs, 'viciously mugged' the song (with permission from the Bernstein estate) under the title of '1994 America'.

● ALBUMS: *Bernstein Conducts Bernstein* (1984)★★★, *Bernstein's America* (1988)★★★, various artists *Leonard Bernstein's New York* (Nonesuch 1996)★★★.

● FURTHER READING: *The Joy Of Music*, Leonard Bernstein. *Leonard Bernstein*, John Briggs. *Leonard Bernstein*, Peter Gadenwitz. *Leonard Bernstein*, Joan Peyser. *Leonard Bernstein*,

Humphrey Burton. *Leonard Bernstein - A Life*, Meryle Secrest. *Leonard Bernstein*, Paul Myers.

BERRY, W.H.

b. William Henry Berry, 23 March 1870, London, England, d. 2 May 1951, London, England. An immensely popular comedian, actor, and singer, who delighted West End audiences for more than 20 years before going into films, Berry initially appeared in the theatre in his spare time while pursuing a financial career in the City of London. After being spotted by the legendary producer George Edwardes, he appeared in several of his musical shows until Edwardes' death in 1915. These included *The Little Cherub* (1906), *Les Merveilleuses* (1906), *The Merry Widow* (1907), *Havana* (1908), *A Waltz Dream* (1908), *The Dollar Princess* (1909), *The Count Of Luxembourg* (1911), and *Gypsy Love* (1912). He remained an important attraction in a variety of musicals such as *A Country Girl* (1914), *Betty* (1915), *Tina* (1915), *High Jinks* (1916), *The Boy* (1917), *The Naughty Princess* (1920), *Who's Hooper?* (1919), *The Golden Moth* (1921), *Head Over Heels* (1923), *Poppy* (1924), *The Blue Kitten* (1925), *The Bamboula* (1925), *Princess Charming* (1926), *Merry Merry* (1929), and *The Girl From Cook's* (1927). In 1934 he made his film debut as the amusing Police Constable Merks in the screen adaptation of Vivian Ellis' stage hit *Mister Cinders* (1934). This was followed by roles in *The Student's Romance* (1935), *Royal Cavalcade* (1935), *Honours Easy* (1935), *Music Hath Charms* (1935), *Once In A Million* (1936), *A Star Fell From Heaven* (1936), and *She Knew What She Wanted* (1936).
● FURTHER READING: *Forty Years In The Limelight*, W.H. Berry.

BEST FOOT FORWARD (FILM MUSICAL)

The story of an ordinary guy inviting a famous movie star to be his date at the school dance has a familiar ring to it. This particular example was adapted from the 1941 Broadway musical of the same name, which had been based on a book by John Cecil Holmes. Lucille Ball was the glamour girl who, in the cause of public relations and personal publicity, answers the call from young Tommy Dix and hastens to the Winsocki Military Academy to join several veterans of the original stage production, who included June Allyson, Nancy Walker, Kenny Bowers, Jack Jordan Jnr., and Dix himself. Also in the cast were William Gaxton, Virginia Weidler, Gloria DeHaven, Beverley Tyler, Chill Wills and Henry O'Neill. Songwriters Hugh Martin and Ralph Blane made their Hollywood debut with a mixture of lively and romantic numbers that included 'Three Men On A Date', 'You're Lucky', 'My First Promise', 'Shady Lady Bird', 'Alive And Kicking', 'The Three 'B's', 'Wish I May Wish I Might', 'Ev'ry Time', and 'Buckle Down, Winsocki'. Two instrumentals, 'Two O'Clock Jump' (Harry James-Count Basie-Benny Goodman) and 'The Flight Of The Bumble Bee' (Rimsky-Korsakov), were used as showcases for guest artist Harry James And His Orchestra. Irving Brecher and Fred Finklehoffe wrote the screenplay, and the imaginative and spirited choreography was designed by Charles Walters. Edward Buzzell was the director, and *Best Foot Forward* was shot in Technicolor by producer Arthur Freed's excellent MGM unit.

BEST FOOT FORWARD (STAGE MUSICAL)

Subtitled 'A Modern Musical Comedy', and set in Winsocki, a prep school in Pennsylvania, *Best Foot Forward* had a book by John Cecil Holmes and a score by the new team of Hugh Martin and Ralph Blane. It opened at New York's Ethel Barrymore Theatre on 1 October 1941, and was directed by George Abbott, who also produced the show with Richard Rodgers (uncredited). The choreographer was Gene Kelly. The story deals with the bewildering complications that arise when Bud Hooper (Gil Stratton Jnr.) mischievously invites the glamorous movie star Gale Joy (Rosemary Lane) to the school prom. Sensing the possibility of a good publicity stunt, she accepts, but, following problems involving Bud's jealous girlfriend, Helen Schlesinger (Maureen Cannon), and a brawl during which she loses her dress as the students demand more than just autographs, she cannot wait to return to Hollywood. The songs included 'Just A Little Joint With A Jukebox', 'What Do You Think I Am?', 'I Know You By Heart', 'Ev'ry Time', 'The Three B's', 'Shady Lady Bird', 'That's How I Love The Blues', and the lively 'Buckle Down, Winsocki', which achieved some popularity and became a hit outside the show for Al Jarrett And His Orchestra. *Best Foot Forward* ran on Broadway for 326 performances, and gave two future stars, Nancy Walker and June Allyson, their first real opportunity to shine. They also appeared in the 1943 film version, with Lucille Ball and William Gaxton. The 1963 stage show revival, which played off-Broadway at Stage 73, gave Liza Minnelli her first theatrical chance, just two years before she came to prominence in *Flora, The Red Menace*.

BEST LITTLE WHOREHOUSE IN TEXAS, THE

The advance publicity for this musical, with just about the most provocative title ever, ensured full houses when it opened off-Broadway at the Entermedia Theatre on 17 April 1978. New York audiences took to the show immediately, and it moved to Broadway's 46th Street Theatre on 19 June. The book, by Peter Masterson and Larry L. King, was based on a magazine article by King which told of the last few days in the life of The Chicken Ranch, a long-serving Texan brothel that was having to close down after its activities had been exposed on an investigative television programme. Clint Allmon played Melvin P. Thorpe, the slick and slimy television front man, complete with bouffant blond wig, gaudy jacket, and a stars and stripes tie, while Carlin Glynn, as Miss Mona, the friendly establishment's 'hostess with the mostess', and Henderson Forsythe (Sheriff Ed Earl Dodd, her ex-lover), both won Tony Awards for their performances. Despite its title, the whole thing turned out to be a highly amusing, raunchy romp, with a few sentimental moments too. The lively, atmospheric score, with its folksy, country quality, was by the former classical music student, Carol Hall, and included 'A Li'l Ole Bitty Pissant Country Place', 'Texas Has A Whorehouse In It', 'Girl, You're A Woman', 'Hard-Candy Christmas, 'Bus From Amarillo', 'Twenty Four Hours Of Lovin'', 'Good Old Girl' and 'Doatsy Mae'. Several of the creative participants, including Masterson, King and Hall, came from Texas, and it was Tommy Tune, another refugee from the 'lone star state', who provided the imaginative choreography. *The Best Little Whorehouse In Texas* surprised a lot of people, and ran on Broadway for 1,584 performances. The 1982 film version starred Dolly Parton and Burt Reynolds.

BEST THINGS IN LIFE ARE FREE, THE

This highly entertaining film biography of De Sylva, Brown And Henderson, one of the top songwriting teams of the 20s and 30s, was released in 1956. The sheer pleasure of listening to the constant stream of singable, happy songs, diverted the attention from a screenplay by William Bowers and Phoebe Ephron that, as usual with biopics, made the subjects' interesting lives seem ordinary. In this case, the composer Ray Henderson (Dan Dailey), gives up teaching children to work with two men who behave like children, Buddy De Sylva (Gordon MacRae) and Ray Brown (Ernest Borgnine). Their tempestuous working relationship results in hit after hit for Broadway shows before De Sylva develops a taste for the Hollywood 'big time' and goes off to produce early films. In no time at all he realizes the error of his ways and is reunited with his two buddies, and with Kitty Kane (Sheree North), the girl he left behind. She has reflected on his absence with the lovely ballad, 'Without Love' (dubbed by Eileen Wilson), a rare quiet moment in an otherwise jolly collection of the composers' numbers, including 'Birth Of The Blues', 'You Try Somebody Else', 'Button Up Your Overcoat', 'Sunny Side Up', 'If I Had A Talking Picture Of You', 'This Is My Lucky Day', 'Black Bottom' and 'The Best Things In Life Are Free'. One of the film's most amusing scenes comes when the songwriters, forced against their will to write a number for Al Jolson (played by Norman Brooks), try to come up with a 'stinker', but it turns out to be 'Sonny Boy'! The film was produced by 20th Century-Fox in CinemaScope and Technicolor and was directed by Michael Curtiz.

BETTER 'OLE, THE

With a subtitle like 'a fragment from France in two explosions, seven splinters and a gas attack', this show has to have been around during World War I. It did, in fact, open at the Oxford Theatre in London on 4 August 1917, with a book by Bruce Bairnsfather and Arthur Eliot, James Hurd's lyrics, and music composed by Herman Darewski. The show was set in the trenches of France, as seen through the eyes of Old Bill (Arthur Bourchier), and his soldier colleagues Alf (Sinclair Cotter) and Bert (Tom Wootwell). All three were characters that had been created by Bairnsworth in his widely enjoyed wartime cartoons. The show's title is taken from one of the drawings in which Old Bill is berating a fellow companion in his muddy pit with: 'If you know of a better 'ole then go to it!'. The show proved to be enormously popular both with the audience at home and those on leave. They left the theatre happily singing songs such as 'From Someone In France To Someone In Somerset', 'Tommy', 'She's My Gal', 'My Word! Ain't We Carrying On?', 'I'm Sick Of This 'Ere War', and 'Let's Dust Together'. One item, by the American songwriters Jimmy Monaco, James McCarthy and

Howard Johnson, was interpolated into the score. It was called 'What Do You Want To Make Those Eyes At Me For', and its appeal endured to such an extent that it was sung by Betty Hutton in the 1945 film, *Incendiary Blonde*, and also entered the UK chart in versions by Emile Ford (1959) and Shakin' Stevens (1987). *The Better 'Ole* ran in London for a remarkable 811 performances, and added a further 353 in New York. The story was made into a silent film in 1918 under the title of *The Romance Of Old Bill*.

BETTY

One of the early hits of World War I, *Betty* opened at Daly's Theatre in London on 24 April 1915. In an effort to vary the London musical theatre's normal fare of European operetta, the American librettist Gladys B. Ungar was engaged to write the book with England's own Frederick Lonsdale. It dealt with the young, high-born, wild and irresponsible Gerald, the Earl of Beverly (Donald Calthrop), who, to spite his ducal father, marries Betty, a kitchen maid (Winifred Barnes). His action causes a good deal of trouble up at the 'big house', especially when the cad neglects the poor girl and carries on as before. Inevitably, with the help of severe paternal financial pressure, he learns the error of his ways, returns to Betty, and true love conquers in the end. Paul Rubens and Adrian Ross's score (with additional songs by Ernest Steffan and Merlin Morgan) contained several appealing ballads, including 'Can It Be Love?', 'The Duchess Of Dreams', 'Cinderella', 'If It Were True', 'It's A Beautiful Day Today', and a charming duet, 'Dance With Me', along with the amusing 'I Love The Girls', 'We Ought To Combine' and 'Opposite The Ducks'. *Betty* stayed in London for nearly a year, a total of 391 performances. A New York production opened in the autumn of 1916, but was not nearly so successful.

BEYOND THE FRINGE

Born in 1960 as a late-night 'fringe entertainment' at the Edinburgh Festival, this four-man satirical revue moved to the tiny Fortune Theatre in London on 10 May 1961. It was written and performed by the cast, consisting of four Oxbridge university graduates: Alan Bennett, Peter Cook, Jonathan Miller and Dudley Moore. Unlike the smart, sophisticated revues popular in the 50s, such as *The Lyric Revue*, *Airs On A Shoestring* and *Look Who's Here!*, *Beyond The Fringe* was, in the words of the distinguished critic Bernard Levin, 'so brilliant, adult, hard-boiled, accurate, merciless, witty, unexpected, alive, exhilarating, cleansing, right, true, and good that my first conscious thought as I stumbled, weak and sick with laughter, up the stairs at the end was one of gratitude.' Moore wrote the music for the 'series of unconnected skits', which included 'The Bollard', 'The Sadder And Wiser Beaver' (based on the press baron Lord Beaverbrook), 'Take A Pew', 'Aftermyth Of War', 'Sitting On A Bench' (a precursor to Cook and Moore's notorious Derek and Clive characters), 'And The Same To You' (shades of David Lean's film, *The Bridge Over The River Kwai*), and 'The End Of The World' (a fashionably anti-nuclear piece). The production was highly acclaimed by public and press alike, and won the London *Evening Standard* award for best musical in 1961. Bennett, Cook, Miller and Moore left early in 1962, but the show continued with a second cast, eventually closing in March 1964 after 1189 performances. The original quartet of performers went to Cape Town, Toronto, Washington and Boston before the Broadway premiere of *Beyond The Fringe* at the John Golden Theatre on 27 October 1962. This edition, which had been revised for US consumption, was widely applauded and the cast received a special Tony Award for 'their brilliance which has shattered all the old concepts of comedy'. Miller stayed with the show for about a year and the other three withdrew soon afterwards. In addition to the New York run of 673 performances, another company toured the USA for seven months. Alan Bennett and Jonathan Miller, the 'serious pair', have devoted much of their time since to the theatre, Bennett as one of the UK's most renowned playwrights, and Miller as a notable director for a variety of productions, including opera. For more than a decade, Peter Cook and Dudley Moore were an immensely popular film and television comedy team, particularly in the series, *Not Only . . . But Also*, before Moore combined a lucrative acting career in Hollywood with occasional flashes of brilliance as an accomplished jazz pianist. Cook continued to be associated with satire through his involvement in the notorious *Private Eye* magazine, as well as being one of Britain's most familiar character actors and chat-show personalities, until his death in 1995. The Original Cast 'live' album of *Beyond The Fringe*, which charted in the UK and the USA, was re-released in 1993 on Broadway Angel.

BIG

Assembled and then premiered in the motor city of Detroit, Michigan, USA, in February 1996, this $10.3 million model went on display at the Shubert Theatre in New York on 28 April of that year. John Weidman's book was based on Gary Ross and Anne Spielberg's screenplay for the immensely successful 1988 film comedy starring Tom Hanks, and faithfully related the charming story of 12-going-on-13-year-old Josh Baskin (Patrick Levis), whose burning ambition to grow up instantly is granted by a carnival fortune-telling machine. However, he soon finds that life within the body of 30-year-old Big Josh (Daniel Jenkins) - a transformation that leads to the job of his dreams at MacMillan Toys, and a (very) close relationship with the company's scheming marketing director Susan (Christa Moore) - is not at all what he thought it would be. Even with an office chock-full of the most amazing toys and an apartment resembling a pinball arcade, he has missed out on an important stage of his life. Fortunately, his pal Billy (Brett Tabisel), who helped Josh to realize his dream in the first place, is still around when things become too difficult. Young Josh also has a fan in Cynthia Benson (Lizzy Mack), who shone in some of choreographer Susan Stroman's spirited and inventive dance sequences, while featured and ensemble members John Sloman, Gene Weygandt, Clent Bowers, Frank Mastron, Frank Vlastnik, Donna Lee Marshall and Jan Neuberger were impressive. The team of David Shire (music) and Richard Maltby Jnr. (lyrics) were responsible for the songs, and Josh's mother (Barbara Walsh) had perhaps the best one, 'Stop, Time'. There were several other musical highlights, such as Moore's 'Dancing All The Time' and 'One Special Man', as well as her duet with Jenkins on the dreamy 'Stars, Stars, Stars'. One of the most touching moments came when, with Josh and Susan about to further their relationship, young Josh begins to sing the tender 'I Want To Know'. The remainder of a varied and polished score included 'Can't Wait', 'Talk To Her', 'The Carnival', 'This Isn't Me', 'I Want To Go Home', 'The Time Of Your Life', 'Dr. Deathstar', 'Here We Go Again', 'Cross The Line', 'It's Time', 'Happy Birthday, Josh', 'Coffee, Black', 'The Real Thing', 'When You're Big', 'Skateboard Romance', and 'Fun', a big production number, which builds impressively as Josh and toy boss MacMillan (Jon Cypher) are gradually joined by an energetic crowd of youngsters. Mike Ockrent was the director, but his name was not among the five Tony Award nominations the show received for book, score, choreography, leading actress (Moore), and featured actor (Tabisel). No winners though, and, significantly, no nomination for best musical. Even so, experienced Broadway watchers were surprised when *Big* closed on 13 October 1996 after a run of nearly six months, losing its total investment. It joined *The Red Shoes*, *My Favorite Year*, *The Goodbye Girl*, and *State Fair*, four other recent failed attempts to adapt hit movies for the musical stage.

● FURTHER READING: *Making It Big*, Barbara Isenberg.

BIG BEAT, THE

One of several films made at the advent of rock 'n' roll, *The Big Beat* contained one of the genre's most expansive casts. The wafer-thin plot, wherein a record company executive, who hates rock 'n' roll, employs his pop music-loving son, allowed scope for a variety of acts. Establishment stars including Harry James, George Shearing and the Mills Brothers, were featured alongside emergent talent, notably the Del Vikings and Fats Domino. This 1957 film is of interest because, whether by accident or design, it showed how the 'new' music was an extension of the 'old', rather than an aberration. Rock 'n' roll's roots in jazz are clearly seen and doo-wop is shown as a successor to 40s vocal harmony groups. The inclusion of white act the Diamonds, who specialized in 'clean-cut' cover versions of songs originally recorded by black singers, demonstrated another facet of the era. Although stilted in its presentation, *The Big Beat* puts 50s music into a historical context.

BIG BEN

This 'light opera' was Vivian Ellis' first post-war West End show, and reunited him with the author A.P. Herbert (b. 24 September 1890, Elstead, England, d. 11 November 1971), and the impresario C.B. Cochran. *Big Ben* opened at the Adelphi Theatre in London on 17 July 1946. Herbert was a noted crusader for justice, and a Member of Parliament from 1935-50, so it was hardly surprising that his somewhat unconventional story for *Big Ben* revolved around a shop girl, Grace Green (Gloria Lynne), who is elected to the House Of Commons. She is a Socialist, and her gentleman friend, the Hon. George Home (Eric Palmer), is a true-blue Conservative, but they are united in their opposition to a bill that would affect the drinking (of alcohol) habits of the community at large. Their unorthodox methods bring about their incarceration in a secure part of Westminster for a time, but the inevitable happy ending is never far away. Vivian Ellis wrote the words and music for what turned out to be one of his most agreeable scores. A fine cast, which included Gabrielle Brune, David Davies, Eric Forte, Trefor Jones, and Yvonne Robinson, excelled in numbers such as 'London's Alight Again', 'Let Us Go Down The River', 'The Sun Is On the City', 'Who's The Lady?', 'Love Me Not', 'Do You Remember The Good Old Days?', 'London Town', and the rousing 'I Want To See The People Happy'. During the show's run of 172 performances, Carol Lynne was replaced in the leading role by one of Cochran's young 'discoveries', a future star of musical comedy and operetta, Lizbeth Webb; Gabrielle Brune gave way to Noele Gordon, who eventually became a national figure in Britain through her involvement in the long-running television soap opera, *Crossroads*.

BIG BROADCAST, THE

By 1932, when this film was released by Paramount, Bing Crosby was the radio sensation of America. His relaxed singing style and self-deprecating humour transferred easily to film, and, later, the more intimate medium of television. In George Marion Jnr.'s screenplay for *The Big Broadcast*, Bing plays a radio crooner who serenades the lovely Leila Hyams, but she prefers well-heeled Texan Stuart Erwin. Crosby loses the girl, but gets a job when the radio station is saved from extinction by Erwin's dollars. There were songs and stars galore in a picture in which several of the performers sang numbers that were to become indelibly identified with them, such as 'Please' and 'Where The Blue Of The Night Meets The Gold Of The Day' (Crosby), 'Trees' (Donald Novis), and 'When The Moon Comes Over The Mountain' (Kate Smith). Among the other musical items played and sung were 'Tiger Rag' (the Mills Brothers), 'Kickin' The Gong Around' (Cab Calloway and his Orchestra), 'It Was So Beautiful' (Smith), 'Shout, Sister, Shout' (Boswell Sisters), 'Minnie The Moocher' (Calloway), 'Marta' (Arthur Tracy), 'Goodbye Blues' (Mills Brothers), 'Dinah' (Crosby), and 'Here Lies Love' (Tracy, Crosby and the Vincent Lopez Orchestra). Also in the cast were George Burns, Gracie Allen, and Eddie Lang. The film, which was directed by Paramount veteran Frank Tuttle, became so successful that it spawned three sequels.

Although Bing Crosby turned up again in *The Big Broadcast Of 1936* (released 1935), Jack Oakie plays the romantic radio crooner this time - except that he actually isn't - because, unknown to his nationwide listening audience, someone else is paid to do the singing for him. Complications arise when a wealthy countess played by Lyda Roberti falls in love with the voice - and whisks him off to her own private Shangri-la. Burns and Allen were in attendance again, and also in the cast were Akim Tamiroff, Wendy Barrie, Henry Wadsworth, and Benny Baker. Brief, but effective contributions came from Amos 'N Andy, Bill 'Bojangles' Robinson, the Nicholas Brothers, the Vienna Boys' Choir, and Ray Noble And His Orchestra. Highlights included Ethel Merman's 'man-hungry' 'It's The Animal In Me', and Crosby's smooth and soulful 'I

Wished On The Moon', which became a big US hit for him, and for Little Jack Little And His Orchestra. The rest of the songs, such as 'Miss Brown To You', 'Double Trouble', 'Why Dream?', and 'Through The Doorway Of Dreams I Saw You', were not particularly memorable, but the whole package, which had a screenplay by Walter DeLeon, Francis Martin and Ralph Spence, and was directed by Norman Taurog, proved to be fast and furious fun, and led to more of the same, or similar, a year later.

Songwriters Ralph Rainger and Leo Robin, who, in association with Richard Whiting and Dorothy Parker, had written most of the songs for the 1936 edition, provided the complete score for *The Big Broadcast Of 1937* (made in 1936). Numbers such as 'You Came To My Rescue', 'Hi-Ho The Radio', 'La Bomba', 'I'm Talking Through My Heart', and 'Here's Love In Your Eye', punctuated Walter DeLeon and Francis Martin's token story, which involved Jack Benny, a great radio favourite at the time, along with a fascinating mixture of comedic and musical talent such as Burns And Allen, Bob Burns, Martha Raye, Benny Fields, Benny Goodman And His Orchestra, Leopold Stokowski and the Philadelphia Orchestra, Eleanore Whitney, Frank Forrest, and mouth organist Larry Adler. The engaging 'Here's Love In Your Eye' became a hit on record for Benny Goodman, and for trumpeter Henry Allen And His Orchestra.

In *The Big Broadcast Of 1938*, Shirley Ross, who, with Ray Milland, had provided the love interest in the 1937 film, joined with screen newcomer Bob Hope, to introduce one of the most enduring of all popular songs, 'Thanks For The Memory'. That number was the highlight of another Robin and Rainger score that included several other memorable moments, such as 'Mama, That Moon Is Here Again' (sung by Martha Raye), 'This Little Ripple Had Rhythm' (Shep Fields And His Orchestra), and 'You Took The Words Right Out Of My Heart' (Dorothy Lamour). Comedian W.C. Fields headlined the cast, which also featured South American singer Tito Guizar and opera diva Kirsten Flagstad. Fields strutted his usual stuff in a story by Walter DeLeon, Francis Martin and Ken Englund that was directed by Mitchell Leisen and set around a transoceanic race. Of course, one of the two large liners had to organize a celebrity radio show during the voyage, thereby justifying the film's title.

All four of Paramount's *Big Broadcast* films were highly entertaining and big money-spinners. Shirley Ross and Bob Hope's big hit from the last of them, 'Thanks For The Memory', won an Academy Award and became the title of another 1938 picture in which they appeared together. In that one, the duo introduced yet another all-time standard, Frank Loesser and Hoagy Carmichael's 'Two Sleepy People' ('Here we are, out of cigarettes . . .').

BIG RIVER

Notable especially for the Broadway debut of the country singer-songwriter Roger Miller, who provided both music and lyrics for this musical adaptation of Mark Twain's immortal book, *The Adventures Of Huckleberry Finn*. The show opened at the Eugene O'Neill Theatre in New York on 25 April 1985, and William Hautman's book was set mainly on the Mississippi River, on which Huck (Daniel

H. Jenkins) and the runaway slave Jim (Ron Richardson) make their bid for freedom. A fine supporting cast included John Short as Tom Sawyer, and Bob Gunton and René Auberjonois as King and Duke, a couple of con-men. Miller's songs, a mixture of bluegrass and blues, with just a touch of gospel, were widely applauded. They included 'Muddy Water', 'You Ought To Be Here With Me', 'Guv'ment', 'Worlds Apart', 'River In The Rain', 'Leaving's Not The Only Way To Go', 'Waiting For The Light To Shine' and 'Worlds Apart'. To the surprise of many, *Big River* enjoyed a run of 1,005 performances, and, in a season almost bereft of new musicals, gained Tony Awards for best musical, score, book, featured actor (Ron Richardson), director (Des McAnuff), lighting (Richard Riddell) and scenic design (Heidi Landesman). The latter's atmospheric sets were one of the production's most attractive features.

BIG TNT SHOW

Star names the Rolling Stones, the Beach Boys and James Brown ensured the *T.A.M.I Show* (aka *Gather No Moss*) became one of the leading pop spectaculars of 1964. A second show was planned for the following year, although its title was later changed to the *TNT Show*. Originally screened on US television on 31 December 1965, it featured some of the era's finest and most innovative acts, notably the Lovin' Spoonful and the Byrds. Their respective versions of 'Do You Believe In Magic' and 'Mr Tambourine Man' are magnificent. Bo Diddley, Ray Charles and Joan Baez also appeared, while the presence of Petula Clark and Roger Miller brought a lighter side of pop to the proceedings. David McCallum, star of cult television series *The Man From U.N.C.L.E.*, introduced the show by leading the house band through versions of 'Satisfaction' and '1-2-3', while revered producer Phil Spector assumed musical direction. Two of the acts from his Philles label - Ike And Tina Turner and the Ronettes - completed the *TNT Show* bill. Spector's notorious perfectionism resulted in several backstage problems - Petula Clark was required to complete several takes of her hit, 'Downtown', before the producer was satisfied. Four and a half hours were set aside for recording the entire show, but only three acts had completed their set by that time and shooting necessarily entered a second day. This painstaking approach was worthwhile - the *Big TNT Show* perfectly captures a vibrant period in pop.

BIKEL, THEODORE

b. 2 May 1924, Vienna, Austria. Bikel was a stage and screen actor as well as a folk-singer. He arrived in the USA having visited Palestine and London. He starred in the film *The African Queen* in 1951. His Jewish background enabled him to build up a comprehensive repertoire of Eastern European, Russian and Yiddish songs. His first album for Elektra Records was the appropriately titled *Folk Songs From Just About Everywhere*. Bikel appeared at the 1960 Newport Folk Festival, and in several films, including *My Fair Lady* in 1964, and Frank Zappa's *200 Motels* in 1971. During the early 60s Bikel had his own radio show, *At Home With Theodore Bikel*. He also co-starred with Mary Martin in the Broadway production of

The Sound Of Music in 1954. Additionally, he appeared in films such as *The Pride And The Passion* in 1957, and *The Russians Are Coming* in 1966. In his film roles, Bikel played a variety of nationalities. Later albums appeared on Reprise Records. In 1977, Bikel was appointed by President Jimmy Carter to the National Council For The Arts.

● ALBUMS: *Folk Songs From Just About Everywhere* (Elektra 1959)★★★, *Bravo Bikel* (1959)★★★, *Folk Songs Of Israel* (1960)★★★, *Actor's Holiday* (1960)★★★, *From Bondage To Freedom* (1961)★★★, *On Tour* (1963)★★★, *Folksingers Choice* (1964)★★★, *Yiddish Theater And Folk Songs* (60s)★★★, *Harvest Of Israeli Folk Songs* (60s)★★★, *Jewish Folk Songs* (60s)★★★, *Songs Of The Russian Gypsy* (60s)★★★, *New Day* (1969)★★★, *Silent No More* (1972)★★★, *Song Of Songs* (70s)★★★.

● COMPILATIONS: *Best Of Theodore Bikel* (1962)★★★.

BIKINI BEACH

Another in a long line of 'beach' films, this 1964 feature starred genre stalwarts Annette Funicello and Frankie Avalon, the latter playing a double role of drag racer and British pop star. 'The Girls Are Bare-ing, The Guys Are Dare-ing, And The Surf's Rare-ing To Go-Go-Go', screamed the advertising by-line, but *Bikini Beach* followed the exploitative formula of its predecessors. Misunderstood teenagers encounter dim-witted adults as the plot follows the accustomed frothy boy-meets-girl motif. Hollywood mainstay Keenan Wynn joined comedian Don Rickles in a cast supplemented by rising Tamla/Motown upstart (Little) Stevie Wonder and instrumental surf combo, the Pyramids, famed for their shaven-headed image. Of interest to 'trash culture' aesthetes, *Bikini Beach* does have a period-piece charm lacking in, for example, contemporaneous Elvis Presley films. These were a waste of talent, where here, Annette and Avalon play up their camp roles to the hilt.

BILLY

The question was this: could a story that had already been the subject of a bestselling novel, and a successful film and play, go one further and be turned into a hit musical show? The answer proved to be a most definite 'yes'. Keith Waterhouse's novel, *Billy Liar*, which had been adapted for the stage and screen by Waterhouse and Willis Hall, proved to be ideal material in the hands of librettists Dick Clement and Ian La Frenais (*The Likely Lads, Porridge, Auf Wiedersehn, Pet*), and songwriters John Barry (music) and Don Black (lyrics). *Billy* opened at the Drury Lane Theatre in London on 1 May 1974. Michael Crawford, who had been acclaimed for his role in the film of *Hello, Dolly!* (1969), and would eventually attain superstardom in Andrew Lloyd Webber's *The Phantom Of The Opera* (1986), played the part of young Billy Fisher, the undertaker's clerk, who is forever dreaming of another life in the fantasy country of Ambrosia, where he is the leader of his own private (female) army, far from reality and the drab environment of his native Yorkshire. His long-suffering parents were played by Avis Bunnage and Bryan Pringle, and his loyal girlfriends, the raunchy Rita, and the more refined Liz, by Elaine Paige and Diana Quick. Billy's flights of fancy were best reflected in the show's hit song,

'Some Of Us Belong To The Stars', 'The Lady From LA,' and the reflective 'I Missed The Last Rainbow', but Barry and Black distributed some fine, lively and pertinent numbers throughout the entire cast, including 'Happy To Be Themselves', 'It Were All Green Hills', 'Remembering', 'Any Minute Now', 'Is This Where I Wake Up?', 'Billy', 'The Witch', 'Aren't You Billy Fisher?', and 'Ambrosia'. *Billy* was the big hit London musical of 1974 and beyond, but audiences dwindled rapidly following Michael Crawford's departure. The multi-talented Roy Castle was in the leading role when the show closed after an impressive run of 904 performances. Plans for a major 1991 West End revival were aborted two weeks before it went into rehearsal, but, in the following year, the National Youth Theatre mounted a well-received production at the Edinburgh Festival Fringe, complete with two new songs. It starred the comedian, magician and television game show host, Andrew O'Connor, in the leading role.

BILLY ROSE'S DIAMOND HORSESHOE

There really was an establishment with this name in New York, owned and operated by the master-showman and songwriter himself, along with the New York Supper Club and two theatres. Much of the action in writer-director George Seaton's screenplay consisted of lavish, set-piece musical numbers, but he provided ample opportunity for the more intimate love scenes between two of 20th Century-Fox's brightest stars, Betty Grable and Dick Haymes. Grable plays one of the showgirls who prefers dollar signs to doctors, which is unfortunate for Haymes who is a typically impoverished medical student. Things improve after Haymes gives her the treatment via two lovely ballads by Harry Warren and Mack Gordon, 'The More I See You' and 'I Wish I Knew'. Warren and Gordon contributed several other numbers, including the rousing 'Welcome To The Diamond Horseshoe', 'Play Me An Old Fashioned Melody', 'A Nickel's Worth Of Jive', 'Cooking Up A Show' and 'In Acapulco'. William Gaxton, a trouper in the old tradition, played Haymes' father, and Phil Silvers was always funny, floating around backstage just as he did in *Cover Girl*. The rest of the cast, which included Margaret Dumont (always good comic value), Carmen Cavallero, and Beatrice Kay, were admirable, but it was the superb baritone voice of Haymes, in only his second leading role, that took the honours. The film was photographed in Technicolor and released in 1945.

BILLY ROSE'S JUMBO

Twenty-seven years after he starred on Broadway in master showman Billy Rose's mixture of circus and musical comedy, Jimmy Durante was present again in this 1962 screen version. Screenwriter Sidney Sheldon's somewhat liberal adaptation of the original stage libretto cast Durante as the owner of a circus with financial problems and ripe for a takeover. First in line as the potential new owner is Dean Jagger, the boss of a rival outfit. Jagger's son, played by Stephen Boyd, gains control of the crippled carnival by devious means, but is eventually won over by the decency of Durante and the delicious charms of his daughter, Doris Day. The film ends on an optimistic note with Durante and his wife (Martha Raye), Day and Boyd

looking to the future and singing 'Sawdust, Spangles And Dreams'(written by Roger Edens), but the rest of the songs - some from the original stage show - were the work of Richard Rodgers and Lorenz Hart. They included Durante's endearing and individual rendering of 'The Most Beautiful Girl In The World' and a tender version of 'This Can't Be Love' by Doris Day, along with several other memorable songs such as 'Little Girl Blue', 'Over And Over Again', 'My Romance', 'The Circus Is On Parade', and 'Why Can't I?'. Fine performances all round, especially from Durante and Raye, and Jumbo the elephant played a big part, too. William Daniels was responsible for the impressive photography in Metrocolor and Panavision, and the director was Charles Walters. The film was the last to be choreographed by the legendary Busby Berkeley.

BING BOYS ARE HERE, THE

This was the first in a series of tremendously popular revues that played continuously at the Alhambra Theatre in London during the last two years of World War I. They all had scores by Nat D. Ayer (music) and Clifford Grey (lyrics), and the book for this initial show was written by George Grossmith Jnr. and Fred Thompson, and had additional songs by Eustace Ponsonby, Philip Braham, and Ivor Novello. It opened on 19 April 1916, and starred the Prime Minister of Mirth, George Robey, and Violet Lorraine, who combined on the lovely ballad, 'If You Were The Only Girl In The World', which became one of the most cherished songs of the day. The score was chock-full of other popular items such as 'Another Little Drink Wouldn't Do Us Any Harm', 'I Stopped, I Looked And I Listened', 'The Kipling Walk', 'The Kiss Trot', 'I Started My Day Over Again', 'Underneath The Stars', 'The Right Side Of Bond Street', 'Ragging The Dog', 'The Languid Melody', and 'Dear Old Shepherd's Bush'. Also in the cast were Gillie Potter, Maidie Andrews, Phyllis Monkman, Alfred Lester, Odette Myrtil and Jack Morrison. *The Bing Boys Are Here* ran for 378 performances and was succeeded by *The Bing Boys Are There* which opened on 24 February 1917, again with a book by Grossmith Jnr. and Thompson, and additional songs by Eric Blore, Melville Gideon, Worton David, and Eustace Ponsonby. Robey was absent from this edition, but Lorraine was back, and she sang the rousing hit, 'Let The Great Big World Keep Turning', as well as others such as 'So He Followed Me', and 'That Dear Old Home Of Mine' and 'Do You Like Me?' (both with Joseph Coyne). The rest of the score included 'The Bond Street Dress Parade', 'I'll Be Nice To You', 'Oh Yes! I Remember', 'Yula Hicki Wicki Yacki Dula', 'When You're Dancing With Me', 'That's What I Call Love', 'Who Taught You All Those Things You Taught Me?', and 'I Bring My Own Girls Along'. Also in the cast were Lorna and Toots Pound, Laddie Cliff, and Wilkie Baird.

The exceptional success of both shows resulted in *The Bing Boys On Broadway*, which made its debut at the Alhambra on 16 February 1918. Robey returned for this final fling which ran for 562 performances, and was still going strong well after the Armistice was signed in November of that year. Violet Lorraine was there too, along with Lorna and Toots Pound, Clara Evelyn, Kitty

Fielder, Dan Agar, and Arthur Finn. This time the book was provided by Fred Thompson and Harry M. Bernon, and, once again, Ayer and Grey came up with another massive hit song, 'First Love, Last Love, Best Love', as well as several other amusing and singable numbers such as 'Hello, New York', 'Take Me Back To Bingville', 'Indian Rag', 'Crinoline Days', 'Something Oriental', 'College Days', 'Day After Day', 'Shurr-up!', and 'Southern Home'. By the time it closed, the soldiers were returning home, but *The Bing Boys* series had served its purpose, and, together with *Chu Chin Chow*, *The Maid Of The Mountains*, and *'The Better 'Ole'*, had provided invaluable entertainment through those dark years.

BIRD

In defence of any biopic about a seminal figure in the arts, it has to be said that depicting on film the creative process and the manner in which an individual can inspire a generation is nearly impossible - so it proves in this account of the life of Charlie Parker. This 1988 film also misses Parker's articulateness and his sharp and ready wit. For all these shortcomings, however, *Bird* is an honestly conceived and well-made attempt at portraying this erratic genius of jazz. Drawing heavily upon Chan Parker's account of her common-law husband's life, rather than upon reminiscences of his musical peers, the film frequently but perhaps misleadingly stresses the turbulent life of one of the half-dozen greatest figures in jazz history, while allowing his importance to jazz slip by as if it were almost incidental to his private life. Nevertheless, director Client Eastwood's admiration and affection for his subject makes up for most of the film's historical uncertainty, and is infinitely superior to the rag-tag 50s biopics of swing era favourites such as Benny Goodman, Gene Krupa and Glenn Miller. Clearly, Eastwood worked on the project for love not money, and with a solid, if uncharismatic, central performance from Forest Whitaker, *Bird* surprisingly proved to have box-office appeal that far transcended the hardcore jazz audience. The soundtrack is a brilliant display of latter-day technology, allied to astute and perceptive musical understanding. Overseen by Lennie Niehaus, Parker's solos from some of his original recordings were detached from their sometimes scrappy surroundings, and provided with newly recorded accompaniment by leading latter-day bop musicians. The end result is musical excellence, even if, predictably perhaps, the film and its re-jigged music was received in some quarters with a marked lack of enthusiasm. Among the musicians appearing on the soundtrack are Monty Alexander, Chuck Berghofer, Ray Brown, Conte Candoli, Ron Carter, Pete Christlieb, Bob Cooper, Walter Davis Jnr., Jon Faddis, John Guerin, Barry Harris, Pete Jolly, Bill Watrous and Red Rodney (portrayed in the film by Michael Zelniker and Charles McPherson, who provided all of the non-original Parker performances).

BIRD ON A WIRE

Taking its title from one of Leonard Cohen's most resonant compositions, *Bird On A Wire* is a *cinéma vérité* documentary, hinged to the singer's 1972 European tour. This was not the first time he had been the subject of a film.

Ladies And Gentlemen: Mr. Leonard Cohen was shot by the National Film Board Of Canada in celebration of the artist's work as a novelist and poet. Since that time he had become internationally known as a composer of melancholic songs, including 'Suzanne', 'Hey That's No Way To Say Goodbye', 'Sisters Of Mercy' and 'So Long Marianne'. Each are featured in this film, alongside masterful newer compositions such as 'Famous Blue Raincoat' and 'Chelsea Hotel', the latter of which is a moving paean to Janis Joplin. Co-director Tony Palmer, previously responsible for *All My Loving*, *Cream's Last Concert* and *Rope Ladder To The Moon*, combined concert footage with scenes backstage and on location, notably at the Eiffel Tower and on the banks of Dutch canals. Although suffering by comparison with D.A. Pennebaker's Bob Dylan film, *Don't Look Back*, *Bird On A Wire* provides a fascinating view of a gifted artist at work.

BIRTH OF THE BEATLES

This entertaining but factually flawed document of the Beatles' early years was originally made for US television in 1979 by Dick Clark's production company. With Stephen McKenna as John Lennon, Rod Culbertson as Paul McCartney, John Altman as George Harrison, Ryan Michael as Pete Best, David Wilkinson as Stuart Sutcliffe and Ray Ashcroft as Ringo Starr, the story of the Beatles' formative period includes scenes drawn from Liverpool's Cavern Club, Hamburg's Reeperbahn and eventually London. Pete Best himself served as technical advisor, but many Beatles fans reacted angrily to the film's liberal treatment of the group's chronology. Among several scenes to raise their ire was the 'competition' between the Beatles and Rory Storm to see who could 'stomp' their way through the stage floor at the Star Club - in the film the Beatles triumph, winning a bottle of champagne, yet historians state categorically that Rory Storm's band were the victors. Despite such problems, the characterizations of the Beatles were largely impressive, with Brian Jameson's portrayal of Brian Epstein particularly memorable. Directed by Richard Marquand and produced by Tony Bishop, the screenplay was written by John Kurland and Jacob E. Shendar, from a story by John Hurland. The soundtrack music (other than the Beatles) was composed by Carl Davis.

BIRTH OF THE BLUES

Released by Paramount in 1941, this film is remembered mainly for one song, Johnny Mercer's 'The Waiter And The Porter And The Upstairs Maid', which was performed in exuberant fashion by Bing Crosby, Jack Teagarden and Mary Martin. Harry Tugend and Walter DeLeon's screenplay was set in New Orleans at a time when the 'devil' jazz music was threatening the cosy world of opulent operettas. Throughout his life, Crosby was associated with jazz and many of its exalted exponents, including Louis Armstrong, with whom he collaborated so memorably in *High Society*. In *Birth Of The Blues*, as well as crooning, Crosby is the clarinet-playing leader of the Hot Shots, a swinging group supposedly based on the Original Dixieland Jazz Band. Brian Donlevy, an actor who later made a career out of playing the tough guy with a heart of gold, was the hot trumpeter for the Hot Shots, and Mary Martin obliged with the cool vocals. The rest of the numbers included 'Wait 'Til The Sun Shines, Nellie' (Harry Von Tilzer, Andrew Stirling), 'My Melancholy Baby' (George A. Norton, Ernie Burnett), 'Cuddle Up A Little Closer' (Karl Hoschna, Otto Harbach), 'By The Light Of The Silvery Moon' (Gus Edwards, Edward Madden), 'The Birth Of The Blues' (De Sylva, Brown And Henderson), 'St. Louis Blues' (W.C. Handy), and several other jazzy oldies. Jack Benny's long-time comic companion, Eddie 'Rochester' Anderson, was also in the cast, and the film was directed by Victor Schertzinger.

BITTER SWEET

After delighting West End audiences with his smart and witty revues, Noël Coward wrote the book, music, and lyrics for this opérette which opened in London at His Majesty's Theatre on 2 July 1929, transferring to the Palace Theatre on 2 March 1931. Following its closure there after a West End run of 697 performances, the show played a further month at the Lyceum Theatre. Set in Vienna in the late nineteenth century, the story is told in flashback, as Sarah Millick (Peggy Wood), looks back over her life. As a teenager she left her fiancé to marry piano teacher Carl Linden (George Metaxa). After changing her name to Sari, they work together - she as a singer - in a Viennese café, One night Sari is assaulted by an army officer, Lieutenant Lutte (Austin Trevor), and Carl is killed when going to her aid. Sari moves on to become a famous prima donna, and after marrying one of her many admirers (Alan Napier) becomes the Marchioness of Shayne. Although contented, she still remains emotionally attached to her first real love, Carl. Their special song was 'I'll See You Again', just one of the richly sentimental numbers in this exceptional score full of incandescent melodies, which also included 'If Love Were All', 'Zigeuner', 'If You Could Only Come With Me', 'Ladies Of The Town', 'Tokay', 'Dear Little Café', 'The Call Of Life', and 'Green Carnation'. Also in the cast were Ivy St. Helier, Billy Milton, Robert Newton, Norah Howard, Alan Napier, and Gerald Nodin. The sumptuous settings and costumes were by G.E. Calthrop and Tilly Losch was the choreographer. Directed by Coward, and presented by master showman Charles B. Cochran, *Bitter Sweet* was a triumph, and transferred to the Ziegfeld Theatre in New York on 5 November 1929. It starred Evelyn Laye and Gerald Nodin (moving up from his London role of Captain Schenzi), and ran for 159 performances. Evelyn Laye subsequently played in the West End production. Since that time, revivals have been rare, and the 1988 production at Sadlers Wells with Valerie Masterson and Martin Smith was said to be the first on the London stage for nearly 60 years. Two 'unsatisfactory' film versions were made, in 1933 with Anna Neagle and Fernand Gravet, and 1940 with Jeanette MacDonald and Nelson Eddy.

BIX 'AIN'T NONE OF THEM PLAY LIKE THAT'

An exceptionally well-researched and presented documentary released in 1981. Canadian film-maker Brigitte Berman traces the life of the legendary Bix Beiderbecke through some film, many stills and numerous interviews, all backed by a sublime soundtrack. The subject's catastrophic decline through alcohol and his habitual disregard of things like sleep and food in favour of playing and drinking, is sympathetically but unglamorously explored. A deeply moving moment emerges with the revelation that on a visit to his disapproving parents' house, Beiderbecke found in a closet all his records, which he had proudly sent home, still enclosed in their wrappings. The standards of jazz documentaries were raised by this film and it is wholeheartedly recommended for its immediacy and understanding.

BLACK AND TAN

Directed by Dudley Murphy in 1929, who, in the same year, made *St. Louis Blues* with Bessie Smith, this early talkie short remains one of the few films to use jazz as its *raison d'être*. A slight but melodramatic storyline has showgirl Fredi Washington literally dancing her life away to ensure her musical colleagues get the big break they have been waiting for. The musicians involved are Duke Ellington And His Orchestra (their screen debut) including Barney Bigard, Harry Carney, Johnny Hodges, Joe Nanton, Artie Whetsol and Cootie Williams. Among the musical numbers are 'The Duke Steps Out', 'Black Beauty' and, of course, an eloquent version of 'Black And Tan Fantasy'.

BLACK JOY

This low-budget but engaging 1977 film told the cautionary tale of Guyanan immigrant Ben Jones. He encounters numerous disappointments and setbacks before coming to terms with his new life in London. Among the cast were Norman Beaton, Trevor Thomas, Floella Benjamin and, somewhat improbably, Viv Stanshall. Director Anthony Simmons provides an entertaining view of black life in Brixton, and the atmosphere of the film is heightened by an excellent soundtrack. It featured material by stellar soul acts Billy Paul, Harold Melvin And The Blue Notes, the Drifters, Aretha Franklin and Gladys Knight, as well as reggae acts Toots And The Maytals, the Cimmerons, the Heptones and Junior Murvin. Black UK performers Linda Lewis, the Real Thing and Jimmy Helms are also featured; the last-named provides the title song to an articulate, entertaining film.

BLACK, DON

b. 21 June 1938, Hackney, London, England. A prolific lyricist for film songs, stage musicals and Tin Pan Alley. One of five children, Black worked part-time as an usher at the London Palladium before finding a job as an office boy and sometime journalist with the *New Musical Express* in the early 50s. After a brief sojourn as a stand-up comic in the dying days of the music halls, he gravitated towards London's Denmark Street, the centre of UK music publishing, where he worked as a song plugger for firms owned by Dave Toff and Joe 'Mr. Piano' Henderson. He met Matt Monro in 1960, shortly before the singer made his breakthrough with Cyril Ornadel and Norman Newell's 'Portrait Of My Love'. Encouraged by Monro, Black began to develop his talent for lyric writing. Together with another popular vocalist, Al Saxon, Black wrote 'April Fool', which Monro included on his *Love Is The Same Anywhere.* In 1964 Black collaborated with the German composer, Udo Jurgens, and together they turned Jurgens' Eurovision Song Contest entry, 'Warum Nur Warum', into 'Walk Away', which became a UK Top 5 hit for Monro. The singer also charted with 'For Mama', which Black wrote with Charles Aznavour. The song was also popular for Connie Francis and Jerry Vale in the USA. In 1965 Black made his break into films with the lyric of the title song for *Thunderball*, the fourth James Bond movie. The song was popularized by Tom Jones, and it marked the beginning of a fruitful collaboration with composer John Barry. As well as providing Bond with two more themes, 'Diamonds Are Forever' (1971, Shirley Bassey, and for which they received an Ivor Novello Award) and 'The Man With The Golden Gun' (1974, Lulu), the songwriters received a second 'Ivor' and an Academy Award for their title song to *Born Free* in 1966. Black has been nominated on four other occasions: for 'True Grit' (with Elmer Bernstein, 1969), 'Ben' (Walter Scharf, a US number 1 for Michael Jackson in 1972, and a UK hit for Marti Webb in 1985), 'Wherever Love Takes Me', from *Gold* (Bernstein, 1972), and 'Come To Me', from *The Pink Panther Strikes Again* (Henry Mancini, 1976). It has been estimated that Black's lyrics have been heard in well over 100 movies, including *To Sir With Love* (title song, with Mark London, 1972, a US number 1 for Lulu), *Pretty Polly* (title song, Michel Legrand, 1967), *I'll Never Forget What's 'Is Name* ('One Day Soon', Francis Lai, 1968), *The Italian Job* ('On Days Like These', Quincy Jones, 1969), *Satan's Harvest* ('Two People', Denis King, 1969), *Hoffman* ('If There Ever Is A Next Time', Ron Grainer, 1970), *Mary Queen Of Scots* ('Wish Was Then', John Barry, 1971), *Alice's Adventures In Wonderland* (several songs with Barry, 1972), *The Tamarind Seed* ('Play It Again', Barry, 1974), *The Dove* ('Sail The Summer Winds', Barry, 1974), and *The Wilby Conspiracy* ('All The Wishing In The World', Stanley Myers, 1975). In 1970, Matt Monro invited Don Black to become his manager, and he remained in that role until the singer died in 1985. Black considered Monro to be one of the finest interpreters of his lyrics, particularly with regard to 'If I Never Sing Another Song', which Black wrote with Udo Jurgens in 1977. It was featured on *Matt Monro Sings Don Black* which was released in 1990. The song became a favourite closing number for many artists, including Johnnie Ray and Eddie Fisher. In 1971, Black augmented his already heavy workload by becoming involved with stage musicals. His first score, written with composer Walter Scharf, was for *Maybe That's Your Problem*, which had a limited run (18 performances) at London's Roundhouse Theatre. The subject of the show was premature ejaculation (Black says that his friend, Alan Jay Lerner, suggested that it should be called *Shortcomings*, but the critics regarded it as 'a dismal piece'). However, one of the performers was Elaine Paige, just seven years before her triumph in *Evita*. Paige was also in *Billy*, London's hit musical of 1974. Adapted from the play *Billy Liar*, which was set in the north of England, Black and John Barry's score captured the 'feel' and the dialect of the original. The songs included 'Some Of Us

Belong To The Stars', 'I Missed The Last Rainbow', 'Any Minute Now', and 'It Were All Green Fields When I Were A Lad', which was subsequently recorded by Stanley Holloway. *Billy* ran for over 900 performances and made a star of Michael Crawford in his musical comedy debut. Black's collaborator on the score for his next show, *Bar Mitzvah Boy* (1978), was Jule Styne, the legendary composer of shows such as *Funny Girl* and *Gypsy*, among others. Although *Bar Mitzvah Boy* had a disappointingly short run, it did impress Andrew Lloyd Webber, who engaged Black to write the lyrics for his song cycle, *Tell Me On Sunday*, a television programme and album that featured Marti Webb. Considered too short for theatrical presentation, on the recommendation of Cameron Mackintosh it was combined with Lloyd Webber's *Variations* to form *Song And Dance*, a two-part 'theatrical concert', and featured songs such as 'Take That Look Off Your Face', which gave Marti Webb a UK Top 5 hit and gained Black another Ivor Novello Award, 'Nothing Like You've Ever Known', 'Capped Teeth And Caesar Salad', and 'Tell Me On Sunday'. The show ran in the West End for 781 performances before being remodelled and expanded for Broadway, where it starred Bernadette Peters, who received a Tony Award for her performance. Black teamed with Benny Andersson and Bjorn Ulvaeus, two former members of Abba, for the aptly titled *Abbacadabra*, a Christmas show that played to packed houses in 1983. Earlier that year, he had written the score for *Dear Anyone* with Geoff Stephens, a successful composer of pop hits such as 'Winchester Cathedral', 'You Won't Find Another Fool Like Me' and 'There's A Kind Of Hush'. The show first surfaced as a concept album in 1978, and one of its numbers, 'I'll Put You Together Again', became a Top 20 hit for the group Hot Chocolate. The 1983 stage presentation did not last long, and neither did *Budgie* (1988). Against a background of 'the sleazy subculture of London's Soho', this show starred Adam Faith and Anita Dobson. Black's lyrics combined with Mort Shuman's music for songs such as 'Why Not Me?', 'There Is Love And There Is Love', 'In One Of My Weaker Moments', and 'They're Naked And They Move', but to no avail - Black, as co-producer, presided over a '£1 million flop'. Two years earlier, Anita Dobson had achieved a UK hit with 'Anyone Can Fall In Love', when Black added a lyric to Simon May and Leslie Osborn's theme for BBC Television's *EastEnders*, one of Britain's top television soap operas. He collaborated with the composers again for 'Always There', a vocal version of their theme for *Howard's Way*, which gave Marti Webb a UK hit. In 1989, Black resumed his partnership with Andrew Lloyd Webber for *Aspects Of Love*. Together with *Phantom Of The Opera* lyricist Charles Hart, they fashioned a musical treatment of David Garnett's 1955 novel that turned out to be more intimate than some of Lloyd Webber's other works, but still retained the operatic form. The show starred Michael Ball and Ann Crumb; Ball took the big ballad, 'Love Changes Everything', to number 2 in the UK, and the score also featured the 'subtle, aching melancholy' of 'The First Man You Remember'. *Aspects of Love* was not considered a hit by Lloyd Webber's standards - it ran for three years in the West End, and for one year on Broadway - but the London Cast recording topped the

UK album chart. In the 90s Black's activities remain numerous and diverse. In 1992, together with Chris Walker, he provided extra lyrics for the London stage production of *Radio Times*; wrote additional songs for a revival of *Billy* by the National Youth Music Theatre at the Edinburgh Festival; renewed his partnership with Geoff Stephens for a concept album of a 'revuesical' entitled *Off The Wall*, the story of 'six characters determined to end it all by throwing themselves off a ledge on the 34th storey of a London highrise building'; collaborated with Lloyd Webber on the Barcelona Olympics anthem, 'Friends For Life' ('Amigos Para Siempre'), which was recorded by Sarah Brightman and Jose Carreras; and worked with David Dundas on 'Keep Your Dreams Alive', for the animated feature, *Freddie As F.R.O.7*. He spent a good deal of the year co-writing the book and lyrics, with Christopher Hampton, for Lloyd Webber's musical treatment of the Hollywood classic, *Sunset Boulevard*. The show, which opened in London and on Broadway in 1993, brought Black two Tony Awards. He adapted one of the hit songs, 'As If We Never Said Goodbye', for Barbra Streisand to sing in her first concert tour for 27 years. Black has held the positions of chairman and vice-president of the British Academy of Songwriters, Composers and Authors, and has, for the past few years, been the genial chairman of the voting panel for the Vivian Ellis Prize, a national competition to encourage new writers for the musical stage. In 1993, 22 of his own songs were celebrated on *The Don Black Songbook*, and in the following year Black branched out into broadcasting, interviewing Elmer Bernstein, and presenting the six-part *How To Make A Musical* on BBC Radio 2. In 1995 he was presented with the Jimmy Kennedy Award at the 40th anniversary Ivor Novello Awards ceremony. In 1996 he received a Lifetime Achievement Award from BMI, and in the following year provided the lyric for 'You Stayed Away Too Long', a song that made the last four of the British heats of the Eurovision Song Contest, but failed to progress further. Another disappointment in 1997 came when the London production of the flop Broadway musical, *The Goodbye Girl*, for which Black wrote seven new songs with composer Marvin Hamlisch, departed after a brief run.

BLACK, STANLEY

b. 14 June 1913, London, England. At the age of seven he began learning the piano and later studied at the Mathay School of Music. His first composition, when he was aged 12, was broadcast by the BBC Symphony Orchestra. In 1929 he won an arranging contest sponsored by the then jazz weekly, *Melody Maker*, and became known as a promising jazz pianist, recording with visiting Americans Coleman Hawkins, Louis Armstrong and Benny Carter, plus the British bands of Lew Stone and Harry Roy. In 1938, he went to South America with Roy's orchestra, and became fascinated with Latin-American music, a subject on which he became an expert. He started recording for Decca in 1944, and in the same year became conductor of the BBC Dance Orchestra, a position that lasted until 1952. Black took part in many vintage radio shows including *Hi Gang* and *Much Binding In The Marsh*. He also composed signature tunes for several radio programmes, including

the legendary *Goon Show*. He also broadcast with ensembles ranging from full symphony orchestras and the BBC Dance Orchestra to a quartet or sextet in his own programmes, such as *Black Magic* and *The Musical World Of Stanley Black*. Black has worked on over a hundred films either as score composer or musical director, and in many cases as both. His credits include *It Always Rains On Sunday* (1948), *The Long And The Short And The Tall* (1961), the Cliff Richard musicals *The Young Ones* (1961) and *Summer Holiday* (1962), and all of the late Mario Zampi's screwball comedies, such as *Laughter In Paradise* (1951), *The Naked Truth* (1957) and *Too Many Crooks* (1958). His albums have sold in huge quantities, not only in the UK, but also in the USA, New Zealand and Japan. In 1994 he joined Stéphane Grappelli in a Charity Gala Performance at the Barbican Hall in London. His many honours include an OBE and Life Fellowship of the International Institute of Arts and Letters. In 1995 he was made life president of the Celebrities Guild of Great Britain.

● ALBUMS: *Exotic Percussion* (Phase 4 1962)★★★, *Spain* (Phase 4 1962)★★★★, *Film Spectacular* (Phase 4 1963)★★★★, *Film Spectacular, Volume Two* (Phase 4 1963)★★★★, *'Bolero'/Polovtsian Dances* (Phase 4 1964)★★, *Grand Canyon Suite* (Phase 4 1964)★★★, *Music Of A People* (Phase 4 1965)★★★, *Russia* (Phase 4 1966)★★★, *Capriccio* (Phase 4 1965)★★★, *Film Spectacular, Volume Three* (Phase 4 1966)★★★★, *Broadway Spectacular* (Phase 4 1966)★★★, *Gershwin Concert* (Phase 4 1966)★★★, *Blockbusters From Broadway* (Phase 4 1967)★★★★, *Tchaikovsky Concert* (Phase 4 1967)★★, *Sputniks For Orchestra* (Phase 4 1967)★★★, *Spectacular Dances For Orchestra* (Phase 4 1967)★★★, *France* (Phase 4 1967)★★★, *Dimensions In Sound* (Phase 4 1968)★★★★, *Overture* (Phase 4 1968)★★★, *Cuban Moonlight* (Eclipse 1969)★★★, *Great Rhapsodies For Orchestra* (Phase 4 1970)★★★, *Plays For Latin Lovers* (Eclipse 1970)★★★, with the London Symphony Orchestra *Grieg Concert* (Phase 4 1971)★★, *Tribute To Charlie Chaplin* (Phase 4 1972)★★★, *Tropical Moonlight* (Eclipse 1972)★★★, *Film Spectacular, Volume Four - The Epic* (Phase 4 1973)★★★, *Cuban Moonlight, Volume Two* (Eclipse 1973)★★★, with the London Festival Orchestra *Spirit Of A People* (Phase 4 1974)★★★, *Film Spectacular, Volume Five - The Love Story* (Phase 4 1975)★★★★, *Twelve Top Tangos* (Eclipse 1976)★★, *Black Magic* (Phase 4 1976)★★★, *Film Spectacular, Volume Six - Great Stories From World War II* (Phase 4 1976)★★★, *Sounds Wide Screen* (Phase 4 1977)★★★, *Satan Superstar* (Phase 4 1978)★★★, *Digital Magic* (Decca 1979)★★★, *Great Love Stories* (Decca 1988)★★★, *ITV Themes* (Hallmark 1988)★★★, *S'Wonderful* (President 1990)★★★, *Nice 'N' Easy* (Decca 1992)★★★.

● COMPILATIONS: *Film World Of Stanley Black* (Decca 1970)★★★★, *Latin World Of Stanley Black* (Decca 1973)★★★, *Focus On Stanley Black* (Decca 1978)★★★★.

BLACKBIRDS OF 1928

The first and most successful of Lew Leslie's all-black revues opened at New York's Liberty Theatre on 9 May 1928. Leslie had mounted something similar in London two years earlier, called simply *Blackbirds*, which by all accounts caused quite a stir in that conventional clime. It starred Florence Mills (who had come to prominence in *Shuffle Along* (1922)), Johnny Hudgins and Lloyd Mitchell. The score for the 1926 *Blackbirds* was written by George

W. Meyer, and included 'Silver Rose', 'Do The Black Bottom With Me' and 'On The Beach At Wika Kiki Blues'. Meyer also provided the songs for Leslie's 'racial reversal', *White Birds*, which starred Maurice Chevalier, and opened in London's West End in May 1927. *Blackbirds Of 1928* was a much grander affair, with an impressive cast that included Adelaide Hall, Aida Ward, Bill 'Bojangles' Robinson, and the 20-year-old Elisabeth Welch. It marked the Broadway debut of songwriters Jimmy McHugh and Dorothy Fields, and introduced one of their biggest all-time hits, 'I Can't Give You Anything But Love', along with several other delightful numbers such as 'Dig-Diga-Doo', 'I Must Have That Man', 'Porgy', 'Doin' The New Low Down', 'Baby!', 'Bandanna Babies', 'Magnolia's Wedding Day' and 'Shuffle Your Feet And Just Roll Along'. Subsequent editions of *Blackbirds* on Broadway all contained some good things, but none of them recaptured the magic of 1928: the 1930 show starred Ethel Waters, Buck & Bubbles, Flournoy Miller, and the Berry Brothers, and featured Minto Cato singing Andy Razaf and Eubie Blakes' lovely ballad, 'Memories Of You'; Bill Robinson returned in the 1934 version in which Kathryn Perry introduced 'A Hundred Years From Today', a song that became a hit for Ethel Waters, and is usually associated with the trombonist and vocalist Jack Teagarden; and *Blackbirds Of 1939*, even with Lena Horne, and songs by such luminaries as George Gershwin, Johnny Mercer, Sammy Fain, Mitchell Parish, Rube Bloom, and others, still did not make it into a second week. Lew Leslie's London edition of *Blackbirds Of 1934* included the haunting 'Moonglow' by Eddie de Lange, Irving Mills, and Will Hudson, and the 1936 version of what are generally regarded now as the premier all-Negro revues, had songs by Mercer and Bloom, and gave West End audiences the opportunity to enjoy the acrobatic dancing of the Nicholas Brothers, who went on to star in many Hollywood musicals of the 40s.

BLAINE, VIVIAN

b. Vivian Stapleton, 21 November 1921, Newark, New Jersey, USA, d. 9 December 1995, New York, USA. A vivacious actress and singer, Vivian Blaine created one of the American musical theatre's best-loved characters, Miss Adelaide, in Frank Loesser's *Guys And Dolls*. She appeared on stage at her local theatre, and later attended the American Academy of Dramatic Art, before touring with various dance bands. From 1942-46, she was under contract to 20th Century-Fox, and played leading roles in musical films such as *Greenwich Village Follies*, *Something For The Boys*, *Nob Hill*, *State Fair* (in which she introduced 'That's For Me' and, with Dick Haymes, 'Isn't It Kinda Fun?'), and *Three Little Girls In Blue* ('Somewhere In The Night'). Blaine also toured in various musicals and in vaudeville before making her Broadway debut in *Guys And Dolls* in 1950. She gave a delightful performance as the dancer who has been waiting for 14 years in the hope that her fiancé, Nathan Detroit, will finally abandon his floating crap game and marry her. Her frustration boiled over in 'Sue Me', and she was splendid in the ensemble numbers 'Take Back Your Mink' and 'A Bushel And A Peck' with the girls at the 'Hot Box' nightclub. However, her stand-out song was 'Adelaide's Lament', in which she

shared the knowledge - just gleaned from a book, of all things - that there seems to be a direct relationship between long engagements and ill-health: 'In other words just from waiting around for that plain little band of gold/A person - can develop a cold'. In 1953 she repeated her success at the London Coliseum, and was back on Broadway five years later with *Say, Darling*, in which she co-starred with Robert Morse, David Wayne and Johnny Desmond. She subsequently appeared in a number of plays such as *A Hatful Of Rain* and *Enter Laughing*, and toured extensively in musical revivals, including *Zorba*, *Follies*, *Hello, Dolly!*, *Gypsy*, and *I Do! I Do!*. She succeeded Jane Russell (who had taken over from Elaine Stritch) in the role of Joanne in the Broadway production of *Company*, and also performed in cabaret. After that, her work consisted of mainly straight roles in plays, movies, and on US television, where she appeared in the ongoing soap-opera parody, *Mary Hartman, Mary Hartman*. She was married three times - one of her husbands was Milton Rackmil, president of Decca Records and Universal Pictures.

● FILMS: *Thru Different Eyes* (1942), *Girl Trouble* (1942), *It Happened In Flatbush* (1942), *He Hired The Boss* (1943), *Jitterbugs* (1943), *Greenwich Village* (1943), *Something For The Boys* (1944), *Nob Hill* (1945), *State Fair* (1945), *Doll Face* (1945), *If I'm Lucky* (1946), *Three Little Girls In Blue* (1946), *Skirts Ahoy* (1952), *Guys And Dolls* (1955), *Mainstream To Broadway* cameo (1955), *Public Pigeon No. 1* (1957), *Richard* cameo (1972), *The Dark* (1979), *Sooner Or Later* television (1979), *Fast Friends* television (1979), *The Cracker Factory* television (1979), *I'm Going To Be Famous* (1981), *Parasite* (1982).

BLAIR, JANET

b. Martha Janet Lafferty, 23 April 1921, Altoona, Pennsylvania, USA. A band singer who went on to become a popular film actress, Blair replaced Nan Wynn in the famous Hal Kemp Band in 1940, and remained until Kemp died in an automobile accident in December of that year. After singing on the Kemp record hits 'So You're The One' and 'Walkin' By The River', and other sides such as 'Meet The Sun Half-Way', 'I Can't Love You Any More', 'The Girl Who Took A Second Look' and 'Talkin' To My Heart', in 1941 she made her film debut in the amusing 'B' picture, *Three Girls About Town*, and subsequently appeared in the screen musicals *Broadway*, *Something To Shout About*, *Tonight And Every Night*, *Tars And Spars*, *The Fabulous Dorseys*, and *The One And Only Genuine Original Family Band*. In 1950 she headed the US touring company of Richard Rodgers and Oscar Hammerstein II's *South Pacific*, staying with the show for approximately three years of its almost five-year run. Later, she sang in nightclubs, and during the late 50s and 60s appeared frequently on US television, featuring prominently in *The Smith Family* series in the early 70s.

● FILMS: *Three Girls About Town* (1941), *Blondie Goes To College* (1941), *Two Yanks In Trinidad* (1942), *Broadway* (1942), *My Sister Eileen* (1942), *Something To Shout About* (1943), *Once Upon A Time* (1944), *Tonight And Every Night* (1945), *Tars And Spars* (1946), *Gallant Journey* (1946), *The Fabulous Dorseys* (1947), *I Love Trouble* (1948), *Black Arrow* (1948), *The Fuller Brush Man* (1948), *Public Pigeon No. 1* (1957), *Island Of Lost Women* (1959), *The Rabbit*

Trap (1959), *The Best Of Everything* (1959), *The Lone Texan* (1959), *Night Of The Eagle* (1962), *Boys' Night Out* (1962), *Burn, Witch, Burn* (1962), *The One And Only Genuine Original Family Band* (1968), *Won Ton Ton, The Dog Who Saved Hollywood* cameo (1976).

BLAKE, EUBIE

b. James Hubert Blake, 7 February 1883, Baltimore, Maryland, USA, d. 12 February 1983, New York, USA. Eubie Blake grew up to the sounds of ragtime music, and before the turn of the century was playing piano in sporting houses and other similar establishments. He was a composer too, and in 1915 joined forces with Noble Sissle; they played in vaudeville as a double act and wrote together extensively. In 1921 Sissle and Blake wrote the score for a Broadway show - a remarkable accomplishment for blacks at that time. *Shuffle Along*, which starred Flournoy Miller, Aubrey Lyles, Gertrude Saunders, and Sissle himself (with Blake on the piano), included several admirable songs, including 'Bandana Days', 'Gypsy Blues', 'Love Will Find A Way', 'Everything Reminds Me Of You', 'Shuffle Along' and 'If You've Never Been Vamped By A Brown Skin (You've Never Been Vamped At All)'. There was also one enormous hit, 'I'm Just Wild About Harry', which became popular at the time for artists such as Marion Harris, Ray Miller, and Paul Whiteman, among others, and gave a boost to Harry S. Truman's election campaign in 1948. Blake contributed to other Broadway musicals and revues such as *Elsie*, *Andre Charlot's Revue Of 1924*, and Lew Leslie's *Blackbirds Of 1930*. For the latter, he and Andy Razaf wrote 'Baby Mine', 'That Lindy Hop', 'My Handy Man Ain't Handy No More', and another substantial hit, the lovely reflective ballad 'Memories Of You'. After one more Broadway musical, *Swing It* (1937), Blake reunited with Sissle for a time, and then spent much of World War II entertaining troops with the USO.

In the 50s Blake demonstrated and lectured on ragtime but his day seemed to be past. Then, in 1969, at the age of 86, Blake's fortunes were revived when John Hammond recorded the old man playing piano and talking about his life. The concurrent vogue for ragtime helped his comeback and the next years were filled with honours, recordings, concerts, festivals and television appearances; in 1978, his life and music were celebrated in a Broadway show, *Eubie*, which was also televised in the USA and later staged in London. In 1983 Blake contributed to the lists of favourite quotations when, on the occasion of his 100th birthday, he said: 'If I'd known I was going to live this long, I would've taken better care of myself.' He died five days later.

● ALBUMS: *The Wizard Of Ragtime* (1959)★★★, *The Eighty-six Years Of Eubie Blake* (Columbia 1969)★★★★, *At The Piano* (1974)★★★, *Eubie Blake In Concert* (Stash 1987)★★★.

● COMPILATIONS: *Eubie Blake, Blues And Rags: His Earliest Piano Rolls* 1917-21 recordings ★★★★.

● FURTHER READING: *Reminiscing With Sissle And Blake*, Robert Kimball and William Bolcom.

BLANE, RALPH

b. Ralph Blaine Hunsecker, 26 July 1914, Broken Arrow, Oklahoma, USA, d. 13 November 1995. The son of a local clothing store proprietor, Blane was educated in Broken Arrow and Tulsa, which had not yet expanded to swallow up the small town. Later, he attended Northwestern University and then pursued his interest in a musical career by studying in New York. He found work as a singer on Broadway, appearing in 1937 in *Hooray For What!*, where he met another young singer, Hugh Martin; together they formed a vocal quartet, the Martins. Blane appeared in other Broadway shows and also began developing his composing abilities, usually in collaboration with Martin. The shows included *Too Many Girls*, *Louisiana Purchase*, *DuBarry Was A Lady*, *Cabin In The Sky*, *Very Warm For May*, *Stars In Your Eyes*, *Pal Joey*, and *Best Foot Forward*, which included the very underrated song, 'Ev'ry Time'. During the early 40s, Blane and Martin moved to Hollywood where they were contracted to MGM. Their film work included occasional songs in *Broadway Rhythm*, *Thousands Cheer* (both 1943), and *Ziegfeld Follies* (1944), for which he and Martin wrote 'Love', sung by Lena Horne, for whom it became an important part of her repertoire. That same year Blane and Martin had their first major venture, the enduringly popular Judy Garland film, *Meet Me In St. Louis*, for which they wrote 'The Trolley Song', which was nominated for an Oscar, 'The Boy Next Door' and 'Have Yourself A Merry Little Christmas'. Blane's music and lyric writing activities were by no means confined to his collaborations with Martin. He also wrote with Harold Arlen, Harry Warren, and many others, and his other film credits include *The Thrill Of A Romance* (1945), *No Leave, No Love, Easy To Wed* (both 1946) and *Summer Holiday* (1946, released 1948), on which his collaborator was Warren. Blane and Warren also wrote the songs for Doris Day's second starring role, *My Dream Is Yours* (1949). Other films of the late 40s and early 50s on which Blane worked included *My Blue Heaven*, *Skirts Ahoy*, *The French Line*, and three films on which he was reunited with Martin, *Athena*, *The Girl Rush*, for which the duo wrote 'An Occasional Man' and 'The Girl Most Likely'. In 1952 he wrote music and lyrics for the Broadway musical *Three Wishes For Jamie*. In 1963, Blane and Martin worked on a revival of *Best Foot Forward*, which had an early starring role for Liza Minnelli, adding a new song, 'You Are For Loving', regarded by Alec Wilder as one of the best ballads ever written for the musical theatre. In 1989 Martin and Blane wrote 10 new songs for a stage version of *Meet Me In St. Louis*, which ran for seven months on Broadway. Blane's voice remained true into his later years and he and Martin recorded a delightful album of their songs. He spent his retirement years in his home town.

● ALBUMS: *Martin And Blane Sing Martin And Blane* 1956 recording (DRG 1994)★★★.

BLANK GENERATION, THE

Co-directed in 1976 by Amos Poe and Ivan Kral, *The Blank Generation* chronicles the emergent punk scene in New York, USA. This pivotal film is comprised of live, black-and-white footage, shot at seminal clubs CBGB's and Max's Kansas City. The use of hand-held cameras complements the *de rigeur* do-it-yourself ethos, although its relevance as a musical documentary is marginally undermined by the fact that the footage is deliberately out of synchronization with the soundtrack. This robs the viewer of seeing such groundbreaking acts as Television, the Patti Smith Group (of which Kral was a member), Talking Heads, the Ramones and Heartbreakers in their formative glory. As an art statement, *The Blank Generation* is a triumph, breaking the rules of what a pop film should be and showing solidarity with the confrontational aims of the music on offer.

BLESS THE BRIDE

An enormously successful and fondly remembered musical, this is the show that immediately comes to mind when the work of the British composer Vivian Ellis is discussed. *Bless The Bride* opened at London's Adelphi Theatre on 26 April 1947, and was still there over two years later. It proved to be the highlight of Ellis' occasional collaborations with the author A.P. Herbert, and the celebrated producer Charles B. Cochran. The female star of Herbert's story, which was set in the 1870s, was Cochran's 'pride and joy', Lizbeth Webb, in her first leading role. She played Lucy Veracity Willow, a young English girl who intends to marry the awfully reliable (and dull) Hon. Thomas Trout (Brian Reece). Leaving Thomas at the altar, she elopes with the dashing and debonair French actor Pierre Fontaine (Georges Guétary). During their subsequent adventures in France at the time of the Franco-Prussian war, they are separated for a time, but, reunited, they return to marry in England. Ellis' music and Herbert's lyrics were applauded from all sides. The lively and engaging score was full of good points, including three of Ellis's biggest hit songs, 'Ma Belle Marguerite' (Guétary), and two outstanding duets, 'This Is My Lovely Day' and 'I Was Never Kissed Before' (Guétary and Webb), along with other fine numbers such as 'Table For Two', 'Oh, What Will Mother Say?', 'Too Good To Be True', 'Silent Heart', 'Ducky', 'God Bless The Family', 'Thomas T.', and 'Bless The Bride'. Brian Reece, who, at that point in his career, was about to become a national figure via the radio series *PC 49*, made the most of his comedy song, the prophetically titled 'My Big Moment'. *Bless The Bride* ran for 886 performances, despite opposition from 'new wave' American shows such as *Oklahoma!* and *Annie Get Your Gun*, and probably would have continued for longer if Cochran had not decided to take it off to make room for his final collaboration with Ellis and Herbert (and his, Cochran's last West End production), *Tough At The Top*, which, in the event, only lasted for 154 performances. A major London revival of *Bless The Bride* was presented at Sadlers Wells in 1987, starring Jan Hartley as Lucy, Bernard Alane as Pierre, and the well-known television actor, Simon Williams, in the role of Thomas.

BLITZ!

Lionel Bart was back at the top of his form with this follow-up to the smash-hit *Oliver!* (1960). For *Blitz!*, which opened at the Adelphi Theatre in London on 8 May 1962, Bart not only wrote the book (with Joan Maitland), music and lyrics, but directed the piece. The show, set in the East End of London during the dark years of World War II, concerns two families: one is Jewish - the other is not.

Mrs. Blitztein (originally played by Amanda Bayntun) runs a pickled herring stall in Petticoat Lane's Sunday market, next to that of Alfred Locke (Bob Grant). Their dislike of each other is such that messages have to be passed between them ('Tell Him-Tell Her') by Mrs Blitztein's daughter Carol (Grazina Frame) and Alfred's son Georgie (Graham James). Inevitably, the two young people fall in love, and express their feelings for each other in 'Opposites'. The small children are evacuated to the countryside ('We're Going To The Country'), while Mrs. Blitztein pours scorn into 'Who's This Geezer Hitler?' ('He's a nasty little basket with a black moustache/And we don't want him here'). Later, Carol is blinded in a air-raid, Georgie deserts from the Army, and there is a typical East End 'knees-up' wedding before a bomb destroys much of the immediate locality. Mrs. Blitztein emerges from the rubble unscathed. Bart's rousing, and sometimes tender score, included 'Our Hotel', 'I Want To Whisper Something', 'Another Morning', 'Be What You Wanna Be', 'Petticoat Lane (On A Saturday Ain't So Nice)', 'Down The Lane', 'So Tell Me', 'Mums And Dads' and 'Is This Gonna Be A Wedding?'. Grazina Frame sang the haunting 'Far Away', which became a UK chart hit for Shirley Bassey, and the voice of Vera Lynn was heard on the 'radio' with 'The Day After Tomorrow'. The entire production was designed by Sean Kenny, whose huge mechanical sets, a mass of girders and metal platforms, was praised by one critic as 'the most remarkable spectacle to hit the London stage in my time.' The show was a tremendous success and ran for well over two years, with a total of 568 performances. Nearly 30 years later, in September 1990, the National Youth Theatre of Great Britain staged a revival of *Blitz!* at London's Playhouse Theatre, and, in the following year, it was presented again, in the north of England. The Original Cast album, which had featured in the UK charts in 1962, was re-released in 1991 with three additional tracks.

BLITZSTEIN, MARC

b. 2 March 1905, Philadelphia, Pennsylvania, USA, d. 22 January 1964, Martinique, West Indies. An important, but little-known composer, early in his life Blitzstein seemed destined for a career in classical music, and attended the Curtis Institute of Music in Philadelphia. While studying composition in Europe, he became influenced and inspired by the innovative work of Kurt Weill and Bertolt Brecht, and from then on his music bore a similar feeling of commitment, energy and social conscience. This was immediately apparent in his first contributions to theatre in New York. His one-act opera, 'Triple Sec', was included in *Garrick Gaieties* (1930), and 'Song For Militia' was perfectly in tune with the left-wing political viewpoint of the 'social revue' *Parade* (1935). In 1937 Blitzstein wrote the book, music and lyrics for the controversial *The Cradle Will Rock*, which was conceived for the Federal Theatre Project of the Works Progress Administration, and directed by Orson Welles. Government pressure forced the production to flit from theatre to theatre, until its commercial opening at the Windsor Theatre in January 1938, where it ran for 104 performances. During the remainder of the 30s and throughout the 40s, Blitzstein continued to be involved with several critically acclaimed and highly ambitious plays and musicals, providing, on various occasions, book, music, or incidental music to productions such as *Julius Caesar, Danton's Death, No For An Answer, Lunchtime Follies, Let Freedom Sing, Another Part Of The Forest, Androcles And The Lion* and *Regina* (1949). The latter was based on Lillian Hellman's play the *Little Foxes*, and was one of several collaborations between Hellman and Blitzstein. He wrote the book, music and lyrics for *Regina*, expanding the piece into a superb operatic production. In the early 50s, after writing the incidental music for *King Lear* (1949), starring Louis Calhern and directed by John Housman, Blitzstein came to the project for which he is generally best known - *The Threepenny Opera*. When it was originally conceived by Blitzstein's early influences, composer Kurt Weill and librettist/lyricist Bertolt Brecht, it ran on Broadway for 12 performances in 1933. More than 20 years later, a revised production, with Weill's music and a new book and lyrics by Blitzstein, opened off-Broadway at the Theatre de Lys in 1954, and, after a break of a few months, ran for a total of 2,706 performances. 'Mack The Knife' was just one of the memorable songs from the score. After *Reuben Reuben* closed out of town in 1955, Blitzstein's wrote his final Broadway score, for *Juno*, four years later. Beset by backstage problems - and Joseph Stein's downbeat book - it closed after 16 performances. Juno was based on 'one of the 20th century's greatest plays', Sean O'Casey's *Juno And The Paycock*, and had what has been called a rich and gorgeous score, including 'We're Alive', 'My True Heart', 'I Wish It So' and 'One Kind Word'. Radically revised, the show was presented in a 'chamber version' at the Vineyard Theatre in New York in October 1992.

● FURTHER READING: *Mark The Music: The Life And Work Of Marc Blitzstein*, E. Gordon.

BLONDEL

After a short provincial tour and a season at the Old Vic, Tim Rice's first stage musical following the break-up of his highly successful partnership with Andrew Lloyd Webber, arrived at the Aldwych Theatre in London on 20 January 1984. Stephen Oliver, the eminent theatre and opera composer, was Rice's collaborator for this anachronistic piece in which the minstrel Blondel (Paul Nicholas) divides his time between rescuing his hero, King Richard I, from a prison in Austria, and attempting to write a hit song. Rice's knack of being able to write lyrics in almost any style ('from mediaeval liturgy to rock 'n' roll', according to *The Stage*), revealed itself particularly in numbers such as 'Blondel And Fiona', 'The Least Of My Troubles', 'No Rhyme For Richard', 'Assassins' Song', 'Saladin Days', 'I Can't Wait To Be King', the deliberately excruciating 'I'm A Monarchist', and 'Running Back For More', which Rice and Oliver probably wrote with an eye on the UK chart. A quartet of monks in the shape of the vocal group Cantabile, got the show on the road, and occasionally kept the audience in touch with the not-so-subtle plot developments, while Sharon Lee Hill as Blondel's beloved Fiona, David Burt as the dastardly Prince John, and Chris Langham in the role of a hilarious hatchet man, led the rest of the cast - including (a typical Rice touch) a singing

group called the Blondettes - in this most amusing romp. Maria Friedman, who by the early 90s had become one of the West End's favourite singing actresses, was in the chorus. The director was Peter James, and the ingenious settings were the work of Tim Goodchild. Critical reaction was mixed, and ranged from 'tawdry showbiz pastiche' to 'the wittiest and funniest musical I have seen in decades'. Unfortunately, *Blondel* failed to appeal, although, with Rice's backing apparently, it managed a run of 278 performances.

BLOOD BROTHERS

After transferring from the Liverpool Playhouse, this distinctly contemporary stage musical opened at the Lyric Theatre in London on 11 April 1983. Its tough and realistic setting - Liverpool in the depths of that city's despairing inner-urban collapse - mirrored the harshly unsentimental tale of twin brothers Eddie (Andrew C. Wadsworth) and Mickey (George Costigan), separated as children, who grow up in radically different situations. Despite being worlds apart in their social lives, they are drawn together, but the reunion ends tragically. With book, music and lyrics by Willy Russell, one of a handful of brilliant chroniclers of Liverpool's contemporary traumas and dramas, the show starred Barbara Dickson as Mrs. Johnstone (the twins' mother), accompanied by what author and critic Sheridan Morley referred to as 'a hit-squad cast capable of slamming Russell's score out across the footlights'. Prominent amongst the performers were Peter Christian (Sammy), Amanda York (Linda), Wendy Murray (Mrs. Lyons), Alan Leith (Mr. Lyons) and Andrew Scholfield (Narrator). *Blood Brothers* was generally well received by the critics (although there was talk of 'a sordid melodrama'), and earned an Ivor Novello Award for Best British Musical, and Laurence Olivier Awards for best musical and actress (Dickson). However, by the time it began to become popular with the public, aided by radio play of Barbara Dickson's 'Tell Me It's Not True', closing notices had been posted, and the show ran for only six months. In the years that followed, many productions were mounted in the UK and abroad. West End impresario Bill Kenwright acquired the national touring rights, and it was his production, headed by Kiki Dee, that opened at London's Albery Theatre on 28 July 1988. With audiences now more familiar with the material, this new *Blood Brothers* was acclaimed from the start. Highlights of the score, which included 'My Child', 'Kids Game', 'Bright New Day', 'That Guy', 'Miss Jones' and 'Light Romance', were the mother's catchy opening 'Marilyn Monroe', the melancholy 'Easy Terms', and the affecting 'Tell Me It's Not True'; Eddie's tender 'I'm Not Saying A Word', Eddie and Mickey's bluesy 'Long Sunday Afternoon', and the Narrator's 'Shoes Upon The Table' were also noteworthy. Con O'Neill (Mickey) won the Olivier Award for Best Actor in a Musical Entertainment, and he and Stephanie Lawrence, with Mark Michael Hutchinson (Eddie) and Warwick Evans (Narrator), led *Blood Brothers* into New York's Music Box Theatre on 25 April 1993. Co-directed by Kenwright and Bob Tomson, it was damned by leading critic Frank Rich ('Not much dancing, and not much to dance about'), and in spite of enjoying regular standing ovations, was about to be withdrawn when leading cast members were succeeded by more mature artists from the world of popular music, such as Petula Clark, David Cassidy and his step-brother Shaun Cassidy. Business then picked up considerably, and the show completed 839 performances before recouping its losses during a US tour headed by Clark and David Cassidy. Meanwhile, the London production had transferred to the larger Phoenix Theatre in December 1991, and continued a remarkable run, celebrating its 10th anniversary in July 1998, having taken nearly £50 million at the box office. Lyn Paul, former member of the New Seekers, was Mrs. Johnstone on that occasion, and others to fill the role in London and/or New York or Australia, have included Angela Richards, Siobhán McCarthy, Helen Reddy, Carole King, and Delia Hannah. Several more stars from the worlds of pop and television have also been in various *Blood Brothers* ensembles, such as Carl Wayne (of 60s pop group the Move), David Soul (*Starsky And Hutch*), and Stefan Dennis (*Neighbours*). Chief albums issued feature the 1988 and 1995 London casts, and *The International Recording*, with Clark and the Cassidy brothers accompanied by the Royal Philharmonic Orchestra.

BLOOMER GIRL

Composer Harold Arlen's biggest Broadway success was way ahead of its time - in subject matter, at least. The book, by Sig Herzig and Fred Saidy, was based on a play by Dan and Lilith James, and dealt with the highly controversial subjects of civil liberties, women's rights - and the 'phasing-in' of ladies' bloomers during the American Civil War. Even before it opened at the Shubert Theatre in New York on 5 October 1944, rumours abounded that the show was attempting to 'cash in' on the success of *Oklahoma!*, which had hit Broadway like a huge breath of fresh air during the previous season. There were similarities: they shared the same costume and set designers, the choreography for both shows was designed by Agnes de Mille (her Civil War ballet depicting the plight of women waiting for their men-folk to return from the conflict, was highly praised), and two of the principals from *Oklahoma!* (in which some garments that looked very much like bloomers were on display), Celeste Holm, who had played Ado Annie, and Joan McCracken (Sylvie), a former member of the American Ballet Company, were together again in *Bloomer Girl*. The setting is Cicero Falls, New York, in 1861, and Evelina Applegate (Celeste Holm), is so outraged when her domineering father - a manufacturer of hoop skirts - demands that she marry one of his salesman, that she joins her crusading aunt, Amelia 'Dolly' Bloomer (Margaret Douglass), in her fight for women's rights in general, and their freedom to wear comfortable clothing in particular. Evelina even converts a Southern slaveholder, Jefferson Calhoun (David Brooks), to her cause. They fall in love, and their duet, 'Right As The Rain', is one of the most appealing numbers in Harold Arlen and lyricist 'Yip' Harburg's score, which also included 'T'morra, T'morra'', 'It Was Good Enough For Grandma', 'Sunday In Cicero Falls', 'When The Boys Come Home', and 'Evelina'. There were also two songs that perfectly encapsulated one of the show's underlying themes, a desire for racial

understanding: 'I Got A Song' and 'The Eagle And Me', which was performed by Dooley Wilson, who had made a big impression in the show *Cabin In The Sky* (1940), and in the film *Casablanca* (1942), in which he ostensibly sang 'As Time Goes By'. 'The Eagle And Me' subsequently became an important element in the repertoire of Lena Horne. *Bloomer Girl* enjoyed an impressive run of 654 performances, and was revived briefly in New York at the City Center in 1947. In 1992, a CD purporting to be the first *complete* Original Cast recording of *Bloomer Girl* since its first 78 issue, was released in MCA's Broadway Gold series.

BLOSSOM TIME (FILM MUSICAL)

This lavish, but idealized film biography of composer Franz Schubert, which was released in 1934, gave the celebrated tenor Richard Tauber his most famous screen role. Set in Vienna in the 1820s, Franz Schulz's romantic screenplay, which was adapted from a story by John Drinkwater, Roger Burford, Paul Perez, and G.H. Clutsam, concerns the struggle for recognition by a middle-aged (Tauber was 42), unknown genius who sacrifices his love for the sweet young Vicki Wimpassinger (Jane Baxter) because he realizes that she is passionately in love with a dashing young officer, Rudi (Carl Esmond). Paul Graetz, as Vicki's father, Alois, provided the comic relief, and also cast were Athene Seyler, Charles Carson, Marguerite Allen, Edward Chapman, Lester Matthews, Gibb McLaughlin and Frederick Lloyd. Schubert's magnificent music was heard throughout, with Tauber providing a thrilling finale with 'Impatience (Thine Is My Heart)', which had a lyric by John Drinkwater. *Blossom Time* was produced in the UK by Walter C. Mycroft for British International Pictures (BIP). The director was Paul Stein, who continued to direct film musicals until after World War II.

BLOSSOM TIME (STAGE MUSICAL)

This was an American version of the Viennese operetta, *Das Dreimäderlhaus*, by A.M. Wilner and Heinz Reichert, adapted from the novel *Schwammerl*, by Dr. R.H. Bartsch, with music arranged by Heinrich Berté. It was based on the life and music of the composer Franz Schubert, and opened at the Ambassador Theatre in New York on 29 September 1921. For the US production, Schubert's music was arranged by the young Sigmund Romberg, and Dorothy Donnelly provided a revised book and lyrics. Her libretto was a tangled web of romantic intrigue in which Franz Schubert (Bertram Peacock) supposedly loses his inspiration, and his girl, Mitzi Krantz (Olga Cook), after his best friend, Baron Franz Von Schober (Howard Marsh), has serenaded her with Schubert's own songs. Marsh was widely applauded for his rendition of 'Serenade', and the complete score was a sheer delight, including as it did the wonderful 'Song Of Love', 'Three Little Maids', 'Peace To My Lonely Heart', 'This Is An Old Vienna Town', 'Tell Me Daisy', 'My Springtime Thou Art', and 'Let Me Awake'. After the remarkable New York run of 592 performances, several road companies toured the USA, and Broadway audiences enjoyed the show again in 1939 and 1943. In 1922, London audiences were offered a different version entitled *Lilac Time*. The musical adaptation was by Heinrich Berté and G.H. Clutsam, with a fresh book and lyrics by Adrian Ross, and several appealing songs emerged such as 'Under The Lilac Bough', 'Three Little Girls', 'The Golden Song', 'My Sweetest Song Of All', 'Yours Is My Heart', and 'Just A Little Ring'. The cast included Dorothy Clayton, Courtice Pounds, and Clara Butterworth, and the show stayed at the Lyric Theatre for well over a year. Several London revivals were presented up to the early 40s. Another production called *Blossom Time*, with a book by Rodney Ackland, and music and lyrics by G.H. Clutsam and Richard Tauber, 'based on the music of Franz Schubert', was presented in London in 1942. It was actually a vehicle for Richard Tauber, the Austrian singer and composer who had been domiciled in England since 1938. He also starred in a film version of *Blossom Time* which was released in 1938. The show itself, in its many variations, remains a favourite of professional and amateur operatic societies throughout the world.

BLOSSOM, HENRY, JNR.

b. 6 May 1866, St. Louis, Missouri, USA, d. 23 March 1919, New York, USA. An important librettist and lyricist during the early years of the 20th century, Blossom left his father's insurance business after he began writing short stories and then, novels, one of which, *Checkers*, he successfully dramatized. His first Broadway musical project as a book writer and lyricist was an early musical comedy, *The Yankee Consul* (1904, music: Alfred Robyn, 'Ain't It Funny', 'What A Difference A Few Hours Make'), which was followed by two immensely popular comic operettas, *Mlle. Modiste* (1905, 'Kiss Me Again', 'I Want What I Want When I Want It', 'If I Were On The Stage'), and *The Red Mill* ('Every Day Is Ladies' Day With Me', 'Because You're You', 'Moonbeams', 'In Old New York'), a vehicle for the ex-vaudeville comedy duo of David Montgomery and Fred Stone. His collaborator on both of them was the great composer Victor Herbert. From then on, Blossom wrote the book and/or lyrics for productions such as *The Hoyden* (1907, music: Paul Rubens), *The Prima Donna* (1908, music: Herbert, 'If You Were I And I Were You', 'I'll Be Married To The Music Of A Military Band'), *The Slim Princess* (1911, music: Leslie Stuart, 'Let Me Live And Die In Dixie'), *Baron Trenck* (1912, music: Felix Albini and Robyn), *The Man From Cook's* (1912, music: Raymond Hubbell), *All For The Ladies* (1912, music: Robyn), *A Glimpse Of The Great White Way* (1913, music: Robyn), *The Only Girl* (1914, music: Herbert, 'When You're Away'), *The Princess Pat* (1915, music: Herbert, 'Two Laughing Irish Eyes'), *The Century Girl* (1916, music: Herbert, *et al*), *Eileen* (1917, music: Herbert, 'Thine Alone', 'When Love Awakes', 'Eileen Alanna Asthore'), *Follow The Girl* (1918, music: Zoel Paranteau), and *The Velvet Lady* (1919, music: Herbert, 'Life And Love', 'Spooky Ookum'). Blossom was also involved with several shows that failed to reach Broadway, and was working until shortly before his death in 1919.

BLOW UP

This much-fêted 1966 film by Italian director Michelangelo Antonioni was an ironic homage to 'swing-ing London', in which David Hemmings starred as a successful photographer, the character loosely modelled on David Bailey and Terence Donovan. Emotionally detached at the outset, Hemmings later becomes obsessed by a series of seemingly casual shots of a couple on Hampstead Heath. When one of the subjects, played by Vanessa Redgrave, goes to great lengths to retrieve the negatives, he makes several 'blow-ups' of one frame in which he perceives the image of a corpse. He returns to the scene - no body is found - and all shreds of 'evidence' are later removed from his studio. He absent-mindedly wanders into a London club before encountering a group of mime artists playing tennis. At one point they ask Hemmings to throw back their 'ball', the noise of which becomes audible as he walks away. *Blow Up* poses questions about reality to telling effect but musicologists revere the film for a cameo appearance by the Yardbirds. The rare Jeff Beck/Jimmy Page line-up is featured as a guitar-smashing group, a part rejected by the Who. They perform 'Stroll On' to an expressionless audience that becomes frenzied when Beck throws the remains of his instrument to them. Hemmings escapes with this totem, then throws it away, whereupon passers-by examine the object only to deem it worthless. 'Stroll On' is featured on an accompanying soundtrack album, which is completed by contributions from jazz musician Herbie Hancock. The soundtrack adds tonal colour to one of the most fascinating films of its, or any other, era.

BLUE FOR A BOY

With a book by Austin Melford, which was based on the German farce, *Hurrah! Eine Junge!*, by Franz Arnold and Ernest Bach, *Blue For A Boy* opened at Her Majesty's Theatre in London on 30 November 1950. Subtitled *What Shall We Do With The Body?*, it purported to be 'a musical romp' involving several well-known comedy performers such as the substantially built Fred Emney (complete with monocle and cigar), Richard Hearne (*not* in his usual character of Mr. Pastry), Bertha Belmore, and the show's author and director, Austin Melford. The plot was extremely complicated and involved step-sons, stepfathers, and stepmothers, female impersonators, and many of the various misconceptions and confused identities essential for a successful farce - and this one was very successful. The engaging songs, by composer Harry Parr Davies and lyricist Harold Purcell, which were delivered with a great deal of verve and panache by the show's leading ladies, Hermene French and Eve Lister, included 'Lying Awake And Dreaming', 'At Last It Happened', and 'Blue For A Boy', which had a life outside of the show, particularly in a recording by Dick James and Pearl Carr. One critic described the production as 'sheer lunatic fun that keeps the theatre rocking', and it continued to do so for 664 performances.

BLUE HAWAII

Blue Hawaii was Elvis Presley's third film after leaving the US Army. Released in 1961, its lush production and romantic theme set the tone for the production-line formula that followed. Here, Presley plays a GI who, having returned home to Honolulu, opts for a life as a beachcomber. Despite this mild 'drop-out' theme, the star's assimilation into conventional life culminates with his marriage and his version of the 'Hawaiian Wedding Song'. Glamorous location shots helped to enhance the film's appeal, particularly in an austere UK where the soundtrack album remained on the charts for over a year. A double-sided single culled from its content, 'Rock A Hula Baby'/'Can't Help Falling In Love With You', topped the UK singles chart for four weeks.

BLUE PARADISE, THE

Composer Sigmund Romberg's first successful musical production opened on 5 August 1915 at the Casino Theatre in New York. It was adapted from Ein Tag Im Paradies, a Viennese operetta by Edmund Eysler, and had lyrics by Herbert Reynolds. Edgar Smith's book tells the sad tale of the shy and gentle Mizzi, played by Vivienne Segal, who works at the Blue Paradise restaurant in Vienna. Her lover, Rudolphe (Cecil Lean), leaves to seek his fortune in America, but when he returns several years later, she has changed beyond belief, and is now cynical and world-weary. Vivienne Segal was enchanting in her first Broadway book musical, and, together with Lean, introduced the show's big hit song, 'Auf Wiedersehn'. The number became widely popular, especially through a recording by Harry Macdonough and Olive Kline. The rest of Romberg's delightfully romantic score included 'One Step Into Love' 'My Model Girl (lyric: Harold Atteridge), and 'A Toast To A Woman's Eyes'. Several of Edmund Eysler's original songs were also retained. The Blue Paradise ran for a profitable 356 performances, and launched both Vivienne Segal and Sigmund Romberg on their memorable Broadway careers.

BLUE SKIES

Released by Paramount in 1946, Blue Skies was similar in style and content to Holiday Inn (1942) in that it starred Bing Crosby and Fred Astaire as a former song-and-dance duo weaving their way through a great bunch of Irving Berlin songs. Arthur Sheekman's screenplay told of Johnny Adams (Crosby), a singer who buys and sells nightclubs on the side, while good old reliable Jed Potter (Astaire) looks on and disapproves. They are both chasing the same girl, Mary O'Hara (Joan Caufield), who marries Johnny, but his instability eventually leads to their divorce and her disappearance. Many years later, the trio are reunited in a radio studio to the strains of 'You Keep Coming Back Like A Song'. The film's many highlights included 'A Couple Of Song And Dance Men' (Crosby and Astaire), 'I've Got My Captain Working For Me Now' (Crosby and Billy De Wolfe), '(I'll See You In) C-U-B-A' (Crosby and Olga San Juan), and 'Puttin' On The Ritz', which was brilliantly danced by Astaire, accompanied by eight other images of himself. The rest of the score featured some of the best of Berlin, and included 'Always', 'You'd Be Surprised', 'A Pretty Girl Is Like A Melody', 'Not For All The Rice In China', 'How Deep Is The Ocean?', 'This Is The Army Mr Jones', '(Running Around In Circles) Getting Nowhere', 'Russian Lullaby', 'White Christmas', and 'Heatwave'. Most of the choreography for the musical numbers was by Hermes Pan. Blue Skies was

photographed in Technicolor and directed by Stuart Heisler. It proved to be a box-office smash, and became one of the Top 10 musicals of the 40s.

BLUEBELL IN FAIRYLAND

This 'musical dream play' opened at the Vaudeville Theatre in London on 18 December 1901. The book was by Seymour Hicks, who also starred with his wife, Ellaline Terris, and the basic score was composed by Walter Slaughter (music) and Aubrey Hopwood and Charles H. Taylor (lyrics), although there were several interpolated songs by other hands. Albert Fitz and William Penn's enduring 'The Honeysuckle And The Bee', was one of those that enhanced the charming story of the little Bluebell (Terris) who travels to fairyland in order to help the King (Hicks) regain his throne. Other popular items were 'I Want Yer, Ma Honey', 'Dreamland', 'Only A Penny, Sir', 'The Sunflower And The Sun', and Leslie Stuart's 'Louisiana Lou'. The piece appealed to children and adults alike, and became a Christmas favourite, being revived in London on several occasions from 1905 through to 1937. Jessie Matthews, who was to become one of the West End's brightest and most loved musical stars, made her professional debut as a speciality dancer at the age of 12 in the 1919 production. One of the youngsters in the original production was Phyllis Dare.

BLUES BROTHERS, THE

John Landis, director of An American Werewolf In London and Michael Jackson's promotional video for Thriller, was responsible for this 1980 feature film. John Belushi (b. 24 January 1949, Chicago, Illinois, USA, d. 5 March 1982, Los Angeles, California, USA), star of a previous Landis project, National Lampoon's Animal House, shared top billing with Dan Aykroyd (b. 1 July 1952, Ottawa, Ontario, Canada) as Jake and Elwood Blues, who re-form their R&B band following the former's release from jail. 'We're on a mission from God', the pair proclaim when, after a vision, they attempt to raise funds for the orphanage in which they were raised. A highly popular slapstick comedy, The Blues Brothers contains some priceless scenes, notably when the band attempt to play soul at a redneck venue. However, it is equally prone to cliché, in particular, the car chase and wrecking sequences, and it is reported that the shot in which one vehicle is dropped from a crane cost more than the rest of the film put together. Despite the presence of former Booker T. And The MGs members Steve Cropper and Duck Dunn, many critics sensed a patronizing, almost pantomime, view of R&B in its content. Cameo roles for James Brown, Ray Charles, Aretha Franklin and John Lee Hooker, however memorable, seemed to marginalize performers actually at the forefront of the genre. However, there is little doubt many of the musicians and singers featured found their careers galvanized by their appearances therein. A successful soundtrack album ensued, while Belushi and Aykroyd, aided by Cropper and Dunn, recorded further albums under the Blues Brothers banner. Belushi's sudden death brought that pastime to a premature end. The film, nevertheless, has retained its appeal and remains one of the most popular musical features of its era. Long planned by

Aykroyd, a sequel, *Blues Brothers 2000*, was released in 1998 to general critical disapproval. Reprising his role as Elwood, Aykroyd was this time paired with ex-*Roseanne* star John Goodman; the film retrod the original virtually step for step, and featured more lazy cover versions of R&B classics.

● FILMS: *The Blues Brothers* (1980).

BLUES IN THE NIGHT (FILM MUSICAL)

The Big Band Era was still in full swing when this unassuming little film was released by Warner Brothers in 1941. The story reflected what had been going on for many years all over the USA - a group of dedicated jazz musicians enduring the grind of one-night stands, with all their attendant problems and temptations. Robert Rossen's screenplay was adapted from the play, *Hot Nocturne*, by Edwin Gilbert, and cast Richard Whorf as the band's leader whose affair with Betty Field - an actress who specialised in neurotic roles - ends in tragedy. Priscilla Lane, Jack Carson, Elia Kazan, Lloyd Nolan, Peter Whitney, Wallace Ford, Bill Halop were in it as well, and there were guest appearances by the real-life orchestras of Jimmy Lunceford and Will Osborne. The top-class score by Harold Arlen and Johnny Mercer contained two of their all-time standards, the beautiful 'Blues In The Night' ('My Momma Done Tol' Me/When I was in knee pants . . .') which was introduced by William Gillespie, and the pretty 'This Time The Dream's On Me'. The other numbers were 'Says Who, Says You, Says Me' and 'Hang On To Your Lids, Kids'. With that kind of music and the snappy dialogue long associated with jazz music fraternity, *Blues In The Night*, which was directed by Anatole Litvak, provided an engaging, if not absorbing, 90 minutes or so of entertainment for the fans.

BLUES IN THE NIGHT (STAGE MUSICAL)

This celebratory revue of blues music first opened on 6 June 1982 off-Broadway at the Rialto Theatre, where it starred Leslie Uggams and ran for 53 performances. Almost exactly five years later, a revised production, which was conceived and directed by Sheldon Epps, was presented in June 1987 at the tiny Donmar Warehouse on the London Fringe. After an enthusiastic critical reception, it transferred to the Piccadilly Theatre in the West End on 23 September of that year. The show is set in a seedy hotel in Chicago in the 30s, and the residents are three women, the Lady from the Road (Carol Woods), the Woman of the World (Debby Bishop), the Girl with a Date (Maria Friedman), and a pianist, The Man in the Saloon, played by Peter Straker. The lovelorn ladies reflect on the vagaries of men through a long anthology of urban blues tunes and bluesy pop standards. Carol Woods gave a sensational performance, shimmying her way through raunchy numbers such as 'Kitchen Man' and 'Take Me For A Buggy Ride'. Some of the other songs in this feast for the blues connoisseurs and discerning pop fans included 'Four Walls (And One Dirty Window) Blues', 'Stomping At The Savoy', 'New Orleans Hop Scop Blues', 'Taking A Chance On Love', 'Wild Women Don't Have The Blues', 'Lush Life', 'I'm Just A Lucky So-And So', 'Blues In The Night', 'Dirty No-Gooder's Blues', and 'Nobody Loves You

When You're Down And Out'. After a London run lasting 11 months, Woods recreated her role for another off-Broadway production that made a brief appearance at the Minetta Lane Theatre in September 1988. Also in the cast were Brenda Pressley, Leilani Jones and Lawrence Hamilton. In 1993, a new version, directed by Clarke Peters and starring Patti Boulaye, toured the UK provinces.

BLYTH, ANN

b Ann Marie Blyth, 16 August 1928, Mount Kisco, New York, USA. An actress and singer with a fine soprano voice and a fresh, engaging style, Blyth starred in several important movie musicals in the 50s. After voice training, Blyth spent some time with the San Carlo Opera Company, and made her Broadway debut at the age of 13 in the play *Watch On The Rhine*. She began her film career in 1944 when she was just 16, joining song and dance man Donald O'Connor in the musicals *Chip Off The Old Block*, *The Merry Monahans* and *Bowery To Broadway*. Having made a good impression with those less than serious affairs, she proved her dramatic ability the following year when she was nominated for an Academy Award for her performance as Joan Crawford's selfish daughter in *Mildred Pierce*. From then on, she mixed non-singing roles with 40s musicals, including *Babes On Swing Street* and *Top O' The Morning*. She eventually came into her own in the major 50s screen musicals *The Great Caruso*, *Rose Marie*, *The Student Prince* and *Kismet*. Many felt that she was miscast as torch singer Helen Morgan in her last film to date, *The Helen Morgan Story*, and indeed her singing voice was dubbed by Gogi Grant. In more recent years, Blyth has appeared frequently in the musical theatre, and received excellent reviews in November 1992 when she partnered Bill Hayes in an elegant tribute to the songs of Broadway and Hollywood at the Rainbow & Stars nightspot in New York.

● FILMS: *Chip Off The Old Block* (1944), *The Merry Monahans* (1944), *Babes On Swing Street* (1944), *Bowery To Broadway* (1944), *Mildred Pierce* (1945), *Swell Guy* (1946), *Brute Force* (1947), *Killer McCoy* (1947), *A Woman's Vengeance* (1947), *Mr. Peabody And The Mermaid* (1948), *Another Part Of The Forest* (1948), *Red Canyon* (1949), *Free For All* (1949), *Top O' The Morning* (1949), *Once More, My Darling* (1949), *Our Very Own* (1950), *The Great Caruso* (1951), *Katie Did It* (1951), *Thunder On The Hill* (1951), *The Golden Horde* (1951), *I'll Never Forget You* (1951), *One Minute To Zero* (1952), *The World In His Arms* (1952), *Sally And Saint Anne* (1952), *All The Brothers Were Valiant* (1953), *Rose Marie* (1954), *The Student Prince* (1954), *Kismet* (1955), *The King's Thief* (1955), *Slander* (1956), *The Buster Keaton Story* (1957), *Jazz Age* (1957), *The Helen Morgan Story* (1957).

BOCK, JERRY

b. Jerrold Lewis Bock, 23 November 1928, New Haven, Connecticut, USA. An important composer for the musical theatre, Bock studied the piano from an early age and was soon able to play quite complicated compositions by ear. He wrote the music for various shows while studying at high school and the University of Wisconsin in the 40s, and subsequently worked on revues at summer camps and for television. In 1955 Bock and lyricist Larry

Holofcener contributed some songs to the Broadway revue *Catch A Star*, and a year later, with George Weiss, they provided the complete score for *Mr. Wonderful*, a musical vehicle for Sammy Davis Jnr., which ran for 383 performances. Bock and Holofcener's last assignment together was for the *Ziegfeld Follies Of 1956*, which closed before it reached New York. Shortly afterwards, Bock met lyricist Sheldon Harnick (b. 30 April 1924, Chicago, Illinois, USA), and they formed what is arguably the most important musical partnership of the 60s. Harnick had been a danceband violinist before moving to New York in 1950 where he had several of his songs performed in revues such as *New Faces Of 1952* ('Boston Beguine') and *Shoestring Revue*. Bock and Harnick's first effort, *The Body Beautiful* (1958), was a failure, but *Fiorello!* (1959) ran for 795 performances. Next came the underrated *Tenderloin* (1960), a humorous exposé of vice in New York with some good songs including 'Little Old New York', 'The Picture Of Happiness' and 'How The Money Changes Hands'. In 1963 the team wrote several numbers for the critically acclaimed marionette show *Man In The Moon*, and later in the same year, came up with what is considered to be their best score, for *She Loves Me*. With delightful songs such as 'Will He Like Me?', 'Ice Cream', 'A Trip To The Library' and 'She Loves Me', plus Broadway's favourite ingénue, Barbara Cook, it warranted a longer stay than just 302 performances. Bock and Harnick's next show clocked up more than 10 times that total in New York, and was a smash hit around the world. *Fiddler On The Roof* (1964), starring Zero Mostel, became one of the most cherished of all Broadway musicals, and gave the world of popular music (and Jewish functions of all kinds) hit songs such as 'Matchmaker, Matchmaker', 'Sunrise, Sunset' and the immortal 'If I Was A Rich Man'. It proved impossible to follow, and for the remainder of the decade the composers worked on a variety of projects including a 'Sherlock Holmes' musical, *Baker Street*, *The Apple Tree*, which was based on stories by Mark Twain and others, and ran for 463 performances, and *Her First Roman*, based on George Bernard Shaw's play *Caesar And Cleopatra*, to which they contributed a few songs. After *The Rothschilds* (1970), which had a strong Jewish theme and was similar in a way to *Fiddler On The Roof*, Bock and Harnick ended their partnership. Bock has been inactive for over 20 years, with no apparent musical work forthcoming. In 1971, Harnick gave his 'observations on the fine art and craft of lyric writing' at a recital in the *Lyrics And Lyricists* series at the 92nd Street 'Y' in New York, and since then his projects have included *Pinocchio* (1973) with music by Mary Rodgers, *Rex* (1976) with music by Richard Rodgers, and an English translation of the *Umbrellas Of Cherbourg* with composer Michel Legrand for an 1979 off-Broadway production.

In the 80s there was a projected musical, *Dragons*, that did not materialize, and in the 90s Harnick collaborated with Joe Raposo on *A Wonderful Life*, and with Thomas Z. Shepard on *Love In Two Countries*, neither of which opened on Broadway following their out-of-town try-outs. In 1997, Harnick contributed the book to *Good Company: Songs That Made It From Shows That Didn't*. Premiered in Stockbridge, Massachusetts, the score included such gems

as 'More Than You Know', 'Time On My Hands' and 'All The Things You Are'.

● ALBUMS: *An Evening With Sheldon Harnick* (Laureate 1977)★★★.

BOLAND, CLAY

b. 25 October 1903, Olyphant, Pennsylvania, USA, d. 23 July 1963, Queens, New York, USA. A composer with a relatively modest output, after attending university Boland practised dentistry for a time while also playing piano in various dance bands. His most enduring song, 'Gypsy In My Soul', which he wrote in 1937 with lyricist Moe Jaffe, was introduced in *Fifty-Fifty*, one of the renowned *University Of Pennsylvania Mask And Wig* shows for which Boland used to write and direct. Mildred Bailey made what many consider to be the definitive recording of the song, and there were several popular versions in Britain by Roy Fox, Nat Gonella, and Jack Harris in the late 30s. Later, an outstanding recording was released by Eydie Gorme on her first album, *Eydie Gorme*, in 1957. She also featured it effectively in her nightclub act, with a special lyric by Fred Elton. Another of Boland's well-known songs, 'Stop Beatin' 'Round The Mulberry Bush', which was adapted from a nursery song, was written with another of his regular lyricists, Bickley Reichner, and was successful in 1938 for Tommy Dorsey (with a vocal by Edythe Wright and Skeets Herfurt), Count Basie (Jimmy Rushing), Kay Kyser, and Al Donohue (Paula Kelly). Benny Goodman had a hit with Boland's 'When I Go A-Dreamin'', and Kay Kyser took another of the composer's *Mask And Wig* numbers, 'Ya Got Me', into the US Hit Parade in 1938. Boland and Reichner's 'Tell Me At Midnight' proved to be another popular item for Tommy Dorsey in 1940, with a Frank Sinatra vocal, and Boland's other compositions included 'An Apple A Day', 'Something Has Happened To Me', 'Midnight On The Trail', 'There's No Place Like Your Arms', 'Stop! It's Wonderful', and 'How I'd Like To Be With You In Bermuda'. After military service in World War II, Boland concentrated mainly on his publishing interests, although he did continue to write some more *Mask And Wig* shows.

BOLES, JOHN

b. 28 August 1895 or 1898, Greenville, Texas, USA, d. 27 February 1969, San Angelo, Texas, USA. An archetypal handsome leading man with a fine baritone voice who was in several popular movie musicals of the 30s. After graduating from the University of Texas, Boles completed military service during World War I before studying singing in Paris and New York. In the early 20s he had minor roles in several Broadway shows including *Little Jessie James* and *Mercenary Mary*, which was followed by a good part in *Kitty's Kisses* (1926). During the late 20s he was suitably strong and manly in silent films, and, at the same time, also came into his own in a string of movie musicals that included *The Desert Song*, *Rio Rita*, *The King Of Jazz*, *One Heavenly Night*, *My Lips Betray*, *Music In The Air*, *Bottoms Up*, *Stand Up And Cheer*, *Curly Top*, *Redheads On Parade*, *Rose Of The Rancho*, *Romance In The Dark* (1938) and *Thousands Cheer* (1943). These films represented only a small fraction of his output which mainly consisted of dramatic, non-musical roles. In the 40s and early 50s he appeared in revivals of well-known stage musicals such as *Show Boat*, and in 1946 co-starred with Mary Martin and Kenny Baker in the Broadway hit musical, *One Touch Of Venus*. After joining other veteran stars such as Paulette Goddard and Gypsy Rose Lee in the poorly received satirical picture *Babes In Baghdad* in 1952, he retired from showbusiness shortly afterwards.

BOLGER, RAY

b. Raymond Wallace Bolger, 10 January 1904, Boston, Massachusetts, USA, d. 15 January 1987, Los Angeles, California, USA. An eccentric, rubber-legged dancer with a style and image that had to be seen to be believed. He started out as a comedian in 1922 with the Bob Ott Musical Repertory Company and four years later gained a small part in a Broadway show called *The Merry Whirl*. After a spell in vaudeville, he returned to Broadway in the late 20s and 30s in shows such as *Heads Up, George White's Scandals, Life Begins At 8:40*, and *On Your Toes* (1936). Bolger shot to stardom in the latter show in which he introduced the lovely 'There's A Small Hotel', and performed an hilarious eccentric dance in Richard Rodgers' famous 'Slaughter On Tenth Avenue' ballet. After leaving the show he moved to Hollywood and appeared in *The Great Ziegfeld, Rosalie, Sweethearts*, and one of the most memorable films of all time, *The Wizard Of Oz* (1939), in which he played the Scarecrow in search of a brain. After returning to New York for the short-lived musical *Keep Off The Grass* (1940), he made one more film, *Sunny* (1941), before leaving for the South Pacific where he entertained troops with the USO during World War II. He was back on Broadway in 1942 for *By Jupiter*, and then the revue *Three To Make Ready*, in which he stopped the show regularly with the charming 'That Old Soft Shoe', complete with straw hat and cane. Frank Loesser's *Where's Charley?* came along in 1948 and gave Bolger his greatest role; he introduced the gentle 'Once In Love With Amy', and it subsequently became his signature tune. During the 40s and 50s he made several more films including *Stage Door Canteen, Four Jacks And A Jill, The Harvey Girls, Look For The Silver Lining, Where's Charley?*, and *April In Paris*. In 1962 and 1969 he appeared in two more stage musicals, *All American* and *Come Summer*, but mostly during the 60s and 70s he mixed feature films such as *Babes In Toyland, The Daydreamer, The Runner Stumbles*, and *Just You And Me Kid*, with television movies that included *The Entertainer, The Captains And The Kings*, and *Only Heaven Knows*. In the MGM extravaganza *That's Entertainment!*, he looked back affectionately on a career that had spanned well over half a century. Three years later he died of cancer at the age of 83.

BOLTON, GUY

b. Guy Reginald Bolton, 23 November 1884, Broxbourne, England, d. 6 September 1979, London, England. An important librettist who was there in the early part of the century when the real American musical was born. Bolton was the son of an American father and an English mother, and, after the family had moved to the USA, he began his adult life as an architect and wrote in his spare time.

Early on he discovered that he worked best with others, and throughout his long and distinguished career his list of co-authors included George Grossmith, Clifford Grey, Philip Bartholmae, George Middleton, W. Somerset Maugham and Eddie Davis. His two principal collaborators were Fred Thompson and P.G. Wodehouse, and, early on, Bolton teamed with Wodehouse and composer Jerome Kern for the famous Princess Theatre musicals which, with their smart and witty integrated books and lyrics, are considered to be a watershed in the evolution of the American musical. The best of these were *Oh, Boy!* (1917), *Leave It To Jane* (1917), and *Oh, Lady! Lady!!* (1918). From 1915 through to 1924, Bolton worked mostly with Kern and various lyricists on shows such as *90 In The Shade, Nobody Home, Very Good Eddie, Miss Springtime, Have A Heart, The Riviera Girl, Miss 1917, Oh, My Dear!, Sally, Tangerine, The Hotel Mouse, Daffy Dill, Sitting Pretty*, and *Primrose* (1924, London). By that time he had become a leading librettist, and so was the logical choice to write the book (with Fred Thomson) for *Lady, Be Good!* (1924), the show that contained George and Ira Gershwin's first complete score. It turned out to be a joyous affair and was a big hit on Broadway and in London, and confirmed Fred Astaire and his sister Adele as musical comedy's premier dance team. During the next six years Bolton worked at a tremendous rate on shows such as *The Bamboula* (London), *Tip Toes, The Ramblers, Oh, Kay!, The Nightingale, Rio Rita, The Five O'clock Girl, She's My Baby, Rosalie, Blue Eyes* (London), *Polly, Top Speed, Simple Simon*, and *Girl Crazy*. The latter production, with its wonderful Gershwin score, was typical Bolton - beautifully constructed, and full of fun and excruciating puns. However, just like the rest of his work, it was never going to win a Pulitzer Prize for drama, and that was the direction in which the Gershwins were heading. Their next show, *Of Thee I Sing*, had a book by George S. Kaufman that satirized America's social and political life and was quite different from the frothy confections that Bolton concocted. He seemed unable or unwilling to change his style, and, leaving Broadway to its own more serious devices, he moved to London, where, for the next decade, he collaborated mostly with Clifford Grey and Fred Thompson on a series of highly successful romps, many of which starred some of the London theatre's top talent, such as Leslie Henson, Jack Buchanan, Elsie Randolph, Bobby Howes and Evelyn Laye. The shows included *Song Of The Drum, Give Me A Ring, Seeing Stars, At The Silver Swan, Swing Along, This'll Make You Whistle, Going Places, Going Greek, Hide And Seek, The Fleet's Lit Up, Running Riot, Bobby Get Your Gun*, and *Magyar Melody* (1939). Bolton did not neglect Broadway entirely, and teamed up with his old friend P.G. Wodehouse in 1934 to write the book for the Cole Porter smash-hit *Anything Goes*, and returned to the USA again during World War II to provide the librettos for *Walk With Music, Hold On To Your Hats, Jackpot*, and *Follow The Girls*. In 1947, he revised the book for a revival of the 1909/10 hit, *The Chocolate Soldier*. In 1955, 50 years after his debut on Broadway with *90 In The Shade*, Old Father Time caught up with him. While the latest of his archaic efforts, *Ankles Aweigh*, was playing at the Mark Hellinger Theatre, just around the corner at the

Royale, Sandy Wilson's *The Boy Friend* was spoofing exactly that kind of thing. Bolton wrote only one more book for Broadway when he adapted his and Marcelle Maurete's *Anastasia* for the 1967 musical production of *Anya*.

● FURTHER READING: *Bring On The Girls!*, Guy Bolton and P.G. Wodehouse. *Bolton And Wodehouse And Kern*, Lee Davis.

BOOTH, SHIRLEY

b. Thelma Booth Ford, 30 August 1898, New York City, USA, d. 16 October 1992, North Chatham, Massachusetts, USA. A distinguished actress and singer, who was once described by the *New York Post* as 'one of the wonders of the American stage; a superb actress, a magnificent comedienne, and an all-round performer of seemingly endless variety', Booth started to act at an early age, and made her professional stage debut in 1923 and her first Broadway appearance two years later. In the Broadway musical theatre she played a gossip columnist in *Hollywood Pinafore* (1945), and excelled as the wonderfully wistful Aunt Cissy with 'Love Is The Reason' and the magnificent 'He Had Refinement', in *A Tree Grows In Brooklyn* (1951). She was a vaudeville star-turned theatrical boarding house proprietor in *By The Beautiful Sea* (1954), took the title role in *Juno* (1959), a musical version of Sean O'Casey's play *Juno And The Paycock*, with a Marc Blitzstein score, and played the Mother Superior in the short-lived *Look To The Lilies* (1970). In the latter, she introduced Sammy Cahn and Jule Styne's 'I, Yes Me! That's Who!' with Al Freeman Jnr. In non-musical areas, Booth won Tony and Academy Awards for her roles in both stage and film versions of *Come Back, Little Sheba*, and two more Tonys for her work in *Goodbye, My Fancy* and *Time Of The Cuckoo*. She also created the role of Dolly Levi in *The Matchmaker*, the play that Jerry Herman musicalized into *Hello, Dolly!* She was probably best known to the public at large for her performance as the gossipy maid Hazel Burke in the sitcom *Hazel* (1961-66), for which she won two Emmys. The first of her two husbands was actor Edward Gardner, with whom she appeared in the popular radio series *Duffy's Tavern*. Until her death, most reference works recorded her date of birth as 1907, but since then sources say that she was born nine years earlier, and was 94 when she died.

● FILMS: *Come Back, Little Sheba* (1952), *Main Street To Broadway* (1953), *About Mrs. Leslie* (1954), *The Matchmaker* (1958), *Hot Spell* (1958).

BOOTH, WEBSTER

(see Ziegler, Anne, And Booth, Webster)

BORDONI, IRENE

b. 16 January 1895, Corsica, d. 19 March 1953, New York, USA. A vivacious actress and singer who has been described as 'petite, chic, coquettish and the epitome of French au-la-la.' After being educated in Paris, she first appeared on the French stage in 1907, and made her Broadway debut five years later in the revue *Broadway To Paris* (1912). After returning to France to work in Parisian revues, she was back on Broadway in 1915, along with the lively Elsie Janis, in the short-lived (47 performances) *Miss Information*, 'a little comedy with a little music', which had a score written mostly by Jerome Kern and

Janis herself. After taking part in two of Raymond Hubbell's *Hitchy-Koo* revues in 1917 and 1918, Bordoni joined ex-vaudeville comedian Sam Bernard, and played four different roles in *As You Were* (1920), 'a fantastic revue' based on Rip's Parisian production *Plus Ça Change*. This was the first of three shows of hers that were produced by her then husband E. Ray Goetz. In 1922 Bordoni introduced George Gershwin and Buddy De Sylva's 'Do It Again' in *The French Doll*, and then sang the risqué 'Let's Do It' in Cole Porter's first hit show, *Paris* (1928). In between those two musicals, she appeared on the London stage in Avery Hopwood's *Little Miss Bluebeard*. In 1938 neither Bordoni or co-stars Norma Terris, Helen Ford, and Tullio Carminati could save the operetta *Great Lady*, even though it had music by Frederick Loewe (pre-Alan Jay Lerner), but her Broadway swan-song, Irving Berlin's *Louisiana Purchase* (1940), in the company of William Gaxton, Vera Zorina, and Victor Moore, was a much better prospect, and ran for 444 performances. Bordini appeared in the movie version in 1942, having been to Hollywood previously to film one of her other stage successes, *Paris* (1929), in which she co-starred with the suave English song and dance man, Jack Buchanan. In the same year she sang 'Just An Hour Of Love' in the lavish all-star movie *The Show Of Shows*. The song was one of her many recordings, and she also had record hits with 'So This Is Love' (1924) and 'This Means Nothing To Me' (1926). Throughout her career, Bordoni also appeared in the non-musical theatre, regional productions, and vaudeville. Towards the end of her life, she took over the role of Bloody Mary from Diosa Costello during the US road tour of *South Pacific*, which set out in 1950 and ran for nearly five years.

BORN TO BOOGIE

The word 'boogie' became synonymous with Marc Bolan's career. As an adjective, it describes the style of music purveyed by his group, T. Rex, who emerged from the UK 'underground' scene to become one of the 70s' leading chart attractions. Bolan loved pop's tradition and was quick to capitalize on this success with a feature film. Released in 1973, *Born To Boogie* encapsulates the phenomenon dubbed 'T. Rextacy', showcasing the singer at the height of his popularity. Former Beatles drummer Ringo Starr - who understood about being the subject of fan worship - guested alongside Elton John. The film itself revolves around a T. Rex concert at Wembley, and features some of the group's most popular numbers, including 'Hot Love', 'Get It On', 'Jeepster' and 'Telegram Sam'. Bolan also recites one of his poems.

BORN TO DANCE

Eleanor Powell, one of the big screen's most accomplished tap dancers, was the star of this 1937 MGM release in which two of Cole Porter's all-time standards, 'I've Got You Under My Skin' and 'Easy To Love', were introduced. James Stewart's charming version of the latter song came during one of the film's quieter moments in Jack McGowan and Sid Silvers' screenplay, during which a group of sailors on shore leave find themselves mixed up in the world of showbusiness. After the usual complications, Stewart ends up with Powell, of course, who gets her big chance on Broadway when replacing Virginia Bruce, the indisposed (and extremely temperamental) star of the show. For maximum enjoyment of this film, the fact that Powell is a dancer and Bruce a singer is an issue that is better ignored. Virginia Bruce is the lucky lady who is given first chance at 'I've Got You Under My Skin', and Powell is particularly scintillating on 'Rap Tap On Wood' and the spectacular finale, 'Swingin' The Jinx Away', which takes place on the foredeck of a battleship populated by an enormous cast and a band that looks as if it should be in *The Music Man*. The rest of the classy Porter numbers included 'Hey, Babe, Hey', 'Rolling Home', 'Entrance Of Lucy James', and 'Love Me, Love My Pekinese', an amusing item given the full treatment by Bruce. Two of Stewart's shipmates, Buddy Ebsen and Sid Silvers, were prominent in a lively cast that also included Frances Langford and Una Merkel. The spirited choreography was by Dave Gould, and the picture was directed by Roy Del Routh.

BORN TO SWING

An outstanding documentary made in 1973 by John Jeremy, which draws on interviews (with Buck Clayton, John Hammond, Andy Kirk, Gene Krupa and others), still photographs (by Valerie Wilmer), archive film of the Count Basie band of the early 40s, and, most tellingly, ex-Basie sidemen in musical action. Among those still playing (in 1972) and swinging magnificently, are Eddie Durham, Jo Jones, Joe Newman, Gene Ramey, Buddy Tate, Earle Warren and Dicky Wells. Made in the UK and first screened on BBC TV, the film has a linking commentary spoken by Humphrey Lyttelton.

BOUBLIL, ALAIN

b. 5 March 1941, Tunis, Tunisia. A librettist and lyricist, Boublil's first musical, the rock opera *La Revolution Francaise* in 1973, marked the beginning of his collaboration with Claude-Michel Schönberg. Boublil co-produced the double-gold record album of the show which sold in excess of 350,000 copies. His original conception of the musical *Les Misérables* brought them together again in 1978, and, after two years of work, the show was produced at the Palais des Sports in Paris in September 1980. Three years later, Boublil was involved with two ex-members of Abba, Björn Ulvaeus and Benny Andersson, in a production of *Abbacadabra* at the Lyric Theatre, Hammersmith. In 1985, *Les Misérables* (with English lyrics by Herbert Kretzmer) began its London run, and, in January 1994, overtook *Jesus Christ Superstar* as the third longest-running London musical. After the show opened on Broadway in 1987, Boublil won two Tony Awards, and a Grammy for best Original Cast album. Boublil and Schönberg's latest blockbuster, *Miss Saigon*, hit the West End in 1989, and repeated its success in New York two years later. Impresario Cameron Mackintosh, who produced both hit shows, premiered two more of Boublil and Schönberg's compositions, 'Rhapsody For Piano And Orchestra' and 'Symphonic Suite', at London's Royal Albert Hall in 1992. In 1996, Boublil, Schönberg, and Mackintosh collaborated on a musical adaptation of the sixteenth-century story of mistaken identity, *Martin Guerre*, which folded after a 20-month run in London, only to be revived at the UK regional West Yorkshire Playhouse in November 1998.

BOUND FOR GLORY

Released in 1976, *Bound For Glory* relates the early years of folk-singer Woody Guthrie, taking its title from his enthralling autobiography. Former *Kung Fu* star David Carradine performs creditably in this representation of the artist's formative years, which he spent traversing the USA of the Depression era. Indeed, the images of dust-bowl drought were so acute that photographer Haskell Wexler was nominated for an Academy Award. Director Hal Ashby made several adjustments for dramatic effect. Guthrie's real-life travelling companion, Cisco Houston, was replaced by fictional character Ozark Blue, and several of the featured songs were actually written after the period in question. These minor quibbles aside, *Bound For Glory* is a fitting tribute to one of the 20th century's most influential musicians. Woody Guthrie was the father of modern American folk-song and brought new perspectives to melody and lyrical content, inspiring the whole folk revival movement of the 50s and 60s. As well as Guthrie's own performances, *Bound For Glory* includes Carradine's versions of classic songs such as 'This Land Is Your Land', 'Do Ri Me', 'Pastures Of Plenty' and 'Roll On Columbia'. In addition, the soundtrack also features performances by Guthrie acolytes Country Joe MacDonald, Odetta, the Weavers and Judy Collins, as well as the subject's son, Arlo Guthrie.

BOWERS, ROBERT HOOD

b. 24 May 1877, Chambersburg, Pennsylvania, USA, d. 29 December 1941, New York, USA. A composer for the musical theatre in the early part of the 20th century, Bowers studied at Franklin & Marshall College in Lancaster, Pennsylvania, and received a thorough musical education. In 1903 he collaborated with librettist and lyricist Raymond Peck on the score for *Rubes And Roses*, which played briefly at the La Salle Theatre in Chicago. In the following year he made his Broadway debut, working with Richard Carle on *The Maid And The Mummy*, which featured veteran Annie Yeamans. From then on, he contributed scores, or occasional songs, to a number of shows of variable quality, including *The Vanderbilt Cup* (1906), *The Hoyden* (1907), *Mary's Lamb* (1908), *The Silver Star* (1909), *The Wife Tamers* (1910, Chicago), *A Certain Party* (1911), *The Red Rose* (1911), *The Spring Maid* (1911), *The Rose Maid* (1912), and *A Lonely Romeo* (1919). His best-known song, 'The Moon Shines On The Moonshine' (written with Francis De Witt), was introduced by ex-*Ziegfeld Follies* star, Bert Williams, making his final Broadway appearance in the revue *Broadway Brevities Of 1920*. After an absence of some years, Bowers' own Broadway swansong was *Oh, Ernest!* (1927), a musical adaptation of Oscar Wilde's *The Importance Of Being Earnest*. Bowers also conducted orchestras on radio and in recording studios, and in the last years of his life served as the musical director of The School of Radio Technique.

BOY FRIEND, THE

Despite a quiet opening at London's Players' Theatre in April 1953, Sandy Wilson's stage musical *The Boy Friend* became a huge popular success after transferring to Wyndham's Theatre in the West End on 14 January 1954. An affectionate pastiche of the musical theatre of the 20s, the show starred Anthony Hayes, Hugh Paddick, Denise Hurst, Joan Gadsdon, Juliet Hunt, Beryl Cooke, Joan Sterndale Bennett, Larry Drew, John Rutland, and Anne Rogers, who came in 48 hours before it was due to open. Wilson wrote the book as well as the delightful score, which included several memorable numbers such as 'It's Never Too Late To Fall In Love', 'Won't You Charleston With Me', 'I Could Be Happy With You', 'Fancy Forgetting', 'The Boy Friend', 'Poor Little Pierrette' and the wistful 'A Room In Bloomsbury'. While *The Boy Friend* settled in for a run of 2,084 performances in London, Julie Andrews made her Broadway debut in the US production which opened at the Royale Theatre on 30 September 1954 and ran for well over a year. A major New York revival was mounted in 1958, and London audiences enjoyed the show again in 1967 and 1984. A 40th anniversary revival opened at the Players' Theatre in April 1994, before embarking on a UK tour. It was directed by Maria Charles who played the role of Dulcie in the 1954 production. Another survivor from the original show was John Rutland, who recreated the part of Lord Brockhurst. The 'disastrous' 1971 film version, which starred Twiggy and future Broadway star Tommy Tune, was directed by Ken Russell.

BOY FROM OZ, THE

Australia's first major home-grown musical since Manning Clark's *History Of Australia* flopped some 10 years previously, the immensely entertaining show *The Boy From Oz* sang and danced its way into Her Majesty's Theatre, Sydney, on 5 March 1998. Playwright Nick Enright researched, wrote, and edited the piece which was based on the life story of Australian singer and composer Peter Allen. Todd McKenney played Allen, who was spotted by Judy Garland (Chrissie Amphlett, 'lights up the stage') in 1964 while he was appearing with a trio at the Hong Kong Hilton, and joined her on concert tours worldwide. He subsequently married her daughter, Liza Minnelli (Angela Toohey) in 1967 (divorced 1970), developed a highly individual cabaret act, and wrote, or co-wrote several hit songs which were recorded by himself and artists such as Olivia Newton-John, Helen Reddy, Melissa Manchester, Ray Peterson and Manfred Mann. He died of an AIDS-related illness in June 1992, after playing his last concert in Sydney, and Enright re-creates the setting, although not the actual occasion, in order to tell Allen's story in a series of non-linear flashbacks. It also gives the perfect excuse for introducing many Allen numbers, including 'I'd Rather Leave While I'm In Love', the Oscar-winning '(Arthur's Theme) Best That You Can Do', 'I Honestly Love You', 'Don't Cry Out Loud', a nod to his hometown, 'Tenterfield Saddler', the Quantas Airlines theme, 'I Still Call Australia Home', his own signature song, 'I Go To Rio', and a tribute to Garland, 'Quiet Please, There's A Lady On Stage'. Jilly

Perryman played Marion Woolnough, Allen's mother, and Murray Bartlett was his boyfriend Greg Connell. Among the other credits were Gale Edwards (director), Anthony Van Laast (choreography), Peter Davidson (sets), and Roger Kirk (costumes).

BOY, THE

This highly successful musical comedy opened at the Adelphi Theatre in London on 14 September 1917. Fred Thompson's book was based on Arthur Wing Pinero's 1885 farce *The Magistrate*, and the score was the work of Lionel Monckton and Howard Talbot (music) and Adrian Ross and Percy Greenbank (lyrics). W.H. Berry played the metropolitan magistrate who goes out on a spree with his 19-year-old step-son (Donald Calthrop). However, the boy's mother (Maisie Gay) has pretended that he is only 14 in order that she should appear younger. Mix in a shabby hotel and a police raid, and it is hardly surprising that amid the ensuing mayhem, the magistrate finds himself in the unfortunate position of sentencing his own wife. Berry's 'I Want To Go To Bye-Bye' was a consistent audience-pleaser, and the other songs included 'Little Miss Melody', 'When The Heart Is Young', 'A Game That Ends With A Kiss', 'Young Folks And Old Folks', 'It's The Drum', and 'I've Always Got Time To Talk To You'. Among the cast were Heather Thatcher, Billie Carleton, C.M. Lowne, Nellie Taylor, and Peter Gawthorne. *The Boy* ran on for an impressive 801 performances, and just a few months before it closed in August 1919, a retitled version, *Good Morning, Judge*, opened on Broadway. It played for 140 performances, and two early George Gershwin numbers, 'I Was So Young (You Were So Beautiful)' (lyric: Irving Caesar, Alfred Bryan) and 'There's More To The Kiss Than XXX' (lyric: Caesar), were interpolated into the score.

BOYS FROM SYRACUSE, THE

Richard Rodgers and Lorenz Hart were in the autumn of their partnership (Rodgers and Oscar Hammerstein II's *Oklahoma!* was only five years away) when they wrote this appealing score for what is said to be the first musical based on a play by William Shakespeare. Librettist-director-producer George Abbott's adaptation of *The Comedy Of Errors* incorporated a variety of characters with names such as Antiphulus, Luce, Dromio, and Luciana, in a scenario that was based in Asia Minor. The story of mixed-up twins bordered on farce: 'Did you bring your harp?'. 'No'. 'Good, then you can pick on me.' The cast included the well-known comedy performer Jimmy Savo, Teddy Hart (Lorenz Hart's brother who, rather conveniently, bore an uncanny resemblance to Savo), Eddie Albert, Wynn Murray, Ronald Graham, Muriel Angelus, Marcy Wescott, Betty Bruce, and Burl Ives (as Tailor's Apprentice). Rodgers and Hart's score contained three of their all-time standards: 'Sing For Your Supper', 'This Can't Be Love', and 'Falling In Love With Love', along with the lovely ballad 'You Have Cast Your Shadow On The Sea'. There were also a few point numbers such as 'What Can You Do With A Man?', 'Dear Old Syracuse', 'The Shortest Day Of The Year', 'Oh, Diogenes', and 'He And She'. The show, which began its run at the Alvin Theatre on 23 November 1938, ran for a somewhat disappointing 235 performances, but the 1963 off-Broadway revival stayed in New York for over twice as long. In November 1963 *The Boys From Syracuse* had its London premiere with a cast that included UK comedians Bob Monkhouse and Ronnie Corbett. Nearly 30 years later, in the summer of 1991, Londoners had another chance to savour the show's zany antics and melodic score when it played a limited season at the Open Air Theatre in Regent's Park, and won a Laurence Olivier Award for best revival. The 1940 film version starred Allan Jones, Joe Penner, and Martha Raye. Other well-known musicals based on Shakespeare's works include *Kiss Me, Kate* (*The Taming Of The Shrew*) and *West Side Story* (*Romeo And Juliet*).

BRAHAM, PHILIP

b. 18 June 1881, London, England, d. 2 May 1934, London, England. Braham studied at Cambridge University before embarking on a career as a composer for the theatre. He wrote music mostly for the smart and sophisticated revues of the day, and also for some musical comedies. Among his collaborators were Fred Thompson, Eric Blore, Sydney Blow, Howard Talbot, Douglas Hoare, Frank Tours, G.H. Clutsam, Herbert Haines, Nat D. Ayer, Kenneth Duffield, Reginald Arkell, Max Darewski, Davy Burnaby, Donovan Parsons, Ronald Jeans, and Noël Coward. He provided occasional songs or complete scores for numerous productions, including *Violet And Pink* (1914), *Beauties* (1914), *Mr. Manhattan* (1916), *See-Saw* (1916), *Back To Blighty* (1916), *Bubbly* (1917), *The Bing Boys Are Here* (1916), *Telling The Tale* (1918), *Tails Up* (1918), *The Officers' Mess* (1918), *Jumble Sale* (1920), *Now And Then* (1921), *Pot Luck* (1921), *Battling Butler* (1922), *Rats!* (1923), *London Calling!* (1923), *Boodle* (1924), *Up With The Lark* (1925), *On With The Dance* (1925), and *The Co-Optimists*, editions of which were presented from 1921-35. His best-known song is 'Limehouse Blues', which he wrote with Douglas Furber. It was introduced by Teddie Gerard in the 1921 West End revue *A To Z*, and drew a sensational response from New York audiences three years later when it was performed by Gertrude Lawrence in the acclaimed *Charlot's Revue*. Subsequently, it more or less became her personal property, and was sung by Julie Andrews in the 1968 Lawrence biopic *Star!* More than 20 years earlier the song had been heard on the soundtrack of *Ziegfeld Follies* (1946) in an effective scene that featured Fred Astaire and Lucille Bremer. After providing the London musical theatre with some of its brightest and most danceable tunes for more than a decade, in the early 30s Braham served as musical director at Wembley Studios for a number of infant talking pictures, such as *City Of Song* (1930), *Wedding Rehearsal* (1932), and *The First Mrs. Fraser* (1932).

BRAMBLE, MARK

b. 7 December 1950, Maryland, USA. A librettist and director for the musical theatre, Bramble was raised on his parents' farm in Maryland. The retired actress Tallulah Bankhead was a neighbour and family friend, and she was instrumental in young Bramble being offered a job in the offices of New York impresario David Merrick. After four years of invaluable work experience, he left and began the long haul of writing shows - and persuading someone to produce them. He began his two major works in the early 70s, but they had to wait. After working off-off-Broadway and in the regional theatre in the mid- to late 70s, he collaborated with veteran librettist and lyricist Michael Stewart on the book for *The Grand Tour*, a show that was based on Franz Werfel's play *Jacobowsky And The Colonel*, and played for 61 performances at the Palace Theatre on Broadway early in 1979. He worked with Stewart again for the 1980 off-Broadway production of *Elizabeth And Essex*, adapted from Maxwell Anderson's *Elizabeth And The Queen*. Bramble's big breakthrough came in April 1980, when the first of those two previously mentioned early works, *Barnum*, for which he had written the book, opened at the St. James Theatre in New York, and ran for 854 performances. There was more to come in August of that same year, when a stage version of the 30s' much loved movie musical, *42nd Street*, with a Stewart-Bramble libretto, began its run of 3,486 performances at the Winter Garden. After this great success, the remainder of the 80s was not so fruitful. In 1983, his revised version of *The Three Musketeers*, which was also his first show as a director, folded after only eight performances. This bitter disappointment, and the experience of being badly mugged on a New York street, persuaded him to relocate to London in 1985. Since then his projects have included *Fat Pig* (1987, Leicester Haymarket), an adaptation of Jérome Savary's Paris production of a musical based on Colin McNaughton's children's book, involving, like *Barnum*, circus tricks and acrobats, and *Notre Dame* (1991, Old Fire Station, Oxford), a musical based on Victor Hugo's *Notre Dame De Paris*. In 1992, Bramble wrote and directed *Someone Else's Rainbow*, a one-woman show about Judy Garland, starring Elaine Loudon, which was presented for the benefit of London Lighthouse. He also spends a great deal of his time overseeing and directing productions of *Barnum* and *42nd Street* around the world.

BRATTON, JOHN W.

b. 21 January 1867, Wilmington, Delaware, USA, d. 7 February 1947, Brooklyn, New York, USA. A composer, producer, and performer, Bratton studied at the Philadelphia College of Music before becoming a singer and actor in various musical shows. Eventually, he joined with Johnny Leffler to form the production company Leffler And Bratton, and in the first decade of the twentieth century also composed all or most of the scores for the musical comedies *Star And Garter* (1900), *Hodge, Podge, & Co.* (1900), *The Liberty Belles* (1901), *The Man From China* (1904), *The Pearl And The Pumpkin* (1905), *Buster Brown* (1905), and *The Newlyweds And Their Baby* (1909). During this period, he also had occasional songs in numerous other projects, and among his appealing numbers were 'In A Cozy Corner' (popularized under the title of 'My Cosey Corner Girl' by Henry Burr, and as 'My Cozy Corner Girl' by Harry Macdonough), 'I'm On The Water Wagon Now', 'The Sunshine Of Paradise Alley', 'A Picture No Artist Can Paint', 'I Love You In The Same Old Way', 'Henrietta, Have You Met Her?', 'He Was A Sailor', 'In A Garden Of Faded Flowers', 'You'll Always Be Sweet Sixteen To Me', 'Sweetheart, Let's Grow Old Together', 'My Sunbeam From The South', 'I'll Be Your Honey', 'Mender Of Broken

Dreams' and 'Loving Time'. His collaborators included Paul West, Chas Noel Douglas, Nat D. Ayer, Walter Ford, and Leo Edwardes. Perhaps his most enduring tune - especially for several generations of children - is 'The Teddy Bears' Picnic'. It was written around 1907, and British songwriter Jimmy Kennedy added the well-known lyric in 1932. The most popular recording of the song in Britain was made by the BBC Dance Orchestra directed by Henry Hall, with a vocal by Val Rosing.

BREAKING GLASS

This 1980 film covers the time-honoured plot of a singer's rise to stardom and the subsequent pressures that cause her to crack. New wave music and clashes between the National Front and the Anti-Nazi League provide the only deviation in this clichéd 'sex and drugs and rock 'n' roll' pot-boiler. Hazel O'Connor took the role of the 'tortured' artist in question, while *Quadrophenia* star Phil Daniels also appeared in a cast that included Zoot Money and former Heavy Metal Kids vocalist Gary Holton. Producer Tony Visconti was the film's musical director while O'Connor sang and composed each of the soundtrack songs, bar one that featured Victy Silva. The *Breaking Glass* album reached number 5 in the UK chart, while 'Eighth Day' reached the same position in the singles chart. For all its punk bravura, *Breaking Glass* owed more to *A Star Is Born* than *Jubilee*.

BRECHT, BERTOLT

b. 10 February 1898, Augsburg, Bavaria, d. 14 August 1956, Berlin, Germany. A controversial playwright, poet and lyricist, Brecht was educated at Munich University and had established himself as a writer by the early 20s. He toured the music halls and cabarets in Germany and Scandinavia during the rest of the decade, singing and playing his own songs. Many of these reflected his outspoken political beliefs, and in 1941 he sought exile in the USA to escape the Nazi regime. Apart from Paul Dessau, who wrote the music for many of his plays, Brecht's main collaborator was composer Kurt Weill. Their most celebrated work was *The Threepenny Opera*, which had its first English language production on Broadway in 1933, and has been revised and revived many times over the years. Brecht's other shows to be seen in New York included *Brecht On Brecht* (1962), *Arturo UI* (a play with incidental music by Jule Styne, 1963), the opera *The Rise And Fall Of The City Of Mahagonny* (1970), and *Happy End* (1977). The latter starred Meryl Streep, and was originally written with Weill for Berlin in 1929. In 1994 a revue entitled *Brecht In Hollywood*, with a cast of three headed by Vanessa Redgrave, played the London Fringe. A year later a caustic biography accused Brecht of being a misogynist and an anti-Semite, and suggested that 80 per cent of *The Threepenny Opera* was, apparently, the work of Elizabeth Hauptmann. Also in 1995, a new production of *The Rise And Fall Of The City Of Mahagonny* was presented by the English National Opera at the Coliseum in London. As the 90s drew to a close, Brecht's straight plays, such as *Mother Courage* and his final masterpiece, *The Caucasian Chalk Circle*, finally seemed to be slowly finding favour again, while artists such as Lotte Lenya, Liliane Montevecchi,

and Eva Meier, continued to perform his songs, most often in cabaret. In 1998, his centenary year, as well as the numerous inevitable revivals of *The Threepenny Opera*, there was a re-staging of *Happy End* by the European Opera Company in Chicago.

● FURTHER READING: *The Life And Lies Of Bertolt Brecht*, John Fuegi.

BREWSTER'S MILLIONS

This 1935 musical is often regarded as British song-and-dance-man Jack Buchanan's best home-grown film - the qualification is necessary because of his appearance with Fred Astaire in the wonderful Hollywood movie of *The Band Wagon* (1953). As Jack Brewster, Buchanan is faced with the farcical task of losing £500,000 in a couple of months in order to inherit the sum of £6 million. Inevitably, everything he invests in - including a musical show which is supposed to be a guaranteed flop - yields a handsome profit. After buying a lavish yacht and taking a large party to Monte Carlo and Italy, he finances a local carnival and evades potential kidnappers by functioning as the rear end of a papier-maché dragon. All this provides a great excuse for some extremely elaborate production numbers, one of which, 'The Caranga', bore an uncanny resemblance to 'The Carioca', a dance that became popular after it was featured in the Fred Astaire-Ginger Rogers movie, *Flying Down To Rio*. Thornton Freeland, the director of that film, also directed *Brewster's Millions*. Composer Ray Noble and lyricist Douglas Furber contributed a further three songs, 'I Think I Can', 'One Good Tune Deserves Another', and 'Pull Down The Blind'. Surrounded by a host of lovely girls and some lovely scenery, Buchanan is in his element, both comically and musically. He receives strong support from Lili Damita and the rest of the cast, which included Nancy O'Neil, Sydney Fairbrother, Ian McLean, Allan Aynesworth, Lawrence Hanray, Dennis Hoey, Henry Wenman, Amy Venesa, Sebastian Shaw, and Antony Holles. Herbert Wilcox was the producer for the British and Dominion Films Corporation. The screenplay, by Arthur Wimperis, Paul Gangelin, Douglas Furber, Clifford Grey, Donovan Pedelty and Wolfgan Wilhem, was based on the 1906 play by George Barr McCutcheon and Winchell Smith, which itself was adapted from McCutcheon's original novel. *Brewster's Millions* was remade in America in 1945 (with Dennis O'Keefe) and 1985 (with Richard Pryor), and another version, entitled *Three On A Spree*, was produced in the UK in 1961 starring Jack Watling. Due no doubt to inflation, Brewster now had to get rid of £1 million in order to inherit £8 million. The 1951 West End musical *Zip Goes A Million*, starring George Formby, was yet another production based on the same format.

BRIAN, DONALD

b. 17 February 1877, St. John's, Newfoundland, d. 22 December 1948, Great Neck, New York, USA. An actor, dancer, and singer, who is usually described by those who saw him as 'handsome, with a round, dimpled face and wavy hair.' After moving to the USA, Brian played in a few straight and musical provincial productions, including *The Chaperons*, before making his first musical appearances on Broadway at the Winter Garden on the roof of the New York Theatre in two frothy confections, *The Supper Club* (1901) and *The Belle Of Broadway* (1902). He also played Captain Arthur Donegal in the 1902 revival of *Floradora* before being noticed by the great showman George M. Cohan, who gave Brian good roles in *Little Johnny Jones* (1904) and *Forty-Five Minutes From Broadway* (1906). After enjoying a personal triumph as the young attaché Prince Danilo, co-starring with Ethel Jackson in the legendary operetta *The Merry Widow* (1907), Brian went on to star in a string of mostly successful musicals, three of them in the company of Julia Sanderson, *The Siren* (1911), *The Girl From Utah* (1914, in which the duo introduced Jerome Kern and Herbert Reynolds' enduring 'They Didn't Believe Me'), and *Sybil* (1916). The remainder included *The Dollar Princess* (1909), *The Marriage Market* (1913), *Her Regiment* (1917), *The Girl Behind The Gun* (1918), *Buddies* (1919), *The Chocolate Soldier* (1921, revival), *Up She Goes* (1922), *No, No, Nanette* (1926, US tour), *Castles In The Air* (1927, replacement), *Yes, Yes, Yvette* (1927), *Music In The Air* (1933, replacement), and *Very Warm For May* (1939, Kern's final theatre score).

BRICE, FANNY

b. 29 October 1891, New York City, New York, USA, d. 29 May 1951. In her early teens Brice appeared on the stage in both legitimate musical shows and in vaudeville. In 1910 she was booked into impresario Florenz Ziegfeld's lavish *Ziegfeld Follies* and was the outstanding star in several subsequent editions of those revues for the next dozen years, gradually rising to become one of Broadway's biggest attractions. She also appeared in other Broadway shows including *The Honeymoon Express* (1913), *Nobody Home* (1915), *Music Box Revue* (1924), *Fioretta* (1929), *Sweet And Low* (1930) and *Crazy Quilt* (1931). For the most part her act consisted of comic patter and novelty songs, such as 'Second Hand Rose', which she sang in a Brooklyn dialect. Despite her plain features and gawky stage presence, or perhaps because of the affinity audiences felt with her for these characteristics, she enjoyed great success with torch songs, including 'When A Woman Loves A Man' and 'My Man', the number with which she was most closely linked. Other songs associated with her include 'I Found A Million-Dollar Baby In A Five And Ten Cent Store', I'm An Indian', and 'I'd Rather Be Blue Over You (Than Be Happy With Somebody Else)'. In 1928 she appeared in her first film, *My Man*, but her real forte was the stage and she made only spasmodic journeys to Hollywood for *Night Club* (1929), *Be Yourself* (1930), *The Great Ziegfeld* (1936), *Everybody Sing* (1938), and *Ziegfeld Follies* (1945). Brice was also successful on radio, appearing in the title role of the popular series *Baby Snooks*, which ran for six years from 1939. She died in 1951, but in 1964 her career and chequered private life (she married gambler Nicky Arnstein and showman Billy Rose) became the subject of a hit Broadway show, *Funny Girl*, which had a score by Jule Styne and Bob Merrill and starred Barbra Streisand. It ran for 1,348 performances in New York, and four years later provided the basis for a successful film, and its 1975 sequel, *Funny Lady*. Two other films were (allegedly) based on her life: *Broadway Thru A Keyhole*

(1933) and *Rose Of Washington Square* (1938).
● FURTHER READING: *The Fabulous Fanny-The Story Of Fanny Brice*, N. Katkov. *Funny Woman: The Life And Times Of Fanny Brice*, Barbara W. Grossman. *Fanny Brice-The Original Funny Girl*, Herbert G. Goldman.

BRICUSSE, LESLIE

b. 29 January 1931, London, England. A composer, lyricist, librettist and screenwriter, Bricusse was influenced by the MGM musicals of the 40s, particularly *Words And Music*, the Richard Rodgers and Lorenz Hart biopic. He originally intended to be a journalist, but, while studying at Cambridge University, started to write, direct and appear in the *Footlights Reviews*. In 1953, he wrote the music and lyrics (with Robin Beaumont) for *Lady At the Wheel*, a musical with the Monte Carlo rally as its setting, which included songs such as 'The Early Birdie', 'Pete Y'Know', 'Love Is' and a comedy tango, 'Siesta'. It was staged at the local Arts Theatre, and, five years later, had a limited run in the West End. From 1954-5, Bricusse had appeared on the London stage himself with a theatrical legend, in *An Evening With Beatrice Lillie*. For a while during the 50s, he was under contract as a writer at Pinewood Film Studios, and in 1954, wrote the screenplay and the songs (with Beaumont) for *Charley Moon*, which starred Max Bygraves. The popular singer/comedian took one of the numbers, 'Out Of Town', into the UK Top 20, and it gained Bricusse his first Ivor Novello Award: he won several others, including one for 'My Kind Of Girl' (words and music by Bricusse), which was a UK Top 5 hit for Matt Monro in 1961. Bricusse also wrote a good deal of special material for Bygraves, including one of his 'catchphrase' songs, 'A Good Idea - Son!'. Early in 1961, Bricusse went to New York to write for another Beatrice Lillie revue, taking Anthony Newley with him to develop ideas for a show of their own. The result, *Stop The World - I Want To Get Off*, written in around three weeks, opened in London's West End in July of that year, and stayed there until November 1962. It later ran for over 500 performances on Broadway, and was filmed in 1966. Book, music and lyrics were jointly credited to Bricusse and Newley, and the latter starred as the central character, Littlechap, in London and New York. The score included several hit songs, including 'What Kind Of Fool Am I?', 'Once In A Lifetime' and 'Gonna Build A Mountain', as well as other, more specialized numbers, such as 'Lumbered', 'Typically English' and 'Someone Nice Like You'. While Newley went off to appear in the offbeat, parochial movie *The World Of Sammy Lee*, Bricusse collaborated with Cyril Ornadel on the score for the musical *Pickwick* (1963), which starred the 'Goon with the golden voice', Harry Secombe, in the title role. His recording of the show's big ballad, 'If I Ruled The World', was a Top 20 hit in the UK, and, later, after the Broadway production had flopped, it became part of Tony Bennett's repertoire. Reunited in 1964, Bricusse and Newley's next major stage project, *The Roar Of The Greasepaint - The Smell Of The Crowd* (1965), appeared similar to their previous effort, a moral tale of a downtrodden little man, bucking the system. It toured (Bricusse: 'We managed to empty every provincial theatre in England'), but did not play the West End. Bricusse, and others, felt that comedian Norman Wisdom was miscast in the central role, and Newley took over for the Broadway run of 232 performances. Once again, however, the hit songs were there - in this case, 'Who Can I Turn To?' and 'A Wonderful Day Like Today', plus other items such as 'This Dream', 'The Beautiful Land', 'The Joker', 'Where Would You Be Without Me?', 'Nothing Can Stop Me Now' and 'Feeling Good'. The latter number was popularized in the USA by Joe Sherman, and received an impressive, extended treatment from Steve Winwood's UK rock group, Traffic, on their live *Last Exit* (1969). In 1964, Bricusse and Newley turned their attention to the big screen, providing the lyric to John Barry's music for the title song to the James Bond movie *Goldfinger* (1964), sung by Shirley Bassey. Bricusse and Barry later wrote another Bond theme for *You Only Live Twice* (1968), popularized by Nancy Sinatra. In 1967, Bricusse contributed the screenplay and the complete song score to *Doctor Dolittle*, which starred Newley, along with Rex Harrison, who sang the Oscar-winning 'Talk To The Animals'. Considered an 'expensive dud', there was no mention of a *Doctor Dolittle II*. Far more to the public's taste was Roald Dahl's *Willy Wonka And The Chocolate Factory* (1971). Bricusse and Newley's score contained 'The Candy Man', a song that gave Sammy Davis Jnr. a US number 1 the following year. Davis was one of the songwriting team's favourite people - Bricusse estimates that he recorded at least 60 of his songs, including a complete album of *Doctor Dolittle*. Davis also starred in a revival of *Stop The World - I Want To Get Off* during the 1978/9 Broadway season.

After writing several numbers for a 1971 US television adaptation of *Peter Pan*, which starred Danny Kaye and Mia Farrow, Bricusse and Newley returned to the stage with *The Good Old Bad Old Days*. Newley directed and starred in the show, which ran for 10 months in London, and included the jolly title song and several other appealing numbers, such as 'I Do Not Love You', 'It's A Musical World', 'The People Tree' and 'The Good Things In Life'. Since then, their back catalogue has been repackaged in productions such as *The Travelling Music Show* (1978), with Bruce Forsyth, and *Once Upon A Song*, in which Newley occasionally appears when he is not singing for big dollars in Las Vegas. Also in 1978, Bricusse collaborated with composer Armando Trovajoli on *Beyond The Rainbow*, an English language version of the Italian musical *Aggiungi Una Posta Alla Tavola*, which ran for six months in London - a good deal longer than his own *Kings And Clowns*. He also wrote some new songs for a Chichester Festival Theatre production of his film score for *Goodbye, Mr Chips* (1982). By then, he was generally wearing his Hollywood hat, and had received Oscar nominations for his work on *Goodbye, Mr Chips* (1969, original song score, with John Williams), *Scrooge* (1970, original song score with Ian Fraser and Herbert W. Spencer, and his own song, 'Thank You Very Much'), *That's Life* (1986, 'Life In a Looking Glass', with Henry Mancini), *Home Alone* (1990, 'Somewhere In My Memory', with John Williams), and *Hook* (1991, 'When You're Alone', with John Williams). He won his second Academy Award in 1982, in collaboration with Mancini, for the original song score to *Victor/Victoria*. Bricusse and Newley were induct-ed into the Songwriters' Hall Of Fame in 1989, a year that otherwise proved something of a disappointment for the partners. For instance, an updated version of *Stop The World*, directed by, and starring Newley, staggered along for five weeks in London, and Bricusse's *Sherlock Holmes*, with Ron Moody and Liz Robertson, opened there as well, to disappointing reviews. *Sherlock Holmes* resurfaced in 1993, and toured the UK with Robert Powell in the title role. In the same year, Bricusse's stage adaptation of *Scrooge*, with Newley in the title role, was presented for the first time. Also in 1993, Harry Secombe recreated his orginal role in *Pickwick* at Chichester and in the West End. In October 1995, a stage version of *Victor/Victoria*, starring Julie Andrews, opened on Broadway, to be followed in April 1997 by *Jekyll And Hyde*, on which librettist/lyricist Bricusse collaborated with composer Frank Wildhorn. In July 1998, a stage version of *Doctor Dolittle*, for which Bricusse wrote the book, music and lyrics, opened at the Labatt's Apollo Theatre in West London.

BRIGADOON (FILM MUSICAL)

Despite the acknowledged brilliance of the MGM team that transferred the 1947 Broadway musical *Brigadoon* to the big screen (notably producer Arthur Freed and director Vincente Minnelli), for many, the magic touch so evident in their other creations was absent in this 1954 film. Alan Jay Lerner's mystical tale is set in a Scottish Highland village that only comes to life once every hundred years, and where two Americans, Tommy Albright (Gene Kelly) and Jeff Douglas (Van Johnson), happen to stray during a hunting holiday. Albright falls in love with Fiona (Cyd Charisse), one of the townspeople; initially, the thoughts of his life and girl back home in the USA draw him away and he is unable to make the sacrifice and remain part of the sleeping village. It is only a minor miracle brought about by the strength of Tommy's love that reawakens the village temporarily so he can once again, and forever, be with his true love. Many reasons have been cited for the rather staged *Brigadoon* not working as effectively as other Freed creations. These include the decisions to photograph the film in Ansco Color and CinemaScope and not on location, owing to financial restraints, which resulted in the use of artificial-looking studio backdrops; the proliferation of highly unconvincing Scottish accents; and the exclusion of some of the show's most endearing numbers such as 'There But For You Go I' and 'Come To Me, Bend To Me'. However, despite these factors, the film, released in September 1954, certainly has its enchanting moments. Some sequences are widely considered to be misjudged, but it is hard to fault Charisse and Kelly (also the film's choreographer) when they are dancing to 'Heather On The Hill' (Charisse dubbed by Carole Richards), or Kelly's expression of joy in 'Almost Like Being In Love'. Other songs in what is a lovely score, written by Frederick Loewe, with charming lyrics from Alan Jay Lerner, included 'Brigadoon', 'Waitin' For My Dearie', 'Once In The Highlands', and the rousing ensemble piece 'I'll Go Home With Bonnie Jean'. Most of the comic moments are left to Van Johnson, who, as Kelly's cynical companion, prefers to dream with the help of alcohol rather than women. Despite its flaws, *Brigadoon*, with its romantic and fairytale atmosphere, is still fondly regarded by many admirers of film musicals.

BRIGADOON (STAGE MUSICAL)

This first major success for the team of Alan Jay Lerner and Frederick Loewe opened at the Ziegfeld Theatre in New York on 13 March 1947. Lerner's whimsical book is set in Scotland, where two Americans on holiday, Tommy Albright (David Brooks) and Jeff Douglas (George Keane), happen upon a quaint village. Tommy falls in love with a local girl, Fiona MacLaren (Marion Bell), only to be told that the village is only visible to earthly beings for one day each century - the rest of the time it sleeps. When Brigadoon vanishes Tommy returns to the USA, but his love for Fiona is so strong that he has to return to Scotland. Once there, the village is brought back to life just long enough for him to re-enter before the mists close around it again. Virginia Bosler played Fiona's sister Jeannie, ripe for marriage with Charlie Dalrymple (Lee Sullivan), and Pamela Britton was the 'marriage happy' Meg Brockie, with her eye on Jeff. All the numbers are highlights in Lerner and Loewe's exquisite score, including 'Almost Like Being In Love', 'The Heather On The Hill', 'I'll Go Home With Bonnie Jean', 'Waitin' For My Dearie', 'Come To Me, Bend To Me', 'The Love Of My Life', 'There But For You Go I', 'My Mother's Wedding Day', 'From This Day On', 'Once In The Highlands', 'Down On MacConnachy Square', and 'Brigadoon'. Agnes De Mille won a Tony Award for her outstanding, versatile dance direction, and the show ran for 581 performances. The 1949 London production, with Philip Hanna (Tommy), Patricia Hughes (Fiona), Hiram Sherman (Jeff), did even better, and stayed at His Majesty's Theatre for 685 performances. *Brigadoon* was revived on Broadway in 1980 - Meg Bussert (Fiona), Martin Vidnovic (Tommy), and in a 1986 production by the New York City Opera. London audiences applauded this delightful fantasy for 387 performances in Roger Redfarn's 1988 Victoria Palace presentation, with Jacinta Mulcahy (Fiona), Robert Meadmore (Tommy), Lesley Mackie (Meg), and Robin Nedwell (Jeff). The New York City Opera re-staged *Brigadoon* in 1991, and again in 1996. For the latter production, conductor John McGlinn reassembled three of the principals from his acclaimed 1992 recording of the show, Rebecca Luker (Fiona), Brent Barrett (Tommy), and Judy Kaye (Meg). *Brigadoon* was filmed in 1954 with Gene Kelly and Cyd Charisse.

BRIGHTMAN, SARAH

b. 14 August 1961, England. An actress and singer who first came to notice in 1978 when, with the dance group Hot Gossip, she made the UK Top 10 with the disco-pop single 'I Lost My Heart To A Starship Trooper'. It was all a far cry from her childhood ambition to become a ballet dancer. Three years after her chart success, she won a part in Andrew Lloyd Webber's musical *Cats*, and was noticed again - this time by the composer himself - and they were married in 1984. The marriage lasted for six years, and, during that time, Brightman became established as one of the premier leading ladies of the musical theatre. After *Cats*, she appeared for a season at the Old Vic in Frank

Dunlop's 1982 adaptation of *Masquerade*, and later in the year she was in Charles Strouse's short-lived musical *Nightingale*. All this time she was taking singing lessons, training her superb soprano voice so that she could undertake more demanding roles than those in conventional musical comedy. In 1984 she appeared in the television version of Lloyd Webber's *Song And Dance*, and also sang on the Top 30 album. A year later, she made her operatic debut in the role of Valencienne in *The Merry Widow* at Sadlers Wells, and gave several concerts of Lloyd Webber's *Requiem* in England and America, which resulted in another bestselling album. It also produced a Top 5 single, 'Pie Jesu', on which Brightman duetted with the 12-year-old Paul Miles-Kingston. In 1986 she enjoyed a great personal triumph when she co-starred with Michael Crawford in *The Phantom Of The Opera*, and recreated her role two years later on Broadway. She had UK Top 10 hits with three songs from the show, 'The Phantom Of The Opera' (with Steve Harley), 'All I Ask Of You' (with Cliff Richard) and 'Wishing You Were Somehow Here Again'. In the late 80s and early 90s, she toured many parts of the world, including Japan and the UK, in a concert production of *The Music Of Andrew Lloyd Webber*. In December 1991, at the end of the American leg of the tour, she took over the leading role of Rose in *Aspects Of Love* for the last few weeks of the Broadway run. She also joined the West End production for a time, but, while her presence was welcomed and her performance critically acclaimed, she was unable to prevent its closure in June 1992. In the same year Brightman was high in the UK chart again, this time duetting with opera singer José Carreras on the Olympic Anthem, 'Amigos Para Siempre (Friends For Life)', which was written, inevitably, by Andrew Lloyd Webber, with lyric by Don Black. In 1993 she made her debut in the straight theatre with appearances in *Trelawny Of The Wells* and *Relative Values*. For some years it had been forecast that Lloyd Webber would write a stage musical or film for her based on the life of Jessie Matthews, the graceful star of many 20s and 30s musicals, and to whom she bears an uncanny facial resemblance. However, in 1994 the composer dropped his option on Michael Thornton's biography of Matthews, and announced that there 'no further plans to develop the project'. Based mostly in Germany in the 90s, Brightman continued to perform in Australia, Canada, America and elsewhere. In 1997 her duet with the blind Tuscan tenor Andrea Bocelli, 'Time To Say Goodbye', topped the charts throughout Europe, and is reported to have 'gone platinum five times'. In the same year, her tour of the UK, in company with the English National Orchestra, included a concert at London's Royal Albert Hall. She had another surprise UK hit single in 1997 when 'Timeless' went near the top of the charts.

● ALBUMS: *Britten Folk Songs* (Angel 1988)★★★, with Peter Ustinov *Howard Blake: Granpa* (Columbia 1988)★★, *The Songs That Got Away* (Really Useful 1989)★★, *As I Came Of Age* (Polydor 1990)★★★, with José Carreras *Amigos Para Siempre* (East West 1992)★★★, *Dive* (1993)★★★, *Sings The Music Of Andrew Lloyd Webber* (Really Useful 1994)★★★, *Surrender: The Unexpected Songs* (Really Useful 1995)★★★, *Fly* (1995)★★★, *Just Show Me How To Love You* (1996)★★★, *Timeless* (1997)★★★,

Time To Say Goodbye (Nemo 1998)★★, *Eden* (Coalition/East West 1998)★★★, and Original Cast recordings.

BRING IN 'DA NOISE, BRING IN 'DA FUNK

Originally subtitled *A Rap/Tap Discourse On The Staying Power Of The Beat*, this revolutionary new musical opened off-Broadway at the 299-seater Joseph Papp Public Theatre on 15 November 1995. A few months later, after enjoying rave reviews and incredible audience reaction, it transferred uptown to the Ambassador Theatre (capacity 1,068) on 25 April. Conceived and directed by George C. Wolfe, from an idea by Wolfe and Savion Glover, it had a book by the poet Reg E. Gaines, and music by Daryl Waters, Zane Mark, and Ann Duquesnay. Glover, only 22 years old, was also responsible for the choreography - and for most of the fuss surrounding the show. He was the dynamic and mesmerizing Terpsichorean star in a production that purported - mainly via high-octane tap-dancing - to trace the history of the African-American experience in the USA. It took the form of a series of thematically linked vignettes dealing visually and musically with seminal events such as slavery and the law making the slaves' use of drums a criminal offence, brutal lynchings in the south, the migration to the industrial north, minstrels, Hollywood's trivialization of black artists, and the urban upheavals of the last 30 years. Also in the cast were four marvellously versatile tap-dancers, Vincent Bingham, Dule Hill, Baakari Wilder, and Jimmy Tate, along with blues singer Duquesnay, Jeffrey Wright, performer of Gaines's poems in-between the numbers, and two street percussionists, Jared Crawford and Raymond King, who performed an amazing duet on pots and pans. The explosive action was accompanied by an irrepressible score consisting of 'Bring In 'Da Noise, Bring In 'Da Funk', 'Slave Ships', 'Som'thin' From Nuthin'/The Circle Stomp', 'The Lynching Blues', 'Chicago Bound', 'I Got The Beat/Dark Tower', 'The Uncle Huck-A-Buck Song', 'The Lost Beat Swing', 'Them Conkheads', 'Hot Fun', 'Gospel/Hip Hop Rant'. The production was rated by critics as a 'brilliant work, a breakthrough . . . a major piece of musical theatre'. It won Tony Awards for best director (Wolfe), choreography (Glover), featured actress (Duquesnay), and lighting design (Jules Fisher and Peggy Eisenhauer). Further recognition included Glover's Outer Critics Circle Award for Outstanding Choreography. Glover returned for the last 40 performances before *Bring In 'Da Noise ...* closed on 10 January 1999, after a two and a half year run.

BRISSON, CARL

b. Carl Pederson, 24 December 1895, Copenhagen, Denmark, d. 26 September 1958, Copenhagen, Denmark. A stylish and romantic singer, actor and dancer in the musical theatre and films, Brisson was an up-and-coming boxer before making his stage debut as a dancer while in his teens. He moved to England in 1921 where he appeared in vaudeville revues, and had leading roles in revivals of *The Merry Widow* (1923) and *The Dollar Princess* (1925), before enjoying great success with two European imports, *The Apache* (1927) and *Wonder Bar* (1930). However, his reputation as something of a matinée

idol is based mainly on his films, many recordings, and cabaret work. After making some early talking pictures in Britain, in 1934 Brisson went to Hollywood to star in the screen adaptation of Earl Carroll's hit stage musical, *Murder At The Vanities*, in which he introduced the song that was to become his theme tune, 'Cocktails For Two' (Sam Coslow-Arthur Johnston). A year later, he took the lead in two more US films, *Ship's Café* and *All The King's Horses*. In the latter he co-starred with the American actress Mary Ellis, and sang another number that became identified with him, 'A Little White Gardenia' (Coslow). In 1936 Brisson made his sole foray onto the New York musical stage in Sigmund Romberg and Otto Harbach's operetta, *Forbidden Melody*. He subsequently devoted himself to international cabaret appearances, and was knighted by the kings of Denmark and Sweden.

● FILMS: *The Ring* (1927), *The Manxman* (1929), *The American Prisoner* (1929), *The Knowing Man* (1930), *Song Of Soho* (1930), *The Prince Of Arcadia* (1933), *Two Hearts In Waltztime* (1934), *Murder At The Vanities* (1934), *All The King's Horses* (1935), *Ship's Café* (1935).

BRISSON, FREDERICK

b. Carl Frederick Brisson, 17 March 1913, Copenhagen, Denmark, d. 8 October 1984, New York, USA. Brisson, the son of Carl Brisson, was a stage and film producer. He grew up in England, and after attending the Rossall College in Lancashire, began his career as a theatrical manager. He co-produced his father's 1930 hit show *Wonder Bar*, and in 1937 moved into films, first as an associate producer. Brisson also opened a talent agency that eventually had offices in London, Paris and Hollywood. Finding himself more or less permanently based in the USA, he served in the American Air Force during World War II, attaining the rank of Lieutenant Colonel. After the war he formed Independent Artists Pictures, and in 1954 turned his attention to Broadway, co-producing the hit musicals *The Pajama Game* (1954), *Damn Yankees* (1955) and *New Girl In Town* (1957). He also mounted numerous straight plays, and was instrumental in introducing several important British writers to American audiences, such as Harold Pinter, Peter Shaffer and Tom Stoppard. His projects during the 60s included two more musicals, *Passion Flower Hotel* (1965, London) and *Coco* (1969, New York). Brisson also produced the film musicals *The Girl Rush* (1955) and the acclaimed screen adaptation of *The Pajama Game* (1958). The former starred Rosalind Russell, who was married to Brisson from 1941 until her death in 1976. Brisson's honours included the US Legion of Merit, the King Christian V Medal (Denmark), and the New York Drama Critics Award for his work on Shaffer's *Five Finger Exercise*.

BROADWAY ANGEL RECORDS

From the 50s onwards, Capitol Records recorded the Original Cast albums for a number of Broadway shows. Some of them, such as *Annie Get Your Gun*, *Kiss Me, Kate*, *The Music Man*, and *Funny Girl*, were enormous hits, while others, including *The Gay Life* and *Kwamina*, were most definitely not. In the early 90s, Broadway Angel began to re-release the material from the original vinyl albums on mid-price CDs, thereby enabling musicals fans to renew their worn-out, dog-eared copies of the originals, and also to discover, perhaps for the first time, that some of the shows that flopped contained some good songs. As well as the productions listed above, early in 1994, the label's Broadway Classics catalogue included *St. Louis Woman, Zorba, Follies, Can-Can, No Strings, The Boys From Syracuse* (25th anniversary revival cast), *The Unsinkable Molly Brown, Flahooley, Pal Joey, Plain and Fancy, A Funny Thing Happened On the Way To The Forum, Beyond The Fringe* (London and Broadway cast), *Top Banana, Little Mary Sunshine, Three Wishes For Jamie, By The Beautiful Sea, Cabin In The Sky, Tovarich, Fiorello, Tenderloin, Golden Boy, A Party With Betty Comden And Adolph Green,* and *Of Thee I Sing.* In addition, the label had also released the Original Cast album of the current Broadway smash-hit, *Crazy For You,* and film soundtracks of *Oklahoma!, The King And I* and *Carousel.* One of the other labels specializing in putting many glorious stage scores back into circulation is Sony Broadway.

BROADWAY MELODY, THE

Al Jolson had already dispensed a few musical morsels in the otherwise silent *The Jazz Singer,* the now legendary first feature-length 'talking' picture in 1927, but this film, which was released by MGM two years later, launched the movie musical proper, and more than lived up to its billing as the first 'All Talking! All Singing! All Dancing!' motion picture. The witty and realistic screenplay by James Gleason, Norman Houston, and Edmund Goulding, tells of a vaudeville sister act, played by Bessie Love and Anita Page, that splits up when handsome song-and-dance-man (Charles King) jilts Love and marries Page. Bessie Love, one of the biggest stars of the silent era, proved more than equal to the talkie challenge and turned in a fine emotional performance. The strong supporting cast included Jed Prouty, Kenneth Thompson, Eddie Kane, Mary Doran, and James Gleason. Nacio Herb Brown and Arthur Freed came up with a first-rate score that included two future standards, 'The Broadway Melody' and the tender 'You Were Meant For Me', both superbly delivered by Charles King, and the remainder of the score included 'The Boy Friend', 'Harmony Babies From Melody Lane', 'Love Boat' and 'The Wedding Of The Painted Doll'. The latter accompanied a sequence shot in two-colour Technicolor. Another song, 'Truthful Parson Brown', written by Willard Robison (he later composed the classic 'Cottage For Sale'), was performed by the Biltmore Trio and Orchestra. George Cunningham staged the dances, and Harry Beaumont was the director. Irving Thalberg produced this historic picture, which, although primitive in many respects, was dramatically and musically wonderful, and inspired a host of similar backstage movie musicals during the 30s, including MGM's own occasional series, which began with *Broadway Melody Of 1936.* Apart from a chorus of 'The Broadway Melody' in the first scene and the presence of songwriters Nacio Herb Brown and Arthur Freed, this 1936 edition bore little resemblance to its predecessor. Jack McGowan and Sid Silvers' screenplay, which was based on a story by Moss Hart, concerns newspaper (and radio) gossip columnist Bert Keeler (Jack Benny). His edi-

tor, fed up with Benny's 'baby arrival' stories, demands 'the sort of stuff you get peeking through keyholes'. Keeler obliges, and becomes involved in a feud with Broadway producer Robert Gordon (Robert Taylor). After booking Mademoiselle Belle Arlette (a figment of Keeler's imagination) as his new leading lady, Gordon's show is saved from disaster by starstruck novice Irene Foster (Eleanor Powell), who, after dancing up a storm in the spectacular 'Broadway Rhythm' finale, dances straight into Gordon's arms. Frances Langford, playing herself, introduced the lovely 'You Are My Lucky Star', and the rest of Brown and Freed's appealing score included 'I've Got A Feeling You're Foolin', 'Sing Before Breakfast' and 'On A Sunday Afternoon'. The latter number was sung and danced by the engaging duo of Buddy and Vilma Ebsen. Among the rest of the supporting cast were Una Merkel, Sid Silvers, June Knight, Harry Stockwell, and Nick Long Jnr. The dances were created and staged by Dave Gould, and the 'Lucky Star Ballet' was staged by Albertina Rasch. Roy Del Routh directed, and the producer was John Considine Jnr. *Broadway Melody Of 1938* was very much a follow-up to the previous edition, with Robert Taylor, Eleanor Powell and Buddy Ebsen on hand again, along with songwriters Nacio Herb Brown and Arthur Freed, choreographer Dave Gould, director Roy Del Routh, and screenwriters Jack McGowan and Sid Silvers. In the latter's slight and samey story, Powell is still trying to make it big in Taylor's Broadway show. However, this time she provides the finance, as well as the talent, when the racehorse that she co-owns (who is partial to opera as well as oats) wins $25,000 after being urged on by a passionate rendering of Rossini's 'Largo Al Factotum' over the racecourse PA system. Also involved were George Murphy, Binnie Barnes, Raymond Walburn, Charles Igor Gorin, Willie Howard, Robert Benchley, Charley Grapewin and Robert Wildhack, but it was 15-year-old Judy Garland who stole the picture with one number - 'Dear Mr. Gable'. Roger Edens added a new verse and some patter to the old Jimmy Monaco-Joseph McCarthy number, 'You Made Me Love You', and when Garland sang it while 'writing' a note to a picture of 'The King' that she kept on her dressing table, there was not a dry eye in movie houses worldwide. Sophie Tucker played Garland's mother, so naturally one of her specialities - 'Some Of These Days' - was in the film, and Tucker also sang Brown and Freed's latest 'Broadway' song, 'Your Broadway And My Broadway'. The rest of the numbers included 'Yours And Mine', 'Everybody Sing', 'I'm Feelin' Like A Million' and 'Sun Showers' (all Brown-Freed). Jack Cummings was the producer.

The highlight of *Broadway Melody Of 1940* was undoubtedly the complicated 'Begin The Beguine' number, which was danced exquisitely by Eleanor Powell and Fred Astaire on a vast mirrored surface - in the tap-dancing section, the couple, dressed in white, are accompanied by Roger Edens' 'swing' arrangement with clarinet lead. However, the rest of the picture was fine, too, with a top-notch Cole Porter score that included the amusing 'Please Don't Monkey With Broadway', 'Between You And Me', 'I've Got My Eyes On You', and the enduring standard, 'I Concentrate On You'. In Leon Gordon and George Oppenheimer's screenplay, which was based on an original story by Jack McGowan and Dore Schary, Astaire and George Murphy are a couple of song and dance men who break up after being involved in a mix-up during which Murphy is chosen for the Broadway role intended for Astaire. The dances were staged by Bobby Connolly, and also taking part in the fun and games were Frank Morgan, Ian Hunter, Florence Rice, Lynne Carver and Ann Morriss. Jack Cummings was the producer and Norman Taurog directed an immensely entertaining climax to this MGM *Broadway Melody* series, which ended on the highest possible note with that 'Begin The Beguine' finale.

BRODERICK, HELEN

b. 1891, Philadelphia, Pennsylvania, USA, d. 25 September 1959, Beverly Hills, California, USA. An actress and singer with a deadpan expression and sardonic manner, Broderick made her Broadway debut in the chorus of the *Follies Of 1907*, the first of the series that came to be known as the *Ziegfeld Follies*. This was followed by further chorus work in *The Girl In Question* (1908) and *The Honeymoon Express*, along with the role of Miss Winston in comedian Richard Carle's vehicle, *Jumping Jupiter* (1911). Broderick then spent several years performing in vaudeville with her husband, Lester Crawford, and appeared in various straight parts, before returning to New York in the revues *Nifties Of 1923* and *Puzzles Of 1925*. After joining Beatrice Lillie, Charles Winninger, and Charles Purcell for a couple of months in *Oh, Please!* (1926), she excelled in the Cole Porter musical comedy *Fifty Million Frenchmen* (1929). She enjoyed further success in *The Band Wagon* (1931, introducing the witty 'Where Can He Be?'), *Earl Carroll Vanities* (1932), and *As Thousands Cheer* (1933), before turning her attention to Hollywood. Signed initially to RKO, Broderick provided the comic relief while Fred Astaire and Ginger Rogers danced delightfully in *Top Hat* and *Swing Time*, and continued to keep cinema audiences laughing for the best part of a decade.

● FILMS: *Top Hat* (1935), *To Beat The Band* (1935), *Swing Time* (1936), *The Life Of The Party* (1937), *Radio City Revels* (1938), *Naughty But Nice* (1939), *No No Nanette* (1940), *Nice Girl?* (1941), *Stage Door Canteen* (1943), *Chip Off The Old Block* (1944).

BROWN, GEORGIA

b. Lillie Klot, 21 October 1933, Whitechapel, London, England, d. 5 July 1992. An exciting and spirited vocalist and actress, on stage, in cabaret, and on television, Brown came from a poor working-class area of the East End and made her way to Broadway in true storybook fashion. Although jazz was her early influence (she adopted her name from 'Sweet Georgia Brown'), the attraction of the British music hall tradition took over and in this she enjoyed great success for four decades. One of her earliest stage show appearances was as Lucy in the Royal Court's 1956 production of *The Threepenny Opera* which transferred to the Aldwych and then to Broadway. In 1960 she enjoyed extraordinary success in Lionel Bart's *Oliver!*, and her performance as Nancy remained her greatest role. Her interpretation of 'As Long As He Needs Me' gave such drama and emotion to the song, that nobody has been able to equal it, and she was equally impressive with her exuberant performance of the music hall-styled 'Oom Pah

Pah'. In 1965 she took over from Rachel Roberts in the title role of another Bart musical, *Maggie May*, and in 1968 was mesmerizing in an hour-long programme of Kurt Weill songs on ITV. She began to make films in the 60s, and her screen credits included *A Study In Terror* (1965), *The Fixer*, *Lock Up Your Daughters*, *The Raging Moon*, *Nothing But The Night*, *Tom Jones*, and *The Seven Per Cent Solution* (1976). After moving to the USA she appeared as a replacement in *Side By Side By Sondheim*, and performed in two other Broadway shows, *Carmelina* (1979) and *Roza* (1987). She returned to London in the 80s to star in the smash hit stage adaptation of *42nd Street* and was critically acclaimed for her performance in Steven Berkoff's play *Greek*. She later starred in her own one-woman show, *Georgia Brown And Friends*, an apt title, as she had many friends and critical admirers and rarely received a bad review throughout her entire career. Georgia Brown made her last live stage appearance in June 1992 at a star-studded tribute to Sammy Davis Jnr. at London's Theatre Royal, Drury Lane.

● ALBUMS: *September Song-The Music Of Kurt Weill* (Decca 1962)★★★, *Sings Gershwin* (Decca 1963)★★★★, *Many Shades Of Georgia* (Capitol 1966)★★★, *Sings A Little Of What You Fancy* (Decca 60s)★★.

BROWN, LEW

b. 10 December 1893, Odessa, Russia, d. 5 February 1958, New York, USA. A prolific lyricist, and a member of one of the all-time great songwriting teams, De Sylva, Brown And Henderson, Lew Brown moved to America with his family when he was five. After writing parodies of popular songs while in his teens, in 1912 he collaborated with the veteran composer Albert Von Tilzer on his first hit, 'I'm The Lonesomest Gal In Town'. The new team followed this with 'Give Me The Moonlight, Give Me The Girl' (which eventually became UK singer Frankie Vaughan's signature tune), 'Oh, By Jingo, Oh By Gee' (from the stage musical *Linger Longer Letty*), 'I Used To Love You But It's All Over Now', 'Chili Bean', and 'Dapper Dan' (1921), among others. In the early 20s Brown also produced 'Oh! Ma-Ma (The Butcher Boy)' (with Rudy Vallee and Paola Citorello), 'Where The Lazy Daisies Grow' (with Cliff Friend), 'Last Night On The Back Porch' (Carl Schraubstader), 'When It's Night Time In Italy, It's Wednesday Over Here' (James Kendis), 'Don't Sit Under The Apple Tree (With Anyone Else But Me)' (Sam Stept and Charles Tobias), 'Shine' (Cecil Mack and Ford Dabney), and 'I Wanna Go Where You Go, Do What You Do, Then I'll Be Happy' (Sidney Clare and Cliff Friend). Around this same time, his meeting with composer Ray Henderson resulted in 'Georgette', 'Why Did I Kiss That Girl' (with Robert King), 'Don't Bring Lulu' (with Billy Rose), and 'The Dummy Song (with Rose). The latter was revived in 1953 by Max Bygraves and ventriloquist Peter Brough with 'Archie Andrews'. In 1925, Brown and Henderson were joined by Buddy De Sylva, and during the next six years or so the trio turned out a string of hit songs with snappy, singable tunes and colloquial lyrics perfectly suited to the lively, carefree 'roaring twenties'. Many of the songs were introduced in the most popular shows and revues of the time, such as *George White's*

Scandals, *Big Boy*, *Good News!*, *Artists And Models*, *Manhattan Mary*, *Hold Everything!*, *Follow Thru*, and *Flying High*, as well as early movie musicals such as *The Singing Fool*, *Sunnyside Up*, *Say It With Songs*, *Just Imagine*, *Show Girl In Hollywood*, and *Indiscreet*. The list of songs that were featured in those productions is a long one, and includes such memorable numbers as 'I Want A Lovable Baby', 'The Black Bottom', 'It All Depends On You', 'Lucky Day', 'The Birth Of The Blues', 'The Girl Is You And The Boy Is Me', 'Broadway', 'Good News', 'He's A Ladies Man', 'Here Am I - Broken Hearted' 'Just Imagine', 'Lucky In Love', 'Magnolia', 'I Wonder How I Look When I'm Asleep', 'The Varsity Drag', 'Button Up Your Overcoat', 'Don't Hold Everything', 'For Old Time's Sake', 'I'm On The Crest Of A Wave', 'Pickin' Cotton', 'Sonny Boy', 'Together', 'What D'ya Say?', 'You Wouldn't Fool Me, Would You?', 'You're The Cream In My Coffee', 'I Want To Be Bad', 'If I Had A Talking Picture Of You', 'Little Pal', 'My Lucky Star', 'I'm a Dreamer, Aren't We All?', 'Sunny Side Up', 'Turn On The Heat', 'Why Can't You (Birdies Sing In Cages Too)', '(There's Something About An) Old Fashioned Girl', 'Don't Tell Her What's Happened To Me', 'Good For You, Bad For Me', 'My Sin', 'Without Love', 'Come To Me', 'You Try Somebody Else, And I'll Try Somebody Else' and 'The Best Things In Life Are Free'. The latter became the title of the team's 1956 Hollywood biopic. After De Sylva departed in 1931, Brown and Henderson collaborated on 'Life Is Just A Bowl Of Cherries', 'That's Why Darkies Are Born', 'My Song' and 'The Thrill Is Gone'; and Brown's association in the 30s and early 40s with various composers and lyricists such as Jay Gorney, Harold Arlen, Sammy Fain, Jaromir Vejvoda, Sam Stept, Charles Tobias, Laurindo Almeida, U. Nesdan and Ralph Freed, resulted in songs such as 'Baby, Take A Bow', 'Broadway's Gone Hill Billy', 'I'm Laughin'', 'First You Have Me High (Then You Have Me Low)', 'The Lady Dances', 'Shake It Off With Rhythm', 'It's Great To Be Alive', 'That Old Feeling', 'Love Is Never Out Of Season', 'Beer Barrel Polka', 'Comes Love', 'Johnny Pedler', 'I Came Here To Talk For Joe' and 'Mississippi Dream Boat' (1943). Several of these came from shows including *George White's Scandals*, *Vogues Of 1938*, *Hot-Cha!*, *Strike Me Pink*, and *New Faces*, and films such as *Stand Up And Cheer*, *Strike Me Pink*, and *Swing Fever*. As well as writing the lyrics for some of the world's most engaging and popular songs, Lew Brown was also an author, publisher, producer and director of note.

BROWN, NACIO HERB

b. 22 February 1896, Deming, New Mexico, USA, d. 28 September 1964, San Francisco, California, USA. After studying piano with his mother (his father was the local sheriff), Brown graduated from Musical Art High School, Los Angeles, but then took a course in business administration. Before long, however, he was playing piano as accompanist to vaudeville singer Alice Doll. A year later he became a tailor in Hollywood, dabbling in real estate on the side, and by 1920 was wealthy enough to hang up his tailors' scissors and start writing songs. His first was 'Coral Sea', written in 1920 with Alice Doll's husband, Jack (who used the pseudonym Zany King).

Later in the decade he collaborated with Richard Whiting (father of singer Margaret Whiting) and Arthur Freed, with whom he wrote songs for the movie *The Broadway Melody* (1929). This collaboration produced the songs 'Broadway Melody', 'You Were Meant For Me' and 'The Wedding Of The Painted Doll'. Another film of the same year, *The Hollywood Revue*, featured 'Singin' In The Rain'. Brown also collaborated with Whiting and Buddy De Sylva on 'Eadie Was A Lady' and 'You're An Old Smoothie' for the 1932 Broadway show *Take A Chance*. Brown continued to collaborate with Freed on film songs, one of which was 'All I Do Is Dream Of You', written for *Sadie McKay* (1934) and reprised in 1953 in *Singin' In The Rain*. Also heard again in that film were the Freed-Brown songs, 'You Are My Lucky Star' and 'I've Got A Feelin' You're Foolin'', written for *Broadway Melody Of 1936*. The team also wrote 'Alone' for the Marx Brothers film *A Night At The Opera* (1935). The 1939 film *Babes In Arms*, which starred Mickey Rooney and Judy Garland, included 'Good Morning', yet another song to delight a later generation of filmgoers in *Singin' In The Rain*. In the early 40s Brown worked with other collaborators such as Gus Kahn on 'You Stepped Out Of A Dream' (from *Ziegfeld Girl*), and Earl Brent and Edward Heyman on the score for the Frank Sinatra/Kathryn Grayson film *The Kissing Bandit*, which included 'Love Is Where You Find It', 'If I Steal A Kiss' and 'Dance Of Fury'.

Brown retired at the end of the 40s, but saw his music revived thanks largely to *Singin' In The Rain*. In celebration of their return to acclaim, they wrote one original song for the film, 'Make 'Em Laugh'. In February 1960 the authorities in Deming celebrated the 64th birthday of their most famous citizen by naming a city park after him.

BRYAN, DORA

b. Dora Broadbent, 7 February 1924, Southport, Lancashire, England. A much-loved singer, actress, and comedienne, Dora Bryan has successfully mixed straight theatre with revue, cabaret, musical comedy, variety, pantomime, television and film, in a career that has endured for more than 60 years. She made her first stage appearance in a Manchester pantomime at the age of 12, and two years later was a member of the Oldham Repertory Company. She met her future husband, professional cricketer Bill Lawton in Oldham, and they were married 12 years later in 1953. Dora Bryan moved to London when she was 21, and was seen by Noël Coward while appearing in the play *No Room At The Inn*. Coward wrote a good character part for her in *Peace In Our Time*, his 1947 drama about a German occupation of London. Subsequently, Bryan was noticed by film director Carol Reed, who introduced her to the film business. Another of her mentors was impresario Binkie Beaumont, a provider of much work for Bryan over the years. During World War II she entertained British Forces abroad with the often derided, but immensely valuable, Entertainments National Service Association (ENSA), and in the 50s starred in a series of intimate and satirical revues. These included Coward's *The Lyric Revue* (1951) and *The Globe Revue* (1952), as well as *At The Lyric* (1953) by Alan Melville, and Arthur MacRae's *Living For Pleasure* (1958).

Her first venture into West End musical comedy with *The Water Gipsies* (1955, Lily Bell) was a personal triumph ('Why Did You Call Me Lily?', 'You Never Know With Men', 'It Would Cramp My Style' [with Roy Godfrey]), and was followed by *Gentlemen Prefer Blondes* (1962, Lorelei Lee). In 1966, she took over the title role in *Hello, Dolly!* from Mary Martin and made it her own. In 1979, a nervous breakdown forced her to withdraw before the opening of *On The Twentieth Century*, and Bryan subsequently spoke of her problems with alcohol. A comeback to the musical stage in 1986 with a revival of the 60s hit *Charlie Girl* (Kay Connor) proved disappointingly brief, even with Hollywood legend Cyd Charisse on board. Far more satisfying was her irresistible portrayal of Ida, 'the ideal leader of a septuagenarian brat pack', in Paul Kerryson's Chichester Festival production of *70, Girls, 70*, which toured and reached London's Vaudeville Theatre in June 1991. It was the beginning of a decade in which Dora Bryan received an honorary MA degree from the University of Manchester (1992), won a Laurence Olivier Award for her role in Harold Pinter's *The Birthday Party* at the Royal National Theatre (1994), and was awarded the OBE (1996). No stranger to awards, back in the 60s Bryan was adjudged best leading actress by the British Film Academy for her performance in *A Taste Of Honey* (1961), and her Top 20 novelty single record, 'All I Want For Christmas Is A Beatle', collected the Best Bad Record prize two years later. In the late 90s she continued to star in productions such as *The School For Scandal* and *When We Are Married*, and also toured her own one-woman show, *Memories Of A Life*.

● FURTHER READING: *According To Dora*, Dora Bryan.

● FILMS: *Odd Man Out* (1946), *Once Upon A Dream* (1947), *The Fallen Idol* (1948), *Traveller's Joy* (1949), *The Perfect Woman* (1949), *The Interrupted Journey* (1949), *The Blue Lamp* (1950), *The Quiet Woman* (1950), *Cure For Love* (1950), *Whispering Smith Hits London* (1951), *High Treason* (1951), *The Scarlet Thread* (1951), *Lady Godiva Rides Again* (1951), *No Highway In The Sky* (1951), *Time Gentlemen Please!* (1952), *The Ringer* (1952), *Mother Riley Meets The Vampire* (1952), *Miss Robin Hood* (1952), *Made In Heaven* (1952), *The Gift Horse* (1952), *13 East Street* (1952), *Street Corner* (1953), *The Fake* (1953), *You Know What Sailors Are* (1954), *Mad About Men* (1954), *Fast And Loose* (1954), *The Intruder* (1955), *As Long As They're Happy* (1955), *Cockleshell Heroes* (1956), *Small Hotel* (1957), *The Man Who Wouldn't Talk* (1958), *Hello London* 1958), *Carry On Sergeant* (1958), *Operation Bullshine* (1959), *Desert Mice* (1959), *The Night We Got The Bird* (1961), *A Taste Of Honey* (1961), *The Sandwich Man* (1966), *The Great St. Trinian's Train Robbery* (1966), *Two A Penny* (1967), *Hands Of The Ripper* (1971), *Up The Front* (1972), *Screamtime* (1983), *Apartment Zero* (1988).

BRYNNER, YUL

b. Youl Bryner, 11 July 1920, Sakhalin, Russia, d. 10 October 1985, New York, USA. Sakhalin is a Siberian island north of Japan, and the date of Brynner's date of birth there is a matter for negotiation; it probably lies somewhere between 1915 and 1920. He spent his early childhood in Peking but was brought up in Paris where he sang in clubs before moving to America in 1941. There he worked in radio and toured as an actor until his Broadway debut with Mary Martin in the short-lived musical *Lute Song* in 1946. Two years later he reprised his role for London and subsequently worked as an actor and director in US television, before creating one of the all-time great roles in Richard Rodgers and Oscar Hammerstein II's *The King And I* in 1951. He shaved his head for the character of the King of Siam, and the completely bald dome became his lifelong trademark - although some said it limited his choice of future parts. His striking, sensual performance opposite the 'terribly English' Gertrude Lawrence earned him a Tony Award, and their duet, 'Shall We Dance?', remains one of the most memorable moments in American musical theatre. Deborah Kerr, another delightful English actress, was his partner in the 1956 film version for which he won an Oscar. For most of the rest of his career he worked in films, and was highly acclaimed for his performances in many of them, particularly *Anastasia*, *The Brothers Karamazov*, *The Magnificent Seven*, *Taras Bulba*, *Westworld* and *Invitation To A Gunfighter*. In the early 60s he settled in Switzerland and spent a good deal of his time making documentary films about refugee children for the United Nations. He returned to America in 1972 and appeared with the English actress Samantha Eggar in the television series *Anna And The King Of Siam*. Five years later came a triumphant Broadway revival of *The King And I* which was also seen in London in 1979. He brought it back to New York again in 1985 even though he was suffering from lung cancer, which entailed regular radiation treatment. It was the biggest hit of the season with Brynner's curtain calls lasting so long that they became known as 'the third act'. In June 1985 he received a special Tony Award in recognition of his 4,525 performances in *The King And I*. He increased that figure by another 100 before he died at the Cornell Medical Centre in New York in October of that year.

● ALBUMS: *The Gypsy And I* (Vanguard 1967)★★★.

BUCHANAN, JACK

b. 2 April 1890, Helensburgh, Strathclyde, Scotland, d. 20 October 1957, London, England. A major UK musical comedy, revue and film star, choreographer, director, producer and manager with a disarming, casual style, Buchanan's career spanned 40 years. He played in amateur dramatics and local music halls before moving to London to work as an understudy and chorus boy. Rejected for military service at the start of World War I because of poor health, he taught himself to dance, and played a leading role in the touring version of the West End hit musical comedy *Tonight's The Night* in 1915. His big break came two years later when he took over from Jack Hulbert in producer André Charlot's revue *Bubbly*, followed by another Charlot show, *A To Z*, in 1921. In the latter Buchanan sang one of his all-time hits, 'And Her Mother Came Too', with Ivor Novello's music and a lyric by Dion Titheradge. Also in the cast were Beatrice Lillie and a young Gertrude Lawrence. After branching out into management with the musical farce *Battling Butler* at the New Oxford Theatre, Buchanan went to New York with Lillie and Lawrence to appear in *André Charlot's Revue Of 1924* at the Times Square Theater. Buchanan was a substantial success on Broadway, and returned in 1926 with another Charlot revue in which he duetted with Lawrence on 'A Cup Of Coffee, A Sandwich, And You'. The recording reached number 5 in the chart and was his only US hit. Back in London in 1926 he was at his peak in Jerome Kern's *Sunny*. With Elsie Randolph as his regular leading lady, he appeared in dancing musicals such as *That's A Good Girl, Mr Whittington, This'll Make You Whistle*, and their last show together in 1943, *It's Time To Dance*. He also went back to New York for *Wake Up And Dream!* with Jessie Matthews, and *Between The Devil* with Evelyn Laye. Songs such as 'Who', 'Goodnight Vienna', 'I Think I Can', 'There's Always Tomorrow', 'Fancy Our Meeting', 'Sweet So And So', 'Weep No More My Baby', 'By Myself' and 'I'm In A Dancing Mood', were delivered in a seemingly fragile, 'typically English' style. In his show *Stand Up And Sing* at the London Hippodrome in 1931, a very young Anna Neagle was discovered by film producer Herbert Wilcox, who started her on the road to a long and distinguished film career by putting her into the Buchanan film *Goodnight Vienna*. Buchanan's own film career proper had started in 1917 with the silent *Auld Lang Syne* (he had previously worked as an extra), and included a series of comedies, light dramas and farces such as *Yes, Mr Brown, Brewster's Millions* and *The Gang's All Here*. His first movie musical was *Paris*, with Corsican actress/singer Irene Bordoni, and he made several more including *Monte Carlo*, directed by Ernst Lubitsch, and co-starring Jeanette MacDonald, plus a few celluloid transfers of his hit stage productions. In 1953, the top UK and US song-and-dance men met in *The Band Wagon*. Buchanan and Fred Astaire's duet, 'I Guess I'll Have To Change My Plan', and their clever version, with Nanette Fabray, of 'Triplets' fame, made this one of MGM's most acclaimed musical films, and the pinnacle of Buchanan's career.

● ALBUMS: with Elsie Randolph *Selections From London Stage Shows* (Retrospect/EMI 1979)★★★.

● COMPILATIONS: *That's A Good Girl* (Retrospect/EMI 1979)★★★, *The Golden Age Of Jack Buchanan* (Golden Age/EMI 1984)★★★, *Elegance* (Living Era 1985)★★★, *This'll Make You Whistle* (Movie Stars 1990).

● FURTHER READING: *Top Hat And Tails*, Michael Marshall.

● FILMS: *Auld Lang Syne* (1917), *Her Heritage* (1919), *The Audacious Mr. Squire* (1924), *Bulldog Drummond's Third Round* (1925), *A Typical Budget* (1925), *Settled Out Of Court* (1925), *The Happy Ending* (1925), *Confetti* (1927), *Toni* (1928), *Paris* (1929), *Monte Carlo* (1930), *The Glee Quartet* (1930), *Man Of Mayfair* (1931), *The Invisible Enemy* (1931), *Goodnight, Vienna* US title *Magic Night* (1932), *That's A Good Girl* (1933), *Yes, Mr. Brown* (1933), *Come Out Of The Pantry* (1935), *Brewster's Millions* (1935), *When Knights Were Bold* (1936), *Limelight* US title *Backstage* (1936), *The Sky's The Limit* (1937), *Smash And Grab* (1937), *This'll Make You Whistle* (1937), *Break The News* (1938), *Sweet Devil* (1938), *The Middle Watch* (1939), *The Gang's All Here* US title *The Amazing Mr. Forrest* (1939), *Bulldog Sees It Through* (1940), *Giselle* (1952), *The Band Wagon* (1953), *Josephine And Men* (1955), *As Long As They're Happy* (1955), *The French They Are A Funny Race* (1957).

BUCKLEY, BETTY

b. Betty Lynn Buckley, 3 July 1947, Fort Worth, Texas, USA. Encouraged by a mother who was a singer and dancer, Buckley became attracted to the musical theatre

after seeing *The Pajama Game* when she was 11 years old. Nevertheless, she graduated with a BA degree in journalism from Texas Christian College, as well as studying voice and acting, and then worked in regional theatre before making her Broadway debut as Martha Jefferson in the musical *1776* in 1969. Having moved to London, in 1969 she starred in the West End production of Neil Simon's *Promises, Promises*, which had a score by Burt Bacharach and Hal David. Back in New York in the 70s and 80s, she mixed straight roles with appearances at various times in musicals such as *Pippin, I'm Getting My Act Together And Taking It On The Road, The Mystery Of Edwin Drood*, and *Song And Dance*, and in 1983 won a Tony Award for her performance as Grizabella in *Cats*. From the security of Andrew Lloyd Webber's longest-running musical to date, five years later Buckley played Margaret White, the fanatically religious mother, in *Carrie*, one of the most famous flops in Broadway history, which closed after only five performances. Coincidentally, she had played the role of the gym teacher, Miss Collins, in Stephen King's 1976 film of *Carrie*. She has made several other movies, including *Tender Mercies* (1983) and *Wyatt Earp* (1994), but is probably best known on screen as the kidnapped wife in the Roman Polanski film *Frantic* (1988). In 1994 Buckley renewed her Lloyd Webber connection and succeeded Patti LuPone as the fading movie queen Norma Desmond in the revised London production of *Sunset Boulevard*. During the run she starred as Desirée, with Keith Michell as Fredrik, in a BBC Radio 2 recording of *A Little Night Music*. She also featured in another broadcast, *Betty Buckley In Concert*, for the same radio station, before taking over the lead from Glenn Close in the Broadway production of *Sunset Boulevard* in July 1995. In addition to a permanently heavy concert schedule, including a sell-out date at Carnegie Hall in 1996, during the late 90s Buckley appeared on Broadway in the short-lived *Triumph Of Love* (1997), and led the cast, as Rose, in a 1998 revival of *Gypsy* at the Paper Mill Playhouse, New Jersey.

● ALBUMS: *Children Will Listen* (Sterling 1993)★★★, *With One Look* (Sterling 1994)★★★, *Buckley: The London Concert* (Sterling 1995)★★★, *An Evening At Carnegie Hall* (Sterling 1996)★★★, *An Evening With Betty Buckley* (Sterling 1996)★★★, *Much More* (Sterling 1997)★★★, and cast albums.

BUDDY

One of the most successful 'pop legend' musical biographies in recent years, this celebration of the brief life and times of Buddy Holly opened at the Victoria Palace Theatre in London on 12 October 1989. From a 'short' list of over 30 eager hopefuls, Paul Hipp was selected to portray the young rock 'n' roll singer-songwriter who made such an enormous impact in his brief spell at the top, before he perished in an air crash in 1959 at the age of 22, along with fellow artists Ritchie Valens and the Big Bopper. Paul Janes' book, which traces Holly's life from his hicksville roots and his first appearance with the Crickets at New York's Apollo theatre (whose management was expecting a black band), through the disputes with greedy managers and cynical record companies, and ending with the final concert at Clear Lake, Iowa, which took place just a few hours before the tragic accident. Long before that comes round, the audience has been letting rip and jiving in the aisles to such favourites as 'That'll Be The Day', 'Peggy Sue' and 'Oh Boy', and smooching, together with Buddy and his wife, to 'True Love Ways' and 'Raining In My Heart'. To the surprise of many, *Buddy* settled in for a long run, and touring companies also flourished. To mark the occasion of the show's 1,001 nights at the Victoria Palace three of the actors who had played the leading role, Paul Hipp, Billy Geraghty and Chip Esten, appeared on the stage together, and, on 7 September 1993, Holly's 57th birthday, all tickets were sold at 50s prices: the best seats costing sixteen shillings (80 pence). *Buddy* opened on Broadway in November 1990, but was unable to sustain a run longer than 225 performances. Meanwhile, in London ('10th Triumphant Year!!') and several other locations, they continued to 'Rave On'.

BUDDY HOLLY STORY, THE

Gary Busey starred as the doomed rock 'n' roll singer in this sympathetic biography. The tenacity he brings to his performance provides the film with much of its strength. The storyline rarely strays from true-life events in which Holly rose from regional obscurity to become one of the bona fide stars of the 50s. Although clearly sympathetic, *The Buddy Holly Story* avoids the trappings of sentimentality, and shows how Holly's ambition led to the break-up of the Crickets. Rather than mime to original tracks, Busey took responsibility for the vocals, ably interpreting such classic material as 'Peggy Sue', 'That'll Be The Day' and 'Rave On'. The events surrounding Holly's fatal aeroplane trip are portrayed sensitively, and honest performances from the entire cast prevent *The Buddy Holly Story* becoming a hagiography. Its artistic merits were echoed in *La Bamba*, an equally convincing resumé of the career of Richie Valens, who perished in the same crash.

BUDGIE

Even with big names in most departments, this show was one of the most spectacular flop musicals in London during the late 80s. It opened on 18 October 1988 at the Cambridge Theatre, with a starry cast that included Adam Faith, Anita Dobson, and John Turner. The book was by Keith Waterhouse and Willis Hall, authors of the 1974 smash-hit, *Billy*, and the music and lyrics were written by Mort Shuman, one half of the celebrated US songwriting team Doc Pomus and Shuman, and Britain's own Don Black. It was hoped that the teaming of Faith, who had played the leading role in the 70s television series on which the show was based, with Dobson, an accomplished actress who created the role of the barmaid Angie Watts in *EastEnders*, one of the UK's top small-screen soaps, would prove to be irresistible. The opposite proved to be true, and the 'over-romanticized, sleazy' story of a small-time Cockney swindler and his reforming girlfriend, set in London's Soho, was dismissed by the critics and ignored by the public. Shuman and Black's score contained some mildly amusing numbers such as 'If You Want to See Palermo Again' and 'They're Naked And They Move', and the engaging ballad, 'There Is Love And There Is Love'.

The remainder of the songs included 'In One Of My Weaker Moments', 'I'm Sure We Won't Fall Out Over This', 'Mary, Doris And Jane', 'Why Not Me?', 'Old Compton Street' and 'I Like That In A Man'. *Budgie* closed on 21 January 1989 after a run of only three months, with estimated losses in excess of over £1 million.

BUGSY MALONE

Alan Parker properly put the old adage 'never work with children' to shame with his 1976 musical gangster spoof *Bugsy Malone*. With all the roles played by young people of varying ages, writer/director Parker tells the tongue-in-cheek tale of gang warfare in 20s New York - where no one is safe from the 'fatal' effects of the dreaded splurge gun. However, in the bitter battle between Fat Sam (goodie) and Dandy Dan (baddie), the guns do not shoot bullets; instead the ammunition is whipped cream. Paul Williams' score was skilfully integrated into the plot, which sees Bugsy (a very young Scott Baio) emerging from an advanced state of apathy to help Fat Sam (John Cassisi), and fall in love with Blousey Brown (a name, he says, that sounds like a stale loaf of bread). 'With an Irish father and an Italian mother,' remarks Fat Sam, 'naturally Bugsy has grown up a little confused.' Made in Britain and released at a time when the Hollywood musical was a thing of the past, young audiences were given a taste of what they had missed with well-choreographed production numbers (the custard pie-throwing finale, 'You Give A Little Love', is sentimental but enchanting), comic sequences such as 'So You Wanna Be A Boxer', and melancholy lost-love songs for Blousey - 'I'm Feeling Fine' and 'Ordinary Fool'. The film received mixed reviews from the critics but was popular with audiences, as was the album, which included songs sung by the composer himself. Made by Rank/Bugsy Malone Productions (producers Allan Marshall and David Puttnam), Parker claims that the inspiration for the musical came in a 'drugstore-come-restaurant' in Las Vegas called Fox's Deli. Considered a novelty film by many, it nevertheless helped to propel a few youngsters to future stardom, notably double Oscar-winner Jodie Foster, whose portrayal of Sam's girlfriend Tallulah is one of the film's highlights. West End audiences have seen two stage versions. For the 1983 show, which was directed by Michael Dolenz (former member of the Monkees), off-stage adult voices sang the songs, but in the National Youth Music Theatre's 1997 production the company (average age 13-14) put over their own numbers with a great deal of gusto and panache. Outstanding amongst the 40-strong cast were Michael Sturges (Bugsy), Elizabeth Avis (Blousey), Sean Parkins (Fizzy), Paul Lowe (Fat Sam), and Sheridan Smith (Tallulah).

BURKE, JOHNNY

b. 3 October 1908, Antioch, California, USA, d. 25 February 1964, New York, USA. Brought up in Chicago, Burke studied piano and drama, and in 1926 worked as a piano salesman with Irving Berlin Inc. in New York. While there, he began writing lyrics, and in 1933 Guy Lombardo had a hit with his 'Annie Doesn't Live Here Anymore' (written with Joe Young and Harold Spina). After collaborating on a string of minor songs with Spina, which were recorded by various popular artists of the day, among them Paul Whiteman, Ozzie Nelson and Ben Pollack, Burke had another hit with 'My Very Good Friend The Milkman', which was recorded by Fats Waller. In 1936 he went to Hollywood, and there began a sustained period of creative activity and success. Burke made his name as a lyricist for Bing Crosby, working with many co-composers such as Arthur Johnston: 'Pennies From Heaven' and 'One, Two, Button Your Shoe' from *Pennies From Heaven* (1936), and 'The Moon Got In My Eyes' and 'All You Want To Do Is Dance' from *Double Or Nothing* (1937); and with Jimmy Monaco, 'I've Got A Pocketful Of Dreams' and 'Don't Let That Moon Get Away' from *Sing You Sinners* (1938), 'An Apple For The Teacher' from *The Star Maker*, 'East Side Of Heaven' and 'Sing A Song Of Moonbeams' from *East Side Of Heaven* (1939), and 'Too Romantic' and 'Sweet Potato Piper' from the first Bob Hope and Bing Crosby 'Road' film, *Road To Singapore* (1940). Burke's most famous collaboration, with Jimmy Van Heusen, began in 1940. The team supplied songs for 16 Crosby films, including *Road To Zanzibar* (1941), *Road To Morocco* (1942), *Dixie* (1943), *Going My Way* (1944) (which featured the Academy Award-winning 'Swinging On A Star'), *The Bells Of St Mary's* (1945), *Road To Utopia* (1945), *Road To Rio* (1947), *A Connecticut Yankee In King Arthur's Court* (1949) and *Riding High* (1950). Besides working on other films, Van Heusen and Burke also wrote the score for the 1953 Broadway musical *Carnival In Flanders*, which contained the songs 'Here's That Rainy Day' and 'It's An Old Spanish Custom'. Other Van Heusen-Burke songs during this period included 'Oh, You Crazy Moon', 'Suddenly It's Spring' and 'Like Someone In Love'. Burke wrote many more very popular songs, including 'Scatterbrain', with Frankie Masters, Kahn Keene and Carl Bean; 'What's New', with Bob Haggart; and 'Misty', with jazz pianist Erroll Garner. He continued working until shortly before his death. In 1994, the Goodspeed Opera House in Connecticut, USA, presented a new musical, *Swinging On A Star*, as a tribute to his prolific career.

BURNETT, CAROL

b. 26 April 1933, San Antonio, Texas, USA. An actress, comedienne, singer, director, producer, and writer, Burnett was raised by her maternal grandmother in Los Angeles and studied theatre arts and English at the University of California. After graduating she worked in summer stock before moving to New York in 1954. Unable to find work as an actress, she staged a show at the Rehearsal Club hotel in which she sang Eartha's Kitt's hit song 'Monotonous' from *New Faces Of 1953*. In 1957 she caused a stir at the Blue Angel nightclub with her rendition of 'I Made A Fool Of Myself Over John Foster Dulles'. This parody aimed at teenage rock 'n' roll groupies was written by Ken Welch, a songwriter and vocal coach whose material was ideally suited to her 'kooky' style. Years later, he and his wife Mitzi wrote medleys for Burnett's television specials with Julie Andrews and others. In 1959 Burnett made an impressive Broadway debut as Princess Winnifred in *Once Upon A Mattress*, a successful musical based on the fairytale *The Princess And The Pea*. At around the same time she began appearing on The

Garry Moore Show, and in the early 60s won an Emmy and several awards as the most popular female performer on television. In 1962 she and Julie Andrews won more Emmys for the special *Julie And Carol At Carnegie Hall*. The two performers were teamed again in similar concerts at the Lincoln Centre (1971) and in Los Angeles (1989). Signed to CBS in 1962, Burnett's television career failed to take off during the next few years, and it was not until she returned to Broadway in the musical *Fade Out-Fade In* (1965) that her fortunes began to improve. Although the show itself - an affectionate look at the Hollywood of the 30s - was not well received, Burnett's 'genial comic impudence' and 'cheerful gaucherie' were singled out for praise, and her impression of Shirley Temple on 'You Mustn't Be Discouraged' was hilarious. From 1967 CBS aired *The Carol Burnett Show*, a weekly prime-time variety show that featured a stellar line-up of guest stars and won 22 Emmys. In 1978, after appearing in approximately 1,500 sketches, Burnett had tired of the weekly grind and turned more to the theatre and feature films. In 1985 she was Carlotta Campion for two nights in the Stephen Sondheim tribute *Follies In Concert*, and performed marvellous renditions of the composer's 'survival anthem' 'I'm Still Here'. She returned to weekly television again in 1990 and chose an anthology format for her new series *Carol And Company*, which added to her list of honours that already included People's Choice, Critics Circle, Photoplay and Golden Globe Awards, along with her induction into the Television Academy Hall of Fame. In 1993 she starred in two productions by the Long Beach Civic Light Opera: Stephen Sondheim and George Furth's *Company*, with Patrick Cassidy, and a new musical entitled *From The Top*. The latter was conceived and written by Ken Welch (of 'I Made A Fool Of Myself Over John Foster Dulles' fame) and his wife Mitzie, and consisted of three one-act musicals. The first, *My Walking Stick*, is a back-stage vaudeville story set at the time of World War I, with songs by Irving Berlin; the second, called *One Night In Marrakech*, has words and music by Cole Porter; and the third and final piece, *That Simpson Woman*, is, naturally enough, an attempt to find a new angle on the famous Duke and Duchess of Windsor-in-exile saga, with a background of songs with lyrics by Ira Gershwin and music by a variety of composers.

Television projects in 1994 included *Carol Burnett: The Special Years*, which featured some of the most memorable moments from her specials, and *Men, Movies & Carol*, a CBS variety programme spoofing the cinema, with Tony Bennett among the guest artists. In 1996 Burnett returned to Broadway after an absence of some 30 years, and received a Tony nomination for her portrayal of Charlotte Hay in Ken Ludwig's crazy comedy *Moon Over Buffalo*. Two years later she was back in Los Angeles, at the Mark Taper Forum, in Cameron Mackintosh's Sondheim revue, *Putting It Together*.

● ALBUMS: *Remembers How They Stopped The Show* (Columbia 1962)★★★★, with Julie Andrews *Julie And Carol At Carnegie Hall* (1962)★★★, *Let Me Entertain You* (Columbia 1964)★★★, *Carol Burnett Sings* (Victor 1967)★★★, *Julie Andrews And Carol Burnett At The Lincoln Center* (Silva 1989)★★.

● FURTHER READING: *One More Time*, Carol Burnett. *Laughing Till It Hurts*, J. Randy Taraborrelli.
● FILMS: *Who's Been Sleeping In My Bed?* (1963), *Star Spangled Salesman* (1966), *Rowan & Martin At The Movies* (1968), *Pete 'N' Tillie* (1972), *The Front Page* (1974), *A Wedding* (1978), *H.E.A.L.T.H.* (1979), *Chu Chu And The Philly Flash* (1981), *Annie* as Miss Hannigan (1982), *Laundromat* (1985), *Noises Off* (1992), *Moon Over Broadway* (1997), *Marriage Fool* (1998).

BURROWS, ABE

b. Abram Solman Borowitz, 18 December 1910, d. 17 May 1985, New York, USA. A distinguished director and librettist with many Broadway musicals and straight plays to his credit. Burrows studied to be a doctor and an accountant before eventually embarking on a career as a salesman. He was diverted from this course when he began to write radio comedy programmes such as *Duffy's Tavern*, and the late 40s hit, *Take Your Word*. He also wrote and recorded a series of comedy songs, but his big break came when he collaborated with Jo Swerling on the witty book for Frank Loesser's *Guys And Dolls*, which is considered to be the quintessential Broadway musical. It gained Burrows the first of his many Tony Awards, and throughout the 50s he wrote or co-wrote the librettos for *Make A Wish*, *Three Wishes For Jamie*, *Can-Can*, *Silk Stockings*, *Say, Darling*, and *First Impressions*. In 1961 he joined with Loesser again to create an hilarious skit on American big-business, *How To Succeed In Business Without Really Trying*, for which he won another Tony, and a share in the Pulitzer Prize for Drama. Burrows also directed *How To Succeed*, as well as several others of the above shows, including *Three Wishes For Jamie*, *Can-Can*, *Say, Darling*, and *First Impressions*. He also staged the Bert Lahr vehicle *Two On The Aisle*, *Happy Hunting*, and *What Makes Sammy Run?*, in which the popular singer Steve Lawrence made his 1964 Broadway debut. In later years, although Burrows was associated with some bizarre flops such as *Breakfast At Tiffany's* and a 1976 version of the classic *Hellzapoppin'!*, both of which failed to reach New York, he was frequently called upon (mostly uncredited) to successfully revise and revive other people's shows that were in trouble.
● FURTHER READING: *Honest Abe*, Abe Burrows.

BY JUPITER

Richard Rodgers and Lorenz Hart's longest-running original Broadway musical opened at the Shubert Theatre on 2 June 1942. The two songwriters also wrote the book, which was based on Julian Thompson's play, *The Warrior's Husband*. *By Jupiter* is set in ancient Greece, and tells the amusing (and archaic) story of the Amazons, a breed of powerful, well-built, muscular women who dominate their own land and everyone who lives in it - male or female - until they are conquered - and absolutely captivated - by a tribe of marauding Greek warriors. Thereafter, the ladies are perfectly happy to forget about their previous superiority and assume a subordinate role. Ray Bolger, who had scored such a big success in Rodgers and Hart's *On Your Toes*, was the first choice for the part of Sapiens, the effeminate husband of the Amazonian chieftain, Queen Hippolyta (Benay Venuta). The leading female role of the Queen's sister, Antiope, was played by Constance Moore, whose passion for the leader of the invading army, Theseus (Ronald Graham), is what causes the Amazonian resistance to crumble in the first place. The score had several good moments, particularly the duet for Bolger and Venuta entitled 'Life With Father', although none of the songs really stood out and took off. The rest of the numbers included 'Nobody's Heart', 'Now That I've Got My Strength', 'Ev'rything I've Got', 'Jupiter Forbid', 'Careless Rhapsody', 'Here's A Hand', 'The Gateway To The Temple Of Minerva', and 'The Boy I Left Behind Me'. There was one beautiful ballad, 'Wait Till You See Her', sung by Ronald Graham, that did endure through the years, although, ironically, it was removed for a time because the show was too long, and only replaced shortly before the end of the run. After Ray Bolger departed to entertain US troops in the Far East, audiences dwindled rapidly, and *By Jupiter* closed after 427 performances. Only one Rodgers and Hart show - the 1952 revival of *Pal Joey* - stayed longer on Broadway. In 1963, *By Jupiter* was presented off-Broadway, where it ran for 118 performances.

BYE BYE BIRDIE (FILM MUSICAL)

Dick Van Dyke, one of the most popular comic actors on US and UK television, made his big screen debut in this 1963 Columbia adaptation of the hit Broadway show. Van Dyke reprised his stage role as Albert Peterson, the flamboyant manager and promoter of Conrad Birdie (Jesse Pearson), the rock 'n' roll singing sensation, who, in one final extravagant publicity stunt before he enters the US Army (*à la* Elvis Presley) sings Albert's latest song, 'One Last Kiss', on the *Ed Sullivan Show* while bestowing same on his biggest fan, Kim McAfee (Ann-Margret). The other members of a particularly strong cast included Janet Leigh (as Albert's secretary), Bobby Rydell, Maureen Stapleton, Paul Lynde, Frank Albertson, and Ed Sullivan himself. As usual, several of the original songs from the stage show were lost in the transfer to film, but the survivors included some of Charles Strouse and Lee Adams' most amusing and entertaining numbers such as 'Put On A Happy Face', 'A Lot Of Livin' To Do', 'Kids', 'Honestly Sincere', 'How Lovely To Be A Woman', 'One Last Kiss', and 'The Telephone Hour', which was performed by Rydell and the 'kids', and is generally held to be the film's musical high spot. Screenplay writer Irving Brecher made only a few changes to Michael Stewart's original libretto, and Onna White, whose work had enhanced *The Music Man* the year before, choreographed the proceedings with style. The film, which was photographed in Eastman Color and Panavision, was directed by Fred Kohlmar.

BYE BYE BIRDIE (STAGE MUSICAL)

Generally regarded as the first Broadway musical to reflect the rock 'n' roll phenomenon of the 50s, *Bye Bye Birdie* opened in New York at the Martin Beck Theatre on 14 April 1960. Michael Stewart's book tells of Albert Peterson (Dick Van Dyke), a rock manager and promoter, whose only client, 'the hip-thrusting' Conrad Birdie (Dick Gautier), is about to be inducted into the US Army. Peterson and his long-suffering and loving secretary, Rose (Chita Rivera), decide to cook up one last publicity stunt:

Birdie will travel to the small town of Sweet Apple, Ohio, where he will kiss Kim MacAfee (Susan Watson) the president of his fan club ('One Last Kiss'), and bid a temporary farewell to the nation - 'live' on the *Ed Sullivan Show* ('Elvis' allusions were everywhere). The sometimes hilarious events leading up to that historical moment when he is knocked cold on prime-time television by Kim's jealous boyfriend, Hugo (Michael J. Pollard), and the subsequent repercussions, involved Albert's overbearing mother, Mae (Kay Medford) and Kim's father, Mr MacAfee (Paul Lynde), who had always had a yen to be on the *Sullivan Show* ('Hymn To A Sunday Evening'). The rest of the score, by composer Charles Strouse and lyricist Lee Adams, was full of bright, lively, amusing, and sometimes satirical numbers. Three of them became familiar outside of the show: 'Put On A Happy Face', 'A Lot Of Livin' To Do', and the parents' plea for understanding, 'Kids' ('Why can't they be like we were, perfect in every way?'). The other songs included 'The Telephone Hour', 'An English Teacher', 'Honestly Sincere', 'One Boy', 'Baby, Talk To Me', 'Rosie', and the engaging ballad, 'How Lovely to Be A Woman'. *Bye Bye Birdie* won the Tony Award for Best Musical in 1961, and Tonys also went to librettist Michael Stewart, and choreographer and director Gower Champion, who won two. The show ran for 607 performances and significantly boosted the careers of Strouse, Adams, Champion, and Rivera. The latter reprised her role in the 1961 London production with Britain's own 'Birdie', Marty Wilde, which ran for 268 performances. Dick Van Dyke starred with Ann-Margret and Janet Leigh in the 1963 film version. A sequel, *Bring Back Birdie* opened on Broadway in 1981, but folded after four nights. In 1990, a 'classy revival' of the original *Bye Bye Birdie*, starring one of the American musical theatre's favourite sons, Tommy Tune, opened in St. Louis before embarking on a highly successful and record-breaking seven-month nationwide tour.

BYNG, DOUGLAS

b. 17 March 1893, Nottingham, England, d. 24 August 1987, Brighton, Sussex, England. An actor and singer in musical comedy, revue, pantomime, and cabaret, Byng worked as a dressmaker and designer of theatrical costumes before beginning his long and distinguished career in showbusiness. After touring in concert parties, and playing in various West End musical productions such as *Theodore & Co.* and *Yes, Uncle!* (both 1917) and *A Night Out* (1920), in 1924 he made the first of more than 50 appearances as a Dame in pantomime at the New Oxford Theatre. Byng's Dame was sophisticated and elegant ('I played the housekeeper-never the cook'), and wore glittering gowns - not at all like the often down-trodden, humble creatures who were often portrayed in that role in the traditional Christmas shows. His stylish performances came to the notice of impresario Charles B. Cochran, who starred him, often in female parts, in several of his glossy revues, such as *On With The Dance* (1925), *Still Dancing!* (1925), *One Dam Thing After Another* (1927), *This Year Of Grace!* (1928), *Cochran's Revue Of 1926* (1926), *Wake Up And Dream!* (1929), and *Cochran's 1930 Revue* (1930). Byng's other London credits included *How D'You Do?*

(1933), *Hi-Diddle-Diddle* (1934, in which Byng introduced Cole Porter's 'Miss Otis Regrets' to London audiences), *Stop-Go!* (1935), *Maritza* (1938), *Strike Up The Music* (1941), *Fine And Dandy* (1942), *Flying Colours* (1943), *The Shephard Show* (1946), *Sauce Piquante* (1950), *The Bells Of St. Martin's* (1952), *The Love Doctor* (1959), and *House Of Cards* (1963). His highly acclaimed and lucrative cabaret act in the 30s and early 40s, at ritzy venues such as the Café de Paris and Monseigneur Restaurant, was considered rather risqué, and he was reported to the authorities on more than one occasion, and banned for a time by the BBC. Noël Coward described his songs, which included items such as 'I'm Doris The Goddess Of Wind' and 'I'm Millie A Messy Old Mermaid', as 'the most refined vulgarity in London'. When the entertainment scene changed forever after World War II, he took to straight acting in plays such as *Lady Windermere's Fan* and *Hotel Paradiso*. He retired from the stage in the late 60s, and resided in Brighton until he was in his 90s, when he went to live in the actors' retirement home, Denville Hall, in Northwood. In 1986, somewhat reluctantly, he teamed up briefly with the legendary variety entertainer Billy Milton for a nostalgic revue, *Those Thirties Memories*. Among subsequent efforts to keep his memory alive was Phillip Leather's one-man show, *Just A Bit Of Stuff And Nonsense*.

● FURTHER READING: *As You Were*, Douglas Byng.

CABARET (FILM MUSICAL)

One of the relatively few film musicals to be considered a vast improvement on the original Broadway show, *Cabaret* underwent substantial revisions before it came to the big screen courtesy of Allied Artists and ABC Picture Corporation in 1972. Screenwriter Jay Presson Allen and his 'research consultant', Hugh Wheeler, reportedly supplemented their adaptation of Joe Masteroff's 1966 stage libretto with further information from its source, Christopher Isherwood's collection of *Berlin Stories*, and John Van Druten's play *I Am A Camera*. Although there were several changes in characterization, the basic story of the decadence and corruption prevalent in Berlin during the emergence of Nazism immediately prior to World War II still came through loud and clear. Liza Minnelli, in her first leading role in a film musical, gave a sensational performance as Sally Bowles, a tawdry American singer who shares her lover, the English writer Brian Roberts (Michael York), with a bisexual aristocrat. Joel Grey recreated the menacing 'Emcee' at the Kit Kat Club, a part that had brought him much acclaim on Broadway, and he joined Minnelli in one of the film's musical high spots, 'Money, Money'; both the latter and the impressive Minelli number, 'Mein Herr', were written especially for the film. The surviving songs from John Kander and Fred Ebb's original Broadway score included Grey's extravagant but sinister 'Willkommen', 'Two Ladies', 'If You Could See Her', 'Tomorrow Belongs To Me', 'Heiraten (Married)', and the title song, which Minnelli made forever her own. She also gave a highly emotional reading of 'Maybe This Time', which Kander and Ebb - who could almost be regarded as her 'personal' songwriters - had composed for her some years previously. Bob Fosse, who was probably still nursing the bruises from the adverse critical reaction to his work on the film of *Sweet Charity*, staged the dances and musical numbers, and won an Academy Award for his inspired direction. Other Oscars went to Minnelli, Grey, Geoffrey Unsworth (for his brilliant Technicolor photography) and Ralph Burns (musical director). *Cabaret* also scooped the technical awards for best sound, film editing, art/set direction, music scoring and cinematography. *Cabaret* was beaten to the Oscar for best film by *The Godfather*; the musical also trailed some $66 million behind the Marlon Brando film at the box-office.

CABARET (STAGE MUSICAL)

Worthwhile new musicals were extremely scarce during the Broadway season 1966-7, so this show was more than welcome when it opened at the Broadhurst Theatre on 20 November 1966. Joe Masteroff's book was set in Berlin, Germany 1929-30 before the start of the Third Reich, and based on the play *I Am A Camera* by John Druten and stories by Christopher Isherwood. Those gaudy, bawdy scenes in the cabaret Kit Kat Club, introduced by the egregious Master of Ceremonies (Joel Grey), are contrasted by the reality of a Berlin in which ordinary people's lives were about to be changed for ever by the rapidly growing insidious menace of Nazi power. Singer Sally Bowles (Jill Haworth) works in that nightclub, and there she meets newly arrived young American writer-turned English teacher, Clifford Bradshaw (Bert Convy). He has just the one pupil, German Ernst Ludwig (Edward Winter). In no time at all, Sally and her toothbrush move in at the flat Cliff has rented from Fräulein Schneider (Lotte Lenya) for 50 marks per week. As if Fräulein Schneider has not enough problems already, with another lodger, Fräulein Kost (Peg Murray), seeming to harbour ambitions of entertaining the entire German naval fleet in her room. She herself has an arrangement with another of her paying guests, fruitstore owner Herr Schultz (Jack Gilford), who usually brings home a few samples. They become engaged, but after his shop is attacked by Nazi sympathisers, Fräulein Schneidercalls it off, afraid that her boarding house licence will be withdrawn if she marries a Jew. He moves to the other side of town. The general mood is ugly, and Cliff urges Sally to return with him to America. She refuses, and as he goes back alone, she is back at the Kit

Kat Club, bored with the politics of it all, and giving the customers the benefit of her own person philosophy . . . come here the music play . . . life is a cabaret. John Kander and Fred Ebb's score complemented perfectly this seedy scenario, and mixed - after 'Wilkommen', MC's three-language greeting - the ominous and satirical with an occasional love song, in amongst 'So What', 'Don't Tell Mama', 'Telephone Song', 'Perfectly Marvelous', 'Two Ladies', 'It Couldn't Please Me More', 'Tomorrow Belongs to Me', 'Why Should I Wake Up?', 'The Money Song', 'Married', 'Meeskite', 'If You Could See Her', 'What Would You Do', and 'Cabaret'. It ran for 1,165 performances, and won Tony Awards for best musical, supporting actor (Grey), supporting actress (Peg Murray), score, director-producer (Harold Prince), choreographer (Ron Field), scenic design (Boris Aronson) and costumes (Patricia Zipprodt). The 1968 London production (336 performances) starred classical actress Judi Dench as Sally Bowles, with Lila Kedrova (Schneider), Peter Sallis (Schultz), Kevin Colson (Cliff), Barry Dennen (Master of Ceremonies), Pamela Strong (Kost), and Richard Owens (Ludwig). Joel Grey recreated his original role on Broadway in a 1987 staging, along with Alyson Reed (Sally), Gregg Edelman (Cliff), David Staller (Ludwig), Regina Resnik (Schneider), Werner Klemperer (Schultz). West End audiences had seen the show again the preceding year, with ballet dancer Wayne Sleep as the MC, Kelly Hunter (Sally), Vivienne Martin (Schneider), Peter Land (Cliff), and Oscar Quitak (Schultz). It ran for some nine months before being terminated by a dispute between management and the musicians' union. In 1993 and 1994, the Donmar Warehouse on the London Fringe presented the show in the manner of a play with music, which prompted *Variety* to comment: 'In taking *Cabaret* away from Broadway, an essential verve that can only be defined as Broadway has been taken from *Cabaret*'. Alan Cumming played the MC in that production, with Jane Horrocks (Sally), Sara Kestelman (Schneider), George Raistrick (Schultz), and Adam Godley (Clifford Bradshaw). Cumming reprised his role when Sam Mendes's controversial production finally arrived at New York's 512-seater Kit Kat Club (aka the Henry Miller Theatre) in March 1998. Natasha Richardson was Sally (and took all the best notices), with Mary Louise Wilson (Schneider), Ron Rifkin (Schultz), John Benjamin Hickey (Clifford Bradshaw), and Denis O'Hare (Ludwig). *Cabaret* won Tony Awards for best revival of a musical, leading musical actress and actor (Richardson and Cumming), and featured musical actor (Rifkin). The 1972 film version starred Liza Minnelli as Sally, with Grey reprising his once-in-a-lifetime role.

CABARET GIRL, THE

With the cabaret style of entertainment just catching on in England in the early 20s, this show, which opened at London's Winter Garden Theatre on 19 September 1922, could hardly have had a more appropriate title. It was an Anglo-American production, with the home-grown P.G. Wodehouse and George Grossmith providing the book and lyrics to music by 'the father of the American musical theatre', Jerome Kern. One of the show's stars, Dorothy Dickson, could claim to have a foot in both camps. She was born in Kansas City, USA, on 26 July 1896, but settled in London following her great success there in shows such as *Sally* (1921), which was also a Grossmith-Kern-Wodehouse affair. As with *Sally*, Dickson played the title role in *The Cabaret Girl*. As Marilynn, an ordinary working girl, her efforts to win the affections of the high-born Jim Paradene (Geoffrey Gwyther) bring her into contact with Mr. Gripps (George Grossmith) and Mr. Gravvins (Norman Griffin), producers of the *All Night Follies*, who, knowing true love when they see it, attempt, in a sometimes misguided way, to bring the couple together. Despite animosity from his snooty aristocratic family, Marilynn wins her man - and a job at the cabaret. One critic suggested that 'Kern's melodies are touched with a certain dreamy and haunting wistfulness, even at their gayest . . . a refreshing holiday from jazz'. The show's two big numbers were 'Dancing Time', a duet for Marilynn and Gravvins, and 'Ka-Lu-A', which Kern borrowed from his recent show, *Good Morning, Dearie*, for Marilynn to sing at the end when she finally becomes a cabaret star. The rest of the score included 'Chopin Ad Lib', 'You Want The Best Seats, We Have 'Em', 'Mr. Gravinns-Mr. Gripps', 'First Rose Of Summer', 'Journey's End', 'Whoop-De-Oodle-Do', 'At The Ball', 'Shimmy With Me', 'Those Days Are Gone Forever', 'Looking all Over For You' and 'London, Dear Old London'. The talented comedienne Heather Thatcher, another refugee from *Sally*, played the part of Little Ada, and performed the charming 'Nerves' with Gravvins and Gripps. Though not Kern at his very best, *A Cabaret Girl* was a bright and entertaining show, and ran for a creditable 361 performances.

CABIN IN THE SKY (FILM MUSICAL)

Adapted from the 1940 Broadway musical, this film version was released by MGM three years later. Joseph Schrank's screenplay is set in the Negro south, with Ethel Waters recreating her stage role as Petunia, the wife of Little Joe (Eddie 'Rochester' Anderson), a no-good gambling man. Little Joe is fatally injured in a fight and is destined for the fiery furnace until Petunia's fervent prayers result in a six-month earthbound extension so that he can mend his ways. After being lobbied by representatives from the various ultimate destinations, the Lawd's General (Kenneth Spencer) and Lucifer Jnr. (Rex Ingram) - with additional interference from one of the Devil's delicious disciples, Georgia Brown (Lena Horne) - Little Joe is eventually allowed through the Pearly Gates, along with Petunia who, by then, has qualified for entry herself. Also in the cast were the jazz greats Louis Armstrong and the Duke Ellington Orchestra. The original stage production's score was by composer Vernon Duke and lyricist John Latouche, but most of their work is lost in the show's transfer to the screen. Fortunately, one of the songs that survived was 'Taking A Chance On Love' (lyric with Ted Fetter), which was given a memorable reading by Ethel Waters. Other songs by various composers included 'Honey In The Honeycomb', 'Cabin In The Sky', 'Shine', 'Life's Full Of Consequences', 'In My Old Virginia Home', and the lovely 'Happiness Is Just A Thing Called Joe', written by Harold Arlen and E.Y. 'Yip' Harburg. That song became an enduring standard and was immortalized by Judy Garland. *Cabin In The Sky* was an Arthur Freed production, and is remembered as the first Hollywood directorial assignment in Vincente Minnelli's distinguished career.

CABIN IN THE SKY (STAGE MUSICAL)

A musical fantasy based on the age-old theme of good and evil, with music by Vernon Duke and lyrics by John Latouche, *Cabin In The Sky* opened at the Martin Beck Theatre in New York on 25 October 1940. Lynn Root's book is set in the Negro south, where the devout Petunia (Ethel Waters) is making an agreement with the Lord regarding her good-for-nothing husband, 'Little Joe' (Dooley Wilson), who has been fatally injured in a street fight. Following her impassioned pleas, a life extension of six months is granted to enable Joe to mend his ways, and thereby give himself a chance of entering heaven. Complications arise when the Lawd's General (Todd Duncan) and the boss man from 'down below', Lucifer Jnr. (Rex Ingram), vie for the soul of the unfortunate Joe, but, despite the occasional lapse (shooting Petunia, for instance), he is eventually forgiven by the Lord, and he and Petunia pass through the Pearly Gates together. Ethel Waters' performance in *Cabin In The Sky* is generally acknowledged to be her finest on Broadway (it was her only 'book' show, as opposed to revues), and she was applauded from all sides, especially for her joyous rendering of 'Taking A Chance On Love' (lyric with Ted Fetter), which brought down the house every night. Duke and Latouche's score contained several other excellent numbers such as 'Do What You Wanna Do', 'Cabin In The Sky', 'Honey In The Honeycomb', 'Savannah' and 'Love Turned The Light Out'. The show, which was choreographed and directed by the innovative George Balanchine, ran for 156 performances, and was revived briefly off-Broadway in 1964. Ethel Waters was also in the 1943 film version, along with an all-star cast that included Lena Horne, Eddie 'Rochester' Anderson, and Louis Armstrong.

CAESAR, IRVING

b. 4 July 1895, New York City, New York, USA, d. 17 December 1996. An important lyricist for stage shows and films during the 20s and 30s, after studying music while at school, Caesar worked in commerce for several years, mostly for the Ford Motor Company. Highly literate, and a graduate of several educational establishments for advanced students, he began writing lyrics for his own amusement, and George Gershwin, a childhood friend, collaborated with him on some mildly successful songs between 1916 and 1919. The pair then had a huge success with 'Swanee', which was sung by Al Jolson in the Broadway musical *Sinbad*, and later became a favourite of Judy Garland. Caesar wrote numerous songs for stage musicals and revues with a succession of collaborators during the 20s, among them 'I Love Her, She Loves Me' (*Make It Snappy*, 1922, written with Eddie Cantor), 'The Yankee Doodle Blues' (*Spice Of 1922*, with Buddy De Sylva and George Gershwin), 'What Do You Do Sunday, Mary?' (*Poppy*, 1923, with Stephen Jones), 'Tea For Two', 'I Want To Be Happy', and 'Too Many Rings Around Rosie' (*No, No*

Nanette, 1925, music by Vincent Youmans), 'Stonewall Moscowitz March' (*Betsy*, 1926, with Richard Rodgers and Lorenz Hart), 'Sometimes I'm Happy' (*Hit The Deck*, 1927, Youmans), and 'Crazy Rhythm' (*Here's Howe*, 1928, music by Joseph Meyer and Roger Wolfe Kahn). Caesar also worked in Hollywood, writing lyrics for 'Sweethearts Forever' (*The Crooner*, 1932, Cliff Friend), 'What A Perfect Combination' (*The Kid From Spain*, 1932, Bert Kalmar, Harry Ruby, Harry Akst), 'Hold My Hand', 'Oh, You Nasty Man' and 'My Dog Loves Your Dog' (*George White's Scandals*, 1934, Ray Henderson and Jack Yellen), 'Count Your Blessings' (*Palooka*, Ferde Grofé and Edgar A. Guest), and 'Animal Crackers In My Soup' (with Ted Koehler and Ray Henderson), which was sung by Shirley Temple in *Curly Top* (1935). In 1936, Caesar co-wrote 'Is It True What They Say About Dixie?' with Sammy Lerner and Gerald Marks, and among his other songs are 'I'm a Little Bit Fonder Of You', 'Lady, Play Your Mandolin', 'It Goes Like This (That Funny Little Melody)', 'My Blackbirds Are Bluebirds Now', Oh, Donna Clara', 'Good Evening Friends', 'Just A Gigolo', 'If I Forget You', '(Oh Suzanna) Dust Off That Old Pianna', and 'Umbriago'. Caesar wrote the latter number with Jimmy Durante, and it became one of the comedian's specialities. During his long career, his many other collaborators have included Oscar Levant, James Melton, Victor Herbert, Rudolph Friml, Louis Hirsch and Cliff Friend. Although he has continued to write throughout most of his life, his best work was done before the outbreak of World War II. In his later years he often wrote to commissions from government departments on such subjects as safety and health.

Caesar's best-known number, 'Tea For Two', has been recorded by numerous artists in a wide variety of styles over the years, and became the title of a film starring Doris Day and Gordon MacRae in 1950. Over 40 years later, in July 1992, the song was the subject of a BBC radio programme in which Caesar related how it came to be written. He died at the remarkable age of 101 in 1996.

CAGNEY, JAMES

b. James Francis Cagney, 17 July 1899, New York, New York, USA, d. 30 March 1986, Stanfordville, New York USA. One of Hollywood's all-time great stars, Cagney was a versatile actor with a tough-guy image - he was particularly renowned for his gangster movies - who appeared in several highly entertaining screen musicals. One of five children of an Irish-American father and an Irish-Norwegian mother, Cagney attended Columbia University but left to find full-time work after his father died in the influenza epidemic of 1918. He had a variety of jobs before finding a place in the chorus of the Broadway musical comedy *Pitter Patter* in 1920. Also in the chorus was Frances Willard Vernon, and the couple were married in 1922 and worked together in vaudeville for a few years before Cagney began to appear in stage melodramas, and musicals such as *The Grand Street Follies* of 1928 and 1929. In 1930 Cagney joined the Warner Brothers Studio in Hollywood and proceeded to make the classic gangster movies for which he is so famous, including *Public Enemy*, *Angels With Dirty Faces* and *The Roaring Twenties*. In 1933 he played the lead in one of the best musicals of the

decade, *Footlight Parade*, and in 1937 kicked up his heels in the lively *Something To Sing About*. The musical high spot of his film career came in 1942 with *Yankee Doodle Dandy*, in which Cagney's magnetic portrayal of the master-showman George M. Cohan won him an Academy Award. He played Cohan again in 1955 when he and Bob Hope (as Eddie Foy) combined in splendid fashion for 'Mary's A Grand Old Name' and 'Yankee Doodle Boy' in *The Seven Little Foys*. Also in the 50s he co-starred with Doris Day in two musicals, *West Point Story* and *Love Me Or Leave Me*. In the latter, the screen biography of torch singer Ruth Etting, Cagney gave a brilliant performance as Martin 'The Gimp' Snyder, Etting's jealous husband and Svengali. In 1960 Cagney retired from films, and despite repeated pleas for his return (Jack Warner, head of Warner Brothers, is said to have begged him to play Alfred P. Doolittle in the 1964 film version of *My Fair Lady*), he emerged only occasionally during the next 20 years to accept honours such as the second American Film Institute's Lifetime Achievement Award and a Kennedy Centre Lifetime Achievement Award. In 1981, at the age of 82, he was tempted back for *Ragtime*, a story of 1906 America in which he played (somewhat ironically in view of his early roles) a New York police commissioner. Parts of the film were shot in Britain and Cagney made a poignant appearance at a Royal Variety Show that was attended by the Queen Mother. He continued to play the occasional role on US television until shortly before his death in 1986.

● FURTHER READING: *Films Of James Cagney*, H. Dickens. *Cagney: The Actor As Auteur*, Patrick McGilligan. *James Cagney: The Authorized Biography*, Doug Warren. *Cagney By Cagney*, James Cagney.

● FILMS: *Blood On The Sun* (1845), *The Steel Highway* (1930), *Doorway To Hell* (1930), *Sinners' Holiday* (1930), *Blonde Crazy* (1931), *Smart Money* (1931), *The Public Enemy* (1931), *Other Men's Women* (1931), *The Millionaire* (1931), *Winner Takes All* (1932), *The Crowd Roars* (1932), *Taxi* (1932), *Lady Killer* (1933), *Footlight Parade* (1933), *The Mayor Of Hell* (1933), *The Picture Snatcher* (1933), *Hard To Handle* (1933), *The St. Louis Kid* (1934), *Here Comes The Navy* (1934), *He Was Her Man* (1934), *Jimmy The Gent* (1934), *Ceiling Zero* (1935), *The Frisco Kid* (1935), *A Midsummer's Night Dream* (1935), *The Irish In Us* (1935), *G-Men* (1935), *Devil Dogs Of The Air* (1935), *Great Guy* (1936), *Something To Sing About* (1937), *Angels With Dirty Faces* (1938), *Boy Meets Girl* (1938), *The Roaring Twenties* (1939), *Each Dawn I Die* (1939), *The Oklahoma Kid* (1939), *City For Conquest* (1940), *Torrid Zone* (1940), *The Fighting 69th* (1940), *The Bride Came C.O.D.* (1941), *The Strawberry Blonde* (1941), *Yankee Doodle Dandy* (1942), *Captains Of The Clouds* (1942), *Johnny Come Lately* (1943), *Rue Madelaine* (1947), *The Time Of Your Life* (1948), *White Heat* (1949), *Kiss Tomorrow Goodbye* (1950), *West Point Story* (1950), *Starlift* (1951), *Come Fill The Cup* (1951), *What Price Glory?* (1952), *A Lion Is In The Streets* (1953), *Mister Roberts* (1955), *The Seven Little Foys* (1955), *Love Me Or Leave Me* (1955), *Run For Cover* (1955), *These Wilder Years* (1956), *Tribute To A Bad Man* (1956), *Man Of A Thousand Faces* (1957), *Short Cut To Hell* (1958), *Shake Hands With The Devil* (1959), *Never Steal Anything Small* (1959), *The Gallant Hours* (1960), *One Two Three* (1961), *Arizona Bushwackers* (1968), *Ragtime* (1981), *Moran, Joe* (1984).

CAHN, SAMMY

b. Samuel Cohen, 18 June 1913, New York, USA, d. 15 January 1993, Los Angeles, California, USA. The son of Jewish immigrant parents from Galicia, Poland, Cahn grew up on Manhattan's Lower East Side. Encouraged by his mother, he learned to play the violin, joined a small orchestra that played at bar mitzvahs and other functions, and later worked as a violinist in Bowery burlesque houses. At the age of 16 he wrote his first lyric, 'Like Niagara Falls, I'm Falling For You', and persuaded a fellow member of the orchestra, Saul Chaplin, to join him in a songwriting partnership. Their first published effort was 'Shake Your Head From Side To Side', and in the early 30s they wrote special material for vaudeville acts and bands. In 1935 they had their first big hit when the Jimmy Lunceford orchestra recorded their 'Rhythm Is Our Business'. The following year Andy Kirk topped the US Hit Parade with the duo's 'Until The Real Thing Comes Along', and Louis Armstrong featured their 'Shoe Shine Boy' in the revue Connie's Hot Chocolates Of 1936. In the following year Cahn and Chaplin had their biggest success to date when they adapted the Yiddish folk song 'Beir Mir Bist Du Schöen'. It became the top novelty song of the year and gave the Andrews Sisters their first million-seller. The team followed this with 'Please Be Kind', a major seller for Bob Crosby, Red Norvo and Benny Goodman. During this time Cahn and Chaplin were also under contract to Warner Brothers Records, and soon after that commitment ended they decided to part company. In 1942, Cahn began his very productive partnership with Jule Styne, with their first chart success, 'I've Heard That Song Before'. Just as significant was Cahn's renewed association with Frank Sinatra, whom he had known when the singer was with Tommy Dorsey. Cahn and Styne wrote the score for the Sinatra films Step Lively (1944), ('Come Out Wherever You Are' and 'As Long As There's Music'), Anchors Aweigh (1945) ('I Fall In Love Too Easily', 'The Charm Of You' and 'What Makes The Sunset?') and It Happened In Brooklyn (1947) ('Time After Time', 'It's The Same Old Dream' and 'It's Gotta Come From The Heart'). Sinatra also popularized several other 40s Cahn/Styne songs, including 'I'll Walk Alone', 'Saturday Night Is The Loneliest Night In The Week', 'The Things We Did Last Summer', 'Five Minutes More', and the bleak 'Guess I'll Hang My Tears Out To Dry', which appeared on his 1958 album, Only The Lonely. Some of their other hits included 'It's Been A Long, Long Time', associated with Harry James and his vocalist Kitty Kallen, 'Let It Snow! Let It Snow! Let It Snow!' (Vaughan Monroe) and 'There Goes That Song Again' (Kay Kyser and Russ Morgan). Cahn and Styne wrote the scores for several other films, including Tonight And Every Night (1945), two Danny Kaye vehicles, Wonder Man (1945) and The Kid From Brooklyn (1946), and West Point Story (1950). They also provided the songs for Romance On The High Seas (1948), the film in which Doris Day shot to international stardom, singing 'It's Magic' and 'Put 'Em In A Box, Tie It With A Ribbon, And Throw 'Em In The Deep Blue Sea'. The two songwriters also wrote the Broadway show High Button Shoes (1947), starring Phil Silvers (later Sgt. Bilko) and Nanette Fabray, which ran for

727 performances and introduced songs such as 'I Still Get Jealous', 'You're My Girl' and 'Papa, Won't You Dance With Me'. After High Button Shoes Cahn went to California, while Styne stayed in New York. Cahn collaborated with Nicholas Brodszky for a time in the early 50s, writing movie songs for Mario Lanza including 'Be My Love', 'Wonder Why', 'Because You're Mine', 'Serenade' and 'My Destiny'. The collaboration also composed 'I'll Never Stop Loving You' for the Doris Day film Love Me Or Leave Me (1955). Cahn and Styne reunited briefly in 1954, ostensibly to write the score for the film Pink Tights, to star Sinatra and Marilyn Monroe, but the project was shelved. Soon afterwards, Cahn and Styne were asked to write the title song for the film Three Coins In The Fountain. The result, a big hit for Sinatra and for the Four Aces, gained Cahn his first Academy Award. Cahn and Styne eventually worked with Monroe when they wrote the score for the comedy The Seven Year Itch (1955). In the same year Cahn started his last major collaboration - with Jimmy Van Heusen and, some would say, with Frank Sinatra as well. They had immediate success with the title song of the Sinatra movie The Tender Trap (1955), and won Academy Awards for songs in two of his movies, 'All The Way', from The Joker Is Wild (1957) and 'High Hopes', from A Hole In The Head (1959). A parody of 'High Hopes' was used as John F. Kennedy's presidential campaign song in 1960. Among the many other numbers written especially for Sinatra were 'My Kind Of Town' (from Robin And The Seven Hoods, 1964) and the title songs for his bestselling albums Come Fly With Me, Only The Lonely, Come Dance With Me!, No One Cares, Ring-A-Ding-Ding! and September Of My Years. Cahn and Van Heusen also produced his successful Timex television series during 1959-60. They won another Oscar for 'Call Me Irresponsible' (from Papa's Delicate Condition, 1963), Cahn's fourth Academy Award from over 30 nominations, and contributed to many other films including 'The Second Time Around' (from High Time) and the title songs from A Pocketful Of Miracles, Where Love Has Gone, Thoroughly Modern Millie and Star. The songwriters also supplied the score for a television musical version of Thorton Wilder's play Our Town, which introduced 'Love And Marriage' and 'The Impatient Years'. In the mid-60s they wrote the scores for two Broadway musicals, Skyscraper ('Everybody Has The Right To Be Wrong' and 'I'll Only Miss Her When I Think Of Her') and Walking Happy, while in 1969 Cahn worked with Styne again on another musical, Look To The Lilies ('I, Yes, Me! That's Who!'). Cahn's other collaborators included Axel Stordahl and Paul Weston ('Day By Day' and 'I Should Care'), Gene De Paul ('Teach Me Tonight'), Arthur Schwartz ('Relax-Ay-Voo'), George Barrie ('All That Love To Waste') and Vernon Duke ('That's What Makes Paris Paree', and 'I'm Gonna Ring The Bell Tonight'). In 1972 Cahn was inducted into the Songwriters Hall Of Fame after claiming throughout his lifetime that he only wrote songs so that he could demonstrate them. Two years later he mounted his 'one man show', Words And Music, on Broadway, and despite his voice being described by a New York critic as that of 'a vain duck with a hangover', the nostalgic mixture of his songs, sprinkled with amusing memories of the way they were created, won the Outer

Circle Critics Award for the best new talent on Broadway. Later in 1974, he repeated his triumph in England, and then re-staged the whole show all over again in 1987. After over six decades of 'putting *that* word to *that* note', as he termed it, he died in January 1993.

● ALBUMS: *I've Heard That Song Before* (EMI 1977)★★.

● FURTHER READING: *I Should Care: The Sammy Cahn Story*, Sammy Cahn.

CALAMITY JANE

Straying from her girl-next-door image, and employing all her substantial wisecracking and musical talents, Doris Day was the definitive Calamity Jane in this 1953 Warner Brothers release. The story of one the most famous characters from the days of the Old West has been filmed several times over the years, but this version was as good as any of them. In James O'Hanlon's screenplay, the residents of Deadwood, right in the heart of good ol' cowboy and Injun territory, drool over cigarette pictures of stage star Adelaide Adams. As a result, naïve but good-hearted Calamity Jane takes the stagecoach to Chicago to persuade Adams to perform at Deadwood's humble theatre - but mistakenly returns with the star's maid instead. Rather conveniently, Katie Brown (Allyn McLerie) proves to be quite an entertainer and wins the hearts of the Deadwood people. Howard Keel is funny and in fine voice as Wild Bill Hickock, a reminder of his performance in *Annie Get Your Gun*, to which *Calamity Jane* was quite naturally compared. However, this film does not match the excellence of that classic, although Day and Keel's wrangling on the song 'I Can Do Without You' was very reminiscent of Keel and Betty Hutton's performance of 'Anything You Can Do' in the earlier film. Sammy Fain and Paul Francis Webster's refreshing score contained several effective comic up-tempo moments, such as 'The Deadwood Stage' and 'Just Blew In From The Windy City', along with other pleasant numbers including 'Higher Than A Hawk', ''Tis Harry I'm Planning To Marry', 'I've Got A Heart Full Of Honey', 'A Woman's Touch' and 'The Black Hills Of Dakota'. The tender 'Secret Love' won the Oscar for best song and went on to become a US number 1 for Doris Day. Also among the cast were Paul Harvey, Dick Wesson, Phil Carey and Chubby Johnson. Jack Donohue staged the spirited dance sequences, and the wide open spaces gave Wilfred M. Cline ample scope for his superb Technicolor photography. The director was David Butler. There have been several stage adaptations, notably a 1961 US regional production with Carol Burnett, who recreated her 'Calam' for a 1963 television special. Most recently in the UK, Leigh McDonald, Louise Gold, and Gemma Craven (1996, at London's Sadler's Wells Theatre), have all ridden that famous 'Deadwood Stage'. A studio recording of the stage version, starring Debbie Shapiro, has been released on a 2-CD set.

CALL ME MADAM (FILM MUSICAL)

Ethel Merman enjoyed her greatest film triumph when she recreated her original role in this 1953 adaptation of Irving Berlin's hit Broadway show. Although she was never considered to be as effective on the screen as she was on stage, the part of the extrovert oil-heiress Sally Adams, the brand new Ambassador to the mythical Duchy of Lichtenburg, suited her down to the ground. In Arthur Sheekman's screenplay, which was faithfully based on Howard Lindsay and Russell Crouse's witty and sometimes satirical libretto, Merman flirted with one of the tiny principality's highest officials, Cosmo Constantine (George Sanders), while enquiring 'Can You Use Any Money Today?'. This was only one of the charming and amusing numbers in a Berlin score that arrived in Hollywood from New York almost intact, although inevitably the reference to 'panties' in Merman's *tour de force*, 'The Hostess With The Mostes'', which had presumably been acceptable to Broadway theatregoers, was removed for worldwide consumption. Merman was also firing on all cylinders with 'That International Rag', 'You're Just In Love' (with Donald O'Connor, who played her press attaché Ken Gibson) and 'The Best Thing For You' (with Sanders). The latter artist was more than adequate on the gentle 'Marrying For Love', and O'Connor had his moments on 'What Chance Have I With Love?', 'Something To Dance About' and the lively 'It's A Lovely Day Today', the last two with Vera-Ellen, whose singing was dubbed by Carole Richards. O'Connor and Vera-Ellen made a charming couple, and their dances together, which were choreographed by Robert Alton, were sublime. The rest of the cast included the always watchable duo, Walter Slezak and Billy De Wolfe. Musical Director Alfred Newman won an Oscar for his 'scoring of a musical picture' which was directed by Walter Lang and released by 20th Century-Fox.

CALL ME MADAM (STAGE MUSICAL)

Inspired by President Harry Truman's controversial appointment of wealthy Washington D.C. hostess and leading party-giver, Perle Mesta, as the US ambassadress to Luxembourg in 1949, this tuneful and witty musical opened at the Imperial Theatre in New York on 12 October 1950. Howard Lindsay and Russell Crouse wrote the book, which had oil heiress Mrs. Sally Adams (Ethel Merman) taking up her post to the European Grand Duchy of Lichtenburg, and immediately establishing a more than friendly relationship with the new foreign minister, Cosmo Constantine (Paul Lukas). Once under his cultured spell, she changes her initial ideas on US foreign aid to Lichtenburg from 'Not a dime!' to 'How much?', and sets about trying to wangle Cosmo the job of Prime Minister. Meanwhile, her young attaché, Ken Gibson (Russell Nype), is working on diplomatic relations of his own with Princess Maria (Galina Talva). After she oversteps the mark once too often, Sally is eventually recalled, but will inevitably return to Cosmo, and the Grand Duchy (partly because, as she remarks, one of her ancestors was Dutch). Irving Berlin's lively and romantic score gave Merman the chance to pull out all the stops on 'The Hostess With The Mostes' On The Ball', before doing the 'Washington Square Dance', inquiring of Cosmo, 'Can You Use Any Money Today?', and all the while insisting that 'The Best Thing For You' ('would be me'). 'Marrying For Love' (duet with Lukas) would give them both 'Something To Dance About'. Lukas also had the welcoming 'Lichtenburg', Nype, the lovely 'Once Upon A Time

Today', Talva, 'The Ocarina', and the young couple shared 'It's A Lovely Day Today'. The amusing 'They Like Ike' was rendered by some visiting political firemen on a fact-finding mission from the USA. The big song - or the 11 O'Clock number as it is called on Broadway - was 'You're Just In Love', in which Sally accurately diagnoses Ken's condition - and comes up with the cure. One of Berlin's finest 'double' numbers, it stopped the show regularly throughout *Call Me Madam*'s highly impressive 644-performance run. Jerome Robbins choreographed the show, it was directed by George Abbott, and won Tony Awards for musical score (Berlin), musical actress (Merman), and supporting or featured actor (Nype). RCA Records secured the rights for the Original Cast album, but Merman was contracted to Decca Records. So Dinah Shore was called in to give her Sally on the official cast recording, and *Ethel Merman: Songs From Call Me Madam*, featured Dick Haymes and Eileen Wilson in the other parts. Elaine Stritch (Sally), Kent Smith (Cosmo), Galina Talva (Princess), and David Daniels (Ken) headed the US touring company, and from 15 March 1952, the London Coliseum saw a production which ran for 485 performances, premiering with Billie Worth (Sally Adams), Anton Walbrook (Cosmo), Jeff Warren (Ken), and Shani Wallis (Princess). Since then, major revivals have been rare. There was a spirited UK staging, with ex-soap opera star Noele Gordon, Basil Hoskins, Veronica Page, and William Relton, which toured the regions before settling into London's Victoria Palace for a short spell in 1983, and just over 10 years later, in September 1994, BBC 2 broadcast a good production in their series of Broadway musicals. Tyne Daly was Sally, with David Kernan (Cosmo), John Barrowman (Ken), and Shona Lindsay (Princess). Early in the following year, Daly was hosting the party again, this time in the New York City Center's *Encores!* series, with Lewis Cleale (Ken) and Melissa Errico (Princess). Charles Repole directed those semi-staged performances, and also helmed a Paper Mill Playhouse, New Jersey, revival in 1996, featuring Leslie Uggams (Sally), Neal Benari (Cosmo), Vanessa Dorman (Princess), and Jonathan Hadley (Ken). *Call Me Madam* was filmed in 1953 with Merman, George Sanders, Vera-Ellen, and Donald O'Connor.

CALL ME MISTER

A post-war revue in which most of the personnel, on- and off-stage, were men and women who had served in the US armed forces or the USO. *Call Me Mister* opened at the National Theatre (now the Nederlander) in New York on 18 April 1946. The sketches, by Arnold Auerbach and Arnold B. Horwitt, and the songs, by Harold Rome, dealt with the problems of servicemen and women adjusting to civilian life after several years of war. Betty Garrett and Jules Munshin, both of whom were soon to join Frank Sinatra and Gene Kelly in a couple of Hollywood classics, *Take Me Out To The Ball Game* and *On The Town*, were two of the stars. Garrett had the show's big number, during which, as a USO hostess tired of a Latin diet of congas, sambas and rhumbas, she implored 'South America, Take It Away' ('That's enough, that's enough, take it back, my spines' out of whack/There's a strange click-clack in the back of my sacroiliac'). The song was recorded success-

fully by many artists, including Bing Crosby with the Andrews Sisters, and Xavier Cugat. Lawrence Winters handled two of the show's more serious moments well - when he sang 'The Face On The Dime', a genuine and moving tribute to President Roosevelt, and in the scene during which, after detailing his experiences in the army Transportation Corps with 'Red Ball Express', he, as a Negro, is unable to find a job as a civilian. Those two numbers also reminded audiences of Harold Rome's established credentials as a writer with a social conscience. The remainder of the score for *Call Me Mister*, however, was more light-hearted and slyly satirical, with only the occasional serious moment, and included such numbers as 'The Drugstore Song', 'Along With Me', 'Little Surplus Me', 'Call Me Mister', 'Going Home Train', 'Love Remains', 'Yuletide, Park Avenue', 'When We Meet Again' and 'Military Life (The Jerk Song)'. In fact, the only really serious aspect of the whole show was the degree of its success, which resulted in a run of 734 performances. The 1951 film version, with a storyline by Auerbach and Horwitt, starred Betty Grable, Dan Dailey and Danny Thomas.

CALLOWAY, CAB

b. Cabell Calloway, 25 December 1907, Rochester, New York, USA, d. 8 November 1994, Cokebury Village, Delaware, USA. Involved in showbusiness from an early age, vocalist Calloway was an occasional drummer and MC, working mostly in Baltimore, where he was raised, and Chicago, where he relocated in the late 20s. He worked with his sister Blanche, and then, in 1929, he became frontman for the Alabamians. Engagements with this band took him to New York; in the same year he fronted the Missourians, a band for which he had briefly worked a year earlier. The Missourians were hired for New York's Savoy Ballroom; although the band consisted of proficient musicians, there is no doubt that it was Calloway's flamboyant leadership that attracted most attention. Dressing outlandishly in an eye-catching 'Zoot Suit' - knee-length drape jacket, voluminous trousers, huge wide-brimmed hat and a floor-trailing watch chain - he was the centre of attraction. His speech was peppered with hip phraseology and his catch phrase, 'Hi-De-Hi', echoed by the fans, became a permanent part of the language. The popularity of the band and of its leader led to changes. Renamed as Cab Calloway And His Orchestra, the band moved into the Cotton Club in 1931 as replacement for Duke Ellington, allegedly at the insistence of the club's Mafia-connected owners. The radio exposure this brought helped to establish Calloway as a national figure. As a singer Calloway proved difficult for jazz fans to swallow. His eccentricities of dress extended into his vocal style, which carried echoes of the blues, crass sentimentality and cantorial religiosity. At his best, however, as on 'Geechy Joe' and 'Sunday In Savannah', which he sang in the 1943 film *Stormy Weather*, he could be highly effective. His greatest popular hits were a succession of songs, the lyrics of which were replete with veiled references to drugs that, presumably, the record company executives failed to recognize. 'Minnie The Moocher' was the first of these, recorded in March 1931 with 'Kicking The Gong

Around', an expression that means smoking opium, released in October the same year. Other hits, about sexual prowess, were Fats Waller's 'Six Or Seven Times' and the Harold Arlen-Ted Koehler song 'Triggeration'. For the more perceptive jazz fans who were patient enough to sit through the razzmatazz, and what one of his sidemen referred to as 'all that hooping and hollering', Calloway's chief contribution to the music came through the extraordinary calibre of the musicians he hired. In the earlier band he had the remarkable cornetist Reuben Reeves, trombonist Ed Swayzee, Doc Cheatham and Bennie Payne. As his popularity increased, Calloway began hiring the best men he could find, paying excellent salaries and allowing plenty of solo space, even though the records were usually heavily orientated towards his singing. By the early 40s the band included outstanding players such as Chu Berry, featured on 'Ghost Of A Chance' and 'Tappin' Off', Hilton Jefferson ('Willow Weep For Me'), Milt Hinton ('Pluckin' The Bass'), Cozy Cole ('Ratamacue' and 'Crescendo In Drums') and Jonah Jones ('Jonah Joins The Cab'). Further musicians included Ben Webster, Shad Collins, Garvin Bushell, Mario Bauza, Walter 'Foots' Thomas, Tyree Glenn, J.C. Heard and Dizzy Gillespie, making the Calloway band a force with which to be reckoned and one of the outstanding big bands of the swing era. In later years Cab worked on the stage in *Porgy And Bess* and *Hello, Dolly!*, and took acting roles in films such as *The Blues Brothers* (1980). His other films over the years included *The Big Broadcast* (1932), *International House*, *The Singing Kid*, *Manhattan Merry Go Round*, *Sensations Of 1945*, *St. Louis Blues*, *The Cincinnati Kid* and *A Man Called Adam* (1966). Calloway enjoyed a resurgence of popularity in the 70s with a Broadway appearance in *Bubbling Brown Sugar*. In the 80s he was seen and heard on stages and television screens in the USA and UK, sometimes as star, sometimes as support but always as the centre of attention. In 1993 he appeared at London's Barbican Centre, and in the same year celebrated his honorary doctorate in fine arts at the University of Rochester in New York State by leading the 9,000 graduates and guests in a singalong to 'Minnie The Moocher'. Calloway died the following year.

● ALBUMS: *Cab Calloway* 10-inch album (Brunswick 1954)★★★★, *Cab Calloway* ii (Epic 1956)★★★, *Hi De Hi, Hi De Ho* (RCA Victor 1958)★★★★, *The Cotton Club Revue Of 1958* (Gone 1959)★★★, *Blues Make Me Happy* (Coral 1962)★★★.

● COMPILATIONS: *Club Zanzibar Broadcasts* (Unique Jazz 1981)★★★, *Kicking The Gong Around* (Living Era 1982)★★★, *The Hi-De-Ho Man* (RCA 1983)★★★★, *Cab & Co.* (RCA 1985)★★★, *Cab Calloway Collection - 20 Greatest Hits* (Deja Vu 1986)★★★★, *Missourians* (1986)★★★, *The Cab Calloway Story* (Deja Vu 1989)★★★★, *Best Of The Big Bands* (Columbia 1991)★★★, *Classics 1941-42* (1993)★★★★, *Jumpin' Jive* (Camden 1998)★★★.

● FURTHER READING: *Of Minnie The Moocher And Me*, Cab Calloway. *The New Cab Calloway's Hepster's Dictionary*, Cab Calloway.

● FILMS: *The Big Broadcast* (1932), *International House* (1933), *Stormy Weather* (1943), *Sensations Of 1945* (1945), *St. Louis Blues* (1958), *A Man Called Adam* (1966), *The Blues Brothers* (1980).

CAMELOT (FILM MUSICAL)

This brave but financially unsuccessful attempt to bring Alan Jay Lerner and Frederick Loewe's underrated Broadway musical to the screen was produced by Jack L. Warner for Warner Brothers in 1967. Lerner's screenplay was adapted from his own stage libretto, which had been based on T.H. White's novel *The Once And Future King*. Richard Harris's portrayal of King Arthur, whose hopes and dreams are shattered when his Queen Guinevere (Vanessa Redgrave) is unfaithful with Sir Lancelot (Franco Nero), was far more sympathetic and less regal and arrogant than Richard Burton's original interpretation on Broadway. He also handled his songs in a most appealing way. Laurence Naismith as Merlin and David Hemmings as Mordred were in a supporting cast that also included Lionel Jeffries, Estelle Winwood, Pierre Olaf, Gary Marshall and Anthony Rogers. Most of the songs in Lerner and Loewe's magnificent score were retained, including 'I Wonder What The King Is Doing Tonight', 'The Simple Joys Of Maidenhood', 'Camelot', 'Follow Me', 'C'est Moi', 'The Lusty Month Of May', 'Then You May Take Me To The Fair', 'How To Handle A Woman', 'If Ever I Would Leave You', 'What Do The Simple Folk Do?', 'I Loved You Once In Silence' and 'Guinevere'. Franco Nero's singing voice was dubbed by Gene Merlina. Joshua Logan directed, and *Camelot* received Academy Awards for its sumptuous costumes and art-set direction (John Truscott, Edward Carrere and John W. Brown), and music scoring (Alfred Newman and Ken Darby). It was photographed in Technicolor and Panavision. Poorly received by the critics, the film went on to become one of the top box-office attractions of the 60s, although with a massive production cost of more than $15 million, it still lost money.

CAMELOT (STAGE MUSICAL)

Nearly two years in making, this musical was beset by all manner of problems - and at least one tragedy - before its try-outs in Toronto and Boston, prior to the New York opening on 3 December 1960 at the Majestic Theatre. The show's costume designer, Gilbert Adrian, who had designed productions for Cecil B. De Mille and shaped the screen images of Greta Garbo and Joan Crawford, died in 1959. In addition, Alan Jay Lerner had periods of ill health, although he was well enough to take over from director Moss Hart when he suffered a severe heart attack. Lerner was, of course, also responsible for the book which was based on T.H. White's novel, *The Once And Future King*. Everyone's first choice to play Queen Guinevere was Julie Andrews, who was then still in the London production of *My Fair Lady*. After she signed on, another actor from the same company, Robert Coote, agreed to play Pellinore, the King who simply cannot find his lost kingdom. In Lerner's conception of White's whimsical story, Guinevere's marriage to King Arthur (Richard Burton) and the establishment of the celebrated Round Table, bring a period of peace and tranquillity to the domain. True, one of the architects of this desirable state, Merlyn (David Hurst), has been lured away by the spirit Nimue, but morale is boosted by the arrival of young Lancelot (Robert Goulet), who strikes up a great affection for Arthur. The problem is, he becomes rather too fond of Guinevere as well. Although he is aware of this situation, Arthur invests Lancelot with the Knighthood of the Round Table in order to preserve the peace, but this is shattered when Arthur's illegitimate son Mordred (Roddy McDowell), with the help of his sorcerer aunt, Morgan LeFay (M'el Dowd), attempts to dishonour him with the intention of ascending the throne. Lancelot and Guinevere escape to France, and Arthur, in an action which is foreign to all he has worked for, is forced to make war against his friend. Highlights of Lerner (lyrics) and composer Frederick Loewe's score were Andrews' 'The Simple Joys Of Maidenhood' and 'I Loved You Once In Silence', Goulet's 'If Ever I Would Leave You', 'C'est Moi', an impressive reading of 'How To Handle A Woman' and 'Camelot' by Burton, along with 'What Do The Simple Folk Do?' (Andrews-Burton), although there were no duds in what was a superb set of songs: 'I Wonder What The King Is Doing Tonight', 'Follow Me', 'The Lusty Month Of May', 'Then You May Take Me To The Fair', 'Before I Gaze At You Again', 'The Seven Deadly Virtues', 'Fie On Goodness', and 'Guinevere'. When Lerner returned from holiday in February 1961, Camelot was on its knees and failing fast. However, a saviour arrived in the person of Ed Sullivan, who wanted to mount a fifth anniversary My Fair Lady tribute to Lerner and Loewe on his top-rated television show. The last 20 minutes of the programme consisted of studio excerpts from Camelot, all in full costume, and the next morning there were queues around the block waiting for tickets. The show went on to run for over two years, winning Tony Awards for musical actor (Burton), conductor-musical director Franz Allers, and - in recognition of this physically stunning production - Oliver Smith's scenic designs (he won for Becket as well), and the costumes of Adrian, and Tony Duquette. The Original Cast album spent more than 150 weeks in the US chart, six of them at number 1. A London production at My Fair Lady's former home, the Theatre Royal, Drury Lane, opened 19 August 1964, and ran for 518 performances. Laurence Harvey, led the cast, along with Elizabeth Larner (Guinevere), Barry Kent (Lancelot), Miles Malleson (Merlyn), Moyra Fraser (LeFay), and Nicky Henson (Mordred). Broadway saw it again in July 1980 when a touring version called in for a limited engagement, with Burton recreating his original role, and Christine Ebersole (Guinevere) and Richard Muenz (Lancelot). Burton was subsequently taken ill, and Richard Harris was in his place when the company paid another visit to New York in November 1981, this time with Meg Bussert as Guinevere. A decade later, the Paper Mill Playhouse, New Jersey, mounted a well-regarded revival with James Brennan (Arthur), Mari Nelson (Guenevere), Joseph Mahowalds (Lancelot), Robert Johanson (Mordred), and Larry Grey (Merlyn, Pellinore). A further 10 years on, the show was revived again on Broadway following a long US tour during the season 1992/3. In this radically revised production, Robert Goulet was now playing King Arthur, and received what were probably some of the worst reviews of his career so far. Also sharing the blame were Patricia Kies (Guenevere), Steve Blanched (Lancelot), Tucker McCrady (Mordred), and James Valentine (Merlyn-Pellinore). The soap opera

actor and pop star Jason Donovan, as Mordred, was the main attraction in a 1996 BOC Covent Garden Festival production, with Paul Nicholas (Arthur), Samantha Jaunts (Guenevere), Robert Meadmore (Lancelot) and Desmond McNamara (Merlyn-Pellinore). The critics did not like that one either. A moderately successful version of Camelot was filmed in 1967 with Richard Harris, Vanessa Redgrave and David Hemmings, and at least two other screen versions of the Arthurian legend have been made - A Connecticut Yankee (1931) and the Bing Crosby-William Bendix musical, A Connecticut Yankee In King Arthur's Court (1949).

CAN'T HELP SINGING

War-weary cinema audiences experienced a welcome breath of fresh air with this 1944 Deanna Durbin vehicle in which she hits the trail to the wide open spaces of the Wild West. Lewis Foster and Frank Ryan's screenplay, set in 1847, finds Universal Studio's favourite female singing star aboard a wagon train bound for California and the man she loves. She fails to make the rendezvous after being waylaid by Robert Paige who is not only handsome - but he can sing as well. Durbin's own voice was as thrilling and spine-tingling as ever on a set of superior songs by Jerome Kern and E.Y. 'Yip' Harburg which included the lovely and lyrical 'Can't Help Singing', 'Californ-i-ay', 'Elbow Room', 'More And More', 'Any Moment Now' and 'Swing Your Sweetheart'. Ray Collins played the disgruntled and possessive father, with Akim Tamiroff and Leonid Kinskey as a pair of wandering adventurers. Also in the cast were Thomas Gomez, David Bruce, June Vincent, Olin Howlin and Clara Blandick. This extremely good-looking picture was photographed by Woody Bredell and W. Howard Greene in glorious Technicolor and directed by Frank Ryan.

CAN'T STOP THE MUSIC

In this pseudo biography of the camp disco group Village People, the story has this motley crew being rounded up on the streets of Greenwich Village by Jack Morell (Steve Guttenberg) and his friend Samantha Simpson (Valerie Perrine) in order to make a demo tape of Jack's songs. Unfortunately, record magnate Steve Waits (Paul Sand) is more interested in Sam's (body) work than either Jack's compositions or the group, but with the aid of Steve's tax lawyer, Ron White (Bruce Jenner), modelling agent Sydney Channing (Tammy Grimes), and Jack's loving mother, Helen Morell (June Havoc), Steve is eventually coaxed into signing Village People to a big deal. Altovise Davis and Russell Nype were also involved, and Arlene Phillips (formerly of dance group Hot Gossip) handled the choreography. Jacques Morali, the man who in reality brought Village People to world-wide prominence in the disco era, wrote the songs in collaboration with Henri Belolo, Phil Hurtt, Beauris Whitehead, Victor Willis, and the Ritchie Family. These included 'Liberation', 'I Love You To Death', 'YMCA', 'Magic Night', 'Milk Shake', 'Give Me A Break', 'Samantha', 'The Sound Of The City', 'Sophistication', and 'I'm A Singing Juggler'. Village People took the title song to number 11 in the UK chart. It was to be their last Top 20 entry, apart from the inevitable remixes, or re-issues. Directed by Nancy Walker, *Can't Stop The Music* was released in 1980, and nominated for seven Razzie Awards. It picked up two - for Worst Picture and Worst Screenplay (Allan Carr and Bronte Woodward).

CAN-CAN (FILM MUSICAL)

This popular, but uninspired screen version of Cole Porter's smash hit Broadway musical was released by 20th Century-Fox in 1960. The all-star cast included Frank Sinatra as a lawyer who defends cabaret club owner Shirley MacLaine's constitutional right to present (and take part in) an immoral dance known as the can-can. He also takes a very personal interest in her welfare, in spite of opposition from Louis Jourdan, and even the judge (Maurice Chevalier), who is expected to protect the public virtue, but finds that his sympathies are most definitely with the attractive defendant. Several of Porter's Broadway songs survived, and a few were added from his other shows, in a score that included 'It's Alright With Me' (Sinatra), 'Come Along With Me' (MacLaine'), 'Live And Let Live' (Chevalier-Jourdan), 'You Do Something To Me' (Jourdan), 'Let's Do It' (Sinatra-MacLaine), 'Montmart'' (Sinatra-Chevalier), 'C'est Magnifique' (Sinatra), 'Maidens Typical Of France' (chorus), 'Just One Of Those Things' (Chevalier), 'I Love Paris' (Sinatra-Chevalier) and 'Can-Can' (orchestral). One of the highest kickers in the business, Juliet Prowse, had her legs in the air and was displaying her frilly underwear, along with Shirley MacLaine and the rest of the chorus, when Russian premier Nikita Krushchev visited the film set - and departed somewhat disgusted. Those responsible for the 'shocking' display (which was shot in Technicolor and Todd-AO) - choreographer Hermes Pan, screenwriters Dorothy Kingsley and Charles Lederer, and director Walter Lang - were found not guilty of any moral offence, but were, perhaps, partly to blame for a fairly dull film.

CAN-CAN (STAGE MUSICAL)

It is a very ancient saying, but not necessarily a true and honest thought, that this show, which opened on 7 May 1953 at the Shubert Theatre in New York, has a hit-filled Cole Porter score, and a lack-lustre, unwieldy book. Abe Burrows, who had triumphed three years earlier with *Guys And Dolls*, and was to do it again in 1961 with *How To Succeed In Business Without Really Trying*, was the guilty guy responsible for this libretto, and he directed the show too. *Can-Can* is set in Paris, France, around the turn of the century. The girls from the Bal du Paradis in Monmartre are up in front of the judiciary again, accused of cavorting to the banned can-can dance. When straight-laced Judge Aristide Forestier (Peter Cookson) goes to the scene of the crime in order to see for himself, he attracts the attention of La Mome Pistache (Lilo), the owner of Bal du Paradis. The events that follow, involve a Bulgarian sculptor by the name of Boris Adzinidzinadze (Hans Conried), Theophile (Phil Leeds) the painter, and Hilaire Jussac (Erik Rhodes), an influential art critic, who decides that the renowned Quatz' Arts Ball should be held at Bal du Paradis. By this time, Aristide has fallen in love with Pistache, and as he is facing suspension by the bar and his legal society, they go into business together. By curtain

time, they are side by side in the dock. Perhaps they were right about Burrow's book after all. Best thing in the show, by general consent, was Gwen Verdon, as the high-kicking Claudine, who was only hired for *Can-Can* because Lilo the leading lady was not a dancer. Verdon's sensational performance in the 'Apache' and 'Garden Of Eden' ballets stopped the show regularly, and shot her to stardom overnight. The rest of the numbers included 'Maidens Typical Of France', 'Never Give Anything Away', 'Quadrille', 'Come Along With Me', 'Live And Let Love', 'I Am In Love', 'If You Love Me Truly', 'Montmart', 'Allez-Vous En, Go Away', 'Never, Never Be An Artist', and 'Every Man Is A Stupid Man'. Best known perhaps are 'C'est Magnifique', 'It's All Right With Me', and Porter's eloquent hymn to the city he adored, 'I Love Paris'. However, the composer's witty lyric to 'Can-Can' ('If a lady in Iran can/If a shady African can/If a Jap with a slap of her fan can/Baby, you can can-can too') was pretty good as well. Cabaret singer-pianist Steve Ross used to have a lot of fun with that one. There were Tony Awards for Michael Kidd's outstanding choreography, and for Verdon, as supporting or featured actress. *Can-Can* ran on Broadway for over two years, and the 1954 London Coliseum production, with Irene Hilda (Pistache), Edmund Hockridge (Forestier), Alfred Marks (Boris), Gillian Lynne (Claudine), Warren Mitchell (Theophile), and George Gee (Jussac), lasted for 394 performances. There were two major revivals in 1988, in Chicago and London. Chita Rivera, as Pistache, headed the Chicago cast, which included Ronald Holgate (Aristide Forestier), Larry Raiken (Boris), Erica L. Paulson (Claudine), and Michael Connolly (Jussac). No additional book writers were credited, but in the London Strand Theatre production with Donna McKechnie (Pistache), Milo O'Shea (Paul), Bernard Alane (Forestier), Jean Michel Dagory (Boris), and Janie Dee (Claudine), Julian More (*Grab Me A Gondola, Expresso Bongo, Irma La Douce*) did an 'adaptation' of Burrows' work. A Goodspeed Opera House staging in 1995 went even further, and commissioned director Martin Charnin to completely revise the libretto. He also cut seven numbers, and added four which Porter wrote but were not used in the original Broadway production. In addition, there were three songs from other Porter sources, 'Give Him The Oo-La-La' (from *DuBarry Was A Lady*), 'They All Fall In Love' (film *The Battle Of Paris*), and 'Under A Dress' (not used in *Silk Stockings*). The Goodspeed cast featured Belle Calaway (Pistache), Jamie Chandler-Torns (Claudine), Jamie Ross (Jacques Forestier), Ed Dixon (Boris), and Bill Ullman (Judge Aristide Forestier). Two years earlier, a re-mastered version of the splendid Broadway Original Cast album was re-released on CD. A 1960 film version starred Frank Sinatra, Shirley MacLaine, Louis Jourdan, and Maurice Chevalier.

CANDIDE

A famous flop when first presented at the Martin Beck Theatre in New York on 1 December 1956, *Candide* was later sympathetically revised and reached a much wider and appreciative audience. From the start, Leonard Bernstein's music, and the lyrics, mostly by Richard Wilbur, have escaped much of the flak. It was the book by

Lillian Hellman, based on Voltaire's novel, that attracted a good deal of criticism. The satirical story involves Candide (Robert Rounseville) and his adored Cunegonde (Barbara Cook), who are brainwashed by their philosophy professor Dr. Pangloss (Max Adrian) into believing that this is 'the best of all possible worlds'. After being confronted with real-life situations worldwide in Lisbon, Venice, Beunos Aires, Paris, and other exotic locations, the lovers come to terms with life as it is - imperfect, but perfectly acceptable. Barbara Cook was a joy, just a year before she captivated Broadway as Marion the librarian in *The Music Man*. The lush and melodic score, with its delightful touches of pastiche, included 'The Best Of All Possible Worlds', 'It Must Be So', 'Oh, Happy We', 'Glitter And Be Gay', 'You Were Dead, You Know', 'I Am Easily Assimilated', 'My Love', 'Ballad Of Eldorado', 'Bon Voyage', 'What's The Use?' and 'Make Our Garden Grow'. Extra lyrics were provided by Bernstein himself, Dorothy Parker and John Latouche, who died shortly before the show opened. Although critically well received, *Candide* lasted for only 73 performances. It contrasted sharply in both content and box-office appeal with the 'darling' of that Broadway season - *My Fair Lady*. The 1974 production at the Broadway Theatre did much better. With a new book by Hugh Wheeler, some additional songs from Stephen Sondheim, and Hal Prince's innovative staging, *Candide* at last realized its potential and ran for 740 performances. In 1982 this 'comic operetta' as it was originally called, was taken into the repertoire of the New York City Opera. A 1959 London production with Denis Quilley and Mary Costa stayed at the Saville Theatre for less than two months, and in 1988 *Candide* was presented by the Scottish Opera for a limited season at the Old Vic. In the following year Bernstein conducted the London Symphony Orchestra in a concert version of the show at the Barbican Theatre, and several members of that cast were on a two-CD recording of the score that was released in 1991. The Scottish Opera version received its American premiere by the Opera Theatre of St. Louis in 1994, with John Stephens (Voltaire/Pangloss), Kevin Anderson (Candide), and Constance Hauman (Cunegonde). There were further revivals in Los Angeles, 1995, Kenn Chester (Candide), Constance Hauman (Cunegonde), William Schallert (Pangloss/Martin), and The Gate Theatre, London, 1997, Justin Salinger (Candide), Rose Keegan (Cunegonde), Andrew Melville (Pangloss). A Broadway mounting starring Jim Dale as Voltaire/Pangloss, Jason Danieley (Candide), and Harolyn Blackwell (Cunegonde), had a disappointingly brief April-July run at the Gershwin Theatre in 1997. It won one Tony Award, for costume design (Judith Dolan).

CANTERBURY TALES

Playwright and producer Martin Starkie conceived the idea of adding music to a new dramatization by himself and Nevill Coghill, of Coghill's acclaimed translation of Geoffrey Chaucer's classic. Starkie had previously adapted the Coghill work for presentation at the Oxford Playhouse in October 1964. The recruitment of composers Richard Hill and John Hawkins, who had been working on a musical project of their own, entitled *Canterbury Pilgrims*,

eventually resulted in *Canterbury Tales* being expanded into a full-scale musical production that opened at London's Phoenix Theatre on 21 March 1968. The 'raciest, bawdiest, most good-hearted and good humoured show in London' appealed to the critics and public alike and settled in for a long run. The 'release of this pre-Puritan inheritance on stage' owed much to the fact that, the previous month, a bill had been passed in the House of Commons abolishing the theatrical censorship powers of the Lord Chamberlain. Significantly, the four tales chosen from Chaucer's originals all reflected the 60s generation's preoccupation with sex: there was at least one case of a kissed backside, a red-hot poker, a severe bout of bed-hopping, and several examples of cuckolding, leading up to the evening's optimistic and idealistic anthem, 'Love Will Conquer All'. The rest of the score echoed the show's main theme: 'I Have A Noble Cock' ('He crows at the break of day'), 'Darling, Let Me Teach You How to Kiss', 'Pilgrims' Riding Music', 'What Do Most Women Desire?', 'I Am For Ever Dated', 'Come On And Marry Me, Honey' and 'Fill Your Glass'. The first-rate cast included Wilfred Brambell (of BBC Television's *Steptoe And Son*) as the Steward, Kenneth J. Warren (the Miller), Jessie Evans (the Wife of Bath), Billy Boyle (the Clerk of Oxenford), Nicky Henson (the Squire), Gay Soper (Alison) and Pamela Charles (the Prioress). It was a rude, riotous romp that went on to become one of London's most popular tourist attractions, although even its most ardent fans were probably surprised that it sustained audiences' interest for a period of five years, closing in 1973 following a run of 2,080 performances. A limited run in 1979 at the Shaftesbury Theatre, in celebration of Coghill's 80th birthday, failed to rekindle the show's original appeal. As if to prove that parochial English humour does not travel well to America (and vice versa), a revised version (which won a Tony Award for costume designer Louden Sainthill) with Hermione Baddeley, Martyn Green, George Rose, and Sandy Duncan, lasted for only 121 performances on Broadway in 1969. New York theatregoers sampled the show again (for two weeks) in 1980, via an 'insipid revival'. However, it has been successful in several other countries around the world, including Sweden, South Africa, Hungary, Czechoslovakia, Canada, Denmark, Germany, New Zealand, and especially Australia, where the show enjoyed wide acceptance. In 1991, *Canterbury Tales In Cabaret* was presented at the tiny Arts Theatre in London as part of Starkie's annual Chaucer Festival. He also directed and appeared in the piece. Since then, there have been other attempts to adapt Chaucer's 'medieval traipse through Kent' for the stage. Michael Bogdanov's adaptation, starring Brian Glover, played the Garrick Theatre in 1994, and three years later John Cotgrave's production, conceived by Richard Hope, who also contributed lyrics to Ron McAllister's 'clever pastiche tunes', began its journey at Yorkshire's Lawrence Batley Theatre, and spent some time at the New End Theatre on the London Fringe.

CANTOR, EDDIE

b. Edward Israel Iskowitz, 31 January 1892, New York, USA, d. 10 October 1964, Hollywood, California, USA. An extremely popular comedian, singer and dancer who was prominent in several areas of showbusiness from the 20s through to the 50s. Cantor's performances were highly animated, seeing him jumping up and down, with hands gesticulating and his eyes popping and swivelling, giving rise to his nickname 'Banjo Eyes'. The son of Russian immigrants, Cantor was orphaned at an early age and reared by his grandmother. He sang on street corners before joining composer Gus Edwards' group of youngsters, and appearing in blackface for *Kid Cabaret* in 1912. George Jessel, another big star of the future, was in the same troupe. Cantor became a top performer in vaudeville before breaking into Broadway in Florenz Ziegfeld's *Midnight Frolics* (1916), leading to starring roles in the *Ziegfeld Follies* 1917-19. In the latter show, completely in character, he sang Irving Berlin's saucy number, 'You'd Be Surprised', and it featured on what is considered to be the earliest 'original cast' album, on Smithsonian Records. After *Broadway Brevities* (1920) and *Make It Snappy* (1922), Cantor appeared in his two most successful Broadway shows. The first, *Kid Boots*, in 1923, ran for 479 performances, introduced two of his most popular songs, 'Alabamy Bound' and 'If You Knew Susie', and was filmed as a silent movie three years later. The second, *Whoopee*, in 1928, teamed Cantor with a young Ruth Etting and was his biggest Broadway hit. The 1930 movie version only retained one song, 'Makin' Whoopee', from the original score, but it established Cantor as a Hollywood star, and was notable for the debut of dance director Busby Berkeley and the use of two-colour Technicolor. During the 30s and 40s, after reputedly losing heavily in the 1929 Wall Street Crash, he concentrated his efforts on films and radio. The extremely successful movies invariably featured him as the poor, timid little man, winning against all the odds after wandering around some of Hollywood's most lavish settings, occasionally in blackface. They included *Glorifying The American Girl* (1929), *Palmy Days* (1931), *The Kid From Spain* (1932), *Roman Scandals* (1932), *Kid Millions* (1934), *Strike Me Pink* (1936), *Ali Baba Goes To Town* (1937), *40 Little Mothers* (1940), *Thank Your Lucky Stars* (1943), *Show Business* and *Hollywood Canteen* (both 1944). In the 30s he was reputed to be radio's highest-paid star via his *Chase & Sanborn* show with its famous theme, Richard Whiting's 'One Hour With You'. It is said that during this period Cantor had been responsible for helping Deanna Durbin, and later, Dinah Shore and Eddie Fisher early in their careers. In 1941 Cantor made his last Broadway appearance in *Banjo Eyes*, which ran for 126 performances and is remembered mainly for his version of 'We're Having A Baby'. After World War II he was on radio with his *Time To Smile* show and on early television in 1950 with the *Colgate Comedy Hour*. In the same year he played himself in the movie *The Story Of Will Rogers*. A heart attack in 1952 impaired his activities, eventually forcing him to retire, although he did appear in the occasional 'special'. He also dubbed the songs to the soundtrack of his biopic, *The Eddie Cantor Story*, in 1953, with Keefe Brasselle in the title role. The film contained some of the songs for which he was famous, such as 'Yes Sir, That's My Baby', 'How Ya Gonna Keep 'Em Down On The Farm', 'Oh, You Beautiful Doll', 'Margie', 'Ma (He's Making Eyes At Me)' and 'You Must Have Been A Beautiful Baby'.

There were many others including 'My Baby Just Cares For Me', 'Everybody's Doing It', 'No, No Nora', 'Now's The Time To Fall In Love', 'Dinah', 'Keep Young And Beautiful' and 'Ida, Sweet As Apple Cider', which he always dedicated to his wife. He also wrote lyrics to some songs including 'Merrily We Roll Along' and 'There's Nothing Too Good For My Baby', and several books, including *Caught Short*, an account of his 1929 financial losses, and two volumes of his autobiography.

● COMPILATIONS: *The Best Of Eddie Cantor* (1981)★★★★, *Makin' Whoopee!* (1989)★★★, *The Original Complete Carnegie Hall Concert* 1950 recording (Original Cast 1993)★★★, *The Show That Never Aired* 1940 recording (Original Cast 1993)★★★, *The Columbia Years 1922-1940* (Sony 1994)★★★★, *The Eddie Cantor Radio Show* (Original Cast 1996)★★★.

● FURTHER READING: *My Life Is In Your Hands*, Eddie Cantor. *Take My Life*, Eddie Cantor and J.K. Ardmore. *The Way I See It*, Eddie Cantor. *As I Remember Them*, Eddie Cantor. *Banjo Eyes: Eddie Cantor And The Birth Of Modern Stardom*, Herbert G. Goldman.

CAPEMAN, THE

This show was intended as the answer to all those who, for many years, had yearned for a successful Broadway score by a major rock composer. Previously, major figures such as Lou Reed, David Byrne and Ray Davies had dabbled in musical dramas, and *The Who's Tommy* was a smash hit in 1993, although it had begun its life as an album nearly 25 years earlier. *The Capeman* was created specifically for Broadway by Paul Simon, who composed the music and collaborated on the book and lyrics with Nobel prize-winning poet Derek Walcott. Ambitiously, Simon brought the piece straight into New York, and after being postponed for three weeks, *The Capeman* opened at the Marquis Theatre on 29 January 1998. It told the true story of Salvador Agron, the cape-wearing member of the Vampires, a Puerto Rican gang, who caused media uproar in 1959 after he was involved in the killing of two white teenagers in New York's Hell's Kitchen district. Sentenced to death at the age of 16, he was subsequently reprieved, became a poet, and spent the next 20 years in jail before being released, and dying of a heart attack in 1986 at the age of 43. The charismatic Rubén Blades and Hispanic salsa star Marc Anthony played the elder and younger Agron, respectively, with the seven-year-old boy Salvi portrayed by Evan Jay Newman. Prominent among the rest of the cast were Sal's girlfriend, Bernadette (Sophia Salguero), the Capeman's accomplice, Tony Hernandez (Renaly Santiago), and his devoted mother, Esmeralda (Ednita Nazario). The 'bewitching and bewitched' sung-through score was a mixture of salsa, doo-wop, rock, gospel and Puerto Rican-style folk songs, and featured 'El Coqui', 'Born In Puerto Rico', 'In Mayaguez', 'The Santero', 'Chimes', 'Satin Summer Nights', 'Bernadette', 'The Vampires', 'Shopliftin' Clothes', 'Dance To A Dream', 'Quality', 'Manhunt', 'Can I Forgive Him', 'Adios Hermanos', 'Jesus Es Mi Senor', 'Sunday Afternoon', 'Time Is An Ocean Of Endless Tears', 'Wahzinak's First Letter', 'Killer Wants To Go To College', 'Virgil', 'Wahzinak's Letter' (duet), 'My Only Defence', 'Virgil And The Warden', 'El Malecon', 'You Fucked Up My Life',

'Lazarus/Last Drop Of Blood', 'Wahzinak's Last Letter', 'Tony Hernandez', 'Carlos And Yolanda', 'Sal's Last Song' and 'Esmeralda's Dream'. Even then, some aficionados bemoaned the absence of the 'Trailways Bus' number that had been featured on Simon's earlier CD 'taster', *Songs From The Capeman*. Although Bob Crowley's stunning 'red-sky' sets were acclaimed, the 'expletive-laced, dramatically inert and inept' book, with its 'drippingly-sentimental picture of Puerto Rican life' was not. Director and choreographer credit went to Mark Morris, but it was common knowledge that veterans Jerry Zaks and Joey McKneely worked on the show in the last three weeks of previews. Nevertheless, the production failed to overcome the mostly negative reviews and protests from the surviving relatives of Agron's victims. *The Capeman* was withdrawn on 28 March after 59 previews and only 68 regular performances. Simon and his fellow investors were reported to have lost a record $11 million.

CAR WASH

A day in the life of the Dee-Lux Car Wash in Los Angeles, in which all manner of strange visitors turn up to plague the close-knit group of African-American employees, who include Lonnie (Ivan Dixon), the philandering Scruggs (Jack Kehoe), T.C. (Franklyn Ajaye), an extravagant, over-the-top homosexual Lindy (Antonio Fargas), the militant Duane (Bill Duke), and the rest. All watched over by Mr. B (Sully Boyar), the white owner and his drop-out son Irwin (Richard Brestoff). The film comprises a series of tenuously connected comedy situations and running gags, involving the enterprising evangelistic Daddy Rich (Richard Pryor), complete with his gold limousine, and a whole host of bizarre characters such as an hysterical lady who can't seem to stop her son vomiting in her car, a suspicious-looking customer whose 'bomb' turns out to be a urine sample, and hooker (Lauren Jones) who comes to an arrangement with one of the workers, Hippo (James Spinks) in exchange for a transistor radio. Not a film for the kiddies. In and around, and in between all this mayhem, is a pulsating soul music score that includes 'Car Wash', 'I Wanna Get Next To You', 'Put Your Money Where Your Mouth Is', 'You Gotta Believe', 'Daddy Rich', 'Keep On Keepin' On', 'Zig Zag', 'Born To Love You', 'Yo Yo', and 'You're On My Mind'. All the numbers were written by Norman Whitfield, with occasional assistance from the vocal-instrumental group Rose Royce, featuring Gwen Dickey, and augmented by Mark Davis, Ben Wilber (keyboards), Melvin Ragin (guitar), and the Pointer Sisters. Joel Schumacher wrote the screenplay, it was niftily directed by Michael Schultz, and released by Universal in 1976. The *Car Wash* soundtrack album made the US Top 20, and won a Grammy for Best Original Score for a Motion Picture or Television Special. There were also two hit singles, 'Car Wash' (number 1) and 'I Wanna Get Next To You' (number 10). Whitfield won the Best Music Award at the Cannes Film Festival, and the 'Car Wash' theme was nominated for a Golden Globe. Rose Royce were still around in the 90s, starring in the *70s Soul Giants Tour*, along with other sequined legends such as KC And The Sunshine Band, Tavares, and the *Real Thing*. Five of the original members were still on board, but to many people's relief, the platform heels and striped, tiger-skin pants were long gone.

CARA, IRENE

b. 18 March 1959, New York City, New York, USA. Having spent most of her childhood as a successful actor, singer and dancer, Cara's role as Coco Hernandez in the 1980 Alan Parker film *Fame* was tailor-made. Based around the lives, loves and ambitions of students at the New York School of Performing Arts, Cara's rendition of the jubilant title song was an Oscar-winning international hit, reaching the number 1 spot, belatedly, in the UK. This sparked off an entire 'Fame' industry and a worldwide boost for sales of leg warmers. Another movie song, 'Flashdance ... What A Feeling', from *Flashdance*, earned Cara a US number 1, a UK number 2 and yet another Oscar for Best Song. Signing to Geffen Records, Cara enjoyed further US hits with 'Why Me' (1983), a further movie hit with 'The Dream (Hold On To Your Dream)' from *DC Cab*, and the Top 10 hit 'Breakdance' (both 1984). Contractual disputes delayed her recording career in the mid-80s, before she re-emerged with a new album in 1987 on Elektra Records.

● ALBUMS: *Anyone Can See* (Network 1982)★★, *What A Feelin'* (Geffen 1983)★★, *Carasmatic* (Elektra 1987)★★.
● FILMS: *Fame* (1980).

CARD, THE

Arnold Bennett's 1909 novel had already been the subject of a 1951 film, starring Alec Guinness, well before Cameron Mackintosh commissioned Keith Waterhouse and Willis Hall to adapt it for the musical stage in 1973. The show, which opened at the Queen's Theatre in London on 24 July of that year, was set in the Potteries area of the Midlands, and told the story of young, thrusting Denry Machin, a washerwoman's mischievous son who wangles his way to the position of Mayor of his town, double-crossing everyone who gets in his way. Jim Dale, the 50s pop star who became a well-known actor, played the wheeler-dealer Denry, with Joan Hickson as his long-suffering mother, Eleanor Bron as the Countess who gives his career a boost, and John Savident as his first boss, the archetypical Potteries capitalist. In the roles of Denry's girlfriends were two future stars of the British musical theatre, Marti Webb and Millicent Martin. *The Card*'s score was written Tony Hatch and Jackie Trent whose catchy compositions during the 60s had provided many artists, notably Petula Clark, with massive worldwide hit records. None of the songs in this show attained chart status, but there were some attractive numbers. Webb had one of the best of them, a strong ballad entitled 'I Could Be the One', and she joined Dale for the beguiling 'Opposite Your Smile' which Hatch and Trent recorded themselves, along with 'Moving On'. The rest of the bright and lively score included 'That Once A Year Feeling', 'That's The Way The Money Grows', 'Nobody Thought Of It', 'Nothing Succeeds Like Success', 'Come Along And Join Us', 'Lead Me', and 'Universal Kid Gloves'. The critics thought that Dale, with his 'innocent cheerfulness', gave a 'virtuoso performance', and the show ran for 130 performances. Dale was soon to be based in America, where he created the title role of *Barnum* on Broadway in 1980. Hatch and Trent, too, soon left Britain to live in Australia, but when they returned in the early 90s, *The Card* was revised and revived. With some new songs, and additional lyrics by Anthony Drewe, the show toured UK provincial theatres in 1992 with the ex-children's television entertainer, Peter Duncan, in the lead. When it called in at the Open Air Theatre, Regent's Park, two years later, he was joined by Jane Lowe (Mrs. Machin), Hayley Mills (Countess), Jenna Russell (Nellie), and Jessica Martin (Ruth), with John Turner as Denry's former employer Duncalf.

CAREFREE

After Ginger Rogers had attempted straight acting and Fred Astaire had endured a rather unsatisfactory (professional) relationship with Joan Fontaine in *A Damsel In Distress*, the screen's all-time favourite dance team were reunited in 1938 for *Carefree*. Old stagers Allan Scott and Ernest Pagano set their story mostly in a plush country club, and cast Astaire as psychiatrist Tony Flagg, who, by means of hypnosis and food-induced dreams, convinces radio singer Amanda Cooper (Ginger Rogers) that she is crazy about him - and not her fiancé Stephen Arden (Ralph Bellamy) - who sent her for treatment in the first place! What Irving Berlin's score lacked in quantity - there were only five numbers, just three of which were sung - it made up for in quality. Astaire's reading of the gently chiding 'Change Partners' ('Must you dance, every dance, with the same fortunate man?') was alone worth the price of a ticket, and his version of 'I Used To Be Colour Blind' was just as good. The instrumental items consisted of two superb dance sequences, the romantic 'The Night Is Filled With Music', the joyfully energetic 'The Yam', along with 'Since They Turned Loch Lomond Into Swing'. The latter number accompanied one of the film's high spots in which Astaire consistently hits a considerable number of golf balls from tee to fairway in the style and manner of a US Masters champion. However, the box-office returns were not so spectacular, and in spite of the presence of regulars such as director Mark Sandrich and dance director Hermes Pan, *Carefree* turned out to be the first Astaire-Rogers movie to lose money.

CARELESS RAPTURE

The first of Ivor Novello's immensely popular musical plays, *Glamorous Night*, was a substantial hit in 1935 at London's Theatre Royal Drury Lane, before the management took it off to make way for a previously arranged (and potentially more lucrative) Christmas pantomime. As a measure of compensation, Novello was invited to submit the next play to follow the pantomime. A few days before *Glamorous Night* closed, he finished writing *Careless Rapture*, but it was turned down by the theatre's directorate. Novello went off to establish himself as a straight actor in *The Happy Hypocrite*, and in the autumn of 1936 he and *Careless Rapture* were invited back to Drury Lane - on his own terms. The show opened on 11 September 1936, with book and music by Novello, and Christopher Hassall's lyrics. Novello played Michael, who is vying for the affections of musical comedy actress Penelope Lee (Dorothy Dickson), with his own brother, Sir Rodney Alderney (Ivan Samson). His quest for this lady's

hand takes him as far afield as China, where he is captured by bandits and also becomes involved in an earthquake, before returning home to claim his true love. Novello surrounded himself with favourite artists such as Zena Dare, Olive Gilbert, Minnie Rayner, Frederick Peisley, Philip Friend, and the highly talented young American dancer named Walter Crisham, who made quite an impression in this show. The musical numbers included 'Why Is There Ever Goodbye?', 'Love Made The Song', 'Wait for Me', 'Music In May', 'Rose Ballet', 'The Manchuko', 'The Miracle Of Nichaow', 'Bridge Of Lovers', and 'We Are The Wives'. This splendidly lavish production was choreographed by Joan Davis and Anthony Tudor, and beautifully staged by Leontine Sagan. It kept Drury Lane occupied for almost a year, a total of 295 performances, and established Novello as a major force in the West End musical theatre.

CARLISLE, ELSIE

b. *c.*1902, Didsbury, Lancashire, England, d. 5 September 1977. A lively young singer, Carlisle first appeared professionally on the variety stages of the UK. In 1920 she became much more widely known owing to many successful recordings and by the end of the decade was a featured artist in top West End productions, including *Wake Up And Dream*, composed by Cole Porter. Her popularity was extended through the medium of radio, where she was billed as 'Radio Sweetheart No 1'. Unusually for British singers of her era, Carlisle habitually used American material without too much self-conscious Anglicizing. Although she featured songs associated with Ruth Etting, her style was closer to that of Annette Hanshaw. Unlike Hanshaw, however, she also tried her hand at the blues, performing numbers that were, by the standards of the day, rather raunchy. During the early 30s, Carlisle, who sometimes recorded as Amy Brunton, was featured with the popular dance band led by Bert Ambrose where she met singer Sam Browne. After the Ambrose stint, she and Browne continued to sing together until the outbreak of World War II. By the time the war had ended, Carlisle had decided to retire. Singing with an airy, delicate voice, Carlisle brought a wistfully engaging quality to her material, usually well chosen from the great songwriters of the day. Thus, it was that her decision to perform songs such as 'My Handy Man' and 'My Man O'War', which, with their sexual overtones, came as something of a shock to the refined sensibilities of inter-war British audiences.

CARMEN JONES (FILM MUSICAL)

This was at least the fifth manifestation of a story that started out as a novel by Frenchman Prosper Mérimeé, then became a grand opera by Bizet, Meilhac and Halévy, a 1943 Broadway musical, a 1948 film *The Loves Of Carmen* starring Rita Hayworth and Glenn Ford, and eventually this, a full-blown film musical that was produced and directed by Otto Preminger for 20th Century-Fox in 1954. Harry Kleiner's screenplay, which was based on Oscar Hammerstein II's libretto for that 1943 musical, follows the dramatic action of its operatic source, but changes the setting of the cigarette factory in Seville to a parachute factory in Chicago, and updates the story to

World War II. Don José becomes Joe (Harry Belafonte), a young soldier destined for flying school before being ruined by Carmen (Dorothy Dandridge); Escamillo, the toreador, is now Husky Miller (Joe Adams), a champion heavyweight prizefighter; Micaëla, the village maid, is transformed into Cindy Lou (Olga James), a small-town maiden who always remains faithful to her Joe; and Frasquita and the smuggler friends of Carmen are now Frankie (Pearl Bailey), Myrt (Diahann Carroll), Dink (Nick Stewart) and Rum (Roy Glenn). The singing voices of Carmen, Joe, Husky, Myrt, Rum and Dink are dubbed by Marilyn Horne, La Vern Hutcherson, Marvin Hayes, Bernice Peterson, Brock Peters and Joe Crawford, respectively. The highly emotional score, with music by Georges Bizet and lyrics by Oscar Hammerstein, was comprised of 'Dat's Love', 'You Talk Jus' Like My Maw', 'Dere's A Cafe On De Corner', 'Dis Flower', 'Beat Out Dat Rhythm On A Drum', 'Stan' Up And Fight', 'Whizzin' Away Along De Track', 'Card Song' and 'My Joe'. Herbert Ross was the choreographer and *Carmen Jones* was photographed by Sam Leavitt in DeLuxe Color and CinemaScope.

CARMEN JONES (STAGE MUSICAL)

Although other musical shows had been adapted from operas, *Carmen Jones*, Oscar Hammerstein II's reworking of Georges Bizet's *Carmen*, made few changes to either score or storyline. The setting was drastically altered, however, from Spain to America's Deep South, with a World War II parachute factory taking the place of the original's cigarette factory. Also dramatically affecting audience response was the fact that all the characters in *Carmen Jones* are black. Hammerstein's lyrics inventively update the original, changing the 'Seguidilia' to 'Dere's A Café On De Corner', the *Habañera* to 'Dat's Love', 'Stan' Up And Fight' in place of the 'Toreador's Song' and 'Dis Flower' for 'The Flower Song'. *Carmen Jones* is a tale of love and jealousy that ends when Joe, a military policeman guarding the factory, stabs Carmen Jones outside the arena where her new lover, prizefighter Husky Miller, is appearing. The resulting show, described by the producers as a musical play, was a powerful drama that lost none of the impact of Bizet's work, itself based upon a short novel by *Prosper Merimée*. For the original production, which opened at the Broadway Theatre in New York on 2 December 1943, two artists were cast in the demanding main roles, alternating between matinée and evening performances. Muriel Smith and Muriel Rahn played Carmen, with Napoleon Reed and Luther Saxon as Joe. *Carmen Jones* ran for just over 500 performances. The first ever London production opened at the Old Vic in 1991 and ran for nearly two years. It won the Laurence Olivier, *Evening Standard*, and Critics' Circle awards for best musical, and its director, Simon Callow, also won an Olivier Award. The 1954 film version starred Dorothy Dandridge and Harry Belafonte, both of whose voices were dubbed (respectively by Marilyn Horne and La Vern Hutcherson).

CARMICHAEL, HOAGY

b. Hoagland Howard Carmichael, 22 November 1899, Bloomington, Indiana, USA, d. 27 December 1981, Palm Springs, California, USA. An important composer, pianist and singer from the 30s through to the 50s, Carmichael grew up in a poor rural community, and was encouraged to play piano by his mother, who accompanied silent films at a local movie theatre. Largely self taught, he continued to play in spite of having ambitions towards a career in law. In 1916, the Carmichaels moved to Indianapolis where Hoagy took lessons from Reginald DuValle, a ragtime pianist. While still at high school he formed a band and continued to lead various groups during his time at Indiana University. In 1922, he met and became friendly with Bix Beiderbecke, then with the Wolverines, for whom Carmichael composed 'Riverboat Shuffle' (with Dick Voynow, Mitchell Parish, Irving Mills), one of his first works. During the mid-20s he wrote occasionally, his music being published while he continued with his law studies. In 1927, he happened to hear a recording by Red Nichols of one of his tunes, 'Washboard Blues' (lyric later, with Fred B. Callahan and Irving Mills). This convinced Carmichael that he should abandon law school and make a career in music. Also in 1927, he composed 'Stardust', which, with a subsequent lyric by Mitchell Parish, became his biggest seller, and one of the most recorded songs of all time. Based in New York from 1929, the year 'Stardust' was published, Carmichael mixed with the jazz community, playing piano, singing and simply hanging out. For their part, the musicians, who included Louis Armstrong, Red Allen, Benny Goodman, Beiderbecke, Bud Freeman, Red Norvo, Glenn Miller, Joe Venuti, Gene Krupa, Tommy and Jimmy Dorsey, Pee Wee Russell, Jack Teagarden and many others, were happy to have him around and they recorded several of his compositions including 'Rockin' Chair', 'Georgia On My Mind' (lyric by Stuart Gorrell), 'Lazy River' (with Sidney Arodin) and 'Lazybones' (lyric by Johnny Mercer). After Beiderbecke's death in 1931, Carmichael's interest in jazz waned although he never lost his affection for the music's early form and its performers. He began to concentrate on songwriting, redirecting his musical thought towards the mainstream of popular songs, many of which were introduced in films. Occasionally he wrote both words and music, but generally he collaborated with some of the leading lyricists of the day. During the 30s his compositions included 'Old Man Harlem' (with Rudy Vallee), 'Judy' (Sammy Lerner), 'Moon Country' (Mercer), 'One Morning In May' (Parish), 'Moonburn' (Edward Heyman), 'Little Old Lady' (from the 1937 Broadway musical *The Show Is On*, Stanley Adams), 'Small Fry' (Frank Loesser), 'Two Sleepy People' (Loesser), 'Kinda Lonesome' (Leo Robin, Sam Coslow), 'Heart And Soul' (Loesser), 'Blue Orchids' (Carmichael), 'I Get Along Without You Very Well' (Carmichael) and 'Hong Kong Blues' (Carmichael). From 1937 onwards, Carmichael also appeared as an actor/performer in films such as *Topper* (1937), *To Have And Have Not* (1944), *Johnny Angel* (1945), *Canyon Passage* (1946), *The Best Years Of Our Lives*, (1946) *Johnny Holiday* (1949), *Young Man With A Horn* (1950), *The Las Vegas Story* (1952), *Belles On Their Toes*, (1952), and *Timberjack* (1955). He also had a featured role in the popular television western series *Laramie* from 1959-62. In 1940, Carmichael wrote 'The Nearness Of You' (Ned Washington), his most frequently recorded song after 'Stardust', as well as 'The Rhumba Jumps' (from the

Broadway musical *Walk With Music*) and 'Can't Get Indiana Off My Mind'. Among his other songs during the 40s were the tender 'Skylark' (Mercer), 'Lamplighter's Serenade', 'Memphis In June', 'Baltimore Oriole', 'Doctor, Lawyer, Indian Chief' (last four, Paul Francis Webster), 'The Old Music Master' (Carmichael), 'How Little We Know' (Mercer), 'Ole Buttermilk Sky' (Jack Brooks), 'Ivy' (Carmichael), 'Casanova Cricket' (Larry Markes, Dick Charles), 'Put Yourself In My Place, Baby' (Frankie Laine), and 'Don't Forget To Say "No", Baby' (Cee Pee Johnson, Lou Victor). In 1951, Carmichael collaborated with Mercer on 'In The Cool Cool Cool Of The Evening', which won an Academy Award after it was sung by Bing Crosby in the movie *Here Comes The Groom*. Two years later he and Harold Adamson added two new songs, 'Ain't There Anyone Here For Love?' and 'When Love Goes Wrong', to Jule Styne and Leo Robin's score for the film adaptation of *Gentlemen Prefer Blondes*. Carmichael also worked with Adamson on 'Winter Moon' and 'My Resistance Is Low'. The latter song was revived successfully in the UK by Robin Sarstedt in 1976.

Shifts in musical tastes gently shunted Carmichael onto the sidelines of contemporary popular music in the 60s, and after the failure of two orchestral works, 'Brown County In Autumn' and 'Johnny Appleseed', he never resumed his role as an active composer. Nevertheless, his place as a major contributor to American popular song had long since become secure. As a singer, Carmichael's intonation was uncertain and his vocal range decidedly limited (he referred to his frequently off-key voice as 'flatsy through the nose'). Nevertheless, as albums of his performances show, he sang with engaging simplicity and a delightful rhythmic gaiety. Carmichael spent the 70s in contented retirement, playing golf near his Palm Springs home. Several artists as diverse as Matt Monro and George Melly have devoted albums to his work, and in the early 90s, two tribute recordings, presenting a 'well-rounded sound picture' of Carmichael's work, were released: *Hoagy's Children* (performed by Bob Dorough, Barbara Lea and Dick Sudhalter) and Malcolm McNeill's *Skylark*.

● ALBUMS: *Stardust Road* 10-inch album (Decca 1950)★★★, *Old Rockin' Chair* 10-inch album (RCA Victor 1953)★★★★, *Hoagy Sings Carmichael* (Pacific Jazz 1956)★★★★, *I Can Dream, Can't I?* (Capitol 1963)★★★.

● COMPILATIONS: with Curtis Hitch *1923-28* (Fountain 1979)★★★, *Hoagy* (RCA 1981)★★★, *16 Classic Tracks* (MCA 1982)★★★, *Ballads For Dancing* (MCA 1986)★★★, *1944-45 V-Discs* (Totem 1988)★★, *The Hoagy Carmichael Songbook* (1988)★★★★, *The Classic Hoagy Carmichael* (Smithsonian/Folkways 1989)★★★★, *Mr. Music Master* (Flapper 1993)★★★★.

● FURTHER READING: *Sometimes I Wonder: The Story Of Hoagy Carmichael*, Hoagy Carmichael with Stephen Longstreet. *The Stardust Road*, Hoagy Carmichael.

CARNIVAL

It is difficult to think of many Hollywood films that have been turned into successful musical shows, but *Carnival* is certainly one of them. It was based on *Lili* (1953), starring Leslie Caron, which had a screenplay by Helen Deutsch (based on a story by Paul Gallico), who also collaborated with composer Bronislau Kaper on the film's only song (as opposed to dance sequences), the enchanting 'Hi-Lili, Hi-Lo'. *Carnival* opened at the Imperial Theatre in New York on 13 April 1961, with a book by Michael Stewart, who had provided the plot for the smash-hit *Bye Bye Birdie* the year before, and a score by Bob Merrill, whose main claim to fame up until that time was as the writer of 50s novelty songs such as 'Feet Up (Pat Him On The Po-Po)' and '(How Much Is That) Doggie In The Window'. The majority of Merrill's numbers for *Carnival* were nothing like those. The show's theme, the gently lilting 'Love Makes The World Go 'Round', is established in the opening scene (there is no overture) in which exhausted members of a shabby French carnival troupe set up the tents and decorations for the next evening's performance. The song continues to insinuate throughout the story which tells of the young waif, Lili (Anna Maria Alberghetti), from the town of Mira, who joins the carnival and is captivated by Marco the Magnificent (James Mitchell), the narcissistic magician, until she realizes - just in time- that her heart really belongs to the lame puppeteer, Paul Berthalot (Jerry Orbach). The puppets were a delightful innovation, and they even had their own songs: 'Golden, Delicious Fish', 'The Rich', and the hilarious 'Yum-Ticky-Tum-Tum', as well as joining Lili in the charming 'Love Makes The World Go 'Round'. The other songs, in a variety of styles and moods, included the rousing 'Grand Imperial Cirque De Paris', 'A Very Nice Man', 'Her Face', 'It Was Always You', 'Mira', 'She's My Love', 'I've Got To Find A Reason', 'Beautiful Candy', 'Everybody Likes You' and 'Humming'. A major contributor to the show's substantial success was its director and choreographer, Gower Champion, who, like Michael Stewart, had also worked on *Bye Bye Birdie*. Gower's imaginative staging and dance direction was acclaimed from all sides, and earned him two Tony Awards. Anna Maria Alberghetti also won a Tony for best actress. The show itself gained the New York Critics Circle Award for best musical. *Carnival* closed in 1963 after a run of 719 performances, and was revived briefly at New York's City Center five years later. A London production lasted only one month. In 1993, another revival, off-Broadway at the Theatre at St. Peter's Church, starred Emily Loesser, daughter of the legendary composer-lyricist Frank Loesser.

CARON, LESLIE

b. 1 July 1931, Paris, France. An elegant, captivating actress and dancer. Caron's mother was Margaret Petit, an American ballet dancer, and her father, Claude Caron, a wealthy chemist with his own pharmacy in Paris. The good life continued until France was occupied during World War II when the Caron family, like so many others, lost their fortune. Even so, Leslie Caron took ballet lessons, and had a ballet called *La Rencontre* written especially for her. She was 17 and dancing professionally with the Ballet des Champs Elysées when she was seen by Gene Kelly who returned to Paris a year later to test her for the film *An American In Paris*. She accepted the ingenue role opposite him in Vincente Minnelli's charming film which won six Academy Awards, including one for best picture. She followed her enchanting performance in that film with others equally appealing in *Lili* (in which she and Mel Ferrer introduced the charming 'Hi-Lili, Hi-Lo'), *The Glass Slipper*, *Daddy Long Legs*, and *Gigi*. By the time she made the latter multi-Oscar winner, Caron was 27 and a mother, but she still managed to retain her fresh, gamine image. Two years after her first marriage to George Hormel, heir to the American Span fortune, was dissolved in 1954, she married the British stage director Peter Hall. He discouraged her from acting, although having developed into a serious actress on the stage and screen in between her musical films, she did manage to do some work, including Jean Giraudoux's play *Ondine* for the RSC in 1961. A romantic relationship with the actor Warren Beatty precipitated her divorce from Hall in 1965, and she and Beatty lived together in the USA for two years. Her third marriage to the much younger American film producer Michael Laughlin lasted for seven years. During the 60s Caron returned to films, and although there were no musicals amongst them, she was acclaimed in the 60s for her dramatic performance in *The L-Shaped Room*, and teamed with Cary Grant for the amusing *Father Goose*. She lives chiefly in Paris and New York, and continues to perform on stage, sometimes in her own plays. In 1982 she published a collection of short stories under the title of *Vengeance*, and in 1991 learnt to speak German so that she could play the role of the fading ballerina Grushinskaya in a stage production of the musical *Grand Hotel*. Two years later Caron opened her own restaurant in the Burgundy town of Villeneuve-sur-Yonne, 75 miles from Paris, having painstakingly converted a group of dilapidated thirteenth-century houses over a period of five years. Towards the end of the 90s she spent some time in Britain, and in 1997 played the female French writer, who adopted the male name of George Sand, in the nineteenth-century play *Nocturne For Lovers* at Chichester's Minerva Theatre. She was also the voice of Saint-Sébastien narrating 'Le Martyre de Saint Sébastien' by Debussy which was performed at the Barbican by the London Symphony Orchestra under Michael Tilson Thomas. A year later, Caron joined a host of other former MGM stars in a salute to those *Magnificent Golden Years Of Musicals* at the London Palladium, and was awarded the Order du Merite to add to the Legion d'Honneur she received from President Mitterand five years earlier.

● FILMS: *The Man With A Cloak* (1951), *An American In Paris* (1951), *Glory Alley* (1952), *Lili* (1953), *The Story Of Three Loves* (1953), *Daddy Long Legs* (1955), *The Glass Slipper* (1955), *Gaby* (1956), *The Doctor's Dilemma* (1958), *Gigi* (1958), *The Man Who Understood Women* (1959), *The Subterraneans* (1960), *Austerlitz* (1960), *Fanny* (1961), *Three Fables Of Love* (1962), *The L-Shaped Room* (1963), *Guns Of Darkness* (1962), *Father Goose* (1964), *A Very Special Favour* (1965), *Promise Her Anything* (1966), *Is Paris Burning?* (1966), *The Head Of The Family* (1968), *Madron* (1970), *Chandler* (1972), *Nicole* (1972), *Purple Night* (1972), *Serail* (1976), *Valentino* (1977), *The Man Who Loved Women* (1977), *Goldengirl* (1979), *Contract* (1980), *Chanel Solitaire* (1981), *Imperatives* (1982), *Dangerous Moves* (1984), *Unapproachable* (1987), *Warriers And Captives* (1989), *Courage Mountain* (1989), *Damage* (1992), *Jean Renoir* (1993), *The Genius* (1993), *Let It Be Me* (1995), *Funny Bones* (1995), *The Reef* (1997).

CAROUSEL (FILM MUSICAL)

It took more than 10 years for Richard Rodgers and Oscar Hammerstein II's second musical to transfer from Broadway to Hollywood in 1956, but the wait was more than worthwhile. The story, with its inherent dark undertones, was always going to be difficult to film, but Henry Ephron and his wife Phoebe wrote a fine screenplay. It was based on the original stage libretto, which itself had been adapted from Ferenc Molnar's play *Liliom*. It was set in Maine, New England, in 1873, and told of the tragic love affair between carousel barker Billy Bigelow (Gordon MacRae) and mill worker Julie Jordan (Shirley Jones). Out of work, and desperate to earn enough money to support his pregnant wife, Billy is persuaded by sly Jigger Craigin (Cameron Mitchell) to take part in a robbery that goes awry. He is killed in the ensuing scuffle when he falls on his own knife. Fifteen years later he is allowed to return to earth for just one day so that he can make his peace with his lovely teenage daughter. An admirable supporting cast included Barbara Ruick and Robert Rounseville as the delightful Carrie Pipperidge and Enoch Snow, Claramae Turner, Susan Luckey, Audrey Christie, Gene Lockhart and Jacques d'Amboise. The classic score remained more or less intact, from the majestic 'Carousel Waltz' through to the inspirational 'You'll Never Walk Alone'. Along the way there are other memorable numbers such as 'You're A Queer One, Julie Jordan', 'If I Loved You', 'Mr. Snow', 'June Is Bustin' Out All Over', 'When The Children Are Asleep', 'Soliloquy', 'Stonecutters Cut It On Stone', 'What's The Use Of Wond'rin'?' and 'A Real Nice Clambake'. Roger Alexander and the legendary Agnes de Mille staged the dances, and the film, which was produced by Henry Ephron for 20th Century-Fox, was photographed by Charles Clarke in DeLuxe Color and CinemaScope. The director was Henry King. Frank Sinatra was the original choice to play Billy Bigelow but he withdrew soon after filming began. However, he did record an impressive version of 'Soliloquy' which stretched to both sides of a 12-inch 78 rpm record.

CAROUSEL (STAGE MUSICAL)

Based on the play *Liliom*, by Hungarian playwright Ferenc Molnar, this show, which opened at the Majestic Theatre in New York on 19 April 1945, marked an important development in the fast-maturing American musical theatre. With the scene of the action shifted from Europe to a late nineteenth-century New England fishing village, Oscar Hammerstein's often dark story tells of the love affair between Billy Bigelow (John Raitt), the handsome, arrogant, carousel barker, and the shy young millworker Julie Jordan (Jan Clayton). When Billy pays too much attention to Julie and her friend Carrie Pipperidge (Jean Darling), he is sacked by the amusement park's jealous owner, Mrs. Mullins (Jean Casto). With Carrie all fixed up to marry the hard-working fisherman Enoch Snow (Eric Mattson), it is Julie who accepts Billy's invitation for a date. After they are married, the couple live with Julie's cousin, Nettie Fowler (Christine Johnson), but Billy becomes more and more depressed when he is unable to get a job, and hits Julie during one especially frustrating argument. After she tells him they are to have a child, he becomes more determined to earn some money, and falls in with no-good Jigger Craigin (Murvyn Vye), who plans to steal the payroll from mill-owner David Bascombe (Franklyn Fox). When they botch the robbery, Billy stabs himself to death rather than spend the rest of his life in jail. However, his problems are really just beginning, for the Starkeeper (Russell Collins) will not let him into Heaven with his kind of record. His only chance is to return to Earth for one day, and try and do something about it. Fifteen years later (Earth, not Heaven time), he goes back and tries to make his daughter Louise (Bambi Linn) understand that her father had some good in him, as well as the bad. He fails, but at her graduation ceremony, when the speaker talks of the right and proper way of life, Billy is there, hoping and praying that his daughter will take the his advice. Richard Rodgers and Oscar Hammerstein's magnificent score, which opened with the unconventional, insinuating 'Carousel Waltz' (no overture), included 'You're A Queer One, Julie Jordan', 'Mister Snow', 'If I Loved You', 'June Is Bustin' Out All Over', 'When The Children Are Asleep', 'Blow High, Blow Low', 'Soliloquy', 'The Highest Judge Of All', 'This Was A Real Nice Clambake', 'Geraniums In The Winder', 'There's Nothin' So Bad For A Woman', 'What's The Use Of Wond'rin'', and 'You'll Never Walk Alone'. There was also an extended 'Ballet' sequence staged by choreographer Agnes De Mille. Rouben Mamoulian directed the production which won the New York Drama Critics Award for best musical, and went on to become a substantial hit. There was a two-year national tour, and a London staging at the Theatre Royal, Drury Lane in 1950, with Stephen Douglass (Billy), Iva Withers (Julie), Margot Moser (Carrie), Eric Mattson (Enoch), Marion Ross (Nettie), Morgan Davies (Jigger), and William Sherwood (Starkeeper), ran for 566 performances. Raitt reprised his role in 1965 at the Lincoln Center opposite Eileen Christy, and Robert Goulet starred in the 1967 US television version. Jan Clayton was back in her original part during the summer run at the US Pavilion of the 1958 Brussels Exposition. In December 1992, a highly acclaimed 're-examination' of *Carousel* ('electrifying piece of theatre . . . devastating emotional impact . . . fully unveiled emotionalism') ran at the Royal National Theatre, subsequently transferring to the West End. The cast included Michael Hayden (Billy), Joanna Riding (Julie), Clive Rowe (Enoch), Janie Dee (Carrie), and Patricia Routledge (Nettie). Choreographed by Kenneth MacMillan and directed by Nicholas Hytner, with Bob Crowley's ingenious sets, it won Laurence Olivier Awards for best musical revival, actress (Riding), director (Hytner), and supporting performance (Dee). Hayden led a Lincoln Center production at the Vivian Beaumont Theatre in 1994, along with Sally Murphy (Julie), Audra McDonald (Carrie), and Eddie Korbich (Enoch). This production gained Tony Awards for best musical revival, featured actress (McDonald), director (Hytner), scenic design (Crowley), choreography (MacMillan), and later toured extensively throughout the USA. The 1956 film version starred Gordon MacRae and Shirley Jones.

CARRIE

There must have been worse shows than *Carrie* - a few even ran for less than *Carrie's* tally of 16 previews and five performances - yet for some reason this show seems to have been selected to represent the 'Broadway flops' - those often misguided, tasteless, and gloriously horrible and expensive short-lived productions, behind many of which have been some of the musical theatre's most illustrious names. It even lent its name to a fascinating book: *Not Since Carrie: 40 Years Of Broadway Musical Flops*, by the American author and critic Ken Mandelbaum, which gives an indication of just how bad it really was. The show was a Royal Shakespeare Company production, and started its life in Stratford-upon-Avon, England, in February 1988, with a three-week run before transferring directly to New York. Lawrence D. Cohen's book, which was adapted from the novel by Stephen King, tells of a repressed, sexually retarded young schoolgirl (Linzi Hateley), with telekinetic powers (her fingers 'spurt fire'), and a 'religious-nut mother' (Barbara Cook). The early part of the show dealt with the girl's first menstruation, a 'nightmare passage to womanhood' (in UK theatrical circles the show was known as *Monthly: A Musical*). Much of what followed was unclear, but, in Act Two, several pigs are slaughtered, and then, in the finale, the mother and daughter appear to kill each other on a white staircase - there was a great deal of blood spilt in this show. The score, by Michael Gore (music) and Dean Pitchford (lyrics) (writers of the Academy Award-winning title song for the *Fame* movie), consisted of a series of 'coarse semi-disco numbers interspersed with some soupy, soppy ballads', and included 'Dream On', 'Open Your Heart', 'Eve Was Weak', 'Don't Waste The Moon', 'Evening Prayers', 'Unsuspecting Hearts', 'Do Me A Favor', 'I Remember How Those Boys Could Dance', 'It Hurts To Be Strong', 'Unsuspecting Hearts', 'I'm Not Alone', 'Carrie', and, of course, 'Out For Blood'. Barbara Cook, Broadway's favourite ingénue of the 50s, who was in the middle of an 80s renaissance, soon realized how awful the whole thing was (she was nearly decapitated by a piece of scenery early on), and withdrew at the end of the Stratford run, which was not well received ('Is there a doctor in the house?') by the critics. Betty Buckley took her role for the Broadway opening on 12 May 1988 at the Virginia Theatre, where the auditorium had been completely painted black - in mourning, perhaps? Most of those concerned in one of the most celebrated disasters in contemporary musical theatre history came in for critical punishment, particularly the director Terry Hands, and choreographer Debbie Allen, who was best known for her work on the television series *Fame*. Linzi Hateley, a 17-year-old drama school graduate, escaped most of the flak, although her acting was compared unfavourably with that of Sissy Spacek in the 1976 film of *Carrie*.

CARROLL, EARL

b. 16 September 1893, Pittsburgh, Pennsylvania, USA, d. 17 June 1948, Mount Carmel, Pennsylvania, USA. A producer, director, author and songwriter, in the 20s and early 30s, Carroll's glamorous revues, 'Featuring The Most

Beautiful Girls In The World' rivalled other similar - although perhaps more up-market - productions such as the *Ziegfeld Follies* and *George White's Scandals*. Carroll was selling programmes in theatres when he was 10 years old, before working his way around the world while still in his teens. From 1912-17 he was a staff writer with the Feist music publishing company, and also contributed material to Broadway shows such as *The Passing Show Of 1912*, the *Ziegfeld Follies Of 1913*, and *Pretty Miss Smith* (with composer Alfred Robyn, 1914). He wrote his first full scores for *So Long Letty* (1916) and *Canary Cottage* (1917). After serving as a pilot in World War II, Carroll worked with the composer Alfred Francis on *The Love Mill* (1918), and then moved into management and production to such an extent that, in 1922, he was able to build his own Earl Carroll Theatre in New York. Between 1923 and 1932 (plus an extra version in 1940), he staged a series of 'girlie' revues under the title of the *Earl Carroll Vanities*, with the exception of 1929 and 1935 when the shows were presented as the *Earl Carroll Sketchbook*. They all had decent runs, but there were notable editions in 1929, when the show ran for 440 performances, and featured songs mostly by E.Y. 'Yip' Harburg and Jay Gorney, such as 'Kinda Cute', 'Like Me Less, Love Me More', and 'Crashing The Golden Gate'; and in 1930, again with Harburg and Gorney's songs such as 'Ring Out The Blues' and 'I Came to Life'. In 1931, several of the numbers were written by Burton Lane and Harold Adamson, including 'Have A Heart', 'Goin' To Town', 'Love Come Into My Heart' and 'Heigh Ho, The Gang's All Here', plus interpolations from other songwriters such as Ray Noble, Reg Connelly and Jimmy Campbell with their 'Goodnight Sweetheart'; and in 1932, when the *Vanities* was staged by the young Vincente Minnelli, Lilian Shade introduced Harold Arlen and Ted Koehler's 'I Gotta Right To Sing The Blues', which Jack Teagarden adopted as his theme tune. 1931 was also the year that the new Earl Carroll Theatre, 'the largest legitimate theatre in the world', opened on the site of the old one, with 3000 seats and a number of features that ranged from black velvet walls, to reconditioned air, to free soft drinks in the intermission. The naked girls and the onstage antics still had the critics fuming at what they considered to be 'a monstrosity of bad taste'. Many famous names appeared in Carroll's shows during the years, including Joe Cook, Sophie Tucker, W.C. Fields, Lillian Roth, Jack Benny, Helen Broderick, Jimmy Savo, Patsy Kelly, William Mahoney, Milton Berle, and one of Britain's brightest stars, Jessie Matthews, who, in the 1927 edition, suffered the indignity of having coins thrown onto the stage by a dissatisfied audience. Carroll was also involved in other Broadway and off-Broadway shows such as *Murder At The Vanities* (1933), and in several movies, *A Night At Earl Carroll's* (1940), *Earl Carroll's Vanities* (1945), and *Earl Carroll's Sketch Book* (1946). One of Broadway's most flamboyant showmen, Carroll died in an air crash in June 1948.

CASSIDY, DAVID

b. 12 April 1950, New York, USA. A singer and actor, the son of Jack Cassidy and actress Evelyn Ward, who achieved worldwide fame as a pop star after appearing with his stepmother, Shirley Jones, in the US television sitcom *The Partridge Family* (1970-74). In the show, Cassidy, along with Susan Dey and Danny Bonaduce, was part of a singing group based on the Cowsills. Almost immediately, *The Partridge Family* began registering hits in their own right. Cassidy was lead singer, with Jones on backing vocals, for the US chart-topper 'I Think I Love You' (1970), which was followed by two more Top 10 entries, 'Doesn't Somebody Want To Be Wanted' and 'I'll Meet You Halfway', along with a few other minor releases. Launched in 1971 as a solo artist, late in the year Cassidy went to US number 1 with a revival of the Association's 'Cherish'. Cassidy was classic teen-idol material, but was ambivalent about the superficiality of his image. He attempted to create a more adult sexual persona by appearing semi-naked in the pages of *Rolling Stone*. The publicity did not help his career at home, but by mid-1972 he was finding even greater acclaim in the UK, where adolescent adoration for pop stars was suddenly in the ascendant. Early in that year he climbed to number 2 in Britain with 'Could It Be Forever'/'Cherish', and topped the chart with his reworking of the Young Rascals' 'How Can I Be Sure'. The more R&B-style 'Rock Me Baby' just failed to reach the UK Top 10, and peaked at number 38 in the US. It was nearly 20 years before Cassidy had another Top 30 hit, 'Lyin' To Myself' (1990), in his home country. By 1973, he was concentrating on the UK market, and his efforts were rewarded with the Top 3 'I'm A Clown'/'Some Kind Of Summer', and his second UK number 1, 'Daydreamer'/'The Puppy Song'. His ability to raid old catalogues and recycle well-known songs and standards to teenage audiences was reflected through further successful reworkings of 'If I Didn't Care' - an Inkspots hit from the 30s - the Beatles' 'Please Please Me', and the Beach Boys' 'Darlin'. After switching from Bell to RCA Records, in 1975 he just failed to reach the UK Top 10 with 'I Write The Songs'/'Get It Up For Love'. There followed a period of alcohol and drugs abuse which led to Cassidy retiring to Los Angeles for about three 'dark' years, but in 1978 he won an Emmy nomination for a leading part on television, and four years later he was on Broadway playing the title role in a long-running revival of Andrew Lloyd Webber and Tim Rice's *Joseph And The Amazing Technicolor Dreamcoat*. In 1985, he made a surprise return to the UK Top 10 with 'The Last Kiss', which featured backing vocals by George Michael, and was followed later in the year by 'Romance (Let Your Heart Go)'. Two years on, he took over the leading role from Cliff Richard in Dave Clark's lavish stage musical, *Time*. At this point, the recording career of one of his step-brothers, Shaun Cassidy, was declining, and in 1993 British theatrical producer Bill Kenwright had the brilliant idea of casting the duo, along with veteran singer Petula Clark, in his ailing New York production of Willy Russell's gritty musical, *Blood Brothers*. The trio's presence averted the show's imminent closure, and David Cassidy recreated the role of Mickey in subsequent productions of *Blood Brothers* in the West End, and on US and UK regional tours. In 1996 Cassidy's next major assignment was on a somewhat larger scale, taking over the lead from Michael Crawford in the multi-million high-tech musical *EFX* at the MGM

Grand Hotel, Las Vegas. Cassidy himself was replaced early in 1999 by Broadway song-and-dance man Tommy Tune. His 1998 album contained several remakes of such 70s hits as 'I Can Feel Your Heartbeat' and 'I Woke Up In Love This Morning', as well as a re-recording of 'I Think I Love You', a song which turned up in the movie *Scream 2* and a Levi's television commercial.

● ALBUMS: *Cherish* (Bell 1972)★★, *Could It Be Forever* (Bell 1972)★★, *Rock Me Baby* (Bell 1973)★★, *Dreams Are Nothin' More Than Wishes* (Bell 1973)★★, *Cassidy Live* (1974)★, *The Higher They Climb The Harder They Fall* (RCA 1975)★★, *Home Is Where The Heart Is* (1976)★★★, *Gettin' It In The Street* (1976)★★★, *Romance* (Arista 1985)★★, *His Greatest Hits, Live* (Starblend 1986)★, *Labor Of Love* (1990)★★★, *David Cassidy* (Enigma 1990)★★, *Didn't You Used To Be ...* (1992)★★★, *Old Trick, New Dog* (1998)★★★.

● COMPILATIONS: *Greatest Hits* (MFP 1977)★★★.

● FURTHER READING: *Meet David Cassidy*, James A. Hudson. *David Cassidy Annual 1974*, no editor listed. *The David Cassidy Story*, James Gregory. *David In Europe: Exclusive! David's Own Story In David's Own Words*, David Cassidy. *C'mon Get Happy ... Fear And Loathing On The Partridge Family Bus*, David Cassidy.

● FILMS: *The Spirit Of '76* (1990), *Instant Karma* (1990).

CASSIDY, JACK

b. John Cassidy, 5 March 1927, Richmond Hill, New York, USA, d. 12 March 1976, Los Angeles, California, USA. A versatile actor and singer who, even in his later years, seemed to retain his youthful appearance, Cassidy made his Broadway debut at the age of 17 in the chorus of the 1943 Cole Porter-Ethel Merman hit musical *Something For The Boys*. More chorus work followed in *Sadie Thompson*, *The Firebrand Of Florence*, *Around The World*, *Music In My Heart*, and *Inside USA*, before Cassidy played a more prominent role, along with others on the brink of success such as Tom Ewell and Alice Pearce, in the stylish revue *Small Wonder* (1948). He was in the short-lived *Alive And Kicking* in 1950, and two years later took over the part of Seabee Richard West in *South Pacific*. Also in 1952, Cassidy had his first leading role as the suave Chick Miller in *Wish You Were Here*, a show that attracted a great deal of publicity owing to the fact that it had a swimming-pool built into the stage. Cassidy introduced the appealing title song, and also sang the underrated 'Where Did The Night Go?'. He subsequently played opposite Betty Oakes in the off-beat *Sandhog* (1954), co-starred with Carol Lawrence in a musical adaptation of James Hilton's novel *Lost Horizon* called *Shangri-La*, and appeared in various musical productions in the US regions and Europe, before returning to Broadway in 1963 with the charming *She Loves Me*. While Barbara Cook and Daniel Massey resolved their complicated relationship, Cassidy, playing the unctuous 'resident ladies man' Steven Kodaly, pursued Barbara Baxley with 'Ilona' and 'Grand Knowing You'. His performance was rewarded with the 1964 Tony Award for Supporting/Featured Actor in a musical. During the remainder of the 60s, Cassidy had another ultra-smooth role as Hollywood leading man Byron Prong in *Fade Out-Fade In* (1964), was egotistical columnist Max Mencken in the comic strip spoof *It's A Bird, It's A Plane, It's Superman* (1966), and played Irishman Phineas Flynn in the Civil

War musical *Maggie Flynn* (1968). In the title role of the latter show was Shirley Jones, the former star of films such as *Oklahoma!*, *Carousel* and *The Music Man*, who was Cassidy's second wife. Cassidy himself also appeared in a number of films, notably as John Barrymore in *W.C. Fields And Me* and as Damon Runyon in *The Private Files Of J. Edgar Hoover*. After his Broadway career declined, he worked in regional theatre, both straight and musical, and appeared on television and in nightclubs. He died at the age of 49 in a fire at his Los Angeles apartment. Three of his sons, Patrick Cassidy and Shaun Cassidy (from his marriage to Shirley Jones), along with David Cassidy (from his earlier marriage to Evelyn Ward), are also in showbusiness.

● ALBUMS: *Show Tunes*, *Love From Hollywood*, *Speaking Of Love*, *Marriage Type Love* (all c. 50s-60s), and Original Cast Recordings.

● FILMS: *Look In Any Window* (1961), *The Chapman Report* (1962), *FBI Code 98* (1964), *Guide For The Married Man* (1967), *The Cockeyed Cowboys Of Calico County* (1970), *Bunny O'Hare* (1971), *The Eiger Sanction* (1975), *W.C. Fields And Me* (1976), *The Private Files Of J. Edgar Hoover* (1978).

CASSIDY, PATRICK

b. 4 January 1962. A singer, actor, and dancer, and the son of Jack Cassidy and Shirley Jones, Cassidy has appeared on Broadway in *Pirates Of Penzance* (1982), as Jeff Barry in Ellie Greenwich's *Leader Of The Pack* (1985), and off-Broadway in Stephen Sondheim's *Assassins* (as the Balladeer, 1990). US regional credits have included *The Sound Of Music*, *Faces On The Wall*, *Little Shop Of Horrors*, *Love Letters*, *Robber Bridegroom*, *Conrack*, *Martin Guerre* (the show with book and lyrics by Laura Harrington and music by Roger Ames, not Cameron Mackintosh's London version), and *Company*. He has also been involved in several television series, such as *Napoleon And Josephine*, *Perversions Of Science*, *The Second Family Tree*, *Dirty Dancing*, and *Here's Boomer* and participated in various cast recordings.

● FILMS: for television *Midnight Offerings* (1981), *Angel Dusted* (1981), *Something In Common* (1986), *Christmas Eve* (1986), *Dress Gray* (1986), *Three On A Match* (1987), *Follow Your Heart* (1990), *Hitler's Daughter* (1990), *How The West Was Won* (1994); feature *Off The Wall* (1983), *Just The Way You Are* (1984), *Nickel Mountain* (1985), *Fever Pitch* (1985), *Love At Stake* (1987), *Longtime Companion* (1990), *I'll Do Anything* (1994), *Man Of Her Dreams* (1996), *Lord Protector* (1997).

CASSIDY, SHAUN

b. 27 September 1959, Los Angeles, California, USA. A singer, actor, writer, and producer, Shaun Cassidy is the son of Broadway and film stars Jack Cassidy and Shirley Jones, and the step-brother of David Cassidy. After singing and composing with the Longfellows group when he was only 14, in the mid-70s Cassidy made an impression on European pop charts with his debut solo single, 'Morning Girl', followed by 'That's Rock 'N' Roll'. Back home in 1977, his re-working of the Crystals' 'Da Doo Ron Ron' topped the US chart, and was followed by two other Top 5 entries, 'That's Rock 'N' Roll' and 'Hey Deanie', as well as the modestly successful 'Do You Believe In Magic'. Around this time Cassidy was also active in the theatre and on television. His stage credits in the 80s included regional productions of *Barefoot In The Park*, *The Subject Was Roses*, *Mass Appeal*, *Pass/Fail*, *A Loss Of Roses*, *Triumph Of The Spider Monkey*, *Dangerous Music*, and *Romance, Romance*. In 1990, he co-starred with model Jerry Hall in a West End version of *Bus Stop*, and later that year appeared in *They're Playing Our Song* at Stage West, Toronto, in Canada. In 1993, Shaun joined David Cassidy and Petula Clark in Bill Kenwright's Broadway production of *Blood Brothers*. This inspired casting reportedly prevented the show's early demise. On television he has had leading roles in top rated series such as *The Hardy Boys*, *Breaking Away*, *General Hospital*, *Roots*, *Alfred Hitchcock Presents*, and *Matlock*, as well as hosting his own *Shaun Cassidy Special*. His television movies have included *Dawn, Portrait Of A Runaway Singer*, *Like Normal People*, and *Once Upon A Texas Train*. In 1993, when David Cassidy took over from Michael Crawford in the spectacular *EFX* at the MGM Grand Hotel in Las Vegas, the two brothers worked together on script revisions. Among Shaun Cassidy's most recent television projects, as a writer, producer, creator, have been *American Gothic* (1995) and *Roar* (1998).

● ALBUMS: *Shaun Cassidy* (Warners 1977)★★★, *Born Late* (Warners 1977)★★, *Under Wraps* (Warners 1978)★★, *Room Service* (70s)★★★, *W.A.S.P.* (80s)★★★, *Live* (80s)★★★.

● COMPILATIONS: *Greatest Hits* (Curb 1992)★★★.

● FURTHER READING: *Shaun Cassidy*, Craig Schumacher.

CASTLE, VERNON AND IRENE

Vernon Castle Blythe (b. Vernon Blyth, 1887, England, d. 1918) and Irene Foote (b. 1893, d. 1969) were the leading dance team pre-World War I. Influential as dancers and trend-setters in their way of life, fashions and coiffures, they were responsible for bringing an air of spontaneity to formal dancing (pre-empting the 'roaring 20s' 15 years early, in fact). Vernon was on Broadway in his teens and appeared in Victor Herbert's *Old Dutch*, where nine-year-old Helen Hayes made her debut. He and Irene met and teamed up in 1911 and had their first big success in Paris the following year, introducing various dancers including the Bunny Hug, Grizzly Bear, Turkey Trot, Maxixe, Fox Trot and the One-Step, later re christened the Castle Walk. In 1914 alone they earned $31,000 on one-night appearances, starred on Broadway in *Sunshine Girl* and Irving Berlin's *Watch Your Step*, opened their own Sans Souci nightclub in Manhattan's Times Square, plus a chain of Castle House dance studios, and started work on their only joint film appearance, *The Whirl Of Life*. When Vernon, an Englishman, volunteered for the Royal Canadian Air Force, Irene co-starred with Vivienne Segal on Broadway in *Miss 1917* and appeared in several films, including *Patria* (1917), *The Hillcrest Mystery* (1918), *The Invisible Bond* (1919), *Broadway Bride* (1921 and *No Trespassing* (1922). With a fine combat record, Vernon was promoted to Captain and returned as an instructor, but was then killed in a training accident in Texas in 1918. Irene went into vaudeville but retired in the 30s, returning to create another dance, the World's Fair Hop, at the New York World's Fair in 1939. The Castles had been a great influence on the young Fred Astaire, so it was only logical that he, with Ginger Rogers, should recreate their lives in *The Story Of Vernon And Irene Castle* (1939). Irene, now Mrs. McLaughlin, an early animal rights campaigner, finally retired to her pet sanctuary, Orphans Of The Storm, in Lake Forest, Illinois, where she died in 1969.

CAT AND THE FIDDLE, THE

Although Jerome Kern's lyricist for this show, Otto Harbach, was steeped in the Viennese-style of music that had influenced the American musical theatre for so long in the early part of the 20th century, *The Cat And The Fiddle*, which opened at the Globe Theatre in New York on 15 October 1931, was a significant and successful attempt by the distinguished composer to update the long-standing, traditional form of operetta, and give it a more believable and accessible storyline. Harbach also wrote the book for the show, which was subtitled 'A Musical Love Story'. The setting is Brussels, where two students find that personally they are completely compatible - but musically they are worlds apart. The prize composition pupil at the local Conservatoire, Victor (Georges Metaxa) is more than aghast when he - mistakenly - thinks that a misguided impresario has introduced several examples of jazzy music, written by Shirley (Bettina Hall), into his score for a serious operetta, *The Passionate Pilgrim*. However, principles eventually dissolve into passion, and the inevitable happy ending ensues (*West Side Story* was over 25 years away). Two songs from the score, 'The Night Was Made for Love' and 'She Didn't Say 'Yes'' ('She loved to be *en rapport* with him/But not behind a bolted door with him'), were hits at the time for Leo Reisman And His Orchestra, and the latter song received an amusing reading, much later, from the husband-and-wife team of Steve Lawrence and Eydie Gorme. The rest of Kern and Harbach's ambitious and progressive score included 'I Watch The Love Parade', 'Poor Pierrot', 'Hh! Cha! Cha!', 'Try To Forget', 'The Breeze Kissed Your Hair', 'One Moment Alone', and 'A New Love Is Old'. *The Cat And The Fiddle* was a welcome hit in the dark days of the Depression, and a ran for 395 performances, rather more than the 1932 London production at the Palace Theatre. The 1934 film version starred Jeanette MacDonald, Ramon Novarro, and Vivienne Segal. A recording of the complete score was never made available, but in 1992, a CD was issued containing Kern's 'Entr'acte', an instrumental selection of songs from the score, and a lengthy two-part medley by the Light Opera Company, which included Peggy Wood's recordings of some of the show's most popular numbers.

CATCH MY SOUL

Catch My Soul, a rock opera based on Shakespeare's *Othello*, was originally a play written and directed by Jack Good, who had produced the television pop music programmes *Oh Boy* and *Boy Meets Girl*. He possessed an intuitive understanding of music's dynamism and image, characteristics he brought to the stage production. Temperamental singer P.J. Proby took the lead role on stage, but he was replaced in this 1974 film by Richie Havens. Lance LeGault reprised his exceptional portrayal of Iago, but the celluloid version was a marked disappointment. Patrick McGoohan, of *The Prisoner* and *Danger*

Man fame, directed. He had already appeared, with Charles Mingus, in a 1961 adaptation of *Othello*, *All Night Long*, but here he undermined the project in hand by turning it into a 'Jesus freak' carnival, changing music and characterizations. Tony Joe White, who played Cassio, supplied much of the background score which was produced by Delaney Bramlett, formerly of Delaney And Bonnie. Unlike its theatrical counterpart, the film version of *Catch My Soul* was not a commercial success.

CATCH OF THE SEASON, THE

An early musical retelling of the Cinderella fable, *The Catch Of The Season* was presented by the renowned producer Charles Frohman, and starred one of London's most familiar theatrical figures in the first part of the 20th century, Seymour Hicks, who also directed the piece. It opened at the Vaudeville Theatre in London on 9 September 1904, with Hicks as the Duke of St. Jermyns ('Prince Charming'), and Zena Dare as Angela Crystal ('Cinderella'). Hicks also collaborated on the book with Cosmo Hamilton, and the score was by Herbert E. Haines and Evelyn Baker (music) and Charles H. Taylor (lyrics). Their songs included 'My Rainbow', 'The Quaint Old Bird', 'Cigarette', 'My Singing Bird', 'Sombrero', 'Butterfly', 'Come Down From That Big Fir Tree' and 'A Wise Old Owl', among others. Intense interest in the show at the time was generated, not by the plot or music, but by 'its brazen introduction of the bare shoulders, padded hips, and upswept hairdos of the newly stylish Gibson Girl, inspired by the artist Charles Dana Gibson', and personified by Camille Clifford who played Sylvia Gibson in the show. Fashion shops of all descriptions were inundated with women demanding copies. Another, more pertinent point regarding this show is the degree of involvement of the young American composer, Jerome Kern. The London production of *The Catch Of The Season* had a song entitled 'Molly O'Halloran', and so did the New York presentation which opened at Daly's Theatre on 28 August 1905. The American version of 'Molly O'Halloran', which is also known as 'Edna May's Irish Song' (May played the lead on Broadway), is definitely credited to Kern (both music and lyrics). He also interpolated several other songs (with various lyricists) into the US show, including 'Raining', 'Take Me On The Merry-Go-Round' and 'Won't You Kiss Me Before I Go?'. This all happened several years before he was engaged to write his first complete score. *The Catch Of The Season* had an extraordinary London run (for those days) of 621 performances, and played for 104 in New York.

CATCH US IF YOU CAN

Clearly inspired by the success of the Beatles' *A Hard Day's Night*, the Dave Clark Five completed this underrated feature in 1965. Ably directed by John Boorman, who later found fame with *Deliverance*, the film revolves around group leader Clark's infatuation with the image of a girl spied on an advertising hoarding. A debt to Richard Lester's fast-paced métier is apparent and although the quintet lack the Beatles' charisma and wit, *Catch Us If You Can* is more than mere pastiche. The Dave Clark Five were never in the same league and this film easily surpasses every other beat group cinematic excursion. If nothing else, the film immortalizes the mini-moke as one of the great fashionable vehicles, alongside the bubble car, scooter and E-type jaguar. The music featured on *Catch Us If You Can* formed the core of the group's second album, which reached number 8 in the album lists in 1965. The title song reached the Top 5 in the USA and UK, while a further selection, 'Over And Over', subsequently topped the latter chart. The Dave Clark Five enjoyed considerable success in the USA, where the film was retitled *Having A Wild Weekend*.

CATS

Following the termination of his partnership with Tim Rice which had resulted in such 70s hits as *Jesus Christ Superstar*, *Joseph And The Amazing Technicolor Dreamcoat*, and *Evita*, in 1980 the composer Andrew Lloyd Webber turned for the source of his next musical to a favourite collection of poems from his childhood, T.S. Eliot's *Old Possum's Book Of Practical Cats*, which was first published in 1939. After hearing some of his songs, the author's widow, Valerie Eliot, gave Lloyd Webber access to her late husband's letters and an unpublished poem about Grizabella the Glamour Cat, who became one of the show's leading characters, and introduced the hit song, 'Memory'. Together with producer Cameron Mackintosh, Lloyd Webber assembled a highly impressive creative team that included the RSC's Trevor Nunn (director), Gillian Lynne (associate director and choreographer), John Napier (designer), and John Hersey (lighting designer). Finance was not easy to come by - not many of the regular 'angels' (theatrical investors) fancied putting money into an English show about cats, but Lloyd Webber toured the television chat-show circuit and provided personal monetary guarantees so that *Cats* could open at London's New London Theatre on 11 May 1981. The show's action is played out on Napier's spectacular (permanent) set representing a gigantic rubbish dump, which, after dark, becomes alive with cats of all types, shapes and sizes. Soon, there are cats all over the place - in the aisles - everywhere, gathering for the Jellicle Ball during which one cat will be selected by the Jellicle leader and allotted an extra precious life. The main contenders in this 'match of the moggies' are Grizabella (Elaine Paige), Rum Tum Tugger (Paul Nicholas), Asparagus (Stephen Tate), Mr Mistoffelees (Wayne Sleep), Deuteronomy and Bustopher Jones (Brian Blessed), Skimbleshanks (Kenn Wells), Griddlebone (Susan Jane Tanner), Rumpleteazer (Bonnie Langford), Mungojerrie (John Thornton) and Munkustrap (Jeff Shankley). Sarah Brightman, who, with the dance group Hot Gossip, had climbed high in the UK chart with 'I Lost My Heart To A Starship Trooper' in 1978, was in the chorus, and subsequently became Lloyd Webber's second wife. The opening night had to be postponed when the celebrated actress Judi Dench suffered a torn Achilles tendon, and Elaine Paige, who had made such an impact in *Evita*, took over the role of Grizabella. She is the one, the former Glamour Cat-turned-dishevelled outcast, who, at the end of the evening, is chosen by Deuteronomy to receive the prized additional life. Paige delivered her big number, 'Memory', a highly dramatic reading, and her

recorded version entered the UK Top 5. The song, with a tune from Lloyd Webber's trunk of unused items, had a lyric by Trevor Nunn that was based on Eliot's poem *Rhapsody On A Windy Night*. Because all the text in the show was taken from Eliot's writings, with a few minor revisions, the only other 'extra lyrics' credit was given to Richard Stilgoe. The remainder of the score included 'Prologue: Jellicle Songs For Jellicle Cats', 'The Naming Of The Cats', 'The Invitation To The Jellicle Ball', 'Moments Of Happiness', 'The Journey To The Heavyside Layer', 'The Ad-Dressing Of Cats', and several numbers in the names of the various characters, such as 'Old Gumbie Cat', 'Gus, Theatre Cat', and 'Growltiger's Last Stand'. Initial reviews were mixed, but word-of-mouth about Napier's environmental set and slinky black cat costumes, as well as Gillian Lynne's exciting and innovative choreography and the show's special effects, ensured full houses for a 'performance extravaganza that was then a radical departure from anything seen on the musical stage'. Napier and Lynne were both involved again in the Broadway production of *Cats* which opened at the Winter Garden Theatre on 7 October 1982, with Betty Buckley in the role of Grizabella. Since those days *Cats* has undertaken several US tours, and played in the major cities of Europe, Canada, Australia, Britain, and many other countries. Its awards have included: 1981 Evening Standard, Laurence Olivier, and Ivor Novello Awards for best musical; 1983 Tonys for best musical, book, score, director (Nunn), supporting actress (Buckley), costumes (Napier), lighting (Hersey), and Drama Desk Awards for music, costumes, lighting; and 1989 Moliere Award for best musical.
In 1992 Lloyd Webber's Really Useful Company announced that it was aware of 150 different recorded versions of 'Memory' (it even listed them). In January 1996 the West End production of his most enduring show, *Cats*, went one step further in justifying its billing of 'Now And Forever' by overtaking *A Chorus Line* as the longest-running musical of all time, having resided at the New London theatre for 6,138 performances. On 19 June 1997, the New York production also reached that magic figure, thereby replacing *A Chorus Line* as the longest-running show (musical or play) in Broadway history. It was then estimated that in the past 16 years, *Cats* had grossed $2.2 billion worldwide and played to more than 50 million people in 42 productions. In 1998 a video version was released. Directed by David Mallet, the cast included Elaine Paige (Grizabella), James Barron (Bustopher), John Mills (Gus), Rosemarie Ford (Bombalurina), Geoffrey Garratt (Skimbleshanks), Jo Gibb (Rumpleteazer), John Partridge (Rum Tum Tugger), Michael Gruber (Munkustrap), Mae (Demeter), Ken Page (Old Deuteronomy), Susie McKenna (Jennyanydots), Jacob Brent (Mistoffolees), and Susan Jane Turner (Jellyorum).
● VIDEOS: *Andrew Lloyd Webber's Cats* (PolyGram 1998).

CAVALCADE

A play with music, rather than a musical, Noël Coward's *Cavalcade* was nevertheless filled with songs. This patriotic epic, one of the most spectacular productions ever to be mounted on the English stage, opened at London's Drury Lane Theatre on 13 October 1931. Its cast of over 200 included Mary Clare, Edward Sinclair, John Mills, Irene Browne, Binnie Barnes, Una O'Connor, Arthur McCrae, and Moyra Nugent. The show depicted some of the important events of the first 30 years of the 20th century - the relief of Mafeking, the sinking of the Titanic, the funeral of Queen Victoria, World War I - seen through the eyes of an English family. Although Coward himself did not appear in the piece, he recorded a medley of many of the popular songs of those days that permeated the action, such as 'Soldiers Of The Queen', 'Goodbye Dolly Gray', 'If You Were The Only Girl In The World', 'Take Me Back To Dear Old Blighty', and two numbers that he wrote especially for the show, 'Twentieth Century Blues', sung by Binnie Barnes, and 'Lover Of My Dreams' ('Mirabelle Waltz'), which was introduced by Stella Wilson. All of those, and Coward's version of the celebrated 'Toast From *Cavalcade*', which occurs towards the end of the show and was originally spoken by Mary Clare, were reissued in 1992 on a 4-CD boxed set, *Noël Coward: His HMV Recordings 1928-1953*. The show ran for well over a year, and was revived, 50 years later in the 80s at Farnham and Chichester in the UK, and in Canada. In 1995, Gabrielle Drake and Jeremy Clyde led a cast of over 300 in a production directed by Dan Crawford at the Sadler's Wells Theatre in London. A 1933 film version made in Hollywood, starring Diana Wynyard and Clive Brook, won three Oscars, including best picture; and the popular 70s television series, *Upstairs, Downstairs*, is said to have been based on the show. Sheridan Morley, the author and critic and Coward's biographer, tells of the occasion when they were seated together at a 'fork luncheon' at the Savoy Hotel in London. Morley remarked that he (Coward) seemed to be the only person in the room in possession of a fork. Coward replied, 'But of course dear boy. You see, I wrote *Cavalcade*.'

CHAMPAGNE CHARLIE

Released by Ealing Studios in 1944, this film was set in the English musical halls of the 1860, and was packed full of traditional songs as well as specially composed items. The screenplay, by Austin Melford, Angus MacPhail, and John Dighton, concerns the rivalry between two of the most popular singers of the time, George Leybourne (Tommy Trinder) and the Great Vance (Stanley Holloway). Before they finally make their peace with each other they become involved in an attempted duel, and spectacular battle of drinking songs. The latter included 'Rum' and 'Old Ale' (both Ernest Irving-Frank Eyton), 'Little Drop Of Gin', 'Burgundy Claret And Port', 'Brandy And Seltzer Boys', 'Sherry Wine' (Billy Mayerl-Frank Eyton), and, of course, 'Champagne Charlie' (Alfred Lee-George Leybourne). Among the other featured numbers were 'Don't Bring Shame', 'It 'Im On The Boko', and 'Not In Front Of Baby' (Irving-Eyton), 'Arf Of Arf And Arf' (Una Bart), 'Norma' (Bellini-Ernest Irving), 'Perfection Polka' (J.H. White-Irving), 'Come On Algernon' (Lord Berners-T.E.B. Clark-Diana Morgan), 'Strolling In The Park' (Mayerl-Eyton), 'Polka' (Berners), 'Concerto' (Weber), 'Man On The Flying Trapeze', (Lee-Leybourne), 'By And By' (Noel Gay-Eyton), 'EE! But It's A Grand And Healthy Life' (George Formby-Harry Gifford-Frederick E. Cliffe), and 'Hunting After Dark' (Mayerl-Clarke-Morgan). However, it is not just the songs that make this film so appealing. It also had a fine supporting cast, which included Betty Warren, Austin Trevor, Jean Kent, Guy Middleton, Frederick Piper, Harry Fowler, Robert Wyndham, and Peter de Greef, and director Alberto Cavalacanti's sympathetic and skilful recreation of the period atmosphere was outstanding.

CHAMPION, GOWER

b. 22 June 1920, Geneva, Illinois, USA, d. 25 August 1980, New York City, New York, USA. One of the most distinguished and influential directors and choreographers in the American musical theatre, Champion was brought up in Los Angeles and took dancing lessons from an early age. When he was 15, he and his friend, Jeanne Tyler, toured nightclubs as 'Gower and Jeanne America's youngest dance team'. After serving in the US Coast Guard during World War II, Champion found another dance partner, Marge Belcher, and they were married in 1947. In the 50s they appeared together on numerous television variety programmes and in their own situation comedy, *The Marge And Gower Champion Show*. They also made several film musicals including *Mr. Music, Lovely To Look At, Give A Girl A Break, Jupiter's Darling, Three For The Show*, and the autobiographical *Everything I Have Is Yours*. Their exuberant dancing to 'I Might Fall Back On You' and 'Life Upon The Wicked Stage' were two of the highlights of the 1951 remake of *Show Boat*, which starred Howard Keel and Kathryn Grayson. During the late 30s and 40s Champion worked on Broadway as a solo dancer and choreographer. In 1948 he began to direct as well, and won a Tony Award for his staging of the musical *Lend An Ear*, the show that introduced Carol Channing to New York theatre audiences. From then on he choreographed and directed a mixture of smash hits and dismal flops in a list that included *Three For Tonight, Bye Bye Birdie, Carnival, Hello, Dolly!, I Do! I Do!, The Happy Time, Sugar, Irene, Mack And Mabel* (1974) and *Rockabye Hamlet* (1976). They earned him another three Tonys and New York Critics and Donaldson Awards. After some years away from Broadway, he returned (uncredited) to 'doctor' *The Act* (1977), but could do nothing to prevent *A Broadway Musical* (1978) folding after only one night. He finished with a smash hit, however, when he choreographed and directed a 1980 stage adaptation of the movie classic *42nd Street*. During the show's try-out in Washington, Champion learnt that he had a rare form of blood cancer, and after the first curtain call on the New York opening night, producer David Merrick informed the cast and the audience that Gower Champion had died that afternoon.

CHANNING, CAROL

b. 31 January 1921, Seattle, Washington, USA. An actress and singer with a style and appearance that are difficult to define, she has been described as 'a blonde, wide-eyed, long-legged, husky voiced, scatty personality' - among other things. The daughter of a Christian Science teacher, Channing moved with her family to San Franciso at an early age, and later attended Bennington College in Vermont, where she majored in drama and dance. In 1941 she appeared in Marc Blitzstein's labour opera *No For An Answer*, but only for three Sunday nights. In the same year she served as an understudy in *Let's Face It!* on Broadway, and had a small part in *Proof Through The Night* (1942). After playing nightclubs around New York, she returned to San Francisco in 1946 and won a part in the Hollywood revue *Lend An Ear*. Her performance in the Broadway version of the show led to her triumph as Lorelei Lee in *Gentlemen Prefer Blondes*, in which she introduced several memorable numbers including 'A Little Girl From Little Rock' and 'Diamonds Are A Girl's Best Friend'. In 1954, she replaced Rosalind Russell in *Wonderful Town*, and in the next year, had her first big flop with *The Vamp*. In the late 50s her nightclub act was so successful that it was turned into a one-woman revue entitled *Show Girl*, which played on Broadway in 1961. Three years later, she had her biggest success in *Hello, Dolly!*, as the matchmaker Dolly Levi, with a Jerry Herman score that included 'So Long, Dearie', 'Before The Parade Passes By', and the insinuating title song. She won a Tony Award for outstanding performance, but Barbra Streisand was preferred for the movie version. Channing's larger-than-life personality is perhaps more suited to the stage than film, although she was hilarious in *Thoroughly Modern Millie* (1967). Other film credits include *Paid In Full, The First Travelling Saleslady, Skidoo* and *Shinbone Alley* (voice only). In 1974 she was back on Broadway in *Lorelei*, which, as the title suggests, was a compilation of the best scenes from *Gentlemen Prefer Blondes*. It lasted for 320 performances and had a reasonable life on the road. At that stage of her career, with suitable musical comedy roles hard to come by, Channing continued to work mostly on US television and in nightclubs, but in 1987 she co-starred with Mary Martin in James Kirkwood's aptly named show *Legends!*. A year later she embarked on a concert tour of locations such as Kansas City and San Diego, accompanied at each stop by the local symphony orchestra. In 1990 she appeared at the Desert Inn, Las Vegas, and two years later toured with Rita Moreno in *Two Ladies Of Broadway*. In 1995, Carol Channing received a special Lifetime Achievement Tony Award, and was back where she belongs, on Broadway starring in a major revival of her greatest success, *Hello, Dolly!*

● ALBUMS: *Carol Channing* (Vanguard 1959)★★★, *Previous Hits* (Vanguard 1959)★★★, *Carol Channing Entertains* (1965)★★★★, *Jazz Baby* (DRG 1994)★★★, and Original Cast and soundtrack recordings.

● FILMS: *Paid In Full* (1950), *The First Travelling Saleslady* (1956), *Thoroughly Modern Millie* (1967).

CHAPLIN, SAUL

b. Saul Kaplan, 19 February 1912, Brooklyn, New York, USA, d. 15 November 1997, Los Angeles, California, USA. A composer, lyricist, musical director and film producer, Chaplin is probably best known to the public for the popular songs he wrote with lyricist Sammy Cahn. While studying at the New York University in the early 30s, Chaplin joined Cahn in the Dixieland band, the Pals Of Harmony. They began to write 10 songs a day together (according to Cahn), and had their first hit in 1934 with 'Rhythm Is Our Business', which also had bandleader

Jimmy Lunceford's name on the song copy. The Lunceford Orchestra's recording of the tune went to number 1 in the USA, and he also had a hand in another of Cahn and Chaplin's successes around that time, '(If I Had) Rhythm In My Nursery Rhymes' (with Don Raye). From then on, until they parted in the early 40s, Chaplin and Cahn collaborated on some of the most appealing songs of the times, including 'Dedicated To You' (with Hy Zaret), 'Shoe Shine Boy', 'Until The Real Thing Comes Along' (with L.E. Freeman-Mann Holiner), a hit for Andy Kirk, Fats Waller and Jan Garber, among others; 'Bei Mir Bist Du Schon' (adapted from a Yiddish song composed by Sholem Secunda and Jacob Jacobs), a number 1 hit for the Andrews Sisters); 'If It's The Last Thing I Do', 'Posin'', 'Joseph! Joseph!' (with Nellie Casman and Sam Steinberg), and 'Please Be Kind', a US number 1 for Red Norvo in 1938. They also wrote songs for films such as *Argentine Nights*, *Time Out For Rhythm* (which starred Rudy Vallee and Ann Miller), *Go West Young Lady* (another Miller starrer) and *Redhead From Manhattan*. By the time the latter film was released in 1943, Chaplin had begun the next phase of his career in Hollywood as a composer-arranger and/or musical director. Among the often legendary movies he worked on were *On The Town*, *The Jolson Story* (with Jolson he also contributed 'The Anniversary Song', adapted from J. Ivanovici's 'Danube Waves'), *Summer Stock* (song: 'You Wonderful You', with Jack Brooks and Harry Warren), *An American In Paris* (Academy Award for scoring with Johnny Green), *Kiss Me Kate*, *Seven Brides For Seven Brothers* (Academy Award for scoring with Adolph Deutsch), *High Society* and *West Side Story* (Academy Award for scoring with Johnny Green, Sid Ramin and Irwin Kostal). Rather less successfully, in 1948 Chaplin was involved in the stage musical *Bonanza Bound*, which starred Gwen Verdon, but folded before it reached Broadway. Starting in the late 50s, he served as associate producer, and sometimes producer on movie musicals such as *Les Girls*, *Merry Andrew* (he also wrote the songs with Johnny Mercer), *Can-Can*, *The Sound Of Music*, *Star!* (Chaplin also contributed the song 'My Garden Of Joy', and hired his first collaborator, Sammy Cahn, to write the title song with Jimmy Van Heusen), and *That's Entertainment, Part Two* (1976).
● FURTHER READING: *The Golden Age of Movie Musicals And Me*, Saul Chaplin.

CHARIG, PHIL

b. 31 August 1902, New York, USA, d. 21 July 1960, New York, USA. A composer and occasional lyricist for the Broadway and London stage, in the early 20s Charig was a protégé of bandleader Ben Bernie. In 1925 he served as rehearsal pianist for Jerome Kern's Broadway musical, *Sunny*, and a year later collaborated with lyricist Ira Gershwin on the novel 'Sunny Disposish' for the first edition of *Americana*. For that same revue, Charig also wrote 'Why Do Ya Roll Those Eyes?' with Morrie Ryskind. It was introduced by Helen Morgan, Lyman Beck, Evelyn Bennett, and Betty Compton, and later popularized by Paul Whiteman And His Orchestra. Bolstered by that success, and his burgeoning friendship with the rapidly rising Gershwins, in 1927 Charig had his name on two book

musicals, *Yes, Yes, Yvette*, (with Irving Caesar), a kind of riposte to *No, No, Nanette* of a couple of years earlier in which Caesar was also involved, and *Just Fancy* (Joseph Meyer-Leo Robin). Neither set Broadway alight, and Charig sought more satisfaction in the late 20s and early 30s in London's West End. *Lucky Girl* (1928, with Douglas Furber-R.P. Weston-Bert Lee) and *Lady Mary* (1928, additional songs) showed promise, before *That's A Good Girl* (1928) made Charig's trip really worth while, running for 363 performances. A quartet of Joseph Meyer, Ira Gershwin, Desmond Carter, and Furber helped out with the songs, which included 'The One I'm Looking For', 'Sweet So-And-So', and 'Fancy Our Meeting'. The latter number was memorably performed by Jack Buchanan and Elsie Randolph in London, and later by Buchanan and Jessie Matthews on Broadway in the 1929 revue *Wake Up And Dream*. Charig and Furber combined again in 1931 for another Buchanan offering, *Stand Up And Sing*, which pleased audiences for almost as long as *That's A Good Girl*. Among the best songs were the lovely ballad 'There's Always Tomorrow' sung by Buchanan and Anna Neagle, 'Its Not You', and the title number, on which British composer Vivian Ellis received a third of the credit. In addition, Ellis composed a few of his own numbers for the show. In parallel with his West End diversion, Charig interpolated some material with Howard Dietz into the popular revue, *Three's A Crowd* (1930), and was also represented on Broadway by *Polly* (1929, Caesar) and *Nikki* (1931). In among Charig and James Dyrenforth's score for *Nikki* were 'On Account Of I Love You', 'Taking Off', and 'Wonder Why', and heading the cast was actress Fay Wray, just two years before she was carried to the top of the Empire State Building in the celebrated movie *King Kong*. Also present in *Nikki* were Archie Leach, who later changed his name to Cary Grant, and, in the chorus, the future stage and film star, Adele Dixon. It was more than a decade before Charig returned to the New York scene, firstly with some material for *Artists And Models* (1943), and then with the score for his most successful Broadway show, *Follow The Girls* (1944). In both cases his collaborators were Dan Shapiro and Milton Pascal, and for *Follow The Girls* they produced the slightly suggestive 'I Wanna Get Married', which was introduced by Gertrude Niesen. Jackie Gleason was also on board this goodtime musical which ran for over two years, considerably longer than Charig's Broadway swan-song, *Catch A Star!*, which folded after three weeks in spite of the combined songwriting talents of Charig, Sammy Fain, Jerry Bock (later the co-composer of *Fiddler On The Roof*), and Larry Holofcener.

CHARISSE, CYD

b. Tulla Ellice Finklea, 8 March 1923, Amarillo, Texas, USA. An elegant, long-legged dancer who appeared in several outstanding film musicals of the 40s and 50s, she took ballet classes from an early age, and was enrolled in the renowned Fanchon and Marco Dance Studio in Hollywood at the age of 12. One of the teachers there was Frenchman Nico Charisse, and four years later, during which time she performed at intervals with the famed Ballet Russes, they were married. Her connections with the Ballet Russes gained Charisse a part in the Columbia film *Something To Shout About* (1943), which led to a contract with MGM. One of the studio's top producers, Arthur Freed, is said to have been responsible for changing her name to Cyd (she had been known as Sid by her friends since childhood). During the late 40s and early 50s she made effective contributions to several straight films, and a number of musicals, which included *Ziegfeld Follies*, *The Harvey Girls*, *Till The Clouds Roll By*, *Fiesta* (in which Ricardo Montalban made his debut), *The Unfinished Dance*, *On An Island With You*, *Words And Music*, *The Kissing Bandit*, *Singin' In The Rain* (with Gene Kelly) and *Easy To Love* (1953). Also in 1953 she had what was arguably her best role in *The Band Wagon* with Fred Astaire and Jack Buchanan. By this time she was at her peak both as an actress and a dancer (although her singing was invariably dubbed in films), and her excellent work during the remaining years of the 50s included *Brigadoon*, *It's Always Fair Weather* and *Invitation To The Dance* (all with Kelly), *Meet Me In Las Vegas* (with Dan Dailey), and *Silk Stockings* (with Astaire). The latter was her last musical, although she did appear in the occasional dance sequence in films such as *Black Tights* (1960) and *The Silencers* (1966). Her screen work since then has been confined to guest appearances and television features. After the break-up of her first marriage in the early 40s, she married the popular singer Tony Martin in 1948, and he travelled with her to London in 1986 when she played the role of Lady Hadwell in a new production of David Heneker's musical *Charlie Girl*. Even then, when she was in her 60s, those famous legs were still the main subject of discussion. Impresario Harold Fielding said: 'They are her trademark, so we're going to insure them for a million, maybe two.' A substantial sum of money must also have changed hands in 1988 when Cyd Charisse agreed to appear in a video to promote a pop single by the two-man group the Blue Mercedes. Their record of 'I Want To Be Your Property' reached the top of the US dance charts. In a rather different vein, four years later Miss Charisse made her Broadway debut when she took over the role of fading ballerina Grushinskaya in the hit musical *Grand Hotel*. Asked about her age, which has always been a subject of some dispute (born 1921 or 1923), she would only say: 'Oh, I feel young!'

● FURTHER READING: *The Two Of Us*, Tony Martin and Cyd Charisse.

● FILMS: *Something To Shout About* (1943), *Mission To Moscow* (1943), *Till The Clouds Roll By* (1946), *Three Wise Fools* (1946), *The Harvey Girls* (1946), *Ziegfeld Follies* (1946), *The Unfinished Dance* (1947), *Fiesta* (1947), *Words And Music* (1948), *On An Island With You* (1948), *Tension* (1949), *East Side West Side* (1949), *The Kissing Bandit* (1949), *Mark Of The Renegade* (1951), *Singin' In The Rain* (1952), *The Wild North* (1952), *The Band Wagon* (1953), *Easy To Love* (1953), *Sombrero* (1953), *Deep In My Heart* (1954), *Brigadoon* (1954), *It's Always Fair Weather* (1955), *Meet Me In Las Vegas* (1956), *Silk Stockings* (1957), *Invitation To The Dance* (1957), *Party Girl* (1958), *Twilight For The Gods* (1958), *Black Tights* (1960), *Five Golden Hours* (1961), *Call Her Mom* (1962), *Two Weeks In Another Town* (1962), *Assassination In Rome* (1963), *The Silencers* (1966), *Maroc 7* (1967), *Warlords Of Atlantis* (1978), *Portrait Of An Escort* (1980), *Swimsuit* (1989), *Private Screening* (1990).

CHARLIE GIRL

One of the biggest blockbusters in the history of the London musical theatre (pre-Andrew Lloyd Webber), *Charlie Girl* opened at the Adelphi Theatre on 15 December 1965. Initial reviews were of the 'it takes geniuses of inspired mediocrity to produce rubbish such as this' variety, but the public loved it from the start. As with that other enormously popular musical, *Me And My Girl*, whose long and glorious run was inconveniently interrupted (temporarily) by World War II, *Charlie Girl* utilizes the age-old formula of mixing the English upper and lower classes, and allowing the latter to come off best. Hugh and Margaret Williams' book (with some humorous help from Ray Cooney) tells the sad tale of Lady Hadwell (Anna Neagle), who was on the stage as one of Cochran's Young Ladies before she married the late earl. It is not enough that she is beset by death duties, leaky roofs, and nosey tourists, but she also has a daughter Charlotte (Christine Holmes), who prefers to be known as Charlie and rides motorcycles. With this kind of laid-back attitude, Charlie is obviously destined to marry Lady Hadwell's Cockney *aide de camp*, Joe Studholme (60s pop star Joe Brown), who wants to be loved for himself alone, and not for his life-enhancing win on the football pools, the news of which has been brought to him by Nicholas Wainright (Derek Nimmo). Charlie's brief (innocent) affair with wealthy Jack Connor (Stuart Damon), the son of Kay Connor (Hy Hazell), Lady Hadwell's buddy from the Cochran days, is only a minor hitch before fireworks in the sky blaze out the message, 'Isn't It Flippin' Well Marvellous!'. Adelphi audiences certainly thought so, and *Charlie Girl* ran there for nearly five and a half years, a total of 2202 performances, and won an Ivor Novello Award for best musical. The show's score, by David Heneker (*Half A Sixpence*) and John Taylor, showcased Brown's charming, cheeky style in numbers such as 'My Favourite Occupation', 'Charlie Girl', 'I 'ates Money' (with Nimmo), 'Fish 'N' Chips', and 'You Never Know What You Can Do Until You Try' (with Neagle). Christine Holmes, had the delightful 'Bells Will Ring', 'I Love Him, I Love Him' and 'Like Love', while Hy Hazell excelled in 'Party Of A Lifetime', 'Let's Do A Deal' (with Neagle), and 'What Would I Get From Being Married?'. Neagle brought down the house regularly at the end of the first act with 'I Was Young'. During the run, this much-loved actress was created a Dame of the British Empire, and the cast borrowed the band parts from *South Pacific*, which was at the Prince of Wales Theatre, and sang 'There Is Nothing Like A Dame' to her at the close of the evening's performance. She stayed with the show throughout, except for holidays, but Joe Brown was replaced by Gerry Marsden, without his Pacemakers (the role was 'tweaked' to explain his Liverpudlian accent). When the show closed in 1971 Neagle and Nimmo joined the successful Australian and New Zealand productions which included John Farnham. In 1986 a revised version of *Charlie Girl* was mounted at London's Victoria Palace, starring Paul Nicholas, Dora Bryan, Mark Wynter, Nicholas Parsons, and Cyd Charisse, but times had changed, and the production lasted for only six months.

CHARLOT, ANDRÉ

b. 26 July 1882, Paris, France, d. 20 May 1956, Woodland, California, USA. A manager, producer and director of sophisticated intimate revues from the 1910s through to the late 30s, in his heyday Charlot, or 'Guv', as he became known, was rivalled only by that other great showman, Charles B. Cochran. Charlot's grandfather Auguste Charlot was a composer, and his father a theatre manager who also invested in shows. From the age of 19, André worked as a general secretary and business manager in various theatres and music halls, gradually learning the French style of revue. At 26 he married Florence Gladman, one half of an English sister act who visited Paris. Charlot was the Paris agent for London's Alhambra Theatre, and when rival West End houses began to introduce ragtime music and other American innovations, Charlot moved to England, and in association with actor-manager George Grossmith, produced the successful revue *Kill That Fly!* in 1912. This was followed by *Eightpence A Mile* (1913), *Keep Smiling* (1913), and *Not Likely!* (1914) in which the young Canadian comedienne Beatrice Lillie, who was to become Charlot's most enduring star, made her West End debut. Two more Charlot discoveries, Gertrude Lawrence and Jack Buchanan, also emerged as the impresario revolutionized the London musical stage with smart shows full of talented artists such as Jack Hulbert, Phyllis Monkman, Melville Gideon, Joyce Barbour, and Binnie Hale. These included *5064 Gerrard* (1915), *Now's The Time!* (1915), *Samples* (1915), *Some* (1916), *This And That* (1916), *See-Saw* (1916), *Three Cheers* (1916), *Cheep* (1917), *Bubbly* (1917), *Tabs* (1918), *Tails Up* (1918), *Buzz-Buzz* (1918, said to be Charlot's longest-running production), *Bran-Pie* (1919), *Just Fancy* (1920), *Jumble Sale* (1920), *Puss-Puss* (1921), *A To Z* (1921), *Pot Luck* (1921), *Snap* (1922), *Dé Dé* (1922), and *Rats!* (1923). Also in 1923, the up-and-coming playwright Noël Coward, who had failed a Charlot audition six years earlier, made his first appearance in revue, co-starring with Gertrude Lawrence in Charlot's *London Calling!* For this important part, Coward was coached by Fred Astaire, who was in town appearing with his sister Adele in *Stop Flirting*. Coward also wrote most of the songs and sketches, and Lawrence introduced the delightful 'Parisian Pierrot', his first popular hit.

By this time, Charlot's name was magic in the West End, and with his two latest offerings, *Yes!* (1923) and *Puppets* (1924), playing there, he moved further afield, conquering Broadway with *Charlot's Revue*. It opened at the Times Square Theatre on 9 January 1924, and contained elements of his most successful London productions, especially *A To Z* and *London Calling!* Jack Buchanan reprised Ivor Novello and Dion Titheradge's charming 'And Her Mother Came Too', Beatrice Lillie regularly stopped the show with another of the same composers' numbers, the glorious 'March With Me', while Gertrude Lawrence had the biggest hit with Douglas Furber and Philip Braham's 'Limehouse Blues'. Among the other numbers were 'Night May Have Its Sadness' (Novello-Collie Knox) and 'There's Life In The Old Girl Yet' (Coward). *Charlot's Revue* ran for 298 performances in New York, and when it went on tour, Jessie Matthews, who was in the chorus, took over

Lawrence's part when she was ill. There was a further edition on Broadway in 1926, while, back in London, *Charlot's Revue* (1924 and 1925), *The Charlot Show Of 1926*, and *Charlot 1928*, kept the master's name on theatre marquees. In 1926 he experienced an unaccustomed hiccup in his career when an ill-advised collaboration with the *Earl Carroll Vanities*, an American series of glamorous revues, led to financial difficulties.

However, he survived, and in 1928 founded the Sunday Play Society and broke into BBC radio with *Charlot's Hour*. After pioneering radio revue, and becoming quite a celebrity on the air, on 4 September 1930 he opened the new Cambridge Theatre with *Charlot's Masquerade*. In the cast were Beatrice Lillie, Anton Dolin, and Florence Desmond, but not Gertrude Lawrence, who had been poached by Noël Coward for his *Private Lives*. That show, along with Cochran's *Ever Green*, starring Jessie Matthews, were Charlot's main competition when he presented a rare book musical, *Wonder Bar*, at the Savoy Theatre in December 1930. In spite of a star-studded cast that included Dorothy Dickson, Elsie Randolph, and the romantic Danish singer Carl Brisson, *Wonder Bar* audiences thought it was not all that wonderful, and Charlot went bankrupt in 1931. He came back in 1933 with *How D'you Do?*, starring Frances Day, Douglas Byng, and Queenie Leonard, and then came *Please* (1933), *Hi-Diddle-Diddle* (1934), *Charlot's Char-A-Bang!* (1935), *Shall We Reverse?* (1935), *Stop ... Go* (1935), *The Town Talks* (1936), *Red, Bright And Blue* (1937), and *Charlot's Stars And Strips* (1937).

The latter show was nearer to run-of-the-mill variety than the stylish, intelligent affairs with which he had made his name, and, shortly after its brief run ended, Charlot sailed to America, eventually settling in Hollywood. He worked there in various capacities, and was technical advisor for Paramount Pictures at one stage. In 1940 he gathered together a number of cast members from his previous shows, and presented *Charlot's Revue* for the British War Relief Association, which was followed by *Charlot's Revuette* in 1941. In the early 40s he appeared in the films *Arabian Nights* and *The Constant Nymph*, and is reported to have acted in more than 20 other, mostly 'B' movies. In 1968 he was portrayed as rather a figure of fun by Alan Oppenheimer in *Star!*, the film biography of Gertrude Lawrence, starring Julie Andrews. Although his name is indelibly associated with revue, Charlot did produce a number of book musicals of variable quality. As well as the aforementioned *Wonder Bar*, these included *Flora* (1918), which in spite of having a score by Herman Darewski and Melville Gideon and a cast headed by Gertie Millar, was still not a success, *Very Good Eddie* (1918), *The Officer's Mess* (1918), *Wild Geese* (1920), *Now And Then* (1921), and *Dancing City* (1935).

CHARNIN, MARTIN

b. Martin Jay Charnin, 24 November 1934, New York, USA. A director, lyricist, composer, producer, author, and actor. In 1957 Charnin played the part of Big Deal, a member of the Jets, in the original Broadway cast of *West Side Story*, and two years later was in the revue *The Girls Against The Boys*, starring Bert Lahr and Nancy Walker.

Around the same time, he began writing lyrics, at first for revues such as *Kaleidoscope Revue* (1957), which began its life at the Provincetown Playhouse in Boston, Massachusetts, and *Fallout Revue*, *Pieces Of Eight* (both 1959), and *Seven Come Eleven* (1961), all three of which opened off-Broadway. In 1963 he wrote the words to Mary Rodgers' music for his first book show, the much-hyped *Hot Spot* starring Judy Holliday, which folded after 43 performances at New York's Majestic Theatre. Also credited on one of the production's best songs, 'Don't Laugh', was Stephen Sondheim. Charnin's next effort, *Zenda* (1963), proved to be composer Vernon Duke's final musical. It closed out of town in San Franciso in spite of having a cast headed by Alfred Drake, Anne Rogers, and Chita Rivera. In 1967 *Mata Hari* suffered the same fate, failing to progress beyond Washington, DC. This 'anti-war operetta', involving Vincente Minnelli (director) and David Merrick (producer), had music composed by Edward Thomas. A year later, it was presented off-Broadway in a scaled-down, revised version entitled *Ballad For A Firing Squad*, which was directed by Charnin himself. Having worked with Mary Rodgers early in his career, in 1970 he collaborated with her legendary father, Richard Rodgers, on *Two By Two*. Peter Stone's book was based on the play *The Flowering Peach* by Clifford Odet, and the show's run of 343 performances was due in no small part to the presence in the cast of Danny Kaye. Only one of the songs attracted much attention, the charming 'I Do Not Know A Day I Did Not Love You'. More directorial assignments followed, including *Nash At Nine* (1973, Charnin's own adaptation of the works of Ogden Nash), *Music! Music!* (1974), and *The National Lampoon Show* (1975), before Charnin achieved his biggest success so far with *Annie*, a musical based on the well-known comic strip, *Little Orphan Annie*. In company with Charles Strouse (music) and Thomas Meehan (book), lyricist Charnin directed what became one of the smash hits of the 70s. It opened at the Alvin Theatre on 21 April 1977 and ran for 2,377 performances. For his work on *Annie*, Charnin won Tony, Drama Desk, and New York Drama Critics' Circle awards, a Grammy for Best Cast Show Album, and a Standard award for the ASCAP 'most performed song of the decade', 'Tomorrow'. Nothing he has been associated with since then has even approached the success of that show. In the late 70s Charnin directed *Bar Mitzvah Boy* (1978, 77 performances) in London, and worked again with Richard Rodgers on *I Remember Mama* (1979, 108 performances). In the 80s his projects as a lyricist and/or director included *The First* (1981), *Lena Horne: The Lady And Her Music* (1981), *Upstairs At O'Neal's* (1982, a cabaret revue conceived and co-produced by Charnin, and for which he also wrote the witty title number), *A Backer's Audition* (1983), *Jokers* (1986, Goodspeed Opera House), *No Frills Revue* (1988), *Mike* (1988, closed out of town), *Café Crown* (1989), *Laughing Matters* (1989), and *Sid Caesar And Company: Does Anyone Know What I'm Talking About?* (1989). In January 1990, two years before the original *Annie* began an acclaimed US national tour, a sequel called *Annie 2: Miss Hannigan's Revenge*, developed by the same creative team, opened in Washington. However, it was to be more than three years before this new concept, eventually retitled *Annie Warbucks* reached New York, where it played for five months off-Broadway. Set free from the traumatic *Annie* saga, Charnin directed *Starcrossed: The Galileo Musical* (1994) and *Loose Lips* (1995), as well as radically rewriting and directing Cole Porter's *Can-Can* for Goodspeed (1995). In 1996 he staged a new version of his 1967 musical, *Mata Hari*, which was produced by the York Theatre Company in New York. In the same year, an intriguing album entitled *Incurably Romantic* was released. It contained 'Seventeen songs from twelve musicals performed by Laurie Beechman, Christy Baron, Sasha Charnin, Anita Jackson, Deborah Lippman, Andrea McCardle, Andrea Marcovicci, Maria Maples Trump, Terri White, Margaret Whiting, Barbara Walsh, and Karen Ziemba, and written by seven composers and one lyricist - Martin Charnin'. The latter also composed the music for several of the songs, including the only non-show number on the set - 'Sing Me Pretty'. Two years later, Charnin was in London directing an *Annie* revival starring Lesley Joseph and Kevin Colson.

Besides his work for the stage, Charnin has also won Emmy awards for television programmes such as *Annie, The Woman In The Life Of A Man* (1970) and *'S Wonderful, 'S Marvellous, 'S Gershwin*, which starred Jack Lemmon. He has produced, directed, and written lyrics for several others, and has been the author and director of nightclub acts for artists such as Nancy Wilson, Dionne Warwick, Shirley Jones, and Abbe Lane. Apart from 'Tomorrow', his most successful song to date is 'Best Thing You've Ever Done' which Barbra Streisand included on her *The Way We Were* album.

CHARRO

Elvis Presley's penultimate Hollywood film, released in 1969, was an attempt to cast the singer as a straight actor. No songs were heard, except for the title track, in a feature that cast the singer as an outlaw framed for the theft of a cannon by his former partners. Presley subverted his clean-cut, on-screen image with facial stubble and, taken in isolation, *Charro* is an entertaining, if lightweight, western. However, the general public had become exhausted by poor-quality Elvis movies and the film was not a success. Its release was completely overshadowed by the superb *Elvis* television spectacular of the previous Christmas.

CHESS

As with two of his big hit shows of the 70s, *Jesus Christ Superstar* and *Evita* (both written with Andrew Lloyd Webber), Tim Rice opted to introduce this show by way of a studio concept album, which made the UK Top 10 in 1984. For *Chess*, Rice wrote the book and lyrics, and the composers were Bjorn Ulvaeus and Benny Andersen, two ex-members of the record-breaking Swedish pop group Abba. The album spawned two hit singles: Murray Head's 'disco-rap-style' 'One Night In Bangkok', which reputedly sold several million copies worldwide and did particularly well in the UK and the USA; and the atmospheric ballad 'I Know Him So Well', a UK number 1 for Elaine Paige with Barbara Dickson. The show itself opened at London's Prince Edward Theatre (replacing *Evita*) on 14 May 1986.

Rice's book was generally considered at the time to be the weakest element in the show. It dealt with the familiar conflict between East and West - the Reds and the rest - but this time the different sides were personified by two chess grandmasters, the US world champion Frederick Trumper (Murray Head) and Anatoly Sergeievsky (Tommy Korgerg) from the USSR. After the prologue ('The Story Of Chess'), Frederick dumps the Russian challenger under the table in the middle of the World Championships which are being held in a Tyrolean township, and eventually loses not only his crown, but his devoted 'second', Florence Vassy (Elaine Paige), to Anatoly, who defects in the best Nureyev tradition. During the dark intrigues that follow, Anatoly defends his title (with the help of a reformed Frederick) against another Russian challenger, and, reversing his original career move, bids a heartfelt farewell to Florence at the airport before flying off into the (red) sunset. The 'part opera - part chorale' score was generally well received for its 'witty, stylish lyrics and consistently listenable music' (although some called it sheer Euro-pop), not only for 'One Night In Bangkok' and 'I Know Him So Well', which were important elements within the context of the show, but for the touching ballad, 'Heaven Help My Heart', and other numbers such as 'Pity The Child' and 'Where I Want To Be', As befitted a musical of the 80s, Chess was full of 'technological glitz' and much of its £4 million budget was visible onstage in the form of an elaborate rolling and revolving hydraulic set, a vast bank of television monitors and various other high-tech gear. Despite the sniping of the critics, Chess ran in London until April 1989, a total of 1102 performances. The show's director, Trevor Nunn, who had taken over from the renowned American director-choreographer, Michael Bennett, when he became ill (he died from AIDS in 1987), also staged the 1988 Broadway version which was savaged by the critics and flopped, despite having been 'Americanized' and fitted with a new cast and book. Chess returned to the USA in 1990 for a 40-week tour, and then, two years later, the musical 'with more past lives than Shirley MacLaine' was reworked yet again for a limited run Off Broadway.

CHEVALIER, MAURICE

b. Maurice Auguste Chevalier, 12 September 1888, Menilmontant, nr. Paris, France, d. 1 January 1972, Paris, France. The ninth of 10 children eventually reduced by death to three males, Chevalier's early ambitions to become an acrobat were thwarted by injury. He toured local cafes and music halls as a singer and broad comedian, and later performed at the Eldorado in Paris. His big break came when he signed a three-year contract with the Folies Bergère, and worked with his idol, Mistinguett. In 1913 he was drafted into the French Army, was captured, and then sent to Alten Grabow prisoner-of-war camp where he learnt to speak English. After the war he developed a more sophisticated act, wearing a tuxedo for his solo spot, and the straw boater that soon became his trademark. In-between the triumphs at the Folies Bergère, Casino de Paris and the Empire in Paris, Chevalier suffered a serious mental breakdown. When he recovered he went to England in 1927 and appeared in the revue White

Birds. Two years later he made his first Hollywood film, Innocents Of Paris, in which he introduced 'Louise', a song forever associated with him ('every little breeze seems to whisper Louise'). He also sang his famous French version of 'Yes, We Have No Bananas'. He then starred in several films, directed by Ernst Lubitsch including Lubitsch's first talkie, The Love Parade (1929). It was also the first of four films that Chevalier made with Jeanette MacDonald. Following The Smiling Lieutenant (1931) with Claudette Colbert, and One Hour With You (1932), Chevalier made what has been described as 'one of the great films of the decade'. Love Me Tonight, directed by Rouben Mamoulian and co-starring MacDonald, was innovative in several ways, especially in its integration of plot and music. It also contained 'Mimi', another speciality Chevalier song. He then appeared in The Merry Widow (1934, MGM) and Folies Bergère (1935, United Artists) in 1935 before returning to France, as one of the world's leading entertainers. During World War II Chevalier lived mostly in seclusion, emerging twice to perform in response to German demands, once in exchange for the release of 10 French prisoners. Rumours and accusations of collaboration with the enemy were emphatically disproved. After the war he projected a more mature image in the film Le Silence Est D'or (1947) directed by René Clair, which won the Grand Prize at the Brussels Film Festival. During the same period, Chevalier toured Europe and the USA with his 'one man show'. Semi-retired during the early 50s, he returned to Hollywood to play a series of character roles in films such as Love In The Afternoon (1957), Gigi (1958), Can-Can (1959), Fanny (1961), In Search Of The Castaways (1962) and I'd Rather Be Rich (1964). Gigi was one of the highlights of Chevalier's career. His idiosyncratic versions of 'Thank Heaven For Little Girls', 'I'm Glad I'm Not Young Any More', and a duet with Hermione Gingold, 'I Remember It Well', charmed the Academy of MPAS into awarding Gigi nine Oscars, including Best Picture. At the age of 70, Chevalier received a special Academy Award for his contribution to the world of entertainment for over half a century. During the 60s he appeared frequently on US television with his own 'specials' such as The World Of Maurice Chevalier, and travelled widely with his 'one man show' until 1968, when, from the stage of the Theatre des Champs Elysees in Paris, he announced his retirement. His honours included the Croix de Guerre (1917), the Belgian Order of Leopold (1943), the Légion d'Honneur (1938) and the Order Mérite National (1964).

● ALBUMS: Maurice Chevalier Sings Broadway (MGM 1959)★★★★, A Tribute To Al Jolson (MGM 1959)★★★, Life Is Just A Bowl Of Cherries (MGM 1960)★★★★, Thank Heaven For Little Girls (MGM 1960)★★★★, Thank Heaven For Maurice Chevalier (RCA Victor 1960)★★★, Maurice Chevalier Sings Lerner, Loewe And Chevalier (MGM 1962)★★★, Paris To Broadway (MGM 1963)★★★★, Maurice Chevalier (Time 1963)★★★.

● COMPILATIONS: Sings (Retrospect 1969)★★★★, The World Of Maurice Chevalier (Decca 1971)★★★★, You Brought A New Kind Of Love To Me (Monmouth Evergreen 1979)★★★, Encore Maurice (Living Era 1982)★★★, Bonjour D'Amour (Karussell 1982)★★★, Ma Pomme (EMI France 1983)★★★, The Golden Age Of Maurice Chevalier (Golden Age 1984)★★★★, Bravo Maurice (Living Era

1986)★★★, *The Maurice Chevalier Collection* (Deja Vu 1987)★★★★, *Maurice Chevalier's Paris* (Compact Selection 1988)★★★, *On Top Of The World* (Flapper 1990)★★★, *Maurice Chevalier* (ASV 1997)★★★.

● FURTHER READING: *The Man In The Straw Hat*, Maurice Chevalier. *With Love*, Maurice Chevalier. *I Remember It Well*, Maurice Chevalier. *Maurice Chevalier: His Life 1888-1972*, James Harding. *Thank Heaven For Little Girls: The True Story Of Maurice Chevalier's Life*, Edward Behr.

● FILMS: *Trop Crédule* (1908), *Par Habitude* (1911), *Un Mariée Récalcitrante* (1911), *Une Mariée Qui Se Fait Attendre* (1911), *La Valse Renversante* (1914), *Une Soirée Mondaine* (1917), *Le Mauvais Garçon* (1921), *Le Match Criqui-Ledoux* (1922), *L'Affaire De La Rue Lourcine* (1923), *Gonzague* (1923), *Jim Bougne Boxeur* (1924), *Par Habitude* remake (1924), *Bonjour New York!* (1928), *Innocents Of Paris* (1929), *The Love Parade* (1929), *Playboy Of Paris* (1930), *The Big Pond* (1930), *Paramount On Parade* (1930), *The Smiling Lieutenant* (1931), *The Stolen Jools (The Slippery Pearls)* (1931), *El Cliente Seductor* (1931), *Love Me Tonight* (1932), *Make Me A Star* (1932), *One Hour With You* (1932), *Toboggan (Battling Georges)* (1932), *The Way To Love* (1933), *Bedtime Story* (1933), *The Merry Widow* (1934), *Folies Bergère* (1935), *The Beloved Vagabond* (1936), *Avec Le Sourire* (1936), *L'Homme Du Jour* (1936), *Break The News* (1938), *Pièges* (1939), *Le Silence Est D'Or* (1945), *Le Roi* (1946), *Paris 1900* (1950), *Ma Pomme* (1950), *Schlager-Parade* (1953), *J'Avais Sept Filles* (1954), *Cento Anni D'Amore* (1954), *Love In The Afternoon* (1957), *Rendezvous With Maurice Chevalier* series of six (1957), *Gigi* (1958), *Count Your Blessings* (1959), *Can-Can* (1959), *Pepe* (1960), *A Breath Of Scandal* (1960), *Un, Deux, Trois, Quatre!* (1960), *Fanny* (1961), *In Search Of The Castaways* (1962), *Jessica* (1962), *A New Kind Of Love* (1963), *I'd Rather Be Rich* (1964), *Panic Button* (1964), *Monkeys Go Home!* (1966).

CHICAGO

Fred Ebb and Bob Fosse's book for this 'Musical Vaudeville', which opened on Broadway at the 46th Street Theatre on 3 June 1975, was based on a play by Maurine Dallas Watkins, and set in the Roaring 20s. A married chorus girl, Roxie Hart (Gwen Verdon), has strayed from husband Amos (Barney Martin), only to dispatch her lover in an unlawful manner (she shot him). She is subsequently banged up in the Cook County Jail - under the tight control of Matron 'Mama' Morton (Mary McCarty) - along with a bunch of 'six merry murderesses' ('And then he ran into my knife - he ran into my knife 10 times!'). In company with Velma Kelly (Chita Rivera), Roxie eventually achieves her freedom due to a talent for self-publicity and the skills of her disreputable, wheeler-dealer lawyer, the flash Billy Flynn (Jerry Orbach). Once on the outside, Velma and Roxy decide to stop bumping people off and form a successful nightclub act. Goody-goody columnist Mary Sunshine (M. O'Haughey) underwent a surprising transformation as well. An unusual musical in some ways - it doesn't have a love story, and an M.C. introduces the numbers in true vaudeville style - the book takes a lot of sly digs at the shortcomings of the often tawdry and corrupt American way of life in general, and its legal system in particular. The tongue-in-cheek score, by Fred Ebb and John Kander, had more than a hint of pastiche, and included numbers such as 'Funny Honey', 'Cell Block Tango', 'When You're Good To Mama', 'All I Care About', 'A Little

Bit Of Good', 'We Both Reached For The Gun', 'Roxie', 'I Can't Do It Alone', 'My Own Best Friend', 'Me And My Baby', 'Mr. Cellophane', 'When Velma Takes The Stand', 'Class', and 'Nowadays'. Two of the songs, the scintillating opener 'All That Jazz' (Velma), and 'Razzle Dazzle' (Billy), had lives of their own outside the show. Gwen Verdon and Chita Rivera were both making their Broadway comebacks after an absence of some years, and their presence, together with that of Bob Fosse, ensured that the show was light on its feet and complete with an array of dances that were popular in those Prohibition times. The New York production ran for 898 performances, and the 1979 London version stayed in the West End for 18 months. Since then *Chicago* has proved to be a popular choice of provincial and stock companies in many parts of the world. In 1991 it was presented at the UK Leicester Haymarket Theatre, the springboard for many successful musicals, and, in the following year, the Long Beach Civic Light Opera Company's classy production starred Juliet Prowse and Kay Ballard. In 1996, the show became such a hit when revived as part of the New York City Centre *Encores!* musicals in concerts, that it was transferred to Broadway in November of that year. Although still more or less in concert form - orchestra on stage, and no changes of sets or costumes - the 'Drop-Dead Musical', as it was called, became a critical and financial blockbuster, winning six Tony Awards, along with Drama Desk, Outer Circle, Astaire, Drama League, and New York Critics Circle honours. Walter Bobbie directed a cast which was led by Bebe Neuwirth (Velma), Ann Reinking (Roxie), Billy (James Naughton), Joel Grey (Amos), and Mama (Marcia Lewis). Reinking also choreographed 'in the style of Bob Fosse'. A year later, *Chicago* repeated its triumph in London with Ute Lemper (Velma), Ruthie Henshall (Roxie), Henry Goodman (Billy), Nigel Planer (Amos), and Meg Johnson (Mama) It won Laurence Olivier Awards for best musical and actress (Lemper). The story itself has been filmed twice, in 1927 under the title of *Chicago*, and again, in 1942, as *Roxie Hart*, starring Ginger Rogers, Adolphe Menjou, and George Montgomery.

CHILDREN OF EDEN

'Excuse me, where's the nearest Exodus?', was one critic's morning-after reaction to this 'new biblical musical', which opened at London's Prince Edward Theatre on 8 January 1991. The staging was by John Caird, the co-director of *Les Misérables*, and his book, adapted from the Old Testament, told the familiar story from the Creation until just after the Flood. The music and lyrics were by Stephen Schwartz, whose *Godspell* had played 1,128 performances just along the road at Wyndhams Theatre 20 years earlier. The critics were quick to point out that God (Ken Page) and Eve (Shezwae Powell) were black, and they, along with Adam (Martin Smith) had somehow got kitted out in 'cute little costumes complete with shoes'; and that Cain's slaying of Abel was presented 'in the humdrum context of a family spat'. Schwartz's score of over 22 numbers, ranging 'from oratorio to gospel', included 'In Pursuit Of Excellence', 'In Whatever Time We Have', 'Let There Be', 'A World Without You', 'Children Of Eden', 'What Is He Waiting For?' and 'Ain't It Good'. Praise was reserved for

John Napier's set and David Hersey's lighting, and especially for Richard Sharples' imaginative animal costumes and the actors' expressive use of them. This 'sentimental and silly' show ran for 10 weeks and reportedly lost its total investment of £2.2 million. Nearly seven years later, a restructured and revised *Children Of Eden* was well received at the Paper Mill Playhouse in New Jersey, USA.

CHINESE HONEYMOON, A

A run of 1000 performances does not seem such a remarkable feat in these days of Andrew Lloyd Webber's megahits, but in the early part of the twentieth century, it was a remarkable achievement. This show, which opened at the Strand Theatre in London on 5 October 1901, was the first local production to pass that magic figure, and went on to add 75 more performances to the total. This musical comedy had a book and lyrics by George Dance, and music by Howard Talbot, with additional songs by others, including Ivan Caryll. It was set in the Chinese Kingdom of Ylang Ylang, where Emperor Hang Chow has decreed that any member of the royal family who kisses another person has to marry them. Unbelievable complications ensue, involving the Lord Chancellor Chippee Choppy, a naval officer who leaves the service for the love of Fi Fi a hotel waitress, the English honeymooners Samuel Pineapple and his young ex-typist wife Marie, and a sweet singer named Soo Soo, who is really a princess. Fortunately, the score was a good deal more straightforward and harmonious, and contained a number of jolly songs such as 'Martha Spank The Grand Pianner', 'I Want To Be A Lidy', 'The À La Girl', 'The Twiddly Bits', 'Sweet Little Sing-Sing', 'Roses Red And White', 'But Yesterday', 'A Paper Fan', 'Daisy With A Dimple On Her Chin', and 'A Chinese Honeymoon'. The cast included Lily Elsie, Marie Dainton, Louie Freear, and Lionel Rignold. The 1902 New York production ran for 376 performances, and there was a London revival in 1915.

CHITTY CHITTY BANG BANG

Made in Britain, this highly successful, but critically derided children's musical is about a more than usually eccentric inventor, Caractacus Potts (Dick Van Dyke), whose crowning achievement is a flying car. This airy form of transportation conveys his two children, Jemima and Jeremy (Heather Ripley and Adrian Hall), and their mutual friend, Truly Scrumptious (Sally Ann Howes), on their mission to bring down the authoritarian regime of a country that does not like children. On their travels they are surrounded by a host of familiar and much-loved characters from UK showbusiness, including Lionel Jeffries, Benny Hill, Anna Quayle, Robert Helpmann, James Robertson Justice, Max Wall, Bernard Spear, Davy Kaye, Barbara Windsor, Stanley Unwin, Victor Maddern, Max Bacon, Richard Wattis and Peter Arne. Gert Frobe, the German actor who made such as impact in Goldfinger a few years earlier, was in it too. Richard M. Sherman and Robert B. Sherman's score was nothing special, and included 'Lovely Lonely Man', 'Hushabye Mountain', 'Toot Sweet', 'Truly Scrumptious', 'Posh!', 'Chu-Chi Face', and the title song. One of the most appealing moments comes when Van Dyke gets caught up with a folk dance group at a fairground. The ensuing number, 'The 'Ole Bamboo', which involves the dextrous use of white bowler hats and lengthy individual poles, is a delight. Comparisons with the blockbuster *Mary Poppins* were inevitable, especially as Dick Van Dyke was in it, and Sally Ann Howes' 'terribly British' image is similar to that of Julie Andrews. However, this film is just not in that class. Roald Dahl and Ken Hughes' sugary screenplay was based on a novel by Ian Fleming, and Hughes also directed. The choreographers were March Breaux and DeeDee Wood, and the film was produced by Albert R. Broccoli and released by United Artists.

CHOCOLATE SOLDIER, THE

Nearly 50 years before Alan Jay Lerner and Frederick Loewe created *My Fair Lady*, the ultimate musical adaptation of a George Bernard Shaw play, a Viennese operetta, *Der Tapfere Soldat*, which had been adapted from Shaw's *Arms And The Man*, was presented in Vienna in 1908. Renamed *The Chocolate Soldier*, with a book and lyrics by Stanislaus Stange who also directed the piece, and music by Oscar Strauss, the show moved to the Lyric Theatre in New York on 13 September 1909. In this satirical look at war and its consequences, Lt. Bumerli (J.E. Gardner), a Swiss soldier who is serving in the Serb army during its invasion of Bulgaria in 1885, is more fond of chocolate than he is of fighting. On the run from the enemy, he conceals himself, and his identity, in the home of the Bulgarian Colonel Popoff (William Pruette), and falls in love with the Colonel's daughter, Nadine (Ida Brooks Hunt). Despite opposition from her ex-boyfriend, the extremely brave Major Alexius Spiridoff (George Tallman), Bumerli's pacifism wins the day. These stories, of course, are made tolerable by the magnificent music that punctuates the sometimes overly dramatic scenes. *The Chocolate Soldier* contained several popular and enduring numbers, such as 'My Hero', 'Sympathy', 'Seek the Spy', 'Falling In Love', 'The Letter Song', 'Thank The Lord The War Is Over', 'Bulgarians', and 'The Chocolate Soldier'. The New York run of 296 performances was exceeded by the 1910 London production, which lasted for exactly 500. Since then, the show has become a much-loved feature in the repertoires of light operatic companies around the world. The main professionals revivals have been on Broadway in 1921, 1930, 1931, and 1947 (a revised version by Guy Bolton), and London audiences were able to enjoy the show again in 1914, 1932 and 1940. The 1941 film of *The Chocolate Soldier*, with Nelson Eddy and Rise Stevens, used a different story based on Molnar's *The Guardsman*.

CHORUS LINE, A (FILM MUSICAL)

Richard Attenborough was the controversial choice of director to attempt the transfer of the longest-running (to date) Broadway production from stage to screen in 1985. General opinion seemed to be that the outcome was unsatisfactory, but then the task was an extremely difficult one. Even Michael Bennett, who conceived the show and was its director-choreographer, declined 'to spend three more years of his life' on a film version. Screenwriter Arnold Shulman adapted the original story of a group of chorus dancers auditioning on a bare stage in an empty theatre for the show's volatile director, Zach (Michael Douglas). One by one they step forward to push their claims to be one of the lucky final eight, revealing more about themselves than they probably realize. One of them, Cassie (Alyson Reed), is an ex-girlfriend of Zach's who is trying to make a comeback as a dancer - despite his opposition. The rest of the hopefuls included Gregg Burke, Cameron English, Vicki Frederick, Audrey Landers, Nicole Fosse, and Janet Jones. Most of Marvin Hamlisch and Edward Kleban's original numbers were retained, and two added, in a score that consisted of 'I Hope I Get It', 'I Can Do That', 'Surprise, Surprise', 'At The Ballet', 'Nothing', 'Dance: Ten, Looks: Three', 'Let Me Dance For You', 'One' and 'What I Did For Love'. Jeffrey Hornaday created the 'lacklustre' choreography and the film was produced by Embassy and PolyGram in Technicolor and Panavision.

CHORUS LINE, A (STAGE MUSICAL)

Conceived, directed and co-choreographed (with Bob Avian) by Michael Bennett, with a book by James Kirkwood and Nicholas Dante, and a score by Marvin Hamlisch (music) and Edward Kleban (lyrics), the show began as a workshop production at producer Joseph Papp's New York Shakespeare Festival Public Theatre on 21 May 1975. After a spell at the Newman Theatre in the same complex, A Chorus Line opened on Broadway at the Schubert Theatre on the 21 July 1975. Set in a bare Broadway theatre, the compelling story tells of a director, Zach (Robert LuPone), and his search for eight dancers from a group of 17 hopefuls that includes his former mistress, Cassie (Donna McKechnie). Assembled on a large, empty stage with just a mirror-covered rear wall, it was 'the quintessential Broadway show, summing up the heartbreak and frustrations of thousands of aspirant stars'. Representing them in this show were Renee Baughman (Kristine), Carole Bishop (Sheila), Pamela Blair (Val), Wayne Cilento (Mike), Clive Clerk (Larry), Kay Cole (Maggie), Baayork Lee (Connie), Priscilla Lopez (Diane), Don Percassi (Al), and Sammy Williams (Paul). The production won the 1976 Pulitzer Prize for Drama, the New York Drama Critics Award for best musical, and Tony Awards for best musical, best musical actress, featured actor, musical, featured actress, and for best director, book, score, lighting (Tharon Musser), and choreography. The songs included 'I Can Do That', 'What I Did For Love', 'Dance: Ten, Looks: Three', 'The Music And The Mirror', 'I Hope I Get It', and the spectacular finale, 'One'. A Chorus Line closed on Broadway on 28 April 1990, following a run of 6,137 performances. After a six-minute standing ovation from the audience on the final evening, members of the 1975 cast joined the current performers on stage, and later, there was a public auction of souvenirs from the show, including some items from the wardrobe and even a sign from the lobby that stated: 'No Photos'. The total Broadway gross was estimated at over $140 million. A Chorus Line reigned as the longest-running Broadway show (musical or play) until 19 June 1997, when it was overtaken by Andrew Lloyd Webber's Cats. A London production opened in July 1976 and ran for near-

ly three years. Since then, productions have been licensed in countries such as Puerto Rico, Europe, South America, the Netherlands, Canada, and the Far East. A film version, directed by Richard Attenborough, was released in 1985. The most complete recording of the show ever to be made available is said to be that which was broadcast by BBC Radio 2 on 30 November 1996. It starred Donna McKechnie in her original role, with David Soul as Zach. A 21st anniversary 50-city tour of the USA was launched in September 1997 with Jilly Slyter (Cassie) and Mark Martino (Zach). It was staged by original 1975 cast member Baayork Lee, as was the UK production led by Adam Faith (Zach) and Maria Laura Baccarini (Cassie), which began its journey in February 1997.

● FURTHER READING: A Chorus Line: The Complete Text, Applause Books. On The Line: The Creation Of A Chorus Line, Baayork Lee, Thommie Walsh and Robert Viagas. A Chorus Line And The Musicals Of Michael Bennett, Ken Mandelbaum. A Chorus Line: The Book Of The Musical, The Complete Book And Lyrics, Frank Rich (Introduction). The Longest Line: Broadway's Most Singular Sensation, A Chorus Line, Gary Stevens and Alan George.

CHU CHIN CHOW

This lavish 'Musical Tale Of The East' was first staged at His Majesty's Theatre in London on 31 August 1916 when Britain was in the midst of World War I. It was written, directed, and produced by Austrian Oscar Asche, who also co-starred with his wife, Lily Brayton. Loosely based on the ancient tale of Ali Baba And The Forty Thieves - although various aspects of the original were embellished or diminished in Asche's version - the piece was set in around Bagdhad, where robber chief Abu Hasan (Asche) is extremely keen on gaining entry to the palatial habitat of Kasim Baba (Frank Cochrane). Hasan's slave, Zahrat Al-Kulub (Lily Brayton), is already in there spying on his behalf. However, Kasim's own slave, Marjanah (Violet Essex), along with her lover Nur Al-Huda Ali (J.V. Bryant) and his father, Ali Baba (Courtice Pounds), turn the tables, and discover Hasan's cave full of riches (say after me: 'Open Sesame'). Hasan kills Kasim, and plans an attack on the occasion of Marjanah and Nur Al-Huda Ali's wedding. Prior to the onslaught, forty of Hasan's thieves are already concealed in the forty oil jars, but the renegade's plans are foiled when Zahrat pours a large measure of the boiling hot black liquid into each jar. She stabs Abu Hasan to death, too. The score, with Frederic Norton's music and Asche's lyrics, matched the colourful, exciting story, and included 'I Am Chu Chin Chow', 'Cleopatra's Nile', 'I'll Sing And Dance', 'Corraline', 'When A Pullet Is Plump', 'Serenade', 'I Love Thee So', 'Behold!', 'The Robbers' March', 'I Long For The Sun', 'Mahbubah', 'I Built A Fairy Palace In The Sky', 'Song Of The Scimitar', 'Anytime's Kissing Time', 'The Cobbler's Song', and 'We Bring Ye Fruits'. This blend of romanticism and the spectacular proved just the thing to give the troops about to leave, or just returning from the horrors of war. Along with The Bing Boys Are Here, Chu Chin Chow was the most popular of all the World War 1 shows, and ran until well after the hostilities had finished, finally closing on 22 July 1921, following a total of 2,235 performances. A sobering thought: it is said to have cost under £5,000 to produce. New York stagings at the Manhattan Opera House and the Century Theatre 1917-18 folded after only 208 performances, even though future film star Tyrone Power played the role of Abu Hasan. This was a show very much for its time - and place. A silent film version was released in 1923, followed by a talkie in 1934. The show was produced as an ice spectacular at the Empire Pool Wembley in 1953. In 1994 a CD containing studio cast recordings of *Chu Chin Chow*, supplemented by a few original cast and revival tracks, was issued on the West End Angel label.

CINDERELLA (FILM MUSICAL)
(see Disney, Walt)

CINDERELLA (STAGE MUSICAL)

This 'delightful and entrancing' musical began its life in 1957 as a CBS television film. Julie Andrews was in the title role, with Howard Lindsay and Dorothy Stickney (the King and Queen), Jon Cypher (Prince Charming), Edie Adams (Fairy Godmother), Ilka Chase, and Kaye Ballard and Alice Ghostley as stepmother and stepsisters. Oscar Hammerstein II wrote the book, and collaborated with Richard Rodgers on a score that contained several appealing numbers, such as 'In My Own Little Corner' and 'When You're Driving In The Moonlight' (Andrews), 'A Lovely Night' (Andrews, Chase, Ballard, Ghostley), an amusing 'Stepsisters' Lament' (Ballard, Ghostley), and the charming instrumental 'Waltz For A Ball'. In 1958, British impresario Harold Fielding presented *Cinderella* as a Christmas-time entertainment at the London Coliseum. The popular rock 'n' roll singer Tommy Steele (as Buttons) headed the cast, with Bruce Trent (the Prince), Yana (Cinderella), Jimmy Edwards (the King), Enid Lowe (the Queen), Betty Marsden (Fairy Godmother), Graham Squire (the Baron), Robin Palmer (Lord Chancellor), and Kenneth Williams and Ted Durante (Stepsisters). This production was a blend of musical comedy and traditional Christmas pantomime fare. Nevertheless, all the aforementioned songs were retained, along with 'A Very Special Day' and 'Marriage Type Love' (Buttons), 'No Other Love' (Prince), 'Do I Love You Because You're Beautiful' and 'Ten Minutes Ago' (Prince and Cinderella), 'Impossible' (Cinderella and Fairy Godmother), 'The Prince Is Giving A Ball' (Lord Chancellor and Chorus), and 'Your Majesties, A List Of The Bare Necessities' (King, Queen and Chorus). There was also another number, 'You And Me', written by Tommy Steele, and sung by him and Jimmy Edwards. 'No Other Love', which had featured earlier in the show *Me And Juliet*, and as part of the background score to the 1952 television documentary *Victory At Sea*, became a big hit for Perry Como in the USA, and a UK number 1 for Ronnie Hilton. In a 1965 telecast Lesley Ann Warren played Cinderella, supported by Stuart Damon (the Prince), and Walter Pidgeon and Ginger Rogers (King and Queen), Celeste Holm (Fairy Godmother), Jo Van Fleet (Stepmother), and Pat Carroll and Barbara Ruick (Stepsisters). In 1993, Rodgers and Hammerstein's *Cinderella* received its first major stage production in America by the New York City Opera, and four years later there was a new television version, starring Bernadette Peters (the Wicked Stepmother), Whoopi Goldberg (the

Queen), Whitney Houston (Fairy Godmother), Paolo Montalban (the Prince), and pop star Brandy (Cinderella). Among the additions to the score were 'The Sweetest Sounds' (from *No Strings*), 'Falling In Love With Love' (*The Boys From Syracuse*), and 'There's Music In You'.

CITY OF ANGELS

'The great American musical is back and showbusiness USA is breathing a little easier', is how one relieved critic put it after *City Of Angels* exploded into view at the Virginia Theatre in New York on 11 December 1989. Larry Gelbart's book, 'an hilarious Hollywood private-eye spoof', together with 'a 40s-era jazz-tinged score' by Cy Coleman (music) and David Zippel (lyrics), dazzled almost everyone, and was hailed as the most brilliantly inventive musical New York had seen for years. Gelbart's clever double-plot concerns the interlocking worlds of the screenwriter named Stine (Gregg Edelman) and the main character in the film he is writing, a tough private-eye named Stone (James Naughton), who is Stine's alter ego. Both Stone and Stine have a weakness for beautiful women, but Stine's main problem is the bully-boy film producer Buddy Fidler (Rene Auberjonois). Buddy's secretary, Donna, and Stone's secretary, Oolie, are both played by Randy Graff who has one of the show's big numbers, the bittersweet 'You Can Always Count On Me' ('I've been the "other woman" since my puberty began/I crashed the junior prom and met the only married man'). Another example of Zippel's witty lyrics comes in the double-entendres of 'The Tennis Song', in which Stone and his beautiful 'client', Alaura Kingsley, play around with lines such as, He: 'I bet you like to play rough'/She: 'I like to work up a sweat'/He: 'And you just can't get enough'/She: 'I'm good for more than one set'. The rest of the fine score included 'Double-Talk', 'What You Don't Know About Women', 'Ya Gotta Look Out For Yourself', 'With Every Breath I Take', 'Ev'rybody's Gotta Be Somewhere', 'Lost And Found', 'You're Nothing Without Me' - Stone and Stine tell each other, 'Stay With Me', and 'It Needs Work'. The show ran for over two years in New York, a total of 878 performances, and won three Outer Critics Circle Awards, eight Drama Desk Awards, and Tony Awards for best musical, book, score, actor (Naughton), featured actress (Graff), and scenic design (Robin Wagner). Director Michael Blakemore repeated his brilliant staging for the London production which opened at the Prince of Wales Theatre in March 1993, but, in spite of attracting ecstatic reviews and winning Critics Circle London Theatre and Laurence Olivier Awards, it never caught on in the West End ('too sophisticated and tricky', some said), and stuttered along until November when it closed with losses estimated at £2.5 million.

CLAMBAKE

By 1967 Elvis Presley was showing dissension about his Hollywood career. Features such as this indicate why. In what was his only film that year, the singer plays an heir who exchanges identities with a water-skiing instructor and becomes infatuated with boat racing. Singer Shelley Fabares, who enjoyed a memorable US chart-topper with 'Johnny Angel' in 1962, was Presley's co-star in this uneventful vehicle. Eight songs were featured in the film, none of which were particularly interesting, but the soundtrack album was bolstered by newer recordings undertaken in September 1967. Among these songs were 'Big Boss Man' and 'Guitar Man', both of which used a tight, stripped-down band and incisive production. Although neither was a major hit single these tracks signalled an artistic rebirth not hinted at in *Clambake*.

CLARK, PETULA

b. 15 November 1932, Epsom, Surrey, England. Her Welsh mother, a soprano, taught Petula to sing, which enabled her to commence a stage career at the age of seven and a broadcasting career two years later. Her youthful image and crystal-clear enunciation were ideal for radio and by 1943, she had her own programme with the accent on wartime, morale-building songs. She made her first film, *Medal For The General*, in 1944 and then signed for the J. Arthur Rank Organization appearing in over 20 feature films, including the *Huggett* series, alongside other young hopefuls such as Anthony Newley and Alec Guinness. By 1949 she was recording, and throughout the 50s had several hits including 'The Little Shoemaker', 'Suddenly There's A Valley' 'With All My Heart' and 'Alone'. Around this period, Clark's success in France led to many concert appearances in Paris and recordings, in French, for the Vogue label. Eventually, in 1959, at the age of 27 and unhappy with the British audiences' reluctance to see her as anything but a sweet adolescent, she moved to France, where she married Vogue's PR representative, Claude Wolff. At the Olympia Theatre, Paris, in 1960, she introduced her new sound, retaining the ultra-clear vocals, but adding to them electronic effects and a hefty beat. Almost immediately her career took off. She had a massive hit with 'Ya-Ya Twist', for which she received the Grand Prix du Disque, and by 1962 was France's favourite female vocalist, ahead even of the legendary Edith Piaf. Meanwhile, in Britain, Clark's versions of 'Romeo', 'My Friend The Sea' and 'Sailor', were chasing Elvis Presley up the charts. Her international breakthrough began in 1964 when the British songwriter/arranger Tony Hatch presented Clark with 'Downtown'. It became a big hit in western Europe, and a year later climbed to the top of the US charts, clinching her popularity in a country where she was previously unknown. The record sold over three million copies worldwide and gained a Grammy Award in the USA as the best rock 'n' roll single. Clark's subsequent recordings of other Hatch songs, frequently written with his lyricist wife, Jackie Trent, including 'Don't Sleep In The Subway', 'The Other Man's Grass', 'I Couldn't Live Without Your Love', 'My Love' and 'I Know A Place', all made the US Top 10. Her recording of 'This Is My Song', written by Charles Chaplin for the Marlon Brando/Sophia Loren epic, *A Countess From Hong Kong* (1967), reached number 1 in the UK charts. Tours of the USA and television guest shots followed. As well as hosting her own BBC Television series, she was given her own US NBC television special *Petula*, in 1968. This was marred by the programme sponsor's request that a sequence in which she touched the arm of black guest Harry Belafonte should be removed in deference to the southern states. The show

was eventually transmitted complete. That same year Clark revived her film career when she appeared as Sharon, the 'Glocca Morra' girl in E.Y. 'Yip' Harburg and Burton Lane's *Finian's Rainbow*, co-starring with Fred Astaire and Tommy Steele. While the film was generally regarded as too old-fashioned for 60s audiences, Clark's performance, with just a touch of the blarney, was well received, as was her partnership with Peter O'Toole in MGM's 1969 remake of *Goodbye, Mr. Chips*, marking her 30 years in showbusiness. She was, by now, not only a major recording star, but an international personality, able to play all over the world, in cabaret and concerts. Between 1981 and 1982 she played the part of Maria in the London revival of Richard Rodgers/Oscar Hammerstein II's *The Sound Of Music*. It ran for 14 months, and was a great personal success. In 1989 PYS Records issued a 'radically remised' version of her 60s hit, 'Downtown', with the original vocal accompanied by 'acid house' backing. It went to number 10 in the UK chart.

To date Clark has sold over 30 million records worldwide and has been awarded more gold discs than any other British female singer. From early in her career she has written songs, sometimes under the pseudonym of Al Grant; so it was particularly pleasing for Clark to write the music, and appear in a West End musical, *Someone Like You*. The show opened in March 1990 to mixed reviews, and had only a brief run. Two years later Clark undertook her first concert tour of the UK for 10 years, and in 1993 took over the starring role of Mrs Johnstone in Willy Russell's musical *Blood Brothers* on Broadway, and then toured it through 26 American cities. In 1995, she played the part of Norma Desmond in the London production of *Sunset Boulevard* for six weeks while Elaine Paige was on holiday, and subsequently led the cast until the show closed in April 1997. A few months on, she was created CBE, 'for services to entertainment', in the New Year's Honours List. Early in 1998 Clark embarked on a UK tour and released *Where The Heart Is*, a collection of personal favourites. It featured 11 new tracks including her versions of 'With One Look', 'As If We Never Said Goodbye', and 'The Perfect Year', three numbers from *Sunset Boulevard* which had been previously issued as a CD maxi-single. There was also 'Home Is Where The Heart Is', a song she co-wrote for the ill-fated *Someone Like You*. Late in 1998/9, Clark starred in a 'pared-down' *Sunset Boulevard* on a major national US tour.

● ALBUMS: *Petula Clark Sings* (Pye Nixa 1956)★★★, *A Date With Pet* (Pye Nixa 1956)★★★, *You Are My Lucky Star* (Pye Nixa 1957)★★★, *Pet Clark* (Pye Nixa 1959)★★★, *Petula Clark In Hollywood* (Pye Nixa 1959)★★★, *In Other Words* (Pye 1962)★★★, *Petula* (Pye 1962)★★★, *Les James Dean* (Pye-Vogue 1962)★★★, *Downtown* (Pye 1964)★★★★, *I Know A Place* (Pye 1965)★★★, *The World's Greatest International Hits!* (Pye 1965)★★★, *The New Petula Clark Album* (Pye 1965)★★★, *Uptown With Petula Clark* (Pye 1965)★★★, *In Love* (Pye 1965)★★★, *Petula '65* (Pye 1965)★★★★, *My Love* (Pye 1966),★★★★ *Petula '66* (Pye 1966)★★★, *Hello Paris, Volume I* (Pye-Vogue 1966)★★★, *Hello Paris, Volume II* (Pye-Vogue 1966)★★★, *Petula Clark Sings For Everybody* (Pye 1966)★★★, *I Couldn't Live Without Your Love* (Pye 1966),★★★★ *Colour My World/Who Am I?* (Pye 1967)★★★,

These Are My Songs (Pye 1967)★★★, *The Other Man's Grass Is Always Greener* (Pye 1968)★★★★, *Petula* (Pye 1968)★★★, *Portrait Of Petula* (Pye 1969)★★★, *Just Pet* (Pye 1969)★★★, *Memphis* (Pye 1970)★★, *The Song Of My Life* (Pye 1971)★★★, *Wonderland Of Sound* (Pye 1971)★★, *Today* (Pye 1971)★★★, *Petula '71* (Pye 1971)★★★, *Warm And Tender* (Pye 1971)★★★, *Live At The Royal Albert Hall* (Pye 1972)★★★, *Now* (Polydor 1972)★★★, *Live In London* (1974)★★★, *Come On Home* (1974)★★★, *C'est Le Befrain De Ma Vie* (1975)★★★, *La Chanson De Marie-Madeleine* (1975)★★★, *I'm The Woman You Need* (1975)★★★, *Just Petula* (Polydor 1975)★★★, *Noel* (Pet Projects 1975)★★, *Beautiful Sounds* (Pet Projects 1976)★★, *Destiny* (Columbia 1978)★★★, *An Hour In Concert With Petula Clark* (1983)★★★, *Here For You* (Varese Sarabande 1998)★★★.

● COMPILATIONS: *Petula's Greatest Hits, Volume 1* (Pye 1968)★★★★, *Petula Clark's Hit Parade* (Pye 1969)★★★★, *Petula Clark's 20 All Time Greatest* (K-Tel 1977)★★★★, *Spotlight On Petula Clark* (PRT 1980)★★★, *100 Minutes Of Petula Clark* (PRT 1982)★★★, *Early Years* (PRT 1986)★★★, *The Hit Singles Collection* (PRT 1987)★★★★, *My Greatest* (MFP/EMI 1989)★★★, *Downtown* (PRT 1989)★★★, *Treasures Volume 1* (1992)★★★, *Jumble Sale: Rarities And Obscurities 1959-1964* 2-CD set (Sequel 1992)★★★★, *The EP Collection Volume 2* (See For Miles 1993)★★★★, *The Nixa Years Volume One* 2-CD set (1994)★★★★, *The Polygon Years Volume One: 1950-1952* (RPM 1994)★★★, *The Polygon Years Volume Two: 1952-1955* (RPM 1994)★★★, *I Love To Sing* 3-CD box set (Sequel 1995)★★★★, *The Nixa Years Volume Two* 2-CD set (1995)★★★★, *Downtown: The Best Of Petula Clark* (Pulse 1995)★★★, *The Pye Years Volume Two* (RPM 1996)★★★, *These Are My Songs* (Start 1996)★★★, *The Pye Years Volume Three* (RPM 1997)★★★★, *The Classic Collection* 4-CD box set (Pulse 1997)★★★, *Where The Heart Is* (Connoisseur Collection 1998)★★★★.

● VIDEOS: *Petula Clark Spectacular* (Laserlight 1996).

● FURTHER READING: *This Is My Song: Biography Of Petula Clark*, Andrea Kon.

● FILMS: *Medal For The General* (1944), *Murder In Reverse* (1945), *I Know Where I'm Going* (1945), *London Town* (1946), *Strawberry Roan* (1947), *Here Come The Huggetts* (1948), *Vice Versa* (1948), *Easy Money* (1948), *Don't Ever Leave Me* (1949), *Vote For Huggett* (1949), *The Huggetts Abroad* (1950), *Dance Hall* (1950), *The Romantic Age* (1950), *White Corridors* (1951), *Madame Louise* (1951), *Made In Heaven* (1952), *The Card* (1952), *The Runaway Bus* (1954), *The Gay Dog* (1954), *The Happiness Of Three Women* (1955), *Track The Man Down* (1956), *The Woman Opposite* (1957), *Daggers Drawn* (1964), *Finian's Rianbow* (1968), *Goodbye Mr Chips* (1969), *Never Never Land* (1981).

CLOONEY, ROSEMARY

b. 23 May 1928, Maysville, Kentucky, USA. A popular singer and actress. Although her heyday was back in the 50s, she has mellowed and matured, and is still close to the peak of her powers in the 90s. Rosemary and her sister Betty sang at political rallies in support of their paternal grandfather. When Rosemary was 13 the Clooney children moved to Cincinnati, Ohio, and appeared on radio station WLW. In 1945 they auditioned successfully for tenor saxophonist Tony Pastor and joined his band as featured vocalists, travelling the country doing mainly one-night shows. Rosemary made her first solo record in 1946 with 'I'm Sorry I Didn't Say I'm Sorry When I Made You

Cry Last Night'. After around three years of touring, Betty quit, and Rosemary stayed on as a soloist with the band. She signed for Columbia Records in 1950 and had some success with children's songs such as 'Me And My Teddy Bear' and 'Little Johnny Chickadee', before coming under the influence of A&R manager Mitch Miller, who had a penchant for folksy, novelty dialect songs. In 1951 Clooney's warm, husky melodious voice registered well on minor hits, 'You're Just In Love', a duet with Guy Mitchell, and 'Beautiful Brown Eyes'. Later that year she topped the US chart with 'Come On-A-My House' from the off-Broadway musical *The Son*, with a catchy harpsichord accompaniment by Stan Freeman. During the next four years Clooney had a string of US hits including 'Tenderly', which became her theme tune, 'Half As Much' (number 1), 'Botcha-Me', 'Too Old To Cut The Mustard' (a duet with Marlene Dietrich), 'The Night Before Christmas Song' (with Gene Autry), 'Hey There' and 'This Ole House' (both number 1 hits), and 'Mambo Italiano'. UK hits included 'Man', with the b-side, 'Woman', sung by her husband, actor/producer/director Jose Ferrer, and the novelty, 'Where Will The Dimple Be'. Her last singles hit was 'Mangos', in 1957. Her own US television series regularly featured close harmony vocal group the Hi-Lo's, leading to their communal album *Ring Around Rosie*. Clooney's film career started in 1953 with *The Stars Are Singing* and was followed by three films the next year, *Here Come The Girls* with Bob Hope, *Red Garters* (1954) with Guy Mitchell and the Sigmund Romberg biopic, *Deep In My Heart*, in which she sang 'Mr And Mrs' with Jose Ferrer. In the same year she teamed with Bing Crosby in *White Christmas*. Highly compatible, with friendly, easy-going styles, their professional association was to last until Crosby died, and included, in 1958, the highly regarded album *Fancy Meeting You Here*, a musical travelogue with special material by Sammy Cahn and James Van Heusen, arranged and conducted by Billy May. Semi-retired in the 60s her psychiatric problems were chronicled in her autobiography, *This For Remembrance*, later dramatized on television as *Escape From Madness*. Her more recent work has been jazz-based, and included a series of tributes to the 'great' songwriters such as Harold Arlen, Cole Porter and Duke Ellington, released on the Concorde Jazz label. In 1991 Clooney gave an 'assured performance' in concert at Carnegie Hall, and duetted with her special guest artist, Linda Ronstadt. Throughout the early 90s she has continued to play US clubs, including her much appreciated annual stint at the Rainbow & Stars in New York. She also made occasional appearances in the US medical drama *ER*.

● ALBUMS: *Hollywood's Best* (Columbia 1952/55)★★★, *Deep In My Heart* film soundtrack (MGM 1954)★★★, *Rosemary Clooney* 10-inch album (Columbia 1954)★★★, *White Christmas* 10-inch album (Columbia 1954)★★★★, *Red Garters* film soundtrack (Columbia 1954)★★★, *Tenderly* 10-inch album (Columbia 1955)★★★★, *Children's Favorites* 10-inch album (Columbia 1956)★★, *Blue Rose* (Columbia 1956)★★★, *A Date With The King* 10-inch album (Columbia 1956)★★★, *On Stage* 10-inch album (Columbia 1956)★★, *My Fair Lady* 10-inch album (Columbia 1956)★★, *Clooney Tunes* (Columbia 1957)★★★, with the Hi-Lo's

Ring A Round Rosie (Columbia 1957)★★★, *Swing Around Rosie* (Coral 1958)★★★, with Bing Crosby *Fancy Meeting You Here* (RCA Victor 1958)★★★★, *Rosemary Clooney In Hi-Fidelity* (Harmony 1958)★★★, *The Ferrers At Home* (1958)★★★, *Hymns From The Heart* (MGM 1959)★★, *Oh Captain!* (MGM 1959)★★, *Rosemary Clooney Swings Softly* (MGM 1960)★★★★, *A Touch Of Tabasco* (RCA Victor 1960)★★★, *Clap Hands, Here Comes Rosie* (RCA Victor 1960)★★★, *Rosie Solves The Swingin' Riddle* (RCA Victor 1961)★★★★, *Country Hits From The Heart* (RCA Victor 1963)★★, *Love* (Reprise 1963)★★★, *Thanks For Nothing* (Reprise 1964)★★★, with Crosby *That Travelin' Two Beat* (Capitol 1965)★★★, *Look My Way* (United Artists 1976)★★★, *Nice To Be Around* (United Artists 1977)★★★, *Here's To My Lady* (Concord 1979)★★★, *With Love* (Concord 1981)★★★, *Sings The Music Of Cole Porter* (Concord 1982)★★★★, *Sings Harold Arlen* (Concord 1983)★★★★, *My Buddy* (Concord 1983)★★★, *Sings The Music Of Irving Berlin* (Concord 1984)★★★★, *Rosemary Clooney Sings Ballads* (Concord 1985)★★★, *Our Favourite Things* (Dance Band Days 1986)★★★, *Mixed Emotions* (Columbia 1986)★★★, *Sings The Lyrics Of Johnny Mercer* (Concord 1987)★★★★, *Sings The Music Of Jimmy Van Heusen* (Concord 1987)★★★★, *Show Tunes* (Concord 1989)★★★, *Everything's Coming Up Rosie* (Concord 1989)★★★, *Sings Rodgers, Hart And Hammerstein* (Concord 1990)★★★, *Rosemary Clooney Sings The Lyrics Of Ira Gershwin* (Concord 1990)★★★★, *For The Duration* (Concord 1991)★★★, *Girl Singer* (Concord 1992)★★★, *Do You Miss New York?* (Concord 1994)★★★, *Still On The Road* (Concord 1994)★★★★, *Demi-Centennial* (Concord 1995)★★★, *Dedicated To Nelson* (Concord 1995)★★★★, *Mothers & Daughters* (Concord Jazz 1997)★★★, *White Christmas* (Concord 1997)★★, with the Count Basie Orchestra *At Long Last* (Concord 1998)★★★★.

● COMPILATIONS: *Rosie's Greatest Hits* (Columbia 1957)★★★★, *Rosemary Clooney Showcase Of Hits* (Columbia 1959)★★★★, *Greatest Hits* (Columbia 1983)★★★★, *The Best Of Rosemary Clooney* (Creole 1984)★★★★, *The Rosemary Clooney Songbook* (Columbia 1984)★★★★, *Come On-A My House* 7-CD box set (Bear Family 1997)★★★★, *Rosemary Clooney 70: A Seventieth Birthday Celebration* (Concord Jazz 1998)★★★.

● FURTHER READING: *This For Remembrance*, Rosemary Clooney.

● FILMS: *The Stars Are Singing* (1953), *Here Come The Girls* (1953), *Red Garters* (1954), *White Christmas* (1954), *Deep In My Heart* (1954).

CLOSE, GLENN

b. 19 March 1947, Greenwich, Connecticut, USA. Although known primarily as an accomplished actress in films such as *The World According To Garp*, *The Big Chill*, *The Natural One*, and especially *Fatal Attraction*, *Dangerous Liaisons*, and *Reversal Of Fortune*, Glenn Close has also made an important contribution to the musical theatre. After majoring in drama at the College of William and Mary, she worked in regional theatre before appearing in Richard Rodgers' ill-fated musical *Rex* in the late 70s. She was nominated for a Tony Award for her performance as P.T. Barnum's feisty wife, Charity, in the Broadway musical *Barnum* (1980), and won Tonys for best actress in Tom Stoppard's play, *The Real Thing* (1984), and Ariel Dorfman's *Death Of A Maiden* (1992). However, Close achieved her greatest triumph so far when she portrayed the ageing film star, Norma Desmond, in the Los Angeles

production of Andrew Lloyd Webber's musical, *Sunset Boulevard* (1993). She repeated her 'untamed, larger-than-life performance' - for which she was hailed as 'the exciting new star of the American musical theatre of the 90s' - on Broadway a year later, and won one of the show's seven Tony Awards, for best actress in a musical.

● FILMS: *The World According To Garp* (1982), *The Big Chill* (1983), *The Stone Boy* (1984), *The Natural* (1984), *Maxie* (1985), *Jagged Edge* (1985), *Fatal Attraction* (1987), *Light Years* voice (1988), *Dangerous Liaisons* (1988), *Immediate Family* (1989), *Reversal Of Fortune* (1990), *Hamlet* (1990), *Meeting Venus* (1991), *Hook* (1991), *The House Of The Spirits* (1993), *The Paper* (1994), *Anne Frank Remembered* voice (1995), *Mary Roberts* (1996), *101 Dalmations* (1996), *Mars Attacks!* (1996), *Paradise Road* (1997), *Air Force One* (1997), *In And Out* (1997).

COATES, ERIC

b. 27 August 1886, Hucknall, Nottingham, England, d. 21 December 1957, Sussex, England. Coates was a major force in light music for over 30 years, and many of his works are still closely associated with the radio and television programmes for which they served as signature tunes. Son of a doctor, his early career found him playing viola in many orchestras, including those of Sir Henry Wood and Sir Thomas Beecham. He was keen to gain recognition as a composer, and persuaded Fred E. Weatherly, the most famous lyric writer of the day, to write him a verse which became 'Stonecracker John'. This was an immediate success, and produced a number of fine sequels, notably 'A Dinder Courtship' and 'Green Hills o' Somerset'. Coates' first success with a purely orchestral work was his 'Miniature Suite' which was premiered by Sir Henry Wood at a Promenade Concert in October 1911. A noticeable weakness in his left-hand caused Coates to worry about his long-term prospects as a viola player, and he was anxious to establish his composing credentials. Ballads still formed an important part of his output: 'I Pitch My Lonely Caravan At Night', 'I Heard You Singing' and 'Bird Songs At Eventide' are still remembered. His suite 'From The Countryside' and the waltz 'Wood Nymphs' were well received, but it was not until 1919 that Coates was able to give up playing and devote himself entirely to writing. Then began an amazing flow of original works: 'Summer Days' (1919), 'Joyous Youth', 'The Merrymakers', 'The Selfish Giant' (1925) - based on the Oscar Wilde tale, 'The Three Bears' (1926), 'Four Ways Suite' (1927), 'Cinderella' (1929), 'By The Tamarisk', 'Mirage', 'Under The Stars' and 'By The Sleepy Lagoon' (1930) inspired by the south coast of England near Bognor, close to his rural retreat in Sussex. This music is still used by the BBC for its *Desert Island Discs* programme. New works continued unabated: 'The Seven Dwarfs' (later rewritten as 'The Enchanted Garden'), 'From Meadow To Mayfair Suite', 'Dancing Nights', 'The Jester At The Wedding' then his 'London Suite' (1932) which included the 'Knightsbridge March', the signature tune for BBC's *In Town Tonight*. The great success of the 'London Suite' spawned 'London Bridge' and, three years later 'London Again Suite'. In between Coates created his 'Three Men Suite' (1935) and the 'Saxo-Rhapsody' given the premiere performance by the Danish virtuoso Sigurd Rascher at the

1936 Folkestone Festival. 'Springtime Suite', 'For Your Delight' 'The Seven Seas', 'Footlights' and 'Last Love' were followed, early in World War II, by 'Calling All Workers', forever remembered as the signature tune for the BBC's *Music While You Work*. 1941 brought 'Four Centuries Suite' and the march 'Over To You', then 'London Calling' (1942) and 'Eighth Army March' (1942). Bouts of illness stemmed Coates' creative flow at times, but he finally completed 'The Three Elizabeths' in time for a premiere performance on Christmas Eve, 1944. In 1966 the BBC used the first movement as theme for *The Forsyte Saga*, which was televised all over the world. In fact television was to be the last major influence on Coates, because many new services asked him to write marches to be played at the start of transmissions, such as BBC's 'Television March' and ATV's 'Sound And Vision'. There was one final success for Coates - his march used in the film *The Dam Busters* (1954). This won him an Ivor Novello Award, and the sheet music sold more copies than any of his other works.
● ALBUMS: *Three Elizabeths/Four Centuries* conducted by the composer (Decca 1950)★★★, *London Suite/London Again* conducted by the composer (Parlophone 1952)★★★★, *The Three Bears/Jester At The Wedding/The Three Men* conducted by the composer (Decca 1950)★★★, *The Music Of Eric Coates* (Classics For Pleasure 1986)★★★★, *The Music Of Eric Coates* (ASV 1991),★★★★ *Eric Coates* re mastered 78s (Pearl 1992)★★, *British Light Music - Eric Coates* (Marco Polo 1993)★★, *Music Of Eric Coates - Volume 2* (ASV 1993)★★, *The Music Of Eric Coates - Volume 1* re mastered 78s (Conifer 1994)★★★★, *BBC Radio Classics* (Pickwick 1995)★★★★, *The Music Of Eric Coates - Volume 2* re mastered 78s (Conifer 1995)★★.

COCHRAN, CHARLES B.

b. Charles Blake Cochran, 25 September 1872, Sussex, England, d. 31 January 1951, London, England. Britain's leading theatrical producer of musicals, revues, plays, operettas, and so much more during the 20s and 30s. A master showman, the like of which has never been seen before or since, he is said to have been annoyed when referred to as 'the English Ziegfeld', but then Florenz Ziegfeld did not present flea circuses, boxing matches, rodeos, or run the Royal Albert Hall. There were similarities though: both men specialised in lavish and spectacular theatrical extravaganzas, and, while the American had his lovely 'Ziegfeld Girls', the London stage was graced by 'Mr. Cochran's Young Ladies'. Many of these talented and delightful 'young things' went on to become stars in their own right. Cochran is credited with discovering or significantly promoting Gertrude Lawrence, Tilly Losch, Jessie Matthews, Anna Neagle, Larry Adler, Evelyn Laye, John Mills, Alice Delysia, Hermione Baddeley, Elisabeth Welch, Binnie Hale, Beatrice Lillie, Pirandello, Douglas Byng, and numerous others. However, Cochran's most famous association was with the 'Master' himself, Noël Coward. After inviting Coward to write the words and music for the revue *On With The Dance* in 1925, during the next nine years Cochran produced some of the composer's most celebrated works, including *This Year Of Grace*, *Bitter Sweet*, *Cavalcade*, *Private Lives*, *Cochran's 1931 Revue*, *Words And Music*, and *Conversation Piece*. They parted in 1934 because Coward thought that the impresario had cheated

him out of his fair share of royalties. From 1914 through to 1949, Cochran's London productions included *Odds And Ends*, *More*, *Half-Past Eight*, *The Better 'Ole*, *As You Were*, *Afgar*, *London, Paris And New York*, *League Of Notions*, *Phi-Phi*, *Music Box Revue*, *Little Nellie Kelly*, *Cochran's Revue Of 1926*, *Blackbirds*, *One Dam Thing After Another*, *Castles In The Air*, *Wake Up And Dream*, *Ever Green*, *Cochran's 1931 Revue*, *Helen!*, *The Cat And The Fiddle*, *Music In The Air*, *Nymph Errant*, *Streamline*, *Anything Goes*, *Blackbirds Of 1936*, *Home And Beauty*, *Paganini*, *Happy Returns*, *Lights Up*, *Big Ben*, *Bless the Bride*, and *Tough At The Top*. Early in 1951 Cochran was involved in a terrible accident at his London home. He scalded himself whilst taking a bath and was taken to the Westminster Hospital, but died on 31 January.
● FURTHER READING: *Secrets Of A Showman*, *I Had Almost Forgotten*, *Cock-A-Doodle-Doo*, *Showman Looks On*, all by Charles B. Cochran. *The Cochran Story*, Charles Graves Allen. *'Cockie'-An Authoritative Life Of C.B. Cochran*, Sam Heppner. *Cochran*, James Harding.

COCOANUTS, THE

Irving Berlin meets the Marx Brothers does not sound like a particularly good idea for a musical, but the production which opened at New York's Lyric Theatre on 8 December 1925, amused and delighted audiences for nearly 400 performances. It was George S Kaufman's book which the Marx Brothers used (and sometimes modified) to create their usual brand of zany mayhem. The story concerns Henry W. Schlemmer (Groucho), a devious Florida hotel owner who deals in a little real estate on the side. He is aided, abetted, and sometimes hindered in his various shady transactions by two hotel guests, Silent Sam (Harpo), Willie The Wop (Chico), and the desk clerk Jameson (Zeppo). Complications arise when jewel thieves, posing as hotel residents, rob the wealthy Mrs Potter, played by Margaret Dumont (Groucho's regular 'stooge'), and try to 'frame' her future son-in-law. Berlin's score was largely unappreciated at the time, but in retrospect the lively, catchy songs such as 'The Monkey Doodle-Doo', 'A Little Bungalow', 'Lucky Boy', 'Florida By The Sea', and 'Why Am I A Hit With The Ladies?', were entirely right for this riotous romp. This was the second of the three Marx Brothers' Broadway musicals - the others were *I'll Say She Is* (1924) and *Animal Crackers* (1928). The Marx Brothers made their feature-film debut in the 1929 screen version of *The Cocoanuts*.

COHAN, GEORGE M.

b. George Michael Cohan, 3 July 1878, Providence, Rhode Island, USA, d. 5 November 1942, New York, USA. A legendary figure in the history of American popular entertainment: a performer, songwriter, playwright, director, producer, and a high-profile patriot. Cohan's paternal grandfather emigrated to America from County Cork, Ireland, and George was baptized in the family's Catholic faith. His parents were vaudevillians, and from an early age, he and his sister, Josephine, joined them on stage as the Four Cohans. By the time he was eight, George had finished his conventional education, but already he was learning the skills that would make him one of the great show business all-rounders. He wrote sketches and dialogue for the family's headline act, and had his first song, 'Why Did Nellie Leave Home?', published when he was 16. Around this time, he also developed his curious dancing style, a straight-legged strut, with the body bent forward; and introduced his famous closing address to the audience: 'My mother thanks you, my father thanks you, my sister thanks you, and I thank you.' In 1899, Cohan married the singer and comedienne Ethel Levey, who joined the Four Cohans. They all appeared, two years later, in George's first Broadway musical comedy, *The Governor's Son*, for which, as with most of his future shows, he wrote the book, music and lyrics. However, neither that show, or the follow-up, *Running For Office* (1903), lasted for over 50 performances.

By 1904 Cohan was into his stride. In partnership with the producer, Sam H. Harris, he presented, starred in, and directed a series of (mostly) hit musical shows during the next 15 years. The first, *Little Johnny Jones*, was not successful initially, despite a score that included 'The Yankee Doodle Boy', 'Life's A Funny Proposition After All', and 'Give My Regards To Broadway', amongst others. Even so, the 'play with music' which told the story of an American jockey wrongfully accused of accepting a bribe to lose the English Derby race, is seen as a watershed in the history of the Broadway musical. With its brash, patriotic, flag-waving style, and a strong, believable plot, it marked the beginning of the indigenous American musical - a real alternative to the country's currently fashionable operettas which had originated in Europe. It was filmed as a silent in 1923, and again in 1930. *Little Johnny Jones* was followed by *Forty-Five Minutes From Broadway*, which contained three enormously popular Cohan numbers: the title song, 'So Long Mary', and 'Mary's A Grand Old Name'. In *George Washington Jnr.* (1906), Cohan initiated one of his famous pieces of business, when he wrapped himself in the American flag during the song, 'You're A Grand Old Flag', which he had originally called 'You're A Grand Old Rag', until he was lobbied by various nationalistic societies. From then, until 1914 and the outbreak of World War I, Cohan's musical comedies were a regular feature of each New York season - he dominated the Broadway musical theatre. In 1907 there was *The Honeymooners*, a revised version of *Running For Office*, with a score that included 'I'm a Popular Man', If I'm Going to Die', and 'I'll Be There In The Public Square'. It was followed by others such as *The Talk Of New York* ('When We Are M-A-Double R-I-E-D', 'When A Fellow's On The Level With A Girl That's On The Square'), *Fifty Miles From Boston* ('Harrigan', 'A Small Town Girl'), *The Yankee Prince* ('Come On Down Town', 'I'm Awfully Strong For You'), *The Man Who Owns Broadway* ('There's Something About A Uniform'), *The Little Millionaire* ('Barnum Had The Right Idea', 'Any Place The Old Flag Flies'). In 1914, with the innovative *Hello Broadway!*, Cohan introduced the modern revue format to New York, later sustained by *The Cohan Revues* of 1916 and 1918. In 1917 he wrote 'Over There', generally considered to be the greatest of all war songs, for which he subsequently received the Congressional Medal. Two years later, he dissolved his partnership with Sam H. Harris and threatened to retire from show business following the strike of the Actors' Equity Association. As a producer as well as an actor, the dispute must have placed Cohan in something of a quandary, but he sided with the management against Equity, who won the bitter month-long dispute. In the process, Cohan lost many long-standing friends at a time when he was beginning to be regarded as old fashioned, in comparison with the more sophisticated writers and performers that were beginning to make their mark in the 20s. It was Cohan's last decade on Broadway as a writer and director of musical shows. These included *Little Nellie Kelly* (filmed in 1940, starring Judy Garland), *The Rise Of Rosie O'Reilly*, *The Merry Malones*, and *Billie* (1928). Ironically, nearly 10 years later, in 1937, Cohan made a triumphant return to the New York musical stage in George S. Kaufman and Moss Hart's political satire, *I'd Rather Be Right*, which had a score by Richard Rodgers and Lorenz Hart, two of the 'upstarts' who had made Cohan and his continual celebration of the American dream, seem 'corny'. In *I'd Rather Be Right*, Cohan played the role of the President of the USA, Franklin D. Roosevelt, his first appearance in a musical that he hadn't written himself. Coincidentally, in Cohan's solitary appearance in a film musical, *The Phantom President* (1932), he played the part of a presidential *candidate*. His biggest impression on the cinema screen was made in 1942, when James Cagney portrayed him in the biopic *Yankee Doodle Dandy*. Cagney's uncanny impersonation of Cohan - the arrogant, dynamic, charismatic performer, complete with that individual dancing style, reviving a clutch of imperishable songs, won him an Academy Award and the New York Drama Critics Award as 'Best Actor'. Cagney reprised his Cohan role in *The Seven Little Foys* (1955), when his bar-top dance with Bob Hope (as Eddie Foy), was the highlight of the picture. Other attempts to recapture, and cash in, on the Cohan larger-then-life image have included *George M!* (1968), a Broadway musical starring Joel Grey (fresh from his *Cabaret* triumph), which ran for over a year; and *Give My Regards To Broadway* another musical anthology which played some US east coast resorts in 1987.

In the latter years of his life, Cohan concerned himself solely with the straight theatre (apart from *I'd Rather Be Right*). His first break, at the age of 13, had been in the play, *Peck's Bad Boy*', and, in parallel with his musical career, he had written some 40 plays, and presented and acted in his own, and other productions, including 13 Broadway credits. One of his critically acclaimed performances came in 1933, when he portrayed the kindly newspaper editor in Eugene O'Neill's, *Ah, Wilderness!*, and his last stage appearance is said to have been in *Return Of The Vagabond* in 1940. However, it is for his musical side, - some 500 songs - and the 'naive, brash, optimistic, jaunty, and patriotic shows, and his participation in them, that caused him to be called 'the greatest single figure the American theatre has produced'. In the early part of the 20th century, one of the early New York theatres was named after him, and his statue overlooks Times Square.
● FURTHER READING: *Twenty Years On Broadway*, George M. Cohan. *George M. Cohan: Prince Of The American Theatre*, Ward Morehouse. *George M. Cohan: The Man Who Owned Broadway*, John McCabe.

COLEMAN, CY

b. Seymour Kaufman, 14 June 1929, New York, USA. A pianist, singer, producer and composer of popular songs and scores for films and the Broadway stage. The youngest of the five sons of emigrants from Russia, Coleman was born and brought up in the Bronx, where his mother owned two tenement buildings. He began to pick out tunes on the piano when he was four years old, irritating his father, a carpenter, to such an extent that he nailed down the lid of the instrument. However, a local teacher was so impressed by Coleman's piano playing that she provided free lessons in classical music. Between the ages of six and nine, Coleman performed in New York at the Town Hall, Steinway Hall and Carnegie Hall. While continuing his classical studies at the High School of Music and Art and the New York College of Music, from which he graduated in 1948, Coleman decided to change course and pursue a career in popular music. After a stint at Billy Reed's Little Club, he spent two years as a cocktail-lounge pianist at the exclusive Sherry Netherland Hotel in Manhattan, and played piano for several television programmes, including *The Kate Smith Show* and *A Date In Manhattan*. In 1950 he appeared with his trio, and singer Margaret Phelan, in the RKO short *Package Of Rhythm*. During the early 50s Coleman began to play in jazz clubs in New York and elsewhere, developing what he called a 'kind of bepoppy style'. By then he had been composing songs for several years. One of his earliest collaborators was Joseph Allen McCarthy, whose father, also named Joseph, wrote the lyrics for shows such as *Irene*, *Kid Boots* and *Rio Rita*. One of their first efforts, 'The Riviera', was included several years later on Johnny Mathis' *Live It Up*, while 'I'm Gonna Laugh You Right Out Of My Life' was recorded by singer-pianist Buddy Greco. Another, 'Why Try To Change Me Now?', received a memorable reading from Frank Sinatra in 1952. In the following year Coleman contributed 'Tin Pan Alley' to the Broadway show *John Murray Anderson's Almanac*, and around the same time, he wrote several songs for a Tallulah Bankhead vehicle, *Ziegfeld Follies*, which never made it to Broadway. From the late 50s until 1962, Coleman had a 'stormy' working relationship with lyricist Carolyn Leigh. Together they wrote several popular numbers such as 'Witchcraft' (Frank Sinatra), 'The Best Is Yet To Come' (Mabel Mercer), 'A Moment Of Madness' (Sammy Davis Jnr.), 'When In Rome (I Do As The Romans Do)' (Vikki Carr/Barbra Streisand), 'You Fascinate Me So' (Mark Murphy), 'Playboy's Theme', 'The Rules Of The Road', 'It Amazes Me', 'I Walk A Little Faster' and 'Firefly'. The latter was written in 1958 for Coleman and Leigh's musical based on the memoirs of stripper Gypsy Rose Lee. The project was later abandoned, but the song became a hit for Tony Bennett, who was instrumental in bringing their work before the public, and included two of their songs in his famous Carnegie Hall concert in 1962. Two years before that, the team wrote the music and lyrics for the Broadway musical *Wildcat*. The score included the show-stopper 'What Takes My Fancy', plus 'That's What I Want For Janie', 'Give A Little Whistle', 'You've Come Home', 'El Sombrero', and the march 'Hey, Look Me Over'. The latter became a hit for Peggy Lee. Coleman and Lee collaborated to write 'Then Is Then And Now Is Now'.

In 1962, Coleman and Leigh were back on Broadway with *Little Me*. The libretto, by Neil Simon, was based on a successful novel by Patrick Dennis, and traced the life of Belle Poitrine. Sid Caesar played all seven of her lovers, from the 16-year-old Noble Eggleston to the geriatric skinflint Mr. Pinchley. The score included 'Love You', 'Deep Down Inside', 'The Other Side Of The Tracks', 'Real Live Girl' and the show-stopper 'I've Got Your Number'. Despite a favourable reception from the critics, *Little Me* did not fulfil its potential, and folded after only 257 performances. In 1964, it was acclaimed in London, where comedian and song and dance man Bruce Forsyth played the lead, and a revised version was presented in the West End in 1984, starring the UK television comic Russ Abbott. After *Little Me*, Coleman and Leigh went their separate ways, collaborating briefly again in 1964 for 'Pass Me By', which was sung by the British writer-performer Digby Wolfe, over the opening titles of the Cary Grant movie *Father Goose*. In the same year, Coleman wrote the catchy 'Take a Little Walk' with Buddy Greco, before teaming with the lyricist and librettist Dorothy Fields. Fields was 25 years older than Coleman, with an impressive track record of standard songs for films and shows, written with composers such as Jimmy McHugh, Jerome Kern and Arthur Schwartz, plus the book for Irving Berlin's smash hit musical *Annie Get Your Gun*. In 1966 the new combination had their own Broadway hit with the score for *Sweet Charity*, a musical version of Federico Fellini's film *Nights Of Cabiria*. The accent was very much on dancing in this 'sentimental story of a New York dancehall hostess, and her desperate search for love'. The Coleman-Fields score included 'Baby, Dream Your Dream', 'Big Spender', 'If My Friends Could See Me Now', 'There's Gotta Be Something Better Than This', 'Where Am I Going?' and 'I'm A Brass Band'. The show ran for 608 performances on Broadway, and for 14 months in London, where it starred Juliet Prowse. The lead in the 1969 movie version was taken by Shirley Maclaine, and it also featured Sammy Davis Jnr. as a hippie evangelist singing 'The Rhythm Of Life', and Stubby Kaye leading the ensemble in 'I Love To Cry At Weddings'. Coleman was nominated for an Academy Award for his musical score. After failing to have several other projects mounted, such as a biography of Eleanor Roosevelt and a stage adaptation of the 1939 James Stewart movie *Mr. Smith Goes To Washington*, Coleman and Fields were back on Broadway in 1973 with *Seesaw*, based on William Gibson's 50s comedy *Two For The Seesaw*. The score included 'Welcome To Holiday Inn', 'Poor Everybody Else' and the blockbusters 'It's Not Where You Start (It's Where You Finish)' and 'Nobody Does It Like Me'. The latter became successful outside the show as a cabaret number for artists such as Shirley Bassey and comedienne Marti Caine. After Dorothy Fields' death in 1974, it was another three years before Coleman returned to Broadway with *I Love My Wife*, with book and lyrics by Michael Stewart. Adapted from Luis Rego's farce 'about two suburban couples and their bumbling attempt to engage in wife swapping', the production ran for 857 performances. It featured a small onstage orchestra whose members sang, dressed in fancy clothes, and commented on the show's action. Coleman won the Drama Desk Award for a score which included 'Hey There, Good Times', 'Something Wonderful I Missed', 'Sexually Free', 'Lovers On Christmas Eve', 'Everybody Today Is Turning On' and the title song. Less than a year after the opening of *I Love My Wife*, Coleman contributed to *On The Twentieth Century*, which was based on a 30s play by Ben Hecht and Charles MacArthur, with lyrics and libretto by Betty Comden and Adolph Green. The production included the songs 'I Rise Again', 'Together', 'Never', 'She's A Nut' and 'Our Private World'. The show ran for over a year, and earned six Tony Awards, including best score of a musical. Coleman's next project, with lyricist Barbara Fried, was *Home Again*, which 'followed an Illinois family from the Depression to the Watergate scandal'. It closed in Toronto during April 1979, two weeks before it was set to open on Broadway.

In complete contrast, *Barnum* (1980), a musical treatment of the life of showman P.T. Barnum, was a smash hit. Coleman's music and Michael Stewart's lyrics were 'catchy and clever, and occasionally very beautiful'. British actor Jim Dale received rave notices for his endearing performance in the title role, which called for him to sing and be a clown, ride a unicycle and walk a tightrope. The part of his wife was played by Glenn Close, on the brink of her 80s movie stardom. The score included 'There's A Sucker Born Ev'ry Minute', 'One Brick At A Time', 'The Colours Of My Life' and 'Come Follow The Band'. *Barnum* ran for 854 performances and captured three Tonys and two Grammies for the Broadway Cast album. Its subsequent run of almost two years at the London Palladium was a triumph for Michael Crawford. During the early 80s Coleman mounted Broadway revivals of *Little Me* and *Sweet Charity* which won four Tonys, including best revival of a play or musical. In 1988 Coleman wrote the music and lyrics, in collaboration with A.E. Hotchner, for *Let 'Em Rot*. It failed to reach New York, and when Coleman did return to Broadway in April 1989 with *Welcome To The Club*, that show was censured by the critics, and only ran for a few performances. It proved to be a temporary setback, for in December of that year, Coleman had one of the biggest hits of his career with *City Of Angels*, utilizing David Zippel's lyrics, and a book by Larry Gelbart that 'both satirized and celebrated the film *noire* genre and the hard boiled detective fiction of the 1940s'. The show garnered six Tonys, three Outer Critics Circle Awards and eight Drama Desk Awards, among them those for best musical, best music and lyrics. The production included the songs 'With Every Breath I Take', 'The Tennis Song', 'What You Don't Know About Women', 'You're Nothing Without Me' and 'Double Talk'. *City Of Angels* ran at the Virginia Theatre in New York for 878 performances. Meanwhile, Coleman had turned his attention to *The Will Rogers Follies*, which related 'the life story of America's favourite humorist in the style of a *Ziegfeld Follies*' (1991). With Keith Carradine in the title role, Peter Stone's book called for 'a mutt act, a world champion roper, four kids, 12 sisters, a ranchful of cowboys, Gregory Peck (his voice only), and girls wearing spangles, and, of course, girls wearing not much of anything at all', which was put together by director-choreographer Tommy Tune. For the

lyrics to his pastiche melodies, Coleman turned again to Comden and Green for 'Never Met A Man I Didn't Like', 'Let's Go Flying', 'Willamania', 'It's A Boy!', 'The Powder Puff Ballet', 'Give A Man Enough Rope' and 'Marry Me Now/I Got You'. Despite initial notices citing 'lapses of taste' and 'a paltry case for a cultural icon', the show ran for 1,420 performances, and gained Tony Awards for best musical and original score. Taste could well have been an issue once more with Coleman's 1997 Broadway project, *The Life*. Based around New York's 42nd Street, habitat of hookers and their pimps, the show had lyrics by Ira Gasman, who collaborated with Coleman and David Newman on the book. Among the best numbers in Coleman's 'most driving big-beat score since *Sweet Charity*', were 'Check It Out!', 'The Oldest Profession', 'My Body', 'Use What You Got', 'Mr. Greed', 'People Magazine', and 'Why Don't They Leave Us Alone'. *The Life* won two Tony Awards, as well as Drama Desk, Outer Critics Circle and Drama League honours. In 1998, *Exactly Like You*, 'a courtroom drama' on which Coleman collaborated with co-lyricist and librettist A.E. Hotchner, had its world premiere at Goodspeed-at-Chester, Connecticut.

In parallel with his Broadway career, Coleman has written several film scores, although they have generally failed to match the critical acclaim of his stage work. His music for *Family Business* was termed by one critic as 'one of the most appalling music scores in recent memory'. Coleman's other film work has included *Father Goose* (1964), *The Troublemaker* (1964), *The Art Of Love* (1965), *The Heartbreak Kid* (1972), *Blame It On Rio* (1984), *Garbo Talks* (1984) and *Power* (1986). He has also worked in television, where he conceived and co-produced Shirley Maclaine's special *If They Could See Me Now* (1974), and produced her *Gypsy In My Soul* (1976), both Emmy-winning presentations. Coleman has also performed with many symphony orchestras, including those of Milwaukee, Detroit, San Antonio, Indianapolis and Fort Worth, and has been a director of ASCAP, and a governor of the Academy of Television Arts And Sciences and the Dramatists Guild. He was inducted into the Songwriters' Hall of Fame, and has served as a member of the Academy of Motion Picture Arts and Sciences and the New York State Advisory Committee on Music. His honours include the La Guardia Award for Outstanding Achievement in Music and the Irvin Feld Humanitarian award from the National Conference of Christians and Jews.

● ALBUMS: as a pianist and vocalist *Cy Coleman* 10-inch album (Benida 1955)★★★, *Jamaica, Playboy's Penthouse, Piano Artistry* (all 50s), *Cool Coleman* (Westminster 1958)★★★★, *Flower Drum Song* (1959)★★★, *Why Try To Change Me* (1959)★★★, *If My Friends Could See Me Now* (1966)★★★, *Barnum* (Rhapsody 1981)★★★, *Coming Home* (DRG 1988)★★★.

COLERIDGE-TAYLOR, SAMUEL

b. 15 August 1875, London, England, d. 1 September 1912, Croydon, Surrey, England. Son of a Negro physician from Sierra Leone (who deserted his family) and an English woman, Coleridge-Taylor survived a disadvantaged childhood to become a much-praised composer in Britain and the USA. The work which brought him fame was 'Hiawatha's Wedding Feast' (1898), the first part of his

'Hiawatha' trilogy based on Longfellow's poem. He is best remembered for his 'Petite Suite De Concert' (1910) which clearly indicated that he could have achieved much as a light music composer, had he lived beyond the age of 37. He regularly conducted his works in the USA and assumed a mission to dignify the Negro through his settings of Negro melodies; at one stage he seriously contemplated emigrating. Commissions in Britain kept him fully employed, and major works included incidental music for Herbert Beerbohm Tree theatrical productions in London's West End. Coleridge-Taylor's most popular song was 'On Away Awake Beloved' from 'Hiawatha' which formed part of the repertoire of almost every concert tenor for the following 50 years.

● ALBUMS: *Coleridge-Taylor* re mastered 78s (Pearl 1992)★★★, *British Light Music - Samuel Coleridge-Taylor* (Marco Polo 1995)★★★★.

COMDEN, BETTY

b. 3 May 1915, New York City, New York, USA. After graduating with a degree in science, Betty Comden strove to find work as an actress. During this period, the late 30s, she met Adolph Green (b. 2 December 1915, New York, USA), who was also seeking work in the theatre. Unsuccessful in their attempts to find acting jobs, Comden and Green formed their own troupe, together with another struggling actress, Judy Holliday. In the absence of suitable material, Comden and Green began creating their own and discovered an ability to write librettos and lyrics. At first their success was only limited, but in the early 40s they were invited by a mutual friend, Leonard Bernstein, to work on the book and lyrics of a musical he planned to adapt from his ballet score *Fancy Free*. The show, in which Comden and Green also appeared, was retitled *On The Town* (1944), and became a huge success; Comden and Green never looked back. *On The Town* was followed by *Billion Dollar Baby* (1945, music by Morton Gould) and an assignment in Hollywood for the musical films *Good News* (1947), *The Barkleys Of Broadway* (1949), *On The Town* and *Take Me Out To The Ball Game* (both 1949). In the 50s and 60s Comden and Green were back on Broadway, collaborating with Bernstein again on *Wonderful Town* (1953), and with Jule Styne on *Two On The Aisle*, *Peter Pan*, *Say, Darling*, *Do Re Mi*, *Subways Are For Sleeping*, *Fade Out-Fade In*, *Halleluja, Baby!*, and most notably, *Bells Are Ringing* (1956), in which the leading role was played by their former associate Judy Holliday. Among their films were *Singin' In The Rain* (1952), for which they wrote the screenplay, incorporating the songs of Nacio Herb Brown, and *The Band Wagon* (1953), again contributing the screenplay which was peppered with the songs of Arthur Schwartz and Howard Dietz. For *It's Always Fair Weather* (1955) they wrote screenplay and lyrics (music by André Previn) and later in the 50s and into the 60s wrote screenplays for *Auntie Mame* (1958) and *Bells Are Ringing* (1960), among others. From the late 50s they also performed their own accomplished two-person stage show. After writing the libretto for *Applause* (1970) they continued to make sporadic returns to the musical stage with *Lorelei* (1974), *On The Twentieth Century* (1978), *A Doll's Life* (1982) and *The Will*

Rogers Follies (1991). Among their best-known songs are 'Just In Time', 'Make Someone Happy', 'Lonely Town', 'Some Other Time', 'Never-Never Land', 'It's Love', 'Long Before I Knew You', 'Lucky To Be Me', 'New York, New York', 'The Party's Over' and The Right Girl For Me'. Regarded as the longest-running creative partnership in theatre history, Comden and Green have gained several Tony Awards, a Grammy and Kennedy Center Awards. They have also been elected to the Songwriters' Hall of Fame and the Theatre Hall of Fame. Albums celebrating their work have been released by Sally Mayes and Blossom Dearie, among others. In 1993, 40 years after they wrote one of their most famous numbers, 'Ohio', for *On The Town*, the Governor of that US State threw an opulent anniversary party, *The Show Must Go On: Fifty Years Of Comden And Green*, in their honour. As well as seeing their musical *On The Town* return to Broadway, they continued to receive tributes and awards throughout the 90s, including the ASCAP Richard Rodgers Lifetime Achievement Award and the Stage Directors And Choreographers President's Award for Outstanding Contribution to the Theatre. A revue of their songs, *Make Someone Happy*, opened the Bay City season in 1997, and a year later they wrote a new book and English dialogue for the Metropolitan Opera's revival of Johann Strauss's *Die Fledermaus*.

● ALBUMS: *A Party With Betty Comden And Adolph Green* (Broadway Angel 1993)★★★★, *Comden And Green Perform Their Own Songs* 1955 recordings (DRG 1998)★★★★.

● FURTHER READING: *Betty Comden And Adolph Green: A Bio-Bibliography*, Alice M. Robinson. *Off Stage*, Betty Comden. *The New York Musicals Of Comden & Green*, Mike Nichols and Aldolph Green.

COMMITMENTS, THE

Alan Parker's highly acclaimed 1991 movie, set in the working-class north side of contemporary Dublin, concerns the efforts of young Jimmy Rabbitte (Robert Arkins) to form the 'World's Hardest Working Band', and bring real soul music to the city. His adverts for musicians in the local press and elsewhere bring forth guitarists Derek Scully (Ken McCluskey) and Outspan Foster (Glen Hansard), saxophone player Dean Fay (Felim Gormley), pianist Steven Clifford (Michael Aherne), and the 45-year-old messianic trumpeter Joey 'The Lips' Fagan (Johnny Murphy), who says that he knows most of the American greats and has toured with Elvis Presley. Last, but definitely not least, there is singer Deco Cuffe (Andrew Strong), whose voice *Variety*'s critic likened to 'a diesel engine'. A gruelling rehearsal schedule pays off, and the band gets through some pub gigs, although arrogant Deco's continual 'harmonising' with backing girl vocalists Bernie McGloughlin (Bronagh Gallagher), Natalie Murphy (Maria Doyle), and Imelda Quirke (Angeline Ball), causes trouble within the ranks. Hopes (and temperatures) soar when Joey promises to ask Wilson Pickett, who is also in town, to join them on stage after he has finished his own performance. He fails to show, and tempers flare, resulting in the band splitting up. As Jimmy wanders disconsolately along the roadway, a limousine pulls up alongside him, and a member of Wilson Pickett's entourage enquires where the Commitments are playing. They were in fact playing superbly all through this film - these unknown musicians Parker preferred to seasoned actors. Amongst their repertoire: 'Mustang Sally', 'Too Many Fish In The Sea', 'Mr Pitiful', 'Bye Bye Baby', 'Show Me', 'Take Me To The River', 'The Dark End Of The Street', 'Hard To Handle', 'Chain Of Fools', 'I Never Loved A Man', 'Try A Little Tenderness', and Wilson Pickett and Steve Cropper's 'In The Midnight Hour'. There was a lot more where that came from, plus some neat touches like the way Jimmy's dad (Colm Meaney), a rabid Elvis fan, keeps a picture of the 'King' on his wall - just *above* one of the Pope. The screenplay was based on Roddy's Doyle's novel, and adapted by Doyle himself, in collaboration with Dick Clement and Ian La Frenais, one of Britain's top comedy writing teams (*Porridge*, *The Likely Lads*). This immensely enjoyable, and thoroughly authentic movie, was nominated for an Oscar (Gerry Hambling's film editing), a Golden Globe for best picture, and won the best director award at the Tokyo International Film Festival for Alan Parker. The soundtrack album and *Commitments Volume 2* spent a total of 131 weeks in the UK chart, and their version of 'Mustang Sally' was a modest singles hit. This film, a joint Irish/UK/US production, was the first of Doyle's Barrytown trilogy, followed by *The Snapper* (1993) and *The Van* (1996). Colm Meaney was in all three.

COMPANY

The first of what are sometimes called Stephen Sondheim's 'concept musicals', on which he collaborated with producer and director Harold Prince, opened at the Alvin Theatre in New York on 26 April 1970. The book, by George Furth, was based on five of his own one-act plays. It concerned Robert (Dean Jones), a bachelor who is extremely reluctant to change that status despite the well-intentioned and loving efforts of five married friends, although by the end of the piece he has begun to realise that a commitment to one woman - for better or worse - is what his life should be all about. This was a brilliant and revolutionary musical, with Sondheim using his words and music to comment on the action as well as being part of it. In their own way, the songs were all memorable and apposite, and included 'Company', 'The Little Things You Do Together', 'Sorry-Grateful', 'You Could Drive A Person Crazy', 'Have I Got A Girl For You?', 'Someone Is Waiting', 'Another Hundred People', 'Getting Married Today', "Side By Side By Side', 'What Would We Do Without You?', 'Poor Baby', 'Tick, Tock', 'Barcelona', 'The Ladies Who Lunch', and 'Being Alive'. Just a few weeks into the run, Dean was succeeded by Lary Kert; the role of Robert had originally been intended for Anthony Perkins. The remainder of the fine cast included Barbara Barrie, George Coe, John Cunningham, Teri Ralston, Charles Kimbrough, Donna McKechnie, Charles Braswell, Susan Browning, Steve Elmore, Beth Howland, Pamela Myers, Merle Louis, and the incomparable Elaine Stritch. *Company* ran on Broadway for 690 performances and won Tony Awards for best musical, music and lyrics, book, and director. Scenic designer Boris Aronson also won for his innovative multi-level skeletal sets and effects. Several of the principals, including Kert, Ralston and Stritch, reprised their roles for the London production which ran for 344 performances. A fascinating videotape which was made of the original cast recording sessions revealed the agonies and the ecstasies involved in such a project, particularly Stritch's valiant attempts to lay down on tape the difficult 'The Ladies Who Lunch' in the early hours of the morning, when she probably would have just preferred to lay down. In 1992 the video was released by RCA under the title of *Original Cast Album: Company*, and, a year later, that same original cast (with the exception of Charles Braswell) assembled at the Vivian Beaumont Theatre in New York for two highly acclaimed concert versions of the show. Two contrasting 25th anniversary revivals opened in London and on Broadway in 1995. The Manhattan version (Criterion Centre/Stage Right, 4 October) remained in the 70s as originally written, while Sam Mendes' Donmar Warehouse production (13 December), which transferred to the West End's Albery Theatre, 'altered the spirit of the show . . . and updated it'. Director Scott Ellis's New York cast had Boyd Gaines as Robert, with Kate Burton, Robert Westenberg, Patricia Ben Peterson, Jonathan Dokuchitz, Diana Canova, John Hillner, Veanne Cox, Danny Burstein, Debra Monk, Timothy Landfield, La Chanze, Charlotte d'Amboise, and Jane Krakowski. Following sell-out business, a transfer to the Brooks Atkinson Theatre on 19 December was abandoned due to a casting dispute involving Boyd Gaines. The Donmar cast, which was led by Adrian Lester (Robert) - said to be the first black man to play a lead role in any major Stephen Sondheim production - included Rebecca Front, Clive Rowe, Clare Burt, Gareth Snook, Liza Sadovy, Teddy Kempner, Sophie Thompson, Michael Simkins, Sheila Gish, Paul Bentley, Anna Francolini, Kiran Hocking, and Hannah James. The show won the Critics Circle Award for best musical, and Laurence Olivier Awards for director, actor in a musical (Lester), and supporting actress in a musical (Gish). After revisions and updatings from both the Broadway and London versions were incorporated, the newly authorized performing version of the musical received its first professional staging in May 1997 at the non-profit Huntington Theatre in Boston.

CONEY ISLAND

With her legs insured for astronomical sums, and that famous pin-up picture pinned on a million or more US (and UK) servicemen's bedside cupboard doors, Betty Grable was box office dynamite in films such as this one which was released by 20th Century-Fox in 1943. With her appeal, any showcase for her shapely song-and-dance talent could get away with the slightest of stories. In this case, George Seaton's screenplay was set at the turn-of-the-century and concerned the efforts of two pleasure park owners, played by George Montgomery and Cesar Romero, to boost their takings by having Miss Grable strut her gaudy stuff in front of their own particular audiences. However, the lady has loftier ambitions - for instance, on Broadway - and eventually, with a touch of class, makes it to the big time. The always amusing Charles Winninger and Phil Silvers were also in the film, along with Matt Briggs, Paul Hurst, Frank Orth, Carmen D'Antonio, Phyllis Kennedy, Hal K. Dawson, and Andrew Tombes. Grable's big number was Karl Hoschna and Otto Harbach's 'Cuddle Up A Little Closer', and the film was jam-packed with several other warm and wonderful songs such as 'Pretty Baby', (Egbert Van Alstyne-Gus Kahn-Tony Jackson), 'The Darktown Strutters' Ball' (Shelton Brooks), 'When Irish Eyes Are Smiling' (George Graff-Ernest Ball-Chauncey Olcott), 'Put Your Arms Around Me, Honey' (Albert Von Tilzer-Junie McCree), 'Let Me Call You Sweetheart' (Beth Slater Whitson-Leo Friedman), and several by Ralph Rainger and Leo Robin, including 'Beautiful Coney Island', 'Lulu From Louisville', 'Take It From There', 'There's Danger In A Dance', 'Get The Money', and 'Old Demon Rum'. Hermes Pan staged the dances, and Walter Lang directed a typical Technicolor mélange of colourful song and dance. Betty Grable reprised her role in the 1950 remake which was entitled *Wabash Avenue*, along with co-stars Victor Mature, Phil Harris, James Barton, and Reginald Gardiner. Once again there were some good songs, including 'Wilhelmina', 'Baby, Won't You Say You Love Me?', and 'Walking Along With Billy', all by Mack Gordon and Josef Myrow.

CONNECTICUT YANKEE, A

Richard Rodgers and Lorenz Hart's biggest Broadway hit of the 20s was adapted by Herbert Fields from Mark Twain's original story of *A Connecticut Yankee In King Arthur's Court*, and opened at the Vanderbilt Theatre on 3 November 1927. The scene is Hartford, Connecticut, and Martin (William Gaxford) has been given a suit of armour as a wedding present. It is a pity that he is not wearing it when his fiancé, Fay Morgan (Nana Bryant), crowns him with a champagne bottle for flirting with the attractive Alice Carter (Constance Carpenter) at his bachelor party. Out like a light, Martin dreams that he is back in the days of Camelot, and he and his friends are all members of the Round Table. Initially treated with suspicion, he ingratiates himself with King Arthur by introducing his own Industrial Revolution and supplying the Court with telephones, radios, and other modern devices. When he comes round, he realises that he was about to marry the wrong girl, and decides to devote himself to Alice, the girl he really loves. Rodgers and Hart's score contained two of their big all-time hits, 'My Heart Stood Still' and 'Thou Swell', along with the amusing 'On A Desert Island With Thee' and 'I Feel At Home With You'. The show ran for 418 performances and found the songwriters at the height of their powers. Sadly, that was not the case when *A Connecticut Yankee* was revived on Broadway in 1943. With an updated book - in which just about everybody was dressed in naval uniform - and some new songs, the show ran for 135 performances, but, five days after the opening, Hart died of pneumonia. One of the extra numbers, a 'list' song entitled 'To Keep My Love Alive', was sung by Vivienne Segal, who gloried in one of Hart's most ingenious lyrics about a much-married lady who reveals her personal system of 'divorce': 'Sir Athelston indulged in fratricide/He killed his dad, and that was patricide/One night I stabbed him by my mattress-side/To keep my love alive.' There was nothing wrong with the score, so it was probably the 'nonsensical, lamentably incoherent' book which prevented the show being constantly revived. That

was certainly the point made by UK critics when *A Connecticut Yankee* was presented at Regent's Park Open Air Theatre in 1993, 64 years after it flopped in London under the title of *A Yankee At The Court Of King Arthur*. The 1949 screen version, starring Bing Crosby and William Bendix, reverted to Mark Twain's original title, *A Connecticut Yankee At King Arthur's Court*.

CONTI, BILL

b. 13 April 1942, Providence, Rhode Island, USA. A composer, conductor and musical director for television and films, Conti was taught to play the piano by his father from the age of seven, and later, after the family had moved to Miami, Florida, took up the bassoon. After leaving high school he studied composition at Louisiana State University, and played in its symphony orchestra, while also playing jazz in local nightspots to defray educational expenses. Subsequently, he gained honours at the Juilliard School Of Music, New York, including a master's degree. Influenced by his major professor at Juilliard, composer Hugo Weisgall, Conti and his wife moved to Italy in 1967. During his seven year stay, he broke into films, arranging, composing and conducting for productions such as *Juliette De Sade*, *Candidate Per Un Assassino (Candidate For Killing)*, *Liquid Subway*, and *Blume In Love* (1973). On his return to the USA in 1974, he settled in California, and, aided by established film composer Lionel Newman, began to make his name all over again. Success was just around the corner, for, after scoring *Harry And Tonto*; *Next Stop, Greenwich Village*, and the documentary *Pacific Challenge*, Conti hit the big time with his music for *Rocky* (1976). The soundtrack album went platinum, and one of the numbers, 'Gonna Fly Now' (lyric by Carol Connors and Ayn Robbins), was nominated for an Oscar and, in an instrumental version by Conti, topped the US singles chart. He also scored the *Rocky* sequels, II, III (gold album), and V (1990). The composer's projects in the late 70s included two more Stallone vehicles, *F.I.S.T.* and *Paradise Alley*; plus others, such as *Citizens' Band (Handle With Care)*, *An Unmarried Woman*, *The Big Fix*, *A Man, A Woman, And A Bank*, *Goldengirl*, and *The Seduction Of Joe Tynan*. In 1981 Conti provided the score for 'one of the best' James Bond movies, *For Your Eyes Only*, starring Roger Moore. UK expatriate, Sheena Easton sang Conti's title song (written with Mick Leeson), and her record made the US Top 5. It gained Conti his second Oscar nomination, and, two years later, he finally won an Academy Award for his music to *The Right Stuff*, 'an off-beat story about America's space programme'. Throughout the rest of the 80s, and early 90s, Conti's music continued to pour out, for films such as *Unfaithfully Yours*, *Mass Appeal*, *The Karate Kid* and its two sequels; *The Bear*, *Nomads* (his first all-electronic score), *Gotcha*, *FIX*, *Masters Of The Universe*, *Baby Boom*, *Broadcast News*, *Lean On Me*, *The Fourth War*, *Year Of The Gun*, *Necessary Roughness*, *Blood In Blood Out*, *The Adventures Of Huck Finn*, and *Rookie Of The Year* (1993). Conti has by no means concentrated on composing just for the big screen - his television credits are formidable. He gained two Emmys as 'creative concept and composer' for the New York City Marathon (1990), and nominations for his music for the popular mini-series

North And South II (1985). His themes for the small screen include *Dallas*, *Falcon Crest*, *Lifestyles Of The Rich And Famous*, *Cagney And Lacey*, *The Colbys*, *O'Hara*, *Our World*, and *Mariah*; he also composed the complete scores for numerous television movies. On several occasions between 1977 and 1995, Conti has served as arranger and musical director for the Academy Awards ceremony. In 1984 he had to relinquish the baton and go on stage to receive the Oscar for his work on *The Right Stuff*. In 1995, he was presented with the Golden Soundtrack Award for lifetime achievement by ASCAP at its 10th Annual Film & Television Music Awards. Conti is the only composer to be honoured at all 10 of the Society's ceremonies.

CONVERSATION PIECE

Noël Coward wrote this 'romantic comedy with music' as a vehicle for the celebrated French actress, Yvonne Printemps. It opened at His Majesty's Theatre in London on 16 February 1934, and was, in fact, a costume operetta set in the upper crust Regency seaside town of Brighton, England, in 1811. The impoverished nobleman, Paul, Duc de Chaucigny-Varennes (Noël Coward) and his ward, Melanie (Yvonne Printemps), have arrived in Brighton with the intention of finding a rich husband for the young lady. The first of several candidates is the Marquis of Sheere (Louis Hayward), and his father, the Duke of Beneden (Athol Stewart), is also a contender. For a while Paul seems to have captured the affections of the well-heeled Lady Julia Charteris, (Irene Browne) but, just before the curtain falls at the end of the final act, Paul and Melanie realise they are really meant for each other. Coward's score contained one of his best-loved songs, the lovely waltz, 'I'll Follow My Secret Heart', which he wrote for Yvonne Printemps, and she also sang the touching 'Nevermore'. The rest of the numbers included 'There's Always Something Fishy About The French', 'Regency Rakes', 'Dear Little Soldiers', 'The English Lesson', 'Brighton Parade', and 'Danser, Danser'. George Sanders, who was destined to play so many smooth and shady characters in a long career in films which began in 1936, was one of the 'Regency Rakes'. *Conversation Piece* had a disappointing run of only 177 performances. More had been expected of Coward, especially after the success of *Bitter Sweet* (1929) which was similar in style to this current show. Pierre Fresnay, who had helped Yvonne Printemps to learn enough English to tackle her role (much of the show's dialogue was in French), and who had substituted occasionally for Coward during the London run, played the lead when *Conversation Piece* played on Broadway for 55 performances. The original London cast recordings were issued on *Noël Coward: The Great Shows*, and when Coward made a new recording of the show in New York 17 years later, the part of the Marquis of Sheere was played by a young British actor who was just beginning to make an impact in films, Richard Burton.

COOK, BARBARA

b. 25 October 1927, Atlanta, Georgia, USA. A celebrated actress and singer, with a style that, as one critic expressed it, 'marries a beautiful and undiminished soprano voice to nuance-rich phrasing and a skilled actress's emotional interpretation'. Cook's first professional engagement was at New York's Blue Angel club in 1950, where she sang mainly standards by the likes of George Gershwin, Jerome Kern and Rodgers And Hart. A year later she was starring on Broadway as Sandy in the offbeat, short-lived musical *Flahooley*. In 1953 she played Ado Annie in a City Centre revival of *Oklahoma!*, followed by a national tour. The following year her performance as Carrie Pipperidge in another Richard Rodgers/Oscar Hammerstein II revival, *Carousel*, gained her the role of Hilda Miller in *Plain And Fancy* which ran for over 400 performances. In 1956 she introduced Leonard Bernstein and Richard Wilbur's 'Glitter And Be Gay' in *Candide*, 'the season's most interesting failure', and, soon afterwards, played the lead in yet another New York revival of *Carousel*, with Howard Keel. The highlight of her early career came in 1957 when she appeared with Robert Preston in Meredith Willson's *The Music Man*, which ran for over 1,300 performances. In the role of Marian Paroo, the stern librarian, for which she won a Tony Award, Cook excelled with numbers such as 'Till There Was You', 'Goodnight My Someone' and 'Will I Ever Tell You', and is reported to have been 'devastated' when Shirley Jones played Marian in the 1962 movie version. After gaining good reviews as a youthful Anna in *The King And I* at the City Centre, *The Gay Life* (1961) gave Cook her most prestigious role to date, with a superior Arthur Schwartz and Howard Dietz score containing 'Something You Never Had Before', 'Is She Waiting There For You?' and 'Magic Moment'. Two years later, she appeared in *She Loves Me*. Bock and Harnick's score gave her the delightful 'Will He Like Me?', 'Dear Friend' and 'Ice Cream', and was released on a double album. This was Cook's final major Broadway musical, although she did appear in the less successful *Something More!* (1964) and *The Grass Harp* (1971). She had been Broadway's favourite ingénue for 10 years and, for a while, continued to tour in well-received revivals such as *Showboat* (1966). She also appeared in several straight plays including *Any Wednesday* and *Little Murders*. In 1973, after starring in a stage show entitled *The Gershwin Years*, she started playing clubs again, including the Brothers & Sisters in New York. In 1975 she made her concert debut at Carnegie Hall in New York, and received a rapturous reception that was repeated in large cities throughout the USA. In complete contrast, on her first visit to the UK in the late 70s she performed at the small Country Cousin club in London, where she had to compete with interference on the PA system from an adjoining taxi cab company. She was back at Carnegie Hall again in 1980 (*It's Better With A Band*) with a programme that included some contemporary material along with the show tunes, and an amusing item co-written by her musical director, Wally Harper, called 'The Ingenue' ('The parts for boys you play against, they bring out all the clones to do/And movie roles you live to play, they give to Shirley Jones to do!'). In 1985 Cook's career received an enormous boost when she appeared in two performances of *Follies In Concert With The New York Philharmonic*, along with other Broadway luminaries such as Lee Remick, George Hearn, Elaine Stritch and Carol Burnett. She scored a personal triumph with the Stephen Sondheim numbers 'Losing My Mind', 'The Girl Upstairs', 'Who's That Woman?' and 'In Buddy's Eyes'. In September 1986, her one-woman show, *Wait 'Til You See Her*, reached London's West End and was acclaimed by critics and public alike. In the following year, she was back on Broadway in *A Concert For The Theatre*, for which she received a Drama Desk Award, and continued to play other US venues such as the Ballroom, New York. Also in 1987, on a recording of *Carousel* produced by Thomas Z. Shepard, she was joined by Sarah Brightman and opera singers Maureen Forrester, David Rendall and Samuel Ramey, and accompanied by the Royal Philharmonic Orchestra. A hiccup occurred in the UK in 1988 when she withdrew from the Royal Shakespeare Company's touring production of the Broadway-bound musical *Carrie*, but she continues to delight international concert and cabaret audiences well into the 90s. In 1994 Barbara Cook was inducted into Broadway's Hall Of Fame.

● ALBUMS: *Songs Of Perfect Propriety* (Urania 1958)★★★, *From The Heart* (Urania 1959)★★★, *Barbara Cook At Carnegie Hall* (Columbia 1975)★★★★, *As Of Today* (Columbia 1977)★★★, *It's Better With A Band* (MMG 1981)★★★, *Sings The Walt Disney Song Book* (MCA 1988)★★★, *Close As Pages In A Book* (DRG 1993)★★★, *A Cabaret Christmas* (DRG 1993)★★★, *Thumbelina* (SBK 1994)★★★, *Live From London* (DRG 1994)★★★, *The Broadway Years* (Koch 1995)★★★, *Oscar Winners: The Lyrics Of Oscar Hammerstein II* (DRG 1997)★★★, and Original Cast and Ben Bagley 'Revisited' albums.

COOTS, J. FRED

b. 2 May 1897, Brooklyn, New York, USA, d. 8 April 1985. A prolific composer in the 20s and 30s, as a young man Coots worked as a song plugger and vaudeville pianist. During the 20s he co-wrote the songs for the Broadway shows *Sally, Irene And Mary* (1922), *Artists And Models Of 1924/25*, *Gay Paree*, *June Days*, *Mayflowers*, *The Merry World*, *A Night In Paris*, and *White Lights*. In 1929 he collaborated with lyricist Benny Davis on several songs, including 'Cross Your Fingers' and 'Why (Is There A Rainbow In The Sky)' for the 1929 hit Broadway musical *Sons O' Guns*, and worked with him again on others such as 'I Still Get A Thrill (Thinking Of You)', 'Alabama Barbecue', 'Doin' The Suzi-Q', 'Dream Time', 'Frisco Flo', 'Copper Colored Gal', and 'Until Today' (with Oscar Levant), some of which were featured in the famous Cotton Club revues. He also teamed with Lou Davis on 'A Precious Little Thing Called Love' for the movie *Shopworn Angel*. Among Coots's best known songs in the 30s were 'Love Letters In The Sand' (with Nick and Charles Kenny), which was a hit in 1931 for Ted Black, and successfully revived in 1957 by Pat Boone; 'Santa Claus Is Comin' To Town' and the all-time standard 'You Go To My Head' (both with Haven Gillespie), and another enduring number, 'For All We Know', and 'A Beautiful Boy In Blue' (both with Sam M. Lewis). Among his other numbers were 'Doin' The Racoon', 'Moonlight Madness', 'You Can Never Tell About Love' (from the 1930 Broadway musical *Ripples*), 'Here's Hoping', 'One Minute To One', 'I Wouldn't Trade The Silver In My Mother's Hair (For All The Gold In The World)', 'I Want To Ring Bells', 'This Time It's Love', 'Two Tickets To Georgia', 'I Knew You When', 'Whose

Honey Are You?', 'Who Loves You?', 'Encore, Cherie', 'In Your Own Little Way', 'My Day Begins And Ends With You', 'There's Honey On The Moon Tonight', and 'Let's Stop The Clock' (1939). His occasional output during the 40s and early 50s included 'Poor Ballerina', 'I'll Wait For You Forever', 'Encore, Cherie', 'Little Johnny Chickadee', and 'If I Should Love Again' (1954). Among his other collaborators were Clifford Grey, Joe Young, Arthur Swanstrom and Little Jack Little.

COPACABANA

It all began in 1978 when Barry Manilow took the infectious 'Copacabana (At The Copa)', into the US Top 10. The song told the sad story of Lola, a young showgirl ('With yellow feathers in her hair/And a dress cut down to there'), whose love affair with bartender Tony ends tragically when he is shot and killed in a scuffle with his rival for her affections, Rico. This storyline was retained for the CBS made-for-television musical film *Copacabana*, which it was claimed was the first musical written for that medium since Richard Rodgers and Oscar Hammerstein II's *Cinderella* (1957). However, by the time *Copacabana* the stage musical opened at the Prince Of Wales Theatre in London on 23 June 1994, the situation had changed somewhat. Set in the 40s, struggling composer Stephen (Gary Wilmot) writes a song ('Copacabana') in which the ambitious Lola (Nicola Dawn) arrives in Manhattan from Oklahoma, intent on becoming a showgirl. She is kidnapped, and whisked off by Rico to Havana. All ends happily though, when Stephen's alter ego, Tony (Wilmot again), rescues her, and this time it is Rico who is transported to that big night club in the sky. The book and lyrics were by Bruce Sussman and Jack Feldman, with music by Barry Manilow, who also collaborated on the book. There were two pleasant ballads, 'Who Needs To Dream?' and 'Sweet Heaven', amongst a score which also included 'Dancin' Fool', 'Man Wanted', 'Just Arrived', 'This Can't Be Real', 'Jump, Shout, Boogie', 'Who Am I Kidding', 'Night On the Town', 'Changing My Tune', and of course the title number. One of the most glitzy shows to hit London for some time, *Copacabana*, with its glowing (white or glittering gold) sets, dazzling costumes, computer-run special effects, and energetic dancing (choreography by Dorian Sanchez) was greeted with disdain by most of the London critics: 'Recommended to those who enjoy watching people wearing pineapples on their heads and lemons round their groins . . . jovially vulgar'. However, by audiences' standards the show was a roaring success - at least for a time. Darren Day took over from Gary Wilmot 10 months into the run, and *Copacabana* was withdrawn shortly afterwards.

COTTON CLUB, THE (FILM MUSICAL)

Made in 1984 this was one of the most expensive films ever produced (reputedly $47 million), it is hard to see just where the money went. Producer Robert Evans and writer-director Francis Ford Coppola lavished everything except sensitivity and foresight on the project. In retrospect, one of their best decisions was to hire Bob Wilber as arranger for the jazz sequences. Given the film's premise - the gangsters, molls and, almost an afterthought, entertainers associated with Harlem's most celebrated uptown nightclub - it is hard to see how it could miss. Yet, somehow, it did. Up front dramatics surrounding a (white, of course!) trumpet player, Richard Gere, were inappropriate, so too were the jokey gangsters, Bob Hoskins and Fred Gwynne. Dancer Gregory Hines did his considerable best but only some aspects of the soundtrack can be treated with unreserved praise. Masterminded by Wilber (who was living and working in the UK at the time and commuted to Los Angeles every few weeks), the arrangements and sound he created for the club's resident orchestra, theoretically Duke Ellington's, were an extraordinary achievement as can be heard on soundtrack albums. Gere's on-screen cornet playing was ostensibly his own, although he was, at least, coached by Warren Vaché Jnr.

COTTON CLUB, THE (STAGE MUSICAL)
This is one of several compilation shows which infiltrated London's West End in the early 90s. They generally took the form of tributes to famous composers such as Cole Porter (A Swell Party), Vivian Ellis (Spread A Little Happiness), and Duke Ellington (Sophisticated Ladies), although the catchment area could be extended to include composer/performers like Louis Jordan (Five Guys Named Mo), Buddy Holly (Buddy), a television producer, Jack Good (Good Rockin' Tonite), and a couple of Chicago gangsters from the world of television and films, A Tribute To The Blues Brothers. This particular production saluted an edifice, or rather what went on in that edifice. The Cotton Club, which opened at 644 Lenox Avenue in the Harlem district of New York in the early 20s, was operated by the Mafia. Throughout the 20s and 30s legendary performers such as Duke Ellington, Lena Horne, Cab Calloway, Jimmy Lunceford, Ethel Waters, Bill 'Bojangles' Robinson, the Nicholas Brothers, and many more, played, sang, and danced there - to strictly white audiences. This latest celebration of the area and the times (Bubbling Brown Sugar covered much the same ground in 1976) opened at London's Aldwych Theatre on 24 January 1992. In an attempt to link the numbers, it has a nominal book by Douglas Barron which involves four fictitious characters: Millie Gibson, whose career as a singing star is terminated by her drug addiction, and her niece, Dinah Andrews who takes over her spot a moment's notice and becomes a star; Jim Carlton, a fellow entertainer whose ambition is to get Millie to Paris; and the bandleader, Andy Chambers, who sings 'Minnie The Moocher' and so must represent Cab Calloway. Good singing performances were forthcoming from Debby Bishop, Joanne Campbell, and Marilyn J. Johnson, and there was some outstanding tap dancing from Marcel Peneux. The choice of songs was sometimes suspect - 'That Old Black Magic' (1942) and 'I Got It Bad And That Ain't Good' (1941) were surely written too late for this shindig - but there is still a lot of mileage left in them, and the other 20-odd numbers joyfully conjured up in this, the 'Feel Good Musical', which ran until June 1992.

COUNTESS MARITZA
Originally titled Gräfin Mariza (no 't') when it was first presented in Vienna 1924, this operetta, with lyrics and book by Harry B. Smith, is generally regarded as composer Emmerich Kálmán's masterpiece. Several of his previous works such as The Gypsy Violinist (1914), The Csardas Princess (1917), and The Bajadere (1922), had been produced in New York before Countess Maritza opened at the Shubert Theatre on 18 September 1926. The action takes place near the Hungarian border, on one of the many estates belonging to Countess Maritza (Yvonne d'Arle). The Countess, who is forever on her guard against fortune-hunters, falls in love with her land superintendent, unaware that he is the aristocratic Count Tassilo (Walter Woolf). Misunderstandings continue to prevail, but they are resolved when, about to leave, he reads the reference his employer has prepared for him - which turns out to be a proposal of marriage. Kálmán composed one of his loveliest melodies for Woolf to sing in 'Play Gypsies - Dance Gypsies', and the song was successful outside the show for the Polish born pianist-bandleader, Fred Rich And His Orchestra. The rest of Smith and Kálmán's sumptuous score included 'I'll Keep On Dreaming', 'The Call Of Love', and 'The One I'm Looking For'. The show had an impressive run of 321 performances. When it was presented in London in 1938, the title was changed to Maritza, but the 1983 West End production reverted to the original Broadway name. There have been three film versions, in 1925, 1932, and 1958.

COUNTRY GIRL, A
A tremendously successful musical play, with a book by James T. Tanner, and a score by Lionel Monkton (music) and Adrian Ross (lyrics), with additional songs by Paul Rubens. A Country Girl opened at Daly's Theatre in London on 18 January 1902. The story concerns the trials and tribulations of Geoffrey Challoner (Hayden Coffin), who leaves England, and the ladies in his life, his true love Marjorie Joy (Lilian Eldée), and the village flirt Nan (Evie Greene), while he seeks his fortune overseas. On his return he brings with him The Rajah of Bhong (Rutland Barrington), and Princess Mehelaneh, who soon makes herself at home, and also makes Geoffrey a royal offer she feels that he can hardly refuse. However - good man - he turns her down, and decides to wed Marjorie, his 'little country girl'. Also in the cast were Huntley Wright, Quinton Raikes, and Ethel Irving. The delightful score contained popular favourites such as the jaunty 'Yo-Ho, Little Girls, Yo-Ho', 'Molly The Marchioness', 'The Pink Hungarian Band', 'Not The Little Girl She Knew', 'Try Again, Johnny', 'Me And Mrs Brown', and 'Under The Deodar'. During the remarkable run of 729 performances, the score underwent drastic revisions, and even more so for the 1914 and 1931 revivals. A Country Girl was produced in New York in 1902 and 1911, and also played the L'Olympia in Paris in 1904.

COURT JESTER, THE
Regarded by many as the best film Danny Kaye ever made, this 1956 Paramount release is the one in which he is perpetually puzzled as to the contents of the 'chalice from the palace' ('the pellet with the poison is in the vessel with the pestle'). The rest of this hilarious mediaeval story is just as complicated, with the red-headed clown

getting mixed up with a gang of Robin Hood-style outlaws led by the Black Fox, inveigling himself into the English court of the evil King (Basil Rathbone), and assisting in the royal downfall. In less hectic moments he finds time to fall for the lovely Maid Jean played by Glynis Johns. She headed a particularly strong supporting cast which included Angela Lansbury, Cecil Parker, Mildred Natwick, Michael Pate, John Carradine, Robert Middleton, and Alan Napier. Danny Kaye's wife, Sylvia Fine, who wrote so many excellent songs for the comedian throughout his career, contributed one clever number 'The Maladjusted Jester', and collaborated with Sammy Cahn on the remaining 'They'll Never Outfox The Fox', 'Life Could Not Be Better', 'My Heart Knows A Love Song', and 'Baby, Let Me Take You Dreaming'. James Starbuck staged the dances and Ray June was responsible for the photography in Technicolor and VistaVision. The witty screenplay was written by producer-directors Norman Panama and Melvyn Frank, and just went to prove that, when Kaye was in the mood, and with material like this, he was unbeatable.

COURTNEIDGE, CICELY

b. Esmeralda Cicely Courtneidge, 1 April 1893, Sydney, Australia, d. 26 April 1980, London, England. Her father, actor, producer and writer Robert Courtneidge, was appearing in the operetta *Esmeralda* when she was born, hence the name. Back in Britain she trained for the stage and at the age of 10 appeared as Fairy Peaseblossom in *Midsummer Night's Dream*, followed by her father's production of *The Arcadians* in 1909. She made her first records in 1911, singing selections from the show in which she was appearing, *(The) Mousme*. Courtneidge married musical comedy star Jack Hulbert in 1914, and while he was engaged in World War I she toured the music halls as a male impersonator and somewhat risqué comedienne. After appearing in several shows together, Courtneidge and Hulbert made their first big impact as a team in the 1925 revue *By The Way*, with music by Vivian Ellis. It ran for over 300 performances before transferring to New York. *Lido Lady*, in 1926, with a Richard Rodgers/Lorenz Hart score, and *Clowns In Clover*, which opened in 1927 and ran for two years, confirmed their enormous popularity in London's West End. By now, Hulbert was also writing and producing. The team split up temporarily, and while he was appearing with Sophie Tucker in the musical play *Follow A Star*, Courtneidge was considered to be at her best in the Vivian Ellis revue *Folly To Be Wise*. For most of the 30s Courtneidge concentrated on making films such as *Ghost Train*, *Jack's The Boy*, *Aunt Sally*, *Soldiers Of The King*, *Me And Marlborough* and *Take My Tip*. She returned to the stage in 1937 in *Hide And Seek* and in the following year the Hulberts reunited for one of their biggest successes, *Under Your Hat*, yet again with music and lyrics by Vivian Ellis. It ran for over two years and was filmed in 1940. During World War II the team had substantial runs in *Full Swing* and their last musical show on the London stage together, *Something In The Air*, as well as undertaking extensive ENSA tours. After the war Courtneidge starred in *Her Excellency*, and *Under The Counter* in London and New York, where it attracted

extremely hostile reviews. In 1951 she undertook probably the best role of her career, playing Gay Davenport in the satirical backstage musical play *Gay's The Word*, by Ivor Novello and Alan Melville. It presented her with several good songs including 'Guards Are On Parade', 'It's Bound To Be Right On The Night' and 'Vitality', a number that epitomized her stage persona throughout her long career. The show ran at the Saville Theatre for 504 performances, and was Novello's last - he died three weeks after the opening. Courtneidge's final West End musical was *High Spirits* in 1964, a musical version of Noël Coward's 1941 play *Blithe Spirit*. Its songs did not suit her as well as others she had introduced over the years, such as 'The King's Horses', 'Home', 'There's Something About A Soldier', 'We'll All Go Riding On A Rainbow' and 'I Was Anything But Sentimental'. During the 60s and 70s she toured in plays and revues including, with Hulbert, the semi-autobiographical *Once More With Music*. She also appeared in several more films including a critically acclaimed character part in Bryan Forbes' *The L-Shaped Room* (1963), and cameos in *Those Magnificent Men In Their Flying Machines* (1965), *The Wrong Box* (1966) and *Not Now Darling* (1972). The latter was released when she was aged 80. In the same year she was created a Dame of the British Empire. In 1986, Courtneidge's history reached a new generation when her 'Take Me Back To Dear Old Blighty' was used as the opening for the Smiths' album *The Queen Is Dead*. In 1995 a tribute show entitled *Vitality*, written by and starring Helen Fraser, was presented on the London Fringe.

● ALBUMS: *The Golden Age Of Jack Hulbert And Cicely Courtneidge* (Golden Age 1984)★★★★.

● FURTHER READING: *The Little Woman's Always Right*, Jack Hulbert. *Cicely: An Autobiography*, Cicely Courtneidge.

COVER GIRL

Although Gene Kelly made an impressive debut in *For Me And My Gal* two years earlier, it is well recorded that he was by no means Columbia studio boss Harry Cohn's first choice to play the lead in this film which was released in 1944. However, his decision to borrow the rising star from MGM proved to be a winner. In Virginia Van Upp's screenplay, Kelly plays Danny McGuire, a performer who owns a nightclub in Brooklyn. The McGuire philosophy towards life, explains one of his chorus girls, is 'that you get to the top on your feet, not your face'. So, when Danny's girlfriend, Rusty Parker (Rita Hayworth), enters a *Vanity* magazine competition to become a cover girl, he feels hurt and betrayed, and even more so when she wins and the club is besieged by her new fans, with Kelly being pushed into the background. What Parker does not realise is that *Vanity*'s ageing publisher (Otto Kruger) (who is ably assisted by Eve Arden) was once in love with her grandmother, a great music hall performer. However, he and his money could not tempt her away from her impoverished piano playing lover - just as many years later Parker eschews her own fame and fortune and returns to McGuire. Kruger remembers Parker's grandmother in flashback, with Hayworth playing both parts of Parker and her grandmother. While *Cover Girl* may not be quite as sophisticated as Kelly's later work at MGM, some of the musical sequences are very entertaining, and provide a foretaste of his innovative and inspired later work. Jerome Kern and Ira Gershwin's score contained the exquisite ballad 'Long Ago And Far Away' (Kelly), as well as 'Make Way For Tomorrow' (lyric: Gershwin-E.Y. 'Yip' Harburg), during which Hayworth, Kelly and Phil Silvers (as amusing as ever) dance through the streets of Brooklyn improvising dance with anything that comes to hand along the way. The film is also remembered for Kelly's 'alter-ego' dance as he tussles with both sides of his conscience. Walking home one night, confused and unhappy, he begins to argue with his reflection in a shop window. The reflection answers back and then jumps out of the window to join him for a frenetic dance. A clever and innovative sequence, it has Kelly and Stanley Donen's stamp on it, despite Val Raset and Seymour Felix being credited for the film's overall choreography. The other numbers included 'Sure Thing' (Hayworth), 'Put Me To The Test' (Hayworth-Kelly), and 'Who's Complaining?' (Silvers). Various sources credit Martha Mears or Nan Wynn as dubbing the singing voice of Hayworth. Also in the cast were Lee Bowman, Jinx Falkenburg, Jess Barker, Leslie Brooks, Curt Bois, Thurston Hall, and Ed Brophy. Charles Victor was the director, and the film was photographed in Technicolor and produced by Arthur Schwartz.

COWARD, NOËL

b. 16 December 1899, Teddington, Middlesex, England, d. 26 March 1973, Jamaica. Coward began his professional career as a child actor, appearing frequently on the stage. As a teenager he made his first film appearance in D. W. Griffiths's *Hearts Of The World* (1918), which was made in England and starred the Gish sisters, Dorothy and Lillian. By 1919 Coward was already writing plays and soon afterwards began his songwriting career. The revue, *London Calling!* (1923), included 'Parisian Pierrot', performed by Gertrude Lawrence, which became one of his most popular songs. In the same show Coward and Lawrence danced to 'You Were Meant For Me', for which special choreography was created by Fred Astaire. Although none was yet produced, Coward's stock of completed plays already included important works such as *The Vortex*, *Fallen Angels*, *Hay Fever* and *Easy Virtue*. When *The Vortex* opened in London in 1924, its frank approach to drug addiction created a sensation, which was repeated the following year when it opened on Broadway. Coward's songwriting progressed with 'Poor Little Rich Girl', composed for the revue, *On With The Dance*. In 1928 he had two productions playing in London's West End: *This Year Of Grace!*, a sparkling revue for which he wrote script, music and lyrics, and *The Second Man*, in which he also starred. In the late 20s and early 30s Coward's output was remarkable in its quantity and high quality. His stage productions in this period included *Bitter Sweet*, from which came the song 'I'll See You Again', *Private Lives*, *Cavalcade*, which included 'Twentieth-Century Blues', *Words And Music*, with its hit song, 'Mad About The Boy', *Design For Living*, *Conversation Piece*, *Fumed Oak*, *Hands Across The Sea* and *Tonight At Eight Thirty*. Apart from their intrinsic qualities, Coward's plays were significant in altering perceptions of how stage dialogue should be written and spoken in the English theatre with his more conversational

approach replacing the previous declamatory style. The success of his stage work ensured that some of his material was brought to the screen. Amongst the films were *Cavalcade* (1933) and *Bitter Sweet* (1940). Towards the end of the 30s he wrote *Present Laughter* and *This Happy Breed*. During the early months of World War II, he wrote the play *Blithe Spirit*, several songs including 'London Pride', and the screenplay and score for *In Which We Serve* (1942), which he also co-directed (with David Lean), in addition to taking the leading role. For his work on this film he received a special Academy Award. Coward's film commitments continued with screenplays for some of his earlier stage pieces including *Blithe Spirit*, *Brief Encounter* (both 1945), *The Astonished Heart* (1950) and *Tonight At Eight Thirty* (1952). By the 50s, Coward's style of writing for the stage was seen as outmoded, but he regained a measure of his earlier West End success with *Relative Values* (1951) and with personal appearances at the Café De Paris, at which he sang his own songs to delighted audiences. In the 30s Coward had written his autobiography, *Present Indicative*, and had also written short stories and novels. In the 50s and early 60s he produced another autobiography, *Future Indefinite*, more novels and short stories and a volume of verse. Coward's spell in cabaret at the Café De Paris had brought him to the attention of the American impresario Joe Glaser (who managed, among others, Louis Armstrong). Glaser was so impressed that he offered Coward an engagement at the Desert Inn, Las Vegas. To the surprise of many, Coward's Desert Inn performances were hugely successful, as was an album recorded live during his run, *Noël Coward At Las Vegas* (1955). Coward's triumph at Las Vegas led to a series of three television spectaculars for CBS. More stage productions followed in the 60s, among them *Nude With Violin* and *A Song At Twilight*. In his last years Coward appeared in numerous films, usually in cameo roles, often sending up his own image of the plummy-voiced, terribly nice, very English gentleman. One of the most gifted writers and entertainers the English theatre has produced, Coward was knighted in 1970 and in the same year was awarded a special Tony Award for distinguished achievement in the theatre. He was honoured with gala performances of his work in London and New York, notably *Oh! Coward* early in 1973. Soon after this, Coward returned to his home in Jamaica, where he died in March 1973.

In 1998, 25 years after his death, a charity CD entitled *Twentieth Century Blues* was released. It contained versions of his songs by a collection of 90s pop celebrities such as Sting, Robbie Williams, Shola Ama, The Divine Comedy and Elton John. Supervised by the Pet Shop Boys' Neil Tennant, televised highlights were shown on British television. The *Noël Coward Trilogy*, a cocktail of archive footage, was also shown over three successive nights. Around the same time, additional verses to 200 of Coward's most famous songs were discovered after languishing in a Swiss bank for 50 years.

● ALBUMS: with Gertrude Lawrence *Noel And Gertie* (RCA Victor 1955)★★★, *Noël Coward At Las Vegas* (1955)★★, *Noël Coward In New York* (1957)★★★.

● COMPILATIONS: *The Masters' Voice: His HMV Recordings (1928-*

53) 4-CD box set (1993)★★★★, various artists *Twentieth Century Blues: The Songs Of Noel Coward* (EMI 1998)★★★.

● FURTHER READING: *Autobiography*, Noel Coward. *Noel Coward: A Talent To Amuse*, Sheridan Morley. *The Life Of Noel Coward*, Cole Lesley. *The Noel Coward Diaries*, Graham Payne and Sheridan Morley. *Noel Coward*, Clive Fisher. *Noel And Cole: The Sophisticates*, Stephen Citron. *My Life With Noel Coward*, Graham Payne with Barry Day. *Noel Coward: A Bio-Bibliography*, Stephen Cole.

CRADLE WILL ROCK, THE

Sub-titled 'A Play In Music', this was one of the most unusual and controversial stage presentations in the pre-World War II era. The book, music, and lyrics were by Marc Blitzstein, who was a piano soloist with the Philadelphia Symphony Orchestra in his teens, and subsequently had been heavily influenced by Kurt Weill and Bertolt Brecht. *The Cradle Will Rock*, which dealt with a trades union's desperate attempt for recognition in a US steel town, was originally conceived for the Federal Theatre Project of the Works Progress Administration, with producer John Housman and director Orson Welles (three years before Citizen Kane). After failing to get on in Washington, the project was moved to New York, and scheduled for the Maxine Elliot Theatre on 16 June 1937. Under severe political pressure from a number of government departments, the Federal Theatre pulled out, and Welles and Housman diverted 800 people to the empty Venice (Jolson) Theatre. Union rules prevented the actors performing on stage, so they gave their performances while seated in the auditorium, and the same rules meant Blitzstein had to provide a piano accompaniment in place of an orchestra. Still beset by all manner of problems, the show ran for 14 performances at the Venice, and gave a few weekend shows at the small Mercury Theatre, before its commercial opening on 3 January 1938 at the Windsor Theatre, where it stayed for 108 performances. The extreme left-wing story set in Steeltown, USA, in the which the young, idealistic union organizer, Larry Foreman (Howard Da Silva) forces his unscrupulous boss, Mr. Mister (Will Geer), to recognize the union, also presented Blitzstein's positive attitude towards prostitution, and was punctuated with such numbers as 'The Freedom Of The Press', 'Joe Worker', 'Art For Art's Sake', 'Honolulu', 'Nickel Under Foot', 'The Cradle Will Rock', 'Drugstore Freedom', 'Croon-Spoon', and 'Doctor And Ella'. In revivals of the show, several well-known actors have played Foreman, including Alfred Drake (1947), Jerry Orbach (1964), and Randle Mell (1983). A rare British production, directed by Mehmet Ergen, was presented at London's Battersea Arts Centre in 1997.

CRASH 'N' BURN

A punk documentary, *Crash 'n' Burn* is a Canadian short - it lasts less than half an hour - which enshrines performances by nominally rebellious US acts the Dead Boys, the Diodes and Teenage Head, and power-pop group, the Boyfriends. Although entertaining enough in its own right, the film lacks the imaginative direction of Amos Poe's *Blank Generation*, or Beth and Scott B.'s fascinating résumé of the 'no-wave' scene, *The Offenders*. *Crash 'n' Burn* lacks ground-breaking acts which would transform the feature from being merely interesting to one of relevance.

CRAWFORD, MICHAEL

b. Michael Patrick Dumble-Smith, 19 January 1942, Salisbury, Wiltshire, England. An actor and singer who came to world-wide fame when he played the leading role in Andrew Lloyd Webber's hit musical, *The Phantom Of The Opera*, in 1986. His father was a fighter pilot during World War II and died six months before his son was born. Crawford sang in the school choir and later toured in the original productions of Benjamin Britten's *Let's Make An Opera* and *Noyes Fluddle*. While still a teenager he changed his name to Crawford (after seeing it on a biscuit box), and worked extensively in radio, and in films and television programmes for children. In the 60s he appeared in the late-night satirical BBC television series *Not So Much A Programme, More A Way Of Life*, and created the character of Byron, a 'rocker' who was thought to be typical of the swinging 60s. He also made a number of films including *The War Lover*, starring Steve McQueen, *Two Left Feet*, Richard Lester's *The Knack*, *A Funny Thing Happened On The Way To The Forum*, and *How I Won The War*. His London stage debut came in Neil Simon's *Come Blow Your Horn* (1962), which was followed by the off-beat comedy-drama *The Anniversary*. In 1967 he moved to New York and appeared in a pair of short plays written by Peter Shaffer entitled *White Lies* and *Black Comedy*. While in the latter piece, he was spotted by film director Gene Kelly who cast him as Cornelius Hackl in the screen version of *Hello, Dolly!* starring Barbra Streisand. It gained him an international following, but subsequent films such as *The Games*, *Hello, Goodbye*, and *Alice's Adventures In Wonderland*, were not so satisfying. In 1971 Crawford returned to the London stage in the long-running farce *No Sex, Please - We're British*, and, soon afterwards, was voted Funniest Man On Television for his performance as the accident-prone Frank Spencer in the situation comedy, *Some Mothers Do 'Ave 'Em*. In 1974 he starred in *Billy*, his first stage musical, and was voted Show Business Personality of the Year and received the Silver Heart Award from the Variety Club of Great Britain. In 1976 he appeared in the American two-hander comedy *Same Time, Next Year*, and, two years later, portrayed a mentally handicapped man who volunteers to be a guinea-pig for a medical experiment in *Flowers For Algernon*. After a further television series, *Chalk And Cheese*, Crawford was back on the London stage for the musical *Barnum*, in which he played the celebrated American showman P.T. Barnum, a role he prepared for by attending the New York Circus School for two months in order to acquire the necessary specialist skills. The show was a smash-hit and Crawford won a Laurence Olivier Award for his outstanding, charismatic performance. He stayed with *Barnum* in various places for several years, and, when he returned with it to London at the Victoria Palace in 1985, it was estimated that more than 2.5 million people had seen the production. Around this time, Andrew Lloyd Webber heard him at singing practice and cast him in the leading role - opposite Sarah Brightman - in *The Phantom Of The Opera*.

Following the show's opening night in October 1986 one critic was moved to write of him: 'It is surely one of the great performances, not only in a musical but on any stage in any year.' Two years later Broadway audiences felt the same, and he won the Tony Award for best actor in a musical. The show gave Crawford's singing career a tremendous boost (he had already made the UK Top 10 with one of the *Phantom*'s hit songs, 'The Music Of The Night'), and he embarked on extensive tours of several countries, including America, Australia, and the UK, with a concert production entitled *The Music Of Andrew Lloyd Webber*, supported by a 37-piece orchestra, soloists, and a back-up chorus. Recognition at home, where he is still unable to shake off the 'Frank Spencer' image, came in 1987 when he was awarded the OBE. In America he is billed as 'the matinee idol of the decade', and must have realised that he had hit the big-time when invited to duet with Barbra Streisand on 'The Music Of The Night' for her 1993 *Back To Broadway* album. The track was also included on his own *A Touch Of Music In The Night*, which proved to be an intriguing mixture of standards ('Stormy Weather'), pop songs ('The Power Of Love'), and show tunes. In April 1995, Crawford opened at the MGM Grand Hotel Las Vegas in *EFX*, a 'gigantic $41 million musical spectacle' in which he played five roles: The EFX Master, Merlin, Houdini, H.G. Wells and Barnum (again). A serious hip injury, sustained in the early days of his involvement with the show, forced Crawford to withdraw from *EFX* in August 1996. He was replaced by American actor and singer David Cassidy, and the production was revamped accordingly. After undergoing a hip replacement operation, Crawford returned to the concert circuit, touring the USA, Australia, and New Zealand in 1998, as well as releasing CDs and a video.

● ALBUMS: *Songs From The Stage And Screen* (1987)★★★, *With Love* (1989)★★★, *Performs Andrew Lloyd Webber* (1992)★★, *A Touch Of Music In The Night* (1993)★★, *The Love Songs Album* (Telstar 1994)★★★, *EFX* (Atlantic 1995)★★★, *With Love* (Atlantic 1995)★★★, *The Songs Of Andrew Lloyd Webber* (Atlantic 1995)★★★, *On Eagle's Wings* (Atlantic 1998)★★★★, *Michael Crawford - Live In Concert* (Atlantic 1998)★★★, and Original Cast and soundtrack recordings.

● FURTHER READING: *Phantom: Michael Crawford Unmasked*, Anthony Howard.

● VIDEOS: *A Touch Of Music In The Night* (1994).

● FILMS: *Soapbox Derby* (1958), *Blow Your Own Trumpet* (1958), *Two Living, One Dead* (1962), *Two Left Feet* (1963), *The War Lover* (1963), *The Knack* (1965), *A Funny Thing Happened On The Way To The Forum* (1966), *The Jokers* (1967), *How I Won The War* (1967), *Hello, Dolly!* (1969), *Hello-Goodbye* (1970), *The Games* (1970), *Alice's Adventures In Wonderland* (1972), *Condorman* voice of Cornelius (1981).

CRAZY FOR YOU

After losing a reported half a million dollars in Washington during its tryout in December 1991, *Crazy For You* exploded into the Shubert Theatre on 19 February 1992, sending shock waves along Broadway, the like of which had not been experienced for some considerable time. It was the kind of musical that America does best, and the perfect riposte to the imported British variety that had held sway on the 'great white way' for so long. The term, 'Loosely based on the 1930 musical *Girl Crazy*', meant that it contained a bunch of great songs by George and Ira Gershwin. A total of four numbers were retained from that production: 'I Got Rhythm', 'Could You Use Me?', 'Bidin' My Time', and the lovely 'But Not For Me'; and another 13 were culled from various other Gershwin shows. The story was changed, too: in Ken Ludwig's new book, which was adapted from the original by Guy Bolton and John McGowan, aspiring performer Bobby Child (Harry Groener), is sent by his wealthy mother (Jane Connell) to foreclose on the old Gaiety theatre in Deadrock, Nevada. He falls for the theatre-owner's daughter, Polly (Jodi Benson), and, in an effort to impress her - and keep the Gaiety open - he imports most of the chorus girls from the fabulous *Zangler Follies*, and they put on a show - right there in the old barn . . . I mean, theatre. The lavish production, which was staged by Mike Ockrent, won the Tony Award for best musical, and other Tonys went to Broadway newcomer Susan Stroman for her superb choreography, and William Ivey Long for his 'sensational' costumes. While the Broadway production was settling in for a long run (1,622 performances), a West End version, starring Ruthie Henshall and Kirby Ward, opened at the 1,600-seater Prince Edward Theatre on 3 March 1993. It gained Laurence Olivier Awards for Stroman and best musical, and was soon being cited as 'one of the biggest - if not *the* biggest - American musical in London history'. Well, not quite, but it did run almost three years, until 24 February 1996.

CREESE, MALCOLM

b. 24 August 1959, Bristol, Avon, England. After singing in the St. John's College, Cambridge choir as a boy, he studied classical cello at the Guildhall School of Music and Drama in London, worked as a freelance with various classical orchestras and then in 1985, switched instruments and style. As a bass player he quickly began to make a name in London jazz circles and in 1990 joined Stan Tracey. The following year he was invited to join the group led by John Dankworth and Cleo Laine. During the 90s he continued playing with Dankworth and Laine and also appeared on numerous recording dates with pop artists, including Sting, Rod Stewart, Depeche Mode, Chris De Burgh and Shara Nelson. In these same years he also played with jazz groups and led his own trio with John Horler and Tony Coe. Creese has also played on many movie soundtracks and on television (shows and commercials). In addition to his extensive jazz and pop work, Creese has continued to work in the classical field. He is also active as a record producer and runs several labels including ABCDs and Black Box Jazz on which he has recorded singer Liz Fletcher, Matt Wates, Coe and Dankworth. Creese's sound musical background and wide experience has resulted in his becoming a much sought-after session player and he brings to all his work a deep sense of commitment and enormous technical and rhythmic skills.

● ALBUMS: *The Malcolm Creese Trio* (ABCDs 1997)★★★.

CRIMSON CANARY, THE

Amongst the ingredients of *film noir* was jazz-inflected music as background to shady on-screen happenings. A low-budget, generally ineffective, and decidedly border-line entry for the genre, this 1945 film went one better by setting the plot in the jazz world. When a band singer is found beaten to death with a trumpet ('how I wish' many trumpet-section members must have cried), two of the band's sidemen are suspected. The detective in charge of the investigation is a jazz fan and digs into the case with finger-snapping enthusiasm. In keeping with Hollywood's tradition of hiring the band for filming one day and the band for the recording another, who you see does not often, if ever, match who you hear. Amongst those you see are Denzil De Costa Best, Coleman Hawkins, Howard McGhee, Oscar Pettiford and Sir Charles Thompson (current winners in the *Esquire* poll). Josh White performs his hit song, 'One Meat Ball'. Oh, yes, the club owner did it.

CRISWELL, KIM

b. Hampton, Virginia, USA. An actress and singer who came to prominence in stage musicals during the 80s, with a style and voice reminiscent of the much-missed Ethel Merman. Criswell grew up in Chattanooga, Tennessee, where, so she says, the 'live' theatre used to arrive in a bus and stay for just two nights. Her early influences were Julie Andrews, Barbra Streisand, and Judy Garland, and, like them, she started performing from an early age. After graduating from high school, she studied musical theatre at the University of Cincinnatti's College Conservatory of Music before moving to New York where she gained a featured part in a revival of *Annie Get Your Gun*. She made her Broadway musical debut in *The First* (1981), and then appeared in *Nine*, which was staged by Tommy Tune and had a cast of 21 women and only one male adult. Her other Broadway credits during the 80s included revivals of the *Three Musketeers* and *The Threepenny Opera* (re-titled as *3 Penny Opera*). In the latter show Criswell played Lucy, one of the leading roles in a production that was headed by the popular rock singer Sting. She has appeared as the featured soloist with several of America's leading symphony orchestras, and took part in concert stagings of Jerome Kern's *Sitting Pretty* at Carnegie Hall, and George and Ira Gershwin's *Girl Crazy* at the Lincoln Centre. She won the Helen Hayes award for her performance in *Side By Side By Sondheim*, and played the role of Grizabella (the feline who sings 'Memory') for six months in the Los Angeles production of Andrew Lloyd Webber's *Cats*. Between 1989 and 1991 Criswell starred in three London studio recordings of famous Broadway shows, *Anything Goes*, *Kiss Me, Kate*, and *Annie Get Your Gun*, accompanied by a large orchestra directed by John McGlinn. He also conducted the London Sinfonietta when Criswell joined Brent Barrett in *Cole Porter And The American Musical* at the Royal Festival Hall. In September 1991 she presented her one-woman show, *Doin' What Comes Naturally*, at the Shaw Theatre in London, and, just over a year later, co-starred with John Diedrich in a West End revival of *Annie Get Your Gun*. The show was acclaimed by the critics ('Criswell is the best Annie we have seen since Dolores Gray') but it folded after less than two months. In 1993 she appeared in two very different kind of shows in the UK. The first, *Elegies For Angels, Punks And Raging Queens*, was a musical play that purported to tell the real-life stories of 33 individuals who have met their death through AIDS; while the other, a touring nostalgia show, *Hollywood And Broadway II*, with Bonnie Langford and Wayne Sleep, found her on more familiar ground. Her 1993 record releases were dissimilar, too: *The Lorelei* contained a mixture of well-known and neglected show tunes, while *Human Cry* turned out to be a pop album in a contemporary, and sometimes funky style, and the single, 'Moment Of Weakness', demonstrated her ability to cross over to the pop scene.

During the remainder of the 90s Criswell has starred in musicals such as *Dames At Sea* (1996, Covent Garden Festival), *The Slow Drag* (1997, Freedom and Whitehall theatres), *Of Thee I Sing* (1998, Opera North), and featured prominently in *Side By Side ... By Cole Porter* (1998), a tribute to the famous composer at London's Palace Theatre, with the BBC Concert Orchestra conducted by John McGlinn. She has also continued to appear regularly on the concert platform, in cabaret with pianist and musical director Wayne Marshall, as well as recording a number of studio cast albums, including Simon Rattle's setting of *Wonderful Town*.

● ALBUMS: with the Cincinnati University Singers *I Wants To Be An Actor Lady* (New World 1978)★★★, *Songs Of New York* (1984)★★★, *Fifty Million Frenchmen* (1986)★★★, *Anything Goes* (Studio Cast 1989)★★★★, *Kiss Me, Kate* (Studio Cast 1990)★★★, *Annie Get Your Gun* (Studio Cast 1991)★★★, *The Lorelei* (1993)★★★, *Human Cry* (1993)★★, *Guys And Dolls* (Jay 90s, Studio Cast)★★★, *On The Town* (Jay 90s, Studio Cast)★★★, *The Pajama Game* (Jay 90s, Studio Cast)★★★, *The Rocky Horror Show* (Jay 90s, Studio Cast)★★★, *Showstoppers From Broadway* (Jay 90s)★★★, *Miss Saigon* (90s, Studio Cast)★★★, *Wonderful Town* (EMI 1998, Studio Cast)★★★, *The Slow Drag* (Jay 1998)★★★, *Back To Before* (1998)★★★, and Original Cast recordings.
● FILMS: *True Colors* (1991).

CROSBY, BING

b. Harry Lillis Crosby, 3 May 1903, Tacoma, Washington, USA, d. 14 October 1977. One of the most popular vocalists of all time, Crosby picked up his nickname through a childhood love of a strip-cartoon character in a local newspaper. After first singing with a jazz band at high school, he sang at university with a friend, Al Rinker. The duo decided to take a chance on showbusiness success, quit school and called on Rinker's sister, Mildred Bailey, in the hope that she could help them find work. Their hopes were fulfilled and they were soon hired by Paul Whiteman. With the addition of Harry Barris they formed the singing trio the Rhythm Boys, and quickly became one of the major attractions of the Whiteman entertainment package. The popularity of the trio on such recordings as 'Mississippi Mud' and 'I'm Coming Virginia', and an appearance in the film *The King Of Jazz* (1930), gave Crosby an edge when he chose to begin a solo career. The late 20s saw a great increase in the use of microphones in public auditoriums and the widespread use of more sophisticated microphones in recording studios. This allowed singers to adopt a more confidential singing style, which became known as 'crooning'. Of the new breed of crooners, Crosby was by far the most popular and successful. Although never a jazz singer, Crosby worked with many jazzmen, especially during his stint with Whiteman, when his accompanists included Jimmy and Tommy Dorsey, Joe Venuti and Bix Beiderbecke. This early experience, and a sharp awareness of the rhythmic advances of Louis Armstrong, brought Crosby to the forefront of popular American singers in an era when jazz styles were beginning to reshape popular music. Another contributory factor to his rise was the fact that the new singing style was very well suited to radio, which at the time dominated the entertainment industry. He made numerous film appearances and many hundreds of records, several of them massive hits. Indeed, sales of his records eclipsed those of any earlier recording artist and by the 40s, these had helped to establish Crosby as the world's biggest singing star. In contrast, his films were usually frothy affairs and he displayed only limited acting ability. However, in the early 40s his film career took an upswing with a series of comedies in which he co-starred with Bob Hope and Dorothy Lamour, while some good light dramatic roles advanced his career still further. Throughout the 50s Crosby continued to work in radio and television, and made regular concert appearances and still more records. During his radio and television career Crosby often worked with other leading entertainers, among them Al Jolson, Connee Boswell, Dinah Shore, Judy Garland, Armstrong, Hope and his brother, Bob Crosby. By the mid-60s he was content to take things a little easier, although he still made records and personal appearances. Despite his carefree public persona, Crosby was a complex man, difficult to know and understand. As a singer, his seemingly lazy intonation often gave the impression that anyone could sing the way he did, itself a possible factor in his popularity. Nevertheless, his distinctive phrasing was achieved by a good ear, selective taste in building his repertoire, and an acute awareness of what the public wanted. Although his countless fans may well regard it as heresy, Crosby's way with a song was not always what songwriters might have wanted. Indeed, some of Crosby's recordings indicate scant regard for the meanings of lyrics and, unlike Frank Sinatra, for instance, he was never a major interpreter of songs. Despite this casual disregard for the niceties of music and lyrics, many of Crosby's best-known recordings remain definitive by virtue of the highly personal stylistic stamp he placed upon them. Songs such as 'Pennies From Heaven', 'Blue Skies', 'White Christmas', 'The Bells Of St Mary's', 'Moonlight Becomes You', 'Love In Bloom', 'How Deep Is The Ocean', 'The Blue Of The Night' and 'Temptation' became his own. Although Sinatra is the major male songstylist of American popular music, and also the one who most influenced other singers, every vocalist who followed Crosby owes him a debt for the manner in which his casual, relaxed approach completely altered audience perceptions of how a singer should behave. Towards the end of his life, Crosby's star had waned but he was still capable of attracting sell-out crowds for his occasional public appearances, even though he preferred to spend as much time as he could on the golf course. It was while playing golf in Spain that he collapsed and died.

● ALBUMS: *Merry Christmas* (Decca 1945)★★★, *Going My Way* film soundtrack (Decca 1945)★★★, *The Bells Of St. Mary's* film soundtrack (Decca 1946)★★★, *Don't Fence Me In* (Decca 1946)★★★, *The Happy Prince* (Decca 1946)★★★, *Road To Utopia* (Decca 1946)★★★, *Stephen Foster Songs* (Decca 1946)★★★, *What So Proudly We Hail* (Decca 1946)★★★, *Favorite Hawaiian Songs Volumes 1 & 2* (Decca 1946)★★★, *Blue Skies* (Decca 1946)★★★, *St. Patrick's Day* (Decca 1947)★★★, *Merry Christmas* (Decca 1948)★★★, *Emperor Waltz* (Decca 1948)★★★, *St. Valentine's Day* (Decca 1948)★★★, *Stardust* (Decca 1948)★★★, *A Connecticut Yankee* (Decca 1949)★★★, *South Pacific* (Decca 1949)★★★, *Christmas Greetings* (Decca 1949)★★★, *Hits From Musical Comedies* (Decca 1949)★★★, *Jerome Kern Songs* (Decca 1949)★★★, with Andrews Sisters *Merry Christmas* (Decca 1949)★★★, *El Bingo* (Decca 1950)★★★, *Drifting And Dreaming* (Decca 1950)★★★, *Auld Lang Syne* (Decca 1950)★★★, *Showboat Selections* (Decca 1950)★★★, *Cole Porter Songs* (Decca 1950)★★★, *Songs By Gershwin* (Decca 1950)★★★, *Holiday Inn* film soundtrack (Decca 1950)★★★, *Blue Of The Night* (Decca 1950)★★★, *Cowboy Songs* (Decca 1950)★★★, *Cowboy Songs, Volume 2* (Decca 1950)★★★, *Bing Sings Hits* (Decca 1950)★★★, *Top O' The Morning* (Decca 1950)★★★, *Mr. Music* (Decca 1950)★★★, *The Small One/The Happy Prince* film soundtrack (Decca 1950)★★★, with Connee Boswell *Bing And Connee* (Decca 1951)★★★, *Hits From Broadway Shows* (Decca 1951)★★★, *Go West, Young Man* (Decca 1951)★★★, *Way Back Home* (Decca 1951)★★★, *Bing Crosby* (Decca 1951)★★★, *Bing And The Dixieland Bands* (Decca 1951)★★★, *Yours Is My Heart Alone* (Decca 1951)★★★, *Country Style* (Decca 1951)★★★, *Down Memory Lane* (Decca 1951)★★★, *Down Memory Lane, Volume 2* (Decca 1951)★★★, *Beloved Hymns* (Decca 1951)★★★, *Bing Sings Victor Herbert* (Decca 1951)★★★, *Ichabod Crane* (Decca 1951)★★★, *Collector's Classics* (Decca 1951)★★★, *Two For Tonight* (Decca 1951)★★★, *Rhythm Of The Range* film soundtrack (Decca 1951)★★★, *Waikiki Wedding* film soundtrack (Decca 1951)★★★, *The Star Maker* film soundtrack (Decca 1951)★★★, *The Road To Singapore* film soundtrack (Decca 1951)★★★, *When Irish Eyes Are Smiling* (Decca 1952)★★★, *Just For You* (Decca 1952)★★★, *The Road To Bali* film soundtrack (Decca 1952)★★, *Song Hits Of Paris/Le Bing* (Decca 1953)★★★, *Country Girl* (Decca 1953)★★★, *Some Fine Old Chestnuts* (Decca 1954)★★★, *A Man Without A Country* (Decca 1954)★★★, *White Christmas* film soundtrack (Decca 1954)★★★★, *Lullabye Time* (Decca 1955)★★★, *Shillelaghs And Shamrocks* (Decca 1956)★★★, *Home On The Range* (Decca 1956)★★★, *Blue Hawaii* (Decca 1956)★★★, *High Tor* film soundtrack (Decca 1956)★★★, *Anything Goes* film soundtrack (Decca 1956)★★★, *Songs I Wish I Had Sung The First Time Around* (Decca 1956)★★★, *Twilight On The Trail* (Decca 1956)★★★, *A Christmas Sing With Bing Around The World* (Decca 1956)★★★, *High Society* film soundtrack (Capitol 1956)★★★★, *Bing Crosby Sings While Bergman Swings* (Verve 1956)★★★, *New Tricks* (Decca 1957)★★, *Ali Baba And The Forty Thieves* (Grand Award 1957)★★★, *Christmas Story* (Grand Award 1957)★★★, *Bing With A Beat* (RCA Victor 1957)★★★, *Around The World* (Decca 1958)★★★, *Bing In Paris* (Decca 1958)★★★, *That Christmas Feeling* (Decca 1958)★★★, with Rosemary Clooney *Fancy Meeting You Here* (RCA Victor 1958)★★★★, *Paris Holiday* film soundtrack (United Artists

1958)★★★, *In A Little Spanish Town* (Decca 1959)★★★, *Ichabod* (Decca 1959)★★★, *Young Bing Crosby* (RCA Victor 1959)★★★, with Louis Armstrong *Bing And Satchmo* (MGM 1960)★★★, *High Time* film soundtrack (RCA Victor 1960)★★★, *Join Bing And Sing Along: 33 Great Songs* (Warners 1960)★★★, *Join Bing And Sing Along: 101 Gang Songs* (Warners 1960)★★★, *Join Bing In A Gang Sing Along* (Warners 1961)★★★, *My Golden Favorites* (Decca 1961)★★★, *Easy To Remember* (Decca 1962)★★★, *Pennies From Heaven* (Decca 1962)★★★, *Pocket Full Of Dreams* (Decca 1962)★★★, *East Side Of Heaven* (Decca 1962)★★★, *The Road Begins* (Decca 1962)★★★, *Only Forever* (Decca 1962)★★★, *Swinging On A Star* (Decca 1962)★★★, *Accentuate The Positive* (Decca 1962)★★★, *But Beautiful* (Decca 1962)★★★, *Sunshine Cake* (Decca 1962)★★★, *Cool Of The Evening* (Decca 1962)★★★, *Zing A Little Zong* (Decca 1962)★★★, *Anything Goes* (Decca 1962)★★★, *Holiday In Europe* (Decca 1962)★★★, *The Small One* (Decca 1962)★★★, *The Road To Hong Kong* film soundtrack (Liberty 1962)★★★, *A Southern Memoir* (London 1962)★★★, *Join Bing And Sing Along: 51 Good Time Songs* (Warners 1962)★★★, *On The Happy Side* (Warners 1962)★★★, *I Wish You A Merry Christmas* (Warners 1962)★★★, *Bing Sings The Great Standards* (MGM 1963)★★★, *Songs Everybody Knows* (Decca 1964)★★★, *Return To Paradise Islands* (Reprise 1964)★★★, with Frank Sinatra, Fred Waring *America, I Hear You Singing* (Reprise 1964)★★, *Robin And The Seven Hoods* film soundtrack (Reprise 1964)★★★, with Clooney *That Travellin' Two-Beat* (Capitol 1965)★★★, *Bing Crosby* (MGM 1965)★★★, *Great Country Hits* (Capitol 1965)★★★, *Thoroughly Modern Bing* (Stateside 1968)★★★, *Hey Jude/Hey Bing!!* (Amos 1969)★★★, *Wrap Your Troubles In Dreams* (RCA 1972)★★★, *Bingo Viejo* (London 1975)★★★, *The Dinah Shore-Bing Crosby Shows* (Sunbeam 1975)★★★, *That's What Life Is All About* (United Artists 1975)★★★, with Fred Astaire *A Couple Of Song And Dance Men* (United Artists 1975)★★★, *Feels Good, Feels Right* (Decca 1976)★★★, *Live At The London Palladium* (K-Tel 1976)★★★, *"On The Air"* (Spokane 1976)★★★★, *At My Time Of Life* (United Artists 1976)★★★★, *Beautiful Memories* (United Artists 1976)★★★★, *Kraft Music Hall December 24, 1942* (Spokane 1978)★★★.

● COMPILATIONS: *Crosby Classics, Volume 1* (Columbia 1949)★★★, *Crosby Classics, Volume 2* (Columbia 1950)★★★, *Bing Crosby Volumes 1 & 2* (Brunswick 1950)★★★, *Bing - A Musical Autobiography* 5-LP box set (Decca 1954)★★★, *Old Masters* 3-LP set (Decca 1954)★★★, *Der Bingle* (Columbia 1955)★★★, *Crosby Classics* (Columbia 1955)★★★, *The Voice Of Bing In The 30s* (Brunswick 1955)★★★, *A Musical Autobiography Of Bing Crosby 1927-34* (Decca 1958)★★★, *A Musical Autobiography Of Bing Crosby 1934-41* (Decca 1958)★★★, *A Musical Autobiography Of Bing Crosby 1941-44* (Decca 1958)★★★, *A Musical Autobiography Of Bing Crosby 1944-47* (Decca 1958)★★★, *A Musical Autobiography Of Bing Crosby, 1947-53* (Decca 1958)★★★, *The Very Best Of* (MGM 1964)★★★, *The Best Of Bing Crosby* (Decca 1965)★★★, *The Bing Crosby Story - Volume 1: Early Jazz Years 1928-32* (Columbia 1968)★★★, *Bing Crosby Remembered: A CSP Treasury* (Fairway 1977)★★★, *Bing Crosby's Greatest Hits* (MCA 1977)★★★★, *Seasons* (Polydor 1977)★★★, *A Legendary Performer* (RCA 1977)★★★★, *Crosby Classics Volume 3* (Capitol 1977)★★★★, *A Bing Crosby Collection Volumes 1 & 2* (Columbia 1978)★★★★, *Christmas With Bing* (Reader's Digest 1980)★★★, *Bing In The Hall* (Spokane 1980)★★★, *Music Hall Highlights* (Spokane 1981)★★★, *Rare 1930-31 Brunswick Recordings* (MCA

1982)★★★, *Bing In The Thirties Volumes 1-8* (Spokane 1984-88)★★★★, *The Radio Years Volumes 1-4* (GNP Crescendo 1985-87)★★★★, *Bing Crosby Sings Again* (MCA 1986)★★★, *10th Anniversary Album* (Warwick 1987)★★★★, *Bing Crosby 1929-34, Classic Years Volume 1* (BBC 1987)★★★★, *Chronological Bing Crosby Volumes 1-10* (Jonzo 1985-88)★★★★, *The Crooner: The Columbia Years 1928-34* (Columbia 1988)★★★★, *The Victor Masters Featuring Bing Crosby (Paul Whiteman And His Orchestra)* (RCA 1989)★★★★, *The All Time Best Of* (Curb 1990)★★★, *Bing Crosby And Some Jazz Friends* (MCA/GRP 1991)★★★★, *The Jazzin' Bing Crosby* (Charly 1992)★★★★, *16 Most Requested Songs Legacy* (Columbia 1992)★★★★, *The Quintessential Bing Crosby* (1993)★★★★, *The EP Collection* (1993)★★★★, *Bing Crosby And Friends* (1993)★★★, *His Legendary Years* 4-CD box set (MCA 1993)★★★★, *Only Forever* (Empress 1994)★★★, *The Complete United Artists Sessions - Special Collectors Edition* 3-CD set (EMI 1997)★★★, with the Andrews Sisters *The Essential Collection* (Half Moon 1998)★★★, *Christmas Is A Comin'* (MCA 1998)★★★.

● VIDEOS: *A Bing Crosby Christmas* (VCI 1997).

● FURTHER READING: *Bing: The Authorized Biography*, Charles Thompson. *The One & Only Bing*, Bob Thomas. *The Complete Crosby*, Charles Thompson. *Bing Crosby: The Hollow Man*, Donald Shepherd. *Bing Crosby: A Discography, Radio Programme List & Filmography*, Timothy A. Morgereth.

● FILMS: *King Of Jazz* (1930), *Reaching For The Moon* (1930), *Confessions Of A Co-Ed* (1931), *The Bif Broadcast* (1932), *College Humor* (1933), *Too Much Harmony* (1933), *Going Hollywood* (1933), *Here Is My Heart* (1934), *She Loves Me Not* (1934), *We're Not Dressing* (1934), *The Big Broadcast Of 1936* (1935), *Two For Tonight* (1935), *Mississippi* (1935), *Pennies From Heaven* (1936), *Rhythm On The Range* (1936), *Anything Goes* (1936), *Double Or Nothing* (1937), *Waikiki Wedding* (1937), *Sing You Sinners* (1938), *Doctor Rhythm* (1938), *The Star Maker* (1939), *East Side Of Heaven* (1939), *Paris Honeymoon* (1939), *Rhythm On The River* (1940), *If I Had My Way* (1940), *Road To Singapore* (1940), *Birth Of The Blues* (1941), *Road To Zanzibar* (1941), *My Favorite Blonde* cameo (1942), *Star-Spangled Rhythm* (1942), *Road To Morocco* (1942), *Holiday Inn* (1942), *Dixie* (1943), *The Princess And The Pirate* (1944), *Here Comes The Waves* (1944), *Going My Way* (1944), *The Bells Of St. Mary's* (1945), *Duffy's Tavern* (1945), *Blue Skies* (1946), *Road To Utopia* (1946), *My Favorite Brunette* cameo (1947), *Variety Girl* (1947), *Road To Rio* (1947), *Welcome Stranger* (1947), *The Emperor Waltz* (1948), *Top O' The Morning* (1949), *A Connecticut Yankee In King Arthur's Court* (1949), *Mr. Music* (1950), *Riding High* (1950), *Here Comes The Groom* (1951), *Son Of Paleface* cameo (1952), *The Greatest Show On Earth* cameo (1952), *Road To Bali* (1952), *Just For You* (1952), *Scared Stiff* cameo (1953), *Little Boy Lost* (1953), *The Country Girl* (1954), *White Christmas* (1954), *High Society* (1956), *Anything Goes* remake (1956), *Man On Fire* (1957), *Alias Jesse James* cameo (1959), *Say One For Me* (1959), *Pepe* cameo (1960), *Let's Make Love* cameo (1960), *High Time* (1960), *The Road To Hong Kong* (1962), *Robin And The Seven Hoods* (1964), *Cinerama's Russian Adventure* narration (1966), *Stagecoach* (1966), *That's Entertainment!* on-screen narration (1974).

CRUMIT, FRANK

b. 26 September 1889, Jackson, Ohio, USA, d. 7 September 1943, Longmeadow, Massachusetts, USA. Crumit's early career took a somewhat unusual route from the Culver Military Academy, Indiana, via the University of Ohio, into vaudeville as the One Man Glee Club. First recording in 1919 for the Columbia label, he later signed for Victor Records in 1924 and shortly after for Decca. Crumit played the ukulele, sang in a soft, warm voice, and was especially noted for his performance of novelty numbers, such as 'A Gay Caballero', 'Abdul Abulbul Amir' (and the follow-ups, 'The Return Of ...' and 'The Grandson Of . . .'), 'The Prune Song', 'There's No One With Endurance Like The Man Who Sells Insurance', 'Connie's Got Connections In Connecticut', 'Nettie Is The Nit-Wit Of The Networks' and 'What Kind Of A Noise Annoys An Oyster?'. He is supposed to have written thousands of songs and adapted many others such as 'Frankie And Johnny' and 'Little Brown Jug' to suit his individual style. Crumit enjoyed great popularity throughout the 20s and 30s, appearing in several Broadway shows, including *Greenwich Village Follies*. He also appeared in *Tangerine* with his future wife, Julia Sanderson. They married in 1927 and retired from show business for two years. Following their comeback in 1929, they were extremely successful together on radio in the 30s as the Singing Sweethearts, and in 1939 began *The Battle Of The Sexes* game show which continued until Crumit's death in 1943.

● ALBUMS: *Mountain Greenery* (1981)★★★, *Everybody's Best Friend* (1988)★★★, *Around The Corner* (1990)★★★.

CUCKOO PATROL

Those wishing to denigrate the style of pop dubbed 'British Beat' found the ideal outlet in Freddie And The Dreamers. Led by the giggling ex-milkman Freddie Garrity, the Manchester quintet brought schoolboy prankishness to the genre with effete, choreographed stage movements and insouciant readings of R&B/rock 'n' roll standards. Garrity's vocal style owed more to Norman Wisdom than John Lennon, yet the group became momentarily popular in the UK and the USA, where novelty songs, including a cover of the Royal Teens' 'Short Shorts' and the dance-based 'Do The Freddy', proved popular. In *Cuckoo Patrol* the quintet played dull-witted boy scouts who encounter wrestlers, criminals and, predictably, girl guides. The film also featured British comedy stalwarts John Le Mesurier, Arthur Mullard and *Carry On* star Kenneth Connor, but *Cuckoo Patrol* lacks even the seaside postcard charm of the last-named's better-known celluloid adventures.

CUGAT, XAVIER

b. Francisco de Asis Javier Cugat Mingall de Bru y Deluefeo, 1 January 1900, Gerona, Spain, d. 27 October 1990, Barcelona, Spain. An immensely popular bandleader and composer who became known as the 'King Of The Rumba' during the 30s and 40s after he introduced some of the most insinuating Spanish and Latin American dance rhythms to the USA. Although details of Cugat's early life are unclear, it would seem that he moved with his family to Cuba when he was between three and five years old, and began to learn to play the violin. He performed in cafes and concert halls before the family was on the move again, this time to the USA. Cugat studied in Berlin, playing with the Berlin Symphony Orchestra, and eventually settled in California, drawing caricatures of early movie stars for the Los Angeles Times. He formed

Xavier Cugat And His Gigolos to play at the Cocoanut Grove, the Chez Paris in Chicago, and New York's Waldorf-Astoria. By the time he reached the Waldorf, a venue he was to return to again and again, he had customised his music, removing the raw elements of these exciting imported rhythms. He had a great flair for showmanship, and employed several elegant and talented dancers and singers, one of whom, Rita Cansino, later changed her name to Rita Hayworth. In 1930 he scored the Ramon Novarro film *In Gay Madrid* (1930), which included the song 'Dark Night' (with Herbert Stothart and Clifford Grey). There were many other numbers, co-composed with a variety of writers, such as 'The Thrill Of A New Romance', 'Yo Te Amo Mucho (And That's That)', 'Rain In Spain', 'El Americano', 'Cougat's Nougat', 'Night Must Fall', 'Illusion', 'Nightingale', 'One-Two-Three-Kick', and his appealing theme, 'My Shawl'. Cugat had a string of record hits from 1935-49, including 'The Lady In Red', 'Night Must Fall', 'Perfidia', 'Chica, Chica, Boom, Chic' (vocal: Lina Romay), 'Babula' (Miguelito Valdes), 'Amor' (Carmen Castillo), 'Good, Good, Good (That's You-That's You)', and 'South America, Take It Away' (Bobby Clark). Two of his best remembered discs are 'The Breeze And I' (vocal: Dinah Shore) and 'Brazil'. In the mid-30s his was one of the bands featured on radio's famous *Let's Dance* three-hour Saturday night dance marathon. During the 40s and 50s he appeared, almost always as himself, in films such as *You Were Never Lovelier* (with Fred Astaire and Rita Hayworth), *Two Girls And A Sailor* (June Allyson and Van Johnson), and *Neptune's Daughter* (Esther Williams, Red Skelton and Ricardo Montalban). He married five times, and two of his wives, Abbe Lane and Charo Baeza (Charo) were singers with his band. A stroke in 1971 forced him into semi-retirement, but in 1987, when The 'New' Xavier Cugat Orchestra conducted by Ada Cavallo was advertising for business, Cugat appeared in the television documentary *Images/Imagenes: Latin Music Special* in 1987. He died three years later of heart failure.

● ALBUMS: *Dance With Cugat* (Columbia 50s), *Cugat's Favorite Rhumbas* (Columbia 50s), *Cugat Cavalcade* (Columbia (50s), *Waltzes-But By Cugat!* (Columbia 50s), *Viva Cugat* (Mercury 1958), *Continental Hits* 1944-45 recordings, reissue 1984 (1959), *To All My Friends* reissue (1986), *Xavier Cugat - The Original Mambo King* (Sony 1996).

● FILMS: shorts *Xavier Cugat And His Gigolos*, *Spanish Serenade*, *The Camp Fire* (all three 1928); features *Go West Young Man* (1936), *You Were Never Lovelier* (1942), *Stage Door Canteen* (1943), *The Heat's On* (1943), *Two Girls And A Sailor* (1944), *Bathing Beauty* (1944), *Weekend At The Waldorf* (1945), *No Leave, No Love* (1946), *Holiday In Mexico* (1946), *This Time For Keeps* (1947), *Luxery Liner* (1948), *On An Island With You* (1948), *A Date With Judy* (1948), *Neptune's Daughter* (1949), *Chicago Syndicate* (1955), *Lo Scapolo* (1955), *Donatella* (1956), *Susana Y Yo* (1957), *Das Feuerschiff* (1962), *The Monitors* cameo (1969), *The Phynx* (1970), *Rosa Al Viento, Una* (1984).

● FURTHER READING: *Rumba Is My Life* (his autobiography).

CURRY, TIM

b. 19 April 1946, Cheshire, England. A versatile actor and singer, with much flair and a dashing style, Curry studied drama and English at Birmingham University. In the 60s, he was a member of the Royal Shakespeare company, and joined the cast of *Hair* early on in its run. After appearing in a supporting role in the 1970 flop musical, *Lie Down, I Think I Love You*, three years later he created the role of the outrageous Frank N. Furter in Richard O'Brien's phenomenally successful *The Rocky Horror Show*. In 1975 he reprised the part in the short-lived New York production, and also starred in the film adaptation which was entitled *The Rocky Horror Picture Show*. In 1981 Curry was nominated for a Tony Award for his performance in the title role of the Broadway production of *Amadeus*, and in the following year received a Variety Club Award when he played the role of the Pirate King, with George Cole and Bonnie Langford, in a West End revival of *The Pirates Of Penzance*. In 1986 he was 'bold, muscular and in fine ample baritone voice' as Macheath in the UK National Theatre's *The Threepenny Opera*, and two years later played Bill Sibson in the US tour of *Me And My Girl*. In 1993, Curry received another Tony nomination for his performance as the ageing and alcoholic swashbuckler Alan Swann in *My Favorite Year*. The musical, which had a book by Joseph Dougherty and a score by Stephen Flaherty and Lynn Ahrens, was based on the 1982 Peter O'Toole movie of the same name. Negative revues forced its closure after 37 performances, but Curry's own film career has flourished since the mid-70s. As well as his on-screen performances, on numerous occasions he has provided the voice for feature and television productions. These have included the voice of the evil spirit Hexxus who sang Thomas Dolby's 'Toxic Love' in *Ferngully: The Last Rainforest* (1992). Three years later he was the voice of the 'macho, strutting Drake' in MGM's animated *The Pebble And The Penguin*. Curry has appeared extensively on television, especially in the USA, in films or series such as *Oliver Twist* (1982, as Bill Sikes), *The Worst Witch* (1986), *Wiseguy* (1987), *Daisy-Head Mayzie* (1995), *Titanic* (1996), and *Over The Top* (1997)

● ALBUMS: *Fearless* (A&M 1979)★★★, *Simplicity* (A&M 1981)★★★.

● FILMS: *The Rocky Horror Picture Show* (1975), *The Shout* (1978), *Times Square* (1980), *Annie* (1982), *The Ploughman's Lunch* (1983), *Clue* (1985), *Legend* (1985), *Pass The Ammo* (1988), *The Hunt For Red October* (1990), *Oscar* (1991), *Passed Away* (1992), *Home Alone 2: Lost In New York* (1992), *National Lampoon's Loaded Wagon 1* (1993), *The Three Musketeers* (1993), *The Shadow* (1994), *Congo* (1995), *Toonstruck* (1996), *Muppet Treasure Island* (1996), *Lover's Knot* (1996), *McHale's Navy* (1997).

CURZON, FREDERIC

b. Ernest Frederic Curzon, 4 September 1899, London, England, d. 6 December 1973, Bournemouth, England. Largely unknown, but highly talented composer, who has contributed several important works to the light music repertoire. Curzon's career began accompanying silent films, but he decided that he would prefer to concentrate on the organ, and was one of the first in Britain to play the 'new' electronic organ, giving many demonstration recitals. After 12 years at top London cinemas, in 1938 he decided to specialize in composing, although he still accepted occasional offers to perform on the BBC Theatre Organ. This decision had been prompted by the success of

his 'Robin Hood Suite' (1937) especially the movement 'March Of The Bowmen' which appeared frequently in broadcasts for the following 20 years. His other important works included 'The Boulevardier' - his best-known piece which was published in 1941 although its fame was not assured until the Sidney Torch 1948 recording for EMI-Columbia, 'Dance Of An Ostracised Imp' (1940), 'Punchinello' (1948), 'Bonaventure', 'Busybodies', 'Cascade', 'Chevalier' 'In Malaga', 'Over The Hills And Far Away', 'Summer Souvenir' and 'Galavant' (1950).

● ALBUMS: *British Light Music - Frederic Curzon* (Marco Polo 1992)★★★★.

DADDY LONG LEGS

Previously filmed in 1919, 1931 and 1935, this 1955 adaptation of Jean Webster's classic novel, by Phoebe and Henry Ephron, strayed somewhat from the original because of the presence of the delightful French actress Leslie Caron. In this version of the story, a wealthy US businessman, played by Fred Astaire, sponsors the education of a French orphan-girl (Caron) - on the strict understanding that he remains anonymous. After his office receives fulsome letters of gratitude from her school, his secretary (a beautifully 'hard-bitten' performance by Thelma Ritter) persuades him to visit her. He is captivated by the charming young woman and they fall in love, although she still has no idea that he is her mysterious benefactor, even when she continues her education in the USA. Their romance blossoms, and Astaire and Caron proved to be a perfect dancing team, accompanied by a score by Johnny Mercer containing two songs that went on to become standards, 'Something's Gotta Give' and 'Dream'. The former gave Astaire the opportunity to convey a perfect lyrical illustration of the difficulties inherent in the 'generation gap' ('When an irresistible force such as you/Meets an old immovable object like me'), and the latter, a lovely ethereal ballad that enhanced the film's dream sequences, was subsequently used for many years by Frank Sinatra as his closing theme. One of the many highlights in *Daddy Long Legs* came in 'Sluefoot', when Astaire demonstrated to a group of college students how this dance business really should be done, backed by trumpeter Ray Anthony And His Orchestra. Astaire also gave a good account of himself on the drums. The rest of a lively and highly entertaining set of songs included 'History Of The Beat', 'C-A-T Spells Cat' and 'Welcome Egghead'. Legendary film composer Alex North was responsible for much of the film's orchestral music. Also in the cast were Terry Moore, Fred Clark, Ralph Dumke and Larry Keating. The film, which was choreographed by David Robel and Roland Petit, and directed by Jean Negulesco, was photographed in DeLuxe Color and CinemaScope and released by 20th Century-Fox.

DAILEY, DAN

b. 14 December 1914 (or 1917), New York City, New York, USA, d. 1978. An elegant and versatile song-and-dance-man with a genial personality, who starred in some of the most entertaining musicals of the 40s and 50s, often as a vaudeville performer or similar. As a youngster, Dailey worked in minstrel shows and vaudeville. In 1937 he got a job in the chorus of Richard Rodgers and Lorenz Hart's Broadway show Babes In Arms, and, two years later, played a supporting role in another stage musical, Stars In Your Eyes, which starred Ethel Merman and Jimmy Durante. His first appearance in a movie musical came in 1941 with the lavish Ziegfeld Girl, which was followed by *Lady Be Good* and *Panama Hattie*. After service in World War II, Dailey signed for 20th Century-Fox and began to play the lead in films such as Mother Wore Tights (the first of several he made with Betty Grable), *You Were Meant For Me*, Give My Regards To Broadway, *When My Baby Smiles At Me* (for which he was nominated for the best actor Oscar, only to be beaten by Laurence Olivier!), *You're My Everything*, *I'll Get By*, *My Blue Heaven*, and *Call Me Mister*. In 1952 his portrayal of baseball star Dizzy Dean in *The Pride Of St. Louis* was highly acclaimed. As well as these occasional, but skilfully played straight roles, he continued to devote most of his time to musicals such as *The Girl Next Door*, There's No Business Like Show Business, It's Always Fair Weather, The Best Things In Life Are Free, *Meet Me In Las Vegas*, and *Pepe* (1960). By then, the lavish, big budget musicals had become old fashioned, and Dailey subsequently worked on stage and in the big US cabaret rooms. In the late 50s he co-starred with Vittorio De Sica, Jack Hawkins and Richard Conte in *The Four Just Men*, a television series which was popular in the US and UK, and his other small screen work included *The Governor And J.J.* in the 60s, and *Faraday And Company* in the 70s.

● FILMS: The Mortal Storm (1940), Dulcy (1940), Susan And God (1940), The Captain Is A Lady (1940), The Mortal Storm (1940), Lady Be Good (1941), Moon Over Her Shoulder (1941), Ziegfeld Girl (1941), Give Out Sisters (1942), Panama Hattie (1942), Mother Wore Tights (1947), When My Baby Smiles At Me (1948), You Were Meant For Me (1948), Give My Regards To Broadway (1948), Chicken Every Sunday (1949), You're My Everything (1949), I'll Get By (1950), A Ticket To Tomahawk (1950), When Willie Comes Marching Home (1950), My Blue Heaven (1950), I Can Get It For You Wholesale (1951), The Pride Of St. Louis (1951), Call Me Mister (1951), What Price Glory? (1952), The Girl Next Door (1953), The Kid From Left Field (1953), Taxi (1953), Meet Me At The Fair (1953), There's No Business Like Showbusiness (1954), It's Always Fair Weather (1955), The Wings Of Eagles (1956), The Best Things In Life Are Free (1956), Meet Me In Las Vegas (1956), The Wayward Bus (1957), Oh Men! Oh Women! (1957), Pepe (1960), Hemingway's Adventures Of A Young Man (1962), The Private Files Of J. Edgar Hoover (1977).

DALE, JIM

b. Jim Smith, 15 August 1935, Kettering, Northamptonshire, England. Dale, a failed impressionist, who wanted to be an all-round entertainer, had a two-year stint with Carrol Levis' touring show as part of a comedy tumbling act. He then became a solo comedian and only turned to singing when he found people preferred his finale song to his tame comedy. He joined the BBC Television series 6.5 Special in April 1957, and shortly afterwards signed to Parlophone Records, where he was produced by George Martin. His only Top 20 hit came with his second single, a cover version of Johnny Madara's 'Be My Girl', which reached number 2 in late 1957. He had three more UK Top 40 entries, the last being a version of the McGuire Sisters' US hit 'Sugartime' in 1958. In the 60s Dale pursued his acting career, and appeared in a string of successful Carry On films, and others, such as Lock Up Your Daughters. He made his West End debut in a musical, The Wayward Way, and appeared at the Edinburgh Festival in a pop version of The Winter's Tale. He also co-wrote the Seekers' smash hit 'Georgy Girl', for which he was nominated for an Academy Award, and contributed to the music for movies such as Shalako and Lola. In the late 60s and early 70s, as member of the National Theatre Company, he appeared in several productions at the Old Vic and the Young Vic. He also made more films, including Adolph Hitler - My Part In His Downfall and Digby, The Biggest Dog In The World. In 1973, Dale played for six months at the Queen's Theatre, London, in the musical The Card, and around the same time, hosted the popular television show, Sunday Night At The London Palladium. In 1974 he went to the USA with the National Theatre Company and created a stir with his performance as an 'ingratiating scamp' in the Molière farce Scapino, which brought him Drama Desk and Outer Critics Circle Awards, and a Tony Award nomination. During the late 70s, by now domiciled in the USA, he appeared in stage productions of Comedians and Privates On Parade, as well as making several other movies, three of them for the Disney Studio.

In 1980 Dale found the ideal vehicle for his talents in Barnum, a musical about the life of the famed US showman, which involved juggling, trampolining and tightrope walking, among other skills. He won a Tony Award for his performance and stayed with the show for over a year, following ecstatic opening reviews. In the 80s he made more films, and appeared on the New York stage in productions as diverse as Peter Nichol's Joe Egg (1985), Me And My Girl (1987), and a revival of Privates On Parade (1989). During the 90s, as well as appearing on the American stage and in television movies such as The American Clock (1993) and The Hunchback (1997), he returned to the UK on occasions, playing the title role in the film Carry On Columbus, Professor Harold Hill in a BBC Radio 2 recording of The Music Man (1995), and Fagin in Cameron Mackintosh's record-breaking revival of Oliver! at the London Palladium (1995 and 1997). He was also nominated for the best leading actor in a musical Tony Award for his performance on Broadway in *Candide* (1997).

● ALBUMS: *Jim!* (Parlophone 1958)★★, and cast recordings.
● FILMS: *6.5 Special* (1958), *Raising The Wind* (1961), *Nurse On Wheels* (1963), *Carry On Cabby* (1963), *Carry On Cleo* (1964), *Carry On Jack* (1964), *Carry On Spying* (1964), *The Big Job* (1965), *Carry On Cowboy* (1965), *Don't Lose Your Head* (1966), *Carry On Screaming* (1966), *Follow That Camel* (1967), *The Plank* (1967), *The Winter's Tale* (1968), *Carry On Doctor* (1968), *Lock Up Your Daughters* (1969), *Carry On Again Doctor* (1969), *Adolph Hitler-My Part In His Downfall* (1972), *The National Health* (1973), *Digby-The Biggest Dog In The World* (1974), *Pete's Dragon* (1977), *Joseph Andrews* (1977), *Hot Lead And Cold Feet* (1978), *Unidentified Flying Oddball* (1979), *Scandalous* (1984), *Carry On Columbus* (1992).

DAMES

Following their triumphs in 42nd Street, Gold Diggers Of 1933, and Footlight Parade, Dick Powell, Ruby Keeler, Busby Berkeley and songwriters Harry Warren and Al Dubin reconvened for more of the same in this Warner release of 1934. The dramatic backstage events this particular time concern the efforts of a wealthy philanthropist (Hugh Herbert) to give away his money, while his cousin (Guy Kibbee) is practically given the 'third degree' by Joan Blondell in an effort to extract cash from him so that Dick Powell can put on his show. In any event, Delmar Daves's screenplay is simply an excuse for Warren and Dubin's marvellous songs and Busby Berkeley's imaginative and spectacular dance sequences. Perhaps the most memorable is the one built around 'I Only Have Eyes For You', which begins with Powell and Keeler on a street corner, and then moves to the subway where, aided by the train's motion, the couple fall asleep. In the dream sequence that follows, every advertisement bears Ruby's face, as does a whole screenful of faces which is transposed into an enormous jigsaw puzzle. Finally, a set consisting of huge revolving Ferris-type wheels and connecting staircases is filled with a host of Berkeley's beauties - all dressed and made-up to look exactly like Ruby Keeler. Dick Powell gives a spirited rendition of the title song, and Joan Blondell has her big moment too with the endearing 'The Girl At The Ironing Board'. The score was supplemented by Sammy Fain and Irving Kahal's 'When You Were A Smile On Your Mother's Lips' and 'Try To See It My Way' by Allie Wrubel and Mort Dixon. The popular comedienne ZaSu Pitts made a significant contribution to a film that was fast-moving, funny, entertaining, and a sumptuous feast for both the ear and the eye.

DAMES AT SEA

New York salutes Hollywood in this affectionate spoof of the Busby Berkeley-Harry Warren and Al Dubin-Dick Powell and Ruby Keeler-style film musicals of the 30s, which opened off-Broadway at the Bouwerie Lane Theatre on 20 December 1968. This time, though, the setting is not 'by a waterfall', but the deck of a battleship where Ruby, the talented tap-dancer from the sticks (Bernadette Peters), climbs on board a youngster, and disembarks a star. The show is being floated because its songwriter, Dick (David Christmas), happens to be a sailor, and is therefore able to offer an alternate venue when under the

nicest kind of pressure from the leading lady, Mona (Tamara Long). Unfortunately for Mona, even a brief spell on the ocean wave does not agree with her - Ruby takes over, and she and Dick set off on life's long voyage together. George Haimsohn and Robin Miller wrote the book and lyrics, and the composer was Jim Wise. Their show's atmosphere and its songs reflected the good-natured send-up of the real thing (is 'Singapore Sue' any relation to 'Shanghai Lil'?), and included 'Choo-Choo Honeymoon', 'That Mister Man Of Mine', 'It's You', 'Good Times Are Here To Stay', 'Sailor Of My Dreams', and 'Star Tar'. It proved to be the first big break, not only for Mona, but also for Bernadette Peters who went on to become a major Broadway star, appearing in such shows as the failed, but fondly remembered, Mack And Mabel, and several Stephen Sondheim musicals. Dames At Sea sailed on for 575 performances - an impressive run for an off-Broadway show - and also played the Plaza 9 Musical Hall for a spell. It was revived again in New York in 1985, and was seen in the 90s at London's Ambassadors Theatre (1996, with Kim Criswell: Mona, Jason Gardiner: Dick, Ruby: Joanne Farrell) and the Marines Memorial Theatre, San Francisco (1998, Ellen Harvey: Mona, Ruby: Andrea Chamberlain, and Joel Carlton: Dick).

DAMN YANKEES (FILM MUSICAL)

Although the original 1955 Broadway show kept that title for the London stage production, the 1958 film version was released in the UK as *What Lola Wants*. Regardless of its title, this story of Joe Boyd (Robert Shafer), an ageing American baseball fan, whose frustration with his team, the Washington Senators, leads him to make a Faustian pact with the Devil, turned out to be a highly entertaining movie musical. Joe's musings along the lines of 'I'd sell my soul for just one long-ball hitter' bring forth a Mr. Applegate (Ray Walston), who, after casually flashing his red socks and lighting a cigarette by spontaneous combustion ('I'm handy with fire'), agrees to turn Joe into a young athlete for one season only in return for his soul. The deal is done, and, sure enough, as the Senators' amazing new discovery Joe Hardy (Tab Hunter), he galvanizes the team into action and leads them to glory, after which he reverts to his former self (his contract with Applegate contains an escape clause), and returns to his humdrum life and wife Meg (Shannon Bolin). Walston was marvellous, as always, and former pop heart-throb Hunter also gave an appealing performance. However, the star of the film without any doubt was the red-headed, long-legged dancer Gwen Verdon. She plays Lola, Applegate's apprentice, whose mission is to retain Joe's soul forever. Her attempt to seduce him in the locker-room to the sexy strains of 'Whatever Lola Wants', was a hilarious send-up of every vamp scene in the history of stage and screen. Verdon was one of the original Broadway team - not including Hunter - who recreated their roles for the screen. Russ Brown, as the Senators' coach, and Rae Allen in the role of Gloria, the nosy, hard-bitten newspaper reporter, were also in the film cast, along with Nathaniel Frey, Jimmie Komack, Jean Stapleton and Albert Linville. Richard Adler and Jerry Ross's splendid score included 'Goodbye, Old Girl', 'Heart' ('You gotta have . . .'), 'Shoeless

Jo From Hannibal, Mo', 'A Little Brains-A Little Talent', 'There's Something About An Empty Chair', 'Two Lost Souls', 'Those Were The Good Old Days' and 'Six Months Out Of Every Year'. Bob Fosse was again responsible for the brilliant choreography, and he also joined Gwen Verdon for the mambo-styled 'Who's Got The Pain?'. George Abbott's screenplay was based on his own stage libretto which was adapted from the novel *The Year The Yankees Lost The Pennant* by Douglass Wallop. Abbott also co-directed the film with Stanley Donen. The film was shot in Technicolor for Warner Brothers.

DAMN YANKEES (STAGE MUSICAL)

Combining the improbable ingredients of a Faustian plot with a baseball setting, *Damn Yankees* opened at the 46th Street Theatre in New York on 5 May 1955. George Abbott and Douglass Wallop's witty book was based on Wallop's novel, *The Year The Yankees Lost The Pennant*. Middle-aged baseball fan Joe Boyd (Robert Shafer) is totally frustrated with the inadequate performance of his team, the Washington Senators, and one day when things get really bad, he vows that he would willingly sell his soul to the Devil if only the Senators could win the pennant. The Devil (Ray Walston, aka Mr. Applegate) promptly appears and grants his wish. A contract is drawn up, and in a flash, Joe Boyd is transformed into Joe Hardy (Stephen Douglass), a handsome, hard hitting young ballplayer who steers the Senators to victory in almost every match. Off the park, he has to deal with the amorous advances of Lola (Gwen Verdon), the Devil's glamorous reincarnated ugly old witch, who gets what she wants - most of the time. Eventually, after the complications that beset his team's triumphs, Joe returns to plump middle-age and his nice, ordinary wife Meg (Shannon Bolin), while Lola gets back on her broomstick. Also prominent amongst the cast were Jean Stapleton, Al Lanti, Eddie Phillips, Nathaniel Frey, Albert Linville, Russ Brown, Jimmie Komack, and Rae Allen. Jerry Ross and Richard Adler's score was full of amusing and thoroughly entertaining numbers, including 'Six Months Out Of Every Year', 'Goodbye, Old Girl', 'Heart', 'Shoeless Joe From Hannibal Mo', 'A Man Doesn't Know', 'A Little Brains - A Little Talent', 'Whatever Lola Wants', 'Not Meg', 'Who's Got The Pain?', 'The American League', 'The Game', 'Near To You', 'Those Were The Good Old Days', and 'Two Lost Souls'. *Damn Yankees* scooped the 1956 Tony Awards, winning for best musical, actress (Verdon), actor (Walston), supporting actor (Brown), choreographer (Bob Fosse), and director (Hal Hastings). Gwen Verdon's powerful and sexy performance swept her to stardom in this show, which ran on Broadway for 1,019 performances, and a further 258 at the London Coliseum, with Belita (Lola), Ivor Emmanuel (Joe Hardy), Bill Kerr (Mr. Applegate), Betty Paul (Meg), and Phil Vickers (Joe Boyd). The show's outstanding ballad, 'Heart', was a big hit in the US for Eddie Fisher and the Four Aces, and in Britain for the Johnston Brothers and Max Bygraves. An acclaimed Broadway revival opened in March 1994, with Bebe Neuwirth (Lola), Dennis Kelly (Joe Boyd), Victor Garber (Applegate), Linda Stephens (Meg), and Jarrod Emick (Joe Hardy). During the run, comedian Jerry Lewis made his Broadway debut when he took over the role of Applegate. He subsequently reprised the part (incorporating a vintage Vaudeville routine) when the touring version called in at London's Adelphi Theatre in 1997. Verdon and Walston were joined by pop heart-throb Tab Hunter in the 1958 film version.

DAMSEL IN DISTRESS, A

Following Ginger Rogers' reported desire to take a rest from musicals, the British-born actress Joan Fontaine became Fred Astaire's new partner in this 1937 RKO release - and proved to be a somewhat disappointing choice. In the screenplay by P.G. Wodehouse, Ernest Pagano and S.K. Lauren, which was adapted from Wodehouse's 1919 novel, Fontaine was cast as a society lady incarcerated in 'Ye olde English castle' complete with a scheming butler (Reginald Gardiner). A swashbuckling dancer (Astaire) - from the 'new' country - goes to the maiden's rescue, and would probably have swept her off into the sunset, singing and dancing - except that Joan Fontaine was not much good at either. The comedy team of George Burns and Gracie Allen (as Astaire's press agent and scatty secretary) were pretty nifty though, and Astaire's best dance moments came with them. As usual with these 30s musicals, the inadequacies of the plot were overcome, and more than compensated for by the marvellous music. The score this time was by George and Ira Gershwin, and included two of their enduring standards, 'A Foggy Day' and 'Nice Work If You Get It', as well as others just as good but not as popular, such as 'I Can't Be Bothered Now', 'The Jolly Tar And The Milkmaid', 'Put Me To The Test', 'Stiff Upper Lip', 'Sing Of Spring', and 'Things Are Looking Up'. Also included was another musical piece, 'Ah, Che A Voi Perdoni Iddio' (from Flowtow's *Marta*). George Stevens directed, and dance director Hermes Pan won an Academy Award for his contribution to a movie which, although vastly entertaining, proved to be Fred Astaire's first box-office failure.

DANCE A LITTLE CLOSER

Alan Jay Lerner's last Broadway show - a one-performance flop - had already been dubbed *Close A Little Faster* during previews, prior to the opening on the 11 May 1983 at New York's Minskoff Theatre. This music adaptation of Robert E. Sherwood's Pulitzer Prize-winning play, *Idiot's Delight*, had a book and lyrics by Lerner, who also directed. The composer, Charles Strouse, was adjudged to be the least guilty of the participating parties for his melodies to such numbers as 'Another Life', 'There's Never Been Anything Like Us', 'I Never Want To See You again', and the enchanting 'Dance A Little Closer', which is preserved in a recording by Liz Robertson, one of the show's stars, and Lerner's eighth wife. Len Cariou played Harry Aikens, a down at heel supper club entertainer who warms again to an old flame, Cynthia Brookfield-Bailey (Liz Robertson), when they are both holed up in an Austrian hotel on New Year's Eve, awaiting World War III. Cynthia was the mistress of a man who bore a remarkable resemblance to the American diplomat Henry Kissinger.

DANCE BAND

The American actor, singer and band leader Charles 'Buddy' Rogers added some welcome authenticity to this amusing comedy of misunderstandings which was produced by British International Pictures (BIP) in 1935. A competition for dance bands with big prize money and a year's recording contract draws Buddy Milton (Rogers) to London. Blonde and beautiful Pat Shelley (June Clyde) and her all-female orchestra are also entered in the contest, but her pianist is injured in an accident and Buddy deputises for him - under an alias. When she finds out who Buddy really is Pat is furious and accuses him of foul play. The happy ending arrives after Buddy's boys come to the rescue when the girls lose their instruments, and the result of the competition is, of course, a tie - with the inevitable romance to follow. The 'scenario and dialogue' by Roger Burford, Jack Davies Jnr., and Denis Waldock, provides plenty of opportunities for some smart set pieces and snappy musical numbers. The dance team of Jack Holland and June Hart introduced what was intended to be the newest dance sensation, 'The Valparaiso', and the three other catchy songs by Mabel Wayne, Desmond Carter, Arthur Young, Sonny Miller, and Jack Shirley were 'Turtle-Dovey', 'I Hate To Say Goodnight', and 'Gypsy Love'. Steve Geray and the Hungarian actress Magda Kun provided the secondary love interest, and other roles went to Fred Duprez, Leon Sherkot, Richard Hearne (as a drunk), Hal Gordon, and Albert Whelan (the music hall favourite). The musical director was Harry Acres, and this light but entertaining film was directed by Marcel Varnel.

DANCIN'

Bob Fosse had probably been waiting all his life for the opportunity to get rid of those tiresome librettos and get down to what the Broadway musical stage was all about for him - Dancin'. Over the years, this super-talented choreographer and director had created memorable dance sequences for such marvellous shows as The Pajama Game, Damn Yankees, Bells Are Ringing, New Girl In Town, Redhead, How To Succeed In Business Without Really Trying, Little Me, Sweet Charity, Pippin, and Chicago, amongst others, as well as performing a similar role for a string of Hollywood musicals. Dancin' opened at New York's Broadhurst Theatre on 27 March 1978, and stayed there for over four years, an incredible run totalling 1, 774 performances. The show had a team of 16 dancers who brilliantly executed Fosse's precision routines based on more than 20 carefully chosen musical numbers that ranged 'from Bach through John Philip Sousa and George M. Cohan to Johnny Mercer to Cat Stevens'. It soon became a popular foreign tourist attraction - you don't have to know the language to enjoy a show like this - and was a triumph for all concerned, especially Fosse, whose death in 1987 coincided with a (hopefully temporary) decline in the fortunes of the traditional Broadway musical in the face of the British invasion.

DANCING LADY

Backstage musicals in which the young chorus girl saves the show by 'going out there on stage a youngster and coming back a star' proliferated in Hollywood in the early 30s, and this one, which was released by MGM in 1933, was really only significant because it marked the film debut of Fred Astaire - complete with his trade-mark top hat, white tie and tails. He played himself, and danced with Joan Crawford to 'Heigh-Ho, The Gang's All Here' and 'Let's Go Bavarian'. Those two numbers and the lovely ballad 'Everything I Have Is Yours', were written by Harold Adamson and Burton Lane. Fresh from their Broadway success, Richard Rodgers and Lorenz Hart, contributed the lively 'That's The Rhythm Of The Day', which was sung by Nelson Eddy, and the always reliable team of Dorothy Fields and Jimmy McHugh provided 'My Dancing Lady', 'Close Your Old Umbrella', and 'Hey, Young Fella'. Clark Gable was perfectly cast as the hard-hearted director who pushed Crawford into the limelight, and Franchot Tone, on the brink of a distinguished film career, was in a cast which also included Al Jarrett, May Robson, Robert Benchley, Winnie Lightner, and the Three Stooges. The screenplay was written by Allen Rivkin and P.J. Wolfson, the choreographers were Sammy Lee and Eddie Prinz, and the picture was directed by Robert Z. Leonard. Although their subsequent careers were in completely different areas of the movie business, Gable and Astaire are both indelibly associated with one particular song - 'Puttin' On the Ritz'. It provided the accompaniment for one of Fred's most memorable moments in Blue Skies (1946), and was also used to great effect in Clark Gable's snappy song-and-dance routine in Idiot's Delight (1939).

DANCING YEARS, THE

Ivor Novello's fourth musical play at Drury Lane, which opened on 23 March 1939, was considered to be his best work for the theatre to date. It was set initially in 1911 Vienna, where the young composer, Rudi Kleber (Novello), leaves his little admirer Grete Schone (Roma Beaumont), when prima donna Maria Ziegler (Mary Ellis) comes to call. The couple run away together despite the protests of Maria's wealthy boyfriend, Prince Charles Metterling (Anthony Nicholls), and are happy until Grete, now a star of English musical comedy, reappears to remind Rudi of his promise never to marry anyone until she has had the chance to refuse. Naturally, Maria overhears his 'mock' proposal, and goes off to marry Charles. Years later, Rudi asks Maria to come back to him, but after she introduces their son, Rudi refuses to ruin the boy's life, and says goodbye. Also prominent in an excellent cast were Peter Graves, Olive Gilbert, Dunstan Hart, Fred Hearne, and Minnie Rayner. Novello's delightful score, with lyrics by Christopher Hassall, included 'My Dearest Dear', 'Waltz Of My Heart', 'I Can Give You The Starlight', 'My Life Belongs To You', 'Leap Year Waltz', 'Primrose', 'Wings Of Sleep', 'Lorelei', and 'Uniform'. After a run of 187 performances, and with World War II looming, The Dancing Years closed on 1 September 1939. Just over a year later, it toured the UK regions, and returned to the West End at the Adelphi Theatre on 14 March 1942 (with Muriel Barron as Maria), where it ran for a further 969 performances, before going the regional road again. It was back in the West End again in 1947 (Barry Sinclair (Rudi), Jessica James (Maria), Nicolette Roeg (Grete)) and 1968

(David Knight (Rudi), Cathy Jose (Grete), June Bronhill (Maria)). An ice spectacular version was presented at the Empire Pool Wembley in 1954. The ubiquitous Dennis Price played the Ivor Novello role in the 1950 film version, (Giselle Preville (Maria), and Patricia Dainton (Grete)), Anthony Valentine took the role of Rudi in a 1981 television production, with Susan Skipper as Grete, and Celia Gregory (sung by Marilyn Hill Smith) playing Maria. In 1995, BBC Radio 2 presented the show in a new performing version, with the popular actor Simon Williams (Rudi), Marilyn Hill Smith (Maria), and Shona Lindsay (Grete).

DANGEROUS WHEN WET

The clue is in the title: this was a vehicle - or a vessel - for Esther Williams, the aquatic queen herself. Whilst on dry land, Esther is member of an Arkansas farming family of keep-fit fanatics, consisting of Ma (Charlotte Greenwood), Pa (William Demarest), and two sisters played by Barbara Whiting and Donna Corcoran. One fine day, a travelling salesman in a body-enhancing elixir named Liquapep, (Jack Carson) shows up, and his marketing skills come in handy when Esther to decides to take the plunge and engage in a sponsored swim of the English channel in order to raise money so that Pa can add a prize Jersey bull to the herd. Seriously handsome Fernando Lamas provides Esther's love interest, and serenades her with the attractive ballad, 'In My Wildest Dreams', Arthur Schwartz and Johnny Mercer wrote that one, and the rest of the songs, including the vigorous 'I Got Out Of Bed On The Right Side', 'Ain't Nature Grand?', and 'I Like Men'. The latter number was sung appealingly by Esther's sister Susie who was played Barbara Whiting, the real-life sister of popular singer Margaret Whiting, and the daughter of composer Richard Whiting. Esther was involved in a couple other underwater escapades, and was joined in one of them - a clever dream sequence - by the animated duo Tom And Jerry. Also in the cast were Denise Darcel, Paul Bryer, Henri Letondel, Bunny Waters, and Richard Alexander. Dorothy Kingsley wrote the amusing screenplay and Charles Walters directed this entertaining film which was shot in Technicolor and released in 1953.

DANIELS, BILLY

b. 12 September 1915, Jacksonville, Florida, USA, d. 7 October 1988. Daniels began his career as a singing waiter before working with dance bands and in vaudeville. In the late 30s he became popular in clubs and on radio. In 1943, during a club appearance, he performed 'That Old Black Magic', giving the song a highly dramatic, visually exciting treatment it had never before received, and from that time onwards, the singer and the song were inseparable. At his best in a cabaret setting, Daniels was a natural for television and from 1950, in partnership with pianist Bennie Payne, appeared regularly in the USA and UK. He made a few film appearances and was also in the television production of Night Of The Quarter Moon. P.J. Proby used much of Daniels' vocal technique with his epic ballads during the 60s. In 1975 he worked with Pearl Bailey in Hello, Dolly! and two years later starred in London in the UK version of Bubbling Brown Sugar. He also appeared with Sammy Davis Jnr. in the revival of Golden Boy.

Offstage, Daniels frequently associated with underworld characters. He was stabbed in one incident and was once charged with a shooting. Late in his life he suffered ill health and twice underwent heart bypass surgery before his death in 1988.

● ALBUMS: Around That Time (50s)★★★, At The Stardust Las Vegas (50s)★★, Love Songs For A Fool (50s)★★★, You Go to My Head (1957)★★★★, The Masculine Touch (1958)★★★, At the Crescendo (1959)★★★, Dance To The Magic (1959)★★★, Bubbling Black Magic (Polydor 1978)★★★.
● COMPILATIONS: The Magic Of Billy Daniels (MFP 1976)★★★.

DARBY, KEN

b. 13 May 1909, Hebron, Nebraska, USA, d. 24 January 1992, Sherman Oaks, California, USA. A prolific composer, arranger and musical director for records and films, Ken Darby's Singers and the John Scott Trotter Orchestra backed Bing Crosby on what is said to be the biggest-selling record of all time - 'White Christmas'. That was in 1942, and Darby's vocal group was present on several other appealing Crosby sides during the 40s, including 'If You Please', 'Riders In The Sky', 'Far Away Places', 'Anniversary Song', and two more million-sellers, 'Sunday, Monday, Or Always' (1943) and 'Now Is The Hour' (1948). By this time Darby was also working in films, having done some of the orchestral and vocal arrangements for the classic The Wizard Of Oz (1939). From then on, he served in various capacities, such as music supervisor, musical associate, choral, vocal or musical director, or arranger, on numerous features which included Step Lively (1944), State Fair (1945), Song Of The South (1946), So Dear To My Heart (1948), The Adventures of Ichabod And Mr. Toad (1949), Rancho Notorious (1952), Tonight We Sing (1952), The Robe (1953), The Egyptian (1954), Hound Dog Man (1959), Elmer Gantry (1960), The Canadians (1961), How The West Was Won (1962), The Greatest Story Ever Told (1965), and many more. Darby also contributed occasional songs or lyrics to films such as Walt Disney's Make Mine Music (1946, 'Casey At The Bat', with Ray Gilbert and Eliot Daniel), Golden Girl (1951, 'Sunday Mornin'', with Daniel), The Guy Who Came Back (1951), With A Song In My Heart (1952, 'Wonderful Home Sweet Home'), River Of No Return (1954), The Garden Of Evil (1954), and Bus Stop (1956, 'The Bus Stop Song', with Frank Skinner).

Throughout much of his career Darby collaborated with Alfred Newman, one of the doyens of Hollywood film music. They were awarded Oscars for their work on The King And I (1956) and Camelot (1967), and were nominated on a further three occasions, for South Pacific (1958), Flower Drum Song (1961), and How The West Was Won (1963). Darby won another Academy Award with André Previn for the scoring of Porgy And Bess (1959). The duo also won Grammys for the Porgy And Bess soundtrack album.

DAVID, MACK

b. 5 July 1912, Brooklyn, New York, USA, d. 30 December 1993, Rancho Mirage, California, USA. Although he was always cast in the shadow of his younger brother, Hal David, Mack was a popular songwriter of considerable merit. After studying law for a time, Mack David himself collaborated with Bacharach on 'Baby, It's You' which was a US Top 10 hit for the Shirelles in 1962. Many years before that - in 1939, he had his first hit with 'Moon Love' which he, Mack Davis and André Kostelanetz adapted from a part of Tchaikovsky's Fifth Symphony. It became successful for Glenn Miller, amongst others, and the next year David and Kostelanetz turned to Tchaikovsky again ('String Quartet In D Major') for inspiration on the Connee Boswell favourite 'On The Isle Of May'. In 1941 David and Vee Lawnhurst contributed 'Do You Believe In Fairy Tales?' to the movie *Pot 'O Gold*, and the rest of the 40s found David writing lyrics for mostly popular songs such as 'A Sinner Kissed An Angel', 'Sweet Eloise', 'Take Me', 'Candy', 'Don't You Know I Care?', 'I'm Just A Lucky So And So', 'I Don't Care If The Sun Don't Shine', and the delightfully nonsensical 'Chi-Baba, Chi-Baba' which was a US chart-topper for Perry Como in 1947. A year later another top crooner of the day, Frank Sinatra, did well with 'Sunflower' (words and music by Mack David), as did Russ Morgan And His Orchestra. This proved to be his best-remembered piece, especially in middle America, where it became the Kansas 'state song'. Subsequent recordings included a popular version by Frank Sinatra, and the song would become the subject of a court battle between David and composer Jerry Herman in 1964. The latter was sued for plagiarising a section of 'Sunflower' for his 'Hello, Dolly'. In 1950 David received his first Oscar nomination for another catchy nonsense song, 'Bibbidi-Bobbidi-Boo', which was part of the score which he, Jerry Livingston and Al Hoffman wrote for the Walt Disney animated feature Cinderella. The other numbers included 'A Dream Is A Wish Your Heart Makes', 'The Work Song', and 'So This Is Love'. During the 60s David was nominated on a further seven occasions for the film title songs *The Hanging Tree*, *Bachelor In Paradise*, *Walk On The Wild Side*, *It's A Mad, Mad, Mad, Mad World*, *Hush, Hush Sweet Charlotte*, and for 'The Ballad Of Cat Ballou', and 'My Wishing Doll' from *Hawaii*. The 50s had seen him working on pictures such as *At War With The Army* ('The Navy Gets The Gravy But The Army Gets The Beans'), *Sailor Beware* ('Never Before' and 'Merci Beaucoup'), and *Those Readheads From Seattle* ('I Guess It Was You All The Time' and 'Baby, Baby, Baby'). He also contributed theme songs to *Shane*, *The Hanging Tree*, *To Kill A Mocking Bird*, *Bachelor In Paradise*, *Hud*, and *The Dirty Dozen* (1967), and added a lyric to Max Steiner's 'Tara's Theme' from *Gone With The Wind*, turning it into 'My Own True Love'. The new version was popularised by Leroy Holmes And His Chorus And Orchestra. David's other notable songs over the years included 'La Vie En Rose', 'Cherry Pink And Apple Blossom White', 'It Must Be Him' (a US and UK hit for Vikki Carr), 'Falling Leaves', 'At The Candlelight Café', 'Johnny Zero', and 'It's Love, Love, Love'. He also wrote the words to several popular television themes, such as *77 Sunset Strip*, *Hawaiian Eye*, *The Roaring Twenties*, *Casper The Friendly Ghost*, and *Surfside 6*. Apart from those already mentioned, his collaborators included Duke Ellington, Joan Whitney, Frankie Carle, Count Basie, Alex Kramer, Henry Mancini, Elmer Bernstein, and Frank DeVol. He was a long-time member of ASCAP and was also inducted into the US Songwriters Hall of Fame.

DAVIS, BENNY

b. 21 August 1895, New York, USA, d. 20 December 1979, Miami, Florida, USA. An important lyricist with a prolific output from the 20s through the 50s, Davis was also a performer of some note. As a youngster, he wrote his own material while touring the leading vaudeville circuits, and then collaborated with C. Francis Reisner and Billy Baskette on the patriotic 'Goodbye, Broadway, Hello France', which was introduced on Broadway in the *Passing Show* of 1917. Three years later, with Con Conrad and J. Russel Robinson, Davis wrote the song that he is probably best-remembered for - 'Margie'. Of all the artists who recorded it, Eddie Cantor had the biggest hit, and 'Margie' became the title of two Hollywood musicals in the 40s, and is as appealing today as when it was first introduced. During the 20s and 30s Davis worked with a variety of composers and co-lyricists, including Milton Ager, Lester Santly, George Price, Abner Silver, Harry Akst, Isham Jones, Abe Lyman, Joe Burke, Mark Fisher, Con Conrad, Arthur Swanstrom, Oscar Levant, Peter De Rose, Harry Tierney, and Al Sherman on numbers such as 'I'm Nobody's Baby', 'Angel Child', 'Say It While Dancing', 'A Smile Will Go A Long, Long Way', 'Indiana Moon', 'Oh, How I Miss You Tonight' (a US number 1 for Ben Selvin), 'Roses Remind Me Of You', 'Yearning (Just For You)', 'Baby Face', 'Lonesome And Sorry', 'Dixiana' (film title song), 'Carolina Moon' (a US number 1 for Gene Austin in 1929, and a UK number 1 for Connie Francis in 1958), 'Who Wouldn't Be Blue?', 'Chasing Shadows', and 'Everything's Gonna Be All Right' (1936). Davis also collaborated with the celebrated composer J. Fred Coots on several songs, including 'Cross Your Fingers' and 'Why (Is There A Rainbow In The Sky)' for the 1929 hit Broadway musical *Sons O' Guns*, and others such as 'I Still Get A Thrill (Thinking Of You)', 'Alabama Barbecue', 'Doin' The Suzi-Q', 'Dream Time', 'Frisco Flo', and 'Until Today' (with Oscar Levant), some of which were featured in the famous Cotton Club revues. In the 40s and early 50s Davis was back with Abner Silver for 'How Green Was My Valley', 'She's A Home Girl', 'It's A Cruel Cruel World', and 'With These Hands', as well as collaborating with Peter De Rose and Mitchell Parish on 'All I Need Is You'. During the remainder of the 50s and early 60s, Davis teamed with Carl Fischer for the title song of the Frankie Laine film *Bring Your Smile Along* (1955), and with Ted Murray (or Murry) for 'There Must Be A Reason', 'Don't Break The Heart That Loves You' (a US number 1 for Connie Francis in 1962), 'Whose Heart Are You Breaking Tonight?', and several numbers, including the title song, for the Connie Francis movie musical Follow The Boys (1963). Also among Davis' impressive catalogue of over a thousand songs are 'That's My Girl', 'It's A Million To One You're In Love', 'Mary Ann', 'So Ashamed', 'I Hate Myself', 'Kiss Me Goodbye', 'Love Tales', 'Yours Is Truly Yours', 'All In Favour Of Swing Say "Aye"', 'A Kiss And A Promise', 'Endless', and There's No Other Girl'. Davis also had extensive business interests, and was renowned for encouraging new talent.

DAVIS, CARL

b. 28 October 1936, Brooklyn, New York, USA. A conductor, and composer, Davis moved to England in 1961, and, after an initial struggle, became a respected figure in films and television during the next 30 years. From 1962, he contributed music to television programmes such as *The Right Prospectus, Mad Jack, The World Of Coppard, Edward II, The Arrangement* (television opera), *The Snowgoose, The Grievance, Hells Angels, Arturo Ui, Catholics, The Merchant Of Venice* (a National Theatre production), *The World At War* (series), *The Pickwick Papers, Prince Regent, Late Starter, The Naked Civil Servant, The Day The Universe Changed, Oscar, Why Lockerbie, The Secret Life Of Ian Fleming, The Accountant, Somewhere To Run, The Far Pavilions, Silas Marner, Hotel Du Lac, Winston Churchill - The Wilderness Years, The Last Romantics, The Crucifer Of Blood, Covington Cross, A Very Polish Practice, Clive James - Fame In The Twentieth Century, A Year In Provence, Genghis Cohn,* and *Hope In The Year Two* (1994). Davis' most memorable work for television, however, is probably his complementary music to *Hollywood*, a major documentary series on the motion picture's formative silent era. His other work in that area included a music score for the 1927 silent *Napoleon*, and 10 more musical pieces to accompany short films made between 1919 and 1924, and released on *The Silents*. He began composing for the talkies in 1967, and his credits have included *The Bofors Gun, Praise Marx And Pass The Ammunition, Up Pompeii, Up The Chastity Belt, What Became Of Jack And Jill, Rentadick, The Lovers, The National Health, The French Lieutenant's Woman* (British Film Academy Award for Davis in 1981), *Champions, King David, The Rainbow, The Girl In A Swing, Scandal* and Roger Corman's *Frankenstein Unbound,* and *Widow's Peak* (1993). In 1985 Davis toured the UK, conducting the Halle Orchestra, the Liverpool Philharmonic, and various other orchestras, in a series of concerts to commemorate the 40th anniversary of VE and VJ days (Victory in Europe and Victory in Japan). The programmes included music composed by Sir William Walton for the film *The Battle Of Britain,* which did not make the final cut. In 1989, Davis provided the incidental music for the London version of the off-Broadway hit play *Steel Magnolias,* and, around the same time, he began collaborating with the world's best-known left-handed guitarist, to create Paul McCartney's Liverpool Oratorio, to mark the 150th anniversary of the Royal Liverpool Philharmonic Society. The piece had its world premiere in the Liverpool Anglican Cathedral in 1991, and featured soloists Dame Kiri Te Kanawa, Jerry Hadley, Sally Burgess and Williard White. Also in 1991, Davis' music accompanied the 'absorbing persuasive' US television film, *Separate But Equal Parts I & II,* and *The Crucifer Of Blood,* in which Charlton Heston was cast, somewhat intriguingly, as Sherlock Holmes.

DAVIS, SAMMY, JNR.

b. 8 December 1925, Harlem, New York, USA, d. 16 May 1990, Los Angeles, California, USA. A dynamic and versatile all-round entertainer, Davis was a trouper in the old-fashioned tradition. The only son of two dancers in a black vaudeville troupe, called Will Mastin's Holiday In Dixieland, Davis made his professional debut with the group at the age of three, as 'Silent Sam, The Dancing Midget'. While still young he was coached by the legendary tap-dancer Bill 'Bojangles' Robinson. Davis left the group in 1943 to serve in the US Army, where he encountered severe racial prejudice for the first, but not the last, time. After the war he rejoined his father and adopted uncle in the Will Mastin Trio. By 1950 the Trio were headlining at venues such as the Capitol in New York and Ciro's in Hollywood with stars including Jack Benny and Bob Hope, but it was Davis who was receiving the standing ovations for his singing, dancing, drumming, comedy and apparently inexhaustible energy. In 1954 he signed for Decca Records, and released two albums, *Starring Sammy Davis Jr.* (number 1 in the US chart), featuring his impressions of stars such as Dean Martin, Jerry Lewis, Johnnie Ray and Jimmy Durante, and *Just For Lovers*. He also made the US singles chart with 'Hey There' from The Pajama Game, and in the same year he lost his left eye in a road accident. When he returned to performing in January 1955 wearing an eye patch, he was greeted even more enthusiastically than before. During that year he reached the US Top 20 with 'Something's Gotta Give', 'Love Me Or Leave Me' and 'That Old Black Magic'. In 1956 he made his Broadway debut in the musical *Mr Wonderful,* with music and lyrics by Jerry Bock, Larry Holofcener and George Weiss. Also in the show were the rest of the Will Mastin Trio, Sammy's uncle and Davis Snr. The show ran for nearly 400 performances and produced two hits, 'Too Close For Comfort', and the title song, which was very successful for Peggy Lee. Although generally regarded as the first popular American black performer to become acceptable to both black and white audiences, Davis attracted heavy criticism in 1956 over his conversion to Judaism, and later for his marriage to Swedish actress Mai Britt. He described himself as a 'one-eyed Jewish nigger'. Apart from a few brief appearances when he was very young, Davis started his film career in 1958 with *Anna Lucasta,* and was critically acclaimed the following year for his performance as Sporting Life in Porgy And Bess. By this time Davis was a leading member of Frank Sinatra's 'inner circle', called, variously, the 'Clan' or the 'Rat Pack'. He appeared with Sinatra in three movies, *Ocean's Eleven* (1960), *Sergeants Three* (1962), and *Robin And The Seven Hoods* (1964), but made, perhaps, a greater impact when he co-starred with another member of the 'Clan', Shirley MacLaine, in the Cy Coleman and Dorothy Fields film musical Sweet Charity. The 60s were good times for Davis, who was enormously popular on records and television, but especially 'live', at Las Vegas and in concert. In 1962 he made the US chart with the Anthony Newley/Leslie Bricusse number 'What Kind Of Fool Am I?', and thereafter featured several of their songs in his act. He sang Bricusse's nominated song, 'Talk To The Animals', at the 1967 Academy Awards ceremony, and collected the Oscar on behalf of the songwriter when it won. In 1972, he had a million-selling hit record with another Newley/Bricusse song, 'The Candy Man', from the film *Willy Wonka And The Chocolate Factory*. He appeared again on Broadway in 1964 in Golden Boy, Charles Strouse and Lee Adams' musical adaptation of Clifford Odet's 1937 drama of a young man torn between the boxing ring and his violin. Also in the cast was Billy Daniels. The show ran for 569 performances in New York, and went to London in 1968. During the 70s Davis worked less, suffering, allegedly, as a result of previous alcohol and drug abuse. He entertained US troops in the Lebanon in 1983, and five years later undertook an arduous comeback tour of the USA and Canada with Sinatra and Dean Martin. In 1989 he travelled further, touring Europe with the show *The Ultimate Event*, along with Liza Minnelli and Sinatra. While he was giving everything to career favourites such as 'Birth Of The Blues', 'Mr Bojangles' and 'That Old Black Magic', he was already ill, although it was not apparent to audiences. After his death in 1990 it was revealed that his estate was almost worthless. In 1992, an all-star tribute, led by Liza Minnelli, was mounted at the Royal Albert Hall in London, the city that had always welcomed him. Proceeds from the concert went to the Royal Marsden Cancer Appeal.

● ALBUMS: *Starring Sammy Davis Jr.* (Decca 1955)★★★, *Just For Lovers* (Decca 1955)★★★, *Mr. Wonderful* film soundtrack (Decca 1956)★★, *Here's Looking At You* (Decca 1956)★★★, with Carmen McRae *Boy Meets Girl* (1957)★★★, *Sammy Swings* (Decca 1957)★★★★, *It's All Over But The Swingin'* (Decca 1957)★★★★, *Mood To Be Wooed* (Decca 1958)★★★, *All The Way And Then Some* (Decca 1958)★★★★, *Sammy Davis Jr. At Town Hall* (Decca 1959)★★★★, *Porgy And Bess* (Decca 1959)★★★, *I Got A Right To Swing* (Decca 1960)★★★★, *Sammy Awards* (Decca 1960)★★★, *What Kind Of Fool Am I And Other Show-Stoppers* (Reprise 1962)★★★★, *Sammy Davis Jr. At The Cocoanut Grove* (Reprise 1963)★★★★, *Johnny Cool* film soundtrack (United Artists 1963)★★★, *As Long As She Needs Me* (Reprise 1963)★★★, *Sammy Davis Jr. Salutes The Stars Of The London Palladium* (Reprise 1964)★★★, *The Shelter Of Your Arms* (Reprise 1964)★★★, *Golden Boy* film soundtrack (Capitol 1964)★★, with Count Basie *Our Shining Hour* (Verve 1965)★★★, *Sammy's Back On Broadway* (Reprise 1965)★★★, *A Man Called Adam* film soundtrack (Reprise 1966)★★, *I've Gotta Be Me* (Reprise 1969)★★★, *Sammy Davis Jr. Now* (MGM 1972)★★★, *Portrait Of Sammy Davis Jr.* (MGM 1972)★★★, *It's A Musical World* (MGM 1976)★★★, *The Song And Dance Man* (20th Century 1977)★★★★, *Sammy Davis Jr. In Person 1977* (RCA 1983)★★★, *Closest Of Friends* (Vogue 1984)★★★.

● COMPILATIONS: *The Best Of Sammy Davis Jr.* (MCA 1982)★★★, *Collection* (Castle 1989)★★★, *The Great Sammy Davis Jr.* (MFP 1989)★★★, *Capitol Collectors Series* (Capitol 1990)★★★.

● VIDEOS: *Mr Bojangles* (Decca/PolyGram Music Video 1991).

● FURTHER READING: *Yes I Can: The Story Of Sammy Davis Jr.*, Sammy Davis Jr. *Hollywood In A Suitcase*, Sammy Davis Jr. *Why Me: The Autobiography Of Sammy Davis Jr.*, Sammy Davis Jr. with Burt Boyar.

● FILMS: The *Benny Goodman Story* (1956), *Anna Lucasta* (1958), *Porgy And Bess* (1959), *Pepe* (1960), *Ocean's Eleven* (1960), *Convicts Four* (1962), *Sergeants Three* (1962), *Johnny Cool* (1963), *The Threepenny Opera* (1963), *Robin And The Seven Hoods* (1964), *Nightmare In The Sun* (1964), *A Man Called Adam* (1966), *Salt And Pepper* (1968), *Man Without Mercy* (1969), *Sweet Charity* (1969), *One More Time* (1970), *Diamonds Are Forever* (1972), *Save The Children* concert film (1973), *Stop The World - I Want To Get Off* (1978), *The Cannonball Run II* (1984), *Moon Over Parador* (1988), *Tap* (1989).

DAY, DORIS

b. Doris Von Kappelhoff, 3 April 1922, Cincinnati, Ohio, USA. One of popular music's premier post-war vocalists and biggest names, Kappelhoff originally trained as a dancer, before turning to singing at the age of 16. After changing her surname to Day, she became the featured singer with the Bob Crosby Band. A similarly successful period with the Les Brown Band saw her record a single for Columbia, 'Sentimental Journey', which sold in excess of a million copies. Already an accomplished businesswoman, it was rumoured that she held a substantial shareholding in her record company. After securing the female lead in the 1948 film Romance On The High Seas, in which she introduced Sammy Cahn and Jule Styne's 'It's Magic', she enjoyed a stupendous movie career. Her striking looks, crystal-clear singing voice and willingness to play tomboy heroines, as well as romantic figures, brought her a huge following. In common with other female singers of the period, she was occasionally teamed with the stars of the day and enjoyed collaborative hits with Frankie Laine ('Sugarbush') and Johnnie Ray ('Let's Walk That A-Way'). She appeared in nearly 40 movies over two decades, including *It's A Great Feeling* (1949), Young Man With A Horn (1950), *Tea For Two* (1950), *West Point Story* (1950), *Lullaby Of Broadway* (1951), *On Moonlight Bay* (1951), *Starlift* (1951), *I'll See You In My Dreams* (1951), *April In Paris* (1952), *By The Light Of The Silvery Moon* (1953), Calamity Jane (1953), Young At Heart (1954), *Love Me Or Leave Me* (1955), *The Man Who Knew Too Much* (1956), *The Pajama Game* (1957), *Pillow Talk* (1959) and *Jumbo* (1962). These films featured some of her best-known hits. One of her finest performances was in the uproarious romantic western Calamity Jane, which featured her enduringly vivacious versions of 'The Deadwood Stage' and 'Black Hills Of Dakota'. The movie also gave her a US/UK number 1 single with the yearningly sensual 'Secret Love' (later a lesser hit for Kathy Kirby). Day enjoyed a further UK chart topper with the romantically uplifting 'Whatever Will Be Will Be (Que Sera, Sera)'. After a gap of nearly six years, she returned to the charts with the sexually inviting movie theme 'Move Over Darling', co-written by her producer son Terry Melcher. Her Hollywood career ended in the late 60s and thereafter she was known for her reclusiveness. After more than 20 years away from the public's gaze, she emerged into the limelight in 1993 for a charity screening of *Calamity Jane* in her home-town of Carmel, California. Two years later she made further appearances to promote *The Love Album*, which was recorded in 1967 but had been 'lost' since that time and never released. An earlier effort to remind her fans of the good old days came in the early 90s, when Leo P. Carusone and Patsy Carver's songbook revue *Definitely Doris* began its life as a cabaret at New York's Duplex. The show subsequently had its 'world premiere' at the King's Head Theatre, Islington, north London, before returning to the USA and entertaining audiences at Boston's 57 Theatre with a host of memorable numbers such as 'Ten Cents A Dance', 'Secret Love', 'When I Fall In Love', 'It's Magic', and the rest. In 1998, a British-born celebration of Doris Day and her work starred popular singer Rosemary Squires, who created the project with Helen Ash, wife of musician Vic Ash. History has made her an icon; her fresh-faced looks, sensual innocence and strikingly pure vocal style effectively summed up an era of American music.

● ALBUMS: *You're My Thrill* (Columbia 1949)★★, *Young Man With A Horn* film soundtrack (Columbia 1950/54)★★, *Tea For Two* film soundtrack (Columbia 1950)★★, *Lullaby Of Broadway* film soundtrack (Columbia 1951)★★, *On Moonlight Bay* film soundtrack (Columbia 1951)★★★, *I'll See You In My Dreams* film soundtrack (Columbia 1951)★★★, *By The Light Of The Silvery Moon* film soundtrack (Columbia 1953)★★★, *Calamity Jane* film soundtrack (Columbia 1953)★★★★, *Young At Heart* (Columbia 1954)★★★★, *Lights Camera Action* (Columbia 1955)★★★, *Boys And Girls Together* (Columbia 1955)★★★, with Peggy Lee *Hot Canaries* (Columbia 1955)★★★, *Lullaby Of Broadway* (Columbia 1955)★★★★, *Day Dreams* (Columbia 1955)★★★, *Day In Hollywood* (Columbia 1955)★★★, *Love Me Or Leave Me* film soundtrack (Columbia 1955)★★★★, *Day By Day* (Columbia 1957)★★★★, *Day By Night* (Columbia 1957)★★★, *The Pajama Game* film soundtrack (Columbia 1957)★★★★, *Hooray For Hollywood* (Columbia 1958)★★★, *Cuttin' Capers* (Columbia 1959)★★★, *Show Time* (Columbia 1960)★★★, *What Every Girl Should Know* (Columbia 1960)★★★, *Listen To Day* (Columbia 1960)★★★, *Bright & Shiny* (Columbia 1961)★★, *I Have Dreamed* (Columbia 1961)★★★, *Love Him!* (Columbia 1964)★★★, *Sentimental Journey* (Columbia 1965)★★★, *Latin For Lovers* (Columbia 1965)★★, *The Love Album* 1967 recordings (1994)★★★★.

● COMPILATIONS: *Doris Day's Greatest Hits* (Columbia 1958)★★★★, *Golden Greats* (Warwick 1978)★★★, *The Best Of Doris Day* (Columbia 1980)★★★★, *It's Magic* 6-CD box set (Bear Family 1993)★★★★, *Hit Singles Collection* (Telstar 1994)★★★★, *Personal Christmas Collection* (1994)★★★, *The Magic Of Doris Day* (Sony 1994)★★★★, *Move Over Darling* 8-CD set (Bear Family 1997)★★★, *The Complete Doris Day With Les Brown* 2-CD set (Sony Music Special Products 1997)★★★.

● VIDEOS: *Magic Of Doris Day* (Warner Home Video 1989).

● FURTHER READING: *Doris Day: Her Own Story*, Doris Day and A.E. Hotcher. *Doris Day*, Eric Braun.

● FILMS: *Romance On The High Seas* (1948), *It's A Great Feeling* (1949), *My Dream Is Yours* (1949), *West Point Story* (1950), *Tea For Two* (1950), *Young Man With A Horn* (1950), *Starlift* cameo (1951), *I'll See You In My Dreams* (1951), *On Moonlight Bay* (1951), *Lullaby Of Broadway* (1951), *Storm Warning* (1951), *April In Paris* (1952), *The Winning Team* (1952), *Calamity Jane* (1953), *By The Light Of The Silvery Moon* (1953), *Lucky Me* (1954), *Young At Heart* (1954), *Love Me Or Leave Me* (1955), *Julie* (1956), *The Man Who Knew Too Much* (1956), *The Pajama Game* (1957), *Teacher's Pet* (1958), *Tunnel Of Love* (1958), *Pillow Talk* (1959), *It Happened To Jane* (1959), *Midnight Lace* (1960), *Please Don't Eat The Daisies* (1960), *That Touch Of Mink* (1962), *Jumbo* (1962), *Lover Come Back* (1962), *Move Over Darling* (1963), *The Thrill Of It All* (1963), *Send Me No Flowers* (1964), *Do Not Disturb* (1965), *The Glass Bottom Boat* (1966), *Caprice* (1967), *With Six You Get Eggroll* (1968), *Where Were You When The Lights Went Out?* (1968), *The Ballad Of Josie* (1968).

DAY, FRANCES

b. Frances Victoria Schenck, 16 December c. 1907, East Orange, New Jersey, USA, d. 29 April 1984, England. An actress and singer, whose glamorous image and appealing voice with its provocative, squeaky inflection, made her an incandescent star of the London stage in the 30s and 40s. While appearing as a dancer in Texas Guinan's famous New York speakeasy in 1924, Frances Schenck was spotted by entrepreneur Beaumont Alexander, who changed her name, and took her to London. In 1925 he managed to get her into the chorus of Rose-Marie at the Theatre Royal, Drury Lane, and two years later they were married. After gaining quite a reputation as a night club performer in London and on the Continent, Day appeared in provincial productions of two musical comedies, *Little Tommy Tucker* (1930) and Fifty Million Frenchmen (1931). In 1932, she finally arrived in the West End in the book musical, *Out Of The Bottle*, the first of several shows in which she co-starred with the comic actor Arthur Riscoe. In *Out Of The Bottle*, they duetted on the attractive 'I've Got The Moon And Sixpence'. From then on, until the mid-40s, Day lit up the London stage in a mixture of musical comedies and revues. *How D'You Do?*, in 1933, was followed a year later by *Jill Darling*, the show which confirmed her as a major star. Among her songs was Vivian Ellis's delightful 'Dancing With A Ghost'. Also in the cast (as well as Arthur Riscoe), was John Mills, and he subsequently joined Day for the 1937 revue, *Floodlight*, in which they sang several more Ellis numbers, including 'A Little White Room'. In *The Fleet's Lit Up* (1938) Day introduced Cole Porter's 'It's De-Lovely' to London audiences. During the next few years she was associated with several other memorable songs, such as 'Music Maestro Please' (from *These Foolish Things*, 1939), 'My Love For You' (*Black And Blue*, 1939), and Michael Carr and Eric Maschwitz's tribute to the Royal Air Force, 'A Pair Of Silver Wings', which she sang in the 1941 George Black revue, *Black Vanities*. During World War II, Day entertained the troops at home and abroad, as well as working regularly in the recording studio and on radio, and appearing in the London production of Du Barry Was A Lady (1942). Shortly after the end of the war, Day starred in *Evangeline* (1946), an adaptation of Nymph Errant, but without Cole Porter's songs. It folded after only 32 performances, and marked the beginning of Day's decline. In 1949, she left the cast of the revue, *Latin Quarter*, at the London Casino to appear in Bernard Shaw's play, *Buoyant Billions*, but the results were disappointing. In the mid-50s she is said to have toured with an act called A Day And Her Knights. Around this time, she cut some tracks for HMV Records, which included the single 'The Wheels Of Love'/'Why Did The Chicken Cross The Road?'. Even before she rose to fame, Day began making a number of films. They were mostly crime features and comedies, but among them was the occasional musical, such as *Public Nuisance No. 1* (1936), in which she sang Vivian Ellis's risqué 'Me And My Dog'. She also co-starred with Tommy Trinder, Sonnie Hale, and Francis L. Sullivan, in an entertaining Roman fantasy romp entitled *Fiddlers Three* (1944). Shortly after her last film, *Climb Up The Wall*, was released in 1960, Day began refusing to acknowledge her previous career. She changed her name to Frankie Day, and often passed herself off as 'Frances Day's daughter'. She continued to perform for a time, and her final stage appearance is thought to have been in 1965 with Bob Monkhouse at London's Jeannetta Cochrane

Theatre in *The Gulls*, in an English version of an eighteenth-century French satirical comedy. In her later years she lived as a recluse just outside London. She was heard briefly again on the screen in 1981, when her recording of the jaunty 'When My Little Pomeranian Met Your Little Pekinese', which she made with Al Bowlly in 1933, was played in the Donald Sutherland movie, *Eye Of The Needle*.

● ALBUMS: *Rose-Marie* studio cast (RCA 1960)★★★.
● FILMS: *The Price Of Divorce* (1927, not released, extracts shown in *Such Is The Law* 1930), *O.K. Chief* (1930), *Big Business* (1930), *The First Mrs Frazer* (1932), *Two Hearts In Waltztime* (1934), *The Girl From Maxim's* (1934), *Temptation* (1934), *Oh Daddy!* (1934), *Public Nuisance No. 1* (1936), *You Must Get Married* (1936), *Dreams Come True* (1936), *Who's Your Lady Friend?* (1937), *The Girl In The Taxi* (1937), *Kicking The Moon Around* (1938), *Room For Two* (1940), *Fiddlers Three* (1944), *Tread Softly* (1952), *There's Always Thursday* (1957), *Climb Up The Wall* (1960).

DE HAVEN, GLORIA

b. 23 July 1924, Los Angeles, California, USA. An accomplished actress and singer, with a fine voice and style and a glamorous personality who appeared in several movie musicals in the 40s and 50s. Her parents were the popular stage entertainers the Carter De Havens, and Gloria entered showbusiness while she was quite young. In the early 40s she sang with acclaimed dancebands lead by names such as Jan Savitt, and was employed as an extra in the Charlie Chaplin films *Modern Times* and *The Great Dictator*. After playing some bit parts, she signed to MGM and made her first impression in Best Foot Forward (1943), and, in the same year, took part in the all-star extravaganza Thousands Cheer. During the rest of the 40s she had mostly good roles in musicals such as *Broadway Rhythm*, *Two Girls And A Sailor*, *Step Lively*, Summer Holiday, and *Yes Sir That's My Baby* (1949), as well as playing several solely dramatic parts. In 1950 Gloria De Haven portrayed her mother and sang 'Who's Sorry Now' in the biopic of songwriters Bert Kalmar and Harry Ruby, and followed that with appearances in Summer Stock, *I'll Get By*, *Two Tickets To Broadway*, *Down Among The Sheltering Palms*, So This Is Paris, and *The Girl Rush* (1955). With the advent of rock 'n' roll, musical films underwent some radical changes in the late 50s, so De Haven turned to television and stage work. In 1955 she co-starred with Ricardo Montalban on Broadway in *Seventh Heaven*, a musical version of the 1927 Janet Gaynor-Charles Farrell silent film classic. In the 70s she was still appearing in dramatic parts in films and US television series. In 1989 she re-launched her career as a cabaret singer at the Rainbow & Stars in New York, where she sang saloon songs and talked of her vaudevillian parents who launched her career so many years ago. It is not reported whether she dwelt on the subject of her several husbands, one of whom was another film star of the golden era of movie musicals, John Payne.

DE MILLE, AGNES

b. 18 September 1905, New York City, New York, USA, d. 6 October 1993, Greenwich Village, New York, USA. An important and influential choreographer, director, and dancer, who 'helped transform the American musical theatre of the 40s and 50s'. After graduating with honours from the University of California, Agnes de Mille gave her first solo dance recital in 1928 at the Republic Theatre in New York. A year later she arranged the choreography for a revival of *The Black Crook* in Hoboken, New Jersey, and subsequently spent several years in London studying the ballet. In 1933 she arranged and staged the dances for Charles B. Cochran's production of Nymph Errant at the Adelphi Theatre in London, and later returned to America to work on shows such as *Hooray For What!* and *Swinging The Dream*, and the film, *Romeo And Juliet*. In 1939 she joined the Ballet Theatre in New York and choreographed productions such as *Black Ritual*, *Three Virgins And A Devil*, and Aaron Copland's *Rodeo*. Her work for the last-named, in which she herself danced the leading role, was highly acclaimed and led to her being hired for Richard Rodgers and Oscar Hammerstein II's first musical, Oklahoma! (1943). Her skilful blending of classical and modern dance which enhanced and developed the show's story, was highlighted by the 'Dream Ballet' sequence, a feature that became the benchmark for many a future musical. The list of her subsequent Broadway assignments, mainly as a choreographer, but occasionally as a director, included One Touch Of Venus (1943), Bloomer Girl, Carousel, Brigadoon, Allegro, Gentlemen Prefer Blondes, *Out Of This World* (1950), Paint Your Wagon, *The Girl In Pink Tights*, Goldilocks, *Juno*, *Kwamina*, 110 In the Shade, and *Come Summer* (1969). Throughout her long and distinguished career Agnes de Mille received many awards, including two Tonys (for *Brigadoon* and *Kwamina*), and numerous other honours and citations. In her best work, her 'gift for narrative dance not only told stories, but each step and gesture came out of an individualized concept of each character's motivation. Her treatment of dancers as individual characters enabled the chorus dancers to become actors in the play'. As well as the Broadway shows, she maintained a full and satisfying career in ballet, performing directing and choreographing, and continued to work even after suffering a stroke in 1975 which left her partially paralysed. Her two final ballets were *The Informer* (1988) and *The Other* (1992).
● FURTHER READING: *Dance To The Piper. And Promenade Home. To A Young Dancer. Book Of The Dance. Speak To Me, Dance With Me*, all by Agnes de Mille. *No Intermissions*, Carol Easton.

DE PAUL, GENE

b. Gene Vincent De Paul, 17 June 1919, New York, USA, d. 27 February 1988, Northridge, California, USA. A pianist, arranger and composer for films during the 40s and 50s, early in his career De Paul performed as a pianist-singer, and also wrote arrangements for vocal groups, before starting to compose in 1940. One of his first published songs was 'Your Red Wagon', written in collaboration with lyricist Don Raye and Richard M. Jones, and based on an instrumental blues theme by Jones. It was sung by Marie Bryant in the RKO film *They Live By Night* (1949), and became a hit for the Andrews Sisters and Ray McKinley. Some years before that, in 1941, the Andrews Sisters, together with Abbott and Costello, and singers Dick Powell and Dick Foran, were the stars of *In The Navy*, the first of many, mostly small-scale, musical movies to which

De Paul and Raye contributed songs during the 40s. *In The Navy* featured songs such as 'Starlight, Starbright', 'A Sailor's Life For Me', 'You're Off To See The World' and 'Hu Ba Lua'. This was immediately followed by *San Antonio Rose* ('Mexican Jumping Beat' and 'You've Got What It Takes'), *Moonlight In Hawaii* ('Aloha Low Down' and 'It's People Like You') and *Keep 'Em Flying* ('You Don't Know What Love Is' and 'Pig Foot Pete'). In the following year, Hellzapoppin', the film adaptation of Olsen and Johnson's successful Broadway musical, included the zany 'Watch The Birdie'. The film's other new songs from De Paul and Raye included 'Putting On The Dog', 'What Kind Of Love Is This?' and 'You Were There'. Also in 1942, De Paul and Raye contributed numbers to *Get Hep To Love* ('Heaven For Two'); *What's Cookin'* ('If' and 'Love Laughs At Anything'), featuring Woody Herman's Band and the Andrews Sisters; and *Ride 'Em Cowboy*, one of the top Abbott and Costello movies which included 'Wake Up Jacob', 'Beside The River Tonto', 'Rockin' and Reelin'' and 'I'll Remember April'. The co-writer on the latter was teenager Patricia Johnston, who died in 1953. The song later became a much-recorded number by artists such as June Christy and Julie London. Other De Paul projects around this time included *Almost Married* ('Just To Be Near You' and 'Mister Five By Five', a novelty number said to have been inspired by the generously built blues singer Jimmy Rushing); *Pardon My Sarong*, another Abbott and Costello vehicle,('Island Of The Moon', 'Lovely Luana' and 'Vingo Jingo'), and *Behind The Eight Ball* ('Don't You Think We Ought To Dance?', 'Riverboat Jamboree' and 'Wasn't It Wonderful?'). After writing 'He's My Guy', a hit for Harry James, which was included in *Hi Ya Chum* (1943), De Paul and Raye briefly turned their attention to World War II with *When Johnny Comes Marching Home* ('This Is It', and 'Say It With Dancing') and *Hi Buddy* ('We're In The Navy'). Another film with a wartime theme was Reveille With Beverly (1943), which starred Frank Sinatra, and featured several musical stars such as the Mills Brothers, Freddie Slack, Bob Crosby and Count Basie. Also in the movie, Ella Mae Morse sang 'Cow-Cow Boogie', written by De Paul, Raye and Benny Carter, and her version became the first release for the newly-formed Capitol label. Other 1943 songs by De Paul and Raye included 'Ain't That Just Like A Man' and 'Short, Fat and 4F' for *What's Buzzin' Cousin?*; 'They Died With Their Boots Laced' and 'Do You Hear Music?' for *Larceny With Music*; 'Get On Board Little Children' (*Crazy House*), and 'Star Eyes', one of the songwriters' most enduring numbers, sung in *I Dood It* by Bob Eberly and Helen O'Connell with Jimmy Dorsey's Orchestra. In 1944 De Paul and Raye contributed 'I Won't Forget The Dawn' to *Hi Good Lookin'* and 'Where Am I Without You' to *Stars On Parade*. They also enjoyed success with 'Who's That In Your Love Life?', 'Irresistible You' and 'Solid Potato Salad'. 'Milkman, Keep Those Bottles Quiet' (from *Broadway Rhythm*) became a hit for Ella Mae Morse, Woody Herman and the King Sisters. Towards the end of World War II, De Paul spent two years in the Armed Forces. He and Don Raye resumed writing their movie songs in 1947 with 'Who Knows?' for *Wake Up And Dream* and 'Judaline' for *A Date With Judy*. In 1948 they contributed to A Song Is Born, Danny Kaye's last film for

Samuel Goldwyn, and also wrote 'It's Whatcha Do With Whatcha Got' for the Walt Disney live-action feature *So Dear To My Heart*. De Paul and Raye's last film work together was in 1949 for another Disney project, the highly acclaimed cartoon *The Adventures Of Ichabod And Mr Toad*. Bing Crosby was one of the narrators and the songs included 'Ichabod', 'Katrina' and 'The Headless Horseman'. De Paul returned to movie musicals in 1954 with the celebrated Seven Brides For Seven Brothers, an exhilarating, dance-orientated musical, on a par with the best of that genre. The choreography was by Michael Kidd, and Johnny Mercer supplied the lyrics for the songs which included 'Bless Your Beautiful Hide', 'Goin' Courtin'', 'June Bride', 'Spring, Spring, Spring', 'Sobbin' Women', 'When You're In Love', 'Wonderful Day' and 'Lonesome Polecat (Lament)'. In 1956 De Paul and Mercer combined again, on the songs for *You Can't Run Away From It*, based on the 1934 Oscar-winning comedy *It Happened One Night*. The film included numbers such as 'Howdy Friends And Neighbours', 'Temporarily', 'Thumbing a Ride' and 'Scarecrow Ballet'. In the same year, De Paul and Mercer were back on Broadway with the smash hit Li'l Abner, based on Al Capp's famous cartoon character, and his life in Dogpatch, a town designated by the Government as 'the most useless piece of real estate in the USA'. The population's efforts to reverse that decision, and Daisy Mae's persistent pursuit of Abner Yokum, were accompanied by songs such as 'If I Had My Druthers', 'The Country's In The Very Best Of Hands', 'Oh, Happy Day' and 'Jubilation T. Cornpone', with which the ever-ebullient Stubby Kaye regularly stopped the show. Another number, 'Namely You', became popular outside the show which ran for nearly 700 performances, and was transferred to the screen in 1959 with most of its original players. In later years De Paul composed a good deal for television, including music for the popular *Sesame Street* series. His other songs included 'Your Eyes', 'I'm In Love With You', 'I Love To Hear A Choo Choo Train' and 'Teach Me Tonight', which he wrote with Sammy Cahn. The latter was a hit for the De Castro Sisters, Jo Stafford and Dinah Washington. De Paul was inducted into the Songwriters Hall of Fame in 1985, and died three years later following a long illness.

DE SYLVA, BROWN AND HENDERSON

(see De Sylva, Buddy; Brown, Lew; Henderson, Ray)

DE SYLVA, BUDDY

b. George G. De Sylva, 27 January 1895, New York City, New York, USA, d. 11 July 1950. Growing up in Los Angeles, De Sylva worked briefly in vaudeville while still a small child. In school and college he was active in theatrical pursuits, played in bands and wrote song lyrics. In his early 20s, De Sylva began a mutually profitable association with Al Jolson, who sang and recorded songs for which De Sylva wrote the lyrics. He collaborated with several composers including Jolson, George Gershwin, Rudolf Friml and Jerome Kern. His first hit was with Kern, 'Look For The Silver Lining', published in 1920. The following year Jolson introduced De Sylva's 'April Showers' (music by Louis Silvers) and in 1924, in his show, *Bombo*,

Jolson sang 'California, Here I Come' (Jolson as co-lyricist, music by Joseph Meyer). Again with Jolson and Meyer, De Sylva wrote 'If You Knew Susie', and another popular success of the mid-20s was 'Keep Smiling At Trouble' (Jolson and Lewis E. Gensler). This same period saw De Sylva writing lyrics, often with other lyricists, to many of George Gershwin's compositions. These included 'I'll Build A Stairway To Paradise' (co-lyricist Ira Gershwin), 'Somebody Loves Me' (Ballard MacDonald), 'Why Do I Love You?' (Ira Gershwin) and 'Do It Again'. He also wrote lyrics to music by Victor Herbert, ('A Kiss In The Dark') and James F. Hanley, ('Just A Cottage Small By A Waterfall'). In 1925 De Sylva began his most fruitful association when he teamed up with composer Ray Henderson and lyricist Lew Brown. Their first success, again introduced by Jolson, was 'It All Depends On You'. Following this, and mostly written for the popular Broadway shows such as Good News, Hold Everything, Follow Through, Flying High, and some of the annual editions of George White's Scandals, came 'The Birth Of The Blues', 'Black Bottom', 'Life Is Just A Bowl Of Cherries', 'Good News', 'The Best Things In Life Are Free', 'The Varsity Drag', 'Luck In Love', 'Broadway', 'You're The Cream In My Coffee', 'Button Up Your Overcoat', 'My Lucky Star', 'Sonny Boy' (written for Jolson's 1928 early talkie, The Singing Fool), 'Aren't We All', 'An Old-fashioned Girl', 'My Sin' and 'If I Had A Talking Picture Of You.' The trio's involvement with talking pictures grew, and from 1929-31 they wrote songs for Sunny Side Up, Say It With Songs, In Old Arizona, Just Imagine, Show Girl In Hollywood, and Indiscreet. They also formed a music publishing house to market their own compositions and those of other songwriters. In 1931 De Sylva split from Brown and Henderson, opting to continue working in films while they wanted to concentrate on writing for the New York stage. The careers of the three songwriters was the subject of The Best Things In Life Are Free, a Hollywood biopic released in 1956. After the split, De Sylva became involved in motion picture production, being successful with a string of musicals featuring child-star Shirley Temple. During the years he was involved in production he still wrote lyrics, but inevitably with much less frequency. At the end of the 30s, De Sylva, too, was in New York, where he engaged in theatrical production, enjoying considerable success with several hit musicals. In addition to producing, De Sylva also co-wrote the books for some of the shows, including Cole Porter's DuBarry Was A Lady (1939) and Panama Hattie (1940). In the early 40s De Sylva returned to film production in Hollywood. In 1942 he teamed up with Glen Wallichs and Johnny Mercer to found Capitol Records. He died, eight years later, in July 1950.

DEAREST ENEMY

Richard Rodgers and Lorenz Hart had interpolated songs into two Broadway shows, Poor Litle Ritz Girl and The Garrick Gaieties, before writing the complete score for this, their first book musical. Dearest Enemy opened at New York's Knickerbocker Theatre on 18 September 1925, with a book by Herbert Fields which was set at the time of the American Revolution of the 18th century, and based

on a supposedly true incident in which a Mrs. Robert Murray (Flavia Arcaro) delayed the British general, Sir William Howe (Harold Crane), by 'using her feminine charms', thereby enabling General Putnam's forces to join those of General Washington's on Harlem Heights. The other, more conventional love interest was provided by the English Captain Sir John Copeland (Charles Purcell) and an Irish-American girl, Betsy Burke (Helen Ford), who meet when her modesty is preserved only by a barrel (she has just emerged from a swimming pool), and later tell of their love for each other in the duet 'Here In My Arms'. That song, and the rest of the score, was a complete delight. Even this early in their partnership Hart was writing such literate, witty and relevant lyrics to Rodgers' surprising and tender melodies. 'Here In My Arms' became popular in recordings by the orchestras of Jack Shilkret and Leo Reisman, and the rest of the score included 'Bye And Bye', 'Cheerio', 'War Is War', 'I Beg Your Pardon', 'The Hermits', 'Where The Hudson River Flows', 'I'd Like To Hide It', 'Sweet Peter', 'Old Enough To Love', and 'Here's A Kiss'. Dearest Enemy was staged by John Murray Anderson, one of Broadway's most innovative directors, and ran for 286 performances.

DEE, KIKI

b. Pauline Matthews, 6 March 1947, Bradford, England. Having begun her career in local dancebands, this popular vocalist made her recording debut in 1963 with the Mitch Murray-penned 'Early Night'. Its somewhat perfunctory pop style was quickly replaced by a series of releases modelled on US producer Phil Spector before Kiki achieved notoriety for excellent interpretations of contemporary soul hits, including Tami Lynn's 'I'm Gonna Run Away From You' and Aretha Franklin's 'Runnin' Out Of Fools'. Her skilled interpretations secured a recording deal with Tamla/Motown Records, the first white British act to be so honoured. However, although lauded artistically, Kiki was unable to attain due commercial success, and the despondent singer sought cabaret work in Europe and South Africa. Her career was revitalized in 1973 on signing up with Elton John's Rocket label. He produced her 'comeback' set, Loving And Free, which spawned a UK Top 20 entry in 'Amoureuse', while Dee subsequently scored further chart success with 'I Got The Music In Me' (1974) and 'How Glad I Am' (1975), fronting the Kiki Dee Band - Jo Partridge (guitar), Bias Boshell (piano), Phil Curtis (bass) and Roger Pope (drums). Her duet with John, 'Don't Go Breaking My Heart', topped the UK and US charts in 1976, and despite further minor UK hits, the most notable of which was 'Star', which reached number 13 in 1981, this remains her best-known performance. She took a tentative step into acting by appearing in the London stage musical, Pump Boys And Dinettes in 1984. Kiki Dee's career underwent yet another regeneration in 1987 with Angel Eyes, which was co-produced by David A. Stewart of the Eurythmics. She has since appeared in Willy Russell's award-winning musical, Blood Brothers in London's West End, and was nominated for an Laurence Olivier Award for her performance in 1989. In 1993 she had a number 2 single with Elton John, 'True Love'. Almost Naked, released in 1995, was her 'unplugged' album and although commercial success continued to elude her it was one of her best albums. Notable tracks were Joni Mitchell's 'Carey' and a slowed down reworking of 'Don't Go Breaking My Heart' which gave the song greater depth than the earlier version.

● ALBUMS: *I'm Kiki Dee* (Fontana 1968)★★, *Great Expectations* (Tamla Motown 1970)★★, *Loving And Free* (Rocket 1973)★★★, *I've Got The Music In Me* (Rocket 1974)★★★, *Kiki Dee* (Rocket 1977)★★★, *Stay With Me* (Rocket 1979)★★★, *Perfect Timing* (Ariola 1980)★★, *Angel Eyes* (Columbia 1987)★★★, *Almost Naked* (Tickety-Boo 1995)★★★.

● COMPILATIONS: *Patterns* (Philips International 1974)★★★, *Kiki Dee's Greatest Hits* (Warwick 1980)★★★, *The Very Best Of Kiki Dee* (Rocket 1994)★★★.

● FILMS: *Dateline Diamonds* (1965).

DEEP IN MY HEART

This film biography of Sigmund Romberg, the composer of more than 50 American stage musicals, was released by MGM in 1954. José Ferrer, who had distinguished himself in movies such as *Joan Of Arc*, *Cyrano De Bergerac*, and *Moulin Rouge*, played Romberg with Doe Avedon as his wife. The screenplay, by Leonard Spigelgass, traced the composer's life from his early days as a musician in a New York café run by Anna Mueller (Helen Traubel), through to his many and varied Broadway triumphs. Among the cast were Walter Pidgeon as J.J. Shubert, the youngest brother of the powerful trio of theatrical producers, Merle Oberon as lyricist Dorothy Donnelly, one of Romberg's principal collaborators, and Paul Henreid, who played impresario Florenz Ziegfeld. Other parts were taken by Tamara Toumanova, Jim Backus and Paul Stewart. What must have been an almost impossible task of selecting musical highlights from such a prolific output, resulted in sequences in which Gene Kelly and his brother, Fred, dance together for the first time on film in 'I Love To Go Swimmin' With Wimmen''; Ann Miller's scintillating dance to 'It'; Ferrer and his real-life wife, actress-singer Rosemary Clooney, with 'Mr. And Mrs.'; Ferrer again in another duet, this time with Helen Traubel, on 'Leg Of Mutton'; and Tony Martin and Joan Weldon's lovely version of 'Lover, Come Back To Me'. One particularly memorable scene had Ferrer taking all the roles in an hilarious musical comedy spoof, *Jazz A Doo*. Squeezed into the film's running time of more than two hours were many more of Romberg's wonderful songs, including 'The Road To Paradise', 'Softly, As In a Morning Sunrise', 'Stouthearted Men', 'Serenade', 'One Alone', 'Your Land And My Land', 'You Will Remember Vienna', 'When I Grow Too Old To Dream', 'One Kiss', 'Auf Wiedersehn', and of course, 'Deep In My Heart'. The list of guest artists featured such illustrious names as Howard Keel, Vic Damone, Jane Powell, Cyd Charisse, James Mitchell and William Ovis. The choreographer was Eugene Loring, and the film, which was shot in Eastman Color, was directed by Stanley Donen. Not a box-office blockbuster by any means, but a diverting film for all that.

DELERUE, GEORGES

b. 12 March 1925, Roubaix, France, d. 20 March 1992, Los Angeles, California, USA. An important composer of film music for well over 150 features, from the early 50s through to the 90s. Delerue won a scholarship to the prestigious Paris Conservatoire, where he was encouraged to develop his interest in music for the screen. In 1952 Delerue composed new scores for two early 20s silent films, *Le Chapeau De Paille De'Italie* and *Les Deux Timides*, and, in 1956, he served as musical director for a series of short films by Alain Resnais, and then for Raymond Rouleau's *The Witches Of Salem* (1957). Two years later he co-composed the scores for *Le Bel Age* (with Alain Goraguer), and *Hiroshima Mon Amour* (with Giovanni Fusco). In 1960 Delerue made *Shoot The Piano Player*, the first of a celebrated series of films with Francois Truffaut, one of France's premier 'new wave' directors. Their other collaborations included *Jules And Jim*; *Love At Twenty*; *The Soft Skin*; *Two English Girls* (in which Delerue made a cameo appearance); *Such A Gorgeous Kid Like Me*; *Day For Night* (Oscar for Best Foreign Language Film (1973)); *Love On The Run*; *The Last Metro*; *The Woman Next Door*; and *Confidentially Yours* (1983). In 1961 Delerue began another important association with director Philippe De Broca, lasting some 16 films. These included *Five Day Lover (Time Out For Love)*; *The Joker*; *Cartouche*; *That Man From Rio*; *Up To His Ears*; *King Of Hearts*, which became a cult item; *Practice Makes Perfect* (1978).

In the early 60s Delerue's career developed further with his involvement in British films. In 1963 he scored *French Dressing*, controversial director Ken Russell's feature debut, and also Russell's *Women In Love* (1969), with its famous nude wrestling sequence. Delerue's other scores for British films included *The Pumpkin Eater*; *It Began In Brighton*; *A Man For All Seasons*; *Our Mother's House*; *Interlude*; *Anne Of The Thousand Days* (the first of his five Oscar nominations); *The Lonely Passion Of Judith Hearne*; *A Summer Story*; and *Paris By Night* (1988). By the early 70s, after completing one of his best scores for *The Conformist*, an Italian-French-West German production, Delerue broke into Hollywood, and subsequently lived in Los Angeles for several years. Even so, for the majority of the time he continued to work in France. His initial US scores included Frankenheimer's *The Horsemen*; *The Day Of The Dolphin*; Fred Zinnemann's *Julia*; and *A Little Romance* (1979), for which Delerue received an Academy Award. During the 80s scores for English-language movies included *Rich And Famous*; *True Confessions*; *A Little Sex*; *The Escape Artist*; *Exposed*; *Man, Woman And Child*; *Agnes Of God*; *Maxie*; *Salvador*; *Maid To Order*; *A Man In Love*; *The House On Carroll Street*; *Memories Of Me*; *Heartbreak Hotel*; and such box-office hits as Mike Nichols' *Silkwood* and *Biloxi Blues*; Oliver Stone's *Platoon* and *Twins* (Schwarzenegger and De Vito); *Beaches* ('Bette Midler is dynamite'); and *Steel Magnolias* (1989).

In 1985, he composed a new score for Alexander Volkov's 1927 silent film *Casanova*. His last few scores, in the early 90s, included *Black Robe*; *Curly Sue*; *Count A Lonely Cadence*; *Mister Johnson*; *American Friends*; and the French production *Dien Bien Phu* (1992). Delerue died shortly after the latter film had been previewed at the Berlin Festival. Besides his work for feature films, he wrote a great deal of music for television, for shows such as *Love Thy Neighbour*; *Silence Of The Heart*; *Aurora*; *Arch Of*

Triumph; *The Execution*; *Amos*; *Deadly Intentions*; *Stone Pillow*; *A Time To Live*; *Sin Of Innocence*; *Women Of Valour*; *Her Secret Life*; *Escape From Sobibor*; and *Queenie* (miniseries). His last few projects for the small screen were *The Josephine Baker Story*; *Without Warning: The James Brady Story*; and *Momento Mori*, based on Muriel Spark's 1958 novel, which received rave reviews when it was shown in Britain in April 1992. Representative recordings include: *The London Sessions* volumes 1-3. Delerue was a Commander of Arts and Letters, one of France's highest honours.

DESERT SONG, THE

Although damned by the critics when it opened at the Casino Theatre in New York on 30 November 1926, *The Desert Song* proved to be one of the most durable of American stage musicals. With music by Sigmund Romberg, and a book and lyrics by Otto Harbach, Oscar Hammerstein II, and Frank Mandel, the show was set in North Africa, where the French occupying forces are striving to capture the Red Shadow (Robert Halliday), leader of the Riffs, an outlaw band of Moroccan tribesmen. The famous renegade is in love with Margot (Vivienne Segal), but she is infatuated with the governor's son, Pierre. Captured by the Red Shadow, she eventually falls in love with him but then he is imprisoned by the governor's soldiers. All ends happily when the Red Shadow is revealed to be Pierre in disguise. *The Desert Song* ran on Broadway for over 450 performances and was revived in 1946 and 1973. Amongst the show's songs are 'One Alone', 'The Riff Song', 'Romance', 'Margot', 'It', 'French Marching Song', 'Then You Will Know', 'Let Love Go', 'The Sabre Song', 'One Flower Grows Alone In Your Garden', and the title number. London audiences enjoyed *The Desert Song* for the first time in 1927, and on a further four subsequent occasions through until 1967. The latter production starred John Hanson who, from the late 50s, appeared in and managed a semi-permanent UK touring company which presented *The Desert Song* and other popular operettas. Film versions were released in 1929 (John Boles, Myrna Loy and Carlotta King), 1943 (Dennis Morgan and Irene Manning), and 1953 (Gordon MacRae and Kathryn Grayson).

DESTRY RIDES AGAIN

To most devotees of popular entertainment that title conjures up the celluloid image of Marlene Dietrich as the dance-hall girl known as Frenchy, driving the cowboys wild with her rendition of 'See What The Boys In the Back Room Will Have'. That was Hollywood in 1939, and 20 years later in New York, this stage version of Max Brand's satirical and entertaining impression of the American Wild West, opened on Broadway at the Imperial Theatre on 23 April 1959, and stayed there for over a year, a total of 472 performances. It came complete with a new book, by Leonard Gershe, and some fresh songs from the veteran composer-lyricist Harold Rome. The time is still the turn of the century, though, and Frenchy is continuing to sashay through the saloon, played this time by Dolores Gray, whose powerful vocal style could not be further away from Dietrich's sexy drawl. Andy Griffith is young

Destry, the mild-mannered sheriff of Bottleneck, hired by the townspeople to get rid of Kent (Scott Brady) and his gang, who are terrorising the town. At first, Frenchy is one of Kent's crowd, but, after saving Destry's life, she defects to the side of law and order - with romantic consequences. Rome's score was not considered to be out of his top drawer - in any event, his subtle and sensitive style of writing rarely produced songs that became chart hits (apart from the out-of-character 'South America, Take It Away' (1946) - but it did contain some pleasing songs, including 'Anyone Would Love You', 'Ballad Of the Gun', 'I Know Your Kind', 'Every Once In A While', 'I Say Hello', 'That Ring On Your Finger', 'Once Knew A Fella', and 'Hoop De Dingle'. However, there was a good deal of approval - and a Tony Award - for choreographer and director Michael Kidd and his exciting dance sequences. He was back in New York after spending several years on the west coast working on classic film musicals such as The Band Wagon, Seven Brides For Seven Brothers, and It's Always Fair Weather. One of the outstanding dancers in *Destry Rides Again* was Swen Swenson, whose triumph in Cy Coleman and Carolyn Leigh's Little Me was just three years away.

DEUTSCH, ADOLPH

b. 20 October 1897, London, England, d. 1 January 1980, Palm Desert, California, USA. A composer, arranger and musical director for films from the 30s to the 60s. Deutsch began to learn music at the age of five, and, while still a schoolboy, studied composition and piano at the Royal College of Music in London. At the age of 13 he was taken to the USA by his uncle and settled in Buffalo. He became a US citizen in 1920. After high school he worked in the accessory department at the Ford Motor Company, at the same time submitting arrangements to various entertainment organizations. He moved to New York, and during the 20s and early 30s, scored and arranged for musical shows, including those of Irving Berlin and George Gershwin; worked in radio, with a three year stint on Paul Whiteman's Music Hall; and served as musical director on a few films, such as *The Smiling Lieutenant* (1931). In 1937 he began to score films, initially for Warner Brothers, such as *They Won't Forget Him*, *The Great Garrick*, *Cowboy From Brooklyn*, *Indianapolis Speedway*, *Three Cheers For The Irish*, *The Fighting 69th*, *They Drive By Night*, *High Sierra*, *The Maltese Falcon*, *Across The Pacific*, *The Great Mr Nobody*, *Action In The North Atlantic*, *Northern Pursuit*, *Uncertain Glory*, *The Mask Of Dimitrios*, and *Three Strangers*. In 1939, Deutsch spent 12 weeks assisting Max Steiner with his score for *Gone With The Wind*. In 1948 he joined MGM, already well into their golden age of musical movies, and was associated with the a studio until 1962. He won Academy Awards for his scores for Annie Get Your Gun (1950) (with Roger Edens), Seven Brides For Seven Brothers (1954) (with Saul Chaplin), Oklahoma! (1955) (with Robert Russell Bennett and Jay Blackton). He won Oscar nominations for his work on Show Boat, The Band Wagon, Deep In My Heart, Some Like It Hot and The Apartment (1960). His other background scores through the 50s, included *Father Of The Bride*, *Mrs O'Malley And Mr Malone*, *The Long Long Trailer*, *The Rack*, *Tea And Sympathy*, Funny Face, *The Matchmaker*, Les Girls and many others. Deutsch also wrote a symphonic piece, the 'Scottish Suite', which was performed by US classical orchestras, and a number of other instrumental works, such as 'March Of The United Nations', 'Clarabelle', 'Three Sister's', 'Piano Echoes', 'Skyride', 'March Eccentrique' 'Margo', 'Stairway' and 'Lonely Room' (theme from *The Apartment*). In 1943 Deutsch formed the Screen Composers Association and was its President Emeritus from 1955 until his death.

DIAMOND HORSESHOE

(see *Billy Rose's Diamond Horseshoe*)

DICKSON, BARBARA

b. 27 September 1947, Dunfermline, Fife, Scotland. Dickson earned her initial reputation during the 60s as part of Scotland's flourishing folk scene. An accomplished singer, she tackled traditional and contemporary material and enjoyed a fruitful partnership with Archie Fisher. In the 70s she encompassed a wider repertoire and became a popular MOR artist in the wake of her contributions to Willy Russell's *John, Paul, George, Ringo And Bert*, a successful London West End musical. She enjoyed a UK Top 10 single in 1976 with 'Answer Me', while two later releases, 'Another Suitcase In Another Hall' (1977) and 'January February' (1980), also broached the UK Top 20. In 1983, the Dickson/Russell combination scored again when she won a Laurence Olivier Award for her portrayal of Mrs Johnstone in his widely applauded musical Blood Brothers. Dickson maintained her popularity through assiduous television and concert appearances and in 1985 had a number 1 hit with 'I Know Him So Well', a duet with Elaine Paige from the London musical Chess. Its success confirmed Barbara Dickson as one of Britain's leading MOR attractions. In 1993 Dickson received renewed critical acclaim when she recreated her original role in the current West End revival of *Blood Brothers*. Two years later she played in cabaret at London's Café Royal, and appeared in the television dramas *Band Of Gold* and *Taggart*. Her recording career is shared with her acting duties and she is able to choose her projects. *Dark End Of The Street* was a personal selection of songs she wanted to record, most notably her credible interpretations of Dan Penn's title track and the Bryants' 'Love Hurts'.

● ALBUMS: with Archie Fisher *The Fate Of O'Charlie* (Trailer 1969)★★★, with Fisher *Thro' The Recent Years* (1969)★★★, *From The Beggar's Mantle* (Decca 1972)★★, *Answer Me* (RSO 1976)★★★, *Morning Comes Quickly* (RSO 1977)★★★, *Sweet Oasis* (Columbia 1978)★★★, *The Barbara Dickson Album* (Epic 1980)★★★, *I Will Sing* (Decca 1981)★★, *You Know It's Me* (Epic 1981)★★, *Here We Go (Live On Tour)* (Epic 1982)★★, *All For A Song* (Epic 1982)★★, *Tell Me It's Not True* adapted from the stage musical *Blood Brothers* (Legacy 1983)★★★, *Heartbeats* (Epic 1984)★★, *The Right Moment* (K-Tel 1986)★★, *After Dark* (Theobald Dickson 1987)★★★, *Coming Alive Again (Album)* (Telstar 1989)★★, with Elaine Paige *Together* (1992)★★, *Don't Think Twice It's Alright* (1993)★★★, *Parcel Of Rogues* (Castle 1994)★★★, *Dark End Of The Street* (Transatlantic 1995)★★★.

● COMPILATIONS: *The Barbara Dickson Songbook* (K-Tel 1985)★★, *Gold* (K-Tel 1985)★★★, *The Very Best Of Barbara*

Dickson (Telstar 1986)★★★, *The Barbara Dickson Collection* (Castle 1987)★★★.

DICKSON, DOROTHY

b. 25 July 1893, Kansas City, Missouri, USA, d. 26 September 1995, London, England. Dickson's father was a famous Chicago journalist who scooped the opposition by interviewing the outlaw Jesse James, while her mother was a notable member of the early American feminist movement. Ironically, in view of that last fact, the enchanting actress Dorothy Dickson became a symbol of eroticism via her delicate good looks, sensual dancing and singing. When she was 21, she married America's number one ballroom dancer, Carl Hyson (born Heisen), and they made their Broadway debut as a dancing team in Jerome Kern's Oh, Boy! in February 1917. In June, they were together again in the Ziegfeld Follies, and Dickson's dancing subsequently received favourable reviews in *Girl O' Mine* (1918), *Rock-A-Bye Baby* (1918), *Ziegfeld Follies* (1918), *The Royal Vagabond* (1919), and *Lassie* (1920). In the following year, the English impresario Charles B. Cochran transported the duo to London, and put them in his 1921 revue, *London, Paris And New York*. Dickson captivated West End audiences later that year with her sensitive portrayal of the title role in Kern's Sally at the Winter Garden, in which she introduced the supremely optimistic 'Look For A Silver Lining' (lyric Buddy De Sylva), a song that was thereafter always identified with her. She continued to dazzle in two more Kern musicals, The Cabaret Girl (1922) and The Beauty Prize (1923), as well as *Patricia* (1924), before playing the title role of Peter Pan in 1925, which she reprised a year later. Also in 1926, Dickson made her straight acting debut opposite Gerald Du Maurier in Edgar Wallace's long-running thriller play, *The Ringer*, before returning to the musical stage with Tip-Toes, in which she sang George and Ira Gershwin's 'Looking For A Boy', and duetted with Allan Kearns on 'That Certain Feeling'. By this time Dickson was one of the West End's favourite musical comedy actresses, mixing in high society, and friendly with leading theatrical personalities such as Noël Coward. Richard Rodgers and Lorenz Hart's Peggy-Ann (1927), in which she created the wistful 'Where's That Rainbow', was just one of a string of hit shows she graced during the next decade. These included *Coo-ee!* (1929), Hold Everything! (1929, in which she replaced Mamie Watson), and two European imports, *The Wonder Bar* (1930) and *Casanova* (1932). In the Irving Berlin revue *Stop Press* (1935), which was a revised version of the composer's Broadway show, As Thousands Cheer, Dickson sang and danced to 'Easter Parade', while in another non-book show, *Spread It Abroad* (1936), she introduced the enduring ballad 'These Foolish Things' (Eric Maschwitz-Jack Strachey-Harry Link), although its popularity in Britain also had a good deal to do with the sophisticated entertainer Leslie 'Hutch' Hutchinson. In the late 30s Dickson returned to musical comedy, co-starring with Ivor Novello in two smash hits, Careless Rapture (1936) and *Crest Of The Wave* (1937) at the Theatre Royal, Drury Lane. The pair were together again in the same theatre for *Henry V* (1938). During the 30s, Dickson had also appeared in a handful of films, the best of which was probably *Channel Crossing* (1933), when her fellow travellers included Matheson Lang, comedian Max Miller, and Constance Cummings. Shortly after the outbreak of World War II, Dickson appeared in the revues *Diversion* (1940), *Diversion No. 2* (1941), and *Fine And Dandy* (1942), before embarking on an ENSA tour of North Africa with Vivien Leigh and Beatrice Lillie. On her return, she began work on a project which eventually came to fruition in 1944. It was the Stage Door Canteen, an enormously popular venue in London's Piccadilly, which provided top entertainment for troops of all nationalities. Among the many stars who appeared there were Bing Crosby and Bob Hope. From then on, Dickson made infrequent excursions into the straight theatre, her last West End appearance being in Jack Buchanan's satire on rock singers, *As Long As They're Happy* (1953). Her last public appearance was in 1980 at the Duke of York's Theatre for a gala performance to commemorate the 75th anniversary of *Peter Pan*. She received an immensely affecting standing ovation. When she was 96, she was presented to Prince Andrew at the National Film Theatre, and alarmed her escorts by performing a full olde worlde curtsey - from which she rose with great style. In any event, her royal connections went back a long way - she was said to be the Queen Mother's oldest friend. They first met after a performance of *The Cabaret Girl* in 1923. Her family and friends had the greatest difficulty in persuading her to acknowledge her 100th birthday, for, being a life-long Christian Scientist, she recognized neither age or illness. Dorothy Dickson was divorced from Carl Hyson in 1936, and their daughter, also named Dorothy, married the celebrated British actor, Anthony Quayle. Dorothy Hyson (b. Dorothy Wardell Heisen, 24 December 1914, Chicago, Illinois, USA, d. 23 May 1996, London, England) was an actress who played mostly straight parts in the theatre and films. However, on the occasions when she did sing and dance, her performance was compared favourably with that of her mother. Her exquisite looks caused Richard Rodgers and Lorenz Hart to dedicate their immensely popular song 'The Most Beautiful Girl In the World' to her.

● FILMS: *Money Mad* (1917), *Channel Crossing* (1933), *Danny Boy* (1934), *Sword Of Honour* (1939).

DIETRICH, MARLENE

b. Maria Magdelene Dietrich, 27 December 1901, Berlin, Germany, d. 6 May 1992, Paris, France. Dietrich's heavily accented, half-spoken vocal style made her a *femme fatale* for nearly half a century. She studied acting with director Max Reinhardt, appearing in Germany on stage and in films during the 20s. Her first major role was in *The Blue Angel*, in which she sang what was to become her theme tune, 'Falling In Love Again'. The international success of the film led to a career in Hollywood, where Dietrich starred as a cabaret singer or bar-girl in numerous movies. Among them were *Morocco* (1930), *The Blonde Venus* (1932), *Song Of Songs* (1933), *Destry Rides Again* (in which she performed 'The Boys In The Back Room'), *Follow The Boys* (1944), and *A Foreign Affair* (1948). She returned to Britain to make *Stage Fright*, which was produced and directed by Alfred Hitchcock and released in 1950. After becoming a US citizen in 1939, Dietrich joined the American war effort in 1941, and became associated with the song 'Lilli Marlene'. Originally a German poem written in World War II, it had been recorded in 1939 by Lale Anderson, whose version was extremely popular in Nazi Germany. In turn, Dietrich's Brunswick recording was a big hit in the USA.

In the 50s, she began a new career as one of the world's most highly paid cabaret artists. With musical direction by Burt Bacharach, Dietrich sang in three languages and performed a wide variety of songs ranging from 'Miss Otis Regrets' to the Pete Seeger anti-war composition 'Where Have All The Flowers Gone ?' In translation, this song was a German hit in 1968. In 1963 Dietrich appeared with the Beatles at the Royal Variety Performance. The media had a field day when they posed together for a photo call. She came out of retirement in 1979 for her final film role with David Bowie in *Just A Gigolo*, in which she sang the title song. After almost a decade as a virtual recluse, she died in 1992. Almost a year later, a new musical about her life, Marlene, Das Musical (originally known as *Sag Mir Wo Die Blumen Sind* (Where Have All The Flowers Gone)), opened in Berlin. In 1997, a play entitled *Marlene*, by Pam Gems, directed by Sean Mathias, and starring Siân Phillips, had a decent run in the West End. In November of that year, an auction of Marlene Dietrich memorabilia, 270 lots of items from her New York apartment, fetched a remarkable £440,000 - twice what experts had anticipated.

● ALBUMS: *Souvenir Album* (Decca 1950)★★★★, *Marlene Dietrich Sings* (Vox 1951)★★★★, *American Songs In German For The OSS* (Columbia 1952)★★★, *Dietrich In Rio* (Columbia 1953)★★★, *Cafe De Paris* (Columbia 1955)★★★, *Marlene Dietrich* (Decca 1957)★★★★, *Lili Marlene* (Columbia 1959)★★★★, *Dietrich Returns To Germany* (1962)★★★, *At The Café De Paris* (1964)★★★, *Marlene* (Capitol 1965)★★★, *Mythos* (1968)★★★, *The Magic Of Marlene* (Capitol 1969)★★★, *The Legendary, Lovely Marlene* (1972)★★★, *The Best Of* (Columbia 1973)★★★★, *Lilli Marlene* (1983)★★★★, *The Cosmopolitan Marlene Dietrich* (Columbia/Legacy 1993)★★★★.

● FURTHER READING: *Dietrich*, Donald Spoto. *Marlene Dietrich: Life And Legend*, Steven Bach. *Marlene My Friend*, David Bret.

DIETZ, HOWARD

b. 8 September 1896, New York City, New York, USA, d. 30 July 1983. Despite attending special schools for pupils of advanced intelligence, Dietz quit formal education while still in his teens. He studied journalism at Columbia University, where his classmates included two other future lyricists, Lorenz Hart and Oscar Hammerstein II. In 1917 he took a job in advertising, where his most lasting contribution to American popular visual culture was his design of a roaring lion logo for a tyro film producer named Samuel Goldwyn. Dietz had begun to dabble in lyric writing and after military service during World War I, he directed much of his energy into this activity. He worked on such Broadway productions as *Poppy* (1923) and *Dear Sir* (1924). Despite the latter having music by Jerome Kern, it was a flop; but Dietz persisted and soon afterwards was introduced to Arthur Schwartz, who suggested that they should work together. Dietz demurred, feeling that he was not up to Schwartz's standard. In any event, Dietz had been offered an important job with a new film production company that Samuel Goldwyn had formed, following a merger with Louis B. Mayer. Dietz became publicity and advertising director for Metro-Goldwyn-Mayer, later rising to vice-president. Soon after his appointment, Dietz met Schwartz again and thus began one of the great partnerships of American popular music.

Over the next dozen years Dietz and Schwartz wrote the scores for several Broadway musicals and revues, such as The Little Show (1929), *Grand Street Follies*, Three's A Crowd, *The Second Little Show*, The Band Wagon, Flying Colors, *Revenge With Music*, At Home Abroad, *Between The Devil*, and Inside USA. The shows contained a string of memorable songs, including 'I Guess I'll Have To Change My Plan', 'Something To Remember You By', 'The Moment I Saw You', 'I Love Louisa', 'New Sun In The Sky', 'Louisiana Hayride', 'A Shine On Your Shoes', 'Alone Together', 'You And The Night And The Music', 'If There Is Someone Lovelier Than You', 'Got A Bran' New Suit', 'Love Is A Dancing Thing', 'I See Your Face Before Me', 'Triplets', and 'Rhode Island Is Famous For You'. Their greatest song of this period, which Dietz used as the title of his 1974 autobiography, was 'Dancing In The Dark'. After 1936 Schwartz worked with other collaborators while Dietz concentrated on his work with MGM. In the early 40s Dietz returned to songwriting, this time with Vernon Duke, in a succession of stage productions, most of which were relative failures. Towards the end of the 40s he again teamed up with Schwartz on a stage show and on films, one of their new hits being 'That's Entertainment', written for the 1953 film The Band Wagon. Their renewed partnership was not as successful as that of the past, although the calibre of Dietz's writing always remained high. In the 50s he wrote the libretto and new English lyrics for the New York Metropolitan Opera productions of *Die Fledermaus* and *La Boheme*. In 1954 Dietz became seriously ill with Parkinson's disease and, although he lived for nearly 30 more years, his songwriting days were over.

DIRTY DANCING

If films that adhered to a conventional musical formula could be counted on the fingers of one hand in the 80s, the excitement of dance never ceased to attract enthusiastic audiences. Following in the dance steps of the success of Footloose and Flashdance, *Dirty Dancing*, released in 1987, caught the imagination of many with its combination of raunchy dancing, romance and upbeat soundtrack. Directed by Emile Ardolino, with a screenplay by Eleanor Bergstein, it tells the story of Baby (Jennifer Grey), her father's favourite daughter, who suffers the ups-and-downs of growing up while on a family holiday at a Catskills resort in the summer of 1963. Baby is an idealistic girl, soon to begin at college, who thinks she can right any problem, and help anyone, whatever the situation. These are all characteristics which one of the resort's leading dancers, Johnny (Patrick Swayze), finds refreshing and attractive. When someone is desperately needed to fill the shoes of Johnny's dancing partner, Penny (Cynthia Rhodes), it's hardly surprising that Baby is chosen to substitute, learning all the steps from scratch - almost a mild modern variation of the chorus girl becomes star routine.

It's at this point that Baby and Johnny begin to fall in love, and despite the protestations of most of the adults around them - particularly Baby's father (Jerry Orbach) - the young lovers are isolated for a time before the inevitable happy ending. The uplifting finalé features the film's biggest song hit, '(I've Had) The Time Of My Life' sung by Bill Medley and Jennifer Warnes, which won an Oscar and a Grammy, and topped the US chart. Many of the other tracks reflect the film's theme of 60s nostalgia with contributions from Frankie Valli, the Four Seasons, Otis Redding, the Shirelles and Mickey And Sylvia. There is even one song on the soundtrack, 'She's Like The Wind', performed and written by Swayze (with Stacy Widelitz). *Dirty Dancing* was the first feature release for the home video company Vestron Pictures. While its plot is simplistic, it's a sensitive and original portrayal of a young girl's coming of age, helped along by fine performances and some great frenetic and exciting dancing.

DISC JOCKEY JAMBOREE

Arguably the most anodyne film of the rock 'n' roll era, this 1957 feature starred Kay Medford and Robert Pastine as two theatrical agents. Once married, now separated, they individually represent 'Pete' and 'Honey', two singers who begin to work together and become 'America's Sweethearts'. During the course of this, the Medford and Pastine characters are reconciled. Amid this sugary plot are performances by rock 'n' roll and rockabilly stars Jerry Lee Lewis ('Great Balls Of Fire'), Buddy Knox ('Hula Love'), Charlie Gracie ('Cool Baby') and Carl Perkins ('Glad All Over'). Fats Domino, Connie Francis and Frankie Avalon - later the star of innumerable 'beach' films - are also featured in this film that at best showcases acts rarely enshrined on celluloid.

DISK-O-TEK HOLIDAY

This 1966 film was a US adaptation of *Just For You*, a UK feature from 1964. In the latter DJ Sam Costa lay in bed watching pop acts perform on television. Among those he saw were Peter And Gordon, the Applejacks, the Merseybeats, Freddie And The Dreamers, Louise Cordet and A Band Of Angels (with Mike D'Abo). For *Disk-O-Tek Holiday* Costa was replaced by US disc jockeys Arnie Ginsburg and Bob Foster. A few lesser-known UK acts were also axed in favour of the Chiffons, Freddie Cannon, the Rockin' Ramrods and the Vagrants, the last-named of which featured future Mountain guitarist, Leslie West.

DISNEY, WALT

b. 23 August 1901, Chicago, Illinois, USA, d. 15 December 1966, New York, USA. Apart from creating legendary cartoon characters such as Mickey and Minnie Mouse, Donald Duck, Goofy and Pluto, the Walt Disney Studio was responsible for a series of phenomenally successful full-length animated feature films, the first of which, Snow White And The Seven Dwarfs, was released in December 1937. It was three years in the making, with 600 artists producing more than two million Technicolor drawings, only about an eighth of which were used. The ravishing fairy story by the brothers Grimm was adapted for the screen by Ted Sears, Dorothy Ann Blank, Otto Englander,

Earl Hurd, Richard Creedon, Dick Richard, Merrill de Maris, and Webb Smith. All the dwarfs, Grumpy, Doc, Sleepy, Happy, Sneezy, Bashful, and Dopey (who Charlie Chaplin said was one of the greatest comedians of all time), were given their own delightful personalities, and the soundtrack voices of Andriana Caselotti, Harry Stockwell, Lucille LaVerne, Roy Atwell, Pinto Colvig, Otis Harlan, Billy Gilbert, Scot Mattraw, and Moroni Olsen were perfectly matched to them and the rest of the characters including the handsome Prince whose kiss brings Snow White back to life after the evil Queen has tried to get rid of her. All this was supplemented by some marvellous songs by Frank Churchill (music) and Larry Morey (lyrics), which included 'Whistle While You Work', 'Heigh-Ho', 'Some Day My Prince Will Come', 'With A Smile And A Song', 'I'm Wishing', 'One Song', and 'Isn't This A Silly Song?'. David Hand was the supervising editor, and, although *Snow White And The Seven Dwarfs* was released late in the 30s, it went on to take more money than any other film at the US box-office during the decade, with the exception of *Gone With The Wind*. In 1938 Walt Disney received a special Academy Award 'in recognition of a significant screen innovation which has charmed millions and pioneered a great new entertainment field for the motion picture cartoon' (one statuette and seven miniature statuettes). More than 50 years later, in 1993, the picture's overall earnings were estimated at £92 million, a record for any animated film until Disney's own *Aladdin* overtook it (with the help of inflation) after being screened for just 11 incredible weeks in the world's cinemas. As just one more example of the enduring interest in this historic picture, in 1992 an original production cel (a hand-painted celluloid still) from the film fetched £115,000 at Sotheby's auction house in New York, three times its estimated price. A digitally restored version of *Snow White* was released in 1994, and in the same year the film appeared in the USA on home-video for the first time. Most of Disney's other full-length animated features have already been made available in that form although usually only for a strictly limited period of time before being withdrawn. In May 1994 it was reported that nine out of 10 of all home-videos sold have been Disney films. These included:

Pinocchio (1940). Inspired by the stories of 19th century author Carlo Collodi, this film concerns a wilful puppet whose habitual 'economy with the truth' results in his nose growing longer and longer. However, by listening to his conscience, in the shape of the loveable character Jiminy Cricket, he mends his ways, bravely rescues his personal Svengali, Geppetto the wood carver from inside Monstro the whale, and eventually achieves his ambition, and is turned into a real live boy by the Blue Fairy. Cliff Edwards, the puckish entertainer, provided the voice for Jiminy Cricket, and he had two of Leigh Harline and Ned Washington's most endearing and enduring songs, 'Give A Little Whistle' and 'When You Wish Upon A Star'. The latter number won an Academy Award, and the two songwriters, together with P.J. Smith, won another Oscar for their original score. The remaining songs were 'Hi-Diddle-Dee-Dee (An Actor's Life For Me)', 'I've Got No Strings', 'Three Cheers For Anything', 'As I Was Say'n' To The

Duchess', and 'Turn On The Old Music Box'. Some of the other voices which, together with the brilliant animation, brought the various characters to life with startling effect, were provided by Dickie Jones (Pinocchio), Christian Rub (Geppetto), Evelyn Venable (the Blue Fairy), Walter Catlett (J. Worthington Foulfellow), Charles Judels (Stromboli), and Frankie Darrow (Lampwick). Ben Sharpsteen and Hamilton Luske were the supervising editors, and the film, which was photographed in Technicolor, took over $40 million in the USA and Canada, becoming the fourth-highest-grossing film of the decade.

Fantasia (1940). This was an astonishingly successful blending of cartoon characters and classical music that featured Leopold Stokowski and the Philadelphia Orchestra. It was narrated by Deems Taylor, and contained eight pieces, 'Toccata And Fugue In D Minor' (Bach), 'The Nutcracker Suite' (Tchaikovsky), 'The Sorcerer's Apprentice' (Dukas), 'The Rite Of Spring' (Stravinsky), 'Pastoral Symphony' (Beethoven), 'Dance Of The Hours' (Ponchielli), 'Night On The Bald Mountain' (Mussorgsky), and 'Ave Maria' (Schubert). Amidst all this wonderful music, there cavorted Mickey Mouse and any number of other animals, including hippopotami, dinosaurs, alligators, elephants, and ostriches, along with nymphs, satyrs, the Goddess of Night, and many more strange and fantastic creations. Ben Sharpsteen was the production supervisor, and this incredible piece of entertainment was filmed in Technicolor and Fantasound. It was the second-highest-grossing 40s picture in the USA. Fifty years after it burst gloriously upon the scene, *Fantasia* was subjected to the currently fashionable desire for 'political correctness' which prevailed in the early 90s. Prior to its video release, and at a reputed cost of hundreds of thousands of pounds, a black 'piccaninny centaurette' seen polishing the hooves of a preening blonde figure was removed from all prints.

Bambi (1942). The general consensus of opinion seems to be that this is the most naturalistic of all Walt Disney's full-length animated features. The animators' skill in their drawing of the animals' graceful movements and charming facial expressions gave the tender, exquisite story of a young deer growing up in a world of changing seasons an awesome sense of reality. Apart from Bambi himself, another star to emerge was Thumper the rabbit, whose amusing voice was dubbed by Peter Behn. Frank Churchill and Larry Morey wrote the score, which included 'Love Is A Song', 'The Thumper Song', 'Let's Sing A Gay Little Spring Song', 'Twitterpated', and 'Little April Showers'. David Hand was the production supervisor, and the screenplay was adapted from a book by Felix Salten. By 1993, according to the *Variety* trade newspaper, *Bambi* was at the head of the US money-earning list of films made in the 40s.

Cinderella (1950). Based on Charles Perrault's traditional fairytale, this was another triumph for the Disney Studio. Once again, as in previous features, the animators came up with some more endearing creatures. This time they were two resourceful rodents, Jaq and Gus, who enlist the help of their friends to make a gorgeous gown so that Cinderella can finally go to the Ball. The dynamic duo were dubbed by James Mcdonald, and the rest of the soundtrack voices were just about perfect, including Ilene Woods as the lovely Cinderella, William Phipps (Prince Charming), Eleanor Audley (wicked stepmother), Verna Felton (fairy godmother), and Luis Van Ruten (King and Grand Duke). Rhoda Williams and Lucille Bliss voiced the ugly stepsisters and were suitably disagreeable on the incongruously titled 'Sing Sweet Nightingale'. The remainder of Mack Gordon, Jerry Livingston and Al Hoffman's score was first-rate, and included 'A Dream Is A Wish Your Heart Makes', 'Bibbidi-Bobbidi-Boo', 'The Work Song', 'So This Is Love', and 'Cinderella'. The Technicolor production was supervised by Ben Sharpsteen, and directed by Wilfred Jackson, Hamilton Luske, and Clyde Geronimi. Some sources, including *Variety*, regard *Cinderella* as a 1949 film because it is said to have been released in December of that year. The newspaper places it third in domestic rental earners during that decade.

Peter Pan (1953). Not regarded as one of the best of Disney's animated features at the time, although it was still an outstanding piece of work. John M. Barrie's classic story was ideal material from which the studio's artists crafted a magical picture. All the much-loved characters were on hand, including Peter himself (dubbed by Bobby Driscoll), Wendy (Kathy Beaumont), the deliciously evil Captain Hook (Hans Conreid), Mrs. Darling (Heather Angel), Mr. Darling ((Paul Collins), Smee (Bill Thompson), John (Tommy Luske), and Tom Conway (narrator) - not forgetting Tinkerbell and the animal that Frank Churchill and Jack Lawrence warned about in their amusing song, 'Never Smile At A Crocodile'. Sammy Cahn and Sammy Fain wrote most of the remaining numbers, including the popular 'You Can Fly', 'Your Mother And Mine', 'The Elegant Captain Hook', and 'What Makes The Red Man Red?', and there were also contributions from Oliver Wallace and Erdman Penner ('A Pirate's Life') and Wallace also collaborated with Winston Hibler and Ted Sears on 'Tee Dum-Tee Dee'. The production and direction credits were the same as *Cinderella*. *Peter Pan* is third in the line of 50s top money-spinners in the USA, just behind the next listed film.

Lady And The Tramp (1955). The first of these full-length animated features to be photographed in Cinemascope was based on Ward Green's waggish tale about a mongrel called Tramp who falls in a big way for Lady, a spoilt pedigree cocker spaniel, while he is helping her to come to terms with the changes that are taking place (such as the arrival of a new baby) in her owners' family. Getting in on the act are Trusty the bloodhound, Lady's owners Jim Dear and Darling, and a sundry collection of hounds such as Toughy, Bull, Boris, Pedro, and an ex-show dog called Peg. Erdman Penner, Joe Rinaldi, Ralph White and Donald Da Gradi wrote the screenplay, while Sonny Burke and Peggy Lee came up with some charming songs that included 'He's A Tramp', 'Siamese Cat Song', 'Bella Notte', 'Peace On Earth', and 'La La Lu'. Lee herself provided the voices for Peg (an ex-show dog), two naughty Siamese cats, and Darling, and other characters were dubbed by Barbara Luddy (Lady), Larry Roberts (Tramp), George Givot, Bill Thompson, Stan Freberg, Bill Baucon, Verna Felton, and Alan Reed. Production and direction credits as for *Cinderella* and *Peter Pan*. A sad aspect of this produc-

tion is that, nearly 40 years after it was made, Peggy Lee was locked in litigation with the Disney organization over disputed amounts of home-video royalties.

Sleeping Beauty (1959). The Disney Studio's preoccupation with live-action feature films, beginning with *Treasure Island* in 1950 and leading to 60s classics such as *Mary Poppins*, meant that this was one of their last animated fairytales - for some time, at least. Extremely expensive to make, it was a box-office failure following its original release, although subsequent re-valuation of the film's outstanding qualities has resulted in substantial earnings from reissues, pushing it into the 50s US Top 6 in more recent times. Like *Cinderella*, the film was based on a Charles Perrault fairytale in which the three good fairies, Flaura, Fauna and Merryweather, care for the Princess Aurora after the wicked fairy, Maleficent, has put a spell on her. After many exciting adventures involving some superb animation and special effects, the seriously handsome Prince Philip ensures that, as always with Disney, good triumphs over evil. Opera singer Mary Costa voiced the Princess, with Bill Shirley (Prince), Eleanor Audley (Maleficent), Verna Felton, Barbara Luddy, Candy Candido, and Bill Thompson as the other main characters. The songs included 'Once Upon A Dream' (Sammy Fain-Jack Lawrence), 'Hail The Princess Aurora' and 'The Sleeping Beauty Song' (both Tom Adair-George Bruns), 'I Wonder' (Winston Hibler-Ted Sears-Bruns), 'The Skump Song' (Adair-Erdman Penner-Bruns), and excerpts from Tchaikovsky's *Sleeping Beauty*. This production, which was supervised by Don da Gradi and Ken Anderson and directed by Clyde Geronomi, was shot in Technicolor and the wide-screen process Super Technirama 70, a combination that enhanced the proceedings for some viewers, but was a disturbing influence for others.

The Jungle Book (1967). After a lean spell - and Walt Disney's death the year before - the Studio was back on top form with this captivating film which was inspired by Rudyard Kipling's *Mowgli* stories. It tells of the boy Mowgli who was raised by wolves in the jungle until he was 10 years old. After it is learned that Shere Khan the tiger intends to kill him, Bagheera the panther undertakes to return the youngster to the safety of the man village. After some scrapes along the way involving Baloo the bear, a band of monkeys led by King Louie of the Apes, and Shere Khan himself, the youngster reaches the village where he really belongs. Major features of this production are the inspired choice of actors to voice these marvellous characters, such as Phil Harris (Baloo), Louis Prima (King Louie), Sebastion Cabot (Bagheera), George Sanders (Shere Khan), and Sterling Holloway (Kaa the Snake), and the jazzy score, which consisted of 'Colonel Hathi's March', 'Trust In Me', 'I Wan'na Be Like You', 'That's What Friends Are For', and 'My Own Home' (all by Richard M. Sherman and Robert B. Sherman), and 'The Bare Necessities' (Terry Gilkyson). This joyous and immensely entertaining Technicolor film had a screenplay by Larry Clemmons, Ralph Wright, Ken Anderson and Vance Gerry, and was directed by Wolfgang Reitherman. Since then, there have been two further attempts to bring the story to the screen: Disney's *Rudyard Kipling's The Jungle Book* (1994) starring Jason Scott Lee, and *The Second Jungle*

Book: *Mowgli & Baloo* (1997, TriStar-MDP).

In the 70s Disney released further full-length animated features, *The Aristocats*, *Robin Hood*, and *The Rescuers*, which, although fine in their way, were not in the same class as many of the Studio's earlier efforts. It was not until 1989 that the great Disney comeback began with *The Little Mermaid*, and continued via *Beauty And The Beast*, *Aladdin*, and *The Lion King*. That money-spinning quartet was soon joined by other major features such as *Pocahontas* (1995), with its strong plea for tolerance, *Toy Story* (1995), *The Hunchback Of Notre Dame* (1996), *Hercules* (1997), and *Mulan* (1998). In 1994, the 'Disneyfication' of Broadway began with an extravagant stage adaptation of *Beauty And The Beast*. This was followed three years later by *King David*, the first Disney musical conceived for the stage. It had a limited run at the re-opened New Amsterdam Theatre on 42nd Street, former home of the *Ziegfeld Follies*, which been derelict for some years before Disney spent an estimated £21 million restoring it to its former Art Nouveau glory. Also in 1997, the New Amsterdam hosted Disney's spectacular stage version of *The Lion King*, which most critics agreed was a 'roaring sensation'. Not so well received was *Elaborate Lives: The Legend Of Aida*, which had its premiere on 7 October 1998 well away from Broadway in Atlanta, Georgia.

● FURTHER READING: *Walt Disney*, Diane Disney Miller. *The Disney Version*, Richard Schickel. *The Art Of Walt Disney*, Christopher Finch. *Walt Disney: Hollywood's Dark Prince*, Marc Eliot. *Walt Disney's Snow White And The Seven Dwarfs*, Jack Solomon. *Disney Animation: The Illusion Of Life*, Frank Thomas and Ollie Johnston. *The Disney Studio Story*, Richard Hollis and Brian Sibley. *Walt Disney - Hollywood's Dark Prince*, Marc Eliot.

DIXON, ADELE

b. Adela Helena Dixon, 3 June 1908, Newington, London, England, d. 11 April 1992, Wythenshawe, Greater Manchester, England. A versatile actress with a pleasing soprano voice who was equally at home in dramatic roles and musical comedies. Her trim figure, attractive red-brown hair, and commanding appearance also made an ideal pantomime Principal Boy. Dixon attended the Italia Conti stage school and made her London stage debut in 1921 at the age of 13 as the First Elf in *Where The Rainbow Ends*. After studying at the Royal Academy of Dramatic Art, she toured in various Shakespearean roles before joining the Old Vic Company where she impressed Sir John Gielgud in *Romeo And Juliet* and *Hamlet*. In 1928 she attracted attention in her first singing role as Princess Beauty in *Adam's Opera*. The music for that production was composed by Richard Addinsell, and three years later, when he wrote the songs for the stage adaptation of J.B. Priestley's novel, *The Good Companions*, Dixon was cast - again opposite Gielgud - in the important role of Susie Dean, the young and enterprising soubrette. Shortly after appearing alongside the high-kicking Charlotte Greenwood in Robert Stoltz's *Wild Violets* (1932), Dixon took over from Evelyn Laye in *Give Me A Ring* (1933), combining with John Mills (who had replaced Ernest Verebes) on the attractive 'A Couple Of Fools In Love'. She survived the farcical goings-on in the Leslie Henson vehi-

cle *Lucky Break* (1934), to co-star later in the year with Stanley Holloway, and again with Greenwood, in *Three Sisters*. Jerome Kern and Oscar Hammerstein's lovely score for this original musical which was presented at Drury Lane, contained the future standard, 'I Won't Dance', on which Dixon duetted with Richard Dolman. The song's lyric was subsequently revised, and the new version featured in several films, including *Roberta* (1935) with Fred Astaire and Ginger Rogers, and the 1952 remake, *Lovely To Look At*. In 1935 Dixon played Hope Harcourt in Cole Porter's *Anything Goes*, an American import full of good songs, and in the following year she introduced, with Eric Fawcett, the delightful 'I Breathe On Windows' in Charles B. Cochran's production of *Over She Goes*, which also starred Stanley Lupino and Laddie Cliff. By this time Dixon was one of the West End's best-loved leading ladies, and in November 1936 she became the first female performer to be seen in Britain on the new medium of television, being chosen to sing the specially composed 'Television' ('Bringing Television To You') when the BBC launched the world's first regular service from Alexandra Palace on 2 November 1936. Her Broadway debut with Jack Buchanan and Evelyn Laye in *Between The Devil* (1937) was not so successful, in spite of a score by Arthur Schwartz and Howard Dietz containing the superior ballad, 'I See Your Face Before Me', which was introduced by Laye, and reprised by Dixon and Buchanan. A further trip to New York in 1948 with Buchanan, to appear in the comedy, *Don't Listen Ladies!*, also proved a disappointment. Back home in 1938, Dixon continued to triumph in the 'musical frolic', *The Fleet's Lit Up*, which had a Vivian Ellis score, plus Frances Day, Stanley Lupino, and Ralph Reader, with whom she combined on 'Hide And Seek'; and the revue, *All Clear*, in company with Bobby Howes, Beatrice Lillie, and Fred Emney. In December 1940 at the Sheffield Empire, Dixon made the first of more than a dozen appearances as Principal Boy in Christmas pantomime, playing Prince Charming to Jack Buchanan's Buttons in *Cinderella*. Constantly mixing roles in both the straight and musical theatre, Dixon joined Sonnie Hale in the short-lived (10 performances at the Piccadilly Theatre) *The Knight Was Bold* in 1943, and said farewell to the London musical stage in an old fashioned romantic piece, with a score by Eric Maschwitz and Jack Strachey, entitled *Belinda Fair* (1949). Two years earlier, she had also concluded her occasional film career, which had included the musical, *Calling The Tune* (1936), featuring guest artists Sir Henry Wood and Reginald Forsyth. West End audiences saw Dixon for the last time as Prince Charming in the 1953 production of *Cinderella*, which starred Julie Andrews just prior to her ascendancy to superstardom on Broadway via The Boy Friend and My Fair Lady. Thereafter Dixon made several forays into the provincial theatre before retiring in the late 50s. Her husband of nearly 50 years, jewel expert Ernest Schwaiger, died in 1976, and some 10 years later Dixon moved from London to a retirement home in Sale, Greater Manchester.

● FILMS: *Uneasy Virtue* (1931), *The Happy Husband* (1932), *Calling The Tune* (1936), *Banana Ridge* (1941), *Woman To Woman* (1947).

DIXON, MORT

b. 20 March 1892, New York, USA, d. 23 March 1956, Bronxville, New York, USA. A leading lyricist for popular songs during the 20s and 30s, as a young man Dixon became an actor in vaudeville, and then served in France during World War I. After the war he directed the famous army show *Whiz Bang*, in France. He began to write songs in the early 20s, and in 1923 collaborated with Ray Henderson on 'That Old Gang Of Mine', which became a big hit for Billy Murray and Ed Smalle, and Benny Krueger, amongst others. Throughout the decade Dixon had more success with 'Wonder Who's Kissing Her Tonight?' and 'If I Had A Girl Like You' (both Krueger), 'Follow The Swallow' (Al Jolson), 'Bam, Bam, Bamy Shore' (Ted Lewis), 'Bye Bye Blackbird' (written with Henderson, and one of Dixon's biggest hits, for Nick Lucas and Gene Austin, and revived later by Helen Merrill), 'I'm Looking Over A Four-Leaf Clover' (written with Harry Woods, and another of Dixon's most enduring numbers, especially in the Al Jolson version), 'Just Like A Butterfly' (Ipana Troubadors), 'Nagasaki' (written with Warren, and a song which epitomized the whole 20s flappers scene) and 'Where The Wild Flowers Grow'. In 1928, 'If You Want A Rainbow (You Must Have The Rain)' (written by Dixon, Billy Rose and Oscar Levant) was included in the early talkie, *My Man*. This was followed by Billy Rose's Broadway revue *Sweet And Low* (1930), for which Dixon, Harry Warren and Rose wrote 'Would You Like To Take A Walk?'. When the show was re-staged the following year under the title of *Crazy Quilt*, 'I Found a Million Dollar Baby (In A Five And Ten Cent Store)' was added. Later the number was associated mostly with Nat 'King' Cole, and was featured in the Barbra Streisand vehicle, *Funny Girl* (1975). Also in 1931, Morton, together with Joe Young and Warren, wrote 'Ooh! That Kiss', 'The Torch Song' and 'You're My Everything'. The latter became the title song of the 1949 movie starring Dan Dailey and Anne Baxter, and was used even later by the popular UK entertainer, Max Bygraves, as the signature tune for his *Sing-Along-A-Max* television series. In the early 30s, Dixon collaborated with composer Allie Wrubel on the songs for several Warner Brothers movies. For the spectacular *Dames* (1934), they merely added 'Try To See It My Way' to the existing Warren-Dubin score, but for *Flirtation Walk* they wrote 'Mr And Mrs Is The Name', 'I See Two Lovers', 'When Do We Eat?' and the title song. Other Dixon-Wrubel scores included *Happiness Ahead* ('Pop! Goes Your Heart', 'All On Account Of A Strawberry Sundae' and the title song), *Sweet Music*, starring Rudy Vallee ('Fare Thee Well Annabelle', 'The Snake Charmer'), *In Caliente* ('To Call My Own', the title song and 'The Lady In Red'), *I Live For Love* ('Mine Alone', 'Silver Wings', 'I Wanna Play House', 'A Man Must Shave', and the title song), and *Broadway Hostess* ('He Was Her Man', 'Let It Be Me', 'Weary', 'Who But You' and 'Playboy Of Paris'). His other songs included 'Under The Ukelele Tree', 'I'm In Love With You, That's Why', 'Is It Possible?', 'Moonbeam', 'In The Sing Song Sycamore Tree', 'Where The Forget-Me-Nots Remember', 'River Stay 'Way From My Door' (a hit in 1931 for Ethel Waters and Kate Smith, and revived by Frank Sinatra over 20 years later), 'Pink Elephants' (George Olsen and Guy Lombardo), 'I Raised My Hat', 'Marching Along Together', 'So Nice Seeing You Again', 'Toddlin' Along With You', 'Did You Mean It?', 'Every Once In A While' and 'Tears From My Inkwell'. In the late 30s, Dixon's output declined, and he retired early to live in Westchester County, New York.

DO I HEAR A WALTZ?

It has been called 'a creative match made in heaven', but for some of the participants it became a living hell. Put another way, the 'dream ticket' of Stephen Sondheim (lyrics), Richard Rodgers (music), and Arthur Laurents (book), became a kind of nightmare. Apparently, Sondheim was reluctant to commit himself to the project from the start, and in the event, he and Rodgers just did not get along. *Do I Hear A Waltz?* opened at the 46th Street Theatre in New York on 18 March 1965. It was based on Laurents' own play, *The Time Of The Cuckoo*, which had also been filmed in 1955 as *Summertime*, with Katharine Hepburn. The story concerns Leona Samish (Elizabeth Allen), 'a virginal spinster lady' who travels to Venice and falls in love with Renato Di Rossi (Sergio Franchi), who she subsequently discovers is a married man. Although, for the first time in her life 'she hears a waltz', she terminates the affair and returns from her holiday a sadder but wiser woman. Sondheim and Rodgers have both expressed their unhappiness and general dissatisfaction with each other, and with the piece, but their collaboration did result in a charming and interesting score. Several of the songs are more than worthwhile, including a tourists' lament, 'What Do We Do? We Fly!' ('If it's white, it's sweet/If it's brown, it's meat/If it's grey, don't eat!'), 'Take The Moment', the ravishing 'Moon In My Window', 'Someone Woke Up', 'Stay', 'Thinking', and the title song a typically lovely Rodgers waltz. Sondheim was forced to change the lyric to 'We're Gonna Be All Right', which was sung by a couple whose marriage was shaky, because it was considered 'not suitable for a Rodgers' musical'. The original surfaced during the 70s in the revue, *Side By Side By Sondheim*, and contained lines such as 'Sometimes she drinks in bed/Sometimes he's homosexual/But why be vicious?/They keep it out of sight/Just so we're gonna be all right'. *Do I Hear A Waltz* staggered along for only 220 performances, but is fondly remembered via its fine cast album. Revivals occasionally emerge particularly in Britain, where, in the early 90s, two concert versions and a production by the Guildhall School of Music were widely applauded.

DO RE MI

Not remotely connected with the famous song of that title written in 1959 by Richard Rodgers and Oscar Hammerstein for their smash-hit musical, The Sound Of Music, this show, which opened a year later on 26 December 1960 at the St. James Theatre in New York, had a much more contemporary theme - and Phil Silvers. He had recently been 'demobilised' from the long-running television series in which he had starred as the conniving Sergeant Bilko, and was returning to the New York musical stage after an absence of nearly 10 years. Prospects looked good for *Do Re Mi* - the book was written by the celebrated author Garson Kanin, and Jule Styne (music), along with Betty Comden and Adolph Green (lyrics), provided the score. Nancy Walker, who had made such an impact on her Broadway debut in *High Button Shoes* nearly 20 years before, was Silvers' co-star in a story that concerned one of America's greatest gifts to the civilised world - jukeboxes. Hubie Cram (Phil Silvers) persuades some old slot machine hoodlums, Brains Berman, Fats O'Rear, and Skin Demopoulos, to come out of retirement and help him to make the big time. When their singer, Tilda Mullen (Nancy Dussault), is poached by rival businessman John Henry Wheeler (John Reardon), it sparks off a bitter jukebox war. In the end, Hubie decides it is better to have his wife, Kay (Nancy Walker), by the hearth (she leaves him for a time), than a jukebox in the Zen Pancake Parlour. Nancy Dussault and John Reardon had the show's big hit, 'Make Someone Happy', and they combined again on the unconventional 'Fireworks'. The rest of the delightful score included 'All You Need Is A Quarter', 'Cry Like The Wind', 'What's New At The Zoo?', 'The Late, Late Show', 'I Know About Love', 'Asking for You', 'All Of My Life', 'Adventure', and 'Ambition'. *Do Re Mi* ran for 400 performances on Broadway, but the London production, which starred Max Bygraves, Maggie Fitzgibbon, Jan Waters, and Steve Arlen, did not appeal much to British audiences.

DOCTOR DOLITTLE

A disaster movie of the wrong kind - this lavish and expensive musical about one man's incredible affinity with animals was released from captivity in 1968 by 20th Century-Fox, and quietly crawled into a corner and died. Rex Harrison, just a few years after his triumph in the screen version of *My Fair Lady*, played the country Doctor who could talk to the animals in more than 400 different languages (courtesy of a parrot named Polynesia), and whose house in the English village Puddleby-on-the-Marsh, resembled London Zoo - only more so. Samantha Eggar and Anthony Newley tried hard to inject some life into the proceedings, and Richard Attenborough, as a much be-whiskered circus promoter confronted by Pushmi-Pullyu, a double-headed llama (one at each end), was suitably incredulous on 'I've Never Seen Anything Like It'. That song was part of an engaging score by Leslie Bricusse that also included 'My Friend The Doctor', 'Beautiful Things', 'When I Look In Your Eyes', 'After Today', 'Fabulous Places', 'I Think I Like You', 'At The Crossroads', 'The Vegetarian', 'Like Animals', 'Where Are The Words?', 'Something In Your Smile', and 'Doctor Dolittle'. Harrison's most effective number, 'Talk To The Animals', won the Academy Award for best song, and the film picked up another Oscar for special effects (L.B. Abbott), the most impressive of these being the Great Pink Sea Snail. Other, more human, roles were taken by Peter Bull, William Dix, Geoffrey Holder, Norma Varden, Muriel Landers and Portia Nelson. Leslie Bricusse was responsible for the screenplay which was based on Hugh Lofting's much-loved stories, and Herbert Ross designed the choreography. Richard Fleischer directed, and the film was shot in DeLuxe Color and Todd AO.

It was reportedly Jim Henson, creator of the Muppets, who first suggested to Bricusse that *Doctor Dolittle* should be turned into a stage show. After Henson's sudden death in 1990, his son Brian took over the British-based Henson Creature Workshop, and in 1998, the organization fulfilled its creator's dream by taking on the £4 million stage version of *Doctor Dolittle*. It created a menagerie of some 92 animals - from an eight-inch long goldfish to an 18ft-tall dinosaur. Using a system known as animatronics, the large creatures contained human operators, with remote controls for the smaller ones. The chief human being, Dr. John Dolittle, was played by Phillip Schofield, making a substantial leap from his comparatively undemanding role in *Joseph And The Amazing Technicolor Dreamcoat*. He is aided, abetted - and sometimes obstructed (a spell in an asylum on the charge of abducting a seal) - in his search for the pink sea snail by, among others, girlfriend Emma Fairfax (Sarah Jane Hassell), 10-year-old local boy Tommy Stubbins (James Paul Bradley/Samuel Carter-Bown/Darien Smith), circus owner Albert Blossom and his wife Gertie (John Rawnsley and Jane Stoggles), Cats fish man Matthew Mugg (Bryan Smyth), fisherman Charlie (Hadrian Delacey), and colleague Straight Arrow (Peter Gallagher). Chee-Chee the chimpanzee (Holli Hoffman) got in on the act as well, and in a real coup for the production, Broadway and West End legend Julie Andrews provided the recorded voice of Polynesia the parrot. Polynesia joined Dolittle, Matthew and Tommy on 'Talk To The Animals', one of several surviving songs from Bricusse's film score. Another making the trip from celluloid to stage was 'When I Look In Your Eyes' (sung by the good Doctor to Sophie the Seal), and there were three newcomers, 'You're Impossible' (Dolittle and Emma), 'Save The Animals' (Straight Arrow and Company), and 'The Voice Of Protest' (Emma and Company). The whole affair was played out on Mark Thompson's exquisite sets, and he was also responsible for the ravishing costumes. Aletta Collins designed the (minimal) choreography, and by the time Dolittle made his hair-raising descent aboard the luminescent Giant Lunar Moth, in order to sort out a pack of raging foxhunters, the evening had a definite feeling of 'Animal Lib Rules OK' about it.

A few days after the show opened, fans of Lofting's stories, who may have found it too sentimental for them, were able to catch the release of a new, non-musical film version starring Eddie Murphy. Henson's Creature Workshop provided the animatronics for this one too, although with the movie's 'lavatorial and butt humour, messages of political correctness and cultural diversity in San Francisco', along with 'an alcoholic marmoset, flatulent rodents, and a suicidal circus tiger', there were few other similarities.

DOLLY SISTERS, THE

The real-life Hungarian Dolly Sisters, Jenny and Rosie, started in American vaudeville before graduating to Broadway musicals and revues such as the Ziegfeld Follies (1911) and the Greenwich Village Follies of 1924. In the latter production they introduced Cole Porter's 'I'm In Love Again', and they were always surrounded by good songs. There were plenty of those, too, in this 1945 film biography which had a screenplay by John Larkin and Marion Spitzer based on John Kenyon Nicholson's story.

Betty Grable and June Haver portray the song-and-dance sister act which, after playing small-time clubs and theatres, catch the attention of producer Oscar Hammerstein (grandfather of Oscar Hammerstein II) played by Frank Middlemass, and zooms right to the top. Along the way - in the film, at least - Haver falls for Frank Latimore, and Grable gets John Payne at last - something she failed to do in Tin Pan Alley (1940). Also in the cast were S.Z. Sakall, Reginald Gardiner, Gene Sheldon, André Charlot, Sig Ruman, Colette Lyons, and Lester Allen. As for the songs, they were a mixture of old and new. Grable, Payne and Haver all had a crack at the best of the newcomers, 'I Can't Begin To Tell You' (Jimmy Monaco-Mack Gordon), and the trio shared the honours on the remainder which included 'I'm Always Chasing Rainbows' (Harry Carroll-Joseph McCarthy, adapted from Chopin), 'Give Me The Moonlight, Give Me The Girl' (Albert Von Tilzer-Lew Brown), 'Darktown Strutters' Ball' (Shelton Brooks), 'The Sidewalks Of New York' (James Blake-Charles Lawlor), 'Powder, Lipstick And Rouge' (Harry Revel-Mack Gordon), 'Carolina In The Morning' (Walter Donaldson-Gus Kahn), 'We Have Been Around' (Gordon-Charles Henderson), and 'The Vamp' (Byron Gay). This lively, colourful and thoroughly enjoyable film - it grossed nearly $4 million and became one of the hit musicals of the 40s - was choreographed by Ernest Palmer and directed by Irving Cummings. It was photographed in Technicolor and produced by 20th Century-Fox.

DON'T BOTHER ME I CANT COPE

Conceived by director Vinnette Carroll at his Urban Arts Corps Thatre, this show, the title of which the authors are said to prefer without traditional punctuation, transferred to the Playhouse Theatre in New York on 19 April 1972. It was performed by an all-black cast, whose generally good-natured, self-effacing exhortations regarding their proclaimed inferior position in the scheme of things - even in the modern world - was supplemented by music and lyrics by Micki Grant which ranged through a variety of musical styles including gospel, jazz, calypso, and downright joyful good-time music. The numbers included 'Don't Bother Me I Cant Cope', 'Good Vibrations', 'Fighting For Pharaoh', 'It Takes A Whole Lot Of Human Feeling', and 'Thank Heaven For You'. In the cast were Alex Bradford, Micki Grant, Hope Clarke, Bobby Hill, and Arnold Wilkerson. Opinions vary as to why this particular mixture of message and music took off, but it did, and in a big way - for nearly two and half years - a total of 1,065 performances. In 1976 Micki Grant , Hope Clarke, and Alex Bradford were the prime movers in another all-black production, *Your Arms Too Short To Box With God* (*sans* punctuation again), which was based on the Gospel according to St. Matthew, and provided the 'best singing and dancing on Broadway' for a time, and was revived twice in the early 80s. Delores Hall won a Tony Award for best featured actress. Another production with all-black entertainers and a book, music, and lyrics by Grant, entitled *It's So Nice To Be Civilized*, closed after one week in 1980.

DON'T KNOCK THE ROCK

The same production team responsible for *Rock Around The Clock* made this 1956 film. Alan Dale played the part of rock 'n' roll singer Arnie Haynes, accused by parents of corrupting impressionable minds when he returns to his home-town. Disc jockey Alan Freed enjoyed a prominent role as Haynes' agent. When a riot breaks out at a concert headlined by Bill Haley And His Comets, the pair stage another show to convince the adults the music is no more controversial than previous fashions. The Treniers and Dave Appell And His Applejacks make appearances, but the film's highlight comes courtesy of Little Richard who contributes explosive versions of 'Long Tall Sally', 'Tutti Frutti' and 'Rip It Up'.

DON'T KNOCK THE TWIST

Mindful of Don't Knock The Rock, a follow-up to Rock Around The Clock, *Don't Knock The Twist* succeeded Twist Around The Clock. Few could accuse its producers of possessing imagination. This 1962 feature revolved around a television executive, who hurriedly stages a twisting marathon to pre-empt a similar plan by a rival station. Chubby Checker contributed the title song and 'Slow Twistin', the latter with the help of Dee Dee Sharp. Inspired by another dance craze, Ms. Sharp offered the memorable 'Mashed Potato Time', while the Dovels sang 'Do The New Continental' and 'Bristol Stomp'. Soul singer Gene Chandler provided the undoubted highlight when, replete with top hat, cape and monocle, he performed the classic 'Duke Of Earl'.

DON'T LOOK BACK

Arguably the finest documentary in rock, *Don't Look Back* is a *cinéma vérité* film of Bob Dylan's 1965 tour of England. Director D.A. Pennebaker shot the proceedings in black and white with a 16mm, hand-held camera. Indeed, the opening scene, in which 'Subterranean Homesick Blues' plays while the singer holds up placards with words from its lyric, has become a much-copied pop legend. The subsequent pace is almost relentless and, having gained access both onstage and off, Pennebaker exposes Dylan in various moods. The concert footage itself is superb, in particular because this would be Dylan's final all-acoustic tour. He performs excellent versions of 'Gates Of Eden' and 'It's Alright Ma (I'm Only Bleeding)', but these are overshadowed by other events captured on film. Dylan's verbal demolition of the *Time* magazine reporter is revelatory, as is his anger when some glasses are thrown from a window at a party. Yet a sense of mischief abounds when, in the company of US companion Bobby Neuworth, a running joke about Donovan only ends when Dylan finally meets his supposed 'rival'. Joan Baez, Marianne Faithfull, Alan Price, John Mayall, Derroll Adams and sundry Pretty Things are also caught on camera, but Dylan is always the focus of attention. *Don't Look Back* was released in 1967, but screenings were generally restricted to independent cinemas. It was withdrawn on Dylan's instructions for a period during the 70s, but was reactivated again in the 80s and finally released on video.

DONALDSON, WALTER

b. 15 February 1893, New York City, New York, USA, d. 15 July 1947. A self-taught pianist, despite his mother being a piano teacher, Donaldson began composing while still attending school. After leaving school he worked in various finance companies, but also held down jobs as a song plugger and piano demonstrator. He had his first small successes in 1915 with 'Back Home In Tennessee' (lyrics by William Jerome), 'You'd Never Know The Old Town Of Mine' (Howard Johnson) and other songs popularizing places and regions. Donaldson's first major success was 'The Daughter Of Rosie O'Grady' in 1918, just before he began a period entertaining at US army camps. After the war he had some minor successes with songs used in Broadway shows, the best known of which was 'How Ya Gonna Keep 'Em Down On The Farm' (Sam M. Lewis and Joe Young). It was another song, written by Donaldson with Lewis and Young, that established him as a major songwriter of the 20s. This was 'My Mammy', popularized by Al Jolson and which ever afterwards became synonymous with the blackface entertainer. Jolson also sang other Donaldson compositions, including 'My Buddy' and 'Carolina In The Morning' (both with Gus Kahn). With Kahn, Donaldson also wrote 'I'll See You In My Dreams', 'Yes Sir, That's My Baby', 'I Wonder Where My Baby Is Tonight', 'That Certain Party', 'Makin' Whoopee' and 'Love Me Or Leave Me'. These last two songs came from the Broadway show, Whoopee, written by Donaldson and Kahn in 1928, where they were sung respectively by Eddie Cantor and Ruth Etting. When the Hollywood version of the show was filmed, in 1930, among additional songs Donaldson and Kahn wrote was 'My Baby Just Cares For Me'. In the 30s Donaldson also contributed numbers to films such as Hollywood Party, Kid Millions, The Great Ziegfeld, Suzy, Sinner Take All, After The Thin Man, Saratoga, and That's Right-You're Wrong. Although his collaboration with Kahn was enormously successful, Donaldson sometimes worked with other lyricists, including George Whiting ('My Blue Heaven'), Howard Johnson ('Georgia'), Cliff Friend ('Let It Rain, Let It Pour') and Abe Lyman ('What Can I Say After I Say I'm Sorry'). On occasions he also wrote lyrics to his own music, notably as 'At Sundown', 'You're Driving Me Crazy' and 'Little White Lies'. In the 30s, Donaldson wrote many songs for films with such collaborators as Kahn and Howard Dietz, and he also worked with Johnny Mercer.

DONEN, STANLEY

b. 13 April 1924, Columbia, South Carolina, USA. The director and choreographer for a string of classic MGM musicals of the 50s, Donen was fascinated by film and theatre from an early age. After graduating from high school he worked on Broadway in the chorus of the Richard Rodgers and Lorenz Hart musical Pal Joey (1940), which starred Gene Kelly, and he assisted Kelly on the choreography for Best Foot Forward (1941) and also appeared in the chorus. Signed to MGM, during the 40s he worked as choreographer, co-choreographer and/or co-director of occasional sequences (often uncredited) on musicals such as Cover Girl, Hey Rookie, Jam Session, Kansas City Kitty,

Anchors Aweigh, Holiday In Mexico, No Leave, No Love, Living In A Big Way, This Time For Keeps, A Date With Judy, The Kissing Bandit and Take Me Out To The Ball Game. In 1949 Donen made his official directorial debut as Gene Kelly's co-director on the acclaimed, groundbreaking musical On The Town, and they worked together on several more memorable films, including Singin' In The Rain, It's Always Fair Weather and The Pajama Game. Donen also brought his skill as a director of breathtakingly fresh and exuberant sequences to pictures such as Wedding Bells, Give A Girl A Break (also choreographed with Gower Champion), Deep In My Heart, Seven Brides For Seven Brothers, Funny Face and Damn Yankees (1958). By that time the golden age of movie musicals was over, and, with the exception of The Little Prince (1974), Donen concentrated on directing (and producing) dramatic and light-comedy films such as Indiscreet, The Grass Is Greener, Arabesque, Two For The Road, Bedazzled, Staircase, Lucky Lady, Movie, Movie, Saturn 3, and Blame It On Rio (1984). Since then, Donen has been rumoured to be trying to bring biographies of Judy Garland and Marlene Dietrich to the screen, but to date nothing has materialized. In 1988 he produced the Academy Awards show, and five years later made his directorial debut on Broadway in the Jule Styne musical The Red Shoes. After the original director, Susan Schulman, bowed out in the early stages of production, Donen took over. Unfortunately, unlike those earlier MGM musicals, there was no happy ending and the show closed after three days. However, in 1998 Donen received an Honorary Academy Award 'in appreciation of a body of work marked by grace, elegance, wit and visual innovation'.

DONOVAN, JASON

b. Jason Sean Donovan, 1 June 1968, Malvern, Melbourne, Australia. Donovan appeared in the Australian television soap-opera Neighbours, which, when shown on British television, commanded a considerable viewing audience of pre-pubescent/teenage girls who instantly took his character, Scott Robinson, to their hearts. His co-star Kylie Minogue had already begun to forge a career in pop music when he also signed to the Stock, Aitken And Waterman label, PWL. In 1988 his first single, 'Nothing Can Divide Us Now', reached the UK Top 5. The follow-up was a collaboration with Kylie, 'Especially For You', which topped the UK charts in January the following year. Donovan consolidated his position as Britain's top teen pin-up by scoring four more Top 10 hits, including 'Too Many Broken Hearts' (a number 1 hit), 'Sealed With A Kiss', 'Every Day (I Love You More)' and 'When You Come Back To Me'. His album, Ten Good Reasons, reached number 1 and became one of 1989's bestsellers. His success the following year was endorsed by Top 10 hits in 'Hang On To Your Love' and a remake of the 1963 Cascades hit, 'Rhythm Of The Rain'. By this time Donovan had left the cast of Neighbours. His performances in the stage show of the Andrew Lloyd Webber/Tim Rice musical Joseph And The Amazing Technicolor Dreamcoat, at the London Palladium, drew sell-out crowds and mostly good reviews, taking many of his regular critics by surprise. A single from the show, 'Any Dream Will Do', reached number 1 in the UK chart, scotching any notion that Donovan was wavering as a hit-maker. He was perceived by many as simply being a teen-idol, yet his obvious talent in acting and singing, and the extent of his loyal following, echoed previous teen-idols made good as all-round entertainers (Tommy Steele for example).

In the spring of 1992, Donovan won a libel action he brought against *The Face* magazine. Later in the same year, his high-profile concert tour was greeted with a good deal of apathy and critical derision ('Jason's big rock dream turns sour'), and it was considered by many to be a retrograde career move when he returned to *Joseph And The Amazing Technicolor Dreamcoat* the following year. For some time he alternated with other leading performers before taking over for the last few weeks before the show closed in February 1994. After he had collapsed several times in public during 1995, there was inevitably speculation in the press regarding drugs and alcohol abuse. However, the following year he was in London playing Mordred in the Covent Garden Festival production of Camelot, and had his first non-singing role as a psychopath who keeps his first victim's head in a hat box, in Emlyn Williams's classic 1935 thriller, *Night Must Fall*, at the Theatre Royal Haymarket. Having also dressed in a black bin liner and Dr. Marten boots in order to host *Mr. Gay UK*, a beauty contest for men, he went one step further and donned the obligatory stockings and suspenders for the role of Frank 'N' Furter in an Australian production of *The Rocky Horror Show*. In 1998, he headed the 25th Anniversary tour of that cult show in Britain.

● ALBUMS: *Ten Good Reasons* (PWL 1989)★★, *Between The Lines* (PWL 1990)★★, *Joseph And The Amazing Technicolor Dreamcoat* stageshow soundtrack (PolyGram 1991)★★★, *All Around The World* (Polydor 1993)★★.
● COMPILATIONS: *Greatest Hits* (PWL 1991)★★★.
● VIDEOS: *Jason, The Videos* (PWL 1989), *The Videos 2* (PWL 1990), *Into The Nineties: Live* (Castle Music Pictures 1991), *Greatest Video Hits* (PWL 1991), *The Joseph Mega-Remix* (PolyGram Music Video 1992), *Live* (1993).

DOUBLE TROUBLE

In this 1967 feature Elvis Presley plays a singer on tour in Europe who falls for two girls; one in Belgium, another, a teenage heiress, in London. Of course the star did not visit Britain; location shots were handled by a second crew. In keeping with the dated air Presley's film career now epitomised, such scenes emphasised a passé 'Swinging London' image, rather than concurrent psychedelia. The soundtrack material was equally lamentable, plumbing new depths with 'Old MacDonald', one of the worst songs ever recorded by an established artist. Of the nine songs featured only 'Long Legged Girl (With The Short Dress On)' showed any merit yet, when issued as a single, the song failed to reach the US Top 50 and UK Top 40. It was the first Presley a-side to do so since he joined RCA from Sun Records in 1956.

DOWN ARGENTINE WAY

Don Ameche and Betty Grable were the headliners in this 1940 20th Century-Fox musical, but, as the opening titles gave way to the action, the first impression was made by Brazilian bombshell Carmen Miranda who began her American film debut with a dynamic interpretation of Jimmy McHugh and Al Dubin's 'South American Way' - or as she insisted on singing it, 'Souse American Way'. Miranda was also involved in two other numbers, which was rather fortunate because there was not a lot to the plot. It concerned a Buenos Aires horsebreeder, played by Don Ameche, who is prevented from selling one of his prized specimens to wealthy New Yorker Glenda Crawford (Betty Grable), because she is the daughter of his father's worst enemy. This is an obstacle that true romance eventually surmounts, and the two lovers, Ameche and Gable - and their respective families - settle their differences with the help of some agreeable locations and an attractive bunch of songs, most of which were written by Harry Warren and Mack Gordon. These included a lovely ballad, 'Two Dreams Met', along with 'Sing To Your Senorita', 'Nenita', and 'Down Argentina Way' which is sung by practically everyone in the film including the Nicholas Brothers who use it as the setting for one of their scintillating acrobatic dance routines. The other songs were 'Mama Yo Quiero' (Jaraca and Vincente Paiva) and 'Doin' The Conga' (Gene Rose). Also in the cast were J. Carroll Naish, Henry Stephenson, Katharine Aldridge, Leonid Kinskey, Chris-Pin Martin, and the ubiquitous Charlotte Greenwood, whose wise-cracking and high-kicking was a joy, as ever. Darrell Ware and Karl Tunberg's screenplay was based on a story by Rian James and Ralph Spencer, and the bright and attractive dances were staged by Nick Castle and Geneva Sawyer. Irving Cummings was the director, and this diverting and tuneful film was photographed in Technicolor.

DOWNS, JOHNNY

b. John Morey Downs, 10 October 1913, New York City, USA, d. 6 June 1994, Coronado, California, USA. An old-styled song and dance man, Downs' contributions to the screen as a dancer and singer may not have stolen the headlines, but in their entirety they added up to a worthy body of work. The son of a navy lieutenant, Downs' family relocated to San Diego when he was eight. Encouraged by his mother to attend film auditions, he made his debut in a silent comedy alongside Charley Chase, before beginning a sequence of *Our Gang* silent movies for Hal Roach. His first grounding in stage work came on the east coast, however, opposite Jimmy Durante in *Strike Me Pink*. Back with Roach, he took a small role in the Laurel & Hardy production of the stage musical hit, *Babes In Toyland*. His subsequent musical films of the 30s (often dubbed teen operas or college musicals) included *College Scandal* (remade as *Sweater Girl* in 1942, giving Betty Jane Rhodes a number 1 hit in 'I Don't Want To Walk Without You'), *College Holiday*, *Pigskin Parade* (both 1936), *Turn Off The Moon* (1937) and *Hold That Co-Ed* (1938). Afterwards he switched to Universal for a further series of low-budget musicals. These began with *Swing, Sister, Swing* (1939, which saw him sing 'The Baltimore Rumble', an intended US answer to 'The Lambeth Walk'), then *Hawaiian Nights* (1939). *I Can't Give You Anything But Love, Baby* from the following year saw him sing the title-song, before he moved to Republic for *Melody And Moonlight*. Another of

Downs' most famous numbers, 'The Aloha Lowdown', was premiered on the cut and paste *Moonlight And Hawaii* soundtrack. After a break from musicals with a leading role in the horror flick *Mad Monster* (1942) he returned to his established stomping ground with *Harvest Melody* in 1943. After which he spent the rest of the 40s and early 50s in Broadway productions such as *Here Come The Girls* and *Are You With It?* He came back to Hollywood in 1953 for his last major role in *Cruisin' Down The River*, before returning to his adopted San Diego home, appearing regularly on television as a host of children's programmes for nearly two decades.

DRAKE, ALFRED

b. Alfredo Capurro, 7 October, 1914, New York City, New York, USA, d. 25 July 1992, New York, USA. An actor, singer, director, and author, Drake will always be associated with that magical moment when the curtain rose on Oklahoma! at the St. James Theatre in New York on 31 March 1943, and he made his entrance singing 'Oh, What A Beautiful Mornin''. The show marked a new and exciting beginning for the American musical theatre, and Drake reigned as its leading male star for more than a decade. After singing in the Glee Club at Brooklyn College, he made his stage debut in July 1935 at the Adelphi Theatre in New York in the chorus of *The Mikado*. A year later, he was in the chorus again, and also understudied one of the leading roles, in a City Centre revival of *White Horse Inn*. In 1937 he introduced the title song in *Babes In Arms*, and was also featured in *Two Bouquets* (1938) with Patricia Morison, an actress who would later share in one of his greatest successes. From 1939-40 Drake also appeared in three Broadway revues, *One For The Money*, *The Straw Hat Revue* (with Danny Kaye), and *Two For The Show*, in which, together with Frances Comstock, he introduced the future standard, 'How High The Moon'. After his magnetic performance in *Oklahoma!*, Drake co-starred with Burl Ives in Walter Kerr's folk music tribute *Sing Out, Sweet Land* (1944), played Macheath in John Latouche and Duke Ellington's contemporary version of *The Beggar's Holiday* (1946), and took the role of Larry Foreman, the union organiser, in a revival of The Cradle Will Rock (1947). In 1948 he enjoyed what is often considered to be his greatest personal success in Kiss Me, Kate. Drake gave a marvellously witty and stylish performance in the role of Fred Graham, the egocentric thespian who is tormented on and off stage by his leading lady (Patricia Morison), who also happens to be his ex-wife, Lilli. His glorious lyric tenor voice delighted audiences on numbers such as 'Where Is the Life That Late I Led?', 'I've Come To Wive It Wealthily In Padua', and 'Were Thine That Special Face'. In 1951 he turned down the leading role in The King And I, but played it for a time in 1953 while Yul Brynner was on holiday. Two years later he completed a hat-trick of great roles when he played Hajj, the public poet in the musical version of Kismet (1955), for which he won New York Drama Critics, Donaldson, and Tony Awards. He reprised his role in the London production and for subsequent revivals. Along with the triumphs, Drake had his flop musicals too, as a performer, director and author. They included *The Liar* (1950),

Courtin' Time (1951), Lock Up Your Daughters (1960), *Kean* (1961), and *Zenda* (1963). He made his final appearance in a Broadway musical in Gigi (1973), a lacklustre adaptation of the classic film which closed after three months. For most of his career he remained active in the straight, non-musical theatre, and was especially applauded for his Shakespearean roles which included Claudius to Richard Burton's Hamlet in John Gielgud's 1964 Broadway production. He bade farewell to the Broadway stage in *The Skin Of Our Teeth* in 1975. Ironically, as is often the case with Hollywood, he was not required to recreate his major stage performances for the screen; Gordon MacRae and Howard Keel took care of those. Drake made only one film, a routine musical called *Tars And Spars* (1946). He appeared on plenty of television productions, though, and there still exists a 90-minute telecast of *Kiss Me, Kate* from 1958, in which he is said to be awesome. In 1990 Drake received his second Tony, a special award for lifetime achievement as perhaps 'the greatest singing actor the American musical theatre has ever produced'.

DREAM

Subtitled '*The Johnny Mercer Musical*', this revue, which was conceived by Louis Westergaard and Jack Wrangler, opened on 3 April 1997 at the Royale Theatre in New York, and contained some 45 prime examples of the work of the great lyricist (and sometime composer). Lesley Ann Warren ('Goody Goody', 'Blues In The Night', 'That Old Black Magic'), Margaret Whiting, and jazz singer/guitarist John Pizzarelli ('Fools Rush In', 'Jeepers Creepers', 'I Thought About You') headed a talented cast that also featured Brooks Ashmanskas, Jonathan Dokuchitz, Charles McGowan, Jessica Molaskey and Darcie Roberts. Over the years, Whiting actually introduced several of Mercer's songs, and she excelled here with 'One For My Baby', 'Day In Day Out' and 'My Shining Hour'. Her father, Richard Whiting, was also one of Mercer's many collaborators, and he was represented by 'Have You Got Any Castles, Baby?', 'Hooray For Hollywood', and the enduring 'Too Marvellous For Words'. Among Mercer's other important composing colleagues were Harold Arlen, Hoagy Carmichael, Harry Warren, Jerome Kern, Rube Bloom, Victor Schertzinger, Henry Mancini - and of course, Mercer himself, who wrote both words and music for standards such as 'Something's Gotta Give' and the show's title number. *Dream* divided Mercer's long career into significant periods: 20s decadent Savannah (The Age of Innocence), 30s at the Rainbow nightclub (The Age of Decadence), 40s Big Band Era, and the golden, Academy Award-winning Hollywood years of the 50s, 60s, and beyond. Packed as it was with wonderful songs, *Dream* failed to register strongly when awards time came around (just one Tony Awards nomination, for director and choreographer Wayne Cilento), and the show closed on 6 July. Although Broadway was not the prime source of Mercer's work over the years, he did write occasional lyrics for musical shows in the 30s, as well as providing the complete score (with Rube Bloom) for the London production of *Blackbirds Of 1936*. He subsequently collaborated on entire scores for St. Louis Woman (with Harold Arlen, 1946), *Texas, L'il Darlin'* (music: Robert Emmett Dolan,

1949), *Top Banana* (Mercer, 1951), Li'l Abner (Gene de Paul, 1956), *Saratoga* (Arlen, 1959), *Foxy* (Dolan, 1964), and *The Good Companions* (André Previn, London 1974). His outstanding film score for Seven Brides For Seven Brothers (with de Paul) was also adapted for the stage in 1982 (Broadway) and 1985 (London). Among the many revues and cabaret shows to celebrate his lyrics, was one by Peggy Herman, whose *2 Marvellous 4 Words* played at New York's Eighty Eight's in the early 90s.

DREAMGIRLS

With a provocative book by Tom Eyen which tells of the peaks and troughs in the life of the Dreams, a black female singing group not a million miles away from the Supremes, *Dreamgirls* opened on Broadway at the Imperial Theatre on 20 December 1981 - and stayed for nearly four years. When it is apparent that they can make it right to the top, their manager, Curtis Taylor Jnr. (Ben Harney), tells the substantially built lead singer, Effie White (Jennifer Holliday), who has been his lover, to move over and to the rear, so that a more attractive girl can take the spotlight. The decision proves to be the right one for the group, and Effie eventually leaves and subsequently achieves her own, solo stardom. Michael Bennett, the doyen of Broadway choreographers and directors, staged the show brilliantly, and there were some stunning moments, especially Effie's dramatic rendering of 'And I Am Telling You I'm Not Going'. That number, and the rest of the score, was the work of Henry Krieger and Tom Eyen, who succeeded in infusing the songs with a genuine Motown quality. They included 'When I First Saw You', 'I Am Changing', 'Fake Your Way To The Top', 'Cadillac Car', 'Hard To Say Goodbye, My Love', 'Dreamgirls', and 'Steppin' On The Bad Side'. *Dreamgirls* ran for 1,522 performances and dominated the Tony Awards ceremony, winning in six categories: book, choreography (Bennett and Michael Peters), best actor (Harney), best actress (Holliday), featured actor (Cleavant Derricks), and lighting (Tharon Musser). Krieger and Eyen, together with producer David Foster, also picked up Grammys for Best Cast Show Album. In 1987, after an extensive road tour, a streamlined version of the show was welcomed back on Broadway for five months. Since that time various other productions have played US regional theatres such as the Paper Mill Playhouse, Marriot's Lincolnshire Theatre, and the Long Beach Civic Light Opera. A national touring company was on the road late 1997-98.

DU BARRY WAS A LADY

Cole Porter's third show with the dynamic Ethel Merman as his leading lady, and the third longest-running book musical of the 30s, opened at the 46th Street Theatre in New York on 6 December 1939. The book, by Herbert Fields and Buddy De Sylva, concerns Louis Blore (Bert Lahr), a washroom attendant at New York's Club Petite. Louis loves May Daly (Ethel Merman), the star of the club's floorshow, and feels that a windfall of $75,000 from a win on the Irish Sweepstakes puts him in with a chance. He tries to improve his odds by preparing a potent potion for May's married boyfriend, Alex Barton (Ronald Graham), but accidentally drinks it himself and passes

out. After waking from the trance, during which he imagines he is Louis XV and May is Du Barry, Louis realises that his place is really in the washroom, and leaves the field clear for Alex. The situation provides some marvellous opportunities for Lahr's inspired clowning and Raoul Péne du Bois's spectacular settings and costumes. 'Do I Love You?', sung by Merman and Graham, was the only one of Porter's songs that became popular outside the show, but his score contained several other witty and memorable numbers such as two Merman and Lahr duets, 'Friendship' (She: 'If they ever hang you, pard, send a card.' He: 'If they ever cut your throat, write a note.' She: 'If they ever make a cannibal stew of you. Invite me too.' Both: 'It's friendship, friendship . . .') and 'But In The Morning, No!'. Merman also had several excellent solo opportunities with 'When Love Beckoned (In Fifty-Second Street)', 'Give Him The Oo-La-La', and 'Katie Went To Haiti'. Another interesting item was 'Well, Did You Evah?', sung in this show by Charles Walters and the future World War II 'pin-up girl', Betty Grable, and later revised for the 1956 film, *High Society*. *Du Barry Was A Lady*, the last Broadway musical of the decade, stayed on for 408 performances, and a London production, with Arthur Riscoe and Frances Day as Louis and May, ran for nearly six months. The 1943 film version starred Gene Kelly, Lucille Ball, Red Skelton, and Virginia O'Brien.

DUBIN, AL

b. Alexander Dubin, 10 June 1891, Zurich, Switzerland, d. 11 February 1945. Brought by his parents to the USA when still a small child, Dubin grew up in Philadelphia. He wrote poetry and song lyrics while attending school, but his aspiration to become a professional songwriter was obstructed by parental hopes that he would follow in his father's footsteps as a surgeon. His education came to an abrupt halt in 1911 when he was expelled for neglecting his studies in favour of hanging out with musicians, gamblers and drunks, and he promptly headed for New York, and a career in music. A number of moderately successful songs were published in the years before World War I. During the war Dubin was gassed while serving in France, and soon afterwards he was back in New York writing songs. His work still met with only mild success until he had the idea of writing lyrics to several popular instrumentals, some of them from the classical field. The resulting songs included 'Humoresque' (music by Anton Dvorak) and 'Song Of India' (Rimsky-Korsakov). More orthodoxly, he wrote lyrics for 'The Lonesomest Gal In Town' (Jimmy McHugh and Irving Mills). By the late 20s Dubin was in Hollywood where he was teamed with Joe Burke, with such popular results as 'Tip Toe Through The Tulips', 'Painting The Clouds With Sunshine', 'Sally', 'Love Will Find A Way' and 'Dancing With Tears In My Eyes'. During the 30s, now collaborating with Harry Warren, Dubin enjoyed his most prolific and creative period, writing for films such as *The Crooner*, Roman Scandals, 42nd Street, *Gold Diggers Of 1933*, Footlight Parade, *Wonder Bar*, *Moulin Rouge*, *Twenty Million Sweethearts*, Dames, Go Into Your Dance, *Gold Diggers Of 1935*, *Broadway Gondolier*, *Shipmates Forever*, *Page Miss Glory*, *Sweet Music*, *Stars Over Broadway*, *Colleen*, *Hearts Divided*, *Sing Me A Love Song*,

Cain And Mabel, Melody For Two, Gold Diggers Of 1937, The Singing Marine, Mr. Dodd Takes The Air, and Gold Diggers In Paris (1939). Among the many successes the duo enjoyed over a five-year period were 'You're Getting To Be A Habit With Me', 'Young And Healthy', 'We're In The Money', 'Shanghai Lil', 'Honeymoon Hotel', 'The Boulevard Of Broken Dreams', 'I'll String Along With You', 'I Only Have Eyes For You', 'Keep Young And Beautiful', Lulu's Back In Town', 'With Plenty Of Money And You', 'Confidentially', 'Lullaby Of Broadway', which won an Oscar, and 'Love Is Where You Find It' (co-lyricist with Johnny Mercer). Dubin's hits with other collaborators included 'Nobody Knows What A Red Headed Mama Can Do' (Sammy Fain and Irving Mills); 'Dancing With Tears In My Eyes', and 'For You' (Joe Burke). Despite a lifestyle in which he indulged in excesses of eating, drinking, womanizing and drug-taking, Dubin wrote with enormous flair and speed. In addition to the foregoing collaborations with Warren, Dubin also wrote 'South American Way' (with McHugh), 'Indian Summer' (Victor Herbert), 'Along The Santa Fe Trail' (Will Grosz) and 'I Never Felt This Way Before' (Duke Ellington). By the end of the 30s, Dubin's lifestyle began to catch up with him and in the early 40s he suffered severe illness, the break-up of two marriages and a final collapse brought on by a drugs overdose.
● FURTHER READING: Lullaby Of Broadway: A Biography Of Al Dubin, P.D. McGuire.

DUKE WORE JEANS, THE

Taking its cue from the plot of The Prince And The Pauper, this 1958 film starred Tommy Steele as the son of a Cockney pearly king who trades lifestyles with his double, the Hon. Tony Whitecliffe. Inevitably, the former falls in love with an aristocrat. The Duke Wore Jeans has little to commend it other than being a vehicle for Steele's chirpy personality. He contributed eight songs to the soundtrack, including 'Happy Guitar', which reached number 20 in the UK charts when issued as a single. If Steele was ever a bona fide rock 'n' roll singer, this film marked his transformation into an all-round entertainer. The Duke Wore Jeans was retitled It's All Happening for the US market. The same title was used for a British 1963 feature film starring Steele, which was known as The Dream Maker in America.

DUKE, VERNON

b. Vladimir Dukelsky, 10 October 1903, Parfianovka, Russia, d. 16 January 1969. A popular composer during the 30s and 40s, Duke was a child prodigy. Initially classically-trained - he studied extensively, mainly at Kiev and Odessa - in the early 20s he began experimenting with songs written in the style of such currently popular composers as Irving Berlin and George Gershwin. For these early efforts at popular song writing, he used pseudonyms, a practice he continued when, in 1921, he emigrated to the USA. For the next three decades he used his real name for his classical compositions and the name Vernon Duke for his popular songs. His first songs in the New World suffered through his lack of a thorough grasp of English and his adherence to the styles of other songwriters. By the mid-20s, Duke was in Paris, pursuing his classical studies and writing music for the piano and the bal-

let. In London in the late 20s, he wrote for the musical stage, mostly for revues and in the field of operetta. Back in the USA before the decade was out, he was hired to write incidental music for films but still hoped to find popular success. This began with 'I Am Only Human After All', with lyrics by E. 'Yip' Harburg and Ira Gershwin, which featured in The Garrick Gaieties (1930). He continued to write for Broadway, with varying levels of success, and in the 1932 show, Walk A Little Faster, introduced his first standard, 'April In Paris' (with Harburg). For the 1934 show Thumbs Up, Duke wrote his own lyric for another song destined to become a standard, 'Autumn In New York', and in the same year contributed 'What Is There To Say?', and 'I Like The Likes Of You' to the Ziegfeld Follies. For the Ziegfeld Follies Of 1936 Duke composed 'An Island In The West Indies', 'That Moment Of Moments', and the magnificent 'I Can't Get Started', which was sung in the show by Bob Hope and Eve Arden. In 1940 he wrote the music for Cabin In The Sky, which opened on Broadway in October and featured an all-black cast. The show's songs included 'Taking A Chance On Love' (lyrics by John Latouche and Ted Fetter), introduced on the stage by Ethel Waters, and destined to become another standard. Duke's shows of the early 40s were not so well received and he followed his military service with a two-year sojourn in Paris. Back in the USA in the early 50s, Duke worked on a number of shows, including Two's Company and The Littlest Revue (both with Ogden Nash), but he was never able to recapture his earlier success. Later in his life he continued to write classical music, including oratorios and ballets. In 1994 Ben Bagley's Vernon Duke Revisited provided a timely reminder of several of his rarely heard, but lovely songs, such as 'Water Under The Bridge', 'Now', 'Lady', 'Roundabout', 'The Theatre Is A Lady', 'We're Having A Baby', 'I Cling To You', and 'If You Can't Get The Love You Want'.

DUNCAN, TODD

b. Robert Todd Duncan, 12 February 1903, Danville, Kentucky, USA, d. 28 February 1998, Washington, DC, USA. (Some sources give this artist's year of birth as 1900.) A splendid baritone singer, actor and teacher, Duncan is remembered particularly for creating the role of Porgy in America's most popular opera, Porgy And Bess. After attending Butler's University and the College of Fine Arts in Indianapolis, he became a music teacher in Louisville, Kentucky. In 1931, he was appointed Professor of Voice at Howard University in Washington (a post he held until 1945), and began his operatic career three years later in a production of Mascagni's Cavalleria Rusticana with the Aeollian Opera. His performance was seen by New York Times critic Olin Downes, who put forward Duncan's name when George Gershwin was auditioning around 100 baritones for the role of Porgy. However, Duncan considered himself to be an opera singer, and thought Gershwin rather 'Tin Pan Alley'. On their first meeting, after Duncan had sung only 12 measures of an Italian aria, Gershwin said: 'Will you be my Porgy?'. Incredibly, Duncan prevaricated, replying: 'Well, Mr. Gershwin, I've gotta hear your music first.' He soon realized the importance of the man and his music, and accepted the part. Duncan stayed with

Porgy And Bess for all 124 performances of its original 1935 Broadway run, introducing immortal numbers such as 'Bess, You Is My Woman Now' and 'I Got Plenty O' Nuttin''. He later co-starred with his Bess (Anne Brown) on the cast album, and in Cheryl Crawford's 1942 revival. In 1938, Duncan joined Stewart Granger, Edna Best and Adelaide Hall at London's Theatre Royal, Drury Lane, in *The Sun Never Sets*, a play adapted from the West Indian stories of Edgar Wallace. Two of his numbers were the suitably atmospheric 'Drums' and 'River God'. Duncan returned to Broadway with distinguished appearances in the musicals *Cabin In The Sky* (1940, as the Lawd's General) and *Lost In The Stars* (1949, as Stephen Kumalo). In the latter, which was adapted from Alan Paton's novel *Cry, The Beloved Country*, he sang the title song, and was acclaimed for his sensitive performance of a black Anglican minister whose son is sentenced to hang after killing a white man. In 1945, the same year he relinquished his post at Howard University, Duncan became the first black artist (in an otherwise all-white cast) to appear at the New York City Opera, when he sang the role of Tonio in Leoncavallo's *Pagliacci*. He was then at the height of his career, and continued to perform in opera and gave recitals in numerous countries as well as teaching at Howard University, the Curtis Institute of Music in Philedphia, and at his home in Washington. In 1942 Duncan was seen briefly on screen in *Syncopation*, a film tracing the history of jazz in fictional form, and in 1955, he played the part of Bill Howard in the prison drama *Unchained*, and sang Hy Zaret and Alex North's 'Unchained Melody', which has endured over the years. Duncan himself remained active for most of his life, but a few months before his death at the age of 95, he was too weak to attend a symposium on *Porgy And Bess* at the University of Michigan. Instead, he sent his good wishes and a rendition of 'Bess, You Is My Woman Now' on tape.

DUNING, GEORGE

b. 25 February 1908, Richmond, Indiana, USA. A composer and conductor for films, from the 40s through to the 80s. Duning studied at the University of Cincinnati, and the Cincinnati Conservatory Of Music, becoming a jazz and symphonic trumpet player. He was a sideman and chief arranger for the Kay Kyser Band in the early 40s when Kyser was one of the biggest attractions in the business. Around the same time, he began to arrange and orchestrate music for films, and in 1946 he collaborated with Irving Gertz to write the score for *The Devil's Mask*. Between then and 1950, he scored some 21 features for Columbia, a mixture of thrillers, melodramas, westerns and comedies. These included *Mysterious Intruder*; *Johnny O'Clock* and *To The Ends Of Earth*, starring Dick Powell, *The Guilt Of Janet James*; *I Love Trouble*; *The Man From Colorado*; *Shockproof*; *The Dark Past*; *The Undercover Man* and *And Baby Makes Three*. Duning also scored *Down To Earth* and *The Gallant Blade*, both starring Larry Parks, and Parks appeared once more in *Jolson Sings Again*, for which Duning gained the first of five Oscar nominations. Three of the others came to Duning in the 50s for his work on *From Here To Eternity*, *The Eddie Duchin Story* and *Picnic* (1955). The latter's theme music, used extremely effectively on the soundtrack in conjunction with the 1934 melody 'Moonglow', became a US number 1 for Morris Stolloff and his orchestra, and a substantial hit for pianist George Cates. A lyric was added by Steve Allen. Duning's other scores during the 50s and 60s included *Lorna Doone*, *Man In The Saddle*, *Scandal Sheet*; *Last Of The Commanches*, *Salome*, *Houseboat*; *Bell, Book And Candle*, *Cowboy*, *The World Of Suzie Wong*, *The Devil At 4 O'Clock*, *Toys In The Attic*, *My Blood Runs Cold* and *Any Wednesday*. In the 60s and 70s, apart from the occasional feature such as *Arnold* (1973), *Terror In The Wax Museum* (1976) and *The Man With Bogart's Face* (1980), which was George Raft's last film, Duning concentrated on writing for television. He scored several films such as *Then Came Bronson*, *Quarantined*, *But I Don't Want To Get Married!*, *Yuma*, *Black Noon*, *Climb An Angry Mountain*, *The Woman Hunter*, *Honour Thy Father*, *The Abduction Of Saint Anne*, *The Top Of The Hill*, *The Dream Merchants* and *Goliath Waits* (1981); he also contributed music to numerous television series, including *Star Trek*, *The Partridge Family* and *Houseboat*.

DURANTE, JIMMY

b. James Francis Durante, 10 February 1893, New York City, New York, USA, d. 29 January 1980, Santa Monica, California, USA. A unique entertainer: a comedian, actor and singer whose straight-legged strut, outsize nose (which brought him the nickname 'Schnozzola') and a penchant for mangling the English language ('Da hours I worked were eight to unconscious') made him a much-loved character throughout the world. The son of immigrant French-Italian parents, Durante taught himself to play ragtime on a piano his father bought him when he was 12. While in his teens he played in New York clubs and gangster hangouts, and later had his own six-piece jazz band in New Orleans.

In the early 20s he ran his own speakeasy, the Club Durant, with his partners, dancer and businessman Lou Clayton and song-and-dance-man Eddie Jackson. When the trio began to receive 'offers that they couldn't refuse' from certain shady characters, they gave up the club and toured as a vaudeville act. They also appeared in the Broadway musicals *Show Girl* and *The New Yorkers* (1930). In 1931 the partnership split up and Durante signed a contract with MGM, going on to make nearly 40 films. In the 30s these included musicals such as *Roadhouse Nights*, *The Cuban Love Song*, *The Phantom President*, *Blondie Of The Follies*, *Broadway To Hollywood*, *George White's Scandals*, *Palooka*, *Strictly Dynamite*, *Hollywood Party*, *She Learned About Sailors*, *Sally, Irene And Mary*, *Little Miss Broadway*, and *Start Cheering* (1938). During that period Durante also starred in several Broadway musicals, *Strike Me Pink*, *Jumbo*, *Red, Hot And Blue!*, *Stars In Your Eyes*, and *Keep Off the Grass* (1940), as well as performing his comedy act at the London Palladium. He was successful on radio, too, and was teamed with straight man Garry Moore in *The Camel Comedy Hour* from 1943-47. After that Durante had his own show for three years before he moved into television with the comedy-variety *All Star Revue* (they called him 'TV's newest and freshest face' - he was 57), and later, *The*

Jimmy Durante Show in a nightclub setting similar to the old Club Durant with his old friend Eddie Jackson. In 1952 he was back at the London Palladium and played other theatres and important clubs. Throughout the 40s and 50s he continued to appear in film musicals such as *Melody Ranch*, *This Time For Keeps*, *Two Girls And A Sailor*, *Music For Millions*, *Two Sisters From Boston*, It Happened In Brooklyn, and *On An Island With You*. In 1960 Durante was one of the guest stars in *Pepe*, and, two years later, co-starred with Doris Day in Billy Rose's Jumbo. His final film appearance was a cameo role in that orgy of slapstick (or slapschtik), *It's A Mad Mad Mad Mad World* (1963), but he remained popular on US television shows in such as *Jimmy Durante Meets The Seven Lively Arts*, *Jimmy Durante Presents The Lennon Sisters* and *The Hollywood Palace*. In 1960, at the age of 67, he was married for the second time (his first wife died in 1943) to the actress Margaret Alice Little, an actress he had been dating for 16 years. Four years later he was honoured for his 50 years in show business with a lavish ceremony at the Hollywood Roosevelt Hotel. His other awards included Best TV Performer (Motion Picture Daily 1951), George Foster Peabody Award (1951), and Citation Of Merit, City Of New York (1956), and Special Page One Award (1962). He was the composer or co-composer of several of his most popular numbers, including his trademark 'Inka Dinka Doo', and others such as 'Umbriago', 'So I Ups To Him', 'Start Off Each Day With A Song', 'Can Broadway Do Without Me?', and 'Jimmy, The Well Dressed Man'. Several of these, and others that he did not write but are indelibly associated with him such as 'September Song', were featured in two tribute shows, both entitled *Durante*, which played in Hollywood and San Francisco in 1982 and 1989. No doubt Durante's immortal protest 'Everybody wants to get into the act' and his closing message 'Goodnight, Mrs, Calabash, wherever you are', also cropped up in these celebrations of this loveable clown who was much-missed after he died in 1980 following several years of ill health.

● ALBUMS: *Jimmy Durante In Person* (Lion 1959)★★★, *Club Durante* (Decca 1959)★★★, *Jimmy Durante At The Copacabana* (Roulette 1961)★★★, *September Song* (Warners 1963)★★★★, *Hello Young Lovers* (Warners 1964)★★★, *One Of Those Songs* (1965)★★★, *Songs For Sunday* (1967)★★★, *The Special Magic Of Jimmy Durante* (1973)★★★, *On the Radio* (Silva Screen 1989)★★★, *I've Got A Million Of 'Em Folks* (1994)★★★.

● FURTHER READING: *Schnozzola*, Gene Fowler. *Goodnight Mrs. Calabash: The Secret Life Of Jimmy Durante*, William Cahn. *Inka Dinka Doo: The Life Of Jimmy Durante*, Jhan Robbins.

● FILMS: *Roadhouse Nights* (1930), *The Cuban Love Song* (1931), *New Adventures Of Get-Rich-Quick Wallingford* (1931), *Blondie Of The Follies* (1932), *The Passionate Plumber* (1932), *The Phantom President* (1932), *Speak Easily* (1932), *The Wet Parade* (1932), *Meet The Baron* (1933), *Broadway To Hollywood* (1933), *The Lost Stooges* (1933), *What! No Beer?* (1933), *Hell Below* (1933), *She Learned About Sailors* (1934), *Student Tour* (1934), *Strictly Dynamite* (1934), *Palooka* (1934), *Hollywood Party* (1934), *George White's Scandals* (1934), *Carnival* (1935), *Land Without Music* (1936), *Little Miss Broadway* (1938), *Sally, Irene And Mary* (1938), *Start Cheering* (1938), *Melody Ranch* (1940), *The Man Who Came To Dinner* (1941), *You're In The Army Now* (1941), *Two Girls And A Sailor* (1944), *Music For Millions* (1945), *Two Sisters From Boston* (1946),

It Happened In Brooklyn (1947), *This Time For Keeps* (1947), *On An Island With You* (1948), *The Milkman* (1950), *The Great Rupert* (1950), *Beau James* (1957), *Pepe* (1960), *Billy Rose's Jumbo* (1962), *It's A Mad Mad Mad Mad World* (1963).

DURBIN, DEANNA

b. Edna Mae Durbin, 4 December 1921, Winnipeg, Canada. A refreshingly natural and spirited actress and singer, with a clear, thrilling soprano voice, who was one of the top box-office stars in film musicals of the late 30s and 40s. The Durbin family moved to Los Angeles, California when Deanna was a baby, and she received voice training from the age of eight. After being spotted by an MGM agent singing at a recital, she was set to portray the opera singer Eva Schumann-Heink as a child in a picture based on the diva's life, but that fell through and instead she co-starred with Judy Garland in the musical short film *Every Sunday* (1936). When MGM boss Louis B. Mayer decided to drop Durbin and keep Garland, she was immediately snapped up for Universal by producer Joe Pasternak. The public's response to her performance in *Three Smart Girls* (1936) was rapturous, and the film's receipts of $2 million saved the studio from bankruptcy. Just before it was released she had made several highly impressive appearances on the Eddie Cantor Radio Hour, so a great many Americans were already familiar with this enchanting 15-year-old with the mature voice and style. During the rest of the 30s, with Pasternak's guidance and skill, audiences were able to follow her gradual evolving from a precocious teenager into a lovely woman in films such as 100 Men And A Girl, Mad About Music, *That Certain Age*, *Three Smart Girls Grow Up*, *First Love*, (in which she had her first screen kiss with Robert Stack), *It's A Date*, and *Spring Parade* (1940). In 1938 she and that other fine young star, Mickey Rooney, were awarded special Oscars 'for their significant contribution in bringing to the screen the spirit and personification of youth, and as juvenile players setting a high standard of ability and achievement'. For most of the 40s she was still Hollywood's top female attraction, via the musicals *Nice Girl?*, *It Started With Eve*, *Hers To Hold*, Can't Help Singing (her only film in colour), *I'll Be Yours*, *Something In The Wind*, and *Up In Central Park* (1948). She tried to change her girl-next-door image by accepting straight parts in pictures such as *Christmas Holiday* and *Lady In A Train*, but Universal, who made all her 22 pictures, were not interested in grooming her for sophisticated dramatic roles, so in 1948 she quit Hollywood for good. With two failed marriages behind her (to producer Vaughn Paul when she was 19, and German-born producer Felix Jackson in 1945), she retired with her third husband, French film director Charles David, to the French village of Neauphle-le-Château near Paris where they still live to this day. Despite the repeated efforts of Pasternak she refused to return, saying 'I can't run around being a Little Miss Fix-it who bursts into song - the highest paid star with the poorest material.' She did have the pick of the leading men, though, including Robert Cummings, Walter Pidgeon, Franchot Tone, and Melvyn Douglas. While refusing to make public appearances, she apparently works tirelessly for UNICEF and remains particularly popular in the UK where the BBC still receives more requests for her films than for any other film star of the 30s and 40s.

● COMPILATIONS: *Movie Songs* (Coral 1982)★★★, *Best Of Deanna Durbin* (MCA 1981)★★★★, *Can't Help Singing* (MFP/EMI 1982)★★★, *Best Of Deanna Durbin Volume 2* (MCA 1983)★★★, *Songs Of The Silver Screen* (MCA 1986)★★★, *20 Golden Greats* (Deja Vu 1987)★★★, *Favourites* (Memoir 1989)★★★, *The Legendary* (Silva Screen 1990)★★★, *With A Song In My Heart* (1993)★★★, *Original Film Soundtracks* (1994)★★★.

EARL CARROLL VANITIES
(see Carroll, Earl)

EASTER PARADE
It is fascinating to think how it would all have turned out if Gene Kelly had not broken his ankle and therefore been able to partner Judy Garland in this 1948 musical. As it was, MGM tempted Fred Astaire out of retirement - and the rest is history. Astaire played Don Hewes, whose partner in a successful dance act, Nadine (Ann Miller), gets the urge to go solo and leaves him in the lurch. More than slightly miffed, especially as he had hoped to marry the lady, Don plucks Hannah Brown (Judy Garland) from the chorus of a small club, and together they form a happy and prosperous relationship - on stage and off. Irving Berlin's wonderful songs - a mixture of the old and the new - revealed the incredible range of his writing as one musical highlight followed another. Astaire, at nearly twice the age of Garland, was singing and dancing as well as ever in numbers such as 'Drum Crazy', 'Steppin' Out With My Baby', and 'It Only Happens When I Dance With You' (with Ann Miller). His moments with Garland were a joy, and included a ragtime vaudeville medley, 'When The Midnight Choo-Choo Leaves For Alabam', 'Snooky Ookums', 'Ragtime Violin', 'I Love A Piano', and, of course 'Easter Parade'. However, their most memorable number was surely 'A Couple Of Swells', in which, dressed as two social-climbing tramps, they mused: 'The Vanderbilts have asked us out to tea/We don't know how to get there, no siree.' Garland had the poignant 'Better Luck Next Time' and 'I Want to Go Back To Michigan', and Miller was scintillating and sizzling on 'Shaking The Blues Away'. Peter Lawford too, as Astaire's best friend, 'The Professor', displayed a pleasant light vocal touch with 'A Fella With An Umbrella'. The supporting cast was particularly fine, and included Clinton Sundberg as Mike, the philosophical barman, and Jules Munshin in the role of the frustrated head waiter. All in all, a triumph for all concerned, including producer Arthur Freed, director Charles Walters, dance director Robert Alton, and screenwriters Sidney Sheldon, Frances Goodrich, and Albert Hackett. Roger Edens and Johnny Green won Academy Awards for 'scoring of a musical picture'. In 1992, *Easter Parade* was issued on a laserdisc in a 'Technicolor restoration' from the original nitrate camera negative, with improved digital sound. The disc also included Judy Garland's performance of 'Mr. Monotony', a number that was cut from the original release. In 1998, Tommy Tune's stage version of *Easter Parade* was out of town, eyeing Broadway.

EASY COME, EASY GO
Elvis Presley starred as a frogman operating off the Californian coast, who discovers treasure in a sunken wreck. The plight of that ship is a perfect metaphor for the singer's career at this point. Eight songs were recorded for *Easy Come, Easy Go*, two of which, 'The Love Machine' and 'Leave My Woman Alone', were omitted from the film and subsequent soundtrack EP, the last such release under Presley's name. The rejected material could not have been much worse than those retained, notably the awful 'Yoga Is As Yoga Does'. However, the sessions were of interest for one reason. They were the first to feature bassist Jerry Scheff, who remained associated with the singer until the latter's death in 1977.

EASY RIDER
Released in 1969, *Easy Rider* is one of the lynchpin films of the 60s, encapsulating the mood of its time upon release. Co-stars Peter Fonda and Dennis Hopper, who also directed, play two bikers who, having finalized a drugs deal, ride to New Orleans to celebrate the Mardi Gras. En route they encounter friendship and animosity in equal doses but as the film progresses, the 'American Dream' - and indeed the idealism of the central characters - gradually sours. 'We blew it', states Fonda in the scene preceding the still numbing finale, referring both to his immediate circle and society in general. Fonda and Hopper apart, *Easy Rider* features a superb performance from Jack Nicholson playing drunken lawyer George Hansen, and the normally reclusive Phil Spector has a small role as the Connection. *Easy Rider* is also a technical triumph. The usually profligate Hopper is remarkably disciplined, although he would later claim 'his' film was cut to ribbons. Laszlo Kovak's photography is breathtaking and Terry Southern's script is suitably economic. *Easy Rider* also boasted a superb soundtrack and two songs in particular, Steppenwolf's 'Born To Be Wild' and the Byrds' 'I Wasn't Born To Follow', are forever linked to the imagery they accompany. Material by the Band, Bob Dylan, Jimi Hendrix, Roger McGuinn, the Holy Modal Rounders, Fraternity Of Man and Electric Prunes is also well selected, creating a new standard for the cinematic use of rock music. Indeed the whole style and content of *Easy Rider* became much copied, but few films came close to emulating it.

EBB, FRED
(see Kander, John)

EDDY, NELSON, AND JEANETTE MACDONALD

Nelson Eddy (b. 29 June 1901, Providence, Rhode Island, USA, d. 6 March 1967) and Jeanette MacDonald (b. 18 June 1901, Philadelphia, Pennsylvania, USA, d. 14 January 1965, Houston, Texas, USA). Often called the most successful singing partnership in the history of the cinema, their series of eight operetta-style films vividly caught the imagination of 30s audiences. Eddy came from a musical family and learned to sing by continually listening to operatic records. After the family moved to Philadelphia, he worked at a variety of jobs including telephone operator, advertising salesman and copy-writer. He played several leading roles in Gilbert and Sullivan operettas presented by the Savoy Company of Philadelphia, before travelling to Europe for music studies. On his return in 1924, he had minor parts at the Metropolitan Opera House in New York, and other concert halls, and appeared on radio. In 1933, he made a brief appearance, singing 'In the Garden Of My Heart', in the film *Broadway To Hollywood*, which featured 10-year-old Mickey Rooney. This was followed by small roles in *Dancing Lady* (1933, in which Fred Astaire made his debut) and *Student Tour* (1934), after which he attained star status with MacDonald in 1935.

MacDonald took singing and dancing lessons as a child, before moving to New York to study, and in 1920 her tap-dancing ability gained her a place in the chorus of the Broadway show *The Night Boat*, one of the year's best musicals, with a score by Jerome Kern. In the same year she served as a replacement in *Irene*, a fondly remembered all-time favourite of the US theatre. Harry Tierney and Joseph McCarthy were responsible for the show's score, which contained the big hit, 'Alice Blue Gown'. MacDonald's other 20s shows included *Tangerine*, *A Fantastic Fricassee*, *The Magic Ring*, *Sunny Days*, and the title roles in *Yes, Yes, Yvette* and *Angela*. However, she appeared in only one real hit, George and Ira Gershwin's *Tip-Toes* (1925), in which she co-starred with Queenie Smith. In 1929 she was teamed with Maurice Chevalier for her film debut in director Ernst Lubitsch's first sound picture, *The Love Parade*. The musical score, by Victor Schertzinger and Clifford Grey, included 'Dream Lover', 'March Of The Grenadiers' and 'My Love Parade'. It was a great success and prompted MacDonald and Chevalier to make three more similar operetta-style films together: *One Hour With You*, (1932; the Oscar Strauss-Richard Whiting-Leo Robin songs included 'We Will Always Be Sweethearts' and the title song); *Love Me Tonight* (1932), one of the most innovative of all movie musicals, directed by Rouben Mamoulian, with a Richard Rodgers and Lorenz Hart score that included 'Lover', 'Isn't It Romantic?', 'Mimi'; and a lavish production of *The Merry Widow* (1934, with Franz Lehar's enduring score being aided by some occasional Lorenz Hart lyrics). MacDonald's other movies during the early 30s were a mixture of musicals and comedies, including *The Lottery Bride*, *Monte Carlo* (both 1930) and *The Cat And The Fiddle* (1934). The latter was another outstanding Lubitsch musical that teamed MacDonald with UK song and dance man, Jack Buchanan, and included 'Beyond The Blue Horizon', one of her first hit recordings.

It was in 1935 that MGM brought Eddy and MacDonald together for the first time in *Naughty Marietta*. They were not at first sight an ideal combination, MacDonald's infectious personality and soprano voice, ideal for operetta, coupled with Eddy, whose acting occasionally lacked animation. Despite being known in some quarters as 'The Singing Capon And The Iron Butterfly', the duo's impact was immediate and enormous. *Naughty Marietta*'s score, by Victor Herbert, included 'Tramp, Tramp, Tramp', 'The Italian Street Song', and the big duet, 'Ah, Sweet Mystery Of Life'. Rudolph Friml's *Rose Marie* (1936) followed, and was equally successful. Sometimes called the quintessential operetta, the original play's plot underwent severe changes to enable MacDonald to play a renowned Canadian opera singer, while Eddy became an extremely heroic mountie. Two of the most popular Friml-Oscar Hammerstein II-Harbach songs were the evergreen 'Rose Marie', and the duet, 'Indian Love Call', which proved to be a major US record hit. Both stars made other films during the 30s besides their mutual projects. In 1936, MGM starred MacDonald in the highly regarded melodramatic musical *San Francisco*, with Clark Gable and Spencer Tracy. The movie's earthquake climax was lampooned by Judy Garland in her legendary 1961 Carnegie Hall Concert, when she sang the film's title song, with a special verse which ran: 'I never will forget Jeanette MacDonald/Just to think of her, it gives my heart a pang/I never will forget, how that brave Jeanette, just stood there in the ruins, and sang - aaaand sang!' Meanwhile, Eddy was somewhat miscast as an American football hero in *Rosalie*, with Eleanor Powell as Princess Rosalie of Romanza. However, he did introduce a Cole Porter classic, 'In The Still Of The Night', the song that is supposed to have moved MGM boss Louis B. Mayer to tears the first time he heard it. Noël Coward is said also to have wept, albeit for a different reason, when he saw MacDonald optimistically playing a girl of 18, and Eddy as a starving Viennese singing teacher in the film version of Coward's *Bitter Sweet* (1940). Several songs from the original stage show were retained including 'Zigeuner' and 'I'll See You Again'. The MacDonald-Eddy partnership attracted much criticism for being over-romantic and far too saccharine. However, 30s audiences loved their films such as *Maytime* (1937), *The Girl Of The Golden West* (1938), *Sweethearts* (1938, MGM's first three-colour technicolour picture); and *New Moon* (1940), one of their biggest box-office hits, with a Sigmund Romberg-Oscar Hammerstein II score, which included the memorable 'Lover Come Back To Me', 'Softly As In A Morning Sunrise' and 'Stout-Hearted Men'. In 1941, MacDonald appeared in *Smilin' Through*, with her husband Gene Raymond, while Eddy's performance that same year in *The Chocolate Soldier* was generally thought to be his best acting on film. By 1942, the team had run out of steam. With the onset of World War II, moviegoers' tastes had changed. Their last film together, *I Married An Angel*, even with songs by Rodgers and Hart, was the least successful of the series. In 1942, MacDonald made her final film at MGM, *Cairo*, with Robert Young. This was followed, later in the 40s, by a brief appearance in *Follow The Boys* (1944) and a starring role in *Three Daring Daughters*, in which, with the trio, she sang an appealing version of 'The Dickey Bird Song', by Sammy Fain and Howard Dietz. In 1949, after a career that had teamed her with many of Hollywood's leading men, she made her last film, *The Sun Comes Up*, with another big star, the wonder dog, Lassie! For several years MacDonald also returned to the concert stage and appeared in operettas, and on television, before eventually disappearing from the limelight. She died from a heart attack in January 1965. After their break-up, Nelson Eddy appeared in the horror-musical *Phantom Of The Opera* (1943) and *Knickerbocker Holiday* (1944), in which he sang 'There's Nowhere To Go But Up'. His final movie appearance was with Ilona Massey in the Rudolph Friml operetta *Northwest Outpost*, in 1947. He returned to the stage, played in nightclubs and stock musicals and on radio, and occasionally television. He was appearing at the Miami Beach Hotel in Florida when he became ill and was taken to hospital. He died shortly afterwards, in March 1967.

● COMPILATIONS: *Favourites In Hi-Fi* (RCA Victor 1958)★★★, *Jeanette MacDonald And Nelson Eddy* (RCA 1984)★★★, *Apple Blossoms* (Mac/Eddy 1989)★★★, *The Christmas Album* (Mac/Eddy 1989)★★★, *The Early Years* (Mac/Eddy 1989)★★★, *Naughty Marietta* (Mac/Eddy 1989)★★★, *Operatic Recital Volume 3* (Mac/Eddy 1989)★★★, *Sing Patriotic Songs* (Mac/Eddy 1989)★★★, *Chase And Sanborn Radio Show* (Mac/Eddy 1989)★★★, *Tonight Or Never* (Mac/Eddy 1989)★★★, *Irene* (Mac/Eddy 1989)★★★, *Songs Of Faith And Inspiration* (Silva Screen 1990)★★★, *When I'm Calling You* (1994)★★★.
Solo: Nelson Eddy *Through Theatreland* (1955)★★★, with Dorothy Kirsten *Rose Marie* (1955)★★★, with Doretta Morrow and Cast *The Desert Song* (1958)★★★, *Stout-Hearted Men* (1958)★★★, *Because* (1959)★★★, *The Lord's Prayer* (1960)★★★, *Story Of A Starry Night* (1961)★★★, *Carols Of Christmas* (1961)★★★, *Of Girls I Sing* (1964)★★★, *Our Love* (1967)★★★, *Till The End Of Time* (1967)★★★, *Greatest Hits* (1967)★★★, *World Favourite Love Songs* (1972)★★★, *Isn't It Romantic?* (1974)★★★, *Love's Own Sweet Song* (1988)★★★, *On the Air* (1988)★★★, *With Friends* (1990)★★★, *Nelson Eddy And Ilona Massey* (1990)★★★, *Phantom Of The Opera* (1990). Jeanette MacDonald *Smilin' Through* (1960)★★★, *Sings 'San Francisco' And Other Silver Screen Favourites* (RCA 1983)★★★, *Dream Lover* (Happy Days 1988)★★★.

● FURTHER READING: *The Films Of Jeanette MacDonald And Nelson Eddy*, E. Knowles. *Jeanette MacDonald: A Pictorial History*, S. Rich. *The Jeanette MacDonald Story*, J.R. Parish. *Jeanette MacDonald*, L.E. Stern. *Sweethearts: The Timeless Love Affair-On Screen And Off-Between Jeanette MacDonald And Nelson Eddy*, Sharon Rich.

EDELMAN, RANDY

This US vocalist won his audience by writing and performing some classic love songs. He made his debut in 1972, with a self-titled album that went largely unnoticed. During the 70s, however, he slowly built up his reputation and finally reached the big time with the worldwide smash, 'Uptown Uptempo Woman'. His highest chart

entry in the UK came with a revival of Unit Four Plus Two's 1965 hit 'Concrete And Clay'. By 1978 his singles career had ground to a halt. During this period one of his songs, 'Weekend In New England', was covered and made into a million-selling record by Barry Manilow. An attempted comeback in 1982 failed, but a new career was found when he was invited to provide the music for a new animated feature, *The Care Bears*. He went on to write and perform the soundtrack for a number of movies and by 1988 was in the big league, writing scores for movies including *Parenthood* and *Kindergarten Cop*. His other credits in the late 80s and early 90s included *Twins* (with George Delarue), *Troop Beverly Hills*, *Ghostbusters II*, *Come See The Paradise*, *Quick Change*, *Drop Dead Fred*, *V.I. Warshawski*, *Beethoven*, *The Last Of The Mohicans*, *The Distinguished Gentlemen*, *Dragon: The Bruce Lee Story*, *Beethoven's Second*, *Gettysburg*, and *The Mask* (1994).
● ALBUMS: *Randy Edelman* (1972)★★★, *Laughter And Tears* (1973)★★★, *Prime Cuts* (20th Century 1975)★★, *Fairwell Fairbanks* (1976)★★, *If Love Is Real* (Arista 1977)★★, *You're The One* (20th Century 1979)★★, *On Time* (Rocket 1982)★★, *... And His Piano* (Elecstar 1984)★★, *The Distinguished Gentlemen* (1993)★★.
● COMPILATIONS: *Uptown, Uptempo: The Best Of ...* (20th Century 1979)★★★.

EDENS, ROGER
b. 9 November 1905, Hillsboro, Texas, USA, d. 13 July 1970, Hollywood, California, USA. An important arranger, songwriter - and later - producer, who was a close associate of MGM producer Arthur Freed from the 30s through to the 50s, when the legendary Freed Unit was turning out one magnificent film musical after another. Edens first came to notice on Broadway in *Girl Crazy* (1930) when he stepped out of the pit orchestra and took over as Ethel Merman's pianist when her regular man became ill. He subsequently became Merman's arranger and accompanist for some time before joining MGM in 1934. After serving as musical supervisor on the Jean Harlow picture *Reckless*, he adapted Freed and Nacio Herb Brown's songs for the studio's big-budget *Broadway Melody Of 1936*, which was released in 1935. In the same year, Edens arranged the music for a party to celebrate the 36th birthday of one of MGM's biggest stars, Clark Gable. The highlight of the affair was 14-year-old Judy Garland's tender version of 'You Made Me Love You', which she prefaced with the 'fan letter' 'Dear Mr. Gable', written by Edens. The response was sensational and Garland reprised the sequence in *Broadway Melody Of 1938*. From then on Edens scored numerous films, winning Academy Awards for his work on *Easter Parade* (with Johnny Green), *On The Town* (with Lennie Hayton), and *Annie Get Your Gun* (with Adolph Deutsch). He also contributed songs to numerous pictures including *Love Finds Any Hardy*, *Babes In Arms*, *Little Nellie Kelly*, *Strike Up The Band*, *Two Girls On Broadway*, *Lady Be Good*, *Ziegfeld Girl*, *Babes On Broadway*, *Girl Crazy*, *Thousands Cheer*, *Good News*, *On The Town*, *Take Me Out To The Ball Game*, *Singin' In The Rain*, *Funny Face*, and *Billy Rose's Jumbo*. Out of these came numbers such as 'In-Between', 'It's A Great Day For The Irish', 'Our Love Affair', 'Nobody', 'Do The Conga',

'My Wonderful One', 'Minnie From Trinidad', 'Caribbean Love Song', 'Carnegie Hall', 'Hoe Down', 'Here's To The Girls', 'Pass That Peace Pipe', 'You're Awful', 'The Right Girl For Me', 'Strictly USA', 'Moses Supposes', 'Sawdust, Spangles And Dreams', and 'Think Pink', 'Bonjour Paris', 'On How To Be Loved' (the last three for *Funny Face*). For much of the time Edens wrote both words and music, but on other occasions his main collaborators were Arthur Freed, Ralph Freed, Hugh Martin, Betty Comden and Adolph Green, Sigmund Romberg and Jimmy Monaco. He was associate producer on *The Harvey Girls* (1946) and many other Freed musicals, but it was not until several years later that he took full producer credit on the Sigmund Romberg biopic *Deep In My Heart* (1954), and *Funny Face* (1957) for which MGM loaned him to Paramount. His last major assignment was as associate producer on *Hello Dolly!* for 20th Century Fox in 1967, although he was also involved in the preliminary work on Irving Berlin's *Say It With Music*, which was to have been made in 1969, but never materialized due to upheavals in Metro's top management. One of the most important aspect of Edens' work was his ability to discover and nurture fresh talent. He gave Lena Horne her break in films which led to appearances in *Cabin In The Sky* and *Stormy Weather*, and he befriended and nurtured Judy Garland through some well-documented difficult times, as well as writing special material for her concerts. According to the trade paper *Variety*, he coached Katharine Hepburn for her starring role in *Coco* which opened on Broadway in December 1969. He died a few months later of lung cancer.
● FURTHER READING: *The Movies' Greatest Musicals-Produced In Hollywood USA By The Freed Unit*, Hugh Fordin.

EDWARDS, CLIFF

b. 14 June 1895, Hannibal, Missouri, USA, d. 18 July 1972, Los Angeles, California, USA. This diminutive, soft-voiced singer became universally known as 'Ukelele Ike', and popularized that instrument during his successful vaudeville career in the early 20s. Before that he had worked in carnivals, St. Louis saloons, and in Chicago with comedian Joe Frisco. As well as vaudeville, Edwards appeared in several Broadway musicals including *Lady, Be Good!* (1924), with Adele and Fred Astaire (in which he sang 'Fascinating Rhythm'), *Sunny* (1925), *Ziegfeld Follies Of 1927* and *George White's Scandals Of 1931*. The beginning of his film career coincided with the transition from silents to 'talkies', and he is reputed to have made over 60 films, which included musicals, romantic comedies and dramas such as *Hollywood Revue Of 1929* (1929) in which he introduced the Arthur Freed/Nacio Herb Brown song, 'Singin' In The Rain', *Parlor, Bedroom And Bath* (1931) with Buster Keaton, *Hell Divers* (1932), *Take A Chance* (1933) in which he sang 'It's Only A Paper Moon', *George White's Scandals* (1934) and *George White's 1935 Scandals* (1935). He had a string of hits between 1924 and 1933 with songs such as 'It Had To Be You', 'All Alone', 'Who Takes Care Of The Caretaker's Daughter?', 'If You Knew Susie (Like I Know Susie)', 'Paddlin' Madelin' Home', 'Remember', 'Dinah', 'Sunday', 'I'm Tellin' The Birds And Bees (How I Love You)', 'Together', 'Mary Ann' and 'I Can't Give You

Anything But Love'. On many records he was joined by top instrumentalists such as Jimmy Dorsey, Miff Mole and Red Nichols, and was credited with playing the kazoo, though it is fairly certain that it was a vocal effect, unaided by any instrument. In the early 30s Edwards' career waned, but was revived in 1940 when he provided the voice of Jiminy Cricket in Walt Disney's animated classic, *Pinocchio*. Two of the movie's most popular numbers, 'Give A Little Whistle' and 'When You Wish Upon A Star' (which won an Oscar for 'Best Song'), were Edwards' first hits for seven years, and his last US chart entries. In 1941 he became the voice of another Disney cartoon character, Jim Crow, in *Dumbo*, and despite poor health and alcohol problems, continued to work for the studio, recording children's songs, and making appearances in the television series, *Mickey Mouse Club*.
● COMPILATIONS: *I Want A Girl* (1978)★★★, *Cliff Edwards And His Hot Combination* (1979)★★, *The Hottest Man In Town* (1981)★★★, *Fascinatin' Rhythm* (1988)★★★, *Shakin' The Blues Away* (1988)★★.

EFX

'You can never keep anything longer than about 15 minutes for a Vegas audience, because their attention span is very short.' So said Michael Crawford, the star of this spectacular $41 million production which opened at the 1,800-seater MGM Grand Theatre in Las Vegas on 22 March 1995. He also pointed out that 'most of them are Asian, and they don't necessarily speak English, so it has to be very visual'. Well, *EFX* was certainly that. Introduced by a mysterious, disembodied voice, Crawford, the original 'Phantom of the Opera', emerged from a vast wall of fog, poised precariously on a flying saucer which zoomed to a height of some 70 feet above the stage, before streaking and strafing the front of the auditorium. At this point in the proceedings, he was wearing the 'hat' (actually, white and gold costume complete with cape) of the EFX! Master, whose task is to link a series of self-contained scenes which transport the audience and himself (via time machine) from the Camelot world of King Arthur, to the science fiction future of H.G. Wells. Crawford himself re-appeared in the guise of historical figures Merlin, P.T. Barnum, Houdini, and Wells. He was supported in this physically onerous task by leading players Tina Walsh (as Morgana, Bess Houdini), Jeffrey Polk (Master of Magic), Kevin Koelbl (Master of Spirits, Vladimir), Rick Stockwell (Master of Time), Stewart Daylida (Master of Laughter), and Lisa Geist (Arthur). They, of course, formed the human element of the show, and were constantly dwarfed by a multitude of the most extravagant special effects (EFX is NASA-speak for technical effects in sound, lighting, and pyrotechnics). Enormous dragons belching forth walls of fire, a little Chinese water torture, a manned rocket, a circus, leafy forests, an invasion of alien beings, a waterfall spurting from a rock face, the odd earthquake, and so much more, were miraculously conjured up, and played out for 90 heart-stopping, head-throbbing minutes (no interval) in a space which Crawford estimated as being 'three times the width of a London stage, and three times the height'. Almost 100,000 watts of stereo amplification belted out the musical numbers which included

'Nexus', 'EFX!', 'The Magic That Surrounds You', 'The Sprite Dance', 'Morgana's Entrance', 'The Wizard's Dual', 'Arrival', 'The Intergalactic Circus Of Wonders', 'The Flying Kaganovich', 'The Greatest Showman In The Universe', 'Intergalactic Circus Finale', 'The Seance', 'Escape', 'Tonight', 'H.G. Wells' Laboratory', '3-D Adventure', 'Morlock Exterior', 'Morlock Interior/Slave Dance', 'Battle With The Morlocks', and 'To The Future'. It was created by Gary Goddard, Tony Christopher and the Landmark Entertainment Group. Goddard and Christopher also wrote the lyrics, and Don Grady was responsible for the music, musical production and musical direction. The director was Scott Faris, with co-direction and choreography by Anthony van Laast. Top of the 'just as important' list were David Mitchell (sets), Theoni V. Aldredge (costumes), Natasha Katz (lighting and special effects), Jonathan Deans (sound), and David Mendoza (illusions). After more that 600 consecutive performances, the majority of them suffering pain from an injury early on, Crawford was forced to withdraw in August 1996. He was replaced by David Cassidy, former 70s pop heart-throb-turned-actor in musicals such as *Blood Brothers*, and the production was tweaked accordingly, with David and Shaun Cassidy, along with Andrew Gold, revising script and songs. Proving the human body can only take so much, David Cassidy finished his stint in *EFX* at the end of December 1998, to be replaced by Broadway director, choreographer, and song-and-dance man Tommy Tune.

ELABORATE LIVES: THE LEGEND OF AIDA

Apparently executives of Walt Disney Theatrical Productions felt the original title of Guiseppe Verdi's *Aida* was rather 'too gloomy and hard to pronounce' for the rock opera audience they wanted to reach with a $15 million spectacular. So they eventually sprawled the somewhat unwieldy *Elton John And Tim Rice's Elaborate Lives: The Legend Of Aida* on the marquee for this show which had its world premiere performances at the Alliance Theatre Company, Atlanta, Georgia, from 7 October to 8 November 1998 (plus previews). The production was 'suggested' by Verdi's 1871 version of his great work - the most famous interpretation - and Linda Woolverton's 'simplistic' book covers familiar ground. With Egypt and Ethiopia at war, Ethiopian slave Aida (Heather Headley, 'outstanding in every way') - who turns out to be a princess - falls in love with the Egyptian general Radames (Hank Stratton). However, Aida's mistress, the Egyptian princess Amneris (Sherie Scott), has designs on Radames herself. Eventually sentenced to die for an act of betrayal, Radames is joined by Aida as a vast pyramid, the central feature of the $10 million laser-powered set, finally entombs the couple for ever. Nekhen (Scott Irby-Ranniar), as an Ethiopian slave boy, gave a notable performance, and the cast also included Neal Benari (Pharaoh), Roger Robinson (Aida's father, Amonasro), Mary Bentley-LaMar (Nehebka), Future Davis (Nenu), Pamela Gold (Shu), Jenny Hill (Hefnut), and Rich Herbert (Zoser). Initial critical reaction suggested that this *Aida* was closer to contemporary television drama than the Metropolitan Opera Company, while one scribe's derision was reserved especially for the second number, 'Our Nation Holds Sway' (reprised as first act finalé), which he described this way: . . . '"Oh-oh-ohhh. Our nation holds sway" (on the word "sway", everyone, got up in gaudy Egyptian togs, wags his butt").' In fact, Elton John and Tim Rice's 'infectious pop-rock score' came out of it far better than Woolverton's storyline, which appeared to be 'a spoof of Ancient Egypt' in the first act, but decidedly more melodramatic in the second. A blend of gospel, blues, 50s rock 'n' roll, a surfeit of love ballads, and the odd amusing moment, were in there amongst 'Every Story Is A Love Story' (reprised at curtain), 'The Past Is Another Land', 'Another Pyramid', 'How I Know You' (and reprise), 'My Strongest Suit', 'Night Of Nights', 'Enchantment Passing Through', 'The Dance Of The Robe', 'Elaborate Lives', 'A Step Too Far', 'Easy As Life', 'Like Father Like Son', 'The Gods Love Nubia', 'Written In The Stars', 'I Know The Truth' (and reprise), 'The Judgement', and 'The Messenger'. Just a week after *Elaborate Lives* closed, Disney dismissed the backstage creative team of director Robert Jess Roth, choreographer Matt West, set designer Stanley Meyer, costume, designer Ann Hould-Ward, and lighting designer Natasha Katz. These were the people behind Disney's first stage musical hit, *Beauty And The Beast*. Whether *Elaborate Lives* will reach Broadway and the commercial heights of *Beauty*, the far superior *The Lion King*, or those other two comparatively recent musicals inspired by operas, *Miss Saigon* (*Madame Butterfly*) and *Rent* (*La Boheme*), only time will tell.

Earlier in 1998 a large scale, visually stunning production of the genuine *Aida* - 500 extras, 1,500 costumes - was presented at the cavernous Earls Court in London. As with *Elaborate Lives*, it too utilised several banks of lasers - projecting shifting kaleidoscopic images along the vast length of the arena - and other sophisticated lighting and scenic effects. The similarities probably ended there though, judging by Tim Rice's reported comments prior to the debut of the Atlanta show: 'A bloke called Verdi had a go with *Aida*. We're slinging out the problem area - Verdi's music - and keeping the story with Elton's music and my words.'

ELEGIES FOR ANGELS, PUNKS AND RAVING QUEENS

After arousing a good deal of interest off-Broadway and on the London Fringe, this highly emotional play-with-music opened in June 1993 at the Criterion Theatre in the heart of the West End. It tells the tale from the point of view of some 30 individuals who died as a result of contracting AIDS from a wide variety of sources - such as 'a regular Joe who dropped into a brothel, to a granny who was given an infected blood transfusion'. The actors step forward one by one and tell their stories in verse and song. Kim Criswell, who gave a stunning performance in the 1992/3 London revival of *Annie Get Your Gun*, was the best-known name in a cast that also featured Kwama Kwei-Armah, Lily Savage, Trudie Styler, and comedian Simon Fanshawe. The score, with music by Janet Hood, and lyrics by the show's author, Bill Russell, was an intensely moving - and sometimes euphoric - blend of jazz, blues, and gospel. It could not run for long at a mainstream theatre, of course, even one as tiny as the

Criterion, and, after a late-night show on 23 July to enable other West End actors to experience this thought-provoking piece, *Elegies* closed the following night.

ELISCU, EDWARD

b. 2 April 1902, New York, USA, d. 18 June 1998, Newton, Connecticut, USA. Some sources give Eliscu's year of birth as 1900. An author, songwriter, director, producer and actor, Eliscu was educated at City College in New York. While there, he became involved in various theatrical pursuits - writing lyrics, directing - and after graduation served as a director of entertainment at summer camps. He made his Broadway acting debut in the Helen Hayes comedy *Quarantine* (1924), and also appeared in *The Racket* and S. Ansky's 'dramatic legend', *The Dybbuk*. After being introduced to Vincent Youmans, in 1928 Eliscu worked (uncredited) with the composer on the musical *Rainbow*. A year later, another collaboration between Eliscu, Youmans, and Billy Rose resulted in the score for *Great Day!*, which included three future standards, 'More Than You Know', 'Without A Song' and the title number. Also in 1929, Eliscu wrote lyrics to Joseph Meyer's music for *Lady Fingers*, and was subsequently represented on Broadway, as a lyricist and sometime librettist, by *The Third Little Show* revue ('You Forgot Your Gloves', with Ned Lehac, 1931), *A Little Racketeer* (1932), a production of Franz Lehar's 1928 hit, *Frederika* ('Kiss To Remind You', 'Why Did You Kiss My Heart Awake?', 'Rose In The Heather', 1937), and a tough political revue, *Meet The People* (with Jay Gorney, 'Four Freedoms' and title number, 1940), among others. There was also an off-Broadway musical, *The Banker's Daughter*, in 1962. With the advent of talking pictures, coupled with often declining Broadway audiences as a result of the great Depression, from 1930 onwards Eliscu spent a good deal of his time in Hollywood. While there, he joined with Nacio Herb Brown, Bruno Granichstaedten, and Clifford Grey for the score to the screen operetta *One Heavenly Night* (1931), starring British musical comedy star Evelyn Laye ('I Belong To Everybody', 'My Heart Is Beating', 'Along The Road Of Dreams', 'Goodnight Serenade', 'Heavenly Night'), and the irresistible *Flying Down To Rio* (1933), which marked the beginning of the legendary partnership of Fred Astaire and Ginger Rogers. Eliscu and Gus Kahn provided the lyrics, and Vincent Youmans the melodies, for the memorable 'Carioca', 'Music Makes Me', 'Orchids In The Moonlight' and 'Flying Down To Rio'. Eliscu's other screen credits through the 30s into the early 40s included Eddie Cantor's *Whoopee!* ('I'll Still Belong To You', with Nacio Herb Brown), *Queen High* ('It Seems To Me', 'I'm Afraid Of You', with Arthur Schwartz and Ralph Rainger), *Follow Thru* ('It Must Be You', with Manning Sherwin), *Rockabye, Paddy O'Day* (screenplay with Lou Breslo, and songs 'Keep That Twinkle In Your Eye', 'I Like A Balalaika', with Harry Akst), the Mae West vehicle *The Heat's On* ('Just A Stranger In Town', 'Hello, Mi Amigo', 'The White Keys', 'There Goes That Guitar', with Henry Myers and Jay Gorney), *The More The Merrier* ('The Torpedo Song', with Myers and Gorney), and *Hey, Rookie* (script by Eliscu, Myers, and Gorney, who composed the songs with J.C. Lewis). Eliscu also wrote the screenplays

for, and produced or co-produced, several non-musical pictures. In the early 50s, Eliscu was named as a subversive by Senator Joe McCarthy's Committee On Un-American Activities, and was unable to work in films or television for around 10 years. This episode in his life provoked right-wing objections to his election for the post of President of the American Guild of Authors and Composers, but they were overcome, and he served a term of five years in the post from 1968-73. He was also inducted into the Songwriters Hall of Fame, and performed a selection of his own works in the renowned *Lyrics And Lyricists* series at the 92nd Street 'Y' in New York City. His prolific output included 'Happy Because I'm In Love', 'A Fellow And A Girl', 'They Cut Down The Old Pine Tree', 'It's No Fun Eating Alone', 'Ankle Up The Altar With Me', 'It's The Same Old South', 'A Kiss To Remind You', 'The Four Rivers', 'Bird Of Paradise', 'You're Perfect!', and 'When The Clock Is Striking Twelve'. Amongst his other collaborators were Johnny Green, Vernon Duke, Richard Myers, and Billy Hill. It was reported at the time of his death that he had almost completed his autobiography, *With Or Without A Song*.

ELLIS, MARY

b. Mary Elsas, 15 June 1900, New York, USA. The date of birth given is the 'official' one, although Mary Ellis is reported to have claimed in 1997 that she was born 100 years ago. A unique and enduring actress and singer, Mary Ellis was an art student for three years and studied singing with the Belgian contralto Madame Freda Ashforth. From 1918-22 she was with the Metropolitan Opera, during which time she shared a stage with the legendary Caruso. She then turned to the dramatic theatre before creating the title role, opposite Dennis King, in the musical *Rose Marie* in 1924. After settling in London, in the early 30s, Mary Ellis played Frieda Hatzfeld in *Music In The Air*, which opened in 1933. Ivor Novello was so enchanted by her performance in the piece, that he wrote two of his most celebrated shows, *Glamorous Night* (1933) and *The Dancing Years* (1939), especially for her. When the latter show was forced to close due to the outbreak of World War II, Ellis became involved in hospital welfare, and spent much of the war years giving concerts for the troops. She and Novello were reunited in 1943 for *Arc De Triomphe*, but for the rest of the decade, and through to the early 50s, Ellis devoted most of her time to the straight theatre. Her association with Noël Coward's *After The Ball* (1954) was, by all accounts, an unhappy one, and proved to be her last London stage musical to date. After watching her performance in that piece, the Master is said to have raged: 'Mary Ellis couldn't get a laugh if she pulled a kipper out of her drawers.' Since making her debut with Conrad Veidt in *Bella Donna* in 1934, she has starred in several films, both in Hollywood and Britain, and many television plays. Amongst her most recent television appearances, was one with Jeremy Brett as Sherlock Holmes in the early 90s.

● FURTHER READING: *Those Dancing Years*, Mary Ellis.
● FILMS: *Bella Donna* (1934), *All The King's Horses* (1934), *Paris In Spring* (1935), *Fatal Lady* (1936), *Glamorous Night* (1937), *The Magic Box* (1951), *The 3 Worlds Of Gulliver* (1960).

ELLIS, VIVIAN

b. 29 October 1904, Hampstead, London, England, d. 19 June 1996, London, England. A highly respected composer, lyricist and author, chiefly celebrated for his fresh, witty and romantic music for revues and musicals in the UK during the period from the 20s through to the 50s. He also wrote the music for several films, including *Jack's The Boy*, starring Jack Hulbert and Cicely Courtneidge ('The Flies Crawled Up The Window'), *Piccadilly Incident* ('Piccadilly 1944'), *Public Nuisance No. 1* ('Me And My Dog') and individual pieces such as 'Coronation Scot', which became the signature tune of the popular BBC radio series *Paul Temple* in the 40s, and emerged again in the 80s in a television commercial for British Rail. As an author, he published a number of novels, and a series of humorous books entitled *How To Make Your Fortune On The Stock Exchange* and *How To Enjoy Your Operation*, etc. Ellis's mother was an extremely talented violinist, and his grandmother, Julia Woolf, was the composer of a 1888 comic opera *Carina*. His early ambition was to be a concert pianist, and he studied the piano with Dame Myra Hess and composition at the Royal Academy of Music, later giving a number of recitals. In his late teens, he developed an interest in light music and did the rounds of London's music publishers with some of his compositions, eventually getting a job as a reader and demonstrator with Francis, Day & Hunter. In the early 20s he composed the music for several numbers in revues such as *The Curate's Egg*, *The Little Revue*, and *The Punch Bowl*, and then, in 1924, wrote most of the songs (with lyrics by Graham John) for the successful Jack Hulbert and Cicely Courtneidge revue *By The Way*. These included 'Three Little Hairs', 'By The Way', and 'Nothing Ever Happens To Me'. A year later, June (née Howard-Tripp) sang his 'Over My Shoulder' (lyric by Graham John) in *Mercenary Mary*, and she was one of several artists to perform Ellis and John's hit 'Little Boy Blues' in another Hulbert and Courtneidge revue *Clowns In Clover* (1927). In the late 20s, Ellis was represented by various compositions in several other West End shows, including *Kid Boots*, *Cochran's 1926 Revue*, *My Son John*, *Merely Molly*, *Palladium Pleasures*, *Blue Skies*, *The Girl Friend*, *Charlot Revue 1928*, *Vogue And Vanities*, *The House That Jack Built*, *A Yankee At King Arthur's Court*, and *Will O' The Whispers* (1928), in which 'I Never Dreamt' (words and music by Ellis), was sung by the popular American vocalist, 'Whispering' Jack Smith.

In 1929 Vivian Ellis moved on from the revue format and had his first musical comedy hit with *Mr Cinders*, which had a book and lyrics by Clifford Grey and Greatrex Newman, and additional music by Richard Myers. The show contained one of Ellis's most enduring numbers, 'Spread A Little Happiness', which was performed by Binnie Hale, and several other favourites, including 'Ev'ry Little Moment' (Binnie Hale and Bobby Howes), and Howes' comedy high spot, 'On the Amazon'. Despite initially cool reviews, the show was an enormous success, running for a total of 529 performances. Ellis himself was unable to attend the opening of the show - he was seriously ill in the South of France. On his return to Britain he collaborated with lyricist Desmond Carter for *Little*

Tommy Tucker ('Let's Be Sentimental'), and again, for the wistful 'Wind In The Willows', which was featured in *Cochran's 1930 Revue* and became an extremely popular item in the repertoire of Leslie 'Hutch' Hutchinson. The show marked the beginning of an association with the impresario C.B. Cochran that was to prove one of the most important in Ellis's professional life. In the early 30s Ellis experienced mixed fortunes. *Follow A Star* was a financial failure despite the presence in the cast of Jack Hulbert, and Sophie Tucker, who sang Ellis and Jack Yellen's powerful, bluesy 'If Your Kisses Can't Hold The Man You Love', which Tucker later used to close her cabaret act. *The Song Of The Drum* ('Within My Heart'), *Blue Roses* ('Dancing In My Sleep', 'If I Had Three Wishes', 'Where Have You Been Hiding?'), and *Out Of The Bottle* (music by Ellis and Oscar Levant), were disappointing too. *Stand Up And Sing*, starring Jack Buchanan and Elsie Randolph, was much more successful, and contained numbers by Ellis, Philip Charig and Douglas Furber, such as 'There's Always Tomorrow', 'It's Not You', and 'Night Time'. By 1934, Ellis was one of the leading figures in the British musical theatre. For the revue *Streamline* (1934), C.B. Cochran teamed him with the author A.P. Herbert (b. 24 September 1890, Elstead, England, d. 11 November 1971), a collaboration that produced 'Other People's Babies' (sung by Norah Howard), among others, which provided a foretaste of their fruitful partnership during the late 40s, and, briefly, in the 50s. In the meantime, Ellis turned once more to Desmond Carter for the lyrics to *Jill Darling* (1934), a charming musical comedy that starred Frances Day, one of Ellis's favourite leading ladies, and included 'Dancing With A Ghost', 'Nonny, Nonny, No', 'Pardon My English', 'Let's Lay Our Heads Together', 'A Flower For You', and another of the composer's all-time standards, 'I'm On A See-Saw', which was performed in vivacious fashion by Louise Browne and John Mills, who later became a celebrated dramatic actor. 'I'm On A See-Saw' was recorded by Fats Waller, in a typically ebullient version, and became successful in America for Ambrose and his orchestra - one of Ellis's rare transatlantic hits. In the late 30s, Ellis began to write more of his own lyrics for songs such as 'Drop In Next Time You're Passing' (*Going Places*), 'The Trees In Bloomsbury Square' and 'London In The Season' (*The Town Talks*), and the delightful 'She's My Lovely', sung by Bobby Howes in *Hide And Seek* (1937), and later adopted by bandleader Billy Ternent as his signature tune. In 1938 he had three hit shows running in the West End: *The Fleet's Lit Up* ('Little Miss Go-As-You-Please', 'Guess It Must Be The Spring', 'How Do You Do, Mr. Right?', 'Hide And Seek'), *Running Riot* ('Take Your Partners For The Waltz', 'When Love Knocks At My Door', 'Doing An Irish Jig'), and *Under Your Hat*, 'the funniest musical comedy for years', which ran for a total of 512 performances in London, and included Cicely Courtneidge's hilariously patriotic 'The Empire Depends On You', and other numbers such as 'Together Again', 'Keep It Under Your Hat', 'and 'If You Want To Dance'.

While those shows were running in London, Vivian Ellis lived for a time in Hollywood, where he wrote film songs for Deanna Durbin. He returned to Britain in the Spring of 1939, and subsequently joined the R.N.V.R. He attained the rank of Lieutenant-Commander, and spent most of World War II as a Command Entertainments Officer for E.N.S.A. After his release in 1945, Ellis resumed his collaboration with A.P. Herbert (book and lyrics) in C.B.Cochran's production of a 'light opera' entitled *Big Ben* (1946). Remembered particularly for introducing the 19-year-old Lizbeth Webb to the London stage, the score included 'Let Us Go Down To The River', 'London Town', 'I Want To See The People Happy', 'Love Me Not', and 'Who's The Lady?', amongst others. One critic wrote that *Big Ben* lacked distinction, something that could never be said about Ellis and Herbert's next effort, *Bless The Bride* (1947), which was probably Vivian Ellis's biggest hit, and the climax of his career. Featuring hit songs such as the 'gaily traditional French pastiche', 'Ma Belle Marguerite', 'This Is My Lovely Day', and 'I Was Never Kissed Before', *Bless The Bride* was essentially a romantic operetta set in Victorian England, and could hardly have been more different to the brash, young American import, *Oklahoma!*, which opened at a nearby London theatre in the same week. Nevertheless, with Georges Guétary and Lizbeth Webb in the leading roles, *Bless The Bride* settled into the Adelphi Theatre, and ran for 886 performances. One of the main reasons it closed in 1949 was that Cochran wanted to replace it with Ellis and Herbert's *Tough At The Top*, a decision that proved to be an expensive mistake - the new show ran for just over four months.

In the 50s, the US invasion of the British musical theatre that had begun with *Oklahoma!* in 1947, intensified. In the face of all that Americana, Vivian Ellis's first score of the decade couldn't have been more parochial. *And So To Bed* (1951) was a musical adaptation of J.B.Fagan's renowned play about the Elizabethan diarist, Samuel Pepys, for which Ellis was called upon to compose music in a variety of styles, such as madrigal, jig, and saraband. A rather unconventional choice for the leading role was 'rubber-faced' comic actor, Leslie Henson, whose idea the whole thing was, and the score included 'Gaze Not On The Swans', 'Moppety Mo', 'Love Me Little, Love Me Long', 'Amo, Amas', and 'Bartholomew Fair'. The show's musical director was Mantovani, later renowned for his 'cascading strings'. *And So To Bed* had a healthy run of 323 performances, and Ellis followed it, two years later, with a revue, *Over The Moon*, before renewing his partnership with A.P. Herbert for *The Water Gipsies* (1955). Ellis had written the melody for one song, 'Little Boat', in the film version of Herbert's 1930 novel, set on London's waterways, and now, over 20 years later, he contributed a complete musical score, which included Dora Bryan's amusing versions of 'Why Did You Call Me Lily?', 'You Never Know With Men', 'I Should Worry', and 'It Would Cramp My Style'. Her presence ensured the show's initial success, but when she became pregnant and had to leave, *The Water Gipsies* folded after a run of 239 performances. It was Vivian Ellis's last major musical production, and he has been quoted as saying that it may have been his best score. Of his other work around that time, his children's musical, *Listen To The Wind* (1954), contained several excellent songs, and he continued to contribute to productions such as *Half In Earnest*, *Four To The Bar*, *Six Of One*, *Mr Whatnot*, and *Chaganog* (1964).

In 1973 Vivian Ellis received the Ivor Novello Award for outstanding services to British music, and, 10 years later, he was presented with the Ivor Novello Lifetime Achievement Award and became the President of the Performing Rights Society. In 1984, at the age of 80, he received the CBE, and, in the same year, the Vivian Ellis Prize, an annual award for the writers of new musicals, was instituted by the PRS. *Bless The Bride* was revived at London's Sadler's Wells Theatre in 1987, and Ellis's first musical comedy hit, *Mr Cinders*, also enjoyed London revivals in 1983 and 1993. The latter show was first produced in America in 1988, at the Goodspeed Opera House, and then, in 1992, it finally had its New York premiere at the Mazur Theatre. The show's hit song, 'Spread A Little Happiness', was sung in the 1982 film *Brimstone And Treacle*, by Sting, the ex-leader of the UK band, Police; it gave him his first solo Top 10 entry. Peter Skellern's version featured in an 80s television commercial for Lurpak butter. *Spread A Little Happiness* also became the title of a 'musical celebration of Vivian Ellis', devised by the author and critic Sheridan Morley, and presented at London's King's Head and Whitehall theatres in 1992. It meant that Vivian Ellis, a contemporary of Ivor Novello and Noël Coward, and one of the most important influences in the British musical theatre during the late 20s and 30s, still had his name up in lights more than 50 years later, alongside present incumbents such as Andrew Lloyd Webber. Up until shortly before his death, Ellis was working with Dan Crawford, artistic director of the King's Head Theatre, on a revival of his 1954 musical, *Listen To The Wind*. He wrote three new songs and the production opened to excellent notices in December 1996.

● ALBUMS: *You've Never Had It So Good* (Decca 1960)★★★, *Spread A Little Happiness* (Past 1996)★★★★.

● FURTHER READING: *Ellis In Wonderland*, Vivian Ellis. *I'm On A See-Saw*, Vivian Ellis.

ELSTREE CALLING

This 'all-star vaudeville and revue entertainment' which was compered by the popular radio comedian Tommy Handley and produced by British International Pictures (BIP) at Elstree Studios in 1930, is reputed to be the first British film musical. A variety of artists, most of whom were drawn from London shows, performed a series of sketches and musical numbers that included 'Ain't Misbehavin'' (Fats Waller-Harry Brooks-Andy Razaf) performed by Teddy Brown with his xylophone and Orchestra; 'My Heart Is Singing' (Ivor Novello-Donovan Parsons, from the current show *The House That Jack Built*), sung by Helen Burnell with the Adelphi Girls; 'Why Am I Always The Bridesmaid' (Fred W. Leigh-Charles Collins) and 'He's Only A Working Man' sung by Lily Morris; 'The Ladies Maid Is Always In The Know' sung by the Charlot Girls; 'The Thought Never Entered My Head' (Novello-Parsons from *The House That Jack Built*) sung by Helen Burnell and Jack Hulbert; 'I've Fallen In Love' sung by Cicely Courtneidge; 'It's Twelve and A Tanner A Bottle' sung by Will Fyffe; and 'Dance Around In Your Bones' which was tap-danced by the Three Eddies dressed as skeletons. The remainder of the music was composed by Vivian Ellis, Reginald Casson, Jack Strachey, and Chick

Endor. Others taking part were Anna May Wong, Bobbie Comber, Hannah Jones, Jameson Thomas, John Longden, Ivor McLaren, Lawrence Green, the Berkoff Dancers, the Kasbeck Singers, and the Balalaika Choral Orchestra. During the proceedings, funny-man Gordon Harker is constantly trying to receive the show on a home-made television set. The screenplay was written by Val Valentine, Walter Mycroft, and Adrian Brunel, who, in his dual role as director, skilfully assembled the whole affair. The sketches and other interpolated items were staged by the 31-year-old Alfred Hitchcock. *Elstree Calling* was photographed by John Maxwell with some of the sequences in colour, including those featuring the Charlot Girls, the Adelphi Girls, and Cicely Courtneidge.

ELVIS - THAT'S THE WAY IT IS

Having announced an artistic rebirth with the *Elvis* television spectacular, Elvis Presley began preparations for his first concert appearances since 1957. His live debut at the International Hotel in Las Vegas yielded tremendous acclaim, and the event was recorded on the *On Stage* album. His third engagement, from 10 to 15 August 1970, along with the rehearsal sessions at MGM Studios, became the subject of *Elvis - That's The Way It Is*. The MGM sequences, which feature Presley's rhythm section including James Burton (guitar), Glen D. Hardin (piano), Jerry Scheff (bass) and Ronnie Tutt (drums) provide an interesting profile of work-in-progress, although the film itself offers little insight into the singer's character. The Las Vegas performances are powerful, showing an artist of renewed confidence. His gentle self-depreciation is amusing, although a rustiness does creep into his stage movements. Dennis Saunders' direction and Lucien Ballard's photography add sparkle to the proceedings, much of which was enshrined on an enduringly popular soundtrack album. It sadly omitted Presley's renditions of his early rock 'n' roll material in favour of newer songs, including his international smash, 'I Just Can't Help Believin'', as well as versions of 'Bridge Over Troubled Water', 'You Don't Have To Say You Love Me' and 'You've Lost That Lovin' Feelin''. Nonetheless, *Elvis - That's The Way It Is* marked a triumphant return to live performances.

ELVIS - THE MOVIE

Originally made for television, *Elvis - The Movie* is a three-hour hagiography starring Kurt Russell in the title role, with vocals provided by Presley impersonator Ronnie McDowell. This sentimental film, released in 1979, provided no insight into its subject, sugaring the tale by emphasizing his impoverished background and the death of his mother, while glossing over Presley's personal and professional traumas and his hedonistic lifestyle. Indeed, *Elvis - The Movie* closes with the singer's 1970's triumphs in Las Vegas, completely ignoring his sorry subsequent decline and death. Director John Carpenter later disowned the entire project, declaring it one of the worst films he had ever seen. That is perhaps too critical, but *Elvis - The Movie* is certainly a lost opportunity.

ELVIS ON TOUR

Pierre Adidge and Robert Abel, who had directed the enthralling Joe Cocker feature, *Mad Dogs And Englishmen*, assumed the same role for this 1972 documentary. 'At last! The first real Elvis Presley movie,' proclaimed an ecstatic review in *Rolling Stone* and indeed the film captures the performer just before his final artistic decline. Superbly shot, *Elvis On Tour* showcases material from Presley's early recordings - 'That's Alright', 'Mystery Train', 'Don't Be Cruel' - as well as presenting several songs pivotal to his late 60s rebirth. These include 'Suspicious Minds', 'Burning Love' and his powerful rendition of Mickey Newbury's 'American Trilogy'. Martin Scorcese (*Taxi Driver*, *The Last Waltz*) was responsible for the inventive montage sequence and the film also contains footage from Presley's appearance on the *Ed Sullivan Show*, where he invests 'Ready Teddy' with awesome exuberance. The Elvis of 1972, replete with white cat-suit and rhinestones, was inevitably incapable of recreating such intensity, but his performances on this film still hold an enthralling magnetism.

ENNIS, SKINNAY

b. Robert Ennis, 13 August 1909, Salisbury, North Carolina, USA, d. 3 June 1963, Beverley Hills, California, USA. Ennis joined the Hal Kemp band as a singer/drummer in the late 20s while still at the University of North Carolina. He became the band's leading attraction because of his unique 'out of breath' vocal style. Ennis left Kemp in 1938 and, after working with Gil Evans and Claude Thornhill, formed his own band with its theme song, 'Got A Date With An Angel', and gained maximum exposure with a prestigious residency on Bob Hope's *Pepsodent Show*. Ennis also featured in the show's comedy routines and became a personality in his own right. After World War II, during which he led a service band, Ennis rejoined Hope until 1946, and then worked on radio with Abbott And Costello in the late 40s. He made several diverting appearances in films including *College Swing* (with Bob Hope), *Follow The Band*, *Swing It Soldier*, *Sleepytime Gal*, *Let's Go Steady* and *Radio Stars On Parade*. During the 50s his band toured the USA, playing the hotel circuit, including, from 1958, a five-year residency at the Statler-Hilton, Los Angeles. During the early 60s he recorded the album *Skinnay Ennis Salutes Hal Kemp*, using many of the musicians who had played in the original Kemp band. He died after choking on a bone while dining in a restaurant.
● COMPILATIONS: *Skinnay Ennis, 1947-1948* (Hindsight 1989)★★★.

ENTER THE GUARDSMAN

This show won Denmark's first Musical Of The Year competition in September 1996, which attracted some 300 entries from around the world. *Enter The Guardsman* won for its creators, Americans Scott Wentworth (book), Marion Adler (lyrics) and Craig Bohmler (music), the substantial sum of £40,000 (approximately $60,000). It had previously attracted some attention when it won the Bernice Cohen Award for Outstanding Presentation Of 1994 by ASCAP, and had appeared at the National Alliance for Musical Theatre's 1995 Festival of New Musicals in the USA. After its success in Denmark, various producers expressed interest in mounting the show in England, and it was Andrew Lloyd Webber's Really Useful Group that sponsored the production, which opened on 17 September 1997 at London's Donmar Warehouse. Set in the 20s, this chamber piece proved to be a sophisticated musical reworking of Ferenc Molnár's 1910 play *The Guardsman*, a comedy of manners that was once a favourite on Broadway, featuring Alfred Lunt and Lynn Fontanne; the story was also filmed in 1931. In this musical treatment, The Actor (Alexander Hanson) has recently married his leading lady, The Actress (Janie Dee). Aware that his new bride is not - by any means - inexperienced in the love department, The Actor decides to test her fidelity. He bombards her with red roses, sent anonymously at first. However, later, enter the guardsman (The Actor in disguise), who discovers, to his horror, that his wife succumbs to another's manly charms rather too easily for his taste. The proceedings are witnessed by the couple's old friend, The Playwright (Nicky Henson), a wryly debonair, but uncertain, character with notebook permanently poised, searching for a satisfying ending to their story. He is ultimately disappointed, because, in answer to his final question as to whether she knew that her soldier-count lover was really her husband, the Actress enigmatically responds: 'On that night - he was.' Also in the fine Donmar cast were Angela Richards (The Dresser), Jeremy Finch (The Assistant Stage Manager), Walter Van Dyk (The Wigs Master) and Nicola Sloane (The Wardrobe Mistress). High points of the witty and tuneful score, which was suitably European in texture, included Angela Richards' 'Waiting In The Wings', 'My One Great Love' (Janie Dee), 'The First Night' (Company), 'Art Imitating Life' (Nicky Henson), and the title number (Company). The remaining, extremely attractive songs, were 'Chopin', 'My One Great Love', 'Language Of Flowers', 'Drama', 'Actor's Fantasy', 'You Have The Ring', 'True To Me', 'She's A Little Off', 'I Can't Go On', 'They Die' and 'In The Long Run'. Jeremy Sands directed the production, which played out its four-week season in the face of generally adverse critical reaction, ranging from 'lacked Stephen Sondheim's cynicism, ironic wit or savage streak' to 'simply gentle, civilized fun.'

ESSEX, DAVID

b. David Albert Cook, 23 July 1947, London, England. Originally a drummer in the semi-professional Everons, Essex subsequently turned to singing during the mid-60s, and recorded a series of unsuccessful singles for a variety of labels. On the advice of his influential manager, Derek Bowman, he switched to acting and after a series of minor roles gained his big break upon winning the lead part in the stage musical *Godspell*. This was followed by the authentic 50s-inspired film *That'll Be The Day* and its sequel *Stardust*. The former reactivated Essex's recording career and the song he composed for the film, 'Rock On', was a transatlantic Top 10 hit. It was in Britain, however, that Essex enjoyed several years as a pin-up teen-idol. During the mid-70s, he registered two UK number 1s, 'Gonna Make You A Star' and 'Hold Me Close', plus the Top

10 hits 'Lamplight', 'Stardust' and 'Rollin' Stone'. After parting with producer Jeff Wayne, Essex continued to chart, though with noticeably diminishing returns. As his teen appeal waned, his serious acting commitments increased, most notably with the role of Che Guevara in *Evita*. The musical also provided another Top 5 hit with the acerbic 'Oh, What A Circus'. His lead part in the film *Silver Dream Racer* resulted in a hit of the same title. Thereafter, Essex took on a straight non-singing part in *Childe Byron*. The Christmas hit, 'A Winter's Tale', kept his chart career alive, as did the equally successful 'Tahiti'. The latter anticipated one of his biggest projects to date, an elaborate musical, *Mutiny!* (based on *Mutiny On The Bounty*). In 1993, after neglecting his showbusiness career while he spent two a half years in the African region as an ambassador for Voluntary Service Overseas, Essex embarked on a UK concert tour, and issued *Cover Shot*, a collection of mostly 60s songs. In the same year he played the part of Tony Lumpkin in Oliver Goldsmith's comedy, *She Stoops To Conquer*, in London's West End. In 1994 he continued to tour, and released a new album produced by Jeff Wayne. It included a duet with Catherine Zeta Jones on 'True Love Ways', and the VSO-influenced 'Africa', an old Toto number. Despite pursuing two careers, Essex has managed to achieve consistent success on record, in films and stage. He was awarded an OBE in the 1999 New Year Honours list.

● ALBUMS: *Rock On* (Columbia 1973)★★★, *David Essex* (Columbia 1974)★★★, *All The Fun Of The Fair* (Columbia 1975)★★, *Out On The Street* (Columbia 1976)★★, *On Tour* (Columbia 1976)★★, *Gold And Ivory* (Columbia 1977)★★, *Hold Me Close* (Columbia 1979)★★, *Imperial Wizard* (Mercury 1979)★★, *The David Essex Album* (Columbia 1979)★★, *Silver Dream Racer* (Mercury 1980)★, *Hot Love* (Mercury 1980)★★, *Be-Bop - The Future* (Mercury 1981)★★, *Stage Struck* (Mercury 1982)★★, *Mutiny!* (Mercury 1983)★★, *The Whisper* (Mercury 1983)★★, *This One's For You* (Mercury 1984)★★, *Live At The Royal Albert Hall* (1984)★★, *Centre Stage* (K-Tel 1986)★★, *Touching The Ghost* (Lamplight 1989)★★, *Cover Shot* (Lamplight 1993)★★, *Back To Back* (Lamplight 1994)★★, *Here We All Are Together* (Lamplight 1998)★★.

● COMPILATIONS: *The David Essex Collection* (Pickwick 1980)★★★, *The Very Best Of David Essex* (TV Records 1982)★★★, *Spotlight On David Essex* (1993)★★★, *The Best Of David Essex* (Columbia 1996)★★★.

● VIDEOS: *Live At The Royal Albert Hall* (PolyGram Music Video 1984).

● FURTHER READING: *The David Essex Story*, George Tremlett.

● FILMS: *That'll Be The Day* (1975), *Stardust* (1976), *Silver Dream Racer* (1980).

ETTING, RUTH

b. 23 November 1907, David City, Nebraska, USA, d. 24 September 1978, Colorado Springs, USA. This famous torch singer sang on radio and in Chicago nightclubs before making her Broadway debut in *Ziegfeld Follies Of 1927* in which she made a tremendous impact with 'Shakin' The Blues Away'. In her next show, *Whoopee* (1928), she introduced 'Love Me Or Leave Me', which was subsequently always associated with her, and titled her 1955 film biography, which starred Doris Day. After launching two more future standards, 'Get Happy' (*Nine-Fifteen Revue*) and 'Ten Cents A Dance' (*Simple Simon*), her sparkling rendition of an old Nora Bayes number, 'Shine On Harvest Moon', in *Ziegfeld Follies Of 1931*, made the song a hit all over again. By then she was one of America's brightest stars with her own radio shows and string of hit records. There were more than 60 of them between 1926 and 1937, including 'Lonesome And Sorry', 'Thinking Of You', 'The Song Is Ended', 'Back In Your Own Back Yard', 'Ramona', 'I'll Get By', 'Mean To Me', 'More Than You Know', 'Ain't Misbehavin'', 'Try A Little Tenderness', 'Love Is Like That', 'I'm Good For Nothing But Love', 'Guilty', 'Smoke Gets In Your Eyes', and 'Life Is A Song'. In the 30s she also made three films, *Roman Scandals*, *Hips Hips Hooray*, and *The Gift Of The Gab*, and in 1936 she appeared on the London stage in *Transatlantic Rhythm*. A year later she split from her husband and manager, Martin ('Moe The Gimp') Snyder, a Chicago 'hood' who had guided her career from the start. James Cagney played Snyder in the biopic *Love Me Or Leave Me*, and the story of his domination of Etting's life and his revenge wounding of her second husband - plus a great bunch of songs - made for an absorbing film. After Ruth Etting's career faded towards the end of the 30s, she entertained at intervals during World War II and enjoyed a brief comeback in the late 40s, when club patrons and radio listeners were reminded that she was one of the outstanding vocalists of her era.

● COMPILATIONS: *On The Air* (1979)★★, *Ten Cents A Dance* (1981)★★★, *America's Radio Sweetheart* (1989)★★★.

EUROVISION

This 'comedy of homosexual manners set against the backdrop of the Eurovision Song Contest', was written and directed by Tim Luscombe, and made its debut in 1992 at the Drill Hall in Bloomsbury, a fringe theatre devoted to lesbian and gay writing. While at the Drill Hall, the piece was brought to the attention of Andrew Lloyd Webber who presented it at his Sydmonton Festival in the summer of 1993, where it was extremely well received. He then decided to finance a London production, which opened at the Vaudeville Theatre on 10 November 1993. It was immediately savaged by the critics who ridiculed the 'preposterous plot in which the ghosts of two gay lovers from ancient Rome materialise in the milieu of a thoroughly modern Eurovision Song Contest'. Anita Dobson, ex-*EastEnders* soap-star, played Katia Europa, 'who is suddenly possessed by something calling itself The Spirit of Europe', and she escaped more or less unscathed from the press hammering, as did James Dreyfus (Gary) and Charles Edwards (Kevin) as the 'two gay young things'. There was one genuine Eurovision song, a former Greek entry entitled 'Bim-Bam-Bom!', and several original songs, including 'Grazie, Macedonia', by Jason Carr. The show's author, Tim Luscombe, was generally held responsible for the 'utter bilge', and he fought back, claiming that the critics seemed to be regarding the show as 'Ibsen' instead of a 'self-mocking entertainment' which had 700 people falling off their chairs every night'. It was all to no avail. Unlike Broadway, where a show can close after only one night, most West End cripples stagger on for a few weeks, but

Andrew Lloyd Webber saw the writing on the wall, and pulled out the financial plug so that *Eurovision* disappeared down the drain after only a run of only three weeks with estimated losses of £275,000.

EVENSONG

Evelyn Laye, who was one of the most enchanting leading ladies of the London musical theatre, especially during the 20s, only made a few films, and this was arguably the best of them. In the poignant and tragic story she plays the young and lovely Maggie O'Neil who leaves her home in England, against her parents' wishes, and runs away to Paris in the hope of becoming a famous opera star. Changing her name to Mm. Irela, she is warned by her manager, Kober (Fritz Kortner), that she cannot have both romance and career. She chooses the latter course, and so loses her first love, George Murray (Emlyn Williams), who is killed in World War I. Many years later she realizes that it was the wrong decision, but by then her constant admirer, Archduke Theodore (Carl Esmond), is an old man, and she herself is embittered. After being upstaged by the young pretender, Baba (Conchita Supervia), she dies in her dressing room while listening to an early recording of her voice on a gramophone record. A particularly fine supporting cast included Muriel Aked, Patrick O'Moore, Dennis Van Norton, Arthur Sinclair, and Browning Mummary. The film was full of music, with both Evelyn Laye and Supervia in superb voice with operatic excerpts such as 'Mimi's Song' and 'Musetta's Song' (from *La Boheme*), the 'Drinking Song' (from *La Traviata*), and 'Carceleras' (from *Las Hijas Del Zebado*). Laye also sings a medley of old favourites that were popular during the 1914-18 war years, such as 'A Perfect Day' (Carrie Jacobs-Bond), 'There's A Long, Long Trail' (Stoddard King-Joe Elliot), 'Keep The Home Fires Burning' (Ivor Novello-Lena Guilbert-Ford), 'I Love The Moon' (Paul Rubens), and 'Love's Old Sweet Song' (G. Clifton Bingham-James L. Molloy). In addition there were two new numbers by Mischa Spoliansky and Edward Knoblock, 'Irela Valse' and 'I'll Wait For You'. In the final analysis, however, as one critic pointed out at the time, this is a tensely dramatic picture that has drama, romance, opera, comedy, tears and all the other surefire ingredients that make a success in showbusiness. It also had a magnificent central performance from Evelyn Laye, whose portrayal of the prima donna from girlhood to her eventual eclipse, in dramatic terms, surpassed anything she had done previously. The screenplay, by Edward Knoblock and Dorothy Farnum, was adapted from Beverley Nichols' novel, which he and Knoblock turned into a successful West End play. This memorable film was photographed by Mutz Greenbaum and impressively directed by Victor Saville.

EVER GREEN

The renowned English impresario C.B. Cochran was taking a big risk in 1930 when he cast Jessie Matthews, one of the most popular stars of the London stage, in *Ever Green*. A year earlier, another of the West End's favourite leading ladies, Evelyn Laye, had cited Mattthews as co-respondent in her petition for divorce from Sonnie Hale, and Jessie Matthews' co-star in *Ever Green* was to be that same Sonny Hale. Would the prim and proper English the-atre-going public accept the situation? Well, they did, and the show proved to be the most successful of Matthews' career. Richard Rodgers and Lorenz Hart came up with a fine score, and it was their original idea that librettist Ben W. Levy used for his story of Harriet Green (Jessie Matthews), a young, somewhat pushy actress, who, to gain publicity for herself, purports to be a woman in her 60s whose looks have been preserved by the miracle of modern cosmetics. The problem is, that the man she loves, Tommy Thompson (Sonnie Hale), does not want to marry someone more than twice his age. As usual with a Cochran show there were some spectacular effects. One of the most delightful of these was the setting for the two stars' big number, 'Dancing On The Ceiling', when an enormous inverted chandelier was mounted on the revolving stage. The song had been cut from a previous Rodgers and Hart show, *Simple Simon*, and went on to become a much-admired standard, particularly in the version by Frank Sinatra on his *In The Wee Small Hours*. *Ever Green*'s pleasing score also contained 'If I Give In To You', 'In The Cool Of The Evening', 'Dear, Dear', and 'No Place Like Home', and the show ran for 254 performances. Jessie Matthews and Sonnie Hale married in 1931, and starred in the 1934 film version of *Evergreen* (one word), which had some different songs and a modified storyline.

EVERGREEN

After delighting West End audiences with her scintillating singing and dancing in the stage musical *Ever Green* (1930), Jessie Matthews recreated her role for this film version (with its slightly different title) in 1934. In the screenplay, which was written by the celebrated actor and playwright Emlyn Williams and Marjorie Gaffney, Miss Matthews plays Harriet Green, the daughter of an Edwardian music-hall singing star, who secretly takes her mother's place after she has gone missing, and triumphs in her own right. Most of the songs from the stage show were dispensed with, but three survived the trip to the Gaumont British Studios at Shepherd's Bush: 'Dear Dear', 'If I Give In To You', and the big hit, 'Dancing On The Ceiling', which gave Jessie Matthews a wonderful oppor-tunity for a fine solo dance which she is reputed to have choreographed herself. Harry Woods contributed two songs that the leading lady immediately made her own: 'When You've Got A Little Springtime In Your Heart', and the lively 'Over My Shoulder' which accompanied a spec-tacular production number atop a 'wedding cake'. Jessie's husband, Sonnie Hale, played stage director Leslie Benn, and also in the cast were Betty Balfour, Barry Mackay, Ivor McLaren, Hartley Power, Patrick Ludlow, Betty Shale, and Marjorie Brooks. Buddy Bradley staged the imaginative dance sequences, and *Evergreen*, which was its leading lady's most successful film, was produced by Michael Balcon and directed by Victor Saville.

EVERYBODY'S CHEERING

(see *Take Me Out To The Ball Game*)

EVERYDAY'S A HOLIDAY

Retitled *Seaside Swingers* for US audiences, *Everyday's A Holiday* revolved around several teenagers who take sea-sonal work at a holiday camp, before entering a television talent contest. The film starred former Joe Meek protégé, John Leyton, famed for the ghostly 'Johnny Remember Me', and light-hearted singer Mike Sarne, creator of early 60s novelty hits 'Come Outside' and 'Will I What?' Pantomime beat group Freddie And The Dreamers were featured in a cast that also included the far superior Mojos. This forgettable feature was billed as including '16 smash hit numbers', a fact that was patently untrue. *Everyday's A Holiday* did contain some good photographic sequences, courtesy of Nicolas Roeg, but offered little for the pop fan. Coincidentally, both Leyton and Sarne would later abandon music for 'serious' acting roles.

EVERYONE SAYS I LOVE YOU

Woody Allen's tribute to the romantic musicals of the 30s, and subsequently, deals with a year in the life of Steffi (Goldie Hawn) and her second husband Bob (Alan Alda), a comfortably liberal, wealthy married couple residing on New York's Upper East Side. Their children and step-chil-dren include Skylar (Drew Barrymore), who is engaged to Holden (Edward Norton), Laura (Natalie Portman), Lane (Gaby Hoffman), Scott (Lukas Haas), who unfortunately has a nasty streak of political conservatism, and DJ (Natasha Lyonne), the film's narrator. Steffi's first hus-band, Joe (Woody Allen), lives in Paris and is mixed up and not very good with women (no surprise there), although (having been given 'inside information'), he manages to woo and win Von (Julia Roberts). Steffi mean-while, as part of her good deed for the day, invites paroled felon Charles Ferry (Tim Roth) to dinner, only for Skylar to have a brief fling with him. All this plot - and more - is enhanced by a clutch of wonderful standard songs, sung by actors who, so it is said, signed their contracts before they knew the movie was going to be a musical. So there are varying degrees of vocal expertise here, with Goldie Hawn and Alan Alda emerging with the greatest credit, and only Barrymore having to be dubbed (in this film, even the spirits down at the funeral parlour leap out of their coffins and sing). Among the many highlights are the mood-setting 'Just You, Just Me', Alda's neat reading of Cole Porter's 'Looking At You', Norton's hilarious spoof-ing of Walter Donaldson and Gus Kahn's 'My Baby Just Cares For Me', 'I'm A Dreamer, Aren't We All?', 'Makin' Whoopee', 'Cuddle Up a Little Closer', 'What A Little Moonlight Can Do', and the final number, 'Hooray For Captain Spalding', sung in French by a group of Groucho Marx imitators (actually by the Helen Miles Singers). That last item was written by Bert Kalmar and Harry Ruby for the Marx Brothers' show *Animal Crackers*, and, coinciden-tally, the song from which this picture takes its title, 'Everyone Says I Love You', is also a Kalmar and Ruby composition which featured in another zany Marx Brothers vehicle, *Horse Feathers*. But the best of the lot - the top of the heap - is Hawn's computer-enhanced song and dance scene with Allen to 'I'm Thru With Love' on the banks of the Seine. An homage to those Fred Astaire-Cyd

Charisse and Gene Kelly-Lesley Caron numbers from MGM's golden age of movie musicals. Arranged and conducted by Dick Hyman, choreographed by Graciela Daniele, with Carlo DiPalma's stunning Technicolor photography, this film was scripted and directed by Woody Allen. It was produced by Mirimax and released in 1996.

EVITA

In the period following their success with *Jesus Christ Superstar*, Andrew Lloyd Webber and Tim Rice went their different ways for a time. While Lloyd Webber was involved with Alan Ayckbourn in an ill-fated attempt to bring P.G. Wodehouse's *Jeeves* to the musical stage, Tim Rice spent well over a year researching the life of Eva Peron. He discovered it to be the ultimate rags to riches fairytale. His book tells of the illegitimate, malnourished, and barely literate young Eva (Elaine Paige) from a poor village in Junin, arriving in Buenos Aires, helped by tango dancer Agustin Magaldi (Mark Ryan), with ambitions to be an actress. Her life changes dramatically in 1944 when she meets Colonel Juan Peron (Joss Ackland) and, after deftly ousting his young mistress (Siobhán McCarthy), becomes his First Lady two years later. Fiercely devoted to her husband, and to her *descamisados* (shirtless ones), she became Argentina's first truly international figure, the most adored - and hated - woman in Latin America, until her death from cancer at the age of 33. When *Evita* opened at the Prince Edward Theatre in London on 21 June 1978, there were howls of protest from some quarters accusing Rice and Lloyd Webber of glorifying 'this wife of the Peronist regime, a loathsome fascist dictatorship', rejecting the subject as quite unsuitable for a West End musical. Many years later, Rice commented: 'You can never really know the truth about Eva Peron, and I think the best way to tell her story is through a musical because she was a larger-than-life actress on a public stage. Her life was insane, and a musical is just the sort of melodramatic document which can capture something of her - much better than a book can.' Rice and Lloyd Webber's device of utilising the character of Che (David Essex) to comment on, and link the scenes was a clever one, and he had two of the best numbers, the mocking 'Oh What A Circus' and 'High Flying, Adored'. Among the other highlights of this recitative score were Eva's 'I'd Be Surprisingly Good For You' (to Peron, that is), her 'Don't Cry For Me Argentina' on the balcony, following Peron's Presidential election victory, and the mistress-on-the-way out's rueful 'Another Suitcase In Another Hall'. The remainder of the numbers included 'Requiem For Evita', 'On This Night Of A Thousand Stars', 'Buenos Aires', 'Goodnight And Thank You', 'A New Argentina', 'Rainbow High', 'And The Money Keeps Rolling In (And Out)', 'Waltz For Eva And Che', 'She Is A Diamond', and 'Lament'. Harold Prince directed, the choreographer was Larry Fuller, and *Evita* ran for nearly eight years (2,900 performances) in London. Paige received a SWET (Society Of West End Theatre) award, and the show won another for best musical. Prior to opening, just as they did with *Jesus Christ Superstar*, Rice and Lloyd Webber introduced the score via a concept album (1976), with principal singers, Julie Covington (Eva), Paul Jones (Peron), Colm Wilkinson (Che), Tony Christie

(Magaldi), and Barbara Dickson (Mistress). Early in 1977, Covington went to number 1 in the UK with 'Don't Cry For Me Argentina', and Barbara Dickson ('Another Suitcase In Another Hall') and David Essex ('Oh What A Circus') also had hits with songs from the show. Evita's success in the West End was echoed in the USA where it became the forerunner of a wave of British stage musicals that helped reverse the transatlantic tide. It opened at the Broadway Theatre in New York on the 25 September 1979, with Bob Gunton (Peron), Jane Ohringer (Mistress), and Mark Syers (Magaldi). The production ran for 1,568 performances, and won Tony Awards for Mandy Patinkin (Che), Patti LuPone (Eva), Harold Prince, David Hersey (lighting), book, score, and best musical. Since then it has been produced all round the world, although banned in Argentina, and a major revival starring Marti Webb, toured the UK in 1995. An acclaimed film version of *Evita*, directed by Alan Parker and produced by Robert Stigwood, was released in 1996. It starred Madonna in the title role, with Antonio Banderas (Che), Jonathan Pryce (Juan Peron), and Jimmy Nail (Agustin Magaldi). Madonna had hits with a 'Don't Cry For Me Argentina' and a new Rice/Lloyd Webber song, the Oscar-winning 'You Must Love Me'. A new Broadway-bound production of the show began a national tour on 6 November 1998 in Detroit. It had four Latin actors in the leading roles - Natalie Toro and Ana Marie Andricain sharing the title role, Raul Esparza (Che), and Raymond Jaramillo McLeod (Peron). Coincidentally, outstanding amongst the rest of the cast was 16-year-old Angela Covington. The coincidences ends there. This Covington plays Peron's mistress, and scores with the highly emotional 'Another Suitcase In Another Hall'.

EXPRESSO BONGO (FILM MUSICAL)

This 1959 comedy feature began life as a stage play loosely based on the rise of British rock 'n' roll star Tommy Steele. Written by Wolf Mankowitz and directed by Val Guest, *Expresso Bongo* starred Laurence Harvey as an unscrupulous Soho agent, determined to make his protégé, ably played by Cliff Richard, into an international success. The film manages to convey some of the exploitative nature of early pop and the nascent teenage subculture spearheaded by the legendary 2I's coffee bar. However, the cynicism of Mankowitz meant the funny moments lacked warmth and the film now merely offers period charm. Although mild-mannered by the standards of today, *Expresso Bongo* was given an X-certificate, confirming the moody, threat-to-society image Richard initially bore. It did nothing to hinder his popularity, however, and in 1960 a soundtrack EP reached the number 14 position in the UK singles chart while the film's finest song, 'Voice In The Wilderness', peaked at number 2.

EXPRESSO BONGO (STAGE MUSICAL)

Considered by many to be 'the most important and original British musical of its time', *Expresso Bongo* opened at the Saville Theatre on 23 April 1958. The book, by Wolf Mankowitz and Julian More, was taken from a newspaper piece by Mankowitz, and is said to have been based on the true-life story of the young ex-merchant seaman Thomas Hicks. He had been discovered in 1956, playing the guitar and singing in a Soho coffee-bar called the 2I's, by his future manager John Kennedy. He, and the agent Larry Parnes, changed Hicks' name to Tommy Steele, and moulded him into Britain's first rock 'n' roller. In this show, Herbert Rudge is also discovered at a trendy coffee-bar, but he is playing bongo drums, not guitar, hence his eventual stage name of Bongo Herbert. With the aid of a crafty agent, Johnnie (Paul Schofield), he quickly climbs the chart with 'Expresso Party', and then, just like Steele, shrewdly broadens his image, in Bongo's case with a magnificently ghastly hymn to his old mum, 'The Shrine On The Second Floor' ('There's a beautiful grey-haired Madonna/Who once taught me what life had in store'). The show was full of accurately drawn, colourful characters such as the stripper who wants to be a singer, Maisie King (Millicent Martin), a recording executive, Mr. Mayer (Meir Tzelniker), and a well-to-do, ageing actress, Dixie Collins (Hy Hazell), who gives Bongo a taste of the high life, and arranges for him to be represented by an 'establishment' agent. Johnnie cannot compete, looks around for new talent, and decides to promote Maisie as a singer. The score, by David Heneker and Monty Norman, both of whom also collaborated on the lyrics with Julian More, was a match for the book. The songs were witty and satirical, including Bongo's wry 'Don't You Sell Me Down The River', and Johnnie's charting of his ups and downs with 'I've Never Had It So Good' and 'The Gravy Train', while Maisie ground her hips (and a good deal more) to 'Spoil The Child'. She also had two poignant ballads, 'Seriously' and 'I Am'. Dixie reflected on her life in and out of the theatre with the touching 'Time', and joined Johnnie and Mr. Mayer for 'Nothing Is For Nothing'. Opinions as to the show's value were mixed, and ran along the lines of 'an adult approach', 'wit, bite and topicality' and 'a raucous paeon of disgust aimed at the shoddy side of society'. It was certainly very different in style from that other British musical, Sandy Wilson's *Valmouth* (set in an English spa town inhabited by centenarians), which came to the Lyric when *Expresso Bongo* closed after a run of 316 performances. Even then, the Tommy Steele connections continued: his brother, Colin Hicks, played the lead in the touring version of *Expresso Bongo*, and the show's co-composer and lyricist, David Heneker, wrote the score for Steele's smash-hit musical *Half A Sixpence*, in 1963. The 1959 film of *Expresso Bongo* starred Laurence Harvey, Cliff Richard, Yolande Dolan and Sylvia Syms. Changes in the score resulted in the inclusion of 'A Voice In The Wilderness', written by Norrie Paramor and Bunny Lewis, which Richard took to number 2 in the UK chart.

FABULOUS DORSEYS, THE

The first jazz-related biopic, this 1947 film also has the dubious distinction of casting its subjects as themselves. Although both Jimmy and Tommy Dorsey managed to avoid appearing too embarrassed by the shaky plot (much of which centred on pleasing Ma and Pa Dorsey), their acting was understandably wooden. Their playing was, of course, excellent as both men, then still in their prime, were amongst the outstanding technicians on their respective instruments. For jazz fans the best moment comes in a cornily-contrived nightclub scene in which a jam session occurs. Apart from Jimmy and Tommy, the mismatched musicians include Charlie Barnet, Ray Bauduc and Ziggy Elman, all of whom get in the way of the superb Art Tatum.

FACE THE MUSIC

Generally considered to be Irving Berlin's best score for some years, it came at a time when both he and America were recovering from the Depression, and the Prohibition bootleggers were about to be put out of business by the newly-elected President Roosevelt. *Face The Music* opened on Broadway at the New Amsterdam Theatre on 17 February 1932. The somewhat satirical book was the work of Moss Hart, who, in collaboration with the show's directors, Hassard Short and George S. Kaufman, fashioned a contemporary story of shady deals, in which Mrs. Martin Van Buren Meshbesher (Mary Boland), the wife of a police sergeant who, in the course of his duty, has accumulated a great deal of money from undisclosed sources. She panics, and tries to lose some of it by investing in a bizarre Broadway show. Unfortunately for her the show is a big success and makes even more money. As usual Berlin captured perfectly the mood and the period - the bitterness and cynicism that prevailed in America at that time: 'Let's Have Another Cup Of Coffee' ('And let's have another piece of pie') was sung by the Rockefeller and Vanderbilt-types - the ex-swells (personified in the show by Katherine Carrington and J. Harold Murray) who are now eating at the Automat instead of the Astor. The song became widely popular through a recording by Fred Waring and his Pennsyvanians, and was sung lustily by Ethel Merman in the 1954 film, *There's No Business Like Show Business*. Carrington and Murray also had 'I Say It's Spinach', 'On A Roof In Manhattan', and the romantic and soothing 'Soft Lights And Sweet Music'. The latter song was also successful for Waring and his 'glee club'. *Face The Music* played for 165 performances and was revived briefly on Broadway in the following year.

FAIN, SAMMY

b. Samuel Feinberg, 17 June 1902, New York, USA, d. 6 December 1989, Los Angeles, California, USA. A prolific composer of Broadway shows and films for over 40 years, early in his career he worked for music publisher Jack Mills, and as a singer/pianist in vaudeville and radio. His first published song, with a lyric by Irving Mills and Al Dubin in 1925, was 'Nobody Knows What A Red-Haired Mamma Can Do', and was recorded, appropriately, by Sophie Tucker. In 1926 he met Irving Kahal (b. 5 March 1903, Houtzdale, Pennsylvania, USA), who was to be his main collaborator until Kahal's death in 1942. Almost immediately they had hits with 'Let A Smile Be Your Umbrella' and 'I Left My Sugar Standing In The Rain'. In 1929 their song, 'Wedding Bells Are Breaking Up That Old Gang Of Mine' was a hit for another singer/pianist, Gene Austin, and surfaced again 25 years later, sung by the Four Aces. Fain contributed songs to several early musical films including The Big Pond (1930) in which Maurice Chevalier introduced 'You Brought A New Kind Of Love To Me', the Marx Brothers' comedy, Monkey Business (1931) 'When I Take My Sugar To Tea', Footlight Parade (1933) 'By A Waterfall', Goin' To Town (1935) in which Mae West sang 'Now I'm A Lady' and 'He's A Bad, Bad Man But He's Good Enough For Me' and Dames (1934) which featured the song 'When You Were A Smile On Your Mother's Lips And A Twinkle In Your Daddy's Eye' - and in which Fain actually appeared as a songwriter. Fain's 30s Broadway credits included Everybody's Welcome, Right This Way (featuring 'I'll Be Seeing You' and 'I Can Dream, Can't I'), Hellzapoppin' (reputedly the most popular musical of the 30s) and George White's Scandals Of 1939 ('Are You Havin' Any Fun?' and 'Something I Dreamed Last Night'). During the 40s and 50s Fain collaborated with several lyricists including Lew Brown, Jack Yellen, Mitchell Parish, Harold Adamson, E.Y. 'Yip' Harburg, Bob Hilliard and Paul Francis Webster. In 1945 he worked with Ralph Freed, brother of the more famous lyricist and movie producer, Arthur Freed. Fain and Freed's 'The Worry Song' was interpolated into the Sammy Cahn/Jule Styne score for the Frank Sinatra/Gene Kelly movie Anchors Aweigh (1945), to accompany Kelly's famous dance sequence with the animated Jerry the mouse. Fain's greatest Hollywood success was in the 50s. He wrote the scores for two Walt Disney classics: Alice In Wonderland (1951), 'I'm Late' with Bob Hilliard; and Peter Pan (1953), 'Your Mother And Mine' and 'Second Star To The Right' with Sammy Cahn. Also with Cahn, Fain wrote some songs for the Three Sailors And a Girl (1953) movie ('The Lately Song' and 'Show Me A Happy Woman And I'll Show You A Miserable Man'). In 1953 Fain, in collaboration with Paul Francis Webster, won his first Academy Award for 'Secret Love', from their score for the Doris Day/Howard Keel movie, Calamity Jane. His second Oscar, the title song for the film Love Is A Many Splendored Thing (1955), was also written in partnership with Webster, as were several other film title songs including 'A Certain Smile', 'April Love', and 'Tender Is The Night', which were all nominated for Academy Awards. Other Fain/Webster movie songs included 'There's A Rising Moon (For Every Falling Star)' from Young At Heart (1954) and 'A Very Precious Love' from Marjorie Morningstar (1958), both sung by Doris Day. Fain's last four Broadway musicals were Flahooley (1951) written with Harburg ('Here's To Your Illusions' and 'He's Only Wonderful'), Ankles Aweigh (1955) with Dan Shapiro, Christine (1960), with Webster, and Something More (1964) with Alan And Marilyn Bergman. Fain continued to write films songs through to the 70s. He also made some vocal records, and had a US chart entry as early as 1926 with Al Dubin and Joe Burke's, 'Painting The Clouds With Sunshine'. He was inducted into the Songwriters Hall Of Fame in 1971, and served on the board of directors of ASCAP from 1979 until his death from a heart attack in December 1989.

FAITH, PERCY

b. 7 April 1908, Toronto, Ontario, Canada, d. 9 February 1976, Ericino, California, USA. During the 30s Faith worked extensively on radio in Canada, and moved to the USA in 1940 to take up a post with NBC. During the 50s he was musical director for Columbia Records, for whom he made a number of popular albums, mostly of mood music. He worked with Tony Bennett, with whom he had three million-selling singles, and, from 1950, also had several hits in his own right, including 'Cross My Fingers', 'All My Love', 'On Top Of Old Smoky' (vocal by Burl Ives), 'Delicado', 'Song From The Moulin Rouge (Where Is Your Heart)' (US number 1 in 1953), 'Return To Paradise' (1953), and 'Theme From A Summer Place', which reached number 1 in the US and number 2 in the UK charts in 1960. In Hollywood in the 50s Faith had composed several background film scores, including Love Me Or Leave Me (1955), the highly acclaimed biopic of singer Ruth Etting, which starred Doris Day. His film credits in the 60s included Tammy Tell Me True (1961), I'd Rather Be Rich (1964), The Third Day (1965) and The Oscar (1966). For The Love Goddesses, Faith wrote the title song with Mack David. His other compositions included 'My Heart Cries For You' (with his main collaborator Carl Sigman), which was a big hit for Guy Mitchell, Dinah Shore, Vic Damone and others in 1951. Faith died of cancer in February 1976. In the mid-90s there has been a renewed interest in Faith's work, particularly in Japan, where many of his albums have been reissued. New performances of his arrangements have been conducted by Nick Perito for a series of CDs.

● ALBUMS: Continental Music (Columbia 1956)★★★, Passport To Romance (Columbia 1956)★★★, Music From My Fair Lady (Columbia 1957)★★★★, Touchdown! (Columbia 1958)★★★, North & South Of The Border (Columbia 1958)★★★, Music Of Victor Herbert (Columbia 1958)★★★, Viva! (Columbia 1959)★★★, Hallelujah (Columbia 1959)★★★, Porgy And Bess (Columbia 1959)★★★, Music Of George Gershwin (Columbia 1959)★★★★, A Night With Sigmund Romberg (Columbia 1959)★★★, Malaguena (Columbia 1959)★★★, Bouquet (Columbia 1959)★★★★, Music From South Pacific (Columbia 1960)★★, Bon Voyage! (Columbia 1960)★★★, Continental Souvenirs (Columbia 1960)★★★, Jealousy (Columbia 1960)★★★★, A Night With Jerome Kern (Columbia 1960)★★★, Camelot (Columbia 1961)★★★★, Carefree (Columbia 1961)★★★, Mucho Gusto! More Music Of Mexico (Columbia

1961)★★, *Tara's Theme* (Columbia 1961)★★★, *Bouquet Of Love* (Columbia 1962)★★★, *Subways Are For Sleeping* (Columbia 1962)★★★, *The Music Of Brazil!* (Columbia 1962)★★★, *Hollywood's Themes* (Columbia 1963)★★★★, *American Serenade* (Columbia 1963)★★★, *Exotic Strings* (Columbia 1963)★★★, *Shangri-La!* (Columbia 1963)★★★, *Great Folk Themes* (Columbia 1964)★★★, *More Themes For Young Lovers* (Columbia 1964)★★★, *Latin Themes* (Columbia 1965)★★★, *Broadway Bouquet* (Columbia 1965)★★★, *Themes For The 'In' Crowd* (Columbia 1966)★★★, *The Academy Award Winner And Other Great Movie Themes* (Columbia 1967)★★★★, *Today's Themes For Young Lovers* (Columbia 1967)★★★, *For Those In Love* (Columbia 1968)★★★, *Angel Of The Morning (Hit Themes For Young Lovers)* (Columbia 1968)★★, *Those Were The Days* (Columbia 1969)★★, *Windmills Of Your Mind* (Columbia 1969)★★, *Love Theme From 'Romeo And Juliet'* (Columbia 1969)★★★, *Forever Young* (Columbia 1970)★★, *Leaving On A Jet Plane* (Columbia 1970)★★, *Held Over! Today's Great Movie Themes* (Columbia 1970)★★★, *The Beatles Album* (Columbia 1970)★★, *A Time For Love* (Columbia 1971)★★★, *I Think I Love You* (Columbia 1971)★★, *Black Magic Woman* (Columbia 1971)★★, *Jesus Christ, Superstar* (Columbia 1971)★★, *Joy* (Columbia 1972)★★★, *Day By Day* (Columbia 1972)★★★.

● COMPILATIONS: *Moods* (Ditto 1983)★★★, *Images* (Knight 1990)★★★, *Music From the Movies* (1994)★★★.

FALSETTOLAND
(see *March Of The Falsettos*)

FAME
Exiled British director Alan Parker (*Bugsy Malone*, *The Commitments*) took the reins for this 1980 film, which followed the lives of young showbusiness aspirants in time-honoured fashion. Set in Manhattan's High School for the Performing Arts, *Fame* charts the lives of a group of teenagers over a period of four years. Parker cast disparate characters - homosexuals, Puerto Ricans, individuals drawn from New York's uptown and downtown environments - in what turned out to be a box-office blockbuster. Star Irene Cara's recording of Michael Gore and Dean Pitchford's title song, which won an Academy Award, went to number 1 in the UK, and there was another Oscar for Gore's exciting score. The rest of the songs included 'Red Light', 'I Sing The Body Electric', 'Dogs In The Yard', 'Hot Lunch Jam', 'Out Here On My Own', and 'Is It OK If I Call You Mine?'. Prominent among the cast were Paul McCrane, Gene Anthony Ray, Lee Carreri, and Barry Miller as a slick and hip Puerto Rican. Produced by David De Silva and Alan Marshall, with a screenplay by Christopher Gore, *Fame* proved popular enough to inspire a spin-off television series, which in turn spawned more chart successes for *The Kids From Fame*. This played in more than 60 countries, and prompted De Silva to conceive and develop a version for the stage. He formed a new creative team that included composer Steven Margoshes, lyricist Jacques Levy, and librettist Jose Fernandez.

Fame: The Musical made its debut at the Coconut Grove Playhouse, Miami, on 21 October 1988. Despite positive audience reaction in Miami, and later, Philadelphia, a Broadway transfer fell through, but *Fame* subsequently proved a hit in Stockholm, Sweden and other European countries. West End audiences were introduced to the show at the Cambridge Theatre on 27 June 1995. Gore and Pitchford's title song was still in there, along with numbers such as 'Hard Work', 'I Want To Make Magic', 'Dance Class' (after Beethoven's 'Spring Sonata'), 'Can't Keep It Down', 'Tyrone's Rap', 'There She Goes', 'Let's Play A Love Scene', 'Bring On Tomorrow', 'The Teachers' Argument', 'Mabel's Prayer', 'Dancin' On The Sidewalk', 'These Are My Children' and 'In L.A.'. Loraine Velez played Carmen with dash and authority, and Sonia Swaby (Mabel) tore into the amusing 'Think Of Meryl Streep'. Also cast were Marcus D'Cruze (Joe), Scott Sherrin (Tyrone), Jonatha Aris (Schlomo), Richard Dempsey (Nick) and Gemma Wardle (Serena). Directed by Runa Borge and choreographed by Lars Bethke, *Fame* ran until 28 September 1996. The UK touring version called in on London's West End for Christmas seasons in 1997 and 1998, while elsewhere productions during 1998/9 were being forecast for Toronto, Paris, Sydney, Berlin, Chicago, Warsaw, Tokyo, Vienna, Oslo, Munich, Caracas, Milan, Budapest, Montreal, and Los Angeles.

FANNY
Based on the Frenchman Marcel Pagnol's film trilogy, *Marius*, *Fanny*, and *César*, which were made in the early 30s, this show marked the musical theatre debut of one of Broadway's most important post-war producers, David Merrick. *Fanny* opened in New York at the Majestic Theatre on 4 November 1954, and stayed around for over two years. Joshua Logan, the show's director, co-wrote the book with the celebrated author and playwright, S. N. Behrman. Some critics felt that the librettists attempted too much - that it was not possible to do full justice to the complicated situations and personal relationships dealt with in the three books, in the space of one musical evening. Audiences were faced with the dramatic story of the young Marius (William Tabbert), who goes to sea against the wishes of his father, César (Ezio Pinza), leaving Fanny (Florence Henderson) to have his child. She marries the affluent sail-maker, Panisse (Walter Slezak), who brings up the boy, Césario, as his own. When Marius returns some years later, Césario wants to get to know his real father, but César insists that he stays with Panisse, and so Marius turns him away. Césario goes back to Panisse, who knowing that he is dying, pleads with Fanny to make a life together with Marius and the boy who means so much to them all. Harold Rome's music and lyrics, usually so full of social conscience and comment, echos the intense emotional and sentimental feelings present in the story, with songs such as 'Restless Heart', 'Why Be Afraid To Dance?', 'Never Too Late For Love', 'To My Wife', 'I Like You', 'Love Is A Very Light Thing', 'Welcome Home', 'I Have To Tell You', and 'Be Kind To Your Parents'. The show's title song had some success in a recording by Eddie Fisher. Walter Slezak won the Tony Award for best actor, and *Fanny* ran for 888 performances on Broadway, and for more than 300 in London. In 1986, a revival was presented at the Goodspeed Opera House in Connecticut, USA. The 1960 film version - without the songs - was directed by Joshua Logan, and starred Leslie Caron, Maurice Chevalier, and Charles Boyer.

FANTASIA
(see Disney, Walt)

FANTASTICKS, THE
The longest running musical in the world opened off-Broadway at the 153-seater Sullivan Street Playhouse on 3 May 1960. Based on the play *Les Romanesques* by Edmund Rostand, the show is all about the illusions and dreams of young love. The simple story tells of Matt Hucklebee, The Boy (Kenneth Nelson) and Luisa Bellamy, The Girl (Rita Gardner), whose fathers, Hucklebee (William Larsen) and Amos Babcock Bellamy (Hugh Thomas) try to ensure that the couple fall in love by building a wall between their two properties, and pretending to disapprove of the romance. Just to emphasise their point, they also hire the bandit El Gallo (Jerry Orbach, who also acts as the narrator) to seemingly attempt an unsuccessful rape of The Girl. The young couple discover the deception, and, disillusioned with the ways of the world, go their separate ways, only to return eventually - much wiser - to each other's arms. Settings and costumes were by Ed Wittstein, and Word Baker was the director. Also in the cast was Tom Jones, who wrote the book and lyrics, with Harvey Schmidt composing a score which contained the gorgeous ballads, 'Soon It's Gonna Rain' and 'Try To Remember', along with other numbers such as 'It Depends On What You Pay', 'I Can See It', 'Plant A Radish', 'Much More', 'They Were You', and 'Round And Round'. To date it has been estimated that the show has played more than 5,000 American cities, and over 70 other countries around the world (put another way: 11,000 US and 700 foreign productions). A 1961 West End production with Terence Cooper (El Gallo), Peter Gilmore (Matt), Stephanie Voss (Luisa), and Michael Barrington and Timothy Bateson as the fathers, fared badly, some critics considering that the engaging intimacy of the original was lost in a regular-sized Apollo Theatre. The Regent's Park Open Air Theatre and various fringe venues, such as the King's Head, Islington, proved more suitable settings when the show was presented in London again during the 90s. In 1992, Jones and Schmidt both participated in an English-speaking Japanese production, and three years later *The Fantasticks* was filmed, with Joseph McIntyre (Matt), Jean Louisa Kelly (Luisa), Jonathon Morris (El Gallo), Brad Sullivan (Matt's father), and Joel Grey (Luisa's father). What is, technically, still the original New York production, clocked up its 16,000th performance on 18 December 1998.

● FURTHER READING: *The Fantasticks: The 30th Anniversary Edition*, Tom Jones and Harvey Schmidt. *The Amazing Story Of The Fantasticks: America's Longest Running Play*, Robert Viagas and Donald C. Farber.

FAREWELL PERFORMANCE
A young pop singer, played by David Kernan, who has made many enemies during his rise to fame, is murdered. A decoy is groomed for stardom, during which the culprit is apprehended. Iconoclast producer/composer Joe Meek provided all the music for this lightweight vehicle, which featured his blond-haired protégé Heinz as the Kernan character's replacement. His former group in real life, the Tornadoes, are also cast in this 1963 'B' feature. *Farewell Performance* has little merit and Meek's wish to launch Heinz as a major attraction faltered at the first hurdle. A second film, *Living It Up*, was equally moribund and the pair quickly sundered their relationship.

FARNON, ROBERT
b. 24 July 1917, Toronto, Ontario, Canada. Gifted with a prodigious musical talent, early in his life Farnon was accomplished on several instruments, and at the age of 11 was playing with the Toronto Junior Symphony Orchestra. In 1932 he joined the Canadian Broadcasting Corporation Orchestra where the musical director, Percy Faith, made him responsible for many of the choral arrangements. In 1941 Farnon's First Symphony was performed by the Philadelphia Symphony Orchestra under Eugene Ormandy. At the start of World War II Farnon enlisted in the Canadian army and was sent to Europe as leader of the Canadian Band of the American Expeditionary Force. After the war, he remained in the UK, writing arrangements for popular bands such as those of Ted Heath and Geraldo. He formed and led a studio orchestra for a long-running BBC radio series and many of his light orchestral compositions became popular, most notably 'Jumping Bean', 'Portrait Of A Flirt', 'The Westminster Waltz' and 'The Colditz March'. His other important compositions have included 'Melody Fair', 'Peanut Polka', 'A La Claire Fontaine', 'Gateway To The West', 'Pictures In The Fire', 'A Star Is Born', 'Manhattan Playboy', 'Journey Into Melody', 'Lake Of The Woods', 'Derby Day', and 'State Occasion'. In the late 40s and early 50s he wrote scores for several films such as *I Live In Grosvenor Square* (1946), *Spring In Park Lane* (1948), *Maytime In Mayfair* (1949), *Lilacs In The Spring* (1949), *Captain Horatio Hornblower RN* (1951), *His Majesty O'Keefe* (1953), *Gentlemen Marry Brunettes* (1955), *The Little Hut* (1957), *The Sheriff Of Fractured Jaw* (1958), *The Road To Hong Kong* (1962), *The Truth About Spring* (1965), *Shalako* (1968), *Bear Island* (1979), and *A Man Called Intrepid* (1980). In 1962, Farnon arranged and conducted for Frank Sinatra's *Great Songs From Great Britain*, the first album the singer had recorded in the UK. Subsequently, he worked in television, composing several television themes for top-rated programmes such as *Panorama*, *Armchair Theatre*, *Colditz*, *The Secret Army*, and *Kessler*, and continued to make occasional radio broadcasts and assemble orchestras for special concerts and recording dates. In 1996, Farnon received the Best Instrumental Arrangement Grammy Award for 'Lament', a track on his *Tangence* album with the famous trombonist J.J. Johnson. In the following year, Farnon's many admirers around the world, including the members of an extremely active British-based appreciation society, were celebrating his 80th birthday. He was awarded the Order Of Canada in 1998, and also completed a new piano concerto to be recorded by the Czechoslovakia Symphony Orchestra in Bratislava.

● ALBUMS: *A Robert Farnon Concert* (Decca 1950)★★★, *Journey Into Melody* (Decca 1950)★★★★, with Eugene Conley *Favourite Songs* (Decca 1950)★★★, *Stephen Foster Melodies* (Decca

1951)★★★, *Music Of Vincent Youmans* (Decca 1951)★★★, *Hoagy Carmichael And Victor Schertzinger Suites* (Decca 1953)★★★, *Songs Of Britain* (Decca 1953)★★★★, *Presenting Robert Farnon* (Decca 1953)★★★★, *Flirtation Walk* (Decca 1954)★★★, *Two Cigarettes In The Dark* (Decca 1955)★★★, *Gentleman Marry Brunettes* film soundtrack (Vogue/Coral 1955)★★★, *Something To Remember You By-Music Of Arthur Schwartz* (Decca 1955)★★★, *Canadian Impressions* (Decca 1956)★★★★, *Melody Fair* (Decca 1956)★★★★, *Pictures In The Fire* (Decca 1957)★★★, *From The Highlands* (Decca 1958)★★★, *From The Emerald Isle* (Decca 1959)★★★, *Gateway To The West/Portrait Of The West* (MGM 1960)★★★, *Captain Horatio Hornblower RN/Rhapsody For Violin And Orchestra* (Delyse 1960)★★★★, *Sensuous Strings Of Robert Farnon* (Philips 1962)★★★★, with Rawicz And Landauer *Robert Farnon And Leroy Anderson Encores* (Philips 1962)★★★, with Frank Sinatra *Great Songs From Great Britain* (Reprise 1962)★★★, *The Road To Hong Kong* film soundtrack (Decca 1962)★★★, *Captain From Castile And Other Great Movie Themes* (Philips 1964)★★★, with Sarah Vaughan *Vaughan With Voices* (Mercury 1964)★★★, *Conducts My Fair Lady And Other Musical Bouquets* (Philips 1965)★★★★, *Portrait Of Johnny Mathis* (Philips 1965)★★★, *Plays The Hits Of Sinatra* (Philips 1965)★★★, *Symphonic Suite-Porgy and Bess* (Decca 1966)★★★, with Tony Bennett *Christmas Album* (Columbia 1969)★★★, with Tony Coe *Pop Makes Progress* (Chapter One 1970)★★★, with Tony Bennett *With Love* (Columbia 1972)★★★, with Tony Bennett *The Good Things In Life* (Philips 1972)★★★, with Tony Bennett and the LPO *Get Happy* (Columbia 1972)★★★, *Showcase For Soloists* (Invicta 1973)★★★, *In A Dream World* (Rediffusion 1974)★★★, with the LPO *At The Festival Hall* (Pye 1974)★★★, with the Singers Unlimited *Sentimental Journey* (MPS 1975)★★★, *Sketches Of Tony Bennett And Frank Sinatra* (Pye 1976)★★★, with Lena Horne *A New Album* (RCA 1976)★★★, *Dreaming* (Peerless 1977)★★★, with the Singers Unlimited *Eventide* (MPS 1978)★★★, with Ray Ellington *I Wish You Love* (Mayfair 1979)★★★, with George Shearing *On Target* (MPS 1982)★★★★, with Jose Carreras *Love Is ...* (Philips 1984)★★★, with Pia Zadora *Pia And Phil* (Columbia 1985)★★★, with Pia Zadora *I Am What I Am* (Columbia 1986)★★★, *At The Movies* (Horatio Nelson 1987)★★★, with Sheila Southern *With Love* (Horatio Nelson (1989)★★★, *Melody Fair* (President (1990)★★★, with Eileen Farrell *This Time It's Love* (Reference 1992)★★★, conducting the Royal Philharmonic Orchestra *Concert Music* (Reference 1992)★★★, with Eileen Farrell *It's Over* (Reference 1992)★★★, *British Light Music-Robert Farnon* (Marco Polo 1992)★★★, with George Shearing *How Beautiful Is Night* (Telarc 1993)★★★, with Eileen Farrell *Here* (Elba 1993)★★★, with Joe Williams *Here's To Life* (Telarc 1994)★★★, with J.J. Johnson *Tangence* (PolyGram-Verve 1995)★★★, with Eileen Farrell *Love Is Letting Go* (DRG 1995)★★★.

FASTEST GUITAR ALIVE, THE

Roy Orbison remains one of pop's consummate voices; time has not diminished the emotional punch of his best recordings. He was not, however, conventionally photogenic, and the singer was one of the few successful chart acts of his era not courted by Hollywood. However, having secured a new recording deal with MGM in 1966 Orbison sought to rectify that fact. *The Faster Guitar Alive* was his sole entry into pop cinema and it was not an auspicious success. The film, set in the American Civil War, cast the

singer as a Confederate agent, plotting to rob a Union mint. Sam The Sham, who with his group, the Pharaohs, created the immortal 'Wooly Bully', co-starred alongside Orbison in a feature in which the star never looked comfortable. Eight songs were included on the soundtrack, none of which were particularly memorable. The same was true of this unconvincing film.

FAYE, ALICE

b. Alice Jeanne Leppert, 5 May 1912, New York City, New York, USA, d. 9 May 1998, Rancho Mirage, California, USA. An attractive blonde actress and singer, Alice Faye symbolized for many the glamorous 20th Century Fox movies musicals of the 30s and 40s. She was noticed by Rudy Vallee in the Broadway chorus of *George White's Scandals Of 1931*, and, after touring and recording with his Connecticut Yankees, she starred with Vallee in the movie *George White's Scandals* (1934), making a strong impression with her version of 'Nasty Man'. She was also cited in Vallee's divorce trial. Over the next 11 years she made more than 30 films, mostly very appealing musicals such as *Poor Little Rich Girl* (1936), *Sing Baby Sing* (1936), *Stowaway* (1936), *On The Avenue* (1937), *In Old Chicago* (1938), *Alexander's Ragtime Band* (1938), *Rose Of Washington Square* (1939), *Hollywood Cavalcade* (1939), *Tin Pan Alley* (1940), *Lillian Russell* (1940), *That Night In Rio* (1941), *The Great American Broadcast* (1941), *Weekend In Havana* (1941), *Hello, Frisco, Hello* (1943), and *The Gang's All Here* (1943). With her deep-throated, sexy voice, Faye serenaded her good-looking leading men, Dick Powell, Tyrone Power, Don Ameche and John Payne, with songs that included 'Goodnight My Love', 'No Love, No Nothing', 'Sing, Baby, Sing', 'You're A Sweetheart', and 'You'll Never Know' the Academy Award winning song for 1943. By this time she was a major star, together with her friend Betty Grable, with an equally loyal following. Faye retired from movies in 1945 after starring in Otto Preminger's *Fallen Angel*, and following a much-publicized rift with 20th Century Fox boss Darryl F. Zanuck, but she returned in 1962 for the second re-make of *State Fair*. Following a first marriage to singer Tony Martin (with whom she co-starred in 1938's *Silly, Irene And Mary*), she re-married in 1941 to bandleader/singer/actor Phil Harris, famous for his delivery of novelty songs such as 'Woodman, Spare That Tree', 'The Darktown Poker Club' and 'That's What I Like About The South'. From 1946-54 they appeared together on a top rated US radio series, and thereafter Faye starred in her own television specials and continued to record, mostly songs forever associated with her. She returned to the stage in 1973 in a revival of *Good News*.

● ALBUMS: *Movie Hits* (Reprise 1962)★★★, *Alice Faye And The Songs Of Harry Warren* (1979)★★★★, *On The Air, Volume One* (1979)★★, *On The Air, Volume Two* (1979)★★, *In Hollywood* (1983)★★★, *All The Gang's Here* (1988)★★★, *This Year's Kisses* (1989)★★★, *Music From Hollywood* (1993)★★★, *Got My Mind On Music* (Jasmine 1997)★★★, *Alice Faye* (Great Movie Themes 1997)★★★.

● FURTHER READING: *Getting Older - Looking Younger*, Alice Faye.

● FILMS: *George White's 1935 Scandals* (1934), *365 Nights In Hollywood* (1934), *She Learned About Sailors* (1934), *Now I'll Tell* (1934), *George White's Scandals* (1934), *Music Is Magic* (1935), *Every Night At Eight* (1935), *Stowaway* (1936), *Sing Baby Sing* (1936), *Poor Little Rich Girl* (1936), *King Of Burlesque* (1936), *Wake Up And Live* (1937), *You're A Sweetheart* (1937), *You Can't Have Everything* (1937), *On The Avenue* (1937), *Alexander's Ragtime Band* (1938), *In Old Chicago* (1938), *Sally Irene And Mary* (1938), *Barricade* (1939), *Hollywood Cavacade* (1939), *Rose Of Washington Square* (1939), *Tailspin* (1939), *Tin Pan Alley* (1940), *Lillian Russell* (1940), *Little Old New York* (1940), *Weekend In Havana* (1941), *The Great American Broadcast* (1941), *That Night In Rio* (1941), *The Gang's All Here* (1943), *Hello Frisco Hello* (1943), *Fallen Angel* (1945), *State Fair* (1962), *The Magic Of Lassie* (1978).

FEINSTEIN, MICHAEL

b. Michael Jay Feinstein, 7 September 1956, Columbus, Ohio, USA. A singer, pianist and musical archivist, Feinstein was a boy prodigy, able to play all manner of show tunes by ear. His mother was an amateur tap dancer and his father a singer and sales executive. After attending high school in Columbus he worked as a piano salesman in California, where he discovered some rare acetate recordings by Oscar Levant. He returned them to the actor/pianist's widow, who secured him a job as archivist and personal assistant to two of popular music's all-time great songwriters, Ira Gershwin and Harry Warren. In the late 70s and early 80s, as well as cataloguing their material, Feinstein unearthed several alternative Gershwin lyrics that had never been printed. Through Gershwin he met the lyricist's god-daughter, Liza Minnelli, and she opened a great many showbusiness doors for him. He also served as her accompanist, and played for other artists such as Rosemary Clooney, John Bubbles, Jessie Matthews, and Estelle Reiner. During the 80s and 90s Feinstein appeared in cabaret in Britain and America. He made his Broadway debut with *Michael Feinstein In Concert* (1988), which later toured major US cities and returned to New York in 1990. Some five years later he presented *An Evening With Michael Feinstein* at London's Comedy Theatre. He also filled the 18,000-seater Hollywood Bowl twice in July 1987. On television, Feinstein has hosted his own *Michael Feinstein And Friends* special, as well as featuring in several tributes to legendary songwriters, including George Gershwin, Irving Berlin and Jule Styne. Therefore, it was entirely appropriate that he was chosen to pay homage to Gershwin in *A Capitol Fourth*, a spectacular Independence Day celebration held in Washington, DC, in 1998 - the centenary of the composer's birth.

On his second album, *Live At The Algonquin*, Feinstein sang Raymond Jessel's 'I Wanna Hear A Show Song' ('Please don't bend my ear with punk or funk - it's junk'), which summed up his musical philosophy perfectly. One of the joys of his performances is that he includes rarely heard songs - and unfamiliar verses to more popular songs - and sings them as he believes the writers intended them to be sung. His voice has been called 'overly stylized - the high notes being rather faint, while the lower register is too loud'. Nevertheless, Michael Feinstein has a good ear for phrasing, and is recognized as a leading expert in and

exponent of the American standard popular song.

● ALBUMS: *Pure Gershwin* (Parnassus 1987)★★★★, *Live At The Algonquin* (Elektra 1987)★★★, *Isn't It Romantic* (Elektra 1987)★★★, *Remember: Michael Feinstein Sings Irving Berlin Songbook* (Elektra 1987)★★★, *The MGM Album* (Elektra 1989)★★★★, *Over There: Songs Of War and Peace c.1900-1920* (EMI Angel 1989)★★★, *Sings The Burton Lane Songbook Volume One* (Elektra Nonesuch 1990)★★★★, *Sings The Burton Lane Songbook Volume Two* (Elektra Nonesuch 1992)★★★, *Sings The Jule Styne Songbook* (Elektra Nonesuch 1991)★★★, *Pure Imagination* (Elektra 1992)★★★, with Andrea Marcovicci *Just Kern* one track only (Elba 1992)★, *Forever* (Elektra 1993)★★, *Sings The Jerry Herman Songbook* (Elektra Nonesuch 1994)★★★, *Sings The Hugh Martin Songbook* (Nonesuch 1995)★★★, *Such Sweet Sorrow* (Atlantic 1995)★★★, *Nice Work If You Can Get It* (Atlantic 1996)★★★, *Michael & George: Feinstein Sings Gershwin* (Concord Jazz 1998)★★★.

● VIDEOS: *Michael Feinstein & Friends* (KulterVideo/Image Entertainment 1994).

● FURTHER READING: *Nice Work If You Can Get It: My Life In Rhythm And Rhyme*, Michael Feinstein. *The Ira Gershwin Songbook*, Michael Feinstein (ed.).

● FILMS: *Scenes From The Class Struggle In Beverly Hills* (1989).

FENTON, GEORGE

b. 19 October 1949, England. An important composer for the British theatre, films and television, from the 70s through to the 90s. After working on minor films in the 70s and early 80s, such as *What Became Of Jack And Jill*, *You're A Big Girl Now* and *Hussy*, Fenton got his big break in 1982, when he collaborated with Ravi Shankar on the score for Richard Attenborough's *Gandhi*. It was nominated for a Grammy and an Oscar, and the theme, 'For All Mankind', won an Ivor Novello Award. Five years later, Fenton, in association with Jonas Gwangwa, won another 'Ivor', and two Oscar nominations (score and title song), for his work on another Attenborough project, *Cry Freedom*. Fenton has scored several other superior British productions, such as *Runners*, *The Company Of Wolves*, *Clockwise*, *White Of The Eye*, *84 Charing Cross Road*, *High Spirits*, *The Dressmaker*, *A Handful Of Dust*, *White Mischief*, *Ladybird Ladybird*, and *The Madness Of King George* (1994, adapted from the works of George Frederic Handel). In the late 80s and early 90s, Fenton worked a good deal in the USA, and won another Academy Award nomination for his score to the Glenn Close-John Malkovich drama, *Dangerous Liaisons* (1988). Apart from *Memphis Belle*, which told an American World War II story, but was actually a UK production, Fenton's other US movies have included *We're No Angels*, *The Long Walk Home*, *White Palace*, *China Moon* and *The Fisher King*, *Hero* (*Accidental Hero* in UK), *Groundhog Day*, *Born Yesterday*, and *Shadowlands* (1993). The latter film brought him an Ivor Novello Award for the best commissioned score.

In 1991, his music for the Richard Gere-Kim Basinger thriller, *Final Analysis*, was compared favourably to 'nearly everything Bernard Herrmann and Miklos Rozsa ever did'. As well as feature films, the composer worked prolifically in television, on some of the most popular and critically acclaimed programmes of their time. By the early 90s these totalled a staggering 80 productions, and included *Shoestring, Fox, The History Man, Going Gently, No Country For Old Men, Bergerac, A Woman Of No Importance, Outside Edge, Natural World, An Englishman Abroad, Saigon-Year Of The Cat, Village Earth, Walter, The Ghost Writer, The Jewel In The Crown, The Monocled Mutineer, The Trials Of Life*, and two sets of six plays and six monologues (*Talking Heads*), by Alan Bennett. He won the BAFTA Award for the best original television music in 1981, 1983 and 1986, and cornered the market in jingles for various daily news bulletins in the BBC's domestic and World Service.

From the early 70s he also worked in provincial theatres, with the Royal Shakespeare Company, and at the National Theatre, composing music and serving as musical director for a variety of productions including *Rosencrantz And Guildenstern Are Dead, A Month In The Country, Don Juan, Bengal Lancer, Kafka's Dick, High Society, Racing Demon, Saki*, and many more. He also composed a children's opera, *Birthday*. Much of his music has been released on records.

FERRY ACROSS THE MERSEY

Released in 1965, *Ferry Across The Mersey* represents the final fling of the genre dubbed 'Mersey Beat'. Gerry And The Pacemakers star as the main contenders hoping to win an international beat group contest. Although hardly innovative in terms of plot, the film retains appeal, largely through the cheeky persona of Gerry Marsden. It also provides a platform for several lesser-known Liverpool acts, including the Blackwells, the Black Knights and Earl Royce And The Olympics, the last-named of whom perform a creditable 'Shake A Tail Feather'. *Ferry Across The Mersey* also features performers drawn from Beatles' manager Brian Epstein's NEMS agency, including the Fourmost, who contribute 'I Love You Too' and Cilla Black, who sings 'Is It Love?' However, the film is plainly a vehicle for Marsden's group, who provide nine songs, notably 'It's Gonna Be Alright' and the memorable title song, which reached number 8 in the UK. Disc jockey Jimmy Saville enjoys a cameo role in a film which captures something of the flavour of the times, albeit in a somewhat clichéd manner.

FESTIVAL

Although not released until two years after the event, *Festival* is a dazzling documentary of the 1965 Newport Folk Festival. Director Murray Lerner captured the spirit of the proceedings, including backstage conversations and riveting in-concert footage. Pete Seeger, Joan Baez, Judy Collins and Peter, Paul And Mary lace acoustic folk music with contemporary 'protest' material, mindful of the music's role within the Civil Rights movement. Donovan introduces 'The Universal Soldier' by declaring it 'the song the BBC wouldn't let me sing', inspiring cheers from an audience weaned on conspiratorial notions. Blues singer Howlin' Wolf generates considerable excitement with the aid of electric instruments and indeed the use of amplification would prove the catalyst for raging controversy. White Chicago group, the Paul Butterfield Blues Band, played a set to considerable behind-the-scenes argument. (A reputed fist-fight between manager Albert Grossman

and folklorist Alan Lomax over electrification was sadly not caught on camera.) Yet such discourse paled in comparison with the reaction to Bob Dylan's set. Aided by Mike Bloomfield (guitar), Jerome Arnold (bass) and Sammy Lay (drums) (all from the Butterfield Band) plus Al Kooper (organ) and Barry Goldberg (piano), he performed three tough, rock-styled songs, one of which, 'Maggie's Farm', is enshrined in this film. Purists were outraged, and the notion of cat-calling Dylan's performances was born with this appearance. However, criticism levelled at the singer's show was not necessarily over amplification per se, but was equally due to a distorted sound obscuring his vocals. It is also evident from the film that many in the audience were in raptures. Dylan returned to sing two acoustic songs; both they and a workshop rendition of 'All I Really Want To Do', filmed the previous day, are preserved in *Festival*. His rendition of 'It's All Over Now, Baby Blue' is prophetic. It answers those expecting Dylan to remain encamped and simultaneously bids farewell to the acoustic muse of his past. The singer's use of an electric sound changed folk music forever - indeed the Newport Folk Festival then transformed itself into a rock event. This enduring film captures this pivotal moment forever.

FIDDLER ON THE ROOF (FILM MUSICAL)

This generally satisfactory screen version of the record-breaking Broadway musical came to the screen in 1971. The Israeli actor Topol, who had enjoyed much success in the London stage production, was chosen to play the role of Tevye, the Jewish milkman in the small town of Anatevka in Russia, who is forever trying to come to terms with his daughters (played by Michele Marsh, Rosalind Harris, and Neva Small) and the lives they are making for themselves, whilst also fighting to retain the traditions that have, for centuries, existed amongst his people. Topol gave a fine charismatic performance, and had excellent support from Norma Crane as his wife, and the celebrated American stage actress Molly Picon in the key role of the Matchmaker. Also in the cast were Zvee Scooler, Michael Glaser, Paul Mann, and Leonard Frey as Motel the tailor, the role he played in the original Broadway production. Swedish actor Tutte Lemkow appeared as the Fiddler, and his playing was dubbed by Isaac Stern. Jerry Bock and Sheldon Harnick's magnificent stage score was mostly retained, and included 'Tradition', 'Matchmaker, Matchmaker', 'If I Were A Rich Man', 'Sabbath Prayer', 'To Life', 'Miracle Of Miracles', 'Tevye's Dream', 'Sunrise, Sunset', 'Wedding And The Bottle Dance', 'Do You Love Me', 'Far From The Home I Love', 'Chava Ballet Sequence', and 'Anatevka'. Tom Abbott based his choreography on Jerome Robbins' Tony Award-winning original work and Joseph Stein's screenplay was adapted from his Broadway libretto. Norman Jewison was the producer-director, and the film won Academy Awards for Oswald Morris's cinematography (DeLuxe Color and Panavision), sound (Gordon K. McCallum and David Hildyard), and adaptation and music scoring (John Williams). According to *Variety*, the film, which grossed nearly $40 million, was one of the hit movies of the decade.

FIDDLER ON THE ROOF (STAGE MUSICAL)

In a Broadway season packed with musicals such as *Golden Boy*, *Ben Franklin In Paris*, *Baker Street*, *Do I Hear A Waltz?*, *Flora, The Red Menace*, and *The Roar Of The Greasepaint - The Smell Of The Crowd*, *Fiddler On The Roof* opened at the Imperial Theatre on 22 September 1964 - and topped them all. Set in 1905 on the eve of the Russian Revolution, Joseph Stein's book is based on Sholom Aleichem's stories which recount episodes in the life of Tevye (Zero Mostel), a dairyman living in the impoverished Jewish village of Anatevka, in Tsarist Russia. Tevye has five daughters, and Yente (Beatrice Arthur), the matchmaker brings his wife Golde (Maria Karnilova) the news that wealthy widower Lazar Wolf (Michael Granger) desires the hand of the eldest, Tzeitel (Joanna Merlin). This is unfortunate, because Tzeitel has already made her own arrangements with childhood sweetheart Motel (Austin Pendleton), admittedly a penniless tailor. In the meantime, Tevye enlists Perchik (Bert Convy), a young student revolutionary, to lecture his daughters in the ways of the Good Book. He does more than that, introducing the spirited Hodel (Julia Migenes) to certain Terpsichorean delights. Although it is strictly against his beloved tradition, Tevye eventually agrees to the wedding of Tzeitel and Motel, and reluctantly accepts that Perchik and Hodel will also be together, but he absolutely refuses to endorse the intention of third daughter Chava (Tanya Everett) to marry outside the faith - but she goes ahead anyway. Perchik is arrested for his political activities, and sent to Siberia. Hodel leaves to be with him, and, as the pogroms advance ever nearer, Tevye, and what is left of his family, seek refuge in America. His problems in coming to terms with the changes in customs, language, and religion, were reflected in Sheldon Harnick and Jerry Bock's splendid score. The music drew upon traditional folk forms, and the lyrics were awash with cultural references that gave audiences a strong sense of social awareness, while simultaneously providing high quality entertainment and a good deal of humour. Musical numbers included 'Tradition', 'Matchmaker, Matchmaker', 'If I Were A Rich Man', 'Sabbath Prayer', 'To Life', 'Miracle Of Miracles', 'The Tailor, Motel Kamzoil', 'Sunrise, Sunset', 'Wedding Dance', 'Now I Have Everything', 'Do You Love Me?', 'I Just Heard', 'Far From The Home I Love', and 'Anatevka'. *Fiddler On The Roof* ran on Broadway for 3,242 performances, winning the New York Drama Critics' Circle Award as best musical, and Tony Awards for best musical, score, book, actor (Mostel), featured actress (Karnilova), director-choreographer (Jerome Robbins), producer (Harold Prince), and costumes (Patricia Zipprodt). In addition, the Original Cast album spent a total of 60 weeks in the US chart. Mostel's was a bravura performance, and his replacements during the record-breaking run included Luther Adler, who also headed the first US tour which lasted over two years, Herschel Bernardi, Paul Lipson, Harry Goz, and veteran operatic tenor, Jan Peerce. Bette Midler, the future 'Divine Miss M', played Tzeitel for three years, 1967-70. Mostel reprised his role opposite Thelma Lee (Golde) in the 1976 revival at the Winter Garden. A 1967 London production, with the Israeli actor Topol as Tevye, along with Miriam Karlin (Golde), Cynthia Grenville (Yente), Paul Whitsun-Jones (Lazar), Sandor Eles (Perchik), Rosemary Nicols (Tzeitel), Linda Gardner (Hodel), Jonathan Lynn (Motel), and Caryl Little (Chava), lasted for 2,030 performances. Topol enjoyed a surprise record hit with 'If I Were A Rich Man' which reached the UK Top 10. He also starred in the 1971 film version, a 1983 staging at London's Apollo Victoria Theatre, a 1990 Broadway revival with Marcia Lewis as Golde, and the show's 30th anniversary world tour which called in at the London Palladium in June 1994 (Sara Kestelman as Golde).

FIELDING, HAROLD

b. 4 December 1916, Woking, Surrey, England. A leading producer of stage musicals from the 50s through to the 80s, Fielding has presented, or co-presented, some of the West End's favourite shows. When he was 10 years old he resisted parental pressure to play the piano, and instead took up the violin, studying in Paris with virtuoso Szigeti. By the time he was 12, Fielding was himself a concert performer, touring as a supporting artist to the diva Tetrazzini. When he was in his early 20s, the impresario who was presenting him died, and Fielding took over the tour management. In a short space of time, he was presenting hundreds of concerts throughout the UK, including his Sunday Concert Series at Blackpool Opera House, which endured for many years. He also mounted a series called *Music For Millions* in collaboration with his wife, Maisie. Among the artists appearing in his productions were Richard Tauber, Grace Moore, Benjamino Gigli, Rawicz and Landauer, Jeanette MacDonald, Paul Robeson, Gracie Fields, and the London Philharmonic Orchestra. Subsequent promotions in the popular field would include Johnnie Ray, Danny Kaye, Nat 'King' Cole, and Frank Sinatra. In January 1949, while returning from the USA after negotiating a contract for the Philadelphia Symphony Orchestra to visit England, Fielding was involved in the famous pick-a-back air crash. A light aircraft collided with the roof of his Constellation airliner, and the dead pilot fell into Fielding's lap. The Constellation made a perfect landing, and, having survived that kind of crash, from then on Fielding believed that flying was the safest form of travel. By the late 50s, with government-sponsored concerts affecting his business, Fielding turned to the legitimate theatre. He had already collaborated with Charles B. Cochran and Jack Hylton, one of his associations with Hylton resulting in the first ever arena concert festival at Harringay, London. They also promoted a classical ballet season. Just prior to Christmas 1958, Fielding launched himself as a solo producer with a spectacular presentation of Richard Rodgers and Oscar Hammerstein II's *Cinderella* at the London Coliseum. Originally conceived for US television, Fielding blended pantomime material with the musical comedy aspect of the piece, and cast rock 'n' roll star Tommy Steele as Buttons. *Cinderella* was followed by another Coliseum extravaganza, *Aladdin*, and from then on Fielding lived a roller coaster existence - producing or co-producing many of the West End's biggest hits, and some of its biggest disasters. *The Music Man*, starring Van Johnson, and Noël Coward's *Sail Away*, led in 1963 to one of Fielding's most fondly remembered shows, *Half A Sixpence*, a musicalization of H.G. Wells's novel, *Kipps*, starring Tommy Steele. However, the success of *Half A Sixpence* in London and New York paled in comparison with *Charlie Girl* (1965, 2,202 performances), which was followed by several more profitable productions in the shape of *Sweet Charity, Mame, The Great Waltz, Show Boat, I Love My Wife, Irene*, stage versions of the popular movies *Hans Andersen* and *Singin' In The Rain* (both with Tommy Steele), as well as *Barnum* (Michael Crawford). At the time, Fielding's 1971 *Show Boat* was the longest-running to date with 910 performances (Hal Prince's 1994 production clocked up 951). Like all the great showmen since Florenz Ziegfeld, Fielding was fond of making extravagant gestures. When Ginger Rogers arrived in the UK to appear in *Mame* (1969), he ensured that the event made the front pages by transporting her from Southampton to London in a special train filled with pressmen, and an orchestra playing tunes from the show. There was also a portable movie theatre showing her old films. The Ziegfeld reference would probably send a shiver up the now-venerable producer's spine, because *Ziegfeld* (1988), with a book by Ned Sherrin, was one of his shows, along with *Man Of Magic, You're A Good Man, Charlie Brown, Phil The Fluter, Gone With The Wind, Beyond The Rainbow, On The Twentieth Century, The Biograph Girl*, and the 1986 revival of *Charlie Girl* with Cyd Charisse, which failed to set the London theatrical scene alight. He was reported to have lost £1.3 million on *Ziegfeld*, and that sum rose to £1.7 million four years later when Petula Clark's American Civil War musical, *Someone Like You*, folded after only a month, ensuring that Harold Fielding Limited went into voluntary liquidation. Since then, understandably, Fielding has not been a major force, partly due to ill health, although he was associated with the West End transfer of *Mack And Mabel* from the Leicester Haymarket Theatre in 1995, which resulted in the show's long-awaited London premiere. Over the years, he has presented a whole range of entertainment, including revues, plays, and variety shows featuring outstanding performers such as The Two Ronnies (Corbett and Barker), Petula Clark, Julie Andrews, Peter Sellers, Benny Hill, Marlene Dietrich, Eartha Kitt, and Shirley Bassey, but it is for his often lavish and immensely likeable musicals that he will be remembered. In 1986 he 'passed' on the opportunity to present the UK version of *La Cage Aux Folles* because 'it wasn't a family show', yet more than 10 years previously he had been associated with the notorious 'sexual musical', *Let My People Come*. A much-loved personality, he belongs to the tradition of great British showman such as Hylton, Bernard Delfont, and Lew Grade. He risked his own money rather than that of theatrical 'angels', and in 1996 received a Gold Badge from BASCA (British Academy of Songwriters. Composers and Authors) in recognition of his special contribution to Britain's entertainment industry.

FIELDS OF AMBROSIA, THE

Enthusiastically received during its try-out early in 1993 at the George Street Playhouse, New Jersey, USA, this 'adventurous black musical comedy' came under heavy fire from most of the London critics when it transferred to the Aldwych Theatre on 31 January 1996 complete with the original leads, Joel Higgins and Christine Andreas. Higgins also wrote the book and lyrics, and the music was composed by Martin Silvestri. Based on the 1970 Stacey Keach film, *The Traveling Executioner*, the story is set in 1918 rural Louisiana in the American deep south. Jonas Candide (Higgins), an ex-carnival hustler-turned State executioner, comforts his 'victims' as he straps them down by painting a rose-coloured musical picture of their paradisaic hereafter - 'The fields of ambrosia/Where everyone knows ya'. When he falls in love with his first female client, the beautiful Austrian countess Gretchen Herzallerliebst (Andreas), he craftily attempts to delay her death by accidentally 'misplacing' Old Reliable, his mobile electric chair. Whiskey-soaked Doc (Michael Fenton Stevens) is also involved in the deception, which sparks off a scene in which 'suspicious guards set on the assembled convicts, viciously beating and throttling and gouging their eyes out while Jonas has gleeful sex with Gretchen on a platform above'. Jonas's main rival for Gretchen's generous favours, Malcolm Piquant (Mark Heenehan), a burly butch warder, 'evidently consoles himself with impressionable male convicts'. Other 'highlights' include the rape of young mortician Jimmy Crawford (Marc Joseph), by two prisoners, an act which moves him to give out with the painful lament 'Alone' ('If it ain't one thing it's another'), and the appearance of Warden Brodsky (Roger Leach) who kindly advises Gretchen that 'your ass is too good to fry', before sexually assaulting her. Among the rest of the participants were Amanda Noar, Caron Skinns, Kevin Rooney, Henry Webster, Michael Neilson, Chris Andrew Mellon, Susie Fenwick, and Peter Gallagher. At the end of this game of musical, or rather, electrical chairs, Jonas is 'shocked' himself, and 'the show's final image reveals its principals united happily in the sweet afterlife represented by the Ambrosian fields'. Although critics were generally either sickened or outraged by the book ('Surely something can be done to discourage the dumping of American theatrical refuse like *The Fields Of Ambrosia* in attractive London theatres?'), there were some kind words for the score, notably the rueful 'Too Bad', 'Continental Sunday' an evocative word-picture of New Orleans, the flag-waving 'All In This Together', the recitative 'My Name's Candide', 'Too Bad', and the impressive production numbers, 'Nuthin'' and 'Step Right Up'. Also present were 'Ball And Chain/Jonas' Theme', 'The Fields Of Ambrosia', 'Some Days/How Could This Happen?', 'Who Are You?', 'Reasonable Man', 'Hungry', 'The Card Game', and 'Do It For Me'. The sets were designed by Deborah Jasien, David Toguri handled the musical staging, and the director was Gregory S. Hurst. Higgins and Andreas, both of whom have solid Broadway credits, emerged from the nightmare with some distinction, particularly in the singing department, but their stay in the West End was brief, and this £1.3 million production, which announced its closure for 17 February, was hastily withdrawn a week earlier.

FIELDS, DOROTHY

b. 15 July 1905, Allenhurst, New Jersey, USA, d. 28 March 1974, New York, New York, USA. A librettist and lyricist; one of the few, and arguably the best and most successful female writers of 'standard' popular songs, and the first woman to be elected to the Songwriters Hall of Fame. The list of her distinguished collaborators includes Jerome Kern, Jimmy McHugh, Sigmund Romberg, Harry Warren, J. Fred Coots, Harold Arlen, Morton Gould, Oscar Levant, Arthur Schwartz, Albert Hague, Cy Coleman, and Fritz Kreisler. Dorothy Fields's parents were Lew and Rose, better known as the famous comedy team, Weber And Fields. She had one sister, and two brothers: Joseph, who became a Broadway playwright, and Herbert (b. 26 July 1898, d. 24 March 1958), a librettist, with whom she worked frequently. Shortly after she was born (while her parents were on holiday in New Jersey), Weber and Fields terminated their partnership, and Lew Fields became a Broadway producer and appeared in several of his own shows. It was because of her father's show business associations that Dorothy Fields, at the age of 15, took the lead in one of Richard Rodgers and Lorenz Hart's earliest musical shows, *You'd Be Surprised*, which played for one night at the Plaza Hotel Grand Ballroom in New York. After graduating from the Benjamin Franklin High School, Fields contributed poetry to several magazines, and worked with J Fred Coots (who went on to write the music for songs such as 'Love Letters In The Sand', 'Santa Claus Is Coming to Town', and 'You Go To My Head'), before being introduced to the composer Jimmy McHugh at Mills Brothers Music. With McHugh, she initially wrote sundry novelty numbers, and some songs for Cotton Club revues. The new team made their Broadway debut with the complete score for Lew Leslie's *Blackbirds Of 1928*, which starred Bill 'Bojangles' Robinson, Aida Ward and Adelaide Hall, and ran for over 500 performances. The songs included 'Porgy', 'I Must Have That Man', 'Doin' The New Low Down', and future standards, 'I Can't Give You Anything But Love' and 'Diga Diga Doo'. In the same year, McHugh and Fields' next effort, *Hello Daddy*, proved to be a family affair, with Fields' brother Herbert as librettist, and her father as the producer and leading man, although the show's comedy hit number, 'In A Great Big Way', was sung by Billy Taylor. In 1930, another of Lew Leslie's lavish productions, *The International Revue*, contained two of McHugh and Fields' most enduring songs: 'On The Sunny Side Of The Street', which was introduced by Harry Richman, and 'Exactly Like You', a duet for Richman and Gertrude Lawrence.

After contributing 'Button Up Your Heart' and 'Blue Again' to the unsuccessful *Vanderbilt Revue* (1930), McHugh and Fields moved to Hollywood, and, during the next few years, wrote songs for movies such as *Love In The Rough* ('Go Home And Tell Your Mother', 'One More Waltz'), *Cuban Love Song* (title number), *Dancing Lady* ('My Dancing Lady'), *Hooray For Love* (title song, 'Livin' In A Great Big Way', 'I'm In Love All Over Again', 'You're An Angel'), and *The Nitwits* ('Music In My Heart'). *Every Night At Eight*, which starred Frances Langford, Harry Barris, Patsy Kelly, and Alice Faye, included two more McHugh and Fields all-time favourites: 'I'm In The Mood For Love' and 'I Feel A Song Coming On'. Another of their standards, 'Don't Blame Me', was interpolated into the Broadway revue *Clowns In Clover* (1933). Two years later, Dorothy Fields began to work with other composers, including Jerome Kern, with whom she collaborated on the score for the film, *Roberta*, which included 'Lovely To Look At', and 'I Won't Dance', a song that had been in Kern's locker for a couple of years, and which, for complex contractual reasons, is usually credited to five songwriters. The Kern/Fields partnership continued with *Swing Time*, the sixth Fred Astaire/Ginger Rogers screen musical. Often regarded as Kern's finest film score, the songs included 'Pick Yourself Up', 'Bojangles Of Harlem', 'Waltz In Swing Time', 'A Fine Romance' ('You're calmer than the seals in the Arctic Ocean/At least they flap their fins to express emotion'), and 'The Way You Look Tonight' ('With each word your tenderness grows/Tearing my fear apart/And that laugh that wrinkles your nose/Touches my foolish heart'), which gained Kern and Fields an Academy Award. During the remainder of the 30s they worked together again on *I Dream Too Much* ('I'm The Echo', and the title song), *When You're In Love* ('Our Song', 'The Whistling Boy'), and others such as *One Night In The Tropics* ('Remind Me') and *Joy Of Living*, which starred Irene Dunne and Douglas Fairbanks Jnr., and included 'Just Let Me Look At You', 'What's Good About Good-Night?', and 'You Couldn't Be Cuter' ('My ma will show you an album of me that'll bore you to tears!/And you'll attract all the relatives we have dodged for years and years'). Dorothy Fields also wrote film songs with Oscar Levant ('Don't Mention Love To Me', 'Out Of Sight, Out Of Mind'), Max Steiner ('I Can't Waltz Alone'), and provided new lyrics to Fritz Kreisler's music in *The King Steps Out*. Before the end of the decade Fields was back on Broadway, working with the composer Arthur Schwartz on *Stars In Your Eyes*. Their score included 'This Is It', 'A Lady Needs A Change', 'Just A Little Bit More', 'I'll Pay The Check', and the show's highlight, 'It's All Yours', a duet by the stars, Ethel Merman and Jimmy Durante. In the early 40s, Dorothy Fields turned from writing lyrics and collaborated with her brother Herbert on the books for three highly successful Cole Porter musicals: *Let's Face It!* (starring Danny Kaye), *Something For The Boys*, (Ethel Merman/Bill Johnson), and *Mexican Hayride* (Bobby Clark/June Havoc), each of which ran for well over a year. In 1945, the Fields partnership again served as librettists, and Dorothy wrote the lyrics, to Sigmund Romberg's music, for the smash-hit, *Up In Central Park*. Not surprisingly, with Romberg's participation, the score had operetta overtones, and included the robust 'The Big Back Yard', two charming ballads, 'April Snow' and 'Close As Pages In A Book', and a skating ballet in the manner of a Currier and Ives print. Towards the end of 1945, Dorothy Fields was set to collaborate again with Jerome Kern, on *Annie Get Your Gun*, a musical loosely based on the life of sharpshooter Annie Oakley. When Kern died in November of that year, Irving Berlin was brought in to write what is generally regarded as his greatest score, while Dorothy and Herbert Fields provided the highly entertaining book for a production which ran for 1,147 performances. In contrast, *Arms And The Girl* (1950) closed after only 134 shows, despite Rouben Mamoulian's involvement with Dorothy and Herbert Fields in a libretto which was based on the play *The Pursuit Of Happiness*. The Dorothy Fields/Morton Gould score included Pearl Bailey's inimitable renderings of 'Nothin' For Nothin'' and 'There Must Be Somethin' Better Than Love', a strange attempt at a tender love song called 'A Cow, And A Plough, And A Frau', and the double entendres of 'That's What I Told Him Last Night'. During the 50s, Dorothy Fields teamed again with Arthur Schwartz for two shows. The first, *A Tree Grows In Brooklyn*, was a critical success, but a commercial failure. Based on Dorothy Smith's best-selling novel, the witty and melodic score included 'If You Haven't Got A Sweetheart', 'I'll Buy You A Star', 'Make The Man Love Me', 'Look Who's Dancing', 'Mine Till Monday', 'I'm Like A New Broom', and 'Growing Pains'. Shirley Booth stopped the show each night with 'He Had Refinement', the story of Harry, her late spouse, who 'only used four-letter words that I didn't understand', and 'undressed with all the lights off until we was wed - a gentleman to his fingernails, was he!'. The show lasted for 270 performances, and so did the second Fields/Schwartz 50s collaboration, *By The Beautiful Sea* (1954), mainly due to the presence, once again, of Shirley Booth. The songs included 'Alone Too Long', 'Happy Habit', 'I'd Rather Wake Up By Myself', 'Hang Up!', 'More Love Than Your Love', 'By The Beautiful Sea', and 'Coney Island'. Far more successful, was *Redhead* (1959), which ran for 452 performances, and won the Tony Award for 'Best Musical'. Dorothy Fields and Albert Hague's score, which also won a Tony, included 'I Feel Merely Marvellous', 'I'm Back In Circulation', 'Just For Once', 'The Uncle Sam Rag', 'The Right Finger Of My Left Hand', 'Look Who's In Love', ''Erbie Fitch's Dilemma', and 'My Girl Is Just Enough Woman For Me'.

Dorothy Fields's last two Broadway scores were written with Cy Coleman, a composer who was 25 years her junior. The first, *Sweet Charity* (1966), a musical version of Federico Fellini's movie *Nights Of Cabiria*, was conceived, directed and choreographed by Bob Fosse, and starred Gwen Verdon as the good-hearted hostess at the Fan-Dango ballroom, who almost - but not quite - realises her dream of being a conventional wife and mother. Fields and Coleman's score produced several popular numbers, including 'Big Spender' ('So let me get right to the point/I don't pop my cork for every guy I see!'), which quickly became associated in the UK with Shirley Bassey, and 'Baby, Dream Your Dream', 'If My Friends Could See Me Now', 'I'm A Brass Band', 'Where Am I Going?', 'There's Gotta Be Something Better Than This', 'Too Many Tomorrows', and 'I Love To Cry At Weddings' ('I walk into a chapel and get happily hysterical'). Fields's Broadway swansong came in 1973, with *Seesaw*. Her lyrics for this musical adaptation of William Gibson's play *Two For The Seesaw*, are regarded as somewhat tougher than much of her previous work, although they continued to have the colloquial edge and the contemporary, witty, 'street-wise' quality that had become her trademark. The songs included 'Seesaw', 'In Tune', 'Spanglish', 'We've Got It', 'Welcome To Holiday Inn', 'Poor Everybody Else', 'I'm Way Ahead',

and the two best-known numbers, 'Nobody Does It Like Me' ('If there's a problem, I duck it/I don't solve it, I just muck it up!'), and Tommy Tune's show-stopper, 'It's Not Where You Start (It's Where You Finish)'. The latter song closed with. . . 'And you're gonna finish on top!'. Dorothy Fields did just that, 45 years after she had her first Broadway hit with 'I Can't Give You Anything But Love'. Shortly before her death in March 1974, she appeared in a programme in the *Lyrics And Lyricists* series at the Kaufmann Concert Hall of The 92nd Street 'Y' in New York City, giving her 'observations on the fine art and craft of lyric writing', and performing several of her own numbers. Her lyrics have rarely been celebrated by artists on record, but two notable exceptions are *The Dorothy Fields Songbook*, by Sally Mayes, and *Close As Pages In A Book*, by Barbara Cook.

● FURTHER READING: *On The Sunny Side Of The Street: The Life And Lyrics Of Dorothy Fields*, Deborah Grace Winer.

FIELDS, GRACIE

b. Grace Stansfield, 9 January 1898, Rochdale, Lancashire, England, d. 27 September 1979, Capri. A singer and comedienne, so popular in the UK during the 30s and 40s that she was its most famous person next to Royalty. Educated occasionally, in-between work in a cotton mill and playing in juvenile troupes, pierrot shows and revues, she took her first big step in 1918 when she won the part of Sally Perkins in the musical *Mr Tower Of London*, which ran for over seven years. Her career took off after she married the show's producer/comedian Archie Pitt. She started recording in 1928, and by 1933 was celebrating the sale of four million records. Guided by stage producer Basil Dean, Fields made her film debut in 1931 with *Sally In Our Alley*, from which came 'Sally', her famous theme song. In other movies such as, *Looking On The Bright Side*, *This Week Of Grace*, *Love, Life And Laughter*, *Sing As We Go*, *Look Up And Laugh*, *Queen Of Hearts*, *The Show Goes On*, *We're Going To Be Rich*, *Keep Smiling*, and *Shipyard Sally* (1939), her vitality and spirit of determination, cheerfulness and courage, endeared her particularly to working-class people during the dark years of the 30s. After divorcing Pitt, she married Italian comedian/dancer Monte Banks in 1940. When she subsequently moved to the USA, taking with her substantial assets, questions were asked in Parliament. The once supportive UK Press even went as far as branding her a traitor. During World War II she toured extensively, entertaining troops and appearing in USA stage shows, nightclubs, some films, including *Stage Door Canteen* (1944), and on her own radio programmes. After the War she was welcomed back to the UK and featured in a series of morale-building radio shows, *Gracie's Working Party*, but still retained her popularity in the USA during the 40s with chart hits 'Forever And Ever' and the Maori song, 'Now Is The Hour'. As early as 1933 she had bought a villa on the Isle of Capri, and during the 50s she went into semi-retirement there with her third husband, Boris Alperovic, emerging only for the occasional concert or record date. She made her final London appearance at her 10th Royal Command Performance in 1978. Her song hits, sung in a fine soprano voice, varied from the comic 'In My Little Bottom Drawer', 'Walter, Walter', 'I Took My

Harp To A Party', 'Fred Fannakapan', and 'The Biggest Aspidistra In The World', through the spirited 'Sing As We Go' and 'Wish Me Luck As You Wave Me Goodbye', to the ballads 'Around The World', 'Pedro The Fisherman', 'Little Donkey', 'La Vie En Rose', and 'Ave Maria'. Some of her more personalized material was studied, as social documents, by the Department of Social History at the University of Lancaster. Throughout her life she worked hard for charities, including the Gracie Fields Orphanage, and was awarded the CBE in 1938. Fields was made Dame Commander of the British Empire shortly before her death in September 1979.

● COMPILATIONS: *The World Of Gracie Fields* (1970)★★★, *Stage And Screen* (1972)★★★, *The Golden Years Of Gracie Fields* (1975)★★★, *Focus On Gracie Fields* (1977)★★★, *The Gracie Fields Story* (1979)★★★, *Amazing Gracie Fields* (1979)★★★, *Gracie Fields - Best Of Her BBC Broadcasts* (1980)★★★, *Life Is A Song* (1983)★★★, *The Biggest Aspidistra In The World* (1985)★★★, *Incomparable* (1985)★★★, *Isle Of Capri* (1987)★★★, *Laughter And Song* (1987)★★★, *Sally* (1988)★★★, *Queen Of Hearts* (1989)★★★, *Last Concert In America* (1989)★★★, *That Old Feeling* (1989)★★★, *Classic Years In Digital Stereo* (1990)★★★, *Sing As We Go* (1990)★★★.

● FURTHER READING: *Sing As We Go, Her Autobiography*, Gracie Fields. *Gracie Fields: Her Life In Pictures*, P. Hudson. *Gracie Fields*, Joan Moules.

FIFTY MILLION FRENCHMEN

That is an awful lot of people to see during 'A Musical Comedy Tour Of Paris' - the subtitle of Cole Porter's first big hit show, which opened at New York's Lyric Theatre on 27 November 1929. Following the critical reaction to his *See America First* (one critic: 'See *See America First* - last!'), Porter switched his milieu to Europe, where he had spent several pleasurable years during the 20s, and found success with *Paris*, which ran for six months on Broadway from October 1928. This second theatrical excursion to the city he loved, had a book by Herbert Fields which once again turned on the familiar theme - a rich man's desire to be loved for himself and not for his money. Peter Forbes (William Gaxton) is the tormented soul this time, and he bets a friend, Michael Cummins (Jack Thompson), that he will be engaged to an attractive tourist, Looloo Carroll (Genevieve Tobin), within a month - and without any recourse to his financial resources. Taking a job as a guide, he conducts Looloo on 'a musical comedy guide of city', which provides Norman Bel Geddes with a marvellous opportunity to display his impressive settings, which include the Longchamps Racetrack, the Eiffel Tower, and the Café de la Paix. Porter's score was a joy, and contained one of his all-time standards, 'You Do Something To Me', as well as the humorous 'You've Got That Thing' ('You've got what Adam craved when he/With love for Eve was tortured/She only had an apple tree/But you, you've got an orchard'), 'Find Me A Primitive Man' ('I don't mean the kind that belongs to a club/But the kind that has a club that belongs to him'), 'The Tale Of An Oyster', 'I Worship You', 'I'm Unlucky At Gambling', and, of course, a couple of affectionate hymns to the city, 'You Don't Know Paree' and 'Paree, What Did You Do To Me?'. The show ran for 254 performances, and launched Porter - who was already

38 years old when it opened - on a glittering career that lasted for another 25 years on Broadway. William Gaxton and Helen Broderick recreated their roles in the 1931 film version of *Fifty Million Frenchmen*, but the Hollywood interpretation was not classed as a musical.

FILLMORE

In 1971 US impresario Bill Graham opted to close his leading venues, the Fillmore East in New York and Fillmore West in San Francisco. The latter had been at the hub of the 60s' Bay Area scene, showcasing almost all the leading rock acts of the era. The final week's proceedings were filmed and *Fillmore* contains notable live performances from Santana, the Grateful Dead, Quicksilver Messenger Service, Hot Tuna and Boz Scaggs. The in-concert appearances are interspersed with interview material in which Graham reminisces about his past. Talkative and opinionated, he makes an interesting subject although his notorious quick temper is also apparent. One now-legendary scene shows guitarist/vocalist Mike Wilhelm asking Graham to find a slot for his group, Loose Gravel. Wilhelm, a former member of the pioneering Charlatans, San Francisco's first 'underground' act, argues that as he was there at the beginning he should be there at the end. Graham refuses, citing the former band's unprofessionalism. 'Fuck you and thanks for the memories', Wilhelm states as he is about to leave, inciting Graham to have him bodily ejected from the premises, vowing to blacklist his group from all future bills. *Fillmore* is a nostalgic tribute to an important period in Graham's life. He continued to work as a leading concert promoter (c/f Live Aid), but this feature expresses the special nature of those early years and captures several acts in their prime. A triple-boxed set, with lavish booklet, was issued in 1972 to complement the film.

● ALBUMS: *Fillmore: The Last Days* (Warner 1972)★★★.
● FURTHER READING: *The Fillmore East*, Richard Kostelanetz.

FINDERS KEEPERS

British character actors Robert Morley and Peggy Mount co-starred alongside Cliff Richard and the Shadows in this poorly executed 1966 film. Based on a real event, the plot involves an atomic bomb, lost off the Spanish coast. The device is washed-up on shore, where it is discovered by Richard and his group. *Finders Keepers* lacks the charm of the singer's previous films, notably *Summer Holiday*. The *joie de vivre* is noticeably false and the entire project seems to mirror the artistic fall of his early mentor, Elvis Presley. The soundtrack proved equally weak, although it did reach number 6 in the UK album chart, Richard's highest such placing since his previous film excursion, *Wonderful Life*. The material seemed contrived; 'Fiesta', 'Paella' and 'Oh Senorita' the obvious worst offenders, but it did yield a Top 10 single in 'Time Goes By'.

FINE AND DANDY

A rather bizarre title for a show, considering that it opened in New York at the height of the Depression, on 23 September 1930. The production was a vehicle for the much-loved ex-vaudevillian, Joe Cook, an extremely versatile and zany comedian whose routines included a range of highly amusing, inventive stories (particularly the one about the 'Four Hawaiians'), and a consistently entertaining display of circus-style skills such as acrobatics, juggling, and balancing - not to mention a degree of proficiency on the ukelele and saxophone. In Donald Ogden Stewart's plot for *Fine And Dandy*, Cook played the role of Joe Squibb, who, like the funny-man himself, was adept at keeping several balls in the air at once (metaphorically speaking). These consisted of his female boss, Mrs. Fordyce (Dora Maughan), his girlfriend, Nancy Ellis (Alice Boulden) - and his wife and children! The show's music and lyrics were by Kay Swift and Paul James (a pseudonym for Swift's husband, a banker named James P. Warburg). Kay Swift (b. 19 April 1897, New York, USA, d. 28 January 1993, Southington, Connecticut, USA) was one of the few female composers of popular songs to have a degree of success on Broadway. With her husband she had contributed 'Can't We Be Friends?' to *The Little Show* in 1929, and was a close personal and professional associate of George Gershwin. For *Fine And Dandy* she and Warburg wrote the jaunty title song which was sung by Cook and Boulden, along with 'Let's Go Eat Worms In The Garden' (Boulden and Joe Wagstaff), and 'Jig Hope', a number that was performed by Eleanor Powell who subsequently tap-danced her way through several entertaining Hollywood musicals, notably *Broadway Melody Of 1940* with Fred Astaire. The show's big romantic ballad, 'Can This Be Love?' (Boulden), became successful through a recording by the pianistic duo Victor Arden and Ohman's Orchestra. They also made the best-sellers with 'Fine And Dandy', as did another rather more famous band led by Tommy and Jimmy Dorsey. On the strength of initial revues such as 'pretty nearly everything you've yearned for in the way of 1930 entertainment', and Cook's renowned inspired clowning, *Fine And Dandy* ran at Erlanger's Theatre (later known as the St. James) for 255 performances. That production is not connected with the 1942 London revue of the same name, which starred Leslie Henson, Stanley Holloway, Dorothy Dickson, and Douglas Byng.

FINGS AIN'T WOT THEY USED T'BE

This show originally opened on 17 February 1959 at the Theatre Royal, Stratford East, London, home of the *avant garde* director Joan Littlewood and her 'repertory company'. During two separate runs there it was completely revised and remodelled, and transferred to the Garrick Theatre in the West End on 11 February 1960. Set in the drab and dreary world of London's Soho district, with its prostitutes, pimps and small-time criminals, Frank Norman's book (Norman was an ex-convict) told of Fred Cochran (Glynn Edwards), one of life's losers, who runs a sleazy gambling club - a haven for the local low-life. He can only dream of owning a big-time venue, but a large win on the horses means that he can at least have his place decorated by the camp decorator Horace Seaton (Wallas Eaton). Unfortunately, the reopening night party is ruined when Fred is beaten up for not providing the police with their usual slice of payola. There is a good deal more trouble and strife before Fred ends up with a knees-up *al fresco* wedding to his girlfriend Lily Smith (Miriam Karlin). The local milieu is populated by a variety of char-

acters such as the crooked copper Sergeant Collins (Tom Chatto), plus two more members of the constabulary, played by Yootha Joyce and George Sewell, a civilian crook, Redhot (Edward Carrick), Tosher (James Booth), the area's premier ponce, and several 'ladies of the night', including Rosie (Barbara Windsor) and Betty (Toni Palmer). Lionel Bart, who had provided just the lyrics for *Lock Up Your Daughters* at the Mermaid Theatre in 1959, wrote both words and music for this exhilarating piece. His songs, which so accurately captured the show's spirit and atmosphere, included 'G'Night Dearie', 'Layin' Abaht', 'Where It's Hot', 'Contempery', 'Meatface', 'The Ceilin's Comin' Dahn', 'Where Do Little Birds Go?', 'The Student Ponce', 'Big Time', 'Polka Dots', 'Cop A Bit Of Pride' and 'Cochran Will Return'. The popular comedian-singer Max Bygraves took a cleaned-up version of the title song into the UK Top 5, and the personality pianist Russ Conway also had a minor hit with the tune. The critics were not enthusiastic about the show, but audiences loved it, and *Fings Ain't Wot They Used T'Be* enjoyed a two-year run of 897 performances. This established Lionel Bart as a real force in the London musical theatre, and won the *Evening Standard Award* for best musical.

FINIAN'S RAINBOW (FILM MUSICAL)

Some Broadway musicals defy even the most determined attempts to transform them into successful movies, and *Finian's Rainbow* falls very much in that category. Twenty one years after the show made its debut at the 46th Street in New York, E.Y. 'Yip Harburg' and Fred Saidy finally adapted their whimsical stage libretto for this film which was released by Warner Brothers in 1968. Their moralistic story told of simple Irishman Finian McLonergan (Fred Astaire), who travels to Rainbow Valley, Missitucky, USA with his daughter Sonia (Petula Clark) and a crock of gold which he has stolen from a leprechaun (Tommy Steele). Finian believes that if he buries the gold in the ground it will increase in value just as it does at Fort Knox. It does not quite work out that way, and the crock causes a heap of trouble - especially to a bigoted Southern Senator (Keenan Wynn) who turns black after tinkering with its 'three wish factor' - before Sonia falls for the leprechaun - who gets his gold back - and Finian takes off by himself to pastures new. The principle of people over profit has by then been clearly established. Most of the engaging and melodic songs from the show, by Burton Lane and Harburg, were retained for the screen version. They included 'How Are Things In Glocca Morra?', 'If This Isn't Love', 'Look To The Rainbow', 'Something Sort Of Grandish', 'That Great Come-And-Get-It Day', 'Old Devil Moon', 'When The Idle Poor Become The Idle Rich', 'When I'm Not Near The Girl I Love', 'Rain Dance', and 'The Begat'. The film, which was Fred Astaire's last musical, was directed by Francis Ford Coppola, with choreography by Hermes Pan, and was photographed in Technicolor and Panavision.

FINIAN'S RAINBOW (STAGE MUSICAL)

Conceived by E. Y. 'Yip' Harburg, this stage musical opened on Broadway on 10 January 1947. With book by Harburg and Fred Saidy, music by Burton Lane and lyrics by Harburg, the show was a fantasy with a strong satirical core. Central to the story was Harburg's desire to express his views on racial bigotry and political persecution. At the time he was blacklisted in Hollywood and had returned to Broadway out of necessity. Set in the Deep South, in Rainbow Valley in the mythical state of Missitucky, the story tells of Og, a leprechaun, who arrives there in search of Finian who has stolen a pot of gold from Glocca Morra in Ireland. The leprechaun grants three wishes, one of which turns Billboard Rawkins, a land-grabbing racist white Senator, into a black evangelist, humanizing him in the process, another gives the power of speech to Susan, a mute, while the third helps the local sharecroppers recover their land from Rawkins. Songs from the show included 'How Are Things In Glocca Morra?', 'When I'm Not Near The Girl I Love', 'If This Isn't Love', 'The Great Come-And-Get-It Day' and 'Look To The Rainbow'. *Finian's Rainbow* starred David Wayne as Og, Albert Sharp as Finian, Anita Alvarez as Susan, Ella Logan as Sharon, Finian's sister, and Donald Richards as Woody, Sharon's boyfriend. With good songs and performances allied to Michael Kidd's exhilarating choreography, the show was a critical and popular success running for 725 performances. The 1968 screen version starred Fred Astaire, Petula Clark and Tommy Steele.

FIORELLO!

With a book by Jerome Weidman and George Abbott which was based on the true story of Fiorello LaGuardia, the aggressive, extrovert US Congressman and Mayor of New York, *Fiorello!* opened at the Broadhurst Theatre on Broadway on 23 November 1959. The show's story began shortly before World War I when LaGuardia was first a conscientious, reforming lawyer, and then a Congressman who became a sworn enemy of the corruption that was endemic in the social and political life of New York. It continued through his time as a pilot during World War I, his initial unsuccessful campaign against James J. Walker, right up to the eve of his election as the Mayor of New York in 1933. Along the way, his wife, Thea (Ellen Hanley) dies, and he eventually finds happiness with his secretary Marie Fischer (Patricia Wilson). The role of the rough, tough, ebullient LaGuardia, was played by Tom Bosley, making his Broadway debut. The actor was subsequently best-known for his work on television, as the indulgent father in the 50s spoof, *Happy Days*, and another long-running series, *Father Dowling Investigates*. *Fiorello!*'s score, by Jerry Bock (music) and Sheldon Harnick (lyrics), included 'On the Side Of The Angels', 'The Name's LaGuardia', 'Politics And Poker', 'I Love A Cop', ''Til Tomorrow', 'When Did I Fall In Love?', 'Gentleman Jimmy', 'The Very Next Man', 'Marie's Law', and 'The Bum Won'. One of the most amusing numbers was 'Little Tin Box'. Setting aside a small sum therein each week apparently enabled certain of the city's apparently less than well-off citizens to buy yachts and Rolls Royces, or as one of them put it, in court: 'I can see your Honour doesn't pull his punches/And it looks a trifle fishy, I'll admit/But for one whole week I went without my lunches/And it mounted up your honour, bit by bit.' Chorus: 'Up your Honour bit by bit . . .' In spite of a few critical carp-

ings *Fiorello!* was a great success and ran for 795 performances. It won Tony Awards for best director (George Abbott) outright, tied with *The Sound Of Music* for best musical, composer, and librettists, and was also voted best musical by the New York Drama Critics. Even more prestigiously, it became only the third musical (not counting *Oklahoma!*'s special award in 1944) to be awarded the Pulitzer Prize for Drama. The 1962 London production stayed at the Princes Theatre for 56 performances. Four concert performances of *Fiorello!* were presented at the New York City Centre in 1994. The starry cast included Faith Prince, Jerry Zaks, Donna McKechnie, Liz Callaway, Philip Bosco, Greg Adelman, Marilyn Cooper, and Adam Arkin.

FIREFLY, THE (FILM MUSICAL)

Remembered particularly for one of Allan Jones's finest film performances and his thrilling rendition of 'The Donkey Serenade', *The Firefly* was released by MGM in 1937. The song itself was based on Rudolph Friml's 'Chanson', a solo piano piece written in 1920, which was arranged for the picture by Herbert Stothart, with a lyric by Robert Wright and Chet Forrest. Most of the songs from the 1912 Broadway show were discarded, and Frances Goodrich and Albert Hackett came up with a new story which was set in Spain at the time of the Napoleonic war. Jones and his co-star, Jeanette MacDonald, were both involved in espionage work during the hostilities, while their personal relationship flourished. The songs that survived from the original stage musical, with music by Rudolph Friml, were 'Giannina Mia' (lyric by Otto Harbach), 'When A Maid Comes Knocking At Your Heart' (lyric Harbach-Robert Wright-Chet Forrest), 'Love Is Like A Firefly' (lyric Wright-Forrest), and 'Sympathy' (lyric Gus Kahn-Harbach), were supplemented by several others including 'He Who Loves And Runs Away' (Friml-Kahn). Also in the cast were Henry Daniell, Warren William, Leonard Penn, Douglas Dumbrille, Billy Gilbert, and George Zucco. The choreographer was Albertina Rasch, and the opulent and entertaining Hunt Stromberg production, which was photographed by Oliver T. Marsh in a sepia tint, was directed by Robert Z. Leonard.

FIREFLY, THE (STAGE MUSICAL)

Composer Rudolph Friml's first Broadway score and the beginning of his partnership with Otto Harbach who wrote the book and lyrics, and with whom he collaborated for 10 musicals. *The Firefly* opened at the Lyric theatre in New York on 2 December 1912, Friml was given the job because Victor Herbert, the original choice of the composer could not get along with Emma Trentini who plays the role of Nina Corelli. As *The Firefly* begins, Geraldine Van Dare (Audrey Maple) is about to sail for Bermuda on her uncle's yacht in the company of her fiancé Jack Travers (Craig Campbell). To escape the clutches of her drunken father, Nina (Trentini), an Italian street singer who lives in New York, disguises herself as a boy and manoeuvres herself aboard. After the most elaborate and complicated plot schemes, and some expert tutorage from the musician Franz (Henry Vogel), she becomes Giannina, a famous prima donna, and, of course, marries

Jack Travers. As usual with operetta, the score, and not the story, is the important item, and this score is regarded as one of the best of its kind. It included lovely songs such as 'When A Maid Comes Knocking At Your Door', 'Sympathy', 'Giannina Mia', 'Love Is Like A Firefly', 'In Sapphire Seas', and 'An American Beauty Rose'. The show ran for 120 performances - a decent total in the early part of the century - and was filmed in 1937. The Hollywood version had a different story which involved spies in Spain, and starred Jeanette MacDonald and Allan Jones.

FIVE GUYS NAMED MOE

This show was playing a limited five-week engagement in October 1990 at the tiny Theatre Royal, Stratford East, in London when it was spotted by superstar impresario Cameron Mackintosh who was so impressed that he negotiated contracts on the spot, enabling the production to transfer to the Lyric Theatre in Shaftesbury Avenue in December of that year. The show, which was conceived and written by Clarke Peters, is a tribute to the jazz-blues-man Louis Jordan, who is sometimes cited as the 'musical father' of Chuck Berry and Bill Haley, and therefore, by implication, of rock 'n' roll itself. The story concerns a lovelorn central character, Nomax (Dig Wayne), drowning his sorrows in drink and listening to the blues on an old-fashioned radio. The apparatus explodes, and he is confronted by the five Moes - these sharp-suited, fast-talking characters from a Jordan song - who set about improving his attitude and putting him straight about women and love. The group consists of: Big Moe (Kenny Andrews), Little Moe (Paul J. Medford), No Moe (Peter Alex Newton), Eat Moe (Omar Okai), and Four-Eyed Moe (Clarke Peters). Nexus's education is delivered via song and dance routines, in some of which he is allowed to participate. At times during the show the story is temporarily dispensed with, and the audience is invited onstage, and led in a conga around the theatre and then through the exits during the interval. The 20 or so songs from the 40s and 50s, which were either written by Jordan or are indelibly associated with him, are delivered joyously with lots of verve and attack. They include 'Saturday Night Fish Fry', 'Ain't Nobody Here But Us Chickens', 'Is You Is, Or Is You Ain't (Ma' Baby)', 'What's The Use Of Getting Sober?' ('When you're gonna get drunk again'), 'Look Out Sister', 'Brother Beware', 'Caldonia', 'It Must Be Jelly ('Cause Jam Don't Shake Like That)', and 'Dad Gum Your Hide, Boy'. *Five Guys Named Moe* won the 1991 Laurence Olivier Award for best entertainment and settled in for a long run. It celebrated its 1,000th performance in June 1993, proclaiming 'The Joint Never Stops Jumpin''. In fact, the London production did stop 'jumpin'' for a time in 1995 (4 March) while the show switched to the Albery Theatre, where it stayed for a further eight months. *Five Guys Named Named Moe* had become the longest-running musical at the Lyric (overtaking *Irma La Douce*) the year before. A Broadway production opened in April 1992, with Frank Rich, the most important critic in New York who has never been enamoured of Cameron Mackintosh's productions, describing the show derisively as 'a British tourist's view of a patch of black American pop music history'. However, it survived that initial onslaught and remained at the

Eugene O'Neill Theatre for over a year, a total of 445 performances. Successful international tours indicate that this show is going to 'party on' for a very long time.

FIVE PENNIES, THE

This schmaltzy biopic of 20s cornet player Red Nichols was released by Paramount in 1959. Danny Kaye plays Nichols, and Barbara Bel Geddes is the wife who, following his early success, stays with him through the emotional traumas of their daughter's illness, until he re-emerges from depression and returns to his beloved world of jazz. On-screen musicians include Shelly Manne (in the role of Dave Tough, the second time in the same year he played the part of the drummer), Bobby Troup, Ray Anthony (in the role of Jimmy Dorsey, despite his being a trumpet player), and Louis Armstrong and his All Stars, who at that time included Peanuts Hucko, Billy Kyle and Trummy Young. Kaye and Armstrong mug their way through a vocal and trumpet duet of 'When the Saints Go Marching In', with Nichols himself dubbing for Kaye. Period songs such as 'Runnin' Wild' (Joe Grey-Leo Wood-A. Harrington Gibbs), 'Out Of Nowhere' (Edward Heyman-Johnny Green), 'After You've Gone' (Henry Creamer-Turner Layton), and 'Indiana' (Ballard MacDonald-James F. Hanley), are supplemented by three new ones written by Kaye's wife, Sylvia Fine - 'The Five Pennies', 'Lullaby In Ragtime' and 'Goodnight Sleep Tight', the last two of which are presented in a charming contrapuntal setting. Leith Stevens won an Oscar nomination for his 'scoring for a musical film', and there were other nominations for Daniel L. Fapp's impressive Vistavision and Technicolor cinematography, and Fine's title song. Melville Shavelson directed the picture, and he and Jack Rose wrote the script.

FIX, THE

The process of preparing the mega-musical *Martin Guerre* for the West End is said to have taken Cameron Mackintosh seven years, but his more satirical and complex piece, *The Fix*, opened at London's Donmar Warehouse on 12 May 1997, only seven months after the producer became aware of it. The American team of John Dempsey (lyrics) and Dana P. Rowe (music) provided the score, and Dempsey also wrote the book, which dealt with what one critic called 'corrupt machinations of a dangerous political dynasty' - of the American kind. Presidential contender Senator Reed Chandler (David Firth) has suffered a fatal heart attack while *in flagrante* with hotel receptionist Donna (Christina Fry), and hot on the heels of his death, his not-so-grieving widow, Violet (Kathryn Evans), and her polio-stricken brother-in-law, Grahame (Philip Quast), prepare to groom Chandler's layabout son, Cal (John Barrowman), to take his place on the White House ladder. This entails an obligatory spell in the US Army, marriage to Deborah (Gael Johnson), the blonde (from a good family), and the formulation of his political creed - basically, the economy, crime and taxes. Enter the Mob, and Cal's life and career go rapidly downhill via his involvement with a voluptuous dancer, Tina McCoy (Krysten Cummings), hard drugs, corruption in high places, and a variety of sexual predilections. A cleaned-up comeback is short-lived, and his inevitable demise is marked by 'crass' Kennedy-Marilyn Monroe overtones. Also cast were Mark Frendo, Carrie Ellis, John Partridge, Bogdan Kominowski, Archie Preston and Christopher Holt. Accompanying the scheming and the rest of the shenanigans was a rock-driven score that incorporated elements of gospel, mock-vaudeville, country and rock 'n' roll, among other genres. The bluesy 'Lonely Is A Two-Way Street', 'Simple Words', and the second-act opener, 'Two Guys At Harvard', were prominent in a score that also included 'Advocate, Architect', 'The Funeral', 'One, Two, Three', 'Embrace Tomorrow', 'Army Chant', 'Control', 'Man And Wife', 'America's Son', 'I See The Future', 'Alleluia', 'Flash, Pop, Sizzle!', 'Making Sense Of Insanity', 'Clandestine Affairs', 'First Came Mercy', 'Bend The Spoon', 'Cleaning House', 'Upper Hand', 'Spin', 'The Ballad Of Bobby "Cracker" Barrel', 'Child's Play', 'Lion Hunts The Tiger' and 'Mistress Of Deception'. Director Sam Mendes ('sure and slick production'), choreographer Charles Augins, Rob Howell (sets and costumes), and Howard Harrison (fierce, yet shadowy, lighting), emerged relatively unscathed, and this £3.5 million '*Manchurian Candidate* without the warmth' played out its month-long season despite a chilly critical reception. Cameron Mackintosh was reportedly furious at the panning, claiming that the critics were unable to deal with changes in musical style. *The Fix* had its US premiere at the Signature Theatre, Washington, D.C. in April 1998, with Linda Balgord, Stephen Bienskie, Sal Mistretta, and Jim Walton.

FLAHOOLEY

Four years after *Finian's Rainbow* its authors E.Y. 'Yip' Harburg and Fred Saidy came up with another piece of whimsy called *Flahooley* which opened on 14 May 1951 at the Broadhurst Theatre in New York, and, unlike that previous show, did not stay around for too long. The action takes place in Capsulanti, Indiana, USA at the business premises of B.G. Bigelow, Inc., manufactures of all manner of dolls, and specialists in novelty items such as exploding cigars and similar playthings. Sylvester (Jerome Courtland), one of the Company's puppet designers, is in love with Sandy (Barbara Cook), a fellow puppet operator. Sylvester has come up with a revolutionary new puppet, but, before he can unveil it, a mission from Arabia arrives at the factory with a problem. Their Aladdin's magic lamp no longer produces a genie; can B.G. Bigelow, Inc. repair it? They can. The new puppet is revealed, and named Flahooley: it chews gum, it reads comic books - and it laughs! B.G. Bigelow (Ernest Truex) is delighted, and puts it on the market, but disaster strikes. A competitor has already developed a cheaper version (industrial spies?), and Sylvester is dismayed - will he ever have enough money to marry Sandy? While the magic lamp is being mended, Flahooley's hand touches it, and the resulting genie, Abou Ben Atom (Irwin Corey), organizes the production of Flahooleys in such numbers that the market is saturated. The citizens of Capsulanti arrange a genie hunt, intending to burn every Flahooley they can find. The lamp is seized by Elsa Bulinger, the leader of the reactionary mob, but Abou escapes and decides to become a Santa Claus. Bigelow flies off on a magic carpet to marry

Najla (Yma Sumac), one of the Arabian delegation. Harburg's books and lyrics always had a social and political edge, although they were never dull or boring, and, as this show was written at the height of the McCarthy witch-hunts in America, it was inevitable that the prevailing climate would be reflected in this work. All the usual targets such as politicians, big business - capitalism in general - were examined and satirized. The show's more conventional - and marvellous - songs were written by Harburg and composer Sammy Fain (a prolific film composer, this was regarded as Fain's best score for the stage). Jerome Courtland, and Barbara Cook in her first Broadway role, introduced 'Here's To Your Illusions', 'Who Says There Ain't No Santa Claus?', 'The World Is Your Balloon', 'He's Only Wonderful', and Cook also had the tender 'Come Back, Little Genie'. Other Harburg-Fain numbers included 'The Springtime Cometh', 'You, Too, Can Be A Puppet', 'Jump, Little Chillun!', and 'Flahooley!'. The remainder of the numbers - written especially for the four-octave range of Yma Sumac by Mosises Vivanco - were 'Birds/Enchantment', 'Najla's Lament', and Najla's Song Of Joy'. *Flahooley* was a charming piece, with an excellent cast - including the delightful Baird puppets - but commercially it failed dismally, and closed after only 40 performances. A second version, entitled *Jollyanna*, with a cast that included Bobby Clark, Mitzi Gaynor, John Beal, and Biff McGuire, opened on 11 September 1952 at the Curran Theatre in San Francisco, but closed during the pre-Broadway tryout. In September 1998, the first major New York revival of the 1951 *Flahooley* was mounted off-Broadway at the Theatre at St. Clement's.

FLAME

Slade were unequivocally one of the most popular acts of the early 70s. Although noted for boisterous singles, including 'Mama Weer All Crazee Now' and 'Cum On Feel The Noize', the quartet boasted a strong grasp of melody, redolent of their 60s' mentors. In this, their only feature film, Slade portray a group from that era, 'Flame', who achieve success only to disband, disillusioned with their management. Ex-Animals members Chas Chandler - Slade's manager/producer in real-life - and John Steele were executive producers in this project, which featured the latter in an acting role as a drummer in a band booked for a wedding. The *Flame* soundtrack album included two UK hit singles, 'Far Far Away' and 'How Does It Feel'. Although the former reached number 2, its successor failed to broach the Top 10 after 12 consecutive such entries. Released in 1974, *Flame* appeared just as Slade's star began to wane, yet it remains a meritorious look at British pop culture.

FLAMING STAR

The second 1960 film to star Elvis Presley, *Flaming Star* caused a minor furore upon release. It arrived soon after the highly-successful *GI Blues*, but this particular feature was a vehicle for Presley the actor, not singer. Director Don Seigel, later famous for his 'Dirty Harry' work with Clint Eastwood, declared there would be no music at all, although the film did included the insouciant, but contextualised 'A Cane And A High-Starched Collar', as well as its popular title song. Set in the US Civil War, *Flaming Star* portrays Presley as a confused half-breed, torn between cultural loyalties and a love triangle when his family is slaughtered by Kiowa Indians. Critics praised his dramatic abilities and indeed Elvis did excel in a part originally written for Marlon Brando. Fans, however, were a little more reserved, particularly in view of the downbeat ending in which Presley's character dies, echoing the close of his first feature, *Lovin' You*. *Flaming Star* was not a spectacular box-office success, paling in comparison with *GI Blues*. This perhaps explains the light-hearted features the singer was forced to complete over the next eight years.

FLANAGAN AND ALLEN

Bud Flanagan (b. Reuben Weintrop [Robert Winthrop], 14 October 1896, Whitechapel, London, England, d. 20 October 1968, Kingston, Surrey, England) and Chesney Allen (b. William Ernest Allen, 5 April 1896, London, England, d. 13 November 1982, Midhurst, Sussex, England). One of Britain's best-loved comedy-singing duos during their heyday in the 30s and 40s. Allen was the straight man, with a neat, well tailored image complete with trilby, while comedian Flanagan wore a voluminous mangy fur coat and a battered straw hat. The son of Jewish refugees from Poland, Flanagan took a job as a call boy at the Cambridge Music Hall when he was 10, and made his first stage appearance at the London Music Hall - as conjuror Fargo, the Boy Wizard - in 1908. After winning singing competitions sponsored by the popular musical hall artist Dora Lyric, Flanagan made up his young mind to run away to America, and, at the age of 14, found himself washing dishes in the galley of the *S.S. Majestic* bound for New York. Once there, he worked as a Western Union messenger, newspaper vendor, and prizefighter (billed as 'Luke McGlook from England'), before forming a vaudeville double act with Dale Burgess. They toured the US, and appeared in Australia, New Zealand, and South Africa, before Flanagan returned to England just after the outbreak of World War I, and enlisted in the Royal Artillery. Posted to Northern France, where he first met Chesney Allen briefly, he took his future stage name from a particularly obnoxious, anti-Semitic Sergeant-Major Flanagan. After his release in 1919, he worked with various stage partners and was a taxi driver for a spell in the early 20s, before taking over from Stan Stanford as Chesney Allen's partner in Florrie Forde's revue and pantomime company in 1924. Allen, whose father was master builder, had been articled to a solicitor before opting for a stage career. As well as performing in Forde's shows, he was also her manager. When Forde decided to retire, Flanagan and Allen's first inclination was to follow their main interest and start up as bookmakers, but they accepted D.J. Clarke's offer of a week in variety at the Argyle Theatre, Birkenhead, in January 1931. Their performances were so well received, especially their rendering of Flanagan's composition, 'Underneath The Arches', that they were swiftly booked for the Holborn Empire and the London Palladium. Flanagan and Allen also appeared at the Palladium in their first Royal Variety Performance in 1932. Flanagan's impulsive appeal for 'three cheers' for their majesties King George V and Queen Mary at the end

of the show, marked the beginning of his long reign as an affectionately regarded 'court jester'. Also on the bill that year were the comic duo, Nervo And Knox, and that pair's subsequent appearances with Flanagan And Allen, Eddie Gray, Caryll And Mundy, and Naughton And Gold in the Palladium's *Crazy Month* revues, saw the birth of the legendary Crazy Gang. The team was reduced to seven after Billy Caryll lost a leg and died. In the 30s, as well as touring in variety and appearing together in their own shows such as *Give Me A Ring*, *Happy Returns*, *Life Begins At Oxford Circus*, and *Swing Is In The Air*, Flanagan And Allen were part of the Crazy Gang (although in most cases the artists were each billed separately) in popular revues such as *Round About Regent Street*, *O-Kay For Sound*, *London Rhapsody*, *These Foolish Things*, and *The Little Dog Laughed* (1939). During World War II Flanagan And Allen entertained the troops with ENSA, and were seen in the revues *Top Of The World*, *Black Vanities* and *Hi-Di-Hi*. They also starred in a series of comedy films - sprinkled occasionally with songs - which had begun in the 30s with *A Fire Has Been Arranged*, *Underneath The Arches*, *Okay For Sound*, *Alf's Button Afloat*, and *The Frozen Limit*, and continued in the early 40s with *Gasbags*, *We'll Smile Again*, *Theatre Royal*, *Here Comes The Sun*, and *Dreaming* (1944). Chesney Allen's ill health brought the illustrious partnership to an end in 1946, and in the same year Flanagan appeared in Robert Nesbitt's revue, *The Night And The Laughter*, before rejoining the re-formed Crazy Gang in 1947 for *Together Again* at the Victoria Palace. It ran for more than two years, and similar productions such as *Knights Of Madness*, *Ring Out The Bells*, *Jokers Wild*, *These Foolish Kings*, and *Clown Jewels* (1959), also enjoyed extended stays, keeping the same theatre fully occupied during the 50s. In the latter show, Flanagan introduced Ralph Reader's 'Strollin'', a perfect addition to the catalogue of songs indelibly identified with Flanagan And Allen, which included 'The Umbrella Man', 'Run, Rabbit, Run', 'Home Town', 'Hey, Neighbour', 'We're Gonna Hang Out The Washing On The Siegfried Line', 'Dreaming', 'Forget-Me-Not Lane', 'Music, Maestro, Please', 'Franklin D. Roosevelt Jones' 'On The Outside Looking In', 'The Oi Song', and, of course, 'Underneath The Arches'. Flanagan received the OBE in 1959, and after the Crazy Gang's farewell show, *Young In Heart*, closed in 1962, he concentrated mainly on his bookmaking and other business interests. However, in 1968 he was persuaded to sing Jimmy Perry and Derek Taverner's 'Who Do You Think You Are Kidding Mr. Hitler' to be used over the opening titles of the brand new television comedy series, *Dad's Army*. Although he died just a few weeks after the first show was transmitted, his voice is still heard in 90s re-runs.

Following his early retirement from the stage, Chesney Allen became the managing director of a theatrical and variety agency, and was the Crazy Gang's manager for a time. He joined Flanagan for two more films, *Life Is A Circus* and *Dunkirk*, in 1958, and made a nostalgic appearance at the 1980 Royal Variety Performance. He also took part in the cast recording of *Underneath The Arches*, a celebration of Flanagan And Allen, starring Roy Hudd (as Flanagan) and Christopher Timothy (as Allen), which played at London's Prince of Wales Theatre in 1982.

● ALBUMS: Flanagan And Allen *Favourites* (Decca 1953)★★★★, *Successes* (Columbia 1953)★★★★, *Down Forget-Me-Not Lane* (Decca 1962)★★★★, *The Flanagan And Allen Story* (Encore 60s)★★★★, *We'll Smile Again* (Ace Of Clubs 1965)★★★★, *Best Of* (Encore 1978)★★★★, *Yesterday's Dreams* (Decca 1981)★★★★, *Arches and Umbrellas* (Flapper 1990)★★★★, *Underneath The Arches* (MFP 1991)★★★★. Bud Flanagan *Maybe It's Because I'm A Londoner* (Columbia 60s)★★★★.

● FURTHER READING: *My Crazy Life* Bud Flanagan.

FLANDERS AND SWANN

The son of an actor father, and a mother who had been a concert-violinist before she married, Michael Flanders (b. 1 March 1922, London, England, d. 14 April 1975), was brought up in a musical household. He learned to play the clarinet and made his stage debut at the age of seven in a singing contest with *Uncle Mac's Minstrel Show*. At Westminster School in London, where Peter Ustinov was one of his classmates, he started to write and stage revues. His search for a pianist led him to Donald Swann (b. Donald Ibrahim Swann, 30 September 1923, Llanelli, Wales, d. 23 March 1994, London, England), and their first revue together was *Go To It*. At Oxford University in 1940 Flanders played in and directed several productions for the Dramatic Society and made his professional debut as Valentine in Shaw's *You Never Can Tell*, at the Oxford Playhouse. In 1943, while serving in the Royal Navy Volunteer Reserve, having survived the infamous convoys to Russia, he was struck down by poliomyelitis. Three years later he was discharged from hospital, in a wheelchair, and with a full beard which he retained for the rest of his life. Unable to resume a normal acting career, Flanders turned to writing and broadcasting. He contributed lyrics to several West End revues, in collaboration with Swann, including *Penny Plain* (1951), *Airs On A Shoestring* (1953) and *Fresh Airs* (1956). Flanders also appeared extensively on radio, and later, television, in programmes ranging from sports commentary to poetry readings, and including a spell of two years as chairman of *The Brains Trust*. His translation of Stravinsky's *Soldier's Tale* (with Kitty Black) became the standard English version, and his concert performance of it with Peter Ustinov and Sir Ralph Richardson was a surprise sell-out at the Royal Festival Hall in 1956. After successfully entertaining their friends at parties with their own songs, Flanders and Swann decided to perform professionally, so on New Year's Eve 1956, they opened their own two-man show, *At The Drop Of A Hat*, at the intimate New Lindsey Theatre, Notting Hill, west London, moving three weeks later into the West End's Fortune Theatre. The show was a smash hit and ran for over two years. It was reported that Princess Margaret attended a performance, and returned the following week with the Queen and the Duke of Edinburgh. With Flanders' urbane image contrasting with Swann's almost schoolboy enthusiasm, they introduced songs such as 'The Hippopotamus ('Mud, Mud, Glorious Mud')', 'Misalliance', 'A Gnu', and 'Madeira M'Dear?'. Two albums from the show were released, the earlier mono recording being preferable to the later stereo issue from the last night of the London run. In 1959 the show opened on Broadway, billed as 'An After-Dinner Farrago', and later

toured the USA, Canada and the UK. In 1963 at the Haymarket Theatre, London, they presented a fully revised version entitled *At The Drop Of Another Hat*, which included songs such as 'The Gas-Man Cometh', 'First And Second Law' and 'Bedstead Men'. During 1964/5 they toured Australia, New Zealand and Hong Kong, before returning to the West End in 1965, and yet again, to New York in the following year. Meanwhile, Flanders was still continuing with his other work, writing, broadcasting and performing theatrical speech recitals. He published *Creatures Great And Small*, a children's book of verses about animals and, together with Swann, released an album of animal songs entitled *The Bestiary Of Flanders And Swann*. Flanders was awarded the OBE in 1964. After the partnership broke up in 1967, Swann, who was born of Russian parents, continued to compose. In the 50s he had written the music for revues such as *Pay The Piper* and *Wild Thyme*, but in later years his music reflected his religious beliefs (he was a Quaker) and his love of Greece, and many other interests. He was still working right up to the time he died from cancer in 1994. In that same year, a musical celebration of the works of Michael Flanders and Donald Swann, entitled *Under Their Hats*, was presented at the King's Head Theatre in London.

● ALBUMS: *At The Drop Of A Hat* (Parlophone 1957)★★★★, *The Bestiary Of Flanders And Swann* (Parlophone 1961)★★★, *At The Drop Of Another Hat* (Parlophone 1964)★★★.

● COMPILATIONS: *A Review Of Revues* (EMI 1975)★★★, *Tried By Centre Court* (Note 1977)★★★, *The Complete Flanders & Swann* 3-CD set (EMI 1991)★★★★.

● VIDEOS: *The Only Flanders And Swann Video* (PMI 1992).

● FURTHER READING: all by Donald Swann *The Space Behind The Bars*. *Swann's Way Out*. *Swann's Way-A-Life In Song* (autobiography).

FLASHDANCE

Alex Owens (Jennifer Beals) yearns to be a ballet star, and is encouraged and coached by former classical dancer, Hanna Long (Lilia Skala). However, until the real thing comes along, there is always the erotic disco dancing in the evening, and a day job working as a female welder in a Pittsburg factory. Nick (Michael Nouri), the foreman, is her boyfriend, and Alex puts a brick through his window just to remind him, after he has been seen with another girl (it was his sister). Life can be tough, but Hanna's death inspires Alex to pass the audition and finally achieve her dream. With a screenplay (Tom Hedley and Joe Eszterhas) like that, no wonder the critics saw this film as a series of rock videos, especially as it is full of slick, gaudy images (choreography: Jeffrey Hornaday) and a super-high energy score, composed mainly by Giorgio Moroder, one of the most successful and inventive dance music producers of the 80s. The numbers include 'Imagination' and 'Gloria' (performed by Laura Branigan), 'Flashdance ... What A Feeling' (Irene Cara), 'I'll Be Here Where The Heart Is' (Kim Carnes), 'Seduce Me Tonight' (Cycle V), 'Lady, Lady, Lady' (Joe Esposito), 'Manhunt' (Karen Kamon), 'Love Theme From Flashdance' (Helen St. John), 'Maniac' (Michael Sembello), 'He's A Dream' (Shandi), 'Romeo' (Donna Summer), 'It's Just Begun' (Jimmy Castor and the Jimmy Castor Bunch), 'I Love

Rock 'N' Roll' (Joan Jett And The Blackhearts), and somewhat incongruously, Hoagy Carmichael and Ned Washington's oldie, 'The Nearness Of You'. Directed by Adrian Lyne and produced by PolyGram Records for Paramount in 1983, *Flashdance* was immensely successful worldwide, grossing over $36 million at the North American box office alone. The soundtrack album won a Grammy Award and spent 10 weeks at the top of the US chart, and there was another Grammy for Moroder's 'Love Theme From Flashdance'. Two number one singles, Irene Cara's 'Flashdance ... What A Feeling' and 'Maniac' sung by Michael Sembello, also came from the score, with the former song (lyric by Keith Forsey) winning an Oscar and other honours. Not surprisingly, there was a Worst Screenplay Razzie nomination for Hedley and Eszterhas.

FLEET'S IN, THE

Blonde bombshell Betty Hutton made her screen debut in this lively, amusing and typically wartime musical which was produced by Paramount in 1942. She plays the best friend of the Countess of Swingland (Dorothy Lamour), a nightclub singer whose methods of dealing with troublesome customers ensure that she does not meet with much aggravation. One of a bunch of visiting sailors, the shy and retiring Casey Kirby (William Holden), is urged by his friends to try to make a breakthrough on behalf of the Navy, which he does - and ends up marrying her. Victor Schertzinger and Johnny Mercer provided a bunch of terrific numbers such as 'Tangerine', which was introduced by vocalists Bob Eberly and Helen O'Connell with the popular Jimmy Dorsey Orchestra, and subsequently proved to be an enormous hit for them. The rest of the songs included 'It's Somebody Else's Moon', 'When You Hear The Time Signal', and 'I Remember You' (all Lamour), 'The Fleet's In' (Betty Jane Rhodes), 'Not Mine' (Hutton and Lamour), and 'If You Build A Better Mousetrap', and 'Arthur Murray Taught Me Dancing In A Hurry' ('To my way of thinkin', it came out stinkin'/I don't know my left from my right') (both Hutton). The other songs were 'Tomorrow You Belong To Uncle Sam' and 'Conga From Honga'. Also in the cast were comedian Eddie Bracken (who winds up with Hutton), Leif Erickson, Cass Daley ('an osteopathic soprano-she sings in the joints'), Barbara Brittan, Gil Lamb, and Rod Cameron. Jack Donahue staged the dances and the director was Victor Schertzinger. Walter DeLeon and Sid Silvers' screenplay was the third time the original story by Walter de Leon had been filmed. Previous efforts in the 30s starred Clara Bow and Mary Carlisle, and there was yet another remake, in 1951, entitled *Sailor Beware*, with Dean Martin and Jerry Lewis.

FLIGHT FROM FOLLY

This bright and breezy musical, one of the last films to be made at Teddington Studios in England, was released by Warner Brothers-First National in 1945. It starred one of the West End's favourite leading ladies, Pat Kirkwood. She plays showgirl Sue Brown who poses as a nurse in order to impress playwright Clinton Clay (Hugh Sinclair) while he is suffering from amnesia. The celebrated British composer Michael Carr contributed the appealing 'Never Like

This Before', 'Miss Brown', and collaborated with Benjamin Frankel on the impressive 'Dream Sequence' during which Sue and Clinton 'find' each other. Frankel composed most of the film's instrumental themes such as 'Symphonic Jazz', 'Harem Dance' and 'Fiesta Dance'. Eric Spear, too, provided much of the film's music, including 'The Sultan', 'Cuban Song', and the spectacular 'The Majorca' song-and-dance finalé. Basil Woon, Lesley Storm, and Katherine Strueby wrote the screenplay which involved chubby comedian Sydney Howard (in his last film role), Marian Spencer, Tamara Desni, A.E. Matthews, Jean Gillie, Charles Goldner and dancers Halama and Konarski. Also taking part were the bands of Edmundo Ros and Don Marino Barreto. The director of this tuneful - and at times, quite hilarious - feature was Herbert Mason.

FLORA, THE RED MENACE

A curious piece in some ways, this show is mainly notable for the first appearance on Broadway of the 19-years-old Liza Minnelli, although she had made her first New York stage appearance two years earlier, Off Broadway, in a revival of *Best Foot Forward*. The production also marked the Broadway debut of the composer John Kander and his lyricist Fred Ebb. Their subsequent enduring relationship with Minnelli would eventually reach its peak in 1972 with the film version of *Cabaret*. *Flora, The Red Menace* opened at New York's Alvin Theatre on 11 May 1965, with a book by George Abbott and Robert Russell, which was based on Lester Atwell's novel, *Love Is Just Around The Corner*. It was set in the early 30s when America was deep in the Depression, and told of Flora (Liza Minnelli), a naive young girl, who, because of her affection for her boy friend, Harry Toukarian (Bob Dishy), joins the Communist Party. She never becomes a totally committed comrade - Charlotte (Cathryn Damon) is far more dedicated to the Red cause, and to Harry for a time - but he resists her advances, and he and Flora resume diplomatic (and affectionate) relations. The best thing about the whole production was the score. Minnelli had several outstanding numbers including the tender 'Dear Love', 'All I Need (Is One Good Break)', 'Knock Knock', and 'Sing Happy'. There was also 'Not Every Day Of The Week', 'Palamino Pal', 'Street Songs', and a few highly hilarious items such as the 'The Flame', 'Express Yourself', and 'Sign Here'. The show existed for 87 performances mainly on the strength of Minnelli, who won the Tony Award for best actress. Somehow it seemed out of place in a Broadway season that included *Fiddler On The Roof, Do I Hear A Waltz?, I Had A Ball*, and *Golden Boy*. A revised production of *Flora, The Red Menace*, with a new book by David Thompson and several additional Kander and Ebb songs, was presented off-Broadway in 1987. That version played in the UK at the Cambridge Arts Theatre (1992) and the Orange Tree Theatre in Richmond, Surrey (1994).

FLORADORA

This is the kind of the show that was all the rage in London and New York as the 20th century dawned. It opened first at the Lyric Theatre in London on 11 November 1899. In Owen Hall's book, *Floradora* is an island in the Phillipines, and also the name of the perfume that is manufactured there by a rich American, Cyrus Gilfain (Charles E. Stevens). The complicated romantic entanglements that take place on the island, and in a castle in Wales - of all places - involve Angela Gilfain (Kate Cutler), Lady Holyrood (Ada Reeve), Dolores (Evie Greene), Frank Abercoed (Melville Stewart), and Arthur Donegal (Edgar Stevens). A private investigator, Arthur Tweedlepunch (Willie Edouin), is instrumental in unravelling the whole thing and making sure that all the lovers find the right and proper partners. The show's score was a collaboration between the composer Leslie Stuart, who also wrote some of the lyrics along with Ernest Boyd-Jones and Paul Rubens. Extra lyrics were provided by Alfred Murray and Frank A. Clement. The production, which ran for an incredible (for the time) 455 performances, attracted a great deal of attention mainly because of its Floradora Girls, a dainty sextette of parasol-twirling young ladies, accompanied by an equal number of straw-hatted young gentlemen. Their speciality song, 'Tell Me Pretty Maiden' ('Are there any more at home like you?'), swept the country, and, when the show reached the USA in 1900, the same number became popular all over again through recordings by Byron G. Harlan, Joe Belmont and the Floradora Girls; and Harry Macdonough with Grace Spencer. *Floradora* did even better in New York than in London, and gave 553 performances at the New Casino Theatre. The show's score contained several other popular items which became the hits of the day on both sides of the Atlantic, including 'I Want to Be A Military Man', 'The Silver Star Of Love', 'When I Leave Town, 'The Shade Of The Palm', 'Tact', 'When You're A Millionaire', and 'The Island Of Love'. There were London revivals in 1915 and 1931, and New York audiences saw the show again in 1920 when it ran for 120 performances.

FLOWER DRUM SONG (FILM MUSICAL)

While being perfectly agreeable - and successful - in the form of the stage musical, which opened on Broadway in 1958, this screen version, released three years later, seemed somewhat precious and quaint, particularly in comparison with the dynamic *West Side Story*, which arrived in US cinemas at around the same time. Joseph Fields and Oscar Hammerstein II were responsible for the stage libretto, which was based on a novel by Chin Y. Lee. Fields' screenplay for the film followed the original closely, telling the story of a mail-order bride, played by Miyoshi Umeki, who travels from Hong Kong to San Francisco for the sole purpose of marrying nightclub owner Sammy Fong (Jack Soo). Ultimately, circumstances work out differently, and she finally finds happiness with student Wang Ta (James Shigeta), while Fong stays true to his long-time girlfriend, Linda Low (Nancy Kwan). Umeki was in the original Broadway cast, and so was Juanita Hall, who gave a delicious performance in the role of Madam Liang. There were several memorable numbers in Richard Rodgers and Oscar Hammerstein's score, including 'I Enjoy Being A Girl' (Kwan), 'You Are Beautiful' (Shigeta), 'Sunday' (Kwan-Soo), 'Love, Look Away' (Sato), 'Chop Suey' (Hall), 'A Hundred Million Miracles' (Umeki-Kam Tong), 'I Am Going To Like It Here' (Umeki), 'Don't

Marry Me' (Umeki-Soo), 'Grant Avenue' (Kwan), and 'The Other Generation' (Fong-Hall-Adiarte). As usual, Hermes Pan's choreography was singled out for praise, as was Russell Metty's photography in Eastman Color and Panavision. Henry Koster was the director for this Universal picture, which, although pleasantly entertaining, dealt with a subject - the problems of adjustment between different generations of the Chinese-American community in the USA - that did not appeal to a wide range of cinema-goers in the early 60s.

FLOWER DRUM SONG (STAGE MUSICAL)

Most of Richard Rodgers and Oscar Hammerstein's blockbuster musicals were adapted from existing works, and this show was based on a novel by Chin Y. Lee. It opened at the St. James Theatre in New York on 1 December 1958, and was the only Broadway show that Gene Kelly directed. Hammerstein's book, written in collaboration with Joseph Fields, is set in San Francisco's Chinatown, and deals in a warm-hearted way with the problems of the Chinese, the Chinese-Americans, and their Americanized children. The difficulties posed by the various generation-gaps and cultures are sympathetically presented in a story of mail-order brides, marriage contracts, and fiendishly clever plot-lines, resulting in the inevitable wedding ceremony. Mei Li (Miyoshi Umeki) is the lady who was delivered via by the US Mail, but she is not the bride. Linda Low (Pat Suzuki) is the lucky married lady, and has one of the show's most popular numbers, 'I Enjoy Being A Girl', as well as the duet 'Sunday', with her groom Sammy Fong (Larry Blyden). The rest of Rodgers and Hammerstein's lovely score included 'You Are Beautiful', 'A Hundred Million Miracles', 'I Am Going To Like It Here', 'Like A God', 'Chop Suey', 'Don't Marry Me', 'Grant Avenue', 'Love Look Away', 'Gliding Through My Memories' and 'The Other Generation'. Juanita Hall played Madame Liang, 'an enthusiastic candidate for American citizenship'. She also starred in Rodgers and Hammerstein's film of *South Pacific*, which was released in the same year as *Flower Drum Song* began its Broadway run of 600 performances. The popular vocalist Anita Ellis was also in the show's cast. She played a nightclub singer, and had the novelty number 'Fan Tan Fannie'. That scene, and the rest of the production, was choreographed by Carol Haney, who introduced 'Hernado's Hideaway' in *The Pajama Game*. The 1960 London production of *Flower Drum Song* had different principal cast members, but Miyoshi Umeki recreated her role for the 1961 film version, which also starred Nancy Kwan.

FLOWERS FOR ALGERNON

Originally tried out in Ontario, Canada, this unusual musical played briefly at the Queen's Theatre in London from 14 June 1979. It was based on the novel of the same name by Daniel Keyes, and had a score by Charles Strouse (music) and David Rogers (lyrics). Rogers also wrote the book, which took most of the blame for the show's early demise. The subject was a tricky one - especially for a musical. Having successfully raised the IQ of a mouse (Algernon), scientists turn their attention to the mentally handicapped Charlie (Michael Crawford). Initially, their experiments turn him into a near-genius, but as the effects of the operation wear off, he returns to his former condition - and makes friends with Algernon. Crawford's sensitive, gentle performance was applauded, and he was well supported by Cheryl Kennedy, the teacher who falls in love with him. The cast also featured Betty Benfield, Sharon Lee Hill, Jeanna L'Esty, George Harris, Ralph Nossek and Aubrey Woods. The score included several admirable songs, such as 'Whatever Time There Is', 'Reading', 'I Got A Friend' and 'No Surprises', along with 'His Name Is Charlie Gordon', 'Some Bright Morning', 'Our Boy Charlie', 'Hey, Look At Me!', 'Midnight Riding', 'Dream Safe With Me', 'I Can't Tell You', 'Now', 'Charlie And Algernon', 'The Maze', 'Charlie' and 'I Really Loved You'. Peter Coe directed, and the show attracted some good notices, but in spite of Crawford's box office appeal, *Flowers For Algernon* was withdrawn after only 28 performances. However, that was a slightly better achievement than the Broadway production, retitled *Charlie And Algernon*, which opened at the Helen Hayes Theatre on 14 September 1980, with P.J. Benjamin and Sandy Faison as the leads, and lasted for only 17 performances. Nevertheless, Strouse and Rogers' score was nominated for a Tony Award, and is preserved in a London cast recording. Cliff Robertson's remarkable performance in the 1968 film version of Daniel Keyes' book, entitled *Charly*, won him an Academy Award.

FLYING COLORS

The American Depression was on the point of ending when this revue opened at the Imperial Theatre in New York on 15 September 1932. With music by Arthur Schwartz and lyrics and sketches by Howard Dietz, who also directed, this was obviously from the same line-up that produced *The Band Wagon*, *Three's A Crowd* and *The Little Show*. The talented cast, an ideal mixture of actors, dancers, comedians, singers, (and one harmonica virtuoso) included Clifton Webb, Charles Butterworth, Tamara Geva, Patsy Kelly, Philip Loeb, Vilma and Buddy Ebsen, Larry Adler, Imogen Coca, and Monette Moore. All the songs were of high quality, but there were three special numbers, 'Alone Together', 'Louisiana Hayride', and the exuberant 'A Shine On Your Shoes', which were destined to endure. The rest of the score included 'Two-Faced Woman', 'A Rainy Day', 'Mother Told Me So', 'Fatal Fascination', 'Meine Klein Akrobat', and 'Smokin' Reefers'. This smart, witty show which dealt with the recent hard times in America, and looked forward to better days (and politicians), was produced by Max Gordon and choreographed by Albertina Rasch. *Flying Colors* stayed around for a decent run of 188 performances, and Buddy Ebsen, a talented hoofer at the time, went on much later to star in the legendary television series *The Beverley Hillbillies*.

FLYING DOWN TO RIO

It is not recorded whether the earth moved, but it certainly should have done when Fred Astaire and Ginger Rogers teamed for the first time in this film which was released in 1933 by RKO. Dolores Del Rio, as the sultry Belinha De Rezende, was supposed to be the star of a story by Cyril Hume, H.W. Hanemann and Erwin Gelsey (from a play by Anne Caldwell), in which she has to choose between the charms of the glamorous American band-leader-aviator Roger Bond (Gene Raymond) and her Brazilian boyfriend Julio Rubeire (Raul Roulien), but Astaire and Rogers stole the film away. The seven white grand pianos on which they danced 'The Carioca', proved to be the launching pad to a glittering future. That number was part of a score by Vincent Youmans (music) and Edward Eliscu and Gus Kahn (lyrics), which also included 'Orchids In The Moonlight' and 'Music Makes Me'. The spectacular 'Flying Down To Rio' sequence featured a bevy of beautiful girls clad in various modes of dress (and undress), performing a series of formation dances while balanced on the wings of biplanes apparently several thousand feet above the city. The choreography for that and the rest of the splendid dance scenes, was by Dave Gould and Hermes Pan, and the film was directed by Thorton Freedland.

FLYING HIGH

Soon after its opening at the Apollo Theatre in New York on 3 March 1930, the celebrated newspaper columnist Walter Winchell dubbed this show, 'The Lindbergh of musical comedies'. That was a reference to its theme which reflected the American public's fascination with the pioneering flights of the late 20s in general, and Charles Lindbergh's 1927 record solo flight to Paris in particular. The creative crew for this trip, composer Ray Henderson, and lyricists Buddy De Sylva and Lew Brown, who also wrote the book with John McGowan, had already had some mileage from other US fads and fancies in previous shows such as *Good News!* (football and dancing), *Hold Everything!* (boxing), and *Follow Thru* (golf). Apparently, the plot was not complete until the show went into rehearsal, but it eventually turned out to be a story about an aeroplane mechanic, Rusty Krause (Bert Lahr), who carelessly takes to the air in a plane that was supposed to be piloted by Tod Addison (Oscar Shaw). Not only does he take off, but he stays up there long enough to create a world endurance record simply because he does not know how to get down again. Todd does get airborne himself, but is forced to make a parachute jump. In the interests of the show's romantic scenario he lands on a New York roof belonging to the lovely Eileen Cassidy (Grace Brinkley). Kate Smith, the powerful singer, was also in the cast, and had a show-stopper with 'Red Hot Chicago'. The rest of the typically De Sylva ballad and Henderson score - lively and entertaining, with the occasional classy balled - included 'I'll Know Him', 'Thank Your Father', 'Good For You - Bad for Me', 'Without Love', 'Mrs. Krauses's Blue-Eyed Baby Boy', and 'Wasn't It Beautiful While It Lasted?' The show was a big hit and ran for 357 performances, mainly owing to Lahr's hilarious antics. He starred with Charlotte Greenwood and Pat O'Brien in the 1931 film version.

FOLIES BERGÈRE DE PARIS

From the moment when the opening titles fade and Maurice Chevalier, complete with familiar straw boater, launches into the jaunty 'Valentine' (Herbert Reynolds-Henri Christine), all sense of belief is necessarily suspended while he plays an entertainer who is hired by a wealthy businessman to substitute for him at a swanky social occasion. He fools all the guests except for the busy executive's wife (Merle Oberon) who would know her husband anywhere, or would she? Chevalier played both leading male roles, of course, and Ann Sothern was his feisty mistress. Also in the cast were Walter Byron, Eric Blore, and Lumsden Hare. Jack Stern and Jack Meskill wrote most of the songs which included 'Rhythm Of The Rain' (with Chevalier and Sothern plus lots of girls and umbrellas), 'I Was Lucky', 'Singing A Happy Song', and 'Au Revoir, L'Amour'. The best of the rest was Burton Lane and Harold Adamson's 'You Took The Words Right Out Of My Mouth'. Bess Meredyth and Hal Long wrote the screenplay which was adapted from a play by Rudolph Lothar and Hans Adler by Jessie Enst, which was also used as the basis for two other movies, *That Night In Rio* (1941) and *On The Riviera* (1951). Roy Del Routh directed *Folies Bergère De Paris*, which was released in 1935, and dance director Dave Gould won an Oscar for his staging of the spectacular 'Straw Hat' finalé.

FOLLIES

Often cited as one of Stephen Sondheim's more 'accessible' shows, *Follies* opened at the Winter Garden Theatre in New York on 4 April 1971. James Goldman's book is set on the stage of the derelict, soon-to-be-demolished Weismann Theatre. For this first, and last, reunion party, showgirls who were part of the legendary *Weismann Follies* some 30 years ago, return - as Dimitri Weismann (Arnold Moss) himself puts it - 'to stumble through a song or two, and lie about ourselves . . . a little'. Two of them, Phyllis Stone (Alexis Smith) and Sally Plummer (Dorothy Collins), married young stage-door-Johnnies way back then. Benjamin Stone (John McMartin) wed Phyllis in spite of having a brief fling with Sally, who eventually ended up with Buddy Plummer (Gene Nelson). In the intervening years, both couples have been desperately unhappy. Although Ben has done well for himself, and risen to be a wealthy diplomat, he looks upon Phyllis as an accessory to his jet-setting lifestyle. Buddy is a salesman, permanently on the road, and with a girl in every town. Sally stays at home reading her Harlequin novels, convinced that she married the wrong man. Now they have returned to this theatre, with all its memories, and as the night progresses each one of them is confronted - in a series of flashbacks - with a ghost of their former selves. The reminiscences and recriminations are constantly interrupted by contributions from other ex-*Follies* performers attending this often dark, soul-searching soirée, some of them pastiche numbers which eerily re-create that half-forgotten era. Solange (Fifi D'Orsay) slinks sexily through 'Ah, Paris'; wheelchair-bound Heidi Schiller (Justine Johnston), accompanied by her younger self (Victoria Mallory), evokes memories of Sigmund Romberg with 'One More Kiss'; and two memorable anthems of survival - Hattie Walker (Ethel Shutta) reveals the desperation and heartbreak of the common chorus girl in the show-stopping 'Broadway Baby', while Carlotta Campion (played by 40s movie star Yvonne De Carlo) triumphantly insists 'I'm Still Here'. And then there are The Whitmans, a song-and-dance duo (Marcie Stringer and Charles Welch) who eagerly take on the tongue-twist-ing 'Listen To The Rain On The Roof', and veteran Stella (Mary McCarty) refusing to believe the image that cruel glass reveals in 'Who's That Woman?' ('the mirror number'). Ben, Phyllis, Buddy, and Sally share 'Don't Look At Me', 'Waiting For The Girls Upstairs', 'The Road You Didn't Take', 'In Buddy's Eyes', 'Too Many Mornings', 'The Right Girl', 'Could I Leave You' (Phyllis finally considers divorce), before having the second section of the final 'Loveland' sequence to themselves. Entitled 'The Folly Of Youth', it consisted of 'You're Gonna Love Tomorrow' (Ben and Phyllis), 'Love Will See Us Through' (Buddy and Sally), 'The God-Why-Don't-You-Love-Me Blues' ('Buddy's Folly'), 'Losing My Mind' ('Sally's Folly'), 'The Story Of Lucy And Jessie' ('Phyllis's Folly'), and 'Live, Laugh, Love' ('Ben's Folly'). As dawn breaks, emotionally shattered and with no illusions left, the two couples go back to try and pick up their previous lives, and find what consolation they can in each other. The bulldozers await: Roscoe (Michael Bartlett) has brought on his 'Beautiful Girls' for the very last time. *Follies* was a spectacular and glamorous production, and opinions vary widely as to why it was not successful. Sondheim himself is said to feel that there were too many pastiche numbers, while co-director (with Hal Prince) and choreographer Michael Bennett blamed the book. In any event, the show ran for 522 performances and collected the kudos: New York Drama Critics Award for best musical, and Tony Awards for best score, director, choreographer, scenic design (Boris Aronson), costumes (Florence Klotz), lighting (Tharon Musser), and actress (Alexis Smith).

Follies In Concert with the New York Philharmonic played two nights, 6 and 7 September 1985, at the Lincoln Centre's Avery Fisher Hall in New York, with an all-star cast which included Barbara Cook (Sally), George Hearn (Ben), Mandy Patinkin (Buddy), Lee Remick (Phyllis), Elaine Stritch, Liliane Montevecchi, Carol Burnett, Phyllis Newman, Betty Comden, and Adolph Green. Two years later, Cameron Mackintosh's fully staged London production, which was streamlined, extensively re-written, and incorporated some different numbers, starred Julia McKenzie (Sally), Diana Rigg (Phyllis), Daniel Massey (Ben), David Healy (Buddy), Dolores Gray, Adele Leigh, Pearl Carr And Teddy Johnson, and ran for 18 months. Productions at the Theater Des Westens in Berlin (1991), and at Britain's Leicester Haymarket Theatre (1994), reverted to the 1971 US concept, with theatre buffs predicting (perhaps unwisely) that Mackintosh's radical revisions would never be seen again. When Julia McKenzie (Sally) and Pearl Carr and Teddy Johnson (The Whitmans), reprised their 1987 London performances for a BBC Radio 2 *Follies* which played the Theatre Royal, Drury Lane, on 8 December 1996, they were among the few artists who have appeared in both versions. Also cast in this broadcast concert were Denis Quilley (Ben), Donna McKechnie (Phyllis), Ron Moody (Buddy), Joan Savage, Elizabeth Seal, Libby Morris, Eileen Page, Shona Lindsay, David Bardsley, Lori Haley Fox, Michael Cahill, Angela Richards, and Carrie Ellis. On 15 April 1998, the Paper Mill Playhouse, New Jersey, presented the first major New York-area staging of the whole show since the 1971 original. It starred as Sally (Donna McKechnie), Phyllis

(Dee Hoty), Ben (Laurence Guittard), Buddy (Tony Roberts), Solange (Liliane Montevecchi), The Whitmans (Donald Saddler and Natalie Mosco), Stella (Phyllis Newman), Carlotta (Ann Miller), Hattie (Kaye Ballard), with Eddie Bracken as Dimitri Weismann. It resulted in *Follies: The Complete Recording*, which contains every piece of music written for the show. There were some items missing on the original 1971 cast album, but this new set not only has the complete score, but includes an appendix of eight numbers, including the famous 'Can That Boy Fox-Trot', that were cut from the show during the various stages of its life. All are orchestrated by Sondheim's long time collaborator, Jonathan Tunick.

FOLLOW A STAR

Although the music and lyrics for this piece were by Vivian Ellis and Douglas Furber, this was by no means a typical Ellis show. The reason was the dominating presence in the cast of the American entertainer Sophie Tucker. It was Tucker's second appearance in the London theatre, (as opposed to music halls and clubs), and her first book musical (she had played in the revue *Round In 50* in 1922). This time she brought along her two regular songwriters, Jack Yellen and Ted Shapiro, just in case Ellis and Furber did not come up with her particular kind of goods. Ironically, and much to Ellis's delight, the hit of the show, and the number which became so popular that she had to close with it, was 'If Your Kisses Can't Hold The Man You Love', which had music by Ellis and a lyric by Yellen. *Follow A Star* opened at the Winter Garden Theatre in London on 17 September 1930, with a book by Furber and Dion Titheradge. It was directed and choreographed by Jack Hulbert who also played a leading role. Hulbert had appeared in so many successful shows with his wife Cicely Courtneidge, but this time she had temporarily deserted musical comedy for the revue *Folly to Be Wise*, and left Hulbert to deal with Tucker, whose role in the show was as a cabaret singer (Georgia Madison) who is elevated to better things when she inherits a title and becomes Lady Bohun. Jack Hulbert played Bobby Hilary, the lover of Georgia's daughter, Merrie Boon (Betty Davies). Ellis's music was as charming and delightful as ever in songs such as 'Don't Wear Your Heart On Your Sleeve', 'The First Weekend In June', 'The English Gentlemen', and 'You Do The Singing'. Tucker's numbers included 'Follow A Star', 'I Can Never Think Of The Words', and 'That's Where The South Begins', but they were cut when she left the show early in December ('If Your Kisses Can't Hold The Man You Love' stayed in) to be replaced by Maisie Gay when it reopened later in the month. The revised production had a disappointing run, closing after only 118 performances, and losing a good deal of its investment.

FOLLOW THAT DREAM

This 1962 venture revealed a further reduction in the quality of Elvis Presley's films. The plot revolves around a group of homesteaders whose business venture on a Florida beach is threatened by local mobsters. Naturally good triumphs over evil, during which Presley contributes seven songs, six of which were recorded on 5 July 1961.

The seventh, 'On Top Of Old Smokey' was cut on the film set itself. 'What A Wonderful Life', 'I'm Not The Marrying Kind', 'Angel' and the film's title track made up the *Follow That Dream* EP which reached number 15 in the US singles' chart and also entered the UK Top 40. 'A Whistling Tune' surfaced on the subsequent *Kid Galahad* EP while 'Sound Advice' appeared on 1965's *Elvis For Everyone*. In a rare deviation from the norm, RCA Records did not issue a single from the soundtrack, suggesting even they felt that nothing from the film's material was strong enough to warrant such a high-profile release.

FOLLOW THAT GIRL

A kind of hectic musical tour of London, this show was adapted by composer Julian Slade and Dorothy Reynolds from their 1952 production, *Christmas In King Street*. It opened at the Vaudeville Theatre in London on 17 March 1960. The light and frothy story concerned Victoria (Susan Hampshire), whose parents, Mr. and Mrs. Gilchrist (James Cairness and Patricia Routledge), want her to marry one of two rich businessmen, Wilberforce (Robert MacBaine) or Tancred (Philip Guard). She gives them the slip, and, after a long and hectic chase, is finally captured by a policeman, Tom (Peter Gilmore), who takes her into custody, and marries her. Slade and Reynolds's score is generally regarded as among their very best work. The songs included 'Tra La La', 'Follow That Girl', 'Life Must Go On', 'Waiting For Our Daughter', 'Shopping In Kensington', 'Solitary Stranger', 'Lovely Meeting You At Last', 'I'm Away', 'Where Shall I Find My Love?', 'Three Victorian Mermaids', 'One, Two, Three, One', 'Doh Ray Me', and 'Taken For A Ride'. Gilmore and Hampshire both went on to television super-stardom, he in *The Onedin Line*, and she in *The Forsyth Saga* and *The Pallisers*. Grazina Frame, who was also in the cast of *Follow That Girl*, had her moment of glory when she starred in Lionel Bart's *Blitz!* in 1962. In spite of its fun story and quality score, *Follow That Girl* received mixed notices, but had a reasonable run of 211 performances. Hardly in the same league as the same authors' *Salad Days* (2,283), but then that sort of success usually only comes along once in a lifetime.

FOLLOW THE BOYS

This 1962 film starred Connie Francis, one of the most popular singers of the pre-Beatles era. She had 16 US Top 10 entries prior to this role which succeeded her part in the previous year's *Where The Boys Are*. Paula Prentiss, Danny Robin and Russ Tamblyn (veteran of *West Side Story* and *Tom Thumb*) were also featured in a light-hearted musical wherein four girls arrange to meet their sweethearts at a port in the south of France. When the ship fails to dock, the quartet travel to its next destination in an old car they buy for the occasion. The appeal of *Follow The Boys* rests on Francis's distinctive *métier* and she contributes six songs including 'Italian Lullaby', 'Waiting For Billy' and 'Tonight's My Night'. Her rendition of the title track provided another US Top 20 entry, the last time the singer achieved this feat. Francis' once pre-eminent position was then taken up by a new generation of acts.

FOLLOW THE FLEET

After their triumph in *Top Hat* in 1935, Fred Astaire and Ginger Rogers did it again with more or less the same artistic team a year later in *Follow The Fleet*. Mark Sandrich (director), Hermes Pan (dance director) and songwriter Irving Berlin, all combined for another feast of song and dance. Apart from one number, 'Let's Face The Music And Dance', Fred traded in his top hat, white tie and tails for a sailor suit in Dwight Taylor and Allan Scott's screenplay which was based on Hubert Osborne's Broadway play *Shore Leave*. The central love story concerns spinster Connie Martin (Harriet Hilliard) who falls for Bilge Smith (Randolph Scott) in such a big way that she arranges for a ship to be salvaged for him after his discharge from the US Navy. Harriet reveals the depths of her love for Bilge via two beautiful but surprisingly melancholy ballads 'Get Thee Behind Me, Satan' and 'But Where Are You?', but that is where the film's heartaches began and ended. On a much brighter note, Fred and Ginger, as Bake Baker and Sherry Martin the former dance team which split up when Bake enlisted in the navy, meet again at the Paradise Ballroom in San Francisco, and rekindle the old magic in an effort to raise money to salvage the ship. They dance everybody's cares away to glorious Berlin numbers such as 'We Saw The Sea', 'I'd Rather Lead A Band', 'Let Yourself Go', and 'I'm Putting All My Eggs In One Basket'. Future stars Tony Martin, Lucille Ball, and Betty Grable made brief but effective appearances in this RKO release which some critics thought was too long at 110 minutes. The public did not seem to agree and flocked to see *Follow The Fleet* in great numbers.

FOLLOW THE GIRLS

This big wartime stage musical hit on both sides of the Atlantic, first saw the light of day at the New Century Theatre in New York on 8 April 1944. Guy Bolton, together with Eddie Davis and Fred Thompson, wrote the libretto which concerns Bubbles LaMarr (Gertrude Niesen in her only book musical), a burlesque stripper whose career takes off in a big way at the Spotlight Club, a sanctuary for servicemen in Long Island, USA. Her boyfriend, Goofy Gale (Jackie Gleason), cannot get in to see her because, physically speaking, the army just does not want him. As this is a Bolton book (he wrote the jolly Princess Theatre japes with P.G. Wodehouse and Jerome Kern), and Gleason is also involved, Goofy complicates the issue by stealing, not an admiral or a colonel's uniform, but one that is worn by a Wave. The show's setting gave ample opportunities for lots of singing and dancing, and some of the supporting characters had 'Damon Runyon'-type names such as Dinky Riley and Spud Doolittle. Niesen made a big impression every night with 'I Wanna Get Married', and the rest of the score, by Phil Charig (music) and Dan Shapiro and Milton Pascal (lyrics), included 'You're Perf', 'Twelve O'Clock And All's Well', 'Follow The Girls', 'I'm Gonna Hang My Hat', 'Out For No Good', and 'Tomorrow Will Be Yesterday Tomorrow'. *Follow The Girls* ran for over two years, a total of 882 performances, in New York, and played 572 shows at His Majesty's Theatre in London, where the popular local comedian Arthur Askey

starred as Goofy, with Evelyn Dall as Bubbles. Another member of the West End Cast was Wendy Toye, who also directed the piece. She went on to become one of the British theatre's most admired and respected directors.

FOLLOW THRU

Opening at New York's 46th Street theatre on 9 January 1929, and sub-titled 'A Musical Slice Of Country Life', this was another in a series of sporty shows (*Good News!* and *Hold Everything!* were about football and boxing) that songwriters De Sylva, Brown And Henderson had such success with in the 20s. *Follow Thru*'s book, by De Sylva and Laurence Schwab, turned the spotlight on golf. The show was the first big break on Broadway for comedian Jack Haley, who made a career out of playing shy diffident characters who are usually pursued by pretty women. This time he is the object of affection for Angie Howard (Zelma O'Neal), and when they do get together they give the evening a big lift with their version of one of the composers' all-time standards, 'Button Up Your Overcoat' ('Eat an apple ev'ry day, Get to bed by three, Take good care of yourself, You belong to me.'). Meanwhile, back on the greens and in the locker-room, Lora Moore (Irene Delroy) and Ruth Van Horn (Madeline Cameron) are locked in combat - for the country club's women's championship, and the chance to go round the course forever with the handsome, good guy, with a low-handicap, Jerry Downs (John Barker). Lora comes out top in both events. Another winner here, who gave the show a big lift, was 19 years old tap-dancer Eleanor Powell in her first book musical, following her Broadway debut in *The Optimists* revue in 1928. She went on to Hollywood fame in the 30s and 40s. De Sylva, Brown And Henderson's songs, which were so typical of the happy-go-lucky 20s period, included 'My Lucky Star', 'You Wouldn't Fool Me, Would You?', 'I Want To Be Bad', 'Then I'll Have Time For You', and, of course, the smash-hit 'Button Up Your Overcoat', which became all the rage through various recordings by Helen Kane, Paul Whiteman, Fred Waring's Pennsylvanians, and Ruth Etting.

The show sang and danced its happy way to an impressive 403 performances in New York, and the London edition, *Follow Through*, which starred Leslie Henson, Ivy Tresmond, and Elsie Randolph, added another 148. Jack Haley and Zelma O'Neal recreated their original roles for the 1930 film version.

FOLLY TO BE WISE

This popular revue, devised by Jack Hulbert and Paul Murray, opened on 8 January 1931 at the Piccadilly Theatre in London. Hulbert did not appear in it himself - at the time he was in the Vivian Ellis musical comedy, *Follow A Star*. His wife, Cicely Courtneidge was present, though, and right at the top of her form. She was joined in the cast by Nelson Keys and Ivor McLaren, together with a couple of visitors from the USA, Mary Eaton and J. Albert Traherne. The music and lyrics were provided by a variety of songwriters, including Vivian Ellis, Noel Gay, Harry Graham, Bert Kalmar, Harry Ruby, Herman Hupfeld, and Dion Titheradge. Probably the best-known song to emerge from the show, at least as far as British audiences are concerned, was 'All The King's Horses' (Noel Gay and Harry Graham), which was given the full Courtneidge treatment, and became extremely popular for artists such as Jack Hylton And His Orchestra, The New Mayfair Orchestra conducted by Ray Noble, The Big Four, and, much later, Dennis Lotis with the Ted Heath Orchestra. Some of the other numbers included 'Looking For A Sunbeam', 'Three Little Words' (Kalmar-Ruby), and 'Sing Something Simple' (Hupfield). The show ran for 257 performances, which, for this kind of production in the days of general economic unrest in Britain during the early 30s, was considered to be a more than satisfactory state of affairs.

FOOTE, IRENE
(see Castle, Vernon And Irene)

FOOTLIGHT PARADE
Following their highly successful teaming in *42nd Street* and *Gold Diggers Of 1932*, Dick Powell and Ruby Keeler were joined by a new boy to musicals - James Cagney - in this backstage saga which was released by Warner Brothers in 1933. Cagney plays a slick, hyperactive dance director of 'prologues', those miniature 'live' productions which were inserted between showings of main feature movies in the early days of the talkies. In Manuel Seff and James Seymour's screenplay for *Footlight Parade*, Chester Kent (Cagney) stages three of these creations, each of which has its own title song. The first, a somewhat saucy piece entitled 'Honeymoon Hotel' (Harry Warren-Al Dubin), is thought to be a follow-up from the 'Shuffle Off To Buffalo' number in *42nd Street*. Just married Powell and Keeler arrive at the hotel (where every guest's name is 'Smith'!), only to find their entire family is there to greet them. 'By A Waterfall' (Sammy Fain-Irving Kahal) is a dream sequence during which Powell and Keeler 'imagine' scores of beautiful girls swimming and relaxing in a gigantic pool which had glass sides so that head of photography George Barnes could shoot the scene from all angles. The 'five tier' finalé rounds off one of the most spectacular production numbers of any film musical. The final 'prologue', the dramatic 'Shanghai Lil' (Warren-Dubin), sees Cagney, as a sailor, scouring Shanghai saloons and opium dens for his Lil (Keeler). When he finds her in a sleazy club they perform a tap dance atop the bar before he is called back to his ship, accompanied by a sailor who looks remarkably like . . . Shanghai Lil. Fain and Kahal also contributed 'Sittin' On A Backyard Fence', and 'Ah, The Moon Is Here'. Among the rest of the cast were Joan Blondell, Guy Kibbee, Frank McHugh, Claire Dodd, Ruth Donnelly, and Hugh Herbert. *Footlight Parade*, which was directed by Lloyd Bacon and choreographed by Busby Berkeley in his own highly innovative style, remains one of the most memorable of all movie musicals.

FOOTLOOSE
Always on the lookout for deep psychological meanings, even in something as frivolous as a film musical, some critics saw this movie as an attempt to combine the frustrations of *Rebel Without A Cause* with the more recent disco-style *Flashdance*. On a less pretentious level, and prefaced by an exciting opening sequence of dancing feet moving to urgent, restless rhythms, Dean Pitchford's screenplay concerns Ethel and Ren MacCormack (Frances Lee McCain and Kevin Bacon), a mother and son who arrive in the small mid-Western US town of Bomont. Once there, they discover that owing to the influence of the 'hellfire' local preacher, the Reverend Shaw Moore (John Lithgow), rock 'n' roll music, dancing, and certain forms of literature, are banned. Big city boy Ren not only refuses to abide by these 'unreasonable' laws, he also attracts the attention of Ariel Moore (Lori Singer), the preacher's daughter, and with friends Willard (Chris Penn) and Rusty (Sarah Jessica Parker), they go to a disco over the state line. On the return journey, it turns out that during a similar trip around five years ago, Ariel's brother - the preacher's son - was killed, thereby invoking the town disco ban. From then on, there is much burning of library books, re-examining of actions and beliefs, and establishing of mutual respect, before Ren is eventually allowed to organize a dance - outside the town limits. Dianne Wiest, John Laughlin, and Elizabeth Gorcey, Jim Youngs, Douglas Dirkson, Lynne Marta, and Arthur Rosenberg, were also amongst the cast, and most of the appealing songs, such as 'Footloose' and 'I'm Free (Heaven Helps The Man)' (performed by Kenny Loggins), 'The Girl Gets Around' (Sammy Hagar), 'Dancing In The Streets' (Shalamar), 'Holding Out For A Hero' (Bonnie Tyler), 'Never' (Moving Pictures), 'Somebody's Eyes' (Karla Bonoff), 'Let's Hear It For The Boy' (Deniece Williams), 'Almost Paradise ... Love Theme From Footloose' (Mike Reno and Ann Wilson, lead singers of Loverboy and Heart, respectively), were written by lyricist Dean Pitchford in collaboration with Loggins, Hagar, Bill Wolfer, Jim Steinman, Michael Gore, Tom Snow, and Eric Carmen. The rest of the numbers included 'Waiting For A Girl Like You', by Mick Jones and Lou Gramm, performed by Foreigner, 'Hurts So Good', by John Mellencamp and George Green, performed by Mellencamp, and 'Bang Your Head (Mental Health)', by Carlos and Tony Cavazo, Kevin DuBrow, and Frankie Banali, performed by Quiet Riot. Directed by veteran Hollywood choreographer-director Herbert Ross, choreographed by Lynne Taylor-Corbett, this likeable 1984 Paramount release was a box office hit, grossing $34 million in the USA and Canada alone. The soundtrack album spent 10 weeks at the top of the US charts, and both 'Footloose' (Loggins) and 'Let's Hear It For The Boy' (Deniece Williams), went to number 1, and were nominated for Oscars. Mike Reno and Ann Wilson's 'Almost Paradise' also charted.

On 22 October 1998, a $6.5 million stage version of *Footloose* opened at the Richard Rodgers Theatre in New York. Adapted by Dean Pitchford and director Walter Bobbie from Pitchford's original screenplay, it had Stephen Lee Anderson (Rev. Shaw Moore), Jeremy Kushnier (Ren McCormack), Catherine Cox (Ethel McCormack), Jennifer Laura Thompson (Ariel Moore), Dee Hoty (Vi Moore, Ariel's mother), Stacy Francis (Rusty), Billy Hartung (Chuck Cranston), and Tom Plotkin (Willard Hewitt). Several of the film songs were retained, including those three former chart entries, with Pitchford and composer Tom Snow providing some new material, 'On Any Sunday', 'I Can't Stand Still', 'Learning To Be Silent', 'Heaven Help Me', 'Still Rockin'', 'Can You Find It In Your Heart?', 'Mama Says', 'Dancing Is Not A Crime', and 'I Confess'. Initial critical reaction compared it unfavourably with the movie.

FOR ME AND MY GAL

If asked to name Judy Garland's most famous movie partner, most people would plump for Mickey Rooney, but her partnership with Gene Kelly in films like this one, together with *Summer Stock* and *The Pirate*, were just as endearing in their way. *For And My Gal*, released by MGM in 1942, was Kelly's first film appearance, although he arrived on set at the age of 30 direct from his success in the title role of Richard Rodgers and Lorenz Hart's Broadway musical *Pal Joey*. In this film, which had a screenplay by Richard Sherman, Fred Finklehoffe, and Sid Silvers, Kelly is cast as Harry Palmer, an ambitious vaudeville song-and-dance-man who falls for Jo Hayden (Garland). They form a double act and dream of winning the ultimate prize - a chance to perform at the Palace Theatre. However, when they eventually achieve their goal, World War I looms large and Kelly receives his draft notice. Desperate not to miss his big career chance, he deliberately cripples his hand. His actions help him to avoid the draft but appall Garland and they split up. After suffering a crisis of conscience, Kelly travels overseas to entertain the troops, and while there becomes something of a hero. His moral transformation complete, the couple are reunited on the stage of the Palace Theatre after the war. George Murphy co-starred, and also featured were Marta Eggerth, Ben Blue, Horace (later Stephen) McNally, Keenan Wynn, and Richard Quine. Garland and Kelly sang a delightful version of 'For Me And My Gal' (Edgar Leslie-Ray Goetz-George W. Meyer), and the rest of the score - a substantial collection of memorable old numbers - included 'When You Wore A Tulip' (Jack Mahoney-Percy Wenrich), 'After You've Gone' (Turner Layton-Henry Creamer), 'Ballin' The Jack' (Jim Burris-Chris Smith), 'Oh You Beautiful Doll' (Seymour Brown-Nat D. Ayer), 'How Ya Gonna Keep 'Em Down On The Farm?' (Walter Donaldson-Sam M. Lewis-Joe Young), and 'It's A Long Way To Tipperary' (Harry Williams-Jack Judge). The many dance sequences were staged by Bobby Connelly (with uncredited assistance from Kelly), and the film, which was a product of Arthur Freed's legendary MGM unit, was directed by Busby Berkeley.

FORBIDDEN BROADWAY

An annual revue conceived by Gerard Alessandrini, who also writes his own, sometimes hilarious, lyrics to popular show tunes in an effort to lampoon everything and anyone who dares to appear on the New York and London musical stage. The show was first performed as a cabaret revue at Palsson's Supper Club in New York on 15 January 1982. It moved off-Broadway in the following year, and settled in the 125-seater Theatre East. Annual editions have followed. Alessandrini's early targets included *Annie* and *Evita* (Andrew Lloyd Webber and Tim Rice were like manna from heaven to this revue), along with Broadway

icons such as Ethel Merman, Mary Martin, Stephen Sondheim, and Tommy Tune. Later, highlights included 'The Ladies Who Screech' by 'Elaine Stritch'; 'My Souvenir Things', sung by 'Cameron Mackintosh' as he flogs T-shirts and coffee mugs; 'I've Strained In Vain To Train Madonna's Brain' (a hint of *My Fair Lady*?); 'I Get A Kick Out Of Me' by 'Patti LuPone'; shades of *On The Town*, and a dig at the celebrated director-choreographer Jerome Robbins, in 'Jerome, Jerome, I'm A Hell Of A Guy'; 'Julie Andrews's' 'I Couldn't Hit That Note' (to the tune of 'I Could Have Danced All Night'); a chandelier and a helicopter, representing *The Phantom Of The Opera* and *Miss Saigon*, in the merry duet 'Anywhere You Can Fly, I Can Fly Higher' (from Irving Berlin's 'Anything You Can Do, I Can Do Better'); and another stab at Lloyd Webber in which a Michael Ball clone converts the powerful ballad, 'Love Changes Everything' (from *Aspects Of Love*) into 'I, I Sleep With Everyone'. Michael Crawford, Barbra Streisand, and Broadway revivals such as *The Most Happy Fella*, *Guys And Dolls*, and the more contemporary shows, especially *Les Misérables*, all get the treatment. The 1992 edition presented some of the 'Best' of the last decade, and in the following year the show won the 1993 Lucille Lortel Award for oustanding musical, and was still going strong - blessed with four 'Carol Channings' (only two of which were female). Alessandrini's 1994 targets included *Kiss Of The Spider Woman*, *Blood Brothers*, *Sunset Boulevard* and *She Loves Me*. In 1989, a slightly Anglicized version had a brief run at London's Fortune Theatre, and a similar production, *Forbidden Pittsburgh*, which was not associated with Alessandrini, reigned in that city in the late 80s. In 1997, *Forbidden Broadway Strikes Back!* ('We shall steal a little bit of every show in our desire . . . to abuse them.') was hailed as Alessandrini's best effort, and targeted the *Show Boat* (*Slow Boat*) revival, *Victor/Victoria*, *Rent*, *State Fair*, *Titanic*, and *Big*, while 'accusing' Donna Murphy of allowing her bleak role in *Passion* to colour her later 'mumsy' one in *The King And I*. The marketing flair of Mackintosh ('the Napoleon of Broadway') still rankled, and his *Les Misérables* was still on the rack, to the tune of Richard Rodgers's 'My Favourite Things': 'Les Mis chocolates/Shaped like orphans/Patches for your sleeve/It costs one hundred dollars/To come see the show/And one hundred more to leave'. Delivering the goods were Bryan Batt, Donna English, Christine Pedi, and David Hibbard. Batt returned for the 1998 edition, entitled *Forbidden Broadway Cleans Up Its Act!*, along with Lori Hammel, Edward Staudenmayer, and Kristine Zbornik. Some of the other extremely talented cast members to have been involved with Alessandrini over the years, include Tom Plotkin, Brad Ellis, Roxie Lucas, Susanne Blakeslee, Jeff Lyons, Michael McGrath, Mary Denise Bentley, Toni DiBuono, Brad Oscar, Craig Wells, and Dorothy Kiara.

FOREVER PLAID

This 'Heavenly Musical Hit' was greeted with rave reviews from every quarter when it opened Off Broadway at Steve McGraw's on 20 May 1990. Written, directed and choreographed by Stuart Ross, it concerns the return to earth of four aspiring crooners, the members of a close-harmony group called Forever Plaid. The guys were on their way to collect four tartan tuxedos in time for their first big gig, when the vehicle in which they were travelling collided with a school bus full of Catholic teenagers on their way to see the Beatles' debut on the *Ed Sullivan Show*. No Catholic casualties, but the Plaids were killed instantly. That was back in 1964, but 26 years later (and several times a week subsequently), 'through the power of Harmony and the expanding holes in the Ozone layer combined with the positions of the Planets and all that Astro-Technical stuff, the Plaids return to perform the show they never got to do in life'. The rejuvenated quartet consisted of Jinx (Stan Chandler), Smudge (David Engel), Sparky (Jason Graae), and Frankie (Guy Stroman). Together with a bass player and pianist, they pay a joyous tribute to the close-harmony groups of the 50s, such as the Four Lads, the Four Preps, and the Four Aces, via a string of potently nostalgic numbers such as 'Three Coins In The Fountain', 'Love Is A Many Splendoured Thing', 'Catch A Falling Star', 'Chain Gang', 'Magic Moments', 'Sixteen Tons', 'Heart And Soul', and some 20-odd more. Perry Como comes in for the treatment as well. There is also a witty and irreverent send-up of the Beatles (the indirect cause of the Plaids' premature retirement) in 'She Loves You - Yes Siree'. Showered with unanimously ecstatic reviews ('37 out 37') along the lines of 'A high octane tour-de-force' and 'Screamingly funny! Entirely enchanting, utterly entertaining, awesome!', *Forever Plaid* settled in for a long New York run, and, during the next three years, repeated its success in 23 US cities. In September 1993 the show opened for a disappointingly short run in London complete with the original cast except for Sparky who was played by Larry Raben. At the West End Apollo Theatre, one aspect of the audience participation consisted of a minute's silence while one brave soul who went up on to the stage was rewarded with a pack of plaid dental floss.

FOREVER TANGO

Conceived and staged by Luis Bravo, this exciting and passionate Argentinian dance revue played many sell-out seasons in Europe, the USA and Canada, before sashaying sexily into the Walter Kerr Theatre in New York on 19 June 1997. During its stopover in London two years earlier, the show resided at the Strand Theatre, just a dance step away from the Savoy Hotel where they served 'Tango Teas' to the Prince of Wales and his cronies as the tango craze raged in Britain prior to World War I. On Broadway in 1997, *Forever Tango* featured a cast of 25 performers, including six brilliant dance couples who slithered, swayed, spun, kicked, and thrust their way around the floor to the music of an 11-piece orchestra led by Lisandro Adrover. The key instrument in that ensemble was the bandoneón, similar to an accordion, which visiting German sailors introduced to Argentina in the late nineteenth century. Its unique, haunting and melancholy sound enhanced perfectly such numbers as 'El Dia Que Me Quieras', one of the most popular songs of the 30s, in which the singer tells of his romantic wish for an unachievable dream. Written by tango singer and composer *par excellence* Carlos Gardel, with his partner Alfredo Le Pera, it was performed in *Forever Tango* by

Carlos Morel, along with 'Balada Para Un Loco', a toast to the 'crazy'. Each selection tells a story, and among the numerous dance and musical highlights were 'A Evaristo Carriego', the eternal fantasy of an older man obsessed with a younger woman, danced by Marcela Duran and Carlos Gavito; 'La Cumparsita', an ensemble tribute to one of the most famous of all tangos; and the insinuating 'Jealousy', played by the *Forever Tango* orchestra. The remaining members of this dazzling, graceful and immensely skilful company comprised Miriam Larici, Diego DiFalco, Luis Castro and Claudia Mendoza, Jorge Torres and Karina Piazza, Guillermo Merlo and Cecilia Saia, Pedro Calveyra and Nora Robles, Carlos Vera and Laura Marcarie, Gabriel Ortega and Sandra Bootz, and Carolina Zokalski. Initially set to close on 9 August, *Forever Tango* repeatedly extended its run, and in April 1998 moved to the Marquis Theatre following the rapid demise of Paul Simon's *The Capeman*. After running for more than a year, this lesson in Latin sensuality was finally withdrawn on 2 August 1998, having played 453 performances. Road companies subsequently proliferated.

FORMBY, GEORGE

b. George Hoy Booth, 26 May 1904, Wigan, Lancashire, England, d. 6 March 1961, Penwortham, Lancashire, England. The son of George Formby, a successful Edwardian Music Hall comedian, George Hoy was an apprentice jockey before following in his father's footsteps when he died in 1921. At first he worked under his real name and offered what he believed to be an imitation of his father's act - although he had never seen him perform. He changed his name to Formby and discarded the old image when he introduced a ukelele into his act, and then, just as significantly, married a dancer, Beryl Ingham. The lady was to mastermind - some would say, dominate - the remainder of his career. In the late 20s he developed a stage personality that was described variously as: 'the beloved imbecile', 'the modern minstrel' and, 'with a carp-like face, a mouth outrageously full of teeth, a walk that seems normally to be that of a flustered hen and a smile of perpetual wonder at the joyous incomprehensibility of the universe'. Self-taught on the ukelele, he developed an individual style, that even years later, was difficult to copy. Apart from a small part in a silent movie in 1915, Formby's film career started in 1934 with *Boots, Boots*, and continued until 1946 with such films as *No Limit* (1935), *Keep Your Seats Please* (1935), *Feather Your Nest* (1937), Keep Fit (1937), *It's In The Air* (1938), *Trouble Brewing* (1939), *Let George Do It* (1940), *Turned Out Nice Again* (1940), *Spare A Copper* (1941), *South American George* (1941), *Bell Bottom George* (1943), and *George In Civvy Street* (1946). As with his music hall act, the films featured a series of saucy songs such as 'With My Little Ukulele In My Hand', 'When I'm Cleaning Windows', 'Fanlight Fanny', 'Auntie Maggie's Remedy', 'She's Got Two Of Everything', 'You Don't Need A Licence For That' and 'Grandad's Flannelette Nightshirt'. Besides his other 'identity' songs such as 'Leaning On A Lamp Post', 'Chinese Laundry Blues' and 'Mr. Wu's A Window Cleaner Now'. His film image was that of a little man, with a very attractive girl friend, fighting evil in the shape of crooks or the

Germans, and coming out on top in the end ('It's turned out nice again!') to the sheer delight of cinema audiences: 'Our George has done it again!' During the 30s and 40s, Formby and Gracie Fields were regarded as the most popular entertainers in the UK. Even in the early 30s his annual earnings were estimated at around £85,000. During World War II Formby toured extensively with ENSA, entertaining troops in Europe, the Middle East and North Africa. In 1946 he was awarded the OBE for his war efforts. In 1951 he appeared in his first 'book' musical at the Palace Theatre in London's West End. The show was *Zip Goes A Million*, a musical adaptation of the George Barr McCutcheon novel, *Brewster's Millions*. It gave Formby the biggest success of his career, but six months into the run he had to withdraw after suffering a heart attack, to be replaced by comedian Reg Dixon. A year later he returned to work in the usual round of revues and summer shows, but throughout the 50s he was plagued by recurring illness. In 1960 he made his first record for 15 years. The single, 'Happy Go Lucky Me', 'Banjo Boy', was also his first to make the UK Top 40. On Christmas Day of that year his wife and manager, Beryl, died. About two months later, his fans, and especially his family, were startled when he announced his engagement to a 36-year-old schoolteacher, Pat Howson. The marriage was arranged for May, but never took place. Formby died in hospital on 6 March 1961. He left most of his fortune to his fiancée, a situation which led to a lengthy period of litigation when his relations contested the will. A musical play set in the period just before he died, entitled *Turned Out Nice Again*, which was written by Alan Randall and Vince Powell, and starred Randall, had its world premiere at the Blackpool Grand Theatre in March 1992.

● COMPILATIONS: *George Formby Souvenir* (Ace Of Clubs 1961)★★★, *Turned Out Nice Again* (Ace Of Clubs 60s)★★★, *The World Of George Formby* (1969)★★★★, *George Formby* (1970)★★★, *The Best Of George Formby* (1975)★★★, *The World Of George Formby, Volume Two* (1976)★★★★, *With My Ukulele* (1981)★★★, with George Formby Snr. *A Chip Off The Old Block* (1981)★★★, *Leaning On A Lamp Post* (1986)★★★, *Easy Going Chap* (1989)★★★.

● FURTHER READING: *George Formby*, Alan Randall and Ray Seaton. *The Entertainer - George Formby*, John Fisher.

● FILMS: *By The Shortest Heads* (1915), *Boots, Boots* (1934), *Off The Dole* (1935), *No Limit* (1936), *Feather Your Nest* (1937), *Keep Your Seats Please* (1937), *I See Ice* (1938), *Keep Fit* (1938), *Trouble Brewing* (1939), *It's In The Air* (1939), *Let George Do It* (1940), *Come On George* (1940), *South American George* (1941), *Turned Out Nice Again* (1941), *Spare A Copper* (1941), *Much Too Shy* (1942), *Get Cracking* (1943), *Bell Bottom George* (1944), *I Didn't Do It* (1945), *He Snoops To Conquer* (1945), *George In Civvy Street* (1946).

FORREST, GEORGE

(see Wright, Robert)

FORTY-FIVE MINUTES FROM BROADWAY

You can get to New Rochelle, New York, in forty-five minutes from the 'great white way', and that's the location George M. Cohan had in mind when he wrote the music, book, and lyrics for this show which opened at the New Amsterdam Theatre on 1 January 1906. As the curtain rises, Tom Bennet (Donald Brian) is expecting to inherit a great deal of money from his recently deceased millionaire uncle, which will enable him to marry the actress, Flora Dora Dean (Lois Ewell), and keep her in a style to which she is rapidly becoming accustomed. However, the important last will and testament is missing - until Tom's secretary, the cocky Kid Burns (Victor Moore), finds it, and discovers that all the money has been left to the millionaire's housekeeper, Mary Jane Jenkins (Fay Templeton). Mary and the Kid fall in love, but, when he shows her the will, she thinks he wants her for the money. Perish the thought: it has never crossed the Kid's mind, and he tells her so in no uncertain terms. He would never contemplate marrying someone with that much money - so Mary eventually tears up the will. Cohan's score contained three of his most successful songs: 'Mary's A Grand Old Name', 'So Long Mary', and the title number. There was also 'Gentlemen Of The Press' and 'I Want to Be a Popular Millionaire'. Moore, who played Kid Burns in the show, played him again in the 1907 musical *Talk Of New York*, before going on to a long and successful Hollywood career. When *Forty-Five Minutes From Broadway* was revived in New York 1912 (at the Cohan Theatre), Cohan himself took the lead. The show's initial run of only 90 performances gives no indication as to how innovative and different Cohan's ideas actually were. When this show was presented, America was still on a diet of European operetta, none of which had the flair or showmanship that this multi-talented personality displayed.

42ND STREET (FILM MUSICAL)

The definitive backstage musical, starring Ruby Keeler as Peggy Sawyer. Warner Baxter played tough guy Julian Marsh who gives her a push into the spotlight after his has-been star, Dorothy Brock (Bebe Daniels), hits the bottle and accidentally descends a long flight of stairs. Tommy Lawer (Dick Powell) is the show's juvenile lead and Peg's biggest fan, but Ginger Rogers, as Anytime Annie, almost steals the film away from everyone. The screenplay was by James Seymour and Rian James, and Harry Warren and Al Dubin contributed some memorable songs, including 'Young And Healthy', 'Shuffle Off To Buffalo', 'You're Getting To Be A Habit With Me', 'It Must Be June', and 'Forty-Second Street'. That score, and the sensational dance routines designed by Busby Berkeley, make this one of the all-time great screen musicals, and are the reasons why it still sounds and looks so good more than 60 years later. Also in the cast were George Brent, Ned Sparks, Guy Kibbee, Allen Jenkins, George E. Stone, and Una Merkel. Warren and Dubin also made brief appearances, as did another well-known songwriter, Harry Akst. *42nd Street* was produced in 1933 for Warner Brothers by Darryl F. Zanuck and directed by Lloyd Bacon. In 1980, a stage version began a run of more than eight years on Broadway, and in 1984 a successful production opened in London.

42ND STREET (STAGE MUSICAL)

Based on one of the most popular film musicals of the 30s, and the novel by Bradford Ropes, *42nd Street* was a kind of twin-edged sword. On the one hand, it was enormously successful, running for 3,486 performances, and on the other, well, perhaps it was a sign that, apart from composers such as Stephen Sondheim and Jerry Herman, there was beginning to be a shortage of home-grown original musicals written for Broadway. When it opened at the Winter Garden Theatre in New York on 24 August 1980, the British invasion had already begun, and, during the next 10 years or so, would intensify until the New York theatre was dominated by 'intruders' such as Andrew Lloyd Webber. The book for *42nd Street*, which was written by Michael Stewart and Mark Bramble, told the old familiar story of a stage-struck chorus girl, Peggy Sawyer (Wanda Richert), from Allentown, Pennsylvania, who gets her big chance when the star, Dorothy Brock (Tammy Grimes), breaks her ankle during show's tryout. Broadway veteran Jerry Orbach plays the frantic producer, Julian Marsh, who tells Dorothy: 'You're going out a youngster, but you've got to come back a star!' Harry Warren and Al Dubin's songs from the original film were supplemented by other numbers of theirs, and the score contained most of the familiar favourites, such as 'Young And Healthy', 'Shadow Waltz', 'Go Into Your Dance', 'You're Getting To Be A Habit With Me', 'Dames', 'We're In The Money', 'Lullaby Of Broadway', 'About A Quarter To Nine', 'Shuffle Off To Buffalo', and 'Forty-Second Street'. The show was produced by David Merrick, and won Tony Awards for best musical, and for Gower Champion's sensational choreography. Sadly, Champion never experienced the public's ecstatic reaction to his work; he died on the day the show opened in New York. In the 1984 London production at Drury Lane, the part of Julian Marsh, the producer, was originally played by James Laurenson. His surprise replacement during the run of 1,823 performances was the veteran popular singer Frankie Vaughan. Vaughan himself was succeeded by Kenneth Nelson, an American actor domiciled in Britain. Nelson also played Marsh in a limited-run revival at London's Dominion Theatre in 1991.

FOSSE, BOB

b. Robert Louis Fosse, 23 June 1927, Chicago, Illinois, USA, d. 23 September 1987, Washington, DC, USA. A director, choreographer, dancer and actor for films and stage, Fosse was renowned particularly for his innovative and spectacular staging, with the emphasis very firmly on the exhilarating dance sequences. He studied ballet, tap and acrobatic dance from an early age, and, while still a youngster, performed with a partner as the Riff Brothers in vaudeville and burlesque houses. After graduating from high school in 1945, he spent two years in the US Navy before moving to New York and studying acting at the American Theatre Wing. He then toured in the chorus of various productions before making his Broadway debut as a dancer in the revue *Dance Me A Song* (1950). He worked on television and in theatres and clubs for a time until Hollywood beckoned, and he moved to the west coast to appear in three films, *Give A Girl A Break*, *The Affairs Of Dobie Gillis* and *Kiss Me, Kate* (1953). On his return to New York, he gained his big break when author and director George Abbott hired him as a choreographer for *The*

Pajama Game (1954). The show was a massive hit, and Fosse was much in demand - for a time at least. He met Gwen Verdon while working on *Damn Yankees* in 1955, and they were married in 1960. He choreographed *Bells Are Ringing* in 1956, and worked with Verdon again on *New Girl In Town* a year later. From then on, with the exception of *How To Succeed In Business Without Really Trying* (1961), he directed his shows as well as staging the dancing. Fosse's dual role is considered by critics to be a major factor in the success of highly popular productions such as *Redhead* (1959), *Little Me* (1962), *Sweet Charity* (1966), *Pippin* (1972), *Chicago* (1975) and *Dancin'* (1978). Throughout all this time he moved back and forwards between New York and Hollywood, working on films such as *My Sister Eileen* (1955), *The Pajama Game* (1957) and *Damn Yankees* (1958), all three of which were well received. However, *Sweet Charity* (1968), which Fosse controlled completely in his role as director and choreographer, was hammered by many critics for Shirley MacLaine's over-the-top performance, and particularly for the director's self-indulgent cinematography, with its looming close-ups, zooms and blurred focus effects. Fosse was in the wilderness for some time, but all was forgiven four years later when *Cabaret*, starring Liza Minnelli and Joel Grey, won eight Academy Awards, one of which went to Fosse. It was a box-office smash, and Fosse also satisfied most of the purists by confining the dance sequences to appropriate locations such as a beer garden and nightclub, rather than flooding the streets of Berlin with terpsichorean tourists. In the early 70s Fosse was applauded for his direction of *Lenny*, a film biography of the comedian Lennie Bruce, which starred Dustin Hoffman. In the light of Fosse's recent heart problems, his record as a workaholic, and his lifelong obsession with perfection, many observers thought that *All That Jazz* (1979) was intended to be Fosse's own film autobiography, with its ghoulish, self-indulgent examination of life and death. However, no one denied the brilliance of the dance routines or the outstanding performance of Roy Scheider in the leading role. In 1983 Fosse wrote and directed his last movie, *Star 80*, which also had a lurid, tragic theme. Three years later, he wrote, staged and choreographed his final Broadway musical, *Big Deal* - which was, in fact, far less than its title suggested. It represented an inappropriate end to a brilliant career, in which Fosse had created some of the most imaginative and thrilling dance routines ever seen on Broadway or in Hollywood, winning eight Tony Awards in the process. In 1987 he revived one of his most successful shows, *Sweet Charity*, and died shortly before the curtain went up on the night of 23 September. A fascinating documentary entitled *Bob Fosse - Steam Heat*, was made by the US company WNET/Thirteen in 1990. The source of one of his greatest triumphs, *Chicago*, was revived to great acclaim on Broadway and in the West End in 1996/7. Anne Reinking's choreography was created, with great respect and affection, 'in the style of Bob Fosse'. His incredibly wit and vitality were remembered again early in 1999, when a retrospective of his dance numbers entitled *Fosse* opened on Broadway. The show was directed by Richard Maltby Jnr. and Ann Reinking, and choreographed by Reinking and Chet Walker.

● FURTHER READING: *Razzle Dazzle: The Life And Works Of Bob Fosse*, Kevin Boyd Grubb. *Bob Fosse's Broadway*, Margery Beddow.

FOUR MUSKETEERS, THE

Over the years, Alexander Dumas's famous story of *The Three Musketeers* has turned up in many forms on stage, television, and at least five films. This comedy musical, which opened at the Theatre Royal, Drury Lane in London on 5 December 1967, gave the highly experienced English writer, Michael Pertwee, the opportunity to turn the legend upside down. In Pertwee's book, the dashing and fearless D'Artagnan (Harry Secombe), is turned into 'Neddy' D'Artagna - a country bumpkin, an accident-prone figure, whose bravest deeds are accomplished purely by chance. His compatriots, portrayed here as womanising sots, were obviously recruited from some of Britains' top low-brow comedy talent, and included Porthos (Jeremy Lloyd), Athos (Glyn Owen) Aramis (John Junkin), with Kenneth Connor as (King Louis XIII). In complete contrast, Elizabeth Larner, whose thrilling voice had last been heard in the West End when she played Guinevere in *Camelot* (1964), was this time cast as Milady. Obviously, the whole affair was an attempt to repeat the success of *Pickwick*, four years earlier, but Laurie Johnson and Herbert Kretzmer's score did not provide Secombe with anything nearly as powerful as 'If I Ruled the World', although its pleasant score did contain songs such as 'A Little Bit Of Glory', 'Think Big', 'What Love Can Do', 'Masquerade', There Comes A Time', 'Nobody's Changing Places With Me', 'Strike While The Iron Is Hot', 'If You Are Looking For A Girl', 'Got A Lot Of Love To Give', 'Give Me A Man's Life', and 'There's A New Face In The Old Town'. The critics did not like it much, and despite a decent run of over a year, a total of 462 performances, *The Four Musketeers* is reported to have lost much of its investment. Herbert Kretzmer, the journalist and lyricist, had his greatest success 20 years later, with *Les Misérables*.

FRANKIE AND JOHNNY

The first of three Elvis Presley films released in 1966, *Frankie And Johnny* boasted a plot loosely based on the traditional jazz song of the same name. Presley plays a gambler aboard a Mississippi paddleboat, down on his luck. He changes girlfriends hoping this will change his fortunes. The feature is better than the rest of that year's output, although the soundtrack material leaves a lot to be desired. A medley of 'Down By The Riverside' and 'When The Saints Go Marchin' In' was an obvious sop to the New Orleans setting, while 'Petunia, The Gardener's Daughter' was another in a line of notoriously terrible songs which marred the singer's movies. The title track was issued as single, but its comparatively low chart placing in the US and UK showed the public was weary of Presley's formula-based output.

FREE AS AIR

Julian Slade and Dorothy Reynolds's follow-up to their 1954 mega-hit *Salad Days*, opened at London's Savoy Theatre on 6 June 1957 - at a time when *Salad Days*, itself, had nearly another three years to run. This musical play was set on the island of Terhou, a location the authors had based on Sark, one of the Channel Islands situated off the north coast of France. A somewhat philosophical piece, it told the story of the beautiful and wealthy Geraldine Melford (Gillian Lewis), who escapes from the press (and a persistent and unwelcome lover), and settles on this isolated island where she finally finds true happiness with one of the residents, Albert Postumous (John Trevor). Along the way (and in line with the play's 'back-to-nature approach') she also foils the attempts of the sophisticated Jack Amersham (Gerald Harper) and the hard-nosed newspaper reporter (Josephine Tewson) to bring 'progress and civilization' to the island. Also in the cast were Michael Aldridge, who played the Lord Paul Postumous, Dorothy Reynolds, Patricia Bredin, and Leonard Rossiter, who became a household name in British television situation comedies such as *Rising Damp* and *The Fall And Rise Of Reginald Perrin*. As usual, Julian Slade and Dorothy Reynolds came up with a delightful and elegant score, the highlight of which was probably the charming 'Let The Grass Grow', sung by Michael Aldridge with two of the islanders, played by Roy Godfrey and Howard Goorney. The other songs included 'I'm Up Early', 'I've Got My Feet On The Ground', 'A Man From the Mainland', 'Nothing But Sea And Sky', 'Free As Air', 'The Girl From London', 'I'd Like To Be Like You', 'We're Holding Hands', and 'Terhou'. *Free As Air* closed on 7 June 1958 after a run of 417 performances, proving that there was still a place in the theatre for the home-grown product, despite the current popularity of imported American shows such as *My Fair Lady*, *Bells Are Ringing*, *Where's Charley?* - and in December 1958 - *West Side Story*.

FREED, ARTHUR

b. Arthur Grossman, 9 September 1894, Charleston, South Carolina, USA, d. 12 April 1973, Los Angeles, California, USA. A distinguished film producer and lyricist, Freed was instrumental in elevating MGM Studios to its position as the king of the film school, and was then already an accomplished pianist, determined to make his way as a songwriter. His first job was as a demonstrator in a Chicago music shop where he met Minnie Marx, mother of the Marx Brothers. With her encouragement he quit his job and joined her sons' show as a singer. He later teamed up with Gus Edwards as a musical act in vaudeville. During this period he wrote many songs with different collaborators and had his first big success in 1923 with 'I Cried For You', written with Gus Arnheim and Abe Lyman. By the end of the 20s Freed was in Hollywood where he contributed the score to *The Broadway Melody* (1929) and *The Hollywood Revue Of 1929*, amongst others. Throughout the 30s he continued to write songs for films such as *Montana Moon*, *Lord Byron Of Broadway*, *Those Three French Girls*, *The Big Broadcast*, *The Barbarian*, *Going Hollywood*, *Sadie McKee*, *Student Tour*, *A Night At The Opera*, *Broadway Melody Of 1936*, *San Francisco*, *Broadway Melody Of 1938*, and *Babes In Arms* (1939). As well as being a hit for all concerned, including its stars, Judy Garland and Mickey Rooney, the latter picture was significant in that it marked the beginning of Arthur Freed's second career, that of a producer. During the next two decades the legendary Freed Unit produced most of

MGM's outstanding musicals, including *The Wizard Of Oz, Strike Up The Band, Lady Be Good, Cabin In the Sky, Meet Me In St. Louis, The Ziegfeld Follies, The Pirate, The Barkleys Of Broadway, Easter Parade, Take Me Out To The Ball Game, Words And Music, Annie Get Your Gun, On The Town, An American In Paris* (1951 Oscar for best film), *Show Boat, Singin' In The Rain, The Band Wagon, Brigadoon, Kismet, Silk Stockings,* and *Gigi,* (1958 Oscar for best film). During his long stay at MGM Freed's closest associate was musical arranger and songwriter Roger Edens. However, his chief composing partner was Nacio Herb Brown, with whom he wrote 'After Sundown', 'Alone', 'The Boy Friend', Broadway Rhythm', 'You Were Meant For Me', 'The Wedding Of The Painted Doll', 'The Broadway Melody', 'Singin' In The Rain', 'Should I?', 'Temptation', 'Fit As A Fiddle', 'Pagan Love Song', 'Alone', 'I Got A Feelin' You're Foolin', 'You Are My Lucky Star', ' Lovely Lady', 'Good Morning', 'All I Do Is Dream Of You', and many others. These were all written for various films before Freed devoted himself to producing, although several of their most popular numbers were reprised in *Singin' In The Rain* (1951), including the title song which was originally introduced in *Hollywood Revue Of 1929*. For *Singin' In The Rain* Freed and Brown wrote a new song, 'Make 'Em Laugh', which Donald O'Connor immediately made his own. Freed's other collaborators included Al Hoffman, Harry Warren, and Burton Lane. For a number of years in the 60s Freed was president of the American Academy of Motion Picture Arts and Sciences, from whom he received the Irving Thalberg Award in 1951 and a further award in 1967 'for distinguished service to the Academy and the production of six top-rated Awards telecasts'. Arthur Freed's brother, Ralph Freed (b. 1 May 1907, Vancouver, Canada, d. 13 February 1973, California, USA), was also a lyricist, and contributed songs, written mainly with composers Burton Lane and Sammy Fain, to several movies during the 30s and 40s. These included *Champagne Waltz* (1937), *College Holiday, Double Or Nothing, Swing High, Swing Low, Cocoanut Grove, She Married A Cop, Babes On Broadway, Ziegfeld Girl, Dubarry Was A Lady, Thousands Cheer, Thrill Of Romance, No Leave, No Love, Two Sisters From Boston,* and *Ziegfeld Follies* (1946). One of his numbers, 'The Worry Song' (with Fain), was featured in the renowned live, action sequence in *Anchors Aweigh* in which Gene Kelly danced with Jerry the cartoon mouse. His other songs included 'How About You?', 'You Leave Me Breathless', 'Love Lies', 'Smarty', 'Little Dutch Mill', 'Hawaiian War Chant', and 'Who Walks In When I Walk Out?'.

● FURTHER READING: *The Movies' Greatest Musicals-Produced In Hollywood USA By The Freed Unit,* Hugh Fordin.

FREEDLEY, VINTON

(see Aarons, Alex A.)

FRIEDHOFER, HUGO WILHELM

b. 3 May 1901, San Francisco, California, USA, d. 17 May 1981. After an early career as a painter, Friedhofer turned to another branch of the arts, taking up the cello and studying composition under Domenico Brescia. He wrote music to accompany silent films and in 1929 went to Hollywood to arrange and direct music for the new sound films. When procedures changed and composers were hired to write specifically for films, Friedhofer was well-suited for a new role, and was called upon to orchestrate the music for *Keep Your Sunny Side Up.* He later orchestrated music composed by acclaimed and much better-known people such as Erich Wolfgang Korngold, Max Steiner and Franz Waxman. The films on which he worked for these composers are numerous and his contribution to their success undoubted, if undervalued. As a film composer in his own right, Friedhofer's first complete score was for the 1938 film, *The Adventures Of Marco Polo.* He also composed for films such as *Brewster's Millions, Joan Of Arc, Body And Soul, No Man Of Her Own, Hondo, Vera Cruz, Young Lions* and *The Best Years Of Our Lives* (for which he won an Oscar), and *One-Eyed Jacks* - just a few of a very long list. Greatly admired by fellow musicians as diverse as Paul Glass and John Lewis, Friedhofer remained almost unknown to the world outside the music business. Gene Lees, a longtime friend, wrote movingly of him in his book, *Singers And The Song.*

FRIEDMAN, MARIA

b. 1960, Switzerland. An actress, musician, singer, and dancer, with a penchant for the works of Stephen Sondheim, Friedman was born into a musical family. Her mother, Claire, is a concert pianist and composer, and her late Russian-Jewish father Leonard Friedman was an accomplished violinist who founded the Scottish Chamber Orchestra and Scottish Opera. The family moved to Germany when she was three on her father's appointment as Leader of the Bremen Philharmonic Orchestra. Shortly afterwards, the marriage broke up and Friedman was subsequently brought up in England. Early training as a cellist was abandoned because 'I quickly realised I didn't have the discipline required', but her musical ability was never in question, and after training at the Arts Educational School, Friedman joined Sonnet, an all-girl trio which backed Vernon Nesbeth, founder of the Southlanders vocal group, on a European tour. On her return to England, she played the chorus role of Doris in Cameron Mackintosh's 1980 revival of *Oklahoma!* at the Palace Theatre (the programme mis-spelled her name as Freedman), and subsequently took over the leading part of Ado Annie in the same show. During the remainder of the 80s, she was in London productions such as *Blondel* (Aldwych), *Small Expectations* (Queen Elizabeth Hall), *By George It's Gershwin* (Purcell Rooms), *Spin Of The Wheel* (Comedy), *April In Paris* (Ambassadors), and *Blues In The Night* (Piccadilly). In the latter show she played the Girl With A Date, more than holding her own in the heady company of Debby Bishop and Carol Woods. Another very important role was that of Hayyah in *Ghetto* (Royal National Theatre 1989), Joseph Sobol's unforgettable play about a theatre created by Jewish inhabitants of the Vilna, Lithuania ghetto during the Holocaust. Friedman first met Stephen Sondheim after singing his 'Broadway Baby' at a charity concert at the Theatre Royal, Drury Lane, and he subsequently cast her as Dot/Marie in *Sunday In The Park With George* (1990). This was followed by a Leicester Haymarket revival of the composer's *Merrily We Roll*

Along (1992). Her big break came when she was seen providing 'a little light entertainment' at her father's annual international music festival in the Hebrides called *Mendelssohn On Mull*, by Caro Newling, the administrator of London's Donmar Warehouse Theatre. Newling booked her to appear at the venue for three Sunday performances in February-March 1994. Her one-woman show, *Maria Friedman By Special Arrangement*, for which she was supported by a group of hand-picked musicians playing brand new arrangements, sent hardened critics into the realms of ecstasy. Her eclectic programme was topped and tailed by Sondheim's 'Our Time' and 'Marry Me A Little', and included two songs from *Ghetto*, 'In The Sky' and 'Springtime'. The show won the 1995 Best Entertainment Laurence Olivier Award, and she encored with *Maria Friedman By Extra Special Arrangement* which played the Whitehall Theatre for a limited season. In 1997, there was another Olivier Award, this time for Best Actress In A Musical, in recognition of her outstanding performance as the disfigured Fosca, opposite Michael Ball, in the London premiere of Sondheim and James Lapine's *Passion*. A year later, she was back at the National's Lyttleton Theatre as Liza Elliot in the first London production of the Ira Gershwin-Kurt Weill-Moss Hart 1941 musical, *Lady In The Dark*. After that, she moved on to something quite different, taking over the 'murderous' role of Roxie Hart in the West End hit production of *Chicago* (1998). As a concert performer Friedman has sung at most of the major venues in the UK, and also appeared frequently on television. On the small screen she is probably best known for her portrayal of social worker Trish Baynes in the top-rated television hospital series *Casualty*, but has also featured in other shows such as *Me And The Girls*, *Blues In The Night*, *Red Dwarf*, *Black Daisies For The Bride*, *Shakers*, *The Ancient Mariner*, and *Frank Stubbs Promotes*.

● ALBUMS: *Maria Friedman* (Carlton Sounds 1996)★★★, as well as studio and stage cast recordings.

FRIML, RUDOLPH

b. 8 December 1879, Prague, Bohemia, d. 12 November 1972, Hollywood, California, USA. An important composer who helped to perpetuate the romantic operetta-style of musical which was so popular in America at the turn of the century. After studying at Prague University, Friml toured Europe and America as a concert pianist and settled in the US in 1906. As a composer his first opportunity came when he took over from Victor Herbert on the score for *The Firefly* (1912) from which came 'Giannina Mia' and 'Sympathy'. His collaborator for that show was Otto Harbach, and the two men worked together on a further nine productions. Throughout his career Friml's other lyricists and librettists included P.G. Wodehouse, Herbert Reynolds, Harold Atteridge, Rida Johnson Young, Oscar Hammerstein II, Brian Hooker, Clifford Grey, Dailey Paskman, Edward Clark, Chisholm Cushing, and Rowland Leigh. He composed the music for some of the most popular songs of the time in a list of shows which includes *High Jinks* ('The Bubble'; 'Love's Own Kiss'; 'Not Now But Later'), *The Peasant Girl* ('Love Is Like A Butterfly'; 'Listen, Dear'; 'And The Dream Came True'), *Katinka* ('Allah's Holiday'; 'I Want to Marry A Male

Quartet'; 'Katinka'), *You're In Love* ('I'm Only Dreaming'; 'You're In Love'), *Glorianna* ('My Climbing Rose'; 'Toodle-oo'), *Sometime* ('Sometime'; 'Keep On Smiling') *Tumble Inn* ('Snuggle And Dream'; 'I've Told My Love'), *The Little Whopper* ('You'll Dream And I'll Dream'; ''Round The Corner'), *June Love* ('June Love'; 'The Flapper And The Vamp'; 'Don't Keep Calling Me Dearie'), *Ziegfeld Follies Of 1921* ('Bring Back My Blushing Rose'; 'Every Time I Hear The Band Play'), *The Blue Kitten* ('When I Waltz With You'; 'Cutie'; 'Blue Kitten Blues'), *Cinders* ('Belle Of The Bronx'; 'I'm Simply Mad About The Boys'), *Rose-Marie* ('Rose-Marie'; 'Indian Love Call'; 'Totem Tom-Tom'; 'Song Of The Mounties'), *The Vagabond King* ('Only A Rose'; 'Song Of The Vagabonds'; 'Some Day'), *The Wild Rose* ('Brown Eyes'; 'One Golden Hour'), *No Foolin'* ('Wasn't It Nice?'; 'Florida, The Moon And You'), *The Three Musketeers* ('March Of The Musketeers'; 'Ma Belle'; 'Queen Of My Heart'; 'Heart Of Mine'), *The White Eagle* ('Gather The Rose'; 'Give Me One Hour'), *Luana* ('My Bird of Paradise'; 'Aloha'), and *Music Hath Charms* (1934) ('My Heart Is Yours'; 'Sweet Fool'). In the lavish 1935 film version of Friml's first show, *The Firefly*, Allan Jones had a big hit with 'The Donkey Serenade' which was adapted from Friml's composition 'Chansonette', a piece he had originally written for the *Ziegfeld Follies Of 1923*. Some of his other shows were filmed and he also wrote the music for the 1947 movie *Northwest Outpost*. Friml's last two shows, *Luana* and *Music Hath Charms*, only ran for some 20-odd performances each and he appeared unable or unwilling to adapt his music to the ever-growing American-style of musical comedy, although he remained active in his later years and appeared frequently on US television.

FROM A JACK TO A KING

With a title borrowed from Ned Miller's 1963 hit record, *From A Jack To A King* opened in London's West End on 20 July 1992 at the Ambassador's Theatre, following a run at the tiny Boulevard Theatre in Soho. Bob Carlton's rock 'n' roll musical spoof of Shakespeare's *Macbeth*, followed his tremendous success in 1989 with *Return To The Forbidden Planet*, a rock version of *The Tempest*. In this show, Eric Glamis (Matthew Devitt) is a stand-in drummer for the Coronets, a band run by Duke Box (Christian Roberts). He aspires to replace the megastar lead singer Terry King (an arrogant Elvis Presley impersonation by Robert Dallas). Goaded by his lover, Queenie (Allison Harding), Glamis tinkers with the King's motorbike ('Is this a spanner I see before me?') with fatal results. He gets the gig, though, and experiences (temporary) glory, but subsequent disillusionment. Large extracts, and sometimes complete speeches and scenes, are extracted from, not only *Macbeth*, but other works by the Bard, such as *Hamlet* and *Romeo And Juliet*. These are absorbed into the story, which is punctuated with lots of classic songs such as 'Shakin' All Over', 'You've Lost That Lovin' Feelin'', 'Keep On Running', 'Leader Of The Pack', 'Stepping Stone'. Unfortunately for Carlton, the show arrived in London at a time when audiences were already being saturated with the old songs in shows such as *Good Rockin' Tonite*, *Buddy*, *The Cotton Club*, *Five Guys Named Moe* - and his own *Return To The Forbidden Planet* - and this may well have been the reason why *From A Jack To A King* was unable to stay around for longer than 202 performances. A 'cabaret-style' revival was presented at the Studio Theatre, in the London suburb of Wimbledon in 1994.

FUN IN ACAPULCO

Elvis Presley's second film of 1963 featured the singer as a former trapeze artist, who, following an accident to his partner, is now afraid of heights. He decamps to Acapulco, ultimately conquering this phobia with a high-dive from the coastal rock. Ursula Andress, thrust into the public eye following her role in the first James Bond feature *Dr. No*, co-starred in this slice of light entertainment. The soundtrack provided 11 songs, including the much-maligned '(There's) No Room To Rhumba In A Sports Car'. It is a terrible composition, but several other tracks, notably 'The Bullfighter Was A Lady' and 'El Toro', were equally poor. *Fun In Acapulco* contained the obligatory spin-off single, but the relatively low chart placings gained by 'Bossa Nova Baby' (number 8 US, number 13 UK) suggested Presley's audience was beginning to tire of sub-standard material. Paradoxically, the course he had embarked upon exacerbated the problem. 1963 was the first year in which the singer did not complete a regular studio album and, in deference to his film schedule, Presley began to overdub vocals on to pre-existing backing tracks, rather than record them with his backing group. He completed his contributions to the songs on *Fun In Acapulco* in one day.

FUNICELLO, ANNETTE

(see Annette)

FUNNY FACE (FILM MUSICAL)

George and Ira Gershwin's 1927 Broadway hit *Funny Face* took 30 years to travel from New York to Hollywood, but the wait was well worthwhile. Screenwriter Leonard Gershe discarded the original story entirely and adapted the plot from his own unproduced musical *Wedding Day*. Five songs survived the trip - and so did Fred Astaire, who had co-starred with his sister Adele in *Funny Face* in both New York and London. In this new scenario, Fred played a fashion photographer who transforms a shy, intellectual Greenwich Village librarian (Audrey Hepburn) into a cover girl for a sophisticated magazine. She agrees to go with him to Paris for the photo-shoot so that she can meet her intellectual mentor, who is portrayed in the film as a Jean-Paul Sartre figure, the founder of the then popular Existentialist movement. However, he and his philosophies are soon forgotten shortly after the elegant Astaire takes her in his arms and the magical music begins. Although Astaire was in his late 50s, the years seemed to fall away as he recreated the wonderful numbers from 30 years earlier, such as 'Funny Face', ''S Wonderful', 'He Loves And She Loves', and 'Let's Kiss And Make Up'. Hepburn, too, was charming on 'How Long Has This Been Going On?', which had been written for the original show but was cut before the New York opening night. Kay Thompson gave an outstanding performance as the magazine editor with lots of pizzazz, and duetted with Astaire on another Gershwin song, 'Clap Yo' Hands', which had been used previously in the musical *Oh, Kay!* (1926).

Leonard Gershe and Roger Edens contributed 'Bonjour Paris', 'On How To Be Lovely' and 'Think Pink', which was the opening number in what is generally regarded as a visually gorgeous movie. Much of the credit for that aspect of the production was owing to fashion photographer Richard Avedon's work as visual consultant. Ray June photographed the film in Technicolor and VistaVision. *Funny Face* was originally conceived by the Arthur Freed Unit at MGM, who, for various reasons, decided not to proceed with it themselves and sold it to Paramount, along with the services of MGM stalwarts such as Edens, Gershe, director Stanley Donen, dance director Eugene Loring, and music arranger Adolph Deutsch. In 1992 *Funny Face* was released on laserdisc with its colour enhanced and featuring a slightly 'letterboxed' format.

FUNNY FACE (STAGE MUSICAL)

When producers Alex A. Aarons and Vincent Freedley built the Alvin Theatre in New York, they each gave the project just a small part of their names ('Al' and 'Vin'), but a great deal of their money. Some of that money had been earned from George and Ira Gershwin's shows such as *Oh, Kay!*, *Tip-Toes*, and *Lady, Be Good*, and now there was more to be made from *Funny Face*, the Gershwins' latest offering, and the first presentation at their new theatre on 2 November 1927. The show's title had originally been *Smarty*, but a change of name was only one of a series of measures that were taken when the production was clearly in trouble during its pre-Broadway tryout. Robert Benchley, the renowned American humorist, and co-writer of the book with Fred Thompson, was replaced by Paul Gerard Smith; several songs were dropped, and five more added; and Victor Moore, who, for 20 years, had been one of Broadway and Hollywood's much-loved bumbling clowns, joined the party. Moore plays one of the two comic burglars caught up in a story of mistakes and mayhem. Frankie Wynne (Adele Astaire) is the ward of the autocratic Jimmie Reeve (Fred Astaire). She persuades her aviator boyfriend, Peter Thurston (Allen Kearns), to retrieve an her incriminating diary that belongs to her, from Jimmie's wall safe, but the silly boy comes away with a bracelet instead. This act of carelessness on his part sets off a mad chase that takes the assembled cast to exotic locations such as Lake Wapatog, New Jersey, and then on to the Paymore Hotel and the Two-Million Dollar Pier, Atlantic City. Fred and his sister, Adele, were together again with another Gershwin score, following their great success in 1924 with *Lady, Be Good!*. The songs were right out of the composers' top drawer - one all-time standard, ''S Wonderful' - and other great numbers such as the lovely ballad, 'He Loves And She Loves', 'Let's Kiss And Make Up', 'Tell The Doc' (an hilarious lampoon of psychiatrists), 'High Hat' (along with the white tie and tails, it became Astaire's trademark in many Hollywood movies), 'My One And Only', the engaging 'Funny Face', and 'The Babbitt And The Bromide', which Astaire later sung with Gene Kelly when they met for the first time on film in *Ziegfeld Follies* (1945). *Funny Face* was a tremendous success, and ran for 250 performances in New York. It played for two weeks longer than that in London, where the Astaires were very popular, especially with British Royalty. They were joined in the West End production by Sydney Howard and Leslie Henson. The 1957 film version, which had a different story but retained some of the songs, and borrowed others from different Gershwin shows, starred Fred Astaire (Adele had retired long since) with Audrey Hepburn and Kay Thompson. The story was overhauled yet again in 1983, when a projected Broadway revival of *Funny Face* underwent such drastic changes, that, although, as with the film, it had some of the original numbers, it turned out to be essentially a quite different show, and the title was changed to *My One And Only*. It starred Twiggy and Tommy Tune, and ran for 767 performances.

FUNNY GIRL (FILM MUSICAL)

Youth and experience were celebrated by the Academy Awards committee in April 1969, when Barbra Streisand and Katharine Hepburn tied for the best actress Oscar. It was Hepburn's third Award, for her 36th film, while Streisand was making her movie debut in what proved to be the role-of-a-lifetime as comedienne Fanny Brice, the most famous star of the *Ziegfeld Follies*. Streisand had already enjoyed much success on Broadway and in London with this saga of Fanny's on-stage triumphs and her turbulent marriage to compulsive gambler Nicky Arnstein (Omar Sharif). Kay Medford, who was in the original Broadway cast, recreated her fine and funny performance as Fanny's typically Jewish mother, and some of the other parts went to Walter Pidgeon (as Florenz Ziegfeld), Anne Francis, Ma Questel, Lee Allen, Tommy Rall, and Gerald Mohr. Three of Brice's genuine hit songs, 'My Man' (Channing Pollock-Maurice Yvain), 'I'd Rather Be Blue Over You (Than Be Happy With Somebody Else)' (Billy Rose-Fred Fisher), and 'Second Hand Rose' (Grant Clarke-James F. Hanley), were added to what remained of Jule Styne and Bob Merrill's splendid stage score and some additional songs they wrote especially for the film. Streisand's big emotional numbers such as 'People', 'His Love Makes Me Beautiful', and 'Don't Rain On My Parade', were all retained, and the rest of the songs, including several comedy items which fitted the 'funny girl' like a glove, were 'I'm The Greatest Star' (Streisand), 'If A Girl Isn't Pretty' (Streisand-Medford-Questel), 'Roller Skate Rag' (Streisand), 'You Are Woman, I Am Man' (Streisand-Sharif), 'Sadie, Sadie' (Streisand), 'The Swan' (orchestral ballet parody), and 'Funny Girl' (Streisand). Styne and Merrill wrote at least one more title song, a lively, up-tempo number which Streisand released on record but was not included in the film. Isobel Lennart, adapted her own witty stage libretto for the screenplay, and Herbert Ross designed the often hilarious choreography. He is also said to have collaborated with director William Wyler on some of the film's spectacular sequences, including the 'Don't Rain On My Parade' number which Streisand performed while tearing around on various modes of transport, ending up on a tugboat in New York harbour. *Funny Girl* was photographed by Harry Stradling in Technicolor and Panavision and released by Columbia in 1968. According to *Variety*, it went on to become the 10th highest-grossing film of the decade.

Barbra Streisand starred in the 1975 sequel, *Funny Lady*, in which Fanny marries producer Billy Rose (James Caan), but is still unable to find enduring happiness. John Kander and Fred Ebb provided most of the songs, including the appealing 'How Lucky Can You Get?', 'Isn't It Better?', 'Blind Date', 'Let's Hear It For Me', and 'So Long, Honey Lamb', and there were also several oldies such as 'More Than You Know' (Billy Rose-Edward Eliscu-Vincent Youmans), 'I Found A Million Dollar Baby' (Rose-Mort Dixon-Harry Warren), and 'Great Day' (Rose-Eliscu-Youmans). Roddy McDowall, Ben Vereen, and Carole Wells were also in the cast, along with Omar Sharif, who made a brief appearance as Fanny's ex-husband who passes briefly through her life again. The screenplay was by Jay Presson Allen and Arnold Shulman, and Herbert Ross was present again, this time as choreographer-director.

FUNNY GIRL (STAGE MUSICAL)

The story goes that agent and producer Ray Stark had the idea that the life of his mother-in-law, the legendary *Ziegfeld Follies* comedienne, actress and singer, Fanny Brice, would be a great subject for a film. That was before she died in 1951. Several screenplays and prospective leading ladies (including Mary Martin, Anne Bancroft, Eydie Gormé, and Carol Burnett) later, *Funny Girl* opened on Broadway at the Winter Garden Theatre on 26 March 1964. Isobel Lennart adapted her draft screenplay for the stage, while regular trips by composer Jule Styne to a Greenwich Village club called the Bon Soir, resolved the leading lady problem, and gave Broadway an outstanding new star - Barbra Streisand. She had attracted some interest in *I Can Get It For You Wholesale* two years before, but this time she was carrying a major musical on those 22-year-old shoulders. Lennart's book has Fanny sitting in her Follies dressing room, looking back over the years to when, as an awkward, plain-looking teenager, she gets a job at Keeney's Music Hall with the aid of dance director Eddie Ryan (Danny Meehan) and gambler Nick Arnstein (Sydney Chaplin). That pleases her mom, Mrs. Brice (Kay Medford) and mom's three-cent poker-playing cronies, who include Mrs. Strakosh (Jean Stapleton), back in 'Henry Street' on New York's East Side. They are even more delighted when Fanny joins the famous *Ziegfeld Follies*. Once there, she constantly tries the patience of The Big Boss, Florenz Ziegfeld (Reginald DeKoven), especially when she leaves to marry and have a baby with the suave and totally gorgeous Arnstein. However, due to Nick's cash flow problem (he speculates on the wrong oil well) he is soon forced to return to the theatre, and then Arnstein's financial antics eventually land him in jail. Back to the present, and as Fanny sits and reflects, Nick, having served his sentence, returns to see her again. This time though, Fanny has had enough. She stands firm, and they part, presumably for ever. The perfect opportunity for a reprise of the Act I finalé number, 'Don't Rain On My Parade'. Jule Styne and Bob Merrill's score was full of funny, disarming, and often poignant songs, including Nick's seduction piece, 'You Are Woman' (Fanny: 'Well, a bit of dinner never hurt/But guess who is gonna be dessert'), the 'Henry Street' mob's soft-shoe shuffle to 'Who Taught Her Everything?' ('She sings like a bird, yes indeed/But who used to stand there and feed her the seed'), Fanny's paean to domesticity, 'Sadie, Sadie' ('The honeymoon was such delight/That we got married that same night'), her aching request for Nick to stay, 'Who Are You Now?' ('Are you someone better for my love?'), as well as 'If A Girl Isn't Pretty', 'I'm The Greatest Star', 'Cornet Man', 'His Love Makes Me Beautiful', 'I Want To Be Seen With You Tonight', 'Henry Street', 'Find Yourself A Man', 'Rat-Tat-Tat-Tat', and 'The Music That Makes Me Dance'. Streisand's recording of the immensely compelling 'People' reached the US Top 10, and, won a Grammy for best vocal performance. Another Grammy went to the Original Cast album, consolation perhaps for the show's inability to convert even one of its eight Tony Awards nominations. *Funny Girl* was choreographed by Carol Haney, and three directors, Bob Fosse, Garson Kanin, and Jerome Robbins, were used on the trip to Broadway, with the last two getting programme credit. Costumes were by Irene Sharaff, and Ralph Burns was responsible for the terrific orchestrations, including an overture which is a mini-show in itself. The New York production ran for a satisfying 1,348 performances, and when Streisand left for London, she was succeeded by Mimi Hines. Streisand's triumph at London's Prince of Wales Theatre in 1966, with Michael Craig (Arnstein), Kay Medford (Mrs. Brice), Lee Allen (Eddie), Stella Moray (Mrs. Strakosh), and Ronald Leigh-Hunt (Ziegfeld), was confined to 112 performances after the star informed the producers that she was pregnant. Since then, regional stagings have proliferated, especially in the USA, and it appeared that Broadway audiences would finally see a major revival before a 1996 production starring Debbie Gibson closed on the road. The 1968 film version starred Streisand, and Omar Sharif as Arnstein.

FUNNY LADY
(see *Funny Girl*)

FUNNY THING HAPPENED ON THE WAY TO THE FORUM, A

Stephen Sondheim's third Broadway show, and the first for which he wrote the music as well as the lyrics. It opened at the Alvin Theatre in New York on 8 May 1962, and was still there over two years later. The book, by Burt Shevelove and Larry Gelbart, was freely adapted from all 21 of the comedies by the Roman playwright, Plautus. Set 'in a street in Rome, on a day in spring, two hundred years before the Christian era', the show has been described variously as 'a funny vaudeville farce . . . a bawdy farcical musical . . . an old-fashioned musical burlesque' . . . and 'a riot of risqué patter'. The Prologus (the slave Pseudolus, played by Zero Mostel addresses the audience and welcomes them with 'Comedy Tonight' ('Something appealing/Something appalling/Something for everyone/A comedy tonight!'). There follows a joyous, fast-moving romp, involving an old man, Senex (David Burns) and his wife Domina (Ruth Kobart), their son Hero (Brian Davies), their slave Hysterium (Jack Gilford), another old man, Erronius (Raymond Walburn), a buyer and seller of courtesans, Marcus Lycus (John Carradine), a warrior, Miles Gloriosus (Ronald Holgate), and a virgin, Philia (Preshy Marker). Mostel, in his role as Pseudolus, slave to

Hero, updates the audience regularly when he is not trying to help the other characters out of various embarrassing situations. Sondheim punctuated the action with songs such as 'Everybody Ought To Have A Maid', 'Bring Me My Bride', 'That'll Show Him', 'Love I Hear', 'Lovely', 'Free', 'I'm Calm', 'Pretty Little Picture', and 'Impossible'. The show ran for 964 performances and scooped the Tony Awards, winning for best musical, book, actor (Mostel), supporting actor (David Burns), director (George Abbott), and producer (Harold Prince) The 1963 London production, which stayed at the Strand Theatre for 762 performances, starred Frankie Howerd as Pseudolus, and a band of renowned British low-farce comedians, including Kenneth Connor, 'Monsewer' Eddie Gray, Robertson Hare, and Jon Pertwee. Howerd reprised his role in the 1986 West End revival which was directed by Larry Gelbart. His co-librettist, Burt Shevelove, staged the show when Broadway audiences saw it for the second time in 1972. Phil Silvers, who had been the original choice for Pseudolus in 1962, appeared in the revival until he had a stroke, and it was forced to close. The production won Tony Awards for Silvers and supporting actor, Larry Blyden. When he recovered, Silvers took the show to the UK provinces at a time when his popularity rating was high due to reruns of the *Sergeant Bilko* television show. In 1991, in an effort to reduce costs but still revive some favourite Broadway musicals, a scaled-down production of *A Funny Thing Happened On The Way To The Forum* was presented at the Church of the Heavenly Rest by the New York Theatre Company. Five years later *Forum* was back on Broadway with 'one of the great actors of the American theatre'. Nathan Lane, in the lead. He won a Tony Award for his outstanding performance, and was succeeded - somewhat controversially - by film actress Whoopi Goldberg. The 1966 film version starred Zero Mostel, Phil Silvers, Jack Gilford, and Buster Keaton.

GANG'S ALL HERE, THE

Although Alice Faye, Carmen Miranda, Phil Baker and Benny Goodman And His Orchestra were top-billed in this 1943 20th Century-Fox release, the real star, by general consent, was director-choreographer Busby Berkeley. Taking full advantage of Edward Cronjager's photography and the Technicolor process, early in the film Berkeley created the famous 'The Lady In The Tutti-Frutti Hat' sequence during which dozens of girls manipulating gigantic bananas dance around Carmen Miranda who is topped by her basket of fruit *chapeau*. Later on, Alice Faye joins a group of snazzily dressed children in the spectacular finalé based on 'The Polka Dot Polka', in which Berkely added a display of pink and other delicately coloured discs and fluorescent rings to his trade-mark kaleidoscopic patterns. In between those two quite stunning set pieces, there was a slight story by Walter Bullock which involved a US Army sergeant (James Ellison) who finds it impossible to resist a nightclub singer (Faye), especially when she sings Harry Warren and Leo Robin's tearful 'No Love, No Nothin'' and 'A Journey To A Star': millions of real-life American (and British) servicemen and civilians knew exactly how he felt. As for the rest, the slim and sassy Charlotte Greenwood's high-kicks were well up to her usual standard, clarinettist Benny Goodman's vocals on 'Minnie's In The Money' and 'Paducah' (with Miranda) were not in the least offensive, and Miranda combined with Baker (and others) for the lively 'You Discover You're In New York'. Among a strong supporting cast were the always amusing Edward Everett Horton, Sheila Ryan, Eugene Pallette, Tony DeMarco, and Dave Willock. Two future movie favourites, Jeanne Crain and June Haver, also made brief appearances.

GARLAND, JUDY

b. Frances Gumm, 10 June 1922, Grand Rapids, Minnesota, USA, d. 22 June 1969. The Gumms were a theatrical family. Parents Frank and Ethel had appeared in vaudeville as Jack and Virginia Lee, and later, with the addition of their first two daughters, Mary Jane and Virginia, they appeared locally as 'The Four Gumms'. 'Baby Frances' joined the troupe when she was just over two years of age, and it was quickly apparent that with her arrival, even at that early age, the Gumm family had outgrown their locale. The family moved to Los Angeles, where all three girls were enrolled in a dance school. When Frank Gumm bought a run-down theatre in Lancaster, a desert town north of Los Angeles, the family moved again. Domestic problems beset the Gumm family throughout this period and Frances's life was further disrupted by Ethel Gumm's determined belief in her youngest daughter's showbusiness potential. The act had become the Gumm Sisters, although Baby Frances was clearly the one audiences wanted to see and hear. In 1933 Ethel Gumm returned to Los Angeles, taking the girls with her. Frances was again enrolled in a theatrical school. A visit to Chicago was an important step for the girls, with the youngest once more attracting the most attention; here too, at the urging of comedian George Jessell, they changed their name to the Garland Sisters. On their return to Los Angeles in 1934 the sisters played a successful engagement at Grauman's Chinese Theater in Hollywood. Soon afterwards, Frances was personally auditioned by Louis B. Mayer, head of MGM. Deeply impressed by what he saw and heard, Mayer signed the girl before she had even taken a screen test. With another adjustment to her name, Frances became Judy Garland. She made her first film appearance in *Every Sunday* (1936), a short musical film that also featured Deanna Durbin. Her first major impact on audiences came with her third film, *Broadway Melody Of 1938*, in which she sang 'Dear Mr Gable' (to a photograph of Clark Gable), seguing into 'You Made Me Love You'. She was then teamed with MGM's established child star Mickey Rooney, a partnership that brought a succession of popular films in the 'Andy Hardy' series. By now, everyone at MGM knew that they had a star on their hands. This fact was triumphantly confirmed with her appearance in *The Wizard Of Oz* (1939), in which she sang 'Over The Rainbow', the song with which she would subsequently always be associated. Unfortunately, this period of frenzied activity came at a time when she was still developing physically. Like many young teenagers, she tended to put on weight, which was something film-makers could not tolerate. Undoubtedly, they did not want a podgy celebrity, and continuity considerations could not allow their star to change appearance during the course of the film. Regardless of the reason, she was prescribed some drugs for weight control, others to ensure she was bright and perky for the long hours of shooting, and still more to bring her down at the end of the day so that she could sleep. This was long before the side effects of amphetamines (which she took to suppress her appetite) were understood, and no one at the time was aware that the pills she was consuming in such huge quantities were highly addictive. Added to the growing girl's problems were emotional difficulties that had begun during her parents' stormy relationship and were exacerbated by the pressures of her new life. In 1941, against the wishes and advice of her mother and the studio, she married David Rose and soon afterwards became pregnant, but was persuaded by her mother and Mayer to have an abortion. With her personal life already on a downward spiral, Garland's successful film career conversely took a further upswing. In 1942 she appeared in *For Me And My Gal*, then made *Presenting Lily Mars*, *Thousands Cheer*, *Girl Crazy* (all 1943), *Meet Me In St Louis* (1944), *The Harvey Girls*, *Ziegfeld Follies* and *Till The Clouds Roll By* (all 1946). Garland's popularity extended beyond films into radio and records, but her private life was still in disarray. In 1945 she divorced Rose and married Vincente Minnelli, who had directed her in *Meet Me In St Louis*. In 1946 her daughter, Liza Minnelli, was born. The late 40s brought more film successes with *The Pirate, Easter Parade, Words And Music* (all 1948) and *In The Good Old Summertime* (1949). Although Garland's career appeared to be in splendid shape, in 1950 her private life was fast deteriorating. Pills, alcohol and severe emotional disturbances led to her failing to appear before the cameras on several occasions and resulted in the ending of her contract with MGM. In 1951 her marriage to Minnelli also dissolved and she attempted suicide. Her subsequent marriage to Sid Luft and his handling of her career brought an upturn both emotionally and professionally. She made a trip to Europe, appearing at the London Palladium to great acclaim. On her return to the USA she played the Palace Theater in New York for a hugely successful 19-week run. Her film career resumed with a dramatic/singing role in *A Star Is Born* (1954), for which she was nominated for an Oscar. By the late 50s, her problems had returned, and in some cases, had worsened. She suffered nervous and emotional breakdowns, and made further suicide attempts. A straight dramatic role in *Judgement At Nuremberg* (1961), for which she was again nominated for an Oscar, enhanced her reputation. However, her marriage was in trouble, although she and Luft made repeated attempts to hold it together (they had two children, Lorna and Joey). Despite the personal traumas and the professional ups and downs, Garland achieved another huge success with a personal appearance at New York's Carnegie Hall on 23 April 1961, the subsequent album of the concert winning five Grammy Awards. A 1963 television series was disappointing and, despite another good film performance in a dramatic role in *A Child Is Waiting*, and a fair dramatic/singing appearance in *I Could Go On Singing* (both 1963), her career remained plagued with inconsistencies. The marriage with Luft ended in divorce, as did a subsequent marriage. Remarried again in 1969, Garland attempted a comeback in a season at London's Talk Of The Town nightclub, but suffered the indignity of having bread sticks and other objects thrown at her when she turned up late for some performances. On 22 June 1969 she was found dead, apparently from an accidental overdose of sleeping pills. She was at her best in such films as *Meet Me In St Louis* and *The Wizard Of Oz* and on stage for the superb Carnegie Hall concert, and had she done nothing else, she would have earned a substantial reputation as a major singing star. To her powerful singing voice she added great emotional depths, which came not only through artifice but from the often cruel reality of her life. When the catalogue of personal tragedies was added to Garland's performing talent she became something else, a cult figure, and a showbusiness legend. She was a figure that only Hollywood could have created and yet, had she been a character in a melodrama, no one would have believed such a life was possible.

● ALBUMS: *Till The Clouds Roll By* film soundtrack (MGM 1950/55)★★★, *Easter Parade* film soundtrack (MGM 1950/55)★★★, *Words And Music* film soundtrack (MGM 1950/55)★★★, *Summer Stock/The Pirate* film soundtracks (MGM 1950/55)★★★, *Judy Garland Sings* (MGM 1951)★★★, *Judy At The Palace* (Decca 1951)★★★, *The Wizard Of Oz* (Decca 1951)★★★★, *Girl Crazy* film soundtrack (Decca 1953)★★★, *If You Feel Like Singing Sing* (MGM 1955)★★★, *Judy Garland's Greatest Performances* (Decca 1955)★★★, *Miss Show Business* (Capitol 1955)★★★, *Judy Garland With The MGM Orchestra* (MGM 1956)★★★, *The Wizard Of Oz* (MGM 1956)★★★★, *Judy* (Capitol 1956)★★★, *Meet Me In St Louis/The Harvey Girls* film soundtracks (Decca 1957)★★★, *Alone* (Capitol 1957)★★★, *A Star Is Born* (Columbia 1958)★★★★, *Judy In Love* (Capitol 1958)★★★, *In Love* (Capitol 1958)★★★, *Garland At The Grove* (Capitol 1959)★★★, with John Ireland *The Letter* (Capitol 1959)★★★, *Judy! That's Entertainment* (Capitol 1960)★★★, *Judy At Carnegie Hall* (Capitol 1961)★★★★★, *Pepe* film soundtrack (Colpix 1961)★★, *The Star Years* (MGM 1961)★★★, *The Magic Of Judy Garland* (Decca 1961)★★★, *The Hollywood Years* (MGM 1962)★★★, *Gay Purr-ee* film soundtrack (Warners 1962)★★, *The Garland Touch* (Capitol 1962)★★★, *I Could Go On Singing* film soundtrack (Capitol 1963)★★★★, *Our Love Letter* (Capitol 1963)★★★, *Just For Openers* (Capitol 1964)★★★, with Liza Minnelli *Live At The London Palladium* (Capitol 1965)★★★, *Judy Garland* (1965)★★★, *Judy Garland At Home At The Palace* (ABC 1967)★★★, *The Last Concert 20-7-68* (Paragon 1984)★★★, *Judy Garland Live!* recorded 1962 (Capitol 1989)★★★, *Judy Garland On Radio: 1936-44, Volume One* (Vintage Jazz Classics 1993)★★★.

● COMPILATIONS: *The Very Best Of Judy Garland* (MGM 1962)★★★, *The Hits Of Judy Garland* (Capitol 1963)★★★★, *The Best Of Judy Garland* (Decca 1964)★★★, *The Judy Garland DeLuxe Set* 3-LP box set (Capitol 1957)★★★★, *The ABC Years* (1976)★★★, *The Beginning* (1979)★★★, *The Young Judy Garland 1938-42* (MCA 1983)★★★, *Golden Greats* (MCA 1985)★★★, *Collection* (Castle 1986)★★★, *The Capitol Years* (Capitol 1989)★★★★, *Great MGM Stars* (MGM 1991)★★★, *The One And Only* 3-CD box set (Capitol 1991)★★★, *The Complete Decca Masters (Plus)* 4-CD box set (1994)★★★★, *Child Of Hollywood* (CDS 1994)★★★, *Collectors' Gems From The M-G-M Films* (R2 1997)★★★, *The Best Of Judy Garland* (Half Moon 1998)★★★.

● VIDEOS: *Best Of Judy Garland* (World Of Video 1988), *Judy Garland In Concert* (RCA/Columbia 1988).

● FURTHER READING: *Judy: The Films And Career Of Judy Garland*, Joe Morella and Edward Epstein. *The Other Side Of The Rainbow: With Judy Garland On The Dawn Patrol*, Mel Tormé. *Weep No More, My Lady: An Intimate Biography Of Judy Garland*, Mickey Deans. *Judy With Love*, Lorna Smith. *Judy*, Gerold Frank. *Rainbow: The Stormy Life Of Judy Garland*, Christopher Finch. *Judy Garland: A Mortgaged Life*, Anne Edwards. *Little Girl Lost: The Life And Hard Times Of Judy Garland*, Al DiOrio. *The Young Judy*, David Dahl and Barry Kehoe. *Judy & Liza*, James Spada and Karen Swenson. *Judy: Portrait Of An American Legend*, Thomas J. Watson and Bill Chapman. *The Complete Judy Garland*, Emily R. Coleman. *Rainbow's End: The Judy Garland Show*, Coyne Stephen Sanders. *Judy Garland*, David Shipman. *Me And My Shadows: Living With The Legacy Of Judy Garland*, Lorna Luft.

● FILMS: *Every Sunday* (1936), *Pigskin Parade* (1936), *Broadway Melody Of 1938* (1938), *Thoroughbreds Don't Cry* (1938), *Everybody Sing* (1938), *Listen Darling* (1938), *Love Finds Andy Hardy* (1938), *The Wizard Of Oz* (1939), *Babes In Arms* (1939), *Andy Hardy Meets A Debutante* (1939), *Strike Up The Band* (1940), *Little Nellie Kelly* (1940), *Ziegfeld Girl* (1941), *Life Begins For Andy Hardy* (1941), *Babes On Broadway* (1941), *For Me And My Gal* (1942), *We Must Have Music* (1942), *Presenting Lily Mars* (1943), *Girl Crazy* (1943), *Thousands Cheer* (1943), *Meet Me In St. Louis* (1944), *Under The*

Clock (1945), *The Harvey Girls* (1946), *Till The Clouds Roll By* (1946), *Ziegfeld Follies* (1946), *The Pirate* (1948), *Easter Parade* (1948), *Words And Music* (1948), *In The Good Old Summertime* (1949), *Summer Stock* (1950), *A Star Is Born* (1954), *Pepe* (1960), *Judgement At Nuremberg* (1961), *A Child Is Waiting* (1962), *I Could Go On Singing* (1963).

GARRETT, BETTY

b. 23 May 1919, St. Joseph, Missouri, USA. After winning a scholarship to a New York theatre company, Garrett enjoyed some success on the stage. She was an accomplished dancer, working with the celebrated Martha Graham troupe, and she also sang in clubs and hotel lounges. She made her Broadway debut in 1942 in the revue *Let Freedom Ring*, and had supporting roles in other stage shows such as *Something For The Boys*, *Jackpot*, and *Laffing Room Only*. After starring in *Call Me Mister* (1946) in which she introduced Harold Rome's 'South America, Take It Away', she was signed to a film contract. In the late 40s she sang and danced with immense zest and vitality in popular movie musicals such as *Big City*, *Words And Music*, *Take Me Out To The Ball Game*, *On the Town*, and *Neptune's Daughter*. After retiring to have children she attempted a comeback but her husband, Larry Parks, who had starred in two bio-pics about Al Jolson, had been blacklisted for refusing to testify before the House Un-American Activities Committee, and her career, too, was severely damaged. Later, Garrett and Parks developed a nightclub act and, later still, they worked in repertory theatres. She made one more film musical in the 50s, *My Sister Eileen*, but was reluctant to be parted from Parks and dropped out of that area of show business. She did appear on television, however, with roles in the long-running comedy *All In The Family*, and *Laverne And Shirley* (1976). In the 80s she toured with Sheree North and Gale Storm in the comedy *Breaking Up The Act*, and returned to Broadway in the short-lived stage adaptation of the hit film musical *Meet Me In St. Louis*. In 1990 her one-woman show, *Betty Garrett And Other Songs*, was acclaimed at the Ballroom in New York, and in the early 90s she presented her cabaret act, which includes Broadway and Hollywood songs old and new - plus a little Jacques Brel - at London's Pizza On The Park.

GARRICK GAIETIES, THE

Sub-titled 'A Bubbling Satirical Musical Revue Of Plays, Problems and Persons', the first of three editions of this satirical revue was presented by the Theatre Guild Junior Players, a group of young Theatre Guild actors, for two Sunday performances on 17 May 1925, in an effort to raise money for their new theatre on 52nd Street in New York. The production aroused such interest, that it began a commercial run at the Garrick Theatre on 8 June that year. It was an irreverent mix of sketches and songs which lampooned the musical theatre in general, and the Theatre Guild in particular (a kind of early *Forbidden Broadway*, perhaps?). The show gave the young songwriters Richard Rodgers and Lorenz Hart their first big Broadway opportunity, and they came through with several outstanding numbers such as 'April Fool', 'Sentimental Me', 'On With The Dance', 'Old Fashioned Girl (lyric by Edith Meiser),

'Do You Love Me? (I Wonder)', 'Black And Blue', and 'Manhattan', a song that was first popularized by Ben Selvin and Paul Whiteman, and eventually became a much-loved standard. That first show ran for 211 performances, and a second edition opened a year later, again at the Garrick Theatre, on 10 May 1926. Once more, the score was by Rodgers and Hart, and included 'Keys To Heaven', 'Back To Nature', 'Say It With Flowers', 'It May Rain', 'What's The Use Of Talking?', 'A Little Souvenir', and an operetta spoof 'The Rose Of Arizona'. The show's big hit was 'Mountain Greenery', which became such a success on record for Mel Tormé, and turned up in the 1948 Rodgers and Hart biopic *Words And Music*, where it was sung by Perry Como and Allyn McLerie. The third, and final version of the *The Garrick Gaieties* was presented at the Guild Theatre in 1930, with songs by a variety of composers and lyricists. Several of the numbers had music by Vernon Duke, including 'I Am Only Human After All' (lyric by Ira Gershwin and Harburg), 'Too, Too Divine' (E.Y. 'Yip' Harburg and Duke), and 'Ankle Up The Altar With Me (Harburg and Richard Myers). Also in the score was 'Triple Sec', a 'progressive opera' by the *avant garde* composer Marc Blitzstein, and 'Out Of Breath And Scared To Death Of You' by Johnny Mercer and Everett Miller, which is said to be Mercer's first published song. Some of the cast who were in the first *Gaieties* and still there at the end, included Sterling Holloway, Edith Meiser, James Norris, Hidegarde Halliday, and Philip Loeb, who also directed. Lee Strasberg, who later opened the famous acting studio, was in one of the shows, as was Libby Holman. Two talented newcomers in the third show were Ray Heatherton and the actress-comedienne Imogen Coca, and the future Hollywood star, Rosalind Russell, made her Broadway debut when the 1930 edition returned briefly to Broadway in October of that same year.

GAY DIVORCE

Opening at New York's Ethel Barrymore Theatre on 29 November 1932, this show was Fred Astaire's first stage musical without his sister, Adele (she retired after *The Band Wagon* in 1931) - and Astaire's own final Broadway appearance before leaving for Hollywood to star in some 30 musical films. Music and lyrics were provided by Cole Porter, and the book was written by Kenneth Webb and Samuel Hoffenstein from Dwight Taylor's adaptation of an unproduced play, *An Adorable Adventure*, by J. Hartley Manners. It seems that Mimi Pratt (Claire Luce) wants to divorce her husband. Guy Holden (Fred Astaire), a British novelist who loves Mimi, is mistaken for Toneti (Erik Rhodes), the professional co-respondent Mimi has hired in an effort to shake herself loose. That kind of story can use a great score, and Porter came up with one of his best. Comedienne Louella Gear had the amusing 'I Still Love The Red, White And Blue' and 'Mister And Missus Fitch'; Erik Rhodes sang 'How's Your Romance?' ('Does he or not love you an awful lot?/Cold, tepid, warm, or hot/How's your romance?'); Eric Blore, who played an immaculate waiter in the show (and later made a career in films, usually as a butler), enquired 'What Will Become Of Our England?' ('When the Prince of Wales finds a wife'); Astaire crooned the haunting 'After You, Who?' ('I could search years but who else could change my tears/Into laughter after you?') and joined Claire Luce in 'I've Got You On My Mind' ('You're not wild enough/You're not gay enough/You don't let me lead you astray enough') and one of Porter's most potent love songs, 'Night And Day'. The composer claimed the music for the latter number was inspired by a Mohammedan call to worship that he had heard in Morocco. Initially, the show had an indifferent response, but the exposure of some of the songs, especially 'Night And Day', soon boosted audiences. The number became a nation-wide hit through recordings by Astaire himself (With Leo Reisman's Orchestra), Eddy Duchin, Charlie Barnet, Frank Sinatra, and Bing Crosby. Gay Divorce played 248 performances on Broadway, and another 180 in London in 1933, where Astaire, Luce, Rhodes, and Blore recreated their roles. It was revived briefly Off Broadway in 1960. Over 30 years later, in 1993, the show was presented in concert by John McGlinn at Carnegie Hall's Weill Recital Hall complete with the original orchestrations by Hans Spialek and Robert Russell Bennett. The 1934 film version, called The Gay Divorcée, starred Astaire and Ginger Rogers, but the only song retained from the original score was 'Night And Day'.

GAY DIVORCEE, THE

It was not just the title that was changed when Cole Porter's 1932 hit Broadway show, The Gay Divorce, was transferred to the screen two years later. The title itself was not seen to be fit for wider consumption in America, and only one song, the incomparable 'Night And Day', survived from the smart and sophisticated stage score. Fortunately, Fred Astaire also made the trip from New York to Hollywood, and the screenplay, by George Marion Jnr., Dorothy Yost and Edward Kaufman, remained reasonably true to the original book. After the plot, which was set in an English seaside town and involved Guy Holden (Astaire) being mistaken for the professional co-respondent hired by Mimi Glossop (Ginger Rogers) in an effort to facilitate her divorce, had got under way, delighted audiences were able to sit back and enjoy the sublime dancing of Astaire and Rogers in their first starring role together. 'Night And Day' would dominate any film musical, especially when it accompanied dancing of this style and grace, The Gay Divorcée was no exception, but there were several other engaging numbers by a variety of composers, including 'A Needle In A Haystack' (Con Conrad-Herb Magidson), and two by Mack Gordon and Harry Revel - 'Don't Let It Bother You' and 'Let's K-nock K-nees'. The latter was punched out with a great deal of zest by Betty Grable, whose 'pin-up' image during the 40s necessitated her own legs being insured for many thousands of dollars. 'Night And Day' may have been the film's major romantic moment, but The Gay Divorcée is probably best-remembered for another song, 'The Continental' (Conrad-Magidson), which was introduced by Fred and Ginger in a spectacular 17-minute sequence, and went on to become all the rage of dance floors everywhere. It also has the distinction of being the first song to win an Academy Award. Meanwhile, back to the plot. As for the details of the prospective divorce, a character by the name of Rodolfo Tonetti (Erik Rhodes) turned out to be the real co-respon-

dent, and the rest of the cast was made up of always reliable and amusing supporting players such as Edward Everett Horton and Alice Brady. Dave Gould and Hermes Pan were responsible for the innovative choreography, and the film, which was released by RKO, was directed by Mark Sandrich. In view of the film's title change, which was apparently demanded by the US censor, it is interesting that his UK equivalent had no such problems, and both the original British cinema and subsequent video release bear the title: The Gay Divorce.

GAY'S THE WORD

A light musical comedy which turned out to be the last production involving Ivor Novello, one of the London musical theatre's favourite sons; he died less than a month after Gay's The Word opened at the Saville Theatre on 16 February 1951. Novello provided the music and libretto, and Alan Melville wrote the sharp, witty lyrics for a show that, in some ways lampooned the composer's previous extravagantly staged operetta-style shows. This was particularly evident in 'Ruritania', the opening number for the chorus, with lines such as 'Since Oklahoma!/We've been in a coma'. Jack Hulbert directed the piece, and his wife, Cicely Courtneidge took the lead as Gay Daventry, a 'star actress in charge of a drama school'. Her young pupils included the lovely Linda (Lizbeth Webb) with her boyfriend, Peter Lynton (Thorley Walters). The school was located in an English seaside town with lots of sea and sand, plus plenty of rocky cliffs, which gave Courtneidge a chance to be 'bossy', and the author an ideal excuse for a sub-plot involving smugglers and their midnight shenanigans. Courtneidge was her usually ebullient self. Even at the age of 57 she had lost none of the energy and enthusiasm for which she was renowned. Novello and Melville summed it up perfectly in 'Vitality', which she delivered with such style, along with another song that, being a seasoned trouper, could well have been her life-long creed, 'It's Bound To Be Right On The Night' ('Over cold pork, pink blancmange and unripe Stilton/You've rather a nasty supper with Jack Hylton'). The rest of the score included the songs 'Gaiety Glad', 'Bees Are Buzzin'', 'Finder, Please Return', 'On Such A Night As This', 'A Matter Of Minutes', and 'Guards On Parade'.

It was fitting, considering Novello's previous contributions to the London theatre, that he should go out with a big hit; Gay's The Word ran for 504 performances. It proved to be Cicely Courtneidge's last musical comedy in the West End (she still continued to appear in other kinds of productions) until 1964, and her appearance as Mme. Arcati in High Spirits, a musical adaptation of Noël Coward's Blithe Spirit.

GAY, NOEL

b. Richard Moxon Armitage, 3 March 1898, Wakefield, Yorkshire, England, d. 3 March 1954, London England. A prolific composer and lyricist, Gay was responsible for many of the most popular and memorable songs in the UK during the 30s and 40s. A child prodigy, he was educated at Wakefield Cathedral School, and often deputized for the Cathedral organist. In 1913 he moved to London to study at the Royal College of Music, and later became the director of music and organist at St Anne's Church in Soho. After four years studying for his MA and B.Mus. at Christ's Church College, Cambridge, he seemed destined for a career in a university or cathedral. However, while at Cambridge he became interested in the world of musical comedy, and started to write songs. After contributing to the revue *Stop Press*, he was commissioned to write the complete score for the *Charlot Show Of 1926*. He was also the principal composer for *Clowns In Clover*, which starred Jack Hulbert and Cicely Courtneidge, and ran for over 500 performances. Around this time he took the name of Noel Gay for his popular work to avoid embarrassment to the church authorities. In 1930, Gay, with Harry Graham, wrote his most successful song to date, 'The King's Horses', which was sung in another Charlot revue, *Folly To Be Wise*. He then collaborated with lyricist Desmond Carter for the score of his first musical show, *Hold My Hand* (1931). Starring Jessie Matthews, Sonnie Hale and Stanley Lupino, the songs included 'Pied Piper', 'What's In A Kiss', 'Hold My Hand' and 'Turn On The Music'. During the 30s Gay wrote complete, or contributed to, scores for popular shows such as *She Couldn't Say No*, *That's A Pretty Thing*, *Jack O'Diamonds*, *Love Laughs!*, *O-Kay For Sound* (one of the early Crazy Gang music hall-type revues at the London Palladium, in which Bud Flanagan sang Gay's 'The Fleet's In Port Again'), *Wild Oats* and *Me And My Girl* (1937). The latter show, with a book and lyrics by L. Arthur Rose, and starring Lupino Lane in the central role of Bill Sibson, ran for over 1,600 performances and featured 'The Lambeth Walk', which became an enormously popular sequence dance craze - so popular, in fact, that when the show was filmed in 1939, it was re-titled *The Lambeth Walk*. In the same year, with Ralph Butler, Gay gave Bud Flanagan the big song, 'Run Rabbit Run', in another Crazy Gang revue, *The Little Dog Laughed*. During the 40s, Gay wrote for several shows with lyrics mostly by Frank Eyton, including *Lights Up* ('Let The People Sing'), 'Only A Glass Of Champagne' and 'You've Done Something To My Heart'); *Present Arms*; *La-Di-Di-Di-Da'*; *The Love Racket*; *Meet Me Victoria*; *Sweetheart Mine*; and *Bob's Your Uncle* (1948). His songs for films included 'All For A Shilling A Day' and 'There's Something About A Soldier', sung by Courtneidge in *Me And Marlborough* (1935); 'Leaning On A Lamp Post' introduced by comedian George Formby in *Feather Your Nest*; 'Who's Been Polishing The Sun', sung by Jack Hulbert in *The Camels Are Coming*; 'I Don't Want To Go to Bed' (Stanley Lupino in *Sleepless Nights*); and 'All Over The Place' (*Sailors Three*). Gay also composed 'Tondeleyo', the first song to be synchronized into a British talking picture (*White Cargo*). His other songs included 'Round The Marble Arch', 'All For The Love Of A Lady', 'I Took My Harp To A Party' (a hit for Gracie Fields), 'Let's Have A Tiddley At The Milk Bar', 'Red, White And Blue', 'Love Makes The World Go Round', 'The Moon Remembered, But You Forgot', 'The Girl Who Loves A Soldier', 'The Birthday Of The Little Princess', 'Are We Downhearted? - No!', 'Hey Little Hen', 'Happy Days Happy Months', 'I'll Always Love You', 'Just A Little Fond Affection', 'When Alice Blue Gown Met Little Boy Blue', 'I Was Much Better Off In The Army' and 'My Thanks To You' (co-written with Norman Newell). His

other collaborators included Archie Gottler, Clifford Grey, Dion Titheradge, Donavan Parsons and Ian Grant. In the early 50s Gay wrote very little, just a few songs such as 'I Was Much Better Off In The Army' and 'You Smile At Everyone But Me'. He had been going deaf for some years, and had to wear a hearing aid. After his death in March 1954, his publishing company, Noel Gay Music, which he had formed in 1938, published one more song, 'Love Me Now'. His son, Richard Armitage (b. 12 August 1928, Wakefield, England, d. 17 November 1986), a successful impresario and agent, took over the company, and extended and developed the organization into one of the biggest television and representational agencies in Europe. His clients included David Frost, Rowan Atkinson, Esther Rantzen, Russ Conway, Russell Harty, Jonathan Miller, John Cleese, the King's Singers and many more. The publishing side had several hit copyrights, including the Scaffold's 'Thank U Very Much'. After mounting several minor productions, Armitage revived his father's most popular show, *Me And My Girl*, in London in February 1985. With the versatile actor Robert Lindsay as Sibson, a revised book, and two other Gay hits, 'The Sun Has Got His Hat On' and 'Leaning On A Lamp Post' interpolated into the score, the new production was an immediate success. It closed in 1993 following a stay of eight years. Around the same time, *Radio Times*, a new show featuring Noel Gay's music, enjoyed a brief West End run. Opening on Broadway in 1986, *Me And My Girl* ran for over 1,500 performances, New York's biggest hit for years. Armitage died just three months after the show's Broadway debut.

GAYNOR, MITZI

b. Francesca Mitzi Gerber, 4 September 1930, Chicago, Illinois. USA. This vivacious and extremely talented actress, singer and dancer, reputedly of Hungarian descent, graced several good movie musicals in the 50s, and is probably best remembered as the girl who tried to 'wash that man (Rossano Brazzi) right out of her hair' in *South Pacific* (1958). After taking ballet lessons from an early age, Gaynor danced with the Los Angeles Civic Light Opera while in her early teens, and made a strong impression with Betty Grable and Dan Dailey in her first movie, *My Blue Heaven* (1950). This was followed by one or two straight parts, and a few musicals such as *Golden Girl*, *Bloodhounds Of Broadway*, *Down Among The Sheltering Palms* and *The 'I Don't Care' Girl* (1953), which were not as satisfying. The situation improved as the 50s progressed and she had excellent roles in *There's No Business Like Show Business*, *Anything Goes*, *The Birds And The Bees*, *The Joker Is Wild* and *Les Girls* (1957). She was good, too, in *South Pacific*, but although it remains, to date, the fourth highest-grossing screen musical of the period in the USA, she was reportedly personally disaffected with the experience. Her particular genre of film musicals was becoming extinct, and, like so many others, she worked more often in television and had her own top-rated specials during the 60s. She also toured in stage musical revivals, and, as an accomplished actress, continued to play the occasional comic or dramatic movie role. Gaynor also built up a polished and highly regarded concert and cabaret act. As recently as 1987 she was acclaimed for her nightclub performances, which included a section devoted to Irving Berlin and Fred Astaire, a satirical version of Harry Von Tilzer and Arthur Lamb's nineteenth century song 'A Bird In A Gilded Cage', and a rousing singalong 'God Bless America' finale. Two years later she embarked on an 11-month, 36-city tour of the USA in a revival of Cole Porter's 1934 show *Anything Goes*, the first time in her long career that she had been on the road in a book musical. The *Daily News*, commenting on a New York performance of hers in the late 90s, wrote: 'She is what show business is all about.'

● ALBUMS: *Mitzi* (Verve 1959)★★★, *Mitzi Gaynor Sings The Lyrics Of Ira Gershwin* (Verve 1959)★★★, and soundtrack recordings.

● FILMS: *My Blue Heaven* (1950), *Take Care Of My Little Girl* (1951), *Golden Girl* (1951), *Bloodhounds Of Broadway* (1952), *We're Not Married!* (1952), *The I Don't Care Girl* (1953), *Down Among The Sheltering Palms* (1953), *Three Young Texans* (1954), *There's No Business Like Show Business* (1954), *Birds And The Bees* (1956), *Anything Goes* (1956), *The Joker Is Wild* (1957), *Les Girls* (1957), *South Pacific* (1958), *Happy Anniversary* (1959), *Surprise Package* (1960), *For Love Or Money* (1963).

GELBART, LARRY

b. Larry Simon Gelbart, 25 February 1928, Chicago, Illinois, USA. A pre-eminent screenwriter, librettist, director, and producer, Gelbert moved as a child with his family to California. His father was a barber, and used to cut the famous comedian Danny Thomas's hair. When Gelbart was 16, he went to work for Thomas, writing jokes, and then moved on to other top radio comics such as Bob Hope and Eddie Cantor. Hope took Gelbart into television, where he met Burt Shevelove, and in 1958 the two men set about the task of working through all 21 of the surviving comedies by the Roman playwright, Plautus. Together with composer Stephen Sondheim, they took four years writing and re-writing what became *A Funny Thing Happened On The Way To The Forum*. The show opened on Broadway in May 1962, and ran for 964 performances. Gelbart and Shevelove both won Tony Awards. Gelbart went to London in 1963 for the West End opening, and stayed for nine years. He wrote for Marty Feldman, and provided the screenplays for a number of movies, many of them uncredited. Back in the USA, Gelbart started work on turning the 1970 film *M*A*S*H* into a television series. He won Emmys for his contributions - writing many of the almost 100 episodes 1972-83, as well as directing and serving as executive producer on the series. Gelbart made his stage debut as a director with a UK revival of '*Forum*', which transferred from the Chichester Festival to the West End in 1986. Three years later, *City Of Angels*, an ingenious and hilarious private eye spoof of a musical, for which Gelbart wrote the book (and won his third Tony), opened on Broadway. It was a stinging satire on Hollywood, and the indignities that screenwriters suffer in 'the ego-fuelled jungle warfare that rages on the West Coast', in particular, Gelbart's experience on the film *Tootsie*, the story of a 'resting' actor who masquerades as a woman in order to get a job in a television soap opera. Of its star, Dustin Hoffman, Gelbart was quoted thus: 'Never argue with a man who is shorter than his Oscar.' A

legend in the business, renowned for his skill and wit, apart from his two big hits, '*Forum*' and *City Of Angels*, Gelbart's credits have included *Sly Fox*, *Mastergate*, *Jump*, and *Power Failure*. He has not emerged unscathed. In 1961, after experiencing immense difficulties getting *The Conquering Hero*, a show based on Preston Sturges's sentimental comedy movie *Hail The Conquering Hero*, into New York for its eight-performance run, he is reported to have said somewhat wearily, 'If Hitler is still alive, I hope he's out of town with a musical.'

● FILMS: as a writer *The Notorious Landlady* (1962), *The Wrong Box* (1966), *Not With My Wife, You Don't* (1966), *A Funny Thing Happened On The Way To The Forum* (1966), *A Fine Pair* (1969), *The Chastity Belt* (1969), *Oh, God!* (1977), *Movie Movie* (1978), *Rough Cut* (1980), *Neighbors* (1981), *Tootsie* (1982), *Blame It On Rio* (1984).

GENE KRUPA STORY, THE

This film, made in 1959, is another jazz biopic that misses its target by a mile. Sal Mineo portrays Gene Krupa as a sulky rebel, quite unlike the real-life drummer. Despite other shortcomings, Mineo convincingly played on-screen drums to Krupa's ghosted backing, and, to his credit, the actor later acknowledged the film's mediocrity. On the strength of this telling of Krupa's tale, no one could have imagined that he was a heart-throb idol of millions and one of the greatest showbiz attractions of his era; but then, any film on Krupa that manages to omit Benny Goodman is more than a little short on veracity. Shot in black and white, the film's director was Don Weis. Musically, there are low and high points. Among the former is a scrappy jam session with Red Nichols; the best of the latter is a wonderful version of 'Memories Of You' sung by Anita O'Day. Shelly Manne appears as Dave Tough (he also played the late drummer in *The Five Pennies*). Krupa's return to the stage after a drugs bust that put him in jail and cost him his highly popular band is quite well represented, with Tommy Pederson playing the role of Tommy Dorsey who hired Krupa in 1944. In 1989 a projected remake was abandoned when a leading Hollywood star, interested in the role of Krupa, had to bow out to meet other obligations. (Alternative title: *Drum Crazy*).

GENTLEMEN MARRY BRUNETTES

(see *Gentlemen Prefer Blondes*)

GENTLEMEN PREFER BLONDES (FILM MUSICAL)

Carol Channing really started something in 1949 when she created the role of diamond-loving Lorelei Lee in the hit Broadway musical *Gentlemen Prefer Blondes*. Ever since then - even into the early 90s - actresses all over the world have endeavoured to purvey the right mixture of sexiness and vulnerability that was Lorelei, and one of them who achieved it, in this 1953 screen version, was Marilyn Monroe. The concept started with Anita Loos' novel, which she turned into a stage show with the help of Joseph Fields. Charles Lederer's screenplay followed the same familiar path: thoroughly modern 20s girls Lorelei and her best friend, Dorothy Shaw (Jane Russell), travel to Paris with the intention of improving Lorelei's finances and Dorothy's marriage prospects. After causing a certain amount of havoc amongst the city's male population, they return to New York having accomplished their aims (and celebrate with a double wedding). The supporting cast was exceptionally fine, and included Charles Coburn, Tommy Noonan, Elliot Reid, Taylor Holmes, Norma Varden, Steven Geray, the seven-year-old 'frog-voiced' George Winslow, and the 20-year-old George (*West Side Story*) Chakiris. Only three of Jule Styne and Leo Robin's songs survived from the original show: the delicious 'Diamonds Are A Girl's Best Friend' (Monroe), 'A Little Girl From Little Rock' - or rather, 'Two Girls From Little Rock' (Monroe-Russell) - and 'Bye, Bye Baby'. Hoagy Carmichael and Harold Adamson contributed two more: 'Ain't There Anyone Here For Love?', Jane Russell's touching plea to a gymnasium full of muscular males, and the reflective 'When Love Goes Wrong' (Monroe-Russell). The whole affair was a delight, with both Monroe and Russell, who were essentially very different in style, giving marvellous performances. Jack Cole designed the spirited choreography, and the director was Howard Hawks. Sol C. Seigel produced the film in Technicolor for 20th Century-Fox. A sequel, *Gentlemen Marry Brunettes*, was released in 1955. Jeanne Crain replaced Marilyn Monroe and played Jane Russell's sister in a lacklustre, pale shadow of the original, which, apart from the title song by Herbert Spencer and Earle Hagen, featured a score consisting of old standards.

GENTLEMEN PREFER BLONDES (STAGE MUSICAL)

This show opened at the Ziegfeld Theatre in New York on 8 December 1949, but the story immediately transported audiences back to the roaring 20s. Working on the basis that 'there's gold in them thar tycoons', Lorelei Lee (Carol Channing), has got herself engaged to Gus Esmond (Jack McCauley), who has made a fortune out of buttons. At midnight, she bids him a tearful farewell on the dockside (He: 'I'll be in my room alone every post meridian/She: 'And I'll be with my diary and that book by Mr. Gideon') as she sails with her best chum, Dorothy Shaw (Yvonne Adair), on the Ile de France. When she hits Paris, her pursuit of a life-style to which she would dearly like to become accustomed, involves a zipper tycoon, Josephus Gage (George S Irving), and sundry other potential goldmines, such as Sir Francis Beekman (Rex Evans), as she takes in most of the glamorous sights of the city. As befits 'A Little Girl From Little Rock', she eventually returns home to marry her Mr. Esmond, and Dorothy also finds her happiness in America, with Philadelphian Henry Spofford (Eric Brotherson). The book, by Anita Loos and Joseph Fields, from Anita Loos's novel was charming and funny. Channing had appeared on Broadway the year before in the revue *Lend An Ear*, but *Gentleman Prefer Blondes* rocketed her to stardom in the space of just a few weeks. The score, by Jule Styne (music) and Leo Robin (lyrics), was full of good songs. As well as the tender 'Bye, Bye Baby' (with McCauley), 'It's Delightful Down In Chile' (with Evans), and two numbers with the ensemble, 'Homesick Blues' and 'Gentlemen Prefer Blondes', Channing also had 'I'm Just A Little Girl From Little Rock'

and the marvellous 'Diamonds Are A Girl's Best Friend' ('He's your guy when stocks go high/But beware when they start to descend/It's then that those louses go back to their spouses/Diamonds are a girl's best friend'). The rest of the songs included 'I Love What I'm Doing', 'Just A Kiss Apart', 'You Say You Care', 'I'm A'Tingle, I'm Aglow', 'Mamie Is Mimi', and 'It's High Time'. The show was a great success and ran on Broadway for 740 performances. A film version of *Gentlemen Prefer Blondes* with extra songs by Hoagy Carmichael and Harold Adamson, and starring Marilyn Monroe and Jane Russell, was released in 1953, and there was a sequel, *Gentlemen Marry Brunettes*, two years later. For some reason, the show was not presented in London until 1962 when Dora Bryan played Lorelei during a run of 223 performances. In 1974, Carol Channing starred on Broadway in the musical, *Lorelei*, which was sub-titled 'Gentlemen Still Prefer Blondes', retained some of the best features of the 1949 original, and incorporated a prologue and an epilogue in which Lorelei appeared as an older woman. The revised book was by Kenny Solms and Gail Parent, and Jule Styne contributed some new songs with lyrics by Betty Comden and Adolph Green. The show enjoyed a run of 320 performances. In April 1995, a revival of the original *Gentlemen Prefer Blondes*, presented by Tony Randall's National Actors Theater in association with the Goodspeed Opera House, opened on Broadway. It starred cabaret singer K.T. Sullivan (Lorelei), Karen Prunzik (Dorothy), Allen Fitzpatrick (Gus), Henry (George Dvorsky), Jamie Ross (Josephus), and David Ponting (Sir Francis). As usual, the score was juggled around quite a bit, and there was one interpolation, the lovely 'A Ride On A Rainbow' which Styne and Robin wrote for a 1957 NBC musical of *Ruggles Of Red Gap*. It later received a memorable treatment on *Lena Horne At The Sands*. London audiences saw Lorelei and her pals again at the Open Air Theatre, Regent's Park in 1998. The gold-digging, not-so-dumb flapper was played by Sara Crowe, with Debby Bishop as Dorothy ('giving a master class in laid-back teasing raunchiness'), and Clive Rowe (Gus).

GEORGE M!

A celebratory musical about the life of the multi-talented George M. Cohan (singer-dancer-author-director, and more), detailing his early days in vaudeville, through his ups and downs, to his final Broadway triumph when he portrayed President Franklin D. Roosevelt in *I'd Rather Be Right* in 1937. With a book by Michael Stewart, and John and Fran Pascal, *George M!* opened at the Palace Theatre in New York on 10 April 1968. After his triumph as the MC in *Cabaret* two years earlier, Joel Grey strutted his stuff somewhat in the manner of Cohan, but did not go for a precise impersonation as James Cagney did in the 1942 film, *Yankee Doodle Dandy*. Most of the songs associated with the master showman - all the flag-waving favourites - were included, many of which he wrote himself, such as 'Yankee Doodle Dandy', 'So Long, Mary', 'Forty-Five Minutes From Broadway', 'Harrigan', 'Over There', 'Mary's A Grand Old Name', 'You're A Grand Old Flag', and 'Give My Regards To Broadway'. The show also featured the future Broadway star, Bernadette Peters, in the relatively minor role of Cohan's sister. She made a sufficiently strong impression to be awarded a Theatre World Citation for her performance. These compilation shows are not everyone's idea of what the musical theatre should be all about, but they can be entertaining, and this one, which ran for 427 performances - over a year - was cited by a US critic as 'The one flicker of light in a drab Broadway season.'

GEORGE WHITE'S SCANDALS
(see White, George)

GERSHWIN, GEORGE

b. 26 September 1898, New York City, New York, USA, d. 11 June 1937, Beverly Hills, California, USA. One of the select group of all-time great American composers, as a youngster George Gershwin was a poor student, happy to spend his days playing in the streets. He eventually took up the piano when the family bought an instrument for his older brother, Ira Gershwin. He quickly showed enormous enthusiasm for music, taking lessons and studying harmony and theory. His taste was eclectic: he listened to classical music and to the popular music of the day, in particular the music of black Americans which was then gaining a widespread appeal. After becoming a professional musician in 1912, he played the piano at holiday resorts in upstate New York, and worked as a song plugger for the renowned Remick Music Company. He continued with his studies and began to write music. His first songs were undistinguished, but attracted the attention of important figures such as Sophie Tucker, Harry Von Tilzer and Sigmund Romberg. Some of his early compositions were influenced by ragtime - 'Rialto Ripples' (1916, with Will Donaldson) was one such example - and he also continued to gain a reputation as a performer. In 1917 he was hired as a rehearsal pianist for the Jerome Kern/Victor Herbert Broadway show Miss 1917, and his own compositions continued to flow, some with lyrics by his brother Ira, and others by Irving Caesar. It was a collaboration in 1919 with Caesar that gave Gershwin his first hit: 'Swanee' had originally been played by the popular Arthur Pryor band, but it was only when Al Jolson sang it in the musical, Sinbad, that it became a success. Also in 1919, George Gershwin collaborated with Arthur J. Jackson and Buddy De Sylva on his first complete Broadway score, for La, La Lucille. In the early 20s, he wrote the exquisite ballad, 'The Man I Love', with Ira, and contributed to revues such as George White's Scandals of 1922 ('I'll Build A Stairway To Paradise' (lyric: Buddy De Sylva and Ira Gershwin), George White's Scandals of 1924 ('Somebody Loves Me' with a lyric: De Sylva and Ballard MacDonald), and the London musical, Primrose (lyrics mostly by Ira Gershwin and Desmond Carter). In complete contrast to his work for the musical theatre, bandleader Paul Whiteman commissioned George to write an extended piece that was to be classical in structure but which would use the jazz idiom. The result was 'Rhapsody In Blue', arranged by Ferde Grofé, and first performed by Whiteman at the Aeolian Hall in New York in 1924, with the composer at the piano. In the same year, George and Ira were back on Broadway with the hit musical Lady, Be Good! ('Fascinating Rhythm',

'The "Half Of It, Dearie" Blues', title song), which was followed throughout the decade by several other delightful productions, including Tip Toes ('Sweet And Low-Down', 'That Certain Feeling'), Oh, Kay! (with Sigmund Romberg and P.G. Wodehouse, 'Clap Yo' Hands', 'Dear Little Girl', 'Do-Do-Do', 'Maybe', 'Someone To Watch Over Me'), Funny Face, with Fred Astaire and his sister Adele ('He Loves And She Loves', 'S Wonderful', title song), Rosalie ('How Long Has This Been Going On?', 'Oh Gee! Oh Joy!'), Treasure Girl ('Feeling I'm Falling'), and Show Girl ('Liza [All The Clouds'll Roll Away]', 1929). During this period the brothers each worked with other collaborators. The Gershwins' success was maintained in the early 30s with Strike Up The Band ('I've Got A Crush On You', 'Soon', title song) and the magnificent Girl Crazy, which starred Ethel Merman ('I Got Rhythm', 'But Not For Me', 'Embraceable You', 'Bidin' My Time', 'Boy! What Love Has Done To Me', 'But Not For Me'). In the pit band for Girl Crazy were up-and-coming musicians such as Benny Goodman, Glenn Miller and Gene Krupa. The Pulitzer Prize-winning Of Thee I Sing ('Love Is Sweeping The Country', 'Who Cares', title song) was another hit, but the Gershwins' next two Broadway shows, Pardon My English! and Let 'Em Eat Cake, were flops. After the success of 'Rhapsody In Blue', George Gershwin had again written music in classical form with 'Concert In F' (1925), the tone poem 'An American In Paris' (1928) and his 'Second Rhapsody' (1930). In 1935, his folk opera Porgy And Bess (lyrics by Ira Gershwin and DuBose Heyward) opened in Boston, Massachusetts, and despite early critical disapproval and audience indifference, it became one of his most performed works. The score included such memorable songs as 'It Ain't Necessarily So', 'Bess, You Is My Woman', 'I Loves You, Porgy', 'I Got Plenty O' Nuttin' (Ira Gershwin, in his book Lyrics On Several Occasions, refers to this song as 'I've Got Plenty O' Nuthin'), 'There's A Boat Dat's Leavin' Soon For New York', and the immortal 'Summertime'. In 1936, the Gershwin brothers returned to Hollywood, after visiting a few years earlier with only modest results. Now they entered into a new phase of creativity, writing the score for the Fred Astaire/Ginger Rogers musical Shall We Dance ('They All Laughed', 'Let's Call The Whole Thing Off', 'They Can't Take That Away From Me'), and A Damsel In Distress ('Nice Work If You Can Get It', 'Stiff Upper Lip', 'Things Are Looking Up', 'A Foggy Day'), in which Astaire was teamed with the English actress, Joan Fontaine. It was while he was working on the next film, The Goldwyn Follies (1938), that George Gershwin was taken ill. He died of a brain tumour in June 1937. Despite the severity of his illness, Gershwin's songs for the film, which included 'Love Walked In', 'I Was Doing all Right', 'I Love To Rhyme', 'Just Another Rhumba', and the beautiful 'Love Is Here To Stay' were among his best work. In 1947, some hitherto unpublished songs, such as 'For You, For Me, For Evermore', 'Aren't You Kind Of Glad We Did', and 'Changing My Tune', were used in the Betty Grable/Dick Haymes movie The Shocking Miss Pilgrim, and other Gershwin numbers were heard on the screen in The Barkleys Of Broadway (1949) and An American In Paris (1951), as well as in the film adaptations of Girl Crazy, Funny Face, and Porgy And

Bess. Although his life span was relatively short, Gershwin's work was not merely extensive but also imperishable. Hardly any of his songs have dated, and they are performed frequently more than 50 years after his death. As with so many of his contemporaries, Gershwin's popular songs adapted to the latest musical developments, in particular incorporating concepts from the jazz world, and, not surprisingly, his work is especially popular among jazz instrumentalists. Another accomplished exponent of the best of Gershwin was pianist Oscar Levant, a valued lifelong friend of the composer. It is, however, with singers that the full glory of Gershwin's music emerges, and he remains a key and influential figure in the story of American popular song. In 1992, many of his most enduring numbers were showcased in two contrasting productions: the intimate New York revue *'S Wonderful, 'S Marvelous, 'S Gershwin!*, and the big budget Broadway musical, *Crazy For You*, which was 'very loosely based' on the Gershwins' 1930 show *Girl Crazy*. In 1993, a West End production of *Crazy For You* opened to rave notices, and looked set for a long residency. In 1994, Elektra Nonesuch released a unique CD entitled *Gershwin Plays Gershwin*, which contained transcribed piano rolls made by the composer between 1916 and 1927. Among the tracks were his earliest versions of immortal melodies such as 'Swanee', 'That Certain Feeling', 'An American In Paris', and 'Rhapsody In Blue'.

After Ira's centennial celebrations in 1996, it was George's turn two years later. One of the highlights was *George Gershwin At 100*, a concert at Carnegie Hall, with the San Francisco Symphony Orchestra conducted by Michael Tilson Thomas, and starring Audra McDonald, Brian Stokes Mitchell, and Frederica Von Stade. Another proved to be Hope Clarke's new ballet based on *Porgy And Bess* which premiered at the Lincoln Center. The Library of Congress also paid tribute to George and Ira by dedicating a room to them. It is dominated by George's grand piano and Ira's portable typewriter. In addition, the team now have a star on the Hollywood Walk of Fame. In Britain, *S'Wonderful: A Celebration Of George Gershwin*, was presented at the London Palladium, and - a rare honour - George was made Composer Of The Week on BBC Radio 3. The BBC also broadcast a concert version of the 1931 Broadway musical, *Of Thee I Sing*.

● ALBUMS: *Plays The Rhapsody In Blue* (50s)★★★, *At The Piano* (50s)★★★, *Gershwin Plays Gershwin* (Elektra Nonesuch 1994)★★★, *I Got Rhythm: The Music Of George Gershwin* 4-CD box set (Koch 1995)★★★★, *George & Ira Gershwin In Hollywood* (Rhino/Turner 1997)★★★, *Gershwin And Grofé* (Pearl GEM 1998)★★★.

● FURTHER READING: *Gershwin*, Edward Jablonski. *The Memory Of All That: The Life Of George Gershwin*, Joan Peyser. *A Journey To Greatness*, David Ewen. *George Gershwin*, Robert Payne. *The Gershwins*, Robert Kimball and Alfred E. Simon. *Gershwin*, Isaac Goldberg. *George Gershwin*, Alan Kendall. *Rhapsody In Blue*, George Gershwin. *Fascinating Rhythm: The Collaborations Of George & Ira Gershwin*, Deena Rosenberg. *A Gershwin Companion A Critical Inventory & Discography 1916-1984*, Walter Rimler. *George Gershwin*, M. Armitage. *George Gershwin: Man And Legend*, M. Armstrong. *George Gershwin*, R. Chalupt. *George Gershwin*, C. Longolius. *George Gershwin*, M. Pasi.

The Life Of George Gershwin, R. Rushmore. *George Gershwin*, A. Gauthier. *George Gershwin: A Selective Bibliography And Discography*, C. Schwartz. *Gershwin: His Life And Music*, C Schwartz. *The Gershwin Years: George And Ira*, Edward Jablonski And Lawrence D. Stewart. *George Gershwin*, Rodney Greenberg.

GERSHWIN, IRA

b. 6 December 1896, New York City, New York, USA, d. 17 August 1983, Beverly Hills, California, USA. A consummate lyricist, whose career spanned some 40 years, like his younger brother George Gershwin, Ira was an indifferent student, but became fascinated by popular music, and particularly the lyrics of songs. He began writing seriously in 1917, sometimes using the pseudonym 'Arthur Francis', and had a number of minor successes, including the score for the stage show, *Two Little Girls In Blue* (music by Vincent Youmans). In the 20s and 30s he was closely associated with his brother, collaborating on numerous Broadway shows such as *Primrose* (with Desmond Carter), *Tell Me More!* (with Buddy De Sylva), *Tip Toes*, *Lady, Be Good!*, *Oh, Kay!*, *Funny Face*, *Rosalie*, *Treasure Girl*, *Show Girl* (with Gus Khan), *Strike Up The Band*, *Girl Crazy*, *Pardon My English*, *Let 'Em Eat Cake*, and *Porgy And Bess*. From those productions came some of the perennial standards of American popular song. Despite the brothers' prolific output, which resulted in hits such as 'That Certain Feeling', 'Someone To Watch Over Me', 'Do, Do, Do', ''S Wonderful', 'How Long Has This Been Going On?', 'I've Got A Crush On You', 'I Got Rhythm', 'But Not For Me', 'It Ain't Necessarily So', 'Embraceable You', and so many more, Ira Gershwin found time to write lyrics for other composers. Among these collaborations were 'Cheerful Little Earful' (from the stage show *Sweet And Low*, with Billy Rose and Harry Warren), 'Let's Take A Walk Around The Block', 'You're A Builder-Upper', 'Fun To Be Fooled', and 'What Can You Say In A Love Song?' (from the revue *Life Begins At 8:40*, with Harold Arlen and E.Y. 'Yip' Harburg), and 'I Can't Get Started', 'He Hasn't A Thing Except Me', and 'Island In The West Indies' (from the revue *Ziegfeld Follies* of 1936, with Vernon Duke). In 1931, the brothers collaborated on the score for the Broadway show, *Of Thee I Sing*, which became the first musical to be awarded a Pulitzer Prize for Drama. Just before George died in 1937 from a brain tumor, he worked with Ira on the movies *A Damsel In Distress* ('A Foggy Day', 'Nice Work If You Can Get It'), *Shall We Dance* ('Let's Call The Whole Thing Off', 'They All Laughed', 'They Can't Take That Away From Me'), and *The Goldwyn Follies* ('Love Is Here To Stay', 'Love Walked In'). Ira finished the score for the latter film with Vernon Duke, and in the years immediately following his brother's early death, wrote very little. When he eventually resumed work, he teamed with Kurt Weill on the Broadway musicals *Lady In The Dark* (1941), which starred Gertrude Lawrence, with Danny Kaye ('My Ship', 'Jenny', 'This Is New' 'Tchaikowsky'), and *The Firebrand Of Florence* (1945), and worked on other stage shows with Aaron Copland (*North Star*, 1945) and Arthur Schwartz (*Park Avenue*, 1946). He also wrote the lyrics for several films, among them the outstanding scores for *Cover Girl*, with Gene Kelly ('Long Ago And Far Away', 'Make Way For Tomorrow', 'The Show

Must Go On', 'Put Me To The Test', with Jerome Kern), *A Star Is Born* with Judy Garland (the unforgettable 'The Man That Got Away', 'Gotta Have Me Go With You', 'It's A New World, with Harold Arlen), and *The Barkleys of Broadway*, starring Fred Astaire and Ginger Rogers ('My One And Only Highland Fling', 'Shoes With Wings On', 'You'd Be Hard To Replace', with Harry Warren). Several of George and Ira Gershwin's stage shows were adapted for the screen, and a collection of their old numbers formed the score for the multi Oscar-winning *An American In Paris* (1951). In 1959, Ira published a delightful collection of his wonderfully witty and colloquial lyrics, entitled *Lyrics On Several Occasions*. He retired in the following year, occasionally working on lyrics of past successes when they needed refining or updating for revivals of the most popular Gershwin shows. Ten years after his death in 1983, some of his most popular lyrics were still being relished in the New York and London productions of *Crazy For You*, a re-hash of the Gershwins' 1930 hit, *Girl Crazy*.

There was a full house in December 1996 when a gala concert was held at Carnegie Hall to celebrate the centennial of Ira's birth. Stars such as a leading Gershwin authority Michael Feinstein, Debbie Gravitte, Vic Damone, Rosemary Clooney, and Maureen McGovern were there, as was Burton Lane, Ira's only living collaborator. Lorna Luft led an all-star cast in the British tribute, *Who Could Ask For Anything More!*, at London's Royal Albert Hall.

● ALBUMS: *George & Ira Gershwin In Hollywood* (Rhino/Turner 1997)★★★.

● COMPILATIONS: various artists *'S Wonderful: Concord Jazz Salutes Ira Gershwin* (Concord Jazz)★★★★.

● FURTHER READING: *Lyrics On Several Occasions*, Ira Gershwin. *The Gershwins*, R. Kimball and A. Simon. *The Complete Lyrics Of Ira Gershwin*, edited by R. Kimball. *Fascinating Rhythm: Collaboration Of George And Ira Gershwin*, Deena Rosenberg. *The Art Of The Lyricist*, Philip Furia. *The Gershwin Years: George And Ira*, Edward Jablonski and Lawrence D. Stewart.

GI BLUES

Art imitated life in this 1960 feature, Elvis Presley's first film since completing military service. His manager, Colonel Tom Parker had skilfully manipulated the singer's career during his absence. What better way of announcing Presley's return than with a film romanticising his period of induction? Elvis portrayed a guitar-playing gunner in the US Army, stationed in West Germany, who woos a cabaret dancer, played by Juliet Prowse, as a bet, before predictably falling in love with her. Considerable publicity was generated by a rumoured off-screen affair, all of which fuelled further interest in the film. *GI Blues* remains one of Presley's most popular and enduring features, although purists murmured disquiet when he sang 'Wooden Heart' to a puppet. That particular song - based on a German composition 'Muss I Den' - became a UK chart-topping single when culled from the film's soundtrack. The *GI Blues* album also reached number 1 in its respective UK chart and remained on the listing for over a year. The joint success of the film and music confirmed that indeed Elvis was back.

GIGI

The golden era of MGM film musicals was drawing to a close when this most delightful of films was released in 1958. The original story, by the French novelist Colette, had previously been adapted into a non-musical film in 1948 starring Daniele Delormé and Gaby Morlay, and a play that was subsequently performed in New York and London. Alan Jay Lerner's screenplay for this musical treatment was set in Paris at the turn of the century and tells of the young, strong-willed Gigi (Leslie Caron), who is being brought up by her grandmother, Mamita (Hermione Gingold), and her great-aunt Alicia (Isabel Jeans) to be a courtesan, but breaks with that family tradition - and actually marries her suitor, Gaston Lachailles (Louis Jourdan). Watching over this somewhat shocking situation is Honoré Lachailles (Maurice Chevalier), Gaston's grandfather and a good friend of Mamita. He is also a gentleman with much experience in the delights of romance, and, therefore, is appalled when Gaston, his well-heeled grandson, who, permanently surrounded by lovely ladies and all the other good things in life, suddenly declares that 'It's A Bore'. This was just one of Alan Jay Lerner and Frederick Loewe's memorable songs that were so skilfully integrated into the charming story. Other highlights included Chevalier's 'Thank Heaven For Little Girls' ('Those little eyes so helpless and appealing/One day will flash, and send you crashing through the ceiling'), 'The Parisians' (Caron), 'Waltz At Maxim's (She Is Not Thinking Of Me)' (Jourdan), 'The Night They Invented Champagne' (Caron-Jourdan-Mamita), 'Say A Prayer For Me Tonight' (Caron), 'I'm Glad I'm Not Young Anymore' (Chevalier) and 'Gigi (Gaston's Soliloquy)' (Jourdan). For many, the most endearing moment came when Honoré and Mamita reminisced about old times with 'I Remember It Well' (He: 'You wore a gown of gold.' She: 'I was all in blue.' He: 'Am I getting old?' She: 'Oh, no - not you.'). Vincente Minnelli directed the film which was mostly shot on location in Paris, and the producer was Arthur Freed. It was magnificently photographed in Metrocolor and CinemaScope by Joseph Ruttenberg, and he won one of the picture's Academy Awards, along with those for Cecil Beaton's sumptuous costumes and best picture, director, writer (Lerner), art direction-set direction (William A. Horning and Preston Ames; Henry Grace and Keogh Gleason), film editing (Adrienne Fazan), best song ('Gigi'), and scoring of a musical picture (André Previn). At the same awards ceremony Maurice Chevalier received a special Oscar 'for his contributions to the world of entertainment for more than half a century'. *Gigi* was one of the Top 10 highest-grossing films of the 50s in the USA, but subsequent stage productions did not appeal. The 1973 Broadway production starring Alfred Drake, Agnes Moorhead, Maria Karnilova and Daniel Massey only ran for three months, and West End audiences saw *Gigi* for seven months in 1985-86.

GIMME SHELTER

Released in 1970, *Gimme Shelter* was directed by brothers David and Albert Maysles, renowned for their work as documentary film makers. Their skills and experience brought a chilling intensity to a project initially viewed as a commemoration of the Rolling Stones 1969 tour of the USA. The tour ended with the ill-fated Altamont Concert, which exposed the dark side of the 60s counter culture dream when Hells Angels, employed as stewards, murdered a member of the audience. The film's focus was changed irrevocably. *Gimme Shelter* provides lighter moments, including a pulsating recording session at the Muscle Shoals studio, but a sense of foreboding sweeps the entire proceedings. Other acts featured include the Flying Burrito Brothers and Jefferson Airplane (whose lead singer, Marty Balin, was knocked unconscious by the Hells Angels), but the power of *Gimme Shelter* rests in its uncompromising documentation of one of rock music's most tragic episodes.

GIRL CAN'T HELP IT, THE

Perhaps the finest film of the rock 'n' roll era, this 1956 outing has much to recommend it. In a plot illiberally borrowed from Judy Holiday's *Born Yesterday*, struggling agent Tom Ewell is charged by mobster Edmund O'Brien to further the career of his girlfriend (Jayne Mansfield). Risqué (for 1956) references to the latter's physical attributes aside - a running gag throughout - the film is fired by comedy veteran Frank Tashlin's script and direction which, for once, matches the pace and rhythm of the musical interludes. Gene Vincent contributes a memorable 'The Girl Can't Help It', the fledgling talent of Eddie Cochran is heard on 'Twenty Flight Rock' and Fats Domino adds a superb 'Blue Monday'. However, the star is undoubtedly Little Richard, who tears through the title song, 'She's Got It' and 'Ready Teddy'. *The Girl Can't Help It* not only showcased such acts without condescension, it was the first rock 'n' roll film shot in colour. However, the film's strength does not solely rest on these pivotal figures. Tom Ewell is superb as the long-suffering agent, and his hallucinations about a former client immortalized Julie London's 'Cry Me A River'. Edmund O'Brien relished his rare excursion into comedy and the gangster-inspired composition he sang, 'Rock Around The Rock Pile', acted as a thinly veiled sideswipe at exploitative releases made to cash in on fads. Few films embraced rock 'n' roll with similar understanding and respect.

GIRL CRAZY (FILM MUSICAL)

(see *Babes In Arms* (film musical))

GIRL CRAZY (STAGE MUSICAL)

The American Depression was biting hard, but Broadway itself was remarkably buoyant when *Girl Crazy* opened at the Alvin Theatre on 14 October 1930. The show's producers, Alex A. Aarons and Vincent Freedley, wanted Bert Lahr as their chief laughter-maker, but they had rather carelessly loaned him out to George White for *Flying Home!*, and could not get him back in time. So they signed the singing comedy team of Willie and Eugene Howard instead, although only Willie appeared in the show. In Guy Bolton and John McGowan's's contemporary tale of cowboy life, Willie plays the role of Gieber Goldfarb, a taxi driver who is hired by a wealthy New Yorker to transport his philandering son, Danny Churchill (Allan Kearns), 3000 miles to Custerville, a town that has not had a female

resident in 50 years. Danny soon changes that situation by turning the family lodge into Buzzards, a dude ranch with imported New York showgirls and a gambling saloon which is managed by Slick Fothergill (William Kent) and his wife Kate (Ethel Merman). Danny himself falls for the local postmistress, Molly Gray (Ginger Rogers), and Goldfarb gives up driving taxis and becomes the town's sheriff (Custerville gets through two of those a week). It was the first time that Ethel Merman had been seen and heard (!) on Broadway, and she excelled with 'Boy! What Love Has Done To Me!', and the smoochy 'Sam And Delilah' which was followed almost immediately by the ebullient 'I Got Rhythm' - just three of the outstanding numbers in this marvellous score by George and Ira Gershwin. Naturally enough, Kearns and Rogers shared the big romantic ballad, 'Embraceable You' and the getting-to-know-you 'Could You Use Me?'. Rogers also had 'Cactus Time In Arizona' and the wistful 'But Not For Me'. The rest of the songs included 'The Lonesome Cowboy', 'Bronco Busters', Geiber's campaign song, 'Goldfarb! That's I'm!', 'Land Of The Gay Caballero', and 'Treat Me Rough'. Another of the show's most endearing numbers, 'Bidin' My Time', was sung at various moments throughout the show by a quartet of cowboys played by the Foursome. That sequence was recreated in the film, *The Glenn Miller Story*, when James Stewart, as Miller, was supposed to be playing in the pit orchestra for *Girl Crazy*. Unlike many of Hollywood's inaccurate representations of Broadway musicals, this one was true. Miller did play in the orchestra along, with Benny Goodman and Gene Krupa, in what was an augmented version of Red Nichols' dance band. Nichols also had big record hits with 'I Got Rhythm' and 'Embraceable You'. With those songs, a bright, colourful production, and its famous curtain line: 'Go on - marry him Molly. It's 11:15 now!.', *Girl Crazy* seemed to be set for a long run, but when Willy Howard and Ethel Merman left for the 1931 edition of *George White's Scandals*, it closed after 272 performances. Three film adaptations were made: an early talkie version in 1932, the definitive version with Judy Garland and Mickey Rooney in 1943, and a 1965 re-hash, *When The Boys Meet The Girls*, starring Connie Francis, Harve Presnell, Herman's Hermits, Louis Armstrong, and Liberace. More than 60 years later, on 24 February 1992, a 'revamp' of the show, entitled *Crazy For You*, conceived by Mike Ockrent and Ken Ludwig, opened on Broadway and became a smash-hit, winning the Tony Award for best musical. It repeated its success in London during the following year. In 1991, a CD recording of *Girl Crazy* was released complete with the original orchestrations by Robert Russell Bennett, and starring Lorna Luft, David Carroll, Judy Blazer, and Frank Gorshin.

GIRL FRIEND, THE

One of Richard Rodgers and Lorenz Hart's earliest shows, *The Girl Friend* opened at the Vanderbilt Theatre in New York on 17 March 1926. After their success with *Dearest Enemy*, the young songwriters teamed again with librettist Herbert Fields for this story of a six-day cycle race in which the apparent long-shot for the title is nobbled by unscrupulous punters, which was a vehicle for the husband and wife dance team Eva Puck and Sammy White. They introduced Rodgers and Hart's Charleston-styled title song ('Isn't she cute?/Isn't she sweet?/An eyeful you'd die full/Of pleasure to meet/In my funny fashion/I'm cursed with a passion/For the girl friend!'), and one of the composers' loveliest ballads, 'The Blue Room' ('We will thrive on/Keep alive on/Just nothing but kisses/With Mister and Missus/On little blue chairs'). Eva Puck also had the amusing 'The Damsel Who Done All The Dirt' ('The greatest of heroes/Would now rank as zeros/If not for the hem of a skirt'), and the rest of the score included 'Good Fellow Mine', 'Why Do I?', 'Hey, Hey', 'The Simple Life', 'Goodbye, Lenny', and 'Creole Crooning Song'. After initially poor audiences, the show picked up and ran for a creditable 301 performances. A different production with a new book, but still called *The Girl Friend*, opened in London on 8 September 1927. It contained several Rodgers and Hart numbers, including the title song, 'The Blue Room, 'What's The Use Of Talking?', and 'Mountain Greenery', and ran for 421 performances.

GIRL FROM UTAH, THE
Even with its sub-title, 'The Acme Of Musical Comedy', this show would not be of any particular interest except that it contains a certain song. That song was not present when *The Girl From Utah* opened in London at the Adelphi Theatre on 18 October 1913 where it played for 195 performances. It was added, along with a few others, when the show was presented nearly a year later in New York. The score for the original West End production was written by Sidney Jones and Paul Robens (music) and Adrian Ross, Percy Greenbank, and Robens (lyrics). It included songs such as 'D'You Follow Me?', 'Una', 'Call Right Here', 'The Girl From Utah', 'Kissing Time', 'At The Bottom Of Brixton Hill', 'The Music Of Love', and 'When We Meet A Mormon'. The last two titles give a good clue as to the location and the subject of the piece. James T. Taylor's book was set in England, and dealt with Una Trance (Ina Claire), an American girl who flees to London in an attempt to avoid being added to a Mormon's wedding list - for wives. Although he pursues her to Europe, she is rescued from a meandering existence with the Mormon by a handsome local hoofer Sandy Blair (Joseph Coyne). When *The Girl From Utah* transferred to the Knickerbocker Theatre on Broadway in August 1914, producer Charles Frohman gave it the American touch, and commissioned some interpolations from an up-and-coming young composer named Jerome Kern, and here is where that special song comes in. Following its introduction in this show by David Brian (Sandy), 'They'll Never Believe Me', with a lyric by Herbert Reynolds, became one of the most enduring standards in the history of popular music. Aside from numerous recordings by some of the world's leading singers, it was featured in two London musicals, *Tonight's The Night* (1915) and *Oh! What A Lovely War* (1963, also the 1969 film), and in films such as the Jerome Kern biopic *Till The Clouds Roll By* (1946, sung by Kathryn Grayson), and *That Midnight Kiss* (1949, Mario Lanza). Kern's other songs for the US version of *The Girl From Utah*, with lyrics by Harry B. Smith, were all of a very high standard, and included 'You Can Never Tell',

'Same Sort Of Girl', 'The Land Of Let's Pretend', 'Alice In Wonderland', 'We'll Take Care Of You' (The Little Refugees)', and the vivacious 'Why Don't They Dance The Polka?'. The rest of the New York cast included Julia Sanderson as Una and Joseph Cawthorn in the role of the Mormon. *The Girl From Utah*, which ran for 120 performances on Broadway, was an early example of the move, spearheaded by Kern, to create a modern American musical which would eventually replace the imported European operettas.

GIRL HAPPY
One of the poorest Elvis Presley films, this 1965 feature portrayed the singer as a pop star charged with chaperoning a group of girl students while on holiday. Shelley Fabares, creator of the sublime 'Johnny Angel', co-starred alongside Bing Crosby's son, Gary. Presley's lack of interest in the project stretched to the material he was required to sing on the attendant soundtrack. The title song, 'Do Not Disturb' and 'Do The Clam' may have been of comparative interest; each paled into insignificance when set beside recordings from the singer's halcyon era. He found little to inspire his talent on the remaining selections; boredom is very palpable in his voice.

GIRLS ON THE BEACH, THE
Taking its cue from a succession of 'quickie' films emanating from the American International Pictures company, *The Girls On The Beach* tied a flimsy plot to a series of pop act cameos. In this 1965 feature, girl students wishing to raise funds decide to organize a concert which they mistakenly believe will feature the Beatles. Fortunately other performers step into the breech, including the Crickets, who offer a version of 'La Bamba', and Leslie Gore. The latter sings three numbers, 'Leave Me Alone', 'It's Got To Be You' and 'I Don't Wanna Be A Loser', the last of which was a minor US hit the previous year. Topping the bill are the Beach Boys with 'Little Honda', 'The Lonely Sea' and the title song itself. Prolific surf and drag music producer/composer Gary Usher was responsible for the bulk of the soundtrack score, but the appeal of the 'beach' genre was waning by the time this film was released. The Byrds' 'Mr. Tambourine Man', also issued in 1965, signalled the rise of an altogether different Californian sub-culture.

GIRLS! GIRLS! GIRLS!
The first signs of a decline in the quality of films starring Elvis Presley could be seen in this 1962 feature. The plot involved the singer's wish to buy a boat, an ambition he finances by performing in nightclubs and fishing for tuna. This noticeably slight premise lacked the spark of *King Creole* or the solid light-heartedness of *GI Blues*, offering little for the star to engage with. More worrying still was the quality of the songs contained in the soundtrack. *Girls! Girls! Girls!* may well have reached the upper echelons of the UK and US album charts, but few could imagine that its content, notably 'Song Of The Shrimp', 'We're Coming In Loaded' and 'Thanks To The Rolling Sea', bore serious comparison with previous recordings. Parsimonious to the end, RCA omitted three tracks featured in the film, but included the concurrent hit, 'Return To Sender', which

topped the UK charts and reached number 2 in the US. Singles inspired interest in the film, which in turn generated an album release. A promotional Presley jigsaw had been established, irrespective of the merits of the pieces.

GLAMOROUS NIGHT (FILM MUSICAL)

When Ivor Novello's hit show opened at the Drury Lane Theatre in London in 1935, critics were quick to compare its story of the king who is so infatuated with a gypsy girl that he is willing to give up his throne, with a similar state of affairs between the King of Rumania and Mme. Lupesco. Two years later, when this film version was released by the Associated British Picture Corporation, a situation much nearer home - the abdication of King Edward owing to his relationship with the American Mrs. Simpson - was still very fresh in the British people's minds. Mary Ellis recreated her stage role as the fiery gypsy, and Otto Kruger gave a fine performance as the weak and confused king. Barry Mackay, in the role originally played by Ivor Novello, was suitably macho as the young Englishman who saves the Romany girl's life, and the villainy and comedy aspects were handled by Victor Jory and Finlay Currie respectively. Other roles went to Trefor Jones, Antony Holles, Maire O'Neill, Charles Carson, and Felix Aylmer. Most of Ivor Novello and Christopher Hassall's lovely stage score survived, including four of the most popular pieces, 'Shine Through Your Dreams', 'Fold Your Wings', 'When A Gypsy Played', and 'Glamorous Night'. The screenplay was adapted from Novello's original play by Dudley Leslie, Hugh Brooke, and William Freshman. Fritz Arno Wagner photographed this lavish and good-looking production which was directed by Brian Desmond Hurst.

GLAMOROUS NIGHT (STAGE MUSICAL)

In his first great stage musical hit, which opened at London's Theatre Royal, Drury Lane on 2 May 1935, Ivor Novello discovered a way of setting before British audiences of the 30s a home-grown version of the highly-popular Viennese operettas of the late nineteenth century. Filling the stage with beautifully-costumed elegant ladies, and with some deliberately heart-tugging music, Novello concocted a fairy-tale world to which audiences flocked consistently. The hugely improbable plot concerned the inventor of a television system (Novello) who is paid handsomely by the head of radio to disappear and take his invention with him. He goes to the Ruritanian-style land of Krasnia, meets the gypsy princess Militza (Mary Ellis), who is about to marry the Krasnian king (Barry Jones), saves her life, falls in love, is almost killed, then gives up his love for the greater good of Krasnia. Also cast were Lyn Harding, Clifford Heatherley, Bettie Bucknelle, Trefor Jones, and Elisabeth Welch. The appropriately operetta-style score included 'Fold Your Wings', 'Shine Through My Dreams', 'When The Gypsy Played', 'Far Away In Shanty Town', 'Glamorous Night', 'Royal Wedding', 'Singing Waltz', and 'Her Majesty Militza'. Christopher Hassall wrote the lyrics, and composer Novello found himself with a show that looked as though it would run forever. In fact, the management of the theatre closed it after only 243 performances because of a prior commitment to stage a

Christmas pantomime. However, after touring for a while, *Glamorous Night* reopened at the London Coliseum for a brief run in 1936, and subsequently became an enduring part of regional theatre repertoires the length and breadth of the land. A 1937 film version starred Mary Ellis, Barry Mackay and Otto Kruger.

GLASS, PHILIP

b. 31 January 1937, Chicago, Illinois, USA. Glass was educated at the University of Chicago and the Juilliard School before going to Paris to study with Nadia Boulanger between 1963 and 1965. By this time he knew that 'playing second fiddle to Stockhausen didn't seem like a lot of fun. . . . There didn't seem to be any need to write any more of that kind of music. The only thing to do was to start somewhere else. . .' He did not know where that point was until he was hired to work on an Ornette Coleman film score. He did not want to change the music so Ravi Shankar was asked to write additional material which Glass orchestrated. As he struggled with the problem of writing this music down, Glass came to see that there was another way that music could be organized. It could be structured by rhythm. Instead of dividing the music up as he had been trying to do to write it down, the Indian musicians added to rhythmic phrases and let the music expand. With Ravi Shankar he had now also worked with a composer who was a performer. Glass travelled to North Africa and Asia before returning to New York in 1967 where he studied with the tabla player Alla Rakha. In 1968 he formed the ensemble he needed to perform the music he was now writing. This was the period of the purest minimalism with extending and contracting rhythmic figures in a stable diatonic framework performed at the kind of volume more often associated with rock music. Glass later described it as music which 'must be listened to as a pure sound event, an act without any dramatic structure.' It did not stay in that abstract world of pure sound for very long. In 1975 he had no record contract and began work with Robert Wilson on *Einstein On The Beach* which turned out to be the first of three operas on 'historical figures who changed the course of world events through the wisdom and strength of their inner vision'. *Einstein On The Beach* was premiered in Europe and reached the Metropolitan on 21 November 1976. He was signed by CBS Records in 1982 and produced the successful *Glassworks*. In 1970 he had been joined by Kurt Munkacsi, sound designer, mixer and engineer and the two explored all the potential studios and new technology on offer. The operas were produced in the studio first so that others could work with them and their final recordings were enhanced by the capabilities of the studio: 'We don't hang a mike in front of an orchestra. . . . Almost every section is extended electronically.' Although Glass's music has stayed close to the method he established in the early 70s, from *Einstein On The Beach* onwards the harmony has been richer and he has been willing to explore orchestral colour because 'the most important thing is that the music provides an emotional framework or context. It literally tells you what to feel about what you're seeing.' Much of his work since has been either for the stage or for film. This includes the two operas *Satyagraha* (1980) and

Ahknaten (1984) and the films with Godfrey Reggio - *Koyaanisqatsi* (1983) and *Powaqqatsi* (1988). In the late 80s and early 90s Glass also wrote film scores for *The Thin Blue Line, Hamburger Hill, Candyman, Compassion In Exile: The Life Of The 14th Dalai Lama* (1992). Glass's plans include a second opera with author Doris Lessing; a theatre work based on Cocteau's *Orphee;* a film based on Stephen Hawking's *A Brief History Of Time,* more work with Wilson and Hydrogen Jukebox; and an opera with Allen Ginsberg. Most recently, he co-operated with Brian Eno on an reappraisal of the latter's *Low* project for David Bowie and repeated the formula with *Heroes* in 1997. At the start of 1998 he gained an Oscar nomination for the score of Martin Scorcese's *Kundun.*

● ALBUMS: *Two Pages* (Folkways 1974)★★★, *Music In 12 Parts 1&2* (Cardine 1976)★★★, *Solo Music* (Shandar 1978)★★★★, *Einstein On The Beach* (Columbia 1979)★★★, *Glassworks* (Columbia 1982)★★★★, *Koyaanisqatsi* film soundtrack (Island 1983)★★★★, *Akhnaten* (1984)★★★, *Mishima* (Nonesuch 1985), *Satyagraha* (1985)★★★, *Songs From Liquid Days* (Columbia 1986)★★★, *Powaqqatsi* film soundtrack (Nonesuch 1988)★★, *North Star* (Virgin 1988)★★★, *The Photographer* (CBS 1988)★★, *1000 Airplanes On The Roof* (Venture 1989)★★★, *Solo Piano* (1989)★★★★, with Ravi Shankar *Passages* (Private Music 1990)★★★, *Low* (Philips 1993)★★★, *Hydrogen Jukebox* (1994)★★★, *Heroes* (Point 1997)★★★★, *Kundun* (Nonesuch 1998)★★★.

GLENN MILLER STORY, THE

Competently directed by Anthony Mann, and featuring a fine James Stewart performance as Miller (portrayed as much more warm-hearted than the real man), this 1953 biopic does not pass up any opportunity for a cliché. Miller's search for a 'new sound' is hounded to death (scratch any ex-sideman of Miller and one would hear a different version of how he achieved it), but the storyline omits the obvious, if dull, solution that it was all a matter of a workmanlike arranger sticking to his trade. The cross-country slogs on a tour of one-night shows are well presented and the studio-assembled band accurately recreates Miller's music. Stewart copes well with his on-screen trombone miming, and off-screen, Joe Yukl (and possibly Murray McEachern) provides the sound. Miller's disappearance, just before Christmas 1944, is tied into a mythical 'gift' to his wife of an arrangement of her favourite tune, 'Little Brown Jug'. In fact, Miller's hit recording of this tune came some years before his death, but in this way, the film can end without a dry eye in the house. In a jazz club sequence, the 1953 edition of the Louis Armstrong All Stars, including Barney Bigard, William 'Cozy' Cole and Trummy Young, teams up with a handful of 30s swing stars, including Gene Krupa and Babe Russin, to knock spots off 'Basin Street Blues'.

GO INTO YOUR DANCE

The only film in which Al Jolson and his wife, Ruby Keeler, starred together was released by Warner Brothers in 1935. Al plays a woman-chasing entertainer on the loose in Chicago, hanging around clubs such as La Cucaracha (complete with sombrero and Mexican shawl), before Keeler is persuaded by a mutual friend to look after

him. After surviving being framed for a murder he probably is not even capable (mostly too drunk) of committing, he and Keeler celebrate the happy ending in their own nightspot. The songs, by Harry Warren and Al Dubin, included a smart little floor-show number for Keeler called 'A Good Old-Fashioned Cocktail', and there were several attractive items for Jolson such as 'She's A Latin From Manhattan', 'Mammy, I'll Sing About You', and 'Go Into Your Dance'. He also strutted with Keeler in the film's highspot, a spectacular production number constructed around the spirited 'A Quarter To Nine', in which, after a brief and slightly incongruous segue into 'Way Down Upon The Swanee River', the faces of Jolson and the male chorus turn black, while their top hats become white. It was almost as if the film was being shown in negative, except that Keeler's face and costume remained white all the time. Torch singer Helen Morgan, who was to make such an impact as Julie in the film of *Show Boat* in 1936, also brought a touch of class to *Go Into Your Dance* with a lovely version of 'The Little Things You Used To Do'. Earl Baldwin wrote the screenplay, Bobby Connolly created the lively and enterprising choreography, and the film was directed by Archie Mayo.

GO JOHNNY GO

Disc jockey Alan Freed, who reputedly coined the phrase 'rock 'n' roll', took part in several 50s genre films, including *Rock Around The Clock* and *Rock Rock Rock.* He assumed the lead role in this 1958 feature, playing to type as a DJ searching for singer Johnny Melody, whose demo recordings proved highly popular with Freed's audience. Chuck Berry also enjoys a (brief) acting part, but is clearly more comfortable performing the title song, plus 'Little Queenie' and 'Memphis, Tennessee', the last of which became a UK Top 10 entry five years later. Rising star Richie Valens contributes 'Ooh My Head' in what would be his only film appearance, while other notable cameos include the Flamingos' 'Jump Children', Eddie Cochran's 'Teenage Heaven', Jackie Wilson's 'You'd Better Know It' and Harvey Fuqua's 'Don't Be Afraid To Love Me'. New Orleans-based singer Jimmy Clanton, who played Melody, provides four songs for the soundtrack, including 'My Own True Love', a US Top 40 entry in 1959. The film did not propel Clanton to stardom, although the singer did enjoy several subsequent hit singles, including 'Go Jimmy Go' (clearly based on his starring feature) and 'Venus In Blue Jeans'.

GODSPELL

One of the first of the rock-type religious musicals that began to emerge in the 70s, *Godspell* opened Off Broadway at the Cherry Lane Theatre in New York on 17 May 1971. It had a book, by John-Michael Tebelak, which was based on the Gospel according to St Matthew, and music and lyrics by newcomer Stephen Schwartz. The cast included Stephen Nathan (Jesus) and David Haskell (Judas), and the score contained songs such as 'All Good Gifts', 'Save The People', 'Prepare Ye The Way Of The Lord', 'Light Of The Best', and 'Day By Day', a number that epitomises this style of production, and which became an enormous US hit in a version by the Broadway original cast. After

2,124 performances, the show moved to a main house, the Broadhurst Theatre, for a further 527. The cast of the London production, which stayed at Wyndham's Theatre for nearly three years, included Julie Covington, David Essex, Marti Webb, and the future movie heartthrob Jeremy Irons. A 1993 revival at the Barbican Hall in London, which starred the actress and singer Gemma Craven, was not helped by the fact that 'Andy Crane, the blond and denimed children's television personality signed up to play Jesus, is strikingly uncharismatic and bland - this resurrection is not good news'. Also in 1993, Los Angeles saw *Godspell - Now!*, a contemporary reinterpretation of the original show, based around the riots in that city in April 1992.

GOING HOLLYWOOD

Bing Crosby was on temporary loan from Paramount for this 1933 MGM release which teamed him with Marion Davies, who, despite being a talented actress, is best-known for her friendship with millionaire newspaper tycoon William Randolph Hearst. Screenwriter Donald Ogden Stewart's slight story concerns a young teacher (Davies), who follows her crooning idol (Crosby) to Hollywood, and masquerades as a maid before playing a starring role in Bing's latest movie (and his subsequent personal life) when his leading lady (Fifi D'Orsay) hits the bottle. Generously built comedienne Patsy Kelly, who had enjoyed success in Broadway revues, made a big impression in her screen debut, and the cast also included Stuart Erwin, Bobby Watson, Ned Sparks and Sterling Holloway. Nacio Herb Brown and Arthur Freed wrote songs, and one of them, the powerful 'Temptation', became popular for Crosby at the time of the picture's release, and was revived by Perry Como some 10 years later. The other songs included the spirited 'Going Hollywood', 'Beautiful Girl', 'After Sundown', 'Our Big Love Scene', and 'We'll Make Hay While The Sun Shines' which became a record hit for Crosby and was also popular with the British dance bands of the period, particularly Billy Merrin And His Commanders. *Going Hollywood* was directed by Raoul Walsh and the choreographer was Albertina Rasch. Bing Crosby did not appear in another film for MGM until *High Society* in 1956.

GOING MY WAY

This enormously successful light-comedy musical was released by Paramount in 1944. It starred Bing Crosby as Father Chuck O'Malley, a young priest whose attempts to introduce order to the run-down St. Dominick's Church in a tough area of New York, bring him into conflict with the crotchety long-time incumbent, Father Fitzgibbon (Barry Fitzgerald). Frank Butler and Frank Cavett's screenplay (from an original story by producer-director Leo McCarey) was warm and tender, without being maudlin, but there was not a dry eye in the house when, towards the end, the two men resolve their differences and Father Fitzgibbon is reunited with his aged mother (Adeline DeWalt Reynolds). Crosby and Fitzgerald were splendid together, and the admirable supporting cast included Risë Stevens, Jean Heather, Frank McHugh, Gene Lockhart, William Frawley, Carl Switzer, Stanley Clements, James Brown,

and the Robert Mitchell Boys' Choir. Jimmy Van Heusen and Johnny Burke wrote three of the songs: 'The Day After Forever' (Crosby-Heather), 'Going My Way' (Crosby-Stevens), and the lively 'Swinging On A Star', which Crosby performed in beguiling style at the piano, surrounded by a group of youngsters. He also gave a memorable reading of the lovely 1914 ballad 'Too-Ra-Loo-Ra-Loo-Ral' (J. R. Shannon). The rest of the score consisted of 'Silent Night' (Franz Gruber), 'Ave Maria' (Schubert), and 'Haberna' (Bizet). Not only was *Going My Way* one of the top money-spinners of the decade, it also scooped the Oscars for 1944, winning for best picture, actor (Crosby), supporting actor (Fitzgerald), director (McCarey), original story (McCarey), and song ('Swinging On A Star').

Bing Crosby reprised his role of Father O'Malley in *The Bells Of St. Mary's* which was released by RKO in 1945. This time he was called upon to win over Sister Benedict (Ingrid Bergman) at the local Catholic school, but luckily still found the time to sing 'Aren't You Glad You're You?' (Van Heusen-Burke). *The Bells Of St. Mary's* was even more successful at the box-office than *Going My Way*.

GOING STEADY

This 1979 Israeli film was a successor to *Lemon Popsicle*. Taking its cue from 50s revival films such as *American Graffiti* and *Grease*, *Going Steady* revolved around the antics of high-school students. However, the film failed to re-create the atmosphere of the times, a feature compounded by a series of anachronisms. The equally expansive soundtrack included material by Jerry Lee Lewis, Brian Hyland, Bobby Darin and Chubby Checker, as well as Debbie Reynolds. Her hit song 'Tammy' inspired the name given to the central character in this largely forgettable film.

GOLD DIGGERS OF BROADWAY

This film, the first in a series of popular backstage musicals produced by Warner Brothers in the early days of sound, was released in 1929. It was adapted from Avery Hopwood's 1919 play *The Gold Diggers*, which the studio originally filmed as a silent in 1923. Robert Lord's charming and amusing screenplay was all about a trio of chorus girls played by Winnie Lightner, Nancy Welford and Anne Pennington, whose feminine charms break down all social barriers in their quest for well-heeled husbands. Al Dubin and Joe Burke's tuneful score contained two enduring numbers, 'Painting The Clouds With Sunshine' and 'Tip Toe Through The Tulips', which were introduced by Nick Lucas, a singer with an appealing, easy-going style. He had enormous record hits with both of them. The rest of the songs included 'What Will I Do Without You?', 'And They Still Fall In Love', 'Go To Bed', 'In A Kitchenette', 'Song Of The Gold Diggers', and 'Mechanical Man'. Also in the cast were Conway Tearle, Lilyan Tashman, William Blakewell, and Helen Foster. The lively dance sequences were staged by Larry Ceballos, and the director was Roy Del Ruth. It was filmed in two-colour Technicolor, a process which, at times, could be surprisingly effective. Even as early as this in the evolvement of movie musicals, different studios were beginning to specialise in their own particular aspects of the genre: Paramount had their operettas with Maurice Chevalier and Jeanette MacDonald, MGM pioneered revue-type features, RKO were to enjoy tremendous success with the Fred Astaire and Ginger Rogers dance diversions, and Warners soon led the way (with MGM in hot pursuit) in memorable backstage sagas such as *42nd Street* and *Footlight Parade* and others in the same vein:

Gold Diggers Of 1933. Dick Powell and Ruby Keeler, who had made such a favourable impression in the aforementioned *42nd Street*, were reunited for this film whose screenplay, by Erwin Gelsey, James Seymour, David Boehm, and Ben Markson, was again based on that Avery Hopwood play. Harry Warren and Al Dubin's songs provided the inspiration for choreographer Busby Berkeley's memorable production numbers, complete with his trademark 'top shots': 'We're In The Money', in which Ginger Rogers, her fellow chorus girls, and the stage on which they are performing, are completely clad in various-sized models of silver dollars (an ironic touch considering America was still in the midst of its worst Depression); 'Shadow Waltz', and a spectacular array of white-wigged girls in double-hooped dresses 'playing' neon-edged violins; and 'Pettin' In The Park', a risqué sequence, during which several apparently nude female forms are tantalisingly silhouetted behind flimsy roller blinds. When the blinds are raised the girls emerge dressed in *metal* costumes, and the scene ends with Dick Powell hard at work with a can opener! The most poignant sequence, though, is 'Remember My Forgotten Man', a powerful portrait of post-World War I disillusionment with the American Dream, which culminates in three sets of armed soldiers marching over a curved bridge set, while, in the foreground, Joan Blondell sings the heart-rending lyric. All in all, with its persistent emphasis on the scarcity of money, the picture was as much a social document as a lively and entertaining musical. Also among the cast were Warren William, Aline MacMahon, Guy Kibbee, Ned Sparks, Sterling Holloway, and Dennis O'Keefe. Mervyn LeRoy directed, and this edition, and the rest of the series, was shot in more conventional black and white.

Gold Diggers Of 1935. Busby Berkeley served as director as well as choreographer, and this picture is mainly remembered for his creation of one of the most outstanding sequences in movie musical history based on the Oscar-winning song 'Lullaby Of Broadway'. It begins as dawn breaks, and ends 24 hours later. The spectacular climax comes when Dick Powell and Wini Shaw, a couple of good-time pleasure seekers, are seated high up in a nightclub looking down on a sensational orgy of power tap dancing, after which the girl falls to her death from a window. Another memorable number is 'The Words Are In My Heart', during which more than 50 girls seated at white pianos are slickly manoeuvred around in time with the music - by very small men, if you look closely enough. Harry Warren and Al Dubin also contributed the appealing 'I'm Going Shopping With You'. Manuel Seff and Peter Milne's slight screenplay (adapted from a story by Robert Lord and Peter Milne), concerns the efforts of the wealthy set to put on a lavish musical show at a country house (makes a change from a barn). Also involved were Adolph Menjou, Frank McHugh, Gloria Stuart, Glenda Farrell, Alice Brady, Joseph Cawthorn, Hugh Herbert, Grant Mitchell, and Virginia Grey.

Gold Diggers Of 1937. Dick Powell's last '*Gold Diggers*' outing found him cast as an insurance salesman who sells a $1 million life-insurance policy to a Broadway producer (Victor Moore)- and ends up starring in the (still healthy) impresario's lavish show. Yet again Busby Berkeley came up with some marvellous production numbers including 'Let's Put Our Heads Together' (Harold Arlen-E.Y. 'Yip' Harburg) with its bevy of girls on rocking chairs, and the razzamatazz finalé, 'All's Fair In Love And War' (Warren-Dubin), in which Joan Blondell puts a kind of all-girl military band, some 70 strong, through their paces, predating the 'Seventy-Six Trombones' sequence in *The Music Man* by some 25 years. Powell also introduced the delightful 'With Plenty Of Money And You' (Warren-Dubin), and the score was completed by 'Life Insurance Song', 'Speaking Of The Weather', and 'Hush Ma Mouth' (Arlen-Harburg). Also cast were Glenda Farrell, Lee Dixon, Osgood Perkins, and Rosalind Marquis. Warren Duff wrote the screenplay and the director was Lloyd Bacon.

Gold Diggers In Paris (1938). Rudy Vallee takes a three-girl dance act to Europe where they are mistaken for a classical troupe - with the inevitable complications. Earl Baldwin and Warren Duff's slight story was just an excuse for more of Berkeley's ingenious ideas based around such numbers as 'I Wanna Go Back To Bali', 'The Latin Quarter', 'Put That Down In Writing', and 'A Stranger In Paree' (all Warren-Dubin), and 'Day Dreaming All Night Long', 'Waltz Of The Flowers' and 'My Adventure' (Warren-Mercer). Rosemary Lane was Vallee's love interest, and supporting the couple were Hugh Herbert, Allen Jenkins, and Gloria Dickson. Ray Enright directed, but the *Gold Diggers* concept was worn out. However, it resurfaced once more (to date) in:

Painting The Clouds With Sunshine (1951). Named after one of the hit songs in the original 1929 film, it was loosely based on Avery Hopwood's story, only this time the girls (Virginia Mayo, Virginia Gibson and Lucille Norman) are sisters, and Las Vegas is the base for the male chase. Most of the songs were old standards, and the creaky screenplay was by Harry Clark, Roland Kibbee, and Peter Milne. Gene Nelson, Dennis Morgan, S.Z. Sakall, Tom Conway, and Wallace Ford tried their best to put some life in it, as did choreographer LeRoy Prince and director David Butler. It was photographed in Technicolor by William Jacobs, and, like the rest of what is regarded as an historic series, produced by Warner brothers.

GOLDEN APPLE, THE

Following its enthusiastic reception at the off-Broadway Phoenix Theatre, New York, USA, in March 1954, *The Golden Apple* was rapidly moved uptown to the Alvin Theatre where it reopened on 20 April. Based on Homer's *Iliad* and *The Odyssey*, John Latouche (book and lyrics) and Jerome Moross (music) transported those epic tales to the state of Washington in the early part of the 20th century. The story concerns the consternation caused in the town of Angel's Roost when a travelling salesman named Paris (Jonathan Lucas) arrives unannounced in a balloon, and takes Helen (Kaye Ballard), the impressionable wife of old Sheriff Menelaus (Dean Michener), off to Rhododendron by-the-sea (not entirely against her will). For some reason, the intrepid Ulysses (Stephen Douglass), who has just returned from the Spanish-American war, leaves his wife Penelope (Priscilla Gillette), and sets off to retrieve the errant Helen. After a decade of excitement and adventure - during which time he engages successfully in fisticuffs with Paris - Ulysses is finally reunited with his incredibly patient spouse. As for the songs - which carried the story almost on their own - Kaye Ballard's languid reading of 'Lazy Afternoon' was one of the high points of a delicious score that is treasured in recordings by stage musical buffs the world over. The other numbers, a mixture of witty spoofs and appealing ballads, included 'Goona-Goona', 'It's The Going Home Together', 'Come Along, Boys', 'Doomed, Doomed Doomed', 'My Picture In The Papers', 'Store-Bought Suit', 'Helen Is Always Willing', 'My Love Is On the Way' and 'Scylla And Charybdis'. This 'brilliant, innovative theatre experience', which was just pipped for a Tony Award by *The Pajama Game*, but which won the New York Drama Critics Award best musical, closed after only 127 performances. It was revived off-Broadway in 1962 (112 performances), and is regarded as something of a musical theatre legend.

GOLDEN BOY

Frank Sinatra is said to have tried to discourage Sammy Davis, a fellow-member of the infamous 60s 'Clan', from continually submitting himself to the discipline of an eight-shows-a-week stint in a Broadway musical. Davis, a major star in nightclubs and on records, had made his debut on the 'great white way' in *Mr. Wonderful* in 1956, and, 12 years later, he ignored Sinatra's advice and opened in *Golden Boy* at the Majestic Theatre on 20 October 1964. Clifford Odets died a few months after he began to adapt his well-known play for this Broadway musical, and the work was finished by his friend, William Gibson. In a neat twist of both name and colour, the writers changed the name of the leading character, a boxer, from an Italian-American named Joe Bonaparte, to a Negro-American named Joe Wellington. Davis was impressive as the young fighter, who is determined to get out, get rich, and make it to the top. One of the oustanding features of the production was Donald McKayle's innovative and exciting choreography, particularly in the opening scene, which simulated a high-energy workout, and a marvellously conceived fight sequence. The score, by Charles Strouse (music) and Lee Adams (lyrics), received a mixed press. There was one show-stopper, 'Don't Forget 127th Street', in which Wellington berates his young fans, telling them to be proud of their Harlem roots. Davis also had a couple of telling ballads, 'Night Song' and 'I Want To Be With You', and the rest of the score included 'Workout', 'Everything's Great', 'Gimme Some', 'Lorna's Here', 'This Is The Life', 'While The City Sleeps', 'Golden Boy', 'Colourful', 'No More', and 'The Fight'. Also in the cast were Kenneth Tobey, who played Tom Moody, the fighter's manager; Paula Wayne in the role of Lorna Moon, a lady who shares her favours with both of them, and Billy Daniels as Eddie Satin. Davis was credited with being the main reason that *Golden Boy* played for well over a year in New York, a total

of 569 performances, but West End audiences were not so impressed, and the London Palladium production folded after nearly four months. A 25th anniversary edition of the show, with a new book by Leslie Lee, reworked music and lyrics, and starring Obba Babatunde, played venues such as Miami's Coconut Grove Playhouse and the Candlewood Playhouse in New Fairfield, Connecticut, in the late 80s-early 90s.

GOLDEN DISC, THE

Titled *The In-Between Age* for the USA, *The Golden Disc* starred ill-fated British rock 'n' roll star Terry Dene. This Jack Good discovery was briefly touted as a bona fide star, although none of his three UK chart entries actually reached the Top 10. A former record packer, Dene briefly enjoyed the limelight upon joining the army, but praise turned to derision when the singer was discharged following a nervous breakdown. The fiancée who 'would wait for him' promptly broke off their engagement and his recording career was left in tatters. He later joined the Salvation Army. Real-life events were certainly more interesting than the plot of this 1957 film, in which the owners of a café turn it into an expresso bar before founding a record label to showcase the acts performing there. With skiffle the fad of the moment, acts including Nancy Whiskey and Sonny Stewart And The Skiffle Kings featured in the cast alongside the disc jockey David Jacobs, crooner Dennis Lotis and the exceptional Phil Seamen Jazz Group. Other performers included future impresario Terry Kennedy, Sheila Buxton and Murray Campbell. *The Golden Disc* is not an auspicious feature, but the film serves as a timely reminder of Terry Dene's all too brief pop ascendancy.

GOLDILOCKS

This show, which opened at the Lunt Fontanne Theatre in New York on 11 October 1958, afforded Broadway audiences their only opportunity to hear the music of Leroy Anderson, who was better known as a composer of light, engaging, and some times humorous works, such as 'Blue Tango', 'Sleigh Ride', 'Forgotten Dreams', and 'The Typewriter'. Anderson's lyricists for *Goldilocks* were John Ford, and Walter and Jean Kerr. The husband-and-wife team also wrote the book, which was set in 1913, and was essentially a sometimes hilarious spoof on the silent-movie business. As the curtain rises, an actress Maggie Harris (Elaine Stritch, in one of her typically 'acerbic' roles), is about to give up the theatre and marry the millionaire George Randolph Brown (Russell Nype). Enter film producer-director Max Grady (Don Ameche) to remind her that she is, in fact, contracted to appear in his movie, *Frontier Woman*, which is about to begin shooting. Max tricks Maggie into filming enough footage for several movies, and, although they admit their feelings for each other, she fully intends to marry George. However, when the unexpected happens, and snow begins falls on the site of Max's latest movie - an Egyptian epic which is being shot in down-state California (in April) - she takes that as a sign that she should do something equally unconventional - so she marries Max instead. Jilted George has to make do with Lois (Pat Stanley), but both Stanley and Nype were consoled by receiving real-life Tony Awards for their performances. 'Never mind the story - the score's the thing,' has been said so many times, and this was yet another of them. The songs were indeed both charming and amusing. Stritch was beautifully served with 'Give The Little Lady', 'Whose Been Sitting In My Chair?', 'The Beast In You', 'I Never Know When', and 'Save A Kiss' (with Nype), and an 'abusive' duet with Ameche, 'No One'll Ever Love You' ('Like you do'). Ameche displayed an impressive singing voice in 'There Never Was A Woman', and the insistent, disbelieving 'I Can't Be In Love' (with the accent very much on the 'can't'), and the rest of the score included 'Lazy Moon', 'Lady In Waiting', 'Shall I Take My Heart And Go?' (Nype), 'Bad Companions', 'Two Years In The Making', and 'Heart Of Stone'. The Broadway veteran choreographer, Agnes de Mille, was acclaimed for her staging of both songs and dances, and she had a great time with the comic 'Pussy Foot'. It all added up to another of those fondly-remembered flops. A run of 161 performances equalled a reported financial loss in the region of $360,000 dollars - and an Original Cast album to treasure.

GOLDSMITH, JERRY

b. Jerrald Goldsmith, 10 February 1929, Los Angeles, California, USA. A prolific composer for films and television, from the late 50s through to the 90s. Besides studying music at the University of South Carolina, Goldsmith also took lessons in office practice and secured a job as a clerk/typist with CBS Television, before moving to the company's music department in Los Angeles in 1950. During the 50s, first as a staffer, and then as a freelancer, he wrote theme music for popular television series such as *Gunsmoke*, *Perry Mason*, *Have Gun Will Travel*, *The Twilight Zone*, *The Man From U.N.C.L.E.*, *Doctor Kildare*, and several more. In the late 50s, Goldsmith started to compose for films such as *Black Patch* and *City Of Fear* and, through the good auspices of film composer Alfred Newman, he came to prominence with his score for *Lonely Are The Brave* (1962). It was the start of a career in which he composed the music for over 150 films, ranging from westerns such as *Rio Conchos*, *Bandolero!* and a remake of *Stagecoach* to the 'shockers', *Poltergeist*, *The Omen*, *Damien: Omen II*, *The Final Conflict*, *Psycho II* and *Seconds*. He was also involved in *Star Trek*, *Gremlins*, *Total Recall*, *Rambo*, *Patton*, *Tora! Tora! Tora!*, *Chinatown*, *Freud*, *Seven Days In May*, *The Secret Of Nimh* and *Islands In The Stream*. The latter film was one of several that he made with his favourite director, Franklin Schaffner. The others included *The Boys From Brazil*, *The Stripper*, *Papillon*, *Planet Of The Apes* and *Patton*. During the 60s it was estimated that Goldsmith was averaging about six films a year. These included *The Prize*, *Seven Days In May*, *The Spiral Road*, *Lilies Of The Field*, *In Harm's Way*, *The Trouble With Angels*, *The Sand Pebbles*, *The Blue Max*, *In Like Flint*, *To Trap A Spy*, *A Patch Of Blue*, *Von Ryan's Express*, *The Satan Bug*, *The Flim-Flam Man*, *The Detective* and *Justine*. Throughout the 70s, 80s and early 90s, he was still one of the busiest film composers, contributing to movies such as *The Mephisto Waltz*, *The Reincarnation Of Peter Proud*, *MacArthur*, *Capricorn One*, *Coma*, *Magic*, *The First Great Train Robbery*, *Outland*, *Raggedy Man*, *Under Fire*, *King*

Solomon's Mines, *Hoosiers*, *Extreme Prejudice*, *Best Shot*, *Innerspace*, *Warlock*, *Rambo III*, *Gremlins: The New Batch*, *Star Trek V The Final Frontier*, *The Russia House*, *Sleeping With The Enemy*, *Not Without My Daughter*, *Total Recall*, *Basic Instinct*, *Mom And Dad Save The World*, *Forever Young*, *Love Field*, *Matinee*, *The Vanishing*, *Dennis*, *Malice*, *Angie*, *Bad Girls*, *The Shadow*, *The River Wild*, and *I. Q.* (1994). By this stage, more than 15 of his scores had been nominated for an Academy Award, but only *The Omen* (1976) received an Oscar. In addition to composing, Goldsmith has conducted orchestras such as the San Diego Symphony and Britain's Royal Philharmonic, playing his music in concert halls around the world.

GONKS GO BEAT

Inspired by the plot from the AIP film, *Pajama Party*, this 1965 feature offered a wafer-thin premise whereby a space-travelling alien versed in the wonder of pop attempts to placate rivalry between Beatland and Balladisle. This is achieved through an unlikely combination of acts, most of which were culled from the Decca Records roster. Although the bulk of the acts were undistinguished - precocious child stars Elaine and Derek were set beside second-string beat groups the Long And The Short and Trolls - the film did include otherwise unavailable recordings by chart acts the Nashville Teens and Lulu And The Luvvers. The latter featured future Stone The Crows and Robin Trower member Jimmy Dewar on bass. However, the highlight of *Gonks Go Beat* was unquestionably an appearance by the Graham Bond Organization, one of the finest - and most influential - 60s groups. Vocalist/keyboard player Bond was herein joined by Jack Bruce and Ginger Baker, both later of Cream, and future Colosseum saxophonist, Dick Heckstall-Smith. Their contribution, 'Harmonica', was shot in a studio bedecked in tropical style, but the ill-fitting setting did not undermine the quartet's charismatic power. It did nothing to salvage the film's commercial prospects and an attendant soundtrack album enjoyed negligible success. Another in a line of British 'quickie' pop films, *Gonks Go Beat* does at least boast one highly memorable sequence.

GOOD NEWS

Twenty years after it became a smash-hit Broadway musical, *Good News* came to the screen in 1947 courtesy of MGM. It was one of songwriters' De Sylva, Brown And Henderson's 'fad' musicals - and the fad this time was US football. Star player Tommy Marlowe (Peter Lawford) might not be able to play for Tait college in the big game because he has been neglecting his studies and concentrating on having fun and games with Pat McClellan (Patricia Marshall). However, after Connie Lane (June Allyson) has helped him to swot, Tommy wins the game and Connie as well. Classy singer Mel Tormé was in the admirable supporting cast, along with Joan McCracken, Donald MacBride, Ray McDonald, Robert Strickland, Tommy Dugan, Clinton Sundberg, and Loren Tindall. The lively and hugely enjoyable 'Varsity Drag' and 'Good News' were two of the songs retained from the original stage production in a score which included 'He's A Ladies Man', 'Lucky In Love', 'The Best Things In Life Are Free',

'Just Imagine' (all De Sylva, Brown And Henderson), 'The French Lesson' (Roger Edens-Kay Thompson), and 'Pass That Peace Pipe' (Edens-Ralph Blane-Hugh Martin) which accompanied just one of the entertaining and energetic dance numbers staged by Robert Alton and Charles Walters. The latter was also making his debut as a director. Betty Comden and Adolph Green's screenplay (their first) was adapted from De Sylva and Laurence Schwab's Broadway libretto, and film was produced by Arthur Freed. A previous version of *Good News* had been made in 1930 as an early talkie. It starred Bessie Love, Stanley Smith, Gus Shy and Mary Lawlor, and used more songs from the stage show than this 1947 version did.

GOOD ROCKIN' TONITE

There was plenty of that when this show opened at the Strand Theatre in London on 28 January 1992. It was devised by Jack Good, the influential producer who gave British television its earliest - and many still say best - pop music programmes, such as *6.5 Special* and *Oh Boy!* Some of the early beneficiaries of his ingenuity were there on the show's opening night - rock 'n' roll survivors such as Cliff Richard, Lonnie Donegan, Joe Brown, Marty Wilde, and Jess Conrad. Brilliantly staged by Good and Ian Kellgran, the story, which was only loosely based on Good's life, was really an excuse to celebrate some 60 of those seminal numbers from the 50s and early 60s, in the onstage company of Tommy Steele (David Howarth), Gene Vincent (Michael Dimitri), Cliff Richard (Tim Whitnall), Eddie Cochrane, the Vernon Girls, and more. There was also an 'uncanny' impression of Billy Fury by Gavin Stanley, and a 'creepy' one of the agent Larry Parnes by David Howarth (again). Good himself, engagingly played by Philip Baird, 'stumbles amusingly through an obsessive relationship with music, and a stormy one with his wife (Anna-Juliana Claire) and the BBC's Head of Light Entertainment, played hilariously by James Compton'. After the show transferred to the Prince Of Wales Theatre in July, the jiving in the aisles (literally) continued until November, when the show closed after a rock 'n' rolling 327 performances.

GOOD TIMES

There was a moment during 1965 when it seemed Sonny And Cher could do little wrong. Singles together, singles apart and archive recordings scaled the US and UK charts with impunity, aurally blending Phil Spector with folk-rock. Visually the pair extolled mutual love and bohemian imagery but their popularity was short-lived. By the time *Good Times* was released in 1966, their star was already waning, although re-invention has allowed Cher's career to prosper. She harboured acting ambitions before becoming a singer and thus this project provided a particularly welcome opportunity. During the film the couple imagine all the movies they could have made, creating genuinely amusing scenes from this unlikely premise. Their international best-seller, 'I Got You Babe', is among the nine songs in a film that has been too quickly overlooked. Despite this, however, few would have predicted this was Cher's first step towards winning a Best Actress Oscar.

GOODBYE GIRL, THE

By the time this musical blew into New York's Marquis Theatre from Chicago on 4 March 1993, it had lost its original director (Gene Saks) and opening number. Rather appropriately for Saks, who was replaced by 73-year-old veteran stager Michael Kidd, the discarded number was called 'I'm Outta Here'. These changes did nothing to dampen the climate of anticipation for what some out-of-town critics regarded as 'a sure-fire winner . . . the funniest new musical for years'. The production certainly had some good things going for it, notably a score by composer Marvin (*A Chorus Line*) Hamlisch and lyricist David (*City Of Angels*) Zippel, as well as a cast headed by Broadway favourite Bernadette Peters and Hollywood and television funny man Martin Short. Best of all (in theory), the book was written by Neil Simon, the most popular playwright of his time. He adapted it from his 1977 romantic film comedy of the same name, starring the one-time Mrs. Simon, Marsha Mason, and the Oscar-winning Richard Dreyfuss. Set in New York City, the story concerns Paula (Peters), a struggling single mother, who is eventually attracted to an unemployed émigré Chicago actor Elliot (Short), after she is forced to share an apartment with him. In his pursuit of Paula, Elliot finds an ally in her daughter, Lucy (Tammy Minoff), extolling his virtues as a prospective father with the vocally impressive 'I Can Play This Part'. The domestic situation is frequently enlivened - and enhanced - by the rhythm-and-blues rantings of landlady Mrs. Crosby (Carol Woods). Making his Broadway musical theatre debut, Short attracted all the best notices, and proved a charismatic, assured performer, especially in the gay 'Richard Interred' sequence, where he is forced by a manic stage director (John Christopher-Jones), to play Richard III as 'a man playing a woman playing a man' rather than a homosexual. Although some critics felt that she was upstaged by Short, the never-less-than-superb Peters had her moments - including one scene in which she danced in a pile of French fries for the sake of a television show - with three big solos and various duets in amongst the rest of the score which comprised 'This Is As Good As It Gets', 'No More', 'A Beat Behind', 'My Rules', 'Good News, Bad News', 'Footsteps', 'How Can I Win?', 'Too Good To Be Bad', '2 Good 2 B Bad', 'Who Would've Thought?', 'Paula (An Improvised Love Song)', 'Jump For Joy', and 'What A Guy'. Musical staging was by Graciela Daniele, and Billy Byers and Torrie Zito were responsible for the lively orchestrations. Despite its earlier promise, *The Goodbye Girl* was immediately faced with a batch of negative reviews which criticized particularly its slim storyline, old-fashioned style, and unimaginative staging. The writing (and closing notice) was on the wall, and, after failing to convert any of its five Tony Award nominations for best musical, actor (Short), actress (Peters), director, and choreography (Daniele), it was withdrawn in August after 188 performances. The original cast album differed in several respects from the score performed on stage, with the new opening number for Broadway, 'This Is As Good As It Gets', going the same way as its predecessor, 'I'm Outta Here'.

The show was the third unsuccessful attempt - along with

Nick And Nora and My Favorite Year - to convert well-known films into stage musicals in the early 90s. Having been jilted in New York, The Goodbye Girl subsequently went back to her Chicago roots early in 1994, when a production starring Kathy Santen and James FitzGerald, directed by Joe Leonardo and David Zippel, played at Marriot's Lincolnshire Theatre. Three years later, West End audiences and critics rejected a new version of the show starring Gary Wilmot and Ann Crumb, which closed after only two months. Hamlisch wrote seven new songs, 'I'll Take The Sky', 'Body Talk', 'Get A Life', 'Am I Who I Think I Am?'/'Are You Who You Think You Are?', 'If You Break Their Hearts', 'Do You Want To Be In My Movie?', and 'the Future Isn't What It Used To Be', with lyricist Don Black. Fortunately, two of the three Zippel numbers to be retained were first act highlights, 'Elliot Garfield Grant' and 'Good News, Bad News'.

GOODNIGHT VIENNA

After a brief foray to Hollywood in 1930 to co-star with Jeanette MacDonald in Ernst Lubitsch's Monte Carlo, Jack Buchanan returned to England for this popular film which was released by the British Dominions company two years later. Set in Vienna in 1914, it concerns a bachelor gay, Captain Maximilian Schlettoff (Buchanan), who falls in love with Viki (Anna Neagle), a pretty young assistant in a flower shop. On the night they are due to elope the gallant Captain is ordered to leave for the war front immediately, and the note he sends to Viki is never delivered. She is distraught when she receives a letter from Maximilian's father (Clive Currie) telling her that his son has entered into an arranged marriage with Countess Helga (Joyce Bland). After the war has ended, the Captain returns to Vienna in reduced financial circumstances and gets a job in a shoe shop where one of his first customers is Viki - now a famous opera star. She is initially aloof, but eventually, according to the film's publicity hand-out at the time, 'they meet again in a charming café set amidst flowering trees, where in the old days they had laughed and sung with carefree joyousness, and their favourite song reunites them.' All four of the songs in the film, 'Just Heaven', 'Living In Clover', 'Marching Song', and 'Goodnight Vienna', were the work of Eric Maschwitz and George Posford, who also adapted the screenplay from the original radio play. Buchanan gave his usual engaging performance, and Anna Neagle, who had come to prominence only the year before in Buchanan's musical comedy Stand Up And Sing, was delightful and obviously a star in the making. Gina Malo as Frieda, headed a supporting cast which included William Kendall, Herbert Carrick, Gibb McLaughlin, Clifford Heatherley, O.B. Clarence, Aubrey Fitzgerald, Peggy Cartwright, and Muriel Akred. The producer-director was Herbert Wilcox. For its release in the USA the film was re-titled Magic Night.

GOODWIN, RON

b. 17 February 1925, Plymouth, Devon, England. An important composer, conductor and arranger, from an early age Goodwin was deeply interested in all things musical, but began his working life outside the business. Eventually, he took a job as a music copier with a firm of music publishers. He also studied trumpet and arranging at the Guildhall School of Music in London, and played trumpet professionally with Harry Gold and wrote arrangements for the bands of Ted Heath and Geraldo. Goodwin made several records, arranging and conducting the backing music for singers, including Petula Clark, and also worked in radio. He has composed music in the classical form, including his 'Drake 400 Concert Suite' and 'New Zealand Suite', but it is as a writer for films that he made his greatest impact. After first writing for documentaries, from the 60s through to the 80s he composed the scores - and generally served as the musical director - for numerous feature films, including Whirlpool, The Witness, I'm All Right Jack, In The Nick, Village Of The Damned, The Trials Of Oscar Wilde, The Man With The Green Carnation, The Man At The Carleton Tower, The Clue Of The New Pin, Partners In Crime, Invasion Quartet, a series of 'Miss Marple' films starring Margaret Rutherford (Murder, She Said, Murder At The Gallop, Murder Most Foul and Murder Ahoy), The Day Of The Triffids, Follow The Boys, Of Human Bondage, Children Of The Damned, 633 Squadron, A Home Of Your Own, Those Magnificent Men In Their Flying Machines, Operation Crossbow, The Alphabet Murders, That Riviera Touch, The Trap (used as the theme for the London Marathon), Mrs. Brown, You've Got A Lovely Daughter, Where Eagles Dare, Battle Of Britain, The Executioner, Frenzy, One Of Our Dinosaurs Is Missing, Escape From The Dark, Ride A Wild Pony, Candleshoe, Force 10 From Navarone, The Spaceman And King Arthur, Clash Of Loyalties and Valhalla (1986). He has won several Ivor Novello Awards, including the Entertainment Music Award in 1972, and a Life Achievement Award in 1993. In the 70s he made concert tours of the UK with an orchestra performing his own film scores. He has continued to broadcast on radio, and has worked extensively in Canada.
● ALBUMS: Film Favourites (Parlophone 1954)★★★★, Music To Set You Dreaming (Parlophone 1956)★★★, Out Of This World (Parlophone 1958)★★★★, Adventure And Excitement/Music For An Arabian Night (Parlophone 1958)★★★, Decline And Fall ... Of A Birdwatcher film soundtrack (Stateside 1968)★★, Monte Carlo Or Bust film soundtrack (Paramount 1969)★★★, Legend Of The Glass Mountain (Studio 2 1970)★★★, Spellbound (Studio 2 1973)★★★, Elizabethan Serenade (MFP 1975)★★★, I'll See You In My Dreams (Studio 2 1976)★★★, Escape From The Dark film soundtrack (EMI 1976)★★★, Rhythm And Romance (Studio 2 1977)★★★, with the New Zealand Symphony Orchestra Going Places (Studio 2 1978)★★★, Christmas Wonderland (One-Up 1978)★★★, with the Bournemouth Symphony Orchestra Ron Goodwin And The Bournemouth Symphony Orchestra (Chandos 1980)★★★, Drake 400 Concert Suite (Chandos 1980)★★★, Sounds Superb (MFP 1981)★★★, with the Royal Philharmonic Orchestra Projections (EMI 1983)★★★, Fire And Romance (EMI 1984)★★★, with the New Zealand Symphony Orchestra New Zealand Suite (Columbia 1984)★★★, Ron Goodwin Plays Bacharach And David (Ideal 1984)★★★, The Love Album (MFP 1985)★★★, with the Bournemouth Symphony Orchestra My Kind Of Music (Chandos 1989)★★★.
● COMPILATIONS: This Is Ron Goodwin (EMI 1973)★★★, Very Best Of Ron Goodwin (Studio 2 1977)★★★, First 25 Years (Studio 2 1978)★★★★.

GORDON, MACK

b. Morris Gittler, 21 June 1904, Warsaw, Poland, d. 1 March 1959, New York, USA. A prolific lyricist, mainly for movie songs during the 30s and 40s, Gordon was taken to the USA at an early age, and grew up in the Brooklyn area of New York. He toured with minstrel shows as a boy soprano, and later became a singer-comedian in vaudeville, before starting to write songs in the late 20s. His 'Aintcha', with music by Max Rich, was featured in the 1929 movie *Painted Heels*, and he also contributed to *The Song Of Love* and *Swing High* (1930). In the same year he teamed with Harold Adamson and Vincent Youmans for 'Time On My Hands', which was performed by Marilyn Miller and Paul Gregory in the Broadway revue *Smiles*. In 1931, Gordon began a collaboration with composer Harry Revel which lasted until 1939. Initially they contributed songs to stage shows such as the *Ziegfeld Follies Of 1931* ('Help Yourself To Happiness' and 'Cigarettes, Cigars') and *Everybody's Welcome* ('All Wrapped Up In You') but, from 1933 onwards, they wrote mainly for the movies - over 30 of them. These included *Broadway Thru A Keyhole*, starring Russ Columbo and Constance Cummings, and featuring 'Doin' The Uptown Lowdown'; *Shoot The Works* ('With My Eyes Wide Open I'm Dreaming'); *Sitting Pretty* ('Did You Ever See A Dream Walking?'); *We're Not Dressing*, with Bing Crosby and Carole Lombard ('May I?', 'Love Thy Neighbour' and 'She Reminds Me Of You'); *The Gay Divorcée*, ('Don't Let It Bother You', sung by Fred Astaire); *College Rhythm* ('Stay As Sweet As You Are'); *Love In Bloom* ('Here Comes Cookie' and 'My Heart Is An Open Book'); *Two For Tonight*, with Crosby and Joan Bennett ('Without A Word Of Warning' and 'From The Top Of Your Head'); *Collegiate* ('I Feel Like A Feather In The Breeze' and 'You Hit The Spot'); *Stowaway* starring Shirley Temple, Alice Faye and Robert Young ('Goodnight My Love' and 'One Never Knows, Does One?'); *Wake Up And Live* ('Never In A Million Years' and 'There's A Lull In My Life'); *You Can't Have Everything* (title song); *Love Finds Andy Hardy*, with Judy Garland and Mickey Rooney ('What Do You Know About Love?' and 'Meet The Beat Of My Heart'); *Thanks For Everything* (title song) and *My Lucky Star* ('I've Got A Date With A Dream'). In 1940 Gordon teamed with Harry Warren, fresh from his Warner Brothers triumphs with Al Dubin. During the next 10 years they wrote some of America's most memorable popular songs, for films such as *Down Argentine Way* (title song and 'When Two Dreams Met'); *Tin Pan Alley* ('You Say The Sweetest Things, Baby'); *That Night In Rio* ('Chica Chica Boom Chic', 'Boa Noite' and 'I, Yi, Yi, Yi, Yi, I Like You Very Much'); *The Great American Broadcast* ('Where You Are' and 'Long Ago Last Night'); and *Weekend In Havana* ('When I Love I Love' and 'Tropical Magic'). They featured some of the biggest stars of the day, including Alice Faye, John Payne, Carmen Miranda, Betty Grable, Don Ameche, the Nicholas Brothers, and many more. In 1941/2, Gordon and Warren contributed perhaps their best known songs to *Sun Valley Serenade* and *Orchestra Wives*, starring the enormously popular Glenn Miller And His Orchestra. They included 'I Know Why', 'Chattanooga Choo Choo', 'It Happened In Sun Valley', 'The Kiss Polka', 'At Last', 'I've

Got A Girl In Kalamazoo' and 'People Like You And Me'. Miller's million-selling record of 'Chattanooga Choo Choo' was the first to be awarded a gold disc. Gordon and Warren continued throughout the 40s, with films such as *Iceland* ('There Will Never Be Another You'); *Sweet Rosie O'Grady* ('My Heart Tells Me' and 'The Wishing Waltz'); *Hello, Frisco, Hello* ('You'll Never Know', the Academy Award-winning song of 1943); *Billy Rose's Diamond Horseshoe*, with Dick Haymes ('I Wish I Knew' and 'The More I See You'); and *Summer Stock*, with Judy Garland ('If You Feel Like Singing, Sing'). Even during the period of almost 20 years with Revel and Warren, Gordon found the time to collaborate with several other composers on songs such as 'Mamselle', 'Time Alone Will Tell', 'I Can't Begin To Tell You', 'Somewhere In The Night', 'This Is Always', 'You Make Me Feel So Young' (with Joseph Myrow), 'You Do', 'Baby, Won't You Say You Love Me?' and 'A Lady Loves To Love'. His last film score, with Myrow, was for *Bundle Of Joy* (1956), starring Eddie Fisher and Debbie Reynolds. Among Gordon's other collaborators were Ray Henderson, Jimmy Van Heusen, Jimmy Monaco, Max Rich, Maurice Abrahams, Ted Snyder, Abner Silver and George Weist.

GOULD, MORTON

b. 10 December 1913, Richmond Hill, New York, USA, d. 21 February 1996, Orlando, Florida, USA. Gould was one of the most important figures in American music in the twentieth century, and his composition 'Pavane' (from his 'American Symphonette No. 2') has become a light-music standard. By the age of 21 he was conducting and arranging a weekly series of orchestral radio shows, which allowed him to introduce many of his lighter works to a wider public. Equally at home in the popular and classical fields, his compositions included 'American Salute', 'Latin-American Symphonette', 'Spirituals For Orchestra', 'Interplay For Piano And Orchestra', 'Tap Dance Concerto', 'Dance Variations For Two Pianos And Orchestra', 'Jekyll And Hyde Variations', plus five symphonies and numerous works for symphonic band. Among many special commissions were 'Fall River Legend', 'Inventions For Four Pianos And Wind Orchestra', 'Declaration', 'St Lawrence Suite', 'Festive Music', 'Venice', 'Columbia', 'Soundings', 'Cheers' (commissioned by the Boston Symphony for Arthur Fiedler's 50th anniversary), 'Burchfield Gallery', 'Celebration '81', 'Housewarming', 'Cello Suite', 'Concerto Concertante', 'Centennial Symphony For Band' and 'Troubador Music For Four Guitars'. Gould's musical scores for Broadway included *Billion Dollar Baby* (1945) and *Arms And The Girl* (1950). For the cinema he scored *Delightfully Dangerous*, *Cinerama Holiday* and *Windjammer*. Ballets included Jerome Robbins' *Interplay*, Agnes De Mille's *Fall River Legend*, George Balanchine's *Clarinade* and Eliot Field's *Santa Fe Saga* and *Halftime*. His television work included a CBS World War 1 documentary series, *F. Scott Fitzgerald In Hollywood* for ABC, the four-part mini-series *Holocaust* (1978) and a role as musical host for the National Educational Network series *The World Of Music With Morton Gould*. His list of recordings is extensive and he received many 'Grammy' nominations. In 1966 his RCA Red Seal recording of Charles Ives with the Chicago

Symphony won the NARAS Grammy Award as the best classical recording of the year. In lighter vein, Gould's mood albums by his own orchestra from the 40s and 50s are collector's items. He also recorded with the London Symphony, London Philharmonic, the American Symphony Orchestra and the Louisville Orchestra. Gould travelled widely in the USA and throughout the world as a guest conductor, and was the recipient of numerous awards from fellow musicians. In March 1986 he became President of the American Society of Composers, Authors and Publishers (ASCAP), holding the post until 1994. Much of his music featured a strong patriotic American flavour, partly explaining why his own compositions were not better known outside the USA. In 1995, at the age of 81, Morton Gould won his first Pulitzer Prize in music for his work 'Stringmusic'. He died suddenly at a hotel in Florida, while attending the Disney Institute as artist-in-residence.

● ALBUMS: *After Dark* (Columbia 1949)★★★, *South Of The Border* (Columbia 50s)★★★, *Rhapsodies For Piano And Orchestra* (Columbia 50s)★★★, *Soft Lights And Sweet Music* (Columbia 50s)★★★, *Strike Up The Band* (Columbia 50s)★★★, *Christmas Music For Orchestra* (Columbia 50s)★★★, *Interplay For Piano And Orchestra - Music Of Morton Gould* (Columbia 50s)★★★, *Family Album/Tap Dance Concerts* (Columbia 50s)★★★, *Manhattan Moods* (Columbia 50s)★★★, *Victor Herbert Serenades* (Columbia 50s)★★★, *Symphonic Serenade* (Columbia 50s)★★★, *Starlight Serenade* (Columbia 50s)★★★, *Music At Midnight* (Columbia 50s)★★★, *Morton Gould Showcase* (Columbia 50s)★★★, *Music Of Morton Gould* (Columbia 50s)★★★, *Curtain Time* (Columbia 1951)★★★, *Morton Gould Programme* (Columbia 1951)★★★, *The Months (Tchaikovsky)* (Columbia 50s)★★★, *Movie Time* (Columbia 50s)★★★, *Memories* (Columbia 50s)★★★, *Wagon Wheels* (Columbia 50s)★★★, *Famous Operettas* (Columbia 50s)★★★, *Oklahoma! And Carousel Suites* (RCA 1955)★★★, *An American In Paris/Porgy And Bess Suite* (RCA 1956)★★★, *Music For Summertime* (RCA 1956)★★★, *Where's The Melody* (RCA 1958)★★★, *Moon, Wind And Stars* (RCA 1958)★★★, *World's Best Loved Waltzes* (RCA 50s)★★★, *Pendagrass* (Columbia 50s)★★★, *High-Fi Band Concert* (Columbia 50s)★★★, *Brass And Percussion* (RCA 50s)★★★, *Blues In The Night* (RCA 1957)★★★, *Temptation* (RCA 1957)★★★, *Batons And Bows* (RCA 1958)★★★, *Coffee Time* (RCA 1958)★★★, *Jungle Drums* (RCA 1960)★★★, *Doubling In Brass* (RCA 1961)★★★, *Living Strings* (RCA 60s)★★★, *Ballet Music By Gould* (RCA 60s)★★★, *Beyond The Blue Horizon* (RCA 1961)★★★, *Kern And Porter Favorites* (RCA 1961)★★★, *Sousa Forever!* (RCA 1961)★★★, *Love Walked In* (RCA 1961)★★★, *Moonlight Sonata* (RCA 1961)★★★, *Goodnight Sweetheart* (RCA 1962)★★★, *Finlandia* (RCA 1963)★★★, *More Jungle Drums* (RCA 1964)★★★, *Spirituals For Strings* (RCA 1965)★★★, *World War I* (RCA 1965)★★★, *Spirituals For Orchestra* (RCA 1965)★★★, *Latin Lush And Lovely* (RCA 1966)★★★, *Two Worlds Of Kurt Weill* (RCA 1966)★★★, *Charles Ives Orchestra Set No. 2* (RCA 1967)★★★, *Morton Gould Makes The Scene* (RCA 1967)★★★, *Discovery* (RCA 1968)★★★, *Musical Christmas Tree* (RCA 1969)★★★, *Holocaust* (RCA 1978)★★★, *Gould Conducts Gould* (1978)★★★, *An American In Paris/Adagio For Strings/American Salute* (Pro Art 1983)★★★, *The Louisville Orchestra First Edition Series - Morton Gould* (Albany 1988)★★★.

GOULET, ROBERT

b. Stanley Applebaum, 26 November 1933, Lawrence, Massachusetts, USA. An actor and singer, Goulet made his first professional engagement in 1951 with the Edmonton Summer Pops in 1951. He also played in *Thunder Rock* and *Visit To A Small Planet*. After appearing in Canadian productions of *South Pacific*, *Finian's Rainbow*, and *Gentlemen Prefer Blondes*, he moved to the US, and made his Broadway debut in 1960, when he played Sir Lancelot in the musical *Camelot*, introducing the poignant 'If Ever I Would Leave You'. He also began launching his singing career during this time, and appeared on the Ed Sullivan television variety programme as well as others of that kind. Goulet signed with Columbia Records in 1962 and had his first chart entry with 'What Kind Of Fool Am I?' from the musical *Stop The World - I Want To Get Off*. He won the Grammy Award for Best New Artist in 1962, and his greatest singles success came in 1965 with the operatic 'My Love Forgive Me (Amore, Scusami)'. By then he had already proven that his strength was in album sales, as was often the case with middle of the road performers at that time. His 1962 Columbia debut, *Always You*, had charted, but it was the following year's *Sincerely Yours...* and 1964's *My Love Forgive Me* that became Goulet's top-performing albums. In 1968 he returned to the Broadway musical theatre in *The Happy Time*, and won a Tony Award for his portrayal of the French-Canadian man-about-the-world Uncle Jacques. In the 70s and 80s he toured in several musical revivals and appeared extensively in concerts, cabaret (with his wife Carol Lawrence), and on his own television series. In 1993, after taking a new production of *Camelot* around the US (in which, more than 30 years on, he played King Arthur instead of Lancelot), Goulet brought the show to New York where it was greeted with enthusiasm.

● ALBUMS: *Always You* (Columbia 1962)★★★, *Two Of Us* (Columbia 1962)★★★, *Sincerely Yours ...* (Columbia 1963)★★★★, *The Wonderful World Of Love* (Columbia 1963)★★★, *Robert Goulet In Person* (Columbia 1963)★★★, *Manhattan Tower/The Man Who Loves Manhattan* (Columbia 1964)★★★, *Without You* (Columbia 1964)★★★, *My Love Forgive Me* (Columbia 1964)★★★★, *Begin To Love* (Columbia 1965)★★★, *Summer Sounds* (Columbia 1965)★★★, *Robert Goulet On Broadway* (Columbia 1965)★★★, *Traveling On* (Columbia 1966)★★★, *I Remember You* (Columbia 1966)★★★, *Robert Goulet On Broadway, Volume 2* (Columbia 1967)★★★, *Woman, Woman* (Columbia 1968)★★★, *Hollywood Mon Amour - Great Love Songs From The Movies* (Columbia 1968)★★★, *Both Sides Now* (Columbia 1969)★★, *Souvenir D'Italie* (Columbia 1969)★★★, *Greatest Hits* (Columbia 1969)★★★★, *I Wish You Love* (Columbia 1970)★★, *Close To You* (Columbia 1992)★★.

GRAB ME A GONDOLA

In the 50s, many years before film actresses such as Barbra Streisand and Bette Midler had their own production companies, the major studios called their young ladies 'starlets', and required them to flaunt their assets at annual film festivals around the world. One of Britain's leading glamour girls was Diana Dors, and she and her mink bikini were a common sight at the cinematic celebrations which took place at various venues such as the Venice Film Festival. The lady, and the location, provided the inspiration for this highly successful musical which was written by Julian More, and opened at the Lyric theatre in London on 26 December 1956. Tom Wilson (Denis Quilley) is a showbiz reporter, and has gone to Venice to interview Virginia Jones (Joan Heal), who is a very 'hot property'. Tom's girlfriend, Margaret Kyle (Jane Wenham), finds it difficult to believe that his interest in Virginia is exclusively professional, and is flattered when the unctuous Prince Luigi Bourbon Corielli (Guido Lorraine) suggests that they sip champagne together. However, Tom is just not the cheating kind, and anyway, Virginia needs the Prince to finance her Shakespearean ambitions ('Cravin' for Avon'), so everyone else is paired-off accordingly. Julian More, together with the composer, James Gilbert, contributed a delightful score, which included Heal's amusing introductory number, 'That's My Biography', and then she, and the rest of the cast, had a ball with numbers such as 'Plain In Love', 'The Motor Car Is Treacherous', 'Bid Him A Fond Goodbye', 'Star Quality', 'Man, Not A Mouse', 'Lonely In A Crowd', 'Jimmy's Bar', 'Chianti', 'What Are The Facts?', 'Rig 'O The Day', 'When I Find That Girl', and 'Rockin' At The Cannon Ball'. Heal, a veteran of the London revue scene, was outstanding, and, generally, the show had a first-rate cast. *Grab Me A Gondola* was light, bright, bubbly stuff - a perfect antidote to the current American musical invasion - a huge hit which eventually ran for 673 performances, and provided Julian More with his first West End success - *Expresso Bongo*, *Irma La Douce*, and *Songbook*, were all still a few years away.

GRABLE, BETTY

b. Ruth Elizabeth Grable, 18 December 1916, St. Louis Missouri, USA, d. 2 July 1973, Santa Monica, California, USA. An actress, singer and dancer in movie musicals of the 30s, 40s and early 50s. A beautiful blonde with a peaches-and-cream complexion, during World War II the famous picture of her wearing a white bathing suit displaying her shapely legs (which were reportedly insured for a million dollars) and looking over her right shoulder, was pinned up on servicemen's lockers the world over. Encouraged by her mother, Grable began to take singing and dancing lessons while she was still very young, and she was part of the chorus in musical films such as *Let's Go Places*, *New Movietone Follies Of 1930*, and *Whoopee!* while still in her early teens. During the 30s, sometimes under the name of Frances Dean, she played roles of varying importance (but never starring ones) in a several comedies such as *Hold 'Em Jail* and *The Nitwits*, and musicals which included *Palmy Days*, *The Kid From Spain*, *Student Tour*, *The Gay Divorcee*, *Old Man Rhythm*, *Collegiate*, *Follow The Fleet*, *Pigskin Parade*, *This Way Please*, *College Swing*, *Give Me A Sailor*, and *Million Dollar Legs* (1939). Also in 1939 she had a good role in the Broadway musical *DuBarry Was A Lady* in which she introduced Cole Porter's famous song of 'social scandal', 'Well, Did You Evah!' with Charles Walters. In 1937 Grable had married former child star Jackie Coogan, and their divorce in 1940 coincided with her elevation to star status when she signed for 20th-Century Fox. After co-starring

with Don Ameche in *Down Argentine Way*, she worked with several other handsome leading men of the day, such as John Payne, Victor Mature, Dan Dailey, George Montgomery, Cesar Romero, Robert Cummings, and Dick Haymes in a string of mostly entertaining and tuneful musicals such as *Tin Pan Alley*, *Moon Over Miami*, *Footlight Serenade*, *Song Of The Islands*, *Springtime In The Rockies*, *Coney Island*, *Sweet Rosie O'Grady*, *Four Jills In A Jeep*, *Pin-Up Girl*, *Billy Rose's Diamond Horseshoe*, *The Dolly Sisters*, *The Shocking Miss Pilgrim*, *Mother Wore Tights*, *That Lady In Ermine*, When *My Baby Smiles At Me*, *The Beautiful Blonde From Bashful Bend*, *Wabash Avenue*, *My Blue Heaven*, *Call Me Mister*, *Meet Me After The Show*, *The Farmer Takes A Wife*, and *Three For The Show* (1955). Several of those were set at the turn of the century, and, by the late 50s, Grable's kind of movie musical was itself a period piece. She played nightclubs, appeared on television, and also worked with her husband, bandleader Harry James, before they divorced in 1964. In 1967 she took over the leading role from Carol Channing in the Broadway production of *Hello, Dolly!*, and subsequently headed a road tour of the show. In 1969 she travelled to London and appeared briefly in the spectacular flop American musical, *Belle Starr*, at the Palace Theatre. On her return to the US, she continued to work on television and in provincial theatre until her death from cancer at the age of only 56. In 1997 came the treat that fans had been waiting for - a collection of 48 original Grable songs from soundtracks dating back to 1930.

● ALBUMS: *The Pin-Up Girl* 2-CD set (Jasmine 1997)★★★.
● FURTHER READING: *Betty Grable: The Reluctant Movie Queen*, D. Warren. *Betty Grable: A Bio-Bibliography*, Larry Billman. *Pin-Up: The Tragedy Of Betty Grable*, Spero Pastos.
● FILMS: *Whoopee* (1930), *New Movietone Follies Of 1930* (1930), *Let's Go Places* (1930), *Palmy Days* (1931), *Kiki* (1931), *Hold 'Em Jail* (1932), *Probation* (1932), *Child Of Manhattan* (1932), *The Kid From Spain* (1932), *The Greeks Had A Word For Them* (1932), *What Price Innocence* (1933), *Cavalcade* (1933), *The Gay Divorcee* (1934), *Student Tour* (1934), *Collegiate* (1935), *Old Man Rhythm* (1935), *The Nitwits* (1935), *Don't Turn 'Em Loose* (1936), *Pigskin Parade* (1936), *Follow The Fleet* (1936), *Thrill Of A Lifetime* (1937), *This Way Please* (1937), *Campus Confessions* (1938), *Give Me A Sailor* (1938), *College Swing* (1938), *The Day The Bookies Wept* (1939), *Million Dollar Legs* (1939), *Man About Town* (1939), *Tin Pan Alley* (1940), *Down Argentine Way* (1940), *I Wake Up Screaming* (1941), *A Yank In The RAF* (1941), *Moon Over Miami* (1941), *Springtime In The Rockies* (1942), *Song Of The Islands* (1942), *Footlight Serenade* (1942), *Sweet Rosie O'Grady* (1943), *Coney Island* (1943), *Pin Up Girl* (1944), *Four Jills In A Jeep* (1944), *The Dolly Sisters* (1945), *Billy Rose's Diamond Horseshoe* (1945), *Mother Wore Tights* (1947), *The Shocking Miss Pilgrim* (1947), *When My Baby Smiles At Me* (1948), *That Lady In Ermine* (1948), *The Beautiful Blonde From Bashful Bend* (1949), *My Blue Heaven* (1950), *Wabash Avenue* (1950), *Meet Me After The Show* (1951), *Call Me Mister* (1951), *How To Marry A Millionaire* (1953), *The Farmer Takes A Wife* (1953), *Three For The Show* (1954), *How To Be Very Very Popular* (1955).

GRACE OF MY HEART

A tribute to the female songwriters of the 60s, particularly the early life of Carole King, who with husband Gerry Goffin turned out classic hits such as 'Will You Love Me

Tomorrow', 'The Loco-Motion', and 'Take Good Care Of My Baby'. In this film, Illeana Douglas plays the King character, Philadelphia-born steel heiress Edna Buxton, who changes her name to Denise Waverly when she starts work in New York's legendary Brill Building. She and husband Howard Caszatt (Eric Stolz) write a string of hits for girl groups, before he cheats on her. From then on, Denise has a torrid time, involved with radio DJ John Murray (Bruce Davison), the Brian Wilson-like destructive genius of a record producer Jay Phillips (Matt Dillon), teen idol and closet lesbian Kelly Porter (Bridget Fonda), and publisher-manager Joel Millner (John Turturro), her mentor. Like Carole King with her *Tapestry*, in the early 70s Denise finally gets to record her own multi-million-selling album, *Grace Of My Heart*. Allison Anders (*Gas, Food Lodging, Mi Vida Loca*) wrote and directed this picture, and apparently it was her idea to ask writers from then and from now to come up with songs that evoked those fabulous 60s sounds. It resulted in a fascinating mix - Burt Bacharach, Elvis Costello, Los Lobos, Carol Bayer Sager, Larry Klein, Dave Stewart, and even Gerry Goffin himself. Stand-out tracks included 'God Give Me Strength' (Bacharach-Costello), 'My Secret Love' (Klein-David Baerwald-Leslie Gore), 'Born To Love That Boy' (Klein-Geffen), and 'Turn Around' (Mike Johnson). Illeana Douglas's singing voice was dubbed by Kristen Vigard. Keith Young was the choreographer, executive producer Martin Scorsese, and *Grace Of My Heart* was a 1996 release produced by Universal Records.

GRADUATE, THE

One of the biggest grossing films of 1968 - and one which has proved enduringly popular - *The Graduate* launched Dustin Hoffman's acting career. He plays the part of the graduate, Benjamin Braddock, unsure about his future. He is seduced by his father's business partner's wife, Mrs. Robinson, played by Anne Bancroft, before falling in love, and eloping with Bancroft's screen daughter (Katherine Ross). A mild comment on US middle-class values, *The Graduate*'s strengths are derived from Hoffman's portrayal of Braddock, suitably lost and decisive when the need arose. The film's charm was enhanced by a soundtrack featuring Simon And Garfunkel. Although the duo had enjoyed chart success with 'Homeward Bound' and 'Sound Of Silence', they were not a household name prior to this film. The latter song enhanced one of the film's most poignant scenes, a feature shared with 'Scarborough Fair' and 'April Come She Will'. The album reached number 3 in the UK charts, while the duo's recording of 'Mrs. Robinson' broached the UK Top 5. Indeed, such was the attendant popularity, an EP comprising the aforementioned four songs peaked at number 9 in the singles chart early the following year. Simon And Garfunkel were no longer viewed as an alternative, if coy, act; their next album *Bridge Over Troubled Waters* effortlessly topped the UK chart and remained on the list for 303 weeks.

GRAINER, RON

b. 11 August 1922, Queensland, Australia, d. 22 February 1981, Sussex, England. A highly successful musical director, and composer for television, films and theatre,

Grainer trained as a musician in Australia before moving to England in 1952 with the intention of working as a pianist and writing classical music. Instead, at first he became part of a knockabout variety act, the Allen Brothers And June, touring the UK music halls, and staying in touch with music by being hit on the head every night by the lid of a grand piano! Later in the 50s, he served as musical director for London's West End musical comedy, *Zuleika*, and spent some time as a rehearsal pianist for television, which led to his contributing music for a few plays. His big break came when he wrote the theme music for the highly popular BBC detective series, *Maigret*. This won him an Ivor Novello Award in 1961, and he also received 'Ivors' for his themes for *Steptoe And Son* (1962); and the satirical *Not So Much A Programme, More A Way Of Life*, in collaboration with writer-director Ned Sherrin and his oft-time partner Caryl Brahms. Grainer's other television music included, *Comedy Playhouse, Dr Who* (on which he pioneered the use of electronic music in the medium as Ray Cathode), *Panorama, Five O'Clock Club, That Was The Week That Was, Oliver Twist, Boy Meets Girl, The Flying Swan, Man In A Suitcase, The Prisoner, Thief, For The Love Of Ada, Paul Temple, South Riding, Kim The Detective, Edward And Mrs Simpson, Malice Aforethought, Rebecca* and *Tales Of The Unexpected*. Grainer's enormous success in television led to continuous film work during the 60s and 70s. His film scores included, *A Kind Of Loving* (1962), *The Moonspinners* (1964), *Night Must Fall* (1964), *The Caretaker* (1964), *Nothing But The Best* (1964), *Station Six-Sahara* (1964), *To Sir With Love* (1967), *Only When I Larf* (1968), *The Assassination Bureau* (1969), *Before Winter Comes* (1969), *Hoffman* (1970), *In Search Of Gregory* (1970), *The Omega Man* (1971), *Cat And Mouse* (1974), *I Don't Want To Be Born* (1975) and *The Bawdy Adventures Of Tom Jones* (1976). For the stage, Grainer contributed some songs for the pasticcio, *Cindy-Ella* in 1962, a Sherrin/Brahms all-black production of the traditional English pantomime, *Cinderella*. Two years later, he wrote the music, with Ronald Millar's lyrics, for *Robert And Elizabeth*, a musical adaptation of *The Barretts Of Wimpole Street*, by Rudolph Besier. It was a great success, running for over 900 performances in the West End, and winning another Ivor Novello Award in 1964, for 'The Year's Outstanding Score Of A Stage Musical'. Grainer's other music for the London theatre included *On The Level*, also with Millar, a tale of contemporary education, which featured an amusing number entitled, 'Thermodynamically Yours'; *Sing A Rude Song*, a musical biography of legendary British Music Hall star, Marie Lloyd; and *Nickleby And Me*, a musical play-within-a-play about the famous Dickens character. Grainer's orchestral albums, mainly of film and television music, included *Tales Of The Unexpected*, which contained the insinuating, 'I've Danced With The Man', sung by Jenny Wren over the titles of *Edward And Mrs. Simpson*; and 'A Touch Of Velvet, A Sting Of Brass', which was a minor chart hit in 1978 for Ron Grainer and his Orchestra.
● ALBUMS: *'Maigret Theme' And Other Themes From BBC Television Series* (early 60s)★★★★, *Edward And Mrs. Simpson* television soundtrack (1978)★★★, *Tales Of The Unexpected And*

Other Themes (1980)★★★★, *Dr. Who And Other Classic Ron Grainer Themes* (Play It Again 1994)★★★★.
● COMPILATIONS: *The A-Z Of British TV Themes - The Ron Grainer Years* (Play It Again 1997)★★★★.

GRAND HOTEL

An impressive stage production, with music and lyrics by Robert Wright and George Forrest (additional numbers by Maury Yeston), and a book by Luther Davis based on the novel by Vicki Baum and the classic 1932 film which starred Greta Garbo, John Barrymore, Joan Crawford and several other well-known Hollywood names. *Grand Hotel* opened at the Martin Beck Theatre in New York on 12 October 1989. The show had begun its life under the title of *At The Grand* in 1958, but on that occasion it failed to reach Broadway. Now set in a ritzy Berlin hotel in 1928 when Germany was already on the brink of Nazism, the main characters in this heavily plotted story whirl through the revolving doors: there is Elizaveta Grushinskaya (Liliane Montevecchi) the ageing Russian ballerina, Felix von Gaigern (David Carroll) the impoverished romantic German nobleman, Otto Kringelein (Michael Jeter) a Jewish bookkeeper dying of cancer and blowing his life savings on a few days of high living, and Flaemmchen (Jane Krakowski) the pregnant typist who is desperate to make it in Hollywood. However, the real star of the piece was Tommy Tune, whose fluid direction and razzle dazzle choreography made this the most visually exciting musical that Broadway had seen for many a year. The songs came in for some severe criticism, although there were several appealing numbers among the score which included 'As It Should Be', 'Some Have, Some Have Not', 'At The Grand Hotel', 'And Life Goes On', 'Fire And Ice', 'I Want To Go To Hollywood', 'Everybody's Doing It', 'Who Couldn't Dance With You?', 'Love Can't Happen', 'I Waltz Alone', 'Roses At The Station', 'Bolero' (brilliantly danced adagio-style by Yvonne Marceau and Pierre Dulaine) and 'How Can I Tell Her?'. One of the highspots towards the end of the piece (there was no interval) came when the book-keeper Kringelein and the Baron Gaigern link arms and kick up their heels in the exuberant 'We'll Take A Glass Together'. After transferring to the Gershwin Theatre early in 1992 to make way for a revival of *Guys And Dolls*, *Grand Hotel* continued its run for 1,018 performances, before closing in May of that year. The show was showered with awards, including five Tonys, for costumes, lighting, and featured actor (Michael Jeter),. Most of the kudos went to Tommy Tune, who won two Tony Awards and several others honours, including a couple of Astaire awards for his brilliant direction and choreography. The London production of *Grand Hotel* opened at the refurbished 2,000-seater Dominion Theatre but, despite initially good reviews, never really took off and closed after three months with losses estimated at around £2 million. The original cast album was not issued until more than two and half years after the show opened. Most of the original principals recreated their roles but a notable exception was David Carroll who played the Baron. He died of AIDS in March 1992, and, as a tribute, the CD contains a live recording of his version of one of the show's most attractive ballads, 'Love Can't Happen'.

GRAY, DOLORES

b. 7 June 1924, Chicago, Illinois, USA. A dynamic, full-bloodied singer, early in her career Gray sang on radio with Milton Berle and Rudy Vallee. Making her Broadway debut in Cole Porter's *Seven Lively Arts* (1944), she went on to appear in *Are You With It* and *Sweet Bye And Bye* in 1946, and was then chosen by Richard Rodgers and Oscar Hammerstein II for the lead in their London production of *Annie Get Your Gun*. That historic opening night in 1947, on her 23rd birthday, she took London by storm with a performance that almost matched Ethel Merman's triumph in the role on Broadway. She was back there herself in 1951 with *Two On The Aisle*, and followed this two years later with *Carnival In Flanders*, for which she won a Tony Award as the oustanding actress in a musical. MGM signed her for *It's Always Fair Weather* (1955) in which she shared the spotlight with Gene Kelly, Dan Dailey Michael Kidd, and Cyd Charisse, and excelled with her vibrant versions of 'Music Is Better Than Words' and 'Thanks A Lot But No Thanks'. She was rewarded with a starring role in *Kismet*, followed by *The Opposite Sex* in 1956, but because film musicals were on the wane, MGM had only the comedy *Designing Woman* to offer, and she returned to Broadway in *Destry Rides Again*. Gray worked steadily in television and clubs and made singles for Capitol showing that she was no mere stage belter but a sensitive interpreter of standards. Apart from the splendid *Warm Brandy*, so far she has been heard only on soundtrack and Original Cast albums. After taking over from Angela Lansbury in the 1973 London production of *Gypsy*, in 1987 she returned to the West End in the role of Carlotta Campion, singing that memorable anthem, 'I'm Still Here', in Stephen Sondheim's *Follies*.
● ALBUMS: *Warm Brandy*. (Capitol 1957)★★★★.

GRAYSON, KATHRYN

b. Zelma Kathryn Hedrick, 9 February 1922, Winston-Salem, North Carolina, USA. An actress and singer with a spectacular soprano voice and a charming and ingenuous personality, who was popular in MGM musicals in the 40s and 50s. She is said to have been discovered while singing on Eddie Cantor's radio show in the late 30s, and made her film debut in 1941 with Mickey Rooney in *Andy Hardy's Private Secretary*. After being teamed with the comedy duo Bud Abbott and Lou Costello in *Rio Rita* (1942), during the rest of the 40s and in the 50s, she co-starred with major stars such as Frank Sinatra, Mario Lanza and Howard Keel in a string of musicals that included *Seven Sweethearts*, *Thousands Cheer*, *Two Sisters From Boston*, *Ziegfeld Follies*, *Till The Clouds Roll By*, *It Happened In Brooklyn*, *The Toast Of New Orleans*, *Show Boat*, *Lovely To Look At*, *The Desert Song*, *Kiss Me Kate* and *The Vagabond King* (1956). In *So This Is Love* (1953), she portrayed opera singer Grace Moore, and in some of her other films, she again played characters attempting to audition for maestros, such as José Iturbi, with the intention of making a career as a classical singer. As the golden age of movie musicals drew to a close in the late 50s, Grayson played concerts and clubs, and also toured in revivals of well-known stage musicals.
● ALBUMS: *Kathryn Grayson* 10-inch album (MGM 1952)★★★,

Kathryn Grayson Sings (MGM 1956)★★★, *Kathryn Grayson* (Lion 1959)★★★, and film soundtracks.
● COMPILATIONS: *20 Golden Favourites* (Bulldog 1984)★★★.

GREASE (FILM MUSICAL)

Released in 1978 and adapted from a stage play, this endearingly simple musical became one of the decade's most spectacular successes. Set in a high school during the early 60s, the plot recalled those of the Annette/Frankie Avalon 'beach' movies. Stars John Travolta and Olivia Newton-John meet during the summer break, but their affair seems doomed when the former plays up to his 'tough-guy' image, fearful of the admonishment of fellow gang members. Naturally, the pair are together at the end and only the occasional sexual innuendo - and co-star Stockard Channing's pregnancy - indicate the film is a product of a later decade. What elevated *Grease* from mere formula was Travolta, then riding on the crest of success from *Saturday Night Fever*, and a succession of memorable songs. He paired with Newton-John on 'You're The One That I Want' and 'Summer Nights', which together topped the UK singles chart in 1978 for a total of 16 weeks. Travolta's solo release, 'Sandy', reached number 2, a position equalled by Newton-John with 'Hopelessly Devoted To You'. Meanwhile, the soundtrack album spent 13 consecutive weeks at the top of the album charts, and climbed high again in 1998 when *Grease* was re-released worldwide. A reminder of its phenomenal success 20 years previously.

GREASE (STAGE MUSICAL)

After starting its life as a five hour amateur production in Chicago in 1971, *Grease* opened in New York, Off Broadway, at the Eden Theatre in February 1972. Following a surprisingly enthusiastic reaction there, it moved to the Broadhurst Theatre on Broadway on 7 June. The book, music and lyrics, by Jim Jacobs (b. 7 October 1942, Chicago, Illinois, USA) and Warren Casey (b. 2 April 1935, Yonkers, New York, USA, d. 8 November 1988), transported excited audiences (but not unimpressed theatre critics) back to the rock 'n' roll days of the 50s, when bored, sexually frustrated teenagers went around in gangs with names like 'Pink Ladies' and 'Burger Palace Boys'. At a reunion of the class of 1959, the assembled group relive the time when Danny Zuko (Barry Bostwick) and Sandy Dumbrowski (Carol Demas) met up again at Rydell High School after an innocent summer romance. At first they seemed to be incompatible - him with his tough, macho image - and her so prim and proper and virginal - quite unlike the seemingly hard-bitten Betty Rizzo (Adrienne Barbeau). However, by the end of the piece, it was Sandy (some years before the advent of women's lib) who changed her attitude and donned the leather jacket and tight pants - along with the rest of the uniform of a 'greaser''s steady girl friend. The satirical and highly entertaining score contained plenty of affectionate digs at the period ('Look at me, I'm Sandra Dee/Lousy with virginity'), and other numbers such as 'Summer Nights', 'Freddie, My Love', 'Beauty School Dropout', 'We Go Together', 'Greased Lightnin'', 'There Are Worse Things That I Could Do', 'Mooning', and 'It's Raining On Prom Night'. *Grease* stayed

on Broadway for 3,388 performances, closing in February 1980. The first London production, in 1973, ran for 236 performances, and starred the then unknown Richard Gere as Danny. Elaine Paige was also in the company as an understudy, and eventually took over the role of Sandy. The show was revived in the West End in 1979, and again, in 1993, when Paul Nicholas, who had succeeded Richard Gere in the original 1973 London production, collaborated with the impresario Robert Stigwood, to present a radically revised version. It starred the Australian soap actor, Craig McLachlan and the popular US singer Debbie Gibson, and incorporated several songs that were written by Barry Gibb, John Farrar, Louis St. Louis, and Scott Simon for the 1978 smash-hit *Grease* movie, such as 'Hopelessly Devoted To You', 'You're The One That I Want', 'Grease', and 'Sandy'. On-screen, Danny and Sandy were played by John Travolta and Olivia Newton-John. The 1994 Broadway revival, directed and choreographed by Jeff Calhoun, and starring Rosie O'Donnell (Rizzo), Susan Wood (Sandy), Ricky Paull Goldin (Danny) and Marcia Lewis (Miss Lynch), did not use the film songs, but interpolated the old Skyliners' hit, 'Since I Don't Have You'. During its 1,501-performance run, which ended in January 1998, producers Fran and Barry Weissler made a practice of introducing stars from various areas of show business into the leading roles. Brooke Shields, Sheena Easton and Debby Boone all took turns as Sandy, Jon Secada served as Danny, and ex-Monkees Davy Jones and Mickey Dolenz played Vince Fontaine, while JoAnn Worley and Sally Struthers were amongst those to lecture as Miss Lynch. Teen Angel, the cameo character who, along with Frenchy and the rest of the company gives out with 'Beauty School Dropout', tempted Chubby Checker and Darlene Love onto the brightly coloured Grease sets. Some of those involved in the David Gilmore-directed long-running West End show included Shane Richie, Ian Kelsey, Luke Goss (ex-Bros), Sonia, Samantha Janus, Marissa Dunlop (Sandy), Sally Ann Triplett and Linzi Hately (Rizzo). In the spring of 1998, an Italian production opened in Rome, and an 'arena spectacular' Grease tour of Australia starred Craig McLachlan (Danny), Danni Minogue (Rizzo), Jane Scali (Sandy) and Australia's original 'Phantom', Anthony Warlow, as Teen Angel.

GREAT AMERICAN BROADCAST, THE

Even before this film was released by 20th Century-Fox in 1941, the American public's fascination with radio had already spawned several entertaining musicals - and Alice Faye had favoured more than one of them with her presence. Here she is again - this time playing a singer whose involvement with radio pioneers Jack Oakie and John Payne, along with businessman Cesar Romero, eventually leads her to stardom. Also cast were Mary Beth Hughes, William Pawley, Lucien Littlefield, Eula Morgan, and guest artists, the Ink Spots, the Nicholas Brothers, and the Wiere Brothers. Mack Gordon and Harry Warren wrote most of the songs which included 'Where You Are', 'I Take To You', 'The Great American Broadcast', 'Long Ago Last Night', 'It's All In A Lifetime', and 'I've Got A Bone To Pick With You'. They were joined by the Ink Spots' theme song 'If I Didn't Care' (Jack Lawrence), 'Give My Regards To

Broadway' (George M. Cohan), and 'Alabamy Bound' (Buddy De Sylva-Bud Green-Ray Henderson). Don Ettlinger, Edwin Blum, Robert Ellis, and Helen Logan provided an entertaining and sometimes witty screenplay, and the director was Archie Mayo.

GREAT BIG RADIO SHOW, THE

One of the most entertaining musical comedies to emerge in the UK during the 90s, this show won a special prize at the Vivian Ellis Awards in 1989. It was subsequently workshopped at the Festival of New Musicals at Buxton Opera House three years later, before having its premiere in 1993 at the Watermill Theatre, Newbury, in England. It was optioned for the West End by one of Britain's leading producers, Harold Fielding, but ill health prevented him from moving forward. The project lost momentum until it resurfaced at London's Bridewell Theatre in May 1997. Philip Glassborow and Nick McIvor's book is set in 1933, on a Saturday night when America's favourite radio variety show is about to go on the air coast to coast. However, producer Bernie Bernstein (Peter Goodwright) has a problem. Only seven minutes to the red light, and Gloria Pilbeam, the golden-voiced 'Songstress of the Airwaves' ('a top recording star who enjoys all kind of sports') has not arrived at the NBS (National Broadcasting System) 'Studio of the Stars'. What is more, Alfred H. Zannenberg (Brian Greene), the show's sponsor, and inventor/proprietor of Nourishvite, the famous nerve tonic and all-round pick-me-up, is due any moment. Orchestra leader Blue Woodword (David Staller) retires to the cafeteria for a shot of caffeine, and hears waitress Freckles Murray (Danielle Carson) singing happily as she works. Great voice, but surely she cannot save the show? Oh yes she can, even though she has picked up the wrong 'violin' case at her previous nightclub job, and is therefore being pursued by two gangsters, Big Louie Rosenbaum (Howard Attfield) and Two-Gun Shapiro (Nick Burnell), who want their machine gun back. They turn out to be a couple of vaudeville hoofers anyway. By curtain time everything is sorted out. Blue and Freckles are harmonising happily, while Alfred H. ('the meal in a spoon') Zannenberg has discovered that the slinky Olga (Elizabeth Counsell) is his long lost childhood sweetheart. Counsell had one of the best songs in the show, 'I Felt Myself Falling', but there was much else to enjoy in Glassborow's score which affectionately recalled a much loved era, and included 'Unmistakably', 'She Ain't Here Yet!', 'Surprises', 'What Can I Do For You?', 'Radio In My Mind', 'No Matter What', 'Where Have I Seen You Before?', 'Pretty As A Picture', 'Suddenly I'm Singing', 'You Came By', 'Nourishvite', 'You Take My Breath Away', 'Then I Bumped Into You', 'The Balalaika', 'Tomorrow Is Another Day', and 'Me And My Stradivarius'. Also joining in the ('Radio') fun were Jerry Palmer (Richard Brightiff), Polly March (Myrtle Gray), Gavin Faulkner-Hackett (Flash Harry), and Carl Patrick (Stanley Wintergreen). The arrangements and dance music were by David Rhind-Tutt, and this 'fast-moving and delightful pastiche, with its agonising puns, hilarious commercials, and fine performances', was directed and choreographed by Angela Hardcastle.

GREAT CARUSO, THE

This lavishly produced biopic of the celebrated Italian opera singer was released by MGM in 1951. Mario Lanza, making his third screen appearance, was the perfect choice to play the lead in a screenplay by Sonia Levian and William Ludwig that, in certain areas of Caruso's life, was somewhat economical with the truth. For instance, the existence of one of his wives was totally ignored in the haste to condense drastically his rise to fame, and to feature as much music on the screen as possible. It was all rather false, and even the hit song that emerged from the film, 'The Loveliest Night Of The Year', was not actually associated with Caruso, being a Mexican instrumental piece, 'Over The Waves' (Juventino Rosas), adapted by Irving Aaronson and lyricist Paul Francis Webster. As for the remainder of the musical fare, it was a collection of songs and operatic excerpts that included 'Last Rose Of Summer' (Thomas Moore-Richard Alfred Milliken), 'Sextet' (Donizetti), 'La Donna E Mobile' (Verdi), 'Celeste Aida' (Verdi), 'Ave Maria' (Bach-Charles Gounod), 'Sweethearts' (Victor Herbert-Robert B. Smith), 'Vesti La Guibba' (Leoncavallo) and 'M'Appari' (Flotow). Anne Blyth played Dorothy Benjamin, Caruso's wife, and among the rest of the cast were Dorothy Kirsten, Jarmila Novotna, Richard Hageman, Eduard Franz, Carl Benton, Ludwig Donath, Ian Wolfe and Mae Clarke.

Joseph Ruttenbergs' Technicolor photography enhanced the whole spectacular affair, which was produced by Joe Pasternak and directed by Richard Thorpe. Musical directors Johnny Green and Peter Herman Adler were nominated for Oscars, and Douglas Shearer won one for sound recording. *The Great Caruso* grossed over $4.5 million in North America (a great deal of money in those days), and proved to be the most popular of Mario Lanza's brief film career (he made only seven films).

GREAT HUSSAR, THE

(see *Balalaika*)

GREAT ROCK'N'ROLL SWINDLE, THE

By the time this film was released in 1979, its progenitors the Sex Pistols had disintegrated owing chiefly to disagreements between group vocalist John Lydon (aka Johnny Rotten) and manager Malcolm McLaren. *The Great Rock'n'Roll Swindle* took the latter's philosophical line, offering his blueprint on methods of how to manipulate the music industry, based on Situationist rhetoric. Different scenes reflect McLaren's pointers for success, drawn on notorious vistas during the Sex Pistols' career. These include the group's appearance on Bill Grundy's show, the loss of contracts with EMI Records and A&M Records while retaining fiscal advances, and the anti-establishment attitude of punk. The film features footage of the Rotten line-up as well as several subsequent incarnations, notably the brief liaison with great train robber Ronnie Biggs. Staged sequences and animation are also included. Edward Tudor-Pole is the featured vocalist on 'Who Killed Bambi', a title briefly mooted for the film during the period McLaren declared it would be directed by controversial exploitation figure Russ Meyer. Long-time

McLaren associate Julien Temple subsequently took charge, but the presence of pornography star Mary Millington in the final print provided a lingering link to that early notion. The absence of Rotten allowed bassist Sid Vicious to assume centrestage. He sang two rock 'n' roll classics first recorded by Eddie Cochran, 'Somethin' Else' and 'C'mon Everybody', but his most memorable contribution was a rendition of 'My Way'. Having begun the song in balladeer fashion, Vicious deconstructs it into a punk-attitude *tour-de-force*. The accompanying visual images, filmed at the Paris Olympia, close with the singer shooting members of the audience before proffering a 'V' sign. Such recordings were at the core of a soundtrack album that reached number 7 in the UK chart. *The Great Rock'n'Roll Swindle* contained other hit singles, including 'Silly Thing', but chief interest in its content lies in archive recordings drawn from the group's early incarnation. Neither a documentary nor fiction, the film is a tribute to McLaren's manifesto. As such, it provides an entertaining insight into one of pop's most mercurial characters.

GREAT WALTZ, THE

In a Broadway season that was dominated by the all-American, smart and sophisticated *Anything Goes*, one of the most spectacular and elaborate stage productions of the 30s, *The Great Waltz*, opened at New York's huge Center Theatre in the Rockefeller Centre on 22 September 1934. A gigantic undertaking - almost 200 performers appeared onstage, including an orchestra of some 50 musicians - the show was based on a London production of the operetta, *Waltzes In Vienna*, and had music and lyrics by Johann Strauss Jnr. and Desmond Carter. The book, by Moss Hart, details the struggles between the younger Strauss (Guy Robertson), and his father, Johann Strauss Snr. (H. Reeves-Smith), which eventually results in the latter relinquishing his position - and his baton - to his son. The score contained several attractive numbers such as 'Like A Star In The Sky', 'Danube So Blue', 'Love Will Find You', and 'While You Love Me'. Audience and critical reactions were mixed, but the show ran for a creditable 298 performances and was revived briefly in 1935. A different version of the *The Great Waltz* opened at London's Drury Lane Theatre in 1970. It had music by both Strauss Snr. and Jnr, with Robert Wright and George Forrest's lyrics, and a book by Jerome Chodorov which was based on a story by Moss Hart and Milton Lazarus. This production ran for more than 600 performances.

GREAT ZIEGFELD, THE

This vastly overblown, but breathtakingly opulent biopic of America's master showman, Florenz Ziegfeld, was produced for MGM by Hunt Stromberg in 1936. William Powell played the leading role, and William Anthony Macguire's screenplay, conveniently omitting the subject's reported excesses and philandering, concentrated on his undoubted charm, and unrivalled fervour and skill in the art of discovering a host of talented artists, before presenting them in the most lavish of settings which displayed those talents to the full. The most impressive - and extravagant - scene involves an enormous fluted spiral structure which is surrounded by an imposing staircase.

Dennis Morgan (dubbed by Alan Jones) sings 'A Pretty Girl Is Like A Melody', which segues into various classical excerpts as dozens of singers, dancers, and 'musicians', dressed in a variety of costumes ranging from white tie and tails, to bewigged Regency-style, 'perform' musical excerpts from the classics. As the sequence draws to a close, Virginia Bruce, as the Spirit of the *Follies*, appears high up on top of the set. Morgan resumes his song, and a circular curtain descends, shrouding everything and everybody, and somehow forms itself precisely on to the spiral surface. An extraordinary experience, and something that has to be seen to be believed. In complete contrast, the other most remarked-on sequence in the film comes when Luise Rainer, as Ziegfeld's first wife, Anna Held, makes a frenzied telephone call to her husband after discovering that he has married Billy Burke (played here by Myrna Loy). However, the film was mostly a feast of lavish spectacle and music featuring some memorable songs, including 'It's Delightful To Be Married' (Vincent Sotto-Anna Held), 'A Circus Must Be Different In A Ziegfeld Show' (Con Conrad-Herb Magidson), 'Shine On Harvest Moon' (Jack Norworth-Nora Bayes), 'Won't You Come And Play With Me' (Held), 'If You Knew Susie' (Buddy De Sylva-Joseph Meyer); and 'She's A Follies Girl', 'You Gotta Pull The Strings', 'Queen Of The Jungle', and 'You Never Looked So Beautiful' (all Walter Donaldson-Harold Adamson). Fanny Brice, the biggest star to emerge from the real-life *Ziegfeld Follies*, sang 'Yiddle On Your Fiddle' (Irving Berlin) and part of another of her all-time favourites, 'My Man' (Maurice Yvain-Channing Pollack) Also among the starry cast were Ray Bolger, Frank Morgan, Reginald Owen, Nat Pendleton, Herman Bing, Raymond Walburn, Ernest Cossart, Joseph Cawthorn, Virginia Grey, Buddy Doyle, Jean Chatburn, and Robert Greig. The credit for the film's splendid photography went to Oliver T. Marsh, Ray June, and George Folsey, and the dance sequences were staged by Seymour Felix. The director was Robert Z. Leonard. *The Great Ziegfeld* won Academy Awards for best picture and actress (Luise Rainer). William Powell played Florenz Ziegfeld again in the 1946 film *Ziegfeld Follies*.

GREEN, ADOLPH

(see Comden, Betty)

GREEN, JOHNNY

b. 10 October 1908, New York City, New York, USA, d. 15 May 1989, Beverly Hills, California, USA. Fascinated by music from childhood, Green studied piano from the age of five. By the time he entered his teens he had mastered orchestration, and throughout his years at Harvard University he greatly advanced his knowledge and understanding of all aspects of musical theory. While at Harvard he led a band which made records. During one vacation he was hired by Guy Lombardo as an arranger. Green's first song, 'Coquette', was written in collaboration with Lombardo's brother, Carmen, and Gus Kahn. After graduating from Harvard, Green worked on Wall Street but continued his musical studies, eventually making the decision in 1928 to concentrate on music for his livelihood. For the next few years he arranged music for films, working in the east coast studios of Paramount. With different lyricists he wrote several songs during the 30s, including 'I'm Yours' (lyrics by E.Y. 'Yip' Harburg), 'Hello, My Lover, Goodbye' (Edward Heyman), 'Out Of Nowhere' (Heyman), 'I Wanna Be Loved' (Heyman and Billy Rose), 'Rain, Rain, Go Away' (Heyman and Mack David), 'I Cover The Waterfront' (Heyman) and the massively successful 'Body And Soul' (Heyman, Frank Eyton and Robert Sour). 'Body And Soul' was introduced by Libby Holman in the 1930 revue *Three's A Crowd*. Also during the 30s, Green led a dance band, appearing regularly on radio and also worked on Broadway as musical director for shows. In 1942 he moved to Hollywood where he began writing scores for motion pictures. He was nominated for an Oscar for *Fiesta* (1947), his music including passages from Aaron Copland's 'El Salón México'. He won an Oscar the following year for his scoring of *Easter Parade*. During the 50s Green was General Music Director at MGM, working either directly or indirectly on many of the best musicals of the period. He won a second Oscar for his arrangements of *An American In Paris* (1951) and a third for his work on *The Merry Wives Of Windsor* (1953). He continued to write songs, including 'The Song Of Raintree County' (lyric by Paul Francis Webster). In the 60s he received two more Oscars for his work on *West Side Story* (1960) and *Oliver!* (1968). Green's musical range was such that he frequently appeared as guest conductor of symphony orchestras, notably the Los Angeles Philharmonic with which he worked regularly for many years. He was the recipient of many honours and awards, and in the late 70s was artist-in-residence at Harvard.

GREEN, PHILIP

b. 1911, England, d. 1983, Dublin, Eire. Although not a big 'name' as far as the public is concerned, Green was one of the most prolific 'backroom-boys' in the British music business. He is believed to have created more original compositions than any other writer, and he scored over 150 British films. His radio credits included the theme for BBC's *Meet The Huggets* ('Horse Feathers') and among the countless television shows which used his music were BBC's *Picture Page* ('Shopping Centre'), ITV's early filmed drama *Ghost Squad* and ATV's *The Golden Shot*. Green's first recording for EMI was in 1933, and from 1935-39 he was closely associated with commercial radio, at times up to 17 shows a week. During the war he was responsible for numerous successful BBC series such as *Salute To Rhythm*, *Band Call*, *Cuban Caballeros* and *Music Society Of Lower Basin Street*. He assisted Gracie Fields' revival after the war (her big hits 'Now Is The Hour' and 'Pedro The Fisherman' were recorded under his musical direction). Green also composed under the names Don Felipe, Louise Duke and Jose Belmonte. Some of his memorable works included his 'Cuban Suite', 'La Maja De Goya', 'Ecstasy - Tango', 'White Orchids', 'Follow Me Around', 'Romance' (from the film *The Magic Bow*), 'Two Mexican Pictures', 'Sensation For Strings', 'Mandolins In The Moonlight', 'Silhouette' and 'Pan American Panorama'. In the cinema his main scores included *Saints And Sinners* (1946), *Man On The Run* (1949), *Ha'penny Breeze* (1950), *Young Wives Tale* (1951), *Isn't Life Wonderful* (1952), *Park Plaza 605*

(1953), *Conflict Of Wings* - US title *Fuss Over Feathers* (1954), *One Good Turn* (1954), *John And Julie* (1955), *The March Hare* (1956), *Carry On Admiral* - US title *The Ship Was Loaded* (1957), *Sea Fury* (1958), *The Square Peg* (1958), *Violent Playground* (1958), *The Golden Disc* - US title *The In-Between Age* (1958), *Operation Amsterdam* (1959), *Sapphire* (1959), *Make Mine Mink* (1960), *The League Of Gentlemen* (1960), *The Singer Not The Song* (1961), *Victim* (1961), *Tiara Tahiti* (1962), *A Stitch In Time* (1963), *Masquerade* (1964), *The Intelligence Men* - US title *Spylarks* (1965), and *The Yellow Hat* (1967). His themes for *John And Julie* and *The March Hare* won Ivor Novello Awards, and he became resident musical director of the Rank Organisation. He also wrote many short pieces for publishers' libraries (Chappell, Francis Day & Hunter, Paxton, Photoplay etc.) especially for radio, film and television use. Green's hundreds of commercial recordings included hit selections, various novelty and jazz numbers, countless accompaniments for popular singers plus special recordings for Decca's wartime *Music While You Work* series and a series of MGM 78s for the American market.
● ALBUMS: *Rhythm On Reeds* (Decca)★★, *Moments In Mayfair* (EMI-Columbia)★★★, *Follow The Sun* (EMI-Columbia)★★★, *Pan-American Panorama* (EMI-Columbia)★★★, *Wings Of Song* (Top Rank)★★, *Music Of Rodgers And Hammerstein* (RCA)★★★, *Jerome Kern* (RCA)★★★, *Irving Berlin* (RCA)★★★★, *Rodgers & Hart* (RCA)★★★, *Great Opera And Ballet Themes* (RCA)★★★.

GREENWICH VILLAGE FOLLIES

The first of these revues, which were similar, but less lavish than the *Ziegfeld Follies*, opened at the Greenwich Village Theatre on 15 July 1919. All of the eight editions, through to 1928, played on Broadway, and were presented by the Bohemians Inc. (Al Jones and Morris Green). Most of them were directed by John Murray Anderson who also contributed sketches and lyrics. The show's satirical targets included most aspects of the Greenwich Village district and its uninhibited, arty inhabitants. The first edition, which ran for 232 performances - the most successful of all - was subtitled 'A Revusical Comedy Of New York's Latin Quarter', and had songs by A. Baldwin Sloane, Arthur Swanstrom and John Murray Anderson which included 'My Marionette', 'I'm Ashamed To Look The Moon In The Face,' 'My Little Javanese', and 'Message Of the Cameo'. An additional number was Irving Berlin's 'I'll See You In C-U-B-A'. Subsequent editions continued to arrive with the occasional appealing song such as Dorothy Terris and Julian Robeldo's 'Three O'Clock In The Morning' (1921), 'Georgette' (1922) by Lew Brown and Ray Henderson (of De Sylva, Brown And Henderson), and Cole Porter's gorgeous 'I'm In Love Again' (1924), but, generally speaking, the music department was not this particular *Follies'* strongest point. However, a great many talented entertainers graced its various productions, including Bobby Edwards, Bessie McCoy, Cecil Cunningham, Ted Lewis And His Orchestra, James Watts, Rex Story, Grace La Rue, Benny Fields, Bobby Watson, Frank Crumit, Howard Marsh, Joe E. Brown, Sammy White and Eva Puck, Vincent Lopez And His Orchestra, Savoy And Brennan, and Florence Moore.

GREENWILLOW

A whimsical, fantasy piece, with music and lyrics by Frank Loesser, and a book by Loesser and Lesser Samuels, *Greenwillow* opened on Broadway at the Alvin Theatre on 8 March 1960. Based on B.J. Chute's novel, it was set in a mythical American village, and told the story of Gideon Briggs (Anthony Perkins) and his reluctance to marry his sweetheart, Dorrie (Ellen McCown), because he is afraid that he may have inherited the family trait - wanderlust - and so may up and leave her. Loesser's songs were tender and charming, and have continued to be admired. They included 'The Music Of Home', 'Summertime Love', 'A Day Borrowed From Heaven', 'Gideon Briggs, I Love You', 'Walking Away Whistling', and 'Faraway Boy'. Anthony Perkins, making his Broadway musical debut, had the reflective 'Never Will I Marry', which attained some popularity. The whole affair was far removed from another of Perkin's projects in 1960, Alfred Hitchcock's terrifying film *Psycho*, in which he gave a performance that will always be remembered. The folksy, thoughtful *Greenwillow* just did not appeal to New York theatre audiences at a time when the entertainment world in general was on the brink of the brash, swinging 60s, and it closed after only 95 performances. By then, Loesser was in the throes of a far different proposition: his 1961 blockbuster, *How To Succeed In Business Without Really Trying*, lasted for 1,417 performances.

GREENWOOD, CHARLOTTE

b. 25 June 1890, Philadelphia, Pennsylvania, USA, d. 18 January 1978, Beverly Hills, California, USA. A tall, slender and immensely likeable musical comedy and film actress who graced several musical pictures in the 40s with her spunky and eccentric style and amazingly loose-jointed high-kick. Greenwood first came to notice on Broadway in *The Passing Show Of 1913*, and in the following year made such an impression with her 'flat-footed' kicks and 'splits' in *Pretty Miss Smith*, particularly in one number, 'Long, Lean, Lanky Letty', that producer Oliver Morosco re-titled the show *Long-Legged Letty*. The 'Letty' character kept Greenwood in occasional employment during the next few years via *So Long, Letty* (1916), *Linger Longer Letty* (1919), and *Letty Pepper* (1922), and there were subsequent film versions. Greenwood also appeared in several Broadway revues in the 20s, but by then she had also established herself in silent movies. In the 30s she easily made the transition into talkies, mostly with comedies, but also in occasional musicals such as *Flying High* (1931) and the Eddie Cantor vehicle *Palmy Days* (1932). In 1940 she co-starred with Shirley Temple and Jack Oakie in *Young People*, and during the rest of the decade made effective and highly entertaining contributions to a number of 20th Century-Fox musicals including *Down Argentine Way*, *Tall, Dark And Handsome*, *Moon Over Miami*, *Springtime In The Rockies*, *The Gang's All Here*, *Wake Up And Dream*, and *Oh, You Beautiful Doll* (1949). She also had her own US networked radio show in the 40s. In 1950 Greenwood returned to Broadway (high-kicks and all) in Cole Porter's musical *Out Of This World*, and stopped the show every night with the plaintive (but hilar-

ious) 'Nobody's Chasing Me' ('Nobody wants to own me/And I object/Nobody wants to 'phone me/Even collect'). Three years later she showed Esther Williams a few aquatic tricks in *Dangerous When Wet*, and in 1957 made her last screen appearance as Aunt Eller in *Oklahoma!*. According to the obituary in *Variety* following her sudden death at the age of 87, the part had originally been written for her by Oscar Hammerstein II, in the historic 1943 Broadway production. For some reason she had been unable to accept it then.

● FURTHER READING: *Never Too Tall* (her autobiography).

GRENFELL, JOYCE

b. Joyce Irene Phipps, 10 February 1910, London, England, d. 30 November 1979, London, England. An actress, singer and author, and a brilliant exponent of the monologue and witty song. The daughter of American parents - her mother's sister was Nancy Astor - Joyce Phipps used to describe herself as 'three fourths American'. She became interested in the theatre at an early age, and spent a term at RADA before marrying Reginald Grenfell in 1929. Subsequently, she worked for a time in commercial art, contributed to *Punch* and *Country Life*, and spent over three years as radio critic for the *Observer*. After impressing the humorist Steven Potter with her own charming recollection of a lecture that she had recently attended at a Women's Institute, she was engaged by the theatrical producer Herbert Farjeon for *The Little Revue* (1939). In the early 40s she appeared in other Farjeon revues, *Diversion*, *Diversion No. 2* and *Light And Shade*, and then, in 1944, toured extensively with ENSA, in the Near and Far East, and in India, entertaining the troops in British forces' hospitals, with comic monologues and songs. Two years later she was awarded the OBE. In *Sigh No More* (1945), at London's Piccadilly Theatre, Grenfell dressed as a schoolgirl for Noël Coward's witty 'That Is The End Of The News', and, in the same show, introduced 'Du Maurier', a song she had written with composer Richard Addinsell. They collaborated again on material for the revues, *Tuppence Coloured* (1947) and *Penny Plain* (1951), in which Grenfell also appeared. It was the beginning of a significant and enduring professional relationship. By the late 40s and early 50s, Grenfell was working more and more in radio - as a panellist on *We Beg To Differ*, and as the British host of *Transatlantic Quiz*. She made a couple of propaganda films during the war, but her movie career proper began in 1943 with a comedy, *The Demi-Paradise*, which starred Laurence Olivier and Margaret Rutherford. Grenfell appeared with Rutherford again, in *The Happiest Days Of Your Life* (1949), which also starred the lugubrious Alastair Sim. He and Grenfell managed to emerge unscathed from the *St. Trinians* film series. during the late 50s. Grenfell's other film roles, some of them highly telling cameos, included appearances in *Here Comes The Bride*, *The Galloping Major*, *Pickwick Papers*, *The Million Pound Note* and *The Americanization Of Emily*. It was on stage, however, that she really came into her own. In 1954 she wrote the book and lyrics, with Addinsell's music, for *Joyce Grenfell Requests The Pleasure*, which ran for nearly a year in London before transferring to Broadway in the following year. In America, Grenfell developed her one-woman show, toured US cities, and appeared on the *Ed Sullivan Show* several times in the late 50s. One Sullivan date saw her on the same bill with Elvis Presley ('a pasty-faced plump boy', as she recalled). She presented her solo effort in London for the first time in 1957, at the Lyric theatre, under the title of *Joyce Grenfell - A Miscellany*, and later took the show to Australia where it was called *Meet Joyce Grenfell*. Throughout the 60s she continued to tour extensively at home and abroad, and went back to Australia three times. In the early 70s she lost the sight in one eye and retired from the stage. During the next six years she published two volumes of autobiography, *Joyce Grenfell Requests The Pleasure* and *In Pleasant Places*, before cancer affected her other eye, and she died in 1979. Always an effective broadcaster, from 1966 she was an essential panel-member on television's *Face The Music*, a general knowledge quiz about music, and had her own television series on UK's BBC2 for a time. As a performer she was unique, and impossible to pigeonhole. Despite her 'terribly English' image, she was incredibly popular around the world, particularly in America. With the gentle 'I'm Going To See You Today', which became her theme, the pomp of 'Stately As A Galleon', and many other favourites such as 'Maude', 'Nursery School', 'A Terrible Worrier', 'Time', 'Three Brothers', 'It's Almost Tomorrow', and two recorded duets with Norman Wisdom, 'Narcissus' and 'I Don't 'Arf Love You', she presented a refined, humorous, perceptive, yet never unkind, view of society. One of her best-remembered pieces is 'I Like Life', which accords with her own philosophy: 'I am not interested in the pursuit of happiness, but only in the discovery of joy'. Her companion on that journey, Reginald Grenfell, died in 1993. In 1988, the revue *Re: Joyce!*, 'a diverting and engaging mixture of anecdotal biography and quintessential sketch material', starring Maureen Lipman with Denis King, opened in London and continued to be presented at intervals into the 90s.

● ALBUMS: *Requests The Pleasure* (1955)★★★★, *At Home* (1957)★★★★,
● COMPILATIONS: *The Collection* (One-Up 1976)★★★★, *George Don't Do That* (Starline 1977)★★★★, *The New Collection* (EMI 1978)★★★, *The Second Collection* (Encore 1979)★★★★, *Joyce Grenfell Talking* (Cube 1981)★★★★, *Keepsake* (Retrospect 1986)★★★, *Re: Joyce* (EMI 1988)★★★, Maureen Lipman and Denis King *Re: Joyce!* stage cast (EMI 1989)★★, *Songs And Monologues Of Joyce Grenfell* (EMI 1991)★★★★, *Joyful Joyce* (1991)★★★★, *Requests The Pleasure* 3-CD set (BBC 1992)★★★★, *More Joyful Joyce* (1994)★★★.
● FURTHER READING: *George - Don't Do That...* (sketches and songs). *Stately As A Galleon* (sketches and songs). *Time Of My Life - Entertaining The Troops: Her Wartime Journals*, Joyce Grenfell. *Joyce Grenfell Requests The Pleasure*, Joyce Grenfell. *In Pleasant Places*, Joyce Grenfell. *Darling Ma: Letters To Her Mother, 1932-1944*, edited by James Roose-Evans. *Joyce: By Herself And Her Friends*, edited by Reggie Grenfell and Richard Garnett. *Joyce And Ginnie: The Letters Of Joyce Grenfell And Virginia Graham*, edited by Janie Hampton.

GREY, CLIFFORD
b. Percival Davis, 5 January 1887, Birmingham, West Midlands, England, d. 25 September 1941, Ipswich,

Suffolk, England. A prolific lyricist and librettist for the London and New York stage, Grey started out as a performer before collaborating with composer Nat D. Ayer on the score for *The Bing Boys Are Here*. This immensely popular revue opened at the Alhambra Theatre in London in April 1916, and contained two of Grey's most enduring numbers, 'If You Were The Only Girl In The World' and 'Another Little Drink Wouldn't Do Us Any Harm'. During the next few years, Grey contributed words to several other revues, such as *Pell-Mell* (Ayer), *The Bing Girls Are There* (Ayer, 'Let The Great Big World Keep Turning'), *The Other Bing Boys* (Ayer), *Hullo, America!* (Herman Finck), *The Bing Brothers On Broadway* (Ayer, 'First Love, Last Love, Best Love'), and *Johnny Jones* (Charles Cuvillier), as well as a few musical plays: *Theodore & Co.* (Ivor Novello-Jerome Kern), *Arlette* (Jane Vieu-Guy Lefeuvre-Novello), *Yes, Uncle!* (Ayer), *Who's Hooper?* (Howard Talbot-Novello), *Kissing Time* (Ivan Caryll-Willie Redstone), and *A Night Out* (Redstone).

In 1920, Grey went to America and renewed his association with Jerome Kern for Florenz Ziegfeld's *Sally*. This lavish production, which starred Marilyn Miller, Leon Errol and Walter Catlett, ran for 570 performances. Among the appealing Kern/Grey numbers were 'Sally', 'Wild Rose', and 'The Church 'Round The Corner' (lyric also with P.G. Wodehouse). Grey remained in the USA for most of the 20s, although, during the early part of the decade, he was also represented in the West End by *Phi-Phi* (1922, Henri Christiné), *The Smith Family* (1922, Ayer), and *The Rainbow* (1923, George Gershwin). As for Broadway, he provided the lyrics - and some occasions the libretti - to a string of musical comedies and revues of variable quality. These included *The Hotel Mouse* (1922, Armand Vecsey-Caryll), *Lady Butterfly* (1923, Werner Janssen), *Vogues Of 1924* (Herbert Stothart), *Majorie* (1924, Stothart-Sigmund Romberg-Stephen Jones), *Artists And Models* (1924, Romberg-J. Fred Coots), *Annie Dear* (1924, Romberg), *Artists And Models* (1925, Alfred Goodman-Coots-Maurice Rubens), *June Days* (1925, Coots), *Gay Paree* (1925, Goodman-Coots), *Mayflowers* (1925, Edward Kunneke), *A Night In Paris* (1926, Coots-Rubens), *The Merry World* (1926, Coots), *The Optimists* (1928, Melville Gideon), *The Madcap* (1928, Rubens), *Sunny Days* (1928, Jean Schwartz), and *Ups-A-Daisy* (1928, Lewis E. Gensler). His most satisfying projects around this time were *Hit The Deck* (1927, Vincent Youmans-Leo Robin), which ran for 352 performances, and produced the rousing 'Hallelujah!'; and *The Three Musketeers* (1928, Rudolph Friml-Wodehouse), a Ziegfeld production, with 'Ma Belle' and 'March Of The Musketeers' outstanding. Grey also wrote the English lyric to José Padilla's spirited 'Valencia', which Hazel Dawn introduced in the 1926 Shubert revue *Great Temptations*. The song went on to become a big hit in the USA for Paul Whiteman, Ben Selvin and the Revelers, amongst others.

With the advent of talking pictures, Grey settled in Hollywood for a spell, collaborating with Victor Schertzinger on the score for the 1929 Maurice Chevalier/Jeanette MacDonald starrer, *The Love Parade* ('Dream Lover', 'Nobody's Using It Now', 'Paris Stay The Same', 'March Of The Grenadiers', 'My Love Parade'), and with Oscar Straus on another Chevalier vehicle, *The Smiling Lieutenant* (1931, 'One More Hour Of Love', 'Jazz Up Your Lingerie', 'Toujours L'Amour In The Army', 'Live For Today'). He also contributed to two Ramon Novarro movies, *Devil May Care* (1929, Stothart, 'Charming') and *In Gay Madrid* (1930, Stothart, 'Dark Night'), as well as *The Rogue Song* (1929, Stothart-Lehar, 'When I'm Looking At You', 'White Dove', 'The Rogue Song'), which had operatic baritone Lawrence Tibbett as its main attraction. Another project with Stothart was *The Floradora Girl* (1930, UK title *The Gay Nineties*), which featured Marion Davies, and songs such as 'Pass The Beer And Pretzels', 'Swingin' In The Lane', and 'My Kind Of Man'.

From then on, apart from having one or two numbers in the disappointing Broadway musical *Smiles*, including 'I'm Glad I Waited' (1930, Youmans-Harold Adamson), which was sung by Fred Astaire and Marilyn Miller, Grey spent the remainder of his career in England. He also served as librettist or co-librettist on the majority of shows he worked on there.

The first of these was the immensely popular *Mr. Cinders*, for which Grey collaborated on the book and lyrics with Greatrex Newman. The music was composed by Vivian Ellis, and the show's most memorable song, 'Spread A Little Happiness', which was sweetly sung by Binnie Hale, has been revived several times over the years by various artists, including the rock star Sting, who took it into the UK Top 20 in 1982. It has even received the ultimate accolade of being featured in a television commercial. Another appealing Grey song, 'Got A Date With An Angel', written with Jack Waller, Sonny Miller and Joseph Tunbridge, was introduced by Bobby Howes in the 'play with tunes', *For The Love Of Mike* (1931). Howes had quite a hit with it in the UK, and the number became popular in the USA for Skinnay Ennis with the Hal Kemp Orchestra.

Gray continued to work consistently during the 30s, on screenplays and songs for British films, and West End shows such as *Out Of The Bottle* (1932, Oscar Levant-Ellis), *The One Girl* (1933, a revised version of *Smiles*, with Youmans and Adamson), *Command Performance* (1933, Waller-Tunbridge), *Mr. Whittington* (1934, Waller-Tunbridge-Green, 'Oceans Of Time'), *Jack O' Diamonds* (1935, Noel Gay), *Love Laughs!* (1935, Gay), *At The Silver Swan*, (1936, Edmond Samuels), *Oh, You Letty* (1937, Paul Sheron), and *Bobby Get Your Gun* (1938, Waller-Tunbridge).

Shortly after the outbreak of World War II, Grey joined ENSA, and ran concert parties for the troops until his death, which was caused by the blast from a bomb.

GREY, JOEL

b. Joel Katz, 11 April 1932, Cleveland, Ohio, USA. A nimble, versatile and dynamic entertainer - an actor, singer and dancer - Grey is the elder son of Mickey Katz, the popular bandleader and comedian in the American Yiddish musical theatre. After making his stage debut in 1941 as Pud in *Borrowed Time*, as a teenager Grey performed featured acts in his father's shows. In 1951, he was spotted by Eddie Cantor who booked him on his network television programme, and this led to prestige nightclub appearances in New York, Chicago, Hollywood, and Miami

Beach. In 1956, Grey made his first appearance on the New York stage in *The Littlest Revue*, and during the next few years played a few minor roles in films and television, and recorded some 'bad rock 'n' roll songs' for Capitol Records. In the early 60s he replaced Warren Berlinger in *Come Blow Your Horn*, Anthony Newley in *Stop The World - I Want To Get* Off, and Tommy Steele in *Half A Sixpence*, before creating the role of the evil Master of Ceremonies in the hit musical *Cabaret* in 1966. Grey's 'cheerful, charming, soulless, and conspiratorially wicked' performance of songs such as 'Willkommen', 'Two Ladies', 'Tomorrow Belongs To Me', 'The Money Song', and 'If You Could See Her', made him a star, and he received a Tony Award for best supporting actor in a musical. He also won an Oscar for his part in Bob Fosse's superior 1972 film version. Grey left the Broadway cast of *Cabaret* in 1968 to star in *George M!*, a musical biography of George M. Cohan. His spirited renderings of the master-showman's 'Give My Regards To Broadway', 'Yankee Doodle Dandy', 'Harrigan', and the rest, were widely acclaimed, and earned him another Tony nomination. *George M!* has been Grey's last real original success on Broadway to date, although he has appeared in New York in *Goodtime Charley* (1975), *The Grand Tour* (1979), and the operatically inclined 'theatre piece', *Silverlake* (1980), as well as off-Broadway shows. He also starred in the 1987 revival of *Cabaret*, and gave a performance which prompted critic US Clive Barnes to note that he is 'at least twice as good as he was'. Nearly a decade later he was acclaimed for his performance as Amos Hart ('Mister Cellophane'), in a smash hit revival of *Chicago* (Broadway 1996, West End 1998). It brought him Drama Desk and Outer Critics Circle Awards for Best Featured Actor In A Musical. In 1993, Grey was inducted into the Theater Hall of Fame, and appeared in the one-man musical *Herringbone* for the Hartford Stage Company. Over the years he has featured extensively in regional theatre, on television, and in some memorable film parts. His highly skilled cabaret act is based around a battered outsized trunk, complete with labels from shows with which has been associated. Grey's daughter, Jennifer Grey, came to prominence in 1987 when she co-starred with Patrick Swayze in the movie musical *Dirty Dancing*.

● ALBUMS: *Songs My Father Taught Me* (Capitol 1957)★★★, *Cabaret* Original Broadway Cast (Columbia 1966)★★★, *Only The Beginning* (Columbia 1967)★★★, *Black Sheep Boy* (Columbia 1968)★★★, *George M!* (Columbia 1968)★★★, *Cabaret* film soundtrack(ABC 1972)★★★★, *Joel Grey Live!* (Columbia 1973)★★★, *Goodtime Charley* (RCA Victor 1975)★★★, *The Grand Tour* (Columbia 1979)★★, *Silverlake* (Elektra Nonesuch 1980)★★★.

● FILMS: *About Face* (1952), *Calypso Heat Wave* (1957), *Come September* (1961), *Cabaret* (1972), *Man On A Swing* (1974), *Buffalo Bill And The Indians* (1976), *The Seven-Per-Cent Solution* (1976), *Remo Williams: The Adventure Begins . . .* (1985), *Kafka* (1991), *The Player* as himself (1992), *The Music Of Chance* (1993), *The Dangerous* (1994), *Venus Rising* (1995), *The Fantasticks* (1995), *The Empty Mirror* (1996), *My Friend Joe* (1996).

GRUSIN, DAVE

b. 26 June 1934, Littleton, Colorado, USA. He played piano semi-professionally while studying at the University of Colorado, and almost abandoned music to become a vet-

erinary surgeon. Grusin stated 'I'm still not sure I made the right decision, a lot of dead cows might still be alive today if I hadn't gone to music school.' His musical associates at the time included Art Pepper, Terry Gibbs and Spike Robinson, with whom he worked extensively in the early 50s. In 1959 Grusin was hired as musical director by singer Andy Williams, a role he maintained into the mid-60s. An eclectic musician, Grusin worked with mainstream artists such as Benny Goodman and Thad Jones and also worked with hard bop players. He made many recording dates, including several in the early 70s, accompanying singers amongst whom were Sarah Vaughan and Carmen McRae. Around this same time Grusin began to concentrate more and more on electric piano and keyboards, recording with Gerry Mulligan, Lee Ritenour in the jazz world and with Paul Simon and Billy Joel in pop. He has arranged and produced for the Byrds, Peggy Lee, Grover Washington Jnr., Donna Summer, Barbra Streisand, Al Jarreau, Phoebe Snow and Patti Austin. He is also co-founder and owner, with Larry Rosen, of GRP Records, a label which they founded in 1976 and has an impressive catalogue of singers, jazz and jazz-rock artists including Diane Schuur, Lee Ritenour, David Benoit, his brother Don Grusin, Michael Brecker, Chick Corea, Steve Gadd, Dave Valentin, Special EFX and Gary Burton. The success of GRP has much to do with Grusin's refusal to compromise on quality. With Rosen he pioneered an all digital recording policy, and using 'state of the art' technology their productions reach a pinnacle of recorded quality. In addition to his activities as a player and producer, Grusin has written extensively for films and television. His portfolio is most impressive; in addition to winning a Grammy in 1984 his film scores have received several Academy Award nominations, and include *Divorce Italian Style*, *The Graduate*, *The Heart Is A Lonely Hunter*, *Three Days Of The Condor*, *Heaven Can Wait*, *Reds*, *On Golden Pond*, *The Champ*, *Tootsie*, *Racing With The Moon*, *The Milagro Beanfield War*, *Clara's Heart*, *Tequila Sunrise*, *A Dry White Season*, *The Fabulous Baker Boys*, *Bonfire Of The Vanities*, *Havana*, *For The Boys*, and *The Firm* (1993). Additionally one of his most evocative songs 'Mountain Dance' was the title song to *Falling In Love*. His American television credits include *St. Elsewhere*, *Maude*, *Roots*, *It Takes A Thief* and *Baretta*. Grusin is a master musical chemist - able to blend many elements of pop and jazz into uplifting intelligent and accessible music. In 1993 he appeared as a performer on the international jazz circuit and in 1997 issued a highly credible album of the music of Henry Mancini.
● ALBUMS: *Candy* soundtrack (1961)★★, *The Many Moods Of Dave Grusin* (1962)★★, *Subways Are For Sleeping* (Epic 1962)★★, *Kaleidoscope* (Columbia 1964)★★, *Don't Touch* (1964)★★★, *Discovered Again* (1976)★★, *One Of A Kind* (GRP 1977)★★★, *Dave Grusin And The GRP All Stars Live In Japan Featuring Sadao Watanabe* (GRP 1980)★★★, *Out Of The Shadows* (GRP 1982)★★★, *Mountain Dance* (GRP 1983)★★★★, *Night Lines* (GRP 1984)★★★, with Lee Ritenour *Harlequin* (GRP 1984)★★, *The NYLA Dream Band* (GRP 1988)★★★, with Don Grusin *Sticks And Stones* (GRP 1988)★★★, *Migration* (GRP 1989)★★, *The Fabulous Baker Boys* film soundtrack (GRP 1989)★★★, *Havana* (GRP 1990)★★★, *The*

Gershwin Collection (GRP 1992)★★★, *Homage To Duke* (GRP 1993)★★★, *Two For The Road: The Music Of Henry Mancini* (GRP 1997)★★★★, *Dave Grusin Presents West Side Story* (N2K 1997)★★★.
● COMPILATIONS: *Cinemagic* (1987)★★★★, *Dave Grusin Collection* (GRP 1991)★★★★.

GUÉTARY, GEORGES

b. Lambros Worloou, 8 February 1915, Alexandria, Egypt, d. 13 September 1997, Mougins (Alpes-Maritimes), France. A singer, dancer, variety and revue artist for more than 50 years, Guétary was the epitome of the charming and romantic Latin lover. His boundless energy, good nature and mischievous air endeared him to audiences in Europe and America. The son of Greek parents, he was sent by his father to Paris in 1934, ostensibly to extend his knowledge of commerce. Instead, he succumbed to his early love of music, and studied at the music school run by the distinguished violinist Jacques Thibaud and pianist Alfred Cordot. He also received vocal training from Ninon Vallin before making his stage debut in 1937 at the Européen with Jo Bouillon And His Orchestra. The legendary Mistinguett spotted him there, and invited him to appear with her at the Casino de Paris. Soon, he was making records - several with accordionist Fredo Gardoni - and touring as a soloist in revue and operetta. During World War II, he changed his name to Georges Guétary, and moved to Toulouse, where he worked as a maître d'hôtel. He continued to sing, however, and, after returning to Paris, starred in a series of operettas. He also became an immensely popular recording artist, and appeared in a number of films during the 50s directed by Gilles Grangier. In November 1946, Guétary returned from singing in Switzerland in order to meet the British impresario Charles B. Cochran, who was in Paris auditioning for his new musical, *Bless The Bride*. Although he could speak hardly any English, Guétary was engaged, and starred opposite Lizbeth Webb, revelling in songs such as 'Ma Belle Marguerite', 'This Is My Lovely Day' and 'I Was Never Kissed Before', from Vivian Ellis and A.P. Herbert's memorable score. Guétary also appeared in Robert Nesbitt's West End revue, *Latin Quarter* (1949), with Frances Day, before making his Broadway debut in *Arms And The Girl* (1950), a musical version of Lawrence Langner and Armina Marshall's play *The Pursuit Of Happiness*. *Arms And The Girl* ran for only about four months, but Guétary's excellent reviews led to him being cast as the 'older man', Henri Baurel, in what was his only American movie, Vincente Minnelli's *An American In Paris*. Screenwriter Alan Jay Lerner had created the role of Baurel specifically for Maurice Chevalier, but the latter was not used, owing to various problems. In company with Gene Kelly and Leslie Caron, Guétary was superb, singing '(I'll Build A) Stairway To Paradise', 'Love Walked In', ''S Wonderful' (with Kelly) and 'By Strauss' (with Kelly and Oscar Levant), while simply musing on 'Nice Work If You Can Get It'. A few years later, Guétary confirmed his ever-youthful image and approach by humorously welcoming the 50s musical revolution with 'Georges Viens Danser Le Rock 'N' Roll'. From then on, he continued to perform and sing regularly on stage, and at the age of 80 returned to the scene of former triumphs, the Bobino music hall in Paris for his final concert. His audience, mostly consisting of elderly ladies whom he had enchanted for many years, were enraptured and he did not disappoint.

GUYS AND DOLLS (FILM MUSICAL)

Producer Sam Goldwyn pulled off quite a coup when he cast Frank Sinatra and Marlon Brando in this 1955 screen version of the smash-hit Broadway show. In Joseph L. Mankiewicz's screenplay, which was based on Abe Burrows' libretto and Damon Runyan's short story *The Idyll Of Miss Sarah Brown*, Sinatra plays Nathan Detroit, the operator of the oldest established permanent floating crap game in New York. Constantly harassed by Inspector Brannigan (Robert Keith), and his fiancé of 14 years, Miss Adelaide (Vivian Blaine), Nathan bets 'the highest roller in town', Sky Masterson (Brando), that he cannot transport Salvation Army stalwart Sarah Brown (Jean Simmons), from the Save Our Souls Mission in New York, to Havana. Against all the odds, Sky and Sarah make the trip, but Nathan subsequently loses nothing - except his precious freedom - when he and Adelaide, along with Sky and Sarah, make it a double wedding in Times Square. There was a rumour that Sinatra wanted to play the Brando role because, in the original, Nathan does not have a solo number. In the event, composer Frank Loesser gave him a new song, 'Adelaide', and he also wrote another new one for Brando, 'A Woman In Love', because the actor reportedly could not handle the tender 'I've Never Been In Love Before'. In fact, both he and Jean Simmons were surprisingly good on 'I'll Know' and 'If I Were A Bell'. The rest of the magnificent score - arguably Loesser's masterpiece - included 'Fugue For Tinhorns' (Sinatra-Silver-Danny Dayton), 'The Oldest Established' (Sinatra-Silver-Kaye-ensemble), 'Pet Me Poppa' (which replaced 'A Bushel And A Peck') (Blaine and chorus), 'Adelaide's Lament' (Blaine), 'Guys And Dolls' (Sinatra-Silver-Kaye), 'Take Back Your Mink' (Blaine and chorus), 'Luck Be A Lady' (Brando), 'Sue Me' (Sinatra-Blaine) and 'Sit Down, You're Rockin' The Boat'. The latter number was performed by the irrepressible Stubby Kaye, recreating his Broadway role of Nicely-Nicely Johnson. Other veterans of the stage show, playing two of the loveable Runyanesque rogues, were Johnny Silver (Benny Southstreet) and B.S. Pully (Big Jule), along with the marvellous Vivian Blaine and choreographer Michael Kidd. Also in the cast were Sheldon Leonard, George E. Stone, Regis Toomey, Kathryn Givney, Veda Ann Borg and Alan Hokanson. Directed by Mankiewicz, and photographed in Eastman Color and CinemaScope for MGM, *Guys And Dolls* was derided by the critics, but welcomed by the cinema-going public who made it one of the top box-office successes of the 50s.

GUYS AND DOLLS (STAGE MUSICAL)

Opening at the 46th Street Theatre in New York on 24 November 1950, the stage musical *Guys And Dolls* was a smash hit. With a book by Abe Burrows and Jo Swerling, and music and lyrics by Frank Loesser, out-of-town tryouts were hugely successful and by the time of its opening night on Broadway, the word was out that the show was a winner. Based upon the risqué yarns of Damon Runyon, the dialogue and lyrics effectively captured the speech patterns of Runyon's larger-than-life characters, and complemented the show's strong characterization and dramatic book. In addition, the music perfectly matched the show's mood. The story tells of two love affairs, the first between compulsive gambler Nathan Detroit (Sam Levene) and the leading dancer at the Hot Box night club, Miss Adelaide (Vivian Blaine), and the second between another - far more successful - gambler, Sky Masterson (Robert Alda), and Miss Sarah Brown (Isabel Bigley), a leading light of the Save-A-Soul Mission. Other Runyonesque characters enhance the milieu, notably Benny Southstreet (Johnny Silver), Big Jule (B.S. Pully), Harry the Horse (Tom Pedi), and Nicely-Nicely Johnson (Stubby Kaye), who stopped the show every night when he led the cast in the exuberant 'Sit Down, You're Rockin' The Boat'. During the course of the play, true love triumphs despite many obstacles, not least of which is the police officer Lieutenant Brannigan's desperate attempts to locate and close down Nathan's floating crap game, the 'oldest established' in New York. By the time the curtain falls, Masterson is a reformed character and has married Sarah, while Nathan and Miss Adelaide are about to marry after a 14-year-long courtship. Loesser's marvellous score included 'Follow The Fold', 'Fugue For Tinhorns', 'The Oldest Established', 'I'll Know', 'A Bushel And A Peck', 'Adelaide's Lament', 'Guys And Dolls', 'Havana', 'If I Were A Bell', 'My Time Of Day', 'I've Never Been In Love Before', 'Take Back Your Mink', 'More I Cannot Wish You', 'Luck Be A Lady', 'Sue Me' and 'Marry The Man Today'. Critics and public loved the show and it ran for some 1,200 performances, winning Tony Awards for best musical, actor (Alda), featured actress (Bigley), director (George S. Kaufman), and choreographer (Michael Kidd). A London production opened on 28 May 1953 at the Coliseum, and ran for over a year (555 performances). Blaine, Levene, Kaye, Pedi and Silver reprised their roles, with Jerry Wayne as Sky and Lizbeth Webb playing Miss Sarah. The show was revived in Britain by the Royal National Theatre in 1982, 1985 (with pop singer Lulu as Miss Adelaide) and 1996. New York audiences enjoyed an all-black production of the show in 1976, and an acclaimed Broadway mounting, starring Nathan Lane, Faith Prince, Peter Gallagher and Josie de Guzman, opened in April 1992 and ran for 1,143 performances. It won Tonys for best revival, actress (Prince) and director (Jerry Zaks). The 1955 film version starred Marlon Brando, Frank Sinatra, Vivian Blaine and Stubby Kaye.

GYPSY (FILM MUSICAL)

This entertaining and faithful screen adaptation of the hit Broadway musical which opened in 1959, was released by Warner Brothers three years later. Rosalind Russell gave a memorable, if controversial, performance as the show-business mother who is determined that if she cannot become a star herself, then one of her daughters, June (Ann Jillian) or Louise (Natalie Wood), damn-well will. Louise is the one who finally makes it in the guise of classy stripper Gypsy Rose Lee, and, while Russell could not be expected to have the vocal power of Ethel Merman who created the role on Broadway, she did manage to bring to the part a mixture of spunky charm and vulnerability that was all her own. Her singing voice on some of the numbers was provided by Lisa Kirk, and Natalie Wood was dubbed by Marni Nixon. Jule Styne and Stephen Sondheim's score, which has long been recognised as one of the finest of all-time, arrived in Hollywood intact. All the songs are classics of their kind, including 'Let Me Entertain You', 'Some People', 'Small World', 'Mr. Goldstone, I Love You', 'Little Lamb', 'You'll Never Get Away From Me', 'If Mama Was Married', 'All I Need Is The Girl', 'Everything's Coming Up Roses', 'You Gotta Have A Gimmick', and 'Rose's Turn'. One of the other splendid songs, 'Together Wherever We Go', was apparently removed by the distributors. Karl Malden was fine as Herbie, Rose's long-suffering fiancé who just wants her to give it all up for a cottage with roses round the door, and among the rest of the strong cast were Paul Wallace, Faith Dane, Betty Bruce, Harry Shannon, Roxanne Arlen, Harvey Korman, Danny Locklin, Guy Raymond, and Parley Baer. Leonard Spigelgass's screenplay was based on Gypsy Rose Lee's memoirs, and Robert Tucker was responsible for the spirited (and sometimes hilarious) choreography. Produced and directed by Mervyn LeRoy, the film was shot in Technicolor and Technirama. Released in 1962, it was not a commercial success.

GYPSY (STAGE MUSICAL)

Based on stripper Gypsy Rose Lee's autobiography, this legendary show opened at the Broadway Theatre in New York on 21 May 1959. Arthur Laurents's book follows Rose (Ethel Merman), the ruthless and ambitious show-biz mother, who is determined that her Baby June (Jacqueline Mayro) will be a star no matter what. Unfortunately for Rose, when she grows older, June (Lane Bradbury) evades her mother's clutches and defects to get married. Unfazed, Rose disregards the advice of manager and long-time fiancé Herbie (Jack Klugman), switches her fanatical attention to June's sister, Louise (Sandra Church), and eventually transforms her from a shy young girl into the classy stripper Gypsy Rose Lee. Laurents suggested that Stephen Sondheim, fresh from his lyrical success with West Side Story, should provide the score but Merman turned him down, preferring to rely on the experience of composer Jule Styne. Laurents eventually persuaded Sondheim to write lyrics only, and the overall result was a triumph. The score is among the most highly regarded in Broadway musical history, and includes 'Let Me Entertain You', 'Together Wherever We Go', 'Small World', 'If Mamma Was Married', 'All I Need Is The Girl', 'You Gotta Have A Gimmick', 'Mr. Goldstone', and Merman's blockbusters, 'Everything's Coming Up Roses' and 'Rose's Turn'. Also cast were Maria Karnilova (Tessie Tura), Paul Wallace (Tulsa), Mort Marshall (Uncle Jocko), Lane Bradbury (June), Joe Silver (Weber), Peg Murray (Miss Cratchitt), and Michael Parks (LA). The David Merrick production, which gave Merman one of her most satisfying roles, both in vocal and acting terms, was directed and choreographed by Jerome Robbins, and ran for 702 performances. The 1973 London version, with Angela Lansbury as Rose, Barrie Ingham (Herbie), and Zan

Charisse (Louise) was directed by Arthur Laurents, and lasted for 300 performances. This production transferred to Broadway in the following year (120 performances) with Rex Robbins taking over as Herbie. In 1989 Gypsy returned to Broadway once again (476 performances), with television star Tyne Daly in the leading role, along with Jonathan Hadary (Herbie) and Crista Moore (Louise). Daly won a Tony Award for best actress, and there was another for best musical revival. A unique opportunity to view this wonderful musical at leisure came in 1993, when Gypsy, starring Bette Midler (Rose), Peter Riegert (Herbie), and Cynthia Gibb (Louise), was shown on US television and later released on video. It purported to be the first film of a complete stage musical to retain the original text, with no material added or altered. The 1998 Paper Mill Playhouse, New Jersey, production had Betty Buckley as Rose, Deborah Gibson (Louise), and Lenny Wolpe (Herbie). The 1962 film version starred Rosalind Russell (Rose), Natalie Wood (Louise), and Karl Malden (Herbie).

HAGUE, ALBERT

b. 13 October 1920, Berlin, Germany. A composer for the musical theatre and films, Hague was educated at the Royal Conservatory in Rome and the College of Music of the University of Cincinnati, from where he graduated with a B.A. Degree in Music in 1942. After writing his first stage score for a regional production of Reluctant Lady in 1948, and contributing songs and incidental music to shows such as The Madwoman Of Chaillot, Dance Me A Song and All Summer Long, in 1955 he collaborated with lyricist Arnold B. Horwitt on the score for Plain And Fancy, which contained the enduring 'Young And Foolish'. Four years later, he worked with Horwitt again (and Richard Lewine) on the revue The Girls Against The Boys, and in the same year he and the celebrated lyricist and librettist Dorothy Fields won Tony Awards for their words and music for Redhead ('Merely Marvellous', 'The Right Finger Of My Right Hand'). Redhead ran for over a year, but Hague's subsequent efforts, including Café Crown (with Marty Brill, 1964), The Fig Leaves Are Falling (with Allan Sherman, 1969), Miss Moffatt (1974), and Surprise! Surprise! (1979) have all failed to appeal. Miss Moffatt, starring Bette Davis, closed out of town. In 1992, The Lady In Question, a musical about Dorothy Parker, with Hague's music and a book and lyrics by Thomas O'Malley, was presented in concert at the Cast Theatre in Hollywood. Hague has also composed music for films and television, and it was in the latter medium that he came to notice in the 80s when he played music teacher Shorofsky in the top-rated US television series *Fame*.

HAIR

Having spent a few months at Joseph Papp's New York Shakespeare Festival Public Theatre and the city's Cheetah nightclub, a revised and recast version of this 'American Tribal Love-Rock Musical' arrived on Broadway at the Biltmore Theatre on 29 April 1968. In jargon not yet in use, *Hair* was what might be described as 'alternative entertainment'. Amongst the many things that made the show different was its forceful stand on matters like sex, politics, drugs, the draft and religion. It purported to be the first musical of the hippie peace and love generation; many of the performers wore wigs as they had yet to grow their own hair. Strong language and some over-rated nudity ensured a measure of shock value, and despite, or perhaps because of, its irreverence and decidedly contemporary attitude, *Hair* was received favourably by many critics. One scribe who disagreed was Milton Shulman of the London Evening Standard, who wrote: 'The effect was like being at an orgy of boy scouts and girl guides.' At the end of each performance, many members of the audience joined those on stage in a spontaneous gesture of their appreciation of the show's themes. The music was composed by Galt MacDermot, and the book and lyrics by Gerome Ragni and James Rado. That book - or non-book, according to their theatre programme biography - cast Ragni and Rado as co-habiting best friends Berger and Claude, the draft-dodger, who puts it around that he comes from Manchester, England. They are in a tribe whose other main members consist of Sheila (Lynn Kellogg), who fancies Berger, and is in turn fancied by Claude. Jeanie (Sally Eaton), girlfriend of Claude, who is pregnant with someone else's child, and seriously into drugs. And then there is Woof (Steve Curry), who is even more seriously into Mick Jagger, and Hud (Lamont Washington). Also around somewhere are Melba Moore (Dionne), Shelley Plimpton (Crissy), and Diane Keaton, who plays a waitress. The often difficult-to-follow goings-on were embellished with a set of songs which included 'Hair', 'Hare Krishna', 'Dead End', 'Easy To Be Hard', 'I Got Life', 'Black Boys', 'White Boys', 'Frank Mills', 'Where Do I Go?', 'Don't Put It Down', 'Good Morning Starshine', 'Prisoners In Niggertown', 'My Conviction', 'Walking In Space', 'Ain't Got No', 'Electric Blues', 'Coloured Spade', 'Going Down', 'Hashish', 'Air', and 'Sodomy'. Several artists had hits with numbers from the show, notably the Fifth Dimension who topped the US chart with a medley which included 'Aquarius' and 'Let The Sunshine In'. *Hair* ran on Broadway for 1,742 performances, and there were several changes to the score for the London production which was timed by the producers to open on Friday 27 September 1968, the day after the Lord Chamberlain's censorship powers were abolished. First audiences into the Shaftesbury Theatre saw Paul Nicholas (Claude), Oliver Tobias (Berger), Michael Feast (Woof), Linda Kendrick (Jeanie), Peter Straker (Hud), Annabel Leventon (Sheila), and Marsha Hunt (Dionne). The respected British musician Alex Harvey played electric guitar in the pit orchestra. This production was terminated when part of the Shaftesbury Theatre roof fell into the stalls in July 1973, on the day of what would have been its 2,000th performance. It reopened for a further 111 performances nearly a year later. By then, several road companies were touring the USA, and the message of love and peace had spread much further afield. It returned briefly to the Biltmore Theatre in 1977, and was in the US regions again in 1994 with what was billed as a 25th anniversary production, directed by James Rado - 'a wilting reminder that much of the flower-power idealism of the 60s comes across as just plain silly in the cynical 90s' (Variety). Cast in that one were Kent Dalian (Berger), Luther Creek (Claude), Catrice Joseph (Dionne), Sean Jenness (Woof), Cathy Trien (Sheila), Ali Zorlas (Jeanie). The London critics were no kinder when another 25th anniversary effort sashayed into the Old Vic Theatre on 14 September 1993, and sashayed out again about two months later. 'This show is about as topical as *The Pirates Of Penzance*,' was a typical response to the efforts of Paul Hipp (Berger), John Barrowman (Claude), Sinitta (Dionne), Lawrie Demacque (Pepsi), Felice Arena (Woof), Paul J. Medford (Hud), Andree Bernard (Sheila), and Katharine Mehrling (Chrissy), who were directed by Michael Bogdanov. Also in 1993, the New York Festival Theatre saluted *Hair*, which was the Festival's inaugural production in their new home, the Public Theatre, back in 1967. Galt MacDermot was the musical director, and performers included Ben Vereen, Kevin Kline, Betty Buckley, Ellen Greene, and James Rado. Five years on, a new French version of *Hair* opened at the Theatre Mogador for a limited run, and another production, with an international cast, set out on a 71-date tour of Europe. A film version of *Hair* was released in 1979.

HAIRSPRAY

A 1988 film set in America in 1962, *Hairspray* featured rock and pop luminaries Deborah Harry (as Velma Von Tussle), Sonny Bono (as Franklin Von Tussle) and Divine (as Edna Turnblad). It is among writer/director John Waters most famous 'schlock classics'. The plot introduced later mainstream chat show host Ricki Lake's character, Tracy Turnblad. By entering the Baltimore *Corny Colins* television show and winning their talent contest, she proves that 'fat girls can dance'. However, jealous school friends and anxious teachers make her life a misery after Tracy becomes the regular star of the show. She and friend Penny travel to Baltimore's black quarter and find boyfriends - Tracy's an Elvis impersonator/look-a-like. However, when their new boyfriends are brought back to the studio their colour causes problems. Eventually it is decided that a live *Corny Colins* show is to be broadcast from Mr and Mrs Von Tussle's amusement arcade. A riot follows and Tracy is arrested. This means she is unable to compete at the car show pageant and Amber Von Tussle (Colleen Fitzpatrick) usurps her place. Predictably, Tracy is returned to her rightful position as queen of the pageant after the students protest. As a nostalgia spoof the film included some nice touches - not least cameos by Ric Ocasek of the Cars as 'the beatnik cat' and an excellent period soundtrack - but failed to convince cinema reviewers. Divine died just two weeks after the film's premiere.

HALE, BINNIE

b. Beatrice Mary Hale-Monro, 22 May 1899, Liverpool, England, d. 10 January 1984, London, England. Arguably the brightest and most successful star of the London musical comedy and revue stage during the 20s and 30s, this versatile and vivacious blonde actress, singer, dancer, and exceptionally gifted mimic, made her stage debut in the musical comedy *Follow The Crowd* at the old Empire Theatre in 1916. Later that year she appeared in the revue *We're All In It* at the same theatre, and then joined the chorus of *Houp-La!*, which opened C.B. Cochran's brand new St. Martin's Theatre. After being seen in a number of run-of-the-mill revues and musical comedies, including *150 Pound*, *The Kiss Call*, *Just Fancy*, *Jumble Sale*, *My Nieces*, *Katinka*, *Puppets*, and *The Odd Spot* (1924), in the late 20s and 30s she excelled in *No, No, Nanette* ('I Want To Be Happy', 'Tea For Two', 'I've Confessed To The Breeze', 'Take A Little One-Step'), *Sunny* ('Who', with Jack Buchanan) *Mr. Cinders* ('Spread A Little Happiness, 'I'm A One-Man Girl', 'Ev'ry Little Moment' - the first of three shows with Bobby Howes), *Nippy*, *Bow Bells*, with her father, actor Robert Hale ('You're Blasé', 'Mona Lisa'), *The Dubarry* (as Jeanne in the UK tour), *Give Me A Ring*, *Yes, Madame?* ('Dreaming A Dream'), *Rise And Shine*, Cochran's Coronation revue *Home And Beauty* ('A Nice Cup Of Tea'), and *Magyar Melody* (1939). In the 40s, and for most of the 50s, she mixed appearances in pantomime (in her day, she was a superb principal boy) and variety theatres with more revues and musicals such as *Up And Doing*, *Flying Colours*, *One, Two, Three!* (with her younger brother Sonnie Hale), *Four, Five, Six!*, *Out Of This World*, and *The Punch Revue* (1955). She also joined her brother in the radio series *All Hale*. Her last West End role is said to have been as the Duchess and Queen of Hearts in *Alice In Wonderland* at the Winter Garden Theatre in 1959.

● ALBUMS: *Binnie Hale In No No Nanette* (World Records 60s)★★.

HALE, SONNIE

b. John Robert Hale-Monro, 1 May 1902, London, England, d. 9 June 1959, London, England. An amiable actor and singer, as well as an author, producer and director, Hale made his West End stage debut in the chorus of the revue *Fun Of The Fayre* at the London Pavilion in 1921. Apart from his undeniable talents as a performer, he is remembered particularly for having been married to two of the London musical theatre's favourite leading ladies, Evelyn Laye and Jessie Matthews. Between 1927 and 1940 he appeared with Matthews in *One Dam Thing After Another*, *This Year Of Grace!* (in which he sang Noël Coward's 'A Room With A View' and 'Dance, Little Lady'), *Wake Up and Dream!*, *Ever Green*, (introducing Richard Rodgers and Lorenz Hart's 'Dancing On The Ceiling'), *Hold My Hand*, and *Come Out To Play*. He was also seen in several other musical comedies and revues, including *Little Nellie Kelly*, *The Punch Bowl*, *Mercenary Mary*, *Queen High*, *The Knight Was Bold*, and *One, Two, Three!* (1947).

He directed and co-produced the latter show - one of his last West End projects - in which he starred with his sister, Binnie Hale. Their father was the actor, Robert Hale. From around 1934-39, Sonnie Hale took time off from the stage to appear in - and later - direct a number of film musicals, such as *On With The Dance*, *Tell Me Tonight*, *Happy Ever After*, *Early To Bed*, *Evergreen*, *My Song For You*, *My Heart Is Calling*, *First A Girl*, *It's Love Again*, *Head Over Heels*, *Gangway*, and *Sailing Along*. He was also in the cast of the movie *London Town* (1946), which starred Sid Field, and his 1955 play, *A French Mistress*, was filmed in 1960 with Cecil Parker and James Robertson Justice. Playing a minor role was a future superstar of the musical theatre - 18-year-old Michael Crawford. Sonnie Hale died before that film was released, after spending the last few years of his career in the regional theatre.

HALF A SIXPENCE (FILM MUSICAL)

Most of the original songs survived, but much of the charm was lost when this British screen version of the West End and Broadway hit show was released by Paramount in 1967. Beverley Cross adapted his original libretto which had been based on H.G. Wells's 1925 novel *Kipps*, and Tommy Steele recreated his stage role - and dominated the whole affair - as the shop assistant who wins a fortune but loses his head and his childhood sweetheart Ann (Julia Foster), before realising that money cannot buy love or happiness. There was still plenty to enjoy in David Heneker's appealing score, including the exuberant 'Flash, Bang, Wallop!' and the tender 'She's Too Far Above Me' and 'Half A Sixpence', along with 'All In The Cause Of Economy', 'If The Rain's Got To Fall', 'I'm Not Talking To You', 'I Know What I Am', 'I Don't Believe A Word Of It', and 'A Proper Gentleman'. Heneker also wrote two additional numbers especially for the film, 'The Race Is On' and 'This Is My World' (with Irvin Kostal). James Villiers, renowned in British films and television shows for his portrayal of upper-class snooty characters, was prominent among a strong supporting cast which also featured Cyril Ritchard, Penelope Horner, Grover Dale, Elaine Taylor, and Hilton Edwards. Gillian Lynne, who came to world-wide fame in the 70s with her contribution to Andrew Lloyd Webber's *Cats*, staged the imaginative and energetic dance sequences, and George Sidney was the director. Marti Webb, the original 'Ann' in the 1963 London production, dubbed the singing voice of Julia Foster.

HALF A SIXPENCE (STAGE MUSICAL)

The chirpy Tommy Steele moved impressively from rock 'n' roll stardom to musical comedy in producer Harold Fielding's engaging adaptation of H.G. Wells's novel, *Kipps*, which opened at the Cambridge Theatre in London on 21 March 1963. Beverley Cross's book told of a young orphan, Arthur Kipps (Steele), who is an apprentice at Shalford's Drapery Emporium. When he inherits a large sum of money he abandons his childhood sweetheart, Ann (Marti Webb), in favour of Helen (Anna Barry), whom he feels is more in keeping with his newly acquired financial status and social-climbing ambitions. Naturally, after losing the cash, he comes back down to earth, returns to Ann - and shrewdly turns down another fortune. A fine supporting cast included James Grout, Jessica James, Anthony Valentine, John Bull, and Colin Farrell. David Heneker's score was a joy, and contained several lovely songs such as the apprentices' anthem to their boss, 'All In The Cause Of Economy', three gentle ballads 'Half A Sixpence', 'She's Too Far Above Me', and 'If The Rain's Got To Fall', and the rousing 'Money To Burn'. Other numbers included 'The Oak And The Ash', 'I'm Not Talking To You', 'The Old Military Canal', 'The One That's Run Away', 'Long Ago', 'I Know What I Am', 'I'll Build A Palace', and 'I Only Want A Little House'. The show's musical highlight, 'Flash, Bang, Wallop!', was an ensemble piece during which Kipps and his bride were married, congratulated, and photographed - all in a flash. Steele was outstanding. The musical numbers and dances were staged by Edmund Balin, and the director was John Dexter. This was probably the best and most satisfying stage role of his long career, although no doubt he would argue with that. After a London run of 679 performances, he took the show to Broadway in 1965 where it stayed at the Broadhurst Theatre for over a year. James Grout also reprised his role, with Polly James (Ann), Carrie Nye, Ann Shoemaker, Grover Dale, Will Mackenzie, Norman Allen, as well as the future author, and television and film star, John Cleese. For this production, Onna White handled the staging of musical numbers and dances, and it was directed by Gene Saks. Steele's co-stars in the 1967 film version were Julia Foster and Cyril Ritchard.

HALL, ADELAIDE
b. Adelaide Louisa Hall, 20 October 1901, Brooklyn, New York City, New York, USA, d. 7 November 1993, London, England. Though not a jazz singer, Hall has become one of the most famous vocalists in jazz history through her wordless vocals on such Duke Ellington recordings as 'Creole Love Call' and 'Blues I Love To Sing'. Other numbers with which she was indelibly associated, included 'Sophisticated Lady', 'Old Fashioned Love', 'Memories Of You', 'Solitude', 'Don't Get Around Much Anymore' and 'Don't Worry 'Bout Me'. Many of the songs she sang were written especially for her. Her fine soprano voice was developed by her father, a music professor. Like her friend, Lena Horne, her name will always be associated with Harlem's famous Cotton Club and the 'greats' who gathered there, such as Ellington, Fats Waller and composer Harold Arlen. Hall, a self-taught tap dancer, played in the Eubie Blake-Noble Sissle show in the early 20s, and appeared in a series of revues, including *Shuffle Along* and *Desires Of 1927*. She starred in Lew Leslie's *Blackbirds Of 1928*, in a cast which also included Bill 'Bojangles' Robinson, and Elisabeth Welch. The Dorothy Fields/Jimmy McHugh score introduced 'Diga Diga Doo', 'Doin' The New Low-Down', 'I Can't Give You Anything But Love' and a pre-Gershwin 'Porgy'. When the show transferred to the Moulin Rouge in Paris, Hall went with it, and stayed on to sing at the Lido. By this time she had married an English seaman, Bert Hicks. He opened a club for her, called La Grosse Pomme (The Big Apple), whose clientele included Django Reinhardt, Maurice Chevalier and Charles Boyer. In the early 30s she recorded with

Duke Ellington and Willy Lewis in the USA, and was also accompanied by pianists Art Tatum and Joe Turner on a New York session which produced 'This Time It's Love'. During the rest of the decade she toured extensively in the USA and Europe, and by the late 30s had settled in Britain, where she lived for over 50 years. In 1938 Hall appeared at London's Theatre Royal, Drury Lane, in *The Sun Never Sets*, a musical in which she impressed audiences and critics with her version of Vivian Ellis's title song. In the same year she recorded four songs with Fats Waller in London: 'That Old Feeling', 'I Can't Give You Anything But Love', 'Smoke Dreams' and 'You Can't Have Your Cake And Eat It'. With her husband, she opened the Florida Club in Bruton Mews, but it was destroyed during a bombing raid in World War II. Later she joined an ENSA company and was one of the first artists into Germany after the liberation. After the war she worked consistently, singing in theatres throughout the country, on cruise liners, and on her own radio show, accompanied by the Joe Loss Orchestra. In 1951 she starred in the London version of Cole Porter's *Kiss Me, Kate*, and, in the following year, sang 'A Touch Of Voodoo' and 'Kind To Animals' in Jack Gray and Hugh Martin's hit musical, *Love From Judy*, at the Saville Theatre. In 1957 she was back on Broadway, with Lena Horne, in *Jamaica*, which ran for over 500 performances. In 1963, shortly after opening a new club, the Calypso, in London's Regent Street, Adelaide's husband Bert died. During the 60s and 70s, Hall was out of the limelight, but in the 80s, came a renaissance, partly sparked by the release of Francis Ford Coppola's film *The Cotton Club*. From then on she was in constant demand for cabaret at the Ritz Hotel, and other UK venues such as the Donmar Warehouse and the King's Head, Islington. In 1988, she presented her one-woman show at New York's Carnegie Hall, and three years later, was joined onstage at London's Queen Elizabeth Hall by artists such as Larry Adler, Ralph McTell and Roy Budd, in a concert to celebrate her 90th birthday.
● ALBUMS: *That Wonderful Adelaide Hall* (1969)★★★, *Hall Of Fame* (1970)★★, *Hall Of Ellington* (1976)★★★, *There Goes That Song Again* (1980)★★★, *Live At The Riverside Studios* (1989)★★★★, *I Touched A Star* (1989)★★★, *Hall Of Memories 1927-1939* (1990)★★★, *Crooning Blackbird* (1993)★★★.

HAMLISCH, MARVIN
b. 2 June 1944, New York City, New York, USA. A pianist, arranger and conductor, who has made an indelible mark as a composer for Broadway musical shows and films, Hamlisch began as a child prodigy, and played the piano by ear at the age of five. When he was seven, he became the youngest student ever to be enrolled at the Juilliard School of Music. One of the first songs he wrote as a teenager was 'Travelin' Man', which was eventually recorded by his friend, Liza Minnelli, on her first album, *Liza, Liza*. Through Minnelli, he was able to obtain work as a rehearsal pianist and assistant vocal arranger for some Broadway shows. Lesley Gore gave him his first song hit in 1965, when she took his 'Sunshine, Lollipops And Rainbows' (lyric: Howard Liebling) into the US Top 20. After majoring in music at Queen's College, Hamlisch wrote the theme music for the 1968 film, *The Swimmer*,

and subsequently moved to Hollywood where he composed the music for two Woody Allen comedies, *Take The Money And Run* (1969) and *Bananas* (1971). He also scored two Jack Lemmon films, *The April Fools* (1969) and *Save The Tiger* (1973). In 1971, his song 'Life Is What You Make It' (lyric: Johnny Mercer), written for *Kotch*, was nominated for an Academy Award. Three years later, in April 1974, he collected an impressive total of three Oscars. For *The Way We Were*, he won Best Original Dramatic Score, and Best Title Song in conjunction with lyricists Alan And Marilyn Bergman. The third Oscar was for his adaptation of Scott Joplin's music for *The Sting*; Hamlisch's piano recording of one of the film's main themes, 'The Entertainer', sold over a million copies. In July 1975, his first Broadway musical, the revolutionary *A Chorus Line*, opened at the Shubert Theatre. Conceived and directed by Michael Bennett, the songs included 'One', 'What I Did For Love', 'Nothing', 'I Can Do That', 'Dance: Ten; Looks: Three', 'Music And The Mirror' and 'I Hope I Get It', with lyrics by the virtually unknown Edward Kleban. They complemented perfectly the poignant and agonizing story of a group of chorus dancers auditioning for an idiosyncratic director. The production was showered with honours, including New York Drama Critics and Drama Desk Awards, nine Tony Awards, and the Pulitzer Prize for Drama. The Original Cast album was estimated to have sold 1,250,000 copies by October 1983. *A Chorus Line* closed in March 1990 after an incredible run of 6,137 performances, and held the record as Broadway's longest-running show until overtaken by Andrew Lloyd Webber's *Cats* in 1997. An 'unsatisfactory' film version was made in 1985, directed by Richard Attenborough.

Hamlisch was back on Broadway in 1979 with *They're Playing Our Song*, which had a book by Neil Simon, and lyrics by Carole Bayer Sager. This two-hander, starring Robert Klein and Lucie Arnaz, about the stormy relationship between two songwriters (with three singing alter egos each), is said to have been based on Hamlisch's and Bayer Sager's own liaison. The songs included 'Fallin'', 'If He Really Knew Me', 'They're Playing Our Song', 'When You're In My Arms' and 'I Still Believe In Love'. The show played over 1,000 performances on Broadway and did well at London's Shaftesbury Theatre. Hamlisch also provided the music (with lyrics by Christopher Adler) for a production of *Jean Seberg*, which enjoyed a brief run at London's National Theatre in 1983. Three years later, he was represented on Broadway again, with *Smile* (lyrics: Howard Ashman), but it closed after only 48 performances. Film music collaborations between Hamlisch and Bayer Sager during the 70s included the Oscar-nominated 'Nobody Does It Better', from the James Bond feature, *The Spy Who Loved Me* (a US number 2 hit for Carly Simon), 'Better Than Ever' (from *Starting Over*), the theme from *Ice Castles*, 'Through The Eyes Of Love' (Academy Award nomination) and 'If You Remember Me' (from Franco Zeffirelli's *The Champ*). Hamlisch also wrote the scores for three Neil Simon film comedies, *Chapter Two*, *Seems Like Old Times* and *I Ought To Be In Pictures*; the 1981 US film version of *Pennies From Heaven* (in collaboration with veteran bandleader Billy May); and *Ordinary People*, an Academy Award-winning film in 1980. He received an ASCAP award for his score to *Three Men And A Baby*, and gained Academy Award nominations for songs written with Alan And Marilyn Bergman, 'The Last Time I Felt Like This' from *Same Time Next Year* (1978), and 'The Girl Who Used To Be Me' from *Shirley Valentine* (1989). He was also nominated for his score for the Oscar-winning film *Sophie's Choice* (1982) and, with Edward Kleban, found himself on the short list again with 'Surprise, Surprise', from the film version of their Broadway show, *A Chorus Line*. Hamlisch's film scores in the early 90s included *Frankie And Johnny* and *Missing Pieces*, which contained the song 'High Energy', written with David Zippel. Hamlisch collaborated with Zippel again, on the score for Neil Simon's *The Goodbye Girl*, which, even with Bernadette Peters in the cast, could only manage a run of 188 performances in 1993. In the same year, Hamlisch conducted the London Symphony Orchestra at the Barbican Hall in the European premiere of his 25-minute work, 'The Anatomy Of Peace'. After serving as Barbra Streisand's musical director on her 1994 comeback tour, Hamlisch worked with her again on the film *The Mirror Has Two Faces* (1996), which produced yet another Oscar-nominated number, 'I've Finally Found Someone' (with Streisand, Robert John Lange, Bryan Adams). In his other career as musical director of the Pittsburg Symphony Pops and the Baltimore Symphony Pops, he has regularly conducted around 70 concerts a year. He is due to leave the latter orchestra in June 2000 after a four-year tenure, and will create a Pops series for the National Symphony in the Kennedy Center, Washington D.C. Constantly on the lookout for another hit stage musical, Hamlisch rewrote most of the score of his 1993 flop, *The Goodbye Girl* (with lyricist Don Black), for a (brief) West End run in 1997.

● ALBUMS: *The Sting* film soundtrack (1974)★★★★, *The Entertainer* (1974)★★★★, *The Way We Were* film soundtrack (1974)★★★★, *A Chorus Line* Broadway Cast (1975)★★★★, *The Spy Who Loved Me* film soundtrack (1977)★★★, *Ice Castles* film soundtrack (1979)★★★, *They're Playing Our Song* Broadway Cast (1979)★★★, *They're Playing Our Song* London Cast (1980)★★★.

● FURTHER READING: *The Way I Was*, Marvin Hamlisch with Gerald Gardner. *The Longest Line*, Gary Stevens and Alan George.

● FILMS: Score and/or songs *The Swimmer* (1968), *Take The Money And Run* (1969), *The April Fools* (1969), *Move* (1970), *Flap* (1970), *Kotch* (1971), *Something Big* (1971), *Bananas* (1971), *The War Between Men And Women* (1972), *Fat City* (1972), *The World's Greatest Athlete* (1973), *The Way We Were* (1973), *The Sting* (1973), *Save The Tiger* (1973), 'Doc Elliot' television series (1973), *The Spy Who Loved Me* (1977), *Same Time, Next Year* (1978), *Ice Castles* (1978), *Starting Over* (1979), *Chapter Two* (1979), *Seems Like Old Times* (1980), *Ordinary People* (1980), *Gilda Live* (1980), *Pennies From Heaven* (1981), *Sophie's Choice* (1982), *I Ought To Be In Pictures* (1983), *Romantic Comedy* (1983), *D.A.R.Y.L..* (1985), *A Chorus Line* (1985), *Three Men And A Baby* (1987), *The Two Mrs. Grenvilles* television (1987), *When The Time Comes* television (1987), *Little Nikita* (1988), *Shirley Valentine* (1989), *The January Man* (1989), *The Experts* (1989), *Women And Men: Stories Of Seduction* television (1990), *Missing Pieces* (1991), *Switched At Birth* television (1991), *Frankie And Johnny* (1991), *Seasons Of The Heart* television (1994), *Open Season* (1995), *The Mirror Has Two Faces* (1996), *Fairy Tales On Ice: Alice In The Looking Glass* television (1996).

HAMMERSTEIN, OSCAR, II

b. 12 July 1895, New York City, New York, USA, d. 23 August 1960. Hammerstein was born into a family with long-standing theatrical associations. His father, William Hammerstein, was manager of New York's Victoria theatre, and an uncle, Arthur Hammerstein, was a Broadway producer. Most famous of all his ancestors was his grandfather, Oscar Hammerstein I, who had made a fortune in industry before becoming one of New York's leading theatrical impresarios and founder of the Manhattan Opera. Although he studied law, the young Oscar's background inevitably affected him and, while still at school, he wrote for shows. He was doubtless also influenced by some of his fellow students, who included future songwriters Lorenz Hart and Howard Dietz. Oscar's showbusiness career began when he was employed by his uncle as assistant stage manager. Soon afterwards, he collaborated with Otto Harbach, Frank Mandel, and composer Herbert Stothart on *Tickle Me* (1920). Subsequently, he and Harbach teamed up again to write the book and lyrics to the season's biggest hit, *Wildflower* (1923), which had music by Stothart and Vincent Youmans. Hammerstein, Harbach and Stothart then had further success, working with Rudolph Friml on *Rose-Marie* (1924), which proved to be a classic of American operetta. Two of the show's most memorable songs were 'Rose-Marie' and 'Indian Love Call'. Hammerstein and Harbach's next composing partner was Jerome Kern, and their liaison resulted in *Sunny* (1925), which had the appealing 'Sunny' and 'Who?' in its score.

In the following year, Hammerstein worked with George Gershwin on *Song Of The Flame*, and the year after that with Harbach and Sigmund Romberg on *The Desert Song*, which produced lasting successes such as 'The Desert Song' and 'One Alone'. Hammerstein teamed up again with Kern in 1927 for *Show Boat*, writing lyrics for such immortal numbers as 'Why Do I Love You?', 'Can't Help Lovin' Dat Man', 'Only Make Believe' and 'Ol' Man River'. In 1928 he rejoined Harbach and Friml to gain further acclaim with *The New Moon*, which featured 'Lover Come Back To Me' and 'Softly As In A Morning Sunrise'. He continued to work with Kern, and during the next few years their shows were full of songs that became standards, among them 'The Song Is You', 'I've Told Ev'ry Little Star' and 'All The Things You Are'.

In the early 30s Hammerstein was lured to Hollywood, where he met with only limited success. Although some of the films on which he worked were box-office failures, he nevertheless co-authored several timeless songs, including, 'When I Grow Too Old To Dream' (with Romberg) and 'I Won't Dance' (with Harbach and Kern), the latter for the 1935 Fred Astaire-Ginger Rogers film *Roberta*. Other songs written with Kern for films were 'Can I Forget You', 'The Folks Who Live On The Hill', 'I'll Take Romance' and 'The Last Time I Saw Paris', which won an Oscar in 1941. In the early 40s Hammerstein's career took a new direction, and the ups and downs of the past were forgotten with the first of a series of smash-hit Broadway shows written with a new partner. He had worked briefly with Richard Rodgers in 1928 and again in

1935, but now, with Rodgers' regular collaborator Lorenz Hart a victim of alcoholism and depression, a new partnership was formed. Rodgers and Hammerstein's first score was for *Oklahoma!* (1943), which was followed by *Carousel* (1945), *Allegro* (1947), *South Pacific* (1949), *The King And I* (1951), *Me And Juliet* (1953), *Pipe Dream* (1955), *Flower Drum Song* (1958) and *The Sound Of Music* (1959). Collectively, these shows were among the most successful in the history of the American musical theatre, with *Oklahoma!* running for 2,212 performances and winning a Pulitzer Prize - as did *South Pacific*, which ran for 1,925 performances. In addition to their stage successes, Rodgers and Hammerstein wrote the score for the film *State Fair* (1945), which included the Oscar-winning song 'It Might As Well Be Spring', and the television show *Cinderella* (1957). A brief list of songs from their stage musicals includes such well-loved hits as 'Oh, What A Beautiful Morning', 'People Will Say We're In Love', 'The Surrey With The Fringe On Top', 'If I Loved You', 'You'll Never Walk Alone', 'Some Enchanted Evening', 'Younger Than Springtime', 'Bali Ha'i', 'Hello, Young Lovers', 'Shall We Dance?', 'No Other Love' and 'Climb Ev'ry Mountain'. Between *Oklahoma!* and *Carousel*, Hammerstein wrote a new book and lyrics for Georges Bizet's opera *Carmen*. The new show, *Carmen Jones*, opened on Broadway in 1943 and was a great success. It was transferred to the screen in 1954 and, most recently, was revived in London's West End in 1991. One of Broadway's most successful lyricists, Hammerstein wrote with engaging simplicity, a trait that set him well apart from his predecessor Hart. His remarkable contribution to America's theatrical tradition was profound, and his irreproachable standards represented the culmination of the traditional, operetta-based style of musical comedy. In 1993, the 50th anniversary of Rodgers and Hammerstein's first collaboration on 'America's most loved musical' was celebrated by the publication of *OK! The Story Of Oklahoma!* and *The Rodgers And Hammerstein Birthday Book*. In addition, the revue *A Grand Night For Singing*, which was packed with their songs, played for a brief spell in New York.

● FURTHER READING: *Some Enchanted Evening: The Story Of Rodgers and Hammerstein*, J.D. Taylor. *The Rodgers And Hammerstein Story*, Stanley Green. *The Sound Of Their Music: The Story Of Rodgers And Hammerstein*, Frederick Nolan. *OK! The Story Of Oklahoma!*, Max Wilk. *Rodgers And Hammerstein Birthday Book*, compiled by Bert Fink. *The Wordsmiths: Oscar Hammerstein & Alan Jay Lerner*, Stephen Citron.

HANS CHRISTIAN ANDERSEN

This extremely popular, but critically slated, musical biopic of the legendary Danish storyteller was produced by Samuel Goldwyn in 1952. Estimates vary as to how many prospective screenplays were rejected by the producer (and the Danish authorities) before Moss Hart came up with the final draft. Eschewing all pretensions of biographical accuracy, this 'fairy tale about a great spinner of fairy tales' set in 1830, told of a simple cobbler (Danny Kaye) who falls in love with a beautiful ballerina (Jeanmaire) after he has made some shoes for her. When his love is rejected, he returns to his home-town and eventually makes a fortune from writing children's stories.

Kaye, whose renowned zany style had made him a controversial choice for the leading role, toned down the histrionics and gave a brilliant performance. He was assisted in no small part by a marvellous Frank Loesser score, much of which was inspired by Andersen's original tales. It included several endearing numbers, such as 'Thumbelina', 'No Two People', 'I'm Hans Christian Andersen', 'The King's New Clothes', 'Wonderful Copenhagen', 'Anywhere I Wander', 'The Ugly Duckling' and 'The Inchworm'. The delightful ballet sequences were choreographed by Roland Petit, who made an appearance in one of them. Also in the cast were Farley Granger, Joey Walsh, John Brown, Philip Tonge, Erik Bruhn and John Qualen. The director was Charles Vidor, and the film was beautifully photographed in Technicolor by Harry Stradling. It grossed $6 million in the USA, and went on to become one of the most celebrated film musicals of the decade. A successful stage production, entitled *Hans Andersen*, with a new book by Beverley Cross and some additional songs from Marvin Laird, was presented at the London Palladium in 1974 and 1977. It starred Tommy Steele on both occasions, and in the later production his leading lady was Sally Ann Howes. Around 20 years later, two entirely different musicals with the same theme, *Hans Christian Andersen* (music: Sebastian, book: Flemming Enevold) and *H.C. Andersen* (Tove Lind and Tommy Jervidal) premiered in Denmark.

HANSON, JOHN

b. John Stanley Watts, 31 August 1922, Oshawa, Ontario, Canada, d. 4 December 1998, Shepperton, Surrey, England. A singer, actor and producer, Watts moved to the UK with his parents in 1925 and was brought up in Dumfries, Scotland. He sang as a boy soprano in his local choir and made several broadcasts in the early 30s. When he left school he became a production engineer before making his professional debut in 1946 in *Night Of A Thousand Stars* in Birmingham. Taking his mother's maiden name of Hanson, he made his name initially on radio programmes such as *Songs From The Shows*, and appeared with the orchestras of Geraldo and Mantovani, and Troise And His Mandoliers. Hanson later became a regular on *Friday Night Is Music Night*, *Fred Hartleys' Hour* and *Ray's A Laugh*. It was Mantovani who gave Hanson his first opportunity on television and he eventually had his own series, *John Hanson Sings*, which was introduced by 'A Song Of Romance', one of his own compositions.

In 1957 he began to organize and appear in touring revivals of romantic musicals from the past. He played the Red Shadow in *The Desert Song*, and the role became indelibly associated with him. It was followed by *The Student Prince*, *The Vagabond King*, *Lilac Time*, *Rose Marie*, and *The Maid Of The Mountains*. In Britain the beat boom was well under way, but Hanson - who by then was being termed 'the last of the matinee idols' - continued to bring a glorious taste of nostalgia to eager and appreciative audiences throughout the UK. In 1965 he took the leading role in *The World Of Ivor Novello* and a year later appeared in *When You're Young* (originally known as *Smilin' Through*), for which he wrote the book, music, and lyrics. In 1967 he made his West End debut in *The Desert Song* which was

succeeded by *The Student Prince*. Both London productions transferred to Blackpool for summer seasons in 1969/70. In 1972 at the Prince of Wales Theatre he played John Carteret in his own *Smilin' Through*. Over the next few years he continued to tour in nostalgic productions such as *Lilac Time*, *Rose Marie*, *The Dancing Years*, and *Glamorous Night*. After producing and directing a farewell tour of *The Desert Song* in 1976/7, he devoted most of his time to concerts and summer seasons, and was still active until the mid-80s when he was forced to retire through ill health.

● ALBUMS: *The Student Prince-Vagabond King* (1961)★★★★, *Lilac Time-Maid Of the Mountains* (1964)★★★, *In Musical Comedy* (1964)★★★, *The Music Of Ivor Novello* (1965)★★★★, *Songs Of Romance* (1965)★★★, with Vanessa Lee *This Is London* (1966)★★★, *Encores* (1966)★★★, *When You're Young* (1966)★★★, *The Desert Song-New Moon* (1967)★★, *Rodgers And Hammerstein Favourites* (1968)★★★, *My Songs Of Love For You* (1969)★★★, *Desert Song-Student Prince* (1970)★★★, *Great Songs From Great Films* (1970)★★★, *Smilin' Through* (1972)★★★, *Lilac Time-Maid Of The Mountain* (1973)★★★, *Sings Friml Favourites* (1973)★★★, *I'll Sing You A Thousand Love Songs* (1973)★★★, *The Dancing Years-White Horse Inn* (Philips 1975)★★, *Sings 20 Showtime Greats* (K-Tel 1977)★★★.

● COMPILATIONS: *Showcase* (1968)★★★, *Favourites* (Philips 1974)★★★, *Sings Songs From His Hit Shows* (Philips 1976)★★★, *Spotlight On John Hanson* (Philips 1977)★★★.

● FURTHER READING: *Me And My Red Shadow: The Autobiography Of John Hanson*, John Hanson.

HAPPY

'A Capital Comedy With New Laughs' was how the studio publicity machine described this vehicle for the broad and British comedian Stanley Lupino when it was released by British International Pictures (BIP) in 1933. Lupino played Frank, a bandleading inventor who comes up with a device that is supposed to scream 'Police!' when his car is stolen. Initial teething troubles cause it to do nothing of the kind. Meanwhile, Frank goes to Paris with his friend George (Laddie Cliff). While there, he meets and falls in love with the beautiful blonde Lillian (Dorothy Hyson), whose father is a millionaire car insurance financier who just might be able to help Frank exploit his brilliant - if erratic - idea. After the most tortured complications, things work out well for everybody.

Scottish comedian Will Fyffe had some funny moments, especially in a scene where he tried to get a gander to lay eggs, and also in the strong supporting cast were Harry Tate, Renee Gadd, Gus McNaughton, Jimmy Godden, Bertha Belmore, and Hal Gordon. The screenplay, by Austin Melford, Frank Launder, Arthur Woods, and Stanley Lupino, was adapted from an original story by Jacques Bachrach, Alfred Hahm, and Karl Notl. Occasionally, there was a pause in the frenetic action in order to accommodate the following songs: 'There's So Much I'm Wanting To Tell You', 'Will You Dance Through Life With Me', 'There Was A Poor Musician', and 'Happy', which were all written by Noel Gay. The man who tried to make sense of it all was the director-producer Fred Zelnik.

HAPPY TIME, THE

Two years after their triumph on Broadway with *Cabaret*, John Kander and Fred Ebb returned with this very different show, which opened on 18 January 1968 at the Broadway Theatre in New York. N. Richard Nash's book, based on the novel by Robert L. Fontaine, told the warm and touching story of a French-Canadian family who find themselves in a state of flux. Jacques (Robert Goulet), an unattached, fancy-free magazine photographer, returns home for a while, and discovers that his nephew, Bibi Bonnard (Mike Rupert), is growing up fast and wants to leave his home and grandpére, (David Wayne), to get out and see the world with his uncle. In the end the boy is persuaded to stay, and Grandpa Bonnard also hangs on to the show's most convivial number, 'The Life Of The Party' ('If your festivities include a soirée/You ought to give it ease, the easiest way/Beside the caviar and chocolate soufflé/You better have me there, the life of the party'). The rest of this affectionately regarded score included 'A Certain Girl', 'The Happy Time', 'Please Stay', 'Tomorrow Morning', 'I Don't Remember You', 'Seeing Things', 'Without Me', 'St. Pierre', and '(Walking) Among My Yesterdays'. During the *The Happy Time*'s run of 286 performances, there was some difference of opinion as to choreographer-director Gower Champion's use of blown-up photographs and filmed sequences for some of the show's scenes. The Tony Awards committee was obviously impressed because they gave him two Awards, and Robert Goulet also received one for best actor.

HARBACH, OTTO

b. Otto Abels Hauerbach, 18 August 1873, Salt Lake City, Utah, USA, d. 24 January 1963, New York City, New York, USA. An important lyricist and librettist for more than 20 years, Harbach was one of the links between traditional operetta and America's indigenous musical comedy. After beginning his career as an academic, Harbach wrote for newspapers and advertising agencies in the early part of the century before collaborating with the composer Karl Hoschna on the score for the successful Broadway musical *The Three Twins* in 1908. One of the show's songs, 'Cuddle Up A Little Closer, Lovey Mine', became popular at the time for Ada Jones and Billy Murray. Harbach and Hoschna worked together on four more shows, *Madame Sherry* ('Every Little Movement'; 'The Smile She Means For Me'), *Dr. Deluxe*, *The Girl Of My Dreams*, and *The Fascinating Widow*. After Hoschna's death in 1911 Harbach collaborated with several notable composers including Oscar Hammerstein II, Rudolph Friml, Herbert Stothart, Louis Hirsch, Aladar Renyi, Alfred Newman, Vincent Youmans, William Daly, Sigmund Romberg, George Gershwin, and Jerome Kern. There are several all-time hits among his list of nearly 40 shows which included *The Firefly* ('Giannina Mia'; 'Sympathy'; 'Love Is Like A Firefly'), *High Jinks* ('Love's Own Kiss'; 'The Bubble'), *Katinka* ('My Paradise'), *You're In Love* ('I'm Only Dreaming'), *Going Up* ('Kiss Me; 'If You Look Into Her Eyes'; 'The Tickle Toe'), *Mary* ('The Love Nest'; 'Waiting'), *Tickle Me* ('If A Wish Could Make It So'), *Wildflower* ('Bambalina'; 'April Blossoms'), *Rose Marie* ('Rose Marie';

'Indian Love Call'; 'Song Of The Mounties'), *No, No, Nanette* ('I've Confessed To The Breeze'; 'No, No, Nanette'), *Sunny* ('Who'; 'D'Ya Love Me?'), *The Desert Song* ('The Desert Song'; 'The Riff Song'; 'One Alone'), *The Wild Rose* ('Brown Eyes'), *Lucky* ('The Same Old Moon'), *The Cat And The Fiddle* ('The Night Was Made For Love'; 'She Didn't Say 'Yes''; 'Try To Forget'), and *Roberta* (1933) ('Smoke Gets In Your Eyes'; 'The Touch Of Your Hand'; 'Yesterdays'). Over the years, several of them such as *The Desert Song*, *The Cat And The Fiddle*, *Roberta*, *Rose Marie*, and *No, No, Nanette*, were turned into popular films. One of Harbach's earliest shows, *Madame Sherry*, was subsequently rewritten following its original run and several popular songs by other composers were added, such as 'Put Your Arms Around Me, Honey', 'Oh! You Beautiful Doll', 'Ciribiribin', and 'Walking the Dog'. This later version was revived at the Goodspeed Opera House, Connecticut, in 1992. The acclaimed production was adapted and directed by Martin Connor who re-staged it at London's Guildhall School of Music in 1993.

HARBURG, E.Y. 'YIP'

b. Edgar Harburg, 8 April 1896, New York City, New York, USA, d. 5 March 1981, Los Angeles, California, USA. An important lyricist during the 30s and 40s, Harburg was born on New York's Lower East Side, the son of Jewish immigrant parents, and given the nickname 'Yipsel' (meaning 'squirrel'). At high school, he worked on the student newspaper with fellow pupil Ira Gershwin, before they both attended the City College of New York, where Harburg began to write light verse. After graduating in 1918, he worked for a time as a journalist in South America, before returning to New York to run his own electrical supply business. Hit by the stock market crash of 1929, he resorted to versifying, and, with composers such as Jay Gorney, Vernon Duke and Lewis Gensler, contributed songs to several Broadway revues and musicals, including *Earl Carroll's Sketch Book*, *Earl Carroll's Vanities*, *The Garrick Gaieties*, *Shoot The Works* and *Ballyhoo Of 1932*. In 1932, in the midst of the Depression, Harburg and Gorney wrote the socially significant 'Brother, Can You Spare A Dime', for the revue *Americana* (or *New Americana*). It became extremely successful on records for Bing Crosby and Rudy Vallee. *Americana* also contained several other Harburg lyrics, including 'Satan's Li'l Lamb', which marked the beginning of his long and fruitful collaboration with the composer Harold Arlen. Another of their early songs, 'It's Only A Paper Moon' (1933), was written in association with Billy Rose. In collaboration with Vernon Duke, Harburg wrote another future standard, 'April In Paris', for the Beatrice Lillie stage musical *Walk A Little Faster*; and 'I Like The Likes Of You' and 'What Is There To Say?' for the *Ziegfeld Follies* of 1934. Also in 1934, together with Arlen and Ira Gershwin, he contributed the score to *Life Begins At 8.40*, which included 'You're A Builder-Upper', 'Fun To Be Fooled', 'What Can You Say In A Love Song' and 'Let's Take A Walk Around The Block'. After that, Harburg moved to Hollywood and worked with Arlen on three Warner Brothers movie musicals: *The Singing Kid*, starring Al Jolson ('You're The Cure For What Ails Me', 'I Love To

Sing-A'), *Stage Struck* ('Fancy Meeting You', 'In Your Own Quiet Way'), and *Gold Diggers Of 1937* ('Let's Put Our Heads Together', 'Speaking Of The Weather').

Around this time, the two writers also produced one of their most memorable songs, 'When The World Was Young', which received a classic reading from Frank Sinatra nearly 20 years later on his *In The Wee Small Hours*. In 1937, Harburg and Arlen contributed the score to the Broadway musical *Hooray For What!* ('God's Country', 'Down With Love'), but they returned to Hollywood soon afterwards to work on one of the most famous and beloved films in the history of the cinema. *The Wizard Of Oz* (1939), starring Judy Garland and such beloved characters as the Tin Man, the Scarecrow, and the Cowardly Lion, was an early example of a movie in which the songs were seamlessly integrated into the plot. Harburg is also said to have made a significant contribution to the screenplay, collecting and blending several different stories together. The film included numbers such as 'Ding Dong The Witch Is Dead', 'We're Off To See The Wizard', 'If I Only Had A Brain', 'Follow The Yellow Brick Road', and the immortal, yearning, 'Over The Rainbow' for which Harburg and Arlen won an Academy Award. It was all a far cry from their next movie project, *The Marx Brothers At The Circus*, which contained the amusing 'Lydia, The Tattooed Lady' ('When her robe is unfurled, she will show you the world/If you step up, and tell-her-where/For a dime you can see Kankakee or Paree/Or Washington crossing the Delaware'). During the 40s Harburg continued to write mostly for films. These included *Babes On Broadway* ('Chin Up, Cheerio, Carry On'), *Ship Ahoy* (with Burton Lane Frank Sinatra sang 'The Last Call For Love', 'Poor You' and 'Moonlight Bay' with the Tommy Dorsey Orchestra), *Cabin In The Sky* (with Arlen, 'Happiness Is Just A Thing Called Joe'), *Thousands Cheer* (with Earl Brent, 'Let There Be Music'), *Can't Help Singing* (with Jerome Kern, starring Deanna Durbin, and songs such as 'More And More', 'Swing Your Sweetheart', 'Cal-i-for-ni-ay'), and *Hollywood Canteen* (1944, with Burton Lane, 'You Can Always Tell A Yank').Harburg teamed up with Lane again in 1947 to write the score for the Broadway musical *Finian's Rainbow*. This time, as well as the lyrics, Harburg collaborated with Fred Saidy on the book - a fantasy laced with social commentary, and a score which included memorable numbers such as 'How Are Things In Glocca Morra?', 'If This Isn't Love', 'Look To The Rainbow', 'Old Devil Moon', 'When I'm Not Near The Girl I Love', 'Something Sort Of Grandish', 'Necessity', 'When The Idle Poor Become The Idle Rich', 'That Great Come-On-And-Get-It Day', and 'The Begat'. The show ran for over 700 performances in New York, but it was 1968 before Hollywood took a chance on the whimsical piece. The film version, directed by Francis Ford Coppola, starred Fred Astaire, Petula Clark, and Tommy Steele. Harburg had always been strongly political, and in the 40s and early 50s, the time of the McCarthy witch hunts, he became even more so. His work for the stage musical *Bloomer Girl*, (1944, with Arlen), which had a Civil War background, included 'The Eagle And Me', a passionate plea for racial equality and freedom; while *Flahooley* (1951) (with Sammy Fain), took a swipe at the incon-

gruities of 'Big Business'. Among its impressive score were songs such as 'Here's To Your Ilusions', 'The Springtime Cometh', and 'He's Only Wonderful'. In *Jamaica* (1957), which starred Lena Horne, and had another Harburg/Saidy libretto, urban life was scrutinized. The Harburg/Arlen songs included 'Coconut Sweet', 'Take It Slow, Joe', 'Ain't It The Truth?', 'Push De Button' and 'Napoleon'. Harburg's last two Broadway shows, *The Happiest Girl In The World* (1961) and *Darling Of The Day* (1968), did not survive for long.

In 1962, after an absence of nearly 20 years, Harburg was invited back to Hollywood to write the songs, with Arlen, for the movie cartoon *Gay Purr-ee*. They included 'Little Drops Of Rain', 'Mewsette', and 'Paris Is A Lonely Town'. The two men also wrote the title song for *I Could Go On Singing* (1963), Judy Garland's last film. Throughout his life Harburg received many awards and citations, including the Humanity in Arts Award from Wayne State University. He died in a car crash in Los Angeles in March 1981. Four years later, a biographical revue entitled *Look To The Rainbow*, devised and directed by Canadian author and broadcaster Robert Cushman, and starring Broadway veteran Jack Gilford, played in London's West End. In 1996, an exhibition entitled 'The Necessity Of Rainbows: Lyrics by 'Yip' Harburg' at the New York Library for the Performing Arts, traced Harburg's remarkable rise from the Lower East Side to Broadway and Hollywood.

● ALBUMS: *An Evening With E.Y. 'Yip' Harburg* (Laureate (70s)★★★, *Yip Sings Harburg* (Koch 1996)★★.

● FURTHER READING: *Rhymes For The Irreverent*, E.Y. Harburg. *At This Point In Rhyme*, E.Y. Harburg. *The Making Of 'The Wizard Of Oz'*, Al Jean Harmetz. *Who Put The Rainbow In The Wizard Of Oz? Yip Harburg, Lyricist*, Harold Meyerson and Ernie Harburg.

HARD DAY'S NIGHT, A

When it was released in 1964, the first Beatles feature broke many pop film taboos. Director Richard Lester, famed for his work with the madcap Goons, brought elements of that tradition to this innovative venture. Shot in black and white with the merest whiff of kitchen-sink realism, it captured the quartet's natural humour and left their Liverpudlian accents intact. Superb support from Wilfred Brambell, as McCartney's 'grandfather', and Victor Spinetti as the harassed television producer, complement the Beatles' performances superbly. If the plot was slight, the imagery and camera work were captivating, buoyed by a slew of superior John Lennon/Paul McCartney compositions. The sequence featuring 'I Should Have Known Better', set in a train, is particularly memorable, but the entire film is a fast-moving kaleidoscope of sound and picture. 'If I Fell', 'Tell Me Why' and 'Can't Buy Me Love' encapsulate Beatlemania at its height, while the six songs completing the *A Hard Day's Night* album, not featured in the film, show its sound and scope maturing. A landmark in British cinema and pop.

HARDER THEY COME, THE

One of the pivotal music films, *The Harder They Come* played a vital role in introducing Jamaican reggae to an international audience. Filmed in 1971 and released in 1973, it has since become a cult movie, and its attendant soundtrack album proved as crucial to reggae's popularization as Bob Marley And The Wailers' *Catch A Fire*. The film starred Jimmy Cliff as Ivan O. Martin, inspired by the Jamaican legend of Vincent 'Rhygin' Martin, a real-life outlaw who hit the Jamaican headlines in 1948. Cliff is superb in his role, and, indeed, the entire film bristles with atmosphere, humour and action. However, the strengths of *The Harder They Come* are equally drawn from its sub-plot: a portrait of the island's music industry. Rivalries between different entrepreneurs, who run labels and recording studios, are pointedly encapsulated. Producer Perry Henzell, who had previously forged a career in Jamaica producing commercials, judiciously chose a soundtrack spanning five years of Jamaican music, including Toots And The Maytals, Scotty, the Slickers - whose 'Johnny Too Bad' pre-empts the film's plot - and Cliff himself.

The film's plot revolves around Martin, an aspiring singer, who, unable to shake off the 'rude boy' subculture, becomes a folk-hero through his often violent brushes with authority. Having travelled to the Kingston ghetto to inform his mother that his grandmother has died, he quickly learns the harsh reality of life in the city. He asks an apparently obliging street vendor for directions, and the man makes off with all his belongings. Penniless, he visits his mother who, unable to support him, arranges accommodation with the local clergy. He works for the minister and is asked to deliver an audio master tape of the church choir to the recording studio. At the studio he witnesses the Maytals performing 'Sweet And Dandy', and is successful in persuading the record company boss Mr. Hilton to give him an audition. He records 'The Harder They Come', but when Hilton offers him $20 he refuses to accept, confident that he can make more money with the song. His efforts in self-promotion are thwarted when the DJs advise him that Hilton has the record industry sown up. Martin reluctantly agrees to sign over his song, but Hilton decides not to promote it, fearing discord. Disillusioned with the recording industry, Martin drifts into dealing in ganja, but soon learns that this industry is also controlled by dominant forces. Martin encourages solidarity among the other dealers, who at first support his stance until they begin to feel pressure. Martin becomes a fugitive and, when exposed, he finds the informant and shoots him. Hilton realizes that Martin's notoriety could prove lucrative and promotes his song, which sails to the top of the charts. While the dealers and Hilton benefit from Martin's self-assurance, he is forced underground. The only solution is for him to catch a boat to Cuba where he can start again, but Martin misses the boat, is hunted down by the police, and is ultimately gunned down. The film also starred Carl Bradshaw and featured comedy act Ed 'Bim' Lewis and Aston 'Bam' Winter with Ken Boothe's elder sister Hyacinth Lewis (née Clover); it also included cameo appearances from Prince Buster and the Maytals. *The Harder They Come* inspired a lengthy piece in *Rolling Stone* magazine, and did much to introduce the history of reggae to the USA. The soundtrack album proved a commercial success in spite of the sensationalist liner notes. In 1996 rumours of a sequel were rife, with claims that Martin was not killed in the closing scenes, and instead serves his time and returns to Kingston in the present.

● ALBUMS: *The Harder They Come* film soundtrack (Island 1972)★★★★★.

HAREM HOLIDAY

Harem Holiday was the UK title for *Harum Scarum*, the second Elvis Presley feature of 1965. Described by one critic as 'the first of the really bad films to star the King of Rock', it confirmed how trends in pop and cinema were swiftly passing the artist by. Presley played a singing movie star who is kidnapped while touring the Middle East. He dresses up Moor style and becomes embroiled in an assassination plot. The action is poor, the backdrops lamentable and the soundtrack uniformly mediocre. Presley repaired to RCA Records' Nashville studio to complete the required 11 songs. These included the woeful 'Shake That Tambourine' and 'My Desert Serenade'. It is rumoured the entire session was completed in one day, which may explain why several of Presley's regular musicians were not employed and why the resultant album was burdened by poor sound quality. Little wonder the singer's popularity slumped during the mid-60s given the contemptuous attitude for fans from all those involved in the entire *Harem Holiday* package. Sadly, there would be worse to come in Elvis' film career.

HAREM SCARUM

Harem Scarum was the USA title of *Harem Holiday*, the second Elvis Presley feature of 1965. Described by one critic as 'the first of the really bad films to star the King of Rock', it confirmed how trends in pop and cinema were passing the artist by. Presley played a singing movie star who is kidnapped while touring the Middle East. He dresses up Moor style and becomes involved in an assassination plot. The acting is poor, the backdrops lamentable and the soundtrack uniformly mediocre. Presley repaired to RCA's Nashville studio to complete the 11 required songs which included the woeful 'Shake That Tambourine' and 'My Desert Serenade'. It is rumoured the entire session was completed in one day, which explains why several regular musicians were not employed and why the resultant album was burdened by poor sound quality. Little wonder Presley's popularity slumped during the mid-60s given the contemptuous attitude of all those involved in the entire *Harem Holiday* package.

HARNICK, SHELDON

(see Bock, Jerry)

HARRIS, PHIL

b. 16 January 1904, Linton, Indiana, USA, d. 11 August 1995, Rancho Mirage, California, USA. A highly individual singer, bandleader, actor, and comedian, as a boy Harris was taught to play a number of instruments by his father, who was a vaudeville musician. Raised in Nashville, Tennessee, he played the drums with Francis Craig's orchestra before forming his own Dixie Syncopators and performing throughout the South. While fronting various outfits on tour and at prestige venues such as the Cocoanut Grove in Los Angeles in the late 20s and early 30s, Harris created a great impression with his fine band

and slick, comedy vocals. He made his film debut in RKO's *So This Is Harris*, which won the 1932/3 Academy Award for Best Short Subject (Comedy). In 1934 he was on radio with *Let's Listen To Harris*, but his big break came two years later when he joined the popular Jack Benny radio programme as a the leader of a 25-piece orchestra. Almost immediately, he began to develop the famous image of a likeable wise-cracking, lazy, hard-drinking womaniser, which became so popular that he stayed with the programme until 1952, and also worked with Benny on television, and in films such as *Buck Benny Rides Again*. In 1941 he married the glamorous film star Alice Faye. Their marriage lasted for 54 years, until Harris's death, and they had their own radio show between 1946 and 1954. Over a period of some 20 years, from 1933, Harris made several famous recordings in that distinctive, hip Southern drawl, including 'The Dark Town Poker Club', 'Woodman, Spare That Tree', 'That's What I Like About The South', 'The Preacher And The Bear', 'Smoke! Smoke! Smoke! (That Cigarette)', 'Is It True What They Say About Dixie?', and 'Deck Of Cards'. In 1950 he had a million-seller with 'The Thing' ('I discovered a boom-boom-boom right before my eyes'), and among his other successful sides were 'What Have We Got To Lose? (Heigh-Ho Lackaway)', 'How's About It?', 'I'd Love To Take Orders From You', 'One-Zy, Two-Zy (I Love You-Zy)', 'The Old Master Painter', 'Chattanoogie Shoe Shine Boy', 'Play A Simple Melody', 'The Musicians' (with Betty Hutton, Dinah Shore, and Tony Martin), and 'Hambone' (with the Bell Sisters). During this time Harris also made further films, notably *Wabash Avenue* (with Betty Grable and Victor Mature, 1950), *The High And The Mighty* (with John Wayne, 1954), and the 1956 re-make of *Anything Goes* (with Bing Crosby and Donald O'Connor). By 1967, when Harris was concentrating more on his golf than most other pursuits, he was asked by the Walt Disney studios to provide the voice of Baloo the Bear in the animated feature *Jungle Book*. Improvising around the existing script, his hilarious performance, which included the Oscar-nominated song 'The Bare Necessities', was a major factor in the film becoming the third-highest grossing feature of the 60s in North America. He was still active in the business into the 70s, but thereafter concentrated mostly on golf commentary and the occasional personal appearances.

● ALBUMS: *You're Blasé* (RCA Victor *c*.50s)★★★, *That's What I Like About The South* (Camden 1958)★★★, *The South Shall Rise Again* (RCA Victor 1959)★★.

● FILMS: *Melody Cruise* (1933), *So This Is Harris* (1933), *Turn Off The Moon* (1937), *Man About Town* (1939), *Buck Benny Rides Again* (1940), *I Love A Bandleader* (1945), *Wabash Avenue* (1950), *Starlift* (1951), *The Wild Blue Yonder* (1951), *The High And The Mighty* (1954), *Anything Goes* (1956), *Goodbye My Lady* (1956), *The Wheeler Dealers* (1963), *The Patsy* (1964), *The Jungle Book* voice only (1967), *The Cool Ones* (1967), *The Aristocats* voice only (1970), *The Gatling Gun* voice only (1972), *Robin Hood* (1973).

HARRISON, REX

b. Reginald Carey Harrison, 5 March 1908, Huyton, England, d. 2 June 1990, Manhattan, New York, USA. A stylish and urbane actor, Harrison had a long and distinguished career in dramatic and light comedy roles both in the theatre and in films, but will probably be remembered by the public at large for his sublime portrayal of Professor Henry Higgins in one of the all-time great musicals, *My Fair Lady*. He made his stage debut in the provincial theatre in 1924, and six years later appeared in the West End and made his first film. From then on he skilfully mixed his stage commitments and movie work until 1956 when he spent two years on Broadway in *My Fair Lady*, a performance which earned him a Tony Award. He reprised the role-of-a-lifetime in London in 1958 and won an Oscar for his part in the 1964 film version. His individual spoken-style of singing was tremendously effective on numbers such as 'The Rain In Spain', 'Why Can't The English?', 'I'm an Ordinary Man', and 'I've Grown Accustomed To Her Face'. In spite of his extraordinary success with the show he made no further stage musicals, and only one other film musical, *Doctor Dolittle* (1967), which proved to be a highly expensive disaster. His many career highlights included an Order of Merit from Italy for his portrayal of Pope Julius II in Carol Reed's film *The Agony And The Ecstasy*, and the knighthood he received from Queen Elizabeth II in honour of his stage career. Only a month before his death he was starring on Broadway opposite two other old stagers, Glynis Johns and Stewart Granger, in Somerset Maugham's *The Circle*. Noel Harrison, Rex Harrison's son from his second marriage to actress Lilli Palmer, was a familiar figure on the London cabaret scene in the 50s, but is probably best-known for his 1969 UK Top 10 single 'Windmills Of Your Mind', the theme from the Steve McQueen movie *The Thomas Crown Affair*, and for his appearances in the highly popular television series *The Girl From UNCLE*. In the late 80s he toured in his new one-man show *Adieu Jacques*, based on the life and songs of the late Jacques Brel, and in 1994 he was set to achieve a lifetime ambition by appearing in the New York Gilbert And Sullivan Players production of *The Pirates Of Penzance*.

● ALBUMS: *His Favourite Songs* (1979)★★, and Original Cast recordings.

● FURTHER READING: *A Damned Serious Business: My Life In Comedy*, Rex Harrison. *Fatal Attraction: A Life Of Rex Harrison*, Alexander Walker.

HART, LORENZ
(see Rodgers, Richard)

HART, MOSS

b. 24 October 1904, New York, USA, d. 20 December 1961, Palm Springs, California, USA. A distinguished librettist, director, and playwright who was particularly renowned for his work with George S. Kaufman. Hart is reported to have written the book for the short-lived *Jonica* in 1930, but his first real Broadway musical credit came three years later when he contributed the sketches to the Irving Berlin revue *As Thousands Cheer*. Subsequent revues for which he co-wrote sketches included *The Show Is On*, *Seven Lively Arts* and *Inside USA*. During the remainder of the 30s Hart wrote the librettos for *The Great Waltz* (adapted from the operetta *Waltzes Of Vienna*), *Jubilee*, *I'd Rather Be Right* (with Kaufman) and *Sing Out The News* (which he also co-produced with Kaufman and Max Gordon). In 1941 he wrote one of his wittiest and most inventive books for *Lady In Dark*, which starred Gertrude Lawrence, and gave Danny Kaye his first chance on Broadway. Thereafter, as far as the musical theatre was concerned, apart from the occasional revue, Hart concentrated mostly on directing, and sometimes producing, shows such as Irving Berlin's *Miss Liberty*, and Alan Jay Lerner and Frederick Loewe's *My Fair Lady* and *Camelot*. He won a Tony Award for his work on *My Fair Lady*. His output for the straight theatre included *Light Up the Sky*, *The Climate Of Eden*, *Winged Victory*, and (with Kaufman) *Once In A Lifetime*, *You Can't Take It With You* (for which they both won the Pulitzer Prize) and *The Man Who Came To Dinner*. Hart also wrote the screenplays for *Hans Christian Andersen* (1952) and the 1954 remake of *A Star Is Born*, starring Judy Garland. His autobiography was filmed in 1963 with George Hamilton as Hart and Jason Robards as Kaufman.

● FURTHER READING: *Act One*, Moss Hart.

HARVEY GIRLS, THE

As the railroads opened up the Wild West in America during the 1880s, in their wake came Fred Harvey's chain of restaurants complete with their immaculate facilities and prim and proper waitresses. They are the ones who are said to have 'conquered the undeveloped territory with a beefsteak and a cup of coffee'. In this story, set in Sandrock, New Mexico, one of those winsome women, Susan Bradley (Judy Garland), gets involved with the opposition - a saloon which is owned and operated by Ned Trent (John Hodiak), and populated with some girls who are really not very nice, especially a floozy named Em (Angela Lansbury). Actually, Hodiak turns out to be all right. It is the evil Judge Sam Purvis (Preston Foster) and his mob of villains who set fire to the Harvey House in an attempt to drive the girls out of town. Susan does board the departing train, but it has not travelled far before Hodiak catches up with it, and their subsequent embrace dissolves into a wedding picture. Ray Bolger with his marvellous eccentric dancing and Virginia O'Brien with her 'dead-pan' humour, led a first-class supporting cast which included Kenny Baker, Marjorie Main, Chill Wills, Cyd Charisse, Selena Royle, and Stephen McNally. Johnny Mercer and Harry Warren's score provided Judy Garland with another of her 'travelling' songs (following soon after 'The Trolley Song' in *Meet Me In St. Louis*). This time it was a train number, 'On The Atcheson, Topeka And The Santa Fe', which won the Oscar for best song. Garland was also involved in 'In The Valley (Where The Evening Sun Goes Down)', 'Swing Your Partner Round And Round' (with Bolger and Main), and 'It's A Great Big World' (with Charisse and O'Brien). The rest of the songs included 'Oh You Kid', 'Wait And See', and 'The Train Must Be Fed'. The screenplay, by Edmund Beloin, Nathaniel Curtis, Samson Ralphaelson, James O'Hanlon, and Harry Crane, was based on Samuel Hopkins Adams' book and a story by Eleanor Griffin and William Rankin. Robert Alton staged the dances and the musical sequences were arranged by Roger Edens, a close colleague of producer Arthur Freed. *The Harvey Girls* was photographed in Technicolor by George Folsey and released by MGM in 1946. The director was George Sidney.

HAVE A HEART

Appropriately sub-titled The-Up-To-The-Minute Musical Comedy, *Have A Heart* marked the beginning of a highly significant partnership. Jerome Kern (music), Guy Bolton (book), and P.G. Wodehouse (book and lyrics), invented their own kind of witty, tuneful, and contemporary musical, far removed from the imported European operetta which ruled in America at the time. The show opened at the Liberty Theatre in New York on 11 January 1917, and only lasted for 76 performances. It's demise was due, in part at least, to the departure of the star comedian, Billy B. Van, who had been hired by Henry W. Savage (an ogre of a producer, apparently) on the condition that Wodehouse and Bolton pay half of his salary for the first three months. At the end of the period, Savage fired him! In *Have A Heart*, Van plays an elevator boy who becomes involved with a couple who decide to be radical, and elope on the eve of their divorce. He scored a big hit with 'Napoleon', and there were several other amusing and tenderly romantic songs which complemented the plot perfectly and gave audiences a foretaste of the delights to come in future shows. These included 'You Said Something' and 'I Am All Alone' (lyrics by Kern and Wodehouse), 'They all Look Alike', 'Daisy', 'The Road That Lies Before', 'Honeymoon Inn', 'Bright Lights', and 'I'm Here, Little Girl, I'm Here'. *Have A Heart* was one of 25 new musicals to open on Broadway during the 1916/7 season. *Oh, Boy!*, the next Kern-Bolton-Wodehouse effort, and the first of their renowned Princess Theatre shows, opened in February 1917 and ran for 475 performances.

HAVER, JUNE

b. June Stovenour, 10 June 1926, Rock Island, Illinois, USA. A vivacious singer and actress in several 20th Century-Fox musicals of the 40s and early 50s, who gave up her career after marrying the highly successful film actor Fred MacMurray. A talented all-round entertainer as a youngster - she is said to have played the piano with the Cincinnati Symphony Orchestra - Haver sang with dance bands before landing the part of a hat-check girl in the Alice Faye movie *The Gang's All Here* in 1943. A year later, when she co-starred with crooner Dick Haymes in *When Irish Eyes Are Smiling*, she was being tipped as the successor to Betty Grable. During the course of *Where Do We Go From Here?* (1945), she lost Fred MacMurray to Joan Leslie - but they were reunited (in real life) some years later. Before then, Haver decorated a series of period musicals - mostly set around the turn of the century - which included *The Dolly Sisters*, *Three Little Girls In Blue*, *Wake Up And Dream*, *I Wonder Who's Kissing Her Now*, *Look For The Silver Lining*, *Oh You Beautiful Doll*, *The Daughter Of Rosie O'Grady* and *I'll Get By* (1950). *The Girl Next Door* (1953), in which Haver co-starred with Dan Dailey, was her last film (and one of her best), and the only one with contemporary costumes and setting. Her decision to leave the movie business while she was still at her peak and enter The Sisters of Charity Convent at Xavier, Kansas, in February 1953, was branded by many as a publicity stunt. This conclusion seemed the more credible when she re-emerged into the outside world after only seven and a half months. However, she claimed that she 'did not have the physical strength to withstand the strain of religious life', and after meeting up with Fred MacMurray again, and marrying him in June 1954, she has not made another motion picture since. Even that union, in view of the difference in their ages (he was 45, she 28), came in for a fair amount of criticism, but they raised their twin daughters and were still together when MacMurray died in 1991 at the age of 83.

HAYMAN, RICHARD

b. 27 March 1920, Cambridge, Massachusetts, USA. As a young man, Hayman taught himself to play the harmonica and accordion, and performed in local bands before moving to the west coast. In the late 30s he worked for three years with Borrah Minevitch's Harmonica Rascals, and later played with Leo Diamond. He also appeared in vaudeville, and had several 'bit' parts in movies. In the early 40s he arranged background music for films such as *Girl Crazy* (1943), *Meet Me In St Louis* (1944) and *State Fair* (1945). In the late 40s he was arranger for Vaughan Monroe for a long spell, and in the early 50s was musical director and arranger for Bobby Wayne, providing the accompaniment on such Wayne hits as, 'Let Me In' and 'Oh Mis'rable Lover'. In 1953 he started recording for Mercury Records with his own orchestra, featuring his own harmonica solos, and others by Jerry Murad, leader of the Harmonicats. His hits included 'Ruby' (from the film, *Ruby Gentry*), 'April In Portugal', 'Limelight (Terry's Theme)', 'Eyes Of Blue' (theme from the film, *Shane*), 'The Story Of Three Loves' (the film title theme), 'Off Shore' and 'Sadie Thompson's Song' (from the Rita Hayworth movie, *Miss Sadie Thompson*). His last chart entry, in 1956, was 'A Theme From *The Threepenny Opera* (Moriat)', featuring pianist Jan August. He also made some recordings under the name of Dick Hayman And The Harmonica Sparklers. He composed several numbers such as 'Dansero', 'No Strings Attached', 'Serenade To A Lost Love', 'Carriage Trade', 'Skipping Along' and 'Valse d'Amour'. In the 80s he was reported playing piano in nightclubs around the USA.

● ALBUMS: *Reminiscing* (50s)★★★, *My Fair Lady* (50s)★★, *Two Tickets To Paris* (50s)★★★, *Around The Campfire* (50s)★★★, *Harmonica Holiday* (50s)★★★, *Love Is A Many Splendored Thing* (50s)★★★★, *Only Memories* (50s)★★★, *Let's Get Together* (50s)★★★, *Two Tickets To Rome* (1957)★★★, *Havana Hi-Fi* (1957)★★, *Great Motion Picture Themes Of Victor Young* (1958)★★★★, *Caramba!* (1959)★★, *Come With Me To Faraway Places* (1960)★★★, *The Sound Of Music* (1960)★★★, *Serenade For Love* (1960)★★★★ *Voodoo* (1960)★★★★, *Pop Concert In Sound* (1961)★★★, *Tender Moments* (1961)★★★, *Era Of Cleopatra* (1963)★★★, *Gypsy* (1964)★★★, *Hits Of The 40s* (1964)★★★★, *Songs Of Wonderful Girls* (1964)★★, *Richard Hayman* (1964)★★★.

HAYMES, DICK

b. Richard Benjamin Haymes, 13 September 1916, Buenos Aires, Argentina, d. 28 March 1980, Los Angeles, California, USA. One of the outstanding ballad singers to emerge from the swing era of the late 30s/early 40s, with a deep, warm baritone voice and a straightforward style similar to Bob Manning, another singer who was popular in the 50s. Son of a Scottish father, and an Irish mother who was a concert singer and vocal coach, Haymes was educated in several countries including France, Switzerland and the USA. After working as a radio announcer, film extra and stuntman, and taking small parts in vaudeville, he replaced Frank Sinatra in the Harry James Band in 1941 and worked briefly for Benny Goodman and Tommy Dorsey before going out as a solo act in 1943. Signed for US Decca, he had a string of hits through to 1951, including 'It Can't Be Wrong' (number 1), 'You'll Never Know' (number 1), 'Wait For Me Mary', 'Put Your Arms Around Me Honey', 'How Blue The Night', 'Laura', 'The More I See You', 'I Wish I Knew', 'Till The End Of Time', 'Love Letters', 'That's For Me', 'It's A Grand Night For Singing', 'It Might As Well Be Spring', 'How Are Thing In Glocca Morra?', 'Mamselle', 'I Wish I Didn't Love You So', 'Little White Lies', 'You Can't Be True Dear', 'It's Magic', 'Room Full Of Roses', 'Maybe It's Because', 'The Old Master Painter' and 'Count Every Star'. During this time he also recorded duets with Judy Garland, such as in 'For You, For Me, Forever More' (1947), as well as joining Bing Crosby and the Andrews Sisters in 'There's No Business Like Show Business' (1947), and Ethel Merman in 'You're Just In Love' (1951). He also had several hits with another ex-Harry James singer, Helen Forrest, which included 'Long Ago And Far Away', 'It Had To Be You', 'Together', 'I'll Buy That Dream', 'Some Sunday Morning', 'I'm Always Chasing Rainbows' and 'Oh! What It Seemed To Be'. Haymes was also successful on radio with his *Here's To Romance* and the *Autolite* shows. His first starring role in films was in *Irish Eyes Are Smiling* (1944), a musical bio-pic of composer Ernest R. Ball ('When Irish Eyes Are Smiling', 'Dear Little Boy Of Mine', 'A Little Bit Of Heaven' and 'Let The Rest Of The World Go By'). His other film musicals included *Billy Rose's Diamond Horseshoe* (1945), *State Fair* (1945), *Do You Love Me?* (1946), *The Shocking Miss Pilgrim* (1947), *Up In Central Park* and *One Touch Of Venus* (both 1948).

His career waned somewhat in the 50s, hampered by tax problems and immigration departments. He also had financial troubles over the years with some of his various wives, who included film stars Rita Hayworth and Joanne Dru, singers Edith Harper and Fran Jeffries, Errol Flynn's ex-wife Nora, and finally, model Wendy Patricia Smith. A switch from Decca to Capitol Records in 1955 produced two albums of standard ballads, *Rain Or Shine* and *Moondreams*, with arrangements by Johnny Mandel and Ian Bernard, which are generally considered to be classics of their kind. Both are now available together on one CD in the UK. During the 60s Haymes lived and worked mostly in Europe, and in 1969 made a UK album entitled *Now And Then*, a mixture of his old favourites and more contemporary material. On his return to the USA in the 70s, he undertook television and cabaret dates, and recorded *Dick Haymes Comes Home! First Stop: The Cocoanut Grove*, on which he was backed by an old name from the swing era, the Les Brown Band of Renown.

● ALBUMS: *Souvenir Album* (Decca 1949)★★★, *Christmas Songs* (Decca 1949)★★, *Dick Haymes Sings Irving Berlin* (Decca 1950)★★★, *Little Shamrocks* (Decca 1950)★★★, *Rain Or Shine*

(Capitol 1956)★★★, *Moondreams* (Capitol 1957)★★★, *Little White Lies* (Decca 1959)★★★, *Richard The Lion-Hearted* (Warwick 1961)★★★, *Dick Haymes Sings* (1964)★★, *Now And Then* (1969)★★, *Dick Haymes Comes Home! First Stop: The Cocoanut Grove* (1972)★★.

● COMPILATIONS: *The Special Magic Of Dick Haymes* (1979)★★★, *The V-Disc Years* (1979)★★★, *The Best Of Dick Haymes* (1982)★★★, *The Last Goodbye* (1983)★★★, *Great Song Stylists, Volume One* (1983)★★★, *Golden Greats* (1985)★★★, *For You, For Me, Forever More* (1994)★★★, *The Very Best Of Dick Haymes Vol 1* (Taragon 1997)★★★, *The Very Best Of Dick Haymes Vol 2* (Taragon 1997)★★.

● FILMS: *Du Barry Was A Lady* (1943), *Four Jill In A Jeep* (1944), *Irish Eyes Are Smiling* (1944), *State Fair* (1945), *Billy Rose's Diamond Horseshoe* (1945), *Do You Love Me?* (1946), *Carnival In Costa Rica* (1947), *The Shocking Miss Pilgrim* (1947), *One Touch Of Venus* (1948), *Up In Central Park* (1948), *St. Benny The Dip* (1951), *Cruisin' Down The River* (1953), *All Ashore* (1953), *Betrayed* television movie (1974).

HAYTON, LENNIE

b. 13 February 1908, New York City, New York, USA, d. 24 April 1971, Palm Springs, California. After formal musical tuition, Hayton turned to danceband work, playing piano for several leading hotel bands in the mid-to late-20s. He was also with Paul Whiteman from 1928-30, and during this period associated with many jazzmen, writing arrangements and sometimes playing piano for recording sessions with artists such as Bix Beiderbecke, Red Nichols and Joe Venuti. In the early 30s he worked on radio shows with Bing Crosby, and the famous *Lucky Strike Hit Parade*. Later in the decade he led his own band, before working for MGM as an arranger, conductor and musical director on movie musicals such as *Ziegfeld Follies*, *The Harvey Girls*, *Till The Clouds Roll By*, *The Pirate*, *On The Town*, *The Barkleys Of Broadway*, and *Singin' In The Rain*. He married Lena Horne in 1947, and thereafter served as her pianist, arranger and musical director. In 1968 he was nominated for an Oscar for his work on the Gertrude Lawrence biopic *Star!*, and two years later was co-musical director, with Lionel Newman, on the lavish *Hello, Dolly!*

HAYWORTH, RITA

b. Margarita Carmen Cansino, 17 October 1918, Brooklyn, New York, USA, d. 14 May 1987, New York, USA. An actress and dancer; one of the most popular and glamorous film stars of the 40s. In Hollywood she was dubbed 'The Love Goddess', and the pin-up picture (from the cover of *Life* magazine) of her on a bed clad only in a sheer negligee rivalled that of another Forces' favourite, Betty Grable, and was stuck on the side of the atom bomb that was dropped on Hiroshima. Hayworth started taking dancing lessons when she was six years old, and later, after the family had moved to Mexico, she formed a dance act with her father Eduardo, a well-known Spanish dancer. From the age of 16, she appeared as a dancer in several low-budget movies until she met the Texan promoter Edward C. Judson. He obtained a contract for her with Columbia Pictures and the couple were married in 1937. After appearing in several movies, including musicals such as *Music In My Heart* and *Strawberry Blonde* (with James Cagney), she made her breakthrough in 1941 when she partnered Fred Astaire in *You'll Never Get Rich*, and they were teamed again the following year for *You Were Never Lovelier*. Around this time she also co-starred with Victor Mature in *My Gal Sal*. Having broken up with Judson, she married the actor Orson Welles in 1943, and a year later made what was arguably her best musical, *Cover Girl*, with Gene Kelly. This was followed in 1945 by *Tonight And Every Night* which was set in London and was supposedly a tribute to the famous Windmill Theatre. After periods of dispute with Columbia during which she refused to make films, and two more marriages - to wealthy playboy Aly Khan and singer Dick Haymes - Hayworth made her final musical film, *Pal Joey*, with Frank Sinatra and Kim Novak, in 1957. Although only a small percentage of her more than 60 movies were musicals, several of the films in which she played dramatic roles contained some memorable musical sequences, such as 'Put The Blame On Mame' from perhaps her most famous film, *Gilda*, and the incredibly erotic 'The Heat Is On' from *Miss Sadie Thompson*. According to the experts she was always dubbed by singers such as Anita Ellis, Martha Mears, Nan Wynn and Jo Ann Greer, and it will be their voices that are heard on the album *The Rita Hayworth Collection: 20 Golden Greats*. After a fifth marriage to producer James Hill from 1958-61, Hayworth continued to make films into the 70s. During that decade her behaviour led people to believe that she was a reclusive alcoholic, and it was only in later years that her daughter, Princess Yasmin Aga Kahn, revealed that her mother had been suffering from Alzheimer's disease. In 1981 she was moved from California to New York and a court placed her in the care of Yasmin until she died in 1987.

● FURTHER READING: *Rita Hayworth: The Time, The Place, And The Woman*, John Kobal.

● FILMS: *Paddy O'Day* (1935), *Charlie Chan In Egypt* (1935), *Under The Pampas Moon* (1935), *Dante's Inferno* (1935), *Rebellion* (1936), *Meet Nero Wolfe* (1936), *A Message To Garcia* (1936), *Human Cargo* (1936), *The Shadow* (1937), *Paid To Dance* (1937), *The Game That Kills* (1937), *Girls Can Play* (1937), *Criminals Of The Air* (1937), *Trouble In Texas* (1937), *Hit The Saddle* (1937), *Old Louisiana* (1937), *Homicide Bureau* (1938), *Juvenile Court* (1938), *Convicted* (1938), *There's Always A Woman* (1938), *Who Killed Gail Preston?* (1938), *Special Inspector* (1939), *Only Angels Have Wings* (1939), *Renegade Ranger* (1939), *The Lone Wolf's Spy Hunt* (1939), *Angels Over Broadway* (1940), *The Lady In Question* (1940), *Susan And God* (1940), *Blondie On A Budget* (1940), *Music In My Heart* (1940), *You'll Never Get Rich* (1941), *Blood And Sand* (1941), *Affectionately Yours* (1941), *The Strawberry Blonde* (1941), *You Were Never Lovelier* (1942), *Tales Of Manhattan* (1942), *My Gal Sal* (1942), *Cover Girl* (1944), *Tonight And Every Night* (1945), *Gilda* (1946), *Down To Earth* (1947), *The Lovers Of Carmen* (1948), *The Lady From Shanghai* (1948), *Affair In Trinidad* (1952), *Miss Sadie Thompson* (1953), *Salome* (1953), *Pal Joey* (1957), *Fire Down Below* (1957), *They Came To Cordura* (1958), *Separate Tables* (1958), *The Story On Page One* (1959), *The Happy Thieves* (1962), *Circus World* (1964), *The Money Trap* (1966), *The Poppy Is Also A Flower* (1967), *Sons Of Satan* (1968), *The Rover* (1968), *The Road To Salina* (1970), *The Naked Zoo* (1971), *The Wrath Of God* (1972).

HEAR MY SONG

To many Britons of a certain age, that title makes them think of the 1938 song 'Hear My Song, Violetta' (Rudolph Luckesch-Othmar Klose-Harry S. Pepper), which was a big hit in the late 40s and 50s for the enormously popular Irish tenor Josef Locke. By the early 60s, after a series of disagreements with the Inland Revenue, Locke had 'retired' to Ireland where, it was revealed many years later, he started a new life as a gentleman farmer. Subsequently, a look-alike billed as Mr. X ('Is he or isn't he Josef Locke?') made a comfortable living touring the UK variety theatres singing all the familiar Locke songs. This film is set in Liverpool in the early 80s. Micky O'Neill (Adrian Dunbar) books Mr. X (William Hootkins) in an effort to boost the takings of the financially troubled night-club he manages. Although the audience are taken in by Mr. X's performance, the impostor fails to convince Locke's former lover, Cathleen Doyle (Shirley Anne Field) - especially when he tries to seduce her. Sacked from his job, Micky tracks down the real Locke (Ned Beatty) and persuades him to perform a free concert in the club. While the customers are still applauding, Locke makes his escape - Chief of Police Jim Abbott (David McCallum) captures Mr. X - and is reunited with Cathleen. Tara Fitzgerald played Nancy Doyle, Mickey's girlfriend (and Cathleen's daughter), and the remainder of a strong supporting cast included Harold Berens, James Nesbitt, John Dare, Stephen Marcus, Britta Smith, Gladys Sheehan, Gina Moxley, and comedian Norman Vaughan as himself. Ned Beatty was dubbed by operatic tenor Vernon Midgely, and Brian Hoey was the voice of Mr. X. Many of Locke's old favourites were given an airing, including 'I'll Take You Home Again Kathleen' (Thomas Westendorf), 'Come Back To Sorrento' (Ernesto De Curtis-Claude Aveling), 'Blaze Away' (Abe Holzmann), 'Goodbye' (Ralph Benatzky-Harry Graham), and, of course, 'Hear My Song, Violetta'. John Altman composed the splendid background score which was performed by his own Jazz Orchestra. Peter Chelsom directed, and co-wrote the screenplay with Adrian Dunbar. It was photographed in Fujicolor by Sue Gibson. This perfectly delightful and thoroughly enjoyable film, which became a surprise smash hit in the USA in 1991, was produced in the UK by Alison Owen-Allen.

HEARN, GEORGE

b. 18 June 1934, St. Louis, Missouri, USA. An actor and singer whose career has spanned some 30 years, Hearn started out playing mainly dramatic roles, despite having vocal training from an early age. After working in regional theatre, he made his Broadway debut in 1966 in the short-lived musical *A Time For Singing*, which was based on the famous novel *How Green Was My Valley*. In the early 70s, he played John Dickenson in *1776* on the US tour and on Broadway, and in 1979 was in the cast of Richard Rodgers's last musical, *I Remember Mama*. A year later, he and Dorothy Loudon took over the leading roles in Stephen Sondheim's *Sweeney Todd*, and Hearn subsequently won an Emmy Award for his portrayal of Sweeney in a telecast of the show. After struggling with the five-performance 'Ibsen disaster', *A Doll's House*

(1983), Hearn won the Tony Award for best actor in a musical in 1984 for his performance as the flamboyant drag queen Albin, in Jerry Herman's smash-hit *La Cage Aux Folles*. In 1985, he played Ben opposite Barbara Cook's Sally, in two highly acclaimed performances of *Follies In Concert* at the Lincoln Center, and was in the cast of Jule Styne's *Pieces Of Eight*, which folded during its try-out in Canada. He then appeared in New York City Opera productions of *Kismet* and *Casanova*, before recreating his role in *La Cage Aux Folles* for London. After returning to Broadway in the 'clumsy' stage adaptation of the legendary film musical *Meet Me In St. Louis* in 1989, Hearn moved to the West Coast for several years. He played the demon barber Sweeney yet again in the 1992 Paper Mill Playhouse revival, and in December 1993 took the role of Max von Mayerling in the Los Angeles premiere of Andrew Lloyd Webber's *Sunset Boulevard*. After the show opened on Broadway nearly a year later, Hearn won the Tony Award for Featured Actor in a musical. Since then, Hearn has featured in several pictures, and made the television movie *Annie: A Royal Adventure* (1995). His stage appearances have included one as Otto Frank, Anne's father, in the James Lapine-directed revival of Frances Goodrich and Albert Hackett's *The Diary Of Anne Frank*, which played for six months on Broadway in 1997/8.

HEARTS OF FIRE

This 1986 film may have tempted fate by casting Bob Dylan as a 'burned out' former rock star. As Billy Parker, he befriends toll-booth attendant and rock 'n' roll aspirant, Molly McGuire (played by singer Fiona). He takes her on tour with him to the UK, but she remains frustrated at her inability to write her own songs. Club owner Jack Rosner (Larry Lamb), who books Parker's band to play at his Soho club, spots her talent. Through him McGuire is introduced to James Colt (played by Rupert Everett), the current star of the UK rock scene. Parker is persuaded to stay to help while Colt produces an album with McGuire. The success of the album, and Colt's relationship with his 'discovery', causes Dylan's character to smash his hotel room and leave the country in a fit of pique. The script, by Scott Richardson and Joe Eszterhas, at this point becomes farcically contrived. While Colt and McGuire tour the USA together a fanatical blind girl points a gun at Colt before shooting herself. Colt flees to New York leaving McGuire to visit Parker at his run-down chicken farm. At her home-town performance later that evening, both Colt and Parker attend. McGuire chooses to stay in America rather than return to England with Colt, thus completing the circle. The critical response to the movie was poor, and its intention to say something profound about the music industry missed the mark completely. However, Dylan's acting was praised. Musicians used on the film included Eric Clapton and Ron Wood, while Wood, Richie Havens and Ian Dury all had small acting roles. Director Richard Marquand died shortly after the completion of the film.

HEATHCLIFF

Originally due to open in November 1994, this spectacular musical, inspired by Emily Brontë's famous romantic epic novel, *Wuthering Heights*, was postponed 'because of recording and production delays'. By the time it finally made its debut at the UK's provincial Birmingham Academy Indoor Arena nearly two years later on 16 October 1996, it had a record-breaking £8.5 million box office advance, having sold more than 340,000 tickets. The show was the brainchild of singer Cliff Richard, the most successful British chart act of all time, who was reported to have invested £2 million of his own money in it. He collaborated on the book with the production's director, Frank Dunlop, and the score was the work of composer John Farrar, a former member of Richard's original backing group, the Shadows, and lyricist Tim Rice. More than 10 years earlier, Richard had realised a long-held ambition to appear in a lavish stage musical when he was perfectly cast as a spiritual rock star in Dave Clark's ambitious *Time*, and now another of his fantasies - to play the part of Heathcliff - was coming true. The critics, who were not invited to the first night, saw it all rather differently, and no amount of mean and moody gestures, hair extensions, clenched fists, and designer stubble was going to convince them that this 56-year-old 'devout Anglican who says that he hasn't had sex for 36 years', could effectively portray 'the brooding, destructive hero - one of the greatest victims of love in English literature' - who dies when he is only 38.

Most other aspects of the show were found wanting, too, particularly the story which 'lacks momentum, tension, force, danger, sex, and much else'. It opens with Cathy's funeral, and her thwarted love affair with Heathcliff is revealed in flashback (Richard also plays the Narrator). The writers had taken some liberties with the original book, inventing an entirely new scene in which Heathcliff, having been spurned by Cathy, dons a range of exotic costumes, and embarks on extensive trips abroad in order to make his fortune (cue song: 'The Journey: India/Africa/China'). The show ends long before the novel does, with Heathcliff joining Cathy in the grave. Along the way, there were nightly gasps from the audience when Heathcliff has to slap his pregnant wife, Isabella, and there was more regular reaction to Cliff (Mr Clean) Richard's line: 'I shall be as dirty as I please, I like being dirty.' Rice's 'ponderous' lyrics and Farrar's 'department store rock music' seemed most acceptable in 'A Misunderstood Man' and bouncy 'I Do Not Love You Isabella'. The remainder of the score consisted of 'Funeral Cortege', 'The Sleep Of The Good', 'Gypsy Bundle', 'The Grange Waltz (The Seduction Of Cathy)', 'Each To His Own', 'Had To Be', 'Mrs Edgar Linton', 'When You Thought Of Me', 'Dream Tomorrow', 'Isabella', 'The Gambling Song' 'Choosing When It's Too Late', 'The Madness Of Cathy', 'Marked With Death', 'Be With Me Always', and 'The Nightmare'. With the spotlight firmly (and, perhaps, hysterically) on Richard's performance, Helen Hobson, who previously had important roles in *Chess*, *Blood Brothers*, *Aspects Of Love*, and *Passion*, hardly rated a mention for her performance as Cathy. Neither did the rest of the cast which consisted of Jimmy Johnston (Earnshaw/Hindley), Darryl Knock (Edgar), Sara Haggerty (Isabella), and Gordon Giltrap (Troubadour), also with the 'Elements' - Geoff David, Chris Holland, Sonia Jones, Niki Kitt, and Suzanne Parry. There were a few words, though, for light-

ing designer Andrew Bridge's computer projections, Brad Jeffries's choreography, Joe Vanek's production designs, and Dunlop's 'static directing style'. None of this criticism mattered, of course, because for every one who sneered at the show and found the casting of Richard as incongruous as 'Julie Andrews playing Lady Macbeth' or 'Perry Como in the role of the Antichrist', there were many thousands more who thought that 'Cliff is completely convincing . . . a real man, a real lover . . . marvellous, bloody marvellous'. Audiences continued to love every minute of the experience at large venues in Edinburgh, Manchester, and the Labatt's Apollo, Hammersmith, London (the nearest it came to the West End) from February-May 1997.

Previous attempts to musicalize Brontë's classic have included several shows which retained the original title. Two American productions of *Wuthering Heights*, one with book, music, and lyrics by Paul Dick, and the other composed by Edward Trach, were presented at small venues in New York in 1992. A European *Wuthering Heights* began life in 1991 as a concept album featuring Dave Willetts, opera diva Lesley Garrett, Bonnie Langford, Clive Carter, Sharon Campbell, and James Staddon, and subsequently had its stage premiere in The Netherlands. It was created by Bernard J. Taylor, who has also written a musical based on another literary masterpiece, Jane Austen's *Pride And Prejudice*. So far there have been no reports of Sir Cliff releasing a version of Kate Bush's haunting 'Wuthering Heights', which spent four weeks at UK number 1 in 1978.

HELLO, DOLLY! (FILM MUSICAL)

From its still-frame sepia beginning on the streets of New York (*c.*1890) through to the triumphant finalé, in which Dolly Levi (Barbra Streisand), widow, and matchmaker supreme, finally meets her own match with wealthy merchant Horace Vandergelder (Walter Matthau) in a white-walled church overlooking the lake, this was a thoroughly enjoyable film. Those who are supposed to know said that, at the age of only 27, Streisand was far too young for the role, but it did not prevent the cinema-going public from making this 1969 20th Century-Fox release one of the 10 most popular musical movies of the decade in the USA. Michael Crawford, as Cornelius Hackle, Horace's head clerk, and Danny Locklin as his assistant, were among a strong supporting cast which also included Marianne McAndrew as milliner Irene Molloy (Horace's date before Dolly decided to have him for herself), E.J. Peaker, Tommy Tune, Fritz Feld, and Joyce Ames. But it was Streisand's film, and she gloried in a marvellous Jerry Herman score which gave her such numbers as 'Just Leave Everything To Me', 'Love Is Only Love', 'Put On Your Sunday Clothes', (with Crawford, Locklin and ensemble), 'So Long, Dearie', 'Before The Parade Passes By', and the title number during which she makes her triumphant entrance into the swell Harmonia Gardens restaurant where she is greeted by none other than Louis Armstrong, who had himself enjoyed a US number 1 hit with the song some years previously. Crawford and Locklin were delightful on 'Elegance' and the tender 'It Only Takes A Moment', and when they joined forces with Matthau for the philosophical 'It Takes A Woman'. Other numbers included 'Ribbons Down My Back', 'Dancing', and 'Waiter's Gavotte'. In a production as lavish and expensive (it cost $24 million) the dance sequences were always going to be spectacular and interesting, especially with director Gene Kelly and choreographer Michael Kidd around, but the finished production was well worthwhile. Adapted from the 1964 Broadway show by producer-screenwriter Ernest Lehman, *Hello, Dolly!* was shot in De Luxe Color and Todd-AO, and won Academy Awards for several of its outstanding qualities, art-set direction, sound, and music direction.

HELLO, DOLLY! (STAGE MUSICAL)

Producer David Merrick already regarded Thornton Wilder's play, *The Matchmaker*, as a potential musical when he presented it on Broadway (in association with the Theatre Guild) during the 1955/6 season. However, it was not until nearly 10 years later, following a series of difficult out of town tryouts involving major warfare between Merrick and director-choreographer Gower Champion, that *Dolly-The Musical* made her debut at the St. James Theatre in New York on 16 January 1964. One of the few things on which Merrick and Gower did agree, was that they wanted Ethel Merman as their star, but she turned them down. Somewhat reluctantly they hired Carol Channing, and the rest, as they say, is musical theatre history. Michael Stewart wrote the book, which was set in the late 1890s. New York matchmaker Dolly Gallagher Levi (Channing) means to marry wealthy Yonkers merchant Horace Vandergelder (David Burns) herself, but until he comes around to her way of thinking she dangles no less than two decoys in his direction - an heiress, no less, and milliner Irene Molloy (Eileen Brennan). While on business in New York, Vandergelder calls on Mrs. Molloy at her shop, but leaves in disgust when he senses that there are other men around. Little does he know that those concealed young men are his long-suffering clerks, Cornelius Hackl (Nelson Reilly) and Barnaby Tucker (Jerry Dodge). They have arrived in New York from Yonkers with an awful lot of living to do. Enter Dolly again, who notices that Cornelius and Mrs. Molloy are already taken with each other, and suggests they make up a foursome with Barnaby and Mrs. Molloy's assistant, Minnie Fay (Sondra Lee), and repair to the Harmonia Gardens Restaurant for dinner. Once there, the atmosphere is electric, as word gets round that Dolly is coming back for the first time since the death of her beloved husband, Ephraim Levi. And as the room is filled with the exultant 'Hello, Dolly!', what an entrance she makes, dressed in a glittering red dress, and every gesture, every nuance of her performance is at her financial future of whom she is really rather fond - Horace Vandergelder. Faced with all this aggravation from Dolly and his disobedient clerks - even his niece, Ermengarde (Alice Playten), is there at the Harmonia Gardens - Horace hightails it back to his Yonkers Hay and Feed Store. Come the morning though, he figures a man would be a fool to let this wonderful woman get away . . . wouldn't he? A splendid set of songs accompanied all that entertaining action, and they included 'I Put My Hand In', 'It Takes A Woman', 'Put On Your Sunday Clothes', 'Ribbons Down My Back', 'Motherhood', 'Dancing', 'Before The Parade Passes By',

'Elegance', 'The Waiters' Gallop', 'It Only Takes A Moment', and 'So Long Dearie'. Although the complete score is publicly credited to Jerry Herman, it would seem that he received aid on 'Elegance' and the 'Motherhood' march from Bob Merrill, and with the idea for 'Before The Parade Passes By' from Charles Strouse and Lee Adams. Herman is also reported to have paid a settlement - estimated to be $275,000 - (without any admission of infringement) to Mack David because of the similarity of the title song for *Hello, Dolly!* to David's 1949 success, 'Sunflower'. Numerous recordings were made of 'Hello, Dolly!', with Louis Armstrong's version topping the US chart. There were also Grammy Awards for Best Song (Herman) and Best Male Vocal (Armstrong). *Hello, Dolly!* was a surefire hit right from the start, and won Tony Awards for best musical, actress (Channing), producer, director, choreographer, composer-lyricist, conductor and musical director (Shepard Coleman), sets (Oliver Smith), and costumes (Freddy Wittop). During the record-breaking 2,844-performance run, Channing was succeeded by Ginger Rogers, Martha Raye, and Betty Grable, amongst others. One of those others was Pearl Bailey, who led an all-black cast of *Dolly* into the St. James from November 1967, just when the old girl was faltering a bit. Merrick finally persuaded Merman to play the lead for around nine months in 1970, and to mark the occasion, Herman came up with some songs he had written especially for her, including 'World, Take Me Back' and 'Love, Look In My Window'. She was joined by Jack Goode (Vandergelder), Russell Nype (Cornelius), Danny Lockin (Barnaby), June Helmers (Mrs. Molloy), and Georgia Engel (Minnie).

Numerous touring productions criss-crossed several continents, and Mary Martin headed the one that arrived at London's Theatre Royal, Drury Lane, on 2 December 1965, and lasted for 794 performances. She was supported by Loring Smith (Vandergelder), Marilynn Lovell (Mrs. Molloy), Coco Ramirez (Minnie), Garrett Lewis (Cornelius), and Johnny Beecher (Barnaby), before being succeeded in May 1966 by Dora Bryan, with Bernard Spear as her Horace. Subsequent stagings have included another all-black version with Pearl Bailey and Billy Daniels (Broadway 1975), with Channing (Broadway 1978, West End 1979), and a 1984 revival at the London's Prince of Wales in which female impersonator Danny La Rue gave his/her own highly individual Dolly. Apparently he/she was still giving it occasionally in 1995. In July of the previous year, at the age of 73, Channing set out from Denver ('Dolly! Does Denver', ran one magazine headline) on yet another extensive tour which reached Broadway in October 1995. Directed by Lee Roy Reams, this revival, which was intended to recreate the show's original production values, was superbly cast with Jay Garner (Vandergelder), Cory English (Barnaby), Michael DeVries (Cornelius), Florence Lacey (Mrs. Molloy), Lori Ann Mahl (Minnie), and Christine De Vito (Ermengarde). As for its leading lady and her vintage musical vehicle, the *Denver Post* critic summed them up rather neatly: 'Channing has become a national monument, sort of like Mount Rushmore. God knows why they made it, and why they put it there. But you've got to see it at least once in your lifetime.' Ironically, the 1969 film version starred

Barbra Streisand, with Walter Matthau, Marianne McAndrew and Michael Crawford.

HELLO, FRISCO, HELLO

This typically lavish 20th Century-Fox period musical reunited the popular team of Alice Faye and John Payne in 1943 for a story which was set in the gaudy, bawdy Barbary Coast area of San Francisco. Payne has a nightspot there, and Faye is his girlfriend and singer until he loses everything following his brief marriage to the high-faluting Lynn Bari. Meanwhile, Faye goes to London where she becomes a big star before returning to help Payne reopen his establishment and resume their romantic relationship. Jack Oakie and June Havoc co-starred, and the supporting cast included Laird Cregar, George Barbier, Ward Bond, John Archer, and Esther Dale. Alice Faye introduced the only new song in the film, Harry Warren and Mack Gordon's lovely ballad, 'You'll Never Know', which went on to win an Academy Award. The rest of the ample score consisted of a mixed bag of good old familiar numbers such as 'By The Light Of The Silvery Moon' (Gus Edwards-Edgar Madden), 'Why Do They Always Pick On Me?' (Harry Von Tilzer-Stanley Murphy), 'When You Wore A Tulip' (Jack Mahoney-Percy Wenrich), 'Has Anybody Here Seen Kelly?' (Charles Moore-C.W. Murphy-William McKenna), 'Ragtime Cowboy Joe' (Lewis Muir-Grant Clarke-Maurice Abrahams), and 'Hello, Frisco, Hello' (Louis Hirsch-Gene Buck). Robert Ellis, Helen Logan and Richard Macauley wrote the screenplay, and the choreographer was Val Raset. H. Bruce Humberstone directed this pleasant and undemanding picture which, with its attractive costumes and settings, was a pleasure to look at.

HELLZAPOPPIN

This highly successful revue vehicle for the old-time vaudeville comedy team of Olsen and Johnson (Ole Olsen and Chic Johnson) opened at New York's 46th Street Theatre, on 22 September 1928, and was quickly transferred to the Winter Garden Theatre when it became obvious to the producers (i.e. Olsen and Johnson) that they had a more than substantial hit on their hands. The dynamic duo were credited with the sketches, too, which involved Barto and Mann, the Radio Rogues, Hal Sherman, and Ray Kinney, but the songs were provided by others, and included the odd opus such as 'Fuddle Dee Duddle' and 'Time To Say Aloha' by Sammy Fain and Charles Tobias, 'Abe Lincoln' by Earl Robinson and Alfred Hayes, and an interesting item entitled 'Boomps-A-Daisy', which was written by Annette Mills, and, more than 50 years later, is still a party-dance favourite when the old, and the not-so-old folks, get together. As for *Hellzapoppin*, its nightly onstage party, with its unsophisticated and deliciously decadent humour, ran on and on for a record 1,404 performances, replacing *Pins And Needles* as the longest-running Broadway musical production. Olsen and Johnson, together with Martha Raye, starred in the 1941 film version. In 1976, an attempted revised revival, with music and lyrics by Cy Coleman, Carolyn Leigh, Hank Bebe, and Bill Heyer, and starring Jerry Lewis, Lynn Redgrave, Joey Faye, and Brandon Maggart, opened in Baltimore, Maryland, but closed during its pre-Broadway tryout.

HELP!

The Beatles' second feature film was, like *A Hard Day's Night*, directed by Richard Lester. His eccentricity was still evident, but the simple plot and location scenes resulted in a finished work closer in style to classic 60s teen movies than its predecessor. This is not to deny *Help!*'s many good qualities, particularly the Beatles' unpretentious performances, superb comedic support by Victor Spinetti and Roy Kinnear and the dazzling array of original songs providing the soundtrack. 'Ticket To Ride', which accompanies antics on an Alpine ski-slope, and 'You've Got To Hide Your Love Away', set in a communal living room, are particularly memorable. The corresponding album is completed by several more superb John Lennon/Paul McCartney compositions, notably 'Yesterday', plus a handful of cover versions, including a rousing take of Larry Williams' 'Dizzy Miss Lizzy'. *Help!*'s breathtaking scope complements the film from which it takes its cue.

HENDERSON, RAY

b. Raymond Brost, 16 December 1896, Buffalo, New York, USA, d. 31 December 1970, Greenwich, Connecticut, USA. Born into a show business family, Henderson studied music but was a self-taught pianist. In 1918 he became a song promoter in New York City and spent his free time writing songs. He met with no success until 1922, when he joined lyricist Lew Brown. They had a string of popular hits with 'Georgette', 'Humming' and 'Annabelle' (all 1922). During the early and mid-20s Henderson worked with various other lyricists on what turned out to be future standards, such as 'That Old Gang Of Mine' (1923, with Billy Rose and Mort Dixon), 'Bye Bye Blackbird' (1926, with Dixon), 'Five Feet Two, Eyes Of Blue' and 'I'm Sitting On Top Of The World' (both 1925, with Sam M. Lewis and Joe Young). In 1925 he began an association with Buddy De Sylva with 'Alabamy Bound'. In the same year Brown joined them, and the three men quickly became one of the most formidable songwriting teams in the USA for their work on Broadway musicals such as *Good News*, *Hold Everything*, *Follow Through*, *Flying High*, *George White's Scandals*. They wrote 'It All Depends On You', 'Lucky Day', 'Black Bottom', 'Broken-Hearted', 'The Birth Of The Blues', 'The Best Things In Life Are Free' (which became the title of a 1956 Hollywood biopic about the trio), 'The Varsity Drag', 'You're The Cream In My Coffee' and 'Good News'. In the late 20s De Sylva, Brown and Henderson went to Hollywood, where they wrote 'Sonny Boy' overnight for Al Jolson to sing in a film that was approaching completion. Although written as a spoof, Jolson sang it straight and it became one of his greatest hits. The team then wrote the score for *Sunny Side Up* (1929), which included the title song, 'If I Had A Talking Picture Of You' and 'I'm A Dreamer Aren't We All'. Other film songs include 'Button Up Your Overcoat' and 'I Want To Be Bad'. In 1931 the partnership was dissolved, with De Sylva becoming a successful film producer. Henderson and Brown remained collaborators for further hit songs such as 'Life Is Just A Bowl Of Cherries', 'My Song' and 'The Thrill Is Gone'. In the late 30s Henderson's other collaborators included Ted Koehler, Irving Caesar and Jack Yellen. Henderson retired in the late 40s, and worked sporadically on a never-completed opera.

● COMPILATIONS: various artist *Songs Of Ray Henderson: The Best Things In Life Are Free* (Living Era 1997)★★★★.

HENEKER, DAVID

b. 31 March 1906, Southsea, Hampshire, England. An eminent composer and lyricist for the British musical theatre - but a late starter - Heneker was already in his early 50s when his first show was produced in the West End. The son of General Sir William Heneker KCB, KCMG, DSO, he was educated at Wellington College and the Royal Military College, Sandhurst, and served as a Regular Army Officer from 1925-48. After writing songs for some years, he had his first hit in 1940 with 'There Goes My Dream', which was recorded by Leslie 'Hutch' Hutchinson. Although he spent much of his time during World War II in Tunisia, Heneker continued to compose, and contributed the occasional number to revues and musicals such as *Scoop*, *Black Vanities*, and *Cockles And Champagne*. He also collaborated with Gordon Thompson and Barbara Gordon on an amusing item entitled 'The Thingummybob' ('She's the girl that makes the thing that drills the hole that holds the spring that drives the rod that turns the knob - that works the thingummybob'), which was a great favourite during the war years, particularly with the women who worked in the munitions factories. Arthur Askey also used to sing it on radio programmes such as *Workers' Playtime*. Following his release from the Army, Heneker worked at several different jobs before becoming the pianist at the Embassy Club in London's Bond Street in the 50s. Around that time he met Julian More and Monty Norman, and the trio, together with author Wolf Mankowitz, collaborated on the innovative musical *Expresso Bongo* which opened at the Saville Theatre in April 1958. Three months later, *Irma La Douce*, a saucy French import with music by Marguérite Monnot, for which Heneker, More and Norman wrote the lyrics and adapted the book, began its run of 1512 performances at the Lyric Theatre. It subsequently played for over a year on Broadway. Since then, Heneker has written the music and lyrics - mostly in association with others - for *Make Me An Offer* (1959), *Art Of Living* (1960), two smash hits, *Half A Sixpence* (1963, complete score) and *Charlie Girl* (1965), *Jorrocks* (1966, complete score), *Phil The Fluter* (1969), *Popkiss* (1972), *The Biograph Girl* (1980), and *Peg* (1982, complete score). The latter show, complete with a new book, was presented under the title of *Peg O' My Heart - The Musical* by the American Stage Festival Theatre at Milford, New Haven, USA, in June 1987. A modest and unassuming man, David Heneker's honours during his career have included an MBE, a *Plays And Players* award for *Jorrocks* (regarded as his most underrated score), and several Ivor Novello Awards, including one for Outstanding Services to British Music in 1987. He has served as both chairman and president of BASCA and is now their President of Honour. In 1996, many leading personalities from British show business, such as Vera Lynn, Marti Webb, Derek Nimmo,

Elizabeth Seal, Joss Ackland, Keith Michell, and Dora Bryan, gathered at the Theatre Museum in London to pay tribute to Heneker on the occasion of his 90th birthday.

HENSHALL, RUTHIE

b. 7 March 1967, Bromley, Kent, England. A singer, dancer, and actress, with a strong mezzo-soprano voice, in the 90s Henshall established herself as one of the brightest stars of the London musical stage. The daughter of a journalist father, and a mother who taught English and drama, Henshall's early ambition was to be a ballet dancer, but her physique was not suitable. She also failed to meet the criteria for a part in the musical, *Annie*, when she was 13, being half an inch too tall. At the age of 19, after studying at the Laine Theatre Arts drama school in Epsom, she got her first big break, winning the role of Maggie in a provincial production of *A Chorus Line*. In the late 80s, Henshall took over as Grizabella in Andrew Lloyd Webber's record-breaking *Cats*, and was in the chorus of the original London production of *Miss Saigon*, subsequently taking over the part of Ellen from Claire Moore. In 1991, her career suffered a temporary setback, although she personally emerged unscathed from the 10-week 'silly and sentimental' flop, *Children Of Eden*. In any case, it hardly mattered, as by now Henshall was on the brink of real success. After a spell in *Les Misérables* as Fantine, in 1993 she played her first leading role, opposite American Kirby Ward, in 'the new [George and Ira] Gershwin musical', *Crazy For You*. The show opened at the Prince Edward Theatre, a fact which fascinated sections of the British press, who were currently obsessed by Henshall's relationship with her 'very good friend', Prince Edward ('the prince and the showgirl'), the Queen's youngest son, whom she met when he was production assistant for Lloyd Webber's Really Useful Company. Henshall's private life provided good copy again in 1994 when she and co-star John Gordon Sinclair announced their engagement during the West End run of *She Loves Me*. The show proved to be the highlight of Henshall's career so far, and she and Sinclair, who first came to notice in the 1981 film comedy *Gregory's Girl*, won Laurence Olivier Awards for their delightful performances. Also in 1994, Henshall gave a concert of Gershwin songs at London's Royal Festival Hall, supported only by tenor Michael Strassen and six boy dancers. In January 1996 she returned from appearing with Mickey Rooney in the Toronto production of *Crazy For You*, to succeed Sally Dexter in the role of Nancy in Cameron Mackintosh's smash hit revival of *Oliver!* at the London Palladium. Later in the year, accompanied by the BBC Concert Orchestra, she recorded a radio programme consisting mostly of classic show songs as a tribute to female singers she admires, such as Barbra Streisand, Ethel Merman, and Julie Andrews. This was later released on CD, although for some reason the applause was removed. However, none of the ecstatic audience reaction was deleted from either the album or video of the lavish 10th anniversary concert performance of *Les Misérables*, which took place in October 1995 at the Royal Albert Hall. Henshall once again played Fantine, and her continual affection for that role led to her being involved in an amusing incident towards the end of 1996.

Owing to illness in the London cast, she had taken over the part again at short notice, but was also committed to switch on the *Evening Standard* Christmas tree lights in Covent Garden. Crowds at the ceremony were unaware that, shortly before Henshall made a brief appearance, she had been 'murdered' on stage during the matinee performance of *Les Misérables*, and was dashing back to reappear as a ghost in the finalé. Early in 1997, Henshall turned her back on the musical theatre, and set out on a UK concert tour. Later in the year she returned to London's Adelphi Theatre, and gave a 'killer-diller' performance as Roxie Hart in the smash hit, *Chicago*.

● ALBUMS: *Love Is Here To Stay* (Bravo/Pickwick 1994)★★★, *The Ruthie Henshall Album* (Tring 1996)★★, and Original Cast recordings.

● VIDEOS: *Les Misérables In Concert* (1996).

HENSON, LESLIE

b. 3 August 1891, Notting Hill, London, England, d. 2 December 1957, Harrow Weald, Middlesex, England. An actor, director, manager, and producer, Henson, with his bulging eyes, facial contortions ('which resembled a mandarin about to sneeze') and croaky voice, was one of the outstanding comedians in British musical comedy in the first half of the century. He attended drama school while in his teens, and toured with concert parties from around 1910. Four years later he went to New York and appeared on Broadway in the musical farce *Tonight's The Night*, and returned with it to the West End in 1915. In 1916 he scored a tremendous personal success in *Theodore And Company*, which was followed by satisfying runs in *Yes, Uncle!*, *Kissing Time*, *A Night Out*, *Sally*, *The Cabaret Girl*, *The Beauty Prize*, *Primrose*, *Tell Me More*, and *Kid Boots* (1926). Most of the shows were presented at the Winter Garden for one of London's leading producers, George Grossmith. From 1927 Henson also served as a manager, director and/or co-producer for a wide variety of shows, including those in which he appeared himself. Among the latter in the late 20s were *Lady Luck*, *Funny Face*, *Follow Through*, *Nice Goings On*, and *Lucky Break* (1934). In 1935 he and Firth Shephard took over control of the Gaiety Theatre and produced four of the comedian's biggest hit shows, *Seeing Stars*, *Swing Along*, *Going Greek*, and *Running Riot* (1938). Following the outbreak of World War II, Henson returned to the UK from a tour of South Africa and, together with Basil Deans, formed the British Forces entertainments unit ENSA (the troops called it 'Every Night Something Awful'), which set up its headquarters in the Drury Lane Theatre, recently vacated by Ivor Novello's musical, *The Dancing Years*. Throughout World War II Henson entertained troops in Europe, the Middle East, and Far East, returning to star in London revues such as *Up And Doing*, *Fine And Dandy*, and *Leslie Henson's Gaieties*. After the war, at the age of 57 he went back to musical comedy in the smash-hit *Bob's Your Uncle* (1948), and then appeared as Samuel Pepys, complete with full-bottomed wig, in *And So To Bed* (1951). His many theatrical roles left little time for films, but he did make a few, including *The Sport Of Kings* (1930), *A Warm Corner* (1934), *The Demi-Paradise* (1943), *Home And Away* (1956).

● FURTHER READING: *My Laugh Story* and *Yours Faithfully*, both by Leslie Henson.

HERBERT, VICTOR

b. 1 February 1859, Dublin, Eire, d. 26 May 1924, New York, USA. An important and influential composer during the transitional period in the early part of the century when the operetta form was overtaken by American musical comedy. Brought up in the south of England, Herbert studied classical music as a youngster. He played cello in various European symphony orchestras, all the while composing music for the concert platform. In 1885 he accepted a teaching post in Stuttgart where he married an opera singer. The following year he accompanied her on a visit to the USA where he also played, taught and studied. Among Herbert's compositions from his early days in the USA were 'An American Fantasy'. He then began writing operettas, and in 1898 one of the first of them, *The Fortune Teller*, became a great success in New York, establishing his reputation. Four years later Herbert became a US citizen. He continued writing classical music and operettas, and, over the next 20 years composed the music for some 30 Broadway shows, including *Babes In Toyland* (1903), *It Happened In Nordland* (1904), *Mlle. Modiste* (1906), *The Red Mill* (1906), *The Prima Donna* (1908), *Naughty Marietta* (1910), *Sweethearts* (1913), *Princess Pat* (1915), *Eileen* (1917), *The Velvet Lady* (1919), *Orange Blossoms* (1922), *The Dream Girl* (1924), and contributed to several editions of the *Ziegfeld Follies*. The shows contained some of the most memorable and popular songs of the day, including 'Gypsy Love', 'Tramp! Tramp! Tramp!', 'Every Day Is Ladies Day With Me', 'Eileen', 'Because You're You', 'Kiss In The Dark', 'Kiss Me Again', 'Italian Street Song', 'Neapolitan Love Song', 'Indian Summer', 'Romany Life', 'Ah, Sweet Mystery Of Life', 'Sweethearts', 'Moonbeams', 'Yesterthoughts', 'Thine Alone', and 'Rose Of The World'. His main lyricist collaborators included Rida Johnson Young, Henry Blossom, Buddy De Sylva, Harry B. Smith, Glen MacDonough, Gene Buck, and Robert Smith. Herbert also wrote musical scores for silent films (usually performed only in those motion picture theatres in main urban centres equipped to house a full orchestra) and grand operas. In February 1924 Herbert's 'A Suite For Serenades' was performed by Paul Whiteman's orchestra at a New York concert which also saw the first public performance of George Gershwin's 'Rhapsody In Blue'. The 1939 movie, the Great Victor Herbert, starred Walter Connolly, Allan Jones and Mary Martin. Herbert's prolific output was achieved despite ill health but he suffered a fatal heart attack in May 1924

● FURTHER READING: *Victor Herbert: American Music Master*, Claire Lee.

HERE WE GO ROUND THE MULBERRY BUSH

Based on Beatles' biographer Hunter Davies' novel of the same name, *Here We Go Round The Mulberry Bush* provided a very British view of sexual awakening. Barry Evans starred as the naive school-leaver determined to lose his virginity; Adrienne Posta and Judy Geeson featured as two objects of desire. Deemed daring at the time of its release

(1967), the film's modish trappings have dated badly. Its myopic view of women is largely unacceptable and the screenplay fails to recreate the angst of adolescence. Indeed, if the film has a place in British cinema history, it is as a stepping-stone between the 'Carry-On' and 'Confessions' series. Chief interest in *Here We Go Round The Mulberry Bush* centres on its soundtrack, the bulk of which was provided by the Spencer Davis Group. The quartet even make a cameo appearance as the featured group at a church dance. Paradoxically, it was another act, Traffic, formed by ex-Spencer Davis singer Steve Winwood, which enjoyed greater success through their association with the film. Their self-penned theme song provided Traffic with their third UK Top 10 hit. It remains more memorable than the film inspiring it.

HERMAN, JERRY

b. 10 July 1933, New York City, New York, USA. One of the leading composers and lyricists for the American musical theatre during the past 30 years, Herman was playing piano by the age of six under the tuition of his mother, a professional piano teacher. After high school, he started to train as a designer, but had second thoughts, and studied drama at the University of Miami. By the mid-50s he was playing piano in New York clubs and writing material for several well-known entertainers. During the late 50s and early 60s, he worked on a number of off-Broadway musical shows, the first of which was *I Feel Wonderful* (1954), and had several songs in the revue *Nightcap*, which ran for nearly a year. He also wrote the book, music and lyrics - and directed - *Parade* (1960), and in the same year contributed the opening number, 'Best Gold', to the short-lived *A To Z*. In 1961, after writing some songs for the 13-performance flop, *Madame Aphrodite*, he enjoyed his first real success with his score for the Broadway musical *Milk And Honey*, which ran for 543 performances. He had a smash hit three years later with *Hello, Dolly!* ('Before The Parade Passes By', 'It Only Takes A Moment', 'It Takes A Woman', 'Put On Your Sunday Clothes', 'Elegance'), which stayed at the St. James Theatre in New York for nearly seven years. The show - with it's Grammy-winning title number - gave Carol Channing her greatest role, and has been constantly revived ever since. In 1966, Herman had another triumph with *Mame*, which is generally considered to be his best score. Once again, there was a marvellous title song, which was accompanied by other delights such as 'If He Should Walk Into My Life', 'We Need A Little Christmas', 'Open A New Window', 'Bosom Buddies', and 'It's Today'. Since then, his infrequent, but classy scores, have included *Dear World* ('And I Was Beautiful', 'The Spring Of Next Year', 1969), *Mack And Mabel* ('I Won't Send Roses', 'When Mabel Comes In The Room', 'Movies Were Movies', 1974), *The Grand Tour* (1979), and *La Cage Aux Folles* ('Song On the Sand (La Da Da Da)', 'With You On My Arm', 'I Am What I Am'). The latter show opened in 1983, and ran for 1,176 performances in New York. Herman won a Grammy for the *Mame* cast album, and Tony Awards for his work on *Hello, Dolly!* and *La Cage Aux Folles*. There was some controversy when Herman's 'old fashioned' music and lyrics for the latter show, triumphed over Stephen Sondheim's typically contemporary score

for *Sunday In The Park With George*. Herman has been inducted into the Theatre Hall of Fame and the Songwriters Hall of Fame. The latter organization honoured him with their Johnny Mercer Award in 1987, and in 1996, he received a lifetime achievement award from the Hollywood Press Club. Herman occasionally presents an evening devoted to his own songs, and many shows have been staged in tribute to him over the years, including *Jerry's Girls*, which played on Broadway in 1986. In 1993, Herman left New York to live in Bel Air on the west coast, but denied rumours of retirement, explaining that his 10-year absence had been due to lack of inspiration: 'Nothing has come along that is fresh and interesting.' Revivals of his earlier works, with which he is usually closely involved, are constantly circulating. In the early 90s, these included US regional productions of *La Cage Aux Folles* and *Mame*, as well as a 30th anniversary international tour of *Hello, Dolly!*, complete with its original leading lady, Carol Channing, which reached Broadway in October 1995. Two months later, Herman's personal favourite of all his own shows, *Mack And Mabel*, made its West End debut. Herman's 'dry' spell finally came to an end in December 1996, when the two-hour musical, *Mrs. Santa Claus*, was transmitted on CBS television. The composer's first creative contribution to the medium, it starred the original Auntie Mame, Angela Lansbury. Among the highlights of Herman's score, were 'Almost Young', 'We Don't Go Together', 'He Needs Me', 'Avenue A', and 'Whistle'. There was no mention of his recent triple bypass and other health problems when in 1998 Herman was joined by old friends Lee Roy Reams and Florence Lacey on stage at the Booth Theatre in New York, playing and singing a mixture of his familiar, and not so well known songs, in *An Evening With Jerry Herman*. Also in 1998, another celebratory revue, *The Best Of Times*, was presented at the Bridewell and Vaudeville theatres in London. Although a generation removed from the past masters of the American musical theatre - whom he admires so much - Herman's style adheres closely to the earlier formulae and he brings to his best work a richness sadly lacking in that of many of his contemporaries.
● ALBUMS: *An Evening With Jerry Herman* (1993)★★★.
● FURTHER READING: *Showtune-A Memoir*, Jerry Herman with Marilyn Stasio.

HERRMANN, BERNARD

b. 29 June 1911, New York, USA, d. 24 December 1975, Los Angeles, USA. One of the most highly regarded composers and arrangers of background music for films, from the early 40s through to the 70s. Herrmann studied at New York University and the Juilliard School of Music, before joining CBS broadcasting in 1933. While serving as a composer conductor for radio documentaries and dramas he became associated with Orson Welles, and began his film career by scoring Welles' legendary *Citizen Kane*, for which he was nominated for an Academy Award in 1941. He did win the Oscar that year, not for *Citizen Kane*, but for his music to *All That Money Can Buy* (also known as *The Devil And Danny Webster* amongst other titles), generally thought of as among his best work. His other early scores included another Welles classic, *The Magnificent*

Ambersons, *Jane Eyre*, *Hangover Square*, *Anna And The King Of Siam*, *The Ghost And Mrs Muir*, *The Day The Earth Stood Still*, *Five Fingers*, *Beneath The 12 Mile Reef*, *King Of The Khyber Rifles*, *Garden Of Evil*, *The Egyptian* (with Alfred Newman), *The Man In The Grey Flannel Suit*, *Prince Of Players* and *The Kentuckian* (1955). Herrmann then proceeded to make several films with Alfred Hitchcock - he became known as the director's favourite movie composer. They included thrillers such as *The Man Who Knew Too Much*, *The Wrong Man*, *Vertigo*, *North By Northwest*, *Psycho* and *Marnie*. He was also a consultant on Hitchcock's sinister *The Birds*. Herrmann was 'gravely wounded' when Hitchcock rejected his score for *Torn Curtain* in favour of one by John Addison; this decision terminated their relationship.

His other dramatic scores included *A Hatful Of Rain*, *The Naked And The Dead*, *Journey To The Centre Of The Earth*, *The Three Worlds Of Gulliver*, *Mysterious Island*, *Cape Fear*, *Tender Is The Night*, *Joy In The Morning*, *Sisters*, *It's Alive*. Between 1965 and 1975, Herrmann spent much of his time based in Britain, and composed the background music for a good many European productions, such as *Jason And The Argonauts*, *Fahrenheit 451*, *The Bride Wore Black*, *Twisted Nerve*, *The Battle Of Nereveta*, *The Night Digger* and *Endless Night*. At the end of his career, as at the beginning, Herrmann was nominated for an Academy Award twice in the same year. This time, however, neither *Taxi Driver* nor *Obsession* won the Oscar for Original Score, and Herrmann died, the day after he completed recording the music for Martin Scorsese's *Taxi Driver* in 1975. The many recordings of his vast output include *Classic Fantasy Film Scores* conducted by Herrmann, *Citizen Kane - Classic Film Scores Of Bernard Herrmann* with the National Philharmonic Orchestra, and *From Citizen Kane To Taxi Driver* (1993) on which Elmer Bernstein conducts the Royal Philharmonic Orchestra. In 1992, an hour-long, analytical documentary, *Music For The Movies: Bernard Herrmann*, which included home movies, interviews, and a scene from Hitchcock's *Torn Curtain* accompanied by Herrmann's original, rejected music, was shown on US television.
● FURTHER READING: *Bernard Herrmann*, E. Johnson. *A Heart At Fire's Center: The Life And Music Of Bernard Herrmann*, Steven C. Smith.

HEY BOY! HEY GIRL!

This slight 1959 feature starred husband and wife team Keely Smith and Louis Prima. The latter was renowned as a jazz vocalist, trumpeter, composer and bandleader, whose rhythmic style provided a stepping-stone towards rock 'n' roll. After their marriage, the pair embraced Smith's MOR inclinations, enjoying residencies in Las Vegas clubs where they were backed by Sam Butera And The Witnesses. The group appeared with the couple in *Hey Boy! Hey Girl!*, in which Smith plays Dorothy Spencer, a singer who joins Prima and the Witnesses on the understanding that the band will help her with a church bazaar. The film featured such numbers as 'Autumn Leaves', 'Fever', 'When The Saints Go Marching In' and 'Lazy River', although it does not include the duo's 1959 US hit, 'That Old Black Magic'. The couple separated in 1961;

Smith later enjoyed a UK hit with 'You're Breaking My Heart' (1965), while Prima enjoyed greater acclaim by providing the voice for King Louis in the Walt Disney cartoon *The Jungle Book*.

HEY LET'S TWIST

Few imagined that when R&B troupe Hank Ballard And The Midnighters placed 'The Twist' on the b-side of 'Teardrops On Your Letter', that the song would inspire an early 60s dance craze. Chubby Checker gained the plaudits for popularizing the craze on record, but the Twist initially sprang from relative obscurity when it was showcased at Manhattan's chic club The Peppermint Lounge. The club's houseband, Joey Dee And The Starlighters, starred in this 1960 film alongside singers Jo-Ann Campbell and Teddy Randazzo. *Hey Let's Twist* offered little in the way of plot; rather it featured the venue and acts performing while clientele swivelled across the dancefloor in 'twisting' fashion. Decried at the time as 'lewd' by the moral majority, the Twist, now looks quaint and faintly ridiculous, adjectives also applicable to this film. However, Dee enjoyed brief success in the US charts with several songs from the soundtrack including the number 1 hit, 'Peppermint Twist', 'Shout', which reached number 6, and 'Hey Let's Twist', which peaked at number 20. 'Peppermint Twist' also entered the UK Top 40, inspiring a British release for the *Hey Let's Twist* soundtrack, as well as a less distinguished follow-up movie, *Two Tickets To Paris*. However, by the time this was achieved the first rumblings of Mersey Beat could be heard. The Twist and its propagators were about to be eclipsed by something of a less transitory nature.

HEYMAN, EDWARD

b. 14 March 1907, New York, USA. A prolific lyricist, whose output during the 30s and 40s included several enduring standards, Heyman studied at the University of Michigan, before collaborating with Ken Smith on 'I'll Be Reminded Of You' for the 1929 Rudy Vallee movie *The Vagabond Lover*. He had his first big hit a year later with the magnificent 'Body And Soul', written with Johnny (later John) Green, Robert Sour and Frank Eyton, which was introduced by Libby Holman in the sophisticated revue *Three's A Crowd*. Green was to compose the music for many of Heyman's songs during the early 30s, including 'Hello, My Lover, Goodbye', 'My Sweetheart 'Tis Of Thee' and 'One Second Of Sex' (all three from the 1931 stage musical *Here Goes The Bride*), 'Out Of Nowhere' (a US number 1 for Bing Crosby), 'I Cover The Waterfront', 'Weep No More My Baby' (from the 1933 stage musical *Murder At The Vanities*), 'You're Mine You', 'Easy Come, Easy Go', and 'I Wanna Be Loved' (with Billy Rose). The latter number was revived in 1950 when it became a US number 1 for the Andrews Sisters. Heyman's other songs during the 30s and 40s included 'Ho Hum' (with Dana Suesse for the Marx Brothers film *Monkey Business*), 'It's Every Girl's Ambition', 'Kinda Like You', 'Kathleen Mine', 'You're Everywhere', 'Drums In My Heart' and 'Through The Years' (all with Vincent Youmans for the 1932 stage show *Through The Years*), 'My Darling' (with Richard Myers for the 1932 *Earl Carroll Vanities*), 'My Silent Love' (with Dana Suesse), 'Blame It On My Youth' (with Oscar Levant), 'You Oughta Be In Pictures' (with Dana Suesse, sung by Jane Froman in the *Zeigfeld Follies* of 1934), 'You're One In A Million, 'Dream Kingdom' and 'Silver Sails (all three with Harden Church for the stage show *Caviar* (1934), several songs with Suesse for the 1935 film musical *Sweet Surrender*, 'Moonburn' (with Hoagy Carmichael, sung by Bing Crosby in the 1936 film *Anything Goes*), 'Boo-Hoo!' (with Carmen Lombardo and John Jacob Loeb), 'Bluebird Of Happiness' (with Harry Parr-Davis and Sandor Harmati), 'Love Letters' (with Victor Young), and 'If I Steal A Kiss' and 'What's Wrong With Me?' (both with Nacio Herb Brown), which were featured, along with others, in the Frank Sinatra-Kathryn Grayson film *The Kissing Bandit* (1948). In the 50s Heyman worked again with Victor Young on the songs for the unsuccessful Olsen and Johnson stage show *Pardon Our French* (1950). They also collaborated on the exquisite ballad 'When I Fall In Love' (1951), which is usually associated with Nat King Cole, and on 'Blue Star' (1955), the theme from the popular *Medic* television series. After that Heyman worked only occasionally, but his old songs continued to be featured in musical films such as *The Five Pennies* and *The Helen Morgan Story* (UK title: *Both Ends Of The Candle*), and in 1963 he adapted composer Mark Lawrence's theme from the movie *David And Lisa*, for 'David And Lisa's Love Song'.

HIGH BUTTON SHOES

Having established themselves as popular songwriters for Tin Pan Alley, and movies such as *Step Lively* and *Anchors Aweigh*, Sammy Cahn and Jule Styne turned to Broadway, and wrote the music and lyrics for this show which opened at the Century Theatre, on 9 October 1947. In Styne's case, it was be the beginning of a long and glorious stage career during which he composed the music for such legendary shows as *Gentlemen Prefer Blondes*, *Bells Are Ringing*, *Gypsy*, *Do Re Mi*, and *Funny Girl*. Stephen Longstreet based the book for *High Button Shoes* on his novel, *The Sisters Liked Them Handsome*, and Phil Silvers, who had appeared on Broadway in *Yokel Boy* (1939), rocketed to stardom as Harrison Floy, a small-time con-man who sells off some of his neighbours' land which turns out to be a useless swamp. He escapes with the money, and throughout the rest of the story, loses it, wins it back, and then loses it again, in a series of hair-brained schemes. Silvers was ideally cast as the accident-prone loser, and the strong supporting cast included Nanette Fabray, Jack McCauley, Joey Faye, and Helen Gallagher. Cahn and Styne's score contained several numbers that became popular hits, such as 'I Still Get Jealous', which was recorded by the Three Suns, Harry James, and Gordon MacRae; 'Papa, Won't You Dance With Me?', Doris Day, Skitch Henderson; and 'You're My Girl', which Frank Sinatra took into the US Hit Parade. Sinatra also made an appealing recording of another song from the show, 'Can't You Just See Yourself?'. The rest of the engaging score included 'There's Nothing Like A Model 'T'', 'Get Away For A Day In The Country', and 'On A Sunday By The Sea'. One of the most spectacular sequences in the show was the 'Bathing Beauty Ballet', which was choreographed by

a young Jerome Robbins who went on to a glittering future on Broadway and in Hollywood. *High Button Shoes* ran for a more than decent 727 performances in New York, and for a further 291 in London.

HIGH SOCIETY

This enjoyable musical adaptation of Philip Barry's stylish play, *The Philadephia Story*, which was filmed (without songs) in 1940 with Katharine Hepburn, Cary Grant and James Stewart, was released by MGM in 1956. Apart from some changes in characterization and locales, John Patrick's screenplay, which was set in swanky Newport, Rhode Island, stayed fairly close to the original and concerns Tracey Lord (Grace Kelly), who is set to marry an insufferable snob, George Ketteridge (John Lund), when her former husband, C.K. Dexter Haven (Bing Crosby), returns to his house next door, ostensibly to organize a jazz festival. This situation is further complicated by the arrival of Mike Connor (Frank Sinatra) and Liz Imbrie (Celeste Holm), two reporters from *Spy* magazine, which has been allowed access to the wedding because it is in possession of certain information regarding the (alleged) philandering of Tracey's father, Seth Lord (Sidney Blackmer). Louis Calhern is especially amusing as Tracey's uncle, and also in the cast were Lydia Reed, Margalo Gillmore, Richard Keene, Hugh Boswell, and jazz giant Louis Armstrong who played - who else but himself? By the end of the film Tracey comes to her senses, sends George off in a huff, and remarries Dexter. It is obvious that Mike and Liz will be making their own arrangements soon. Cole Porter's score contained several pleasing numbers such as 'High Society Calypso' (Armstrong), 'Now You Has Jazz' (Crosby-Armstrong), 'Little One' (Crosby), 'Who Wants to Be A Millionaire?' (Sinatra-Holm), 'You're Sensational' (Sinatra), 'I Love You, Samantha' (Crosby) and 'Well, Did You Evah?' (Crosby-Sinatra). Bing Crosby and Grace Kelly's record of 'True Love' made the Top 5 in both the UK and US charts, and Sinatra's version of 'Mind If I Make Love To You?' remains one of his most endearing recorded performances. The director-choreographer was Charles Walters, and, in a decade that produced a feast of film musicals, *High Society* grossed nearly six million dollars.

A 1987 UK stage adaptation of the movie, starring Trevor Eve (Dexter), Stephen Rea (Mike), Natasha Richardson (Tracey), Angela Richards (Liz), Ronald Fraser (Uncle Willie) and Robert Swales (George), had a revised book by Richard Eyre, and interpolated into the score some of Porter's other numbers, including 'Give Him The Oo-La-La', 'Hey, Good Lookin'', 'Most Gentlemen Don't Like Love' and 'In The Still Of The Night'. Another version, adapted by Carolyn Burns, dipped further into the Porter song catalogue, and toured the English provinces in 1996. A year later, an American *High Society* started out in San Francisco on its journey to Broadway, where it opened in April 1998. This staging, with Melissa Errico (Tracey), Daniel McDonald (Dexter), Stephen Bogardus (Mike), Randy Graff (Liz), Marc Kudisch (George) and John McMartin (Uncle Willie), supplemented the original film score with Porter numbers such as 'I Love Paris', 'Just One Of Those Things', 'It's All Right With Me' and 'Let's

Misbehave'. Additional lyrics were credited to Susan Birkenhead, and Arthur Kopit provided the book.

HIGH SPIRITS

Yes, it most definitely was, as the subtitle suggested, 'An Improbable Musical Comedy'. Any show in which a zany spiritualist - in this case, the infamous Mme. Arcati (Beatrice Lillie) - arranges for the spectre of a man's first wife Elvira (Tammy Grimes), to return to earth for one last lap of honour, is surely nearer to farce than *Fiddler On The Roof*. The latter show, along with *Funny Girl*, *Hello, Dolly!*, and *She Loves Me*, was the kind of opposition that *High Spirits* was up against during its Broadway run which began at the Alvin Theatre on 7 April 1964. The show was based on Noël Coward's 1941 play *Blithe Spirit*, and Coward himself directed at first, but is said to have been replaced at a later stage by Gower Champion. It was to be Coward's last connection with the New York musical theatre. Edward Woodward played Charles Condomine, the poor unfortunate earthly soul whose second marriage to Ruth (Louise Troy), is terminated when she (Ruth) is accidentally killed by wife number one in the course of trying to take her husband back with her to the 'other side'. Woodward, one of the UK's most respected actors, and a more than competent singer, would eventually achieve world-wide renown on television as *The Equalizer*, following on from his earlier small-screen break in *Callan*. The men responsible for adapting *Blithe Spirit* for the stage were Hugh Martin and Timothy Gray, and they also contributed the pretty, though unexciting score which gave Lillie some amusing moments with 'The Bicycle Song', 'Go Into Your Trance', 'Talking To You', 'Madame Arcati's Tea Party', and 'The Exorcism', while Grimes had the appealing 'Something Tells Me', 'Faster Than Sound', 'Home Sweet Heaven', and 'You'd Better Love Me', which attained some sort of popularity, and is probably better known as 'You'd Better Love Me (While You May)'. Also sung by various members of the company were 'If I Gave You', 'Was She Prettier Than I?', 'Where Is The Man That I Married?', 'The Sandwich Man', 'Forever And A Day', 'I Know Your Heart', and 'What In The World Did You Want?'. No show-stoppers there, and the reason for the production's 375 performance run was no doubt due to the presence of the redoubtable and irrepressible Beatrice Lillie in what what was to be her final Broadway show. The dances and musical numbers were staged by Danny Daniels, and he was one of the show's eight Tony Award nominations, none of which were converted. A production moved into London's Savoy Theatre on 3 November 1964, with Cicely Courtneidge (Mme. Arcati), Denis Quilley (Charles), Marti Stevens (Elvira), and Jan Waters (Ruth). Like Beatrice Lillie, Ms. Courtneidge was also bidding farewell to musical theatre audiences, in the West End at least, who had followed her glorious career for more than 50 years.

HIGH, WIDE AND HANDSOME

This film is usually mentioned in conjunction with two of the acknowledged masterpieces of the musical theatre, *Show Boat* and *Oklahoma!*. This is partly, although not solely, because Oscar Hammerstein II wrote the book (or in the case of the film, the screenplay) and lyrics for all three projects. The other common factor is that each, in its own way, succeeds in musicalizing a slice of cherished American history. In the case of *High, Wide And Handsome*, which is set in the state of Pennsylvania in the year 1859, the story concerns the efforts of a group of militants led by a crooked railway mogul (Alan Hale), to prevent a farmer (Randolph Scott) and his showgirl sweetheart (Irene Dunne) from setting up a pipeline to transport the newly discovered oil from their land to the refinery. Irene Dunne introduced two of Jerome Kern and Oscar Hammerstein's most enduring standards, 'The Folks Who Live On The Hill' and 'Can I Forget You?', and the score also included 'Will You Marry Me Tomorrow, Maria?', 'Allegheny Al', 'The Things I Want', and the spirited title song. Dorothy Lamour - just three years before she donned her sarong and joined Bob Hope and Bing Crosby on the *Road To Singapore* - was also in the cast, along with Akim Tamiroff, William Frawley, Charles Bickford, Raymond Walburn, Elizabeth Patterson, and Ben Blue. *High, Wide And Handsome*, which was choreographed by LeRoy Prinz and directed by Rouben Mamoulian, was released by Paramount in 1937. A sobering thought: neither 'The Folks Who Live On The Hill' or 'Can I Forget You?' was even nominated for an Academy Award in 1937. The Oscar for best song went to 'Sweet Leilani' from the film *Waikiki Wedding*.

HIGHER AND HIGHER

Idol of the bobby-soxers Frank Sinatra made his acting debut - as himself - in this 1944 screen version of the Broadway show, which was released by RKO in 1944. The screenplay, by Jay Dratler and Ralph Spence, stayed close to Gladys Hurlbut and Joshua Logan's original stage book in which a group of servants, headed by butler Jack Haley, plan to turn one of their number, a kitchen maid (Michele Morgan), into a debutante in order to raise money for their bankrupt boss (Leon Errol), to whom they owe so much (and vice-versa). For probably the only time in his film life, Sinatra did not get the girl - Michele preferred Haley - but he did get to sing a bunch of marvellous songs by Jimmy McHugh and Harold Adamson, including 'I Couldn't Sleep A Wink Last Night', 'This Is A Lovely Way To Spend An Evening', 'The Music Stopped', 'You're On Your Own', and 'I Saw You First'. The rest of the numbers consisted of 'It's A Most Important Affair', 'Today I'm A Debutante', 'Minuet In Boogie'; and 'Disgustingly Rich', the only song retained from Richard Rogers and Lorenz Hart's original stage score. Another fine singer, Mel Tormé, made the first of his infrequent screen appearances, and also in the sprightly cast were Victor Borge, Mary Wickes, Marcy McGuire, Elizabeth Risdon, Barbara Hale, Paul and Grace Hartman, Ivy Scott, and Dooley Wilson. Additional dialogue was provided by William Bowers and Howard Harris, and the lively dance sequences were choreographed by Ernest Matray. The producer-director was Tim Whelan.

HIRED MAN, THE

Howard Goodall's skilful adaptation of Melvyn Bragg's novel, *The Hired Man*, brought to the musical stage a powerful story of mining and farming life around the English Lake District in the early years of the century. It opened at the Astoria Theatre in London on 31 October 1984, and traced one family's domestic tribulations against the disturbing background of World War I, pit disasters and the birth of trades unionism - the plot was strong meat. Appropriately, Goodall took his musical inspiration from a powerful English tradition. His absorption of the grandeur of the choral work of Edward Elgar gave the show an impressive undercurrent, although the unique-sounding orchestral accompaniment featuring a harpsichord and trumpet, was only a five-piece unit. Sweeping along plot and characterization, the music counterpointed major national and international events even as it highlighted such domestic affairs as work in the mines, and day-to-day country life as experienced at the hiring fairs. Among the cast were Claire Burt, Paul Clarkson, Julia Hills, Gerard Doyle, Michael Mawby, Sarah Woollett, Christopher Wild, Stephen Earle, Billy Hartman, Joe Lloyd-Collatin, and Richard Walsh. The director was David Gilmore, and choreographer Anthony Van Laast. The songs included 'Song Of The Hired Men', 'Work Song', 'I Wouldn't Be The First', 'Fade Away', 'Hired Men', 'Black Rock', 'So Tell Your Children (War Song)', 'No Choir Of Angels', 'The Rehiring', 'If I Could', 'Men Of Stone (Union Song)', 'What A Fool I've Been', and 'When You Next See That Smile'. Clarkson won the Laurence Olivier Award for best actor in a musical, but despite general critical approval the Andrew Lloyd Webber production folded after 164 performances, with substantial financial losses. The show was subsequently seen off-off Broadway in 1988, and in the 90s continued to circulate in the English regional theatre, and on the London Fringe. In March 1992, the 'entire original cast', with additional orchestrations by John Owen Edwards for 10 musicians, gave a concert performance of *The Hired Man* at the Palace Theatre in London in aid of the Cancer Relief Macmillan Fund. A live recording of the occasion was later released on a 2-CD set.

HIT THE DECK (FILM MUSICAL)

Considering the wealth of talent on board, this 1955 screen adaptation of the 1927 Broadway musical proved to be a pretty disappointing affair, mainly owing to a lack-lustre screenplay by Sonya Levien and William Ludwig. It told the by now familiar story of three off-duty sailors, (Tony Martin, Russ Tamblyn and Vic Damone) and their search for three lovely gals (Ann Miller, Debbie Reynolds and Jane Powell) with whom to embark on the voyage of life. Fortunately, there were plenty of musical highlights in composer Vincent Youmans' score, such as the lovely 'More Than You Know' (Tony Martin) (lyric: Billy Rose-Edward Eliscu), 'Sometimes I'm Happy' (Vic Damone-Jane Powell) (lyric: Clifford Grey-Irving Caesar), 'Hallelujah' (Martin-Tamblyn-Damone) (lyric: Grey-Leo Robin), 'I Know that You Know' (Damone-Powell) (lyric: Anne Caldwell), and 'Keepin' Myself For You' (Martin-Ann Miller) (lyric: Sidney Clare). The other songs included 'Join The Navy', 'Why, Oh Why', and 'Lucky Bird' (all with lyrics by Robin and Grey), and 'Lady From The Bayou' and 'A Kiss Or Two' (lyrics: Robin), and 'Ciribiribin' (Albert Pestalozza). Hermes Pan staged the dance sequences with his usual imagination and flair (especially in the sequences which involved Ann Miller) and Roy Rowland directed a cast which also included Walter Pidgeon, Kay Armen, Gene Raymond, J Carrol Naish, and Allan King. *Hit The Deck* was photographed in Eastman Color and Cinemascope, and produced for MGM by Joe Pasternak. Hubert Osborne's play *Shore Leave*, which was the basis for this film and the original Broadway musical, had been filmed before in 1930 with Jack Oakie, Polly Walker and Roger Gray.

HIT THE DECK (STAGE MUSICAL)

Herbert Fields's book for this 'Nautical Musical Comedy' was based on the 1922 play, *Shore Leave*, by Hubert Osborne. With music by Vincent Youmans, and lyrics by Clifford Grey and Leo Robin, it began the 'stage phase' of its existence on 25 April 1927 at the Belasco theatre in New York, and stayed around for 352 performances. Field's story turned out to be yet another reworking of that familiar musical comedy saga of a boy (or girl) discovering that his (or her) beloved is blessed with a big bundle of cash. The marriage is always immediately called off - true happiness, they always agree, is based on love, and not lucre. Of course, they also invariably have second thoughts. Looloo Martin (Louise Groody) owns a coffee shop in Newport, Rhode Island, USA, and a lot of her customers are sailors. She is completely besotted by one of them, Bilge Smith (Charles King), and, in an effort to tie the marriage knot, is perfectly prepared to follow him to the ends of the earth - in Bilge's case that means China. Even out there, the sailor is reluctant to restrict himself to just one girl (Looloo) in one port (Rhode Island), particularly when he finds out that Looloo is wealthy. Matters are resolved when the lady agrees to assuage his pride and assign all the money to their first offspring. Youmans' songs with Grey and Robin included 'Join The Navy', 'Loo-Loo', 'Harbour Of My Heart', 'Why, Oh Why?', 'Lucky Bird', and 'Hallelujah!' which became something of a hit through recordings by Nat Shilkret, the Revelers, and Cass Hagen. Another of Youmans' numbers for the show, 'Sometimes I'm Happy' (with a lyric by Irving Caesar), also became popular at the time via Roger Wolfe Kahn, and a recording by two members of the original cast, Louise Groody and Charles King. The song, which was not at all like the smart, sophisticated material that Cole Porter, for instance, was writing at the time, had a charming, artless lyric: 'Sometimes I'm happy, sometimes I'm blue/My disposition, depends on you/I'll never mind the rain from the sky/If I can see the sun in your eye'. It endured, and was included, along with 'Hallelujah', in the 1930 and 1955 screen versions of the show, but omitted from the 1936 film, *Follow The Fleet* (which was also based on the original concept), in favour of an Irving Berlin score. The 1927 London stage production, which starred Stanley Holloway and Ivy Tresmand, used more or less the same songs, and ran for 277 performances.

HOCKRIDGE, EDMUND

b. 9 August 1923, Vancouver, British Columbia, Canada. One of the UK's most popular leading men in the imported US musicals of the 50s, with rugged looks, a sure manner, and a big, strong, baritone voice. Hockridge first visited the UK in 1941 with the Royal Canadian Air Force, and helped set up the Allied Expeditionary Forces Network which supplied entertainment and news for troops in Europe. He also sang on many of the broadcasts, several of them with fellow Canadian Robert Farnon who was leader of the Canadian Allied Expeditionary Force Band. After the war, he featured in his own coast-to-coast show for the CBC, playing leading roles in operas such as *La Bohème*, *Don Giovanni* and Gilbert And Sullivan operettas. After seeing some Broadway musical shows, such as *Brigadoon* and *Carousel*, on a visit to New York, he decided that there was more of a future for him in that direction. That was certainly the case, for on his return to the UK in 1951, he replaced Stephen Douglass as Billy Bigelow in *Carousel* at the Drury Lane Theatre, London, and, when the run ended, took over from Jerry Wayne as Sky Masterson in *Guys And Dolls* at the Coliseum. He stayed at that theatre for two more shows, playing Judge Aristide Forestier in *Can-Can* and Sid Sorokin in *The Pajama Game*. A song from *The Pajama Game*, 'Hey There', gave him one of his biggest record hits. His other 50s singles included 'Young And Foolish', 'No Other Love', 'The Fountains Of Rome', 'Sixteen Tons', 'The Man From Laramie', 'A Woman In Love', 'More Than Ever' and 'Tonight'. Extremely popular in theatres and on television, he played a six-month season at the London Palladium, appeared in six Royal Command Performances, and was Canada's representative in the Westminster Abbey Choir at the Queen's Coronation in 1953. He headlined the cabaret on the liner QE2's maiden voyage, and toured Europe extensively, both in revivals of musicals, and his own one-man show, which contained over 30 songs.

In the early 80s he toured the UK with successful revivals of *The Sound Of Music* and *South Pacific*, before returning to Canada in 1984 for a concert tour with Robert Farnon and the Vancouver Symphony Orchestra. In 1986, 35 years after he strode onto the Drury Lane stage as young, arrogant Billy Bigelow, he played the part of senior citizen, Buffalo Bill, in a major London revival of *Annie Get Your Gun*, with pop star, Suzi Quatro, in the role of Annie. In the early 90s, Hockridge toured regularly with *The Edmund Hockridge Family*, being joined onstage by his wife, Jackie, and their two sons, Murray and Stephen.

● ALBUMS: *Edmund Hockridge Sings* (Pye 1957)★★★, *In Romantic Mood* (Pye 1957)★★★, *Hooray For Love* (Pye 1958)★★★, *Hockridge Meets Hammond* (1975)★★★, *Make It Easy On Yourself* (1984)★★★, *Sings Hits From Various Musicals* (1985)★★★★, with Jackie Hockridge *Sings Favourites Of Yours* (1991)★★★.

HODGES, EDDIE

b. 5 March 1947, Hattiesburg, Mississippi, USA. In the mid-50s child star Hodges appeared in television programmes *The Jackie Gleason Show* and *Name That Tune* and was seen on Broadway 405 times in the hit musical *The Music Man*. In 1959 he starred alongside Frank Sinatra and Edward G. Robinson in the film *A Hole In The Head* and can be heard on Sinatra's hit from the film, 'High Hopes'. He also had a major role in the film of *Huckleberry Finn*, starred with Hayley Mills in *Summer Magic* and even had his own television show, *The Secret World Of Eddie*

Hodges. His youthful revival of the Isley Brothers' 'I'm Gonna Knock On Your Door' on Cadence, not only took him into the US Top 20 in 1961 but also gave the 14-year-old an Australian and Canadian chart-topper and a small UK hit. He returned to the US Top 20 with an endearing song written by Phil Everly, '(Girls, Girls, Girls) Made To Love' in 1962. He had releases on Columbia in 1963 and MGM in 1964 before 'New Orleans' on Aurora in 1965 gave him his last US chart entry. It seems that, for Hodges, maturity brought a halt to his recording career.

HOLD EVERYTHING!

College football having proved to be a winning formula for De Sylva, Brown And Henderson in their *Good News!* (1927), two years later they placed their collective fingers firmly on the pulse of the New York theatre-going public, and deduced - quite rightly - that the noble art of boxing would be good for a few rounds as the subject matter for another amusing musical comedy. The result, *Hold Everything!*, opened at the Broadhurst Theatre on 10 October 1929, with a book by De Sylva and John McGowan in which 'Sonny Jim' Brooks (Jack Wilding), a welterweight contender, is temporarily estranged from his girlfriend, Sue Burke (Ona Munson), when she discovers that he is being coached in various aspects of his technique by the young and extremely sociable Norine Lloyd (Betty Compton). Sue may be down, but she is not out, and when she is bad-mouthed by his opponent, the reigning champ, 'Sonny Jim' bounces off the ropes, clinches the title, and signs her to a long-term contract. Much of the show's humour was provided by Victor Moore and Bert Lahr, who made a big impact in the role of Gink Schiner, a punch-drunk fighter who rather carelessly floors himself instead of his opponent. As usual, De Sylva, Brown And Henderson's lively, carefree songs fitted the action like a glove. They included 'To Know You Is To Love You', 'Don't Hold Everything', 'Too Good To Be True', and one of the songwriters' all-time big ones, the zippy 'You're The Cream In My Coffee', which became popular for a great many artists and bands, particularly Ben Selvin, Ted Weems, and Ruth Etting. It all added up to a lot of fun, and America would soon be in need of a lot more of that particular commodity - the Wall Street Crash and the Depression were just around the corner. With the Roaring 20s rapidly running out of steam, *Hold Everything!* held on for 413 performances in New York, and added another 173 to that total in London. The 1930 film version, which starred Joe E. Brown, was considered to one of the best of the early talkie comedies.

HOLD MY HAND

Another in the series of comedy musicals starring the popular British funny-man Stanley Lupino. This one, which was released by the Associated British Picture Corporation in 1938, cast Lupino as Eddie Marston, a soft-hearted gentleman who secretly finances a newspaper which is run by his dependant, Paula (Polly Ward), who thinks he is after the profits. Further farcical complications ensue when Eddie's fiancée, Helen (Sally Gray), falls in love with Pop Currie (Jack Melford) the paper's editor; his friend Bob Crane (John Wood) is attracted by Polly;

and his secretary, Jane (Barbara Blair) find it difficult to keep her hands off him! While all this is going on, Eddie gets involved in a bizarre cat burglary with Lord Milchester (Fred Emney), and the others joining in the fun and games included Bertha Belmore (as Lady Milchester), Syd Walker, Arthur Rigby, and Gibb McLaughlin. Polly Ward and John Wood handled most of the songs which included 'Turn On The Love-light', 'As Long As I Can Look At You', and 'Hold My Hand'. Clifford Grey, Bert Lee, William Freshman, adapted the screenplay from Stanley Lupino's original story. American Thornton Freeland, a leading exponent of this zany kind of musical entertainment in the US and UK, directed with flair.

HOLD ON!

The first of two films starring Herman's Hermits, this 1966 feature was funded and shot in the US where the group enjoyed considerable popularity. The plot was risible - an employee of NASA follows the quintet on tour to decide whether or not they merit having a space-ship named after them. The soundtrack was equally anodyne, featuring a version of the George Formby standard 'Leaning On A Lampost'. Herman's Hermits' interpretation reached number 9 in the US, but the single was not issued in the UK. *Hold On!* co-starred singer Shelley Fabares, who at that point was married to Lou Adler, owner of Dunhill Records. One of the label's major talents, P.F. Sloan, co-composed several songs featured on film, including 'Where Were You When I Needed You?' and 'A Must To Avoid'. The latter was a Top 10 hit in the US and UK.

HOLIDAY INN

The cinema's favourite (male) singer and dancer of the 30s and 40s, Bing Crosby and Fred Astaire, co-starred for the first time in this Paramount release of 1942. Irving Berlin contributed a wonderful score, and he is also credited with the original idea for what turned out be a novel story, which was adapted for the screen by the distinguished playwright, Elmer Rice. Claude Binyon's screenplay concerned a couple of song and dance men, Jim Hardy (Crosby) and Ted Hanover (Astaire), who were doing all right before Jim gets tired of the nightly grind and takes up farming. That proves a little too taxing too, so he turns a large New England farmhouse into a night club that will only be open on holidays. The Holiday Inn has it's gala opening on New Year's Eve, and proves to be a tremendous success. Berlin celebrated that holiday by writing 'Let's Start The New Year Right', and each of the other seven important annual American vacations, such as Lincoln's Birthday and Valentine's Day, was allocated it's own song, with the Fourth of July getting two. Two of the numbers, 'Lazy' and 'Easter Parade', had been used before in other productions, but the rest of the score was new, and included 'I'll Capture Your Heart Singing', 'You're Easy To Dance With', 'Happy Holiday', 'Holiday Inn', 'Abraham', 'Be Careful, It's My Heart', 'I Can't Tell A Lie', 'Let's Say It With Firecrackers' (an explosive Astaire solo dance), 'Song Of Freedom', 'Plenty To Be Thankful For', and 'White Christmas'. The latter song won an Academy Award, was inducted into the NARAS Hall of

Fame, and went on to become an enduring Christmas favourite. Crosby's recording is reputed to have sold in excess of 30 million copies. In the film, he and Astaire were perfect together - each with his own relaxed and easygoing style, and a mutual flair for comedy. Their characters, Jim and Ted, clash for a while - over a girl, naturally - but eventually Jim finds happiness with Linda (Marjorie Reynolds), and Ted settles for Lila (Virginia Dale). Also in the cast were Bing's brother Bob and his Bobcats, and Harry Barris, a former member, with Bing and Al Rinker, of the famous Rhythm Boys. The dance director was Danny Dare, and *Holiday Inn*, which took nearly $4 million at the US box-office, was produced and directed by Mark Sandrich, who had worked so successfully with Fred Astaire at RKO.

HOLLIDAY, JENNIFER

b. 19 October 1960, Houston, Texas, USA. This powerful vocalist first attracted attention as lead in the Broadway show *Your Arm's Too Short To Box With God*. She is, however, better known for her Tony-winning role in the musical *Dreamgirls*, a thinly disguised adaptation of the Supremes' story, which former member Mary Wilson took as the title of her autobiography. The show's undoubted highlight was Holliday's heart-stopping rendition of 'And I Am Telling You I'm Not Going', one of soul's most emotional, passionate performances. The single's success in 1982 prompted Holliday's solo career, but subsequent work was overshadowed by that first hit. She returned to the stage in 1985 in *Sing, Mahalia Sing* and has also acted in the television series *The Love Boat*. Holliday was also part of the backing choir on Foreigner's 1984 UK number 1 hit single, 'I Wanna Know What Love Is'. *Say You Love Me* won her a second Grammy award in 1985. She appeared in the musical *Grease* in the 90s and has recorded only sporadically. Holliday possesses an outstandingly powerful and emotional voice, the range of which has seen her compared to Aretha Franklin.
● ALBUMS: with Loretta Devine, Cleavant Derricks *Dreamgirls* Original Broadway Cast (Geffen 1982)★★★, *Feel My Soul* (Geffen 1983)★★★, *Say You Love Me* (Geffen 1985)★★★, *Get Close To My Love* (Geffen 1987)★★★, *I'm On Your Side* (Arista 1991)★★★, *On And On* (Inter Sound 1994)★★★.
● COMPILATIONS: *The Best Of Jennifer Holliday* (Geffen 1996)★★★★.

HOLLIDAY, JUDY

b. Judith Tuvim, 21 June 1922, New York, USA, d. 7 June 1965, New York, USA. An actress and singer with an endearing quality and a warm, unique comic style, Holliday's first attempt to break into showbusiness was with Orson Welles and John Houseman at the Mercury Theatre, but she only succeeded in getting a job there as a telephone operator - ironic considering her later memorable role in the musical theatre. Holliday joined some more young hopefuls, Betty Comden, Adolph Green, John Frank and Alvin Hammer, in a nightclub act called the Revuers, who attracted a good deal of attention. In 1945 she made her Broadway debut in the play *Kiss Them For Me*, and a year later was acclaimed for her performance in the Garson Kanin comedy *Born Yesterday*. She had taken over the dizzy blonde role after the producers' original choice, Jean Arthur, withdrew during the Philadelphia try-out. In 1950 Holliday won an Academy Award when she recreated her part for the Columbia film version. In the previous year she had almost stolen the glory from stars Katharine Hepburn and Spencer Tracey in *Adam's Rib*, which also had a screenplay by Kanin and his wife Ruth Gordon. In 1956 Holliday returned to Broadway in the musical *Bells Are Ringing*. The book and lyrics were by her old friends, Comden and Green (music by Jule Styne), and Holliday played Ella Peterson, a telephone operator who cannot help becoming emotionally involved with the clients who subscribe to Susanswerphone, the answering service where she works. *Bells Are Ringing* was a smash hit, and Holliday introduced several of its delightful songs, including 'The Party's Over', 'Drop That Name', 'Just In Time' and 'Long Before I Knew You' (both with Sydney Chaplin), and the immortal 'I'm Goin' Back (To The Bonjour Tristesse Brassiere Company)'. Her unforgettable performance won her Tony and New York Drama Critics awards.

In 1948 she had married musician David Oppenheim, who became head of the classical division of Columbia Records, but they divorced in 1957. Holliday's subsequent partner was another musician, a giant of the jazz world, Gerry Mulligan. He played one of her boyfriends in the 1960 screen adaptation of *Bells Are Ringing*, in which she co-starred with Dean Martin, and they also wrote songs together. Four of the best of these, 'What's The Rush?', 'Loving You', 'It Must Be Christmas' and 'Summer's Over', were included among the standards on an album they recorded in 1961. In spite of its tender and poignant quality, and the presence of accompanying luminaries such as Bob Brookmeyer, Mel Lewis and Al Klink, Holliday was reported to be unhappy with the result, and the album was not released until 1980. In 1960 she was out of town with the play *Laurette*, based on the life of the former Broadway star Laurette Taylor, when she found that she was unable to project her voice properly. It was the first sign that she had cancer. After surgery, she returned to New York in 1963 with the musical *Hot Spot*, but it folded after only 43 performances. She died just two weeks before her forty-third birthday.

● ALBUMS: with Gerry Mulligan *Holliday With Mulligan* 1961 recording (DRG 1980)★★★★, and Original Cast and soundtrack recordings.

● FURTHER READING: *Judy Holliday*, W. Holtzman. *Judy Holliday*, G. Carey.

● FILMS: *Greenwich Village* (1944), *Something For The Boys* (1944), *Winged Victory* (1944), *Adam's Rib* (1949), *Born Yesterday* (1950), *The Marrying Kind* (1952), *It Should Happen To You* (1954), *Phffft* (1954), *The Solid Gold Cadillac* (1956), *Full Of Life* (1956), *Bells Are Ringing* (1960).

HOLLOWAY, STANLEY

b. Stanley Augustus Holloway, 1 October 1890, London, England, d. 30 January 1982, Littlehampton, Sussex, England. A much-loved comedian, actor, singer, at the age of 10 Holloway was performing professionally as Master Stanley Holloway-The Wonderful Boy Soprano. He then toured in concert parties before studying in Milan for a period in 1913 with the intention of becoming an opera singer. After serving in the Connaught Rangers during World War I, Holloway played the music halls and made his London stage musical debut as Captain Wentworth in *Kissing Time* at the Winter Garden Theatre in 1919. This was followed by roles in *A Night Out* (1920), *Hit The Deck* (1927), *Song Of The Sea* (1928) and *Coo-ee* (1929). During the 20s Holloway received much acclaim for his appearances in several editions of the renowned *Co-Optimists* shows which were produced at various London theatres, beginning with the Royalty in London in 1921, and toured the provinces. He also became extremely popular on radio, especially for his monologues which involved characters such as Albert, who is eventually eaten by a lion at a zoo; and soldier Sam, who refuses to participate in the Battle of Waterloo until he has been approached by the Duke of Wellington himself. Throughout the 30s and 40s he continued to appear in the West End in revues and musicals such as *Savoy Follies*, *Three Sisters*, *Here We Are Again*, *All Wave*, *London Rhapsody*, *Up And Doing* and *Fine And Dandy*. He also worked occasionally in the straight theatre, and it was while playing the role of Bottom in *A Midsummer Summer Night's Dream* in New York that Holloway was offered the role of philosophical dustman Alfred P. Doolittle in Alan Jay Lerner and Frederick Loewe's musical, *My Fair Lady*, which opened on Broadway in March 1956. It proved to be the highlight of his career, and his ebullient performance of the show-stopping numbers 'Get Me To The Church On Time' and 'I'm Getting Married In The Morning' earned him a Tony nomination. He reprised his role in the 1958 London production, and again in the 1964 film for which he was nominated for an Oscar. Holloway's film career had begun in 1921 with *The Rotters*, a comedy, as were many of the other upwards of 60 films he made. He is particularly renowned for his outstanding work in the series of post-war Ealing comedies such as *Passport To Pimlico*, *The Lavender Hill Mob* and *The Titfield Thunderbolt*, but also shone in more serious pictures such as *This Happy Breed* and *The Way Ahead* (both 1944), *Brief Encounter* (1945), *No Love For Johnnie* (1961) and the musicals *Champagne Charlie* (1944) in which he co-starred with another top comic, Tommy Trinder, and *The Beggar's Opera* (1952) with Laurence Olivier. Holloway was awarded the OBE in 1960, and two years later found nationwide fame in America when he starred as an English butler trying to come to terms with the American way of life in the television situation comedy *Our Man Higgins*. From then on he continued to be active, making films and occasional stage appearances, and in 1977 toured Australia and the Far East in a tribute to Noël Coward entitled *The Pleasure Of His Company*. After a long and distinguished career, he is said to have told his actor son Julian that his only regret was that he had not been asked to do the voice-over for a television commercial extolling the virtues of Mr. Kipling's cakes.

● ALBUMS: *Famous Adventires With Old Sam And The Ramsbottoms* (Columbia 1956)★★★, *'Ere's 'Olloway* (Philips 1959)★★★, *Join In The Chorus* (Nixa 1961)★★★, *Stanley Holloway's Concert Party* (Riverside 1962)★★★, *Stanley, I Presume* (Columbia 60s).

● COMPILATIONS: *World Of* (Decca 1971)★★★, *Best Of* (Encore 1979)★★★, *More Monologues And Songs* (Encore 1980)★★★, *Brahn Boots* (Decca 1982)★★★, *Many Happy Returns* (Movie Stars 1989)★★★, *Nostalgic Memories* (Savage 1989)★★★.
● FURTHER READING: *Wiv A Little Bit O' Luck*, Stanley Holloway.

HOLLYWOOD HOTEL

A slice of Hollywood hokum starring crooner Dick Powell and directed by Busby Berkeley. The film's wan plot is centred around a small-town boy's attempt to hit the big-time via a radio show broadcast from the hotel of the title. The film's one virtue for the fans of big band swing (and quite a big virtue at that) is the appearance of the current sensation of the era, Benny Goodman And His Orchestra. The quartet of Goodman, Teddy Wilson, Lionel Hampton and Gene Krupa is featured. Showing an integrated group like this on screen in 1937 was as much a departure for Hollywood as it was for the music business when Goodman first presented Wilson a year earlier. The quartet plays 'I've Got A Heartful Of Music' and the big band, including Harry James, Ziggy Elman, Chris Griffin, Murray McEachern, Red Ballard, Vido Musso, Hymie Schertzer and Jess Stacy, performs several numbers including the film's title song and a short, breakneck version of the Goodman-Krupa showstopper, 'Sing, Sing, Sing'.

HOLMAN, LIBBY

b. Elsbeth Holzman, 23 May 1904, Cincinnati, Ohio, USA, d. 18 June 1971, Stamford, Connecticut, USA. Holman was regarded by some as the first great white torch singer, and by others as 'a dark purple menace', because of her tempestuous private life. She played minor roles in Broadway musicals such as Richard Rodgers and Lorenz Hart's *The Garrick Gaieties* (1925), but became a featured star in *Merry-Go-Round* (1927), and *Rainbow* (1928), in which she gave a languorous performance of 'I Want A Man'. After making the US Top 10 in 1929 with 'Am I Blue?', she was acclaimed a major star following her performance in *The Little Show*, in which she sang 'Can't We Be Friends' and 'Moanin' Low'. Holman received rave reviews for her sultry renditions of 'Body And Soul' and 'Something To Remember Me By' in *Three's A Crowd* (1930). Her career declined following the shooting of her husband Zachary Smith Reynolds. She was accused of his murder but the case was declared *nolle prosequi*, and never came to court. Holman returned to Broadway in *Revenge With Music* (1934), in which she introduced Arthur Schwartz and Howard Dietz's insinuating 'You And The Night And The Music', and subsequently appeared in Cole Porter's *You Never Know* (1938). Sadly, she never achieved her former heights. During the early 40s she caused a furore by appearing as a double-act with black folk singer Josh White, playing clubs and concerts in an era when a black male and white female stage relationship was frowned upon by many bookers and critics. Holman continued touring during the 50s presenting a programme called *Blues, Ballads And Sin Songs*, but still controversy followed her when she befriended ill-fated screen idol, Montgomery Clift. Mainly inactive in her later years, she is said to have died of carbon monoxide poisoning.

● COMPILATIONS: *The Legendary Libby Holman* (Evergreen 1965)★★★, *Something To Remember Her By* (1979)★★★.
● FURTHER READING: *Libby*, Milt Machlin. *Dreams That Money Can Buy: The Tragic Life Of Libby Holman*, Jon Bradshaw.

HONK!

This musical which has a book and lyrics by Anthony Drewe and music by George Stiles, had its world premiere under the title of *The Ugly Duckling (Or The Aesthetically Challenged Farmyard Fowl)* in December 1993 at the Watermill Theatre, Newbury, England, and was produced in a concert version two years later at the Bay Street Festival, Long Island, USA. Heading the impressive American cast were Evan Pappas, Debra Monk, Michael Mandell, Kate Burton, Tim Ewing, Peter Slutsker, Veanne Cox, and Ruth Williamson. However, on the journey back to England, the show changed its name to *Honk!* for an engagement at Alan Ayckbourn's Stephen Joseph Theatre, Scarborough, late in 1997. In Drewe's book, which is adapted from Hans Christian Andersen's famous fairy-tail, 'Honk', rather than the traditional 'Quack', is the noise made by the strange grey creature which emerges from the inordinately large egg hatched by mother duck Ida (Kristin Marks). The Ugly Duckling/Honk (Richard Dempsey) soon becomes the subject of ridicule around the farmyard, and sets off on a series of adventures with the pin-stripe suited Tom Cat (Paul Sharma), whose intentions, quite frankly, are culinary rather that honourable. He manages to escape, temporarily, from Cat's clutches, when Tom's attention is distracted by the feline charms of Queenie (Leigh McDonald). As winter turns to spring, Ida finally catches up with her errant son, only to find that the Ugly Duckling has grown to be a beautiful swan. Naturally, she and her partner Drake, the Mallard Duck (Michael McLean), are delighted when he decides to return to the duckyard, and set up nest with a beautiful young swan called Penny (Elizabeth Renihan). Along the way, there were some 'genuinely hummable tunes, with splendidly witty lyrics, ranging from novelty numbers to yearning love songs', in a score which included 'A Poultry Tale Of Folks Down On The Farm', 'The Joy Of Motherhood', 'Different', 'Hold Your Head Up High', 'Look At Him', 'You Can Play With Your Food', 'The Elegy', 'Every Tear A Mother Cries', 'The Wild Goose Chase', 'It Takes All Sorts To Make A World', 'Together', 'The Collage', 'Now I've Seen You', 'Warts And All', and 'The Blizzard'. Critics felt it was 'full of idiosyncratic charm', and particularly liked the way the cast - Honk's siblings were dressed in Doc Martens boots and baseball caps - did not fall into the trap of pretending to be animals. Much dancing of course, which was choreographed by Aletta Collins, and this colourful and entertaining production was directed by Julia McKenzie. Previous attempts to bring Andersen's work to film and stage have included the 1952 movie *Hans Christian Andersen*, starring Danny Kaye, the stage show *Hans Andersen*, with Tommy Steele (London Palladium 1974 and 1977), and two entirely different musicals with the same theme, *Hans Christian Andersen* and *H.C. Andersen*, which emerged during the 90s in Denmark.

HOORAY FOR WHAT!

A toned-down political and anti-war musical satire, *Hooray For What!* opened at New York's Winter Garden Theatre on 1 December 1937, nearly two years before World War II itself opened - in Europe at least. The book by Howard Lindsay and Russel Crouse, told of Chuckles (Ed Wynn), a horticultural scientist who invents a gas that kills appleworms - unfortunately it also kill humans as well. The discovery sparks off a string of diplomatic and political incidents and high-level conferences, culminating in Chuckles's appearance at the Geneva Peace Convention. While he is there, agents from an 'unfriendly power' steal the formula with the aid of a mirror, and so get it backwards. The result is a harmless laughing gas, which enables the world to breath a sigh of relief. During the pre-Broadway tryout, the show's originally powerful messages were modified somewhat - Agnes de Mille's anti-war ballet was cut - but with E.Y. 'Yip' Harburg providing the lyrics to Harold Arlen's music, there was always going to be an irreverent, and more 'sideways' look at issues and songs. Not content with coming up with 'In The Shade Of The *New* Apple Tree' in place of the cosy 1905 number, 'In the Shade of The *Old* Apple Tree', he actually had the tongue-in-cheek effrontery to question the basic ingredient of popular music itself - love. His witty 'Down With Love' contained lines such as 'Down with songs that moan about night and day . . . give it back to the birds and bees - and the Viennese . . . down with songs romantic and stupid/Down with sighs, and down with Cupid/Brother, let's stuff that dove/Down with love'. The rest of the fine score included 'Moanin' In The Mornin'', 'I've Gone Romantic On You', 'Life's A Dance', and 'God's Country', which was featured in the 1939 Judy Garland-Mickey Rooney film *Babes In Arm*s, and also became a hit in 1950 for both Frank Sinatra and Vic Damone. *Hooray For What!* stayed around for 200 performances - a reasonable run - and besides Ed Wynn, with his zany, crazy antics, the cast included Jack Whiting, Paul Haakon, June Clyde, Vivian Vance (who went on to become an important member of the 50s hit television show, *I Love Lucy*), and singers Hugh Martin and Ralph Blane, who were to make an impact on Broadway with their own songs in the 1941 show *Best Foot Forward*.

HOPE, BOB

b. Leslie Townes Hope, 26 May 1903, Eltham, England. One of the all-time great entertainers; an actor and comedian, whose singing ability has usually been sadly underrated. Hope was taken to the USA at the age of four and grew up in Cleveland. As a teenager he tried his hand at various jobs including boxing, and toured in vaudeville as a song-and-dance-man for a time. In the late 20s and early 30s he had small parts and some chorus work in a few Broadway shows before making a big impression in *Roberta* in 1933. He had the amusing duet, 'Don't Tell Me It's Bad', with Linda Watkins in *Say When* (1934), and in 1936 introduced the lovely 'I Can't Get Started' in the *Ziegfeld Follies*, and (with Ethel Merman) Cole Porter's amusing 'It's De-lovely' in *Red, Hot And Blue*. By this time he had broken into radio, and in 1938 he was given his own show. In the same year he made his first feature film, *The Big Broadcast Of 1938*, in which he introduced (with Shirley Ross) yet another durable song, Leo Robin and Ralph Rainger's 'Thanks For The Memory', which won an Oscar and went on to become his life-long theme tune. In 1939 Hope was highly acclaimed for his performance in the comedy-thriller *The Cat And The Canary*, and he continued to appear in musicals such as *College Swing*, *Give Me A Sailor*, and *Some Like It Hot*. In 1940 he teamed up with Bing Crosby and Dorothy Lamour for *Road To Singapore*, the first of seven comedy musicals which took the trio to Zanzibar, Morocco, Utopia, Rio, Bali, and finally, in 1962, to Hong Kong. Over the years the comedy pictures far outweighed the musicals, but during the 40s and 50s Hope still appeared in a few, such as *Louisiana Purchase* (1941), *Star Spangled Rhythm* (1942), *Let's Face It* (1943), *My Favourite Spy* (1951), *Here Come The Girls* (1953), *The Seven Little Foys* (1955), and *Beau James* (1957). He also sang the occasional engaging number in other films, including two by Jay Livingston and Ray Evans: 'Buttons And Bows', another Oscar-winner, from *The Paleface* (1948), and 'Silver Bells' from *The Lemon Drop Kid* (1950). In 1958 he joined Crosby for one of their 'insulting' duets, 'Nothing In Common', which Sammy Cahn and Jimmy Van Heusen composed for the zany *Paris Holiday*. Hope's ongoing 'feud' with Crosby has been a permanent feature of his act since the 30s, and has featured prominently on the comedian's annual trips overseas to entertain US troops, events that were particularly newsworthy during the years of the Vietnam War. He also spent much of World War II in the South Pacific war zone, along with artists such as Jerry Colonna and Frances Langford. Hope has been with NBC radio and television since 1934, the year his first *Pepsodent* show was aired - his 1992 Christmas TV Special was his 43rd - and there was a good deal of speculation when, following the 1993 tribute *Bob Hope: The First 90 Years*, his annual contract was not immediately renewed. During his career he has been showered with awards from many organizations and countries, including Emmys, a Peabody, 50 honorary academic degrees, and five special Academy Awards for humanitarianism and contributions to the film industry. He has also hosted the Academy Awards ceremony itself on numerous occasions. In 1994 he appeared at the Royal Albert Hall in London as part of the D-Day 50th Anniversary celebrations, and called in at the American Embassy to collect a Supreme Headquarters Allied Expeditionary Forces plaque to commemorate his wartime work. Two years later, he hosted *Bob Hope . . . Laughing With Presidents*, 'his 284th and final special for NBC television'.

On 18 May 1998 Hope was awarded an honorary knighthood. It was presented by the British Ambassador Sir Christopher Meyer on behalf of the Queen, in recognition of his long service as an entertainer, particularly for troops in wartime. In the following month he received an apology from Congress after a false report led to the premature announcement of his death. He is supposed to be 'the most wealthy entertainer who has ever lived', a point which was touched on by fellow comedian Milton Berle at a Friar's Club Roast in Hope's honour in 1989. Berle noted:

'This guy owns so much property in America he should be Japanese.'

● FURTHER READING: *The Amazing Careers Of Bob Hope*, Joe Morelli, Edward Epstein, Eleanor Clarke. *The Secret Life Of Bob Hope*, Arthur Marx. *Have Tux Will Travel. I Owe Russia $1,200. They Got Me Covered. I Never Left Home. The Road To Hollywood* (autobiography), all by Bob Hope.

● FILMS: *Thanks For The Memory* (1938), *Give Me A Sailor* (1938), *The Big Broadcast Of 1938, College Swing* (1938), *The Cat And The Canary* (1939), *Some Like It Hot* (1939), *Never Say Die* (1939), *The Ghost Breakers* (1940), *Road To Singapore* (1940), *Louisiana Purchase* (1941), *Nothing But The Truth* (1941), *Caught In The Draft* (1941), *Road To Zanzibar* (1941), *They Got Me Covered* (1942), *Star Spangled Rhythm* (1942), *Road To Morocco* (1942), *My Favorite Blonde* (1942), *Let's Face It* (1943), *The Princess And The Pirate* (1944), *Road To Utopia* (1945), *Monsieur Beaucaire* (1946), *Variety Girl (cameo)* (1947), *Where There's Life* (1947), *My Favorite Brunette* (1947), *The Paleface* (1948), *Road To Rio* (1948), *The Great Lover* (1949), *Sorrowful Jones* (1949), *Fancy Pants* (1950), *My Favorite Spy* (1951), *The Lemon Drop Kid* (1951), *Road To Bali* (1952), *The Greatest Show On Earth* cameo (1952), *Son Of Paleface* (1952), *Here Come The Girls* (1953), *Off Limits* (1953), *Casanova's Big Night* (1954), *The Seven Little Foys* (1955), *The Iron Petticoat* (1956), *That Certain Feeling* (1956), *Beau James* (1957), *Paris Holiday* (1958), *Alias Jesse James* (1959), *The Facts Of Life* (1960), *Bachelor In Paradise* (1961), *The Road To Hong Kong* (1962), *Call Me Bwana* (1963), *Critics Choice* (1963), *A Global Affair* (1964), *I'll Take Sweden* (1965), *The Oscar* cameo (1966), *Boy Did I Get A Wrong Number* (1966), *Eight On The Lam* (1967), *The Private Navy Of Sgt O'Farrell* (1968), *How To Commit Marriage* (1969), *Cancel My Reservation* (1972), *The Muppet Movie* cameo (1979), *Spies Like Us* cameo (1985).

HORNE, LENA

b. 30 June 1917, Brooklyn, New York, USA. Horne is a dynamic performer, of striking appearance and elegant style. The daughter of an actress and a hotel operator, she was brought up mainly by her paternal grandmother, Cora Calhoun Horne. She made her professional debut at the age of 16 as a singer in the chorus at Harlem's Cotton Club, learning from Duke Ellington, Cab Calloway, Billie Holiday and Harold Arlen, the composer of a future big hit, 'Stormy Weather'. From 1935-36 she was featured vocalist with the all-black Noble Sissle's Society Orchestra (the same Noble Sissle who, with Eubie Blake, wrote several hit songs including 'Shuffle Along' and 'I'm Just Wild About Harry') and later toured with the top swing band of Charlie Barnet, singing numbers such as 'Good For Nothin' Joe' and 'You're My Thrill'. Sometimes, when Barnet's Band played the southern towns, Horne had to stay in the band bus. She made her Broadway debut in 1934 as 'A Quadroon Girl' in *Dance With Your Gods*, and also appeared in Lew Leslie's *Blackbirds Of 1939*, in which she sang Mitchell Parish and Sammy Fain's 'You're So Indifferent' - but only for the show's run of nine performances.

After a spell at the Café Society Downtown in New York, she moved to Hollywood's Little Troc Club and was spotted by Roger Edens, musical supervisor for MGM Pictures, and former accompanist for Ethel Merman, who introduced her to producer Arthur Freed. In her first film for MGM, *Panama Hattie* (1942), which starred Merman, Horne sang Cole Porter's 'Just One Of Those Things', and a rhumba number called 'The Sping'. To make her skin appear lighter on film, the studio used a special make-up called 'Light Egyptian'. Horne referred to herself as 'a sepia Hedy Lamarr'. Her next two films, *Cabin In The Sky* and *Stormy Weather*, both made in 1943, are generally regarded as her best. In the remainder of her 40s and 50s movie musicals (which included *Thousands Cheer, Swing Fever, Broadway Rhythm, Two Girls And A Sailor, Ziegfeld Follies, Till The Clouds Roll By, Words And Music, Duchess Of Idaho* and *Meet Me In Las Vegas*), she merely performed guest shots that were easily removable, without spoiling the plot, for the benefit of southern-state distributors.

Her 40s record hits included her theme song, 'Stormy Weather', and two other Arlen songs, "Deed I Do' and 'As Long As I Live'. She also recorded with several big swing era names such as Artie Shaw, Calloway and Teddy Wilson. During World War II, she became the pin-up girl for many thousands of black GIs and refused to appear on US tours unless black soldiers were admitted to the audience. In 1947 she married pianist, arranger and conductor Lennie Hayton, who also became her manager and mentor until his death in 1971. For a time during the 50s Lena Horne was blacklisted, probably for her constant involvement with the Civil Rights movement, but particularly for her friendship with alleged Communist sympathizer Paul Robeson. Ironically, she was at the peak of her powers at that time, and although she was unable to appear much on television and in films, she continued to make records and appear in nightclubs, which were regarded as her special forte. Evidence of that was displayed on *Lena Horne At The Waldorf Astoria*. The material on this classic album ranged from the sultry 'Mood Indigo', right through to the novelty 'New Fangled Tango'. *Lena At The Sands* featured a medley of songs by Richard Rodgers/Oscar Hammerstein II, Jule Styne and E.Y. 'Yip' Harburg. Other US Top 30 chart albums included *Give The Lady What She Wants* and *Porgy And Bess*, with Harry Belafonte. Horne also made the US Top 20 singles charts in 1955 with 'Love Me Or Leave Me', written by Gus Kahn and Walter Donaldson for Ruth Etting to sing in the 1928 Broadway show *Whoopee*.

In 1957 Horne had her first starring role on Broadway when she played Savannah, opposite Ricardo Montalban, in the Arlen/Harburg musical *Jamaica*. In the 60s, besides the usual round of television shows and records, she appeared in a dramatic role, with Richard Widmark, in *Death Of A Gunfighter* (1969). After Hayton's death in 1971 she worked less, but did feature in *The Wiz*, an all-black film version of *The Wizard Of Oz*, starring Diana Ross and Michael Jackson, and in 1979 she received an honorary doctorate degree from Harvard University. In May 1981, she opened on Broadway in her own autobiographical show, *Lena Horne: The Lady And Her Music*. It ran at the Nederland Theatre to full houses for 14 months, a Broadway record for a one-woman show. Horne received several awards including a special Tony Award for 'Distinguished Achievement In The Theatre', a Drama Desk Award, New York Drama Critics' Special Award, New York City's Handel Medallion, Dance Theatre of Harlem's

Emergence Award, two Grammy Awards and the NAACP Springarn Award. She took the show to London in 1984, where it was also acclaimed. In 1993, after not having sung in public for several years, Lena Horne agreed to perform the songs of Billy Strayhorn at the US JVC Jazz Festival. She included several of the same composer's songs on her 1994 album *We'll Be Together Again*, and, in the same year, surprised and delighted her fans by appearing in concert at Carnegie Hall. In 1996 she won a Grammy for the best vocal jazz performance on her album *An Evening With Lena Horne*. In 1998, she sang a superb version of 'Stormy Weather' on US television's top-rated *Rosie O'Donnell Show*, and introduced what is said to be her fortieth album, *Being Myself*.

● ALBUMS: *Lena Horne Sings* 10-inch album (MGM 1952)★★★, *This Is Lena Horne* 10-inch album 10-inch album (RCA Victor 1952)★★★★, *Moanin' Low* 10-inch album (Tops 1954)★★, *It's Love* (RCA Victor 1955)★★★, *Stormy Weather* (RCA Victor 1956)★★★★, with Ivie Anderson *Lena And Ivie* (Jazztone 1956)★★★, *Lena Horne At The Waldorf Astoria* (RCA Victor 1957)★★★★, *Jamaica* film soundtrack (RCA Victor 1957)★★, *Give The Lady What She Wants* (RCA Victor 1958)★★★, with Harry Belafonte *Porgy And Bess* film soundtrack (RCA Victor 1959)★★★★, *Songs Of Burke And Van Heusen* (RCA Victor 1959)★★★, *Lena Horne At The Sands* (RCA Victor 1961)★★★★, *Lena On The Blue Side* (RCA Victor 1962)★★★, *Lena ... Lovely And Alive* (RCA Victor 1963)★★★, *Lena Goes Latin* (RCA Victor 1963)★★★, with Gabor Szabo *Lena And Gabor* (Skye 1970)★★★, *Lena* (1974)★★★, *Lena, A New Album* (RCA 1976)★★★, *Lena Horne: The Lady And Her Music* stage cast (Qwest 1981)★★★, *A Song For You* (1992)★★★, *We'll Be Together Again* (Blue Note 1994)★★★, *An Evening With Lena Horne: Live At The Supper Club* (Blue Note 1995)★★★★, *Being Myself* (Blue Note 1998)★★★★.

● COMPILATIONS: *Twenty Golden Pieces Of Lena Horne* (Bulldog 1979)★★★, *Lena Horne* (Jazz Greats 1979)★★★, *Lena Horne And Pearl Bailey* (Jazz Greats 1979)★★★, shared with Ella Fitzgerald, Billie Holiday, Sarah Vaughan *Billie, Ella, Lena, Sarah!* (Columbia 1980)★★★★, *Lena Horne And Frank Sinatra* (Astan 1984)★★★, *The Fabulous Lena Horne* (Cambra 1985)★★★, *Being Myself* (Blue Note 1998)★★★★.

● FURTHER READING: *In Person*, Lena Horne. *Lena*, Lena Horne with Richard Schikel. *Lena: A Personal And Professional Biography*, J. Haskins and K. Benson.

● FILMS: *The Duke Is Tops* (1938), *Panama Hattie* (1942), *I Dood It* (1943), *Swing Fever* (1943), *Stormy Weather* (1943), *Thousands Cheer* (1943), *Cabin In The Sky* (1943), *Two Girls And A Sailor* (1944), *Broadway Rhythm* (1944), *Till The Clouds Roll By* (1946), *Ziegfeld Follies* (1946), *Words And Music* (1948), *Duchess Of Idaho* (1950), *Meet Me In Las Vegas* (1956), *Death Of A Gunfighter* (1969), *The Wiz* (1978).

HORNER, JAMES

b. 1953, Los Angeles, California, USA. A prolific composer, arranger and conductor for films from the late 70s through to the 90s, Horner studied at the Royal College Of Music in London, at USC Los Angeles, and UCLA. In the late 70s he worked on several films for Roger Corman's New World production company, including *Up From The Depths*, *The Lady In Red*, *Battle Beyond The Stars* and *Humanoids From The Deep* (1980); reminders of Corman's Z Grade movies of the 50s. During the 80s he scored some 35 feature films,

mainly with recurring themes of grisly tales of horror, violence, science-fiction, fantasy, and sinister drama. These included *Deadly Blessing*, *The Hand*, *Wolfen*, *Star Trek II: 48 Hours* (Eddie Murphy's screen debut), *The Wrath Of Khan*; *Brainstorm*; *Krull*, *Testament*; *Gorky Park*, *Star Trek III: The Search For Spock*, *Cocoon*, *Commando*, *The Name Of The Rose*, *Project X*, *Batteries Not Included*, *Willow*, *Red Heat*, *Cocoon: The Return* and *Honey, I Shrunk The Kids* (1989). In 1986 Horner was nominated for an Academy Award for his *Aliens* score, and for the song 'Somewhere Out There' (written with Barry Mann and Cynthia Weil), for the animated feature *American Tail*. Both compositions gained ASCAP Awards. Horner was nominated again for an Oscar in 1989 for his music for another fantasy, *Field Of Dreams*, starring Kevin Costner, and, in the same year, won a Grammy for his score to *Glory*. Horner's 90s feature film credits include *Thunderheart*, *My Heroes Have Always Been Cowboys*, a tribute to the 'Wild West'; the live-action *Rocketeer*, two animated features, *An American Tail: Fievel Goes West* and *Fish Police* (1992), *Patriot Games*, *Unlawful Entry*, *Sneakers*, *House Of Cards*, *Jack The Bear*, *Swing Kids*, *A Far Off Place*, *Once Upon A Forest*, *The Man Without A Face*, *Innocent Moves*, *The Pelican Brief*, *Clear And Present Danger*, *Legends Of The Fall*, *Apollo 13* and *Braveheart*. In 1998, he won two Oscars for his work on *Titanic*, 'Best Original Dramatic Score', and 'Best Song' for 'My Heart Will Go On' (lyric: Will Jennings). Horner has also worked in television, composing music for such as *Angel Dusted*, *A Few Days In Weasel Creek*, *Rascals And Robbers - The Secret Adventures Of Tom Sawyer And Huck Finn*, *A Piano For Mrs Cimino*, *Between Friends* and *Surviving*.

HOT MIKADO

During the 30s, when President Roosevelt inaugurated his New Deal to help America emerge from its crippling Depression, the Federal Theatre Project became an important part of his plan to absorb the unemployed - in this case actors and technicians - in government-sponsored jobs. In 1938, the Federal Theatre in Chicago launched a particularly successful production, *The Swing Mikado*. It was a jazzy Negro version of what many consider to be the best of all W.S. Gilbert and Arthur Sullivan's operas, *The Mikado* or *The Town Of Titipu*, which was first presented at the Savoy Theatre in London on 14 March 1885. The flamboyant showman Mike Todd offered to buy the project and take it to New York, but he was informed that it was public property, and not for sale. However, the Federal Theatre organization itself subsequently moved *The Swing Mikado* to Broadway, where it opened on 1 March 1939 at the New Yorker Theatre. Not to be outdone, Todd responded by assembling a cast of more than 100 African-American actors, including the renowned 60-year old tap dancer, Bill 'Bojangles' Robinson, and installing them in *The Hot Mikado* which moved into the nearby Broadhurst Theatre a few weeks later on 23 March. *The Hot Mikado* was directed by Hassard Short, who had previously staged such prominent musicals and revues as *Three's A Crowd*, *The Band Wagon*, *As Thousands Cheer*, *Roberta*, and Irving Berlin's *Music Box Review* series. Garbed all in gold - even down to his cane - Robinson played the Mikado, the title given by foreigners to the Emperor of Japan, and scored a big hit with his version of 'The Punishment Fit The Crime'. Early each evening he performed at Harlem's famous Cotton Club, before donning his Emperor's robes to go on stage at the Broadhurst. Members of the press especially liked the Jitterbug Girls in their snazzy slacks, and reported that the creators of *The Hot Mikado* 'have done amazing and agreeably absurd things with Gilbert and Sullivan's score, leaving large chunks out entirely. Everything has been chucked overboard except the basic melodies, but it is very entertaining to have Katisha (an elderly lady in love with the Emperor's son) sing to torch rhythms.' Both shows ran through the summer, but while *The Swing Mikado* faded, Todd shrewdly took *The Hot Mikado* to the New York World's Fair at Flushing Meadow, and then on tour until April 1940. By that time, it was considered the most successful black musical show since *Shuffle Along* (1921), although, ironically, all the members of the orchestra were white.

Towards the end of World War II, in May 1945, two more shows adapted from another Gilbert and Sullivan opera, *H.M.S. Pinafore* or *The Lass That Loved A Sailor*, made brief visits to Broadway. The first of them, *Memphis Bound!*, had Bill 'Bojangles' Robinson again, and stayed fairly close to its source material, but *Hollywood Pinafore*, which starred William Gaxton and Victor Moore, was more up to date, and had a witty book by George S. Kaufman. Neither of them lasted for very long.

Some 40 years after they both went down, David H. Bell, the Artistic Director of Ford's Theatre, Washington, decided to present *Hot Mikado* as its 1986 Spring Musical. Unable to track down any of the material from the 1939 show, he and his collaborator Rob Bowman decided to adapt the material themselves. Most of the titles of the songs they included seemed familiar, and Gilbert and Sullivan aficionados will be able to judge how close to the 1885 original this production was - as far as the score was concerned at least - by browsing the following list: 'We Are The Gentlemen Of Japan', 'A Wand'ring Minstrel I', 'I Am Right', 'The Brass Will Crash', 'The Lord High Executioner', 'A Little List', 'Three Little Maids', 'This I'll Never Do', 'A Cheap And Chippy Chopper', 'With Joyous Shout', 'Katisha's Warning', 'Braid The Raven Hair', 'The Sun And I', 'Swing A Merry Madrigal', 'A How-Dee-Doo', 'The Punishment Fit The Crime', 'The Criminal's End', 'Alone And Yet Alive', 'Tit Willow', and 'Beauty In The Bellow'. Prominent among the cast were Robin Baxter (Pitti-Sing), Raymond Bazemore (Pooh-Bah), Steve Blanchard (Nanki Poo), Merwin Foard (Pish-Tush), Lawrence Hamilton (Mikado), Frank Kopyc (Ko-Ko), Kathleen Mahony-Bennett (Yum-Yum), Val Scott (Peep-Bo), Helena-Joyce Wright (Katisha), and Gregg Hellems and Mona Wyatt (both Swing). *Hot Mikado* was well received in Washington, and had stagings in several other US locations (but not on Broadway) before venturing to England - the heartland of Gilbert and Sullivan - at London's Queen's Theatre on 18 May 1995. Lawrence Hamilton recreated his fine tap-dancing performance as Washington's *Mikado*, and also singled out for praise were Ross Lehman, as the reluctant executioner Ko-Ko, for his

superb clowning in the style of American vaudevillians such as Eddie Cantor and Phil Silvers, as well as his compelling rendition of 'Tit Willow', and Sharon Benson, who transformed Katisha from an ageing battleaxe into 'a sensational vamp in an hourglass suit of pillar-box red, singing 'The Hour Of Gladness' with barely controlled sexual rage as a fierce blues number'. Among the rest of a high class cast were Neil Couperthwaite (Junior), Veronica Hart (Peep-Bo), Paulette Ivory (Yum-Yum), Alison Jiear (Pitti-Sing), Richard Lloyd King (Pooh-Bah), Paul Manuel (Nanki-Poo), and Ben Richards (Pish-Tush). With the production set in the late 30s-early 40s, traditional Japanese costumes were eschewed in favour of 'snappy zoot suits and the skin tight skirts of jitterbuggers', modes of dress entirely suitable for performing a score consisting of elements of gospel, jazz, blues and swing, as well as the odd Andrews Sisters take-off. So, more than 50 years after its inception, *Hot Mikado* 1995-style was generally acclaimed as 'more fun than you can shake a chopstick at'. By now employing several white actors, its re-creators justified the 'brash attack' on this particular Savoy opera by claiming that even the original show was a Victorian, non-authentic interpretation of Japan. Sadly, it failed to secure an audience in the West End, and closed on the 19 August 1995.

Among the other attempts to up-date, jazz-up, or generally play around with *The Mikado* on stage, have been the highly successful *The Black Mikado*, which had a long run in London during 1975/6, a *Cool Mikado*, and a Berlin jazz *Mikado*, in which Nanki-Poo 'Charlestoned in Oxford Bags'.

HOUND-DOG MAN

Fabian was one of several 50s rock 'n' roll singers styled on Elvis Presley, but boasting only a slim resemblance to their role model. 'Turn Me Loose' and 'Tiger' were among his US Top 10 entries, but the sexual bravura of their titles was undermined by unconvincing vocals. However, he was quickly plucked from the singles chart and presented in a series of blithe Hollywood films. Released in 1959, *Hound-Dog Man* provided Fabian's first starring role, in which he plays one of two teenagers star-struck by a wayward acquaintance. The light comedy feature was set in 1912, demanding that Fabian act rather than simply perform, while rising director Don Seigel, later famed for Clint Eastwood's *Dirty Harry* series, brought a sharper focus to the proceedings than many contemporary releases of its type. The title song became one of Fabian's five US Top 30 entries during 1959, but the appeal of his recordings waned as quickly as it arose.

HOUSE OF FLOWERS

Truman Capote is said to have got the idea for this show while visiting Port-au-Prince in Haiti in the late 40s. In an event, he wrote the libretto, and collaborated with composer Harold Arlen on the lyrics for what was a short-lived, but fondly remembered production. It opened at New York's Alvin Theatre on 30 December 1954, and told of the trials and tribulations of two brothels on an unidentified West Indies island. Madame Fleur (Pearl Bailey) tends the House of Flowers, while Madame Tango (Juanita Hall) performs a similar service for a rival concern. One of Madame Fleur's young blooms, Ottilie (Diahann Carroll), turns down the opportunity of real career advancement in favour of an exclusive love contract with the young and innocent Royal (Rawn Spearman), and eventually, Madame Fleur corners the terra firma market franchise when Madame Tango's operation is floated (on a world cruise). However, it is the unusual, but somehow overwhelming score that makes this a memorable show. It contained the delightful calypso-styled 'Two Ladies In De Shade Of De Banana Tree', along with 'I Never Has Seen Snow', 'I'm Gonna Leave Off Wearin' My Shoes', 'Smellin' Of Vanilla', 'Has I Let You Down?', 'One Man Ain't Quite Enough', and 'A Sleepin' Bee' which was sung in the show by Ottilie and Royal, and received what was probably its definitive version from Barbra Streisand on her first album. There was another lovely ballad, 'Don't Like Goodbyes', which was given a smooth treatment by Frank Sinatra on his *Close To You*. During the pre-Broadway tryout there were rumours of backstage battles involving several of the principals, and, indeed, some particularly volatile personalities and egos assembled for this production. Diahann Carroll and Truman Capote both made highly impressive Broadway debuts, and Pearl Bailey was her usual dominating self. Oliver Messel's pastel-coloured sets, which somehow gave the whole affair a kind of ethereal quality, were singled out for special praise. *House Of Flowers* had a disappointing run of 165 performances, and a 1968 Off Broadway revival was brief and to the point.

HOW TO STUFF A WILD BIKINI

Another in a string of 'beach' movies undertaken by the American International Pictures group in the wake of *Beach Party*, *How To Stuff A Wild Bikini* (1965) showed the genre was flagging badly. Annette Funicello took the lead role. The former Disney Mouseketeer starred as Dee Dee, whose boyfriend, played by Dwayne Hickman, is called up on naval reserve duty. Fearful of the attentions of predatory males, the Hickman character employs a witch-doctor to watch over her. Silent veteran Buster Keaton took the latter role in a film which also featured Mickey Rooney, and Harvey Lembeck, who portrayed the 'bad guy', Erich Von Zipper. Beach Boys' leader Brian Wilson enjoyed a non-singing cameo role, while guest act the Kingsmen, popularizers of 'Louie Louie', contributed the title song and 'Give Her Lovin''. The film was retitled *How To Fill A Wild Bikini* in the UK, but such machinations were unnecessary as this sorry featured failed to gain a British release.

HOW TO SUCCEED IN BUSINESS WITHOUT REALLY TRYING

If *Guys And Dolls* is considered to be composer and lyricist Frank Loesser's masterpiece, then this show must be right up there in second place. After its world première at the Shubert Theatre in Philadelphia on 4 September 1961, it opened on Broadway at the 46th Street Theatre just over a month later on 14 October. The libretto, by Abe Burrows, Jack Weinstock, and Willie Gilbert, based on a book of the same title by Shepheard Mead, was 'a witty satire on the methods and mores of Big Business in general, and in par-

ticular, on the wiles and ways of Big Business in new glass-enclosed office buildings on Park Avenue'. The story concerns a young man, J. Pierpont Finch (Robert Morse), who climbs from his position as a window-washer to the position of Chairman of the Board of the World Wide Wickets Company, Inc. His rapid rise is not due to diligence or hard work. He simply follows the rules in a book called *How To Succeed In Business Without Even Trying*, which he pauses to consult whenever he is faced with an obstacle to his success ('How To'). With its aid, he is able to defeat his main rival, Bud Frump (Charles Nelson Reilly), the boss's oily nephew, and avoid the usual traps such as the office wolf, the office party, the dangerous secretary, and the big boss himself, J.B. Biggley (Rudy Vallee). Finch's girlfriend and main supporter is the attractive secretary Rosemary Pilkington (Bonnie Harris), who makes it clear that she would be 'Happy To Keep His Dinner Warm', while he goes onward and upward. When stuck for a time in the mailroom ('Coffee Break'), he emphasises that he considers the best route to advancement is 'The Company Way', while always bearing in mind, of course, that 'A Secretary Is Not A Toy' - even if she is Biggley's mistress. Additionally, although he agrees with Rosemary and her best friend Smitty (Claudette Sutherland), that it has 'Been A Long Day', it does not prevent him from being slumped over his desk, looking as though he has been working all night, when Biggley calls into the office on a Sunday morning en route to his round of golf. With cries of 'Groundhog!', they unite in Biggley's hymn to his alma mata, 'Grand Old Ivy' (Rip the Chipmunks off the field!'). From then on, Finch's onward and upward progress is positively phenomenal, and his self-assurance is undisguised as he sings 'I Believe In You' to his reflection in the executive washroom mirror. There are still some awkward moments to survive, including a treasure hunt during which the company's offices are wrecked, but Finch surmounts them all to become the Chairman, to marry Rosemary, and to watch his ex-rival Frump washing the office windows while reading a book entitled *How To Succeed In Business Without Even Trying*. 'I Believe In You', sung as a love song and not a soliloquy, achieved some popularity outside the show, particularly in a recording by Peggy Lee. The rest of the outstanding score included 'Paris Original', 'Rosemary', 'Cinderella, Darling', 'Love From A Heart Of Gold', and 'Brotherhood Of Man'. Rudy Vallee, the enormously popular singing idol of the 30s, and Robert Morse, who had previously appeared on Broadway in *Say, Darling* and *Take Me Along*, were perfectly cast, and the show reunited Frank Loesser, Abe Burrows, and producers Cy Feuer and Ernest Martin, 11 years after their collective triumph with *Guys And Dolls*. It was to be Loesser's final Broadway score, and he could not have gone out on a higher note. The show ran in New York for 1,417 performances, and was showered with awards: the prestigious Pulitzer Prize for Drama (1962), the New York Drama Critics Award for best musical, and Tony Awards for best musical, actor (Morse), lyrics, librettists, and director (Burrows). The 1963 London production, starring Warren Berlinger (Finch), Billy De Wolfe (Biggley), David Knight (Bud), Josphine Blake (Smitty), and Patricia Michael (Rosemary), ran at the Shaftesbury Theatre for well over a year, and Rudy Vallee and Robert Morse reprised their original performances in the 1967 film version. In March 1995, a 'wonderful' Broadway revival had the popular film and stage actor Matthew Broderick as Finch (Tony Award), with Ronn Carroll (Biggley), Megan Mullally (Rosemary), Victoria Clark (Smitty), and Jeff Blumenkrantz (Bud).

HOWARD, JAMES NEWTON

b. USA. Although he is regarded as a prolific composer of film music, Howard began his musical career as a musician (keyboards, synthesizer, mellotron) during the 70s, and played on record sessions with rock artists such as Ringo Starr, Neil Diamond, Melissa Manchester, Harry Nilsson, Neil Sedaka, Yvonne Elliman and Boz Scaggs. From 1975-80, he was member of Elton John's Band (Mark II), and served as his studio arranger. Howard, and another American, bassist Joe Passarelli, were part of the new John line-up which was introduced to the 75,000 crowd at Wembley Stadium in 1975. He was on Elton John's *Rock Of The Westies*, *Blue Moves*, *21 At 33* and *The Fox* (1980) and, in the same year, played at John's free concert in New York's Central Park to an estimated audience of 400,000. Howard was also a member of the band, China, and John produced one of their albums. In the 80s Howard began composing music for films. His first feature credit, Ken Finkleman's comedy *Head Office*, was followed by *Wildcats* (co-composed with Hawk Wolinski), *Never Too Young To Die*, *8 Million Ways To Die*, *Nobody's Fool*, *Tough Guys*, *Campus Man*, *Five Corners* ('an appropriately moody score'), *Russkies*, *Promised Land*, *Off Limits*, *Some Girls*, *Everybody's All-American*, *Tap*, a tribute to tap dancing, starring Gregory Hines and Sammy Davis Jnr. in the latter's last feature film; *Major League* and *The Package* (1989). In the 90s, Howard became known as 'hot' in Hollywood, with his scores for movies such as *Pretty Woman*, *Flatliners*, *King Ralph*, *Marked For Death*, *Guilty By Suspicion*, *Dying Young*, *Three Men And A Little Lady*, *Coupe De Ville*, *The Man In The Moon*, *My Girl*, *American Heart*, *A Private Matter* (television), *Grand Canyon*, *Diggstown*, *Glengarry Glen Ross*, *Night And The City*, *Alive*, *Falling Down*, *The Fugitive*, *Dave*, and *The Saint Of Fort Washington* (1993). His status was not diminished when Barbra Streisand chose him to replace UK composer John Barry on *The Prince Of Tides* (1991).
● ALBUMS: *James Newton Howard & Friends* (1988)★★.

HOWES, BOBBY

b. Robert William Howes, 4 August 1895, Battersea, London, England, d. 27 April 1972. An actor, singer and dancer with a charming, disarming style, Howes was apprenticed to be an electrical engineer before realising his ambition to go on to the stage. While in his teens he performed at music halls and with concert parties, before spending three years in the Army during World War I. After the war he had difficulty getting work, but he made his West End debut in 1923 in *The Little Revue Starts At 9*, and from then on, for the next 25 years, his inimitable comic style allied to an appealing way of putting over a song and dance, ensured that he stayed at the top in the British musical theatre. Among the shows and revues he

appeared in were *The Second Little Revue* (1924), *The Punch Bowl*, *The Blue Kitten*, *Vaudeville Vanities*, *The Blue Train*, *The Yellow Mask*, *Mr. Cinders* - the first of three in which he starred with Binnie Hale ('I'm A One-Man Girl' and 'Ev'ry Little Moment'), *Sons O' Guns*, *Song Of The Drum*, *For The Love Of Mike* ('Who Do You Love?' and 'Got A Date With An Angel'), *Tell Her The Truth*, *He Wanted Adventure*, *Yes, Madame?*, *Please, Teacher*, *Big Business*, *Hide And Seek* ('She's My Lovely'), *Bobby Get Your Gun*, *All Clear*, *Shephard's Pie*, *Lady Behave*, *Let's Face It!*, *Here Come The Boys*, *Four, Five, Six!*, *Roundabout*, and *Finian's Rainbow* (New York replacement 1960). In 1953 he starred with his daughter, Sally Ann Howes (b. 20 July 1930, London, England) in *Paint Your Wagon*. She had made her first appearance on the London musical stage two years earlier in *Fancy Free*, and subsequently developed into an elegant and charming leading lady. Her principal appearances in musicals have included *Bet Your Life* (1952), *Romance In Candlelight*, *Summer Song*, *My Fair Lady* (1958 Broadway replacement), *Kwamina*, *Brigadoon* and *Wonderful Town* (both New York City Centre revivals), *What Makes Sammy Run?* (introducing 'A Room Without Windows'), *The King And I* (1973 London replacement), *The Sound Of Music* (US regional production 1973/4), and *Robert And Elizabeth* (1976 UK regional revival), and *Hans Anderson* (with Tommy Steele, London Palladium 1977). She has toured consistently in shows throughout the world, both musicals and straight theatre, and has appeared extensively on television, especially in America. She was married for a time to the US composer Richard Adler. Like her father, Sally Ann Howes has made a number of films, including the musical, *Chitty Chitty Bang Bang*. In the early 90s, her cabaret act was receiving enthusiastic reviews in London and New York.
● ALBUMS: with Binnie Hale, Sally Ann Howes *She's My Lovely* (World Records 60s)★★.

HOWES, SALLY ANN

(see Howes, Bobby)

HULBERT, JACK

b. 24 April 1892, Ely, England, d. 25 March 1978, London, England. A popular actor, singer, dancer, director, author choreographer, and producer, whose jaunty onstage image was of the 'terribly British, "I say, old chap"' variety. Hulbert began to develop his various skills in undergraduate productions while he was studying at Cambridge University. In 1913, while appearing in *The Pearl Girl* in the West End, he met Cicely Courtneidge, the daughter of producer Robert Courtneidge, and they were married in 1916. *The Pearl Girl* was the first of 13 musicals in which they appeared together. During the next few years Hulbert established himself in a mixture of musical comedies and revues such as *The Cinema Star*, *The Arcadians*, *The Light Blues* (for which he was also co-librettist), *See-Saw*, *Bubbly*, *Bran-Pie*, *A Little Dutch Girl*, *Ring Up*, *Pot Luck*, and *The Little Revue Starts At 9* (1923). From 1925 onwards he co-produced and/or directed (and sometimes choreographed) a range of productions, particularly those in which he also acted. These included *By The Way* (in London and New York), *Lido Lady*, *Clowns In Clover*, *The*

House That Jack Built, *Follow A Star* (1930), *Under Your Hat*, *Full Swing*, and *Something In The Air* (1943). After World War II, with *Oklahoma!* and the other American blockbusters on the horizon, Hulbert's smart and sophisticated style of musical comedy was less in demand, although he directed Cicely Courtneidge in the highly successful *Gay's The Word* in 1951. Over the years he introduced several popular songs, including 'The Flies Crawled Up The Window', 'My Hat's On The Side Of My Head', 'She's Such A Comfort To Me', and 'I Was Anything But Sentimental', a duet with his wife from their film *Take My Tip* (1937). Hulbert made several other light comedy movies during the 30s, - he and Courtneidge were just as popular on the screen as on the stage - such as *Elstree Calling* (1930), *The Ghost Train*, *Jack's The Boy*, *Bulldog Jack*, *Paradise For Two*, and *Kate Plus Ten*. From then on there were only occasional releases which included *Under Your Hat* (1940), *Into The Blue* (1951) *Spider's Web* (1960), and *Not Now Darling* (1973).

● ALBUMS: *The Golden Age Of Cicely Courtneidge And Jack Hulbert* (1984)★★★.

● FURTHER READING: *The Little Woman's Always Right*, Jack Hulbert. *Cicely*, Cicely Courtneidge.

110 IN THE SHADE

If only this show had not opened in the same 1963-64 Broadway season as *Hello, Dolly!* and *Funny Girl*, things might have been different; it would probably have won some awards for a start. Even so, when it made its debut at the Broadhurst Theatre on 24 October 1963, *110 In The Shade* met with almost universal acclaim. The odd man out was Walter Kerr of the New York Herald Tribune, who called the song 'Little Red Hat' 'dirty and salacious'; lines such as 'I find us a spot/Where no one is at/Then I reach across and grab her little red hat' would hardly raise an eyebrows today. That song, and the rest of the score, was written by Tom Jones and Harvey Schmidt, whose first collaboration in 1960 had resulted in *The Fantasticks*, the record-breaking off-Broadway production. N. Richard Nash's book was adapted from his own 1954 play, *The Rainmaker*, and it was only after seeing that on US television that Jones and Schmidt came up with this musical. A feature film version, with Burt Lancaster and Katharine Hepburn had been released in 1956. The story is set in a bleak town in the American Midwest, where a self-styled rainmaker, the handsome Bill Starbuck (Robert Horton), has arrived to cure the problem ('Rain Song'). Lizzie Curry (Inga Swenson) has a problem of her own - she cannot find a husband ('Love Don't Turn Away'). Her father and brothers try to fix her up with the town's sheriff, File (Stephen Douglass), a shy divorcee ('A Man And A Woman'), but she prefers the glamorous Starbuck. He indulges in all the rigmarole that is needed to bring the much-needed rain, but is eventually revealed to be a con-man on the run. Even so, Lizzie is about to run away with him ('Is It Really Me?') until File at last reveals his own love for her ('Wonderful Music'). She decides to accept him, and settle for the quiet life. At that moment, the heavens open . . . Jones and Schmidt's lovely, tuneful score, complemented perfectly the folksy, sentimental feeling of the piece. The rest of the songs included 'Gonna

Be A Hot Day', 'Lizzie's Comin' Home', 'Poker Polka', 'Hungry Men', 'You're Not Foolin' Me', 'Raunchy', 'Old Maid', 'Everything Beautiful Happens At Night', 'Little Red Hat', 'Melisande', and 'Simple Little Things'. *110 In The Shade* had a decent run of 330 performances, and Inga Swenson's performance was outstanding. She was widely tipped to win a Tony Award, but *Hello, Dolly!* swept the board. In 1992 the show was revived by the New York City Opera, with Karen Ziémba as Lizzie. It was taped for transmission on the *Great Performances* television series.

HUNSECKER, RALPH BLANE
(see Blane, Ralph)

HUNTER, TAB

b. Arthur Gelien, 11 July 1931, New York City, New York, USA. This blond-haired, blue-eyed pop vocalist/actor used his mother's maiden name, Gelien, until he was spotted in 1948, working at a stable, by talent scout Dick Clayton. He introduced him to Rock Hudson's Hollywood agent Harry Wilson, who said 'We've got to tab you something', then named him Tab Hunter. He made his screen debut in the 1950 film *The Lawless* and two years later co-starred with Linda Darnell in the British film *Saturday Island* (US title: *Island Of Desire*). In late 1956 he received a phone call from Randy Wood, president of Dot Records, asking him to record a song recently cut by US country star Sonny James, the lilting ballad 'Young Love'. Both versions made the US charts, Hunter reaching number 1 and James peaking at number 2. Hunter also topped the UK chart, but James lagged behind at number 11. He continued recording for Dot and hit with the slightly up-tempo '99 Ways', which narrowly missed the US Top 10 but made the UK Top 5 (1957). In the following year he appeared in the film version of the Broadway show *Damn Yankees*, with Gwen Verdon and Ray Walston. As Warner Brothers had him under contract to make films, they resented him recording for Dot and established their own record label in 1958. He signed, with moderate success, and in 1960 starred in his own NBC US television series. He continued his acting and appeared opposite Fabian in the 1964 'beach party' film *Ride The Wild Surf*. He was still acting in the 80s, notably with the late Divine in *Polyester* and *Lust In The Dust*, and also in the *Grease* sequel, *Grease 2*. In the late 80s Hunter moved to Mexico to write, and set up a film production company, one of the fruits of which was the 'family' picture *Dark Horse* (1992).

● ALBUMS: *Tab Hunter* (Warners 1958)★★, *When I Fall In Love* (Warners 1959)★★, *R.F.D. Tab Hunter* (Warners 1960)★★, *Young Love* (Dot 1961)★★.

● FILMS: *The Lawless* (1950), *Saturday Island* (1952), *Island Of Desire* (1952), *The Steel Lady* (1953), *Gun Belt* (1953), *Return To Treasure Island* (1953), *Track Of The Cat* (1954), *Battle Cry* (1955), *The Sea Chase* (1955), *The Girl He Left Behind* (1956), *The Burning Hills* (1956), *Gunman's Walk* (1958), *Damn Yankees* (1958), *Hell Bent For Glory* (1958), *That Kind Of Woman* (1959), *They Came To Cordura* (1959), *The Pleasure Of His Company* (1961), *Operation Bikini* (1963), *Ride The Wild Surf* (1964), *The Golden Arrow* (1964), *War Gods Of The Deep* (1965), *The Loved One* (1965), *Birds Do It* (1966), *Hostile Guns* (1967), *The Fickle Finger Of Fate* (1967), *Shotgun* (1968), *The Last Chance* (1968), *Legion Of No Return*

(1969), *Sweet Kill* (1970), *The Life And Times Of Judge Roy Bean* (1972), *Timber Tramps* (1973), *Won Ton Ton, The Dog Who Saved Hollywood* (1976), *Polyester* (1981), *Pandemonium* (1982), *Grease 2* (1982), *Lust In The Dust* (1985), *Out Of The Dark* (1988), *Cameron's Closet* (1989), *Dark Horse* (1992), *Wild Bill: Hollywood Maverick* (1996).

HUNTING OF THE SNARK, THE

Prior to 24 October 1991, Mike Batt was best-known in Britain as the arranger and producer of a highly successful series of children's novelty records (on which he also sang) involving the Wombles, a mythical group of small, furry, friendly creatures, who apparently lived on Wimbledon Common in south east London. Soon after that date he became renowned as an obstinate entrepreneur who had poured several years of his life, and a good deal of his own money, into a spectacular flop musical called *The Hunting Of The Snark*. The project, which was based on Lewis Carroll's epic nonsense poem, first surfaced in 1987 as a concept album which was narrated by Sir John Gielgud and John Hurt, and performed by such luminaries as Roger Daltrey, Art Garfunkel, Julian Lennon, Cliff Richard, Deniece Williams *et al.* Four years later, a concert version was well-received at the State Theatre in Sydney, Australia, and the full West End production opened at the Prince Edward Theatre in October 1991. It was Mike Batt's baby all along; he wrote the book, music, and lyrics, staged the show with James Hayes, and was also credited with the design and the orchestrations. The story concerned the search for an 'improbable beast', and involved the Bellman (Philip Quast) and his crew which consisted of the Beaver (Veronica Hart), the Butcher (John Partridge), the Barrister (Allan Love), the Banker (David Firth), the Baker (Mark McGann), the Bandmaster (Jae Alexander), the Broker (Peter Leadbury), and the Bishop (Gary Martin). The disc jockey and television presenter, Kenny Everett, made his West End musical theatre debut as the Billiard Marker, and the role of the author-narrator was played by the film and television actor, David McCallum. Quast, McGann, John Partridge, and Veronica Hart, were all singled out by the critics for special praise. Most of the reputed £2.1 million investment was up there on the stage for all to see in the shape of a 50 piece orchestra and the high-tech computerized scenic projections. The score, with its 'prosaic music and portentous lyrics', contained some 26 numbers including 'Children Of The Sky', 'Hymn To The Snark', 'Who'll Join Me On This Escapade?', 'Nursery Pictures', 'The Pig Must Die', 'As Long As The Moon Can Shine', and the prophetically titled 'Dancing Towards Disaster'. Audiences stayed away in their thousands (the Prince Edward is a medium-sized house with a capacity of 1,666), and, throughout November, Batt refused to bring the curtain down despite heavy losses. It was rumoured that Andrew Lloyd Webber, Tim Rice, and Cameron Mackintosh were contributing to the diminishing kitty. Some people loved what they regarded as 'one of the most unusual and intriguing musicals to be seen in the West End', and an angry exchange of opposing views raged in the letters column of *The Stage* newspaper. Finally, on 14 December, Batt could take no more and closed the show after only seven weeks, incur-

ring personal losses that were estimated to be in excess of £600,000.

HUPFELD, HERMAN

b. 1 February 1894, Montclair, New Jersey, USA, d. 8 June 1951, Montclair, New Jersey, USA. A little-known songwriter, pianist and conductor, who, although he did not compose complete scores, was particularly adept in interpolating the occasional superior song into stage shows and films of the 20s and 30s. After being sent to Germany at the age of nine to study the violin, Hupfeld returned to the USA and completed his education at the local Montclair high school. After serving in the US Navy during World War I, he worked as a pianist-singer before contributing songs such as 'Baby's Blue', 'Sort Of Lonesome', and 'The Calinda' to the smart and fashionable Broadway revues of the day. In 1930 his 'Sing Something Simple' attracted some attention when it was introduced by Ruth Tester, with Arline Judge and Fay Brady, in *The Second Little Show*. A year later, as well as contributing the amusing 'When Yuba Plays The Rumba On His Tuba' to *The Third Little Show*, he wrote the song for which he will always be remembered - 'As Time Goes By'. It was first sung by the popular platinum blonde singer Frances Williams in the musical *Everybody's Welcome*, and subsequently recorded by Jacques Renard and Rudy Vallee, amongst others. However, it came to world-wide prominence in the 1943 film *Casablanca*, when it was memorably performed by Dooley Wilson. More than 50 years later, it still conjures up the bitter-sweet romance between Humphrey Bogart and Ingrid Bergman in the movie, and that magical moment when Bergman requests the pianist to 'Play it Sam. Play 'As Time Goes By''. In 1932 Hupfeld had another of his best-known numbers, 'Let's Put Out The Lights And Go To Sleep', featured in *George White's Music Hall Varieties* stage show, and during the remainder of the 30s his other songs included 'Wouldn't That Be Wonderful' (*Hey Nonny Nonny!* revue), 'Savage Serenade' (Earl Carroll's *Murder At The Vanities*), and 'Buy Yourself A Balloon' (*The Show Is On* revue). He also placed songs in movies such as *Moonlight And Pretzels* ('Gotta Get Up And Get To Work' and 'Are You Makin' Any Money ?') and *Take A Chance* ('Night Owl'). During World War II Hupfeld travelled widely, entertaining the troops in the USA and Europe. In 1950 he had one last fling at Broadway, contributing material to the musical *Dance Me A Song*. The show was notable only for an early appearance of dancer Bob Fosse, and was quickly withdrawn.

HUTCHINSON, LESLIE 'HUTCH'

b. c.1900, Grenada, West Indies, d. 18 August 1969. In his early teens Hutchinson was in New York where he studied law. In 1924 he was in Paris where he played piano and sang at various bars and restaurants, including Joselli's. He became friendly with many other ex-patriots and visitors including Bricktop and Cole Porter. In 1927 he was heard by UK impresario C. B. Cochran who invited him to London to appear in the Richard Rodgers/Lorenz Hart show, *One Dam Thing After Another*. Hutchinson remained in London, appearing at the best hotels and restaurants including long residencies at Quaglino's and

Café De Paris, and making the occasional stage appearance in shows such as Porter's *Wake Up And Dream!* During the 30s and 40s he was frequently heard on radio, but in 1949 he retired, making a comeback in 1953, and playing at Quaglino's again in the following year. Although best known for his work in the UK, Hutchinson also appeared in Kenya where he was popular with the white Anglo-Kenyan community. Leslie Hutchinson played the piano simply and discreetly, singing in a huskily confidential manner which befitted the type of venue with which he was customarily associated. (This artist should not be confused with the trumpeter Leslie 'Jiver' Hutchinson who led and played in several dance bands in London during the same period.)

● ALBUMS: *Moonlight Cocktail* (30s-40s recordings)★★★, *Hutch At The Piano* (30s-40s recordings)★★★, *With A Song In My Heart* (30s-40s recordings)★★★, *The Magic Of Hutch* (30s-40s recordings)★★★.

HUTTON, BETTY

b. 26 February 1921, Battle Creek, Michigan, USA. A dynamic and vivacious singer and actress, while still a small child Hutton began singing in the streets to help support her impoverished family. By her early teens she was already beginning to make a name for herself when she was hired by Vincent Lopez, then leader of a popular radio band. In 1940, by then known as 'The Blonde Bombshell' in recognition of her fizzing vitality, Hutton appeared on Broadway in *Panama Hattie*, and the following year was snapped up by Hollywood. During the 40s she appeared in a string of popular musicals including *Star Spangled Rhythm, Happy Go Lucky, Let's Face It, And The Angels Sing, Here Comes The Waves, Incendiary Blonde, Duffy's Tavern, The Stork Club, Cross My Heart, The Perils Of Pauline, Dream Girl* and *Red Hot And Blue*. However, it was her sensational performance in the title role of *Annie Get Your Gun* in 1950 that established her as a major star. It gained her an international reputation, which she enhanced with roles in *Let's Dance* (1950), *The Greatest Show On Earth* and *Somebody Loves Me* (both 1952). Subsequent contractual difficulties with the studio resulted in her career coming to an abrupt halt, and although she made a brief appearance in the 1957 film *Spring Reunion*, she was declared bankrupt in 1967. In 1971, the last of her four marriages, to trumpeter Pete Candoli, ended in divorce, and after suffering a nervous breakdown and problems with drugs and alcohol, she worked for several years as a cook and housekeeper in a rectory in Portsmouth, Long Island. She made a triumphant comeback in 1980 when she took over the role of Miss Hannigan in the hit Broadway musical *Annie*. Later, she enrolled as a student at a New England college, before settling in Los Angeles. Her sister, Marion, two years her senior, was also a singer who worked with Glenn Miller's civilian band. In 1994 Capitol issued a collection of some of her most entertaining tracks, and a year later singer Björk included one of Hutton's specialities, 'It's Oh So Quiet', on her *Post* album.

● ALBUMS: *Square In The Social Circle* 10-inch album (Capitol 1950)★★★, *Annie Get Your Gun* film soundtrack (MGM 1950/55)★★★, *Somebody Loves Me* film soundtrack (RCA 1952)★★★, *Satins And Spurs* TV soundtrack (Capitol 1954)★★, *At The Saints And Sinners Ball* (Warners 1959)★★★.

● COMPILATIONS: *Great Ladies Of Song: Spotlight On Betty Hutton* (Capitol 1994)★★★.

● FILMS: *The Fleet's In* (1942), *Star Spangled Rhythm* (1942), *The Miracle Of Morgan's Creek* (1943), *Let's Face It* (1943), *Here Comes The Waves* (1944), *And The Angels Sing* (1944), *Incendiary Blonde* (1945), *The Stork Club* (1946), *Cross My Heart* (1946), *The Perils Of Pauline* (1947), *Dream Girl* (1948) *Annie Get Your Gun* (1950), *Let's Dance* (1951), *Somebody Loves Me* (1952), *The Greatest Show On Earth* (1952), *Spring Reunion* (1957).

HYLTON, JACK

b. 2 July 1892, Lancashire, England, d. 29 January 1965, London, England. Hylton was the leader of an outstanding showband, often called 'Britain's answer to Paul Whiteman' because their repertoire included popular songs, novelties, light classical pieces and a few 'hot' jazz numbers. Hylton sang as a boy soprano in his father's bar before turning to the piano and organ. After playing in a small band at the Queen's Hall Roof in London, he took over, enlarged the group, and started recording in 1921. Although broadcasting occasionally, Hylton concentrated on 'live' performances, and built his showband into a major stage attraction. During the late 20s he toured Europe extensively, while still recording prolifically under several other names such as the Kit-Cat Band, the Hyltonians and the Rhythmagicians. He sold over three million records in 1929 alone, sometimes using gimmicks like flying low over Blackpool in an aircraft, to publicize Joe Gilbert's novelty song, 'Me And Jane In A Plane'. During the 30s his band became the first to broadcast directly to America. Subsequently, he toured the USA using local musicians, while still remaining the premier European showband. Hylton also made two films, *She Shall Have Music* (1935) and *Band Waggon* (1940) the movie version of the highly popular radio programme featuring Arthur Askey and Richard Murdoch. The band broke up in 1940, when several of the members were drafted into the forces. Hylton had used some of the best musicians, such as Ted Heath, Eric Pogson, Jack Jackson, Lew Davis, arranger Billy Ternent, jazzman Coleman Hawkins, and singers Jack Plant, Sam Browne and Peggy Dell. With his vast experience, Hylton then moved on to become an impresario, presenting countless West End productions such as *Annie Get Your Gun, Kiss Me, Kate, Call Me Madam, Camelot* and many more. One of his most endearing legacies was the legendary series of Crazy Gang shows at the Victoria Palace, London.

● COMPILATIONS: *Jack Hylton And His Orchestra* (1966)★★★, *Bands That Matter* (Eclipse 1970)★★★, *The Band That Jack Built* (Retrospect 1973)★★★, *Plays DeSylva, Brown & Henderson* (Retrospect 1974)★★★, *A Programme Light Orchestra Favour's* (1978)★★★, *From Berlin - 1927/31* (1979)★★★, *Jack's Back* (Living Era 1982)★★★, *Breakaway* (Joy 1982)★★★, *Swing* (Saville 1983)★★★, *The Talk Of The Town* (Saville 1984)★★★, *The Golden Age Of Jack Hylton* (Golden Age 1984)★★★, *I'm In A Dancing Mood* (Retrospect 1986)★★★, *Song Of Happiness 1931-33* (Saville 1987)★★★, *This'll Make You Whistle* (Burlington 1988)★★★, *Cream Of Jack Hylton* (Flapper 1992)★★★.

I CAN GET IT FOR YOU WHOLESALE

Notable mainly for the Broadway debut of the 19-year-old Barbra Streisand, who, in her role as an overworked secretary, stopped the show nightly with 'Miss Marmelstein', this production opened at the Shubert Theatre in New York on 22 March 1962. The 'wholesale' aspect referred to librettist Jerome Weidman's story, based on his own book, which was set in the 30s Depression days of the 'dog-eat-dog' world of New York's rag trade. Harry Bogen (Elliot Gould) is the tough small-time businessman, who will stop at nothing to get to the top, even though his mother, (Lillian Roth) and his girlfriend, Ruthie Rivkin (Marilyn Cooper) plead with him to change his ways. Ruthie is replaced by the flashy nightclub singer, Martha Mills (Sheree North), and, in the end, Harry gets his just deserts. Streisand was low down in the billing, but she was given another effective number, 'What Are They Doing To Us Now?', in a what was generally considered to be a lacklustre Harold Rome score that also included 'Have I Told You Lately?', 'Momma, Momma', 'The Sound Of Money', 'A Gift for Today', 'On My Way To Love', 'Too Soon', 'What's In It For Me?', and 'Who Knows'. Even during the show's run of 300 performances, the young, self-assured lady who married the leading man (Gould), was recording her breakthrough *The Barbra Streisand Album*, complete with its prophetic sleeve-note by no less a person than Harold Arlen, part of which ran: 'I advise you to watch Barbra Streisand's career. This young lady has a stunning future'. How right he was.

I COULD GO ON SINGING

Nine years elapsed between Judy Garland's critically acclaimed performance in *A Star Is Born* and this, her next musical film, which was released in 1963 and provoked an entirely different response. Mayo Simon's often poignant story was about a star American singer, Jenny Bowman (Garland), who travels to England for a concert tour and, while there, engineers a meeting with Harley Street surgeon David Donne (Dirk Bogarde), in an effort to get to know their illegitimate son, Matt (Gregory Phillips). Jenny's craving for the boy's affection, and his sudden realization that she is his mother, bordered on the maudlin and was generally unconvincing. Not so the musical sequences, however, in which Garland was at the top of her form. She pulled all the stops out on E.Y. 'Yip' Harburg and Harold Arlen's highly appropriate title song, and on the other lovely numbers such as 'It Never Was You' (Kurt Weill-Maxwell Anderson), 'By Myself' (Arthur Schwartz-Howard Dietz), and 'Hello, Bluebird' (Cliff

Friend). Dirk Bogarde himself provided some additional (and much-needed) extra dialogue, and gave his usually efficient performance. Also in the cast were Jack Klugman as George Kogan (Jenny's long-suffering manager), Aline MacMahon, Pauline Jameson, and Russell Waters. Ronald Neame directed what sadly proved to be Garland's last film. It was produced by Stuart Millar and Laurence Turman in Eastman Color and Panavision for Barbican Films in Great Britain, and released by United Artists.

I DO! I DO!

This musical opened at the 46th Street Theatre in New York on 5 December 1966 with a cast consisting of just two people. However, they were two extraordinary people - each of them a theatrical legend. Robert Preston had burst onto the Broadway scene some nine years previously as the conniving Professor Harold Hill in *The Music Man*, and Mary Martin's glorious career in musicals such as *One Touch Of Venus*, *South Pacific*, *Peter Pan*, and *The Sound Of Music*, was destined to end with this unusual two-hander. Tom Jones's book, which was adapted from the 1951 play *The Fourposter* by Jan de Hartog, told of a couple's 50 years of marriage, from their wedding day at the turn of the century, through the good times and bad, the arrival of the children, his affair, and finally, their exit from the large house to make way for a young couple with, no doubt, the same kind of aspirations that she (Agnes) and he (Michael) had all those years ago. Tom Jones and Harvey Schmidt's score augmented the story with appropriate numbers such as 'I Love My Wife', 'My Cup Runneth Over', 'Love Isn't Everything', 'Nobody's Perfect', 'Together Forever', 'What Is A Woman?', 'The Honeymoon Is Over', 'Where Are The Snows?', 'When The Kids Get Married', 'Someone Needs Me', 'Roll Up the Ribbons', and the title song. Carol Lawrence and Gordon MacRae succeeded the two original stars during the New York production which ran for over a year, a total of 560 performances. Jones and Schmidt are familiar with long runs - their off-Broadway show, *The Fantasticks*, has reigned for over 30 years. The London production of *I Do! I Do!*, with Ian Carmichael and Anne Rogers, played for 166 performances in 1968, and a short-lived 1976 West End revival starred Rock Hudson and Juliet Prowse. Twenty years on, New Yorkers saw a 30th anniversary production which opened off-Broadway at the Lamb's Theatre in March 1996. Still struggling to cope with the ups and downs of married life, were Michael (David Garrison) and Agnes (Karen Ziemba).

I GIVE MY HEART

This film version of the celebrated 1931 German operetta *The Dubarry* by Paul Knepler and J.M. Welleminsky, with music by Carl Millöcker adapted by Theo Mackeben, was released by British International Pictures in 1935. The story is set in France in 1769, where the delightful Gitta Alpar, who starred in the original production, recreates her role as Jeanne, the little milliner who dispenses her favours rather freely to, among others, her compatriot René (Patrick Waddington), and husband Count Dubarry (Arthur Margetson), in an effort to achieve her ambition of becoming the mistress of Louis XV (Owen Nares). The

Marechale de Luxembourg (Margaret Bannerman) and Choiseul (Hugh Miller) plot together to rouse the Paris mob against her, but they are overwhelmed by the majority of people who have come to love their little Jeanne. Other roles were taken by Gibb McClaughlin, Iris Ashley, and Hay Petrie. All the famous songs were retained, and Gitta Alpar excelled in a cast of all-round excellent vocal talents. A charming and appealing film, it had a screenplay by Frank Launder, Roger Burford, Kurt Siodmak, and Paul Perez, adapted from the original play. After this film, director Marcel Varnel left the world of operetta and devoted all his energies to creating classic comedy films starring Will Hay, George Formby, the Crazy Gang and Arthur Askey.

I LOVE MY WIFE

Wife-swapping in Trenton, New Jersey, USA (population a healthy 92,124), was the slightly old-fashioned subject of Michael Stewart's book for this show which opened at the Ethel Barrymore Theatre on Broadway on 17 April 1977. The two couples, initially intent on being 'Sexually Free', 'Lovers On A Christmas Eve', where 'Everybody Is Turning On' because they each feel there is 'Something Wonderful I've Missed', were Ileen Graff, Lenny Baker, Joanna Gleason, and James Naughton. Of course, being decent, upright citizens, they changed their minds at the last minute - one of the men takes an age to undress - and even then has to finish his dessert - with both husbands affirming: 'I Love My Wife'. Those songs, and the show's outstanding number, 'Hey There, Good Times', were the work of Cy Coleman (music) and Michael Stewart (lyrics). A small onstage orchestra dressed in various fancy clothing, comments on the action in the manner of a Greek chorus, a device that was also used by Richard Rodgers and Oscar Hammerstein II in *Allegro*. *I Love My Wife* caught on, and had a good run of 872 performances. The London production, which opened in October 1977, also did well. It starred Richard Beckinsale, an extremely popular actor in British television comedy programmes such as *Porridge*, who died so tragically young.

I LOVE YOU, YOU'RE PERFECT, NOW CHANGE

With not a single new musical opening on Broadway in the latter half of 1996, many of those fans in search of their regular 'fix' went downtown and upstairs to the Westside Theater on West 43rd Street for this musical revue which opened on 1 August. Originally produced by the American Stage Company, the show had called in at the Long Wharf Theatre in New Haven, Connecticut, on its way to New York City. Initial concerns (and low groans) that it was yet another revue about 'relationships' were dispelled within moments, as the highly talented cast of Jordan Leeds, Robert Roznowski, Jennifer Simard, and Melissa Weil, took a fresh, witty, and often hilarious look at the trials and tribulations of the first date ('Cantata For A First Date', 'A Stud And A Babe', 'Single Man Drought'), and the subsequent smooth segue through breakup ('Hey There, Single Guy/Gal', 'He Called Me'), into marriage ('Wedding Vows', 'Always A Bridesmaid', 'Marriage Tango'), the arrival of that 'absurd bird with a

bundle hung on his nose' ('The Baby Song'), to the final difficult funeral home scenario ('I Can Live With That'). Joe Dipietro wrote the book and lyrics to Jimmy Roberts' music, and the rest of their numbers, interspersed with Dipietro's sketches revealing more about the agonies and ecstasies regarding the whole darn man and woman, sex and romance thing, included 'Why? 'Cause I'm A Guy', 'Tear Jerk', 'I Will Be Loved Tonight', 'On The Highway Of Love', 'Waiting Trio', 'Shouldn't I Be Less In Love With You?', and 'I Love You, You're Perfect, Now Change'. Violinist Diane Montalbine brought a novel touch to the whole proceedings which were skilfully directed by Joel Bishoff. *I Love You, You're Perfect, Now Change* must have touched some kind of a nerve, because it was still running more that two years later.

I MARRIED AN ANGEL

Originally intended for Hollywood, this adaptation by Richard Rodgers and Lorenz Hart of a Hungarian play by John Vaszary, changed course and flew into New York, landing at the Shubert Theatre on 11 May 1938. It turned out to be a satirical, comic-fantasy concerning a banker in Budapest, Count Willi Palaffi (Dennis King), who breaks off his engagement to Audrey Christie (Anna Murphy), swearing that he will only ever marry an angel. Lo and behold, an apparition answering to the name of Angel (Vera Zorina), flies in through Willi's window. They are married, but Angel's open and honest winning ways cause chaos and confusion until she is taken in hand by Willi's sister, Countess Palaffi (Vivienne Segal). Walter Slezak, the Austrian character actor who later had a successful Hollywood career, played the financial backer who bailed Willi out when he was in trouble. Vivienne Segal was a revelation. For more than 20 years she had valiantly hung on to her honour in operettas such as *The Desert Song* and *The Yankee Princess*, and yet, here she was in *I Married An Angel*, shining in a sophisticated comedy role. King too, was a classically trained singer and came from a similar background. The duo combined on one of Rodgers and Hart's loveliest ballads, the bleak 'Spring Is Here' ('Stars appear!/Why doesn't the night invite me?/Maybe it's because nobody loves me/Spring is here/I hear!'). Ex-ballet dancer Vera Zorina was graceful and charming, but Audrey Christie had the show-stopper, 'At The Roxy Music Hall', a hilarious send-up of that vast, venerable institution: 'Where they change the lights a million times a minute/Where the stage goes up and down when they begin in it/It's a wonder Mrs. Roosevelt isn't in it.' The rest of the composers' songs in a high-quality score included 'Did You Ever Get Stung?', 'I'll Tell The Man In The Street', 'How To Win Friends And Influence People', and 'A Twinkle In Your Eye'. This was an unusual show in many ways; for instance, there was a full-scale ballet in each of the two acts, and some of the dialogue leading up to the songs was rhymed and sung. The production was also notable as the Broadway debut of director Joshua Logan. He was associated with subsequent Rodgers and Hart shows, as well as Rodgers and Oscar Hammerstein's *South Pacific*, and Irving Berlin's *Annie Get Your Gun* and *Mr. President*. Miss Segal's impact, too, earned her the plum role of Vera Simpson in *Pal Joey* in 1940. *I Married An*

Angel enjoyed a good run of 338 performances, which was followed by a satisfying road tour. The 1942 film version starred Jeanette MacDonald and Nelson Eddy.

I'D RATHER BE RIGHT

Even before it opened, this eagerly awaited show, which marked George M. Cohan's return to the Broadway musical stage after an absence of nearly 10 years, had more than the usual set of problems. The composer, Richard Rodgers, who wrote the score with lyricist Lorenz Hart, did not like Cohan (the loathing was mutual) - and he did not care much for the director George S. Kaufman (*he* did not like musicals) either, who co-authored the book with Moss Hart. Cohan, in turn, could not stand President Franklin D. Roosevelt, the somewhat controversial figure he had been chosen to play in his comeback vehicle. However, with the exception of Roosevelt, the rest of the combatants assembled on 2 November 1937 at the Alvin Theatre for the opening of what promised to be an historic event: it was the first time that a President had been portrayed in a book musical - as opposed to a revue - and a satirical one, at that. As the curtain rises, the setting is New York's Central Park on 4 July. Peggy (Joy Hodges) and Phil (Austin Marshall) are in love, but are waiting to get married until Phil gets an increase in salary - which his boss has refused to give him until Roosevelt balances the budget. Phil falls asleep, and in his dreams the two young people meet Roosevelt who promises to do what he can to help, but all his efforts, which include the introduction of hundred dollar postage stamps, come to nothing. Phil and Peggy decide to get married anyway. In spite of fears that the show might turn out to be an attack on the President, it was, in fact, a warm-hearted piece that poked fun at most of the prominent political figures of the day, with the notable exception of Eleanor Roosevelt (she was on holiday at the time). Initially, Cohan, who was appearing for the first time in a musical that he had not written himself, took some liberties with the material, particularly 'Off The Record', a song about Al Smith the Democratic candidate who had lost to Herbert Hoover in the 1928 election. In any event, Rodgers' music was not considered to be anywhere near his best, although Hart's lyrics were as sharp and witty as ever in songs such as 'We're Going To Balance The Budget', 'Sweet Sixty-Five', 'I'd Rather Be Right', 'Take And Take And Take', and the charming 'Have You Met Miss Jones?'. The latter number was the nearest the show came to having a love song, and it went on to become something of a minor standard. *I'd Rather Be Right* played for 290 performances in New York before undertaking a successful road tour.

I'LL BE YOUR SWEETHEART

This film was regarded at the time of its release in 1945 as Britain's answer to the highly popular 20th Century-Fox musicals. Set in London in 1900, it deals with the bitter struggle between the popular songwriters of the day and the pirates who copy their sheet music and sell it for a fraction of the true price. Screen newcomer Michael Rennie plays the young, idealistic song publisher Bob Fielding, who leads the fight for justice - that is when he is not vying with fellow songwriter Jim Knight (Peter

Graves) for the hand of music-hall star Edie Storey, who is played by Margaret Lockwood (singing voice dubbed by Maudie Edwards). Vic Oliver and Moore Marriott, as songwriters Sammy Kahn and George Le Brunn, led a strong supporting cast that includes Frederick Burtwell, Maudie Edwards, Garry Marsh, and George Merritt. Several of the songs in the film were hits, such as 'I'll Be Your Sweetheart' (Harry Dacre), 'Oh! Mr. Porter' (Thomas Le Brunn-George Le Brunn), 'Honeysuckle And The Bee' (W.H. Penn-A.H. Fitz), 'I Wouldn't Leave My Little Wooden Hut For You' (Tom Mellor-Charles Collins), and 'Liza Johnson' (George Le Brunn-Edgar Bateman). These were supplemented by three compositions written by Manning Sherwin and Val Guest: 'I'm Banking Everything On You', 'Sooner Or Later', and 'Mary Anna'. The musical numbers were devised by Robert Nesbitt and choreographed by Wendy Toye. Director Val Guest, who wrote the screenplay with Val Valentine, captured the style of the period perfectly, and although not *quite* in the class of the Fox movies, *I'll Be Your Sweetheart* was certainly an extremely diverting film. The producer for Gainsborough Pictures was Louis Levy.

I'LL GET BY
(see *Tin Pan Alley*)

I'M GETTING MY ACT TOGETHER AND TAKING IT ON THE ROAD

Produced by Joseph Papp at his New York Shakespeare Festival Public Theatre, the launchpad for several successful musical productions through the years, including *A Chorus Line*, this show opened on 14 June 1978. Nancy Ford (music) and Gretchen Cryer (lyrics and libretto) were well known in the US feminist movement, and their work consistently reflected their beliefs. In this piece, Ford plays a divorced 39-year-old pop singer on the comeback trail, who, with the help of her manager, played by Joe Fabiani, discovers her true self, and becomes a completely liberated person through her songs. These included 'Happy Birthday', 'Dear Tom', 'Natural High', 'Old Friend', 'Miss America', and 'Strong Woman Number'. After six months, the show transferred to the Circle in the Square Theatre in Greenwich Village, and eventually ran for 1,165 performances. During that time, other well-known names such as Betty Buckley, Phyllis Newman, Carol Hall, and Virginia Vestoff played the leading role. In 1981, a London production starring Ben Cross, Nicky Croydon, Diane Langton, Greg Martyn, and Megg Nichol, played briefly at the Apollo Theatre.

I'VE GOTTA HORSE

In 1964 pop singer Billy Fury purchased a racehorse, Anselmo. When it came fourth in that year's Derby race, the seeds were sewn for this anachronistic 1965 feature. Art mirrored life in the plot; Fury played a pop star distracted from his career by his devotion to animals, in particular his horse, Armitage, which emulates Anselmo in the cheery finale. Michael Medwin and Amanda Barrie co-starred with Fury in this largely forgettable film, which compounded a cosy view of pop by including passé vocal group the Bachelors. Mike Leander directed a score composed by David Heneker, who had previously written the music for Tommy Steele's highly successful *Half A Sixpence*. The songs on *I've Gotta Horse* were, however, below par, reaching a nadir with 'I Like Animals (Much Better Than Human Beings)'. The film, unimaginatively retitled *Wonderful Day* for the USA, was a waste of Fury's talents. Arguably one of Britain's finest pop talents of the 50s and 60s, he cried out for a vehicle that would enhance his moody, vulnerable image, rather than blithe, inconsequential fare. The Beatles, Rolling Stones and Byrds were taking pop into new arenas. *I've Gotta Horse* ensured that Fury remained criminally trapped in the past.

IDLE ON PARADE

Taking inspiration from Elvis Presley's induction into the US Army, Anthony Newley starred as the drafted pop star Jeep Jones in this 1959 British feature. Comedy stalwarts Sid James and Lionel Jeffries were also cast, but this jaundiced film owed more to television's *The Army Game* than rock 'n' roll. The soundtrack material, including 'Idle Rock-A-Boogie' and 'Saturday Night Rock-A-Boogie', consisted of little more than poorly formed pastiches, lacking neither the charm of Newley's Goons-inspired hits, 'Strawberry Fair' and 'That Noise', nor the wistfulness of his two UK chart-toppers, 'Why' and 'Do You Mind'. The four-track *Idle On Parade* EP nonetheless reached number 13 in the UK singles chart, reflecting the singer's popularity rather than the success of the film itself. Newley later became a celebrated songwriter for West End and Broadway productions, having bade farewell to his pop-styled inclinations.

IF YOU FEEL LIKE SINGING

(see *Summer Stock*)

IMAGINE

Between 1968 and 1972 John Lennon and Yoko Ono completed numerous *avant garde* films including *Smile*, *Self Portrait* and *Erection*. Shot largely at the couple's home in Ascot, England and released in 1972, *Imagine* was based around Lennon's album of the same title, his 'Power To The People' single, and portions of Ono's concurrent *Fly*. 'We're putting the picture to the sound, not the other way round', the former Beatle later explained and indeed there were several interludes where visual and aural impressions matched to perfection. This was especially true of 'Imagine' itself, which featured Lennon at a white piano while Ono gradually opened up shutters to allow light to penetrate the room. Indeed the entire *Imagine* project evolved from this particular sequence. Other notable moments include the pair's attempt at rowing a boat on the lake within their grounds and a game of chess where all the pieces are white, itself based on one of Ono's early art works. Newsreel footage was intercut into the free-flowing, dreamlike images and George Harrison and Phil Spector were among those momentarily appearing in the tableaux. A party scene featuring Andy Warhol was shot by Jonas Mekas, the director of *Guns Of The Trees* and a fellow member of the Fluxus Group with Ono during the early 60s. The first print of *Imagine* lasted 81 minutes, although this represented only 20% of the actual footage

shot. The film was not well received upon release and this first print was withdrawn and trimmed to 55 minutes. The bulk of Ono's contributions - 'Mind Train' and 'Midsummer New York' - were removed, but fortunately her haunting 'Mrs. Lennon' was retained. *Imagine* was edited further for video release during the 80s; clips and out-takes were also included in posthumous projects undertaken following Lennon's death.

IMAGINE (STAGE MUSICAL)

Devised by Keith Strachen and Ian Kellgren (who also directed) from an original idea by Bob Eaton, with additional material by Liam Lloyd, this tribute to John Lennon played the Liverpool Playhouse Theatre late in 1992. Mark McGann, who portrayed the late Beatle in the play *Lennon*, in the early 80s, and on film in *John And Yoko - A Love Story*, once again gave a performance that 'nurtures the shrewd, enquiring mind of John behind his eyes, and masters not only his native arrogance, his comic manner, bearing and stance, but his grim lips in repose'. In *Imagine*, the direct narrative was shared by Cynthia Lennon (Caroline Dennis), Yoko Ono (Ava de Souza), and composite characters such as an American fan (Francine Brody). Some 40 Beatles numbers were played and sung 'live' by McGann, along with Karl Lorne (Paul), Peter Ferris (George), and Paul Case (Ringo). Andy Walmsley's setting varied between a New York skyline and a section of the Cavern Club, and the evening provided 'moments of glorious affirmation as John Lennon's career describes its meteoric curve from rock musician to freaked-out martyr - with some marvellous songs along the way'.

IN DAHOMEY

A significant production in the history of the musical theatre on both sides of the Atlantic, *In Dahomey* is said to be the first full-length musical written and performed by black Americans to play a major Broadway theatre, and, perhaps rather less importantly, it introduced sophisticated New Yorkers to the current dance craze - a syncopated predecessor to ragtime - the cakewalk. In fact, one of the most popular moments in the show came when the audience was invited to judge a cakewalk competition by the level of its applause. *In Dahomey* opened on 18 February 1903 at the New York Theatre, with a book by Jesse A. Shipp that told of a gang of Boston con-men who plan to colonize Africa with the money they inveigle out of a geriatric millionaire. The popular ex-vaudeville team of Bert Williams and George. W. Walker supplied most of the comedy, and a lively score by Will Marion Cook (music) and Paul Lawrence Dubar (lyrics), included 'I'm A Jonah Now', 'I Want to Be A Real Lady', and 'On Emancipation Day'. *In Dahomey* only ran for 53 performances in New York, but, somewhat surprisingly, none of the expected racial tensions materialized, and the production was acclaimed for its verve and enthusiasm. Those factors also took London by surprise. Audiences there were not used to that level of exuberance, but they liked it, and the show stayed at the Shaftesbury Theatre for 251 performances during 1903, with Williams and Walker in their original roles.

INSIDE U.S.A.

The last of the seven always entertaining revues with music and lyrics by Arthur Schwartz and Howard Dietz opened at the New Century Theatre in New York on 30 April 1948. The show, which was also produced by Schwartz, is said to have been 'suggested' by John Gunther's famous book, but that was not apparent in the sketches by Arnold Auerbach, Arnold B. Horwitt, and Moss Hart. The indomitable Beatrice Lillie skylarked around along with Jack Haley in a series of comical geographical situations in which they, as two Indians in Alberquerque, resolutely refuse the offer of the whole country ('We Won't Take It Back'), and become involved with members of a choral society who are intent on solving the problems of pollution in Pittsburgh. 'Haunted Heart' was the song that achieved some popularity outside the show in recordings by Perry Como and Jo Stafford, and another ballad, 'First Prize At The Fair', was also singled out for praise. However, the novelty show-stopper was a United States list song, 'Rhode Island Is Famous For You', which was performed in the show by Haley, and seemed fairly conventional early on: 'Old whiskey, comes from old Kentucky/Ain't the country lucky?/New Jersey gives us glue' . . . 'Grand Canyons, come from Colorada/Gold comes from Nevada/Divorces also do' . . . but then 'declined' into the amusingly excruciating: 'Pencils come from Pencilvania/Vests from Vest Virgina/And tents from Tentassee'. The composer himself gave the song a more than adequate reading nearly 30 years later on his *From The Pen Of Arthur Schwartz*. The show's other numbers were 'Blue Grass', 'My Gal Is Mine Once More', and 'At The Mardi Gras', and the chorus contained some famous names: Jack Cassidy, who went on to star in *Wish You Were Here* and *She Loves Me*, and become the father of pop star David Cassidy before marrying Shirley Jones; and Carl Reiner, who achieved fame in the 60s as the writer of television's *The Dick Van Dyke Show*. *Inside U.S.A.* enjoyed a run of 399 performances, and, shortly after it closed, Schwartz devised a television variety programme based on the idea, which used the same songs, and starred Peter Lind Hayes and Mary Healy.

INTO THE WOODS

Once again Stephen Sondheim came up with something surprising and original for this show, which made its debut at the Martin Beck Theatre in New York on 5 November 1987. He and director-librettist James Lapine transformed a series of nursery rhyme characters, Cinderella (Kim Crosby), Red Riding Hood (Danielle Ferland), Jack (Ben Wright) And The Beanstalk, and Rapunzel (Pamela Winslow) into what one critic called 'a symbolic world of adulthood and self-discovery'. The tales are linked by the Baker (Chip Zien) and his wife (Joanna Gleason), who desperately want a child. A nearby Witch (Bernadette Peters) offers to solve their sterility problem if the baker will deliver to her within three days: Cinderella's slipper, Red Riding Hood's cape, Jack's cow, and Rapunzel's hair. The Baker obliges, and his wife duly becomes pregnant. Thereafter, the story takes on Freudian overtones, and becomes a 'timely moral allegory for adults'. Red Riding Hood is swallowed by the wolf but later emerges unscathed; Rapunzel goes mad; Jack's mother and Red Riding Hood's grandmother die suddenly; and the witch is transformed into her younger self. Sondheim's score was regarded as 'melodic and lyrically rich', and included such numbers as the recurring 'Into The Woods', 'Any Moment', 'Children Will Listen', 'It Takes Two', 'I Know Things Now', 'Moments In The Woods', and 'No More'. Another song that attracted some attention was 'Agony', a duet for two princes (Robert Westenberg and Chuck Wagner) who decide that adultery is more fun than fidelity. *Into The Woods* ran for 764 performances, slightly over-par for Sondheim, and won Tony Awards for the score, book, and best actress (Joanna Gleason), despite *The Phantom Of The Opera* running off with most of them in that year. It also gained the New York Drama Critics Circle and Drama Desk Awards for best musical. The 1990 London production, which ran for five months, starred Julia McKenzie as the Witch, NIcholas Parsons (Narrator), Jacqueline Dankworth (Cinderella), Richard Dempsey (Jack), Ian Bartholemew (Baker), Mary Lincoln (Rapunzel), Tessa Burbridge (Red Riding Hood), and Patsy Rowlands (Jack's Mother), It won Laurence Olivier Awards for the director (Richard Jones) and best actress (Imelda Staunton as the Baker's wife). An acclaimed revival was presented by the Long Beach Civic Light Opera in 1993, and five years later London audiences saw a Donmar Warehouse production with Frank Middlemass (Narrator), Jenna Russell (Cinderella), Christopher Pizzey (Jack), Nick Holder (Baker), Sophie Thompson (Baker's Wife), and Claire Burt (Witch).

INVITATION TO THE DANCE

Filming began on this ambitious Gene Kelly project in 1952, but the finished product was only presented to the public four years later. Produced by Arthur Freed for MGM, the picture was a gallant but unsuccessful attempt by Kelly to bring ballet to the cinema-going masses. There was no dialogue, and the film consisted of three individual ballet sequences (another, featuring several popular songs, had been cut prior to release). The first, 'Circus', in which Kelly plays a Pierrot character whose love for a ballerina (Claire Sombert) ends in tragedy, had music by Jacques Ibert. The second, 'Ring Around The Rosy', with music by André Previn, had overtones of La Ronde in its story of a bracelet which, after being presented by a husband to his wife, then passed through the hands of an artist, a nightclub singer, and a whore, among others, is finally returned to the husband. The final sequence, 'Sinbad The Sailor', composed by Rimsky-Korsakov, revived memories of Kelly's innovative dance with Jerry the cartoon mouse in *Anchors Aweigh* (1945). This time he was a sailor once more, involved with animated characters as well as the real-life Carol Haney and David Kasday. Other artists featured in the first two scenes were Igor Youskevitch, Claude Bessey, Tommy Rall, Tamara Toumanova, Belita, Irving Davies, Diana Adams and David Paltenghi. Gene Kelly was also the overall director-choreographer, and the film was beautifully photographed in Technicolor by Freddie Young and Joseph Ruttenberg, and shot mostly in England. Although it was critical and financial flop, the picture became something of a cult item, especially in Europe where it was awarded the Grand Prize in the 1958 West Berlin film festival. It is invariably included in Gene Kelly retrospectives.

IRENE

Yet another show based on the familiar Cinderella rags-to-riches story, this is, nevertheless, one of America's most treasured musical productions. It opened at the Vanderbilt Theatre in New York on 18 November 1919. James Montgomery's book, based on his own play, *Irene O'Dare*, told of a poor young girl (Edith Day), who works for an upholsterer. She is sent by her employer to do some work for Donald Marshall (Walter Regan) at his grand home in Long Island. Impressed by the personable girl, Donald arranges a job for her at an establishment belonging to a male fashion designer, Mme. Lucy (Bobby Watson). She charms everyone, including the extra-snobbish J.P. Bowden (Arthur Burckly), who gives a her a party, and becomes stricken with love for her, until he discovers that she is from 'the other side of the tracks'. Donald, however, has no such prejudice, and, after the usual trouble with his high-falutin' family, he and Irene eventually marry. The memorable score, by Harry Tierney (music), who was making his Broadway debut, and Joseph McCarthy (lyrics), produced one enormous hit, 'Alice Blue Gown', which was introduced by Edith Day, and later became popular through recordings by Day herself, and Frankie Masters, Ozzie Nelson, and Glenn Miller. There were some other good songs, too, such as 'Castle Of Dreams', 'The Talk Of The Town', 'Sky Rocket', 'To Be Worthy Of You', 'Irene', and the exuberant 'The Last Part Of Every Party'. During the show's run of 670 performances, a record for a Broadway musical, which it held for 18 years, Edith Day left to recreate her role in the London production which stayed at the Empire Theatre for almost a year. The show's incredible popularity continued via road companies which at one stage were estimated to be around 17 in number. In 1973, more than 50 years after it had first been produced, *Irene* was revived in New York with the popular film actress Debbie Reynolds, making her Broadway debut. In the revised book by Joseph Stein, Hugh Wheeler, and Harry Rigby, Irene O'Day's days as a model were long gone, and she was now - of all things - a piano tuner. Several changes were made to the score, including the addition of some songs by Charles Gaynor, Fred Fisher, and Otis Clements; and two others, both with lyrics by Joseph McCarthy, 'You Made Me Love You' (music by Jimmy Monaco), and 'I'm Always Chasing Rainbows' (music by Harry Carroll), which was originally used in the show *Oh Look!* (1918). Once again, the show endeared itself to the public, and stayed around for 604 performances. Two films of *Irene* were made, a silent version in 1926, with Colleen Moore, and another, in 1940, starring Anna Neagle, Ray Milland, and Roland Young.

IRMA LA DOUCE

This show originally opened at the tiny Theatre Gramont in Paris on 12 November 1956, and gave the city a new star - young Colette Renard - in the leading role. The book and lyrics were written by the ex-taxi driver and novelist Alexandre Breffort, and the music was provided by Marguerite Monnot, who had written several songs for Edith Piaf, including 'Poor People Of Paris', which became a big hit in France, and gave the personality pianist, Winifred Atwell, a UK number 1. Serious doubts were expressed as to whether this tender, typically French love story between a prostitute and her pimp, could weather the Channel crossing, and survive the trip to London's West End. In the event, it did so triumphantly. The production arrived at the Lyric Theatre, via the seaside town of Bournemouth, on 17 July 1958, with an English book and lyrics by three comparative newcomers to the musical theatre, Julian More, David Heneker, and Monty Norman. Rather than 'Anglicize' the show completely, the writers inserted a glossary of terms in the theatre programme, a device which had also been found to be necessary in France. The list of 'translations' included, Milieu (underworld), Poule (tart), Mec (pimp), and Grisbi (money). The story is set in the backstreets, off the Pigalle ('Valse Milieu'), with its small-time crooks ('Tres Tres Snob') and the poules, such as Irma-la-Douce (Elizabeth Seal). She falls in love with an impoverished law student, Nestor-le-Fripe (Keith Michell) ('The Bridge Of Caulaincourt'), and they live together ('Our Language Of Love') while Irma continues to work so that Nestor can continue his studies ('She's Got The Lot'). Nestor disguises himself as Monsieur Oscar, and becomes her sole client ('Dis-Donc'), but he soon becomes disenchanted with the double life ('The Wreck Of A Mec'), and dispenses with his alter ego ('That's A Crime'). He is found guilty of murder ('Le Grisbi Is Le Root Of Le Evil In Man') and sent to Devil's Island ('From A Prison Cell'), but he escapes ('There Is Only One Paris For That'), and returns to Irma just in time for the birth of their baby ('Christmas Child'). The production was a triumph all round, with a particularly strong supporting cast which included Clive Revill (Bob-le-Hontu), John East (Polyte-le-Mou), Julian Orchard (Police Inspector), and Gary Raymond (Frangipane). It ran for more than three and half years in London, a total of 1,512 performances, and the New York edition, in which several of the principals recreated their roles, played for over a year. Elizabeth Seal won the Tony Award for best actress, and Elliot Gould, who was on the brink of a successful film career at the time, played an Usher, a Priest, and a Warder. The 1963 film of *Irma La Douce* starred Shirley MacLaine and Jack Lemmon, but deleted all the songs, and used some of the music as background themes.

IRON MAN, THE

With the smash hit, razzle-dazzle production of the Who's *Tommy* doing 101.1% business on Broadway, its creator, Pete Townshend, turned his hand to this much smaller project which opened for a three month season at the Young Vic in London on 25 November 1993. Together with the show's director David Thacker, he adapted Poet Laureate Ted Hughes' 1968 book of children's fairytales into a musical production 'which is pitched somewhere between a children's show with a strong ecological message and one of those hippy musicals which surfaced in the late 60s and early 70s'. On a set 'that makes the rubbish dump in *Cats* look like an assembly line in a Japanese car factory', there emerges from time to time a 12 feet-high figure with vast headlamps for eyes, spanners for hands, and huge cans for feet. In between all of that is another load of junk. Actually none of the critics went that far, but, with hardly any exceptions, they did not like the show much. One of the main quibbles was the 'watering down' of certain characters such as the Star Spirit (Josette Bushell-Mingo), who, in Hughes' book, is a giant male dragon, and in this production is 'prettified and turned into a female sex symbol'. As to the plot, for most of the time the huge metal giant, accompanied by the Spirit of the Iron Man (Trevor Michael Georges), eats every piece of metal he can find ('cannibalism', one reviewer called it) and threatens to dominate the earth until a young boy named Hogarth (Anthony Barclay), together with some of his friends, pacifies him by singing 'Let's Have A Ball-Bearing Ball'. Townshend's music was deemed to be a good deal stronger than his lyrics in a score which contained numbers such as 'Over The Top We Go', 'Man Makes Machines', 'Dig!', 'Every Young Kid Has To Train', 'When Eyes Meet In Silence', 'I Eat Heavy Metal', 'I Awake Deep In The Night', 'Fast Food', 'I'm Not Gonna Run Anymore', 'Was There Life Before This Love?', and a typical 60s 'flower-power' plea for love and understanding, 'What We Want Is A Brand New Year'. Not an auspicious event, but, following *Tommy*'s triumph, it may be wise not to bet against Townshend eventually getting it right.

ISHAM, MARK

b. *c*.50s, New York City, New York, USA. Born into a musical family that encouraged him to learn the piano, violin and trumpet at an early age, Mark Isham began studying the jazz trumpet while at high school and then explored electronic music while in his early 20s. For a time he pursued parallel careers as a classical, jazz and rock musician, performing, for instance, with the San Francisco Opera, the Beach Boys and Pharoah Sanders, but by he early 70s, he concentrated his efforts on jazz. As co-leader of pianist Art Lande's Rubisa Patrol, he recorded two albums on ECM Records in the late 70s, continuing his partnership with Lande through to the late 80s. Together with guitarist Peter Mannu, Synthesizer player Patrick O'Hearn and drummer Terry Bozzio, he set up the Group 87 ensemble in 1979, releasing a self-titled debut album in 1981. At the same time, Isham continued his links with rock music, recording and touring as part of Van Morrison's band, where his trumpet and flugelhorn set off the saxophone of Pee Wee Ellis to good effect. During the 80s, Isham developed his compositional skills, using a synthesis of brass, electronics and his own plaintive trumpet to produce a very visual, narrative form of music. He recalls that 'my mother once told me that, as a kid, even before I really played music, I tried to tell stories with music. So, whether it's in the vocabulary of heavy metal or Stravinsky, the thread has to do with images.' Isham has taken that thread into film music, scoring the Academy winning documentary *The Life and Times Of Harvey Milk*, the film *Mrs Soffel* (both recorded on *Film Music*), and writing music to accompany children's fairy tales. His feature credits include *Trouble In Mind*, *Everybody Wins*, *Reversal*

Of Fortune, *Billy Bathgate*, *Little Man Tate*, *Cool World*, *Of Mice And Men*, *Sketch Artist*, *The Public Eye*, *A River Runs Through It*, *Nowhere To Run*, *Fire In The Sky*, *A Midnight Clear*, *Made In America*, *Romeo Is Bleeding*, *Short Cuts*, *Quiz Show*, *The Getaway*, *The Moderns*, *The Browning Version*, *Timecop*, *Mrs. Parker And The Vicious Circle*, *Nell*, *Quiz Show* (1994) and *Gotti* (1996). Throughout his career, Isham has remained a prolific session man, whose work encompasses recordings with artists as varied as saxophonist David Liebman, guitarist David Torn, and singers Suzanne Vega, Tanita Tikaram and Marianne Faithfull. Isham is blessed with an instantly memorable trumpet sound, one that is burnished, resonant, in places lush but which can, at times, be bleakly powerful, relying on minimalist fragments to achieve its subdued effect.

● ALBUMS: with Art Lande *Rubisia Patrol* (ECM 1976)★★, with Lande *Desert Marauders* (ECM 1978)★★★, *Group 87* (1981)★★, *Vapour Drawings* (Windham Hill 1983)★★★★, *A Career In Dada Processing* (1984)★★★, with Lande *We Begin* (1987)★★★, *Film Music* (Windham Hill 1987)★★★★, *Fire In The Sky* (1993)★★★, *Blue Sun* (Columbia 1995)★★★, *Afterglow* (Columbia 1998)★★★★.

IT HAPPENED AT THE WORLD'S FAIR

The second 1962 film to star Elvis Presley, *It Happened At The World's Fair* had a typically slight plot. Using the contemporaneous Seattle World's Fair as a backdrop, the singer falls in love, despite inevitable mix-ups, to provide a suitable happy last frame. A mere 10 songs were recorded for the accompanying soundtrack, described by one Presley biographer as 'the first in a string of albums that had fans despairing of him ever doing any decent material again'. Indeed, its playing time was barely 20 minutes. The track selected as a single, 'One Broken Heart For Sale', lasted a mere 1 minute 43 seconds, and failed to reach the Top 10 in either the USA or UK.

IT HAPPENED IN BROOKLYN

This pleasant MGM musical was released in 1947, and had a typically post-war story. Isobel Lennart's screenplay told of a shy ex-GI (Frank Sinatra) who returns to his beloved Brooklyn in New York, determined to make it to the top as a singer. As in the earlier *Anchors Aweigh*, he meets up with Kathryn Grayson (this time playing a music teacher) who, as usual, feels that she is destined for great things in the operatic vocal department. Jimmy Durante - the old scene stealer himself - is a kindly school caretaker who makes it his business to boost Sinatra's self confidence (!) in the film's high spot, 'The Song's Gotta Come From The Heart'. In this joyous hymn to sincerity and success, Sinatra spoofs Durante's straight-legged strut, and even manages to work in an excerpt from the traditional Russian folk song 'Orchi Chornya' ('Dark Eyes'). Apart from that piece, and the obligatory classical extracts from Grayson, the rest of the score was provided by Sammy Cahn and Jule Styne, and contained some lovely ballads for Sinatra such as 'Time After Time', 'It's The Same Old Dream', and 'The Brooklyn Bridge', as well as the livelier 'I Believe' and 'Whose Baby Are You?'. They did not do the singer much good, though, because his best friend, played by Peter Lawford, ended up with Grayson, and, when last seen, Sinatra was on the trail of a nurse (Gloria Grahame) he left behind in the US Army. Also in the cast were Aubrey Mather, Marcy McGuire, Tamara Shayne, Bobby Long and Billy Roy. Jack Donahue staged the dance sequences, and Richard Thorpe directed this unpretentious little film, which became quite a hit.

IT'S A BIRD, IT'S A PLANE, IT'S SUPERMAN

A camp version of the famous comic strip, with a book by David Newman and Robert Benton, this show zoomed into the Alvin Theatre in New York on 29 May 1966, and zoomed out again just four months later. In the stage musical phase of his varied and interesting life - as opposed to the film or printed page - Clark Kent (Bob Holiday), the meek and mild newspaper reporter on the *Daily Planet*, is still prepared to strip off to reveal that famous suit, complete with large letter 'S', at the merest hint of a national emergency. Surely Superman should have suspected foul play when the mad scientist, Dr. Sedgwick (Michael O'Sullivan), invites him to a dedication ceremony in his honour at the physics hall, while he (Sedgwick) sneaks away to blow up the Metropolis city hall? What a stroke of luck that he is in the power station to rescue Lois Lane (Patricia Marand), before streaking into the atmosphere to intercept a missile in mid-air that is destined for the city. Throw in an egotistical columnist, Max Mencken (Jack Cassidy), and an amusing score by Charles Strouse (music) and Lee Adams (lyrics), and somehow it is difficult to understand why the show did not run for more than 129 performances. One of the songs, 'You've Got Possibilities', received a much attention, and most of the other numbers were enjoyable, including 'It's Superman', 'We Don't Matter At All', 'The Woman For The Man', 'Ooh, Do You Love You!', 'What I've Always Wanted', 'You've Got What I Need', 'Pow! Bam! Zonk!', and 'It's Super Nice'. In the 80s there was the famous series of big blockbuster movies, starring Christopher Reeve, and then, in 1992, the stage show resurfaced in a production by the Godspeed Opera House, Connecticut, USA. The roles of Superman/Clark Kent and Lois were played by Gary Jackson and Kay McClelland, Strouse and Adams contributed several new songs, including 'Thanks To You', 'Karabitz!', and 'It's Up To Me', but the best notices went to 'Flying By Foy', 'the world's largest flying effects company', whose aerial manoeuvring of Superman over the heads of the audience was, by all accounts, sensational.

IT'S ALL HAPPENING

British singer and all-round entertainer Tommy Steele starred in this 1963 feature. In a plot that even in 1963 inspired a sense of *déjà vu*, a talent scout gathers together acts signed to his record label in order to stage a fund-raising concert for a local orphanage. This weak storyline is hampered further by his uninspiring roster, which included anachronistic stalwarts the George Mitchell Minstrels, pianist Russ Conway and vocalist Marion Ryan, mother of pop-singing twins, Paul And Barry Ryan. Shane Fenton And The Fentones, Carol Deen and the Clyde Valley Stompers do nothing to enliven proceedings which are

saved, albeit only momentarily, by the presence of John Barry. *It's All Happening* was renamed *The Dream Maker* in the US, a title derived from the insouciant song during which Steele is accompanied by a trilling children's chorale. Hopelessly out of date - this was, after all, the year of the Beatles' 'She Loves You' and 'I Want To Hold Your Hand' - *It's All Happening* is undoubtedly one of the most inappropriately titled films in cinema history.

IT'S ALL OVER TOWN

This 1964 film was a homage to a pre-'Swinging' London that revolved around Lance Percival and Roy Kinnear, two members of the team responsible for UK television's *That Was The Week That Was*. Sadly, the satirical elements of that pivotal weekly revue were not on offer herein and the travelogue merely provided famous landmarks in which to feature a succession of 'family'-orientated acts. 50s heart-throb Frankie Vaughan, clarinettist Acker Bilk and harmony trio the Bachelors were among those on offer. Pulses were raised slightly by the appearance of the Springfields, paradoxically about to disband to facilitate Dusty Springfield's solo career. Wayne Gibson And The Dynamic Sounds contributed a reading of Richie Valens' 'Come On Let's Go', but the film's real highlight came from the Hollies, who performed 'Now's The Time' to the backdrop of Covent Garden's fruit market. However, *It's All Over Town* neither captures a moment in time nor retains kitsch value.

IT'S ALWAYS FAIR WEATHER

As the opening titles fade in this entertaining and somewhat satirical musical, released by MGM in 1955, three US soldier buddies, back home in New York after serving together in World War II, have a final drink and sing the poignant 'The Time For Parting' as they pledge to meet again 10 years later. However, when the threesome, played by Gene Kelly, Dan Dailey and Michael Kidd, reunite in their favourite bar after 10 years, things have changed. Dailey is conceited, continually stressed and hates his job in advertising; Kelly has turned into a tough city dweller with one eye on the fight scene and the other looking over his shoulder; and Kidd is the only one who seems reasonably content with his life as the owner of a provincial diner grandly named the Cordon Bleu. High-powered executive (and boxing fan) Cyd Charisse deviously manoeuvres them and their 'fascinating' story onto the tacky television show *The Throb Of Manhattan*, which is hosted by the gorgeously over-the-top Dolores Gray. When Kelly is threatened by some unsavoury colleagues in the fight racket and Dailey and Kidd jump in to defend him with all fists blazing, the years roll back and it is just like old times for the three pals again. Originally conceived by screenwriters Betty Comden and Adolph Green as a sequel to *On The Town* (1949), *It's Always Fair Weather* turned out to be quite different from that project, with a marked cynical edge, especially in regard to the burgeoning US television industry. The basic creative team remained the same, however, with Arthur Freed producing and Gene Kelly and Stanley Donen sharing the director-choreographer credit. The score, by composer André Previn and Comden and Green (lyrics), had some marvellous moments, such as 'Situation-Wise', Dailey's exposé of the advertising industry; Kelly's escape from a gang of hoodlums via a song, dance and a pair of roller skates in 'I Like Myself'; Gray's magnificently syrupy and effusive 'Thanks A Lot But No Thanks'; and Charisse boxing clever in 'Baby You Knock Me Out'. The three male stars come together for a split screen rendition of 'Once Upon A Time' (the Cinemascope effect is generally destroyed when shown on television), and for an exhilarating dance routine through the streets, at one point using dustbin lids as improvised tap shoes. The other numbers included 'March, March' (Kelly-Dailey-Kidd), 'Stillman's Gym' (Charisse and boxers), and 'Music Is Better Than Words' (lyric: Comden-Green-Roger Edens; ensemble). Also featured were Jay C. Flippen, David Burns, Hal March and Lou Lubin.

IT'S GREAT TO BE YOUNG

Although rock 'n' roll was gathering pace throughout the world in 1956, this engaging British musical, which was released by AB-Pathé-Marble Arch, showed no sign of any such influence. Set in a co-educational school, it concerns the charismatic Mr Dingle (John Mills), a teacher whose interest in the school orchestra leads to a clash with the newly appointed (and very square) headmaster Mr Frome (Cecil Parker). Dingle is eventually dismissed, and his infuriated pupils stage a massive sit-in in order to get him reinstated. All ends happily when the combatants realize that a bit of give and take is all that is needed to live and learn in harmony together. The most memorable song remains the pretty ballad, 'You Are My First Love' (Paddy Roberts-Lester Powell), which is sung over the opening titles by Ruby Murray, and reprised during the sit-in by Paulette (Dorothy Bromiley, dubbed by Edna Savage). She aims it straight at Nicky (Jeremy Spenser), the young man to whom she has decided to give her adolescent heart. Other songs include 'Rhythm Is Our Business' (Sammy Cahn-Saul Chaplin-Jimmy Lunceford), performed engagingly by a group of pupils, singing and dancing on the sidewalk (dubbed by the Coronets). John Mills was perfectly cast in the role of the trumpet-playing music master who 'moonlights' on the piano in the local pub. Jazzman Humphrey Lyttelton helped out on the trumpet, and it was pianist Winifred Atwell's excellent version of 'The Original Dixieland One-Step' that was heard on the soundtrack. The film's musical director, Ray Martin, contributed the title song, the rousing 'Marching Strings', and the film's background score. In fact he also co-wrote the big ballad, 'You Are My First Love', because 'Lester Powell' was just one of his several aliases. It's Great To Be Young was directed by Cyril Frankel, produced by Victor Skutezky and had a screenplay by Ted Willis. Among the cast of this immensely enjoyable, unpretentious (and rare) British musical were Eleanor Summerfield, John Salew, Bryan Forbes, Brian Smith, Carole Shelley, Derek Blomfield, and a 13-year-old Richard O'Sullivan.

IT'S IN THE AIR

Another George Formby vehicle - and this time the vehicle is a motorcycle that George (wearing a friend's RAF uniform) borrows in order to post a letter. Mistaken for a dispatch rider, he is forced to drive around the Commanding Officer (Garry Marsh) of the RAF station, and eventually has to take an experimental aeroplane into the air and demonstrate it to a Government official, Sir Philip Bargrave (C. Denier Warren). The slapstick fun is fast and furious, with George getting involved in many complicated adventures, one of which concerns certain nocturnal experiences in an NCO's bedroom. Throughout it all, he wears that endearing toothy grin and ingenuous expression, and pauses occasionally to pull out his ukulele and slip in the odd song, such as 'They Can't Fool Me', 'It's In The Air', and 'Our Sergeant Major' (George Formby-Fred E. Cliffe-Harry Gifford). Polly Ward was his long-suffering fiancée, and among the other familiar names were Julien Mitchell, Jack Hobbs, Jack Melford, Hal Gordon, Frank Leighton, Michael Shepley, Ilena Sylva, and O.B. Clarence. Anthony Kimmins wrote the story and directed, and Basil Dean produced the film for Associated Talking Pictures in Britain in 1938.

IT'S LOVE AGAIN

Having captivated London theatre audiences with her enchanting dancing and singing during the 20s, in the next decade Jessie Matthews established herself as one of Britain's brightest film stars. In this picture, which was released by Gaumont in 1936, she plays Elaine Bradford, an ambitious but frustrated young performer who impersonates the alluring and mysterious Mrs. Smythe-Smythe, a dashing pilot, big-game hunter and friend of maharajahs, whose exciting exploits are constantly being revealed in the Daily Record. Unbeknown to her, Mrs. Smythe-Smythe does not in fact exist, and has been dreamed up by gossip columnist Peter Carlton (Robert Young) in an effort to boost the paper's circulation. Even when he acquaints her with the facts, Elaine still perpetuates the masquerade, and, after performing the sensational 'Temple Dance Of The East' at a party, she is engaged by impresario Archibald Raymond (Ernest Milton) for his new revue. Threatened with exposure by one of Peter's rival columnists (Cyril Raymond), she resigns, but is rehired as Elaine Bradford, a name she changes soon enough to Mrs. Peter Carlton. Jessie Matthews' real-life husband, Sonnie Hale, led a supporting cast that also included Robb Wilton, Sara Allgood, Warren Jenkins, Glennis Lorimer, and Athene Seyler. Marion Dix and Lesser Samuels wrote the screenplay, and American songwriters Sam Coslow and Harry Woods came up with some snappy numbers, including 'Gotta Dance My Way To Heaven', 'I Nearly Let Love Go Slipping Through My Fingers', 'Tony's In Town', and 'It's Love Again'. The musical score was written by Louis Levy and Bretton Byrd, and the dances were arranged by Buddy Bradley. It was directed by Victor Saville and produced by Michael Balcon.

IT'S MAGIC
(see Romance On The High Seas)

IT'S TRAD DAD

Clearly taking its cue from US films inspired by the Twist craze (Twist Around The Clock, Hey Let's Twist), this 1962 feature drew upon the 'trad jazz' boom then gripping

British pop. Its title came from a popular television show and, forsaking any notion of plot, *It's Trad Dad* (called *Ring A Ding Rhythm* in the USA) presented a succession of acts playing their current bestsellers. Although directed by Richard Lester, later to find fame for his work with the Beatles, the film is curiously reserved, lacking the spontaneity of its television counterpart. The cast included Kenny Ball, Acker Bilk, Terry Lightfoot and Chris Barber, each of whom was firmly in the New Orlean's revivalist camp, as well as the memorably eccentric Temperance 7. British pop acts featured included Helen Shapiro and Craig Douglas, but performances by US imports Gene Vincent, Gary U.S. Bonds and Del Shannon showed how staid their UK counterparts were. John Leyton, a protégé of iconoclast producer Joe Meek, was the sole British act offering something unique, largely through his mentor's bizarre fix on science-fiction pop. Meek, however, was an exception; a better measure of UK pop was emerging from Liverpool *It's Trad Dad* crossed the country.

IT'S YOUR THING

Popularizers of the seminal 'Twist And Shout', the Isley Brothers subsequently spent a frustrating period signed to Tamla/Motown before leaving the label to found their own outlet, T-Neck. Their first release on the label, 'It's Your Thing', topped the US R&B charts and reached number 2 in the corresponding pop listing. Energized by this new-found success, the group produced this 1969 feature film the following year which features moments from a soul music concert held in New York's Yankee Stadium. Ike And Tina Turner, themselves enjoying an artistic rebirth at the time, contributed powerful versions of 'Proud Mary', 'Honky Tonk Woman' and '(I Want To Take You) Higher'. The Edwin Hawkins Singers perform a memorable rendition of their international hit, 'Oh Happy Day', while the Five Stairsteps, Brooklyn Bridge and Patti Austin display contrasting contemporary soul styles. The Isley Brothers close the event with an exhilarating performance. Buoyed by artistic freedom, their melange of gospel, pop, R&B and Jimi Hendrix-styled guitar work, provides a suitably exciting finale to a film capturing a musical genre as it moved out of the shadows of Tamla/Motown and Stax Records to fully engage with rock.

IVES, BURL

b. Burl Icle Ivanhoe Ives, 14 June 1909, Hunt Township, Jasper County, Illinois, USA, d. 14 April 1995, Anacortes, Washington, USA. One of the world's most celebrated singers of folk ballads, with a gentle, intimate style, Ives was also an actor on the stage and screen, and an anthologist and editor of folk music. The son of tenant farmers in the 'Bible Belt' of Illinois, he was singing in public for money with his brothers and sisters when he was four years old. Many of the songs they sang originated in the British Isles, and were taught to them by their tobacco-chewing grandmother. After graduating from high school in 1927 Ives went to college with the aim of becoming a professional football coach. Instead, he left college early, in 1930, and hitch-hiked throughout the USA, Canada and Mexico, supporting himself by doing odd jobs and singing

to his own banjo accompaniment, picking up songs everywhere he went. After staying for a time in Terre Haute, Indiana, attending the State Teachers College, he moved to New York and studied with vocal coach Ekka Toedt, before enrolling for formal music training at New York University. Despite this classical education, he was determined to devote himself to folk songs. In 1938 he played character roles in several plays, and had a non-singing role on Broadway in the Richard Rodgers and Lorenz Hart musical *The Boys From Syracuse*, followed by a four-month singing engagement at New York's Village Vanguard nightclub. He then toured with another Rodgers and Hart show, *I Married An Angel*. In 1940 Ives performed on radio, singing his folk ballads to his own guitar accompaniment on programmes such as *Back Where I Come From*, and was soon given his own series entitled *Wayfaring Stranger*. The introductory 'Poor Wayfaring Stranger', one of America's favourite folk songs, and by then already over 100 years old, became his long-time theme. Drafted into the US Army in 1942, Ives sang in Irving Berlin's military musical revue *This Is The Army*, both on Broadway and on tour. In 1944, after medical discharge from the forces, Ives played a long stint at New York's Cafe Society Uptown nightclub, and also appeared on Broadway with Alfred Drake in *Sing Out Sweet Land*, a 'Salute To American Folk And Popular Music'. For his performance, Ives received the Donaldson Award as Best Supporting Actor. During the following year, he made a concert appearance at New York's Town Hall, and played a return engagement in 1946. Also in that year he made his first film, *Smoky*, with Fred McMurray and Anne Baxter, and appeared with Josh White in a full-length feature about folk music. Ives' other movies, in which he played characters ranging from villainous to warmly sympathetic, included *So Dear To My Heart* (1948), *East Of Eden* (1955) and *Cat On A Hot Tin Roof* (1958), in which he played Big Daddy, recreating his highly acclaimed Broadway performance in the Tennessee Williams play; he also appeared in *Wind Across The Everglades* (1958), *Desire Under The Elms* (1958) and *The Big Country* (1958), for which he received an Oscar as the Best Supporting Actor; and *Our Man In Havana* (1960). In 1954 Ives appeared as Cap'n Andy Hawkes in a revival of Jerome Kern and Oscar Hammerstein II's *Show Boat* at the New York City Center. In the 60s and 70s he appeared regularly on US television, sometimes in his dramatic series, such as *OK Crackerby* and *The Bold Ones*, and several musical specials. In the 80s, he continued to contribute character roles to feature films and television, and performed in concerts around the world. Back in 1948, his first chart record, 'Blue Tail Fly', teamed him with the Andrews Sisters. The song, written by Dan Emmett in 1846, had been in the Ives repertoire for some years. Other US Top 30 hits through to the early 60s included 'Lavender Blue (Dilly Dilly)', 'Riders In The Sky (Cowboy Legend)', 'On Top Of Old Smokey', 'The Wild Side Of Life', 'True Love Goes On And On', 'A Little Bitty Tear', 'Funny Way Of Laughin'' and 'Call Me Mr In-Between'. Many other songs became associated with him, such as 'Foggy Foggy Dew', 'Woolie Boogie Bee', 'Turtle Dove', 'Ten Thousand Miles', 'Big Rock Candy Mountain', 'I Know An Old Lady (Who Swallowed A Fly)', 'Aunt Rhody' and

'Ballad Of Davy Crockett'. Ives published several collections of folk ballads and tales, including *America's Musical Heritage - Song Of America*, *Burl Ives Song Book*, *Tales Of America*, *Burl Ives Book Of Irish Songs*, and for children, *Sailing On A Very Fine Day*. In 1993, in the distinguished company of Tom Paxton, Pete Seeger, Theodore Bikel, the Chad Mitchell Trio, Oscar Brand and Paul Robeson Jnr., Burl Ives performed in an emotional and nostalgic concert at the 92nd Street 'Y' Theatre in New York. Ives died in April 1995.

● ALBUMS: *The Wayfaring Stranger* 10-inch album (Stinson 1949)★★★★, *Ballads And Folk Songs Volume 1* 10-inch album (Decca 1949)★★★★, *Ballads And Folk Songs Volume 2* 10-inch album (Decca 1949)★★★★, *The Return Of The Wayfaring Stranger* 10-inch album (Columbia 1949)★★★★, *Ballads, Folk And Country Songs* 10-inch album (Decca 1949)★★★★, *More Folksongs* 10-inch album (Columbia 1950)★★★, *Christmas Day In The Morning* 10-inch album (Decca 1952)★★★, *Folk Songs Dramatic And Dangerous* 10-inch album (Decca 1953)★★★★, *Women: Folk Songs About The Fair* 10-inch album (Decca 1954)★★★, *Children's Favorites* 10-inch album (Columbia 1954)★★★, *Coronation Concert* (Decca 1956)★★★, *The Wild Side Of Life* (Decca 1956)★★★, *Men* (Decca 1956)★★★, *Down To The Sea In Ships* (Decca 1956)★★★★, *Women* (Decca 1956)★★, *In The Quiet Of Night* (Decca 1956)★★★, *Burl Ives Sings For Fun* (Decca 1956)★★, *Burl Ives Sings Songs For All Ages* (Columbia 1957)★★, *Christmas Eve With Ives* (Decca 1957)★★, *Songs Of Ireland* (Decca 1958)★★★, *Old Time Varieties* (Decca 1958)★★★, *Captain Burl Ives' Ark* (Decca 1958)★★★, *Australian Folk Songs* (Decca 1958)★★★, *Cheers* (Decca 1959)★★★, *Little White Duck* (Fontana 1960)★★, *Burl Ives Sings Irving Berlin* (1961)★★, *The Versatile Burl Ives!* (Decca 1962)★★, *It's Just My Funny Way Of Laughin'* (Decca 1962)★★★, *Songs Of The West* (Brunswick 1962)★★★, *Sunshine In My Soul* (Brunswick 1963)★★★, *Singin' Easy* (Brunswick 1963)★★★, *Walt Disney Presents Burl Ives - Animal Folk* (1964)★★, *Pearly Shells* (Decca 1964)★★★, *Rudolph The Red Nosed Reindeer* (Decca 1966)★, *Something Special* (Brunswick 1966)★★★, *Times They Are A-Changin'* (Columbia 1968)★★, *Animal Folk* (Castle Music 1974)★, *Chim Chim Cheree* (Castle Music 1974)★, with the Korean Children Choir *Faith And Joy* (Sacred/Word 1974)★, *How Great Thou Art* (Word 1974)★★, *Songs I Sang In Sunday School* (Sacred/Word 1974)★★, *I Do Believe* (Word 1974)★★★, *Shall We Gather At The River* (Sacred/Word 1978)★★★, *Talented Man* (Bulldog 1978)★★★, *Live In Europe* (Polydor 1979)★★★, *Bright And Beautiful* (Word 1979)★★, *Christmas At The White House* (Caedmon 1979)★★, *Stepping In The Light* (Word 1984)★★★, *Love And Joy* (Word 1984)★★★, and the 50s film and audio series *Historical America In Song* for Encyclopedia Britannica.

● COMPILATIONS: *The Best Of Burl Ives* (MCA 1965)★★★, *Junior Choice* (MFP 1979)★★, *The Best Of Burl's For Boys And Girls* (MCA 1980)★★, *The Very Best Of* (1993)★★★, *A Little Bitty Tear: The Nashville Years 1961-65* (1993)★★★.

● FURTHER READING: *Wayfaring Stranger*, Burl Ives.

● FILMS: *Smoky* (1946), *So Dear To My Heart* (1948), *East Of Eden* (1955), *Cat On A Hot Tin Roof* (1958), *Wind Across The Everglades* (1958), *Desire Under The Elms* (1958), *The Big Country* (1958), *Our Man In Havana* (1960), *The Brass Bottle* (1964), *Rocket To The Moon* (1967).

JACQUES BREL IS ALIVE AND WELL AND LIVING IN PARIS

This cabaret-style revue which celebrates the songs of the well-known Belgian composer, author, and performer, opened Off Broadway at the Village Gate on 22 January 1968, and ran for an incredible 1,847 performances. The show was conceived by Americans Mort Shuman and Eric Blau, who also wrote the lyrics and sundry other additional material. Jacques Brel's original critical and satirical approach to his life and work was impressively reflected in the upwards of 20 numbers that were used in the piece. These included some tender ballads, 'Marieke', 'Old Folks', and 'You're Not Alone', along with an impressive variety of other songs, such as the exuberant 'Carousel' and 'Brussels'. Shuman himself was in the cast of four, along with Shawn Elliot, Alice Whitfield, and Elly Stone, who got to sing most of the best songs, and received all the best notices. She also starred in the London production, along with Shuman, Elliot, and June Gable, but that folded after only 41 performances. Some 20 years later, Stone's connection with the show was renewed when she directed a revival which ran briefly at the Town Hall, New York in 1988. The performers then were Karen Akers, Shelle Ackerman, Kenny Morris, and Elmore James. By then the title was an anachronism - Jacques Brel had died in 1978. Even so, it has become a cult item over the years, so it was fitting that, in 1993, a 25th anniversary production was mounted at its original birthplace, the Village Gate, directed of course, by Elly Stone. In 1995, the show returned to Britain and played theatres on the London Fringe.

JAILHOUSE ROCK

Although hamstrung by mediocre films throughout much of his Hollywood career, Elvis Presley did complete some outstanding early features. In *Jailhouse Rock* he was aided by a superior plot in which the singer is taught to play guitar while serving in prison for manslaughter. Fame and egotism follow suit until his former cell-mate returns to haunt him and, eventually, prick his conscience. The film also provides an insight into record company practices during the 50s and has a visual impact many other contemporary works lacked. The highly choreographed scene that the title track accompanies has passed into pop cinema history. The Leiber And Stoller songwriting team, famed for their work with the Coasters, provided all of the soundtrack material, which ranges from the electric 'Baby I Don't Care' to the ballad-styled 'Young And Beautiful'. Taken together, the album and film represent a high-water mark in Presley's output.

JAMAICA

Making her only appearance in a Broadway book musical, Lena Horne was the main attraction when this show opened at the Imperial Theatre in New York on 31 October 1957. Ironically, it is sometimes claimed that Harry Belafonte was first choice for the leading role until he became unwell (Horne herself says: 'There's always been talk of a slight resemblance!'). If that is so, then the book, by E.Y. 'Yip' Harburg and Fred Saidly, obviously underwent some radical changes to enable Savannah (Lena Horne), to become the object of affection for Koli (Ricardo Montalban), a fisherman who lives on a mythical, magical tropical paradise known as Pigeon Island. Savannah is dissatisfied with that particular island, and would much prefer to move to another one where there is a bit more action - like Manhattan, for instance. However, after briefly flirting with an example of the civilization from that area in the shape of Joe Nashua (Joe Adams), she thinks better of it, and decides to settle for what she has got. The show had a top-notch score by Harburg and composer Harold Arlen, which included the outstanding ballad, 'Cocoanut Sweet', along with 'I Don't Think I'll End It Today', 'Ain't It The Truth', 'Pretty To Walk With', 'Little Biscuit', 'Incompatibility', 'Take It Slow, Joe', 'Napoleon', an amusing 'list' song, and Savannah's hymn to Manhattan, 'Push De Button'. A few years later, another of the songs, 'What Good Does It Do?', received a sensitive reading from Tony Bennett on an album he recorded in concert at Carnegie Hall in New York. On the strength of Lena Horne's box-office appeal (she was at her peak around this time), the show ran for nearly a year and a half, a total of 559 performances.

JAMBOREE

(see *Disc Jockey Jamboree*)

JAMES, HARRY

b. 15 March 1916, Albany, Georgia, USA, d. 5 July 1983, Las Vegas, Nevada, USA. Harry James's father played trumpet in the band of a touring circus, and at first Harry played the drums, but then he, too, took up the trumpet and at the age of nine was also playing in the circus band. He showed such enormous promise that his father had soon taught him everything he knew. Harry left the circus and played with various bands in Texas before joining Ben Pollack in 1935. Early in 1937 James was hired by Benny Goodman, an engagement which gave him maximum exposure to swing era audiences. Heavily featured with Goodman and, with Ziggy Elman and Chris Griffin, forming part of a powerful and exciting trumpet section, James quickly became a household name. He remained with Goodman a little under two years, leaving to form his own big band. James popularity increased and his public image, aided by his marriage to film star Betty Grable, reached remarkable heights for a musician. The band's popularity was achieved largely through James own solos, but a small part of its success may be attributed to his singers, Louise Tobin, to whom he was briefly married before Grable, Frank Sinatra, who soon left to join Tommy Dorsey, Dick Haymes and Kitty Kallen. James maintained his band throughout the 40s and into the early 50s, establishing a solid reputation thanks to distinguished sidemen such as Willie Smith, Buddy Rich, Corky Corcoran and Juan Tizol. Owing chiefly to the recorded repertoire, much of which featured James playing florid trumpet solos on tunes such as 'The Flight Of The Bumble Bee', 'The Carnival of Venice', 'I Cried For You' and 'You Made Me Love You', his band was at times less than popular with hardcore jazz fans. This view should have altered when, in the mid-50s, after a period of re-evaluation, James formed a band to play charts by Ernie Wilkins and Neal Hefti. One of the outstanding big bands, this particular group is often and very unfairly regarded as a copy of Count Basie's, a point of view which completely disregards chronology. In fact, James band can be seen to have pre-empted the slightly later but much more widely recognized middle-period band led by Basie, which also used Wilkins' and Hefti's charts. James continued leading into the 60s and 70s, dividing his time between extended residencies at major hotel and casino venues, mostly in Las Vegas, Nevada, and touring internationally. Amongst the first-rate musicians James used in these years were Willie Smith again, a succession of fine drummers (including Rich, Sonny Payne and Louie Bellson) and lead trumpeter Nick Buono, who had joined in December 1939 and showed no signs of relinquishing his chair and would, indeed, remain until the end. In his early years James was a brashly exciting player, attacking solos and abetting ensembles with a rich tone and what was at times an overwhelmingly powerful sound. With his own band he exploited his virtuoso technique, performing with great conviction the ballads and trumpet spectaculars that so disconcerted his jazz followers but which delighted the wider audience at whom they were aimed. Over the years James appeared in several movies - with his band in *Private Buckaroo* (1942), *Springtime In The Rockies*, *Best Foot Forward*, *Bathing Beauty*, *Two Girls And A Sailor*, *Do You Love Me?*, *If I'm Lucky*, *Carnegie Hall*, and *I'll Get By* (1950) - and as a solo artist in *Syncopation* (1942) and *The Benny Goodman Story* (1956). He also played trumpet on the soundtrack of *Young Man With A Horn* (1950). Later in his career, James work combined the best of both worlds - jazz and the more flashy style - and shed many of its excesses. He remained popular into the 80s and never lost his enthusiasm, despite suffering from cancer, which eventually claimed him in 1983.

● ALBUMS: *All Time Favorites* (Columbia 1950)★★★★, *Trumpet Time* (Columbia 1950)★★★, *Dance Parade* (Columbia 1950)★★★★, *Your Dance Date* (Columbia 1950)★★★★, *Soft Lights And Sweet Trumpet* (Columbia 1952)★★★, *One Night Stand* (Columbia 1953)★★★★, *At The Hollywood Palladium* (Columbia 1954)★★★★, *Trumpet After Midnight* (Columbia 1954)★★★, *Juke Box Jamboree* (Columbia 1955)★★★, *Man With The Horn* (Columbia 1995)★★★, *Harry James In Hi-Fi* (Capitol 1955)★★★★, *More Harry James In Hi-Fi* (Capitol 1956)★★, *Wild About Harry* (Capitol 1957)★★★, *The New James* (1958)★★★, *Harry's Choice!* (Capitol 1958)★★★, *Harry James And His New Swingin' Bands* (1959)★★★, *Harry James Today* (MGM 1960)★★★, *The Spectacular Sound Of Harry James* (1961)★★★, *Harry James Plays Neal Hefti* (1961)★★★★, *The Solid Trumpet Of*

Harry James (1962)★★★, *Double Dixie* (MGM/Verve 1962)★★★, *On Tour In '64* (1964)★★★, *Harry James Live At The Riverboat* (1966)★★★, *Live From Clearwater, Florida Vols 1-3* (1970)★★★★, *Live In London* (1971)★★★, *King James Version* (1976)★★★, *Still Harry After All These Years* (1979)★★★.
● FILMS: *The Big Beat* (1957).

JAMMIN' THE BLUES

Held by many movie buffs to be the finest jazz short ever filmed, and with considerable justification. The film, released in 1944, features superbly evocative photography by Gjon Mili, who also directed, and was supervised by Norman Granz. The musicians include Red Callender, Big Sid Catlett, Harry Edison, Illinois Jacquet, Jo Jones, Barney Kessel and the magnificent Lester Young. Timeless music by these assembled giants, allied to moody, smoky chiaroscuro makes this a must for any self-respecting jazz fan.
● VIDEOS: *Swing! Swing! Swing!* (1997).

JANIS

Released in 1974 and directed by Howard Alk and Seaton Findlay, *Janis* is an entertaining documentary on rock singer Janis Joplin. However, the film was made with the co-operation of the Joplin family and, although not a hagiography, *Janis* avoids controversial aspects of the singer's life, notably her bisexuality and the heroin addiction which brought her life to a premature end. Nevertheless, *Janis* does excel as a musical biography with the bulk of the in-concert footage left intact. These include Joplin's dazzling performance at the 1967 Monterey Pop Festival as a member of Big Brother And The Holding Company and an exciting rendition of 'Move Over' with her final group, the apply-titled Full Tilt Boogie Band. Behind-the-scenes footage at the recording of *Cheap Thrills* - where the tension is almost tangible - is equally revealing.

JARRE, MAURICE

b. 13 September 1924, Lyons, France. An important composer for films for over 40 years, as a youngster Jarre intended to become an electrical engineer, but changed his mind and studied music at the Paris Conservatoire in 1944. He joined the orchestra of the Jean Louise Barrault Theatre, and in 1951, composed the music for Kleist's *Le Prince De Homburg*. Soon afterwards he moved into films, and during the 50s, wrote the scores for such French productions as *Hotel Des Invalides*, *Le Grand Silence*, *Le Tetre Contre Les Murs* and *Les Yeux Sans Visage (Eyes Without A Face)*. During the early 60s, he began to score the occasional non-Gallic movie, such as *Crack In The Mirror*, starring Orson Welles, *The Big Gamble* and 'the last great epic of World War II', *The Longest Day* (1962). In the same year, Jarre won his first Academy Award for his memorable score for *Lawrence Of Arabia*, and was honoured again, three years later, for his music to *Doctor Zhivago*, featuring the haunting 'Lara's Theme' ('Somewhere, My Love'), which, with a lyric by Paul Francis Webster, became a Top 10 singles hit for the Ray Conniff Singers, and was the title track of one of their million-selling albums. Jarre's other 60s scores for English-speaking films included *Behold A*

Pale Horse, *The Collector*, *Is Paris Burning?*, *The Professionals*, *Grand Prix*, *Gambit*, *The Night Of The Generals*, *Villa Rides!*, *Five Card Stud*, *The Fixer*, *Isadora*, *The Damned* and Alfred Hitchcock's *Topaz* (1969). He continued to write prolifically in the 70s for films such as director George Steven's swan-song, *The Only Game In Town*, one of Neil Simon's funniest comedies, *Plaza Suite*, and many others, such as *The Effect Of Gamma Rays On Man-In-The-Moon Marigolds*, *The Life And Times Of Judge Roy Bean*, in which Andy Williams sang Jarre's 'Marmalade, Molasses And Honey' (lyric by Alan and Marilyn Bergman), *The Mackintosh Man*, *Great Expectations*, *Posse*, *The Man Who Would Be King*, *The Last Tycoon*, *Mohammed, Messenger Of God*, *March Or Die* and *Winter Kills*. His third Oscar came in 1984 for his 'anachronistic' score for David Lean's *A Passage To India*, and he was nominated in the following year for his work on *Witness*, starring Harrison Ford. His other 80s scores included *Resurrection*, *Lion Of The Desert*, *Taps*, *The Year Of Living Dangerously*, *Dreamscape*, *The Bride*, *Mad Max And The Thunderdrome*, *Enemy Mine*, *The Mosquito Coast*, *No Way Out*, *Fatal Attraction*, *Distant Thunder*, *Gorillas In The Mist* (another Academy Award nomination for Jarre), *Moon Over Parador*, *Chances Are*, *Dead Poets Society* (BAFTA Award, 1989), *Prancer* and *Enemies, A Love Story*. In 1991, Jarre received an ASCAP Award as the composer of the music for *Ghost*, the 'top box office film of 1990'. His other early 90s work included *After Dark, My Sweet*, *School Ties*, *Shadow Of The Wolf* (aka *Agaguk*), *Only The Lonely*, *Fearless* and *Mr. Jones* (1994). Apart from feature films, Jarre also wrote extensively for television. His credits included *The Silence*, *Jesus Of Nazareth* (mini-series), *Ishi, The Last Of His Tribe*, *Shogun* (mini-series), *Enola Gay*, *Coming Out Of The Ice*, *The Sky's No Limit*, *Samson And Delilah*, *Apology*, *The Murder Of Mary Phagan* (mini-series) and *Robinson Crusoe And Man Friday*.
● ALBUMS: *Jarre By Jarre* (Silva Screen 1989)★★★, *Only The Lonely* (Colosseum 1991)★★.

JAZZ DANCE

In 1954 an excellent idea took director Roger Tilton and a film crew into New York City's Central Plaza Dance Hall. Without gimmickry, they filmed the dancers and the end result is a marvellous feeling for the occasion. The band on the stand features Jimmy Archey, George 'Pops' Foster, Jimmy McPartland, Willie 'The Lion' Smith, Pee Wee Russell and George Wettling.

JAZZ IN EXILE

American jazz musicians in Europe have been the cynosure of fascinated interest not only by audiences but also by jazz historians. Magazine articles abound and there have been several good books on the subject. There have also been a number of films but none as good or effective as this exceptional documentary directed by Chuck France released in 1978. There are many interviews with musicians such as Gary Burton, Richard Davis, Dexter Gordon, Freddie Hubbard, Ben Sidran, McCoy Tyner and Phil Woods. There is some fine music to be heard, notably from Davis and Woods.

JAZZ IS OUR RELIGION

Directed by John Jeremy, this excellent USA documentary released in 1972 features the idiosyncratic photography of Valerie Wilmer. There are numerous audio interviews with Art Blakey, Bill Evans, Jimmy Garrison, Dizzy Gillespie, Johnny Griffin, Jo Jones, Blue Mitchell, Sunny Murray and Dewey Redman, amongst many. Music by Griffin, Dizzy Reece, Jon Hendricks, Lol Coxhill and the Clarke-Boland Big Band and others fills the soundtrack. Altogether a satisfactory mixture that goes a long way to confirming the premise of the film's title and creating an understanding of its meaning.

JAZZ ON A SUMMER'S DAY

From its opening moments, depicting reflected sailboats while Jimmy Giuffre's 'The Train And The River' bubbles on the soundtrack, this film sets out to create an unforgettable record of the 1958 Newport Jazz Festival. Directed by Bert Stern in 1960, repeated viewing might make some of the 60s photo-gimmickry a little trying and there are certainly too many audience cutaways during performances, but, overall, the concept is very well-realized. And the music is magnificent. Amongst the assembled giants are Louis Armstrong, Bob Brookmeyer, Ben Webster, Thelonious Monk, Roy Haynes, Rex Stewart, Sonny Stitt, Dinah Washington singing superbly and also clowning very musically on vibes with Terry Gibbs, Max Roach, Gerry Mulligan, Art Farmer, Chico Hamilton seen in rehearsal, Eric Dolphy, George Shearing, Jack Teagarden, Buck Clayton and Jo Jones. Mahalia Jackson brings the show to a sacred finale but for most people the outstanding moment is the considerably less-sacred sight of Anita O'Day, in high heels, cartwheel hat, gloves, and tight dress, struggling up onto the stage where she memorably recomposes 'Sweet Georgia Brown' and 'Tea For Two' in her own image. The video of this film should be on every jazz fan's shelf.

JAZZ SINGER, THE

Al Jolson, one of the world's all-time great entertainers, spoke a few words and sang a few songs in this, the first feature length talking picture which was released by Warner Brothers in 1927, and the screen musical was born. Alfred A. Cohen's screenplay was adapted from the short story, *The Day Of Atonement*, by Samson Raphaelson, which had been produced as a play on Broadway in 1925. It told of Jakie Rabinowitz (Jolson), a cantor's son who breaks his parents' hearts when he gives up his life in the synagogue for a career as a popular singer. Of course it was all pure schmaltz, and cinema audiences wept when, after his father has died, he returns to his beloved mother and tries to explain to her his love of music and his need to perform. Jolson, who appeared in blackface for the theatre sequences, was sensational, especially on songs which he had previously introduced in various stage productions such as 'My Mammy' and 'Toot Toot Tootsie'. The rest of the numbers included 'Dirty Hands, Dirty Face', 'Blue Skies', 'Mother Of Mine, I Still Have You', 'My Gal Sal', and the traditional Jewish 'Yahrzeit'. Also in the cast were Warner Oland, May

McAvoy, Otto Lederer, Eugenie Besserer, Bobby Gordon, and Myrna Loy. The sound, which was only heard on the musical sequences and some short pieces of dialogue -the rest of the film was silent - was recorded on the Vitaphone sound-on-disc system, and the film was directed by Alan Crosland and produced by Darryl F. Zanuck.

The exciting and extremely complicated changeover from silents to talkies was brilliantly spoofed in one of the world's favourite musicals, *Singin' In The Rain*, which was made in 1952. A year later, Warner released a remake of *The Jazz Singer* starring Danny Thomas, Peggy Lee, and Mildred Dunnock. This time the sentimental screenplay dealt with the return of US soldier from the Korean war. The score consisted of a bunch of well-tried musical standards. A third version, with Neil Diamond as Jess Rabinovitch and Laurence Olivier as his father, was made in 1980. The story remained fairly true to the 1927 original, and the cast included Lucie Arnaz, Catlin Adams, and Paul Nicholas as a particularly unpleasant recording artist. Diamond took three of the film's songs, 'America', 'Love On The Rocks', and 'Hello Again', all co-written by him, into the US Top 10.

JEEVES

This show is the skeleton in the cupboard of Andrew Lloyd Webber, the most successful composer of stage musicals during the past 20 years. Most of the creative giants of Broadway and the West End have had their superflops - Alan Jay Lerner (*Dance A Little Closer*), Lionel Bart (*Twang!!*), and Stephen Sondheim (*Anyone Can Whistle*), to mention only a few - and *Jeeves* proved that Lloyd Webber is no exception. The débâcle occurred at Her Majesty's Theatre in London on 22 April 1975, and was despatched, 38 performances later, on 24 May. The composer had already tasted substantial success with *Jesus Christ Superstar* and *Joseph And The Amazing Technicolor Dreamcoat* - and another smash-hit, *Evita*, was only three years into the future. Tim Rice, his collaborator on all three of those productions, was conveniently unavailable for *Jeeves* , so Lloyd Webber turned for the book and lyrics to the celebrated comedy playwright Alan Ayckbourn. One critic claimed that the result was 'like a dream of all the P.G. Wodehouse novels combined in the ultimate ghastly weekend', although Ayckbourn maintained that he 'tried to 'narrow in'' on one book, *The Code Of The Woosters*, and adapt that, with a few references to other books'. Jeeves (Michael Aldridge) and Bertie Wooster (David Hemmings) were joined by the usual Drones Club crowd, along with a veritable gaggle of girlfriends, and various other comical characters. Members of the cast included Betty Marsden, Gordon Clyde, Christopher Good, John Turner, Bill Wallis, Angela Easterling, Graham Hamilton, and Gabrielle Drake. It was widely felt that Lloyd Webber's music failed to capture the lively, happy-go-lucky flavour of the 20 and 30s period with a score which contained such songs as 'Code Of The Woosters', 'Travel Hopefully', 'Today', 'S.P.O.D.E.', 'Eulalie', 'Banjo Boy', 'Female Of The Species', 'When Love Arrives', 'Half A Moment', 'Summer Day', and 'Jeeves Is Past His Peak'. It must have seemed such a good idea at the time, but this 'straggling, heavy-handed affair' - the book of which, all concerned admitted, was a 'huge dinosaur' and far too long - proved to be only a slight hiccup in the careers of both Andrew Lloyd Webber and Alan Ayckbourn.

Almost exactly 20 years later, the bruises had apparently healed sufficiently for the duo to take a look at the subject again, and consequently 'an almost entirely new musical' entitled *By Jeeves* made its debut at the recently converted Stephen Joseph Theatre-in-the-round in Scarborough, Yorkshire, on 1 May 1996. Reaction was generally enthusiastic, and the production transferred to the fairly intimate (654-seater) Duke Of York's Theatre on 2 July for a 12-week season, which was extended at the Lyric in Shaftesbury Avenue until February 1997. It featured a radically revised (and down-sized) book, with an entirely original plot by Ayckbourn, who also directed (much of the blame for *Jeeves'* failure had been apportioned to director Eric Thompson, father of film actress Emma). This time round, in a classic mistaken identity plot, Bertie (Steven Pacey), is foiled in his commendable (but questionable) intention to entertain an expectant village hall audience with his banjo playing in aid of charity, when some music lover - Jeeves (Malcolm Sinclair) - hides the offending instrument. Undeterred, Bertie launches into a programme of 'this has been my life' anecdotes, which results in a series of hilarious escapades involving Gussie Fink-Nottle (Simon Day), Bingo Little (Nicholas Haverson), Harold 'Stinker' Pinker (Richard Long), the inevitable American house guest, jam millionaire Cyrus Budge III Junior (Nicolas Colicos), a grim magistrate, Sir Watkyn Bassett (Robert Austin), and female admirers Madeline Bassett (Diana Morrison), Stiffy Byng (Cathy Sara), and Honoria Glossop (Lucy Tregear). Regretfully, there was no sign of any of Bertie's eccentric aunts. However, whether impersonating a hat-stand, being 'driven' through the countryside on an up-turned table pulled by Jeeves, or burgling Madeline's home disguised in a pig's mask, Pacey's ebullient Wooster was a 'delightful mixture of silliness, charm, and bemusement'. He was aided and abetted by Sinclair's 'wonderfully supercilious Jeeves - sleek, calm, and ostentatiously unobtrusive', and the jolly choreography of Sheila Carter. The score, which gave a nod in the direction of Sandy Wilson and Vivian Ellis, amongst others, contained eight new songs, 'A False Start', 'That Was Nearly Us', 'Love's Maze', 'The Hallo Song', the jaunty second act opener, 'By Jeeves', 'What Have You Got To Say, Jeeves?', 'It's A Pig', and 'The Wizard Rainbow Finale'. Five numbers from the 1975 *Jeeves* were retained - some of which were re-lyricised by Ayckbourn - 'Code Of The Woosters', 'Travel Hopefully', 'When Love Arrives', 'Banjo Boy', and the appealing 'Half A Moment'. According to Lloyd Webber, the melody of another song from that earlier ill-fated production, 'Summer Day', was re-used by the composer in *Evita* as 'Another Suitcase In Another Hall'. After accomplishing 'one of the slickest comebacks since Lazarus', *By Jeeves* was nominated for three Laurence Olivier Awards, but failed to convert any. It had its American premiere at the Norma Terris Theatre, Goodspeed-at-Chester, Connecticut, in November 1996. Heading the cast were John Scherer (Bertie), Richard Kline (Jeeves), Merwin Goldsmith (Sir Watkyn), Emily Loesser (Stiffy), Donna Lynne Champlin (Honoria),

Randy Redd (Bingo), Kevin Ligon (Gussie), Nancy Anderson (Madeline), Ian Knauer (Stinker), and Jonathan Stewart (Cyrus).

JEKYLL & HYDE

This musicalization of Robert Louis Stevenson's famous 1886 novella, *The Strange Case Of Dr. Jekyll And Mr. Hyde*, first saw the light in the form of a concept album in 1990. It featured pop versions of the songs, performed by Colm Wilkinson as Jekyll/Hyde and Linda Eder as Lucy, the prostitute who has a love/hate relationship with the celebrated split personality. Soon after its release, in June 1990 the stage show had its world premiere at the Alley Theatre in Houston, Texas, but failed to generate enough interest to warrant a tour or Broadway transfer. However, boosted by a second (double) album, on which Eder was joined by Anthony Warlow, the Australian star of *The Phantom Of The Opera* and *Les Misérables*, as well as former Broadway legend John Raitt, a much-expanded production played Houston and Seattle in the spring of 1995, before touring extensively prior to Broadway. Robert Cuccioli assumed the dual roles of Jekyll/Hyde in December 1994, and he was still leading the cast when the show finally opened at New York's Plymouth Theatre on 28 April 1997. The show was conceived for the stage by Steve Cuden and Frank Wildhorn, with book and lyrics by Leslie Bricusse, and music by former pop composer Wildhorn. Although the original story had inevitably been reworked, Bricusse's book followed the familiar tale, set in Victorian London, of the upstanding Dr. Henry Jekyll (Cuccioli), who has developed a potion that, once and for all, will separate good from evil in humanity - and cure mental illness. After an asylum's board of governors refuses to test the brew on their patients, Jekyll swallows it (along with his pride), turns into Edward Hyde, and sets out to execute each member of the board. Fortunately, he omits to inform his fiancée, Emma Carew (Christiane Noll), of his intentions, and she continues to support him. Eder's 'stunning show-stopping voice', and considerable stage presence as the prostitute, attracted the best notices, and she was blessed with some of the best numbers, such as the soaring 'A New Life', 'Someone Like You' and 'In His Eyes' (with Noll). Cuccioli duetted with Noll on 'Take Me As I Am', and with himself for the dramatic 'Confrontation', as well as handling the impressive 'This Is The Moment'. Also included in the score, which was described by one critic as having a 'romantic pop-synth twist', were 'Lost In The Darkness', 'Facade', 'Jekyll's Plea', 'Emma's Reasons', 'Letting Go', 'No One Knows Who I Am', 'Good 'n' Evil', 'Alive', 'His Work And Nothing More', 'Murder, Murder', 'Once Upon A Dream', 'Obsession', 'Dangerous Game', 'The Way Back', 'Sympathy, Tenderness' and 'Dear Lord And Father Of Mankind'. Robin Phillips was the director, and Joey Pizzi the choreographer. The cast also featured George Merritt (John Utterson), Barrie Ingham (Sir Danvers Carew), Raymond Jaramillo McLeod (Mr. Simon Stride), Michael Ingam (Rupert, Bishop of Basingstoke), Brad Oscar (Archibald Proops), Martin Van Treuren (Lord Savage), Emily Zacharias (Lady Beaconsfield, Guinevere) and Geoffrey Blaisdell (General Lord Glossop). Bricusse received his usual generous dose of poison from the New York critics, and the show failed to win any of its four Tony Award nominations, although Cuccioli won FANY (Friends of New York Theatre), Drama Desk and Outer Critics Circle prizes for best actor in a musical. Two other musical adaptations of Stephenson's tale began prowling around in 1996: *Dr. Jekyll And Mr. Hyde* with book and lyrics by David Levy and Leslie Eberhard, and music by Phil Hall played Beverly, Massachusetts, and *Jekyll*, with a score by Tony Rees and Gary Young toured the UK provinces with ex-Phantom *Dave Willetts* in the lead. When the former reached the Paper Mill Playhouse, New Jersey, late in 1998, two actors played Jekyll (Richard White) and Hyde (Marc Kudisch).

JELLY'S LAST JAM

Although full to the brim with the music of the legendary pioneer jazz composer, pianist, and bandleader Jelly Roll Morton, this is an original book musical, and not just a run-down of a bunch of songs, most of which are over 60 years old. *Jelly's Last Jam* opened at the Virginia Theatre in New York on 26 April 1992. The book, by a newcomer to Broadway, George C. Wolfe who also directed the piece, opens with Morton (Gregory Hines) recently demised. Up (or down) there, in the anti-room in which the big decisions as to the eventual direction (eternity-wise) are made, the Chimney Man (Keith David), reviews the evidence as to Morton's earthly behaviour - from his early piano-playing days in Storyville brothels, through his self-appointed position as the 'inventor of jazz', to his controversial rejection of his African ancestry. Morton's own compositions are supplemented by some additional material from Luther Henderson, who also adapted and orchestrated the musical side of the whole production, and a set of sometimes saucy and sardonic lyrics by Susan Birkenhead. Naturally, with Hines on board, the tap dancing is sensational, but the entire cast, including Savion Glover as the young Morton, Stanley Wayne Mathis in the role of Jack the Bear, Morton's best friend, and Tonya Pinkins as his sexy girlfriend, were all outstanding. With the benefit of some memorable musical numbers such as 'Lovin' Is A Lowdown Blues', 'Play The Music For Me', 'The Last Chance Blues', 'The Chicago Stomp', 'Dr. Jazz', and many more, *Jelly's Last Jam* sang and danced its way into 1993, but after May of that year, when Hines was replaced by Brian Mitchell, things were never quite the same, although the highly popular Ben Vereen took over the role of the Chimney Man around the same time. However, the show still ran for a year and a half, closing in September 1993. Considering that it opened in the same season as *Falsettos*, along with *Crazy For You* and a revival of *Guys And Dolls*, the last two of which showcased three of America's favourite composers, *Jelly's Last Jam* did remarkably well in the kudos stakes. In the Drama Desk Awards, Gregory Hines tied with Nathan Lane (*Guys And Dolls*) for best actor, and the show won outright for featured actress (Tonya Pinkins), lyrics, orchestrations-musical adaptations, and book. Tony Awards went to Hines, Pinkins, and lighting designer Jules Fisher. US television viewers were given a rare opportunity to see the creators and performers discussing the show's roots and

relevance, in *Jammin': Jelly Roll Morton On Broadway*, which was transmitted in November 1992. Maurice Hines, brother of Gregory, headed the touring road company which rolled late in 1994.

JESUS CHRIST SUPERSTAR

While their 'pop cantata' *Joseph And The Amazing Technicolor Dreamcoat* was making the rounds of schools and festivals in the UK, Andrew Lloyd Webber and Tim Rice were creating the score for this rock opera which purported to tell the story of the last seven days of Christ. It was first released as a double album in 1970 (US number 1), with an all-star line-up of singers which included Ian Gillan (Jesus Christ), Murray Head (Judas), Yvonne Elliman (Mary), and Mike D'Abo (Herod). This was followed by a number of US concert tours, which led to a Broadway production opening at the Mark Hellinger Theatre on 12 October 1971. Tom O'Horgan's book (he also directed) was based on the New Testament, and heading the cast were Jeff Fenolt (Jesus), Yvonne Elliman (Mary Magdalene), Ben Vereen (Judas), and Barry Dennen (Pontius Pilate). 'Superstar', the number that inspired the whole concept, and 'I Don't Know How To Love Him', were prominent in a score which also included 'What's The Buzz?', 'Everything's All Right', 'This Jesus Must Die', 'Damned For All Time', 'The Last Supper', 'King Herod's Song', 'Heaven On Their Minds', 'Hosanna', and 'I Only Want To Say' ('Gethsemane'). Criticism from religious leaders and others who were offended by the show's alleged equating of Christ with a pop star on the decline, only helped to arouse more interest, and it ran for 711 performances. A London production opened at the Palace Theatre on 9 August 1972, with Paul Nicholas (Jesus), Dana Gillespie (Mary), Stephen Tate (Judas), and John Parker (Pontius Pilate). It ran until August 1980, a total of 3,358 performances, and reigned as the third-longest-running musical in the history of the London theatre (after *Cats* and *Starlight Express*) until it was overtaken by *Les Misérables* in January 1994. The 1973 film version, which starred Ted Neeley (Jesus), Carl Anderson (Judas), Yvonne Elliman (Mary), Barry Dennen (Pontius Pilate), and Josh Mostel (Herod), was not a box-office winner. Over the years *Jesus Christ Superstar* has enjoyed phenomenal success throughout the world, and in 1992 a 20th anniversary concert production toured the UK, starring one of the original performers, Paul Nicholas. Also in that year, a highly distinctive Japanese-language version by the Shiki Theatrical Company of Tokyo ('a kabuki-style production') was presented at the Dominion Theatre in London. Critical comments ranged from 'A memorable evening' to 'Seeing this ghastly show once 20 years ago was bad enough, but here it is again, banal and garish as ever.' In 1994, the show was seen in South Korea, when that country staged the first full-length Japanese theatrical production in Seoul since World War II. A year later, *Jesus Christ Superstar* grossed $3.5 million in two weeks at Madison Square Garden in New York. In November 1996, a major West End revival opened at the Lyceum Theatre, which had undergone a £15 million revamp. In the leading roles were Zubin Varla (Judas), Joanna Ampil (Mary), Nick Holder (Herod), David Burt (Pontius Pilate), and an unknown Welsh rock singer Steve Balsamo (Jesus), who went on to win the Variety Award for Outstanding New Talent of 1996. Earlier that year, a BBC Radio 2 production starred Roger Daltrey (Judas), Tony Hadley (ex-Spandau Ballet) (Jesus), Frances Ruffelle (Mary), Jeff Shankly (Pontius Pilate), and comedian Julian Clary (Herod). Also in 1996, Ted Neeley, who played Jesus in the 1973 film version, reprised his role for a US production at Stamford, Connecticut.

JILL DARLING

After touring the UK provinces under the title of *Jack And Jill*, the re-named and revised *Jill Darling* opened in the West End at the Saville Theatre on 19 December 1934. The composer Vivian Ellis had gone to extreme lengths to bring together his 'dream couple', Frances Day and Arthur Riscoe, in this musical comedy by Marriot Edgar. His story told of a young girl, Jill Sonning (Frances Day), who, for reasons that are not entirely clear, is masquerading as an Hungarian cabaret performer, while Arthur Riscoe has a double role - as Pendleton Brown, who is running for Parliament on an 'anti-booze' ticket, and Jack Crawford, who substitutes for Brown when he gets drunk. Vivian Ellis and Desmond Carter wrote a lovely score which gave the two leading players 'Let's Lay Our Heads Together' and 'I'd Do The Most Extraordinary Thing', and several other charming pieces such as 'Dancing With A Ghost' (Riscoe), along with 'I'm In Budapest' and 'Pardon My English' (Day). The second leads, Louise Brown and John Mills (later to become a celebrated straight actor), had the jolly 'Nonny, Nonny, No', as well as the surprise hit of the show, 'I'm On a See-Saw', which became successful for Ambrose And His Orchestra in America, and was subsequently recorded by Fats Waller. In a scene reminiscent of a 40s Hollywood movie, the show's backer, a young South African by the name of Jack Eggar, 'suggested' that there might part in *Jill Darling* for his wife, Teddi St. Dennis, and Ellis and Carter obligingly whipped up 'Bats In The Belfrey' for the lady to sing with the young Edward Molloy. The show was a great success, but, after Frances Day had to leave in the early summer of 1935 to fulfil a filming commitment (she was replaced by a *real* Hungarian), business fell off, and the production closed after a run of 242 performances. There was a revival at the Winter Garden Theatre in 1944, with Riscoe in his original role, and Carol Lynne as Jill, but it only lasted for two months.

JIVIN' IN BEBOP

Forget the amateur-night quality of the storyline and concentrate instead on the musical numbers which include a dozen powerful performances by Dizzy Gillespie's big band. Given the relatively short life of this outstanding band, and the fact that it made only a handful of records, this 1946 film thus gains a value far in excess of its other shaky qualities. Milt Jackson, John Lewis and James Moody are on hand as is the inimitable Helen Humes.

JOHNSON, LAURIE

b. 7 February 1927, England. A bandleader, musical director, and composer for the stage, television and films,

Johnson studied at the Royal College Of Music in London, and spent four years in the Coldstream Guards, before establishing himself on the UK entertainment scene in the late 50s and 60s. One of his first major projects early in 1959, was to write the music, and act as musical director, for *Lock Up Your Daughters*, a musical adaptation of Henry Fielding's *Rape Upon Rape*, which opened Bernard Miles' Mermaid Theatre in the City of London. Johnson's score, in collaboration with lyricist Lionel Bart, won an Ivor Novello Award. The show returned to the Mermaid in 1969 for a 10th anniversary season, and also played around the world, including a spell at the Godspeed Opera House in Connecticut, USA. The film version omitted the songs and featured a score by Ron Grainer. Johnson's other work for the West End stage has included music for the Peter Cook revue *Pieces Of Eight* (1959), and the score, with lyrics by Herbert Kretzmer, to *The Four Musketeers* (1967), which starred singer-comedian Harry Secombe. Despite attracting venomous reviews, *The Four Musketeers* ran for over a year. In 1961 the Laurie Johnson Orchestra had a UK Top 10 chart entry with the Latin-styled 'Sucu Sucu', written by Tarateno Rosa, the theme from the UK television series *Top Secret*. On the b-side was a Johnson composition, the title theme for another television production, *Echo Four-Two*. This is one of over 50 themes and scores that he wrote for television, a list that included *No Hiding Place*, *When The Kissing Had To Stop*, *Jason King*, *Shirley's World*, *The Adventurers*, *Thriller*, *The Avengers*, *The New Avengers* and *The Professionals*. The latter two were produced by Johnson's company, Avengers (Film And TV) Enterprises, formed with Albert Fennell and Brian Clemens. Johnson has also composed extensively for the cinema, from the late 50s. His film scores include *The Moonraker* (1958), *No Trees In The Street* (1958), *Tiger Bay* (1959), *I Aim At The Stars* (1960), *Spare The Rod* (1961), *Dr Strangelove - Or: How I Learned To Stop Worrying And Love The Bomb* (1964), *The First Men In The Moon* (1964), *The Beauty Jungle* (1966), *East Of Sudan* (1966), *Hot Millions* (1968), *And Soon The Darkness* (1970), *The Belstone Fox* (1976), *Diagnosis: Murder* (1976), *It's Alive II (It Lives Again)* (1978), *It Shouldn't Happen To A Vet* (1979) and *Bitter Harvest* (1981). Among his other works was the music for the television movie *Jericho*, which involved many of the original *Avengers* team, including Patrick MacNee. Late in 1994, Johnson announced the formation of the London Big Band, 'the largest band in Britain', consisting of the 'cream' of the music business, and led by veteran Jack Parnell.

● ALBUMS: *Operation Orchestra* (1959)★★★, *Songs Of Three Seasons* (1959)★★, *A Brass Band Swinging* (1961)★★★★, *Top Secret* (1962)★★★, *Two Cities Suite* (1963)★★★, *The Avengers* (1963)★★★★, *The New Big Sound Of Johnson* (1964)★★★, *Something's Coming* (1968)★★★, *Themes And...By Laurie Johnson* (1969)★★★, with Sir Bernard Miles *The Conquistadors* (1971)★★, *Laurie Johnson With The London Philharmonic And London Jazz Orchestras* (1973)★★★★, with the London Studio Orchestra *Music From the Avengers, New Avengers & The Professionals* (KPM 1980)★★★★, *Film Music Of Laurie Johnson* (Unicorn-Kanchana 1981)★★★, *Digital Film Scores Volumes 1-3* (1981)★★★, with the London Studio Symphony Orchestra *Rose And The Gun - The*

Music Of Laurie Johnson (Unicorn-Kanchana 1992)★★★, Laurie Johnson's London Big Band (1994)★★.
● COMPILATIONS: The Professional: The Best Of Laurie Johnson (1998)★★★.

JOKER IS WILD, THE

One of the first artists that Frank Sinatra signed to his own new Reprise label in the early 60s was nightclub comedian Joe E. Lewis. Before then, the two had been close friends, so it seemed logical, when Paramount decided in 1957 to make the film biography of a singer with a slick line in patter, that Sinatra's name would be to the fore. Shot in black and white, presumably to heighten the dramatic effect, the film turned out to be a hard-hitting, realistic account as to the likely fate of a young man in the Roaring 20s if he declined to co-operate with men in dark overcoats carrying violin cases. Young Lewes' career is progressing well in one particular nightspot, singing songs such as 'At Sundown' (Walter Donaldson) and 'I Cried For You' (Arthur Freed-Gus Arnheim-Abe Lyman). After ignoring warnings against moving elsewhere, he manages to impress audiences in the new venue ('where they carry the drunks out - they don't just toss 'em out into the street') with 'If I Could Be With You One Hour Tonight' (Henry Creamer-Jimmy Johnson) and 'All The Way' (Sammy Cahn-Jimmy Van Heusen), before his vocals cords are slashed and he finds a new career as a comedian. Subsequent fractured vocalizing is confined to parodies of songs such as 'Out Of Nowhere' (music-John Green), 'Swinging On A Star' (music-Van Heusen), and 'Naturally' (music-Flotow), all with new lyrics by Harry Harris. Before he finally kicks the bottle, Lewis has become a physical wreck and ruined the lives of the two women who love him, played by Jeanne Crain and Mitzi Gaynor. Eddie Albert plays Lewes' accompanist, whose wife (Beverly Garland) forces him to give up on the comedian, and the cast also included Jackie Coogan, Barry Kelley, Ted de Corsia, Valerie Allen, Hank Henry and Sophie Tucker. Oscar Saul's screenplay was adapted from a book by Art Cohn, and the film, which was photographed in VistaVision, was directed by Charles Vidor. The song 'All The Way' won an Academy Award, and gave Frank Sinatra a number 2 hit in the USA.

JOLSON - THE MUSICAL

After originating at the Theatre Royal in Plymouth in August 1995, and enjoying record-breaking business in the provinces en route to London, the biographical Jolson opened at the Victoria Palace on 26 October. The previous tenant of that theatre for almost six years had been another anthology musical, the smash-hit Buddy (also begat in Plymouth), which continued to post 'House Full' notices after transferring to the Strand Theatre, nearer to the heart of the West End. Inevitably, comparisons were drawn between the two productions, with many doubting the appeal - in the Politically Correct generation - of a show featuring an egotist with an often turbulent domestic life, who not only appeared regularly in blackface, but actually hit the big time in 1911 singing a song called 'Paris Is A Paradise For Coons'. In the event, Francis Essex and Rob Bettinson's book, which was developed from an original idea by Jolson biographer Michael Freedland, dealt with the blacking-up in a perfunctory manner, and even included 'a mawkishly implausible scene' in which Jolson (superbly portrayed by the popular television personality, Brian Conley), uncharacteristically gives a little encouragement (in the shape of a hug and some cash) to a young black boy, Sammy (Timothy Walker or Sean Parkins), who sings for him. The first act is set in the 20s, and deals with Jolson 'arrogantly steamrolling his career through the wishes of exasperated managers and agents' on his way to Broadway stardom, replacing obsolete wife number two with nifty hoofer Ruby Keeler (Sally Ann Triplett), as well as his involvement in the first talking picture, The Jazz Singer. Act II jumps forward to cover his decline in the 40s, and closes with a re-creation of the famous Radio City Concert, thereby providing a good excuse for Conley to belt out the few Jolson blockbusters remaining from the past couple of hours. Triplett's share of the goodies included 'By The Light Of The Silvery Moon', 'You Made Me Love You', 'I'm Just Wild About Harry', and 'I Only Have Eyes For You', and she combined with Conley on the insinuating 'About A Quarter To Nine'. Prominent amongst the cast were John Bennett, who gave a fine performance as Louis Epstein, the singer's long-suffering agent, Brian Greene (Lee Shubert), John Conroy (Frankie Holmes), Craig Stevenson (Harry Akst), Chrissy Roberts (Eugenie Besserer), Kit Benjamin (Pat Levin), Gareth Williams (Harry Cohn), Corinna Richards (Henrietta), David Bacon (Sam Warner), and Julie Armstrong, Alison Carter, and Helen McNee as the Rooney Sisters. Tudor Davies was the choreographer, the 'sumptuously contrived period settings' were designed by Robert Jones, and director Rob Bettinson moved the show along at great pace. However, it was Conley, with his brash, swaggering, incandescent performance, accurately incorporating many of Jolson's vocal mannerisms, who kept the coach parties turning up consistently, and it was a good idea to record the Original Cast CD 'live' at the theatre. The versatile Allan Stewart took over when the star was occasionally absent. Overall, Jolson was greeted by the critics with grudging admiration, although the general opinion seemed to be that, despite the billboards' claim that 'You truly ain't seen nothing yet', the show was 'not worth walking a million miles to see'. As with Jerry Herman's Mack And Mabel, Jolson proved once again that it is extremely difficult to mount a successful musical about an unsympathetic central character (except Evita?). Even so, it won the 1996 Laurence Olivier Award for Best Musical, and was also nominated for best actor (Conley) and supporting actor (Bennett). After the London run came to an end in March 1997, Conley and the show enjoyed a sell-out season in Toronto, Canada. Mike Burstyn (Ain't Broadway Grand) was in the lead when Jolson had its American premiere on 13 October 1998 at the newly-restored Allen Theatre in Cleveland, Ohio, prior to a national tour. On course to make it a possible head-to head clash on Broadway was another Jolson musical vehicle, The Jazz Singer. Two 'Jolsons' on Broadway in one season? 'Jolie' would have liked that. Regarding the controversial question of blacking-up, theatre-watchers pointed out that, ironically, Jolson played at the same London theatre where the renowned (but now redundant) *Black And White Minstrel Show* reigned between 1962 and 1972.

JOLSON SINGS AGAIN
(see *Jolson Story, The*)

JOLSON STORY, THE
This enormously successful, sanitised film biography of 'The World's Greatest Entertainer', who was actually in at the birth of screen musicals with *The Jazz Singer*, was released by Columbia in 1946. In fact, Stephen Longstreet's screenplay for *The Jolson Story* was very much along the lines of that earlier pioneering film: a cantor's son, Asa Yoelson (Al Jolson), breaks his father's heart by leaving home to make a successful career in show business as the black-faced entertainer who had an extraordinary effect on audiences all over the world. After countless actors had been tested for the leading role (Jolson put forward himself [aged 60] and James Cagney), Larry Parks got the part, with Evelyn Keyes as his wife Julie Benson (Ruby Keeler would not allow her name to be used). So it was Parks who strutted and gestured in that electrifying manner, but, at his insistence, it was Jolson's own voice that was heard on the carefully selected favourites that he had, over the years, made his own - songs such as 'My Mammy' (Joe Young-Sam Lewis-Walter Donaldson), 'California, Here I Come' (Joseph Meyer-Buddy De Sylva), 'Let Me Sing And I'm Happy' (Irving Berlin), 'Swanee' (George Gershwin-Irving Caesar), 'I'm Sitting On Top Of The World' (Ray Henderson-Lewis-Young), 'April Showers' (Louis Silvers-De Sylva), 'Toot Toot Tootsie' (Robert King-Ted Fiorito-Gus Kahn), 'Avalon' (Jolson-Vincent Rose), 'The Spaniard That Blighted My Life' (Billy Merson), 'Rock-A-Bye Your Baby With A Dixie Melody' (Lewis-Jean Schwartz-Young), 'Liza' George Gershwin-Ira Gershwin-Kahn), and the rest. There was also a new number, 'Anniversary Song', which was based on 'Danube Waves' and credited to Jolson, Saul Chaplin and Ion Ivanovici. William Demarest played the part of Jolson's mentor, Steve Martin, and the rest of the cast included Tamara Shayne, Ludwig Donath, Bill Goodwin, and Scotty Beckett as the boy Jolson. Jolson himself managed to make a brief appearance, albeit in long shot. Jack Cole staged the dances, and director Alfred E. Green skilfully blended all the various elements into a Technicolor film of blockbuster proportions. It grossed in excess of $7.5 million and was the seventh most popular film of the decade in the USA (after *This Is The Army*, *The Bells Of St. Mary's* and four Walt Disney animated features).
The inevitable sequel, *Jolson Sings Again*, which was almost, but not quite as successful as the original, came along in 1949 complete with a screenplay by Sidney Buchman in which Jolson (again played by Larry Parks) is seen entertaining US troops during World War II before retiring, initially because of ill-health. Permanently bored with his inactivity, it does not take a lot of persuading for him to agree to appear at a benefit show - which leads to a comeback, which leads to negotiations for a film of his life . . . *The Jolson Story*. Ludwig Donath and Tamara Shayne, who played his parents in that film were in this one too, and so was William Demarest. Barbara Hale was the nurse who helped Jolson to recover after his illness, and then married him, and also featured were Myron McCormick and Bill Goodwin. As before, the score provided a welcome opportunity to wallow in the Jolson songbook. The songs included 'When The Red, Red Robin Comes Bob, Bob Bobbin' Along' (Harry Woods), 'Carolina In The Morning' (Gus Kahn-Walter Donaldson), 'I'm Looking Over A Four Leaf Clover' (Woods-Mort Dixon), 'Sonny Boy' (De Sylva, Brown And Henderson), 'Back In Your Own Back Yard' (Billy Rose-Dave Dreyer), and many more. Henry Levin directed, and the film, which would have been known in more contemporary times as *The Jolson Story II*, grossed over $5 million in the US and was another worldwide hit.

JOLSON, AL
b. Asa Yoelson, *c*.1885, Snrednicke, Lithuania, d. 23 October 1950. Shortly before the turn of the century, Jolson's father, Moses Yoelson, emigrated to the USA. In a few years he was able to send for his wife and four children, who joined him in Washington DC. Moses Yoelson was cantor at a synagogue and had hopes that his youngest son, Asa, would adopt this profession. After the death of their mother, the two sons, Asa and Hirsch, occasionally sang on street corners for pennies. Following the example of his brother, who had changed his name to Harry, Asa became Al. When family disagreements arose after his father remarried, Al went to New York where his brother had gone to try his luck in show business. For food-money, he sang at McGirk's, a saloon/restaurant in New York's Bowery and later sang with military bands during the time of the Spanish-American War. Back in Washington, he attracted attention when, as a member of the audience at the city's Bijou Theater, he joined in the singing with entertainer Eddie Leonard. The vaudevillian was so impressed he offered the boy a job, singing from the balcony as part of the act. Al refused but ran away to join a theatrical troupe. This venture was short-lived and a week or so later he was back home but had again altered the spelling of his name, this time to Al Joelson. In the audience, again at the Bijou, he sang during the stage act of burlesque queen Aggie Beeler. Once more he was made an offer and this time he did not refuse. This job was also brief, because he was not content to merely sing from the balcony and Beller would not allow him to join her on the stage.
Joelson moved to New York and found work as a singing waiter. He also appeared in the crowd scenes of a play which survived for only three performances. Calling himself Harry Joelson, he formed a double act with Fred E. Moore but abandoned this when his voice broke. Reverting to the name Al he now joined his brother Harry and formed an act during which he whistled songs until his voice matured. The brothers teamed up with Joe Palmer to form the act Joelson, Palmer and Joelson, but again changed the spelling to shorten the space taken on playbills. In 1905 Harry dropped out of the act and the following year Al Jolson was on his own. In San Francisco he established a reputation as an exciting entertainer and coined the phrase which later became an integral part of his performance: 'All right, all right, folks - you ain't heard

nothin' yet!' In 1908 Jolson was hired by Lew Dockstader, leader of one of the country's two most famous minstrel shows, and quickly became the top attraction. Around this time he also formed a lifelong association with Harry Akst, a song plugger who later wrote songs including 'Dinah', 'Baby Face' and 'Am I Blue?'. Akst was especially useful to Jolson in finding songs suitable for his extrovert style. In 1911 Jolson opened at the Winter Garden in New York City, where he was a huge success. That same year he made his first records, reputedly having to be strapped to a chair as his involuntary movements were too much for the primitive recording equipment. Also in 1911 he suggested that the Winter Garden show be taken on tour, sets and full cast, orchestra and all, something that had never been done before. In 1912 he again did something new, putting on Sunday shows at the Garden so that other show business people could come and see him. Although he sang in blackface for the regular shows, local bylaws on religious observance meant that the Sunday shows had to be put on without sets and make-up. He devised an extended platform so that he could come out in front of the proscenium arch, thus allowing him to be closer to his audience with whom he was already having a remarkable love affair.

Among his song successes at this time were 'The Spaniard That Blighted My Life' and 'You Made Me Love You'. One night, when the show at the Garden was overrunning, he sent the rest of the cast off stage and simply sang to the audience who loved it. From then on, whenever he felt inclined, which was often, he would ask the audience to choose if they wanted to see the rest of the show or just listen to him. Invariably, they chose him. Significantly enough, on such occasions, the dismissed cast rarely went home, happily sitting in the wings to watch him perform. By 1915 Jolson was being billed as 'America's Greatest Entertainer' and even great rivals such as Eddie Cantor and George Jessel had to agree with this title. In 1916 Jolson made a silent film but found the experiment an unsatisfactory experience. Jolson's 1918 Broadway show was Sinbad and his song successes included 'Rockabye Your Baby With A Dixie Melody', 'Swanee' and 'My Mammy'. In 1919 he again tried something unprecedented for a popular entertainer, a concert at the Boston Opera House where he was accompanied by the city's symphony orchestra. Jolson's 1921 show was Bombo which opened at a new theatre which bore his name, Jolson's 59th Street Theater. The songs in the show included 'My Mammy', 'April Showers', 'California Here I Come' and 'Toot, Toot, Tootsie (Goo' Bye)'.

During the mid-20s Jolson tried some more new departures; in 1925 he opened in Big Boy, which had a real live horse in the cast, and in 1927 he performed on the radio. Of even more lasting significance, in 1926 he returned to the film studios to participate in an experimental film, a one-reel short entitled April Showers in which he sang three songs, his voice recorded on new equipment being tested by Vitaphone, a company which had been acquired by Warner Brothers Records. Although this brief film remained only a curio, and was seen by few people, the system stirred the imagination of Sam Warner, who believed that this might be what the company needed if it

was to stave off imminent bankruptcy. They decided to incorporate sound into a film currently in pre-production. This was The Jazz Singer which, as a stage show, had run for three years with George Jessel in the lead. Jessel wanted more money than the Warners could afford and Eddie Cantor turned them down flat. They approached Jolson, cannily inviting him to put money into the project in return for a piece of the profits. The Jazz Singer (1927) was a silent film into which it was planned to interpolate a song or two but Jolson, being Jolson, did it his way, calling out to the orchestra leader, 'Wait a minute, wait a minute. You ain't heard nothin' yet!' before launching into 'Toot, Toot, Tootsie'. The results were sensational and the motion picture industry was revolutionized overnight. The Warner brothers were saved from bankruptcy and Jolson's piece of the action made him even richer than he already was. His follow-up film, The Singing Fool, (1928) included a song especially written for him by the team of De Sylva, Brown And Henderson. Although they treated the exercise as a joke, the results were a massive hit and Jolson's recording of 'Sonny Boy' became one of the first million sellers. Although Jolson's films were popular and he was one of the highest paid performers in Hollywood, the cinema proved detrimental to his career. The cameras never fully captured the magic that had made him so successful on Broadway. Additionally, Jolson's love for working with a live audience was not satisfied by the film medium. His need to sing before a live audience was so overpowering that when his third wife, the dancer Ruby Keeler, opened on Broadway in Show Girl, he stood up in his seat and joined in with her big number, 'Liza'. He completely upstaged Keeler, who would later state that this was one of the things about him that she grew to hate the most. Jolson continued to make films, among them Mammy (1930) which included 'Let Me Sing And I'm Happy', and Big Boy (1930), generally cited as the film which came closest to capturing the essence of his live performances. Back on Broadway in 1931 with The Wonder Bar, Jolson was still popular and was certainly an extremely rich man, but he was no longer the massive success that he had been in the 20s. For a man who sang for many reasons, of which money was perhaps the least important, this was a very bad time. Fuelling his dissatisfaction was the fact that Keeler, whose film career he had actively encouraged and helped, was a bigger box-office attraction. Despite spreading a thin talent very wide, Keeler rose while Jolson fell. In 1932 he stopped making records and that year there were no shows or films, even though there were still offers. He made a film with Keeler, Go Into Your Dance (1935) in which he sang 'About A Quarter To Nine', and participated in an early television pilot. Not surprisingly for a man who had tried many new ventures in show business, Jolson was impressed by the medium and confidently predicted its success, but his enthusiasm was not followed up by producers. He made more films in the late 30s, sometimes cameos, occasionally rating third billing but the great days appeared to be over. Even his return to Broadway, in 1940 in Hold Onto Your Hats, was fated to close when he was struck down with pneumonia. The same year Jolson's marriage to Keeler ended acrimoniously.

On 7 December 1941, within hours of learning of the Japanese attack on Pearl Harbor, Jolson volunteered to travel overseas to entertain troops. Appearing before audiences of young men, to whom he was at best only a name, Jolson found and captured a new audience. All the old magic worked and during the next few years he toured endlessly, putting on shows to audiences of thousands or singing songs to a couple of GIs on street corners. With Harry Akst as his accompanist, he visited Europe and the UK, Africa and the Near and Far East theatres of war. Eventually, tired and sick, he returned to the USA where doctors advised him not to resume his overseas travels. Jolson agreed but instead began a punishing round of hospital visits on the mainland. Taken ill again, he was operated on and a part of one lung was removed. The hospital visits had a happier ending when he met Erle Galbraith, a civilian X-ray technician on one of the army bases he visited, who became his fourth wife. The war over, Jolson made a cameo appearance in a film and also performed on a couple of records, but it appeared as though his career, temporarily buoyed by the war, was ended. However, a man named Sidney Skolsky had long wanted to make a film about Jolson's life and, although turned down flat by all the major studios, eventually was given the go-ahead by Harry Cohn, boss of the ailing independent Columbia Pictures, who happened to be a Jolson fan. After surmounting many difficulties, not least that Jolson, despite being over 60 years old, wanted to play himself on the screen, the film was made. Starring Larry Parks as Jolson and with a superb soundtrack on which Jolson sang all his old favourites in exciting new arrangements by Morris Stoloff, *The Jolson Story* (1946) was a hit. Apart from making a great deal of money for Columbia, who thus became the second film company Jolson had saved, it put the singer back in the public eye with a bang. He signed a deal with Decca Records for a series of records using the same Stoloff arrangements and orchestral accompaniment. All the old songs became hugely popular as did 'The Anniversary Song' which was written especially for a scene in the film in which his father and mother dance on their wedding anniversary (Hollywood having conveniently overlooked the fact that his real mother had died when he was a boy). The film and the records, particularly 'The Anniversary Song', were especially popular in the UK.

In the USA Jolson's star continued to rise and after a string of performances on radio, where he became a regular guest on Bing Crosby's show, he was given his own series, which ran for four years and helped encourage Columbia to create another Jolson precedent. This was to make a sequel to a bio-pic. *Jolson Sings Again* (1949) recaptured the spirit and energy of the first film and was another huge success. In 1950 Jolson was again talking to television executives and this time it appeared that something would come from the discussions. Before anything could be settled, however, the US Army became involved in the so-called 'police action' in Korea and Jolson immediately volunteered to entertain the troops. With Harry Akst again accompanying him, he visited front-line soldiers during a punishing tour. Exhausted, he returned to the USA where he was booked to appear on Crosby's radio

show which was scheduled to be aired from San Francisco. On 23 October 1950, while playing cards with Akst and other long-time friends at the St. Francis hotel, he complained of chest pains and died shortly afterwards.

Throughout the 20s and into the mid-30s, Jolson was the USA's outstanding entertainer and in 1925 his already hyperbolic billing was changed to 'The World's Greatest Entertainer'. Unfortunately, latterday audiences have only his films and records to go on. None of the films can be regarded as offering substantial evidence of his greatness. His best records are those made with Stoloff for the soundtrack of the biographical films, by which time his voice was deeper and, anyway, recordings cannot recapture the stage presence which allowed him to hold audiences in their seats for hours on end. Although it is easy to be carried away by the enthusiasm of others, it would appear to be entirely justified in Jolson's case. Unlike many other instances of fan worship clouding reality, even Jolson's rivals acknowledged that he was the best. In addition, most of those who knew him disliked him as a man, but this never diminished their adulation of him as an entertainer. On the night he died they turned out the lights on Broadway, and traffic in Times Square was halted. It is hard to think of any subsequent superstar who would be granted, or who has earned, such testimonials. There has been only a small handful of entertainers, in any medium, of which it can be truly said, we shall never see their like again. Al Jolson was one of that number.

● ALBUMS: *Jolson Sings Again* soundtrack (Decca 1949)★★★, *In Songs He Made Famous* (Decca 1949)★★★, *Souvenir Album* (Decca/Brunswick 1949)★★★★, *Souvenir Album Vol 2* (Decca 1949)★★★, *Al Jolson* (Decca 1949)★★★, *Souvenir Album Vol 4* (Decca 19490, *Stephen Foster Songs* (Decca 1950)★★★★, *Souvenir Album Vol 5* (Decca 1951)★★★, *Souvenir Album Vol 6* (Decca 1951)★★★, *You Made Me Love You* (Decca 1957)★★★★, *Rock A Bye Your Baby* (Decca 1957)★★★★, *Rainbow Round My Shoulder* (Decca 1957)★★★, *You Ain't Heard Nothing Yet* (Decca 1957)★★★, *Memories* (Decca 1957)★★★, *Among My Souvenirs* (Decca 1957)★★★, *The Immortal Al Jolson* (Decca 1958)★★★★, *Overseas* (Decca 1959)★★★, *The Worlds Greatest Entertainer* (Decca 1959)★★★★, *Al Jolson With Oscar Levant At the Piano* (Decca 1961)★★★, *The Best Of Jolson* (1963)★★★, *Say It With Songs* (1965)★★★, *Jolson Sings Again* (1974)★★★, *You Ain't Heard Nothin' Yet* (1975)★★★, *Immortal Al Jolson* (1975)★★★, *20 Golden Greats* (1981)★★★★, *20 More Golden Greats* (1981)★★★, *The Man And The Legend Vols 1 & 2* (1982)★★★, *The Man And The Legend Vol 3* (1983)★★★, *Al Jolson Collection Vols. 1 & 2* (1983)★★★★, *The World's Greatest Entertainer* (1983)★★★★, *You Ain't Heard Nothin' Yet: Jolie's Finest Columbia Recordings* (Sony 1994)★★★★.

● FURTHER READING: *Jolie: The Story Of Al Jolson*, Michael Freedland. *Jolson: The Legend Comes To Life*, Herbert Goldman.

JONES, ALLAN

b. 14 October 1908, Scranton, Pennsylvania, USA. d. 27 June 1992, New York, USA. A popular, romantic tenor star in movies in the late 30s and early 40s, Jones studied singing in Paris, before returning to the USA and working in provincial operettas. He appeared on Broadway in *Roberta* (1933) and the 1934 revival of *Bitter Sweet* before gaining a part in the film *Reckless* (1935). In the same year he made a big impression singing 'Alone' in the Marx

Brothers film *A Night At The Opera*. This was followed by leading screen roles in *Rose-Marie*, *Show Boat* (1936), *A Day At The Races*, *The Firefly* (in which he introduced his signature tune 'The Donkey Serenade'), *Everybody Sing*, *The Great Victor Herbert*, *The Boys From Syracuse*, *One Night In The Tropics*, *There's Magic In Music*, *True To The Army*, *Moonlight In Havana*, *When Johnny Comes Marching Home*, *Larceny With Music*, *Rhythm Of The Islands*, *Crazy House*, *You're A Lucky Fellow Mr. Smith*, *The Singing Sheriff*, *Honeymoon Ahead*, and *Senorita From The West* (1945). Jones married actress Irene Hervey and their son, Jack Jones, went on to become a popular singer with big hits in the 60s. Allan Jones quit Hollywood in 1945 following a dispute with MGM boss Louis B. Mayer, and took to the nightclub circuit. In the 50s he starred in a major US tour of *Guys And Dolls*, and in the 70s he toured with *Man Of La Mancha*. He had recently returned from tour of Australia when he died of lung cancer in June 1992.

JONES, TOM
(see Schmidt, Harvey)

JONES, QUINCY

b. Quincy Delight Jones Jnr., 14 March 1933, Chicago, Illinois, USA. Jones began playing trumpet as a child and also developed an early interest in arranging, studying at the Berklee College Of Music. When he joined Lionel Hampton in 1951 it was as both performer and writer. With Hampton he visited Europe in a remarkable group that included rising stars Clifford Brown, Art Farmer, Gigi Gryce and Alan Dawson. Leaving Hampton in 1953, Jones wrote arrangements for many musicians, including some of his former colleagues and Ray Anthony, Count Basie and Tommy Dorsey. He mostly worked as a freelance but had a stint in the mid-50s as musical director for Dizzy Gillespie, one result of which was the 1956 album *World Statesman*. Later in the 50s and into the 60s Jones wrote charts and directed the orchestras for concerts and record sessions by several singers, including Frank Sinatra, Billy Eckstine, Brook Benton, Dinah Washington (an association that included the 1956 album *The Swingin' Miss 'D'*), Johnny Mathis and Ray Charles, whom he had known since childhood. He continued to write big band charts, composing and arranging albums for Basie, *One More Time* (1958-59) and *Li'l Ol' Groovemaker...Basie* (1963). By this time, Jones was fast becoming a major force in American popular music. In addition to playing he was busy writing and arranging, and was increasingly active as a record producer. In the late 60s and 70s he composed scores for around 40 feature films and hundreds of television shows. Among the former were *The Pawnbroker* (1965), *In Cold Blood* (1967) and *In The Heat Of The Night* (1967), while the latter included the long-running *Ironside* series and *Roots*. Other credits for television programmes include *The Bill Cosby Show*, *NBC Mystery Series*, *The Jesse Jackson Series*, *In The House* and *Mad TV*. He continued to produce records featuring his own music played by specially assembled orchestras. As a record producer Jones had originally worked for Mercury's Paris-based subsidiary Barclay, but later became the first black vice-president of the company's New York division. Later, he spent a dozen

years with A&M Records before starting up his own label, Qwest. Despite suffering two brain aneurysms in 1974 he showed no signs of reducing his high level of activity. In the 70s and 80s, in addition to many film soundtracks, he produced successful albums for Aretha Franklin, George Benson, Michael Jackson, the Brothers Johnston and other popular artists. With Benson he produced *Give Me The Night*, while for Jackson he helped to create *Off The Wall* and *Thriller*, the latter proving to be one of the best-selling albums of all time. He was also producer of the 1985 number 1 charity single 'We Are The World'. Latterly, Jones has been involved in film and television production, not necessarily in a musical context. As a player, Jones was an unexceptional soloist; as an arranger, his attributes are sometimes overlooked by the jazz audience, perhaps because of the manner in which he has consistently sought to create a smooth and wholly sophisticated entity, even at the expense of eliminating the essential characteristics of the artists concerned (as some of his work for Basie exemplifies). Nevertheless, with considerable subtlety he has fused elements of the blues and its many offshoots into mainstream jazz, and has found ways to bring soul to latter-day pop in a manner that adds to the latter without diminishing the former. His example has been followed by many although few have achieved such a level of success. A major film documentary, *Listen Up: The Lives Of Quincy Jones*, was released in 1990, and five years later Jones received the Jean Hersholt Humanitarian Award at the Academy Awards ceremony in Los Angeles. This coincided with *Q's Jook Joint*, a celebration of his 50 years in the music business with re-recordings of selections from his extraordinarily varied catalogue. The album lodged itself at the top of the *Billboard* jazz album chart for over four months. The film *Austin Powers* prompted a release of his 60s classic 'Soul Bossa Nova' in 1998.

● ALBUMS: *Quincy Jones With The Swedish/U.S. All Stars* (Prestige 1953)★★★, *This Is How I Feel About Jazz* (ABC-Paramount 1957)★★, *Go West Man* (ABC-Paramount 1957)★★★, *The Birth Of A Band* (Mercury 1959)★★★, *The Great Wide World Of Quincy Jones* (Mercury 1960)★★, *Quincy Jones At Newport '61* (Mercury 1961)★★★★, *I Dig Dancers* (Mercury 1961)★★★, *Around The World* (Mercury 1961)★★★, *The Quintessence* (Impulse! 1961)★★★, with Billy Eckstine *Billy Eckstine & Quincy Jones At Basin St. East* (Mercury 1962)★★★, *Big Band Bossa Nova* (Mercury 1962)★★★, *Quincy Jones Plays Hip Hits* (Mercury 1963)★★, *The Boy In The Tree* (1963)★★★, *Quincy's Got A Brand New Bag* (Mercury 1964)★★, *Quincy Jones Explores The Music Of Henry Mancini* (Mercury 1964)★★★, *Golden Boy* (Mercury 1964)★★★, *The Pawnbroker* (Mercury 1964)★★★, *Quincy Plays For Pussycats* (Mercury 1965)★★★, *Walk Don't Run* (Mainstream 1966)★★, *The Slender Thread* (Mercury 1966)★★★, *The Deadly Affair* (Verve 1967)★★★, *Enter Laughing* (Liberty 1967)★★★, *In The Heat Of The Night* film soundtrack (United Artists 1967)★★★★, *In Cold Blood* film soundtrack (Colgems 1967)★★★, *Banning* (1968)★★★, *For The Love Of Ivy* (ABC 1968)★★, *The Split* (1968)★★★, *Jigsaw* (1968)★★★, *A Dandy In Aspic* (1968)★★★, *The Hell With Heroes* (1968)★★★, *MacKennas Gold* (RCA 1969)★★★, *The Italian Job* film soundtrack (Paramount 1969)★★★★, *The Lost Man* (1969)★★★, *Bob & Carol & Ted & Alice* (Bell 1969)★★★, *John And Mary* (A&M 1969)★★★, *Walking*

In Space (A&M 1969)★★, *Gula Matari* (A&M 1970)★★★, *The Out Of Towners* (United Artists 1970)★★★, *Cactus Flower* (Bell 1970)★★★, *The Last Of The Hot Shots* (1970)★★★, *Sheila* (1970)★★, *They Call Me Mr Tibbs* (United Artists 1970)★★★, *Smackwater Jack* (A&M 1971)★★★, *The Anderson Tapes* (1971)★★★★, *Dollars* (1971)★★★, *Man And Boy* (1971)★★★, *The Hot Rock* (Prophesy 1972)★★★, *Ndeda* (Mercury 1972)★★★, *The New Centurians* (1972)★★★, with Donny Hathaway *Come Back Charleston Blue* film soundtrack (Atco 1972)★★, *You've Got It Bad Girl* (A&M 1973)★★, *Body Heat* (A&M 1974)★★★★, *This Is How I Feel About Jazz* (Impulse! 1974)★★★, *Mellow Madness* (A&M 1975)★★★, *I Heard That!* (A&M 1976)★★★, *Roots* (A&M 1977)★★★, *Sounds ... And Stuff Like That* (A&M 1978)★★, *The Wiz* (MCA 1978)★★★, *The Dude* (A&M 1981)★★★, *The Color Purple* film soundtrack (Qwest 1985)★★★★, *Back On The Block* (Qwest 1989)★★★, *Listen Up, The Lives Of Quincy Jones* (Qwest 1990)★★★, with Miles Davis *Live At Montreux* recorded 1991 (Reprise 1993)★★★★, *Q's Jook Joint* (Qwest 1995)★★★★.
● COMPILATIONS: *Compact Jazz: Quincy Jones* (Phillips/PolyGram 1989)★★★★, *Best Of Quincy Jones* (Spectrum 1998)★★★.
● VIDEOS: *Miles Davis And Quincy Jones: Live At Montreux* (1993).
● FURTHER READING: *Quincy Jones*, Raymond Horricks.
● FILMS: *Listen Up: The Lives Of Quincy Jones* (1990).

JONES, SHIRLEY

b. 31 March 1934, Smithton, Pennsylvania, USA. An actress and singer whose film portrayals of sweet and wholesome ingénues in the 50s contrasted sharply with her Academy Award-winning performance as Burt Lancaster's prostitute girlfriend in *Elmer Gantry* (1960). After taking singing lessons from an early age, Jones performed in stage productions before making her film debut opposite Gordon MacRae in the excellent film version of Richard Rodgers and Oscar Hammerstein II's *Oklahoma!* (1955). So successful was the collaboration that the two stars came together again a year later for another Rodgers and Hammerstein project, *Carousel*. After appearing with Pat Boone in *April Love* (1957), Jones turned in an impressive acting performance alongside James Cagney in the musical comedy-drama *Never Steal Anything Small*, joined a host of other stars in *Pepe*, and made one or two lacklustre features before partnering Robert Preston in another fine screen adaptation of a Broadway show, *The Music Man* (1962). From then on, Shirley Jones eschewed musical films for dramatic roles in big-screen features and on television. She was married for a time to the actor and singer Jack Cassidy, and she co-starred with her step-son, David Cassidy, in the top-rated television series *The Partridge Family* in the early 70s. Later in the decade she had her own show entitled *Shirley*. She continued to sing in nightclubs and concerts, and in the late 80s undertook a 14-week tour of the USA in *The King And I* with David Carradine. In the summer of 1994 she appeared with Marty Ingels in a provincial production of A.R. Gurney's two-hander *Love Letters*, and also starred in a Detroit revival of *The King And I*.

JOSEPH AND THE AMAZING TECHNICOLOR DREAMCOAT

Andrew Lloyd Webber's eventual domination of musical theatre throughout the world started with this show. It was initially a 20-minute 'pop cantata' based on the biblical character of Joseph, which he wrote with Tim Rice for an end-of-term concert at Colet Court Boys' School in the City of London. That was in March 1968, and, during the next five years, it was gradually revised and expanded during performances in the UK at a variety of venues including the Central Hall Westminster, St. Paul's Cathedral, the Edinburgh Festival, the Roundhouse, and the Young Vic. On 17 September 1973, a production opened at London's Albery Theatre, with Gary Bond as Joseph, and ran for 243 performances. Throughout the 70s, the show was often presented in and around London, generally with pop stars such as Paul Jones and Jess Conrad in the lead, and in 1976 it had its New York premiere at the Brooklyn Academy of Music. Five years later, in November 1981, *Joseph* opened on Broadway, and ran for 824 performances. However, it was not until Lloyd Webber decided to present it at the London Palladium in June 1991, that the piece was finally developed into its present two-hour, two-act form. A significant factor which contributed to its sensational reception in the 2,271-seater house, was the inspired casting of the teeny-boppers' idol Jason Donovan, ex-star of the popular Australian television soap, *Neighbours*. When Donovan went on holiday, Lloyd Webber did it again, and replaced him with Philip Schofield, another highly popular television personality. He and Donovan proceeded to alternate during much of the run. While he was associated with the show, Donovan sued a fringe magazine, *The Face*, for inferring that he was homosexual. The High Court heard that the hit song from *Joseph*, 'Any Dream Will Do', which Donovan took to the top of the UK chart, was adapted by gays to become 'Any Queen Will Do'. The whole affair has travelled a long way from its inception in 1968. According to one critic, the simple story of Joseph, son of Jacob, and his brothers, which is narrated in this production by Linzi Hately, is 'a lurid, synthetic Joseph, accompanied by spoofs of sentimental American ballads, calypso, and Presley rock', with 'Joseph's prison cell filled with bopping lovelies', and 'an Elvis lookalike in Tutankhamun gear emerging from a vast sphinx, to sing at inordinate length', while 'Donovan, a macho Goldilocks, makes a climactic entrance in primeval batmobile with lion-heads and wings'. Nevertheless, the score which contained Lloyd Webber's tongue-in-cheek pastiches and some of Rice's deceptively ingenuous lyrics retained its appeal, with songs such as 'One More Angel To Heaven', 'Joseph's Coat', 'Go, Go, Go, Joseph', and 'Pharaoh's Story'. When it closed in January 1994, *Joseph* had become the longest-running show ever at the London Palladium. In the early 90s, Joseph fever spread quickly, and productions were mounted throughout the world. Donny Osmond - who once, just like Joseph, was part of a brother act - played the lead in the Canadian production which toured North American breaking records wherever it went, especially in Chicago and Minneapolis. An American production, with Michael

Damien in the leading role, opened on Broadway in November 1993 for a limited season. Joseph was played by Darren Day and ex-boy soprano Aled Jones, amongst others, in 1994 and 1995 UK regional productions.

JOURNEY THROUGH THE PAST

Singer-songwriter Neil Young was riding a crest of popularity thanks to his 1972 release, *Harvest*, and his involvement in the supergroup, Crosby, Stills, Nash And Young. Mercurial to the end, he confronted the notion of commercial success with this self-indulgent film. 'Every scene meant something to me, though with some of them, I can't say what', he later gave as some kind of explanation about this sprawling 1973 feature. Directed by Young under his 'Bernard Shakey' pseudonym, *Journey Through The Past* is a surreal autobiography, combining elements of Americana with moments drawn from the singer's life as a performer. It included elements from his first successful group, Buffalo Springfield, as well as alternative versions of songs from concurrent projects, notably lengthy interpretations of 'Words' and 'Alabama'. The soundtrack also featured 'Ohio', a song inspired by the slaying of four students at Kent State campus, pitted against a reading of 'God Bless America', sung by evangelist Billy Graham and US President Richard Nixon. Variously described as 'pretentious' and 'technically inept', *Journey Through The Past* was withdrawn soon after release. Given public acceptance of Young's now notorious obdurism, it seems ripe for re-appraisal.

JUAN DARIEN, A CARNIVAL MASS

Not by any means a conventional stage musical, *Juan Darien* had enjoyed a couple of outings off-off and off-Broadway in the late 80s before a Lincoln Centre production opened on 24 November 1996 at the Vivian Beaumont Theatre in New York for a two-month run. This one-act 'performance piece', based on a tale by Uruguayan Horacio Quiroga, was the work of Julie Taymor and Elliot Goldenthal. Portrayed in Taymor's trademark style, utilizing masks and puppets of different designs, the story concerns an orphaned jaguar cub, nurtured by a woman whose own baby has been killed by the plague. The cub is miraculously transformed into a human child, Juan Darien, but after his secret is betrayed, he is flogged and crucified by a mob before being resurrected in his feline form. A visual and aural feast (sets and costumes, G.W. Mercier and Taymor), with a strange, haunting ambience, complemented by a mix of religious, South American, and fiesta-style sounds, most of the words in the fervent, sung-through score were taken from the Latin Requiem Mass, with music and original lyrics by Goldenthal. His film music during the 80s and 90s was featured in movies such as *Alien 3*, *Interview With The Vampire* and the *Batman* series. The *Juan Darien* cast included Ariel Ashwell, Andrea Frierson-Toney, Kristofer Batho, Bruce Turk, Stephen Kaplin, Andrea Kane, Barbara Pollitt, Martin Santangelo, David Toney, Sophia Salguero, Irma-Estel LaGuerre, and the youngster Daniel Hodd, who for a time during the production, superseded a puppet figure and portrayed Juan Darien. Almost exactly a year later, Julie Taymor, who directed this affecting and often disturbing

piece, found a much wider audience - and won two Tony Awards - for her skill with puppetry and masks in the sensational stage adaptation of Walt Disney's *The Lion King*.

JUBILEE

The story goes that the celebrated composer Cole Porter took librettist Moss Hart and director Monty Woolley on a round-the-world cruise to think up ideas for this show. The jaunt lasted for about five months, but the resulting show was unable to stay around for that long. Perhaps the ship docked for a while in England, because the inspiration for the plot is said to have been the Silver Jubilee of Britain's King George V and Queen Mary. The result of the trio's deliberations commenced at the Imperial Theatre in New York on 12 October 1935, and posed the question as to what might happen to an imaginary (Anglicised) royal family, also about to celebrate their jubilee, who have been advised to take off their tiaras for a while, and go incognito to avoid the embarrassment of a left-wing coup. The King (Melville Cooper) and the Queen (Mary Boland), along with their children, welcome this break from conformity, and revel in their new-found freedom which gives the King an opportunity to perfect his rope tricks. In the course of their travels they meet up with several characters bearing a remarkable resemblance to celebrities of the day: there's Charles Rausmiller ('Johnny Weissmuller') played by Mark Plant, and Eric Dare ('Noël Coward') as portrayed by Derek Williams (the Queen has a crush on both of those); and Eve Standing ('Elsa Maxwell'), who was played to a 'T' by May Boley. Another famous real-life name in the cast was Montgomery Clift the future cult film actor. Aged only 15, he played the good Prince Peter, and on the first night of the show, out of town in Boston, he received a kidnap threat. It turned out to be from a woman whose son had failed the audition for his part. One more cast member of the Moss Hart's mythical royal family, over 50 years before she became a reality in England, was the prophetically named Princess Diana. However, Mary Boland was the box-office draw, and when she left after four months to resume her film career, her replacement, Laura Hope Crews, was unable to create sufficient impact to prevent the show closing after 169 performances. So, only a limited number of privileged theatre-goers were able to listen to that outstanding Cole Porter score which included 'Mr. And Mrs. Smith', 'Me And Marie', 'When Love Comes Your Way', 'A Picture Of Me Without You', 'The Kling-Kling Bird On The Divi-Divi Tree', and three of the composer's all-time standards, 'Why Shouldn't I?', 'Just One Of Those Things', and 'Begin The Beguine', which became such a big hit for Artie Shaw in 1938. Regional theatres in the UK and US continued to look at *Jubilee* again, and there was an off-off-Broadway production at the Medicine Show Theatre in 1994. Ian Marshall Fisher revived it in his *Lost Musicals* series at London's Barbican in 1992, where the guest speakers included Moss Hart's widow, Kitty Carlisle. There was a gala benefit concert staging at Carnegie Hall, New York, on 10 October 1998. The starry cast included Michael Jeter (King), Beatrice Arthur (Queen), Damien Woetzel (Prince), Alice Ripley (Princess), Stephen Spinella (Eric Dare), Sandy Duncan (Karen O'Kane), Tyne Daly (Eva

Standing), Bob Paris (Mowgli), Philip Bosco (Prime Minister), Daniel A. Barrios (Prince Peter), and Craig Lee Thomas (Prince Rudolph).

JUMBO (FILM MUSICAL)
(see *Billy Rose's Jumbo*)

JUMBO (STAGE MUSICAL)
Beset by all kinds of troubles, and undecided for a time whether it was a musical or a circus (it was finally classed as the latter), Jumbo eventually lumbered into the newly renovated Hippodrome in New York, several weeks late, on 16 November 1935. The book, by Ben Hecht and Charles McArthur, told the story of the feuding male figureheads of two circus families who are brought to their senses by the love between the son of one, and the daughter of the other. The show was an extravagant spectacle, and an enormous undertaking, costing upwards of $300,000, with equestrian, acrobatic, and aerial dances, a cast of nearly a hundred, and almost as many animals. Gloria Grafton and Donald Novis played the young lovers, and they shared the three classic songs that emerged from Richard Rodgers and Lorenz Hart's lovely score, 'Little Girl Blue', 'My Romance' ('Wide awake, I can make my most fantastic dreams come true/My romance, doesn't need a thing but you'), and 'The Most Beautiful Girl In The World'. The other numbers included 'Over And Over Again' and 'The Circus Is On Parade', both of which were sung by Bob Lawrence and Henderson's Singing Razorbacks. The star of the show was one of the world's greatest clowns - in the widest sense - Jimmy Durante, who played the role of press agent Claudius B. Bowers and introduced the lively and amusing 'Laugh' and 'Women'. Paul Whiteman And His Orchestra were another big attraction in this magnificent spectacle which was directed by John Murray Anderson, and ran for just over seven months, 233 performances. Inevitably it lost money for flamboyant producer Billy Rose. The 1962 film version, which is generally known as *Billy Rose's Jumbo*, had a revised storyline, and starred Durante, Doris Day, Stephen Boyd, and Martha Raye.

JUNGLE BOOK, THE
(see Disney, Walt)

JUST A GIGOLO
'My 30 Elvis Presley films in one,' was how David Bowie once described his starring role in *Just A Gigolo*. Actor David Hemmings directed and played a part in this 1978 feature, which also featured Kim Novak and Marlene Dietrich in its cast. Bowie played a disillusioned Prussian, entrenched in Berlin, in this costly West German production. Despite the chameleon qualities he brought to his recordings, the singer is obviously ill-at-ease in the role, undermining any merits the film may have. A glossy soundtrack included material by Manhattan Transfer and the Rebels, who perform Bowie's 'Revolutionary Song'.

JUST FOR FUN
1963 was a pivotal year in British pop. It was the time of Beatlemania, the Mersey Boom and beat groups, when a new generation changed the face of music forever. Although one of that period's transitional acts, Brian Poole And The Tremeloes, was included in its cast, *Just For Fun* rather reflected the immediate past, one of brylcreem and beehive hairstyles. The plot, in which teenagers try to win the right to vote, is largely irrelevant, hampered by a wooden script and acting. The film is, however, notable for the appearance of a string of acts about to be eclipsed. American stars Bobby Vee and the Crickets contribute 'The Night Has A Thousand Eyes' and 'My Little One' respectively, Freddie Cannon and Johnny Tillotson are also on hand, while Kitty Lester provides her memorable version of 'Love Letters'. Nevertheless, the cast chiefly comprises of UK performers. These include the Springfields, Mark Wynter, Joe Brown and Kenny Lynch, but the highlights are provided by three instrumental groups. Former Shadows, Jet Harris And Tony Meehan, were captured at their peak; the former's growling basslines offset by the latter's flashy drumming. The Tornadoes, protégés of iconoclast producer Joe Meek, unleashed a view of science-fiction pop adopted wholesale of Swedish quartet the Spotniks. Dressed in spacesuits and using guitars linked to amplifiers through radio waves rather than leads, the group took their chosen genre to its limits. *Just For Fun* is worthwhile simply to see this band in action, but it also captures pop in its final innocent moments.

JUST SO
This musical, which was created by George Stiles (music) And Anthony Drewe (book and lyrics), was the first winner of the inaugural Vivian Ellis Awards in 1985. It attracted the interest (and financial assistance) of producer Cameron Mackintosh, who went to see a semi-professional production at the Barbican Theatre, Plymouth. He is said to have told the composers that the show 'was 60% right - now go away and write the other 40%'. Stiles and Drewe continued to revise and add new songs, and in 1989 it was presented at the Watermill Theatre, Newbury (an important launching pad for many a new musical), with Julia McKenzie directing. A year later, Mike Ockrent staged it at the Tricycle Theatre, on the London Fringe. Associates of film director Steven Spielberg saw it there, and the show was optioned for feature animation, although the film has yet to be made. Various US productions were planned, including one at Ford's Theatre, Washington, in 1992, (where it was replaced prior to opening by *Five Guys Named Moe*), before the show eventually had its American premiere on 5 November 1998 at the Norma Terris Theatre, Goodspeed-at-Chester, Connecticut. Drewe's book draws from several of Kipling's stories, and comes up with the tale of The Eldest Magician (Tom Nelis), who creates a brave new world in which the animals find themselves threatened when a crab named Pau Amma plays around with the sea, and consequently floods the land. The Elephant's Child (Cory Shafer) sets out for the Limpopo River, hitched up with the cynical Kolokolo Bird (Sheri Sanders), intent on finding the evil decapoda. Along the way he discovers how the leopard got his spots, the elephant got his trunk, and the rhinoceros got his skin, as well as other Kipling-esque fascinating

facts. Also involved are the Cooking Stove (Timothy Gulan), Rhino (Ben Lipitz), Zebra (Katy Grenfell), Giraffe (Amy Bodnar), Leopard (Stephen Bienskie), Jaguar (Curtiss I. Cook), Dingo (Julia Haubner), Kangaroo (Timothy Gulan), and the Parsee Man (Gabriel Barre), who naturally takes a leading part in 'The Parsee Cake Walk', 'the wildest number, a kind of reggae romp given a psychedelic touch, with actors decked out as dancing cake ingredients and stoves.' Other highlights in a 'rock-based score, which ranges from British music hall and rock to Caribbean rhythms and a faux-operatic quartet', include 'We Want To Take The Ladies Out', 'Thick Skin', 'Pick Up Your Hooves And Trot', and the 'genuinely moving' 'The Limpopo River'. The rest of the songs were fun too, and included 'A World Of Possibilities', 'Just So', 'Another Tempest', 'There's No Harm In Asking', 'Living On This Island', 'The Crime', 'Jungle Light', 'Putting On Appearances', 'The Argument', 'Roll Up, Roll Up', 'Leaps And Bounds', 'Wait A Bit', 'Take Your Time', 'Please Don't Touch My Stove', 'Little One Come Hither', 'Does The Moment Ever Come', and 'If-The Crab'. Goodspeed is renowned for its commitment to new musicals, and so the local critics are accustomed to viewing a wide variety of ideas and themes. In this case, most of them seem charmed by this 'droll, touching and imaginative collaboration', which was ingeniously choreographed by Jennifer Paulson Lee, and directed by Lou Jacob.

In the early 90s the Mermaid Theatre of Nova Scotia, one of Canada's leading theatre companies for young people, toured Graham Whitehead's adaptation of Kipling's *Just So* stories, with music by Steven Naylor. It featured puppets and masks designed by Tom Miller. The best-known musicalization of Kipling is, of course, Walt Disney's 1967 animated movie, *The Jungle Book*, which featured the voices of Phil Harris, Louis Prima, and George Sanders, as, respectively, Baloo the Bear, King Louie, and Shere Khan.

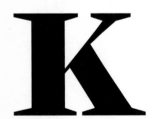

KAHN, GUS

b. 6 November 1886, Koblenz, Germany, d. 8 October 1941, Beverly Hills, California, USA. A prolific lyricist during the 20s and 30s for Tin Pan Alley, stage and films. Not particularly well known by the public, but highly regarded in the music business, he was once rated by a trade magazine as the second most popular US songwriter after Irving Berlin. After being taken to the USA by his immigrant parents in 1891 when they settled in Chicago, he started writing songs while still at school. However, it was not until 1908 when he collaborated with his future wife, the composer Grace LeBoy, that he had some success with 'I Wish I Had A Girl'. His first big hit came in 1915 with 'Memories', written with composer Egbert van Alstyne. In the following year, Kahn collaborated with him again, and Tony Jackson, for 'Pretty Baby', which became one of Kahn's biggest hits, and was featured in the bio-pics *Jolson Sings Again* (1949) and *The Eddie Cantor Story* (1953); two artists who benefited substantially from Kahn's output. 'Pretty Baby' was just one of a series of Kahn 'baby' songs which evoke the 'jazz age' of the 20s. These included 'Yes Sir, That's My Baby', 'There Ain't No Maybe In My Baby's Eyes', 'My Baby Just Cares for Me', 'I Wonder Where My Baby Is Tonight' and 'Sing Me A Baby Song', all written with composer Walter Donaldson, Khan's major collaborator. Donaldson, with his playboy image, was the antithesis of Kahn with his sober, family background. Other songs by the team included 'That Certain Party', 'Carolina In The Morning', 'My Buddy' and 'Beside A Babbling Brook'. Some of their best work was contained in the 1928 Broadway show *Whoopee!*. Starring Ruth Etting and Eddie Cantor, it introduced 'I'm Bringing A Red Red Rose', 'Love Me Or Leave Me', 'My Baby Just Cares for Me' and 'Makin' Whoopee', the lyric of which is considered to be one of Kahn's best. The show later became an early sound movie in 1930. In 1929, Kahn contributed to another Broadway musical, *Show Girl*. This time his collaborators were George and Ira Gershwin. The trio produced 'Liza', for the show's star, Ruby Keeler. It is said that, during at least one performance, Keeler's husband, Al Jolson, stood up in the audience and sang the song *to her*. In 1933, Kahn went to Hollywood to work on various movies, from the Marx Brothers' *A Day At The Races* ('All God's Chillun Got Rhythm'), to *Spring Parade*, starring Deanna Durbin, singing 'Waltzing In The Clouds'. In 1933, his first Hollywood project, with composer Vincent Youmans, was *Flying Down To Rio*, which featured the title song and 'The Carioca'. It was also the first film to bring together Fred Astaire and Ginger Rogers. It was Youmans' last original film score before he died in 1946. For the next eight years Kahn's output for films was prolific. They included *Bottoms Up* ('Waiting At The Gate For Katy'), *Caravan* ('Ha-Cha-Cha' and 'Wine Song'), *Hollywood Party* ('I've Had My Moments'), *Kid Millions* ('Okay Toots', 'When My Ship Comes In' and 'Your Head On My Shoulder'), *One Night Of Love*, *The Girl Friend*, *Love Me Forever*, *Thanks A Million* (Dick Powell singing the title song), *San Francisco* (Jeanette MacDonald singing the title song), *Rose Marie* ('Just For You' and 'Pardon Me, Madame'), *Three Smart Girls* (Deanna Durbin singing 'Someone To Care For Me'), *Everybody Sing* ('The One I Love'), *Girl Of The Golden West* ('Shadows On The Moon' and 'Who Are We To Say'), *Lillian Russell* (a bio-pic of the famous 1890s entertainer) and *Ziegfeld Girl* ('You Stepped Out Of A Dream', written with composer Nacio Herb Brown, sung by Tony Martin). Kahn's realised a life-long ambition to write with Jerome Kern with his last song, 1941's 'Day Dreaming'.

Throughout his career Kahn had many different collaborators, including bandleader Isham Jones ('I'll See You In My Dreams', 'The One I Love Belongs To Somebody Else', 'Swingin' Down The Lane', and 'It Had To Be You'), Richard Whiting ('Ukulele Lady'), Whiting and Ray Egan ('Ain't We Got Fun'), Whiting and Harry Akst ('Guilty'), Ted Fio Rito ('I Never Knew', 'Charley My Boy' and 'Sometime'), Ernie Erdman, Elmer Schoebel and Billy Meyers ('Nobody's Sweetheart Now'), Erdman and Dan Russo ('Toot Toot Tootsie, Goodbye'), Wilbur Schwandt and Fabian Andre ('Dream A Little Dream Of Me' - a later hit for 'Mama' Cass Elliot), Charlie Rossoff ('When You And I Were Seventeen'), Carmen Lombardo and Johnny Green ('Coquette'), Neil Moret ('Chloe'), Wayne King ('Goofus'), Matty Malneck and Fud Livingston ('I'm Through With Love'), Malneck and Frank Signorelli ('I'll Never Be The Same') and Victor Schertzinger ('One Night Of Love'). In the 1951 movie, *I'll See You In My Dreams*, based on his life, Kahn was portrayed by Danny Thomas, and Grace LeBoy by Doris Day.

KALMAR, BERT

b. 10 February 1884, New York City, New York, USA, d. 18 September 1947, Los Angeles, California, USA. Ill-educated and a runaway before he was in his teens, Kalmar's life was completely immersed in showbusiness. In the years before World War I he wrote lyrics for a number of songs with various composers, among them Harry Ruby. For the next few years each wrote with other collaborators, but by the beginning of the 20s they recognized the special qualities of their work together. Throughout the 20s they wrote for Broadway musicals such as *Ladies First*, *Broadway Brevities Of 1920*, *Ziegfeld Follies Of 1920*, *Midnight Rounders Of 1921*, *Greenwich Village Follies Of 1922*, *Helen Of Troy-New York*, *Puzzles Of 1925*, *The Ramblers*, *Five O'Clock Girl*, *Lucky*, *Good Boy*, and *Animal Crackers*. The latter score was written for the Marx Brothers, and contained songs such as 'Who's Been Listening To My Heart?', 'Watching The Clouds Roll By', and 'Hooray For Captain Spaulding'. Other songs from those shows included 'Oh! What A Pal Was Mary', 'So Long, Oo-long', 'Who's Sorry Now?', 'Thinking Of You', 'The Same Old Moon', 'Dancing The Devil Away', 'Some Sweet Someone', and 'I Wanna Be Loved By You'. By the 30s Kalmar and Ruby were writing songs for films and one of their first, and the song by which they are best remembered, was 'Three Little Words' (from *Check And Double Check*). It became the title of the songwriters' 1950 film biography when they were played by Fred Astaire and Red Skelton. Their other film work included *The Cuckoos*, *Horse Feathers*, *The Kid From Spain*, *Hips Hips Hooray*, *Kentucky Kernels*, *Thanks A Million*, and *The Story Of Vernon And Irene Castle*. They contained numbers such as 'I Love You So Much', 'What A Perfect Combination', 'Only When You're In My Arms', and 'Keep Romance Alive'. Most of their songs were written for either stage or screen but among their great successes were 'Nevertheless' and 'A Kiss To Build A Dream On' - written for neither medium. (The latter did not become popular until the 50s after some rewriting by Oscar Hammerstein II.)

KAMEN, MICHAEL

b. 1948, New York, USA. A former member of the 60s band the New York Rock 'n' Roll Ensemble. A prolific composer, conductor, and arranger, particularly for films, from the 70s through to the 90s. After studying at the Juilliard School Of Music, Kamen contributed some music to the off-beat rock Western film *Zachariah* in 1971. Later in the 70s, he wrote the complete scores for *The Next Man*, *Between The Lines*, and *Stunts* (1977). During the 80s he scored co-composed the music for several films with some of contemporary pop music's most illustrious names, such as Eric Clapton (*Lethal Weapon*, *Homeboy*, and *Lethal Weapon II* (also with David Sanborn), George Harrison (*Shanghai Surprise*), David A. Stewart (*Rooftops*), and Herbie Hancock (*Action Jackson*). Subsequently, Kamen scored some of the period's most entertaining and diverting UK and US movies, which included *Venom*, *Pink Floyd-The Wall*, *Angleo, My Love*, *The Dead Zone*, *Brazil* (supposedly his favourite score), *Mona Lisa*, *Riot*, *Sue And Bob, Too*, *Someone To Watch Over Me*, *Suspect*, *Die Hard* and *Die Hard II*, *Raggedy Rawney*, *Crusoe*, *For Queen And Country*, *The Adventures Of Baron Munchausen*, *Dead-Bang* (with Gary Chang), *Road House*, *Renegades*, and *Licence To Kill* (1989), Timothy Dalton's second attempt to replace Connery and Moore as James Bond. In the early 90s Kamen composed the music for *The Krays* and *Let Him Have It*, two films that reflected infamous criminal incidents in the UK, and others such as *Nothing But Trouble*, *Hudson Hawk*, *The Last Boy Scout*, *Company Business*, *Blue Ice*, *Lethal Weapon 3*, *Shining Through* (1992), *Blue Ice*, *Splitting Heirs*, *Last Action Hero*, *The Three Muskateers*, *Circle Of Friends*, and *Don Juan DeMarco* (1995). In several instances, besides scoring the films, Kamen served as musical director, music editor, and played keyboards and other instruments. In 1991, he provided the music for the smash hit Kevin Kostner movie, *Robin Hood: Prince Of Thieves*, and, with lyricists Bryan Adams and Robert John 'Mutt' Lange, composed the closing number, '(Everything I Do) I Do For You'. Adams' recording of the song enjoyed phenomenal success, staying at the top of the UK chart for an unprecedented 16 weeks. It was nominated for an Academy Award, and Kamen received two Grammys and a special Ivor Novello Award. Three years later the trio of songwriters repeated their success with 'All For Love', which was recorded by Adams, together with Sting and Rod Stewart, and turned up at the end of *The Three Musketeers* and at the top of the UK chart. Kamen has also composed music for televison films such as *Liza's Pioneer Diary*, *S*H*E*, *Shoot For The Sun*, and two television miniseries, *The Duty Men* (theme: 'Watching You' (with Sashazoe)), and *Edge Of Darkness*. The theme from the latter, written with Eric Clapton, gained another Ivor Novello Award (1985). He has written a guitar concerto for Clapton, a saxophone concerto for David Sanborn, and composed several scores for the Joffrey Ballet and the La Scala Opera Company.

● ALBUMS: with Orbital *Event Horizon* film soundtrack (London 1997)★★★.

KANDER, JOHN

b. 18 March 1927, Kansas City, Missouri, USA. An important composer for the American musical theatre from the early 60s, Kander studied music as a child, continued at college and was determined to make his way in the musical theatre. He had some successes in the early 50s with various lyricists before meeting Fred Ebb in 1962. Ebb (b. 8 April 1932, New York, USA) had already dabbled with lyric writing, and had collaborated with Jerry Herman on some songs for the short-lived musical *From A To Z* (1960). Among Kander and Ebb's first efforts were 'My Coloring Book' and 'I Don't Care Much', both of which were recorded by Barbra Streisand. The new team made their Broadway debut in 1965 with the score for *Flora, The Red Menace*, which included an eye-catching, Tony Award-winning performance, by Liza Minnelli, who would subsequently perform much of their work, and become indelibly associated with them. Although *Flora* was relatively unsuccessful, Kander and Ebb were invited to write the score for *Cabaret* (1966), which starred Joel Grey and Jill Haworth, and won seven Tony Awards including best score. They wrote two additional songs, 'Money, Money' and 'Mein Herr', for the 1972 film version in which Liza Minnelli gave a sensational performance and won an Oscar. The television special produced by Ebb for Minnelli, *Liza With A Z*, also won an Emmy award, with a Grammy later going to the recorded highlights album. Ebb's television work continued with the production of *Ol' Blue Eyes Is Back* (1972) for Frank Sinatra. Other Broadway shows followed, including *The Happy Time*, *Zorba*, *70, Girls, 70*, and *Chicago*, which opened in 1975 and ran for 923 performances. In the same year, the duo wrote two songs for the film *Funny Lady*, which starred Barbra Streisand, and followed this with music for two Minnelli films, *A Matter Of Time* (1976) and *New York, New York* (1977). The theme from the latter became an enormous, enduring hit for Frank Sinatra in 1980. Back on Broadway, Kander and Ebb wrote scores for *The Act* (1977) with Minnelli, *Woman Of The Year* (1981), which starred Lauren Bacall, and *The Rink* (1984), yet another Minnelli (and Chita Rivera) vehicle. In 1991 they were inducted into the New York Theatre Hall of Fame, and a revue, *And The World Goes 'Round*, which celebrated some 30 of their songs, opened Off Broadway and ran for nearly a year. Another musical anthology, *Sing Happy*, played on the London Fringe in the following year. In 1993 their spectacular musical *Kiss Of The Spider Woman*, starring Chita Rivera, won several Tony Awards in New York following its transfer from the West End. During the 1996/7 Broadway season, a superb concert version of the 20 year old *Chicago* won six Tonys, while *Steel Pier*, a new Kander and Ebb musical about a dance marathon held in Atlantic City in 1933 at the height of the Depression, failed to convert any of its 11 nominations, and closed after only two months. In 1996, the songwriters were among the recipients of the Stage Directors & Choreographers Foundation's 12th annual Mr. Abbott Awards. It was an appropriate gesture, because George Abbott directed Kander and Ebb's first Broadway musical, *Flora, The Red Menace*. The two men were also recipients of Kennedy Center Honours in

1998. Apart from their work together, both Kander and Ebb have enjoyed successful independent careers. Kander has written music for film soundtracks, including *Kramer Vs. Kramer* (1980), and Ebb has continued to produce and co-produce numerous television specials, including *Gypsy In My Soul* (1976) and *Baryshnikov On Broadway* (1980).
● ALBUMS: *An Evening With John Kander & Fred Ebb* (DRG 1993)★★.

KANE, HELEN

b. Helen Schroder, 4 August 1904, New York, USA, d. 26 September 1966. Kane is remembered these days as the singer portrayed by Debbie Reynolds in *Three Little Words*, the 1950 film biography of songwriters Bert Kalmar and Harry Ruby. Kane, (who dubbed Reynolds' vocals), was the baby-voiced singer who rose to fame on Broadway in the late 20s. She began her career in vaudeville and night clubs but was much-acclaimed for an appearance with Paul Ash And His Orchestra at New York's Paramount Theatre. She was then featured in such Broadway shows as *A Night In Spain* (1927) and *Good Boy* (1928) in which she sang 'I Wanna Be Loved By You', the 'Boop-Boop-A-Doop' hit that was re-created by Reynolds. After her Broadway success she moved to Hollywood in the late 20s, appearing in several films, including *Nothing But The Truth* (1929), featuring one of her biggest hits, 'Do Something', plus *Sweetie* (1929), *Pointed Heels* (1930), *Dangerous Nan McGrew* (1930), *Heads Up* (1930), and the all-star spectacular, *Paramount On Parade* (1930). Meanwhile, she continued to make hit records such as 'That's My Weakness Now', 'Get Out And Get Under The Moon', 'Me And The Man In The Moon' and 'Button Up Your Overcoat'. Often acknowledged to have been a major influence in the creation of Grim Natwick's cartoon character Betty Boop, Kane continued her career throughout the 30s playing nightclubs. Kane was, for the most part, largely forgotten until the arrival of *Three Little Words*, at which point she became a minor celebrity amid a new generation.

KAPER, BRONISLAW (BRONISLAU)

b. 5 February 1902, Warsaw, Poland, d. 26 April 1983, Beverly Hills, California, USA. A composer, arranger and conductor for films, from the mid-30s through to the late 60s. Kaper studied at the Warsaw Conservatory of Music and in Berlin before working as a composer in several European countries, including London and Paris. In 1935, after moving to the USA, he began a collaboration with Walter Jurmann, and sometimes with Gus Kahn and Ned Washington, on songs for movies such as *A Night At The Opera* ('Cosi Cosa'), *Mutiny On The Bounty* ('Love Song Of Tahiti'), *Escapade* ('You're All I Need'), *San Francisco* (the title song and 'Happy New Year'), *A Day At The Races* ('All God's Chillun Got Rhythm'), 'A Message From The Man In The Moon', 'Tomorrow Is Another Day', *Three Smart Girls* ('Someone To Care For Me' and 'My Heart Is Singing'), and *Everybody Sing* ('The One I Love' and 'Swing, Mr. Mendelssohn'). With Kahn, Kaper also wrote 'Blue Lovebird' for the bio-pic, *Lillian Russell* (1940). During the 40s, Kaper composed complete scores for films such as *Johnny Eager*, *The Chocolate Soldier*, *Two Faced Woman*,

Keeper Of The Flame, Somewhere I'll Find You, Gaslight, Mrs. Parkinson, Without Love, Green Dolphin Street (the song, 'One Green Dolphin Street', became a jazz standard), and contributed 'I Know, I Know I Know', to Mario Lanza's debut movie, That Midnight Kiss. In 1953, Kaper won an Academy Award for his score to Lili, which also contained the song 'Hi-Lili, Hi-Lo' (lyric by Helen Deutsch). Sung by Leslie Caron and Mel Ferrer in the movie, the song later became a hit for both Richard Chamberlain and Alan Price. In the following year, Kaper, Caron and Deutsch were together again for the film musical The Glass Slipper, which included 'Take My Love'. Kaper's other movie music in the 50s and 60s included A Life Of Her Own, The Red Badge Of Courage, The Wild North, The Naked Spur, Them, Somebody Up There Likes Me, The Swan, Don't Go Near The Water, Auntie Mame, The Brothers Karamazov, Butterfield 8, Green Mansions, The Angel Wore Red, Two Loves, Mutiny On The Bounty (the 1962 version, containing 'Follow Me', with a lyric by Paul Francis Webster, which was nominated for an Oscar), Kisses For My President, Lord Jim, The Way West, Tobruk, Counterpoint and A Flea In Her Ear (1968). Kaper also composed for television programmes such as The F.B.I., and, in 1945, adapted music by Chopin for the score of the Broadway show Polonaise. His collaborators included Herbert Stothart, Bob Russell and Hector Villa-Lobos.

KARAS, ANTON

b. 7 July 1906, Vienna, Austria, d. 9 January 1985, Vienna, Austria. The man who arguably did more to popularize the zither than anyone before or after him, is best remembered as the sound behind the famous 'Third Man Theme' (Harry Lime). Carol Reed's classic 1949 film, The Third Man, utilized Karas' music throughout, and it was no surprise that film-goers made the song and its accompanying album a number 1 hit in 1951. Although Karas was a virtuoso, he remains one of the more famous one-hit-wonders of our time.

● ALBUMS: Anton Karas (Decca 1951)★★★.
● COMPILATIONS: World Of Anton Karas (Decca 1971)★★★, Folk Songs Of Austria (1974)★★★, Harry Lime Theme (The Third Man) (1974)★★★, Bons Bons De Vienne (1977)★★★.

KAUFMAN, GEORGE S.

b. 14 November 1889, Pittsburg, Pennsylvania, USA, d. 2 June 1961, New York, USA. For a man who was supposed to hate music and musicals with considerable fervour, George S. Kaufman made significant contributions as a librettist and director to a variety of productions in the American musical theatre from the 20s through to the 50s. Early in his career he worked as a newspaper columnist for several years in Washington and later in New York where he became one of the brightest young talents in the early 30s, many of whom, including Kaufman, Ring Lardner, Dorothy Parker, Alexander Woollcott, and Robert Benchley, were members of the Algonquin Hotel's Round Table set. After co-writing the book with Marc Connelly in 1923 for Helen Of Troy, New York, which had a score by Bert Kalmar and Harry Ruby, Kaufman contributed sketches or was the librettist or co-librettist on a number of other Broadway musical productions including The

Music Box Revue (Third Edition), Be Yourself!, The Cocoanuts, Animal Crackers, The Little Show, Strike Up The Band, Nine-Fifteen Revue, and The Band Wagon (1931). By now an established figure, he also directed most of the subsequent productions on which he worked. In the 30s and 40s these included Of Thee I Sing, for which he won a Pulitzer Award, Face The Music (director only), Let 'Em Eat Cake, I'd Rather Be Right, Sing Out The News, Seven Lively Arts, Hollywood Pinafore, and Park Avenue (1946). In 1950 Kaufman earned a Tony Award for his direction of the superb Guys And Dolls, and, five years later, collaborated with his second wife, the actress Leueen MacGrath, on the book for the Cole Porter musical Silk Stockings. His work in the musical theatre was just a part of his wider output. He is credited with 45 plays written in conjunction with some 16 known collaborators who included Edna Furber, Ring Lardner, and his principal later collaborator Moss Hart. With Hart he wrote some of the American theatre's most enduring comedies - Once In A Lifetime, You Can't Take It With You (for which he won his second Pulitzer Prize), and The Man Who Came To Dinner.
● FURTHER READING: George S. Kaufman: An Intimate Portrait, Howard Teichmann. George S. Kaufman And His Friends, Scott Meredith.

KAYE, DANNY

b. David Daniel Kominsky, 18 January 1913, Brooklyn, New York, USA, d. 3 March 1987, Los Angeles, California, USA. Kaye was an extraordinary entertainer and an apparently inexhaustible comedian, mimic and dancer who seemed to be able to twist his face and body into any shape he wanted. As a singer, he specialized in very fast double talk and tongue-twisters, but could present a gentle ballad equally well. He was also an indefatigable ambassador for numerous charities, especially the United Nations International Children's Emergency Fund (now UNICEF), for which he travelled and worked for many years. A son of Jewish immigrant parents from Russia, Kominsky originally wanted to join the medical profession, but dropped out of high school when he was 14 years old, and hitch-hiked to Florida with his friend, Louis Eilson, where they sang for money. On their return to New York, they formed an act called Red And Blackie, and performed at private functions. During the day, Kominski worked as a soda-jerk, and then as an automobile appraiser with an insurance company. The latter job was terminated after he made a mistake which is said to have cost the company some $40,000. Kominski and Eilson then obtained summer work as 'toomlers', creators of tumult or all-round entertainers, in the Borscht Circuit summer hotels and camps in the Catskill Mountains. After five years, Kominski was earning $1,000 per season.
In 1933, he joined David Harvey and Kathleen Young on the vaudeville circuit in their dancing act, the Three Terpsichoreans, and was billed for the first time as Danny Kaye. An early onstage accident in which he split his trousers, elicited much laughter from the audience and was incorporated into the act. Signed by producer A.B. Marcus, the group toured the USA for five months in the revue La Vie Paree, before sailing for the Orient in February 1934. It is often said that this period of playing

to non-English speaking audiences in Japan, China and Malaya, was when Kaye first developed his face-making and pantomiming techniques, and his 'gibberish' singing with the occasional recognized word. Back in the USA in 1936, Kaye worked with comedian Nick Long Jnr. and toured with Abe Lyman's Band, before being booked by impresario Henry Sherek, to appear in cabaret at London's Dorchester Hotel. The engagement, in 1938, was not a success. Kaye commented: 'I was too loud for the joint'. (Ten years later in London, it would be an entirely different story.) While appearing in Max Liebman's *Sunday Night Varieties* in New York, Kaye met pianist-songwriter Sylvia Fine (b. 29 August 1913, New York, USA, d. 28 October 1991, New York, USA), who had been raised in the same Brooklyn neighbourhood, and majored in music at Brooklyn College. She became a powerful influence throughout his career, as his director, coach and critic. Working with Liebman's Saturday night revues at Camp Taimiment in the Pennsylvania Hills, during the summer of 1939, they started their collaboration, with Fine accompanying Kaye on the piano, and writing special material that included three of his most famous numbers, 'Stanislavsky', 'Pavlova' and the story of the unstable chapeau designer, 'Anatole Of Paris'. The best of the material was assembled in *The Straw Hat Revue* in which Kaye appeared with Imogene Coca, and which opened on Broadway in September 1939. The show also featured a young dancer named Jerome Robbins. After Fine and Kaye were married in January 1940, Kaye appeared in a smash hit engagement at La Martinique nightclub in New York, which led to a part in *Lady In The Dark*, starring Gertrude Lawrence. On the first night, Kaye stopped the show with the Kurt Weill and Ira Gershwin tongue-twister 'Tchaikovsky', in which he reeled off the names of 50 real, or imagined, Russian composers in 38 seconds. After playing a return engagement at La Martinique, and a five-week stint at the Paramount Theatre, Kaye appeared again on Broadway, starring in the Cole Porter musical *Let's Face It!*, which opened in October 1941. Porter allowed Sylvia Fine and Max Liebman to interpolate some special material for Kaye, which included a 'jabberwocky of song, dance, illustration and double-talk' called 'Melody In 4F'. Kaye had to leave the show early in 1942, suffering from nervous exhaustion, but having recovered, he toured on behalf of the war effort and is said to have sold a million dollars' worth of government bonds in six months. Rejected by the US Army because of a back ailment, he entertained troops with his two-hour shows in many theatres of operations including the South Pacific.

In 1944, Kaye made his feature film debut in *Up In Arms*, the first in a series of five pictures for Sam Goldwyn at RKO. His performance as a hypochondriac elevator boy, involving yet another memorable Fine-Liebman piece, 'Manic Depressive Pictures Presents: Lobby Number', moved one critic to hail his introduction as 'the most exciting since Garbo's'. Goldwyn was criticized, however for having Kaye's red hair dyed blonde. His remaining films for the studio included *Wonder Man*, in which he gave his impression of a sneezing Russian baritone with 'Orchi Tchornya'. This was the first of several films in which he

played more than one character; *The Kid From Brooklyn* (1946), which featured 'Pavlova', *The Secret Life Of Walter Mitty* (1947), one of his best-remembered roles (six of them), and *A Song Is Born* (1948), one of his least remembered. In 1945, Kaye appeared for a year on his own CBS radio show with Harry James and Eve Arden, and during the following year the Kayes' daughter, Dena, was born. When Kaye recorded the old standard 'Dinah', he changed some of the 'i' sounds to 'e', so that the song ran: 'Denah, is there anyone fener? In the State of Carolena . . .', etc. His other hit songs included 'Tubby The Tuba', 'Minnie The Moocher', 'Ballin' The Jack', 'Bloop Bleep', 'Civilization' and 'The Woody Woodpecker Song', both with the Andrews Sisters; 'C'est Si Bon'; and 'Blackstrap Molasses', recorded with Jimmy Durante, Jane Wyman and Groucho Marx. In 1948, Kaye returned to England to appear at the London Palladium. His enormously successful record-breaking performances began an affectionate and enduring relationship with the British public. He is said to have received over 100,000 letters in a week. His shows were attended by the Royal Family; he met both Winston Churchill and George Bernard Shaw, and was cast in wax for London's Madame Tussaud's Museum. He returned in 1949 for the first of several Royal Command Performances, and also toured provincial music-halls throughout 1952. He endeared himself to the British by singing some of their parochial songs such as the novelty 'I've Got A Lovely Bunch Of Coconuts' and 'Maybe It's Because I'm A Londoner'. During one performance at the Palladium, when a member of the audience enquired after the state of Kaye's ribs following a car accident, he ordered the lights to be lowered while he displayed the actual X-ray plates! Kaye went to Canada in 1950 and became the first solo performer to star at the Canadian National Exhibition, where he sold out the 24,000-seater stadium for each of his 14 performances.

He returned to his multiple roles in films such as *The Inspector General* (1949) and *On The Riviera* (1951), before embarking on the somewhat controversial *Hans Christian Andersen* (1952). After 16 different screenplays over a period of 15 years, and protests in the Danish press about the choice of Kaye to play their national hero, the film, with a final screenplay by Moss Hart, became a huge money-spinner. Frank Loesser's score produced several appealing songs, including 'No Two People', 'Anywhere I Wander', 'Inchworm', 'Thumbelina', 'The Ugly Duckling' and 'Wonderful Copenhagen', the latter reaching the UK Top 5. Kaye's other films during the 50s and early 60s included *Knock On Wood* (1954), said to be his favourite, in which he sang two more Fine numbers, the title song, and 'All About Me', *White Christmas* (1954), co-starring with Bing Crosby, Rosemary Clooney and Vera-Ellen, *The Court Jester* (1956), *Me And The Colonel* (1958), *Merry Andrew* (1958), *The Five Pennies* (1959), a biopic of 20s cornet player Red Nichols (including a rousing version of 'When The Saints Go Marching In' with Louis Armstrong), *On The Double* (1961) and *The Man From The Diners' Club* (1963). After a break, he came back for *The Madwoman Of Challiot* (1969), and the following year, returned to Broadway in the role of Noah, in the Richard Rodgers and Martin Charnin musical *Two By Two*. Shortly after the show opened, Kaye tore a ligament in his leg during a performance, and subsequently appeared on crutches or in a wheelchair, in which he tried to run down the other actors, adapting the show to his injury, much to the distaste of producer and composer Richard Rodgers.

During the 70s and 80s, Kaye conducted classical orchestras and appeared on several television shows including *Peter Pan*, *Pinocchio* and *Danny Kaye's Look At The Metropolitan Opera*. He also played dramatic roles on television in *Skokie* and *The Twilight Zone*, but concentrated mainly on his charity work. He had started his association with UNICEF in the early 50s, and in 1955 made a 20-minute documentary, *Assignment Children*. He eventually became the organization's ambassador-at-large for 34 years, travelling worldwide on their behalf, and entering the *Guinness Book Of Records* by visiting 65 US and Canadian cities in five days, piloting himself in his own jet plane. During his career he received many awards including the French Légion d'Honneur, the Jean Hersholt Humanitarian Award, and the Knight's Cross of the First Class of the Order of Danneborg, given by the Danish Government. Other awards included a special Academy Award in 1954, along with Tonys for his stage performances, plus Emmys for his successful 60s television series. He died in 1987, following a heart attack.

● ALBUMS: *Danny Kaye* (Columbia 1949)★★, *Danny Kaye Entertains* (Columbia 1949)★★★, *Gilbert And Sullivan And Danny Kaye* (Decca 1949)★★, *Hans Christian Andersen* film soundtrack (1953)★★★★, *Danny At The Palace* (Decca 1953)★★★, *Mommy, Gimme A Drink Of Water* (Capitol 1958)★★★, *Merry Andrew* film soundtrack (Capitol 1958)★★★, with Louis Armstrong *The Five Pennies* film soundtrack (1958)★★★, *The Court Jester* (Decca 1959)★★★, *For Children* (Decca 1959)★★, with Ivor Moreton *Happy Fingers* (1977)★★★.

● COMPILATIONS: *The Best Of Danny Kaye* (Decca 1962)★★★, *The Very Best Of Danny Kaye - 20 Golden Greats* (MCA 1987)★★★.

● FURTHER READING: *The Danny Kaye Saga*, Kurt Singer. *Nobody's Fool - The Secret Lives Of Danny Kaye*, Martin Gottfried. *The Life Story Of Danny Kaye*, D. Richards. *Fine And Danny*, Sylvia Fine.

● FILMS: *Up In Arms* (1944), *Wonder Man* (1945), *The Kid From Brooklyn* (1946), *The Secret Life Of Walter Mitty* (1947), *A Song Is Born* (1948), *The Inspector General* (1949), *On The Riviera* (1951), *Hans Christian Anderson* (1952), *Knock On Wood* (1953), *White Christmas* (1954), *Assignment Children* (1954), *The Court Jester* (1956), *Me And The Colonel* (1957), *Merry Andrew* (1958), *The Five Pennies* (1959), *On The Double* (1962), *The Man From The Diner's Club* (1963), *The Madwoman Of Chaillot* (1969).

KAYE, STUBBY

b. 11 November 1918, New York City, New York, USA, d. 14 December 1997. An actor and singer who carved himself an instant slice of musical history by stopping the show as Nicely-Nicely Johnson in the original Broadway production of *Guys And Dolls* - and then doing it all over again three years later in London. Kaye had his first break when he came first on the Major Bowes Amateur Hour on US radio in 1939. During the late 30s and early 40s he toured as a comedian in vaudeville, and made his London debut in USO shows during World War II. His role in *Guys And Dolls* (1950) was not a leading one, but he was outstanding

in numbers such as 'Fugue For Tinhorns', 'The Oldest Established', 'Guys And Dolls', and the rousing 'Sit Down You're Rockin' The Boat'. He had one more big success on Broadway in 1956 as Marryin' Sam in *Li'l Abner*, and subsequently toured in revivals, played nightclubs as a comedian, and appeared on the television series *Love And Marriage* and *My Sister Eileen*. Unlike many stage performers he moved easily into films, and appeared in a variety features including *Guys And Dolls*, *Li'l Abner*, *40 Pounds Of Trouble*, *Cat Ballou* (with Nat King Cole), *Sweet Charity*, *The Cockeyed Cowboys Of Calico County*, *The Dirtiest Girl I Ever Met*, *Six Pack Annie* and *Who Framed Roger Rabbit?*. The ample figure and sunny disposition he displayed as Nicely-Nicely in 1953 endeared him to London audiences and he made frequent appearances in the UK, including one in the musical *Man Of Magic* in 1956. Eventually he settled in Britain and married Angela Bracewell, who came to fame in the 50s in her role as the hostess of the audience participation game 'Beat The Clock' in the top-rated television variety show *Sunday Night At The London Palladium*. After appearing in the West End in 1983 in the short-lived musical *Dear Anyone*, Kaye returned to Broadway two years later and won the only good notices in the musical *Grind*, a complete disaster that was described by one critic as 'art slaughter'. He continued to work in the UK and in 1986 starred as Ring Lardner in the radio play *Some Like Them Cold*. His voice also featured in 1988's partly-animated *Who Framed Roger Rabbit?* Kaye died in December 1997.

● ALBUMS: *Music For Chubby Lovers* (1962)★★★, and Original Cast and film soundtrack recordings.

KEEL, HOWARD

b. Harry Clifford Leek, 13 April 1917, Gillespie, Illinois, USA. A popular singer in films and on the musical stage, with a rich, powerful baritone voice and commanding presence. After starting his career as a singing waiter in Los Angeles, Keel became an 'in-house entertainer' for the huge Douglas aircraft manufacturing company. In 1945, he appeared in *Carousel* on the west coast and then travelled to the UK to appear in the London production of *Oklahoma!*. At this time he was known as Harold Keel, having reversed the spelling of his last name. He subsequently changed his first name and after making a non-singing appearance in the film *The Small Voice* (1948), he returned to the USA where he landed the role of Frank Butler in the film *Annie Get Your Gun* (1950). He continued to make films, mostly musicals, including *Show Boat* (1951), *Kiss Me Kate* and *Calamity Jane* (both 1953), *Rose Marie* and *Seven Brides For Seven Brothers* (both 1954) and *Kismet* (1955). By the 60s he was touring the USA in revivals of popular shows, and appearing in non-musical low-budget western movies. In 1981 his acting career received a boost when he started to appear in the long-running television soap opera *Dallas*. This revived interest in his singing, particularly in the UK, and in 1984 he recorded his first solo album. In 1993, with tongue firmly in his cheek, he announced his farewell tour of the UK, but subsequently returned 'by public demand' for encores.

● ALBUMS: *And I Love You So* (Warwick 1984)★★★★,

Reminiscing (Telstar 1985)★★★, *Live In Concert* (BBC 1989)★★★, *The Collection* (Castle 1989)★★★, *The Great MGM Stars* (MGM 1991)★★★, *An Enchanted Evening With Howard Keel* (Music Club 1991)★★★, *Close To My Heart* (Premier 1991)★★★, and the soundtrack albums from the above musicals.

● VIDEOS: *Close To My Heart* (PMI 1991).

● FURTHER READING: *A Bio-Bibliography*, Bruce R. Leiby.

● FILMS: *The Small Voice* (1948), *Pagan Love Song* (1950), *Annie Get Your Gun* (1950), *Texas Carnival* (1951), *Three Guys Named Mike* (1951), *Show Boat* (1951), *Lovely To Look At* (1952), *Desperate Search* (1952), *Callaway Went Thataway* (1952), *Calamity Jane* (1953), *Fast Company* (1953), *I Love Melvin* (1953), *Kiss Me Kate* (1953), *Ride Vaquero!* (1953), *Deep In My Heart* (1954), *Seven Brides For Seven Brothers* (1954), *Rose Marie* (1954), *Jupiter's Darling* (1955), *Kismet* (1955), *Floods Of Fear* (1958), *The Big Fisherman* (1959), *Armoured Command* (1961), *Day Of The Triffids* (1963), *The Man From Button Willow* voice only (1965), *Waco* (1966), *Red Tomahawk* (1967), *The War Wagon* (1967), *Arizona Bushwackers* (1968).

KEELER, RUBY

b. Ethel Keeler, 25 August 1909, Halifax, Nova Scotia, Canada, d. 28 February 1993, Rancho Mirage, California, USA. A charming and petite actress and singer renowned for the Busby Berkeley 'Depression-era' musicals she made with Dick Powell in the 30s, particularly for *42nd Street* in which Warner Baxter barked at her: 'You're going out a youngster but you've got to come back a star.' That is exactly what she did do, some time after taking dance lessons as a child and tap-dancing in the speakeasies of New York while she was still a teenager. In 1927 she danced her way into three Broadway musicals *Bye, Bye Bonnie*, *Lucky*, and *The Sidewalks Of New York*, and Florenz Ziegfeld offered her an important role with Eddie Cantor and Ruth Etting in *Whoopee!*. While the show was being cast she travelled to Hollywood to make a short film, and there met Al Jolson. He followed her back to New York, and they were married in September 1928. At her husband's request, Keeler left *Whoopee!* before it reached Broadway, and for the same reason she only spent a few weeks in *Show Girl* (in which she was billed as Ruby Keeler Jolson). While she was performing in the latter show, Jolson rose from his seat in the stalls and serenaded his wife with a song. For the next few years she stepped out of the spotlight and concentrated on being just Mrs. Jolson. That is, until 1933, when Darryl F. Zanuck at Warner Brothers saw a film test she had made some years before, and signed her for the ingenue role *42nd Street*. All her years of training paid off as she and Dick Powell and those marvellous Busby Berkeley dance routines (coupled with a tremendous Harry Warren and Al Dubin score) made the film a smash hit. Keeler's most memorable moment came with a soft shoe number, 'Shuffle Off To Buffalo', but her demure, sincere personality and fancy footwork delighted audiences throughout the picture. *42nd Street* was followed by more of the same in the form of *Gold Diggers Of 1933*, *Footlight Parade*, *Flirtation Walk*, *Shipmates Forever*, and *Colleen*. In 1934 she and Jolson starred in their only film together, *Go Into Your Dance*. Keeler made her last film for Warners, *Ready Willing And Able* in 1937. It contained what is supposed to

be one of her favourite sequences in which she dances with co-star Lee Dixon on the keys of a giant typewriter. After playing a straight dramatic role in *Mother Carey's Chickens* (1938) and appearing in one more musical, *Sweetheart Of The Campus* (1941), she retired from the screen. In between making those two films, she had divorced Jolson in 1940, and, a year later, married John Homer Lowe, a wealthy broker from California, and they raised four children. Apart from making some guest appearances on television during the 50s and 60s, and playing in a brief revival tour of the play *Bell, Book And Candle*, Keeler stayed well away from the public eye until 1970, a year after Lowe died. She was tempted back to Broadway for a revival of the 1925 musical *No, No Nanette*, partly because she was assured that it would not ridicule the old musicals, and also because Busby Berkeley was to be the production supervisor. The show was a triumph, running for 871 performances and winning several Tony Awards. US television viewers were reminded of her prowess in 1986 when Ruby Keeler made her last major public appearance in the ABC special *Happy Birthday Hollywood*.

KEEP ON ROCKIN'

Released in 1972, *Keep On Rockin'* was an abridged version of an earlier release, *Sweet Toronto* (1970), which chronicled a rock 'n' roll festival from the previous year. The performance by the Plastic Ono Band, featuring John Lennon, Yoko Ono and Eric Clapton was dropped from the first draft at the former Beatle's behest. (Lennon's first on-stage appearance since 1966 was nonetheless immortalised on the album *Live Peace In Toronto*.) Despite this loss, *Keep On Rockin'* is a sometimes dazzling film, partly through the skilled direction D.A. Pennebaker, famed for his work on Bob Dylan's *Don't Look Back*, but principally for sensational sets rock 'n' roll veterans Bo Diddley, Jerry Lee Lewis, Little Richard and Chuck Berry. Their years as creative forces had ebbed, but they invested their best-known material with passion and urgency. Doubtlessly fired by sharing a bill together, each claimed the spotlight with rekindled vigour. Janis Joplin and Jimi Hendrix also appeared, but their individual personal problems undermined their performances. Indeed the latter was arrested for drugs' possession during his visit to Canada. *Keep On Rockin'* is thus a testament to rock 'n' roll's origins and the enduring power of some of its early acts and songs.

KELLY, GENE

b. Eugene Curran Kelly, 23 August 1912, Pittsburgh, Pennsylvania, USA, d. 1 February 1996, Los Angeles, California, USA. An actor, dancer, singer, choreographer, director, producer, and one of the most innovative and respected figures in the history of the screen musical. Kelly took dance lessons at the age of eight - albeit against his will - and excelled at sports when he was at high school. During the Depression he had a variety of jobs, including gymnastics instructor, and, with his brother Fred, performed a song-and-dance act at local nightclubs. In the early 30s, he spent a few months at law school before opening the Gene Kelly Studios of the Dance, and discovering that he had a real aptitude for teaching, which would manifest itself throughout his career in some of the most creative choreography ever seen on the big screen. In 1937 Kelly moved to New York, and gained a small part as a dancer in the musical comedy *Leave It To Me!*, in which Mary Martin also made her Broadway debut. A larger role followed in the revue *One For The Money*, and he also played Harry, the 'good natured hoofer', in the Pulitzer prize-winning comedy, *The Time Of Your Life*. In 1940, after working in summer stock, and serving as a dance director at Billy Rose's Diamond Horseshoe club, Kelly won the title role in the new Richard Rodgers and Lorenz Hart musical, *Pal Joey*. His portrayal of the devious, unscrupulous nightclub entertainer made him a star overnight in New York, but, after choreographing another Broadway hit show, *Best Foot Forward*, he moved to Hollywood in 1942, and made his screen debut with Judy Garland in *For Me And My Gal*. He appeared in two more musicals for MGM, *Du Barry Was A Lady* and *Thousands Cheer*, before the company loaned him to Columbia for *Cover Girl* (1944). Co-starring with Rita Hayworth and Phil Silvers, the film was a major landmark in Kelly's career, and an indication of the heights he would achieve during the next 10 years. It was memorable in many respects, particularly for Kelly's sensitive rendering of Jerome Kern and Ira Gershwin's 'Long Ago And Far Away', and the 'Alter Ego' dance, during which Kelly danced with his own reflection in a shop window. Back at MGM, he was called upon to play several dramatic roles as well as appearing in *Anchors Aweigh* (1945), for which he received an Oscar nomination for best actor. In the film, as a couple of sailors on leave, Kelly and Frank Sinatra were accompanied by Kathryn Grayson, a Sammy Cahn and Jule Styne score - and Jerry - an animated mouse, who joined Kelly in a live-action/cartoon sequence that is still regarded as a classic of its kind.

After spending two years in the real US Navy during World War II, supervising training films, Kelly resumed at MGM with *Ziegfeld Follies* (1946), in which he sang and danced with Fred Astaire for the first time on screen, in 'The Babbitt And The Bromide'. Two years later he was reunited with Judy Garland for *The Pirate*, a somewhat underrated film, with a score by Cole Porter that included 'Be A Clown'. He then choreographed the 'Slaughter On Tenth Avenue' sequence in the Rodgers and Hart biopic *Words And Music*, in which he danced with Vera-Ellen, before joining Sinatra and Jules Munshin, first for the lively *Take Me Out To The Ball Game* (1949), and again for *On The Town*, 'the most inventive and effervescent movie musical Hollywood had thus far produced'. Although criticized for its truncation of the original Broadway score, *On The Town*, with its integrated music and plot, and the athletic dance sequences on the streets of New York, was acclaimed from all sides. After his triumph in *On The Town*, Kelly went on to *Summer Stock*, with Judy Garland again, before turning to what many consider to be the jewel in MGM's musical crown - *An American In Paris* (1951). Directed by Vincente Minnelli, and set in an idealized version of Paris, Kelly and his partner, Leslie Caron, danced exquisitely to a Gershwin score that included 'I Got Rhythm', 'Our Love Is Here To Stay', ''S Wonderful' and 'I'll Build A Stairway To Paradise'. The film ended with

a 17-minute ballet sequence, a 'summation of Gene Kelly's work as a film dancer and choreographer, allowing him his full range of style - classical ballet, modern ballet, Cohanesque hoofing, tapping, jitterbugging, and sheer athletic expressionism'. It won eight Academy Awards, including one for best picture. Kelly received a special Oscar 'in appreciation of his versatility as an actor, singer, director, and dancer, and specifically for his brilliant achievements in the art of choreography on film'. If *An American In Paris* was MGM's jewel, then *Singin' In The Rain* (1952), was probably its financial plum - arguably the most popular Hollywood musical of them all. Produced by Arthur Freed, who also wrote the songs with Nacio Herb Brown, the film's witty screenplay, by Betty Comden and Adolph Green, dealt with the Hollywood silent movie industry trying to come to terms with talking pictures. Debbie Reynolds and Donald O'Connor joined Kelly in the joyous spoof, and sang and danced to a score that included 'You Were Meant For Me', 'Make 'Em Laugh', 'Good Mornin'' and 'Moses Supposes'. The scene in which Kelly sings the title song, while getting completely drenched, is probably the most requested film clip in the history of the musical cinema.

For *Deep In My Heart* (1955), the Sigmund Romberg biopic, Kelly went back to his roots and danced with his younger brother, Fred, in one of the film's high spots, 'I Love To Go Swimmin' With Wimmen'. Kelly's final major musical projects for MGM were *Brigadoon* (1954) and *It's Always Fair Weather* (1955). In the former, 'the magical story of a Scottish village long lost to history and coming to life once every hundred years for a single day', Kelly co-starred with Cyd Charisse and Van Johnson in a production that was criticized for being shot in Cinemascope, and in the studio, rather than on location. For the latter film in 1955, Kelly co-starred with Dan Dailey and Michael Kidd for what was essentially a satirical swipe at the cynical commercialism of the US television industry - with music. His next project, *Invitation To The Dance* (1956), with script, choreography, and direction by Kelly, consisted of three unrelated episodes, all entirely danced, with Kelly accompanied by a classically trained troupe. A commercial failure in the USA, it was acclaimed in some parts of Europe, and awarded the grand prize at the West Berlin film festival in 1958. Following its success there, Kelly choreographed a new ballet for the Paris Opera's resident company, and was made a Chevalier of the Legion of Honor by the French government. *Les Girls* (1957) was Kelly's final MGM musical, and Cole Porter's last Hollywood score - the golden era of screen musicals was over. Subsequently, Kelly played several straight roles in films such as *Marjorie Morningstar* and *Inherit The Wind*, but spent much of his time as a director on projects such as Richard Rodgers and Oscar Hammerstein's Broadway musical *Flower Drum Song*, and 20th Century Fox's $24,000,000 extravaganza, *Hello, Dolly!* (1969), which starred Barbra Streisand, Walter Matthau and a young Michael Crawford. In 1974, he was back on the screen in *That's Entertainment!*, 'a nostalgia bash, featuring scenes from nearly 100 MGM musicals'. It became a surprise hit, and two years later, Kelly and Fred Astaire hosted the inevitable sequel, *That's Entertainment, Part 2*. After viewing all that vintage footage, it would be interesting to know Kelly's real opinions on a more modern musical film, such as *Xanadu* (1980), in which he appeared with Olivia Newton-John. By then, together with director Stanley Donen, the complete Arthur Freed Unit, and the rest of the talented personnel who produced most of his musicals at MGM, Kelly, with his athletic performance, choreography and direction, had completed a body of work that was only equalled by the other master of dance on film, Fred Astaire - but in a very different style. Whereas Astaire purveyed the image of a smooth man about town, with top hat, white tie and tails, Kelly's preferred to appear casual in sports shirt, slacks and white socks. As he said himself: 'Astaire represents the aristocracy when he dances - I represent the proletariat!'.

● ALBUMS: *Song And Dance Man* (1954)★★★★, *Singin' In The Rain Again* (Decca 1978)★★, *Best Of Gene Kelly - From MGM Films* (MCA 1988)★★★, *Great MGM Stars* (MGM 1991)★★★, *Gotta Dance! The Best Of Gene Kelly* (1994)★★★, and film soundtracks.

● FURTHER READING: *Gene Kelly: A Biography*, Clive Hirschhorn. *The Films Of Gene Kelly*, Tony Thomas. *Gene Kelly*, J. Basinger.

● FILMS: *For Me And My Gal* (1942), *Pilot No. 5* (1943), *Du Barry Was A Lady* (1943), *Thousands Cheer* (1943), *The Cross Of Lorraine* (1943), *Cover Girl* (1944), *Christmas Holiday* (1944), *Anchors Aweigh* (1945), *Ziegfeld Follies* (1946), *Living In A Big Way* (1947), *The Pirate* (1948), *The Three Musketeers* (1948), *Words And Music* (1948), *Take Me Out To The Ball Game* (1949), *On The Town* (1949), *The Black Hand* (1950), *Summer Stock* (1950), *An American In Paris* (1951), *It's A Big Country* (1952), *Singin' In The Rain* (1952), *The Devil Makes Three* (1952), *Brigadoon* (1954), *Crest Of The Wave* (1954), *Deep In My Heart* (1955), *It's Always Fair Weather* (1955), *Invitation To The Dance* (1956), *The Happy Road* (1957), *Les Girls* (1957), *Marjorie Morningstar* (1958), *The Tunnel Of Love* as director (1958), *Inherit The Wind* (1960), *Gigot* as director (1962), *Let's Make Love* (1960), *What A Way To Go* (1964), *The Young Girls Of Rochefort* (1968) *A Guide For The Married Man* as director (1967), *Hello, Dolly!* as director (1969), *The Cheyenne Social Club* as director and producer (1970), *40 Carats* (1973), *That's Entertainment!* as narrator (1974), *That's Entertainment, Part 2* as narrator (1976), *Viva Knievel!* (1977), *Xanadu* (1980), *Reporters* (1981), *That's Dancing!* (1985).

KERN, JEROME

b. 27 January 1885, New York City, New York, USA, d. 11 November 1945, New York, USA. One of the most important composers in the history of American popular music, Kern was taught to play the piano by his mother, and proved to be a gifted musician with a remarkable ear. While still at junior school he was dabbling with composition, and by his mid-teens was simultaneously studying classical music and writing songs in the popular vein. He became a song plugger in New York's Tin Pan Alley and occasionally accompanied leading entertainers of the day. Some of his early songs were picked up by producers of Broadway shows and were also used in London, a city Kern visited first in 1902/3 and thereafter held in great affection. During the next few years Kern became a familiar figure at theatres in London and New York, working on scores and acting as a rehearsal pianist. He had his first hit in 1905 with 'How'd You Like To Spoon With Me?' (lyric:

Edward Laska), which was interpolated in the score for *The Earl And The Girl*. Throughout this period, Kern continued to contribute songs to various shows, and in 1912 wrote his first complete score, with lyrics by Paul West, for *The Red Petticoat*. Two years later, his most accomplished work so far, *The Girl From Utah*, contained the delightful 'They Didn't Believe Me' (lyric: Herbert Reynolds), and in 1915 Kern had his second song hit, 'Babes In The Wood' (lyric: Kern and Schuyler Greene), from *Very Good Eddie*. In 1916, Kern contributed a few songs to *Miss Springtime*, an operetta, with lyrics by P.G. Wodehouse, and a book by Guy Bolton. This marked the beginning of the partnership which, with its witty books and lyrics, and songs cleverly integrated, into the story, is credited with helping to create America's own indigenous musical comedy format, as opposed to the imported European operetta. Kern, Bolton and Wodehouse's first complete show together, *Have A Heart* (January 1917), ran for only 76 performances, but *Oh, Boy!* (February 1917), the first and most successful of their renowned Princess Theatre Musicals, stayed at the tiny 299-seater house for more than a year. It's charming score included 'Words Are Not Needed', 'An Old Fashioned Wife', 'A Pal Like You', 'You Never Knew About Me', 'Nesting Time In Flatbush', and 'Till The Clouds Roll By' (lyric: Kern and Wodehouse). The latter song was a tremendous hit for Anna Wheaton, one of the stars of the show, and James Harrod. The success of *Oh, Boy!* meant that the trio's *Leave It To Jane* ('The Crickets Are Calling', 'The Siren's Song', 'Wait Till Tomorrow', 'Leave It To Jane', 'Cleopatterer'), which opened in August 1917, had to be accommodated in the much larger Longacre Theatre. After *Oh Lady! Lady!!* ('Do Look At Him', 'Before I Met You', 'Not Yet', 'It's A Hard Hard World'), which made its debut at the Princess Theatre in February 1918, Kern, Bolton and Wodehouse, went their separate ways, reuniting briefly in 1924 for the disappointing *Sitting Pretty*. During the early 20s Kern was perhaps the most prolific composer on Broadway, with numerous show scores to his credit. These included *The Night Boat* (1920), *Sally* (1920, 'Look For The Silver Lining', lyric: Buddy De Sylva), *The Cabaret Girl* (London 1921), *Good Morning Dearie* (1921), *The Beauty Prize* (London 1923), *The Stepping Stones* (1923, 'Raggedy Ann', lyric: Anne Caldwell), and *Sunny* (1925, 'Who?', lyric: Oscar Hammerstein II). In 1927, Kern composed his masterpiece, *Show Boat*, which ran on Broadway for 575 performances. Oscar Hammerstein wrote the lyrics for the magnificent score which included 'Ol' Man River', 'Make Believe', 'Why Do I Love You?', and 'Can't Help Lovin' Dat Man'. Also present was 'Bill' (lyric: Wodehouse and Hammerstein), which had been cut from *Oh Lady! Lady!!* nearly 10 years previously. Naturally enough, Kern's subsequent Broadway shows were unable to match the enormous success of *Show Boat*, but fine songs were invariably found in the scores for most of them, such as *Sweet Adeline* (1929, 'Why Was I Born?', lyric: Hammerstein), *The Cat And The Fiddle* (1931, 'She Didn't Say "Yes"', lyric: Otto Harbach), *Music In The Air* (1932, 'I've Told Ev'ry Little Star', 'The Song Is You', lyrics: Hammerstein), *Roberta* (1933, 'The Touch Of Your Hand', 'Yesterdays', 'Smoke Gets In Your Eyes', lyrics: Harbach), and *Very Warm For May* (1939, the exquisite 'All The

Things You Are' [lyric: Hammerstein]). Four years before the latter show drew a line under Kern's prolific and distinguished Broadway career, the composer had begun to compose the music for a number of extremely popular film musicals. These included *Roberta* (1935), for which 'Lovely To Look At' (lyric: Dorothy Fields and Jimmy McHugh) and 'I Won't Dance' (lyric: Harbach and Hammerstein) were added to the original stage score), *Swing Time* (1936, 'The Way You Look Tonight' [Academy Award], 'A Fine Romance', 'Pick Yourself Up', 'Bojangles Of Harlem', lyrics: Fields), *High, Wide And Handsome* (1937, 'The Folks Who Live On The Hill', 'Can I Forget You?', lyrics: Hammerstein), *Joy Of Living* (1938, 'You Couldn't Be Cuter', 'Just Let Me Look At You', lyrics: Fields), *One Night In The Tropics* (1940, 'Remind Me', lyric: Fields), *Lady Be Good* (1941, 'The Last Time I Saw Paris' [Academy Award], lyric: Hammerstein), *You Were Never Lovelier* (1942, 'Dearly Beloved', 'I'm Old Fashioned', 'You Were Never Lovelier', lyrics: Johnny Mercer), *Cover Girl* (1944, 'Long Ago And Far Away', lyric: Ira Gershwin), Can't Help Singing (1944, 'Cali-for-ni-ay', 'More And More', 'Any Moment Now', 'Can't Help Singing', lyric: E.Y. 'Yip' Harburg), and *Centennial Summer* (1946, 'In Love In Vain', 'The Right Romance', lyrics: Leo Robin). Kern and Hammerstein also wrote some new numbers, including 'I Have The Room Above' and 'Ah Still Suits Me', for the 1936 film version of *Show Boat*. That show, along with many of Kern's other marvellous songs, was showcased in the 1946 biopic *Till The Clouds Roll By*, in which the composer was portrayed by Robert Walker. Having conquered Broadway and Hollywood, Kern turned to writing music for the concert platform, composing a classical suite based upon his music for *Show Boat*, and another suite entitled 'Mark Twain: A Portrait For Orchestra'. He had agreed to write the music, with Hammerstein's lyrics, for a new Broadway show entitled *Annie Get Your Gun*, when he collapsed and died in November 1945. An outstanding songwriter with an ability to find beautiful, lilting and emotional melodies with deceptive ease while At the same time incorporating elements of ragtime and syncopation into his lively dance tunes, Kern's work has remained popular with singers and jazz musicians. More than half a century after his last great songs were written, the music remains fresh and undated. In 1994, a highly acclaimed revival of *Show Boat*, directed by Harold Prince, opened on Broadway and won five Tony Awards. Several leading artists such as Ella Fitzgerald have recorded albums in tribute to him, and there are compilations of Kern's music including *Capitol Sings Jerome Kern* (1992), currently available.

● VIDEOS: *The Legends Collection: Showboat Composer Jerome Kern* (Simitar 1995).
● FURTHER READING: *The World Of Jerome Kern*, David Ewen. *Jerome Kern: A Biography*, Michael Freedland. *Jerome Kern: His Life And Music*, Gerald Bordman. *Bolton And Wodehouse And Kern*, Lee Davis.

KID FROM SPAIN, THE

One of the most lavish and successful musicals of the early 30s, and 'the kid' in question was, of course, the irrepressible Eddie Cantor. On this hilarious occasion, while on the run from the US Federal authorities, he winds up in Spain where, through no fault of his own, he is somehow mistaken for a famous bullfighter. His efforts to justify this exalted position - actually in the bullring - are delightful to see. Robert Young and Lyda Roberti gave him all the support they could, and the rest of the cast included Ruth Hall, John Miljan, Noah Beery, and J. Carrol Naish. Soon-to-be-familiar faces in the chorus were those of Betty Grable and Paulette Goddard. Cantor's most engaging vocal moment came with 'What a Perfect Combination' (Bert Kalmar-Irving Caesar [lyric]; Harry Ruby-Harry Askst [music]), and Ruby and Kalmar also contributed 'The College Song', 'Look What You've Done', and 'In The Moonlight'. The two songwriters also wrote the screenplay in collaboration with William Anthony McGuire. Busby Berkeley was the choreographer so the dance sequences were imaginative and high-class, and Samuel Goldwyn produced the film so the Goldwyn Girls were present - and pretty. Leon McCarey was responsible for directing a kind of musical and comedy masterpiece.

KID GALAHAD

Elvis Presley starred in this 1962 film, which was a remake of Edward G. Robinson's 1937 vehicle. In a plot later echoed by the *Rocky* series, an unrated fighter rises from obscurity to become a boxing champion. It was not an artistic success, although Presley's popularity ensured greater box-office returns than the action merited. Six songs, including 'King Of The Whole Wide World' and 'I Got Lucky', were completed for the soundtrack. These were compiled on the *Kid Galahad* EP, which remained on the US singles chart for seven weeks.

KID MILLIONS

In fact, all of $77 millions - that is the sum the naive kid from Brooklyn (Eddie Cantor) inherits from his archaeologist father early on in this 1934 Samuel Goldwyn picture (released by United Artists). Naturally, as soon as the word gets around regarding his windfall, several unsavoury individuals come crawling out of the woodwork - or rather, the stonework, as in this case the loot is hidden somewhere in Egypt. Arthur Sheekman, Nat Perrin, and Nunnally Johnson wrote the screenplay, but it was all academic anyway, because, as usual with a Cantor vehicle, it is Eddie's infectious humour and a batch of peppy numbers that propel the film along. A talented supporting cast helps as well, and in this case, Ann Sothern, Ethel Merman, George Murphy, Jesse Block, Warren Hymer, the Nicholas Brothers and Eve Sully, along with Goldwyn girls Lucille Ball and Paulette Goddard, more than filled the bill. Cantor managed to don his traditional blackface for some of the time, and he had four splendid songs, 'When My Ship Comes In' and 'Okay Toots' (both Walter Donaldson-Gus Kahn), 'I Want To Be A Minstrel Man' (Burton Lane-Harold Adamson) featuring the marvellous dancing Nicholas Brothers, and 'Mandy' (Irving Berlin). Merman was thrilling on 'An Earful Of Music' (Donaldson-Kahn), and Murphy and Sothern tender on 'Your Head On My Shoulder' (Lane-Adamson). Cantor, Merman, Hymer, and the Goldwyn Girls were all involved in the spectacular 'Ice Cream Fantasy' finale which was filmed in Technicolor. Seymour Felix was the choreographer, and *Kid Millions* was directed by Roy Del Routh.

KIDD, MICHAEL

b. Milton Greenwald, 12 August 1919, New York City, New York, USA. An important choreographer and director who pioneered a joyful and energetic style of dancing. Kidd was a soloist with the Ballet Theatre (later called the American Ballet Theatre) before making his Broadway debut as choreographer with *Finian's Rainbow* in 1947. He won a Tony Award for his work on that show, and earned four more during the 50s for *Guys And Dolls* (1950), *Can-Can* (1953), *Li'l Abner* (1956) and *Destry Rides Again* (1959). His other shows around that time were *Hold It*, *Love Life* and *Arms And The Girl*. From *Li'l Abner* onwards he also directed, and sometimes produced, most of the shows on which he worked, but it was as a choreographer of apparently limitless invention that he dominated the Broadway musical during the 50s. In the 60s and early 70s he worked on productions such as *Wildcat*, *Subways Are For Sleeping*, *Here's Love*, *Ben Franklin In Paris*, *Skyscraper*, *Breakfast At Tiffany's* (which closed during previews), *The Rothschilds* (1970), *Cyrano*, and a revival of *Good News* (1974). Kidd also filled the big screen with his brilliant and exuberant dance sequences in classic Hollywood musicals such as *The Band Wagon*, *Seven Brides For Seven Brothers*, *It's Always Fair Weather* and *Hello, Dolly!* He co-starred with Gene Kelly and Dan Dailey in *It's Always Fair Weather*, and appeared in several other films, including *Movie Movie*, an affectionate parody of a typical 30s double-feature that went largely unappreciated in 1979. However, recognition of his immense contribution to the screen musical came in 1997 when he received a special Honorary Academy Award.
● FILMS: *It's Always Fair Weather* (1955), *Movie Movie* (1979).

KIDS ARE ALRIGHT, THE

Taking its title from one of guitarist/composer Pete Townshend's early songs, this 1978 documentary of the Who is a fine resume of one of rock's most fascinating acts. Having begun life in 1964 as an aspiring R&B group, the quartet fell under the influence of Peter Meadon who turned them into a leading exponent of the Mod subculture. The film charts their innovative pop-art period, smashing instruments in auto-destructive manner to the strains of early hits 'I Can't Explain' and 'My Generation'. Townshend's rise as a distinctly English songwriter is shown in period television appearances, drawn from UK, USA and European sources. (Mild controversy arose when the compiler allegedly failed to return these archive shots.) The Who's rise from pop to rock attraction is shown through their appearance at the Monterey Pop Festival and part of their set on the hitherto unscreened *Rolling Stones' Rock 'n' Roll Circus* is also exhumed. Their pounding performance of 'A Quick One While He's Away' sets the scene for the rock opera *Tommy*, which was at the core of their live shows during the late 60s/early 70s. By that point the Who had become one of the world's most popular live attractions, as footage drawn from albums, notably *Who's Next*, attests. Promotional shorts for concurrent singles, including 'Joined Together' are spliced

with interview material, such as a memorable appearance on UK television's *Russell Harty Show* during which Keith Moon removed his clothes. The drummer's eccentric behaviour became the stuff of legend, but the road of excess brought his life to a premature end. Film shot during the recording of his last album with the group, *Who Are You*, adds poignancy to this resume. *The Kids Are Alright* is dedicated to the memory of the person who lay at the heart of this leading rock attraction.

KIDS FROM FAME, THE

In 1980, British film director Alan Parker made his Hollywood debut with a movie about the New York City High School for Performing Arts called *Fame*. The movie did not make that much of an impression at the box office, but American television network NBC bought the rights and developed the original idea into a weekly serial. The series was originally dropped in the USA, but subsequently hit the top of the ratings in the UK and further episodes were produced. In the UK, the success crossed over to the record industry where a soundtrack album of songs from the first series was compiled. Written by top writers such as Rick Springfield, Gary Portnoy and Carole Bayer Sager, the series produced five top-selling albums, and three Top 20 singles, including the US number 4/UK number 1 hit, 'Fame' for Irene Cara. Each song was sung by a different cast member and backed by top session musicians. The series ran for a couple of years before UK interest declined. The series turned out to be a showcase for many aspiring young actors.
● ALBUMS: *The Kids From Fame* (1982)★★★, *The Kids From Fame, Again* (1982)★★, *The Kids From Fame, Live* (1983)★, *The Kids From Fame, Songs* (1983)★★★, *The Kids From Fame, Sing For You* (1983)★★.
● COMPILATIONS: *Best Of Fame* (1984)★★★.

KILEY, RICHARD

b. 31 March 1922, Chicago, Illinois, USA. An actor and singer, with an imposing bearing and inimitable voice, Kiley studied at Loyala University and spent more than three years in the US Navy, before moving to New York in 1947. Although he appeared out of town with Nancy Walker in the musical *A Month Of Sundays*, during the late 40s and early 50s Kiley worked mostly in dramatic parts off-Broadway and in first-class televisions productions such as *Patterns* (*Kraft Television Theatre*) and *P.O.W.* (*United States Steel Hour*). His career in the musical theatre really began in 1953 when he created the role of Caliph in *Kismet*, in which he introduced, with others, several memorable numbers, including 'Stranger In Paradise' and 'And This Is My Beloved'. Following a gap of six years, Kiley returned to Broadway in the murder mystery musical *Redhead* (1959), for which he and his co-star Gwen Verdon won Tony Awards. *No Strings* followed in 1962, and with Diahann Carroll he sang the lovely 'The Sweetest Sounds'. After taking over from Craig Stevens in Meredith Willson's *Here's Love*, Kiley played pitchman Sam the Shpieler in *I Had A Ball* (1964) - and then came the role of a lifetime. Kiley won a second Tony Award for his memorable portrayal of Don Quixote in *Man Of La Mancha* (1965), and introduced Mitch Leigh and Joe Darion's 'The Impossible

Dream', a song with which he is always identified. He reprised the part on several occasions, including the 1969 London revival, two further New York productions, and on tour. Since his triumph in *Man Of La Mancha*, Kiley's appearances in musical productions have been limited. He played Julius Caesar in *Her First Roman* (1968), an adaptation of Bernard Shaw's *Caesar And Cleopatra*; took part in the one-night tribute, *A Celebration Of Richard Rodgers* (1972); played an aviator in Alan Jay Lerner and Frederick Loewe's poorly received fantasy movie, *The Little Prince* (1974); appeared in a brief revival of *Knickerbocker Holiday* (1977) at Town Hall, New York; and starred out of town in a musical version of *A Christmas Carol* (1981), with music and lyrics by Michel Legrand and Sheldon Harnick. However, he has continued to appear in dramatic roles in films, the theatre, and on television. He won an Emmy in 1984 for his performance as Paddy Cleary in *The Thorn Birds*, and in 1999 was inducted into The Theatre Hall of Fame.

● ALBUMS: *The Rodgers And Hammerstein Songbook* (RCA Camden 1960)★★★, and Original Cast and spoken word recordings.

● FILMS: *The Mob* (1951), *Eight Iron Men* (1952), *The Sniper* (1952), *Pickup On South Street* (1953), *The Blackboard Jungle* (1955), *The Phenix City Story* (1955), *Spanish Affair* (1958), *Pendulum* (1969), *AKA Cassius Clay* (1970), *The Little Prince* (1974), *Looking For Mr. Goodbar* (1977), *Endless Love* (1981), *Howard The Duck* voice only (1986), *Chameleon Street* (1991), *Jurassic Park* voice only (1993), *Phenomenon* (1996), *Time To Say Goodbye* (1997), *Patch Adams* (1998).

KING

'The road to opening night, now shifted to April 18, has been the bloodiest of any musical in recent memory. Writers, directors, a producer, and even a leading actor, have either walked out or been fired after rows over racial politics and money.' That was the kind of advance publicity that this show received prior to its first performance which eventually took place at the Piccadilly Theatre in London on 23 April 1990. The £2.5 million production, which was directed by Clarke Peters, and based on the life of the controversial civil rights leader, Martin Luther King Jnr., had a book by Lonnie Elder III, music by Richard Blackford, and lyrics by Maya Angelou and Alistair Beaton. Just prior to the opening, Angelou left in a huff, and demanded that her name be removed from the credits, but that was refused, and although Elder is credited with the final libretto, the completed work was the product of many hands. Apparently, one of Angelou's objections was that 'it takes a black man to write about a black man and there hasn't been a single black man in the writing of this show.' That was also the reported attitude of King's widow, Coretta Scott King, who initially withheld her approval from the project. Most critics savagely dismissed the book and the production in general as 'an insignificant little offering' . . . 'of such banality it is in itself a crime against humanity' . . . 'evoking a pocket history of bloody protest marches, political intrigue, factionalism, melodramatic Jim Crowism, and character defamation, but with little dramatic flair and less depth'. American opera singers Simon Estes (King) and Cynthia

Haymon (Coretta) were absolved from the blame - in the singing department, at least. The score, 'a mix of jazz, gospel, and showbiz pizzazz', consisted of some 24 numbers, along the lines of 'Cotton's My Momma', 'Bus Boycott', 'Welcome To Atlanta', 'Equal Rights', 'No More Sorrow', 'The Price Of Freedom'. 'They're After You're Vote', 'Sacrifice', 'For I Am An American', 'Safe In Your Arms', and one inspired by King's immortal words, 'I Have A Dream' ('so did I,' said one cynic, 'but I fought against temptation and stayed awake.'). More money was ploughed in, but to no avail. Not many shows could withstand that sort of battering, and *King* closed after six weeks, with losses estimated at between £2.6 million and £3.3 million.

KING AND I, THE (FILM MUSICAL)

Yul Brynner became a legend in the 1951 Broadway show, and no other actor could even have been considered for the leading role in this 1956 screen version. Brynner's stage partner, Gertrude Lawrence, died during the Broadway run, and his co-star for this film, the British actress Deborah Kerr, proved to be an ideal replacement. She plays Anna, the widowed English governess, who is engaged by King Mongkut of Siam (Brynner) to educate his many children. In spite of their fundamental differences and principles, they fall in love, but are parted by the King's death. The film's other love story is that between one of the King's daughter's, Tuptim (Rita Moreno) and Lun Tha (Carlos Rivas), but that romance, too, is destined to end unhappily. Other parts were taken by Martin Balsam, Rex Thompson, Terry Saunders, Alan Mowbray, Patrick Adiarte, Yuriko, Michiko, Geoffrey Toone, and Charles Irwin. The highly emotional story was complemented by Richard Rodgers and Oscar Hammerstein II's magnificent score, which included 'I Whistle A Happy Tune' (Kerr), 'March Of The Siamese Children' (instrumental), 'Hello, Young Lovers' (Kerr), 'A Puzzlement' (Brynner), 'Getting To Know You' (Kerr with the children), 'We Kiss In A Shadow' (Moreno-Rivas), 'Something Wonderful' (Saunders), 'The Small House Of Uncle Thomas' (ballet) and 'Song Of The King' (Brynner). Perhaps the film's most memorable moment comes when Anna tries to teach the King how to dance, and they - awkwardly at first - and then exuberantly, whirl around the floor to the sublime 'Shall We Dance?'. Deborah Kerr's singing voice was dubbed by Marni Nixon. Ernest Lehman's screenplay was based on Hammerstein's original libretto and Margaret Landon's novel *Anna And The King Of Siam*. Jerome Robbins was the choreographer and the film, which was directed by Walter Land, was superbly photographed by Leon Shamroy in DeLuxe Color and CinemaScope. It won Oscars for best actor (Brynner), its sumptuous costumes (Irene Shariff), sound recording, artset decoration and scoring of a musical picture (Alfred Newman and Ken Darby), and went on to gross well over $8 million in the USA.

KING AND I, THE (STAGE MUSICAL)

The fifth stage musical to emerge from the partnership between Richard Rodgers and Oscar Hammerstein II, and the first of them to be suggested by an artist who wanted to play the leading role. It was Gertrude Lawrence who made it known to the composers early in 1951 that she would like to star in a musical version of *Anna And The King Of Siam*, and after viewing the 1946 movie which was based on Margaret Landon's novel, Rodgers and Hammerstein, too, became enthusiastic about the project. They even considered Rex Harrison, who had played the King in the film, for the leading role, and *Oklahoma!*'s Alfred Drake was high on the list as well In the end, they settled for a bald Russian, with a great deal of presence, who turned up at the auditions looking rather ferocious. His name, of course, was Yul Brynner, and he was about to create one of the all-time great roles in the history of the musical theatre. *The King And I* opened on 29 March 1951 at the St. James Theatre in New York, Set in the early 1860s, Hammerstein's book tells of the immense effect the arrival in Bangkok of the widowed Anna Leonowens (Lawrence) has on the King of Siam (Brynner), and the members of his court. Disapproved of initially by the Prime Minister, The Kralahome (John Juliano), befriended by the King's chief wife, Lady Thiang (Dorothy Sarnoff), and adored by the 67 children, including eldest son Prince Chulalongkorn (Johnny Stewart), she has been hired to teach, Anna struggles to come to terms with this strange and often brutal culture. However, to the surprise of both of them, she and the King learn from each other in roughly equal measure, and by curtain time, as he lies sick and dying, their relationship has developed into something quite wonderful. Rodgers and Hammerstein's score was full of splendid songs, including 'We Kiss In A Shadow' and 'I Have Dreamed' for the ill-fated young lovers Tuptim (Doretta Morrow) and Lun Tha (Larry Douglas), Tuptim's 'My Lord And Master', Lady Thaing's 'Something Wonderful', and the King's only solo, 'A Puzzlement'. Rodgers was careful to compose the music for Lawrence's songs to accommodate her limited vocal range, and they were all a joy: 'I Whistle A Happy Tune', 'Hello, Young Lovers!', 'Getting To Know You', 'The Royal Bangkok Academy', 'Shall I Tell You What I Think Of You?', and the climactic 'Shall We Dance', with Brynner. Among the other items were 'Western People Funny', a long narrative ballet sequence - 'The Small House Of Uncle Tom' - and 'March Of The Siamese Children' (orchestrations Robert Russell Bennett). The sumptuous production, which ran for 1,246 performances, was choreographed by Jerome Robbins, directed by John Van Druten, and won Tony Awards for best musical, actress (Lawrence), featured actor (Brynner), costumes (Irene Sharaff), and sets (Jo Mielziner). Sadly, around 18 months into the run, Gertrude Lawrence died of cancer at the age of 54, and was succeeded by Constance Carpenter. Alfred Drake, an early contender for the King, played the role for three months while Brynner was on holiday in 1952. Just over a year later, a London production opened at the Theatre Royal, Drury Lane, on 8 October 1953, and lasted for 926 performances. Valerie Hobson and Herbert Lom led the cast, with Muriel Smith (Lady Thiang), Doreen Duke (Tuptim), Jan Mazarus (Lun Tha), Timothy Brooking (Prince Chulalongkorn), Martin Benson (The Kralahome). Since then there have been numerous revivals of this much-loved piece, including several at New York's City Center, and at Lincoln Center. Brynner toured with the show frequently, and returned to Broadway in 1977 (a lavish affair, with Constance Towers as Anna) and 1985 (with Mary Beth Peil as Anna), took it to the London Palladium in 1979 with Virginia McKenna. Other West End revivals have included Adelphi Theatre 1973 with Peter Wyngarde and Sally Ann Howes, Sadler's Wells 1991 with Susan Hampshire and Japanese Koshiro Matsumoto IX and later David Yip, and the Covent Garden Festival 1995 with Liz Robertson and the Royal Ballet's Russian star Irek Mukhamedov making his singing and acting debut. Robertson had toured the USA six years previously playing opposite Mukhamedov's fellow countryman, Rudolph Nureyev. In 1996, an acclaimed Australian production - said to be that country's first stage musical export to Broadway - opened at the Neil Simon Theatre, starring Donna Murphy and Lou Diamond Phillips. It won Tony Awards for best musical revival, leading musical actress (Murphy), scenic design (Brian Thomson), and costumes (Roger Kirk), and subsequently toured with Hayley Mills and Vee (Victor) Talmadge (1997) and Marie Osmond and Talmadge (1998). The Broadway production closed after 781 performances, making it the longest-running revival ever of *The King And I*. In 1992, Julie Andrews, who many consider would have made the perfect Anna, sang the role for a studio cast CD, with British actor Ben Kingsley as the King. The 1956 film version starred Yul Brynner and Deborah Kerr. A 1999 animated movie will be voiced by Christiane Noll (Anna), Martin Vidnovic (the King). This is the first animated original Broadway musical ever.

KING CREOLE

This 1958 film is, for many, the best of Elvis Presley's Hollywood career. Based on the Harold Robbins novel *A Stone For Danny Fisher*, it afforded him a first-rate plot - that of a singer performing in a New Orleans club owned by mobsters - providing Presley with a dramatic role equal to the memorable soundtrack. 'Trouble', 'Crawfish' and the title track itself rank among the finest tracks he recorded and the content ranged from compulsive rock 'n' roll numbers to melodic ballads. Presley's singing is self-assured yet unmannered and only his induction into the US Army thwarted the direction both his acting and music were taking.

KING DAVID

On the 18 March 1997, Walt Disney Theatrical Productions marked the unofficial opening of their beautifully restored New Amsterdam Theatre on 42nd Street in New York with the world premiere of this epic 'pop oratorio'. Staged in a concert setting by Mike Ockrent for a limited run of nine performances, it had a score by Alan Menken (music) and Tim Rice (book and lyrics). This was Rice's third - and most solemn - delve into Biblical waters. Some theatre watchers missed the level of irony and irreverence that he brought to his previous work with Andrew Lloyd Webber on *Joseph And The Amazing Technicolor Dreamcoat* and *Jesus Christ Superstar*. Menken's music too, it was felt, could perhaps have been 'lightened up' a degree or so. As for the book, David's general, Joab

(Stephen Bogardus), narrated the story in which the young shepherd's victories against the Philistines, and his slaying of Goliath (Bill Nolte), arouse the jealousy of Saul (Martin Vidnovic), Israel's first king. After the death of Saul and his brother Jonathan (Roger Bart), David (Marcus Lovett) is crowned King of all Israel. Michal (Judy Kuhn), Saul's daughter, becomes one of several wives, but David's reign is marred by the death of his rebellious son Absalom (Anthony Galde). At the final curtain, he himself is dying, to be succeeded by Young Solomon (Daniel Hodd), a son born of his adulterous relationship with Bathsheba (Alice Ripley). The stellar cast performed the often exciting and moving sung-through score in great style. Highlights included Kuhn's plaintive love ballads 'Sheer Perfection' and 'Never Again', Lovett's cool, jazzy, 'Warm Spring Night', the anthem 'This New Jerusalem', Ripley's gorgeous 'When In Love', and the gospel-tinged crowd-pleaser, 'Saul Has Slain His Thousands'. The remainder of the score consisted of 'Israel And Saul', 'Samuel Confronts Saul', 'Samuel Anoints David', 'The Enemy Within', 'There Is A View', 'Psalm 8', 'Genius From Bethlehem', 'The Valley Of Elah', 'You Have It All', 'Psalm 23', 'Hunted Partridge On The Hill', 'The Death Of Saul', 'How Are The Mighty Fallen', 'David & Michal', 'The Ark Brought To Jerusalem', 'How Wonderful The Peace', 'Off Limits', 'Uriah's Fate Sealed', 'Atonement', 'The Caravan Moves On', 'Death Of Absalom', 'Absalom My Absalom', 'Solomon', 'David's Final Hours', and 'The Long Long Day'. Not surprisingly, the latter number gave critics a good excuse to comment that it was also a long night as well - some two hours forty-five minutes-worth. A 54-piece orchestra and chorus joined the principals on Tony Walton's admirable stepped-platform set which was lit by David Agress. Costume design was by William Ivey. The CD recording, containing approximately half of the material performed, gives an insight into a show whose future remains uncertain. Another *King David* musical, by Pepe Cibrian and Angel Mahler, made its debut at Buenos Aires' Teatro El Liceo on the 2 April 1998.

KING OF JAZZ, THE

The title of this lavish and spectacular musical revue which was released by Universal in 1930 refers, of course, to Paul Whiteman, who led the most popular orchestra of his time. Although not a jazzman himself, he did promote that brand of music by employing many fine jazz musicians over the years, such as Joe Venuti, Eddie Lang, and Frankie Trumbauer. That trio are all featured prominently in this film along with Whiteman's most famous vocalist, Bing Crosby and his fellow Rhythm Boys Harry Barris and Al Rinker, plus a host of other artists including John Boles, Jeannie Lang, the Brox Sisters, William Kent, Grace Hayes, Stanley Smith, Jeanette Loff, Walter Brennan, Laura La Plante, and Slim Summerville. Inevitably the spotlight is very firmly on Paul Whiteman And His Orchestra throughout, from the opening 'Rhapsody In Blue' (George Gershwin), during which the entire orchestra seated inside - and at the keyboard - of a gigantic grand piano, through to the breathtaking finalé when, beginning with 'D'Ye Ken John Peel' and 'Santa Lucia', the music from various countries around the world is symbolically

blended together in 'The Melting Pot Of Music'. In between those two amazing sequences, and introduced every time by a caption card giving song title and performer details, were well over 50 musical items ranging from folk and classical pieces to popular songs such as 'Mississippi Mud' (Harry Barris-James Cavanaugh), 'It Happened In Monterey' (Mabel Wayne-Billy Rose), 'So The Bluebirds And The Blackbirds Got Together' (Barris-Billy Moll), 'Ragamuffin Romeo' (Wayne-Harry DeCosta); and 'A Bench In The Park', 'Happy Feet', 'Music Hath Charms', and 'Song Of The Dawn' (all by Milton Ager and Jack Yellen). As well as conducting the orchestra, Whiteman appeared at other times in a variety of costumes (including baby clothes, complete with feeding bottle), mugging to the camera and looking not unlike Oliver Hardy *sans* Stan Laurel. Russell Markert staged the dances, and the sketches were written by John Murray Anderson who had enjoyed a great deal of success on Broadway with several editions of the *Greenwich Village Follies*, and his own *John Murray Anderson's Almanac*. He was also the director, the man responsible for assembling this whole marvellously original concept, parts of which eventually influenced many a future screen musical. Hal Mohr, Jerome Ash and Ray Rennahan photographed the film in two-colour Technicolor which gave the film a charm of its own, and contributed to the desire to watch it over again, if only to catch some of the details and bits of business missed the first time around.

KING'S RHAPSODY

With this show, Ivor Novello maintained the high standard of his spectacular, romantic musicals which had graced the West End for almost 15 years. King's Rhapsody opened at the Palace Theatre in London on 15 September 1949, and was set in the mythical Central European country of Murania. It is the late nineteenth century, and the young prince, Nikki (Novello), breaks free from the family ties that bind, and sets off for the good life in Paris. However, some years later when his father dies, King Nikki reluctantly returns to his homeland and an arranged marriage with Queen Christiane (Vanessa Lee), taking his mistress, Marta Karillos (Phyllis Dare) along with him. His court is not a happy one, and he is prevented from introducing certain laws and reforms - especially by his mother, Queen Elena (Zena Dare). So it is back to Paris and Marta, with Queen Christiane taking over the reins of the country, and raising their child to take his place. Also prominent amongst the cast were Olive Gilbert and Denis Martin. Novello's music, with lyrics by Christopher Hassall, was of the highest quality, with Vanessa Lee introducing the beautiful 'Someday My Heart Will Awake', from a score which also included 'The Violin Began To Play', 'If This Were Love', 'Fly Home, Little Heart', 'The Gates Of Paradise', 'Take Your Girl', 'Mountain Dove', and 'The Night You Were Mine'. The show was still playing to packed houses when Novello died suddenly on 5 March 1951. Jack Buchanan assumed his role, and *King's Rhapsody* continued to run for 881 performances, closing on 6 October of that year. A 1955 film version starred Errol Flynn and Anna Neagle, and Vanessa Lee recreated her original role when the show was presented on BBC

Television in 1957, with Griffith Jones as Nikki. To commemorate the centenary of Novello's birth, in 1993 BBC Radio 2 transmitted a complete performance of the show. Nikki was played by Jeremy Nicholas, with Queen Elena (Margaret Courtney), Cristiane (spoken by Charlotte Attenborough, sung by Marilyn Hill Smith), and Marta (spoken by Mel Martin, sung by Meriel Dickinson).

KING, DENNIS

b. Dennis Pratt, 2 November 1897, Coventry, England, d. 21 May 1971, New York, USA. An actor and singer who enjoyed considerable success in the USA during the 20s and 30s, King began his career, like so many others, with the Birmingham Repertory Theatre Company. After touring in the UK provinces, he made his West End debut in Frederick Lonsdale's romantic opera, Monsieur Beaucaire (1919, as Townbrake), and moved to the USA two years later. His first few appearances on Broadway were in straight plays, but in 1924 he played fur trapper Jim Kenyon, opposite Mary Ellis, in Rose Marie ('Indian Love Call', title song). His next show, The Vagabond King (1925, François Villon), once again with Rudolph Friml's splendid melodies ('Only A Rose', 'Some Day'), made him a star overnight. King's recording of another of the show's numbers, 'Song Of The Vagabonds', on which he was accompanied by Rosario Bourdon's Orchestra, climbed high in the US bestsellers. He reprised his role as Villon, co-starred with Jeanette MacDonald, in the early talkie version of The Vagabond King in 1930. King starred in both Broadway (1928) and London (1930) productions of his third Friml show, The Three Musketeers (D'Artagnan), before appearing as Gaylord Ravenal opposite Norma Terris (Magnolia) in the 1932 revival of Show Boat. In the following year he was back on the West End stage, as Peter Mali, an actor masquerading as a prince, in C. Stafford Dickens' short-lived musical romance, Command Performance. At this point, King began to devote himself to the straight theatre, although did appear in two more Broadway musicals during the 30s - a staging of Franz Lehár's 1928 Berlin hit, Frederike (1937, the poet Goethe) and I Married An Angel (1938, Count Willi Palaffi). His subsequent work in the legit. theatre was often extremely impressive, with starring roles in plays such as A Doll's House (1937), The Three Sisters (1942), The Searching Wind (1944), Medea (1947, taking over from John Gielgud), The Devil's Disciple (1950), Billy Budd (1951), Lunatics And Lovers (1954), and Photo Finish (1963). He did return to the musical theatre in the 50s for a brief revival of Music In The Air (1951, Bruno), and an ever briefer (less than three weeks) outing for the musicalization of James Hilton's famous novel, Lost Horizon, tantalizingly retitled Shangri-la (1956, Hugh Conway). King was also permanently in demand on radio, particularly during the 30s, and graduated to television programmes such as Twelfth Night (1957), via several late 40s guest spots on the Philco Television Playhouse, Alfred Hitchcock Presents, and The Alcoa Hour. On the big screen he sang 'Nichavo' in the all-star Paramount On Parade (1930), and was no doubt amused and bemused with his involvement in Fra Diavolo (1933, aka The Devil's Brother), a Laurel And Hardy vehicle, adapted from Daniel Auber's 1830 operetta.

Dennis King's son, John Michael King, made his Broadway debut in the last of the Arthur Schwartz and Howard Dietz's acclaimed New York revues, Inside U.S.A (1948), then took minor or chorus parts in musicals such as Courtin' Time (1951), Me And Juliet (1953), Hit The Trail (1954), and Ankles Aweigh (1955). In 1956 he created his first major role, Freddy Eynsford-Hill, in My Fair Lady (1956), in which he introduced the 'shamelessly romantic' 'On The Street Where You Live'. He was also in the 1977 Broadway revival of The King And I (Sir Edward Ramsay) and played GI Carlton Smith in the Alan Jay Lerner-Joseph Stein-Burton Lane musical Carmelina (1979). Later in his career he appeared frequently on television, and toured.

● FILMS: The Vagabond King (1930), Paramount On Parade guest star (1930), The Devil's Brother (1933), Between Two Worlds (1944), Aladdin (1958), The Miracle (1959), Some Kind Of A Nut (1969).

KIRKWOOD, PAT

b. 24 February 1921, Manchester, England. An actress and singer; one of the premier leading ladies of 40s and 50s West End musicals, British films, and Christmas pantomimes. Her frequent appearances in the latter medium earned her the title of 'the greatest principal boy of the Century', and the critic Kenneth Tynan called her legs 'the eighth wonder of the world'. She started her career at the age of 14 at the Salford Hippodrome, and a year later appeared in pantomime in Cardiff. When she was 16 she made her West End debut as Dandini in Cinderella at London's Princes' Theatre. In 1939 at the age of only 18, Pat Kirkwood headlined the revue Black Velvet at the London Hippodrome and sang a sizzling version of 'My Heart Belongs To Daddy', a song that is forever identified with her. Further West End successes followed, including Top Of The World (1940), Lady Behave (1941), Let's Face It! (1942), Starlight Roof (1947), Ace Of Clubs (1950) (in which she introduced Noël Coward's witty song 'Chase Me Charlie'), Fancy Free (1951), Wonderful Town (1955), and Chrysanthemum (1956). It was while she was appearing in Starlight Roof (in which the 12-years-old Julie Andrews made her West End debut) that Kirkwood was introduced to Prince Philip, consort of Queen Elizabeth, by her boyfriend, the fashion photographer Baron. Rumours that they had an affair - always strenuously denied by the actress - continue to surface even in the 90s. Her film career began in 1938 with Save A Little Sunshine, and continued with Me And My Pal (1939), Band Waggon (with Arthur Askey and Richard Murdoch) (1939), Come On George (with George Formby) (1939), Flight From Folly (1944), No Leave, No Love (made in America with Van Johnson) (1946), Once A Sinner (1950), Stars In Your Eyes (1956), and After The Ball (1957). Miss Kirkwood also appeared in several Royal Command Performances, in cabaret, and on radio and television. On the small screen during the 50s she portrayed the renowned musical hall performers Marie Lloyd in All Our Yesterdays and Our Marie; and Vesta Tilley in The Great Little Tilley. Two years after her second husband wealthy Greek-Russian ship-owner Spiro de Spero died in 1954, she married the actor-broadcaster-songwriter ('Maybe It's Because I'm A Londoner', 'I'm Going To Get Lit Up') Hubert Gregg. They were divorced in 1976, and Kirkwood went to live in Portugal for four years where she met the solicitor Peter Knight who subsequently became her fourth husband. They retired to Yorkshire, where Pat Kirkwood consistently turned down offers to return to the stage. Even Cameron Mackintosh was unable to tempt her with the prime role of Carlotta Campion in the 1987 London production of *Follies*. Eventually, however, she did emerge into the spotlight again with her own show, *Glamorous Nights Of Music*, which opened to excellent reviews at the Wimbledon Theatre on the outskirts of London in April 1993. In the following year, she stole the show when making a rare guest appearance in a revue which celebrated the music and lyrics of Cole Porter and Noël Coward entitled *Let's Do It!*, which was presented at Chichester and beyond.

KISMET (FILM MUSICAL)

This opulent but rather unsatisfying adaptation of the hit Broadway musical reached the screen in 1955, courtesy of Arthur Freed's renowned MGM production unit. Although the show's librettists, Charles Lederer and Luther Davis, were entrusted with the screenplay, much of the magic in this Arabian Nights saga was somehow lost in the transfer. For some strange reason, Alfred Drake, who had enjoyed such a triumph in the stage production, was replaced by Howard Keel. He plays the public poet-turned-beggar Hajj, who lives on the streets of old Baghdad, and embarks on a hectic day-long adventure during which his daughter (Ann Blyth) is married to the young Caliph (Vic Damone), while he elopes with the lovely Lalume (Dolores Gray) after getting rid of her husband, the evil Wazir (Sebastian Cabot). Robert Wright and George Forrest's majestic score was based on themes by Alexander Borodin, and there were several memorable songs in the score, including 'Baubles, Bangles, And Beads', 'The Olive Tree', 'Stranger In Paradise', 'And This Is My Beloved', 'Not Since Ninevah', 'Fate', 'Bored', 'Sands Of Time', 'Night Of My Nights', 'Rhymes Have I' and 'Gesticulate'. While perhaps regretting the absence of Drake (he only ever made one film), there is no doubt that Keel was in fine voice and he made an adequate substitute. Also taking part were Jay C. Flippen, Monty Woolley, Jack Elam, Ted De Corsia and Aaron Spelling. Jack Cole was the choreographer, and the film was directed by Vincente Minnelli. Whatever its faults, the film did at least look beautiful, owing in no small part to the Eastman Color and Cinemascope photography of Joseph Ruttenberg. The source of *Kismet* - the 1911 play by Edward Knoblock - has also been adapted into three other, non-musical films, in 1920, 1930 and 1944.

KISMET (STAGE MUSICAL)

Skilled practitioners in the art of adapting the romantic music of classical and operetta composers for their lavish stage musicals, Robert Wright and George Forrest borrowed from Borodin for this show which travelled from San Francisco across America for its Broadway opening at the Ziegfeld Theatre on 3 December 1953. It arrived in the middle of a newspaper strike, which did not appear to harm the production at all. Word of mouth ensured that potential punters knew the combination of Charles

Lederer and Luther Davis' book, based on Edward Knoblock's 1911 Arabian fantasy, and the work of Wright and Forrest, was a splendidly melodic crowd-pleaser. Like *On The Town*, which had delighted New York audiences almost a decade earlier, the action in *Kismet* takes place in one period of 24 hours. Only on this occasion, the setting is Baghdad, not New York. Squeezed into that relatively short space of time is the story of the street poet Hajj (Alfred Drake), who masquerades as a relative of senior beggar Old Hajj, foils the dreaded Wazir (Henry Calvin) - well, drowns him, actually - manages to get his daughter Marsinah (Doretta Morrow) married to the Caliph (Richard Kiley) when everyone knows the Caliph has the pick of several foreign princesses, and ends up by being sentenced by the same Caliph to dally in the desert with Wazir's wife Lalume (Joan Denier). What you might call a perfect day. They carried on like that for 583 performances, in order to perform a collection of delightful songs, which included 'And This Is My Beloved', 'Stranger In Paradise', 'Baubles, Bangles And Beads', 'He's In Love', 'Night Of My Nights', 'Sands Of Time', 'Rhymes Have I', 'Rahadlakum', 'Fate', 'Gesticulate', 'Not Since Nineveh', 'Was I Wazir?', and 'The Olive Tree'. These numbers, and others, were adapted from themes Alexander Borodin composed for works such as 'Polovtsian Dances', 'String Quartet In D', 'In The Steppes Of Central Asia', 'Second String Quartet', 'Symphony Number 2 In B-Minor', and 'Serenade'. Lemuel Ayres designed the opulent sets and costumes, Jack Cole handled the choreography, and the show was directed by Albert Marre. *Kismet* won Tony Awards for best musical, musical actor (Drake), producer (Charles Lederer), author, composer (Borodin), and musical conductor (Louis Adrian). Drake, Morrow, and Denier reprised their performances at London's Stoll Theatre, beginning 20 April 1955, along with Peter Grant (Caliph) and Paul Whitsun-Jones (Wazir). This time the fun continued for 648 performances. A 1965 revival was mounted by the Lincoln Center (with Alfred Drake and Anne Jeffreys), and in 1978 a Civic Light Opera production arrived at London's Shaftesbury Theatre with John Reardon, Lorna Dallas, and Clifton Todd. A 1978 version of the show, retitled *Timbuktu*, featured an all-black cast, which included Eartha Kitt, Gilbert Price, and Melba Moore. The 1955 film version starred Howard Keel, Ann Blyth, Dolores Gray and Vic Damone. BBC Radio 2 broadcast the original in December 1994, with Julia Migenes (Lalume), Ethan Freeman (Hajj), Stephen Hill (Caliph), David Alder (Wazir), and Katrina Murphy (Marsinah).

KISS ME KATE (FILM MUSICAL)

This film had most of the elements of a great screen musical - an outstanding score, a witty screenplay, and a fine cast. The original Broadway show from which it was adapted is generally considered to be Cole Porter's masterpiece, and this 1953 version only served to emphasize and reaffirm that view. The story of thespians Fred Graham (Howard Keel) and his ex-wife, Lilli Vanessi (Kathryn Grayson), who allow their onstage conflict in an out-of-town production of *The Taming Of The Shrew* to spill over into their own tempestuous private lives, was both hilarious and musically thrilling. The dance sequences, which were choreographed by Hermes Pan and his assistant Bob Fosse, were stunning, involving high-class hoofers such as Ann Miller, Bobby Van, Tommy Rall and Carol Haney. Most observers cite Miller's scintillating 'Too Darn Hot' as the film's high spot, but all the songs were performed memorably, including 'I Hate Men' (Grayson), 'So In Love', 'Wunderbar' and 'Kiss Me Kate' (Grayson-Keel), 'I've Come To Wive It Wealthily In Padua', 'Were Thine That Special Face' and 'Where Is The Life That Late I Led?' (Keel), 'Always True To You In My Fashion' and 'Why Can't You Behave? (Miller-Rall), 'We Open In Venice' (Keel-Grayson-Miller-Rall), and 'From This Moment On' (Miller-Rall-Haney-Van-Fosse-Jeannie Coyne). One other item, which would have stopped the show every night if it had been performed in a similar fashion on stage, was 'Brush Up Your Shakespeare', in which James Whitmore and Keenan Wynn, as a couple of affable debt-collecting gangsters, mangle the Bard, courtesy of Porter, in lines such as 'If your blonde won't respond when you flatter 'er/Tell her what Tony told Cleopaterer'. George Sidney directed, and the film was photographed in Ansco Color. Dorothy Kingsley's screenplay was based on Bella and Sam Spewack's original libretto. Some sequences appear slightly puzzling and unnerving - even unnatural - until one realizes that certain effects, such as characters throwing items towards the camera, were inserted to take advantage of the 3-D process in which the film was originally shot.

KISS ME, KATE (STAGE MUSICAL)

The original idea for this show came from stagehand Arnold Saint Subber after he noticed that, when Alfred Lunt and Lynn Fontanne were appearing in a production of William Shakespeare's The Taming Of Shrew, they fought almost as much off-stage as their characters Petruchio and Katherina did on. When, several years later, Subber and set designer Lemuel Ayers decided that this situation might be the basis for a musical, as co-producers they were fortunate enough to acquire the services of librettists Bella And Sam Spewack, and composer Cole Porter. Kiss Me, Kate opened on Broadway at the New Century Theatre 30 December 1948, with a story that went something like this: Fred Graham (Alfred Drake) and Lilli Vanessi (Patricia Morison) are divorced (although they are obviously meant for each other) and now ready for new love. However, they are currently involved in the try-out of a musical version of The Taming Of The Shrew at the Ford Theatre, Baltimore. Fred has hired the nubile Lois Lane (Lisa Kirk) to play the role of Bianca, and sends her a bouquet of flowers which somehow ends up in Lilli's dressing room. She reads the note and threatens to leave. Meanwhile, Lois' friend, Bill Calhoun (Harold Lang), who is supposed to be playing Lucentio, signs a $10,000 IOU for his gambling debts with the name Fred Graham. Two Runyon-esque gangsters (Harry Clark and Jack Diamond) call at the theatre to collect, but when it is explained to them that the money will have to come out of the takings which will inevitably plummet if the leading lady flies the coop, they chaperone her carefully and plug the production - but subtly: 'It's entertaining, vivacious and calculated to please the discerning theatre-goer. You can quote me.' Fred and Lilli's rift continues onstage, where, as Petruchio and Katharine, they attempt to knock six bells out of each other. Good news from the gangsters though. Their boss has been suddenly 'deposed', so the debt is void. Lilli appears to leave, but as the curtain descends on The Taming Of The Shrew - she's back. Cole Porter's score was superb. His 'Shrew' songs blending splendidly with the backstage numbers, and including 'Another Op'nin', Another Show', 'Why Can't You Behave', 'Wunderbar', 'So In Love', 'We Open In Venice', 'Tom, Dick Or Harry', 'I've Come To Wive It Wealthily In Padua', 'I Hate Men', 'Were Thine That Special Face', 'Too Darn Hot', 'Where Is The Life That Late I Led?', 'Always True To You (In My Fashion)', 'Bianca', and 'I Am Ashamed That Women Are So Simple'. Several standards there, and there was also a real live soft-shoe shuffle of a show-stopper for the gangster duo, 'Brush Up Your Shakespeare' ('If she says your behaviour is heinous/Kick her right in the 'Coriolanus''). Choreographer was Hanya Holm, the director John C. Wilson, and it ran for 1,077 performances - making it Porter's most successful show. There were Tony Awards for best musical, producers, authors, composer-lyricist, and costumes (Ayers). Patricia Morison took her Lilli to the London Coliseum in March 1951 for Sam Spewack's restaged version (501 performances), along with Bill Johnson (Fred), Julie Wilson (Lois), Walter Long (Bill), Danny Green and Sydney James (gangsters). Adelaide Hall played Lilli's maid, Hattie. London audiences saw revivals in 1970 (English National Opera, with Emile Belcourt as Fred, Ann Howard as Lilli, Judith Bruce and Teddy Green), 1987 (Royal Shakespeare Company at the Old Vic, with Paul Jones, Nichola McAuliffe, Fiona Hendley, Tim Flavin), and 1997 (Open Air Theatre, Regent's Park, Andrew C. Wadsworth, Louise Gold, Issy Van Randwyck, Graeme Henderson). In the USA it has been seen on television and at the New York City Center. There was also a production at the Goodspeed Opera House, Connecticut, in 1994, with Steve Barton (Fred), Marilyn Caskey (Lilli), Leah Hocking (Lois) and Michael Gruber (Bill). Some musical theatre buffs blame the absence of a major Broadway revival on the inadequacies of the Spewacks' book, but one has been rumoured for some years now, and it is almost certain to happen in 1999. The 1953 film version starred Howard Keel and Kathryn Grayson.

KISS OF THE SPIDER WOMAN

'And the curtain will shake, and the fire will hiss, here comes her kiss' - read the cobwebbed publicity handouts prior to the show's debut at London's Shaftesbury Theatre on 20 October 1992. Extensively revised following its New York/Purchase workshop in 1990, this production of Kiss Of The Spider Woman had received its world premiere in June 1992 in Toronto, Canada. Considered by many to be an unlikely - even unsuitable choice for a musical - it was adapted by Terrence McNally from Manuel Puig's 1976 novel, which was also made into an acclaimed film in 1984. The story concerns two cellmates in a prison somewhere in Latin America, the gay window dresser, Molina (Brent Carver), and the single-minded Marxist revolutionary, Valentin (Anthony Crivello). The two men are gradually drawn together and eventually become lovers. For some of the time, Molina lives in a fantasy world in which his childhood idol, film star, Aurora (Chita Rivera), frequently comes to life in a series of gaudy routines from her tacky 40s B-movies. Rivera is also the black-clad Spider Woman, the temptress who lures men to their death. In this way, the grim reality of the torture and persecution of life in the jail (almost too realistically created) is contrasted effectively with the unreal world outside. John Kander and Fred Ebb's score switched from 'serious' numbers such as 'The Day After That' and 'You Could Never Shame Me', to the spectacular 'Gimme Love', and more conventional and good-humoured songs which included the lovely 'Dear One', along with 'Dressing Them Up', 'Russian Movie', 'Morphine Tango', 'Gimme Love', and 'Only In The Movies'. Critical reaction was mixed, although both Brent Carver and Chita Rivera, making her first appearance in London for 30 years, were both highly acclaimed. Harold Prince's 'triumphant' direction and Jerome Sirlin's 'staggering scenic design, with the steel bars of the cells fading into fanciful projections of tropical jungles and glittering palaces of pleasure' were also applauded. Although it was voted best musical in the *Evening Standard* Drama Awards, *Kiss Of The Spider Woman* had a disappointingly short West End stay of nine months. In May 1993, a Broadway production, with Chita Rivera and Brent Carver, began its run at the Broadhurst Theatre, and scooped the Tony Awards, winning for best musical, score (tied with the *The Who's Tommy*), book, actress (Chita Rivera), actor (Brent Carver), and featured actor (Anthony Crivello). It also gained the New York Critics' prize for Best Musical, ran for 906 performances, and became a popular touring attraction.

KISS THE BOYS GOODBYE

Screen adaptations of Broadway plays and musicals generally make alterations to the story which are considered to be desirable. In this case one of the changes at least was essential, because the central topic of Clare Booth's 1938 play *Kiss The Boys Goodbye* was the all-consuming question of who was going to play the role of Scarlett in the film of *Gone With The Wind*. So, three years later, that had to go, and along with it went a lot of the play's bite and satire. What was left turned out to be a more or less conventional backstage story in which Broadway producer Don Ameche falls for chorus girl Mary Martin. She introduced most of Frank Loesser and Victor Schertzinger's songs, including 'I'll Never Let A Day Pass By', 'That's How I Got My Start', and the lively title song, but Connee Boswell provided the film's musical highlight with her sultry rendering of 'Sand In My Shoes'. Oscar Levant, who invariably raised the laughter (and musical) quota of any film in which he appeared, was in the supporting cast, along with Eddie (Rochester) Anderson, Raymond Walburn, Virginia Dale, Barbara Jo Allen, and Elizabeth Patterson. Harry Tugend and Dwight Taylor wrote the screenplay, and it was directed by Victor Schertzinger.

KISSIN' COUSINS

Trusting that two would prove more popular than one, director Gene Nelson cast Elvis Presley in a dual role for this 1964 feature. The singer played a GI and also a dim-witted hillbilly (donning a wig for the latter) in a plot involving plans to build an ICBM base in the backwoods. The title song reached number 10 (UK) and number 12 (US) when issued as a single; an alternate version, 'Kissin' Cousins (Number Two)', was one of 11 songs from the film featured on an attendant soundtrack album. Fearful, for once, of seeming parsimonious, RCA added 'Echoes Of Love' and 'Long Lonely Highway', two tracks from an earlier session, to enhance the playing time. Sadly, little was being done to halt the artistic decline in Presley's films.

KISSING BANDIT, THE

Frank Sinatra himself is among the many (including his friend Dean Martin) who have been known to mock this 1948 MGM release in which he co-starred (yet again) with Kathryn Grayson. At least on this occasion Grayson was not trying to make it to the top as an operatic singer - that would have been rather difficult anyway because the setting for Isobel Lennart and John Briard Harding's screenplay was way out west in old California. Sinatra, with long hair and even longer sideburns, was in the middle of his early 'shy' period (*Anchors Aweigh*, *Step Lively*, *It Happened In Brooklyn*, *On The Town*). He played the young and retiring son of an infamous womanizing bandit who is reluctantly forced to follow in his father's footsteps. Two of the screen's favourite dancing ladies, Ann Miller and Cyd Charisse, were also in the cast, along with Ricardo Montalban, J. Carrol Naish, Mildred Natwick, Billy Gilbert, Mikhail Rasumny, and Clinton Sundberg. Most of the songs, by Nacio Herb Brown, Earl K. Brent and Edward Heyman were romantic ballads tailored for Sinatra, such as 'Siesta', 'If I Steal A Kiss', 'Senorita', 'What's Wrong With Me?', but things livened up a lot when Charisse, Miller and Montalban got together for the scintillating 'Dance Of Fury'. Grayson had the best song, 'Love Is Where You Find It' (Brown-Brent). Laszlo Benedek directed this Technicolor flop which gave no indication whatsoever that Sinatra was just a few years away from the sophisticated comedy of *The Tender Trap*, and an Oscar-winning performance in *From Here To Eternity*.

KITT, EARTHA

b. 26 January 1928, Columbia, South Carolina, USA. Raised in New York's Harlem, Kitt attended the High School for Performing Arts before joining Katharine Dunham's famed dancing troupe. At the end of a European tour Kitt decided to stay behind, taking up residence in Paris. Having added singing to her repertoire, she was a success and on her return to New York appeared at several leading nightclubs. She appeared on Broadway in *New Faces Of 1952* introducing 'Monotonous', and was later seen more widely in the film version of the show. Her other Broadway shows around this time included *Mrs. Patterson* (1954) and *Shinbone Alley* (1957). She continued to work in cabaret, theatre and television, singing in her uniquely accented manner and slinkily draping herself across any available object, animate or otherwise. She made a few more films over the years, playing a leading role in *St Louis Blues* (1958), with Nat 'King' Cole, and in an all-black version of *Anna Lucasta* (1959), opposite

Sammy Davis Jnr. Although her highly mannered presentation of songs is best seen rather than merely heard, Kitt has made some songs virtually her own property, among them 'I Want To Be Evil', 'An Englishman Needs Time', 'Santa Baby' and 'I'm Just An Old-Fashioned Girl', a claim which is patently untrue. Her other record successes over the years have included 'Uska Dara - A Turkish Tale', 'C'est Si Bon', 'Somebody Bad Stole De Wedding Bell', 'Lovin' Spree', 'Under The Bridges Of Paris', 'Where Is My Man', 'I Love Men' and 'This Is My Life'. In 1978 Kitt appeared on Broadway with Gilbert Wright and Melba Moore in an all-black version of *Kismet* entitled *Timbuktu*. Her career has continued along similar lines on both sides of the Atlantic throughout the 80s and into the 90s, although she was courted by a much younger audience (witness her collaboration on 'Cha Cha Heels' with Bronski Beat in 1989) who were suitably impressed by her irreverent coolness. In 1988 Kitt played the role of Carlotta Campion in the London production of *Follies* and sang Stephen Sondheim's legendary anthem to survival, 'I'm Still Here', which, appropriately, became the title of her second volume of autobiography. In the early 90s she performed her one-woman show in London and New York and appeared as a witch in the comedy/horror movie *Ernest Scared Stupid*. She also toured Britain with the Ink Spots in the revue *A Night At The Cotton Club*. In 1993 Kitt appeared in cabaret at several international venues, including London's Café Royal, and in the following year she played the role of Molly Bloom, the heroine of James Joyce's novel *Ulysses*, in 'an erotic monologue punctuated with songs by the French crooner, Charles Aznavour', which proved to be a cult hit at the Edinburgh Festival.

● ALBUMS: *New Faces Of 1952* original cast (RCA Victor 1952)★★★, *Songs* 10-inch album (RCA Victor 1953)★★★, *That Bad Eartha* 10-inch album (RCA Victor 1953)★★★★, *Down To Eartha* (RCA Victor 1955)★★★, *Thursday's Child* (RCA Victor 1956)★★★, *St. Louis Blues* (RCA Victor 1958)★★★, *The Fabulous Eartha Kitt* (Kapp 1959)★★★, *Eartha Kitt Revisited* (Kapp 1960)★★★, *Bad But Beautiful* (MGM 1962)★★★, *At The Plaza* (1965)★★★, *Eartha Kitt Sings In Spanish* (Decca 1965)★★★, *C'est Si Bon* (IMS 1983)★★★, *I Love Men* (Record Shack 1984)★★★, *Love For Sale* (Capitol 1984)★★, *The Romantic Eartha Kitt* (Pathe Marconi 1984)★★, *St. Louis Blues* (RCA Germany 1985)★★★, *That Bad Eartha* (RCA Germany 1985)★★★, *Eartha Kitt In Person At The Plaza* (GNP 1988)★★★★, *I'm A Funny Dame* (Official 1988)★★★, *My Way* (Caravan 1988)★★★, *I'm Still Here* (Arista 1989)★★★, *Live In London* (Arista 1990)★★★★, *Thinking Jazz* (1992)★★★, *Back In Business* (1994)★★★.

● COMPILATIONS: *At Her Very Best* (RCA 1982)★★★, *Songs* (RCA 1983)★★★, *Diamond Series: Eartha Kitt* (Diamond 1988)★★★, *Best Of Eartha Kitt* (MCA 1990)★★★.

● FURTHER READING: *Thursday's Child*, Eartha Kitt. *Alone With Me: A New Biography*, Eartha Kitt. *I'm Still Here*, Eartha Kitt.

KNICKERBOCKER HOLIDAY

Not a particularly successful show, but notable for the participation of two much-admired American citizens, the distinguished character actor Walter Huston, and the celebrated playwright Maxwell Anderson; and the introduction of one most cherished songs in the history of popular music, 'September Song'. *Knickerbocker Holiday*

opened on 12 October 1938 at the Ethel Barrymore Theatre in New York, with a book by Anderson which was based on Washington Irving's *Knickerbocker History Of New York*. The show begins as Irving, played by Ray Middleton, is beginning to write his book, and then flashes back to New Amsterdam in 1647. The author himself is also transported back in time, and actually takes part in, and occasionally comments on certain aspects of the story that he is supposed to be writing. The piece, in which an all-powerful town council select the knife-sharpener Brom Breck (Richard Kollmar), as the candidate for their 'hanging day', only to see him reprieved by the incoming governor, Peter Stuyvesant (Walter Huston), was considered by many at the time to be a bitter attack on the US President, Franklin D. Roosevelt and his cabinet. *Knickerbocker Holiday* was the first production by the Playwrights Company, an organization which was made up of five distinguished (and sometimes, disillusioned) American dramatists, which included Maxwell Anderson. The show's score, with Anderson's lyrics and music by Kurt Weill, was different in many respects from conventional Broadway show music. The songs were completely integrated into the plot, and included 'How Can You Tell An American?', 'Will You Remember Me?', 'The One Indispensable Man', "You People Think About Love", 'There's Nowhere To Go But Up', 'Sitting In Jail', 'Our Ancient Liberties', 'No Ve Vould'nt Gonnto To Do It' (much of the dialogue is spoken in a strong Dutch accent), and a lovely ballad, 'It Never Was You'. Walter Huston sang the poignant 'September Song', and his recorded version became widely popular. The show itself was unable to sustain a long run, and closed after only 168 performances. After Huston's death in 1950, his version of 'September Song' was played in the film, *September Affair*, and was acclaimed all over again. It was also selected for the US National Academy of Recording Arts and Sciences (NARAS) Hall of Fame. In the 1944 film version of *Knickerbocker Holiday* the song was sung by Charles Coburn.

KNIGHT, PETER

b. 23 June 1917, Exmouth, Devon, England, d. 30 July 1985. An arranger, composer and musical director, Knight played the piano by ear as a young child, and studied piano, harmony and counterpoint privately before making his first broadcast on BBC Radio's *Children's Hour* in 1924. After working in semi-professional bands at venues such as London's Gig club, he won the individual piano award with Al Morter's Rhythm Kings in the 1937 *Melody Maker* All London Dance Band Championship. Three years later he played with the Ambrose Orchestra at the Mayfair Hotel before joining the Royal Air Force for service in World War II. On his discharge, he worked with Sydney Lipton at the Grosvenor House in London for four years before forming a vocal group, the Peter Knight Singers, which became popular on stage and radio. His wife Babs was a founder member and remained with the group for over 30 years. Besides operating the Singers, Knight also worked for Geraldo for a year before becoming a musical director for London West End shows such as *Cockles And Champagne* and *The Jazz Train*, a revue which gave American actress Bertice Reading her first London success. In the late 50s, Knight became musical director for Granada Television, and worked on popular programmes such as *Spot The Tune* and *Chelsea At Nine*. When he resumed freelance work, he arranged and conducted records by artists such as Harry Secombe, Petula Clark, Sammy Davis Jnr. and the Moody Blues (*Days Of Future Passed*). Knight was musical director for a 1964 touring version of Leslie Bricusse and Anthony Newley's show, *The Roar Of The Greasepaint - The Smell Of The Crowd*, and for several series of the extremely popular *Morecambe And Wise Show* on television. In the late 70s, Knight spent some time in Hollywood, and conducted the Los Angeles Philharmonic Orchestra in concerts by the Carpenters. In 1979, he scored and conducted the music for Roman Polanski's Oscar-nominated film *Tess*. His other film credits include the scores for *Sunstruck* (1972) and *Curse Of The Crimson Altar* (1968). Shortly after his death in 1985, Yorkshire television inaugurated the annual Peter Knight Award which 'celebrates and rewards the craft of musical arranging'. Knight rarely put a foot wrong throughout his career and is remembered still with the utmost respect and affection.

● ALBUMS: with the Peter Knight Singers *Vocal Gems From My Fair Lady* (1959)★★★, with his orchestra *A Knight Of Merrie England* (1960)★★★, with two pianos and orchestra *The Best Of Ivor Novello And Noël Coward* (1961)★★★, with the Peter Knight Singers *Voices In The Night* (Deram 1967)★★★, *Sgt Pepper* (Mercury 1967)★★, with the Moody Blues *Days Of Future Passed* (Deram 1967)★★★★, with Bob Johnson *The King Of Elfland's Daughter* (1977)★★★.

KORNGOLD, ERICH WOLFGANG

b. 29 May 1897, Brno (Brunn), Czechoslovakia, d. 29 November 1957, Hollywood, California, USA. An important composer, conductor and arranger for films, from the mid-30s into the 50s. Korngold was a child prodigy, and, in his teens, wrote short operas, such as *The Ring Of Polycrates* and *Violant*. He performed as a pianist in concerts, and was the resident conductor at the Hamburg Opera House for several years. He also re-scored vintage operetta classics, giving them a new lease of life. During the 20s, his own operatic compositions, including *Die Tote Stadt (The Dead City)*, and *The Miracle Of Heliane*, played European opera houses, and his enormous popularity on that continent led him to move to the USA in 1934, where he subsequently became an American citizen in 1943. In 1935, he worked on the first of a series of films for Warner Brothers Studio, when he adapted Mendelssohn's music for the highly regarded film *A Midsummer Night's Dream*, starring Dick Powell and James Cagney. In the same year, he composed the score for *Captain Blood*, the movie that made Errol Flynn a star. Such was his prestige, Korngold was able to pick and choose which movies he cared to work on. During the 30s, his film scores included *Give Us This Night*, *Anthony Adverse*, for which Korngold won his first Academy Award (1936), *The Green Pastures*, *The Prince And The Pauper*, *Another Dawn*, *Of Human Bondage*, *The Adventure Of Robin Hood*, (another Oscar for Korngold), *Juarez* and *The Private Lives Of Elizabeth And Essex*. In 1940, Korngold composed some of his most stir-ring music for *Sea Hawk*, his last for an historical adventure, and was nominated for another Academy Award. His other scores during the 40s included *Sea Wolf*, *King's Row*, *The Constant Nymph*, *Between Two Worlds*, *Devotion*, *Deception* and *Escape Me Never* (1947). In 1944, he conducted and adapted Offenbach's music for the Broadway show, *Helen Goes To Troy*, and added a few things of his own. In the late 40s, Korngold became disenamoured with movies, and turned again to classical composing. These included 'Piano Sonata In E', 'Violin Concerto In D', 'Piano Trio', and 'Piano Concerto For The Left Hand', and the opera, *Die Kathrin*, which flopped in Vienna in 1950. He returned to films in 1955 with his score for the 'uninspired' Richard Wagner bio-pic, *The Magic Fire*, but died two years later in 1957. In spite of his relatively small output, he is still regarded as the leader of his craft. Recordings include: *Elizabeth And Essex* and *The Sea Hawk*, both played by the National Philharmonic Orchestra, and *Music Of Erich Wolfgang Korngold*, conducted by Lionel Newman.

● FURTHER READING: *Erich Wolfgang Korngold* by R.S. Hoffman. *Erich Wolfgang Korngold: Ein Lebensbild* by L. Korngold.

KRETZMER, HERBERT

b. 5 October 1925, Kroonstad, South Africa. A distinguished journalist and lyricist, Kretzmer left his home country in the late 40s, and drifted for a few years. He lived in Paris for a time, playing the piano in a bar on the Left Bank, before settling in London in 1954. Pursuing twin careers, he served as drama critic for the *Daily Express* and television critic for the *Daily Mail*, as well as collaborating with Dave Lee on two novelty hits for Peter Sellers and Sophia Loren, 'Goodness Gracious Me' and 'Bangers And Mash'. The former went to number 4 in the UK chart, and won an Ivor Novello Award. Kretzmer and Lee were commissioned to write a topical song each week for BBC television's satirical *That Was The Week That Was*, and their 'In The Summer Of His Years', which was performed by Millicent Martin within hours of the assassination of President Kennedy, was swiftly covered in America by Mahalia Jackson, Kate Smith, and Connie Francis. Kretzmer then wrote the book and lyrics for the West End musical *Our Man Crichton* (1964), and contributed lyrics only to *The Four Musketeers* (1967) and Anthony Newley's cult musical film *Can Heironymus Merkin Ever Forget Mercy Humppe And Find True Happiness?* From the latter, 'When You Gotta Go' has become a closing song for many cabaret singers, while 'On The Boards', performed in the film by Bruce Forsyth, is a skilfully-worded tribute to music hall. Kretzmer's English lyrics for the Charles Aznavour songs, 'Yesterday When I Was Young', 'Happy Anniversary' and 'She' (from the ITV series *The Seven Faces Of Woman*), were brought to the attention of Cameron Mackintosh, who invited Kretzmer to write the lyrics for the London production of the French musical *Les Misérables*. This was done by adapting into English the original text by Alain Boublil and Jean-Marc Natel, and involved expanding the two-hour piece into a three-hour show. The all-sung musical has been a West End success since 1985, and includes the witty and ingenious rhymes of 'Master Of The House' as well as the familiar ballads, 'I Dreamed A Dream', 'On My Own' and 'Bring Him Home'. In 1988 Kretzmer was made a Chevalier of the Order of Arts and Letters by the French Government. His lyrics have been translated into several languages to enable *Les Misérables* to be performed with enormous success throughout the world.

KRISTOFFERSON, KRIS

b. 22 June 1936, Brownsville, Texas, USA. Kristofferson, a key figure in the 'New Nashville' of the 70s, began his singing career in Europe. While studying at Oxford University in 1958 he briefly performed for impresario Larry Parnes as Kris Carson, while for five years he sang and played at US Army bases in Germany. As Captain Kristofferson, he left the army in 1965 to concentrate on songwriting. After piloting helicopters part-time he worked as a cleaner at the CBS Records studios in Nashville, until Jerry Lee Lewis became the first to record one of his songs, 'Once More With Feeling'. Johnny Cash soon became a champion of Kristofferson's work and it was he who persuaded Roger Miller to record 'Me And Bobby McGee' (co-written with Fred Foster) in 1969. With its atmospheric opening ('Busted flat in Baton Rouge, waiting for a train/feeling nearly faded as my jeans'), the bluesy song was a country hit and became a rock standard in the melodramatic style of Janis Joplin and the Grateful Dead. Another classic among Kristofferson's early songs was 'Sunday Morning Coming Down', which Cash recorded. In 1970, Kristofferson appeared at the Isle of Wight pop festival while Sammi Smith was charting with the second of his major compositions, the passionate 'Help Me Make It Through The Night', which later crossed over to the pop and R&B audiences in Gladys Knight's version. Knight was also among the numerous artists who covered the tender 'For The Good Times', a huge country hit for Ray Price, while 'One Day At A Time' was a UK number 1 for Lena Martell in 1979. Kristofferson's own hits began with 'Loving Her Was Easier (Than Anything I'll Ever Do Again)' and 'Why Me', a ballad that was frequently performed in concert by Elvis Presley. In 1973, Kristofferson married singer Rita Coolidge and recorded three albums with her before their divorce six years later. Kristofferson had made his film debut in *Cisco Pike* (1971) and also appeared with Bob Dylan in *Pat Garrett And Billy The Kid*, but he achieved movie stardom when he acted opposite Barbra Streisand in a 1976 remake of the 1937 picture *A Star Is Born*. For the next few years he concentrated on his film career (until the 1979 disaster *Heaven's Gate*, the same year he split from Coolidge), but returned to country music with *The Winning Hand*, which featured duets with Brenda Lee, Dolly Parton and Willie Nelson. A further collaboration, *Highwaymen* (with Nelson, Cash and Waylon Jennings), headed the country chart in 1985. The four musicians subsequently toured as the Highwaymen and issued two further collaborative albums. A campaigner for radical causes, Kristofferson starred in the postnuclear television drama *Amerika* (1987) and came up with hard-hitting political commentaries on *Third World Warrior*. Kristofferson compered and performed at the Bob Dylan Tribute Concert in 1992, during which he gave Sinead O'Conner a sympathetic shoulder to cry on after

she was booed off stage. His recording career took an upturn with the release of *A Moment Of Forever* in 1995.

● ALBUMS: *Kristofferson* (Monument 1970)★★, *The Silver-Tongued Devil And I* (Monument 1971)★★★, *Me And Bobby McGee* (Monument 1971)★★★, *Border Lord* (Monument 1972)★★★, *Jesus Was A Capricorn* (Monument 1972)★★★, with Rita Coolidge *Full Moon* (A&M 1973)★★★, *Spooky Lady's Sideshow* (Monument 1974)★★★, with Coolidge *Breakaway* (A&M 1974)★, *Who's To Bless ... And Who's To Blame* (Monument 1975)★★, *Surreal Thing* (Monument 1976)★★, five tracks on *A Star Is Born* film soundtrack (Monument 1976)★★★, *Easter Island* (Monument 1977)★★, with Coolidge *Natural Act* (A&M 1979)★★, *Shake Hands With The Devil* (Monument 1979)★★★, *To The Bone* (Monument 1981)★★, with Dolly Parton, Brenda Lee, Willie Nelson *The Winning Hand* (Monument 1983)★★★, with Willie Nelson *Music From Songwriter* film soundtrack (Columbia 1984)★★★, with Nelson, Johnny Cash, Waylon Jennings *Highwayman* (Columbia 1985)★★★★, *Repossessed* (Mercury 1986)★★, *Third World Warrior* (Mercury 1990)★★, with Nelson, Cash, Jennings *Highwayman 2* (Columbia 1990)★★★, *Live At The Philharmonic* (Monument 1992)★★★, with Nelson, Cash, Jennings *The Road Goes On Forever* (Liberty 1995)★★, *A Moment Of Forever* (Justice 1995)★★★.

● COMPILATIONS: *The Songs Of Kristofferson* (Monument 1977)★★★, *Country Store* (Starblend 1988)★★★, *The Legendary Years* (Connoisseur Collection 1990)★★★, *Singer/Songwriter* (Monument 1991)★★★, *The Best Of Kristofferson* (Sony 1995)★★★★, *The Country Collection* (Spectrum 1998)★★★.

● FURTHER READING: *Kris Kristofferson*, Beth Kalet.

● FILMS: *The Last Movie* (1970), *Cisco Pike* (1972), *Blume In Love* (1973), *Pat Garrett And Billy The Kid* (1973), *Bring Me The Head Of Alfredo Garcia* (1974), *Alice Doesn't Live Here Any More* (1975), *The Sailor Who Fell From Grace With The Sea* (1976), *A Star Is Born* (1976), *Vigilante Force* (1976), *Semi-Tough* (1978), *Convoy* (1978), *Heaven's Gate* (1980), *Rollover* (1981), *Flashpoint* (1984), *Songwriter* (1984), *Trouble In Mind* (1985), *Blood And Orchids* television movie (1986).

KYSER, KAY

b. James King Kern Kyser, 18 June 1906, Rocky Mount, North Carolina, USA, d. 23 July 1985, Chapel Hill, North Carolina, USA. A popular bandleader in the USA during the 30s and 40s, Kyser was born into an academically excellent family, and he too became a 'professor', though hardly in the conventional sense. Whilst at high school he developed a flair for showmanship, and entered the University of North Carolina in 1924 with the intention of studying law. The subject was soon discarded in favour of music, and Kyser took over the leadership of the campus band from Hal Kemp when Kemp departed to form one of the most popular 'sweet' bands of the 30s. Kyser was soon on the road himself, and in 1927 he recruited George Duning, a graduate of the Cincinnati Conservatory of Music, as the chief arranger of what was originally a jazz unit. This turned out to be a smart move, because Kyser could not read or write a note of music. Duning stayed with the Kyser band for most of its life, before going on to write films scores as diverse as *Jolson Sings Again* and *Picnic*. By 1933, when Kyser played the Miramar Hotel in Santa Monica, California, the band had developed a 'sweeter' style, and had become a major attraction. Kyser, the showman, also injected several gimmicks. For example, instead of a having a spoken introduction to a song, the vocalist would *sing* the title at the beginning of each number; and later, just before the vocal chorus, the band would play a few bars of its theme, Walter Donaldson's 'Thinking Of You', while Kyser announced the singer's name. It was simple, but highly effective. In the following year, Kyser took over from Hal Kemp yet again, this time at the Blackhawk Restaurant in Chicago. The band's sell-out performances at the venue were supplemented by regular radio broadcasts, and so the renowned *Kay Kyser's Kollege Of Musical Knowlege* was born. It was a zany, comedy quiz programme in which the Blackhawk's patrons' skill in identifying song titles was rewarded with prizes (there were rarely any losers). NBC's networked airings brought Kyser (by then known as the 'old perfesser'), national recognition, and in the late 30s he and the band had several hit records, including 'Did You Mean It?', 'Cry, Baby, Cry', 'Music, Maestro, Please!', 'Ya Got Me', 'Two Sleepy People', 'I Promise You', 'Cuckoo In The Clock', 'The Tinkle Song', 'The Little Red Fox', 'The Umbrella Man', 'Three Little Fishies', and 'Stairway To The Stars'. Throughout its life, Kyser's band had a string of popular vocalists, including Harry Babbitt, Ginny Simms (d. 4 April 1994, Palm Springs, California, USA, aged 81), Sully Mason, Gloria Wood, Julie Conway, Trudy Erwin, Dorothy Dunn, Lucy Ann Polk, and Ish Kabibble. The latter name was a pseudonym for trumpeter Merwyn Bogue (d. 5 June 1994, Joshua Tree, California, USA, aged 86), and he featured on most of the band's many novelty numbers, and in their series of comedy films which included *That's Right, You're Wrong* (1939), *You'll Find Out*, *Playmates*, *My Favorite Spy*, *Around The World*, *Swing Fever*, and *Carolina Blues* (1944). Mike Douglas, who later became a popular television talk show host, also sang with the band in the 40s, and for a few months in the 50s. In the early 40s, the recruitment of Van Alexander, who had arranged the Chick Webb-Ella Fitzgerald recording of 'A-Tisket A-Tasket', coincided with a critical reappraisal of Kyser's musical output. As well as winning polls in the 'corn' category, the band came to be regarded as a genuine swing unit that also had a way with a ballad. During World War II, Kyser toured extensively for the USO, entertaining troops in over 500 service camps and hospitals over a wide area. In 1944, he married the blonde Hollywood model, Georgia Carroll, who had decorated such movies as *Ziegfeld Girl* and *Du Barry Was A Lady*. She was a singer, too, and provided the vocals on one of the band's 1945 hits, 'There Goes That Song Again'. Throughout the decade the Kyser band was almost invariably in the US Top 20 with a variety of titles such as 'You, You, Darlin'', 'Playmates', 'With The Wind And The Rain In Your Hair', 'Friendship', 'Blue Love Bird', 'Tennessee Fish Fry', 'Who's Yehoodi?', 'Blueberry Hill', 'Ferryboat Serenade', 'You Got Me This Way'. 'Alexander The Swoose (Half Swan, Half Goose)', '(Lights Out) 'Til Reveille', 'Why Don't We Do This More Often?', '(There'll Be Bluebirds Over) The White Cliffs Of Dover', 'A Zoot Suit (For My Sunday Girl)', 'Who Wouldn't Love You', 'Johnny Doughboy Found A Rose In Ireland', 'Got The Moon In My Pocket', 'Jingle, Jangle, Jingle', 'He Wears A Pair Of Silver Wings', 'Strip

Polka', 'Ev'ry Night About This Time', 'Praise The Lord And Pass The Ammunition' (the band's biggest hit), 'Can't Get Of This Mood', 'Let's Get Lost', 'Bell Bottom Trousers', 'One-Zy, Two-Zy (I Love You-Zy)', 'Ole Buttermilk Sky', 'The Old Lamp-Lighter', 'Huggin' And Chalkin'', 'Managua, Nicaragua', 'Woody Woodpecker', and 'Slow Boat To China' (1948). During that period *The Kollege Of Musical Knowlege* continued to delight and amuse American radio audiences who knew that when Kyser welcomed them with: 'Evenin' Folks. How y'all?', in that strong southern accent, he was dressed in his professor's white gown and mortarboard, 'jumping, cavorting, mugging, and waving his arms like a dervish', just for the benefit of the few in the studio. In 1949, while the show was still high in the ratings, it was unexpectedly cancelled by the sponsors, and Kyser switched the concept to television, but it made little impact. By 1951 he had lost interest, and retired to North Carolina a wealthy man. He devoted the rest of his life to Christian Science, a subject in which he was an authorised practitioner.

● ALBUMS: *Greatest Hits* (50s)★★★, *Dance Date* (80s)★★, *The Songs Of World War II* (1993)★★★★.

L'AVENTURE DU JAZZ

An outstanding film documentary produced and directed in 1969 by Louis and Claudine Panassie, this film features numerous leading mainstream musicians. Amongst the artists on view are Eddie Barefield, Buck Clayton, William 'Cozy' Cole, Jimmy Crawford, Vic Dickenson, Sister Rosetta Tharpe, Milt Hinton, Pat Jenkins, Budd Johnson, Jo Jones, Eli Robinson, Zutty Singleton, Willie 'The Lion' Smith, Tiny Grimes, Buddy Tate and Dick Vance. Also on hand are blues singers John Lee Hooker and Memphis Slim and the exciting dance team, Lou Parks' Lindy Hoppers. Rarely seen, this film is a major achievement and worth a place on the shelf of any collector lucky enough to come across a copy. Soundtrack excerpts were issued as a double album on the Jazz Odyssey label.

LA BAMBA

In this 1986 musical biopic of Ritchie Valens, the first Hispanic-American rock star, director Luis Valdez's screenplay initially explores the teenager's relationships with his mother (Rosanna DeSoto), delinquent, dope-smoking half-brother Bob (Esai Morales), friend Rosie (Elizabeth Peña), and the rich white girl he meets at high school, Donna Ludwig (Danielle von Zerneck). Lou Diamond Phillips plays Valens (then named Richard Valanzuela), who replaces Rudy Castro (Geoffrey Rivas) as vocalist with a local group, the Silhouettes, and is then offered a solo contract by Bob Keene (Joe Pantoliano) of Del-Fi Records. After changing his name, Valens hears a band in a Tijuana brothel playing a Mexican nonsense song called 'La Bamba', and persuades Keene to put his (Valens') recording on the b-side of his own composition, 'Donna'. Shortly after its release, Valens, who has a phobia about flying, goes on tour with Buddy Holly (Marshall Crenshaw) and the Big Bopper (Stephen Lee). All three are killed in a plane crash following a concert in Clear Lake, Iowa. Valens was not quite 18 years old. The soundtrack is full of popular songs of the period, such as 'Chantilly Lace', 'Summertime Blues', 'Oh Boy', 'Ready Teddy', 'Goodnight My Love', 'Lonely Teardrops', 'Come On Let's Go', and 'Rip It Up'. These are performed by the original artists, the actors who are portraying those artists, or the Los Lobos rock quintet. Los Lobos sang most of the Valens material. In addition, there was some music written specially for the film by Carlos Santana and Miles Goodman. Also portrayed on screen were Alan Freed (Alan Chandler), Eddie Cochran (Brian Setzer), and Jackie Wilson (Howard Huntsberry). After being featured in this movie, the Los Lobos version of 'La Bamba' spent three weeks at the top of the US chart in the summer of 1987. Around nine years later, Lou Diamond Phillips played the King of Siam, with Donna Murphy as Anna, in the 1996 revival of Richard Rodgers and Oscar Hammerstein II's musical, *The King And I*. 'A wonderful old musical, and a major new star.'

LA CAGE AUX FOLLES

After experiencing his biggest hits with the all-frills and femininity of *Hello, Dolly!* and *Mame*, composer and lyricist Jerry Herman gave Broadway a dose of effeminacy in 1983 with its first homosexual musical, *La Cage Aux Folles*. It opened at the Palace Theatre on 21 August with a book by Harvey Fierstein based on the play by Jean Poiret and the cult 1978 French-Italian movie, which itself was inspired by the real-life Les Allonges by the harbour in St. Tropez. The La Cage Aux Folles nightclub is owned by Georges (Gene Barry), whose cosy 20 years 'marriage' to his transvestite star Albin (George Hearn), is disturbed when Jean-Michel (John Weiner), Georges' son from his 'closet days', announces that he is to be married to the daughter of a family who would just not understand or appreciate his father's long-standing domestic relationship. Albin (stage name Zaza) has to fade into the background for a time, but returns to the scene masquerading as Georges' wife. Despite the show's highly contemporary theme, Herman's score was good old-fashioned musical comedy with a couple of beautifully poignant ballads, 'Song On The Sand (La Da Da Da)' and 'Look Over There', the jaunty 'With You On My Arm', the defiant 'I Am What I Am', a rousing 'The Best Of Times', plus 'A Little More Mascara', 'Masculinity', and an hilarious tour of 'La Cage Aux Folles': 'It's slightly bawdy and a little bit 'new

wave'/You may be dancing with a girl who needs a shave . . . Eccentric couples always punctuate the scene/A pair of eunuchs and a nun with a marine.' The show was a tremendous success, and stayed on Broadway for 1,176 performances and toured throughout the USA. Gene Barry, who has a reputation in America as a song-and-dance man but whose main claim to fame internationally is due to television programmes such as *Burke's Law*, was a revelation. He was nominated for a Tony for best actor but the award went to George Hearn, and the show also won for best musical, score, book, director (Arthur Laurents), and costumes. Hearn recreated his role for the 1986 London production, which also starred British actor Denis Quilley and ran for nine months. In 1994, a new US national touring company starred Walter Charles as Georges and Lee Roy Reams as Albin.

LA VALLEE

Barbet Schroeder directed this 1972 film in which the French cast travels to New Guinea seeking the lost valley of its title. Its idealistic view of back-to-nature hippie lifestyles proved some five years out-of-date and *La Vallee* would have inspired little interest but for the involvement of Pink Floyd. The group had already scored a previous Schroeder feature, *More* (1969) and he invited them to contribute to this project. The results were issued on *Obscured By Clouds*, a release sandwiched between ground-breaking albums *Meddle* and *Dark Side Of The Moon*. Although worthwhile in its own right, *Obscured By Clouds* contained several short pieces of mood music ideally suited for airplay on US FM stations. This facilitated acceptance of its successor's lengthier, more complex, compositions.

LADIES AND GENTLEMEN...THE ROLLING STONES

The Rolling Stones' 1972 US tour has assumed legendary proportions. Undertaken in the wake of two acclaimed albums, *Sticky Fingers* and *Exile On Main Street*, it captured the band at the height of its creative and performing powers. The offstage hedonism that accompanied life on the road was graphically described in Robert Greenfield's book *Stones Touring Party* and Robert Frank's rarely seen documentary *Cocksucker's Blues*. The warts-and-all premise of the latter was not apparent on *Ladies And Gentlemen*, released in 1974. This straightforward film focused on the Rolling Stones' music, showcasing 15 of their best-known and most popular numbers. Executive producer Marshall Chess, then head of Rolling Stones' Records' ensured that the film celebrated music and not lifestyle excess. *Ladies And Gentlemen* confirmed that the sobriquet 'the world's greatest rock 'n' roll band' was not misplaced during this era.

LADY AND THE TRAMP

(see Disney, Walt)

LADY IN THE DARK

For his first Broadway book musical following his brother George's death in 1937, Ira Gershwin teamed with composer Kurt Weill for this show which arrived in New York at the Alvin Theatre on 23 January 1941. Moss Hart's book had started out as a straight play, *I Am Listening*, and when it became obvious that the piece would work better as a musical, Katherine Cornell, the original choice for leading lady, was replaced by Gertrude Lawrence. She played Liza Elliott, the editor of a highly successful fashion magazine who seeks psychiatric help in an effort to allay her feelings of insecurity, and to explain the extraordinary dreams that she is constantly experiencing. These generally concern four men: Kendall Nesbitt (Bert Lytell) her lover and professional patron; Randy Curtis, a Hollywood star played by Victor Mature, who was on the brink of a lucrative movie career himself, during which he became known as 'The Hunk'; Russell Paxton, the magazine's photographer (Danny Kaye making his Broadway musical comedy debut), and Charley Johnson (Macdonald Carey), Liza's cantankerous advertising manager, and the man she eventually falls for. All the songs, except one, are presented in four dream sequences, linked together with Gershwin and Weill's beautifully ethereal ballad, 'My Ship', a song which subsequently received sensitive readings over the years from popular singers such as Tony Bennett and Buddy Greco. *Lady In The Dark* contained at least two more memorable songs, 'The Saga Of Jenny' and 'Tschaikowsky'. The former, performed in the 'Circus Dream' by Gertrude Lawrence, stopped the show every night, and concerned a lady who, throughout her life, just could not make up her mind: 'Jenny made her mind up when she was twelve/That into foreign languages she would delve/But at seventeen to Vassar it was quite a blow/That in twenty-seven languages she couldn't say no.' The number has been described as 'a sort of blues bordello', and, it is said, was written especially so that Lawrence could 'follow' the immense impact made by Danny Kaye with the tongue-twisting 'Tschaikowsky', in which he listed the names of 49 Russian composers in 39 seconds. The remaining songs in what was a classy score included 'One Life To Live', 'Girl Of The Moment', 'This Is New', 'The Princess Of Pure Delight', and 'Tributes To Liza Elliott'. Following several cast changes in June 1941, *Lady In The Dark* completed a run of 467 performances, and then toured before returning to Broadway for another two and half months in 1943. A year later, a film version was released starring Ginger Rogers and Ray Milland, but minus several of the songs. Ten years after that, there was a US television production with Anne Sothern and Carleton Carpenter. The show endured in various presentations, including a tour of the UK provinces in 1981, and an appearance at the Edinburgh Festival in 1988. After taking more than 50 years to reach London, *Lady In The Dark* opened at the Royal National Theatre's Lyttleton house on 11 March 1997. Maria Friedman played Liza, with James Dreyfus in the Danny Kaye role of Russell Paxton, and Adrian Dunbar (Charley), Paul Shelley (Kendall), and Steven Edward Moore (Randy). The choreographer was Quinny Sacks, and the director Francesca Zambello. In 1992, a CD was released of Gertrude Lawrence recreating her original role for a 1950 *Theatre Guild Of The Air* broadcast.

LADY IS A SQUARE, THE

This was Britain's high-kicking 50s heart-throb Frankie Vaughan's third picture - and his first musical. He played Johnny Burns, a pop singer who poses as a butler in the service of a hard-up society lady, Frances Baring (Anna Neagle), and secretly helps her to prolong the life of her husband's symphony orchestra. Janette Scott plays the dutiful daughter, and other roles went to Anthony Newley, Wilfred Hyde White, Ted Lune, Christopher Rhodes, Kenneth Cope, and Josephine Fitzgerald. Vaughan sang the lovely Ray Noble ballad, 'Love Is The Sweetest Thing', as well as the more contemporary 'The Lady Is A Square' (Raymond Dutch-Johnny Franz), 'That's My Doll' (Dick Glasser-Ann Hall), and 'Honey Bunny Baby'. The last number is credited to 'Frank Able', which sounds suspiciously like an abridged version of Vaughan's real name of Frank Abelson. Harold Purcell, Pamela Bower and Nicholas Phipps adapted the screenplay from a story by Purcell, and the director was Herbert Wilcox. He and his wife, Anna Neagle, produced the picture in 1959 for Everest Films in the UK.

LADY SINGS THE BLUES

Roundly criticized at the time of its release in 1972 (in some instances before it was even seen), this bio-pic purports to tell the life story of Billie Holiday. Loosely based upon Lady Day's autobiography, which was itself only linked tenuously with reality (though this is an assertion contested by research in the 90s), the film misses the essential tragedy while simultaneously failing to establish the young Holiday's often over-exuberant love of life. Instead, the film settles for gloomy melodrama. One of the men in Holiday's later life was on hand in an advisory capacity and, predictably, the plot line suffered as axes were ground and excuses made. In the end the film offers a sanitised version of the singer's life, adding a sheen to her heroin addiction and troubled personal relationships. Most of the initial critical flak came from the casting of Diana Ross in the lead (the production originated with Motown to whom Ross was contracted). In fact, Ross's performance was excellent and she was nominated for an Oscar in this, her first acting role. Ross also drastically altered her singing style to leave behind her Tamla/Motown origins and move towards jazz. Of course, she did not sound at all like Holiday but that was never her intention.

LADY, BE GOOD!

George and Ira Gershwin introduced a refreshingly new style and 'feel' to the musical theatre with this, their first Broadway show together. It opened at the Liberty Theatre on 1 December 1924, with a book by Guy Bolton and Fred Thompson which had wealthy Josephine Vanderwater (Jayne Auburn) arranging to evict Dick Trevor (Fred Astaire) and his sister Susie (Adele Astaire) from their home in the hope that Dick will marry her, and her money. Tired of living on the sidewalk, Dick and Susie turn up at Jo's posh party where Susie is persuaded by shady lawyer J. Watterson 'Watty' Watkins (Walter Catlett) to impersonate an indisposed (she is in jail) Mexican lady client of his so that she can collect on her late husband's estate. As it transpires, not only is he still alive, but her husband, Jack Robinson (Alan Edwards), is not really her husband at all - one of these illegal Mexican marriages, you know. He is loaded though, and smitten with Susie. With that kind of money in the family, Dick can safely wave goodbye to Jo, and marry Shirley Vernon (Kathlene Martyn), the girl he has loved all along. One other thing, towards the end, house detective Bertie Bassett (Gerald Oliver Smith) handcuffs himself to Watty - but that is another story. As a consolation, Watty gets to introduce the title song from the Gershwins' wonderfully witty score, with its jazzy harmonies, captivating rhythms, and colloquial lyrics. The numbers included 'Hang On To Me', 'So Am I', 'End Of A String', 'Linger In The Lobby', 'The Half Of It, Dearie, Blues', 'Juanita', 'Oh, What A Lovely Party', and 'So Am I',. 'Fascinating Rhythm', one of the show's big hits, was given the nifty dance treatment by the Astaires, who were helped out ('with agitation') on the vocal by Cliff Edwards (Ukulele Ike). Edwards had his own speciality, 'Little Jazz Bird', in Act II, just before Fred and Adele danced their famous 'oompah trot' to 'Swiss Miss' (lyric with Arthur Jackson). One of the songwriters' all-time big standards, 'The Man I Love', was dropped when the show was in Philadelphia on its way to Broadway, but survived to be used in the first version of Strike Up The Band (1927). Choreographed by Sammy Lee, and featuring Norman Bel Geddes' snazzy art déco sets, this swinging affair was directed by Felix Edwardes, and ran for a very creditable 330 performances. It did almost as well in London (326), despite opening on 14 April 1926, three weeks before the start of the General Strike, and might have done even better if it not been forced to vacate the Empire theatre which was due to close. Fred and Adele Astaire became the toast of the town when they reprised their roles with William Kent (Watty) and George Vollaire (Jack). Three songs were added for this production, 'Buy A Little Button From Us', 'I'd Rather Charleston' (lyric by Desmond Carter), and 'Something About Love' (lyric by Lou Paley). The latter was originally used in The Lady In Red (1919). The show was revived in London with Lionel Blair and Aimi Macdonald in 1968, and seen again in 1992 at the Open Air Theatre, Regent's Park, with Joanna Riding (Susie). Simon Green (Dick) and Bernard Cribbins (Watty). The Goodspeed Opera House, Connecticut, has mounted two revivals: in 1967 (Richard Cooper Bayne, Bonnie Schon and John Remme) and 1987 (Ray Benson, Nikki Sahagen and Russell Leib). The 1941 film entitled Lady, Be Good!, starring Ann Sothern and Robert Young, had a different storyline and many of the songs came from other sources.

LAHR, BERT

b. Irving Lahrheim, 13 August 1895, d. 4 December 1967, New York, USA. An actor, comedian and singer, with his rubber-faced expression and noisy antics - which included his trademark expression 'gnong-gnong' - Lahr was one of the all-time great clowns of the American musical theatre. After working for a good many years in vaudeville and burlesque - some of the time with his first wife in an act called Lahr And Mercedes - he appeared on Broadway in the revue Harry Delmar's Revels (1927), before making an immediate impact as an erratic prize fighter in the musical comedy Hold Everything! in 1928. He repeated his success, this time as airport mechanic who accidentally sets an endurance flying record because he cannot land the plane, in Flying High (1930). During the remainder of the 30s, Lahr spent most of his time in revues, such as Hot-Cha! (1932), George White's Music Hall Varieties (1932), Life Begins At 8:40 (1934), George White's Scandals (1935), and The Show Is On (1936), in which he introduced the hilarious 'Song Of The Woodman' (E.Y. 'Yip' Harburg-Harold Arlen). In 1939, he played a nightclub washroom attendant who dreams that he is Louis XV, in the Cole Porter book musical, Du Barry Was A Lady, and duetted with co-star Ethel Merman on 'But In The Morning, No!' and the lively 'Friendship'. By this time Lahr had modified his raucous image somewhat, and he brought his new, softer - but often satirical - personality to the character of the Cowardly Lion, in the classic 1939 movie, The Wizard Of Oz. He had two solo numbers, 'Lions And Tigers And Bears' and the splendid 'King Of The Forest', as well as ensemble pieces with Judy Garland, Ray Bolger and Jack Haley. Throughout the 40s and 50s he continued to appear in revues, including Seven Lively Arts (1944), Meet The People (1944), Make Mine Manhattan (1948), Two On The Aisle (1950), and The Boys Against The Girls (1959), as well as starring on radio, television and in films. Towards the end of his career, he also worked extensively in the straight theatre in highly regarded productions such as Waiting For Godot, Hotel Paradiso, and The Beauty Part. Lahr made his final Broadway appearance in Foxy (1964), a musical comedy adaptation of Ben Jonson's Volpone, in which the action was switched from Venice to the Klondike gold rush. His film career, which had begun with the screen version of one his first stage hits, Flying High, and peaked with The Wizard Of Oz, ended, appropriately enough, with a movie in which he played a burlesque comic, The Night They Raided Minsky's. Lahr died during the filming. Two years after his death, he was the subject of a biography written by his son.

● FURTHER READING: Notes On A Cowardly Lion, John Lahr.
● FILMS: Flying High (1931), Mr. Broadway (1933), Merry-Go-Round Of 1938 (1937), Love And Hisses (1937), Just Around The Corner (1938), Josette (1938), Zaza (1939), The Wizard Of Oz (1939), Sing Your Worries Away (1942), Ship Ahoy (1942), Meet The People (1944), Always Leave Them Laughing (1949), Mr. Universe (1951), Rose-Marie (1954), The Second Greatest Sex (1955), The Night They Raided Minsky's (1968).

LAI, FRANCIS

b. 1932, Nice, France. A composer and conductor for films from the early 60s. After scoring Circle Of Love, Roger Vadim's re-make of Ophuls' classic La Ronde, starring Jane Fonda, Lai won an Academy Award for his music to director Claud Lelouch's classic love story A Man And A Woman (1966). He also scored Lelouch's follow-up, Live For Life, before going on to something lighter with the comedy-drama, I'll Never Forget What's 'Is Name; followed by others in the late 60s such as Three Into Two Won't Go, Mayerling and Hannibal Brooks. In 1970, Lai won his second Oscar for Love Story, one of the most popular movies of the decade. The soundtrack album stayed at number 2 in the US album chart for six weeks, and the film's theme, 'Where Do I Begin?' (lyric by Carl Sigman), was a singles hit in the USA for Andy Williams, Henry Mancini and Lai himself; and in the UK for Williams and Shirley Bassey. In the same year, Lai, with his Orchestra, had a big hit in Japan with the title music for the film *Le Passager De La Pluie (Rider Of The Rain)*. During the 70s, Lai's cosmopolitan career included several more films for Lelouch, such as *The Crook, Money, Money, Money, Happy New Year, Cat And Mouse, Child Under A Leaf, Emmanuelle II* and *Another Man, Another Chance*; and others, such as . . . *And Hope To Die, Visit To A Chief's Son, And Now My Love, International Velvet* and the sequel to *Love Story, Oliver's Story* (1979) (music written with Lee Holdridge). In the 80s and early 90s the majority of Lai's music continued to be for French productions, and the Lelouch connection was maintained through films such as *Bolero* (in conjunction with Michel LeGrand), *Edith And Marcel, Bandits, La Belle Histoire (The Beautiful Story)* (co-composer Philippe Servain) and *Les Cles Du Paradis (The Keys To Paradise)* (1992). His work for other directors included *Beyond The Reef, Marie; A Man And A Woman: 20 Years Later* and *My New Partner II*. Besides his scores for feature films, Lai also contributed music to television programmes such as *Berlin Affair* and *Sins* (mini-series). Recordings include: *Great Film Themes; A Man, A Woman And A Love Story*; and the soundtracks, *Bilitis* and *Dark Eyes*.

LAINE, FRANKIE

b. Frank Paul LoVecchio, 30 March 1913, Chicago, Illinois, USA. Laine had been a chorister at the Immaculate Conception Church in his city's Sicilian quarter before entering showbusiness proper on leaving school. For nearly a decade he travelled as a singing waiter, dancing instructor (with a victory in a 1932 dance marathon as his principal qualification) and other lowly jobs, but it was as a member of a New Jersey nightclub quartet that he was given his first big break - replacing Perry Como in Freddie Carlone's touring band in 1937. This was a springboard to a post as house vocalist with a New York radio station until migration to Los Angeles, where he was 'discovered' entertaining in a Hollywood spa by Hoagy Carmichael. The songwriter persuaded him to adopt an Anglicized *nom de theatre*, and funded the 1947 session that resulted in 'That's My Desire', Laine's first smash. This was followed by 'Shine' (written in 1924) and a revival again in Louis Armstrong's 'When You're Smiling'. This was the title song to a 1950 movie starring Laine, the Mills Brothers, Kay Starr and other contributors of musical interludes to its 'backstage' plot. His later career on celluloid focused largely on his disembodied voice carrying main themes of cowboy movies such as *Man With A Star*, the celebrated *High Noon, Gunfight At The OK Corral* and the *Rawhide* television series. Each enhanced the dramatic, heavily masculine style favoured by Laine's producer, Mitch Miller, who also spiced the artist's output with generous pinches of country and western. This was best exemplified in the extraordinary 1949 hit 'Mule Train', one of the most dramatic and impassioned recordings of its era. Other early successes included 'Jezebel', 'Jalousie' and

'Rose Rose, I Love You', an adaptation by Wilfred Thomas of Hue Lin's Chinese melody 'Mei Kuei'.

Laine proved a formidable international star, particularly in the UK, where his long chart run began in 1952 with 'High Noon'. The following year he made chart history when his version of 'I Believe' topped the charts for a staggering 18 weeks, a record that has never been eclipsed since, despite a valiant run of 16 weeks by Bryan Adams 28 years later. Laine enjoyed two further UK chart-toppers in 1953 with 'Hey Joe' and 'Answer Me'. Incredibly, he was number 1 for 27 weeks that year, another feat of chart domination that it is difficult to envisage ever being equalled. No less than 22 UK Top 20 hits during the 50s emphasized Laine's popularity, including such memorable songs as 'Blowing Wild', 'Granada', 'The Kid's Last Fight', 'My Friend', 'Rain Rain Rain', 'Cool Water', 'Hawkeye', 'Sixteen Tons', 'A Woman In Love' and 'Rawhide'. Laine was also a consummate duettist and enjoyed additional hits with Johnnie Ray, Doris Day and Jimmy Boyd. After his hit-parade farewell with 1961's 'Gunslinger', he pursued a full-time career commuting around the world as a highly paid cabaret performer, with a repertoire built around selections from hit compilations, one of which (*The Very Best Of Frankie Laine*) climbed into international charts as late as 1977. New material tended to be of a sacred nature - though in the more familiar 'clip-petty-clop' character was 'Blazing Saddles', featured in Mel Brooks' (the lyricist) 1974 spoof-western of the same name. By the mid-80s, he was in virtual semi-retirement in an opulent ocean-front dwelling in San Diego, California, with his wife, former actress Nanette Gray. With sales in excess of 100 million copies, Laine was a giant of his time and one of the most important solo singers of the immediate pre-rock 'n' roll period.

● ALBUMS: *Favorites* (Mercury 1949)★★★, *Songs From The Heart* (Mercury 1949)★★, *Frankie Laine* (Mercury 1950)★★★, *Mr Rhythm Sings* (Mercury 1951)★★★, *Christmas Favorites* (Mercury 1951)★★, *Listen To Laine* (Mercury 1952)★★★, *One For My Baby* (Columbia 1952)★★★★, with Jo Stafford *Musical Portrait Of New Orleans* (Columbia 1954)★★, *Mr Rhythm* (Columbia 1954)★★★, *Songs By Frankie Laine* (Mercury 1955)★★★★, *That's My Desire* (Mercury 1955)★★★★, *Lovers Laine* (Columbia 1955)★★★, *Frankie Laine Sings For Us* (Mercury 1955)★★★, *Concert Date* (Mercury 1955)★★★, *With All My Heart* (Mercury 1955)★★★, *Command Performance* (Columbia 1956)★★★, *Jazz Spectacular* (Columbia 1956)★★, *Rockin'* (Columbia 1957)★★, *Foreign Affair* (Columbia 1958)★★★, *Torchin'* (Columbia 1960)★★★, *Reunion In Rhythm* (Columbia 1961)★★★, *You Are My Love* (Columbia 1961)★★★, *Frankie Laine, Balladeer* (Columbia 1961)★★★, *Hell Bent For Leather!* (Columbia 1961)★★★, *Deuces Wild* (Columbia 1962)★★★, *Call Of The Wild* (1962)★★★, *Wanderlust* (1963)★★, *I'll Take Care Of Your Cares* (ABC 1967)★★★, *I Wanted Someone To Love* (ABC 1967)★★★, *To Each His Own* (ABC 1968)★★, *You Gave Me A Mountain* (ABC 1969)★★★, with Erich Kunzel And The Cincinnati Pops Orchestra *Round Up* (1987)★★★.
● COMPILATIONS: *Greatest Hits* (Columbia 1959)★★★★, *Golden Hits* (Mercury 1960)★★★★, *Golden Memories* (Polydor 1974)★★★, *The Very Best Of Frankie Laine* (Warwick 1977)★★★★, *American Legend* (Columbia 1978)★★★, *Songbook* (World Records 1981)★★★★, *All Of Me* (Bulldog 1982)★★★,

Golden Greats (Polydor 1983)★★★, *The Golden Years* (Phillips 1984)★★★, *His Greatest Hits* (Warwick 1986)★★★, *The Uncollected* (Hindsight 1986)★★★, *Rawhide* (Castle 1986)★★★, *20 Of His Best* (The Collection 1987)★★★, *Sixteen Evergreens* (Joker 1988)★★★, *Country Store: Frankie Laine* (Country Store 1988)★★★, *Portrait Of A Song Stylist* (Masterpiece 1989)★★★, *21 Greatest Hits* (Westmoor 1989)★★★, *Memories In Gold* (Prestige 1990)★★★, *All Time Hits* (MFP 1991)★★★, with Jo Stafford *Goin' Like Wildfire* (Bear Family 1992)★★★, *On The Trail Again* (1993)★★★.

● FURTHER READING: *That Lucky Old Son*, Frankie Laine and Joseph F. Laredo.

LAMOUR, DOROTHY

b. Mary Leta Dorothy Stanton (or Kaumeyer), 10 December 1914, New Orleans, Louisiana, USA, d. 22 September 1996, Los Angeles, California, USA. An actress and singer particularly remembered for the series of 'Road' films with Bing Crosby and Bob Hope in which she invariably wore her trademark sarong. Crowned Miss Orleans at the age of 14, she moved to Chicago in the early 30s and worked in clubs and on radio, becoming known as the 'Sultry Songstress of the Airwaves' even though the listeners were unaware that she had 'a stunning statuesque figure'. She married bandleader Herbie Kay in 1934 and they were divorced in 1939. A subsequent marriage to millionaire business William Ross Howard survived for 35 years until his death in 1978. She made her breakthrough into films in 1936 with *The Jungle Princess*, the first of what she calls 'those silly, but wonderful jungle pictures', which included *Her Jungle Love* and *Moon Over Burma*. In the late 30s she appeared in several musical films, including *Swing High Swing Low*, *College Holiday*, *High Wide And Handsome*, *Thrill Of A Lifetime*, *The Big Broadcast Of 1938*, and *Tropic Holiday*. One of her best roles came in *St. Louis Blues* (1939), in which she played an ex-Broadway star and sang several appealing numbers such as 'Blue Nightfall', 'I Go For That', 'Let's Dream In The Moonlight', and the title song. She joined Crosby and Hope on *The Road To Singapore* in 1940, and continued to travel with them along other 'Roads' to Zanzibar (1941), Morocco (1942), Utopia (1946), Rio (1947), and Bali (1953). Rumour has it that she nearly did not make the trip to Hong Kong in 1962, but Hope is said to have insisted on her presence in the picture, although Joan Collins played the main female role. Over the years, in between the 'Roads', she made several other mostly entertaining musicals including *The Fleet's In*, *Star Spangled Rhythm*, *Dixie*, *Riding High*, *And The Angels Sing*, *Rainbow Island*, *Duffy's Tavern*, *Variety Girl*, *Lulu Belle*, *Slightly French*, and *The Greatest Show On Earth* (1952). This was in addition to films in which she played straight roles - a total of more than 60 in all. She was still making the occasional feature film and television appearance into the 80s. In her one-woman show she poked fun at her image - the sarongs and all that - and told of the occasion when she received a standing ovation from 5,000 people while heading a touring company of *Hello, Dolly!* in the late 60s. All the sarongs have been auctioned off for charity, and there is a rumour that one resides in the Smithsonian Museum.

● COMPILATIONS: *The Moon Of Manakoora* (ASV 1997)★★★.

● FURTHER READING: *My Side Of The Road*, Dorothy Lamour and D. McInnes.
● FILMS: *The Jungle Princess* (1936), *Swing High Swing Low* (1937), *The Last Train From Madrid* (1937), *College Holiday* (1937), *High Wide And Handsome* (1937), *Thrill Of A Lifetime* (1937), *The Hurricane* (1937), *The Big Broadcast Of 1938* (1938), *Spawn Of The North* (1938), *Her Jungle Love* (1938), *Tropic Holiday* (1938), *Man About Town* (1939), *St. Louis Blues* (1939), *Disputed Passage* (1939), *Johnny Apollo* (1940), *Road To Singapore* (1940), *Typhoon* (1940), *Moon Over Burma* (19440), *Chad Hanna* (1940), *Caught In The Draft* (1941), *Road To Zanzibar* (1941), *Aloma Of The South Seas* (1941), *The Fleet's In* (1942), *Beyond The Blue Horizon* (1942), *Road To Morocco* (1942), *They Got Me Covered* (1943), *Star Spangled Rhythm* (1943), *Dixie* (1943), *Riding High* (1943), *And The Angels Sing* (1944), *Rainbow Island* (1944), *Duffy's Tavern* (1945), *Masquerade In Mexico* (1945), *A Medal For Benny* (1945), *Road To Utopia* (1946), *Road To Rio* (1947), *My Favourite Brunette* (1947), *Wild Harvest* (1947), *Variety Girl* (1947), *On Our Merry Way* (aka *A Miracle Can Happen*, 1948), *The Girl From Manhattan* (1948), *Lulu Belle* (1948), *Slightly French* (1949), *Manhandled* (1949), *Lucky Stiff* (1949), *Here Comes The Groom* (1951, cameo), *The Greatest Show On Earth* (1952), *Road To Bali* (1953), *The Road To Hong Kong* (1962), *Donovan's Reef* (1963), *Pajama Party* (1964), *The Phynx* (1970, cameo), *Creepshow 2* (1987).

LANE, BURTON

b. 2 February 1912, New York City, New York, USA, 5 January 1997. Lane was a distinguished composer for films and the stage. After studying piano as a child, he later played stringed instruments in school orchestras. Some early compositions written for the school band attracted attention, and while still in his early teens he was commissioned to write songs for a projected off-Broadway revue, which never came to fruition. In his mid-teens Lane joined the staff of the Remick Music Company where he was encouraged in his songwriting career by George Gershwin. In 1929 he worked with Howard Dietz on some songs for the Broadway revue *Three's A Crowd*, and with Harold Adamson on *Earl Carroll's Vanities Of 1931*. When the effects of the Depression hit Broadway, Lane went to Hollywood and wrote for numerous musical films, often with Adamson. During the 30s his screen songs included 'Heigh Ho, The Gang's All Here', 'You're My Thrill', 'Stop, You're Breaking My Heart', 'Says My Heart' and his first major hit, 'Everything I Have Is Yours'. Perhaps the most popular of his songs of this period were 'The Lady's In Love With You' (Frank Loesser), from the film *Some Like It Hot*, 'I Hear Music' (Loesser) and 'How About You?' (Ralph Freed). The latter was sung by Judy Garland and Mickey Rooney in *Babes On Broadway* (1940). Lane also contributed scores or single songs to other movies such as *Dancing Lady*, *Bottoms Up*, *Her Husband Lies*, *Love On Toast*, *Artists And Models*, *Champagne Waltz*, *College Holiday*, *Swing High, Swing Low*, *Cocoanut Grove*, *College Swing*, *St. Louis Blues*, *Spawn Of The North*, *She Married A Cop*, *Dancing On A Dime*, *Ship Ahoy*, *Du Barry Was A Lady*, *Hollywood Canteen*, *Royal Wedding*, and *Give A Girl A Break* (1952). *Royal Wedding* contained one of the longest song titles ever - 'How Could You Believe Me When I Said I Love You When You Know I've Been A Liar All My Life?', as well as the lovely 'Too Late Now' and

'Open Your Eyes' (all Alan Jay Lerner). Among the other songs in those aforementioned pictures were 'I Hear Music', 'Poor You', 'Last Call For Love', 'I'll Take Tallulah', 'Tampico', 'Moonlight Bay', 'Madame, I Love Your Crepe Suzettes', 'You Can Always Tell A Yank', 'What Are You Doing The Rest Of Your Life?', and 'I Dig A Witch In Witchita'. In the 40s Lane wrote the score for the Broadway musicals *Hold On To Your Hats* (with E.Y. 'Yip' Harburg), *Laffing Room Only* (with Al Dubin), and the whimsical *Finian's Rainbow* (Harburg). The latter show, which opened in 1947 and ran for more than 700 performances, contained a fine set of songs including 'That Great Come-And-Get-It Day', 'Old Devil Moon', 'How Are Things In Glocca Morra?', 'When I'm Not Near The Girl I Love', 'If This Isn't Love', and 'Look To The Rainbow'. It was 18 years before Lane was back on Broadway with *On A Clear Day You Can See Forever* (Lerner) from which came 'Come Back To Me', 'Hurry! It's Lovely Up Here!', 'Melinda', and several other fine numbers. Lane and Lerner were teamed again in 1978 for *Carmelina*, which, despite the engaging 'One More Walk Around The Garden', 'Someone In April', 'I'm A Woman', and 'It's Time for A Love Song', was a resounding flop.

Throughout his long career Lane worked with many partners. As well as the men already mentioned, these included Ted Koehler, Sam Coslow, Ira Gershwin, and Sammy Cahn with whom he collaborated on songs such as 'Can You Imagine?' and 'That's What Friends Are For' for the Hanna-Barbera animated film *Heidi's Song* in 1982. Ten years after that, at the age of 80, Burton Lane was inducted into the US Theatre Hall Of Fame and was presented with the Berkshire Festival Theatre's fourth American Theatre Award at a benefit performance appropriately entitled *Hold On To Your Hats*. One of the stars of the show, singer and music archivist Michael Feinstein, released two CDs of Lane's songs in the early 90s. On each one he was accompanied by the composer himself on the piano. A long-time member of the Songwriters Hall of Fame, Burton was honoured in the Lyrics and Lyricists series at New York's 92nd Street 'Y' in April 1995.

LANE, LUPINO

b. Henry George Lupino, 16 June 1892, London, England, d. 10 November 1959, London, England. An actor, singer, dancer, choreographer, author, and director. Lane was born into a theatrical family which could trace its connections with the stage back to 1632 - one of his famous ancestors was the clown Grimaldi. At the age of four he was performing in theatres, and soon earned the nickname 'Nipper'. He developed his own individual style of extremely skilful, and sometimes dangerous comic acrobatic dancing, and appeared in many English and American two-reelers. However, his greatest impact was made in stage musicals where his trademark bowler hat and Cockney persona endeared him to audiences, especially those in London. From 1915 through to 1934 he appeared in the West End in musical productions such as *Watch Your Step*, *Follow The Crowd*, *Extra Special*, *Afgar*, *League Of Notions*, *Puss-Puss* (1920), *Brighter London*, *Turned Up*, *Silver Wings* (1930), *The One Girl*, and *The Golden Toy*. In 1935, *Twenty To One*, a musical with a plot

about horse racing, was Lane's first show as director and producer as well as actor. Two years later he had the biggest hit of his career with *Me And My Girl* (1937) in which he introduced the enormously popular 'Lambeth Walk'. In the 40s Lane continued on the London stage with *La-Di-Da-Di-Da*, *Meet Me Victoria*, and *Sweetheart Mine* (1946). Although he had enjoyed success in silent films during the 20s, he was unable to recreate his later stage appeal in talkies. However, he and Lillian Roth were acclaimed for their performances as second leads in *The Love Parade* (1929), which starred Maurice Chevalier and Jeanette MacDonald. Another well-known member of Lane's show business family was Stanley Lupino (b. 15 May 1894, London, England, d. 10 June 1942, London England), who was also an athletic dancer and a talented all-round performer. He appeared in a number of London musical productions from 1917 until 1941, and introduced several amusing songs including Leslie Sarony's 'I Lift Up My Finger And I Say 'Tweet Tweet'' in *Love Lies* (1929). Among his other shows were *Suzette*, *Arlette*, *Hullo, America!*, *Cinderella*, *Jig-Saw*, *The Peep Show*, *Phi-Phi*, *Dover Street To Dixie*, *Puppets*, *Better Days*, *So This Is Love*, *The Love Race*, *Hold My Hand*, *Sporting Love*, *Over She Goes*, *Crazy Days*, *The Fleet's Lit Up*, *Funny Side Up*, *Lady Behave*. He also made nearly 20 films. Stanley Lupino was the father of the actress Ida Lupino, who went to Hollywood and starred in numerous films from the 30s through to the 80s, including *They Drive By Night*, *High Sierra*, and *Roadhouse*. Lupino Lane's only child, Lauri Lupino Lane, who appeared with his father in *Me And My Girl*, was a regular performer in UK variety theatres until television closed them down in the early 60s. He died at the age of 64 in 1986, and is reckoned to be the last in the line of the celebrated family of entertainers.

● FURTHER READING: *Born To Star - The Lupino Lane Story*, J.D. White. *From The Stocks To The Stars*, Stanley Lupino.

LANGFORD, FRANCES

b. 4 April 1913, Tampa, Florida, USA. An accomplished singer with an easy, friendly style, who was popular from the 30s through the 50s. Langford began singing as a child, could have conceivably had a career in opera, but her voice was affected by a throat operation. After some stage work, mostly in vaudeville, she established a reputation as a nightclub singer. By the mid-30s her light, sweet singing voice had made her a popular recording and broadcasting star and she was invited to Hollywood. Some of her films were merely vehicles in which she played supporting roles and sang a couple of songs, such as in *Hollywood Hotel* and *Follow The Band*, the latter an early Robert Mitchum film. Occasionally, she was the female lead as in *Palm Springs*, where she played opposite David Niven in his first leading role in Hollywood, and *Girl Rush*, a Wally Brown-Alan Carney comedy, in which she worked again with Mitchum. In her first feature movie in 1935, *Every Night At Eight*, she introduced Dorothy Fields' and Jimmy McHugh's 'I'm In The Mood For Love'. That was one of several hit records she had during the late 30s, which also included 'I Feel A Song Comin' On', 'Easy To Love', 'Was It Rain?', 'Harbor Lights', 'So Many Memories', and 'Falling In Love With Love'. During World War II she toured extensively, entertaining US troops with Bob Hope, Jerry Colonna, and a few friends. 'We were just a small group, but we would go into places real close to the front. If they had a foxhole with men in it, we'd do a show for 'em.' While she was in the South Pacific, Langford also wrote a column for Hurst newspapers entitled 'Purple Heart Diary', in which she reported the 'gripes' gleaned from the troops while entertaining in hospital wards. She continued her commitment later in Korea. Back home, Langford appeared consistently on radio, and she was a regular for many years on Hope's top-rated show. After the war she continued to broadcast, make records, and guest on early television shows hosted by such as Perry Como, Jackie Gleason, and Hope. She had television series of her own in 1959 and 1960. In 1954 Langford played herself in *The Glenn Miller Story*, but by then rock 'n' roll was taking over, and she moved elegantly - as always - into semi-retirement. Still remembered though, and in 1996 an album was issued containing tracks she recorded in the 30s and 40s, including 'You're Nearer' (from the film *Too Many Girls*), 'Then You've Never Been Blue' (*Every Night At Eight*), and 'Easy To Love' (*Born To Dance*).

● ALBUMS: *Rainbow Rhapsody* (Mercury 50s)★★★, *Sings Old Songs For Old Friends* (Capitol 50s)★★★, with Don Ameche *The Bickersons Fight Back* (Columbia 50s)★★★, *Gettin' Sentimental* (Conifer 1988)★★★, *Sweet Heartaches* (Flare 1996)★★★.

● FILMS: *Every Night At Eight* (1935), *Broadway Melody Of 1936* (1935), *Collegiate* (1936), *Palm Springs* (1936), *Sunkist Stars At Palm Springs* (1936), *Born To Dance* (1936), *Hollywood Hotel* (1937), *Hit Parade Of 1937* (1937), *Dreaming Out Loud* (1940), *Hit Parade Of 1941* (1940), *Too Many Girls* (1940), *All American Co-Ed* (1941), *Swing It Soldier* (1941), *Mississippi Gambler* (1942), *Yankee Doodle Dandy* (1942), *Combat America* (1943), *Career Girl* (1943), *Follow The Band* (1943), *Cowboy In Manhattan* (1943), *This Is The Army* (1943), *Never A Dull Moment* (1943), *Memo For Joe* (1944), *Dixie Jamboree* (1944), *Girl Rush* (1944), *Tropical Moon* (1945), *Some Day When The Clouds Roll By* (1945), *A Dream Came True* (1945), *Radio Stars On Parade* (1945), *People Are Funny* (1946), *Bamboo Blonde* (1946), *Beat The Band* (1947), *Melody Time* voice (1947), *Make Mine Laughs* (1949), *Deputy Marshall* (1949), *Purple Heart Diary* (1951), *The Glenn Miller Story* (1954), *Entertaining The Troops* (1989).

LANSBURY, ANGELA

b. Angela Brigid Lansbury, 16 October 1925, London, England. An actress and singer who enjoyed a prolific career in Hollywood before blossoming into a star of Broadway musicals in the 60s. Angela Lansbury's grandfather was George Lansbury, the legendary social reformer, and leader of the British Labour Party for a time during the 30s. She was taken to America in 1942 by her widowed mother, a popular actress named Moyna MacGill. After attending drama school in New York, Lansbury received an Oscar nomination for her first film performance in *Gaslight* (1944). It was the beginning of a long career in Hollywood during which she appeared in several musicals including *The Harvey Girls* (1946), *Till The Clouds Roll By* (1947), *The Court Jester* (1956), *Blue Hawaii* (1961, as Elvis Presley's mother), and *Bedknobs And Broomsticks* (1971). For much of the time she played characters a good deal older than herself. From 1957 onwards, Lansbury played

several straight roles on Broadway, but it was not until 1964 that she appeared in her first musical, *Anyone Can Whistle*, which had a score by Stephen Sondheim. It only ran for nine performances, but Lansbury's subsequent excursions into the musical theatre proved far more successful. She won wide acclaim, and Tony Awards, for her roles in *Mame* (1966), *Dear World* (1969), *Gypsy* (1974 revival), and *Sweeney Todd* (1979). She also took *Gypsy* to London in 1973. In the 80s, Lansbury began to work more in television and created the part of the writer-come-supersleuth, Jessica Fletcher, in the US series *Murder, She Wrote*. The programme's long-term success resulted in her being rated as one of the highest-paid actresses in the world by the early 90s. In 1991 she received a Lifetime Achievement Award from the British Academy of Film and Television Arts (BAFTA), and, in the same, year, she lent her voice to Mrs Potts, the character that sang the Academy Award-winning title song in the highly acclaimed Walt Disney animated feature *Beauty And The Beast*. In 1992 Angela Lansbury was back to her Cockney roots playing a charlady in the television film *Mrs 'Arris Goes To Paris*, and two years later she was awarded a CBE in the Queen's Birthday Honours List. During the remainder of the 90s she led the cast in a concert version of *Anyone Can Whistle* at Carnegie Hall (1995), played the title role in the television musical comedy *Mrs. Santa Claus* (1996), and was honoured in *Angela Lansbury-A Celebration*. The latter gala benefit was held in November 1996 at the Majestic Theatre, the same house which launched her first musical, *Anyone Can Whistle*. Paying tribute were Barbara Cook, George Hearn, Tyne Daly, and a host of other stars from theatre and film.

● FURTHER READING: *Angela Lansbury - A Biography*, Margaret Wander Bonanno. *Balancing Act: The Authorised Biography Of Angela Lansbury*, Martin Gottfried.

● FILMS: *National Velvet* (1944), *Gaslight* (1945), *The Picture Of Dorian Gray* (1945), *Till The Clouds Roll By* (1946), *The Hoodlum Saint* (1946), *The Harvey Girls* (1946), *If Winter Comes* (1947), *The Private Affairs Of Bel Ami* (1947), *Tenth Avenue Angel* (1948), *State Of The Union* (1948), *The Three Musketeers* (1948), *The Red Danube* (1949), *Samson And Delilah* (1949), *Kind Lady* (1951), *Mutiny* (1952), *Remains To Be Seen* (1952), *A Life At Stake* (1954), *The Key Man* (1955), *The Purple Mask* (1955), *Please Murder Me* (1956), *The Court Jester* (1956), *The Reluctant Debutante* (1958), *The Long Hot Summer* (1958), *Summer Of The Seventeenth Doll* (1959), *The Dark At The Top Of The Stairs* (1960), *A Breath Of Scandal* (1960), *Four Horses Of The Apocalypse* voice only (1961), *Blue Hawaii* (1961), *The Manchurian Candidate* (1962), *All Fall Down* (1962), *In The Cool Of The Day* (1963), *The World Of Henry Orient* (1963), *Dear Heart* (1964), *Mister Buddwing* (1965), *The Greatest Story Ever Told* (1965), *Harlow* (1965), *The Amorous Adventures Of Moll Flanders* (1965), *Something For Everyone* (1970), *Bedknobs And Broomsticks* (1971), *Death On The Nile* (1978), *The Lady Vanishes* (1979), *The Mirror Crack'd* (1980), *The Last Unicorn* voice only (1982), *The Pirates Of Penzance* (1983), *The Company Of Wolves* (1984), *Beauty And The Beast* voice only (1991), *Your Studio And You* (1995), *The Films Of John Frankenheimer* (1995), *Anastasia* voice only (1997).

LANZA, MARIO

b. Alfredo Arnold Cocozza, 31 January 1921, Philadelphia, Pennsylvania, USA, d. 7 October 1959. An enormously popular star in film musicals and on records during the 50s, with a magnificent operatic tenor voice. The son of Italian immigrants, he took his stage name from the masculine version of his mother's maiden name, Maria Lanza. From the age of 15, Lanza studied singing with several teachers, and was introduced into society circles with the object of gaining a patron. He was signed to Columbia Artistes Management as a concert singer, but their plans to send him on an introductory tour were quashed when Lanza was drafted into the US Army in 1943. He appeared in shows, billed as 'the Service Caruso', and sang in the chorus of the celebratory Forces show *Winged Victory*. After release, he lived in New York, gave concerts and worked on radio shows. One of the audition recordings that he made for RCA found its way to the MGM Film Studios, and when he deputized for another tenor at the Hollywood Bowl, MGM chief Louis B. Mayer was in the audience. Soon afterwards Lanza was signed to a seven-year MGM contract by Hungarian producer Joe Pasternak, who was quoted as saying: 'It was the most beautiful voice I had ever heard - but his bushy hair made him look like a caveman!' Lanza's contract allowed him to continue with his concert career, and in April 1948 he made his first, and last, appearance on the professional operatic stage, in two performances of *Madame Butterfly*, with the New Orleans Opera. In Lanza's first film in 1949 for MGM, *That Midnight Kiss*, he co-starred with Kathryn Grayson and pianist Jose Iturbi; the musical contained a mixture of popular standards as diverse as 'They Didn't Believe Me' and 'Down Among The Sheltering Palms', and classical pieces, including 'Celeste Aida' (from Verdi's *Aida*), which gave Lanza one of his first record hits. The film was a big box-office success, and was followed by *The Toast Of New Orleans*, also with Grayson, which, along with the operatic excerpts, contained some songs by Sammy Cahn and Nicholas Brodszky, including one of Lanza's all-time smash hits, the million-seller, 'Be My Love'. Lanza starred in the biopic *The Great Caruso* (1951), performing several arias associated with his idol. He also introduced 'The Loveliest Night Of The Year', a song adapted by Irving Aaronson from 'Over the Waves', by Juventino Rosas, with a new lyric by Paul Francis Webster; it gave Lanza his second million-selling record.

By this point, he was one of Hollywood's hottest properties, and as his career blossomed, so did his waistline. There were rumours of breakfasts consisting of four steaks and six eggs, washed down with a gallon of milk, which caused his weight to soar to 20 stone. He claimed that 'nervousness' made him eat. In 1951, Lanza embarked on a country-wide tour of 22 cities, and also appeared on his own CBS radio series. Back in Hollywood, he initially rejected MGM's next project, *Because You're Mine*, because of its 'singer-becomes-a-GI' storyline. After some difficulties, the film was eventually completed, and was chosen for the 1952 Royal Film Premiere in the UK. The title song, by Cahn and Brodszky, was nominated for an Academy Award in 1952, and became Lanza's third, and last, million-selling single. He had already recorded the songs for his next MGM project, *The Student Prince*, when he walked out on the studio following a disagreement with the director. He avoided damaging breach of

contract lawsuits by allowing MGM to retain the rights to his recordings for the film. British actor Edmund Purdom took his place, miming to Lanza's singing voice. Ironically, Lanza's vocal performances for the film were considered to be among his best, and *Songs From The Student Prince And Other Great Musical Comedies* (containing 'The Drinking Song'), was number 1 in the USA for several weeks. Beset by problems with alcohol, food, tranquillizers and the US tax authorities, Lanza became a virtual recluse, not performing for over a year, before appearing on CBS Television with Betty Grable and Harry James. He was criticized in the press for miming to his old recordings on the show, but proved the voice was still intact by resuming his recording career soon afterwards. In 1956, Lanza returned to filming, this time for Warner Brothers. *Serenade*, adapted from the novel by James M. Cain, in which Lanza co-starred with Joan Fontaine, was considered by the critics to be one of his best movies. Once again, the operatic excerpts were interspersed with some romantic songs by Cahn and Brodszky, including 'Serenade' and 'My Destiny'. In 1957, tired of all the crash diets, and disillusioned by life in the USA, Lanza moved to Italy, and settled in Rome. He made one film there, *The Seven Hills Of Rome* (1958). Apart from the sight of Lanza playing an American entertainer doing impersonations of Dean Martin, Frankie Laine and Louis Armstrong, the film is probably best remembered for the inclusion of the 1955 hit song 'Arrivederci, Roma', written by Renato Rascel (Ranucci) and Carl Sigman, impressively sung in the film by Lanza, and which has become the accompaniment to many a backward glance by tourists ever since. In 1958, Lanza visited the UK, making his first stage appearances for six years, in concert at London's Royal Albert Hall and on the Royal Variety Show. From there, he embarked on a European tour. While on the Continent, he made *For The First Time* (1959), which was the last time he was seen on film. He appeared relatively slim, and was still in excellent voice. In the autumn of 1959 he went into a Rome clinic; a week later, he died of a heart attack. Much later it was alleged that he was murdered by the Mafia because he refused to appear at a concert organized by mobster Lucky Luciano. The city of Philadelphia officially proclaimed 7 October as 'Mario Lanza Day', and subsequently established a museum that still preserves his memory in the 90s. Opinions of his voice, and its potential, vary. José Carreras is quoted as saying that he was 'turned on' to opera at the age of 16 by seeing Lanza in *The Great Caruso*, and he emphasized the singer's influence by presenting his *Homage To Mario Lanza* concert at London's Royal Albert Hall in March 1994. Arturo Toscannini allegedly described it as the greatest voice of the twentieth century. On the other hand, one critic, perhaps representing the majority, said: 'He just concentrated on the big "lollipops" of the opera repertoire, he had a poor musical memory, and would never have been an opera star.' Ironically, it was one of the world's leading contemporary opera singers, Placido Domingo, who narrated the 1981 television biography *Mario Lanza-The American Caruso*.

● ALBUMS: *The Great Caruso* (HMV 1953)★★★★, *Operatic Arias*

(HMV 1954)★★★, *Songs Of Romance* (HMV 1955)★★★, *Serenade* (HMV 1956)★★★★, *Songs From The Student Prince* film soundtrack (RCA 1956)★★★★, *Lanza On Broadway* (HMV 1957)★★★★, *The Touch Of Your Hand* (HMV 1957)★★★, *In A Cavalcade Of Show Tunes* (RCA 1957)★★★, *Seven Hills Of Rome* film soundtrack (RCA 1958)★★★, *Songs From The Student Prince/The Great Caruso* (1958)★★★★, *Sings A Kiss And Other Love Songs* (RCA 1959)★★★, *For The First Time* film soundtrack (RCA 1959)★★★, *Lanza Sings Christmas Carols* (RCA 1959)★★★, *Mario Lanza Sings Caruso Favourites/The Great Caruso* (RCA 1960)★★★★, *You Do Something To Me* (RCA 1969)★★★.

● COMPILATIONS: *I'll Walk With God* (1962)★★, *His Greatest Hits, Volume 1* (RCA 1971)★★★★, *Art And Voice Of Mario Lanza* (RCA 1973)★★★, *Pure Gold* (RCA 1980)★★★, *His Greatest Hits From Operettas And Musicals, Volumes One, Two & Three* (RCA Classics 1981)★★★★, *The Legendary Mario Lanza* (K-Tel 1981)★★★★, *Collection* (RCA Red Seal 1982)★★★, *20 Golden Favourites* (RCA 1984)★★★★, *Magic Moments With Mario Lanza* (RCA 1985)★★★, *Forever* (RCA 1986)★★★, *A Portrait Of Mario Lanza* (Stylus 1987)★★★★, *Diamond Series: Mario Lanza* (Diamond Series 1988)★★★★, *Be My Love* (RCA 1991)★★★, *The Ultimate Collection* (1994)★★★★, *With A Song In My Heart: The Love: Collection* (Camden 1997)★★★★.

● FURTHER READING: *Mario Lanza*, Matt Bernard. *Mario Lanza*, Michael Burrows. *Lanza - His Tragic Life*, R. Strait and T. Robinson. *Mario Lanza*, Derek Mannering.

LAST OF THE BLUE DEVILS, THE

A superior USA film documentary, worth its place in any collection, this film celebrates the remarkable contribution to jazz provided by Kansas City-based musicians. Extensive interviews and live performances filmed especially for the documentary mingle effectively with archive film clips. Amongst the artists displaying their considerable talents are Count Basie, Jimmy Forrest, Dizzy Gillespie, Budd Johnson, Gus Johnson, Jo Jones, Jay McShann, Charlie Parker, Jesse Price, Buster Smith, Joe Turner and Lester Young.

LAST WALTZ, THE

By 1976, years of road life coupled with personal excess had taken its toll of the Band. Famed as Bob Dylan's backing group and creators of milestone albums, *Music From Big Pink* and *The Band*, the group was beset by internal problems. They decided to host a farewell Thanksgiving Day concert at San Francisco's Winterland Ballroom which would be filmed for posterity by Martin Scorsese. The extravaganza not only featured some of the Band's best-known material, including 'The Night They Drove Old Dixie Down' and 'The Weight', the group was clearly inspired to invest the songs with renewed vigour. *The Last Waltz* was also a showcase for acts with whom they associated themselves. One of their early inspirations, Muddy Waters, provided a searing rendition of 'Mannish Boy' and Ronnie Hawkins, whom the Band backed in an earlier incarnation, the Hawks, offered an explosive 'Who Do You Love'. San Francisco-based poet Lawrence Ferlingetti brought a literary air to the proceedings - much to Band drummer Levon Helm's chagrin - whereas contributions from Joni Mitchell, Neil Young, Eric Clapton and Van Morrison were more in keeping with the notion of a rock

concert. The arrival of Bob Dylan wrought images of his tours with the Band in 1966 and 1972, and the event closed with an all-cast version of the hymnal 'I Shall Be Released'. A commemorative three-album set formed a précis of the evening's proceedings. *The Last Waltz* film also featured newly recorded material, shot in a studio some months following the concert. Interview footage with Band members was also included, much of which reflected a jaded perception of their history and the project itself. Only guitarist/composer Robbie Robertson, the prime mover of the film, showed real enthusiasm. Nonetheless, *The Last Waltz* is an endearing tribute to one of rock's most fascinating groups and, given the advent of punk the following year, acts as a eulogy to an entire generation of musicians.

● ALBUMS: *The Last Waltz* 3-LP set (Warners 1977)★★★.
● VIDEOS: The *Last Waltz* (Warner Home Video 1988).

LAUDER, HARRY

b. 4 August 1870, Portobello, near Edinburgh, Scotland, d. 26 February 1950, Strathaven, Scotland. This popular singer, comedian and composer was a minstrel of the British music halls. The son of a potter, Lauder worked in a flax mill, and for 10 years in a coal mine. He made his first stage appearance in 1882, and continued to perform as an amateur, before turning professional in 1894. After touring Scotland in concert parties, he ventured to England, first with appearances in the Newcastle area, and then London, where he made his debut at Gatti's, Westminster in 1900. A short, stocky, bandy-legged figure, dressed in the tartan kilt complete with sporran, and carrying his 'crummock' (a stick with a curved head), Lauder exuded vitality and good humour. He sang his own songs, such as 'Tobermory' and 'The Lass Of Killiecrankie', and performed a sketch about an Irish tailor named 'Callaghan'. Despite his Scottish burr amid what was basically a Cockney form of entertainment, Lauder soon became one of the leading figures and highest paid entertainers in such London music halls as the Oxford, Royal Holborn and London Pavilion. In 1908 he performed for King Edward VII at Rufford Abbey. He toured abroad, including the USA, and had his first record hit there in 1907 with his theme song, 'I Love A Lassie', followed (through until 1916) with 'The Wedding Of Sandy McNab', 'When I Get Back To Bonnie Scotland', 'She Is My Daisy', 'He Was Very Kind To Me', 'Stop Your Tickling Jock', 'The Bounding Bounder', 'We Parted On the Shore', 'The Blarney Stone', 'Roamin' In The Gloamin'', 'The Picnic (Every Laddy Loves A Lassie)', 'She's The Lass For Me' and 'My Bonnie, Bonnie Jean'. Several of those were his own songs, written mostly in collaboration with Gerald Grafton. Others included 'Early In The Morning', 'The Last Of The Sandies', 'The Saftest O' The Family', 'Bonnie Hielan Mary', 'Glasgow Belongs To Me', 'That's The Reason Noo I Wear A Kilt', 'A Wee Deoch-An-Doris', 'It's Nice To Get Up In The Morning' and the rousing 'End Of The Road'.

During World War I, Lauder raised large sums of money for charity through his concerts, entertained the troops on the French front and, in 1919, received a knighthood for his services. He lost his only son in the conflict. In 1916 he starred in Harry Gratton's revue, *Three Cheers*, at London's Shaftesbury Theatre, and during the 20s and 30s continued to appear in variety theatres in London and the provinces, as well as touring South Africa, New Zealand, Australia and the Dominions. In 1932 he made his 25th tour of the USA.

Lauder also made several films, including *Huntingtower* (1927), *Auld Lang Syne* (1929) and the musical, *The End Of The Road* (1936). He wrote several novels and collected his own reminiscences in *Harry Lauder: At Home And On Tour*. Other books included *Roamin' In The Gloamin'*, *A Minstrel In France* and *Wee Drappies*. His biographies included *Great Scot: The Life Of Sir Harry Lauder* by G. Irving. Vocal evidence of his pre-eminence in the music hall era, rivalled only, perhaps, by Dan Leno, has been preserved on several recent compilations. After his death, the Harry Lauder Society continued to flourish, with members throughout the world. In 1991, over 40 years later, the Society became affiliated to the Clyde Valley Tourist Board.

● COMPILATIONS: *Sir Harry Lauder Sings Scottish Songs* (1974)★★★, *The Very Best Of Sir Harry Lauder* (1976)★★★★, *I Love A Lassie* (1980)★★★, *The Golden Age Of Sir Harry Lauder* (1983)★★★★, *We Parted On The Shore* (1988)★★★, *Roamin' In The Gloamin'* (1990)★★★.

● FURTHER READING: *Great Scot: The Life Of Harry Lauder*, G. Irving.

LAURENTS, ARTHUR

b. 14 July 1918, New York, USA. A distinguished stage director, author and screenwriter, Laurents has enjoyed equal success in both the musical and legitimate theatre. His parents did not approve of his early ambitions to be a playwright, and young Laurents went alone to New York theatres in the Depression-hit early 30s. He made his name as the author of plays such as *Home Of The Brave* (1945) and *The Time Of The Cuckoo* (1952), before writing the libretto for the landmark musical *West Side Story* (1957). The 50s were troubled times for Laurents: blacklisted during the McCarthy witch hunts, he was nearly bankrupted by the lawyers fees incurred in securing the return of his passport. He and composer Leonard Bernstein auditioned Stephen Sondheim as lyricist for *West Side Story*, enabling him to make his Broadway debut. Laurents and Sondheim collaborated again in 1959 on *Gypsy* (music: Jule Styne), *Anyone Can Whistle* (1964, Laurents also directed) and *Do I Hear A Waltz?* (1965). Laurents made his debut as the director of a musical in 1962 with *I Can Get It For You Wholesale*, in which Barbra Streisand made an enormous impact, stopping the show every night with the comic 'Miss Marmelstein'. Since then, Laurents has experienced mixed fortunes. *Hallelujah, Baby!* (1967), with his libretto and a score by Jule Styne, Betty Comden and Adolph Green, was considered a failure in New York, but the first West End production of *Gypsy* in 1973, starring Angela Lansbury, which Laurents directed, was acclaimed, and subsequently transferred to Broadway. Laurents also directed another New York revival of his favourite musical in 1989, with Tyne Daly. In 1979, *The Madwoman Of Central Park West*, a one-woman entertainment that Laurents wrote with and for Phyllis

Newman, played off-Broadway at the 22 Steps Theatre. After being nominated for a Tony Award for his direction of the original *Gypsy*, Laurents' staging of *La Cage Aux Folles* finally won him an Award in 1983. However, there were no Tonys awarded to *Nick And Nora* (1991); Laurents was associated with this colossal flop as author and director, but ironically, for him personally, some good came from it. Disillusioned with musical productions, he immediately launched into the creation of a series of plays, their content spanning four decades: *Jolson Sings Again*, a piece about politics and principles set in Hollywood during the McCarthy era, a comedy of manners entitled *The Radical Mystique*, *My Good Name*, and *Two Lives*. He also settled on two venues sympathetic to his work, Seattle Rep and the Manhattan Theatre Club. Laurents' other notable contributions to the straight theatre over the years have included *Invitation To A March* (1960), which had incidental music by Sondheim, *The Way We Were*, *Scream*, *A Clearing In The Woods*, and the homosexual-themed *The Enclave* (1973). One of his earliest efforts, *The Time Of The Cuckoo*, had already provided the basis for the musical *Do I Hear A Waltz?*, before it was filmed in 1955 as *Summertime*, starring Katharine Hepburn, while *The Way We Were* came to the big screen in 1973, with Barbra Streisand and Robert Redford in the leading roles. Laurents wrote the screenplay for the latter, and he also scripted *The Snake Pit* (1948), *Rope* (1948), *Caught* (1948), *Anna Lucasta* (1949, with Philp Yordan), *Anastasia* (1956), *Bonjour Tristesse* (1958) and *The Turning Point* (1977). In 1995, the York Theatre Company presented Laurents with its sixth annual Oscar Hammerstein II Award, and his many other honours have included Golden Globe, Drama Desk, National Board of Review, Writers Guild of America, National Institute of Arts and Letters, Screen Writers Guild, Sydney Drama Critics awards. He has been inducted into the Theatre Hall of Fame.

LAWRENCE, GERTRUDE

b. Gertrud Alexandra Dagmar Lawrence Klasen, 4 July 1898, London, England, d. 6 September 1952. An actress, singer, dancer, comedienne, one of the most vivacious and elegant performers in the history of West End and Broadway theatre. Coming from a showbusiness family, her mother was an actress and her father a singer, Lawrence studied dancing under Madame Espinosa. She made her first proper stage appearance at the age of 12, as a child dancer in the pantomime *Babes In The Wood* at the south London, Brixton Theatre. In 1913, while studying acting and elocution under Italia Conte, where her cockney accent was obliterated, she met the 12-year-old Noël Coward who was to have such an important influence on her later career. After appearing in various provincial theatres in shows such as *Miss Lamb Of Canterbury* and *Miss Plaster Of Paris*, Lawrence made her West End debut in 1916 at the Vaudeville Theatre as principal dancer and understudy in Andre Charlot's revue, *Some*. In 1920, after taking a variety of roles in other revues such as *Cheep*, *Tabs* and *Buzz-Buzz*, she appeared as leading lady at Murray's Club, London's first cabaret entertainment. Later, she toured variety theatres with Walter Williams, before taking the lead, with Jack Buchanan, in *A-To-Z*

(1921), followed by *De-De*, *Rats* and Noël Coward's *London's Calling!* (1923), in which she introduced his bitter-sweet 'Parisian Pierrot'. She then co-starred on Broadway with Beatrice Lillie in the successful *Andre Charlot's Revue of 1924*, giving America its first taste of 'Limehouse Blues'. In 1926, after more Charlot associations, including his *Revue Of 1926*, in which she sang 'A Cup of Coffee, A Sandwich And You', Lawrence became the first English actress to originate a role on Broadway before playing it in London, when she took the lead in her first 'book' musical, *Oh, Kay*, with a score by George and Ira Gershwin, which included 'Someone To Watch Over Me', 'Maybe', and 'Do-Do-Do'. After repeating her triumph in the West End, Lawrence appeared in several other musicals productions in the late 20s, although none were as lavish as the *International Revue* (1930) in New York, in which she sang Jimmy McHugh and Dorothy Fields' catchy 'Exactly Like You' with Harry Richman. In the same year she was back in London, co-starring with Coward in his sophisticated light comedy *Private Lives*, fondly remembered for lines such as 'Strange how potent cheap music is', and the waltz, 'Someday I'll Find You'. During the 30s Lawrence appeared in a number of successful straight plays, including *Can The Leopard?*, *Behold We Live*, *This Inconsistancy*, *Heavy House*, *Susan And God* and *Skylark*. One musical highlight of the decade was *Nymph Errant* (1933), in which she sang the title song 'Experiment', 'How Could We Be Wrong?', 'It's Bad For Me' and one of Cole Porter's most amusing 'list songs', 'The Physician' ('He said my epidermis was darling/And found my blood as blue as could be/He went through wild ecstatics when I showed him my lymphatics/But he never said he loved me'). Another, *Tonight At 8.30* (1936), saw her reunited with Coward in his series of one-act plays, two of which, *Shadowplay*, ('Then', 'Play Orchestra Play' and 'You Were There') and *Red Peppers* ('Has Anybody Seen Our Ship?' and 'Men About Town'), are particularly celebrated. That was the last time Lawrence was seen in a musical production in London. She and Coward took *Tonight At 8.30* to New York in 1936, and, five years later, Lawrence had her biggest Broadway success to date when she appeared in *Lady In The Dark*, with a score by Kurt Weill and Ira Gershwin, which gave her the droll 'Jenny' and the haunting 'My Ship'.

For much of the 40s she toured countries such as Belgium, France, Holland and the Pacific Ocean Area, on behalf of the USO and ENSA, entertaining the Allied Troops. At the end of World War II, Lawrence began a three-year engagement as Eliza in a revival of *Pygmalion*, which played New York and toured the USA. She also appeared in various other straight plays in the UK and the USA, including *September Tide* (1949), and completed *The Glass Menagerie*, the last in a series of films she made, beginning with *The Battle Of Paris* (1929). In March 1951, she opened on Broadway in 'the most satisfying role of my career', Richard Rodgers and Oscar Hammerstein II's spectacular musical *The King And I*, playing the part of the children's Governess, Anna for well over a year before being taken ill with a rare form of cancer. She died in September 1952, within a week of being admitted into hospital. Rodgers subscribed to the view, widely held throughout her life-time, that Lawrence sang flat. 'Just the same', he said, 'whenever I think of Anna, I think of Gertie'.

In 1968, the movie *Star!*, purported to relate her life story. Starring Julie Andrews and Daniel Massey as Noël Coward, it ran for almost three hours ('cost \$14 million and took four'), and was subsequently trimmed to two and re-titled *Those Were The Happy Times*. In the early 80s, UK critic and author Sheridan Morley devised the after-dinner entertainment *Noel And Gertie*, which, revised and expanded, toured abroad and played in the West End in 1989 with Patricia Hodge as Gertie and Simon Cadell as Coward. Subsequently, the leading roles were played by Susan Hampshire and Edward Petherbridge, amongst others, and - off-Broadway in 1992 - by Jane Summerhays and Michael Zaslow.

● ALBUMS: *A Souvenir Album* (Decca 1952)★★★, *Noël And Gertie* (1955)★★★, *A Remembrance* (Decca 1958)★★★, *The Incomparable Gertrude Lawrence* (1964)★★★.

● FURTHER READING: *Gertrude Lawrence: A Bright Particular Star*, Sheridan Morley.

LAWRENCE, JACK

b. 7 April 1912, New York, USA. Although mainly a lyricist, as well as a singer and conductor, Lawrence wrote both words and music for some of his most popular songs. He studied at Long Island University, and sang on various radio stations, before having his first efforts published in the early 30s. One of these, 'Play, Fiddle, Play' (1932, written with Emery Deutsch and Arthur Altman), was made popular in the USA by the bands of George Olsen and Ted Lewis, and in the UK by Al Bowlly with the New Mayfair Dance Orchestra. During the remainder of the 30s, Lawrence's output resulted in record success for artists such as Glen Gray and the Casa Loma Orchestra and Glenn Miller ('Sunrise Serenade', 1938, with Frankie Carle), Ella Fitzgerald ('All Over Nothing At All', 1937), Ella Fitzgerald with the Mills Brothers ('Big Boy Blue', 1937), Andy Kirk And His Clouds Of Joy and Bing Crosby ('What's Your Story, Morning Glory?', 1938, with Paul Francis Webster-Mary Lou Williams), Horace Heidt and Crosby with Jimmy Dorsey ('What Will I Tell My Heart?' (1937, with Peter Tinturin-Irving Gordon), Heidt, the Andrews Sisters and Dick Barrie ('Tu-li-Tulip Time', 1938, with Maria Grever), Raymond Scott ('Huckleberry Duck', with Scott), and Guy Lombardo ('In An Eighteenth Century Drawing Room', 1939, with Scott). One of the songs for which Lawrence composed both words and music was the enduring ballad 'If I Didn't Care', which was a big hit in 1939 for the Ink Spots, and later revived by the Hilltoppers (1954), Connie Francis (1961), the Platters (1970), and David Cassidy (UK 1974). Lawrence was also solely responsible for 'It's Funny To Everyone But Me', and collaborated with Arthur Altman on 'All Or Nothing At All'. Both of those numbers were recorded by Frank Sinatra in 1939 when he was with the Harry James band, but they only entered the US Hit Parade in the early 40s after the singer began to attract a lot of attention during his stint with Tommy Dorsey.

Glenn Miller made the bestseller lists in 1940 with two Lawrence numbers, 'Vagabond Dreams' (with Hoagy Carmichael) and 'Handful Of Stars' (Ted Shapiro), while in the same year Larry Clinton had a hit with 'Johnson Rag' (Guy H. Hall-Henry Kleinkauf), and Kay Kyser and Bob Chester, did well with 'With The Wind And Rain In Your Hair' (Clara Edwards). In the following year Lawrence wrote 'Yes, My Darling Daughter', which was introduced in the revue *Crazy With The Heat* by Gracie Barrie. It subsequently became popular for Dinah Shore and Glenn Miller, and was revived by Eydie Gorme in 1962. Also in 1941, Lawrence adapted Tchaikovsky's 'Piano Concerto Number 1' for 'Concerto For Two', and wrote the English lyric for Toots Camarata and Isaac Albeniz's adaptation of Albeniz's 'Tango In D', which was entitled 'Moonlight Masquerade'. He also provided a lyric for the old Eric Coates composition '(By The) Sleepy Lagoon', which was then recorded by Harry James and Dinah Shore, and became the title number of a 1943 movie starring Judy Canova and Ruth Donnelly. During World War II, Lawrence served in the US Coastguard and the US Navy-US Maritime Service. He wrote the official song for the latter organization, 'Heave Ho, My Lads, Heave Ho', which subsequently appeared in the 1944 film *Moonlight And Cactus*. Lawrence also organized various service bands, welfare and morale units, and worked overseas for a time. After the war, he provided the English lyrics for European numbers such as 'Symphony' (1945, music: Alex Alstone), 'Beyond The Sea' (1947, adapted from Charles Trenet's 'La Mer', and a big hit in 1960 for Bobby Darin), 'Choo Choo Train' (1953, music: Marc Fontenoy), and 'The Poor People Of Paris (1954, music: Marguerite Monnet). In 1946, with composer Walter Gross, Lawrence produced what is arguably his most enduring song, the lovely ballad 'Tenderly', which Rosemary Clooney adopted as her signature number. There were also many other popular items, such as 'Hand In Hand' (1947), 'Linda' (1947), 'Hold My Hand' (1950, with Richard Myers, sung in the film *Susan Slept Here* by Don Cornell, and nominated for an Academy Award), 'Delicado' (1952, Waldyr Azevado, a US number 1 for Percy Faith), and 'No One But You', written with Nicholas Brodszky for the 1954 Lana Turner movie *The Flame And The Flesh*, and given a memorable recording by Billy Eckstine. Lawrence's work was featured in several other films, including *Outside Of Paradise* (1938, 'A Little Bit Of Everything', 'All For One', 'Outside Of Paradise', 'A Sweet Irish Sweetheart Of Mine', 'Doing Shenanigans', with Peter Tinturin), *Hullabaloo* (1940, 'A Handful Of Stars', with Ted Shapiro), *The Great American Broadcast* (1941), *Doughboys In Ireland* (1943), *Stars On Parade* (1944, 'My Heart Isn't In It'), *Weekend Pass* (1944), *This Is The Life* (1944), *Peter Pan* (1953, 'Never Smile At A Crocodile', with Frank Churchill), *So This Is Love* (1953, 'Ciribiribin', with Harry James), and *Sleeping Beauty* ('Once Upon A Dream', with Sammy Fain). He was also represented on Broadway with the musicals *Courtin' Time* (1951, 'Heart In Hand', with Don Walker), *Torch Song* (1953), and *I Had A Ball* (1964, 'The Fickle Finger Of Fate', 'The Other Half Of Me', with Stan Freeman), starring Buddy Hackett, as well as the aforementioned *Crazy With The Heat*. Among his other collaborators have been John Green, John Barry and Victor Young.

● ALBUMS: *Come To The Circus* (50s)★★★.

LAYE, EVELYN

b. Elsie Evelyn Lay, 10 July 1900, London, England, d. February 1996. An actress and singer - one of the most celebrated leading ladies of the English musical stage. Her father was the actor and composer Gilbert Laye (he added the 'e' on to the family name for stage appearances) and her mother the actress Evelyn Stewart. Known as 'Boo' from when she was a baby, Evelyn Laye was constantly performing as a child, and made her professional stage debut at the age of 15 as a Chinese servant in a production entitled *Mr. Wu*. After appearing in *The Beauty Spot*, *Going Up*, and *The Kiss Call*, she had her first West End success in 1920 with *The Shop Girl*, in which she was backed by a chorus of real guardsmen as she sang 'The Guards' Parade'. In the early 20s she delighted London audiences in shows such as *Phi-Phi*, and *The Merry Widow. Madame Pompadour* (1923), her first show for C. B. Cochran, was a significant landmark in her career, and was followed by more good roles in stylish productions such as *Cleopatra*, *Betty In Mayfair*, *Merely Molly*, and *Blue Eyes*. By 1929, when Evelyn Laye introduced Drury Lane audiences to 'Lover, Come Back To Me' in Sigmund Romberg's musical *The New Moon*, she had become the brightest star on the London theatre scene; Cochran called her 'the fairest prima donna this side of heaven' ('I think he must have had a little too much champagne', says Miss Laye). Around this time she was separated from her husband, the comedian Sonnie Hale, and he later married one of her main 'rivals', the enchanting Jessie Matthews. She turned down the leading role in the London production of Noël Coward's *Bitter Sweet*, but triumphed in the 1929 Broadway production, and later succeeded Peggy Wood in the West End version. Her success on Broadway resulted in a trip to Hollywood and appearances in *One Heavenly Night* with John Boles, and *The Night Is Young*, in which she co-starred with Ramon Novarro and sang Sigmund Romberg and Oscar Hammerstein II's enduring 'When I Grow Too Old To Dream'. While in America she married the British actor, Frank Lawton, and they were together until he died in 1969. On her return to England she made more film musicals, including *Princess Charming*, *Waltz Time*, and *Evensong* (1934). The latter is regarded as perhaps the most accomplished of her relatively few screen appearances. Even in the 90s it continues to be re-shown in cinema retrospective seasons, and on television, providing a tantalising glimpse of an artist who lit up the screen whenever she chose to neglect her beloved stage for a while. During the remainder of the 30s, Evelyn Laye was a 'ravishing' Helen of Troy in *Helen!*, appeared with the embryonic John Mills in *Give Me A Ring*, co-starred with the far more mature Viennese tenor Richard Tauber in *Paganini*, and returned to Broadway in 1937 with Jack Buchanan and Adele Dixon for *Between The Devil*. The show made history when it was presented for one night at the National Theatre in New York on the occasion of President Roosevelt's birthday, thereby becoming the first American Command Performance. In 1940 she sang 'You've Done Something To My Heart', 'Only A Glass Of Champagne', and 'Let The People Sing' in Ronald Jeans' revue, *Lights Up*. During the remainder of World War II

she appeared in the 1942 revival of *The Belle Of New York* and another Romberg/Hammerstein show, *Sunny River*. She also served as Entertainments Director for the Royal Navy, and led the first-ever concert party for the troops based in the remote Scapa Flow in the Orkneys. In 1945 Evelyn Laye returned to the London stage in *Three Waltzes*. Immediately after the war, when suitable parts in the musical theatre were few and far between, she played straight roles in plays throughout the UK and on a 1951 tour of Australia, but made a triumphant comeback to the London musical stage in *Wedding In Paris* in 1954. More straight plays followed before she starred in the musical, *Strike A Light* (1966), and replaced Anna Neagle for a time in the long-running *Charlie Girl*. In her last West End musical (to date), *Phil The Fluter* (1969), she reflected on a better, more civilised age, in the memorable 'They Don't Make Them Like That Any More', a number that was so perfectly suited to her. In 1971 she appeared with Michael Crawford in the comedy, *No Sex, Please - We're British*, and two years later was awarded the CBE. During the rest of the 70s and 80s she made several more films, including *Say Hello To Yesterday* with Jean Simmons, and *Never Never Land* with Petula Clark. She also did a good deal of television work, and appeared in the provinces in *A Little Night Music* with Honor Blackman in 1979/80. In 1992, at the age of 92, she toured parts of the UK with the nostalgia show *Glamorous Nights At Drury Lane*, and received standing ovations. In July of that year, in *A Glamorous Night With Evelyn Laye At The London Palladium*, the élite of British show-business gathered to pay tribute and nod in agreement as she sang 'They Don't Make Them Like That Any More'.
● ALBUMS: *Golden Age Of Evelyn Laye* (1985)★★★★, *When I Grow Too Old To Dream* (1991)★★★, *Gaiety Girl* (ASW Living Era 1996)★★★★.
● FURTHER READING: *Boo To My Friends*, Evelyn Laye.

LAYTON, TURNER

b. 1894, Washington, DC, USA, d. 2 February 1978. Although born into a musical family, Layton studied medicine for a few years before becoming a professional pianist. He appeared in New York where he teamed up with Henry Creamer, forming a duo to play in vaudeville and in several musical shows and revues. Creamer also wrote lyrics for many songs composed by Layton, one of which, 'Dear Old Southland', became Louis Armstrong's signature tune. Amongst their other songs, several of which also became very popular with jazz musicians, were 'Everybody's Crazy About The Doggone Blues', 'After You've Gone', 'Way Down Yonder In New Orleans' (popularized by Blossom Seeley) and '(If I Could Be With You) One Hour Tonight'. In 1922, Layton formed another partnership, this time with Clarence Nathaniel Johnstone. They settled in London the following year and quickly became popular with audiences at theatres and the hotels, restaurants and nightclubs frequented by the elite. They also appealed to a wider audience thanks to broadcasts on the radio. Although Layton had recorded in New York in the early 20s, the collaboration with Johnstone was hugely successful and their records, especially 'Alabamy Bound', 'Bye Bye Blackbird' and 'The Song Is Ended', sold

extremely well. In 1935, when their combined record sales were running into several millions, Johnstone was named as co-respondent in the divorce of a well-known classical musician. Despite Johnstone's popularity, London society of that era could not sanction an affair between a black man and a white woman. Bookings plummeted and the partnership of Layton and Johnstone was forced to end. Johnstone returned to the USA where he died in obscurity and poverty in 1953. Layton continued to perform, this time as a solo artist, into the late 40s.
● ALBUMS: by Layton And Johnstone *Alabamy Bound (1920-30)* (1980)★★★, *The Song Is Ended (1920-30)* (1983)★★★, *When You're Smiling* (1986)★★.

LEAVE IT TO JANE

One of the five engaging and tuneful musicals that the team of Jerome Kern (music), Guy Bolton (book), and P.G. Wodehouse (book and lyrics) turned out in 1917, this particular production could not get into their favourite 499-seater Princess Theatre, situated on the corner of Broadway and 48th Street, because their *Oh, Boy!*, was still playing to packed houses for an incredible (in those days) 467 performances. So, *Leave It Jane* made its debut at the Longacre Theatre on 28 August 1917. Based on George Ade's play, *The College Widow*, and set in the football-mad Atwater College, the story concerns Jane Witherspoon (Edith Hallor), the daughter of the college president. When the highly talented and extremely supple Billy Bolton (Robert Pitkin) announces that he intends to devote his footballing talents to Atwater's deadly rivals, Bingham, Jane persuades Billy to play for Atwater under an assumed name - and inevitably, she eventually changes hers to Bolton. The breezy, optimistic score included 'The Crickets Are Calling', 'I'm Going To Find A Girl', 'It's A Great Big Land', 'Just You Watch My Step', 'A Peach Of A Life', 'Poor Prune', 'Sir Galahad', 'The Siren's Song', 'The Sun Shines Brighter', 'There It Is Again', 'Wait Till Tomorrow', 'What I'm Longing To Say', and 'Why?'. The novelty number that usually stopped the show was a highly amusing mock-Egyptian piece called 'Cleopatterer', which was sung by Georgia O'Ramey, and had a typical Wodehouse lyric. He had the knack of noticing and using the current fad phrases, like 'ginks' and 'Oh, you kid!': 'She gave those poor Egyptian ginks/Something else to watch beside the Sphinx . . . They'd take her hand and squeeze it, and murmur, "Oh, you kid!"/But you bet they never started to feed, till Cleopatterer did'. That song, and 'Leave It To Jane', were sung by June Allyson in the Jerome Kern biopic *Till The Clouds Roll By* (1946). *Leave It To Jane* ran for 167 performances in 1917, and was revived, over 40 years later in May 1959, when it remained Off Broadway at the Sheridan Square Playhouse for over two years, a remarkable 928 performances. The show was presented again at the Goodspeed Opera House, Connecticut, in 1985, and at the Guildhall School of Music and Drama in London 10 years later.

LEAVE IT TO ME!

Just a year after his riding accident, during which both his legs were very badly injured, Cole Porter came up with a terrific score for this funny and satirical show which opened at the Imperial Theatre in New York on 9 November 1938. With a book by Bella and Sam Spewack which was based on their play, *Clear All Wires*, it heralded the Broadway debut of Mary Martin, who went on to become one of the American musical theatre's cherished leading ladies. Her big moment came as she sat on a trunk at a Siberian railway station clad in furs which she slowly and deliberately removed during Porter's wonderful 'My Heart Belongs To Daddy'. Closely in attendance were five male dancers, and the one visible over Martin's right shoulder in the publicity shots is Gene Kelly. After the show had been running for three months she received feature billing. Her saucy first impression is interesting because, it is said, that in subsequent shows she was extremely reluctant to be involved with material that was anywhere 'near the knuckle'. The Spewacks' story for *Leave It To Me!* told of the meek and mild Alonzo P. Goodhue (Victor Moore), whose wife, played by Sophie Tucker, raised such a big bundle of cash for President Roosevelt's re-election campaign, that Alonzo is made the American ambassador to the Soviet Union. This is precisely what he does not want, and he sets out make a real hash of things so that he will be recalled. Unfortunately for him, everything he touches turns out right - until he gets together with foreign correspondent Buckley Joyce Thomas (William Gaxton) to inaugurate a plan that will guarantee world peace. This, of course, is in nobody's interest, and he is immediately removed, and returned to the USA. Gaxton and Tamara, who played his girlfriend, Colette, combined in two romantic duets, 'From Now On' and 'Far, Far Away', and she sang one of Porter's most potent love songs, 'Get Out Of Town'. The composer gave Sophie Tucker, appearing in her only Broadway book musical, one of her early 'advice to young ladies' numbers with the clever 'Most Gentlemen Don't Like Love', and she and the chorus also had 'Tomorrow'. There was lots of larking about in Red Square, and other appropriate locations, particularly by funny-men Gaxton and Moore who teamed in several other Broadway musicals. After its initial run of 291 performances, *Leave It To Me!* returned to New York for another two weeks in September 1939 when Mary Martin was succeeded by Mildred Fenton. During the subsequent tour, the character of Stalin was removed from the piece following the Russian dictator's signing of non-aggression pact with Hitler. Many years later, the show still retained some interest, and it was revived as recently as 1991 at the Arts Theatre in Cambridge, England.

LEGRAND, MICHEL

b. 24 February 1932, Paris, France. Legrand grew up in a musical environment - his father was an orchestra leader and film composer - and studied formally at the Paris Conservatoire. In the 50s he was an active pianist but was most successful as an arranger. Later in the decade he moved to New York and continued to arrange, but now with a strong orientation towards the contemporary jazz scene, for leading artists such as Miles Davis and John Coltrane. In France he had occasionally led his own bands and did so again in the USA. In these years he was also a prolific composer, writing material performed by Stan Getz, Phil Woods and others, and occasionally playing with jazzmen such as Shelly Manne. He had begun to compose music for French films in 1953, and, in the 60s, developed this area of his work on productions such as *Lola*; *Cleo From 5 To 7*, which he also appeared in, and *My Life To Live*. In 1964 he received the first of his many Academy Award nominations, for the score to *The Umbrellas Of Cherbourg*, which contained 'I Will Wait For You' and 'Watch What Happens' (English lyrics by Norman Gimbel). His second Oscar came for his work on the follow-up, *The Young Ladies Of Rochefort* (1968). In the late 60s he began to compose for US and British films. His score for one of the first of these, *The Thomas Crown Affair*, included 'The Windmills Of Your Mind' (lyric by Alan and Marilyn Bergman), which became popular for Noel Harrison (son of actor Rex) and Dusty Springfield, and won an Academy Award in 1968. Another collaboration with Alan and Marilyn Bergman produced 'What Are You Doing The Rest Of Your Life?', from *The Happy Ending* (1969). Throughout the 70s, Legrand continued to write prolifically for films such as *The Go-Between*, *Wuthering Heights*, *Summer Of 42* (another Oscar), *Lady Sings The Blues*, *One Is A Lonely Number* and *The Three Musketeers*. He teamed with the Bergmans yet again for Barbra Streisand's film *Yentl* (1983). Two of their 12 songs, 'Papa, Can You Hear Me?' and 'The Way He Makes Me Feel' were nominated, and the complete score won an Academy Award. Legrand's other film music included *Never Say Never Again*, Sean Connery's eagerly awaited return to the role of James Bond; *Secret Places* (title song written with Alan Jay Lerner); the amusing *Switching Channels* (theme written with Neil Diamond), *Fate* and *The Burning Shore*, and *Pret-A-Porter* (1994). In 1991 Legrand was back to his jazz roots for the score to *Dingo*, which he wrote with Miles Davis. Davis also gave an impressive performance in the movie. At his best with lyrical and sometimes sentimental themes, Legrand's writing for films remains his major contribution to popular music. Besides his feature film credits, Legrand also worked extensively in television, contributing music to *Brian's Song*, *The Adventures Of Don Quixote*, *It's Good To Be Alive*, *Cage Without A Key*, *A Woman Called Golda*, *The Jesse Owens Story*, *Promises To Keep*, *Sins* (mini-series), *Crossings*, *Casanova* and *Not A Penny More, Not A Penny Less*.

● ALBUMS: *Legrand Jazz* (Philips 1958)★★★★, *At Shelly's Manne Hole* (1968)★★★★, *Michel Legrand Recorded Live At Jimmy's* (1973)★★, *Themes And Variations* (1973)★★★, *After The Rain* (1982)★★★, *Live At Fat Tuesday's* (Verve 1985)★★★★, ★★★ (Verve 1993), *Douce France* (Verve 1997)★★★, and film soundtracks.

LEIGH, CAROLYN

b. Carolyn Paula Rosenthal, 21 August 1926, New York, USA, d. 19 November 1983, New York, USA. An important lyricist in the late 50s and 60s, Leigh began writing verse and doggerel when she was only nine. She later studied at Queens College and New York University. She began her career by writing announcements for radio station WQXR and working as a copywriter. By the time she was 25 years old Leigh is reputed to have written about 200 songs, although none had been published. In 1951, she wrote 'I'm Waiting Just For You' (with Lucky Millinder and Henry Glover), which was modestly successful for Millinder, Rosemary Clooney, and later, Pat Boone. Her first big hit came in 1954, when Frank Sinatra took 'Young At Heart', written with Johnny Richards, to number 2 in the USA, and it became the title and theme of a film in which he co-starred with Doris Day. This led to Leigh being offered the chance to write most of the songs, with composer Mark 'Moose' Charlap, for the Broadway show *Peter Pan* (1954, 'I'm Flying', 'I've Gotta Crow' and 'I Won't Grow Up'). She also contributed to the off-Broadway revue *Shoestring '57*. Leigh's other work around this time included 'The Day The Circus Left Town' (with E.D. Thomas), which was recorded by Eartha Kitt, 'Stowaway' (with Jerry Livingston, a UK Top 20 entry for Barbara Lyon), '(How Little It Matters) How Little We Know' (Philip Springer) and 'Witchcraft' (Cy Coleman). The last two songs were chart hits for Frank Sinatra. Leigh's fruitful - and, apparently, stormy - collaboration with the composer Cy Coleman lasted from the late 50s into the early 60s. During that time they wrote the scores for the Broadway musicals *Wildcat*, a Lucille Ball vehicle (1960, 'Hey, Look Me Over', 'Give A Little Whistle', 'You've Come Home', 'What Takes My Fancy'), and the marvellous *Little Me* (1962, 'I've Got Your Number', 'Real Live Girl', 'On The Other Side Of The Tracks', 'Deep Down Inside'). Another number intended for *Little Me*, 'When In Rome', was recorded by Barbra Streisand and Vikki Carr. The team also worked on an abortive musical adaptation of the memoirs of stripper Gypsy Rose Lee (later immortalized as *Gypsy* with a score by Jule Styne and Stephen Sondheim), from which came 'Firefly'. It gave Tony Bennett a bestselling record, and he included the song, along with Leigh and Coleman's sensitive ballad 'It Amazes Me', on *Tony Bennett At Carnegie Hall*. After they split up, Leigh and Coleman worked together again on the charming 'Pass Me By', which was sung over the titles of the 1964 Cary Grant movie *Father Goose*; and 'A Doodlin' Song', which was recorded by Peggy Lee. In 1967, Leigh teamed with composer Elmer Bernstein on the score for *How Now, Dow Jones* ('Live A Little', 'Walk Away', 'He's Here!' and 'Step To The Rear'), and in later years continued to write occasionally for the stage, television and films. She wrote the lyrics for the Bicentennial show *Something To Do*, and for the television special *Heidi*. Her other songs included 'Stay With Me', 'Love Is A Melody (Short And Sweet)', 'Disenchanted Castle', 'Playboy Theme', 'On Second Thought', 'In The Barrio', 'Westport' and 'Bouncing Back For More'. Among her collaborators were Morton Gould, Lee Pockriss and Marvin Hamlisch. She was working on a musical adaptation of *Smiles* with Hamlisch when she died from a heart attack in 1983.

LEIGH, MITCH

b. Irwin Mitchnick, 30 January 1928, Brooklyn, New York, USA. A composer, producer and director for the musical theatre and television, Leigh studied music at Yale, graduating with a B.A. and M.A. In the late 50s he formed Music Makers, a company which eventually became the prime source of television and radio jingles in the USA. In the

early 60s, Leigh wrote the incidental music for two plays, *Too Good To Be True* and *Never Live Over A Pretzel Factory*, before collaborating with lyricist Joe Darion (b. 30 January 1917, New York, USA.) on the musical *Man Of La Mancha* in 1965. It ran for 2,328 performances in New York and won five Tony Awards, and one of its songs, 'The Impossible Dream', was awarded the Contemporary Classic Award by the Songwriters Hall of Fame. Since then, Leigh has been unable to attain anywhere near that degree of success with Broadway shows such as *Cry For Us All* (1970), *Home Sweet Homer* (one performance in 1976), *Sarava* (1979), *Chu Chem* (1989), and *Ain't Broadway Grand* (1993). Indeed, they were all flops, and one or two more of Leigh's efforts closed out of town. A 25th anniversary production of *Man Of La Mancha*, starring Raul Julia and Sheena Easton, toured the US, and played 108 performances on Broadway in 1992.

LEND AN EAR

Notable mainly for the Broadway debut of Carol Channing, the blonde comedienne with a the wide-eyed look and a voice that no-one has ever described satisfactorily, this revue opened at the National Theatre in New York on 16 December 1948, after stop-overs during the previous few years in Pittsburgh and Los Angeles. *Lend An Ear* was also the first Broadway musical to be directed and choreographed by the former dancer, Gower Champion, and Charles Gaynor, another new boy in the 'back-stage' department, contributed the witty music, lyrics, and sketches. Gaynor went through the card, pointing-up and lampooning a variety of targets, but some of the funniest moments came when he concentrated on a pair of celebrities who lived their lives according to the columnists, the effect on society by the growing influence of psychoanalysts, an opera company that just reads the librettos because it cannot afford an orchestra, and a wicked 20s spoof concerning a theatrical touring company that has sent out several versions of *The Gladioli Girl* over the years, none of which has returned. The songs, too, were affectionate parodies of the kind from days gone by, and included 'Give Your Heart A Chance To Sing', 'Doin' The Old Yahoo Step', 'Molly O'Reilly', 'Who Hit Me?', 'In Our Teeny Weeny Little Nest', 'Where Is The She For Me?'. The lively, young and talented cast consisted of William Eythe, Yvonne Adair, Jennie Lou Law, Gloria Hamilton, Bob Scheerer, and Gene Nelson, the song-and-dance man who had begun his film career in 1947, and will be affectionately remembered for his performances in musicals such as *Lullaby Of Broadway*, *Tea For Two*, and especially *Oklahoma!*. In some ways, a surprising and gratifying production for its time, *Lend An Ear* enjoyed a good run of 460 performances.

LEONARDO

Early in 1993, residents of the UK could have been forgiven for consulting their calendars to see if the date was April 1 after reading reports that the Republic of Nauro, a small island in the Pacific (population 8,000), was financing a West End musical show with the proceeds from its major export - bird droppings (they are high in phosphates). *LEONARDO - THE MUSICAL - A PORTRAIT OF*

LOVE, which opened at the Strand Theatre in London on 3 June 1993, was the brainchild of Duke Minks, an advisor to the Nauruan government, and a former road manager with the 60s pop group, Unit Four Plus Two, which had a UK number 1 in 1965 with 'Concrete And Clay'. Tommy Moeller, the co-writer of 'Concrete And Clay', is credited with Leonardo's music and lyrics, along with Greg Moeller, Russell Dunlop, and Minks, who also produced the piece. John Kane's book ('half fact-half guesswork') begins and ends with the hero, Leonardo da Vinci (Paul Collis), on his deathbed - his masterpiece, the Mona Lisa, by his side. In Kane's scenario, Leonardo is commissioned by nobleman Francesco Del Giocondo (James Barron) to paint a portrait of his fiancé, Lisa (Jane Arden), but the artist falls in love with his model, and makes her pregnant. She cannot marry him, but must pretend that the child is Del Giocondo's or he will have them both killed. Eventually, she returns to the by now successful Leonardo, and begs his forgiveness, but he is accidentally killed by her husband in a jealous rage. Kane also hints at a homosexual relationship between the painter and his devoted friend, Melzi (Hal Fowler). Some 20 musical numbers accompanied this sad tale, and they included 'Who The Hell Are You?', 'Firenza Mia', 'Part Of Your Life', 'Just A Dream Away', 'Her Heart Beats', 'Endless As My Love', 'Just One More Time', 'Goodbye And No One Said A Word', 'Forever Child', 'Portrait Of Love', and 'She Lives With Me'. The President of Nauru hosted a first night party while the critics polished their prose: 'A great deal of risible tosh' . . . 'Only six months to Christmas and the first turkey has arrived', were typical tabloid comments. In addition, bearing in mind the source of the show's reported £2 million investment, there was a good deal of talk about fertiliser, and 'dropping us all in it'. Leonardo folded on 10 July after a run of just over four weeks. From his house in Cannes, Duke Minks, the instigator of it all, was quoted as saying: 'Leonardo died in Italy in 1519, and again in the Strand in 1993.'

LERNER, ALAN JAY

b. 31 August 1918, New York, USA, d. June 1986. A lyricist and librettist, and one of the most eminent and literate personalities in the history of the Broadway musical theatre, Lerner played the piano as a child, and studied at the Juilliard School of Music, the Bedales public school in England, and Harvard University, where he took a Bachelor of Science degree in the late 30s. After working as a journalist and radio scriptwriter, he met composer Frederick Loewe at the Lamb's Club in 1942. Also a pianist, Loewe had moved to the USA in 1924, and had previously been involved in some unsuccessful musical shows. The new team's first efforts, What's Up? and The Day Before Spring (1945; 'A Jug Of Wine', 'I Love You This Morning'), did not exactly set Broadway alight, but two years later, they had their first hit with Brigadoon. Lerner's whimsical fantasy about a Scottish village that only comes to life every 100 years, contained 'Waitin' For My Dearie', 'I'll Go Home To Bonnie Jean', 'The Heather On The Hill', 'Come To Me, Bend To Me', 'From This Day On', and the future standard, 'Almost Like Being In Love'. A film version was made in 1954, starring Gene Kelly, Cyd Charisse

and Van Johnson. After Brigadoon, Lerner collaborated with Kurt Weill on the vaudeville-style Love Life (1948), and then spent some time in Hollywood writing the songs, with Burton Lane, for Royal Wedding (1951). Among them was one of the longest-ever titles, 'How Could You Believe Me When I Said I Loved You (When You Know I've Been A Liar All My Life?)', expertly manipulated by Fred Astaire and Jane Powell. Another of the numbers, 'Too Late Now', sung by Powell, was nominated for an Academy Award. In the same year, Lerner picked up an Oscar for his story and screenplay for George and Ira Gershwin's musical film An American In Paris (1951). Also in 1951, Lerner reunited with Loewe for the 'Gold Rush' Musical, Paint Your Wagon. The colourful score included 'They Call The Wind Maria', 'I Talk To The Trees', 'I Still See Elisa', 'I'm On My Way' and 'Wand'rin' Star', which, in the 1969 movie, received a lugubrious reading from Lee Marvin. Precisely the opposite sentiments prevailed in My Fair Lady (1956), Lerner's adaptation of Pygmalion by George Bernard Shaw, which starred Rex Harrison as the irascible Higgins, and Julie Andrews as Eliza ('I'm a good girl, I am'). Sometimes called 'the most perfect musical', Lerner and Loewe's memorable score included 'Why Can't The English?', 'Wouldn't It Be Loverly?', 'The Rain In Spain', 'I Could Have Danced All Night', 'On The Street Where You Live', 'Show Me', 'Get Me To The Church On Time', 'A Hymn To Him', 'Without You' and 'I've Grown Accustomed To Her Face'. 'Come To The Ball', originally written for the show, but discarded before the opening, was, subsequently, often performed, particularly by Lerner himself. After a run of 2,717 performances on Broadway, and 2,281 in London, the show was filmed in 1964, when Andrews was replaced by Audrey Hepburn (dubbed by Marni Nixon). The Broadway Cast album went to number 1 in the US charts, sold over five million copies, and stayed in the Top 40 for 311 weeks. In 1958 Lerner was back in Hollywood, with a somewhat reluctant Loewe, for one of the last original screen musicals, the charming Gigi. Lerner's stylish treatment of Colette's turn-of-the-century novella, directed by Vincente Minnelli, starred Maurice Chevalier, Leslie Caron, Louis Jourdan and Hermione Gingold, and boasted a delightful score that included 'The Night They Invented Champagne', 'Say A Prayer For Me Tonight', 'I'm Glad I'm Not Young Anymore', 'Thank Heaven For Little Girls', 'Waltz At Maxim's', 'She Is Not Thinking Of Me' and the touching 'I Remember It Well', memorably performed by Chevalier and Gingold. Lerner won one of the film's nine Oscars for his screenplay, and another, with Loewe, for the title song.

Two years later, Lerner and Loewe returned to Broadway with Camelot, a musical version of the Arthurian legend, based on T.H. White's The Once And Future King. With Julie Andrews, Richard Burton and Robert Goulet, plus a fine score that included 'C'Est Moi', 'The Lusty Month Of May', 'If Ever I Would Leave You', 'Follow Me', 'How To Handle A Woman' and the title song, the show ran on Broadway for two years. During that time it became indelibly connected with the Kennedy presidency: 'for one brief shining moment, that was known as Camelot'. The 1967 movie version was poorly received. In the early 60s, partly because of the composer's ill health, Lerner and Loewe ended their partnership, coming together again briefly in 1973 to write some new songs for a stage presentation of *Gigi*, and, a year later, for the score to the film *The Little Prince*. Lerner's subsequent collaborators included Burton Lane for *On A Clear Day You Can See Forever* (1965) ('Come Back To Me', 'On The S.S. Bernard Cohn', and others). Lerner won a Grammy award for the title song, and maintained that it was his most frequently recorded number. He wrote with Lane again in 1979 for *Carmelina*. In the interim he collaborated with André Previn for *Coco* (1969), which had a respectable run of 332 performances, mainly due to its star, Katherine Hepburn, and with Leonard Bernstein for *1600 Pennsylvania Avenue* (1976). Lerner's last musical, *Dance A Little Closer* (1983), which starred his eighth wife, English actress Liz Robertson, closed after one performance. They had met in 1979 when he directed her, as Eliza, in a major London revival of *My Fair Lady*. Shortly before he died of lung cancer in June 1986, he was still working on various projects, including a musical treatment of the 30s film comedy *My Man Godfrey*, in collaboration with pianist-singer Gerard Kenny, and *Yerma*, based on the play by Federico Garcia Lorca. Frederick Loewe, who shared in Lerner's triumphs, and had been semi-retired since the 60s, died in February 1988. In 1993, New Yorkers celebrated the 75th anniversary of Lerner's birth, and his remarkable and fruitful partnership with Loewe, with *The Night They Invented Champagne: The Lerner And Loewe Revue*, which played for a season at the Rainbow and Stars.

● ALBUMS: *An Evening With Alan Jay Lerner* (Laureate 1977)★★★.

● FURTHER READING: *The Musical Theatre: A Celebration*, Alan Jay Lerner. *The Street Where I Live: The Story Of My Fair Lady, Gigi And Camelot*, Alan Jay Lerner. *A Hymn To Him: The Lyrics Of Alan Jay Lerner*, Benny Green (ed.). *The Wordsmiths: Oscar Hammerstein & Alan Jay Lerner*, Stephen Citron.

LES GIRLS

To many it must have seemed like the end of an era when Gene Kelly completed his very last MGM musical. The string of hits he left behind are firmly registered in the vaults of film musical history. His last project, *Les Girls*, released in October 1957, and adapted by John Patrick from a Vera Caspery story, struggles to live up to Kelly's own high standards, but there are enough entertaining sequences to maintain the momentum. Directed by George Cukor and produced by Sol C Siegel, the film is set in Paris 1949. It follows the adventures of Kelly, a musical performer, and his female trio, Les Girls, played by Mitzi Gaynor, Kay Kendall and Taina Elg. The unusual story is revealed in a series of flashbacks. The first of them concerns the courtroom battle between two of the girls that opens the film. Lady Wren (Kay Kendall) has included an account of her experiences with Les Girls in her memoirs, and stands in the dock defending her words, while furious Taina Elg refuses to accept any of the book as the truth. As the film continues, the viewer begins to wonder who is really telling the truth, and with which one of the girls Kelly is in love. Or did he have flings with all of them? It is only towards the conclusion of the movie that it is revealed that Mitzi Gaynor is the girl he truly desires.

Indeed, during one of the flashbacks he reveals a whole wall of photos of Gaynor, and pretends he is terribly ill in order to win his way into her affections. In the aftermath of the court case, she demands Kelly's assurance that his flings with the other girls were purely fictional. With all these complications, it is hardly surprising that the film becomes rather weighed down, but one or two individual performances and the words and music of Cole Porter save the day (*Les Girls* was his last original score for the big screen). The musical highlights included Kelly and Gaynor's tongue-in-cheek send-up of Marlon Brando in 'Why Am I So Gone About That Gal?' and Kendall's almost music-hall routine with Kelly, 'You're Just Too, Too'. Other songs were 'Ladies In Waiting' and 'Ca, C'est L'Amour'. Among the supporting cast, which had a definite European flavour, were Leslie Phillips, Jacques Bergerac, Henry Daniell and Patrick MacNee. Jack Cole was the choreographer, and it was photographed in Metrocolor and CinemaScope.

LES MISÉRABLES

According to Alain Boublil, who wrote the book (with Claude-Michel Schönberg) and original lyrics for this show, it all began one night in London when he saw the Artful Dodger on stage in the 1978 West End revival of Lionel Bart's *Oliver!* From then on, he became obsessed with the image of young Gavroche, and all the other wonderful characters in Victor Hugo's classic novel, *Les Misérables*. Boublil's subsequent musical adaptation, in collaboration with composer Schönberg and poet Jean-Marc Natel, was originally released as a best-selling double album before being staged in Paris by Robert Hossein at the 4,500-seater Palais des Sports. As with so many other musicals in the past two decades, the key moment in the development of *Les Misérables* came when producer Cameron Mackintosh announced his involvement. After hearing the recording, he set about the immense task of adapting it into something suitable for British audiences, with the aid of directors Trevor Nunn and John Caird, journalist and lyricist Herbert Kretzmer, and Oxford Professor of Poetry James Fenton. (The latter's work was later rejected, although he still retains a credit and a percentage of the gross). The result, a co-production between Mackintosh and the Royal Shakespeare Company, opened at the Barbican Theatre on 8 October 1985. It was one hour longer than the Paris show, and had six new songs and a 20-minute prologue. The year is 1815, and an embittered Jean Valjean (Colm Wilkinson) is released on a ticket of leave after 19 years in prison. Eight years later, Valjean has broken his parole. He now owns a factory and has become Mayor, but is forced to sack one of his workers, Fantine (Patti LuPone), because she has borne an illegitimate child. Meanwhile, hot on Valjean's trail throughout the piece, is policeman Javert (Roger Allam). Fantine is dead, and her daughter Cosette (a role shared between a child and soprano Rebecca Caine) has been abused for several years by the Thénardiers (Alun Armstrong and Susan Jane Tanner). Valjean inveigles her away to Paris, where, several years later, there is great political unrest. Cosette is now a young woman, and in love with Marius (Michael Ball), one of a band of students preparing for the revolution. The barricades go up, and the revolutionaries face an army warning they must surrender or die. The Thénardiers' daughter, Eponine (Frances Ruffelle), is killed, as is the urchin Gavroche along with the rest of the rebels, including their leader Enjolras (David Burt). Valjean refuses the opportunity to dispose of Javert, and escapes with the injured Marius. Shattered by Valjean's enlightened attitude, Javert throws himself into the Seine. Cosette nurses Marius back to health, and after they are married - just before the old man's death - she learns of the debt she owes to Valjean. Highlights of the sung-through score included Valjean's thrilling 'Who Am I?' and his Act 2 show-stopper, 'Bring Him Home', Fantine's 'I Dreamed A Dream', Marius' poignant 'Empty Chairs At Empty Tables', along with 'Dog Eats Dog', delivered by Alun Armstrong's repellent Thénardier ('a sewer rat with wit'). The remainder of the highly dramatic and emotional numbers were 'At The End Of The Day', 'Lovely Ladies', 'Come To Me', 'Confrontation', 'Castle On A Cloud', 'Master Of The House', 'Look Down', 'Stars', 'Little People', 'Red And Black', 'Do You Hear The People Singing', 'I Saw Him Once', 'In My Life', 'One Day More', 'On My Own', 'The Attack', 'A Little Fall Of Rain', 'Drink With Me To Days Gone By', 'Soliloquy', 'Wedding Chorale', 'Beggars At The Feast', and 'Finale'. Critical reaction was not favourable ('Victor Hugo on the garbage dump . . . few glimmers of fun . . . Hugo-ago-go . . push-button emotionalism at the expense of character and content'), although *The Times* had no reservations about John Napier's set 'that assembly of rotting timber and ironwork, locking together like two ungainly monsters to form the Gorbeau tenement or the barricades'. Mackintosh hesitated before transferring the show to the West End, but after learning that the Barbican box office was constantly under siege, he went ahead, opening at the Palace Theatre, on the 4 December 1985. A New York production made its debut at the Broadway Theatre on 12 March 1987 to an entirely different critical reception (Clive Barnes: 'This is magnificent, red-blooded, two-fisted theatre'). Wilkinson and Ruffelle reprised their roles, and also in the cast were Terrence Mann (Javert), David Bryant (Marius), Judy Kuhn (Cosette), Michael Maguire (Enjolras), Randy Graff (Fantine), and Jennifer Butt and Leo Burmester (Thénardiers). The show scooped the Tony Awards, winning for Best Musical, Book, Score, Director (Nunn and Caird), Featured Actress (Ruffelle), Featured Actor (Maguire), Sets (Napier), and Lighting (David Hersey). Since that time, *Les Misérables* has been seen by more that 40 million people, grossing over $1.6 billion worldwide. Ironically, the only country to resist its appeal has been France, where a 1991 staging at the Théâtre de Mogador was withdrawn after only seven months. In January 1994, the show overtook *Jesus Christ Superstar* as the third-longest-running musical (after *Cats* and *Starlight Express*) in the history of the London musical theatre. A 10th anniversary concert performance was presented at London's Royal Albert Hall on 8 October 1995. It featured the Royal Philharmonic Orchestra, and a company of over 250 performers from many of the worldwide productions, with principals: Colm Wilkinson (Jean Valjean), Philip Quast (Javert), Ruthie Henshall (Fantine),

Jenny Galloway (Madame Thenardier), Alun Armstrong (Thenardier), Lea Salonga (Eponine), Michael Ball (Marius), Michael Maguire (Enjolras), and Judy Kuhn (Cosette). Towards the end of 1996, as the New York production neared its own 10th anniversary, there was much anger and indignation when Mackintosh sacked most of the cast on the grounds that the production had got 'flabby', and the actors had simply outgrown the student-aged characters. Generous pay-offs soon quelled a potentially inflammable situation which the press dubbed the 'Bloodbath On Broadway'. Other changes were made to the Broadway show (which moved to the Imperial Theatre in October 1990), and they were incorporated into the London production when it closed for a week in September 1997. *Les Misérables* now has its own Internet website, magazine (*Barricade*), and about 30 different cast albums. The best remembered of all the films based on Victor Hugo's novel would appear to be the 1935 version starring Fredric March and Charles Laughton. The latest was released in 1998, with Liam Neeson, Geoffrey Rush, Uma Thurman, and Claire Danes.

LET GEORGE DO IT

In the early years of World War II, George Formby's comedy-musical films raised the spirits of millions of people in the Britain. This one was typical of the genre: George is about to join his fellow members of the Dinkie Doo Concert Party when he is whisked off to Bergen in Norway to replace a ukulele player (a member of British Intelligence) who has died in mysterious circumstances while playing in a hotel band. George discovers that its leader, Mark Mendez (Garry Marsh), is a German spy who is transmitting shipping information by code in his band's broadcasts. With the help of Mary Wilson (Phyllis Calvert), George breaks the code, warns the Admiralty, and as a result five U-Boats are sunk. Not surprisingly, he flees the country - in a German submarine! In the midst of all that derring-doo, he found the time to introduce two of his best-known novelty numbers, 'Grandad's Flannelette Nightshirt' and 'Mr Wu's A Window Cleaner Now', as well as the cheery 'Count Your Blessings And Smile' and 'Oh, Don't The Wind Blow Cold' (Formby-Fred E. Cliffe-Harry Gifford). Ronald Shiner, a leading star of the famous Whitehall farces after the war, had a minor role as a clarinettist in this picture, and other parts went to Romney Brent, Bernard Lee (he played 'M' in the James Bond films), Ian Fleming (an Australian character, not the Bond author), Coral Browne, Percy Walsh, Diana Beaumont, Donald Calthrop, Torin Thatcher, Hal Gordon, Jack Hobbs, and Alec Clunes. The screenplay was written by John Dighton, Austin Melford, Angus Macphail, and Basil Dearden. The latter was also the Associated Producer for Ealing-Associated Talking Pictures. The director was Marcel Varnel, and this invaluable little morale booster was released in 1940.

LET IT BE

The concept for *Let It Be* was, on paper, simple. The Beatles, who were about to record a new album, would have a feature film of the proceedings to show them at work, 'warts and all'. Michael Lindsay-Hogg, who had previously worked on television's seminal *Ready, Steady, Go!*, was brought in as director and on 2 January 1969, the group convened in a cold studio in Twickenham to begin recording. Unfortunately, relations between the individual members were strained and, despite bonhomie when jamming and playing 'oldies' from their Hamburg days, it seemed the camera was chronicling a wake rather than a celebration. Paul McCartney's attempts at marshalling proceedings alienated the others, in particular George Harrison, who walked out when instructed on how to play a solo. Within weeks the Beatles opted to move to the basement of their Apple offices, where they hoped to create a better atmosphere. Such events make watching *Let It Be* a sad experience, although circumstances do brighten up when pianist/organist Billy Preston joins their ranks. The infamous live rooftop scene, where they perform 'Don't Let Me Down' and 'Get Back', is a glorious moment, both musically and emotionally and although it closes the film on a positive note, in reality further sessions for the album followed. However, all work was suspended at the end of January and the following month the Beatles began work on what became *Abbey Road*. The *Let It Be* film was released in 1970, by which time the relevant recording had been 'post-produced' by Phil Spector to create a corresponding album, which initially came complete with a lavish book of photographs from the recording session.

LET THE GOOD TIMES ROLL

Perhaps one of the finest paeans to classic rock 'n' roll, *Let The Good Times Roll* is a sumptuous amalgamation of documentary footage and memorable concert performances. At its core was a 1972 marathon, hosted at Madison Square Gardens by New York impresario Richard Nader. Directors Sid Levin and Robert Abel blended footage from that event with television appearances, newsreels, interviews and demonstration films. Scenes from 50s genre movies *The Wild One* and *I Was A Teenage Werewolf* help to place the music in a broader cultural context, while intelligent use of split-screen techniques facilitated then-and-now scenarios. One particular clip of Little Richard, in monochrome from the 50s and in colour from the 70s, is particularly memorable. 'Good Golly Miss Molly', 'Rip It Up' and 'Lucille' are among the songs he performs as part of a cast that also includes Fats Domino, Chuck Berry, the Coasters, Danny And The Juniors, the Five Satins, Shirley And Lee, Bo Diddley, the Shirelles, Chubby Checker and Bill Haley And His Comets. 'Blueberry Hill', 'Reelin' And Rockin'', 'At The Hop', 'Poison Ivy', 'I'm A Man' and, of course, 'Rock Around The Clock', are among the songs featured in this endearing tribute to rock's first golden era.

LET'S FACE IT!

Danny Kaye confirmed the star qualities he had shown earlier in the year in *Lady In The Dark* when he played his first leading role on Broadway in this show which opened at the Imperial Theatre in New York on 29 October 1941. In *Lady In The Dark*, Kaye had been called upon to sing a song, listing 49 Russian composers, in 39 seconds; in *Let's Face It!*, he stopped the show with 'Melody In 4-F', which encapsulated a rookie soldier's first few weeks in the army - this time in 90 seconds. That particular piece of special material was written by Kaye's wife, Sylvia Fine and Max Liebman. Herbert and Dorothy Fields' book, which was based on the 1925 hit comedy, *The Cradle Snatchers*, deals with three wives who suspect that their husbands' sporting activities may be of the indoor, rather the outdoor variety, so they enlist the help of three soldiers from the local army camp to assist them in their own night-time manoeuvres. However, serious complications arise when the husbands return - with the girlfriends of the soldiers on their arms. With Kaye in the cast, were Eve Arden, Benny Baker, Edith Meiser, Vivian Vance, Mary Jane Walsh, and, in a minor role, Nanette Fabray, who later had success in other Broadway musicals such as *High Button Shoes*, and in several films, particularly *The Band Wagon* (1953) with Fred Astaire and Jack Buchanan. Cole Porter's score was smart and witty as usual, and included 'Ace In The Hole', 'Farming', 'Ev'rything I Love', 'A Little Rhumba Numba', 'A Lady Needs A Rest', and 'I Hate You Darling'. The composer's riposte to Kaye's 'Melody In 4-F' that he (Porter) allowed to be interpolated from another source, was another equally vocally taxing piece which Kaye shared with Eve Arden: 'Let's Not Talk About Love' ('Why not discuss, my dee-arie, the life of Wallace Bee-ery/Or bring a jeroboam on, and write a drunken poem on/Astrology, mythology, geology, philology/ Pathology, psychology, electro-physiology/Spermology, phrenology/I owe you an apology/But let's not talk about love.'). During the show's New York run of 547 performances, Danny Kaye was succeeded by José Ferrer, and, when *Let's Face* it began its 10 months' stay at the London Hippodrome, it starred Bobby Howes, Joyce Barbour, Jack Stamford, and Pat Kirkwood. The 1943 film version featured Bob Hope, Betty Hutton, and Eve Arden.

LET'S MAKE LOVE

The story worked well in *On The Avenue* (1937), so screenwriter Norman Krasna adapted it slightly for this 20th Century-Fox release some 23 years later. A seriously wealthy businessman (Yves Montand) discovers that he is going to be lampooned in a satirical off-Broadway revue, so, after honing his almost non-existent performing skills with the help of Gene Kelly (dancing), Bing Crosby (singing), and Milton Berle (comedy), he joins the show as a lookalike of himself and immediately falls for the leading lady (Marilyn Monroe). Her boyfriend-in-residence is British singer Frankie Vaughan, but after Montand turns on the Gallic charm he does not stand a chance and might as well go home. (In fact that is what Vaughan did shortly after filming was finished - Mrs Vaughan had explained that when Monroe offered to help him with his lines that was not really what she meant). Sammy Cahn and Jimmy Van Heusen's were pleasant but uninspired, and included 'Let's Make Love', 'Incurably Romantic' (which Monroe sang with both Vaughan and Montand), 'Latin One', 'Specialization', 'Hey You With The Crazy Eyes', and 'Strip City'. However, the film's musical highlight was Monroe's sizzling version of Cole Porter's 'My Heart Belongs To Daddy'. Tony Randall was his usual amusing self as Montand's long-suffering personal assistant, and other parts went to Wilfred Hyde White, David Burns, Michael David, and Mara Lynn. Jack Cole staged the smart and contemporary dances, and the director was George Cukor. This good-looking picture was photographed in DeLuxe Color and CinemaScope by Daniel L. Fapp.

LEVANT, OSCAR

b. 27 December 1906, Pittsburgh, Pennsylvania, USA, d. 14 August 1972, Beverly Hills, California, USA. Hypochondriac, witty, neurotic, grouchy, melancholic, acidic, and eccentric, are just a few of the adjectives that have been used over the years in a desperate attempt to accurately describe one of the most original characters in films, radio, and popular and light classical music. All the above definitions apparently apply to his personal as well as his public image. After graduating from high school, Levant struggled to make a living as pianist before moving to New York where he studied with Sigismund Stojovkskis and Arnold Schoenberg. He also played in clubs, and appeared on Broadway in the play, *Burlesque* (1927), and in the movie version entitled *The Dance Of Life*, two years later. In 1930 Levant worked with Irving Caesar, Graham John and Albert Sirmay on the score for another Broadway show, the Charles B. Dillingham production of *Ripples*, which starred Fred and Dorothy Stone and included songs such as 'Is It Love?', 'There's Nothing Wrong With A Kiss', and 'I'm A Little Bit Fonder Of You'. In the same year Levant collaborated with Irving Caesar again on 'Lady, Play Your Mandolin' which was successful for Nick Lucas and the Havana Novelty Orchestra, amongst others. He wrote his best-known song, 'Blame It On My Youth', with Edward Heyman in 1934, and it is still being played and sung 60 years later. Levant spent much of the late 20s and 30s in Hollywood writing songs and scores for movies such as *My Man* (Fanny Brice's film debut in 1928), *Street Girl*, *Tanned Legs*, *Leathernecking*, *In Person*, *Music Is Magic*, and *The Goldwyn Follies* (1938). Out of those came several appealing songs, including 'If You Want A Rainbow (You Must Have Rain)', 'Lovable And Sweet', 'Don't Mention Love To Me', 'Honey Chile', and 'Out Of Sight Out Of Mind'. His collaborators included Ray Heindorf, Mort Dixon, Billy Rose, Sam M. Lewis, Vernon Duke, Sidney Clare, Dorothy Fields, Stanley Adams, and Joe Young. Beginning in the late 30s, Levant also demonstrated his quick wit on the long-running radio series *Information Please*, and brought his grumpy irascible self to the screen in films such as *In Person* (1935), *Rhythm On The River*, *Kiss The Boys Goodbye*, *Rhapsody In Blue* (in which he played himself), *Humoresque*, *Romance On The High Seas*, *You Were Meant For Me*, *The Barkleys Of Broadway*, *An American In Paris*, and *The Band Wagon* (1953). In the last two pictures, both directed by Vincente Minnelli, he seemed to be at the peak of his powers, especially in the former which has a famous dream sequence in which Levant imagines he is conducting part of George Gershwin's Concert In F and every member of the orchestra is himself. Levant was a life-long friend and accomplished exponent of Gershwin's works. His final musical, *The 'I Don't Care Girl'*, was a fairly dull affair, and his last picture of all, *The Cobweb* (1955), was set in a mental hospital. That was both sad and ironic, because for the last 20 years of his life Levant suffered from failing mental and physical health, emerging only occasionally to appear on television talk shows. In 1989 a one-man play based on the works of Oscar Levant entitled *At Wit's End* ('An Irreverent Evening'), opened to critical acclaim in Los Angeles.

● ALBUMS: *Plays Levant And Gershwin* (1994)★★★, and other soundtrack and classical recordings.

● FURTHER READING: *A Smattering Of Ignorance. Memoirs Of An Amnesiac. The Unimportance Of Being Oscar* all by Oscar Levant. *A Talent For Genius: The Life And Times Of Oscar Levant*, Sam Kashner and Nancy Schoenberger.

LEVENE, SAM

b. 28 August 1905, Russia, d. 28 December 1980, New York, USA. Some sources suggest that this popular stage and screen character actor was born in New York. However, it seems more likely that he was taken to the USA in 1907, and became a naturalized citizen some 30 years later. After graduating from high school, Levene attended the American Academy of Dramatic Art in New York from 1925-27, and made his Broadway debut almost immediately in *Wall Street* (1927). The Depression made work scarce, but Levene persevered, and after making an impression in *Dinner At Eight* (1932), he established himself as a fine actor with *Three Men On A Horse* (1935). His hustling, fast-talking, streetwise style meant he was a natural choice for the role of Nathan Detroit, the operator of 'the oldest established permanent floating crap game in New York', in *Guys And Dolls* (1950). Levene reprised his role for London audiences in 1953, but was overlooked by producers of the film version, who preferred Frank Sinatra in the part. Although the remainder of his career was mostly spent in Hollywood film studios and the straight theatre, where he is particularly remembered for his performances in *The Devil's Advocate* (1961, Tony Awards nomination) and Neil Simon's 1972 hit, *The Sunshine Boys*, Levene did star in two more Broadway musicals, *Let It Ride* (1961, as Patsy) and *Café Crown* (1964, as Hymie). He continued to sigh and shrug in projects of variable quality on stage and screen until shortly before his death.

● FILMS: *Three Men On A Horse* (1936), *After The Thin Man* (1936), *Yellow Jack* (1938), *The Mad Miss Manton* (1938), *The Shopworn Angel* (1938), *Golden Boy* (1939), *Married Bachelor* (1941), *Shadow Of The Thin Man* (1941), *Grand Central Murder* (1942), *Sunday Punch* (1942), *Sing Your Worries Away* (1942), *The Big Street* (1942), *I Dood It* (1943), *Action In the North Atlantic* (1943), *Whistling In Brooklyn* (1943), *Gung Ho!* (1943), *The Purple Heart* (1944), *The Killers* (1946), *Brute Force* (1947), *Boomerang!* (1947), *Killer McCoy* (1947), *The Babe Ruth Story* (1948), *Leather Gloves* (1948), *Dial 1119* (1950), *Guilty Bystander* (1950), *Three Sailors And A Girl* (1953), *The Opposite Sex* (1956), *Sweet Smell Of Success* (1957), *A Farewell To Arms* (1957), *Designing Woman* (1957), *Slaughter On Tenth Avenue* (1957), *Kathy O* (1958), *Act One* (1963), *A Dream Of Kings* (1969), *Such Good Friends* (1971), *The Money* (1976), *God Told Me So* (1976), *Demon* (1977), *Last Embrace* (1979), *And Justice For All* (1979).

LI'L ABNER (FILM MUSICAL)

Probably because most of the original cast of the 1956 hit Broadway show recreated their roles, this 1959 screen version was a satisfying and entertaining affair. Norman Panama and Melvin Frank adapted their libretto, which was based on Al Capp's popular cartoon character, and the community of Dogpatch - one of the most underrated areas in the whole of the USA - was up there on the screen in Technicolor and VistaVision. When they learn that their town has been earmarked as a testing site for atom bombs, the residents, Daisy Mae (Leslie Parrish), Abner Yokum (Peter Palmer), Pappy and Mammy Yokum (Joe E. Marks and Billie Hayes), Marryin' Sam (Stubby Kaye), Earthquake McGoon (Bernie Hoffman), Stupifyin' Jones (Julie Newmar) and the rest, discover that, many years ago, their beloved Dogpatch was designated a national shrine. Johnny Mercer and Gene De Paul's witty score sounded as good as ever and included 'If I Had My Druthers', 'Jubilation T. Cornpone', 'The Country's In The Very Best Of Hands', 'Put 'Em Back', 'Namely You', 'Room Enuff For Us', 'A Typical Day', 'Don't Take That Rag Off'n The Bush', 'I'm Past My Prime', 'Unnecessary Town', and 'I Wish It Could Be Otherwise'. Dee Dee Wood and Michael Kidd's exuberant and exhilarating choreography, coupled with Panama and Frank's skilful and sympathetic direction, made this a film to savour and remember. Another, non-musical, version of Al Capp's tale was released in 1940.

LI'L ABNER (STAGE MUSICAL)

The wonderful world of Dogpatch, a rural community somewhere in the south of the USA, came to The St. James Theatre on Broadway in November 1956 when librettists Norman Panama and Melvin Frank adapted Al Capp's famous comic strip, Li'l Abner, for the musical stage. All the familiar characters made the trip, including Daisy Mae (Edith Adams) who is still trying to catch Abner Yokum (Peter Palmer) in the annual Sadie Hawkins' Day Chase (if you catch 'em, Marryin' Sam [Stubby Kaye] will do the rest). Then there is Appassionata von Climax (Tina Louise) - she's after Li'l Abner as well - Earthquake McGoon (Bern Hoffman - he's after Ellie Mae, General Bullmoose (Howard St. John), Mammy Yokum (Charlotte Rae), Stupefyin' Jones (Julie Newmar), Romeo Scragg (Mark Breaux), Clem Scragg (James Hurst), Moonbeam McSwine (Carmen Alvarez), and many more. All of them are shocked when they hear that the US Government has such a low opinion of Dogpatch that they want to test an atom bomb there. Fortune smiles on the town and its amiable inhabitants when they discover that, back in Abraham Lincoln's time, the town was designated a national shrine. The lively and exhilarating score, by Johnny Mercer and Gene De Paul, was full of good things, including what could be said to be the community's theme song, 'Progress Is The Root Of All Evil', along with 'Past My Prime', 'Put 'Em Back', 'Oh Happy Day', 'Unnecessary Town', the rousing 'The Country's In The Very Best Of Hands', and a hymn to the founder of Dogpatch, the incompetent 'Jubilation T. Cornpone', which was sung by Stubby Kaye who was ousanding throughout, as usual. There was also the tender ballad, 'Love In A Home', and 'Namely You', which achieved some popularity through recordings by Lawrence Welk and Carmen McRae. Another of the songs, 'If I Had My Druthers', was included by Johnny Mercer on Two Of A Kind, an album he made with Bobby Darin in 1961. Michael Kidd won a Tony Award for his spirited choreography (just two years after

his tremendous work in Hollywood on Seven Brides For Seven Brothers) and Li'l Abner enjoyed a run of 693 performances. The 1959 film version starred Peter Palmer, Leslie Parrish, Stubby Kaye, and some of the other actors from the show.

LIEBERSON, GODDARD

b. 5 April 1911, Hanley, Staffordshire, England, d. 29 May 1977, New York City, New York, USA. A record company executive, composer, author, and musician, Lieberson was four years old when his family moved to Seattle, Washington, USA. After graduating from the local university, he studied at the Eastman School of Music in New York, and originally intended to pursue a career as a composer. Financial reality intervened, and in 1939, he became the assistant director of the Masterworks division of Columbia Records, part of the CBS group. During the 40s he recorded plays, operas, and other classical works, while at the same time rising to the position of executive vice-president of Columbia. In the late 40s, he was influential in the decision to select the 33 1/3 speed as the standard for the new long-playing record. The development also contributed directly towards his greatest success as a pioneering producer of original cast recordings of hit Broadway shows. He began in 1949 with South Pacific, for which he won the first of seven Gold Discs. The other award winners were Flower Drum Song, Camelot, West Side Story, Mame, The Sound Of Music and My Fair Lady. He was so impressed by the score for the latter show that he persuaded CBS to become the sole investor - and, with sales of over six million units, they made a fortune. His 'amazing ear, his enthusiasm for theatre music, and his respect for the work he was doing' made him a legendary figure in the industry. Lieberson also recorded many shows when they had closed after only a few performances, convinced, quite rightly in most cases, that the scores were worth preserving. He was responsible for recording the vast majority of the shows that have been re-released in CD form on the Sony Broadway label. During a long and distinguished career, Lieberson is credited with having signed many important artists, including Simon And Garfunkel and Bob Dylan. He rose to become the president of Columbia Records (1955-56), of the CBS/Columbia Group (1966-71 and 1973-75), but he will be remembered mainly for his sensitive and brilliant work in preserving so much wonderful Broadway music. His final recordings, in the early 70s, were A Little Night Music, Billy and the record-breaking A Chorus Line.

LIFE BEGINS AT 8:40

One of the outstanding revues of the 30s, Life Begins At 8:40 opened at the Winter Garden Theatre in New York on 27 August 1934. There was high quality throughout, in every department. The backstage team included directors Philip Loeb and John Murray Anderson who was renowned for his work on several editions of the Greenwich Village Follies, and his own John Murray Anderson's Almanac, and much else; the sketches were mainly written by David Freedman, and the songs provided by the classy trio of Harold Arlen (music) with Ira Gershwin and E.Y. 'Yip' Harburg (lyrics). They included

'Let's Take A Walk Around The Block', 'What Can You Say In A Love Song?', 'Things', 'Fun To Be Fooled', 'Shoein' the Mare', 'I Couldn't Hold My Man', and 'You're A Builder-Upper', which had some success via recordings by Leo Reisman (with Arlen), Henry King, and Glen Gray. Two of America's funniest song-and-dance men, Bert Lahr and Ray Bolger, led the cast, which included Luella Gear, Frances Williams, Dixie Dunbar, Earl Oxford, and Brian Donlevy, the Irish-American actor who went on to become one of Hollywood's top tough guys. The combination of good songs and a series of sometimes hilarious sketches ensured a decent run of 237 performances.

LIFE, THE

Having been workshopped almost seven years previously, announced for Broadway on several occasions, and had more than half its score performed on a concept album by a wide variety of artists, *The Life* finally surfaced at the Ethel Barrymore Theatre on 26 April 1997. It was set in the pre-AIDS awareness late 70s, in and around 42nd Street, when that whole area of New York had become a neon-lit haven of porn parlours, whores and pimps. This is the *milieu* of *The Life*, where hooker Queen (Pamela Isaacs) works flat out (literally) in order to service the drug habit of her husband (and pimp) Fleetwood (Kevin Ramsey). Fleetwood is attempting to block out the memories of his time in Vietnam, but the arrival in town of pretty, fresh-faced blonde Mary (Bellamy Young) also provides some relief from those horrors. After he has given Mary the benefit of his personal attention, Queen, consoled by her best friend, the ageing prostitute Sonja (Lillias White), jumps ship and lands up with Memphis (Chuck Cooper), the nastiest pimp of them all. Mary, on the other hand, turns out to be a surprisingly shrewd, hard-headed career woman, intent on a Hollywood career as a porn star, by way of go-go dancing. Also involved in this compelling mixture of sleaze, violence and incongruity ('The Hookers' Ball', for example) were Carmen (Lynn Sterling), Chichi (Sharon Wilkins), Frenchie (Katy Grenfell), Tracy (Judine Richard), Bobby (Mark Bove), Oddjob (Michael Gregory Gong), Silky (Rudy Roberson), Slick (Mark Anthony Taylor), April (Felicia Finlay), Snickers (Gordon Joseph Weiss), Lacy (Vernel Bagneris), Lou (Rich Herbert) and Doll House Dancer (Stephanie Michels). It was written by David Newman, Ira Gasman, and Cy Coleman, and augmented by a melodic, jazzy, dynamic score, composed by Coleman (music) and Gasman (lyrics), which lifted the piece out of the gutter into a world of sheer entertainment. As well as Sonja's hilarious 'The Oldest Profession', there were numerous other highlights in a fine set of songs that included 'Check It Out!', 'Use What You Got', 'A Lovely Day To Be Out Of Jail', 'A Piece Of The Action', 'Don't Take Much', 'Go Home', 'You Can't Get To Heaven', 'My Body', 'Why Don't They Leave Us Alone', 'Easy Money', 'He's No Good', 'Was That A Smile', 'I'm Leaving You', 'Step Right Up', 'Mr. Greed', 'My Way Or The Highway', 'People Magazine', 'We Had A Dream', 'Someday Is For Suckers', 'My Friend', and 'We Gotta Go'. The director was Michael Blakemore, choreographer Joey McKneely, and set designer Robin Wagner.
The Life won Tony Awards for featured actor and actress

(Chuck Cooper and Lillias White), and was voted best musical in the Drama Desk, Outer Critics Circle and Drama League awards. Despite the honours and general critical approval, it closed early in June 1998 after only 466 performances, losing a reported $7 million.
The aforementioned concept album featured artists such as Liza Minnelli, Jennifer Holliday, Jack Jones, Lou Rawls, and Billy Preston, as well as comedian George Burns in his last recording.

LILAC TIME
(see *Blossom Time*)

LILI

Just two years after she made her Hollywood debut in Vincente Minnelli's *An American In Paris* (1951), Leslie Caron delighted cinema audiences once again with this enchanting film which was also released by MGM. She plays a 16-year-old French orphan who joins a carnival and falls madly in love with a handsome magician (Jean-Pierre Aumont). After she is fired for devoting too much her time to him and his illusions, she finds consolation in talking to a group of puppets operated by a disillusioned cripple (Mel Ferrer), and their subsequent, touching relationship makes this a rather special film. One of the highlights came when Caron danced a dream ballet with the puppets to the lovely, haunting music of Bronislau Kaper for which he won an Oscar. He and lyricist Helen Deutsch also wrote the song 'Hi-Lili, Hi-Lo', which was performed in captivating fashion by the puppets, and later became quite a hit. Helen Deutsch was also responsible for the screenplay which she adapted from a novel by Paul Gallico. Charles Walters and Dorothy Jarnac were responsible for the imaginative choreography, and Walters also directed. Zsa Zsa Gabor led a strong supporting cast which also included Kurt Kasznar, Alex Gerry, Amanda Blake, and Wilton Graff. The film was produced by Edwin H. Knopf and photographed in Technicolor. In 1961 the magic of *Lili* was transferred to the stage in *Carnival*, the first Broadway musical show to be adapted from a screen musical. With a score by Bob Merrill, and starring Anna Maria Alberghetti, it became a popular hit and ran for 719 performances.

LILLIE, BEATRICE
b. 29 May 1894, Toronto, Canada, d. 20 January 1989, Henley-On-Thames, England. An incomparable artist - a comedienne, actress, and singer - who was known in the 20s and 30s as 'the funniest woman in the world.' After leaving school at the age of 15 to form a singing trio with her mother and sister, Lillie moved to England just prior to World War I. From 1914-1922, she starred in a series of West End revues, mostly produced by André Charlot. These included *Not Likely!* (1914), *5064 Gerrard* (1915), *Samples* (1916), *Some* (1916), *Cheep* (1917), *Tabs* (1918), *Bran Pie* (1919), *Now And Then* (1921), *Pot Luck* (1921), and *The Nine O'Clock Revue* (1922). She also took the comic lead in the Jerome Kern-Guy Bolton-P.G. Wodehouse musical comedy, *Oh, Joy!* (1919), which had played at the Princess Theatre in New York under the title of *Oh, Boy!* In 1920 Lillie married Robert Peel, a descendant of the

founder of the Metropolitan Police, and became Lady Peel five years later when his baronet father died. Two years later she made her Broadway debut, with Gertrude Lawrence and Jack Buchanan, in the smash hit *André Charlot's Revue*, and almost stopped the show every night with the splendidly chaotic 'March With Me' number. After more Charlot revues in London and New York, Lillie appeared in two musical comedies. She duetted with Charles Purcell on Anne Caldwell and Vincent Youmans' 'I Know That You Know' in *Oh, Please!* (New York 1926), and brought the house down every night with her rendering of Richard Rodgers and Lorenz Hart's 'A Baby's Best Friend' (is his mother) in *She's My Baby* (New York 1928). Returning to revue, she co-starred with Noël Coward, and sang the enduring 'World Weary', in his immensely successful *This Year Of Grace!* (New York 1928). A brief foray into the West End with *Charlot's Masquerade* (1930), was followed by *The Third Little Show* (New York 1931), in which she introduced American audiences to another Coward classic, 'Mad Dogs And Englishmen'. During the 30s Lillie was one of the most sought after of celebrities, the darling of the social set, and the toast of two continents. She continued to excite and delight theatregoers on both sides of the Atlantic in productions such as *Walk A Little Faster* (New York 1932), *Please* (London 1933), *At Home Abroad* (New York 1935), *The Show Is On* (New York 1936), *Happy Returns* (London 1938), and *All Clear* (London 1939). It is said that Cole Porter wrote his 'story of a nightmare weekend', 'Thank You So Much, Mrs. Lowsborough-Goodby', for Lillie, and Coward gave her his delightfully gossipy 'I've Been To A Marvellous Party' in *Set To Music* (1939). She made her cabaret debut in 1939 at London's Café Royal, and then - apart from appearing in Herbert Farjeon's revue, *Big Top* (London 1942), and some straight theatre - spent most of World War II entertaining the troops at home and abroad. She was decorated by General de Gaulle with the French Liberation Medal, and throughout the 40s continued to criss-cross the Atlantic, appearing in revues such as *Seven Lively Arts* (New York 1944), *Better Late* (London 1946), and *Inside USA* (New York 1948), as well as working regularly on radio and in cabaret. In 1953 she won a Tony Award for the New York production of *An Evening With Beatrice Lillie*, which was also presented at the Globe Theatre in London a year later. Among the West End cast then was composer/librettist Leslie Bricusse, who retained his association with her for some years. In fact, he and Anthony Newley wrote their smash hit musical, *Stop The World-I Want To Get Off*, early in 1961, while Bricusse was working with Lillie in New York. Before that, she was the best thing in a generally disappointing Golden Jubilee edition of the *Ziegfeld Follies* (1957), a superbly eccentric aunt in *Auntie Mame* in London (1958), as well as being her anarchic self in *Late Evening With Beatrice Lillie* at the 1960 Edinburgh Festival. She made her final Broadway appearance, as Madame Arcati, in *High Spirits*, the 1964 musical based on Noël Coward's play *Blithe Spirit*. Although her career spanned the period from silent features to *The Sound Of Music*, Lillie made only a few films - she needed a live audience to inspire her. Probably her most telling screen appearance was as an hilarious oriental white slave trader

in *Thoroughly Modern Millie* (1967). Shortly after suffering a stroke in 1975 which left her partly paralysed, she returned to England and spent the remainder of her life in poor health at her home in Henley. After her death, Sir John Gielgud paid a touching tribute, and said that he regarded her as The Mistress of the Absurd, recalling her in performance at the Winter Garden Theatre, in New York, 'standing dramatically against a pillar dressed in a flowing gown which she lifted suddenly to reveal her feet shod in roller skates on which she gravely skidded across the stage'. With her trademark Eton crop topped with a smart cap, and bearing a long cigarette holder, she was a true original - the enemy of pomposity, and a murderer of the sentimental - much to the delight of her audience. Fortunately, many of her satirical and surrealistic comic numbers and skits, such as 'There Are Fairies At The Bottom Of My Garden', 'Double Damask', 'Weary Of It All', 'Wind Round My Heart', and 'This Is My First Affair' ('so please be kind' - which during the course of her version, became 'please be quick'), are preserved on record.
- ALBUMS: *Auntie Bea* (Decca 1959)★★★, *Queen Bea* (1970)★★★★, *The Unique! The Incomparable!* (Pavilion 1995)★★★★.
- FILMS: *Exit Smiling* (1926), *The Show Of Shows* (1929), *Are You There?* (1929), *Dr. Rhythm* (1938), *On Approval* (1943), *Around The World In 80 Days* (1956), *Thoroughly Modern Millie* (1967).
- FURTHER READING: *Every Other Inch A Lady*, Beatrice Lillie. *Beatrice Lillie: The Funniest Woman In The World*, B. Laffey.

LION KING, THE

'Prepare to be awed', was *Time* magazine's warning when the latest Walt Disney blockbuster was preparing to dominate the world's cinema screens in 1994. Unlike the Studio's previous feature length animated triumphs, *The Lion King* is not based on an established fairy tale or children's book. Instead, the witty screenplay, by Irene Mecchi, Jonathan Roberts and Linda Woolverton, weaves a timeless tale of 'monarchical principal, family unity and male supremacy', and has 'lions dancing with zebras, monkeys aping around with warthogs and ostriches, and giraffes performing as in the *Folies Bergère*'. With a soundtrack full of perfectly selected, familiar voices, the Hamlet-style hero, Simba the lion cub (Jonathan Taylor Thomas), is cheated out of his inheritance by his wicked Uncle Scar (Jeremy Irons), after he has seen his regal father, Mufasa (James Earl Jones), killed while trying to rescue him from a stampeding herd of hyenas and wildebeests. It takes a long period in the wilderness, where he meets up with Pumbaa, the weird and wonderful warthog (Ernie Sabella) and Timon, the marvellous meercat (Nathan Lane), before the grown Simba (now voiced by Matthew Broderick), urged by the ghost of his dead father, returns to dispose of his murdering uncle and take his rightful place in the scheme of things. Also contributing their vocal talents to a heart-warming range of characters, are Rowan Atkinson (as Zazu the hornbill) and Whoopi Goldberg, Cheech Marin (ex-Cheech And Chong) and Jim Cummings as a trio of a leering hyenas. The critics were unanimous in their praise of the film's 'technical wizardry and rich imagery, the late 20th century sophistication', and 'the lurid colours, that are so right for the African subject matter', although some of them had reservations about the degree of violence involved in some scenes, and the lack of political correctness. The general feeling seemed to be that the film's music was not in the same class as that which graced two of Disney's other recent animated successes, *The Little Mermaid* and *Beauty And The Beast*. Even so, Hans Zimmer's score, and one of Elton John and Tim Rice's songs, 'Can You Feel The Love Tonight', won Oscars, and the soundtrack was awarded two Grammys. With forecasts in the order of 'this will be the most successful film of the century', *The Lion King*, which was directed by Roger Allers and Rob Minkoff, grossed £21 million over the first weekend of its release.

LISBON STORY, THE (FILM MUSICAL)

Released by British National in 1946, this war-time story of intrigue set in Lisbon and Paris in 1940, was adapted by Jack Whittingham from Harold Purcell's long-running musical which opened in London in 1943. The delightful Patricia Burke recreated her stage role as Gabrielle Gerard, a French actress and singer, who risks accusations of collaborating with the invading Germans to assist a member of British Intelligence, David Warren (David Farrar), in his successful efforts to smuggle atom scientist Pierre Sargon (John Ruddock) back to England. David returns to Gabrielle after Paris has been liberated by the Allies, and they are married. The celebrated tenor, Richard Tauber, played Andre Joubert, Gabrielle's singing partner, and Walter Rilla was suitably evil as Karl von Schriner, Director of German Propaganda in Paris. Other roles went to Lawrence O'Madden, Austin Trevor, Harry Welchman, Paul Bonifas, Esme Percy, Noele Gordon, John Ruddock, and Joan Seton. Violin virtuoso Stéphane Grappelli was in it too, and so were two of the original show's hit songs, 'Pedro the Fisherman', 'Never Say Goodbye' (music Harry Parr-Davies, lyrics Harold Purcell). The former song was enormously popular during and after the war, especially in a recording by Gracie Fields. The picture itself, which was directed by Paul Stein, was pretty popular as well.

LISBON STORY, THE (STAGE MUSICAL)

One of the most popular West End musicals during World War II, *The Lisbon Story* opened at the London Hippodrome on 17 June 1943. Fifty years on, it is still recalled fondly because of the inclusion of the jaunty 'Pedro The Fisherman', which almost immediately became an enormous hit. The song was part of a score written by composer Harry Parr-Davies and lyricist Harold Purcell, who also provided a book in which wartime drama was mixed with sentimental music and lavish dance sequences in a spectacular and entertaining fashion. The story concerns a Parisian prima ballerina, Gabrielle Gerard (Patricia Burke), who colludes with the Nazis in an effort to secure the release of an important French scientist. When her deceit is discovered, she is executed. Albert Lieven played her German go-between, Carl von Shriner, and the cast also included Arséne Kiriloff, Zulia, Noele Gordon, Jack Livesey, Margaret McGrath, Reginald Long, and Joseph Dollinger. There were two major dance scenes and a lovely operetta sequence. The

score contained several attractive numbers, including the waltz, 'Someday We Shall Meet Again', 'Never Say Goodbye', 'For The First Time (I've Fallen In Love)', 'Follow The Drum', 'Happy Days', and 'A Serenade For Sale', but it was 'Pedro The Fisherman', which was sung in the show by Vincent Tildsley's Master Singers, in sailor rig, that audiences were whistling when they left the theatre. Patricia Burke made a successful recording of the song, as did the distinguished tenor, Richard Tauber, who appeared with her in the 1946 film of *The Lisbon Story*. Probably the version that endured the most, and which received consistent exposure on BBC Radio's *Family Favourites* programme, was that by Gracie Fields.

LISZTOMANIA

In his early career the maverick British film director Ken Russell made several controversial biographies of revered classic composers. These early films were notable for introducing previously unknown aspects of the composers' private lives. This reached a peak with the Tchaikovsky feature, *The Music Lovers*. Russell's later work was often criticised as excessive, particularly in the wake of his film of the Who's rock-opera, *Tommy* (1975). The group's lead singer, Roger Daltrey, starred in *Lisztomania*, which was released that same year. However, the director's attempt to portray the composer as a hedonistic rock star was artistically unsatisfying, and did much to undermine Russell's reputation. Ringo Starr and Paul Nicholas were part of an uninspired cast while ex-Yes keyboard player Rick Wakeman provided a score comprised of heavy-handed treatments of Liszt and Wagner compositions. *Lisztomania* played upon the artistic flaws of all the participants.

LITTLE JOHNNY JONES

George M. Cohan's first Broadway hit, and the beginning of his long association with producer Sam H. Harris. The show opened at the Liberty Theatre in New York on 7 November 1904, and, as was to become the norm throughout his career, Cohan provided the book, music and lyrics, as well directing and appearing in the piece. He is said to have got the idea for the plot from a newspaper account about an American jockey, Tod Sloane, who rode in the English Derby race in 1903. In Cohan's version, Johnny Jones refuses to be bribed to throw the race, but he loses anyway. When he arrives at Southampton docks to board a ship for his return to America, he is besieged by an angry crowd. Eventually they disperse and he is left alone waiting for a signal from his friend on the ship, now some way out at sea, to indicate that his innocence has been proved. The moment when the rocket soars into the sky and Jones goes into an exuberant rendering of 'Give My Regards To Broadway', is one of the most memorable sequences in musical comedy history. It was recreated superbly by James Cagney when he starred in the George M. Cohan biopic, *Yankee Doodle Dandy*, in 1942. The latter film got it's title from 'The Yankee Doodle Boy', which Cohan introduced in *Little Johnny Jones*, along with other numbers such as 'Life's A Funny Proposition After All', 'If Mr. Boston Lawson Got His Way', and 'I'm Might Glad I'm Living And That's All'. Cohan's wife, Ethel Levy, had a leading role, and so did his mother and father, Helen and Jerry Cohan. Also in the cast was Donald Brian, the actor, singer, and dancer who was to appear in Cohan's next Broadway musical, *Forty-Five Minutes From Broadway*, before going on to star in other important shows such as *The Merry Widow* and *The Girl From Utah*, in which he introduced Jerome Kern and Herbert Reynolds' lovely song, 'They Didn't Believe Me'. Although Cohan is often criticized for his sentimental, flag-waving approach, *Little Johnny Jones*, with its strong score and solid, believable book is considered to a be significant landmark in development of the indigenous American musical. It ran for only 52 performances in its first outing on Broadway, but Cohan brought it back twice during 1905, and toured it extensively. The 1930 film version starred Alice Day and Eddie Buzzell. A 1981 revival of the show which began its life at the Goodspeed Opera House, Connecticut, amended the original plot and introduced some other Cohan songs. After using several actors in the lead role during its pre-Broadway tour, Donny Osmond was chosen to play the part at the Alvin Theatre in New York - but for the one-night run only.

LITTLE MARY SUNSHINE

On first sight a show with a title like that, and characters with names such as Mme. Ernestine Von Liebedich and General Oscar Fairfax, plus songs with titles like 'Do You Ever Dream Of Vienna?', the casual observer could be forgiven for thinking that this is an operetta. It is the date that gives the game away: *Little Mary Sunshine* opened Off Broadway (another clue) at the Orpheum Theatre on 19 November 1959. With rock 'n' roll already into its stride, there was not much of an audience in those days for genuinely new operetta, and, sure enough, this show turned out to be an elaborate spoof of the real thing. Sub titled *A New Musical About An Old Operetta*, *Little Mary Sunshine* unmercifully sends up prime examples of the genre such as *Rose Marie* and *Naughty Marietta*. Set in the upper reaches of the Colorado Rockies, Rick Besoyan's book tells the hot-blooded story of Mary Potts (Eileen Brennan), the hostess of the local hostelry, who makes it quite clear to the Rangers' Captain Big Jim Warrington (William Graham), that there is always plenty of room at her inn, for him. However, Big Jim is more interested in capturing the despicable Indian, Yellow Feather (Ray James), who has indicated on more than one occasion that he would like to get Mary into his wigwam. Fortunately for our heroine, she and Big Jim give out with the 'Colorado Love Call', which proves to have more of a deterrent effect on amorous, ambitious Indians than a whole company of cavalry. The sub-plot involves another young loving couple Nancy Twinkle (Elmarie Wendel) and Corporal Billy Jester (John McMartin), who promise to be true to each other 'Once In A Blue Moon'. The remainder of Rick Besoyan's score was in that same mocking vein, and included 'Look For Sky Of Blue', 'Playing Croquet', 'Tell A Handsome Stranger', 'Every Little Nothing', 'Naughty Naughty, Nancy', and 'Such A Merry Party', and 'In Izzenschnooken On The Lovely Ezzenzook Zee', which is 'authentically' rendered by a visiting opera star of yesterday (or the day before), Mme. Ernestine Von Liebedich

(Elizabeth Parrish). It all must have touched the right nerve, because *Little Mary Sunshine* became one of the longest-running Off Broadway musicals ever, during its run of 1,143 performances. Londoners did not seem to see the joke, and, despite the presence in the cast of comedy stalwarts such as Patricia Routledge and Bernard Cribbins, the show folded after five weeks.

LITTLE ME

Conceived as a vehicle for one of US television's favourite performers, Sid Caesar, the versatile comedian needed all his skills and ingenuity to cope with a scenario that called upon him to play seven different characters. The leading female role, on the other hand, is shared by two different actresses. *Little Me* opened at the Lunt-Fontanne Theatre in New York on 17 November 1962. Neil Simon's book, which was based on the play by Patrick Dennis, opens with the older Belle Poitrine (Nancy Andrews), 'queen of the silver screen', dictating her memoirs ('The Truth'). The young, ambitious Belle Schlumpfort (Virginia Martin) then relives the scenes as they actually occurred, and in each one she is accompanied by a male admirer played by Caesar. These range from her first love, the snobby 16-years-old Noble Eggleston, from whom she gets a taste for the high-life ('Rich Kids Rag') and yearns to be 'On The Other Side Of The Tracks', to the geriatric banker Amos Pinchley, who is surely a good person 'Deep Down Inside', the 'great French entertainer', Val du Val, ('Boom-Boom'), her temporary husband, Fred Poitrine a World War I sad soldier who yearns for a 'Real Live Girl', a dominating film director, ('Poor Little Hollywood Star'), and Prince Cherney 'the expiring regent of Rosenzweig' ('Goodbye'). George Musgrove (Swen Swenson), a childhood admirer of Belle's, and now a big-time gambler, comes back into her life at one point and tries to seduce her with the sensuous 'I've Got Your Number'. This was the only major male role not played by Sid Caesar. At the end, the two Belles get together to try and make sense of it all and unite in 'Little Me'. The older Belle is then left alone, seated in her Beverly Hill mansion, realising that she has achieved her aims of 'wealth, culture and social position' - but not, unfortunately, Noble Eggleston. Cy Coleman and Carolyn Leigh's score was, in turn, witty and tender, especially in numbers such as 'Real Live Girl' ('Speaking of miracles, this must be it/Just when I started to learn how to knit/I'm all in stitches from finding what riches a waltz, can reveal/With a real, live girl'), and 'The Other Side Of The Tracks', which became popular through a recording by Tony Bennett. It was directed by Cy Feuer and Bob Fosse, and Fosse won a Tony Award for his ingenious choreography. After a Broadway run of only 257 performances, the show received a much better reception in London, and stayed at the Cambridge Theatre for 10 months. It proved to be a personal triumph for Bruce Forsyth, the young comedian and television compère. Swenson reprised his mock strip to the delight of the female members of the audience, and also in the cast were Avril Angers (Miss Poitrine, older Belle), Eileen Gourlay (Belle), and Bernard Spear, who had as many roles as Forsyth, albeit modest ones. In 1982, a revised Broadway revival introduced a new opening number, 'Don't Ask A

Lady', dropped some of the others, and split the leading role between James Coco and Victor Garber. It only lasted for a month, but two years later London audiences approved of the show again (423 performances), with Russ Abbot, Lynda Baron, and Sheila White. For this production, 'Dimples', which had been cut in 1982, was back as 'Oh Dem Doggone Dimples'. The version of *Little Me* which opened at the Criterion Center Stage Right in November 1998, starring Martin Short and Faith Prince, appeared to be a hybrid of what had gone before. Back in 1993, another, more 'intimate' musical entitled *Little Me*, with a score by Brad Ross, Ellen Greenfield, Hal Hackady, *et al*, played at Steve McGraw's in New York.

LITTLE MERMAID, THE

Based on the Hans Christian Andersen fairytale, this 1989 Walt Disney release was the Studio's 28th animated feature, and a reminder of that golden era during which cinema audiences of all ages all over the world were enchanted with the immortal stories of *Snow White And The Seven Dwarfs*, *Peter Pan*, *Cinderella*, and *Sleeping Beauty*. This particular tale concerns the 16-year-old mermaid Ariel, who, after a series of exciting watery adventures, takes on a human form and marries the handsome and heroic Prince Eric. The action is enhanced by the 'contemporary songs and score ranging from English folk to French cabaret, from lively Caribbean to showstopping Broadway'. The composer Alan Menken won an Academy Award for his original score, and he and lyricist Howard Ashman gained another Oscar for the song, 'Under The Sea'. 'Kiss The Girl' was also nominated, and there were other attractive numbers such as 'Poor Unfortunate Souls' and 'Part Of Your World'. All these contributed to a soundtrack album which won a Grammy for the 'Best Recording For Children'. The film's spectacular animation, particularly in the underwater sequences, was widely applauded, and as usual the Disney organization selected appropriate voices for characters such as Ariel (Jodi Benson), her father King Triton (Kenneth Mars), Ursula (Pat Caroll), Prince Eric (Christopher Daniel Barnes), and Flotsam/Jetsam (Paddi Edwards). No one could mistake the distinctive tones of Ariel's friend Scuttle the seagull, which were provided by comedian Buddy Hackett. He has also made several impressive on-screen performances in movies such as *The Music Man* and *It's A Mad Mad Mad Mad World*. *The Little Mermaid*, which was directed by John Musker and Ron Clements who also wrote the screenplay, enjoyed substantial success in the US and abroad, and set up audiences nicely for Disney's sensational early 90s trio of *Beauty And The Beast*, *Aladdin* and *The Lion King*.

LITTLE MISS MARKER

That old show-biz maxim about not working with animals or children must have crossed Adolphe Menjou's mind more than once during the filming of this Paramount musical which was released in 1934. He was top-billed, but, although she was only six years old, Shirley Temple dominated this Damon Runyon story in which she is adopted by bookmaker Sorrowful Jones (Menjou), after being used as security for a losing bet. Shirley then proceeds to look after Jones while having a far more beneficial effect on the New York gambling fraternity than any government commission could hope for. Shell-shocked as he must have been, Menjou gave a creditable performance under heavy fire. Also suffering from the tremendous impact of this little blonde bombshell were Charles Bickford, Dorothy Dell, Lynne Overman, Willie Best, and Frank McGlynn Snr. Leo Robin and Ralph Rainger wrote the songs which included 'Low Down Lullaby', 'I'm A Black Sheep Who Is Blue', and 'Laugh, You Son-Of-A-Gun'. William R. Lipman, Sam Hellman and Gladys Lehman were responsible for the neat screenplay, and the director was Alexander Hall. The 'marker' of the title being an indigenous American term for IOU, the name of the film was changed to *The Girl In Pawn* for UK distribution. *Little Miss Marker* was remade in 1949 as *Sorrowful Jones*, in 1963 as *40 Pounds Of Trouble*, and again in 1980 under its original title, but none of them made anything like the impact of the 1934 version.

LITTLE NIGHT MUSIC, A

Suggested by Ingmar Bergman's film, *Smiles Of A Summer Night*, *A Little Night Music* opened at the Shubert Theatre in New York on 25 February 1973. The music and lyrics were by Stephen Sondheim, and Hugh Wheeler's book followed an intricate series of love affairs set in turn-of-the-century Sweden. Mature lawyer Fredrik Egerman (Len Cariou) has a young wife, Anne (Victoria Mallory), who has so far shown no inclination to consummate their relationship. Fredrik's former mistress, the actress Desirée Armfeldt (Glynis Johns), is in the neighbourhood with her touring show. Her daughter Fredrika (Judy Kahan), the fruit of an earlier Fredrik-Desirée dalliance, is back home with grandmother Madame Armfeldt (Hermione Gingold). Desirée's current companion is the hustling hussar, Count Carl-Magnus Malcolm (Laurence Guittard). He and his wife, Countess Charlotte (Patricia Elliott), join Desirée and various other family members and friends - including Fredrik's teenage son, Henrik (Mark Lambert) - for a weekend at Madame Armfeldt's country estate. Attended by their host and the often bemused servants, Petra (D. Jamin-Bartlett) and Frid (George Lee Andrews), the resulting *ménage* finds Anne inclined towards Henrik, Carl-Magnus attempting a reconciliation with Charlotte, while Desirée and Fredrik lie back and think of the old days. The show was elegantly staged by Harold Prince (choreography by Patricia Birch), and filled with Sondheim's delightful, waltz-time tunes. The superb score included 'Liaisons', 'The Miller's Son', 'Night Waltz', 'Now', 'Later', 'Soon', 'In Praise Of Women', 'A Weekend In The Country', 'The Sun Won't Set', 'Perpetual Anticipation', 'Every Day A Little Death', 'Remember?', 'It Would Have Been Wonderful', 'You Must Meet My Wife' and 'The Glamorous Life'. There was also a rarity - a Sondheim number that became popular outside the context of its show setting. 'Send In The Clowns', which was sung in a quiet, touching, contemplative manner by Desirée at the house party, soon entered the repertoires of both accomplished and mediocre vocalists around the world, notably those of Judy Collins and Frank Sinatra.

A Little Night Music ran on Broadway for 601 performances

and won Tony Awards for best musical, score, book, leading actress (Johns), supporting actress (Elliott), and costumes (Florence Klotz), along with the New York Critics' Circle Award for Best Musical. Gingold reprised her role as the aged dowager who manipulates happy endings for the various love affairs, for the 1975 London production, with a cast that also included Jean Simmons (Desirée), Joss Ackland (Fredrik), Terry Mitchell (Henrik), Maria Aitken (Charlotte), Veronica Page (Anne), Christine McKenna (Fredrika), David Kernan (Carl-Magnus), Diane Langton (Petra), and Michael Harbour (Frid). A 1989 West End revival starred Susan Hampshire (Charlotte), Lila Kedrova (Mme. Arnfeldt), Peter McEnery (Fredrik), Eric Flynn (Carl-Magnus), and Dorothy Tutin (Desirée), and in 1991, Glynis Johns, the original Desirée, portrayed Mme. Armfeldt in Los Angeles. In 1995, Betty Buckley gave her rendition of 'Send In The Clowns' when she led the cast of a BBC Radio 2 concert version of *A Little Night Music*, and Judi Dench was acclaimed for a highly individual reading of the number in a splendid 1995 Royal National Theatre repertory production. Among the rest of the distinguished cast were Patricia Hodge (Charlotte), Sîan Phillips (Madame Armfeldt), Brenda O'Hea (Henrik), Joanna Riding (Anne), Lambert Wilson (Carl-Magnus), Paul Kynman (Frid), and Issy van Randwyck (Petra). Laurence Guittard, who created the role of Carl-Magnus in the original Broadway production, played Fredrik. The score was supplemented by one additional song, Charlotte's 'My Husband The Pig'. Ironically, although *A Little Night Music* has been produced successfully by theatre companies throughout the world, a 1978 film version, which starred Elizabeth Taylor, vanished from public gaze before it could do any lasting harm to Sondheim's reputation.

LITTLE SHOP OF HORRORS (FILM MUSICAL)

As a film to put audiences off gardening for life, *Little Shop Of Horrors*, released in December 1986, is top of the heap. It tells the story of Seymour (Rick Moranis), a rather sweet but accident-prone character - a sort of Norman Wisdom of the 80s - whose working life at Mushnik's Skid Row flower shop just is not going to plan. On to the scene comes Audrey II, named after the girl Seymour adores, who changes from a tiny shrub to a sinister blood sucking flytrap. When Seymour has bled his fingers dry in an attempt to feed it, the plant forces him to find some human meat to satisfy its hunger. In return Seymour is to have as much success in love and life as he can handle. Eventually, realizing that the man-eating plant really wants to take over the world, Seymour faces up to its menace and, with the help of a few volts of electricity, blows Audrey II into oblivion. *Little Shop Of Horrors* was first seen off-Broadway in 1982, and that production itself was based on Roger Corman's 60s low-budget horror movie. Directed by Frank Oz, and produced by David Geffen for the Geffen Company, the show's author and lyricist, Howard Ashman, also wrote the movie's screenplay. It is interesting to note that the film's ending is distinctly different in tone to its stage predecessor, when Seymour and Audrey are both eaten and Audrey II succeeds. It appears the preview audiences preferred a happy ending and so it

was changed. Ashman was joined by Alan Menken to write the quirky, clever and often extremely funny score. Highlights included 'Skid Row', the film's only real production number of any sorts, involving most of the cast, and 'Suddenly Seymour', by no means an average love song. A host of guest stars joined in the fun, among them Steve Martin, James Belushi, John Candy, and Bill Murray. Ellen Greene recreated her stage role as Audrey. Martin plays Audrey's sadistic dentist boyfriend (in 'Somewhere That's Green', she sings 'I know Seymour's the greatest, but I'm dating a semi-sadist'). Consequently, it is not surprising that Martin becomes Audrey II's first human victim. The plant's big number is 'Mean Green Mother From Outer Space' (the voice is that of the Four Tops' Levi Stubbs). The song was written especially for the film, and is quite a treat, especially its flower bud chorus. The rest of the score included 'Little Shop Of Horrors', 'Grow For Me', 'Dentist', 'Feed Me', and 'Suppertime'. Pat Garrett was the choreographer, and the film was photographed in Technicolor and Panavision by Robert Paynter.

LITTLE SHOP OF HORRORS (STAGE MUSICAL)

After making its debut at the tiny WPA Theatre in New York, *Little Shop Of Horrors* moved to the Orpheum Theatre on the Lower East Side on 27 July 1982. The book, by Howard Ashman, was based on Charles Griffith's screenplay for the 1960 spoof of the horror movie genre, which had become a cult classic. Hardly the usual Broadway - or off-Broadway - fare, the grisly tale tells of Seymour Krelbourn (Lee Wilkof), an assistant at Mushnik's florist shop on Skid Row, who decides to boost sales by producing a strange house plant. He names it Audrey II, because of his love for sales assistant Audrey (Ellen Greene), and finds that it grow faster if it is fed with a few drops of blood - and subsequently, human flesh. Things rapidly get out of hand as the monster - and the business - thrives, eventually devouring just about everything and everyone in sight. The amusing and imaginative score by Ashman and composer Alan Menken had some 'good rock in the Phil Spector Wall of Sound idiom', and included 'Grow For Me', 'Suddenly Seymour', 'Skid Row', 'Somewhere That's Green', and 'Little Shop Of Horrors'. The show's bizarre humour caught on in a big way, as Audrey II and *Little Shop Of Horrors* became a sort of phenomenon. It continued to amaze and delight off-Broadway audiences for 2,209 performances, and was awarded the New York Drama Critics Circle Award for best musical. The 1984 London production, which ran for over a year, also received the Evening Standard prize for outstanding musical. Ellen Greene reprised her role in London, and for the 1986 film version, which also starred Rick Moranis, Vincent Gardenia and Steve Martin. In 1994, a 'gorgeously funny' revival toured the UK starring Sue Pollard, better know for her role as Peggy, the zany chalet maid, in the popular television comedy series *Hi-Di-Hi*.

LITTLE SHOW, THE

Composer Arthur Schwartz and lyricist Howard Dietz, one of the top Broadway songwriting teams of the 30s, got together for the first time to write several songs for this smart, classy revue which opened at the Music Box Theatre on 30 April 1929. Dietz also wrote most of the sketches, along with George S. Kaufman and others. He and Schwartz contributed 'I've Made A Habit Of You', 'Hammacher-Schlemmer, I Love You', and 'I Guess I'll Have To Change My Plan', ('I should have realized there'd be another man/Why did I buy those blue pajamas/Before the big affair began?'), which, for obvious reasons became known as 'The Blue Pajama Song', and, while never becoming a big hit, was one of the songwriters' hardy standards. It was very effectively sung by a couple of song-and-dance-men, Fred Astaire and Jack Buchanan in the film of The Band Wagon in 1953. It was introduced in The Little Show by Clifton Webb, who finally became recognized as a star in this revue, as did the resident funny man, 'dead-pan' Fred Allen. The third leading player, Libby Holman, had 'Can't We Be Friends?' (written by Kay Swift and Paul James - a pseudonym for her husband, James P. Warburg), which was quite a jolly little song for many years until Frank Sinatra turned it into a lonely ballad on his In The Wee Small Hours. Holman also sang the show's big hit, 'Moanin' Low', which had music and lyric by Ralph Rainger and Dietz. One of the other songs, 'A Little Hut In Hoboken', was one of a the relatively few numbers written by Herman Hupfield in his career; two years later he produced another, 'As Time Goes By', which was later immortalised in the film, Casablanca. The Little Show ran for 321 performances. Without Holman, Webb, and Allen neither of the sequels did well. The Second Little Show (1929), again had some songs by Schwartz and Dietz ('You're The Sunshine', 'What A Case I've Got On You', and 'Lucky Seven') and one by Hupfield ('Sing Something Simple'), but only ran for 63 performances; and The Third Little Show (1930), starred Beatrice Lillie who introduced Noël Coward's 'Mad Dogs And Englishmen' to the American public. The show also contained another rare Hupfield number, 'When Yuba Plays The Rhumba On His Tuba', and stayed at Music Box Theatre for four months.

LITTLE VOICE

Adapted from Jim Cartwright's 1992 play The Rise And Fall Of Little Voice, this movie faithfully recreates the sleaze, romance, and broad comedy of the original. Jane Horrocks reprises her performance as LV (for Little Voice), the shy, young Yorkshire (north of England) girl who spends so much of the time playing records inherited from her deceased father, that she can mimic the voices of singers such as Judy Garland, Billie Holiday, Marilyn Monroe, Shirley Bassey, and Gracie Fields, with uncanny accuracy. One night, LV's man-hungry mother, Mari Hoff (Brenda Blethyn), brings show business agent Ray Say (Michael Caine) back home, and he immediately sees LV as his last chance to grab a piece of the 'good time'. Mr. Boo (Jim Broadbent) stages her triumphant debut at his shabby club, but she refuses to make any subsequent appearances. When last seen she is leaving to meet her telephone engineer boyfriend Billy (Ewan McGregor), after standing up to her mother for the first time in her life. As with the play, Horrocks stole the notices with those unbelievable impressions - 'The Man That Got Away', 'I Wanna

Be Loved By You', 'Lover Man', 'Big Spender' - but Blethyn's blowsy, raucous, mother-from-hell was not far behind, and some thought that Caine's performance - particularly in his self-abusive, over-the-top drunken version of Roy Orbison's 'It's Over', following LV's rejection of his overtures to get her back on the stage - was the best thing he had done since Educating Rita. Director Mark Herman and Jim Cartwright wrote the screenplay, and Little Voice, which was photographed in Deluxe London, and distributed by Buena Vista International (UK) in 1998.

LIVING IT UP

One of the best films that Dean Martin and Jerry Lewis made together in the mid-50s, this 1954 Paramount release was twice blessed - with an amusing story and a set of good songs. Jack Rose and Melville Shavelson's screenplay was based on James Street's story Letter To The Editor and the 1937 movie Nothing Sacred, which starred Fredric March and Carole Lombard. Proving that nothing is sacred in Hollywood, Lombard's role was played this time by Jerry Lewis, who gave a typically zany performance as a man who thinks he has had a hefty dose of radiation poisoning. Encouraged by his doctor (Martin), who knows very well it is only a sinus condition, and a newspaper reporter (Janet Leigh), who believes he is going to die and knows a good story when she sees one, Lewis takes a press-sponsored trip to New York for one final all-out binge. It was all very entertaining, but much of the original film's bite and satire seemed to be lost on the way. Two of Jule Styne and Bob Hilliard's songs, 'How Do You Speak To An Angel?' and 'Money Burns A Hole In My Pocket', became popular record hits, and Martin's relaxed and easy manner was ideal for the engaging 'That's What I Like' and a duet with Lewis, 'Ev'ry Street's A Boulevard (In Old New York)'. The other songs were 'Champagne And Wedding Cake' and 'You're Gonna Dance With Me, Baby'. Also featured were Edward Arnold, Fred Clark, Sheree North, Sig Ruman and Sammy White. Norman Taurog was the director and the film was shot in Technicolor. Styne and Hilliard also wrote the score for a 1953 Broadway musical based on this story. It was called Hazel Flagg, and ran for just 190 performances.

LIVINGSTON, JAY

b. 28 March 1915, Pittsburgh, Pennsylvania, USA. After studying music at school, Livingston attended the University of Pennsylvania where he met and formed a lasting friendship with Ray Evans (b. 4 February 1915, Salamanca, New York, USA) with whom he worked in shipboard bands on transatlantic and cruise liners. Their joint careers as songwriters were barely under way when they were interrupted by World War II. In the post-war years Livingston and Evans worked in Hollywood, writing songs for films. Their major success during this period was the title song from To Each His Own (1946). Other films they contributed to included The Cat And The Canary, On Stage Everybody, The Stork Club, My Favourite Brunette, Dream Girl, Whispering Smith, Samson And Delilah, Bitter Victory, The Great Lover, Sorrowful Jones, My Friend Irma, Fancy Pants, The Lemon Drop Kid, Here Comes The Groom, Aaron Slick From Punkin Crick, Thunder In The

East, Here Come The Girls, and *Red Garters*. While continuing their partnership, in which Livingston usually wrote the music and Evans the words, both men occasionally worked with other composers. Their joint successes included the Oscar-winning songs 'Buttons And Bows' (*The Paleface* 1948) and 'Mona Lisa' (*Capt. Carey, USA* 1950). Among their other movie songs were 'Golden Earrings' (music by Victor Young), 'My Love Loves Me', 'Silver Bells', 'I'll Always Love You', 'Home Cookin'', 'A Place In The Sun' (music by Franz Waxman), 'Never Let Me Go', and another Oscar winner and Doris Day hit, 'Whatever Will Be, Will Be (Que Sera, Sera)'. Throughout the 50s Livingston and Evans continued to turn out film songs such as 'Tammy' and 'Almost In Your Arms'. In 1958 they wrote the score for a Broadway show *Oh, Captain!*, which included 'Femininity'. In the 60s came 'The Arms Of Love' and 'Wait Until Dark', and the duo also wrote the themes for the television series *Bonanza* and *Mr. Ed*. In the 70s Livingston and Evans continued to write occasional material for films and television, and contributed to the Broadway musical *Sugar Babies*.

LLOYD WEBBER, ANDREW

b. 22 March 1948, London, England. The 'Sir Arthur Sullivan' of the rock age was born the son of a Royal College of Music professor and a piano teacher. His inbred musical strength manifested itself in a command of piano, violin and French horn by the time he had spent a year at Magdalen College, Oxford, where he penned *The Likes Of Us* with lyricist (and law student) Tim Rice. As well as his liking for such modern composers as Hindemith, Ligeti and Penderecki, this first musical also revealed a captivation with pop music that surfaced even more when he and Rice collaborated in 1967 on *Joseph And The Amazing Technicolor Dreamcoat*, a liberal adaptation of the scriptures. Mixing elements of psychedelia, country and French *chanson*, it was first performed at a London school in 1968 before reaching a more adult audience, via fringe events, the West End theatre (starring Paul Jones, Jess Conrad and Maynard Williams), an album, and, in 1972, national television.

In the early 70s, Lloyd Webber strayed from the stage, writing the music scores for two British films, *Gumshoe* and *The Odessa File*. His next major project with Rice was the audacious *Jesus Christ Superstar* which provoked much protest from religious groups. Among the studio cast were guest vocalists Michael D'Abo, Yvonne Elliman, Ian Gillan and Paul Raven (later Gary Glitter), accompanied by a symphony orchestra under the baton of André Previn - as well as members of Quatermass and the Grease Band. Issued well before its New York opening in 1971, the tunes were already familiar to an audience that took to their seats night after night as the show ran for 711 performances. A less than successful film version was released in 1973. After the failure of *Jeeves* in 1975 (with Alan Ayckbourn replacing Rice) Lloyd Webber returned to form with *Evita*, an approximate musical biography of Eva Peron, self-styled 'political leader' of Argentina. It was preceded by high chart placings for its album's much-covered singles, most notably Julie Covington's 'Don't Cry For Me Argentina' and 'Oh! What A Circus' from David Essex.

Evita was still on Broadway in 1981 when *Cats*, based on T.S. Eliot's *Old Possum's Book Of Practical Cats*, emerged as Lloyd Webber's most commercially satisfying work so far. It was also the composer's second musical without Rice, and included what is arguably his best-known song, 'Memory', with words by Eliot and the show's director, Trevor Nunn. Elaine Paige, previously the star of *Evita*, and substituting for the injured Judi Dench in the feline role of Grizabella, took the song into the UK Top 10. Subsequently, it became popular for Barbra Streisand, amongst others. With *Song And Dance* (1982), which consisted of an earlier piece, *Tell Me On Sunday* (lyrics by Don Black), and *Variations* composed on a theme by Paganini for his cellist brother, Julian, Lloyd Webber became the only theatrical composer to have three works performed simultaneously in both the West End and Broadway. Two items from *Song And Dance*, 'Take That Look Off Your Face' and 'Tell Me On Sunday' became hit singles for one of its stars, Marti Webb. Produced by Cameron Mackintosh and Lloyd Webber's Really Useful Company, it was joined two years later by *Starlight Express* (lyrics by Richard Stilgoe), a train epic with music which was nicknamed 'Squeals On Wheels' because the cast dashed around on roller skates pretending to be locomotives. Diversifying further into production, Lloyd Webber presented the 1983 comedy *Daisy Pulls It Off*, followed by *The Hired Man*, *Lend Me A Tenor* and Richard Rodgers and Lorenz Hart's *On Your Toes* at London's Palace Theatre - of which he had become the new owner.

Like Sullivan before him, Lloyd Webber indulged more personal if lucrative artistic whims in such as *Requiem*, written for his father, which, along with *Variations*, became a best-selling album. A later set, *Premiere Collection*, went triple platinum. A spin-off from *Requiem*, 'Pie Jesu' (1985), was a hit single for Paul Miles-Kington and Sarah Brightman, the composer's second wife. She made the UK Top 10 again in the following year, with two numbers from Lloyd Webber's *The Phantom Of The Opera* (adapted from the Gaston Leroux novel), duetting with Steve Harley on the title theme, and later with Cliff Richard on 'All I Ask Of You'. The original 'Phantom', Michael Crawford, had great success with his recording of another song hit from the show, 'The Music Of The Night'. Controversy followed, with Lloyd Webber's battle to ensure that Brightman re-created her role of Christine in the Broadway production in 1988. His US investors capitulated, reasoning that future Lloyd Webber creations were guaranteed box office smashes before their very conception. Ironically, *Aspects Of Love* (lyrics by Charles Hart and Don Black), which also starred Brightman (by now Lloyd Webber's ex-wife), was rated as one of the failures (it did not recoup its investment) of the 1990/1 Broadway season, although it eventually ran for over 300 performances. In London, the show, which closed in 1992 after a three year run, launched the career of Michael Ball, who had a UK number 2 with its big number, 'Love Changes Everything'. In April 1992, he intervened in the Tate Gallery's attempt to purchase a Canaletto. Anxious, that it should remain in Britain, he bought the picture for £10 million. He was reported as commenting 'I'll have to write another musical before I do this again'. That turned out to be *Sunset Boulevard*, a stage adaptation of Billy Wilder's 1950 Hollywood classic, with Lloyd Webber's music, and book and lyrics by Don Black and Christopher Hampton. It opened in London on 12 July 1993 with Patti LuPone in the leading role of Norma Desmond, and had its American premiere in Los Angeles five months later, where Desmond was played by Glenn Close. Legal wrangles ensued when Lloyd Webber chose Close to star in the 1994 Broadway production instead of LuPone (the latter is said to have received 'somewhere in the region of $1 million compensation'), and there was further controversy when he closed down the Los Angeles production after having reservations about the vocal talents of its prospective new star, Faye Dunaway. She too, is said to have received a 'substantial settlement'. Meanwhile, *Sunset Boulevard* opened at the Minskoff Theatre in New York on November 17 with a record box office advance of $37.5 million. Like *Cats* and *The Phantom Of The Opera* before it, the show won several Tony Awards, including best musical, score and book. Lloyd Webber was living up to his rating as the most powerful person in the American theatre in a list compiled by *TheaterWeek* magazine. His knighthood in 1992 was awarded for services to the theatre, not only in the US and UK, but throughout the world - at any one time there are dozens of his productions touring, and resident in main cities. Among his other show/song honours have been Drama Desk, Grammy, Laurence Olivier, and Ivor Novello Awards. *Cats*, together with *Starlight Express* and *Jesus Christ Superstar*, gave Lloyd Webber the three longest-running musicals in British theatre history for a time, before the latter show was overtaken by *Les Misérables.*. He is also the first person to have a trio of musicals running in London and New York. *Jesus Christ Superstar* celebrated its 20th anniversary in 1992 with a UK concert tour, and other Lloyd Webber highlights of that year included a series of concerts entitled *The Music Of Andrew Lloyd Webber* (special guest star Michael Crawford), a smash hit revival of *Joseph And The Amazing Technicolor Dreamcoat* at the London Palladium, and the recording, by Sarah Brightman and José Carreras, of Lloyd Webber and Don Black's Barcelona Olympic Games anthem 'Friends For Life' ('Amigos Para Siempre').

Since those heady days, Lloyd Webber admirers have waited in vain for another successful theatrical project, although there has been no shortage of personal kudos. He was inducted into the Songwriters Hall of Fame, presented with the Praemium Imperiale Award for Music, became the first recipient of the ASCAP Triple Play Award, and in 1996 received the Richard Rodgers Award for Excellence in the Musical Theatre. In the same year a revised version of his 1975 flop, *Jeeves*, entitled *By Jeeves*, was well received during its extended West End season, but a new work, *Whistle Down The Wind* (lyrics: Jim Steinman, book: Patricia Knop), failed to transfer to Broadway following its Washington premiere. After being extensively re-worked, it arrived in the West End in 1998. A revival of *Jesus Christ Superstar* re-opened the old Lyceum, just off the Strand, and a film version of *Evita*, starring Madonna, was released, containing a new Lloyd Webber-Rice song, 'You Must Love Me', for which they won Academy Awards. Elevated to the peerage in 1997,

Baron Lloyd-Webber of Sydmonton disclosed that the New York and London productions of *Sunset Boulevard*, which both closed early in that year, 'lost money massively overall', and that his Really Useful Group had reduced its staff and suffered substantial financial setbacks. On the brighter side, in January 1996 the West End production of his most enduring show, *Cats*, took over from *A Chorus Line* as the longest-running musical of all time, and in June 1997, the show's New York production replaced *A Chorus Line* as the longest-running show (musical or play) in Broadway history. Early in 1998, Lloyd Webber was honoured with *Variety*'s first British Entertainment Personality Of The Year Award.

● COMPILATIONS: *The Very Best Of ... Broadway Collection* (Polydor 1996)★★★.

● VIDEOS: *The Premier Collection Encore* (1994).

● FURTHER READING: *Andrew Lloyd Webber*, G. McKnight. *Fanfare: The Unauthorized Biography Of Andrew Lloyd Webber*, J. Mantle. *Andrew Lloyd Webber: His Life And Works*, M. Walsh.

LOCK UP YOUR DAUGHTERS

This show was the first to be presented at the new Mermaid Theatre in the City of London, on 28 May 1959, and was, appropriately enough, the brainchild of the Mermaid's founder, Bernard (later, Sir Bernard) Miles. His adaptation of Henry Fielding's *Rape Upon Rape* was an extremely bawdy tale in which a gentle maiden, Hilaret (Stephanie Voss), and her would-be rapist, Ramble (Frederick Jaeger), appear before the lecherous Justice Squeezum (Richard Wordsworth). Squeezum's efforts to inflict his own individual brand of custodial sentence on Hilaret lead to highly complicated manoeuvres that involve the far-from-innocent Mrs Squeezum (Hy Hazell), and result in the Justice himself going to prison. The object of his affections is then reunited with her true love, Captain Constant (Terence Cooper). The score, by two young newcomers, composer Laurie Johnson and lyricist Lionel Bart (Bart's *Fings Ain't Wot They Used T'Be* was just starting out at the Theatre Royal Stratford), complemented perfectly the lusty outrages of the story, in songs such as 'Lock Up Your Daughters' ('Here comes a rake!'), 'When Does The Ravishing Begin?', 'Red Wine And A Wench' and 'I'll Be There'. Hilaret *almost* seduces Squeezum in 'On A Sunny Sunday Morning', and the other delights included 'Lovely Lover', 'Kind Fate', 'A Proper Man', 'It Must Be True', ''Tis Plain To See' and 'Mr. Jones'. The show ran for 330 performances, and subsequently had its US premiere in New Haven in April 1960. *Lock Up Your Daughters* returned to the Mermaid two years later before transferring to the Her Majesty's theatre in the West End for a stay of some 16 months; it returned to the Mermaid in 1969 for a brief stay. Another American production, with 50s film star Carleton Carpenter as Squeezum, was presented at the Goodspeed Opera House in 1982.

LOCKYER, MALCOLM

b. Malcolm Neville Lockyer, 5 October 1923, Greenwich, London, England, d. 28 June 1976, England. Trained as an architect, Lockyer's interest in dance music dated from the age of 12, and he played semi-professionally until called up for war service as a musician in the Royal Air

Force at the age of 19. He played with Sid Phillips And His Quintet, and in 1944 he joined the Buddy Featherstonehaugh Sextet and recorded with them for Radion and HMV. After leaving the RAF, Lockyer worked as pianist with Ambrose, Cyril Stapleton and Robert Farnon. He started with BBC radio in 1945, and during his career he worked on almost 6,000 broadcasts. He formed his own orchestra in 1951. A prolific composer (often under the pseudonym Howard Shaw), his biggest successes were 'Friends And Neighbours' (for the 1954 BBC television series), 'Fiddler's Boogie' and 'The Big Guitar' (for the BBC television series *Stranger Than Fiction* - 1955). Lockyer scored over 30 feature films and also the television series *The Pursuers* and *The Pathfinders*. Together with Reg Owen he made a collection of albums for Top Rank with the Knightsbridge Strings and the Cambridge Strings. He succeeded Harry Rabinowitz as conductor of the BBC Revue Orchestra in 1960, and was associated with many radio shows, among them *Mid-day Music Hall*, *Take It From Here* and *Beyond Our Ken*. When the Revue and Variety orchestras were amalgamated in 1966 to form the new Radio Orchestra, Lockyer became associate conductor. His connection with Glenn Miller began in 1944, when he was stationed in Bedford at the same time as the famous American band leader. He was able to study at first-hand how that unmistakeable sound was achieved. Shortly before his death in 1976 he conducted the Million Airs Orchestra in 26 highly-successful Glenn Miller Tribute Concerts.

LOESSER, FRANK

b. Frank Henry Loesser, 29 June 1910, New York City, New York, USA, d. 28 July 1969. A leading songwriter for the stage, films and Tin Pan Alley from the 30s through to the 60s. Initially, he only wrote lyrics, but later in his career he provided both words and music, and sometimes co-produced through his Frank Productions. Born into a musical family (his father was a music teacher, and his brother a music critic and pianist), Loesser rejected a formal musical education, and trained himself. During the Depression years of the early 30s, following a brief spell at City College, New York, Loesser worked in a variety of jobs including city editor for a local newspaper, jewellery salesman and waiter. His first published song, written with William Schuman in 1931, was 'In Love With A Memory Of You'. Loesser also wrote for vaudeville performers and played piano in nightclubs around New York's 52nd Street. In 1936, he contributed some lyrics to *The Illustrators Show*, with music by Irving Actman, including 'Bang-The Bell Rang!' and 'If You Didn't Love Me', but the show closed after only five Broadway performances. In 1937, Loesser went to Hollywood and spent the next few years writing lyrics for movies such as *Cocoanut Grove* ('Says My Heart'), *College Swing* ('Moments Like This' and 'How'dja Like To Make Love To Me?'), *Sing You Sinners* (Bing Crosby singing 'Small Fry'), *Thanks For The Memory* (Bob Hope and Shirley Ross singing 'Two Sleepy People'), *The Hurricane* (Dorothy Lamour singing 'Moon Of Manakoora'), *Man About Town* ('Fidgety Joe' and 'Strange Enchantment'), *Some Like It Hot* (1939 film starring Bob Hope and Shirley Ross singing 'The Lady's In Love With

You'), *Destry Rides Again* (Marlene Dietrich with a memorable version of 'See What The Boys In The Backroom Will Have'), *Dancing On A Dime* ('I Hear Music'), *Las Vegas Nights* ('Dolores'), *Kiss The Boys Goodbye* ('I'll Never Let A Day Pass By', 'Sand In My Shoes' and the title song), *Sweater Girl* ('I Don't Want To Walk Without You' and 'I Said No'), *Forest Rangers* ('Jingle Jangle Jingle'), *Happy-Go-Lucky* ('Let's Get Lost' and "Murder' She Says'), *Seven Days Leave* ('Can't Get Out Of This Mood') and *Thank Your Lucky Stars* ('They're Either Too Young Or Too Old', sung by Bette Davis, and featuring one of Loesser's most amusing lyrics, including the couplet: 'I either get a fossil, or an adolescent pup/I either have to hold him off, or have to hold him up!'). These songs were written in collaboration with composers Burton Lane, Hoagy Carmichael, Alfred Newman, Matty Malneck, Frederick Hollander, Louis Alter, Victor Schertzinger, Jule Styne, Joseph Lilley, Jimmy McHugh and Arthur Schwartz. The first song for which Loesser wrote both music and lyrics is said to be 'Praise The Lord And Pass The Ammunition', and when he left Hollywood for military service during World War II he added some more service songs to his catalogue, including 'First Class Private Mary Brown', 'The Ballad Of Roger Young', 'What Do You Do In The Infantry?' and 'Salute To The Army Service Forces'. He also continued to write for films such as *Christmas Holiday* (1944, 'Spring Will Be A Little Late This Year') and *The Perils Of Pauline* (1947), the biopic of silent-movie queen Pearl White, with Loesser's songs 'Poppa Don't Preach To Me' and 'I Wish I Didn't Love You So', the latter of which was nominated for an Academy Award. Loesser finally received his Oscar in 1949 for 'Baby It's Cold Outside', from the Esther Williams/Red Skelton movie *Neptune's Daughter*. In 1948, Loesser wrote 'On A Slow Boat To China', which became a hit for several US artists including Kay Kyser, Freddy Martin, Eddy Howard and Benny Goodman. In the same year he again turned his attention to the Broadway stage, writing the score for a musical adaptation of Brandon Thomas's classic English farce, *Charley's Aunt*. *Where's Charley?*, starring Ray Bolger, included the songs 'My Darling, My Darling', 'Once In Love With Amy', 'The New Ashmoleon Marching Society And Student Conservatory Band' and 'Make A Miracle'. The show ran for a creditable 792 performances.

Far more successful, two years later, was *Guys And Dolls*, a musical setting of a Damon Runyon fable, starring Robert Alda, Vivian Blaine, Sam Levene, Isabel Bigley and Stubby Kaye. It ran for 1,200 performances, and is generally considered to be Loesser's masterpiece. As with *Where's Charley?*, he was now writing both music and lyrics, and the show is such a legend that it is worth listing the principal songs: 'Fugue For Tinhorns', 'The Oldest Established', 'I'll Know', 'A Bushel And A Peck', 'Adelaide's Lament', 'Guys And Dolls', 'If I Were A Bell', 'My Time Of Day', 'I've Never Been In Love Before', 'Take Back Your Mink', 'More I Cannot Wish You', 'Luck Be A Lady', 'Sue Me', 'Sit Down, You're Rockin' The Boat' and 'Marry The Man Today'. The original cast album is still available in the 90s, and among the other associated issues was an all-black cast album, released on the Motown label, and *Guys And Dolls: The Kirby Stone Four*. A film adaptation of *Guys*

And Dolls was released in 1955, starring Frank Sinatra, Marlon Brando, Jean Simmons and Vivian Blaine. The movie version left out some of the original songs, and Loesser replaced them with 'A Woman In Love' and 'Adelaide'. In 1952, *Where's Charley?* was released as a film version, and the same year saw a movie of *Hans Christian Andersen*, starring Danny Kaye in the title role, and featuring a Loesser score that included 'Wonderful Copenhagen', 'No Two People', 'Anywhere I Wander', 'Inchworm' and 'Thumbelina'. Loesser's next Broadway project was *The Most Happy Fella*, for which he also wrote the libretto. The show was adapted from the original story *They Knew What They Wanted*, by Sidney Howard, which told the tale of an elderly Italian winegrower living in California, who falls in love at first sight with a waitress. Loesser created what has been called 'one of the most ambitiously operatic works ever written for the Broadway musical theatre'. Arias such as 'Rosabella' and 'My Heart Is So Full Of You' contrast with more familiar Broadway fare such as 'Standing On the Corner', 'Big D' and 'Happy To Make Your Acquaintance'. The show ran for 676 performances, far more than Loesser's 1960 production of the folksy *Greenwillow*, which closed after less than three months. It starred Anthony Perkins in his first musical, and contained a religious hymn, the baptism of a cow, and wistful ballads such as 'Faraway Boy' and 'Walking Away Whistling', along with 'Never Will I Marry' and 'Summertime Love', both sung by Perkins. A three-album set was issued, containing the complete score. In terms of number of performances (1,417), Loesser's last Broadway show, which opened in 1961, was his most successful. *How To Succeed In Business Without Really Trying* was a satire on big business that starred Robert Morse as the aspiring executive J. Pierpont Finch, and Rudy Vallee as his stuffy boss, J.B. Biggley. The songs, which most critics agreed, fitted the plot neatly, included 'The Company Way', 'A Secretary Is Not A Toy', 'Grand Old Ivy', 'Been A Long Day', 'I Believe In You' and 'Brotherhood Of Man'. The show became one of the select band of American musicals to be awarded a Pulitzer Prize; a film version was released in 1967. Loesser died of lung cancer on 28 July 1969, with cigarettes by his side. A lifelong smoker, with a contentious, volatile temperament, he is regarded as one of the most original, innovative men of the musical theatre. In the early 90s *The Most Happy Fella*, *Guys And Dolls* and *How To Succeed In Business Without Really Trying*, were all revived on Broadway, and Loesser's second wife, Jo Sullivan, and one of his daughters, Emily Loesser, appeared in a provincial production of *Where's Charley?* In 1993, the two ladies also featured on the album *An Evening With Frank Loesser*, singing medleys of songs from his shows. Of even more interest, in the same year a fascinating album consisting of demo recordings by Loesser himself was released.

● ALBUMS: *An Evening With Frank Loesser* (1993)★★★, *Loesser By Loesser* (DRG 1993)★★★★.

● FURTHER READING: *A Most Remarkable Fella*, Susan Loesser.

LOEWE, FREDERICK

b. 10 June 1901, Vienna, Austria, d. 14 February 1988, Palm Springs, Florida, USA. A distinguished composer for the musical theatre, Loewe was born into a musical family (his father was a professional singer). He studied piano as a child, appearing with the Berlin Symphony Orchestra in 1917. In 1924, he visited the USA, but was unable to find work in a classical environment. Instead, he eked out a living playing piano in restaurants and bars, then roamed throughout the USA, tackling a variety of jobs, including boxing, prospecting and cowpunching. As a young teenager he had written songs and he resumed this activity in New York in the early 30s. Later in the decade he contributed to various musical shows, and in 1942 began to collaborate with lyricist Alan Jay Lerner. Their first Broadway score was for *What's Up?* in 1943, which was followed two year later with *The Day Before Spring*. From that point onwards, they wrote the music and lyrics (Lerner also contributed the librettos) for some of the most memorable productions in the history of the American musical theatre. They had their first hit in 1947 with *Brigadoon*, from which came 'The Heather On The Hill', 'From This Day On' and 'Almost Like Being In Love', and the association was renewed in 1951 with *Paint Your Wagon*, containing such lovely songs as 'They Call The Wind Maria', 'I Talk To The Trees' and 'Wand'rin' Star'. In 1956, the team had a major triumph with the legendary *My Fair Lady*, which ran on Broadway for 2,717 performances. The score included such lasting favourites as 'On The Street Where You Live', 'Get Me To The Church On Time', 'With A Little Bit Of Luck', 'Wouldn't It Be Loverly?', 'The Rain In Spain', 'Why Can't The English?', 'I'm An Ordinary Man' and 'I Could Have Danced All Night'. After the huge success of *My Fair Lady*, Lerner and Loewe were invited to write the script, music and lyrics for a musical film, and while Lerner was enthusiastic about the idea, Loewe was somewhat reluctant. Eventually he agreed, and together they created the incomparable *Gigi* (1958), one of the final flourishes of the old-style Hollywood musical. The magnificent score included 'Thank Heaven For Little Girls', 'I'm Glad I'm Not Young Anymore', 'I Remember It Well', 'The Night They Invented Champagne', and the charming title song. After being hospitalized with serious heart trouble, Loewe collaborated with Lerner on *Camelot*, which opened in 1960, and ran for over two years. Although the show's pre-production was marred with problems, the result was another success, with such outstanding songs as 'If Ever I Would Leave You' and 'How To Handle A Woman'. Afterwards, Loewe decided to retire, emerging briefly in the early 70s to work with Lerner on two unsuccessful projects - a stage adaptation of *Gigi* and the film *The Little Prince*.

LOGAN, ELLA

b. *c*.1913, Glasgow, Scotland, d. 1 May 1969. A member of a well-known theatrical family, Logan first appeared on the stage at the age of three, singing 'The End Of A Perfect Day' at the Grand Theatre in Paisley, Scotland. She became a popular singer during the 20s, performing with various bands and at many theatres in the UK and Europe. In 1932 she went to the USA to appear with Fred Waring's band and worked on radio, the stage and in films. Accompanying her to Hollywood was her three-year-old niece, Annie Ross. Logan appeared in a small number of musical films, including *Top Of The Town* (1937), *52nd Street* (1937) and *The Goldwyn Follies* (1938). Her stage appearances were more successful and included *Calling All Stars*, *George White's Scandals* and *Sons O'Fun*. During World War II Logan entertained troops in Africa, Italy and various other parts of the European campaign and then returned to the USA. In 1947 she appeared on Broadway, playing the role of Sharon McLonergan (Finian's daughter) in *Finian's Rainbow* at the 46th St Theatre, running for more than 500 performances. In the 50s and 60s she appeared at clubs and on television. A dynamic singer with great flair, Logan's varied career perhaps prevented her from attaining stardom in any one area. Apart from Ross, another famous relative is her nephew, Scottish comedian Jimmy Logan.

LONDON CALLING!

The name 'Noël Coward' went up in West End lights for the first time when this André Charlot revue opened at the Duke of York's Theatre on 4 September 1923. Coward also co-wrote the book, with Ronald Jeans, and the music and lyrics with Philip Braham. Also in the cast was Coward's favourite leading lady, Gertrude Lawrence, along with Maisie Gay, Eileen Molyneux, and comedian Tubby Edlin. Fred Astaire, who was appearing with his sister Adele in *Stop Flirting* at the Shaftesbury Theatre, arranged some of the dances. The songs included 'What Love Means To Girls Like Me', 'Carrie', 'Life In The Old Girl Yet', 'Sentiment', and 'Other Girls'. Gertrude Lawrence introduced one of Coward's most enduring numbers, 'Parisian Pierrot', and together they sang 'You Were Meant For Me', another future standard, written by Arthur Freed and Nacio Herb Brown. The show was a great success and Charlot decided to transfer Gertrude Lawrence and several other members of the company to the Broadway production of *André Charlot's London Revue Of 1924* which opened in January. After Joyce Barbour replaced Lawrence, *London Calling!* soon ran out of steam.

LONDON TOWN

This 1946 release, the first picture be made at 'Sound City Studios', Shepperton, England, after World War II, was an attempt to mount a lavish Technicolor British musical to rival the legendary Hollywood productions. It failed dismally, even though the American producer-director Wesley Ruggles was joined by several of his fellow countrymen including highly experienced songwriters Johnny Burke and Jimmy Van Heusen, and musical director-arranger Salvador 'Tutti' Camarata. The dreary and overly sentimental screenplay by Elliot Paul and Siegfried Herzig concerns ambitious comedian Jerry Ruggles (Sid Field), who is merely the understudy for star Charlie DeHaven (Sonnie Hale) in the West End production of *London Town*, until his fawning daughter, Peggy (14-years-old Petula Clark), gets to work. She persuades Charlie's dresser, Belgrave (Claude Hulbert), to feed him a potion which makes his face go green. Naturally, he cannot go on stage like that, so, step forward Jerry, the world of show business is at your feet. The delectable Kay Kendall rose above it all, and also trying their best were Greta Gynt, Tessie

O'Shea, Sonnie Hale, and Mary Clare. Jerry Desmonde, Sid Field's regular straight man, was also on hand to assist him in several of the celebrated comedian's classic routines, including his famous golfing sketch. 'My Heart Goes Crazy' was the big number, and it was reprised several times. Burke and Van Heusen's other songs consisted of an appealing ballad, 'So Would I' (introduced by Beryl Davis) 'You Can't Keep A Good Dreamer Down', and 'Any Way The Wind Blows'. Drummer-singer Jack Parnell turned up in 'The 'Amstead Way' production number which topped and tailed a knees-up medley of Cockney favourites such as 'Don't Dilly Dally On The Way' (Fred W. Leigh-Charles Collins), 'Any Old Iron' (Collins-Fred Terry-E.A. Sheppard), and 'Wot Cher' ('Knock 'Em In The Old Kent Road') (Albert Chevalier-Charles Ingle). The finalé, which featured an enormous grand piano with 10 men seated at the keyboard, reminded many of previous films in which the instrument was featured in a visually effective fashion, such as *King Of Jazz* and *Gold Diggers Of 1935*. Unfortunately, *London Town* was just not in the same class as either of those pictures. In America it was re-titled *My Heart Goes Crazy*

LOOKING THROUGH A GLASS ONION

Subtitled 'John Lennon In Word And Music', this one-man show consisted of 'a series of wry monologues spliced with the singer's songs, which attempted to unearth the man beneath the mythology'. It was written by the Australian-based, British-born actor John Waters, and toured successfully for two years in Australia before opening at the 600-seater newly-refurbished subterranean Criterion Theatre in London on 18 October 1993. Waters himself starred in the piece, backed by a band which included Stewart D'Arrietta on keyboards and Hamish Stewart on drums. The title image, from the song 'Glass Onion', 'seems to promise a peeling away of the layers of a crystal ball', but what actually transpires is a non-chronological narrative framework around the songs, beginning at the end with Lennon at the door of his New York apartment block watching an autograph hound coming towards him. Waters' 'exaggerated Liverpudlian twang' in the spoken passages, supplemented by a 'good bluesy voice' for the classic Beatles and later, subtler songs, brought him some critical appreciation, but the concept as a whole was generally considered to be 'charmless and depressing - a fraction of the real thing'. Reportedly capitalised at £160,000 and expected to make a profit after three months, closure on 1 January 1994 presumably resulted in a small loss.

LOST IN THE STARS

Following their collaboration on *Knickerbocker Holiday* in 1938, composer Kurt Weill and librettist and lyricist Maxwell Anderson renewed their association more than a decade later for this show which opened at the Music Box Theatre in New York on 30 October 1949. It was a musical adaptation of Alan Paton's novel, *Cry, The Beloved Country*, which was set in apartheid South Africa, and told the powerful story of a black Anglican minister, Stephen Kumalo (Todd Duncan), whose son, Absalom (Julian Mayfield), is sentenced to hang after accidentally killing a young white man - a liberal - during an attempted robbery in Johannesburg. A few minutes before Absalom is due to die, the victim's father, James Jarvis (Leslie Banks), who is a supporter of apartheid, calls at Stephen Kumalo's house, and the two men unite in their grief. The music score reflected the show's brooding, tragic mood, and included ''Thousands Of Miles', 'Cry, The Beloved Country', 'The Hills Of Ixipo', 'Train To Johannesburg', 'Stay Well', 'The Little Gray House', 'Trouble Man', 'Big Mole', 'A Bird Of Passage', 'The Wild Justice, 'Who Will Buy', and the haunting ballad, 'Lost In The Stars', which was sung in the piece by Todd Duncan, and has been recorded many times over the years by artists such as Tony Bennett, Vic Damone, Dick Haymes, Frank Sinatra, Lotte Lenya, and Singers Unlimited. It was to be Kurt Weill's last Broadway show - he died during the run of 273 performances, on 3 April 1950. Eight years later, *Lost In The Stars* entered the repertory of the New York City Opera, and, in 1972, it returned to Broadway for a month, starring Brock Peters as Stephen Kumalo. He also appeared in the 1974 film version, along with Melba Moore, Raymond St. Jacques, Clifton Davis, and Paula Kelly. The Long Wharf Theatre, New Haven, Connecticut, presented a 'chamber version' of the show in 1986, and the work received its UK professional premiere in a production by the New Sussex Opera at the Gardner Centre, Brighton, in 1991. Three years later, a new musical adaptation of Alan Paton's novel, by Frank Galati, was presented by the Goodman Theatre in Chicago. It used the book's title, *Cry, The Beloved Country*, and re-arranged the original score to such an extent that the Kurt Weill Foundation demanded that an apology be included in the showbill. Also in 1993, a 'fine new recording' of the score was issued, with a cast which included Arthur Woodley, Gregory Hopkins, Cynthia Clarey, Reginald Pindell, and Carol Woods, who had impressed in recent years in *Blues In The Night* and *The Goodbye Girl*.

LOUISIANA PURCHASE

This show, which made its debut at the Imperial Theatre in New York on 28 May 1940, was Irving Berlin's first Broadway score since his successful revue *As Thousands Cheer* brightened up America's gradual emergence from the Depression in 1933. In the intervening years, the prolific songwriter had scored several Hollywood films, including the classic Fred Astaire-Ginger Rogers musicals, *Top Hat*, *Follow The Fleet*, and *Carefree*. Morrie Riskin's humorous and satirical book was based on a story by B.G. 'Buddy' De Sylva, and was said to have been influenced by a recent political scandal involving Huey Long, a well-known Louisiana politician. The upstanding and incorruptible Senator Oliver P. Loganberry (Victor Moore), travels to New Orleans in an effort to disentangle the somewhat unconventional business methods practised by the Louisiana Purchase Company. The firm's lawyer, Jim Taylor (William Gaxton), tries to deflect the heat by putting the Senator in a series of compromising situations with the titillating trio of Marina Van Linden (Vera Zorina), Mme. Boredelaise (Irene Bordoni), and Beatrice (Carol Bruce). Happily, Loganberry emerges with his honour intact. As usual, Berlin's score complemented the

story perfectly. Two of the numbers, 'It's A Lovely Day Tomorrow', sung by Bordoni, and 'You're Lonely And I'm Lonely', which served as a duet for Moore and Zorina, became quite popular - the latter for Tommy Dorsey's Orchestra, with a vocal by the young Frank Sinatra. Carol Bruce made a memorable musical comedy debut, and sang the chirpy title song. The rest of the score included 'Outside Of That I Love You', 'Latins Know How', 'The Lord Done Fixed Up My Soul', 'Fools Fall In Love', 'What Chance Have I?', and 'You Can't Brush Me Off'. Chorus members, Hugh Martin and Ralph Blane, later went on to write the scores for *Best Foot Forward* on Broadway, and *Meet Me In St. Louis* in Hollywood. The presence of the familiar team of Gaxton and Moore ensured that *Louisiana Purchase* had a lot of laughs, and a successful run of 444 performances.

LOVE IN LAS VEGAS
(see *Viva Las Vegas*)

LOVE LIFE

A most unusual show, with music by Kurt Weill, and a book and lyrics by Alan Jay Lerner, *Love Life* opened at the 46th Street Theatre in New York on 7 October 1948 - just 18 months after *Brigadoon*, the author's first big Broadway success with Frederick Loewe. Contrasting sharply with *Kiss Me, Kate*, and *South Pacific*, which both made their debut in the same season, this unconventional show deals with a fantasy situation in which a married couple, Sam and Susan Cooper (Nanette Fabray and Ray Middleton) with their two children, reflect on their lives from the year 1791 until the present day - initially a happy, satisfying relationship, which declines into a pointless cynical arrangement - but without the protagonists aging at all. The individual scenes are linked by vaudeville acts, and no attempt is made to integrate the songs into the plot, such as it is - rather, they provide a commentary on the action that is taking place on the stage. Fabray had 'Green-Up Time' and 'Here I'll Stay' (which became a hit for Jo Stafford), and she won the 1949 Tony Award for best actress in a musical. The rest of the score included 'Progress', 'Economics', 'Mr. Right', and 'I Remember It Well', a title that Lerner remembered well enough to use it again in the Oscar-winning film, *Gigi*, in 1958. Considering the style and tone of the piece, a run of 252 performances seems to have been a reasonable outcome. In 1996, Weill and Lerner's 'vaudeville' received its 'first production outside the USA for 48 years'. The occasion was the show's European premiere at the Grand Theatre Leeds. Caroline Gawn directed an Opera North staging which starred Margaret Preece (Susan) and Alan Oke (Sam), with Geoffrey Dolton in the role of the *Cabaret*-style MC.

LOVE ME OR LEAVE ME

This realistic biopic of the popular 20s and 30s torch singer Ruth Etting was produced by Joe Pasternak for MGM in 1955. Daniel Fuchs won an Oscar for his original story which he and Isobel Lennart adapted for the absorbing screenplay. Doris Day shrugged off her 'goody-goody' image and gave a fine performance as the singer whose dramatic rise from dancehall hostess to nightclub and Ziegfeld star was masterminded by her gangster husband Martin 'Moe the Gimp' Snyder. James Cagney was outstanding as the domineering Snyder, whose response to his wife's relationship with her pianist (Cameron Mitchell) is to shoot him. Although cinematic convention (and box office returns) required a happy ending, there was enough reality left to make this a distinctive film. Most of the songs were authentic Etting favourites, and included 'Ten Cents A Dance' (Richard Rodgers-Lorenz Hart), 'Shaking The Blues Away' (Irving Berlin), 'It All Depends On You' (De Sylva, Brown And Henderson), 'You Made Me Love You' (Jimmy Monaco-Joseph McCarthy), 'Everybody Loves My Baby' (Jack Palmer-Spencer Williams), 'Mean To Me' (Roy Turk-Fred Ahlert), 'Sam The Old Accordion Man' (Walter Donaldson), 'My Blue Heaven' (Donaldson-George Whiting), 'At Sundown' (Donaldson) and the singer's theme song, 'Love Me Or Leave Me' (Donaldson-Gus Kahn). One of the new songs, 'I'll Never Stop Loving You', which was written by Nicholas Brodszky and Sammy Cahn, became a US Top 20 record hit for Doris Day. The strong supporting cast featured Robert Keith, Tom Tully, Harry Bellaver, Claude Stroud, Richard Gaines, Peter Leeds and Audrey Young. Alex Romero was the choreographer and Charles Vidor directed this popular, and sometimes intriguing, film that grossed over $4 million in the USA alone.

LOVE ME TENDER

Elvis Presley's first feature, released in 1956, cast the singer as one of three brothers who rob a bank. Strife over a share of the spoils is compounded by conflicting love interests, culminating with the Presley character's slaying, although he appears as a wraith in the final reel. Although cast as a miscreant, the singer had opted for a more conservatively styled film, a western, rather than embracing contemporary teen subcultures in the manner of *Rebel Without A Cause*. Indeed, he did not enjoy top billing - Richard Egan was the star - but interest naturally focused on Presley's performance. Critics were generally impressed, citing great potential, something tossed to the wind by much of the singer's subsequent film output. Although not a musical, the film's mournful title track gave the singer his third US chart-topper and *Love Me Tender* also featured the well-known 'weepie' 'Old Shep'. Again, by avoiding 'controversial' musical content, the Presley industry showed that, even at this early stage, a wider audience was being courted.

LOVE ME TONIGHT

This stylishly adventurous musical which was released by Paramount in 1932, bore many of the hallmarks of Ernst Lubitsch. However, it was, in fact, superbly directed by Rouben Mamoulian whose innovative work on dramatic films such as *Applause*, *City Streets* and *Dr. Jekyll And Mr. Hyde*, had already marked him out as a master of the medium. The sometimes risqué and satirical screenplay, by Samuel Hoffenstein, Waldemar Young, and George Marion Jnr., was set in France where a simple tailor (Maurice Chevalier) is passed off as a baron by the Vicomte de Vareze (Charlie Ruggles) who owes him a

great deal of money. Chevalier is eventually paid in full and also wins the hand of Princess Jeanette (Jeanette MacDonald). The film is brimful of memorable scenes, such as in the early moments when the city of Paris rouses itself from sleep, and especially the sequence in which one song, 'Isn't It Romantic?', is used to transport the action from place to place - a technique which was, at the time, entirely original. The lyric for that song was inextricably linked to the film's story, referring as it did to Chevalier's occupation as a 'tailor', and its composers, Richard Rodgers and Lorenz Hart, wrote a new set of words for the number's wider publication. Their score also contained another enduring standard, 'Lover', which was introduced by Jeanette MacDonald, and she had 'The Son Of A Gun Is Nothing But A Tailor', as well as duetting with Chevalier and others on 'A Woman Needs Something Like That', 'Love Me Tonight', and 'Song Of Paree'. Chevalier was his charming self on 'The Poor Apache', and, especially, 'Mimi'. Also among the cast were Charles Butterworth, Myrna Loy, C. Aubrey Smith, Elizabeth Patterson, and George 'Gabby' Hayes, who would eventually become a respected character actor in Western movies. *Love Me Tonight*, which is regarded by film buffs all over the world as one of the most perfect and important films in the history of the cinema, was photographed by Victor Milner and produced, as well as directed, by Rouben Mamoulian.

LOVE PARADE, THE

Sometimes called 'the first truly cinematic screen musical in America', *The Love Parade* was released by Paramount in 1929. Jeanette MacDonald, who was making her screen debut, co-starred with Maurice Chevalier in Ernest Vajda and Guy Bolton's adaptation of the French play, *Le Prince Consort*. The somewhat bawdy story concerned the Queen of Sylvania (Macdonald), who, having heard on the royal grapevine that her emissary-at-large, Count Alfred (Chevalier), is engaging in the wrong kind of foreign affairs, recalls him so that he can devote more of his energies to her. After he has measured up to her exacting standards, they marry, although her domination extends to the marriage certificate which reads 'wife and man'. Among the rest of the cast were British comedian Lupino Lane, Lillian Roth, Edgar Norton, Lionel Belmore, Virginia Bruce, and Jean Harlow. The score was written by Victor Schertzinger (music) and Clifford Grey (lyrics), and included 'Paris, Stay The Same', 'Dream Lover', 'Nobody's Using It Now', 'The Queen Is Always Right', 'March Of The Grenadiers', and 'Let's Be Common'. Chevalier and MacDonald excelled on 'Anything To Please The Queen' and 'My Love Parade', and the combination of the jaunty boulevardier and the unsophisticated, shrill soprano helped *The Love Parade* to become an enormous box-office winner. Much of the film's success was due to the innovative direction of Ernst Lubitsch, whose lavish settings, and consummate skill in the seamless blending of music, dialogue and action is constantly admired.

LUBITSCH, ERNST

b. 28 January 1892, Berlin, Germany, d. 30 November 1947, Bel Air, Los Angeles, California, USA. A celebrated

film director who took Hollywood by storm after moving to America in 1923. His reputation was based on a series of sophisticated comedies, first with silents, and then with talkies such as *Trouble In Paradise* (1932). In the early 30s, he did grace several immensely successful Paramount musicals - all of which starred Maurice Chevalier - with his highly individual, innovative and delightfully risqué 'Lusbitsch touch'. These were *The Love Parade, Paramount On Parade* (co-directed), *Monte Carlo, The Smiling Lieutenant, One Hour With You*, and *The Merry Widow* (1934). For a time during the 30s Lubitsch was the director of production at Paramount, and he continued work as a director on a variety of films into the 40s. The sole musical among them was 20th Century-Fox's *That Lady In Ermine*, starring Betty Grable, Douglas Fairbanks Jnr., and Cesar Romero. Sadly, it had to be completed by Otto Preminger after Lubitsch's death from a heart attack in 1947. A year earlier he had received a special Academy Award for 'his distinguished contributions to the art of the motion picture'.
● VIDEOS: *The Lubitsch Touch* (Universal Home Video/Image Entertainment 1997).

LUND, ART

b. Arthur London, 1 April 1915, Salt Lake City, Utah, USA, d. 2 June 1990, Salt Lake City, Iowa, USA. An actor and singer, with a fine, strong baritone voice and rugged good looks, Lund sang with Jimmy Joy's Band, before attracting the attention of Benny Goodman, in the late 30s. During his two spells with Goodman in the 40s, which were separated by a four-year stint with the US Navy in the South Pacific, he duetted with Peggy Lee on a recording of 'Winter Weather', and also sang on other band sides such as 'Don't Be A Baby, Baby', 'I Don't Know Enough About You' and 'Blue Skies'. When he went solo in 1947, Lund immediately had a US number 1 with Mack Gordon and Edmund Goulding's ballad, 'Mam'selle', which he followed, through until 1953, with other hits such as 'Peg O' My Heart', 'And Mimi', 'But Beautiful', 'Love Is So Terrific', 'Hair Of Gold' (with the Crew Chiefs), 'You Call Everybody Darling', 'On A Slow Boat To China', 'I've Got My Love To Keep Me Warm', 'Mona Lisa', 'Cincinatti Ding Dong', and 'Crying In The Chapel'. During the early 50s Lund appeared in a number of provincial productions of musicals such as *Wonderful Town, Fiorello!*, and *No Strings*, as well as various straight plays. In 1956, he created the role of Joey in *The Most Happy Fella*, on Broadway. He also appeared in the 1960 London production, starred in two New York City Center revivals. Lund's other Broadway musicals, *Donnybrook!* (1963), and *Sophie* (1963), a celebration of the life of Sophie Tucker, both flopped. From the 50s onwards, he appeared on US television in programmes such as *Gunsmoke, Little House On The Prairie*, and *The Rockford Files*, and in the late 60s he began to appear in feature films. In later years, Lund sang at Swing Era nostalgia nights, and was reported to be working in cabaret shortly before he died.
● ALBUMS: *This Is Art* (Brunswick 50s)★★, and Original Cast Recordings.
● FILMS: *The Molly Maguires* (1970), *Bucktown* (1975), *The Last American Hero* (1973).

LUPINO, STANLEY

(see Lane, Lupino)

LUPONE, PATTI

b. 21 April 1949, Northport, New York, USA. An actress and singer who left several well-known Hollywood and Broadway stars feeling bitterly disappointed and distraught when she won the role of Norma Desmond in Andrew Lloyd Webber's 1993 London production of *Sunset Boulevard*. LuPone made her stage debut, tap dancing, at the age of four, and later took dancing classes with Martha Graham. She trained for the stage at the Juilliard School where she met the actor Kevin Kline. A six-year personal relationship was supplemented by a joint association with John Housman's Actor's Company, which gave them both invaluable experience in the straight theatre, and resulted in their appearance together - as the bride and bridegroom - in a short-lived Broadway musical, *The Robber Bridegroom* (1975). After several other flops, including *The Baker's Wife* (1976) and *Working* (78), LuPone won Tony and Drama Desk Awards for her performance in the leading role of *Evita* (1979) on Broadway, and stayed with the show 'until the strain of being obnoxious and dying from cancer every night got too much'. She returned to serious theatre in the provinces and had occasionally effective roles in films such as *1941* and *Witness*. In 1985 LuPone moved to London and appeared firstly in *The Cradle Will Rock*. In the same year, she became the first American actress and singer to gain a principal role with the Royal Shakespeare Company, in the hit musical *Les Misérables*. The names of both shows appeared on her 1985 Olivier Award. In complete contrast to those two roles, in 1986 she played Lady Bird Johnson in a US mini-series based on the ex-President's life, and, a year later, was back on Broadway in an acclaimed revival of *Anything Goes*. In the late 80s and early 90s LuPone had a major role in the popular US situation comedy *Life Goes On*, and experienced some difficulty breaking free from her contract when the call came from Lloyd Webber. She first played Norma Desmond at the composer's Sydmonton Festival in the summer of 1992. Declining the use of the book on stage, she learnt the part and gave what was regarded as a 'sensational' performance. Soon afterwards it became obvious that she had stolen the role-of-a-lifetime from 'under the noses' of bigger names such as Meryl Streep, Angela Lansbury, Liza Minnelli, and Julie Andrews. *Sunset Boulevard* opened in the West End in July 1993, and although LuPone enjoyed a personal triumph, her contract to take the show to Broadway was cancelled, resulting in a pay-off 'in the region of $1 million'. During the remainder of the 90s LuPone appeared in New York in her own *Patti LuPone On Broadway* (1995) and as opera diva Maria Callas in Terrence McNally's *Master Class* on Broadway (1996) and in London (1997). Early in 1999, she took her acclaimed new concert act, *Matters Of The Heart*, to the Sydney Opera House, in Sydney, Australia. The eclectic programme included works by John Lennon And Paul McCartney, Richard Rodgers And Oscar Hammerstein, Randy Newman, and Cole Porter.
● ALBUMS: *Patti LuPone Live* 2-CD set (RCA Victor 1993),★★★★

Heatwave: Sings Irving Berlin (Philips 1995)★★★, and Original Cast recordings.
● FILMS: *1941* (1979), *Fighting Back* (1982), *Witness* (1985), *Wise Guys* (1986), *Driving Miss Daisy* (1989), *Family Prayers* (1993), *24-Hour Woman* (1998).

LYNNE, GILLIAN

b. 1926, Bromley, Kent, England. An internationally acclaimed director and choreographer with over 40 London and Broadway shows to her credit. Gillian Lynne was originally a dancer and made her stage debut with the Sadlers Wells Ballet in 1944, remaining with the company for seven years, during which time she played several leading roles. During the 50s she danced many times at the London Palladium, and played Claudine in *Can-Can* at the Coliseum. In 1960 she appeared in John Cranko's *New Cranks* at the Lyric, Hammersmith, and choreographed her first ballet, *Owl And The Pussycat*, for the Western Theatre Ballet. Since that time Lynne has worked as a choreographer and/or director on musical productions such as *The Roar Of The Greasepaint - The Smell Of The Crowd*, *The Match Girls*, *Pickwick*, *How Now Dow Jones*, *Tonight At Eight*, *Songbook*, *Tomfoolery*, *Once Upon A Time*, *My Fair Lady*, *Cabaret*, *Cats*, and *The Phantom Of The Opera*. Her work on *Cats* earned her an Laurence Olivier Award - one of four she owns - and the Austrian Government's Order of Merit for a production of the show which was presented in Vienna and subsequently played in East Berlin and Moscow. Her Paris production won the prestigious Moliére Award. She has also worked extensively for the Royal Shakespeare Company, the Royal Opera House, Covent Garden, and on more than 10 films including *Half A Sixpence*, *Man Of La Mancha*, and *Yentl*. Her television credits include *The Muppet Show* series, her own creation, *The Fool On The Hill*, which was based on the Beatles' music, and her BAFTA award-winning ballet *A Simple Man*. In the early 90s, as well as supervising and working on many other productions world-wide, she re-staged and choreographed the 1993 UK revival of Leslie Bricusse and Cyril Ornadel's musical, *Pickwick*, starring Harry Secombe and Roy Castle, and devised her first full-length ballet, *The Brontës*, which had its world premiere in Leeds early in 1995. Two years later, a series of workshop productions of 'a contemporary musical fable', *Anyone Who Had A Heart*, celebrating the works of Burt Bacharach and Hal David, based on an idea by Lynne and Kenny Solms and directed and choreographed by Lynne, were presented at New York's Roundabout Theatre. Also in 1997, Lynne was created a CBE for 'services to dance'. She was married to actor/producer Peter Land for 17 years before they separated in 1997.

MACDERMOT, GALT

b. 18 December 1928, Montreal, Canada. Nostalgia reared its grey and grizzly head at the Palace Theatre in New York when *George M!*, a celebration of the life and works of George M. Cohan, opened on 10 April 1968. Just under three weeks later, audiences at the nearby Biltmore Theatre came face to face (and other parts of the anatomy) with what many theatregoers felt was the 'grim reality' of the present and future, in the full-frontal shape of *Hair*, the 'American Tribal Rock Musical'. Galt MacDermot wrote the music for what was not so much a show as a social phenomenon, and the book and lyrics were by Gerome Ragni (b. 1943, Pittsburg, USA, d. 10 July 1991, New York, USA) and James Rado. The trio won Grammy Awards for the cast album which spent over a year in the US chart and spawned several hit singles, the most successful of which was probably the Fifth Dimension's 'Aquarius/Let The Sunshine In'. During the 1970s, MacDermot's compositions featured in a variety of productions, including *Isabel's A Jezebel* (1970, London), *Two Gentlemen Of Verona* (Tony Award), *Dude, Via Galactica, Take This Bread*, an oratorio, *Vieux Carré, I Took Panama*, and *The Sun Always Shines On The Cool* (1979). In 1984, his musical *The Human Comedy*, lasted for less than two weeks on Broadway, and was revived by the West Coast Ensemble in Hollywood as part of their 1993 season. For some considerable time during the late 80s MacDermot collaborated with the West Indian poet and playwright Derek Walcott on the score for *Steel*, which eventually had its world premiere at Cambridge, Massachusetts, in May 1991. His music for the show was a cosmopolitan mixture of calypso, blues, gospel, and ballads. A reminder, perhaps, of his early days - even before *Hair* - when his instrumental composition, 'African Waltz', won two Grammys and an Ivor Novello Award, and became a UK hit in 1961 for British jazzman Johnny Dankworth.
● ALBUMS: *Disin-Hair-ited* (*c.*70s)★★★, *Haircuts* (*c.*70s)★★★.

MACDONALD, JEANETTE

(see Eddy, Nelson, And Jeanette MacDonald)

MACK AND MABEL

High up on the list of fondly remembered flops - mainly through the medium of its superb Original Cast recording - this show ran on Broadway for only two months. It opened at the Majestic Theatre in New York on 6 October 1974, with what must have seemed a stellar cast. It had David Merrick, the premiere producer of musicals throughout the 60s, director and choreographer Gower

Champion, a book by Michael Stewart, a score by Jerry Herman (*Mame* and *Hello, Dolly!*), and, best of all, two outstanding performers, Robert Preston and Bernadette Peters, supported by Lisa Kirk and James Mitchell - and it still failed. The story is told in flashback: one of the great comedy silent movie innovators, Mack Sennett (Preston), remembers the early days and his first studio in Brooklyn ('Movies Were Movies'). He takes a sandwich delivery girl, Mabel Normand (Bernadette Peters), and puts her into pictures, but neither their private or professional relationship is satisfactory ('I Won't Send Roses'), and when Mabel gets the offer of a serious part, she walks out on him. The story ends in 1938, with Sennett leaving the movie business for ever. As well as Preston's 'Movies Are Movies' and 'I Won't Send Roses', (which is reprised as 'Who Needs Roses?' by Peters), the delightful and lively score included 'Look What Happened To Mabel', 'Big Time', 'I Wanna Make The World Laugh', 'Wherever He Ain't', 'Hundreds Of Girls', 'When Mabel Comes Into The Room', 'My Heart Leaps Up', 'Time Heals Everything', 'Tap Your Troubles Away', and 'I Promise You A Happy Ending'. In spite of receiving several Tony nominations (none of which were for Herman), it just did not catch on and closed after 65 performances, losing an estimated $800,000. Two years later a new production, with a revised book, toured with David Cryer, Lucie Arnez, and Tommy Tune, and, since that time, there have been several US provincial presentations, including one at the Paper Mill Playhouse in 1988, with Lee Horsley as Sennett and Janet Metz as Mabel. In the UK, interest was aroused in the show when its overture was used by Torvill and Dean, in their successful bid for a gold medal in the Olympic Ice Dancing Championship in 1984. A BBC Radio 2 disc jockey, David Jacobs, began playing tracks from the album, and 'I Won't Send Roses', in particular, became one of the station's easy-listening favourites. However, it was not until November 1995 that *Mack And Mabel* travelled to London's West End, via the Leicester Haymarket Theatre. Paul Kerryson's production, which starred Howard McGillin and Caroline O'Connor, had some revisions to the book (which has always been considered to be the problem with this show), including the introduction of a more upbeat ending, and no mention of Mabel's death in 1930. There were also two additional songs, 'Mack And Mabel' and 'Hit 'Em On The Head', which were not on the original album. Critical reviews were mixed, although O'Connor was generally hailed as 'a new star', and the show settled in long enough for McGillin to be replaced by James Smillie.

MACKINTOSH, CAMERON

b. 17 October 1946, Enfield, England. 'The Czar of theatrical producers' - that is what the American magazine *TheatreWeek* called him in 1993 when they rated him number 3 in their list of the 100 Most Powerful People in American Theatre. The son of a Maltese-born mother and a Scottish father, Mackintosh attended a small public school in Bath and became obsessed by the musical theatre at the age of eight after being taken to see a production of Julian Slade's *Salad Days* at Bristol Old Vic in 1954. After leaving school, where he was known as Darryl F.

Mackintosh, he attended the Central School for Speech and Drama for a year before becoming an assistant stage manager at the Theatre Royal, Drury Lane when *Camelot* was running. His first forays into producing came with some budget-priced touring shows before he moved into the West End in 1969 with a revival of *Anything Goes*. It proved to be a disaster and was withdrawn after 27 performances. *Trelawny* (1972) and *The Card* (1973) fared better, and, after a number of provincial productions of varying degrees of profitability, Mackintosh's breakthrough finally came in 1976 with *Side By Side By Sondheim*.

During the next few years he mounted successful revivals of *Oliver!*, *My Fair Lady*, and *Oklahoma!*, before his meeting with Andrew Lloyd Webber resulted in *Cats* in 1981. The show transformed the lives of both men, and became the prototype for future productions which overthrew the old style of musical and provided a simple and vivid theatrical experience that did not rely on big name stars, and was easily exportable. In the 80s Mackintosh went from strength to strength with *Song And Dance*, *Les Misérables*, *The Phantom Of The Opera*, and *Miss Saigon* (1989). In 1990 the latter show provided an example of just how powerful Mackintosh had become when American Equity initially objected to the casting of Jonathan Pryce in the Broadway production 'because it would be an affront to the Asian community'. After the producer threatened to withdraw the show altogether - and one or two others as well - capitulation was more or less immediate. The incident did nothing to improve the producer's ruthless (he prefers 'relentless') reputation with the New York theatre community, many of whom object to his dictatorial attitude and 'flashy' marketing methods. For some reason he deliberately did not use those ploys when his London hit, *Five Guys Named Moe*, transferred to Broadway, and that may well be one of the reasons for its relatively poor showing.

In 1992 Mackintosh was involved with a rare flop which some say marked the beginning of his decline. *Moby Dick* ('a damp squib . . . garbage') is reported to have cost him £1 million and a great deal of pride during its 15-week run, and he hinted at the time that he may be past his peak. However, the highly impressive monetary facts continued to emerge: a personal salary of over £8 million in 1991, the 39th richest man in Britain, and the acquisition of a substantial stake in two West End theatres, the Prince of Wales and the Prince Edward. His love of musicals - that is all he seems to be interested in producing - has caused Mackintosh to divert some of his reported £300 million wealth to a number of extremely worthy causes. As well as numerous donations to small theatrical projects, he provided £2 million to endow Oxford University's first professorship in drama and musical theatre, and his £1 million gift to the Royal National Theatre has enabled it to mount highly acclaimed revivals of *Carousel* and *Sweeney Todd*, the first two in a series of five classic musicals. It is not all philanthropy: Mackintosh is reported to retain the rights to the productions when they are eventually produced in the commercial sector. His kudos have included the 1991 *Observer* Award for Outstanding Achievement, and the prestigious Richard Rodgers Award for Excellence in Musical Theatre (1992). Previous recipients have been Harold Prince, Julie Andrews and Mary Martin. In 1994, Mackintosh's major revival of *Oliver!* opened at the London Palladium, starring Jonathan Pryce, and in 1995 his production company, Cameron Mackintosh Limited, earned a Queen's Award for Export Achievement. Two years earlier, for the benefit of an awe-struck journalist, he had attempted to remember all the musicals he had running in various parts of the world. They included six *Cats*, 20 *Phantom Of The Opera*, 12 *Les Misérables*, seven *Miss Saigon*, four *Five Guys Named Moe*, two *Follies* . . . et cetera, et cetera, as Yul Brynner used to say.

In July 1996, following on from *Les Misérables* and *Miss Saigon*, a third collaboration between Mackintosh and the creative team of Alain Boublil and Claude-Michel Schönberg, entitled *Martin Guerre*, opened in London. However, it failed to live up to its illustrious predecessors, and folded after a 20-month run. On a rather smaller scale, Mackintosh's *The Fix*, a 'daring new musical', also incurred the critics' wrath when presented at the Donmar Warehouse in 1997. Mackintosh received a knighthood for 'services to the musical theatre' in the 1995 New Year Honours List, and three years later was presented with the Bernard Delfont Award by the Variety Club of Great Britain. In June 1998, two charity performances of *Hey Mr Producer! The Musical World Of Cameron Mackintosh* at London's Lyceum Theatre saluted the impresario's 30 years in showbusiness. Later in the year, he was supervising the Sondheim revue *Putting It Together* (Mark II, with Carol Burnett) in Los Angeles, *Martin Guerre* (Mark III) in Yorkshire, England, and the US premiere of George Stiles and Anthony Drewe's Vivian Ellis Award-winning musical, *Just So* (Mark numerous), at Goodspeed, Connecticut.

● ALBUMS: *Hey Mr Producer!* 2-CD set (First Night 1998)★★★.

● VIDEOS: *Hey Mr Producer!* (VCI 1998).

● FURTHER READING: *Hey Mr Producer!: The Musicals Of Cameron Mackintosh*, Sheridan Morley and Ruth Leon.

MacRae, Gordon

b. 12 March 1921, East Orange, New Jersey, USA, d. 24 January 1986, Lincoln, Nebraska, USA. A popular singer on record, radio and in films during the 50s, MacRae was the son of local radio celebrity Wee Willie MacRae, and often worked on radio as a child actor before joining the Millpond Playhouse in New York. There he met actress Sheila Stephens who became his first wife in 1941. After winning an amateur singing contest at the 1939/40 New York World's Fair, he sang for two weeks with the Harry James and Les Brown bands. While working as a pageboy at NBC Radio, he was heard by bandleader Horace Heidt who signed him for two years, during which time he appeared with Heidt, James Stewart and Paulette Goddard in a movie about Heidt's radio giveaway show, *Pot O' Gold*. After serving in the US Army Air Force Corps in World War II, MacRae returned to New York to take a singing role in the 1946 Broadway revue *Three To Make Ready*, starring Ray Bolger. In 1947, he signed to Capitol Records and had a string of hits up to 1954, including 'I Still Get Jealous', 'At The Candlelight Cafe', 'It's Magic', 'Hair Of Gold, Eyes Of Blue', 'So In Love', 'Mule Train'/'Dear Hearts And Gentle People' and 'Rambling Rose'. After a four-year gap, he

entered the US charts again in 1958 with 'The Secret'. MacRae also made a series of successful singles with ex-Tommy Dorsey singer Jo Stafford. These included 'Say Something Sweet To Your Sweetheart', 'Bluebird Of Happiness', 'My Darling, My Darling' (a US number 1), 'A-You're Adorable', 'Need You', 'Whispering Hope', 'Bibbidi-Bobbidi-Boo' and 'Dearie'. MacRae's film career, mostly for Warner Brothers, started in 1948 with a non-singing role in *The Big Punch*. This was followed by a series of musicals that included *Look For The Silver Lining* (1949) and *The Daughter Of Rosie O'Grady* (1950), both co-starring June Haver, and four films in which he was partnered by Doris Day: *Tea For Two* (1950), *West Point Story* (1950), *On Moonlight Bay* (1951) and *By The Light Of The Silvery Moon* (1953). Among his other screen appearances were roles in *The Desert Song* (1953), co-starring Kathryn Grayson, and *Three Sailors And A Girl* (1953), with Jane Powell. In 1955 and 1956 he had the two most satisfying film parts of his career, when he played opposite Shirley Jones in highly successful adaptations of the Broadway shows *Oklahoma!* and *Carousel*. Also in 1956, MacRae appeared in his last film musical as Buddy De Sylva in *The Best Things In Life Are Free*, a biopic of the 20s/30s songwriting team of De Sylva, Brown And Henderson. In 1979, he made one final film appearance, in a dramatic role in *The Pilot*. In the mid-50s, MacRae was also popular on US television as the singing host of *The Railroad Hour*, *The Colgate Comedy Hour*, and his own *Gordon MacRae Show*. After divorcing his first wife, he was remarried in 1967 to Elizabeth Lambert Schrafft. In the same year, he made his first Broadway musical appearance since 1946, replacing Robert Preston in *I Do! I Do!* In the 70s he struggled with alcoholism and, in the early 80s, claimed that he had won the battle. He died from cancer of the mouth and jaw in January 1986.

● ALBUMS: with Jo Stafford *Songs Of Faith* 10-inch album (Capitol 1950)★★, *Prisoner Of Love* film soundtrack (MGM 1952)★★★, with various artists *Roberta* 10-inch album (Capitol 1952)★★★, with various artists *Merry Widow* 10-inch album (Capitol 1952)★★★, with Lucille Norman *New Moon/Vagabond King* film soundtrack (Capitol 1952)★★★, with Stafford *Sunday Evening Songs* 10-inch album (Capitol 1953)★★★, with various artists *The Desert Song* (Capitol 1953)★★★★, with various artists *Student Prince* 10-inch album (Capitol 1953)★★★, *By The Light Of The Silvery Moon* film soundtrack (Capitol 1953)★★, *The Red Mill* film soundtrack (Capitol 1954)★★★, with Stafford *Memory Songs* (Capitol 1954)★★★, *Romantic Ballads* (Capitol 1955)★★★, *Oklahoma!* film soundtrack (Capitol 1955)★★★★★, *Carousel* film soundtrack (Capitol 1956)★★★★★, *Operetta Favourites* (Capitol 1956)★★★★, *The Best Things In Life Are Free* (Capitol 1956)★★★, *Motion Picture Soundstage* (Capitol 1957)★★★, *Cowboy's Lament* (Capitol 1957)★★★, *Gordon MacRae In Concert* (Capitol 1958)★★, *This Is Gordon MacRae* (Capitol 1958)★★★★, *Seasons Of Love* (Capitol 1959)★★★, with Stafford *Whispering Hope* (Capitol 1962)★★★, with Stafford *Peace In The Valley* (Capitol 1963)★★, with Stafford *Old Rugged Cross* (Capitol 1963)★★★.

● COMPILATIONS: *Best Of The Capitol Years* (Capitol 1990)★★★★.

● FURTHER READING: *Hollywood Mother Of The Year: Sheila MacRae's Own Story*, Sheila MacRae with Paul Jeffers.

MAD ABOUT MUSIC

Deanna Durbin was only 17 years old when she made this film in 1938, but her 'significant contribution in bringing to the screen the spirit and personification of youth', gained her a special Academy Award in the same year. In *Mad About Music* she once again plays a character bursting with imagination and energy, who, after being deposited in a swanky Swiss finishing school by her narcissistic actress mother (Gail Patrick), comes up with a father who is simply the product of that same fertile imagination. Invited to produce him for inspection, the youngster offers a rather puzzled visitor (Herbert Marshall) as her partner in the collusion. It was all good fun, and also taking part were Jackie Moran, Arthur Treacher, William Frawley, Helen Parrish, Marcia Mae Jones. The musical highlight was Miss Durbin's spirited rendering of 'I Love To Whistle' with Cappy Barra's Harmonica Band. Harold Adamson and Jimmy McHugh wrote that tune, along with 'Serenade To The Stars', 'Chapel Bells', and 'There Isn't A Day Goes By'. Durbin also joined the Vienna Boys' Choir in a beautiful version of 'Ave Maria' (Charles Gounod). Norman Taurog directed this highly popular feature which attracted several Oscar nominations, two of which went to Marcella Burke and Frederick Kohner, the writers of the story on which Bruce Manning and Felix Jackson's screenplay was based. It received another airing in 1956 when *Mad About Music* was remade as *Toy Tiger* starring Jeff Chandler and Laraine Day, with Tim Hovey in the Deanna Durbin part.

MADAME SHERRY

With music by Hugo Felix and a book by Maurice Ordonneau, this 'Musical Vaudeville' or 'French Vaudeville', was presented in Paris and Berlin in 1902, and in London a year later. By the time it opened at the New Amersterdam Theatre in New York on 30 August 1910, it had been radically reworked, and had music by Karl Hoschna and a book and lyrics by Otto Harbach. The complicated story involves Edward Sherry (Jack Gardner), whose wealthy uncle Theophilus (Ralph Herz), sets him up in his own Sherry School of Aesthetic Dancing. Edward succeeds in convincing his uncle that his housekeeper, Catherine (Elizabeth Murray), is his wife and two of the dancing pupils are his children. At the time, Edward loves Lulu (Frances Demarest), one of his terpsichorean teachers, but, by the end of the piece he has transferred his affections to Yvonne (Lina Abarbanell), who, fresh from the convent school, accedes to the title of Madame Sherry. Hoschna and Harbach's score contained 'Every Little Movement' ('Has a meaning of its own'), which became an enormous hit and a firm favourite in vaudeville and music halls through the years. The Dorsey Brothers Orchestra had some success with it, and the number was also featured in several 40s film musicals such as *Presenting Lily Mars* (Judy Garland), *Shine On Harvest Moon*, and *The Jolson Story*. The rest of the composers' score included 'The Smile She Means For You, 'I Want To Play House With You', and 'The Birth Of Passion'. Another song, 'Put You Arms Around Me Honey', which was written by Albert Von Tilzer and Junie McCree, and interpo-lated into the show, became extremely popular. It also turned up in several movie musicals including two Betty Grable vehicles, *Coney Island* and *Mother Wore Tights*. Lina Abarbanell was the main star of the piece, but comedienne Elizabeth Murray also made a strong impression, and helped the show enjoy a run of 231 performances. She went on to further success in *High Jinks, Watch Your Step*, and *Sidewalks Of New York*.

MADDIE

She got around quite a bit, this lady, after her early development at Stephen Sondheim's Oxford University master classes. There were workshops in London at the Lilian Bayliss Theatre, the Players Theatre, and the Royal National Theatre studio that is dedicated to trying out new work, before she was 'picked up' by producer Kenny Wax. He gave her a full professional production at the regional Salisbury Playhouse in the autumn of 1996. A year later, *Maddie* moved into the West End's Lyric Theatre on the 29 September 1997. Eight years had passed since co-author and lyricist Steven Dexter had been impressed by the movie *Maxie*, starring Glenn Close and Mandy Patinkin, which was based on Jack Finney's novel *Marion's Wall*. Dexter and Shaun McKenna's libretto for this show also takes that book as its source. Set in 1981, it concerns San Francisco residents Nick Cheyney (Graham Bickley), a museum curator, and his wife Jan Cheyney (Summer Rognlie). Their marriage is in the doldrums, but while scraping the old paper off the walls of their apartment, they discover a message scrawled underneath which reads: 'Madeline Marsh - Read It and Weep - June 14 1926'. Nick becomes obsessed with Ms. Marsh, especially after the couple's ageing piano-playing landlord Al Turner (Kevin Colson), explains that Madeline was a 20s flapper who was on the brink of stardom when she was killed on the way to a crucial screen test. Having been re-discovered, Madeline (Summer Rognlie again of course) - all liberation and passion - takes possession of Jan's prim and uptight body for her comeback. This situation causes all sorts of complications, not least for Nick, who has to look on while the 80-year-old Al, in turn, takes possession of his young wife. Lynda Baron - marvellous as usual - played the 'superannuated predatory sexpot' Cordelia Van Arc, and there were other excellent performances from Beth Tuckey (Bernice Klein), Jon Rumney (Irving), Russell Wilcox (Hugo Dahl), Michael A. Elliott (O'Hara), Paddy Glynn (Natalie Brownlow), Louise Davidson (Saffron), Nicola Filshie (Young Maddie), and Martin Parr (Young Al). Stephen Keeling and Shaun McKenna's score included 'Don't Look Back', 'Maddie Dancing', 'Knick Knacks' (lyric: Anthony Drewe), 'Ghost', 'I'll Find Time For You', 'Easy', 'I'll Have My Way', 'The Time Of My Life', 'Star', 'One More Day', 'I've Always Known', 'Suzi's', 'From Now On', 'Afraid', 'Star Reprise', 'At The Gates', and 'If Not For Me'. Musical staging was by David Toguri and Jenny Arnold, and the director was Martin Connor. This was an 'old fashioned musical comedy', i.e. not 'sung through', and the London scribes were unimpressed, comparing it unfavourably to Noël Coward's *Blithe Spirit*. Summer Rognlie was either the next Ethel Merman, or 'loud, brash, and in your face', while the production as a whole seemed to be 'babble, balderdash and baloney . . . the silliness and soppiness of it all beggars belief'. This was particularly unfortunate because one of their number, a respected broadsheet critic, had raved about the Salisbury production to such an extent that the newspaper's readers came up with £150,000 to help finance the West End production. That sum, and more, went down the drain when this 'Magical New Musical' did a disappearing trick on 8 November with estimated losses of £500,000.

MADE

A cheerless 1972 film, *Made* starred Carol White (*Cathy Come Home*, *Poor Cow*) as a struggling single parent mistreated by those around her. The role of her musician lover was initially offered to Marc Bolan, but it was desolate folk singer Roy Harper who secured the part. Both he and White were excellent in their roles, although the depressing situation of the latter ensures that watching *Made*, although thought-provoking, is not a pleasurable experience. Harper contributed several songs, marked by *de rigueur* personal ruminations, but the power of the film is derived from its script and John Mackenzie's sympathetic direction. A minor classic, *Made* continues the atmosphere of early 60s' 'kitchen sink' drama.

MAGGIE MAY

Lionel Bart, who liked to have a hand in most aspects of his shows, concentrated on writing just the music and lyrics for this one which opened at the Adelphi Theatre in London on 22 September 1964. His librettist was the Liverpudlian playwright Alun Owen, an appropriate choice considering that the story was set in and around the Liverpool Docks. Bart's project was inspired by the traditional ballad about a local prostitute, which was sung by the sailors and dockworkers in the area. In Owen's dramatic book dealing with trades union ethics and disputes, the streetwalker, Margaret Mary Duffy (Rachel Roberts), loses her childhood sweetheart, Patrick Casey (Kenneth Haigh), after he dies trying to prevent a shipload of arms going to South America. As in previous shows such as *Fings Ain't Wot They Used T'Be*, *Blitz!*, and *Oliver!*, Bart's score caught the mood and the style of the piece perfectly. The songs ranged from attractive ballads such as 'It's Yourself', 'The Land Of Promises', 'Lullaby', 'I Love A Man', and 'The Ballad Of The Liver Bird', to the more lively 'I Told You So', 'Dey Don't Do Dat T'day', 'Leave Her, Johnny, Leave Her', 'Shine, You Swine', 'We Don't All Wear D'Same Size Boots', 'Maggie, Maggie May', and 'It's Yourself'. The critics were divided, but the public took to the show, partly perhaps because anything to do with Liverpool was of interest while the Beatles, and several other local groups, were constantly storming the pop charts. *Maggie May* had a highly respectable run of 501 performances, and also introduced a future star to the West End in the shape of Julia McKenzie who took over from Rachel Roberts occasionally. Part of Bart's score reached a wider audience when Judy Garland recorded four of the songs from the show, 'Maggie May', 'There's Only One Union', 'Land Of Promise', and 'It's Yourself', on an EP record. In 1992, nearly 30 years later, the National Youth Theatre of Great Britain mounted an acclaimed pro-

duction of *Maggie May* at London's Royalty Theatre. It was a welcome feature of Lionel Bart's UK renaissance.

MAGIC SHOW, THE

Proof of the unpredictability of musical theatre audiences, this show, which was merely a series of spectacular setpiece magical illusions linked by a flimsy plot, opened at the Cort Theatre in New York on 28 May 1974, and closed over four-and-a-half years later after an incredible 1,920 performances. Stephen Schwartz, who can usually be relied upon to conjure up something out of the ordinary himself, wrote the music and lyrics, and the book was the work of Bob Randall. The latter dealt with the sad tale of a New Jersey nightspot, The Passaic Top Hat, which is saved from debt and the road to the depths of degradation, by the arrival of a magic act. Doug Henning was the wizard who made everything well, and he really was the star of the show, with a supporting cast made up of Dale Soules, David Ogden Stiers, and Anita Morris. The songs included 'Up To His Old Tricks', 'Lion Tamer', 'Style', 'West End Avenue', and 'The Goldfarb Variations'. 'Goldfarb' is a familiar name in musical comedy history. George and Ira Gershwin immortalised the taxi driver-turned sheriff in *Girl Crazy* (1930), with their song, 'Goldfarb! That's I'm!'

MAGICAL MYSTERY TOUR

Originally made for television and first screened by the BBC on Boxing Day 1967, *Magical Mystery Tour* was mauled by critics upon release. Yet the film has much to commend it, not least several excellent songs by the Beatles, who wrote, produced and directed the entire proceedings. However, the bulk of responsibility fell upon Paul McCartney, who mooted the idea. *Magical Mystery Tour* has a very simple premise, that of a coach trip to places unknown, but given the period in which it was filmed, events inevitably take on a psychedelic hue. Indeed, it has been claimed the plot was inspired by Ken Kesey's Merry Pranksters, who traversed the USA in a painted bus consuming hallucinogenics on the way. Given the Beatles' eminent position and the era's penchant for self-indulgence, several scenes meander to little purpose, but equally there are many memorable moments and characters. These include the wonderful outdoor scenes accompanying 'The Fool On The Hill', the cornucopia of images surrounding 'I Am The Walrus' and John Lennon's hilarious role as the waiter serving spaghetti with a spade to Ringo Starr's Aunt Jessie. The Bonzo Dog Doo-Dah Band make an excellent cameo appearance and Scottish raconteur Ivor Cutler is superb as Buster Bloodvessel. Over the years since its release, *Magical Mystery Tour* has been the subject of re-evaluation and it is now held in greater esteem. Yet if opinion over the film's merits were largely negative in 1967, this was not the case with the soundtrack (double) EP collection which reached number 2 in the UK charts while the Beatles' 'Hello Goodbye' held the top spot. In the USA a proper album was issued, bolstered by the inclusion of strong tracks such as 'Penny Lane', 'Strawberry Fields Forever', 'All You Need Is Love' and 'Baby You're A Rich Man'. It became a huge hit, spending two months at number 1. Imported copies of the album flowed into the UK in sufficient quantities that it also reached the album chart (number 31). Eventually, the obvious dawned on the record company and it got a belated UK release.

MAGIDSON, HERB

b. 7 January 1906, Braddock, Pennsylvania, USA, d. 5 January 1986, Beverly Hills, California, USA. A leading composer and lyricist in the 30s and 40s, particularly remembered for 'The Continental', which he wrote Con Conrad for the Fred Astaire-Ginger Rogers picture *The Gay Divorcée*. It became the first winner of the 'Best Song' Academy Award in 1934. The team also wrote another good song for Astaire to sing in the film - 'Needle In A Haystack'. Magidson studied journalism at the University of Pittsburg before moving to New York and writing special material for Sophie Tucker. In the late 20s and early 30s he contributed a few numbers to Broadway shows such as *Earl Carroll's Vanities Of 1928* and *George White's Musical Hall Varieties*, but the majority of his output was for movies. Through to 1939 he wrote single songs or complete scores for *The Time, The Place And The Girl* (1929), *Show Of Shows*, *Little Johnny Jones*, *No, No, Nanette*, *I Like It That Way*, *The Gift Of Gab*, *George White's 1935 Scandals*, *Here's To Romance*, *The Great Ziegfeld*, *Hats Off*, *Music For Madame*, *Life Of The Party*, *Radio City Revels*, and *George White's Scandals Of 1939*. From these films came songs such as 'The Racoon', 'Somebody To Love', 'Dance Of The Wooden Shoes', 'Singin' In The Bathtub', 'Talkin' To Myself', 'Oh, I Didn't Know', 'According To The Moonlight', 'Here's To Romance', 'Midnight In Paris', 'Twinkle, Twinkle, Little Star' (not the nursery rhyme), 'Where Have You Been All My Life?', 'Let's Have Another Cigarette', 'Roses In December', 'Goodnight Angel', 'When The Cat's Away', and 'Something I Dreamed Last Night'. In the 40s, two of Magidson's wartime songs, 'Say A Prayer For The Boys Over There' (written with Jimmy McHugh for *Hers To Hold*) and 'I'll Buy That Dream' (with Allie Wrubel for *Sing Your Way Home*) were nominated for Oscars, and he also had numbers in *Sleepy Time Gal*, *Music In Manhattan*, *Do You Love Me?*, and *Make Mine Laughs*, amongst others. Throughout his career Magidson did not neglect Tin Pan Alley, and several of his best songs, not associated with either films or shows, have been sung and played by the finest vocalists and bands. Among them are 'Gone With The Wind', 'Music, Maestro Please!', '(I'm Afraid) The Masquerade Is Over', 'How Long Has This Been Going On?', 'I Can't Love You Anymore', 'A Pink Cocktail For A Blue Lady', 'I'm Stepping Out With A Memory Tonight', 'I'll Dance At Your Wedding', 'Enjoy Yourself (It's Later Than You Think)', and one of his earliest successes, 'Black-Eyed Susan Brown'. Other collaborators included Carl Sigman, Michael Cleary, Sammy Fain, Ben Oakland, Sam Stept, and Jule Styne. Like so many of the Old Guard, he seems to have been a casualty of rock 'n' roll, and there is no apparent record of him composing songs after the early 50s.

MAHOGANY

Released in 1975, *Mahogany* reunited Diana Ross and Billy Dee Williams, co-stars of the Billie Holiday biopic, *Lady Sings The Blues*. Tamla/Motown founder Berry Gordy pro-

duced this rather insubstantial vehicle and assumed the role of director when a disaffected Tony Richardson walked out of the project. The wafer-thin plot - Ross rises from department store secretary to top-line model while falling in and out of love - recalled those of the 'classic' Hollywood era, but the film lacked wit and charm while the actors seemed uninspired. However, the theme from the film, 'Do You Know Where You're Going To', written by Gerry Goffin and Michael Masser, secured an Academy Award as Best Song. It provided Ross with a US chart-topper and an ensuing UK number 5 hit, giving commercial boost to a part of her career in temporary abeyance.

MAID OF THE MOUNTAINS, THE

A favourite with amateur operatic societies throughout the world, this show was first presented in London at Daly's Theatre on 10 February 1917. The score was mainly by Harold Fraser-Simpson and James Tate (music) and Harry Graham (lyrics), with additional songs by F. Clifford Harris, James W. Tate, and (Arthur) 'Valentine'. Frederick Lonsdale's book was set in the high mountains of 'brigand land', and concerned the lovely Teresa (José Collins) who is arrested by General Malona (Mark Lester), the Governor of Santo, and is promised her freedom if her lover, the outlaw Baldasarre (Arthur Wontner), is captured. Complications arise when Teresa learns that Baldasarre has eyes for another, and in a fit of pique, she exposes him. Whereupon he is captured, and incarcerated on Devil's Island. All ends well when Teresa engineers his release, and they board a small boat and sail to the mainland - and into the sunset. The enchanting score included memorable songs such as Fraser-Simpson and Graham's 'Love Will Find A Way'and 'Live For Today', along with the engaging 'A Bachelor Gay', 'My Life Is Love', and 'A Paradise For Two' by Tate, Harris, and Valentine. the show was an enormous success and ran for a record 1,352 performances - even longer than the other big London hit of World War I, *Chu Chin Chow*. It made a star of the fiery José Collins, who had already enjoyed a prosperous Broadway career before she appeared in *The Maid Of The Mountains*, but is always remembered for introducing 'Love Will Find A Way'. Perhaps if she had recreated her role in New York, the 1918 production of *The Maid Of The Mountains* would have stayed at the Casino Theatre more than 37 performances. In the event Collins did appear in the 1921 London revival, the first of several that were produced through until 1942. Thirty years after that, a revised version, with additional songs by Harry Parr-Davies, Harold Purcell, Rudolph Friml, and Brian Hooker, and starring Lynne Kennington, Gordon Clyde, Neville Jason, Jimmy Thompson, and Janet Mahoney, was presented at London's Palace Theatre. Compared to contemporary musicals such as *Jesus Christ Superstar* it was considered to be out of place and somewhat old-fashioned. The original concept was nicely captured in the 1932 film with Nancy Brown and Harry Welchman.

MAKE ME AN OFFER

One of that band of typically English musicals that were around in the late 50s, which included *Fings Ain't Wot They Used T'Be* and *Expresso Bongo*. The creative team behind the latter came together again for this show which began its life at the innovative Theatre Royal, Stratford East, before opening in the West End at the New Theatre on 16 December 1959. The book was adapted by Wolf Mankowitz from his own slim 1952 novel and the 1959 film starring Peter Finch and Adrienne Corri, and was set in the world of small-time antique dealers based around London's Portobello Road market. Charlie (Daniel Massey), an expert in Wedgwood china, longs to own a beautiful piece for himself. His chance comes when he is involved with an auction (a particularly effective scene) for a complete (fake) Wedgwood room - and he ends up with a valuable (genuine) vase. Charlie's main rival dealer in the saga is the stunning Redhead (Dilys Laye), and his wife, Sally, was played by Diana Coupland. Some 20 songs, by David Heneker and Monty Norman, were skilfully incorporated into the plot, pointing up the various characters and situations as they occurred. They consisted of a blend of amusing and sentimental items, such as 'Make Me An Offer', Redhead's proposal that Charlie gallantly turns down; 'The Pram Song', 'I Want A Lock-Up', 'Portobello Road', 'Business Is Business', 'Whatever You Believe', 'It's Sort Of Romantic', 'If I Was A Man', 'Dog Eat Dog', 'All Big Fleas', and 'Love Him'. *Make Me An Offer* had decent run of 267 performances, and won the 1959 *Evening Standard* Award for best musical.

MAKE MINE MANHATTAN

Sid Caesar, a comedian who specialized in subjects satirical, was on the brink of television super-stardom when he appeared with a clutch of fellow clowns, including Joshua Shelley and David Burns, in this show which opened at the Broadhurst Theatre in New York on 15 January 1948. It was Caesar's debut on Broadway, and in a format - the revue - that was on its last legs. The music was by Richard Lewine, with lyrics and sketches by Arnold B. Horwitt, and it went for all the usual New York targets in a pleasant and amusing way. The songs included 'Saturday Night In Central Park', 'Subway Song', 'Phil The Fiddler', 'Gentleman Friend', 'My Brudder And Me', and 'I Fell In Love With You'. It is ironic that a fairly simple, lightweight production such as this should run for 429 performances, when Caesar's triumphant return to Broadway 14 years later in *Little Me* could only manage 257.

MALTBY, RICHARD, JNR.

(see Shire, David)

MAMA, I WANT TO SING

Conceived, so it said, on a beach in Jamaica in 1980, and subsequently showcased at various provincial theatres in the USA, this 'multi-cultural gospel musical' finally opened in New York, off-Broadway, at the Heckscher Theatre, the former home of Joseph Papp's New York Shakespeare Festival, on 23 March 1983. Set in Harlem in the late 40s and 50s, Vy Higginsen and Ken Wydro's book is based the life of Doris Troy, Higginsen's sister, who emerged from her gospel church choir to become an accomplished R&B songwriter and session singer with one or two substantial hits of her own, including 'Just One Look' in 1963. Early in 1984, Doris Troy herself joined the

cast in the role of her mother, and stayed with the company over the years. She is credited, along with Rudolph V. Hawkins, Pat Holley and Stephen Taylor, with composing the music to Higginsen and Wydro's lyrics for the 'rhythmical foot-stomping, hand-clapping score', which is supplemented by some familiar gospel tunes. The musical numbers included 'You Are My Child', 'Faith Can Move A Mountain', 'My Faith Looks Up To Thee', 'I Don't Worry About Tomorrow', 'God Will Be', 'Gifted Is', 'What Do You Win When You Win?', 'Precious Lord', 'Know When To Leave The Party', 'The One Who Will Love Me', and the title song. With audiences flocking to see 'this morally uplifting entertainment', by the end of 1984 *Time Magazine* had selected *Mama, I Want To Sing* as one of the Top 10 theatrical productions of the year, and 1985 saw the show playing 10 performances a week with two different casts. A year later, while the New York cast was still in residence at the Heckscher Theatre, the first US national tour opened. This was followed over the next few years by productions in Tokyo, Osaka, Athens, Zurich, Munich, Venice, Berlin, Frankfurt, Palermo, Sicily, Istanbul and many other cities around the world. When the New York production closed in 1991 (after playing in repertory for a while with *Mama, I Want To Sing Part II*) the show had played more than 2,400 performances over eight consecutive years, and become 'the longest-running, best-loved black off-Broadway musical in the history of the American theatre'. Four years later, when it arrived in London, it was estimated that *Mama, I Want To Sing* had played to more than 3,000,000 people and grossed £38 million. Doris Troy was still present when the West End production opened at the Cambridge Theatre on 1 February 1995, with Stacy Francis as the young Doris, and soul star Chaka Khan, in the principal role of Sister Carrie, singing 'a couple of real stompers'.

MAMBO KINGS, THE

Adapted by Cynthia Cidre from Oscar Hijuelos' Pulitzer Prize-winning novel *The Mambo Kings Play Songs Of Love*, this 1992 Warner Brothers production tells of two Cuban brothers, trumpet player Nestor and mambo singer and percussionist Cesar Castillo (Antonio Banderas and Armand Assante). In 1952 they leave Cuba for New York where Cesar demonstrates his skills at the swish Palladium club with the renowned Tito Puente Orchestra. After forming their own group The Mambo Kings, fellow Cuban Desi Arnaz - who is played by his real-life son Desi Arnaz Jnr. - hears them singing Nestor's composition 'Beautiful Maria Of My Soul' (Robert Kraft-Arne Glimcher) and invites them to appear on the top-rated *I Love Lucy* television show. Their subsequent rise to fame and fortune is shattered when Nestor dies in a car crash. Cesar buys a bar of his own, the Club Havana, and on the opening night, at the request of his late brother's girl, Delores Fuentes (Maruschka Detmers), he sings Nestor's lovely bolero 'Beautiful Maria Of My Soul'. The song had been dedicated to Maria Rivera (Talisa Soto) Nestor's former lover in Cuba. Other roles in the large cast went to Cathy Moriarty, Pablo Calogero, Scott Cohen, Mario Grillo, Ralph Irizzary, Pete MacNamara, and Jimmy Medina. The mostly South American songs included 'Mambo Caliente'

(Arturo Sandoval), 'Tanga, Rumba-Afro-Cubana' (Mario Bauza), 'Guantanamera' (Fernandez Diaz', 'Perfidia' (Alberto Dominguez), 'Quiereme Mucho' (Gonzalo Roig-Augustin Rodriguez), and 'Cuban Pete' (José Norman). The exotic background score was written by Robert Kraft and Carlos Franzetti. Michael Peters was the choreographer, and the film was photographed in Technicolor by Michael Ballhouse. The director was Arne Glimcher. 'Beautiful Maria Of My Soul' was nominated for the best song Oscar, but, unlike the original book, no other prizes came the way of this brash and colourful film.

MAME

Broadway legend Mary Martin was the producers' first choice for the lead in this musical, but she was living in Brazil at the time, and turned the opportunity down. Composer Jerry Herman pushed hard for Angela Lansbury, and, eventually, after a great struggle, had his way. *Mame* opened on the 24 May 1966 at the Winter Garden Theatre, New York, with a book by Jerome Lawrence and Robert E. Lee, based on the novel *Auntie Mame* by Patrick Dennis, and the play by Lawrence and Lee. The action takes place in Mame's New York Beekman Place Apartment and various locales in which she becomes involved during a period from 1928-46. The glamorous, madcap and extremely liberal Mame (Lansbury) is toting a bugle, and hosting one of her famous celebrity parties ('The moon's full, the gin's in the bathtub, and all my dearest friends are here - even the ones I haven't met yet'), when nanny Agnes Gooch (Jane Connell) arrives on her doorstep with the orphaned Patrick Dennis (aged 10: Frankie Michaels, aged 19-29: Jerry Lanning). Mame's plans to educate him herself go by the board when the 1929 Wall Street Crash leaves her without a dime. Her 'bosom buddy', Vera Charles (Beatrice Arthur), gets Mame a part in her new musical, but she falls off a 'pretend' moon, and is dismissed. A job as a manicurist miraculously leads to marriage with Southern gentleman Beauregard Burnside (Charles Braswell), but only after she has proved her worth in a fox hunt (she captures the fox). Sadly, Beauregard falls off a mountain during their honeymoon, and widowed Mame gets down to her memoirs. Agnes take her advice to live a little rather too literally, and returns pregnant. Patrick, meanwhile has got himself a girl, Gloria Upson (Diane Walker), from a snobby family of which Mame does not approve. She deals with the situation neatly by inviting the Upsons back to her place for a party, then announces her intention to build a home for single mothers right next door to their property. Patrick marries the far more suitable Pegeen Ryan (Diane Coupe), and a decade or so later Mame is ready to show *their* son all the wonders of the world, as she did Patrick. His father demurs at first - but you cannot really say 'no' to Auntie Mame. Apart from the exuberant title number, other highlights from Herman's score included 'If He Walked Into My Life' ('Where's that boy with the bugle . . ?') and Mame and Vera's wonderfully bitchy 'Bosom Buddies' ('If I say that your tongue is vicious, if I call you uncouth/It's simply that, who else but a bosom buddy will sit down and tell you the truth?'). 'We Need A Little Christmas' was great too, along with 'St.

Bridget', 'It's Today', 'Open A New Window', 'The Man In The Moon', 'My Best Girl', 'The Fox Hunt', 'Gooch's Song', 'That's How Young I Feel' (orchestrations Philip J. Lang). It was choreographed by Onna White, and Gene Saks directed the show which ran for 1,508 performances, winning Tony Awards for best actress (Lansbury) and supporting actor and actress (Michaels and Arthur). Herman also won a Grammy for Best Score From An Original Cast Album. When Lansbury was about to leave after around two years, Judy Garland was considered, but rejected, as her replacement. The producers finally settled on Janis Paige, Jane Morgan, and when *Mame* was getting a little middle-aged - Ann Miller. Other stars to play Auntie Mame on various tours have included Susan Hayward, Janet Blair, Celeste Holm. Former Hollywood superstar Ginger Rogers headed the 1969 London production at the Theatre Royal, Drury Lane (443 performances), along with Margaret Courtney (Vera), Tony Adams (Patrick), Ann Beach (Agnes), and Barry Kent (Beauregard). Julia McKenzie played Patrick's unsuitable Gloria Upson, and she was Mame in the BBC Radio 2 30th anniversary in May 1996, in company with Libby Morris (Vera), Robert Meadmore (Patrick), Claire Moore (Agnes), and David Kernan (Beauregard). Angela Lansbury and Jane Connell reprised their roles for the short-lived (41 performances) 1983 Broadway revival, with Byron Nease (Patrick) and Anne Francine (Vera). The 1974 film, which Jerry Herman did not like at all, had Beatrice Arthur and Jane Connell from Broadway, as well as Lucille Ball (Mame), Robert Preston (Beauregard), and Kirby Furlong (Patrick).

MAMOULIAN, ROUBEN

b. 8 October 1898, Tbilisi, Georgia, Russia, d. 4 December 1987, Los Angeles, California, USA. A distinguished stage and film director whose name is particularly associated with two masterpieces of the American musical theatre - *Porgy And Bess* and *Oklahoma!*- and a legendary Hollywood movie, *Love Me Tonight*. Mamoulian spent part of his childhood in Paris before studying at Moscow University, and running his own drama school in Tbilisi. In 1920 he toured Britain with a Russian theatre group and subsequently studied drama at London University. He moved to the USA in 1923 and operettas at the George Eastman Theatre in Rochester, New Jersey, before going to New York where he became a leading light with the prestigious Theatre Guild. His reputation as a theatre director led him to Hollywood at the beginning of the talkie era, and he immediately impressed with his innovative and audacious approach to the medium. His first film, *Applause* (1929) starring Helen Morgan, was followed by a series of highly acclaimed pictures - sophisticated comedies, dramas, gangster movies - featuring the biggest stars of the day, including Fredric March, Marlene Dietrich, Tyrone Power, and Greta Garbo. Among them were several musicals, such as the charming *Love Me Tonight* (1932) with Jeanette MacDonald and Maurice Chevalier (which Mamoulian also produced), *The Gay Desperado* (1936), *High, Wide And Handsome* (1937), *Summer Holiday* (1947), and the elegant *Silk Stockings* (1957) starring Fred Astaire and Cyd Charisse. His relatively small cinema output is said to be due to persistent disagreements and confrontations with producers. He was hired and quickly fired from movies such as *Laura*, *Porgy And Bess*, and the Elizabeth Taylor-Richard Burton epic *Cleopatra* (1963). In parallel with his Hollywood career, Mamoulian directed major works on Broadway, including *Porgy And Bess* (1935), *Oklahoma!* (1943), *Sadie Thompson* (1944), *Carousel* (1945), *St. Louis Woman* (1946), *Lost In The Stars* (1949), and *Arms And The Girl* (1950). On the latter show, and on *Sadie Thompson*, he also served as co-librettist, and in later years wrote and adapted several plays and children's stories.

MAN OF LA MANCHA

Staged at the ANTA Washington Square Theater, and hence just a little off-Broadway, *Man Of La Mancha* opened on 22 November 1965. Dale Wasserman's book combined elements of Miguel de Cervantes's classic novel, *Don Quixote*, with the troubled life of the author. Wasserman had earlier written a straight dramatic play which was televised in 1959, and was persuaded by producer-director Albert Marre to adapt it into a musical version. With music by Mitch Leigh and lyrics by Joe Darion, the show opened to good reviews and quickly built a following at the comparatively small ANTA Theater. Starring Richard Kiley as Cervantes/Quixote and Joan Diener as Aldonza, the story interweaved episodes in the life of Cervantes, who endured slavery and imprisonment, often for debt, before achieving success with the publication of his masterpiece. It proved to be an unexpected hit and won Tony Awards for best musical, actor (Kiley), score, director (Marre), and scenic design (Howard Bay). The careful integration of songs and lyrics into the development of the plot made it difficult for most of them to gain life outside the show, but there were several admirable numbers, including 'I'm Only Thinking Of Him', 'The Dubbing', 'Little Bird, Little Bird', 'What Do You Want From Me?', and 'I Really Like Him'. Another of the songs, 'The Impossible Dream', did achieve some measure of popularity especially in a recording by Jack Jones. It endured, and became a UK hit in 1992 for the local eccentric band Carter USM. *Man Of La Mancha* stayed at the ANTA until March 1968, when it transferred to the larger Martin Beck Theatre and continued its run for a total of 2,328 performances. The London production which opened at the Piccadilly Theatre on 24 April 1968, with Joan Diener (Aldonza) and Keith Michell (Quixote), ran for 253 performances. In July of the following year, it reopened with Kiley and Ruth Silvestri as the leads, and stayed for a further 118 performances. Michell went to the USA and took over as Quixote on Broadway in December 1969. A 1992 Broadway revival, which starred Raul Julia and pop singer Sheena Easton, folded after 108 performances. Peter O'Toole appeared in the 'plodding, abysmal' film version in 1972.

MAN WHO FELL TO EARTH, THE

Nicolas Roeg, already responsible for *Performance*, *Walkabout* and *Don't Look Now*, directed this elliptical 1976 feature. His decision to cast David Bowie as Thomas Jerome Newton, an angel/alien on an ill-defined mission, was inspired. The singer's gaunt features and flaxen hair combined well with his chameleon musical persona. Bowie's chillingly austere *Station To Station* appeared the same year as *The Man Who Fell To Earth*, and an atmosphere of disengagement permeates both projects. Roeg's camerawork and direction are suitably enigmatic, resulting in one of the era's most perplexing, but absorbing, films. John Phillips, formerly of the Mamas And The Papas, helped assemble the soundtrack selections, which included four of his own performances; 'Hello Mary Lou', 'Boys From The South', Rhumba Boogie' and 'Bluegrass Breakdown', as well as material by Japanese percussionist Stomu Yamash'ta, 50s' college-folk act the Kingston Trio and Roy Orbison. This beguiling collection was completed by MOR songs, excerpts from Holtz's *Planet Suite* and recordings of the humpback whale. The music proved as eclectic as the film itself.

MANCINI, HENRY

b. Enrico Mancini, 16 April 1924, Cleveland, Ohio, USA, d. 14 June 1994, Los Angeles, California, USA. Prompted by his father, a steelworker who loved music, Mancini learned to play several musical instruments while still a small child. As a teenager he developed an interest in jazz and especially music of the big bands. He wrote some arrangements and sent them to Benny Goodman, from whom he received some encouragement. In 1942, he became a student at the Juilliard School of Music, but his career was interrupted by military service during World War II. Immediately following the war he was hired as pianist and arranger by Tex Beneke, who was then leading the Glenn Miller orchestra. Later in the 40s Mancini began writing arrangements for studios, prompted initially by a contract to score for a recording date secured by his wife, singer Ginny O'Connor (of the Mel-Tones). He was also hired to work on films (the first of which was the Abbott and Costello comedy *Lost In Alaska*), and it was here that his interest in big band music paid off. He wrote the scores for two major Hollywood bio-pics, *The Glenn Miller Story* (1954) and *The Benny Goodman Story* (1956), as well as Orson Welles' *Touch Of Evil* classic (1958). Mancini also contributed jazz-influenced scores for television, including those for the innovative *Peter Gunn* series and *Mr Lucky*. His film work continued with scores and songs for such films as *Breakfast At Tiffany's* (1961), from which came 'Moon River' (the Oscar winner that year), and the title songs for *Days Of Wine And Roses* (1962), which again won an Oscar, and *Charade* (1963). His other film compositions included 'Baby Elephant Walk' from *Hatari!* (1962), the theme from *The Pink Panther* (1964), 'Sweetheart Tree' from *The Great Race* (1965), and scores for *Man's Favourite Sport?*, *Dear Heart*, *Wait Until Dark*, *Darling Lili*, *Mommie Dearest*, *Victor/Victoria* (1982), for which he won an Oscar for 'Original Song Score' with Leslie Bricusse, *That's Dancing*, *Without A Clue*, *Physical Evidence*, *Blind Date*, *That's Life*, *The Glass Menagerie*, *Sunset*, *Fear*, *Switch*, and *Tom And Jerry: The Movie*, on which he again teamed with Leslie Bricusse. One of the most respected film and television composers - and the winner of 20 Grammy Awards - Mancini acknowledged his greatest legacy to be '. . . my use of jazz - incorporating various popular idioms into the mainstream of film scoring. If that's a contribution, then that's mine'. In addition he also regularly conducted orchestras in the USA and UK in concerts of his music, most of which stood comfortably on its own merits outside the context for which it was originally conceived. In the months prior to his death from cancer, Mancini was working with Leslie Bricusse on the score for the stage adaptation of *Victor/Victoria*.

● ALBUMS: *The Versatile Henry Mancini* (Liberty 1959)★★★, *March Step In Stereo And Hi-Fi* (Warners 1959)★★★, *The Music From Peter Gunn* (RCA Victor 1959)★★★, *The Blues And The Beat* (RCA Victor 1960)★★★, *The Mancini Touch* (RCA Victor 1960)★★★, *Music From Mr Lucky* (RCA Victor 1960)★★★, *The Original Peter Gunn* (RCA Victor 1960)★★★, *Mr Lucky Goes Latin* (RCA Victor 1961)★★★, *Breakfast At Tiffany's* (1961)★★★, *Hatari* (1962)★★★, *Combo!* (1962)★★★, *Uniquely Mancini* (1963)★★★, *Our Man In Hollywood* (1963)★★★, *The Second Time Around* (1963)★★★, *Marches* (1963)★★★, *The Concert Sound Of Henry Mancini* (1964)★★★, with his orchestra and chorus *Dear Heart And Other Songs About Love* (1965)★★★, *The Latin Sound Of Henry Mancini* (1965)★★★, *Sounds And Voices* (1966)★★★, *Two For The Road* (1967)★★★, *Encore!* (1967)★★★, *A Warm Shade Of Ivory* (1969)★★★, *Mancini Country* (1970)★★★, *Themes From Love Story* (1971)★★★, *This Is Henry Mancini* (1971)★★★, *The Mancini Generation* (1972)★★★, with Doc Severinsen *Brass, Ivory & Strings* (1973)★★★, *The Academy Award Winning Songs* (1975)★★★, *Mancini's Angels* (1977)★★★, *Just You And Me Together Love* (1979)★★★, *Pure Gold* (1980)★★★, *Victor/Victoria* (1982)★★★, *Best Of* (1984)★★★, *A Man And His Music* (1985)★★★, with James Galway *In The Pink* (1985)★★★, *Merry Mancini Christmas* (1985)★★★, *At The Movies* (1986)★★★, with Johnny Mathis *The Hollywood Musicals* (1986)★★★, *Henry Mancini And The Royal Philharmonic Pops Orchestra* (1988)★★★, *Diamond Series* (1988)★★★, with the Royal Philharmonic Pops Orchestra *Premier Pops* (1988) and *Mancini Rocks The Pops* (1989)★★★, *Theme Scene* (1989)★★★, *Mancini In Surround Sound* (1990)★★★, and various other film and television soundtracks.

● COMPILATIONS: *In The Pink: The Ultimate Collection* (RCA Victor 1995)★★★, *Romantic Movie Themes* (Camden 1997)★★★, *Martinis With Mancini* (BMG 1998)★★★.

● FURTHER READING: *Henry Mancini*, Gene Lees. *Did They Mention The Music?*, Henry Mancini and Gene Lees.

MANDEL, JOHNNY

b. 23 November 1935, New York, USA. After playing trumpet and trombone while still in his pre-teenage years (a period in which he began to write music), Mandel played with various bands in and around New York, including those led by Boyd Raeburn and Jimmy Dorsey. In the mid- to late 40s Mandel played in the bands of Buddy Rich, Alvino Rey and others, and in the early 50s, he worked with Elliott Lawrence and Count Basie. He began to establish himself both as an arranger, contributing charts to the Basie and Artie Shaw bands, and also as a songwriter. By the mid-50s he was writing music for films and was working less in the jazz field, although his film music often contained echoes of his background. Much respected by singers and jazz instrumentalists, Mandel has a particular facility for ballads. He also orchestrated scores for Broadway and for television specials. His film work, from the 50s through to the 80s, includes music for *I Want To Live*, *The Third Voice*, *The Americanization Of*

Emily, *The Sandpiper*, *The Russians Are Coming*, *Point Blank*, *MASH*, *The Last Detail*, *Escape To Witch Mountain*, *Freaky Friday*, *Agatha*, *Being There*, *The Baltimore Bullet*, *Caddyshack*, *Deathtrap*, *The Verdict*, *Staying Alive*, and *Brenda Starr* (1987). He also scored for television movies such as *The Trackers*, *The Turning Point Of Jim Molloy*, *A Letter To Three Wives*, *Christmas Eve*, *LBJ - The Early Years*, *Assault And Matrimony*, *Foxfire*, *Agatha*, *The Great Escape II - The Untold Story*, and *Single Men - Married Women* (1989). Among his songs are 'Emily', 'A Time For Love' and, perhaps his best-known, 'The Shadow Of Your Smile' (lyrics by Paul Francis Webster), written for *The Sandpiper* (1965). The latter won a Grammy for song of the year, and the Oscar for best song.

MANN, BARRY

b. 9 February 1939, Brooklyn, New York, USA. One of the leading pop songwriters of his generation. Although trained as an architect, Mann began his career in music following a summer singing engagement in the Catskills resort. He initially composed material for Elvis Presley's publishers Hill & Range, before briefly collaborating with Howie Greenfield. In 1961, he enjoyed a Top 10 hit in his own right with 'Who Put The Bomp?', but thereafter it was as a composer that he dominated the Hot 100. During the same year as his solo hit, Mann found a new songwriting partner in Cynthia Weil, whom he soon married. Their first success together was Tony Orlando's 'Bless You' (1961), a simple but effective love song, which endeared them to their new employer, bubblegum genius Don Kirschner, who housed a wealth of songwriting talent in the cubicles of his Brill Building offices. With intense competition from those other husband-and-wife teams Jeff Berry and Ellie Greenwich, and Gerry Goffin and Carole King, Mann and Weil responded with a wealth of classic songs which still sound fresh and impressive to this day. Like all great songwriters, they adapted well to different styles and themes, and this insured that their compositions were recorded by a broad range of artists. There was the evocative urban romanticism of the Crystals' 'Uptown' (1962) and the Drifters' 'On Broadway' (1963), novelty teen fodder such as Eydie Gorme's 'Blame It On The Bossa Nova' (1963) and Paul Petersen's 'My Dad' (1963), the desolate neuroticism of Gene Pitney's 'I'm Gonna Be Strong' (1964) and the Righteous Brothers' 'You've Lost That Lovin' Feelin'' (1964), and classic mid-60s protest songs courtesy of the Animals' 'We Gotta Get Out Of This Place', Jody Miller's 'Home Of The Brave', 'Only In America' (Jay And The Americans) and 'Kicks' (Paul Revere And The Raiders)

By the late 60s, Mann and Weil left Kirschner and moved to Hollywood. Throughout this period, they continued to enjoy hit success with Bobby Vinton's 'I Love How You Love Me' (written with Larry Kolber in 1968), Jay And The Americans' 'Walking In The Rain' (1969) and B.J. Thomas' 'I Just Can't Help Believing' (1970). Changes in the pop marketplace subsequently reduced their hit output, but there were some notable successes such as Dan Hill's 'Sometimes When We Touch' (1977). Mann himself still craved recognition as a performer and won a recording contract, but his album work, most notably 1977's aptly titled *Survivor* failed to match the sales of his and his wife's much covered golden hits. *Survivor* was produced by Bruce Johnson and Terry Melcher, and was regarded as a leading example of the 70s' singer/songwriter oeuvre. They wrote the original songs for the *Muppet Treasure Island* movie in 1996.

● ALBUMS: *Who Put The Bomp* (ABC 1963)★★, *Lay It All Out* (1971)★★, *Survivor* (1975)★★.

MARCH OF THE FALSETTOS

The second in a series of musicals with music and lyrics by William Finn, all of which began Off Broadway at the experimental and innovative centre, Playwrights Horizons. The first of what is sometimes called 'The Marvin Trilogy', *In Trousers*, played for 16 performances from 26 March 1985 at the Promenade Theatre in New York, and has rarely been presented since. The third, and last, in the trilogy is entitled *Falsettoland*, and that piece is sometimes combined with *March Of The Falsettos* under the title of *Falsettos*.

March Of The Falsettos, a piece which William Finn himself has called 'a passionate work about being scared to death of love', gave a total of 298 performances at Playwrights Horizons and the West Side Arts Centre from April 1981. It was set in 1979, and told of a Jewish father, Marvin (Michael Rupert), who discovers that he is homosexual, and leaves his wife, Trina (Alison Fraser) and young son, Jason (James Kushner), to go and live with his male lover, Whizzer Brown (Stephen Bogardus). In a neat twist, Marvin's wife marries his psychiatrist, Mendel (Chip Zien), and he is left alone. What has been called 'the most powerful and emotional score of the 80s, (there is no spoken dialogue) included 'Four Jews In A Room Bitching', 'This Had Better Stop', 'The Games I Play', 'The Chess Game, 'I Never Wanted To Love You', 'Trina's Song', 'This Had Better Come To A Stop', 'Love Is Blind', 'My Father's A Homo', and 'The Thrill Of First Love'.

Falsettoland, which opened in 1990, begins two years after *March Of The Falsettos*. Rupert, Bogardus and Zien recreated their original roles, and added to the cast was a doctor, Charlotte (Heather MacRae), and her lesbian lover, Cordelia (Janet Metz). After the excruciatingly difficult adjustments that all the characters had been forced to make in the previous show, the early mood in *Falsettoland* is one of 'whimsical goofiness', but that changes swiftly when Whizzer is diagnosed as having a deadly disease soon to be identified as AIDS. The family gather round his bedside, and the show culminates in young Jason's bar mitzvah in Whizzer's hospital room. The songs included 'Falsettoland', 'Year Of The Child', 'The Baseball Game', 'Everyone Hates His Parents', 'What More Can I Say?', 'Something Bad Is Happening', 'Days Like This', 'Unlikely Lovers,' 'You Gotta Die Sometime', and 'What Would I Do?'. Opinions as to the two shows' merit and value varied widely. To many, *March Of The Falsettos* was 'not just a musical about gay life in modern times, but a masterly feat of comic storytelling and a visionary musical theatre work', while others dismissed both *March Of The Falsettos* and *Falsettoland* as 'overrated Off Broadway cult items'. *Falsettoland* won Tony Awards for best book (Finn and James Lapine, who also directed) and score, and ran for a

total of 245 performances. After over a decade on the Fringe, Finn and Lapine's audacious and original concept finally graduated to Broadway in April 1992, when *March Of The Falsettos* and *Falsettoland* were presented under the title of *Falsettos* at the John Golden Theatre for nearly 500 performances, and was rewarded with Tony Awards for book and score. A London production of *March Of The Falsettos*, with Simon Green, Paddy Navin, Barry James, Martin Smith, and Damien Walker, played 29 performances at the Albery Theatre in 1987. In 1998, the National Asian-American Theater Company presented *Falsettoland* off-off-Broadway at the Vineyard Theatre in New York. Alan Muraoka directed an all Asian-American cast which included Jason Ma (Marvin), Kennedy Kanagawa (Jason), Ann Harada (Trina), and Welly Yang (Whizzer), with Christine Toy Johnson and Mimosa as the lesbian lovers. In June 1998, Finn collaborated with James Lapine again on *A New Brain*, a musical about a songwriter wrongly diagnosed as having a brain tumour.

MARDI GRAS

Pop crooner Pat Boone forged his career by recording antiseptic cover versions of R&B hits. He became the clean-cut face of rock 'n' roll, acceptable to a moral majority fearful of black musicians and the ebullient talent of, for example, Elvis Presley and Jerry Lee Lewis. Boone was thus quickly embraced by Hollywood, but his ventures into pop films proved equally insubstantial. *Mardi Gras*, released in 1958, co-starred aspiring singers Gary Crosby (the son of Bing Crosby) and Tommy Sands, the first husband of Nancy Sinatra. Boone portrays a cadet who wins a date with a movie star; the film's title is inspired by footage of the New Orleans festival which provides momentary relief from this anodyne plot. The soundtrack includes the risible 'A Fiddle, A Rifle, An Axe And A Bible', the last of which Boone grasped in real life when he opted to record religious material.

MARLENE, DAS MUSICAL

Originally titled *Sag Mir Wo Die Blumen Sind* (Where Have All The Flowers Gone?), this musical is based on British author Laurence Roman's biography of the legendary entertainer Marlene Dietrich. It opened at the small (785-seater) Theatre am Kurfürstendamm, Berlin, Germany, on 7 April 1993, almost a year after her death. Somewhat optimistically, in the light of subsequent events, the show's producer, Friedrich Kurz, booked the theatre, where Dietrich herself had performed in 1928, until the year 2000. Reportedly capitalized at between £1.5-2 million and directed by Terry Hands, formerly Artistic Director of the Royal Shakespeare Company, the production 'fast-frames 40 years of Dietrich's life, interspersed with a contemporary sub-plot about a troupe of drama students planning a tribute to her'. Along with the 'clumsy political allegories', there is a scene in which Dietrich romps in bed with her husband and his mistress, and, towards the end, Edith Piaf, played by a man wearing a white wedding dress, is brought on in a wheel chair. The 'charming, slightly plump' Jutta Habicht plays Dietrich in a cast of six which is accompanied by seven musicians. Most of the 20 songs are by Frederick Hollander, and include his bitter-sweet 'Falling In Love Again' from the memorable Dietrich film, *The Blue Angel*. Two months after the show opened it was retitled *Marlene, Das Musical* and drastically revised so that it became a more straight forward chronological life story, while still retaining plenty of sex and innuendo. More songs were added, but the enormous helium-filled Dietrich model which almost seemed to fill the stage was now missing. In any event, the changes were to no avail, and the show, which it was hoped would go some way towards re-establishing Marlene Dietrich's reputation in a city that once reviled her, closed on 30 June 1993. Nearly four years later, a play, entitled *Marlene*, by Pam Gems (*Piaf*), starring Siân Phillips, was presented to appreciative audiences for an extended season at London's Lyric Theatre. Four years later, a play, entitled Marlene, by Pam Gems (Piaf), starring Siân Phillips, was presented to appreciative audiences for an extended season at London's Lyric Theatre.

MARTIN GUERRE

The debut of this much-hyped third collaboration, following on from *Les Misérables* and *Miss Saigon*, between producer Cameron Mackintosh and the creative team of Alain Boublil and Claude-Michel Schönberg, was postponed for three weeks in order 'to develop the special choreographic style of the production'. This delay hardly seemed significant in view of the fact that it had already taken six years to prepare the '£3.5 million' mega-musical for the West End ('Six years!' exclaimed one critic. 'Good grief, Irving Berlin wrote *Annie Get Your Gun* in six days.'). *Martin Guerre* finally opened at London's Prince Edward Theatre on 10 July 1996. The true story of the sixteenth-century French husband who abandoned his young wife only to be replaced by an imposter seven years later, had previously inspired the 1982 French film *The Return Of Martin Guerre* starring Gerard Depardieu, and the 1993 remake *Sommersby* with Richard Gere and Jodie Foster. However, both movies kept audiences guessing about the identity of the man who appeared out of the blue claiming to be the real Martin Guerre, and was eventually accused of impersonating him, found guilty and executed. In Boublil and Schönberg's book, when Arnaud de Thil (Iain Glen) turns up in the village of Artigat posing as Guerre, Bertrande de Rols (Juliette Caton) sees through him right away (cue the big number 'All I Know'). This implausible reunion, along with an overwhelming emphasis on religious bigotry and a generally confusing plot, was supplemented by typically soaring Schönberg music and ordinary lyrics by Edward Hardy (additional lyrics: Boublil and Herbert Kretzmer). As well as 'All I Know', and another dramatic duet, 'Tell Me When To Go', the score also contained 'When We Were Young', 'Here Comes The Morning', 'Martin Guerre', and 'Why Won't You Love Me?', amongst others, but no obvious hits. Choreographer Bob Avian staged some spirited stomping pagan dance rituals, and the director and co-adaptor was Declan Donnellan. Royal Shakespeare Company star Glen, making his first appearance in the musical theatre, headed a cast which included Jérôme Pradon (Guillaume), Matt Rawle (Martin Guerre), Michael Matus (Benoit), Ann Emery (Hortense), Sheila Reid, Julia Sutton, Susan Jane Tanner, and Martin

Turner. Despite a set of decidedly unenthusiastic reviews, *Martin Guerre* soldiered on, with receipts sometimes dropping below the break-even mark, until October when Mackintosh closed the show for three days so that extensive changes could be introduced. On 7 November *Martin Guerre* (Mark II) faced the critics again, and they pronounced the patient cured - well almost. Some inherent faults remained, and there was still a lack of humour to contrast with the overall darkness of the piece, but the general opinion seemed to be that this was about as good as it was going to get. The reported sum of £500,000 had been spent on re-writing 50-60% of the production and incorporating a completely revised first act and extra songs. These included a new opening number, 'Working On The Land', and involved yet another lyricist, Stephen Clark. A far more romantic story was now refocused around Bertrande, whose role was expanded to such an extent that it was to be shared between Juliette Caton and Rebecca Lock. *Martin Guerre* had been given a second chance, but in spite of winning Laurence Olivier Awards for Best New Musical and Best Theatre Choreographer, it failed to attract a consistent audience, and closed in February 1998, 'a $7 million write-off'. The creative team continued to work on the show, and on 30 November 1998, a sharper and more focused version, slimmed down for touring, opened at the West Yorkshire Playhouse. Directed by Conall Morrison, with musical staging and choreography by David Bolger, and John Napier's production design, the cast included Stephen Weller (Guerre), Matthew Cammelle (Arnaud du Thil), Joanna Riding (Bertrande de Rols), Maurice Clarke (Guillaume), Michael Bauer (Pierre Guerre), Kerry Washington (Madame de Rols), Gareth Snook (Father Dominic), Terry Kelly (Benoit), Jonathan Penton (André), Lisa Peace (Catherine), and Geoffrey Abbott (Judge Coras). There was a new orchestrator, William David Brohn, for a score which included 'Live With Somebody You Love', 'Your Wedding Day', 'The Deluge', 'I'm Martin Guerre', 'Without You as A Friend', 'How Many Tears', 'The Conversion', 'God's Anger', 'Dear Louison', 'Welcome To The Land', 'The Confession', 'The Seasons Turn', 'Don't', 'All The Years', 'The Holy Fight', 'The Dinner', 'The Revelation', 'The Day Has Come', 'If You Still Love Me', 'The Courtroom', 'Who?', 'All That I Love', 'The Imposter Is Here', 'The Final Witness', 'The Verdict', 'Justice Will Be Done', 'Benoit's Lament', and 'You Will Be Mine'.

By the mid-90s the Guerre legend had been the basis for at least two other stage musicals: *Martin Guerre*, with book and lyrics by Laura Harrington and music by Roger Ames, starring Patrick Cassidy, Judy Kuhn, Peter Samuels, and Beth Fowler, played at the Hartford Stage, Connecticut, USA, early in 1993; and *The House Of Martin Guerre*, with music and lyrics by Leslie Arden, who co-wrote the book with Anna Theresa Cascio, which originated in Toronto, Canada, and won the 1994 Dora Mavor Moore Award for Best New Musical. It was subsequently presented to much acclaim at Chicago's Goodman Theatre in the summer of 1996, and gained the Joseph Jefferson Award for Best Musical. The show returned to its Toronto roots in 1997 under the title of *Martin Guerre*. Ironically, Arden's mentor is Cameron Mackintosh, who several years ago gave her the opportunity to attend an Oxford masterclass with Stephen Sondheim.

● VIDEOS: *Martin Guerre - A Musical Journey* (VCI 1998).

MARTIN, DEAN

b. Dino Paul Crocetti, 7 June 1917, Steubenville, Ohio, USA, d. 25 December 1995. An extremely popular ballad singer and light comedian with a relaxed and easy style, who developed into an accomplished dramatic actor. After leaving school in the 10th grade, he worked as a shoe-shine boy and a gas station attendant before becoming an 'amateur' welterweight boxer, 'Kid Crochet', earning 10 dollars a fight. When he retired from the boxing arena, he became a croupier at a local casino. His first singing job is said to have been with the Sammy Watkins band in 1941, when he was initially billed as Dino Martini, but the name was soon changed to Dean Martin. His earliest recordings were for the Diamond label, and included 'Which Way Did My Heart Go'/'All Of Me' and 'I Got the Sun In The Morning'/'Sweetheart Of Sigma Chi'. He also recorded some tracks for the Apollo label, well known for its impressive roster of black talent. The Martin recordings included 'Walkin' My Baby Back Home', 'Oh Marie', 'Santa Lucia', 'Hold Me', 'Memory Lane' and 'Louise'. In 1946, Martin first worked with comedian Jerry Lewis at the 500 Club in Atlantic City. Together they developed an ad-libbing song and comedy act that became very popular on US television and radio in the late 40s. In 1949, they appeared in supporting roles in the film *My Friend Irma*, and in the sequel, *My Friend Irma Goes West*, the following year. The team then starred in another 14 popular comedies, with Martin providing the songs and romantic interest, and Lewis contributing the zany fun. These films included *At War With The Army* (1950), *Jumping Jacks* (1952), *Sailor, Beware!*, *The Stooge*, *Scared Stiff* (1953), *The Caddy* (1953), *Living It Up* (1954), *Pardners* (1956) and *Hollywood Or Bust* (1956). Their parting was somewhat acrimonious, and it was widely felt that Martin would be the one to suffer most from the split. In fact, they both did well. After a shaky start in the comedy movie *Ten Thousand Bedrooms* (1957), Martin blossomed as a dramatic actor in *The Young Lions* (1958), *Some Came Running* (1958), *Rio Bravo* (1959), *Ada* (1961), *Toys In The Attic* (1963), *The Sons Of Katie Elder* (1965) and *Airport* (1970). He still retained his comic touch in *Who Was That Lady?* (1960) and *What A Way To Go* (1964), but made surprisingly few musicals. The most notable were *Bells Are Ringing* (1960), with Judy Holliday, and *Robin And The Seven Hoods* (1964).

Meanwhile, Martin had signed to Capitol Records in 1948, and for the next 10 years had a series of US Top 30 chart entries, including 'That Certain Party' (duet with Jerry Lewis), 'Powder Your Face With Sunshine', 'I'll Always Love You', 'If', 'You Belong To Me', 'Love Me, Love Me', 'That's Amore', 'I'd Cry Like A Baby', 'Sway', 'Money Burns A Hole In My Pocket, 'Memories Are Made Of This' (number 1), 'Innamorata', 'Standing On The Corner', 'Return To Me', 'Angel Baby' and 'Volare' ('Nel Blu Dipinto Di Blu'). Martin's version of 'That's Amore' resurfaced when it was featured in the 1987 hit movie *Moonstruck*. Although Martin was still a big attraction on film and in

nightclubs, his records found difficulty in making the singles charts during the early part of the 60s. In 1961, Frank Sinatra, who had also been with Capitol Records, started his own Reprise Records. Martin, who was a member of Sinatra's 'Clan', or 'Ratpack', was one of the first recruits to the new label. In 1964, Martin returned to the US singles charts with a bang. His recording of 'Everybody Loves Somebody', produced by Jimmy Bowen, had a commercial country 'feel' to it, and knocked the Beatles' 'A Hard Day's Night' off the top of the chart. Martin's subsequent Top 30 entries were all in the same vein - records such as 'The Door Is Still Open To My Heart', 'You're Nobody Till Somebody Loves You', 'Send Me The Pillow You Dream On', 'Houston', 'In The Chapel In The Moonlight' and 'Little Ole Wine Drinker, Me'. The latter number was a fitting selection for an artist whose stage persona was that of a man more than slightly inebriated. 'Everybody Loves Somebody' became the theme song for *The Dean Martin Show* on NBC TV which started in 1964, ran for nine seasons and was syndicated worldwide. As well being a showcase for Martin's singing talents, the show gave him the opportunity to display his improvisational skills in comedy. He continued to be a big draw in clubs, especially in Las Vegas, and played the London Palladium in the summer of 1987 to favourable reviews. Later that year, he joined ex-Rat Pack colleagues Sinatra and Sammy Davis Jnr. in the 'Together Again' tour, involving 40 performances in 29 cities, but had to withdraw at an early stage because of a kidney ailment. In the autumn of 1993 it was reported that Martin had lung cancer and he died on Christmas Day 1995.

● ALBUMS: *Capitol Presents Dean Martin* (Capitol 1953)★★★, *Swingin' Down Yonder* (Capitol 1955)★★★, *Dean Martin Sings, Nicolini Lucchesi Plays* (Britone 1956)★★, *The Stooge* film soundtrack (Capitol 1956)★★, *Pretty Baby* (Capitol 1957)★★★, *This Is Dean Martin* (Capitol 1958)★★★, *Sleep Warm* (Capitol 1959)★★★, *Winter Romance* (Capitol 1959)★★★, *Bells Are Ringing* film soundtrack (Capitol 1960)★★★, *This Time I'm Swingin'* (Capitol 1961)★★★, *Dino Goes Dixie* (Encore 1961)★★, *Dean Martin* (Capitol 1961)★★★, *Dino - Italian Love Songs* (Capitol 1962)★★★, *French Style* (Reprise 1962)★★★, *Cha Cha De Amor* (Capitol 1962)★★★, *Dino Latino* (Reprise 1963)★★★, *Dean Martin Country Style* (Reprise 1963)★★, *Dean 'Tex' Martin Rides Again* (Reprise 1963)★★, *Everybody Loves Somebody* (Reprise 1964)★★★, *Hey Brother, Pour The Wine* (Reprise 1964)★★★, *Dream With Dean* (Reprise 1964)★★★, *The Door Is Still Open To My Heart* (Reprise 1964)★★★, *Dean Martin Hits Again* (Reprise 1965)★★★, *Dean Martin Sings, Sinatra Conducts* (1965)★★★, *Southern Style* (1965)★★★, *Dean Martin Month* (Reprise 1965)★★★, *Holiday Cheer* (1965)★★★, *I'm Yours* (Sears 1965)★★★, *Lush Years* (1965)★★★, *(Remember Me) I'm The One Who Loves You* (Reprise 1965)★★★, *Houston* (Reprise 1965)★★★, *Somewhere There's A Someone* (Reprise 1966)★★★, *Relaxin'* (1966)★★★, *Happy In Love* (1966)★★★, *Sings Songs From The Silencers* (Reprise 1966)★★★, *The Hit Sound Of Dean Martin* (Reprise 1966)★★★, *The Dean Martin TV Show* (Reprise 1966)★★★, *The Dean Martin Christmas Album* (Reprise 1966)★★★, *At Ease With Dean* (Reprise 1967)★★★, *Happiness Is Dean Martin* (Reprise 1967)★★★, *Love Is A Career* (Stateside 1967)★★★, *Welcome To My World* (Reprise 1967)★★★, *Gentle On My Mind* (Reprise 1969)★★★, *I Take A Lot*

Of Pride In What I Am (Reprise 1969)★★★, *My Woman, My Wife* (Reprise 1970)★★★, *For The Good Times* (Reprise 1971)★★★, *Dino* (Reprise 1972)★★★, *Sittin' On Top Of The World* (Reprise 1973)★★★, *You're The Best Thing That Ever Happened To Me* (Reprise 1974)★★★, *Once In A While* (Reprise 1978)★★★, *The Nashville Sessions* (Warners 1983)★★.

● COMPILATIONS: *The Best Of Dean Martin* (Capitol 1966)★★★, *Deluxe Set* 3-LP box set (Capitol 1967)★★★, *Dean Of Music* (MFP 1967)★★★, *Dean Martin's Greatest Hits! Volume 1* (Reprise 1968)★★★, *Dean Martin's Greatest Hits! Volume 2* (Reprise 1968)★★★, *The Best Of Dean Martin* (Capitol 1969)★★★, *The Best Of Dean Martin, Volume 2* (Capitol 1970)★★★, *One More Time* (World Record Club 1970)★★★, *20 Original Dean Martin Hits* (Reprise 1976)★★★, *The Classic Dino* (Capitol 1979)★★★, *Dean Martin* 4-LP box set (World Record Club 1981)★★★, *The Very Best Of Dean Martin* (Capitol 1983)★★★, *20 Love Songs* (Black Tulip 1988)★★★, *The Dean Martin Collection* (Deja Vu 1989)★★★, *The Collection* (Castle 1988)★★★, *That's Amore* (Entertainers 1988)★★★, *The Best Of The Capitol Years* (Capitol 1989)★★★, *Capitol Collectors Series* (Capitol 1990)★★★, *Singles* (1994)★★★, *The Capitol Years* (Capitol 1996)★★★, *Memories Are Made Of This* 8-CD box set (Bear Family 1997)★★★.

● FURTHER READING: *Everybody Loves Somebody*, Arthur Marx. *Dino: Living High In The Dirty Business Of Dreams*, Nick Tosches.

● FILMS: *My Friend Irma* (1949), *My Friend Irma Goes West* (1950), *At War With The Army* (1950), *That's My Boy* (1951), *Sailor Beware* (1951), *The Stooge* (1952), cameo *Road To Bali* (1952), *Jumping Jacks* (1952), *Money From Home* (1953), *Scared Stiff* (1953), *The Caddy* (1953), *Living It Up* (1954), *Three Ring Circus* (1954), *You're Never To Young* (1955), *Artists And Models* (1955), *Hollywood Or Bust* (1956), *Pardners* (1956), *Ten Thousand Bedrooms* (1957), *Some Came Running* (1958), *The Young Lions* (1958), *Career* (1959), *Rio Bravo* (1960), cameo *Pepe* (1960), *Who Was That Lady?* (1960), *Bells Are Ringing* (1960), *Ocean's Eleven* (1960), *All In A Night's Work* (1961), *Ada* (1961), *Who's Got The Action?* (1962), *Sergeants 3* (1962), guest star *The Road To Hong Kong* (1962), *Who's Been Sleeping In My Bed?* (1963), *Toys In The Attic* (1963), *Canzoni Nel Mondo* (1963), *Come Blow Your Horn* (1963), *4 For Texas* (1963), *Kiss Me, Stupid* (1964), *What A Way To Go!* (1964), *Robin And The 7 Hoods* (1964), *Marriage On The Rocks* (1965), *The Sons Of Katie Elder* (1965), *Murders' Row* (1966), *The Silencers* (1966), *Texas Across The River* (1966), *Rough Night In Jericho* (1967), *Rowan & Martin At The Movies* (1968), *How To Save A Marriage (And Ruin Your Life)* (1968), *The Ambushers* (1968), *Bandolero!* (1968), *5 Card Stud* (1968), *The Wrecking Crew* (1969), *Airport* (1970), *Something Big* (1971), *Showdown* (1973), *Mr. Ricco* (1975), *The Cannonball Run* (1981), *L.A. Is My Lady* (1984), *Cannonball Run II* (1984).

MARTIN, HUGH

b. 11 August 1914, Birmingham, Alabama, USA. From the age of five Martin took piano lessons and attended local public school, and also studied at Birmingham Southern College. Despite his classical training, however, he was inspired by the music of George Gershwin and gravitated towards the popular music of the day. In 1937 he appeared in a singing role in *Hooray For What!* on Broadway, where he met another young singer, Ralph Blane. Together with Blane, he and two others formed a vocal quartet named the Martins, who were distinguished by their jazzy harmonizing. Martin and Blane appeared with their group on Fred Allen's popular radio show at the end of the decade, but most of Martin's time and energies were directed towards Broadway, and he was active onstage and increasingly involved with offstage activities in the musical theatre. Among the shows with which he was associated were Irving Berlin's *Louisiana Purchase*, for which he was vocal director and arranger, Richard Rodgers and Lorenz Hart's *The Boys From Syracuse*, Cole Porter's *DuBarry Was A Lady*, Vernon Duke's *Cabin In The Sky*, and *High Button Shoes*, *Gentlemen Prefer Blondes*, and the Phil Silvers vehicle, *Top Banana*. Martin was eager to write music for Broadway and in Blane he had found an ideal partner. The nature of their collaborations was unusual, as Martin explained: 'Ralph and I both wrote music and we both wrote lyrics. Almost always, each of us wrote songs unassisted by the other and simply pooled our work.' In 1941 they were commissioned by Rodgers, who was involved in the production of George Abbott's *Best Foot Forward*, a show that starred Nancy Walker, to write songs. Among their songs for this show were 'Buckle Down, Winsocki', a big hit of that year, and the now lesser known 'Ev'ry Time'. The following year, Martin and Blane joined the long procession of Broadway songsmiths lured by Hollywood. At MGM they worked with other songwriters on several films, including *Broadway Rhythm* (1943), for which they wrote 'Brazilian Boogie', performed by Lena Horne, *Thousands Cheer* (1943) and *Ziegfeld Follies* (1944), writing 'Love', memorably sung by Horne. That same year they had their first largely unassisted venture, the hugely popular Judy Garland film, *Meet Me In St. Louis*. For this film the duo wrote 'The Trolley Song', which was nominated for an Academy Award, 'The Boy Next Door' and 'Have Yourself A Merry Little Christmas'. After wartime service, during which Martin served in Europe, he returned to Hollywood and Broadway. In the film *Good News* (1947), he and Blane received another Oscar nomination, together with Roger Edens, for 'Pass That Peace Pipe', and in 1948 Martin wrote music and lyrics for *Look, Ma, I'm Dancin'!*, which starred Walker on Broadway. His score included 'Gotta Dance' and 'I'm The First Girl In The Second Row'.

In 1950 Martin was vocal arranger for a James Cagney movie, *West Point Story*, and he also wrote the music for a movie short about the primitive artist Grandma Moses. This music was later adapted by the composer for the 'New England Suite', orchestrated by Alec Wilder, who was given co-composer credit because, as Martin says, he 'brought so much new beauty and enhancement to it'. The following year Martin was again responsible for music and lyrics, this time for *Make A Wish*, from which came 'What I Was Warned About', 'Suits Me Fine' and 'When Does This Feeling Go Away?'. In 1952 he was in London's West End for *Love From Judy*, which starred Jeannie Carson, and later in the decade worked on Hollywood's *Athena*, with Blane, *The Girl Rush*, for which he and Blane wrote 'An Occasional Man', *The Girl Most Likely*, also with Blane, and in 1954 was vocal director and arranger for Garland's *A Star Is Born*. He also appeared with Garland as her piano accompanist, notably at her first New York Palace Theatre show, and he accompanied Eddie Fisher at the London Palladium. Martin also worked in television, including the series *Washington Square*, with Ray Bolger, and the *Patrice Munsel Show*. During his years in Hollywood he acted as vocal coach for several artists, including Garland, Horne, Bolger, Rosalind Russell and Nanette Fabray. In 1963, Martin and Blane worked on a revival of *Best Foot Forward*, adding a new song, 'You Are For Loving', which Wilder, in his book, *American Popular Song*, ranked 'among the best theatre ballads ever written'. The following year, in collaboration this time with Timothy Gray, Martin wrote the music for *High Spirits*, including 'If I Gave You' and 'You'd Better Love Me'. In 1979 Martin was musical director for *Sugar Babies*, starring Mickey Rooney and Ann Miller, which played on Broadway and in London and which used music written by Jimmy McHugh. In 1989 Martin and Blane again collaborated, this time to write 10 new songs for a stage version of *Meet Me In St. Louis*, which opened at the Gershwin on 2 November and ran for seven months. Among numerous recordings of Martin's work are excellent albums by him and Blane, *Michael Feinstein Sings the Hugh Martin Songbook*, and Marlene VerPlanck's *You'd Better Love Me*. In 1998 Martin was living in retirement in California where, far from being idle, he was preparing a book about his life and career, and in particular, his long and fruitful relationship with Blane. Martin should not be confused with composer, arranger and singer Hugh E. Martin (1929-76).

● ALBUMS: *Martin & Blane Sing Martin & Blane* 1956 recording (DRG 1994)★★★.

MARTIN, MARY

b. Mary Virginia Martin, 1 December 1913, Weatherford, Texas, USA, d. 3 November 1990, Rancho Mirage, California, USA. A legendary star of the Broadway musical theatre during the 40s and 50s, and one of its most charming, vivacious and best-loved performers. Her father was a lawyer, and her mother a violin teacher. She took dancing and singing lessons from an early age, married at 16, and eventually ran a dancing school herself before moving to Hollywood where she auditioned constantly at the film studios, and worked in nightclubs and on radio. After being spotted by the producer Lawrence Schwab, her first big break came on Broadway in 1938 when she won a secondary role, as Dolly Winslow, in the Cole Porter musical *Leave It To Me*. Almost every night she stopped the show with her 'sensational' rendering of 'My Heart Belongs To Daddy' while performing a mock striptease perched on top of a large cabin trunk at a 'Siberian' railway station. On the strength of her performance in that show she was signed to Paramount, and made 10 films over a period of four years, beginning with *The Great Victor Herbert* in 1939. Although her delightfully warm personality and theatrical star quality, were not so effective on film, she did have her moments, particularly in *Rhythm On The River* (with Bing Crosby and Oscar Levant) and *Birth Of The Blues*, in which she joined Crosby and Jack Teagarden for 'The Waiter, And The Porter And The Upstairs Maid'. She also sang the title song in *Kiss The Boys Goodbye*, which became a big hit for Tommy Dorsey, and duetted with Dick Powell on 'Hit The Road To Dreamland' in *Star Spangled Rhythm*. Other film appearances included *Love Thy Neighbour*, *New York Town*, *Happy-Go-Lucky*, *True To*

Life, and *Main Street To Broadway* (1953). While on the west coast, she married for the second time, to a Paramount executive Richard Halliday, who became her manager. In 1943 she returned to the stage, and, after failing to reach Broadway with *Dancing In The Streets*, scored a great success with *One Touch Of Venus* which ran for 567 performances. The role of a glamorous statue that comes to life and falls in love with a human had originally been intended for Marlene Dietrich, but it fell to Martin to sing the haunting 'Speak Low', and the show established her as a true star. She followed it with *Lute Song*, the show which introduced Yul Brynner to Broadway, before returning to Hollywood to reprise 'My Heart Belongs To Daddy' for the Cole Porter biopic *Night And Day*. A trip to London in 1947 for an appearance in Noël Coward's *Pacific 1860*, proved an unsatisfactory experience, and Martin returned to the USA to play the lead in a touring version of *Annie Get Your Gun*. Richard Rodgers and Oscar Hammerstein's smash hit *South Pacific* was next, and Martin's memorable performance, funny and poignant in turns, won her a Tony Award. Starred with opera singer Ezio Pinza, she introduced several of the composers' most endearing numbers, including 'I'm Gonna Wash That Man Right Out Of My Hair' (sung while she shampooed her hair on stage), 'A Wonderful Guy', 'A Cockeyed Optimist', and the hilarious 'Honeybun'. *South Pacific* ran for 1,925 performances in New York, and Martin recreated her role for the 1951 London production at Drury Lane where she was equally well received. During the rest of the 50s Mary Martin appeared in several straight plays, two highly regarded television spectaculars - one with Ethel Merman (which included a 35-song medley), and the other with Noël Coward - as well as starring on Broadway with Cyril Ritchard in a musical version of *Peter Pan* (1954) which was taped and shown repeatedly on US television. In November 1959 Martin opened at the Lunt-Fontanne Theatre in New York in what was to prove yet another blockbuster hit. Rodgers and Hammerstein's musical about the Trapp family of Austrian folk singers, *The Sound Of Music*, immediately produced reactions ranging for raves to revulsion, but it gave Martin another Tony Award and the chance to display her homespun charm with songs such as 'My Favourite Things' and 'Do-Re-Mi'. From the 'hills that were alive with music', Mary Martin plummeted to the depths in *Jennie* (1963), her first real flop. Thereafter, she and her husband spent more time at their home in Brazil, but in 1965 she was persuaded to embark on a world tour in *Hello, Dolly!* which included a visit to Vietnam, and a five-month stay in London. Her final appearance in a Broadway musical was in 1966 with Robert Preston in the two-hander *I Do! I Do!* which ran for 560 performances. In the 70s she did more straight theatre and won a Peabody Award for the television film *Valentine*. After her husband's death in 1973, Martin moved to Palm Springs to be near her friend Janet Gaynor, but returned to New York in 1977 to star with Ethel Merman in a benefit performance of *Together Again*. In the early 80s, Martin and Janet Gaynor were severely injured in an horrific taxicab crash in San Franciso which took the life of her longtime aide Ben Washer. Martin recovered to receive the applause of her peers in *Our*

Heart Belongs To Mary, and to make her final US stage appearance in 1986 with Carol Channing in a national tour of James Kirkwood's comedy *Legends*. For much of the time she had to wear a shortwave radio device to prompt her when she forgot her lines. Mary Martin made her final appearance on the London stage in the 1980 Royal Variety Performance when she performed a delightful version of 'Honeybun', and then had to suffer the embarrassment of watching her son from her first marriage, Larry Hagman (the notorious J. R Ewing from the television soap opera, *Dallas*), forget his lines in front of the celebrity audience.

● ALBUMS: *Adventures For Readers* (Harcourt 1958)★★, *Mary Martin Sings-Richard Rodgers Plays* (RCA 1958)★★★, *Sings For You* (Columbia c.50s)★★★★, *A Spoonful Of Sugar* (Kapp 1964)★★★, with Danny Kaye, Ethel Merman and others *Cole Porter Sings And Plays Jubilee* (Columbia 1972)★★★, with Noël Coward *Together With Music* (AMR 1976)★★★★, *On Broadway* (Silva Screen 1989)★★★, *16 Most Requested Songs* (Columbia 1993)★★★★, and stage cast recordings.

● FURTHER READING: *Mary Martin On Stage*, S. P. Newman, *My Heart Belongs*, Mary Martin.

MARTIN, RAY

b. Raymond Stuart Martin, 11 October 1918, Vienna, Austria, d. February 1988, South Africa. A composer, arranger, musical director and author, after studying violin, composition and orchestration at the State Academy for Music and Fine Arts in Vienna, Martin moved to Britain in 1937. He joined the *Carroll Levis Discoveries* show as a solo violin act, touring the UK variety circuit, and was then chosen as the 'New Voice' in the popular BBC radio series *Bandwaggon*, which starred Arthur Askey and Richard Murdoch. After appearing in several editions of *Sidney Torch's Half Hour*, he enlisted in the British Army in 1940 and worked in the Intelligence Corps, aided by his fluency in German, French and English. Later, he became musical director of the Variety Department for the British Forces Network in Hamburg, Germany. He started broadcasting his *Melody From The Sky* programme from there, with a German string orchestra culled from the Hamburg Philharmonic Orchestra, and transferred the show to the BBC in December 1946, where it ran for over 500 broadcasts. Martin was also instrumental in founding the BBC Northern Variety Orchestra, and, from 1949-51, conducted at least six shows a week. He started recording for Columbia Records in 1949 with his own Concert Orchestra accompanying other artists including Julie Andrews, Steve Conway and Jimmy Young. Eventually he became the company's recording manager. His 50s instrumental hits included Leroy Anderson's 'Blue Tango', 'Swedish Rhapsody' and 'Carousel Waltz'. Some of his many compositions and film scores are difficult to locate because, besides his own name, he wrote under several pseudonyms, such as Tony Simmonds, Buddy Cadbury, Lester Powell and Marshall Ross. In 1956 he wrote the background score, and served as musical director, for a British musical film called *It's Great To Be Young*, starring John Mills. In addition to the title track, written under his own name, the film contained Martin's (as Marshall Ross) 1952 composition 'Marching Strings'; and his (as Lester

Powell) romantic ballad 'You Are My First Love' (in collaboration with Paddy Roberts). Martin's other compositions included 'Melody From The Sky', 'Once Upon A Winter Time', 'Muriella', 'Begorra', 'Parlour Game', 'Blue Violins' (a US hit for Hugo Winterhalter's Orchestra), 'Any Old Time', 'Waltzing Bugle Boy', 'Airborne', 'Ballet Of The Bells', 'Tango Of The Bells', 'Big Ben Blues', 'Never Too Young' and 'Sounds Out Of Sight'. He composed the incidental music for over 20 BBC Sound cartoons, and wrote the scores for several films, including *Yield To The Night*, a prison melodrama in which ex-'glamour girl' Diana Dors gave a highly acclaimed dramatic performance, and the 1956 version of *My Wife's Father*. In 1957 Martin moved to America to work in New York and Hollywood. His US film scores included *The Young Graduates* and *The Hoax*. In 1972 he returned to work in the UK and, in 1980, appeared as himself in *The Baltimore Bullit*. During the 80s he settled in South Africa, and died there in 1988.

● ALBUMS: *Music In The Ray Martin Manner* (Columbia 1953)★★★★, *Music In The Ray Martin Manner Volume 2* (Columbia 1954)★★★★, *Lehar, Strauss And Novello Melodies* (Columbia 1956)★★★, *High Barbaree-12 Famous Sea Shanties* (Columbia 1957)★★, *Olives, Almonds And Raisins* (Columbia 1958)★★★, *Million Dollar Melodies* (Columbia 1959)★★★, *Melodies D'Amour* (Columbia 1961)★★★, *Boots And Saddles* (Columbia 1961)★★, *I Could Have Danced All Night* (1961)★★★, *Dynamica* (RCA 1961)★★★, *We* (1962)★★★, *Spotlight On Strings* (1962)★★★, *Sounds Out Of Sight* (1963)★★★, *The Sound Of Sight* (Phase 4 1964)★★★, *London Under The Stars* (1966)★★★, *Favourite TV Themes* (Decca 1973)★★★, *Favourite TV Themes, Volume 2* (Decca 1975)★★★, *Viva Mariachi* (Gold Star 1975)★★★, *Welcome Home* (Goldstar 1975)★★★.

MARTIN, TONY

b. Alvin Morris, 25 December 1912, Oakland, California, USA. A popular singer and film actor from the 30s until the late 50s, with a powerful tenor voice and an easy, romantic style. As a teenager, Martin learnt to play the saxophone and formed his own band, the Clarion Four. For some years he worked at the Palace Hotel, in the San Francisco area, playing and singing with the bands of Anson Weeks, Tom Coakley, and Tom Guran - whose outfit included Woody Herman. Morris drove across country with Herman and other members of the band to the 1933 Chicago World Fair, and afterwards performed at the city's Chez Paree Club. In 1934 he changed his name to Tony Martin, and tried unsuccessfully to break into films. Two years later he landed a 'bit' part in the Fred Astaire-Ginger Rogers hit movie *Follow The Fleet*, along with two other young hopefuls, Lucille Ball and Betty Grable. Later, in 1936, he signed for 20th Century-Fox, and sang 'When I'm With You' in *Poor Little Rich Girl*, and 'When Did You Leave Heaven?' in *Sing, Baby, Sing*. The following year he married one of the film's stars, Alice Faye. During the late 30s he had leading roles in film musicals such as *Pigskin Parade* (with Judy Garland and Betty Grable), *Banjo On My Knee* (Barbara Stanwyck and Joel McCrea), *The Holy Terror* and *Sing And Be Happy* (Leah Ray) *You Can't Have Everything* and *Sally, Irene And Mary* (Alice Faye), *Ali Baba Goes To Town* (starring Eddie Cantor), *Kentucky Moonshine*, and *Thanks For Everything*. When Martin left

Fox he appeared with Rita Hayworth in *Music In My Heart*, and introduced Robert Wright and George Forrest's 'It's A Blue World' which was nominated for an Academy Award in 1940. In 1941, Martin appeared with the Marx Brothers in *The Big Store*, and sang 'The Tenement Symphony'. Although it was described, somewhat unkindly, as the comedy highlight of the film, the song endured to become one of his identity numbers. Martin's other movie that year was *Ziegfeld Girl*, with some spectacular Busby Berkeley production numbers, and starring, amongst others, Judy Garland, Hedy Lamarr and Lana Turner. After the Japanese attack on Pearl Harbor in December 1941, Martin enlisted in the US Armed Forces, serving first in the Navy, and then with the Army in the Far East. He also sang for a time with the Army Air Forces Training Command Orchestra directed by Glenn Miller, and received several awards, including the Bronze Star and other citations. After his release, he returned to Hollywood, starring in the Jerome Kern bio-pic, *Till The Clouds Roll By* (1946). This was followed by *Casbah* (1948), in which he played the spy Pepe Le Moko, thought by many to have been his best role. The songs were by Harold Arlen and Leo Robin, and included another Martin all-time favourite, the Oscar-nominated 'For Every Man There's A Woman'. In the same year, having divorced Alice Faye, Martin married dancer-actress Cyd Charisse, and later appeared with her in *Easy To Love* (1953). Martin's other films during the 50s included *Two Tickets To Broadway* (with Janet Leigh), *Here Come The Girls* (with Bob Hope and Rosemary Clooney), the all-star Sigmund Romberg bio-pic *Deep In My Heart*, the 1955 MGM re-make of *Hit The Deck,* and a guest appearance in *Meet Me In Las Vegas* (which starred Cyd Charisse and Dan Dailey). In 1957 Martin joined with Vera-Ellen in *Let's Be Happy*, an unsuccessful British attempt to recreate the Hollywood musical. In addition to his film work, Martin has had a very successful recording career. His first hits, 'Now It Can Be Told' and 'South Of The Border', came in the late 30s, and continued through to the mid-50s with songs such as 'It's A Blue World', 'Tonight We Love', 'To Each His Own', 'Rumours Are Flying', 'It's Magic', 'There's No Tomorrow', 'Circus', 'Marta (Rambling Rose Of The Wildwood)', 'I Said My Pyjamas (And Put On My Prayers)' and 'Take A Letter, Miss Smith' (both duets with Fran Warren), 'La Vie En Rose', 'Would I Love You (Love You Love You)', 'I Get Ideas' (adapted from the Argentine tango 'Adios Muchachos' and thought to be quite racy at the time), 'Over A Bottle Of Wine', 'Domino', 'Kiss Of Fire', 'Stranger In Paradise', 'Here', 'Do I Love You (Because You're Beautiful)' and 'Walk Hand In Hand'. He was also very active on radio in the 30s-50s on shows such as Walter Winchell's *Lucky Strike Hour*, and others featuring Burns And Allen, André Kostelanetz and David Rose, along with his own programmes. He subsequently moved to television, and from 1954-56 hosted *The Tony Martin Show*. In 1964, he formed a night club act with his wife, and for many years they toured the cabaret circuit in the USA and abroad. In 1986 Martin accompanied Charisse to London when she re-created the role of Lady Hadwell in the David Heneker-John Taylor stage musical *Charlie Girl* at the Victoria Palace, a part created by Anna Neagle over

20 years earlier. Martin and Charisse had first visited London in 1948 on their honeymoon when he was playing the first of several London Palladium seasons. Martin has come a long way since then, and is still regarded as one of the most accomplished and stylish vocalists of his era. He returned to London yet again in the 90s for cabaret appearances at the Café Royal.

● ALBUMS: *Tony Martin Sings Volume 1* (Brunswick 1955)★★★★, *Tony Martin Favourites* (Mercury 1956)★★★★, *A Night At The Copacabana* (RCA 1956)★★★★, *Our Love Affair* (1957)★★★★, *Speak To Me Of Love* (HMV 1957)★★★, *In The Spotlight* (1958)★★★★, *Dream Music* (Mercury 1959)★★★★, *Mr. Song Man* (1960)★★★★, *At The Desert Inn* (RCA 1960)★★★★, *Tonight* (1960)★★★★, *Fly Me To The Moon* (1962)★★★★, *At Carnegie Hall* (Stateside 1967)★★★★.

● COMPILATIONS: *Greatest Hits* (London 1961)★★★★, *Golden Hits* (1962)★★★★, *Best Of* (1984)★★★★, *Tenement Symphony* (1984)★★★★, *Something In The Air* (1989)★★★★, *This May Be The Night* (ASV 1993)★★★★.

● FILMS: *Sing, Baby, Sing* (1936), *Poor Little Rich Girl* (1936), *Murder On The Bridle Path* (1936), *Banjo On My Knee* (1936), *Follow The Fleet* (1936), *Back To Nature* (1936), *You Can't Have Everything* (1937), *Sing And Be Happy* (1937), *Life Begins In College* (1937), *Ali Baba Goes To Town* (1937), *Up The River* (1938), *Sally, Irene And Mary* (1938), *Kentucky Moonshine* (1938), *Thanks For Everything* (1938), *Winner Take All* (1939), *Music In My Heart* (1940), *Ziegfeld Girl* (1941), *The Big Store* (1941), *Till The Clouds Roll By* (1946), *Casbah* (1948), *Two Tickets To Broadway* (1951), *Here Come The Girls* (1953), *Easy To Love* (1953), *Deep In My Heart* (1954), *Hit The Deck* (1955), *Quincannon-Frontier Scout* (1956), *Meet Me In Last Vegas* cameo (1956), *Let's Be Happy* (1957).

● FURTHER READING: *The Two Of Us*, Tony Martin and Cyd Charisse with Dick Kleiner.

MARY POPPINS

There have been many occasions when performers who have triumphed in Broadway shows have been overlooked when the movie adaptations came along. While Julie Andrews would have no doubt dazzled as Eliza Doolittle in the film version of *My Fair Lady*, it was not to be. Instead, Andrews made up for the disappointment in a big way by making her first screen appearance in this 1964 Walt Disney classic. With supreme irony, Andrews won the best actress Oscar for her debut performance, while Audrey Hepburn, who 'took her place' in the film of Alan Jay Lerner and Frederick Loewe's masterpiece, was not even nominated. With a screenplay by Bill Walsh and Donald Da Gradi, adapted from the children's story by Pamela Travers, the action of *Mary Poppins* evolves around the Banks family, residents of 17 Cherry Tree Lane, London. Mr George Banks (David Tomlinson) is a banker by name, nature and occupation. He rules his house with a rod of iron, while Winifred, his wife (Glynis Johns), spends most of the time fighting for the Suffragettes' cause (the year is 1910). Both spend little time with their children Michael (Matthew Garber) and Jane (Karen Dotrice). Many nannies have come and gone (six in four months), and as the film begins, the time has come to employ another one. The children draw up their own advertisement, outlining what they want most in the new employee. In disgust Mr Banks throws the piece of paper into the fireplace, and unbeknown to him, it travels up the chimney, and, before you can say 'Mary Poppins', she floats down to earth, carrying her trusty umbrella, and appoints herself as the new nanny, giving the family a week's trial! Before long Mary has won the hearts of the children, tidying up by magic, and taking them on many an adventure. During one such trip she bumps into an old friend, Bert (Dick Van Dyke) who plays a number of different roles in the film, entertaining with his one-man band and drawing pictures on the pavement. As if by magic, Mary, Bert and the children escape from reality and step into the street painting. Here the movie really comes into its own as humans mix with all kinds of animated characters and animals. It is great fun to watch, as we see the group being waited on by penguins, and wooden horses galloping with freedom. Only when the pavement picture is washed away by rain, do the happy foursome have to return home. However, fun is frivolous to Mr Banks, and he decides to take the children along to his workplace to see what the real world is all about. Here Michael and Jane meet the bank president, Mr Dawes, (Dick Van Dyke again), but the trip turns into a disaster, and as a result their father is sacked. By the time he eventually gets his job back, the family have become much happier and tolerant of each other. Mary Poppins sees that her job has been accomplished and flies back to her cloud. Also among the cast were Hermione Baddeley, Ed Wynn, Arthur Treacher, Elsa Lanchester, Reginald Owen, and Reta Shaw.

Directed by Robert Stevenson, this is an enchanting fairy tale, never losing its musical and comic pace for a moment. Richard M. and Robert B Sherman's outstanding score included 'A Spoonful Of Sugar', 'Feed the Birds', the infamous 'Supercalifragilisticexpialidocious', 'The Perfect Nanny', 'Sister Suffragette', 'The Life I Lead', 'Fidelity Feduciary Bank', 'Lets' Go Fly A Kite', and 'Chim Chim Cheree' which won the Oscar for best song. One of the film's highlights comes when the energetic Dick Van Dyke (complete with an amusingly artificial Cockney accent) leads a band of chimney sweeps in a dance to 'Step In Time' over the rooftops of London. The scene is a joy, and a credit to choreographers Marc Breaux and DeeDee Wood. *Mary Poppins* won Academy Awards for its music score and (predictably) for special effects and film editing. Photographed in Technicolor by Edward Colman, it went on to become the third-highest grossing musical of the 60s.

MATADOR

This show, which was 'inspired' by the life of the Spanish bullfighter El Cordobes, first surfaced in the form of a concept album recorded by Tom Jones in 1987. One of the tracks, 'A Boy From Nowhere', climbed to number 2 in the UK singles chart, and Jones was originally set to take the leading role in the stage production. Things did not work out that way, and when *Matador* opened at the Queens theatre in London on 16 April 1991, the central character of Domingo Hernandez was played by the young unknown John Barrowman, with Nicky Henson as his crafty manager. In an attempt to give the production some glamour, the actress Stephanie Powers, well-known in

England for her appearances with Robert Wagner in the television series *Hart To Hart*, was brought in to play the part of an American film star Laura-Jane Wilding. The character was thought to be based on Ava Gardner with whom El Cordobes is said to have had an affair. The score was by Michael Leander and Edward Seago, who had written hits for Gary Glitter, Engelbert Humperdinck and Cliff Richard, and the book, by Peter Dukes, was based on Leander and Seago's original storyline. Domingo's rise from the obscure village of Andalucia to the top of the bullfighting world despite a background of illiteracy, was thrillingly staged against a background of spectacular sets, but it was the dancing - particularly the flamenco dancing choreographed by Rafael Aguilar - which proved to be the outstanding feature of the whole production. The score, which contained nothing else as memorable as 'A Boy From Nowhere', also included 'Panama Hat', 'No Way Out Of This Town', 'I Was Born To Be Me', 'I'll Take You Out To Dinner', 'Paseo And Corrida', 'To Be a Matador', 'Children Of The Sun', 'I'll Dress You In Mourning', and 'I'm You, You Are Me'. Critical reaction was mixed ('Risibly awful . . . a load of bull', was the worst), but the show never captured an audience and closed after three months with losses 'approaching £1 million'.

MATTHEWS, JESSIE

b. 11 March 1907, London, England, d. 19 August 1981, Pinner, Middlesex, England. A member of a large and poor family, Matthews became a professional dancer at the age of 10. After a few years in the chorus of several shows in London's West End, she achieved recognition with a series of ingenue roles and some bit parts in films. After appearing in stage production such as *André Charlot's Revue Of 1926*, *Earl Carroll's Vanities Of 1926*, *Jordan*, *This Year Of Grace*, *Wake Up And Dream* (London and New York), *Hold My Hand*, and *Sally Who?*, by the early 30s she had become one of London's most popular stars. At the height of her career, in such shows as the 1930 London production of *Ever Green*, with a score by Richard Rodgers and Lorenz Hart, Matthews was the epitome of the English musical comedy star: her delicate build and translucent beauty fully matched songs such as that show's ethereal 'Dancing On The Ceiling'. Her film work also grew, and she made several British movies in which she shone effortlessly. Despite an appearance in the 1934 film version of her stage hit, slightly retitled as *Evergreen* - in which she introduced 'Over My Shoulder', one of 'identity songs - few of Matthews' film musicals were worthy of her talent. They included *Out Of The Blue*, *Waltzes From Vienna*, *First A Girl*, *It's Love Again*, *Head Over Heels*, *Gangway*, and *Sailing Along* (1938). An outstanding dancer, the variable quality of her films militated against her continuing for long and by the 40s, her career was all but over. Her last appearance on a London stage in this part of her career was in the 1942 production of *Wild Rose*. After many years away from the public eye, spent mostly in Australia, she returned to the screen in 1958 as the mother in *Tom Thumb*, and in 1963 took over the title role in the daily BBC radio serial *Mrs Dale's Diary*. In the 70s she was seen on the London stage in *The Water Babies* and *Lady Windemere's Fan*, and also appeared on television in the series *Edward And Mrs. Simpson*. Her one-woman show *Miss Jessie Matthews In Concert*, which was produced in Los Angeles in 1979, won the US Drama Critics Award. In 1993/94, when the Adelphi Theatre in London was being lavishly restored under the supervision of its co-owner, the celebrated composer and producer Andrew Lloyd Webber - a great admirer of Jessie Matthews, one of the bars in the theatre was named in her honour.

● FURTHER READING: *Over My Shoulder: An Autobiography*, Jessie Matthews with Muriel Burgess. *Jessie Matthews - A Biography*, Michael Thornton.

MAURIAT, PAUL

b. 1925, France. A conductor, arranger and composer, descended from generations of classical musicians, Mauriat began to study music at the age of four, and continued his studies at the Conservatoire in Paris when his family moved there in 1935. His initial ambition to become classical pianist gave way to an interest in popular music and jazz. When he was 17, Mauriet formed his own orchestra and, for several years, toured concert halls and theatres in Europe. His big break came when he began arranging and conducting for recordings by Charles Aznavour, a relationship which endured, and led to him working with other French artists. In the 60s his distinctive, melodic, arrangements on his own instrumental albums with a contemporary beat, gained him a substantial following. In 1962, under the pseudonym Del Roma, Mauriat co-wrote 'Chariot', which, sung in French, became a big Continental hit for Petula Clark. In the following year, with an alternative lyric by Norman Gimbel and Arthur Altman, the song was re-titled 'I Will Follow Him', and was taken to the top of the US chart by Little Peggy March. Mauriat's own success in America was sparked off in 1968, when his enormous international hit version of 'L'Amour Est Bleu' ('Love Is Blue'), Luxembourg's entry in the 1963 Eurovision Song contest, spent five weeks in the number 1 spot. He repeated the feat with *Blooming Hits*, a collection of 60s favourites, including Eurovision winner 'Puppet On A String' and John Lennon/Paul McCartney's 'Penny Lane', which is reputed to have sold well over two million copies. This all led to major television appearances and tours throughout the USA and Mexico, Latin America, Japan, and many other countries. Mauriat had two other minor US hit singles, 'Love In Every Room' and 'Chitty Chitty Bang Bang', but his albums continued to sell in large quantities.

● ALBUMS: *Memories of Russia* (1962)★★, *Rhythm And Blues* (1963)★★, *A Taste Of Paul Mauriat* (1963)★★★★, *Blooming Hits* (1967)★★★★, *More Mauriat* (1968)★★★, *Mauriat Magic* (1968)★★★, *The Soul Of Paul Mauriat* (Philips 1968)★★★, *Prevailing Airs* (1968)★★★, *Doing My Thing* (1969)★★, *L.O.V.E.* (1969)★★, *Gone Is Love* (1970)★★★, *El Condor Pasa* (1971)★★, *Tout Pour La Musiique* (1982)★★★, *Magic* (1984)★★★ *I Love Breeze* (1984)★★★, *Penelope* (1984)★★★, *Magic Laser Hits* (1985)★★★, *The Seven Seas* (1985)v, *Windy* (1986)★★.

● COMPILATIONS: *Love Is Blue* (Spectrum 1998)★★★★.

MAYTIME (FILM MUSICAL)

Although this 1937 screen version retained hardly anything from the 1917 stage operetta other than the title and one of the songs, it remains one of the most accomplished and enjoyable films of its kind. Noel Langley's story, which is told in flashback, concerns the famous opera star Marcia Mornay (Jeanette MacDonald), who puts her career before her true love, Paul Allison (Nelson Eddy), and marries Nicolai Nazaroff (John Barrymore), the dominant figure in her life. The somewhat melodramatic climax comes when Allison, having been killed by Nazaroff while in a jealous rage, materialises in spiritual form and is serenaded by a remorseful Marcia. Among a strong supporting cast were Herman Bing, Lynne Carver, Tom Brown, Sig Ruman, Billy Gilbert, Harry Davenport, Walter Kingsford, Ivan Lebedeff, and Leonid Kinskey. The lovely 'Will You Remember (Sweetheart)?' (Rida Johnson Young-Sigmund Romberg), the song that survived from the original stage show, was sung with a glorious passion by Eddy and MacDonald, a feeling they also brought to bear on 'Czaritza', which consisted of excerpts from Tchaikovsky's Fifth Symphony, arranged by Robert Wright and George Forrest. The latter duo also wrote new lyrics to the folk song, 'Vive L'Opera', and the rest of the score, a mixture of songs and operatic excerpts, included 'Carry Me Back to Old Virginny' (James Bland), 'Love's Old Sweet Song' (James L. Molloy-G. Clifton Bingham), 'Le Regiment De Sambre Et Meuse' (Robert Planquette), and 'Ham And Eggs' (Herbert Stothart-Wright-Forrest). This lavish production, considered to be one of the best of Jeanette MacDonald and Nelson Eddy's eight films together, was produced by Hunt Stromberg for MGM and directed by Robert Z. Leonard. *Variety* reported that it grossed three and a half million dollars in US domestic theatre rentals, putting it among the most successful films of the decade.

MAYTIME (STAGE MUSICAL)

With his score for this highly popular operetta, which was based on a German production, *Wie Einst In Mai*, Sigmund Romberg finally stepped out of Victor Herbert's shadow, and established himself as the leading composer of these gloriously musical, sentimental sagas. Rida Johnson Young wrote the book and lyrics, and the show's role-reversal story was set in New York, where well-off Ottilie Van Zandt (Peggy Wood) is prevented by her father, Matthew Van Zandt (William Norris), from marrying her true love, Richard Wayne (Charles Purcell), because, quite frankly, he comes from 'the other side of the tracks'. They go on to each marry their respective partners, although they meet socially and affirm their love for each other. When Ottilie's husband dies, she is left destitute, and her house and all her belongings are auctioned. Richard buys the house, and many years pass before their grandchildren encounter each other, and presumably find happiness together. The grandchildren were also played by Peggy Wood and Charles Purcell. The sweeping, romantic score included 'The Road To Paradise', 'Jump Jim Crow', 'In Our Little Home Sweet Home', 'Only One Girl For Me', and 'Will You Remember?', a lovely song which achieved wider recognition. One of the other numbers, 'Dancing Will Keep You Young', had music by Romberg and a lyric by Cyrus Wood. An enormously popular show - America's biggest hit of World War I - which all the soldiers aimed to see before they departed for the conflict. Its run of 492 performances in 1917 was, for the time, astounding. The 1937 film changed the story and discarded all the songs except for 'Will You Remember?'. The song was sung superbly by Jane Powell and Vic Damone in the 1954 Sigmund Romberg bio-pic, *Deep In My Heart*.

McCARTHY, JOSEPH

b. 27 September 1885, Somerville, Massachusetts, USA, d. 18 December 1943, New York, USA. An important lyricist in the 20s and 30s, McCarthy sang in cafes and worked for music publishers before writing songs such as 'That Dreamy Italian Waltz', 'That's How I Need You' and 'I Miss You Most Of All'. In 1913, with Jimmy Monaco, he produced one of popular music's all-time standards, 'You Made Me Love You', memorably sung and recorded by hundreds of artists, including Al Jolson, Harry James, Judy Garland and Grace La Rue. Three years later, again with Monaco, and Howard Johnson, McCarthy wrote 'What Do You Want To Make Those Eyes At Me For?' for Betty Hutton to sing in the 1945 movie *Incendiary Blonde*, the bio-pic of nightclub queen Texas Guinan. The song resurfaced in the UK in 1959, as a number 1 for Emile Ford And The Checkmates, and again in 1987, when it was a hit for rock 'n' roll revivalist, Shakin' Stevens.

In 1919, McCarthy and Harry Tierney contributed songs to the *Ziegfeld Follies* of that year, and wrote the score for the hugely successful *Irene*, which was filmed in 1940, starring Anna Neagle and Ray Milland, and successfully revived at the Minskoff Theatre in 1973, with Debbie Reynolds as Irene. In 1920, Tierney and McCarthy had several numbers, including 'Why Don't You?', interpolated in the European score of Charles Cuvillier's *Afgar* when it was staged on Broadway, starring the toast of London and Paris, Alice Delysia. They also contributed to the revues *The Broadway Whirl*, *Up She Goes* and *Glory*, before writing the score for Florenz Ziegfeld's 1923 hit, *Kid Boots*. After a brief break, McCarthy resumed his association with Tierney in 1927 for the operetta *Rio Rita*, the season's biggest musical success. McCarthy and Tierney's songs included 'The Rangers' Song', 'If You're In Love, You'll Waltz', 'You're Always In My Arms', 'Following The Sun Around', 'The Kinkajou' and the main duet, 'Rio Rita', which was sung by Ethelind Terry and J. Harold Murray. It ran for nearly 500 performances and was filmed in 1929, and again in 1942. Tierney and McCarthy's last Broadway show together was *Cross My Heart* in 1928, which closed after only eight weeks.

In the 30s, McCarthy collaborated with James Hanley on the songs for the film *High Society Blues* ('I'm In The Market For You', 'Eleanor', 'Just Like A Story Book', 'I Don't Know You Well Enough For That') and *Listen, Darling*, starring Judy Garland ('Ten Pins In the Sky'), and in 1940 had 'You Think Of Ev'rything and 'When The Spirit Moves Me' in *Billy Rose's Aquacade* water carnival. McCarthy's other songs included the poignant ballad 'I'm Always Chasing Rainbows' (with Harry Carroll), 'They Go Wild, Simply Wild, Over Me' (a hit for Marion Harris), 'Through', 'Ireland Must Be Heaven For My Mother Came From There', Night Time In Italy', 'I'm In The Market For You', and 'Underneath The Arches'. Among his other collaborators were Fred Fisher and Al Piantadosi.

McHUGH, JIMMY

b. James Francis McHugh, 10 July 1894, Boston, Massachusetts, USA, d. 23 May 1969, Beverly Hills, California, USA. A prolific composer for films and the Broadway stage, McHugh was educated at St. John's Preparatory School and Holy Cross College, where he graduated with an honours degree in music. After receiving professional tuition, he worked as a rehearsal pianist at the Boston Opera House, and later as a song-plugger for the Boston office of Irving Berlin Music. Moving to New York, he wrote for Harlem's Cotton Club revues, and had some success with 'When My Sugar Walks Down The Street' (lyric by Irving Mills and Gene Austin) and 'I Can't Believe That You're In Love With Me' (lyric by Clarence Gaskill). His first Broadway success came with the score for the all-black revue, *Blackbirds Of 1928*, in collaboration with Dorothy Fields, who became his first main lyricist. The songs included 'I Can't Give You Anything But Love', 'Diga Diga Doo', 'I Must Have That Man', 'Doin' The New Low-Down' and 'Porgy'. The original stars, Adelaide Hall and Bill 'Bojangles' Robinson were joined by the Mills Brothers, Ethel Waters, and the orchestras of Cab Calloway, Duke Ellington, and Don Redman on a rare reissue album. The McHugh/Fields team wrote the scores for two more Broadway shows, *Hello Daddy* (1929, 'In A Great Big Way' and 'Let's Sit And Talk About You'), and *International Revue* (1930), which starred Gertrude Lawrence and Harry Richman, and featured two important McHugh numbers, 'On The Sunny Side Of The Street' and 'Exactly Like You'. McHugh and Fields also contributed songs to the Chicago revue *Clowns In Clover* (1933), in which Jeanette Leff introduced the lovely ballad 'Don't Blame Me'. During the 30s and 40s McHugh is said to have written songs for over 50 films, initially with Fields. These included *The Cuban Love Song* and *Dinner At Eight* (title songs), *Singin' The Blues* (title song, 'Its The Darndest Thing'), *Have A Heart*, ('Lost In A Fog'), *Every Night At Eight*, starring Alice Faye ('I'm In The Mood For Love', 'I Feel A Song Coming On'), *Dancing Lady* (title song), and *Roberta* ('Lovely To Look At', 'I Won't Dance', with Jerome Kern). McHugh's other chief collaborator was Harold Adamson. Together they wrote numerous songs for films such as *Banjo On My Knee* ('There's Something In The Air'), *You're A Sweetheart*, starring Alice Faye and George Murphy (title song, 'My Fine Feathered Friend'). *That Certain Age* ('My Own'), *Mad About Music*, starring Deanna Durbin ('A Serenade To The Stars', 'I Love To Whistle'), *Four Jills In A Jeep*, starring Dick Haymes, Alice Faye, and Betty Grable ('How Blue The Night'), *Higher And Higher*, an early Frank Sinatra film ('The Music Stopped', 'I Couldn't Sleep A Wink Last Night', 'A Lovely Way To Spend An Evening', 'I Saw You First'), *Calendar Girl* ('Have I Told You Lately That I Love You', 'A Lovely Night To Go Dreaming'), *Smash Up* ('Red Hot And Beautiful', 'Hushabye Island'), *Something For The Boys* ('In The Middle Of Nowhere', 'Wouldn't It Be Nice?'). Two other well-known McHugh/Adamson songs were 'Comin' In On A Wing And A Prayer', and 'Love Me As Though There Were No Tomorrow'. In 1939, McHugh collaborated with Al Dubin on 'South American Way', which was introduced by Carmen Miranda, Ramon Vinay, Della Lind, and the Hylton Sisters in the Broadway revue *Streets Of Paris*. Miranda gave it the full treatment again in the 1940 movie *Down Argentine Way*. In the same year, McHugh and Dubin worked with Howard Dietz on the score for the stage musical *Keep Off the Grass*, which included 'Clear Out Of This World' and 'A Latin Tune, A Manhattan Moon, And You'. Other popular McHugh songs include 'I'm Shooting High', 'Let's Get Lost', I'd Know You Anywhere', 'You've Got Me This Way', 'Sing A Tropical Song, "Murder" She Says', 'Say A Prayer For The Boys Over There', 'Can't Get Out Of This Mood', 'In A Moment Of Madness', 'Blue Again', 'Goodbye Blues', 'I've Just Found Out About Love And I Like It', 'Warm and Willing', 'The Star You Wished Upon Last Night', 'Where The Hot Wind Blows' and 'Massachusetts'. McHugh's collaborators during his long career included Ted Koehler, Frank Loesser, Johnny Mercer, Herb Magidson, Ralph Freed, Ned Washington and Arnold Johnson.

During World War II, McHugh wrote several US Government-commissioned 'War Savings Bond' songs such as 'Buy, Buy, Buy A Bond' and 'We've Got Another Bond To Buy'. For his work during the war he was awarded the Presidential Certificate Of Merit. He continued writing well into the 50s, and in 1955 had a hit with 'Too Young To Go Steady' (with Adamson), which was recorded by Patti Page and Nat 'King' Cole.

McKechnie, Donna

b. November 1940, Pontiac, Michigan, USA. An outstanding dancer, singer, and actress, McKechnie grew up in Detroit and decided she wanted to be a dancer after seeing the classic 1948 British film *The Red Shoes*. Her parents were opposed to the idea, but when she was 15 she moved to New York to try out for the American Ballet Theatre, but was turned down. There followed a brief and unhappy spell at Radio City Music Hall, before she discovered the world of the musical theatre. After touring in *West Side Story* in which she played one of the 'Cool girls', and various other productions, she made her Broadway debut as a dancer in *How To Succeed In Business Without Really Trying* in 1961. This was her first meeting with choreographer Bob Fosse, and Gwen Verdon who was the dance captain. McKechnie was involved in several numbers, including 'A Secretary Is Not A Toy' and 'Coffee Break'. She subsequently toured as Philia in *A Funny Thing Happened On The Way To The Forum*, before becoming one of the six gyrating girl dancers on the popular television programme *Hullabaloo*. Also in the show was Michael Bennett, who was to become an immensely influential figure in her life. In April 1968, McKechnie was back on Broadway as Kathy McKenna in the short-lived musical version of Leo Rosent's collections of short stories *The Education Of H*Y*M*A*N K*A*P*L*A*N*, and in December of that year she played Vivien Della Hoya in Burt Bacharach and Hal David's *Promises, Promises*, performing the Act One closer, 'Turkey Lurkey Time'. This was followed by a spell as the Princess in the touring company of *Call Me Madam* which was headed by the legendary Ethel Merman. Michael Bennett had done the choreography for *Promises, Promises*, and he showcased

McKechnie again in the acclaimed 'Tick Tock' number in Stephen Sondheim's innovative *Company* which opened in 1970. She was also a member of the girl trio that sang the ingenious 'You Could Drive A Person Crazy'. After leaving the New York show, McKechnie reprised her role in Los Angeles and London, and also toured as Ivy in a 1971 revival of *On The Town*. In March 1973 she choreographed and performed in the renowned one night only concert *Sondheim: A Musical Tribute* at the Shubert Theatre, and in the following year appeared in the New York City Center revue *Music! Music!*, as well as joining Richard Kiley and Bob Fosse in the movie *The Little Prince*. In 1975 McKechnie created her most memorable role to date, that of Cassie in *A Chorus Line*, which Michael Bennett conceived, directed and choreographed. Her big number was 'The Music And The Mirror', and she won the Tony Award for Best Actress in a Musical. She married Bennett in 1976, but the marriage broke up after a only few months. After appearing in further productions of *A Chorus Line*, in 1980 McKechnie was diagnosed as suffering from arthritis and told she would never dance again. She pursued various physical and psychological healing remedies, and returned to the Broadway company of *A Chorus Line* in 1986. During the remainder of the 80s she toured in *Sweet Charity* and *Annie Get Your Gun*, and appeared in the 1988 London revival of *Can-Can*. In the early 90s she was off-Broadway, firstly with Georgia Engel and Barbara Feldon in the revue *Cut The Ribbons*, and then as Mrs. Kelly, 'one of the romantic interests' in *Annie Warbucks*. In 1993 she, and all of the original 1970 New York cast of *Company*, except one, assembled for three special nostalgic concert performances. In 1996 she received the Fred Astaire Award for Best Female Dancer for her portrayal of Emily Arden, a 'city-slicker singer', in a Broadway adaptation of Richard Rodgers and Oscar Hammerstein II's much-loved film *State Fair*. Later that year she took her one-woman show, *Inside The Music*, to London, and while there recreated her part of Cassie for a BBC Radio 2 production of *A Chorus Line*. Since then, McKechnie has starred in *I Do, I Do* (Queen's Theatre in the Park, New York), *The Goodbye Girl* (Walnut Street Theatre, Philadelphia), and the gala *Standing Ovations: An Evening With The Great Ladies Of Broadway* (New York's 92nd Street YMHA), in which was joined by legendary artists such as Carol Channing, Liliane Montevecchi, Leslie Uggams, and Marilyn Horne. In February 1997 she played Phyllis in a special concert performance of *Follies* at London's Drury Lane Theatre, and just over a year later switched to the role of Sally in a highly acclaimed production of that same Stephen Sondheim classic at the Paper Mill Playhouse, New Jersey.

● FURTHER READING: *A Chorus Line And The Musicals Of Michael Bennett*, Ken Mandelbaum.

McKenzie, Julia

b. 17 February 1941, Enfield, Middlesex, England. An actress, singer, and director, Julia McKenzie is one of the most accomplished leading ladies in the British (and occasionally Broadway) musical theatre. She started to perform at an early age, and attended the Sylvia Spriggs Dancing School. She was about to begin training to become a French teacher when she was offered a scholarship to study opera. After spending four years at the Guildhall School Of Music, she performed in provincial theatres and toured in operettas and musical comedies for a good number of years before coming to prominence in 1969 in the London production of *Mame*, which starred Ginger Rogers. In the early 70s she had her first introduction to Stephen Sondheim's work - with which she has since become indelibly associated - when she took over one of the leading roles in *Company*. She also replaced Patricia Routledge in *Cowardy Custard*, and, in 1974, appeared in *Cole*, another of the Mermaid Theatre's excellent anthology productions. McKenzie's biggest break came two years later when she co-starred with Millicent Martin, David Kernan, and Ned Sherrin in yet another celebratory revue - *Side By Side By Sondheim* . A surprise hit in London, the show was also well-received in New York where it ran for 384 performances. During the 80s, McKenzie gave a 'dazzling performance' as Lily Garland in *On The Twentieth Century*, won Variety Club and Laurence Olivier Awards for her portrayal of Miss Adelaide in *Guys And Dolls* at the National Theatre, and resumed her association with Sondheim in *Follies* (Sally Plummer) and *Into The Woods* (Witch). The composer played a major part in her life during the 90s too, beginning in 1993 when she played Mrs. Lovett in the Royal National Theatre's highly acclaimed production of *Sweeney Todd*. The performance earned McKenzie another Olivier Award. In the same year she directed the New York premiere of *Putting It Together*, a revue based on Sondheim's songs, which tempted Julie Andrews back to the New York musical stage for the first time since *Camelot* (1960). Julia McKenzie has also worked extensively in the straight theatre, and on television where she was voted Favourite Comedy Performer three times in the 80s for her appearances in situation comedies such as *Maggie And Her*, *Fresh Fields*, and *French Fields*. In 1994, she devised (with Kit Hesketh-Harvey) and directed the well-received *Mercury Workshop Musical Revue* at London's Jermyn Street Theatre. Since then she has directed the 1996 Danish Musical Of The Year competition, the West End musical *Stepping Out* (1997), re-created her Sally for BBC Radio 2's special concert performance of *Follies* (1997), as well as staging (with Bob Avian) *Hey Mr Producer!* (1998), the all-star Cameron Mackintosh charity gala at London's Lyceum Theatre.

● ALBUMS: *Show Stoppers* (Telstar 1993)★★★, and Original Cast recordings.

ME AND JULIET

Perhaps because it emerged into the bright lights of Broadway in the same season as hits such as *Wish You Were Here*, *Wonderful Town*, and *Can-Can*, Richard Rodgers and Oscar Hammerstein's *Me And Juliet* was regarded by critics and public alike to be well below their par. Certainly, after blockbusters such as *Oklahoma!*, *Carousel*, and *The King And I*, a run of 358 performances was not remarkable by their standards. Unlike those three shows, *Me And Juliet* was not adapted from an existing work, but had an original book by Hammerstein. It opened at the Majestic Theatre in New York on 28 May 1953. The setting is a theatre, onstage and off, where a

musical entitled *Me And Juliet* is playing. Jeannie (Isabel Bigley), a singer in the chorus, is being pleasantly pursued by Larry (Bill Hayes), the assistant stage manager, until electrician Bob (Mark Dawson), a nasty hard-drinking character, tries to muscle in on the romance to such an extent that he tries to murder her. The traditional 'fun-romance' situation that usually crops up in these kind of shows, in this case involves a dancer, Betty (Joan McCracken) and the stage manager, Mac (Ray Walston). The latter artist proved to be a memorable Luther Billis in the film of Rodgers and Hammerstein's *South Pacific*, and he also gave a 'devil' of a good performance in *Damn Yankees* on both stage and screen. The score for *Me And Juliet* was light, and contained none of the composers' 'deeply meaningful songs' (such as 'You'll Never Walk Alone', 'Carefully Taught', etc.), but there were some pleasant songs, including 'Keep It Gay', 'It's Me', 'The Big Black Giant', 'A Very Special Day', 'I'm Your Girl', and 'Do I Love You Because You're Beautiful' and 'Marriage-Type Love', both of which achieved some modest popularity. Rodgers had used the melody of one of the other numbers, 'No Other Love', before, as part of the background score for the television documentary series, *Victory At Sea* (1952). The song became a big hit for Perry Como in America, and a UK number 1 for Ronnie Hilton. Rodgers remembered the song again, in 1957, and interpolated it into a US television version of *Cinderella*.

ME AND MY GIRL

The 'Lambeth Walk Musical' as it became known, opened at the Victoria Palace in London on 16 December 1937. L. Arthur Rose and Douglas Furber wrote the simple but endearing book in which Bill Snibson (Lupino Lane), from Lambeth, south London, inherits the title of the Earl of Hereford. Naturally, the estate's snooty executors, the Duchess (Doris Rogers) and Sir John (George Graves), are aghast. Bill takes his girlfriend Sally (Teddie St. Denis) to view the family pile, which does not go down too well with Lady Jacqueline (Betty Frankiss), who already has her mince pies (Cockney rhyming slang for 'eyes' - Bill uses it all the time) trained on him. All ends happily, when Bill returns to his beloved roots, only to find that Sir John has done a Professor Higgins and arranged for Sally to be turned into a lady. Noel Gay composed the music, with Rose and Furber's lyrics, for a singable, hummable, set of songs which included 'Thinking Of No One But Me', 'The Family Solicitor', 'Take It On The Chin', 'I Would If I Could', 'A Domestic Discussion', and, of course, 'The Lambeth Walk', which when brought to life by Lane, was the very embodiment of the Cockney spirit. Bill and Sally also had the warm and charming 'Me And My Girl' early in the show, ensuring audiences knew that, come curtain time, they would still be together. The show did not take off immediately, and it was only after a live radio broadcast from the theatre, that the box office was besieged. In 1938 it was featured on the *Royal Variety Performance* at the London Coliseum, with some 250 artists joining in 'The Lambeth Walk' finalé, including Harry Champion, Will Fyffe, Florrie Forde, Tommy Handley, Harry Tate, and Vesta Victoria. After closing for three weeks at the outbreak of World War II, *Me And My Girl* continued on its happy-go-lucky way for a total of 1,646 performances, before being withdrawn in June 1940. Lane, who presented and directed the original show, led revivals at the London Coliseum (1941), Victoria Palace (1945), and Winter Garden Theatre (1949), and also starred in the 1939 film version, entitled *The Lambeth Walk*, with Sally Gray (Sally) Seymour Hicks (Sir John), Norah Howard (Duchess), and Enid Stamp-Taylor (Jacqueline). On the 4 February 1985, a Leicester Haymarket production took up residence at the Adelphi Theatre in London. Actor and author Stephen Fry had revised and expanded the book, and additional Noel Gay songs were introduced, notably 'The Sun Has Got His Hat On' (lyric: Ralph Butler), 'Leaning On A Lamp Post', 'Once You Lose Your Heart', and 'If Only You Had Cared For Me'. The latter number was amusingly duetted by Frank Thornton and Ursula Smith, who played Sir John and the Duchess. Also cast were Robert Lindsay (Bill), Emma Thompson (Sally), and Susannah Fellows (Jacqueline). Once again, 'The Lambeth Walk' provided the finalé for the *Royal Variety Performance* - and at the original home of *Me And My Girl*, the Victoria Palace. This production, which was produced by Noel Gay's son Richard Armitage, won Laurence Olivier Awards for best musical and actor Lindsay, and ran for almost eight years. It subsequently toured the UK to sell-out houses, When Lindsay took the show to Broadway, he and Maryann Plunkett, along with choreographer (Gillian Gregory) earned Tony Awards, and the production stayed in New York for 1,420 performances.

MEDICINE BALL CARAVAN

This 1971 film followed several rock groups as they travelled across America. The guiding force behind the project was San Franciscan disc-jockey Tom Donahue, former proprietor of Autumn Records. Alternately known as *We Have Come For Your Daughters* after the motto pinned to the touring bus - which drew the ire of feminists - *Medicine Ball Caravan* was a thinly-veiled way of promoting Donahue's management clients, Stoneground. This expansive, revue-styled act was led by Sal Valentino, formerly of the Beau Brummels, and it also included several well-respected Bay Area musicians. B.B. King, Alice Cooper, Delaney And Bonnie and Doug Kershaw are among the other featured acts, but Stoneground remain at its core. Interesting rather than essential, *Medicine Ball Caravan* suggests a last-gasp attempt at exposing a 'gypsy-esque' notion of rock. It was not a great success and an attendant soundtrack album was also poorly received. Paradoxically, several portions featuring Stoneground were exhumed by Warner Brothers Records in a bid to help launch the group in Britain.

MEET ME IN ST. LOUIS

Released by MGM in 1944, this enchanting film traces the adventures of the Smith family as the seasons change from summer through spring in the US city of St. Louis during 1903/4. Based on *The Kensington Stories* by Sally Benson, Irving Brecher and Fred Finklehoffe's screenplay focuses on one of the Smiths' teenage daughters, Esther (Judy Garland), and her romance with the boy who lives next door to her in Kensington Avenue, John Truitt (Tom Drake). The cast was particularly fine: Esther's three sisters, Rose, Tootie and Agnes, were played by Lucille Bremer, Margaret O'Brien, and Joan Carroll; and the family group was completed by brother Lon Jnr. (Henry H. Daniels Jnr.), father and mother (Leon Ames and Mary Astor), grandpa (Harry Davenport) - and their long-time maid Katie (Marjorie Main). Also featured were June Lockhart, Hugh Marlowe, Robert Sully, and Chill Wills. The seemingly ordinary day-to-day happenings involving collusion between Rose, her mother and Katie to advance the time of the evening meal by an hour so that it will not coincide with a long-distance telephone call from Rose's boyfriend, Tootie's Halloween night escapades, Esther and John's mutual joy at the Christmas dance, and the possibility of the whole family moving to New York, resulted in a most extraordinary film. The move away from their beloved home does not materialize, and the whole family celebrate at the opening of 1904 St. Louis World Fair, singing 'Meet Me In St. Louis, Louis' (Andrew Sterling-Kerry Mills). Hugh Martin and Ralph Blane contributed three memorable songs for Judy Garland to sing: 'The Boy Next Door', 'Have Yourself A Merry Little Christmas', and the immortal 'The Trolley Song', which accompanied one of the most endearing sequences in any film musical. Garland also joined O'Brien for the charming 'Under The Bamboo Tree' (Bob Cole-J. Rosamond Johnson), and she and the rest of the young people (and audiences all over the world) brushed a tear from their eyes as Leon Ames (dubbed by Arthur Freed) and Mary Astor rendered the poignant 'You And I' (Freed-Nacio Herb Brown). The dances were staged by Charles Walters, and the film, which was directed with his usual style and flair by Vincente Minnelli, was photographed in Technicolor by George Folsey. *Meet Me In St. Louis* was an enormous commercial success, grossing over $5 million in US domestic theatre rentals alone - a fitting return for what is generally considered to be a masterpiece. Unfortunately, the magic did not extend to the 1989 Broadway stage adaptation which one critic called 'a lumbering and graceless project'. It ran for only 253 performances at the time, but revivals, complete with additional songs, were mounted in St. Louis in 1960 and 1991.

MENKEN, ALAN

(see Ashman, Howard)

MERCER, JOHNNY

b. John Herndon Mercer, 18 November 1909, Savannah, Georgia, USA, d. 25 June 1976, Los Angeles, California, USA. A distinguished lyricist, composer and singer, Mercer was an important link with the first generation of composers of indigenous American popular music such as Jerome Kern and Harry Warren, through to post-World War II writers like Henry Mancini. Along the way, he collaborated with several others, including Harold Arlen, Hoagy Carmichael, Gene DePaul, Rube Bloom, Richard Whiting, Victor Schertzinger, Gordon Jenkins, Jimmy Van Heusen, Duke Ellington, Billy Strayhorn, Matty Malneck, Arthur Schwartz and more. Most of the time, Mercer wrote the most literate and witty lyrics, but occasionally the melody as well. He moved to New York in the late 20s and worked in a variety of jobs before placing one of his first songs, 'Out Of Breath And Scared To Death Of You', (written with Everett Miller), in the *The Garrick Gaieties Of 1930*. During the 30s, Mercer contributed the lyrics to several movie songs, including 'If You Were Mine' from *To Beat The Band*, a record hit for Billie Holiday with Teddy Wilson, 'I'm An Old Cowhand' (words and music) (*Rhythm On The Range*), 'Too Marvellous For Words' (co-written with Richard Whiting for *Ready, Willing And Able*), 'Have You Got Any Castles, Baby?' (*Varsity Show*), 'Hooray For Hollywood' (*Hollywood Hotel*), 'Jeepers Creepers' (*Going Places*) and 'Love Is Where You Find It' (*Garden Of The Moon*). Mercer's other songs during the decade included 'Fare-Thee-Well To Harlem', 'Moon Country', 'When A Woman Loves A Man' (with Gordon Jenkins and Bernard Hanighan), 'P.S. I Love You', 'Goody Goody', 'You Must Have Been A Beautiful Baby', 'And The Angels Sing', 'Cuckoo In The Clock', 'Day In - Day Out' and 'I Thought About You'. In the 30s he appeared frequently on radio, as MC and singer with Paul Whiteman, Benny Goodman and Bob Crosby. With his southern drawl and warm, good-natured style, he was a natural for the medium, and, in the early 40s, had his own show, *Johnny Mercer's Music Shop*. During this period, Mercer became a director of the songwriter's copyright organization, ASCAP. Also, in 1942, he combined with songwriter-turned-film-producer, Buddy De Sylva, and businessman, Glen Wallich, to form Capitol Records, which was, in its original form, dedicated to musical excellence, a policy which reflected Mercer's approach to all his work.

He had previously had record hits with other writers' songs, such as 'Mr Gallagher And Mr Sheen' and 'Small Fry', along with his own 'Mr. Meadowlark' (a duet with Bing Crosby), and 'Strip Polka'. For Capitol, he continued to register in the US Hit Parade with popular favourites such as 'Personality', 'Candy'; and some of his own numbers such as 'G.I. Jive', 'Ac-Cent-Tchu-Ate The Positive', 'Glow Worm'; and 'On The Atchison, Topeka, And The Santa Fe', which was also sung by Judy Garland in the film *The Harvey Girls* (1946), and gained Mercer his first Academy Award. His other 40s song successes, many of them from movies, included 'The Waiter And The Porter And The Upstairs Maid' (from *Birth Of The Blues*); 'Blues In The Night' and 'This Time's The Dream's On Me' (*Blues In The Night*); 'Tangerine', 'I Remember You' and 'Arthur Murray Taught Me Dancing In A Hurry' (*The Fleet's In*), 'Dearly Beloved' and 'I'm Old Fashioned' (*You Were Never Lovelier*) (Kern); 'Hit The Road To Dreamland' and 'That Old Black Magic', Billy Daniels' identity song, (*Star Spangled Rhythm*), 'My Shining Hour' (*The Sky's The Limit*) and 'Come Rain Or Come Shine', 'Legalize My Name' and 'Any Place I Hang My Hat Is Home', from the stage show *St. Louis Woman* (Arlen).

Two particularly attractive compositions were 'Fools Rush In' (with Rube Bloom), which was a big hit for Glenn Miller and the movie title song 'Laura', with Mercer's lyric complementing a haunting tune by David Raksin. Mercer's collaboration with Hoagy Carmichael produced some of his most memorable songs, such as 'Lazybones', 'The Old Music Master', 'Skylark', 'How Little We Know' and the Oscar-winning 'In The Cool, Cool, Cool Of The

Evening', sung by Bing Crosby and Jane Wyman in the film *Here Comes The Groom* (1951). In the same year, Mercer provided both the music and lyrics for the Broadway show, *Top Banana*, a 'burlesque musical' starring Phil Silvers and a host of mature funny men. The entertaining score included the witty 'A Word A Day'.

The 50s were extremely productive years for Mercer, with songs such as 'Here's To My Lady', 'I Wanna Be Around' (later successful for Tony Bennett), and yet more movie songs, including 'I Want To Be A Dancing Man', 'The Bachelor Dinner Song' and 'Seeing's Believing', sung by Fred Astaire in *The Belle Of New York*; 'I Like Men' (covered by Peggy Lee), 'I Got Out Of Bed On The Right Side' and 'Ain't Nature Grand' from *Dangerous When Wet;* and 'Something's Gotta Give' and 'Sluefoot' (words and music by Mercer) from another Fred Astaire film, *Daddy Long Legs*. Mercer also provided additional lyrics to 'When The World Was Young' ('Ah, The Apple Trees'), 'Midnight Sun', 'Early Autumn' and 'Autumn Leaves'. The highlight of the decade was, perhaps, *Seven Brides For Seven Brothers* (1954). Starring Howard Keel and Jane Powell, Mercer and Gene DePaul's 'pip of a score' included 'Spring, Spring, Spring', 'Bless Your Beautiful Hide', 'Sobbin' Women', 'When You're In Love', and 'Goin' Courtin', amongst others. Two years later Mercer and DePaul got together again for the stage show *Li'l Abner*, starring Stubby Kaye, and including such songs as 'Namely You', 'Jubilation T. Cornpone' and 'The Country's In The Very Best Of Hands'. It ran on Broadway for nearly 700 performances and was filmed in 1959.

The early 60s brought Mercer two further Academy Awards; one for 'Moon River' from *Breakfast At Tiffany*'s (1961), and the other, the title song to *The Days Of Wine And Roses* (1962). 'Moon River' was the song in which Mercer first coined the now-famous phrase, 'my huckleberry friend'. Danny Williams took the former song to the UK number slot in 1961, while namesake Andy Williams and Mercer's co-composer Henry Mancini both scored US Top 40 hits with the latter in 1963. Mancini also wrote other movie songs with Mercer, such as 'Charade', 'The Sweetheart Tree' (from *The Great Race*) and 'Whistling Away The Dark' (*Darling Lili*). In the early 70s, Mercer spent a good deal of time in Britain, and, in 1974, wrote the score, with André Previn, for the West End musical *The Good Companions*. He died, two years later, in 1976.

Several of his 1,000-plus songs became an integral part of many a singer's repertoire. In 1992, Frank Sinatra was still using 'One For My Baby' (music by Harold Arlen), 'the greatest saloon song ever written', as a moving set-piece in his concert performances. 'Dream' (words and music by Mercer), closed Sinatra's radio and television shows for many years, and the singer also made impressive recordings of lesser-known Mercer items, such as 'Talk To Me, Baby' and 'The Summer Wind'. Memories of his rapport with Bing Crosby in their early days were revived in 1961, when Mercer recorded *Two Of A Kind* with Bobby Darin, full of spontaneous asides, and featuring Mercer numbers such as 'Bob White' and 'If I Had My Druthers', plus other humorous oldies, like 'Who Takes Care Of The Caretaker's Daughter' and 'My Cutie's Due At Two-To-Two Today'. Several artists, such as Marlene VerPlanck, Susannah

McCorkle, and Nancy LaMott, have devoted complete albums to his work, and in 1992 Capitol Records celebrated its 50th anniversary by issuing *Too Marvellous For Words: Capitol Sings Johnny Mercer*, which consisted of some of the label's most eminent artists singing their co-founder's popular song lyrics. Five years later, the soundtrack of the movie *Midnight In The Garden Of Good And Evil*, starring Clint Eastwood and Kevin Spacey, featured a host of Johnny Mercer songs.

● ALBUMS: *Capitol Presents Johnny Mercer* (Capitol 1953)★★★, *Capitol Presents Johnny Mercer Volume 2* (Capitol 1954)★★★, *Capitol Presents Johnny Mercer Volume 3* (Capitol 1954)★★★, *Capitol Presents Johnny Mercer Volume 4* (Capitol 1954)★★★, with Bobby Darin *Two Of A Kind* (Capitol 1961)★★★, *Johnny Mercer Sings Johnny Mercer* (Capitol 1972)★★★, *Ac-Cent-Tchu-Ate The Positive, Johnny Mercer's Music Shop, My Huckleberry Friend* (Pye 1974)★★★, *An Evening With Johnny Mercer* (Laureate 1977)★★★.

● COMPILATIONS: various artists *Too Marvellous For Words: Capitol Sings Johnny Mercer* (Capitol 1992)★★★★.

● FURTHER READING: *Our Huckleberry Friend: The Life, Times And Song Lyrics Of Johnny Mercer*, B. Back and G. Mercer.

MERCER, MABEL

b. 3 February 1900, Birmingham, Staffordshire, England, d. 20 April 1984, Pittsfield, Massachusetts, USA. A celebrated and influential cabaret singer, as a young girl Mercer was educated at convent school, and underwent classical voice training. Her mother was a white variety singer and actress, her father a black American jazz singer who died before she was born. Her mother remarried and became popular in music hall in the UK, sometimes touring overseas. In her teens, Mercer became a professional dancer, and made one of her first appearances in a London production of Lew Leslie's *Blackbirds*, which starred Florence Mills. By the early 20s, she had become a singer, performing in various parts of Europe and the Middle East. Before the end of the decade she had settled in Paris, and was soon a featured attraction at the renowned Bricktop's nightclub, mixing with and entertaining the 'lost generation' of American expatriates which included songwriters Cole Porter and Vincent Youmans, as well as leading literary figures such as Gertrude Stein and Ernest Hemingway. In 1938 Mercer visited New York, and by 1941 had begun the first of two long residencies in the city, at Tony's, and later at the Byline Room, which continued until 1957. In later years she also became associated with the Café Carlyle where Bobby Short regularly holds court, and recorded two live albums with him. In the 70s she worked at the St. Regis Room, appeared at Carnegie Hall and on UK television in *Miss Mercer In Mayfair*. In 1974 she received *Stereo Review Magazine*'s Award of Merit, which was renamed the Mabel Mercer Award in 1984. On being chosen as its first recipient, Frank Sinatra said: 'Mabel Mercer taught me everything I know, she is the finest music teacher in the world'. She retired in 1979, but was back on stage at the 1982 Kool Jazz Festival, singing a programme of songs by Alec Wilder. The composer is said to have written one of his most appealing songs, 'While We're Young', especially for her. Her final performance was at a charity benefit in November 1983, and in the same year she was awarded the Presidential Medal of Freedom, the nation's highest civilian award, by President Reagan. One of the most respected singers, greatly admired by fellow artists and also by the composers whose work she performs, Mercer's voice had a good range and a deep, melodious sound. Although she would sometimes use jazz phrasing, she was never a jazz singer, but remained one of the finest cabaret or supper-club singers of her generation. Her greatest talent lay in her masterly delivery of lyrics to which she brought intimacy and affection.

● ALBUMS: *Mabel Mercer Sings Cole Porter* (1955),★★★ *Midnight At Mabel Mercer's* (50s)★★★, with Bobby Short *At Town Hall* (Atlantic 1968)★★★★, with Bobby Short *Second Town Hall Concert* (Atlantic 1969)★★★, *The Art Of Mabel Mercer* (c.60s)★★★, *Echoes Of My Life* (c.70s)★★★.

● FURTHER READING: *Mabel Mercer: A Life*, James Haskins.

MERMAN, ETHEL

b. Ethel Agnes Zimmermann, 16 January 1909, Astoria, New York, USA, d. 15 February 1984, New York, USA. One of the most celebrated ladies of the Broadway musical stage, a dynamic entertainer, with a loud, brash, theatrical singing style, flawless diction, and extravagant manner, who usually played a gutsy lady with a heart of gold. She worked first as a secretary, then sang in nightclubs, eventually graduating to the best spots. Noticed by producer Vinton Freedley while singing at the Brooklyn Paramount, she was signed for George and Ira Gershwin's Broadway show *Girl Crazy* (1930), and was a great success, stopping the show with her version of 'I Got Rhythm', a song which became one of her life-long themes. She was equally successful in *George White's Scandals* (1931), in which she co-starred with Rudy Vallee, and sang 'My Song' and 'Life Is Just A Bowl Of Cherries'; and *Take A Chance* (1932), when her two big numbers were 'Eadie Was A Lady' and 'Rise 'N' Shine'. In 1934, Merman starred in *Anything Goes*, the first of five Cole Porter musical shows in which she was to appear. The score was top drawer Porter, full of song hits such as 'I Get A Kick Out Of You', 'All Through The Night', 'You're The Top' (one of the composer's renowned 'list' songs), 'Anything Goes' and 'Blow, Gabriel, Blow'. Merman also appeared in the 1936 film version of the show with Bing Crosby. The other Porter productions in which she appeared were *Red, Hot And Blue!* (1936), co-starring Jimmy Durante and Bob Hope, with the songs, 'Down In The Depths (On The Ninetieth Floor)', 'It's De-Lovely' and 'Ridin' High'; *DuBarry Was A Lady* (1939), with 'But In The Morning, No!', 'Do I Love You?', 'Give Him The Oo-La-La', 'Katie Went To Haiti' and 'Friendship'; *Panama Hattie* (1940), featuring 'I've Still Got My Health', 'Let's Be Buddies', 'Make It Another Old-Fashioned, Please' and 'I'm Throwing A Ball Tonight'; and *Something For The Boys* (1943) with 'Hey, Good Lookin'', 'He's A Right Guy', 'Could It Be You' and 'The Leader Of A Big Time Band'. Merman's longest-running musical was Irving Berlin's *Annie Get Your Gun* (1946), which lasted for 1,147 performances. As the sharp-shooting Annie Oakley, she introduced such Berlin classics as 'They Say It's Wonderful', 'Doin' What Comes Naturally', 'I Got The Sun In The Morning', 'You Can't Get A Man With A Gun', and the song which was to become another of her anthems,

'There's No Business Like Show Business'. Merman's next Broadway show, *Call Me Madam*, again had an Irving Berlin score. This time, as Sally Adams, ambassador to the mythical country of Lichtenburg, she triumphed again with numbers such as 'Marrying For Love', 'You're Just In Love', 'The Best Thing For You', 'Can You Use Any Money Today?', and 'The Hostess With The Mostes' On The Ball'. She also starred in the 1953 film version of the previous show, with George Sanders, Donald O'Connor, and Vera-Ellen. Often cited as the peak of Merman's career, *Gypsy* (1959), with a magnificent score by Jule Styne and Stephen Sondheim, saw her cast as the domineering mother of the legendary stripper Gypsy Rose Lee, and Merman gave the kind of performance for which she had never before been asked. Her songs included 'Some People', 'Small World', 'You'll Never Get Away From Me', 'Together', 'Rose's Turn', and her triumphant hymn, 'Everything's Coming Up Roses'. Apart from a brief revival of *Annie Get Your Gun* (1966), and a spell as a replacement in *Hello, Dolly!*, (she had turned down the role when the show was originally cast), *Gypsy* was Merman's last Broadway musical appearance. Although the stage was her *metier*, she made several successful Hollywood films such as *We're Not Dressing* (1934), *Kid Millions* and *Strike Me Pink* (both 1935 with Eddie Cantor) *Alexander's Ragtime Band* (1938), with Tyrone Power, Alice Faye, and Don Ameche; and *There's No Business Like Show Business* (1954), in which she co-starred with Dan Dailey, Donald O'Connor and Marilyn Monroe.

There were also non-singing roles in comedy films such as *It's A Mad, Mad, Mad, Mad World* (1963), *The Art Of Love* (1965) and *Airplane!* (1980). Merman appeared regularly on television from the 50s through to the 70s in specials and guest spots, merely because she was Ethel Merman, and also starred in cabaret. In 1953 she teamed up with another Broadway legend, Mary Martin, for the historic Ford 50th Anniversary Show, highlights of which were issued on a Decca album. On the same label was her *Musical Autobiography* (2-album set). Besides the many hits from her shows, her record successes included 'How Deep Is The Ocean', 'Move It Over', and four duets with Ray Bolger, 'Dearie', 'I Said My Pajamas (And Put On My Prayers)', 'If I Knew You Were Comin' I'd've Baked A Cake', and 'Once Upon A Nickel'. After a distinguished career lasting over 50 years, Merman's final major appearance was at a Carnegie Hall benefit concert in 1982. A year after her death in 1984, a biographical tribute show entitled *Call Me Miss Birdseye: Ethel Merman - The Lady And Her Music*, was presented at the Donmar Warehouse Theatre in London. In 1994 the US Post Service somewhat optimistically mounted a search for an 'Ethel Merman Soundalike' ('no lip-synching!') in conjunction with the release of the Legends of American Music stamps. The first prize was, appropriately enough, an appearance in the Broadway hit musical *Crazy For You*.

● ALBUMS: *Songs She Made Famous* (Decca 1950)★★★, with Dick Haymes, Eileen Wilson *Call Me Madam* (Decca 1956)★★★, *A Musical Autobiography Volumes 1 & 2* (Decca 1956)★★★★, *Merry-Go-Round* (A&M 1967)★★★, *Merman Sings Merman* (Decca 1973)★★★, *Ethel's Ridin' High* (Decca 1975)★★★.

● COMPILATIONS: *Ethel Was A Lady* (MCA 1984)★★★, *The World Is Your Balloon* (MCA 1987)★★★, *Ethel Merman* (Nostalgia 1988)★★★, *Red. Hot And Blue!/Stars In Your Eyes* (AEI 1991)★★★, *Ethel Sings Merman-And More* (Decca/Eclipse 1992)★★★, *An Earful Of Merman* (Conifer 1994)★★★, *There's No Business Like Show Business: The Ethel Merman Collection* (Razor And Tie 1997)★★★★.
● FURTHER READING: *Who Could Ask For Anything More?* Ethel Merman and P. Martin. *Don't Call Me Madam*, Ethel Merman. *Merman*, Ethel Merman. *I Got Rhythm: The Ethel Merman Story*, B. Thomas.
● FILMS: *Follow The Leader* (1930), *Kid Millions* (1934), *We're Not Dressing* (1934), *Strike Me Pink* (1936), *The Big Broadcast Of 1936* (1936), *Anything Goes* (1936), *Straight Place And Show* (1938), *Alexander's Ragtime Band* (1938), *Happy Landing* (1938), *Stage Door Canteen* (1943), *Call Me Madam* (1953), *There's No Business Like Show Business* (1954), *It's A Mad Mad Mad Mad World* (1963), *The Art Of Love* (1965), *Journey Back To Oz* voice only (1974), *Won Ton Ton, The Dog Who Saved Hollywood* cameo (1976), *Airplane!* (1980).

MERRICK, DAVID

b. David Margulois, 27 November 1911, St. Louis, Missouri, USA. One of the most colourful and controversial theatrical producers and impresarios in the post-World War II years, Merrick is said to believe that his life began on 4 November 1954, the night a musical called *Fanny* opened at New York's Majestic Theatre. After an early, insecure life as the son of a weak father and mentally disturbed mother, Merrick trained as a lawyer before moving into the world of theatre as an associate producer in the late 40s. His production of *Fanny* ran for 888 performances on Broadway, and was followed by a series of successful shows, including the musicals *Jamaica*, *Destry Rides Again*, *Take Me Along*, *Vintage '60*, *Irma La Douce*, *Do Re Mi*, *Carnival*, *I Can Get It For You Wholesale*, *Stop The World - I Want To Get Off*, *110 In The Shade*, *The Roar Of The Greasepaint - The Smell Of The Crowd*, *How Now, Dow Jones*, *The Happy Time*, *Sugar*, *Mack And Mabel* and *Very Good Eddie* (1975 revival). Among his greatest triumphs were *Gypsy* (1959), *Oliver!*, *Hello, Dolly!* (1964), *I Do! I Do!* (1966), *Promises, Promises* (1968) and *42nd Street* (1980). The latter ran for 3,486 performances, his most enduring Broadway production to date. Along the way, there were several failures, such as *Oh, What A Lovely War!* (1964), *Foxy* (1964) and *Pickwick* (1965). In addition, *Breakfast At Tiffany's* (1966) folded during previews, while *Mata Hari* (1967) and *The Baker's Wife* (1976) closed out of town. However, with his sheer determination and flair for publicity, Merrick managed to wring every ounce of possibility out of even the most ailing shows. One of his most famous stunts came in 1961 during the run of the disappointing *Subways Are For Sleeping*. A member of his staff arranged for seven members of the public, with the same names as the leading New York drama critics, to be quoted in newspaper advertisements for the show ('7 Out Of 7 Are Ecstatically Unanimous About Subways Are For Sleeping', ran the copy). When it was published, each of these 'namesakes' appeared opposite a rave quote that the Merrick organization had apparently culled from old reviews of some of Broadway's greatest hits. Such outrageous, but immensely profitable, behaviour came to a temporary halt in February 1983, when Merrick suffered a debilitating stroke that seriously impaired his powers of speech. After initially handing over the reins to others, in 1985 he regained control of his affairs, and has subsequently presented an all-black revival of *Oh, Kay!* (1990), and a stage adaptation of the popular movie *State Fair* (1996). The last of the great American showmen, throughout his career Merrick has been admired, feared, detested and respected - but never ignored. His several Tony Awards and nominations have included one for *Hello, Dolly!*, and special Tonys in 1961 and 1968 'in recognition of his fabulous production record'.

● FURTHER READING: *The Abominable Showman*, Howard Kissell.

MERRILL, BOB

b. Henry Robert Merrill Levan, 17 May 1920, Atlantic City, New Jersey, USA, d. 17 February 1998, Beverly Hills, California, USA. A popular songwriter for Tin Pan Alley, a screenwriter, and a distinguished composer, lyricist and librettist for the musical theatre. Merrill grew up in Philadelphia, and was educated at Temple University. Having enjoyed his first taste of the theatre when he took a temporary job at the Buck's County Playhouse, Merrill moved to New York in 1942, and performed as a comedian and mimic in nightclubs and vaudeville. While serving in the US Army during World War II, he wrote and produced troop shows, and subsequently moved to Hollywood to work as a scriptwriter for NBC Television and Columbia Pictures. He also spent some time as a dialogue coach and casting director, and acted in a few movies. In the late 40s, encouraged by the country-style comedienne Dorothy Shay, who asked him to write some songs for her, Merrill collaborated on 'Lover's Gold' (music: Morty Nevins), 'The Chicken Song' (with Terry Shand) and 'Fool's Paradise' (words and music: Merrill). In 1950, he had his first success with the lively 'If I Knew You Were Comin', I'd Have Baked A Cake' (Al Hoffman and Clem Watts), which was a hit in the USA for Eileen Barton, Georgia Gibbs, Benny Strong, Ethel Merman with Ray Bolger, and Art Mooney. Merrill teamed again with Hoffman on 'Where Will The Baby's Dimple Be?', but he provided his own words and music to Guy Mitchell novelty hits such as 'Sparrow In The Tree Top', 'My Truly, Truly Fair', 'Belle, Belle, My Liberty Belle', 'Pittsburgh, Pennsylvania', 'Feet Up (Pat Him On The Po-Po)', 'She Wears Red Feathers', 'Look At That Girl', 'Chicka Boom' and 'Cuff Of My Shirt'. Several other artists, both in the USA and UK, had chart successes with Merrill numbers, including the Caravelles ('You Don't Have To Be A Baby To Cry'), Lita Roza and Patti Page (('How Much Is That) Doggie In The Window?' - UK and US number 1), Rosemary Clooney ('Mambo Italiano'), Dickie Valentine ('All The Time And Everywhere'), Sarah Vaughan ('Make Yourself Comfortable'), Teresa Brewer ('Sweet Old Fashioned Girl'), Sammy Kaye And His Orchestra ('Walkin' To Missouri'), Arthur Godfrey, Mindy Carson ('Candy And Cake'), and more.

Progressing from pop songs to the musical theatre was difficult, and Merrill's first Broadway show, *New Girl In Town*, began as a projected film. When MGM decided against his musical adaptation of Eugene O'Neill's play, *Anna Christie*, Merrill took it to the distinguished author and director, George Abbott. He wrote the book, and with Merrill's sprightly score ('Flings', 'If That Was Love', 'Yer My Friend Aintcha?', 'Did You Close Your Eyes?'), *New Girl In Town* opened on Broadway in May 1957. Producer David Merrick was more than impressed, and some two years later he was at the helm when Merrill and librettists Joseph Stein and Robert Russell musicalized another O'Neill play, *Ah, Wilderness*. *Take Me Along* (1959) had a charming, nostalgic score, including 'But Yours', 'Little Green Snake', 'We're Home' and 'Promise Me A Rose'. Like *New Girl In Town*, it ran for more than 400 performances, but Merrill's next show, *Carnival* (1961), did even better, residing in New York for 719 performances. Based on a Paul Gallico story, which was turned into the 1953 hit film *Lili*, starring Leslie Caron, Merrill and book writer Michael Stewart created a magical musical comedy containing a delightful variety of songs, such as 'Yes, My Heart', 'Her Face', 'Yum-Ticky-Tum-Tum', and the gently swaying 'Love Makes The World Go Round'. In 1964, Merrill contributed 'Elegance' and 'Motherhood March' to Jerry Herman's Carol Channing vehicle, *Hello, Dolly!*, before collaborating with composer Jule Styne on the score for the smash hit *Funny Girl* ('People', 'Don't Rain On My Parade', 'You Are Woman, I Am Man', 'The Music That Makes Me Dance'). Ironically, *Funny Girl* lost out to *Hello, Dolly!* in the Tony Awards, but the show elevated Barbra Streisand to stardom, and the cast album won Grammy awards for Merrill and Styne. Although the pair wrote the music and lyrics for the animated television special *Mr. Magoo's Christmas Carol* (1963) and a television musical starring Liza Minnelli, *The Dangerous Christmas Of Red Riding Hood* (1965), Merrill's later stage projects proved disappointing. *Breakfast At Tiffany's* (1966) closed during previews, *Henry, Sweet Henry* (1967) folded after only 80 performances, and *Prettybelle* (1971, with Styne) failed to reach Broadway. However, *Sugar* (1972, Styne), based on the highly successful Billy Wilder film *Some Like It Hot*, ran for 505 performances, and in a production that reverted to the title of the movie, became a short-lived showcase for the popular UK entertainer Tommy Steele in 1992. Completing the sad sequence, *The Prince Of Grand Street* (1978), starring Robert Preston, closed during its pre-Broadway try-out and *Hannah ... 1939*, in which Julie Wilson gave a thrilling performance as a dressmaker in Nazi-occupied Czechoslovakia, had a brief stay off-Broadway in 1990. Three years later Merrill teamed with Styne once more (under the pseudonym of Paul Stryker) to provide extra lyrics for *The Red Shoes*, which lasted for just three days. Failures these later shows certainly were, but there was always a song or two in each of them that bore the Merrill stamp of style and humour. In 1984, 37 selections from his prolific output were assembled in a four-character off-Broadway musical entitled *We're Home*. In between the forays to Broadway, Merrill continued to be associated with the film world, co-writing screenplays such as *Mahogany* (1975), starring Diana Ross, and *W.C. Fields And Me* (1976) with Rod Steiger. He also wrote the songs for *The Wonderful World Of The Brothers Grimm*

(1962). Despite suffering from a chronic illness, Merrill was still working through the 90s until his death from 'self inflicted gunshot wounds while sitting in a car outside his Los Angeles home'.

MERRILY WE ROLL ALONG

Two of the musical theatre's current heavyweights went into the Broadway ring during the 1981/2 season, and the result of the contest gave theatre-goers on both sides of the Atlantic a foretaste of the significant shift in the balance of power that was about to take place during the next 10 years. The English champion, Andrew Lloyd Webber with his *Joseph And The Amazing Technicolor Dreamcoat* scored 747 performances, and the native New Yorker, Stephen Sondheim, with *Merrily We Roll Along*, only 16 performances. Prior to the latter show's debut at the Alvin Theatre on 16 November 1981, the smart money was on a Sondheim show that eschewed his usual brittle exposition of contemporary life, in favour of a more traditional style of entertainment - musical comedy - and that is what Sondheim claimed it was originally intended to be. George Furth's book was based on the 1934 play by George S. Kaufman and Moss Hart.

The story, which is told in flashback, tells of a successful composer, Franklin Shepard (as a young man - Jim Walton; aged 43 - Geoffrey Horne), a lyricist, Charles Kringas (Lonny Price), and a mutual friend of the pair, Mary Flynn (Ann Morrison). Shepard is the central character, and the details of his wasted life - the betrayal of his wife and friends in the pursuit of money and glory over a period of some 20 years - are revealed before the final scene, in which - because in this piece the end is the beginning - the friends are meeting in 1957 for the first time. Sondheim constructed the score in what he called 'modular blocks' - the release of one song would be the verse of another, and the chorus of that one could serve as the release of the next, and so on. Some of the songs, such as 'Opening Doors', 'The Hills Of Tomorrow', and 'Good Thing Going'. were based on the same tune - it was Sondheim at his most inventive, and, at least, the composer was nominated for a Tony Award. The rest of the numbers included 'Not A Day Goes By', 'Franklin Shepard Inc.', 'Bobby And Jackie And Jack', 'Like It Was', 'It's A Hit', 'Now You Know', 'Meet The Blob', and 'Merrily We Roll Along'.

Most aspects of the production came in for severe criticism: Eugene Lees' sparse sets, Larry Fuller's choreography, and a cast that was considered by many to be far too young and inexperienced. The celebrated partnership between Sondheim and director and producer Hal Prince came - perhaps temporarily to an end - with this production. As with most, if not all, Sondheim shows, this one continued to live on far beyond its two-weeks run in New York, via the excellent Original Cast album, and various provincial productions. One such, was mounted by the Leicester Haymarket Theatre in England, in 1992, the starting-off point for many fine original musicals and revivals. It starred Michael Cantwell, Maria Friedman, Evan Pappas, Gareth Snook, and Jacqueline Dankworth, the daughter of jazz musicians John Dankworth and Cleo Laine. The 1994 Off Broadway revival reminded *Variety*'s theatre critic that this is 'one of the best scores of any contemporary musical'.

MERRY WIDOW, THE

A perfect example of the kind of Viennese operetta that was so popular in the early part of the 20th century before it was overtaken by the more contemporary shows of Jerome Kern and the other pioneers of musical comedy. With it's superb score by Franz Lehár, *The Merry Widow* was first offered to the public at the Theatre an der Wien in Vienna, on 30 December 1905, under the title of *Die Lustige Witwe*. The book, by Victor Leon and Leo Stein, was based on Henri Meilhac's play *L'Attaché d'Ambassade*. Eighteen months later, on 8 June 1907, when it was presented by George Edwardes at Daly's Theatre in London, the show had a new book by Basil Hood (who declined to be credited), and English lyrics by Adrian Ross. The classic story concerns the arrival in France of Sonia Sadoya (Lily Elsie), a wealthy widow from Marsovia, who is hunting for a husband. If she marries a Frenchman, her millions will be lost for ever to the impoverished principality, and Ambassador Baron Popoff (George Graves) will be out of a job. Prince Danilo (Joseph Coyne), a secretary to the legation, is instructed to make sure that a Franco-Marsovian union does not take place, preferably by marrying the lady himself. The joyous and memorable score contained several enduring favourites such as 'Maxim's', 'I Love You So' (also know as the 'Merry Widow Waltz'), 'Love In My Heart Awakening', 'Vilia', 'Women', 'Home', 'A Dutiful Wife', 'The Girls At Maxim's, and 'Silly, Silly Cavalier'. Enthusiastic audiences, with the ladies dressed in their 'Merry Widow' attire, flocked to the theatre for 778 performances - it was a tremendous success. The 1907 New York production, with Ethel Jackson, ran for a year, and was followed by several Broadway revivals through to the 40s. West End audiences, too, saw the show on many occasions, including 1958 (with June Bronhill), 1969 (with Lizbeth Webb), and 1985 (Helen Kuchareck). All the revivals to date have had revised books and scores. Many other professional and amateur productions are taking place constantly throughout the world, one of the most recent being that mounted by the Paper Mill Playhouse, New Jersey, USA, in 1991. Three film versions have been released: in 1925 (silent), in 1934 with Jeanette Macdonald and Maurice Chevalier, and a 1952 remake with Fernando Lamas and Lana Turner.

METRO

Although several important American producers made the trip to Poland to view this musical which debuted at the Teatr Dramatyzezny in Warsaw in January 1991, it was finally transferred to New York's Minskoff Theatre on 16 April 1992 by its original impresario, Wiktor Kubiak. Touted as a cross between *Hair* and *A Chorus Line*, the show had music composed by Janusz Stoklosa, who also provided the musical direction, as well as vocal and orchestral arrangements, and a score by Agata and Maryna Miklaszewska. Mary Bracken Phillips wrote the English lyrics, and collaborated on the English book with Janusz Jozefowicz, who handled the choreography and directed. Set in post-communism Eastern Europe, the story concerns two brothers, Philip (Olek Krupa) and Jan (Robert Janowski). Philip administers a state theatre which attempts to put on commercial productions, while Jan struggles with his conscience in his subway habitat. He is joined deep down below by several more similarly tortured performing souls who have failed to qualify for Philip's current musical production, *Europe Without Borders*. Among them is Anka (Katarzyna Groniec), a more than usually weird character, who writes intense poems and falls for Jan in a big way. Miffed by Philip's rejection of their talents, the Subway Players mount their own musical which attracts the attention of the press - and Philip - who offers to produce it at his theatre. The moment of truth has arrived: will these hippie types put aside their principles and sell out? Never fear, after a nominal period of soul-searching, of course they do. The score, which was nominated for a Tony Award, was a mishmash of contemporary pop, and bore the unmistakable influence of Andrew Lloyd Webber. It consisted of 'Metro', 'My Fairy Tale', 'But Not Me', 'Windows', 'Bluezwis', 'Love Duet', 'Tower Of Babel', 'Benjamin Franklin', 'Uciekali', 'Waiting', 'Pieniadze', 'Love Duet II', and 'Dreams Don't Die'. Much of the $3 million budget was obviously blown on high-tech effects, with lots of lasers, synthesizers, and a revolving platform that seemed to be in perpetual motion. Actors' Equity, understandably concerned about the large cast of around 40 foreign actors jeopardizing US members' jobs, gave the show their blessing, with the proviso that Americans would take over after the initial 16-week run. They need not have worried - *Metro* collapsed after 24 previews and 13 performances.

METROPOLIS

Inspired by Fritz Lang's 1926 classic silent film of the same name, this lavish stage musical went on display at the Piccadilly Theatre in London on 8 March 1989. Native New Yorker Joe Brooks was the main creative force behind the project, and he composed the music, as well as collaborating with Dusty Hughes on the book and lyrics. Despite a few shifts in emphasis, the story, 'part sci-fi spectacle, part romance-thriller', stays close to the original movie, and is set around the year 2000. In a towering high-tech city populated by two classes, a vast underground machine centre full of workers supplies the idle rich on the surface with all their power. This carefully organized and terrifying system hits a snag when Steven (Graham Bickley), son of John Freeman, Master of the Metropolis, a Citizen Kane-type figure played by Brian Blessed, goes slumming deep down below and falls in love with revolutionary leader Maria (Judy Kuhn). Meanwhile, the ruthless Master is in possession of a robot clone of Maria called Futura, and is scheming to use her against the workers. In this kind of situation a happy ending is too much to expect, but by curtain time the nuclear winter, brought about by the serf uprising, is tempered with a certain feeling of optimism, with nature slowly coming back to life. In the middle of all this revolutionary symbolism and expressionism, was the scientist Warner (Jonathan Adams), and a cast which also included Paul Keown, Stifyn Parri, Lindsey Danvers, Colin Fay, Megan Kelly, Robert Fardell, and Lucy Dixon. However, the star of the

piece was Ralph Koltai's spectacular set, an hydraulic masterpiece involving a vast conglomeration of stairways, pipes, and ramps, with circular, see-through elevators gliding silently up and down. This was enhanced by David Hersey's stunning lighting display, and a high-decibel, rock-flavoured score which featured '101.11', 'Hold Back The Night', 'The Machines Are Beautiful', 'He's Distant From Me Now', 'Elitists Dance', 'Children Of Metropolis', 'One More Morning', 'It's Only Love', 'Bring On The Night', 'You Are The Light', 'The Sun', 'There's A Girl Down Below', 'Futura', 'Nothing Really Matters', 'This Is My Time', 'Listen To Me', 'Learning Song', 'This City's On Fire', 'When Maria Wakes', 'Futura's Promise', 'Haven't You Finished With Me?', 'Let's Watch The World Go To The Devil', 'One Of These Nights', and 'Metropolis'. The imaginative choreography was by Tom Jobe, and the epic production was impressively staged by the prolific French director, Jérome Savary. Faced with critical reaction ranging from 'a triumph of visual style' to 'plumbed new depths', *Metropolis* could only manage a six-month run before closing early in September with the reported loss of its complete £2.5 million investment. Ironically, Lang's original movie nearly bankrupted UFA, Germany's largest film production company. In the early 90s there were several reports of US productions of *Metropolis* - the stage musical - at locations such as Chicago, the University of Texas at El Paso, East Peoria, Illinois, and Charlotte in North Carolina.

MEXICAN HAYRIDE

Master showman Mike Todd was renowned for his spectacular productions, and this show, one of the most lavish and successful of the World War II period, was certainly no exception. It opened at the Winter Garden Theatre in New York on 28 January 1944, and was still around well over a year later. The book, by Herbert and Dorothy Fields, follows Joe Bascom (Bobby Clark), an ex-numbers racketeer from the USA who is on the run in Mexico from the police - and various ladies - through a series of hilarious adventures and disguises. Cole Porter's Latin-styled score was full of good things such as 'I Love You', which was sung in the show by Wilbur Evans, and later became a US number 1 record for Bing Crosby. The other lively and attractive numbers included 'Sing To Me, Guitar', 'Abracadabra', 'Carlotta', 'There Must Be Someone For Me', 'Girls', and 'Count Your Blessings'. Bobby Clark was the man they all came to see, and he was at the top of his form. The veteran comedian had spent around 17 years in vaudeville in partnership with Paul McCullough before he broke through on Broadway in 1922. June Havoc, sister of the legendary Gypsy Rose Lee, was also in the cast of *Mexican Hayride*, along with George Givot, Luba Malina, Corinna Mura, Edith Meiser, Bill Callahan, Paul Haakon, and Candy Jones. The 1948 film version starred Abbott And Costello, but Porter's songs were dropped so the film was not classed as a musical.

MEYER, JOSEPH

b. 12 March 1894, Modesto, California, USA, d. 22 June 1987, New York, USA. A composer of popular songs, mainly for films and the stage, from the early 20s through the

40s, Meyer studied the violin in Paris and worked as a cafe violinist when he returned to the USA in 1908. After military service in World War I, he spent some time in the shipping business before taking up songwriting. In 1922, with Harry Ruby, he wrote 'My Honey's Lovin' Arms', which became a hit for Benny Goodman, Isham Jones and the California Ramblers, and was successfully revived on Barbra Streisand's debut album in 1963. During the 20s and 30s, Meyer composed the songs for several stage shows, including *Battling Buttler* ('You're So Sweet' and 'As We Leave The Years Behind') and *Big Boy* (starring Al Jolson singing 'California, Here I Come'). Another song from *Big Boy*, 'If You Knew Susie', was later associated with Eddie Cantor. Meyer also contributed to *Gay Paree* ('Bamboo Babies'), *Andre Charlote's Revue Of 1925* ('A Cup Of Coffee, A Sandwich, And You'), *Sweetheart Time* ('Who Loves You As I Do?'), *Just Fancy* ('You Came Along'), *Here's Howe* ('Crazy Rhythm' and 'Imagination'), *Lady Fingers* ('There's Something In That', 'An Open Book' and 'I Love You More Then Yesterday'), *Wake Up And Dream*, *Jonica*, *Shoot The Works* ('Chirp, Chirp'), the *Ziegfeld Follies Of 1934* and *New Faces Of 1936* ('It's High Time I Got The Low-Down On You'). His film songs included 'I Love You, I Hate You' (*Dancing Sweeties*), 'Can It Be Possible?' (*The Life Of The Party*), 'Oh, I Didn't Know', 'It's An Old Southern Custom', 'It's Time To Say Goodnight', 'I Got Shoes, You Got Shoesies' and 'According To The Moonlight' (George White's 1935 *Scandals*). His other popular numbers included 'Clap Hands, Here Comes Charley' (the signature tune of pianist, Charlie Kunz), 'Sweet So And So', 'Just A Little Closer', 'How Long Will It Last?' (used in the 1931 Joan Crawford-Clark Gable drama *Possessed*), 'Isn't It Heavenly?', 'I Wish I Were Twins', 'And Then They Called It Love', 'Hurry Home', 'Love Lies', 'Let's Give Love A Chance', 'Passe', 'But I Did', 'Fancy Our Meeting', 'I've Got A Heart Filled With Love', 'There's No Fool Like An Old Fool', 'Idle Gossip' and 'Watching The Clock'. His collaborators included Billy Moll, Billy Rose, Al Dubin, Jack Yellen, Cliff Friend, Buddy De Sylva, Herb Magidson, Al Jolson, Phil Charig, Irving Caesar, Carl Sigman, Frank Loesser, Eddie De Lange, and Douglas Furber.

MICHELL, KEITH

b. Keith Joseph Michell, 1 December 1926, Adelaide, South Australia. A distinguished, versatile actor and singer, who, in addition to his work in the classical and musical theatre, is also a talented painter. Michell gave up his job as an art teacher after successfully auditioning for Laurence Olivier and Vivian Leigh when they toured Australia in 1948. In the following year he moved to England, trained at the Old Vic Theatre School, and spent several years performing the works of the Bard with the Shakespeare Memorial Theatre Company at Stratford-on-Avon. Director-choreographer Wendy Toye subsequently gave him the role of Charles II in the 1951 Vivian Ellis musical *And So To Bed*, after which Michell continued to work in the classical theatre, returning to the musical stage only infrequently. In 1958 he did so for the smash hit English version of *Irma La Douce*, in which he played the poor law student Nestor-le-Fripe, a role he reprised on Broadway in 1960. Four years later, Toye tempted him

back again to co-star with June Bronhill in the critically acclaimed *Robert And Elizabeth*. Since then - apart from a Christmas entertainment - his only appearances in West End musicals have been as Don Quixote in *Man Of La Mancha* (1968, London Critics Award for Best Actor), and in the role of the has-been Broadway producer Oscar Jaffee in *On The Twentieth Century* (1980). He replaced Richard Kiley, the original New York Don in *Man Of La Mancha*, in December 1969 during the show's 2,328-performance Broadway run. As for *On The Twentieth Century*, despite the presence of Michell and Julia McKenzie, it folded after only a few months. Throughout the 80s and 90s he continued to appear occasionally in musicals such as *La Cage Aux Folles* and *Aspects Of Love* - but only abroad, in countries such as Australia, America and Canada. The aforementioned Christmas entertainment was *Captain Beaky's Musical Christmas*, which opened at London's Apollo Theatre in December 1981, starring Michell, Eleanor Bron, Twiggy, and Jeremy Lloyd (Lloyd had written the original children's poems on which the show was based, for which Michell provided the illustrations). Michell's recording of 'Captain Beaky'/'Wilfred The Weasel' made the UK Top 5 (1980), and he had modest success with the Beaky-associated 'The Trial Of Hissing Sid' (1980), as well as the earlier 'I'll Give You The Earth (Tous Les Bateaux, Tous Les Oiseaux)' (1971). Captain Beaky also crossed over into television, a medium in which Michell excelled. In the early 70s he won BAFTA and Emmy Awards for the mini-series *The Six Wives Of Henry VIII*, and his extensive work for the small screen has included *Pygmalion* (1956), *Tiger At The Gates* (1960), *Wuthering Heights* (1962), *The Spread Of The Eagle* (1963), *Julius Caesar* (1979-81), *The Day Christ Died* (1980), *The Miracle* (1985), *My Brother Tom* (series, 1986), *Captain James Cook* (series, 1987), *Murder, She Wrote* (series, 1990-91), and his own variety and concert specials. In 1996, he portrayed Henry VIII for the fifth time in his career in a BBC production of Mark Twain's classic tale of *The Prince And The Pauper*. In the same year he was reunited with his *Irma La Douce* co-star Elizabeth Seal at the 90th birthday celebrations of composer David Heneker. They sang the show's big romantic ballad, 'Our Language Of Love'. Michell served as artistic director of the Chichester Festival Theatre 1972-76, and among his other awards have been those from the Society of Film and Television, Sun Television, the Royal Academy of Television Arts, the *Evening News*, and the Grand Order of Water Rats (Show Business Personality of the Year).

● ALBUMS: *Ancient And Modern* (Spark 1971)★★★, *At The Show* (Spark 1972)★★★, and several spoken-word releases.

● FILMS: *True As A Turtle* (1956), *Dangerous Exile* (1957), *The Gypsy And The Gentleman* (1958), *The Hellfire Club* (1960), *All Night Long* (1961), *Dominatore Dei Sette Mari, II* (1962), *Prudence And The Pill* (1968), *House Of Cards* (1968), *The Executioner* (1970), *Moments* (1974), *Cross Creek* (1983), *The Deceivers* (1988), *The Tales Of Helpmann* as himself (1990).

MIDDLETON, RAY

b. 8 February 1907, Chicago, Illinois, USA, d. 10 April 1984, Panorama City, California, USA. A good looking singer and actor with a rich, powerful, baritone voice, Middleton

seemed destined for a career in opera, before being diverted into musical comedy. He gained a degree in music
from the University of Illinois, and also studied at the
Juilliard School of Music. After venturing on to the professional stage for the first time at the Detroit Civic Opera
House, he made his first appearance in New York in
December 1931 as the Giant in *Jack And The Beanstalk*, off-
Broadway at the 44th Street Theatre. His Broadway musical debut came with *Roberta* (1933, John Kent), followed
by *Knickerbocker Holiday* (1938, Washington Irving), and,
very briefly, *George White's Scandals* (1939). During this
period Middleton also sang leading roles with the Chicago
Opera. He moved to Hollywood in 1940, and over the next
three years made several movies, mostly with murder or
adventure themes, although he received excellent reviews
for his performance as minstrel man E.P. Christy in *I
Dream Of Jeannie* (1952), the third movie biopic of composer Stephen Foster. During World War II, he served with
the US Armed Forces, and appeared in Moss Hart's
morale-boosting play, *Winged Victory*. In 1946, already
nearly 40 years of age, he enjoyed the greatest success of
his career when cast as Frank Butler opposite Ethel
Merman in *Annie Get Your Gun*, one of the all-time great
stage musicals. Middleton introduced such memorable
Irving Berlin numbers as 'They Say It's Wonderful' and
'Anything You Can Do' (both with Merman), 'The Girl
That I Marry', and 'My Defences Are Down'. Following the
razzmatazz of *Annie Get Your Gun*, in 1948 Middleton co-
starred with Nanette Fabray in the unconventional *Love
Life* ('Here I'll Stay', with Fabray), took over from Ezio
Pinza as Emile de Becque in *South Pacific* (1950), and
toured with *America In Song And Story*. He was cast as the
Governor when the musical *Man Of La Mancha* tried out
at the Goodspeed Opera House, Connecticut, in June
1965, but by the time the show reached Broadway in
November, he had become the Innkeeper. Middleton
played the part continuously, so it is said, until the play's
closing in June 1971. In the following year he was in the
movie version of the hit Broadway musical *1776*, portraying Colonel Thomas McKean, but subsequently worked
infrequently.

● FILMS: *Gangs Of Chicago* (1940), *Mercy Island* (1941), *Lady For
A Night* (1941), *Lady From Louisiana* (1941), *Hurricane Smith*
(1941), *The Girl From Alaska* (1942), *I Dream Of Jeannie* (1952),
Jubilee Trail (1954), *The Road To Denver* (1955), *1776* (1972).

MIDLER, BETTE

b. 1 December 1945, Paterson, New Jersey, USA. As a
singer, comedienne and actress, Midler rose to fame with
an outrageous, raunchy stage act, and became known as
'The Divine Miss M', 'Trash With Flash' and 'Sleaze With
Ease'. Her mother, a fan of the movies, named her after
Bette Davis. Raised in Hawaii, as one of the few white students in her school, and the only Jew, she 'toughened up
fast', and won an award in the first grade for singing 'Silent
Night'. Encouraged by her mother, she studied theatre at
the University of Hawaii, and worked in a pineapple factory and as a secretary in a radio station before gaining her
first professional acting job in 1965 in the movie *Hawaii*,
playing the minor role of a missionary wife who is constantly sick. Moving to New York, she held jobs as a glove

saleswoman in Stern's Department Store, a hat-check girl,
and a go-go dancer, before joining the chorus of the hit
Broadway musical *Fiddler On The Roof* in 1966. In
February 1967, Midler took over one of the leading roles,
as Tzeitel, the eldest daughter, and played the part for the
next three years. While singing late-night after the show at
the Improvisation Club, a showcase for young performers,
she was noticed by an executive from the David Frost television show, and subsequently appeared several times
with Frost, and on the *Merv Griffin Show*. After leaving
Fiddler On The Roof, she performed briefly in the off-
Broadway musical *Salvation*, and worked again as a go-go
dancer in a Broadway bar, before taking a $50-a-night job
at the Continental Baths, New York, singing to male homosexuals dressed in bath towels. Clad in toreador pants, or
sequin gowns, strapless tops and platform shoes - uniforms of a bygone age - she strutted her extravagant stuff,
singing songs from the 40s, 50s, and 60s - rock, blues, novelties - even reaching back to 1929 for the Harry
Akst/Grant Clarke ballad 'Am I Blue?', which had been a
hit then for Ethel Waters. News of these somewhat bizarre
happenings soon got round, and outside audiences of both
sexes, including show people, were allowed to view the
show. Offers of other work flooded in, including the
opportunity to appear regularly on Johnny Carson's
Tonight show.

In May 1971, she played the dual roles of the Acid Queen
and Mrs Walker in the Seattle Opera Company's production of the rock opera *Tommy* and, later in the year, made
her official New York nightclub debut at the Downstairs At
The Upstairs, the original two-week engagement being
extended to 10, to accommodate the crowds. During the
following year, she appeared with Carson at the Sahara in
Las Vegas, and in June played to standing room only at
Carnegie Hall in New York. In November, her first album,
The Divine Miss M, was released by Atlantic Records, and
is said to have sold 100,000 copies in the first month. It
contained several of the cover versions that she featured
in her stage act, such as the Andrews Sisters' 'Boogie
Woogie Bugle Boy', the Dixie Cups' 'The Chapel Of Love',
the Shangri-Las' 'The Leader Of The Pack' and Bobby
Freeman's 'Do You Want To Dance?'. The pianist on most
of the tracks was Barry Manilow, who was Midler's accompanist and musical director for three years in the early
70s. The album bears the dedication: 'This is for Judith'.
Judith was Midler's sister who was killed in a road accident on her way to meet Bette when she was appearing in
Fiddler On The Roof. Midler's second album, *Bette Midler*,
also made the US Top 10. In 1973, Midler received the
After Dark Award for Performer Of The Year, and soon
became a superstar, able to fill concert halls throughout
the USA. In 1979, she had her first starring role in the
movie *The Rose*, which was loosely based on the life of
rock singer Janis Joplin. Midler was nominated for an
Academy Award as 'Best Actress', and won two Golden
Globe Awards for her performance. Two songs from the
film, the title track (a million-seller), and 'When A Man
Loves A Woman', and the soundtrack album, entered the
US charts, as did the album from Midler's next film, *Divine
Madness*, a celluloid version of her concert performance
in Pasadena, California. After all the success of the past

decade, things started to go wrong in the early 80s. In 1982, the aptly named black comedy, *Jinxed!*, was a disaster at the box office, amid rumours of violent disagreements between Midler and her co-star Ken Wahl and director Don Siegel. Midler became *persona non grata* in Hollywood, and suffered a nervous breakdown. She married Martin Von Haselberg, a former commodities broker, in 1984, and signed to a long-term contract to the Walt Disney Studios, making her comeback in the comedy *Down And Out In Beverly Hills* (1985), with Nick Nolte and Richard Dreyfuss.

During the rest of the decade she eschewed touring, and concentrated on her acting career in a series of raucous comedy movies such as *Ruthless People* (1986), co-starring Danny De Vito, *Outrageous Fortune* (1987) and *Big Business* (1988). In 1988, *Beaches*, the first film to be made by her own company, All Girls Productions (their motto is, 'We hold a grudge'), gave her one of her best roles, and the opportunity to sing songs within the context of the story. These included standards such as 'Ballin' The Jack', Cole Porter's 'I've Still Got My Health', 'The Glory Of Love', 'Under The Boardwalk', and 'Otto Titsling'. Also included was 'Wind Beneath My Wings', by Larry Henley and Jeff Silbar, which reached number 1 in the US charts. Midler's recording won Grammys in 1990 for 'Record Of The Year' and 'Song Of The Year'. In 1990, Midler appeared in *Stella*, a remake of the classic weepie, *Stella Dallas*, in which she performed a hilarious mock striptease among the bottles and glasses on top of a bar, and *Scenes From A Mall*, a comedy co-staring Woody Allen. Her appearance as a USO entertainer in World War II, alongside actor James Caan, in *For The Boys* (1991), which she also co-produced, earned her a Golden Globe award for Best Actress. The movie showed her at her best, and featured her very individual readings of 'Stuff Like That There' and 'P. S. I Love You'. In the same year, she released *Some People's Lives*, her first non-soundtrack album since the 1983 flop, *No Frills*. It entered the US Top 10, and one of the tracks, 'From A Distance', had an extended chart life in the USA and UK. By the early 90s she was planning to revive her musical career, and in 1993 brought a spectacular new stage show to Radio City Music Hall. The lavish three-hour concert, her first for 10 years, was called *Experience The Divine*, and seemed as 'gaudy and outrageously tasteless as ever'. In 1994 Midler won an Emmy Nomination, along with Golden Globe and National Board of Review Awards for her outstanding performance as Rose in a CBS television musical production of *Gypsy*. In 1995 she released *Bette Of Roses*, her first studio album for five years, and continued to play sell-out concerts and make acclaimed movies. On television, *Bette Midler In Concert: Diva In Las Vegas*, aired in 1997, and in the following year chat show queen Roseanne hosted a nostalgic reunion between Midler and her original vocal and musical support, the Harlettes and Barry Manilow.

● ALBUMS: *The Divine Miss M* (Atlantic 1972)★★★★, *Bette Midler* (Atlantic 1973)★★★, *Songs For The New Depression* (Atlantic 1976)★★, *Live At Last* (Atlantic 1977)★★★, *Broken Blossom* (Atlantic 1977)★★, *Thighs And Whispers* (Atlantic 1979)★★, *The Rose* film soundtrack(Atlantic 1979)★★★, *Divine Madness* film soundtrack (Atlantic 1980)★★, *No Frills* (Atlantic 1983)★★, *Mud Will Be Flung Tonight* (Atlantic 1985)★★, *Beaches* film soundtrack (Atlantic 1989)★★, *Some People's Lives* (Atlantic 1990)★★, *For The Boys* (Atlantic 1991)★★, *Bette Of Roses* (Atlantic 1995)★★.
● COMPILATIONS: *Best Of* (Atlantic 1978)★★★.
● FURTHER READING: *Bette Midler*, Rob Baker. *A View From A Broad*, Bette Midler. *The Saga Of Baby Divine*, Bette Midler. *An Intimate Biography Of Bette Midler*, George Mair.
● FILMS: *The Thorn* (1971), *The Rose* (1979), *Divine Madness!* (1980), *Jinxed!* (1982), *Bette Midler's Mondo Beyondo* (1982), *Down And Out In Beverly Hills* (1986), *Ruthless People* (1982), *Outrageous Fortune* (1987), *Beaches* (1988), *Big Business* (1988), *Oliver & Company* (1988) voice *Stella* (1990), *Scenes From The Mall* (1991), *For The Boys* (1991), *Hocus Pocus* (1993), *A Century Of Cinema* (1994), *Get Shorty* (1995), *The First Wives Club* (1996), *That Old Feeling* (1997).

MILK AND HONEY

Jerry Herman's first Broadway score, and reputedly the first Broadway musical ever to have an Israeli setting - the block buster *Fiddler On The Roof* came along three years after *Milk And Honey* opened on Broadway at the Martin Beck Theatre on 10 October 1961. Don Appel's book deals mainly with the romantic relationship between Phil (Robert Weede) and Ruth (Mimi Benzell), two middle-aged American tourists in Israel. At the end of the piece, their on-off affair is still unresolved, mainly due to Ruth's not unreasonable misgivings concerning Phil's wife. Molly Picon played another American tourist - but one with a mission - a widow in determined pursuit of a new husband in the shape of Mr. Horowitz (Juki Arkin). Picon, a veteran of the Yiddish theatre, also starred in the film of *Fiddler On The Roof*. Other members of the cast included Tommy Rall and Lanna Saunders. Herman's score was acclaimed as 'melodically inventive', and particular praise was reserved for Phil and Ruth's touching 'Shalom'. However, the rest of the songs, such as 'There's No Reason In The World', 'That Was Yesterday', 'Let's Not Waste A Moment', 'Like A Young Man', 'As Simple As That', 'Chin Up, Ladies', and 'Independence Day Hora', were extremely impressive, and lingered in the memory. *Milk And Honey* ran for 543 performances - without making a profit. Still, the money would soon be rolling in for Herman: his first smash-hit, *Hello Dolly*, was set to make its elegant entrance on Broadway in 1964.

MILLER, ANN

b. Lucille Ann Collier, 12 April 1919 or 1923, Chireno, Texas, USA. A vivacious, long-legged tap dancer (500 taps per minute) who achieved stardom rather late in her career via several classic film musicals of the late 40s and early 50s. After her parents were divorced when she was about 10 years old, Miller, who is of Irish, French and Cherokee descent, moved with her mother to California and supplemented the family's finances by dancing in clubs. An RKO talent scout spotted her there, and in the late 30s she made a few films for the studio, including *New Faces Of 1937*, The *Life Of The Party*, *Stage Door*, *Having A Wonderful Time*, *Tarnished Angel*, *Room Service*, and *Radio City Revels*. In 1938 she was loaned out to Columbia for the Frank Capra comedy *You Can't Take It*

With You which won the Oscar for best picture. A year later she thrilled Broadway audiences by dancing 'The Mexiconga', accompanied by the Loo Sisters and Ella Logan in *George White's Scandals*. During the early 40s she was often one of the few artists worth watching in a series of mostly low-budget features which included *Melody Ranch, Time Out For Rhythm, Go West Young Lady, Reveille With Beverley, What's Buzzin' Cousin?, Jam Session, Carolina Blues*, and *Eadie Was A Lady* (1945). In 1948 she had good role in *Easter Parade* with Fred Astaire, Judy Garland, and Peter Lawford, and provided one of the film's highlights with her scintillating solo dance number 'Shaking The Blues Away'. Her performance in that film merited a seven year MGM contract, and after performing a frenetic 'Dance Of Fury' with Ricardo Montalban and Cyd Charisse in *The Kissing Bandit*, joined Frank Sinatra, Gene Kelly, Vera-Ellen, Betty Garrett and Jules Munshin in one of the all-time great movie musicals, *On The Town* (1949). She led them all a fine dance around the anthropology museum with the clever and amusing 'Prehistoric Man'. Although she was by now around 30 years of age, Miller continued to shine during the early 50s in movies such as *Texas Carnival, Two Tickets To Broadway, Lovely To Look At* (which included her highly individual interpretation of 'I'll Be Hard To Handle'), and *Small Town Girl* in which she excelled again, this time with 'I Gotta Hear That Beat'. In *Kiss Me Kate* (1953) she played what is said to be her favourite role of Bianca, and this film was arguably the highlight of her whole career. Her memorable performances of Cole Porter's marvellous 'Too Darn Hot', 'From This Moment On', 'Tom, Dick And Harry', 'Why Can't You Behave?', 'Always True To You Darling In My Fashion', and 'We Open In Venice' were a joy to behold. By now, the golden era of MGM musicals was almost over, and after guesting in the Sigmund Romberg biopic *Deep In My Heart*, and emphasising just how good she still was with a top-class routine to 'The Lady From The Bayou' in *Hit The Deck*, Miller signed off in 1956 with the ordinary *The Opposite Sex* and the non-musical *The Great American Pastime* (about baseball, of course). Like so many others, in the 60s she turned to television and nightclubs and toured in stage revivals of shows such as *Hello, Dolly!, Panama Hattie*, and *Can-Can*. She also made a television commercial for soup in which she danced on the top of an enormous can, surrounded by water fountains, a large orchestra, and a bevy of chorus girls. In 1969 she returned to Broadway after an absence of 30 years and took over the leading role in the hit musical *Mame* to wide critical acclaim. In the early 70s her extensive tours in *Anything Goes* were interrupted for more than a year while Miller recovered from an accident in which she was struck by a sliding steel curtain. In 1979 she joined Mickey Rooney in *Sugar Babies*, a celebration of the golden era of American vaudeville which ran on Broadway for 1,208 performances before touring the US for several years, and spending a brief time in London's West End in 1988. Her honours include the George M. Cohan Award for Best Female Entertainer, the Sarah Siddons Award for Best Actress, and an award for Best Dance Number given to her by the Dance Awards of America. The University of California presented her with its Lifetime Award and endowed a

yearly drama award and scholarship in her honour. Miller's colourful private life, which has involved admirers such as Conrad Hilton and Louis B. Mayer, and failed marriages to three American oil millionaires, is documented in her autobiography. She is also interested in the paranormal and is said to believe implicitly that she is a reincarnation of the first female Pharaoh of Egypt. However, for a limited season in 1998, Miller exchanged the mysteries of the Middle East for the more mundane Paper Mill Playhouse, New Jersey, where she played Carlotta ('I'm Still Here') in a decent revival of *Follies*.

● FURTHER READING: *Miller's High Life*, Ann Miller.

MINEO, SAL

b. Salvatore Mineo, 10 January 1939, New York City, New York, USA, d. 12 February 1976. After a difficult childhood, Mineo studied dancing and made his Broadway debut in *The Rose Tattoo*. He followed this with an appearance in *The King And I* in 1952. In the mid-50s he went to Hollywood and began making films, usually appearing as a troubled teenager. Among his best-known films were *Rebel Without A Cause* (1955), for which he was nominated for an Oscar as Best Supporting Actor, *Somebody Up There Likes Me* and *Giant* (both 1956), and *Exodus* (1960), another unsuccessful Oscar nomination. He also played the title role in *The Gene Krupa Story* (1959). In the late 50s, Mineo made a number of records, including 'Love Affair', 'Start Moving (In My Direction)', 'Lasting Love' and 'You Shouldn't Do That'. He continued making films during the 60s and also returned to stage work. He directed and starred in *Fortune And Men's Eyes*, a play that reflected Mineo's own homosexuality. He was returning home from the theatre when he was stabbed to death in a Hollywood street.

● ALBUMS: *Sal* (Epic 1958)★★.

● COMPILATIONS: *The Secret Doorway: The Ultimate Collection* (Fireball 1998)★★.

MINNELLI, LIZA

b. Liza May Minnelli, 12 March 1946, Los Angeles, California, USA. An extremely vivacious and animated actress, singer and dancer, in films, concerts, musical shows and television. She was named Liza after the George and Ira Gershwin-Gus Kahn song- and May after the mother of her film-director father, Vincente Minnelli. Liza's mother was show-business legend Judy Garland. On the subject of her first name, Miss Minnelli is musically quite precise: 'It's Liza with 'zee', not Lisa with an 's'/'Cos Liza with a 'zee' goes 'zzz', not 'sss'. She spent a good deal of her childhood in Hollywood, where her playmates included Mia Farrow, although she also reputedly attended over 20 schools in the USA and Europe. At the age of two-and-a-half, she made her screen debut in the closing sequence of *In The Good Old Summer Time*, as the daughter of the musical film's stars, Garland and Van Johnson. When she was seven, she danced on the stage of the Palace Theatre, New York, while her mother sang 'Swanee'. In 1962, after initially showing no interest in a show-business career, Minnelli served as an apprentice in revivals of the musicals, *Take Me Along* and *The Flower Drum Song*, and later played Anne Frank in a stock production. By the following year she was accomplished enough to win a Promising Personality Award for her third lead performance in an off-Broadway revival of the 1941 Ralph Blane/Hugh Martin Musical *Best Foot Forward*, and later toured in road productions of *Carnival*, *The Pajama Game*, and *The Fantasticks*. She also made her first album, *Liza! Liza!* which sold over 500,000 copies shortly after it was released in 1964. In November of that year, Minnelli appeared with Judy Garland at the London Palladium. Comparatively unknown in the UK, she startled the audience with dynamic performances of songs such as 'The Travelin' Life' and 'The Gypsy In My Soul' - almost 'stealing' the show from the more experienced artist. Her Broadway debut in *Flora, The Red Menace* (1965), marked the beginning of a long association with songwriters John Kander and Fred Ebb, gained her a Tony Award, although the show closed after only 87 performances. In 1966 she made her New York cabaret debut at the Plaza Hotel to enthusiastic reviews, and in 1967 married Australian singer/songwriter, Peter Allen. Her film career started in 1968 with a supporting role in Albert Finney's first directorial effort, *Charlie Bubbles*, and in 1969, she was nominated for an Academy Award for her performance as Pookie Adams in the film of John Nichols' novel, *The Sterile Cuckoo*. She took time off from making her third film, *Tell Me That You Love Me, Junie Moon*, to attend the funeral of her mother, who died in 1969. In the following year she and Peter Allen announced their separation.

In 1972, Liza Minnelli became a superstar. The film of Kander and Ebb's Broadway hit, *Cabaret*, won nine Oscars, including Best Film, and for her role as Sally Bowles, Minnelli was named Best Actress and appeared on the front covers of *Newsweek* and *Time* magazines in the same week. She also won an Emmy for her television special *Liza With A Z*, directed by Bob Fosse. Her concerts were sell-outs; when she played the Olympia, Paris, they dubbed her 'la petite Piaf Americano'. In 1973 she met producer/director Jack Haley Jnr. while contributing to his film project *That's Entertainment!* Haley's father had played the Tin Man in Judy Garland's most famous picture, *The Wizard Of Oz*. Haley Jnr and Minnelli married in 1974, and in the same year she broke Broadway records and won a special Tony Award for a three-week series of one-woman shows at the Winter Garden. Her next two movies, *Lucky Lady* and *A Matter Of Time* received lukewarm reviews, but she made up for these in 1977, with her next film project, *New York, New York*. Co-starring with Robert DeNiro, and directed by Martin Scorsese, Minnelli's dramatic performance as a young band singer in the period after World War II was a personal triumph. This was the last film she made until *Arthur* (1981), in which she played a supporting role to Dudley Moore. The musical theme for *Arthur*, 'Best You Can Do', was co-written by her ex-husband, Peter Allen. A renewed association with Kander and Ebb for the Broadway musical *The Act* (1977), was dismissed by some critics as being little more than a series of production numbers displaying the talents of Liza Minnelli. In brought her another Tony Award, but she collapsed from exhaustion during the show's run. In 1979, she was divorced from Jack Haley Jnr., and married Italian sculptor, Mark Gero. Rumours were appearing in

the press speculating about her drug and alcohol problems, and for a couple of years she was virtually retired. In 1984 she was nominated for yet another Tony for her performance on Broadway in *The Rink*, with Chita Rivera, but dropped out of the show to seek treatment for drug and alcohol abuse at the Betty Ford Clinic in California. She started her comeback in 1985, and in the following year, on her 40th birthday, opened to a sold-out London Palladium, the first time she had played the theatre since that memorable occasion in 1964; she received the same kind of reception that her mother did then. In the same year, back in the USA, Minnelli won the Golden Globe Award as Best Actress in *A Time To Live*, a television adaptation of the true story, *Intensive Care*, by Mary-Lou Weisman. During the late 80s she joined Frank Sinatra and Sammy Davis Jnr. for a world tour, dubbed *The Ultimate Event!*, and in 1989 collaborated with the UK pop group, the Pet Shop Boys, on the album *Results*. A single from the album, Stephen Sondheim's 'Losing My Mind', gave Liza Minnelli her first UK chart entry, at number 6. She also appeared with Dudley Moore in the film *Arthur 2: On The Rocks*. In 1991 her marriage to Mark Gero ended. In the same year, after co-starring with Julie Walters in the British musical comedy *Stepping Out*, Minnelli used the film's title for a series of concerts she gave at Radio City Music Hall in New York which broke the venue's 59-year box office record. She later took the show to London's Royal Albert Hall, where she returned a year later for a one-off gala charity concert dedicated to the memory of her late friend Sammy Davis Jnr. Her other work in the early 90s included concerts with Charles Aznavour at the Palais des Congress and Carnegie Hall, and serving as host for the 1993 Tony Awards ceremony, during which she sang a medley of Broadway songs with her step-sister Lorna Luft. In June 1994 Minnelli was in Moscow, giving shows as part of the D-Day commemorations. Later in the year she underwent surgery to replace her right hip, after 'being in pain for 10 years'. In 1996, she released *Gently*, her first 'proper' album in years. It featured some lush duets with Donna Summer and Johnny Mathis. After some much-publicized troubles and health scares, in January 1997 Minnelli was back on Broadway for the first time in more than 12 years. Standing ovations became the norm when she played the lead role in *Victor/Victoria* while its star, Julie Andrews, took a break. Later in the year she returned to the concert stage in America, but was forced to withdraw from a series of UK concerts in May 1998 amid growing fears for her health. However, she was fit enough to lead the on-stage tributes (and render a typically flamboyant version of 'New York, New York') to Kander and Ebb when the songwriters received their Kennedy Center Honours early in 1999. Liza Minnelli's roller coaster career in film and music has enabled her to transcend the title, 'Judy Garland's daughter'.

● ALBUMS: *Best Foot Forward* off-Broadway cast (Cadence 1963)★★, *Liza! Liza!* (Capitol 1964)★★★, *It Amazes Me* (1965)★★, *The Dangerous Christmas Of Red Riding Hood* film soundtrack (1965)★★, with Judy Garland *'Live' At The London Palladium* (Capitol 1965)★★★★, *Flora, The Red Menace* Broadway cast (RCA Victor 1965)★★, *There Is A Time* (1966)★★★, *New Feelin'* (A&M

1970)★★, *Cabaret* film soundtrack (1972)★★★★, *Liza With A 'Z'* (1972)★★★★, *Liza Minnelli The Singer* (Columbia 1973)★★★★, *Live At The Winter Garden* (Columbia 1974)★★★, *Lucky Lady* (1976)★★★, *Tropical Nights* (1977)★★★, *Live! - At Carnegie Hall* (Telarc 1988)★★★, *Results* (Epic 1989)★★★, *Live From Radio City Music Hall* (1992)★★★, *Aznavour/Minnelli Paris-Palais Des Congrès* (EMI 1995)★★★, *Gently* (Angel 1996)★★★.

● COMPILATIONS: *The Collection* (Spectrum 1998)★★★.

● VIDEOS: *Visible Results* (1990), *Live At Radio City Music Hall* (1994), with Frank Sinatra, Sammy Davis Jnr. *The Ultimate Event!* (1996).

● FURTHER READING: *Liza*, James Robert Parish. *Judy And Liza*, James Spada. *Liza - Born A Star*, Wendy Leigh. *Liza: Her Cinderella Nightmare*, James Robert Parish. *Me And My Shadows: Living With The Legacy Of Judy Garland*, Lorna Luft. *Under The Rainbow: The Real Liza Minnelli*, George Mair.

● FILMS: *In The Good Old Summertime* child cameo (1949), *Charlie Bubbles* (1967), *The Sterile Cuckoo* (1969), *Tell Me That You Love Me Junie Moon* (1970), *Cabaret* (1972), *That's Entertainment!* on-screen narrator (1974), *Journey Back To Oz* (1974), *Lucky Lady* (1975), *A Matter Of Time* (1976), *Silent Movie* cameo (1976), *New York New York* (1977), *Arthur* (1981), *The King Of Comedy* cameo (1983), *The Muppets Take Manhattan* cameo (1984), *That's Dancing!* co-narrator (1985), *Rent-A-Cop* (1988), *Arthur 2: On The Rocks* (1988), *Stepping Out* (1991).

MINNELLI, VINCENTE

b. 28 February 1903, Chicago, Illinois, USA, d. 25 July 1986, Los Angeles, California, USA. A distinguished film director with a sophisticated style and flair, particularly in the use of colour and the innovative filming of the most exquisite dance sequences. Minnelli is credited, in collaboration with Gene Kelly, with being the main influence on the classic MGM musicals of the 50s. As a young child Minnelli appeared in plays produced by the family Minnelli Bros. Tent Theatre, which toured the American Midwest. After leaving school at 16 he studied at the Art Institute of Chicago, and worked as a window and costume designer before moving to New York to design the scenery and costumes for two 1932 Broadway shows, the *Earl Carroll Vanities* and *The DuBarry*. From 1933-35 Minnelli was art director at the Radio City Music Hall where he staged a series of ballets and musicals. In 1935 he directed as well as designed the Beatrice Lillie musical *At Home Abroad*, and throughout the 30s worked successfully on productions such as *Ziegfeld Follies*, *The Show Is On*, *Hooray For What!* and *Very Warm For May* (1939). From 1940-42, under the aegis of MGM producer Arthur Freed, Minnelli trained in various aspects of Hollywood film techniques and supervised speciality numbers in a number of films including *Strike Up The Band*, *Babes On Broadway* and *Panama Hattie*. He made his debut as a director in 1943 with the all-black musical *Cabin In The Sky*, which was followed by *I Dood It* a year later. Then came *Meet Me In St. Louis* (1944), a delightful piece of nostalgic Americana that became one of the most beloved musicals of all time. Minnelli married its star, Judy Garland, in 1945 (divorced 1951), and in the following year their daughter, Liza Minnelli, was born. Over the next 25 years Minnelli directed a number of musicals that met with varying degrees of success. *Yolande And The*

Thief (1945), which starred Fred Astaire, was followed by the all-star spectacular *Ziegfeld Follies* (1946), and two films with Gene Kelly, the underrated *The Pirate* (1948), and *An American In Paris* (1951), which is often considered to be Minnelli's masterpiece. However, many would argue that another of the director's collaborations with Fred Astaire, *The Band Wagon* (1953), or the delightful *Gigi* (1958), were equally important events in the director's distinguished career. Certainly, whatever their merits - and they were not inconsiderable - few would suggest *Brigadoon* (1954), *Kismet* (1955), *Bells Are Ringing* (1960) or *On A Clear Day You Can See Forever* (1970) as being prime examples of Vincente Minnelli's art. The latter film was made for Paramount after he had ended an association with MGM that had lasted for more than 25 years. However, the majority of Minnelli's films were not musicals. Over the years he made many other pictures in a wide variety of styles and moods, and finally achieved his ambition to work with daughter Liza Minnelli in 1976 on his last film, *A Matter Of Time*. By then, Minnelli's style of films - particularly musicals - were anachronistic, and he lived quietly in retirement until his death at his home in Beverly Hills in 1986. The year of his birth has always been the subject of speculation. The one cited above is that which was printed in the excellent obituary notice in *Variety*. In 1993 the young cabaret entertainer Jeff Harnar presented his solo revue *Dancing In The Dark - Vincente Minnelli's Hollywood* in New York.

● FURTHER READING: *I Remember It Well*, Vincente Minnelli.

● FILMS: as director *I Dood It* (1943), *Cabin In The Sky* (1943), *Meet Me In St. Louis* (1944), *Yolande And The Thief* (1945), *The Clock* (1945), *Till The Clouds Roll By (Judy Garland's sequences only)* (1946), *Ziegfeld Follies* (1946), *Undercurrent* (1946), *The Pirate* (1948), *Madame Bovary* (1949), *Father Of The Bride* (1950), *An American In Paris* (1951), *Father's Little Dividend* (1951), *The Story Of Three Loves (Mademoiselle Sequence)* (1952), *The Bad And The Beautiful* (1952), *The Band Wagon* (1953), *Brigadoon* (1954), *The Long Long Trailer* (1954), *The Cobweb* (1955), *Kismet* (1955), *Lust For Life* (1956), *Tea And Sympathy* (1956), *Designing Woman* (1957), *Some Came Running* (1958), *The Reluctant Debutante* (1958), *Gigi* (1958), *Bells Are Ringing* (1960), *Home From The Hill* (1960), *Two Weeks In Another Town* (1962), *The Four Horsemen Of The Apocalypse* (1962), *The Courtship Of Eddie's Father* (1963), *Goodbye Charlie* (1964), *The Sandpiper* (1965), *On A Clear Day You Can See Forever* (1970), *A Matter Of Time* (1976).

MIRANDA, CARMEN

b. Maria do Carmo Miranda da Cunha, 9 February 1909, near Lisbon, Portugal, d. 5 August 1955, California, USA. A flamboyant singer, dancer and actress with an animated style and a penchant for exotic, colourful costumes, 10 inch-heeled shoes, and turbans decorated with significant amounts of artificial fruit. She was raised in Rio de Janeiro and began her career there on local radio. Later she made several films and appeared in nightclubs and theatres throughout South America. Lee Shubert, the oldest of the famous trio of producer brothers, took Miranda to the USA in 1939 where she introduced Al Dubin and Jimmy McHugh's catchy 'South American Way' in the Broadway musical *The Streets Of Paris*. She sang it again (her peculiar accent turned it into 'Souse American Way') when she made her spectacular film debut with Betty Grable and Don Ameche in *Down Argentine Way* (1940). A year later she joined the comedy team of Olsen and Jolsen in another Broadway show, *Sons O' Fun*. However, her real impact was made in a series of film musicals in the 40s when she became known as the 'Brazilian Bombshell'. These included *That Night In Rio*, *Weekend In Havana*, *Springtime In The Rockies*, *The Gang's All Here*, *Four Jills In A Jeep*, *Greenwich Village*, *Doll Face*, *If I'm Lucky*, *Copacabana*, and *A Date With Judy*. By then her star had faded, and she made only two more pictures, *Nancy Goes To Rio* (1950) and *Scared Stiff* (1953), although in the late 40s and early 50s she continued to perform in theatres and nightclubs. She died suddenly of a heart attack in 1955 shortly after appearing with Jimmy Durante on his television show. A dynamic, much impersonated entertainer - Mickey Rooney's wickedly accurate takeoff in *Babes On Broadway* immediately comes to mind - Carmen Miranda was indelibly associated with several lively and diverting songs, including 'The Lady With The Tutti Frutti Hat', 'I Yi Yi Yi Yi (I Like You Very Much)', 'Chica Boom Chic', 'When I Love, I Love', 'Cuanto La Gusta', 'Mama, Eu Quero (I Want My Mama)', and 'The Wedding Samba' (the last two with the Andrews Sisters).

● ALBUMS: *South American Way* (c.50s, re-released 1982),★★★ *By Popular Demand* (MCA 1995)★★★.

● FURTHER READING: *Brazilian Bombshell: The Biography Of Carmen Miranda*, M. Gil-Montero.

MISS HOOK OF HOLLAND

One of the most popular London musicals in the early part of the century, this show was sub-titled a 'Dutch musical incident in two acts', when it opened at the Prince of Wales Theatre in London on 31 January 1907. The score was the work of Paul Rubens who had enjoyed great success five years earlier with *A Country Girl*. Rubens collaborated with Austen Hurgon on the book which concerns Mr. Hook (G.P. Huntley), a liqueur distiller in Amsterdam. His daughter, Sally (Isabel Jay) boosts the company's sales by inventing a liqueur made of 61 different ingredients, which she calls 'Cream In The Sky'. However, the important recipe is stolen and passed from hand to hand during a romantic, but sometimes bewildering plot, before it is returned to Hook's safe. None of the songs endured, but there were several pleasant numbers including 'Little Miss Wooden Shoes', 'The Sleepy Canal', 'A Little Pink Petty From Peter', 'Tra-La-La', 'The House That Hook Built', and 'Cream Of The Sky'. An excellent London run of 462 performances was followed by a further 119 at the Criterion Theatre in New York in 1907. In the same year the show was presented in Vienna, and there were London revivals in 1914 and 1932.

MISS LIBERTY

Three years after his biggest success with *Annie Get Your Gun* in 1946, Irving Berlin came up with the score for this show, which, on the face of it, had all the right credentials: a book by Pulitzer Prize-winning playwright Robert E. Sherwood, choreography by Jerome Robbins, direction by Moss Hart, and, of course, music and lyrics by Berlin himself. It opened at the Imperial Theatre in New York on 15 July 1949, with Sherwood's cosy, patriotic story set in New York and Paris in 1885. The plot tells of how Horace Miller (Eddie Albert), an inept newspaper photographer, travels to France to find the model who posed for the Statue Of Liberty. He returns with the wrong one, and all sorts of complications have to be overcome before everyone gathers at the statue's dedication ceremony to sing 'Give Me Your Tired, Your Poor', Berlin's musical adaptation of the poem by Emma Lazarus. Monique Dupont, played by the accomplished ballerina, Allyn McLerie, was the lady that Horace fell for in Paris and took back with him to America, only to find that, waiting for him there was his girlfriend, Maisie Dell (Mary McCarty). Berlin's score contained two songs that became popular: 'Let's Take An Old Fashioned Walk' was a big hit for Perry Como, and for Doris Day with Frank Sinatra; and both Como and Jo Stafford took 'Just One Way To Say I Love You' into the US Hit Parade. The rest of the numbers included 'Little Fish In A Big Pond', 'I'd Like My Picture Took', 'Homework', 'Falling Out Of Love Can Be Fun', 'Paris Wakes Up And Smiles', 'Only For Americans', and 'You Can Have Him', an untypical ballad containing 'truth and sarcasm, and dedicated to the "other woman"' - ('You can have him/I don't want him/He's not worth fighting for/Besides, there's plenty more where he came from'), which received a sophisticated reading on the 1965 album *The Nancy Wilson Show!* Despite its virtues, and its patriotic theme, *Miss Liberty* did not start any parades, and closed after 308 performances.

MISS LONDON LTD.

Released by Gainsborough Pictures in 1943, this comedy-musical is a typical example of the cheery, tuneful fare British cinema audiences flocked to see during the dark war years. It starred Arthur 'Hallo Playmates!' Askey, one of the country's most popular funny-men. He played Arthur Bowman, the manager of the Miss London Ltd. escort agency which is visited by its attractive American owner, Terry Arden (Evelyn Dall). The business needs a shake-up, and Arthur goes on a recruitment drive and comes up with railway station announcer Gail Martin (Anne Shelton). The ensuing complications involve some of Britain's top comedy talent, such as Jack Train as Arthur's right-hand man, Max Bacon as an hilariously coy head waiter, and Richard Hearne, who plays a jitterbugging commodore in the Navy, the service into which Arthur himself is being co-opted (by another fine comic actor, Ronald Shiner) when the closing titles roll. Other parts were taken by Peter Graves and Jean Kent. Manning Sherwin and Val Guest, wrote the songs, and Evelyn Dall had one of the film's best musical moments with the punchy 'Keep Cool, Calm - And Collect!'. She also joined Askey for the lively 'It's A Fine How-Do-You-Do'. Anne Shelton, who had the distinction of singing with the Glenn Miller Orchestra during the war, was splendid on 'If You Could Only Cook', 'You Too (Can Have a Lovely Romance)', and 'The Eight Fifty Choo Choo'. Val Guest and Marriott Edgar wrote the screenplay, and Guest also directed. The producer was Edward Black.

MISS SAIGON

A re-working of Puccini's enduring *Madame Butterfly* as a Vietnam war tale, set in Saigon during the last days of the American presence there in 1975. The music was by Claude-Michel Schönberg, with lyrics by Richard Maltby Jnr. and Alain Boublil (adapted from the original French lyrics by Boublil) with additional material by Maltby. *Miss Saigon* opened at the Theatre Royal, Drury Lane in London on 20 September 1989. The dramatic story concerns a young marine, Chris (Simon Bowman), who falls in love with a would-be prostitute Kim (Lea Salonga). However, partly owing to the chaotic troop evacuation (aided by a stunning helicopter effect), he goes back to America without her. As with Puccini, the wartime liaison ends in tragedy, with the soldier returning to Saigon only to find the girl has committed suicide. The show was hailed as being 'savagely objective . . . a critical shot at the destabilizing and corrupting American role in Vietnam . . . more than a mature musical, a tough popular opera, clear-headed but romantic, warm as well as sordid and brutal'. Jonathan Pryce played the central role of the Engineer, the cynical and ruthless owner of the sleazy Dreamland Bar, and he had the show's big number, 'The American Dream', a savage attack on US commercialism. The remainder of a score containing some 24 songs, with lyrics that were 'sharp, hard-hitting, elegantly but bitterly sardonic', included 'The Heat Is On In Saigon', 'The Movie In My Mind', 'Why God, Why?', 'The Last Night Of The World', 'You Will Not Touch Him', 'I'd Give My Life For You', 'Sun And Moon', 'Now That I've Seen Her', and 'The Sacred Bird'. Jonathan Pryce and Lea Salonga both won Laurence Olivier Awards for their outstanding performances, and *Miss Saigon* was widely acclaimed, and settled in for a long stay. The Broadway transfer was in doubt for some time when American Equity banned Pryce from reprising his role because 'it would be an affront to the Asian community'. When producer Cameron Mackintosh reportedly threatened to cancel the production, they relented, and, after opening in April 1991, the show recouped its $10.9 million investment in 39 weeks. Tony Awards went to Pryce, Salonga, and featured actor (Hinton Battle).

Since then, *Miss Saigon* has been successfully presented in many countries throughout the world, including Stuttgart and Toronto, where new theatres were designed specifically to house the German and Canadian productions. In December 1994, when *Miss Saigon* became the Theatre Royal's longest-running musical, eclipsing the 2,281-performance record set by *My Fair Lady*, it was estimated that the show had taken over £65 million at the London box office, and more than £400 million worldwide.

● FURTHER READING: *The Story Of Miss Saigon*, Edward Behr and Mark Steyn.

MISTER ROCK AND ROLL

US DJ Alan Freed was a pivotal figure in the development of 50s rock 'n' roll. His radio programmes helped to expose the emergent music to a generation of teenagers and he later showcased many acts live in revue-styled concerts. A cavalcade of performers populated the films with which Freed was involved, including *Rock Around The Clock* and *Rock Rock Rock*, a premise equally prevalent on this 1957 feature. *Mister Rock And Roll* boasted a plot wherein Freed pondered why the record industry had hit a slump. Salvation arrived in the shape of R&B, but Freed must first incur parental wrath, before trying to convert his denigrators. 'Young people. Show your parents how exciting your music is. Take them to see this picture,' ran the publicity blurb for a film showcasing Little Richard, Chuck Berry, Frankie Lymon, LaVern Baker and the Moonglows. Each performance was meritorious in itself, inspiring continued interest in the feature, but the notion of grafting memorable performances to witless plots was already undermining the true potential of celluloid pop.

MLLE. MODISTE

Composer Victor Herbert's first collaboration with librettist and lyricist Henry Blossom was a tremendous success. - in the long term. After its debut at the Knickerbocker Theatre in New York on 25 December 1905, it ran for 202 performances. That was a decent enough run in those days anyway, and it gained in popularity over the years mainly due to the its star, the lovely Fritzi Scheff, and her close identification with the operetta during its many tours and subsequent Broadway revivals. Scheff played the role of Fifi, who works in a hat shop owned by Mme. Cecil (Josephine Bartlett). She is in love with Captain Etienne de Bouvray (Walter Percival), but their romance is disapproved of by her employer, and the gentleman's uncle, Compte. de St. Mar (William Pruett). Josephine would also like to sing on the stage, and she confides her ambitions to a visiting American, the wealthy Hiram Bent (Claude Gillingwater). He is so taken by her charm and manner, that he offers to pay for an extensive course of singing lessons. Inevitably, when the dissenters hear her beautiful voice, they protest no more, and the marriage is allowed to take place. Fritzi Scheff, who had been with the Metropolitan Opera before she made her Broadway debut in the title role of Babette in 1903, introduced 'Kiss Me Again', one of the most cherished ballads in the history of operetta, and she also excelled on the delightful 'If I Were On The Stage' and 'The Mascot Of The Troops'. Pruett had the resolute 'I Want What I Want When I Want It', and Percival sang the engaging 'The Time, The Place And The Girl'. The rest of the score included 'Love Me, Love My Dog', 'When The Cat's Away', and 'The Nightingale And The Star'. Fritzi Scheff, who was born in Vienna in 1879, made her last Broadway appearance as Mlle. Modiste in 1929 when she was 50 years old. She died in New York on 8 April 1954.

MOBY DICK

'A Whale Of A Tale' according to the publicity hand-outs - but 'a whale of a mistake', according to the critics. They harpooned the show right at the start, and even the financial clout of Cameron Mackintosh could not heal the wounds. *Moby Dick* was tried out at the tiny Old Fire Station in Oxford in the autumn of 1991, before opening at London's Piccadilly Theatre on 17 March 1992. In Robert Longden's book, sixth-form members of a girls' school bearing a remarkable resemblance to the infamous St.

Trinian's, stage a production of Herman Melville's classic story in the school swimming pool. As one critic noted: 'The degree of camp, of music-hall smut and anachronism is extreme.' Cabaret singer Tony Monopoly played Miss Dorothy Hymen, the establishment's headmistress, who in turn played Captain Ahab (with a cricket pad where his peg leg should be) in the musical production of *Moby Dick*. When Ahab's ship sets sail, the schoolgirls, who are supposed to be sailors, appear scantily clad in gymslips and sexy stockings, and utter ancient jokes such as 'three years at sea and no sign of Dick'. Director and librettist Longden also wrote the lyrics, and the music was composed by Hereward Kaye. Their score, which contained more than 20 numbers - but no items that stood out - included 'Hymn', 'Forbidden Seas', 'Primitive', 'Love Will Always', 'Mr. Starbuck', 'Building America', 'Save The Whale', and 'Heave'. In the face of a vicious critical reaction and dwindling audiences, Mackintosh remained committed to the production until he was forced to close after a run of 15 weeks. He sanctioned the release of a double-CD which contained a recording of the show made over the sound system as a souvenir for the cast, and indicated that *Moby* was not sunk for ever. In 1993, a production was mounted by a theatre company in Boston, Massachusetts, and in the same year, a scaled-down, revised version, entitled *Moby!*, was presented in the English city of Exeter. The show surfaced again in 1995 at Hof, a small town in Northern Bavaria, with 'a new concept worked out by the authors and director Steven Dexter'.

MONACO, JAMES V.

b. 13 January 1885, Genoa, Italy, d. 16 October 1945, Beverly Hills, California, USA. A prolific composer, particularly for movies, whose career spanned more than 30 years. After moving to the USA with his family when he was six years old, Monaco taught himself to play piano, and began earning his living playing in Chicago clubs while still in his teens. By 1910 he was resident in New York, playing in saloons. The following year, he began writing songs, some of which were recorded and others used in Broadway shows. In 1912, he had his first hits with 'Row, Row, Row' (lyrics by William Jerome) and 'You Made Me Love You' (Joseph McCarthy). The latter was taken up by Al Jolson, a fact which ensured its enduring popularity. Monaco continued to compose, and his songs of the next few years included 'I Miss You Most Of All', (McCarthy) 'What Do You Want To Make Those Eyes At Me For?' (McCarthy), 'Caresses' and 'Dirty Hands, Dirty Face' (Edgar Leslie and Grant Clarke), which Jolson sang in the 1927 film *The Jazz Singer*. Among Monaco's songs of the late 20s were 'Me And My Boyfriend' (Sidney Clare), 'Me And The Man In The Moon' (Leslie) and 'Through' (McCarthy). In the 30s, Monaco was active in Hollywood, where he began a fruitful collaboration with Johnny Burke. Among the results were a string of hits sung in films and recorded by Bing Crosby, including 'On The Sentimental Side', 'I've Got A Pocketful Of Dreams', 'An Apple For The Teacher', 'Too Romantic', 'That's For Me' and 'Only Forever'. He contributed to films such as *The Golden Calf*, *Doctor Rhythm*, *Sing You Sinners*, *East Side Of Heaven*, *The Star Maker*, *If I Had My Way*, *Road To Singapore*, *Rhythm On The River*, *Stage Door Canteen*, *Pin-Up Girl*, and *The Dolly Sisters* (1945). In the early 40s, Monaco had more popular successes with 'Six Lessons From Madame La Zonga' (Charles Newman), 'I Can't Begin To Tell You' (Mack Gordon), 'Ev'ry Night About This Time' (Ted Koehler), 'We Mustn't Say Goodbye' (Al Dubin), and 'Time Will Tell' (Gordon). Monaco died from a heart attack in 1945.

MONROE, MARILYN

b. Norma Jean Mortenson, 1 June 1926, Los Angeles, California, USA, d. 5 August 1962, Brentwood, California, USA. As well as being a talented comedienne and the number 1 sex symbol in movies during the 50s, Monroe proved to be an appealing interpreter of flirtatious ballads in several of her most popular films. As one of the *Ladies Of The Chorus* (1948), she made a promising start with Lester Lee and Allan Roberts' 'Every Baby Needs A Da-Da-Daddy', which, with its reference to 'Tiffany's', was a precursor to one of her most celebrated performances a few years later, when the same New York store cropped up in 'Diamonds Are A Girl's Best Friend', from Jule Styne and Leo Robin's score for *Gentlemen Prefer Blondes* (1953). In that film Monroe duetted with another of Hollywood's top glamour girls, Jane Russell, on 'Two Little Girls From Little Rock', 'Bye Bye Baby' and a Hoagy Carmichael/Harold Adamson number, 'When Loves Goes Wrong'. Co-starring with Robert Mitchum in *River Of No Return* (1954), Monroe's role as a saloon singer conveniently gave her the opportunity to perform the title song and 'I'm Gonna File My Claim', among others, and, in the same year, she registered strongly with a bundle of Irving Berlin numbers in *There's No Business Like Show Business*. These included 'A Man Chases A Girl' (with Donald O'Connor), 'After You Get What You Want You Don't Want It', 'Heatwave', 'Lazy' and 'You'd Be Surprised'. In 1959 she made what became her most commercially successful film - and arguably the highlight of her career. The classic *Some Like It Hot*, with Tony Curtis, Jack Lemmon and Joe E. ('nobody's perfect') Brown, featured some of Monroe's most effective vocal performances, such as 'I'm Through With Love', 'I Wanna Be Loved By You' and 'Running Wild'. She sang for the last time on screen in *Let's Make Love* (1960). Apart from contributing the film's high spot, a compelling version of 'My Heart Belongs To Daddy', Monroe duetted with two European heart-throbs, Yves Montand and Frankie Vaughan, on Sammy Cahn and Jimmy Van Heusen's 'Specialization', 'Incurably Romantic' and the title song. Her final performance, a sultry rendering of 'Happy Birthday Mr. President' and 'Thanks For The Memory', was given in May 1962 for President Kennedy's birthday celebrations in Madison Square Garden. Just over two months later she died as the result of an overdose of barbiturates, at the age of 36 (Monroe's death has since been the subject of numerous conspiracy theories, most of which concern her alleged affair with John F. Kennedy). One of the musical selections chosen for her funeral service was a recording of 'Over The Rainbow' sung by Judy Garland, another show-business legend who met a tragic end. Since her death, it has been estimated that over 100 Monroe biographies have been published. She was also the subject of several songs, the most famous being Elton John's 'Candle In the Wind'. Others included James Cunningham's 'Norma Jean Wants To Be A Movie Star' and 'Elvis And Marilyn' by Leon Russell.

● COMPILATIONS: *Marilyn* (20th Century Fox 1962)★★★, *Collection: 20 Golden Greats* (Deja Vu 1985)★★★★, *Marilyn Monroe -The Complete Recordings* (Rare 1988)★★★, *The Marilyn Monroe Story* (Deja Vu 1989)★★★.

● VIDEOS: *Marilyn And The Kennedys (Say Goodbye To The President)* (Weinerworld 1998).

● FURTHER READING: *Marilyn*, Norman Mailer. *Marilyn Monroe: The Biography*, Donald Spoto. *Goddess: Secret Lives Of Marilyn Monroe*, Anthony Summers. *The Complete Films Of Marilyn Monroe*, Mark Ricci and Michael Conway, *Young Marilyn Becoming The Legend* James Haspiel. *Marilyn Monroe*, Barbara Leaming.

● FILMS: *Dangerous Years* (1948), *Ladies Of The Chorus* (1948), *Love Happy* (1950), *A Ticket To Tomahawk* (1950), *The Asphalt Jungle* (1950), *All About Eve* (1950), *The Fireball* (1950), *Right Cross* (1950), *Home Town Story* (1951), *As Young As You Feel* (1951), *Love Nest* (1951), *Let's Make It Legal* (1951), *We're Not Married* (1952), *Clash By Night* (1952), *Full House* (1952), *Monkey Business* (1952), *Don't Bother To Knock* (1952), *Niagara* (1952), *Gentlemen Prefer Blondes* (1953), *How To Marry A Millionaire* (1953), *River Of No Return* (1954), *There's No Business Like Show Business* (1954), *The Seven-Year Itch* (1955), *Bus Stop* (1956), *The Prince And The Showgirl* (1957), *Some Like It Hot* (1959), *Let's Make Love* (1960), *The Misfits* (1960).

MONSIEUR BEAUCAIRE

A romantic operetta with music and lyrics by André Messager and Adrian Ross, and a book by Frederick Lonsdale, which was based on the novel by Booth Tarkington. Set in the stylish city of Bath, England, in the early eighteenth century, when it was ruled by the so-called King of Bath, Richard 'Beau' Nash, the familiar plot concerned yet another nobleman disguised as a commoner. In this instance, the Duc d'Orléans (Marion Green), son of the King of France, is masquerading as the barber Monsieur Beaucaire. In spite of stern opposition from the Duke of Winterset (Robert Parker - a bounder who cheats at cards), the ducal barber wins the heart of Lady Mary Carlisle (Maggie Teyte), and eventually accedes to the throne of France. Future Broadway leading man Dennis King made his West End debut in the minor role of Lord Townbrake. After opening at the Prince's Theatre in London on 19 April 1919, the show transferred to the Palace Theatre in July, and ran for 221 performances. The lively score included songs such as 'Honour And Love', 'That's A Woman's Way', 'Lightly, Lightly', 'Say No More', 'Gold And Blue And White', 'Red Rose', 'The Honours Of War', 'Going To The Ball' and 'I Love You A Little'. Maggie Teyte, who had sung in leading operatic roles before turning to the musical stage, was outstanding. *Monsieur Beaucaire* was presented on Broadway in December 1919, and produced in Paris in 1925, 1929, 1935 and 1954. A London revival played Daly's Theatre in 1931. The first (silent) film version (1924) starred Rudolph Valentino, and the second (1946) featured Bob Hope and Joan Caulfield.

MONTE CARLO

Slightly less risqué than *The Love Parade* (1929), *Monte Carlo*, which was released by Paramount a year later, was nevertheless a hot-bed of romance and intrigue in the hands of director-producer Ernst Lubitsch. Jeanette Macdonald, who had raised temperatures and blood pressures with her sizzling scenes in *The Love Parade*, exchanged her European co-star in that film for another - Britain's premiere suave and sophisticated song-and-dance man Jack Buchanan. In Ernest Vajda and Vincent Lawrence's screenplay, which was adapted from the play *The Blue Coast* by Ernest Mueller, MacDonald plays a countess who leaves her intended (titled) husband waiting at the church while she boards the Blue Express which takes her to Monte Carlo. After falling for a barber (Buchanan), her penchant for gambling pays off when he turns out to be a wealthy count. By this stage in his career, director Lubitsch was well into his stride as the leader in intelligent and integrated musicals. Acclaimed highlights of this particularly example of his outstanding work include his setting of the song 'Beyond The Blue Horizon', which MacDonald sings aboard the famous train accompanied by familiar sounds and movements of the train itself; and a novel operatic sequence which was based on Booth Tarkington's story *Monsieur Beaucaire*. The film's engaging score was written by Richard Whiting and W. Franke Harling (music) and Leo Robin (lyrics), and included a variety of numbers such as 'Trimmin' With Women', 'Give Me A Moment Please', 'Whatever It Is, It's Grand', 'Always In All Ways', and 'She'll Love Me And Like It'. Also in the cast were Claud Allister, ZaSu Pitts, Tyler Brooke, and Lionel Belmore.

MONTENEGRO, HUGO

b. 1925, New York City, New York, USA, d. 6 February 1981. An accomplished and prolific composer, arranger and orchestral conductor for film music. After two years in the US Navy where he arranged for Service bands, Montenegro graduated from Manhattan College and entered the record industry in 1955. He served as staff manager to André Kostelanetz, and was conductor-arranger for several artists, including Harry Belafonte. Montenegro also made his own orchestral albums such as *Arriba!, Bongos And Brass, Boogie Woogie And Bongos, Montenegro And Mayhem, Pizzicato Strings, Black Velvet* and *American Musical Theatre 1-4*. After moving to California he wrote the score for Otto Preminger's 1967 film *Hurry Sundown*, a racial melodrama starring Jane Fonda and Michael Caine. In 1968, with his orchestra and chorus, he recorded Ennio Morricone's theme from the Italian film *The Good, The Bad And The Ugly*. The record went to number 2 in the US, topped the chart in the UK, and sold well over a million copies. The instrumental contrasted with Montenegro's big, romantic string sound, and the effects were startling. From the haunting introduction featuring Arthur Smith on the ocarina, the unusual instruments used included an electric violin, electric harmonica and a piccolo trumpet, aided by a vocal group which featured the whistling of Muzzy Marcellino reinforced by grunting vocals. In 1969 Montenegro had a minor UK hit with the theme from *Hang 'Em High*, the film with which Hollywood attempted to match the brutal style of the 'spaghetti' originals, partly by using the same star, Clint Eastwood. The soundtrack album, *Music From 'A Fistful Of Dollars' & 'For A Few Dollars More' & 'The Good, The Bad And The Ugly'* made the US Top 10. There was a refreshing change from the usual film themes on *Broadway Melodies*, where the material included standards such as 'Varsity Drag', 'Thou Swell', 'Tea For Two' and 'I Got Rhythm'. Throughout the late 60s and 70s he continued to provide music for films such as *The Ambushers* (1968) and *The Wrecking Crew* (1969), both Matt Helm adventures starring Dean Martin; *Lady In Cement*, featuring Frank Sinatra as private eye Tony Rome; *Charro!* (1969), an Elvis Presley western; *The Undefeated* (1969), starring John Wayne; *Viva Max!* (1969); *Tomorrow* (1972); and *The Farmer* (1977).

● ALBUMS: *Original Music From 'The Man From UNCLE'* (RCA Victor 1966)★★★, *More Music From 'The Man From UNCLE'* (RCA Victor 1966)★★★, *Hurry Sundown* (RCA Victor 1967)★★★, *Music From 'A Fistful Of Dollars' & 'For A Few Dollars More' & 'The Good, The Bad And The Ugly'* (RCA Victor 1968)★★★★, *Hang 'Em High* (1968)★★★, *Moog Power* (RCA Victor 1969)★★★, *Lady In Cement* (Stateside 1969)★★★ *Arriba!* (70s/80s)★★★, *Bongos And Brass* (70s/80s)★★★, *Boogie Woogie And Bongos* (70s/80s)★★★, *Montenegro And Mayhem* (80s)★★★, *Pizzicato Strings* (80s)★★★, *Black Velvet* (80s)★★★, *American Musical Theatre 1-4* (80s)★★★, *Plays For Lovers* (1981)★★★.

● COMPILATIONS: *The Best Of Broadway* (1977)★★★, *The Best Of Hugh Montenegro* (1980)★★★.

MOODY, RON

b. Ronald Moodnick, 8 January 1924, London, England. An accomplished and versatile actor, singer, author and composer, Moody nursed an ambition to be an entertainer from a very early age. The urge was strengthened during his time as an accounts clerk in the offices of the British National Studios at Elstree, where he managed to sneak a look at stars such as Will Hay and Alastair Sim making some of their memorable films. However, his first break came much later when he was spotted performing in a student musical at the London School of Economics by revue specialists Ronnie Cass and Peter Myers. They put him into *Intimacy At Eight* (1952), which was followed by *More Intimacy At Eight* (1953), *Intimacy At Eight-Thirty* (1954), *For Amusement Only* (1956), and *For Adults Only* (1958). Moody subsequently played the Governor of Buenos Aires in the short-lived London production of *Candide* (1959), before landing the role of a lifetime in Lionel Bart's *Oliver!* (1960). His portrayal of the evil Fagin, marshalling a motley band of adolescent pickpockets throughout the streets of London, is regarded as definitive. He relished great Bart numbers such as 'You've Got To Pick A Pocket Or Two', 'Be Back Soon', 'It's A Fine Life' - and especially 'Reviewing The Situation'. To many people's surprise (because he was not an international star) Moody was chosen to head the cast in the 1968 film version, for which he was nominated for an Oscar, and received several Best Actor honours, including Golden Globe and Variety Awards. He also played Fagin for short London and New York seasons in 1984. After leaving the stage *Oliver!*, in the 60s Moody wrote the musical, *Joey*

(1962), in which he took the part of legendary clown, Joe Grimaldi. A few years later it was revised and re-staged as *The Great Grimaldi* and *Joey, Joey*. He was also involved, as Aristophanes, in *Liz* (1968), Myers and Cass's regional musicalization of the 2,500-year-old classic battle of the sexes, Lysistrata. With the dawning of the age of Aquarius, and theatrical censorship a thing of the past, Moody came up with *Saturnalia* (1971), presumably in an effort to transpose the hippie world of *Hair* to the Yorkshire Moors - but not the West End. During the 80s he toured the USA and Canada successfully as Sir Joseph Porter in Gilbert And Sullivan's *HMS Pinafore*, and played the title role in Leslie Bricusse's *Sherlock Holmes - The Musical* (1988). In 1992, Moody withdrew from *Spread A Little Happiness*, a tribute to songwriter Vivian Ellis, shortly before it was due to open at the Whitehall Theatre. Ironically, in the same year, his musical, *Rasputin*, reached the final of the Vivian Ellis Awards for writers of new musicals, the first year there was no age restriction. In 1993 Moody played Harry Ball, the father of Vesta Tilley (Anita Harris), in *Bertie*, a stage musical based on the life of the immensely popular male impersonator famed for her rendition of 'Burlington Bertie'. During the provincial run, Moody suffered a stroke, and the magazine *Hello!* reported that he had died. Still very much alive and kicking, in his seventies Moody gave his Alfred P. Doolittle in a Radio 2 version of *My Fair Lady*, and played Buddy in the same station's special concert performance of *Follies*, in company with Julia McKenzie, Donna McKechnie, and Denis Quilley. He also sang Pangloss in Leonard Bernstein's *Candide* for Radio 3's *Towards The Millennium* series. Looking back on such a varied career, which included Variety, cabaret, television (*David Copperfield*, *Nobody's Perfect*, *Dial M For Murder*, *Othello* [Iago]), as well as straight theatre and films, he regrets not doing more Shakespeare in Britain. Asked if he minds being so closely identified with the part of Fagin, he replied: 'I'm very pleased to be associated with such a successful part, but I wish it was one of a dozen.' Ron Moody has also published two novels, *The Devil You Don't* and *Very Very Slightly Imperfect*.

● ALBUMS: Original and studio cast recordings.
● FILMS: *Follow A Star* (1959), *Make Mine Mink* (1960), *Five Golden Hours* (1961), *A Pair Of Briefs* (1962), *Summer Holiday* (1963), *Ladies Who Do* (1963), *The Mouse On The Moon* (1963), *Every Day's A Holiday* (1964), *Murder Most Foul* (1964), *Every Day's A Holiday a.k.a. Seaside Swingers* (1965), *The Sandwich Man* (1966), *San Ferry Ann* (1966), *Oliver!* (1968), *The Twelve Chairs* (1970), *Flight Of The Doves* (1971), *Legend Of The Werewolf* (1975), *Dogpound Shuffle* (1975), *The Strange Case Of The End Of Civilisation As We Know It* (1977), *Dominique* (1978), *Unidentified Flying Oddball* (1979), *Othello* (1981), *Arthur* (1981), *Wrong Is Right* (1982), *A Kid In King Arthur's Court* (1995).

MOON OVER MIAMI

This typically lavish 1941 20th Century-Fox Technicolor extravaganza was a remake of the same studio's somewhat less opulent *Three Blind Mice* which was produced three years earlier in 1938. The slight story concerns sisters Kay and Barbara Latimer (Betty Grable and Carole Landis) and their Aunt Charlotte (Charlotte Greenwood), who anxiously anticipate a substantial legacy. When the original

$55,000 is whittled down to $4,287 and 96 cents (to be split three ways), the trio give up their jobs at a roadside diner and set off for Miami with the intention of finding Kay a rich husband. After going through the usual charades and complications, Kay lands the young well-heeled smoothie (Robert Cummings) - and then turns him down for the equally smooth but less well-off Don Ameche. In the sparkling supporting cast were funny-man Jack Haley, Cobina Wright Jnr., Robert Conway, Lynne Roberts, George Lessey, and dancers Jack Cole, the Condos Brothers and Hermes Pan (who also staged the dances). Leo Robin and Ralph Rainger came up with a bright and lively score which included 'You Started Something', 'Kindergarten Conga', 'I've Got You All To Myself', 'What Can I Do For You?', 'Oh Me, Oh Mi-ami', 'Is That Good?', 'Loveliness And Love', and 'Hurrah For Today'. The screenplay was written by Vincent Lawrence and Brown Holmes, and adapted by George Seaton and Lynn Starling from a 1938 English play by Stephen Powys. The director for this entertaining and colourful film was Walter Lang. Another remake appeared in 1946 entitled *Three Little Girls In Blue* and starring June Haver, George Montgomery and Celeste Holm.

MOORE, DUDLEY

b. 19 April 1935, Dagenham, Essex, England. Although severely hampered by having a deformed foot and spending a great deal of his childhood in hospital, this did not deter Moore from becoming passionately interested in music from an early age. The young Dudley played piano in a local youth club and organ at his church. He wore an old brown boot strapped over his normal shoe to give his bad foot extra length to touch the pedals easily. As a young teenager Moore played semi-professionally in various jazz clubs. He studied music at Oxford University, graduating in the late 50s and thereafter playing with Vic Lewis. Early in the following decade he worked with John Dankworth before forming his own trio with Pete McGurk (bass) and Chris Karan (drums). For a while he successfully performed jazz while concurrently appearing in *Beyond The Fringe* in London and New York. During this time he forged a partnership with comedian Peter Cook. With the trio, he also made records and appeared on television in the seminal *Not Only But Also* (with Cook). By the mid-60s Moore's acting career had begun to take precedence over his jazz work and he later moved to Hollywood. His musical interests continued with the writing of scores for feature films including *The Wrong Box* (1966), *30 Is A Dangerous Age Cynthia* (1967), *Inadmissible Evidence* (1968), *Bedazzled* (1968) and *Staircase* (1969), and also for stage shows, plays and ballet. His own acting career took off to such an extent that 'Cuddly Dudley' became a huge Hollywood star in such films as *10* (1979), *Wholly Moses* (1980), *Arthur* (1981), *Six Weeks* (1982), *Lovesick* (1983), *Best Defence* (1984), *Micki And Maude* (1984) and *Santa Claus* (1985). Additionally, he made three hilarious albums with Cook of pure filth and bad language as Derek And Clive. Moore has cited Erroll Garner and Oscar Peterson as two of his main influences. His jazz playing is notable for its lightness of touch and deft right-hand filigrees although his eclecticism, allied to his absorption with other interests, has inhibited the development of a truly identifiable personal style. In recent years, having achieved everything as a 'movie star', Moore has returned to recording and performing, and has resurrected the definitive Dudley Moore Trio. In a revealing biography published in 1997 Moore disclosed a troubled soul who has seemingly succeeded at everything, but remains deeply unfulfilled. Leaving behind him a trail of broken marriages and a number of critically slammed films during the 80s and 90s, Moore has always returned to music in times of stress. His brilliance as both jazz and classical pianist has been constantly undermined by his personal life.

● ALBUMS: *Beyond The Fringe* (Parlophone 1961)★★★, *Theme From Beyond The Fringe And All That Jazz* (Atlantic 1962)★★★, *Beyond The Fringe; Original Broadway Cast* (Capitol 1962)★★★, *The Other Side Of The Dudley Moore Trio* (Decca 1965)★★★★, *Genuine Dud* (Decca 1966)★★★★, *Bedazzled* soundtrack (Decca 1968)★★★, *The Dudley Moore Trio* (Decca 1968)★★★★, *The Music Of Dudley Moore* (Decca 1969)★★★, *Today With The Dudley Moore Trio* (Atlantic 1971)★★★, *Dudley Moore At The Wavendon Festival* (Black Lion 1976)★★★, *The Dudley Moore Trio* (Warners 1978)★★★, *Dudley Down Under* (1978)★★★, *Smilin' Through* (Finesse 1982)★★★, *Orchestra* (Decca 1991)★★★, *Songs Without Words* (GRP 1991)★★★, *Concerto!* (RCA Victor 1992)★★★, *Grieg Piano Concerto In A Minor* (EMI 1995)★★★.

● FURTHER READING: *Dudley*, Paul Donovan. *Off Beat: Dudley Moore's Book Of Musical Anecdotes*, Dudley Moore. *Dudley Moore: The Authorized Biography*, Barbra Paskin.

MOORE, GRACE

b. 5 December 1901, Slabtown, Tennessee, USA, d. 26 January 1947. Gifted with a remarkable singing voice, Moore first made her name on Broadway in musical comedies. The quality of her singing brought her to the attention of New York's Metropolitan Opera Company and from there she went to Hollywood where her physical beauty enhanced a number of 30s musicals. Moore's lyrical soprano voice was far better than anything offered by most singing actresses in Hollywood, as he demonstrated in *A Lady's Morals* (1930), *New Moon* (1931), *One Night Of Love* (for which she was nominated as Best Actress, 1934), *Love Me Forever* (1935), *The King Steps Out* (1936), *When You're In Love* (1937), *I'll Take Romance* (1937), and *Louise* (1940). In the 20s and 30s she made several successful recordings, including 'Listening', 'Tell Her In The Springtime', 'One Night Of Love', and 'Ciribiribin'. While on a concert tour of Europe, Moore was killed when the aircraft in which she was travelling crashed near Copenhagen. The 1953 film *So This Is Love* (UK title: *The Grace Moore Story*), in which she was portrayed by Kathryn Grayson, gave a reasonable account of her career and times.

● ALBUMS: *The Art Of Grace Moore* (RCA 1987)★★★.

● FURTHER READING: *You're Only Human Once*, Grace Moore.

MORE AMERICAN GRAFFITI

American Graffiti was not only a milestone in pop-orientated cinema, it remains one of the finest films of its era. Sadly, this 1979 sequel lacks its charm, atmosphere and characterization. Ron Howard, Paul LeMat and Candy

Clark reprise their earlier roles as the action shifts from 1962 to a late 60s dominated by the Vietnam War, protest and counter-culture idealism. Where the canvas of *American Graffiti* was tight - the action unfolded over a single night - the attempt to compress several years of changing attitudes into the follow-up robbed it of potential resonance. However, appearances by Country Joe And The Fish, with their anti-war anthem 'I Feel Like I'm Fixin' To Die', and Doug Sahm, enliven the proceedings, while legendary disc jockey Wolfman Jack makes another welcome cameo. *More American Graffiti* did boast another stellar soundtrack. A succession of Tamla Motown classics, including 'Heatwave' (Martha And The Vandellas), 'Stop! In The Name Of Love' (the Supremes) and 'My Guy' (Mary Wells) are set beside folk-rock from the Byrds, Bob Dylan and Simon And Garfunkel. Garage bands Sam The Sham And The Pharaoh's and ? And The Mysterions give way to 'west coast' acolytes the Doors, Grateful Dead and Frank Zappa in a collection which, in microcosm, charts the development of US music during a highly-prolific decade.

MORE, JULIAN

b. 1929, England. A librettist and lyricist for some of the most successful British hit musical shows of the late 50s, More became interested in the theatre while at Cambridge University. He was involved as a performer and writer in undergraduate revues, and contributed the occasional item to the Watergate Theatre. In 1953 he wrote some material for the West End revue *Airs On A Shoestring*, which starred Max Adrian, Moyra Fraser and Betty Marsden. Two years later, he collaborated with composer James Gilbert for the Windsor Theatre production of a 'revusical', *The World's The Limit*, and in the following year, they had a smash hit with *Grab Me A Gondola*. Set at the Venice Film Festival, with the character of the film star heroine 'moulded' on Britain's Diana Dors, the show starred Joan Heal, Denis Quilley and June Wenham. It featured numbers such as 'That's My Biography', 'Cravin' For The Avon', 'A Man, Not a Mouse' and 'New To Me'. Even more successful was *Irma La Douce* (1958) for which More, with Monty Norman and David Heneker, provided the English book and lyrics translation to Marguerite Monnot's music. The story included such songs as 'Our Language Of Love' and 'Dis-Donc', and ran for 1,512 performances in London, and over 500 in New York. The More-Heneker-Norman team combined with Wolfe Mankowitz later in 1958 for *Expresso Bongo*. The 'most important British musical for years' starred Paul Schofield, Hy Hazell and James Kenny, and ran for nine months. The score, which included 'The Shrine On The Second Floor' and 'I've Never Had It So Good', virtually disappeared from the innovative 1960 film version starring Cliff Richard and Laurence Harvey. The lead in the road version was taken by Colin Hicks, the brother of Tommy Steele. London's theatrical scene was changing and More was unable to match previous achievements. Throughout the 60s and 70s his offerings included *The Golden Touch* (with Gilbert), *The Art Of Living* (his last collaboration with both Norman and Heneker), *The Perils Of Scobie Prilt* (with Norman), *The Man From The West* (with David

Russell), *Quick, Quick, Slow* (Norman), *Good Time Johnny* (Gilbert), *R Loves J* (with Alexander Ferris) and *Bordello* (with Americans Al Frisch and Bernard Spiro). In 1979 he was back with Monty Norman for *Songbook*, 'a burlesque tale' of the work of the prolific songwriter Mooney Shapiro. Subsequently, More settled in France, with homes in Paris and Provence, and became a successful writer of travel books. Since then, he has re-emerged occasionally, and wrote the book and lyrics to Gilbert Becaud's music for the Broadway show *Roza* (1987), 'a maudlin and awkwardly constructed story with inferior songs'. He also adapted Abe Burrows' original book for a London revival of Cole Porter's *Can-Can* in 1988.

MORENO, RITA

b. Rosita Dolores Alverio, 11 December 1931, Humacao, Puerto Rico. Sometimes called the 'Latin spitfire', this exciting, dynamic actress, dancer and singer was the first performer to win all four premiere entertainment awards, for film (Oscar), theatre (Tony), television (Emmy), and recording (Grammy). Moreno was taken to New York by her parents when she was a baby, and at the age of four was learning Spanish dancing from that celebrated exponent of the art, Paco. After making her first public appearance as a child in a Greenwich Village nightspot, at the age of 13 she acted on Broadway in the play *Skydrift*. Later in her teens, Moreno dubbed voices for films to be exported to Spanish-speaking countries, including those of Elizabeth Taylor and Margaret O'Brien. She made her first movie appearances under the name of Rosita Moreno, but then adopted the more familiar title for a combination of screen dramas, comedies, and musicals such *The Toast Of New Orleans*, *Singin' In The Rain*, *The Vagabond King*, and *The King And I* (as Tuptim). For her electrifying performance as the fiery Anita in *West Side Story*, she won the 1961 'Supporting Actress' Academy Award. After that, she hardly worked in films for the next seven years, and so turned to the stage, playing the second female lead, Ilona, in the London premiere of the new musical *She Loves Me*, opposite popular UK balladeer Gary Miller: 'They wrote a special song for me - 'Heads I Win' - such a scene-stealer.' She also had the amusing 'A Trip To The Library'.
Other theatrical highlights over the years have included her 1975 Tony Award-winning performance as Googie Gomez, an untalented, star-struck, gay bath-house entertainer in *The Ritz*, *The Sign In Sidney Brustein's Window* (with Gabriel Dell), Neil Simon's *Last Of The Red Hot Lovers* (with Dom Deluise), and Simon's reworking of his comedy classic *The Odd Couple* (with Sally Struthers) in a female version, which was a hit on Broadway in 1985. More recently she was in Anne Meara's comedy *After-Play* (1995) and *The Size Of The World* (1996). Late in 1996, she took over the leading role in the London production of *Sunset Boulevard* from the holidaying Petula Clark. Moreno was the fifth (and, at the time, oldest) Norma Desmond. Along with theatre and film, for most of her long career Moreno has also been active in television. She won Emmys for her appearances in *The Muppet Show* (1977) and 'The Paper Palace' episode of *The Rockford Files* (1978). The Grammy came for her part, along with Lee Chamberlain and Bill Cosby, in *The Electric Company*

(voted Best Album For Children in 1972). She starred in *The Electric Company* PBS children's show from 1971-76. Other notable work in television series included *9-5* (1982), the Burt Reynolds series *B.L Stryker* (1989), *Top Of The Heap* (1991), *Cosby Mysteries* (1994), and *Oz* (1997), as well as numerous other films and guest appearances. In the 90s her hectic schedule also involved cabaret, a regional production of the musical *Gypsy*, and a tour of 42 cities in 48 days co-starring with Carol Channing in *Two Ladies Of Broadway*.

● FILMS: as Rosita Moreno *A Medal For Benny* (1946), as Rosita Moreno *So Young, So Bad* (1950), *The Toast Of New Orleans* (1950), *Pagan Love Song* (1950), *Singin' In The Rain* (1952), *Cattle Town* (1952), *The Ring* (1952), *Fort Vengeance* (1953), *Ma And Pa Kettle On Vacation* (1953), *Latin Lovers* (1953), *El Alamein* (1953), *Jivaro* (1954), *Garden Of Evil* (1954), *The Yellow Tomahawk* (1954), *Untamed* (1955), *Seven Cities Of Gold* (1955), *The King And I* (1956), *The Lieutenant Wore Skirts* (1956), *The Vagabond King* (1956), *The Deerslayer* (1957), *This Rebel Breed* (1960), *West Side Story* (1961), *Summer And Smoke* (1961), *Cry Of Battle* (1963), *The Night Of The Following Day* (1969), *Popi* (1969), *Marlowe* (1969), *Carnal Knowledge* (1971), *The Ritz* (1976), *The Boss' Son* (1978), *Happy Birthday, Gemini* (1980), *The Four Seasons* (1981), *Age Isn't Everything* (1991), *Carmen Miranda: Bananas Is My Business* (1994), *Blackout* (1994), *Italian Movie* (1994), *I Like It Like That* (1994), *Angus* (1995), *The Slums Of Beverly Hills* (1998), *Stuffed Dolls* (1998).

MORGAN, HELEN

b. Helen Riggins, 2 August 1900, Danville, Ohio, USA, d. 8 October 1941, Chicago, Illinois, USA. One of the first, and certainly one of the most accomplished torch singers in the history of popular music. After working at a number of unskilled jobs, Morgan began singing in small Chicago clubs. She graduated to revue, appearing in New York in *George White's Scandals* (1925), and *Americana* (1926) in which she was noticed by Florenz Ziegfeld, who signed her to play the role of Julie La Verne in the original production of Jerome Kern's *Show Boat* (1927). Her performance of 'Bill' (lyric by P.G. Wodehouse and Oscar Hammerstein II) was a show-stopper. In fact, the song had been cut from *Oh Lady! Lady!!* (1918) and *Zip, Goes A Million* (1919), before Morgan gave it immortality in *Show Boat*. In the same show she also sang 'Can't Help Lovin Dat Man', and, 10 years later, introduced 'Why Was I Born?' and 'Don't Ever Leave Me' in another Kern-Hammerstein show, *Sweet Adeline*. She later appeared on Broadway in *Ziegfeld Follies* (1931) and the 1932 revival of *Show Boat*, and was in the 1929 and 1936 screen versions of *Show Boat*. Here other film appearances included *Applause*, *Roadhouse Nights*, *Glorifying The American Girl*, *Marie Galante*, *You Belong To Me*, *Sweet Music*, *Go Into Your Dance*, and *Frankie And Johnny* (1936). As well as the above songs from the shows, she had several hit records in the late 20s and early 30s, such as 'A Tree In The Park', 'Mean To Me', 'Body And Soul'. She is also particularly remembered for her version of George and Ira Gershwin's 'The Man I Love'. By the late 30s her career was in disarray and she was heavily dependent upon alcohol. As owner of a number of Prohibition-era speakeasies she had ready access to liquor and her health rapidly deteriorated

until she died of cirrhosis of the liver. Her life story was the subject of a 1957 biopic, *The Helen Morgan Story* (UK title: *Both Ends Of The Candle*), in which she was played by Ann Blyth. In 1998, with *Show Boat* back in the West End, Helen Morgan's unique interpretations of 'Bill' and 'Can't Help Lovin' Dat Man', along with other ballad classics such as 'Why Was I Born', were re-issued on a celebratory album.

● ALBUMS: *Helen Morgan* (Audio Rarities 1962)★★★, *The Glory Of Helen Morgan* (MCI 1998)★★★★.

● FURTHER READING: *Helen Morgan, Her Life And Legend*, Gilbert Maxwell.

MORLEY, ANGELA

In the 50s, 60s and into the 70s, Wally Stott was a highly respected conductor, arranger and composer on the UK music scene. In the early 70s he underwent a sex-change operation, and was subsequently known professionally as Angela Morley. Stott was born in 1924 in Sheffield, England. He attended the same Mexboro school as Tony Mercer, who went on to become one of the principal singers with the *Black And White Minstrel Show*. Mercer sang and played the piano accordion, while Stott concentrated on the saxophone. On leaving school, they each spent some time with Archie's Juveniles and Oscar Rabin's Band. Stott's route to Rabin was via the bands of Billy Merrin and Bram Martin. By 1944, after some years with the Rabin Band, Stott was leading the saxophone section on alto, and had become the band's sole arranger: a great future was already being forecast for him. Stott's next move was to Geraldo, with whom he stayed for about four years, leaving in late 1948 to 'pursue arranging and film music work, which he is to make his future career'. He still managed to find the time to play the saxophone for outfits such as Jack Nathan's Coconut Grove Orchestra. In the early 50s Stott joined Philips Records, and soon became one of their key arrangers, along with Peter Knight and Ivor Raymonde. During the next 20 years he arranged and conducted for some of the UK's most popular artists, such as Frankie Vaughan ('Green Door', 'The Garden Of Eden' and 'The Heart Of A Man'), Anne Shelton ('Lay Down Your Arms' and *My Heart Sings*), Harry Secombe ('This Is My Song'), the Beverley Sisters ('Somebody Bad Stole De Wedding Bell' and 'Happy Wanderer'), Roy Castle (*Newcomer*), Ronnie Carroll ('Say Wonderful Things' and *Carroll Calling*), the Kaye Sisters ('Paper Roses'), Shirley Bassey ('Banana Boat Song' and 'As I Love You'), Muriel Smith ('Hold Me, Thrill Me, Kiss Me'), the Polka Dots (*Nice Work & You Can Buy It*) and many more, plus a few 'foreigners', too, as on *Mel Tormé Meets The British* (1959). Stott also made several of his own instrumental albums, sometimes augmented by a vocal chorus. He began writing music early in his career, and his first significant piece came to light in November 1954, when *Hancock's Half Hour* began. It proved to be one of BBC Radio's most popular programmes, later moving to television, and its opening theme, played on a tuba over Tony Hancock's stuttering introduction, was composed by Stott. He also wrote and arranged the show's instrumental links, and conducted the orchestra for many other radio programmes, including *The Last Goon Show Of All*. Stott composed numerous pieces of mood music for London publishers, especially Chappell's, which included 'A Canadian In Mayfair' (dedicated to Robert Farnon, who gave Stott valuable advice on arranging and composition), 'Mock Turtles', 'Quiz', 'Travelling Along', 'Miss Universe', 'Flight By Jet', 'Casbah', 'Commonwealth March', 'Practice Makes Perfect', 'China', 'Focus On Fashion' and 'Skylight'. In the late 60s and early 70s, Stott wrote the music for several films, including *The Looking Glass War*, *Captain Nemo And The Underwater City* and *When Eight Bells Toll*, and for television productions such as *Hugh And I*, and the *The Maladjusted Busker*. Around that time, credits began to be given in the name of Angela Morley, and these include two Academy Award nominations, for her arrangements of Alan Jay Lerner and Frederick Loewe's score for *The Little Prince* (1974), and Richard M. and Robert B. Shermans' score for *The Slipper And The Rose* (1977). Morley also composed for the animated feature *Watership Down*, the Italian production *La Colina Dei Comali*, and for television films such as *Friendships*, *Secrets And Lies*, *Madame X*, *Summer Girl*, *Two Marriages* and *Threesome* (1984). Most of this work has been completed in the USA, where Morley is reported to have been living for most of the last 20 years.

● ALBUMS: *Wally Stott Tribute To George Gershwin* (Parlophone 1955)★★★★, *Tribute To Irving Berlin* (Parlophone 1956)★★★, *Tribute To Jerome Kern* (Parlophone 1957)★★★★, *London Pride* (1959)★★★, *Chorale In Concert* (1967)★★, *Christmas By The Fireside* (1969)★★.

MOROSS, JEROME

b. 1 August 1913, Brooklyn, New York, USA, d. 25 July 1983, Miami, Florida, USA. A highly regarded composer who wrote symphonic works as well as scores for films and Broadway shows. After graduating from New York University at the age of 18, Moross contributed some incidental music to the theatre, and then composed most of the score for the short-lived Broadway revue *Parade* in 1935. Later in that same year he was engaged by George Gershwin as assistant conductor and pianist for the last few weeks of the New York run of *Porgy And Bess*, and subsequently for the west coast production. Moross moved to Hollywood in 1940 and spent the next decade orchestrating scores for a great many films, including *Our Town*, *Action In The North Atlantic* and *Conflict*. He also worked on Hugo Friedhofer's Oscar-winning score for *The Best Years Of Our Lives* (1946). In 1948 he was given the opportunity to compose his own original score for *Close-Up*, which was followed during the 50s and 60s by others such as *When I Grow Up*, *Captive City*, *The Sharkfighters*, *Hans Christian Andersen* (ballet music only), *Seven Wonders Of The World* (with David Raksin and Sol Kaplan), *The Proud Rebel*, *The Jayhawkers*, *The Adventures Of Huckleberry Finn* (1960), *The Mountain Road*, *Five Finger Exercise*, *The Cardinal*, *The War Lord*, *Rachel Rachel*, *Valley Of The Gwang!* and *Hail, Hero!* (1969). His most acclaimed work during that time was undoubtedly for William Wyler's dramatic western, *The Big Country* (1958), for which he was nominated for an Academy Award. The music, and particularly its electrifying main theme, is considered to be among the most memorable in the history of the cine-

ma. His work was also heard regularly on television in such popular programmes as *Lancer* and *Wagon Train*. On Broadway, Moross collaborated twice with the author and librettist John Latouche, firstly in 1948 for *Ballet Ballads*, a musical adaptation of three one-act plays, and again in 1954, for the innovative *The Golden Apple*, which, although it folded after only 127 performances, won the New York Drama Critics Circle Award for best musical, and has since become a cult piece. One of its songs, the ballad 'Lazy Afternoon', has been recorded by several artists, including Tony Bennett. During his long and distinguished career, Moross also won two Guggenheim fellowship awards, in 1947 and 1948. He brought his own individual brand of folksy homespun Americana to his music for ballets such as *American Patterns*, *The Last Judgement* and *Frankie And Johnny*, along with numerous orchestral works which included 'Biguine', 'A Tall Story', 'Paeans', 'Those Everlasting Blues' and 'First Symphony'. His last completed work was a one-act opera, *Sorry, Wrong Number!*

MORRICONE, ENNIO

b. 11 October 1928, Rome, Italy. A distinguished and prolific composer, whose revolutionary scores for 'spaghetti Westerns' have made him one of the most influential figures in the film music world. He studied trumpet and composition before becoming a professional writer of music for radio, television and the stage as well as the concert hall. During the 50s he wrote songs and arrangements for popular vocalist Gianni Morandi and he later arranged Paul Anka's Italian hit 'Ogni Volta' (1964). Morricone's first film score was for the comedy *Il Federale* in 1961. Three years later he was hired by Sergio Leone to compose music for *A Fistful Of Dollars*. Using the pseudonym Dan Savio, Morricone created a score out of shouts, cries and a haunting whistled phrase, in direct contrast to the use of pseudo-folk melodies in Hollywood Westerns. His work on Leone's trilogy of Italian Westerns led to collaboration with such leading European directors as Pontecorvo (*Battle Of Algiers* 1966), Pasolini (*Big Birds, Little Birds*, 1966) and Bertolucci (*1900*, 1976). In the 70s he began to compose for US films, such as *Exorcist II* (1977), *Days Of Heaven* (1978), *The Untouchables* (1987) and *Frantic* (1988). Morricone won an Oscar for Roland Joffe's *The Mission* (1986), where he used motifs from sacred music and native Indian melodies to create what he called 'contemporary music written in an ancient language'. In 1992 Morricone's score for *Bugsy* received an Oscar nomination. The composer's other scores in the early 90s included *Husbands And Lovers*, *City Of Joy*, *Tie Me Up! Tie Me Down!*, *Everybody's Fine*, *Hamlet*, *State Of Grace*, *Octopus 6 - The Force Of The Mafia*, *Jonah Who Lived In A Whale*, *In The Line Of Fire*, and *Cinema Paradiso - The Special Edition*, *La Scorta*, *Wolf*, and *Disclosure* (1994). The Spaghetti western sound has been a source of inspiration and samples for a number of rock artists including BAD, Cameo and John Zorn (*Big Gundown*, 1987). Morricone has recorded several albums of his own music and in 1981 he had a hit with 'Chi Mai', a tune he composed for a BBC television series. A double album for Virgin Records in 1988 included Morricone's own selection from the over 100 films which he has scored, while in the same year Virgin Venture issued a recording of his classical compositions.

● ALBUMS: *The Good, The Bad And The Ugly* film soundtrack (Capitol 1968)★★★★, *Moses* film soundtrack (Pye 1977)★★★, *This Is …* (EMI 1981)★★★, *Chi Mai* (BBC 1981)★★★, *The Mission* film soundtrack (Virgin 1986)★★★★, *Chamber Music* (Venture 1988)★★★, *Frantic* film soundtrack (Elektra 1988)★★★, *The Endless Game* television soundtrack (Virgin 1989)★★★, *Live In Concert* (Silva Screen 1989)★★★, *Casualties Of War* (1990)★★★, *Morricone '93 Movie Sounds* (1993)★★★, *Wolf* film soundtrack (Columbia 1994)★★★, *Disclosure* film soundtrack (Virgin 1995)★★★, *Ninfa Plebea* film soundtrack (AM Original Soundtracks 1995)★★★, *Concerto: Premio Rota 1995* (AM Original Soundtracks 1996)★★★.

● COMPILATIONS: *Film Hits* (RCA 1981)★★★, *Film Music 1966-87* (Virgin 1988)★★★★, *The Very Best Of* (1992)★★★, *The Ennio Morricone Anthology (A Fistfull Of Film Music)* (Rhino 1995)★★★★, *His Greatest Themes* (Allegro 1995)★★★, *The Singles Collection, Volume Two* (Cinemavox 1997)★★★.

MOST HAPPY FELLA, THE

Any show that opened in the same season as *My Fair Lady* was bound to be somewhat overshadowed by Alan Jay Lerner and Frederick Loewe's masterpiece, which was destined to be a smash hit. However, *The Most Happy Fella* was, in some ways, a more ambitious work than its female counterpart, and enjoyed a satisfactory run of 676 performances on Broadway. The show opened on 3 May 1956 at the Imperial Theatre, and immediately confused many of the critics: was it an opera? A play with music, perhaps? Frank Loesser, who wrote the music, lyrics, and libretto, settled on 'an extended musical comedy'. His adaptation of Sidney Howard's 1924 Pulitzer Prize-winning play, *They Knew What They Wanted*, was set in Napa Valley, California, and tells of an Italian vintner, Tony (Robert Weede, a former opera singer, making his Broadway debut), who is maturing rather more quickly than the grapes in his vineyard. He longs for a wife, and proposes by post to Rosabella (Jo Sullivan, who later became Loesser's wife), a waitress he has noticed in a San Francisco restaurant. To increase his chances of success, he includes a photograph of his handsome young foreman, Joey (Art Lund), and she hurried there to meet him. Even though he has deceived her, she still marries Tony - but tarries with Joey. When she discovers that she is pregnant with Joey's child she is determined to leave, but Tony forgives her and adopts the child as his own. With spoken dialogue at a minimum, *The Most Happy Fella* is a virtually sung-through show, and Loesser's score has moments of high emotion in songs such as 'Somebody Somewhere', My Heart Is Full Of You', and 'Joey, Joey'. Rosabella's friend Cleo (Susan Johnson), who follows her out from San Francisco, becomes fairly friendly herself with one of the ranch hands, Herman (Shorty Long), and leads the company in a hymn to Dallas, the rousing 'Big D'. The show's big hit song was 'Standing On The Corner', which became popular in the USA for Dean Martin, and the Four Lads who repeated their success in the UK, in competition with the King Brothers. Another of the show's lighter numbers, 'Happy To Make Your Acquaintance', also entered the UK chart in a version by Sammy Davis Jnr.

and Carmen McRae. The rest of Loesser's highly distinguished score, which contained well over 30 songs in a wide variety of musical styles such as arias and choral pieces, included 'Ooh! My Feet', 'Mama, Mama', 'Warm All Over', 'I Like Everybody', 'Song Of A Summer Night', 'Sposalizio', 'How Beautiful The Days', 'Rosabella', 'The Most Happy Fella' and 'Abbondanza'. *The Most Happy Fella* was not everybody's idea of what a Broadway musical should be, but during a 20-month stay on Broadway, it won the New York Drama Critics Award for best musical, and subsequently ran for 288 performances at the London Coliseum. Lund reprised his role in the West End, during which time he became a favourite of audiences there, and returned with Richard Rogers' *No Strings* in 1963. *The Most Happy Fella* was revived on Broadway in 1979, and presented by the New York City Opera in 1991, with Giorgio Tozzi in the lead. In the following year the show was back on Broadway again, via the Goodspeed Opera House and Los Angeles, this time with just a two-piano orchestration, which Loesser himself had commissioned some years previously. Although critically acclaimed, the production ran for only 229 performances and lost most of its $1.4 million investment. It was nominated for four Tony Awards, but won just one - Scott Waara for best featured actor - being pipped at the post for 'best revival' by *Guys And Dolls*, which is, of course, another Frank Loesser show. Unusually, the Original Cast album was recorded in 'real time' - in two long takes - just as the show was performed in the theatre. Even with part-retakes, the recording took only one day to complete, in comparison with the 1956 three-album set which needed a week of session time. In 1993, a concert performance of *The Most Happy Fella* became 'the first of its kind to be broadcast on BBC radio in England'.

MOTHER WORE TIGHTS

20th Century-Fox teamed their top pin-up girl, Betty Grable, with one of their most popular and likeable song-and-dance-men, Dan Dailey, in this 1947 release which was produced by Lamar Trotti. He was also responsible for the screenplay which was based on a book by Miriam Young. Set in the early part of the century and told in flashback, it was a warm-hearted tale about a married vaudeville couple, Burt and McKinley (Grable and Dailey) whose hoity-toity elder daughter (Mona Freeman) derides her parents' performing lifestyle ('my friends go to the opera and things') until the entire class of her swanky music school go to see the 'old folks' show' - and actually enjoy it. The wayward miss then realises what a fool she has been, and at her graduation ceremony sings 'You Do', one of her father and mother's big hit songs. Josef Myrow and Mack Gordon wrote that one, and several of the others, including 'There's Nothing Like A Song', 'This Is My Favourite City', 'Kokomo, Indiana', 'Rolling Down To Bowling Green', and 'On A Little Two-Seat Tandem'. Gordon also collaborated with Harry Warren on 'Tra-la-la', and there were several more nostalgic numbers by various composers, such as 'Burlington Bertie From Bow' (William Hargreaves). Musical director Alfred Newman won an Oscar for his work on the score. Connie Marshall played the younger (but more mature) daughter, and there were excellent performances from Vanessa Brown, Robert Arthur, Sara Allgood, William Frawley, Ruth Nelson, Anabel Shaw, Michael Dunne, George Cleveland, Veda Ann Borg, Sig Ruman, Lee Patrick, and especially the highly amusing Señor Wences. Seymour Felix and Kenny Williams handled the olde worlde dance sequences and the director was Walter Lang. *Mother Wore Tights* was one of the Top 20 musicals of the 40s, and Betty Grable's most financially successful picture.

MR. CINDERS

The distinguished English composer, Vivian Ellis, enjoyed his first hit with this show which opened on 11 February 1929 at the Adelphi Theatre in London. Ellis's co-composer was Richard Myers, and the book and lyrics were by Greatrex Newman and Clifford Grey, with additional lyrics by Vivian Ellis and Leo Robin. As the title suggests, the book is a gender-reversal of the well-worn *Cinderella* story with Bobby Howes as Jim Lancaster, a young man whose father has married again, thereby providing Jim with two ugly step-brothers. Binnie Hale is the rich girl masquerading as a parlour maid who becomes his 'fairy godmother', and sings the show's big hit song, 'Spread A Little Happiness', while 'dressed as a parlour maid, high-kicking around the stage with a feather duster'. The rest of the songs in a delightful and engaging score included 'On the Amazon', 'I'm A One-Man Girl', 'Ev'ry Little Moment', 'I've Got You', 'I Could Be True To Two', and 'I Want The World To Know'. Basil Howes, Jack Melford, and Lorna Lubbard were also in the cast, and *Mr. Cinders* was a tremendous hit right away. After five months at the Adelphi, the show transferred to the London Pavilion in March 1929, and continued to run for a total of 529 performances. A film version with Kenneth and George Western (the Western Brothers), Clifford Mollison and Zelma O'Neal, was released in 1934. A London revival of *Mr. Cinders* opened at Dan Crawford's King's Head Theatre Club in 1982, before transferring to the West End's Fortune Theatre where it stayed for two performances short of the original run. Its star, Denis Lawson, won the Laurence Olivier Award for best actor in a musical or entertainment. Crawford staged it again at the King's Head in 1993, with Samuel West, Sally Ann Triplett, Helen Hobson, Christopher Villiers, and Charles Edwards. All the revivals 'borrowed' the occasional Vivian Ellis song from his various other shows. This was also the case when *Mr. Cinders* was produced in 1988 at the Goodspeed Opera House in Connecticut, USA. The piece was finally given its New York premiere at the Mazur Theatre, East 90th Street, from 5 November 1992. That most appealing song, 'Spread A Little Happiness', has endured and surfaces frequently. Sting, the ex-lead singer with the Police, sang it in the 1982 film *Brimstone And Treacle*, and it became his first solo chart hit in the UK. It was also used during the 80s in television commercials for margarine.

MRS BROWN YOU'VE GOT A LOVELY DAUGHTER

As well as being popular in their native country, British beat group Herman's Hermits also enjoyed considerable success in the USA. Their impish pop singles seemed to suggest a vision of 'Swinging England', one exacerbated by smash-hit recordings of music-hall standards, "I'm Henry XIII, I Am' and 'Leaning On The Lamp Post', neither of which were issued as singles in the UK. Another exclusive song, 'Mrs Brown You've Got A Lovely Daughter', topped the US charts in 1965, the theme of which inspired this 1968 film. The group had already completed a 'quickie' feature, *Hold On* in 1966, but its jejune plot and direction were at least related to the era inspiring it. *Mrs Brown You've Got A Lovely Daughter* surfaced amid rock films exposing drugs, protest, psychedelia and the counter-culture, none of which touched this misguided vehicle. Here the group acquire a greyhound and travel to London to race it in the Greyhound Derby. The presence of veterans Stanley Holloway and Mona Washbourne only served to enhance its anachronistic premise. If there was ever any possibility that Herman's Hermits would slip from pop to rock in the manner of the Pretty Things or Spencer Davis Group, it ended with this film.

MUCH ADO

(see Taylor, Bernard J.)

MUPPET MOVIE, THE

Jim Henson's irresistibly engaging characters enjoyed world-wide acclaim via television's *Sesame Street* from 1969, and their own British series 1976-81, before graduating to the big screen with this film in 1979. Jerry Juhl and Jack Burns wrote the script, which has Kermit the Frog crossing America with his big bulging eyes set on Hollywood stardom. Hitching a lift at various points along the route are cheap comic and bad driver Fozzie Bear, the Great Gonzo, Miss Piggy, Rowlf the Dog, Camilla the Chicken, and other sundry hangers-on. On their arrival they are immediately offered a lucrative contract by Lew Lord. Naturally, they meet up with some pretty famous guest artists, including Mel Brooks, Bob Hope, Telly Savalas, Orson Welles, James Coburn, Milton Berle, Edgar Bergen, and Steve Martin. Paul Williams and Kenny Ascher wrote the songs, 'Frogs' Legs So Fine', 'Can You Picture That?', 'Movin' Right Long', 'Never Before', 'This Looks Familiar', 'Something Better', 'I'm Going To Go Back There Some Day', and 'The Rainbow Connection', which was nominated for an Oscar, as was Williams and Ascher's original score. Jim Frawley directed, and *The Muppet Movie* was produced for ITC by Jim Henson. Voicing the main characters are Henson, Frank Oz, Dave Goelz, Steve Whitmire, Richard Hunt, and Jerry Nelson. It was enormously successful, taking £32 million in North America, ahead of such popular features as *The Godfather Part II*, *All The President's Men*, *The Omen*, and *The Deerhunter*. Two years later came the sequel, *The Great Muppet Caper*, in which the gang accidentally become involved in jewel robberies, whilst also paying a musical tribute to Hollywood (think Miss Piggy as Esther Williams) via a Joe Raposo score which includes 'The First Time It Happens'. Raposo had previously written 'Bein' Green' for Kermit way back in the *Sesame Street* days. On this occasion, Diana Rigg, John Cleese, Robert Morley, Peter Ustinov, and Charles Grodin, provide the human element. Since then Kermit and Co. have attempted to create a Broadway blockbuster in *The Muppets Take Manhattan* (1984, with a Jeffrey Moss music score), turned their attention to Charles Dickens in *The Muppet Christmas Carol* (1992, songs by Paul Williams), and searched for buried treasure in the company of Tim Curry (Long John Silver), Billy Connolly (Billy Bones), and Jennifer Saunders (innkeeper Mrs. Bluveridge) for *Muppet Treasure Island* (1996). Grammy Award-winning songwriters Barry Mann and Cynthia Weil wrote an appropriately swashbuckling score, which included Curry's thigh-slapping 'A Professional Pirate' and 'Sailing For Adventure', Kermit and Miss Piggy's touching love duet, 'Love Led Us Here', along with 'Shiver My Timbers', 'Something Better', 'Cabin Fever', and 'Love Power'. Other Muppet television series include *Muppet Babies* (1984) and *Muppets Tonight!* (1996).

MUSCLE BEACH PARTY

This 1964 entry to the American International Pictures production line of 'beach' movies starred genre stalwarts Frankie Avalon and Annette Funicello. The path of true love is threatened when the former becomes attracted to a wealthy socialite - much to the chagrin of her bodybuilding beau, Mr. Galaxy - but Avalon returns to Funicello in time for the closing reel. Rising Tamla/Motown star 'Little' Stevie Wonder provides a welcome cameo, performing 'Happy Street', while surf guitar maestro Dick Dale plays the title tune and 'My First Love'. Brian Wilson of the Beach Boys and then-partner Gary Usher composed much of the soundtrack material, including Donna Loren's superbly rumbustious 'Muscle Bustle'. Annette subsequently re-recorded several songs from the film for a solo outing, *Muscle Beach Party*, issued on the Disney outlet, Buena Vista.

MUSIC BOX REVUE

Irving Berlin and producer Sam H. Harris built their brand new Music Box Theatre on New York's West 45th Street as a showcase for Berlin's prolific output of songs. The composer had contributed many of his early numbers, such as 'A Pretty Girl Is Like A Melody' and 'You'd Be Surprised', to Florenz Ziegfeld's elegant productions, and this lavish revue, a stylish mixture of comedy and songs, was the first of four annual editions to play at his own cosy 1,010-seater Music Box. It opened on 22 September 1921, with a cast that included William Collier, Wilda Bennett, Paul Frawley, Ivy Sawyer, Joseph Santley, Sam Bernard, and the Brox Sisters. Berlin himself, made a brief appearance in a scene with Miriam Hopkins, an actress who went on to a successful Hollywood career in the 30s, in films such as *Dr Jekyll And Mr Hyde*, *Trouble In Paradise*, and *Becky Sharp*. 'Say It With Music' was the show's outstanding number, sung by Bennett and Frawley, and it became a recurring theme during the rest of the series. The other songs included 'Everybody Step', 'The Schoolhouse Blues', 'In A Cozy Kitchenette Apartment', 'My Little Book Of Poetry', 'They Call It Dancing', and 'The Legend Of The Pearls'. Hassard Short, who was just starting out on a career during which he would be acclaimed for his imaginative design and staging, was responsible for this show, and the next two, giving way to John Murray Anderson for the final edition. Short's innovative work was recognized

as a major factor in the *Music Box Revue*'s impressive run of 440 performances. The 1922 production marked the Broadway debut of several future Broadway favourites, including the actor and singer William Gaxton, who later made a habit of appearing in musicals with one of America's most cherished clowns, Victor Moore, and the comedy team of ex-vaudevillians Bobby Clark and Paul McCullough. Comedienne Charlotte Greenwood, another artist who subsequently spent much of her time in Hollywood and will be remembered particularly for her portrayal of Aunt Eller in the film of *Oklahoma!*, was also in the cast, along with Grace La Rue, Margaret and Dorothy McCarthy, and the Fairbanks Twins. The songs included 'I'm Looking For A Daddy Long Legs', 'Crinoline Days', 'Will She Come From The East?', 'Pack Up Your Sins And Go To The Devil', and 'Lady Of The Evening', and the show ran for 330 performances. *The Music Box Revue of 1923* - Mark III - had some sketches by George S. Kaufman and Robert Benchley, who also personally introduced his famous 'Treasurer's Report'. Among the rest of the cast were Frank Tinney, Joseph Santley, and Ivy Sawyer. Grace Moore, who sang with the Metropolitan Opera in the late 20s, had the charming 'Tell Me A Bedtime Story', and 'The Waltz Of Long Ago', and she duetted with John Steel on 'An Orange Grove In California' and the plaintive 'What'll I Do?'. The latter song, one of Berlin's all-time standards, was interpolated during the run of the show. Audiences for these revues were gradually declining - the 1923 version ran for 273 performances, and the final, 1924 edition, only lasted for 184. For that one, Moore was back again, as were Clarke and McCullough, along with Claire Luce, Carl Randall, and Ula Sharon. The star was funny girl Fanny Brice, who sang 'Don't Send Me Back To Petrograd' and 'I Want To Be A Ballet Dancer'. Moore had the lovely 'Tell Her In Springtime' and 'Rockabye Baby', and, with Oscar Shaw, she also introduced the wistful 'All Alone'. The 1923 edition also played at the Palace Theatre in London, where it starred Jessie Matthews, Fred Duprez, and Joseph Santley. This series of shows served as a launching pad for Irving Berlin's long and illustrious career which peaked with *Annie Get Your Gun* in 1946, but endured for much longer than that.

MUSIC IN THE AIR

This delightful musical comedy, with just a hint of operetta, and a score by Jerome Kern and Oscar Hammerstein, opened at the Alvin Theatre in New York on 8 November 1932. With America staggering to its feet following the terrible Depression, Hammerstein chose to set the story in modern-day Bavaria. Music teacher Dr. Walter Lessing (Al Shean) travels from his home in Edenhorf to the big city of Munich, in an effort to impress an old colleague with his new composition, 'I've Told Ev'ry Little Star'. He is accompanied by his daughter, Sieglinde (Katherine Carrington), who loves to perform her father's compositions, and her friend, Karl (Walter Slezak). They are all introduced to the fiery actress and singer, Frieda Hatzfeld (Natalie Hall), who is rehearsing a musical show which has been written by her long-time lover, Bruno Mahler (Tullio Carminati). When Frieda flounces out just before the opening night, Bruno, who is quite partial to the young Sieglinde, tells her to 'go out there and come back a star'. Unfortunately, the young girl is totally lacking in star quality, and she and her father realise this, and decide to return to their quiet life in the country. The score is regarded as one of Kern's finest, with the songs skilfully and sympathetically integrated into the plot. They included 'The Song Is You', 'There's A Hill Beyond A Hill', 'One More Dance', 'In Egern On The Tegern Sea', 'And Love Was Born', 'I'm Alone', 'I Am So Eager', 'We Belong Together', 'When Spring Is In The Air', and, of course, 'I've Told Ev'ry Little Star', which was introduced by Walter Slezak. *Music In The Air*'s Broadway run of 342 performances was followed by a further 275 in London, where Mary Ellis took the role of Frieda. The show returned to New York, with a revised book, for a brief spell in 1951. The 1934 film version starred Gloria Swanson, John Boles and Al Shean.

MUSIC MAN, THE (FILM MUSICAL)

Despite studio chief Jack Warner's reported efforts to get a male superstar such as Cary Grant to play the lead, Robert Preston was eventually invited to recreate his magnificent Broadway performance for this enjoyable screen version which was released in 1962. So filmgoers the world over were able to enjoy this former B picture actor in the once-in-a-lifetime role of Professor Harold Hill, a con-man of the highest order, who descends on the town of River City, Iowa. Ostensibly, his intention is to sell musical instruments, instruction books, and uniforms to the parents of the parish in order that their children can form a brass band - which he will lead. Unfortunately, he cannot read a note of music. Such is his charm, however, that after overcoming the initial resistance of Balzac-loving librarian Marian Paroo (Shirley Jones), they not only fall in love, but he is absolved of all charges of deception following his decision not to make a run for it after all. There were some lovely performances in the supporting roles, such as the Professor's assistant and look-out man (Buddy Hackett), the always-blustering mayor (Paul Ford) along with his lady wife (Hermione Gingold), and Marian's mother-with-the-blarney (Pert Kelton). Other parts were played by Ronnie Howard, Timmy Everett, Susan Luckey, Mary Wickes, and the barber-shop harmonising Buffalo Bills. Meredith Willson's score underwent a few changes on the journey from New York to Hollywood, but the new and old songs were all gems in their way, and included 'Rock Island', 'Iowa Stubborn', 'Piano Lesson', 'If You Don't Mind Me Saying So', 'Goodnight My Someone', 'Sincere', 'The Sadder-But-Wiser Girl', 'Pick-A-Little, Talk-A-Little', 'Marian The Librarian', 'Being In Love', 'Gary, Indiana', 'The Wells Fargo Wagon', 'Lida Rose'-'Will I Ever Tell You?', 'Shipoopi', and 'Till There Was You'. Preston's musical highlight came with 'Ya Got Trouble', in which he warned the River City population about the perils of having a pool table in their midst, and, in the film's exuberant finalé, he was at the head of the triumphant procession during the rousing 'Seventy-Six Trombones'. Onna White was the choreographer, and musical director Ray Heindorf won an Oscar for his scoring. Marian Hargrove's screenplay was adapted from Meredith Willson's stage libretto, which itself was based

on the story he wrote with Franklin Lacey. Morton Da Costa was producer-director, and the film was shot in Technicolor and Technirama. There was some dismay at the time that Barbara Cook, who created the role of Marian on stage, was not asked to repeat her role on the screen. As it transpired, Shirley Jones was just fine - and Robert Preston sensational.

MUSIC MAN, THE (STAGE MUSICAL)

Not many people have been brave (or foolish?) enough to write the book, music, and lyrics for a stage musical, but two major exponents, one from either side of the Atlantic, come to mind. However, the advantage that Meredith Willson had over Frank Loesser and Noël Coward when he created *The Music Man* (from a story by Willson and Franklin Lacey), was that in many ways the piece was autobiographical. So for this show, which opened at the Majestic Theatre in New York on 19 December 1957, Willson's hometown of Mason City, Iowa, becomes River City, Iowa (population 2,212). It is there, that the Music Man - or rather, 'con-man' - descends from the Rock Island steam train in search of suckers just in time for the 4 July celebrations. The name is Professor Harold Hill (Robert Preston), a smooth operator who convinces the good citizens of various (preferably small and remote) townships to cough up the cash for musical instruments, uniforms, and instruction books, he will teach their kids to play. Further, he will form these budding prodigies into a band with himself as leader. Problem is, as one of his fellow-salesman puts it: 'He don't know one note from another. He can't tell a bass drum from a pipe organ.' However, things work out differently than usual during the Professor's visit to River City. After meeting up with former sidekick Marcellus Washburn (Iggie Wolfington), he charms Eulalie Shinn (Helen Raymond), wife of the highly suspicious Mayor Shinn (David Burns), and her fellow members of the Ladies' Auxiliary for the Classic Dance. He also endears himself to Mrs. Paroo (Pert Kelton), her young son, Winthrop (Eddie Hodges), and - after some kind of struggle - her daughter, the music teacher and local librarian Marian Paroo (Barbara Cook). A happy ending then, but not before the Professor has warned the residents of River City of the moral danger of introducing a pool table into the community ('That game with the fifteen numbered balls is the Devil's tool') in 'Ya Got Trouble'. That was the highlight of a score which was chock-full of engaging old-fashioned charm, such as the Buffalo Bills' barbershop-style 'Sincere' ('How can there be any sin in sincere?/Where is the good in goodbye?'), along with 'Overture And Iowa Stubborn', 'Piano Lesson', 'Goodnight My Someone', 'Seventy-Six Trombones', 'The Sadder-But-Wiser Girl', 'Pick-A-Little, Talk-A-Little', 'Goodnight Ladies', 'Marian The Librarian', 'My White Knight', 'The Wells Fargo Wagon', 'It's You', 'Shipoopi', 'Lida Rose', 'Will I Ever Tell You?', 'Gary, Indiana', and 'Till There Was You'. The producers took a big chance casting Robert Preston, a film actor who was more familiar with roping cattle, than singing and dancing on Broadway, but he made his way delightfully through a minefield of counter melodies, rhythmic dialogue and strutting dance routines. Onna White was the choreographer for those dances, the period costumes were by Raoul Péne du Bois, and the entire production was staged by Morton Da Costa. *The Music Man* proved to be a copper-bottomed hit, and ran for 1,375 performances, winning Tony Awards for best musical, actor (Preston), featured actress (Cook), featured actor (Burns), author (Willson/Lacey), composer-lyricist (Willson), the show's producers, and conductor-musical director (Herbert Greene). The 1961 London production, with Van Johnson (Hill), Patricia Lambert (Marian), C. Denier Warren (Mayor), Ruth Kettlewell (Mrs. Paroo), Bernard Spear (Marcellus), Nan Munro (Eualalie), and the Iowa Four singing quartet, only lasted for 395 performances. Winthrop was played by Dennis Waterman, later renowned for his parts in UK television shows such as *The Sweeney* and *Minder*. Subsequent major revivals have been rare, but included one at New York's City Center in 1980, which was headed by Dick Van Dyke. Marriott's Lincolnshire Theatre in Chicago also staged a production in 1993, with Kurt Johns, Pamela Harden, Ross Lehman, Arlene Robertson, and Don Forston. Two years later, at the attractive Open Air Theatre in London's Regent's Park, Brian Cox's Harold Hill was still in love with Liz Robertson's Marian. In the same year, a BBC Radio 2 presentation was led by Jim Dale (Hill) and Claire Moore (Marian). Robert Preston reprised his marvellous performance for the 1962 film version, with Shirley Jones as Marian.

MUTINY!

It started with a concept album, this musical adaptation of *Mutiny On The Bounty* - a marketing ploy which had been used successfully by several authors and composers in the 70s, notably Andrew Lloyd Webber and Tim Rice. This time it was the British actor and singer David Essex who was behind the release of the 1983 recording of *Mutiny!*, which spawned his Top 10 hit 'Tahiti'. Essex wrote the music and collaborated with librettist Richard Crane on the lyrics for the stage production which eventually sailed into the Piccadilly Theatre in London on 18 July 1985. The distinguished actor Frank Finlay played Captain Bligh, with Essex as Fletcher Christian, but the main character was a fully rigged HMS Bounty which was mounted on an hydraulic system and spectacularly recreated the high seas by rocking and rolling the entire stage to and fro. The score turned out to be 'a sequence of pastiche modal folk songs, shanties, ominous marches, and one effectively syncopated hornpipe', and included 'New World', 'Friends', 'Failed Cape Horn', 'Saucy Sal', 'Will You Come Back?', 'Falling Angels Riding', 'I'll Go No More A-Roving', and, of course, 'Tahiti'. First night reviews such as 'Bounty in blunderland . . . caught in the doldrums . . . a very leaky showboat' should really have heralded the end of the voyage, but *Mutiny!* rode the storm for a considerable time. Just as it was about to be recast with the American pop singer David Cassidy taking over from Essex, the show floundered and closed in September 1986 after a run of 526 performances without recovering its investment.

MY FAIR LADY (FILM MUSICAL)

Alan Jay Lerner and Frederick Loewe's Broadway masterpiece came to the screen in 1964 complete with a contro-versial choice of leading lady. Julie Andrews, who created the part of Eliza Doolittle on stage, had only just made her film debut in *Mary Poppins*, and Audrey Hepburn (whose singing was dubbed by Marni Nixon) won the coveted role. Thankfully, after some bizarre alternative casting suggestions, Rex Harrison was once again the irascible confirmed bachelor, Professor Henry Higgins, who bets his companion, Colonel Pickering (Wilfred Hyde-White), that he can take an ordinary cockney flower girl and pass her off in high society just by teaching her to 'speak like a lady'. This he does in triumphant fashion, but only after much hard work and frustration, and some delicate negotiations with the girl's philosophical dustman father, Alfred P. Doolittle, who is superbly played by Stanley Holloway reprising his stage performance. Gladys Cooper as Higgins' mother (who sides with Eliza in all disputes) and Jeremy Brett as the toff who worships the pavements that Eliza walks on, were among the supporting cast which also included Mona Washbourne, Theodore Bikel, Isobel Elsom, Charles Fredericks, and John Holland. Not surprising with Lerner writing the screenplay, all the songs from the stage production were retained. The by-now classic overture preceded this extraordinary score: 'Why Can't The English?', 'Wouldn't It Be Loverly?', 'With A Little Bit Of Luck', 'I'm An Ordinary Man', 'Just You Wait', 'The Rain In Spain', 'I Could Have Danced All Night', 'Ascot Gavotte', 'On the Street Where You Live', 'Embassy Waltz', 'You Did It', 'Show Me', 'Get Me To The Church On Time', 'A Hymn To Him', 'Without You', and the sublime 'I've Grown Accustomed To Her Face'. That last number was part of an ending to the story contrary to the one in Bernard Shaw's *Pygmalion* on which the stage and film musicals were based. Shaw refused to have a happy resolution to Higgins's relationship with Eliza, but in *My Fair Lady*, the famous curtain line, 'Where the devil are my slippers?,' does seem to indicate that the teacher and his prize pupil are destined to stay together. Jack L. Warner produced the film for Warner Brothers and the choreographer was Hermes Pan. It was photographed in Technicolor and Super Panavision 70 and won eight Academy Awards including best picture, actor (Harrison), director (George Cukor), scoring (André Previn), and costumes and sets (Cecil Beaton). The latter's work, especially in such scenes as the marvellous 'Ascot Gavotte', was a major factor in the film's success - even without Julie Andrews. Some 30 years after its release, *My Fair Lady*, which had deteriorated to a great extent in the vaults, was brilliantly restored - visually and aurally - by experts Robert A. Harris and James C. Katz, and reissued in a letterbox format. On the new print Marni Nixon's voice on 'Wouldn't It Be Loverly?' was replaced by Audrey Hepburn's. The actress had apparently recorded several tracks for the film which were never used.

MY FAIR LADY (STAGE MUSICAL)

One of the most successful shows in the history of the American musical theatre, *My Fair Lady* opened to rave reviews at the Mark Hellinger Theatre in New York on 15 March 1956. Alan Jay Lerner's book is based on *Pygmalion* by George Bernard Shaw, and deals with the attempts of Professor Henry Higgins (Rex Harrison) to transform a

Cockney flower girl, Eliza Doolittle (Julie Andrews), into a society lady simply by teaching her to speak correctly. In the course of the story Higgins and Eliza fall in love and all ends happily, if a little differently from the way Shaw intended. In the strong supporting cast were Stanley Holloway (Alfred P. Doolittle, Eliza's father), Robert Coote (Colonel Pickering, friend of Higgins), Michael King (Freddie Eynsford-Hill, Eliza's would-be suitor), and Cathleen Nesbitt (Mrs. Higgins, mother of the Professor). Alan Jay Lerner and Frederick Loewe's score was full of marvellous songs which included 'Why Can't The English?', 'I'm An Ordinary Man', 'A Hymn To Him', and 'I've Grown Accustomed To Her Face', which found Higgins, in turns, exasperated, defensive, perplexed, and (perish the thought) in love; Eliza's dreamy 'Wouldn't It Be Loverly?', defiant 'Just You Wait' and 'Without You', demanding 'Show Me' (in answer to Freddie's wet, but enchanting, 'On The Street Where You Live'), and exuberant 'I Could Have Danced All Night'. That number came towards the end of Act One, well before Eliza had convinced everyone at the Embassy Ball, including the dreaded Zoltan Karparthy (Christopher Hewett), that she was the genuine high-born article. Even her father, dustman Doolittle, does not recognize her ('Blimey, it's Eliza.'), when he calls in at 27a Wimpole Street and admits to Higgins that he is one of the undeserving poor, although: 'I don't need less than a deserving man, I need more. I don't eat less hearty than he does, and I drink a lot more.' Poor or (eventually) rich, Doolittle certainly has two terrific songs, 'With A Little Bit O' Luck', and 'I'm Getting Married In The Morning', in a score which also included 'Ascot Gavotte' (the famous sequence in which Eliza urges her chosen horse Dover on with the immortal words: 'Move your bloomin' arse!'). In those early shows, Harrison and Andrews, in particular, were both superb. Their delight and joy as they, and Pickering, realised that Eliza had finally 'got it' - celebrating their triumph with 'The Rain In Spain' - remains a magical and endearing theatrical moment equal to that in Richard Rodgers and Oscar Hammerstein's *The King And I*, when the King of Siam and Anna take the floor for 'Shall We Dance?'. *My Fair Lady* ran on Broadway for six-and-a-half years, a total of 2,717 performances, and won Tony Awards for best musical, actor (Harrison), director (Moss Hart), musical director (Franz Allers), Oliver Smith (scenic design) and Cecil Beaton (costumes). Numerous road companies toured the show across the USA and it was subsequently presented in many other countries around the world. Four of the principals, Harrison, Andrews, Holloway and Coote, recreated their roles for the London production (with Zena Dare as Mrs. Higgins, and Leonard Wier playing Freddie) which stayed at the Drury Lane Theatre Royal for five and a half years. The Broadway cast album spent nearly 300 weeks in the US chart, 15 of them at number 1. It was also inducted into the NARAS (Grammy) Hall of Fame in 1977. New York City Center brought the show back to New York a couple of times, before Broadway audiences saw a 20th anniversary staging in 1976 with Ian Richardson as Higgins and Christine Andreas as Eliza. There was a West End revival three years later, starring Tony Britton (Higgins), Liz Robertson (Eliza) and the much-loved Anna

Neagle as Mrs. Higgins. The 1981 revival with 73-year-old Harrison, and Cathleen Nesbitt who by then was 92, toured the USA before spending nearly four months in New York. By all accounts it attempted to stay true to the original version, which is more than can be said for some of the later efforts. A 1991 UK provincial production, with a cast headed by Edward Fox (Higgins) and Helen Hobson (Eliza), was described by its director Simon Callow, as 'a politically correct' version, and the 1993 Broadway revival, directed by Howard Davies, with Richard Chamberlain (Higgins), Melissa Errico (Eliza), and Stanley Holloway's son Julian as Doolittle, was 'stripped almost entirely of its romanticism and honed to a provocative post-modern edge', according to the *Variety* theatre critic. He went on: 'The famous 'Ascot Gavotte' scene is recreated as a living Magritte canvas, the actors in colourful finery descending from the flies to hover above the action against a field of brilliant blue'. The 1964 film version was reasonably faithful to the original stage show though, and starred Harrison, Holloway, and - somewhat controversially - Audrey Hepburn as Eliza. As well as the various cast albums, in 1987 Decca Records issued a studio recording with Kiri Te Kanawa (Eliza), Jeremy Irons (Higgins), John Gielguid (Pickering), Jerry Hadley (Freddie), the London Voices, and the London Symphony Orchestra conducted by John Mauceri.

MY FAVORITE YEAR

Following on from the disaster of *Nick And Nora* almost exactly a year earlier, *My Favorite Year* was yet another attempt to adapt a successful movie for the musical stage. The 1982 film of the same name starred the charismatic Peter O'Toole, a fact that made this project all the more vulnerable. A Lincoln Center production, it opened at New York's Vivian Beaumont Theatre on 10 December 1992. Stephen Flaherty (music) and Lynn Ahrens (lyrics) wrote the score, and Joseph Dougherty's book, based on Norman Steinberg and Dennis Palumbo's original screenplay and Palumbo's story, was set in 1954 Manhattan, when television was a live, dangerous, and exciting medium. Fading movie star Alan Swann (Tim Curry in the O'Toole role), whose hell-raising days are just a distant (and hazy) memory, is invited to guest on the small screen's *King Kaiser Comedy Cavalcade*. Fledgling sketch writer Benjy Stone (Evan Pappas), who happens to be a big fan of the movies and Swann in particular (they help compensate for his father's rather sudden departure when Benjy was just a child), is elected to be Swann's minder with orders to keep him and the bottle apart in the days prior to the *Cavalcade*'s transmission, Early on in the show Benjy describes his celluloid influences in the joyous 'Larger Than Life', and in Act 2 has another of the best numbers, 'Shut Up And Dance', in a duet with his girlfriend, K.C. Dowling (Lannyl Stephens). Swann's songs are not so strong, but Curry's performance as the well-oiled smoothie now well past his sell-by date, trying to deal with the guilt of his abandoned daughter, was convincing and won him a Tony Award nomination. Also nominated were Lainie Kazan, who reprised her film role as Belle Steinberg Carroca, Benjy's extremely vulgar but kind hearted mother, and Andrea Martin, the winner of the supporting actress Tony for her hilarious portrayal of Alice Miller, the sole female presence among King Kaiser's (Tom Mardirosian) gang of writers. Amongst the rest of the cast were Josh Mostel, Ethan Phillips, Paul Stolarsky, Thomas Ikeda, Katie Finnerman, David Lipman, and Mary Stout. Flaherty and Ahrens's score, which began in great style with '20 Million People' and finished on a high note with 'My Favorite Year', contained some clever numbers in amongst 'The Musketeer Sketch', 'Waldorf Suite', ''Rookie In The Ring', 'Manhattan', 'Naked In Bethesda Fountain', 'The Gospel According To King', 'Funny/The Duck Joke', 'Welcome To Brooklyn', 'If The World Were Like The Movies', 'Exits', 'Professional Show Business Comedy', 'The Lights Come Up', and 'Maxford House'. Critical reaction was tepid, with the thin book, Thommie Walsh's musical staging, and Ron Lagomarsino's direction taking much of the blame. Overall, partly perhaps because of the inevitable amount of shtick involved, *My Favorite Year* was written off as an old-fashioned musical. It closed after a run of just over a month - and a period of four-and-a-half years in the melting pot. Subsequent productions included one staged by the drama department of London's Guildhall School of Music in 1994, when, along with various other changes, the chorus number 'Pop! Fizz! Happy!' was restored to Act 2.

MY GAL SAL

Another screen biography that played fast and loose with the true facts about its subject - in this case the late 19th century songwriter Paul Dresser. The screenplay, by Seton I. Miller, Darrell Ware and Karl Tunberg, was loosely based on Theodore Dreiser's book *My Brother Paul*, and purported to trace the rise of Dresser (he changed his name from Dreiser early in his career) from his time as a performer in medicine shows and as a blackface comedian in vaudeville, to fame and fortune as a great songwriter. In fact, Dresser was never a commercial success and he wrote his best-known song 'My Gal Sal' in 1905 just a year before he died of heart failure. Victor Mature, an actor guaranteed to make the hearts of female members of the audiences go all-a-flutter, played the composer, and Rita Hayworth was the musical comedy star he fell for in a big way. No wonder, because Hayworth (whose vocals were dubbed by Nan Wynn), looked beautiful and gave one of the best and most joyful performances of her illustrious career. Other roles were played by Carole Landis, John Sutton, James Gleason, Phil Silvers, Walter Catlett, Andrew Tombes, Curt Bois, and Mona Maris. Hermes Pan also made an appearance, and he and Val Raset staged the delightful dance sequences. Several of Dresser's own numbers were featured, including 'On The Banks Of The Wabash', 'Come Tell Me What's Your Answer', 'Liza Jane', 'The Convict And The Bird', 'Mr. Volunteer', 'If You Want Me', and, of course, 'My Gal Sal'. These were supplemented by others, by Ralph Rainger and Leo Robin, such as 'Me And My Fella', 'On The Gay White Way', 'Oh! The Pity Of It All', and 'Midnight At The Masquerade'. It all added up to a colourful and entertaining period piece, which was photographed in Technicolor by Ernest Palmer and produced by Robert Bassler for 20th Century-Fox in 1942. The director was Irving Cummings.

MY HEART GOES CRAZY
(see *London Town*)

MY ONE AND ONLY

This production was similar in many ways to *Crazy For You*, which came along nine years later. Both productions were based on vintage shows with scores by George and Ira Gershwin: in *Crazy For You*, the producers went back to *Girl Crazy* (1930), and for *My One And Only*, which opened at the St. James Theatre in New York on 1 May 1983, librettists Peter Stone and Timothy S. Mayer reached back even further, and used the 1927 Fred Astaire hit, *Funny Face*, as their role model. *My One And Only* starred Tommy Tune, Broadway's contemporary equivalent of Astaire, and he also shared the choreography chores with Thommie Walsh, so the accent was very definitely on the dance. Tune's co-star was Twiggy, the English 60s fashion model, who had appeared in Ken Russell's film of *The Boy Friend* in 1971. Tune and Charles 'Honi' Coles stopped the show each night with their terpsichorean treatment of the title song, and some other numbers were retained from the original *Funny Face*, including 'He Loves And She Loves', ''S Wonderful', and 'Funny Face'. The rest of the score was culled from other Gershwin shows including 'I Can't Be Bothered Now', 'How Long Has This Been Going On?', and 'Nice Work If You Can Get It'. The story, such as it was, had Twiggy as a record-breaking swimmer and Tune as an intrepid pilot, getting mixed up with some Prohibition-busting bootleggers in the late 20s world of Charles Lindbergh and non-stop flights to various capital cities of the world. Tommy Tune won the 1983 Tony Award for best actor, and shared the prize for choreography with Thommie Walsh. The elegant tap dancer, Charles 'Honi' Coles, an ex-vaudevillian who dropped out of the performing business for a while in the 60s and 70s, made a triumphant Broadway comeback in this show at the age of 73, and won the Tony for best supporting actor in a musical. He died in 1992, shortly after receiving the National Medal of the Arts from President Bush. *My One And Only* continued for a total of 767 performances.

MYERS, STANLEY

b. 6 October 1930, London, England, d. 9 November 1993, London, England. A composer, arranger and musical director for films and television from 1966. In the 50s Myers worked in the theatre, and contributed music to several London West End shows including *A Girl Called Jo* and served as musical director for the Julian More-James Gilbert hit musical *Grab Me A Gondola* (1956). In 1966 he scored his first film, a comedy entitled *Kaleidoscope*, which teamed Warren Beatty with English actress Susannah York. Two other early projects included *Ulysses* and *Tropic Of Cancer* for the US director, John Strick. Throughout a career spanning over 60 feature films, Myers worked in several countries besides the UK, including the USA, Canada, Australia, and in Europe, particularly France and Germany. In the 70s his credits included *The Walking Stick, Age Of Consent, A Severed Head, Long Ago Tomorrow (The Raging Moon), Summer Lightning, X, Y And Z, Little Malcolm And His Struggle Against The*

Eunuchs, The Apprenticeship Of Dudley Kravitz, The Wilby Conspiracy, Absolution and *Yesterday's Hero* (1979). In 1978 Myers won his first Ivor Novello Award for the theme from the five times Oscar-winner *The Deer Hunter*. It was a UK Top 20 entry for classical guitarist John Williams, and was also successful for the Welsh singer Iris Williams under the title of 'He Was Beautiful', with a lyric by Cleo Laine. In the 80s, Myers collaborated on the music for several films with Hans Zimmer. Together they scored Jerzy Skolimowski's highly-acclaimed *Moonlighting*, starring Jeremy Irons, *Success Is The Best Revenge, Eureka, Insignificance, Taffin, The Nature Of The Beast* and *Paperhouse*, amongst others. Myers' solo scores during the 80s included *The Watcher In The Woods, Blind Date* (Bruce Willis' big screen success), *The Chain, The Lightship, Conduct Unbecoming, Dreamchild, Castaway, Sammy And Rosie Get Laid, Wish You Were Here, The Boost* and *Scenes From The Class Struggle In Beverly Hills* (1989). In 1987 Myers received an award for 'the best artistic contribution' at Cannes for his music to *Prick Up Your Ears*, Steven Frear's 'realistic and evocative look' at the life of playwright Joe Orton, which included the song 'Dancing Hearts' (written with Richard Myhill). Two years later, Myers won his second Ivor Novello Award for his score for *The Witches*, director Nicholas Roeg's treatment of a story by Roald Dahl. In the early 90s Myers' credits included *Rosencrantz And Guildenstern Are Dead, Iron Maze, Claude, Sarafina!*, and the French-German production *Voyager*. Myers also worked extensively in television, on UK programmes such as *All Gas And Gaiters, Never A Cross Word, Robin Hood, Dirty Money, Widows I And II, Diana, Nancy Astor, Wreath Of Roses, Scoop, Here To Stay, The Russian Soldier, The Most Dangerous Man In The World, My Beautiful Laundrette, Christabel* and many more. For US network television he composed music for *Summer Of My German Soldier, The Gentleman Bandit, The Martian Chronicles, Florence Nightingale, Monte Carlo, Tidy Endings* among others. In the early 90s Myers was working with the saxophonist John Harle. They had just finished recording Myers' specially written piece, 'Concerto For Soprano Saxophone', when he died of cancer. In the same year Myers won another Ivor Novello Award for his Stalag Luft television theme, and in 1995 there was a posthumous BAFTA Award and yet another 'Ivor' for his original television music (written with Christopher Gunning) for the highly popular *Middlemarch* series.

MYROW, JOSEPH

b. 28 February 1910, Russia, d. 24 December 1987, Los Angeles, California, USA. A popular composer from the 40s to the late 50s, mostly for movies, Myrow was educated at the University of Pennsylvania, Philadelphia Conservatory of Music and the Curtis Institute of Music. He graduated as an accomplished pianist, and served as a guest soloist with several symphony orchestras, including those of Cleveland and Philadelphia. After working as musical director for some Philadelphia radio stations, Myrow started composing for nightclub revues in cities on the east coast. His early songs in the late 30s included 'Haunting Me', 'Overheard In A Cocktail Lounge', 'The Fable Of The Rose' and 'I Love To Watch The Moonlight'.

In the early 40s he wrote 'Autumn Nocturne' (a big hit for Claude Thornhill) and 'Velvet Moon'. In 1946, he and Eddie De Lange contributed several songs to the movie *If I'm Lucky*. In the same year, Myrow began what was to be a 10-year association with lyricist Mack Gordon. Together they wrote eight songs for *Three Little Girls In Blue*, including 'Somewhere In The Night', 'Always A Lady', 'On The Boardwalk In Atlantic City' and 'You Make Me Feel So Young'; the latter eventually became indelibly linked with Frank Sinatra. From 1947-50 the team provided the songs for four movies starring Betty Grable, including *Mother Wore Tights* ('Kokomo, Indiana', 'There's Nothing Like A Song' and 'You Do', which was nominated for an Academy Award, and became a hit for Dinah Shore and Vaughn Monroe), *When My Baby Smiles At Me* ('By The Way' and 'What Did I Do?'), *The Beautiful Blonde From Bashville Bend* ('Every Time I Meet You') and *Wabash Avenue* ('Baby Won't You Say You Love Me' and 'Wilhelmina', which was also nominated for an Oscar). Myrow and Gordon continued into the 50s with *The I-Don't-Care Girl* ('This Is My Favorite City'); *I Love Melvin* starring Donald O'Connor and Debbie Reynolds ('A Lady Loves', 'Where Did You Learn To Dance?' and 'There You Are'); and *Bundle Of Joy*, in which Reynolds appeared with husband Eddie Fisher. Myrow also contributed several numbers to *The French Line*, with Ralph Blane ('Comment Allez-Vous?', 'What Is This I Feel?', 'Well, I'll Be Switched' and 'Wait Till You See Paris'). His other compositions included 'Five O'Clock Whistle' (a hit for Glenn Miller, Erskine Hawkins, Ella Fitzgerald); 'It Happens Every Spring' (movie title song), 'Endless Love', 'Love Is Eternal', 'Five Four Blues', 'Soft And Warm', 'Three Quarter Blues' and 'Someday Soon'. His other collaborators included Kim Gannon, Jean Stone and Bickley Reichner. Myrow died of Parkinson's disease in 1987.

MYSTERY OF EDWIN DROOD, THE

In this innovative musical which was 'suggested by the unfinished novel of the same name by Charles Dickens', a newcomer to Broadway, the author and songwriter Rupert Holmes, invited the audience themselves to vote for what they thought should be the outcome at the end of the evening - and it proved to be a popular notion. The show opened at the Imperial Theatre in New York on 2 December 1985, and the story was told as if it was being performed as a play within a play at a London music hall in the late 19th century. The traditional figure of the emporium's Chairman was played by George Rose, and the rest of the cast was led by Betty Buckley, who played Drood, Cleo Laine as Princess Puffer the keeper of an infamous opium den, and Howard McGillin. Holmes' songs included 'Perfect Strangers', 'The Wages Of Sin', 'Moonfall', 'Don't Quit While You're Ahead', 'Both Sides Of The Coin', 'Ceylon', 'Off To The Races', and 'No Good Can Come From Bad'. The show had a good run of 608 performances, and, in a very poor season for new musicals, scooped the Tony Awards, winning for Best Musical, Book, Score, Actor (Rose), and Director (Wilford Leach). The short-lived London production starred Julia Hills, the pop singer Lulu, and Ernie Wise, the surviving partner of one of Britain's comedy double acts, Morecambe And Wise.

NAUGHTY MARIETTA (FILM MUSICAL)

Jeanette MacDonald, who had enjoyed much success with Maurice Chevalier in early musicals such as *The Love Parade*, *One Hour With You*, and *Love Me Tonight*, co-starred in this 1935 film with a new partner with whom she would always be indelibly associated - Nelson Eddy. In the screenplay, by John Lee Mahin, Frances Goodrich, and Albert Hackett, which was based on the 1910 stage operetta of the same name, Macdonald plays a French princess who avoids an arranged marriage by boarding a ship bound for the Colonies. The brave Capt. Warrington (Eddy) saves her from a fate worse than death, and the couple find sanctuary in New Orleans before eventually settling down together 'Neath The Southern Moon'. That was just one of the numbers in Victor Herbert's sumptuous score which included such delights as 'Ah! Sweet Mystery Of Life', 'Italian Street Song', 'I'm Falling In Love With Someone', and 'Tramp! Tramp! Tramp!' (all with lyrics by Rida Johnson Young), and 'Chansonette' (lyric by Gus Kahn). Veteran character actor Frank Morgan lead the supporting cast, which also included Elsa Lanchester, Joseph Cawthorn, Akim Tamiroff, Douglas Dumbrille, Edward Brophy, and Walter Kingsford. This first episode in the Macdonald-Eddy series, during which they became the screen's favourite romantic singing duo, was produced by Hunt Stromberg for MGM and directed by W.S. Van Dyke. The MGM studios were awarded an Oscar for the sound recording.

NAUGHTY MARIETTA (STAGE MUSICAL)

A comic operetta with music by Victor Herbert and a book and lyrics by Rida Johnson Young. It opened on 7 November 1910 at the New York theatre with a story set in New Orleans in 1870, where Naples-born Marietta d'Altena (Emma Trentini) has travelled in search of a husband. She finds the man of her dreams (in more ways than one) when the upstanding Captain Dick Warrington (Orville Harrold) finds that he too has been dreaming of the same song, 'Ah! Sweet Mystery Of Life'. It was only one of several numbers that endured from the attractive and tuneful score. The remainder included 'Tramp! Tramp! Tramp!', 'I'm Falling In Love With Someone', ''Neath The Southern Moon', 'Italian Street Song', 'Naughty Marietta', and 'Live For Today'. Even with the magnificent Trentini, *Naughty Marietta* folded after only 136 performances, but was revived on Broadway in 1912. Since then it has been frequently performed throughout the world, and is a part of the repertoire of the New York City Opera.

NEAGLE, ANNA

b. Marjorie Robertson, 20 October 1904, Forest Gate, London, England, d. 3 June 1986, Surrey, England. One of the most beloved and durable artists in the history of British showbusiness, Neagle was an actress, dancer and singer in West End musicals and British films, with a career spanning more than 60 years. She took dancing lessons as a child, and appeared in the chorus of *Charlot's Revue* and a similar production, *Tricks*, in 1925. In the late 20s she undertook more chorus work in *Rose Marie*, *The Charlot Show Of 1926*, *The Desert Song* and two London Pavilion revues as one of 'Mr Cochran's Young Ladies'. Up until then she had been primarily a dancer, but she developed further in 1931 when she took the ingenue lead opposite Jack Buchanan in the hit musical comedy *Stand Up And Sing*, duetting with him on the lovely 'There's Always Tomorrow'. Herbert Wilcox produced and directed her first film musical, *Goodnight Vienna*, in 1932, and most of her subsequent pictures, and the two were married in 1943. As well as making a number of acclaimed dramatic films during the 30s, Anna Neagle continued to appear in screen musicals such as *The Little Damozel*, *Bitter Sweet*, *The Queen's Affair*, *Limelight* and *London Melody* (1939). From 1940-41 she and Wilcox were in America to make films such as *Irene* (in which she sang and danced to the delightful 'Alice Blue Gown'), *No, No, Nanette* and *Sunny*. They returned to England to make a series of light and frothy romantic comedies, with the occasional musical number, which included *Spring In Park Lane*, *The Courtneys Of Curzon Street* and *Maytime In Mayfair* (1949). Anna Neagle's leading man was Michael Wilding, and this magical partnership ensured that the films were among the British cinema's top box office attractions of the time. In the 50s Anna Neagle returned to the stage for *The Glorious Days* (1953), co-starred with Errol Flynn (of all people) in the film version of that show, *Lilacs In The Spring*; and also appeared in the screen adaptation of *King's Rhapsody*. She then kicked up her heels with popular singer Frankie Vaughan in *The Lady Is A Square* (1958). That was her last appearance on screen, although she did produce three more of Vaughan's films, *These Dangerous Years*, *Wonderful Things!* and *Heart Of A Man*. In the early 60s Wilcox went bankrupt when his film company and several of the couple's other business ventures failed. Part of their salvation came in the form of David Heneker's smash hit musical *Charlie Girl* (1965). Neagle stayed with the show - apart from the occasional holiday - for the duration of its run of over 2,000 performances and subsequent tours. On the day it was announced that she was to be made a Dame of the British Empire, the cast of *Charlie Girl* surprised her by singing 'There Is Nothing Like A Dame' at the end of the evening's performance. In 1973 the new Broadway production of *No, No, Nanette* arrived in London, and Anna Neagle played the role that had been taken by Ruby Keeler in New York. Four years later Herbert Wilcox died, but Anna Neagle continued to work. In 1977 she was back in the West End with the musical *Maggie*; in 1978 she toured as Henry Higgins' mother in a revival of *My Fair Lady*, and in 1982 she played in the pantomime *Cinderella* at the Richmond Theatre. It was as the

Fairy Godmother in *Cinderella* that she made her final stage bow at the London Palladium at Christmas 1986. A few weeks after it closed she went into a Surrey nursing home to rest, and died there in June.

● FURTHER READING: *It's Been Fun*, Anna Neagle. *There's Always Tomorrow*, Anna Neagle.

NELSON, GENE

b. Leander Berg, 24 March 1920, Seattle, Washington, USA, d. 16 September 1996, Woodland Hills, California, USA. An actor, director and athletic dancer in the Gene Kelly style who was in several popular musicals of the 50s. Nelson grew up in Los Angeles and attended the renowned Fanchon and Marco dancing school there. After graduating from high school when he was 18, he took up ice-skating and joined Sonja Henie's touring company and appeared in two of her films, *Second Fiddle* and *Everything Happens At Night*. After enlisting in the US Signals Corps early in World War II, he became a member of the cast of Irving Berlin's celebrated wartime musical *This Is The Army*, which opened on Broadway in 1942 and was then filmed before touring the UK and US military bases throughout the world. Following his discharge, Nelson went to Hollywood in 1947 and made the musical, *I Wonder Who's Kissing Her Now*, with June Haver. Ironically, it was while he was starring in the hit Broadway revue *Lend An Ear* (1949), that Nelson was noticed by a representative of Warner Brothers Pictures. After playing a minor role in *The Daughter Of Rosie O'Grady*, he was signed to a long-term contract and given the third-lead to Doris Day and Gordon MacRae in *Tea For Two* (1950). From then on, he appeared in a string of musicals for the studio, including *The West Point Story*, *Lullaby Of Broadway* (his first starring role, opposite Doris Day), *Painting The Clouds With Sunshine*, *She's Working Her Way Through College*, *She's Back On Broadway*, *Three Sailors And A Girl*, *So This Is Paris*, and *Oklahoma!* (1955). In the latter film he had the best role of his career - and two great numbers, 'Kansas City' and 'All Er Nothin'' (with Gloria Grahame as Ado Annie). In the late 50s Nelson appeared on television until he suffered a horse-riding accident that put an end to his dancing - at least for a while. He turned to directing, and in the 60s worked on some melodramas, and two musical films starring Elvis Presley, *Kissin' Cousins* (which he also co-wrote) and *Harum Scarum*. He also directed *Your Cheatin' Heart*, a film biography of country singer Hank Williams. In 1971 he was back on Broadway with other veteran entertainers such as Yvonne De Carlo and Alexis Smith in Stephen Sondheim's *Follies*. Nelson played Buddy Plummer and performed one of the show's outstanding numbers, the rapid-fire 'Buddy's Blues'. He continued to direct in the 70s and 80s, mostly for television, and worked on the top-rated series *Washington Behind Closed Doors*. In 1993 his projects included staging a US provincial production of Richard Harris's popular comedy *Stepping Out*.

● FILMS: *I Wonder Who's Kissing Her Now* (1947), *Apartment For Peggy* (1948), *Tea For Two* (1950), *The West Point Story* (1950), *The Daughter Of Rosie O'Grady* (1950), *Painting The Clouds With Sunshine* (1951), *Lullaby Of Broadway* (1951), *She's Back On Broadway* (1952), *She's Working Her Way Through College* (1952), *Three Sailors And A Girl* (1953), *Crime Wave* (1954), *The Way Out* UK title *Dial 999* (1955), *The Atomic Man* UK title Timeslip (1955), *Oklahoma!* (1955), *So This Is Paris* (1955), *20,000 Eyes* (1961), *The Purple Hills* (1961), as director *Hand Of Death* (1962), as director *Hootenanny Hoot* (1963), *Thunder Island* (1963), as director *Your Cheatin' Heart* (1964), as director *Kissin' Cousins* (1964), as director *Harum Scarum* (1965), as director *The Cool Ones* (1967), *S.O.B.* (1981).

NEPTUNE'S DAUGHTER

Following their successful portrayal of a pair of twins in the bullfighting musical *Fiesta* (1947), MGM reunited Esther Williams and Ricardo Montalban two years later for this Jack Cummings Technicolor production which proved to be one of the top screen musicals of the decade, grossing $3.5 million in North America alone. Williams plays an up-market swimsuit designer who falls for millionaire Montalban, a member of a visiting South American polo team. The two stars nearly had the film stolen away from them via an hilarious sub-plot that involved Betty Garrett and comedian Red Skelton. He is a simple polo club masseur, but she is convinced that he is the wealthy Montalban, and wants to play her own kind of games with him. Joining in the fun were Keenan Wynn, Mel Blanc, Ted De Corsia, Mike Mazurki, and Xavier Cugat And His Orchestra. Jack Donahue staged the dance sequences and the obligatory underwater ballet. Frank Loesser's songs included 'My Heart Beats Faster', 'I Love Those Men', and the enduring 'Baby, It's Cold Outside', which was introduced by Williams and Montalban, and went on to win an Oscar. Dorothy Kingsley, who wrote the witty screenplay, later worked on major musicals such as *Kiss Me Kate, Seven Brides For Seven Brothers*, and *Pal Joey*. This bright and entertaining film was directed by Edward Buzzell.

NEW GIRL IN TOWN

Bob Merrill, previously known for writing novelty songs such as 'Sparrow In The Treetop', 'Feet Up (Pat Him On the Po-Po)', 'If I Knew You Were Comin' I'd've Baked A Cake' and '(How Much Is That) Doggie In The Window?', some of which became hits for Guy Mitchell, made his Broadway debut with this show, which opened at the 46th Street Theatre in New York on 14 May 1957. George Abbott's book, which was based on Eugene O'Neill's 1921 play, *Anna Christie*, was set in New York at the turn of the century and told of a prostitute, Anna (Gwen Verdon), who returns to live with her bargee father (Chris Christopherson). He is unaware of her occupation, but is soon informed by his unsavoury ladyfriend, Marthy (Thelma Ritter). Matt Burke (George Wallace), a sailor with whom Anna falls in love, leaves her when he, too, discovers the truth about her lifestyle, but he eventually returns in the hope that they can enjoy a more conventional life together. The lively score included 'It's Good To Be Alive', 'Sunshine Girl', 'Did You Close Your Eyes?', 'If That Was Love', 'You're My Friend Ain'tcha?', 'Look At 'Er', 'At the Check Apron Ball', 'Roll Yer Socks Up' and 'There Ain't No Flies On Me'. The engaging and reflective 'Flings' ('Are meant to be flung' . . . 'As a girl, you start seethin'/Over guys just finished teethin'/Now if they're alive and breathin'/That's enough!') was given an amusing treatment on record from Carol Burnett and Martha Raye. When she starred in this piece, Gwen Verdon, one of the American musical theatre's favourite gypsies (dancers), was in the middle of a purple patch with shows such as *Can-Can*, *Damn Yankees* and *Redhead* - with *Sweet Charity* and *Chicago* in the future. She shared the 1958 Tony Award for best actress with Thelma Ritter. *New Girl In Town* ran for 431 performances - an encouraging start for Merrill, who followed it in 1959 with *Take Me Along*, another adaptation of an O'Neill play, *Ah, Wilderness*.

NEW MOON, THE

This romantic musical which arrived at the Imperial Theatre in New York on the 19 September 1928, was created by the same team that had launched *The Desert Song* some two years earlier. However, since its troubled opening in Philadelphia, there had been enforced cast changes, as well as a new book and fresh songs. The story, by Oscar Hammerstein II, Frank Mandel and Lawrence Schwab, now began in 1792 New Orleans, where French nobleman Robert Misson (Robert Halliday) is being pursued by Vicomte Ribaud (Max Figman), suspected of being a party to the murder of the King's cousin. To avoid detection, Robert has been working as a bondsman, together with his former servant Alexander (Gus Shy), on the estate of the wealthy Monsieur Beaunoir (Pacie Ripple). While there, he has fallen in love with Beaunoir's daughter Marianne (Evelyn Herbert). Alexander, meanwhile, is eyeing Marianne's maid Julie (Marie Callahan), who has also caught the eye of Captain Paul Duval (Edward Nell Jnr.), master of the *New Moon*. It is Duval's ship on which Ribaud imprisons Robert *en route* to a French jail. However, before they reach those shores, Robert - and Marianne - are rescued by friends and taken to the Isle of Pines where Robert dreams of setting up his own Utopian society. It thrives, and after the French Revolution, he is made governor of the island.

Sigmund Romberg and Hammerstein's beautiful and often moving score, with its soaring melodies, included 'Lover, Come Back To Me', 'One Kiss', 'Marianne', 'The Girl On The Prow', 'Softly, As In A Morning Sunrise', 'Tavern Song', 'Wanting You', 'Love Is Quite A Simple Thing', and 'Stouthearted Men'. This lavish and spectacular production ran for 509 performances, and was presented at London' Theatre Royal, Drury Lane, on 4 April 1929 (148 performances). Evelyn Laye made a delightful Marianne, with Howett Worster (Robert), Gene Gerard (Alexander), Edmund Willard (Ribaud), Ben Williams (Phillippe), and Dolores Farris (Julie). Since then, as well as becoming an essential element of amateur and professional operetta companies throughout the world, *The New Moon* has been revived, in various revisions, in New York at Carnegie Hall (1942), City Center (1944), State Theatre (1986), and by the New York City Opera (1986 and 1988). A film version, which changed the plot but retained most of the music, was released in 1930 with Grace Moore and Lawrence Tibbett, and the popular singing duo of Jeanette MacDonald and Nelson Eddy were in the 1940 remake.

NEW ORLEANS

Jazz fans watching this US feature film, made in 1947, are torn between embarrassment (at the corny jazz vs. classics storyline) and frustration at the waste of the talent available to the film's makers. Billie Holiday and Louis Armstrong have acting roles (as servants - what else in 1947?) and also perform on screen. Alongside them are musicians such as Barney Bigard, Meade 'Lux' Lewis, Kid Ory, Zutty Singleton, Lucky Thompson and Woody Herman And His Orchestra. Billie Holiday had longed to act in films and when she was cast for this part she expressed her disappointment: 'I fought my whole life to keep from being somebody's damn maid. It was a real drag . . . to end up as a make-believe maid.'

NEW YORK, NEW YORK

Although greeted with mixed reviews at the time of its release in 1977, Martin Scorcese's vibrantly directed film has two major virtues: Robert De Niro is extremely convincing as a big band tenor saxophonist who wants to play bop, and the simulation of the musical ethos of the era (the late 40s) which is remarkably accurate. Otherwise, much of the criticism might be thought fair, the film is too long and the leading roles (the other is Liza Minnelli as a band singer-turned-superstar) are rather unsympathetic. Georgie Auld dubbed for De Niro and the film's musical director was Ralph Burns.

NEW YORKERS, THE

This early Cole Porter show is probably best remembered for the inclusion of the notorious 'Love For Sale'. With a lyric containing such lines as 'Appetizing young love for sale.' . . . 'If you want to buy my wares/Follow me and climb the stairs.', this 'threnody in which a frightened vocalist, Miss Kathryn Crawford, impersonates a lily of the gutters, vending her charms in trembling accents, accompanied by a trio of melancholy female crooners', was banned for some years by radio stations on both sides of the Atlantic. Subtitled 'A Sociological Musical Satire', *The New Yorkers* opened at the Broadway Theatre on 8 December 1930. Herbert Fields' book, based on an idea of cartoonist Peter Arno's, propelled characters, swanky and seedy, around various Manhattan locations, both up-town and down. High society lady, Alice (Hope Williams), loves bootlegger and hoodlum, Al (Charles King), and they have 'Where Have You Been' and one of the score's best numbers, the supremely optimistic 'Let's Fly Away' ('And find a land that's so provincial/We'll never hear what Walter Winchell/Might be forced to say.'). The cast also included Frances Williams, who sang 'The Great Indoors' and 'Take Me Back To Manhattan'; and Barrie Oliver and Ann Pennington, who joined Frances Williams and Charles King for the witty 'I'm Getting Myself Ready For You'. The much-loved clown, Jimmy Durante, together with his vaudeville partners, Eddie Jackson and Lou Clayton, played three hoods. Durante stopped the show most nights with one of his own songs, an item called 'Wood', during which he littered the stage with a wide range of wood products. The clean-cut vocal instrumental group, Fred Waring And His Pennsylvanians, who had been discovered by the show's producer, Ray Goetz, while playing in Los Angeles, also used some of their own material, but, musically, the show belonged to Porter. Shortly after it opened, he interpolated a hymn to the 'Big Apple', 'I Happen To Like New York' ('I like the sight and the sound and even the stink of it.'), which was sung by Oscar 'Rags' Ragland. *The New Yorkers* ran for 168 performances, and despite being banned from airplay, 'Love For Sale' was a hit for Libby Holman, Fred Waring, and later, Hal Kemp. It also became widely heard in a version by Ella Fitzgerald on one of her *Cole Porter Songbooks*.

NEWLEY, ANTHONY

b. 24 September 1931, London, England. A highly successful songwriter, actor and singer, Newley attended the Italia Conti Stage School in London before working as a child actor in several films, including *The Little Ballerina*, *Vice Versa*, and David Lean's acclaimed version of *Oliver Twist* (1948) in which he played the Artful Dodger. He made his London theatrical debut in John Cranko's revue, *Cranks* in 1955, and had character parts in well over 20 films before he was cast as rock 'n' roll star Jeep Jackson in *Idle On Parade* in 1959. Newley's four-track vocal EP, and his version of the film's hit ballad, Jerry Lordan's 'I've Waited So Long', started a three-year UK chart run that included 'Personality', 'If She Should Come To You', 'And The Heavens Cried', the novelty numbers 'Pop Goes The Weasel' and 'Strawberry Fair' and two UK number 1 hits, 'Why' and Lionel Bart's 'Do You Mind'. Newley also made the album charts in 1960 with his set of standards, *Love Is A Now And Then Thing*. He made further appearances in the charts with *Tony* (1961), and the comedy album *Fool Britannia* (1963), on which he was joined by his wife, Joan Collins, and Peter Sellers. In 1961 Newley collaborated with Leslie Bricusse on the book, music and lyrics for the offbeat stage musical, *Stop The World - I Want To Get Off*. Newley also directed, and played the central role of Littlechap. The show, which stayed in the West End for 16 months, ran for over 500 performances on Broadway, and was filmed in 1966. It produced several hit songs, including 'What Kind Of Fool Am I?', 'Once In A Lifetime' and 'Gonna Build A Mountain'.

In 1964 Bricusse and Newley wrote the lyric to John Barry's music for Shirley Bassey to sing over the titles of the James Bond movie, *Goldfinger*. The team's next musical show in 1965, *The Roar Of The Greasepaint - The Smell Of The Crowd*, with comedian Norman Wisdom in the lead, toured the north of England but did not make the West End. When it went to Broadway Newley took over (co-starring with Cyril Ritchard), but was not able to match the success of *Stop The World*, despite an impressive score that contained such numbers as 'Who Can I Turn To?', 'A Wonderful Day Like Today', 'The Joker', 'Look At That Face' and 'This Dream'. In 1967 Newley appeared with Rex Harrison and Richard Attenborough in the film musical *Doctor Dolittle*, with script and songs by Bricusse. Despite winning an Oscar for 'Talk To The Animals', the film was considered an expensive flop, as was Newley's own movie project in 1969, a pseudo-autobiographical sex-fantasy entitled *Can Heironymus Merkin Ever Forget Mercy Humppe And Find True Happiness?* Far

more successful, in 1971, was *Willy Wonka And The Chocolate Factory*, a Roald Dahl story with music and lyrics by Bricusse and Newley. Sammy Davis Jnr. had a million-selling record with one of the songs, 'The Candy Man'. Bricusse and Newley also wrote several numbers for the 1971 NBC television musical adaptation of *Peter Pan*, starring Mia Farrow and Danny Kaye. The team's last authentic stage musical to date, *The Good Old Bad Old Days*, opened in London in 1972 and had a decent run of 309 performances. Newley sang some of the songs, including 'The People Tree', on his 1972 album, *Ain't It Funny*. In 1989, a London revival of *Stop The World - I Want To Get Off*, directed by Newley, and in which he also appeared, closed after five weeks, and, in the same year, he was inducted into the Songwriters' Hall Of Fame, along with Leslie Bricusse. In 1991, Newley appeared on UK television with his ex-wife, Joan Collins, in Noël Coward's *Tonight At 8.30*, with its famous 'Red Peppers' segment. In the following year, having lived in California for some years, Newley announced that he was returning to Britain, and bought a house there to share with his 90-year-old mother. In the early 90s he presented *Once Upon A Song*, an anthology of his own material, at the King's Head Theatre in London, and occasionally played the title role in regional productions of the musical *Scrooge*, which Leslie Bricusse had adapted for the stage from his 1970 film. During the remainder of the 90s Newley continued to perform his accomplished cabaret act (in which he amusingly bemoans the fact that he has not had a hit with one of his own songs) at venues such as the Rainbow & Stars in New York and London's Café Royal. In 1998 he worked in a rather less sophisticated environment when playing crooked car dealer Vince Watson in one of the UK's top-rated television soap operas, *Eastenders*. Tara Newley, the daughter of Newley and Joan Collins, has worked as a radio and television presenter, and in 1994 released her first record entitled 'Save Me From Myself'.

● ALBUMS: *Love Is A Now And Then Thing* (Decca 1960)★★★, *Tony* (Decca 1961)★★★, the London Cast *Stop The World - I Want To Get Off* (1962)★★★★, with Peter Sellers, Joan Collins *Fool Britannia* (1963)★★★, *In My Solitude* (Decca 1964)★★★, *Newley Delivered* (Decca 1965)★★★, the Broadway Cast *The Roar Of The Greasepaint - The Smell Of The Crowd* (1965)★★★★, *Who Can I Turn To* (RCA Victor 1965)★★★★, *Newley Recorded* (RCA Victor 1967)★★★, *Ain't It Funny* (1972)★★★, *The Singer And His Songs* (1978)★★★.

● COMPILATIONS: *The Romantic World Of Anthony Newley* (Decca 1970)★★★, *The Lonely World Of Anthony Newley* (Decca 1972)★★★, *Anthony Newley: Mr. Personality* (1985)★★★, *Greatest Hits* (Deram 1990)★★★★, *Once In A Lifetime: The Anthony Newley Collection* (Razor And Tie 1997)★★★★.

● FILMS: as an actor *Vice Versa* (1948), *The Guinea Pig* (1948), *Oliver Twist* (1948), *Vote For Huggett* (1949), *Don't Ever Leave Me* (1949), *A Boy, A Girl And A Bike* (1949), *Highly Dangerous* (1950), *The Little Ballerina* (1951), *Top Of the Form* (1953), *Up To His Neck* (1954), *The Blue Peter* (1954), *Above Us The Waves* (1955), *High Flight* (1956), *Cockleshell Heroes* (1956), *Port Afrique* (1956), *X The Unknown* (1956), *How To Murder A Rich Uncle* (1957), *Fire Down Below* (1957), *The Small World Of Sammy Lee* (1958), *The Man Inside* (1958), *Tank Force* (1958), *The Lady Is A Square* (1959), *Idle On Parade* (1959), *The Heart Of A Man* (1959), *Bandit Of Zhobe*

(1959), *Killers Of Killimanjaro* (1959), *Jazz Boat* (1960), *In The Nick* (1960), *Doctor Dolittle* (1967), *Sweet November* (1968), *Can Hieronymous Merkin Ever Forget Mercy Humppe And Find True Happiness?* (1969), *The Old Curiosity Shop* (1975), *It Seemed Like A Good Idea At The Time* (1975), *The Garbage Pail Kids Movie* (1987). As a composer *High Flight* songs (1956), *Jazz Boat* songs (1960), *Stop The World-I Want To Get Off* (1966), *Can Hieronymous Merkin Ever Forget Mercy Humppe And Find True Happiness?* also screenplay, director, producer (1969), *Willy Wonka And The Chocolate songs Factory* (1971).

NEWMAN, ALFRED

b. 17 March 1901, New Haven, Connecticut, USA, d. 17 February 1970, Hollywood, California, USA. An important figure in the history of film music, Newman was a composer, conductor, arranger and musical director. A child prodigy on the piano, he went to New York before he was 10 years old, to study piano and harmony. At the age of 13 he was playing in several vaudeville shows a day, while also fitting in appearances as a soloist with various classical orchestras. In the 20s he conducted for the Broadway Theatre, and contributed the occasional song to shows such as *Jack And Jill* ('Voodoo Man', 1923). In 1930 he moved to Hollywood shortly after the movies had started to talk, and worked as an arranger and then a composer for United Artists, on films such as *The Devil To Pay*, *Indiscreet*, *The Unholy Garden* and *Arrowsmith*. His 'immortal' melancholy title theme for *Street Scene* (1931), echoed through the years in many a later film depicting urban decay. His scores for other 30s films included *I Cover The Waterfront* (1933), *Nana* (1934), *The Count Of Monte Cristo* (1934), *Clive Of India* (1935), *Les Miserables* (1935), *Dodsworth* (1936), *The Prisoner Of Zenda* (1937), *The Goldwyn Follies* (1938), *The Cowboy And The Lady* (1938), *Trade Winds* (1938), *Gunga Din* (1939), *Wuthering Heights* (1939), *Young Mr. Lincoln* (1939) and *Beau Geste* (1939). He also served as musical director for Sam Goldwyn (1933-39), and won Academy Awards for his work on *Alexander's Ragtime Band* (1938), *Tin Pan Alley* (1940), *Mother Wore Tights* (1947), *With A Song In My Heart* (1952), *Call Me Madam* (1953), *The King And I* (1956, with co-writer Ken Darby), *Camelot* (1967, again with Darby) and *Hello, Dolly!* (1969, with Lennie Hayton). He gained further Oscars for his complete background scores to *The Song Of Bernadette* (1943) and *Love Is A Many Splendoured Thing* (1955). His film credits during the 40s included *The Grapes Of Wrath* (1940), *The Blue Bird* (1940), *Lillian Russell* (1940), *How Green Was My Valley* (1941), *Charley's Aunt* (1941), *Life Begins At Eight Thirty* (1942), *The Black Swan* (1942), *Heaven Can Wait* (1943), *Claudia* (1943), *The Keys Of The Kingdom* (1944), *Wilson* (1944), *Leave Her To Heaven* (1945), *A Tree Grows In Brooklyn* (1945), *The Razor's Edge* (1946), *Captain From Castille* (1947), *Centennial Summer* (1946), *Unfaithfully Yours* (1948), *The Snake Pit* (1948), *A Letter To Three Wives* (1949), *Yellow Sky* (1948), *Twelve O'Clock High* and *Pinky* (1949). During the 40s Newman spent several years as musical director for 20th Century Fox with his brothers, Lionel and Emil, working for him. In 1950 while still at Fox, Newman wrote the score for 'the wittiest, most devastating, adult and literate motion picture ever made', *All About Eve*, starring Bette Davis and George Sanders. The remainder of his 50s music was of a superb standard, too, for films such as *Panic In The Streets* (1950), *David And Bathsheba* (1951), *What Price Glory?* (1952), *The Snows Of Kilimanjaro* (1952), *The Robe* (1953), *The Seven Year Itch* (1955), *Anastasia* (1956), *Bus Stop* (1956, with Cyril Mockridge), *A Certain Smile* (1958), *The Diary Of Anne Frank* (1959) and *The Best Of Everything* (1959). The latter film's title song (lyric by Sammy Cahn) became popular for Johnny Mathis, and several other earlier pieces of Newman's film music had lives of their own apart from the soundtracks. These included 'Moon of Manakoora' (lyric by Frank Loesser), sung by Dorothy Lamour in *The Hurricane*, and popularized by her fellow 'Road' traveller, Bing Crosby; 'Through A Long And Sleepless Night' (lyric by Mack Gordon), from *Come To The Stable*; and the title songs from *How Green Was My Valley*, *Anastasia* and *The Best Of Everything*. In the 60s his rousing scores for *How The West Was Won* and *The Greatest Story Ever Told* spawned best-selling albums. His music for the melodramatic *Airport* (1970), which featured the popular theme, was the last of Newman's works for the big screen. His son, David Newman (b. 1954), composed a number of television and feature film scores in the 80s and 90s, including *The Kindred*, *The Brave Little Toaster*, *Throw Momma From The Train*, *My Demon Lover*, *The Big Picture*, *Prince Of Pennsylvania*, *Heathers*, *Bill And Ted's Excellent Adventure*, *The War Of The Roses*, *Madhouse*, *The Freshman*, *Meet The Applegates*, *The Marrying Man*, *Bill And Ted's Bogus Journey*, *Don't Tell Momma The Babysitter's Dead*, *Paradise*, *Honeymoon In Las Vegas*, *The Mighty Ducks*, *That Night*, *Hoffa*, *Champions*, *The Sandlot*, *Undercover Blues*, *My Father, The Hero*, *The Air Up There*, *The Flintstones*, *The Sandlot Kids*, *I Love Trouble*, and *Boys On the Side* (1995).

NEWMAN, DAVID

(see Newman, Alfred)

NEWMAN, LIONEL

b. 4 January 1916, New Haven, Connecticut, USA, d. 3 February 1989, California, USA. A distinguished composer, musical director, conductor and arranger for movies for more than 30 years, Newman was a talented pianist as a child, and while in his teens started as a rehearsal pianist for *Earl Carroll's Vanities*, graduating to the position of musical director. He toured with other shows, played piano for Mae West for a while, and performed the same function at 20th Century-Fox when he joined them in 1943. Earlier in 1938, he had composed the title song (lyric by Arthur Quenzer) for the movie *The Cowboy And The Lady*, which had a score by his elder brother, Alfred Newman. In the late 40s Newman's songs included 'As If I Didn't Have Enough On My Mind' (with Harry James), sung by Dick Haymes in *Do You Love Me?*, as well as 'The Morning Glory Road', 'Ramblin' Around' and 'Sentimental Souvenirs'. He had a smash hit in 1948 with the romantic ballad 'Again' (lyric by Dorcas Cochrane), from the film *Road House*. It was successful at the time for Doris Day, Gordon Jenkins and Vic Damone, among others. Another of his numbers, *Never* (lyric by Eliot Daniel), sung by

Dennis Day in *Golden Girl* (1951), was nominated for an Oscar. In his career as a musical director, Newman worked on such films as *Cheaper By The Dozen* (1950), *Mother Didn't Tell Me* (1950), *I'll Get By* (1950), *Dangerous Crossing* (1953), *Love Me Tender* (1956, Elvis Presley's first film), *The Best Things In Life Are Free* (1956), *Mardi Gras* (1958), *Doctor Dolittle* (1967), *The Great White Hope* (1970) and *The Saltzburg Connection* (1972). He supervised all Marilyn Monroe's movies for 20th Century-Fox, such as *Gentlemen Prefer Blondes* (1953), *River Of No Return* (1954) and *There's No Business Like Show Business* (1954). As the studio's general music director, and senior vice-president in 1982, he was a powerful influence on the Fox output. His original music scores included *Don't Bother To Knock* (1952), *The Proud Ones* (1956), *A Kiss Before Dying* (1956), *Compulsion* (1959), *North To Alaska* (1960), *Move Over Darling* (1963), *The Pleasure Seekers* (1964, with Alexander Courage) and *Do Not Disturb* (1965). He was nominated for 11 Academy Awards, and won the Oscar, with Lennie Hayton, in 1969 for his adaptation of Jerry Herman's score for the film version of *Hello, Dolly!*. During the early 80s he conducted the Boston Pops Orchestra in the USA, and performed at London's Royal Albert Hall. He retired in 1985, but was persuaded by MGM to return to the business in 1987. He died two years later.

NEWTON-JOHN, OLIVIA

b. 26 September 1948, Cambridge, England. Her showbusiness career began when she won a local contest to find 'the girl who looked most like Hayley Mills' in 1960 after the Newton-Johns had emigrated to Australia. Later she formed the Sol Four with schoolfriends. Though this vocal group disbanded, the encouragement of customers who heard her sing solo in a cafe led her to enter - and win - a television talent show. The prize was a 1966 holiday in London during which she recorded her debut single, Jackie DeShannon's 'Till You Say You'll Be Mine' after a stint in a duo with Pat Carroll. Staying on in England, Olivia became part of Toomorrow, a group created by bubblegum-pop potentate Don Kirshner, to fill the gap in the market left by the disbanded Monkees (not to be confused with Tomorrow). As well as a science-fiction movie and its soundtrack, Toomorrow was also responsible for 'I Could Never Live Without Your Love,' a 1970 single, produced by the Shadows' Bruce Welch - with whom Olivia was romantically linked. Although Toomorrow petered out, Newton-John's link with Cliff Richard and the Shadows was a source of enduring professional benefit. A role in a Richard movie, tours as special guest in *The Cliff Richard Show*, and a residency - as a comedienne as well as singer - on BBC Television's *It's Cliff!* guaranteed steady sales of her first album, and the start of a patchy British chart career with a Top 10 arrangement of Bob Dylan's 'If Not For You' in 1971. More typical of her output were singles such as 'Take Me Home Country Roads', penned by John Denver, 'Banks Of The Ohio' and, from the late John Rostill of the Shadows, 1973's 'Let Me Be There'. This last release was sparked off by an appearance on the USA's *The Dean Martin Show* and crossed from the US country charts to the Hot 100, winning her a controversial Grammy for Best Female Country Vocal. After an uneasy performance in 1974's Eurovision Song Contest, Newton-John became omnipresent in North America, first as its most popular country artist, though her standing in pop improved considerably after a chart-topper with 'I Honestly Love You,' produced by John Farrar, another latter-day Shadow (and husband of the earlier-mentioned Pat Carroll), who had assumed the task after the estrangement of Olivia and Bruce. Newton-John also became renowned for her duets with other artists, notably in the movie of the musical *Grease* in which she and co-star John Travolta performed 'You're The One That I Want'. This irresistibly effervescent song became one of the most successful UK hit singles in pop history, topping the charts for a stupendous nine weeks. The follow-up, 'Summer Nights' was also a UK number 1 in 1978. 'Xanadu', with the Electric Light Orchestra, the title song of a film in which she starred, was another global number 1. However, not such a money-spinner was a further cinema venture with Travolta (1983's 'Two Of A Kind'). Neither was 'After Dark', a single with the late Andy Gibb in 1980, nor *Now Voyager*, a 1984 album with his brother Barry. With singles such as 'Physical' (1981) and the 1986 album *Soul Kiss* on Mercury Records she adopted a more raunchy image in place of her original perky wholesomeness. During the late 80s/early 90s much of her time was spent, along with Pat (Carroll) Farrar, running her Australian-styled clothing business, Blue Koala. Following *The Rumour*, Newton-John signed to Geffen for the release of a collection of children's songs and rhymes, *Warm And Tender*. The award of an OBE preceded her marriage to actor and dancer Matt Lattanzi. She remains a showbusiness evergreen, although her life was clouded in 1992 when her fashion empire crashed, and it was announced that she was undergoing treatment for cancer. She subsequently revealed that she had won her battle with the disease, and in 1994 released an album that she had written, produced and paid for herself. At the same time, it was estimated that in a career spanning nearly 30 years, she has sold more than 50 million records worldwide. Sales rocketed in 1998, when the *Grease* movie was re-released, and both the soundtrack and single 'You're The On That I Want', returned to the upper reaches of the charts.

● ALBUMS: *If Not For You* (Pye 1971)★★★, *Let Me Be There* (MCA 1973)★★★, *Olivia Newton-John* (1973)★★, *If You Love Me Let Me Know* (MCA 1974)★★★, *Music Makes My Day* (Pye 1974)★★, *Long Live Love* (1974)★★, *Have You Never Been Mellow?* (MCA 1975)★★★, *Clearly Love* (MCA 1975)★★, *Come On Over* (MCA 1976)★★, *Don't Stop Believin'* (MCA 1976)★★, *Making A Good Thing Better* (MCA 1977)★★, with various artists *Grease* film soundtrack (1978)★★★★, *Totally Hot* (MCA 1978)★★★, with Electric Light Orchestra *Xanadu* film soundtrack (MCA 1980)★★, *Physical* (MCA 1981)★★★, with various artists *Two Of A Kind* film soundtrack (1983)★★, *Soul Kiss* (MCA 1986)★★, *The Rumour* (MCA 1988)★★, *Warm And Tender* (Geffen 1990)★★, *Gaia: One Woman's Journey* (1994)★★, *Back With A Heart* (MCA 1998)★★★.

● COMPILATIONS: *Olivia Newton-John's Greatest Hits* (MCA 1977)★★★, *Greatest Hits* i, (EMI 1978)★★★, *Olivia's Greatest Hits, Volume 2* (MCA 1982)★★, *Greatest Hits* ii, (EMI 1982)★★, *Back To Basics: The Essential Collection 1971-1992* (Phonogram 1992)★★★, *Country Girl* (EMI 1998)★★★.

● VIDEOS: *Physical* (PMI 1984), *Live: Olivia Newton-John* (Channel 5 1986), *Down Under* (Channel 5 1989), *Soul Kiss* (Spectrum 1989).

● FURTHER READING: *Olivia Newton-John: Sunshine Supergirl*, Linda Jacobs. *Olivia Newton-John*, Peter Ruff.

● FILMS: *Grease* (1978), *Xanadu* (1980), *Two Of A Kind* (1983).

NICHOLAS BROTHERS

Fayard Nicholas (b. *c*.1918) and Harold Nicholas (b. *c*.1924), constituted what was, without a doubt, the most talented and spectacular power tap-dancing duo in the history of showbusiness. They grew up in Philadelphia where their parents played in the orchestra at the Standard Theatre, a vaudeville house for blacks. The brothers were soon in vaudeville themselves, billed initially as the Nicholas Kids. By 1932 they had graduated to the renowned Cotton Club in Harlem, where, for the next two years they delighted the all-white audiences and rubbed shoulders with great black entertainers such as Ethel Waters, Duke Ellington, and Cab Calloway. In 1936 the Nicholas Brothers made their Broadway debut with Bob Hope and Fanny Brice in *Ziegfeld Follies*, and also appeared in London in Lew Leslie's revue *Blackbirds Of 1936*. A year later they were back on Broadway in the Richard Rodgers and Lorenz Hart hit musical *Babes In Arms*. Their film career had begun in 1932 with two short films, *Black Network* and *Pie Pie Blackbird* (featuring Eubie Blake And His Band), and it continued via *Calling All Stars* (1936), and the Don Ameche-Betty Grable musical *Down Argentine Way* (1940), in which the brothers did a breathtaking dance to the lively number 'Down Argentina Way'. The sequence was choreographed by Nick Castle who worked with the duo on most of their subsequent pictures, and gained them a five year contract with 20th Century-Fox. During the rest of the 40s the Nicholas Brothers contributed some electrifying and superbly acrobatic dances to films such as *Tin Pan Alley*, *The Great American Broadcast*, *Sun Valley Serenade*, *Orchestra Wives*, *Stormy Weather*, and *The Pirate* (1948). In 1946 they both starred in the Broadway musical *St. Louis Woman* in which Harold introduced Harold Arlen and Johnny Mercer's appealing 'Ridin' On The Moon' and (with Ruby Hill) the all-time standard, 'Come Rain Or Come Shine'. Of course, as blacks, in films they were only allowed to be a speciality act and were never considered for leading roles. This is apparently one of the main reasons why, in the 50s, they worked in Europe for several years where audiences and managements were more racially tolerant. When Fayard decided to return to the USA, Harold stayed in France and carved out a solo career for himself there. After seven years they were reunited in America and played in nightclubs and on television until Fayard contracted arthritis and underwent two hip-replacement operations. Harold continued as a solo performer and was top-billed in the musical *Back In The Big Time* (1986). Fayard was still active in non-performing areas of the business and won a Tony Award when he co-choreographed the 1989 Broadway musical *Black And Blue*, with Cholly Atkins, Henry LeTang and Frank Manning. In 1991 the Nicholas Brothers received Kennedy Center Honours for their outstanding work over a period of more than 60 years. A year later, a documentary film *We Sing & We Dance*, celebrated their wonderful careers and included tributes from Mikhail Baryshnikov, Gregory Hines, M.C. Hammer, and Clarke Peters. In 1994, members of the cast of *Hot Shoe Shuffle*, London's 'New Tap Musical', also paid tribute to their 'inspiration' - the Nicholas Brothers.

NICHOLAS, PAUL

b. Paul Beuselinck, 3 December 1945, London, England. An actor, singer, and producer, Nicholas is the son of the flamboyant former show business lawyer Oscar Beuselinck who represented artists such as John Osborne, Richard Harris, and Sean Connery. Nicholas served his musical apprenticeship as pianist with Screaming Lord Sutch And The Savages. Then known as Paul Dean, he embarked on a singing career in 1964, and later had access to exclusive songs by Pete Townshend ('Join My Gang') and David Bowie ('Over The Wall We Go'). Nicholas finally achieved pop single success in 1976/7 with several disco-style numbers for Robert Stigwood's RSO label, including 'Reggae Like It Used To Be', 'Dancing With The Captain', 'Grandma's Party', and 'Heaven On The 7th Floor'. His long association with Stigwood resulted in appearances in some of the most popular stage productions of the era. His debut in the love-rock musical *Hair* (1968, Claude), was followed by *Jesus Christ Superstar* (1972, Jesus), and in 1981 he created the role of Rum Tum Tugger in Andrew Lloyd Webber's *Cats*. He subsequently took the title role in Tim Rice and Stephen Oliver's shortlived *Blondel* (1983), philosophised with Cyd Charisse on 'You Never Know What You Can Do Until You Try' in the 1986 revival of *Charlie Girl*, and walked the high wire in *Barnum* (1992, P.T. Barnum). Also in 1992, Nicholas toured as the Pirate King with *The Pirates Of Penzance*, the first of several forays he made into the regions with this particular vessel. While out there in 1992, he met fellow performer David Ian, and they formed a producing partnership which mounted, sometimes in association with Stigwood, an impressive list of musical shows. These included the 20th anniversary concert tour of *Jesus Christ Superstar*, a compilation of hits from the musicals called *The Greatest Shows In Town*, *Grease*, *The Rocky Horror Show*, *Ain't Misbehavin'*, and UK tours of *Singin' In The Rain* (1995, in which he also starred), *Evita* and *Chess*, as well as the premiere of *Saturday Night Fever* at the London Palladium (1998). Nicholas and Ian presented their first West End production, *Grease*, some 20 years after Nicholas himself had succeeded Richard Gere as Danny Zuko in the original London version. Nicholas has also enjoyed considerable success on television, particularly as turf accountant Vince Pinner in the top-rated series *Just Good Friends*, co-starred with Jan Francis. His other television work has included *Bust* (1987) and *Close To Home* (1989). On the big screen he was in *Stardust* (1974, Johnny), and two Ken Russell projects, *Lisztomania* (1975, Richard Wagner) and *Tommy* (1975, Cousin Kevin).

● ALBUMS: *Paul Nicholas* (RSO 1977)★★★, *Just Good Friends* (K-Tel 1986)★★★, *That's Entertainment* (1993)★★, *Colours Of My Life* (First Night 1994)★★★.

● FILMS: *Cannibis* (1969), *See No Evil* (1971), *What Became Of Jack And Jill?* (1972), *Three For All* (1974), *Lisztomania* (1975), *Tommy*

(1975), *Sgt. Pepper's Lonely Hearts Club Band* (1978), *The World Is Full Of Married Men* (1979), *The Jazz Singer* (1980), *Nutcracker* (1982), *Invitation To The Wedding* (1985), *Alice* (1986).

NICK AND NORA

This show was based on Dashiell Hammett's witty 30s comedy-drama movie, *The Thin Man*, which starred William Powell and Myrna Loy, and spawned several sequels. Its transfer from Hollywood to Broadway provided yet another insight into the agonizing trials and tribulations endured by the creators - and, some would say, the audiences - concerned with a contemporary musical production. After several postponements, the show actually started its previews at the Marquis Theatre in New York on 8 October 1991. These continued for 71 performances - an unprecedented nine weeks - while the highly experienced team of Arthur Laurents (director and librettist), Charles Strouse (music) and Richard Maltby Jnr., strove to get the show ready. After numerous changes to the cast, score and book, *Nick And Nora* finally faced the critics on December 8. The story, still set in the film world of the 30s, has Nora Charles (Joanna Gleason) doing a favour for her old girlfriend, the actress Tracy Gardner (Christine Baranski), by trying to find the murderer of studio book keeper, Lorraine Bixby (Faith Prince). Eventually, she gives way to husband Nick (Barry Bostwick), who comes out of retirement to solve the case himself. Not a show to appeal to feminists. There were high hopes for the score. Richard Maltby Jnr. was co-lyricist on *Miss Saigon*, and his collaborations with David Shire, such as *Baby* and *Starting Here, Starting Now*, had been duly noted. Charles Strouse had composed the music for several big Broadway hits, but his record revealed six flops in a row since *Annie* in 1977. Their songs met with a mixed reception. They included 'Is There Anything Better Than Dancing?', 'Everybody Wants To Do A Musical', 'Swell', 'Not Me', 'As Long As You're Happy', 'Look Whose Alone Now', and 'Let's Go Home', which some unkind critics took literally. The number that attracted the most attention was 'Men', which was sung by Faith Prince, and that too, with its lyric, 'I was nuts . . . dropped my pants like a putz', was regarded as 'astonishingly coarse' by one critic, and 'absolute dynamite' by another. There was an air of doom surrounding the production, anyway, and it folded after only nine performances (not forgetting the 71 previews) with estimated losses in excess of $2.5 million.

NIGHT AND DAY

Benny Green, the British author and critic, has often commented that if only the screenwriters of these lavish Hollywood film biographies had told the subject's real life story instead of writing the usual insipid puff, some fascinating pictures would have resulted. This theory could have been especially true in the case of *Night And Day* which was released by Warner Brothers in 1946. It was supposed to be a celebration of the smart and sophisticated songwriter Cole Porter, but hardly any of the important incidents in his life - apart from his tragic accident - were touched upon. The inclusion of a good many of his magnificent songs more than made up for the omissions, though, and these included 'I've Got You Under My Skin',

'Night And Day', 'Miss Otis Regrets', 'In The Still Of The Night', 'Begin The Beguine', 'What Is This Thing Called Love?', 'Just One Of Those Things', 'I Get A Kick Out Of You', 'Easy To Love', 'You Do Something To Me', 'Let's Do It', 'Old Fashioned Garden', 'Love For Sale', 'You've Got That Thing', and 'Anything Goes'. Mary Martin reprised 'My Heart Belongs To Daddy' which she originally introduced to rapturous acclaim in *Leave It To Me!* back in 1938, and several of the other numbers were sung by Ginny Simms and Jane Wyman. Cary Grant played Porter, and it was interesting, if unsatisfying, to hear his version of 'You're The Top', one of the composer's all-time great 'list' songs. Alexis Smith was Mrs. Porter, and also cast were Monty Woolley (as himself), Eve Arden, Alan Hale, Victor Francen, Dorothy Malone, Selena Royle, Donald Woods, Henry Stephenson, Sig Rumann, and Carlos Ramirez. Charles Hoffman, Leo Townsend and William Bowers were responsible for the screenplay, and the dances were staged by Leroy Prinz. Arthur Schwartz, a legendary songwriter himself, was the producer and Michael Curtiz provided the lacklustre direction. It was photographed in Technicolor by J. Peverell Marley and William Skall. In spite of their obvious drawbacks, these kind of films were always crowd-pullers, and *Night And Day* proved to be no exception, grossing $4 million in North America alone.

NINE

This musical adaptation of Federico Fellini's 1963 movie *Eight And A Half*, had a book by Arthur Kopit, and music and lyrics by the Broadway newcomer Maur y Yeston. It opened on 9 May 1982 at the 46th Street Theatre in New York. The story follows film director Guido Contini (Raul Julia) to Europe in his quest to recharge his physical and emotional batteries, and revitalize his personal life and career. This applies particularly to his continually changing relationships with the women in his life, such as his wife (Karen Akers), his first love, Saraghina (Kathi Moss), his mother (Taina Elg), his close friend and professional colleague, Liliane LaFleur (Liliane Montevecchi), his latest discovery, (Shelley Burch), and his current mistress, Carla (Anita Morris). Yeston's innovative and tuneful score was greeted with enthusiasm, and contained songs such as 'Be Italian', 'My Husband Makes Movies', 'Only With You', 'Be On Your Own', 'Folies Bergéres', 'A Call From The Vatican', 'Nine', 'Unusual Way', 'Simple', 'Getting Tall', and 'The Grand Canal'. Tommy Tune and Thommie Walsh were responsible for the choreography and reprised their collaboration a year later for *My One And Only*. Tune also directed the piece, and his extraordinary staging of a production which only included one adult male, four boys, and 21 women, was generally acclaimed. He won a Tony Award for his work, and *Nine* gained further Tonys for best musical, score, and featured actress (Liliane Montevecchi). The show surprised many critics, and ran for 732 performances. Productions were mounted in other countries, including Australia, where it starred John Diedrich. A concert version was presented at London's Festival Hall in 1992, with Liliane Montevecchi and Jonathan Pryce, the versatile actor who came to prominence as the Engineer in *Miss Saigon*. The resulting two-CD set featured Ann Crumb, Elaine Paige, and a chorus of over 100, and is regarded as the most complete recorded version of Yeston's score .In 1996 London audiences saw a Donmar Warehouse production, with Larry Lamb as Guido, heading an impressive cast which included Sara Kestelman, Susannah Fellows, Jenny Galloway, Clare Burt, Eleanor David, Dilys Laye, Kiran Hocking, and Ria Jones.

NO NUKES

This 1980 documentary revolved around a series of events staged in New York the previous year. Five nights of benefit concerts were held at Madison Square Gardens between 19 and 23 September 1979, which in turn were succeeded by an outdoor gathering in Battery Park, in order to raise funds for Musicians United for Safe Energy. MUSE was a charity headed by John Hall, formerly of the Ozark Mountain Daredevils, who was determined to lobby for the replacement of nuclear power by solar energy. Many well-known 70s US artists lent support to the cause, and *No Nukes* captured several strong performances. Bruce Springsteen contributed the title song to the as yet unreleased *The River*, as well as powerful readings of Gary 'U.S.' Bonds' 'A Quarter To Three' and his own 'Thunder Road'. Crosby, Stills And Nash offer 'Suite Judy Blue Eyes' while Jackson Browne completed resonant versions of 'Running On Empty' and 'Before The Deluge'. The Doobie Brothers, Bonnie Raitt, Jesse Colin Young, James Taylor and Carly Simon are among the others featured in an all-star cast brought together by a common ecological concern. Several guested on each other's sets, notably on the 60s protest anthem, 'Get Together', which featured Browne, Nash and Stills alongside Young, whose group the Youngbloods first popularized the song. *No Nukes* was also the subject of an expansive three-record set which, when combined with the scale of the event itself, showed commitment from all those involved in the project.

● VIDEOS: *No Nukes* (CBS Fox 1980).

NO STRINGS

When Oscar Hammerstein died in 1960, composer Richard Rodgers lost the second of only two lyricists with whom he had worked throughout his illustrious career - the first, of course, being Lorenz Hart. Shortly after Hammerstein's death, Rodgers wrote both words and music to five new songs for the second re-make of the film *State Fair*, and then in 1962 he undertook the complete score for *No Strings* which opened at the 54th Street Theatre in New York on 15 March. Rodgers also produced the piece, for which the book was written by the celebrated playwright Samuel Taylor, who had impressed the composer with his comedies such as *Sabrina Fair* and *The Pleasure Of His Company*. The black actress Diahann Carroll, who was spotted by Rodgers on US television in the *Jack Paar Show*, was cast as an American fashion model, Barbara Woodruff, who has moved to Paris. While there, she falls in love with the former Pulitzer Prize-winning novelist David Jordan (Richard Kiley), whose life has disintegrated to the point that he has given up writing and is just living on hand-outs. She helps in his process of rehabilitation, but they decide to go their separate ways.

Rodgers himself hinted later that the reason that the characters split up is because they anticipate racial prejudice on their return to the USA, although the authors were careful not to mention it directly. The director and choreographer, Joe Layton, introduced several innovative features, such as placing the orchestra onstage instead of in the pit, and having members of the cast move the mobile sets in full view of the audiences. Another neat idea was for Kiley and Carroll to sing the show's lovely hit song, 'The Sweetest Sounds', each accompanied by their own individual instrumental soloist, and this technique was also used on some of the other numbers. Carroll excelled throughout on such as 'Loads Of Love', 'You Don't Tell Me', 'An Orthodox Fool', and joined with Kiley for 'Nobody Told Me', 'Maine', 'Look No Further', and the title song. While not in the same money-making class as *The Sound Of Music* and the other Rodgers and Hammerstein blockbusters, *No Strings* had a decent run of 580 performances. Rodgers won the Tony Award for outstanding music - but not, ironically for lyrics - and joint Tonys also went to Diahann Carroll, who shared hers with Anna Marie Alberghetti (*Carnival*); and Joe Layton, whose choreography was adjudged to be equally as excellent as that of Agnes de Mille's for *Kwamina*. In 1963, *No Strings* was presented at Her Majesty's Theatre in London, where it starred Hy Hazell and Art Lund, and ran for 135 performances.

NO, NO, NANETTE

It was during the early part of its year-long Chicago run, prior to Broadway, that this show was picked up by a couple of visiting British producers, Herbert Clayton and Jack Waller. They presented it at the Palace Theatre in London on 11 March 1925, and soon found that they had a big hit on their hands. Otto Harbach and Frank Mandel's book is based on the play *My Lady Friends* by Mandel and Emile Nyitray, which was adapted from May Edgington's novel, *Oh James!* The entire action takes place on a weekend in early summer, 1925. Jimmy Smith (Joseph Coyne) has become wealthy by publishing bibles, but his wife Sue (Marie Hemingway) refuses to go out and spend the prophets . . . sorry . . . profits. So he fritters away some of the cash on friendships with the various ladies he meets on his business travels. These perfectly innocent liaisons lead to a minefield of complications involving Jimmy and Sue's teenage ward, Nanette (Binnie Hale), whose boyfriend Tom Trainor (Seymour Beard) thinks she and Jimmy are having an affair; Lucille Early (Irene Browne), the wife of Jimmy's best friend and known philanderer Billy (George Grossmith), who imagines that Jimmy's platonic girls belong to Billy; and Jimmy's own wife Sue, who figures that Jimmy has been covering up for Billy all the time. At the final curtain, everyone has found their proper partner, including Tom and Nanette, while Sue has finally splashed out on several decent outfits for herself. The tuneful, light-hearted and danceable score had music by Vincent Youmans, with Irving Caesar and Otto Harbach's lyrics, and the songs included 'You Can Dance With Any Girl', 'I've Confessed To The Breeze', 'Call Of The Sea', 'No, No, Nanette', 'Too Many Rings Around Rosie', 'Telephone Girlie', 'Peach On the Beach', 'Take A

Little One-Step', and "Where Has My Hubby Gone' Blues'. Silly-ass specialist Grossmith was outstanding and the rest of the cast was splendid too, but the star of this zippy production which changed the face of musical comedy with its contemporary humour, bright, colloquial lyrics and vivacious bare-legged girls, was Binnie Hale. It made her a star overnight, and she introduced the show's two big numbers, 'I Want To Be Happy' (with Coyne) and 'Tea For Two' (with Beard). *No, No, Nanette* ran for a terrific 665 performances in London, but did less well in 1925 on Broadway (321), with Louise Groody (Nanette), Charles Winninger (Jimmy), Eleanor Dawn (Sue), Josephine Whittell (Lucille), Wellington Cross (Billy), and Jack Barker (Tom). It is not too often that a revival runs on Broadway longer than the original, but the 1971 revised *No, No, Nanette* did just that, staying around for 861 performances. Heading the cast as Sue Smith was former 30s movie star Ruby Keeler, aided and abetted by Jack Gilford (Jimmy), Helen Gallagher (Lucille), Bobby Van (Billy), Susan Watson (Nanette), and Roger Rathburn (Tommy). It won Tony Awards for best actress (Gallagher), supporting actress (Patsy Kelly), choreographer (Donald Saddler), and costumes (production designer Raoul Péne du Bois). Several other famous film personalities were prominent in the subsequent road tours, such as June Allyson, Virginia Mayo, Evelyn Keyes, Dennis Day, and Don Ameche. The 1971 Tony-winner Helen Gallagher switched to the Ruby Keeler role for the 1997 Paper Mill Playhouse, New Jersey, production, which also had Eddie Bracken, Lee Roy Reams, Kaye Ballard, Debra Wiseman, Virginia Sandifur, and Daniel Herron. The show returned to the West End in 1936, and again in 1973 with Anna Neagle, Anne Rogers, Tony Britton, Teddy Green, Barbara Brown, and Thora Hird. There have been two film versions: in 1930 with Alexander Gray and Bernice Claire, and in 1940 with Anna Neagle and Victor Mature.

● FURTHER READING: *The Making Of No, No, Nanette*, Don Dunn.

NOEL AND GERTIE
(see Lawrence, Gertrude)

NORTH, ALEX
b. 4 December 1910, Chester, Pennsylvania, USA, d. 8 September 1991, Pacific Palisades, California, USA. An important composer for films, theatre, television, ballet and classical music, whose career stretched from the late 30s through to the 80s. After studying at Juilliard with the distinguished composer Aaron Copland, as well as at the Moscow Conservatory (1933-35), North composed for the Federal Theatre Project in the late 30s. During those years, through to 1950, he wrote the scores for government documentary and information films, and served in the US Army in World War II. In 1948 he composed the incidental score for Arthur Miller's landmark play *Death Of A Salesman*, on Broadway, and repeated the role for the film version in 1951. For that, and for his innovative jazz-tinged score to *A Streetcar Named Desire* (1951), he gained the first two of his 15 Academy Award nominations. Other early 50s film music included *The 13th Letter*, *Viva Zapata!* (considered an early milestone in his career), *Les*

Miserables, the ballet music for Fred Astaire and Leslie Caron in *Daddy Long Legs*, and *Unchained* (1955). The latter featured 'Unchained Melody' (lyric by Hy Zaret), a ballad of yearning that was nominated for an Academy Award, and became popular at the time for Les Baxter (US number 1), Al Hibbler and Jimmy Young (UK number 1), among others, and through the years was constantly remembered and revived. The Righteous Brothers' 1965 smash-hit version accompanied an erotic scene in the popular 1990 movie *Ghost*, and in 1995 the song topped the UK chart once again in a version by Robson Green and Jerome Flynn, two actors from the popular television series *Soldier, Soldier*. North's other 50s scores included *The Man With The Gun* (1955), *I'll Cry Tomorrow* (1955), *The Rose Tattoo* (1955), *The Bad Seed* (1956), *The Rainmaker* (1956), *Four Girls In Town* (1956), *The King And Four Queens* (1956), *The Bachelor Party* (1957), *The Long Hot Summer* (1958), *Stage Struck* (1958), *Hot Spell* (1958), *The Sound And The Fury* (1959) and *The Wonderful Country* (1959). Early in the 60s North began an association with director John Huston that lasted until Huston's death in 1987. Together they worked on such films as *The Misfits* (1961), *Wise Blood* (1979), *Under The Volcano* (1984), *Prizzi's Honor* (1985) and *The Dead* (1987), Huston's swan-song. North's 60s film work began with the epic *Spartacus* ('magnificent score, staggering battle scenes'), followed, in complete contrast, by *The Children's Hour*. His other scores of the decade included another epic, *Cleopatra*, John Ford's *Cheyenne Autumn*, *The Agony And The Ecstasy*, *Who's Afraid Of Virginia Woolf?*, *The Shoes Of The Fisherman*, *Hard Contract* and *A Dream Of Kings*. In the 70s, as his style of spectacular, dramatic scores went out of fashion, North worked less for the big screen. However, in later years he composed the music for movies such as *Pocket Money*, *Once Upon A Scoundrel*, *Bite The Bullet* and *Somebody Killed Her Husband*. In the 80s, besides his collaborations with Huston, North was still being critically acclaimed for scores such as *Carny*, *Dragonslayer*, *Under The Volcano*, *Good Morning Vietnam*, and his final film, *The Penitent* (1988). In 1986 he became the first composer to receive an honorary Academy Award 'in recognition of his brilliant artistry in the creation of memorable music for a host of distinguished motion pictures'. He died, five years later, in 1991. As well as films, his occasional television work included the feature documentary *Africa* (1967), music for the mini-series *The Word*, which was nominated for an Emmy, and *Rich Man, Poor Man*, which won two, the television feature *Death Of A Salesman* (again), and music for other programmes, such as *Your Show Of Shows*, *77 Sunset Strip*, *Playhouse 90* and *The F.D.R. Story*. Many of North's scores were made available on albums, and several individual items, such as the title themes from *I'll Cry Tomorrow* and *The Long Hot Summer*, and 'Unchained Melody', of course, endure.

NORWORTH, JACK
b. 5 January 1879, Philadelphia, Pennsylvania, USA, d. 1 September 1959, Laguna Beach, California, USA. A songwriter, producer, and all-round entertainer in the musical theatre, Norworth started out as a black-faced comedian, and spent several years in minstrel shows and vaudeville

at the turn of the twentieth century. In 1906, he appeared in Lew Fields's elaborate vaudeville revue *About Town*, and two years later joined contralto Nora Bayes - his second wife - in Florenz Ziegfeld's *Follies Of 1908*. They introduced their most famous composition, 'Shine On Harvest Moon', in that show, and were together again in *Follies Of 1909*, *The Jolly Bachelors* (1910), *Little Miss Fix-It* (1911), and *Roly Poly* (1912). In the early years of World War I Norworth was in London, where he starred in productions such as *Hullo Tango* (taking over during the run in 1914), *Rosy Rapture-The Pride Of the Beauty Chorus* and *Looking Around* (both 1915), specializing in tongue-twisting numbers such as 'Sister Susie's Sewing Shirts For Soldiers' (R.P. Weston-Herman Darewski) and 'Which Switch Is The Switch, Miss, For Ipswich?' (Darewski-F.W. Mark). He made his final Broadway appearance in *Odds And Ends* (1917), which he also co-produced. Norworth's other compositions with Bayes included 'Turn Off Your Light, Mr. Moon-Man', 'Fancy You Fancying Me', 'I'm Sorry', and 'Young America'. He also wrote the lyrics for composer Albert von Tilzer's immensely popular 'Take Me Out To The Ball Game', and other numbers such as 'Honey Boy', 'Smarty', and 'Good Evening, Caroline'. Norworth and Bayes's most famous song, 'Shine On Harvest Moon', was sung by Ruth Etting in the *Ziegfeld Follies Of 1931*, and it was the title of the Norworth-Bayes 1944 film biography, which starred Ann Sheridan and Dennis King. In 1948 Norworth was still reported to be active in benefit shows, as well as running a novelty shop in California.

NOVELLO, IVOR

b. David Ivor Davies, 15 January 1893, Cardiff, Wales, d. 6 March 1951, London, England. A much-loved composer, lyricist, librettist and actor, Novello was born into a musical family, and was encouraged by his mother, a singing teacher. He soon became musically proficient, and quickly established a local reputation. That reputation spread throughout the UK with the publication of a song that encapsulated the feelings of many families torn apart by World War I. Setting to music a poem by the American Lena Guilbert-Ford, Novello's 'Keep The Home Fires Burning' (1915) was a huge popular success. He continued to write songs while serving in the Naval Air Service, but in 1919 turned mainly to acting and appeared in a number of silent films. With a classic profile that gained him matinee idol status amongst the film-going public, his screen career continued into the 30s, although he persisted in his desire to write for the stage. He contributed material to *Theodore & Co.* (1916) and *Arlette* (1917), before writing the music for *Tabs* (1918) and *Who's Hooper?* (1919). These were followed during the 20s by *The Golden Moth*, *Puppets*, *Our Nell*, and *The House That Jack Built* (1929), but real success eluded him until 1935 when he teamed up with lyricist Christopher Hassall for the hugely popular *Glamorous Night* ('Shine Through My Dreams', 'Fold Your Wings'), which was followed by equally lush and romantic productions such as *Careless Rapture* ('Love Made The Song', 'Why Is There Ever Goodbye?', 1936), *Crest Of The Wave* ('Rose Of England', 'The Haven Of Your Heart', 1937), *The Dancing Years* ('I Can Give You The Starlight', 'Primrose', 'Waltz Of My Heart', 'My Dearest Dear', 'My

Life Belongs To You', 1939), *Arc De Triomphe*, ('Man Of My Heart', 'Waking Or Sleeping', 1943), *Perchance To Dream* ('We'll Gather Lilacs', 'Love Is My Reason', 1945), and *King's Rhapsody* ('Someday My Heart Will Awake', 'Take Your Girl', 1949). His last show, *Gay's The Word* (lyrics by Alan Melville), in which Cicely Courtneidge introduced 'It's Bound To Be Right On The Night' and 'Vitality', opened in London in 1951, three weeks before Novello died. In a way, it lampooned the kind of lavish, brilliantly staged productions with which Novello had captured the imagination of London theatre audiences, and successfully challenged the ever-present American invasion. By customarily taking the non-singing romantic lead in several of his own productions, Novello also built an immense following with the female audience, despite the fact that in his private life he was homosexual. Apart from Hassall, who was the lyricist for six of his shows, Novello's other collaborators included P.G. Wodehouse, Clifford Grey, Harry Graham, Ronald Jeans, Howard Talbot, Dion Titheradge (especially for the song 'And Her Mother Came Too'), Adrian Ross, and Douglas Furber. In 1993, the centenary of his birth was marked by several celebratory shows around the UK, including one at the Players Theatre in London, and the tribute album, *Marilyn Hill Smith Sings Ivor Novello*, which contained 20 of his loveliest melodies.

● FURTHER READING: *Perchance To Dream: The World Of Ivor Novello*, Richard Rose. *Ivor Novello*, Sandy Wilson. *Ivor Novello: Man Of The Theatre*, Peter Noble.

NUNN, TREVOR

b. 14 January 1940, Ipswich, Suffolk, England. Nunn was educated at Downing College, Cambridge, and in 1962 won an ABC Director's Scholarship to the Belgrade Theatre in Coventry where he produced a musical version of *Around The World In 80 Days*. In 1964 he joined the Royal Shakespeare Company, was made an associate director in 1965, and became the company's youngest-ever artistic director in 1968. He was responsible for the running of the RSC until he retired from the post in 1986. As well as his numerous productions for the RSC, he co-directed *Nicholas Nickleby* (winner of five Tony Awards), *Peter Pan*, and *Les Misérables*, which became one of the most-performed musicals in the world. Outside of the RSC he has directed the Tony Award-winning *Cats*, along with other musicals including *Starlight Express*, *Chess*, and *The Baker's Wife*, and operas such as *Cosi Fan Tutte* and *Peter Grimes*. His 'magnificent' 1986 Glyndebourne Festival Opera production of *Porgy And Bess*, which later transferred to the London Royal Opera House, became the first television version of George Gershwin's masterpiece in 1993. He has also worked in television and directed several films including *Hedda* and *Lady Jane*. Nunn is credited, along with Andrew Lloyd Webber and the late poet T.S. Eliot, with the writing of 'Memory', the hit song from *Cats* which has been recorded by hundreds of artists. In 1992 he directed the RSC's highly acclaimed production of Pam Gems' musical play *The Blue Angel*, and a year later became the ninth recipient of the 'Mr. Abbott Award' given by the US Stage Directors and Choreographers Foundation. In the early 90s he was back with Lloyd

Webber again, staging the London, Los Angeles and Broadway productions of *Sunset Boulevard*. It was also reported that Nunn had decided to take a break from the theatre, and had signed a two-year deal to produce films for the New Line Cinema studio. However, in 1995, he did co-direct and supervise a one-night only all-star 10th anniversary concert performance of *Les Misérables* at London's Royal Albert Hall. A year later the movie *Twelfth Night*, which he scripted and directed, was released. In September 1997, Nunn took over from Richard Eyre as the artistic director of the Royal National Theatre, and in July of the following year his 'triumphant' staging of Richard Rodgers and Oscar Hammerstein II's *Oklahoma!* opened at the National's Olivier Theatre, subsequently transferring to the Lyceum in the West End. On behalf of the show, Nunn collected the *Evening Standard*/Carlton Television Award for Best Musical.

NUNSENSE

Originally presented at the Duplex nightspot in Greenwich Village in 1984, this spoof on the Catholic sisterhood - 'The Habit Forming Musical Comedy' - transferred to the off-Broadway Cherry Lane Theatre on 12 December 1985. It was the brainchild of Dan Goggin, who wrote the book (from an original libretto by Steve Hayes), music, and lyrics, and also staged it. The story concerns the efforts of the convent's five surviving nuns to raise money so that they can bury the last few of their 52 companions who died of botulism after having eaten a meal of vichyssoise prepared by the convent chef, Sister Julia. The quintet are still around because they went out to bingo that night. Sister Julia is preparing a cook book containing some of her best recipes (including barbecued spare-ribs), while the rest of the nuns decide to put on a musical so as to raise enough money to get rid of the bodies, thereby leaving more space in the deep-freeze. The energetic Mother Superior was played by comedienne Marilyn Farina, and the rest of a highly talented cast included Suzi Winston, Christine Anderson, Semina De Laurentis, and Vicki Belmonte. Among the lively and extremely relevant songs were 'Nunsense Is Habit-Forming', 'So You Want To Be A Nun', 'Tackle That Temptation', 'Growing Up A Catholic', 'I Want To Be A Star', 'Just A Coupl'a Sisters', 'I Could've Gone To Nashville', and 'Holier Than Thou'. The show ran and ran, and, in 1992, when it entered its eighth 'everlasting' year, was advertising itself as 'The longest-running show in off-Broadway history'. But what about *The Fantasticks*, which opened in 1960? An explanatory rider was attached which stated: '*The Fantasticks* is more than a show, it is an institution!'. In the early 90s, *Nunsense II: The Second Coming* was out of town on its way to New York, with the Mother Superior demanding more audience participation on numbers such 'Oh Dear, What Can The Matter Be', in which Franciscan nuns get locked in the lavatory. Meanwhile, the off-Broadway production of *Nunsense* closed in October 1994, ending a phenomenal run of 3,672 performances. It had also toured extensively. London audiences first saw a version in 1987, and sampled the show again in 1996. In that same year, the Chanhassen Theatre, Minneapolis, was Goggin's chosen launching pad

for *Sister Amnesia's Country And Western Nunsense Jamboree*, the third lively and engaging chapter in the Nunsense saga. An original member of the convent from way back, Sister Amnesia does not remember her real name ever since a crucifix fell on her head. In 1998 the Little Sisters of Hoboken hired the 47th Street Theatre off-Broadway for another fund-raising musical variety show entitled *Nunsense A-Men*. Only this time, the little sisters were actually little brothers.

NYMAN, MICHAEL

b. 23 March 1944, London, England. A composer, pianist, orchestra leader, and author, Nyman studied at the London Academy of Music (of which he is a Fellow) and at King's College, London. To the public at large, he is probably best known for his music to Jane Campion's award-winning 1993 film, *The Piano*, and for the 18 'propulsively pounding' film scores he composed for the idiosyncratic director and screenwriter, Peter Greenaway. Most notable amongst these are *The Draughtsman's Contract* (1982), *A Zed And Two Noughts* (1985), *Drowning By Numbers* (1988), *The Cook, The Thief, His Wife And Her Lover* (1989), and *Prospero's Books* (1991). The two men parted after Nyman discovered that his original score for *Prospero's Books* had been overlaid with what he called 'awful phoney electronic music'. Nyman's film music is just a part of a prolific and extremely varied output that has consisted of several operas (including *The Man Who Mistook His Wife For A Hat*), string quartets, a saxophone concerto ('Where The Bee Dances'), the libretto for Harrison Birtwhistle's dramatic pastoral, *Down By The Greenwoodside*, other classical works, and numerous commissions. He also collaborated on the Channel 4 film, *The Final Score*, in which he paid tribute to the game of football, and in particular to his own favourite club, Queen's Park Rangers. Nyman's score for *The Piano* received the Australian Film Institute Award for Best Original Music, was nominated for a Golden Globe Award, and won the first-ever Chicago Film Critics Award for Best Musical Score. Although the film was nominated for eight Oscars, Nyman's brilliant score was ignored. In 1995, London's South Bank Centre presented a celebratory festival, *Nyman On The South Bank*, which opened with an all-night showing of a number of films associated with him. It continued with performances by his various ensembles, which 'showed off the grandeur of Nyman's orchestral writing, the amplified power of the Michael Nyman Big Band, and the intimate delights of his chamber music'. Among the works performed at the festival were premieres of 'The Upside-Down Violin', with the Orquesta Andalusi de Tetuan from Morocco, Nyman's score for the film *Carrington*, as well as his 'Harpsichord Concerto' with Elisabeth Chojnacka, and 'Six Celan Songs', sung by Hilary Summers. His music, which effortlessly spans the pop/classical divide, has attracted great attention from concert-goers and critics alike, making him a unique figure in UK contemporary music.

● ALBUMS: *Decay Music* (Obscure 1978)★★★, *Michael Nyman* (Sheet 1982)★★★★, *The Kiss And Other Movements* (Editions EG 1987)★★★, *Michael Nyman: Box Set* (Venture 1989)★★★★, *And*

They Do/Zoo Caprices (TER 1988)★★★, *The Essential Michael Nyman* (Argo/Decca 1992)★★★★, *Time Will Pronounce* (Argo/Decca 1993)★★★, *The Piano* (Virgin 1993)★★★★, *Michael Nyman Live* (Virgin 1995)★★★, *Carrington* (Argo 1995)★★★, *AET (After Extra Time)* (Virgin 1996)★★★, Harpsicord, *Bassoon And Horn Concertos* (EMI Classics 1997)★★, *Gattaca OST* (Virgin 1998)★★★, *The Suit & The Photograph* (EMI 1998)★★★.
● FURTHER READING: *Experimental Music: Cage And Beyond*, Michael Nyman.

NYMPH ERRANT

A vehicle for the talented and glamorous Gertrude Lawrence, this show was unusual in that it was written specifically for the London stage by the celebrated American composer Cole Porter. It opened at the Adelphi Theatre on 6 October 1933, with book by Romney Brent which was based on James Laver's somewhat risqué novel. The story told of Evangeline Edwards (Gertrude Lawrence), who, after graduating from a Lausanne finishing school, travels around Europe in a fruitless, but amusing search for a man who will love her. Unsuitable candidates include a Russian violinist, a Greek slave trader and a Count of the Holy Roman Empire. The Adelphi's revolving stage was used to excellent effect by costume and set designer Doris Zinkeisen to conjure up stylish locations such as the Carnival at Venice, Athens by moonlight, and the stage of the Folies de Paris. Elisabeth Welch as Haidee Robinson, Austin Trevor as the French impresario André de Croissant, and Morton Selton in the role of a devilish rake, were all outstanding, but the evening belonged to Gertrude Lawrence. As usual, Porter's songs were both tuneful and witty, especially 'The Physician', in which Lawrence complained: 'He said my maxillaries were marvels/And found my sternum stunning to see/He did a double hurdle/When I shook my pelvic girdle/But he never said he loved me.' The rest of the songs, including 'It's Bad For Me', 'How Could We Be Wrong?', 'Nymph Errant', 'Solomon', and 'If You Like Les Belles Poitrines' were all of similarly high quality. The show was presented by impresario Charles B. Cochran, so it was inevitable that his 'Young Ladies' should turn up from time to time. Considering the quality of performers and the production, he must have been disappointed with a run of only 154 performances.

O LUCKY MAN

Noted British film director Lindsay Anderson (*This Sporting Life*, *If*) cast Malcolm McDowell in the leading role of this enthralling 1973 feature. Arthur Lowe, Ralph Richardson, Rachel Roberts and Helen Mirren were among the first-class supporting players. Screened at the Cannes Film Festival in its original three-hour form, *O Lucky Man* was later trimmed for US audiences. The plot revolved around the antics of a self-serving young man, initially intent on gratification, who later attempts to make amends for his perceived wrong-doings. The proceedings were suitably enhanced by a taut score from former Animals pianist/vocalist Alan Price. Aided by guitarist Colin Green, formerly of Georgie Fame's Blue Flames, Dave Markee (bass) and ex-Jethro Tull drummer Clive Bunker, Price committed some of his finest songs and performances to the project, notably 'Poor People', 'My Home Town' and the ironic title song. One of the finest British films of the early 70s, *O Lucky Man* demonstrates Price's maturity as a songwriter as well as Anderson's considerable cinematic gifts.

O'CONNOR, DONALD

b. Donald David Dixon Ronald O'Connor, 30 August 1925, Chicago, Illinois, USA. One of the most likeable and nimble of all Hollywood's song-and-dance-men, who seems to have retained his youthful looks and casual charm throughout a career spanning well over 50 years. O'Connor was the seventh child of parents who were circus and vaudeville performers. After his father died, Donald (aged three) joined his mother and two of his brothers in the family act until he made his film debut in the minor musical *Melody For Two* in 1937. A year later, at the age of only 13, he made a big impact in *Sing You Sinners* in which he completely captivated cinema audiences in his role as the younger brother of Fred MacMurray and Bing Crosby. The trio's version of 'Small Fry' was the highlight of the picture. After a few straight parts and one other musical, *On Your Toes*, O'Connor went back to vaudeville until 1941 when he signed a contract with Universal which resulted in supporting roles in musicals such as *What's Cookin'?*, *Private Buckaroo*, *Get Hep To Love*, and *Give Out Sisters*. These led to better parts in *It Comes Up Love*, *When Johnny Comes Marching Home*, *Strictly In The Groove*, and especially *Mister Big*. He was top-billed for the first time in *Top Man* (1943) with soprano Susanna Foster. Funny-girl Peggy Ryan was also in *Top Man*, and she joined O'Connor in several other films around this time, including *Chip Off The Old Block*, *This Is*

The Life, Follow The Boys, Bowery To Broadway, The Merry Monahans (all 1944) and *Patrick The Great* (1945). After service in the US Army, O'Connor 'stole' *Something In The Wind* from Universal's premiere female star, Deanna Durbin, and further re-established himself in *Are You With It?*, *Feudin' Fussin' And A-Fightin'*, and *Yes Sir, That's My Baby* for which he was teamed with Gloria DeHaven. He was paired with a rather more unusual partner next - a 'talking mule' named Francis. The popular series, which began with *Francis* (1950), continued until O'Connor called a halt, saying: 'When you've made six pictures and the mule still gets more mail than you do . . .' In 1950 O'Connor starred at the London Palladium, and, on his return to the USA, joined Gene Kelly and Debbie Reynolds for what is probably his best-remembered film - *Singin' In The Rain*. All the routines are classics, but O'Connor's marvellous solo moment, 'Make 'Em Laugh', a series of pratfalls and back-flips performed in the company of a headless dummy, was improvised by O'Connor himself, and remains one of the all-time great sequences from any movie musical. Ironically, he revealed recently that the first take was ruined by 'foggy film' in the camera, and he had to do the whole thing over again three days later. The early 50s were good times for O'Connor. He featured on television's *The Colgate Comedy Hour* for three years, and continued to sing, dance and clown his way through *Call Me Madam*, *I Love Melvin*, *Walking My Baby Back Home*, *There's No Business Like Show Business*, and *Anything Goes* (1956). After that, with the glossy big screen musical in a state of terminal decline, he returned to television, and played the big cabaret rooms and clubs throughout the USA. He continued to appear in the occasional straight roles in films such as *The Buster Keaton Story* (1957), *Ragtime* (with James Cagney in 1981), and *Toys* (1992). In the 80s he toured in revivals of immortal stage musicals such as *Show Boat*, and, later in the decade, was attracting enthusiastic reviews in Las Vegas for his shows with fellow movie legends Debbie Reynolds and Mickey Rooney. In June 1994 he brought his classy cabaret act to London for the opening of the capital's latest (ill-fated) cabaret space, the Connaught Room.

● FILMS: *Tom Sawyer, Detective* (1938), *Sing You Sinners* (1938), *Sons Of The Legion* (1938), *Men With Wings* (1938), *Unmarried* (1939), *Million Dollar Legs* (1939), *Night Work* (1939), *Boy Trouble* (1939), *Death Of A Champion* (1939), *Beau Geste* (1939), *On Your Toes* (1939), *When Johnny Comes Marching Home* (1942), *Private Buckaroo* (1942), *What's Cookin'?* (1942), *Give Out, Sisters* (1942), *Get Hep To Love* (1942), *Mister Big* (1943), *Top Man* (1943), *It Comes Up Love* (1943), *The Merry Mohahans* (1944), *This Is The Life* (1944), *Chip Off The Old Block* (1944), *Follow The Boys* (1944), *Bowery To Broadway* (1944), *Patrick The Great* (1945), *Something In The Wind* (1947), *Are You With It?* (1948), *Feudin', Fussin' And A'Fightin'* (1948), *Yes Sir, That's My Baby* (1949), *Francis* (1949), *The Milkman* (1950), *Double Crossbones* (1950), *Curtain Call At Cactus Creek* (1950), *Francis Goes To The Races* (1951), *Francis Goes To West Point* (1952), *Singin' In The Rain* (1952), *Francis Covers The Big Town* (1953), *Walking My Baby Back Home* (1953), *Call Me Madam* (1953), *I Love Melvin* (1953), *There's No Business Like Show Business* (1954), *Francis Joins the WACS* (1954), *Francis In The Navy* (1955), *Anything Goes* (1956), *The Buster Keaton Story* (1957), *The Wonders Of Aladdin* (1961), *Cry For Happy* (1961),

That Funny Feeling (1965), *That's Entertainment!* on-screen narrator (1974), *Ragtime* (1981), *Pandemonium* (1982), *A Time To Remember* (1987), *Toys* (1992), *Out To Sea* (1997).

OF THEE I SING

After George S. Kaufman's uncompromising book for *Strike Up The Band* had been replaced by a less contentious one by Morrie Ryskind, the two writers collaborated on the libretto for this show which has been called 'the greatest of all American musicals'. It opened at the Music Box Theatre in New York on 26 December 1931, complete with a sharp and witty plot in which most American institutions, especially family life and politics, come in for their fair share of satirical attention. John P. Wintergreen (William Gaxton) and his prospective Vice-President, Alexander Throttlebottom (Victor Moore), have discarded issues such as home and foreign affairs, and are running for office on a ticket of LOVE. In fact, Wintergreen issues a statement that he will propose to his Mary (Lois Moran) in every one of the 48 states. They are elected to the White House with a landslide victory, but, like so many presidents that followed him, Wintergreen's future is threatened by an indiscreet dalliance with the fairer sex - in his case, Diana Devereaux (Grace Brinkley), the current Miss America. Impeachment looms, but Wintergreen keeps his job after Throttlebottom offers to marry the beauty queen because, under the Constitution: 'When the President of the United States is unable to fulfil his duties, his obligations are assumed by the Vice President.' Gaxton and Moore were marvellous, and went on to star in several other musicals together, including *Anything Goes*, *Leave It To Me!*, and *Louisiana Purchase*. Once again, George and Ira Gershwin wrote a score that was both tuneful and entirely complementary to the action. Two of the songs matured into standards, 'Who Cares?' and 'Love Is Sweeping The Country', and the spirited 'Of Thee I Sing (Baby)' was also a hit at the time for Ben Selvin. The remainder of the score consisted of 'Wintergreen For President', 'Hello, Good Morning', 'The Illegitimate Daughter', and 'Because, Because'. As one of 29 new Broadway musicals that season, *Of Thee I Sing* enjoyed an excellent run of 441 performances, and returned two years later for a brief spell at the Imperial theatre. The show became the first musical to be awarded the prestigious Pulitzer Prize for Drama, although composer George Gershwin's music and name was omitted from the citation. Over the years, *Of Thee I Sing* was a leading candidate for revival in the US, especially at election time. When the Arena Stage in Washington presented the show in November 1992, each patron received a voting slip in their programme. The running total was chalked on the back wall of the auditorium, and, even early on in the campaign, there was a hint of things to come, with the Clinton-Gore ticket regularly beating Bush-Quayle by about four to one. In 1998, to mark the centenary of George Gershwin's birth, Britain's Opera North mounted a production, with William Dazeley (Wintergreen), Steven Beard (Throttlebottom), Margaret Preece (Mary), and Kim Criswell (Diana). It toured, and was broadcast on BBC Radio 3. In America, *Of Thee I Sing* was the last show in the 1998 Los Angeles *Reprise!* concert series, and featured Gregory Harrison (Wintergreen), Maureen McGovern (Mary), Heather Lee (Diana), and Charlie Dell (Throttlebottom).

OH! CALCUTTA!

A musical revue, devised in 1969 by Kenneth Tynan, the drama critic, and literary manager of Britain's National Theatre for 10 years, *Oh! Calcutta!* is rarely discussed in theatrical reference books. One of the excuses given for its omission is that it was not very good; but the main reason is surely that in most of the sketches the artists appear in the nude, and perform simulated sex acts. Tynan recruited John Lennon, Samuel Beckett, Jules Feiffer, Joe Orton, Sam Shepard, and others, to write material that reflected the sexual revolution that was taking place in the 'swinging sixties'; music and lyrics were credited to Open Window. The show opened in New York in June 1969 at the off-Broadway Eden Theatre, and was such a success that within a few months it was promoted to Broadway, where it stayed for 1,314 performances. The 1970 London production, taking advantage of the abolition of theatre censorship in 1968, ran for 3,918 performances. However, that impressive total paled in comparison with the 1976 Broadway revival which notched up an incredible total of 5,852. For many years that production was in second place in the Broadway long-running stakes, just behind *A Chorus Line* (6,137), but was overtaken by Andrew Lloyd Webber's *Cats* late in 1996. More than 20 years after its inception, *Oh! Calcutta!* continues to be controversial. In 1991, a judge in Chattanooga, Tennessee, overruled local officials and allowed the show to go on in a city-owned theatre. In both London and New York, its prolonged existence was often attributed to the patronage of visiting Japanese businessmen, so it was somewhat ironic that an American production opened in Tokyo in 1993 - albeit with some concessions involving partial body stockings and body paint.

OH, BOY!

This was the second musical comedy to be written by the young Anglo/American team of Jerome Kern (music), Guy Bolton (book), and P.G. Wodehouse (book and lyrics), and their first to be presented at the tiny Princess Theatre in New York. When *Oh, Boy!* opened there on 20 February 1917, it blew like a wind of change through the cobwebs of operetta that were hanging around most of the other Broadway shows. It was a jolly, contemporary production, unpretentious and thoroughly entertaining. There were elements of farce, too - people did seem to enter and leave through windows rather a lot - but the story was really about George Budd (Tom Powers). His main problem is to prevent his guardian, Aunt Penelope (Edna May Oliver), from discovering that he has just got married to Lou Ellen (Marie Carroll). If she does - there goes his allowance. When they learn of her imminent arrival, the newlyweds decided to part for a time - Lou Ellen's parents have not been informed of the situation either - and from that moment on, a series of complicated events ensues, during which Tom rescues the lovely actress, Jackie Sampson (Ann Wheaton), from the clutches of an amorous Judge Carter ('Tootles' to her), who eventually turns out to be his

(Tom's) father-in-law, and Aunt Penelope gives the happy couple (George and Lou Ellen) her blessing while under the influence of a glass of spiked lemonade. The cast played it all with great style, aided by a marvellous score that included the romantic couple's naive and wistful 'You Never Knew About Me' ('I'd have let you feed my rabbit/Till the thing became a habit, Dear!/But I never knew about you/Or what might have been/And you never knew about me.'). Jackie and Tom's best chum, Jim (Hal Forde), combined on another of the best numbers, 'Nesting Time In Flatbush', but there was not a dud among the rest of the bunch, which included 'Ain't It A Grand And Glorious Feeling', 'Be A Little Sunbeam', 'Every Day', 'The First Day Of May', 'FlubbyDub, The Cave Man', 'Land Where The Good Songs Go', 'A Pal Like You', 'Words Are Not Needed', 'An Old-Fashioned Wife', and 'A Package Of Seeds.' Another of the songs, 'Till the Clouds Roll By', became popular through recordings by Ann Wheaton with James Harrod, the Prince's Orchestra, and Vernon Dalhart. The tremendous success of *Oh, Boy!*, which ran for 475 performances, meant that the next Kern-Bolton-Wodehouse show, *Leave It To Jane*, which was originally intended for the Princess, had to be diverted to the much larger Longacre Theatre. In 1919, when the show was presented in London, it was retitled *Oh, Joy!*, and starred Beatrice Lillie in her first book musical. The title *Oh, Boy!* did eventually go up in lights in London's West End 60 years later, when a show starring pop stars such as Joe Brown, Shakin' Stevens, and Alvin Stardust that was based on the television show, played the Astoria Theatre.

OH, JOY!
(see *Oh, Boy!*)

OH, KAY!

This show provides the perfect argument for those who believe that 'they don't write them like that any more'. George and Ira Gershwin introduced four of the their all-time standards in *Oh, Kay!* which opened at the Imperial Theatre in New York on 8 November 1926, and the rest of the score was in the same class. Guy Bolton and P.G. Wodehouse, fresh from their successes with Jerome Kern, wrote the book in which the Kay of the title (Gertrude Lawrence in her first Broadway book musical) helps her hard-up ducal brother (Gerald Oliver Smith) - a bootlegger - illegally to import alcoholic beverages into the USA. They stash the booze on the Long Island estate of young and wealthy Jimmy Winter (Oscar Shaw), who is normally away and too busy enjoying himself at various shindigs to notice their comings and goings. However, when he returns, complications ensue, and Kay actually has to take a job in the household for a time, before Jimmy - cold sober - rejects his legion of admirers and decides to marry his 'Dear Little Girl'. Although not one of the hits from the show, it was a charming number, which Julie Andrews reprised in the Gertrude Lawrence biopic, *Star!* (1968). Kay and Jimmy's romance can only flourish, of course, after the two lovers have duetted on 'Maybe' and 'Do, Do, Do', and danced the night away with 'Clap Yo' Hands'. A more poignant moment occurs when, disguised as a housemaid, Kay 'meditates musically' - as Ira Gershwin put it - with the tender ballad, 'Someone To Watch Over Me'. 'Fidgety Feet' was another lively number by the two Gershwin brothers, but 'Oh, Kay!' and 'Heaven On Earth' both had lyrics by Howard Deitz who helped out when Ira Gershwin was ill. Victor Moore, one of America's favourite funny-men, returned to Broadway for the first time in 15 years in *Oh, Kay!*, and the cast also included Harland Dixon, Marion and Madeleine Fairbanks, Gerald Oliver, and Sascha Beaumont. The show ran for 256 performances, and Gertrude Lawrence recreated her role in the 1927 London production which lasted for six months. *Oh, Kay!* was revived off-Broadway in 1960, and was back in a main house, the Richard Rodgers Theatre, in 1990. The latter production, which started out at the Goodspeed Opera House in 1989, moved the show's location from Long Island to Harlem, and included an all-black cast. It closed after 77 performances, and producer David Merrick's attempt to re-stage it ended during previews. A reasonably successful West End revival was mounted in 1974, and 10 years later the show was a big hit when it played a season in England at the Chichester Festival Theatre, with the highly acclaimed Michael Siberry as Jimmy.

OH, LADY! LADY!!

Another of the celebrated Princess Theatre shows with a score by Jerome Kern and P.G. Wodehouse, and a book by Wodehouse and Guy Bolton It opened at the tiny theatre in New York on 1 February 1918, and proved to be the last really successful show that the team wrote together. This time the plot centres on the well-to-do Long Island home belonging to the parents of Mollie Farrington (Vivienne Segal). She is about to marry Willoughby 'Bill' Finch (Carl Randall), that is until May Barber (Carroll McComas) turns up and announces that, in the past, she and Bill have been more than just good friends. Mollie is aghast: could Bill really have a female skeleton in his closet? Actually, it's not Bill that May is after at all, but Mollie's parents' jewels. All ends happily when May is apprehended by Bill's associate (and former crook), Spike Hudgins (Edward Ebeles). A thoroughly entertaining score contained no immediately identifiable hits, although Kern's music and Wodehouse's lyrics were far superior than those of their contemporaries - always relevant to the libretto - and continually pushing musical comedy forward. The songs included 'Before I Met You', 'Dear Old Prison Days', 'Do Look At Him', 'Do It Now', 'I'm To Be Married Today', 'It's A Hard, Hard World For A Man', 'Little Ships Come Sailing Home', 'Moon Song' 'Not Yet', 'Our Little Nest', 'A Picture I Want To See Of You', 'Some Little Girl', 'Waiting Round The Corner', 'You Found Me And I Found You', and 'Greenwich Village'. The latter number was featured in a spectacular rooftop sequence set in that New York location. One song was discarded during rehearsals because it was not considered suitable for Vivienne Segal's voice. It almost got to Broadway via *Zip Goes A Million* in 1919, but eventually had to wait until 1927 before it was introduced to the world by Helen Morgan in the magnificent *Show Boat*. The song in question was 'Bill'. Even without it, *Oh, Lady! Lady!!* had an excellent run of 219 performances.

OH, WHAT A LOVELY WAR!

This 'British musical entertainment' started out at the Theatre Royal, Stratford East in March 1963 before transferring to Wyndham's Theatre on 29 June that year. The cast consisted mainly of members of the Theatre Royal's 'repertory company', such as George Sewell, Avis Bunnage, Brian Murphy, Victor Spinetti, *et al*. Some of them collaborated with librettist Charles Chilton on the book, which purported to reflect the misery and sheer waste of human life during World War I from the coercive recruitment methods ('We Don't Want To Lose You, But We Think You Ought To Go') to the grim reality of the trenches. This was achieved in an intelligent and humorous fashion by the use of more than 20 popular songs of the period, such as 'Your King And Country Need You', 'I'll Make A Man Of You', 'Goodbye ee', 'When This Lousy War Is Over', 'Hush, Here Comes A Whizzbang', 'Belgium Put The Kibosh On the Kaiser', 'Keep The Home Fires Burning', 'I Want To Go Home', and Jerome Kern's lovely ballad 'They Didn't Believe Me'. Although some aspects of what started out at Stratford as a bitter anti-war tract were softened somewhat for West End audiences, the message remained loud and clear, and *Oh, What A Lovely War!* continued to spell it out for more than two years, during which time it won the *Evening Standard* Award for best musical. The appeal proved not to be so great in America, although Victor Spinetti won a Tony Award for best supporting actor, and the show folded after three and a half months. The 1969 film, directed by Richard Attenborough, adopted a different, star-studded approach. A rare revival of *Oh, What A Lovely War!* was presented by the UK National Youth Theatre in 1994 at the Bloomsbury Theatre in London. Four years later, exactly 35 years after the show's Stratford East premiere, a Royal National Theatre production, directed by Fiona Laird, embarked on a UK tour. On arrival in London, the show settled in at the Round House, giving that venue its first period of sustained life for nearly two decades.

OKLAHOMA! (FILM MUSICAL)

The show that opened on Broadway in 1943, and is credited with being a significant turning point in the history of the musical theatre, was transferred to the screen in the less than glorious Todd-AO widescreen process in 1955. The skilful integration of Richard Rodgers and Oscar Hammerstein II's wonderful songs into the sentimental but sincere story for which the stage production was so rightly admired, was equally impressive in this celluloid version. The action takes place just after the turn of the century, on and around a ranch in the Oklahoma Territory, where Laurey (Shirley Jones) lives with her Aunt Eller (Charlotte Greenwood). The handsome and decent Curly (Gordon MacRae) and the evil-looking and devious Jud (Rod Steiger) both want to take Laurey to the 'box social'. Her decision to spite Curly (with whom she actually wants to go) by accepting Jud's invitation, sets off a train of events that culminates in Jud's death, for which Curly is immediately blamed, but just as swiftly exonerated. Jones and MacRae were perfect together, and the supporting cast was exceptionally fine, with Gene Nelson as

Will Parker and Gloria Grahame as his girlfriend Ado Annie, who 'just cain't say no'. Eddie Albert played a travelling peddler-man, Ali Akim, whose indiscriminate use of a kissing technique known in his native country as 'A Persian Goodbye', results in a shotgun wedding. Other parts were taken by James Whitmore, Marc Platt, Barbara Lawrence and Roy Barcroft. Dancers James Mitchell and Bambi Lynn were stunning in the ballet sequence to the music of 'Out Of My Dreams'. Most of the rest of Rodgers and Hammerstein's rich and varied score was retained, and included all the favourites such as 'Oh, What A Beautiful Mornin'', 'The Surrey With The Fringe On Top', 'Kansas City', 'I Cain't Say No', 'Many A New Day', 'People Will Say We're In Love', 'Poor Jud Is Dead', 'The Farmer And The Cowman', 'All Er Nothin'', and the rousing 'Oklahoma'. Choreographer Agnes de Mille and musical arranger Robert Russell Bennett adapted their original stage work for the film, and Russell Bennett, together with Jay Blackton and Adolph Deutsch, won Oscars for 'scoring of a musical picture'. It was photographed in Technicolor and produced by Magna by Arthur Hornblow Jnr. The director was Fred Zinnemann. Sonya Levian and William Ludwig's screenplay was adapted from the original libretto by Oscar Hammerstein II, which was based on Lynn Riggs' play *Green Grow The Lilacs*.

OKLAHOMA! (STAGE MUSICAL)

If one show can be said to mark the turning-point in the history of the American musical theatre then it must be *Oklahoma!* Although some of its innovative features had been attempted previously, sometimes successfully, never before had such features as a ballet sequence and a serious plot blended so well into a production that had such great dramatic merit and was filled with so many wonderful songs. Conceived by the Theatre Guild, *Oklahoma!* is set just after the turn of the century, at the time when a section of Indian territory is about to become a US state. Oscar Hammerstein II's book, which was based on Lynn Riggs' play *Green Grow The Lilacs*, traces the love affairs of two contrasting couples. Upstanding Curly McLain (Alfred Drake) eventually wins the hand of Laurey Williams (Joan Roberts) in spite of menacing opposition from disreputable farmhand Jud Fry (Howard Da Silva), watched over by no-nonsense Aunt Eller Murphy (Betty Garde). Travelling tinker Ali Hakim (Joseph Buloff), on the other hand, comes up against a furious father with a shotgun when he tries to woo Ado Annie Carnes (Celeste Holm) away from Will Parker (Lee Dixon), who demands 'All Er Nothin''. She, unashamedly - and delightfully - confesses 'I Cain't Say No'. The remainder of Richard Rodgers and Hammerstein's fine score included the memorable opening 'Oh, What A Beautiful Mornin'', 'The Surrey With The Fringe On Top', 'Kansas City', 'Many A New Day', 'People Will Say We're In Love', 'The Farmer And The Cowman', 'Pore Jud Is Daid', 'Out Of My Dreams', and the rousing finale, 'Oklahoma'. Prior to the Broadway opening on 31 March 1943 at the St. James Theatre, many theatre watchers had reservations about the show, feeling that the combination of an only moderately successful play source, along with the first collaboration between Hammerstein, who had been without

a hit for some time, and Rodgers, now without his long-time partner Lorenz Hart, was a shaky foundation. After that memorable first night all doubts vanished. The superb staging by Rouben Mamoulian, supplemented by Agnes De Mille's wonderful choreography, and above all that now-famous score, made this the most momentous musical event of several decades. During the run of 2,212 performances, Howard Keel was one of the artists to take over the role of Curly, and he headed the cast of the 1947 London production, which also featured Betty Jane Watson (Laurey), Mary Marlo (Aunt Eller), Henry Clarke (Jud), Marek Windheim (Ali), Dorothea MacFarland (Ado Annie), and Walter Donahue (Will). The production ran for 1,548 performances. London audiences - still rooted in the 30s sophistication of Noël Coward and Ruritania operetta of Ivor Novello - were overwhelmed. *Oklahoma!* was prominent in the first wave of the one-way transatlantic musical tide that would take three decades to reverse. The show became a permanent feature on the theatrical scene throughout the world, with touring companies seemingly forever on the road. In 1969, there was a Lincoln Center revival with Bruce Yarnell (Curly), Leigh Beery (Laurey), Margaret Hamilton (Aunt Eller), April Shawhan (Ado Annie), and Lee Roy Reams (Will). A decade later, a brand new production directed by Oscar's son, William Hammerstein, with Laurence Guittard (Curly), Christine Andreas (Laurey), Mary Wickes (Aunt Eller), Martin Vidnovic (Jud), Christine Ebersole (Ado Annie), and Harry Groener (Will), spent nine months on Broadway. A 1980 London mounting, directed by another Hammerstein son, James - starring John Diedrich (Curly), Rosamund Shelley (Laurey), Madge Ryan (Aunt Eller), Jillian Mack (Ado Annie), Mark White (Will), Alfred Molina (Jud), Linal Haft (Ali) - gave impresario Cameron Mackintosh one of the first of his many West End successes. In 1993, the show's 50th anniversary was marked by a special Tony Award, and several more productions worldwide. Five years later, Trevor Nunn's acclaimed Royal National Theatre revival starred another Australian, Hugh Jackman (Curly), Josefina Gabrielle (Laurey), Maureen Lipman (Aunt Eller), Jimmy Johnston (Will), Shuler Hensley (Jud), Vicki Simon (Ado Annie), and Peter Polycarpou (Ali). For what is said to be the first time in the lifetime of this 55-year-old show, the Rodgers And Hammerstein estate allowed Agnes De Mille's original choreography to be replaced by that of Susan Stroman. Her new work was greeted warmly from all sides, and the show won the 1998 *Evening Standard*/Carlton Television Award for Best Musical. The 1955 film version of *Oklahoma!* starred Gordon MacRae and Shirley Jones.
● FURTHER READING: *OK! The Story Of Oklahoma!*, Max Wilk.

OLIVER! (FILM MUSICAL)

'Please sir, can I have some more' was not just the tragic cry of the young orphan in Charles Dickens' famous story, but the plea of theatregoers both in Britain and on Broadway when they witnessed the tremendous success of Lionel Bart's stage musical *Oliver!* in the early 60s. Therefore, it was not surprising that the film adaptation of the stage hit, released in December 1968, with just two songs missing from the original score, did so well and became such a favourite with adults and children alike. Adapted for the screen by Vernon Harris, this musical version of the Dickens story follows young Oliver (Mark Lester) as he runs away from his desperately unhappy existence in a poor-house and his job as an undertaker's assistant, only to find himself lost in the big city. Here he meets the worldly wise Artful Dodger (Jack Wild), and falls in with a group of young pickpockets. At the head of this gang is Fagin (Ron Moody in the part he originally played on stage), a scoundrel who always keeps one eye on his 'bank' balance and the other on the boys in his charge. It is in Fagin's hideout that Oliver has his first stealing lessons, but the innocent boy gets caught on one of his first attempts. His subsequent arrest leads to the discovery of a loving and wealthy relative, and, eventually a happy ending to the story. Oliver Reed gives a truly villainous performance as Bill Sikes, and Shani Wallis is more than adequate in the role of Nancy, the girl who loves despite his evil nature. Directed by Carol Reed, and produced by John Woolf, *Oliver!* is an enchanting film full of great musical sequences and emotional drama. Mark Lester is perfectly innocent in the leading role. His rendition of the plaintive 'Where is Love?' tugs at the audience's heartstrings, and the scene in Fagin's den when he joins Nancy for 'I'd Do Anything' is gentle and touching. Other highlights include Nancy's powerful reaffirmation of her love for Bill in 'As Long As He Needs Me', and Fagin's 'You've Got To Pick A Pocket Or Two' which is a quirky and irresistible celebration of villainy, while his indecision and frustration are perfectly captured in the witty lyrics of 'Reviewing The Situation'. However, it is not just the individual performances that make the film so successful. The ensemble musical numbers are often breathtaking, ranging from the fantasizing of 'Food Glorious Food' to the brotherhood of 'Consider Yourself'. The rest of the fine score includes 'Boy For Sale', 'Who Will Buy?', and the joyous 'Oom-Pah-Pah'. Among the excellent supporting cast were Harry Secombe, Leonard Rossiter, Hugh Griffith, Fred Emney and James Hayter. The film was beautifully photographed in Technicolor and Panavision by Oswald Morris. *Oliver!* won five Oscars, for best picture, director, choreographer (Onna White), and remains one of the all-time great British movies.

OLIVER! (STAGE MUSICAL)

Soon after it opened at the New Theatre in London on 30 June 1960, *Oliver!* was an instant success, winning rave reviews and ecstatic audiences. With book, music and lyrics by Lionel Bart, the show's storyline was reasonably faithful to *Oliver Twist*, the Charles Dickens novel upon which it was based. Filled with memorable songs, from sweet ballads to comic masterpieces, the show had the benefit of a strong cast and one performance that ranks among the genre's finest - Ron Moody's Fagin was worth the price of admission alone. Well supported by a cast that included Georgia Brown as Nancy, Danny Sewell (Bill Sikes), Barry Humphries (Mr. Sowerberry), Sonia Fraser (Mrs. Sowerberry), Paul Whitsun-Jones (Mr. Bumble), Hope Jackman (Mrs. Corney), Betty Turner (Old Sally), Trevor Ray (Noah Claypole), Dian Grey (Bet), George Bishop (Mr. Brownlow), Claude Jones (Mr. Grimwig),

Madeline Newbury (Mrs. Bedwin), and a succession of good Olivers (Keith Hampshire, Royston Thomas, Martin Stephens) and Artful Dodgers (Martin Horsey, Tony Robinson, Michael Goodman), *Oliver!* was excellent entertainment, although the book, which followed young Oliver's journey from the workhouse, via 'employment' in Fagin's gang of thieves, to eventual security with newfound members of his own family, was considered rather lightweight compared to the original Dickens. However, no such reservations were expressed about Bart's thrilling songs, which included 'As Long As He Needs Me', 'Where Is Love?', 'Food, Glorious Food', 'Consider Yourself', 'You've Got To Pick A Pocket Or Two', 'Come Back Soon', 'I Shall Scream', 'Who Will Buy?', 'Oom-Pah-Pah', 'I'd Do Anything' and 'Reviewing The Situation'. The show also had the benefit of extraordinary sets by Sean Kenny, much-admired to the point of outright copying in later years. *Oliver!* ran for 2,618 performances in London, while Georgia Brown, Barry Humphries, and Danny Sewell reprised their roles, with Clive Revill as Fagin, for the 1963 New York production which ran at the Imperial and Shubert Theatres for nearly two years. The Broadway production won Tony Awards for composer and lyricist (Bart), scenic designer (Kenny), and musical director-conductor (Donald Pippin). The 1968 film version dropped a song or two, inexplicably replaced Brown with Shani Wallis, but fortunately preserved Moody's performance for all time. There were also good child actors in Mark Lester as Oliver and, particularly, Jack Wild as the Artful Dodger. Other young stars in the latter role have included Phil Collins and Steve Marriott. Not surprisingly, *Oliver!* has been revived many times over the years by amateur and professional companies alike, most recently in Cameron Mackintosh's major production at the London Palladium which opened on 8 December 1994 with a £7 million box office advance. Directed by Sam Mendes, it starred Jonathan Pryce as Fagin, Sally Dexter as Nancy, Miles Anderson (Bill), Gregory Bradley/James Daley (Oliver), and Paul Bailey/Adam Searles (Dodger). Searles virtually stole the show on the first night. The lavish £3.5 million presentation was generally enthusiastically received by the critics - and Lionel Bart - who, courtesy of Cameron Mackintosh, recouped a portion of the show's rights which he had sold many years earlier. Subsequent cast changes included Claire Moore, Ruthie Henshall, and Sonia Swaby (the first time a black actress had played the role in the West End) as Nancy, and in the part of Fagin - George Layton (a holiday replacement), Jim Dale, Russ Abbott, and Robert Lindsay, who won a Laurence Olivier Award for his outstanding performance. In May 1997, Barry Humphries, by now well known worldwide for his portrayal of Australian superstar Dame Edna Everage, took over the role of Fagin. After creating the part of undertaker Sowerberry in the original London production, Humphries had played Fagin in the 1967 revival of *Oliver!* at the Piccadilly Theatre. Some 30 years later, on 8 July 1997, he was leading the cast when *Oliver!* became the longest-running show in the history of the London Palladium.

OLIVIER, LAURENCE, AWARDS

These awards are presented by the Society of West End Theatre in recognition of distinguished artistic achievement in West End Theatre. They were established in 1976 as the Society of West End Theatre Awards. Lord Olivier agreed to have his name associated with them in 1984 and they are now regarded as the highlight of the British theatrical year. The Awards are judged by three separate panels; for theatre, opera, and dance. The Theatre Panel comprises seven people chosen for their specialist knowledge and professional experience, plus six members of the theatre-going public. Anyone who applies to be included in the latter group should be prepared to see some 80 productions during the Awards year. The musical categories consist of: best director choreographer, actress, actor, supporting performance, revival, and the American Express Award for Best Musical. A musical production, or those associated with it, can also conceivably win in other sections such as best entertainment, costume design, lighting design, set design, outstanding achievement, and lifetime achievement. In 1993, the musicals prizes all went to the highly acclaimed British productions of the American shows *Carousel*, *Crazy For You*, and *Assassins*. The bronze Laurence Olivier Award itself was specially commissioned by the Society from the sculptor Harry Franchetti and represents the young Laurence Olivier as Henry V at the Old Vic in 1937.

ON A CLEAR DAY YOU CAN SEE FOREVER

Alan Jay Lerner's long-time partnership with Frederick Loewe had lapsed by the early 60s partly owing to the composer's ill-health, when he decided to write a Broadway show based on his absorbing interest in the subject of extrasensory perception (ESP). Lerner's first choice for a project that was originally entitled *I Picked A Daisy*, was Richard Rodgers, who had been searching for a new partner since the death of Oscar Hammerstein II in 1960. According to reports, the collaboration resulted in the irresistible force meeting the immovable object, so Lerner turned instead to Burton Lane. The new show, now called *On A Clear Day You Can See Forever*, made its debut at the Mark Hellinger theatre on 17 October 1965. In Lerner's book, Dr. Mark Bruckner (John Cullum) discovers that one of his patients, Daisy Gamble (Barbara Harris), can not only foresee the future and persuade her plants to grow by just talking to them, but is prepared to go into details about her life as Melinda, an early feminist, who lived in 18th century London. They fall in love, but when Daisy begins to believe (mistakenly) that Mark is more interested in Melinda than in her, she walks out. Although miles away, she hears and responds when he gives out with 'Come Back To Me' ('Leave behind all you own/Tell your flowers you'll telephone/Let your dog walk alone/Come back to me!'). McCallum also had two lovely ballads, the title song, 'On A Clear Day (You Can See Forever)', and 'Melinda'. The remainder of a fine score included the delightful 'Hurray! It's Lovely Up Here', 'She Wasn't You', 'Wait Till We're Sixty-Five', 'When I'm Being Born Again', 'What Did I Have That I Don't Have?', 'Don't

Tamper With My Sister', and 'Tosy And Cosh'. The show ran for an unsatisfactory 280 performances and, as usual, while Lerner's lyrics were admired, his book came in for a deal of criticism. Barbara Harris was particularly applauded for her work, but, in the 1970 film, her role was taken by Barbra Streisand, who co-starred with Yves Montand.

ON THE AVENUE

After enjoying tremendous success in partnership with several American leading ladies in movie musicals such as *42nd Street*, *Dames* and the *Gold Diggers* series, Dick Powell teamed with English actress Madeleine Carroll for this picture, which was released by 20th Century-Fox in 1937. Carroll plays wealthy socialite Mimi Caraway who objects violently to being lampooned in a satirical revue by Gary Blake (Dick Powell). Naturally, they eventually resolve their differences and fall in love. This leaves Blake's previous girlfriend, Mona Merrick (Alice Faye), out in the cold, but she consoles herself by singing the lion's share of Irving Berlin's wonderful score, including the enduring 'This Year's Kisses', 'He Ain't Got Rhythm' and 'Slumming On Park Avenue' (the last two with the Ritz Brothers); and 'I've Got My Love To Keep Me Warm' and 'The Girl On The Police Gazette' (both with Dick Powell). Powell himself had the superior 'You're Laughing At Me', which later became popular for Fats Waller. Also among the cast of *On The Avenue* were Alan Mowbray, George Barbier, Cora Witherspoon, Walter Catlett, Billy Gilbert, and Stepin Fetchit. Gene Markey and William Conselman wrote the amusing screenplay, the stylish dances were staged by Seymour Felix, and the film was directed by Roy Del Ruth. The basic plot of this film was used again in *Let's Make Love* (1960) starring Marilyn Monroe, Yves Montand and Frankie Vaughan.

ON THE RIVIERA

Post-war cinema audiences were given a double ration of Danny Kaye in this Sol C. Siegel Technicolor production when it was released by 20th Century-Fox in 1951. Henry and Phoebe Ephron's screenplay concerned a well-known nightclub entertainer who is the spitting image of a philandering businessman. If that plot sounds familiar, it is because it cropped up on the screen in *Folies Bergère De Paris* (1934) and *That Night In Rio* (1941), and, with a slight twist and another change in location, formed the basis of *On The Double* (1961). Kaye played both roles, of course, and had a great time with all the complications that naturally spring from this kind of situation. Gene Tierney was the businessman's wife who could not tell the difference between her real husband and his stand-in, and also taking part in the hilarious shenanigans were Corinne Calvert, Marcel Dalio, Clinton Sundberg, Henri Letondal, Sig Ruman, and Joyce McKenzie. Future dancing star Gwen Verdon was in the chorus. Sylvia Fine, Kaye's wife, tailored four songs especially for him: 'Popo The Puppet', 'Rhythm Of Romance', 'Happy Ending', 'On The Riviera', and he also sang one of his much-loved favourites, the 1913 number 'Ballin' The Jack' (James Henry Burris-Chris Smith). Jack Cole staged the imaginative dance sequences, and the film was directed by Walter Lang.

ON THE ROAD WITH DUKE ELLINGTON

A remarkable film record, made originally in 1967 and updated after Duke Ellington's death in 1974. In addition to Ellington talking about his life there are sequences showing him receiving honorary doctorates, rehearsing and recording his orchestra, playing the piano and, most intriguing of all, composing and arranging. If anything, the casual manner in which he does this simply adds to the mystique. Sprawled out on a couch, feet up, he and Billy Strayhorn put together a piece of music with such deceptive ease as to make even a Hollywood songwriter biopic seem forced. Apart from the Maestro, musicians such as Harry Carney, Jimmy Hamilton, Johnny Hodges, Paul Gonsalves and Louis Armstrong also make appearances.

ON THE TOWN (FILM MUSICAL)

Remembered particularly for its innovative staging of some of the musical sequences on the streets of New York, *On The Town* was released by MGM in 1949. Betty Comden and Adolph Green's screenplay (they also wrote all the lyrics) was based on their book for the 1944 stage musical, which itself was inspired by choreographer-director Jerome Robbins' ballet *Fancy Free*. From the moment that the three sailors, played by Gene Kelly, Frank Sinatra, and Jules Munshin, come dashing from their ship to the strains of the rousing 'New York, New York' (music-Leonard Bernstein), eager to enjoy the delights of New York on their 24 hours' leave, the film sings and dances along in an exhilarating fashion. Naturally, they each find their ideal partner: Kelly first sees the girl of his dreams, Vera-Ellen, on a poster in the subway, and their delightful *pas-de-deux*, 'Main Street' (music-Roger Edens), is one of the film's many high spots; Munshin is pursued through the Museum of Natural History by the anthropological Ann Miller who considers him to be a perfect example of a 'Prehistoric Man' (music-Edens); while the ingenuous Sinatra is invited to 'Come Up To My Place' (music-Bernstein) by the amusingly man-hungry taxi driver Betty Garrett. Stage musical buffs were offended by the way Bernstein's original Broadway score was 'decimated', with only five numbers surviving - the two already mentioned, plus 'I Feel Like I'm Not Out Of Bed Yet' and two ballets, 'Miss Turnstiles' and 'A Day In New York'. The substitutes, with music by Roger Edens, included 'You're Awful' and 'On The Town'. Edens was also co-musical director with Lennie Hayton, and both men won Oscars for music scoring. Alice Pearce recreated her original stage role as Betty Garrett's flatmate, a girl with a permanent cold, and also in the cast were Florence Bates, Carol Haney, Hans Conried, and George Meader. Gene Kelly and Stanley Donen's first film together was photographed in Technicolor and produced by Arthur Freed.

ON THE TOWN (STAGE MUSICAL)

Opening on 28 December 1944, *On The Town* was based on the 20-minute ballet, *Fancy Free*, by choreographer Jerome Robbins and composer Leonard Bernstein. Robbins had been on Broadway before, as a dancer, but for Bernstein, and librettists and lyricists Betty Comden and Adolph Green, *On The Town* was their first taste of the glamorous New York musical theatre. The 'almost non-existent book' concerns three sailors, Gaby (John Battles), Ozzie (Adolph Green), and Chip (Cris Alexander) who are on leave in New York for just 24 hours. They meet three girls, Ivy (Sono Osato), Hildy (Nancy Walker), and Claire (Betty Comden), and all enthusiastically take in tourist spots such as Coney Island, the Museum of Natural History, Central Park, Carnegie Hall, Times Square, and a dive called Diamond Eddie's. The thrilling score ranged from the rousing 'New York, New York', through the amusing 'Ya Got Me', 'Come Up To My Place', 'I Can Cook, Too', and 'I Get Carried Way', to the lovely ballads, 'Lonely Town', 'Lucky To Be Me', and 'Some Other Time'. At the end of the boys' day of freedom, the girls see them off at the quay - and another batch of sailors come careering down the gangplank singing 'New York, New York', and the whole process begins all over again. *On The Town* enjoyed a run of 463 performances and was revived twice in New York, off-Broadway in 1959 (Harold Lang, Wisa D'Orso, and Pat Carroll), and in a main house in 1971, with Ron Husman, Donna McKechnie, Bernadette Peters and Phyllis Newman (Mrs. Adolph Green). A 1963 London production folded after 53 performances. There was renewed interest in the show almost 30 years later, when, in June 1992, a semi-staged version, narrated by Comden and Green, was presented at London's Barbican Hall, and then, in 1993, the Goodspeed Opera House in Connecticut, USA, mounted a well-received production. In August 1997, the Joseph Papp Public Theatre/New York Shakespeare Festival presented a revival that was performed out of doors in Central Park's Delacorte Theatre. Directed by George C. Wolfe ('arguably the hottest producer and director in US theatre'), the cast consisted mostly of unknowns - and admission was free. When the show transferred to Broadway's Gershwin Theatre on 21 November 1998, the cast included Robert Montano (Ozzie), Jesse Tyler Ferguson (Chip), Perry Laylon Ojeda (Gaby), Tai Jimenez (Ivy Smith), Lea DeLaria (Hildy), and Sarah Knowlton (Claire DeLoone). As with the production in the Park, Robbins' original choreography was replaced - the credited Broadway choreographer was Keith Young. Despite an expensive television advertising campaign, *On The Town* closed on 17 January after a run of less than two months. The 1949 film starred Frank Sinatra, Gene Kelly, Jules Munshin, Vera-Ellen, Ann Miller, and Betty Garrett.

ON THE TWENTIETH CENTURY

In the long history of the musical theatre, this was probably not the first occasion on which the critics inferred that 'the audience left the theatre whistling the scenery'. However, that phrase did crop up a lot (along with 'it ran out of steam') in the reviews for this show which opened at the St. James Theatre in New York on 19 February 1978, and was set mostly aboard the fondly remembered train, the Twentieth Century Limited, which used to run from Chicago to New York. The set was certainly spectacular - a splendid art-deco affair - designed by Robin Wagner. The book, by Betty Comden and Adolph Green, which was based on Ben Hecht and Charles MacArthur's farce, *Twentieth Century*, concerns the legendary producer-director, Oscar Jaffee (John Cullum), a Broadway legend - but not recently. He is at the bottom of the barrel, but his former lover and protegée, the temperamental movie star Lily Garland (Madeline Kahn), is at the top of the tree. His efforts to sign her for a project that will ensure his reha-bilitation bring him into contact with the current rivals for her attention, actor Bruce Granit (played by Kevin Kline, himself a film heart-throb of the 80s and 90s), and the film producer Max Jacobs (George Lee Andrews). The veteran Broadway comedienne Imogene Coca, making a welcome comeback to the New York musical stage after an absence of over 30 years, played a kooky religious character with a great deal of fervour. The score was written by Comden and Green together with composer Cy Coleman. His music, which is usually jazz-based, like the man himself, was regarded this time as being too flamboyant and out of character, 'alternating much of the time between early nineteenth century comic-opera mannerisms and early twentieth century operetta', in songs such as 'I Rise Again', 'Veronique', 'On The Twentieth Century', 'Our Private World', 'Repent', 'We've Got It', 'She's A Nut', 'Legacy', 'Never', 'Life Is Like A Train', 'Together', 'Stranded Again', and 'Mine'. In spite of the criticism, the show won Tony Awards for score, book, Cullum, and Kline, and stayed on the rails for 449 performances. Cullum is said to have based his portrayal of the mogul on John Barrymore, who appeared with Carole Lombard in the 1934 film *Twentieth Century*. The 1980 West End pro-duction of *On The Twentieth Century* starred Julia McKenzie, one of the outstanding leading ladies of the London musical theatre, but it still ground to a halt after only 165 performances.

ON WITH THE DANCE

Noël Coward's first revue for impresario Charles B. Cochran opened at the Pavilion, in London's Piccadilly Circus, on 30 April 1925. Coward wrote the book and most of the songs, with Philip Braham providing a few extra numbers. The cast included Hermione Baddeley, Douglas Byng, Ernest Thesiger, Greta Fayne, and Lance Lister. The star was Alice Delysia, who introduced 'Poor Little Rich Girl', a song which Cochran thought 'dreary' and threat-ened to remove at the show's dress rehearsal. It survived, and went on to become one of Coward's most enduring copyrights. Among the other Coward numbers were 'That Means Nothing To Me', 'Lady Bird', and 'First Love'. The lavish, superbly presented show also contained two bal-lets created and danced by Leonide Massine, and enjoyed a run of 229 performances.

ON YOUR TOES

Ballet came to Broadway in a big way, courtesy of choreo-grapher George Balanchine, in this show which opened at the Imperial Theatre in New York on 11 April 1936. Richard Rodgers and Lorenz Hart wrote the book, along with George Abbott, and their complex plot involved Junior Dolan (Ray Bolger), who has given up the grind of the vaudeville circuit in favour of teaching music at the Knickerbocker University. When the Russian Ballet stage

a production of a jazzy, insinuating ballet, 'Slaughter On Tenth Avenue', in the locale, Junior becomes involved, both onstage and off, with its prima ballerina, Vera Barnova (Tamara Geva). This Pavlovian *pas de deux* offends both Junior's girlfriend, Frankie Frayne (Doris Carson), and Vera's regular dancing partner, who tries to have Junior bumped off. Bolger, in a part that was origi-nally created for Fred Astaire, was sensational in his first Broadway role, and soon became one of America's most cherished clowns. Balanchine's choreography, which included a second ballet, 'Princess Zenobia', was highly praised. The show also marked the acting debut of the for-mer Yale professor, Monty Woolley, as the director of the ballet company. Rodgers and Hart's lively and tuneful score was right up to their highest standard, and contained the delightful 'There's A Small Hotel' and It's Got to Be Love', sung by Carson and Bolger, a poignant ballad, 'Glad To Be Unhappy', the comical 'Too Good For The Average Man', and other pleasing numbers such as 'The Heart Is Quicker Than The Eye', 'The Three B's', 'On Your Toes', and 'Quiet Night'. *On Your Toes* danced along for 315 per-formances, and in 1937 was presented at the Palace Theatre in London with Vera Zorina in the leading role. She also starred in a 1954 Broadway revival with Bobby Van and Elaine Stritch. When *On Your Toes* returned to Broadway again in 1983, the role of Vera was played by the celebrated ballerina, Natalia Makarova, during the early part of a run of 505 performances. Both revivals were staged by George Abbott. Makarova also co-starred with Tim Flavin in a successful West End presentation in 1984. 'Slaughter On Tenth Avenue' reached a wider audience when it was danced by Gene Kelly and Vera-Ellen in the Rodgers and Hart biopic, *Words And Music* (1948).

ONCE UPON A MATTRESS

This is an expanded musical adaptation of the comical fairy tale, *The Princess And The Pea*, with music by Mary Rodgers, daughter of the famous composer, Richard Rodgers, and lyrics by Marshall Barer. The show opened off-Broadway at the Phoenix Theatre in New York on 11 May 1959, transferring to the Alvin Theatre on Broadway in November. The book, by Jay Thompson, Dean Fuller, and Barer, told of Princess Winnifred (Carol Burnett), who is unable to marry Prince Dauntless the Drab (Joseph Bova), until she can prove to his mother, Queen Agravain (Jane White), that she is a genuine princess of royal blood. She triumphs during a series of tests, the last of which is to get no sleep at all during a night spent on a heap of mat-tresses with just one pea underneath the bottom one. Comedienne extraordinaire Carol Burnett, who later went on to star in her own top-rated television series via the Gary Moore Show, made an auspicious Broadway debut, and the cast also included that ever-reliable funny-man, Jack Gilford. No hits emerged from the score, but there were several pleasant songs, such as 'Shy', 'Sensitivity', 'Normandy', 'Man To Man Talk', 'Many Moons Ago', 'Very Soft Shoes', 'In A Little While', 'Happily Ever After', 'The Swamp Of Home', and 'Yesterday I Loved You'. An encour-aging New York run of 460 performances was followed by a brief, one month stay in London. A Broadway revival opened at the Broadhurst Theatre in December 1996, and hung on for 187 performances mainly due to clever targeting of family audiences. Directed by Gerald Gutierrez, it starred Sarah Jessica Parker (Princess Winnifred), Mary Lou Rosato (the Queen), David Aaron Baker (Prince Dauntless), and Heath Lamberts (the King).

ONE DAM THING AFTER ANOTHER

This C.B. Cochran revue, written by Ronald Jeans, opened at the London Pavilion on 20 May 1927. The impressive cast included Sonnie Hale, Leslie 'Hutch' Hutchinson, Melvin Cooper, the accomplished American pianist Edythe Baker, and the delightful, vivacious Jessie Matthews in her first leading role. One song, 'The Birth Of The Blues', was written by De Sylva, Brown And Henderson, but the remainder were provided by Richard Rodgers and Lorenz Hart, and included 'My Lucky Star', 'I Need Some Cooling Off', and the enduring standard, 'My Heart Stood Still', which was introduced by Jessie Matthews. The latter number, with Hart's emotional and affecting lyric, played a significant part in the show's success. After the Prince of Wales attended the opening night, he asked for the song to be played at a subsequent function. The orchestra did not know it, so the royal personage hummed it for them. Naturally, the press gave the incident extensive coverage, and also printed the words and music of the song's first 16 bars. The royal seal of approval helped *One Dam Thing After Another* to overcome initially lukewarm reviews, and it became a hit, running for 237 performances.

ONE HOUR WITH YOU

This highly acclaimed musical, a delightful and sophisticated picture which was released by Paramount in 1932, reunited Maurice Chevalier and Jeanette MacDonald following their joint triumph two years earlier in *The Love Parade*. As with that film, *One Hour With You* bore the unmistakable touch of director Ernst Lubitsch, and was, in fact, a remake of his 1924 silent, *The Marriage Circle*. Samson Raphaelson's screenplay told of a happily married couple, played by Chevalier and MacDonald, whose domestic bliss is shattered when he becomes far too friendly with her flirtatious best friend (Genevieve Tobin). Also in the cast were Roland Young, Charlie Ruggles, Josephine Dunn, Donald Novis, and George Barbier. The songs, with music by Oscar Straus and Richard Whiting and lyrics by Leo Robin, included 'Three Times A Day', 'One Hour With You', 'We Will Always Be Sweethearts', 'What Would You Do?', 'It Was Only a Dream Kiss', 'Oh, That Mitzi', and 'What A Little Thing Like A Wedding Ring Can Do'. For various complicated reasons, Lubitsch shared directorial credit with George Cukor on a film that is considered a classic of its kind.

ONE HUNDRED MEN AND A GIRL

'Anything can be achieved if you just try hard enough', was the message that came through loud and clear in this charming and delightful Deanna Durbin film which was produced by Charles Rogers and Joe Pasternak for Universal in 1937. In the wonderfully optimistic screenplay, by Bruce Manning, Charles Kenyon, and Hans Kraly, the 16-year-old female star uses all her unbounded energy and enthusiasm to persuade the celebrated maestro Leopold Stokowski to conduct an orchestra consisting of her father (Adolph Menjou) and a number of other out-of-work musicians. Given that scenario, the songs such as 'It's Raining Sunbeams' (Sam Coslow-Frederick Hollander) and 'A Heart That's Free' (Alfred Robyn-Thomas T. Reilly), were joined by several classical pieces including '2nd Hungarian Rhapsody' (Liszt), '*Lohengrin* Prelude' (Wagner), 'Alleluja' (Mozart), and 'La Traviata' (Verdi). Charles Previn, head of Universal Studio's music department, won an Oscar for the film's score. In the strong supporting cast were Alice Brady, Eugene Pallette, Mischa Auer, and Billy Gilbert. Henry Koster directed the film, which immediately proved to have enormous box-office appeal and touched the hearts of all who saw it.

ONE IN A MILLION

Forty years before John Curry, and then others such as Robin Cousins and Torvill And Dean, caused television ratings to soar with their graceful and imaginative ice dancing, Norwegian champion Sonja Henie was delighting cinema audiences with her own individual brand of ice skating. She made he screen debut in this 1936 film, playing the daughter of a Swiss innkeeper who trains her for the Winter Olympic Games. Naturally, after some hitches along the way, she wins a medal - and the heart of press reporter Don Ameche. He headed an impressive cast along with Adolph Menjou as a band-leading impresario, the always hilarious Ritz Brothers, Jean Hersholt, Arline Judge, Dixie Dunbar, Ned Sparks, Montagu Love, Leah Ray, and Borrah Minevitch and his Harmonica Rascals. Sidney Mitchell and Lew Pollack's songs, which cropped up occasionally throughout an amusing and entertaining picture, included 'We're Back In Circulation Again', 'The Moonlight Waltz', 'Who's Afraid Of Love?', 'Lovely Lady In White', and 'One In A Million'. Producer Darryl F. Zanuck, who produced the film for 20th Century-Fox, is credited with the inspiration for bringing Sonja Henie to Hollywood - an idea that paid off handsomely at the box-office. Leonard Praskins and Mark Kelly wrote the screenplay, the choreographers were Jack Haskell and Nick Castle, and *One In A Million* was directed by Sidney Lanfield.

ONE NIGHT OF LOVE

Grace Moore brought her wonderful world of opera to the screen for the first time proper in this classic musical which was released by Columbia in 1934. In the uncomplicated story, by S.K. Lauren, James Gow, and Edmund North, she plays a young American soprano whose eventual worldwide fame is mainly due to the efforts of her music mentor and guru played impressively by Tullio Carminati. Also in the cast were Lyle Talbot, Mona Barrie, Jessie Ralph, and Jane Darwell. The score was a mixed bag of extracts from popular operettas and arias, along with some classical songs such as 'Ciribiribin' (Rudolph Thaler-Alberto Pestalozza) and 'None But The Lonely Heart' (Peter I. Tchaikovsky). The title number, by the film's director Victor Schertzinger (music) and Gus Kahn (lyric), won an Academy Award for Thematic Music although the award went to Louis Silvers, head of

Columbia's music department - that was the custom in those days. *One Night Of Love* won another Oscar for sound recording, and was nominated for best film, actress (Moore), and director.

ONE TOUCH OF VENUS

After making her initial impact on Broadway in 1938 with Cole Porter's 'My Heart Belongs To Daddy' in *Leave It To Me!*, Mary Martin shot to stardom five years later in this show which opened at the Imperial Theatre in New York on 7 October 1943. The music was written by Kurt Weill, a familiar name in the American musical theatre following his flight from Germany in 1933, but for the two celebrated humorists, poet Ogden Nash (lyrics) and his fellow librettist, S.J. Perelman, *One Touch Of Venus* was their first, and only, book musical. The authors' story, which was based on F. Anstey's *The Tinted Venus*, was a contemporary 'sophisticated and witty variation on the Pygmalion-Galatea myth'. Whitelaw Savory (John Boles) has discovered a 3,000 year-old statue of Venus which he has put on display at his New York museum. While viewing the piece, Rodney Hatch (Kenny Baker), a barber from Ozone Heights, puts his fiancée's ring on Venus's finger, and the statue immediately springs to life in the classic shape of Mary Martin. Complex, and sometimes hilarious situations then develop, during which Whitelaw falls for Venus, but she prefers Rodney - that is until she finds out that he is just a simple barber. Eventually, disillusioned with her animated existence, Venus returns to her marble state, and Rodney falls in love with a girl who looks remarkably like . . . Mary Martin. Weill and Nash's score in which the words and music are always in perfect sympathy, is usually remembered for the haunting torch song, 'Speak Low', but there were several other attractive numbers including 'I'm A Stranger Here Myself', 'How Much I Love You', 'One Touch Of Venus', 'West Wind', 'That's Him', 'Foolish Heart', 'The Trouble With Women', 'Wooden Wedding', 'Very, Very, Very', and two beautiful and highly effective ballets sequences, 'Forty Minutes For Lunch' and 'Venus In Ozone Heights', both of which were choreographed by Agnes de Mille. Elia Kazan directed a brilliant all-round cast which included Paula Laurence, Teddy Hart, Ruth Bond, Sono Osato, and Harry Clark. The show ran for a respectable 322 performances, and is regarded as one of the classic musical comedies. Surprisingly, revivals have been few and far between, but the Goodspeed Opera House mounted an acclaimed production in 1987 which starred Richard Sabellico, Semina De Laurentis, Michael Piontek, and Lynnette Perry.

ONLY THE LONELY

This 'throbbing tribute' to Roy Orbison, which was conceived and produced by the ubiquitous Bill Kenwright for the Liverpool Playhouse, opened at London's Piccadilly Theatre on 27 September 1994. In Shirlie Roden and Jon Miller's 'inept' book, Orbison's life is retold for the benefit of his son, Wesley (Stephen Tremblay), by the late singer's best friend, Bobbie Blackburn (James Carroll Jordan). The 'Big O' himself was played by an uncanny sound- and look-alike, Larry Branson, a Canadian who toured North America for several years in shows which gave him plenty of opportunities to sing 'Running Scared', 'It's Over', 'Crawlin' Back', 'Oh, Pretty Woman', 'In Dreams', 'Blue Bayou', 'Only The Lonely' and the rest of the nearly 30 songs featured during the evening. Not content with noting Branson's 'unnervingly similar Orbison characteristics - wide, plump cheeks, unsmiling mouth, and dark glasses' - some unkind critics also thought that they saw a likeness to the notorious terrorist Carlos the Jackal! Martin Glyn Murray gave a riveting performance as Bruce Springsteen, and the rest of the cast pretended to be Dusty Springfield, Patsy Cline, Bob Dylan, and the Beatles, amongst others. No pretence was needed in May 1995 when a real-life survivor from the 60s - a genuine icon - P.J. Proby joined the cast, and delighted audiences with his own 15-minute spot during each performance. After changing its name to *The Roy Orbison Story*, the show rocked on for almost another year, closing in February 1996.

ORBACH, JERRY

b. 20 October 1935, Bronx, New York, USA. An actor and singer who created a handful of important roles for the Broadway musical theatre, before turning mostly to films and television. Orbach studied acting with Lee Strasberg, and singing with Mazel Schweppe. After making his professional debut as the Typewriter Man in a 1952 Illinois version of *Room Service*, he continued to work in regional theatre, appearing in stock productions of musicals such as *The King And I* and *The Student Prince*. He made his Broadway debut taking over the roles of the Streetsinger (1957) and Macheath (1958), in the long-running revival of *The Threepenny Opera* that opened at the Theatre De Lys in 1955. In 1960 he played the dual role of the Narrator and the bandit El Gallo off-Broadway in Harvey Schmidt and Tom Jones's historic epic *The Fantasticks*, introducing the show's hit song, 'Try To Remember'. During the 60s he created the character of cynical puppeteer Paul Berthalet in *Carnival* (1961) on Broadway and on tour, played in revivals of *The Cradle Will Rock* (1964 as Larry Foreman), *Guys And Dolls* (1965 as Sky Masterson, with Alan King and Sheila MacRae), *Carousel* (1965 as Jigger Craigin), and *Annie Get Your Gun* (1966 as Charlie Davenport), as well as appearing in several straight plays. In 1969 Orbach won a Tony Award for his portrayal of Chuck Baxter, the sad, lowly office worker who lends out his apartment to senior executives in *Promises, Promises*, and introduced (with Jill O'Hara) Burt Bacharach and Hal David's 'I'll Never Fall In Love Again'. In 1974, he played in the Neil Simon revue *The Trouble With People ... And Other Things* in Miami. Orbach subsequently returned to Broadway, full of assurance, singing 'All I Care About' and 'Razzle Dazzle', as Gwen Verdon and Chita Rivera's smart lawyer, the silver-tongued prince of the courtroom, Mr. Billy Flynn, in *Chicago* (1975). Orbach's last major stage musical role to date came in 1980, when he portrayed tough producer Julian Marsh in the long-running Broadway adaptation of the famous 1932 Busby Berkeley movie *42nd Street*. Since then, he has continued to appear in dramatic parts in the theatre, but seems to have concentrated mostly on television (*Perry Mason*, *Murder, She Wrote*, *Law And Order*, etc.) and films. The music connection has continued though, and in more recent years moviegoers have seen him as the disapproving doctor/father figure in the hit film *Dirty Dancing* (1987), and heard his voice behind the hospitable candelabra, Lumiere, singing Alan Menken and Howard Ashman's Oscar-nominated 'Be Our Guest', in Walt Disney's animated feature *Beauty And The Beast* (1991). Orbach did other voice work for video productions of *Aladdin And The King Of Thieves* (1996), *Belle's Magical World* (1997), and *Beauty And The Beast: The Enchanted Christmas* (1997).

● FILMS: *Cop Hater* (1958), *Mad Dog Coll* (1961), *John Goldfarb, Please Come Home* (1964), *The Gang That Couldn't Shoot Straight* (1971), *A Fan's Notes* (1972), *Foreplay* (1975), *The Sentinel* (1977), *Prince Of The City* (1981), *Brewster's Millions* (1985), *F/X* (1986), *The Imagemaker* (1986), *I Love N.Y.* (1987), *Dirty Dancing* (1987), *Someone To Watch Over Me* (1987), *Last Exit To Brooklyn* (1989), *Crimes And Misdemeanors* (1989), *Dead Women In Lingerie* (1990), *Toy Soldiers* (1991), *Out For Justice* (1991), *Delusion* (1991), voice of Lumiere *Beauty And The Beast* (1991), *Delirious* (1992), *Straight Talk* (1992), *Mr. Saturday Night* (1992), *Universal Soldier* (1992), *Gnome Named Gnorm* (1994).

ORCHESTRA WIVES

The marvellous music more than made up for a dull plot in this, the second of only two films in which the enormously popular Glenn Miller Orchestra appeared. The story concerns the glitz and the grind of a band on the road in the heyday of the Swing Era. Glamour-boy trumpeter George Montgomery cannot bear to leave his young sweetheart Ann Rutherford behind so he marries her and brings her aboard the bus - much to the chagrin of the hard-bitten wives of the other orchestra members who give the poor girl a hard time. After providing the Miller band with several hits in their previous movie, *Sun Valley Serenade*, Harry Warren and Mack Gordon came up trumps in this 1942 release with 'At Last', 'Serenade In Blue', 'People Like You And Me', and 'I Got A Gal In Kalamazoo'. The latter number was a speciality for Tex Beneke And The Modernaires, and they were joined by most of Miller's regular sidemen, including Hal McIntyre, Ray Anthony, Billy May, and singers Marion Hutton and Ray Eberle. Also in the cast were Cesar Romero, Lynn Bari, Carole Landis, Mary Beth Hughes, Jackie Gleason, Virginia Gilmore, Tamara Geva, Harry Morgan, and the marvellously athletic dancing team, the Nicholas Brothers. Karl Tunberg and Darrell Ware wrote the screenplay, and Nick Castle choreographed the dances. The director was Archie Mayo and the film was released in 1942. A film to watch again and again - just for those historic musical sequences.

ORNADEL, CYRIL

b. 2 December 1924, London, England. A composer, arranger and conductor for the theatre and films, Ornadel studied piano, double bass, and composition at the Royal College of Music. He was with ENSA for a while, and later toured Europe with the popular singer Dorothy Carless. He led his own all-female band at Murray's Club in London, and later worked as a concert party pianist. After providing some musical and vocal arrangements for the Players' Theatre, he was appointed musical director of the touring show *Hello Beautiful*, which led to his first London assignment as the conductor of a pantomime at the People's Palace in the Mile End Road. In 1950, he became the West End's youngest pit conductor when he took over the baton for the musical revue *Take It From Us* at the Adelphi Theatre. During the remainder of the 50s he conducted for the London productions of several successful American musicals, such as *Kiss Me, Kate, Call Me Madam, Paint Your Wagon, Wish You Were Here, Pal Joey, Wonderful Town, Kismet, Plain And Fancy*, and *My Fair Lady*. Ornadel also collaborated with David Croft on the scores for regional productions of *Star Maker, The Pied Piper*, and the London Palladium's 1956 pantomime, *The Wonderful Lamp* (with Phil Park). For much of the 50s he was the resident musical director for the top-rated television programme, *Sunday Night At The London Palladium*. In 1960, he and lyricist Norman Newell won Ivor Novello Awards for their delightful ballad, 'Portrait Of My Love', which gave Matt Monro his first UK chart hit. Ornadel's other 'Ivors' (to date) came in 1963 for 'If I Ruled The World' (lyric by Leslie Bricusse), the hit song from his score for the immensely successful musical, *Pickwick*, starring Harry Secombe; and the scores for two 'Best British Musicals', *Treasure Island* (1973) and *Great Expectations* (1975), both with Hal Shaper. After playing its initial UK dates and in several Canadian cities, Ornadel and Shaper rewrote the score for *Great Expectations*, and the revised version was presented at the Liverpool Playhouse (1989) and in Sydney, Australia (1991). Ornadel's other stage musicals have included *Ann Veronica* (1969, with Croft), *Once More, Darling* (1978, with Newell), *Winnie* (1988, additional songs with Arnold Sundgaard), *Cyrano: The Musical* (with Shaper), and *The Last Flower On Earth* (1991, with Kelvin Reynolds). Over the years, Ornadel has also conducted and/or composed and orchestrated the music for numerous radio, film and television productions, including *Some May Live, Subterfuge, The Waiters, I Can't, I Can't, Wedding Night, Man Of Violence, Europa Express, Cool It Carol, Die Screaming Marianne, Yesterday, The Flesh And The Blood Show, The Strauss Family* (series), *Edward VII* (series), *Christina, Brief Encounter* (1974 remake), and many more. His albums, especially those on which his Starlight Symphony Orchestra celebrated the great popular composers, have been extremely successful, especially in America. He also composed a series of children's records for EMI, and was the musical supervisor for the *Living Bible* records with Sir Laurence Olivier, and created the 'Stereoaction Orchestra' for RCA Records. A genial, and much-liked man, in the early 90s Cyril Ornadel was living and working in Israel. His many albums include: *Musical World Of Lerner And Loewe, Opening Night-Broadway Overtures, Bewitched, Camelot, Carnival, Dearly Beloved, Enchanted Evening, Gone With The Wind, Musical World Of Jerome Kern, Musical World Of Cole Porter, Musical World Of Rodgers And Hammerstein, So Nice To Come Home To*, and *The Music Man* .

OSMOND, DONNY

b. Donald Clark Osmond, 9 December 1957, Ogden, Utah, USA. The most successful solo artist to emerge from family group the Osmonds, Donny was particularly successful at covering old hits. His first solo success came in the summer of 1971 with a version of Billy Sherrill's 'Sweet And Innocent', which reached the US Top 10. The follow-up, a revival of Gerry Goffin/Carole King's 'Go Away Little Girl' (previously a hit for both Steve Lawrence and Mark Wynter) took Osmond to the top of the US charts. 'Hey Girl', once a success for Freddie Scott, continued his US chart domination, which was now even more successful than that of the family group. By the summer of 1972, Osmondmania reached Britain, and a revival of Paul Anka's 'Puppy Love' gave Donny his first UK number 1. The singer's clean-cut good looks and perpetual smile brought him massive coverage in the pop press, while a back catalogue of hit songs from previous generations sustained his chart career. 'Too Young' and 'Why' both hit the UK Top 10, while 'The Twelfth Of Never' and 'Young Love' both reached number 1. His material appeared to concentrate on the pangs of adolescent love, which made him the perfect teenage idol for the period. In 1974, Donny began a series of duets with his sister Marie Osmond, which included more UK Top 10 hits with 'I'm Leaving It All Up To You' and 'Morning Side Of The Mountain'. It was clear that Donny's appeal was severely circumscribed by his youth and in 1977 he tried unsuccessfully to reach a more mature audience with Donald Clark Osmond. Although minor hits followed, the singer's appeal was waning alarmingly by the late 70s. After the break-up of the group in 1980, Donny went on to star in the 1982 revival of the musical Little Johnny Jones, which closed after only one night on Broadway, and ceased recording after the mid-70s. A decade later, a rugged Osmond returned with 'I'm In It For Love' and the more successful 'Soldier Of Love', which reached the US Top 30. Most agreed that his attempts at mainstream rock were much more impressive than anyone might have imagined. Osmond proved his versatility again in the 90s by playing the lead in Canadian and North American productions of Andrew Lloyd Webber and Tim Rice's musical Joseph And The Amazing Technicolor Dreamcoat. When he hung up his loincloth at Toronto's Elgin Theatre in May 1997, after almost five years and 2,000 performances as the biblical son of Jacob, it was to join the cast of the 60th Hill Cumorah Pageant, America's Witness To Christ. In this upstate New York outdoor production, Osmond portrayed a prophet of the Mormon faith.

● ALBUMS: The Donny Osmond Album (MGM 1971)★★, To You With Love, Donny (MGM 1971)★★, Portrait Of Donny (MGM 1972)★★, Too Young (MGM 1972)★★, My Best Of You (MGM 1972)★★, Alone Together (MGM 1973)★★, A Time For Us (MGM 1973)★★, Donny (MGM 1974)★★, Discotrain (Polydor 1976)★★, Donald Clark Osmond (Polydor 1977)★★, Donny Osmond (Virgin 1988)★★★, Eyes Don't Lie (Capitol 1990)★★. With Marie Osmond I'm Leaving It All Up To You (MGM 1974)★★, Make The World Go Away (MGM 1975)★★, Donny And Marie - Featuring Songs From Their Television Show (Polydor 1976)★★, Deep Purple (Polydor 1976)★★, Donny And Marie - A New Season (Polydor 1977)★★, Winning Combination (Polydor 1978)★★, Goin' Coconuts (Polydor 1978)★★.

OSSER, GLENN
b. 28 August 1914, Munising, Michigan, USA. The son of Russian immigrants, Osser has had a successful career

arranging and conducting for many leading bands and singers. He has also achieved a distinctive string sound through his clever scoring, which he describes as 'voicing register, and composition of the counterpoint'. In his early career Osser concentrated on arranging, and his scores were accepted by Bob Crosby, Charlie Barnet, Bunny Berigan, Paul Whiteman, Les Brown and Red Nichols. During the 50s, while still regularly working with Whiteman (who was Musical Director of the ABC Network at that time), Osser was in demand to back many singers for albums, including Georgia Gibbs, Vic Damone, Jack Jones, Frankie Laine, John Raitt, Maurice Chevalier and Guy Mitchell. Osser was also recording his own instrumental albums, notably some with Bobby Hackett and Joe Bushkin. Further albums found Osser backing Johnny Mathis, Jerry Vale, Tony Bennett, Robert Goulet and Leslie Uggams. Leaving US Columbia and moving to RCA, Osser worked with Della Reese and Sam Cooke. Until 1987 he was Music Director and arranger for the Miss America Beauty Pageant on television, with Osser and his wife contributing various original songs including 'Miss America, You're Beautiful' and 'Look At Her'. He has also written many works for concert bands that are still regularly performed by many high school and college bands in the USA.

● ALBUMS: as Glenn Osser Orchestra But Beautiful (Kapp 1956)★★★, with Joe Bushkin Midnight Rhapsody (Capitol 1957)★★★, March Along Sing Along (Marching Band And Chorus) (United Artists 1960)★★★, Be There At Five (Mercury 1960)★★★. As accompanist: Marian McPartland With You In Mind (Capitol 1957)★★★, Georgia Gibbs Swingin' With Her Nibs (Mercury 1957)★★★, Vivian Blaine Songs From Ziegfeld Follies (Mercury 1957)★★★★, Jerry Vale I Remember Buddy (Columbia 1958)★★, Red Buttons, Barbara Cook Hansel And Gretel (MGM 1958)★★★, Maurice Chevalier Maurice Chevalier Sings Songs Of Yesterday/Today (MGM 1958)★★★, Guy Mitchell A Guy In Love (Columbia/Philips 1959)★★★, Vic Damone Angela Mia (Columbia 1959)★★★, Johnny Mathis Heavenly (Columbia 1959)★★★★, Leslie Uggams The Eyes Of God (Columbia 1959)★★★, Della Reese Della By Starlight (RCA 1960)★★★★, Sam Cooke Cooke's Tour (RCA 1960)★★★, Tony Bennett Tony Bennett Sings A String Of Harold Arlen (Columbia 1960)★★★, Diana Trask Diana Trask (Columbia 1961)★★★★, Dona Jacoby Swinging Big Sound (Decca 1962)★★★, Bobby Hackett The Most Beautiful Horn In The World (Columbia 1962)★★★, Jack Jones Gift Of Love (Kapp 1962)★★★, George Maharis Portrait In Music (Epic 1962)★★★, Robert Goulet Two Of Us (Columbia 1962)★★★, Jerry Vale Arrivederci Roma (Columbia 1963)★★★★, Barbara Carroll Fresh From Broadway (Warners 1964)★★★, Brook Benton That Old Feeling (RCA 1966)★★★, Jerry Vale The Impossible Dream (Columbia 1967)★★★, Johnny Mathis Up Up And Away (Columbia 1967)★★★, Bob Thiele Those Were The Days (Flying Dutchman 1972)★★★.

OUR MISS GIBBS
Another vehicle for the vivacious actress and singer Gertie Millar, with music written for her by her husband, Lionel Monkton, in collaboration with Ivan Caryll. Our Miss Gibbs opened at the Gaiety Theatre in London on 23 January 1909, and dwelt, like so many similar productions of the time, on the life and loves of the common shop girl.

This time the shop is in the county of Yorkshire, England, and sells flowers. Mary Gibbs (Gertie Miller) loves bank clerk Harry Lancaster (J. Edward Fraser), and the romance is going swimmingly until she discovers he is really the well-heeled Lord Eynsford, who has made certain commitments, marriage-wise, to Lady Elizabeth Thanet (Julia James). Wanting to be alone, she dashes off to the 1908 Franco-British Exhibition at London's White City Stadium (capacity 70,000), and emerges to accept the good Lord's apology and nuptial proposal. Most of the songs were written by Monkton or Caryll with lyricists Adrian Ross and Percy Greenbank, but the popular 'Yip-I-Addy-I-Ay', which was sung in the show by George Grossmith Jnr. (as the Hon. Hughie Pierrepoint), was the work of Grossmith Jnr. himself, with Will Cobb and John Flynn. The bulk of the score consisted of 'My Yorkshire Lassie', 'Not That Sort Of Person', 'Yorkshire', 'Mary', 'Hats', 'Country Cousins', 'White City', and 'Our Farm'. The song that created quite a stir, and endured, was the charming 'Moonstruck', which was introduced by Gertie Millar, dressed as a Pierrot, in a party scene. *Our Miss Gibbs* had - for those days - a prodigious run of 636 performances, but, understandably, given its subject matter and setting, flopped in New York, even with Pauline Chase as Mary, and some interpolated songs from Jerome Kern.

OUT OF THE BLUE

'More like into the red', wrote one critic, after attending the opening night of this musical drama on 23 November 1994 at the Shaftesbury Theatre in London. Another scribe remarked on 'the wild courage it takes to create a West End musical in which America's atomic bombing of Nagasaki in 1945, and a terminal case of radiation sickness are the catalysts for catastrophe.' The brave (or foolhardy) person who conceived this epic and wrote the sung-through score, was Tokura Shun-Ichi, one of Japan's leading composers of contemporary music. Paul Sand, the British rock musician-turned composer, lyricist, and director, was responsible for the libretto. His story concerns Father Marshall (James Graeme), a Boston Roman Catholic priest, whose wartime memories comes flooding back to him when he receives a request from the Japanese Dr. Akizuki (Michael McCarthy) to speak at his Boston church on the 25th anniversary commemoration of the dropping of the bomb on Nagasaki. As a young American GI in Japan after the war, Marshall (Greg Ellis) had married a local girl, Hideko (Meredith Braun), who died of radiation sickness. After he returned to the USA, Marshall received a letter from her fanatically nationalistic brother, Hayashi (Simon Burke/David Burt), telling him that their daughter, Hana (Paulette Ivory), had also died. However, during his visit to Boston, Akiszuki reveals that Hana did not perish, but is alive and working in his hospital in Nagasaki. In the second act, father and daughter are finally reunited at the Nagasaki Peace Park. Accompanying this worthy and well-meaning, if often sententious, tale with its inevitable reliance of flashbacks between the 40s, early 50s and 1970, was a score 'which mixed the styles of East and West, and combined frenzied percussion and whispering synthesisers with fragments of haunting melody', sung by some of the most beautiful voices in

London. No individual song titles were listed in the programme. Ironically, set and costume designer Terry Parsons' dramatically angular stage, and chorus of hooded, visored, samurai-like figures, gave the David Gilmore production a kind of space-age look. John Combe was the choreographer. Lighting designer Mark Henderson won a Laurence Olivier Award for his work on this show and others during the year.

As with the other current oriental-type musical, *Miss Saigon*, some critics recognized echoes of Puccini's *Madame Butterfly* in *Out Of The Blue*. That may well be true, but the similarity ended there. For, when the latter closed on 10 December after a run of less than three weeks, *Miss Saigon* was in the process of overtaking *My Fair Lady* to become the longest-running musical in the history of the Theatre Royal Drury Lane.

PACIFIC OVERTURES

Sometimes known as Stephen Sondheim's 'kabuki musical', this ambitious production opened at the Winter Garden, New York, on 11 January 1976. The book was by John Weidman, a student of law at Yale University. It traced the history of Japan from 1852, when naval officer Commander Matthew Perry, and four warships, attempted to establish 'friendly' relations with a 'isolated and peaceful country', through a period of some 120 years of continual change, culminating in the country's emergence as a dominant trading force in the western world. The story was told in an imaginative and original manner, with every aspect of the production heavily influenced by the traditional form of Japanese Kabuki theatre. Most of Sondheim's music was written in the Japanese pentatonic scale, and his lyrics used extremely simple language, with very few rhymes. The songs included 'Pretty Lady', 'Four Black Dragons', "There Is No Other Way", 'Chrysanthemum Tea', 'Please Hello', 'A Bowler Hat', 'Welcome To Kanagawa', 'Someone In A Tree', 'Next'. 'The Advantages Of Floating In The Middle Of The Sea', and 'Poems'. The actors, who included Mako, Soon-Teck Oh, Yukis Shimoda, and Sab Shimono, were all Asians, even those who played Americans. Director Hal Prince was prominent among the show's several Tony Award nominees for his staging of a project that was both daring and completely different from anything Broadway had seen in living memory, but the only winners were Florence Klotz (costumes) and Boris Aronson (scenic design). The show also won the New York Drama Critics' Circle Award for best musical. It ran for 193 performances, and was presented in a revised, small-scale version Off Broadway in 1984, and in a far more lavish Paul Kerryson production at England's Leicester Haymarket Theatre in 1993.

PAIGE, ELAINE

b. Elaine Bickerstaff, 5 March 1951, Barnet, Hertfordshire, England. An actress and singer, often called the first lady of contemporary British musical theatre, Elaine Paige was trained at the Aida Foster Stage School in Golders Green, north London. She had already appeared in several stage musicals in the 60s and 70s, including The Roar Of The Greasepaint-The Smell Of The Crowd, Hair (her first West End show), *Maybe That's Your Problem*, *Rock Carmen*, Jesus Christ Superstar, Grease, Billy, and before she was chosen to portray Eva Peron in Tim Rice and Andrew Lloyd Webber's Evita in 1978. Although Julie Covington had sung the part on the original concept album and had a UK number 1 hit with 'Don't Cry For Me Argentina', Paige went on to make the role her own. In spite of the disappointment of being unable to play the part on Broadway (because of American union rules), *Evita* made Paige into a star almost overnight. She won a Society of West End Theatres Award for her outstanding performance, and was also voted Show Business Personality of the Year. In the 80s she starred in Cats (as Grizabella, singing 'Memory'), *Abbacadabra*, Chess, and a West End revival of Cole Porter's Anything Goes. She topped the UK chart with a number from *Chess*, 'I Know Him So Well', in a duet with Barbara Dickson. Her first solo album, which came in 1981, featured a variety of songs, mostly with lyrics by Tim Rice. It was recorded with the assistance of Stuart Elliot (ex-Cockney Rebel), Ian Bairnson and David Paton from Pilot, and Mike Moran. As well as a version of Paul Simon's 'How The Heart Approaches What It Yearns', there was a rare Paul McCartney instrumental ('Hot As Sun') with words by Rice. She was voted 'Recording Artist of the Year' by the Variety Club of Great Britain. Her most unusual album was released in 1988, and consisted of cover versions of Queen songs. In 1989 she turned her attention more to straight acting, and made two films for the BBC including the acclaimed *Unexplained Laughter*, with Diana Rigg. She had previously worked in television programmes such as *Crossroads*, *Lady Killers*, *Ladybirds*, *A View Of Harry Clark*, and *Tales Of The Unexpected*, as well as musical specials such as *Elaine Paige In Concert*. In 1990 her long-term relationship with Tim Rice dissolved and she threw herself into her work. During the 80s and 90s she embarked on concert tours of Europe, the Middle East, Scandinavia and the UK, most recently accompanied by a 26-piece symphony orchestra. In 1993 she was highly acclaimed for her powerful and dramatic performance as the legendary Edith Piaf in Pam Gems' play with music, Piaf, at the Piccadilly Theatre in London. In May 1995, she took over from Betty Buckley in the leading role of Norma Desmond in the West End hit musical Sunset Boulevard, and later in the year received an OBE in the Queen's Birthday Honours List. In 1996 she finally appeared on Broadway when she replaced Betty Buckley in the New York production of *Sunset Boulevard*. Returning to the West End two years later, she made a daring career move by successfully taking on the role of the duplicitous widow Celimene in Molière's scathing comedy, *The Misanthrope*.

● ALBUMS: with Peter Oliver *Barrier* (Euro Disk 1978)★★, *Elaine Paige* (Warners 1982)★★★, *Stages* (K-Tel 1983)★★, *Cinema* (K-Tel 1984)★★, *Sitting Pretty* (Warners 1985)★★, *Love Hurts* (Warners 1985)★★, *Christmas* (Warners 1986)★★, *The Queen Album* (Virgin 1988)★★, *Love Can Do That* (1991)★★, with Barbara Dickson *Together* (1992)★★, *Romance And The Stage* (RCA 1993)★★, *Piaf* (Warners 1995)★★★, *Encore* (Warners 1995)★★★, *Performance* (BMF 1996)★★★, and Original Cast recordings.

● COMPILATIONS: *Memories - The Best Of Elaine Paige* (Telstar 1987)★★★, *The Collection* (Pickwick 1990)★★★.

PAINT YOUR WAGON (FILM MUSICAL)

Opinions vary widely as to the quality of this film, but, in general, the 'noes' seem to have it. *Paint Your Wagon* started its musical journey on Broadway in 1951, with music by Frederick Loewe and a book and lyrics by Alan Jay Lerner. Lerner's screenplay for this 1969 version was based on a fresh adaptation of the story by Paddy Chayevsky. The action still takes place during the California gold rush of the late 1800s, but the sometimes droll story now concerns the relationship between the lovely young Elizabeth (Jean Seberg) and the two men in her life, Ben Rumson (Lee Marvin) and 'Pardner' (Clint Eastwood). She wants to live in No Name City with both of them, which does not please Ben because he used part of his stake to buy her from a Mormon, and then made her his wife. Also up to their knees in the mud of the goldfields were Harve Presnell ('Rotten Luck Willie), Ray Walston ('Mad Jack' Duncan), Tom Ligon, Alan Dexter, William O'Connell, Ben Baker, Alan Baxter, Paul Truman, and a whole heap of others. Several of Lerner and Loewe's songs survived from the stage score, including the rousing 'Main Title (I'm On My Way)', and the contrasting 'They Call The Wind Maria' and 'There's A Coach Comin' In', both of which were sung admirably by Presnell. Eastwood surprised and delighted with his handling of 'I Still See Elisa' and 'I Talk To The Trees', and Marvin brought his very own individual treatment to 'Hand Me Down That Can O' Beans', and 'Wand'rin Star'. The latter number gave him a number 1 hit in the UK, but did not make the Top 40 in the USA. The rest of the numbers, with Lerner's lyrics and music by André Previn, consisted of 'The First Thing You Know', 'A Million Miles Away Behind The Door', 'The Gospel Of No Name City', 'Best Things', and 'Gold Fever'. Nelson Riddle and his impressive musical arrangements were nominated for an Oscar. Jack Baker staged the energetic dance sequences and the director was Joshua Logan. Alan Jay Lerner produced for Paramount, and the film was photographed in Technicolor and Panavision by William Fraker. In spite of the critics' reservations, *Paint Your Wagon* grossed well over $14 million in the USA, and was just outside the Top 10 musicals of the decade.

PAINT YOUR WAGON (STAGE MUSICAL)

This musical morality play, set in the goldfields of North California around the mid-1800s, opened at the Shubert Theatre in New York on 12 November 1951. The central characters in Alan Jay Lerner's book are Ben Rumson (James Barton) and his daughter Jennifer. (Olga San Juan). After they accidentally discover gold, a heap of hard-bitten characters flock to Rumson Town from miles around. As the only female around, this makes life difficult for Jennifer - and anyway she has become far too fond of the Mexican dreamer Julio Valvera (Tony Bavaar). So she is sent back east to school, although sadly not before she has witnessed her father bidding successfully for a Mormon's spare wife. On her return, she finds a ghost town. The gold has dwindled to nothing, and the fevered prospectors have moved on. Ben's wife has gone too, but when Julio turns up, having finally discovered there is no pot at the end of that mythical rainbow, he and Jennifer can at last settle down and begin to build a life together. Frederick Loewe (music) and Lerner (lyrics) came up with a perfect score for this lively, rumbustious, but often poignant scenario, which included 'Another Autumn', 'I Still See Elisa', 'I'm On My Way', 'Wand'rin Star', 'Hand Me Down That Can O' Beans', 'What's Goin' On?', 'Whoop-Ti-Ay', 'How Can I Wait?', 'Carino Mio', 'There's A Coach Comin' In', and 'All For Him'. Two of the numbers, 'They Call The Wind Maria' and 'I Talk To The Trees', quickly became popular, but the show, which was directed by Daniel Mann, had a disappointing run of only 289 performances. Choreographer Agnes De Mille was in her element with all those prancing miners, and there were the inevitable ballet sequences. From 11 February 1953, London audiences at Her Majesty's Theatre liked it much better, and it played there 477 times, with an initial cast led by Bobby Howes and his real-life daughter Sally Ann Howes, with Ken Cantril as Julio. There was a spirited revival in 1992 at the Goodspeed Opera House, Connecticut, starring George Ball (Ben), Maria Schaffel (Jennifer). and David Bedella (Julio). Four years later, in the rather appropriate setting of the Open Air Theatre, Regent's Park, Tony Selby (Ben), Claire Carrie (Jennifer), Chook Sibtain (Julio), and the remainder of a splendid cast, gloried in what has finally come to be regarded as a marvellous score. The Californian characters were still searching for that elusive rainbow, but at least Lerner and Loewe found their own pot of gold some four years and a few months after the show first opened on Broadway. It was called *My Fair Lady*. A film version of *Paint Your Wagon* was released in 1969, with Lee Marvin, Clint Eastwood, Jean Seberg, and Harve Presnell.

PAJAMA GAME, THE (FILM MUSICAL)

Hardly any screen version of a hit Broadway musical is considered to be better than the original, but this one in 1957 was an exception. This was possibly because several members of the original stage team made the trip to Hollywood to recreate their original roles. Two of them, George Abbott and Richard Bissell, adapted their libretto (which had been based on Bissell's novel *Seven And A Half Cents*) for the screenplay. Based in and around the Sleep Tite Pajama Factory in Iowa, it concerns the efforts of union leader Babe Williams (Doris Day) and her Grievance Committee to extract a rise in pay of seven and a half cents for their members, from the new (and extremely dishy) superintendent, Sid Sorokin (John Raitt). Naturally, Babe falls for Sid, in spite of her protests ('I'm Not At All In Love'), and the negotiations are satisfactorily concluded. This was one of only two scores that Richard Adler and Jerry Ross wrote together (the other was *Damn Yankees*) before the latter's tragic death, and it was a complete joy. Not only did the principals, Day and Raitt, share 'Hey, There', 'Small Talk' and 'There Once Was A Man', but the gifted singer and dancer Carol Haney dazzled with 'Steam Heat' and 'Hernando's Hideaway', while Eddie Foy Jnr. was delightfully unconvincing as he assured Reta Shaw 'I'll Never Be Jealous Again'. In addition, there were pleasing ensemble pieces such as 'Once-A-Year-Day' and 'Racing With The Clock'. Also in the cast were Buzz Miller, Peter Gennaro, Barbara Nicholls, Thelma Pelish and Kenneth LeRoy. Bob Fosse, a veteran of the stage show, was responsible for the lively and imaginative choreography (much of it alfresco), and the producer-directors were George Abbott and Stanley Donen. The film was shot in WarnerColor.

PAJAMA GAME, THE (STAGE MUSICAL)

The new songwriting team of Richard Adler and Jerry Ross joined with Bob Fosse, who was making his Broadway debut as a choreographer, and veteran George Abbott, to help create this immensely enjoyable musical which opened at the St. James Theatre in New York on 13 May 1954. Abbott and Richard Bissell's book, which was based on Bissell's novel *7 1/2 Cents*, deals with a dispute between workers and management in the Sleep Tite Pajama Factory in Cedar Rapids, Iowa. New factory superintendent Sid Sorokin (John Raitt) gets on well with the head of the Grievance Committee, Babe Williams (Janis Paige), but is forced to dismiss her - although their non-industrial relations are progressing quite nicely - when she sabotages the production line. Sid sorts out her, and everyone else's grievances, when he discovers that the big bad boss has been including the requested 7 1/2 cent rise in his costings for ages - even though the workers have not been receiving it. Now, everyone is delighted - even time and motion man Hines (Eddie Foy Jnr.), who is constantly consulting Mabel (Reta Shaw) about the (imagined) unfaithfulness of his girlfriend Gladys (Carol Haney), and union freak Prez (Stanley Prager), who would be unfaithful with any of the female staff if only they would let him. Adler and Ross's sparkling score included 'The Pajama Game; Racing With The Clock', 'A New Town Is A Blue Town', 'I'm Not At All In Love', 'I'll Never Be Jealous Again', 'Her Is', 'Once-A-Year-Day', 'Small Talk', 'There Once Was A Man', 'Think Of The Time I Save', and 'Seven-And-A-Half Cents'. Raitt had a neat scene in which he duetted with his own voice on a dictation machine for 'Hey There', and Haney made a great impression with the sensual 'Steam Heat' and the dimly-lit 'Hernando's Hideaway'. George Abbott and Jerome Robbins directed this smash hit production which ran for 1,063 performances, and won Tony Awards for best musical, featured musical actress (Haney), producers (more Broadway new-comers, Frederick Brisson, Robert E. Griffith and Harold Prince), authors, composer and lyricist, and choreographer. Joy Nichols (Babe), Edmund Hockridge (Sid), Max Wall (Hines), Elizabeth Seal (Gladys), Joan Emney (Mabel), and Frank Lawless (Prez) led the 1955 London show which played 588 times at the Coliseum and is remembered with a great deal of affection. Hockridge had considerable success with his recording of 'Hey There', and it became one of his signature songs. Richard Adler's 1973 Broadway revival introduced a little racial romanticism into the piece, with a black Babe (Barbara McNair) and white Sid (Hal Linden), along with Sharron Miller (Gladys), Cab Calloway (Hines), and Mary Jo Catlett (Mabel). In 1958, the musical *Say, Darling*, allegedly based on Richard Bissell's experiences with *The Pajama Game*, opened on Broadway and ran for 332 performances. The cast was headed by Vivian Blaine, David Wayne, and Johnny Desmond sang and danced to the music and lyrics of Jule Styne, Betty Comden and Adolph Green. The 1985 Leicester Haymarket production toured the UK regions with Paul Jones and Fiona Hendley, and Adler wrote Hendley a new song, a reflective little waltz called 'If You Win, You Lose'. A different number, but with the same title, featured in the 1998 Goodspeed Opera House revival, which had Sean McDermott (Sid), Colleen Fitzpatrick (Babe), Bob Walton (Hines), Valerie Wright (Gladys), Nora Mae Lyng (Mabel), and Casey Nicholaw (Prez). John Raitt, Carol Haney, and Eddie Foy Jnr. were among members of the stage cast who recreated their roles for the 1957 film version, which also starred Doris Day.

PAL JOEY (FILM MUSICAL)

This somewhat sanitized version of the 1940 Broadway show and John O'Hara's witty essays on which it was based, came to the screen in 1957. Frank Sinatra proved to be the ideal choice for the role of 'the heel of all-time', Joey Evans, the nightclub singer and compere, whose apparent mission in life is to seduce each 'mouse' in the chorus with the offer of 'shrimp cocktail, a steak, french fries, a little wine - the whole mish-mosh', so that he can 'help her with her arrangements'. The ingenuous Linda English (Kim Novak) accepts his offer, and, after the usual complications, and to the surprise of many who had read O'Hara's original short stories, goes off with him into the sunset. The musical high spot comes when Joey sings an electrifying version of 'The Lady Is A Tramp' to the wealthy widow Vera Simpson (Rita Hayworth), who had been known as 'Vanessa The Undresser' in her former life as a stripper. London film critics at the time thought it slightly ridiculous when some of their number actually applauded a piece of celluloid, but it was that kind of performance. Hank Henry, as the grumpy owner of the Barbary Coast nightspot where Joey 'operates', and Bobby Sherwood as the leader of its orchestra, headed a supporting cast that also included Barbara Nicholls and Elizabeth Patterson. The majority of Richard Rodgers and Lorenz Hart's fine stage score was retained, with four additional songs from their other shows. Sinatra was in great voice on 'I Could Write A Book', 'There's a Small Hotel' and

'What Do I Care For A Dame?', while Hayworth shimmied her way through 'Zip' and 'Bewitched' (vocals dubbed by Jo Ann Greer). Trudy Erwin's voice was behind Novak's sultry rendering of 'My Funny Valentine' and 'That Terrific Rainbow'. Hermes Pan was the choreographer, and Dorothy Kingsley's screenplay was adequate - O'Hara's version of events would never have been acceptable even in the late 50s - and this entertaining film grossed nearly $5 million in US rentals alone. It was produced in Technicolor for Columbia by Fred Kohlmar. The director was George Sidney.

PAL JOEY (STAGE MUSICAL)

It was John O'Hara who wrote to composer Richard Rodgers suggesting that a series of pieces he had been writing for the *The New Yorker* magazine might be the basis for a stage musical. They were in the form of letters from a skirt-chasing master of ceremonies in seedy nightclubs to a successful bandleader friend of his, and were signed, 'From your pal, Joey'. Rodgers and his lyric-writing partner Lorenz Hart immediately saw this as an opportunity to create something more realistic and mature than the usual Broadway fare - and it certainly turned out that way. *Pal Joey* made its debut at the Ethel Barrymore Theatre on 25 December 1940, with a book by O'Hara which was set in late 30s Chicago. Joey Evans (Gene Kelly) has surfaced at a cheap club on the south side of the city. His reputation as a heel has preceded him, so singer Gladys Bumps (June Havoc) is not impressed with his tired line of talk. Linda English (Leila Ernst) does not work there, so she could well be available. Not for the time being though, as Joey loses all interest in her when wealthy Vera Simpson (Vivienne Segal) and her party arrive at the club. In return for what he can give her, she sets him up with his own nightclub - he is even interviewed by Melba Snyder (Jean Casto), a hack from the *Herald* - but it all turns sour when Vera finds out that Gladys and phoney agent Ludlow Lowell (Jack Durant) are threatening to tip off her husband about the Joey situation. That is blackmail, so it is goodbye to Joey, the club, and his charge accounts - Love, Vera. As the final curtain hovers, the not-to-bright 'mouse' Linda invites him up to her place - but no, there is this important job waiting back in New York . . . Rodgers and Hart's by-now classic score contained a collection of witty, world-weary, phoney-sentimental, vengeful and sleazy numbers which included 'You Mustn't Kick It Around', 'I Could Write A Book', 'That Terrific Rainbow', 'What Is A Man', 'Happy Hunting Horn', 'What Do I Care For A Dame', 'Ballet' (instrumental), 'Zip', 'Plant You Now, Dig You Later', 'Do It The Hard Way', and 'Take Him'. Vera and Joey were delightfully naughty on 'In Our Little Den Of Iniquity', while Vera's 'Bewitched' ('He's kept enough/He's slept enough/And yet where it counts/He's adept enough/Bewitched, bothered and bewildered am I') left very little to the imagination. It was presented and directed by George Abbott, and choreographed by Robert Alton. The critical reaction was - yes, again - mixed - the famous quote being that of Brooks Atkinson of the *New York Times*, who called the show 'odious', and queried: 'Although it is expertly done, can you draw sweet water from a foul well'. Much later, Rodgers himself wrote in his autobiography that, 'There wasn't one decent character in the entire play except for the girl who briefly fell for Joey - her trouble was simply that she was stupid.' Even so, it had a reasonable run of 374 performances, followed by a three-month tour. A recording of 'Bewitched' by Leo Reisman and his orchestra, with Anita Boyer on vocal, was a modest US hit, and almost a decade later the song received a unique piano-led treatment from the Bill Snyder Orchestra. All of a sudden, there were seven other versions around, both vocal and instrumental. It is said that this outburst prompted Columbia Records to release a long-player of *Pal Joey* with Vivienne Segal and Harold Lang as Vera and Joey. Two years later, the pair headed a 1952 revival which ran for much longer than the original - 54 performances - and won Tony Awards for featured musical actress (Helen Gallagher as Gladys) choreographer (Robert Alton) and conductor and musical director (Max Meth). London audiences finally saw the show 245 times in March 1954 at the Princes Theatre, with Carol Bruce (Vera), Harold Lang (Joey), Jean Brampton (Gladys), and Sally Bazely (Linda). A second opportunity came when a production starring Denis Lawson (Joey), Sîan Phillips (Vera), and Danielle Carson (Linda), travelled from the New Half Moon Theatre to the West End in 1980. There have been further UK regional revivals, but one planned for the Royal National Theatre, with Diana Rigg as Vera, never materialised. In the US regions during the 90s, *Pal Joey* was seen at the Goodspeed Opera House (1990, with Peter Reardon: Joey, Florence Lacey: Vera), Long Beach Opera (1991, Reardon: Joey, Dixie Carter: Vera), and Boston University Theatre (Robert Knepper: Joey, Donna Murphy: Vera). Early in 1998, a revised revival was announced with a new book by playwright Terrence McNally (*Kiss Of The Spiderwoman*), but that was before senior members of its production company, Livent Inc., were accused of serious financial irregularities. The 1957 film version of *Pal Joey* starred Frank Sinatra, Rita Hayworth, and Kim Novak.

PAN, HERMES

b. Hermes Panagiotopulos, between 1905 and 1910, Memphis, Tennessee, USA, d. 19 September 1990, Beverly Hills, California, USA. A dancer and legendary choreographer who worked closely with Fred Astaire on most of his film musicals and television specials. Pan danced in clubs and in the singing chorus of the Broadway musical *Top Speed*, which featured Ginger Rogers, before moving to Hollywood in the early 30s. After serving as assistant to dance director Dave Gould on Flying Down To Rio, Astaire and Rogers' first picture together, and the follow-up, The Gay Divorcee, Pan choreographed all of Astaire's films at RKO, including Roberta, Top Hat, Follow The Fleet, Swing Time, Shall We Dance, Carefree, and The Story Of Vernon And Irene Castle. He won an Oscar for his imaginative staging of the 'Fun House' sequence in another RKO feature, A Damsel In Distress (1937), in which Astaire appeared with George Burns and Gracie Allen. Pan also worked with Astaire on *Second Chorus*, Blue Skies, The Barkleys Of Broadway (with Ginger Rogers again), *Three Little Words*, *Let's Dance*, Silk Stockings, and *Finian's Rainbow* (1968) which was their last movie together. Pan

also made one of his rare on-screen appearances in that one. Over the years, he had occasionally danced in films such as My Gal Sal, *Sweet Rosie O'Grady*, Moon Over Miami, Kiss Me Kate, and *Pin-Up Girl*. However, for most of his career, he was content to make major stars - Betty Grable, Rita Hayworth, Don Ameche, Howard Keel, Juliet Prowse, Alice Faye, Carmen Miranda, Ann Miller, Kathryn Grayson and many others - look good in a variety of mostly entertaining musical pictures such as Billy Rose's Diamond Horseshoe, *Song Of The Islands*, *That Night In Rio*, Footlight Serenade, *Springtime In The Rockies*, Coney Island, *Lovely To Look At*, *That Lady In Ermine*, Hit The Deck, The Student Prince, *Meet Me In Las Vegas*, Pal Joey, Can-Can, Flower Drum Song, My Fair Lady, *Darling Lili*, and *Lost Horizon*. He also staged Cleopatra's spectacular entry into Rome for the Elizabeth Taylor-Richard Burton epic *Cleopatra* in 1963. Pan won Emmy Awards for his work on the highly acclaimed television specials *An Evening With Fred Astaire* (1959) and *Astaire Time* (1961). In 1981 he received the National Film Award for achievement in cinema, and six years later was presented with the prestigious Joffrey Ballet Award. A true innovator, many of the films in which he mixed ballet, jazz and tap, are now rightly regarded as classics.

PANAMA HATTIE

Considered to be similar in some ways to Dubarry Was A Lady (1939), this show was nevertheless felt to be inferior to that one, although it employed the same creative team, and ran for some four months longer. *Panama Hattie* opened at the 46th Street Theatre on 30 October 1940, with a Cole Porter score, a book by Herbert Fields and B.G. 'Buddy' DeSylva, and with the dynamic Ethel Merman on hand to belt out the songs. She plays Hattie Maloney, the owner of a nightclub in Panama City. Outwardly cynical, but a real pussy-cat deep down inside (a perfect Merman character) her prospective marriage to well-heeled divorcé, Nick Bullitt (James Dunn), hangs on the approval of Geraldine - sometimes known as Jerry - (Joan Carroll), the precocious eight-year-old daughter from his first marriage. Hattie wins her over during the conciliatory 'Let's Be Buddies' (Hattie: 'Would you like a big box of chocolate creams?'/Jerry: 'No, for candy I never did care'/Hattie: 'Then will you let me get you a cute little dog?'/Jerry: 'Would you mind making it a bear?'). Merman had several other clever Porter numbers, including 'Make It Another Old Fashioned, Please', 'I'm Throwing A Ball Tonight', and 'I've Still Got My Health' ('I can't count my ribs, like His Nibs, Fred Astaire/But I've still got my health, so what do I care!'). The rest of the songs included 'All I've Got To Get Now Is My Man', 'Fresh As A Daisy', 'My Mother Would Love You', 'Who Would Have Dreamed?', and 'Visit Panama'. The cast included some familiar names of the future such as Betty Hutton, along with June Allyson and Vera-Ellen who were both in the chorus. *Panama Hattie*, which was the fourth in a series of five musicals that Porter and Merman did together, enjoyed a run of 501 performances. It marked the beginning of a decade during which they both produced some of their finest work: Porter with Kiss Me, Kate (1948), and Merman with Annie Get Your Gun (1946). *Panama Hattie* also had a decent run of 308 performances in London's West End, where it starred Bebe Daniels, Max Wall, Ivan Brandt, Claude Hulbert, and Richard Hearne.

PARADE

A controversial slice of American history was retold in this musical which opened for a limited run at the Lincoln Center's Vivian Beaumont Theatre on 17 December 1998. The author, Alfred Uhry, is a native of Atlanta, Georgia, the city where one of the worst acts of anti-Semitic violence this century took place in 1913. In the early hours of 27 April, the body of factory girl Mary Phagan (Christy Carlson Romano) was discovered by a black night watchman, Newt Lee (Ray Aranha). Not until a month later did black 27-year-old janitor Jim Conley (Rufus Bonds Jnr.) tell detectives that the pencil factory's manager, Jewishborn Leo Frank (Brent Carver) from Brooklyn, had killed Mary and then enlisted him to dispose of the body. During Frank's trial, the mood in Atlanta was volatile, but after Judge Roan (Don Chastain), sentenced him to death, there were celebrations throughout the city. In this show, the trial comes at the end of Act I, and consists of nine scenes in a variety of song styles in front of a jury made up of cardboard figures The way in which choreographer Patricia Birch arranged the dancing, exultant crowd surrounding the terrified Leo and his wife, Lucille (Carolee Carmello), made for stunning theatre. The campaign to overturn the conviction began almost immediately, and on 20 June 1915, Georgia's Governor Slaton (John Hickok) commuted the sentence to life imprisonment. Within two months, Frank was lynched - pulled from his bed at the Milledgeville prison, and hung from an oak tree near Phagan's home. In this show, a similar, large leafless tree, dominated Riccardo Hernandez's sets, as other pieces of scenery were arranged round it to suggest the courthouse, factory, etc. Carver and Carmello's impressive performances as Frank and Lucille, were supplemented by excellent portrayals from Luther Rosser (J.B. Adams, Frank's attorney), Herndon Lackey (ambitious prosecutor Hugh Dorsey), and John Leslie Wolfe as satanic newspaper publisher Tom Watson. Other leading roles were played by Jeff Edgerton (Fiddlin' John), Kirk McDonald (Frankie Epps), Evan Pappas (newspaperman Britt Craig), and Jessica Molaskey as Mrs Phagan. A young Broadway newcomer, Jason Robert Brown, wrote the music and lyrics, and critics mentioned particularly Leo and Lucille's poignant 'All The Wasted Time', Leo's 'How Can I Call This Home?', and Lucille's 'Do It Alone'. The remainder of the score, which was full of 'subtle and appealing melodies that drew on a variety of influences from poprock, to R&B and gospel', included 'The Old Red Hills Of Home', Anthem: 'The Dream Of Atlanta', 'The Picture Show', 'Leo At Work/What Am I Waiting For?', Interrogation: 'I Am Trying To Remember', 'Big News', 'Watson's Lullaby', 'Somethin' Ain't Right', 'Real Big News', 'You Don't Know This Man', 'It Goes On And On', 'A Rumblin' And A Rollin'', 'Pretty Music', 'Letter To The Governor', 'This Is Not Over Yet', Blues: 'Feel The Rain Fall', 'Where Will You Stand When The Flood Comes', and 'There Is A Fountain/It Don't Make Sense' (incorporating 'There Is A Fountain' traditional hymn by William

Cowper, melody by Lowell Mason 1772). Jason Robert Brown's music was brilliantly orchestrated by jazz veteran Don Sebesky, former ex-Buddy Rich arranger, and Harold Prince's role as co-conceiver proved to be a pivotal one. His concept of staging the piece around three Confederate Day parades was inspired.

In 1986, Leo Frank was given a posthumous pardon after a former office boy at the factory came forward and said that he saw Jim Conley carrying Mary's body. Conley had died in 1962, but author Alfred Urhy believes he committed the crime, and this musical reflects that view. It is the third part of Uhry's trilogy about the Jewish community in Atlanta, preceded by *Driving Miss Daisy* and *Last Night Of Ballyhoo*. The murder helped launch the Knights Of Mary Phagan, a new incarnation of the Klu Klux Klan, and led to the formation of the Anti-Defamation League of B'nai B'rith. *Parade* is not the first attempt to dramatize the case. Four months after the lynching, the film *Thou Shalt Not Kill*, loosely based on the tragic affair, was released, and the 1937 movie *They Won't Forget*, in which Lana Turner had her first screen role, was a fictionalized adaptation. More recently, there was a television miniseries *The Murder Of Mary Phagan*, and a play produced in Chicago entitled *The Lynching Of Leo Frank*.
● FURTHER READING: *Night Fell On Georgia*, Charles and Louise Samuels.

PARADISE - HAWAIIAN STYLE

Elvis Presley's 60s film career was hampered by poor plots between which it is hard to distinguish. This 1966 feature compounds the problem by simply revisiting the location of one of the singer's most popular movies, Blue Hawaii. It is there the comparisons end; *Paradise - Hawaiian Style* had little of the former's attractive points. Here Presley plays a helicopter pilot flitting from one mini-crisis to another on the way to true love. A soundtrack album, comprising a meagre 10 songs, was hastily recorded. Seen by Presley aficionados as one of his worst albums, it featured material of remarkably poor quality, notably 'Queen Wahine's Papaya', and also, interestingly, two 'out-takes' (of 'Datin'' and 'A Dog's Life') that featured studio chat that betrayed Presley's dissatisfaction with the material he was required to sing.

PARIS BLUES

For a few moments at the beginning, hopes are raised that this is a film that will take seriously the problems of racial intolerance. Soon, however, jazz musicians Paul Newman and Sidney Poitier drift into stereotypes and there is little left for the audience to do except enjoy the scenes of Paris and the music. Fortunately, much of the latter, including the film's score, is in the hands of Duke Ellington, which almost makes up for the disappointment in the dramatics. Apart from Ellington And His Orchestra, which includes Cat Anderson, Willie Cook, Johnny Hodges, Ray Nance, Clark Terry and Sam Woodyard, other musicians include Max Roach, Philly Joe Jones and local boys Joseph Reinhardt and Guy Lafitte. Louis Armstrong puts in an appearance and locks horns with the Ellington ensemble in a rowdy nightclub sequence. The playing of Newman and Poitier was dubbed, respectively, by Murray

McEachern and Paul Gonsalves. Directed by Martin Ritt, this 1961 film was based upon the novel by Harold Flender that did not dodge the issues and in which the black musician was the sole protagonist, his white side-kick being very much a minor character.

PARTY PARTY

An unconvincing farce, the chief attraction of the 1983 film *Party Party* is the soundtrack. Punk, new wave and alternative acts such as the Rezillos, Clash, Go-Gos, Selecter, Bad Manners, Undertones, Stranglers, Sex Pistols, X-Ray Spex and Elvis Costello all make appearances, as do Chas And Dave, Jeff Beck and David Bowie. Daniel Peacock and Tony Winsor's plot concerns Larry's (Perry Fenwick) New Year's Eve Party. Around this singular event director Winsor constructs a series of light anec-dotes about teenage romance and sexual conquest, led by writer Daniel Peacock's portrayal of the hapless Toby. As their ambitions are confounded - everyone desires some-one who desires someone else - Sharon (Sally Anne Law) attempts to drown herself in the bath, before a food fight breaks out in the kitchen. With the party in full swing, Larry's parents return home 'unexpectedly'. Failing to notice the party detritus in the dark as the miscreants hide in the dark, they proceed to make love on the sofa. Toby, however, wanders into the room and turns the light on following his conquest of Brenda (Kim Thomson). The 'game is up', but Larry's parents elect to join in the party spirit rather than chastise their offspring's friends. Trite even by the standards of the party movie genre, among the later notables in the cast were Caroline Quentin and soap opera singing star Nick Berry.

PASSION

Stephen Sondheim's third collaboration (following *Sunday In The Park With George* and *Into The Woods*) with librettist and director James Lapine opened at the Plymouth Theatre in New York on 9 May 1994. Set in the late 19th century, and based on Ettore Scola's 1981 film *Passione d'Amore*, which was adapted from the 1869 novel *Fosca* by Igino Tarchetti, *Passion* opens with a 10-minute sequence in which Giorgio (Jere Shea), a handsome young army officer, and Clara (Marin Mazzie) are making rapturous love, naked on a bed. What follows is a complex and absorbing piece in which Giorgio, after being posted to a far outpost, finds himself the object of the obsessive desire of the unattractive Fosca (Donna Murphy), who is dying. Before the curtain falls, Fosca has changed Giorgio's whole conception as to what real love should be, even inveigling him into writing the kind of love letter she believes he should send to her. Sondheim's score, which critics noted contained some of his most 'direct' love songs, consisted of 'Happiness', 'First Letter', 'Second Letter', 'Third Letter', 'Fourth Letter', 'I Read', 'Transition', 'Garden Sequence', 'Trio', 'I Wish I Could Forget You', 'Soldiers' Gossip', 'Flashback', 'Sunrise Letter', 'Is This What You Call Love?', 'Forty Days', 'Loving You', 'Farewell Letter', 'No One Has Ever Loved You' and Finalé. As usual, Jonathan Tunick's arrangements were singled out for spe-cial praise, as were Jane Greenwood's sumptuous costume designs. *Passion* won Tony Awards for best musical, book,

score, leading actress (Donna Murphy), and a Grammy for Best Musical Show album in 1995, but despite being hailed by *Variety* as 'the most emotionally engaging new musical Broadway has had in years', the show closed on January 1995 after 280 performances. An 'extraordinarily poignant' London production, directed by Jeremy Sams, opened in March 1996. Its stellar cast, which included Michael Ball (Giorgio), Maria Friedman (Fosca), and Helen Hobson (Clara), soldiered on until 28 September with only the *Evening Standard* Award for Best Musical for consolation. In an unusual move, most of the cast re-assembled in the following June in order to record a con-cert version of the show. The resulting CD included an additional 20 minutes of Sondheim's score which was not on the original Broadway cast album. An altogether dif-ferent perspective was provided by the Trotter Trio, with their *Stephen Sondheim's Passion ... In Jazz.*.

PAT GARRETT AND BILLY THE KID

This 1973 feature starred James Cockburn and Kris Kristofferson in the respective title roles. Sam Peckinpah directed the film in customary fashion; violent, blood-splattered images pepper many of the scenes. Critical reaction was divided; Stanley Kauffman declared it showed 'what Peckinpah can do when he doesn't put his mind to it.' The presence of Kristofferson and Rita Coolidge helped bring the rock and movie worlds togeth-er. However, interest in the film from music fans was owing to the presence of Bob Dylan. His role as the mono-syllabic 'Alias' was initially much larger, but his scenes were among many cut from the final print. Dylan also contributed the low-key, but atmospheric soundtrack music. His album of the same name reached the UK Top 30 and although the main theme from the film, 'Knocking On Heaven's Door' was only a minor Top 20 hit when issued as a single, the song has since become one of the artist's most popular compositions, inspiring several cover versions. Its appeal has outlasted the film it is drawn from. If *Pat Garrett And Billy The Kid* retains any fascination, it is because of Dylan's role, rather than being the product of a director responsible for the superior *The Wild Bunch* and *Straw Dogs*.

PATINKIN, MANDY

b. Mandel Patinkin, 30 November 1952, Chicago, Illinois, USA. An actor and singer with a 'wonderfully expressive voice', as a boy Patinkin sang in the choir at his Jewish temple, and performed in musicals such as *Anything Goes*, *Stop The World - I Want To Get Off* and *Carousel* at the local youth centre. After attending the University of Kansas and studying drama at the Juilliard School of Music, he worked in regional theatre before spending most of the late 70s with the New York Festival Theatre. In 1980 he won a Tony Award for his portrayal of Che in the Broadway production of *Evita*, and was nominated again, four years later, for his performance in the leading role of *Sunday In The Park With George*. In 1985 Patinkin was one of the many stars of *Follies In Concert* which played for two nights only at the Avery Fisher Hall in New York. His version of 'Buddy's Blues', in particular, is one of the cast CD's many highlights. A year later, Patinkin featured on another fine album, a new CBS studio recording of Richard Rodgers and Oscar Hammerstein II's classic South Pacific, on which he was joined by opera singers Kiri Te Kanawa and Jose Carreras. The album went to number 5 in the UK chart, and Patinkin's sensitive version of 'Younger than Springtime' was released as a single. In 1989, his one-man show, *Mandy Patinkin In Concert: Dress Casual* played for a four week season at the Helen Hayes Theatre, in New York, and in 1990 Patinkin co-starred with Claire Moore in the world premiere of the Jason Carr/Julian Barry/Peter Hall musical *Born Again*, based on Eugene Ionesco's play *Rhinoceros*, at the Chichester Festival Theatre in England. Since making his film debut in *The Big Fix* in 1978, Patinkin has made highly effective appearances in several other movies, including *Ragtime*, *Yentl*, *Dick Tracy* (in the role of 88 Keys, Madonna's pianist), *True Colours*, *The Doctor*, and *The Music Of Chance* (1993). In 1991 he was back on Broadway, playing the hunchbacked uncle, Archibald Craven, in *The Secret Garden*, and in January 1993 he succeeded Michael Rupert as Marvin in *Falsettos*. In 1994 Patinkin played Sky Masterson in a BBC Radio 2 recording of *Guys And Dolls*, and in 1994/5 was on international television screens, starring in the medical drama series *Chicago Hope*, winning Emmy and Golden Globe nominations. He subsequently appeared in concert at the Almeida Theatre in London (1996) and on Broadway (1997), 'wrapping all of the songs in an emotionally charged melodrama that works because of his undeniable vocal talent'. Also in 1997, Patinkin joined an impressive cast, which included Henry Goodman and Margot Leicester, in a BBC Television adaptation of Arthur Miller's *Broken Glass*. In the following year, supported by just a violinist and pianist, Patinkin starred on Broadway in a musical entertainment entitled *Mamaloshen*. Almost all the songs, a collection of old European folk tunes, laments of the Holocaust, and the occasional show number, were sung in Yiddish.

● ALBUMS: *Mandy Patinkin* (CBS 1989)★★★, *Dress Casual* (CBS 1991)★★★★, *Experiment* (Elektra Nonesuch 1994)★★★, *Oscar And Steve* (Nonesuch 1995)★★★, *Mamaloshen* (Nonesuch 1998)★★★★, and many Original Cast recordings.

● FILMS: *The Big Fix* (1978), *French Postcards* (1979), *Last Embrace* (1979), *Night Of The Juggler* (1980), *Ragtime* (1981), *Yentl* (1983), *Daniel* (1983), *Maxie* (1985), *The Princess Bride* (1987), *Alien Nation* (1988), *The House On Carroll Street* (1988), *Dick Tracy* (1990), *Impromptu* (1991), *True Colors* (1991), *The Doctor* (1991), *The Music Of Chance* (1993), *Life With Mikey* (1993), *Squanto: A Warrior's Tale* (1994), *Men With Guns* (1997), *Lulu On The Bridge* (1998).

PEGGY-ANN

With a score by Richard Rodgers and Lorenz Hart, and a book by Herbert Fields, this show opened at the Vanderbilt Theatre in New York on 27 December 1926. It was sandwiched between *Lido Lady* and *Betsy*, two fairly unsatisfactory Rodgers and Hart shows that were produced in the same year. *Peggy-Ann* was sub-titled 'The Utterly Different Musical Comedy', and, in some respects, that proved to be true. To begin with, it was a hit, and although Fields's book was based on the Edgar Smith and

A. Baldwin Sloane's 1910 musical *Tillie's Nightmare*, in which Marie Dressler had enjoyed great success, it had highly topical overtones. 1926 was the year of the Surrealists, a new movement in poetry and painting whose members believed in the 'omnipotence of the dream', and were heavily influenced by Sigmund Freud. The libretto for *Peggy-Ann* was liberally sprinkled with Freudian references, and follows Peggy-Ann Barnes (Helen Ford), a domestic servant in a boarding house in Glen Falls, New York, into her own private fantasy world. In a trice, she is travelling the globe, tasting the high-life at the race track, aboard a yacht, shopping on New York's Fifth Avenue - and getting married in her underwear. There were some other unusual touches, too: no songs were sung in the opening 15 minutes of the show, and there was no rousing finale. Also, the sets and props were moved around in full view of the audience, a device used by Rodgers again, 36 years later, in No Strings. The songs, when they eventually came, were a pleasing bunch, and one of them, 'A Tree In The Park', achieved some popularity through recordings by Helen Morgan and Frank Black. 'Where's That Rainbow?' also endured, and is often performed by supper-club singers such as Bobby Short. The rest of the score included 'A Little Bird Told Me So' 'and 'Maybe It's Me'. A New York run of 333 performances was followed by a further 130 in London, where the role of Peggy-Ann was played by Dorothy Dickson.

PERCHANCE TO DREAM

When this stage musical opened at the London Hippodrome on 21 April 1945, it was conceived as Ivor Novello's 'victory presentation', although the longed-for actual end to World War II was still some months away. As an antidote to the dreary, weary state of post-war Britain, Novello set out to recreate the kind of musical nostalgia with which he had been linked so successfully during the late 30s and early 40s. For some time, he had envisaged a play which would be set in and around an English stately home named Hunter's Moon (or Huntersmoon). The story would then trace the occupants from early in the nineteenth century via the middle of that century, to the present day, and *Perchance To Dream* gave him the opportunity to put the idea into practice. It also gave him a further opportunity, in that he - and his leading ladies - were able to play three characters. Novello's first was Sir Graham Rodney, a Regency roué who pays his debts by moonlighting as a highwayman, ditches his mistress, Lydia Lyddington (Muriel Barron), for the lovely Melinda Fayre (Roma Beaumont), but soon comes to a sticky end. In Act II, the current owner of Huntersmoon, choirmaster Valentine Fayre (Novello), is married to Veronica Lyddington (Barron), but is about to elope with Melanie (Beaumont) when his wife tells him she is pregnant. Melanie commits suicide. In the contemporary scene, the descendants of these tragic liaisons finally find happiness when Bay Fayre (Novello) marries Melody Fayre (Beaumont). The delightful Margaret Rutherford, whose movie heyday was yet to come, played the dowager Lady Charlotte Fayre, and also in the cast were Olive Gilbert, Dunstan Hart, and Robert Andrews. Olive Gilbert and Muriel Barron introduced the show's big hit, 'We'll Gather

Lilacs', Barron had 'Love Is My Reason', and the rest of this gorgeous, and often playful score, included 'A Woman's Heart', 'The Glo-Glo', 'Highwayman Love', 'The Path My Lady Walks', 'When The Gentlemen Get Together', and 'Curtsy To The King'. The songs were all the more remarkable because *Perchance To Dream* was the only one of Novello's musicals for which he wrote his own lyrics. His regular man, Christopher Hassall, was still on Forces duty. The show ran for a remarkable 1,022 performances, before touring South Africa (with Zena Dare taking over from Margaret Rutherford) to great acclaim, and then spent 10 months visiting the British regions while Novello was preparing his final orgy of beautiful music and romance - *King's Rhapsody*.

PERCY

This 1971 British film, directed by Ralph Thomas, starred Hywel Bennett as the recipient of a penis transplant. Intrigued as to who the donor was, he embarks on a series of adventures to try to find out. Elke Sommer and Britt Ekland also feature in the cast of this sex comedy, packed with *double entendre* and innuendo, typical of the *Carry On* and *Confessions of a...* genres. The formula wore thin long before the film's conclusion, but a sequel, *Percy's Progress*, followed in 1974. However, *Percy* did boast a fine soundtrack, courtesy of Ray Davies and his group, the Kinks. 'Lola', the 1970 UK number 2 hit which effectively relaunched their career, was one notable inclusion. The score also featured some of Davies' best work from this period, such as 'Willesden Green', a satirical country and western number, and the poignant 'God's Children'. The set was far superior to the film from which it was derived.

PERFORMANCE

One of the most beguiling rock-related films, *Performance* allowed Mick Jagger to exorcise the ghost of the hapless Ned Kelly and play a role suited to his complex persona. Directed by Nicolas Roeg and Donald Cammell - the latter of whom also wrote the screenplay - *Performance* features James Fox as a vicious gangster who takes refuge in Jagger's flat. The Rolling Stones vocalist plays the failing pop star to perfection and his decaying, bohemian lifestyle at first repulses, then absorbs, Fox. Their identities become intertwined and although Fox is latterly taken away by mobster enemies, it is Jagger's face which peers out from the rear window of the car. Randy Newman took charge of the soundtrack music, contributing his own memorable 'Gone Dead Train' and assembling work from such disparate acts as Ry Cooder, Merry Clayton and the Last Poets. Meanwhile, Jagger's own contribution, 'Memo From Turner', was an explosive song which accompanied one of the film's most powerful segments. In the first inkling of alter egos, Jagger repulsively imagines himself crime boss. Released in 1970, *Performance* is a dense, impressive film which bears - and is enhanced - by repeated viewings.

PETE KELLY'S BLUES

A marvellous opening sequence, depicting the funeral of a New Orleans jazz musician, is the best moment in what is otherwise a fairly predictable movie tale of jazzmen and gangsters in the 20s. Other bright spots are appearances by singers Peggy Lee and Ella Fitzgerald. Teddy Buckner plays in the opening scene and elsewhere can be heard the likes of Nick Fatool, Matty Matlock, Eddie Miller, George Van Eps and Joe Venuti. The role of Pete Kelly is played by Jack Webb, who also directed, and his trumpet playing was dubbed by Dick Cathcart. Lee Marvin made the most unlikely-looking clarinettist in jazz history, with the possible exception of Pee Wee Russell. Four years later, in 1959, a television spin-off lasted 13 episodes.

PETER PAN (FILM MUSICAL)
(see Disney, Walt)

PETER PAN (STAGE MUSICAL)

A musical adaptation of J.M. Barrie's classic story was presented in New York as early as 1905 when Maude Adams and Ernest Lawford starred in a Charles Frohman production. It was revived in 1924, with Marilyn Miller in the leading role, and included two Jerome Kern songs, 'The Sweetest Thing In Life' and 'Just Because You're You'. The 1950 version, which ran for 321 performances, starred Jean Arthur and Boris Karloff. Leonard Bernstein wrote the music and lyrics for several songs, such 'Who Am I?', 'Never-Land', 'Peter, Peter' and 'My House', and Alec Wilder also provided some incidental music. In the fourth interpretation, which opened at the Winter Garden in New York on 20 October 1954, Mary Martin, returning to Broadway for the first time since her triumph in South Pacific, played a spirited, high-flying Peter, to Cyril Ritchard's amusingly degenerate Captain Hook. The initial score, which was written by Moose Charlap and Carolyn Leigh, contained songs such as 'Tender Shepherd', 'I've Got To Crow', 'I'm Flying', and 'I Won't Grow Up'. Before the show reached Broadway, director and choreographer Jerome Robbins asked Jule Styne, Betty Comden and Adolph Green to provide the music and lyrics for several additional numbers, including 'Captain Hook's Waltz', 'Wendy', 'Mysterious Lady', and the lovely 'Never Never Land', which is still sung occasionally, and received a sensitive reading from Lena Horne on her *Lena At The Sands*. Mary Martin received the Tony Award for best actress, and this version ran for 152 performances before it was taped and shown on US television, giving non theatre-going audiences a rare opportunity to see a Broadway show. A 1979 New York revival, starring Sandy Duncan and George Rose, beat all the previous versions and lasted for 551 performances. Six years later, the same production played London's West End, with Joss Ackland, Judith Bruce and Bonnie Langford. In 1990, Cathy Rigby and Stephen Hanan were Peter and Hook/Darling when *Peter Pan* looked in on Broadway again for a limited six-week engagement as part of its nationwide tour. Later in the 90s Cathy Rigby (by now a mother of four) was back on the road again with a new production (Paul Schoeffler as Hook/Darling) which spent Christmas 1998 in New York at the Marquis Theatre. Earlier that year the much acclaimed *Peter And Wendy*, Liza Lorwin's adaptation of the Barrie fantasy, was presented at New York's Victory Theatre by the Mabou Mines troupe. It 'melded movement, theatre, imagery and music into a rich theatrical tapestry', and featured an extraordinary performance by Karen Kandel. She narrated the action and provided the voices for all the characters, including Peter Pan, Captain Hook, and Mr. and Mrs. Darling, which were represented by Bunraku puppets. Johnny Cunningham's Celtic music score enhanced this delightful show perfectly, and Karen Kandel won a Village Voice Obie Award for oustanding work. Numerous other, quite different adaptations of J. M. Barrie's *Peter Pan* have been presented in the UK, including two major London productions: one with music and lyrics by Stephen Oliver at the Barbican Theatre in 1982; and another, *Peter Pan: The British Musical*, with a score by Piers Chater-Robinson, which starred Ron Moody (Hook) and Nicola Stapleton (Peter), and played at the Cambridge Theatre in 1994. In 1997, John Caird directed a Royal National Theatre revival of their 1982 version of *Peter Pan*, with Ian McKellen's Hook sparring with a male Peter, Daniel Evans. In 1996, Varése Sarabande released *The Musical Adventures Of Peter Pan*, which featured 'Great songs from Mary Martin's *Peter Pan*, Walt Disney's *Peter Pan*, Leonard Bernstein's *Peter Pan*, Anthony Newley and Leslie Bricusse's *Peter Pan*, *Hook* by John Williams, and more!' Several classic numbers were included, plus rare cut items by Broadway singers such as Susan Egan, Liz Larsen, Christa Moore, and Jonathan Freeman.

● FURTHER READING: *The Peter Pan Chronicles*, Bruce K. Hanson.

PETERS, BERNADETTE

b. Bernadette Lazzara, 28 February 1948, Ozone Park, Queens, New York City, New York, USA. Often called 'the finest singing actress since Barbra Streisand', Bernadette Peters is certainly one of the few leading ladies of the last decade or so whose name on a Broadway marquee can cause box-office queues to form before the show has gone into previews. She was tap-dancing and acting at an early age, and joined Actors' Equity when she was nine. Soon afterwards she changed her name to Peters, and played Tessie in the 1959 revival of *The Most Happy Fella* at the New York City Centre. After appearing in the role of Baby June in a road tour of *Gypsy*, she gave up performing for a time, and studied acting and singing in her teens, before returning to the stage in two off-Broadway shows, *The Penny Friend* (1966) and a Shirley Temple parody, *Curley McDimple* (1967). In 1968 she received favourable notices, and a Theatre World citation, for her portrayal of George M. Cohan's sister in *George M!*, and, in the same year, won a Drama Desk Award for her 'hilarious performance' as the zany Ruby in *Dames At Sea*, a 30s movie-spoof that enjoyed a good run off-Broadway. Several of the projects with which Peters was involved in the late 60s and early 70s had only brief runs, including *La Strada* (one performance). Nevertheless, she gained Tony Awards nominations for her part in a New York revival of *On The Town* and *Mack And Mabel*. In the latter she played silent movie star Mabel Normand, opposite Robert Preston as Mack Sennett. The show may have only lasted for two months, but the cast album endured to become a cult item. She turned to films and television, often playing straight roles, but without any really notable success. Over the years, her television work has included series such as *All's Fair*

(1976), *The Martian Chronicles* (1980), *The Carol Burnett Show* (1991), voice for the popular animated *Animaniacs* (1993), and *The Odyssey* (1997), as well as television films; *The Islander* (1978), *David* (1988), *Fall From Grace* (1990), *The Last Best Year* (1990), *What The Deaf Man Heard* (1997), *Holiday In Your Heart* (1997), and the third major small screen production of Richard Rodgers and Oscar Hammerstein II's *Cinderella*, in which Peters played the Wicked Stepmother. In 1977 Peters formed a private and professional partnership with the comedian Steve Martin, and they appeared together in two movies, *The Jerk* (1979), and the highly expensive box-office disaster *Pennies From Heaven* (1981), for which Peters won a Golden Globe Award. Her other films around this time included the musical *Annie*, in which she played Lily, the fiendish social worker. In the 80s she excelled in three Broadway musicals, two of which had scores by Stephen Sondheim, *Sunday In The Park With George* (1984, Tony nomination) and *Into The Woods* (1987). She finally won the Actress (Musical) Tony Award for her brilliant solo performance in Andrew Lloyd Webber and Don Black's *Song And Dance* (1985). During the latter part of the decade, Peters developed her cabaret act, which revolved around Broadway show tunes but also contained a lovely version of Hank Williams' 'I'm So Lonesome I Could Cry', and a highly effective Harold Arlen medley. In 1993 she was back on Broadway with Martin Short and Carol Woods in the eagerly awaited *The Goodbye Girl*. In spite of Neil Simon's witty book and a score by Marvin Hamlisch and David Zippel, the show folded after only 188 performances, but Peters departed with another Tony nomination. After being inducted into the Theater Hall of Fame in 1995, a year later she was acclaimed in concert at Carnegie Hall. Sondheim material, such as 'Not A Day Goes By', 'There Won't Be Trumpets', 'Being Alive', 'Move On', 'No One Is Alone', and 'Happiness', formed the core of her performance, and the resulting 'live' album was appropriately entitled *Sondheim, Etc.* In September 1998, she made her UK solo concert debut at London's Royal Festival Hall with a similar show. This followed on from her 'knock-out' rendition of 'Unexpected Song' (from *Song And Dance*) and other numbers, in the Cameron Mackintosh royal gala *Hey Mr Producer!*, earlier in the year. Early in 1999, Peters was due to star on Broadway as sharp-shooter Annie Oakley in the Irving Berlin-Herbert and Dorothy Fields classic musical, *Annie Get Your Gun*.

● ALBUMS: *Bernadette Peters* (1980)★★★, *Now Playing* (1981)★★★, *I'll Be Your Baby Tonight* (Angel 1996)★★★★, *Sondheim, Etc.* (Angel 1997)★★★, and Original Cast and film soundtrack recordings.

● FILMS: *Ace Eli And Rodger Of The Skies* (1973), *The Longest Yard* (1974), *W.C. Fields And Me* (1976), *Vigilante Force* (1976), *Silent Movie* (1976), *The Jerk* (1979), *Pennies From Heaven* (1981), *Heartbeeps* (1981), *Tulips* (1981), *Annie* (1982), *Pink Cadillac* (1989), *Slaves Of New York* (1989), *Alice* (1990), *Impromptu* (1991), voice only *Anastasia* (1997).

PETULIA

Richard Lester, famed for his work with the Beatles, directed this 1968 film which starred Julie Christie, George C. Scott and Richard Chamberlain. Set in San Francisco, the thin plot revolved around marital problems between Christie and Scott and her attempts to find succour with the recently-divorced Chamberlain. The gifted Lester worked miracles with this slight premise and composer John Barry contributed a suitably evocative score. However, musical interest revolves appearances by two seminal San Franciscan bands. Big Brother And The Holding Company (featuring Janis Joplin) perform a mesmerising version of 'Road Block' at a society party, while the Grateful Dead are filmed onstage in full, acid rock flow. Members of the group can also be spotted in a crowd scene near the film's close. Such interludes have ensured *Petulia* its lasting reputation.

PHANTOM OF THE OPERA, THE

This is probably Andrew Lloyd Webber's most highly regarded and critically acclaimed work to date. Of course, the vast majority of his other productions, including those he wrote with Tim Rice and the later ones where people pretend to be cats and trains, have been enormously successful all over the world for many years now, but *The Phantom Of The Opera* seems to be the show that gives audiences the deepest and most enduring satisfaction. It opened at Her Majesty's Theatre in London on 9 October 1986. The score was by Lloyd Webber (music) and Charles Hart (lyrics), with additional lyrics by Richard Stilgoe. Lloyd Webber and Stilgoe also wrote the book, which was based on Gaston Leroux's classic 1911 novel. The familiar story is set in the Paris Opera House during the 19th century, where the facially disfigured masked Phantom (Michael Crawford) haunts and terrorizes the occupants. He is obsessed with the young and beautiful soprano, Christine (Sarah Brightman or Claire Moore), and whisks her away below the theatre, steering her through the candlelit sewers to his richly furnished rooms deep under the streets of the city. He teaches her to sing 'like an angel' and she initially becomes entranced by him, but she still loves another. In his rage, the Phantom threatens to blow up the opera house if she refuses to stay with him. She agrees to his blackmail, but when she kisses him without any apparent sign of revulsion at his deformity, he is so moved that he releases her into the arms of Raoul (Steve Barton), her leading man. Lloyd Webber's 'ravishing' music was his most romantic and overtly operatic so far - and arguably his best. The score contained two outstanding love songs, 'All I Ask Of You', sung by Brightman and Barton, and 'The Music Of The Night', impressively rendered by Crawford, but there were others equally attractive, including 'Masquerade', 'Wandering Child', 'The Phantom Of The Opera', 'Angel Of Music', 'Think Of Me', 'Wishing You Were Somehow Here Again', and 'The Point Of No Return'. Hal Prince's highly impressive staging featured the by-now famous scene in which the great chandelier crashes down from the ceiling on to the stage - one of the Phantom's pranks in reprisal for his protegée not being given the lead. Crawford, who maintains that he only got the job because Lloyd Webber heard him singing while waiting to collect his then wife, Sarah Brightman, from her own lesson, dominated in the leading role. After appearing on the London stage in the musicals Billy and Barnum, and on film in Hello, Dolly!, this show marked a new beginning in his career. He had a UK Top 10 hit with 'The Music Of The Night', and won the Laurence Olivier Award for best actor in a musical. The show itself won for best musical, while Sarah Brightman and Cliff Richard almost made the top of the UK chart (number 3) with their duet of 'All I Ask Of You'. While *The Phantom Of The Opera* settled in for a long London run, Crawford, Brightman, and Barton recreated their roles for the Broadway production which opened at the Majestic Theatre on 26 January 1988. 'A muted triumph' was the consensus of opinion, but there was nothing muted about the show's appeal when Tony Awards time came round. *The Phantom Of The Opera* won for best musical, actor (Crawford), featured actress (Judy Kaye), sets, costumes, lighting, and director (Prince). Since that time, both the UK and US productions have continued to be the hottest tickets in town, and touring versions have proliferated in many countries. In 1993, as the London production celebrated its seventh anniversary, a second company was dispatched to the provinces, and, in the same year, it was estimated that the show had grossed over $1 billion worldwide.

There have been several other musical adaptations of Gaston Leroux's famous story. The two best-known versions are *Phantom Of The Opera* by Ken Hill, and *Phantom* with a book by Arthur Kopit and music and lyrics by Maury Yeston. Ken Hill's show, which is billed as 'The Original Stage Musical', was first seen in 1984 at the Theatre Royal, Stratford East in London. After revisions, and the negative impact of the Lloyd Webber version, it ran for six months at the Shaftesbury Theatre in the West End from 1991-92, with Peter Straker as the Phantom, music by composers such as Offenbach, Gounod, Verdi, Weber, Bizet, and Mozart, and witty and original lyrics by Hill. The Yeston-Kopit version ('A New Musical Thriller') first emerged in 1990 as a four-hour mini-series on US television with Burt Lancaster and Charles Dance, and was later presented on stage at such venues as the Music Hall, Texas, and the Paper Mill Playhouse, New Jersey. The *Phantom* phenomenon continues in many forms, but as far as the public at large are concerned it probably all started with the 1925 film which starred Lon Chaney. Subsequent screen versions were released in 1943 (with Claude Rains, Susanna Foster and Nelson Eddy), 1962 (Herbert Lom, Heather Sears, and Thorley Walters), 1983 (Maximilian Schell, Jane Seymour and Michael York), and 1989 (Robert Englund, Jill Schoelen and Alex Hyde-Whyte).

● FURTHER READING: *The Complete Phantom Of The Opera*, George Perry.

PHIL THE FLUTER

This show began its life in Dublin as a radio play by Donal Giltinan, based on the life of the celebrated Irish entertainer Percy French, who composed such memorable songs as 'The Mountains Of Mourne' and 'Phil The Fluter's Ball'. The radio show evolved into the stage musical *The Golden Years* which was presented successfully at the Gaiety Theatre in Dublin where it caught the eye of one of London's leading theatrical producers, Harold Fielding. He determined to produce the show in London, and engaged Beverly Cross to collaborate with Giltinan on the book, and composer David Heneker, of Half A Sixpence fame, to supplement Percy French's original score. The result, *Phil The Fluter*, opened in the West End at the Palace Theatre on 13 November 1969. The popular singer Mark Wynter, in the role of Percy French, was retained from the cast of *The Golden Years*, and he was joined by comedian and impressionist Stanley Baxter and one of the most celebrated leading ladies of the London musical stage, Evelyn Laye. Her rendition of Heneker's poignant 'They Don't Make Them Like That Any More' ('In those days men gave orchids by the dozen/Today they think forget-me-nots will do') still burns brightly in the memory more than 20 years later. She also had a charming duet with Wynter, 'You Like It'. The remainder of the score, a mixture of French and Heneker, included 'If I Had A Chance', 'Mama', 'A Favour For A Friend', 'Good Money', 'How Would You Like Me?', 'Abdoul Abulbul Ameer', 'I Shouldn't Have To Be The One To Tell You', 'Follow Me', 'Are You Right There, Michael?', 'That's Why The Poor Man's Dead', and 'Wonderful Woman'. Following a set of mixed reviews, the show never really caught on with the public, and closed after 125 performances.

PIAF

Legend has it that when Pam Gems was writing this musical play about Edith Piaf, 'the mid-20th century chanteuse who took to young men, drugs and fame, and regretted nothing', she saw Elaine Paige in a West End show and decided that she would be the ideal choice for the lead. But in the early 70s Paige was too young, and had yet to make a name for herself, so the role went to Jane Lapotaire, whose nerve-shattering performance earned her a Tony Award when the show transferred to Broadway. Since then, Elaine Paige has established herself as one of the outstanding leading ladies on the London musical stage, and was therefore first in line to star in Peter Hall's revival which began its limited run on 13 December 1993. However, Miss Paige was not too happy with Hall's choice of theatre - the Piccadilly - because of its recent association with a series of flop musicals which included Mutiny!, *Metropolis*, King, Moby Dick, and Which Witch. She need not have worried: the critics were unanimous in their praise for her 'astonishingly poignant performance as the tiny, black-garbed creature - a powerhouse of emotion'. She matched Piaf vulgarity for vulgarity, but her finest moments came when she sang those resounding anthems, 'Mon Dieu', 'Je Ne Regrette Rein', and the impassioned aria of loss, 'Hymne A L'Amour'. Lapotaire still lingers in the memory but, with her powerful vocal range and heart-rending, emotional vibrato, Elaine Paige was Edith Piaf to the life. In May-June 1998, at the Drill Hall, London, Elizabeth Mansfield gave a 'thrilling performance' in *Homage To Love*, a musical homage to Piaf by Steve Stafford, who was also responsible for translating most of the songs into English.

PICKWICK

Devised as a vehicle for the popular British comedian and singer Harry Secombe, *Pickwick* had a book by Wolf Mankowitz which was based on Charles Dickens' novel,

The Pickwick Papers. Leslie Bricusse, fresh from his triumph with Stop The World - I Want To Get Off, wrote the lyrics, and the music was composed by Cyril Ornadel. *Pickwick* opened at the Saville Theatre in London on 4 July 1963, and was what one critic described as 'comic-strip Dickens'. Secombe made a jovial, likeable Pickwick, and his adventures with familiar characters such as Sam Weller (Teddy Green), Tony Weller (Robin Wentworth), Mrs. Bardell (Jessie Evans), Augustus Snodgrass (Julian Orchard), and Mr. Jingle (Anton Rodgers), made for an extremely enjoyable evening. The score, a mixture of lively and amusing numbers and one or two spirited ballads, included 'There's Something About You', 'That's What I Want For Christmas', 'The Trouble With Women', 'You Never Met A Feller Like Me', 'A Bit Of Character', 'Look Into Your Heart', 'Talk', 'Learn A Little Something', and 'Do As You Would Be Done By'. The show's big number, 'If I Ruled The World', is sung by Mr. Pickwick when he is mistaken for a parliamentary candidate. It gave Secombe a UK Top 20 hit, and is probably the song most associated with him. After a satisfying London run of some 20 months, *Pickwick* travelled to New York, via a successful stop-over in San Francisco, but Broadway audiences were unimpressed, and the show folded after only 56 performances. Roy Castle, the much-admired UK all-round entertainer, and a good friend of Secombe's, played the role of Sam Weller in the American production. Thirty years later, when *Pickwick* was revived at the Chichester Festival Theatre, prior to a season at London's Sadler's Wells, Castle joined Secombe again - this time as Sam's father, Tony.

PICTURES AT AN EXHIBITION

Progressive rock of the early 70s was epitomised by Emerson, Lake And Palmer, a supergroup formed by Keith Emerson (organ, ex-Nice), Greg Lake (bass/vocals, ex-King Crimson) and Carl Palmer (drums, ex-Crazy World Of Arthur Brown, Atomic Rooster). In 1972 the trio released a classics/rock fusion of Mussorgsky's *Pictures At An Exhibition* which in turn inspired this film. Comprising in-concert footage interspersed with images from *Marvel* comics, this feature included some of the group's best-known compositions, including 'Take A Pebble', 'Knife Edge' and 'The Barbarian', drawn from their albums *Emerson, Lake and Palmer* and *Tarkus*, as well as the title piece. As if to prove they were not devoid of humour, the trio also offer a reading of 'Nut Rocker', a jokey adaptation of part of Tchaikovsky's 'Nutcracker Suite', originally recorded by B. Bumble And The Stingers. Ably directed, the strength of *Pictures At An Exhibition* depends on the viewer's enjoyment of the group's chosen *métier*.

PIED PIPER, THE

'Come, children of the Universe. Let Donovan take you away,' ran the faintly hysterical by-line of this 1971 feature, directed by French auteur, Jacques Demy. Donovan did indeed take centre stage, playing the title role, composing the soundtrack music and singing lead on each one. The meticulously hand-picked cast included Donald Pleasance, Michael Horden, Diana Dors and John Hurt, but despite some memorable cinematography, the final results veered awkwardly between *passé*, hippie-styled fantasy and self-conscious seriousness. Perhaps if the star had not passed his artistic peak the film may have proved more interesting. However an earlier feature, *Brother Sun, Sister Moon*, proved equally flawed.

PINK FLOYD AT POMPEII

This 1971 film featured a performance by Pink Floyd in the deserted amphitheatre of the Roman city. The surrounding ruins added a chilling atmosphere to the quartet's performance, which included versions of their most popular live numbers, including 'A Saucerful Of Secrets', 'Set The Controls For The Heart Of The Sun', and 'Careful With That Axe, Eugene', as well as material which would later appear on *Meddle*: 'One Of These Days' and 'Echoes'. *Pink Floyd At Pompeii* captures the group at the peak of their improvisatory period. Dave Gilmour's guitar work and Rick Wright's organ playing are particularly well-served, helping to define this era's Pink Floyd sound. Spilt-screen shots and psychedelic imagery, although predictable, add to the atmosphere, although the interview material suggests the band speak best through their music. Ably directed by a joint French/Belgian/German company, *Pink Floyd At Pompeii* quickly became a firm favourite of late-night cinema audiences and while dated by today's standards, it remains a valuable aural and visual testament to the group's considerable power.

PINK LADY, THE

After writing the music for several successful shows on the London stage between 1894 and 1909, Ivan Caryll moved to America and collaborated with C.M.S. McLellan on the celebrated operetta, *The Pink Lady*, which opened at the New Amsterdam theatre in New York on 13 March 1911. McLellan's book was based on a French play, *Le Satyre*, by Georges Berr and Marcel Guillemand, and concerns Lucien Garidel (William Elliot), who is soon to marry Angele (Alice Dovey). Before he 'puts the ball and chain on', he decides that he would like to 'bring champagne on', and invites an old flame, Claudine (Hazel Dawn), for one last farewell dinner. Unluckily for him, his future wife is dining at the same restaurant, and cannot help noticing Lucien's companion, who is known as 'The Pink Lady' because of her blushing wardrobe. The embarrassing situation leads to some bewildering twists and turns in the plot, culminating in the reunion of the happy couple as Lucien sings 'My Beautiful Lady' to his Angele. The lovely waltz became widely successful through versions by Lucy Isabelle Marsh, Grace Kerns, and Elizabeth Spencer, and another song from the show, 'By The Saskatchewan' ('Flow river, flow, down to the sea'), was made popular by Reinald Werrenrath and the Hayden Quartet, amongst others. The rest of a romantic and tuneful score included 'The Kiss Waltz', 'The Right To Love', 'Parisian Two-Step', 'Bring Along The Camera', 'The Hudson Belle', 'I Like It', and 'Donny Didn't, Donny Did'. Critics agreed that, unlike most operettas, the songs emerged quite naturally from the plot. It all added up to a tremendous success, and a run of 312 performances. Hazel North, who not only sang and danced in a charming manner, but also played the violin, delighted London audi-

ences when *The Pink Lady* opened at the Globe theatre in 1912. Since those days it has been revived on many occasions.

PINOCCHIO
(see Disney, Walt)

PINS AND NEEDLES

Originally presented by members of the USA International Ladies Garment Workers Union at New York's tiny Labor Stage (formerly the Princess Theatre) for the enjoyment of their fellow workers, this revue subsequently transferred to the Windsor Theatre (which had nearly three times as many seats), and ran for a (then) record 1,108 performances. Armed with a liberal, pro-union point of view, it opened on 27 November 1937, and proceeded to take a satirical swipe at the usual targets, Fascists, Nazis, and Britain's injustice to its long-established Empire. Anyone who could 'Sing Me A Song Of Social Significance', as its most popular number demanded, was OK, of course, and if you could take your partner for 'Doin' The Reactionary', well, that was even better. The sketches were by the show's director, Charles Freidman, amongst several others, and the music and lyrics were provided by a newcomer to Broadway, Harold Rome. His other songs included 'Sunday In The Park', 'Nobody Makes A Pass At Me', 'One Big Union For Two', 'I've Got The Nerve To Be In Love', 'Chain Store Daisy (Vassar Girl Finds A Job)', 'It's Better With A Union Man', 'Not Cricket To Picket', and 'Four Little Angels Of Peace'. When it moved to the Windsor Theatre in 1939, the show was retitled *New Pins And Needles*, and continued on its honest, angry, but good-humoured way, constantly updating the material as it went.

PIPPIN

Director and choreographer Bob Fosse was mainly responsible for bringing this Stuart Ostrow production to Broadway some five years after its conception. He also collaborated with librettist Roger O. Hirson in expanding and revising the original material so that it immediately captured the imagination of Broadway audiences following *Pippin*'s debut at the Imperial Theatre on 23 October 1972. Following hard on the heels of the second, hippie half of the 60s, during which the search for freedom, peace, fulfilment, and - most importantly - one's own true identity, was paramount, Hirson's hero Pippin (John Rubinstein) is also out to find himself. The difference being that he is the son (Pepin) of the Holy Roman Emperor Charlemagne, and the date is '780 AD or thereabouts'. The ultimate idealist, he sets out on his journey to discover and achieve, accompanied by the Mephistophelean Leading Player (Ben Vereen). It takes him from 'The Opening' and 'Home', through 'War', 'The Flesh', 'Revolution', 'Encouragement', to 'The Hearth' and 'The Finale'. When it is over, he realises that his father was right all along, and that 'home is where the heart is' - especially when living with someone as loving and supportive as Catherine (Jill Clayburgh). Also involved in the action were Eric Berry (Charles), Leland Palmer (Fastrada), Irene Ryan (Berthe), Christopher Chadman (Lewis),

Roger Hamilton (The Head/Field Marshall), Shane Nickerson (Theo), Gene Foote (Noble), and John Mineo (Musician). Along with his usual innovative and dynamic choreography, Fosse adopted a *commedia dell'arte* approach - an Italian Renaissance comedy improvisational technique - which freed his ensemble 'Players', one of whom, Ann Reinking, went on to become a distinguished choreographer herself - particularly with the 1996 smash hit revival of *Chicago*. The score had a definite 60s - rather 'Motown-ish' 'feel' about it, which was hardly surprising as the music and lyrics were the work of Stephen Schwartz whose *Godspell* had begun its long pilgrimage the year before. The Leading Player's 'Magic To Do' and 'Simple Joys', along with Pippin's 'Corner Of The Sky', and his wicked stepmother Fastrada's funky 'Spread A Little Sunshine', were among the song highlights, but there were further joys to be had in 'Welcome Home', 'War Is A Science', 'Glory', 'No Time At All', 'With You', 'Morning Glow', 'On The Right Track', 'Kind Of Woman', 'Extraordinary', 'Love Song', and 'I Guess I Miss The Man'. *Pippin* won Tony Awards for best actor (Vereen), director and choreographer (Fosse), scenic design (Tony Walton), lighting design (Jules Fisher), and ran for a remarkable 1,944 performances. Irene Ryan, who was well known for her portrayal of Granny in television's *The Beverly Hillbillies*, died a few months into the run, and was replaced by Dorothy Stickney. The 1973 London (October 30) production at Her Majesty's Theatre simply did not appeal, and folded after 85 performances. This in spite of a cast featuring Paul Jones (Pippin), Northern J. Calloway (Leading Player), Diane Langton (Fastrada), Patricia Hodge (Catherine), Elisabeth Welch (Berthe), and John Turner (Charles). No rival to *Rose Marie* in the seemingly limitless number of worldwide productions stakes, nevertheless *Pippin* has been seen in several countries and in the US regions. In recent times, charity concert performances have also been staged at the Majestic Theatre, New York (1995) and the Royal George Theatre, Chicago (1996). There was also a US television version in 1981, with Vereen as the Leading Player, and William Katt (Pippin), Leslie Denniston (Catherine), Martha Raye (Berthe), Benjamin Rayson (Charlemagne), Christopher Chadman (Lewis), Carmine Rizzo (Theo), and - inspired casting - Chita Rivera (Fastrada). London audiences saw the show twice in the 90s: a National Youth Theatre production at the Bloomsbury Theatre (1995), was followed by a full professional staging at the Bridewell Theatre (1998). The latter had David Burt (Leading Player), James Gillan (Pippin), Juliette Caton (Catherine), Mazz Murray (Berthe), Paul Hawkyard (Charlemagne), and Nadia Strahan (Fastrada).

PIRATE, THE

Released by MGM in 1948, *The Pirate* is set on a Caribbean island in the early part of the 19th century, and tells the colourful story of Manuela (Judy Garland) who is betrothed to the fat and arrogant mayor, Don Pedro (Walter Slezak). Serafin (Gene Kelly), the leader of a group of wandering actors, discovers that Manuela dreams of being with the famous pirate Macoco - Mack the Black to his friends - and so he claims to be the renegade himself.

At first Manuela is taken in by his ruse, but when Don Pedro is hypnotised by Serafin at one of the troupe's performances, he admits he is the real Mack the Black. Not surprisingly, Manuela then loses her overwhelming passion for pirates and realises that she really loves Serafin. Although not a commercial success by any means, the film is impressive, not only for its exuberant music and dance sequences, but for its attempt to do something different. Both Garland and Kelly gave appropriately stylised performances (Garland's furious antics when Serafin's disguise is revealed are hilarious - probably one of the best tantrums ever to be seen in a Hollywood musical). Cole Porter's sophisticated score contained several good numbers including 'Nina', which accompanied a scintillating dance sequence during which Kelly makes his way through the town serenading every pretty young woman he meets; 'Mack The Black', a dream sequence in which Kelly imagines he is the awesome Macoco (somewhat reminiscent of Kelly's vision of serenading Kathryn Grayson in Anchors Aweigh); 'You Can Do No Wrong' and 'Love Of My Life', two ballads which are handled beautifully by Garland; and 'Be A Clown', performed early in the film by Kelly and the amazing Nicholas Brothers, and later given the full circus treatment by Kelly and Garland. Also featured were Reginald Owen, Gladys Cooper, George Zucco, Lola Albright, Lester Allen, and Cully Richards. The spirited and innovative choreography was designed by Robert Alton and Gene Kelly, and Frances Goodrich and Albert Hackett's screenplay was adapted from a play by S.N. Behrman. Vincente Minnelli was the director, and the film, which was brilliantly photographed in Technicolor by Harry Stradling, was produced by the Arthur Freed MGM unit. All in all it proved to be an interesting and frenetic experience for all concerned - almost experimental in parts - and was certainly different from other musicals of that era.

PLAIN AND FANCY

Rock 'n' roll music had begun to take a hold in America by the mid-50s, but the 1954/5 Broadway season was full of more traditional fare, such as The Boy Friend, Peter Pan, Silk Stockings, and Damn Yankees, amongst others. One of the others was *Plain And Fancy*, which opened at the Mark Hellinger Theatre on 27 January 1955. Joseph Stein and Will Glickman's book was set in Bird-in-Hand, Pennsylvania, the home territory of the Amish people, members of a fundamentalist religious sect who have no time or use for even the most basic modern aids. Don King (Richard Derr) has inherited a farm in the area, and he travels there from New York with Ruth Winters (Shirl Conway) to try to sell it to an Amish farmer, Papa Yoder (Stefan Schnabel). Yoder's daughter, Katie (Gloria Marlowe), is about to go through with an arranged marriage to Ezra Reber (Douglas Fletcher Rodgers), but she is still in love with an old flame, Ezra's brother, Peter (David Daniels). Peter has left the Amish community, and, when he returns just before the wedding, he is shunned by the traditionalists. Matters resolve themselves when Peter's bravery in a crisis gains him the respect of Katie's father, and the young people are allowed to marry. Don and Ruth make it a double wedding. The score, by composer Albert

Hague - whose first full Broadway score this was - and lyricist Arnold Horwitt, contained a ballad that many feel to be one of the loveliest of all popular songs, 'Young And Foolish'. It was introduced by Daniels and Marlowe, and they also had 'Follow Your Heart' with Barbara Cook, who made a favourable impression in the role of Hilda Miller. Cook sang 'This Is All Very New To Me', 'I'll Show Him', and 'Take Your Time And Take Your Pick' (with Richard Kerr and Shirl Conway). The remainder of the delightful and romantic score included 'You Can't Miss It', 'It Wonders Me', 'Plenty Of Pennsylvania', 'Why Not Katie?', 'It's A Helluva Way To Run A Love Affair', 'Plain We Live', 'How Do You Raise A Barn?' (a spectacular scene to open Act II), 'Follow Your Heart', and 'City Mouse, Country Mouse'. Sophisticated New York audiences obviously loved this folksy view of their country cousins, and *Plain And Fancy* had a decent run of 461 performances. Barbara Cook went on to become Broadway's favourite ingénue during the 50s in shows such as Candide, The Music Man, The Gay Life and She Loves Me.

PLAY IT COOL

Released in 1962, *Play It Cool* starred Billy Fury as rock 'n' roll singer Billy Universe. While not leading his group, the Satellites, he takes a feisty heiress around London haunts as she seeks to find her brother. Michael Winner, later famed for violent, vigilante-styled films starring Charles Bronson, directed this low-key feature which sadly failed to capture Fury's vulnerable image and talent. *Play It Cool* did allow the singer space to perform and its most notable inclusion, 'Once Upon A Dream', gave Fury a UK Top 10 hit when issued as a single. Among the other featured performers were Helen Shapiro, Shane Fenton And The Fentones, Danny Williams and US star Bobby Vee, included by the producers with a highly-optimistic eye on the American market. Each of these acts were about to be eclipsed by the emergent Mersey Beat, although Shapiro re-emerged some 20 years later as an accomplished jazz singer. Fenton meanwhile reinvented himself as Alvin Stardust during the glam-rock 70s, successfully capturing a further 15 minutes of fame.

PLAY ON!

Sheldon Epps conceived and directed this musical, which marries the songs of Duke Ellington with William Shakespeare's *Twelfth Night*, when he was in residence at the Old Globe Theatre, San Diego. Epps originally intended simply to present the play with incidental jazz music. However, seeking more of a challenge, he subsequently decided to utilize the plot and characters of *Twelfth Night* as the source and adapt it into a legitimate musical, and it opened on 20 March 1997 at the Brooks Atkinson Theatre in New York. Cheryl L. West's book relocated Shakespeare's seventeenth-century comedy to the 'swinging 40s' in New York's 'Magical Kingdom of Harlem', with new 'hip' variations on the participants' names - for instance, Viola is now Vy (Cheryl Freeman), a would-be songwriter, just arrived from the 'sticks'. Informed by her politically incorrect uncle Jester (Shakespeare's Feste the Clown - played by Andre De Shields) that songwriting is really men's work, she dons a zoot suit, and hurries to that fountain of musical wisdom, Duke (originally Duke Orsino, Duke of Illyria - played by Carl Anderson). He recommends she seek the services of his 'main squeeze', nightclub singer Lady Liv (the former Lady Olivia - portrayed by Tonya Pinkins), who immediately and predictably falls for the cross-dressed Vy. Also involved in the Harlem hurly-burly were Rev (Lawrence Hamilton), Sweets (Larry Marshall), Miss Mary (Yvette Cason) and CC (Crystal Allen). Some 23 examples of Ellington's musical excellence were on display, including such classics as 'Don't Get Around Much Anymore', 'Love You Madly', 'I Got It Bad (And That Ain't Good)', 'Solitude', 'Mood Indigo', 'Take The "A" Train', 'I'm Beginning To See The Light', 'In A Mellow Tone' and 'I Let A Song Go Out Of My Heart', as well as some lesser-known items such as 'Rocks In My Bed'. The lovely 1939 ballad 'Something To Live For' was also included, but absent from the cast album for contractual reasons. Luther Henderson offered some excellent arrangements, and the choreography was designed by Mercedes Ellington, the composer's granddaughter. Despite seeming a good idea at the time, and earning three Tony Award nominations, *Play On!* played out on 11 May 1997, after only 61 performances. Later in the year, a new production was presented for a short season at the Goodman Theatre in Chicago.

Play On! was by no means the first time Broadway had felt the influence of Ellington's music. As well as leading his orchestra in several productions, the Duke collaborated with John La Touche for an updating of *The Beggar's Opera*, retitled *Beggar's Holiday* (1946), and composed the music for the 'Sun Tanned Revu-sical' *Jump For Joy* (Los Angeles, 1941), a Stratford, Ontario production of *Timon Of Athens*, and *Pousse-Café* (with Jerome Weidman, 1966). He also composed all the music, words and orchestrations for a major piece, *My People* (1963), as well as directing and appearing in it. In 1981 (London, 1992) his work was celebrated in the revue Sophisticated Ladies. Other musicals that have turned to *Twelfth Night* for their inspiration have included *Your Own Thing*, a highly successful rock adaptation, and *Love And Let Love* (both off-Broadway, 1968), and *Music Is*, which played eight performances on Broadway in 1976. An outstanding example of how great theatrical craftsman can use Shakespeare to great effect remains the Cole Porter-Bella And Sam Spewack masterpiece, Kiss Me, Kate (1948).

POCAHONTAS

The first of all the many Walt Disney animated features to be based on the life of a real, historical figure, this 1995 release is darker in tone, and more tragic that the Studio's usual product. This is only partly due to the absence of the usual Disney menagerie of wisecracking animals. Set in the early seventeenth century, the screenplay, by Carl Binder, Susannah Grant, and Philip LaZebnik, tells a Colonial story of the love affair between John Smith (voiced by Mel Gibson) and native American girl Pocahontas (Irene Bedard, singing voice Judy Kuhn). Smith is the captain of a British ship which has brought Governor Ratcliffe (David Ogden Stiers) of the Virginia Company, and a bunch of greedy, violent men, to the New World in search of gold. Pocahontas' father, Chief

Powhatan (Russell Means), wants her to marry the tribe's bravest warrior, Kocoum (James Apaumut Fall), but after consulting Grandmother Willow (Linda Hunt), the young woman is set on Smith, and their joint plea for peace between settlers and tribe is the movie's most powerful message. Smith begs Pocahontas to return to England with him, but she insists on staying with her own people. Among the other main characters are Meeko the raccoon (John Kassir), Thomas (Christian Bale), Percy (Danny Mann), Ben (Billy Connelly), Lon (Joe Baker), Flit (Frank Welker), Nakomo (Michelle St. John), and Kekata (Gordon Tootoosis). Alan Menken (music) and lyricist Stephen Schwartz provide the score, highlights of which include the robust 'The Virginian Company' (performed by Chorus, Mel Gibson) and 'Just Around The Riverbend' (Judy Kuhn), the bitter 'Savages Part 1' (David Ogden Stiers, Jim Cummings, Chorus) and 'Savages Part 2' (David Ogden Stiers, Jim Cummings, Judy Kuhn, Chorus), in which the settlers and tribe describe each other in exactly the same way, 'Mine, Mine, Mine' (David Ogden Stiers, Mel Gibson, Chorus), an anthem of stupidity and avarice, and Pocahontas' heartfelt message of tolerance, 'Colours Of The Wind' (Judy Kuhn). Also on the soundtrack: 'If I Never Knew You' (Jon Secada, Shanice), 'Steady As The Beating Drum' (Chorus, Jim Cummings), 'Listen With Your Heart, I, II, III' (Linda Hunt, Bobbi Page), and 'Death Song', by Hawk Pope. Mike Gabriel and Eric Goldberg directed the film which attracted its share of criticism for what one critic called 'playing fast and loose with the known facts of Pocahontas' life'. What he meant was that although she saved Smith's life twice, there is no historical evidence of any romance between them, and the real Pocahontas travelled to England with her husband, plantation owner John Rolfe, died there, and was buried in Gravesend, Kent. 'Colours Of The Wind' (performed by Vanessa Williams), won a Grammy Award and reached number 4 in the US chart, and the film received Oscars for Best Song ('Colours Of The Wind') and Original Musical or Comedy Score.

POINT, THE

Much-heralded singer/songwriter Harry Nilsson wrote the screenplay and score for this 1970 animated feature. First produced as a 90-minute film for television, *The Point* revolves around the tale of Oblio, a boy with a round head born into a world where a triangular shape is the norm. Dustin Hoffman narrated the original version, but Alan Barzman took his place for this new version of an engaging fable posing questions about racial prejudice. Nilsson's music was suitably captivating. It included the melodic 'Me And My Arrow', a US Top 40 entrant, 'Think About Your Troubles' and 'Are You Sleeping?', each of which exhibited the singer's craftsmanship. Such material was issued on an concurrent album, and the film's legacy continued to prosper into the next decade. A theatrical version was staged in London featuring Mickey Dolenz, formerly a member of the Monkees, for whom Nilsson had written several songs. *The Point* remains a captivating project, appealing to both children and adults alike.

POOR COW

Poor Cow was based on the novel of the same name, written by Nell Dunn, author of Up The Junction. Director Ken Loach brought a politically acerbic eye to this 1967 feature which starred Carol White (*Cathy Come Home*) and Terence Stamp. They play a married couple, but as the husband is in jail, the wife is required to survive in a harsh world portrayed as the antithesis of concurrent flower-power trivialities. Paradoxically, wan singer/songwriter Donovan provided the score, which included the haunting title track, issued on the b-side of his 1968 hit 'There Is A Mountain'. His music was incidental in the best sense of the word; *Poor Cow* is an excellent work, invoking the spirit of British 'kitchen sink' drama from earlier in the decade.

POOR LITTLE RICH GIRL

By the time she made this film in 1936, Shirley Temple was an eight-year-old superstar with nearly 20 pictures to her credit. Cinema audiences all over the world had taken her to their hearts, and she did not disappoint them in this latest outing which continued along the familiar well-trodden path. In the screenplay, by Sam Hellman, Gladys Lehman, and Harry Tugend, Shirley runs away from her wealthy workaholic father (Michael Whalen) and is co-opted into a vaudeville act (Alice Faye and Jack Haley). Family reconciliation is eventually accomplished, but only after the loveable youngster has wowed the crowds with numbers such as 'You Gotta Eat Your Spinach, Baby', 'Military Man', 'But Definitely', and 'When I'm With You'. Harry Revel and Mack Gordon wrote those, and some others including 'Oh, My Goodness' and 'Wash Your Necks With A Cake Of Beck's' (Shirley did a lot of work on sponsored radio shows). Gloria Stuart, Sara Haden, Claude Gillingwater, Jane Darwell, and Henry Armetta were in the cast, and future singing heart-throb Tony Martin also made a brief appearance. The dance directors were Jack Haskell and Ralph Cooper, and the film, which was directed by Irving Cummings, was produced for 20th Century-Fox by Darryl F. Zanuck and Buddy De Sylva.

POP DOWN

Released in 1968, this rarely-screened British film was an indulgent, flower-power-influenced yarn involving creatures from outer space. There was little new in what the hapless aliens encountered, bar the garb of the Earthlings on view, as this tired plot had already been well-mined by the US American International Pictures Company. Interest lies in the pop performers on view, many of which were rarely captured on film. One-man band/busker Don Partridge, famed for the memorable hit, 'Rosie', and soul singer Brenton Wood appear alongside raver-turned-psychedelic acolyte Zoot Money, who plays Sagittarius, and former John's Children vocalist Andy Ellison, who portrays Mr. Love. The former subsequently became a character actor on television, while the latter occasionally took work as a stunt man. However, it is two acts from the newly-founded Marmalade label which prove most captivating. Julie Driscoll with Brian Auger And The Trinity and Blossom Toes were two of the era's more engaging attractions and *Pop Down* enshrines their brief moment in the limelight. They inhabit an off-beat world inhabited by several unusual individuals, including Miss Offkey, Miss Withit, Perpetual Kisser and Nude On Camel. Cut from 96 minutes to 54 for release, *Pop Down* is an interesting period-piece, thanks to the music on offer, but a far cry from the 'film that turns on tomorrow', despite that contemporaneous publicity line.

POP GEAR

Mindful of the growing British Beat phenomenon, the Pathe film company filmed a succession of acts, spliced them with introductions from DJ Jimmy Saville, and added footage of the Beatles performing 'She Loves You' and 'Twist And Shout' live in Manchester. The cross-section of performers reflected the era's transitional nature and the inclusion of Matt Monro and Susan Maughan brought an MOR slant to the proceedings. Several of the acts were drawn from Brian Epstein's NEMS stable, including Billy J. Kramer And The Dakotas, Tommy Quickly, Sounds Incorporated and the Fourmost, while Herman's Hermits, the Four Pennies, Honeycombs and Rockin' Berries encapsulated the period's unashamedly commercial air. Despite the sterile studio atmosphere, in which the groups and singers mimed, *Pop Gear* contained several memorable performances, including the Animals' 'House Of The Rising Sun', the Nashville Teens' 'Tobacco Road' and the Spencer Davis Group powerful rendition of 'Strong Love'. In an era of black-and-white television, the film allowed fans a rare glimpse of their idols in colour and *Pop Gear* was a popular adjunct to the main feature in British cinemas in 1965. It was released in the USA under a new title, *Go Go Mania*, and portions still surface to this day on archive resumes of a career or era.

POPPY

After a brief career in vaudeville, and appearances in several editions of the Ziegfeld Follies, W.C. Fields, the bulbous-nosed comic with the 'never-give-a-sucker-an-even-break' attitude, came to Broadway in this production which opened at the Apollo Theatre in New York on 3 September 1923. The star was supposed to be Madge Kennedy who plays Fields's foster child, Poppy, but, during the New York run and the subsequent tour, the comedian gradually emerged as the principal attraction. In Dorothy Donnelly's book, Professor Eustace McGargle (Fields) is a card-sharp, a juggler (Fields used to juggle in vaudeville), and an all-round trickster and con-man around the carnivals. Poppy is an orphan girl from the same background, who eventually discovers that she is an heiress. Donnelly also wrote the lyrics for several of the songs, with music by Stephen Jones and Arthur Samuels. These included 'Two Make A Home', 'Steppin' Around', 'Hang Your Sorrows In The Sun', 'When You Are In My Arms', and 'A Picnic Party With You'. However the most popular numbers were the interpolated 'What Do You Do Sunday, Mary?' (music: Jones, lyric: Irving Caesar), which was introduced by Luella Gear and Robert Woolsey, and became a hit for the American Quartet; and 'Alibi Baby' (music: Samuels, lyric: Howard Dietz). 'Alibi Baby' was Howard Dietz's first successful song. Years later, when he

was doing some of his best work with Arthur Schwartz, it turned up in the US Hit Parade in a version by Tommy Dorsey. Fans of W.C. Fields continued to flock to see *Poppy* for 346 performances, and the London production, which starred W.H. Berry and Annie Croft, stayed at the Gaiety Theatre for five months. Fields dominated the two films that were based on the show: a 1925 silent, renamed *Sally Of The Sawdust*, and the 1936 *Poppy*, with Rochelle Hudson. Another, quite different show named *Poppy*, with music by Monty Norman and a book and lyrics by Peter Nichols, played in London's West End in 1982.

PORGY AND BESS (FILM MUSICAL)

The last film of producer Sam Goldwyn's illustrious career, released by Columbia in 1959, proved to be an expensive and troubled affair. After various disputes with his first choice director, Rouben Mamoulian (who had staged the original 1935 Broadway production), Goldwyn replaced him with Otto Preminger, whose work on this occasion was considered to be somewhat laboured and uninspired. For some reason, the well-known story of the crippled beggar Porgy (Sidney Poitier), who lives in the Catfish Row slum area and loves the tempestuous Bess (Dorothy Dandridge), did not transfer successfully to the big screen. The supporting cast was excellent, with Sammy Davis Jnr. (Sportin' Life), Pearl Bailey (Maria), Brock Peters (Crown), Diahann Carroll (Clara) and Ruth Attaway (Serena) all turning in outstanding performances. Other roles were taken by Leslie Scott, Clarence Muse and Joel Fluellen. Because of the extremely demanding operatic score by composer George Gershwin and lyricists DuBose Heyward and Ira Gershwin, several of the principals were dubbed, including Poitier (Robert McFerrin), Dandridge (Adele Addison), Carroll (Loulie Jean Norman), and Attaway (Inez Matthews). Even so, there were some reservations regarding the vocal quality of the production, but these were swept aside by the sheer magnificence of the songs, which included 'Summertime', 'Bess, You Is My Woman', 'There's A Boat Dat's Leavin' Soon For New York', 'I Loves You Porgy', 'A Woman Is A Sometimes Thing', 'I Got Plenty O' Nuttin'', 'It Ain't Necessarily So', 'My Man's Gone Now' and 'Oh Bess, Oh Where's My Bess'. André Previn and Ken Darby both won Oscars for 'scoring a dramatic picture', and Leo Shamroy was nominated for his superb photography in Technicolor and Panavision. Hermes Pan, who had been associated with many top musical films in his long career including the Fred Astaire and Ginger Rogers RKO series, staged the dances. The screenplay, by N. Richard Nash, was based on the original Broadway libretto and novel by Heyward, and his and Dorothy Heyward's play *Porgy*. In the early 90s, this film remained one of the few major musicals not to have been released on video. Cinema distribution has also been curtailed; the Gershwin estate has had this film firmly under lock and key for some years now.

● FURTHER READING: *DuBose Heyward-The Man Who Wrote 'Porgy'*, Frank Durham. *The Life And Times Of Porgy And Bess*, H. Alpert.

PORGY AND BESS (STAGE MUSICAL)

One of the greatest and best-loved musical theatre experiences of all time, *Porgy And Bess* opened at the Alvin Theater in New York on 10 October 1935. It was the culmination of a long-held dream for composer George Gershwin, who had first read DuBose Heyward's novel, *Porgy*, in October 1926. He suggested to the author that they collaborate on a musical version, but Heyward and his wife Dorothy were already in the process of adapting *Porgy* into a highly successful play for the Theatre Guild. Work began on *Porgy And Bess* late in 1933, and in the summer of the following year Gershwin moved to Folly Island, just off the coast of South Carolina. This was near to Heyward's home-town of Charleston, where *Porgy* had been set. For months, Gershwin mixed with the Gulla Negroes, immersing himself in their music with its insinuating and turbulent rhythms and melodies, along with the singing, 'stomping' and 'shouting' that characterized their prayer meetings. To these he added aspects of his own unique musical genius, and with a libretto by Heyward, who co-authored the lyrics with George's brother Ira Gershwin, the 'folk opera' *Porgy And Bess* was enthusiastically received at the Colonial Theatre in Boston on 30 September 1935. Two weeks later, the Broadway critics were not so keen, being unable to decide whether this fascinating new work was an opera, an operetta, or simply a musical comedy. It was certainly different from the usual Broadway fare, this powerful story of Porgy (Todd Duncan), a black, crippled goat-cart beggar living in the slum known as Catfish Row. He and Bess (Anne Brown) fall in love when her man Crown (Warren Coleman) takes flight after murdering a fellow gambler. When Crown eventually returns to claim his woman, Porgy kills him in self-defence. Believing that Porgy will never be released from jail, Bess elopes to New York with the villainous dope peddler, Sportin' Life (John Bubbles). Porgy bids farewell to the other residents of Catfish Row, as, with the perhaps overly optimistic 'Oh Lawd, I'm On My Way' (Gershwin), he boards his goat cart intent on finding and retrieving her. This represents just the bare bones of an immensely dramatic scenario, which Gershwin enhanced with his magnificent score, and in the process gave the world of popular music some its most enduring melodies. These included Clara's (Abbie Mitchell) haunting, scene-setting 'Summertime' (Heyward), Porgy's serene 'I Got Plenty O' Nuthin'', his despairing 'Oh, Bess, Oh Where's My Bess?' (Gershwin), and the tragic lovers' fervent duets, 'Bess, You Is My Woman Now' and 'I Loves You Porgy'. Among the other highlights were Jake's (Edward Matthews) 'A Woman Is A Sometime Thing' (Heyward), 'My Man's Gone Now' (Heyward), Serena's (Ruby Elzy) grief-stricken outburst over the body of her murdered husband, and two by the struttin' Sportin' Life: his cynical view of certain biblical figures (Jonah, Methuselah, Moses, *et al.*), 'It Ain't Necessarily So' (Gershwin), and a tempting offer he thinks that Bess can hardly refuse - 'There's A Boat Dat's Leavin' Soon For New York' (Gershwin). Directed by Rouben Mamoulian, who also staged DuBose Heyward's original *Porgy* for the Theatre Guild, *Porgy and Bess* ran for only 124 performances and lost its total investment. Cheryl Crawford's 1942 production did more than twice as well (286 performances), and was acclaimed as 'America's Greatest'. Most of the principals, including Duncan, Brown, Coleman and Matthews, reprised their roles, and were joined by Avon Long as Sportin' Life. In 1952, a US State Department-sponsored version set out on a four-year tour of 29 countries, including Vienna, Latin America, the USSR, the Middle East, and the USA and Canada. When it called in at London's Stoll Theatre for 142 performances in 1952, William Warfield (Porgy) and Leontyne Price (Bess) headed the cast, with Cab Calloway as Sportin' Life. Calloway was also present when the touring company began a run of 305 performances at New York's Ziegfeld Theatre in March 1953. Otto Preminger directed a lavish film version in 1959, with Sidney Poitier (Porgy), Dorothy Dandridge (Bess), Sammy Davis Jnr. (Sportin' Life), Brock Peters (Crown) and Pearl Bailey (Maria).

The numerous stagings of *Porgy And Bess* since then have included the opera's first New York Metropolitan Opera production (1985), with Grace Bumbry (Bess), Simon Estes (Porgy), Gregg Baker (Crown), Charles Williams (Sportin' Life), and Trevor Nunn's Glyndebourne Festival Opera setting. The latter highly praised production, superbly conducted by Simon Rattle, repeated its triumph at the Royal Opera House, Covent Garden, in 1992. It was televised a year later, with Willard White (Porgy), Cynthia Haymon (Bess), Gregg Baker (Crown) and Damon Evans (Sportin' Life). This television film meant that Gershwin's masterpiece was made available to a worldwide audience, making up for the fact that the 1959 movie has not been seen in public for many a year; presumably, it is locked up in the Gershwin vaults.

Although in the 1935 original only the white people spoke their lines, and the Negro singers delivered theirs in the form of a spoken recitative, since George Gershwin's death his estate has ruled that *Porgy And Bess* must be performed exclusively by black singers. This makes it difficult for mainstream European companies to mount productions, although a fine American touring production, mounted by New York impresario Peter Klein, started out in 1993, and played 140 cities in the USA alone, also taking in Australia, New Zealand, Japan and Taiwan. No doubt even this version has the perennial *Porgy And Bess* problem of bringing in the show under three hours. Also still in contention is whether George Gershwin's masterpiece was (white view) a significant step on the road to emancipation, or (black view) an exercise in reinforcing stereotypes. To most people the question is academic - they simply think that *Porgy And Bess* is a great opera.

● FURTHER READING: *DuBose Heyward-The Man Who Wrote 'Porgy'*, Frank Durham. *The Life And Times Of Porgy And Bess*, H. Alpert.

PORTER, COLE

b. 9 June 1891, Peru, Indiana, USA, d. 15 October 1964, Santa Monica, California, USA. One of the outstanding composers and lyricists of the 20th century, Porter was born into a rich family, and studied music from an early age. In his teens he excelled in many academic subjects, and wrote songs and played the piano for his own amusement - activities he later pursued at Yale University. Later he attended Harvard Law School, but his interest in music overcame his legal studies, and while he was still at college, some of his songs were used in Broadway productions. In 1916, his first complete score, for *See America First* ('I've A Shooting Box In Scotland'), closed after just 15 performances. The Porter family's wealth allowed him to travel extensively and he visited Europe both before and after World War I, developing a life-long affection for Paris. He wrote several numbers for *Hitchy-Koo 1919*, including the moderately successful 'Old Fashioned Garden', and, during the 20s, contributed to several other musicals, including Greenwich Village Follies (1924, 'I'm In Love Again'), before having his first real hit with the slightly risqué 'Let's Do It, Let's Fall In Love', which was introduced by Irene Bordoni and Arthur Margetson in *Paris* (1928). That delightful 'Musicomedy' also contained another attractive number, 'Don't Look At Me That Way'. There followed a series of mainly successful shows, each containing at least one, and more often, several sophisticated and witty numbers. They included *Wake Up And Dream* (1919, London and New York, 'What Is This Thing Called Love?', 'Looking At You'), *Fifty Million Frenchmen* (1929, 'You Do Something To Me', 'You've Got That Thing', 'You Don't Know Paree'), The New Yorkers (1930, 'I Happen To Like New York', 'Let's Fly Away', 'Love For Sale'), Gay Divorce (1932, 'Night And Day', 'After You', 'How's Your Romance?', 'I've Got You On My Mind'), and Nymph Errant (1933). The score for the latter show, which starred Gertrude Lawrence, Elisabeth Welch, and David Burns, and ran for 154 performances, contained several Porter gems, such as 'Experiment', 'It's Bad For Me', 'Solomon', and 'The Physician'. A year later, in the play, *Hi Diddle Diddle*, London audiences were introduced to 'Miss Otis Regrets', one of the songs Porter used to write simply for his friends' amusement. Later in 1934, back on Broadway Porter had his first smash hit with Anything Goes. In that show, Ethel Merman, who had taken New York by storm four years previously in George and Ira Gershwin's Girl Crazy, triumphed all over again with Porter's terrific 'Anything Goes', 'Blow, Gabriel, Blow', 'I Get A Kick Out Of You' and 'You're The Top' (both with William Gaxton). Her dynamic presence and gutsy singing style gave a tremendous lift to four more Porter musicals. The first, Red, Hot And Blue! (1936, 'Down In The Depths (On The Ninetieth Floor)', 'It's De-Lovely', 'Ridin' High'), which also starred Jimmy Durante and Bob Hope, was not particularly successful, but the others such as Du Barry Was A Lady (1939, 'Friendship' [one of Porter's wittiest 'list' songs], 'Do I Love You?'), Panama Hattie (1940, 'Make It Another Old Fashioned, Please', 'I've Still Got My Health'), and Something For The Boys (1943, 'Hey, Good Lookin'', 'The Leader Of A Big-Time Band'), were all substantial hits. Although not all of Porter's shows in the 30s and 40s were long runners by any means (*Around The World*, which had book and direction by Orson Welles, was a 75-performance flop in 1946), almost every one continued to have at least one memorable and enduring song, such as 'Begin The Beguine', 'Just One Of Those Things', and 'Why Shouldn't I?' (1935, Jubilee), 'At Long Last Love', (1938, *You Never Know*), 'Get Out Of Town', 'My Heart Belongs To Daddy', and 'Most

Gentlemen Don't Like Love' (1938, Leave It To Me!), 'Ev'rything I Love', 'Ace In The Hole', and 'Let's Not Talk About Love' (1941, Let's Face It!), 'I Love You' (1944, Mexican Hayride), and 'Ev'ry Time We Say Goodbye' (1944, *Seven Lively Arts*). After a rather lean period in the mid-40s, in 1948 Cole Porter wrote the score for Kiss, Me Kate, which is considered to be his masterpiece. It starred Alfred Drake, Patricia Morison, Harold Lang, and Lisa Kirk, and contained superb numbers such as 'Another Op'nin', Another Show', 'Brush Up Your Shakespeare', 'I Hate Men', 'Always True To You In My Fashion', 'So In Love', 'Too Darn Hot', 'Why Can't You Behave?', 'Were Thine That Special Face', and several more. *Kiss Me, Kate* ran for 1,077 performances on Broadway, and a further 501 in London. Another song, 'From This Moment On', which Porter wrote for the stage production of *Kiss Me, Kate*, was eventually used in the 1953 film version. Before that, it was tried out in *Out Of This World* (1950), a show which, in spite of the presence of the high-kicking Charlotte Greenwood, and a mixture of attractive ballads and novelties such as 'I Am Loved', 'Where, Oh Where?', 'Nobody's Chasing Me', and 'Cherry Pies Ought To Be You', ran for less than six months. Porter's last two shows for Broadway were Can-Can (1953, 'I Love Paris', 'It's All Right With Me', 'C'est Magnifique') and Silk Stockings (1955, 'All Of You', 'Josephine', 'Stereophonic Sound'). The first was a resounding hit, running for 892 performances, but although the latter was generally an unfortunate affair, it still stayed around for over a year.

As well as his work for Broadway, Cole Porter also enjoyed a prolific and equally satisfying career in Hollywood. He wrote his first film songs, 'They All Fall In Love' and 'Here Comes The Bandwagon', for the Gertrude Lawrence movie, *The Battle Of Paris*, in 1929. Thereafter, some of his most outstanding work was featured in Born To Dance (1936, 'Easy To Love' [introduced by James Stewart], 'I've Got You Under My Skin', 'Swingin' the Jinx Away', 'Rap-Tap On Wood'), Rosalie ('In The Still Of The Night', 'Rosalie'), Broadway Melody Of 1940 (1940, 'I've Got My Eyes On You', 'I Concentrate On You', 'Please Don't Monkey With Broadway'), You'll Never Get Rich (1941, 'So Near And Yet So Far', 'Dream Dancing', 'Since I Kissed My Baby Goodbye'), *Something To Shout About* (1943, 'You'd Be So Nice To Come Home To'), *Hollywood Canteen* (1944, 'Don't Fence Me In'), Night And Day (1946, a Porter biopic, in which he was played by Cary Grant), The Pirate (1948, 'Be A Clown', 'Love Of My Life', 'Nina'), *Stage Fright* (1950, 'The Laziest Gal In Town', sung by Marlene Dietrich), High Society (1956, 'True Love', 'You're Sensational', 'I Love You, Samantha', 'Well, Did You Evah?', 'Now You Has Jazz'), and Les Girls (1957, 'All Of You', 'Ladies In Waiting', 'Paris Loves Lovers'). In addition, several of Porter's original stage shows were adapted for the screen (twice in the case of *Anything Goes*), and several of his songs were revived in the 1975 Burt Reynolds/Cybill Shepherd movie, At Long Last Love.

In 1937 Porter was seriously injured in a riding accident. Astonishingly, a series of more than two dozen operations, several years in a wheelchair, and almost constant pain seemed to have little effect on his creative ability. His right leg was amputated in 1958, and in the same year he wrote what is said to have been his last song, 'Wouldn't It Be Fun?' ('not to be famous'), for the television spectacular *Aladdin*. Marked by wit and sophistication often far ahead of the times in which he lived, Porter's music and lyrics set standards which were the envy of most of his contemporaries. When he died in 1964, his fellow songwriters in the American Society of Composers and Authors paid this tribute: 'Cole Porter's talent in the creation of beautiful and witty songs was recognized as unique throughout the world. His brilliant contributions in the field of musical theatre made him an international legend in his lifetime.' Although he ceased writing in the late 50s, his music continued to be used in films and on television, and he was the subject of television specials and numerous honours and awards. In 1991, the centenary of his birth, there were tributes galore. In a gala concert at Carnegie Hall, artists such as Julie Wilson, Kathryn Grayson, and Patricia Morison paid tribute to him, as did songwriters Jule Styne, Sammy Cahn, and Burton Lane. Among the other special events were an Off Broadway revue, *Anything Cole*, the West End production of *A Swell Party*, and a UK touring show entitled *Let's Do It*, starring Elaine Delmar and Paul Jones. The special occasion was also marked by the release of new recordings of his scores for *Nymph Errant* and *Kiss Me, Kate*, and the album *Red Hot And Blue*, which featured a number of well known rock stars, with the proceeds going to AIDS research. In May 1998, *Side By Side By Porter*, yet another celebration of Porter's works took place, at the Palace Theatre in London. It was later broadcast on Radio 2, and starred Nickolas Grace, Rebecca Caine, Kim Criswell, Frank Hernandez, and George Dvorsky. The programme included lesser-heard gems such as the 1911 Yale Football Song, 'Bull Dog', and 'There He Goes, Mr Phileas Fogg', from *Around The World* (1946). The BBC Concert Orchestra was conducted by John McGlinn, who ensured the all the arrangements were as close to the originals as possible. Later that year, on 10 October, a charity concert performance of Porter and Moss Hart's 1935 show *Jubilee* took place at Carnegie Hall in New York. In the cast were Bea Arthur, Bob Paris, Tyne Daly, Alice Ripley, Sandy Duncan, Stephen Spinella, Michael Jeter, Damien Woetzel and Philip Bosco.

● ALBUMS: *Cole Porter Sings Cole Porter* (Koch International 1995)★★.

● FURTHER READING: *The Cole Porter Story*, David Ewen. *Cole: A Biographical Essay*, Brendan Gill and Richard Kimball. *The Cole Porter Story*, Cole Porter and Richard Hubler. *Cole Porter: The Life That Late He Led*, George Eells. *Travels With Cole Porter*, Jean Howard. *Cole*, Brendan Gill. *Cole Porter*, Cole Schwarz. *Cole Porter: The Definitive Biography*, William McBrien.

POWELL, DICK

b. Richard Ewing Powell, 14 November 1904, Mountain View, Arkansas, USA, d. 3 January 1963, Hollywood, California, USA. Powell was an extremely popular singing star of major 30s film musicals, with an appealing tenor voice, and 'matinee-idol' looks. He sang firstly as a boy soprano, and later, tenor, in school and church choirs, and learnt to play several musical instruments including the cornet, saxophone and banjo. In his late teens he was a

member of the Royal Peacock Orchestra in Kentucky, and in the late 20s sang and played for Charlie Davis, with whom he made some early recordings, and other midwest bands. In the early 30s he worked as a Master of Ceremonies and singer at the Circle Theatre, Indianapolis, and the Stanley Theatre in Pittsburg, where he was discovered by a Warner Brothers talent scout, and signed to a film contract. He made his film debut in *Blessed Event* (1932), followed by *Too Busy To Work* and *The King's Vacation* (1933), before making an enormous impact, along with another young newcomer, Ruby Keeler, in the spectacular Busby Berkeley back-stage musical *42nd Street* (1933). The film's score, by Harry Warren and Al Dubin, included the title song; 'Shuffle Off To Buffalo', 'You're Getting To Be A Habit With Me' and 'Young And Healthy'. Co-starring with Keeler, his wife Joan Blondell, and several more glamorous leading ladies, Powell embarked on a series of, mostly, lavish movie musicals for Warners, 20th Century-Fox, and other studios, through to the mid-40s.

Containing some of the classic popular songs of the time, the films included Gold Diggers *Of 1933* (1933), ('We're In The Money', 'Shadow Waltz', 'I've Got To Sing A Torch Song' and 'Pettin' In The Park'); Footlight Parade (1933), ('By A Waterfall'); *Twenty Million Sweethearts* (1934), ('I'll String Along With You'); Dames (1934), (the title song and 'I Only Have Eyes For You'); *Gold Diggers Of 1935* (1935), ('Lullaby Of Broadway' and 'The Words Are In My Heart'); *Broadway Gondolier* (1935), ('Lulu's Back In Town' and 'The Rose In Her Hair'); *Gold Diggers of 1937* (1936), ('With Plenty Of Money And You' and 'All's Fair In Love And War'); On The Avenue (1937), ('The Girl On The Police Gazette', This Year's Kisses', 'I've Got My Love To Keep Me Warm', Slumming On Park Avenue' and 'You're Laughing At Me'); *Varsity Show* (1937), ('Have You Got Any Castles Baby?') and *Going Places* (1938), ('Jeepers Creepers'). During this period, Powell was also very active on US radio, with programmes such as the *Old Gold* show with the Ted Fio Rito Band (1934), Hollywood Hotel (1934-37, with Frances Langford), *Your Hollywood Party* (1938, the show that gave Bob Hope's career a big boost), *Tuesday Night Party* (1939), *American Cruise* (1941) and *Dick Powell Serenade* (1942-43). He also had several hit records, mostly with songs from his films.

During the early 40s Powell concentrated more and more on comedy and dramatic film roles. In 1944, a year before he married actress June Allyson, he confirmed his change of direction when he appeared as private-eye Philip Marlowe in the highly-acclaimed movie *Farewell My Lovely* (aka *Murder My Sweet*). From then on, singing was abandoned, as he undertook a series of 'tough guy' roles in crime and detective movies, becoming just as popular as he had been in the musicals of the 30s. He was also a pioneer of early US television drama in the 50s, directing and producing, as well as performing. From 1959-61, he presented the popular television series *Dick Powell Theatre*. Despite some pressure, Powell never went back to singing, but was still working up to his death from cancer in 1963.

● ALBUMS: *Song Book* (Decca 1958)★★★, *Themes From Original*

TV Soundtracks (Dot 1962)★★★, Dick Powell In Hollywood (Columbia 1966)★★★.
● COMPILATIONS: 16 Classic Tracks (1982)★★★, Lullaby Of Broadway (London 1986), Lullaby Of Broadway (Living Era 1986)★★★, On The Avenue (1988)★★★, Rare Recordings 1934-1951 (1989)★★★.

POWELL, ELEANOR

b. 21 November 1912, Springfield, Massachusetts, USA, d. 11 February 1982, Beverly Hills, California, USA. Often billed as 'the world's greatest female tap dancer', Powell is regarded by many as the most accomplished of Fred Astaire's screen partners, but without, of course, the indefinable magic of Ginger Rogers. She studied ballet at an early age and later took up tap dancing. After only a few lessons she is said to have achieved 'machine-gun rapidity' - up to five taps per second. Powell moved to New York in 1928 and appeared in The Optimists revue at the Casino de Paris Theatre, and a year later made her Broadway debut in the musical Follow Thru. This was followed by more stage shows, such as Fine And Dandy, Hot-Cha, and George White's Scandals (1932). A small, but highly impressive role in the film of George White's Scandals (1935), led to Powell being elevated to star status immediately after the release of Broadway Melody Of 1936. Signed to a seven year contract with MGM, her exhilarating tap dancing was on display in musicals such as Born To Dance, Broadway Melody Of 1938, Rosalie, Honolulu, Broadway Melody Of 1940, Lady Be Good, Ship Ahoy, Thousands Cheer, I Dood It, and Sensations Of 1945. By that stage, Powell, who married the actor Glenn Ford in 1943, had retired from show business to devote more time to her family. She made just one more film, The Duchess Of Idaho, in 1950. A devout Presbyterian, she became a Sunday school teacher in the 50s and starred in her own religious television programme, Faith Of Our Children, which won five Emmy Awards. After she and Ford were divorced in 1959, Powell made a brief comeback playing large clubs and showrooms in Las Vegas and New York with a classy cabaret act. Reminders of her remarkable terpsichorean skills flooded back in 1974, when the marvellous 'Begin The Beguine' routine she did with Fred Astaire in Broadway Melody Of 1940 was included in MGM's That's Entertainment!. As Frank Sinatra said when he introduced the sequence in that film: 'You know, you can wait around and hope, but I'll tell you - you'll never see the likes of this again.'
● FURTHER READING: Eleanor Powell: A Bio-Bibliography, Margie Schultz.

POWELL, JANE

b. Suzanne Burce, 1 April 1929, Portland, Oregon, USA. A petite, vivacious, actress and singer with a thrilling soprano voice who excelled in several popular MGM musicals of the 50s. After singing a mixture of classical and popular songs on local radio, she won a film contract with MGM when she was just 15 years old. Her debut in Song Of The Open Road was followed in the 40s and early 50s by Delightfully Dangerous, Holiday In Mexico, Three Daring Daughters, A Date With Judy, Luxury Liner, Nancy Goes To Rio, Two Weeks With Love, Rich, Young And Pretty, Small

Town Girl and Three Sailors And A Girl (1953). In 1951 she co-starred with Fred Astaire in Royal Wedding, and they duetted on one of the longest song titles ever - 'How Could You Believe Me When I Said I Love You When You Know I've Been A Liar All My Life?'. Their recording became a million-seller. Later, in 1956, Powell made the US Top 20 on her own with 'True Love' from High Society. Her best film role was in 1954 when she joined Howard Keel in the marvellous Seven Brides For Seven Brothers, and she continued to appear on the screen into the late 50s, in musicals such as Athena, Deep In My Heart, Hit The Deck and The Girl Most Likely (1957). The golden era of movie musicals was drawing to a close by then, and Powell turned to provincial theatre and nightclubs. In the 70s she was active on US television in programmes such as Murdoch, The Letters and Mayday At 40,000 Feet. She also succeeded Debbie Reynolds in the leading role of the 1973 Broadway revival of Irene. In 1988 Powell married her fifth husband, Dick Moore, who was a child star himself, and is an authority on the genre, having written a book entitled Twinkle, Twinkle Little Star (But Don't Have Sex Or Take The Car). In the same year she appeared in concert at Carnegie Hall with Skitch Henderson and the New York Pops. In the mid-90s, she co-hosted Cabaret Sings The Movies at the Cabaret Convention at New York's Town Hall. This special evening featured Frank Loesser's widow, Jo Sullivan, singing his Oscar-winning 'Baby, It's Cold Outside' from Neptune's Daughter (1949), and David Staller recreating 'Isn't It Romantic' from Love Me Tonight (1932), amongst other good things. Powell also hosted the television special Nelson And Jeanette (1992) and appeared as herself in The Making Of Seven Brides For Seven Brothers (1997).
● ALBUMS: Romance 10-inch album (Columbia 1949)★★★, A Date With Jane Powell 10-inch album (Columbia 1949)★★★, Alice In Wonderland (Columbia 1950)★★, Nancy Goes To Rio film soundtrack (MGM 1950)★★, Two Weeks With Love film soundtrack (MGM 1950)★★★, Royal Wedding film soundtrack (MGM 1951)★★★, Rich, Young And Pretty film soundtrack (MGM 1951)★★★, Three Sailors And A Girl film soundtrack (MGM 1953)★★★, Seven Brides For Seven Brothers film soundtrack (MGM 1954)★★★, Athena film soundtrack (Mercury 1954)★★, Can't We Be Friends? (Verve 1956)★★★, Something Wonderful (MGM 1957)★★★.
● COMPILATIONS: Songs From Her Films (1989)★★★★.
● FILMS: Song Of The Open Road (1944), Delightfully Dangerous (1945), Holiday In Mexico (1946), Luxury Liner (1948), Three Daring Daughters (1948), A Date With Judy (1948), Two Weeks With Love (1948), Nancy Goes To Rio (1950), Rich, Young And Pretty (1951), Royal Wedding (1951), Three Sailors And A Girl (1953), Small Town Girl (1953), Seven Brides For Seven Brothers (1954), Athena (1954), Deep In My Heart guest star (1954), Hit The Deck (1955), The Female Animal (1957), The Girl Most Likely (1957), Enchanted Island (1958), Marie (1985).

PRESLEY, ELVIS

b. Elvis Aaron Presley, 8 January 1935, Tupelo, Mississippi, USA, d. 16 August 1977, Memphis, Tennessee. The most celebrated popular music phenomenon of his era and, for many, the purest embodiment of rock 'n' roll, Elvis Presley's life and career have become part of rock legend. The elder of twins, his younger brother, Jesse Garon, was stillborn, a tragedy that partly contributed to the maternal solicitude dominating his childhood and teenage years. Presley's first significant step towards a musical career took place at the age of eight when he won $5 in a local song contest performing the lachrymose Red Foley ballad, 'Old Shep'. His earliest musical influence came from attending the Pentecostal Church and listening to the psalms and gospel songs. He also had a strong grounding in country and blues and it was the combination of these different styles that was to provide his unique musical identity.

By the age of 13, Presley had moved with his family to Memphis, and during his later school years began cultivating an outsider image, with long hair, spidery sideburns and ostentatious clothes. After leaving school he took a job as a truck driver, a role in keeping with his unconventional appearance. In spite of his rebel posturing, Presley remained studiously polite to his elders and was devoted to his mother. Indeed, it was his filial affection that first prompted him to visit Sun Records, whose studios offered the sophisticated equivalent of a fairground recording booth service. As a birthday present to his mother, Gladys, Presley cut a version of the Ink Spots' 'My Happiness', backed with the Raskin/Brown/Fisher standard 'That's When Your Heartaches Begin'. The studio manager, Marion Keisker, noted Presley's unusual but distinctive vocal style and informed Sun's owner/producer Sam Phillips of his potential. Phillips nurtured the boy for almost a year before putting him together with country guitarist Scotty Moore and bassist Bill Black. Their early sessions showed considerable promise, especially when Presley began alternating his unorthodox low-key delivery with a high-pitched whine. The amplified guitars of Moore and Black contributed strongly to the effect and convinced Phillips that the singer was startlingly original. In Presley, Phillips saw something that he had long dreamed of discovering: 'a white boy who sang like a negro'. Presley's debut disc on Sun was the extraordinary 'That's All Right (Mama)', a showcase for his rich, multi-textured vocal dexterity, with sharp, solid backing from his compatriots. The b-side, 'Blue Moon Of Kentucky', was a country song, but the arrangement showed that Presley was threatening to slip into an entirely different genre, closer to R&B. Local response to these strange-sounding performances was encouraging and Phillips eventually shifted 20,000 copies of the disc. For his second single, Presley recorded Roy Brown's 'Good Rockin' Tonight' backed by the zingy 'I Don't Care If The Sun Don't Shine'. The more roots-influenced 'Milkcow Blues Boogie' followed, while the b-side, 'You're A Heartbreaker', had some strong tempo changes that neatly complemented Presley's quirky vocal. 'Baby Let's Play House'/'I'm Left, You're Right, She's Gone' continued the momentum and led to Presley performing on *The Grand Old Opry* and *Louisiana Hayride* radio programmes. A series of live dates commenced in 1955 with drummer D.J. Fontana added to the ranks. Presley toured clubs in Arkansas, Louisiana and Texas billed as 'The King Of Western Bop' and 'The Hillbilly Cat'. Audience reaction verged on the fanatical, which was hardly surprising given Presley's semi-erotic performances. His hip-swivelling

routine, in which he cascaded across the stage and plunged to his knees at dramatic moments in a song, was remarkable for the period and prompted near-riotous fan mania. The final Sun single, a cover version of Junior Parker's 'Mystery Train', was later acclaimed by many as the definitive rock 'n' roll single, with its chugging rhythm, soaring vocal and enticing lead guitar breaks. It established Presley as an artist worthy of national attention and ushered in the next phase of his career, which was dominated by the imposing figure of Colonel Tom Parker. The Colonel was a former fairground huckster who managed several country artists including Hank Snow and Eddy Arnold. After relieving disc jockey Bob Neal of Presley's managership, Parker persuaded Sam Phillips that his financial interests would be better served by releasing the boy to a major label. RCA Records had already noted the commercial potential of the phenomenon under offer and agreed to pay Sun Records a release fee of $35,000, an incredible sum for the period. The sheer diversity of Presley's musical heritage and his remarkable ability as a vocalist and interpreter of material enabled him to escape the cultural parochialism of his R&B-influenced predecessors. The attendant rock 'n' roll explosion, in which Presley was both a creator and participant, ensured that he could reach a mass audience, many of them newly affluent teenagers.

It was on 10 January 1956, a mere two days after his 21st birthday, that Presley entered RCA's studios in Nashville to record his first tracks for a major label. His debut session produced the epochal 'Heartbreak Hotel', one of the most striking pop records ever released. Co-composed by Hoyt Axton's mother Mae, the song evoked nothing less than a vision of absolute funereal despair. There was nothing in the pop charts of the period that even hinted at the degree of desolation described in the song. Presley's reading was extraordinarily mature and moving, with a determined avoidance of any histrionics in favour of a pained and resigned acceptance of loneliness as death. The economical yet acutely emphatic piano work of Floyd Cramer enhanced the stark mood of the piece, which was frozen in a suitably minimalist production. The startling originality and intensity of 'Heartbreak Hotel' entranced the American public and pushed the single to number 1 for an astonishing eight weeks. Whatever else he achieved, Presley was already assured a place in pop history for one of the greatest major label debut records ever released. During the same month that 'Heartbreak Hotel' was recorded, Presley made his national television debut displaying his sexually enticing gyrations before a bewildered adult audience whose alleged outrage subsequently persuaded producers to film the star exclusively from the waist upwards. Having outsold his former Sun colleague Carl Perkins with 'Blue Suede Shoes', Presley released a debut album that contained several of the songs he had previously recorded with Sam Phillips, including Little Richard's 'Tutti Fruitti', the R&B classic 'I Got A Woman' and an eerie, wailing version of Richard Rodgers/Lorenz Hart's 'Blue Moon', which emphasized his remarkable vocal range.

Since hitting number 2 in the UK lists with 'Heartbreak Hotel', Presley had been virtually guaranteed European success and his profile was increased via a regular series of releases as RCA took full advantage of their bulging back catalogue. Although there was a danger of overkill, Presley's talent, reputation and immensely strong fanbase vindicated the intense release schedule and the quality of the material ensured that the public was not disappointed. After hitting number 1 for the second time with the slight ballad 'I Want You, I Need You, I Love You', Presley released what was to become the most commercially successful double-sided single in pop history, 'Hound Dog'/'Don't Be Cruel'. The former was composed by the immortal rock 'n' roll songwriting team of Leiber And Stoller, and presented Presley at his upbeat best with a novel lyric, complete with a striking guitar solo and spirited handclapping from his backing group the Jordanaires. Otis Blackwell's 'Don't Be Cruel' was equally effective with a striking melody line and some clever and amusing vocal gymnastics from the hiccuping King of Western Bop, who also received a co-writing credit. The single remained at number 1 in the USA for a staggering 11 weeks and both sides of the record were massive hits in the UK.

Celluloid fame for Presley next beckoned with *Love Me Tender*, produced by David Weisbert, who had previously worked on James Dean's *Rebel Without A Cause*. Presley's movie debut received mixed reviews but was a box-office smash, while the smouldering, perfectly enunciated title track topped the US charts for five weeks. The spate of Presley singles continued in earnest through 1957 and one of the biggest was another Otis Blackwell composition, 'All Shook Up', which the singer used as a cheekily oblique comment on his by now legendary dance movements. By late 1956 it was rumoured that Presley would be drafted into the US Army and, as if to compensate for that irksome eventuality, RCA, Twentieth Century Fox and the Colonel stepped up the work-rate and release schedules. Incredibly, three major films were completed in the next two-and-a-half years. *Loving You* boasted a quasi-autobiographical script with Presley playing a truck driver who becomes a pop star. The title track became the b-side of '(Let Me Be Your) Teddy Bear' which reigned at number 1 for seven weeks. The third movie, Jailhouse Rock, was Presley's most successful to date with an excellent soundtrack and some inspired choreography. The Leiber and Stoller title track was an instant classic that again topped the US charts for seven weeks and made pop history by entering the UK listings at number 1. The fourth celluloid outing, King Creole (adapted from the Harold Robbins novel, *A Stone For Danny Fisher*), is regarded by many as Presley's finest film and a firm indicator of his sadly unfulfilled potential as a serious actor. Once more the soundtrack album featured some surprisingly strong material such as the haunting 'Crawfish' and the vibrant 'Dixieland Rock'. By the time *King Creole* was released in 1958, Elvis had already been inducted into the US Forces. A publicity photograph of the singer having his hair shorn symbolically commented on his approaching musical emasculation. Although rock 'n' roll purists mourned the passing of the old Elvis, it seemed inevitable in the context of the 50s that he would move towards a broader base appeal and tone down his rebellious image. From 1958-60, Presley served in the US Armed Forces, spending much of his time in Germany where he was regarded as a model soldier. It was during this period that he first met 14-year-old Priscilla Beaulieu, whom he later married in 1967. Back in America, the Colonel kept his absent star's reputation intact via a series of films, record releases and extensive merchandising. Hits such as 'Wear My Ring Around Your Neck', 'Hard Headed Woman', 'One Night', 'I Got Stung', 'A Fool Such As I' and 'A Big Hunk O' Love' filled the long, two-year gap and by the time Presley reappeared, he was ready to assume the mantle of all-round entertainer. The change was immediately evident in the series of number 1 hits that he enjoyed in the early 60s. The enormously successful 'It's Now Or Never', based on the Italian melody 'O Sole Mio', revealed the King as an operatic crooner, far removed from his earlier raucous recordings. 'Are You Lonesome Tonight?', originally recorded by Al Jolson as early as 1927, allowed Presley to quote some Shakespeare in the spoken-word middle section as well as showing his ham-acting ability with an overwrought vocal. The new clean-cut Presley was presented on celluloid in *GI Blues*. The movie played upon his recent army exploits and saw him serenading a puppet on the charming chart-topper 'Wooden Heart', which also allowed Elvis to show off his knowledge of German. The grandiose 'Surrender' completed this phase of big ballads in the old-fashioned style. For the next few years Presley concentrated on an undemanding spree of films, including *Flaming Star, Wild In The Country, Blue Hawaii, Kid Galahad, Girls! Girls! Girls!, Follow That Dream, Fun In Acapulco, It Happened At The World's Fair, Kissin' Cousins, Viva Las Vegas, Roustabout, Girl Happy, Tickle Me, Harem Scarum, Frankie And Johnny, Paradise - Hawaiian Style* and *Spinout*. Not surprisingly, most of his album recordings were hastily completed soundtracks with unadventurous commissioned songs. For his singles he relied increasingly on the formidable Doc Pomus/Mort Shuman team who composed such hits as 'Mess Of Blues', 'Little Sister' and 'His Latest Flame'. More and more, however, the hits were adapted from films and their chart positions suffered accordingly. After the 1963 number 1 'Devil In Disguise', a bleak period followed in which such minor songs as 'Bossa Nova Baby', 'Kiss Me Quick', 'Ain't That Lovin' You Baby' and 'Blue Christmas' became the rule rather than the exception. Significantly, his biggest success of the mid-60s, 'Crying In The Chapel', had been recorded five years earlier, and part of its appeal came from the realization that it represented something ineffably lost.

In the wake of the Beatles' rise to fame and the beat boom explosion, Presley seemed a figure out of time. Nevertheless, in spite of the dated nature of many of his recordings, he could still invest power and emotion into classic songs. The sassy 'Frankie And Johnny' was expertly sung by Presley, as was his moving reading of Ketty Lester's 'Love Letters'. His other significant 1966 release, 'If Everyday Was Like Christmas', was a beautiful festive song unlike anything else in the charts of the period. By 1967, however, it was clear to critics and even a large proportion of his devoted following that Presley had seriously lost his way. He continued to grind out pointless movies such as *Double Trouble, Speedway, Clambake* and *Live A Little, Love A Little*, even though the box office returns were increasingly poor. His capacity to register instant hits, irrespective of the material was also wearing thin, as such lowly placed singles as 'You Gotta Stop' and 'Long Legged Woman' demonstrated all too alarmingly. However, just as Elvis' career had reached its all-time nadir he seemed to wake up, take stock, and break free from the artistic malaise in which he found himself. Two songs written by country guitarist Jerry Reed, 'Guitar Man' and 'US Male', proved a spectacular return to form for Elvis in 1968, such was Presley's conviction that the compositions almost seemed to be written specifically for him. During the same year, Colonel Tom Parker had approached NBC-TV about the possibility of recording a Presley Christmas special in which the singer would perform a selection of religious songs similar in feel to his early 60s album *His Hand In Mine*. However, the executive producers of the show vetoed that concept in favour of a one-hour spectacular designed to capture Elvis at his rock 'n' rollin' best. It was a remarkable challenge for the singer, seemingly in the autumn of his career, and he responded to the idea with unexpected enthusiasm. The *Elvis TV Special* was broadcast in America on 3 December 1968 and has since become legendary as one of the most celebrated moments in pop broadcasting history. The show was not merely good but an absolute revelation, with the King emerging as if he had been frozen in time for 10 years. His determination to recapture past glories oozed from every movement and was discernible in every aside. With his leather jacket and acoustic guitar strung casually round his neck, he resembled nothing less than the consummate pop idol of the 50s who had entranced a generation. To add authenticity to the proceedings he was accompanied by his old sidekicks Scotty Moore and D.J. Fontana. There was no sense of self-parody in the show as Presley joked about his famous surly curled-lip movement and even heaped passing ridicule on his endless stream of bad movies. The music concentrated heavily on his 50s classics but, significantly, there was a startling finale courtesy of the passionate 'If I Can Dream' in which he seemed to sum up the frustration of a decade in a few short lines. The critical plaudits heaped upon Elvis in the wake of his television special prompted the singer to undertake his most significant recordings in years. With producer Chips Moman overseeing the sessions in January 1969, Presley recorded enough material to cover two highly praised albums, *From Elvis In Memphis* and *From Memphis To Vegas/From Vegas To Memphis*. The former was particularly strong with such distinctive tracks as the eerie 'Long Black Limousine' and the engagingly melodic 'Any Day Now'. On the singles front, Presley was back in top form and finally coming to terms with contemporary issues, most notably on the socially aware 'In The Ghetto', which hit number 2 in the UK and number 3 in the USA. The glorious 'Suspicious Minds', a wonderful song of marital jealousy, with cascading tempo changes and an exceptional vocal arrangement, gave him his first US chart-topper since 'Good Luck Charm' back in 1962. Subsequent hits such as the maudlin 'Don't Cry Daddy', which dealt with the death of a marriage, ably demonstrated Presley's ability to read a song. Even his final few films seemed less disastrous than expected.

In 1969's *Charro*, he grew a beard for the first time in his portrayal of a moody cowboy, while *A Change Of Habit* dealt with more serious subject matter than usual. More importantly, Presley returned as a live performer at Las Vegas, with a strong backing group including guitarist James Burton and pianist Glen D. Hardin. In common with John Lennon, who also returned to the stage that same year with the Plastic Ono Band, Presley opened his set with Carl Perkins' 'Blue Suede Shoes'. His comeback was well received and one of the live songs, 'The Wonder Of You', stayed at number 1 in Britain for six weeks during the summer of 1970. There was also a revealing documentary film of the tour - *That's The Way It Is* - and a companion album that included contemporary cover versions, such as Tony Joe White's 'Polk Salad Annie', Creedence Clearwater Revival's 'Proud Mary' and Neil Diamond's 'Sweet Caroline'.

During the early 70s Presley continued his live performances, but soon fell victim to the same artistic atrophy that had bedevilled his celluloid career. Rather than re-entering the studio to record fresh material he relied on a slew of patchy live albums that saturated the marketplace. What had been innovative and exciting in 1969 swiftly became a tedious routine and an exercise in misdirected potential. The backdrop to Presley's final years was a sordid slump into drug dependency, reinforced by the pervasive unreality of a pampered lifestyle in his fantasy home, Gracelands. The dissolution of his marriage in 1973 coincided with a further decline and an alarming tendency to put on weight. Remarkably, he continued to undertake live appearances, covering up his bloated frame with brightly coloured jump suits and an enormous, ostentatiously jewelled belt. He collapsed onstage on a couple of occasions and finally on 16 August 1977 his tired body expired. The official cause of death was a heart attack, undoubtedly brought on by barbiturate usage over a long period. In the weeks following his demise, his record sales predictably rocketed and 'Way Down' proved a fittingly final UK number 1.

The importance of Presley in the history of rock 'n' roll and popular music remains incalculable. In spite of his iconographic status, the Elvis image was never captured in a single moment of time like that of Bill Haley, Buddy Holly or even Chuck Berry. Presley, in spite of his apparent creative inertia, was not a one-dimensional artist clinging to history but a multi-faceted performer whose career spanned several decades and phases. For purists and rockabilly enthusiasts it is the early Presley that remains of greatest importance and there is no doubting that his personal fusion of black and white musical influences, incorporating R&B and country, produced some of the finest and most durable recordings of the century. Beyond Elvis 'The Hillbilly Cat', however, there was the face that launched a thousand imitators, that black-haired, smiling or smouldering presence who stared from the front covers of numerous EPs, albums and film posters of the late 50s and early 60s. It was that well-groomed, immaculate pop star who inspired a generation of performers and second-rate imitators in the 60s. There was also Elvis the Las Vegas performer, vibrant and vulgar, yet still distant and increasingly appealing to a later generation brought up on the excesses of 70s rock and glam ephemera. Finally, there was the bloated Presley who bestrode the stage in the last months of his career. For many, he has come to symbolize the decadence and loss of dignity that is all too often heir to pop idolatry. It is no wonder that Presley's remarkable career so sharply divides those who testify to his ultimate greatness and those who bemoan the gifts that he seemingly squandered along the way. Twenty years after his death, in August 1997, there was no waning of his power and appeal. Television, radio, newspapers and magazines all over the world still found that, whatever was happening elsewhere, little could compare to this anniversary.

● ALBUMS: *Elvis Presley* (RCA Victor 1956)★★★★, *Elvis* (RCA Victor 1956)★★★★★, *Rock 'N' Roll* UK release (HMV 1956)★★★★, *Rock 'N' Roll No. 2* UK release (HMV 1957)★★★★, *Loving You* film soundtrack (RCA Victor 1957)★★★★, *Elvis' Christmas Album* (RCA Victor 1957)★★★, *King Creole* film soundtrack (RCA Victor 1958)★★★★, *For LP Fans Only* (RCA Victor 1959)★★★★, *A Date With Elvis* (RCA Victor 1959)★★★★, *Elvis Is Back!* (RCA Victor 1960)★★★★, *G.I. Blues* film soundtrack (RCA Victor 1960)★★★, *His Hand In Mine* (RCA Victor 1961)★★★, *Something For Everybody* (RCA Victor 1961)★★★, *Blue Hawaii* (RCA Victor 1961)★★★, *Pot Luck* (RCA Victor 1962)★★★, *Girls! Girls! Girls!* film soundtrack (RCA Victor 1963)★★★, *It Happened At The World's Fair* film soundtrack (RCA Victor 1963)★★, *Fun In Acapulco* film soundtrack (RCA Victor 1963)★★, *Kissin' Cousins* film soundtrack (RCA Victor 1964)★★, *Roustabout* film soundtrack (RCA Victor 1964)★★, *Girl Happy* film soundtrack (RCA Victor 1965)★★, *Harem Scarum* film soundtrack (RCA Victor 1965)★★, *Frankie And Johnny* film soundtrack (RCA Victor 1966)★★, *Paradise, Hawaiian Style* film soundtrack (RCA Victor 1966)★★, *Spinout* film soundtrack (RCA Victor 1966)★★, *How Great Thou Art* (RCA Victor 1967)★★★, *Double Trouble* film soundtrack (RCA Victor 1967)★★, *Clambake* film soundtrack (RCA Victor 1967)★★, *Speedway* film soundtrack (RCA Victor 1968)★★, *Elvis - TV Special* (RCA Victor 1968)★★★, *From Elvis In Memphis* (RCA Victor 1969)★★★★, *From Memphis To Vegas/From Vegas To Memphis* (RCA Victor 1969)★★★, *On Stage February 1970* (RCA Victor 1970)★★★★, *Elvis Back In Memphis* (RCA Victor 1970)★★★, *That's The Way It Is* (RCA 1970)★★★, *Elvis Country (I'm 10,000 Years Old)* (RCA 1971)★★★, *Love Letters From Elvis* (RCA 1971)★★★, *Elvis Sings The Wonderful World Of Christmas* (RCA 1971)★★★, *Elvis Now* (RCA 1972)★★★, *He Touched Me* (RCA 1972)★★★, *Elvis As Recorded At Madison Square Garden* (RCA 1972)★★★, *Aloha From Hawaii Via Satellite* (RCA 1973)★★★, *Elvis* (RCA 1973)★★★, *Raised On Rock/ For Ol' Times Sake* (RCA 1973)★★★, *Good Times* (RCA 1974)★★★, *Elvis Recorded Live On Stage In Memphis* (RCA 1974)★★★★, *Having Fun With Elvis On Stage* (RCA 1974)★, *Promised Land* (RCA 1975)★★★, *Elvis Today* (RCA 1975)★★★, *From Elvis Presley Boulevard, Memphis, Tennessee* (RCA 1976)★★★, *Welcome To My World* (RCA 1977)★★★, *Moody Blue* (RCA 1977)★★★, *Guitar Man* (RCA 1980)★★★, *The Ultimate Performance* (RCA 1981)★★★, *The Sound Of Your Cry* (RCA 1982)★★★, *The First Year* (Sun 1983)★★★, *Jailhouse Rock/Love In Las Vegas* (RCA 1983)★★★, *Elvis: The First Live Recordings* (Music Works 1984)★★★, *The Elvis Presley Interview Record: An Audio Self-Portrait* (RCA 1984)★★, with Carl Perkins and Jerry Lee Lewis *The Million Dollar Quartet* (RCA 1990)★★★, *The Lost Album* (RCA 1991)★★★, *If Every Day Was Like Christmas* (RCA 1994)★★★, *Elvis Presley '56* (RCA 1996)★★★★★, *Essential Elvis, Volume 4: A Hundred Years From Now* (RCA 1996)★★★, *Essential Elvis, Volume 5: Rhythm And Country* (RCA 1998)★★★, *Tiger Man* 1968 recording (RCA 1998)★★★★.

● COMPILATIONS: *The Best Of Elvis* UK release (HMV 1957)★★★★, *Elvis' Golden Records* (RCA Victor 1958)★★★★★, *50,000,000 Elvis Fans Can't Be Wrong: Golden Records, Volume 2* (RCA Victor 1960)★★★★★, *Elvis' Golden Records, Volume 3* (RCA Victor 1963)★★★★, *Elvis For Everyone!* (RCA Victor 1965)★★★, *Elvis' Golden Records, Volume 4* (RCA Victor 1968)★★★★, *Elvis Sings 'Flaming Star' And Other Hits From His Movies* (RCA Camden 1969)★★, *Let's Be Friends* (RCA Camden 1970)★★★, *Almost In Love* (RCA Camden 1970)★★, *Worldwide 50 Gold Award Hits, Volume 1 - A Touch Of Gold* 4-LP box set (RCA Victor 1970)★★★★★, *You'll Never Walk Alone* (RCA Camden 1971)★★★, *C'mon Everybody* (RCA Camden 1971)★★★, *The Other Sides - Worldwide 50 Gold Award Hits, Volume 2* 4-LP box set (RCA Victor 1971)★★★★, *I Got Lucky* (RCA Camden 1971)★★★, *Elvis Sings Hits From His Movies, Volume 1* (RCA Camden 1972)★★★, *Burning Love And Hits From His Movies, Volume 2* (RCA Camden 1972)★★★, *Separate Ways* (RCA Camden 1973)★★★, *Elvis - A Legendary Performer, Volume 1* (RCA 1974)★★★★, *Hits Of The 70s* (RCA 1974)★★★, *Pure Gold* (RCA 1975)★★★, *Easy Come Easy Go* (RCA Camden 1975)★★★, *The U.S. Male* (RCA Camden 1975)★★★, *Elvis Presley's Greatest Hits* 7-LP box set (Readers Digest 1975)★★★, *Pictures Of Elvis* (RCA Starcall 1975)★★, *Elvis - A Legendary Performer, Volume 2* (RCA 1976)★★★★, *Sun Sessions* (RCA 1976)★★★★★, *Elvis In Demand* (RCA 1977)★★★, *The Elvis Tapes* interview disc (Redwood 1977)★★, *He Walks Beside Me* (RCA 1978)★★★, *Elvis Sings For Children And Grownups Too!* (RCA 1978)★★★, *Elvis - A Canadian Tribute* (RCA 1978)★★★, *The '56 Sessions, Volume 1* (RCA 1978)★★★★, *Elvis' 40 Greatest* (RCA 1978)★★★★★, *Elvis - A Legendary Performer, Volume 3* (RCA 1979)★★★★, *Our Memories Of Elvis* (RCA 1979)★★★, *Our Memories Of Elvis Volume 2* (RCA 1979)★★★, *The '56 Sessions, Volume 2* (RCA 1979)★★★★, *Elvis Presley Sings Leiber And Stoller* (RCA 1979)★★★★, *Elvis - A Legendary Performer, Volume 4* (RCA 1980)★★★★, *Elvis Aaron Presley* 8-LP box set (RCA 1980)★★★, *This Is Elvis* (RCA 1981)★★★, *Elvis - Greatest Hits, Volume 1* (RCA 1981)★★, *The Elvis Medley* (RCA 1982)★★★, *I Was The One* (RCA 1983)★★★, *Elvis' Golden Records, Volume 5* (RCA 1984)★★★★, *Elvis: A Golden Celebration* 6-LP box set (RCA 1984)★★★, *Rocker* (RCA 1984)★★★★, *Reconsider Baby* (RCA 1985)★★★★, *A Valentine Gift For You* (RCA 1985)★★★, *Always On My Mind* (RCA 1985)★★★★, *Return Of The Rocker* (RCA 1986)★★★, *The Number One Hits* (RCA 1987)★★★★★, *The Top Ten Hits* (RCA 1987)★★★★, *The Complete Sun Sessions* (RCA 1987)★★★★★, *Essential Elvis* (RCA 1988)★★★★, *Stereo '57 (Essential Elvis Volume 2)* (RCA 1988)★★★★, *Known Only To Him: Elvis Gospel: 1957-1971* (RCA 1989)★★★★, *Hits Like Never Before: Essential Elvis, Volume 3* (RCA 1990)★★★, *Collector's Gold* (RCA 1991)★★★★, *The King Of Rock 'n' Roll: The Complete '50s Masters* 5-CD box set (RCA 1992)★★★★★, *From Nashville To Memphis: The Essential '60s Masters* 5-CD box set (RCA 1993)★★★★★, *Amazing Grace: His Greatest Sacred Songs* (RCA 1994)★★★★, *Heart And Soul* (RCA 1995)★★, *Walk A Mile In My Shoes: The Essential '70s Masters* 5-CD box set (RCA 1995)★★★★, *Presley - The All Time Greats* (RCA 1996)★★★★, *Great Country Songs* (RCA 1997)★★★, *Platinum - A Life In Music* 4-CD box set (RCA 1997)★★★★.

● VIDEOS: *Elvis On Tour* (MGM/UA 1984), *Elvis Presley In*

Concert (Mountain Films 1986), 68 Comeback Special (Virgin Vision 1986), One Night With You (Virgin Vision 1986), Aloha From Hawaii (Virgin Vision 1986), '56 In the Beginning (Virgin Vision 1987), Memories (Vestron Music Video 1987), This Is Elvis (Warner Home Video 1988), Graceland (Video Gems 1988), Great Performances Volume 1 (Buena Vista 1990), Great Performances Volume 2 (Buena Vista 1990), Young Elvis (Channel 5 1990), Sun Days With Elvis (MMG Video 1991), Elvis: A Portrait By His Friends (Qube Pictures 1991), The Lost Performances (BMG 1992), Private Elvis (1993), Elvis In Hollywood (1993), The Alternate Aloha Concert (Lightyear 1996), Elvis 56 - The Video (BMG 1996), Elvis - That's The Way It Is (1996), Private Moments (Telstar 1997), The Great Performance (Wienerworld 1997), The Legend Lives On (Real Entertainment 1997), Collapse Of The Kingdom (Real Entertainment 1997), The King Comes Back (Real Entertainment 1997), Wild In Hollywood (Real Entertainment 1997), Rocket Ride To Stardom (Real Entertainment 1997), Elvis: All The Kings Men (Real Entertainment 1997), NBC T.V. Special (Lightyear 1997).

● FURTHER READING: I Called Him Babe: Elvis Presley's Nurse Remembers, Marian J. Cocke. The Three Loves Of Elvis Presley: The True Story Of The Presley Legend, Robert Holmes. A Century Of Elvis, Albert Hand. The Elvis They Dig, Albert Hand. Operation Elvis, Alan Levy. The Elvis Presley Pocket Handbook, Albert Hand. All Elvis: An Unofficial Biography Of The 'King Of Discs', Philip Buckle. The Elvis Presley Encyclopedia, Roy Barlow. Elvis: A Biography, Jerry Hopkins. Meet Elvis Presley, Favius Friedman Elvis Presley, Paula Taylor. Elvis, Jerry Hopkins. The Elvis Presley Scrapbook 1935-1977, James Robert Paris. Elvis And The Colonel, May Mann. Recording Sessions 1954-1974, Ernst Jorgensen and Erik Rasmussen. Elvis Presley: An Illustrated Biography, W.A. Harbinson. Elvis: The Films And Career Of Elvis Presley, Steven Zmijewsky and Boris Zmijewsky. Presley Nation, Spencer Leigh. Elvis, Peter Jones. Presley: Entertainer Of The Century, Antony James. Elvis And His Secret, Maria Gripe. On Stage, Elvis Presley, Kathleen Bowman. The Elvis Presley American Discography, Ron Barry. Elvis: What Happened, Red West, Sonny West and Dave Hebler. Elvis: Tribute To The King Of Rock, Dick Tatham. Elvis Presley, Todd Slaughter. Elvis: Recording Sessions, Ernst Jorgensen, Erick Rasmussen and Johnny Mikkelsen. The Life And Death Of Elvis Presley, W.A. Harbinson. Elvis: Lonely Star At The Top, David Hanna. Elvis In His Own Words, Mick Farren and Pearce Marchbank. Twenty Years Of Elvis: The Session File, Colin Escott and Martin Hawkins. Starring Elvis, James W. Bowser. My Life With Elvis, Becky Yancey and Cliff Lindecker. The Real Elvis: A Good Old Boy, Vince Staten. The Elvis Presley Trivia Quiz Book, Helen Rosenbaum. A Presley Speaks, Vester Presley. The Graceland Gates, Harold Lloyd. The Boy Who Dared To Rock: The Definitive Elvis, Paul Lichter. Eine Illustrierte Dokumentation, Bernd King and Heinz Plehn. Elvis Presley Speaks, Hans Holzer. Elvis: The Legend Lives! One Year Later, Martin A. Grove. Private Elvis, Diego Cortez. Bill Adler's Love Letters To Elvis, Bill Adler. Elvis: His Life And Times In Poetry And Lines, Joan Buchanan West. Elvis '56: In The Beginning, Alfred Wertheimer. Elvis Presley: An Illustrated Biography, Rainer Wallraf and Heinz Plehn. Even Elvis, Mary Ann Thornton. Elvis: Images & Fancies, Jac L. Tharpe. Elvis In Concert, John Reggero. Elvis Presley: A Study In Music, Robert Matthew-Walker. Elvis; Portrait Of A Friend, Marty Lacker, Patsy Lacker and Leslie E. Smith. Elvis Is That You?, Holly Hatcher. Elvis: Newly Discovered Drawings Of Elvis Presley, Betty Harper. Trying To Get To You: The Story Of Elvis Presley, Valerie Harms. Love Of Elvis, Bruce Hamilton and Michael L. Liben. To Elvis With Love, Lena

Canada. The Truth About Elvis, Jess Stearn. Elvis: We Love You Tender, Dee Presley, David Rick and Billy Stanley. Presleyana, Jerry Osborne and Bruce Hamilton. Elvis: The Final Years, Jerry Hopkins. When Elvis Died, Nancy Gregory and Joseph. All About Elvis, Fred L. Worth and Steve D. Tamerius. Elvis Presley: A Reference Guide And Discography, John A. Whisle. The Illustrated Discography, Martin Hawkins and Colin Escott. Elvis: Legend Of Love, Marie Greenfield. Elvis Presley: King Of Rock 'N' Roll, Richard Wooton. The Complete Elvis, Martin Torgoff. Elvis Special 1982, Todd Slaughter. Elvis, Dave Marsh. Up And Down With Elvis Presley, Marge Crumbaker with Gabe Tucker. Elvis For The Record, Maureen Covey. Elvis: The Complete Illustrated Record, Roy Carr and Mick Farren. Elvis Collectables, Rosalind Cranor. Jailhouse Rock: The Bootleg Records Of Elvis Presley 1970, Lee Cotten and Howard A. DeWitt. Elvis The Soldier, Rex and Elisabeth Mansfield. All Shook Up: Elvis Day-By-Day, 1954-1977, Lee Cotten. Elvis, John Townson, Gordon Minto and George Richardson. Priscilla, Elvis & Me, Michael Edwards. Elvis On The Road To Stardom: 1955-1956, Jim Black. Return To Sender, Howard F. Banney. Elvis: His Life From A To Z, Fred L. Worth and Steve D. Tamerius. Elvis And The Colonel, Dirk Vallenga with Mick Farren. Elvis: My Brother, Bill Stanley with George Erikson. Long Lonely Highway: 1950's Elvis Scrapbook, Ger J. Rijff. Elvis In Hollywood, Gerry McLafferty. Reconsider Baby: Definitive Elvis Sessionography, E. Jorgensen. Elvis '69, The Return, Joseph A. Tunzi. The Death Of Elvis: What Really Happened, Charles C. Thompson and James P. Cole. Elvis For Beginners, Jill Pearlman. Elvis, The Cool King, Bob Morel and Jan Van Gestel. The Elvis Presley Scrapbooks 1955-1965, Peter Haining (ed.). The Boy Who Would Be King. An Intimate Portrait Of Elvis Presley By His Cousin, Earl Greenwood and Kathleen Tracy. Elvis: The Last 24 Hours, Albert Goldman. The Elvis Files, Gail Brewer-Giorgio. Elvis, My Dad, David Adler and Ernest Andrews. The Elvis Reader: Texts And Sources On The King Of Rock 'n' Roll, Kevin Quain (ed.). Elvis Bootlegs Buyer's Guide, Pts 1 & 2, Tommy Robinson. Elvis: The Music Lives On - The Recording Sessions 1954-1976, Richard Peters. The King Forever, no author listed. Dead Elvis: A Chronicle Of A Cultural Obsession, Greil Marcus. Elvis People: Cult Of The King, Ted Harrison. In Search Of The King, Craig Gelfand, Lynn Blocker-Krantz and Rogerio Noguera. Aren Med Elvis, Roger Ersson and Lennart Svedberg. Elvis And Gladys, Elaine Dundy. King And I: Little Gallery of Elvis Impersonators, Kent Barker and Karin Pritikin. Elvis Sessions: The Recorded Music Of Elvis Aron Presley 1953-1977, Joseph A. Tunzi. Elvis: The Sun Years, Howard A. DeWitt. Elvis In Germany: The Missing Years, Andreas Schroer. Graceland: The Living Legend Of Elvis Presley, Chet Flippo. Elvis: The Secret Files, John Parker. The Life And Cuisine Of Elvis Presley, David Adler. Last Train To Memphis: The Rise Of Elvis Presley, Peter Guralnick. In His Own Words, Mick Farren. Elvis: Murdered By The Mob, John Parker. The Complete Guide To The Music Of..., John Robertson. Elvis' Man Friday, Gene Smith. The Hitchhiker's Guide To Elvis, Mick Farren. Elvis, The Lost Photographs 1948-1969, Joseph Tunzi and O'Neal. Elvis Aaron Presley: Revelations From The Memphis Mafia, Alanna Nash. The Elvis Encyclopaedia, David E. Stanley. E: Reflections On The Birth Of The Elvis Faith, John E. Strausbaugh. Elvis Meets The Beatles: The Untold Story Of Their Entangled Lives, Chris Hutchins and Peter Thompson. Elvis, Highway 51 South, Memphis, Tennessee, Joseph A. Tunzi. Elvis In The Army, William J. Taylor Jr. Everything Elvis, Pauline Bartel. Elvis In Wonderland, Bob Jope. Elvis: Memories And Memorabilia, Richard Bushkin. Elvis Sessions II: The Recorded Music Of Elvis Aron Presley 1953-1977, Joseph A.

Tunzi. *The Ultimate Album Cover Book*, Paul Dowling. *The King Of The Road*, Robert Gordon. *That's Alright, Elvis*, Scotty Moore and James Dickerson. *Raised On Rock: Growing Up At Graceland*, David A. Stanley and Mark Bego. *Elvis: In The Twilight Of Memory*, June Juanico. *The Rise And Fall And Rise Of Elvis*, Aubrey Dillon-Malone. *In Search Of Elvis: Music, Race, Art, Religion*, Vernon Chadwick (editor). *The Complete Idiot's Guide To Elvis*, Frank Coffey. *The Elvis Encyclopedia: An Impartial Guide To The Films Of Elvis*, Eric Braun. *Essential Elvis*, Peter Silverton.
● FILMS: *Love Me Tender* (1956), *Loving You* (1957), *Jailhouse Rock* (1957), *King Creole* (1958), *G.I. Blues* (1960), *Flaming Star* (1960), *Wild In The Country* (1961), *Blue Hawaii* (1961), *Kid Galahad* (1962), *Girls Girls Girls* (1962), *Follow That Dream* (1962), *It Happened At The World's Fair* (1963), *Fun In Acapulco* (1963), *Roustabout* (1964), *Viva Las Vegas* (1964), *Kissin' Cousins* (1964), *Tickle Me* (1965), *Harem Scarum a.k.a. Harem Holiday* (1965), *Girl Happy* (1965), *Spinout* (1966), *Paradise Hawaiian Style* (1966), *Frankie And Johnny* (1966), *Easy Come Easy Go* (1967), *Clambake* (1967), *Live A Little Love A Little* (1968), *Speedway* (1968), *Stay Away Joe* (1968), *Double Trouble* (1968), *The Trouble With Girls* (1969), *Charro!* (1969), *Change Of Habit* (1969), *This Is Elvis* compilation (1981).

PRESTON, ROBERT

b. Robert Preston Meservey, 8 June 1918, Newton Highlands, Massachusetts, USA, d. 21 March 1987, Santa Barbara, California, USA. An actor and singer, Preston had already enjoyed a busy, but undistinguished career in Hollywood for nearly 20 years when he landed the role of a lifetime on Broadway in The Music Man (1957). He grew up in Hollywood, and spent several of his teenage years in the theatre before signing for Paramount and making his first movie, *King Of Alcatraz*, in 1938. From then, until 1942, he made some 15 films, including *Union Pacific*, *Beau Geste*, *Typhoon*, *Moon Over Burma*, *Northwest Mounted Police*, and *This Gun For Hire* (1942). After serving in the US Army Air Force during World War II, Preston resumed his film career in features such as *The Macomber Affair*, *Tulsa* and *When I Grow Up*, until 1951 when he moved to New York. He appeared on Broadway in a number of straight plays including *Twentieth Century*, *The Tender Trap* and *Janus*, and was out of town in Philadelphia with *Boy Meets Girl* when he was asked to audition for *The Music Man*. His portrayal of the likeable con man, Harold Hill, who travels to small US towns such as Iowa, selling band instruments (which never materialize) to parents for their children to play, made Preston a gilt-edged Broadway star. Meredith Willson's fine score featured numbers such as 'Seventy-Six Trombones', ''Til There Was You', and Preston's *tour de force*, 'Ya Got Trouble'. He won the Tony Award for best actor in a musical, and stayed with the show for over two years. After being virtually ignored during initial casting, he recreated the part in the 1962 film version. Cary Grant was one of the actors to whom the role was offered, and he reportedly said: 'Not only won't I play it, but unless Robert Preston plays it, I won't even go see it.' After appearing in several more straight parts, Preston returned to the musical stage in 1964 with *Ben Franklin In Paris*, but, unlike the large onstage floating balloon in which Preston rode, the show did not really take off. Much more satisfying was I Do! I

Do!, a two-hander with Mary Martin for which Preston won another Tony. His final Broadway musical appearance came in 1974 with Mack And Mabel, which, despite a splendid Jerry Herman score, only lasted for six weeks. During the 50s and 60s he had continued to make films, and in the 70s and early 80s he appeared in several more, including the musical Mame (1973), with Lucille Ball, and *S.O.B.* and *Victor/Victoria* (1982), both with Julie Andrews. He also starred in several television movies, including the highly regarded *Finnegan Begin Again*, a poignant story of the love of an older man for a young woman played by Mary Tyler Moore. Preston died of lung cancer in 1987, and in the same year was awarded a special posthumous Tony, the Lawrence Langner Memorial Award for Distinguished Lifetime Achievement in the American Theatre.

PRIDE AND PREJUDICE
(see Taylor, Bernard J.)

PRINCE OF EGYPT, THE
In a year when the Walt Disney Studio's long-time supremacy in the world of animated features had already been challenged by 20th Century-Fox with its saga of the Russian Revolution entitled *Anastasia*, DreamWorks increased the Mouse's discomfiture with the release of this $75 million (at least) cartoon version of the Biblical book of *Exodus*. Well, just half of *Exodus* really, according to disaffected ex-Disney executive, Jeffrey Katzenberg. He formed the new DreamWorks Hollywood office with media mogul David Geffen and director Stephen Spielberg. 'We only went up to the crossing of the Red Sea, because whereas Cecil B. De Mille had almost four hours for his version (*The Ten Commandments*), we had just 90 minutes.' After consulting nearly 700 religious advisors, Philip Lazebnik's screenplay therefore begins with an Israelite woman setting her son Moses (voiced by Val Kilmer) adrift in a rush basket on the Nile, after hearing of the cull ordered by the Pharaoh Seti (Patrick Stewart), and ends when Moses delivers the Ten Commandments from Mount Sinai to the Israelites. During that 90-minutes journey, Moses is adopted by the Queen (Helen Mirren), mistakenly thinks that heir to the throne Rameses (Ralph Fiennes) is his blood-brother rather than his step-brother, recognizes the slave girl Miriam (Sandra Bullock) to be his sister, and marries the nomadic shepherd woman Tzipporah (Michelle Pfeiffer). Retaining Katzenberg's movie metaphor: among the supporting cast were Aaron (Jeff Goldblum), Jethro (Danny Glover), Hotep (Steve Martin), and Huy (Martin Short). It is of course essential for epics on this scale to have a music score (Hans Zimmer) and some original songs to complement the drama. Those provided by Broadway and Hollywood composer Stephen Schwartz included 'Deliver Us', 'All I Ever Wanted', 'Queen's Reprise', 'Through Heaven's Eyes', 'Playing With The Big Boys', 'The Plagues', and 'When You Believe', and were generally thought to be disappointing (actually, 'weedy, unadventurous, and full of ethnic twangs'). An additional number, 'I Will Get There', performed by Boyz II Men, was the work of Diane Warren. Soundtrack album sales were sprightly, while Whitney

Houston and Maria Carey's record of 'All I Ever Wanted', quickly climbed the charts on both sides of the Atlantic. Initial critical reaction was extremely favourable, especially for the film's 'pictorially splendid use of computer-generated imagery and special effects that carry the kind of impact you would expect from a live-action adventure'. These include one sequence towards the end in which the Red Sea is drained in order to allow the chosen ones to cross, followed by Pharaoh getting drenched. No dancing teapots in this one. *The Prince Of Egypt* was directed by Brenda Chapman, Steven Hickner, and Simon Wells, and released in 1998.

PRINCE, HAROLD (HAL)

b. Harold Smith Prince, 30 January 1928, New York, USA. A distinguished director and producer - the supreme Broadway showman - whose career has lasted for nearly 40 years, and is still going strong. Prince served his theatrical apprenticeship in the late 40s and early 50s with the esteemed author, director, and producer George Abbott. In 1954, he presented his first musical, The Pajama Game, in collaboration with Robert E. Griffith and Frederick Brisson. His association with Griffith continued until the latter's death in 1961, mostly with hits such as *Damn Yankees*, *New Girl In Town*, *West Side Story*, and *Fiorello!* (1959). *Tenderloin* (1960) was a disappointment, as was Prince's first assignment as a director, *A Family Affair* (1962). From then on, he has been the producer or co-producer and/or director for a whole range of (mostly) successful musicals such as *A Funny Thing Happened On The Way To The Forum* (1962), *She Loves Me* (1963), *Fiddler On The Roof* (1964), *Baker Street* (1965), *Flora, The Red Menace* (1965), *It's A Bird, It's A Plane, It's Superman* (1966), *Cabaret* (1966), *Zorba* (1968), *Company* (1970), *Follies* (1971), *A Little Night Music* (1973), *Candide* (1974), *Pacific Overtures* (1976), *On The Twentieth Century* (1978), *Evita* (1978), *Sweeney Todd* (1979), *Merrily We Roll Along* (1981), *A Doll's Life* (1982), *Grind* (1985), *The Phantom Of The Opera* (1986), *Roza* (1987), and *Kiss Of The Spider Woman* (1992). The list does not include re-staging and directing the original productions in several different countries, nor his work with American opera companies such as the New York Opera, the Houston Opera, and the Chicago Lyric Opera. For his innovative concepts, the ability to find the exact visual framework for the musical-narrative content, and his role, notably with Stephen Sondheim, in the drastic reshaping of the modern theatre musical, Prince has received more Tony Awards than anyone else, including one for his superb staging of the Broadway revival of *Show Boat* (1995). This was followed by a disappointingly brief run for Prince's revival of the 1974 version of *Candide* (1997) and *Parade* (1998).

● FURTHER READING: *Contradictions*, Harold Prince. *Harold Prince And The American Musical Theatre*, Foster Hirsch. *From Pajama Game To The Phantom Of The Opera And Beyond*, Carol Ilson.

PRINCESS THEATRE MUSICALS

A short but legendary series of significant musical productions presented at the tiny 299-seater house in New York in the period leading up to the Roaring Twenties. The Princess Theatre was built in 1913 at the corner of 39th Street and Sixth Avenue as a home for intimate one-act plays. However, in 1915 the theatre's owner, F. Ray Comstock, decreed that there should be musicals, so Jerome Kern, Guy Bolton and lyricist Schuyler Greene created *Nobody Home*, which, although it contained several interpolated numbers, was the first of what were subsequently regarded as landmarks in the history of American musical comedy. Instead of the usual old-fashioned, scarcely credible operettas, the new shows were funny and fast-moving, with the stylish, contemporary songs and situations integrated to an extent never attempted before. Kern, Bolton and Greene came together later that year for Very Good Eddie, before Schuyler was replaced by P.G. Wodehouse and the magic really began. Not straight away though, because the new team considered that it would be inappropriate to add music and lyrics to Charles Hoyt's play, *A Milk White Flag*, and so the third Princess Theatre musical, *Go To It* (1916), had a score by John Golden and Anne Caldwell. However, Kern, Bolton and Wodehouse came into their own with Oh, Boy! (1917) and Oh, Lady! Lady!! (1918). Another of their shows, Leave It To Jane (1917), was also a contender for the Princess Theatre but was unable to play there because *Oh, Boy!* was in residence for over a year. When it was finally withdrawn, Bolton and Wodehouse collaborated with composer Louis Hirsch for Oh, My Dear! (1918), and the final show in the Princess series was Toot Sweet, a revue with a score by Richard Whiting and Raymond B. Egan. Some 75 years later it is hardly credible that just a few small productions had such an influence on the future course of Broadway, and by definition, world musical theatre, but it is said to be so. In later years the Princess Theatre presented straight plays, and was also used for extended periods as a cinema. In 1936 the theatre was re-named the Labor Stage when it was taken over by the International Ladies Garment Workers Union who produced the popular revue Pins And Needles there, and was finally demolished in the 50s.

PRISONER CELL BLOCK H - THE MUSICAL

This camp send-up of the antipodean cult television series created by Reg Watson and starring Liverpudlian drag artist Lily Savage, opened at - where else? - the Queens Theatre in London on 30 October 1995. With concept, music and lyrics by Don Battye and Peter Pinne for Grundy Intl. Operations Ltd, and additional lyrics and dialogue by Lily Savage, the action takes place in a women's detention centre in Victoria, Australia. On holiday 'down under', Lily (no need to give her character a different name) is locked up after being falsely accused, amongst other things, of murdering her sister and stealing a fondue set. Ruling the roost with a rod of iron is butch warder Joan 'The Freak' Ferguson (Maggie Kirkpatrick reprising her television role), a cross between Goering and Hitler, with a disturbing fondness for strip-searching. She spikes the prison governor's (Penny Morrell) tea with LSD, stirs up a riot, and takes on the top job herself. From then on, the inmates soon get to know what *real* discipline is all about. Prominent amongst them were little Minnie (Liz

Smith), big and burly Steff (Terry Neason), pig-tailed Patsy (Sara Stephens), Twinkie (Emma Kershaw), Babs (Christine Glen), the two Silent Prisoners, Alix Longman and Kathryn Otto, The Man From The Department (Jeffrey Perry), and Mrs Austin, played by Alison Jiear, who sung up such a storm in *The Hot Mikado*, the previous show at the Queens. Stephens was the composer and lyricist of 'Teddy', which she sang while reassembling a teddy bear after it had been decapitated in the course of a drugs search. Cast members Longman and Perry, along with Winston Eade, Simon Lee, and Lesley Hayes, also had a hand in a lively set of songs, which included 'The Freak', 'Life On The Inside', 'Top Dog', 'I Like You', 'Gimme Me A Man', 'Twinset And Pearls', 'Feel I Wanna Boogie', 'Stir Crazy Blues', 'Gloves', 'I Never Told I Love Him', 'I'm Innocent', 'Love Will Set Us Free', 'Style', and 'Why Not For Me'. Augmenting the proceedings were the prison band, the Well Oiled Sisters, but this was Lily Savage's show, and her fans yelled their appreciation throughout, especially during the Wentworth Follies sequence when she emerged in an unbelievably extravagant blue-sequinned creation. Kevin Knight was credited with the costumes and the (flimsy) scenery, Peter Titus handled the choreography, and overseeing this 'mildly amusing rubbish' was director David McVicar. Some of the critics got the joke, but the show only really appealed to the cult-worshippers. It played out its advertised season, closing in January 1996. More than a year later, Lily and her kitsch chums were still on the loose in various British regional theatres.

The *Prisoner* television series had been musicalized before, in the five-performance *The Outside Tour*, organized by a fan of the show, Roz Vecsey, in 1990. She persuaded four of the cast to travel to the town of Derby in the UK, where they were also treated to a civic reception. Other stage musicals set in prisons have included Chicago and Kiss Of The Spider Woman.

PRIVILEGE

This enigmatic British film starred former Manfred Mann vocalist Paul Jones as a pop singer who becomes a Christ-like figure following a highly-successful, but contentious, publicity campaign. Written by Johnny Speight, later famed for the television series *Till Death Us Do Part*, *Privilege* was directed by the controversial Peter Watkins, creator of *The War Game*, a chilling view of Britain following nuclear war, banned by the BBC. Watkins' political leanings doubtlessly attracted him to the underlying theme of manipulation permeate this feature, but such ambitions were only partially realised. Segments of *Privilege* were genuinely powerful, particularly when Jones is manacled and jailed onstage by authoritarian figures. Yet where the singer copes well with his role, co-star Jean Shrimpton, famed as a model, is an unconvincing actress. The cast also featured George Bean, a former protégé of Rolling Stones' manager Andrew Loog Oldham. The soundtrack for *Privilege* was composed by Mike Leander, who later scored success as musical director for Gary Glitter. Although the attendant album did not chart, Paul Jones enjoyed a Top 5 hit single with one of the songs from the film, 'I've Been A Bad, Bad, Boy'. Such success,

however, did not help the fate of *Privilege*, which is now viewed only as a period-piece curio.

PROMISES, PROMISES

Although they had previously enjoyed enormous success writing popular songs, and music for television shows and films, *Promises, Promises* was the first Broadway musical with a score by Burt Bacharach and Hal David. The show, which opened at the Shubert Theatre in New York on 1 December 1968, was adapted by Neil Simon from the successful Billy Wilder film *The Apartment* (1960). The story follows the tormented love affair of Chuck Baxter (Jerry Orbach), a clerk who achieves promotion by renting his room to his bosses for their extra-marital affairs. In the course of his career rise, Chuck learns that one of these 'temporary tenants', J. D. Sheldrake (Edward Winter), is having an affair with Fran Kubelik (Jill O'Hara), the girl he loves. Marian Mercer, A. Larry Haines, Paul Reed, Dick O'Neill. and Norman Shelly, were also among the strong cast which included the future Broadway star Donna McKechnie. The score contained many delightful songs, including 'Whoever You Are', 'Knowing When To Leave', 'You'll Think Of Something', 'Wanting Things', 'Upstairs', 'She Likes Basketball', 'Our Little Secret', and 'I'll Never Fall in Love Again', which became a hit for Dionne Warwick in the US, and was a UK number 1 for Bobby Gentry. *Promises, Promises* won Tony Awards for best actor (Orbach) and supporting actress (Mercer), and ran for a remarkable 1,281 performances. Betty Buckley, Anthony Roberts, and James Congdon starred in the 1969 London production which was in residence at the Prince of Wales Theatre for well over a year, a total of 560 performances. Evan Pappas (Chuck) and Juliet Lambert (Fran) led a well received revival at the Goodspeed Opera House, Connecticut, in 1993, and there were London Fringe productions at the Bloomsbury Theatre (1994, with 60s pop star-turned jazz singer Helen Shapiro and Christopher Ryan) and the Bridewell Theatre (1996, Marcus Allen Cooper and Vanessa Cross). In 1997, the show was featured in both the New York City Center *Encores!* (Martin Short, Kerry O'Malley) and Los Angeles *Reprise!* series of semi-staged productions.

PURLIE

With a score by two newcomers to the New York musical theatre, Gary Geld (music) and Peter Udell (lyrics), this amusing satire on the serious subject of racial bigotry opened at the Broadway Theatre on 15 March 1970. The book, by Ossie Davis, Philip Rose, and Peter Udell, was based on Davis' 1961 play *Purlie Victorious*, and set in southern Georgia. It deals mainly with the struggle between the young evangelist, Purlie (Cleavon Little), who wants to take over the Big Bethel Church, and the intolerant plantation owner, Cap'n Cotchipee (John Heffernan). Fortunately, the Cap'n's son, Charlie (C. David Colson), has not inherited his father's twisted views, and he defects to Purlie's cause. In the end, the new preacher man not only gets the church - but the girl as well Her name was Lutiebelle, and she was played by Melba Moore, an actress who made a big impression in Hair (1968), and has since had several hits in the wider world of pop music. In *Purlie*, Moore gave a beautiful, understated performance, and introduced the tender 'I Got Love'. There was also the spirited 'New Fangled Preacher Man', which celebrates the Cap'n's death early on (the story is told in flashback), and sets the scene for one of those feel-good, 'hallelujah'-style evenings complete with songs such as 'Walk Him Up The Stairs', 'Purlie', 'Skinnin' A Cat', 'First Thing Monday Mornin', 'He Can Do It', 'Big Fish, Little Fish', 'The Harder They Fall', and 'God's Alive'. Cleavon Little and Melba Moore won Tony Awards for their work in a show that, naturally enough, attracted more black audiences than usual to Broadway, and ran for 688 performances. Gary Geld and Peter Udell went on to further success with Shenandoah (1975), another show with a relevant, contemporary theme. Melba Moore was joined by Ron Richardson (a 1985 Tony winner for his performance in Big River) in the 1993 US revival tour of *Purlie*.

PURPLE RAIN

Pop maverick Prince made his film debut in this glamorous, visually stunning release which, not surprisingly, was set in his home town of Minneapolis. Albert Magnoli and William Blinn's screenplay has The Kid (Prince) vying for the attentions of Apollonia (Patricia Kotero), whilst also battling for musical superiority with funky rival Morris Day's the Time outfit. Helping or hindering him in these aims are Olga Karlatos (Mother), Clarence Williams III (Father), Jerome Benton, Billy Sparks, Jill Jones, Charles Huntsberry, Brenda Bennett, Sandra Claire Gershman, and Kim Upsher. Dez Dickerson, the guitarist who featured in Prince's original 1979 line-up, was one of many familiar faces in the movie, and he also contributed one number, 'Modernaire'. The remainder of the songs were almost all composed and performed by Prince, including 'Let's Go Crazy', 'Purple Rain', 'I Would Die 4 U', 'Baby I'm A Star', 'Computer Blue' (written with Wendy And Lisa), 'Take Me With You' (performed with Apollonia), 'The Beautiful Ones', 'God (Love Theme From Purple Rain)', 'When Doves Cry', and 'Darling Nikki'. Also here were 'Father's Song' (by John L. Nelson), 'Sex Shooter' by Apollonia 6 And The Starr Company, performed by Apollonia 6, as well as 'Jungle Love' and 'The Bird', by Morris Day and Jesse Johnson, performed by the Time. It all added up to an Oscar-winning score, with the soundtrack album winning a Grammy and spending 24 weeks at US Number 1. Two singles, 'When Doves Cry' and 'Let's Go Crazy', also topped the chart, and there was further success for 'Purple Rain', 'I Would Die 4 U, and 'Take Me With U'. Directed by Albert Magnoli and released by Columbia-EMI-Warner in 1984, *Purple Rain* proved a real winner, and was one of the top five musical movies of the 80s.

QUADROPHENIA

Released in 1979, *Quadrophenia* is based upon the Who album of the same title in which Pete Townshend paid tribute to the Mod movement inspiring his group. Phil Daniels starred as Jimmy, rootless and disillusioned, who seeks solace and thrills in this vibrant subculture. Director Francis Roddam captures the atmosphere of the time to perfection, whether it is parties, fumbled sex, clubs or fights. Realistic and unflinchingly unsentimental, *Quadrophenia* portrays amphetamine-fuelled aggression, the Bank Holiday skirmishes between Mods and Rockers on seaside beaches and an intoxicating love of fashion and scooters. The Who's musical contributions apart, the soundtrack features bluebeat star Derrick Morgan, James Brown, Marvin Gaye and Booker T And The MGs, whose seminal 'Green Onions' scaled the UK Top 10 following the film's release, 17 years after it was first issued. Leslie Ash and Toyah Willcox are among the supporting cast, while Sting excels as the 'Ace Face', later reduced to the role of bellboy, much to Jimmy's chagrin. Rodham's evocative settings apart, *Quadrophenia*'s main strength is derived from Daniels' remarkable portrayal of a pained, frustrated teenager. It remains one of the most powerful films in rock music history.

QUAKER GIRL, THE

Lionel Monkton was one of the most successful composers for the London musical stage at the turn of the century and for several years afterwards. He wrote the score for this show with lyricists Adrian Ross and Percy Greenbank just 18 months after one of his biggest hits, *The Arcadians*, began its West End run. Presented by George Edwardes, *The Quaker Girl* opened at London's Adelphi Theatre on 5 November 1910. The book was by James T. Tanner, and Gertie Millar starred as Prudence Pym, an English girl who has been brought up in the Quaker faith by her strict aunt and uncle. She is entranced by a visiting American, Tony Chute (Joseph Coyne), and he tempts her to taste some of the 'forbidden' champagne at a wedding reception. Disowned by her family for the dreadful act, she travels to Paris where Tony is a naval attaché at the American Embassy, and works for a time as a mannequin at a fashion house. She attracts the attention of a well-known roué, Prince Carlo (George Carvey), who tries to seduce her, and she and Tony part for a time, before meeting up again at a masked ball when all their misunderstandings are forgotten as they go into 'The First

Dance'. The happy and melodious score was full of delightful numbers such as 'Take A Step', 'Tony From America', 'The Quaker Girl', 'A Bad Boy And A Good Girl', 'I Wore A Little Grey Bonnet', 'Tip Toe', and the ravishing 'Come To The Ball', which was introduced by George Carvey. *The Quaker Girl* played for a remarkable 536 performances in London, and added another 240 to that total in New York, when Ina Claire took the role of Prudence. One London revival was presented in 1938, and two more in the 40s. Since then, *The Quaker Girl* has been kept alive through many amateur productions.

QUEEN OF HEARTS

After the successful teaming of handsome Old Etonian John Loder with the far more down-to-earth Gracie Fields in *Love Life And Laughter* (1933) and *Sing As We Go* (1934), producer Basil Dean brought them together again for this Associated Talking Pictures release, which eager British audiences enjoyed in 1936. Early in the film there is a famous scene in which seamstress Grace Perkins (Fields) pursues the famous (inebriated) actor Derek Cooper (Loder) for his autograph, and gets involved in a hair-raising car drive through London streets, during which she is thrown 'from the running board into the dicky seat'. Next day, at the theatre where Cooper is appearing in *Queen Of Hearts*, Grace is mistaken for the wealthy Mrs. Vandeleur who has promised to invest money in the show if she can have a small part in it. The ensuing events are even more complicated than usual, with Grace appearing as La Perkinosa (she has to do an Apache dance), and the whole thing ending with a wild police chase through the theatre, after which Derek takes Grace into his own personal custody. At intervals amid the chaos, Gracie Fields managed to sing three appealing ballads, 'My First Love Song', 'Why Did I Have To Meet You?', 'Queen Of Hearts', along with the amusing 'One Of The Little Orphans Of The Storm'. A strong supporting cast included Enid Stamp-Taylor, Fred Duprez, Jean Lister, Edward Rigby, Julie Suedo, Jean Lister, Hal Gordon, Madelaine Seymour, Syd Crossley, Tom Payne, and Vera Hilliard. Monty Banks, who subsequently married Gracie Fields, had a small role, and he also directed the picture. The screenplay was written by Anthony Kimmins, Douglas Furber and Gordon Wellesley. It was another box-office success for 'Our Gracie', the most popular British entertainer of her time. Some 60 years after this film was released, its title was being attributed to Princess Diana, wife of Prince Charles, heir to the British throne, in recognition of her charity work and caring image. Following her death in 1997, a musical entitled *Queen Of Hearts*, which purported to be 'a musical experience that takes its audience on the fairy tale journey of Princess Diana's life', opened in October 1998 at the Grove Street Playhouse, off-off-Broadway. It closed, amid a flurry of lawsuits, a few days later. Other attempts to mount stage tributes to the Princess included *Candle In The Wind*, a compilation of her favourite music and ballet excerpts performed by the National Festival Singers and the English Dance Company in Manchester early in 1998.

QUILLEY, DENIS

b. 26 December 1927, London, England. An extremely versatile, popular actor and singer, mostly for the classical stage, but also on television and in films, Quilley joined the Birmingham Repertory Theatre Company as an Assistant Stage Manager straight from school. From 1945 onwards, he appeared with that Company, Nottingham Rep, and the Old Vic Company, in a predictably wide variety of parts. When he was in his 20s, choreographer-director Wendy Toye urged him to have voice lessons so that he could compete for leading roles. He took her advice, and over the years the big baritone has served him well, especially in musical comedy. During the 50s he was a member of the Royal Court Theatre revue, *Airs On A Shoestring* (1953), which ran for over 700 performances, played showbiz reporter Tom Wilson in another long-runner, *Grab Me A Gondola* (1956), and took the title role, with Mary Costa as Cunegonde, in *Candide* (1959). In the following year Quilley took over the part of Nestor-le-Fripe in *Irma La Douce*, and subsequently took Nestor to Broadway, and on a US tour with Taina Elg as his Irma. In 1963 he was Antipholus of Ephesus in *The Boys From Syracuse*, a wife-troubled Charles Condamine in *High Spirits* (Hugh Martin and Timothy Gray's 1964 musicalization of Noël Coward's *Blithe Spirit*), and Robert Browning in Australian productions of the West End hit, *Robert And Elizabeth* (1966). Shortly after portraying Alec Hurley, one of the onstage husbands (the other was Maurice Gibb, from the Bee Gees pop group) of musical hall entertainer Marie Lloyd in *Sing A Rude Song* (1970), Quilley was recruited to the National Theatre by Laurence Olivier. While there, he appeared in many outstanding productions, including *Long Day's Journey Into Night* (Jamie), *Tamburlaine* (Bajazeth), and *The Front Page*, which features one of his favourite parts, ace reporter Hildy Johnson. Mike Westbrook and Adrian Mitchell's *Tyger* (Scofield), based on the works of William Blake, was an early 70s project. In Peter Nicholls' *Privates On Parade* (1977), as a leading member of a Combined Services Song and Dance Unit in the post-war Malayan jungle, Quilley created a hero, Captain Terri Dennis, who was also an outrageously camp drag queen. His hilarious impersonations included a top-hatted Marlene Dietrich, a suitably fruity Carmen Miranda - and even a taste of Vera Lynn and Noël Coward. His splendid performance earned him the Society Of West End Theatres (SWET) award for Comedy Performance Of The Year. Three years later, he received another SWET prize, this time for Best Performance in the musical, *Sweeney Todd*, although overall this Drury Lane production of Stephen Sondheim's 'musical thriller' was thought unsatisfactory in several respects. There were no such reservations about Declan Donnellan's 'spare, razor-sharp' 1993 Royal National Theatre production of the Sondheim classic, in which Quilley initially played Judge Turpin, with Julia McKenzie as the pie-making Mrs. Lovett. Quilley subsequently succeeded Alun Armstrong as Sweeney when the latter went off to work in film and television. Prior to that, Quilley had launched into his second 'gay role', as Georges, to George Hearn's Albin, in the West End version of *La Cage Aux Folles* (1986, 'Song On

The Sand', 'Look Over There'). He also took part in an all-star, one-night only, charity performance at the Theatre Royal Drury Lane, of *Mack And Mabel*. Quilley had Mack Sennett's bittersweet ballad, 'I Won't Send Roses'. Since the early 90s and *Sweeney Todd*, he has concentrated mainly on a range of parts in plays that have included *The Merry Wives Of Windsor* (1995, Falstaff, Royal National Theatre), *The Tempest* (1996 Prospero, Open Air Theatre, Regent's Park), and *Racing Demon* (1998, Bishop of Southwark, Chichester). In 1997, he also played the German composer in *Brahms On A Slow Train* for BBC Radio 3. He has worked in television in programmes such as *The Merchant Of Venice* (1955), *Beast With Two Backs* (1968), *Long Day's Journey Into Night* (1973), *The Shell Seekers* (1989), *A Dangerous Man: Lawrence After Arabia* (1990), and *Rich Tea And Sympathy* (1991), as well as the series *Undermind* (1965), *Timeslip* (1970), *Clayhanger* (1976), *Masada* (1981), and *The Return Of Sherlock Holmes* (1988). He occasionally reflects on this distinguished career in his one-man show, *The Best Of Times*, 'a series of songs and anecdotes recalling a lifetime in the theatre'.

● FILMS: *Life At The Top* (1965), *Anne Of The Thousand Days* (1970), *The Black Windmill* (1974), *Murder On The Orient Express* (1974), *Privates On Parade* (1982), *Evil Under The Sun* (1982), *Memed My Hawk* (1984), *King David* (1985), *Foreign Body* (1986), *Cassidy* (1989), *Mister Johnson* (1991), *Storia Di Una Capinera* (1993).

R

RADIO ON

Released in 1979 and directed by Christopher Petit, *Radio On* is a low-key British film, shot in black and white, indebted in equal terms to road movies and contemporary German cinema. David Beams stars as a disc jockey who travels from London to Bristol to investigate the death of his brother. Engaging, if wilfully obscure, *Radio On* also features Sting as a garage mechanic, obsessed by the life and work of Eddie Cochran. Sting performs a rendition of 'Three Steps To Heaven' in the film. The soundtrack also features music by David Bowie, Kraftwerk, Robert Fripp and a succession of new-wave starts including Devo, Lene Lovich, Ian Dury and Wreckless Eric. These contributions emanate from jukeboxes and radios Beams encounters on his journey. Critically well-received upon release, *Radio*

On captures something of the uncertainty pervading late 70s culture and life.

RAGA

This 1971 documentary charted the life and work of Indian master musician, Ravi Shankar. His stellar early 60s recordings were largely responsible for introducing the sitar to Western audiences, partly through the patronage of several pop musicians, notably George Harrison, who makes a brief appearance in *Raga*, as does ex-Monkees drummer/vocalist Mickey Dolenz. Their cameos are, however, incidental as the film charts Shankar's evolution from Oriental classicist to his adoption by rock audiences at such events as the Monterey Festival, Woodstock and the Concert For Bangladesh. A sumptuously-packaged soundtrack album was issued in the US by the Beatles' record label Apple, but the set was denied a UK pressing.

RAGTIME

Having already conquered audiences in Toronto (December 1996) and Los Angeles (June 1997), *Ragtime* brought the house down in New York even before it opened there on 18 January 1998. Two houses, in fact, because the old Lyric and Apollo Theatres between 42nd and 43rd Street were demolished in order to provide *Ragtime* with a sumptuous new home in the Ford Centre for the Performing Arts. Livent (US) Inc.'s $10 million production was immediately hailed by some as marking the regeneration of the Broadway musical after years of British domination. Tony Awards-winning playwright Terrence McNally adapted E.L. Doctorow's 1975 novel, which was filmed in 1981. *Ragtime*'s story, set at the turn of the century, portrays an era in terms of three families with entirely different backgrounds. As these fictional characters interact with each other, they also become involved with real-life legendary figures, such as Henry Ford (Larry Daggett), Harry Houdini (Jim Corti), J.P. Morgan (Mike O'Carroll), Emma Goldman (Judy Kaye), Booker T. Washington (Tommy Hollis), and the infamous Evelyn 'Crime of the Century' Nesbit (Lynnette Perry). Librettist McNally adopts a Brechtian approach to the narrative, which allows the various characters to speak to the audience occasionally, in the third person and past tense, referring to themselves as the story unfolds. The privileged American family from ritzy New Rochelle, consists of Little Boy (Alex Strange), Younger Brother (Steven Sutcliffe), Grandfather (Conrad McLaren), and the typically unfeeling Father (Mark Jacoby), who departs on his Arctic expedition leaving love-starved Mother (Marin Mazzie), to express her longing with the poignant 'Goodbye, My Love'. While he is gone, Mother discovers a newly born baby buried in her garden, and gives comfort and refuge to its mother, the black servant Sarah (Audra McDonald). She then allows the father, ragtime pianist Colehouse Walker Jnr. (Brian Stokes Mitchell), to come a-calling on Sarah until he eventually wins back her affections. The young couple's inspirational duet, 'Wheels Of A Dream', sung on a hillside overlooking New Rochelle, signified that momentous period between slavery and the dawning political consciousness of African Americans.

Meanwhile, the third family in this complex social melting pot has arrived on the scene. Latvian immigrant Tateh (Peter Friedman), a Jewish widower, with his Little Girl (Lea Michele), initially endures the inevitable hardship borne by so many of his kind, but survives to become - of all things - a successful silent movie director. Lynn Ahrens And Stephen Flaherty's extraordinary score, a blend of ragtime, early jazz, gospel, marches, work songs, and a whole variety of American musical styles, includes the splendidly syncopated title number, 'Journey On', 'The Crime Of The Century', 'What Kind Of Woman', 'A Shtetl Iz Amereke', 'Success', 'Gettin' Ready Rag', the highly stylised 'Henry Ford', 'Nothing Like The City', 'Your Daddy's Son', 'New Music', 'The Night That Goldman Spoke At Union Square', 'Lawrence Massachusetts', 'Gliding', 'Justice', 'President', 'Till We Reach That Day', 'Harry Houdini, Master Escapist', 'Coalhouse's Soliloquy', 'Coalhouse Demands', 'What A Game', 'Atlantic City', 'Atlantic City, Part II', 'Buffalo Nickel Photoplay, Inc.', 'Our Children', 'Sarah Brown Eyes', 'He Wanted To Say', 'Back To Before', 'Look What You've Done', and 'Make Them Hear You'. Graciela Daniele's choreography, Santo Loquasto's costumes, and thrilling sets by Eugene Lee - a backdrop of sepia-tinted period postcards for Atlantic City, a Victorian doll's house personifying the New Rochelle house - combine in a brilliant musical, sensitively and intelligently directed by Frank Galati. Producer Garth Drabinski and Livent received rave notices, and *Ragtime* won Los Angeles Drama Critics Circle, Theatre Ovation, New York Drama League, Drama Desk honours, as well as Tony Awards for best score, book, featured actress (Audra McDonald), and orchestrations (William David Brohn). The eagerly anticipated West End production of *Ragtime* was delayed by reports of 'financial irregularities' within the Livent production company.

RAHMAN, A.R.

b. A.S. Duleep Kumar, 1967, India. The son of a musical director for Indian films, he took to music at an early age, initially on local television and, from the age of nine (following his father's death), as a keyboard player on Indian film soundtracks. As a teenager he accompanied other Indian artists and played in a rock band on the Indian college campus circuit. He gained a scholarship to Trinity College of Music, London, and following the completion of his studies, worked for six years in the Indian advertising industry, composing a number of successful jingles. In 1992 he began to work as a musical director for Indian film soundtracks. His music for the film *Roja*, the soundtrack of which sold 2.5 million copies and spawned two hit singles, was the first of a string of hugely successful soundtracks that also included *Gentleman* (1993), *Duet* (1995), *Bombay* (1995), *Rangeela* (1995) and *Indian* (1996). Rahman has also played keyboards with a number of well-known artists, including David Byrne, Apache Indian and Zakir Hussain. In 1997 he contributed a track to Talvin Singh's *Anokha* compilation and in the same year Sony Records released *Vande Mataram*, Rahman's international debut. An ambitious combination of Indian film soundtrack and folk elements with modern high-tech production values and global pop influences, the album featured an international line-up of musicians, with a guest appearance by Nusrat Fateh Ali Khan on one track.
● ALBUMS: *Vande Mataram* (Sony 1997)★★★.

RAINBOW BRIDGE

Chuck Wein directed this 1971 feature which blended fact and fiction. At the heart of the film was an occult research centre, sited in Hawaii, but any interest *Rainbow Bridge* generated was due to the presence of Jimi Hendrix. Mitch Mitchell (drums) and Buddy Cox (bass) accompany the guitarist on footage shot at a concert held on the side of the Haleakala Volcano. However, a large portion of the soundtrack was recorded the previous year at Hendrix' New York studio, Electric Ladyland. 'Ezy Rider', 'Star Spangled Banner', 'Purple Haze', 'Dolly Dagger' and 'Voodoo Chile' are among the songs on offer, many of which were enshrined on a later soundtrack album. *Rainbow Bridge* also features interview material with Hendrix, including a chilling passage wherein he discusses his death - an event which transpired some three months later. Although hardly a cinematic landmark, *Rainbow Bridge* does at least afford the chance to watch one of rock music's greatest talents in action.

RAINGER, RALPH

b. 7 October 1901, New York City, New York, USA, d. 23 October 1942, near Palm Springs, California, USA. After studying classical music as a child Rainger won a scholarship to New York's Institute of Musical Art. Despite his academic success and enthusiasm, his family disapproved and persuaded him to study law. By the mid-20s, however, he had become a professional pianist, playing in dance and jazz bands. He was also in several pit orchestras in Broadway theatres and worked briefly with Paul Whiteman. While playing in a revue, *Little Show*, in 1929, Rainger wrote 'Moanin' Low' (lyrics by Howard Dietz), which was sung in the show by Libby Holman. After the success of this song, Rainger and Dietz continued their collaboration with 'Got A Man On My Mind' and 'I'll Take An Option On You', and Rainger also wrote 'Breakfast Dance' (lyrics by Edward Eliscu). In the early 30s Rainger was drawn to Hollywood, where he wrote 'When A Woman Loves A Man' (lyrics by Billy Rose) and began a fruitful collaboration with Leo Robin. Many of their joint efforts were sung by Bing Crosby, among them 'Please', 'Love In Bloom', 'June In January', 'With Every Breath I Take' and 'Blue Hawaii'. The team's 'Thanks For The Memory' won the Oscar after it was sung by Bob Hope and Shirley Ross in *Big Broadcast of 1938*. Robin and Rainger's film work included *The Big Broadcast* (1932), *Little Miss Marker*, *She Loves Me Not*, *Here Is My Heart*, *The Big Broadcast Of 1937*, *Palm Springs*, *Three Cheers For Love*, *Rhythm On The Range*, *College Holiday*, *Waikiki Wedding*, *Ebb Tide*, *Artists And Models*, *Give Me A Sailor*, *Paris Honeymoon*, *Moon Over Miami*, *Tall, Dark And Handsome*, *My Gal Sal*, *Footlight Serenade*, *Coney Island*, and *Riding High* (1943). Rainger was killed in a flying accident in October 1942 shortly before the last film was released.

RAISE THE ROOF

This is reputed to be the first British musical comedy film - as opposed to the revue-style *Elstree Calling* which was simply a collection of songs and sketches not linked by a story; both features were released in 1930 by British International Pictures. Walter Summers and Philip MacDonald's simple screenplay concerns Rodney Langford (Maurice Evans) whose ambitions to enter show business are realised when he becomes the owner of an unsuccessful touring company. One of its members, Maisie Gray (Betty Balfour), is on his side from the start, but his parents (played by Sam Livesey and Ellis Jeffreys) are totally opposed to this new venture. Their efforts to ruin the show with the assistance of the company's corrupt leading man, Atherley Armitage (Jack Raine), fail miserably and inspire the company to even greater success. On the opening night, Rodney is reconciled with his father, and he and Maisie embark on their own (personal) long-running partnership. The attractive and tuneful score was complemented by a supporting cast which included Arthur Hardy, Louie Emery, the Plaza Tiller Girls, and specialities Dorothy Minto and Malandrinos, and Josephine Earle. Betty Balfour, who enjoyed a successful career as a comedienne in 20s silent films, proved to be a pleasing singer and dancer, and had one of the best numbers, 'I'm Trembling On The Brink Of Love'. The director, Walter Summers, also worked on silents, and he went on to write and direct the unconventional and highly acclaimed *The Return Of Bulldog Drummond*, starring Ralph Richardson.

RAISIN

During a Broadway season in which good original musicals were scarce, and one-person shows by such as Sammy Davis Jnr., Liza Minnelli, and Sammy Cahn proliferated, *Raisin* came as a welcome relief. It opened at the 46th Street Theatre on 18 October 1973, with a book by Robert Nemiroff and Charlotte Zaltzburg which was based on Lorraine Hansbury's 1959 play *A Raisin In The Sun*. Set in a Chicago ghetto during the 50s, the story told of the efforts of a black family to change their lives once and for all. Newly widowed Lena Younger (Virginia Capers), decides to use her late husband's inheritance to buy a liquor store for her son Walter (Joe Morton), put her daughter Beneatha (Deborah Allen), through medical school, and buy a house somewhere away from the ghetto. Lena's plans are in jeopardy for a time when Walter's sometime business partner flees with part of the money, but her ambitious plans eventually come to fruition, and the family moves into the house of their dreams. It was a moving, heart-warming story, complemented perfectly by a score from Broadway newcomers, Judd Woldin (music) and Robert Brittan (lyrics). Songs such as 'Sweet Time', 'He Come Down This Morning', 'Whose Little Angry Man', 'Not Anymore', 'Measure The Morning', and 'A Whole Lotta Sunlight', were put over with a great deal of verve and zeal by a high-quality cast, which also included Ernestine Jackson, Ralph Carter, Ted Ross, and Robert Jackson. Virginia Capers won a Tony Award for her outstanding performance, and the show itself won for best musical. No doubt the kudos helped *Raisin* to surprise a lot of people, and stay in New York for two years.

RAITT, JOHN

b. John Emmett Raitt, 19 January 1917, Santa Ana, California, USA. An actor and singer with a fine baritone voice, Raitt sang in light opera and concerts before playing the lead in a Chicago production of *Oklahoma!* (1944). In the following year he made his Broadway debut, playing Billy Bigelow, and introducing immortal songs such as 'If I Loved You' and 'Soliloquy', in Richard Rodgers and Oscar Hammerstein II's magnificent *Carousel*. Three years later, he appeared on Broadway again in the short-lived and 'unconventional' *Magdalena*. This was followed in 1952 by the 'whimsical' *Three Wishes For Jamie*, which was 'too treacly' to run for long. *Carnival In Flanders* (1953), despite a score by Johnny Burke and Jimmy Van Heusen that contained 'Here's That Rainy Day', provided less than a week's employment, but his next job, as the factory superintendent in *The Pajama Game* (1954), lasted nearly two and a half years. Raitt's spirited and sensitive renditions of Richard Adler and Jerry Ross's 'There Once Was A Man' and 'Small Talk' (both with Janis Paige), plus 'Hey There', a duet with a dictaphone machine, made sufficient impact in Hollywood for him to be cast opposite Doris Day in the 1957 film version, despite his being a complete newcomer to the big screen. In the 50s and 60s Raitt appeared frequently on US television, and in 1960 toured with the satirical musical *Destry Rides Again*. In the spring of 1966 he recreated his original role in a New York Music Theater revival of *Carousel* and, later in the year, dwelt for a brief spell amid the 'newly created folk songs' of *A Joyful Noise*. Thereafter, Raitt devoted much of his time to touring, and in 1975 was back on Broadway, along with Patricia Munsell, Tammy Grimes, Larry Kert, Lillian Gish and Cyril Ritchard, in *A Musical Jubilee*, a 'potpourri' claiming to demonstrate the development of the American musical. By that time, his daughter, Bonnie Raitt, was gaining recognition as one of the best female singer/guitarists of the 70s and 80s. John Raitt himself continued to be active, and in 1992 he received an Ovation Award in Hollywood for services to the Los Angeles theatre scene. A year later he was inducted into New York's Theater Hall Of Fame, and celebrated the 50th anniversary of *Oklahoma!* by singing the show's title song on the stage of the St. James Theatre in New York (the theatre in which *Oklahoma!* first opened in 1943) prior to a performance of a very different kind of musical - *The Who's Tommy*. In 1998, Raitt appeared in a London concert, and received a Lifetime achievement award from the Los Angeles Critics Circle.
● ALBUMS: *Highlights Of Broadway* (Capitol 1955)★★★★, *Mediterranean Magic* (Capitol 1956)★★★, *Under Open Skies* (Capitol 1958)★★★, *Songs The Kids Brought Home* (Capitol 1959)★★★, with Bonnie Raitt *Broadway Legend* (Angel 1995)★★★★, and many Original Cast recordings.

RAKSIN, DAVID

b. 4 August 1912, Philadelphia, Pennsylvania, USA. A composer, lyricist, and arranger for film background music, whose career has spanned more than 50 years. Raksin was originally taught to play the clarinet by his father, and, after further studying at Pennsylvania University, where he was a soloist with the band, he performed and arranged for society outfits, and on the radio station WCAU. After further stints as a sideman-arranger with New York bands, and a spell with Harms Publishing House in the early 30s, he broke into the movie business in 1936 when he arranged Charlie Chaplin's music for *Modern Times*. In the late 30s and early 40s he worked on several films as co-composer, including *San Quentin*, *Suez*, *Hollywood Cavalcade*, *Stanley And Livingstone*, *The Magnificent Dope* and *The Undying Monster*, and had a few solo credits such as *The Man In Her Life* and *Tampico*. In 1944, Raksin's score for Otto Preminger's highly acclaimed murder mystery *Laura* included the haunting title theme, which, complete with a later lyric by Johnny Mercer, became popular for Dick Haymes, Johnnie Johnston and Freddie Martin, among others, and endured as an all-time standard. Raksin's other 40s film music included another Preminger project *Fallen Angel* (1945) (which contained 'Slowly', a hit for Kay Kyser), and *Where Do We Go From Here?*, *Smoky*, *The Shocking Miss Pilgrim*, *The Secret Life Of Walter Mitty*, *Apartment For Peggy*, *Force Of Evil* and *Forever Amber* (1947), for which Raksin was nominated for an Academy Award. Johnny Mercer again added words to Raksin's title theme. In the 50s and 60s Raksin scored movies with a wide variety of themes, such as courtroom dramas (*The Magnificent Yankee* and *Until They Sail*), boxing (*Right Cross*), Frank Sinatra as an assassin (*Suddenly*), gangsters galore (*Al Capone* and *Pay Or Die*), Westerns (*Invitation To A Gunfighter*), a Jerry Lewis comedy (*The Patsy*), and others such as *The Girl In White*, *Carrie*, *Seven Wonders Of The World (Cinerama)*, *Love Has Many Faces*, including some of the most highly acclaimed productions of their time, such as *The Bad And The Beautiful*, (containing 'Love Is For The Very Young', with Dory Previn), *Two Weeks In Another Town*, *Sylvia*, *A Big Hand For The Little Lady*, *Will Penny* and *Separate Tables* for which Raksin won another Oscar nomination. In 1962 Raksin contributed a jazz-oriented score to *Too Late Blues*, in which John Cassavetes made his Hollywood debut. It featured musicians such as Benny Carter, Shelly Manne and Red Mitchell, and numbers like 'Sax Raises Its Ugly Head' and 'Benny Splits, While Jimmy Rowles'. In the 70s and 80s, apart from occasional feature films such as *What's The Matter With Helen?* and *Glass Houses*, Raksin worked more and more in television on such as *The Over-The Hill Gang Rides Again*, *The Ghost Of Flight 401*, *The Day After* and *Lady In A Corner*. His earlier work for the small screen had included music for *Ben Casey* and *The Breaking Point*. He also scored several movie cartoons including *Sloppy Jaloppy*, *Madeline*, *Giddyap* and *The Unicorn In The Garden*, and has written several serious works.

RANDOLPH, ELSIE

b. Elsie Florence Killick, 9 December 1904, London, England, d. 15 October 1982, London, England. A dancer, comedienne, and singer, Randolph first met Jack Buchanan, with whom her name is always indelibly associated, at the *Queen's Hall Roof Follies Cabaret* in London. She had recently taken over from the show's leading lady

after appearing in the chorus of West End productions such as *The Girl For A Boy* (1919), *The Naughty Princess* (1920), *My Nieces* (1921), and *His Girl* (1922). Buchanan offered her the small dual roles of flapper and maid in his next musical, *Battling Butler* (1922). During the run, she also impressed when deputising temporarily for his co-star, Sylvia Leslie, and Buchanan promoted her to the second lead in *Toni* (1924), in which she joined him in the pleasing song and dance number, 'Don't Love Me'. It was the beginning of a musical comedy partnership, much-loved by West End and film audiences, which, on and off, spanned some 20 years. Initially, in *Boodle* (1925) and *Sunny* (1926), Randolph continued to play second lead, but by the time they combined for the casual yet elegant 'Fancy Our Meeting' in *That's A Good Girl* (1928), she was firmly in the lead opposite Buchanan. Even so, it was not a conventional musical comedy arrangement, as one critic noted: 'Because of her piquancy, she was more of a soubrette than a romantic lead. And she was a brilliant foil for Jack. She could tackle the broadest comedy - even burlesque.' So, while Buchanan was invariably expected to woo and win the ingénue, he and Randolph continued to swap wisecracks, and combine in the most exquisite dance routines in highly successful 30s shows such as *Stand Up And Sing* (1931), *Mr. Whittington* (1934), and *This'll Make You Whistle* (1936). Not so successful was their union in the revue, *Top Hat And Tails*, staged in the Imperial Theatre which Buchanan built in Brighton. As she apparently posed no threat to Buchanan's status as 'Britain's most eligible bachelor', the couple's fans were often disappointed on the occasions when they worked apart. In Randolph's case, this included appearances in musicals such as *Madame Pompadour* (1924), *Peggy-Ann* (1927), *Follow Through* (1929), *The Co-Optimists* (1930), *The Wonder Bar* (1930), and *Charlot's Char-a-Bang* (1935), as well as various stage comedies. In the year after she played the role of Vittoria in the 1942 revival of the World War I hit, *The Maid Of The Mountains*, Randolph and Buchanan were reunited for *It's Time To Dance* (1943) which clocked up a creditable total of 259 London performances. The team also appeared together in four films, *Yes, Mr. Brown*, *That's A Good Girl*, *This'll Make You Whistle*, and *Smash And Grab* (a comedy), and performed, along with several more 'old-timers', in a nostalgic segment of the twenty-fifth *Royal Variety Performance* in 1954. Three years later Buchanan died, but Randolph continued to appear in provincial theatres for some years, and made a late comeback to films, two of which, *Reach For The Sky* (Czech) and *Charleston* (Italy), were non-British. Several of the delightful duets she sang with Buchanan, which included 'Oceans Of Time' and 'Who Do You Think You Are?' (both from *Mr. Whittington*), 'The One I'm Looking For' (*That's A Good Girl*), 'There's Always Tomorrow' (*Stand Up And Sing*), and, of course, 'Fancy Our Meeting', have been released on record.

● ALBUMS: *The Debonair Jack Buchanan* (Music For Pleasure 1967)★★★★, *Jack Buchanan* (World Records 60s)★★★★, *Selections From London Stage Shows* (Retrospect 1979)★★★.

● FILMS: *Rich And Strange* (1931), *Brother Alfred* (1932), *Life Goes On* (1932), *Yes, Mr. Brown* (1933), *Night Of The Garter* (1933), *That's A Good Girl* (1933), *This'll Make You Whistle* (1936), *Smash*

And Grab (1937), *Cheer The Brave* (1951), *Riders Of The Sky* (1968), *Frenzy* (1972), *Charleston* (1977).

RAYE, DON

b. Donald McRae Wilhoite Jnr., 16 March 1909, Washington, D.C., USA, d. January 1985. A popular songwriter from the 30s through to the 50s, Raye was as accomplished dancer as a boy, and won the Virginia State Dancing Championship. From the mid-20s he worked as a singer and dancer in vaudeville, and later toured theatres and nightclubs in France and England, whilst also writing songs for himself and other performers. In 1935 he collaborated with Sammy Cahn, Saul Chaplin and band leader Jimmie Lunceford on 'Rhythm In My Nursery Rhymes' and in the late 30s worked for a New York music publishing house. After moving to Hollywood in 1940, Raye was commissioned to write the songs for *Argentine Nights*, in which the Andrews Sisters made their screen debut. Together with Hughie Prince and the Sisters' arranger, Vic Schoen, Raye wrote 'Hit The Road' and 'Oh! How He Loves Me'. Another collaboration with Prince resulted in 'Rhumboogie', the first of a series of 'boogie woogie' numbers, several of which became hits for the Andrews Sisters, pianist Freddie Slack, and Will Bradley and his Orchestra. Raye and Prince's next assignment was *Buck Privates*, which also featured the Andrews Sisters, and rocketed the comedy duo Abbott And Costello to movie stardom. The songs included 'You're A Lucky Fellow, Mr Smith', 'Bounce Me Brother With A Solid Four' and 'Boogie Woogie Bugle Boy From Company B'. The latter number was nominated for an Academy Award, and revived successfully in 1973 by Bette Midler. Raye's other boogie ballads included 'Beat Me Daddy (Eight To The Bar)', 'Rock-A-Bye The Boogie', 'Down The Road A Piece' and 'Scrub Me, Mamma, With A Boogie Beat'. His long partnership with Gene De Paul, which began in the early 40s, resulted in songs for films such as *In The Navy, San Antonio Rose, Moonlight In Hawaii, Keep 'Em Flying, Hellzapoppin', What's Cookin', Ride 'Em Cowboy, Almost Married, Pardon My Sarong, Behind The Eight Ball, When Johnny Comes Marching Home, Hi Buddy, Reveille With Beverley, What's Buzzin' Cousin?, Larceny With Music, Crazy House, I Dood It, Hi Good Lookin'* and *Stars On Parade*. The team also enjoyed success in 1944 with 'Who's That In Your Love Life?', 'Irresistible You', 'Solid Potato Salad', and 'Milkman, Keep Those Bottles Quiet' from *Broadway Rhythm*. Towards the end of World War II De Paul spent two years in the Armed Forces, before he and Don Raye resumed writing their movie songs in 1947 with 'Who Knows?' for *Wake Up And Dream* and 'Judaline' for *A Date With Judy*. In 1948 they contributed to *A Song Is Born* and also wrote 'It's Whatcha Do With Whatcha Got' for the Walt Disney live-action feature *So Dear To My Heart*. De Paul and Raye's last film work together was for the highly acclaimed Disney cartoon *The Adventures Of Ichabod And Mr Toad* (1949). During the time he worked with De Paul, Raye also collaborated with others on 'Yodelin' Jive', 'Why Begin Again?', 'This Is My Country', 'I Love You Too Much', 'Music Makers', 'The House Of Blue Lights', 'Your Home Is In My Arms', 'Domino', 'They Were Doin' The Mambo' (a US hit for Vaughn Monroe),

'Roses And Revolvers', 'I'm Looking Out The Window' and 'Too Little Time'. Although he wrote just the occasional song after the mid-50s, Raye's 'Well, All Right' (with Frances Faye and Dan Howell) became a hit for the Andrews Sisters in 1959, and was also interpolated into the 1978 bio-pic *The Buddy Holly Story*.

RED MILL, THE

As an operetta with a sense of humour, this has to be one of the most cherished productions of its time. *The Red Mill* opened at the Knickerbocker Theatre in New York on 24 September 1906, and was a vehicle for the ex-vaudeville comedy duo of David Montgomery and Fred Stone who had made their first impact on Broadway in *The Wizard Of Oz* (1903). Their adventures as a couple of naïve American tourists, Kid Connor and Con Kidder, stranded without money in Katwyk-aan-Zee, Holland, involve them in some hair-raising situations, and force them to adopt a number of disguises, one of which finds them masquerading as Sherlock Holmes and Doctor Watson. Henry Blossom's book and lyrics, and Victor Herbert's fine music combined in a score that is generally considered to have crossed the divide from operetta into musical comedy. Romantic and engaging songs such as 'Every Day Is Ladies Day With Me', 'Because You're You', 'When You're Pretty And The World Is Fair', 'The Isle Of Our Dreams', 'Moonbeams', and 'The Streets Of New York' (which became a hit for Billy Murray), ensured a run of 274 performances, the longest for any of Victor Herbert's book musicals. The 1945 revival, which starred Eddie Foy Jnr. and Michael O'Shea, and had additional lyrics by Forman Brown, did even better and stayed at the Ziegfeld Theatre for well over a year. A 1919 London production, with Little Tich as Kid Connor, folded after only 64 performances. A 1947 radically revised revival with 'a tedious new libretto', and starring one of Britain's top comedy double acts, Jewel And Warriss, lost a lot of money in a very short time.

RED SHOES, THE (FILM MUSICAL)

One of the most outstanding films in the history of the British cinema. *The Red Shoes*, which was produced and directed by Michael Powell and Emeric Pressburger, was released in 1948 to worldwide acclaim. Pressburger also wrote the screenplay which was based on a story by Hans Christian Andersen. It told the tragic and romantic tale of Vicky Page (Moira Shearer in her film debut), a gifted young dancer who is forced by the Svengali-like impresario Boris Lermontov (Anton Walbrook), to choose between a glittering career in the ballet and her love for the brilliant composer Julian Craster (Marius Goring). After enjoying spectacular success in *The Red Shoes* ballet, Vicky assures Lermontov that dancing will be the sole purpose of her life. However, her conceptions change as soon as she falls in love with the ballet's composer. When Lermontov discovers their liaison, Julian is immediately dismissed from the company, and, despite the impresario's protestations, Vicky goes with him. Some time later, still intoxicated by glamour of the theatre, she returns to dance *The Red Shoes* ballet once more. She is still torn between going on stage or re-joining Julian, but the shoes themselves seem to take control and they whisk her out of the theatre where she falls to her death under the wheels of a passing train. Opinions in the film world are divided as to whether she committed suicide. Robert Helpmann plays Boleslawsy, the company's leading dancer, and he was also responsible for the film's outstanding choreography which was so skilfully integrated into the story. The part of the shoemaker was created and danced by Leonide Massine, and the remainder of the fine supporting cast included Albert Basserman, Ludmilla Tcherina, Esmond Knight, Irene Browne, Austin Trevor, Jerry Verno, Marcel Poncin, and Hay Petrie. Brian Easdale, who first came to prominence for his work on GPO film shorts, composed, arranged and conducted the music, which was played by the Royal Philharmonic Orchestra. Sir Thomas Beecham conducted the orchestra for The Red Shoes ballet. Easdale won an Academy Award for his memorable score, and other Oscars went to Hein Heckroth and Arthur Lawson for colour art direction-set direction. The film was also nominated for best picture, story, and film editing, although not, strangely, for Jack Cardiff's stunning Technicolor photography. This exquisite and thrilling picture, which has inspired so many young people over the years with its revealing glimpse of the backstage world of ballet, is still viewed with a mixture of awe and admiration to this day. Not so the Broadway musical which was based on the film and Hans Christian Andersen's original story. It opened on 16 December 1993, and closed three days later.

RED SHOES, THE (STAGE MUSICAL)

'Cobbling' and 'cobbled', two words that are dangerously close to 'cobblers' - which does not perhaps have the same connotations in America as is it does in Britain - were prominent in several US critics' reviews of this 'mishmash musical version of the beloved 1948 ballet film The Red Shoes', which opened at the Gershwin Theatre in New York on 16 December 1993. The score was mostly the work of veteran composer Jule Styne and his lyricist and librettist Marsha Norman, but Styne brought in Paul Stryker (a nom de guerre for his Funny Girl collaborator Bob Merrill) at a late hour to help out with the lyrics. Other pre-Broadway changes resulted in director Susan Schulman being replaced by Hollywood legend Stanley Donen, and the departure of Roger Rees, one of the principals. The well-known story tells of a young dancer, Victoria Page (Margaret Illman) who is torn between the impresario who has made her a star, Boris Lermontov (Steve Barton), and the young and dashing composer Julian Craster (Hugh Panaro). He falls passionately in love while creating her 'role of a lifetime', The 'banal and melodramatic' score included 'Swan Lake', 'Corps de Ballet', 'When It Happens To You', 'It's A Fairy Tale', 'Be Somewhere', 'The Rag', 'Come Home', and 'When You Dance For A King'. Lyric lines such as 'Now we learn what no one's known/The shoes have passions of their own', and 'Most of us are bound to a lifetime on the ground/You won't stop 'til you reach the top of the sky', were seized upon with derisory glee by the critical fraternity. The meeting of classical dance and musical comedy just did not work, although Margaret Illman was applauded for her performance overall (in a role that was immortalised in the film by Moira Shearer), and in particular for her elegance and style in the second-act showpiece, 'The Red Shoes Ballet' - the longest dance sequence of its kind since Richard Rodgers' 'Slaughter On Tenth Avenue' for On Your Toes (1936). Heidi Landesman's sets, which featured a baroque false proscenium, were complimented too. But the knives were out, and The Red Shoes was withdrawn after only three days. At the time, the reported loss of $8 million was said to be a Broadway record.

RED, HOT AND BLUE!

This attempt to repeat the success of Anything Goes (1934), went wrong somewhere on the road to the Alvin Theatre in New York, where it opened on 20 October 1936. Victor Moore and William Gaxton, two of the reasons for the earlier show's appeal, were absent this time, but librettists Howard Lindsay and Russel Crouse (who wrote a very amusing book) and songwriter Cole Porter were on hand, and Ethel Merman's presence ensured that the audience heard every word and note. Her co-star was comedian Jimmy Durante, and disagreement over top billing resulted in a design in which their names formed a cross, with 'Jimmy' appearing on the upper left-hand diagonal arm, and 'Merman' on the right. Bob Hope's name was below and in the middle, and a good deal easier to read. Together with Merman, he introduced 'You've Got Something', as well as one of Porter's most durable standards, 'It's De-Lovely'. Merman had the first stab at two more of the composer's most memorable songs, the exuberant 'Ridin' High', and 'Down In The Depths (On the Ninetieth Floor)' ('When the only one you wanted wants another/What's the use of swank and cash in the bank galore?/Why, even the janitor's wife/Has a perfectly good love life/And here am I/Facing tomorrow/Down in the depths on the ninetieth floor'). Durante had 'A Little Skipper From Heaven Above', as part of his role as 'Policy' Pinkle, the captain of the polo team at Lark's Nest Prison. 'Policy' is one of several inmates who are released in an effort to assist with a national lottery organized by 'Nails' O'Reilly Duquesne (Ethel Merman) and her lawyer, Bob Hale (Bob Hope). The winner of the lottery has to find the whereabouts of Hale's childhood sweetheart. The search is made easier by the knowledge that the girl sat on a waffle iron when she was four, so identification should prove to be a fairly simple matter. The whole thing becomes academic anyway when the Supreme Court rules that any such contest which benefits the American people is unconstitutional. The show's political overtones and other aspects of the production, meant that Red, Hot And Blue! was often compared to the 1931 political musical satire Of Thee I Sing. It was not nearly as successful though, and closed after only 183 performances.

REDHEAD

Composer Albert Hague and veteran lyricist and librettist Dorothy Fields came together for the first time to write the score for this musical, which opened at the 46th Street Theatre in New York on 5 February 1959. Fields, together with her brother, Herbert, and their fellow authors, Sydney Sheldon and David Shaw, came up with what was an unusual subject for a Broadway musical - a murder mystery. Set in Victorian London at around the time of the Jack the Ripper killings, the story has Essie Whimple (Gwen Verdon) and Tom Baxter (Richard Kiley) chasing suspects around various parts of the metropolis, including a waxworks museum bearing a remarkable resemblance to Madame Tussaud's emporium. A red-bearded gentleman proves to be the culprit - but which one? Sir Charles Willingham (Patrick Horgan) or George Poppett (Leonard Stone)? Hague and Fields' score is not considered to be remarkable, but any show that contains such engaging songs as 'I Feel Merely Marvellous', 'The Right Finger Of My Right Hand' and 'Look Who's In Love', merits serious consideration. Add to those Verdon's music hall version of 'Erbie Fitch's Twitch', and several other bright numbers, including 'I'm Back In Circulation', The Uncle Sam Rag', 'My Girl Is Just Enough Woman For Me' and 'We Loves Ya, Jimmy', and it was not all bad news. The Tony Awards committee certainly did not think so, and their kudos went to Verdon, Kiley, and Hague, along with others for best musical, libretto, costumes (Rouben Ter-Arutunian) producers (Robert Fryer and Lawrence Carr), as well as Bob Fosse's brilliant choreography. The public gave the show their vote, too, and it ran for well over a year, a total of 452 performances. Almost 40 years after this musical whodunit made its Broadway debut, in September 1998 the Goodspeed Opera House in Connecticut staged a rare revival. Directed by Christopher Ashley, the cast included Valerie Wright (Essie), Timothy Warmen (Tom), Eddie Korbich (Poppett), and James Coyle (Willingham).

RENALDO AND CLARA

Having completed recording sessions for what became *Desire*, Bob Dylan began rehearsals for an informal cavalcade-style tour, later dubbed the Rolling Thunder Revue. Joan Baez, Roger McGuinn, Mick Ronson, T-Bone Burnette and Scarlet Rivera were among the featured artists on a venture which suggested the camaraderie of the 60s coffee-house era inspiring the venture's leading participants. The revue lasted from October 1975 until the following January, before being reconvened between April and May 1976. Several concerts were filmed and, when intercut with acted sequences, the results were released as this intriguing film. First screened in January 1978, *Renaldo And Clara* is still the subject of fierce debate. Many critics pronounced it over-long and self-indulgent, particularly with respect to Dylan's confused 'plotline'. Taking a cue from Spanish director Louis Bunuel, he cast two women, Joan Baez and Ronnee Blakley, as 'Mrs. Dylan' while his 'part' was played by rock 'n' roll singer Ronnie Hawkins. This surreal role-playing was enhanced by Dylan's increasing use of white face paint during live performances, but any intended metaphor was either confused or too trite to be of relevance. Stung by the negative response, Dylan re-edited the film later in the year, in the process trimming a version of 'Knockin' On Heaven's Door' recorded at New Jersey's Clinton Correctional Institution For Women, two songs from an appearance at Boston's Music Hall and an informal reading of 'House Of The Rising Sun' undertaken in a Quebec hotel room. However, despite unwieldy qualities, both versions of

Renaldo And Clara reward the patient viewer with many memorable scenes. Former folk singer David Blue is a joy as the narrator and cameo appearances by Ramblin' Jack Elliott, Gordon Lightfoot, Arlo Guthrie and Allen Ginsberg accentuate the notion of friendship which binds the project. The last-named's beard is symbolically shaven during the film and the portion where the poet joins Dylan for an informal threnody at the grave of novelist Jack Kerouac is highly moving. The musical highlights are many, notably Roger McGuinn's powerful rendition of the Byrds' classic 'Eight Miles High', although the bulk of Dylan's contributions were taped in New York during rehearsals for the tour. Curiously, the film did not inspire a soundtrack album, although four songs were culled from its soundtrack to provide a promotional EP. *Renaldo And Clara* is a frustrating feature, yet is sits alongside the Band's *The Last Waltz* as a tribute to a generation of musicians about to feel the blast of punk rock.

RENT

Regarded by many as the most exciting musical to hit New York for years, if not decades, this electrifying 'rock-opera for the 90s' opened off-Broadway at the New York Theatre Workshop on 13 February 1996. It broke all box office records at the small house, enjoyed saturation press coverage, and had already won the esteemed Pulitzer Prize for Drama by the time it transferred to Broadway's 1,173-seater Nederlander Theatre on 29 April. With book, music, and lyrics by Jonathan Larson, from an original concept and with additional lyrics by Billy Aronson, *Rent* was inspired by Puccini's opera *La Bohème*. Updated, and relocated from the Parisian Left Bank, it is now set in New York's East Village with its contemporary problems of AIDS, drugs, and abject poverty. The action takes place during the period from one Christmas to the next, and the central characters are the ex-junkie punk singer and composer Roger Davis (Adam Pascal), his fellow squatter, videographer Mark Cohen (Anthony Rapp), who cannot resist filming his friends, and their 'landlord', Benny Coffin III (Taye Diggs). Benny's wife has money, and he wants to turn the building into a cyber studio. Roger is HIV-positive, as are his new love, the beautiful Mimi Marquez (Daphne Rubin-Vega), who is a heroin addict and exotic dancer at a sadomasochist club, and Angel Schunard (Wilson Jermaine Heredia), a transvestite street drummer who falls in love with former academic Tom Collins (Jesse L. Martin). Mark's performance-artist girlfriend, Maureen Johnson (Idina Menzel), has left him for another woman, Joanne Jefferson (Fredi Walker). As the curtain rises, Roger is recovering from his former girlfriend's suicide (she too was HIV-positive), and striving to write one really great song before he dies ('One Song Glory'). Larson's score was a fascinating blend of rock, blues, soul, gospel, and echoes of Caribbean and African music. Among the other highlights were the Act 2 opener, 'Seasons Of Love', with the entire company singing about the time you have left when you only have a year to live ('Five hundred twenty-five thousand/Six hundred minutes'), Mimi's highly emotional 'Light My Candle', 'Without You', and 'Out Tonight', and Angel and Tom's blues love-ballad, 'I'll Cover You'. The remainder of the score, which, while firmly set in the rock idiom, was genuinely theatrical and skilfully advanced the complex narrative, consisted of 'Tune Up/Voice Mail No. 1', 'Rent', 'You Okay Honey?', 'Voice Mail No. 2', 'Today 4 U', 'You'll See', 'Tango: Maureen', 'Life Support', 'Another Day', 'Will I?', 'On The Street', 'Santa Fe', 'We're Okay', 'Christmas Bells', 'Over The Moon', 'La Vie Bohème/I Should Tell You', 'Happy New Year/Voice Mail No. 3', 'Take Me Or Leave Me', 'Voice Mail No. 4', 'Contact', 'Halloween', 'Goodbye, Love', 'What You Own', 'Voice Mail No. 5', 'Finale/Your Eyes'. Seamlessly directed by Michael Greif, and choreographed by Marlies Yearby, *Rent* was showered with awards, including Tony and Drama Desk Awards for best musical, book, original score, and featured actor (Heredia), Outer Critics Circle Award for Outstanding Off-Broadway musical, and a Drama Desk Award for orchestrations (Steve Skinner). By the time *Rent* had settled into London's Shaftesbury Theatre, after opening on 12 May 1997, three touring companies were on the road in the USA and Canada, with more productions in the pipeline. The phenomenal impact of *Rent*, with its innovative use of rock music, invited comparisons with previous unconventional Broadway fare such as the sensational *Hair*, the first musical of the hippie peace and love generation (1968), and the Motown-influenced *Dreamgirls* (1981). However, experienced US critics dismissed these notions, claiming that *Rent*'s depth of characterization in both book and score made it far superior to either. Certainly, it will be the first musical in years to reach a non-theatre audience, and have its songs covered by rock artists. Only time will tell whether this is an isolated instance of a musical dealing with truly contemporary personal and musical themes, or one that will inspire other composers and authors to work in that area. If the latter proves to be the case, sadly the creator of *Rent*, Jonathan Larson, will not be among them. Having lived with the project since 1989 when he first met playwright Billy Aronson, and working as a waiter in a diner to support himself, Jonathan Larson died suddenly of an aortic aneurysm on 25 January 1996, the day before previews of his masterpiece were due to begin.

● FURTHER READING: *Rent*, Jonathan Larson.

RETURN TO THE FORBIDDEN PLANET

Based very loosely on the 1956 film *Forbidden Planet* which was a sci-fi version of William Shakespeare's play, *The Tempest*, this show - 'it's all a-Bard for an intergalactic rock extravaganza' - opened at the Cambridge Theatre in London on 18 September 1989. It was written and directed by Bob Carlton, who had mounted a miniature production for the Bubble Theatre Company in the mid-80s. The story, which retains only three names from the original source, Prospero, Miranda, and Ariel, is set on a spaceship that lands on the uncharted planet D'Illyria, the very place that the mad scientist Doctor Prospero (Christian Roberts) and his daughter Miranda (Allison Harding) had ended up several years previously, after the Doctor's wife had rather carelessly tinkered with his formula which was about to change the world. The spaceship's commander is Captain Tempest (John Ashby), 'a square-jawed, *Boys Own*-paper-hero and pipe-smoker', and the antithesis of the devilishly devious Prospero. Examples of the fractured

Shakespearean dialogue included 'Two bleeps, or not two bleeps? That is the question', and 'Shall I compare thee to a chemist's shop?' But it was the music and the high-tech effects (credited to *Thunderbirds* creator Gerry Anderson) that gave the show its wide appeal. Rock classics such as 'Wipeout', 'Telstar', 'Great Balls Of Fire', 'Don't Let Me Be Misunderstood', 'Good Vibrations', 'A Teenager In Love', 'Go Now', 'We've Gotta Get Out Of This Place', and many more, accompanied the crazy antics aboard the space vehicle. Patrick Moore, the doyen of the high-powered telescope and star of UK television's long-running *The Sky At Night*, materialised in video form as a galactic guide, and, of all the comic-book characters, Kraig Thornbar excelled as Ariel, the roller-skating robot. The show won the 1990 Laurence Olivier Award for best musical and went on to become a tremendous success, running for 1,516 performances before its closure in January 1993. A 1991 off-Broadway production stayed at the Variety Arts Theatre for six months.

REVEILLE WITH BEVERLY

A fluffy but engaging US wartime musical film, made in 1943, about a radio station DJ, Ann Miller, who plays swing music for the boys in local army camps. Several leading musicians of the era appear, including the orchestras of Count Basie, Bob Crosby and Duke Ellington. Amongst the singers on hand are the Mills Brothers, Ella Mae Morse, Betty Roché and Frank Sinatra.

REVEL, HARRY

b. 21 December 1905, London, England, d. 3 November 1958, New York City, New York, USA. An important composer, mostly remembered for the series of appealing songs that he and his chief collaborator Mack Gordon contributed to movie musicals of the 30s. After demonstrating a remarkable ability on the piano as a young child, Revel studied at the Guildhall School of Music and seemed destined for a career as a classical musician. Instead, he went to Europe at the age of 15 and toured with dance orchestras, later composing light and operatic music. In 1929 he moved to America where he met vaudevillian Mack Gordon, and in the early 30s they contributed some songs to mostly unsuccessful Broadway shows such as *Fast And Furious* (with Harold Adamson), the 1931 *Ziegfeld Follies* (with Harry Richman), *Everybody's Welcome*, *Marching By*, and *Smiling Faces*. In 1932, Joe Rines, Don Redman, Chick Bullock and Fletcher Henderson all had hits with Revel and Gordon's 'Underneath The Harlem Moon', and in the following year they wrote the score for their first movie, *Broadway Thru A Keyhole*. This was followed during the remainder of the 30s by scores or single songs for a string of mostly entertaining features which included *Sitting Pretty*, *We're Not Dressing*, *Shoot The Works*, *She Loves Me Not*, *The Gay Divorcee*, *College Rhythm*, *Love In Bloom*, *Paris In The Spring*, *Two For Tonight*, *Stowaway*, *Collegiate*, *Poor Little Rich Girl*, *You Can't Have Everything*, *Head Over Heels In Love*, *Wake Up And Live*, *Thin Ice*, *Ali Baba Goes To Town*, *My Lucky Star*, *Rebecca Of Sunnybrook Farm*, *Sally, Irene And Mary*, *In Old Chicago*, *Thanks For Everything*, *Josette*, *Tailspin*, *Love Finds Andy Hardy*, *Love And Hisses*, and *Rose Of Washington Square* (1939). From out of those pictures came many popular and appealing numbers such as 'Did You Ever See A Dream Walking?', 'Good Morning Glory', 'You're Such A Comfort To Me', 'It Was A Night In June', 'May I?', 'Love Thy Neighbour', 'She Reminds Me Of You', 'With My Eyes Wide Open, I'm Dreaming', 'Don't Let It Bother You', 'Stay As Sweet As You Are', 'My Heart Is An Open Book', 'Here Comes Cookie', 'Without A Word Of Warning', 'I Feel Like A Feather In The Breeze', 'When I'm With You', 'Oh, My Goodness', 'Goodnight, My Love', 'One Never Knows, Does One?', 'Never In A Million Years', 'There's A Lull In My Life', 'You Can't Have Ev'rything', 'An Old Straw Hat', 'I've Got A Date With A Dream', 'Meet The Beat Of My Heart', 'It Never Rains But It Pours', and 'I Never Knew Heaven Could Speak'. After working on *The Rains Came* in 1939, the team split up and Gordon went off to write with Harry Warren. Revel worked in an administrative capacity for US Forces entertainment units during World War II and continued to write film songs in the 40s, mostly with lyricist Mort Greene, although he was unable to match his previous success. He provided several numbers, including 'You Go Your Way (And I'll Go Crazy)' and 'I'm In Good Shape (For The Shape I'm In)', for the Ray Bolger picture *Four Jacks And A Jill*, and also worked on *Call Out The Marines, Joan Of Arzak, Midnight Masquerade, Hit The Ice, The Dolly Sisters, I'll Tell The World, It Happened On Fifth Avenue*, and *The Stork Club*. Two of Revel and Greene's songs, 'There's A Breeze On Lake Louise' (from *The Mayor Of Forty-Fourth Street*) and 'Remember Me To Carolina' (from *Minstrel Man*) were nominated for Oscars. There were no awards for Revel and Arnold B. Horwitt's score for the 1945 Broadway show *Are You With It?*, but it enjoyed a reasonable run. Revel's other collaborators included Paul Francis Webster, Bennie Benjamin and George Weiss with whom he wrote one of his last songs, 'Jet', in 1951. It became a modest hit for Nat 'King' Cole.

● FURTHER READING: *Meet The Musikids-They Wrote Your Songs*, Harry Revel.

REVOLUTION

This rarely screened 1969 film was directed by Jack O'Connell who 'discovered' its star, Today Malone, dancing at San Fransciso's Avalon Ballroom. Taking its cue from that city's 'flower-power' era, *Revolution* focuses on such hippie-styled tracts as a back-to-the-woods commune, a Krishna temple, a celebration of the Summer Solstice and a ballet performed by the San Franciscan Workshop in which the participants are naked. Bay Area musicians are also very much in evidence and the soundtrack includes material by three groups in their formative stages. A five-piece Quicksilver Messenger Service contribute 'Babe I'm Gonna Leave You' and 'Codine', the only tracks this line-up recorded. The Steve Miller Band offer the equally nascent 'Mercury Blues', 'Superbyrd' and 'Your Old Lady', while Texan act Mother Earth provide 'Without Love', 'Stranger In My Home Town' and the title track. None of these performances are available on other contemporary releases, inspiring interest in the attendant soundtrack album. Indeed, when the lustre of the film ebbed, the set was repackaged as a release showcasing three fascinating acts in their formative years. An interesting view of west coast alternative lifestyles, *Revolution* is interesting, if only for the rare music on offer.

REYNOLDS, DEBBIE

b. Mary Frances Reynolds, 1 April 1932, El Paso, Texas, USA. A popular actress and singer, particularly in movies. After moving to California in 1940 she became a majorette and played French horn with the Burbank Youth Orchestra. It was there she was spotted by talent scouts at a Miss Burbank competition in 1948. She quickly became a leading light in film musicals such as *The Daughter Of Rosie O'Grady* (1950), *Three Little Words* (as 'Boop-Boop-A-Doop' girl Helen Kane), *Two Weeks With Love, Singin' In The Rain* (perhaps her most memorable role), *Skirts Ahoy!, I Love Melvin, The Affairs Of Dobie Gillis, Athena, Give A Girl A Break, Hit The Deck, The Tender Trap* (comedy with music), *Bundle Of Joy, Meet Me In Las Vegas, Say One For Me, Pepe* and *The Unsinkable Molly Brown* (1964, Oscar nomination). In 1951 she recorded her first million-selling single, 'Abba Daba Honeymoon' (from the film *Two Weeks With Love*), on which she duetted with Carleton Carpenter. She also went to the top of the US charts in 1957 with the million-selling 'Tammy' (from *Tammy And The Bachelor*). She married the singer and actor Eddie Fisher in September 1955, and their daughter Carrie has since become an established actress and writer. They divorced in 1959 when Fisher married Elizabeth Taylor. In 1966 Reynolds appeared in *The Singing Nun* (a fictionalized story about Soeur Sourire), and three years later starred in her own television series, *Debbie*. As her film career declined, she made an acclaimed Broadway debut in the 1973 revival of the much-loved American musical *Irene*, and appeared in her own nightclub revue. In later years, she survived severe financial problems when her second husband's business failed, and she and Carrie were estranged after Carrie's hard-hitting novel, *Postcards From The Edge*, which was supposedly based on their lives together, was filmed in 1990. Always the trouper, she bounced right back, launching two keep-fit videos, and headlining at venues such as Harrah's in Reno, and Caesar's Palace in Las Vegas, often in the company of her former film co-stars, such as Harve Presnell (*The Unsinkable Molly Brown*) and Donald O'Connor (*Singin' In The Rain*). In 1993 she opened the Debbie Reynolds Hotel on the fringe of the Las Vegas Strip, where she presents her two-hour autobiographical one-woman show, which contains often bawdy impressions of Zsa Zsa Gabor, Mae West and Barbra Streisand. The complex also houses Reynolds' museum of Hollywood memorabilia. After struggling for nearly five years to make it a success, Reynolds filed for bankruptcy, two months after an agreement to sell the hotel for $10 million fell through. In 1997 she unveiled her second star on the Hollywood Walk of Fame. This latest one honours her stage revivals of *Woman Of The Year, Annie Get Your Gun*, and *The Unsinkable Molly Brown*. She received her first star in 1960 for film roles such as *Singin' In The Rain*.

● ALBUMS: *Debbie Reynolds* (Dot 1959)★★★, *Am I That Easy To Forget* (Dot 1960)★★★ *Fine & Dandy* (Dot 1960)★★, *From Debbie With Love* (Dot 1960)★★, *Tammy* (Dot 1963)★★★, *Raising A*

Ruckus (Metro 1965)★★★, *Debbie* (Jasmine 1985)★★, and film soundtrack recordings.

● FURTHER READING: *Debbie - My Life*, Debbie Reynolds with David Patrick Columba.

● FILMS: *June Bride* (1948), *Three Little Words* (1950), *Two Weeks With Love* (1950), *The Daughter Of Rosie O'Grady* (1950), *Mr. Imperium* (1951), *Singin' In The Rain* (1952), *Skirts Ahoy!* (1952), *Give A Girl A Break* (1953), *The Affairs Of Dobie Gillis* (1953), *I Love Melvin* (1953), *Susan Slept Here* (1954), *Athena* (1954), *The Tender Trap* (1955), *Hit The Deck* (1955), *Bundle Of Joy* (1956), *The Catered Affair* (1956), *Meet Me In Las Vegas* (1956), *Tammy And The Bachelor* (1957), *This Happy Feeling* (1958), *It Started With A Kiss* (1959), *The Mating Game* (1959), *Say One For Me* (1959), *Pepe* (1960), *The Rat Race* (1960), *The Gazebo* (1960), *The Pleasure Of His Company* (1961), *The Second Time Around* (1961), *How The West Was Won* (1962), *My Six Loves* (1963), *Mary, Mary* (1963), *The Unsinkable Molly Brown* (1964), *Goodbye Charlie* (1964), *The Singing Nun* (1966), *Divorce American Style* (1967), *How Sweet It Is* (1968), *What's The Matter With Helen?* (1971), *Charlottes's Web* (1973), *That's Entertainment!* (1974), *The Bodyguard* (1992), *Heaven And Earth* (1993), *That's Entertainment! III* (1994), *Wedding Bell Blues* (1996), *Mother* (1996), *In And Out* (1997), *Fear And Loathing In Las Vegas* voice only (1998), *Zack And Reba* (1998).

RHAPSODY IN BLUE

Yet another film biography which bears little resemblance to reality. Fortunately, in this case the subject is composer George Gershwin and so the music more than makes up for the inadequacies and fantasies of the screenplay. Robert Alda, the well-known Broadway and radio actor, made his film debut as Gershwin, and Joan Leslie and Alexis Smith played two of the important women in his life. Leslie, whose singing voice was dubbed by Louanne Hogan, handled several of the songs in a predictably glorious score which included 'Fascinating Rhythm', 'I Got Rhythm', 'Love Walked In', 'Embraceable You', 'An American In Paris', 'Someone To Watch Over Me', 'Mine', 'The Man I Love', 'Oh, Lady, Be Good', 'Bidin' My Time', and 'Clap Yo' Hands' (all with lyrics by Ira Gershwin); and 'Summertime' (Du Bose Heyward), 'Swanee' (Irving Caesar), 'Somebody Loves Me' (Buddy De Sylva-Ballard Macdonald), 'Do It Again' (DeSylva), and 'I'll Build A Stairway To Paradise' (DeSylva-Ira Gershwin). Oscar Levant played the celebrated 'Concerto In F' and 'The Rhapsody In Blue' (conducted by Paul Whiteman), and among the other artists who appeared as themselves were Al Jolson, Hazel Scott, George White and Anne Brown. Rosemary DeCamp and Morris Carnovsky played Gershwin's mother and father, and other roles were taken by Charles Coburn (as music publisher Max Dreyfuss), Albert Basserman, Julie Bishop, Herbert Rudley, Mickey Roth, Johnny Downs, Tom Patricola, Stephen Richard, Darryl Hickman, Martin Noble, and Will Wright. Howard Koch and Elliot Paul dreamed up the screenplay, and LeRoy Prinz was responsible for the choreography which, like the rest of the picture, benefited from some fine black and white photography by Sol Polito. Irving Rapper was the director, and *Rhapsody In Blue*, which was produced for Warner Brothers in 1945 by Jesse L. Lasky, still retains its appeal to this day.

RICE, TIM

b. Timothy Miles Bindon Rice, 10 November 1944, Amersham, Buckinghamshire, England. A lyricist, librettist, journalist, broadcaster and cricket captain. Around the time he was briefly studying law, Rice met the 17-year-old Andrew Lloyd Webber, and in 1965, they collaborated on *The Likes Of Us*, a musical version of the Dr. Barnardo story. Lloyd Webber then went off to concentrate on serious music, and Rice worked for EMI Records, progressing later to the Norrie Paramor Organization. In 1968 they resumed their partnership with *Joseph And The Amazing Technicolor Dreamcoat*, a 20-minute 'pop cantata' based on the biblical character of Joseph, for an end-of-term concert at Colet Court boys' school in the City of London. Subsequently, the piece reached a wider audience with performances at the Edinburgh Festival, and venues such as the Old Vic, St. Paul's Cathedral, and the Central Hall, Westminster, where Rice played the part of Pharaoh. In 1970, Rice and Lloyd Webber raided the 'good book' again for the score of *Jesus Christ Superstar*, a 'rock opera', presented on a double album, which, when exploited by producer Robert Stigwood, topped the US chart, and spawned successful singles by Murray Head ('Superstar'), and Yvonne Elliman ('I Don't Know How To Love Him'). After several concert performances of the piece in the USA, some of them unauthorized and unlicensed the show was 'extravagantly' staged on Broadway in 1972, and ran for over 700 performances despite some reviews such as 'nearer to the rock bottom than rock opera', and a good deal of flak from the religious lobby. It did even better in London, running for a total of 3,358 performances over a period of eight years. In 1992 a concert version, celebrating the show's 20th anniversary, toured the UK, starring Paul Nicholas and Claire Moore. The 1973 film version, in one critic's opinion, was 'one of the true fiascos of modern cinema'.

Meanwhile, *Joseph And The Amazing Technicolor Dreamcoat* had risen again, and when extended, and paired with a new one-act piece, *Jacob's Journey*, played in the West End for nearly 250 performances during 1973. Lengthened even further, it became extremely popular throughout the world, and stayed on Broadway for 20 months in 1981, during which time Joseph was personified by pop stars such as Andy Gibb and David Cassidy. Hardly any subject could have been further from Joseph, Jesus and Jacob, than Rice and Lloyd Webber's next collaboration, *Evita*, 'an opera based on the life of Eva Peron'. Conceived as an album in 1976, Julie Covington, who sang the part of Eva, went to number 1 in the UK with 'Don't Cry For Me Argentina', and 'Another Suitcase, Another Hall' was successful for Barbara Dickson. When the project reached the West End in 1978, Elaine Paige became a star overnight as Eva, and David Essex, in the role of Che, made the Top 10 with 'Oh What a Circus'. Four years later, Essex climbed to the UK number 2 spot with Rice's 'A Winter's Tale', written in collaboration with Mike Batt. The original production of *Evita* was 'a technical knockout, a magnificent earful, a visual triumph', which stayed at the Prince Edward Theatre for nearly eight years, and spent almost half that time on Broadway. Rice's next musical, with composer Stephen Oliver, was *Blondel* (1983), 'a medieval romp' which ran for eight months. Three years later Rice was back in the West End with *Chess* (1986), which replaced *Evita* at the Prince Edward Theatre. Written with Benny Andersson and Bjorn Ulvaeus, both ex-members of Abba, the score was released two years earlier on an album which produced 'I Know Him So Well', a UK number 1 for Elaine Paige And Barbara Dickson, and 'One Night In Bangkok', a Top 20 entry for Murray Head. *Chess* ran for three years in London, but was 'a £5 million flop' in New York. Over the years, Rice tinkered with various aspects of the show, and the 1992 off-Broadway version had a drastically revised book. At that stage of his career, *Chess* remained Rice's last major production. In the same year, his first, albeit small theatrical effort, *Joseph And The Amazing Technicolor Dreamcoat* was restaged at the London Palladium, starring, at various times, the children's television entertainer Phillip Schofield, and actor/pop star Jason Donovan. The latter topped the UK chart with the show's big number, 'Any Dream Will Do'. Schofield also had a UK chart hit with another song from the show, 'Close Every Door'. It was estimated that Rice and Lloyd Webber were each receiving £16,000 each week from the box office, besides the peripherals.

Rice's projects on a rather smaller scale have included *Cricket* (1986) (with Andrew Lloyd Webber) and *Tycoon*, an English-language version of Michel Berger's hit French musical *Starmania* (1991). He has also contributed songs to several non-musical films, including *The Fan*, *The Odessa File*, *Gumshoe* and *The Entertainer*, and worked with composers such as Francis Lai, Vangelis, Rick Wakeman and Marvin Hamlisch. In 1993, Rice took over from the late Howard Ashman as Alan Menken's lyricist on the Walt Disney movie *Aladdin*, and won a Golden Globe Award and an Academy Award for 'A Whole New World', The number went to the top of the US charts in a version by Peabo Bryson and Regina Belle. In the early 90s Rice's worked again with Alan Menken on additional songs for the Broadway stage production of *Beauty And The Beast*, and his collaboration with Elton John on the score for the Disney film *The Lion King*, earned him a second Oscar, a Golden Globe, and an Ivor Novello Award for the charming 'Circle Of Life'. He has won several other 'Ivors', along with and Grammy and Tony Awards and gold and platinum records. A tribute album, *I Know Them So Well*, containing a selection of his most successful songs performed by various artists, was released in 1994. In 1996, the highly successful Cliff Richard musical *Heathcliff*, which Rice co-wrote with John Farrar, toured the UK, while in the same year a revival of *Jesus Christ Superstar* re-opened London's Lyceum Theatre, and a film version of *Evita*, starring Madonna, was finally released. It contained a new Lloyd Webber-Rice song, 'You Must Love Me', for which they won Academy Awards.

In June 1997, a concert version of *King David*, for which Rice served as lyricist-librettist with composer Alan Menken, played a limited, nine-performance run at Broadway's refurbished New Amsterdam Theatre, and in November a stage version of *The Lion King* made its triumphant Broadway debut at the same theatre. Almost a year on, 'Elton John & Tim Rice's' *Elaborate Lives: The Legend Of Aida* opened in Atlanta, Georgia, USA, and back home in England, a series entitled *Tim Rice-Superstar* aired on BBC Radio 2.

As a journalist, Rice has written regular columns for UK national newspapers and for cricket magazines, reflecting his abiding interest in the game which resulted in him forming and leading his own regular side, the Heartaches, complete with team colours and year-book. His other more lucrative publications include co-authorship, with his brother Jonathan, and Paul Gambaccini, of the *The Guinness Book Of British Hit Singles* and over 20 associated books. His interest in, and knowledge of, popular music was rewarded with the title of 'Rock Brain Of The Year' on BBC Radio in 1986. He also wrote the script for a 15-part series on the history of Western popular music. His other radio and television work includes *The Musical Triangle*, *Many A Slip*, *American Pie*, *Lyrics By Tim Rice*, *Just A Minute* and *Three More Men In A Boat*. In 1994, Rice was awarded a Knighthood for services to the arts, particularly music, and sport.

● COMPILATIONS: *Tim Rice Collection: Stage And Screen Classics* (Rhino 1997)★★★.

RICHARD, CLIFF

b. Harry Roger Webb, 14 October 1940, Lucknow, India. One of the most popular and enduring talents in the history of UK showbusiness, Richard began his career as a rock 'n' roll performer in 1957. His fascination for Elvis Presley encouraged him to join a skiffle group and several months later he teamed up with drummer Terry Smart and guitarist Ken Payne to form the Drifters. They played at various clubs in the Cheshunt/Hoddesdon area of Hertfordshire before descending on the famous 2I's coffee bar in London's Soho. There, they were approached by lead guitarist Ian Samwell and developed their act as a quartet. In 1958, they secured their big break in the unlikely setting of a Saturday morning talent show at the Gaumont cinema in Shepherd's Bush. It was there that the senatorial theatrical agent George Ganyou recognized Richard's sexual appeal and singing abilities and duly financed the recording of a demonstration tape of 'Breathless' and 'Lawdy Miss Clawdy'. A copy reached the hands of EMI producer Norrie Paramor who was impressed enough to grant the ensemble an audition. Initially, he intended to record Richard as a solo artist backed by an orchestra, but the persuasive performer insisted upon retaining his own backing group. With the assistance of a couple of session musicians, the unit recorded the American teen ballad 'Schoolboy Crush' as a projected first single. An acetate of the recording was paraded around Tin Pan Alley and came to the attention of the influential television producer Jack Good. It was not the juvenile 'Schoolboy Crush' that captured his attention, however, but the Ian Samwell b-side 'Move It'. Good reacted with characteristically manic enthusiasm when he heard the disc, rightly recognizing that it sounded like nothing else in the history of UK pop. The distinctive riff and unaffected vocal seemed authentically American, completely at odds with the mannered material that usually emanated from British recording studios. With Good's ceaseless promotion, which included a full-page review in the music paper *Disc*, Richard's debut was eagerly anticipated and swiftly rose to number 2 in the UK charts. Meanwhile, the star made his debut on Good's television showcase *Oh Boy!*, and rapidly replaced Marty Wilde as Britain's premier rock 'n' roll talent. The low-key role offered to the Drifters persuaded Samwell to leave the group to become a professional songwriter, and by the end of 1958 a new line-up emerged featuring Hank B. Marvin and Bruce Welch. Before long, they changed their name to the Shadows, in order to avoid confusion with the black American R&B group, the Drifters. Meanwhile, Richard consolidated his position in the rock 'n' roll pantheon, even outraging critics in true Elvis Presley fashion. The *New Musical Express* denounced his 'violent, hip-swinging' and 'crude exhibitionism' and pontificated: 'Tommy Steele became Britain's teenage idol without resorting to this form of indecent, short-sighted vulgarity'. Critical mortification had little effect on the screaming female fans who responded to the singer's boyish sexuality with increasing intensity.

1959 was a decisive year for Richard and a firm indicator of his longevity as a performer. With management shake-ups, shifts in national musical taste and some distinctly average singles his career could easily have been curtailed, but instead he matured and transcended his Presley-like beginnings. A recording of Lionel Bart's 'Living Doll' provided him with a massive UK number 1 and three months later he returned to the top with the plaintive 'Travellin' Light'. He also starred in two films, within 12 months. *Serious Charge*, a non-musical drama, was banned in some areas as it dealt with the controversial subject of homosexual blackmail. The Wolf Mankowitz-directed *Expresso Bongo*, in which Richard played the delightfully named Bongo Herbert, was a cinematic pop landmark, brilliantly evoking the rapacious world of Tin Pan Alley. It remains one of the most revealing and humorous films ever made on the music business and proved an interesting vehicle for Richard's varied talents. From 1960 onwards Richard's career progressed along more traditional lines leading to acceptance as a middle-of-the-road entertainer. Varied hits such as the breezy, chart-topping 'Please Don't Tease', the rock 'n' rolling 'Nine Times Out Of Ten' and reflective 'Theme For A Dream' demonstrated his range, and in 1962 he hit a new peak with 'The Young Ones'. A glorious pop anthem to youth, with some striking guitar work from Hank Marvin, the song proved one of his most memorable number 1 hits. The film of the same name was a charming period piece, with a strong cast and fine score. It broke box office records and spawned a series of similar movies from its star, who was clearly following Elvis Presley's cinematic excursions as a means of extending his audience. Unlike the King, however, Richard supplemented his frequent movie commitments with tours, summer seasons, regular television slots and even pantomime appearances. The run of UK Top 10 hits continued uninterrupted until as late as mid-1965. Although the showbiz glitz had brought a certain aural homogeneity to the material, the catchiness of songs such as 'Bachelor Boy', 'Summer Holiday', 'On The Beach' and 'I Could Easily Fall' was undeniable. These were neatly, if predictably, complemented by ballad releases such as 'Constantly', 'The Twelfth Of Never' and 'The Minute You're Gone'. The formula looked likely to be rendered redundant by the British beat boom, but Richard expertly rode that wave, even improving his selection of material along the way. He bravely, although relatively unsuccessfully, covered a Rolling Stones song, 'Blue Turns To Grey', before again hitting top form with the beautifully melodic 'Visions'. During 1966, he had almost retired after converting to fundamentalist Christianity, but elected to use his singing career as a positive expression of his faith. The sparkling 'In The Country' and gorgeously evocative 'The Day I Met Marie' displayed the old strengths to the full, but in the swiftly changing cultural climate of the late 60s, Richard's hold on the pop charts could no longer be guaranteed. The 1968 Eurovision Song Contest offered him a chance of further glory, but the jury placed him a close second with the 'oom-pah-pah'-sounding 'Congratulations'. The song was nevertheless a consummate Eurovision performance and proved one of the biggest UK number 1s of the year. Immediately thereafter, Richard's chart progress declined and his choice of material proved at best desultory. Although there were a couple of solid entries, Raymond Froggatt's 'Big Ship' and a superb duet with Hank Marvin, 'Throw Down A Line', Richard seemed a likely contender for Variety as the decade closed.

The first half of the 70s saw him in a musical rut. The chirpy but insubstantial 'Goodbye Sam, Hello Samantha' was a Top 10 hit in 1970 and heralded a notable decline. A second shot at the Eurovision Song Contest with 'Power To All Our Friends' brought his only other Top 10 success of the period and it was widely assumed that his chart career was over. However, in 1976 there was a surprise resurgence in his career when Bruce Welch of the Shadows was assigned to produce his colleague. The sessions resulted in the best-selling album *I'm Nearly Famous*, which included two major hits, 'Miss You Nights' and 'Devil Woman'. The latter was notable for its decidedly un-Christian imagery and the fact that it gave Richard a rare US chart success. Although Welch remained at the controls for two more albums, time again looked as although it would kill off Richard's perennial chart success. A string of meagre singles culminated in the dull 'Green Light', which stalled at number 57, his lowest chart placing since he started singing. Coincidentally, his backing musicians, Terry Britten and Alan Tarney, had moved into songwriting and production at this point and encouraged him to adopt a more contemporary sound on the album *Rock 'N' Roll Juvenile*. The most startling breakthrough, however, was the attendant single 'We Don't Talk Anymore', written by Tarney and produced by Welch. An exceptional pop record, the song gave Richard his first UK number 1 hit in over a decade and also reached the Top 10 in the USA. The 'new' Richard sound, so refreshing after some of his staid offerings in the late 70s, brought further well-arranged hits, such as 'Carrie' and 'Wired For Sound', and ensured that he was a chart regular throughout the 80s.

Although he resisted the temptation to try anything radical, there were subtle changes in his musical approach. One feature of his talent that emerged during the 80s was a remarkable facility as a duettist. Collaborations with

Olivia Newton-John, Phil Everly, Sarah Brightman, Sheila Walsh, Elton John and Van Morrison added a completely new dimension to his career. It was something of a belated shock to realize that Richard may be one of the finest harmony singers working in the field of popular music. His perfectly enunciated vocals and the smooth texture of his voice have the power to complement work that he might not usually tackle alone. The possibility of his collaborating with an artist even further from his sphere than Van Morrison remains a tantalizing challenge. Throughout his four decades in the pop charts, Richard has displayed a valiant longevity. He parodied one of his earliest hits with comedy quartet the Young Ones and registered yet another number 1; he appeared in the stage musicals *Time* and *Heathcliff*; he sang religious songs on gospel tours; he sued the *New Musical Express* for an appallingly libellous review, far more vicious than their acerbic comments back in 1958; he was decorated by the Queen; and he celebrated his 50th birthday with a move into social commentary with the anti-war hit 'From A Distance'. Richard was nominated to perform at the celebrations for VE day in 1995, appearing with Vera Lynn, and has now been adopted as her male equivalent. It was no surprise, therefore, to learn that he was to be knighted for his services to popular music in May 1995. One of his most recent albums, *Songs From Heathcliff*, was drawn from the John Farrar and Tim Rice stage musical *Heathcliff*. Richard's long-held belief that most UK pop radio stations have an official veto on his tracks seemed to be proven in September 1998, when he distributed a heavily remixed promo. of his soon-to-be-released single, 'Can't Keep This Feeling In', under the pseudonym Blacknight. It was instantly playlisted by youth-orientated stations all over the country, and went to number 10 in the chart. The singer was further angered when DJ Chris Evans, owner of Virgin Radio, announced that he wanted the station's entire stock of Richard's records 'thrown out'. In an unprecedented move, BBC Radio 1 responded by clearing its morning schedules for a four-hour tribute 'Stand Up For Cliff Day' hosted by Jill Dando. Such was the demand for tickets to his November/December 1998 Royal Albert Hall concerts celebrating 40 years in show business, that a further 12 performances were scheduled for March 1999. And so he goes on - Sir Cliff Richard has outlasted every musical trend of the past four decades with a sincerity and commitment that may well be unmatched in his field. He is British pop's most celebrated survivor.

● ALBUMS: *Cliff* (Columbia 1959)★★★, *Cliff Sings* (Columbia 1959)★★★★, *Me And My Shadows* (Columbia 1960)★★★★, *Listen To Cliff* (Columbia 1961)★★★, *21 Today* (Columbia 1961)★★★, *The Young Ones* (Columbia 1961)★★★, *32 Minutes And 17 Seconds With Cliff Richard* (Columbia 1962)★★★★, *Summer Holiday* (Columbia 1963)★★★, *Cliff's Hit Album* (Columbia 1963)★★★★, *When In Spain* (Columbia 1963)★★★, *Wonderful Life* (Columbia 1964)★★★, *Aladdin And His Wonderful Lamp* (Columbia 1964)★★★, *Cliff Richard* (Columbia 1965)★★★, *More Hits By Cliff* (Columbia 1965)★★★, *When In Rome* (Columbia 1965)★★, *Love Is Forever* (Columbia 1965)★★★, *Kinda Latin* (Columbia 1966)★★★, *Finders Keepers* (Columbia 1966)★★, *Cinderella* (Columbia 1967)★★, *Don't Stop Me Now* (Columbia 1967)★★★,

Good News (Columbia 1967)★★★, *Cliff In Japan* (Columbia 1968)★★★, *Two A Penny* (Columbia 1968)★★★, *Established 1958* (Columbia 1968)★★★, *Sincerely Cliff* (Columbia 1969)★★★, *It'll Be Me* (Regal Starline 1969)★★★, *Cliff 'Live' At The Talk Of The Town* (Regal Starline 1970)★★★, *All My Love* (MFP 1970)★★★, *About That Man* (Columbia 1970)★★★, *Tracks 'N' Grooves* (Columbia 1970)★★★, *His Land* (Columbia 1970)★★★, *Cliff's Hit Album* stereo reissue of 1963 album (EMI 1971)★★★★, *Take Me High* (EMI 1973)★★★, *Help It Along* (EMI 1974)★★★, *The 31st Of February Street* (EMI 1974)★★★, *Everybody Needs Someone* (MFP 1975)★★★, *I'm Nearly Famous* (EMI 1976)★★★, *Cliff Live* (MFP 1976)★★★, *Every Face Tells A Story* (EMI 1977)★★★, *Small Corners* (EMI 1977)★★★, *Green Light* (EMI 1978)★★★, *Thank You Very Much* (EMI 1979)★★★, *Rock 'N' Roll Juvenile* (EMI 1979)★★★, *Rock On With Cliff* (MFP 1980)★★★, *Listen To Cliff* (MFP 1980)★★★, *I'm No Hero* (EMI 1980)★★★, *Love Songs* (EMI 1981)★★★, *Wired For Sound* (EMI 1981)★★★, *Now You See Me, Now You Don't* (EMI 1982)★★★, *Dressed For The Occasion* (EMI 1983)★★★, *Silver* (EMI 1983)★★★, *Cliff In The 60s* (MFP 1984)★★★, *Cliff And The Shadows* (EMI 1984)★★★, *Thank You Very Much* (MFP 1984)★★★, *The Rock Connection* (EMI 1984)★★★, *Walking In The Light* (Myrrh 1985)★★★, *Time* (EMI 1986)★★★, *Hymns And Inspirational Songs* (Word 1986)★★★, *Always Guaranteed* (EMI 1987)★★★, *Stronger* (EMI 1989)★★★, *From A Distance ... The Event* (EMI 1990)★★★, *Together With Cliff* (EMI 1991)★★★, *The Album* (EMI 1993)★★★, *Songs From Heathcliff* (EMI 1995)★★★, *Real As I Wanna Be* (EMI 1998)★★★.

● COMPILATIONS: *The Best Of Cliff* (Columbia 1969)★★★★, *The Best Of Cliff Volume 2* (Columbia 1972)★★★★, *The Cliff Richard Story* 6-LP box set (WRC 1972)★★★, *40 Golden Greats* (EMI 1979)★★★★, *The Cliff Richard Songbook* 6-LP box set (WRC 1980)★★★, *Private Collection 1979-1988* (EMI 1988)★★★, *20 Original Greats* (EMI 1989)★★★, *The Hit List* (EMI 1994)★★★★, *At The Movies 1959-1974* (EMI 1996)★★★, *The Rock 'N' Roll Years 1958-1963* 4-CD box set (EMI 1997)★★★, *On The Continent* 5-CD box set (Bear Family 1998)★★★, *1960s* (EMI 1998)★★★, *1970s* (EMI 1998)★★★, *1980s* (EMI 1998)★★★.

● VIDEOS: *Two A Penny* (1978), *The Video Connection* (PMI 1984), *Together* (PMI 1984), *Thank You Very Much* (Thorn-EMI 1984), *Rock In Australia* (PMI 1986), *We Don't Talk Anymore* (Gold Rushes 1987), *Video EP* (PMI 1988), *The Young Ones* (1988), *Summer Holiday* (1988), *Wonderful Life* (1988), *Take Me High* (Warner Home Video 1988), *Private Collection* (PMI 1988), *Always Guaranteed* (PMI 1988), *Live And Guaranteed* (PMI 1989), *From A Distance . . . The Event Volumes 1 and 2* (PMI 1990), *Together With Cliff Richard* (PMI 1991), *Expresso Bongo* (1992), *Cliff-When The Music Stops* (1993), *Access All Areas* (1993), *The Story So Far* (1993), *The Hit List* (PMI 1995), *The Hit List Live* (PMI 1995), *Finders Keepers* (1996), *Cliff At The Movies* (1996), *The 40th Anniversary Concert* (VCI 1998).

● FURTHER READING: *Driftin' With Cliff Richard: The Inside Story Of What Really Happens On Tour*, Jet Harris and Royston Ellis. *Cliff, The Baron Of Beat*, Jack Sutter. *It's Great To Be Young*, Cliff Richard. *Me And My Shadows*, Cliff Richard. *Top Pops*, Cliff Richard. *Cliff Around The Clock*, Bob Ferrier. *The Wonderful World Of Cliff Richard*, Bob Ferrier. *Questions: Cliff Answering Reader And Fan Queries*, Cliff Richard. *The Way I See It*, Cliff Richard. *The Cliff Richard Story*, George Tremlett. *New Singer, New Song: The Cliff Richard Story*, David Winter. *Which One's Cliff?*, Cliff Richard with Bill Latham. *Happy Christmas From Cliff*, Cliff Richard. *Cliff In His Own Words*, Kevin St. John. *Cliff*, Patrick Doncaster and Tony

Jasper. *Cliff Richard*, John Tobler. *Silver Cliff: A 25 Year Journal 1958-1983*, Tony Jasper. *Cliff Richard, Single-Minded*, no author listed. *Cliff Richard: The Complete Recording Sessions, 1958-1990*, Peter Lewry and Nigel Goodall. *Cliff: A Biography*, Tony Jasper. *Cliff Richard, The Complete Chronicle*, Mike Read, Nigel Goodall and Peter Lewry. *Cliff Richard: The Autobiography*, Steve Turner. *Ultimate Cliff*, Peter Lewry and Nigel Goodall. *A Celebration: The Official Story Of 40 Years In Show Business*, André Deutsch.

● FILMS: *Serious Charge* (1959), *Expresso Bongo* (1960), *The Young Ones* (1961), *Summer Holiday* (1962), *Wonderful Life* (1964), *Thunderbirds Are Go!* (1966), *Finders Keepers* (1966), *Two A Penny* (1968), *Take Me High* (1973).

RICHARDSON, CLIVE

b. 23 June 1909, Paris, France (of British parents), d. 11 November 1998, London, England. Pianist and composer of light orchestral music. Richardson trained as a doctor before switching to the Royal Academy Of Music, studying several instruments as well as orchestration and conducting. His early career during the 30s included working in Andre Charlot reviews in London's West End, with artists such as Beatrice Lillie, Lupino Lane and Hermione Gingold. As the singer Hildegarde's accompanist and musical director, he spent several years touring Britain and Europe, culminating in a triumphant season at New York's prestigious Rainbow Room. In 1936 Richardson joined Gaumont-British Films as arranger and assistant musical director to Louis Levy, working alongside Charles Williams, Leighton Lucas, Jack Beaver, Bretton Byrd and Mischa Spoliansky, although almost every film gave screen credits to Levy who did little conducting and no composing at all. With Charles Williams, Richardson wrote the scores for most of the Will Hay comedies, including *Oh Mr Porter* (1937), and he also scored *French Without Tears* (1939) which was officially credited to Nicholas Brodszky. Richardson served in the Royal Artillery Regiment during World War II, but managed to keep his musical career active. He contributed arrangements to BBC Radio's most popular show *ITMA*; novel arrangements by leading writers of folk songs, nursery rhymes and traditional melodies, played by the BBC Variety Orchestra conducted by Charles Shadwell, were a popular feature of each programme. Richardson's scores for this feature included 'A-Hunting We Will Go', 'Baa! Baa! Black Sheep', 'British Grenadiers', 'Camptown Races', 'Come Lassies And Lads', 'Grand Old Duke Of York', 'Irish Washerwoman', 'John Peel', 'Lincolnshire Poacher', 'Little Brown Jug', 'Oh Susannah', 'O Where O Where Has My Little Dog Gone', 'On Ilka Moor Baht' At', 'Polly-Wolly-Doodle' and 'Sing A Song Of Sixpence'. Following the success of Richard Addinsell's 'Warsaw Concerto', Richardson's publisher asked him to compose a sequel, which was originally called 'The Coventry Concerto', as a tribute to the Midlands city which had suffered from saturation bombing. Eventually in 1944 this work emerged as 'London Fantasia', and it was recorded by Sidney Torch (Parlophone Records) and Charles Williams (Columbia Records) - both with the composer at the piano, and also by the Mantovani Orchestra with Monia Liter (Decca Records). Other major works at this time included 'Salute To Industry' (1945) and a nautical overture 'White Cliffs'

(1946). Between numerous composing assignments, Richardson developed a performing career with fellow pianist Tony Lowry as Four Hands In Harmony, which topped variety bills and notched up over 500 broadcasts. Today Richardson is best remembered for his light orchestral works: 'Holiday Spirit', 'Shadow Waltz' (written under the *nom de plume* Paul Dubois), 'Running Off The Rails', 'Melody On The Move', 'Road To Rio', 'Tom Marches On' (the ITMA march), 'Chiming Strings', 'Continental Galop', 'Elixir Of Youth', 'Valse Bijou', 'Romantic Rhapsody' and many others. In 1988 he received a BASCA Gold Award for lifetime services to the music business.

RICHMAN, HARRY

b. Harry Reichman, 10 August 1895, Cincinnati, Ohio, USA, d. 3 November 1972, Hollywood, California, USA. An actor, singer, and nightclub entertainer, Richman was a flamboyant character, with a debonair 'man-about-town' image, complete with top hat, or straw boater and cane, he had an uninhibited vocal style which was often compared to that of Al Jolson. At the age of 12, together with a friend, he formed a musical act, Remington and Reichman, and appeared at the Casino Theatre, Chicago. When he was 18 he changed his name to Richman and played regular cafe engagements in San Francisco as a comedian, then appeared in vaudeville as a song and dance man, and as a pianist for headliners such as the Dolly Sisters, Mae West and Nora Bayes. In 1922 he made his Broadway debut, with Bayes, in *Queen O' Hearts*, which ran for only 39 performances. Much more successful was *George White's Scandals Of 1926*, in which Richman introduced the songs 'Lucky Day' and 'The Birth Of the Blues' which was one of his biggest hits. Richman also starred in the 1928 edition of the *Scandals*, in which he sang 'I'm On the Crest Of A Wave'. His next Broadway appearance was in Lew Leslie's lavish *International Revue* in 1930, which was another comparative flop, despite the presence of England's Gertrude Lawrence, dance director Busby Berkeley, and Richman's renditions of two of Dorothy Fields and Jimmy McHugh's best songs, 'Exactly Like You' and 'On The Sunny Side Of The Street'. He introduced another all-time standard, Joseph McCarthy and Jimmy Monaco's 'You Made Me Love You', in the *Ziegfeld Follies* of 1931, which also had Helen Morgan and Ruth Etting in the cast. A year later, in *George White's Musical Hall Varieties*, his big numbers were 'I Love A Parade' and Herman Hupfeld's 'Let's Put Out The Lights And Go To Sleep'. Richman's last 30s Broadway musical was *Say When*, in 1934.

From early in his career he had co-written songs and made hit recordings of some of them, including 'Walking My Baby Back Home', 'There's Danger In Your Eyes, Cherie', 'Singing A Vagabond Song', 'Miss Annabelle Lee', 'C'est Vous (It's You)' and 'Muddy Water'. As well as records and stage appearances, he was enormously popular during the 30s in cabaret and on radio. He also made a few films, including *Putting On The Ritz* (1930), *The Music Goes Round* (1936) and *Kicking The Moon Around* (1938). The latter movie was made in England, and co-starred top bandleader Ambrose and his Orchestra. Richman was very popular in the UK, playing the London Palladium

and other theatres several times. During the 40s, he appeared in the revue *New Priorities Of 1943*, and continued to play clubs and theatres. By the late 40s he had become semi-retired, but emerged to give the occasional performance until the early 60s. Always a high-living individual, it is said that, at the peak of his career, he drove along Broadway in his Rolls Royce, dispensing 10 dollar gold pieces to his admirers. He also owned a speak-easy establishment, Club Richman, in New York. In his leisure time he was an accomplished pilot, and in 1935 set the world altitude record for a single-engine amphibious plane. A year later, with his partner Dick Merrill, he created another record by flying from New York to the UK, and back again, in a single-engine plane. They reputedly packed the aircraft with 50,000 ping-pong balls as an aid to buoyancy in case they ditched in the sea. After all that, the title of Richman's autobiography, *A Hell Of A Life*, would seem to be a reasonable one. Still remembered in 1993, a cabaret entertainment entitled *Puttin' On the Ritz: An Evening At The Club Richman*, starring Joe Tonti, was presented at Don't Tell Mama in New York.
● ALBUMS: *Harry Richman And Sophie Tucker* (1979)★★★.
● FURTHER READING: *A Hell Of A Life*, Harry Richman.

RIDE THE WILD SURF

Pop singers Fabian, Tab Hunter and Shelley Fabares feature alongside television's *I Dream Of Genie* star Barbara Eden in this 1964 outing. The plot involved three friends who travel to Ohahu in Hawaii to tackle some of the world's biggest heads of surf. True love and dexterity naturally triumph by the close of this lacklustre vehicle, which lacks the guest appearances by hit artists salvaging similar films from the American International Pictures group. Surf singing duo Jan And Dean, who were managed by Ms. Fabares' husband Lou Adler, provide the rousing title song. This Brian Wilson/Jan Berry/Roger Christian composition brought the duo their final US Top 20 hit. It provides *Ride The Wild Surf*'s sole saving grace.

RINK, THE

Considered by many of the US critics to be simply a vehicle for the singing and dancing talents of Chita Rivera and Liza Minnelli, *The Rink* made its debut at the Martin Beck Theatre in New York on 9 February 1984. Terrence McNally's story, much of it told in flashback, deals with the tussle between the hard-hearted Anna (Rivera) and her confused daughter Angel (Minnelli) over the fate of the family-owned run-down seaside roller skating rink. Anna has sold it for development, and the arrival of the demolition men drives the two women into a frenzy of bitter regrets and recriminations about the past and what might have been - and the immediate future. John Kander and Fred Ebb's fine - and at times, often touching and wryly amusing - score, gets off to a flyer with Minnelli's rousing 'Coloured Lights', which is followed splendidly by 'Chief Cook And Bottle Washer', 'Don't "Ah, Ma" Me', 'Blue Crystal', 'Under The Roller-Coaster', 'Not Enough Magic', 'We Can Make It', 'After All These Years', 'Angel's Rink And Social Centre', 'What Happened To The Old Days?', 'Marry Me', 'Mrs. A.', 'The Rink', 'Wallflower' and 'All The Children In A Row'. 'The Apple Doesn't Fall', a rare

moment of harmony between mother and daughter, is a particular delight. The members of the supporting cast, Jason Alexander, Mel Johnson Jnr., Scott Holmes, Scott Ellis, Frank Mastrocola and Ronn Carroll, each played several roles, and the inevitable - and highly entertaining - roller skating scene was choreographed by Graciela Daniele. The director was A.J. Antoon. Chita Rivera won the best actress Tony Award, but audiences dwindled rapidly following Minnelli's departure, and *The Rink* closed after 204 performances. A UK production, directed and choreographed by Paul Kerryson which originated at Manchester's Library Theatre, transferred to the Cambridge Theatre in London on 17 February 1988. Starring Diane Langton and Josephine Blake, it was acclaimed by the critics but immediately began to lose money. In spite of an all-night sit-in at the theatre by members of the cast and sympathetic actors and actresses from musicals such as *Starlight Express* and *Les Misérables*, *The Rink* was withdrawn on 19 March.

RIO RITA

An historic show, in that it was the first to be presented at New York's brand new Ziegfeld Theatre, on 2 February 1927. Florenz Ziegfeld himself produced this hybrid of musical comedy and operetta, so it goes without saying that it was a colourful and spectacular affair, populated by lots of beautiful girls. Guy Bolton and Fred Thomson's story is firmly in the operetta tradition, and concerns the hunt for a desperado known as the Kinkajou. The search across the Rio Grande is led by Capt. James Stewart (J. Harold Murray), with his Texas Rangers. Captain Stewart is in love with the wild and passionate Rita Ferguson (Ethelind Terry), but has to wait for her hand until her other suitor, General Esteban (Vincent Serrano), has been revealed as the Kinkajou. Composer Harry Tierney and lyricist Joseph McCarthy were collaborating on their third, and last, successful Broadway musical, following *Irene* and *Kid Boots*. Their score was notable for the rousing 'Rangers' Song' and the delightful 'If You're In Love, You'll Waltz'. Terry and Murray combined on another lovely ballad, 'Rio Rita', and the rest of the songs included the lively 'The Kinkajou', 'Following The Sun Around', and 'You're Always In My Arms'. *Rio Rita* was an enormous hit, and ran for 494 performances - even longer than *The Desert Song* which had opened earlier in that same season. Coincidentally, when the show reached London, where it starred Edith Day, it inaugurated yet another theatre, the Prince Edward, but only stayed there for 59 performances. Many more people had the opportunity to enjoy the early-talkie film version, with Bebe Daniels and John Boles, which was released in 1929.

RIOT ON SUNSET STRIP

Released in 1967, *Riot On Sunset Strip* was one of several films, alongside *The Wild Angels*, in which the notorious American International Pictures company used storylines drawn from California's emergent underground subcultures. Famed for a lengthy series of 'beach' films starring Annette Funicello, AIP brought the same exploitative, 'quickie' practices to these new features, grafting moral punchlines to plots involving drugs and sex on the same surface level as their predecessors had shown 'bad guys' and kissing. *Riot On Sunset Strip* was inspired by real-life events on the fabled Los Angeles thoroughfare when curfews and legislation prohibiting assembly resulted in an infamous demonstration. Indeed, newsreel footage of the event was dropped into film near its close. Whereas the fall-from-grace and retribution of 'Andy' (Mimsy Farmer) - the daughter of a police lieutenant and an alcoholic mother - provides a cardboard framework, *Riot On Sunset Strip* is revered for appearances by US garage bands the Standells, who sing the title theme, and Chocolate Watchband. The latter's second contribution, 'Sitting There Standing', was actually written in the on-set bathroom during a break in shooting. Both groups are featured playing in a reconstruction of the Strip's fabled club, Pandora's Box. Their cameos lift the entire film although wooden acting, laughable script and stereotypical scenes ensure its cult status. Entrepreneur Mike Curb assembled a soundtrack which included the aforementioned acts as well as several who did not feature in the final print. These included the Mugwumps, the Sidewalk Sounds and Mom's Boys although contractual obligations precluded an appearance by the Enemies, who are in the film. Unpretentious at the outset, *Riot On Sunset Strip* still retains its charm.

RIVERA, CHITA

b. Dolores Conchita Figueroa del Rivero, 23 January 1933, Washington, DC, USA. A vivacious singer, dancer, and actress - an exciting and explosive performer - Rivera was born to Puerto Rican parents and grew up in the Bronx. She started dancing when she was seven, and from the age of 11, trained for a career in classical ballet. After studying at the New York City Ballet via a scholarship from choreographer George Balanchine, in 1952 she turned from classical dance and joined the chorus of *Call Me Madam* on Broadway. Further chorus work in *Guys And Dolls* and *Can-Can* was followed by appearances in *Shoestring Revue*, *Seventh Heaven*, and *Mr. Wonderful* (1956). She rocketed to stardom in 1957 as Anita in *West Side Story*, and stopped the show nightly by singing and dancing herself into a frenzy to the whooping rhythms of 'America'. She caused even more of a sensation when *West Side Story* opened in London on 12 December 1958; it is still regarded by many as the most exciting first night of the post-war years. Two years later she was back on Broadway as Dick Van Dyke's secretary Rose, in the first successful rock 'n' roll musical, *Bye Bye Birdie*, and she recreated her role in London the following year. A musical adaptation of the *The Prisoner Of Zenda* (1963), in which she starred with Alfred Drake, folded before it reached New York, but a year later, Rivera was acclaimed for her role as a gypsy princess in *Bajour* on Broadway. In the late 60s, she toured in various productions including *Sweet Charity*, and also appeared in the 1969 film version with Shirley MacLaine. After more national tours in the early 70s in musicals such as *Jacques Brel Is Alive And Well And Living In Paris* and *Kiss, Me Kate*, in addition to several straight roles, she co-starred with Gwen Verdon in the 'sinfully seductive' *Chicago* (1975). John Kander and Fred Ebb wrote the score, and they also devised and developed Chita Rivera's cabaret

act, which included a number called 'Losing', a reference to the number of Tony Award nominations she had received. She gained one more nomination for her performance in *Bring Back Birdie* (1981), which closed after only four nights, and *Merlin* (1983) was also unsuccessful. Rivera was finally awarded the coveted Tony - and a Drama Desk Award - when she co-starred with Liza Minnelli in *The Rink* (1984), another of Kander and Ebb's projects. Shortly afterwards, she was involved in a serious car accident which 'mangled my leg from the knee down'. After having 12 bolts inserted in the bones, she was back on Broadway, along with Leslie Uggams, Dorothy Loudon, and others, in *Jerry's Girls*, a tribute to the composer Jerry Herman. During the rest of the 80s, she performed in cabaret and continued to tour in America and other countries including the UK. In 1988/9, she joined the Radio City Music Hall Rockettes in a national tour of *Can-Can* that lasted for over a year. In 1991, she was inducted into New York's Theatre Hall Of Fame, along with Kander and Ebb. She was subsequently widely applauded - and won London *Evening Standard* and Tony Awards - for her outstanding dual performance as the movie star Aurora and the Spider Woman in Kander and Ebb's musical *Kiss Of the Spider Woman*. After 749 performances in Toronto, London and New York, in November 1994 she set out on the show's two-year road tour of North America. Her outstanding contribution to the musical theatre was recognized in the early 90s by the Drama Desk's Annual Achievement Award, and the first annual Bandai Musical Award for Excellence in Broadway Theatre. While in Washington D.C. during 1996 with *The Kiss Of The Spider Woman*, she was presented with an honorary Gold Record by the Recording Industry Association of America for her contribution to American sound recording. In the late 90s, Rivera co-starred with Carol Channing on stage in *Broadway Legends* ('Together At Last!') and toured her own revue, *Chita & All That Jazz*, through the US regions. In June 1998 she also appeared in a unique reunion of *Sweet Charity* at the Avery Fisher Hall at New York's Lincoln Centre.

ROAD TO SINGAPORE

The first in the enormously successful Paramount series starring Bing Crosby, Bob Hope and Dorothy Lamour was released in 1940. Frank Butler and Don Hartman's screenplay concerns Josh Mallon (Crosby), the easy-going heir to a shipping fortune, and his buddy Ace Lannigan (Hope), who decide to get away from it all. After ending up in Singapore, they rescue the lovely Mima (Lamour) from a seedy nightspot act in which she has a lighted cigarette removed from her mouth every night by Caesar (Anthony Quinn), her swarthy South American partner. After the usual complications, Lamour chooses Crosby for her romantic partner as she did in all the 'Road' trips, although Hope was in there pitching right up to the final episode in 1962. The main reason for Crosby's continued success with the lady in the sarong may well be that he always had the big love ballad - in this case, 'Too Romantic'. Johnny Burke and Jimmy Monaco wrote that one, along with 'Sweet Potato Piper' and 'Kaigoon', while Burke and the film's director, Victor Schertzinger, contributed 'Captain Custard' and 'The Moon And The Willow Tree'. LeRoy Prinz handled the choreography, and the producer was Harlan Thompson. The general critical opinion at the time was that this film was nothing special, although it rated highly at the box-office. However, subsequent journeys to *Zanzibar* 1941, *Morocco* 1942, *Utopia* 1945, *Rio* 1947, and *Bali* 1952, were acclaimed for the outrageous laid-back humour and zany antics of the two male stars. Generally cast as a couple of likeable swindlers, with Crosby as the 'brains' and Hope in the role of the incredibly gullible fall guy, they were able to extricate themselves from any scrape simply by facing each other and going into their 'Patta-cake' routine which always ended with one of their captors, or similar adversaries, being knocked to the ground. As well as the fun and games, each of the above films in the series had some good songs by Jimmy Van Heusen and Johnny Burke, an engaging mixture of ballads and lively comedy numbers. Over the years these included 'You Lucky People You', 'It's Always You', 'Birds Of A Feather', 'Road To Morocco', 'Ain't Got A Dime To My Name (Ho-Hum)', 'Constantly', 'Moonlight Becomes You', 'Personality', 'Put It There, Pal', 'But Beautiful', 'You Don't Have To Know The Language', 'Experience', 'The Merry Go Runaround', 'Chicago Style', 'Hoot Mon', and 'To See You'. After *Road To Bali* there was a gap of 10 years before the trio were reunited for *The Road To Hong Kong* (1962) which was made in England by Melnor Pictures (producer Melvin Frank and director Norman Panama). At the time, Hope and Crosby were both 59, and in spite of the inclusion of the young and attractive Joan Collins (Lamour still came along for the ride - as herself), as well as a starry list of guest artists such as Frank Sinatra, Dean Martin, Peter Sellers, David Niven, and Jerry Colonna, it was too much to ask that things would be the same. The magic just was not there any more, and it was obviously the end of the 'Road' - and of an era - although the film did well financially. Even the songs, by Van Heusen and Sammy Cahn, were not in the previous class, but the veteran performers did their best with 'Let's Not Be Sensible', 'Teamwork', 'It's The Only Way To Travel', 'We're On The Road To Hong Kong', and 'Warmer Than A Whisper.' No matter, the memories of that historic, much-loved series still remain.

ROADIE

Ebullient vocalist Meat Loaf rose to stardom thanks to *Bat Out Of Hell*, one of the most successful albums in rock history. Its standing inspired the singer's starring role in this 1980 film, in which he plays the roadie. *Roadie* was not Meat Loaf's first on-screen venture, he previously played a part in *The Rocky Horror Picture Show*, but this venture was built around his amiable personality. As the Meat Loaf character rises through rock's multi-layered echelons, he encounters various performers including Alice Cooper, Blondie, Roy Orbison and Ramblin' Jack Elliott. Many were featured on the soundtrack which also contained contributions from Cheap Trick, Teddy Pendergrass, Pat Benatar, Styx and Asleep At The Wheel. Comedian Art Carney co-starred in this engaging feature and proved an excellent foil. *Roadie* remains an amusing picture, taking a wry view of life on the road.

ROAR OF THE GREASEPAINT- THE SMELL OF THE CROWD, THE

Leslie Bricusse and Anthony Newley's follow-up to their smash-hit *Stop The World - I Want To Get Off* floundered in the UK provinces with the popular knockabout comedian Norman Wisdom in the leading role. Adjudged unfit to face the West End critics in its present condition, producer David Merrick persuaded Newley to take over from Wisdom, and sent the show on a successful three month tryout tour of the USA and Canada before the Broadway opening at the Shubert Theatre on 16 May 1965. It proved to be very similar in style to its predecessor - an allegorical piece in which the irrepressible Cocky (Newley) and the imperious Sir (Cyril Ritchard) play the 'game' (of life) in a small arena-like area. Cocky, the little man, always plays by the rules, while the conniving Sir simply ignores them and goes his own way. Towards the end of the piece, Cocky, with the help of the Negro (Gilbert Price), begins to assert himself, and eventually he and Sir agree that the 'game' should be a tie. The British actress Sally Smith made her Broadway debut as The Kid, and Murray Tannenbaum was pretty scary as The Bully. Bricusse and Newley's score was full of good things, not all of them immediately appreciated. 'Who Can I Turn To? (When Nobody Needs Me)', which was introduced by Newley, emerged as the biggest hit, particularly in a version by Tony Bennett. Price created quite an impact with 'Feeling Good', and Ritchard, with a group of 'urchins', sang 'A Wonderful Day Like Today'. The remainder of the fine score consisted of 'The Beautiful Land', 'It Isn't Enough', 'Things To Remember', 'Put It In The Book', 'This Dream', 'Where Would You Be Without Me', 'Look At That Face', 'My First Love Song', 'The Joker', 'A Funny Funeral', 'That's What It's Like To Be Young', 'What A Man', 'Nothing Can Stop Me Now', and 'Sweet Beginning'. Several them were recorded by Sammy Davis Jnr., an enthusiastic promoter of the composers' work. Newley directed the show himself, and the musical staging was by Gillian Lynne, the choreographer and director, whose subsequent credits included Andrew Lloyd Webber's mega-hits *Cats* and *The Phantom Of The Opera*. *The Roar Of The Greaspaint* could only manage a disappointing run of 232 performances, but, fortunately for David Merrick, most of the show's original costs had been recouped during the pre-Broadway tour. A West End production in the near future would seem unlikely.

ROBBINS, JEROME

b. Jerome Rabinowitz, 11 October 1918, New York, USA, d. 29 July 1998, New York, USA. An important director, choreographer and dancer, Robbins began his career with the celebrated Ballet Theatre in New York, and subsequently appeared as a dancer on Broadway in shows such as *Great Lady*, *The Straw Hat Revue* and *Stars In Your Eyes*. In 1944, he and composer Leonard Bernstein conceived a short ballet, *Fancy Free*, which, with the participation of Betty Comden and Adolph Green, evolved into the musical *On The Town*. During the 40s and early 50s he was constantly acclaimed for his stylish and original choreography for shows such as *Billion Dollar Baby* (1945), *High*

Button Shoes (1947, Tony Award), *Look Ma, I'm Dancing* (1948), *Miss Liberty* (1949), *Call Me Madam* (1950), *The King And I* (1951) and *Two's Company* (1952). From then on, he also served as the director on series of notable productions: *The Pajama Game* (1954), *Peter Pan* (1954), *Bells Are Ringing* (1956), *West Side Story* (1957; Tony Award), *Gypsy* (1959), *A Funny Thing Happened On The Way To The Forum* (1962), *Funny Girl* (1964) and *Fiddler On The Roof* (1964). For the last-named show, one of his greatest achievements, he won Tony Awards as choreographer and director. He and Robert Wise were also awarded Oscars when they co-directed the film version of *West Side Story* in 1961. After working on the London productions of *Funny Girl* and *Fiddler On The Roof* in 1966 and 1967, Robbins turned away from the Broadway musical theatre and announced that he was devoting his life to ballet. He had worked with the New York City Ballet since 1948 as dancer, choreographer and associate artistic director, and in 1958 briefly formed his own chamber-sized company Ballets: USA. He returned to the popular field in February 1989 to direct a celebratory revue of his work entitled *Jerome Robbins' Broadway*. In a season that was so bereft of original musicals that *Kenny Loggins On Broadway* and *Barry Manilow At The Gershwin* were catagorized as such, this reminder of Broadway's glory days was greeted with relief and rejoicing (and six Tony Awards). It featured extended sequences from *West Side Story* and *Fiddler On The Roof*, along with other delights such as the gloriously incongruous 'You Gotta Have A Gimmick' from *Gypsy*, and the famous Keystone Cops chase from *High Button Shoes*, all sandwiched between excerpts from Robbins' first hit, *On The Town*, which opened and closed the show. An enormously expensive investment at $8 million, the show reportedly lost around half of that, even though it ran for 538 performances. Robbins continued to work on ballets until his death in July 1998.

ROBERT AND ELIZABETH

A musical adaptation of the 1930 play *The Barretts Of Wimpole Street* by Rudolph Besier, with music by Ron Grainer and a book and lyrics by Ronald Millar. The source of this piece was an unproduced musical, *The Third Kiss*, by the American composer and lyricist Fred G. Moritt. *Robert And Elizabeth*, which opened at the Lyric theatre in London on 20 October 1964, was set in 1845-46 and based on the true story of two poets, the bed-ridden Elizabeth Moulton-Barrett (June Bronhill) and Robert Browning (Keith Michell). After corresponding with each other for some time, they fall in love and eventually marry in spite of stern opposition from Elizabeth's tyrannical father, Edward Moulton-Barrett (John Clements). The production, directed and choreographed by Wendy Toye, captured the period perfectly, with Bronhill and Michell leading an outstanding cast. They made the most of Grainer and Millar's highly romantic score which included 'The Girls That Boys Dream About', 'I Know Now', 'The World Outside', 'Escape Me Never', 'In A Simple Way', and 'I Said Love'. *Robert And Elizabeth* ran for well over two years, a total of 948 performances. To date, the show has not played on Broadway, but was presented in Chicago (1974), Maine (1978), and at the Paper Mill

Playhouse (1982). An acclaimed production was mounted in England at the Chichester Festival Theatre in 1987, starring Mark Wynter and Gaynor Miles.

ROBERTA (FILM MUSICAL)

The Fred Astaire and Ginger Rogers bandwagon gathered pace with this 1935 adaptation of another successful Broadway musical. Naturally, the original libretto, which itself was based on Alice Duer Miller's book *Gowns By Roberta*, was tinkered with by screenwriters Jane Murfin, Sam Mintz, Glen Tryon and Allan Scott, but the basic plot remained. This concerned all-American footballer John Kent (played by Randolph Scott without a horse), who inherits his aunt's Parisian dress salon and falls in love with her assistant, a Russian princess (Irene Dunne). The latter lady was top-billed, but, as usual, Astaire and Rodgers dominated proceedings - in the nicest possible way. Four of Jerome Kern and Otto Harbach's songs from the show were retained: 'Smoke Gets In Your Eyes', 'Let's Begin', 'Yesterdays', and 'I'll Be Hard To Handle' - the latter number being given a new lyric by Bernard Dougall. Three other numbers were added: 'Indiana' (written by Ballard MacDonald and James F. Hanley in 1917), the delightful ballad 'Lovely To Look At' (Kern-Dorothy Fields), which was introduced by Irene Dunne and decorated the film's gigantic fashion parade finale, and 'I Won't Dance' (Kern-Fields-Oscar Hammerstein II) - an Astaire *tour de force*. He also served as the film's (uncredited) dance director with Hermes Pan, and this RKO production was directed by William A. Seiter. Another version of *Roberta* entitled *Lovely To Look At*, starring Howard Keel and Kathryn Grayson, was released in 1952.

ROBERTA (STAGE MUSICAL)

Opening at the New Amsterdam Theatre in New York on 18 November 1933, this show was based on Alice Duer Miller's novel *Gowns By Roberta*, and set, appropriately enough, in the high fashion capital of the world - Paris. Otto Harbach's book concerned John Kent (Ray Middleton), who used to be an All-American full-back before he inherited an interest in a dress shop named Roberta, which is operated by his Aunt Minnie (Fay Templeton). He takes on a partner, Stephanie (Tamara), who leaves it until they are almost married before revealing that she is a Russian Princess. This was a visually stunning production, the highlight of which was an elegant, lavishly mounted fashion show. Jerome Kern and Otto Harbach's score was pretty spectacular, too. It contained a ravishing trio of songs 'Smoke Gets In Your Eyes', 'The Touch Of Your Hand', and 'Yesterdays' which was introduced by Fay Templeton, who was making her final Broadway appearance in a career that had lasted for 50 years. Most of the laughs were provided by Bob Hope and George Murphy, prior to them both going off to Hollywood. They were involved in 'Let's Begin' (with Tamara), and Hope also had the amusing 'You're Devastating', and 'Something Had To Happen' with Ray Middleton and Lyda Roberti. The latter, who was described as 'a supple, Polish-accented blond', also registered strongly with 'I'll Be Hard To Handle' (lyric by Bernard Dougall). This was Jerome Kern's last Broadway hit, and although 295 performances was acceptable, it could have been better The composer who had been the catalyst for what became accepted as America's own popular music, as opposed to the European imported variety, was to spend most of the rest of his life writing music for films. Hollywood had two attempts at filming *Roberta*. The first, in 1935, starred Irene Dunne, Fred Astaire and Ginger Rogers, and the second, retitled *Lovely To Look At*, had Howard Keel, Kathryn Grayson and Ann Miller.

ROBERTS, PADDY

b. 1910, South Africa, d. September 1975, England. A songwriter, pianist and singer, Roberts' early education took place in England. He subsequently attended university in South Africa before joining a law practice. Intent on becoming a songwriter, he returned to the UK where he had some success in the late 30s with songs such as 'Angel Of The Great White Way' (written with Elton Box, Desmond Cox and Don Pelosi), and 'Horsey, Horsey' (with Box, Cox and Ralph Butler) which became popular for Jack Jackson, Billy Cotton and Henry Hall. During World War II Roberts flew with the RAF, and when peace came he became an airline captain on BOAC Constellations. Subsequently, he returned to songwriting, and during the 50s, had several UK chart hits, including 'The Book' (David Whitfield), 'Heart Of A Man' (Frankie Vaughan), 'Lay Down Your Arms' (Anne Shelton), 'Meet Me On The Corner' (Max Bygraves), 'Pickin' A Chicken' (Eve Boswell); and 'Evermore', 'Softly, Softly' (number 1) and 'You Are My First Love' (the last three sung by Ruby Murray). The latter song was featured in the British musical film *It's Great To Be Young*, and Roberts wrote several other movie songs, including 'In Love For The Very First Time' (for *An Alligator Named Daisy*, starring Diana Dors) and the title number to *The Good Companions*. His other 50s compositions included 'Johnny Is The Boy For Me', 'It's A Boy', 'That Dear Old Gentleman', 'Send For Me' and 'The Three Galleons (Las Tres Carabelas)'. Most of the aforementioned songs were written in collaboration with others, such as Hans Gottwald, C.A. Rossi, Geoffrey Parsons, Peggy Cochran, Jack Woodman, Gerry Levine, Ake Gerhard, Leon Land, Peter Hart, Garfield De Mortimer, Derek Bernfield, Augusto Alguego, G. Moreu and Lester Powell. However, towards the end of the decade, he was beginning to write unaided more and more frequently, and during the 60s he included several of his own, often wry, witty and sophisticated, numbers in an accomplished cabaret act. Probably the best-known of these is 'The Ballad Of Bethnal Green', which enjoyed a good deal of airplay, but there were many others too, including 'The Belle Of Barking Creek', 'The Big Dee-Jay', 'Follow Me', 'Country Girl', 'I Love Mary', 'The Tattooed Lady', 'What's All This Fuss About Love?', 'The Lavender Cowboy' and 'Don't Upset The Little Kiddywinks'. Roberts won several Ivor Novello Awards, and held high office in the Performing Right Society and the Song Writers Guild.

● ALBUMS: *Paddy Roberts At The Blue Angel* (Decca 1961)★★.
● COMPILATIONS: *Best Of Paddy Roberts* (MFP 1968)★★★.

ROBESON, PAUL

b. 9 April 1898, Princeton, New Jersey, USA, d. 23 January 1976, Philadephia, Pennsylvania, USA. Robeson's father was born into slavery, but he escaped at the age of 15 and eventually studied theology and became a preacher. His mother was a teacher, but she died in 1904. Education was of paramount importance to the Robeson family, one son became a physician, and the daughter was a teacher. Of all the family, Paul Robeson was by far the most gifted. In 1911 he was one of only two black students at Somerville High School in New Jersey, yet maintained a potentially dangerous high profile. He played the title role in *Othello*, sang in the glee club and also played football. He graduated with honours and won a scholarship to Rutgers University. A formidable athlete, he played football at All-American level and achieved scholastic success. In the early 20s, while studying law at Columbia University, he took part in theatrical productions and sang. In 1922 he visited England where he toured in the play *Taboo* with the noted actress Mrs Patrick Campbell. During this visit he also met pianist Lawrence Brown, with whom he was to have a close professional relationship for the rest of Brown's life. In 1923 Robeson was in the chorus of Lew Leslie's *Plantation Revue*, which starred Florence Mills, and the following year made his first film, *Body And Soul*, for Oscar Micheaux, one of the earliest black film-makers. He appeared in prestigious stage productions, including *All God's Chillun Got Wings* (1924) and *The Emperor Jones* (1925).

In 1924 he had his first brush with the Ku Klux Klan over a scene in *All God's Chillun* in which he was required to kiss the hand of a white woman. In 1925 he made his first concert appearance as a singer. The impact of this concert, which awakened Americans to the beauty of his rich bass-baritone voice, was such that he was invited to tour Europe, appearing in London in 1928 in *Show Boat* with Alberta Hunter. Also in 1928 he played the title role of Porgy in the play by DuBose and Dorothy Heyward which formed the basis of George Gershwin's *Porgy And Bess*. In 1930 he was again in London, where he took the leading role in *Othello*, playing opposite Peggy Ashcroft and Sybil Thorndike. During the 30s he made a number of films including, *The Emperor Jones* (1933) and several in the UK, among them *Sanders Of The River* (1935) and *The Proud Valley* (1939) and in 1936 he made the screen version of *Show Boat*. As in the stage production, his part was small but his rendition of 'Ol' Man River' was one of the outstanding features. The 30s also saw his first visit to Russia and he travelled to Spain to sing for the loyalist troops. He also developed an amazing facility with languages, eventually becoming fluent in 25, including Chinese and Arabic. He incorporated folk songs of many nations in his repertoire, singing them in the appropriate language. This same period saw Robeson's political awareness develop and he extended his studies into political philosophy and wrote on many topics. In 1939 he again played Othello in England, this time at Stratford-upon-Avon, and also played the role in Boston, Massachusetts, in 1942 and on Broadway in 1943. In the 40s Robeson's politicization developed, during another visit to Russia he embraced communism, although he was not blind to the regime's imperfections and spoke out against the anti-Semitism he found there. Reaction in his home country to his espousal of communism was hostile and a speech he delivered in Paris in 1949, in which he stated that although he loved America he loved Russia more than he loved those elements of America which discriminated against him because of his colour, was predictably misunderstood and widely misquoted. Also in 1949, Robeson led protests in London against the racist policies of the government of South Africa.

The FBI began to take an interest in Robeson's activities and conflict with right-wing elements and racists, especially during a rally at Peekskill in upstate New York, which drew the attention of the media away from his artistic work. An appearance before the Un-American Activities Committee drew even more attention to his already high political profile. In 1950 his passport was withdrawn because the State Department considered that his 'travel abroad at this time would be contrary to the best interests of the United States'. Ill health in the mid-50s allied to the withdrawal of his passport, severely damaged his career when he was in his vocal prime. He continued to address rallies, write extensively on political matters and make occasional concert performances by singing over telephone links to gatherings overseas. Repeated high-level efforts by other governments eventually caused the US State Department to reconsider and during his first New York concert in a decade, to a sell-out audience at Carnegie Hall, he was able to announce that his passport had been returned. This was in May 1958 and later that year he appeared on stage and television in the UK and in Russia. His comeback was triumphant and he made several successful tours of Europe and beyond. He was away for five years, returning to the USA in 1963 for more concerts and political rallies. However, pressures continued to build up and he suffered nervous exhaustion and depression. His wife of 44 years died in 1965.

Another comeback, in the late 60s, was greeted with considerable enthusiasm, but the power and quality of his voice had begun to fade. During the final years of his life Robeson toured, wrote and spoke, but his health was deteriorating rapidly and he died on 23 January 1976. Although Robeson possessed only a limited vocal range, the rich coloration of his tone and the unusual flexibility of his voice made his work especially moving. He brought to the 'Negro spiritual' an understanding and a tenderness that overcame their sometimes mawkish sentimentality, and the strength and integrity of his delivery gave them a quality no other male singer has equalled. His extensive repertoire of folk songs from many lands was remarkable and brought to his concert performances a much wider scope than that of almost any regular folk singer. Although beyond the scope of this work, Robeson's career as actor, writer and political activist cannot be ignored. His independence and outspokenness against discrimination and political injustice resulted in him suffering severely at the hands of his own government. Indeed, those close to him have intimated a belief that his final illness was brought about by the deliberate covert action of government agents. Perhaps as a side-effect of this, he is frequently omitted from reference works originating in his own country, even those which purport to be black histories. For all the dismissiveness of his own government, Robeson was highly regarded by his own people and by audiences in many lands. His massive intellect, his powerful personality and astonishing charisma, when added to his abilities as a singer and actor, helped to make him one of the outstanding Americans of the 20th century. In 1995, the Missouri Repertory Company in Missouri, Kansas, presented a play 'illustrating the extent of the man's talent and life of controversy', entitled *Paul Robeson*, which starred Don Marshall in the title role. Three years later, to mark the centenary of his birth, Robeson received a posthumous Grammy Award for lifetime achievement, and the UK National Film Theatre mounted a retrospective season, focusing on some his rarely seen British films and television programmes.

● ALBUMS: *Swing Low Sweet Chariot* (Columbia 1949)★★★, *Spirituals* (Columbia 1949)★★★, *The Incomparable Voice Of Paul Robeson* (HMV 1957)★★★, *Emperor Song* (HMV 1957)★★★, *Spirituals And Folksongs* (Vanguard 1959)★★★, *The Legendary Moscow Concert* (Revelation 1998)★★★★.

● COMPILATIONS: *Best Of Paul Robeson* (Note 1979)★★★★, *Songs Of My People* (RCA 1979)★★★, *The Essential Paul Robeson* (Vanguard 1983)★★★★, *Paul Robeson Collection - 20 Golden Greats* (Deja Vu 1987)★★★, *A Lonesome Road* (Living Era 1984)★★★, *Sings Ol' Man River And Other Favourites* (Retrospect 1985)★★★★, *Songs Of Free Men* (Columbia 1985)★★★, *Green Pastures* (Living Era 1987)★★★, *Songs Of The Mississippi - 20 Greatest Hits* (Platinum 1987)★★★★, *Golden Age Of Paul Robeson* (MFP 1988)★★★★, *The Mighty Voice Of Paul Robeson* (1988)★★★★, *The Essential Paul Robeson* (Start 1989)★★★, *Glorious Voice Of Paul Robeson* (EMI 1990)★★★★, *Paul Robeson I* (Pearl 1990)★★★, *Paul Robeson II* (Pearl 1990)★★★, *The Power And The Glory* (Sony 1991)★★★, *Paul Robeson* (Flapper 1993)★★★, with Elisabeth Welch *Songs From Their Films 1933-1940* (Conifer 1994)★★★.

● FURTHER READING: *Here I Stand*, Paul Robeson. *Paul Robeson Speaks: Writings Speeches Interviews 1918-1974*, Paul Robeson. *Paul Robeson*, Martin Baumi Duberman.

● FILMS: *Body And Soul* (1925), *The Emperor Jones* (1933), *Sanders Of The River* aka *Bosambo* (1935), *Song Of Freedom* (1936), *Show Boat* (1936), *King Solomon's Mines* (1937), *Big Fella* (1937), *Jericho* aka *Dark Sands* (1937), *The Proud Valley* (1940), *Tales Of Manhattan* (1942), *Native Land* narrator (1942), *Song Of The Rivers* singing voice (1954), *Paul Robeson: Portrait Of An Artist* (1979).

ROBIN, LEO

b. 6 April 1895, Pittsburgh, Pennsylvania, USA, d. 29 December 1984. After studying law, Robin turned to writing lyrics for songs. In the mid-20s, in collaboration with various composers, he had a number of minor successes including 'Looking Around' (music by Richard Myers) and one major hit with 'Hallelujah' (Vincent Youmans), written for the 1927 show, *Hit The Deck*. After a few uncertain years on Broadway, Robin went to Hollywood where he came into his own. Amongst his songs written for films during the next few years were 'Louise', 'Beyond The Blue Horizon' (both with Richard Whiting), 'My Ideal' (Newell Chase), 'True Blue Lou' (Sam Coslow), 'If I Were King' (Chase and Coslow), 'Prisoner Of Love' (Clarence Gaskill and Russ Columbo), 'Whispers In The Dark' (Frederick

Hollander), 'Zing A Little Zong', 'No Love, No Nothin'' (both Harry Warren) and an often-overlooked little gem, written with Jerome Kern, 'In Love In Vain'. Many of Robin's best Hollywood songs were written with composer Ralph Rainger. This collaboration produced 'Please', 'Here Lies Love', 'Give Me Liberty Or Give Me Love', 'June In January', 'With Every Breath I Take', 'Here's Love In Your Eye', 'Blue Hawaii', 'Here You Are' and two songs which became theme songs for two of America's best-known comedians, Jack Benny and Bob Hope, 'Love In Bloom' and 'Thanks For The Memory'. They were featured in pictures such as *The Big Broadcast* (1932), *International House*, *Little Miss Marker*, *Shoot The Works*, *She Loves Me Not*, *Here Is My Heart*, *The Big Broadcast Of 1936*, *The Big Broadcast Of 1937*, *Palm Springs*, *Three Cheers For Love*, *Rhythm On The Range*, *Artists And Models*, *College Holiday*, *St. Louis Blues*, *The Big Broadcast Of 1938*, *Give Me A Sailor*, *Paris Honeymoon*, *Moon Over Miami*, *My Gal Sal*, *Footlight Serenade*, and *Coney Island* (1943). After Rainger's death in 1943, Robin collaborated with other composers including Jule Styne, Harry Warren, Arthur Schwartz and Sigmund Romberg. With Styne he wrote the score for the memorable stage musical *Gentlemen Prefer Blondes*, which included songs such as 'Bye Bye, Baby', 'A Little Girl From Little Rock' and 'Diamonds Are A Girl's Best Friend'. He also worked on several films including *The Gang's All Here*, *Centennial Summer*, *The Time, The Place And The Girl*, *Casbah*, *Meet Me After The Show*, *Just For You*, *Latin Lovers*, and *Small Town Girl*. Out of these came notables songs such as 'Paducah', 'The Lady In The Tutti-Frutti Hat', 'Oh, But I Do', 'A Gal In Calico', A Rainy Night In Rio', 'What's Good About Goodbye?', 'It Was Written In The Stars', 'My Flaming Heart', 'Lost In Loveliness', and Love Is The Funniest Thing'. The last two numbers were the result of a partnership with Sigmund Romberg on the stage show *The Girl In Pink Tights* (1954), although the score had to be completed by Don Walker after Romberg's death. In 1982, in sprightly disregard of his age, Robin appeared in New York in a presentation of many of his songs.

ROBINSON, BILL 'BOJANGLES'

b. 25 May 1878, Richmond, Virginia, USA, d. 25 November 1949. As a child Robinson worked in racing stables, nursing a desire to become a jockey. He danced for fun and for the entertainment of others, first appearing on stage at the age of eight. Three years later he decided that dancing was likely to prove a more lucrative career than horseback riding. He became popular on the black vaudeville circuit and also appeared in white vaudeville as a 'pick', from pickaninny, where his dancing skills gave a patina of quality to sometimes second-rate white acts. As his reputation grew so did his prominence in showbusiness. In 1921 while working at the Palace in New York, he danced up and down the stairs leading from the stage to the orchestra pit and out of this developed his famous 'stair dance'. Although Robinson was not the first to dance on stairs, he refined the routine until it was one of the most spectacular events in the world of vernacular dance. Towards the end of the decade, though he was now 60-years-old, he was a huge success in the smash-hit production of Lew

Leslie's *Blackbirds Of 1928*. In the mid-30s he appeared at nightclubs in revues, musical comedies and other stage shows, amongst which was *The Hot Mikado*. He was so active in these years that he sometimes played different shows in different theatres on the same night. Robinson had no doubts that he was the best at what he did, a self-confidence that some took to be arrogance and which was mixed with a sometimes brooding depression at the fact that, because he was black, he had to wait until he was in his 60s before he could enjoy the fame and fortune given to less talented white dancers. In fact, he appears to have been a remarkably generous man and in addition to his massive work-load, he never refused to appear at a benefit for those artists who were less successful or ailing. It has been estimated that in one year he appeared in a staggering 400 benefits. In 1930 Robinson had made a film, *Dixiana*, but it was not until he went to Hollywood in the middle of the decade that he made a breakthrough in this medium.

He danced in a string of popular films, including some with Shirley Temple. By 1937 Robinson was earning $6,600 a week for his films, a strikingly high sum for a black entertainer in Hollywood at the time. In 1943 he played his first leading role in *Stormy Weather*, an all-black musical in which he starred opposite Lena Horne. Despite being in his early 70s when he made the film he performed his stair dance and even if he was outclassed by the Nicholas Brothers, his was a remarkable performance. In addition to dancing, Robinson also sang in a light, ingratiating manner, memorably recording 'Doing The New Low Down' in 1932 with Don Redman And His orchestra. Although his high salary meant that he was estimated to have earned more than $2 million during his career, Robinson's generosity was such that when he died in November 1949 he was broke. Half a million people lined the funeral route of the man who was known with some justification as the Mayor of Harlem. In 1993, a potential Broadway show entitled *Bojangles*, with a book by Douglas Jones and a score by Charles Strouse and the late Sammy Cahn, was being workshopped in various provincial theatres.

● FURTHER READING: *Mister Bojangles*, Jim Haskins and N.R Mitgang.

ROCK 'N' ROLL HIGH SCHOOL

Directed by Alan Arkush and produced by exploitation king Roger Corman, *Rock 'n' Roll High School* starred P.J. Soles in yet another reworking of the 'campus' formula. Although released in 1979, the film bore the stylistic trappings of the 50s, grafting contemporary pop styles on a tired plot. Where the Twist and surfing had provided past genres, here it was punk, with the Soles' character's love of the Ramones the key to the plot. The US quartet played a succession of their best-known songs, including 'Sheena Is A Punk Rocker', 'Pinhead', 'Blitzkrieg Bop' and 'I Wanna Be Sedated', but *Rock 'n' Roll High School* frustratingly failed to exploit the cartoon-like qualities of the group's music and image. Such facets were equally drawn from the era inspiring the film itself. Records by Devo, the Velvet Underground and MC5 were also heard on the soundtrack, alongside distinctly non-new wave acts

Fleetwood Mac, Wings and Chuck Berry. *Rock 'n' Roll High School* failed to encapsulate punk nor invoke a cross-generation sense of rebellion.

ROCK 'N' ROLL REVUE

Jazz and R&B performers were at the fore of this 1956 film, despite its grossly misleading title. Also known as *Harlem Rock 'n' Roll*, it was shot at New York's fabled Apollo Theatre. Lionel Hampton, Duke Ellington and Nat 'King' Cole headed a star-studded cast that also featured the Clovers, Joe Turner and Ruth Brown. Shot in sepia-inspired yellow and brown - known as Wondercolour - the film captures several performers at their peak and provides a fascinating insight into several acts inspiring, although not recording, rock 'n' roll. Curiously, the portion featuring Dinah Washington was cut from the UK print, but *Rock 'n' Roll Revue* remains a highly interesting feature.

ROCK AROUND THE CLOCK

Fred Sears directed this 1956 second feature, inspired by the reaction generated by Bill Haley And The Comets' contribution to *The Blackboard Jungle*. Although not seen on-screen, the group's recording of 'Rock Around The Clock' had been heard over the opening credits, provoking riots in cinemas. The same occurred when this film was screened, prompting several local authorities to ban it from municipal screens. The first feature wholly devoted to rock 'n' roll music, *Rock Around The Clock* cast Haley's group as a small-town act that a bank manager tries to turn into a national attraction, despite the efforts of a booking agent to sabotage his plans. The Comets naturally provide the lion's share of the material, including 'Rock A Beatin' Boogie', 'See You Later Alligator' and the title track. The Platters, Little Richard and Freddie Bell And His Bellboys are among the other acts included, as is disc jockey Alan Freed in the first of a string of roles in rock 'n' roll films. Although hardly innovatory in terms of plot or acting, for better or worse, *Rock Around The Clock* opened the doors for celluloid pop.

ROCK ROCK ROCK

Manifestly another formula 'quickie' made to cash in on rock 'n' roll, *Rock Rock Rock* nonetheless contains several points of interest to pop historians. This 1957 film, reportedly shot in two weeks, starred Tuesday Weld as the girlfriend of an aspiring entrepreneur who organizes a concert. Famed disc jockey Alan Freed makes an obligatory appearance - herein leading an 18-piece band - but *Rock Rock Rock* is notable for the acts it enshrines. Frankie Lymon And The Teenagers offer the memorable 'I'm Not A Juvenile Delinquent', while doo-wop acts the Flamingos and Moonglows perform 'Would I Be Crying' and 'Over And Over Again', respectively. Chuck Berry makes his celluloid debut with 'You Can't Catch Me' and vibrant rockabilly act the Johnny Burnette Trio roar through 'Lonesome Train' in what was their only appearance on film. LaVern Baker, the Three Chuckles and the Bowties are among the others on offer. Ms. Weld contributes 'I Never Had A Sweetheart' and 'Little Blue Wren', but her 'voice' was provided by the then-unknown Connie Francis. Much of the material aired in *Rock Rock Rock* was released by the Chess label, who advertised the set as the first rock soundtrack album. Although failing to break new ground as far as plot and style were concerned, the film showcases several seminal acts at the height of their creative powers.

ROCK-A-BYE BABY

Frank Tashlin, who directed the seminal rock film *The Girl Can't Help It*, took charge of this 1958 feature. It starred comedian Jerry Lewis, former partner of Dean Martin, who excelled in zany, 'misfit' roles, notably *The Nutty Professor*. In *Rock-A-Bye Baby* he plays a nanny, responsible for a film star's triplets, who finds time to satirize rock 'n' roll and US television. The film is largely forgettable, although Lewis does perform a duet, 'In The Land Of La La La', with his 12-year old son, Gary. In the following decade, Gary Lewis became a pop star in his own right as leader of Gary Lewis And The Playboys, who enjoyed a number 1 US hit with 'This Diamond Ring', following it with six further Top 10 entries.

ROCKERS

Rockers is the story of drummer Leroy 'Horsemouth' Wallace and his fictional attempt to become involved in the Jamaican music business. The film featured a host of reggae stars, including Big Youth, Jacob Miller, Gregory Isaacs, Richard 'Dirty Harry' Hall, Robbie Shakespeare and Kiddus I. The film also included cameos from Burning Spear, the Mighty Diamonds, Doctor Alimantado, Leroy Smart, Big Joe, Jack Ruby and Joe Gibbs, to name but a few. The story begins with Horsemouth buying a motorbike which he decorates with the Lion Of Judah. Once his bike is suitably embellished, he successfully attempts to secure records from Joe Gibbs and Jack Ruby. His music business aspirations are encouraged by a host of Jamaican stars, including Tommy McCook, who is seen rehearsing in his backyard with Herman Marquis and Bobby Ellis. In addition to selling records, Horsemouth is asked to support Inner Circle for a regular booking. While at the venue, he trifles with the affections of the owner's daughter, Sunshine, which leads to a violent confrontation. In addition, Horsemouth's bike is stolen by an organized crime group led by Sunshine's father. Horsemouth discovers that his bike is in a warehouse along with an extraordinary haul. Supported by the all-star line-up, he recovers his bike along with the spoils, and in a clandestine operation distributes the 'ill-gotten' gains around Trenchtown. The film's soundtrack featured classic songs from Bunny Wailer, Peter Tosh, Junior Byles, the Mighty Maytones, the Heptones, Junior Murvin, Third World, the Upsetters, Kiddus I, Burning Spear, Gregory Isaacs and Jacob Miller. Though not earning the cult status of *The Harder They Come*, the movie was greeted with enthusiasm in Jamaica, particularly on account of the numerous cameo appearances. In promoting the film Horsemouth made a triumphant appearance at the One Love Peace Concert, where he was hailed as Jamaica's biggest movie star.

● ALBUMS: Various Artists *Rockers* (Island 1979)★★★★.

ROCKY HORROR PICTURE SHOW, THE (FILM MUSICAL)

Borrowing themes from Hammer Horror films and pop, *The Rocky Horror Show* was a huge success as a stage production. Tim Curry reprised his starring role as Frank N. Furter in this 1975 film version which also featured its author Richard O'Brien, Susan Sarandon (later in *Thelma And Louise*) and Meat Loaf in its cast. The premise - a young couple take refuge from a storm in a Gothic castle populated by aliens from the planet Transylvania - was a slight variation on a well-worn theme, but Curry's outrageously camp performance provided the film's memorable qualities. Released in the wake of rock's androgynous period, headed by David Bowie, *The Rocky Horror Picture Show* quickly became a cult favourite, a standing it has retained over the ensuing years. Many of the songs were peppered with sexual innuendo, tickling an audience imagining they were watching something daring. However, *The Rocky Horror Picture Show* is as traditional as the ideas inspiring it. The 21st birthday release of the movie on video included outtakes, alternative takes, the original trailer, and interviews with the stars.

ROCKY HORROR SHOW, THE (STAGE MUSICAL)

One of the phenomenons of the UK musical theatre in the 70s and 80s, this rock musical opened at the Royal Court Theatre Upstairs on 19 June 1973. The book, music and lyrics were by Richard O'Brien who had played a minor role in the London production of *Jesus Christ Superstar*. The abolition of theatrical censorship in Britain nearly five years previously, provided the opportunity to present what turned out to be a jumble of 50s and 60s sexual deviation, drug abuse, horror and science fiction movies, rock 'n' roll music, and much else besides.

The story followed a young all-American couple, Brad (Christopher Malcolm) and Janet (Julie Covington), who take refuge in a remote castle. It is the home of several weird characters, including Frank 'N' Furter (Tim Curry), a 'sweet transvestite from Transsexual, Transylvania', Magenta (Patricia Quinn), an usherette, Columbia (Little Nell), who tap-danced a lot, and the satanic Riff Raff (Richard O'Brien). The outrageously charismatic Frank 'N' Furter, dressed in the obligatory black stockings and suspenders, creates his perfect man, Rocky Horror, when he is not ravishing both Brad and Janet, and the remainder of the plot has to be experienced to be believed. The mostly 50s-style songs included 'Science Fiction, Double Feature', 'Dammit, Janet', 'Over At The Frankenstein Place', 'Sweet Transvestite', 'Time Warp', 'Sword Of Damocles', 'Hot Patootie (Bless My Soul)', 'Touch-A-Touch-A-Touch-A-Touch Me', 'Once In A While', 'Rose Tint My World', 'I'm Going Home', and 'Superheroes'. This 'harmless indulgence of the most monstrous fantasies' caught on in a big way, especially when it moved in August 1973 to the ideal environment of a seedy cinema in the trendy King's Road, Chelsea. After an incredible period of five and a half years, Frank 'N' Furter and his pals finally made it to the West End's Comedy Theatre in April 1979, where they stayed until September of the following year. The total London run amounted to 2,960 performances, but New York audiences demurred, and that production closed after only 45 performances at the Belasco theatre in 1975. In the following year, several of the original cast reassembled to film the *The Rocky Horror Picture Show* which proved to be a critical and financial disaster in the UK, but, ironically, in the USA where the original show had flopped, the movie became a hot cult item on university campuses. However, legend has it that the Waverly Theatre in New York was the scene of the first example of the audience participation craze which has since become the norm. Fanatical fans in America and many other countries in the world, including Britain, who return again and again to see the movie, now dress up in clothes similar to those worn on the screen, and join in with the dialogue and lyrics, as well as constantly heckling and introducing their own ad-lib material. The movie's success helped the stage show's survival in the UK, where, on various provincial tours, the audiences repeated the excesses of the cinema. One of the 'highlights' comes when Brad and Jane are married, and a barrage of rice and various other celebratory souvenirs are despatched from the auditorium, threatening the life and limbs of the participating thespians. It even happened when the show was revived briefly at the Piccadilly Theatre in London in 1990, where, when Frank 'N' Furter sang 'The chips are down, I needed a break', the audience tended to hurl bars of KitKat on to the stage. Two years later, in addition to *The Rocky Horror* fan clubs that have sprung up around the world, the first convention of the British version, snappily called 'Timewarp', was held in London.

A 1991 Dublin production of the piece was halted when Frank 'N' Furter's costume fell foul of the Irish decency laws. The 21st Birthday Anniversary production of *The Rocky Horror Show* took place at the Duke of York's Theatre in 1994, with Jonathon Morris as Frank 'N' Furter, and the celebrations began all over again in the following year when the leading character, who 'teeters between Princess Margaret and an outrageous queen in black suspenders', was played by ex-ice skating champion Robin Cousins. Former 'Joseph' Jason Donovan swapped his loincloth for the extravagant Frank 'N' Furter gear in a 1997 Australian production, and he also headed the cast of a Birmingham Repertory Theatre staging which toured the UK a year later. Other 25th anniversary stagings took place in Sydney, Australia, where Frank 'N' Furter was played by Tim Ferguson, a former member of the comedy group the Doug Anthony All Stars, Italy (US actor and singer Bob Simon), and Los Angeles (David Arquette, known for his performance as an inept policeman in the 1996 movie *Scream*).

● FURTHER READING: *The Rocky Horror Show: Participation Guide*, Sal Piro and Michael Hess.

RODGERS, MARY

(see Rodgers, Richard)

RODGERS, RICHARD

b. 28 June 1902, Hammells Station, Arverne, Long Island, USA, d. 30 December 1979, New York, USA. One of the all-time great composers for the musical theatre, Rodgers was raised in a comfortable middle-class family and developed an early love of music. Encouraged by his parents, he was able to pick out a tune on the piano at the age of four, and wrote his first songs, 'Campfire Days' and 'Auto Show Girl' (lyric: David Dyrenforth), when he was 14. Many years later, when he was asked what he had done before he began composing music, he is supposed to have said: 'I was a baby.' In 1919, Rodgers was introduced to the lyricist Lorenz Hart, and they collaborated on the scores for two well-received Columbia University Varsity shows, *Fly With Me* and *You'll Never Know*, and on songs for other productions, such as the Broadway musicals *A Lonely Romeo* (1919, 'Any Old Place With You') and *Poor Little Ritz Girl* (1920). The early 20s presented few further opportunities, and a frustrated Rodgers was contemplating taking a job as a wholesaler in the baby-wear business, when, in 1925, he and Hart were asked to write the score for a benefit show in aid of the Theatre Guild, the prestigious theatrical production organization. The resulting revue, *The Garrick Gaieties*, was so successful that it began a commercial run that lasted for 211 performances. Rodgers and Hart's lively and amusing score included the charming 'Sentimental Me' as well as one of their most enduring standards, 'Manhattan'. A second edition of the *Gaieties* in 1926, featured another of the songwriters' brightest and inventive numbers, 'Mountain Greenery', which was associated in later years with the distinguished jazz singer Mel Tormé. From this point, Rodgers and Hart were off and running, and during the next few years, wrote some of their most romantic and innovative songs for a series of musical shows that met with varying degrees of success. They included *Dearest Enemy* (1925, 'Here In My Arms'), *The Girl Friend* (1926, 'The Blue Room', 'The Girl Friend'), *Lido Lady* (London 1926, 'Try Again Tomorrow'), *Peggy-Ann* (1926, 'Where's That Rainbow?', 'A Tree In The Park'), *Betsy* (a 39 performance flop in 1926, 'This Funny World'), *One Dam Thing After Another* (London 1927, 'My Heart Stood Still'), *A Connecticut Yankee* (1927, 'Thou Swell', 'On A Desert Island With Thee!', 'Nothing's Wrong'), *She's My Baby* (1928, 'You're What I Need'), *Present Arms!* (1928, 'You Took Advantage Of Me', 'A Kiss For Cinderella'), *Chee-Chee* (a 31-performance flop in 1928, 'Better Be Good to Me'), *Lady Fingers* (1929, 'I Love You More Than Yesterday'), *Spring Is Here* (1929, 'With A Song In My Heart', 'Why Can't I?', 'Baby's Awake Now'), *Heads Up!* (1929, 'A Ship Without A Sail'), *Simple Simon* ('Ten Cents A Dance', 'He Was Too Good To Me'), and *Ever Green* (London 1930, 'Dancing On The Ceiling', 'No Place But Home', 'The Colour Of Her Eyes'). When the team wrote the optimistic 'I've Got Five Dollars' for Ann Sothern and Jack Whiting to sing in *America's Sweetheart* in 1931, the USA was in the middle of the Depression. Although more than 20 new musicals were being produced each season on Broadway, Rodgers and Hart's previous five shows had been relatively unsuccessful, and they spent much of the early 30s in Hollywood writing some memorable songs for early film musicals such as *The Hot Heiress* (1931, 'You're The Cats'), *Love Me Tonight* (1932, 'Isn't It Romantic?', 'Mimi', 'Lover'), *The Phantom President* (1932, 'Give Her A Kiss'), *Hallelujah, I'm A Bum* (1933, 'You Are Too Beautiful'), *Hollywood Party* (1934, 'Hello'), *Nana* (1934,

'That's Love'), and *Mississippi* (1935, 'It's Easy To Remember', 'Soon', 'Down By The River'). They also contributed a song called 'The Bad In Every Man' (previously known as 'Prayer') to the Oscar-winning screen thriller *Manhattan Melodrama*. After Hart wrote a new lyric, it was retitled 'Blue Moon', and became one of their biggest hits. That song, alongside many of their other successful numbers, was featured in the 1948 biopic *Words And Music*, in which Rodgers was played by Tom Drake and Hart by Mickey Rooney.

Rodgers and Hart returned to New York in 1935, and embarked on a body of work that surpassed even their previous achievements. *Jumbo* (1935), with a score containing three outstanding numbers, 'My Romance', 'Little Girl Blue' and 'The Most Beautiful Girl In The World', was followed by the splendid *On Your Toes* (1936, 'Glad To Be Unhappy', 'There's A Small Hotel', 'Too Good For The Average Man', 'Slaughter On Tenth Avenue'), *Babes In Arms* (1937, 'I Wish I Were In Love Again', 'The Lady Is A Tramp', 'My Funny Valentine', 'Where Or When', 'Johnny One Note'), *I'd Rather Be Right* (1937, 'Have You Met Miss Jones?'), *I Married An Angel* (1938, 'Spring Is Here', 'I Married An Angel', 'At The Roxy Music Hall'), *The Boys From Syracuse* (1938, 'Falling In Love With Love', 'This Can't Be Love', 'Sing For Your Supper', 'You Have Cast Your Shadow On The Sea'), *Too Many Girls* (1939, 'I Didn't Know What Time It Was', 'Give It Back To The Indians', 'I Like To Recognize The Tune', 'You're Nearer'), *Higher And Higher* (1940, 'It Never Entered My Mind'), *Pal Joey* ('Bewitched', 'I Could Write A Book', 'Den Of Iniquity') and *By Jupiter* (1942, 'Wait Till You See Her', 'Nobody's Heart', 'Careless Rhapsody'). *Pal Joey*, in particular, was regarded as a landmark in Broadway history, partly because it was the first musical in which the leading character, played by Gene Kelly, was a villain - an anti-hero. Rodgers and Hart's final work together was probably on the songs for a revised production of their 1927 hit, *A Connecticut Yankee*, which contained the witty 'To Keep My Love Alive'. By the time that show opened on 3 November 1943, Hart's physical condition, which had been worsening for several years, had deteriorated to such an extent that he was unable to work, and he died some two weeks later.

In the previous year, Rodgers had been asked by the Theatre Guild to write the score for what eventually became *Oklahoma!* (1943). With Hart unavailable, he began a collaboration with Oscar Hammerstein II that produced some of the biggest blockbusters in the (pre-Andrew Lloyd Webber) history of the musical theatre. Marvellous songs such as 'Oh, What A Beautiful Mornin'', 'People Will Say We're In Love', 'The Surrey With The Fringe On Top', and the rousing title number, were cleverly integrated into the story, and *Oklahoma!* won a special Pulitzer Prize, and ran for 2,212 performances in New York. Next came the magnificent *Carousel* (1945, 'If I Loved You', 'June Is Bustin' Out All Over', 'What's The Use Of Wond'rin'', 'You'll Never Walk Alone', 'Soliloquy'), which is often regarded as Rodgers and Hammerstein's best score. Also in 1945, the partners wrote their only original film score for the highly popular *State Fair*, which featured the exuberant 'It's A Grand Night For Singing' and the lovely ballad 'It Might As Well Be Spring'. Back on Broadway, the uncharacteristic *Allegro* (1947, 'A Fellow Needs A Girl', 'The Gentleman Is A Dope'), complete with its Greek chorus, was a disappointment. However, there were more triumphs just around the corner in the shape of *South Pacific* (1949, 'I'm Gonna Wash That Man Right Outa My Hair', 'Bali Ha'i', 'Some Enchanted Evening', 'This Nearly Was Mine', 'There Is Nothin' Like A Dame'), which ran for nearly five years and won the Pulitzer Prize for Drama, and *The King And I* (1951, 'Hello, Young Lovers', 'I Have Dreamed', 'Shall We Dance?', 'We Kiss In A Shadow', 'Getting To Know You').

In 1952, Richard Rodgers wrote the music for the NBC documentary television series *Victory At Sea*, for which he was awarded the US Navy's Distinguished Public Service Medal. A musical theme from one of the episodes entitled 'Beyond The Southern Cross', attracted a great deal of interest, and Rodgers used it, with a lyric by Hammerstein, as a part of the score for their next Broadway show, *Me And Juliet* (1953). The song was called 'No Other Love', and featured again in television and stage versions of *Cinderella*. Neither *Me And Juliet*, or Rodgers and Hammerstein's Broadway follow-up, *Pipe Dream* (1955, 'All At Once You Love Her', 'The Next Time It Happens'), are considered to be among their best work. Nor, for that matter, is *Flower Drum Song* ('I Enjoy Being A Girl', 'Sunday', 'Love, Look Away'), but the show did endure for 602 performances, and was still running when the final Rodgers and Hammerstein smash hit, *The Sound Of Music* ('Climb Ev'ry Mountain', 'Edelweiss', 'Do-Re-Mi', 'My Favourite Things', 'The Sound Of Music') opened in November 1959 and ran for nearly three and a half years in New York, and more than five and a half in London. The film versions of this and several other Rodgers and Hammerstein shows were among the highest-grossing movie musicals of the 50s and 60s. Less than a year after *The Sound Of Music* opened, Hammerstein was dead. Rodgers subsequently contributed five new songs (music and lyrics) to the 1962 remake of *State Fair*, and wrote the complete score for the Broadway musical *No Strings* ('The Sweetest Sounds'), which ran for 580 performances. For his work on that show he won a Tony Award for Outstanding Composer, and a Grammy for the Original Cast album. From then on, apart from providing both words and music for a US television adaptation of *Androcles And The Lion* (1967), starring Noël Coward and Norman Wisdom, for the remainder of his career Rodgers worked with established lyricists. These included Stephen Sondheim (in 1965 for *Do I Hear A Waltz?*, 'We're Gonna Be All Right', 'Do I Hear A Waltz'), Martin Charnin (in 1970 for *Two By Two*, 'I Do Not Know A Day I Did Not Love You'), Sheldon Harnick (in 1976 for *Rex*), and Martin Charnin (in 1979 for *I Remember Mama*). When he was working on the last two shows, which were both dismal failures at the box office, Rodgers was a sick man, and he died in December 1979. The emotionally uplifting and often witty melodies he left behind - written in collaboration with two supremely gifted, but temperamentally opposite partners - played an important part in the development of American's own indigenous popular music, and in the acceptance of the musical as an important and respected art form. His honours included special Tonys in 1962 and 1972, a Trustee Grammy Award, and the 1979 Lawrence Langner Award for Distinguished Lifetime Achievement in the Theatre. In 1993, on the 50th anniversary of the birth of his second momentous partnership, a celebratory revue entitled *A Grand Night For Singing*, which was crammed with Rodgers and Hammerstein's songs, was presented in New York.

Richard Rodgers' elder daughter, Mary Rodgers (b. 11 January 1931, New York, USA), enjoyed substantial success in the musical theatre with her music for *Once Upon A Mattress* (1959). Earlier, she had studied harmony and counterpoint and written numerous songs for children's records. Rodgers collaborated with lyricist and librettist Marshall Barer on *Once Upon A Mattress*, which was based on the fairytale *The Princess And The Pea*. It ran for 216 performances off-Broadway, and a further 244 at Broadway's Alvin Theatre. Her next effort on Broadway was a musical about the Peace Corps, *Hot Spot* (1963), which had lyrics by Martin Charnin. It folded rapidly, in spite of the presence in the cast of Judy Holliday. Rodgers worked with Barer again in 1966 on *The Mad Show*, which was inspired by the immensely popular *Mad* magazine. The *Mad Show* stayed at the New Theatre, off-Broadway, for 871 performances, and included one song that Rodgers wrote with Stephen Sondheim, entitled 'The Boy From', which mocked the worldwide bossa nova hit, 'The Girl From Ipanema'. In 1978 Rodgers contributed material to the New York musical *Working*, along with others such as Stephen Schwartz, and has also been involved with several projects that were not developed. One that was developed, however, was *The Griffin And The Minor Canon*, which was described as 'a folk tale about the bonding friendship between the last griffin on earth and a minor church official in a small French village.' It had a book by Wendy Kesselman and lyrics by Ellen Fitzhugh, and was presented at Stockbridge, Massachusetts, in August 1988. Over the years, Rodgers has also written several children's books, including the classic teen novel *Freaky Friday*. She later adapted it into a movie and a children's musical.

In 1993, the revue *Hey, Love: The Songs Of Mary Rodgers*, played at Eighty-Eight's in New York. The show, named after a song from *Hot Spot*, was conceived and directed by Richard Maltby Jnr. It contained some of his lyrics, and those of Martin Charnin, Marshall Barer, John Forster, Stephen Sondheim and William Shakespeare.

● ALBUMS: *Mary Martin Sings Richard Rodgers Plays* (1958)★★★.
● FURTHER READING: *Musical Stages: His Autobiography*, Richard Rodgers. *With A Song In His Heart*, David Ewen. *The Rodgers And Hammerstein Story*, Stanley Green. *Rodgers And Hart: Bewitched, Bothered And Bedevilled*, S. Marx and J. Clayton. *The Sound Of Their Music: The Story Of Rodgers And Hammerstein*, Frederick Nolan. *Richard Rodgers*, William G. Hyland.

ROGERS, GINGER

b. Virginia Katherine McMath, 16 July 1911, Independence, Missouri, USA, d. 25 April 1995, Rancho Mirage, California, USA. A charming and vivacious actress, dancer and singer, Ginger Rogers became a movie legend after partnering Fred Astaire in a series of memorable musicals between 1933 and 1949. She grew up in

Fort Worth, Texas, and, after winning a Charleston contest at the age of 15, worked in vaudeville for a time before making a big impression in the 1929 Guy Bolton-Bert Kalmar-Harry Ruby Broadway musical *Top Speed*. A year later she played the lovelorn postmistress Molly Gray, introducing George and Ira Gershwin's lovely song 'But Not For Me', in *Girl Crazy*. Also in 1930, Rogers made her first feature film, *Young Man Of Manhattan*, which was followed by several others, in which she generally played streetwise blondes (after dying her hair), including *42nd Street* (as Anytime Annie) and *Gold Diggers Of 1933*. That was also the year in which she was teamed with Astaire in RKO's *Flying Down To Rio*, the first of 10 light-hearted and tuneful musicals, through which they became the most beloved dance duo in movie history. The films were *The Gay Divorcee*, *Roberta*, *Top Hat*, *Follow The Fleet*, *Swing Time*, *Shall We Dance*, *Carefree*, *The Story Of Vernon And Irene Castle*, and - after a break of 10 years - *The Barkleys Of Broadway* (1949). Even before the two stars went their separate ways in 1939, Ginger Rogers had been playing critically acclaimed dramatic roles in films such as *Stage Door*, and, during the rest of her film career, she continued to excel in both serious and comedy parts, winning the best actress Oscar for her outstanding performance in *Kitty Foyle* (1940). After making her last picture, *Harlow*, in 1964, she returned to the stage in the following year, taking over the leading role from Carol Channing on Broadway in *Hello, Dolly!*, and subsequently touring with the show. In 1969 she opened at London's Theatre Royal Drury Lane in another Jerry Herman musical, *Mame*, the first time British audiences had been given the opportunity to see the show. On her return to the USA she formed the *Rogue River Revues*, out of which came the *Ginger Rogers Show* which toured major cities in the USA in the late 70s and played two weeks at the London Palladium. In later years she became a fashion and beauty consultant and also spent a good deal of time pursuing her hobby of painting. In 1986 Rogers attempted to block the distribution of Federico Fellini's film *Ginger And Fred*, which told of two small-time entertainers who do an impression of Astaire and Rogers, because 'it depicted the film's dance team as having been lovers'. In real life Ginger Rogers was married five times, first to Jack Pepper with whom she danced for a time in the early days, and then to actor Lew Ayres, US marine Jack Briggs, actor Jacques Bergerac, and finally actor-director-producer William Marshall. In 1993, more than 60 years after she came to prominence when playing Molly in *Girl Crazy*, Ginger Rogers attended a performance of the hit Broadway production *Crazy For You*, which was adapted from that very same Gershwin show. She made another rare public appearance in December 1994 to receive a dedication at the European launch of the annual International Achievement in Arts Awards at London's Dominion Theatre.

● ALBUMS: *Miss Ginger Rogers* (1978)★★★, *20 Golden Greats* (1986)★★★★, *Curtain Calls* (1988)★★★, *Rare Recordings 1930-1972* (1989)★★★★, *Fred Astaire And Ginger Rogers Story* (1989)★★★★.

● FURTHER READING: *The Fred Astaire And Ginger Rogers Book*, Arlene Croce. *Ginger: My Story* (her autobiography).

ROGERS, WILL

(see Will Rogers Follies, The)

ROLLING STONES ROCK 'N' ROLL CIRCUS, THE

The 60s most enigmatic rock film, *The Rolling Stones Rock 'n' Roll Circus*, although completed, has never been screened. Shot in 1968, it was the subject of considerable publicity, notably a lengthy feature in *Rolling Stone* magazine. Stills photographer Michael Cooper documented the proceedings, which were set in a carnival big top, with the participants dressed in costume as clowns and ringmasters. John Lennon, Yoko Ono and Marianne Faithfull are among the assembled cast; the first-named completed a ravaged reading of 'Yer Blues' with the aid of Keith Richard and Eric Clapton. Other musical contributions were drawn from Jethro Tull, Taj Mahal, Dick Heckstall-Smith, Stephen Stills, the Who and, of course, the Rolling Stones themselves. Part of the Who's set - a virulent version of their mini-opera, 'A Quick One While He's Away' - surfaced later on the group's own documentary, *The Kid's Are Alright*. So powerful was the Who's performance, it has been suggested the Stones withheld the *Rock 'n' Roll Circus*, as they feared being upstaged. In subsequent interviews they admitted giving a sub-par set as they were tired from the day's events. The film finally surfaced in 1996; on video and as an album, the Stones' last live show with Brian Jones is a historically important piece of rock indulgence.

● ALBUMS: *Rock 'n' Roll Circus* (Abkco 1996).

ROMAN SCANDALS

This Eddie Cantor vehicle, which was produced by Samuel Goldwyn and released by United Artists in 1933, proved to be one the most entertaining of all the comedian's 15 or so films. The screenplay, which was the work of William Anthony McGuire, George Oppenheimer, Nat Perrin, and Arthur Sheekman, cast Cantor as a law-abiding resident of a small town in Oklahoma. Concerned at the level of bribery and corruption all around him, he joins in the political process to try and change things for the better. Most of the film is concerned with a dream in which he is transported back in time to ancient Rome where he discovers what *real* corruption is all about! Cantor ran the full gamut of his energetic, eye-rolling shtick, and director Frank Tuttle managed to manoeuvre his star into blackface (even in ancient Rome), a chariot race, and a scene in which the modesty of a gaggle of gorgeous girls (including the 23-year-old Lucille Ball) is only maintained by their fashionably long tresses. Broadway torch singer Ruth Etting, making her movie debut, introduced the lovely ballad 'No More Love', and Cantor's high-pitched voice was heard to great effect on Harry Warren and Al Dubin's other songs, 'Keep Young And Beautiful', 'Build A Little Home', and 'Put A Tax On Love' (lyric also with L. Gilbert Wolfe). Also among the cast were Gloria Stuart, David Manners, Edward Arnold, Veree Teasdale, and Alan Mowbray.

ROMANCE ON THE HIGH SEAS

Songwriter Sammy Cahn used to claim much of the credit for bringing band singer Doris Day to the attention of the Warner Brothers studio which led to her feature film debut in this movie released in 1948. Whatever the facts of the case, Day just about stole the film from under the noses of top-billed stars Janis Paige, Jack Carson and Don DeFore. Her light comedy touch was evident right from the start of this slight and corny story about mistaken identities on a luxurious Caribbean cruise. Oscar Levant was in the supporting cast - which is always an encouraging sign - along with S.Z Sakall, Eric Blore, Fortunio Bonanova, William Bakewell, Franklin Pangborn, and guest artists the Page Cavanaugh Trio, Sir Lancelot, the Samba Kings and Avon Long. Jule Styne and that same Sammy Cahn produced an enjoyable score which gave Day two big record hits, 'It's Magic' and 'Put 'Em In A Box, Tie 'Em With A Ribbon', as well as 'I'm In Love' and 'It's You Or No One'. The rest of the score consisted of 'Run, Run, Run', 'The Tourist Trade', and 'Cuban Rhapsody' (Levant-Ray Heindorf). The musical numbers were created and directed by Busby Berkeley and the screenplay was written by Philip G. Epstein (with additional dialogue by I.A.L. Diamond) from a story by S. Pondal Rios and Carlos A. Olivari. Michael Curtiz directed this bright, entertaining Technicolor film which was re-titled *It's Magic* for UK distribution.

ROMANCE, ROMANCE

On the 1 May 1988, a few weeks after *The Phantom Of The Opera* had conquered New York's theatre land with a sensational opening night at the Majestic Theatre, *Romance, Romance* took up residence nearby at the 499-seater Helen Hayes Theatre, Broadway's smallest house. *Romance, Romance* had transferred from off-Broadway's Actor's Outlet Theatre, where it began its life in the fall of the previous year. There could hardly have been a greater contrast: Andrew Lloyd Webber's mega-musical, with its famous chandelier and hi-tech special effects, and this charming, witty, and sometimes cynical production, containing two one-act musical comedies. Both are independent of each other, yet fit neatly together. In the first, *The Little Comedy*, which is based on Arthur Schnitzler's short story of the same name, two wealthy and worldly Viennese - Alfred Von Wilmers (Scott Bakula) and Josefine Weninger (Alison Fraser) - masquerade as members of the bourgeoisie (he, a struggling poet; she, a seamstress). Both are hoping of course that someone will love them for themselves - not for their position or money. They meet, they love, they get bored on a trip to the country, they part. What relief! Robert Hoshour and Deborah Graham played 'Him' and 'Her', the couple's alter egos. The beguiling songs that accompanied their brief affair were written by Keith Herrman (music) and Barry Harman (lyrics and book), and included 'The Little Comedy', 'Goodbye, Emil', 'It's Not Too Late', 'Great News', 'Oh, What A Performance!', 'I'll Always Remember The Song', 'Happy, Happy, Happy', 'Women Of Vienna', 'Yes, It's Love', 'A Rustic Country Inn', 'The Night It Had To End', 'The Little Comedy' (finalé). *Summer Share*,

adapted from the one-act play, *Le Pain De Menage*, written in 1899 by Frenchman Jules Renard, was the second piece. Two contemporary couples, Sam and Barb (Scott Bakula and Deborah Graham) and Lenny and Monica (Robert Hoshour and Alison Fraser) agree to get away from the city and relocate to a beach house for the weekend. Sam and Monica have always been really good friends, but on this particular occasion in the wee small hours, fuelled with a few drinks, and with empty marriages on both sides, their self-restraint reaches breaking point. They set out with the intention of having an affair, but return guilt-ridden and awkward after only a few minutes. Later, they and their partners resign themselves to accepting life (imperfect) as it is. It included another fine set of numbers: 'Summer Share', 'Think Of The Odds', 'It's Not Too Late' (reprise), 'Plans A & B', 'Let's Not Talk About It', 'So Glad I Married Her', 'Small Craft Warnings', 'How Did I End Up Here?', 'Words He Doesn't Say', 'My Love For You', 'Moonlight Passing Through A Window', 'Now', 'Romantic Notions', and 'Romance, Romance'. Barry Harman staged the complete show, which was choreographed by Pamela Sousa, nominated for five Tony Awards, and won four Outer Critics Circle Awards. It closed on January 1989 after a run of 297 performances. On 11 September 1996, a production of *Romance, Romance*, directed by Steven Dexter was presented at the Bridewell Theatre on the London Fringe for a short season. The cast of Mark Adams (Alfred/Sam), Ria Jones (Josephine/Monica), 'Him' (Stee Billingsley), 'Her' (Beth Robson), Lenny (Tony Timberlake), and Barb (Anne Wood), received excellent reviews, and the show was transferred to the West End's Gielgud Theatre. Mark Adams and Beth Robson were retained for the move, but rising star Ria Jones was unaccountably dropped. Despite more favourable reviews, it was withdrawn after only seven weeks.

ROMBERG, SIGMUND

b. 29 July 1887, Nagykanizsa, Hungary, d. 9 November 1951. After formal training as a violinist, Romberg began writing music while in his late teens. Despite these early interests, Romberg's main studies were in engineering and it was not until 1909, after completing a period of service in the Hungarian army, most of which was spent in Vienna, that he decided to make his career in music. Romberg showed a practical streak by recognizing that he would do better away from the Viennese 'hot house', which already contained numerous important composers. He emigrated to the USA, taking up residence in New York City where he found work in a factory, supplementing his income playing piano in restaurants and bars. He graduated to leading an orchestra, which proved very popular but his heart was set on composing for the musical stage. His first show, written in collaboration with lyricist Harold Atteridge, was *The Whirl Of The World*, which opened in 1914, the year in which Romberg became an American citizen. Romberg and Atteridge continued their partnership for several years, creating numerous shows, few of which were especially successful despite starring such leading theatrical personalities as Marilyn Miller, Nora Bayes and Al Jolson. The shows that fared best were *The Blue*

Paradise (1915) and *Maytime* (1917); for both Romberg drew upon his musical heritage, writing waltzes in the Viennese manner. This was a practice he utilised in 1921 with *Blossom Time*, which told a fanciful version of the life of classical composer Franz Schubert. The score included 'Song Of Love', by far Romberg's most popular song up to this time. Convinced that the operetta was where he was most at ease, Romberg turned increasingly to this form even though he was obliged to write in other contexts to make a living. It was not until 1924 and the opening of *The Student Prince*, that he was able to prove conclusively that he was right in his belief. *The Student Prince*, in which Romberg was joined by lyricist Dorothy Donnelly, included such major song successes as 'Deep In My Heart', 'Serenade', 'Golden Days' and the 'Drinking Song'. With the evidence of this show as his guide, he concentrated on operettas and, despite some failures, soon became America's leading exponent of this type of musical theatre. In 1926 he wrote *The Desert Song* (lyrics by Otto Harbach and Oscar Hammerstein II), from which came 'Blue Heaven', 'One Alone' and the rousing 'Riff Song'. Romberg followed this with *The New Moon* (1928, with Hammerstein). Both on stage and as a film, in 1930, *The New Moon* was hugely popular, with hit songs such as 'Lover, Come Back To Me', 'One Kiss', 'Stouthearted Men' and 'Softly, As In A Morning Sunrise'. Inevitably, Romberg's inclination towards operetta endangered his continuing popularity through the 30s. Changing musical tastes conspired against him, although he still wrote many engaging songs, among them 'When I Grow Too Old To Dream', written with Hammerstein for the 1934 film *The Night Is Young*. In 1935 he adapted to the vogue for musical comedy with *May Wine*, before settling in California to write for films. In the early 40s he was relatively inactive but he made a comeback on Broadway in 1945 with *Up In Central Park*. With lyrics by Dorothy Fields, the show included such songs as 'Close As Pages In A Book' and 'Carousel In The Park'. Despite this show's success, Romberg's subsequent work drifted between operetta and musical comedy and met with little interest from audiences.

ROME, HAROLD

b. 27 May 1908, Hartford, Connecticut, USA, d. 26 October 1993, New York, USA. While still attending school Rome played piano in local dance bands and was already writing music. Despite this early interest in music, he went on to study architecture and law at Yale. In 1934 he practised as an architect in New York City, but studied piano and composition in his spare time. This was a fortunate decision because by the following year, with work opportunities diminishing with the Depression, he was obliged to turn more and more to his second string activity for support. Much of the music Rome was writing at this time was socially conscious and was thus of little interest to Tin Pan Alley. Nevertheless, he was engaged to write a revue for the International Garment Workers' Union. To everyone's surprise, the revue, *Pins And Needles* (1937), staged for members of the union, became a popular success and one song, 'Sunday In The Park', established a life outside of the show. Rome was now much sought-after, although his

next show displayed similarly political concerns. This was *Sing Out The News* (1939) and, once again, there was a universally accepted hit song, 'F.D.R. Jones'. In the early 40s Rome wrote songs for several revues and shows, but it was not until after the end of World War II that he had his first major success. This was *Call Me Mister* (1946), from which came 'South America, Take It Away'. More revues followed until his first fully fledged musical show, *Wish You Were Here*, in 1952. Two years later he wrote *Fanny*, his most popular Broadway show, which included 'Love Is A Very Light Thing'. This was followed by *Destry Rides Again* (1959) and *I Can Get It For You Wholesale* (1962), in which Barbra Streisand made her Broadway debut. In the mid-60s Rome showed that the social conscience that had marked his early work was still intact when he wrote *The Zulu And The Zayda* (1965), which dealt with racial and religious intolerance. In 1970 he wrote *Scarlett*, based upon the novel *Gone With The Wind*, for a Japanese production in Tokyo. More than with any other American composer in the field of mainstream popular music, Rome's work consistently demonstrated an awareness of social issues, often to the extent that it kept him from the massive successes enjoyed by many of his contemporaries. He was also a gifted painter and a dedicated art collector.

ROONEY, MICKEY

b. Joe Yule Jnr., 23 September 1920, Brooklyn, New York, USA. A five feet three-high bundle of dynamite - an actor, singer, comedian, dancer, songwriter - and much else. The son of vaudevillian parents, Rooney made his stage debut when he was 18 months old, and was taken to Hollywood by his mother soon afterwards. He got his big break at the age of six when he made the first of over 50 two-reel comedies featuring the comic-strip character Mickey McGuire. For most of the 30s he was cast in mainly minor roles, but received critical acclaim for his performances in *Ah Wilderness!* and as Puck in *A Midsummer Night's Dream* (both 1935). The year 1937 marked the beginning of two important associations for Rooney. In *Thoroughbreds Don't Cry* (1937) he was teamed for the first time with Judy Garland, and he also made *A Family Affair*, the first in a highly successful series of 'Andy Hardy' pictures which continued until 1946. In 1938 he created 'cinema's first punk kid' in *Boys' Town*, with Spencer Tracy. In the same year Garland joined him in one of the Hardy pictures, *Love Finds Andy Hardy*, but their real impact together came in the enormously popular musicals *Babes In Arms* (1939), *Strike Up the Band* (1940), *Babes On Broadway* (1941), and *Girl Crazy* (1943). By then, Rooney was at the peak of his career, topping box-office charts in the US and all over the world. However, after an appearance in *Thousands Cheer*, MGM's tribute to the US Armed Forces - and then a stint in the real thing during World War II - he made only two more musicals, *Summer Holiday* and *Words and Music* (both 1948). After that, for many different reasons, his career declined rapidly, although he turned in fine dramatic performances in several films during the 50s. After filing for bankruptcy in 1962 his life hit rock bottom, but he continued to work in movies, nightclubs, dinner-theatres and on television, and in 1979, after being nominated for an Oscar for his role in the adventure movie *Black Stallion*, made a sensational comeback on Broadway with *Sugar Babies*. This celebration of the golden age of American burlesque with its old song favourites and many examples of classic schtick, was perfect for Rooney, and, with co-star Ann Miller, he toured with the show for several years following its New York run of nearly 1,500 performances, and took it to London in 1988. In 1981 he won an Emmy for the television film *Bill*, and a year later received an Honorary Oscar 'in recognition of his 60 years of versatility in a variety of memorable film performances'. He had received a special Academy Award 44 years earlier, when he and Deanna Durbin had been cited for 'their significant contribution in bringing to the screen the spirit and personification of youth, and as juvenile players setting a high standard of ability and achievement'. He continues to film in the 90s, and is estimated to have made in excess of 200 pictures. In 1990, he returned to Broadway, and played the role of Will Rogers' father Clem during the final weeks of the musical *The Will Rogers Follies*. He remains an immensely likeable character who has continually bounced back at every stage of adversity. A good deal of the money he earned from his films up until 1965 (estimated box-office taking $3, 000 million - Rooney's share $12 million) went on alimony to ex-wives. He has (to date) been married eight times: ranging from Ava Gardner ('We were both under contract to MGM, and I was dressed as Carmen Miranda at the time, so she could hardly refuse'), through Barbara Thomason (she was murdered by her lover), to his present wife for more than 15 years, country singer Jan Chamberlain. Although at the time of writing he is almost 80, much else can be expected of Mickey Rooney, especially if he abides by the US Mickey Rooney Old People's Association's principal motto which is: 'Never Retire But Inspire'. Taking his own advice, he was back on the road again in 1998, starring in a stage version of the legendary 1939 film *The Wizard Of Oz*. He played the Wizard, and Eartha Kitt was the Wicked Witch, in a production which toured before dropping in on New York's Madison Square Garden.

● FURTHER READING: *The Nine Lives Of Mickey Rooney*, Arthur Marx. *I.E.* and *Life Is Too Short* (his autobiographies).

● FILMS: *Not To Be Trusted* (1926), *Orchids And Ermine* (1927), *Sin's Pay Day* (1932), *My Pal, The King* (1932), *Emma* (1932), *High Speed* (1932), *The Beast Of The City* (1932), *Fast Companions* (1932), *The World Changes* (1933), *Love Birds* (1933), *The Chief* (1933), *Broadway To Hollywood* (1933), *The Big Chance* (1933), *The Big Cage* (1933), *The Life Of Jimmy Dolan* (1933), *Upperworld* (1934), *Hide-Out* (1934), *Half A Sinner* (1934), *Death On The Diamond* (1934), *Blind Date* (1934), *I Like It That Way* (1934), *Manhattan Melodrama* (1934), *Riffraff* (1935), *A Midsummer Night's Dream* (1935), *The County Chairman* (1935), *Ah, Wilderness!* (1935), *Reckless* (1935), *Little Pal* (1935), *Little Lord Fauntleroy* (1936), *Down The Stretch* (1936), *Devil Is A Sissy* (1936), *Thoroughbreds Don't Cry* (1937), *Slave Ship* (1937), *Live, Love And Learn* (1937), *A Family Affair* (1937), *Captains Courageous* (1937), *Hoosier Schoolboy* (1937), *You're Only Young Once* (1938), *Stablemates* (1938), *Out West With The Hardys* (1938), *Love Is A Headache* (1938), *Lord Jeff* (1938), *Judge Hardy's Children* (1938), *Hollywood Handicap* (1938), *Hold That Kiss* (1938), *Andy Hardy's Dilemma* (1938), *Boy's Town* (1938), *Judge Hardy And Son* (1939),

The Hardys Ride High (1939), *Andy Hardy Gets Spring Fever* (1939), *The Adventures Of Huckleberry Finn* (1939), *Babes In Arms* (1939), *Young Tom Edison* (1940), *Andy Hardy Meets A Debutante* (1940), *Strike Up The Band* (1940), *Life Begins For Andy Hardy* (1941), *Babes On Broadway* (1941), *Andy Hardy's Private Secretary* (1941), *Men Of Boys Town* (1941), *A Yank At Eton* (1942), *The Courtship Of Andy Hardy* (1942), *Andy Hardy's Double Life* (1942), *Thousands Cheer* (1943), *Show Business At War* (1943), *The Human Comedy* (1943), *Girl Crazy* (1943), *National Velvet* (1944), *Andy Hardy's Blonde Trouble* (1944), *Love Laughs At Andy Hardy* (1946), *Killer McCoy* (1947), *Words And Music* (1948), *Summer Holiday* (1948), *The Big Wheel* (1949), *He's A Cock-Eyed Wonder* (1950), *The Fireball* (1950), *Quicksand* (1950), *The Strip* (1951), *My Outlaw Brother* (1951), *Sound Off* (1952), *A Slight Case Of Larceny* (1953), *Off Limits* (1953), *All Ashore* (1953), *Drive A Crooked Road* (1953), *Bridges At Toko-Ri* (1954), *The Atomic Kid* (1954), *The Twinkle In God's Eye* (1955), *Magnificent Roughnecks* (1956), *Francis In The Haunted House* (1956), *The Bold And The Brave* (1956), *Baby Face Nelson* (1956), *Operation Mad Ball* (1957), *Nice Little Bank That Should Be Robbed* (1958), *Andy Hardy Comes Home* (1958), *The Big Operator* (1959), *The Last Mile* (1959), *Platinum High School* (1960), *The Private Lives Of Adam And Eve* (1961), *King Of The Roaring 20s* (1961), *Everything's Ducky* (1961), *Breakfast At Tiffany's* (1961), *Requiem For A Heavyweight* (1962), *It's A Mad Mad Mad Mad World* (1963), *The Secret Invasion* (1964), *Twenty-Four Hours To Kill* (1965), *How To Stuff A Wild Bikini* (1965), *The Devil In Love* (1966), *Ambush Bay* (1966), *Skidoo* (1968), *The Extraordinary Seaman* (1969), *The Comic* (1969), *80 Steps To Jonah* (1969), *Hollywood Blue* (1970), *Cockeyed Cowboys Of Calico County* (1970), *The Manipulator* (1971), *Richard* (1972), *Pulp* (1972), *The Godmothers* (1973), *Thunder County* (1974), *Rachel's Man* (1974), *Ace Of Hearts* (1974), *That's Entertainment!* (1974), *Find The Lady* (1976), *The Domino Principle* (1977), *Pete's Dragon* (1977), *The Magic Of Lassie* (1977), *The Black Stallion* (1979), *Arabian Adventure* (1979), *The Emperor Of Peru* (1981), *Lighting, The White Stallion* (1986), *Erik The Viking* (1989), *Home For Christmas* (1990), *My Heroes Have Always Been Cowboys* (1991), *The Milky Life* (1992), *Sweet Justice* (1992), *Silent Night, Deadly Night 5: The Toymaker* (1992), *The Legend Of Wolf Mountain* (1992), *Revenge Of The Red Baron* (1994), *Radio Star-The AFN Story* (1994), *Making Waves* (1994), *The Legend Of O.B. Taggart* (1994), *A Century Of Cinema* (1994), *That's Entertainment! III* (1994), *Michael Kael In Katango* (1997), *Boys Will Be Boys* (1997), *Animals* (1997), *The First Of May* (1998), *The Face On The Barroom Floor* (1998), *Sinbad: The Battle Of The Dark Knights* (1998).

ROOTS, ROCK AND REGGAE

Jeremy Marre's 1978 documentary about Jamaican music is a fine examination of reggae culture. He includes interviews, live material and sound system rivalry, interspersing these with brief histories of record company practices and the role of radio stations. The music is provided by Bob Marley And The Wailers (including 'Trenchtown Rock' and 'Lively Up Yourself'), Junior Murvin, Third World and Jimmy Cliff. The role of harmony groups in the development of Jamaican music is heard in the Mighty Diamonds' 'When The Right Time Comes' and the Gladiators' 'Hearsay', while the importance of Rastafarianism is captured in the Abyssinians' 'Satta Massanga'. Toots And The Maytals also contribute five wonderfully ebullient songs to a highly engaging film.

ROPE LADDER TO THE MOON

This is the film biography of former Cream bassist/vocalist Jack Bruce and takes its title from a track on his first solo album, *Songs For A Tailor*. Director Tony Palmer, who was responsible for *All My Loving* and *Cream's Last Concert*, charted this stellar musician's rise from poverty in Glasgow's disingenuously-named Harmony Row to millionaire status. Bruce, who won a scholarship to Edinburgh's Royal Academy Of Music, embraced jazz as a member of Jack McHarg's Band, before moving to London where he joined Alexis Korner's Blues Incorporated, the Graham Bond Organization and John Mayall's Bluesbreakers. Mayall is one of the musicians paying tribute to Baker, as is the jazz drummer Tony Williams, who later partnered Bruce in Lifetime. Baker's manager, Robert Stigwood, produced this fitting feature, which largely draws its soundtrack from *Goodbye Cream* and the aforementioned *Songs For A Tailor*.

ROSALIE

Two composers representing entirely different worlds of popular music contributed to this lavish Florenz Ziegfeld production which opened at the New Amsterdam Theatre in New York on 10 January 1928. George Gershwin and Sigmund Romberg squeezed this show into their busy schedules, and were rewarded with an excellent run of 335 performances. The book, by William Anthony McGuire and Guy Bolton, capitalised on the American public's fascination with early aviators in general, and Captain Charles Lindbergh's record-breaking solo flight to Paris in particular. No doubt the latter's achievement pales in comparison with the exploits of West Point high flyer, Lieutenant Richard Fay (Oliver McLennan), who loves Princess Rosalie of Romanza (Marilyn Miller), and risks life and limb to make a trans-Atlantic flight to be near her. However, she is unable to marry a commoner unless her father, King Cyril (Frank Morgan), abdicates. As this appears to be the European thing to do, the King is pleased to oblige. One of the George Gershwin songs, a future standard, 'How Long Has This Been Going On?' (lyric: Ira Gershwin), which had been cut from *Funny Face*, resurfaced here, but did not catch on, and another of the brothers' numbers, 'Ev'rybody Knows I Love Somebody', was also in the score. The rest of the songs included 'Say So!' and 'Oh Gee! Oh Joy!' (music: George Gershwin, lyrics: Ira Gershwin and P.G. Wodehouse), and 'West Point Song' (music: Sigmund Romberg, lyric: Wodehouse). The highly commercial combination of Ziegfeld's elegant production, a singable, danceable score, and the enormous box-office appeal of the petite and lovely Marilyn Miller, ensured that *Rosalie* stayed on Broadway for over 10 months. An attempt by Hollywood to make a film version with Marion Davies was never released, but some of the footage was used in the 1937 movie of *Rosalie* which starred Nelson Eddy and Eleanor Powell. Several pieces of classical music were incorporated, and the orginal stage score was neatly removed in favour of one by Cole Porter - and *Rosalie* got a title song at last.

ROSE-MARIE (FILM MUSICAL)

Previously filmed in 1928 as a silent, this MGM adaptation of the highly successful Broadway operetta was released in 1936. Starring Jeanette MacDonald and Nelson Eddy, it came to the screen with a radically revised plot and minus most of the original songs. In the new story, by Frances Goodrich, Albert Hackett, and Alice Duer Miller, MacDonald is a famous Canadian opera star whose brother (James Stewart) is on the run from the law. Nelson Eddy plays the Mountie intent on bringing him to justice, which interrupts his romance with MacDonald for a time, but the inevitable happy ending is always just around the bend. As for the score, there were four survivors from the stage show, 'Indian Love Call' and 'Rose Marie' (Rudolph Friml-Oscar Hammerstein II-Otto Harbach), and 'The Mounties' and 'Totem Tom-Tom' (Herbert Stothart-Hammerstein-Harbach). They were joined by several others including 'Just for You' (Friml-Gus Kahn), 'Pardon Me, Madame' (Stothart-Kahn), 'Some Of These Days' (Shelton Brooks), and 'Dinah' (Sam M. Lewis-Joe Young-Harry Akst). The names of two future film idols also appeared in the credits, Allan Jones, whose marvellous voice was heard in many a screen musical, and the young David Niven who went on to become the epitome of the dashing and debonair Englishman abroad. Other members of the large cast included Reginald Owen, Alan Mowbray, Una O'Connor, Robert Greig, George Regas, and Herman Bing. Chester Hale was the choreographer, and the film was directed by MGM stalwart W. S. Van Dyke. *Rose-Marie* was re-made again in 1954 with Howard Keel, Ann Blyth, Fernando Lamas, Bert Lahr, and Marjorie Main. This version was choreographed by Busby Berkeley and directed by Mervyn LeRoy.

● VIDEOS: *Memories Of Home* (Telstar 1995).

ROSE MARIE (STAGE MUSICAL)

After resolving to concentrate on an acting career in the legitimate theatre, former opera diva Mary Ellis was persuaded by producer Arthur Hammerstein - and his nephew Oscar Hammerstein II - to take the leading role in this musical of some significance, which opened at the Imperial Theatre in New York on 2 September 1924. Ellis played Rose Marie La Flamme, a charming, young French-Canadian girl, who sings like a bird ('yes indeed') up there in the Rockies. Rose Marie is herself serenaded by miner Jim Kenyon (Dennis King), although her brother Emile (Edward Ciannelli) would much rather she settled down with the suave, well-off city gent, Edward Hawley (Frank Greene). Little does Emile know that Wanda (Pearl Regay) has sensual plans of her own regarding Hawley, and even saves his life by stabbing Blackeagle (Arthur Ludwig) to death when the two men get into a fight. However, things being how they are, an accusing finger points at Jim Kenyon, and he is just about to have his collar felt by Mountie Sergeant Malone (Arthur Deagon) when Wanda does the decent thing and confesses. Rose Marie and Jim can pick out curtains for their cabin after all, and, yes, Lady Jane (Dorothy Mackaye) does marry Hard-Boiled Herman (William Kent) too. Oscar Hammerstein and Otto Harbach wrote the book and lyrics, while Rudolph Friml and Herbert Stothart composed the music. There was a concerted effort by all concerned to integrate the songs into the story, which, unusually for a musical comedy - or 'musical piece' as this was known - contained the aforementioned murder. 'Rose Marie' (introduced by Dennis King) and 'Indian Love Call' (Ellis and King) - both with music by Friml - are the most familiar numbers in a score which also had 'Hard-Boiled Herman', 'The Mounties', 'Totem Tom-Tom', 'Why Shouldn't We', 'Lak Jeem', 'The Door Of My Dreams', 'Pretty Things', 'Only A Kiss', 'I Love Him', and 'One Man Woman'. David Bennett's choreography was played out on spectacular sets by Gates and Morange - locations such as Saskatchewan, Kootenay Pass - and Paul Dickey was the director. A run of 557 performances in those days meant that *Rose Marie* was a big hit, and warranted two road companies. London audiences flocked to see it as well after the opening on 20 March 1925 at the Theatre Royal, Drury Lane. Following Mary Ellis's triumph in New York, it needed considerable persuasion by Oscar Hammerstein before Edith Day agreed to lead the cast of Derek Oldham (Jim), Billy Merson (Herman), Clarice Hardwicke (Lady Jane), John Dunsmure (Malone), Michael Cole (Emile), Ruby Morriss (Wanda), and a 100-strong chorus which made quite an impression, especially in 'Totem Tom-Tom' (and probably a good deal of noise as well). In the event, Edith Day also enjoyed a tremendous personal success, and *Rose Marie* ran for around two years - 851 performances. Ms. Day recreated her role for the 1929 revival, after being christened 'The Queen of Drury Lane' for her splendid performances there in *The Desert Song* (1927), and *Show Boat* (1928). It was the beginning of a decade leading up to World War II, during which the Theatre Royal became the Mecca for lovers of romantic operettas. There were further London stagings of *Rose Marie* in 1942 (Marjorie Brown and Raymond Newell), and 1960 (David Whitfield and Stephanie Voss). Film versions were released in 1928 (silent, with Joan Crawford, 1936 (Jeanette MacDonald and Nelson Eddy), and 1954 (Ann Blyth, Fernando Lamas and Howard Keel). In 1955, Slim Whitman took 'Rose Marie' to the top of the UK chart for an incredible 11 weeks, and enjoyed a successful follow-up with 'Indian Love Call'.

ROSE OF WASHINGTON SQUARE

More than 30 years before Barbra Streisand shot to screen stardom in *Funny Girl* (1968), this unauthorised version of the Fanny Brice story starred Alice Faye and Tyrone Power - and attracted a successful writ for invasion of privacy from the subject herself. According to this story, As Power goes steadily downhill, eventually ending up in prison, Faye's career goes from strength to strength supported by a great bunch of songs which included 'I Never Knew Heaven Could Speak' (Mack Gordon-Harry Revel), 'The Curse Of An Aching Heart' (Al Piantadosi-Henry Fink), 'I'm Just Wild About Harry' (Noble Sissle-Eubie Blake), 'Rose Of Washington Square' (Ballard MacDonald-James F. Hanley) and 'My Man' (Channing Pollock-Maurice Yvain). The last two are especially associated with Fanny Brice. Although Faye and Power were top-billed, their star status was threatened by Al Jolson, who gave typically dynamic performances of favourites such as 'Toot Toot Tootsie' (Gus Kahn-Ernie Erdman-Ted Fio Rito-Robert A. King), 'California, Here I Come' (Buddy De Sylva-Jolson-Joseph Meyer), and 'Pretty Baby' (Kahn-Egbert Van Alstyne-Tony Jackson). Also in the cast were William Frawley, Hobart Cavanaugh, Joyce Compton, and Louis Prima with his band. The screenplay that caused all the legal problems was by Nunnally Johnson, and Gregory Ratoff directed this thoroughly entertaining film which was released by 20th Century-Fox in 1936.

ROSE, BILLY

b. William Samuel Rosenberg, 6 September 1899, New York, USA. d. 10 February 1966, Jamaica. An important lyricist and impresario, Rose was a small, dynamic man, once called 'the little Napoleon of showmanship'. He was married twice, firstly to star comedienne Fanny Brice, and then to champion swimmer Eleanor Holm. As a lyric writer, it is sometimes said that he often insisted on collaborating with songwriters who were contributing to shows that he was producing. His first successful songs came in the early 20s. 'Barney Google', based on the popular cartoon strip, and 'You've Got To See Mama Every Night', were both written with Con Conrad in 1923. 'Does The Spearmint Lose Its Flavor On The Bedpost Overnight?', on which Rose collaborated with Marty Bloom and Ernest Brever in 1924, was also hits, along with 'Spearmint', for US radio's popular tenor-baritone team of Ernest Hare and Billy Jones. With a slightly modified title, the latter song resurfaced in the US charts in 1961, sung by UK artist, Lonnie Donegan. Hare and Jones again, and Billy Murray (the 'Denver Nightingale'), also had success with 'Don't Bring Lulu', which Rose wrote with Lew Brown and Ray Henderson. Among Rose's other well known songs were 'The Night Is Young And You're So Beautiful' (Irving Kahal and Dana Suesse), 'I've Got A Feeling I'm Falling' (Fats Waller and Harry Link), 'That Old Gang Of Mine' (Mort Dixon and Ray Henderson), 'Clap Hands! Here Comes Charley' (Ballard MacDonald and Joseph Meyer), 'Tonight You Belong To Me' (Lee David), 'It Happened In Monterey' (Mabel Wayne), 'Back In Your Own Backyard', 'There's A Rainbow 'Round My Shoulder' and 'Me And My Shadow' (written with Al Jolson and Dave Dreyer).

In 1926 Rose started to contribute songs to Broadway shows and revues, including 'A Cup Of Coffee, A Sandwich And You', for Gertrude Lawrence to sing in the *Charlot Revue* of that year. Three years later he wrote his first Broadway score for *Great Day!*, with Edward Eliscu and Vincent Youmans. This included the songs 'More Than You Know', 'Happy Because I'm In Love', 'Without A Song' and 'Great Day'. Rose's first Broadway production, in 1930, was the revue *Sweet And Low*, which also contained two of his songs, 'Cheerful Little Earful' (with Ira Gershwin and Harry Warren) and 'Would You Like To Take A Walk?' (with Mort Dixon and Warren). When the show was revised in 1931 as *Crazy Quilt*, Rose, Warren and Dixon had added another song, 'I Found A Million Dollar Baby (In A Five And Ten Cent Store)', which was sung by Rose's wife, Fanny Brice. Rose's 1935 Broadway project, *Jumbo*, was not quite a 'million-dollar-baby', but it apparently did cost somewhere in the region of $350,000 to produce - a lot of money for a show in those days. For this musical comedy-vaudeville-circus extravaganza, much of the cash was spent in gutting Broadway's Hippodrome Theatre and refitting it to resemble a circus arena, with a circular revolving stage, and the audience seating sloping in grand-stand fashion. *Jumbo* was spectacular in every way. The extravaganza featured Jimmy Durante, bandleader Paul Whiteman seated on a white horse, an elephant named Big Rosie, a human cast of around 90, and almost as many animals. Despite a book by Ben Hecht and Charles MacArthur, a Richard Rodgers/Lorenz Hart score (no Rose lyrics in this one) which featured songs such as 'The Most Beautiful Girl In The World', 'My Romance', and 'Little Girl Blue', and a healthy New York run of five months, *Jumbo* closed without getting near to recovering its costs. From the excesses of *Jumbo*, Rose's next production was Hecht and MacArthur's play *The Great Magoo*, the story of a Coney Island barker, which contained only one song, 'It's Only A Paper Moon', written by Rose, E.Y. 'Yip' Harburg, and Harold Arlen. Rose, in collaboration with Maceo Pinkard, also contributed one additional song, 'Here Comes The Showboat', to the original Jerome Kern/Oscar Hammerstein II/P.G. Wodehouse score for the 1936 film version of the musical *Show Boat*.

During the 40s, Rose's two main Broadway productions were *Carmen Jones* (1943) and *Seven Lively Arts* (1944). Despite his failure to get Sir Thomas Beecham, his first choice conductor for *Carmen Jones*, Oscar Hammerstein II's re-setting of Georges Bizet's opera *Carmen* was extremely well received by critics and public alike. In direct contrast, *Seven Lively Arts*, with a concept embracing opera, ballet, Broadway, vaudeville, jazz, concert music, and modern painting, along with a Cole Porter score which included 'Ev'ry Time We Say Goodbye', was thought to be somewhere between a 'disappointment' and a 'disaster'. As well as his Broadway projects, Rose produced aquacades at many locations including the *New York World's Fair* in 1937, and the *San Francisco World's Fair* in 1940. He also owned two top New York night-spots, (the New York Supper Club and the Diamond Horseshoe) and two Broadway theatres, the Ziegfeld and the Billy Rose Theatre. One of the most colourful show business characters of his time, Rose retired in the 50s, and repeated his previous success, this time as a stock market speculator.

● FURTHER READING: *Billy Rose: Manhattan Primitive*, Earl Conrad. *The Nine Lives Of Billy Rose*, Pearl Rose Gottlieb (Billy Rose's sister). *Wine, Women And Words*, Billy Rose.

ROSE, DAVID

b. 15 June 1910, London, England, d. 23 August, 1990, Burbank, California, USA. A distinguished orchestra leader, composer, and arranger in the 40s and 50s, Rose was taken to the USA when he was just four-years-old. After graduating from the Chicago College of Music at the age of 16, he joined Ted Fio Rito's dance band, and three years later became a pianist/arranger/conductor for NBC Radio. In 1936 he provided the arrangement for Benny Goodman's big hit 'It's Been So Long', before moving to Hollywood, where he formed his own orchestra in 1938

for the Mutual Broadcasting System, and featured on the programme *California Melodies*. In the same year Rose married comedienne/singer Martha Raye and backed her on her hit record 'Melancholy Mood'. The marriage was later dissolved, and, after meeting Judy Garland when she was appearing on Bob Hope's radio show, he became the first of her five husbands from 1941 until 1945. During military service in World War II Rose was composer/conductor for the Army/Air Force morale-boosting stage musical *Winged Victory*, which was filmed in 1944. In 1943 he had a big hit with his own composition 'Holiday For Strings' and, a year later, with 'Poinciana (Song Of The Tree)'. By the late 40s he was a regular on Red Skelton's radio show, moving with him into television. He later wrote scores and themes for over 20 television series and won Emmy awards for his 14 year stint on *Bonanza*, 10 years with *Little House On The Prairie* and his work on three much-acclaimed Fred Astaire specials, beginning with *An Evening With Fred Astaire* in 1959.

Rose began working in movies in 1941, and is credited with scoring 36 films through to the 60s including *Texas Carnival* (1951), *Rich, Young And Pretty* (1951), *Everything I Have Is Yours* (1952), *Operation Petticoat* (1959), *Please Don't Eat The Daisies* (1960) and *Never Too Late* (1965). He received an Oscar nomination for his song 'So In Love', with a lyric by Leo Robin, which was featured in the 1944 Danny Kaye movie *Wonder Man*. His other compositions included 'Our Waltz' (which he is said to have written for Judy Garland), 'Dance Of The Spanish Onion', 'Manhattan Square Dance', 'Deserted City', 'Holiday For Trombones', 'Rose Of Bel-Air', 'Holiday For Flutes', 'Four Twenty AM', 'Waltz Of The Bubbles', 'Like Young', 'Taco Holiday', 'The Tiny Ballerina', 'Gay Spirits', 'Parade Of The Clowns', 'The Christmas Tree' (familiar to millions of Americans through its traditional use each Yuletide on *The Red Skelton Show*), and a collection of 32 piano solos entitled *Music For Moderns*. After chart success with 'Calypso Melody' in 1957 and his accompaniment for the Connie Francis 1959 hit 'My Happiness', Rose had a worldwide smash hit in 1962 with another of his own tunes, a humorous and satirical piece called 'The Stripper', which was written for a television show called *Burlesque*, starring Dan Dailey. Naturally, it was included on *The Stripper And Other Fun Songs For The Family*, which reached number 3 in the US album chart in 1962. Among Rose's other reported 50 or so albums, were the best-selling *Like Young* and *Like Blue*, recorded with André Previn. Apart from his record, film and television work, Rose was guest conductor with several symphony orchestras. His 'Concerto For Flute And Orchestra' was first played by the Los Angeles Philharmonic Orchestra and later by the Boston Pops.

● ALBUMS: *Autumn Leaves* (MGM 1957)★★★★, *Gigi* (1958)★★★, *Jamaica* (1958)★★★, *Reflections In The Water* (MGM 1958)★★, *Songs Of The Fabulous 30s* (MGM 1958)★★★, *Great Waltzes* (MGM 1958)★★★, *Holiday For Strings* (MGM 1959)★★★, *Fiddlin' For Fun* (MGM 50s)★★, *Let's Fall In Love* (MGM 50s)★★, *Love Walked In* (MGM 50s)★★, *Music From Motion Pictures* (MGM 50s)★★★★, *Sentimental Journey* (MGM 50s)★★★, *Concert With A Beat* (1960)★★★, *Bonanza* (MGM 1961)★★★, *Spectacular Strings* (MGM 1961)★★★, *Box-Office Blockbusters* (MGM 1961)★★★★,

Cimarron And Others (MGM 1961)★★★, *21 Channel Sound* (1962)★★, *The Stripper And Other Fun Songs For The Family* (MGM 1962)★★★★, *Velvet Beat* (MGM 1965)★★★, *Like Young, Like Blue* (1974)★★★, *In The Still Of The Night* (1976)★★★, *Melody Fair* (1977)★★★, *Great Orchestras Of The World* (1978)★★, *Very Thought Of You* (1984)★★★.

● COMPILATIONS: *16 Original Hits* (1984)★★★★.

ROSE, THE

This 1979 film starred Bette Midler in the role of a self-destructive singer, loosely based on the career of Janis Joplin. Midler was already renowned as a brassy interpreter who injected personality into her performances and parallels between the two artists' approach, as opposed to lifestyles, were not outlandish. Eschewing the blues-based métier marking Joplin's work, Midler performed material more akin to conventional 'show-biz' styles and *The Rose* thus functions as cautionary 'rise and fall' tale akin to *A Star Is Born*. British actor Alan Bates appears as the singer's manager, mavericks Harry Dean Stanton and Frederick Forrest are also featured, but the film revolves around Midler's powerful Oscar-nominated portrayal of a hedonistic, self-destructive individual but brilliant person.

● VIDEOS: *1991: The Year Punk Broke* (1993).

ROSENMAN, LEONARD

b. 7 September 1924, Brooklyn, New York, USA. A composer and arranger for films and television, who only studied music seriously after serving in the US Air Force during World War II. His first film score, *East Of Eden* (1955), was followed in the same year by another James Dean vehicle, *Rebel Without A Cause*. Rosenman's other 50s scores included dramas such as *Bombers B-52*, *Edge Of The City*, *The Young Stranger*, *Lafayett Escadrille*, *Pork Chop Hill* and *The Savage Eye*. After providing music for more in the same genre in the 60s, such as *The Rise And Fall Of Legs Diamond*, *The Bramble Bush*, *The Chapman Report*, *A Covenant With Death* and *Hellfighters*, plus essays into science-fiction with *Countdown* and *Fantastic Voyage*, Rosenman received much critical acclaim for his score to *A Man Called Horse* and *Beneath The Planet Of The Apes* (1970). He also scored two 'Apes' sequels. During the 70s Rosenman received two Academy Awards for his adaptation of the scores to *Barry Lyndon* (1975) and *Bound For Glory* (1976). Rosenman's original background scores around that time included *Birch Interval*, *The Car*, *Race With The Devil*, *Prophecy*, *Promises In The Dark* and the animated feature *The Lord Of The Rings*. In the 80s and early 90s, apart from the occasional feature film such as *Hide In Plain Sight*, *Making Love*, *Cross Creek* (Oscar nomination), *Robocop 2*, *Heart Of The Stag* and *Ambition* (1992), Rosenman wrote more and more for television, although he still managed to score the occasional big feature, such as *The Jazz Singer* and *Star Trek IV: The Voyage Home*. Rosenman's music for television included *Stranger On The Run*, *Shadow Over Elveron*, *Any Second Now*, *Banyon*, *Vanished*, *In Broad Daylight*, *The Bravos*, *The Cat Creature*, *The Phantom Of Hollywood*, *Nakia*, *Lanigan's Rabbi*, *Kingston: The Power Play*, *The Possessed*, *Friendly Fire*, *City In Fear*, *The Wall*, *Murder In Texas*, *Celebrity* (mini-series),

Heartsounds, *First Steps*, *Promised A Miracle*, *Where Pigeons Go To Die*, the popular series *The Defenders*, *Marcus Welby MD*, its sequel, *The Return Of Marcus Welby MD* and the television film *Keeper Of The City* (1991). He also composed several classical works.

ROSS, JERRY

(see Adler, Richard)

ROTA, NINO

b. 3 December 1911, Milan, Italy, d. 10 April 1979, Rome, Italy. A prolific composer for films, from the early 30s to the late 70s. A child prodigy, Rota wrote an oratorio and an opera before he was aged 15. He studied at the Curtis Institute in Philadelphia, and, later, at the Liceo Musicale in Bari, eventually becoming its director from 1950-78. He began composing for Italian movies in 1933, but had enormous success in Britain in 1949 with his score for *The Glass Mountain* starring the husband and wife team, Michael Denison and Dulcie Gray. By 1950, when he started collaborating with Federico Fellini, he had composed the scores to some 30 films. His association with the influential Italian director lasted nearly 30 years and included movies such as *Lo Sceicco Bianco*, *I Vitelloni*, *La Strada* (including the 'Love Theme'), *Il Bidone*, *La Dolce Vita* (including 'The Sweet Life'), *Boccaccio*, *Eight And A Half* (with its popular 'Love Theme'), *Juliet Of The Spirits*, *Fellini-Satyricon*, *The Clowns*, *Casanova*, *The Orchestra Rehearsal* and more. Meanwhile, for other directors, Nino provided the music for *The Hidden Room* ('Obsession'), *Anna*, *The White Sheik*, *Star Of India*, *War And Peace*, *Rocco And His Brothers*, *Shoot Louder, Louder ... I Don't Understand*, Franco Zefferelli's *Romeo And Juliet* (1968), and *Waterloo* (1970). In 1972 Rota composed the scores for Francis Ford Coppola's *The Godfather*, 'the 70s' answer to *Gone With The Wind*'. Oscar-laden as it was, Rota had to wait for the sequel, *The Godfather, Part Two* (1974), for his Academy Award. Andy Williams had a minor hit in the USA and UK with the 'Love Theme' from the original movie, entitled 'Speak Softly Love' (lyric by Larry Kusik). Rota's other 70s film music included *The Abdication*, *Boys From The Suburbs*, *Casanova*, *Hurricane* and *Death On The Nile* (1978), with Peter Ustinov as Agatha Christie's Poirot. Rota's last, of an impressive number of scores, was for Fellini's *Orchestra Rehearsal* (1979), which was originally made for television.

ROTH, LILLIAN

b. Lillian Rutstein, 13 December 1910, Boston, Massachusetts, USA, d. 1980. Entering showbusiness while still a tiny child, she appeared on the stage and also in films. Billed as 'Broadway's Youngest Star', she sang and danced in shows staged by leading showmen such as Earl Carroll and Florenz Ziegfeld. She made silent films as early as 1918 but was invited to Hollywood when Paramount boss Jesse L. Lasky heard her sing the blues during a New York show designed to introduce Maurice Chevalier to American audiences before his film debut. She appeared with the Marx Brothers in *Animal Crackers* (1930), *Paramount On Parade* (1930) and *Ladies They Talk About* (1933), a feature for Barbara Stanwyck.

Unfortunately, Roth's private life was in turmoil through failed relationships and drink, and by the end of the 30s she had succumbed to alcoholism and was soon a forgotten figure. Then, in 1953, she was featured on television's *This Is Your Life*. The show, together with the publication of Roth's autobiography, *I'll Cry Tomorrow*, convinced Hollywood that here was a story worth telling. The similarly titled film, released in 1955 and starring Susan Hayward as Lillian, was a rare example of a Hollywood biopic that told a tragic tale without unnecessary sensationalism. Roth was able to fashion a new career out of this appraisal of her life and she worked regularly in clubs and on television for the rest of her life. In 1977, half a lifetime after her last film, she appeared in a minor role in the Brooke Shields debut feature film *Communion (Holy Terror/Alice, Sweet Alice)*. Roth's singing of the blues was for the time a rarity for a white woman and she contrived to deliver this material with a fair degree of authenticity.

ROTHSCHILDS, THE

Six years after their smash-hit *Fiddler On The Roof*, Jerry Bock (music) and Sheldon Harnick (lyrics) collaborated with librettist Sherman Yellen on another tale which centred on the plight of oppressed Jews in Europe. *The Rothschilds* opened at the Lunt-Fontanne Theatre in New York on 19 October 1970. Yellen's book was based on a best-selling biography by Frederic Morton, which detailed the rise of the Rothschilds, the fabulously wealthy banking family, and, in particular, one of its driving influences, Mayer Rothschild (Hal Linden). Paul Hecht, as the son Nathan, and Keene Curtis, who took on several roles throughout the piece, both gained favourable notices. Unlike *Fiddler On The Roof*, *The Rothschilds'* score contained no durable hits, but apposite and engaging songs such as 'He Tossed A Coin', 'Rothschild And Sons', 'One Room', 'Sons', 'I'm In Love! I'm In Love!', 'In My Own Lifetime', 'Everything', and 'Pleasure And Privilege', ensured a run of 507 performances. Linden won a Tony Award for his vigorous performance, and Bock and Harnick split up after writing seven scores together.

ROUND MIDNIGHT

A long step (if not exactly a leap) forward in the treatment of jazz and jazz musicians in feature films, this film, released in 1986, loosely traces the life and times of Bud Powell in Paris. Centring upon the characters of an alcoholic American jazzman and his Parisian fan-cum-mentor, the film contains an excellent performance from Dexter Gordon as the saxophonist, a role for which he was unsuccessfully nominated for an Oscar. The music, an approximation of late 50s bop, is generally well realized by Gordon and musicians such as Ron Carter, Billy Higgins, Bobby Hutcherson, Freddie Hubbard, John McLaughlin, Pierre Michelot, Wayne Shorter, Cedar Walton, Tony Williams and Herbie Hancock (who was also responsible for the score). The mostly restrained, unmelodramatic development of an essentially tragic storyline was the responsibility of director Bernard Tavernier, yet there is rather too much reliance upon stereotype and cliché to warrant the accolades heaped upon the film. Undoubtedly, it is an important improvement upon many

jazz-based films but, as so often in the past, film-makers seem unwilling, or unable, either to leave historical context undamaged or acknowledge the fact that most musicians do what they do because they are musicians. They play to hear the music; film-makers apparently feel obliged to give them non-musical motivation which, as often or not, diminishes them when, presumably, the intention is to uplift.

ROUSTABOUT

Elvis Presley's Hollywood career had become a treadmill by the time this 1964 feature was completed. The obligatory early-reel fight-scene over, the plot took the singer into a travelling carnival where, following mishaps and misunderstandings, he finds the inevitable true love. Presley's punishing schedule left him little space to develop acting skills, but in *Roustabout* he is lifted from stupor by the craft of co-star Barbara Stanwyck. Rightfully feted for her performances in a string of excellent films, notably *Double Indemnity* and *Sorry, Wrong Number*, she uses her talent to great effect herein, despite its flimsy premise. Her presence gives the film status it would otherwise lack and Presley rose to the occasion by contributing two superior recordings; the title track and a reading of the Coasters' 'Little Egypt'. However, *Roustabout* proved but a temporary pause in the decline of his once-promising acting career.

ROYAL WEDDING

Inspired by the wedding of Princess Elizabeth to Philip Mountbatten in 1947, this film, which was released by MGM four years later in 1951, was also loosely based on the experiences of one of its stars, Fred Astaire. In 1928, he and his sister Adele appeared in the London production of the stage musical *Funny Face*. They were fêted by the city's fashionable high society, and, eventually, Adele broke up their double act and married Lord Charles Cavendish in 1932. Alan Jay Lerner's screenplay for *Royal Wedding* also concerns a brother and sister dance team, Tom and Ellen Bowen (Astaire and Jane Powell), who take their hit Broadway show, *Every Night At Seven*, to the British capital where Ellen marries Lord John Brindale (Peter Lawford) and gives up her showbusiness career. Tom also finds happiness in London with a music hall performer (played by Sarah Churchill, daughter of Britain's new Prime Minister in 1951), and all three couples (including Elizabeth and Philip) are married on the same November day. Burton Lane (music) and Alan Jay Lerner (lyrics) wrote the score which contained one of the longest song titles ever: 'How Could You Believe Me When I Said I Love You When You Know I've Been A Liar All My Life.' That number provided a humorous, no-punches-pulled, knockabout duet for Astaire and Powell, a young and up-and-coming singer-actress who surprised many people with her all-round versatility in this film. She also had the tender 'Too Late Now' and 'Open Your Eyes', while Fred, amazingly innovative as usual, danced with a hat stand in 'Sunday Jumps', and appeared to dance on the floor, walls and ceiling of a room filled with furniture, accompanied by 'You're All The World To Me'. Illustrated lectures have since been given as to how that last feat was accomplished. Nick Castle (with uncredited assistance from Astaire) was responsible for the choreography. The rest of the score included 'I Left My Hat In Haiti', 'Open Your Eyes', 'Ev'ry Night At Seven', 'The Happiest Day Of My Life' and 'What A Lovely Day For A Wedding'. Stanley Donen directed the film, which was photographed in Technicolor and retitled *Wedding Bells* when it was released in the UK.

ROZSA, MIKLOS

b. 18 April 1907, Budapest, Hungary, d. 27 July 1995. An important composer for films from the early 30s until the early 80s, who had an equally distinguished career in the world of classical music, Rozsa began to play the piano at the age of five and soon added the violin to his studies. He gave his first public performance when he was seven, playing a movement from a Mozart violin concerto and conducting a children's orchestra in Haydn's 'Toy Symphony'. In his teens Rozsa attended Leipzig University and, during his four years there, completed his first serious compositions. His big breakthrough came in 1934 with his 'Theme, Variations, And Finale (Opus 13)'. A year later he moved to London to write a ballet, and was invited to compose the music for Alexandra Korda's film *Knight Without Armour*, starring Robert Donat and Marlene Dietrich. The successful outcome marked the beginning of Rozsa's five-year association with Korda, which, in the late 30s, produced *The Squeaker*, *The Divorce Of Lady X*, *The Spy In Black* and *The Four Feathers*. In 1940, Rozsa went to Hollywood to finish work on *The Thief Of Baghdad* and then scored *Sundown* and *The Jungle Book*. All three films gained him Oscar nominations, and together with *The Four Feathers*, were designated as his 'Oriental' period. Rozsa was nominated again, for *Lydia*, before Korda shut down London Films for the duration of World War II. Rozsa moved to Paramount where he provided the 'stark, powerful, dissonant score' for 'the archetypal film noir of the 40s', Billy Wilder's *Double Indemnity* (1944), followed by other Wilder movies such as *Five Graves To Cairo* and *The Lost Weekend* (1945). In the latter, Rozsa introduced a new instrument, the theremin, 'an ideal accompaniment to torture'. It was one of around 10 'psychological' movies with which Rozsa was involved during his career. Another, in the same year, was Alfred Hitchcock's *Spellbound*, for which Rozsa won his first Academy Award for a 'bleak and exciting' score. In the late 40s, besides Paramount, Rozsa worked mostly for United Artists and Universal on films such as *Because Of Him*, *The Strange Love Of Martha Ivers*, *The Killers* (Burt Lancaster's first movie), *The Red House*, *The Macomber Affair*, *Brute Force*, *The Naked City* (with Frank Skinner) and *A Double Life* (1947), for which he won another Oscar. At the end of the decade Rozsa began to work for MGM, and embarked on his 'religious and historical epic' period, with monumental scores for *Quo Vadis*, *Ivanhoe*, *Julius Caesar*, *Knights Of The Round Table*, *Valley Of The Kings* and *Ben Hur* (1959 - his third Academy Award, and his last major assignment for MGM). Rozsa pursued the epic into the 60s with the blockbusters *King Of Kings* and *El Cid* (1961), both of which were made in Spain. By no means all of Rozsa's scores in the 50s and 60s were of such gigantic proportions; he also provided the

music for movies with a wide variety of subjects, such as *The Asphalt Jungle*, *Crisis*, *The Story Of Three Loves*, *Moonfleet*, *Tribute To A Bad Man*, *Bhowani Junction*, *Lust For Life*, *Something Of Value*, *The World*, *The Flesh And The Devil*, *The V.I.P.'s*, *The Power*, *The Green Berets*, and many more. In 1970 Rozsa made his last film with Billy Wilder, *The Private Life Of Sherlock Holmes*, and played a cameo role as a ballet conductor. His other 70s film music included *The Golden Voyage Of Sinbad*, *The Secret Files Of J. Edgar Hoover*, *Fedora*, *The Last Embrace*, *Time After Time* and *Providence*, described as his 'most inspiring project for years'. Somewhat ironically, during the 70s and 80s, when the demand for elaborate orchestral movie scores had declined, to be replaced by a montage of pop records, renewed interest in Rozsa's earlier classic film works caused record companies to make new recordings of his scores. In 1981, Rozsa's music for *Eye Of The Needle*, suggested, for some, shades of Korda's *The Spy In Black* over 40 years earlier, and *Dead Men Don't Wear Plaid* (1982), a parody of the 40s film noir which included footage from classics of the genre, found Rozsa writing music for scenes that he had originally scored many years previously. Even though he was partially paralyzed by a stroke in 1982, he continued to compose classical works and, on his 80th birthday, was presented with a Golden Soundtrack Award by ASCAP. The anniversary was declared 'Miklos Rozsa Day' in Los Angeles, and the composer was presented with greetings from President Reagan, Queen Elizabeth, and other luminaries such as Margaret Thatcher and Pope John Paul II. Later in 1987 Rozsa was the guest of honour at a gala charity concert of his music given by the Royal Philharmonic Orchestra at London's Royal Festival Hall.

● ALBUMS: *Miklos Rozsa Conducts His Great Film Music* (Polydor 1975)★★★★, *Spellbound-The Classic Film Scores Of Miklos Rozsa* (RCA 1975)★★★★, *Miklos Rozsa Conducting The Royal Philharmonic Orchestra* (Polydor 1976)★★★.

● FURTHER READING: *Miklos Rozsa: A Sketch Of His Life And Work*, C. Palmer. *Double Life: The Autobiography Of Miklos Rozsa*, Miklos Rozsa.

RUBY, HARRY

b. Harry Rubinstein, 27 January 1895, New York, USA, d. 23 February 1974, Woodland Hills, California, USA. A successful composer for stage shows and films, mostly in collaboration with lyricist Bert Kalmar, Ruby played the piano in publishing houses, and accompanied vaudeville acts such as the Messenger Boys, before starting to write songs. He had an early hit in 1919 with 'And He'd Say Oo-La-La, Wee-Wee', written with comedian George Jessel, which became popular for specialist novelty singer Billy Murray. From 1918-28 Kalmar and Ruby wrote songs for Broadway shows, with Ruby sometimes contributing to the libretto. These included *Helen Of Troy, New York* ('I Like A Big Town', 'Happy Ending'); *The Ramblers* ('All Alone Monday', 'Just One Kiss', 'Any Little Tune'); *Five O'Clock Girl* ('Thinking Of You', 'Up In The Clouds'); *Good Boy* ('Some Sweet Someone', 'I Wanna Be Loved By You', the latter memorably revived by Marilyn Monroe in the 1959 Billy Wilder movie *Some Like It Hot*); and *Animal Crackers* ('Watching The Clouds Roll By, 'Who's Been Listening To My Heart?', 'Hooray For Captain Spaulding').

While working on *Animal Crackers*, Kalmar and Ruby formed a friendship with the Marx Brothers, and, after moving to Hollywood in 1928, supplied songs for some of the Brothers' early movies, including *Horse Feathers* (1932) and *Duck Soup* (1933), and the film version of *Animal Crackers*. Groucho Marx later used their 'Hooray For Captain Spaulding' as a theme for his radio and television shows. While in Hollywood, Kalmar and Ruby wrote what was probably their most popular song, 'Three Little Words', for the comedy film *Check And Double Check* (1930), featuring radio's famous double-act, Amos 'N Andy. The songwriting team continued to write consistently for films through the 30s, including *The Cuckoos* (1931, 'I Love You So Much', 'Dancing The Devil Away'), *The Kid From Spain* (1932, 'Look What You've Done', 'What A Perfect Combination'), *Hips, Hips, Hooray* (1934, 'Keep On Doin' What You're Doin''), and *Kentucky Kernels* (1934) ('One Little Kiss'). Their last film work together, in 1939, was for *The Story Of Vernon And Irene Castle* ('Only When You're In My Arms', 'Ain'tcha Comin' Out?'), starring Fred Astaire and Ginger Rogers, although their 1947 song 'A Kiss To Build A Dream On', written with Oscar Hammerstein II, featured in the 1951 movie *The Strip*, and was nominated for an Academy Award. In 1941, they also contributed to another Broadway show, *The High Kickers* ('You're On My Mind', 'A Panic In Panama', 'Time To Sing'). In the 1950 bio-pic *Three Little Words*, Red Skelton played Ruby, and Fred Astaire was cast as Kalmar. The film featured most of their big hits including 'Who's Sorry Now', 'Nevertheless', and the novelty, 'So Long, Oo-Long (How Long You Gonna Be Gone?)'. During the 40s, Ruby also wrote songs with other lyricists, including Rube Bloom ('Give Me The Simple Life'), and provided both music and lyrics for the title song to the Dick Haymes-Maureen O'Hara film *Do You Love Me?* (1946). After the early 50s Ruby was semi-retired, emerging occasionally to appear on television programmes to celebrate songwriters and associated artists. In 1992, the Goodspeed Opera House in Connecticut presented a revival of *Animal Crackers*, with Frank Ferrante in the role of Groucho Marx.

SAILING ALONG

Released in 1938, this was the last of the three films in which Jessie Matthews appeared under the direction of her husband Sonnie Hale. She plays 'water gypsy' Kay Martin, the ambitious step-daughter of bargemaster Skipper Barnes (Frank Pettingell), who is in love with Skipper's studious son, Steve (Barry Mackay). In an effort to attract his attention, she breaks into showbusiness and is rapidly propelled to stardom by eccentric millionaire Victor Gulliver (Roland Young) and producer and song-and-dance-man Dick Randall (Jack Whiting). Meanwhile, Steve is also taking Victor's advice, and makes a killing on the Stock Exchange. It all ends with Kay fending off the advances of the pushy American press agent, Windy (Noel Madison), and sailing off to foreign climes with Steve in his new yacht. The frothy story, which was adapted by Lesser Samuels from a story by Selwyn Jepson, gave Jessie Matthews and Jack Whiting ample opportunity for some slick dance routines which were staged by Buddy Bradley. There were also several appealing songs by Arthur Johnston and Maurice Sigler, including 'My River', 'Souvenir Of Love', 'Trusting My Luck', 'Your Heart Skips A Beat', and the delightful 'Sailing Along'. Athene Seyler and Alastair Sim (the future star of Ealing comedies and St. Trinian's films), provided the comic relief, and also in the cast were Margaret Vyner, Peggy Novak, and William Dewhurst. The screenplay was adapted by Lesser Samuels from a story by Selwyn Jepson.

SAKAMOTO, RYÛICHI

b. 17 January 1952, Tokyo, Japan. Sakamoto studied composition and electronic music at Tokyo College of Arts and took a Master of Arts degree in 1976 before forming the Yellow Magic Orchestra with Haruomi Hosono and Yukihiro Takahashi two years later. It was with the YMO that he first achieved international recognition with 'Computer Game (Theme From The Invaders)' reaching number 17 in the UK charts in 1980. Sakamoto's first solo *One Thousand Knives*, was recorded in 1978, but not released until 1982 and only then in The Netherlands. The first widely-distributed recording was *B-2 Unit*, made while he was still a member of the Yellow Magic Orchestra in 1980 with the help of Andy Partridge (XTC) and Dennis Bovell. Robin Scott was given equal billing on *Left Handed Dream* on which he provided vocals, with US session guitarist Adrian Belew (Talking Heads, Frank Zappa and David Bowie) also featured. *The End Of Asia* was recorded with Danceries, a Japanese classical ensemble which specialized in recreating medieval music. Working alongside

David Sylvian (to whose work Sakamoto became a key contributor), he scored two UK hit singles with 'Bamboo Houses' (1982) and 'Forbidden Colours' (1983). Since the mid-80s, Sakamoto has established a successful career as a solo recording artist, a film composer and an film actor. His evocative soundtrack to Nagisa Oshima's *Merry Christmas, Mr Lawrence* - in which he made his acting debut - received critical acclaim; his contribution to the soundtrack of Bernardo Bertolucci's *The Last Emperor* (with David Byrne and Cong Su) earned him an Academy Award. In September 1985 at the Tsukaba Expo, he collaborated with Radical TV on a spectacular live performance of *TV WAR*, a science fiction show involving music, video and computer graphics. He has constantly attracted a variety of leading musicians in studio work, varying from Iggy Pop to Brian Wilson and Robbie Robertson and was assisted by Thomas Dolby on *Musical Encyclopedia* and the single 'Field Work' (1986). He has also contributed to Public Image Limited's *Album* and Arto Lindsey's *Esperanto*. His own solo albums have consistently displayed a hi-tech integration of western pop music with traditional music from Japan, the Middle East and Africa. After releasing *Beauty*, which incorporated Okinawan music, Sakamoto toured the USA and Europe and established his international fame with his highly eclectic style. He conducted and arranged the music at the opening ceremony for the 1992 Barcelona Olympic Games. *Discord* marked his first attempt at orchestral composition, and was marketed as a multimedia package.

● ALBUMS: *B-2 Unit* (Island 1980)★★, *Hidariudeno (A Dream Of The Left Arm)* (1981)★★★, *Merry Christmas, Mr. Lawrence* film soundtrack (Virgin 1983)★★, *Coda* (1983)★★★, *Ongaku Zukan (A Picture Book Of Music)* (1984)★★★, *Esperanto* (1985)★★★, *Miraiha Yarô (A Futurist Chap)* (1986)★★★, *Media Bahn Live* (1986)★★, *Oneamisno Tsubasa (The Wings Of Oneamis)* (1986)★★★, *Musical Encyclopedia* (Ten 1986)★★, *Neo Geo* (Columbia 1987)★★★, with David Byrne, Cong Su *The Last Emperor* film soundtrack (Virgin 1987)★★★, *Playing The Orchestra* (1988)★★, *Gruppo Musicale* (1989)★★★, *Beauty* (Virgin 1989)★★★, *Heartbeat* (Virgin 1991)★★★, *Wild Palms* film soundtrack (1993)★★★, *Sweet Revenge* (Elektra 1994)★★★, *1996* (Milan 1996)★★★, *Smoochy* (Milan 1997)★★★, *Discord* (Sony Classical 1998)★★★, *Love Is The Devil* film soundtrack (Asphodel 1998)★★★.

● COMPILATIONS: *Tokyo Joe* (Denon 1988)★★★, *Sakamoto Plays Sakamoto* (Virgin 1989)★★★.

● FURTHER READING: *Otowo Miru, Tokiwo Kiku (Seeing Sound And Hearing Time)*, Ryûichi Sakamoto and Shôzô Omori. *Seldom-Illegal*, Ryûichi Sakamoto.

SALAD DAYS

Hastily assembled to fill a three-week gap in the schedule of the Bristol Old Vic in 1954, *Salad Days* was swiftly transferred to London where it opened at the Vaudeville Theatre on 5 August that same year. Julian Slade wrote the music and collaborated on the book and lyrics with Dorothy Reynolds. The simple story told of story of two young university graduates, Jane (Eleanor Drew) and Timothy (John Warner). He is trying to find a job, while Jane's mother is urging her to get married. They meet a tramp (Newton Blick) in the park, and agree to take care

of his mobile piano for a month in return for a payment of £7 per week. The instrument is a magic one, and makes everybody dance. They lose the instrument, and their efforts to find it involve blackmail, a flying saucer, and several of Timothy's uncles. Whimsical stuff, but some shrewd observers recognized a serious underlying message decrying indolence and emphasizing the desirability of work satisfaction. Also in the cast were James Cairncross (Sir Clamsby Williams, Manager of the Night Club, Zebediah Dawes), Michael Aldridge (Mr. Dawes, Police Inspector, Augustine Williams, Ambrose), Christine Finn (Fiona), Pat Heywood (Aunt Prue, Rowena, Waitress), Michael Meacham (Fosdyke, Nigel Danvers), Yvonne Coulette (Lady Raeburn, Dancer), Joe Greig (PC Boot, Electrode), Bob Harris (Troppo, Slave), and Dorothy Reynolds (Mrs. Dawes, Asphinxia, Heloise). The endearing score consisted of a mixture of lively and gentle songs, and included 'The Things That Are Done By A Don', 'It's Easy To Sing', 'We're Looking For A Piano', 'We Said We Wouldn't Look Back', 'Sand In My Eyes', 'I Sit In The Sun', 'Oh, Look At Me', 'Out Of Breath', 'Find Yourself Something To Do', 'Hush-Hush', 'The Saucer Song', 'Cleopatra', and 'The Time Of My Life'. Julian Slade himself played one of the two accompanying pianos, and Salad Days ran on and on for 2,283 performances - a remarkable achievement in the days long before the Andrew Lloyd Webber blockbusters. Sophisticated New Yorkers were not so impressed, and the 1958 US production folded after only 10 weeks. Londoners retained their enormous affection for this curiously British phenomenon, and there were West End revivals in 1961, 1964, and again in 1976. In 1983, a television version was screened in the UK. The 40th anniversary of this charming entertainment was celebrated in 1994 with a new production which was broadcast on BBC Radio 2. James Cairncross, a member of the 1954 cast, played Uncle Augustine, with Janie Dee (Jane), Simon Green (Timothy), Timothy West (Father), Josephine Tewson (Mother), Prunella Scales (Aunt Prue), John Warner (Tramp), Valerie Masterson (Lady Raeburn), Leslie Phillips (Uncle Clam), Samuel West (Fosdyke), Roy Hudd (Manager), Lynda Baron (Asphinxia), and Willie Rushton (Uncle Zed). An Yvonne Arnaud Theatre, Guildford, production, directed by Ned Sherrin, returned to the Vaudeville, its original London home, starring Kit and the Widow, Simon Connolly (Tim), Nicola Fulljames (Jane), and Elizabeth Counsell, Edward Baker-Duly, Chris Dickins, Gary Fairhall, Doug Fisher, Sarah Mortimer, David Morton, Diane V. Parrott, Nova Skipp, and Gay Soper.

SALLY

One of the most popular musicals of the 20s, this was really another version of the Cinderella rags-to-riches story that has been used in shows such as Irene, Mlle. Modiste, My Fair Lady, and 42nd Street, among others. *Sally* opened at the New Amsterdam Theatre in New York on 21 December 1921, and was intended as a showcase for producer Florenz Ziegfeld's current protegée, Marilynn (later Marilyn) Miller. Guy Bolton's book portrayed Miss Miller as poor Sally Green, who dreams of becoming a famous dancer while washing dishes at a Greenwich Village cafe.

One of the waiters (who, not surprisingly, is the exiled Duke of Czechogovinia in disguise) encourages her when a theatrical agent, Otis Hopper (Walter Catlett), suggests that she masquerades as prima ballerina Mme. Nookarova at an elegant party. Of course, it is her big chance, and leads to a starring role in the Ziegfeld Follies, where she dances the 'Butterfly Ballet' with music by Victor Herbert. Leon Errol, as the disguised Duke, provided most of the comedy, along with Walter Catlett. The score was rather a mixed-up affair. All the music was written by Jerome Kern, but several lyricists were involved. P.G. Wodehouse, who, at one stage, was to have written all the song lyrics, ended up by collaborating with Clifford Grey on just two: 'The Church 'Round The Corner' and 'You Can't Keep A Good Girl Down' (Joan Of Arc). Grey also wrote the words for 'Wild Rose', 'Sally', 'On With The Dance', and 'The Schnitza Komisski'. Two of the numbers, with lyrics by Buddy De Sylva, came from *Zip Goes A Million* which folded before it reached Broadway. One of them, 'Whip-Poor-Will', did not cause much of a stir, but the other, 'Look For The Silver Lining', eventually became a sentimental standard. One more song, 'The Lorelei' (lyric: Anne Caldwell), was also 'borrowed' from an earlier Kern score for *The Night Boat*. It all added up to a tremendous hit. 570 performances in a season when 42 other musicals made their Broadway debut, was quite phenomenal. When *Sally* returned to New York in 1948 with Bambi Linn in the leading role, it was only for a brief run. London audiences took to the show in 1921, when it starred Dorothy Dickson and Leslie Henson, and stayed at the Winter Garden for nearly a year. They also enjoyed a revised version, entitled *Wild Rose*, which spent six months at the Prince's Theatre in 1942 with Jessie Matthews as Sally. There have been two films of the story: a silent version in 1925, and the 1929 early talkie, with Marilyn Miller.

SALLY IN OUR ALLEY

Gracie Fields was already the talk of the north of England, when she made her film debut in this 1931 Basil Dean production for Associated Talking Pictures. The screenplay, by Miles Malleson, Archie Pitt, and Alma Reville, was based on the play *The Likes Of 'Er* by Charles McEvoy. Gracie Fields plays Sally Winch, a lively young lady who has left Rochdale in Lancashire for a job in a coffee shop in London's Mile End Road which is run by Sam Bilson (Ben Field). After many years of waiting she has given up all hope of seeing her true love, George Miles (Ian Hunter), again, fearing him lost in action during World War I. However, George's terrible wounds have healed, and, in spite of the efforts of jealous Florrie Small (Florence Desmond), 'a child of the gutter - cunning suspicious and pretty', to keep them apart, he and Sally are eventually reunited. Renee Macready and Helen Ferrers play Lady Daphne and the Duchess of Wexford, a couple of toffs who try, without success, to turn Sally's head, and also among a strong supporting cast were Fred Groves, Gibb McLaughlin, Ivor Barnard, Barbara Gott, and Florence Harwood. Rising above the action was Gracie Fields' thrilling voice on songs such as 'Following The Sun Around' (Joseph McCarthy-Harry Tierney), 'Moonlight On The Alster' (Osacar Fetras), 'Lancashire Blues', 'Fred

Fernackerpan', and the immortal 'Sally' (Will Haines-Harry Leon-Leo Towers), the number that became her life-long theme. This film, which was directed by Maurice Elvey, helped Gracie on her way to becoming one of the best-loved British entertainers of all time.

SALSA

Twenty-one-year old Rico (Robby Rosa) and his girlfriend Vicki (Angela Alvarado) enter the annual dance contest at the La Luna nightclub in Los Angeles. Rico's eye is firmly set on the first prize of a trip to Puerto Rico, but unfortunately the club's owner, Luna (Miranda Garrison), a former Queen of Salsa, has *her* eyes set firmly on him. As if Rico has not enough trouble already, trying to cope with the attentions of sexy Lola (Moon Orana), his mother (Loyda Ramos), and sister Rita (Magali Alvarado) who is dating Rico's best friend Ken (Rodney Harvey). OK, so Luna teaches him a thing or two, but when the chips are down and the music strikes up, the girl in Rico's arms is Vicki. The hot Latin score that accompanied director Boaz Davidson's screenplay, included 'Son Matamoros', performed by Celia Cruz, 'Chicos Y Chicas' (Mavis Vegas Davis), 'Cali Pachanguero' (Grupo Niche), and 'Salsa Heat' (Michael Sembello), along with the less predictable 'Blue Suede Shoes' (Robby Rosa) and 'Maybe Baby' (Buddy Holly And The Crickets). The original music was composed by Wojciech Kilar, and Kenny (*Dirty Dancing*) Ortego designed the choreography. *Salsa* was released by Cannon Films in 1988, and nominated for the Razzie Worst New Star: Robby Rosa.

SAN FRANCISCO

Jeanette MacDonald arranged a temporary 'divorce' from her celebrated singing partner Nelson Eddy, and co-starred with Clark Gable in this film which must have qualified as one of the very first 'disaster' movies (at least with sound), when it was released by MGM in 1936. In Anita Loo's superb screenplay (based on a story by Robert Hopkins), Macdonald plays singer Mary Blake, whose association with Blackie Norton (Gable), a cabaret club owner in the rough, tough Barbary Coast area of San Francisco, leads to a career in opera and a temporary suspension of their romantic affair. They get back together again after the earth moves for them - and all the other residents of the city - in a spectacular earthquake sequence towards the end of the picture. Spencer Tracy gave an excellent performance as Gable's best buddy, and also in the cast were Jessie Ralph, Jack Holt, Shirley Ross, Ted Healy, Edgar Kennedy, Al Shean, and Richard Carle. The songs were a mixed bag of operatic excerpts and popular numbers, and included 'Would You?' (Nacio Herb Brown-Arthur Freed), 'Sempre Libera' (from Verdi's *La Traviata*), 'A Heart That's Free' (Alfred J. Robyn-T. Railey), 'The Holy City' (Stephen Adams-F.E. Weatherley), and the title song which was mercilessly lampooned by Judy Garland in her celebrated Carnegie Hall concert recording in 1961. *San Francisco*, which was produced by John Emerson and Bernard Hyman, and skilfully directed by W.S. Van Dyke, is considered to be a classic of its kind and a fine example of the film maker's art.

SATCHMO THE GREAT

Made for television by Ed Murrow, this 1956 film follows Louis Armstrong on a tour of Europe and Africa. Intercut with scenes of live performance by Armstrong And His All Stars, and their reception, often by tens of thousands of well-wishers, at airports, are interviews with Armstrong. Although one of the finest and most respected journalists of his, or any other, era, Murrow's questions are sometimes a shade naïve, but Armstrong takes it all in his stride. The film ends with a New York concert performance of 'St Louis Blues' in which Armstrong and his men are joined by Leonard Bernstein and the New York Philharmonic to play to a capacity audience that includes W.C. Handy. One moving moment shows Handy, then over 80, removing his hat to take his handkerchief from his head to mop a tear from his blind eyes. The All Stars featured are Trummy Young, Edmond Hall, Billy Kyle, Jack Lesberg and Barrett Deems with singer Velma Middleton.

SATURDAY NIGHT

Written in the early 50s, this musical should have marked Stephen Sondheim's Broadway debut as a composer and lyricist. However, due to a variety of circumstances, it remained unproduced for more than 40 years. A chance meeting between Sondheim and Lemuel Ayres set the ball rolling. Ayres, who co-produced, and designed the costumes and sets for *Kiss Me, Kate!*, had bought a play called *Front Porch In Flatbush* from the distinguished Hollywood screenwriting twins Julius J. Epstein and Philip G. Epstein. After winning Oscars for their *Casablanca* screenplay (1942), Philip died 10 years later. While Sondheim was writing the score for *Saturday Night*, Julius J. Epstein and producer John Barry Ryan III assembled a cast which included Jack Cassidy, Alice Ghostley, Leila Martin, and Joel Grey. The opening was set, and then in August 1955 Ayers died of leukaemia at the age of 40. The production died with him when the rights to the play passed to his widow, who was not inclined to continue with the project. Later that year, Sondheim used *Saturday Night* for his successful audition with Leonard Bernstein and Arthur Laurents, composer and librettist respectively for *West Side Story*. Some five years on, after Sondheim had collaborated with Jule Styne on *Gypsy*, Styne himself wanted to produce *Saturday Night*, with Bob Fosse directing and playing the lead. They actually went as far as auditioning the cast before Sondheim called a halt. 'I suddenly got the feeling in the pit of my stomach that I didn't want to back to old work - I wanted to go on to something new.' He certainly achieved that aim, and in the process became arguably the most innovative and controversial musical theatre composer of the latter half of the century. A self-confessed Anglophile, Sondheim was present at the Bridewell Theatre (of which he is patron) in London when a group of students from the University of Birmingham presented a concert version of *Saturday Night* in 1995. Asked if he would allow the Bridewell to produce the first full production, he responded positively, and the world premiere took place on the 17 December 1997. In view of the introspection and sombre tone of much of his work,

Saturday Night proved to be a charming, optimistic and upbeat comedy. Sondheim calls it a farce, 'There's only one villain, and he's a comic villain.' His name is Gene (Sam Newman), a thinly disguised version of the Epstein twins' third brother. Gene is the ringleader of a group of young Brooklyn blades, all of whom dream of meeting (cheap) weak and willing women on a Saturday night, and making a killing on the soaring stock market every Monday morning. The time is early in 1929 - pre-Wall Street Crash - and Gene, the son of a travelling salesman, has his own special dream of donning the Brooks Brothers tails suit, and moving uptown to a fancy Park Avenue apartment. Problem is, he rents it with the money he is supposed to be investing for his buddies. Everything turns out OK though, because Gene repents, and settles for his childhood roots and a girlfriend, Helen (Anna Francolini), who isn't really the Southern belle he first took her for. In fact, she's from Brooklyn too. Joining in the fun were Tracie Bennett (Celeste), James Millard (Bobby), Maurice Yeoman (Dino), Jeremy David (Artie), Simon Greiff (Ray), Mark Haddigan (Hank), Ashleigh Sendin (Mildred), as well as Gavin Lee, Rae Baker, and Paul Brereton, all of whom played multiple roles. Several numbers from Sondheim's splendid, tuneful and witty score, had featured in other shows, and tributes to the composer over the years, notably 'Marry Me A Little' 'Saturday Night', and 'So Many People', a trio which formed an important part of the 1981 revue, *Marry Me A Little*. They were now being heard in their proper context, along with 'Class', 'Love's A Bond', 'Isn't It?', 'In The Movies', 'Exhibit A', 'One Wonderful Day', 'I Remember That', 'All For You', 'It's That Kind Of Neighbourhood', 'What More Do I Need?', and one of Sondheim's most delightful ballads, 'A Moment With You'. Tim Flavin staged the musical sequences, sets and costumes were by Bridget Kimak, and this first proper look at the middle-aged musical entitled *Saturday Night*, was directed by Carol Metcalfe and Clive Paget.

SATURDAY NIGHT FEVER

One of the most popular films of the 70s, *Saturday Night Fever* (1977) launched John Travolta as a teen idol. He starred as a member of a Brooklyn street gang, obsessed by dancing, which provides a release from his impoverished background. Travolta's routines were remarkable - inspiring numerous pastiches - and his portrayal of the inarticulate central character is highly convincing. Travolta's co-star was Karen Lynn Gorney, and also cast were Barry Miller, Joseph Cali, Paul Pape, and Bruce Ornstein. Some felt that several external factors robbed *Saturday Night Fever* of its undoubted strengths, inasmuch as an expurgated version, undertaken to reach a younger audience, has become the print through which many encounter the film. This trimming served to rob it of dramatic purpose, editing 'bad' language, sex scenes and violence integral to the plot. More crucially, disco music did not enjoy critical popularity and many disparaged *Saturday Night Fever* on this premise alone. This did not stop the soundtrack becoming, for a while, the bestselling album of all time, retaining the UK number 1 spot for 18 consecutive weeks. Songs were performed by artists such as Tavares, Trammps, Yvonne Elliman, David Shire, KC

And The Sunshine Band, and the Bee Gees, and it is chiefly remembered for several excellent tracks composed by the latter, brothers Barry, Maurice and Robin Gibb. Four selections, 'How Deep Is Your Love', 'More Than A Woman', 'Staying Alive' and 'You Should Be Dancing' reached the UK Top 10 in their own right as singles, while 'Night Fever' held the top spot in 1978. Other numbers, written by Walter Murphy, Shire, R. Bell, Kool And The Gang, W. Eaton, C. Hearndon, Leroy Green/Ron Kersey, M. Mussorgsky, and Harry Casey/Richard Finch, included 'If I Can't Have You', 'Jive Talkin'', 'A Fifth Of Beethoven', 'Calypso Breakdown', 'Open Sesame', 'Boogie Shoes', 'Disco Inferno', 'Manhattan Skyline', 'Night On Disco Mountain' and 'Salsation'. Robert Stigwood produced, and John Badham directed what remains a taut, absorbing teen-orientated film.

Norman Wexler's screenplay was based on a story by Nick Cohn, and their work was the source for the stage version, which opened at the London Palladium on 5 May 1998. This adaptation, which was credited to Nan Knighton, in collaboration with co-producers Stigwood and Paul Nicholas, and the show's director and choreographer Arlene Phillips, starred West End newcomer, Australian Adam Garcia, in the Travolta role (Tony Manero). Joining him in a slick, and occasionally spectacular production, were Anita Louise Combe, Tara Wilkinson, Simon Greiff, Richard Calkin, David Payton-Bruhl, Jonathan Avery, Susan Fay and John Stacey. Amendments to the original film score involved several additional Bee Gees numbers, such as 'Tragedy', 'It's My Neighbourhood', 'First And Last' and 'Immortality', as well as 'Disco Duck' (Rick Dees) and 'What Kind Of Fool' (Barry Gibb/A. Galuten). In spite of mixed reviews ('More Sunday morning than Saturday night'), this predictably anodyne reincarnation of the landmark movie set out to cash in on the late 90s retro chic, aiming firmly at the nostalgic Grease-Fame-Buddy audience.

SAUCY JACK AND THE SPACE VIXENS

Conceived by a group of young people for the 1995 Edinburgh Fringe Festival, this award-winning 'intergalactic camp-fest' was presented by Counterpoint Theatre at regional venues in the UK and America, before beaming down into London's Queen's Theatre on 25 March 1998. The action takes place on the planet Frottage III, a KY Class planet in Sector 6 of the Throbb System, where there is a serial killer at large. Talented cabaret artists from Saucy Jack's seedy bar have been cruelly slain with the heel of a sequinned slingback. Enter the Space Vixens, a team of highly trained crime fighters, led by Jubilee Climax (Catherine Porter), Bunny Lingus (Johanna Allitt), and Anna Labia (Nastasha Bain). Clad in catsuits with conical breastplates, and glitter boots imbued with the power of disco, they groove around searching for the guilty one until Jubilee and Saucy Jack (David Schofield) begin to rekindle the embers of an old romance. After that, it is everyone to the Vibro Chamber. Also involved were Booby (David Ashley), Whackoff (Adam Meggido), Mitch (Mark Oxtoby), Chesty/Shirley (Hannah Waddingham), and Sammy (Daniel Wexler). Charlotte Mann wrote the book, and collaborated on the lyrics with Michael Fidler. Robin

Forrest composed the music with Jonathan Croose, and amid all the lasers, PVC, kitsch references (*This Is Spinal Tap*, *Blake's Seven*, *Return To The Forbidden Planet*), and an extremely high double-entendre count, were several pretty good songs, including 'Glitter Boots Saved My Life', 'All I Need Is Disco', and Catherine Porter's torchy ballad, 'Living In Hell'. The remainder of the score consisted of 'Saucy Jack's', 'Plastic Leather And Love', 'Park My Bike', 'Thrill Me', 'Nowhere To Run', 'I'm Just A Tortured Plaything', 'Cheer Up Bunny', 'Crime Fighting Mamas', 'Fetish Number From Nowhere', 'Let's Make Magic', and 'Space Trucking'. Christina Avery and Iain Stuart-Ferguson handled the musical staging, it was designed by David Blight, and directed by Keith Strachan. The main London critics were not amused ('hopelessly amateurish . . . makes *Dan Dare* look like a masterpiece of sophistication'), and *Saucy Jack* departed the Queen's Theatre planet of this universe on the 6 June. Up until that time the adverts had been reading: '*Red Dwarf* meets *The Rocky Horror Show* in this wacky dollop of theatrical bubblegum.' That sounds about right.

SAVAGE SEVEN, THE

Richard Rush, veteran of the American International Pictures' treadmill, directed this 1969 feature which drew upon the legacy of 'biker' movies The Wild Angels and *Hells Angels On Wheels*. A Californian shanty town provides the setting for battles between a motorcycle gang and Native Americans, paying lip-service to the former's standing as 'outlaws of America.' Guitarist Duane Eddy, responsible for a string of late 50s/early 60s hits, including 'Rebel Rouser', 'Cannonball' and 'Shazam', is unaccustomably featured in an acting role, portraying one of the unruly misfits. Mike Curb, whose Sidewalk company was responsible for scoring many of the exploitation movies from the AIP group and others, assembled a soundtrack which included 'Anyone For Tennis (The Savage Seven Theme)' by Cream. This lilting pop song, which grazed the UK Top 40 when issued as a single, had nothing to do with the film plot, suggesting it was a recording the group would otherwise have held in abeyance. Clearly inspired by *The Magnificent Seven*, the *Savage Seven* has little of the former's lasting qualities.

SCARLET PIMPERNEL, THE

Based on the 1905 novel by Baroness Orczy, this swashbuckling 'New Musical Adventure' swept into the Minskoff Theatre in New York on 9 November 1997. Although Nan Knighton's book 'clarifies' the Baroness's story in several respects, this romantic romp through England and France in the summer of 1794, has most of the hallmarks of the Baroness's musty old tome. Taking as his emblem the small red flower so common in the English countryside, disguised nobleman Sir Percy Blakeney (Douglas Sills, making an impressive Broadway debut) and his band of cronies masquerade as a bunch of fops in order to wreck the French Revolution, quell the horrors of the Reign of Terror, and save many innocent members of the French aristocracy from the guillotine. As if that were not trouble enough, Percy believes his new French actress wife Marguerite (Christine Andreas) to be a spy for the terrorists. Little does he know, however, that the heat is on the poor girl, courtesy of an old flame, the villainous Chauvelin (Terrence Mann). Maybe her brother, Armand St. Just (Gilles Chiasson), will think of something. The pleasant but uninspired score, which accompanied all this good-natured, and often tongue-in-cheek, derring-do, was the work of lyricist Nan Knight and composer Frank Wildhorn (*Jekyll & Hyde*). Among its highlights were the rousing opening number, 'Madame Guillotine' (French Chorus), 'Into The Fire' (Percy and his men), the fiery 'Vivez!' (Marguerite, Percy, Lady Digby [Sandy Rosenberg], Lady Lewellyn [Pamela Burrell *et al*]), the French saloon song 'Storybook' (Leontine, French Chorus), 'When I Look At You' (Marguerite), and 'Falcon In The Dive' (Chauvelin). The remainder of the numbers included 'Believe', 'Prayer', 'The Scarlet Pimpernel', 'Where's The Girl?', 'The Creation Of Man', 'The Riddle', 'They Seek Him Here', 'Only Love', 'She Was There', 'Lullaby' and 'You Are My Home'. Critics were quick to point out that predictably there were several 'repetitive, broken hearted songs suitable for pop divas' in there. As an established pop songwriter (Whitney Houston's US number 1, 'Where Do Broken Hearts Go?'), Wildhorn likes his tunes to have a life outside the theatre. He also believes in concept albums. The one in 1992 that introduced *The Scarlet Pimpernel* to the world featured Chuck Wagner and Dave Clemmons, as well as Peabo Bryson and Linda Eder, who had some success with 'You Are My Home', the show's curtain number. Adam Pelty was the choreographer, and also played the role of Elton, the beautiful costumes were by Jane Greenwood, and Andrew Jackness won a FANY Award for his scenic design which included an awesome-looking guillotine, and a Pimpernel insignia that glowed in the dark. *The Scarlet Pimpernel* was directed by Peter Hunt, returning to Broadway for the first time since he won a Tony Award for his work on *1776* (1969). Andreas and Sills were among the Drama League outstanding artists of the 1997/8 season. After playing consistently to less that 50% capacity, the show was acquired by Radio City Entertainment in a joint venture with financier Theodore Forstmann. They closed the production from 2-9 October 1998, and reopened with Rachel York and Rex Smith replacing Mann and Andreas, but with Sills still in the lead. Robert Longbottom took over as director and choreographer.

SCHERTZINGER, VICTOR

b. 8 April 1880, Mahanoy City, Pennsylvania, USA, d. 26 October 1941, Hollywood, California, USA. A leading composer, conductor and director for movies, from the early days of silents, through the 30s and 40s. A gifted violinist as a child, Schertzinger toured as a concert soloist and studied music in Europe before returning and becoming a well-known conductor by the time he was 30. A few years later he began to compose the music for popular songs such as 'Marcheta' and 'My Wonderful Dream', and in 1916 moved to Hollywood to write scores for a series of silent movies, including Thomas Ince's revolutionary *Civilization*. Almost immediately he began to direct as well, and from then, throughout his career, he successfully combined the two occupations. With the advent of

sound in the late 20s, Schertzinger contributed complete scores or individual songs to musicals such as The Love Parade, *Heads Up*, One Night Of Love, *Love Me Forever*, *Follow Your Heart*, The Music Goes 'Round, *Something To Sing About*, Road To Singapore, *Rhythm On The River*, Kiss The Boys Goodbye, and The Fleet's In. Several of his most appealing songs, with lyrics by Johnny Mercer, came from that last movie which was released in 1942, shortly after his death. These included 'I Remember You', 'Tangerine', 'If You Build A Better Mousetrap', 'Arthur Murray Taught Me Dancing In A Hurry', 'When You Hear The Time Signal', and 'The Fleet's In'. Among his other songs from that period were 'Magnolias In The Moonlight', 'Life Begins When You're In Love', 'Captain Custard', 'The Moon And The Willow Tree', 'I Don't Want To Cry Anymore', 'Kiss The Boys Goodbye', 'Sand In My Shoes', and 'I'll Never Let A Day Pass By'. Schertzinger also directed several of the above musicals, as well as numerous dramatic features. After directing Bing Crosby, Bob Hope and Dorothy Lamour in *Road To Singapore*, the first of the popular 'Road' pictures, Schertzinger worked again with the 'Old Groaner' on *Road To Zanzibar* - arguably the best of the series - *Rhythm On The River*, and Birth Of The Blues. As well as Mercer, Schertzinger's songwriting collaborators included Clifford Grey, Johnny Burke, Gus Kahn, and Frank Loesser. They all shared his ability to write lively, optimistic and amusing numbers, with the occasional memorable ballad as well.

SCHIFRIN, LALO

b. 21 June 1932, Buenos Aires, Argentina. Schifrin was taught classical piano from the age of six but later studied sociology and law at university. He won a scholarship to the Paris Conservatoire where he studied with Olivier Messiaen. In 1955 he represented Argentina in the Third International Jazz Festival in Paris. He met Dizzy Gillespie first in 1956 when the trumpeter was touring South America. Schifrin had founded the first Argentine big band in the Count Basie tradition and in 1957 wrote his first film music. He moved to New York in 1958 and toured Europe in 1960 with a Jazz At The Philharmonic ensemble, which included Gillespie, with whom he played between 1960 and 1962. He had become increasingly interested in large-scale compositions and wrote two suites for Gillespie - *Gillespiana* and New Continent. He worked with Quincy Jones when he left Gillespie, but became more and more involved in scoring for television and feature films including *The Cincinnati Kid* (1965), *Bullitt* (1968), *Dirty Harry* (1971), and the distinctive theme from the television series *Mission Impossible*. His more than 150 scores over a period of nearly 30 years have also included *The Liquidator, Cool Hand Luke, The Fox, Coogan's Bluff, Kelly's Heros, Hit!, Magnum Force, Voyage Of The Damned, The Eagle Has Landed, Rollercoaster, The Amityville Horror, The Competition, The Sting II, Hollywood Wives* (television mini-series), *The Fourth Protocol, F/X2 - The Deadly Art Of Illusion, The Dead Pool, Return From The River Kwai, A Woman Called Jackie* (1992 television series), and *The Beverly Hillbillies* (1993). He lectured in composition at the University of California, Los Angeles (1968-71), and has spent a good deal of his career searching for common ground between jazz and classical music. In 1995, he conducted the London Philharmonic Orchestra at London's Festival Hall, in *Jazz Meets The Symphony*, 'an evening of jazz-symphonic fusion'.

● ALBUMS: *Bossa Nova - New Brazilian Jazz* (Audio Fidelity 1962)★★★, *New Fantasy* (Verve 1966)★★★, *The Dissection And Reconstruction Of Music From The Past As Performed By The Inmates Of Lalo Schiffrin's Demented Ensemble As A Tribute To The Memory Of The Marquis De Sade* (Verve 1966)★★★, *Music From 'Mission: Impossible'* (1967)★★★, *Insensatez* (Verve 1968)★★★, *Towering Toccata* (1977)★★, *Black Widow* (CTI 1976)★★★, *Free Ride* (1979)★★, *Guitar Concerto* (1985)★★, *Anno Domini* (1986)★★, with Jimmy Smith *The Cat Strikes Again* (Verve 1986)★★★, *Jazz Meets The Symphony* (Atlantic 1993)★★★★, *More Jazz Meets The Symphony* (Atlantic 1994)★★★ *Firebird* (Four Winds 1996)★★★, *Gillespiana* (Aleph 1998)★★.

● COMPILATIONS: *Mission: Impossible . . . And More! The Best Of Lalo Schifrin 1962-1972* (Motor 1997)★★★★, *Dirty Harry Anthology* (Aleph/Koch 1998)★★★.

SCHMIDT, HARVEY

b. 12 September 1929, Dallas, Texas, USA. An important composer for the musical theatre from the early 60s, Schmidt was majoring in art at the University of Texas when he met lyricist Tom Jones (b. 17 February 1928, Littlefield, Texas, USA). Jones was studying to be a stage director, and the two men collaborated on college shows before joining the US Army. They subsequently met up again in New York, where Schmidt was working as a commercial artist while Jones was directing a series of nightclub revues produced by Julius Monk. In 1959, Schmidt and Jones contributed several songs to one of these revues, *Demi-Dozen*, and in the following year, on 3 May 1960, the show for which they will always be remembered, *The Fantasticks*, opened off-Broadway at the Sullivan Street Playhouse. With music and lyrics by Schmidt and Jones, and a book by Jones, this simple, romantic comedy, with two memorable songs, 'Try To Remember' and 'Soon It's Gonna Rain', eventually became the world's longest-running musical, and New York's answer to London's *The Mousetrap*. After writing the scores for two successful mainline Broadway productions, *110 In The Shade* (1963) and *I Do! I Do!* (1966), Schmidt and Jones turned their attention to the allegorical *Celebration* (1960), which folded after some three months. Since then their innovative and often experimental work has been presented off-Broadway and in regional theatre. These productions have included *Philemon* (1975), *Grover's Corners* (1987), and several attempts to musicalize the stories of the French author Colette. A national tour of *Grover's Corners*, which was based on Thornton Wilder's play *Our Town*, was announced with a full-page advertisement in *Variety* in 1989, but had to be called off because of the illness of its star, Mary Martin. In 1992, Schmidt and Jones led an English-speaking tour of *The Fantasticks* throughout the Japanese mainland, with Jones reprising the role he played in the 1960 production, and Schmidt playing the piano. In the same year, Schmidt's 'Monteargentario: Seven Dances For Solo Piano' was released on Bay Cities' *Classical Broadway*.

In 1996, a 'new family musical' entitled *Mirette*, with a Schmidt-Jones score, and libretto by Elizabeth Diggs based on Emily Arnold McCully's award-winning book *Mirette On The High Wire*, had its world premiere at Goodspeed-at-Chester's Norma Terris Theatre. In the following year as *The Fantasticks* celebrated its 37th anniversary, the two songwriters starred off-Broadway in *The Show Goes On*, a pot-pourri of their work which included the appealing numbers, 'My Cup Runneth Over' (*I Do! I Do!*) and 'Love Don't Turn Away' (*110 In The Shade*). In 1999, Schmidt and Jones were inducted into The Theatre Hall of Fame.

● FURTHER READING: *The Fantasticks: The 30th Anniversary Edition*, Tom Jones and Harvey Schmidt. *The Amazing Story Of The Fantasticks: America's Longest Running Play*, Robert Viagas and Donald C. Farber. *Making Musicals*, Tom Jones.

SCHOFIELD, PHILLIP

b. 1962, Oldham, Lancashire, England. When Schofield took over the leading role of Joseph And The Amazing Technicolor Dreamcoat at the London Palladium while Jason Donovan went on holiday early in 1992, it proved to be one of Andrew Lloyd Webber's most (commercially) inspired decisions. Having been obsessed with broadcasting from an early age, Schofield eventually secured a job as a bookings clerk with the BBC in 1979. Later that year he emigrated to New Zealand with his family, and began his television career there on a pop show called *Shazam!*. He stayed in New Zealand for three and a half years, and, on his return, landed a late-night spot on Capital Radio in London. During the 80s he became one of the most popular presenters on children's television, especially on the Saturday morning programme *Going Live!*, and other shows such as the travelogue *Schofield's Europe*, and *Television's Greatest Hits*. He also had his own record programmes on BBC Radio One. In October 1991, while hosting the *Smash Hits Pollwinners Party* on live television, he was 'assaulted' by the guitarist Fruitbat, a member of the eccentric pop group Carter USM. When he recovered, he revealed that Jason Donovan had been voted best male singer - and, just under three months later, took over from Donovan in *Joseph* at the Palladium on 13 January 1992. The theatre's box-office was besieged, and, from then on until Donovan returned for the last few weeks prior to the show's closure in January 1994, Schofield played the role for extended periods and was widely acclaimed - particularly by the young girls who arrived by the coachload. Undoubtedly, many of them bought his record of 'Close Every Door', one of the songs from the show, pushing it into the UK Top 30. Since then, Schofield has continued to front television programmes such as the 'investigative series,' *Schofield's Quest*, *Now We're Talking*, and *Talking Telephone Numbers*. Voted the BBC/SOS Top Man On TV for three years running, and winner of *TV Times* Awards for four years, he was honoured with The Variety Show Business Personality Of The Year Award in 1993. Following his personal triumph in *Joseph* he eventually toured with the production, returning to London in 1996, this time at the Labatt's Apollo Theatre, Hammersmith. At that same theatre, on the 14 July 1998, Schofield led the cast, attracting excellent reviews, in the world premiere of Leslie Bricusse's stage musical, *Doctor Dolittle*.

SCHÖNBERG, CLAUDE-MICHEL

b. 6 July 1944, Vannes, France. A composer, author, and record producer, Schönberg began his collaboration with Alain Boublil in 1973 with the first-ever staged French rock opera *La Revolution Francaise*, which played to capacity audiences and sold over 350,000 double albums. A year later he sang his own music and lyrics on an album which spawned the hit single 'Le Premier Pas'. In 1978, he and Boublil started work on the musical Les Misérables which was presented at the Palais des Sports in Paris in September 1980. The concept album won two gold discs in 1981. *Les Misérables* (with English lyrics by Herbert Kretzmer) opened at the Barbican Theatre in London on 30 September 1985, and transferred to the Palace Theatre in December of that year before settling in for a long run. When the show was produced on Broadway in 1987, Schönberg won Tony Awards for best score and book, and a Grammy for Best Original Cast recording. In January 1994, *Les Misérables* became the third longest-running musical in London theatre history. Schonberg and Boublil's next project, Miss Saigon, was acclaimed both in London (1989) and New York (1991), and has been successfully presented in many countries throughout the world. In December 1994, it became the longest-running musical ever at the Theatre Royal, Drury Lane, eclipsing the 2,281-performance record set by My Fair Lady. A later joint project, *Martin Guerre* (London 1996), was not so enduring and closed after a 20-month run, but was revived in December 1998 at the West Yorkshire Playhouse in the north of England. Two more of the partners' compositions, 'Rhapsody For Piano And Orchestra' and 'Symphonic Suite', were premiered at London's Royal Albert Hall in 1992.

SCHWARTZ, ARTHUR

b. 25 November 1900, New York City, New York, USA, d. 3 September 1984. A distinguished composer and film producer, Arthur Schwartz was prohibited by his family from learning music, so he began composing while still a teenager at high school. He studied law and continued to write as a hobby, but in 1924 he met Lorenz Hart, with whom he immediately began to collaborate on songs. They enjoyed some modest success but not enough to turn Schwartz from his path as a lawyer. In the late 20s he practised law in New York City, continuing to write songs in his spare time with a string of lyricists as collaborators, until Hart convinced him that he could make a career in music. He took time off from his practice and was advised to seek a permanent collaborator. He was introduced to Howard Dietz, with whom he established an immediate rapport. Among their first joint efforts to the revue, *The Little Show* (1929), was one of the songs that Schwartz had written with Hart, 'I Love To Lie Awake In Bed'. After being given a new lyric by Dietz, it became 'I Guess I'll Have To Change My Plan' - also known as 'The blue pajama song'. Later songs for revues included 'Something To Remember You By' and 'The Moment I Saw You'. In 1931, Schwartz and Dietz had a major success with The Band Wagon, which starred Fred Astaire and his sister Adele. The partners' score included their most important song

success, 'Dancing In The Dark'. Other shows of the 30s were less successful but there were always excellent songs: 'Louisiana Hayride', 'Alone Together', 'A Shine On Your Shoes', 'What A Wonderful World', 'Love Is A Dancing Thing' and 'You And The Night And The Music'. The pair also wrote for radio and interspersed their collaborations with songs written with other partners. Schwartz wrote songs for shows such as *Virginia* (1937) and *Stars In Your Eyes* (1939). During the 40s and 50s he wrote songs with various collaborators for several film musicals, including *Navy Blues*, *Thank Your Lucky Stars* ('They're Either Too Young Or Too Old' with Frank Loesser), *The Time, The Place And The Girl* ('Gal In Calico', 'A Rainy Night In Rio' with Leo Robin), and *Excuse My Dust* (1951). He also served as producer on pictures such as Cover Girl, Night And Day, and *The Band Wagon*. Schwartz was reunited with Dietz in 1948 on a revue *Inside USA*, and in 1953 they wrote a new song, 'That's Entertainment', for the screen version of The Band Wagon. In 1951, Schwartz collaborated with Dorothy Fields on *A Tree Grows In Brooklyn*, from which came 'Love Is The Reason' and 'I'll Buy You A Star'. Schwartz and Fields also wrote *By The Beautiful Sea* (1954), which included 'Alone Too Long'. Later Broadway shows by Schwartz and Dietz proved unsuccessful and although their songs, such as 'Something You Never Had Before' and 'Before I Kiss The World Goodbye', were pleasant and lyrically deft, they were not of the high standard they had previously set themselves. In the late 60s Schwartz settled in London, England, for a while where he wrote *Nicholas Nickleby* and *Look Who's Dancing* (a revised version of *A Tree Grows In Brooklyn* with several new songs). He also recorded an album of his own songs, *From The Pen Of Arthur Schwartz*, before returning to live in the USA.
● ALBUMS: *From The Pen Of Arthur Schwartz* (1976)★★.

SCHWARTZ, STEPHEN

b. 6 March 1948, New York, USA. One of the few new theatrical composers and lyricists to emerge in the 70s, Schwartz studied at the Carnegie-Mellon University, where he majored in drama, and at Juilliard. He worked as a record producer for RCA Records before deciding to make a career as a songwriter. In 1969 he contributed the title song to Leonard Gershe's play *Butterflies Are Free*, which ran on Broadway for more than 1000 performances, and was filmed in 1972. In 1971, Schwartz had a smash hit with his rock-pop score for the off-Broadway 'biblical' musical Godspell, which ran for over 2,500 performances in New York, and featured the hit song 'Day By Day'. He also produced the Grammy-winning Original Cast album. Later that year, Schwartz collaborated with Leonard Bernstein on additional text for Bernstein's 'theatre piece', *Mass*, which was commissioned for the opening of the John F. Kennedy Center for the Performing Arts. During the early 70s, Schwartz enjoyed more success with Pippin (1972), which had another agreeable song, 'Magic Do', and The Magic Show (1974). Each show ran for nearly five years in New York. Subsequently, he seemed to lose the magic formula. The Baker's Wife (1976) closed out of town although it has since become something of a cult item, and *Working* (1978), *Rags* (1986), and Children Of Eden (London 1991), could only manage 132 performances

between them. However, most theatre observers feel that, like composer Charles Strouse, with whom he worked in a lyrical capacity on *Rags*, Schwartz will almost certainly be back on Broadway. In the meantime, he turned his attention to the screen, and collaborated profitably with Alan Menken on the Walt Disney animated features *Pocahontas* (1995) and *The Hunchback Of Notre Dame* (1996). For *Pocahontas*, the duo won Oscars for 'Original Musical or Comedy Score' and 'Original Song' - 'Colours Of The Wind' (Schwartz was also given an ASCAP award for Most Performed Motion Picture Song) - and were nominated for their work on The *Hunchback Of Notre Dame*. In 1998, Schwartz provided the songs for DreamWorks' animated bible epic, *The Prince Of Egypt*. Having successfully demoed his material for some years, in 1997 he released a compelling album on which he sang all non-show songs, with the exception of 'The Hardest Part Of Love', from *Children Of Eden*.
● ALBUMS: *Reluctant Pilgrim* (Midder 1997)★★.

SCROOGE

By all accounts, Albert Finney was by no means the first choice to play the lead in this musical version of Charles Dickens' celebrated novel *A Christmas Carol*, which was released in 1970. As it turns out, he makes a wonderfully crotchety Ebenezer Scrooge, the miserable miser who becomes a totally reformed character following eerie visitations by his late partner, Jacob Marley (Alec Guinness), and the ghosts of Christmases Past, Present and Yet To Come (Edith Evans, Kenneth More and Paddy Stone). The main beneficiaries of this new-found munificence are Scrooge's clerk, Bob Cratchit (David Collings) and his son Tiny Tim (Richard Beaumont). Also taking part in this extremely good-looking production, which was designed by Terry Marsh and photographed in Technicolor and Panavision by Oswald Morris, were Michael Medwin, Laurence Naismith, Anton Rodgers, Suzanne Neve, Frances Cuka, Roy Kinnear and Gordon Jackson. Leslie Bricusse, who co-produced the film with Robert Solo in the UK for Cinema Center, also wrote the screenplay and the songs. His rather uninspired score included the lively 'Thank You Very Much', 'Father Christmas', 'I'll Begin Again', 'A Christmas Carol', 'December The 25th', 'Happiness', 'I Like Life' and 'The Beautiful Day'. Paddy Stone staged the dances and the director was Ronald Neame. In 1992 Bricusse adapted his screen musical for the stage. It had its world premiere in November 1992 in Birmingham, England, with Bricusse's old writing partner, Anthony Newley, in the leading role.

SEAL, ELIZABETH

b. Elizabeth Anne Seal, 28 August 1933, Genoa, Italy. A dynamic, vivacious dancer, singer, and actress, Elizabeth Seal won a scholarship to the Royal Academy of Dancing at the age of five. As a teenager she was in the chorus of several shows, including *Gay's The Word* in the West End, and in the mid-50s made a big impression in two US musicals at the London Coliseum - *The Pajama Game* (Gladys) and *Damn Yankees* (Lola). In the latter she took over from Belita shortly after the opening. However, she enjoyed her greatest success in the English adaptation of *Irma La*

Douce (1958), and reprised her role in New York, winning the 1961 best actress Tony Award in the face of competition from Julie Andrews, Carol Channing, and Nancy Walker. Out of the limelight for some years after that triumph, she was set to make her West End comeback as Cassie in *A Chorus Line* (1976), but was 'sacked' during rehearsals by Michael Bennett, the show's director. The appearance on the scene of Bennett's wife, Donna McKechnie, who had played Cassie on Broadway, sparked off furious protests within the profession. They resulted in McKechnie's withdrawal, and radical rule changes by Equity, the actor's union. Ironically, three years after Seal appeared in the 1976 revival of *Salad Days*, she was involved in another Equity dispute. Having taken over the role of Roxie Hart in *Chicago* at the Cambridge Theatre, she and other members of the cast were threatened with blacklisting after they offered to take wage cuts in an attempt to keep the show running. The outcome was that Equity invested its own funds in an effort to keep their members in work. Thereafter she devoted much of her time to teaching and directing, but continued to make occasional appearances in regional theatre, including one in *Stepping Out* (1991), which she also choreographed. In 1996, to the delight of those attending the celebrations for composer David Heneker's 90th birthday, Elizabeth Seal reunited with her *Irma La Douce* co-star Keith Michell in the show's big ballad, 'Our Language Of Love'. In the following year, Seal played the role of Solange in a special concert performance of *Follies* at London's Theatre Royal, Drury Lane.
● FILMS: *Radio Cab Murder* (1954), *Town On Trial* (1956), *Cone Of Silence* (1961), *Vampire Circus* (1971), *Philby, Burgess And Maclean* for television (1977), *Mack The Knife* (1989).

SECOMBE, HARRY

b. Harold Donald Secombe, 8 September 1921, Swansea, West Glamorgan, Wales. Harry Secombe's development as an all-round entertainer began as a product of the postwar 'fair play' policy of London's West End Windmill Theatre. This ensured that men recently, or soon to be, demobbed from the armed forces, were given the chance to prove themselves to an audience and get noticed by agents. Secombe worked at the theatre before becoming a regular on the variety circuit in the late 40s. In 1949 he teamed up with Peter Sellers, Spike Milligan and Michael Bentine to form the highly influential British radio comedy team, the Goons, taking on characters created by Spike Milligan, such as the popular Neddy Seagoon. With his large build, gentle humour and resonant Welsh baritone, which he put to good effect on light operatic arias as well as popular tunes, Secombe became a regular fixture at the London Palladium, including Royal Command performances, from the 50s through to the 80s. His frequent screen appearances, in both comedy and 'straight' roles, came in films such as *Helter Skelter* (1949, his debut), *Fake's Progress* (1950), *Down Among The Z Men* (1952), *Davy* (1957), *Oliver!* (1968), *The Bedsitting Room* (1968), *Song Of Norway* (1969), *Rhubarb* (1969) and *The Magnificent Seven Deadly Sins* (1971). He appeared regularly on UK television screens, in variety shows and his own series in the 60s and 70s. In 1963, Secombe created the leading role in the musical Pickwick, which had a book by Wolf Mankowitz, and music and lyrics by Leslie Bricusse and Cyril Ornadel. He took the show's big ballad, 'If I Ruled The World', into the UK Top 20, and it has since become indelibly associated with him. Four years later he appeared in The Four Musketeers, which had a score by Laurie Johnson and Herbert Kretzmer, and ran for over a year. He had scored his first solo UK chart hit with 'On With The Motley' in 1955, and achieved his biggest record success to date in 1967 with Charlie Chaplin's 'This Is My Song', which was prevented from reaching the number 1 slot by Petula Clark's version of the very same song.

Following a massive reduction in his weight (for medical reasons) a trimmed-down Secombe has in recent years carved out a career since 1983 as the presenter of Independent Television's religious programme Highway. He has over the years been actively involved in charity organizations and fund-raising and, after being awarded the CBE in 1963, Harry Secombe was knighted in 1981. In 1993, 30 years after creating the leading role in Pickwick, he appeared in a UK revival of the show with Roy Castle.

● ALBUMS: (excluding Goons and other comedy albums): At Your Request (1957)★★★★, Operatic Arias (1958)★★★, Richard Tauber Favourites (1959)★★★★, Secombe Sings (1959)★★★, Harry Secombe Showcase (1960)★★★★, Sacred Songs (1961)★★, Vienna, City Of My Dreams (1962)★★★, Show Souvenirs (1963)★★★★, Immortal Hymns (1963)★★, Secombe's Personal Choice (1967)★★★, If I Ruled The World (1971)★★★★, Songs For Sunday (1972)★★, This Is Harry Secombe, Volume Four (1974)★★★, A Man And His Dreams (1976)★★★, Far Away Places (1977)★★★, Twenty Songs Of Joy (1978)★★, Bless This House (1979)★★★, Songs Of My Homeland (1979)★★★★, These Are My Songs (1980)★★★, with Moira Anderson Golden Memories (1981)★★★, reissued as This Is My Lovely Day, A Song And A Prayer aka How Great Thou Art (1981)★★★★, The Musical World Of Harry Secombe (1983)★★★★, Highway Of Life (1986)★★, The Highway Companion (1987)★★, Onward Christian Soldiers (1987)★★, Yours Sincerely (1991)★★★, Sir Harry (1993)★★★.

● COMPILATIONS: Spotlight On Harry Secombe (1975)★★★★, The Harry Secombe Collection (1976)★★★★, Portrait (1978)★★★.

● FURTHER READING: Arias And Raspberries, Sir Harry Secombe.

SECOND CHORUS

This 1940 film is an enjoyable piece of hokum about two swing band trumpeters, Fred Astaire and Burgess Meredith, vying for the affections of Paulette Goddard. The musicians play with Artie Shaw's band and there are some excellent musical sequences featuring the leader's clarinet, backed in a performance of 'Concerto For Clarinet' by Nick Fatool's drums, and the trumpets of Bobby Hackett and Billy Butterfield ghosting for Astaire and Meredith.

SECRET GARDEN, THE

This charming and stylish musical was welcomed by one critic as 'one of the most aggressively pretty shows ever to grace a Broadway stage' when it opened at the St. James Theatre in New York on 25 April 1991. Marsha Norman's book was based on the much-loved Edwardian children's novel by Frances Hodgson Burnett, and tells of Mary Lennox (Daisy Eagan), who returns to England and the custody of her hunchbacked uncle, Archibald Craven (Mandy Patinkin), after her family, who were in the Colonial Service in India, are wiped out by an outbreak of cholera. Mary discovers Craven's sickly young son Colin (John Babcock), who is being left to wither and die in a secluded room in the large, dreary mansion on the Yorkshire moors. She also finds the key to the secret walled garden that has been locked up since Craven's wife, Lily (Rebecca Luker), died in childbirth some 10 years earlier. Lily returns to the scene in saintly form, and has one of the show's most effective numbers, 'Come To My Garden'. Several other departed souls also materialize, including Mary's parents and several of the young victims of the cholera outbreak who form the chorus. The spirits lead Mary, Colin, and Craven 'towards vitality and joy' in such captivating numbers as 'I Hear Someone Crying' and 'Come Spirit, Come Charm'. The remainder of composer Lucy Simon and lyricist Marsha Norman's 'sentimental and old-fashioned' score included 'Opening Dream', 'There's A Girl', 'The House Upon A Hill', 'A Girl In the Valley', 'Lily's Eyes', 'The Girl I Mean To Be', 'A Bit Of Earth', 'Letter Song', 'Where In The World', and 'How Could I Ever Know?'. General opinion was that the whole show was 'warm and wonderful', especially the gorgeous costumes, and designer-producer Heidi Landesman's ingenious placing of the action inside a toy theatre complete with drops and wings. She won a Tony Award for her dazzling effects, as did 11-year old Daisy Eagan for her lovely open performance. For a children's story The Secret Garden did pretty well - even with a $60 top price - and ran until January 1993, a total of 706 performances.

A touring company broke records in several US cities, and was also highly successful in other countries such as Japan. Another, much smaller adaptation of Frances Hodgson Burnett's story, with a book and lyrics by Diana Morgan and music by Steven Markwick, was presented more than once in the early 90s at the King's Head, Islington, on the London Fringe, and other, regional venues. The novel has been filmed at least three times: as a feature film with Margaret O'Brien in 1949, a television movie with Gennie James and Derek Jacobi in 1987, and another feature film in 1993 with Maggie Smith, Kate Maberly, John Lynch, and Haydon Prowse.

SEGAL, VIVIENNE

b. 19 April 1897, Philadelphia, Pennsylvania, USA, d. 29 December 1992, Los Angeles, California, USA. One of the brightest stars of the American musical theatre - an actress and singer who made her name in operetta, before moving on to the sophisticated world of Richard Rodgers and Lorenz Hart. She studied voice, and sang the title role in Carmen at the local opera house, before making her Broadway debut in 1915 in The Blue Paradise. Her father was one of the backers for this operetta, and when the original leading soprano failed to impress at rehearsal, 18 year old Segal took over at short notice. She gave a memorable performance, and introduced Sigmund Romberg and Herbert Reynolds's delightful waltz, 'Auf Wiedersehn'. After the success of The Blue Paradise, which she also toured, Segal's next two shows, My Lady's Glove (1917) and

the Charles Dillingham/Florenz Ziegfeld revue *Miss 1917*, were rather unsatisfactory, but Segal had excellent roles in Jerome Kern's Oh, Lady! Lady!! (1918), Rudolph Friml's *The Little Whopper* (1919), and an adaptation of Emmerich Kálmán's operetta *Die Bajadere*, entitled *The Yankee Princess* (1922). Subsequent projects such as *Adrienne* (1923), Ziegfeld Follies (1924), *Florida Girl* (1925), and *Castles In The Air* (1926) were followed by the triumphant The Desert Song (1926), in which she introduced the gorgeous 'Romance' and the title song (with Robert Halliday). Two years later, she played Lady Constance opposite Dennis King as D'Artagnan in Friml's *The Three Musketeers*, and from then on was absent from Broadway for about 10 years. During that period she starred in several provincial productions of musicals, including No, No, Nanette and Music In The Air, as well as appearing frequently on radio. She also made a number of films - all operettas - the best of which was probably the two-colour Technicolor *Viennese Nights* (1930), in which she co-starred with Alexander Gray and Walter Pidgeon. Its sumptuous score, by Romberg and Oscar Hammerstein II, contained several impressive numbers, including 'I Bring A Love Song', 'You Will Remember Vienna', and 'Here We Are'. While she was in Hollywood Segal met Rodgers and Hart, and they were responsible for her Broadway renaissance in 1938. In their witty musical comedy, I Married An Angel, she excelled with numbers such as 'A Twinkle In Your Eye', 'Did You Ever Get Stung?' (with Dennis King and Charles Walters), 'I'll Tell The Man In The Street' (with Walter Slezak), and the bleak but beautiful 'Spring Is Here' (with King). Two years later, Segal took the role of Vera Simpson, the 'mature' socialite, who is tempted - and even 'Bewitched' (bothered and bewildered) - for a while, by the charms of a smooth-talking heel, played by Gene Kelly, in Rodgers and Hart's controversial masterpiece, Pal Joey. Segal's involvement in the revival of that team's 1927 production, *A Connecticut Yankee*, is particularly interesting in that one of the new songs, the ingenious 'To Keep My Love Alive' ('When I'm ill at ease/I kill at ease'), was written especially for her, and is said to be Hart's last work. He died just five days after the show's opening on 17 November 1943. As for Segal, there followed the 'Tchaikovsky-style' operetta *Music In My Heart* (1947) and the ghostly *Great To Be Alive* (1950), before she returned to New York in great style with the 1952 revival of *Pal Joey*, in which her portrayal of Vera received even more acclaim than before. Harold Lang played Joey (his understudy was Bob Fosse), in a production which ran for longer than the original - 542 performances - and is preserved on a fine cast album. *Pal Joey* was Vivienne Segal's Broadway swan song, although she continued to appear on television for some time, notably in prestige drama presentations such as *Alfred Hitchcock Presents* and *Studio One*.
- ALBUMS: *Pal Joey* Broadway Cast (Columbia 1952)★★★★.
- FILMS: *Song Of The West* (1930), *Bride Of The Regiment* (1930), *Golden Dawn* (1930), *Viennese Nights* (1930), *The Cat And The Fiddle* (1934).

SEVEN BRIDES FOR SEVEN BROTHERS

Adapted from Stephen Vincent Benet's short story *The Sobbin' Women*, which was 'inspired' by Plutach's *Rape Of The Sabine Women*, this film was released by MGM in 1954 and, somewhat surprisingly, went on to become one of the most successful screen musicals of the decade. Frances Goodrich, Albert Hackett, and Dorothy Kingsley wrote the screenplay, which told of Adam Pontipee (Howard Keel), who leaves his six scruffy brothers to the squalor of their farmhouse in Oregon (*c*.1850s) to go in search of a hard-working wife. He finds her in the shape of Milly (Jane Powell), and their subsequent life together, during which Milly successfully advises the slovenly sextet on how to live and love, makes for an endearing and entertaining film. Her first 'lesson' is 'Goin' Co'tin', just one of the many musical highlights in Gene De Paul and Johnny Mercer's spirited and exuberant score. Others included the optimistic 'Bless Your Beautiful Hide' (Keel), 'Wonderful, Wonderful Day' (Powell), 'When You're In Love' (Powell-Keel), 'Sobbin' Women' (Keel-brothers), 'June Bride' (Powell-brides), and 'Spring, Spring, Spring' (Powell-brothers-brides). The six virile brothers, named by their god-fearing mother as Benjamin, Caleb, Daniel, Ephram, Frankincense and Gideon, were played by Russ Tamblyn, Tommy Rall, Marc Platt, Jeff Richards, Matt Mattox and Jacques d'Amboise. In the end, they all find their brides (Virginia Gibson, Julie Newmeyer, Betty Carr, Nancy Kilgas, Norma Doggett and Rita Kilmonis) by somewhat unconventional methods, after displaying exceptionally brilliant dancing skills in the contrasting languorous 'Lonesome Polecat' and spectacular 'barn-raising' scenes. The choreography for those, and the rest of the innovative dance numbers, was designed by Michael Kidd. Saul Chaplin and Adolph Deutsch won Academy Awards for 'scoring of a musical picture'. Stanley Donen directed with style and vigour. George Folsey was responsible for the breathtakingly beautiful photography in Amsco and CinemaScope. This film is considered by many to be among the all-time great musicals, but a 1982 stage version was not welcomed in New York and folded after five performances. Four years later, a West End production fared a little better.

1776

America's obsession with its own history had already resulted in at least two Broadway musicals based on momentous national events before this show opened at the 46th Street Theatre on 16 March 1969. Exactly 20 years before that, Miss Liberty, with a score by Irving Berlin, concerned itself with the period leading up to the dedication ceremony for the lady with the torch, and, in 1925, songwriters Richard Rodgers and Lorenz Hart, together with librettist Herbert Fields, offered Dearest Enemy, which was 'inspired' by the American Revolution. Naturally, with a title like *1776*, Peter Stone's book and Sherman Edwards' score relates to the culmination of that Revolution - the signing of the Declaration of Independence. Edwards, a newcomer to Broadway, had worked on the project for several years before collaborating with the more experienced Stone on the final draft. It stayed closely to historical fact, both in regard to the dramatic circumstances, and the personalities involved in them. The performances of Howard Da Silva (Benjamin Franklin), William Daniels (John Adams), and Ken

Howard (Thomas Jefferson) were particularly applauded. In many ways, the show was more like a straight play - a powerful and emotional piece of theatre. Edwards' sympathetic, and sometimes poignant score included songs such as 'Momma Look Sharp', 'Cool, Cool Considerate Man', 'Sit Down, John', 'But Mr. Adams', 'The Lees Of Old Virginia', 'He Plays The Violin', 'Is Anybody There?', 'Yours, Yours, Yours!', 'Molasses To Rum', and 'Till Then'. The show was acclaimed from the start, and became a tremendous success, running for 1,217 performances. It won three Tony Awards: for best musical, supporting actor (Ronald Holgate in the role of Richard Henry Lee) and director (Peter Hunt). There was a short-lived London production in 1970, and in 1991 the show was revived at the Williamstown Theatre Festival in the USA. Six years later, an acclaimed revival of *1776* opened at the non-profit Roundabout Theatre in New York. Directed by Scott Ellis, and starring *Star Trek: The Next Generation* actor Brent Spiner (John Adams), Pat Hingle (Benjamin Franklin), Paul Michael Valley (Thomas Jefferson), Michael Cumpsty (John Dickinson), and Gregg Edelman (Edward Rudledge), it subsequently transferred to the commercial sector's Gershwin Theatre. A 1972 film version retained several members of the Broadway cast, and the laserdisc version contains several items cut from the cinema release.

70, GIRLS, 70

Another celebrated flop, this show closed some five weeks after it emerged into the lights of the Broadhurst Theatre on 15 April 1971. Some critics attributed its failure to Stephen Sondheim's Follies, which had arrived on Broadway just 11 days earlier, and also concerned itself with the celebration of old troupers from the past. However, the glamorous settings of the 'Wiesmann Follies', and a group of veteran vaudevillians returning to Broadway, could hardly be compared to the more down-to-earth situation in *70, Girls, 70*, in which some equally venerable old-time performers live at The Sussex Arms, a senior Citizens' run-down hotel in New York City. One of that establishment's favourite residents, Ida Dodd (Mildred Natwick), forms a shop-lifting gang to get her own back on rude traders. The resulting profits enable the 'crooks' to refurbish their quarters and take in more poor, but deserving cases. After one job the aged criminals just make their getaway, but Ida gets caught. Before they can put her away, she escapes - by dying. The book, by Fred Ebb and Norman L. Martin, was based on the English comedy, *Breath Of Spring*, which was filmed as *One Touch Of Mink*. The show opened with a rousing, defiant anthem: 'Old Folks' . . . 'don't go out, strangers make them ill at ease/Old folks stay at home, nursing their infirmities' . . . 'So take a look at the old folks, they're quite an interesting sight/But if you want to see old folks/You're in the wrong hall tonight!'). From then on, Fred Ebb and composer John Kander cleverly interpolated numbers such as 'Broadway, My Street', 'Go Visit' and 'Coffee In A Cardboard Cup' by the old vaudeville performers, Melba (Lillian Hayman) and Fritzi (Goldye Shaw), among the 'plot' songs which included 'Home', 'The Caper', 'You And I, Love', 'Do We?', 'Hit It, Lorraine', 'See The Light', 'Boom

Ditty Boom', 'Believe', 'The Elephant Song', and 'Yes'. Whatever the reason for the show's miserable run of 35 performances (*Follies* scooped the Tony Awards), it certainly was not the fault of the score, which was witty and entertaining throughout. Twenty years later, *70, Girls, 70* finally reached the West End, where Dora Bryan was 'irresistible' in the leading role.

SHAG

This 1985 film, set in America during 1963, concerned the attempts of southern belles Melaina, Pudge and Carson (Bridget Fonda, Annabeth Gish and Phoebe Cates) to find boyfriends. Instead of taking a trip to colonial Fort Sumter for educational purposes, as they have informed their parents, they attend the Sun Fun festival at Myrtle Beach. The boys they meet are then taught to 'shag' (as in the dance, rather than the euphemism for sexual congress). Later, Melaina enters a beauty contest, to be judged by pop star Jimmy Valentine. The trio then organise a party at the house they are staying at, in Valentine's honour. Riotous party scenes ensue. The narrative then breaks until the following morning, when the housekeeper arrives at the scene of devastation to inform the occupants that the owners, Senator and Mrs Clutterbucket, are due to arrive at noon. Disaster is averted with the announcement of another 'shag' contest, with Senator and Mrs Clutterbucket as judges, alongside Jimmy Valentine. Pudge and her boyfriend Chip (Scott Coffey) win the contest. Thin on narrative development, characterisation and plot, the film encompassed a soundtrack drawing on artists from the 50s onwards, including material from LaVern Baker, the Sensations, Chris Isaak, k.d. lang, Hank Ballard, Jackie Wilson, Randy Newman and the Voltage Brothers, who appeared on the film as the house band, Big Dan And The Sand Dollars.

SHAKE, RATTLE AND ROLL

Taking its title from a bestselling single by Bill Haley And The Comets, this 1956 'B' film attempted to capitalize on rock 'n' roll. In a plot that would quickly become overused, conservative adults attempt to ban the new music, but are challenged to a television trial by teenagers. R&B singer Joe Turner performs 'Lipstick, Powder And Paint' and 'Feelin' Happy', and Fats Domino adds 'Ain't That A Shame', 'Honey Chile' and 'I'm In Love Again'; otherwise, *Shake, Rattle And Roll* is largely forgettable. Clumsily scripted hip parlance - 'dig', 'dad', 'man' and 'the most' - renders the youths' arguments laughable, while the use of subtitles as translation verges on spiteful. It is difficult to imagine the motives behind director Edward Cahn's ideas, but the final sensation is of a film desperate to exploit a genre while apparently at the same time belittling it and its adherents.

SHALL WE DANCE?

Screenwriter Allan Scott, whose name was a familiar feature on the credits of Fred Astaire and Ginger Rogers movies, excelled himself with the plot for this 1937 vehicle for the popular duo's delightful dance routines. Together with Ernest Pagano, Scott fashioned a story in which ballet dancer Pete Rogers (Astaire) falls for

Broadway musical star Linda Keen (Rogers) in Paris - serenades her on the liner back to New York - and later, with her help, fulfils his lifetime ambition by mixing his beloved ballet with modern tap-dancing. Before that happens - and this is where Scott and Pagano really score - the couple dispel constant rumours that they are married by *getting* married - so that they can divorce! There was nothing as complicated as that about the sublime songs by George and Ira Gershwin. They were all simply terrific, and included three of the composers' all-time standards, 'They All Laughed', 'Let's Call The Whole Thing Off' (Fred and Ginger on roller-skates!), and 'They Can't Take That Away From Me', along with the lively '(I've Got) Beginner's Luck' and 'Slap That Bass', the rhythmic title song, and a catchy little instrumental piece, set on the deck of the liner, 'Walking The Dog'. Directed by Mark Sandrich, with dance sequences choreographed by Hermes Pan and Harry Losee, *Shall We Dance?* was the seventh Fred Astaire-Ginger Rogers film, and, while they were as great as ever, and the supporting cast which included Edward Everett Horton and Eric Blore were always amusing, somehow things were beginning to pall. In fact, to some, this picture marked the beginning of their decline.

SHE DONE HIM WRONG

Mae West's second - and some say her best - film was adapted by screenwriters Harvey Thew, John White, and West herself from her own play, *Diamond Lil*, which was set in the late 19th century. The trio toned down the erotic element somewhat, but with West's laconic delivery and skin-tight gowns, wholesomeness was just not possible - and not even desirable. Ironically, as saloon hostess Lady Lou, she directed her first invitation to 'Come up and see me . . . ?' to Cary Grant ('Mr. Clean'), who played a federal agent masquerading as a church mission man intent on terminating her various nefarious activities. Among the accomplished cast were Noah Beery, Owen Moore, Gilbert Roland, Fuzzy Knight, Grace La Rue, and Rochelle Hudson. The songs came from various composers and included 'I Like A Guy What Takes His Time', 'Maisie', and 'Haven't Got No Peace Of Mind' (all with words and music by Ralph Rainger); 'Silver Threads Among The Gold' (Eben E. Rexford-Hart Pease Danks), 'I Wonder Where My Easy Rider's Gone' (Shelton Brooks), and 'Frankie And Johnny' (traditional). Directed by Lowell Sherman, *She Done Him Wrong* shocked and disgusted some sections of the public in 1933, but still took a remarkable $3 million at the box-office.

SHE LOVES ME

This 'chamber musical' set in Budapest in the mid-30s, was the first to be both produced and directed by Harold Prince. It was based on the play *Parfumerie*, by Miklos Laszlo, which had been filmed twice, as *The Shop Around The Corner* and *In The Good Old Summertime*. *She Loves Me* opened at the Eugene O'Neill Theatre in New York on 23 April 1963, with a score by Jerry Bock (music) and Sheldon Harnick (lyrics). Joe Masteroff's book concerns certain members of the sales staff at Maraczek's Parfumerie - Mr. Maraczek himself (Ludwig Donath), mid-

dle-aged salesman Ladislav Sipos (Nathaniel Frey), teenage delivery boy Arpad Laszlo (Ralph Williams), and in particular, the shop's manager, Georg Nowack (Daniel Massey), and brand new salesgirl Amalia Balash (Barbara Cook). The couple bicker with each other all day long, little knowing that each is the other's penfriend. Georg is the first to realize that they have been pouring their hearts out to each other via the US Mail. He finally reveals the true situation - and his feelings for Amalia - by presenting her with some 'Ice Cream' (vanilla kind), and then reading aloud one of the letters she has written to her 'correspondent', to whom she always refers as 'Dear Friend'. Amalia's confidante in the shop, Ilona Ritter (Barbara Baxley), is also in for a surprise - boyfriend Steven Kodaly (Jack Cassidy), a smooth operator and Maraczek's resident ladies' man, has also been romancing Mrs. Maraczek. The charming and tender story was perfectly complemented by the score, which has become one of the most cherished of all Broadway musicals. The musical numbers, which were staged by Carol Haney, included 'Good Morning, Good Day', 'Sounds While Selling', 'Thank You, Madam', 'Days Gone By', 'No More Candy', 'Three Letters', 'Tonight At Eight', 'I Don't Know His Name', 'Perspective', 'Goodbye Georg', 'Will He Like Me?', 'Ilona', 'I Resolve', 'Romantic Atmosphere', 'Tango Tragique', 'Dear Friend', 'Try Me', 'Where's My Shoe', 'Ice Cream', 'She Loves Me', 'A Trip To The Library', 'Grand Knowing You', 'Twelve Days To Christmas' and 'Curtain Call'. She *Loves Me* ran for 301 performances, and gained one Tony Award for featured actor (Cassidy), but lost out in the remainder of the categories to the brash and brassy *Hello, Dolly!* The 1964 London production, with Anne Rogers (Amalia), Gary Raymond (Georg), popular singer Gary Miller (Kodaly), and US movie star Rita Moreno (Ilona), lasted for nearly six months. Bock and Harnick wrote a new song for Moreno, 'Heads I Win', which replaced 'I Resolve'.
In 1993, a 30th anniversary revival, starring Judy Kuhn (Amalia), Tony Award-winning Boyd Gaines (Georg), Sally Mayes (Ilona), and Howard McGillin (Kodaly), directed by Scott Ellis, was welcomed with open arms by Broadway audiences starved of good, original American musicals. Ellis also directed the 1994 West End production, with Ruthie Henshall (Amalia), John Gordon-Sinclair (Georg), Tracie Bennett (Ilona), and Gerard Casey (Kodaly). It received a remarkable five Laurence Olivier Awards, and the London Critics Circle Award for best musical. In 1998, another movie based on the show's original source material was released. *Entitled You've Got Mail*, it reunited the team of Tom Hanks and Meg Ryan from the highly successful 1993 picture *Sleepless In Seattle*.

SHENANDOAH

This musical was based on the critically acclaimed movie of the same name which starred James Stewart and was released in 1965. James Lee Barrett, the author of the screenplay, collaborated with Philip Rose and Peter Udell on the libretto for the stage adaptation which opened at the Alvin Theatre in New York on 7 January 1975. Set in the Shenandoah Valley at the time of the American Civil War, the strongly anti-war story concerns a widowed Virginian farmer, Charlie Anderson (John Cullum), who refuses to allow the North versus South conflict to intrude upon his life until some Yankee troops abduct his youngest son (Joseph Shapiro) because he is wearing a Rebel cap. Several members of Anderson's family are killed in tragic circumstances in the days that follow. The score, by Peter Udell (lyrics) and Gary Geld (music), had a rousing 'wide open spaces' feel about it, with numbers such as 'Raise The Flag Of Dixie', 'I've Heard It All Before', 'Why Am I Me', 'Over The Hill', 'The Pickers Are Comin'', 'Meditation', 'We Make A Beautiful Pair', 'Freedom', 'Violets And Silverbells', 'Papa's Gonna Make It Alright', and 'Meditation'. Two of the most appealing numbers were the exuberant 'Next To Lovin' (I Like Fightin')', and the tender ballad 'The Only Home I Know'. It is sometimes said that *Shenandoah*'s remarkably long run of 1,050 performances owed something to the feelings of revulsion towards war in general - and Vietnam in particular - that were prevalent in America around that time. At any rate, the show won Tony Awards for its book, and for John Cullum's fine, sensitive performance. He recreated his original role when *Shenandoah* was revived for a limited period on Broadway in 1989. In 1994, a 20th anniversary production was presented by the Goodspeed Opera House in Connecticut.

SHERLOCK HOLMES · THE MUSICAL

Without a stage musical hit to his name since Pickwick in 1963, Leslie Bricusse failed once again to find the magic formula with this show which opened at London's Cambridge Theatre on 24 April 1989. In his book, which was based on characters created by Sir Arthur Conan Doyle, Bricusse ensures that Professor Moriarty (Terry Williams) meets a watery end in the traditional manner via the Reichenbach Falls, before his lovely daughter, Bella (Liz Robertson), plots an over-ambitious revenge by attempting to frame Sherlock Holmes (Ron Moody) for murder. Needless to say, she is no match for the master detective, who is not aided by a 'miscast' Doctor Watson (Derek Waring), along with Mrs. Moriarty (Eileen Battye), Lestrade (Roger Llewellyn), Martingdale (Colin Bennett), Duchess (Sally Mates), and Sir Jevons (Lewis Barber). Fred Wiggins (James Francis-Johnston) led the young Baker Street Irregulars in a series of predictable hip-jerking gyrations, while Julia Sutton in the role of housekeeper Mrs. Hudson, almost stopped the show nightly with 'Down The Apples 'N' Pears', an inevitable Cockney 'knees-up'. Hardly a 'plot-advancement' number, but its zest appealed far more than the remainder of Bricusse's 'leaden tunes and lyrics' which included 'Sherlock Holmes', 'Without Him, There Can Be No Me!', 'Vendetta',. 'Look Around You', 'Anything You Want To Know', 'Her Face', 'Men Like You', 'I Shall Find Her', 'No Reason', 'Halcyon Days', 'The Lord Abides In London', 'He's Back!', 'A Million Years Ago - Or Was It Yesterday?', and 'The Best Of You, The Best Of Me', as well as two items the composer had aired before: 'London Is London' (from the 1969 Peter O'Toole-Petula Clark film, *Goodbye, Mr. Chips*) and 'A Lousy Life' (from the 1981 Toronto production of the stage musical, *Say Hello To Harvey!*). This 'misdirected endeavour' was staged by George Roman, and Christine Cartwright choreographed the 'derivative dance routines'.

Given the overwhelming evidence ('this singing detective hasn't a clue'), the solution to the problem was clear, and *Sherlock Holmes* was withdrawn after a run of 97 performances. Not far away, at Wyndham's Theatre, the new stage thriller, *The Secret Of Sherlock Holmes*, with Jeremy Brett (Holmes), and Edward Hardwicke (Watson), did much better, staying around for about a year.

For some reason, perhaps because Bricusse was in the news with a 30th anniversary revival of *Pickwick*, and the premiere of his stage adaptation of the film Scrooge, in March 1993 Bristol Old Vic mounted a revival of his *Sherlock Holmes* musical, starring Robert Powell (Holmes), Roy Barraclough (Watson), and Louise English (Bella). Although well received at the Theatre Royal, Bristol, the show was scrapped in the middle of its seven-month UK tour.

An earlier, more satisfying attempt to musicalize Holmes, entitled *Baker Street*, opened at the Broadway Theatre in New York in 1965. It had a book by Jerome Coopersmith, and music and lyrics mostly by Marian Grudeff and Raymond Jessel, with interpolations from Jerry Bock and Sheldon Harnick, and ran for 313 performances. A German Sherlock Holmes musical, *Ein Fall Für Sherlock Holmes*, conceived by Gerd Natschinski and Jürgen Degenhardt in 1982, was based on just one famous Conan Doyle tale, *The Hound Of The Baskervilles*.

SHERMAN, RICHARD M., AND ROBERT B.

Richard M. Sherman (b. 12 June 1928, New York, USA) and Robert B. Sherman (b. 19 December 1925, New York, USA) followed in their father, Al Sherman's footsteps as songwriters who collaborated on complete scores, mainly for Walt Disney movies of the 60s and 70s. After providing Johnny Burnette with the hit song 'You're Sixteen', they contributed to several films in the early 60s, including *The Parent Trap*, *In Search Of The Castaways*, *Summer Magic* and *The Sword In The Stone*. Massive success came in 1964 with the music and lyrics for Mary Poppins. The Oscar-winning score included 'A Spoonful Of Sugar', 'Feed The Birds', 'Jolly Holiday', 'Let's Go Fly A Kite' and 'Chim Chim Cher-ee' (which won the Academy Award for 'Best Song'). When the brothers accepted their award they commented: 'There are no words. All we can say is: "Supercalafragelisticexpialidocious"' - which was the title of another famous song from the film. *Mary Poppins* was dubbed the 'best and most original musical of the decade', and 'the best live-action film in Disney's history'. The soundtrack album went to number 1 in the US and remained in the charts for 18 months. Julie Andrews, appearing in her first feature film, was voted 'Best Actress' for her performance in the title role. Another British performer, Tommy Steele, was not so fortunate in *The Happiest Millionaire*. It was called 'miserable and depressing' despite a lively score by the Shermans, which included 'Fortuosity'. The film was the last to be personally supervised by Walt Disney before he died in 1966. Much more to the critics' liking was the delightful animated feature, The Jungle Book, which was inspired by the Rudyard Kipling *Mowgli* stories. The Shermans' songs, including 'I Wan'na Be Like You' and 'That's What Friends Are For', were amusingly delivered by the voices of Phil Harris, Sebastian Cabot, Louis Prima, George Sanders and Sterling Holloway. The songs and much of the dialogue were released on a lavishly illustrated album.

The late 60s were extremely fertile years for the Sherman brothers. Among the films to which they contributed music and lyrics were *The One And Only Genuine Original Family Band* (another highly acclaimed animal animation), *The Aristocats*, *Bedknobs And Broomsticks*, and Chitty Chitty Bang Bang. In 1974 the Sherman brothers' score for the Broadway musical *Over Here*, starred the two survivors from the Andrews Sisters, Maxene and Patti. The show, which echoed the styles and sounds of World War II and the swing era, ran for a year.

Throughout the 70s, and beyond, the Shermans continued to write songs and scores for films, including *Charlotte's Web*, *Tom Sawyer*, *Huckleberry Finn*, The Slipper And The Rose and *The Magic Of Lassie*. Several songs from those films were nominated for Academy Awards, and the Sherman brothers were also involved in writing some of the screenplays. In 1995, *Stage Door Charley* (later known as *Busker Alley*), a musical adaptation of the 1938 Vivien Leigh-Charles Laughton movie *St. Martin's Lane*, for which they wrote the music and lyrics, toured the US regions. Despite having Tommy Tune as its star, it failed to reach Broadway.

SHEVELOVE, BURT

b. Burton George Shevelove, 19 September 1915, Newark, New Jersey, USA, d. 8 April 1982, London, England. A librettist, lyricist, and director, Shevelove made his first impression on Broadway in 1948, directing the stylish revue, *Small Wonder*. He also wrote sketch material and lyrics (under the *nom de plume* Billings Brown) for the show, whose cast included future stars, Tom Ewell, Jack Cassidy, Alice Pearce, and Joan Diener. For more than two decades thereafter he worked in the rapidly growing medium of television, producing, writing, and directing hundreds of top-rated shows, starring Art Carney ('Meets Peter And The Wolf'), Judy Garland, Richard Rodgers, Red Buttons, Frank Sinatra, Jack Benny, and numerous others. During this period he returned to the theatre occasionally, sometimes in collaboration with composer Albert Selden, with whom he had worked on *Small Wonder*. However, nothing of any significance came along until 1962, when *A Funny Thing Happened On The Way To The Forum*, the musical he co-authored with Larry Gelbart, opened on Broadway. Both men won Tony Awards, and the show ran for 964 performances in New York, and 762 in London. Shevelove directed the 1972 Broadway revival. In 1965 he took over as director of Lionel Bart's *Twang!!* from Joan Littlewood, prior to its transfer from Manchester to the West End, where it lasted just 43 performances. In the following year, Shevelove and Gelbart adapted their libretto of *A Funny Thing Happened On The Way To The Forum*, for the film version, and worked together again on the screenplay to Bryan Forbes's black farce movie, *The Wrong Box*. Returning to Broadway in 1967, Shevelove directed *Hallelujah, Baby!*, a musical by Arthur Laurents, with a Betty Comden and Adolph Green score. Impressive performances from Leslie Uggams,

Lillian Hayman, Allen Case, and Robert Hooks, ensured a decent run of 293 performances. Four years later, Shevelove reconstructed the lengthy and involved book of the original 1925 *No, No, Nanette* into the fast-moving 1971 version 'without losing a laugh-line'. Starring ex-movie actress Ruby Keeler, Bobby Van, Jack Gilford, Patsy Kelly, and Helen Gallagher, 'Nanette' won four Tony Awards and ran for 861 performances. Shevelove found himself working frequently with Stephen Sondheim in the early 70s - having been friendly with the composer since they worked together on 'Forum' back in the 60s. Shevelove was called in to direct *Sondheim: A Musical Tribute*, which played at the Shubert Theatre in New York for one night in March 1973, and the duo combined again for *The Frogs*, which was based on the play by Aristophanes, and played eight performances in the Yale University swimming pool from 20 May 1974. Among the members of the chorus on that occasion were Meryl Streep and Sigourney Weaver. Shevelove's final Broadway stint was helming *Happy New Year* (1980), a musical he created from Cole Porter songs and Philip Barry's play, *Holiday*. He was to have directed the West End musical, *Windy City* (1982), with a cast led by Dennis Waterman and Anton Rodgers, but died shortly before the show went into rehearsal.

SHIRE, DAVID

b. 3 July 1937, Buffalo, New York, USA. A prolific composer for films, television and the stage, Shire studied piano as a youngster, and played in his father's dance band at local functions. While at Yale he majored in music, and wrote two musicals with Richard Maltby Jnr., *Cyrano* and *Grand Tour*. He subsequently studied briefly at Brandeis University where he was the first recipient of the Eddie Fisher Fellowship Award. In 1961, again with Maltby, Shire wrote some songs for the off-Broadway revue *Sap Of Life*, and the new team also had two of their numbers, 'Autumn' and 'No More Songs For Me', recorded by the up-and-coming Barbra Streisand. This led to Shire spending nearly two years playing piano in the orchestra pit for *Funny Girl*, and serving as assistant arranger on Streisand's early television specials. In the late 60s, after his stage musical *Love Match* failed to reach Broadway, Shire began to write the scores for popular television programmes such as *The Virginian*, and eventually moved out to Hollywood in 1969. The majority of his more than 40 feature film scores - for a wide variety of genre such as westerns, comedies, thrillers, melodramas and love stories - were written in the 70s, and included *One More Train To Rob* (1971), *Summertree*, *Skin Game*, *Drive, He Said*, *Two People*, *Showdown*, *Class Of '44*, *The Conversation*, *Farewell, My Lovely*, *The Hindenburg*, *All The President's Men*, *The Big Bus*, *Saturday Night Fever*, *Straight Time*, and *Norma Rae* (1979). Throughout the 80s and early 90s he continued to write the background music for movies such as *Only When I Laugh* (1981), *The Night The Lights Went Out In Georgia*, *Paternity*, *Max Dugan Returns*, *Oh, God! You Devil*, *2010*, *Return To Oz*, *Short Circuit*, *'Night Mother*, *Backfire*, *Vice Versa*, *Monkey Shines*, *Paris Trout*, *Bed And Breakfast*, *Texan*, *One Night Stand*, and *I Married A Monster From Outer Space* (1998). Shire has also scored numerous television films, and miniseries such as *Echoes In The*

Darkness (1987), *The Women Of Brewster Place* (1989), and *The Kennedys Of Massachusetts, Heartbeat, Remember, Once In A Lifetime, Reunion, Jake's Women, Heidi, Almost Golden: The Jessica Savitch Story, Streets Of Laredo, Alone,* and *Ms. Scrooge* (1997). In 1979 he won an Oscar for the song 'It Goes Like It Goes' (lyric by Norman Gimbel) which was sung on the soundtrack of the film *Norma Rae* by Jennifer Warnes. He was also awarded two Grammys for his contributions to the *Saturday Night Fever* soundtrack album. As well as Streisand, his songs have been recorded by numerous other artists, including Johnny Mathis, Melissa Manchester, and Judy Collins, and he has had several US chart successes, including 'Washington Square' (written with Bob Goldstein, and a US number 2 in 1963 for the Dixieland-styled band, the Village Stompers), and 'With You I'm Born Again' (lyric by Carol Connors), an international hit in 1980 for Billy Preston and Syreeta. Shire has also composed songs and incidental music for Joseph Papp's New York Shakespeare Festival Theatre, and other acclaimed theatrical productions. He was married for a time to actress Talia Shire, the sister of director Francis Ford Coppola, and star of several *Rocky* movies.

Richard Maltby Jnr. (b. 6 October 1937, USA), Shire's main collaborator and the son of the celebrated composer and bandleader Richard Maltby, worked as a director in the legitimate theatre during the 70s before collaborating again with Shire on two successful off-Broadway revues, *Starting Here, Starting Now...* (1977) and *Closer Than Ever* (1989), both of which became cult attractions and have been presented in several countries, including Britain. The duo combined again for the Broadway musicals *Baby* (1983) and *Big* (1996), as well as an off-Broadway project, *Urban Blight* (1988). Maltby also won a Tony Award in 1978 as Outstanding Director for *Ain't Misbehavin'*, a musical celebrating songs written and associated with Fats Waller, which he conceived with Murray Horwitz. His other Broadway credits include directing, adapting, and providing extra lyrics for *Song And Dance* (1985); as well as writing the lyrics (with Alain Boublil) for *Miss Saigon* (1989), and the spectacular 1991 Broadway flop *Nick And Nora*. In November 1998, *The Story Goes On*, a revue surveying the music of Shire and Maltby opened at the Kaufman Theatre, New York. Singer Loni Ackerman performed most of the material, accompanied by Shire on the piano. Maltby is also known for the 'fiendishly difficult' crosswords he contributes to *Harpers* magazine.

● ALBUMS: with Maureen McGovern *David Shire At The Movies* (Bay Cities 1992)★★★, and soundtrack and Original Cast albums.

SHOCKING MISS PILGRIM, THE

Difficult to believe in these more enlightened times, that the lady was shocking because she had the temerity to work in an office. After Mr. Remington came up with his new-fangled invention in 1874, the thoroughly modern Miss Cynthia Pilgrim (Betty Grable) comes top of her class at a New York business school and takes a position as a 'typewriter' (typist) with the Pritchard Shipping Company in Boston. After overcoming initial opposition from her boss, John Pritchard (Dick Haymes), and the office manager (Gene Lockhart), Miss Pilgrim then compounds the

felony by becoming leader of the local suffragette movement. However, this only postpones the inevitable romantic union between worker and management. Somewhat unusually, audiences were accorded only a very brief glimpse of the famous Grable legs - when she lifted her skirt to check a run in her stockings. The charming score had lyrics by Ira Gershwin to what he called 'posthumous' music. He and the composer-musician Kay Swift spent several weeks going through his late brother George Gershwin's manuscripts, and the result was several delightful songs which included two outstanding duets for Grable and Haymes, 'For You, For Me, For Evermore' and 'Aren't You Kind Of Glad We Did?', along with several other appropriate items such as 'The Back Bay Polka', 'One Two Three', 'Waltz Me No Waltzes', Demon Rum', 'Changing My Tune', 'But Not In Boston', 'Waltzing Is Better Than Sitting Down', 'Sweet Packard', and 'Stand Up And Fight'. Hermes Pan staged the dances, and the screenplay, which was adapted from a story by Ernest and Frederica Maas, was written by George Seaton who also directed. The splendid supporting cast included Ann Revere, Allyn Joslyn, Elizabeth Patterson, Elizabeth Risdon, Arthur Shields, Charles Kemper, and Roy Roberts. *The Shocking Miss Pilgrim* was photographed in Technicolor by Leon Shamroy and produced for 20th Century-Fox by William Perlberg.

SHORE, DINAH

b. Frances Rose Shore, 1 March 1917, Winchester, Tennessee, USA, d. 24 February 1994, Los Angeles, California, USA. One of her country's most enduring all-round entertainers, Shore staked her first claim to fame while still at school, on Nashville radio. Further broadcasting and theatre engagements in New York soon followed. She recorded with Xaviar Cugat and Ben Bernie, and sang on some of Cugat's early 40s hits, such as 'The Breeze And I', 'Whatever Happened To You?', 'The Rhumba-Cardi' and 'Quierme Mucho (Yours)', initially under the name Dinah Shaw. Shore was one of the first vocalists to break free from the big bands (she had been rejected at auditions for Benny Goodman and Tommy Dorsey) and become a star in her own right. She became extremely popular on radio, and made her solo recording debut in 1939. Her smoky, low-pitched voice was especially attractive on slow ballads, and from 1940-57 she had a string of some 80 US chart hits, including 'Yes, My Darling Daughter', 'Jim', 'Blues In The Night', 'Skylark', 'You'd Be So Nice To Come Home To', 'Murder, He Says', 'Candy', 'Laughing On The Outside (Crying On The Inside)', 'All That Glitters Is Not Gold', 'Doin' What Comes Natur'lly', 'You Keep Coming Back Like A Song', 'I Wish I Didn't Love You So', 'You Do', 'Baby, It's Cold Outside' (with Buddy Clark), 'Dear Hearts And Gentle People', 'My Heart Cries For You', 'A Penny A Kiss', 'Sweet Violets', and number 1s with 'I'll Walk Alone', 'The Gypsy', 'Anniversary Song' and 'Buttons And Bows'. She made a number of film appearances, including *Thank Your Lucky Stars* (1943), *Up In Arms* (1944), *Follow The Boys* (1944), *Belle Of The Yukon* (1945), *Till The Clouds Roll By* (1946) and *Aaron Slick From Punkin Crick* (1952). She also lent her voice to two Walt Disney animated features, *Make Mine*

Music (1946) and *Fun And Fancy Free* (1957), and was last seen on the big screen in the George Burns comedy *Oh God!* (1977), and Robert Altman's quirky political satire *H.E.A.L.T.H.* (1979). In 1951 Shore began appearing regularly on television, making several spectaculars. Later, it was her continuing success on the small screen that brought about a career change when she became host on a highly rated daytime talk show, a role she maintained into the 80s. Her popularity on television barely declined throughout this period, and she won no less than 10 Emmys in all. The late 80s saw her performing on stage once more, though she returned to the television format for *Conversation With Dinah*, which ran from 1989-91.

● ALBUMS: *Dinah Shore Sings* 10-inch album (Columbia 1949)★★★, *Reminiscing* 10-inch album (Columbia 1949)★★★, *Bongo/Land Of The Lost* (Columbia 1950)★★, *Call Me Madam* 10-inch album (RCA Victor 1950)★★, *The King And I* 10-inch album (RCA Victor 1951)★★★, *Two Tickets To Broadway* 10-inch album (RCA Victor 1951)★★★, *Aaron Slick From Punkin Crick* film soundtrack (RCA Victor 1952)★★, *Dinah Shore Sings The Blues* 10-inch album (RCA Victor 1953)★★★, with Buddy Clark *'SWonderful* (1953)★★★★, *The Dinah Shore TV Show* 10-inch album (RCA Victor 1954)★★, *Holding Hands At Midnight* (RCA Victor 1955)★★★, *Bouquet Of Blues* (RCA Victor 1956)★★★, *Moments Like These* (RCA Victor 1957)★★★, *Buttons And Bows* (1959)★★★★, *Dinah, Yes Indeed!* (Capitol 1959)★★★, with André Previn *Dinah Sings, Previn Plays* (Capitol 1960)★★★, *Lavender Blue* (Capitol 1960)★★★, with Red Norvo *Dinah Sings Some Blues With Red* (Capitol 1960)★★★★, *Dinah, Down Home!* (Capitol 1962)★★★, *Fabulous Hits Newly Recorded* (Capitol 1962)★★★, *Lower Basin St. Revisted* (1965)★★★, *Make The World Go Away* (1987)★★★, *Oh Lonesome Me* (1988)★★★.

● COMPILATIONS: *Best Of Dinah Shore* (RCA 1981)★★★, *'Deed I Do (1942-1952)* (Hep Jazz 1988)★★★, *Dinah Shore's Greatest Hits* (Capitol 1988)★★★★, *The Capitol Years* (Capitol 1989)★★★★.

● FURTHER READING: *Dinah!*, B. Cassidy.

● FILMS: *Thank Your Lucky Stars* (1943), *Up In Arms* (1944), *Follow The Boys* (1944), *Belle Of The Yukon* (1945), *Till The Clouds Roll By* (1946), *Make Mine Music* (1946), *Aaron Slick From Punkin Crick* (1952), *Fun And Fancy Free* (1957), *Oh God!* (1977), *H.E.A.L.T.H.* (1979).

SHOW BOAT (FILM MUSICAL)

The first screen adaptation of Jerome Kern and Oscar Hammerstein II's Broadway show was a part-talkie released in 1929. Seven years later, Hammerstein himself wrote the screenplay which retold the familiar story of life on the Mississippi showboat operated by Captain Andy Hawks. This version starred several of the artists who had, at one time or another, appeared on stage in this beloved American classic. Irene Dunne and Allan Jones play the young ingenue Magnolia Hawks and Gaylord Ravenal, her no-good gambler of a husband; Helen Morgan is the mulatto Julie (she also took the role in the 1929 film), with Donald Cook as her husband Steve; Charles Winninger plays the jovial and understanding Captain Hawks, and Paul Robeson, as Joe, sings the immortal 'Ol' Man River'. Most of the songs from the original score were retained, including 'Make Believe' (Dunne and Jones), 'Can't Help Lovin' Dat Man' (Morgan), 'Bill' (lyric also with P.G. Wodehouse) (Morgan), and 'You Are Love' (Dunne and

Jones). In addition, Kern and Hammerstein wrote three new ones, 'Ah Still Suits Me' (Robeson), 'Gallivantin' Around' (Dunne), and the lovely 'I Have The Room Above Her' (Dunne and Jones). LeRoy Prinz choreographed the spirited and imaginative dance sequences, and the film was produced for Universal by Carl Laemmle Jnr. and directed by James Whale. From the opening titles with their cardboard cut-out figures and models on a carousel, through to the film's final moments when Ravenal, reduced to working as theatre doorman, is reunited with Magnolia and their daughter Kim, this picture is a total delight.

Show Boat was remade in 1951 by the renowned Arthur Freed Unit at MGM. This extremely satisfying version starred Kathryn Grayson (Magnolia), Howard Keel (Ravenal), Ava Gardner (Julie, singing dubbed by Annette Warren), and Joe E. Brown (Captain Hawks). William Warfield sang 'Ol' Man River', and Marge and Gower Champion's song-and-dance routines based around 'I Might Fall Back On You' and 'Life Upon The Wicked Stage' were utterly charming. Those two songs were from the 1927 stage show, and another of the original numbers, 'Why Do I Love You?', which not used in the 1936 film, was sung here by Grayson and Keel. John Lee Mahin's screenplay differed in some respects from Hammerstein's earlier effort, but remained generally faithful to the spirit of the piece. The choreography was the work of Robert Alton, the film was directed by George Sidney.

SHOW BOAT (STAGE MUSICAL)

A major theatrical triumph of the 20s that revolutionized the stage musical, integrating songs, dance and story into one cohesive unit, *Show Boat* opened at the Ziegfeld Theatre in New York on 27 December 1927. The magnificent score was the work of Jerome Kern and Oscar Hammerstein II. Hammerstein also wrote the libretto, which was based on Edna Ferber's novel about the lives and loves of the residents and travelling entertainers on the Cotton Blossom Mississippi showboat in the late 19th century. Charles Winninger played Cap'n Andy Hawks, the kindly husband of irascible Parthy Ann Hawks (Edna May Oliver), who spends most of her time trying to prevent their attractive young daughter, Magnolia (Norma Terris), from falling into the clutches of handsome, good-for-nothing showboat gamblers such as Gaylord Ravenal (Howard Marsh). The latter couple's marriage is followed by separation due to Gaylord's excessive gambling. These developments, along with the Broadway stardom of Magnolia and her daughter Kim, are set against the poignant story of the mulatto Julie (Helen Morgan) and her (then) illegal relationship with white husband Steve Baker (Charles Ellis). Also aboard this floating palace of intrigue and entertainment are the black maid Queenie (Tess Gardella) and the song and dance duo, Frank Schultz (Sammy White) and Ellie May Chipley (Eva Puck). Frank and Ellie, together and separately, regularly delight passengers with amusing numbers such as 'I Might Fall Back On You' and 'Life Upon The Wicked Stage'. However, it is for its wonderful ballads that *Show Boat* is particularly treasured. These included Ravenal and Magnolia's 'Where's The Mate For Me?'/'Make Believe', 'You Are

Love' and 'Why Do I Love You?', Julie and Magnolia's 'Can't Help Lovin' Dat Man' and Julie's 'Bill' (lyric with P.G. Wodehouse), as well as 'Ol' Man River', the black dockworker Joe's (Jules Bledsoe) powerful anthem of indignity and survival on the Mississippi River. Also present in this all-time classic score were 'Cotton Blossom', 'Till Good Luck Comes My Way', 'Queenie's Ballyhoo', 'At The Fair', 'Goodbye, My Lady Love', 'After The Ball' (Charles K. Harris) and 'Hey, Feller'. When it was staged at London's Drury Lane Theatre in 1928, Paul Robeson played Joe, and was subsequently forever associated with 'Ol' Man River'. Also in the cast were Edith Day (Magnolia), Howett Worster (Gaylord), Cedric Hardwicke (Cap'n Andy), Marie Burke (Julie), Viola Compton (Parthy), and Alberta Hunter (Queenie). After touring, in 1932 Show Boat returned to Broadway for 180 performances at the Casino Theatre, complete with most of the 1927 cast, Robeson and Dennis King (Ravenal) joining Terris, Morgan, and Winninger as leads.

London audiences saw it again for 264 performances in 1943 - Gywnneth Lascelles (Magnolia), Bruce Carfax (Ravenal), Pat Taylor (Julie), Leslie and Sylvia Kellaway (Frank and Ellie), Malcolm McEachern (Joe) - and in Harold Fielding's 1971 long-running (910 performances) revival - André Jobin (Ravenal), Lorna Dallas (Magnolia), Cleo Laine (Julie), Thomas Carey (Joe), and Kenneth Nelson and Jan Hunt (Frank and Ellie). For the 1946 Broadway revival, which ran for 418 performances - starring Jan Clayton (Magnolia), Charles Fredericks (Ravenal), Carol Bruce (Julie), Buddy Ebsen and Colette Lyons (Frank and Ellie) - Kern and Hammerstein added a new song, 'Nobody Else But Me', which is said to have been Kern's last composition. The show was produced in 1966 at the Lincoln Center with Barbara Cook, Stephen Douglass, David Wayne, Constance Towers, and William Warfield, and in 1983 by the Houston Grand Opera with a cast that included Donald O'Connor, Sheryl Woods, and Ron Raines. In 1990, a version by Opera North and the Royal Shakespeare Company toured the UK and played a limited season at the London Palladium with Janis Kelly (Magnolia), Peter Savidge (Gaylord), Sally Burgess (Julie), Margaret Courtenay (Parthy), Philip Gould and Janie Dee (Frank and Ellie). Four years later, in October 1994, an 'enormously affecting production', directed by Hal Prince, which had previously been ecstatically received in Toronto, opened at the Gershwin Theatre on Broadway and ran for 951 performances. It won Tony Awards for best musical revival, director, choreography (Susan Stroman), and featured actress (Gretha Boston). Also cast were Rebecca Luker (Magnolia), Mark Jacoby (Ravenal), John McMartin (Cap'n Andy [Robert Morse in Toronto]), Lonette McKee (Julie), Doug LaBrecque (Steve), Dorothy Stanley (Ellie), Joel Blum (Frank), Michel Bell (Joe), and Broadway legend Elaine Stritch (Parthy). Eyebrows were raised in some quarters when Stritch was given 'Why Do I Love You' to open Act Two, and there were other changes to book and score, including the introduction of Queenie's 'Mis'ry's Comin' Aroun'', which was cut from the original 1927 production, along with an import from the first film version, 'I Have The Room Above Her'. However, during its long lifetime, Show Boat has been continually reworked to suit the climate of the times in which it was presented, and Prince's version, which has boldness and conviction, may well become the definitive one.

Three touring versions fanned out across North America, and it was these companies, as well as the former Broadway production, that provided the 57 actors, singers, and dancers for the London Show Boat, which opened at the Prince Edward Theatre in April 1998. Cast principals were George Grizzard (Cap'n Andy), Carole Shelley (Parthy), Teri Hansen (Magnolia), Hugh Panaro (Ravenal), Terry Burrell (Julie), Michel Bell (Joe), Gretha Boston (Queenie), Joel Blum (Frank) and Clare Leach (Ellie). Recordings include one of the 1946 revival, which has been issued on CD (Sony), and 'the first ever complete recording of Jerome Kern and Oscar Hammerstein II's great musical, as heard on the opening night at the Ziegfeld Theatre in 1927' (EMI UK). Released in 1988, it featured Frederica von Stade, Jerry Hadley, Teresa Stratas, Bruce Hubbard, Karia Burns, Lillian Gish, and the London Sinfonietta conducted by John McGlinn.

Several film versions have been made, the first in 1929 as a silent with sound added. The 1936 release starred Morgan, Robeson, Allan Jones and Hattie McDaniel, and in the 1951 remake the leads were sung by Howard Keel and Kathryn Grayson.

● FURTHER READING: Show Boat: The Story Of A Classic American Musical, M. Kreuger. Enchanted Evenings: The Broadway Musical From Show Boat To Sondheim, Geoffrey Block.

SHOW IS ON, THE

One of the last of the smart and sophisticated Broadway revues that were so popular in the late 20s and early 30s. This one, which was a vehicle for the extravagant comedic talents of Beatrice Lillie and Bert Lahr, opened at the Winter Garden in New York on 25 December 1936. David Freedman and Moss Hart wrote the sketches which emphasised the production's celebration of 'show business', and lampooned contemporary figures such as John Gielgud and Leslie Howard, who were both offering their 'Hamlets' in New York. The songs came from a variety of composers and lyricists, but 'Little Old Lady' (Hoagy Carmichael and Stanley Adams) and 'By Strauss' (George Gershwin-Ira Gershwin) are probably the best-remembered items from the score. There were several other appealing numbers, including 'Long As You've Got Your Health' (Will Irwin-E.Y. 'Yip Harburg-Norman Zeno', 'Song Of The Woodman' (Harold Arlen-Harburg), 'Now' (Vernon Duke-Ted Fetter), 'Rhythm' (Richard Rodgers-Lorenz Hart), and 'Buy Yourself A Balloon' (Herman Hupfield). During the latter, Beatrice Lillie distributed garters to gentlemen members of the audience while perched on a 'moon seat', which was swung out into the auditorium. The show was stylishly directed by Edward Clark Lilley and Vincente Minnelli, several years before the beginning of Minnelli's distinguished Hollywood career. It ran for 237 performances, and, in some ways, marked the end of an elegant and rather special era.

SHUFFLE ALONG

This show started its life in America as a vaudeville sketch, and was then adapted into the 'longest-running musical to be produced, directed, written, and acted by Negroes'. Naturally, given the era in which it was created and the kind of people who were concerned with it, *Shuffle Along* was not invited to occupy a prime site. Rather it was shuffled off to the 63rd St. Music Hall at the northern end of Broadway, where it opened on 23 May 1921. Much to everyone's surprise, the show was a big hit, and ran for 504 performances. This was not necessarily due to the book, which was written by Flournoy Miller and Aubrey Lyles, and provided the authors with two of the leading roles. Their story of political corruption in Jimtown, Dixieland, tells of how the leading candidates for the office of mayor, Steve Jenkins (Miller) and Sam Peck (Lyles), fix it so that whichever one of them wins - the other cannot lose. Eventually they are both kicked out of office by a knight in shining armour, the high-principled Harry Walton (Roger Matthews). Noble Sissle and Eubie Blake also took part in the show, but their main role was to write the score which contained one enormous hit, 'I'm Just Wild About Harry', as well as a varied selection of songs including the charming 'Love Will Find A Way', 'Bandana Days', 'If You've Never Been Vamped By a Brownskin (You've Never Been Vamped At All)', 'Everything Reminds Me Of You', 'Low Down Blues', 'Shuffle Along', and several more. Paul Robeson joined the Broadway cast for a time in as member of a vocal group, and, when the show eventually went on the road, Joséphine Baker was a member of the chorus. This was a tremendous, fast moving production, with a lot of style, humour, and pulsating music. Subsequent attempts to recreate the formula in 1928, 1932, and 1952, were all unsuccessful. Eubie Blake lived to be over 100, and a musical anthology of some of his work, entitled *Eubie!*, played on Broadway in 1978.

SHUMAN, MORT

b. 12 November 1936, Brooklyn, New York, USA, d. 2 November 1991, London, England. After studying music, Shuman began writing songs with blues singer Doc Pomus in 1958. Early in 1959 two of their songs were Top 40 hits: 'Plain Jane' for Bobby Darin, and Fabian's 'I'm A Man'. During the next six years, their catalogue was estimated at over 500 songs, in a mixture of styles for a variety of artists. They included 'Surrender', 'Viva Las Vegas', 'Little Sister' and 'Kiss Me Quick' (Elvis Presley), 'Save The Last Dance For Me', 'Sweets For My Sweet' and 'This Magic Moment' (the Drifters), 'Teenager In Love' (Dion And The Belmonts), 'Can't Get Used To Losing You' (Andy Williams), 'Suspicion' (Terry Stafford), 'Seven Day Weekend' (Gary 'U.S.' Bonds) and 'Spanish Lace' (Gene McDaniels). Around the time of the team's break-up in 1965, Shuman collaborated with several other writers. These included John McFarland for Billy J. Kramer's UK number 1, 'Little Children', Clive Westlake for 'Here I Go Again' (the Hollies), ex-pop star Kenny Lynch, for 'Sha-La-La-La-Lee' (Small Faces), 'Love's Just A Broken Heart' (Cilla Black), producer Jerry Ragovoy for 'Get It While You Can' and 'Look At Granny Run, Run' (Howard Tate). Subsequently, Shuman moved to Paris, where he occasionally performed his own one-man show, and issued solo albums such as *Amerika* and *Imagine ...*, as well as

writing several songs for Johnny Halliday. In 1968 Shuman translated the lyrics of French composer Jacques Brel; these were recorded by many artists including Dusty Springfield, Scott Walker and Rod McKuen. Together with Eric Blau, he devised, adapted and wrote lyrics for the revue Jacques Brel Is Alive And Well And Living In Paris. Shuman also starred in the piece, which became a worldwide success. In October 1989, *Budgie*, a musical set in London's Soho district, with Shuman's music and Don Black's lyrics, opened in the West End. It starred former pop star, turned actor and entrepreneur, Adam Faith, and UK soap opera actress, Anita Dobson. The show closed after only three months, losing more than £1,000,000. Shuman wrote several other shows, including *Amadeo, Or How To Get Rid Of It*, based on an Ionesco play, a Hong Kong portrayal of *Madame Butterfly* and a reworking of Bertolt Brecht and Kurt Weill's opera *Aufstieg Und Fall Der Stadt Mahogonny*. None has yet reached the commercial theatre. After undergoing a liver operation in the spring of 1991, he died in London.

● ALBUMS: *Amerika, Imagine ..., Distant Drum.*

SIDE SHOW

This eagerly awaited musical, which was inspired by the lives of the English Siamese twins Daisy and Violet Hilton, opened on the 16 October 1997 at the Richard Rodgers Theatre in New York. Daisy and Violet appeared in two films, *Freaks* (1932) and *Chained For Life* (1951), and the story goes that this whole thing started when *Side Show* director and choreographer Robert Longbottom saw *Chained For Life* in the mid-80s. He brought it to the attention of librettist and lyricist Bill Russell (*Elegies For Angels, Punks And Raving Queens*), who eventually collaborated with composer Henry Krieger (of *Dreamgirls* fame) for this production. Set in the 20s and 30s, *Side Show* follows Violet Hilton (Alice Ripley) and Daisy Hilton (Emily Skinner) as they progress from a cheap and nasty carnival show ('Come Look At The Freaks'), to star attractions on the prestige vaudeville circuit. Aspiring musician Buddy Foster (Hugh Panaro) and talent scout Terry Connor (Jeff McCarthy) overcome the objections of sideshow Boss (Ken Jennings) and the girls' friend and protector, an African-American 'Cannibal King', Jake (Norm Lewis) (gospel-style 'The Devil You Know'), and whisk them off to enjoy the first of many triumphant tours and lavish *Ziegfeld Follies*-style shows ('Rare Songbirds On Display'). This being a musical, rather than a documentary, romance blossoms when ambitious Daisy takes up with Terry, while homeloving Violet falls for tunesmith Buddy. The ensuing complications result in only one wedding - Terry just can't face it - and the twins finally admit that they can only really find solace in each other ('I Will Never Leave You'). Curtain time finds them reprising 'Come Look At The Freaks' as they decamp to Hollywood in order to join the Human Skeleton, Half-Woman, Half-Man, Armless Girl, and the rest, in Todd Browning's movie, *Freaks* (tagline: 'Can a full grown woman truly love a MIDGET?'). Daisy and Violet's poignant 'Feelings You've Got To Hide', 'When I'm By Your Side', 'Who Will Love Me As I Am?' (as well as the impossibly suggestive 'Leave Me Alone'), rank with Jake's aching 'You Should Be Loved' among the highlights of an appealing score, which also included 'Like Everyone Else', 'You Deserve A Better Life', 'Crazy, Deaf and Blind', 'More Than We Bargained For', 'Say Goodnight To The Freak Show', 'Overnight Sensation', 'We Share Everything', 'The Interview', 'New Year's Day', 'Private Conversation', 'One Plus One Equals Three', 'Tunnel Of Love', 'Beautiful Day For A Wedding', and 'Marry Me, Terry'. Gregg Barnes's good looking costumes, Robin Wagner's simple but significant sets, and Robert Longbottom's direction and choreography, combined with two outstanding lead performances from Ripley and Skinner, made this a show to remember. Not many people will do, however, because *Side Show* closed on the 3 January 1998 after only 91 performances. Estimated losses were in the region of $5-7 million. A spokesman for the show's publicity department commented: 'Strong audience resistance seemed based on a wide perception that the production would be a 'freak show', a forbidding, unsettling experience. Attempts to overcome this formidable marketing problem were not effective.' Another Siamese twins show, *Chang & Eng - The Musical*, based on Burton Cohen's play, *The Wedding Of The Siamese Twins*, was presented by Singapore's Action Theatre for the June 1997 Festival of Asian Arts. Daisy and Violet Hilton, who were joined at the hip, died in 1969 aged 60.

SILK STOCKINGS (FILM MUSICAL)

Two years after Silk Stockings began its successful run on Broadway, MGM released this screen version which reunited Fred Astaire with one of his most thrilling dancing partners, Cyd Charisse. Leonard Gershe and Leonard Spigelgass's screenplay was adapted from the show's libretto, which itself was based on the 1939 Greta Garbo movie *Ninotchka* and a story by Melchior Lengyel. The plot concerns a beautiful Russian emissary, Nina (Ninotchka), played by Charisse, who eventually falls for an American businessman (Astaire) after being sent to the USA in an effort to discover why three previous 'comrades' have failed to retrieve a Russian composer who is believed to be contemplating defection to the West. However, by then, the trio of messengers, Jules Munshin, Peter Lorre and Joseph Buloff, are themselves well on the way to capitulating to the capitalist way of life. Most of Cole Porter's songs from the stage show were retained and two new ones, 'Fated To Be Mated' and 'The Ritz Roll And Rock', added. The dancing, predictably, was 'out of this world', and Astaire was his usual charming vocal self on numbers such as 'All Of You', 'Paris Loves Lovers' and 'It's A Chemical Reaction, That's All' (with Charisse, dubbed by Carol Richards), and 'Stereophonic Sound' (with Janis Paige). Other numbers included 'Too Bad', 'Silk Stockings', 'Satin And Silk', 'Without Love', 'Josephine' and 'The Red Blues'. After helping themselves to generous portions of Western liquid hospitality, the three reluctant Reds, Munshin, Lorre and Buloff, are hilarious as they muse - musically - on the subject of 'Siberia'. *Silk Stockings*, which turned out to be Fred Astaire's last musical film (apart from the generally unsatisfactory Finian's Rainbow, made when he was nearly 70), was a fine affair. The choreographers were Hermes Pan and Eugene Loring (with Astaire,

as usual, uncredited) and the director was Rouben Mamoulian. The musical director was André Previn, and the film was photographed in Metrocolor and Cinemascope.

SILK STOCKINGS (STAGE MUSICAL)

Cole Porter's final Broadway show was based on the 1939 film *Ninotchka*, which starred Greta Garbo. During the out-of-town try-outs, Abe Burrows' name was added to those of librettists George S. Kaufman and Leueen McGrath, and Kaufman was replaced as director by Cy Feur. *Silk Stockings* opened at the Imperial Theatre in New York on 24 February 1955. In this musical version of the by now familiar story, Ninotchka (Hildegarde Neff) is seduced by a glib Hollywood talent agent, Steve Canfield (Don Ameche), who is trying to persuade a famous Russian composer, Peter Ilyich Boroff (Philip Sterling), to expand his 'Ode To A Tractor' into the score for a ritzy movie version of *War And Peace*. The score was not top-drawer Porter by any means, but there were some worthwhile numbers, especially the gorgeous ballad 'All Of You', the amusing and contemporary 'Stereophonic Sound', and several more varied and entertaining items including 'Paris Loves Lovers', 'Without Love', 'It's A Chemical Reaction, That's All', 'Too Bad', 'Silk Stockings', 'The Red Blues', 'As On The Seasons We Sail', 'Satin And Silk', 'Josephine' and 'Siberia'. The show enjoyed a run of 478 performances and was filmed in 1957 with Fred Astaire and Cyd Charisse.

SILVER DREAM RACER

David Essex starred in this 1980 film in which he portrayed a garage storeman given a newly-designed motorcycle with which he attempts to win a championship race at the Silverstone circuit. Some excellent action sequences apart, *Silver Dream Racer* is as antiquated as its plot and it failed to recreate the success of earlier Essex ventures *That'll Be The Day* and *Stardust*. The singer wrote most of the soundtrack material with some help from John Cameron, formerly of the rock band CCS, and he was rewarded when the title song reached number 4 in the UK singles chart.

SILVESTRI, ALAN

b. New York, USA. A prolific composer of film music, from the 70s through to the 90s. Silvestri studied at the Berklee College Of Music in Boston, Massachusetts, before scoring some low-budget movies and working on the US television series *Chips* In the late 70s and early 80s he composed the music for *Las Vegas Lady*, *The Amazing Dobermans* (starring Fred Astaire in an off-beat role), and *Par Ou Tes Rentre?* (1984). Subsequently he scored blockbuster productions such as *Romancing The Stone*, *Back To The Future*, and the remarkable live-action *Who Framed Roger Rabbit* (1988). His other credits during the 80s included *Fandang*, *Summer Rental*, *Delta Force*, *Flight Of The Navigator*, *No Mercy*, *Outrageous Fortune*, *Predator*, *Overboard*, *My Stepmother Is An Alien*, *She's Out Of Control*, *The Abyss*, and *Back To The Future Part II* (1989). In the following year, Silvestri also scored the third and final episode of director Robert Zemeckis' time-travel series, *Back To The Future*

Part III, starring Michael J. Fox. During the early 90s Silvestri continued to compose for highly commercial movies such as *Young Guns II*, *Predator 2*, *Dutch*, *Soapdish*, *Ricochet*, *Shattered*, *Driving Me Crazy*, *Father Of The Bride* (a re-make of the 1950 classic starring Steve Martin), *Stop! Or My Mom Will Shoot*, *Death Becomes Her*, *The Bodyguard*, *Cop And A Half*, *Super Mario Brothers*, *The Abyss: Special Edition*, *Grumpy Old Men*, *Blown Away*, *Forrest Gump*, and *Richie Rich* (1994). In 1992, following Ashman and Menken's recent success with *The Little Mermaid* and *Beauty And The Beast*, Silvestri composed the music for the animated feature, *Ferngully...The Last Rainforest*, based on Diana Young's stories, *Ferngully*. In 1995, he was honoured by BMI with its Richard Kirk Award for career achievement.

SIMPLE SIMON

One of America's most cherished clowns, Ed Wynn, brought his fumbling style, nervous laugh, and excruciating puns to this Florenz Ziegfeld production which opened at the impresario's own Broadway theatre on 18 February 1930. Wynn also collaborated with Guy Bolton on the book in which he was cast as a newspaper vendor who, rather than accept that bad news exists, spends his time in a kind of fairy-tale land. This gave Ziegfeld and his designer Joseph Urban the opportunity to display the lavish sets and costumes for which he was justifiably famous. Richard Rodgers and Lorenz Hart wrote the score, and it contained one of their most enduring numbers, 'Ten Cents A Dance', which was emphatically introduced by Ruth Etting. She had a big record hit with the song, and it figured prominently in her film biography, *Love Me Or Leave Me*, in which she was played by Doris Day. Ironically, the song 'Love Me Or Leave Me' (Gus Kahn-Walter Donaldson) was added to the score of *Simple Simon* a couple of months after the show opened. One of the numbers that was cut during the Broadway try-out, 'Dancing On The Ceiling', was later sung by Jessie Matthews in the London production of *Ever Green*, and became forever associated with her. The remainder of the score for *Simple Simon* included 'I Can Do Wonders With You', 'Don't Tell Your Folks', 'Send For Me', and 'I Still Believe In You'. The show ran for 135 performances, and returned early in 1931 for a further brief engagement.

SINATRA, FRANK

b. Francis Albert Sinatra, 12 December 1915, Hoboken, New Jersey, USA, d. 15 May 1998, Los Angeles, California, USA. After working for a time in the office of a local newspaper, *The Jersey Observer*, Frank Sinatra decided to pursue a career as a singer. Already an admirer of Bing Crosby, he was impelled to pursue this course after attending a 1933 Crosby concert, and sang whenever and wherever he could, working locally in clubs and bars. Then, in 1935 he entered a popular US radio talent show, *Major Bowes Amateur Hour*. Also on the show was a singing trio, and the four young men found themselves teamed together by the no-nonsense promoter. The ad-hoc teaming worked, and the group, renamed 'The Hoboken Four', won first prize. Resulting from this came a succession of concert dates with the Major Bowes trav-

elling show, along with club and occasional radio dates. By 1938 Sinatra was singing on several shows on each of a half-dozen radio stations, sometimes for expenses - often for nothing. The experience and, especially, the exposure were vital if he was to be recognized. Among the bands with which he performed was one led by songwriter Harold Arlen but in 1939, shortly after he married his childhood sweetheart, Nancy Barbato, he was heard and hired by Harry James, who had only recently formed his own big band. James recognized Sinatra's talent from the beginning and also identified the source of his determination to succeed, his massive self-confidence and powerful ego. During their brief association, James remarked to an interviewer, 'His name is Sinatra, and he considers himself the greatest vocalist in the business. Get that! No one's even heard of him! He's never had a hit record, and he looks like a wet rag, but he says he's the greatest.' In 1939 and early 1940 Sinatra made a number of records with James and began to develop a small following. His records with James included 'My Buddy' and 'All Or Nothing At All'.

In 1940 Sinatra was approached with an offer by Tommy Dorsey, then leading one of the most popular swing era bands. Only some six months had expired on Sinatra's two-year contract with James, who must have realized he was parting with a potential goldmine, but he was a generous-spirited man and let the singer go. Sinatra had many successful records with Dorsey including 'Polka Dots And Moonbeams', 'Imagination', 'Fools Rush In', 'I'll Never Smile Again', 'The One I Love', 'Violets For Your Furs', 'How About You?' and 'In The Blue Of Evening', some of which became fixtures in his repertoire. One record from this period became a major hit a few years later when the USA entered World War II. This song, recorded at Sinatra's second session with Dorsey in February 1940, was 'I'll Be Seeing You', and its lyric gained a special significance for servicemen, and the women they had left behind. Sinatra's popularity with the young female population, achieved despite, or perhaps because of, his gangling, unheroic and rather vulnerable appearance, prompted him to leave Dorsey and begin a solo career. In spite of the tough line taken by Dorsey over the remaining half of his five-year contract (Dorsey allegedly settled for 43% of the singer's gross over the next 10 years), Sinatra quit. Within months his decision proved to be right. He had become the idol of hordes of teenage girls, his public appearances were sell-outs and his records jostled with one another for hit status. In the early 40s he had appeared in a handful of films as Dorsey's vocalist, but by the middle of the decade he began appearing in feature films as an actor-singer. These included lightweight if enjoyable fare such as *Higher And Higher* (1944), *Anchors Aweigh* (1945), *It Happened In Brooklyn* (1947), *The Kissing Bandit* (1948) and *Double Dynamite* (1951).

By the 50s, however, Sinatra's career was in trouble; both as a singer and actor, he appeared to have reached the end of the road. His acting had suffered in part from the quality of material he was offered, and had accepted. Nevertheless, it was his film career that was the first to recover when he landed the role of Angelo Maggio in *From Here To Eternity* (1953) for which he won an

Academy Award as Best Supporting Actor. Thereafter, he was taken seriously as an actor even if he was rarely given the same standard of role or achieved the same quality of performance. He continued to make films, usually in straight acting roles, but occasionally in musicals. Among the former were *The Man With The Golden Arm* (1955), one of the roles that matched his breakthrough performance as Maggio, *Johnny Concho* (1956), *Kings Go Forth* (1958), *A Hole In The Head* (1959), *The Manchurian Candidate* (1962), *Von Ryan's Express* (1965), *Assault On A Queen* (1966), *Tony Rome* (1967) and *The Detective* (1968). His musicals included Guys And Dolls (1955), High Society (1956), Pal Joey (1957), The Joker Is Wild (1957), Can-Can (1960) and *Robin And The 7 Hoods* (1964). Later, he appeared in an above average television movie, *Contract On Cherry Street* (1977), and *The First Deadly Sin* (1980).

Soon after his Oscar-winning appearance in *From Here To Eternity*, Sinatra made a comeback as a recording artist. He had been recording for Columbia, where he fell out of step when changes were made to the company's musical policy, and in 1953 he was signed by Capitol Records. Sinatra's first session at Capitol was arranged and conducted by Axel Stordahl whom Sinatra had known in the Dorsey band. For the next session, however, he was teamed with Nelson Riddle. Sinatra had heard the results of earlier recording sessions made by Nat 'King' Cole at Capitol on which Riddle had collaborated. Sinatra was deeply impressed by the results and some sources suggest that on joining Capitol he had asked for Riddle. The results of this partnership set Sinatra's singing career firmly in the spotlight. Over the next few years classic albums such as *Songs For Young Lovers*, *This Is Sinatra*, *A Swingin' Affair*, *Come Fly With Me*, *Swing Easy!*, *In The Wee Small Hours* and the exceptional *Songs For Swingin' Lovers* set standards for popular singers that have rarely been equalled and almost never surpassed. The two men were intensely aware of one another's talents and although critics were unanimous in their praise of Riddle, the arranger was unassumingly diffident, declaring that it was the singer's 'great talent that put him back on top'. For all Riddle's modesty, there can be little doubt that the arranger encouraged Sinatra's latent feeling for jazz, which helped to create the relaxed yet superbly swinging atmosphere that epitomized their work together. On his albums for Capitol, his own label Reprise, and other labels, sometimes with Riddle, other times with Robert Farnon, Neal Hefti, Gordon Jenkins, Quincy Jones, Billy May or Stordahl, Sinatra built upon his penchant for the best in American popular song, displaying a deep understanding of the wishes of composer and lyricist.

Fans old and new bought his albums in their tens of thousands and several reached the top in the *Billboard* charts. The 1955 album *In The Wee Small Hours* was in the charts for 29 weeks, reaching number 2; the following year's *Songs For Swingin' Lovers* charted for 66 weeks, also reaching the second spot. *Come Fly With Me*, from 1958, spent 71 weeks in the charts, reaching number 1, and other top positions were attained by 1958's *Only The Lonely* (120 weeks), 1960's *Nice 'N' Easy* (86 weeks), and in 1966, *Strangers In The Night* (73) weeks. The title song from this latter album also made number 1 in *Billboard*'s singles charts, as did the following year's million-selling 'Something Stupid' on which he duetted with his daughter, Nancy Sinatra. At a time in popular music's history when ballads were not the most appealing form, and singers were usually in groups and getting younger by the minute, these represented no mean achievements for a middle-aged solo singer making a comeback. The secret of this late success lay in Sinatra's superior technical ability, his wealth of experience, his abiding love for the material with which he worked and the invariably high standards of professionalism he brought to his recordings and public performances. During his stint with Dorsey, the singer had taken a marked professional interest in the bandleader's trombone playing. He consciously learned breath control, in particular circular breathing, and the use of dynamics from Dorsey. Additionally, he employed Dorsey's legato style, which aided the smooth phrasing of his best ballad work. Complementing this, Sinatra's enjoyment of jazz and the company of jazz musicians prompted him to adopt jazz phrasing, which greatly enhanced his rhythmic style. More than any other popular singer of his or previous generations, Sinatra learned the value of delayed phrasing and singing behind the beat, and he and his arrangers invariably found exactly the right tempo. His relaxed rhythmic style contrasted strikingly with the stiffer-sounding singers who preceded him. Even Crosby, whose popularity Sinatra eventually surpassed, later accommodated some of Sinatra's stylistic devices. (Crosby's habitual lazy-sounding style was of a different order from Sinatra's and until late in his career he never fully shook off his 2/4 style, while Sinatra, almost from the start, was completely comfortable with the 4/4 beat of swing.)

Sinatra's revived career brought him more attention even than in his heyday as the bobby-soxers' idol. Much of the interest was intrusive and led to frequently acrimonious and sometimes violent clashes with reporters. With much of what is written about him stemming from a decidedly ambivalent view, the picture of the man behind the voice is often confused. Undoubtedly, his private persona is multi-faceted. He has been described by acquaintances as quick-tempered, pugnacious, sometimes vicious and capable of extreme verbal cruelty, and he has often displayed serious lack of judgement in the company he has kept. In marked contrast, others have categorically declared him to be enormously generous to friends in need and to individuals and organizations he believes can benefit from his personal or financial support. His political stance has changed dramatically over the years and here again his judgement seems to be flawed. At first a Democrat, he supported Roosevelt and later Kennedy with enormous enthusiasm. His ties with the Kennedy clan were close, and not always for the best of reasons. Sinatra was unceremoniously dropped by the Kennedys following allegations that he had introduced to John Kennedy a woman who became simultaneously the mistress of the President of the United States and a leading figure in the Mafia. Sinatra then became a Republican and lent his support as fund-raiser and campaigner to Richard Nixon and Ronald Reagan, apparently oblivious to their serious flaws.

An immensely rich man, with interests in industry, real estate, recording companies, and film and television production, Sinatra chose to continue working, making frequent comebacks and presenting a never-ending succession of 'farewell' concerts, which, as time passed, became less like concerts and more like major events in contemporary popular culture. He continued to attract adoring audiences and in the late 80s and early 90s, despite being in his mid- to late seventies, could command staggering fees for personal appearances. In 1992, a two-part television biography, *Sinatra*, was transmitted in the USA, produced by Tina Sinatra, and starring Philip Casnoff in the leading role. Almost inevitably, it topped the weekly ratings. In 1993 Capitol Records re-signed Sinatra after 30 years with Reprise Records and announced a new album as 'the recording event of the decade'. *Duets* was a brilliant piece of marketing: it had Sinatra teamed with a varied all-star cast, including Aretha Franklin, Carly Simon, Barbra Streisand, Tony Bennett, Natalie Cole, Kenny G. and U2's Bono. A subsequent volume, *Duets II*, featuring artists such as Stevie Wonder, Antonio Carlos Jobim, Chrissie Hynde, Willie Nelson, Lena Horne, Gladys Knight and Patti LaBelle, was released in 1994. However, rumours of ill health persisted through 1996 and 1997, and although it was not confirmed, Alzheimer's disease was cited as the most likely condition. The voice of the century was finally silenced on 15 May 1998. There were countless tributes from fans, world leaders and musicians.

When an assessment has to be made of his life, it is not the money or the worship of his fans that matters; neither is it the mixed quality of his film career and the uncertainties surrounding his personal characteristics and shortcomings. What really matters is that in his treatment of the classics from the Great American Songbook, Sinatra made a unique contribution to 20th-century popular music. Despite an occasional lapse, when carefully crafted lyrics were replaced with his own inimitable (yet all too often badly imitated) phrases, over several decades he fashioned countless timeless performances. There are some songs that, however many singers may have recorded them before or since Sinatra, or will record them in the future, have become inextricably linked with his name: 'I'll Walk Alone', 'It Could Happen To You', 'I'll Never Smile Again', 'Violets For Your Furs', 'How About You?', 'Jeepers Creepers', 'All Of Me', 'Taking A Chance On Love', 'Just One Of Those Things', 'My Funny Valentine', 'They Can't Take That Away From Me', 'I Get A Kick Out Of You', 'You Make Me Feel So Young', 'Old Devil Moon', 'The Girl Next Door', 'My One And Only Love', 'Three Coins In The Fountain', 'Love And Marriage', 'Swingin' Down The Lane', 'Come Fly With Me', 'Fly Me To The Moon', 'The Tender Trap', 'Chicago', 'New York, New York', 'Let Me Try Again', 'Night And Day', 'Here's That Rainy Day', 'Strangers In The Night', 'I Thought About You', 'Lady Is A Tramp', 'Anything Goes', 'All The Way', 'One For My Baby' and 'I've Got You Under My Skin'. Not all these songs are major examples of the songwriters' art, yet even on lesser material, of which 'My Way' is a notable example, he provided a patina of quality the songs and their writers may not have deserved and that no one else could have supplied. Since the 70s Sinatra's voice showed

serious signs of decay. The pleasing baritone had given way to a worn and slightly rusting replica of what it once had been. Nevertheless, he sang on, adjusting to the changes in his voice and, as often as not, still creating exemplary performances of many of his favourite songs. In these twilight years he was especially effective in the easy-swinging mid-tempo he had always preferred and that concealed the inevitable vocal deterioration wrought by time.

In assessing Sinatra's place in popular music it is very easy to slip into hyperbole. After all, through dedication to his craft and his indisputable love for the songs he sang, Sinatra became the greatest exponent of a form of music that he helped to turn into an art form. In so doing, he became an icon of popular culture, a huge achievement for a skinny kid from Hoboken. Writing in the *Observer*, when Sinatra's retirement was thought, mistakenly, to be imminent, music critic Benny Green observed: 'What few people, apart from musicians, have never seemed to grasp is that he is not simply the best popular singer of his generation . . . but the culminating point in an evolutionary process which has refined the art of interpreting words set to music. Nor is there even the remotest possibility that he will have a successor. Sinatra was the result of a fusing of a set of historical circumstances which can never be repeated.' Sinatra himself never publicly spoke of his work in such glowing terms, choosing instead to describe himself simply as a 'saloon singer'. Deep in his heart, however, Sinatra must have known that Green's judgement was the more accurate and it is one that will long be echoed by countless millions of fans all around the world. Musically at least, it is a world better for the care that Frank Sinatra lavished upon its popular songs.

On his death the newspapers were ready to bring up his dark side, although fortunately the music, and his gigantic contribution to it, was acknowledged. Sinatra was the greatest interpreter of the popular song the world has known. As Gore Vidal remarked, it was likely that 50% of the current population of North America was conceived while Frank Sinatra was singing in the background. He was quite possibly right.

● ALBUMS: *The Voice Of Frank Sinatra* 10-inch album (Columbia 1949)★★★, *Christmas Songs By Frank Sinatra* 10-inch album (Columbia 1950)★★★, *Frankly Sentimental* 10-inch album (Columbia 1951)★★★, *Songs By Sinatra, Volume 1* 10-inch album (Columbia 1951)★★★, *Dedicated To You* 10-inch album (Columbia 1952)★★★, *Sing And Dance With Frank Sinatra* 10-inch album (Columbia 1953)★★★, *I've Got A Crush On You* 10-inch album (Columbia 1954)★★★, *Songs For Young Lovers* 10-inch album (Capitol 1954)★★★★, *Swing Easy* 10-inch album (Capitol 1954)★★★★★, *In The Wee Small Hours* (Capitol 1955)★★★★★, *Songs For Swingin' Lovers!* (Capitol 1956)★★★★★, *High Society* film soundtrack (Capitol 1956)★★★★, *Frank Sinatra Conducts Tone Poems Of Colour* (Capitol 1956)★★★, *Close To You* (Capitol 1957)★★★★, *A Swingin' Affair!* (Capitol 1957)★★★★★, *Where Are You?* (Capitol 1957)★★★★, *Pal Joey* film soundtrack (Capitol 1957)★★★, *A Jolly Christmas From Frank Sinatra* (Capitol 1957)★★★, *Come Fly With Me* (Capitol 1958)★★★★★, *Frank Sinatra Sings For Only The Lonely* (Capitol 1958)★★★★★, *Come Dance With Me!* (Capitol 1959)★★★★★, *No One Cares* (Capitol

1959)★★★★, *Can-Can* film soundtrack (Capitol 1960)★★, *Nice 'N' Easy* (Capitol 1960)★★★★★, *Sinatra's Swinging Session!!!* (Capitol 1961)★★★★, *Ring-A-Ding Ding!* (Reprise 1961)★★★★, *Sinatra Swings* (Reprise 1961)★★★★, *Come Swing With Me!* (Capitol 1961)★★★★, *I Remember Tommie ...* (Reprise 1961)★★★, *Sinatra And Strings* (Reprise 1962)★★★★, *Point Of No Return* (Capitol 1962)★★★★, *Sinatra And Swingin' Brass* (Reprise 1962)★★★★★, *All Alone* (Reprise 1962)★★★, with Count Basie *Sinatra-Basie* (Reprise 1963)★★★, *The Concert Sinatra* (Reprise 1963)★★★★★, *Sinatra's Sinatra* (Reprise 1963)★★★, *Days Of Wine And Roses, Moon River, And Other Academy Award Winners* (Reprise 1964)★★★, with Bing Crosby, Fred Waring *America I Hear You Singing* (Reprise 1964)★★, with Basie *It Might As Well Be Swing* (Reprise 1964)★★★, *Softly As I Leave You* (Reprise 1964)★★★, *Sinatra '65* (Reprise 1965)★★★, *September Of My Years* (Reprise 1965)★★★★★, *My Kind Of Broadway* (Reprise 1965)★★★, *Moonlight Sinatra* (Reprise 1965)★★★★, *A Man And His Music* (Reprise 1965)★★★★, *Strangers In The Night* (Reprise 1966)★★★, with Basie *Sinatra At The Sands* (Reprise 1966)★★★★, *That's Life* (Reprise 1966)★★★, with Antonio Carlos Jobim *Francis Albert Sinatra And Antonio Carlos Jobim* (Reprise 1967)★★★★, *Frank Sinatra (The World We Knew)* (Reprise 1967)★★, with Duke Ellington *Francis A. And Edward K.* (Reprise 1968)★★★, *Cycles* (Reprise 1968)★★★, *The Sinatra Family Wish You A Merry Christmas* (Reprise 1968)★★, *My Way* (Reprise 1969)★★★, *A Man Alone And Other Songs By Rod McKuen* (Reprise 1969)★★, *Watertown* (Reprise 1970)★★, with Antonio Carlos Jobim *Sinatra And Company* (Reprise 1971)★★★, *Ol' Blue Eyes Is Back* (Reprise 1973)★★★, *Some Nice Things I've Missed* (Reprise 1974)★★, *Sinatra - The Main Event Live* (Reprise 1974)★★★, *Trilogy: Past, Present, Future* (Reprise 1980)★★★, *She Shot Me Down* (Reprise 1981)★★, *LA Is My Lady* (Qwest 1984)★★, *Duets* (Capitol 1993)★★, *Sinatra And Sextet: Live In Paris* (Reprise 1994)★★★, *From Hoboken NJ To The White House* (1994)★★★, with Dean Martin *A Swingin' Night At The Sabre Room* (1994)★★★, *Old Gold Shows 1946* (1994)★★★, *Duets II* (Capitol 1994)★★, with Red Norvo *Live In Australia, 1959* (Blue Note 1997)★★★.

● COMPILATIONS: *Frankie* (Columbia 1955)★★★, *That Old Feeling* (Columbia 1956)★★★, *This Is Sinatra!* (Capitol 1957)★★★★, *Adventures Of The Heart* (Columbia 1957)★★★, *This Is Sinatra, Volume 2* (Capitol 1958)★★★★, *The Frank Sinatra Story In Music* (Columbia 1958)★★★★, *Look To Your Heart* (Capitol 1958)★★★, *Put Your Dreams Away* (Columbia 1958)★★★, *Love Is A Kick* (Columbia 1958)★★★, *The Broadway Kick* (Columbia 1959)★★★, *Come Back To Sorrento* (Columbia 1959)★★★, *Reflections* (Columbia 1959)★★★, *All The Way* (Capitol 1961)★★★★, *Sinatra Sings ... Of Love And Things* (Capitol 1962)★★★★, *Tell Her You Love Her* (Capitol 1963)★★★, *Sinatra: A Man And His Music (1960-65)* (Reprise 1965)★★★★★, *The Essential Frank Sinatra, Volumes 1-3* (Columbia 1966)★★★★, *The Movie Songs (1954-60)* (Capitol 1967)★★★, *Greatest Hits - The Early Years* (Columbia 1967)★★★, *Frank Sinatra In Hollywood 1943-1949* (Columbia 1968)★★★, *Frank Sinatra's Greatest Hits!* (Reprise 1968)★★★★, *Frank Sinatra's Greatest Hits, Vol. 2* (Reprise 1972)★★★★, *The Dorsey/Sinatra Sessions, 1940-42* (RCA 1972)★★★★, *Round # 1* (Capitol 1974)★★★, *The Best Of Ol' Blue Eyes* (Reprise 1975)★★★, *Classics* (Columbia 1977)★★★★, *Portrait Of Sinatra (400 Songs From The Life Of A Man)* (Reprise 1977)★★★★, *20 Golden Greats* (Capitol 1978)★★★★, *The Rare Sinatra* (Capitol 1978)★★★, *Screen Sinatra* (Capitol 1980)★★★, *20 Classic Tracks* (MFP 1981)★★★★, with Tommy Dorsey *The Dorsey/Sinatra Radio Years* (RCA 1983)★★★★, *Lena Horne And Frank Sinatra* (Astan 1984)★★★, *The Capitol Years* 20-LP box set (Capitol 1985)★★★★, *Collection* (Castle 1986)★★★, *Now Is The Hour* (Castle 1986)★★★, *All-Time Classics* (Pair 1986)★★★★, *The Voice: The Columbia Years (1943-1952)* 6-LP box set (Columbia 1986)★★★★, *Sinatra: The Radio Years 1939 - 1955* (Meteor 1987)★★★, *Hello Young Lovers* (Columbia 1987)★★★, with Dorsey *Tommy Dorsey/Frank Sinatra All-Time Greatest Hits, Volumes 1-4* (RCA 1988-90)★★★★, *Sinatra Rarities* (Columbia 1988)★★★, *Rare Recordings 1935-70* (Sandy Hook 1989)★★★, *Capitol Collectors Series* (Capitol 1990)★★★★, *The Capitol Years* 3-CD box set (Capitol 1990)★★★★, *The Reprise Collection* 4-CD box set (Reprise 1990)★★★★, *Sinatra Reprise - The Very Good Years* (Reprise 1991)★★★★, *Gold Collection* (1993)★★★, *Sings The Songs Of Cahn And Styne* (1993)★★★★, *This Is Frank Sinatra 1953-57* (1994)★★★★, with Dorsey *The Song Is You* 5-CD box set (Columbia 1994)★★★★, *The Soundtrack Sessions* (Bravura 1994)★★★, *Two From Sinatra* (Capitol 1995)★★★, *The Columbia Years* (Sony 1995)★★★★, *Sinatra 80th: Live In Concert* (EMI 1995)★★★, *All The Best* 2-CD (EMI 1995)★★★★, *Swing And Dance With Frank Sinatra* (Legacy 1996)★★★★, *Sinatra Sings Rodgers And Hammerstein* (Legacy 1996)★★★, *The Complete Capitol Singles Collection* 4-CD set (Capitol 1996)★★★★★, with Dorsey *Love Songs* (RCA 1997)★★★★, *My Way: The Best Of Frank Sinatra* (Reprise 1997)★★★, *Sinatra Swings* 3-CD set (Delta 1997)★★★, *The Frank Sinatra Story* (Carlton 1998)★★, *The Capitol Years* 21-CD box set (Capitol 1998)★★★★★.

● VIDEOS: *Old Blue Eyes* (World Of Video 1988), *A Man And His Music (1965)* (Braveworld 1990), *A Man And His Music Part II (1966)* (Braveworld 1990), *A Man And His Music + Ella + Jobim (1967)* (Braveworld 1990), *Francis Albert Sinatra Does His Thing (1968)* (Braveworld 1990), *Sinatra (1969)* (Braveworld 1990), *Sinatra In Concert: Royal Festival Hall (1970)* (Braveworld 1990), *Ol' Blue Eyes Is Back (1973)* (Braveworld 1990), *The Main Event: Madison Square Garden (1974)* (Braveworld 1990), *Sinatra And Friends (1977)* (Braveworld 1990), *The First 40 Years (1979)* (Braveworld 1990), *Sinatra: The Man And His Music (1981)* (Braveworld 1990), *Concert For The Americas (1982)* (Braveworld 1990), *Sinatra In Japan (1985)* (Braveworld 1990), *His Way* (PolyGram 1995), *My Way - Sinatra's Greatest Ever Performance* (VCI 1997).

● FURTHER READING: *The Voice: The Story Of An American Phenomenon*, E.J. Kahn. *Sinatra And His Rat Pack: A Biography*, Richard Gehman. *Sinatra*, Robin Douglas-Home. *Sinatra: Retreat Of The Romantic*, Arnold Shaw. *The Films Of Frank Sinatra*, Gene Ringold. *Sinatra And The Great Song Stylists*, Ken Barnes. *Songs By Sinatra, 1939-1970*, Brian Hainsworth. *Frank Sinatra*, Paula Taylor. *On Stage: Frank Sinatra*, Harriet Lake. *Frank Sinatra*, Anthony Scaduto. *The Sinatra File: Part One*, John Ridgway. *Sinatra: An Unauthorized Biography*, Earl Wilson. *The Sinatra File: Part Two*, John Ridgway. *Sinatra*, Alan Frank. *The Revised Complete Sinatra: Discography, Filmography And Television Appearances*, Albert I. Lonstein. *Frank Sinatra*, John Howlett. *Sinatra In His Own Words*, Frank Sinatra. *The Frank Sinatra Scrapbook: His Life And Times In Words And Pictures*, Richard Peters. *Frank Sinatra: My Father*, Nancy Sinatra. *His Way: The Unauthorized Biography Of Frank Sinatra*, Kitty Kelly. *Frank Sinatra*, Jessica Hodge. *Frank Sinatra: A Complete Recording History*, Richard W. Ackelson. *The Recording Artistry Of Francis Albert Sinatra 1939-1992* , Ed O'Brien and Scott P. Sayers. *Frank Sinatra Reader: Seven Decades Of American Popular Music*, Steven Petkov and Leonard Mustazza (eds.).

Sinatra! The Song Is You: A Singer's Art, Will Friedwald. *Sinatra: His Life And Times*, Fred Dellar.

● FILMS: *Major Bowes' Amateur Theatre Of The Air* (1935), *Las Vegas Nights* (1941), *Ship Ahoy* (1942), *Reveille With Beverley* (1943), *Higher And Higher* (1943), *Step Lively* (1944), *The Road To Victory* (1944), *The House I Live In* (1945), *Anchors Aweigh* (1945), *The All Star Bond Rally* (1945), *Till The Clouds Roll By* (1946), *It Happened In Brooklyn* (1947), *The Miracle Of The Bells* (1948), *The Kissing Bandit* (1948), *Take Me Out To The Ball Game* (1949), *On The Town* (1949), *Double Dynamite* (1951), *Meet Danny Wilson* (1952), *From Here To Eternity* (1953), *Suddenly* (1954), *Young At Heart* (1955), *Not As A Stranger* (1955), *The Tender Trap* (1955), *Guys And Dolls* (1955), *The Man With The Golden Arm* (1955), *Meet Me In Las Vegas* cameo (1956), *Johnny Concho* (1956), *High Society* (1956), *Around The World In 80 Days* cameo (1956), *The Pride And The Passion* (1957), *The Joker Is Wild* (1957), *Pal Joey* (1957), *Kings Go Forth* (1958), *Some Came Running* (1958), *A Hole In The Head* (1959), *Invitation To Monte Carlo* travelogue (1959), *Never So Few* (1959), *Can-Can* (1960), *Ocean's Eleven* (1960), *Pepe* cameo (1960), *The Devil At 4 O'Clock* (1961), *Sergeants 3* (1962), *The Road To Hong Kong* cameo (1962), *The Manchurian Candidate* (1962), *Sinatra In Israel* (1962), *The List Of Adrian Messenger* (1963), *Come Blow Your Horn* (1963), *4 For Texas* (1963), *Robin And The 7 Hoods* (1964), *None But The Brave* (1965), *Von Ryan's Express* (1965), *Marriage On The Rocks* (1965), *The Oscar* cameo (1966), *Cast A Giant Shadow* (1966), *Assault On A Queen* (1966), *The Naked Runner* (1967), *Tony Rome* (1967), *The Detective* (1968), *Lady In Cement* (1968), *Dirty Dingus Magee* (1970), *That's Entertainment!* on-screen narrator (1974), *Contract On Cherry Street* (1977), *The First Deadly Sin* (1980), *Cannonball Run II* (1984), *Who Framed Roger Rabbit?* voice of Singing Sword (1988), *Listen Up: The Lives Of Quincy Jones* (1990).

SINBAD

This vehicle for the ebullient entertainer Al Jolson, opened at the Winter Garden in New York on 14 February 1918. His regulation blackface came in handy as he travelled to the exotic locations demanded by Harold Atteridge's book which was apparently something to do with the Arabian Nights. In Jolson's shows a simple plot was essential anyway because he continually stopped the action to sell the songs, and the evening always threatened to become a one-man concert. The basic score was credited to Sigmund Romberg and Harold Atteridge, but the interpolated numbers were far more popular, and several of them became Jolson specialities. They included 'Rock-A-Bye Your Baby With A Dixie Melody' and 'Why Do they All Take The Night Boat To Albany?', both written by Jean Schwartz, Sam M. Lewis, and Joe Young; and 'N Everything' by Buddy De Sylva and Gus Kahn. During the show's run of 388 performances, two more songs were added, 'Avalon' (Jolson-Vincent Rose) and 'My Mammy' (Lewis-Joe Young-Walter Donaldson). On the subsequent road tour of *Sinbad*, Jolson introduced yet another one of his enormous crowd-pleasers, 'Swanee', which had a lyric by Irving Caesar, and gave composer George Gershwin his first big hit. Many years later the song became identified with Judy Garland after she performed it so memorably in the film *A Star Is Born*.

SING AS WE GO

Regarded by many as the best of the films that the popular Lancashire entertainer Gracie Fields appeared in, *Sing As We Go* was presented to highly appreciative audiences in 1934 courtesy of producer-director Basil Dean and Associated Talking Pictures. Not just an amusing and tuneful musical, this picture was also something of a social document as well, touching as it did on the difficulties of unemployment in the north of England. Grace Platt (Fields) leads her fellow workers out in style when the Greybeck Mill is forced to close. Not one to sit around and wait for something to happen, Grace 'gets on her bike' and cycles to Blackpool where she (briefly) works as a waitress in a boarding house, a palmist's assistant and 'The Human Spider' in a magician's show at the Pleasure Beach. She is delighted when her new-found friend, Phyllis (Dorothy Hyson), wins first prize in the Bathing Belles competition, but less than pleased when Phyllis becomes attracted to her friend from the mill, assistant manager Hugh Phillips (John Loder), who is also in Blackpool trying to drum up business. Not one to hold a grudge, Grace helps Hugh in his efforts to re-open the mill, and, as the new Welfare Officer, is at the head of the exultant march back to work, singing (not unexpectedly) 'Sing As We Go'. That song, and 'Just A Catchy Little Tune', were the work of the Welsh songwriter Harry Parr-Davies who wrote several other numbers for Gracie Fields, and was her accompanist for a time. The other songs in *Sing As We Go* were 'Thora' (Stephen Adams-Frederick E. Weatherly) and 'Little Bottom Drawer' (Will Haines-Jimmy Harper). As usual with these small but significant British films, the supporting parts were beautifully cast. In this instance the players included Frank Pettingell as Grace's fun-loving Uncle Murgatroyd, Stanley Holloway as a policeman, Lawrence Grossmith, Arthur Sinclair, Morris Harvey, Maire O'Neill, Ben Field, Norman Walker, Margaret Yarde, and Olive Sloane. Gordon Wellesley and the distinguished English author, J.B. Priestley, adapted the screenplay from an original story by Priestley.

SING YOU SINNERS

One of the screen's all-time favourite song-and-dance men, Donald O'Connor, made his debut - at the age of 13 - in this Paramount release of 1938. In Claude Binyon's heart-warming story, he plays the kid brother of Bing Crosby and Fred MacMurray, two guys who never see eye-to-eye - except for music. MacMurray is a thrifty 'small town Galahad, the breakfast-eating, four button type' (as Sky Masterson says in Guys And Dolls), while Crosby is a gambler who continually wastes the family's money until one day he manages to buy a horse, which, with O'Connor aboard, romps home first in the big race. Ellen Drew provided the love interest, and Elizabeth Patterson was amusing (and patient) as the trio's mother. Also in the cast were William Haade, Irving Bacon, and Harry Barris. Johnny Burke and Jimmy Monaco contributed several agreeable songs including 'Laugh And Call It Love', 'Where Is Central Park?', 'I've Got A Pocketful Of Dreams', and 'Don't Let That Moon Get Away', the last two of which became hits for Crosby, and endured. However, the film's musical highlight was probably Hoagy Carmichael and Frank Loesser's 'Small Fry', which the three brothers (who gig together in the evenings) turned into an easy-going, charming routine. Bing Crosby and his friend, lyricist Johnny Mercer, also made a popular recording of the number. *Sing You Sinners*, which was directed by Wesley Ruggles, went on to make beautiful music at the box-office.

SINGIN' IN THE RAIN

Regarded by many as the most entertaining film musical of all time, this MGM classic was released in 1952. Betty Comden and Adolph Green's witty screenplay parodies that momentous and painful period in Hollywood movie history when talkies took over from silent pictures. Don Lockwood (Gene Kelly) and Lina Lamont (Jean Hagen) are Monumental Studio's brightest silent stars. Lockwood, encouraged by his ex-dancing partner Cosmo Brown (Donald O'Connor), has no problem making the transition, while Lina's voice is so squeaky and sharp it could break glass. Luckily, aspiring actress Kathy Selden (Debbie Reynolds) pops out of a giant cake and provides a dubbing service - and Kelly's love interest. The team's first attempt at a sound film is a total disaster, but Kelly and O'Connor turn it into a musical, and, at the triumphant premiere, Reynolds is revealed as the hidden starlet, while Hagen is hilariously disgraced. *Singin' In The Rain* is indeed one of the greatest film musicals of all time, and its comedy exists apart from, and within, the musical numbers. The scenes poking fun at the changeover to sound are very effective, particularly when irate director Roscoe Dexter (Douglas Fowley) is attempting to place Hagen's microphone in a strategic position, desperate to find a place on the set ('It's in the bush!') or on her person where a consistent level of sound can be obtained. Most of the score consisted of a collection of songs written by Arthur Freed and Nacio Herb Brown for early MGM musicals, and every one of them is performed brilliantly. O'Connor is marvellously athletic and funny on 'Make 'Em Laugh' (most critics noted the similarities with Cole Porter's 'Be A Clown'), and on two duets with Kelly, 'Fit As A Fiddle' (Al Goodhart-Al Hoffman) and 'Moses Supposes' (Roger Edens-Comden-Green). Reynolds joins both of them for the uplifting 'Good Morning', and then, just with Kelly, milks the lovely 'You Were Meant For Me' for all its worth. Other highlights include the spectacular 'Broadway Ballet' which is presented as part of the film within a film featuring Cyd Charisse and Kelly, and 'All I Do Is Dream Of You', 'Beautiful Girl', 'I've Got A Feelin' You're Foolin'', 'Should I' and 'Would You?'. However, the moment from the film people always remember, and the clip that most frequently crops up in nostalgia programmes, is the one in which Kelly splashes around in the teeming rain, viewed by a rather bemused and soaking-wet policeman, creating a truly memorable moment from a memorable film. The film was photographed in Technicolor by Harold Rosson and produced by Arthur Freed's MGM unit; the director-choreographers were Gene Kelly and Stanley Donen.

In 1983 Comden and Green adapted the film into a stage musical that ran at the London Palladium for over three years, breaking all theatre records. It starred Tommy Steele (who also directed), Roy Castle, Sarah Payne and Danielle Carson, and featured several additional songs. A 1985 Broadway production failed to recover its costs. Ten years later, Steele directed a highly successful UK revival tour, with Paul Nicholas in the leading role.

SINGING FOOL, THE

According to the American trade paper *Variety*, this part-talkie film - Al Jolson and Warner Brothers' follow-up to The Jazz Singer - grossed nearly $4 million in the US and Canada alone following its release in 1928. C. Graham Baker's screenplay was even more schmaltz-laden than Jolson's previous trail-blazing effort, with that film's tear-jerking 'My Mammy' being more than matched on the maudlin scale by 'Sonny Boy', which Jolson croons to his three-year-old screen son (Davey Lee) when he knows the boy is dying. Songwriters De Sylva, Brown And Henderson are said to have written the cliché-ridden number for a laugh, but there was nothing funny about the character who sang it. Even before his son's illness, the successful singer's wife (Josephine Dunn) had walked out on him, and he was going rapidly downhill before a nightclub cigarette girl (Betty Bronson) gave him some loving and self respect. Once again Jolson was tremendous, his magnetic personality overwhelming every other aspect of the production as he punched out song after song. These included 'It All Depends On You' and 'I'm Sitting On Top Of The World' (De Sylva, Brown And Henderson), 'There's a Rainbow 'Round My Shoulder' (Dave Dreyer-Billy Rose-Al Jolson), 'Golden Gate' (Dreyer-Joseph Meyer-Rose-Jolson), 'Keep Smiling At Trouble' (Jolson-De Sylva-Lewis Gensler), and 'The Spaniard That Blighted My Life' (Billy Merson). The dance director for *The Singing Fool* was Larry Ceballos, and the film was directed by Lloyd Bacon and produced by Darryl F. Zanuck.

SISSLE, NOBLE

b. 10 July 1889, Indianapolis, Indiana, USA, d. 17 December 1975. Sissle's early career was spent largely in vaudeville as a singer and he also sang with the orchestra of James Reese Europe. However, his talents as a song-writer gradually drew him to Broadway where, in collaboration with Eubie Blake, he achieved a major break-through. Before Sissle and Blake it was rare for a black entertainer to gain acceptance along the 'Great White Way', but the success of their 1921 show, *Shuffle Along*, changed all that. *Shuffle Along* starred Florence Mills and among its memorable tunes were 'In Honeysuckle Time', 'Love Will Find A Way' and the hit of the show, 'I'm Just Wild About Harry'. In this and succeeding shows, such as *Chocolate Dandies*, the collaborators presented a succession of songs, dances and sketches that were attuned to the new musical sounds of the day - unlike most other Broadway shows which also performed by all-black casts, had ignored ragtime and the emergence of jazz. In these and later years Sissle led a number of fine orchestras that featured some of the best musicians available, among them Sidney Bechet, Otto 'Toby' Hardwicke, Tommy Ladnier and Buster Bailey. In the late 20s Sissle led a band in Paris and London and during the 30s led successful bands in New York and elsewhere in the USA. He continued touring during the 40s and 50s but gradually directed his attention to music publishing.

● ALBUMS: *Sissle And Blake's 'Shuffle Along'* (1921) (80s)★★★, *Sissle And His Sizzling Syncopators* (1930-31) (80s)★★★★.

1600 PENNSYLVANIA AVENUE

The title, of course, is the location of the White House in Washington, where, in 1974, the current resident, Richard Nixon, reluctantly vacated the premises. Two years later, on 4 May 1976, the show bearing that fancy address took up residence at the Mark Hellinger Theatre in New York - and was evicted after only seven performances. The early departure was all the more surprising because those mainly responsible for its existence were two of the American musical theatre's most illustrious names: Leonard Bernstein (music) and Alan Jay Lerner (book and lyrics). As usual in this kind of debacle, the book got most of the blame. It was a fascinating idea to tell the White House story - the first 100 years of its history from George Washington to Theodore Roosevelt - through the eyes of three generations of Lud Simmons, a family dynasty of black servants who worked at the White House. In this piece, they oversee the action, and represent the American people. Gilbert Price stood in for all the servants, and the presidents were played by one actor, Ken Howard. The British actress Patricia Routledge portrayed all The First Ladies. It is impossible to say where it all went wrong - after all, not many people saw it - but at least the score contained several engaging numbers such as 'Duet For One', 'Take Care Of This House', and 'We Must Have A Ball'. Sixteen years later, on 11 August 1992, a major revival opened - appropriately enough at the John F. Kennedy Centre for the Performing Arts in Washington DC. In 1997, what has become to be regarded as a 'glorious' score received its first full-length recording when BBC Radio 3 broadcast *A White House Cantata* from the Barbican Centre in London. This event, billed as a world premiere, featured the London Symphony Orchestra under Kent Negano, with opera singer Dietrich Henschel singing all the Presidents, soprano Nancy Gustafson all the First Ladies, and Thomas Young as Lud. Although time would not allow all the songs written for the show at the various stages of its development to be performed, 'Take Care Of This House', 'The Mark Of A Man', 'Duet For One', 'This Time', and 'Seena', were among those singled out for praise.

SLACK, FREDDIE

b. Frederic Charles Slack, 7 August 1910, La Crosse, Wisconsin, USA, d. 10 August 1965, Hollywood, California, USA. A composer, pianist and bandleader, prominent from the late 30s until the mid-40s, who specialized in the jazz rhythm style, boogie-woogie. After attending the American Conservatory of Music in Chicago, Slack worked as a pianist and arranger with Ben Pollack and Jimmy Dorsey during the late 30s, before joining trombonist Will Bradley's band in 1939. Together with drummer Ray McKinley (he was the band's co-leader) and arranger Leonard Whitney, Slack was instrumental in changing the band's style from ballads to boogie-woogie,

and a year later they had their biggest hit with 'Beat Me, Daddy, Eight To The Bar'. Other successful recordings included 'Scrub Me, Mama, With A Boogie Beat', 'Down the Road A Piece', 'Rock-Bye-Boogie', 'Bounce Me, Brother, With A Solid Four', 'Fry Me, Cookie, With A Can Of Lard'. Slack left Bradley early in 1941 and started his own outfit on the west coast. In 1942 he had a big hit with 'Cow Cow Boogie', which had a vocal by the orchestra's regular singer, Ella Mae Morse. The record was the first of two initial releases on the brand new Capitol label; the other was 'Strip Polka' sung by one of the label's co-owners, Johnny Mercer. In the following year, Slack provided the backing for another Mercer hit, 'I Lost My Sugar In Salt Lake City', while his own successful records, through until 1946, included 'Hit The Road To Dreamland', 'That Old Black Magic' and 'Silver Wings In The Moonlight', the latter two with vocals by Slack's protégé, Margaret Whiting. 'Mr. Five By Five', 'Get On Board, Little Chillun'' and 'The House Of The Blue Lights', all featured vocals by Ella Mae Morse. The latter song was written by Slack; his other compositions included 'Cuban Sugar Mill', 'Riffette', 'A Cat's Ninth Life', 'Mr. Freddie's Boogie', 'Rib Joint', 'Rock-A-Bye The Boogie', 'A Kiss Goodnight' (a hit for Slack, and Woody Herman'); and Slack's theme, 'Strange Cargo'. During the early 40s the orchestra featured in several musical movies, including Reveille With Beverly (in which Frank Sinatra had his first starring role); *Hat Check Girl, The Sky's The Limit, Seven Days Ashore, Follow The Boys, Babes On Swing Street* and *High School Hero*. In the early 50s Slack gave up the orchestra, and for the next decade played in a piano-duo team and with his own trio, in clubs and lounges, mostly around Nevada and the San Fernando Valley. In 1965 he died, of 'inconclusive causes', in his Hollywood apartment.

● ALBUMS: *Boogie-Woogie On The Eighty-Eight* (EmArcy 50s)★★★, *The Hits Of Ella Mae Morse And Freddie Slack* (Capitol 50s)★★, with Will Bradley *Boogie Woogie* (Epic 50s)★★★.

SLADE, JULIAN

b. 28 May 1930, London, England. A composer, lyricist, librettist and pianist, Slade began to write when he was at Cambridge University, and his first two musicals, *The Meringue* and *Lady May*, were presented by the Cambridge Amateur Dramatic Club. He then went to the Bristol Old Vic Theatre School, and in 1952 was invited by Denis Carey to join the company as a minor role actor and musical director. In the same year he composed the music for a highly successful version of Sheridan's *The Duenna*, and it was at Bristol that he met Dorothy Reynolds, a leading actress, who collaborated with him on libretto and lyrics. Their long association began with *Christmas In King Street* and *The Merry Gentlemen*, written for the Theatre Royal, Bristol, and then, in 1954, Salad Days, which transferred to the Vaudeville Theatre in London. It continued to delight audiences until 1960, becoming the longest-running British musical of its era. Slade played the piano in the pit for the first 18 months, while onstage, a magic piano in a London park caused passers-by to dance uncontrollably. The piece was typical Slade - a simple plot and inconsequential humour, accompanied by charming, hummable songs, such as 'We Said We Wouldn't Look

Back', 'I Sit In The Sun', 'It's Easy To Sing', 'The Time Of My Life' and 'Cleopatra'. In 1956, *The Comedy Of Errors*, a comic operetta adapted from Shakespeare's play, for which Slade wrote the music, played a season at the Arts Theatre. It had originally been performed on BBC Television two years earlier. In 1957, Slade and Reynolds wrote *Free As Air*, which lasted for over a year. This was succeeded by *Follow That Girl*, *Hooray For Daisy* and *Wildest Dreams*, which even contained a 'rock' number. However, these shows seemed out of place in the theatre of the 'angry young men'. 'Our shows went well out of town, but London didn't seem to want them', Slade recalled. *Vanity Fair*, with lyrics by Roger Miller, faded after 70 performances at the Queen's Theatre, and Slade's first solo effort, *Nutmeg And Ginger* (1963), based on Francis Beaumont's 1609 comedy, *The Knight Of The Burning Pestle*, did not play the West End. Neither did some of the others, such as *The Pursuit Of Love* and *Out Of Bounds* (1973), although *Trelawney* (1972) stayed at the Prince of Wales Theatre for over six months. Slade received his warmest reviews for that show, the last time London saw his work until 1991, when a revival of his *Nutmeg And Ginger* opened to enthusiastic reviews on the Fringe, at the Orange Tree Theatre in Richmond, Surrey, England.

SLEEPING BEAUTY
(see Disney, Walt)

SLICE OF SATURDAY NIGHT, A

After a stay of nearly two years at London's tiny Arts Theatre, and many other productions worldwide, the Heather Brothers' most successful musical finally opened in the West End at the Strand theatre on 6 September 1993 for a limited run of 12 weeks. Set in the Club A Go-Go on a typical Saturday night, the story concerns itself with the teenage mating habits that were currently in vogue around 1964. The message is spread via some 30 songs which sound as though they might have been written in the 60s, and hardly any dialogue. There are several amusing and engaging numbers, including 'Love On Our Side', 'The Boy Of My Dreams', 'Oh, So Bad', 'Baby I Love You', 'Please Don't Tell Me', and 'Twiggy'. The 70s UK pop star, Alvin Stardust, played the club's manager, Eric 'Rubber Legs' Devine, in the provinces, but Dennis Waterman, renowned for his work in top-rated television programmes such as *Minder* and *The Sweeney*, took over for the West End run. Also added to the London production were Danny McCall (from the television soap opera *Brookside*), and Sonia, the UK entrant in the 1993 Eurovision Song Contest. The remainder of the energetic young cast, most of whom had been with the show for some time, consisted of Nikki Brooks, Judith Ellis, Joanne Engelsman, Peter Heppelthwaite, and Sean Oliver. In April 1995, *A Slice Of Saturday Night* had its US premiere at Boston's Charles Playhouse.

SLIPPER AND THE ROSE, THE

Generally regarded as a disappointing attempt to musicalize the traditional *Cinderella* fairy tale, this film was made in the UK by Paradine Co-Productions (Executive produc-er David Frost; producer Stuart Lyons). Director Bryan Forbes' screenplay (written with Richard M. and Robert B. Sherman) had some delightful and endearing moments, but there were more than a few dull periods too in the running time of nearly two and a half hours. Richard Chamberlain was a suitably regal Prince Edward, and Gemma Craven gave a charming performance as the young girl who did - eventually - go to the ball. The list of supporting players contained some of the best and most distinguished actors in British films, theatre and television, including Annette Crosbie (Fairy Godmother), Edith Evans (Dowager Queen), Michael Hordern (King of Euphrania), Margaret Lockwood (Stepmother), Kenneth More (Chamberlain), and Christopher Gable, Julian Orchard, John Turner, Roy Barraclough, Valentine Dyall, and André Morell. The talented and prolific Sherman Brothers provided the score, which consisted of 'Why Can't I Be Two People?', 'What Has Love Got To Do With Getting Married?', 'Once I Was Loved', 'What A Comforting Thing To Know', 'Protocoligorically Correct', 'A Bride-Finding Ball', 'Suddenly It Happens', 'Secret Kingdom', 'He/She Danced With Me', 'Position And Positioning', 'Tell Me Anything (But Not That I Love Him)', and 'I Can't Forget The Melody'. It all looked beautiful, due in no small part to production designer Ray Simm and the Technicolor and Panavision photography by Toni Imi. It was reissued in 1980 with 20 minutes cut.

SLOW DRAG, THE

Carson Kreitzer's 'jazz musical', set in and around a jazz cabaret club, is based on the true story of Billy Tipton, the American bandleader, pianist, and saxophone player, who was discovered to be a woman following 'his' death from a stomach ulcer in 1989 at the age of 74. It would appear that only the first of five real-life 'wives' were aware of his secret (a 'terrible car accident' meant that much of 'his' body had to be permanently bandaged). The last marriage lasted 18 years, and they adopted three children. In this piece, which opened off-Broadway at the American Place on 17 April 1996, June Wedding (Ann Crumb), plays the final, estranged, spouse of Johnny Christmas (Peggy Shaw), and she is definitely aware of Johnny's gender. Told in flashback, the emphasis is mainly on June and Johnny's relationship, and their association with Chester Kent (Vernel Bagneris). In a way, Johnny and Chester are two of a kind, for while Johnny adopts a disguise in order to play jazz ('the only females in jazz are girl singers'), the coffee-coloured Chester is really a black musician who is also living a lie, and avoiding the racist lobby by passing himself off as white. One other connection: Chester may be helping June and Johnny's marriage by being more than a friend to June, but that is another story. A play with a sensitive subject such as this, could have become an object of ridicule if the role of Johnny Christmas had not been completely believable. Fortunately, Shaw's performance was absolutely credible in every way, excelling with the slicked-back hair and tough-talking side of her character, as well as in the poignant and tragic aspects too. This diverting and intriguing show was directed by Elise Thoron, and choreographed by Stormy Brandenberger, with a four-piece on-stage combo supplementing the action with some appropriate 30s and 40s tunes. By the time *The Slow Drag* arrived at London's Whitehall Theatre on the 5 November 1997, following a spell at Soho's Freedom Theatre fringe venue, the band had grown into a hot quintet, led by James Pearson. Heading the cast now were Kim Criswell (June Wedding), Liza Sadovy (Johnny Christmas), and Christopher Colquhoun (Chester Kent). Other credits included Bill Deamer (musical staging) and Lisa Forrell (director). Criswell had a hand in choosing the songs for this version, and when she gave out with numbers such as 'More Than You Know', 'Blame It On My Youth', and 'Blues In The Night', more than one male member of the audience was reported to be glancing nervously in the direction of the Whitehall's fire extinguishers. There was another song, 'Sweet Melinda', co-written in 40s style for the show by author Carson Kreitzer. 'It was not the genuine article,' noted critic Jack Massarik, 'but as Billy Tipton knew better than anybody, sometimes you can't really tell.' The extraordinary story of Dorothy Lucille Tipton, who passed as man for more than 50 years, has also inspired a two-act opera, a short documentary film, and a biography written by a Stamford University English professor.

● FURTHER READING: *Suits Me: The Double Life Of Billy Tipton*, Diane Wood Middlebrook.

SMASHING TIME

Released in 1967 and scripted by George Melly, *Smashing Time* features Lynn Redgrave and Rita Tushingham as two starry-eyed girls from the north of England hoping to find fame in 'Swinging' London. While offering obligatory shots of Carnaby Street, dolly birds and mini-cars, the film has little to commend it other than the slapstick scene which features proto-psychedelic act Tomorrow as a pop group, the Snarks. The soundtrack music was written and recorded by another emergent unit, Skip Bifferty, but they and all the other participants are recalled better for other endeavours, rather than this lightweight exercise.

SMOKEY JOE'S CAFE: THE SONGS OF LEIBER AND STOLLER

This celebratory musical revue devoted to the works of the immensely influential songwriting team of the 50s and early 60s, was originally conceived by Stephen Helper and Jack Viertel, with assistance from Otis Sallid. It opened at the Virginia Theatre in New York on 2 March 1995. Nine singers - five men and four women - perform nearly 40 songs on Heidi Landesman's glitzy set, reminding those who needed reminding, that two white men, Jerry Leiber and Mike Stoller, who were seeped in black music, wrote and produced some of the greatest blues-influenced records of their time. One of them, 'Hound Dog', which was written for Willie Mae 'Big Mama' Thornton, and later popularized by Elvis Presley, was given the full treatment by the marvellous B.J. Crosby, who also had a ball with 'Fools Fall In Love'. Other outstanding performances came from DeLee Lively ('Teach Me How To Shimmy'), Victor Trent Cook ('I Who Have Nothing' and 'Searchin''), Pattie Darcy Jones ('Pearl's A Singer'), and Adrian Bailey ('Love Me'). Together with the rest of the splendid cast, which included Ken Ard, Brenda

Baxton, Frederick B. Owens, and Michael Park, they evoked memories of legendary groups such as the Coasters and the Drifters, together with so many other artists who had hits with Leiber and Stoller's terrific songs. Among the rest of the nearly 40 songs on display were 'Love Potion Number Nine', 'Jailhouse Rock', 'Spanish Harlem', 'On Broadway', 'Yakety Yak', 'Charley Brown', 'Poison Ivy', 'Keep On Rollin'', 'There Goes My Baby', and, of course, 'Smokey Joe's Cafe'. Jerry Zaks was the director, and the show, which was superbly choreographed by newcomer Joey McNeely, received seven Tony Award nominations but failed to convert one, although the original cast album did win a Grammy. As it turned out, the Tony famine hardly mattered because the show continued to thrive and was still 'smoking' when it passed the 1,600 performances mark late in 1998. A US national touring company set out in August 1996, and a British production, whose all-star American cast included Crosby, Cook, and Lively, opened to extremely favourable reviews in October 1996 and ran for almost two years. An earlier tribute to Leiber And Stoller, entitled *Only In America*, was devised by the British director and author Ned Sherrin, and presented at the Roundhouse Theatre in London in 1980. In the cast was Clarke Peters, who conceived the long-running Louis Jordan musical anthology, *Five Guys Named Moe*.

SOLDIERS OF THE KING

Although the popular British actress, singer and comedienne Cicely Courtneidge was not accompanied on the screen in this 1933 Gainsborough release by her husband, Jack Hulbert, he did co-write the screenplay with W. P. Lipscomb and John Horton, and is said to have assisted Maurice Elvey with the direction. In this adaptation of an original story by Douglas Furber, Courtneidge plays the dual roles of retired music hall artist Jenny Marvello and her daughter Maisie, the reigning queen of a variety troupe. In the latter part she runs through her impressive range of male impersonations and comic business, while as the older woman she demonstrates an hitherto unseen dramatic acting ability. There were several well-known names such as Edward Everett Horton, Anthony Bushell, Bransby Williams, Dorothy Hyson, Frank Cellier, and Leslie Sarony in a the supporting cast which also included Rebla, Herschel Henlere, Arty Ash, Ivor McLaren, David Deveen, and Olive Sloan. The two most memorable songs were 'The Moment I Saw You' (Noel Gay-Clifford Grey) and the rousing 'There's Something About A Soldier' (Gay). This solo outing for Courtneidge enjoyed considerable success, but, even so, the old team were back together again later in the same year with *Falling For You*.

SOME LIKE IT HOT

(see *Sugar* (stage musical))

SOME PEOPLE

Clive Donner directed this 1962 feature, the profits from which were donated to the Duke Of Edinburgh's Award Scheme. This is hardly the stuff of rebellious cinema. The plot of *Some People* did offer hint of excitement; three bikers who have lost their respective licences form a rock 'n' roll group to play at a youth club only to have one of their number leave to lead a gang which attacks them. However, any potential drama is wasted during what evolves into an antiseptic view of teenage life. Kenneth More stars as the patrician figure watching over rising stars Ray Brooks and David Hemmings, while musical interludes are provided by British instrumental unit the Eagles. Singer Carol Deene, famed for the hits 'Short Movies' and 'Norman', performed the title song to *Some People* and in so doing garnered her final UK chart entry.

SOMEONE LIKE YOU

This musical, which opened 22 March 1990 at the Strand Theatre in London, was set in the aftermath of the American Civil War, and seemed a risky proposition for a London theatre scene containing the indigenous *Me And My Girl* and *Blood Brothers*, along with Andrew Lloyd Webber's operatic efforts, and so it proved. The choice of subject was all the more surprising because the show was based on an original idea by the British actress and singer Petula Clark in collaboration with Ferdie Pacheco. Clark also starred in the piece, and wrote the music to lyrics by Dee Shipman. The book was the work of novelist Fay Weldon and director Robin Midgley. The story concerns Abigail, an English nurse (Clark), who, with her young son Andy (Lewis Rae), roves the field hospitals in search of her long-lost preacher husband Kane (Clive Carter), only to fall in love with a military doctor The Major (Dave Willetts). The evils of slavery and the desirability of sexual liberation are just two of the issues that crop up before the inevitable happy ending. Joanne Campbell, as a black mammy character, Michael Seraphim in the role of Andy's acrobatic friend, and Jane Arden as the tempestuous mistress, were outstanding among a cast which also included Euan Milne, Michael G. Jones, Richard D. Sharp, Calum MacPherson, and Alan Gill. The score, a mixture of romantic ballads, gospel, blues and lively dance numbers, consisted of 'Home Is Where The Heart Is', 'Look Where The Journey Led', 'Empty Spaces', 'Picking Up The Pieces', 'Liberty', 'What Can One Person Do?', 'Someone Like You', 'What You Got!', 'Amen', 'All Through The Years', 'Soldiers' Blues', 'So Easy', 'Getting The Right Thing Wrong', 'I Am What You Need', 'It's A Big Country', 'Young 'Un', 'Without You', 'The Women's Credo', and 'The Fight'. The critics applauded the voices of Clark, Willetts, and Carter, but not much else, and after a run of one month the production suddenly folded. It was reported that its producer, Harold Fielding, was going into liquidation after 48 years in the business.

SONDHEIM, STEPHEN

b. Stephen Joshua Sondheim, 22 March 1930, New York, USA. Sondheim is generally regarded as the most important theatrical composer of the 70s and 80s - his introduction of the concept musical (some say, anti-musical) or 'unified show', has made him a cult figure. Born into an affluent family, his father was a prominent New York dress manufacturer, Sondheim studied piano and organ sporadically from the age of seven. When he was 10 his parents divorced, and he spent some time at military school. His mother's friendship with the Oscar

Hammerstein II family in Philadelphia enabled Sondheim to meet the lyricist, who took him under his wing and educated him in the art of writing for the musical theatre. After majoring in music at Williams College, Sondheim graduated in 1950 with the Hutchinson Prize For Musical Composition, a two-year fellowship, which enabled him to study with the innovative composer Milton Babbitt. During the early 50s, he contributed material to television shows such as *Topper*, and wrote both music and lyrics for the musical, *Saturday Night* (1954), which was abandoned due to the death of producer Lemuel Ayres. Sondheim also wrote the incidental music for the play *Girls Of Summer* (1956). His first major success was as a lyric writer, with Leonard Bernstein's music, for the 1957 Broadway hit musical *West Side Story*. Initially, Bernstein was billed as co-lyricist, but had his name removed before the New York opening, giving Sondheim full credit. The show ran for 734 performances on Broadway, and 1,039 in London. The songs included 'Jet Song', 'Maria', 'Something's Coming', 'Tonight', 'America', 'One Hand, One Heart', 'I Feel Pretty', 'Somewhere' and 'A Boy Like That'. A film version was released in 1961 and there were New York revivals in 1968 and 1980. Productions in London during in 1974 and 1984 were also significant in that they marked the first of many collaborations between Sondheim and producer Harold Prince. It was another powerful theatrical personality, David Merrick, who mounted *Gypsy* (1959), based on stripper Gypsy Rose Lee's book, *Gypsy: A Memoir*, and considered by some to be the pinnacle achievement of the Broadway musical stage. Sondheim was set to write both music and lyrics before the show's star Ethel Merman demanded a more experienced composer. Jule Styne proved to be acceptable, and Sondheim concentrated on the lyrics, which have been called his best work in the musical theatre, despite the critical acclaim accorded his later shows. *Gypsy's* memorable score included 'Let Me Entertain You', 'Some People', 'Small World', 'You'll Never Get Away From Me', 'If Momma Was Married', 'All I Need Is The Girl', 'Everything's Coming Up Roses', 'Together, Wherever We Go', 'You Gotta Have A Gimmick' and 'Rose's Turn'. Merman apparently refused to embark on a long London run, so the show was not mounted there until 1973. Angela Lansbury scored a personal triumph then as the domineering mother, Rose, and repeated her success in the Broadway revival in 1974. In 1989, both the show and its star, Tyne Daly (well known for television's *Cagney and Lacey*), won Tony Awards in the 30th anniversary revival, which ran through until 1991. Rosalind Russell played Rose in the 1962 movie version, which received lukewarm reviews. For *Gypsy*, Sondheim had interrupted work on *A Funny Thing Happened On The Way To The Forum* (1962), to which he contributed both music and lyrics. Based on the plays of Plautus, it has been variously called 'a fast moving farce', 'a vaudeville-based Roman spoof' and 'a musical madhouse'. Sondheim's songs, which included the prologue, 'Comedy Tonight' ('Something appealing, something appalling/Something for everyone, a comedy tonight!') and 'Everybody Ought To Have A Maid', celebrated moments of joy or desire and punctuated the thematic action. The show won several Tony Awards, including 'Best Musical' and 'Best Producer' but nothing for Sondheim's score. The show was revived on Broadway in 1972 with Phil Silvers in the leading role, and had two London productions (1963 and 1986), both starring British comedian Frankie Howerd. A film version, starring Zero Mostel and Silvers, dropped several of the original songs. *Anyone Can Whistle* (1964), 'a daft moral fable about corrupt city officials', with an original book by Laurents, and songs by Sondheim, lasted just a week. The critics were unanimous in their condemnation of the musical with a theme that 'madness is the only hope for world sanity'. The original cast recording, which included 'Simple', 'I've Got You To Lean On', 'A Parade In Town', 'Me And My Town' and the appealing title song, was recorded after the show closed, and became a cult item.

Sondheim was back to 'lyrics only' for *Do I Hear A Waltz?* (1965). The durable Broadway composer Richard Rodgers, supplied the music for the show that he described as 'not a satisfying experience'. In retrospect, it was perhaps underrated. Adapted by Arthur Laurents from his play, *The Time Of The Cuckoo*, the show revolved around an American tourist in Venice, and included 'Moon In My Window', 'This Week's Americans', 'Perfectly Lovely Couple', 'We're Gonna Be All Right', and 'Here We Are Again'. Broadway had to wait until 1970 for the next Sondheim musical, the first to be directed by Harold Prince. *Company* had no plot, but concerned 'the lives of five Manhattan couples held together by their rather excessively protective feelings about a 'bachelor friend'. Its ironic, acerbic score included 'The Little Things You Do Together' ('The concerts you enjoy together/Neighbours you annoy together/Children you destroy together...'), 'Sorry-Grateful', 'You Could Drive A Person Crazy', 'Have I Got A Girl For You?', 'Someone Is Waiting', 'Another Hundred People', 'Getting Married Today', 'Side By Side By Side', 'What Would We Do Without You?', 'Poor Baby', 'Tick Tock', 'Barcelona', 'The Ladies Who Lunch' ('Another chance to disapprove, another brilliant zinger/Another reason not to move, another vodka stinger/I'll drink to that!') and 'Being Alive'. With a book by George Furth, produced and directed by Prince, the musical numbers staged by Michael Bennett, and starring Elaine Stritch and Larry Kert (for most of the run), *Company* ran for 690 performances. It gained the New York Drama Critics' Circle Award for Best Musical, and six Tony Awards, including Best Musical, and Best Music and Lyrics for Sondheim, the first awards of his Broadway career. The marathon recording session for the original cast album, produced by Thomas Z. Shepard, was the subject of a highly-acclaimed television documentary.

The next Prince-Bennett-Sondheim project, with a book by James Goldman, was the mammoth *Follies* (1971), 'the story of four people in their early 50s: two ex-show girls from the *Weismann Follies*, and two stage-door-Johnnies whom they married 30 years ago, who attend a reunion, and start looking backwards...'. It was a lavish, spectacular production, with a cast of 50, and a Sondheim score which contained 22 'book' songs, including 'Who's That Woman?' (sometimes referred to as the 'the mirror number'), 'Ah Paris!', 'Could I Leave You?', 'I'm Still Here' ('Then you career from career, to career/I'm almost through my

memoirs/And I'm here!'); and several 'pastiche' numbers in the style of the 'great' songwriters such as George Gershwin and Dorothy Fields ('Losing My Mind'); Cole Porter ('The Story Of Lucy and Jessie'); Sigmund Romberg and Rudolph Friml ('One More Kiss'); Jerome Kern ('Loveland'); Irving Berlin (the prologue, 'Beautiful Girls') and De Sylva, Brown, And Henderson ('Broadway Baby'). Although the show received a great deal of publicity and gained the Drama Critics Circle Award for Best Musical, plus seven Tony awards, it closed after 522 performances with the loss of its entire $800,000 investment. A spokesperson commented: 'We sold more posters than tickets'. *Follies In Concert*, with the New York Philharmonic, played two performances in September 1985 at the Lincoln Center, and featured several legendary Broadway names such as Carol Burnett, Betty Comden, Adolph Green, Lee Remick, and Barbara Cook. The show was taped for television, and generated a much-acclaimed RCA album, which compensated for the disappointingly truncated recording of the original show. The show did not reach London until 1987, when the young Cameron Mackintosh produced a 'new conception' with Goldman's revised book, and several new songs replacing some of the originals. It closed after 600 performances, because of high running costs. *A Little Night Music* (1973), was the first Sondheim-Prince project to be based on an earlier source; in this instance, Ingmar Bergman's film *Smiles Of A Summer Night*. Set at the turn of the century, in Sweden it was an operetta, with all the music in three quarter time, or multiples thereof. The critics saw in it echoes of Mahler, Ravel, Rachmaninov, Brahms, and even Johann Strauss. The score contained Sondheims' first song hit for which he wrote both words and music, 'Send In The Clowns'. Other songs included 'Liaisons', 'A Weekend In The Country', 'The Glamorous Life', 'In Praise Of Women', 'Remember' and 'Night Waltz'. The show ran for 601 performances, and was a healthy financial success. It gained the New York Drama Critics Award for Best Musical, and five Tony awards, including Sondheim's music and lyrics for a record third time in a row. The London run starred Jean Simmons, while Elizabeth Taylor played Desiree in the 1978 movie version.

On the back of the show's 1973 Broadway success, and the composer's increasing popularity, a benefit concert, *Sondheim: A Musical Tribute*, was mounted at the Shubert Theatre, featuring every available performer who had been associated with his shows, singing familiar, and not so familiar, material. *Pacific Overtures* (1976), was, perhaps, Sondheim's most daring and ambitious musical to date. John Weidman's book purported to relate the entire 120 years history of Japan, from Commodore Perry's arrival in 1856, to its emergence as the powerful industrial force of the 20th century. The production was heavily influenced by the Japanese Kabuki Theatre. The entire cast were Asian, and Sondheim used many Oriental instruments to obtain his effects. Musical numbers included 'Chrysanthemum Tea', 'Please Hello', 'Welcome To Kanagawa', 'Next', 'Someone In A Tree' and 'The Advantages Of Floating In The Middle Of The Sea'. The show closed after 193 performances, losing its entire budget of over half-a-million dollars, but it still won the

Drama Critics Circle Award for Best Musical. It was revived off-Broadway in 1984.

The next Broadway project bearing Sondheim's name was much more successful, and far more conventional. *Side By Side By Sondheim* (1977), an anthology of some of his songs, started out at London's Mermaid Theatre the year before. Starring the original London cast of Millicent Martin, Julia McKenzie, David Kernan and Ned Sherrin, the New York production received almost unanimously favourable notices, and proved that many of Sondheim's songs, when presented in this revue form and removed from the sometimes bewildering librettos, could be popular items in their own right. In complete contrast, was *Sweeney Todd, The Demon Barber Of Fleet Street* (1979), Hugh Wheeler's version of the grisly tale of a 19th century barber who slits the throats of his clients, and turns the bodies over to Mrs Lovett (Angela Lansbury), who bakes them into pies. Sondheim's 'endlessly inventive, highly expressive score', considered to be near-opera, included the gruesome, 'Not While I'm Around', 'Epiphany', 'A Little Priest', the more gentle 'Pretty Women' and 'My Friends'. Generally accepted as one of the most ambitious Broadway musicals ever staged ('a staggering theatrical spectacle'; 'one giant step forward for vegetarianism'), *Sweeney Todd* ran for over 500 performances, and gained eight Tony Awards, including Best Musical, Score and Book. In 1980, it played in London for four months, and starred Denis Quilley and Sheila Hancock, and was successfully revived by the Royal National Theatre in 1993.

According to Sondheim himself, *Merrily We Roll Along* (1981), with a book by George Furth, was deliberately written in 'a consistent musical comedy style'. It was based on the 1934 play by George S. Kaufman and Moss Hart, and despite a run of only 16 performances, the pastiche score contained some 'insinuatingly catchy numbers'. It also marked the end, for the time being, of Sondheim's association with Harold Prince, who had produced and directed nearly all of his shows. Depressed and dejected, Sondheim threatened to give up writing for the theatre. However, in 1982, he began working with James Lapine, who had attracted some attention for his direction of the off-Broadway musical, *March Of The Falsettos* (1981).

The first fruits of the Sondheim-Lapine association, *Sunday In The Park With George* also started off-Broadway, as a Playwrights Horizon workshop production, before opening on Broadway in 1984. Inspired by George Seurat's 19th century painting, *Sunday Afternoon On The Island Of La Grande Jatte*, with book and direction by Lapine, the two-act show starred Mandy Patinkin and Bernadette Peters, and an 'intriguingly intricate' Sondheim score that included 'Finishing The Hat', 'Lesson No.8', and 'Move On'. The run of a year-and-a-half was due in no small part to energetic promotion by the *New York Times*, which caused the theatrical competition to dub the show, *Sunday In The Times With George*. In 1985, it was awarded the coveted Pulitzer Prize for Drama, and in 1990 became one of the rare musicals to be staged at London's Royal National Theatre. In 1987, Sondheim again received a Tony award for *Into the Woods*, a musical fairy tale of a baker and his wife, who live under the curse of a wicked witch, played by Bernadette Peters. The critics called it Sondheim's most accessible show for many years, with a score that included 'Cinderella At The Grave', 'Hello, Little Girl' and 'Children Will Listen'. It won the New York Drama Critics Circle, and Drama Desk Awards, for Best Musical, and a Grammy for Best Original Cast album. 'Angry', rather than accessible, was the critics' verdict of *Assassins*, with a book by John Weidman, which opened for a limited run Off Broadway early in 1991, and played the Donmar Warehouse in London a year later. Dubbed by *Newsweek*: 'Sondheim's most audacious, far out and grotesque work of his career', it 'attempted to examine the common thread of killers and would-be killers from John Wilkes Booth, the murderer of Lincoln, through Lee Harvey Oswald to John Hinckley Jnr, who shot Ronald Reagan'. The pastiche score included 'Everybody's Got The Right', 'The Ballad Of Booth' and 'The Ballad Of Czolgosz'. In 1993, a one-night tribute *Sondheim: A Celebration At Carnegie Hall*, was transmitted on US network television in the 'Great Performers' series, and, on a rather smaller scale, the Off Broadway revue *Putting It Together*, which was packed with Sondheim songs, brought Julie Andrews back to the New York musical stage for the first time since *Camelot*. In May 1994, *Passion*, the result of Sondheim's third collaboration with James Lapine, opened on Broadway and ran for 280 performances. Meanwhile, in April of that year, Sondheim's first non-musical play, *Getting Away With Murder* (previously known as *The Doctor Is Out*), was withdrawn from the Broadhurst Theatre in April after only 17 performances, while a revival of *A Funny Thing Happened On The Way To The Forum*, starring Nathan Lane, began a highly successful run, just across West 44th Street at the St. James Theatre. In December 1998, *Saturday Night*, for which Sondheim wrote the score more than 40 years earlier - it would have marked his Broadway debut - had its world premiere at the tiny, but important, Bridewell Theatre in London.

Besides his main Broadway works over the years, Sondheim provided material for many other stage projects, such as the music and lyrics for *The Frogs* (1974), songs for the revue *Marry Me A Little* and a song for the play *A Mighty Man Is He*. He also contributed the incidental music to *The Girls Of Summer*, 'Come Over Here' and 'Home Is the Place' for Tony Bennett. In addition, Sondheim wrote the incidental music for the play *Invitation To A March*, the score for the mini-musical *Passionella*, the lyrics (with Mary Rodgers' music) for *The Mad Show* and new lyrics for composer Leonard Bernstein's 1974 revival of *Candide*. Sondheim's film work has included the music for *Stavinsky*, *Reds*, and *Dick Tracy*. He received an Oscar for his 'Sooner Or Later (I Always Get My Man)', from the latter film. Sondheim also wrote the screenplay, with Anthony Perkins, for *The Last Of Sheila*, a film 'full of impossible situations, demented logic and indecipherable clues', inspired by his penchant for board games and puzzles of every description. For television, Sondheim wrote the music and lyrics for *Evening Primrose*, which starred Perkins, and made his own acting debut in 1974, with Jack Cassidy, in a revival of the George S. Kaufman-Ring Lardner play *June Moon*.

While never pretending to write 'hit songs' (apparently

the term 'hummable' makes him bristle), Sondheim has nevertheless had his moments in the charts with songs such as 'Small World' (Johnny Mathis); 'Tonight' (Ferrante And Teicher); 'Maria' and 'Somewhere' (P.J. Proby); 'Send In The Clowns' (Judy Collins), and 'Losing My Mind' (Liza Minnelli). Probably Sondheim's greatest impact on records, apart from the Original Cast albums which to date have won seven Grammys, was Barbra Streisand's *The Broadway Album* in 1985. Seven tracks, involving eight songs, were Sondheim's (two in collaboration with Bernstein), and he re-wrote three of them for Streisand, including 'Send In The Clowns'. *The Broadway Album* stayed at number 1 in the US charts for three weeks, and sold over three million copies. Other gratifying moments for Sondheim occurred in 1983 when he was voted a member of the American Academy and the Institute of Arts and Letters, and again in 1990, when he became Oxford University's first Professor of Drama. As for his contribution to the musical theatre, opinions are sharply divided. John Podhoretz in the *Washington Times* said that 'with *West Side Story*, the musical took a crucial, and in retrospect, suicidal step into the realm of social commentary, and created a self-destructive form in which characters were taken to task and made fun of, for doing things like bursting into song'. Others, like Harold Prince, have said that Stephen Sondheim is simply the best in the world.

● ALBUMS: various artists *Sondheim: A Celebration At Carnegie Hall* (RCA Victor 1994)★★★, various artists *Putting It Together* original cast recording (RCA Victor 1994)★★★.

● FURTHER READING: *Sondheim & Co.*, Craig Zadan. *Sondheim And The American Musical*, Paul Sheran and Tom Sutcliffe. *Song By Song By Sondheim (The Stephen Sondheim Songbook)*, edited by Sheridan Morley. *Sunday In the Park With George*, Stephen Sondheim and James Lapine. *Sondheim*, Martin Gottfried. *Art Isn't Easy: Theatre Of Stephen Sondheim*, Joanne Gordon. *Sondheim's Broadway Musicals*, Stephen Banfield. *Stephen Sondheim: A Life*, Meryle Secrest.

SONG AND DANCE

A 'concert for the theatre', consisting of the 'song cycle' *Tell Me On A Sunday*, with music by Andrew Lloyd Webber and lyrics by Don Black, and *Variations*, composed by Lloyd Webber on a theme of Paganini for his 'cellist brother Julian. *Tell Me On A Sunday* was first performed at Lloyd Webber's Sydmonton Festival in 1979. When it subsequently played to an invited audience at London's Royalty Theatre in January 1980, and was broadcast by BBC television during the following month, the piece was sung by Marti Webb. In the same year, she had UK chart hits with two of the songs, 'Tell Me On A Sunday' and 'Take That Look Off Your Face'. The latter number also won an Ivor Novello Award. She was cast again when *Tell Me On A Sunday* was expanded to 50 minutes and became the first part of *Song And Dance*, while Wayne Sleep, with his team of eight dancers, performed *Variations* in the second half. The complete work opened at the Palace Theatre in London on 7 April 1982. *Tell Me On A Sunday* is a simple tale of a young English woman in New York, and the trials and tribulations she experiences during a series of unhappy love affairs. The songs are considered to be among the composer's - and Don Black's -

very best work, and included 'You Made Me Think You Were In Love', 'I Love New York', 'Come Back With The Same Look In Your Eyes', 'I'm Very You, You're Very Me', 'Let's Talk About Me', and 'When You Want To Fall In Love'. Black, who had spent some time in America, came up with what he thought was an apposite song title that apparently pleased him considerably - 'Capped Teeth And Caesar Salad'. *Song And Dance* enjoyed a run of 781 performances, closing in March 1984. During the run, Marti Webb was replaced by several actresses including Gemma Craven, Lulu, and Liz Robertson. Sarah Brightman played the lead when the show was transmitted on UK television in August 1984. In 1985, much to the reported chagrin of Don Black, *Song And Dance* was expanded even further (adaptation and new lyrics by Richard Maltby Jnr.) and presented at the Royale Theatre in New York, where it stayed for over a year. Bernadette Peters won a Tony Award for her performance in the leading role. Singer/songwriter Melissa Manchester was an interesting choice to play the lead in a 1987 Dallas production of the show, but the two original stars, Marti Webb and Wayne Sleep, recreated their roles in a new production which toured the UK and played a six-week season at London's Shaftesbury Theatre in 1990.

SONG IS BORN, A

A lame remake, seven years later, by director Howard Hawks of his own 1941 film, *Ball Of Fire*. A group of professors, locked away for years writing an encyclopedia, discover that the world of music has moved on and send one of their number out to discover what has been going on. Unfortunately for the dramatics, Danny Kaye and Virginia Mayo are no match for the original's Gary Cooper and Barbara Stanwyck. Fortunately for jazz lovers, there is rather a lot of talent on display. As might be expected, who you see on the screen is not always who you hear on the soundtrack but, amongst others, there is the significance presence of Louis Armstrong, Lionel Hampton, Tommy Dorsey, Charlie Barnet, Mel Powell and Louie Bellson. Benny Goodman has an acting role as one of the professors who is also a dab hand on the clarinet.

SONG OF NORWAY

The first of several shows in which Robert Wright and George Forrest adapted works by classical composers for Broadway. In this case they turned to the life and music of Edvard Grieg. *Song Of Norway* played in the San Francisco and the Los Angeles Opera companies, before opening at the Imperial Theatre in New York on 21 August 1944. The book by Milton Lazarus, based on a play by Homer Curran, tells a fanciful story in which Grieg (Lawrence Brooks) and his poet friend, Rikard Nordraak (Robert Shafer), are diverted from their work by the tempestuous Italian prima donna Louisa Giovanni (Irra Petina). After the poet's death, Grieg is supposedly inspired to write the A-Minor Piano Concerto. Wright and Forrest's music and lyrics combined with Grieg's music in a score which included 'Freddy And His Fiddle', 'Midsummer's Eve', 'Three Loves', 'Hill Of Dreams', 'The Legend', 'Strange Music', 'Now!', 'Hymn Of Betrothal', and 'I Love Thee'. *Song Of Norway* was one of Broadway's biggest wartime hits, running for 860 performances. The 1946 London production, featuring John Hargreaves, ran for over a year. A film version, starring Florence Henderson and Toralv Maurstad was released in 1970. In 1981, the show was revived on Broadway by the New York City Opera. Many recordings have been issued over the years, but the complete score was not available until 1992, when a version with Valerie Masterson, Diana Montague, David Rendall, and Donald Maxwell, was released on two CDs.

SONY BROADWAY

The Masterworks division of Columbia Records under the leadership of Goddard Lieberson, dominated the recording of Original Broadway Cast albums from the early 50s onwards. By that time, Columbia Records had become part of the Columbia Broadcasting System (CBS), having been bought out in 1938 for the sum of $700,000. Exactly 50 years later, the Japanese conglomerate, Sony Music, reportedly paid $2 billion for CBS. In the early 90s, the Sony Broadway label was in a position to begin to re-release all those (mostly) marvellous musicals from the genre's vintage years on mid-price CDs. By 1994 the list was substantial, and included *Goldilocks*, *Miss Liberty*, *Mr. President*, *Candide*, *West Side Story*, *Wonderful Town*, *The Apple Tree*, *The Rothschilds*, *On The Twentieth Century*, *The Girl Who Came To Supper*, *1776*, *Ballroom*, *Dear World*, *70, Girls, 70*, *The Most Happy Fella*, *Bajour*, *Irma La Douce*, *Out Of This World*, *Do I Hear A Waltz?*, *Flower Drum Song*, *The Sound Of Music*, *South Pacific*, *Two By Two*, *A Tree Grows In Brooklyn*, *Over Here*, *All American*, *It's a Bird, It's a Plane, It's Superman*, *Gentlemen Prefer Blondes*, *Hallelujah, Baby!*, *Irene*, *Here's Love*, *Dames At Sea*, and *Raisin*. The CD booklet covers are reconstructions of the original album sleeve graphics, but the liner notes are all newly written by contemporary experts such as Ken Mandelbaum. The label has also released several studio recordings of Broadway shows, and compilations such as *There's No Business Like Show Business - Broadway Showstoppers*, *There's Nothing Like A Dame - Broadway's Broads*, *Embraceable You - Broadway In Love*, *The Party's Over - Broadway Sings The Blues*, and tributes to leading songwriters, including Stephen Sondheim, Richard Rodgers and Oscar Hammerstein II, and Betty Comden and Adolph Green. Another label devoted to re-issuing Broadway musicals, most of which have only been available for many years, second-hand and at inflated collectors' prices, is Broadway Angel.

SOPHISTICATED LADIES

This revue which celebrated the music of the great American composer Duke Ellington, was conceived by Donald McKayle and opened at the Lunt-Fontanne Theatre in New York on 1 March 1981. McKayle was also one of the choreographers, along with director Michael Smuin and Henry LeTang, for what was essentially a dynamic song and dance show with an awful lot of class. From a large on-stage orchestra led by Mercer Ellington, Duke's son, there flowed a constant stream of classics from the world of popular music and jazz, such as 'I'm Beginning To See The Light', 'Satin Doll', 'Mood Indigo',

'Take the 'A' Train', 'I Got It Bad (And That Ain't Good)', 'It Don't Mean A Thing (If It Ain't Got That Swing)', and some 30 more. Tap dancer extraordinaire, Gregory Hines, headed a cast of dedicated singers and dancers including Gregg Burge, Judith Jamison, Hinton Battle, P.J. Benjamin, Phyllis Hyman, and Terri Klausner. The original book was dispensed with, and it was left to the superb music to carry the evening. This it did - and for a remarkable 767 performances. For some reason, it was 1992 before the show reached London, and by that time the West End was full of tributes to icons such as Buddy Holly, Louis Jordan, and Cole Porter. *Sophisticated Ladies* joined them for just three months.

SOUND OF JAZZ, THE

An outstanding achievement in the presentation of jazz on US television, this 1957 film was conceived and produced by Robert Herridge with the advice of jazz writers Nat Hentoff and Whitney Balliett. Directed by Jack Smight, the film shows the musicians playing in an atmosphere of complete relaxation and achieving an exceptionally high standard of performance. Regardless of who the musicians might have been, the concept and format would have been commendable. The fact that the musicians on display are some of the greatest figures in the history of jazz make this an hour of continuous joy. The all-star bands led by Count Basie and Red Allen feature Doc Cheatham, Freddie Green, Coleman Hawkins, Jo Jones, Roy Eldridge, Joe Newman, Gerry Mulligan, Rex Stewart, Earle Warren, Dicky Wells, Ben Webster, Lester Young, singer Jimmy Rushing, Vic Dickenson, Danny Barker, Milt Hinton, Nat Pierce (who also contributed the arrangements played by the Basie-led band) and Pee Wee Russell. Also on hand is the Jimmy Giuffre trio with Jim Hall and Jim Atlas playing 'The Train And The River', and Thelonious Monk plays 'Blue Monk' accompanied by Ahmed Abdul-Malik and Osie Johnson. If all this were not enough there is Billie Holiday accompanied by Mal Waldron. She sings her own composition, 'Fine And Mellow', in what must be this song's definitive performance, backed by many of the listed musicians, with Lester Young contributing a poignant solo. Four decades after its making, this film remains a high-water mark in jazz and its standards remain those to which all other film-makers aspire.

SOUND OF MILES DAVIS, THE

Produced and directed by the same team responsible for *The Sound Of Jazz* (Robert Herridge and Jack Smight), this 1959 film was originally entitled *Theater For A Song*. Davis is presented with his quintet (John Coltrane, Wynton Kelly, Paul Chambers and Jimmy Cobb) and also with Gil Evans And His Orchestra. The performance captures Davis in eloquent form and the contributions from the other musicians on hand help to make this an important filmed record of one of the music's most important figures.

SOUND OF MUSIC, THE (FILM MUSICAL)

Dubbed 'The Sound Of Mucus' by some for its almost overwhelming sentimentality and sweetness, in the early

90s this film was still hovering around the Top 40 highest-earning movies of all-time in the USA, and that level of success has been reiterated around the world. Ernest Lehman's screenplay, which was based on the 1959 Broadway musical and the real-life story of the Austrian Von Trapp family of folk singers. Maria (Julie Andrews), a postulant nun in a Saltzburg convent, whose unconventional ways drive her fellow nuns to despair, is engaged by widower Captain Von Trapp (Christopher Plummer) as governess to his seven children. After one or two domestic disagreements (such as when she cuts up the curtains to make clothes for the children), they eventually fall in love and marry. Their happiness is disturbed by the imminence of World War II and the presence of the Nazi army in Austria. When Von Trapp is required to report for military service, the whole family escape from the soldiers' clutches at the end of a concert performance, just as the real Von Trapp family did. Some of the film's most charming moments came when Maria is teaching the children music, and also when they are operating a marionette theatre together. Julie Andrews gave a tender, most appealing performance as the young girl maturing into a woman, and Plummer was bombastic and tender in turns. Eleanor Parker (as the Captain-hungry Baroness) and Richard Haydn (in the role of Max Detweiler, a man who would go anywhere in the world for a free bed and breakfast), led a supporting cast which included Peggy Wood, Charmian Carr, Anna Lee, Portia Nelson, and Marni Nixon. Most of Richard Rodgers and Oscar Hammerstein II's songs from the stage show were retained, along with two new ones, 'Something Good' and 'I Have Confidence In Me', in a score that consisted of 'The Sound Of Music', 'Maria', 'Sixteen Going On Seventeen', 'My Favourite Things', 'Climb Ev'ry Mountain', 'The Lonely Goatherd', 'Do-Re-Mi', 'Edelweiss', and 'So Long, Farewell'. Bill Lee dubbed Plummer's vocals. Marc Breaux and Dee Dee Wood choreographed the delightful dance sequences, and the producer-director for 20th Century-Fox was Robert Wise. The memorable opening alpine aerial shot was credited to Ted McCord, who photographed the film superbly in DeLuxe Color and Todd-AO. The Sound Of Music won Academy Awards for best film, director, and music scoring (Irwin Kostal), and became the highest-grossing film in the USA during the 60s. Its soundtrack album spent a total of 70 weeks at number 1 in the UK, and was over a year in the US chart.

● FURTHER READING: The Sound Of Music: The Making Of America's Favorite Movie, Antopol Hirsch.

SOUND OF MUSIC, THE (STAGE MUSICAL)

Even before its Broadway opening at the Lunt-Fontanne Theatre on 16 November 1959, The Sound Of Music was set to become a financial success. Advance sales exceeded three million dollars and with numerous touring versions, bestselling albums and a blockbuster film, it made a fortune for its composers, Richard Rodgers and Oscar Hammerstein II. The show had a strong narrative book, by Howard Lindsey and Russel Crouse, that was based upon the real-life story of Maria Rainer, her marriage to George von Trapp and her relationship with his family of

singing youngsters. The family's evasion of capture by the Nazis during World War II gave the story a tense dramatic core and the fact that the family became professional singers meant that music and song blended well into the narrative, even if, at times, there seemed to be rather more sentiment than reality would have allowed. Starring Mary Martin as Maria, Theodore Bikel (Von Trapp), Marion Marlowe (Elsa Schraeder), Kurt Kasznar (Max Detweiler), and Patricia Neway (Mother Abbess), the show was filled with marvellous songs, including the title song, 'Do-Re-Mi', 'My Favorite Things', 'Edelweiss', 'So Long, Farewell', 'Sixteen Going On Seventeen', 'How Can Love Survive?', 'Maria', 'The Lonely Goatherd', and 'Climb Ev'ry Mountain'. Sentimental or not, it is hard to imagine that at the time he was working on this show, Hammerstein was a sick man; less than a year after the Broadway opening he was dead. The Sound Of Music played for 1,443 performances, and won Tony Awards for best musical (tied with Fiorello!), actress (Martin), featured actress (Neway), musical director (Frederick Dvonch), and scenic design (Oliver Smith). Jean Bayliss and Roger Dann headed the cast of the 1961 London production, which surpassed the original and ran for 2,385 performances. New York revivals included one in 1967 at the City Centre, and another in 1990, presented by the New York City Opera, in which the ex-chart-topper Debby Boone played Maria. London audiences saw the show again in 1992 when it was presented at Sadlers Wells, with Liz Robertson and Christopher Cazenove. Paul Kerryson's 1997 Leicester Haymarket production had Kathyrn Evans as Maria and Richard Willis as Von Trapp, while the cast of the 1998 Broadway revival, directed by Susan H. Schulman, was headed by Rebecca Luker and the classy British actor Michael Siberry. The 1965 film version, which starred Julie Andrews, won three Oscars and spawned one of the bestselling soundtrack albums of all time.

SOUTH PACIFIC (FILM MUSICAL)

This immensely successful screen version of Richard Rodgers and Oscar Hammerstein's 1949 Broadway hit musical was released by 20th Century-Fox in 1958. Paul Osborn's screenplay, which was adapted from the stage production and James A. Michener's Tales Of The South Pacific, told the story of life on a South Sea island that is temporarily occupied by American troops during World War II. Two love stories run in parallel: that between the mature, sophisticated French planter, Emile de Becque (Rossano Brazzi), and a young nurse, Nellie Forbush (Mitzi Gaynor); and the other, which involves Lt. Joe Cable (John Kerr) and Liat (France Nuyen), the Polynesian daughter of Bloody Mary (Juanita Hall). Some felt that Oscar Hammerstein and Joshua Logan, who wrote the original libretto, fudged the 'racial issue' by allowing Cable to be killed in action so that he could not marry Liat. On the other hand, Nellie, after much personal torment and heart-searching, found herself able to accept de Becque's ethnic children from a previous marriage. The supporting cast was excellent, with Ray Walston outstanding as Luther Billis. Early on in the film he led a group of fellow marines in the rousing, but poignant, 'There Is Nothing

Like A Dame', one of the songs in Rodgers and Hammerstein's marvellous score that came from Broadway intact - with the addition of one other number, 'My Girl Back Home', which had been written, but not used, for the 1949 show. The remainder of the film's much-loved songs were 'Dites-moi', 'A Cockeyed Optimist', 'Twin Soliloquies', 'Some Enchanted Evening', 'Bloody Mary', 'Bali Ha'i', 'I'm Gonna Wash That Man Right Outa My Hair', 'A Wonderful Guy', 'Younger Than Springtime', 'Happy Talk', 'Honey Bun', 'Carefully Taught' and 'This Nearly Was Mine'. The singing voices of Rossano Brazzi, John Kerr, and Juanita Hall were dubbed by Giorgio Tozzi, Bill Lee, and Muriel Smith, respectively. The choreographer was LeRoy Prinz, and Joshua Logan directed, as he had done on Broadway. *South Pacific* was photographed by Leon Shamroy in Technicolor and the Todd-AO wide-screen process. There was a good deal of adverse criticism regarding the use of colour filters in the various musical sequences. The soundtrack album proved to be one of the bestsellers of all time, spending an unprecedented (to date) total of 115 weeks at the top of the UK chart, and 31 weeks at number 1 in the USA.

SOUTH PACIFIC (STAGE MUSICAL)

Opening on Broadway at the Majestic Theatre on 7 April 1949, *South Pacific* became one of the best-loved and most successful of the fruitful collaborations between Richard Rodgers and Oscar Hammerstein II. The libretto, by Hammerstein and Joshua Logan, was based on stories in James Michener's book *Tales Of The South Pacific*. Its story was set during World War II and dealt in part with racism, a subject not exactly commonplace in American musical comedies. Mary Martin starred as Nellie Forbush, an American nurse who falls in love with a middle-aged French planter, Emil de Becque (Ezio Pinza), but is disturbed by the fact that he has two children by a Polynesian woman who is now dead. Meanwhile, a US Navy lieutenant, Joe Cable (William Tabbert), is attracted to an island girl, Liat (Betta St. John), but, like Nellie, his underlying racial fears cause him to reject her (or it could just be that is scared stiff of her mother, Bloody Mary [Juanita Hall]). In any event, Joe dies in action and Nellie comes to terms with the colour issue and is reunited with Emile. The marvellous score, which contained several big hits, included 'Some Enchanted Evening', 'Younger Than Springtime', 'Wonderful Guy', 'I'm Gonna Wash That Man Right Outa My Hair', 'Honey Bun', 'There Is Nothin' Like A Dame', 'A Cockeyed Optimist', 'You've Got To Be Carefully Taught', 'This Nearly Was Mine', and two songs which were sung by Juanita Hall, 'Bali Ha'i' 'Dites-moi', and 'Happy Talk'. Myron McCormick played the endearing character of US marine Luther Billis, and he was the only member of the cast to appear in every one of *South Pacific*'s 1,925 performances. The show scooped the Tony Awards, winning for best musical, score, libretto, actress (Martin), actor (Pinza), supporting actress (Hall), supporting actor (McCormick), and director (Joshua Logan). It also became only the second musical (not counting *Oklahoma!*'s special award) to win the prestigious Pulitzer Prize for Drama. Mary Martin reprised her role in 1951 at the Drury Lane Theatre, with Wilbur Evans as de Becque.

London audiences were delighted with her performance, and were particularly intrigued by her nightly ritual of washing her hair on-stage. Over the years American regional revivals have proliferated, and it was also seen at New York's State Theatre (1967, with Florence Henderson and Giorgio Tozzi). A 1988 London revival with Gemma Craven (Nellie), Emile Belcourt (de Becque), Bertice Reading (Bloody Mary), and Andrew C. Wadsworth (Cable), ran for over 400 performances, and in 1995 the London Fringe mounted one with Peter Polycarpou (Emile), Joanna Maddison (Nellie), Christopher Howard (Cable), and Patti Boulaye (Bloody Mary). The enormously popular 1958 screen version starred Mitzi Gaynor and Rossano Brazzi.

SPEND SPEND SPEND!

In 1961, a 23-year-old coal miner named Keith Howard Nicholson, who lived and worked in the northern English county of Yorkshire, won £152,319 on the football pools. When his wife, Viv, was asked what they intended to do with the money (reputed to be worth about £3 million in the 90s), she announced: 'I want to spend and spend and spend.' Three husbands, some Cadillacs, and a whole lot of living later, in 1976 she was back in her own back yard, existing on just £30 a week. This musical, which was inspired by the life of Viv Nicholson, from the book by Viv Nicholson and Stephen Smith, has a book and lyrics by its director Justin Greene and composer Steve Brown. The world premiere took place at the West Yorkshire Playhouse in Leeds on 23 May 1998. The story is told in flashback, and the initial setting a present-day beauty salon, where the older (and presumably, wiser) Viv (Rosemary Ashe) has come to work. She proceeds to look back in wonder over the years, without a smidgen of regret, confronting her younger self (the insolent and sexy Diana Dors-type, Sophie-Louise Dann), and revelling in her reputation as the great survivor. Green and Brown's book celebrates the renowned Yorkshire grit, whilst gently puncturing it on occasions. And the sometimes bawdy humour (one number, 'Sexual Happening', contains most of the slang terms for coitus), is nicely balanced by several moving and poignant moments such as the one when Viv pours her heart into 'Who's Gonna Love Me?' after her Keith dies. Among the 'memorably melodic and often witty' new songs were reminders of 50s and 60s pop hits, mining and folk tunes, as well as a clever Gilbert And Sullivan pastiche during which the Inland Revenue tie Viv up with red tape. Her favourite colour is actually pink, pink, pink. In a way, the list of items in the sung-through score charts the landmarks of the story in itself: 'Salon Mystique', 'Ice Cream Girl', 'I'll Take Care Of Thee', 'Bread And Jam Man', 'Special Day', 'How To Win Your Man', 'Scars Of Love', 'John Collier', 'The Win', 'Two Rooms', 'Spend, Spend, Spend', 'Miners Arms', 'Big American Car', 'Drinking In America', 'Canary I and II', 'Dance Of The Suits I and II', and 'A Brand New Husband'. Prominent amongst the rest of the cast, which included colliers, superficial gold-laméd types, and the inevitable spongers, were Jonathan D. Ellis (Bank Manager), Michelle Fine (Mrs. Waterman), Melissa Jacques (Beautician/Air Hostess), Andrew Kennedy (Johnny Love), Neil McCaul

(George), Nigel Richards (Keith), Paul Thornley (Solicitor/Matt), and Sara Williams (Sue). Pat Garrett handled the musical staging and choreography, and the designer was Niki Turner. *Spend Spend Spend!* won the award for Best Musical in the annual Barclays Theatre Awards. In 1977, Viv Nicholson's book was adapted by Jack Rosenthal into an award-winning television play, and eight years later Claire Luckman and Chris Bond 'arranged' it into a 'half-baked musical', entitled *Spend, Spend, Spend*, by re-writing the pop songs of the period, such as Chuck Berry's 'You Never Can Tell' and the Rolling Stones' 'Satisfaction'. It was presented at the Half Moon Theatre in London, with Victoria Hardcastle as Viv, and Neil Pearson playing husband Keith. Pearson later found fame in 90s television series such as *Drop The Dead Donkey* and *Between The Lines*.

SPEWACK, BELLA AND SAM

Authors and screenwriters Bella Spewack (b. Bella Cohen, 25 March 1899, Bucharest, Romania, d. 27 April 1990, New York, USA) and Sam Spewack (b. 16 September 1899, Bachmut, Russia, d. 14 October 1971, New York, USA) will be forever remembered in the theatrical world for their work with Cole Porter on one of the outstanding musical comedies in Broadway history, *Kiss Me, Kate*. They each moved to live in New York as children, and later pursued journalistic careers before meeting in 1921. After marrying the following year, the couple worked together as foreign correspondents, and then co-authored several mostly successful comedy (sometimes called 'wacky comedy') plays for Broadway from the mid-20s onwards. These included *The Solitaire Man*, *Poppa*, *The War Song*, *Clear All Wires*, *Spring Song*, *Boy Meets Girl*, *Miss Swan Expects*, *Woman Bites Dog*, and *My Three Angels* (from the French of Albert Husson). In 1938, they converted their script for *Clear All Wires* into the libretto for the musical *Leave It To Me!* Sam Spewack directed this clever satire on communism and US diplomacy, which had a Cole Porter score and introduced Mary Martin and Gene Kelly to Broadway. A decade on, the Spewacks collaborated with Porter again, winning Tony Awards for their witty and skilful adaptation of William Shakespeare's play *The Taming Of The Shrew* for *Kiss Me, Kate*. This landmark musical ran for 1,077 performances in New York, and in 1951 Sam restaged it for the West End where it played at the London Coliseum for more than a year. Since then it has been constantly revived, and was filmed in 1953. Bella and Sam enjoyed more success in Hollywood with screenplays for *The Nuisance*, *The Cat And The Fiddle*, *Rendezvous*, *Vogues Of 1938*, *Three Loves Has Nancy*, *Boy Meets Girl*, *My Favorite Wife* (Oscar nomination, with Leo McCarey, 1940), and *Weekend At The Waldorf*. *My Favorite Wife* was remade in 1963 as *Move Over Darling*, starring Doris Day and James Garner. In later years Sam Spewack wrote plays on his own, which Bella often produced, and in 1965, he and Frank Loesser wrote the book for the musical *Pleasures And Palaces*, based on Sam's play *Once There Was A Russian*. However, in spite of being directed and choreographed by Bob Fosse, and starring Phyllis Newman and Jack Cassidy, the show closed out of town during its Broadway tryout.

SPIELMAN, FRED

b. Fritz Spielman(n), 20 November 1906, Vienna, Austria, d. 21 March 1997. A composer of popular songs for the stage, films, and Tin Pan Alley, Spielman studied composition with Joseph Marx at the Academy of Music in Vienna. After graduating with a Master Degree in Piano he gave some recitals, but then eschewed the classics in favour of earning a living playing the piano in nightclubs and writing his own songs. The prevailing economic climate was ironically reflected in one of his most notable efforts around this time, 'Warum Spielt Bei Den Schinkenfleckerl Alleweil Das Fleisch Versteckerl?', which, roughly translated, means: 'Why is the meat always playing hide and seek in the noodle and ham dish?' Shortly after the German entry into Austria in March 1938, Spielman went to Paris, and then, with World War II imminent, managed to board one of the last ships to Cuba. There he married, and took his wife to New York in 1939. Rapidly coming to terms with the American culture and language, by the early 40s he was composing the music for many popular songs, one of the first of which, 'Shepherd Serenade' (lyric: Kermit Goell), was recorded successfully by Horace Heidt And His Musical Knights, Art Jarrett, and Bing Crosby. He collaborated with Goell again on 'You Better Give Me Lots Of Loving' for the 1943 Andrews Sisters movie, *Swingtime Johnny*, and for 'Every Time I Give My Heart', 'All You Gotta Do', and 'I Love It Out Here In The West', which were delivered by Ann Dvorak, playing a warm-hearted saloon singer, in the robust Randolph Scott western, *Abiline Town* (1946). By this time Spielman was signed to the MGM studio, and in the late 40s he worked with Janice Torre to provide occasional numbers for films such as *Big City* (1948, 'I'm Gonna See A Lot Of You'), *Luxury Liner* (1948, 'Spring Came Back To Vienna', sung by the 20-year-old Jane Powell), and *In The Good Old Summertime* (1949), in which Judy Garland rendered their spirited 'Merry Christmas'. Spielman's other film work included 'Time And Time Again' (with Earl Brent), for another Jane Powell picture, *Nancy Goes To Rio* (1950), several numbers with Goell and Torre for *Tom Thumb* (1958), starring Russ Tamblyn, Peter Sellers, and Terry-Thomas, and 'I Don't Want To' (with Torre) for the Elvis Presley vehicle *Girls! Girls! Girls!* (1962). In 1950, Goell and Al Hoffman adapted a tune that Spielman had composed during his teenage years for the gentle 'One Finger Melody', and Frank Sinatra's recording of it spent 16 weeks in the US Hit Parade. Other prominent numbers among Spielman's prolific output were 'Go To Sleep, Go To Sleep, Go To Sleep' (1950, with Sammy Cahn, a novelty recorded in the USA by Mary Martin and Arthur Godfrey, and in the UK by Lita Roza and Jack Parnell with the Ted Heath Orchestra), 'It Only Hurts For A Little While' (1956, Mack David), 'The Longest Walk' (Eddie Pola), a 1955 US hit for Jaye P. Morgan, and the country-styled 'Paper Roses', written with Janice Torre in 1960, and profitably revived by Marie Osmond in 1973. There was also 'Who Killed 'Er', an amusing piece for which Spielman collaborated with Torre and Hoagy Carmichael, who gave it an inimitable reading on record. In addition, Spielman provided some material with

George Gershwin's brother, Arthur, for the unsuccessful 1945 Broadway musical, *A Lady Says Yes*, and worked on various off-Broadway projects. In 1969, he and Torre supplied the music and lyrics for the television musical *The Stingiest Man In Town*, which was based on Charles Dickens' *A Christmas Carol*. Walter Matthau dubbed the voice of Scrooge, and also involved were Theodore Bikel, Robert Morse, and Dennis Day. When it was adapted for the stage, the Chicago production won the Joseph Jefferson Award. This was a rare instance of recognition for a composer whose work often went unappreciated. Further recognition came in 1990, when the renowned American jazz singer, Shirley Horn, recorded Spielman and Goell's 'You Won't Forget Me', after spotting it in the 1953 Joan Crawford movie *The Torch Song*, on late-night television. The number was also part of the score for the 1950 Esther Williams-Van Johnson picture, *The Duchess Of Idaho*.

SPINOUT

'Singing-swinging-racing-romancing-hitting the curves with no brakes on the excitement,' proclaimed the publicity machine about this 1966 Elvis Presley film. If only. In truth *Spinout* (UK title *California Holiday*) was another sub-standard, routine feature in which the singer played a bandleader and sports-car driver trying to avoid the attentions of four star-struck admirers. As if to confirm the unadventurous nature plaguing Presley's films, singer Shelley Fabares made yet another appearance as his co-star. Nine largely unremarkable tracks were recorded for the soundtrack, but the resultant album was bolstered by three numbers not featured in the film. The best of these was a haunting version of Bob Dylan's 'Tomorrow Is A Long Time', the inclusion of which suggested that Presley was not immune from the changes occurring in contemporary pop. It is an awareness that could not be gleaned from the meagre fare offered in this feature.

SPRING PARADE

Remembered particularly for the joyous 'Waltzing In The Clouds' (Robert Stolz and Gus Kahn), this Deanna Durbin vehicle was released by Universal in 1940. A 'veteran' of eight films in the space of four years - and still only 19 years old - Durbin was cast as a baker's assistant in old Vienna. She falls for a handsome would-be composer (Robert Cummings), who plays the drums in the army while waiting for his music to be appreciated. S.Z. Sakall, as the baker, and Henry Stephenson, in the role of Emperor Franz Joseph, turned Bruce Manning and Felix Jackson's light-hearted (and lightweight) screenplay into an amusing and entertaining movie. Also contributing to the pleasure were Mischa Auer, Henry Stephenson, Anne Gwynne, and the lively duo, Butch And Buddy. The music helped a lot, too. As well as 'Waltzing In The Clouds', which was nominated, but beaten for the Oscar that year by 'When You Wish Upon A Star' (from *Pinocchio*), Stolz and Kahn wrote 'When April Sings' and another catchy bit of nonsense, 'It's Foolish But It's Fun'. The other numbers were 'In A Spring Parade' (Charles Previn-Kahn), 'The Dawn Of Love' (Previn-Ralph Freed), and 'Blue Danube Dream' (Johann Strauss II-Kahn). Henry Koster directed

yet another in the long line of Durbin hits which would continue for a few years to come.

ST LOUIS BLUES

One of the first talkies, and one of few early films to feature jazz or blues artists, this offers the only screen appearance of Bessie Smith, the Empress of the Blues. Directed by Dudley Murphy (who in the same year made *Black And Tan*), this 1929 film features an extended performance of the title song built around a thin story that fully exploits elements of pathos in the lyrics. There is an excellent accompanying band, including Joe Smith and Kaiser Marshall, mostly drawn from the ranks of Fletcher Henderson's band but led on this occasion by James P. Johnson. For all such attractions, however, this film's value lies in this solitary opportunity to see Smith, one of the greatest figures in the history of American popular music and through it to glean some fleeting understanding of the manner in which she commanded attention and dignified the blues.

NB: The same title was used for a 1939 feature film, which includes performances by Maxine Sullivan, and for the 1958 biopic based upon the life of W.C. Handy and starring Nat 'King' Cole.

ST. LOUIS WOMAN

After collaborating with Hoagy Carmichael on the flop *Walk With Music* (1940), lyricist Johnny Mercer teamed with Harold Arlen on this musical which opened at the Martin Beck Theatre in New York on 30 March 1946. Although it ran only a little longer than his previous effort, it did contain at least one song that is still remembered nearly 50 years later. Arna Bontemps and Countee Cullen wrote the book which was based on Bontemps novel *God Sends Sunday*. The setting is St. Louis in 1898, where Della Green (Ruby Hill), is happily in harness with saloon owner Biglow Brown (Rex Ingram) before jockey Little Augie (Harold Nicholas) experiences a phenomenal winning streak. Della is impressed, and switches her affections to the jockey. However, Biglow puts a curse on them both just before he dies, which ruins both the racing and their relationship for a time. 'Come Rain Or Come Shine' is the song from the show that has endured more than any other, but Pearl Bailey, who played the comical character, Butterfly, also delighted audiences with the witty 'Legalize My Name' and 'A Woman's Prerogative'. The remainder of a fine score included 'Any Place I Hang My Hat Is Home', 'I Had Myself A True Love', 'Ridin'' On the Moon', 'Sleep Peaceful, Mr. Used-To-Be', 'Lullabye', 'Leavin'' Time', and 'Cakewalk My Lady'. The Nicholas Brothers, Harold and Fayard, the acrobatic dancers who featured in several Hollywood musicals during the 40s, performed some extraordinary feats, but, for some reason - certainly not because of the score - the public just would not turn up, and *St. Louis Woman* closed after only 113 performances. Arlen and Mercer persevered, and adapted some of the material into a 'blues opera', *Free And Easy*, which spent a brief time in Europe in 1959. The original score - totalling only 29 minutes - was released on CD in 1993.

STAGE DOOR CANTEEN

Released in 1943, this film was a paper-thin excuse for Hollywood to bring onto the screen a stream of front-rank entertainers to alleviate wartime gloom. Alongside screen stars are Benny Goodman And His Orchestra, including Jack Jenney, Conrad Gozzo, Jess Stacy, Louie Bellson and Peggy Lee, perform two numbers. Count Basie And His Orchestra, including Buck Clayton, Freddie Green, Walter Page, Harry Edison, Dicky Wells, Buddy Tate, Don Byas, Earle Warren and Jo Jones, perform one number backing Ethel Waters.

STAMPING GROUND

Released in 1971 and also known as *Love And Music*, this West German film documented the 1970 Rotterdam Pop Festival. Director Hansjurgen Pohland provides a largely low-key view of the proceedings, which are occasionally interspersed with English language interviews. Many of the acts on offer had travelled to Holland from a previous appearance at England's Bath Festival. These include Jefferson Airplane, It's A Beautiful Day, Santana, Pink Floyd and the Byrds. Soft Machine, Family, Dr. John, Al Stewart and Tyrannosaurus Rex are among the others featured in a film which provides live footage of some of the era's most exciting attractions.

STAND UP AND SING

After their tremendous success together in *That's A Good Girl* (1928), Jack Buchanan and Elsie Randolph teamed up again for this delightful musical comedy which was presented at the London Hippodrome on 5 March 1931. The score was by Phil Charig and Vivian Ellis (music) and Douglas Furber (lyrics). Furber also collaborated with Buchanan on a book which turned out to be the story of a mini-world tour. Much of the action takes place on the cruise ship S.S. Ambrosia and in Egypt where Buchanan, who is pretending to be a valet but is really a toff, goes to retrieve some important papers for his girl's father. The ingénue was played by Anna Neagle in her first important stage role before launching into a long and distinguished stage and film career. She duetted with Buchanan on 'There's Always Tomorrow', the show's big ballad, but he and Elsie Randolph (who rather conveniently was a maid to his valet) handled most of the other songs, which included 'Take It Or Leave It', 'Mercantile Marine', 'I Would If I Could', 'It's Not You', 'Nobody To Take Care Of Me', 'Keep Smiling', 'Night Time', and Buchanan's speciality 'inebriated dance' routine, 'Hiccup Time In Burgundy'. Also in the cast were familiar names such as Sylvia Leslie, Richard Dolman, Richard Murdoch, Vera Pearce, Morris Harvey, and Anton Dolin who occasionally brought his brilliant brand of dancing from the ballet theatre to revue and musical comedy. *Stand Up And Sing* was an instant hit - West End audiences rejoiced in having Buchanan back on stage after a break of three years. The show ran for 325 performances at the Hippodrome and then toured successfully. During the run the entire second act was broadcast by the BBC, and several years later, in 1945, the complete show, still with Jack Buchanan and Elsie Randolph, was adapted for radio.

STAR!

While this 1968 movie biography of London-born actress Gertrude Lawrence failed to even nearly recoup its massive $12 million investment, and was generally considered to be far too long, it is by no means a poor picture mainly because the central role is played by Julie Andrews. Wisely, she does not attempt an impersonation, but rather gives an impression of what this darling of London and Broadway musical shows and revues, from the 20s through to the 50s, must have been like. William Fairchild's screenplay begins with Lawrence's childhood days in Clapham when she was part of the family music hall act along with her father (Bruce Forsyth) and his 'lady friend' (Beryl Reid). Director Robert Wise places the adult Lawrence in a projection room watching (and commenting on) the rushes of a biography being compiled about her career and the men in her life, including Richard Crenna as her second husband Richard Aldrich. Noël Coward was probably her greatest influence, and Daniel Massey's portrayal of 'The Master' as an amiable and sophisticated character is one of the movie's most appealing features. His elegant version of 'Forbidden Fruit' which Coward often used as his 'audition song', is a delight. The two stars combine for the 'Red Peppers' sequence from Coward's play *Tonight At 8.30*, and Andrews handles most of the remaining songs with great flair and panache. They included 'Someone to Watch Over Me', 'Do Do Do', and 'Dear Little Boy' (all George Gershwin-Ira Gershwin), ''N' Everything' (Buddy De Sylva-Gus Kahn-Al Jolson), 'Limehouse Blues' (Douglas Furber-Philip Braham), 'Burlington Bertie From Bow' (William Hargreaves), 'Jenny' and 'My Ship' (both Kurt Weill-Ira Gershwin), 'The Physician' (Cole Porter), and 'Parisian Pierrot', 'Someday I'll Find You' and 'Has Anybody Seen Our Ship?' (all Coward). The brand new title number was by James Van Heusen and Sammy Cahn. Also among the cast were Michael Craig, Robert Reed, Garrett Lewis, Don Knoll, John Collin, and Alan Oppenheimer, Richard Anthony, and J. Pat O'Malley. Michael Kidd was the choreographer and the film was superbly photographed by Ernest Laszlo in DeLuxe Color and Todd-AO. It was directed by Robert Wise and produced for 20th Century-Fox by Saul Chaplin. *Star!* was eventually cut from nearly three hours to just over two, and re-released under the title of *Those Were The Happy Times*. That version lost money too.

STAR IS BORN, A

Over the years, several films have attempted to strip the veneer of glamour from Hollywood, the film capital of the world, and expose the sadness and bitterness that sometimes lay beneath. *Sunset Boulevard* (1950) is, perhaps, the prime example of the genre, and, more recently, *The Player* (1992) dwelt on the greed and double-dealing inherent in the movie business. Adela Rogers St. John's original story, which eventually evolved into the 1954 Warner Brothers musical picture *A Star Is Born*, first came to the screen in 1932 under the title of *What Price Hollywood?*. Five years later, it was adapted for an Academy Award-winning dramatic film entitled *A Star Is Born*, which had a story by William A. Wellman, a screenplay by Dorothy Parker, Alan Campbell and Robert Carson, and starred Janet Gaynor and Fredric March. Moss Hart's superbly crafted screenplay for the 1954 musical version, which stayed fairly close to the plot of the previous film, tells of Norman Maine (James Mason), a has-been movie actor, whose temperamental and brutish behaviour results in him being ostracized from Hollywood studios and society. While taking solace in the bottle, he is forced to become dependent on his wife, Esther Blodgett (professional name Vicki Lester), played by Judy Garland. Mainly through his influence (and her talent), she becomes a big star herself. Eventually, unable to cope with life at the bottom of the barrel, he drowns himself. Garland was outstanding throughout - this was probably her greatest film role - and Mason, who is said to have been the fifth choice for the part, was wonderful, too. Charles Bickford, as the studio head who is reluctant to let Maine go, and Jack Carson, in the role of the studio's publicity chief who is only too glad to be rid of him, featured in a fine supporting cast, along with Lucy Marlow, Grady Sutton, Tommy Noonan, Amanda Blake, Irving Bacon and James Brown. Harold Arlen and Ira Gershwin wrote most of the songs, including the compelling 'The Man That Got Away', 'Gotta Have Me Go With You', 'Someone At Last', 'It's A New World' and two that were cut because of the film's excessive length, 'Lose That Long Face' and 'Here's What I'm Here For'. The remainder were 'Swanee' (George Gershwin-Irving Caesar), and 'Born In A Trunk' (Leonard Gershe-Roger Edens) which effectively topped and tailed a medley of old songs. The choreographer was Richard Barstow, and the film was produced by Sidney Luft (at that time Garland's husband), directed by George Cukor, and photographed in Technicolor and CinemaScope. One of the all-time great film musicals, *A Star Is Born* was re-released in the 80s complete with the two songs that were cut from the original print, and with some other scenes restored. In the 1976 remake of *A Star Is Born*, starring Barbra Streisand and Kris Kristofferson, screenwriters John Gregory Dunne, Frank Pierson and Joan Didion set their new plot in the world of rock music, with an appropriate score that included such numbers as 'Lost Inside Of You' (Streisand-Leon Russell), 'I Believe In Love' (Kenny Loggins-Alan And Marilyn Bergman), 'Queen Bee' (Rupert Holmes) and 'The Woman In The Moon' (Paul Williams-Kenny Ascher). Streisand and Williams also collaborated on 'Love Theme (Evergreen)', which won an Academy Award and topped the US chart. The film was released by Warner Brothers and photographed in Metrocolor and Panavision. The director was Frank Pierson, and *A Star Is Born* (Mark III) was a smash hit, grossing nearly $40 million in the USA and Canada alone.

● FURTHER READING: *The Making Of The 1954 Movie And Its 1983 Reconstruction*, Ronald Haver.

STAR SPANGLED RHYTHM

Just the thing for the troops - a rousing, star-studded spectacle that must have raised the spirits of war-weary forces and civilians alike when it was released by Paramount in December 1942. For what it was worth, Harry Tugend's screenplay had the Paramount gatekeeper (Victor Moore)

pretending to be an important studio executive in order to impress the buddies of his sailor son (Eddie Bracken). The latter's efforts to organize a massive show is the perfect hook on which to hang a bundle of songs and sketches performed by many of Paramount's principal players. Joining in the fun and games were Betty Hutton, Bing Crosby, Bob Hope, Dorothy Lamour, Franchot Tone, Vera Zorina, Fred MacMurray, Jerry Colonna, Veronica Lake, Alan Ladd, Marjorie Reynolds, Eddie 'Rochester' Anderson, Paulette Goddard, Arthur Treacher, Cass Daley, Susan Hayward, Macdonald Carey, William Bendix, Sterling Holloway, Marjorie Reynolds, Gil Lamb, Edward Fielding, Walter Abel, and many more. Harold Arlen and Johnny Mercer's appealing score contained two of their all time standards, 'That Old Black Magic', introduced by Johnny Johnston, and 'Hit The Road To Dreamland' which was given a fine treatment by Mary Martin, Dick Powell and the Golden Gate Quartet. The rest of the songs were 'I'm Doing It For Defence', 'On The Swing Shift', 'A Sweater, A Sarong And A Peek-A-Boo Bang', 'He Loved Me Till The All-Clear Came', 'Sharp As A Tack', and 'Old Glory'. Danny Dare and George Ballanchine staged the dances, and the director of this lively and entertaining affair was George Marshall. Joesph Sistrom produced, and it was photographed in black and white by Leo Tover.

STARDUST

Directed by Michael Apted in 1974 and starring David Essex, *Stardust* continued the exploits of pop singer Jim Maclaine, first unveiled on the superior *That'll Be The Day*. This follow-up charted Maclaine's inexorable rise from member of 60s' beat group the Stray Cats to solo star in the early part of the subsequent decade. A life of selfish hedonism - sex, drugs and calculated misanthropy - leaves the star in lonely isolation at the film's close, but the predictable outcome undermines any implied moral statement. Adam Faith co-stars memorably as Maclaine's long-suffering associate, providing much-needed warmth in several scenes. Dave Edmunds, who appears as a member of the Stray Cats, provided a portion of the soundtrack music, creating empathetic renditions of several pop staples, including 'Some Other Guy' and 'A Shot Of Rhythm 'n' Blues' while the remainder is culled from original material by a variety of 60s acts.

STARLIGHT EXPRESS

Andrew Lloyd Webber is quoted as saying that this show, which was nick-named 'Squeals On Wheels' by one unkind critic, started out in 1975 as an entertainment intended for children. In 1983 he rewrote it for the benefit of his own children, Imogen and Nicholas, and then, with the help of lyricist Richard Stilgoe, it became the full-blown musical which opened at the Apollo Victoria in London on 27 March 1984. The theatre's interior had to be completely re-designed to accommodate a series of racetracks, gantrys, ramps, and bridges which encircled and dominated the auditorium. More than 20 roller skaters, pretending to be trains, zoom along the tracks enacting a story in which, after a number of races, Rusty (Ray Shell), a shy little steam engine, triumphs over Greaseball (Jeff Shankley) the flashy diesel locomotive, and gets hitched up to his favourite carriage, Pearl (Stephanie Lawrence). The high-tech effects, plus Arlene Phillips' imaginative choreography and Trevor Nunn's direction, created what seemed almost like a giant computer game. The loudly amplified score contained elements of rock, blues, country, and many other influences, in songs such as 'Call Me Rusty', 'Only He (Has The Power To Move Me)', 'Pumping Iron', 'U.N.C.O.U.P.L.E.D', 'AC-DC', 'Right Place, Right Time', 'One Rock 'N' Roll Too Many', and 'Light At The End Of The Tunnel'. The show proved to be a consistently popular attraction, and, in April 1992, became the second longest-running British musical after *Cats*. Later in the year the production was revised and re-choreographed, and five new songs added, before it resumed its record-breaking journey. One member of the new cast, Lon Satton, had played Poppa the old steam locomotive since the first night in 1984. *Starlight Express* was also reworked for its Broadway run which began in March 1987 and lasted for 761 performances. In September 1993, a 90 minute edition of the show opened at the Las Vegas Hilton, the first major legitimate production ever to play the US gambling capital.

STATE FAIR (FILM MUSICAL)

This warm-hearted, idealistic slice of Americana came to the screen in 1945 courtesy of producer William Perlberg and 20th Century-Fox. It contained the only score that Richard Rodgers and Oscar Hammerstein II wrote especially for a film, and Hammerstein also contributed the screenplay (based on the novel by Phil Stong) which was short on narrative and seemed to consist simply of a series of relationships. Abel Frake (Charles Winninger) and his wife Melissa (Fay Bainter) of Brunswick, Iowa, spend a few days at the state fair with their children, Margie (Jeanne Crain), Wayne (Dick Haymes), and Abel's temperamental boar, Blue Boy. By the time they return to their farm, Blue Boy has won the prestigious blue ribbon, Melissa's sour pickle and mincemeat have both gained first prize, Margie has fallen for a small-time (soon to be a Chicago columnist) newspaper reporter Pat Gilbert (Dana Andrews), and Wayne is serenading band singer Emily Edwards (Vivian Blaine) with 'It's A Grand Night For Singing' in the middle of the day. Blaine had two nice songs, 'That's For Me' and 'Isn't It Kinda Fun?', (with Haymes), but the best number in the score was the lovely 'It Might As Well Be Spring', which was introduced by Jeanne Crain (dubbed by Louanne Hogan) and went on to win the Oscar for best song. Other numbers were the celebratory 'Our State Fair' and 'All I Owe Ioway'. The film's charming and affectionate style extended to the supporting cast which contained many familiar faces including Donald Meek, Frank McHugh, Percy Kilbride, William Marshall, and Harry Morgan. Leon Shamroy photographed it beautifully in Technicolor, and the director, Walter Lang, captured the mood of the times perfectly. There had been a previous (non-musical) film of *State Fair* in 1933 starring Will Rogers and Janet Gaynor, and there was a further musical version in 1962. This featured Tom Ewell, Alice Faye, Pamela Tiffin, Bobby Darin, Pat Boone, Ann-Margret, and some additional songs with both music and lyrics by Richard Rodgers. The premiere of a new

stage version of *State Fair* took place at the Stevens Centre in Winston-Salem, North Carolina, in July 1992, and was later presented at the Long Beach Civic Light Opera. A Broadway production was expected early in 1996.

STATE FAIR (STAGE MUSICAL)

This stage adaptation of Richard Rodgers and Oscar Hammerstein II's much-loved film musical, *State Fair*, began its life in Winston-Salem, North Carolina, and Long Beach, California, in 1992. However, as it evolved, there were several fundamental changes in the creative process, and the revised production set out on its seven month pre-Broadway tour from Des Moines, Iowa, the setting of the original movie and the site of its opening in 1945. When *State Fair* opened at the Music Box Theatre in New York on 27 March 1996, it was rated a new musical because the story had never been presented on the Broadway stage. Tom Briggs and Louis Mattioli's fresh and witty book was based on the screenplay by Hammerstein and Phil Stong's novel, and told the familiar story of the Frake family who, all in their various ways, find happiness and contentment at the Iowa State Fair. Abel Frake (John Davidson) sees his hog win a ribbon, while his wife, Melissa (Kathryn Crosby), returns home with a cookery prize. As for their restless offspring, Margy (Andrea McArdle) falls for the up-and-coming (and fancy-dancing) newspaper reporter, Pat Gilbert (Scott Wise), and Wayne (Ben Wright) goes completely out of his depth with the sophisticated singer from the big city, Emily Arden (Donna McKechnie), before surfacing and settling for the charms of a more homely model. Also in featured roles were Jackie Angelescu, Peter Benson, J. Lee Flynn, Darren C. Ford, Newton R. Gilchrist, Charles Goff, Jacquiline Rohrbacker, and John Sloman. The show incorporated songs from both the 1945 film and the 1962 remake as well as lesser known works from other parts of the Rodgers and Hammerstein catalogue. From 1945 came 'Our State Fair', 'It Might As Well Be Spring', 'That's For Me', 'Isn't It Kinda Fun?', 'It's A Grand Night For Singing', 'All I Owe Ioway', while the much-derided 1962 screen version yielded 'More Than Just A Friend' which was written by Richard Rodgers alone. The remainder of the score consisted of fairly unfamiliar songs from various Rodgers and Hammerstein stage productions: 'That's The Way It Happens' (*Me And Juliet*), 'The Man I Used To Be' and 'The Next Time It Happens' (*Pipe Dream*), two songs cut from *Oklahoma!*, 'Boys And Girls Like You And Me' and 'When I Go Out Walking With My Baby', 'So Far' (from *Allegro*), and 'You Never Had It So Good' (cut from *Me And Juliet*). Oscar Hammerstein's son, James Hammerstein, directed with Randy Skinner who was also the choreographer. *State Fair* was welcomed by the critics for some excellent performances, plus its 'old fashioned simplicity' and 'crowd-pleasing charms', but in a Broadway season which was dominated by such radical productions as *Rent* and *Bring In 'Da Noise, Bring In 'Da Funk*, its folksy charm failed to appeal, and after receiving Tony Award nominations for best original score (with only the songs 'Driving At Night', 'You Never Had It So Good', 'When I Go Out Walking With My Baby', and 'Boys And Girls Like You And Me' eligible), and best featured actor in a musical (Scott Wise), it went rapidly downhill, closing after only three months. A completely different adaptation of *State Fair* was presented at the St. Louis Municipal Opera in 1969 starring Harriet and Ozzie Nelson in the roles taken in the current production by Davidson and Crosby.

STAY AWAY JOE

By the time this Elvis Presley vehicle appeared in 1968, it was abundantly clear his Hollywood treadmill had undermined his entire career. Only die-hard aficionados welcomed a plot wherein the singer portrayed a Native American rodeo rider who returns to his reservation to help fight unwanted federal interference. Only five songs were featured on the soundtrack. That two of them are entitled 'Stay Away' and 'Stay Away Joe' indicates the ambivalent attitude present in Presley's 60s' Hollywood work. Fortunately, *Stay Away Joe* was quickly eclipsed later in the year by the *Elvis* television special, which revived a too-long moribund artist.

STEEL PIER

One of the major disappointments of the 1996/7 Broadway season, *Steel Pier*, a new musical with a score by veterans John Kander and Fred Ebb, opened at the Richard Rodgers Theatre on 24 April 1997. It was set in Atlantic City's Steel Pier dance hall in 1933, when Depression-torn America was in the throes of marathon dancing mania. David Thompson's book for *Steel Pier* related the tale of Bill Kelly (Daniel McDonald), who has died in a plane crash. However, having won a contest for a date with Rita Racine (Karen Ziemba) just prior to the fatal accident, some kind divine authority has given him three weeks of 'extra life' so that he can collect his prize. Rita, who is known as 'Lindy's Lovebird', because she once kissed aviator Charles Lindbergh, is a dance marathon veteran. She - and Bill - could feasibly win the $2,000 jackpot, chiefly because Rita is married to the sleazy M.C., Mick Hamilton (Gregory Harrison), who arranges these things. Also involved in the high (and low) jinks are the tough and bawdy ex-logging camp cook, Shelby Stevens (Debra Monk), vaudeville hoofers Buddy and Bette Becker (Joel Blum and Valerie Wright), a country couple, Happy and Precious McGuire (Jim Newman and Kristin Chenoweth), and snooty Dora Foster (Alison Bevan), escorted by the personable ex-Olympic contender Johnny Adel (Timothy Warmen). Song highlights included Ziemba's captivating 'Willing To Ride', Debra Monk's raunchy burlesque number 'Everybody's Girl', the second act dream sequence, 'Leave The World Behind', featuring Hamilton, Ziemba and the Company, in which a covey of chorus girls strut their stuff on the wings of aircraft thousands of feet above the ground - reminiscent of the famous aerial ballet scene in the film *Flying Down To Rio*, Monk's wistful ballad 'Somebody Older', Ziemba with 'Running In Place', and the jaunty 'Second Chance' (Hamilton). Also in the score were 'A Powerful Thing', 'Everybody Dance', 'Montage I', 'Dance With Me'/'The Last Girl', 'Montage II', 'Lovebird', 'Montage III', 'Running In Place', 'Two Little Words', 'First You Dream', and 'Steel Pier', which reminded many of Kander and Ebb's title song for their 1966 masterpiece, *Cabaret*. Susan Stroman's dynamic and imaginative choreography was played out on Tony Walton's lightbulb-infested set, and the whole affair was directed with style by Scott Ellis. Mixed critical reaction, and the failure to win any of its 11 Tony Awards nominations (although it was voted Outstanding Musical in the Friends Of New York Theatre [FANY] Awards, 'the people's choice' of theatre kudos), resulted in *Steel Pier* being withdrawn on 28 June after 33 previews and 76 regular performances. Ironically, in 1975 another Kander and Ebb show, *Chicago*, had also received 11 nominations and lost them all - mostly to *A Chorus Line*. In 1997 however, the Broadway smash hit revival of *Chicago* won six Tonys.

STEELE, TOMMY

b. Thomas Hicks, 17 December 1936, Bermondsey, London, England. After serving as a merchant seaman, Hicks formed a skiffle trio called the Cavemen, with Lionel Bart and Mike Pratt, before being discovered by entrepreneur John Kennedy in the 2I's coffee bar in Soho, London. A name change to Tommy Steele followed, and after an appearance at London's Condor Club, the boy was introduced to manager Larry Parnes. From that point, his rise to stardom was meteoric. Using the old 'working-class boy makes good' angle, Kennedy launched the chirpy cockney in the unlikely setting of a debutante's ball. Class-conscious Fleet Street lapped up the idea of Steele as the 'Deb's delight' and took him to their hearts. His debut single, 'Rock With The Caveman', was an immediate Top 20 hit and although the follow-up, 'Doomsday Rock'/'Elevator Rock', failed to chart, the management was unfazed. Their confidence was rewarded when Steele hit number 1 in the UK charts with a cover version of Guy Mitchell's 'Singing The Blues' in January 1957. By this point, he was Britain's first and premier rock 'n' roll singer and, without resorting to sexual suggestiveness, provoked mass teenage hysteria unseen since the days of Johnnie Ray. At one stage, he had four songs in the Top 30, although he never restricted himself to pure rock 'n' roll. A minor role in the film *Kill Me Tomorrow* led to an autobiographical musical, *The Tommy Steele Story*, which also spawned a book of the same title. For a time, Steele combined the twin roles of rock 'n' roller and family entertainer, but his original persona faded towards the end of the 50s. Further movie success in *The Duke Wore Jeans* (1958) and *Tommy The Toreador* (1959) effectively redefined his image. His rocking days closed with cover versions of Ritchie Valens' 'Come On Let's Go' and Freddy Cannon's 'Tallahassee Lassie'. The decade ended with the novelty 'Little White Bull', after which it was farewell to rock 'n' roll.

After appearing on several variety bills during the late 50s, Steele sampled the 'legit' side of showbusiness in 1960 when he played Tony Lumpkin in *She Stoops To Conquer* at the Old Vic, and he was back in straight theatre again in 1969, in the role of Truffaldino in *The Servant Of Two Masters* at the Queen's Theatre. In the years between those two plays, he experienced some of the highlights of his career. In 1963, he starred as Arthur Kipps in the stage musical *Half A Sixpence*, which ran for 18 months in the West End before transferring to Broadway in 1965. Steele recreated the role in the 1967 film version. A year later, he appeared in another major musical movie, *Finian's Rainbow*, with Fred Astaire and Petula Clark. His other films included *Touch It Light*, *It's All Happening*, *The Happiest Millionaire* and *Where's Jack?*. In 1974, Steele made one of his rare television appearances in the autobiographical *My Life, My Song*, and appeared at the London Palladium in the musical *Hans Andersen*. He also starred in the revival three years later. In 1979/80 his one-man show was resident at London's Prince of Wales Theatre for a record 60 weeks - the Variety Club Of Great Britain made him their Entertainer Of The Year. He was also awarded the OBE. Steele was back at the Palladium again in 1983 and 1989, heading the cast of the highly popular *Singin' In The Rain*, which he also directed. In the latter capacity he tried - too late as it transpired - to save impresario Harold Fielding's *Ziegfeld* (1988) from becoming a spectacular flop. Fielding had originally cast Steele in *Half A Sixpence* some 25 years earlier. Off-stage in the 80s, Steele published a thriller called *The Final Run*, had one of his paintings exhibited at the Royal Academy, was commissioned by Liverpool City Council to fashion a bronze statue of 'Eleanor Rigby' as a tribute to the Beatles, and composed two musical pieces, 'A Portrait Of Pablo' and 'Rock Suite - An Elderly Person's Guide To Rock'. After *Hans Andersen* and *Singin' In The Rain*, the third, and least successful of Steele's stage adaptations of memorable musical movies, was *Some Like It Hot* (1992). A hybrid of Billy Wilder's classic film, and the Broadway stage musical *Sugar* (1972), it received derisory reviews ('The show's hero is Mr Steele's dentist'), and staggered along for three months in the West End on the strength of its star's undoubted box-office appeal. In 1993, Steele was presented with the Hans Andersen Award at the Danish Embassy in London, and two years later he received the Bernard Delfont Award from the Variety Club of Great Britain for his 'outstanding contribution to show business'. By that time, Tommy Steele was back on the road again with 'A Dazzling New Song & Dance Spectacular' entitled *What A Show!*.

● ALBUMS: *The Tommy Steele Stage Show* 10-inch album (Decca 1957)★★★, *The Tommy Steele Story* 10-inch album (Decca 1957)★★★★, *Stars Of 6.05* (Decca 1958)★★★, *The Duke Wore Jeans* film soundtrack (Decca 1958)★★, *Tommy The Toreador* film soundtrack (1959)★★★, *Light Up The Sky* (1959)★★★, stage cast *Cinderella* (1959)★★★, *Get Happy With Tommy* (Decca 1960)★★★, *It's All Happening* (Decca 1962)★★★, London stage cast *Half A Sixpence* (Decca 1963)★★★, *So This Is Broadway* (1964)★★★, *Everything's Coming Up Broadway* (1967)★★★, *The Happiest Millionaire* (1967)★★, *My Life My Song* (Buena Vista 1974)★★★, London stage cast *Hans Andersen* (Decca 1978)★★★, with Sally Ann Howes *Harold Fielding's Hans Andersen* (1985)★★★.

● COMPILATIONS: *The Happy World Of Tommy Steele* (Decca 1969)★★★, *The World Of Tommy Steele, Volume 2* (Decca 1971)★★★, *Focus On Tommy Steele* (Decca 1977)★★★, *The Family Album* (Ronco 1979)★★★, *The Tommy Steele Story* (Decca 1981)★★★, *20 Greatest Hits* (Spot 1983)★★★, *Tommy Steele And The Steelmen - The Rock 'N' Roll Years* (See For Miles 1988)★★★, *Very Best Of Tommy Steele* (Pickwick 1991)★★★, *The EP Collection* (See For Miles 1992)★★★, *Handful Of Songs* (1993)★★★.

● FILMS: *Kill Me Tomorrow* (1955), *The Tommy Steele Story* (1957), *The Duke Wore Jeans* (1959), *Light Up The Sky* (1959),

Tommy The Toreador (1960), *It's All Happening* (1962), *The Happiest Millionaire* (1967), *Half A Sixpence* (1967), *Finian's Rainbow* (1968), *Where's Jack?* (1969).

● FURTHER READING: *Tommy Steele: The Facts About A Teenage Idol And An Inside Picture Of Show Business*, John Kennedy.

STEELYARD BLUES

Although made several years after such classic 'outlaw' statements as *Easy Rider* or *Two Lane Blacktop*, this 1972 feature for Warner Brothers contains elements of anti-establishment rhetoric. Donald Sutherland starred as a mischievous ex-criminal and demolition derby driver, while Jane Fonda, at that point viewed as the scourge of US society, played a genial call-girl. Their exploits to bring an ageing Catolina flying boat out of disrepair and into working order forms the core of the plot while Sutherland's continued harassment of his brother, a district attorney, provides its mild 'protest' theme. Peter Boyle is memorable as their deranged accomplice and the presence of Howard Hesseman is the link between the film's visual and aural dimensions. Hesseman was formerly associated with two radical troupes, the San Francisco Mime Company and the Committee, both of which occasionally shared billings with rock groups in San Franciscan ballrooms. One such act, the Electric Flag, had already scored Peter Fonda's drug-orientated feature, *The Trip*, and its vocalist/songwriter, Nick Gravenites was commissioned to proved a soundtrack for *Steelyard Blues*. He in turn introduced former Electric Flag guitarist Mike Bloomfield to the project. Bloomfield's bluesy style added atmosphere to the film and the attendant album proved popular in its own right. Yet neither musician could capitalise on this success. Gravenites resumed live work and although Bloomfield did write music for other films, his services were confined to porn features.

STEINER, MAX

b. Maximilian Raoul Steiner, 10 May 1888, Vienna, Austria, d. 28 December 1971, Hollywood, California, USA. A composer and conductor for some 300 films, from the late 20s through to the 60s, Steiner was often called the leader in his field. He studied at the Imperial Academy Of Music in Vienna, and was awarded the Gold Medal. In his teens he wrote and conducted his own operetta before travelling to London in 1904, and conducting in music halls in England and on the Continent. He moved to the USA in 1914 and conducted on Broadway, for concert tours, and spent some time as chief orchestrator for the Harms music publishing house. Steiner joined RKO in Hollywood in 1929, a couple of years after the movies began to talk, and worked, uncredited on *Rio Rita*, a 'lavish musical Western', starring Bebe Daniels and John Boles. From then, until 1934, his name appears on the titles of over 80 productions, mostly as the composer of the background music. They included *Check And Double Check* (film debut of Amos 'n' Andy), *Cimarron*, *Beau Ideal*, *A Bill Of Divorcement*, *The Half Naked Truth*, *The Lost Squadron*, *Little Women* and *Morning Glory*, both starring the young Katharine Hepburn, and *King Kong* 'the greatest monster movie of all'. In 1934, Steiner was nominated for an Academy Award for his score to *The Lost Patrol*, and, in the following year, won the Oscar for his work on John Ford's *The Informer*. His other scores in 30s included *Of Human Bondage*, *Alice Adams* (Hepburn again), *The Charge Of The Light Brigade*, (1936, Steiner's first, in a long series of films for Warner Brothers), *A Star Is Born* (1937), *The Garden Of Allah*, *The Life Of Emile Zola*, *Tovarich*, *Jezebel*, *The Adventures Of Tom Sawyer*, *Crime School*, *The Amazing Dr Clitterhouse*, *Four Daughters*, *The Sisters*, *Angels With Dirty Faces*, *The Dawn Patrol*, *The Oklahoma Kid*, *Dark Victory*, *We Are Not Alone*, and *Gone With The Wind*. Steiner's memorable score for the latter film included the haunting 'Tara's Theme', which became a hit for Leroy Holmes and his Orchestra, and as 'My Own True Love' with a lyric by Mack David, for Johnny Desmond as well.

During the 30s, Steiner also served as musical director on several classic RKO Fred Astaire-Ginger Rogers musicals, such as *The Gay Divorcee*, *Follow The Fleet*, *Roberta*, and *Top Hat*. In the 40s, especially during the years of World War II, Steiner scored some of the most fondly remembered films in the history of the cinema, such as *Now Voyager* (1942, Steiner's second Academy Award), which included the persuasive theme, 'It Can't Be Wrong' (lyric Kim Gannon, a smash hit for Dick Haymes), *Casablanca*, *The Corn Is Green*, *Johnny Belinda*, and *The Letter*. Other significant 40s films for which Steiner provided the music were *All This And Heaven Too*, *Sergeant York*, *They Died With Their Boots On*, *In This Our Life*, *Desperate Journey*, *Mission To Moscow*, *Watch On The Rhine*, *Passage To Marseilles* (including 'Someday I'll Meet You Again'), *The Adventures Of Mark Twain*, *Since You Went Away* (1944, starring Claudette Colbert and Joseph Cotton - Steiner's third Academy Award), *Arsenic And Old Lace*, *The Conspirators*, *Mildred Pearce*, *Saratoga Trunk* (including 'As Long As I Live'), *The Big Sleep*, *My Wild Irish Rose*, *Life With Father*, *The Treasure Of The Sierra Madre*, *Key Largo*, *The Adventures Of Don Juan*, and *White Heat* (1949). In 1950, Steiner received another of his 22 Academy Award nominations for his work on *The Flame And The Arrow*, starring Burt Lancaster, and, in the same year, he scored Tennessee Williams' *The Glass Menagerie*, with the vivacious UK musical comedy star Gertrude Lawrence. His other 50s film music included *Operation Pacific*, *On Moonlight Bay*, *The Miracle Of Our Lady Fatima*, *The Jazz Singer*, *By The Light Of The Silvery Moon*, *The Caine Mutiny*, *Battle Cry* (including 'Honey-Babe'), *Marjorie Morningstar*, *The F.B.I. Story*, and *A Summer Place* (1959, the theme was a US hit for Percy Faith and his Orchestra, and, with a lyric by Mack Discant, for the Lettermen in 1965). Even though he was over 70, Steiner continued to work into the 60s on such movies as *The Dark At The Top Of The Stairs*, *Spencer's Mountain*, *Youngblood Hawk*, and *Two On A Guillotine*, although demand for his kind of romantic, powerful, yet tender, background music had declined. His contributions to television included the theme music for the popular *Perry Mason* series which starred Raymond Burr.

● ALBUMS: *Now Voyager - The Classic Film Scores Of Max Steiner* (RCA 1973)★★★★, *King Kong* (1980)★★★, *Revisited* (1988)★★★★.

STEPPIN' OUT

Lyndall Hobbs directed, and appeared in, this 1979 short which was based around concurrent London teen sub-cultures. Roller disco enthusiasts, punks and mods are presented in favoured haunts with music provided by a variety of acts including Ian Dury And The Blockheads, Bryan Ferry, Sylvester and the Who. Two Mod revival groups are featured live in-concert, the Merton Parkas ('You Need Wheels'), and Secret Affair ('Time For Action'). However, as both punk and disco were better-served elsewhere, any laurels *Steppin' Out* possesses rests on the questionable contributions of these short-lived bands.

STEPT, SAM

b. Samuel H. Stept, 18 September 1897, Odessa, Russia, d. 1 December 1964, Los Angeles, California, USA. A popular composer during the 30s and 40s, Stept was taken to the USA in 1900 and grew up in Pittsburgh, Pennsylvania. After playing the piano for a local music publishing house, he served as an accompanist in vaudeville for artists such as Mae West, Ann Chandler and Jack Norworth, and then led a dance band in Cleveland, Ohio, in the early 20s. A few years later he started composing, and in 1928, in collaboration with Bud Green, had a big hit with 'That's My Weakness Now', which Helen Kane made into one of her special numbers. It was featured in Rouben Mamoulian's critically acclaimed movie *Applause* (1929), and has since become a standard. During the late 20s and early 30s, Stept and Green combined on several songs for films, including 'Love Is A Dreamer', 'For The Likes O' You And Me', 'When They Sing "The Wearing Of The Green" In Syncopated Blues' (all from *Lucky In Love*), 'The World Is Yours and Mine' (*Mother's Boy*), 'There's A Tear For Every Smile In Hollywood' (*Showgirl*), and 'Tomorrow Is Another Day' and 'Liza Lee' (*Big Boy*). With Green and Herman Ruby, Stept contributed 'Do Something' and 'I'll Always Be In Love With You' to the RKO backstage movie *Syncopation* (1929).

During the 30s his other compositions included 'Congratulations', 'Please Don't Talk About Me When I'm Gone' (popular for Gene Austin and later, Johnnie Ray), 'I Beg Your Pardon', 'Mademoiselle', 'London On A Rainy Night', 'I'm Painting The Town Red', 'Tiny Little Fingerprints' and 'My First Impression Of You'. He also wrote songs for films with Sidney Mitchell, such as 'All My Life', 'Laughing Irish Eyes' (title track); 'Recollections Of Love' (*Dancing Feet*), and 'How Am I Doin' With You?' (*Sitting On The Moon*). Stept's other collaborators around this time included Ted Koehler, with whom he wrote 'We've Come A Long Way Together' (*Hullabaloo*), and 'Goodnight My Lucky Day', 'We Happen To Be In The Army', 'Now You're Talking My Language', and 'It Must Be Love' (all from *23 And 1/2 Hours To Leave*). Stept also worked with Sidney Mitchell on 'All My Life' (*Johnny Doughboy*) and 'And Then' (*Twilight On The Prairie*); Ned Washington for 'Sweet Heartache' (*Hit Parade*); and Charles Newman on 'The Answer Is Love' (*That's Right - You're Wrong*). For 30s stage shows Stept wrote 'Swing Little Thingy' (with Bud Green) for *Shady Lady*, 'So I Married The Girl' (with Herb Magidson) for *George White's*

Music Hall Varieties, and most of the songs, with Lew Brown and Charles Tobias, for the 1939 hit, *Yokel Boy*. The score included 'I Can't Afford To Dream', 'Let's Make Memories Tonight', and 'Comes Love'. *Yokel Boy* was filmed in 1942, with Eddie Foy Jnr in the title role. In the same year Stept, again with Brown and Tobias, wrote 'Don't Sit Under The Apple Tree' for the Andrews Sisters to sing in *Private Buckaroo*. The song became a big record hit for the Sisters, as well as Glenn Miller. Stept also contributed numbers to other early 40s movies such as *When Johnny Comes Marching Home* ('This Is Worth Fighting For', lyric by Eddie De Lange) and *Stars On Parade* ('When They Ask About You'). In the late 40s he was less active, but was still composing ballads such as 'I Was Here When You Left Me', and 'Next Time I Fall In Love'. He also contributed 'Yo Te Amo Mucho' to the movie *Holiday In Mexico* in 1946. In 1950, with Dan Shapiro, he wrote several numbers for the Broadway revue, *Michael Todd's Peep Show*, including 'We've Got What It Takes', and 'A Brand New Rainbow In The Sky'. After composing songs such as 'If You Should Leave Me', 'Star-Gazing' and 'Don't You Care A Little Bit About Me?' in the early 50s, Stept concentrated on his music publishing interests. In 1961 his 'Please Don't Talk About Me When I'm Gone' received a carefree rendering from Frank Sinatra on *Swing Along With Me*, the singer's second album for Reprise.

STILES, GEORGE, AND ANTHONY DREWE

A leading songwriting team for the British theatre, composer George Stiles (b. 9 August 1961, Sussex, England) and lyricist Anthony Drewe (b. 22 March 1961, Berkshire, England), first met when they were students at Exeter University in 1980. After graduating (George in Music, Anthony in Zoology), they wrote their first show together, *Tutankhamun*, which was based on the discovery of the Boy-King's tomb. It was well received at the Northcott Theatre on the University campus, and later in a spectacular concert version at the Imagination Building in London. Stiles and Drewe first came to notice in 1985, when their musical, *Just So*, inspired by Rudyard Kipling's *Just So* stories, won the final of that year's Vivian Ellis Awards. With encouragement and financial support from producer Cameron Mackintosh, *Just So* was subsequently presented at the Watermill Theatre, Newbury, the Tricycle Theatre, London, and had its American premiere in November 1998 at the Norma Terris Theatre, Goodspeed-at-Chester, Connecticut. Stiles and Drewe's next musical began its life in 1993 as *The Ugly Duckling, (Or The Aesthetically Challenged Farmyard Fowl)*. Based on Hans Andersen's tale of *The Ugly Duckling*, it had changed its name to *Honk!* by the time it reached the Stephen Joseph Theatre, Scarborough, two years later. The team were then commissioned to write the score for (yet another) new musical version of *Peter Pan* ('Just Beyond The Stars', 'Neverland', 'Good Old Captain Hook', 'The Lost Boys'), with bookwriter Willis Hall. It won Best Song (Hook's *tour de force*, 'When I Kill Peter Pan') and the Orchestra's Prize at the 1996 Musical Of The Year awards in Denmark. Second place in the competition went to *The Three Musketeers* ('Lilacs', 'Any Day', 'The Life Of A Musketeer', 'Riding To Paris', 'The Challenge'), a collaboration between Stiles, Paul Leigh, and Peter Raby. Stiles and Leigh had collaborated earlier on Clare Luckham's adaptation of the Daniel Defoe novel, *Moll Flanders*, for which Stiles used *The Beggar's Opera* as the source of his tunes. When the production played the Lyric Theatre, Hammersmith, in 1993, leading cast members included Josie Lawrence, Issy Van Randwyck, Angela Richards, Peter Woodward, and Darryl Knock. It won the 1995 Martini TMA for Best Musical, and Stiles and Leigh worked together again on another time-honoured eighteenth-century classic, Henry Fielding's bawdy, satirical novel, *Tom Jones*, which premiered in 1996. In the same year Stiles composed the music for *Habeas Corpus*, which Sam Mendes directed at the Donmar Warehouse. Drewe's work apart from Stiles has involved him in writing lyrics for the 1992 revival of *The Card*, the musical which had a score by Tony Hatch and Jackie Trent when it played the West End in 1973, and for *The Canterville Ghost* (with James McConnell, co-winner of the Vivian Ellis Awards in 1987). He has also appeared in *Rogues To Riches*, a musical version of *The Beau Stratagem*, written and starred in the murder mystery musical, *A Twist Of Fate* (Singapore Repertory Theatre, Raffles Hotel, 1997 and 1998), and directed revivals of *Snoopy* (Watermill) and *Cowardy Custard* (Royal Academy of Music). Stiles and Drewe took their own show to the Edinburgh Fringe in 1987, and have since appeared on many television and radio programmes. They also created and starred in two revues, *Navel Fluff And Other Trivial Pursuits* and *Warts And All*, and contributed material to the RSC's *Shakespeare Revue*.

STILGOE, RICHARD

b. 28 March 1943, Camberley, Surrey, England. Now known as a television presenter and entertainer, Richard Stilgoe came into showbusiness via the Cambridge Footlights. He also played piano in a 60s beat group called Tony Snow And The Blizzards. Arriving at the BBC in the 70s, he appeared regularly on shows such as *A Class By Himself*, *Nationwide*, *That's Life*, and *Stilgoe's Around*, often performing a self-written, highly topical little ditty. Extremely talented - he plays 14 instruments and sings in opera - Stilgoe broke new ground in the 80s when he teamed up with composer Andrew Lloyd Webber, and wrote the lyrics for the hit musical *Starlight Express*, and contributed additional lyrics to *Cats* and *The Phantom Of The Opera*. In 1985, he joined Peter Skellern for *Stilgoe And Skellern Stompin' At The Savoy*, a show in aid of The Lords Taverners charity organization. This led to the two entertainers working together on several successful tours, and in their two-man revue, *Who Plays Wins*, which was presented in the West End and New York. Stilgoe has also had his own BBC 1 children's series, and is a patron of the National Youth Music Theatre, for whom has written the words and music for *Bodywork*, a musical that takes place inside the human body. It had its premiere at the Brighton Festival in 1987. In 1991, Stilgoe was also devoting much of his time to a small forest which he is growing for the sole purpose of making musical instruments.

● ALBUMS: *Live Performance* (1977)★★★, *Bodywork* (1988)★★.

STILL CRAZY

The reviewer who described this British movie as 'The Full Monty meets This Is Spinal Tap', got it just about right. There are elements of both in this tale of Strange Fruit, the rock band that called it a day in the late 70s. More than two decades later, keyboard player Tony Costello (Stephen Rea) succeeds in getting most of the guys together again, including guitarist Les Wickes (Jimmy Nail), tax-dodging drummer Beano Baggot (Timothy Spall), and Hughie the roadie (Billy Connolly). Luke Shand (Hans Matheson) has to be recruited in place of the other guitarist, Brian Lovell (Bruce Robinson), who is missing, presumed dead, but vocalist Ray Simms (Bill Nighy), whose mental facilities have declined somewhat, not necessarily because he is now married to a Swedish ex-groupie Astrid Simms (Helena Bergström), also embarks on the band's tour of Holland. Naturally (and hilariously), old tensions and ego problems surface between these ageing lotharios, but everything gets sorted out in time for the comeback concert when the lads are joined on stage by their surprisingly fit former guitarist Brian. He has been tracked down by PA Karen Knowles (Juliet Aubrey), after she discovers that his British royalties have been paid into a cancer foundation. By general consent, the best thing in the film is the permanently exhausted Nighy, who seems to be almost out of it for most of the time. If he shouts, 'Hello Holland!', you can be sure you're in Belgium. Nighy and Nail shared most of the vocal work, on numbers such as 'What Might Have Been', 'The Flame Still Burns', 'Scream Freedom', 'All Over The World', 'Bird On A Wire', 'Dangerous Things', 'Dirty Town', and 'Black Moon'. 'A Woman Like That' (performed by Bernie Marsden), 'Stealin' (arranged and performed by Billy Connolly), and 'Live For Today' (Hans Matheson), made up the remainder of the score. Screenwriters Dick Clement and Ian La Frenais (Auf Wiedersehen, Pet, Porridge) wrote the screenplay, and the director was Brian Gibson. Released in 1998, Still Crazy attracted some criticism because its production was aided by well over £1 million of National Lottery money.

STOP THE WORLD - I WANT TO GET OFF

This fresh, novel - some say unique - entertainment, with book music and lyrics by the new team of Anthony Newley and Leslie Bricusse, opened at the Queen's Theatre in London on 20 July 1961. Newley also directed, and played the leading role of Littlechap whose travels through the Seven Ages of Man - from factory teaboy to an Earldom - inevitably end in disillusionment. After taking the first step by marrying his boss's daughter, Evie (Anna Quayle), Littlechap's rise to fame and power is swift. His new life-style brings him into contact with other women (all played by Quayle), including an athletic Russian, Anya ('I will come to your room at two o'clock. Please be ready - I'm playing football at half past'), the American nightclub singer Ginnie, and Ilse, an au pair from Germany. He is unable to find true happiness for himself and his family, or father the son he constantly yearns for. All the action took place on a set designed by Sean Kenny, which resembled a section of a circus tent with bare planks representing the seating. Newley, dressed like a clown with white face, and wearing baggy pants held up by big braces, sang the show's three big numbers, 'Gonna Build A Mountain', 'Once In A Lifetime', and 'What Kind Of Fool Am I?', and he also had the amusing 'Lumbered', and a lovely ballad, 'Someone Nice Like You'. The score also included 'I Wanna Be Rich', 'Glorious Russia', 'Meilinki Meilchick', 'Typische Deutsche', 'Nag Nag Nag', 'All-American', and 'Mumbo Jumbo'. The London run of 556 performances was followed by an almost identical stay in New York, where Anna Quayle won a Tony Award, but Newley was beaten by Zero Mostel's bravura performance in A Funny Thing Happened On The Way To The Forum. Sammy Davis Jnr., who had a hit with 'What Kind Of Fool Am I?' in the US and UK, starred in a revised revival of the show on Broadway in 1978, and Newley recreated his original role in a 1989 West End production which lasted for five weeks and reportedly lost £600,000. There have been two unsuccessful film versions: in 1966 with Tony Tanner and Millicent Martin; and a 1979 'disaster' entitled Sammy Stops The World, with Sammy Davis Jnr. and Marian Mercer.

STORMY WEATHER

Hollywood being what it was then, director Andrew Stone led an almost 'all-white' team behind the cameras for this otherwise 'all-black' musical. Never mind the routine and rather trite backstage storyline, the cast is superb. Led by Bill 'Bojangles' Robinson and Lena Horne, they romp through some magnificent musical numbers including spots by Cab Calloway and his Orchestra, including Shad Collins, Illinois Jacquet and J.C. Heard, Katharine Dunham and her dancers, and the fabulous Nicholas Brothers. For all this remarkable talent, however, the show is stolen by Fats Waller. In addition to acting in a couple of scenes he and an all-star band, including Slam Stewart, Benny Carter, the film's musical director (and the only black person in an off-camera role), and Zutty Singleton, the band's nominal leader, back Ada Brown for one number and are featured in two: 'Ain't Misbehavin'' and 'Moppin' And Boppin''. It was while returning east from Hollywood after appearing in this film that Waller died. Adding to this 1943 film's many marvels is the fact that at the time of its making, Robinson, who was born around 1873, was long past his youthful prime.

STORY OF VERNON AND IRENE CASTLE, THE

All good things must come to an end, and this picture, which was released in 1939, was Fred Astaire and Ginger Rogers' last for RKO, although they reunited for MGM's The Barkleys Of Broadway some 10 years later. The 'Barkleys' were a product of writers Betty Comden and Adolph Green's fertile imagination, but Vernon and Irene Castle were the famous real-life dance team who became all the rage in America during World War I. The screenplay, by Richard Sherman, Oscar Hammerstein II, and Dorothy Yost, traced the couple's tremendously successful career from their first meeting until Vernon's tragic death in an aircraft training accident in 1918. There was only one new song in the film's score, the charming 'Only When You're In My Arms', by Harry Ruby, Con Conrad and Bert Kalmar. The remainder consisted of carefully selected numbers from the dancing duo's heyday, and included several of their specialities such as 'Too Much Mustard (Castle Walk)', 'Rose Room (Castle Tango)', 'Little Brown Jug (Castle Polka)', 'Dengoza (Maxixe)', 'When They Were Dancing Around', 'Pretty Baby (Trés Jolie)', 'Millicent Waltz', 'Night Of Gladness', 'Missouri Waltz', and numerous other memories of bygone days. Astaire and Rogers excelled, especially in the ballroom dancing sequences, and Edna May Oliver as the couple's agent, was also outstanding. However, the sight of Fred Astaire dying in a film was not most people's idea of fun, and the film reportedly lost some $50,000 dollars. Ever-present dance director Hermes Pan was still there at the end, but producer Pandro S. Berman and director Mark Sandrich, who had contributed so much to the historic series, were replaced this time by George Haight and H.C. Potter. As one legendary dance team (Fred Astaire and Ginger Rogers) portrayed another (Vernon and Irene Castle), one half of a future highly talented duo was waiting to pick up the torch. Marge Belcher (later Marge Champion), who danced so delightfully with her husband Gower Champion in films such as *Show Boat* (1951), had a small part in *The Story Of Vernon And Irene Castle*.

STOTHART, HERBERT

b. 11 September 1885, Milwaukee, Wisconsin, USA, d. 1 February 1949, Los Angeles, California, USA. A composer for the musical stage in the 20s, Stothart subsequently became a legendary name at MGM Pictures for his work on the background music to numerous Hollywood classics. After studying music in Europe and spending some time teaching in the USA, he made his composing debut on Broadway in 1920 with *Always You*. His lyricist was Oscar Hammerstein II, who was also making his Broadway bow. *Always You* was presented by Oscar's uncle, Arthur Hammerstein, and he produced most of Stothart's subsequent stage works, including *Tickle Me* (lyrics: Hammerstein-Otto Harbach) and *Jimmie* (Hammerstein-Harbach), both of which also opened in New York in 1920. Up to this point, and for *Daffy Dill* (1922, Hammerstein), Stothart served as sole composer, but thereafter he generally worked in collaboration with others. In some cases it is difficult to be certain which composer was responsible for each individual song, although it would seem that in most instances Stothart wrote the least popular numbers. In 1923, he teamed with the up-and-coming Vincent Youmans for the immensely successful (477 performances) *Wildflower* (Hammerstein-Harbach) and *Mary Jane McKane* (William Cary Duncan-Hammerstein) A year later, as well as contributing to the popular revue, *Vogues Of 1924* (Clifford Grey), Stothart worked alongside two of the most accomplished composers of operettas, Sigmund Romberg and Rudolph Friml, for *Marjorie* (Romberg-Grey, 'You're Never Too Old To Learn', 'Twilight Rose', 'Happy Ending') and *Rose-Marie* (Friml-Harbach-Hammerstein, 'Hard-Boiled Herman', 'The Mounties', 'Totem Tom-Tom', 'Only A Kiss'). The latter show starred Mary Ellis and Dennis King, and ran for 557 performances on Broadway, and over two years at London's Theatre Royal, Drury Lane, with Edith Day and Derek Oldham in the leading roles. Following the triumph of *Rose-Marie*, Stothart's composing partners in the late 20s included George Gershwin for *Song Of The Flame* (1925, Harbach-Hammerstein, 'Cossak Love Song', 'Far Away', 'Vodka', 'Song Of The Flame'), and Emmerich Kalman for *Golden Dawn* (1927, Harbach-Hammerstein, 'Dawn', 'When I Crack My Whip', 'We Two'). In 1928, his collaboration with lyricist Bert Kalmar and composer Harry Ruby on *Good Boy*, produced the catchy 'I Wanna Be Loved By You', which was introduced by the 'boop-boop-a-doop' girl, Helen Kane, and memorably revived by Marilyn Monroe in the 1959 Billy Wilder comedy movie, *Some Like It Hot*.

Apart from some involvement in *Polly* (1929), Stothart's Broadway career was at an end, and he turned his attention to Hollywood, writing single songs or scores for musical movies such as *Devil May Care* (1929, Clifford Grey, 'Bon Jour', 'Charming', 'March Of The Old Guard', 'Louie'), *The Rogue Song* (1930, Grey, 'When I'm Looking At You', 'The Rogue Song', 'Song Of The Shirt'), *Montana Moon* (1930, Grey, 'Montana Call', 'Let Me Give You Love', starring Joan Crawford), *The Floradora Girl* (1930, Grey, 'Pass The Beer And Pretzels', 'Swingin' In The Lane', 'My Kind Of Man'), *Call Of The Flesh* (1930, Grey), *Madame Satan* (1930, Grey), *The Cuban Love Song* (1931, Dorothy Fields-Jimmy McHugh, 'Cuban Love Song'), *Here Comes The Band* (1935, Ned Washington, 'Heading Home'), *Balalaika* (1939, Eric Maschwitz-Robert Wright-George Forrest, 'At The Balalaika'), *I Married An Angel* (1942, Wright-Forrest, 'But What Of Truth?'), *Music For Millions* (1944, Helen Deutsch, 'Summer Holidays'). For the 1937 film version of the stage hit, *The Firefly*, Stothart arranged Rudolph Friml's lovely melody, 'Chansonette', which, with a lyric by Robert Wright and George Forrest, became 'The Donkey Serenade'. It was sung in the movie by Allan Jones, and is usually interpolated into revivals of the original show. Stothart also contributed numbers to films that were not strictly speaking musicals, such as the delightful 'Sweetheart, Darling' (Gus Kahn) from *Peg O' My Heart* (1933) and 'How Strange' (Kahn-Earl Brent) from the Clark Gable-Norma Shearer feature *Idiot's Delight* (1939).

However, the bulk of Stothart's work at MGM, which he continued until shortly before his death in 1949, was as composer and/or arranger, conductor, and musical director for more than 100 background scores. Several of these were nominated for Academy Awards, including *Mutiny On the Bounty* (1935), *Maytime* (1937), *Marie Antoinette* (1938), *Sweethearts* (1938), *Waterloo Bridge* (1940), *The Chocolate Soldier* (1941), *Random Harvest* (1942), *Thousands Cheer* (1944), *Madame Curie* (1944), *Kismet* (1944), and *The Valley Of Decision* (1945), while his original score for *The Wizard Of Oz* won the Oscar in 1939. Among the rest were *Rasputin And The Empress* (1932), *Night Flight* (1933), *The Barretts Of Wimpole Street* (1934), *The Merry Widow* (1934), *Chained* (1934), *A Night At The Opera* (1935), *A Tale Of Two Cities* (1935), *David Copperfield* (1935), *Naughty Marietta* (1935), *China Seas* (1935), *Ah! Wilderness* (1935), *San Francisco* (1936), *Romeo And Juliet* (1936), *After The Thin Man* (1937, with Edward Ward), *The Gorgeous Hussy* (1936), *The Good Earth* (1937), *The Girl Of The Golden West* (1938), *Northwest Passage*

(1940), *Pride And Prejudice* (1940), *Blossoms In The Dust* (1941), *Ziegfeld Girl* (1941), *Rio Rita* (1942), *Mrs. Miniver* (1942), *Cairo* (1942), *The Human Comedy* (1943), *A Guy Named Joe* (1944), *The White Cliffs Of Dover* (1944), *Thirty Seconds Over Tokyo* (1945), *National Velvet* (1945), *The Picture Of Dorian Gray* (1945, with Mario Castelnuovo-Tedesco), *They Were Expendable* (1945), *Undercurrent* (1946), *The Yearling* (1947), *The Three Musketeers* (1948, based on music by Tchaikovsky), *Hills Of Home* (1948), and *Big Jack* (1949).

STOWAWAY

Alice Faye had the two best songs, Mack Gordon and Harry Revel's 'Goodnight My Love' and 'One Never Knows, Does One?', but it was Shirley Temple's picture - clutching a pooch- that appeared on the sheet music for both numbers. Actually, she does flirt with 'Goodnight My Love' in the film - but not to any great effect. As usual, she plays her 'orphan of the storm' character, this time accidentally stowing away on a luxury yacht out of Shanghai. During the voyage, millionaire playboy Robert Young takes such a shine to her that he actually marries fellow passenger Alice Faye so that he can adopt the little darling - although the impression is given that the nuptials would probably have taken place anyway, even if the curly-headed one had not been around. Naturally, she speaks Chinese fluently, although best wishes such as 'May the bird of prosperity continue to nest in your rooftop' are purveyed in English. When the ship reaches Hong Kong she becomes involved in a kind of Oriental talent contest, taking off Al Jolson and Ginger Rogers (complete with Fred Astaire dummy) while singing 'You've Gotta S-M-I-L-E If You Want To Be H-A-Double P-Y'. It all ends in suitably sentimental style around the festive tree as Shirley gives forth with 'That's What I Want For Christmas' (Irving Caesar-Gerald Marks). Also involved in the shenanigans are Eugene Pallette, Helen Westley, Arthur Treacher, J. Edward Bromberg, Allan Lane, Astrid Allwyn, and Jayne Regan. William Conselman, Arthur Sheekam, and Nat Perrin wrote the screenplay from a story by Samuel G. Engel, and director William A Seiter kept it all moving along at good pace. Darryl F. Zanuck was in charge of production (executive producers Earl Carroll and Harold Wilson) and Arthur Miller photographed the film splendidly in black and white. It was released by 20th Century-Fox in 1936, and went on to become one of the year's biggest money-spinners.

STRACHEY, JACK

b. 25 September 1894, London, England, d. 27 May 1972, London, England. A composer for the London stage from the mid-20s through to the late 40s, Strachey was responsible for writing the music for two all-time great British popular songs. Educated at Marlborough and Oxford University, he played the piano with various concert parties, touring around the country, before contributing to the first of what turned out to be an extensive series of West End revues. These included *The Punch Bowl* and *Charlot's Revue* (both 1924), *Shake Your Feet* (1927), *Moonshine* (1940), *Apple Sauce* (1941), *Flying Colours* (1941), *The Boltons Revue* (1948). One of Strachey's num-

bers from *The Boltons Revue*, 'No Orchids For My Lady' (with Alan Stranks), was played and sung a good deal on both sides of the Atlantic, and received an impressive reading from Frank Sinatra, while in the 1936 revue *Spread It Abroad*, Dorothy Dickson introduced the wistful 'These Foolish Things' (written with Eric Maschwitz and Harry Link). Four years later, another classic Strachey ballad, 'A Nightingale Sang In Berkeley Square' (Maschwitz-Manning Sherwin), emerged from *New Faces*. The last two numbers were particularly successful at the time for the cabaret entertainer Leslie 'Hutch' Hutchinson, as well as Ray Noble, Glenn Miller, Anne Shelton with the Ambrose Orchestra, Carroll Gibbons And The Savoy Orpheans with a vocal by Anne Lenner, and Dorothy Carless with Geraldo. It has since been recorded by a great many artists, in a variety of styles, over the years. Strachey also provided the music for a number of highly successful frothy musical comedies, such as *Dear Little Billie* (1925, H.B. Hedley-Desmond Carter), *Lady Luck* (1927, Hedley-Carter), *So This Is Love* (1928, 'Hal Brody'-Carter), *Love Lies* (1929, 'Hal Brody'-Stanley Lupino-Arthur Rigby), as well as the more romantically inclined *Belinda Fair* (1949, Maschwitz-Gilbert Lennox). The somewhat American-sounding title 'Hal Brody' was a collective *nom de plume* used for a time by Strachey, Hedley, Stanley Lupino and perhaps others, in order to give the impression of US involvement in a particular project. In the 60s, Strachey and Eric Maschwitz, his collaborator on those two memorable songs, served as Vice-Presidents of The Songwriters' Guild Of Great Britain.

STRAWBERRY STATEMENT, THE

A real life sit-in and subsequent riot by students at Columbia University inspired this 1970 film. The one-dimensional plot and pacing leaves no doubt as to where director Stuart Hagmann expects sympathies to fall, resulting in a feature which, while worthy, remains dull. Its graphic ending, wherein the forces of authority exact vengeance with billy-club and boot, while powerful, is clichéd. The soundtrack includes contributions from Buffy Sainte-Marie ('The Circle Game'), Thunderclap Newman ('Something In The Air') and Crosby, Stills Nash And Young ('Our House' and 'Helpless'). The same group, without Young, supply 'Long Time Gone' while two solo Neil Young songs, 'The Loner' and 'Down By The River', are also featured. Such quality music ensured that the soundtrack album, released by Reprise Records in the UK and US, enjoyed a popularity greater than the film itself.

STREISAND, BARBRA

b. 24 April 1942, New York City, New York, USA. A celebrated actress, singer, and film producer, from childhood Streisand was eager to make a career in show business, happily singing and 'playacting' for neighbours in Brooklyn, where she was born and raised. At the age of 15, she had a trial run with a theatrical company in upstate New York and by 1959, the year she graduated, was convinced that she could make a success of her chosen career. She still sang for fun, but was set on being a stage actress. The lack of opportunities in straight plays drove her to try singing instead and she entered and won a talent contest at The Lion, a gay bar in Greenwich Village. The prize was a booking at the club and this was followed by more club work, including an engagement at the Bon Soir which was later extended and established her as a fast-rising new singer. Appearances in off-Broadway revues followed, in which she acted and sang. Towards the end of 1961 she was cast in *I Can Get It For You Wholesale*, a musical play with songs by Harold Rome. The show was only moderately successful but Streisand's notices were excellent (as were those of another newcomer, Elliott Gould), and she regularly stopped the show with 'Miss Marmelstein'. She was invited to appear on an 'original cast' recording of the show, which was followed by another record session, to make an album of Rome's *Pins And Needles*, a show he had written 25 years earlier. The records and her Bon Soir appearances brought a television date, and in 1962, on the strength of these, she made her first album for Columbia Records. With arrangements by Peter Matz, who was also responsible for the charts used by Noël Coward at his 1955 Las Vegas appearance, the songs included 'Cry Me A River', 'Happy Days Are Here Again' and 'Who's Afraid Of The Big, Bad Wolf?'. Within two weeks of its release in February 1963, Streisand was the top-selling female vocalist in the USA. Two Grammy Awards followed, for Best Album and Best Female Vocalist (for 'Happy Days Are Here Again'). Streisand's career was now unstoppable.

She had more successful club appearances in 1963 and released another strong album, and then opened for Liberace at Las Vegas, and appeared at Los Angeles's Coconut Grove and the Hollywood Bowl. That same remarkable year she married Elliott Gould, and she was engaged to appear in the Broadway show *Funny Girl*. Based upon the life of Fanny Brice, *Funny Girl* had a troubled pre-production history, but once it opened it proved to have all the qualities its principal producer, Ray Stark, (who had nurtured the show for 10 years), believed it to have. Jule Styne and Bob Merrill wrote the score, which included amongst which were 'People' and 'Don't Rain On My Parade', the show was a massive success, running for 1,348 performances and giving Streisand cover stories in *Time* and *Life* magazines. Early in 1966 Streisand opened *Funny Girl* in London but the show's run was curtailed when she became pregnant. During the mid-60s she starred in a succession of popular and award-winning television spectaculars. Albums of the music from these shows were big-sellers and one included her first composition, 'Ma Premiere Chanson'. In 1967, she went to Hollywood to make the film version of *Funny Girl*, the original Styne-Merrill score being extended by the addition of some of the songs Fanny Brice had performed during her own Broadway career. These included 'Second-Hand Rose' and 'My Man'. In addition to *Funny Girl*, Streisand's film career included roles in *Hello, Dolly!* and *On A Clear Day You Can See Forever*. *Funny Girl* earned Streisand one of two Oscars awarded in 1968 for Best Actress (the other winner was Katharine Hepburn).

By the time she came to the set to make her second Hollywood film, *Hello, Dolly!* (1969), Streisand had developed an unenviable reputation as a meddlesome perfectionist who wanted, and usually succeeded in obtaining, control over every aspect of the films in which she appeared. Although in her later films, especially those which she produced, her demands seemed increasingly like self-indulgence, her perfectionism worked for her on the many albums and stage appearances which followed throughout the 70s. This next decade saw changes in Streisand's public persona and also in the films she worked on. Developing her childhood ambitions to act, she turned more and more to straight acting roles, leaving the songs for her record albums and television shows. Among her films of the 70s were *The Owl And The Pussycat* (1970), *What's Up, Doc?* (1972), *The Way We Were* (1973), *Funny Lady* (1975), a sequel to *Funny Girl*, and *A Star Is Born* (1976). For the latter she co-wrote (with Paul Williams) a song, 'Evergreen', which won an Oscar as Best Song. Streisand continued to make well-conceived and perfectly executed albums, most of which sold in large numbers. She even recorded a set of the more popular songs written by classical composers such as Debussy and Schumann.

Although her albums continued to attract favourable reviews and sell well, her films became open season for critics and were markedly less popular with fans. The shift became most noticeable after *A Star Is Born* was released and its damaging self-indulgence was apparent to all. Nevertheless, the film won admirers and several Golden Globe Awards. She had an unexpected number 1 hit in 1978 with 'You Don't Bring Me Flowers', a duet with Neil Diamond, and she also shared the microphone with Donna Summer on 'Enough Is Enough', a disco number which reached Platinum, and with Barry Gibb on the album, *Guilty*. Her film career continued into the early 80s with *All Night Long* (1981) and *Yentl*, (1983) which she co-produced and directed. By the mid-80s Streisand's career appeared to be on cruise. However, she starred in and wrote the music for *Nuts* (1987), a film which received mixed reviews. Growing concern for ecological matters revealed themselves in public statements and on such occasions as the recording of her 1986 video/album, *One Voice*. In 1991 she was criticized for another directorial assignment on *Prince Of Tides*. As a performer, Streisand was one of the greatest showbiz phenomenons of the 60s. Her wide vocal range and a voice which unusually blends sweetness with strength, helps make Streisand one of the outstanding dramatic singers in popular music. Her insistence upon perfection has meant that her many records are exemplars for other singers. Her 1991 movie, *Prince Of Tides*, which she also directed, was nominated for seven Oscars. Two years later, she was being talked of as a close confidante and advisor to the newly elected US President Clinton, although she still found the time to return - on record at least - to where it all started, when she released *Back To Broadway*. In November 1993 it was reported that the singer had given away her £10 million Californian estate 'in an attempt to save the earth'. The 26 acres of landscaped gardens with six houses and three swimming pools would become the Barbra Streisand Centre For Conservancy Studies. She recouped the money early in January 1994, by giving two 90-minute concerts at MGM's new Grand Hotel and theme park in Las Vegas for a reported fee of £13 million. Later in the year she received mixed critical reviews for the four British concerts she gave at Wembley Arena in the course of a world tour. Her share of the box-office receipts - with tickets at an all-time high of £260 - and expensive merchandise is reported to have been in the region of £5 million. In 1997 she duelled with Celine Dion on the hit single 'Tell Him' and released *Higher Ground*, her first studio album for four years.

● ALBUMS: *I Can Get It For You Wholesale* (Columbia 1962)★★, *Pins And Needles* (Columbia 1962)★★, *The Barbra Streisand Album* (Columbia 1962)★★★★, *The Second Barbra Streisand Album* (Columbia 1963)★★★★, *Barbra Streisand: The Third Album* (Columbia 1964)★★★★, *Funny Girl* (Columbia 1964)★★★★, *People* (Columbia 1964)★★★★, *My Name Is Barbra* (Columbia 1965)★★★★, *Color Me Barbra* (Columbia 1966)★★★★, *Je M'appelle Barbra* (Columbia 1966)★★★, *Simply Streisand* (Columbia 1967)★★★, *A Happening In Central Park* (Columbia 1968)★★, *What About Today* (Columbia 1969)★★, *Stoney End* (Columbia 1970)★★★★, *On A Clear Day You Can See Forever* (Columbia 1970)★★, *Barbra Joan Streisand* (Columbia 1971)★★★, *The Owl And The Pussycat* (Columbia 1971)★★, *Live Concert At The Forum* (Columbia 1972)★★★, *And Other Musical Instruments* (Columbia 1973)★★, *Classical Barbra* (Columbia 1974)★★★, *The Way We Were And All In Love Is Fair* (Columbia 1974)★★★★, *Butterfly* (Columbia 1975)★★★, *Lazy Afternoon* (Columbia 1975)★★★, *Funny Lady* (Arista 1975)★★★, *A Star Is Born* (Columbia 1976)★★★★, *Streisand Superman* (Columbia 1977)★★★★, *Songbird* (Columbia 1978)★★★★, *Wet* (Columbia 1979)★★★★, *Guilty* (Columbia 1980)★★★★, *Memories* (Columbia 1981)★★★, *A Christmas Album* (Columbia 1981)★★, *Yentl* film soundtrack (Columbia 1983)★★★★, *Emotion* (Columbia 1984)★★★, *The Broadway Album* (Columbia 1985)★★★★, *One Voice* (Columbia 1986)★★★★, *Nuts: Original Motion Picture Soundtrack* (1987)★★★, *Til I Loved You* (Columbia 1988)★★★★, *Just For The Record ...* (Columbia 1991)★★★, *The Prince Of Tides* film soundtrack (1991)★★★, *Back To Broadway* (Columbia 1993)★★★★, *The Concert* (Columbia 1994)★★★, *The Concert Highlights* (Columbia 1995)★★, *The Mirror Has Two Faces* film soundtrack (Columbia 1996)★★, *Higher Ground* (Columbia 1997)★★★★.

● COMPILATIONS: *Greatest Hits* (Columbia 1970)★★★, *Greatest Hits Volume 2* (Columbia 1982)★★★, *A Collection: Greatest Hits ... And More* (Columbia 1989)★★★.

● VIDEOS: *Barbra - The Concert* (Columbia 1994), *One Voice* (1994).

● FURTHER READING: *Barbra Streisand*, Patricia Mulrooney Eldred. *On Stage Barbra Streisand*, Debra Keenan. *Streisand: Unauthorized Biography*, Rene Jordan. *The Films Of Barbra Streisand*, David Castell. *Barbra Streisand: An Illustrated Biography*, Frank Brady. *Streisand: The Woman And The Legend*, James Spada. *Barbra: A Biography Of Barbra Streisand*, Donald Zec and Anthony Fowles. *Streisand Through The Lens*, Frank Teti and Karen Moline. *Barbra: The Second Decade*, Karen Swenson. *Barbra Streisand, The Woman, The Myth, The Music*, Shawn Considine. *Barbra: An Actress Who Sings*, James Kimbrell. *Barbra Streisand: A Biography*, Peter Carrick. *Barbra: An Actress Who Sings Volume II*, Cheri Kimbrell (ed.). *Her Name Is Barbra*, Randall Reise. *The Barbra Streisand Scrapbook*, Allison J. Waldman. *Streisand: The Intimate Biography*, James Spada.

● FILMS: *Funny Girl* (1968), *Hello Dolly* (1969), *On A Clear Day You Can See Forever* (1970), *The Owl And The Pussycat* (1970), *What's Up Doc?* (1972), *Up The Sandbox* (1972), *The Way We Were* (1973), *For Pete's Sake* (1974), *Funny Lady* (1975), *A Star Is Born* (1976), *The Main Event* (1979), *All Night Long* (1981), *Yentl* (1983), *Nuts* (1987), *The Mirror Has Two Faces* (1996).

STRICTLY BALLROOM

Made in Australia, this film was the hit of the 1992 Cannes Festival, and is probably the most enjoyable dance film to emerge since John Travolta strutted his extravagant stuff in *Saturday Night Fever* (1977). It was the brainchild of Baz Luhrmann who is better known 'down under' as the wunderkind of the Sydney Opera House. As director and screenwriter (with Craig Pearce), he presented the original 30 minute, and then 50 minute versions on stage before reshaping the concept for the screen. In this form it tells the story of Scott Hastings (Paul Mercurio) who has been preparing for the Australian Ballroom Dance Federation Championships since he was a young child. Having reached the semi-finals, he blows his chances by breaking the rules and improvising his own steps on the dance floor. This infuriates Scott's partner, Liz Holt (Gia Carides), and she walks away. Also fuming are his domineering mother, Shirley, and coach, Les Kendall (Pat Thompson and Peter Whitford), who together run the local dance school, and the powerful Federation President, Barry Fife (Bill Hunter). Out in the cold, Scott finds a new partner in Fran (Tara Morice), an unattractive beginner, and together, with the help of Fran's Spanish father and grandmother, they perfect a flamenco routine for the Pan-Pacific Grand Prix. As expected, it proves anathema to the judges, but the audience love the sequence and go wild, joining the couple - who by now are preparing to dance off into the sunset together - on the floor for a spectacular celebration. It is not quite as simple as that - there are darker aspects involving Scott's father, Doug (Barry Otto), who, it turns out, was quite an innovative dancer himself in the old days, a fact which led to his wife Shirley turning to the cosy safety of Les Kendall. Also among the cast were John Hannan, Sonia Kruger, Kris McQuade, Pip Munshin, Leonie Page, Antonio Vargas (as Fran's father, Rico), Armonia Benedito, Jack Webster, and Lauren Hewett. John 'Cha Cha' O'Connell was the choreographer and the music score was composed by musical director David Hirschfelder. The songs used ranged from 'Perhaps, Perhaps, Perhaps (Quizas, Quizas, Quizas)' (Osvaldo Farres), 'La Cumparsita' (Rodriguez Ravern), 'Espana Carne' (Pascual Narro-Marquina), and 'Rhumba De Burros' (Baz Luhrmann), to 'Time After Time' (Cyndi Lauper), 'Happy Feet' (Jack Yellen-Milton Ager), and 'Love Is In The Air' (Harry Vanda-George Young). It was beautifully photographed in Eastman Color by Steve Mason, and produced by Tristram Maill. This immensely likeable, charming and amusing film, with fine performances, especially from Scott Hastings, principal dancer and choreographer with the Sydney Dance Company, proved to be a box-office winner, not only in Australia, but worldwide.

STRIKE UP THE BAND

Regarded by some as having been ahead of its time, this somewhat bitter satirical spoof on war, big business, and politics in America at the time of the Depression, proved too much for the public to take first time round. In 1927, it closed during out-of-town tryouts, and only made Broadway in a revised and toned-down version some three years later. By the time the show opened at the Times Square Theatre on 14 January 1930, George S. Kaufman and his acerbic book about a 'cheese tariff' war between the US and the Swiss, had been replaced by Morrie Ryskind and a sweeter plot about chocolate. Nevertheless, it was still a radical departure from the usual 'moon and June' style of musical comedy, and paved the way for other more socially relevant shows such as *Of Thee I Sing*, *I'd Rather Be Right*, and *Let 'Em Eat Cake*. The comedy team of Bobby Clark and Paul McCullough led the cast, along with Blanche Ring, Jerry Goff, Dudley Clements, and Doris Carson. George and Ira Gershwin wrote the score which contained at least three enduring items: the rousing title song; 'Soon', which has received many memorable readings over the years, including one by Ella Fitzgerald on her tribute album to the composers; and 'I've Got A Crush On You', affectionately remembered in 1993 by Frank Sinatra and Barbra Streisand on the album *Duets*. The rest of the numbers, which included 'Madamoiselle In New Rochelle', 'Hanging Around With You', 'If I Became President', 'I Mean To Say', and the highly amusing 'A Typical Self-Made American', were played in fine style by Red Nichols Orchestra, whose personnel included Glenn Miller, Gene Krupa, Jimmy Dorsey, Jack Teagarden and Benny Goodman. Given the show's innovative and original approach, a run of 191 performances was probably as much as the producers could have expected.

Among the subsequent revivals was one in 1995 by the Goodspeed Opera House, Connecticut, which kept the 1927 book but incorporated elements of the 1930 score, and another three years later at the Barbican Centre, London. This latest Ian Marshall Fisher concert production was unadulterated - utilizing the book, songs, and original arrangements from the 1927 version - as part of the worldwide celebrations making the centenary of George Gershwin's birth.

STRIP, THE

A would-be jazz drummer, Mickey Rooney, fresh out of the army, tangles with criminals. Directed by Leslie Kardos in 1951, all is very predictable but the pleasures in this film centre upon the band he joins, no less than Louis Armstrong And His All Stars. To meet some Hollywood executive's misconceived ideas on racial integration, apart from Rooney, another white face appears on-screen in the band, behind the string bass. However, part of what you see and all of what you hear is the real All Stars back in the days when Armstrong's group truly merited the term: Jack Teagarden, Barney Bigard, Earl Hines, Arvell Shaw and William 'Cozy' Cole (the last two dubbing for their on-screen counterparts). Armstrong recorded one of the film's songs, 'A Kiss To Build A Dream On', which became a minor hit for him. He also sings 'Shadrack' and the band plays a handful of other 'good old good ones' including 'Ole Miss'/'Bugle Call Rag' which is a feature for Rooney/Cole. In some scenes without the band Rooney may have played drums himself, something at which he was rather good, although he was no Cozy Cole.

STRITCH, ELAINE

b. 2 February 1925, Detroit, Michigan, USA. An inimitable actress and singer with a magnetic appeal, who has combined a career in the musical theatre with another in drama, films and on television. Stritch has been called caustic, sardonic, witty, tough, and much else besides. She is said to have sung for the first time on stage in the Long Island revue *The Shape Of Things!*, in June 1947, and a few months later introduced 'Civilization (Bongo, Bongo, Bongo)' on Broadway in another revue, *Angels In The Wings*. Stritch subsequently understudied Ethel Merman in Irving Berlin's hit musical *Call Me Madam*, and played Merman's role of ambassador Sally Adams in the 1952/3 US tour. Also in 1952, she was Melba Snyder in a revival of *Pal Joey* at the Broadhurst Theatre, and gave a memorable reading of the amusing 'Zip'. During the remainder of the 50s, Stritch appeared on Broadway in the 1954 revival of *On Your Toes* (rendering a 'drop dead' version of the interpolated 'You Took Advantage Of Me') and with Don Ameche and Russell Nype in *Goldilocks* (1958). In 1961, she sang 'Why Do The Wrong People Travel?', amongst other songs, in Noël Coward's *Sail Away*, and in the following year went with the show to London. Although she starred as Vera Charles in the US tour of *Mame*, and appeared in a US television version of the legendary revue *Pins And Needles*, Stritch did not appear on Broadway again until *Company* (1970), the show which gave her cult status. The television programme documenting the agonies involved in recording its Original Cast album, particularly the sequence in which a weary Stritch struggles to lay down a Stephen Sondheim-pleasing version of 'The Ladies Who Lunch', proved to be riveting viewing, and was eventually released on videotape and laserdisc. After reprising her role for the 1972 London production of *Company*, Stritch lived in England for about 10 years, appearing in various plays, and co-starring with Donald Sinden in the top-rated television series *Two's Company*. In 1985, she returned in triumph to New York for the two-performance *Follies In Concert* at the Lincoln Center. She played Hattie, and very nearly stopped the show with her 'sensational' rendering of 'Broadway Baby'. In the early 90s, she was back at the Lincoln Center with the original cast of *Company* for benefit concerts, made her cabaret debut at New York's Rainbow & Stars, and played the role of Parthy in the 1994 Tony Award-winning revival of *Show Boat* on Broadway. Stritch was inducted into The Theatre Hall of Fame in 1995, and two years later made a rare working trip to London in order to join a host of stars celebrating Barbara Cook's 70th birthday at the Royal Albert Hall. In May 1998 she withdrew from the cast of Bob Kingdom's play *Elsa Edgar* at the Bay Street Theatre, Long Island, just a few hours before its scheduled opening. Stritch was to portray socialite Elsa Maxwell in the first act, and FBI director J. Edgar Hoover in the second.

● ALBUMS: *Stritch* re-released 1995 (Dolphin 1955)★★★, Original and Studio Cast recordings, and Painted Smiles *Revisited* albums.

● FILMS: *The Scarlet Hour* (1956), *Three Violent People* (1956), *A Farewell To Arms* (1957), *The Perfect Furlough* (1958), *Kiss Her*

Goodbye (1958), Who Killed Teddy Bear? (1965), Too Many Thieves (1966), Pigeons (1971), Providence (1977), September (1987), Cocoon: The Return (1988), Cadillac Man (1990), Out To Sea (1997), Krippendorf's Tribe (1998).

STROUSE, CHARLES

b. 7 June 1928, New York City, New York, USA. A composer who has experienced the sweet taste of Broadway success - but not for some considerable time. When Strouse graduated from the Eastman School of Music he intended to make a career in the classical field, and studied for a time with Aaron Copland. After meeting lyricist Lee Adams in 1949 he changed course, and during the early 50s they contributed songs to revues at the popular Green Mansions summer resort, and in 1956 they had some numbers interpolated into the Off Broadway shows The Littlest Revue and Shoestring '57. Their big break came in 1960 with Bye Bye Birdie, which is often cited as the first musical to acknowledge the existence of rock 'n' roll. It starred Dick Van Dyke and Chita Rivera and ran for 607 performances. The witty and tuneful score included 'Kids!', 'A Lot Of Livin' To Do', and 'Put On A Happy Face'. Ironically, two years earlier, Strouse, with Fred Tobias, had written a bona fide rock 'n' roll hit, 'Born Too Late', which the Poni-Tails took to number 7 in the US chart. As for Strouse and Adams' shows, All American (1962), a musical about college football, failed to score heavily, but Golden Boy (1964) lasted for 569 performances on the sheer strength of Sammy Davis Jnr.'s appeal. It's A Bird, It's A Plane, It's Superman (1966), which was based on the syndicated comic-strip, came down to earth with a bump after only 129 performances. It was four years before Strouse and Adams took off again with Applause, their second big hit which ran for over two years, and, like Golden Boy, had a gilt-edged box office star in Lauren Bacall. In 1971 Strouse wrote his own lyrics for Six - which ran for eight - performances, that is, Off Broadway. The composer collaborated once again with Adams for I And Albert in 1972 - presented in London only - but audiences there were definitely not amused. Strouse's hit-of-a-lifetime came five years later - but not in collaboration with Lee Adams. Martin Charnin provided the lyrics for another Strouse show that was based, like It's A Bird, It's A Plane, on a comic-strip - in this case Little Orphan Annie. Together with librettist Thomas Meehan they turned it into Annie (1977), the hottest Broadway ticket of the 70s which ran for 2,377 performances. Since then, over a period of some 15 years, Strouse has had a string of flops - and some real beauties at that: A Broadway Musical (one performance), Flowers For Algernon (London 28 performances) - adapted for New York as Charley And Algernon (17), Bring Back Birdie (four), Dance A Little Closer (one), Mayor (268, but still a failure), Rags (four), Lyle (didn't reach Broadway), Annie 2, the follow-up to his mega-hit (closed in Washington), and Nick And Nora (nine). In 1991, the 1986 disaster, Rags - which has a truly delectable score - was revived Off Broadway, and two years later a scaled-down version of Annie 2, retitled Annie Warbucks, was also presented there. Experienced Broadway watchers say that in spite of all the setbacks, the musical theatre has not seen the last of Charles Strouse. During the remainder of the

90s Strouse hosted An Evening With Charles Strouse in the renowned Lyrics And Lyricists series and at the Lincoln Center, as well as working on a variety of projects reported to include a musical adaptation of Theodore Dreiser's 1924 novel, An American Tragedy (with Adams) and a new musical based on the film comedy, The Night They Raided Minsky's (with Susan Birkenhead). There were also several projects honouring his previous works, such as the revues Simply Strouse at New York's Rainbow & Stars (1996) and Barbara Siman's A Lot Of Living! at London's Jermyn Street Theatre (August 1997), with Dave Willetts, Bonnie Langford, Joanna John, and Chris Coleman. Cabaret performer Jason Graae also released a 'sensational' collection of Strouse's songs on You're Never Fully Dressed Without A Smile. His career honours have included three Tony Awards for his work on Bye Bye Birdie, Applause and Annie, a Grammy for the Annie Original Cast album, and an Emmy for the song 'Let's Settle Down' (with Adams) from the 1996 television version of Bye Bye Birdie. Strouse has also composed several operas, a piano concerto, various chamber music, and several film scores, including Bonnie And Clyde (1967), The Night They Raided Minsky's (1968), There Was A Crooked Man (1970), Just Tell Me What You Want (1980), and All Dogs Go To Heaven (1989). The concerto for piano and orchestra, which he wrote when he was in his twenties, finally received its world premiere in October 1995 when Barbara Irvine played it with the Maryland Symphony Orchestra. In 1998, the piece was included in a programme called The Other Side Of Broadway, in which Irvine also previewed works by Harvey Schmidt (The Fantasticks) and David Shire (Big). As for musical theatre itself, experienced watchers say that, in spite of all the setbacks, Broadway has not yet seen the last of Charles Strouse.

STROMAN, SUSAN

b. c.1955, Wilmington, Delaware, USA. Broadway's leading choreographer of the 90s, Stroman's inventive and snappy work has enhanced several highly successful Broadway revivals, breathing new life into the American musical following a long period of British dominance. She started dancing at the age of five, studying ballet, jazz and tap, whilst also taking piano lessons. Inspired by Fred Astaire movies, and the George Balanchine ballets she went to see on trips to New York, Stroman choreographed school plays at high school before majoring in theatre at the University of Delaware. After graduation, in the late 70s she worked as a dancer in regional productions of Hit The Deck, Chicago, and Whoopee (also Broadway), before serving as assistant director/choreographer, with Scott Ellis, on the 14-performance 1980 off-Broadway flop, Musical Chairs. More choreographic work on off-Broadway shows such as Broadway Babylon, Sayonara, Slasher, and Rhythm Ranch, was followed by a reunion with Ellis, and librettist David Thompson, for the 1987 revival of Flora, The Red Menace at the tiny Vineyard Theatre in New York. The revised production became a cult hit, and so impressed Flora's composer and lyricist, John Kander and Fred Ebb, that they consented to a retrospective revue of their work created by Stroman, Ellis, and Thompson. Stroman won Outer Critics Circle and Drama Leauge awards for the resulting *And The World Goes 'Round,* and in the same year - 1991 - Liza Minnelli, who co-starred in original 1956 *Flora*, commissioned Stroman to stage the dances for Minnelli's *Stepping Out At Radio City*, an event which broke the venue's 59-year box office record. Prior to this, Stroman had choreographed Hal Prince's production of *Don Giovanni* at the New York City Opera, the first of several projects, including *110 In The Shade* and *A Little Night Music*, she would undertake for that company. Stroman was also in at the very beginning of Prince's 1992 musical, *Kiss Of The Spider Woman*. It proved 'a disastrous experience', and she jumped ship before the voyage had hardly begun. She turned instead to *Crazy For You* (1992), winning Tony, Drama Desk, and Outer Critics awards, for the electrifying contribution to the Broadway production, and a Laurence Olivier Award for the West End version. This was the big one for Stroman: 'It certainly exposed me to the masses. It did change my life.' In more ways than one it seems, because she met her future husband, Mike Okrent, while he was directing *Crazy For You*. More success, and another Tony, plus the Theatre Development Fund Astaire Award for Excellence in dance on Broadway, followed with the 1994 revival of *Show Boat*. Not so hot - in fact they were flops - were two subsequent major Stroman shows, *Big* (1994) and *Steel Pier* (1997). Even with the failures, this immensely talented artist, whose work has been compared favourably to Balachine himself by legendary New York Times critic Frank Rich, brought something extra-special to the dance process - whether it be her trademark props and big, exciting production numbers, or the sexy, lyrical stuff - they all have the Stroman pizzazz. Other shows to benefit from her dedication and skill have been *The Roar Of The Greasepaint-The Smell Of The Crowd* (1990) and *Gypsy* (1991), as well as a number of special events including the annual Madison Square Garden annual spectacular *A Christmas Carol*, and the television specials, *An Evening With The Boston Pops-A Tribute To Leonard Bernstein* (1989) and *Sondheim-A Celebration At Carnegie Hall* (1992). In 1998, Stroman received what many in musical theatre would consider to be the ultimate accolade. Called in by Trevor Nunn to work on his Royal National Theatre revival of *Oklahoma!*, she was given *carte blanche* by the Richard Rodgers and Oscar Hammerstein estate to change Agnes De Mille's original 1943 choreography. No other professional company had been granted that freedom in over half a century.

STUDENT PRINCE IN HEIDELBERG, THE

The geographical qualification 'In Heidelberg' was dropped from the title after the original production which opened at the Jolson Theatre in New York on 2 December 1924, and went on to become the longest-running Broadway musical of the 20s. With music by Sigmund Romberg and book and lyrics by Dorothy Donnelly, this operetta was based on the play *Old Heidelberg*, by Rudolf Bleichman, which was adapted from Wilhelm Meyer-Forster's *Alt Heidelberg*. Set in 1860, the story concerns Prince Karl-Franz of Karlsberg (Howard Marsh), who takes lodgings at the Inn of the Three Golden Apples while he is studying at Heidelberg University. He falls in love with a waitress there, Kathie (Ilse Marvenga), and is about to

elope with her when he hears that his father, the king, is dying. Karl-Franz must leave to assume his regal responsibilities. Re-united two years later, they realise that, although they still love each other, their lives will be better spent apart. Romberg and Donnelly's score was in the grand operetta style, and contained several memorable numbers, including 'The Drinking Song', 'Serenade', 'Deep In My Heart, Dear', 'Just We Two', and 'Golden Days'. After an impressive run of 608 performances, Ilse Marvenga recreated her role in the 1926 London production which folded after less than three months. Rather more successful revivals were presented in 1929, 1944, and particularly in 1968 when a revised version, with extra songs, and starring the popular actor-manager John Hanson, played at the Cambridge Theatre. Broadway audiences saw the show again in 1931 and 1943, and there was a production by the New York City Opera in 1980. Film versions were released in 1927, with Ramon Navarro and Norma Shearer, and in 1954, with Edmund Purdom (sung by Mario Lanza) and Ann Blyth.

STUDENT PRINCE, THE

Mario Lanza walked out on MGM producer Joe Pasternak before filming had even started on Sigmund Romberg and Dorothy Donnelly's epic operetta, which eventually reached the screen in 1954. Fortunately for all concerned, Lanza had recorded all the songs before he left, so it was simply a matter of matching his voice to the performing style of Edmund Purdom, the British actor chosen to co-star with Ann Blyth in this tale located in old Heidelberg. Set in the late 1800s, Sonia Levien and William Ludwig's screenplay, which was based on Donnelly's Broadway libretto and Wilhelm Meyer-Forster's play, told the familiar story of the brief romance between the Student Prince, Karl Franz (Purdom), and the waitress, Kathy (Blyth), to the accompaniment of immortal songs from the 1924 hit stage production, such as 'Serenade', 'Deep In My Heart, Dear', 'Drinking Song', 'Come Boys, Let's All Be Gay Boys' and 'Golden Days'. To these were added three new ones by Nicholas Brodszky and Paul Francis Webster, 'I Walk With God', Summertime In Heidelberg' and 'Beloved'. Louis Calhern, S.Z. Sakall, Edmund Gwenn, John Williams, Evelyn Vardon, Richard Anderson and John Hoyt were among those taking part in this lavish production which was expertly photographed in Ansco Color and CinemaScope by Paul Vogel and directed by Richard Thorpe. An earlier, silent film of *The Student Prince*, directed by Ernst Lubitsch and starring Ramon Navarro and Norma Shearer, was released in 1927.

STYNE, JULE

b. Julius Kerwin Stein, 31 December 1905, London, England, d. 20 September 1994, New York, USA. A highly distinguished composer for the musical theatre, films and Tin Pan Alley, Styne spent his early life in the east London district of Bethnal Green, where his father ran a butter and eggs store. He used to do Harry Lauder impressions, and when he was five, he was taken by his parents to see the great entertainer at the London Hippodrome. He climbed up on stage, and Lauder lent him his crook and encouraged him to sing 'She's My Daisy'. Something of a child prodigy, he was a competent pianist even before he emigrated with his family to the USA at the age of eight. They settled in Chicago, and Styne studied harmony and composition, and played with the Chicago Symphony Orchestra, but had to abandon a classical career because 'my hands were too small - my span was inadequate'. While he was still at high school, Styne played the piano at burlesque houses, and composed his first two songs, 'The Guy In the Polka-Dot Tie' and 'The Moth And The Flame'. After graduating, he worked in nightclubs and for various pick-up groups, and in 1927, had a hit with the catchy 'Sunday' (written with Ned Miller, Chester Conn and Bennie Kreuger). In the late 20s, Styne was a member of Ben Pollack's big-time Chicago Band, which at various times included legendary names such as Benny Goodman, Glenn Miller and Charlie Spivak. By 1932, he had formed his own band, which played at the nightclubs and speakeasies in Chicago. During the 30s he moved to Hollywood, via New York, and worked as a vocal coach at 20th Century Fox ('I taught Shirley Temple and Alice Faye how to sing!'), and wrote some songs for low-budget movies such as *Hold That Co-Ed* (1938, 'Limpy Dimp' with Sidney Clare and Nick Castle). He transferred to Republic Studios, the home of Gene Autry and Roy Rogers, and continued to contribute to shoestring productions such as *Hit Parade Of 1941* ('Who Am I?', with Walter Bullock), *Melody Ranch*, *Rookies On Parade* and *Angels With Broken Wings*. On loan to Paramount, Styne teamed with Frank Loesser for 'I Don't Want To Walk Without You' and 'I Said No', which were featured in the Eddie Bracken movie *Sweater Girl* (1942). The former number was an enormous wartime hit, particularly for Harry James and his Orchestra, with a vocal by Helen Forrest. While at Republic, Styne met lyricist Sammy Cahn, and during the 40s they collaborated on numerous appealing songs, mostly for films, including 'I've Heard That Song Before', 'Five Minutes More', 'Victory Polka', 'Poor Little Rhode Island', 'Saturday Night (Is The Loneliest Night Of The Week)', 'Zuyder Zee', 'Guess I'll Hang My Tears Out To Dry' (from the 1944 flop musical *Glad To See You*), 'Anywhere', 'Can't You Read Between The Lines?', 'When The One You Love (Simply Won't Come Back)', 'I've Never Forgotten', 'The Things We Did Last Summer', 'Let It Snow! Let It Snow! Let It Snow!', 'I Gotta Gal I Love In North And South Dakota', 'It's Been A Long, Long Time', 'Ev'ry Day I Love You (Just A Little Bit More)', 'I'm In Love', 'It's Magic', 'It's You Or No One', 'Put 'Em In A Box (Tie It With A Ribbon And Throw 'Em In the Deep Blue Sea' (the last three were from Doris Day's first movie, *Romance On The High Seas*), 'Give Me A Song With A Beautiful Melody' and 'It's A Great Feeling' (1949).

During that period, Styne also collaborated with others, including Herb Magidson ('Barrelhouse Bessie From Basin Street' and 'Conchita, Marquita, Lolita, Pepita, Rosita, Juanita Lopez') and Walter Bishop ('Bop! Goes My Heart'). Many of those songs were immensely successful for Frank Sinatra, and Styne and Cahn wrote the scores for three of the singer's most successful films of the 40s, *Step Lively* ('As Long As There's Music', 'Come Out, Wherever You Are', 'Some Other Time'), *Anchors Aweigh* ('The Charm Of

You', 'I Fall In Love Too Easily', 'I Begged Her'), and *It Happened In Brooklyn* ('It's The Same Old Dream', 'Time After Time', 'I Believe', 'The Brooklyn Bridge'). Sinatra also introduced Styne and Cahn's Oscar-winning 'Three Coins In The Fountain' in 1954. Some years before that, Styne and Cahn had moved to New York to work on the score for the stage musical *High Button Shoes* ('Papa, Won't You Dance With Me', 'I Still Get Jealous', 'Can't You Just See Yourself?'). It starred Phil Silvers and Nanette Fabray, and ran for 727 performances. After returning briefly to Hollywood, at the age of 44 Styne embarked on an illustrious Broadway career, composing the music for a string of mostly highly successful shows, including *Gentlemen Prefer Blondes* (1949, 'Diamonds Are A Girl's Best Friend', 'Bye, Bye, Baby'), *Two On The Aisle* (1951, 'Hold Me-Hold Me-Hold Me', 'If You Hadn't But You Did'), *Hazel Flagg* (1953, 'Ev'ry Street's A Boulevard', 'How do You Speak To An Angel?'), *Peter Pan* (1954, 'Never Never Land', 'Distant Melody'), *Wake Up Darling* (1956, a five-performance flop, 'L'il Ol' You And L'il Ol' Me'), *Bells Are Ringing* (1956, 'Just In Time', 'The Party's Over', 'Long Before I Knew You'), *Say, Darling* (1958, 'Dance Only With Me'), *Gypsy* (1959, 'Small World', 'Everything's Coming Up Roses', 'Rose's Turn', 'All I Need Is The Girl'), *Do Re Mi* (1960, 'Make Someone Happy', 'Fireworks'), *Subways Are For Sleeping* (1961, 'I Just Can't Wait', 'Comes Once In A Lifetime', 'Be A Santa'), *Funny Girl* (1964, 'The Music That Makes Me Dance', 'Sadie, Sadie', 'People', 'Don't Rain On My Parade'), *Fade Out-Fade In* (1964, 'You Mustn't Feel Discouraged'), *Hallelujah, Baby!* (1967, 'My Own Morning', 'Now's The Time'), *Darling Of The Day* (1968, 'Let's See What Happens', 'That Something Extra Special'), *Look To The Lilies* (1970, 'I! Yes, Me! That's Who!'), *Prettybelle* (1971, closed out of town), *Sugar* (1972, 'It's Always Love', 'We Could Be Close' [revised for London as *Some Like It Hot* in 1992]), *Lorelei* (1974, a revised version of *Gentlemen Prefer Blondes*), *Hellzapoppin'!* (1976, closed out of town, 'Only One To A Customer'), *Bar Mitzvah Boy* (London 1978, 'You Wouldn't Be You', 'The Sun Shines Out Of Your Eyes', 'Where The Music Is Coming From'), *One Night Stand* (1980, closed during previews, 'Too Old To Be So Young', 'Long Way From Home'), *Pieces Of Eight* (1985, closed during regional try-out in Canada), and *The Red Shoes* (1993, closed after three days). Styne's chief collaborators for Broadway were Betty Comden and Adolph Green, and he also worked with Leo Robin, E.Y 'Yip' Harburg, Sammy Cahn and Bob Hilliard, among others. His two longest-running (and legendary) shows were written with Bob Merrill (*Funny Girl*) and Stephen Sondheim (*Gypsy*). Styne also co-produced several musicals, and composed the scores for television specials, and films such as *West Point Story*, *Two Tickets To Broadway* and *My Sister Eileen*. One of the most talented, and prolific ('I believe in perspiration - not inspiration') all-round songwriters in the history of American popular music, Styne won many awards and honours, and was inducted into the Songwriters Hall of Fame and the Theatre Hall of Fame. Several artists have devoted complete albums to his songs, and in 1995, *Everything's Coming Up Roses-The Overtures Of Jule Styne*, played by the National Symphony Orchestra conducted by Jack Everly, was released. ASCAP's memorial tribute to Styne in February of that year included a Stephen Sondheim lyric that ran: 'Jule/You never took things coolly/Your syntax was unduly/Unruly/But Jule/I love you truly.'

● ALBUMS: *My Name Is Jule* (United Artists 1958)★★, with Michael Feinstein *Michael Feinstein Sings The Jule Styne Songbook* (Elektra Nonesuch 1991)★★★.

● FURTHER READING: *Jule*, Theodore Taylor.

SUBTERRANEANS, THE

This adaptation of a Jack Kerouac novel came too early for it to be successful. When it was released in 1960, Hollywood was then still hidebound by its own peculiar code of sexual ethics. What could and could not be shown on the screen was a tangle that this film, directed by Ranald MacDougall, failed to unravel. Jazz fans have an excuse for watching it, however, as there are good moments from musicians such as André Previn, the film's musical director, Dave Bailey, Chico Hamilton, Art Farmer, Art Pepper, Bob Enevoldson, Russ Freeman, Red Mitchell, Shelly Manne, Bill Perkins and Gerry Mulligan, who also acts in the film.

SUCCESS!

(see Taylor, Bernard J.)

SUGAR

Based on the enormously popular 1959 film, *Some Like It Hot*, this musical, which had a score by the *Funny Girl* team of Jule Styne and Bob Merrill, opened at the Majestic Theatre in New York on 9 April 1972. Peter Stone's book stayed closely to the original story of two musicians who, having accidentally witnessed the notorious St. Valentine's Day Massacre in Chicago, flee to Miami disguised as members of an all-female orchestra. Robert Morse and Tony Roberts played the roles that were taken in the film by Jack Lemmon and Tony Curtis, Cyril Ritchard was the eccentric millionaire who found himself completely beguiled by Morse in drag, and Elaine Joyce did her best to make people forget the unforgettable Marilyn Monroe. The score was suitably 20s in style, and included numbers such as 'When You Meet A Man In Chicago', '(Doing It For) Sugar', 'Sun On My Face', 'What Do You Give To A Man Who's Had Everything?', 'Beautiful Through And Through', 'We Could Be Close', 'It's Always Love', 'Hey, Why Not!', and 'Penniless Bums'. Gower Champion contributed some slick choreography, and *Sugar* stayed around for 505 performances. Twenty years later a revised edition with the original film title, *Some Like It Hot*, reached London's West End. The emphasis was switched from the character of Sugar to the show's star, Tommy Steele, and when he had to leave the cast for a time following an on-stage accident, the production went rapidly downhill and closed after a run of three months with losses estimated at around £2 million.

SUGAR BABIES

This celebration of the golden age of American burlesque entertainment between 1905 and 1930, opened at the Mark Hellinger Theatre in New York on 8 October 1979. It was conceived by Ralph G. Allen and Harry Rigby, two students of the burlesque form, who based several of the numbers directly on famous historic routines. Most of the music came from the catalogue of the distinguished American composer Jimmy McHugh, with lyrics by Dorothy Fields, Harold Adamson, and Al Dubin. Additional music and lyrics were by Arthur Malvin. The obvious choice for the role of comedian and song-and-dance man, to follow in the oversized footsteps of legendary burlesque comics such as Bert Lahr, Bobby Clark, and W.C. Fields, was one of America's most cherished clowns, Mickey Rooney. His co-star was Ann Miller, whose long legs and precision dancing style showed no noticeable signs of deterioration since she appeared in movies such as *Kiss Me, Kate* and *On The Town* more than 25 years previously. The sketch material was strictly 'adults only', but the songs, which included classics such as 'Exactly Like You', 'I Feel A Song Comin' On', 'I'm In The Mood For Love', and 'On The Sunny Side Of The Street', appealed to young and old alike. The show ran for a remarkable 1,208 performances and then undertook successful US road tours. The 1988 London production, with Rooney and Miller, appealed at first, but then went under after a run of just over three months.

SUMMER HOLIDAY (1948)

Another wallow in turn-of-the-century small-town Americana of the kind that hardly ever failed at the US box-office. This one was based on Eugene O'Neill's comedy *Ah, Wilderness!*, and was released by MGM in 1948. Frances Goodrich and Albert Hackett's screenplay retained much of the warmth and gentleness which had made the original so appealing, and Mickey Rooney, as a youngster making the often bewildering transition into manhood, was superb. Gloria De Haven was fine as his girlfriend, and so were parents Walter Huston and Selena Royle. The remainder of a strong cast included Frank Morgan, Agnes Moorehead, Jackie 'Butch' Jenkins, Marilyn Maxwell, and Anne Francis. Harry Warren and Ralph Blane's score was skilfully integrated into the story, and included 'Our Home Town', 'Independence Day', 'Afraid To Fall In Love', 'Weary Blues', 'I Think You're The Sweetest Kid I've Ever Known', 'All Hail Danville High', and the lively 'Stanley Steamer'. Charles Walters, who was renowned for his exuberant choreography, staged the dances, and Rouben Mamoulian, who set the standard for movie musicals with his *Love Me Tonight* (1933), directed with his usual flair and attention for detail and character. It was photographed brilliantly in Technicolor by Charles Schoenbaum, and produced by the Arthur Freed Unit. The modestly successful 1959 Broadway musical, *Take Me Along*, which had a score by Bob Merrill, was also based on O'Neill's *Ah, Wilderness!*

SUMMER HOLIDAY (1962)

Cliff Richard's second 'teenage' feature, released in 1962, maintained the light-hearted nature of its successful predecessor, *The Young Ones*. *Summer Holiday* revolves around four London Transport mechanics who borrow a double-decker bus and embark for the Continent. Pursuit, love, capture and an inevitable happy ending ensue, but Peter Yates' snappy direction and location shots result in a film no less slight than much British light comedy of its time. Indeed, the appearance of the singer's backing group, the Shadows, in various different guises, was one of the films endearing features. However, the presence of established stalwarts Ron Moody and David Kossoff alongside Richard, Una Stubbs and Mervyn Hayes help place the musical within the framework of all-round entertainment. Winter season pantomime was the next logical step. *Summer Holiday* contained some of the singer's most enduring hit singles, including the double-sided chart topper, 'Bachelor Boy'/'The Next Time' and the title track itself, which also reached number one in the UK. Cliff Richard (and the Shadows), were arguably at the peak of their collective popularity at this point. In February 1963 the *Summer Holiday* album took over the number 1 spot on the album list from *Out Of The Shadows*. It reigned there for 14 unbroken weeks, until being replaced, prophetically, by the Beatles' *Please Please Me*. A stage version of *Summer Holiday*, directed and designed by Ultz, starring Darren Day, Ross King, Clare Buckfield, and Hilary O'Neil, had its world premiere in 1996 at the Blackpool Opera House, where it ran for six months. It subsequently toured, and spent July-September 1997 on the London Fringe at Labatt's Apollo, Hammersmith. Several of Cliff Richard's early hits were interpolated into the score, including 'In The Country', 'Do You Wanna Dance?', 'Move It' and 'Livin' Doll'. Day's recording of 'Summer Holiday Medley' entered the UK Top 20 in 1996.

SUMMER STOCK

Of the three films in which Judy Garland and Gene Kelly starred together, their final project, *Summer Stock*, is the least impressive. Yet this 1950 MGM release still remains a favourite for many, and has some genuinely charming moments. It tells the tale of the two Falbury sisters - Jane (Garland) has remained at home in New England to run the farm, while Abigail (Gloria DeHaven), has left the roost to pursue a showbiz career. To her sister's horror, Abigail brings the people, props and paraphernalia of a whole new show, written and organised by Joe D. Ross (Kelly), to rehearse on the farm. Jane insists that if the whole gang is going to live there and use the barn for rehearsals, they had better earn their keep. This results in some amusing shenanigans, with cows, chickens and an accident with a brand new tractor - disasters which Phil Silvers normally has something to do with. When Abigail suddenly leaves the production, Jane steps into her place, and does so with a hard working attitude and passion that her sister never displayed. When Abigail returns to apologise half way through the opening night of the show, she not only finds that Jane's performance has been a triumph, but that Jane and Joe have fallen in love. Jane's fiancé, Orville (Eddie Bracken), is left out in the cold, but it looks like Abigail is going to help him recover from the blow. George Wells and Sy Gomberg's screenplay is a happy bundle of clichés - let's put a show on in a barn . . . you've only got a few days to learn the part etc. Not that anyone cared much, because *Summer Stock*, directed by Charles Walters and produced by Joe Pasternak, was good fun, and several of the sequences are still quite memorable. Garland's singing and dancing in 'Get Happy'

(Harold Arlen/Ted Koehler) combine to create one of her all-time best and sophisticated performances. During the rest of the film she was obviously overweight, but 'Get Happy' was shot two months after filming had officially ended, and by then she was back in fine condition. Whatever her physical problems, Garland's voice did not seem to be affected on the uplifting 'If You Feel Like Singing, Sing' and the poignant 'Friendly Star'. They were both written by Harry Warren and Mack Gordon, who also contributed 'Happy Harvest', 'Blue Jean Polka', 'Dig-Dig-Dig For Your Dinner' and Mem'ry Island'. Garland and Kelly were perfect together, and Kelly and Silvers also had a great time with the more comical material, as they did in *Cover Girl* six years earlier. Kelly's own personal mark of genius showed itself in the sequence when, while walking on the stage, he stepped on a squeaky floorboard. Simply by using this, a sheet of newspaper and the accompaniment of 'You Wonderful You' (Warren-Jack Brooks-Saul Chaplin), he devised one of the film's most enchanting dances. Nick Castle handled the rest of the choreography, and the film was shot in Technicolor by Robert Planck. For UK audiences the title was changed to *If You Feel Like Singing*.

SUN VALLEY SERENADE

Such was the popularity of the Glenn Miller Band by 1941 that it just had to appear in a film, even if the story was as light as a feather and Miller himself was definitely no actor. Robert Ellis and Helen Logan's screenplay (from a story by Art Arthur and Robert Harari) was about a cute Norwegian refugee (Sonja Henie) whose arrival in America startles the band's pianist (John Payne) simply because he had agreed to sponsor a child. Inevitably, surprise turns to love on the snowy slopes of Sun Valley, Idaho. The musical sequences were tremendous, especially choreographer Hermes Pan's staging of 'Chattanooga Choo-Choo' (Harry Warren-Mack Gordon) which begins conventionally enough with Tex Beneke, Paula Kelly and the Modernaires singing with the band, and then segues into a spectacular song-and-dance routine featuring the amazing Nicholas Brothers and Dorothy Dandridge. Warren and Gordon contributed three other popular numbers, 'The Kiss Polka', 'I Know Why (And So Do You)', and 'It Happened In Sun Valley', while Joe Garland's 'In The Mood' also got an airing. Milton Berle supplied the wisecracks, and Lynn Bari and Joan Davis were in it too. Henie's big moment came in the impressive 'black ice' finalé when, accompanied by numerous white-clad couples, she gave a stunning display of ballet-style ice dancing. H. Bruce Humberstone directed, and *Sun Valley Serenade* was produced by Milton Sperling for 20th Century-Fox. Not much footage of the Miller Band exists, so this film and *Orchestra Wives* are continually re-viewed by lovers of the Swing Era.

SUNDAY IN THE PARK WITH GEORGE

Stephen Sondheim and his librettist and director James Lapine, used a painting by the 19th century impressionist painter, Georges Seurat, as the basis for this innovative musical which opened at the Booth Theatre in New York on 2 May 1984. 'A Sunday Afternoon On The Island Of La

Grande Jatte' has been described as 'a multi-layered panorama of Parisian life and a masterpiece of pointillism - the method of building a painting from minute dots of blending colours'. In the show's first act the painting gradually comes to life as George (Mandy Patinkin) obsessively creates the characters and places them on the canvas, eventually progressing to the complete tableau. Meanwhile, the relationship with his mistress/model Dot/Marie (Bernadette Peters) falls apart, and although they are expecting a child, she leaves him to marry someone else. The second act advances the plot by 100 years. The setting is now present-day New York, and Seurat and Dot's great-grandson, also named George, is 'an American multimedia sculptor likewise bedevilled by a philistine society'. Sondheim and Lapine's point of view about 'the angst of artistic creation' comes over loud and clear throughout. Sondheim's score was complex and intricate, and included 'Sunday In The Park With George', 'No Life', 'Colour And Light', 'Gossip', 'The Day Off', 'Everybody Loves Louis', 'Finishing The Hat', 'We Do Not Belong Together', 'Beautiful', 'Sunday', 'It's Hot Up Here', 'Chromolume No. 7', 'Putting It Together', 'Children And Art', 'Lesson No. 8', and 'Move On'. Considering the quality of the piece, a run of 604 performances was somewhat disappointing. There were Tony Awards for the brilliant scenic design (Tony Straiges) and lighting (Richard Nelson), and the show was voted best musical by the New York Drama Critics Circle. It also won the 1985 Pulitzer Prize for Drama. Five years later, *Sunday In The Park With George* was presented in London for a season by the Royal National Theatre. It won the *Evening Standard* Special Award, and Laurence Olivier Awards for best musical and actor, Philip Quast, who co-starred as George opposite Maria Friedman's Dot/Marie. To honour the show's 10th anniversary, a 'perfect' concert performance was held at the St. James Theatre in New York on 15 May 1994. James Lapine directed most of the original cast, headed by Mandy Patinkin and Bernadette Peters.

SUNNY

After Marilyn Miller's great success in Florenz Ziegfeld's *Sally* (1920), another distinguished American producer, Charles Dillingham, arranged for her to board this vehicle for her singing and dancing talents which arrived at the New Amsterdam Theatre in New York on 22 September 1925, and stayed for 517 performances. Otto Harbach and Oscar Hammerstein II wrote the more than fanciful book in which Sunny Peters (Miller), a star equestrian performer in an English circus, stows away on an ocean liner to be near her beloved, Tom Warren (Paul Frawley). Almost 70 years later, it is difficult to understand why Sunny has to marry - not Tom - but his best friend, Jim Deming (Jack Donahue), in order to disembark in the USA. Also in the cast were Clifton Webb, Mary Hay, Joseph Cawthorn, Cliff Edwards, and George Olsen And His Orchestra. The score, with music by Jerome Kern and lyrics by Harbach and Hammerstein, included 'Let's Not Say Goodnight Till It's Morning', 'Sunny', 'D'Ye Love Me?', 'Two Little Bluebirds', 'I Might Grow Fond Of You', and 'Who'. Jack Buchanan made the latter number his own when *Sunny* opened in London at the Hippodrome in

1926. Joining him in the West End production which ran for 363 performances, were Elsie Randolph, Binnie Hale, Maidie Hope, and Claude Hulbert. An early 'talkie' version of *Sunny* released in 1930 starred Marilyn Miller, Lawrence Grey, and Jack Donahue, and there was a remake in 1941 with Anna Neagle and Ray Bolger.

SUNSET BOULEVARD

Composer Andrew Lloyd Webber's long-awaited musical adaptation of Billy Wilder's classic black-and-white film that starred Gloria Swanson and William Holden, finally surmounted a host of technical problems and opened at the refurbished Adelphi Theatre in London on 12 July 1993. The book and lyrics were by Don Black, who had previously collaborated with Lloyd Webber, and the author Christopher Hampton who was making his debut in the musical theatre. Their libretto, which remained faithful to the original screenplay, told the familiar story of Norma Desmond (Patti LuPone), the ageing silent movie queen, who enlists the help of failed and penniless scriptwriter Joe Gillis (Kevin Anderson) in her attempts to make a comeback. Too late he discovers that he is hopelessly trapped. The score contained several powerful ballads, particularly 'With One Look' and 'As If We Never Said Goodbye', and there were others which had the potential to be similarly durable, such as 'Surrender', 'New Ways To Dream', 'The Perfect Year', and 'Too Much In Love To Care'. There were also a couple of amusing comedy numbers, 'The Lady's Paying' and 'Let's Have Lunch', as well as 'Salome', 'The Greatest Star Of All', 'Girl Meets Boy', 'This Time Next Year', 'Sunset Boulevard', and 'Eternal Youth Is Worth A Little Suffering'. The £3 million production received generally good, if not enthusiastic reviews. Most critics thought that Patti LuPone looked too young for the role, but there were no reservations about her voice. There was also praise for John Napier's 'wonderfully elaborate rococo set'. Prominent amongst the cast were Daniel Benzali (Max von Mayerling), Meredith Braun (Betty Schaefer), and Michael Bauer (Cecil de Mille). Going against convention, *Sunset Boulevard* had its US premiere, not on Broadway, but in Los Angeles. By the time the show opened there at the Shubert Theatre on 9 December 1993, it had been drastically reworked, and a new song, 'Every Movie's A Circus', added. There was a first night standing ovation for film actress Glenn Close who played Norma, with Alan Campbell (Joe), Judy Kuhn (Betty), and George Hearn (Max), and the lavish post-premiere party was held at Paramount Studios where the original 1950 film was made. Lloyd Webber subsequently closed the London production for a '$1.5 million revamp'. When it reopened, Betty Buckley and John Barrowman had taken over the leading roles. Buckley was eventually replaced by Elaine Paige, who was followed by Petula Clark. An interesting choice of holiday replacement for Clark was multi-award-winning actress, Rita Moreno. When Lloyd Webber announced that Glenn Close was to star in the Broadway production of *Sunset Boulevard*, which opened on 17 November 1994, he was faced with the threat of legal action from Patti LuPone who maintained that she had been promised the part. The case was settled out of court, with LuPone receiving a substantial sum. Close took the 'best actress in a musical' Tony Award, and the show also won for best musical, book and score (both unopposed), featured actor (Hearn), scenic design (Napier), and lighting design (Andrew Bridge). Campbell reprised his Los Angeles role, and Alice Ripley played Betty. Norma was later portrayed in New York by Buckley and Elaine Paige (making her Broadway debut). Karen Mason was an frequent understudy for the leading role In June 1994 the curtain fell on the Los Angeles production after film star Faye Dunaway, who was contracted to take over the role of Norma, was judged to be 'unable to fulfil the musical demands of the role' - more litigation. However, during the next two years, *Sunset Boulevard* made its bow in Toronto, Canada (with Diahann Carroll as Norma, Rex Smith as Joe, and Walter Charles as Max), Frankfurt, Germany (Helen Schneider), and Melbourne, Australia (Debra Bryne). The 1996 US national tour was headed by the virtually unknown Linda Balgord.

Early in 1997 Lloyd Webber's Really Useful Group announced that 'because of difficulties in casting the leading role', both the London and New York productions would close almost immediately. The West End show, which had been seen by two million people over four years, gave the last of its 1,530 performances at the Adelphi on 5 April, and Broadway's Norma and Co. went off into the sunset on 22 March after 977 outings. The latter production was reported to have lost £200,000 in one recent month. Lloyd Webber blamed the show for much of his company's financial problems, saying: 'Sunset has lost money massively overall.' A pared-down production of Sunset Boulevard, with a cheaper design, began a 60-week US tour in the autumn of 1998, with a cast headed by Petula Clark.

● FURTHER READING: *Sunset Boulevard - From Movie To Musical*, George Perry.

SUPERFLY

This 1972 release was one of several films starring African-American actors in a genre dubbed 'blaxploitation'. The first, and best, of these was *Shaft*, which featured a taut score by Isaac Hayes. *Superfly* featured the less fêted Jeff Alexander as its musical director, but he proved astute in enlisting former Impressions leader Curtis Mayfield to contribute several excellent compositions. Two powerful songs, 'Freddy's Dead' and the title track itself, reached the US Top 10, providing a boost to their creator's solo career. Their success helped to promote *Superfly* and gave it a prominence that the one-dimensional plot did not deserve. Ron O'Neal starred as a drug-pusher looking for the one big deal that would enable him to retire, but the ambiguous script suggested that violent New York cocaine dealers were merely behaving like noble outlaws. Indeed, black self-help groups picketed several cinemas showing the film. Mayfield himself later expressed disquiet about the theme, preferring the cautionary 'Freddy's Dead' than other, more celebratory, inclusions. The singer later wrote the scores for *Claudine* and *Short Eyes*, neither of which enjoyed the commercial approbation of *Superfly*. The film itself inspired an even more lacklustre follow-up, *Superfly TNT*.

SURF PARTY

Released in 1963, *Surf Party* was an early entrant into the 'beach' genre largely propagated by American International Pictures. This was not one of their vehicles, but it featured a similarly asinine plot. Three girls arrive in California from Arizona, hoping to find one of their number's drop-out brother. Pop singer Bobby Vinton ('Blue Velvet') stars as a surfer aiding their quest, but in now-accustomed fashion, interest lies in the film's musical content. Prolific composer/performer Jackie DeShannon contributed the *de rigeur* 'Glory Wave', one-hit wonders the Routers (Let's Go') offered 'Crack Up', while surf act the Astronauts added 'Fire Water' as well as the title track.

SVEN KLANG'S KVINTETT

Based upon a stage play by Henric Holmberg and Ninne Olsson, this film made in 1976, directed by Stellan Olsson, tells the story of an amateur, and not-very-good, traditional jazz band in Sweden in the late 50s. The band is joined by an alto saxophonist who is not only a vastly superior musician but is also eagerly experimenting with bop. This character, portrayed by Christer Boustedt (who really does play alto), is loosely based upon alto and baritone saxophonist Lars Gullin who died in the year of the film's release. The film offers one of the best accounts of life on the road for jazz musicians, whatever their nationality.

SWANN, DONALD

b. Donald Ibrahim Swann, 30 September 1923, Llanelli, Wales, d. 23 March 1994, London, England. Swann was the progeny of a union between a Russian doctor and Turkoman nurse who fled St. Petersburg, Russia, during the Revolution. He attended school at Westminster where he proved a popular member of the revue team alongside Michael Flanders (see Flanders And Swann) and stage manager and future UK MP Tony Benn, before beginning studies at Oxford University. While working with the Friends' Ambulance Unit he visited Greece, whose serenity and sense of community, alongside his Russian heritage, greatly influenced his music. However, he soon returned to London to contribute material to West End revues, linking again with Michael Flanders. Both were soon buoyed by the success of ventures such as *Penny Plain* (1951), *Airs On A Shoestring* (1953) and *Fresh Airs* (1956). However, it was their own two-man show, *At The Drop Of A Hat*, that propelled them to nationwide fame after it opened on New Year's Eve in 1956. A massive hit, the show ran for over two years in London, before playing on Broadway and touring the USA and Canada. It was followed in 1963 by *At The Drop Of Another Hat*. However, Swann grew discontented with the endless cycle of engagements and touring that followed, leading to the dissolution of his first marriage. He remained in his house in Battersea, collaborating with Flanders on an album of animal songs for children, and scoring adaptations of the works of his friends C.S. Lewis and J.R.R. Tolkien. He also composed music as a backdrop to his favourite poet, Emily Dickinson, and formed less successful partnerships with John Amis, Frank Topping, Ian Wallace and Lili

Malandraki, following the death of Flanders in 1975. Fortunately, he was able to complete his autobiography with the help of second wife Alison Smith before he succumbed to cancer at the age of 70. At that time he was also working on material for a new revue, *Swann Amongst The Sirens*, based on his wartime experiences in Greece (to have been staged by the Cherub Theatre Company).

● FURTHER READING: *Swann's Way: A Life In Song.*

SWEENEY TODD

A 'Musical Thriller' which is often regarded as Stephen Sondheim's most satisfying work to date - certainly his most grisly - *Sweeney Todd* opened at the Uris Theatre in New York on 1 March 1979. Sondheim and librettist Hugh Wheeler based their musical adaptation of the legendary 'demon barber of Fleet Street' on Christopher Bond's play, *Sweeney Todd*, which played at the Theatre Royal, Stratford East in 1973. As Wheeler's story begins, the barber Sweeney Todd (Len Cariou) is just returning to London after 15 years in enforced exile. He discovers that his wife has been driven to her death (or so he thinks) and his daughter made a ward of court by the man who sentenced him - the evil Judge Turpin (Edmund Lyndeck). Intent on revenge, he rents a room above a shop run by Mrs. Lovett (Angela Lansbury), who sells 'The Worst Pies In London'. While waiting for his chance to dispose of Judge Turpin, Todd lures other unsuspecting victims to his barbers' chair. He slits their throats, before passing them over to Mrs. Lovett, who uses her meat grinder and oven to turn them into pies. Although he gets the Judge in the end, justice is seen to be done when Sweeney Todd is slain with one of his own razors, and lies beside the body of his wife whom he has inadvertently murdered. Sondheim's superb 'near-operatic' score, which has been called 'Grand Guignol' and 'quasi-Brechtian' in style, ranged from the witty list song 'A Little Priest', to tender ballads such as 'Not While I'm Around' and 'Johanna', along with other numbers such as 'Pretty Women', 'By The Sea', 'Epiphany', 'Poor Thing', 'God, That's Good', and 'The Ballad Of Sweeney Todd'. The show ran for 558 performances and won eight Tony Awards, including best musical, book, score, actor (Cariou), actress (Lansbury) and director (Harold Prince). A New York revival was presented at the Circle In the Square in 1989, with Bob Gunton (Sweeney) and Beth Fowler (Mrs. Lovett), and the Paper Mill Playhouse, New Jersey, offered a version with George Hearn and Judy Kaye in 1992. Steve Barton and Brooks Almy played the leads in a 1996 Pittsburg Public Theatre production, and in the same year the Goodspeed Opera House mounted the show (said to be its first Sondheim musical) with Timothy Nolen and Barbara Marineau). The 1980 London production at Drury Lane, with Denis Quilley and Sheila Hancock, was generally held to be unsatisfactory. However, Declan Donnellan's 1993 'chamber version', at the Royal National Theatre, starring Julia McKenzie and Alun Armstrong, was widely acclaimed, and won Laurence Olivier Awards for best musical revival, actress (McKenzie). actor (Armstrong), and director (Donnellan). The original 1980 London Sweeney, Denis Quilley, initially played Judge Turpin in the National's production, but later returned to the razors

when Armstrong left. Other professional UK stagings have included the Leicester Haymarket (1996) with Dave Willetts and Jeanette Ranger), and Opera North's 1998 tourer (Stephen Page and Beverley Klein). The 'lifers' of 'D' Wing in Wormwood Scrubs prison were presumably not doing it for the money when (aided by members of the Pimlico Opera) they mounted a full-scale production of the Sondheim-Wheeler classic in November 1991.

● FURTHER READING: *Sweeney Todd: The Demon Barber Of Fleet Street*, Peter Haining.

SWEET ADELINE

Following her tremendous success in *Show Boat* (1927), Jerome Kern and Oscar Hammerstein II wrote the score for this 'Musical Romance Of the Gay Nineties' for Helen Morgan, the torch singer who could wring a tear from even the most innocuous ballad. Not that there were any of those in this show. 'Why Was I Born?', one of the composers' most heart-felt and enduring numbers, was introduced by Morgan, along with 'Here Am I', 'Don't Ever Leave Me', and ''Twas Not So Long Ago'. *Sweet Adeline* opened at the Hammerstein Theatre in New York on 3 September 1929, with a book by Hammerstein set in 1898, and concerns Addie Schmidt who leaves her father's beer garden in Hoboken, New Jersey, for singing stardom on Broadway. There were several more appealing numbers in what is accepted as one of the loveliest of Kern's early scores, including a bluesy piece, 'Some Girl Is On Your Mind' which was sung by a group of Addie's boyfriends, the waltz ballad 'The Sun Is About To Rise', 'Spring Is Here', 'Out Of The Blue', and the lively 'Play Us A Polka Dot'. *Sweet Adeline* was an immediate success and looked set for a long run. Then came the Wall Street Crash, and although the show rode out the storm for a while, it was forced to close in April 1930 after a total of 234 performances. The 1935 film version had a revised book, and Irene Dunne.

SWEET AND LOW-DOWN

Only one good reason for staying up late to watch this 1944 film (if it is ever shown on television) and that is Benny Goodman. Fortunately, he and his orchestra and quartet are on-screen rather a lot in this tale of a swing band on tour. Although this was not Goodman's best band, there are still several good musicians on hand. Some are seen, others only heard while actors mime their instruments. Amongst the musicians are Bill Harris, Zoot Sims, Morey Feld, Jess Stacy, Sid Weiss, Allan Reuss, Heinie Beau and Al Klink. (Alternative title: *Moment For Music*).

SWEET BEAT

This low-budget 1959 British film was produced by Jeff Kruger who co-owned London's fabled Flamingo nightclub and subsequently operated the Ember label. It starred Julie Amber as a beauty queen-turned-singer who is offered a lucrative spot in a New York venue by a promoter seeking sexual favours in return. The title song was performed by Tony Crombie who, as leader of Tony Crombie And His Rockets, was one of the first UK musicians to embrace nascent rock 'n' roll earlier in the decade. Fred Parris And His Satins, Cindy Mann, Jeri Lee and Lee Allen And His Band were among the other acts featured in a film that promptly sank with little trace.

SWEET CHARITY (FILM MUSICAL)

Director-choreographer Bob Fosse's 1969 screen adaptation of the hit Broadway musical was heavily criticized at the time of release in 1969, for its over-use of gimmicky cinematic trickery and the over-the-top central performance of Shirley MacLaine. However, in retrospect many observers feel that it wasn't so bad after all. Peter Stone's screenplay stayed closely to Neil Simon's stage libretto which told of dance hall hostess Charity Hope Valentine (MacLaine) who is all set achieve her ambition and marry strait-laced Oscar Lindquist (John McMartin) until he finds out where she works. At first he appears to be coming to terms with Charity's somewhat unconventional lifestyle, but after attending her rowdy farewell party at the Fan-Dango ballroom, he finds that he can't go through with the ceremony and jilts her at the very last minute. There were strong supporting performances from Ricardo Montalban as film star Vittorio Vidal, Sammy Davis Jnr. in the role of Big Daddy, an hilarious hippy evangelist, Stubby Kaye as the owner of the Fan-Dango, and Paula Kelly, Chito Rivera and the rest of the girls at the club who all want to get out themselves, but still hate to see Charity go. Also among the cast were Barbara Bouchet, Suzanne Charney, Alan Hewitt, Dante D'Paulo, Bud Vest, Ben Vereen, Lee Roy Reams, Al Lanti, John Wheeler, and Leon Bing. Most of Cy Coleman and Dorothy Fields' outstanding songs survived the journey from Broadway to Hollywood, and the team added some new ones to form a score which consisted of 'Big Spender', 'If My Friends Could See Me Now', 'My Personal Property', 'Rhythm Of Life', 'There's Gotta Be Something Better Than This', 'I'm a Brass Band', 'Rich Man's Frug', 'The Hustle', 'Where Am I Going?', 'I Love To Cry At Weddings', 'It's a Nice Face', and the title number. In spite of the carping of the critics, much of Bob Fosse's choreography and direction was superb and stands repeated viewing. Robert Arthur was the producer for Universal, and the picture was photographed in Technicolor and Panavision by Robert Surtees.

SWEET CHARITY (STAGE MUSICAL)

Veteran lyricist Dorothy Fields was teamed with the much younger composer Cy Coleman on the score for this warm-hearted musical which opened at the Palace Theatre in New York on 29 January 1966. Neil Simon's book was based on Bob Fosse's original conception, and a screenplay by Federico Fellini, Tullio Pinelli, and Ennio Flaiano. Set in the 60s, it changed the movie's main character from a prostitute to a dance hall hostess, and named her Charity Hope Valentine (Gwen Verdon). In her desperate quest for love, marriage, and respectability, Charity becomes involved with an Italian film star, Vittorio Vidal (James Luisi), and a neurotic accountant, Oscar Lindquist (John McMartin). She is all set to marry Oscar, thinking that finally she has found something better in life than the Fan-Dango Ballroom, when - wouldn't you know it - he has 'this neurosis and mental block'. In vain, Charity reassures him that 'there's a lot of that going around,' but it's no

good. It seems he also has 'this childish, incomprehensible, idiotic fixation about purity'. In short, the wedding's off. Director-choreographer Fosse won a Tony Award for his innovative, exciting work, and his setting of 'Big Spender' in particular, with the dancehall 'girls' arrayed in a line, trying to attract the attention of each prospective terpsichorean punter, was quite something to see. There were no dull moments in Fields and Coleman's score which contained a whole range of marvellous songs, including 'You Should See Yourself', 'The Rescue', 'Big Spender', 'Charity's Soliloquy', 'Rich Man's Frug', 'If My Friends Could See Me Now', 'Too Many Tomorrows', 'There's Gotta Be Something Better Than This', 'I'm The Bravest Individual', 'Rhythm Of Life', 'Baby Dream Your Dream', 'Sweet Charity', 'Where Am I Going', 'I'm A Brass Band', and 'I Love to Cry At Weddings' (orchestrations, Ralph Burns). Gwen Verdon's portrayal of the loveable Charity was both funny and tender, but she was edged out of the Tonys by Angela Lansbury who triumphed for her performance in *Mame*. Also cast were Helen Gallagher and Thelma Oliver as Charity's best friends Nickie and Helene, John Wheeler as Fan-Dango boss Herman, along with Arnold Soboloff, the hip hippie Evangelist Daddy Johann Sebastian Brubek. *Sweet Charity* ran for 608 performances and was revived on Broadway in 1986 with Debbie Allen (Charity), Mark Jacoby (Vittorio), Michael Rupert (Oscar), Bebe Neuwirth (Nickie), and Allison Williams (Helene). This time there were Tony Awards for reproduction (revival), featured actor and actress (Rupert and Neuwirth), and costumes (Patricia Zipprodt). The 1967 London production starred the South African actress Juliet Prowse (Charity), Rod McLennan (Oscar), Josephine Blake (Nickie), Paula Kelly (Helene), and John Keston (Vittorio). Charity Hope Valentine was back in the West End in 1998, with Bonnie Langford, Cornell John (Oscar), Johanne Murdock (Nicky), Jane Fowler (Helene), and Mark Wynter (Vittorio). In the same year, a star-studded charity performance of *Sweet Charity* took place at the Avery Fisher Hall, Lincoln Center, in New York. For this unique occasion, Verdon, Rivera, Neuwirth, Allen, and Donna McKechnie, alternated in the role of Charity, with other parts also being shared by artists such as Carol Channing, Robert Goulet, Jim Dale, John McMartin, Jerry Orbach, and Betty Buckley. A memorable evening. A film version was released in 1969 with Shirley MacLaine, John McMartin, Chita Rivera, and Sammy Davis Jnr.

SWEET LOVE, BITTER

Alternative title: *It Won't Rub Off, Baby.* A film directed by Herbert Daniels in 1966, this is an attempt to examine racial problems in the USA through the life of a jazz musician. Based upon the novel *Night Song*, by John Alfred Williams, the story loosely portrays Charlie Parker's final years. Dick Gregory stars as the saxophone player, dubbed by Charles McPherson. Also heard are Chick Corea and Steve Swallow. The musical director was Mal Waldron.

SWEET RIDE, THE

Despite an 'adult' cast - which included Tony Franciosa and Jacqueline Bissett - *The Sweet Ride* invokes the spirit of the 'beach movie'. Surfers, drop-outs and miscued romances inhabit this 1968 feature which is largely forgettable barring a cameo role from Lee Hazlewood and footage of Moby Grape playing live. The San Franciscan group perform 'Never Again', a thinly-veiled rewriting of Jimi Hendrix's 'Foxy Lady', with real aplomb. Dusty Springfield contributes the lightweight title song, but it is the all-to-brief club shots which provide the film's only moments of excitement.

SWEETHEARTS (FILM MUSICAL)
Jeanette MacDonald and Nelson Eddy's fifth film together, which was released by MGM in 1938, eschewed the familiar costumes and wigs for a far more contemporary setting. Dorothy Parker and Alan Campbell's screenplay cast them as a successful musical comedy team in the long-running Broadway hit show, *Sweethearts*. Like so many stars in those days, the duo are attracted by the big money that Hollywood has to offer, but, in their case, it all goes sour, and they soon return to the theatre. Also among the strong cast were Ray Bolger, Frank Morgan, Herman Bing, Reginald Gardiner, Mischa Auer, and Florence Rice. The plot bore no relationship to the book of the real Broadway show called *Sweethearts*, which opened in 1913, although four of Victor Herbert's lovely songs were retained for the film version, albeit with new lyrics by Robert Wright and George Forrest. These were 'Pretty As A Picture', 'Wooden Shoes', 'Every Lover Must Meet His Fate', and the title number. The same team also contributed 'Summer Serenade', 'On Parade', and 'Game Of Love', and there were several other songs by various composers such as 'Little Grey Home In The West' (Herman Loehr-D. Eardly Wilmott) and 'Happy Day' (Herbert Stothart-Wright-Forrest). Albertina Rasch was the choreographer, and W.S. Van Dyke directed what was an effervescent and good natured affair in which MacDonald and Eddy were at their peak. It was the first MGM picture to be photographed in three-colour Technicolor, and Oliver T. Marsh and Allen Davey were awarded a special Oscar for their cinematography.

SWEETHEARTS (STAGE MUSICAL)
Most operettas are cherished for their sometimes glorious music, and gently mocked for their 'you cannot be serious' librettos. *Sweethearts*, which opened at the New Amsterdam Theatre in New York on 8 September 1913, was typical of the genré. Even so, Harry B. Smith and Fred De Gresac's book for this show stretched credibility to breaking point and beyond. The romantic story begins when the infant Sylvia (Christie MacDonald) is found in a tulip garden by Dame Paula (also known as Mother Goose) who is in charge of the Laundry of the White Geese. Sylvia is raised as her daughter until one day, purely by chance, she meets Prince Franz (Thomas Conkey) and they fall in love. Everything works out well because Sylvia is really the Crown Princess of the Kingdom of Zilania, so there is a big royal wedding and the couple ascend the vacant throne together. In contrast to that somewhat bizarre tale, the score, by Victor Herbert (music) and Robert B. Smith (lyrics), was rich and grand. Christie Macdonald introduced the gorgeous waltz,

'Sweethearts', and there were other numbers almost as fine, including 'The Angelus', 'Every Lover Must Meet His Fate', 'Pretty As A Picture', 'The Cricket On the Hearth', and 'Jeannette And Her Little Wooden Shoes'. The show ran for 136 performances and returned to New York briefly in 1929. A far more successful Broadway revival was mounted in 1947, when, following the successful resuscitation of Herbert's *The Red Mill* two years before, *Sweethearts* enjoyed a run of 288 performances at the Shubert Theatre. With a revised book by John Cecil Holm, the show was now a vehicle for comedian Bobby Clark, whose own particular brand of mayhem gave the piece a lighter and funnier touch. The 1938 film version starred Jeanette MacDonald and Nelson Eddy.

SWIFT, KAY
b. Kay Faulkner Swift, 19 April 1897, New York City, New York, USA, d. 28 January 1993, Southington, Connecticut, USA. A composer, lyricist and writer for Broadway, whose small but impressive catalogue of work is often overshadowed by her close association with the composer George Gershwin. After studying at Juilliard, Swift became an accomplished pianist and often performed on the concert platform, before making her breakthrough on Broadway in 1929 with the song 'Can't We Be Friends?', which was introduced by Libby Holman in the hit revue *The Little Show*. The sophisticated sombre lyric to what is essentially a spirited, jaunty tune, was written by Paul James, a *nom de plume* for Swift's first husband, banker James P. Warburg. The duo repeated their success in the following year with the score for the musical *Fine And Dandy*, which included 'Let's Go Eat Worms In The Garden', 'Jog Hop', the appealing title number, and Swift's best-remembered song, 'Can This Be Love'. Her relationship with George Gershwin, which eventually led to the break-up of her marriage, was intense and fruitful. As a rich socialite, she made his transition from Tin Pan Alley to concert hall all the smoother, and they spent many hours working together at the piano. In June 1937, after spending nine months in Hollywood with his brother Ira, George told Swift he was returning so that they could be together, but shortly afterwards he died before he could make the trip. Swift subsequently collaborated with Ira Gershwin in turning the best of George's unpublished - and often only partly finished - manuscripts into complete songs. Several of these comprised the score for the 1947 film musical *The Shocking Miss Pilgrim*, starring Betty Grable and Dick Haymes, the best known of which are 'For You, For Me, For Evermore' and 'Aren't You Kind Of Glad We Did?'. Swift's own credits included 'Up Among The Chimney Pots' for the *9:15 Revue* (1930), 'I'm All Washed Up With Love' (with Albert Silverman) for the left-wing musical *Parade* (1935), music and lyrics for Cornelia Otis Skinner's one-woman revue *Paris 90*, the score for celebrated choreographer George Balanchine's ballet *Alma Mater* - a spoof on the Harvard-Yale football game (1935), and the song cycle *Reaching For The Brass Ring*. Among her other songs for revues and shows were 'A Moonlight Memory', 'One Little Girl' ('Campfire Girls' 50th Anniversary Song'), the 1962 Seattle World's Fair song 'Century 21', 'Calliope', 'Sagebrush Lullaby' and 'Forever And A Day'. Swift's sec-

ond husband was rodeo cowboy Faye Hubbard, and details of their life together were revealed in her memoir *Who Could Ask For Anything More?*, published in 1943. It was filmed in 1950 with Irene Dunne and Fred MacMurray. Swift's third marriage, which ended in divorce, was to radio announcer Hunter Galloway.

● FURTHER READING: *Who Could Ask For Anything More?*, Kay Swift.

SWING TIME

Released in August 1936, just a few months after *Follow the Fleet*, *Swing Time* gave Fred Astaire and Ginger Rogers fans another feast of sensational dance routines and marvellous songs. Screenwriters Howard Lindsay and Allan Scott's vivid imagination resulted in a story in which dancer and gambler John 'Lucky' Garnett (Astaire) goes to New York to make his fortune after his future in-laws have rejected him as financially unsuitable for their daughter Margaret (Betty Furness). After meeting dance instructress Penny Carrol (Ginger Rogers), Margaret and money are forgotten, and the new team sing and dance their way to stardom. Jerome Kern and Dorothy Fields' score was full of outstanding numbers such as 'Pick Yourself Up', 'A Fine Romance', 'Never Gonna Dance', 'Waltz In Swing Time', and 'Bojangles Of Harlem' for which Astaire donned blackface for the only time in his long career. The lovely, tender ballad 'The Way You Look Tonight', which Fred sang to Ginger while she was shampooing her hair, won the Academy Award for best song. Most of the laughs were provided by the bumbling ex-vaudevillian Victor Moore and two of the comical characters from previous Astaire-Rogers extravaganzas, Helen Broderick and Eric Blore. *Swing Time*, which was another big box-office hit for RKO, was directed by George Stevens. The dance director - almost inevitably - was Hermes Pan.

SWINGING UK

Swinging UK was the first of two shorts directed by Frank Gilpin in 1964; the second was *UK Swings Again*. The premise of both features was identical; disc jockeys Kent Walton, Alan Freeman and Brian Matthews introduced several popular acts, all bar one of whom mimes to a current hit and a less-feted selection. Thus the Four Pennies offer the chart-topping 'Juliet', Millie sings the perennial 'My Boy Lollipop' and the Merseybeats play 'Don't Turn Around'. The Wackers are the sole exception, their version of 'Love Or Money' failed to chart and on this evidence, it is not hard to fathom why. Both of Gilpin's features were amalgamated with a third film, *Mods And Rockers* for US release. The composite was entitled *Go, Go Big Beat*, with actors Marlon Brando and Rod Steiger improbably standing in for the British disc jockeys.

SWINGMEN IN EUROPE

A film with a succession of bandstand performances by visiting American jazzmen. Directed by Jean Mazeas, this 1977 film features Milt Buckner, Teddy Buckner, Gene 'Mighty Flea' Conner, Illinois Jacquet, Jo Jones, Sammy Price, J.C. Heard and Doc Cheatham.

SYMPHONY IN BLACK

A very short but fascinating film made in 1934 that offers an opportunity to see and hear Duke Ellington And His Orchestra and Billie Holiday. Ellington's musicians include Artie Whetsol, Cootie Williams, Joe Nanton, Lawrence Brown, Johnny Hodges, Harry Carney and Sonny Greer. Holiday, in the first of her few film appearances, sings 'Saddest Tale'.

SYNCOPATION

Directed by William Dieterle, this 1942 film offers a Hollywood eye-view of the story of jazz. Predictably, accuracy is a minor consideration but there are some nice musical moments from a band of winners of a poll held by the *Saturday Evening Post*, whose readers seem to have heard of Benny Goodman and a few other swing era musicians but very little else. Apart from Goodman there are Harry James, Jack Jenney, Charlie Barnet, Joe Venuti, Bob Haggart and Gene Krupa. Stan Wrightsman dubbed the soundtrack for Bonia Granville, Bunny Berigan for Jackie Cooper, and Rex Stewart for Todd Duncan.

TAKE A CHANCE

The stories of the changes that are made to shows on the road during their pre-Broadway or West End try-outs are legendary, but not many can have undergone such radical reforms as this one. In September 1932 it was a revue entitled *Humpty Dumpty* with sketches and songs that dealt in an amusing way with certain aspects of American history. The material was linked by two members of the company seated in one of the theatre boxes, but the remainder of the audience in Pittsburg, Pennsylvania did not see the joke, and *Humpty Dumpty* had a great fall after just five days up there on the wall. However, when the show - retitled *Take A Chance* - opened at the Apollo Theatre on Broadway on 26 November, it had been turned into a conventional book musical, in which the stars, Jack Whiting and June Knight, are appearing together in a revue called *Humpty Dumpty* with songs and sketches that, naturally enough, deal in an amusing way with certain aspects of American history. The original score by Richard Whiting and Nacio Herb Brown (music) and Buddy De Sylva (lyrics) had been supplemented by several numbers by the composer Vincent Youmans. There were also some important changes in the cast, but fortunately Ethel Merman survived to sing (clearly and fairly loudly) the pick of the output from this impressive array of songwriters. She introduced the show's three big hits, 'Eadie Was A Lady' (De Sylva-Whiting-Roger Edens), 'Rise 'n' Shine' (De Sylva-Youmans), and 'You're An Old Smoothie' (De Sylva-Whiting-Brown) on which she duetted with 'innocent-abroad' comedian Jack Haley. The love-interest, Jack Whiting and June Knight, shared most of the other numbers which included 'Should I Be Sweet?', 'Oh, How I Long to Belong To You' and 'So Do I' (all three by De Sylva and Youmans), along with 'Turn Out The Lights' (De Sylva-Whiting-Brown), for which Whiting and Knight were joined by Haley and the show's other funny man, Sid Silvers. He also collaborated on the book with De Sylva and Laurence Schwab. With America emerging slowly from the Depression, Take A Chance was just the tonic that Broadway audiences needed, and they kept on coming for 243 performances. Towards the end of the run, Haley and Silvers were replaced by Olsen and Johnson, the vaudeville comedy team, who were making their debut in a legitimate Broadway musical. June Knight appeared in the 1933 film version, which came up with yet another variation on the original theme, along with Lillian Roth, James Dunn, and Cliff Edwards ('Ukelele Ike').

TAKE ME ALONG

Bob Merrill, the composer and lyricist for a host of pop hits during the 50s, wrote his first Broadway score in 1957 for New Girl In Town, a musical adaptation of Eugene O'Neill's classic drama Anna Christie. Two years later, for Take Me Along, he tackled another of the playwright's works, but one with a much lighter theme - Ah, Wilderness! It opened at the Shubert Theatre in New York on 22 October 1959 with a strong cast that was headed by a legendary Hollywood leading man of the 30s and 40s, Walter Pidgeon, and Jackie Gleason, whose main claim to fame at that time was as a comedian on US television. Joseph Stein and Robert Russell wrote the book, which was set in the homely town of Centerville, Connecticut, in 1910. Pidgeon plays Ned Miller, the publisher of the local newspaper, and the father of Richard, whose adolescent problems with his girlfriend, Muriel Macomber (Susan Luckey), and the devil drink, are resolved when he enters the hallowed halls of Yale University. The sub-plot concerns Sid Davis (Jackie Gleason), a far more serious drinker, who would like to settle down with Ned's sister, Lily (Eileen Herlie), but has to sober up before she will accept him. Pidgeon and Gleason duetted on the lively 'Take Me Along', and the rest of Merrill's score, which has been described as 'wistful and enchanting', included 'I Would Die', 'Staying Young', 'I Get Embarrassed', 'Sid Ol' Kid', 'We're Home', 'Promise Me A Rose', 'Nine O'Clock' and 'But Yours'. Pidgeon and Gleason were both nominated for the Tony Award for best actor, and Gleason won for the most satisfying stage role of his career. He was succeeded during the show's run of 448 performances by William Bendix, a movie tough-guy with a heart of gold.

Take Me Along returned to Broadway during the 1984/5 season, which, according to experienced Broadway watchers, was one of the worst in living memory. The climate was not right for the show's warm and charming approach, and it closed after only one performance.

TAKE ME HIGH

Following a period of reticence, Cliff Richard re-entered the world of celluloid with this 1973 exercise. However, the plot of Take Me High suggested the singer had learned nothing from the years since The Young Ones and Summer Holiday. The story revolves around the exploits of a merchant banker as he attempts to defeat a rival for a prized account but in the meantime opens a hamburger restaurant in Birmingham. Respite cannot be salvaged from Richard's musical contributions which reach a nadir with 'The Brumburger Duet'. Take Me High has barely nothing to commend it; few artists of Cliff's standing and experience have made such a professional blunder and yet survived with career intact.

TAKE ME OUT TO THE BALL GAME

A kind of a rehearsal for the historic On The Town, which was also released in 1949, except that Frank Sinatra, Gene Kelly and Jules Munshin are dressed mostly in baseball gear in this one, instead of their more familiar sailor suits. Actually, at the beginning of the film, Dennis Ryan (Sinatra) and Eddie O'Brien (Kelly), are clad in natty striped suits and straw boaters while engaging in their off-season occupation as a song-and-dance team in vaudeville. When they rejoin Nat Goldberg (Munshin) and the rest of their Wolves team-mates at the Florida training camp, it is to find that the team has a new boss - Miss K.C. (Katharine) Higgins (Esther Williams). She takes the job so seriously that she is only spotted in the hotel swimming pool once. Under her strict supervision, the team is well on the way to winning the pennant when a bunch of racketeers try to knobble O'Brien, and his performance suffers. However, a little love and affection from Katharine soon raises his batting average again, and the Wolves go on to glory. Betty Garrett chases (and catches) Sinatra - as she does in On The Town - and their duet, 'It's Fate Baby, It's Fate' (Roger Edens), is one of the film's highlights. Sinatra is suitably romantic with 'The Right Girl for Me' (Betty Comden-Adolph Green-Edens), and Kelly has his moments - along with other members of the cast - in 'Yes Indeedy', 'O'Brien To Ryan To Goldberg', 'Strictly USA', (all Comden-Green-Edens), 'The Hat My Father Wore Upon St. Patrick's Day' (Jean Schwartz-William Jerome), and 'Take Me Out To The Ball Game' (Albert Von Tilzer-Jack Norworth). Also involved in Harry Tugend and George Wells's turn-of-the-century screenplay (adapted from a story by Kelly and Stanley Donen) were Edward Arnold, Richard Lane, Sally Forrest, Murray Alper, William Graff, and the Blackburn Twins. Kelly and Donen also staged some nifty dance routines, and the whole affair was presided over by another ace choreographer, director Busby Berkeley. George Folsey photographed the picture splendidly in Technicolor, and it was produced by Arthur Freed's MGM unit. It was retitled Everybody's Cheering in the UK.

TAKE MY TIP

Billed as a musical, but more of a farce, this immensely entertaining vehicle for the husband-and-wife team of Cicely Courtneidge and Jack Hulbert was produced by Gaumont-British Pictures in 1937. Lord and Lady Pilkington, otherwise known as George and Hattie (Hulbert and Courtneidge), have fallen on hard times due to George's extravagance and naiveté. The crunch finally comes when he purchases a non-existent oil well for £15,000 from a cove called Buchan (Harold Huth), after meeting him in a Turkish Bath. Happily, help is at hand in the person of George and Hattie's trusted servant, Paradine (Frank Cellier), who has recently bought an hotel in Dalmatia with the money he has made backing horses that his boss (George) *didn't* fancy. He offers his former employers jobs in the hotel as head waiter (George) and hostess (Hattie). While there they adopt various disguises (and somewhat devious means) to retrieve their money from Buchan - complete with a handsome £5,000 profit. All ends satisfactorily (and democratically) with Paradine, George and Hattie going into partnership together. Incidentally, Hattie is an ex-musical comedy actress and George is a nifty hoofer, so there is plenty of excuse for the inclusion of songs such as 'Birdie Out Of A Cage', 'Colonel Bogey' (Kenneth J. Alford), 'The Sleepwalker', 'Sentimental Agitation', 'I'm Turning The Town Upside Down', 'Everybody Dance', and the delightful duet, 'I Was Anything But Sentimental' (Sammy Lerner-Al Hoffman-Al Goodhart). Also taking part in the fun and games were Frank Pettingell, comedian Robb Wilton, Philip Buchel, H.F. Maltby, Elliot Makeham, and Paul Sheridan. In charge of the mayhem was director Herbert Mason.

TAYLOR, BERNARD J.

b. 16 December 1944, Cape Town, South Africa. A versatile and prolific composer of powerful, romantic musicals since the late 80s, Taylor's early musical tastes ranged from rock 'n' roll to the works of the great theatre songwriters. Taylor's only formal musical education came when he spent a year in the South African Army. At the Army's musical school, he learnt to read music, and play flute and piccolo. After establishing himself as an arts journalist, he moved to Britain in 1969. Unable to break into the world of theatre, he worked as a writer and editor for the Shell Oil Company for more than 10 years. His first musical show, *Neigbours And Lovers*, for which he wrote both music and lyrics, failed to arouse any interest even from amateur dramatic groups, so he produced it himself at the Oast Theatre, Tonbridge, in 1987. Although it attracted a good deal of attention and favourable reaction, Taylor decided to abandon it in favour of creating a musical based on a universally known story. He selected Emily Brontë's classic *Wuthering Heights*, composing the music, and collaborating on the lyrics with Eric Vickers. A concept album was released in 1991 with an excellent cast, including a former 'Phantom Of The Opera', Dave Willetts, as Heathcliff, opera diva Lesley Garrett (Cathy Earnshaw), Bonnie Langford (Isabella Linton), Clive Carter (Hindley Earnshaw), Sharon Campbell (Ellen

'Nellie' Dean) and James Staddon (Edgar Linton). The romantic, sweeping score contained several appealing melodies, particularly the impassioned 'I Belong To The Earth'. Endorsed by the Brontë Society, *Wuthering Heights* was initially beset by contractual difficulties, but eventually received its world premiere in Holland. Around the same time, two more musical adaptations of Brontë's saga were on the boards in small off-off Broadway venues, while the long-awaited *Heathcliff*, starring UK pop star Cliff Richard, was still in the pipeline. Meanwhile, Taylor turned his attention to something entirely different. *Success!* was a backstage musical, loosely based on Faust, and set in New York. Peppered with parody and pastiche, with additional lyrics by Vivian Wadham, its typical, and often cynical, view of the ups and downs of showbusiness was accompanied by a jazzy and sometimes tender score, with Claire Moore, Lon Satton, Kathryn Evans, Jessica Martin and Maurice Clarke forming the CD cast. By the time *Success!* made its debut at the Civic Theatre, Rotherham, in September 1995, Taylor had returned to the classics, in the form of Jane Austen's *Pride And Prejudice*. With Claire Moore as Elizabeth Bennet and Peter Karrie in the role of Darcy, the concept album also featured Gay Soper, Janet Mooney, James Staddon and Christopher Biggins as Mr. Collins. Stand-out tracks were considered to be 'Through The Eyes Of A Child', 'Good Breeding' and 'Thank God They're Married'. *Pride And Prejudice* was introduced to US audiences, complete with five new songs, by the Public Theatre Company of Peoria, Illinois, in January 1995. Taylor's musical interpretation of the Austen novel was considered to be closer to its source than the 1959 Broadway version, *First Impressions* (Austen's original title for the book), which starred Hermione Gingold. In direct contrast to the subtleties of *Pride And Prejudice*, Taylor's *Nosferatu: The Vampire* (lyrics with Eric Vickers) proved a haunting, sombre affair. It was based on the silent black-and-white film of the Dracula tale by the German director F.W. Murnau. Prominent in its sung-through score was the opening 'Wild Talk Of Vampires', along with mysterious and unsettling items such as 'And Sheep Shall Not Safely Graze', 'Worms Feed On My Brains', 'Ship Of The Dead', 'Blasphemy' and 'Somewhere At The Edges Of Creation'. Once again, the album cast was led by Claire Moore (as Mina) and Peter Karrie (as Nosferatu), supported by Mario Frangoulis, Mark Wynter, Barry James, Annalene Beechey and Simon Burke. The world premiere was staged at the Madison Theatre, Illinois, in September 1995, and the show had its first European performances a month later in Eastbourne. Both productions were extremely well received. Having achieved considerable success with his adaptations of Brontë and Austen, Taylor did what several other composers, notably Cole Porter (*Kiss Me, Kate*), and Leonard Bernstein and Stephen Sondheim (*West Side Story*), had done before him - looked to the works of William Shakespeare. In this case it was the bard's *Much Ado About Nothing*, abbreviated to *Much Ado* (additional lyrics: Vickers), that came in for the Taylor treatment. Once again, there was a stellar CD cast, which included Paul McGann (Benedick), Claire Moore (Beatrice), Simon Burke (Claudio), Janet Mooney (Hero), Barry James

(Leonato), David Pendelbury (Dogberey) and Peter Karrie (Don John). Once again, Taylor's skill in writing convincing period music was apparent in songs such as 'If I Could Write A Sonnet', 'I'll Never Love Again', 'The Sweetest Kiss', 'Now I Hear Symphonies', and 'This Strange Affliction Called Love', as well as the humorous 'The Officers Of The Watch' and 'Never Satisfied'.

As the 90s drew to a close, Taylor, in collaboration with orchestrator Gareth Price, attempted 'to portray some of the key developments in the advance of civilization over the past 1,000 years' via his *Millenium Suite*. Performed on CD by the Polish State Philharmonic Orchestra of Latowice, conducted by Jerzy Swoboda, the suite consisted of 'The Birth Of Chivalry', 'The Age Of Oppression', 'The Enlightenment', 'The Road To Democracy' and 'The Triumph Of Democracy'. The climax of the programme came with 'Victory Overture', a celebration of the end of World War II. After featuring on the majority of Taylor's concept albums, Claire Moore, who has starred in the West End in shows such as *Aspects Of Love* and *The Phantom Of The Opera*, released the solo CDs *Songs From The Musicals Of Bernard J. Taylor* and *Child Of The Earth*. The latter consisted of Taylor compositions, apart from John Lennon's 'Imagine'.

TEMPLE, SHIRLEY

b. 23 April 1928, Santa Monica, California, USA. By the time this actress, singer, and dancer was six years old, she was a movie star of the first magnitude. Four years later, she became 20th Century-Fox's - and Hollywood's - top box-office attraction, with reported annual earnings of $300,000. Her poise, acting and dancing, plus her incredible screen presence, even gave rise to scurrilous rumours to the effect that she was a dwarf. After taking dancing lessons from the age of three, she appeared in short films and played bit parts in several minor features before coming to prominence singing 'Baby Take A Bow' in the 1934 musical *Stand Up And Cheer*. Her nine pictures in 1934, including *Little Miss Marker*, which made her a major film attraction, earned her a special (miniature) Academy Award 'in grateful recognition of her outstanding contribution to screen entertainment during the year'. Throughout the rest of the 30s she sparkled in musicals such as *Bright Eyes*, *Curly Top*, *The Littlest Rebel*, *Captain January*, *Poor Little Rich Girl*, *Dimples*, *Stowaway*, *Rebecca Of Sunnybrook Farm*, *Little Miss Broadway*, *Just Around The Corner*, *The Blue Bird*, and *Young People* (1940). From out of these simple, yet mostly enormously popular films, came songs such as 'On The Good Ship Lollipop', 'Animal Crackers In My Soup', 'When I Grow Up', 'Curly Top', 'At The Codfish Ball', 'Picture Me Without You', 'Oh, My Goodness', 'But Definitely', 'That's What I Want For Christmas', 'When I'm With You', 'We Should Be Together', 'Swing Me An Old-Fashioned Love Song' 'This Is a Happy Little Ditty', and 'I Want To Walk In The Rain'. By the end of the 30s Shirley Temple's career was in decline; the most successful child star of all-time could not sustain her appeal as a teenager. She left Fox and appeared throughout the 40s in a number of films for other studios - but only in straight roles. There were to be no more musicals. After marrying businessman Charles Black in 1950, she

became known as Shirley Temple Black and retired from showbusiness for a time, concentrating on her family and working extensively for charity. In the late 50s and into the early 60s, she appeared on US television in *The Shirley Temple Storybook* and *The Shirley Temple Show*. Later in the 60s she was prominent in politics and ran unsuccessfully for Congress as a Republican candidate. She subsequently served as US Ambassador to the United Nations and Ghana, and US Chief of Protocol. In 1990 she was appointed US Ambassador to Czechoslovakia, and, two years later, received a career achievement award at the annual D.W. Griffith Awards in Manhattan. In 1992, she attended a lavish retrospective tribute to her films organized by the Academy of Motion Picture Arts and Sciences, and was presented with a new, full-size Oscar to replace the miniature she received in 1934. In 1994 it was announced that some of her most popular films were being computer-coloured and released on video, and in 1998 - her 70th year - Shirley Temple was the recipient of Kennedy Center Honours.

● ALBUMS: *America's Sweetheart* (Pavillion/Flapper 1996)★★★, *On The Good Ship Lollipop* (President 1996)★★★, *The Songs Of Shirley Temple's Films* (Chanson Cinema/France 1998)★★★.

● FURTHER READING: *Shirley Temple*, L.C. Eby. *Temple*, J. Basinger. *Films Of Shirley Temple*, R. Windeler. *Shirley Temple: American Princess*, Anne Edwards. *Child Star* (her autobiography).

● FILMS: *War Babies* (1932), *The Red-Haired Alibi* (1932), *Polly Tix In Washington* (1932), *Pie Covered Wagon* (1932), *Kid's Last Stand* (1932), *Kid In Hollywood* (1932), *Glad Rags To Riches* (1932), *Kid In Africa* (1932), *To The Last Man* (1933), *Out All Night* (1933), *As The Earth Turns* (1933), *Now And Forever* (1934), *Little Miss Marker* (1934), *Change Of Heart* (1934), *Carolina* (1934), *Bright Eyes* (1934), *Baby Take A Bow* (1934), *Stand Up And Cheer* (1934), *Now I'll Tell* (1934), *Mandalay* (1934), *Our Little Girl* (1935), *The Little Colonel* (1935), *Curly Top* (1935), *The Littlest Rebel* (1935), *Stowaway* (1936), *Poor Little Rich Girl* (1936), *Captain January* (1936), *Dimples* (1936), *Wee Willie Winkie* (1937), *Heidi* (1937), *Rebecca Of Sunnybrook Farm* (1938), *Just Around The Corner* (1938), *Little Miss Broadway* (1938), *Susannah Of The Mountains* (1939), *The Little Princess* (1939), *The Blue Bird* (1940), *Young People* (1940), *Kathleen* (1941), *Miss Annie Rooney* (1942), *I'll Be Seeing You* (1944), *Since You Went Away* (1944), *Kiss And Tell* (1945), *That Hagen Girl* (1947), *Honeymoon* (1947), *The Bachelor And The Bobby-Soxer* (1947), *Fort Apache* (1948), *The Story Of Seabiscuit* (1949), *Mr Belvedere Goes To College* (1949), *Adventure In Baltimore* (1949), *A Kiss For Corliss* (1949).

THANK GOD IT'S FRIDAY

After *Saturday Night Fever* at the 2001 Odyssey disco inferno, welcome to Friday night at a rather more down-market establishment, The Zoo in Hollywood. Strutting their funky stuff we have Nicole Simms (Donna Summer), a future star singer if there ever was one; teacher Shirley (Hilary Beane) and her blind date, refuse-collector Gus (Chuck Sacci); schoolgirl Frannie (Valerie Landsburg) who leaves her friend Jeannie (Terri Nunn) so that she can win the dance contest with Marv 'The Leatherman' Gomez (Chick Vennera); and accountant Dave (Mark Lonow), who chats up pill-popping Jackie (Marya Small), while The Zoo's oily proprietor Tony Di Marco (Jeff Goldbum) is chatting up *his* wife. A motley menagerie. Also around somewhere are DJ Bobby Speed (Ray Vitte), along with Ken (John Friedrich) and Jennifer (Debra Winger). Accompanying all these shenanigans is a hot soundtrack featuring the Commodores ('Brickhouse', 'Too Hot Ta Trot', 'Easy'), Donna Summer ('Love To Love You Baby', 'Try With Your Love', 'Je T'Aime (Moi Non Plus)', 'Last Dance'), the Fifth Dimension ('You're The Reason I Feel Like Dancing'), Thelma Houston ('I'm Here Again', 'Love Masterpiece'), Diana Ross ('Lovin', Livin' And Givin''), Village People ('I Am What I Am'), Wright Brothers Flying Machine ('Leatherman's Theme'), Pattie Brooks ('After Dark'), Cameo ('It's Serious'), G.C. Cameron and Syreeta ('Let's Make A Deal'), and many more. Not a classic, this movie, which was directed by Robert Klane and produced by Casablanca/Motown for Columbia in 1978. Even so, the soundtrack album reached the US Top 10, and 'Last Dance' (music and lyric by Paul Jabara) won an Oscar. 'Last Dance' also won Grammys for best R&B song, and Donna Summer's performance of it.

THANKS A MILLION

Taking a break from Warner Brothers, Ruby Keeler and the *Gold Diggers*, Dick Powell co-starred with the delightful Ann Dvorak in this bright and entertaining musical which was released by 20th Century-Fox in 1935. The distinguished writer, producer, and director Nunnally Johnson, came up with a pip of a satirical script in which Powell plays Eric Land, a crooner with a small troupe of travelling entertainers. They get stranded in a small town, and - just to pass the time - Powell reads the speech for the Commonwealth Party candidate for State Governor, A. Darius Culliman (Raymond Walburn), after the old boy is taken ill with indigestion (drunk). Powell is so impressive that leading members of the Party persuade him to run for the office himself. Naturally, they will expect cushy jobs for themselves after he wins. However, he will have no part in their corruption, and, after exposing them, is triumphantly elected on a four-point ticket - one of which is that none of his political addresses will last for more than 30 seconds. Ann Dvorak played Powell's adoring girlfriend, of course, and radio star Fred Allen was fine as his manager - a bit of a hustler who is intent on bringing some pizzazz into politics. Also among the cast were Paula Kelly, Benny Baker, Alan Dinehart, Paul Harvey, Edwin Maxwell, and Margaret Irving. Paul Whitman and his Band with Zorina, and Rubinoff and the Yacht Club Boys made guest appearances. Gus Kahn and Arthur Johnston wrote the tuneful score which included 'Thanks A Million', 'Sittin' On A Hilltop', 'Pocketful Of Sunshine', 'New O'leans', 'Sugar Plum', 'Sing Brother', and 'The Square Deal Party'. Roy Del Ruth directed with verve and style, and it was nicely photographed in black and white by Peverell Marley. The producer was Darryl F. Zanuck. It was remade in 1946 as *If I'm Lucky*.

THAT NIGHT IN RIO

One of the most familiar (and entertaining) plots in movie musicals - it was also the basis of *Folies Bergère De Paris* (1935) and *On The Riviera* (1951) - was utilized in this lively Technicolor 20th Century-Fox, musical which burst onto the screen in 1941. Perhaps the reason why screen-writers George Seaton, Bess Meredyth, and Hal Long (and others before them) used Rudolph Lothar and Hans Adler's original play for their inspiration, is because it entails the (inevitably) good-looking leading man playing two roles. The story goes something like this: a nightclub entertainer (Don Ameche) resembles a philandering businessman (Don Ameche) so closely that he is hired to take the tycoon's place when he is out of town 'on business' with a 'client' (Carmen Miranda). The deception is so convincing that even the neglected wife (Alice Faye) does not know the difference. In only her second American film, Miranda had already got into the habit of stealing the honours from under the noses of the more established stars. In this particular case she was aided and abetted by songwriters Harry Warren and Mack Gordon, who presented her with two stunning numbers, 'I, Yi, Yi, Yi, Yi (I Like You Very Much)' and 'Chica Chica Boom Chic'; and director Irving Cummings who (as he had done in *Down Argentine Way*) gave her the opening number. Choreographer Hermes Pan helped her too, by designing some splendid settings in which to showcase her very individual talents. The rest of the score included 'They Met In Rio', 'Boa Noite', and 'The Baron Is In Conference' (Warren-Gordon), along with 'Cae Cae' (Roberto Martins-Pedro Berrios). The admirable supporting cast contained some very familiar names, including S.Z. Sakall, J. Carrol Naish, Curt Bois, Leonid Kinskey, along with the Banda Da Lua (Carmen Miranda's orchestra), and guest artists the Flores Brothers.

THAT SUMMER

Genre movies hitched to passing fads are the stuff of pop's cinematic history. Rock 'n' roll, surfing and psychedelia all spawned corresponding, often quickie, films, and 70s punk was no different. Two hitherto unknown actors, Emily Moore and Julie Shipley, play factory hands escaping drudgery in Leeds for a summer of seasonal work in Torquay. Here they meet two Londoners, portrayed by Tony Winstone and Ray London, and encounter the usual travails associated with teenage life. Engaging performances coupled with sympathetically paced direction from Harley Cokliss ensures *That Summer*, although hardly innovatory, rises above mere formula. The soundtrack, culled from music heard on jukeboxes, radios and in clubs, emphasises the 'new-wave' aspect of punk with songs by the Boomtown Rats, Elvis Costello, Ian Dury and Nick Lowe. US acts Patti Smith, Richard Hell and the Ramones are among the others featured in a low-key, but meritorious, film.

THAT THING YOU DO!

Set in the early 60s, this story of the Wonders, a four-piece beat group from a small town in Pennsylvania, was written and directed by Tom Hanks. He also plays Mr White, the sharp-suited executive who signs the not-so fab four to Play-Tone Records after hearing their recording of 'That Thing You Do!' (incessantly). Their rise to brief stardom on the back of that disc is almost as difficult to understand as their eventual demise, when the group's leader, Jimmy (Johnathon Schaech), flies the coop because White will not allow the Wonders to record a song of his. Admittedly, the bass player (Ethan Embry), is also threatening to join the Marines, and drummer Guy, the former appliance (electrical-type) salesman, played by Hanks lookalike Tom Everett Scott, has been making (non-musical) overtures to Jimmy's girlfriend, Faye (Liv Tyler). Even so, the Beatles, to whom the Wonders bear more than a passing resemblance (in a superficial kind of way), weathered far worse storms than that. Hanks also had a hand in writing several songs in a score which consisted of, 'Lovin' You Lots And Lots', 'It's Not Far', 'La Senora De Dos Costas', 'Sad Sad Boy', 'Back Together', 'Mr. Downtown', 'Voyage Around The Moon', 'Hold My Hand, Hold My Heart', 'Will You Marry Me?', 'All My Only Dreams', 'Dance With Me Tonight', 'Drive Faster', 'She Knows It', 'I Need You (That Thing You Do)', 'Little Wild One', 'Spartacus', 'Time To Blow', 'Hollywood Showcase Theme', 'Blue Spot', 'My World Is Over', 'Shrimp Shack', 'Twangin'', 'Cock 'N Bull', and 'Watch Your Money'. This bland, *'Happy Days'* kind of film, was produced by 20th Century-Fox and released in 1996.

THAT'LL BE THE DAY

One of the best British films of the early 70s, *That'll Be The Day* was a sometimes bitter look at teenage life in the pre-Beatles era. David Essex starred as the disaffected Jamie MacLean, an aspiring rock 'n' roll singer, who rejects the values of his parents in favour of fairgrounds and holiday camps. He meets and befriends Mike, memorably portrayed by Ringo Starr, who in real life spent a season at Butlins with his early group, Rory Storm And The Hurricanes. Billy Fury plays vocalist Stormy Tempest, leading a group that included Graham Bond and Who drummer Keith Moon, who also collaborated on the soundtrack music with former Beatles road manager, Neil Aspinall, and Wil Malone, latterly of pop groups Orange Bicycle and the Smoke. The Essex character is inspired by Tempest's performance and shows little regard for others in his quest for fame. His affairs are casual and he shows little regard for Mike when the latter is severely beaten. A shallow individual, MacLean steps on the first rung of success as the film closes; his subsequent career is chronicled on a follow-up film, *Stardust. That'll Be The Day* blends strong characterization with the drabness of British late 50s culture. This unflinchingly unsentimental feature contextualizes the importance of concurrent pop as a release for pent-up frustration.

THAT'S A GOOD GIRL

The first of several highly popular and successful musical comedies in which Jack Buchanan and Elsie Randolph starred together and delighted London theatre audiences with their elegant and graceful blend of song and dance - and the usual frothy plot. *That's A Good Girl* opened at the London Hippodrome on 5 June 1928 with a book by Douglas Furber in which Buchanan was pursued throughout England and the South Of France by Randolph in the role of a detective who adopted so many disguises that she probably didn't know who she was herself. There were plenty of smart and witty lines, but the audiences really came to see the 'dynamic duo', Britain's answer to Fred Astaire and his sister Adele. The music for *That's A Good*

Girl was composed by the Americans Phil Charig and Joseph Meyer, and another distinguished American, Ira Gershwin, provided some of the lyrics, along with Douglas Furber and Desmond Carter. The big hit song, introduced by the two stars, was 'Fancy Our Meeting', and this remained forever associated with Jack Buchanan. The rest of the numbers included another duet, 'The One I'm Looking For', along with 'Sweet So-And-So', 'Tell Me Why', 'Chirp, Chirp', 'Marching Song', 'Let Yourself Go', and 'Parting Time'. This show found Buchanan at the peak of his powers. It's sometimes difficult to realise how enormously popular and versatile he was. As well as performing in *That's A Good Girl*, he also presented the show, and choreographed and directed it as well. It ran for nearly a year, a total of 363 performances, and Jack Buchanan and Elsie Randolph recreated their roles for the film version which was released in 1933.

THEODORAKIS, MIKIS

b. 29 July 1925, Khios, Greece. A poet, patriot, politician and composer of numerous film scores, Theodorakis was seven years old when he learned to sing Byzantine hymns and Greek folk songs. His first film music of note was for *Barefoot Battalion* (1954), the true story of Greek orphans' struggle against the Germans during World War II; an apt theme in view of his own subsequent strife. His other movie scores, during the 50s and early 60s, included *Night Ambush*, *The Shadow Of The Cat*, *The Lovers Of Tereul*, *Phaedra*, *Electra* and *Five Miles To Midnight*. In 1964, the composer's memorable score for *Zorba The Greek* contributed to the film's enormous success. It was to be one of his last projects before his life changed dramatically in April 1967. Following the fascist colonels' military *coup d'etat* in Greece, Theodorakis, as a Communist, was forced underground, and eventually imprisoned and tortured. By Army Order, the people were banned from listening to and performing his works, although his music became a symbol of resistance for the his fellow islanders. In 1969, John Barry, a fellow composer for films, smuggled out tapes of Theodorakis singing new songs, reciting his own poems and describing prison conditions, and sent them to U Thant, the then Secretary General of the United Nations. Theodorakis's own version of his appalling experiences were detailed in his book, *Journals Of Resistance*, in 1973. After his escape from Greece, the composer was exiled for several years in Paris, and started writing for films again in the early 70s. These included *Biribi*, *Serpico*, *State Of Seige*, *Sutjeska*, *Partisans*, *Letters From Marusia*, *Iphighenia* and *Easy Road*. For a number years Theodorakis was a Member of Parliament in Greece, but in the late 80s he began to give concerts in Europe and elsewhere, and resumed composing for projects such as the Turkish film *Sis* (1989). In 1992 it was reported that he had resigned his post as a minister without portfolio in the Greek government.

● ALBUMS: *Zorba The Greek* (1983) ★★★★, *The Bouzoukis Of Mikis Theodorakis* (1984)★★★, *Ballad Of Mauthausen* (1986)★★★, *Canto General* (1986)★★★, *All Time Greatest Hits* (1993)★★★★.

THERE'S NO BUSINESS LIKE SHOW BUSINESS

Incongruous is perhaps an appropriate word to describe the casting of the 'Nabob of Sob', pop singer Johnnie Ray, in this film, which was one of the last of the truly lavish screen musicals and was released by 20th Century-Fox in 1955. Ray plays one of the Donahues, a vaudeville act consisting of his brother and sister (Mitzi Gaynor and Donald O'Connor) and their parents (Dan Dailey and Ethel Merman). Ray even manages to induce a few of his trademark tears, although in this instance they swell up in the eyes of his proud old Mom and Dad after he has announced his decision to become a priest. That scene, and his strangulated version of 'If You Believe', one of the two new songs in Irving Berlin's otherwise entertaining score, should surely have won someone a bad-taste Oscar. Instead, the only whiff of an Academy Award was the nomination for Lamar Trotti's story (adapted for the screen by Henry and Phoebe Ephron). It deals with the triumphs and crises experienced by the family group, and O'Connor's initially ill-fated love affair with a cabaret singer played by Marilyn Monroe. After spending some time in the US Navy 'growing up', O'Connor joins the rest of the clan for the finale and a rousing version of the title song. Before going away to sea, he has some of the best numbers, singing and dancing delightfully in 'A Man Chases A Girl (Until She Catches Him)' and (with Gaynor and Monroe) 'Lazy'. He also adopted a Scottish accent for his part in a spectacular setting of 'Alexander's Ragtime Band'. Gaynor gave the number a touch of the Parisian, Merman was gamely Germanic, and Johnnie Ray . . . well, his intended articulation was unclear. Other highlights of the film were Monroe's sizzling versions of 'Heat Wave' and 'After You Get What You Want You Don't Want It', and Merman and Dailey's 'Play A Simple Melody', 'A Pretty Girl Is Like A Melody', 'Let's Have Another Cup Of Coffee' and 'You'd Be Surprised'. Jack Cole, who had worked with Monroe on *Gentlemen Prefer Blondes* two years earlier, staged her dances, and the remainder of the film's spirited routines were choreographed by Robert Alton. Sol C. Siegel was the producer, and it was directed by Walter Lang. The impressive DeLuxe Color and CinemaScope photography was by Leon Shamroy.

THEY'RE PLAYING OUR SONG

After composer Marvin Hamlisch's tremendous success with the long-running *A Chorus Line* (1975), he turned to his real-life partner, Carole Bayer Sager, for the lyrics to this minuscule musical which opened at the Imperial Theatre in New York on 11 February 1979. Minuscule that is, as regards the cast, for there were only two principal players, Lucie Arnaz and Robert Klein, although they each had three singing alter egos. Neil Simon's book, which is said to have been based on Hamlisch and Sager's own stormy relationship, concerns Vernon Gersch (Klein) and Sonia Walsk (Arnaz), two hip young songwriters whose developing romantic entanglement is hampered by Sonia's ex-boyfriend's telephone calls at any time of the day or night, and the feeling that they should keep things on a professional level anyway. The pleasing, melodic

score included 'Fallin'', 'Workin' It Out', 'If He Really Knew Me', 'They're Playing My Song', 'Just For Tonight', 'When You're In My Arms', 'Right', and 'I Still Believe In Love'. No doubt the absence of a large chorus and similar overheads contributed to the show's ability to last out for 1,082 performances. Subsequent road shows were equally successful, and the West End production with Tom Conti and Gemma Craven was the highlight of the 1980 London theatre season.

THIS IS THE ARMY

Apart from George M. Cohan, no personality in American show business could wave the stars and stripes quite like Irving Berlin. He did it to great effect during World War I with the stage show *Yip Yip Yaphank*, and he rekindled the patriotic flames again in 1942 with *This Is The Army*. This all-soldier revue, which opened at the Broadway Theatre in New York on July 4 (naturally), was a mixture of songs and sketches designed to spread the belief that it was just a matter of time before the boys would all be home - and for good. Most of the songs were new, but Berlin himself sang one of fondly remembered oldies, 'Oh, How I Hate To Get Up In the Morning', surrounded by his buddies dressed in 1917 soldiers' uniforms, just as he had in *Yip Yip Yaphank* all those years ago. The rest of the fine score included 'This Is The Army, Mr. Jones' ('You've had your breakfast in bed before/But you won't get it there anymore'), 'The Army's Made A Man Of Me', 'I'm Getting Tired So I Can Sleep', 'This Time', and 'American Eagles'. For the 'I Left My Heart At The Stage Door Canteen' number, male cast members impersonated female celebrities such as Gypsy Rose Lee and Lynn Fontanne, representing the stars who really did wait on members of the US Armed Services at the real-life Stage Door Canteen in New York. Among those taking part in the show at various times, were Ezra Stone, Burl Ives, Robert Sidney, Earl Oxford, Gary Merrill, and Alan Manson. The rousing finale, with everyone dressed in full uniform, was guaranteed to bring a tear to the eye every night. *This Is the Army* ran for 113 performances in New York, and then toured in the US and overseas until the end of the war. The 1943 film version starred George Murphy and Joan Leslie (and Irving Berlin).

THIS YEAR OF GRACE!

One of the most popular of the Noël Coward - Charles B. Cochran revues, *This Year Of Grace!* opened at the London Pavilion on 22 March 1928. The book, music and lyrics were by Coward, and the all-star cast included Sonnie Hale, Douglas Byng, Maisie Gay, Tilly Losch, Jessie Matthews, Lance Lister, and Moya Nugent. The score contained several memorable numbers, such as 'Dance, Little Lady', 'A Room With A View', 'Teach Me To Dance Like Grandma', 'Lorelei', 'Mary Make-Believe', 'I'm Mad About You', and 'Try To Learn To Love'. It ran for 316 performances in London, and Coward himself starred in the Broadway edition which began its run of 158 performances in November 1928. With him in the New York cast were Florence Desmond, and Beatrice Lillie who introduced an extra Coward composition, 'World Weary'.

THIS'LL MAKE YOU WHISTLE

After appearing in various films such as *Brewster's Millions*, *Come Out Of The Pantry*, and *When Knights Were Bold*, with the glamorous Hollywood actresses Fay Wray and Lili Damita, Jack Buchanan was reunited with his best-known partner, the very English Elsie Randolph, for this 1937 General Film Distributors' screen adaptation of the hit West End musical. In Guy Bolton and Paul Thompson's screenplay, which was based on their original book, Bill Hopping (Buchanan) splits from his fiancé, Laura (Marjorie Brooks), because she is more passionate about horses than she is about him. Laura wants him back, and despatches her guardian uncle (Antony Holles) to look him over and give his approval. Having made alternative romantic arrangements with Joan (Jean Gillie), Bill and his pals Reggie and Archie (William Kendall and David Hutcheson), throw a 'Bohemian' party in order to put the uncle off. Unfortunately, this particular uncle entirely approves of this kind of behaviour; even the presence of Bobbie Rivers (Elsie Randolph), an artist's model who is in the habit of removing her clothes even when she isn't working, fails to put him off. However, after the action moves to Le Touquet, Reggie is the one who ends up with Laura. Maurice Sigler, Al Goodhart, and Al Hoffman were responsible for the lively and tuneful score which included 'I'm In Dancing Mood', 'There Isn't Any Limit To My Love', 'Without Rhythm', and 'This'll Make You Whistle'. The producer-director was Herbert Wilcox.

THOROUGHLY MODERN MILLIE

This thoroughly entertaining pastiche of the 20s and the world of silent movies was released by Universal in 1967. Julie Andrews is Millie, the 'modern' of the title, and eager to marry one of New York's rich and eligible bachelors. She has a room at a boarding house which is reserved for single young women. Here she meets, and takes under her wing, a new resident, Miss Dorothy Brown (Mary Tyler Moore), who immediately attracts the attention of the landlady Mrs. Meers (Beatrice Lillie), a sinister (but hilarious) character with a serious interest in white slave trading. Millie sets out to capture her granite-jawed boss, Trevor Graydon (John Gavin), but he falls for Miss Dorothy and Millie is happy to end up with Jimmy Smith (James Fox), who (by heck) makes up dance-steps like 'The Tapioca' (Jimmy Van Heusen-Sammy Cahn) right there on the spot. Carol Channing as the wealthy Muzzy (step-mother of Miss Dorothy and Jimmy, as it turns out), makes one of her rare screen appearances, and renders delightful versions of 'Jazz Baby' (M.K. Jerome-Blanche Merrill) and 'Do It Again' (George Gershwin-Buddy De Sylva). Julie Andrews was splendid as Millie, especially when handling 'period' numbers such as 'Jimmy' (Kay Thompson), 'Baby Face' (Harry Askst-Benny Davis), 'Poor Butterfly' (Raymond Hubbell-John Golden), and the scene-setting title song by Cahn and Van Heusen. Her delicious all-round performance is some indication of how impressive she must have been on Broadway in 1954 when she starred in *The Boyfriend* - a pastiche in a similar vein. This upbeat, jolly movie had a screenplay by Richard Morris and was directed by George Roy Hill. The choreographer was Joe Layton, and it was photographed in Technicolor and Panavision by Russell Metty. Elmer Bernstein won an Oscar for his background music score.

THOSE WERE THE HAPPY TIMES

(see *Star!*)

THOUSANDS CHEER

Another lavish film effort by Hollywood in 1943 to lighten the war years by parading many of the most popular entertainers across the screen with only the most tenuous storyline to hold things together. Paul Jarrico and Richard Collins' script concerns the love affair between a former circus aerialist (Gene Kelly), who becomes a US army private and falls for the colonel's daughter (Kathryn Grayson). John Boles and Mary Astor play her father and mother, and most of MGM's galaxy of stars perform a dazzling array of musical party pieces, including Lena Horne ('Honeysuckle Rose'), Judy Garland, with Jose Iturbi ('The Joint Is Really Jumpin' In Carnegie Hall'), and Virginia O'Brien ('In A Little Spanish Town'). Gene Kelly danced 'The Mop Dance' delightfully, and Kathryn Grayson sang several numbers, notably 'Three Letters In A Mailbox', 'Daybreak', and 'Let There Be Music'. Also cast were Mickey Rooney, Red Skelton, Eleanor Powell, Margaret O'Brien, June Allyson, Gloria De Haven, Lucille Ball, and Frank Morgan. Guest stars included Marilyn Maxwell, Ann Sothern, and Marsha Hunt. Some of the best musical moments were provided by the bands of Bob Crosby, Kay Kyser, and Benny Carter. There were Oscar nominations for George Folsey's colour cinematography, Herbert Stothart's 'scoring of a musical picture', and Cedric Gibbons and Daniel Cathcart's interior direction. George Sidney directed *Thousands Cheer*, which grossed $3.5 million at the box office in the USA and Canada alone, making it one of the most successful musicals of the decade.

THREE'S A CROWD

Just a year after they appeared together in the legendary revue *The Little Show*, the main participants in that show were reunited for this similar kind of song and sketch entertainment which opened at the Selwyn Theatre in New York on 15 October 1930. Most of the numbers were by Arthur Schwartz and Howard Dietz, who combined with the suave and sophisticated song-and-dance man Clifton Webb, deadpan comedian Fred Allen, and torch singer *extraordinaire* Libby Holman, to make this an amusing and innovative show. The sketches came from a variety of writers such as Dietz himself, Laurence Schwab, William Miles, Donald Blackman, Groucho Marx, and Arthur Sheekman. Schwartz and Dietz's musical numbers included 'The Moment I Saw You', 'Right At The Start Of It', and the gentle and wistful 'Something To Remember You By', which was introduced by Holman and became popular via her recording, and another, several years later, by Dinah Shore. Holman also sang the most enduring song in the piece, the lovely ballad 'Body And Soul', which was the work of Johnny Green, Edward Heyman, Frank Eyton and Robert Sour. After early recordings by Paul Whiteman, Leo Reisman with Eddy Duchin at the piano, and Ruth Etting, it went on to become an all-time standard in the popular field, and has proved to be a particular favourite of jazz artists such as the pioneering tenor saxophonist Coleman Hawkins. The rest of the score for *Three's A Crowd* included 'Talkative Toes' (Dietz-Vernon Duke), 'Out In The Open Air' (Dietz-Burton Lane), 'All The King's Horses' (Dietz-Edward Brandt-Alec Wilder), and 'Yaller' (Richard Myers-Charles Schwab). The show ran for 272 performances, and set the mood and style for many other musical productions of the 30s.

THREEPENNY OPERA, THE

A dramatic play with music by Kurt Weill, and a book and lyrics by Bertolt Brecht, this three-act production was first presented at the Theatre am Schiffbauerdam in Berlin on 31 August 1928 under the title of *Die Dreigroschenoper*. That was 200 years after the show on which it was based, *The Beggar's Opera* by John Gay, was first seen in London. *The Threepenny Opera* had its first English language production on Broadway in 1933, and then returned to New York in 1954. This revised version, with an English book and lyrics by Marc Blitzstein, opened off-Broadway at the Theatre de Lys on 10 March, and ran for just three months. Public demand caused it to return in September 1955, and this time it stayed for an incredible 2,706 performances. The cynical and satirical tale of morality that had seemed so appropriate, yet futile, in the Germany of the 20s, remained the same, with its familiar characters including the outlaw Macheath, otherwise known as Mack the Knife (Scott Merrill), his wife Polly Peachum (Jo Sullivan), the police chief's daughter Lucy Brown (Beatrice Arthur), and Jenny Diver, the whore, played by Lotte Lenya (Weill's widow), the actress who had created the role in Germany. The score included 'The Ballad Of Mack The Knife', 'Love Song', 'Army Song', 'Pirate Jenny', 'Tango-Ballad', 'Useless Song', 'Ballad Of The Easy Life', 'Barbara Song', 'Solomon Song' and 'Instead-Of-Song'. During the show's extremely long run, many well-known actors and actresses took part, including Charlotte Rae, James Mitchell, Jerry Orbach, Carole Cook, Nancy Andrews, and Edward Asner. The English actress Georgia Brown played Lucy for a time, and she recreated her role, along with Bill Owen, Daphne Anderson, Lisa Lee, Eric Pohlmann and Warren Mitchell for the 1956 London production, which ran for 140 performances. Thirty years later in March 1986, a UK National Theatre production starred Tim Curry. A new adaptation of the piece, by Ralph Manheim and John Willett, spent 10 months on Broadway in 1976, and yet another version, billed as *3 Penny Opera* and translated by Michael Feingold, gave 65 performances at the Lunt-Fontanne Theatre in November 1989. Perhaps in an attempt to attract a different kind of audience, the cast for that production included rock star Sting as Macheath, along with popular singers Maureen McGovern and Kim Criswell. A 1994 London revival at the Donmar Warehouse, starring Tom Hollander and Sharon Small as Macheath and Polly Peachum, was set in the year 2001. Several film versions have been released, notably in 1931 with Lotte Lenya, and in 1964 with Hildegarde Neff and Curt Jurgens. The show is best remembered by many people for one song - 'Mack the Knife' (originally entitled 'Moriat'). It was introduced by Lotte Lenya in the tinkly Victorian-style of most of the show's music, and became successful in 1956 in the USA for several artists including the Dick Hyman Trio, Richard Hayman with Jan August, Lawrence Welk, Louis Armstrong and Billy Vaughn. Three years later the song became a massive number 1 hit on both sides of the Atlantic in a superb swinging version by Bobby Darin. Shortly afterwards, Ella Fitzgerald made a popular recording, and in 1984, yet another version, by the vocal-instrumental group King Kurt, entered the UK chart.

THUNDER ALLEY

By 1967 the now-profligate American International Pictures was balancing 'quickies' based on the billowing counter-culture (*The Trip*, *Psyche-Out*) with anachronistic features revolving around beach and dragster themes. *Thunder Alley* starred Fabian as a stock car racer haunted by a childhood guilt-complex - he ran over his brother with a go-kart. Also immersed in this risible story-line was AIP stalwart Annette Funicello, but by this point little distraction could be gleaned by a parade of contemporary pop acts. The suitably anonymous Group With No Name offered the title song and 'Time After Time', but it was clear that even Mike Curb, who had been responsible for numerous 'exploitation' film soundtracks, was tiring of the treadmill. *Thunder Alley* was one of the last such projects he undertook before becoming the youngest-ever president of MGM Records.

TICKLE ME

Elvis Presley's 1965 film maintained the insouciant qualities of its immediate predecessors. The singer played an unemployed rodeo star who takes a job at a health ranch, where he becomes embroiled in a search for hidden treasure, helping co-star Julia Adams escape a gang equally intent on finding the booty. In an unexpected finale, the climax takes place in a haunted ghost town, adding a rare twist to a formula crippling Presley's acting promise. The soundtrack was, however, superior to several previous releases. It was comprised of out-takes from earlier sessions - some dating back to 1960 - rather than songs penned to fit the storyline. In isolation, *Tickle Me* offers the same light-hearted appeal as contemporary 'beach' films, but repetition undermined whatever charms it possessed.

TIERNEY, HARRY

b. Harry Austin Tierney, 21 May 1890, Perth Amboy, New Jersey, USA, d. 22 March 1965, New York, USA. A popular composer for the Broadway musical stage during the 20s, Tierney intended to study classical music, and attended the Virgil School of Music in New York. After touring the USA and other countries as a concert pianist, he worked for some time at the famous Remick's publishing house in New York, and started to write popular songs. From 1916-18, he had several songs interpolated into Broadway shows, including *The Passing Show Of 1916* ('So This Is Paris'); *Hitchy-Koo* ('M-I-S-S-I-S-S-I-P-P-I', a hit for Ann Wheaton and Ada Jones); *Everything* ('On Atlantic Beach' and 'Honky Tonk Town'); *The Canary* ('Jazz Marimba' and

'Oh, Doctor'); *So Long Letty* and *Follow Me*. With his chief collaborator Joseph McCarthy, Tierney contributed 'My Baby's Arms' to the *Ziegfeld Follies Of 1919*, which is generally held to be the best edition of the series. In the same year, Tierney and McCarthy wrote the songs for *Irene*, the season's biggest hit, which starred Edith Day, and featured musical numbers such as 'Alice Blue Gown', 'Talk Of The Town' and 'Castle Of Dreams'. It went on to become one of America's most treasured musicals, and was filmed in 1940, starring Anna Neagle and Ray Milland, and successfully revived at the Minskoff Theatre in 1973 with Debbie Reynolds as Irene. In 1920, Tierney and McCarthy added several songs to the European score of Charles Cuvillier's *Afagar* when it was staged on Broadway, starring the toast of London and Paris, Alice Delysia. After contributing to the revue *The Broadway Whirl* ('All Girls Are Like A Rainbow' and 'Oh, Dearie'); *Up She Goes* ('Let's Kiss And Make Up', 'Journey's End' and 'Lady Luck, Smile On Me') and the disappointing *Glory*, the team wrote the score for Florenz Ziegfeld's 1923 hit, *Kid Boots*, with songs such as 'Someone Loves You', 'After All' and 'If Your Heart's In The Game'. In 1924, Tierney teamed with Sigmund Romberg to 'doctor' Clare Kummer's score to another Ziegfeld show, *Annie Dear*, and he also wrote 'Adoring You' for the impresario's *Follies* of that year. Three years later, he was back with McCarthy for *Rio Rita*, one of the highlights of the theatrical year, which was the first show to be staged at 'the finest musical playhouse ever constructed in America', the Ziegfeld Theatre. Tierney's robust and romantic score included 'The Rangers' Song', 'If You're In Love, You'll Waltz', 'You're Always In My Arms', 'Following The Sun Around', 'The Kinkajou' and the main duet, 'Rio Rita', sung by the show's stars, Ethelind Terry and J. Harold Murray. It ran for nearly 500 performances and was filmed in 1929, starring Bebe Daniels, John Boles and Wheeler and Wolsey, and again in 1942, with Abbott and Costello, Kathryn Grayson and John Carroll. Tierney and McCarthy's last Broadway show was *Cross My Heart* in 1928, which ran for only eight weeks. After that, Tierney worked in Hollywood during the 30s on films such as *Dixiana* , which produced the title song (with Benny Davis), 'Here's To The Old Days', 'A Tear, A Kiss, A Smile', 'My One Ambition Is You', and 'A Lady Loved A Soldier' (with Anne Caldwell); and *Half Shot At Sunrise* (the Bert Wheeler/Robert Woolsey comedy). Further attempts by Tierney to write another Broadway show were unsuccessful, and his career declined in what, ironically, was a golden era of popular song.

TIL THE BUTCHER CUTS HIM DOWN

A documentary film directed by Phillip Spalding in 1971, which shows many of the fine New Orleans veterans still around at the time of its making. Central to the film is Ernest 'Punch' Miller and also seen and heard are Kid Thomas Valentine, Kid Sheik Cola, Raymond Burke, Don Ewell, Emmanuel Sayles and Kid Ory. Amongst non-New Orleans musicians filmed are Bobby Hackett and Dizzy Gillespie. At the time of the film's making, Miller was terminally ill (he died in December 1971), but he plays to a festival audience with astonishing, and inevitably moving, verve and enthusiasm.

TILL THE CLOUDS ROLL BY

That was the title of a song from the 1917 hit musical *Oh, Boy!*, and its distinguished composer, Jerome Kern, is the subject of this film biography which was released by MGM in 1946. As usual, in these celebrity celebrations, the story owes more to the screenwriters not-so-vivid imagination than to reality, but the songs and their performers can always be relied upon to provide a feast of entertainment. Particularly in this case, when the tasty morsels on offer from the pen of 'the father of American popular music' are memorably performed by Lena Horne ('Can't Help Lovin' Dat Man' and 'Why Was I Born?'), Judy Garland ('Who?' and 'Look For The Silver Lining'), Dinah Shore ('They Didn't Believe Me' and 'The Last Time I Saw Paris'), June Allyson 'Leave It To Jane' and 'Cleopatterer'), Angela Lansbury ('How'd You Like To Spoon With Me?'), Kathryn Grayson and Tony Martin ('Make Believe'), and Virginia O'Brien ('Life Upon The Wicked Stage'). In spite of those, and others equally as wonderful such as 'Long Ago And Far Away', 'A Fine Romance', 'All The Things You Are', and 'She Didn't Say Yes', the image most people seem to retain from this picture is the sight of a white-suited Frank Sinatra singing 'Ol' Man River' while standing on a lofty pedestal in the finalé. Robert Walker played Kern, with Dorothy Patrick as his wife, and also on hand were Lucille Bremer, Van Johnson, Van Heflin, Gower Champion, Cyd Charisse, Caleb Patterson, Ray McDonald, Sally Forrest, Wilde Twins, Mary Nash, Joan Wells, Paul Langton, and Harry Hayden. Myles Connolly and Jean Holloway were responsible for the storyline, and Robert Alton staged the dances. It was directed by Richard Whorf and Vincente Minnelli and produced by the Arthur Freed unit. Harry Stradling and George Folsey's Technicolor photography helped to make the whole thing look pretty good. *Till The Clouds Roll By* grossed nearly $5 million in the USA, and was highly placed in the Top 20 musicals of the 40s.

TIME

Cliff Richard, the UK 'Peter Pan of Pop', finally realised a long-cherished ambition to star in a lavish stage musical when this production opened at the Dominion Theatre in London on 9 April 1986. It was devised and produced by Dave Clark, leader of the popular 60s group the Dave Clark Five who had major chart hits with 'Glad All Over' and 'Bits And Pieces'. Clark also wrote the book and lyrics with David Soames, and composed the music with Jeff Daniels. The show's theme is one of human survival. Earth itself is on trial before the High Court of the Universe, and Cliff Richard, in the role of a spiritual rock star, is beamed out to the Andromeda galaxy to face the music on Earth's behalf. The planet is saved from extinction by the intervention of a galactic sage, known as the universe's Ultimate Word of Truth, in the shape of a huge holographic speaking image of the distinguished British actor Laurence Olivier. All this was enhanced by the use of spectacular sets and sensational special effects, the like of which London had never seen before. Arlene Phillips, formerly of the pop dance group Hot Gossip, engineered some appropriately high-tech choreography, and the score included several cosmic musical numbers such as 'Time Talkin'', 'The Music Of The Spheres', 'Law Of The Universe', 'What On Earth', and 'We're The UFO'. Despite a luke-warm reception from the critics, *Time* became a popular tourist attraction particularly for its imaginative use of the space-age technology, and stayed at the Dominion for two years, a total of 777 performances. During the run Cliff Richard was succeeded by David Cassidy.

TIN PAN ALLEY

Pin-up girl Betty Grable followed up her splendid performance in *Down Argentine Way* (1940) with a more modest, but highly effective appearance later in the same year in this typical 20th Century-Fox musical. Set in the latter period of World War I, Robert Ellis and Helen Logan's screenplay concerns the singing Blane Sisters, Katie (Alice Faye) and Lily (Grable), who help a couple of songwriters, Harrigan and Calhoun, played by John Payne and Jack Oakie, to build up their own music publishing firm in New York's Tin Pan Alley. The boys and girls are parted for a time while the former 'do their bit' at the Front in France, but they are reunited following the Armistice, and march along together singing the latest Harrigan and Calhoun hit, 'K-K-K-Katie'. In fact, that song was actually written by Geoffrey O' Hara, and was one of the film's group of standards which included 'Honeysuckle Rose' (Andy Razaf-Fats Waller), 'Goodbye Broadway, Hello France' (Benny Davis-Francis Reisner-Billy Baskette), 'Moonlight Bay' (Percy Wenrich-Edward Madden), and 'America, I Love You' (Archie Gottler-Edgar Leslie). There was one new song, the appealing 'You Say The Sweetest Things, Baby' (Mack Gordon-Harry Warren), but the picture's musical highlight, which was staged by choreographer Semour Felix, was a sequence featuring another oldie, 'The Sheik Of Araby' (Ted Snyder-Harry B. Smith-Francis Wheeler). Billy Gilbert, as the Sheik, was serenaded by the hip-swaying Blane Sisters, and entertained in terpsichorean fashion by the scintillating be-turbaned and bare-torsoed Nicholas Brothers. Walter Land was the director who kept the whole thing moving at a smart rate, and the film, which was photographed in black and white by Leon Shamroy, was produced by Darryl F. Zanuck and Kenneth MacGowan. Alfred Newman won an Oscar for his music score. *Tin Pan Alley* was remade as *I'll Get By* in 1950, starring June Haver and Gloria de Haven.

TIOMKIN, DIMITRI

b. 10 May 1894, St. Petersburg, Russia, d. 11 November 1979, London, England. An important composer of film music from the 30s through to the 60s. After being coached in music by his mother as a small child, Tiomkin later studied at the St. Petersburg Conservatory. He worked as a professional musician, playing on the concert platform and as a pianist in silent-movie theatres, before moving to Berlin in 1921 to continue his studies. He gave numerous concert performances in Europe as a soloist, and duetting with another pianist. In 1925 he made his first visit to the USA, and returned in 1930 when his wife, a ballet dancer and choreographer, was hired to work on some Hollywood films. Tiomkin was also engaged to write music for films, and was soon in great demand. His first major film score was for *Alice In Wonderland* (1933). By now an American citizen, Tiomkin quickly became one of the most successful and prolific film composers, writing scores and incidental music in the late 30s, 40s and 50s for films such *Lost Horizon, The Great Waltz, You Can't Take It With You, Lucky Partners, The Westerner, Meet John Doe, The Corsican Brothers, Twin Beds, A Gentleman After Dark, The Moon And Sixpence, Unknown Guest, The Bridge Of San Luis Rey, The Imposter, Forever Yours, Dillinger, Pardon My Past, Duel In The Sun, The Dark Mirror, Whistle Stop, The Long Night, It's A Wonderful Life, Red River, So This Is New York, Champion, Home Of The Brave, Cyrano De Bergerac, Champagne For Caesar, Strangers On A Train, Bugles In The Afternoon, High Noon* (1952, Oscars for best score and title song with lyric by Ned Washington), *The Big Sky, The Four Poster, Angel Face, The Steel Trap, Return To Paradise, The High And The Mighty* (1954, another Oscar), *Dial M For Murder, Blowing In the Wind, Take The High Ground, Land Of The Pharaohs, Giant, Friendly Persuasion, Wild Is The Wind, Search For Paradise, Gun Fight At The O.K Corral, The Old Man And The Sea* (1958, his fourth Oscar) and *Rio Bravo* (1959). In the late 50s Tiomkin composed the theme music for the popular television series *Rawhide*, and throughout the 60s provided scores for some of the most popular and spectacular movies of the decade, including *The Alamo, The Sundowners, The Unforgiven, The Guns Of Navarone, Town Without Pity, 55 Days At Peking, The Fall Of The Roman Empire, Circus World, 36 Hours, The War Wagon* and *Great Catherine*. Among the songs that came from these and other films were 'Friendly Persuasion (Thee I Love)' and 'The Green Leaves Of Summer' (both with lyrics by Paul Francis Webster) and 'Wild Is The Wind' and 'Strange Are The Ways Of Love' (with Washington). He also worked as executive producer on the Russian film *Tchaikowsky* (1970), arranging the music of the film's subject. After moving to London in the 70s, Tiomkin died there in 1979.

● COMPILATIONS: *Lost Horizon-The Classic Film Scores Of Dimitri Tiomkin* (RCA 1976)★★★★.

TIP-TOES

Although this show, which opened at the Liberty Theatre in New York, on 28 December 1925, had more or less the same creative team as the 1924 hit, *Lady, Be Good!*, one of the reasons why it was not nearly so successful, must surely have been that the brilliant dance team of Fred and Adele Astaire were not present this time round. Guy Bolton and Fred Thompson's book was not considered to be up to much either - another rags-to-riches story, this time about a hard-up family vaudeville trio, consisting of Tip-Toes Kaye (Queenie Smith) and her two uncles, who are stranded in Palm Beach. One route to financial security would be for Tip-Toes to marry someone rich, but she loves Steve Burton (Allen Kearns), and he maintains that he is penniless - or his he? Surely he's that guy who made fortune out of glue? Andrew Tombes and Harry Watson Jnr. played Tip-Toes' vaudevillian uncles, and also in the cast was the young singer Jeanette MacDonald, just four years before she burst onto the Hollywood scene in the *The Love Parade*. George and Ira Gershwin's score was delightful in every way - a perfect blend of appealing melodies and witty and sentimental lyrics. Queenie Smith introduced the lovely 'That Certain Feeling' and 'Looking For A Boy', and joined in with 'These Charming People' and the gentle 'Nightie Night'. The rest of the score included the rousing 'Sweet And Low-Down', which was 'sung, kazooed, tromboned, and danced by the entire ensemble at a Palm Beach party'; 'Harlem River Shanty', 'When Do We Dance?', and 'Nice Baby'. *Tip-Toes* was yet another of those 'feel-good' musicals that proliferated during the 20s, and it attracted appreciative audiences for 194 performances. Allen Kearns briefly recreated his role for the London production which also starred Dorothy Dickson and ran for 194 performances. The 1927 film version was made in England with Dorothy Gish and Will Rogers.

TITANIC

With a provocative title that must have left the critics drooling in anticipation, this $10 million musical vessel, based on the legendary and tragic maiden voyage of the luxury liner Titanic, navigated some stormy seas (it occasionally refused to 'sink' on cue during previews) before finally sailing into New York's Lunt-Fontanne Theatre on 23 April 1997. In Peter Stone's book, the action takes place between 10 and 15 April 1912, and all the characters and events are based on factual events: the supposedly unsinkable luxury liner sank after hitting an iceberg, killing more than 1,500 and leaving some 700 survivors. Stone concentrated on the classic disaster-epic route, highlighting the manner in which people from various classes and walks of life temporarily united in a crisis, while pointing an accusing finger at those held to be responsible for the tragedy - in this case, the master, Captain E.J. Smith (John Cunningham), ship owner Thomas Andrews (Michael Cerveris) and builder J. Bruce Ismay (David Garrison). However, it was Maury Yeston's 'ravishing' score that raised the show above the rest of the season's new musicals, and accurately reflected the flavour and period of the piece. It began with an opening montage containing six songs, followed by 'Godspeed Titanic' sung by the Company. Subsequently, there were several other impressive numbers, including 'Still', a poignant ballad sung by the Macy's department store owners, Isador and Ida Straus (Larry Keith and Alma Cuervo), 'Barrett's Song' (Brian d'Arcy James as stoker Frederick Barrett), 'Lady's Maid' (Erin Hill, Theresa McCarthy and Jennifer Piech as a trio of Irish girls), 'Dressed In Your Pyjamas In The Grand Salon' (the Company), 'No Moon', sung by the ship's lookout, Frederick Fleet (David Elder) and the Company, 'We'll Meet Tomorrow', by second-class passenger Charles Clarke (Don Stephenson), and 'The Proposal'/'The Night Was Alive'. The rest of the score included 'In Every Age', 'How Did They Build Titanic?', 'There She Is', 'Loading Inventory', 'The Largest Moving Object', 'I Must Get On That Ship', 'The First Class Roster', 'Barrett's Song', 'What A Remarkable Age This Is', 'To Be A Captain', 'I Give You My Hand', 'A Hymn', 'Doing The Latest Rag', 'Autumn', 'Wake Up, Wake Up!', 'The Staircase', 'The Blame', 'Getting In The Lifeboat' and 'Mr. Andrews' Vision'. Among the remainder of the 43 named characters on board, accompanied by numerous passen-gers and members of the crew, were J.J. Astor (William Youmans) and his 19-year-old wife Madeline (Lisa Datz), an ambitious Indiana housewife, Alice Beane (Victoria Clark), and Caroline Neville (Judy Blazer), a British aristocrat, intent on beginning a new life in the USA with the man she loves. Stewart Laing's ingenious scenic design allowed audiences to view the action taking place in different parts of the ship, the bridge, boiler room, cabins, and so on, via rectangular 'windows' cut into a large black wall. Hydraulic lifts were also used to tilt the set to simulate the Titanic's final moments. Richard Jones was the director, and choreography was by Lynne Taylor-Corbett. Despite mixed reviews, *Titanic*'s future was ensured - at least in the short term, when the show gained five Tony Awards (from five nominations) for book, orchestrations (Jonathan Tunick), score, and scenic design. Tunick's award was the first in Tony Awards history for orchestration. *Titanic* was also represented in the Outer Critics, Drama Desk, and FANY Awards. As further proof of the show's high profile, Titanic launched its own website on the Internet, and the New York restaurant Serendipity 3 introduced a dessert called 'Broadway's *Titanic* Sundae' to its menu. Later in 1997, a 20th Century-Fox production of *Titanic*, costing $200 million and said to be 'the most expensive movie ever made', had its world premiere. It subsequently tied with *Ben Hur*, as the winner of the most Academy Awards.

● FURTHER READING: *Titanic: The Complete Book Of The Musical*, Peter Stone.

TOBIAS BROTHERS

This family group of songwriters comprised Charles Tobias (b. 15 August 1898, New York, USA, d. 7 July 1970), Harry Tobias (b. 11 September 1895, New York, USA, d. 15 December 1994, St. Louis, Missouri, USA), and Henry Tobias (b. 23 April 1905, Worcester, Massachusetts, USA). Charles Tobias was the most prolific of the trio, writing mainly lyrics, and occasionally music. After singing for publishing houses, on radio, and in vaudeville, he formed his own New York publishing company in 1923, and started writing songs soon afterwards. In the late 20s these included 'On A Dew-Dew-Dewy Day' and 'Miss You' (with brothers Henry and Harry), which became hits for Dinah Shore, Bing Crosby and Eddy Howard. From 1928 through to the early 40s, Charles wrote sundry songs for Broadway shows, such as *Good Boy*, *Earl Carroll's Sketch Book* (1929 and 1935), *Earl Carroll's Vanities Of 1932*, *Hellzapoppin*, *Yokel Boy* and *Banjo Eyes*. His contributions to films continued for another 10 years, until the early 50s. These included *Life Begins In College* (1937), *Private Buckaroo* (1942), *Shine On, Harvest Moon* (1944), *Saratoga Trunk* (1945), *Tomorrow Is Forever* (1946), *Love And Learn* (1947), *The Daughter Of Rosie O'Grady* (1950), *On Moonlight Bay* (1951), and *About Face* (1952). From the shows, films and Tin Pan Alley, came popular songs such as 'When Your Hair Has Turned To Silver', 'Throw Another Log On The Fire', 'Don't Sweetheart Me', 'No Can Do', 'A Million Miles Away', 'Coax Me A Little Bit', and 'The Old Lamplighter'. His collaborators included Joe Burke, Murray Mencher, Sam Stept, Peter DeRose, Cliff Friend, Sammy Fain, Nat Simon, Jack Scholl, Lew Brown, Roy

Turk and Charles Newman. In 1962, after a period of relative inactivity, Charles Tobias wrote 'All Over The World' (with Al Frisch) and 'Those Lazy, Hazy, Crazy Days Of Summer' (with Hans Carste), both of which were successful for Nat 'King' Cole.

Charles's older brother Harry, one of America's most beloved songwriters who died in 1995 aged 99, wrote lyrics for some songs in 1916, including 'That Girl Of Mine' and 'Take Me To Alabam' (both with Will Dillon). After military service in World War I, he spent several years in the real estate business before returning to songwriting in the late 20s. In 1931, with bandleader Gus Arnheim and Jules Lemare, he wrote 'Goodnight My Love' (featured in the film *Blondie Of The Follies*), and 'Sweet And Lovely', which became Arnheim's theme song, and a big hit in the UK for Al Bowlly. In the same year he collaborated Harry Barris and Bing Crosby on 'At Your Command', which gave Crosby one of his earliest successes. During the next 20 years, many of Tobias's lyrics were heard in films such as *Gift Of The Gab, Dizzy Dames, The Old Homestead, With Love And Kisses, Swing While You're Able, It's A Date, Stormy Weather, You're A Lucky Fellow, Mr. Smith, Sensations Of 1945, Brazil*, and *Night Club Girl*. His best-known songs included 'It's A Lonesome Old Town', 'Sail Along Sil'vry Moon', 'Wait For Me, Mary', 'Miss You', 'No Regrets', 'Love Is All', 'Fascinating You', 'Go To Sleep, Little Baby', 'Oh Bella Maria' and 'Take Me Back To Those Wide Open Spaces'. Among his collaborators were Al Sherman, Roy Ingraham, Pinky Tomlin, Harry Barris, Neil Moret, Percy Wenrich, and his brothers. In the 50s he concentrated more on his music publishing interests.

The youngest of the three brothers, Henry Tobias, had a varied career. He wrote special material for artists such as Sophie Tucker, Eddie Cantor and Jimmy Durante, was a producer and director for summer stock shows, and also worked for CBS Television as a producer and musical director. With his brother Charles he contributed to the Earl Carroll revues in the 30s, and also wrote many other popular numbers with Will Dillon, David Ormont, David Oppenheim, Don Reid, Milton Berle, Little Jack Little, and his two brothers. Among these were 'Katinka', 'Cooking Breakfast For The One I Love', 'We Did It Before And We Can Do It Again', 'The Bowling Song, 'You Walked Out Of The Picture', 'Easter Sunday With You', and 'I've Written A Letter To Daddy' (with Larry Vincent and Mo Jaffe), which was featured in the 1979 Janis Joplin bio-pic *The Rose*, starring Bette Midler.

TOBIAS, CHARLES

(see Tobias Brothers)

TOMMY (FILM MUSICAL)

Although predated by the Pretty Things' *SF Sorrow*, the Who's *Tommy* is generally granted the dubious distinction of being the first rock opera. Iconoclast director Ken Russell transformed its content into this opulent film in 1975. It combined the excess and self-indulgence of his work and its subject, resulting in a visual feast guaranteed to raise hackles. Given that the original storyline is confused - a child struck deaf, dumb and blind following the murder of his father becomes a messianic figure - *Tommy* relies on outrageous scenes for its effect. These include Elton John's barnstorming version of 'Pinball Wizard', performed in grossly exaggerated platform boots, Tina Turner's dramatic rendition of 'The Acid Queen' and, taking its cue from the Who's pop-art iconography, Ann-Margret's immersion in baked beans. Cameos by Eric Clapton (with 'Eyesight To The Blind') and Arthur Brown are of note, while Paul Nicholas enjoys his role as the sadistic Cousin Kevin. However, two members of the Who steal the limelight; vocalist Roger Daltrey is admirable as Tommy, and drummer Keith Moon excels as the perverted Uncle Ernie. Maligned by many critics upon release, *Tommy* remains of interest if only for its camp scenarios and gross interludes.

TOMMY (STAGE MUSICAL)

(see *Who's Tommy, The*)

TOMMY STEELE STORY, THE

Former merchant seaman Tommy Hicks was discovered while performing in Soho's legendary 2 I's coffee bar. Renamed by manager Larry Parnes, Tommy Steele became Britain's first bona fide rock 'n' roll star with two 1956 hit singles, 'Rock With The Caveman' and 'Singing The Blues', the latter of which was a chart-topper. Although touted as the antidote to Elvis Presley, it was quickly clear that Steele lacked sex appeal or sultry menace, offering instead a clean-cut, boy-next-door image, ripe for his subsequent mutation into all-round entertainer. For many years he remained a peculiarly British institution; indeed, the film was retitled *Rock Around The World* for the USA. Steele was an unknown quantity there and his name had little significance. Released in 1957, *The Tommy Steele Story* retold the artist's rise from rags to riches, while offering a glimpse of music popular in the UK during this transitional period. The influence of jazz on rock 'n' roll was acknowledged by an appearance by Humphrey Lyttelton's band, while the concurrent skiffle craze allowed for the inclusion of Chas McDevitt's Skiffle Group, who, with Nancy Whiskey, were high in the UK charts with the memorable 'Freight Train'. Chris O'Brien's Caribbeans and Tommy Etie's Calypso Band reflected London's nascent interest in West Indian music, yet the film's lacklustre style and pace meant that its symbolism was greater than the audio/visual experience. Indeed, its star's appeal was already undergoing a transformation by the time *The Tommy Steele Story* reached the cinema. His last rock 'n' roll hit, 'Tallahassie Lassie', was succeeded by 'Little White Bull' from the singer's 1959 feature, *Tommy The Toreador*. His mutation into a peculiarly adult attraction was all but complete, and was finally accomplished with Steele's subsequent role in *Half A Sixpence*.

TONIGHT AT 8.30

A series of nine one-act plays written by Noël Coward, and presented in two groups at London's Phoenix Theatre in successive weeks in January 1936, starring Coward and Gertrude Lawrence. After the curtain-raiser, *We Were Dancing*, with its title song, three of the other pieces were significant because of their musical content: *Shadow Play*, a romantic musical fantasy, which contained 'Then', 'Play Orchestra, Play', and 'You Were There'; *Red Peppers*, the most popular item in the set which dealt with a sleazy, quarrelsome music-hall duo in terminal decline, and included 'Has Anybody Seen Our Ship?' and 'Men About Town'; and *Family Album*, a 'mock-Victorian comedy about a missing will' with two songs, 'Here's A Toast' and 'Hearts And Flowers'. This was Coward at his versatile best, both in writing and performing. After a run of 157 performances, he and Gertrude Lawrence enjoyed similar success later in the year in New York. Lawrence also starred with one of Coward's protégés, Graham Payn, in a brief 1948 Broadway revival. Four years later, three of the plays, including *Red Peppers*, were filmed under the collective title of *Meet Me Tonight*, with Ted Ray and Kay Walsh. In 1991, the actress Joan Collins and her ex-husband Anthony Newley, appeared in the complete series of nine plays on UK television.

TONIGHT LET'S ALL MAKE LOVE IN LONDON

Arguably the definitive 'Swinging London'-cum-psychedelic British film, *Tonight Let's All Make Love In London* is a visual kaleidoscope of impressionistic vistas and documentary footage. Director Peter Whitehead had been responsible for *Wholly Communion*, a film that chronicled a poetry recital, and two projects featuring the Rolling Stones; the rarely screened *Charlie Is My Darling* and a promotional short for 1967's 'We Love You'. Released the same year, this 72-minute feature included pop art, miniskirts, contemporary music and the emergent counterculture. Appearances by 60s icons Julie Christie, Vanessa Redgrave and Michael Caine nestle alongside contributions by painter David Hockney, poet Allen Ginsberg and actor Lee Marvin. Mick Jagger and producer/manager Andrew Loog Oldham are also featured; the latter overseeing recording sessions by Twice As Much and Vashti, both of whom were signed to his Immediate label. Two other acts from this roster, the Small Faces and Chris Fallow, contribute music, and Pink Floyd provide a memorable, early rendition of their pivotal instrumental, 'Interstellar Overdrive'. A soundtrack album was briefly issued on Immediate subsidiary Instant. It was reissued in 1993 amid plans to issue *Tonight Let's Make Love In London* on video.

TONIGHT'S THE NIGHT

World War I was just a few months old when this British musical opened - not in London - but at the Shubert Theatre in New York on 24 December 1914. Fred Thompson's book, which was based on the popular 19th century farce *The Pink Dominoes* by James Albery, was typical of the genre and involved a 'did-they-know-or-not' story about two society chaps, Dudley Mitten (George Grossmith) and his pal Albert (Dave Burnaby), who are cajoled into romancing a certain two young ladies at a masked ball. When it is revealed that the female duo are the men-about-towns' current girlfriends, June (Emmy Wehlen) and Beatrice (Iris Hoey), they staunchly insist that they were aware of the joke all the time - and went along with it. *Tonight's The Night* had a reasonably suc-

cessful New York run of 108 performances, but found its true audience when it returned to London and the Gaiety Theatre on 28 April 1915. Paul Rubens and Percy Greenbank' score, which included 'Murders', 'The Only Way', 'Boots And Shoes', 'I'm A Millionaire', 'Dancing Mad', 'Please Don't Flirt With Me', 'When the Boys Come Home To Tea', 'Too Particular', and 'Round The Corner', was strengthened by the scatty 'I'd Like To Bring My Mother', and two interpolated songs, 'Any Old Night (Is A Wonderful Night)' (music by Otto Motzan and Jerome Kern, lyric by Schuyler Greene and Harry B. Smith), and 'They Didn't Believe Me' (music by Kern, lyric by Herbert Reynolds). Comedian Leslie Henson, who had originally had a minor part in the Broadway production, was elevated to the role of Henry, 'a naughty schoolboy out for a spree and a flirt with a pretty maid', and was oustanding in the first of his many West End successes. *Tonight's The Night* ran on and on for 460 performances, and was revived at the Winter Garden in 1924 with several of the original cast, including Leslie Henson.

TONY AWARDS

The Antoinette Perry Awards, America's most prestigious theatrical awards - the equivalent to the Hollywood Oscars - were inaugurated in 1947. Their fascinating history began during World War I when an obscure playwright, Rachel Crothers, and a few other women, organized theatre people to sell Liberty Bonds and run a canteen for servicemen in Times Square. In 1939 Crothers and her voluntary workers, including an actress-director named Antoinette Perry, surfaced again and formed the American Theatre Wing War Service. The Wing founded two famous institutions: the Stage Door Canteen, where stars of stage, screen and radio served coffee and doughnuts and entertained visiting service personnel, and which was immortalized in the 1943 film of the same name; and the annual award given in memory of Antoinette Perry's pioneering work both for women and young people in the theatre, and for the American Theatre Wing itself, which still organizes the Awards. As an example, in 1993 the nominations for the 19 categories were selected by an independent committee of 12 theatre professionals, and they in turn were voted on by 670 theatre professionals and journalists. In that year the specific musical sections consisted of best musical, book, original score, performance by a leading actor, leading actress, featured actor, and featured actress; and best direction and choreography. Musical productions could also win in the best scenic, costume, and lighting design categories, and the best revival of a play or musical. In most years one or more special Tonys are awarded for outstanding service to the theatre, and in 1993 one of these celebrated the 50th anniversary of Richard Rodgers and Oscar Hammerstein II's *Oklahoma!*. Over the years the Award itself has taken many forms. The current honour is in the shape of a Tony Medallion, the product of a Stage Designer's Union competition won by Herman Rose in 1950. In 1997, a new category was introduced, Best Orchestrations. The first winner was Jonathan Tunick, whose name is indelibly associated with the shows of Stephen Sondheim, amongst others. An annual live television audience of some 10 million

watch the ceremony, the outcome of which often means the difference between success and failure on Broadway.
● FURTHER READING: *The Tony Award Book*, Lee Alan Morrow. *The Tony Award*, Crown Publishers USA.

TOO LATE BLUES

Director and star John Cassavetes, uncharacteristically turning out a Hollywood studio film in 1961, carefully evokes the personal and professional relationships between members of a jazz group. Cassavetes, who also appeared in the *Johnny Staccato* television series, not only loves the music but clearly cares for the musicians who play it. Among the participating musicians, mostly off-screen, are Milt Bernhardt, Benny Carter, Slim Gaillard, Shelly Manne, Red Mitchell, Jimmy Rowles and Uan Rasey, who dubs for Bobby Darin who has an acting role.

TOO MANY GIRLS

Another musical set at an American college where football consistently scores over schoolbooks, the lively and entertaining *Too Many Girls* opened at the Imperial Theatre in New York on 19 October 1939. George Marion Jnr.'s book concerns Consuelo (Marcy Westcott), whose wealthy father, Harvey Casey (Clyde Fillmore), sends her to Pottawatomie College in New Mexico in search of a little discipline. Just to be on the safe side he hires four All-American footballers, Manuelito (Desi Arnaz), Jojo Jordan (Eddie Bracken) Al Terwilliger (Hal LeRoy), and Clint Kelley (Richard Kollmar), to serve as her bodyguards. Complications ensue when Consuelo falls for Clint, but everything is sorted out by the day of the BIG GAME!!. Richard Rodgers and Lorenz Hart's score was full of good things although there was only one enduring number, 'I Didn't Know What Time It Was', which was introduced by Westcott and Kollmar. It became popular for Benny Goodman and Jimmy Dorsey, and Frank Sinatra gave the song a pleasant reading when it was interpolated into the film score of *Pal Joey* (1957). Westcott and Kalmar also duetted on 'Love Never Went To College', and the rest of the score consisted of lively and amusing numbers such as the Latin-styled 'All Dressed Up (Spic And Spanish)', 'She Could Shake The Maracas', in which Arnaz, quite naturally, was involved; 'Give It Back To The Indians', and the songwriters' witty plea - in the face of the blare of the Big Band Era - for a return to musical sanity in 'I Like To Recognize The Tune' ('A guy Krupa plays the drums like thunder/But the melody is six feet under'). Mel Tormé made an excellent recording of that one. Rumour has it that Lorenz Hart was frequently absent during preparations for this show and Rodgers had to write some of his own lyrics. The future movie heartthrob Van Johnson was in the chorus, and he succeeded Richard Kollmar when the show toured directly after its New York run of 249 performances. Several of the original cast were in the 1940 film version, including Desi Arnaz, whose meeting on the set with Lucille Ball led to their stormy marriage, and the long-running television series *I Love Lucy*.

TOP HAT

Probably the most fondly remembered of all the 10 movies Fred Astaire and Ginger Rogers made together, *Top Hat* was released by RKO in 1935. Dwight Taylor and Allan Scott's screenplay finds Jerry Travers (Astaire) falling for swanky socialite Dale Tremont (Rogers) in London, and following her to Venice where she mistakes him for her best friend's husband. Jerry's problem is to divert Dale from the oily embraces of dress designer Alberto Beddini (Erik Rhodes), which he does in spite of being surrounded by the mayhem caused by other regular members of RKO's consistently droll 'repertory' company which included - besides Rhodes - Edward Everett Horton, Eric Blore and Helen Broderick. What made this musical so special and different to Astaire and Rogers' previous work, was the way in which the songs emerged so smoothly and naturally out of the story. And what songs! Irving Berlin came up with one of his best-ever film scores, and, in the process, gave Astaire his life-long identity number - 'Top Hat, White Tie And Tails'. There were four other marvellous dance sequences: 'Cheek To Cheek', during which, apparently, Fred became rather annoyed and frustrated because the feathers from Ginger's dress kept flying off and getting up his nose; 'No Strings', an Astaire solo which he reduced to a soft-shoe-shuffle after complaints from a sleepy Ginger in the apartment below; 'Isn't This A Lovely Day?', where the two are stranded in a bandstand during a thunder storm, a situation which leads to one of the most endearing all-time great movie moments; and 'The Piccolina', a lively dance finalé that gives Ginger a rare solo vocal opportunity. Director Mark Sandrich and dance director Hermes Pan, along with an outstanding cast and Irving Berlin's wonderful music, all combined to make this a very special film.

TOUCHABLES, THE

Australian Robert Freeman, known chiefly for taking the photographs for the sleeves of several Beatles albums, directed this 1968 feature. Pop star Christian, played by David Anthony, is kidnapped by four mini-skirted models, who then enact sexual fantasies with their captive in a pleasure dome. The title song, 'All Of Us', was written and performed by Island Records act Nirvana, while stablemate Wynder K. Frog contributed 'Blues For A Frog' and 'Dancing Frog'. The Ferris Wheel (with Linda Lewis) and Roy Redman are also featured on a soundtrack superior to its setting.

TRAVOLTA, JOHN

b. 18 February 1954, Englewood, New Jersey, USA, of Italian-Irish ancestry. Travolta left school at the age of 16 to become an actor. After working in off-Broadway productions and Hollywood bit-parts, he landed a lead in *Welcome Back Cotter*, a nationally transmitted television series. Hating to see this exposure go to waste, Midsong Records engaged the handsome young thespian as a recording artist. Three singles, notably 1976's 'Let Her In', cracked the US Top 40 which, with his film roles in such as *Devil's Rain* (1975), *The Boy In The Plastic Bubble* (1976) and *Carrie* (1976), readied the public for his *pièce de résistance* as the star of *Saturday Night Fever* which turned disco into a multinational industry. Travolta's pop and cinema interests combined in 1978's *Grease*, for which he was singularly well prepared, having once toured in a stage version of this musical. From the soundtrack, his duets with co-star Olivia Newton-John, 'You're The One That I Want' and 'Summer Nights', were worldwide number 1 hits with Travolta's solo highlights, 'Sandy' and 'Greased Lightning', also selling well. His solo chart career ended (perhaps temporarily) after the fall of *Sandy* from the UK album lists in 1979. *Staying Alive*, a sequel-of-sorts to *Saturday Night Fever*, and *Two Of A Kind* (in which he teamed again with Newton-John) were made during the 80s when his career was in decline. Travolta found himself replaced by a new wave of actors who included Tom Cruise, Tom Hanks, and Kevin Costner. His comeback came in 1994 courtesy of director Quentin Tarantino's smash hit *Pulp Fiction*, which earned Travolta a second Best Actor Oscar nomination to add to the one for *Saturday Night Fever*. Since then his star has been in the ascendancy, and the musical magic started all over again in 1998, when the *Grease* soundtrack, and the single, 'You're The One That I Want', returned to the charts following the film's 20th anniversary re-release. In the same year, Travolta received a lifetime achievement award at the 34th Chicago International Film Festival.

● ALBUMS: *John Travolta* (Midland Int. 1976)★★, *Sandy* (1978)★★, *Whenever I'm Away From You* (1978)★★, *Girl Like You* (Polydor 1982)★★, *Two Of A Kind* film soundtrack (1983)★★.

● COMPILATIONS: *20 Golden Pieces* (1981)★★, *The Best Of ...* (Essential Gold 1996)★★★.

● FURTHER READING: *Saturday Night Fever: A Novelisation*, H.B. Gilmour, *The John Travolta Scrapbook: An Illustrated Biography*, Suzanne Munshower, *Grease*, Ron De Christoforo, *John Travolta*, Craig Schumacher. *Urban Cowboy: A Novel*, Aaron Latham.

● FILMS: *The Devil's Rain* (1975), *The Tenth Level* (1976), *Carrie* (1976), *Saturday Night Fever* (1977), *Moment By Moment* (1978), *Grease* (1978), *Urban Cowboy* (1980), *Blow Out* (1981), *Two of A Kind* (1983), *Staying Alive* (1983), *Perfect* (1985), *Look Who's Talking* (1989), *The Experts* (1989), *Look Who's Talking Too* (1990), *Shout* (1991), *Eyes Of An Angel* (1991), *Look Who's Talking Now* (1993), *Pulp Fiction* (1994), *White Man's Burden* (1995), *Get Shorty* (1995), *Broken Arrow* (1996), *Phenomenon* (1996), *Michael* (1996), *She's So Lovely* (1997), *Face/Off* (1997), *Mad City* (1997), *Primary Colors* (1998), *The Thin Red Line* (1998), *A Civil Action* (1998).

TREE GROWS IN BROOKLYN, A

With a book by George Abbott and Betty Smith which was adapted from Smith's best-selling novel of the same name, this sentimental story of an ordinary, working-class Brooklyn family opened at the Alvin Theatre in New York on 19 April 1951. Set in the early 1900s, the story follows the fortunes of the hard-drinking Johnny Nolan (Johnny Johnston), a singing waiter, who meets and marries Katie (Marcia Van Dyke). She has a sister named Cissy who 'collects' husbands and calls them all Harry. Eventually, her current spouse becomes so used to the name that he objects to being called by his real name of Oscar. Meanwhile, Johnny and Katie have a daughter, Francie (Nomi Mitty), but Johnny's drinking is getting worse. He loses his job and leaves home to find other work, only to get killed in the process. However, he has left sufficient money to enable Francie to finish her education, and the curtain falls on the celebrations following her graduation. In Smith's original book, and in the 1945 film, the story focused on the daughter Francie, but for this musical treatment the authors shifted the emphasis on to the older players, particularly Shirley Booth who gave a wonderfully humorous performance, particularly when reflecting on her 'late' Harry in 'He Had Refinement' ('One time he said: "May I suggest/You call a lady's chest, a chest/Instead of her points of interest?"/Dainty, ain't he?'). The remainder of Dorothy Fields and Arthur Schwartz's warmly romantic and sometimes lively score, included the lovely 'Make The Man Love Me', 'Look Who's Dancing', 'Love Is The Reason', 'I'm Like A New Broom', 'Growing Pains', 'Mine 'Til Monday', 'Don't Be Afraid', and 'If You Haven't Got A Sweetheart'. One of the other numbers, 'I'll Buy You A Star', was sung by Johnny Mathis on his 1961 album of the same title. *A Tree Grows In Brooklyn* had a decent run of 270 performances, but is rarely revived.

TRENT, BRUCE

b. William Butters, 21 August 1912, St. Helier, Jersey, d. 19 November 1995, Burgh Heath, Surrey, England. An actor and singer with a fine, baritone voice and matinée idol good looks, Trent was one of the British theatre's most popular romantic leading men in the 40s and 50s. After singing with local dance groups, in the late 30s he spent two years touring the UK with Jack Hylton's famous show band, before joining Jack Payne's new BBC orchestra in 1940. He left Payne in 1942 in order to co-star with Frances Day, Arthur Riscoe, Jackie Hunter and Bud Flanagan in Cole Porter's musical *Du Barry Was A Lady* at His Majesty's Theatre in London. Trent subsequently returned to the West End, and then toured, in *The Student Prince*, before joining the army and entertaining the troops in the company of the Stars In Battledress. He was also a guest artist, along with Dorothy Carless, on a BBC broadcast with Glenn Miller's Band of the AEF. After the war, Trent took over the leading roles in *Carissima* (1948) and *Brigadoon* (1950), as well as starring in London in *Rainbow Square* (1951), *Wish You Were Here* (1953) and *The Burning Boat* (1955, Royal Court Theatre). He also toured in various other productions, including *Lilac Time*, *Good-Night Vienna* and *The Desert Song*. In 1958, Trent joined the all-star cast of Tommy Steele, Jimmy Edwards, Yana, and Ted Durante, in Richard Rodgers and Oscar Hammerstein II's lavish *Cinderella* at the Coliseum. As the dashing Prince, he sang the show's big ballad, 'No Other Love', and duetted with Yana on the equally splendid 'Do I Love You Because You're Beautiful?'. In later years he continued to tour in numerous revivals, both at home and abroad, notably as Arthur in *Camelot* in 1966. He also participated in re-recordings of favourite musicals, and was a regular broadcaster on BBC light music programmes. After retiring in the 70s, he worked tirelessly for the Grand Order of Water Rats charity.

TRENT, JACKIE

b. Jacqueline Trent, 6 September 1940, Newcastle-Under-Lyme, Staffordshire, England. A singer and lyricist who has achieved much of her success in collaboration with her husband, Tony Hatch. After performing in amateur productions from an early age, Trent started singing with local bands at the age of 13, and turned professional when she was 17. She toured parts of Europe and the Middle East, and played in cabaret in London, and traditional seaside shows. In the early 60s she recorded for the Oriole label before successfully auditioning for Pye Records producer Tony Hatch in 1964. Hatch had already written several successful compositions, including the theme to the television UK soap opera, *Crossroads*. Together, they wrote the melodic 'Where Are You Now (My Love)', which Trent took to number 1 in the UK chart in 1965. During the late 60s they composed several major hits for Petula Clark, including 'Don't Sleep In The Subway', 'The Other Man's Grass', 'I Couldn't Live Without Your Love', and 'Colour My World'. Scott Walker also made the chart with their 'Joanna' in 1968. For their wedding day in 1967, Pye issued 'The Two Of Us', an incidental item they had recorded months before. Its success, particularly in Australia, caused them to form a double act for cabaret, and make frequent trips to the Antipodes. In 1970 Trent starred as Nell Gwynne in the regional musical *Nell!*, with Hatch as co-producer and musical director. Two years later, the couple wrote the score for Cameron Mackintosh's first West End production, *The Card*, a musical adaptation of Arnold Bennett's novel, which starred Jim Dale, Marti Webb, Eleanor Bron and Millicent Martin. The songs included 'I Could Be The One', 'That's The Way The Money Goes' and 'Opposite Your Smile'. Another project, *Rock Nativity* (1974), proved to be 'one biblical musical too many'. Around the same time they released *Two For The Show*. Since 1982, Hatch and Trent have spent the majority of each year living and working in Australia, and in 1986 they wrote the theme song for *Neighbours*, a television soap set in Melbourne. Its success spread to the UK, and it was even introduced into the USA in 1991. They have composed several other UK television themes, including *Mr & Mrs*. Hatch and Trent's most successful stage project, *The Card*, was revived at the Open Air Theatre in London's Regent Park in 1992. In the same year the couple celebrated their 25th wedding anniversary, and also received the British Association of Songwriters Authors and Publishers' prestigious Award for Services to British Music, to add to their several Ivor Novello Awards. After their marriage ended in 1995, Trent returned to England to pick up her solo career, and in 1996 was touring with a provincial production of the musical *High Society*.

● ALBUMS: *The Magic Of Jackie Trent* (Pye 1965)★★★★, *Once More With Feeling* (Pye 1967)★★★, *Stop Me And Buy One* (Pye 1967)★★★, *Yesterdays* (Pye 1968)★★★★, *The Night, The Music And...* (1979)★★★, with Tony Hatch *Two For The Show* (1973)★★★, with Hatch *Our World Of Music* (1980)★★★.

● COMPILATIONS: *The Best Of Jackie Trent* (1973)★★★★, *Golden Hour Of Jackie Trent And Tony Hatch* (Pye 1976)★★★★.

TRIBUTE TO THE BLUES BROTHERS, A

Inspired by the American television satire-comedy institution *Saturday Night Live*, which spawned the cult 1980 film *The Blues Brothers*, this 'couple of hours of high-octane serious partying' began as a pub (or bar) entertainment in the English seaside town of Brighton, before moving to the up-market London suburb of Hampstead. From there it was just a short distance to the West End and the Whitehall Theatre, where this 'good-time' entertainment opened on 12 August 1991. Jake and Elwood Blues, two Chicago petty crooks-turned R&B singers, complete with dark blue suits, narrow-brim hats, and Ray Ban shades, were the creations of film actors John Belushi and Dan Aykroyd. Their on-stage counterparts, played by Con O'Neill and Warwick Evans, retain the uniform, but claim to come from Halifax in Yorkshire, and have hobbies which include train-spotting and collecting cardigans ('a couple of nerds'). The story remains nominal, but the music more than makes up for it. A dazzling array of mostly great old songs include 'Hey Bartender', 'I Need You, Flip Flop Fly', 'I Can Dance', 'Gimme Some Lovin'', 'Minnie The Moocher', 'Soul Man', 'Cell Block No.9', 'Jailhouse Rock', 'Who's Making Love To Your Old Lady While You're Out Making Love?', and, somewhat surprisingly, the 'Theme From Rawhide' and a rap version of the Rolf Harris hit 'Two Little Boys'. The 'brothers' are supported by singers Greg Brown, who gives an immaculate reading of 'In The Midnight Hour', Ian Roberts, whose outstanding solo is 'On The Boardwalk', Liza Spenz, and a hot six-piece band. The 'initial onslaught' was greeted enthusiastically by the critics, and the singing and dancing on the stage (and in the aisles) continued for 10 months at the Whitehall, prior to UK and European tours. On its return to the West End in September 1994, the show was retitled *The Official Tribute To The Blues Brothers*. This apparently meant that David Leland's world-touring production had received the blessing of Dan Aykroyd and the widow of the late John Belushi (d. 1982). Apart from the amended billing, everything seemed much the same, and black shades and trilby hats could still be purchased in the foyer.

TRIP, THE

Released in the USA in 1967, but denied a UK certificate, *The Trip* was an exploitative feature, typical of Roger Corman's American International Pictures. The film starred Peter Fonda as a director of television commercials who takes a trip on LSD, encountering good and bad effects. The widespread ban which the film encountered was based largely on its subject matter, rather than an appraisal of its moralistic conclusion. Written by Jack Nicholson, *The Trip* also featured Dennis Hopper, both of whom teamed with Fonda two years later in *Easy Rider*. The plot of *The Trip* was largely insubstantial, but it served as a vehicle for Peter Gardiner's striking psychedelic effects. The soundtrack was provided by the Electric Flag, a new act formed by blues guitarist Mike Bloomfield. Their hallucinogenic-inspired music was aptly suited to *The Trip*'s visual images, particularly when the group was augmented by violinist Sandy Konikoff. Curiously, the Electric Flag did not appear in the film. The International Submarine Band, a country/pop quartet led by Gram Parsons were featured, although they mimed to one of the former group's songs. Parsons and Fonda were close friends, which perhaps explains their inclusion. Although revered as a genre classic, limited distribution has enhanced *The Trip*'s reputation as much as its content.

TRIUMPH OF LOVE

With the mighty *Les Misérables* heading relentlessly towards its 5,000th performance at the Imperial Theatre on New York's West 45th Street, this chamber-size farcical romantic musical comedy opened just along the way at the Royale Theatre on 23 October 1997. James Magruder's book, which was based on the eighteenth-century play by Pierre Marivaux, tells the charming tale of headstrong Princess Léonide (Susan Egan) and her often outrageous efforts to gain the favour of philosophy student (he's really a prince), Agis (Christopher Sieber). Aided and abetted by her wisecracking maid, Corine (Nancy Opel), she inveigles herself into a garden retreat in Sparta, where Agis lives with his stern and dominating uncle and aunt, philosopher Hermocrates (F. Murray Abraham) and his sister, the seriously repressed Hesione (Betty Buckley). After recruiting servants Harlequin (Roger Bart) and Dimas (Kevin Chamberlin) to her cause, the covert operation involves the Princess in some hilarious escapades, including one in which she bends her gender, and, disguised as a man, seduces Hesione. On another occasion, she comes on strongly to Hermocrates à la Marilyn Monroe. The delightful, irreverent romp, which had its moments of irony and poignancy - particularly when, in true Marivaux fashion, dry old Hesione and Hermocrates gradually come to terms with the beginnings of love. Among the highlights of composer Jeffrey Stock and lyricist Susan Birkenhead's witty and tuneful score were 'Serenity', a haunting tour de force for Buckley, Abrahams's 'Emotions', Egan's two big numbers, 'Anything' and 'What Have I Done?', the amusing 'Mr. Right', with which Opel attempts to seduce Harlequin, Abraham and Buckley's 'The Tree', and 'Henchmen', an opportunity for the servants to give their point of view. Also featured were 'This Day Of Days', 'The Bond That Can't Be Broken', 'You May Call Me Phocion', 'The Sad And Sordid Saga Of Cecile', 'Issue In Question', 'Teach Me Not To Love You', 'Have A Little Faith', 'Love Won't Take No For An Answer'. Heidi Ettinger's exquisite garden mural set, Doug Varone's laidback choreography, and fine direction from Michael Mayer making an impressive Broadway debut, all conspired to create a show to treasure. Unfortunately, audiences did not attend in sufficient numbers, and *Triumph Of Love* was withdrawn on the 4 January 1998 after a run of just two and a half months. Michael Mayer directed the first of what must surely be many subsequent productions at Philadelphia's Walnut Street Theatre in September-October 1998. Four years earlier, Mayer and librettist Magruder had worked on a Classic Stage Company presentation of Marivaux's 1732 three-act play, *The Triumph Of Love*, *sans* musical score, off-Broadway.

TROUBLE WITH GIRLS, THE

The success of the *Elvis* television spectacular of Christmas 1968 rendered redundant Elvis Presley's Hollywood career. Contractual obligations necessitated three more films, the first of which was this 1969 offering. In this the singer plays a member of a 20s travelling educational show, a Chautauqua, which becomes embroiled in a murder during a visit to a small town. Aware of the negligible return Presley's films now created, RCA sanctioned the recording of five songs, only two of which were ever released. The most notable of those was the protest-inspired 'Clean Up Your Own Back Yard', a minor hit in the UK and US. Its comparatively low chart placing made no difference to Presley's artistic rebirth. The single was preceded by 'In The Ghetto' and succeeded by 'Suspicious Minds', two crowning points in the singer's rejuvenated career. The era of sub-standard Presley films was now thankfully drawing to a close.

TUCKER, SOPHIE

b. Sophie (or Sonia) Kalish-Abuza, 13 January 1884, in transit between Russia and Poland, d. 9 February 1966, New York, USA. A legendary performer of generous proportions, brassy and dynamic, who claimed to be 'The Last Of The Red-Hot Mamas'. The daughter of Russian parents, Tucker was taken to the USA when she was three years old. Sophie's father took the man's name and papers in an attempt to evade the Russian authorities. By the time she was 10-years-old Tucker was a singing waitress in her father's cafe in Hartford, Connecticut, and in 1906 she moved to New York to work at the Café Monopole, the German Village Cafe and then in burlesque, vaudeville and cabaret. Sometimes, because of her plain appearance she was persuaded to work in blackface, and made a reputation as a 'Coon-Shouter' in the ragtime era. After a teenage marriage failed (as did two later attempts), she added 'er' to her ex-husband's name of 'Tuck' to create her new stage name. In 1909 she played a small, but telling part in the *Ziegfeld Follies*. By 1911 she was a headliner, and was able to drop the dreaded blackface for good. In the same year she made her first recording of the song which was to become her life-long theme, forever associated with her. 'Some Of These Days' was written by composer-pianist Shelton Brooks, who also wrote 'The Darktown Strutters Ball' and special material for Nora Bayes and Al Jolson. Other hits around this time were 'That Lovin' Rag', 'That Lovin' Two-Step Man', 'That Loving Soul Kiss' and 'Knock Wood'. When jazz music became the new craze during World War I, Tucker became known as 'The Queen Of Jazz', and toured with the band 'Sophie Tucker And Her Five Kings Of Syncopation'.

In 1919 she replaced 'shimmy dance' specialist, Gilda Gray in the Broadway show *Shubert Gaieties*, and in 1921 hired pianist Ted Shapiro, who as well as writing some of her risque material, became her accompanist and musical director for the rest of her career. In the following year she made the first of many performances in London in the revue, *Round In 50*, based on the novel *Around The World In 80 Days*, by Jules Verne. She was back on Broadway in 1924 for the *Earl Carroll Vanities*, and was by now a major star. Her hits during the 20s included 'High Brown Blues', 'You've Gotta See Mama Ev'ry Night (Or You Won't See Mama At All)', 'Aggravatin' Papa', 'The One I Love Belongs To Somebody Else', 'Red-Hot Mama', 'Bugle Call Rag' (with Ted Lewis and his band), 'Fifty Million Frenchmen Can't Be Wrong', 'After You've Gone', 'I Ain't Got Nobody', 'Blue River', 'There'll Be Some Changes Made', 'The Man I Love', 'I'm The Last Of The Red-Hot Mamas', and two reputed million-sellers, a re-recording of her trademark song, 'Some Of These Days', and 'My Yiddishe Momme', written for her by Jack Yellen and Lew Pollack. She recorded the song in English on one side of the record, and in Yiddish on the other.

In 1929 Tucker made her movie debut in an early talkie, *Honky Tonk*, with songs by Yellen. She made several more films until 1944, including *Gay Love*, *Follow The Boys* and *Sensations Of 1945* - usually as a guest artist playing her larger-than-life self - although she gave critically acclaimed performances in *Thoroughbreds Don't Cry* and *Broadway Melody Of 1938*, co-starring with Judy Garland. In 1930 she returned to London's West End to star with Jack Hulbert in the musical comedy, *Follow A Star*. The London *Observer*'s theatre critic wrote: 'She hurls her songs like projectiles, in a very explosive manner'. Composer Vivian Ellis and Yellen tailored one of the show's outstanding numbers, 'If Your Kisses Can't Hold The Man You Love', especially for Tucker, and it proved to be such a powerful piece that she used it to close her cabaret act for some time afterwards. Four years later she was back in London for the first of several Royal Command Performances, besides regular appearances at London's Kit Kat Club, music hall tours and cabaret. She made her final Broadway appearances in Cole Porter's *Leave It To Me!* (1938), in which she sang 'Most Gentlemen Don't Like Love (They Just Like To Kick It Around')' and *High Kickers* (1941). Her fame faded somewhat in the 50s and 60s, although she still worked in clubs and occasionally on television, including several appearances on the *Ed Sullivan Show*. She also played an effective cameo role in *The Joker Is Wild* (1957) a biopic of comedian Joe E. Lewis. In her later years, when her voice declined, she specialized in half-sung, half-spoken, philosophical songs and monologues, many written by Jack Yellen, sometimes in partnership with Ted Shapiro or Milton Ager. Her specialities included 'Life Begins At 40', 'I'm Having More Fun Now I'm 50', 'I'm Having More Fun Since I'm 60', 'I'm Starting All Over Again', 'The Older They Get', 'You've Got To Be Loved To Be Healthy', 'No One Man Is Ever Going To Worry Me' and 'He Hadn't Till Yesterday'. Her last appearances included New York's Latin Quarter, and The Talk Of The Town in London. The 1963 Broadway musical *Sophie*, was based on her life.

● ALBUMS: *My Dream* (Mercury 1954)★★★, *Cabaret Days* (Mercury 1954)★★★, *Latest And Greatest Spicey Saucy Songs* (Mercury 1954)★★★, *The Great Sophie Tucker* (Brunswick 1957)★★★, *Bigger And Better Than Ever* (Mercury 1957)★★★.

● COMPILATIONS: *Miff Mole's Molers 1927* (1971)★★★, *The Great Sophie Tucker* (1974)★★★, *Some Of These Days* (1976)★★★, *Harry Richman And Sophie Tucker* (1979)★★★, *Last Of The Red-Hot Mamas* (1983)★★★, *The Golden Age Of Sophie Tucker* (1985)★★★, *Follow A Star* (1987)★★★, *The Sophie Tucker Collection* (1987)★★★.

● FURTHER READING: *Some Of These Days*, Sophie Tucker.

TUNE, TOMMY

b. Thomas James Tune, 28 February 1939, Wichita Falls, Texas, USA. An actor, dancer, choreographer, and director. His father worked in the oil industry, and Tune grew up in Houston, Texas. He took dancing lessons from the age of

five, directed and choreographed musicals at high school, and majored in performing arts at the University of Texas. Soon after he moved to New York, he moved right out again with a touring version of *Irma La Douce*. Ironically, his height of six feet nine inches, which he thought might be a hindrance, helped him to gain his first part on Broadway - as one of three tall men in the chorus of the musical *Baker Street* (1965). After further modest roles in *The Joyful Noise* and *How Now Dow Jones*, he choreographed the 1969 touring version of *Canterbury Tales*, and appeared in two films, *Hello, Dolly!* (1969) and *The Boyfriend* (1971). His big break came firstly as a performer in *Seesaw* (1973), in which he stopped the show almost every night with 'It's Not Where You Start (It's Where You Finish)', a number that he choreographed himself. He won a Tony Award for best featured actor, and then did not work on a Broadway musical for five barren years ('I couldn't even get arrested'). His role as choreographer-director on *The Best Little Whorehouse In Texas* (1978) changed all that, and, during the next decade, Tune became the natural successor to past masters in that field, such as Bob Fosse, Jerome Robbins, Gower Champion, and Michael Bennett. He brought his own brand of 'infectious, eye-popping pizzazz' to a string of hit shows: *A Day In Hollywood, A Night In The Ukraine* (1980), *Nine* (1982), *My One And Only* (1983, in which he also co-starred with Twiggy), *Grand Hotel* (1989), and *The Will Rogers Follies* (1991). They gained him a total of nine Tony Awards, and induction into New York's Theatre Hall of Fame in 1991. In the following year, Tune took time out from appearing in a lucrative US tour of *Bye Bye Birdie*, to stage the London production of *Grand Hotel* which was greeted with apathy by the critics and public alike. In December 1992 he presented his own *Tommy Tune Tonight!* on Broadway for a limited period, prior to a 20-week 1993 national tour. Also in 1993, he directed the Takarazuka Theatre Company in Japan, and two years later, his new production of *Grease* opened on Broadway. During the remainder of the 90s, he toured with *Tommy Tune And The Rhythm Kings: Everything Old Is New Again*, but withdrew from the musicals *Busker Alley* and *The Royal Family* while they were still on the road. He also experienced problems with the Broadway-bound stage version of the highly successful movie *Easter Parade* in which he was set to play the Fred Astaire role. However, things looked up in January 1999, when Tune took over from David Cassidy as the star of the special-effects musical spectacular *EFX* in Las Vegas.

● ALBUMS: *Slow Dancin'* (RCA Victor 1997)★★★, and Original Cast recordings.

● FURTHER READING: *Footnotes*, Tommy Tune.

TWANG!!

The Robin Hood legend has been the subject of many a musical production since it was presented, usually as a comic operetta, in both the USA and England in the late 19th, and early 20th century. The 'burlesque' version which opened at London's Shaftesbury Theatre on the 20 December 1965, had music and lyrics by Lionel Bart, who also wrote the book in collaboration with an American talent agent and television personality, Harvey Orkin. Several members of Bart's successful 1960 production,

Fings Ain't Wot They Used T'Be, were involved in his new venture, including Joan Littlewood (director), James Booth (Robin Hood, a con-man), and Barbara Windsor (Delphina, a nymphomaniac). In addition, the diminutive Ronnie Corbett played Will Scarlett, and Long John Baldry, who was to have a UK number 1 hit with 'Let The Heartaches Begin' two years later, was billed as 'Mystery Voice'. Bart said it was all supposed be a 'giggle'. From an early stage, *Twang!!* was perceived to be in trouble, and the persistent rumours were confirmed when, after being set for a provincial tryout in October in Birmingham, the show was reluctantly presented to the public for the first time on the 3 November - in Manchester. On the following day, Littlewood departed, to be replaced by American Burt Shevelove. Booth was said to be suffering from nervous exhaustion, and soon afterwards, Bernard Delfont Ltd withdrew its financial backing. Bart was determined to open in London, and, disregarding his friend Noël Coward's advice, invested his own money in the show. It was the beginning of his slide into bankruptcy, which preceded many years in the wilderness. Naturally, the script changed daily, as did the score. At various stages in the production the songs included 'Make An Honest Woman Out Of Me', 'Roger The Ugly', 'Whose Little Girl Are You?', 'Follow Your Leader', 'With Bells On', and a delicate piece called 'Sighs'. The critics had a field day: 'The worst musical for years' . . . 'a dank, bedraggled, feeble thing', were two of the more favourable reviews. The word 'shambles' was used a lot, as *Twang!!* staggered on for 43 performances. Perhaps there's a jinx on the whole Robin Hood musical concept, because in 1993, *Robin, Prince Of Sherwood* ('a doomed farrago'), with music and lyrics by Rick Fenn and Peter Howarth and directed by Bill Kenwright - an impresario with the 'magic touch' - closed in London after a run of eight weeks, losing £500,000.

TWIST AROUND THE CLOCK
It was Columbia Pictures who launched the notion of cinematic pop with *Rock Around The Clock*, the first film wholly devoted to rock 'n' roll. In 1961 the same company disinterred the same flimsy plot in an attempt to cash-in on the current Twist dance craze. *Twist Around The Clock* has become an abject lesson in differentiating between a fad and something of substance, with the Twist clearly one of the former. Popularizer Chubby Checker starred in this flimsy vehicle which was barely saved from stupor by its guest artists. A rare on-screen outing for Dion provided the film's sole saving grace. His readings of 'Runaround Sue' (US Number 1) and 'The Wanderer' (US number 2) were highly memorable, easily eclipsing performances by the Marcels and Vicki Spencer. Sadly, *Twist Around The Clock* was viewed as an outlet for Checker's questionable talent and as such fails to excite. Perhaps if it had featured the superior Hank Ballard And The Midnighters, who recorded the original 'The Twist', as a b-side, in 1959, the film would have been of greater interest.

TWO GENTLEMEN OF VERONA
Galt MacDermot, who burst on the Broadway scene in 1967 with his music for *Hair*, collaborated with lyricist John Guare on the score for this rock musical version of William Shakespeare's play which concerns, according to one critic, 'two sets of lovers, who are by turns, skittish, treacherous, endearing and eccentric'. This modern conception of the *Two Gentlemen Of Verona* was first presented as part of a series of open-air productions in New York's Central Park in the summer of 1971, and proved to be so successful that it transferred to Broadway at the St. James Theatre on December 1 that year. Librettists John Guare and the show's director Mel Shapiro, skilfully interpolated contemporary language and references into the original and well-worn story of odious Proteous (Raul Julia), who not only plays fast and loose with his lady friend Julia (Diana Davila), but also tries to muscle in on Silvia (Jonelle Allen), the mistress of his best friend Valentine (Clifton Davis). The cast also included Stockard Channing who was to blossom into a fine stage actress, and made such an impact as the cynical Rizzo in the film of *Grease*. The score was not considered by the critics to be in the same class as *Hair*, but numbers such as 'Bring All The Boys Back Home', 'Follow The Rainbow', 'Night Letter', 'Who Is Silvia?' (lyric: Shakespeare), and 'Calla Lily Lady', when reproduced at extremely high levels of sound, appealed sufficiently to sustain a run of 627 performances. To the surprise of many the show won Tony Awards for best musical and book, but *Follies* took most of the rest of the prizes that season. More than 20 years later, in October 1993, the Royal Shakespeare Company in Britain approached *Two Gentlemen Of Verona* in quite a different way. Their much-praised production at the Barbican in London was conceived by David Thacker, and gave the piece an elegant and stylish 30s setting, in which singer Hilary Cromie accompanied by a seven-piece band, drifted in and out of the action with bitter-sweet songs of the era, such as 'Love Is The Sweetest Thing', 'More Than You Know', 'What'll I Do?', 'Heartaches', and 'In The Still Of The Night'. As with the Broadway production, the song 'Who Is Silvia?' was present, although this time the melody was by Guy Woolfenden who composed the original music for the entire production.

200 MOTELS
Rock iconoclast Frank Zappa wrote the story, screenplay and music for this 1971 film. Tony Palmer, famed for his documentaries *All My Loving* and *Cream's Last Concert*, directed the project with considerable aplomb, shooting the scenes on video before transferring the results onto film using newly discovered optical effects. The result was a surreal pantomime based around the on-the-road experiences of a touring band staying at a motel in Centreville, USA. The freewheeling imagery centred on Zappa's group, the Mothers Of Invention, which he reassembled for this project with several new members, including Aynsley Dunbar and two former Turtles, Mark Volman and Howard Kaylan. The latter pair, known as the Phlorescent Leech And Eddie (or Flo And Eddie), to escape contractual wrangles, brought a new visual/verbal aspect to the band, one this madcap film exploits to great effect. Former Mother Jimmy Carl Black stars as the Lonesome Cowboy, folk-singer Theodore Bikel drifts in and out of the proceedings, Keith Moon of the Who features dressed as a nun and Ringo Starr appears memorably as Frank Zappa.

In-concert footage, including the Mothers' collaboration with the Royal Philharmonic Orchestra, crosscuts satirical scenes of sexual conquest and hedonism and in the manner of many of Zappa's 'documentary' projects, the attendant soundtrack album, which includes material not in the film and omits some that is, mixes dialogue with music. Disjointed and self-indulgent, *200 Motels* articulates the madness surrounding rock's first generation.

TWO LANE BLACKTOP

Released by a major studio, Universal, in the wake of *Easy Rider, Two Lane Blacktop* (1971) avoids 'cash-in' trappings thanks to the underplayed acting of novices James Taylor and Dennis Wilson. The casting of a winsome singer-songwriter and disenchanted Beach Boys' member raised contemporary eyebrows, but the pair's portrayal of two drifters was genuinely affecting. Skilfully directed by Monte Hellman, the film's car races between nihilistic hippie (Taylor) and flash Southerner (Warren Oates) provided its scant action, but the largely unspoken communication between the former and Wilson provides much of the lasting power. Neither boasts a name - they are billed as 'the Driver' and 'the Mechanic' - and the tenuous relationship between them is sundered with the arrival of 'the Girl' (Laurie Bird). Underlying tensions explode in the film's dramatic finale. Curiously, despite the involvement of two well-known musicians, neither was featured on the soundtrack. Atmospheric accompaniment was directed by Billy James, previously a publicist at the Columbia and Elektra labels.

UK SWINGS AGAIN

A follow-up to *Swinging UK*, this was the second 1964 short directed by Frank Gilpin. Disc jockeys Kent Walton (host of television's *Discs A Go Go*), Alan Freeman and Brian Matthews introduced a succession of British acts miming to contemporaneous releases. Among the cast were Brian Poole And The Tremeloes, the Applejacks, the Tornadoes and Swinging Blue Jeans, but the highlights were provided by Lulu And The Luvvers ('Shout'), the Hollies ('Here I Go Again') and the Animals ('Baby Let Me Take You Home'). Released in UK cinemas as a second feature, *UK Swings Again* was amalgamated with *Swinging UK* and a third short, *Mods And Rockers*, for US consumption. The

composite, titled *Go Go Big Beat*, was somewhat improbably hosted by actors Marlon Brando and Rod Steiger in place of the British trio.

UNDER YOUR HAT (FILM MUSICAL)

This was one of the best - and the last - of the popular series of Cicely Courtneidge and Jack Hulbert musicals, although they did make the occasional comedy and dramatic picture together later in their careers. It was adapted from the successful couple's hit West End musical, and released in 1940 by Grand National (British Lion) Pictures. Courtneidge and Hulbert play film stars Kay and Jack Millett who get caught up in a web of espionage. A glamorous spy, Carole Markoff (Leonora Corbett), heads off to Europe with the intention of passing a top secret carburettor to Russian agent Boris Vladimir (Austin Trevor). Jack is despatched by the authorities to use his renowned charm on the lady in an effort to retrieve the stolen property, but Kay is not aware that his interest in Carole is purely platonic and in the national interest. However, she and her husband, with the help of some hilarious disguises, eventually wrestle the booty from the Reds. Also involved in the fun and games were Cecil Parker, Charles Oliver, H.F. Maltby, Glynis Johns, Myrette Morvan, and Don Marino Barretto's Band. Most of the original stage score was dispensed with, and the songs in the film consisted of 'Keep It Under Your Hat' (Clive Erard-Claude Hulbert), 'I Won't Conga' (F. King-Hulbert), 'Tiger Rag' (Larocca), and 'Sur Le Pont D'Avignon' (Traditional). The well-known bandleader Lew Stone composed the atmospheric background music. Maurice Elvy was the director, and this amusing and typically English picture was produced by Jack Hulbert.

UNDER YOUR HAT (STAGE MUSICAL)

This musical comedy reunited the husband-and-wife team of Cicely Courtneidge and Jack Hulbert on the West End stage for the first time since they appeared together in the revue *The House That Jack Built* (1929). It opened on 24 November 1938 at the Palace Theatre, and, after being withdrawn for two months at the beginning of World War II, ran until April 1940, a total of 512 performances. The book was the result of a collaboration between Archie Menzies, Arthur Macrae, and Jack Hulbert, and the music and lyrics were by Vivian Ellis, with additional numbers by the Rhythm Brothers and Claude Hulbert. Almost inevitably, Cicely Courtneidge and Jack Hulbert were once again cast as husband and wife, this time as the smart film-star twosome Kay Porter and Jack Millet. The plot has them travelling to various home and foreign locations on behalf of the British Government in an effort to retrieve a valuable carburettor which has been stolen by the glamorous spy, Carol Markoff (Leonora Corbett), who has given it to the Russians' representative, Boris Vladimir (Frank Cellier). Also among the cast were Madeline Gibson, Peter Haddon, John Byron, Pamela Rosemary, Henry Thompson, Lena Maitland, and Jevan Brandon-Thomas. The whole thing was an ideal excuse for everyone to dress up in a variety of disguises, especially Courtneidge, who provided one of the show's many highlights when her impersonation of a waitress in a red wig develops into an hilarious burlesque of a French cabaret performer in the number, 'La Danse C'est Moi'. The consistently tuneful and witty score also included 'Together Again', 'If You Want To Dance', 'Rise Above It', 'They're Wearing Them This Way Now', 'Cook's Ballet', 'I've Lost My Way', 'Hostesses Of The Air', 'Crocodile On Parade', 'Keep It Under Your Hat', and 'The Hat Ballet'. As usual there was one particularly outstanding song for Cicely Courtneidge. This time it was Ellis's 'The Empire Depends On You', in which she lectured the chorus, not necessarily severely, thus: 'Now I'm a soldier's daughter, our family thrive on war/Why, all my folk were Army, they fought at Agincourt/My dear old Dad, the Major, he served at Crecy too/A touch of gout just put him out/He was late for Waterloo'. This 'lavish, witty, fool-proof entertainment . . . the funniest musical comedy for years' lightened the early, uneasy years of the war, and was filmed under the title of *Grand National* in 1940, when Courtneidge and Hulbert recreated their roles.

UNION CITY

Based on Cornell Woolrich's novel *The Corpse Next Door*, *Union City* starred Dennis Lipscomb and Blondie vocalist Deborah Harry. They play a married couple, living in a claustrophobic apartment, whose orderly lives are upset when milk is constantly stolen from outside their door. Lipscomb's character, a mannered businessman, murders the culprit, resulting in scenes of black humour. Mark Reichert directs the proceedings in a low-key, dispassionate manner, reminiscent of Jim Jarmusch or David Lynch, yet lacking Lynch's wilful surrealism or Jarmusch's absurd humour. *Union City* is nonetheless a fascinating, if downbeat, film that benefits from a score by Chris Stein, another Blondie member. It provides a wider view of both their talents.

UNSINKABLE MOLLY BROWN, THE

Not as successful or as satisfying as Meredith Willson's earlier smash-hit, *The Music Man*, but then that show was all his own work and is considered to be a masterpiece of the American musical theatre. Willson only provided the music and lyrics for this one, and left the book to Richard Morris, who also collaborated with him on *1491*, Willson's final musical, which did not reach Broadway. *The Unsinkable Molly Brown* opened at the Winter Garden in New York on 3 November 1960. The story was set in the early part of the 20th century and concerned the indefatigable Molly Brown, a legendary figure in US history, who was born on the wrong side of the tracks in Hannibal, Missouri, but is determined to progress swiftly from that unfortunate condition. She moves to the mining town of Colorado, and marries Johnny 'Leadville' Brown (Harve Presnell), a prospector with the 'golden touch'. Their initial attempts to break into Denver high society fail dismally, but after conquering Europe - especially Monte Carlo - with her personality and Johnny's money, and becoming something of a hero (and a survivor) during the *Titanic* disaster, she returns to find that Denver and its high-falutin' citizens are at her feet. Willson's score had the same kind of folksy, all-American down-home charm that had worked so well in *The Music Man*. The highlight

was Molly's spirited anthem to survival, 'I Ain't Down Yet', and there were several other rousing numbers among the rest of the songs, which included 'My Own Brass Bed', 'Belly Up To The Bar, Boys', 'I'll Never Say No', 'Colorado, My Home', 'Are You Sure?', 'Bea-u-ti-ful People Of Denver', 'Chick-A-Pen', and 'Dolce Far Niente'. Tammy Grimes won a Tony Award for her lively and gutsy performance, and New York theatregoers liked this glimpse of their pioneering past sufficiently for the show to run for 15 months. Harve Presnell reprised his role for the 1964 film in which he co-starred with Debbie Reynolds.

UP IN ARMS

Considering the impact Danny Kaye made in this, his first feature film, it could well have been retitled *A Star Is Born*. Produced by Sam Goldwyn in Technicolor and released by RKO in 1944, *Up In Arms* is the story of a zany hypochondriac who leaves his job as an elevator boy and winds up in the US Army on an island in the South Pacific. With him is his buddy (Dana Andrews) and their girlfriends, played by Dinah Shore and Constance Dowling. The hectic storyline is interrupted occasionally by similarly hectic numbers such as 'Melody In 4-F' and 'The Lobby Song' ('Manic-Depressive Pictures presents . . .'), both written by Sylvia Fine and Max Liebman, and performed by Kaye in his own highly individual and brilliant style. If it was all getting a bit too frantic, audiences could relax for a few moments in the company of Dinah Shore and her lovely renderings of Harold Arlen and Ted Koehler's 'Now I Know' and 'Tess's Torch Song'. Not many were heard to complain, though, and this film launched the red-haired unique entertainer on his way to well-deserved worldwide acclaim. Joining in the fun were Louis Calhern, Lyle Talbot, Benny Baker, George Matthews, Walter Catlett, Margaret Dumont, Elisha Cook Jnr., and 24-year-old Virginia Mayo in only her second film. Danny Dare handled the choreography and the director was Elliot Nugent. *Up In Arms*, which had a screenplay by Don Hartman, Allan Boretz and Robert Pirosh, is sometimes considered to be a remake of *Whoopee!* (1930), which was based on Owen Davis' play *The Nervous Wreck*, and starred Eddie Cantor.

UP IN CENTRAL PARK

More than 15 years had passed since composer Sigmund Romberg's last big hit, *New Moon*, when he teamed with lyricist Dorothy Fields to write the score for this show which opened at the New Century Theatre in New York on 27 January 1945. Fields also collaborated with her brother Herbert on the book, a tale of intrigue and corruption set in the late 19th century in which newspaper reporter John Matthews (Wilbur Evans) is intent on exposing an infamous Tammany Hall political group, led by William Macey Tweed (Noah Beery), who are siphoning off monies that have been allotted for the creation of Central Park. Complications ensue when Matthews falls for Rosie Moore (Maureen Cannon), the daughter of one of the fraudsters. Naturally, the lovers have the show's outstanding ballad, the lovely 'Close As Pages In A Book', which became a bestseller for Benny Goodman at the time, and was later given memorable readings by

Margaret Whiting and Maxine Sullivan, amongst others. It also titled Barbara Cook's 1993 tribute album to Dorothy Fields. Evans and Cannon introduced yet another superior song, 'April Snow', and the remainder of Romberg's typically 'operetta-tinged' score included 'Carousel In The Park', 'When You Walk In The Room', and 'The Big Back Yard'. The outstanding moment came with the celebrated 'Currier And Ives Ballet', a stunning sequence set in the Park, and choreographed by Helen Tamaris. The show, which is said to have some basis in fact, ran for 504 performances, and was filmed in 1948 with Dick Haymes and Deanna Durbin.

UP ON THE ROOF

Following a brief run at the Theatre Royal, Plymouth, this show spent a few weeks at London's Donmar Warehouse before transferring to the Apollo theatre in the West End on 8 June 1987. The play, which was written by Simon Moore and Jane Prowse (who also directed), was originally developed from improvisation with Beverley Hills, Mark McGann, Felicity Montagu, Michael Mueller, and Gary Olsen. Olsen has gone on to various UK television successes, including *2point4 Children*, and Mark McGann, one of the four theatrical brothers from Liverpool, is renowned for his portrayal of John Lennon in several productions. McGann was also present in 1991 when *The Hunting Of The Snark* proved to be a fruitless expedition. As *Up On The Roof* opens, the time is the summer of 1975. Five university students have had their examination results, and are spending their last night on the roof of their student house, discussing life and what the future holds for them. They decide to meet up for a reunion in 10 years time at a villa in the south of France, and the story follows them through those years, reflecting in a dramatic and often amusing way, the gradual changes in their attitudes and ideals. The 70s songs that accompany this journey are performed appealingly by the cast, a cappella, and include 'Never Can Say Goodbye', 'When Will I See You Again', 'Sad Sweet Dreamer', 'Band Of Gold', 'What Becomes Of The Broken Hearted?', 'My Eyes Adored You', and, of course, 'Up On The Roof. The production gained three Laurence Olivier Award nominations, including best musical, and, in the subsequent touring version, Steve McGann replaced his brother Mark, and also served as the musical director.

UP THE JUNCTION

Released in 1967, *Up The Junction* starred Suzi Kendall as an affluent, middle-class young woman who crosses the Thames - and social barriers - to live in Clapham, south London. Although her assimilation into working-class culture is highly contentious - Kendall remains stoically detached from her new surroundings - the film remains an interesting, if mildly patronising, period-piece. Adapted by Roger Smith from Nell Dunn's book of the same name, *Up The Junction* was inspired by a television documentary drama, fleshed out with references to casual sex, abortion, motorcycles and dancing. Maureen Lipman and Adrienne Posta excel in their individual roles and the cast is aided by contributions from British film veterans Alfie Bass, Liz Fraser and Hylda Baker. *Up The Junction* also provided former child star Dennis Waterman with his first significant adult part. Mike Hugg, drummer in Manfred Mann, completed an excellent soundtrack album with the aid of his group's nominal leader. Although Manfred Mann were renowned for scoring hits with other writers' material, Hugg had proved himself an excellent composer on the band's albums and flipsides. His ear for quirky, but memorable melodies is apparent on *Up The Junction*, which is the equal of the group's 'official' releases.

VAGABOND KING, THE

With music by Rudolph Friml and lyrics by Brian Hooker, this operetta was presented at the Casino Theatre in New York on 21 September 1925. The book, by Hooker, Russey Janney, and W.H. Post, was based on the play and novel *If I Were A King*, and was a highly imaginative piece - even for this era. It was set in 15th century Paris and concerned the outlaw Francois Villon (Dennis King) who escapes the guillotine by becoming the King of France for a day and defeating the Duke of Burgundy. His reward is the hand in marriage of the lovely Katherine de Vaucelles (Carolyn Thompson). The score was a mixture of rousing songs and ballads, and included such enduring favourites as 'Song Of the Vagabonds', 'Only A Rose', 'Some Day', 'Hugette Waltz', 'Love Me Tonight', and 'Love For Sale'. The New York run of 511 performances was followed by a further 480 in London in 1927, and the show has remained a staple item in the repertoires of amateur and professional operatic societies ever since. Two film versions have been released: in 1930 with Dennis King and Jeanette MacDonald, and 1956 with Oreste and Kathryn Grayson.

VALLEE, RUDY

b. Hubert Prior Vallee, 28 July 1901, Island Pond, Vermont, USA, d. 3 July 1986, North Hollywood, California, USA. An immensely popular singer during the 20s and 30s, Vallee sang through a megaphone and is generally regarded as the first 'crooner' - a precursor of Russ Columbo and Bing Crosby. He was also one of the first entertainers to generate mass hysteria among his audiences. Vallee was brought up in Westbrook, Maine, and learnt to play the saxophone in his teens, taking the name 'Rudy' because of his admiration for saxophonist Rudy Weidoft. During 1924/5 he took a year off from university to play the saxophone in London with the Savoy Havana Band led by Reginald Batten. At this time his singing voice, which was rather slight and nasal, was not taken seriously. In 1928 he led his first band, at the exclusive Heigh-Ho Club on New York's 53rd Street. Billed as Rudy And His Connecticut Yankees, Vallee made an excellent frontman, complete with his famous greeting: 'Heigh-ho everybody', and his smooth vocal delivery of his theme song at that time, Walter Donaldson's 'Heigh-ho Everybody, Heigh-ho'. When radio stations started to carry his shows in the club, he became an instant success and admitted that he was 'a product of radio'. His next venue was the Versaille Club on 50th Street. After a few weeks, business was so good they renamed it the Villa Vallee. His success continued when he transferred his show to vaude-ville. In 1929 he starred in his first feature film, the poor-ly received *Vagabond Lover*, and in the same year began a weekly NBC network radio variety show sponsored by the Fleischmann's Yeast company (*The Fleischmann Hour*), which became a top attraction and ran for 10 years. His theme song for this production was 'My Time Is Your Time'. Artists he promoted on the show included radio ventriloquist Edgar Bergen, Frances Langford, and Alice Faye. In 1931 and 1936 Vallee appeared on Broadway in *George White's Scandals*, and in 1934 starred in a film ver-sion of the show. From early in his career he had co-writ-ten several popular songs, such as 'I'm Still Caring', 'If You Haven't Got A Girl', 'Don't Play With Fire', 'Two Little Blue Little Eyes' and 'Oh, Ma-Ma'. He had big hits with some of his own numbers including 'I'm Just A Vagabond Lover', 'Deep Night', 'Vieni Vieni' and 'Betty Co-ed' (a song men-tioning most of the US colleges).

Other record successes included 'Marie', 'Honey' (a num-ber 1 hit), 'Weary River', 'Lonely Troubadour', 'A Little Kiss Each Morning (A Little Kiss Each Night)', 'Stein Song (University Of Maine)', 'If I Had A Girl Like You', 'You're Driving Me Crazy', 'Would You Like To Take A Walk?', 'When Yuba Plays The Rhumba On The Tuba', ' Let's Put Out The Lights', 'Brother Can You Spare A Dime?', 'Just An Echo In The Valley', 'Everything I Have Is Yours', 'Orchids In The Moonlight', 'You Oughta Be In Pictures', 'Nasty Man', 'As Time Goes By', and 'The Whiffenpoof Song'. During the 30s, Vallee appeared in several popular musical films including *Glorifying The American Girl*, *International House*, *Sweet Music*, *Gold Diggers Of Paris*, and *Second Fiddle*. However, after *Time Out For Rhythm*, *Too Many Blondes*, and *Happy-Go-Lucky* (1943), he launched a new movie career as a comedy actor. Discarding his romantic image, he began portraying a series of eccentric, strait-laced, pompous characters in films such as *The Palm Beach Story*, *Man Alive!*, and *It's In The Bag*. During World War II, Vallee led the California Coastguard orchestra which he augmented to 45 musicians. After the war he was back on the radio, in nightclubs, and making more movies, including *The Bachelor And The Bobbysoxer*, *I Remember Mama*, *So This Is New York*, *Unfaithfully Yours*, and *The Beautiful Blonde From Bashful Bend*. During the 50s he appeared regularly on television, especially in talk shows, and featured in the films *Gentlemen Marry Brunettes* and *The Helen Morgan Story*. In 1961 he enjoyed a triumph in the role of J.B. Biggley, a caricature of a col-legiate executive figure, in Frank Loesser's smash hit musical *How To Succeed In Business Without Really Trying*. Vallee re-created the part in the 1967 movie, and in a San Francisco stage revival in 1975. In 1968 he contributed the narration to the William Friedkin film *The Night They Raided Minsky's*. He continued to make movies into the 70s (his last feature was the 1976 film *Won Ton Ton, The Dog Who Saved Hollywood*), and performed his one-man show up until his death from a heart attack.

● ALBUMS: *Let's Do It* (50s)★★★, *Stein Songs* (50s)★★★, *Young Rudy Vallee* (RCA Victor)★★★, original cast *How To Succeed In Business Without Really Trying* soundtrack (1961)★★.
● COMPILATIONS: *Best Of* (1967)★★★, *Rudy Vallee And His Connecticut Yankees* (1986)★★★, *'Heigh-ho Everybody, This Is Rudy Vallee* (1981)★★★, *Sing For Your Supper* (1989)★★★.
● FURTHER READING: all by Rudy Vallee *Vagabond Dreams Come True*, *My Time Is Your Time*, *I Digress*.

VALMOUTH

A British cult musical that shocked some, is fondly remembered by many, and - so the story goes - is under-stood by relatively few. *Valmouth* opened on 2 October 1958 at the Lyric Theatre, Hammersmith, which is locat-ed a few miles away from the glamorous West End. It was adapted from the 'scandalous' works of Ronald Firbank by Sandy Wilson, whose smash-hit *The Boy Friend* was com-ing to the end of its five-year run at Wyndhams Theatre. Many wise and learned beings have attempted unsuccess-fully to fathom the mysteries of this show, but what seems to be clear is that Valmouth is one of those essentially English spa towns, where life-enhancing benefits of a somewhat bizarre kind can be had by visitors and resi-dents alike. In the case of Valmouth, the residents are mostly centenarians, and the main benefits involve an abnormally long and active sex life. The inhabitants include Mrs. Yajnavalka (Bertice Reading), the black masseuse with the 'magic fingers', who provides a variety of advice and services to Grannie Took (Doris Hare) and her granddaughter Thetis (Patsy Rowlands). Thetis imag-ines she is to be the bride of Captain Dick Thoroughfare (Alan Edwards), heir to Mrs Hurstpierpoint (Barbara Couper), the Catholic châtelaine of Hare Hatch House ('the former favourite of a King, but for just a few min-utes'). In actual fact, Captain Dick has already married Mrs. Yajnavalka's niece, Niri-Esther (Maxine Daniels). It's that complicated. Another familiar figure in the area is Lady Parvula de Panzoust (Fenella Fielding), an ageing nymphomaniac - but she is just visiting.

The song mostly associated with the show is 'My Big Best Shoes', joyously performed by Bertice Reading, but there were other memorable moments too in Wilson's wonder-fully witty score. These included 'Just Once More' and 'Only A Passing Phase' (both Fielding), 'Magic Fingers', 'Mustapha', 'The Cry Of The Peacock', 'Little Girl Baby' (all Reading), 'I Will Miss You' (Hare and Reading), and 'I Loved A Man', 'What Then Can Make Him Come So Slow', 'All The Girls Were Pretty', 'Lady Of The Manor', 'What Do I Want With Love', 'Where The Trees Are Green With Parrots', and 'My Talking Day'. *Valmouth* ran for 84 perfor-mances at the Lyric, but by the time the show transferred to the Saville Theatre in the West End on 27 January 1959,

Bertice Reading had returned to America, to be replaced by the young up-and-coming jazz singer Cleo Laine. A further run of 102 performances to frequently puzzled and offended audiences, was followed by complete rejection in New York where the show was withdrawn after less than two weeks. Over 20 years later in May 1982, *Valmouth* was revived at the Chichester Festival Theatre with several of the original cast, including Bertice Reading and Fenella Fielding, who were joined by pop-star-turned-actor Mark Wynter as Captain Dick. The production was highly acclaimed, and although it is inconceivable that audiences would be even slightly outraged by this show nowadays, no impresario has so far stepped forward to present it in London.

VAN HEUSEN, JIMMY

b. Edward Chester Babcock, 26 January 1913, Syracuse, New York, USA, d. 6 February 1990, Rancho Mirage, California, USA. Van Heusen was an extremely popular and prolific composer from the late 30s through to the 60s, particularly for movies. He was an affable, high-living, fun-loving character. His main collaborators were lyricists Johnny Burke and Sammy Cahn. While still at high school, Van Heusen worked at a local radio station, playing piano and singing. He changed his name to Van Heusen, after the famous shirt manufacturer. In the early 30s he studied piano and composition at Syracuse University, and met Jerry Arlen, son of composer Harold Arlen. Arlen Snr. gave Van Heusen the opportunity to write for Harlem's *Cotton Club Revues*. His big break came in 1938 when bandleader Jimmy Dorsey wrote a lyric to Van Heusen's tune for 'It's The Dreamer In Me'. Ironically, the song was a big hit for rival bandleader Harry James. In the same year Van Heusen started working with lyricist Eddie DeLange. Their songs included 'Deep In A Dream', 'All This And Heaven Too', 'Heaven Can Wait' (a number 1 hit for Glen Gray), 'This Is Madness' and 'Shake Down The Stars' (a hit for Glenn Miller). In 1939 they wrote the score for the Broadway musical *Swingin' The Dream*, a jazzy treatment of Shakespeare's *A Midsummer Night's Dream*. Despite the presence in the cast of the all-star Benny Goodman Sextet, Louis Armstrong, Maxine Sullivan, and the Deep River Boys, plus the song 'Darn That Dream', the show folded after only 13 performances. In 1940 Van Heusen was placed under contract to Paramount Pictures, and began his association with Johnny Burke. Their first songs together included 'Polka Dots And Moonbeams' and 'Imagination', both hits for the Tommy Dorsey Orchestra, with vocals by Frank Sinatra, who was to have an enormous effect on Van Heusen's later career. After contributing to the Fred Allen-Jack Benny comedy film *Love Thy Neighbor* (1940), Van Heusen and Burke supplied songs for 16 Bing Crosby films through to 1953, including 'It's Always You' (*Road To Zanzibar*), 'Road To Morocco', 'Moonlight Becomes You' (*Road To Morocco*), 'Sunday, Monday Or Always' (*Dixie*), 'Swinging On A Star' (which won the 1944 Academy Award, from the film *Going My Way*), 'Aren't You Glad You're You?' (*The Bells Of St Mary's*), 'Personality' (*Road To Utopia*), 'But Beautiful', 'You Don't Have To Know The Language', 'Experience' (*Road To Rio*), 'If You Stub Your

Toe On the Moon', 'Busy Doing Nothing' (*A Connecticut Yankee In King Arthur's Court*) and 'Sunshine Cake' (*Riding High*). Besides working on other films, Van Heusen and Burke also wrote the score for the 1953 Broadway musical *Carnival In Flanders*, which contained the songs 'Here's That Rainy Day' and 'It's An Old Spanish Custom'. Other Van Heusen songs during this period include 'Oh, You Crazy Moon', 'Suddenly It's Spring' and 'Like Someone In Love' (all with Burke). The last song received a memorable delivery from Frank Sinatra on his first album, *Songs For Young Lovers*, in 1953, as did 'I Thought About You', on Sinatra's *Songs For Swinging Lovers*. Van Heusen also wrote, along with comedian Phil Silvers, one of Sinatra's special songs, dedicated to his daughter, 'Nancy (With The Laughing Face)'.

When Burke became seriously ill in 1954 and was unable to work for two years, Van Heusen began a collaboration with Sammy Cahn. Cahn had recently ended his partnership with Jule Styne in style by winning an Oscar for their title song to the film *Three Coins In The Fountain* (1954). The new team had immediate success with another title song, for the 1955 Sinatra comedy, *The Tender Trap*, and then won Academy Awards for their songs in two more Sinatra films: 'All The Way' (from the Joe E. Lewis biopic, *The Joker Is Wild*) in 1957, and 'High Hopes' (from *A Hole In The Head*) in 1959. They also contributed songs to several other Sinatra movies, including 'Ain't That A Kick In The Head' (*Ocean's 11*), 'My Kind Of Town', 'Style' (*Robin And The Seven Hoods*), the title songs to *A Pocketful Of Miracles*, *Come Blow Your Horn* and several of Sinatra's bestselling albums, such as *Come Fly With Me*, *Only The Lonely*, *Come Dance With Me*, *No One Cares*, *Ring-A-Ding-Ding* and *September Of My Years*. Van Heusen and Cahn also produced his successful *Timex* television series (1959-60). They won their third Academy Award in 1963 for 'Call Me Irresponsible', from the film *Papa's Delicate Condition*, and contributed songs to many other movies, including 'The Second Time Around' (*High Time*), and the title songs for *Say One For Me*, *Where Love Has Gone*, *Thoroughly Modern Millie* and *Star!*. The duo also supplied the songs for a musical version of Thornton Wilder's classic play *Our Town*, which included 'Love And Marriage' and 'The Impatient Years'. They wrote the scores for two Broadway musicals, *Skyscraper* in 1965 ('Everybody Has The Right To Be Wrong', 'I'll Only Miss Her When I Think Of Her') and *Walking Happy* in 1966, starring Norman Wisdom. From then on, Van Heusen concentrated on his other interests such as music publishing (he had formed a company with Johnny Burke in 1944), photography, flying his own aeroplanes, and collecting rare manuscripts by classical composers. He also continued to make television appearances, especially on tribute shows for composers. He died in 1990, after a long illness.

VAN HOVE, FRED

b. 19 February 1937, Antwerp, Belgium. As a child Van Hove studied piano formally but in his teens was diverted from the classics by be-bop. Ever forward-thinking in his approach, he responded to new concepts, including modality and in the late 60s began a long association with Peter Brötzmann that also involved Han Bennink. These three played as a trio into the mid-70s, although during this period Van Hove also continued to develop a reputation as a soloist and for his performances in duo with saxophonists Cel Overbeghe (early 70s) and Lol Coxhill (late 70s/early 80s). During the 80s he continued his contemporary jazz-playing alongside a successful career as a composer of music for motion pictures and also for the theatre. In addition to playing piano, he also occasionally plays organ. Although not as readily accessible as many pianists of his era, Van Hove's work repays the commitment needed by his audiences fully to engage with its often deeply introspective complexities.

● ALBUMS: with Peter Brötzmann, Han Bennink *Outspan No. 2* (FMP 1974)★★★★, *Live At The University* (Vogel 1974)★★★, *Verloren Maandag* (FMP 1977)★★★, *Church Organ* (FMP 1979)★★★, *Suite For B City* (FMP 1998)★★★★.

VANISHING POINT

This 1971 feature successfully rekindled the 'outlaw' motif of *Easy Rider*. Barry Newman starred as a former racing driver who delivers cars, cross country, for a living. Liberally dosed with amphetamines, he takes one vehicle across the Nevada Desert, pursued by an ever-increasing number of police cars. The metaphor of authority versus free expression is well struck as Newman encounters unexpected friendships during his journey. As the chase intensifies he is aided by a disc jockey, who relays messages and warnings during his programme. The car radio is the source of much of the soundtrack music, although Delaney And Bonnie make an appearance on film, performing on a makeshift stage, many miles from 'civilisation'. This sometimes beguiling film was not a box-office success, yet it remains an above-average example of its genre. It inspired Primal Scream's 1997 album of the same title.

VAUGHAN, FRANKIE

b. Frank Abelson, 3 February 1928, Liverpool, England. While studying at Leeds College of Art, Vaughan's vocal performance at a college revue earned him a week's trial at the Kingston Empire music hall. Warmly received, he went on to play the UK variety circuit, developing a stylish act with trademarks that included a top hat and cane, a particularly athletic side kick, and his theme song 'Give Me The Moonlight' (Albert Von Tilzer-Lew Brown). His Russian-born maternal grandmother inspired his stage name by always referring to him as her 'Number Vorn' grandchild. After registering strongly in pre-chart days with 'That Old Piano Roll Blues', 'Daddy's Little Girl', 'Look At That Girl', and 'Hey, Joe', during the mid to late 50s Vaughan was consistently in the UK Top 30 with hits such as 'Istanbul (Not Constantinople)', 'Happy Days And Lonely Nights', 'Tweedle Dee', 'Seventeen', 'My Boy Flat Top', 'Green Door', 'Garden Of Eden' (number 1), 'Man On Fire'/'Wanderin' Eyes', 'Gotta Have Something In the Bank Frank' (with the Kaye Sisters), 'Kisses Sweeter Than Wine', 'Can't Get Along Without You'/'We Are Not Alone', 'Kewpie Doll', 'Wonderful Things', 'Am I Wasting My Time On You', 'That's My Doll', 'Come Softly To Me' (with the Kaye Sisters), 'The Heart Of A Man' and 'Walkin' Tall'. In spite of the burgeoning beat boom, he continued to flour-

ish in the 60s with hits including 'What More Do You Want', 'Kookie Little Paradise', 'Milord', 'Tower Of Strength' (number 1), 'Don't Stop Twist', 'Loop-De-Loop', 'Hey Mama', 'Hello Dolly', 'There Must Be A Way', 'So Tired' and 'Nevertheless' (1968). With his matinée idol looks he seemed a natural for films, and made his debut in 1956 in the Arthur Askey comedy, *Ramsbottom Rides Again*. This was followed by a highly acclaimed straight role in *These Dangerous Years*, and a musical frolic with the normally staid Anna Neagle in *The Lady Is A Square*. Other screen appearances included *Wonderful Things! Heart Of A Man* with Anne Heywood, Tony Britton and Anthony Newley, and *It's All Over Town*, a pop extravaganza in which he was joined by then-current favourites such as Acker Bilk, the Bachelors, the Springfields, and the Hollies. In the early 60s, Vaughan began to experience real success in America, in nightclubs and on television. He was playing his second season in Las Vegas when he was chosen to star with Marilyn Monroe and Yves Montand in the 20th Century-Fox picture *Let's Make Love*. Although he gave a creditable performance, especially when he duetted with Monroe on Sammy Cahn and Jimmy Van Heusen's 'Incurably Romantic', his disaffection with Hollywood ensured that a US film career was not pursued. At home, however, he had become an extremely well-established performer, headlining at the London Palladium and enjoying lucrative summer season work, appealing consistently to mainly family audiences. In 1985, he was an unexpected choice to replace James Laurenson as the belligerent Broadway producer Julian Marsh in the West End hit musical, *42nd Street*. A one-year run in the show ended with ill-health and some acrimony. His career-long efforts for the benefit of young people, partly through the assignment of record royalties to bodies such as the National Association of Boys' Clubs, was recognized by an OBE in 1965 and a CBE in 1996. He was also honoured in 1993 when the Queen appointed him Deputy Lord Lieutenant of Buckinghamshire. In the preceding year he had undergone a life-saving operation to replace a ruptured main artery in his heart. However, in cabaret at London's Café Royal in 1994, the legendary side-kick was still (gingerly) in evidence. He continues to perform occasionally, and in 1998, BBC Radio 2 celebrated his 70th birthday with a documentary entitled *Mr. Moonlight*.

● ALBUMS: *Happy Go Lucky* (Philips 1957)★★★, *Showcase* (Philips 1958)★★★, *At The London Palladium* (Philips 1959)★★★, *Let Me Sing And I'm Happy* (Philips 1961)★★★, *Warm Feeling* (Philips 1961)★★★, *Songbook* (1967)★★★, *There Must Be A Way* (Columbia 1967)★★★, *Double Exposure* (Columbia 1971)★★★, *Frankie* (Columbia 1973)★★★, *Frankie Vaughan's Sing Song* (One Up 1973)★★★, *Sincerely Yours, Frankie Vaughan* (Pye 1975)★★★, *Sings* (Columbia 1975)★★★, *Someone Who Cares* (Pye 1976)★★, *Seasons For Lovers* (Pye 1977)★★★, *Moonlight And Love Songs* (SRT 1979)★★, *Time After Time* (Hour Of Pleasure 1986)★★★.

● COMPILATIONS: *The Very Best Of Frankie Vaughan* (EMI 1975)★★★, *Spotlight On Frankie Vaughan* (Philips 1975)★★★, *100 Golden Greats* (Ronco 1977)★★★, *Golden Hour Presents* (Golden Hour 1978)★★★, *Greatest Hits* (Spot 1983)★★★, *Love Hits And High Kicks* (Creole 1985)★★★, *Music Maestro Please* (PRT

1986)★★★, *The Best Of The EMI Years* (EMI 1990)★★★, *The Essential Recordings 1955-65* (1993)★★★.

VELVET GOLDMINE

Initial critical reaction to this UK/US produced movie, which is set around that brief, curiously British musical phenomenon of the early 70s known as glam rock, was sharply divided. 'Glorious' or 'a huge disappointment' were just a couple of the reactions to director Todd Haynes' screenplay in which Brian Slade (Jonathan Rhys Meyers), a young lad from Birmingham, reinvents himself as the pouting, catsuited David Bowie-like Maxwell Demon. In 1974, at the height of his fame, he fakes his own 'assassination' on stage, and then disappears. Ten years later, New York based English journalist Arthur Stuart (Christian Bale) starts digging around, and utilising a flashback technique which reminded most critics of *Citizen Kane*, interviews a number of Slade's close friends and associates. These include wife Mandy (Toni Collette, à la Angie Bowie), his lover, the self-destructive American singer Curt Wilde (Ewan McGregor), who comes over as a combination of Iggy Pop and Lou Reed (with a Kurt Cobain, of Nirvana, hairstyle), and manager Jerry Divine (Eddie Izzard). Also swanning around, a bit like Marc Bolan, is Jack Fairy (Micko Westmoreland), while Oscar Wilde is delivered into his mother arms by a flying saucer (one critic called the film 'densely plotted' - he was right). A virtually continuous soundtrack which mixes original recordings of the glam rock (and a touch later) songs, such as Roxy Music's 'Virginia Plain', Slade's 'Coz I Luv You', Gary Glitter's 'Do You Want To Touch Me? (Oh Yeah)', T-Rex's, 'Band Of Gold' (that's Freda Payne, not Don Cherry or Sylvester), and 'Make Me Smile (Come Up And See Me)' (Steve Harley And Cockney Rebel), with contemporary covers, and a few newly written numbers. The three bands which were assembled to perform some of the material, The Venus In Furs, Shudder To Think, and The Wylde Rattz, featured top musicians such as Bernard Butler, Thom Yorke, Mark Arm, Ron Asheton, and Thurston Moore. In the role of another musician, Polly Small, was Elastica's Donna Matthews. Bowie himself, the most important glam rock star of them all, withheld permission for his songs to be used. No matter, the rock critics had a field day, wallowing in this celebration of a garish, chaotic time - an interlude between the late 60s flower power and the punk explosion a decade later - when cross-dressing became the norm, and teenagers emerged blinking from the safety of the closet. Michael Stipe of R.E.M. was one of the executive producers for this movie which won awards for its director/conceiver Todd Haynes at both the Cannes and Edinburgh International Film festivals shortly after its release in 1998.

VERA-ELLEN

b. Vera-Ellen Westmeyer Rohe, 16 February 1926, Cincinnati, Ohio, USA, d. 30 August 1981, Los Angeles, California, USA. A charming actress, and one of the finest dancers in the film musicals of the 40s and 50s. After taking dance lessons from the age of 10, as a teenager Vera-Ellen toured with the Major Bowes talent show before joining the Rockette line at the famous Radio City Musical

Hall in New York. She made her Broadway debut in *Very Warm For May* (1939), and followed that with other roles in *Higher And Higher* (1940), *Panama Hattie* (1940), *By Jupiter* (1942), and *A Connecticut Yankee* (1943). After being spotted by producer Samuel Goldwyn, she moved to Hollywood and made *Wonder Man* and *The Kid From Brooklyn* (both with Danny Kaye), *Three Little Girls In Blue* and *Carnival In Costa Rica* (1947). The latter proved to be fairly forgettable, but things improved when she signed a seven-year contract with MGM. It began with the Richard Rodgers and Lorenz Hart biopic *Words And Music* (1948), in which she and Gene Kelly provided the film's high spot with the classic ballet sequence, 'Slaughter On Tenth Avenue'. She was teamed with Kelly again a year later in the splendid *On The Town*, and then danced with that other great movie song-and-dance-man Fred Astaire in *Three Little Words* (1950) and *The Belle Of New York* (1952). In between those last two pictures, she made *Happy-Go-Lovely* with David Niven in the UK. Her final two films for MGM cast her opposite a pair of completely contrasting personalities: in *The Big Leaguer* (1953) her co-star was Edward G. Robinson, and for *Call Me Madam*, which was released in the same year, she danced delightfully with the bright and breezy Donald O'Connor. During most of the 50s Vera-Ellen appeared in cabaret, and made guest appearances on some of the top-rated US television variety shows, including the one hosted by Perry Como. In 1959, 10 years after she made her debut with him in *Wonder Man*, she was reunited with Danny Kaye in the immensely popular *White Christmas*, which also starred Bing Crosby and Rosemary Clooney. Her final film, *Let's Be Happy* (1957), was made in England, but even with Tony Martin, and songs by Nicholas Brodszky and Paul Francis Webster, it was an unsatisfactory affair. At the end of the decade she retired from the screen, and, after she was divorced from her second husband, the oil company executive Victor Rothschild, in 1966, she lived in seclusion at her Hollywood home.

VERDON, GWEN

b. Gwyneth Evelyn Verdon, 13 January 1926, Culver City, California, USA. A vivacious, red-headed dancer, actress and singer, Verdon can be funny or tender, sassy or seductive, depending on the music and the mood. She studied dancing from an early age, and, after assisting the notable choreographer Jack Cole on *Magdalena* (1948), made her first appearance on Broadway two years later in *Alive And Kicking*. However, it was Cole Porter's *Can-Can* that made her a star in 1953. Her thrilling performance as the (very) high-kicking Claudine gained her a Tony Award, and she won another two years later for her portrayal of the bewitching Lola in *Damn Yankees* ('Two Lost Souls', 'Whatever Lola Wants [Lola Gets]', 'Who's Got The Pain'), a show that was brilliantly choreographed by her future husband, Bob Fosse. He restaged his innovative dance sequences for the 1958 film version, for which, instead of casting an already established film star, Verdon was invited to reprise her Broadway role. From then on, Fosse choreographed and/or directed all Verdon's shows. In 1957 she played Anna Christie in *New Girl In Town* ('Ven I Valse', 'On The Farm', 'It's Good To Be Alive', 'If That Was

Love'), a musical adaptation of Eugene O'Neill's 1921 play, and on this occasion she shared the Tony with fellow cast member Thelma Ritter - the first time there had been a Tony-tie. In 1959, Verdon won outright - and for the last time (so far) - when she starred with Richard Kiley in *Redhead*. After that, Broadway audiences had to wait another seven years before they saw Verdon on the musical stage, but the wait was more than worthwhile. In *Sweet Charity* (1966) she played a dancehall hostess with a heart of gold who yearns for marriage and roses round the door. Cy Coleman and Dorothy Fields provided her with some lovely songs, including 'If My Friends Could See Me Now' and 'There's Gotta Be Something Better Than This'. Verdon's final Broadway musical (to date) was *Chicago* (1975), a razzle-dazzle affair set in the roaring 20s, full of hoods and Chita Rivera. In more recent times she has turned once more to films. She had appeared in several during the 50s, including *On The Riviera*, *Meet Me After The Show*, *David And Bathsheba*, *The Merry Widow*, *The I Don't Care Girl*, *The Farmer Takes A Wife*, as well as *Damn Yankees*. In 1983, she played a choreographer in the television movie *Legs*, and had several other good roles in big-screen features such as *The Cotton Club*, *Cocoon*, *Nadine*, *Cocoon-The Return* and *Alice* (1990). In 1992 she donated a substantial amount of material documenting her own career and that of her late husband, Bob Fosse (he died in 1987), to the Library of Congress. A year later, Gwen Verdon received the 1993 New Dramatists Lifetime Achievement Award at a ceremony in which fellow Broadway legends such as Richard Adler, Chita Rivera, Cy Coleman, John Kander, and Fred Ebb, gathered to pay tribute. She continued to be honoured throughout the 90s, with the Broadway Theatre Institute's award for Lifetime Achievement in the Theatre, the Actors' Fund of America's Julie Harris Lifetime Achievement Award, and the National Medal of Arts, which she received from the US President in November 1998. During that year Verdon had been serving as Artistic Director on a tribute to her late husband entitled *Fosse: A Celebration In Dance And Song* which opened on Broadway in January 1999.

VERY GOOD EDDIE

The second of the renowned Princess Theatre shows written by Jerome Kern and Guy Bolton immediately before they began their fruitful partnership with P.G. Wodehouse. It was an early attempt to write jolly, tuneful musical comedies on a small, inexpensive scale, which would be quite different from the prevailing imported operettas. Bolton's book, written with Philip Bartholomae, and adapted from the latter's play, *Over Night*, told of two honeymoon couples on a Hudson River cruise boat, who become embarrassingly separated when the husband from one couple and the wife from the other pair are accidentally left on shore. Explanations are offered and accepted when the quartet are subsequently reunited at the Rip Van Winkle Inn. The young and talented cast included Ernest Truex, Oscar Shaw, Alice Dovey, Helen Raymond, and John E. Hazzard. Kern's light-hearted and appealing score, with lyrics mostly by Schuyler Greene and Herbert Reynolds, contained two of his early hits, 'Some Sort Of Somebody' and 'Babes In The Wood', along

with others such as 'I'd Like To Have A Million In The Bank', 'Nodding Roses', 'On The Shore At Le Lei Wi', 'Isn't It Great To Be Married?', 'Thirteen Collar', 'Old Boy Neutral', and 'If I Find The Girl'. The plausible book and the skilfully integrated songs attracted a great deal of approval for a show which is now considered to be a landmark in the history of the American musical. *Very Good Eddie* ran for 341 performances in New York, but the 1918 London production could only add another 46 to that total. The show was successfully revived on Broadway in 1975.

VICTOR/VICTORIA (FILM MUSICAL)

In 1982, after finally breaking free from her 'goody goody' image by going topless in *S.O.B.* a year earlier, Julie Andrews went in for a touch of 'gender-bending' in this MGM release for which her husband, Blake Edwards, served as screenwriter, director and co-producer (with Tony Adams). Andrews plays singer Victoria Grant, down on her luck in Paris during the 30s. Desperate for work, and encouraged by a gay friend (Robert Preston), she takes a job as a female impersonator called Victor (i.e., as a woman, she impersonates a man who is masquerading as a woman). No wonder the businessman-hood (James Garner) who has just blown in from Chicago is confused. After seeing Vicki in cabaret, he falls for her/him before being entirely certain of the gender situation. Edwards invariably handles these kinds of situations well, and there are several marvellous moments in the film, such as when Garner sneaks into Vicki's room to try and discover once and for all whether she is male or female, and another scene in which Garner's girlfriend, played by Lesley Ann Warren, having discovered Vicki's secret, thinks that he (Garner) may be homosexual. Henry Mancini and Leslie Bricusse won Academy Awards for their song score, which included 'The Shady Dame From Seville', 'Le Jazz Hot', 'Crazy World', 'You And Me', 'Gay Paree', and 'Chicago, Illinois'. Paddy Stone was the choreographer, and the film, which was either charming or crude depending on your point of view, was photographed in Metrocolor and Panavision. In 1995, following her successful comeback off-Broadway in the Stephen Sondheim revue *Putting It Together*, Julie Andrews reprised her film role in the stage adaptation of *Victor/Victoria*, which opened on Broadway in October of that year, and Toni Tenille, one half of the popular 70s act, Captain And Tenille, headed the 1998 tour.

VICTOR/VICTORIA (STAGE MUSICAL)

Following years of speculation as to whether it would ever happen, the stage adaptation of Blake Edwards' 1982 film, which starred his wife Julie Andrews, finally commenced public try-outs at the Orpheum Theatre, Minneapolis, in June 1995. As with the movie, it was based on German actor and director Rheinhold Schunzel's play and 1933 film, *Viktor Und Viktoria*, which also inspired the 1935 Jessie Matthews/Sonnie Hale British film musical, *First A Girl*. Andrews reprised her movie role as Victoria Grant, a singer down on her luck in 30s Paris. With the help of her good and gay friend, Toddy (Tony Roberts), she finds a new career in cabaret as Victor, a 'male' drag queen, while falling for gangster King Marchan (Michael Nouri).

Among the other characters involved in the fast-paced comings and goings amid Robin Wagner's classy sets, were Marchan's bodyguard, Squash (Gregory Jbara), who eventually falls - believe it or not - for Toddy, agent/promoter Andre Cassell (Richard B. Shull), Henri Labisse (Adam Heller), and Richard Di Nardo (Michael Cripe). Also present was Rachel York as Norma Cassidy, Marchan's zany blonde girlfriend, who almost stole the show from Andrews, especially during her two specialities, 'Chicago, Illinois' and 'Paris Makes Me Horny'. By the time *Victor/Victoria* reached Broadway on 25 October 1995, after radical revisions on the road, 'Chicago, Illinois', along with 'You And Me' (a delightful duet for Victor and Toddy), 'Crazy World' (Victoria's closing song of the first act), and 'Le Jazz Hot' (Victor's sizzling debut), were the only survivors from lyricist Leslie Bricusse and composer Henry Mancini's film score. 'Paris Makes Me Horny' was one of several new songs that Mancini had completed before his death in June 1994. Other Mancini melodies to make it to the New York opening were 'Paris By Night', 'If I Were A Man', 'The Tango', 'King's Dilemma', 'Apache', 'Almost A Love Song', and 'Victor/Victoria'. These were supplemented by three numbers with music composed by Broadway newcomer Frank Wildhorn - 'Trust Me', 'Louis Says', and 'Living In The Shadows'. They, too, had lyrics by Bricusse, whose general contributions were labelled 'witless' by one critic. There was little praise, either, for Edwards' book (he also directed), or Rob Marshall's 'lacklustre' choreography. Indeed, as far as most scribes were concerned, the only positive factor in the show was Andrews, returning to Broadway after an absence of three decades. The Tony Awards committee concurred, and gave her a nomination for Best Musical Actress, which she refused (from the Marquis stage) in protest at the lack of recognition for her fellow cast members. The show did better in other directions, winning Outer Critics Circle Awards for Outstanding Broadway Musical and Outstanding Actress in a Musical, and Drama Desk Awards for Musical Actress (Andrews) and Featured Musical Actress (York). More controversy followed when Liza Minnelli stood in for Andrews while she took a holiday - leading man Tony Roberts walked out in protest at her poor performance. Eyebrows were raised yet again in June 1997, when Andrews finally withdrew from the Broadway production. Many felt that the choice of voluptuous film star Raquel Welch to replace her (in the role of a man, remember) presented an unfair challenge to the costume department, and required a complete suspension of disbelief on the part of the audience. Without its legendary star, *Victor/Victoria* went rapidly downhill, and was withdrawn on 27 July after a total of 738 performances. A major US touring version set out in September 1998, with Toni Tennille, one half of the popular 70s duo Captain And Tennille, in the lead.

VIVA LAS VEGAS

Released by MGM in 1964, this was one of Elvis Presley's best film musicals, mainly due to the presence of Ann-Margret as his leading lady. They proved to be an irresistible combination in a screenplay that has Presley as an ambitious racing driver who takes a temporary job in a hotel after losing his bankroll when Ann-Margret pushes him into the swimming pool. Upon their first meeting she had mistaken him for a mechanic - She: 'I'd like you to check my motor - it whistles.' He: 'I don't blame it.' His persistent pursuit of her is aided by some pretty good songs, the best of which is their amusing love/hate duet, 'The Lady Loves Me' (He: 'The lady's dying to be kissed.' She: 'The gentleman needs a psychiatrist.'). Sid Tepper and Roy C. Bennett wrote that one, and the rest of the score included 'I Need Somebody To Lean On' (Doc Pomus), 'Appreciation' and 'My Rival' (both Marvin Moore-Bernie Wayne), 'If You Think I Don't Need You' (Red West), 'Come On, Everybody' (Stanley Chianese), 'What'd I Say?' (Ray Charles), and 'Today, Tomorrow And Forever' (Bill Giant-Bernie Baum-Florence Kaye). Naturally, Elvis wins the big race and the girl, and winds the whole thing up with the bustling 'Viva Las Vegas' (Pomus-Mort Shuman). Cesare Danova was his arch-rival for both prizes, and also among the cast were William Demarest, Nicky Blair, and Jack Carter. Sally Benson wrote the thin but diverting screenplay, David Winters was the choreographer, and director George Sidney kept up a lively pace. Sidney was also co-producer with Jack Cummings. According to *Variety*, this was the most commercially successful of all the Presley films, grossing well over 5 million dollars. For the UK it was retitled *Love In Las Vegas*. This was probably because the 1956 Dan Dailey-Cyd Charisse musical *Meet Me In Las Vegas* was called *Viva Las Vegas* when it the UK.

VON TILZER, ALBERT

b. Albert Gumm, 29 March 1878, Indianapolis, Indiana, USA, d. 1 October 1956, Los Angeles, California, USA. An important composer and publisher, Albert changed his name from Gumm following his elder brother, Harry Von Tilzer's success as a composer and song publisher, and worked for him for a while as a song-plugger. In 1903 he started his own publishing company with another brother, Jack, and in the following year wrote his first song hit, 'Teasing', with lyricist Cecil Mack. He contributed songs to several Broadway shows, including *About Town* ('I'm Sorry'), *The Yankee Girl* ('Nora Malone') and *Madame Sherry* ('Put Your Arms Around Me Honey', lyric by Junie McCree). The last number was a big hit in 1911 for several artists, including Arthur Collins, Byron Harlan and Ada Jones, and was revived in 1943 after it was featured in the Betty Grable movie *Coney Island*. The composer also contributed to the 1917 revue *Hitchy-Koo* in which Albert's war song, 'I May Be Gone For A Long, Long Time', written with Lew Brown, was the main hit, and *Linger Longer Letty* which included another collaboration with Brown, 'Oh, By Jingo'. Von Tilzer's complete Broadway scores included *The Happiest Night Of His Life* (lyrics by Junie McCree), *Honey Girl*, (an impressive score, written with Neville Fleeson), *The Gingham Girl*, *Adrienne* and *Bye Bye Bonnie*. His many other successful compositions included 'Honey Boy' (with Jack Norworth), which was successful in 1907 for the Peerless Quartet and Billy Murray, 'Smarty' (Ada Jones and Billy Murray), 'Take Me Out To The Ball Game' (with Norworth), sung at the time by Billy Murray And The Haydn Quartet and revived by Frank Sinatra and

Gene Kelly in the 1949 film of the same name; and 'I'll Be With You In Apple Blossom Time' (with Fleeson), recorded by Charles Harrison, Henry Burr and Albert Campbell in 1920. Other hits included a big wartime speciality for the Andrews Sisters (1941), 'My Cutey's Due At Two-To-Two Today', a 'tale of amatory fidelity', amusingly performed by Bobby Darin and Johnny Mercer on their 1961 album *Two Of A Kind*, and several songs with lyrics by Lew Brown, such as 'Give Me The Moonlight, Give Me The Girl' (the theme song of UK entertainer Frankie Vaughan), 'I Used To Love You (But It's All Over Now)' and 'Dapper Dan', a hit in 1921 for the singer of comic novelties, Frank Crumit.

Albert Von Tilzer's other collaborators included Arthur J. Lamb and Edward Madden. In the late 20s, after the *Bye Bye Bonnie* show, Von Tilzer's songwriting output declined, although he did write a few minor film scores in the 30s, including *Here Comes The Band* (1935), which included 'Roll Along Prairie Moon'. The latter had a lyric by Ted Fio Rito and Cecil Mack, and became successful for the singing bandleader Smith Ballew. In the early 50s, he wrote 'I'm Praying To St. Christopher' with Larry McPherson, which was recorded in the UK by Anne Shelton, Joyce Frazer and Toni Arden.

VON TILZER, HARRY

b. Harold Gumm, 8 July 1872, Detroit, Michigan, USA, d. 10 January 1946. A prolific composer, publisher, and producer, and the elder brother of songwriter Albert Von Tilzer, Harry Von Tilzer grew up in Indianapolis where he learned to play the piano. As a teenager he worked in a circus, touring in shows, singing and playing the piano, and performing his own material. In 1892 he moved to New York and started writing special material for vaudeville performers, and in 1898 had his first song hit, 'My Old Hampshire Home' (lyric by Andrew B. Sterling, his chief collaborator). This was followed soon afterwards by 'I'd Leave My Happy Home For You' (with Will A. Heelan). For a time Von Tilzer worked for music publishers Shapiro & Bernstein, and while there wrote 'A Bird In A Gilded Cage' (with Arthur J. Lamb) which sold over two million copies as sheet music. With his share of the royalties, Harry set up his own music publishing company on West 28th Street, New York, in 1902, becoming one of the first residents in what became known as 'Tin Pan Alley', a term that, it is claimed, was coined in his office. In the same year he wrote 'Down Where The Wurzburger Flows' (with Vincent Bryan), which was a hit for the flamboyant entertainer Nora Bayes, who became known as the 'Wurzburger Girl'. A year later Harry composed his first and only complete Broadway score, for the comic opera *The Fisher Maiden*; it closed after only a month.

Later, he contributed the occasional number to several other musicals, including *The Liberty Belles*, *The Girls Of Gottenburg*, *The Kissing Girl*, *The Dairy Maids*, *Lifting The Lid* and *The Honeymoon Express* (1913), but it was with the individual songs that he had his biggest hits. These included the extremely successful 'The Mansion Of Aching Hearts' 'On A Sunday Afternoon', 'Please Go 'Way And Let Me Sleep', 'Wait Till The Sun Shines, Nellie', 'Cubanola Glide', 'I Want A Girl (Just Like The Girl That Married

Dear Old Dad)', 'In The Evening By The Moonlight' and 'They Always Pick On Me'. He also wrote 'Under The Anheuser Tree' with Sterling, Percy Krone and Russell Hunting, better known in its rearranged version as 'Down At The Old Bull And Bush', a perennial singalong favourite in the UK. Also popular was the anti-Prohibition number, 'If I Meet The Guy Who Made This Country Dry' (1920). Harry Von Tilzer's last big song was 'Just Around The Corner' (1925). When it was followed a year later by 'Under The Wurzburger Tree', a throwback to one of his biggest early hits, the end of his songwriting career was in sight, and he retired to supervise his publishing interests. Some of his songs were used in the 1975 Broadway musical *Doctor Jazz*, starring Bobby Van. His other collaborators included William Dillon, William Jerome, Bert Hanlon and Arthur J. Lamb.

VOYEURZ

It must have crossed the minds of some members of this show's first night audience on 22 July 1996 - those of a certain age, at least - that for many years London's Whitehall Theatre was the home of farce. The undisputed King of the genre, Brian Rix, used to drop his trousers on the stage nightly, and according to most of the critics, *Voyeurz*, for all its promise of 'a raunchy mix of simulated sex, rock music, and nudity', was hardly more erotic. Produced by Michael White, who shocked West End patrons in 1969 with *Oh! Calcutta!*, *Voyeurz* was developed by its directors, Michael Lewis and Peter Rafelson, from a concert album that the 'outrageous lipstick lesbian' band Fem 2 Fem (Chris Minna, L.D., LaLa Hamparsomian, Christine Salata) performed at the London Astoria in March 1995. Lewis and Rafelson are credited as writers of the music and lyrics, as well as a slight book that tells of Jane (Sally Anne Marsh), a virgin from Virginia, USA, who leaves the farm and sets out for New York intent on broadening her mind. En route, lesbianism rears its head in the shape of Andi (Krysten Cummings), a temptress in a blue miniskirt, while the company moan 'Jane, Jane, sex on a train'. In New York, Jane winds up in a cage in the fetishistic night club Voyeurz (motto: 'Sex, Control. Pain. Pleasure. Lust. Distress. Shame.'), where she attracts the desirous attentions of Eve (Natasha Kristie), and (on the occasions when she is not blindfolded or handcuffed) focuses her camcorder on the club's members fondling themselves, each other, and various pieces of scaffolding. Rubber is also an issue here, and in one number a milky white sheet of the material is skilfully manipulated in such a fashion that it conceals the nudity of four of the girls. When the company does wear anything, they are costumes designed by Joseph Corre. All this takes place amid set designer Geoff Rose's steel-framed stage, which is illuminated by Ian Peacock's old-fashioned psychedelic light show. Krysten Cummings sang powerfully, and there were other impressive voices among what was an all-female cast, apart from two of the dancers, Robert Nurse (Pretty Boy Lloyd) and Marcus J. McCue (Zephyr). The score was predictably full of blatant seduction songs choreographed by Bunty Matthias and Annabel Haydn, who were presumably responsible for the subtle manipulation of the whips and chains. One critic confessed that the ingenious use of a corn on the cob was new to him. The songs included 'Intro/Dreamtime', 'Come To Me/Sin', 'Reflections', 'Out In Style', 'The Hole', 'Xtropia', 'Swing', 'Kinda Slow Now', 'Insatiable', 'Go For The Kill', 'Cruel And Unusual', 'Until The Dawn', 'Tantric Trance (Animus)', 'I'd Die For You', 'Stand Back', 'Dark Dance', 'I'm So Sorry', 'Compulsive Jane', 'Evil', 'Worship', and 'Where Did Love Go'. At curtain time, Jane finally wakes up blissfully in bed with Andi, and the whole nightmare ended when *Voyeurz*, a show 'totally devoid of genuine wit and comedy', was withdrawn on 14 September after a run of less than two months, with reported losses of £1 million.

WABASH AVENUE
(see *Coney Island*)

WALLER, FATS

b. Thomas Wright Waller, 21 May 1904, Waverley, New York, USA, d. 15 December 1943, Kansas City, Missouri, USA. Influenced by his grandfather, a violinist, and his mother, Waller was playing piano at students' concerts and organ in his father's church by the time he was 10 years old. In 1918, while still in high school, he was asked to fill in for the regular organist at the Lincoln Theatre, and subsequently gained a permanent seat at the Wurlitzer Grand. A year later he won a talent contest, playing ragtime pianist James P. Johnson's 'Carolina Shout'. While a protégé of Johnson's, Waller adopted the Harlem stride style of piano playing, 'the swinging left hand', emphasizing tenths on the bass, to which Waller added his own distinctive touch. In 1919, while on tour as a vaudeville pianist, he composed 'Boston Blues' which, when the title was later changed to 'Squeeze Me', with a lyric by Clarence Williams, became one of his best-known songs. In the early 20s, with the USA on the brink of the 'jazz age', and Prohibition in force, Waller's piano playing was much in demand at rent-parties, bootleg joints, in cabaret and vaudeville. Inevitably, he mixed with gangsters, and it is said that his first 100 dollar bill was given to him by Al Capone, who fortunately enjoyed his piano playing. Around this time Waller made his first records as accompanist to one of the leading blues singers, Sara Martin. He also recorded with the legendary Bessie Smith, and toured with her in 1926. His first solo piano recording was reputedly 'Muscle Shoal Blues'.

From 1926-29 he made a series of pipe organ recordings in a disused church in Camden, New Jersey. Having studied composition from an early age with various teachers, including Leopold Godowski and Carl Bohm, Waller collaborated with James P. Johnson and Clarence Todd on the music for the Broadway revue *Keep Shufflin'* (1928). This was a follow-up to Noble Sissle and Eubie Blake's smash hit *Shuffle Along* (1921), which starred Joséphine Baker, and was the show that is credited with making black music acceptable to Broadway audiences. Although not on stage in *Keep Shufflin'*, Waller made a considerable impression with his exuberant piano playing from the show's orchestra pit at Daly's Theatre. Andy Razaf, who wrote most of the show's lyrics, including the outstanding number, 'Willow Tree', would become Waller's regular collaborator, and his closest friend. Just over a year later, in June 1929, Waller again combined with Razaf for *Hot Chocolates*, another Negro revue, revised for Broadway. In the orchestra pit this time was trumpeter Louis Armstrong, whose role was expanded during the show's run. The score for *Hot Chocolates* also contained the plaintive '(What Did I Do To Be So) Black, And Blue?', and one of the team's most enduring standards, 'Ain't Misbehavin'', an instrumental version of which became Waller's first hit, and years later, was selected for inclusion in the NARAS Hall of Fame. Both *Keep Shufflin'* and *Hot Chocolates* were first staged at Connie's Inn, in Harlem, one of the biggest black communities in the world. Waller lived in the middle of Harlem, until he really hit the big-time and moved to St. Albans, Long Island, where he installed a built-in Hammond organ. In the late 20s and early 30s he was still on the brink of that success. Although he endured some bleak times during the Depression he was writing some of his most effective songs, such as 'Honeysuckle Rose', 'Blue, Turning Grey Over You' and 'Keepin' Out Of Mischief Now' (all with Razaf); 'I've Got A Feeling I'm Falling' (with Billy Rose and Harry Link); and 'I'm Crazy 'Bout My Baby' (with Alexander Hill). In 1932 he toured Europe in the company of fellow composer Spencer Williams, and played prestigious venues such as London's Kit Kat Club and the Moulin Rouge in Paris. Worldwide fame followed with the formation of Fats Waller And His Rhythm in 1934. The all-star group featured musicians such as Al Casey (b. 15 September 1915, Louisville, Kentucky, USA; guitar), Herman Autrey (b. 4 December 1904, Evergreen, Alabama, USA, d. 14 June 1980; trumpet), Gene Sedric (b. 17 June 1907, St. Louis, Missouri, USA, d. 3 April 1963; reeds), Billy Taylor or Charles Turner (string bass), drummers Harry Dial (b. 17 February 1907, Birmingham, Alabama, USA, d. 25 January 1987) or Yank Porter (b. Allen Porter, c.1895, Norfolk, Virginia, USA, d. 22 March 1944, New York, USA) and Rudy Powell (b. Everard Stephen Powell, 28 October 1907, New York City, New York, USA, d. 30 October 1976; clarinet). Signed for Victor Records, the ensemble made over 150 78 rpm records between May 1934 and January 1943, in addition to Waller's output of piano and organ solos, and some big-band tracks. The Rhythm records were a revelation: high-class musicianship accompanied Waller's exuberant vocals, sometimes spiced with sly, irreverent asides on popular titles such as 'Don't Let It Bother You', 'Sweetie

Pie', 'Lulu's Back In Town', 'Truckin'', 'A Little Bit Independent', 'It's A Sin To Tell A Lie', 'You're Not That Kind', 'Until The Real Thing Comes Along', 'The Curse Of An Aching Heart', 'Dinah', 'S'posin', 'Smarty', 'The Sheik Of Araby', 'Hold Tight' and 'I Love To Whistle'.

Waller had massive hits with specialities such as 'I'm Gonna Sit Right Down And Write Myself A Letter', 'When Somebody Thinks You're Wonderful', 'My Very Good Friend The Milkman' and 'Your Feet's Too Big'. He recorded ballads including 'Two Sleepy People' and 'Then I'll Be Tired Of You', and several of his own compositions, including 'Honeysuckle Rose' and 'The Joint Is Jumpin'' (written with Razaf and J.C. Johnson). In 1935, Waller appeared in the first of his three feature films, *Hooray For Love*, which also featured Bill 'Bojangles' Robinson. In the following year he received excellent reviews for his rendering of 'I've Got My Fingers Crossed' in *King Of Burlesque*. In 1938, he toured Europe again for several months, this time as a big star. He played concerts in several cities, performed at the London Palladium, and appeared in an early television broadcast from Alexandra Palace. Waller also became the first - and probably the only - jazz musician to play the organ of the Notre Dame de Paris. He returned to England and Scotland the following year. Back in the USA, Waller toured with a combo for a while, and during the early 40s performed with his own big band, before again working as a solo artist. In 1942 he tried to play serious jazz in concert at Carnegie Hall - but was poorly received. In 1943, he returned to Broadway to write the score, with George Marion, for the bawdy musical *Early To Bed*. The comedy high-spot proved to be 'The Ladies Who Sing With The Band'.

Waller teamed with 'Bojangles' Robinson once again in 1943 for the film of *Stormy Weather*, which included a version of 'Ain't Misbehavin''. Afterwards, he stayed in California for an engagement at the Zanzibar Club in Los Angeles. On his way back to New York on the Santa Fe Chief railway express, he died of pneumonia as it was pulling into Kansas City. His life had been one of excess. Enormous amounts of food and liquor meant that his weight varied between 285 and 310 lbs - 'a girthful of blues'. Days of carousing were followed by equal amounts of sleeping, not necessarily alone. Jazz continually influenced his work, even when he was cajoled into recording inferior material. He worked and recorded with leading artists such as Fletcher Henderson, Ted Lewis, Alberta Hunter, Jack Teagarden, Gene Austin and Lee Wiley. Waller felt strongly that he did not receive his fair share of the songwriting royalties. He was said to have visited the Brill Building, which housed New York's most prominent music publishers, and obtained advances from several publishers for the same tune. Each, however, had a different lyric. He sold many numbers outright, and never received credit for them. Two songs that are sometimes rumoured to be his, but are always definitely attributed to Jimmy McHugh and Dorothy Fields - 'I Can't Give You Anything But Love' and 'On The Sunny Side Of The Street' - were included in the 1978 Broadway show *Ain't Misbehavin'*. Most of the numbers in that production were genuine Waller, along with a few others like 'Mean To Me', 'It's A Sin To Tell A Lie', 'Fat And Greasy' and 'Cash For Your Trash', which, in performance, he had made his own. The majority of his recordings have been reissued and appear on a variety of labels such as RCA Records, Saville, Halcyon, Living Era, President, Swaggie (Australia) and Vogue (France).

● COMPILATIONS: *Fats Waller 1934-42* 10-inch album (RCA Victor 1951)★★★, *Fats Waller Favorites* 10-inch album (RCA Victor 1951)★★★, *Swingin' The Organ* 10-inch album (RCA Victor 1953)★★★, *Rediscovered Fats Waller Piano Solos* 10-inch album (Riverside 1953)★★★, *Fats Waller At The Organ* 10-inch album (Riverside 1953)★★★, *Jiving With Fats Waller* 10-inch album (Riverside 1953)★★★, *Fats Waller Plays And Sings* (RCA Victor 1954)★★★, *Fats Waller Radio Transcriptions* 2-LP box set (RCA Victor 1955)★★★, *Rhythm And Romance With Fats Waller* (HMV 1954)★★★, *The Young Fats Waller* 10-inch album (X 1955)★★★, *Fun With Fats* (HMV 1955)★★★, *The Amazing Mr Waller* 10-inch album (Riverside 1955)★★★, *Thomas Fats Waller Vols. 1 And 2* (HMV 1955)★★★, *Ain't Misbehavin'* (RCA Victor 1956)★★★, *Handful Of Keys* (RCA Victor 1957)★★★, *Spreadin' Rhythm Around* (HMV 1957)★★★, *Fats* (RCA Victor 1960)★★★, *The Real Fats Waller* (RCA Victor 1965)★★★, *Fats Waller '34/'35* (RCA Victor 1965)★★★, *Valentine Stomp* (RCA Victor 1965)★★★, *Smashing Thirds* (RCA Victor 1966)★★★, *African Ripplets* (RCA Victor 1966)★★★, *Fine Arabian Stuff* 1939 recording (Muse 1981)★★★, *20 Golden Pieces* (Bulldog 1982)★★★, *Piano Solos (1929-1941)* (RCA 1983)★★★, *Live At The Yacht Club, Vol. 1* (Giants Of Jazz 1984)★★★, *Live At The Yacht Club, Vol. 2* (Giants Of Jazz 1984)★★★, *Fats Waller In London* 1922-1939 recordings (Disques Swing 1985)★★★, *My Very Good Friend The Milkman* (President 1986)★★★, *Armful O'Sweetness* (Saville 1987)★★★, *Dust Off That Old Piano* (Saville 1987)★★★, *Complete Early Band Works* 1927-1929 recordings (Halcyon 1987)★★★, *Take It Easy* (Saville 1988)★★★, *Fats Waller And His Rhythm 1934-1936* (Classic Years In Digital Stereo) (BBC 1988)★★★, *Spreadin' Rhythm Around* (Saville 1989)★★★, *Ragtime Piano Entertainer* (Vogue 1989)★★★, *Loungin' At The Waldorf* (1990)★★★, *1939/40 - Private Acetates And Film Soundtracks* (1993)★★★, *The Ultimate Collection* (Pulse 1997)★★★★, *Piano Masterworks, Vol. 1* 1922-1929 recordings (EPM)★★★, *Giants Of Jazz* 3-LP box set (Time-Life)★★★★, *Classic Jazz From Rare Piano Rolls* 1923-1929 recordings (Music Masters)★★★, *Fats At The Organ* 1923-1927 recordings (ASV/Living Era)★★★, *Turn On The Heat: The Fats Waller Piano Solos* 1927-1941 recordings (Bluebird)★★★★, *Fats Waller And His Buddies* 1927-1929 recordings (Bluebird)★★★, *Greatest Hits* 1929-1943 recordings (RCA Victor)★★★, *Here 'Tis* 1929-1943 recordings (Jazz Archives)★★★, *Jugglin' Jive Of Fats Waller And His Orchestra* 1938 recordings (Sandy Hook)★★★, *Breakin' The Ice: The Early Years, Part 1* 1934/1935 recordings (Bluebird)★★★★, *I'm Gonna Sit Right Down: The Early Years, Part 2* 1935/1936 recordings (Bluebird)★★★★, *Fractious Fingering: The Early Years, Part 3* 1936 recordings (Bluebird 1997)★★★★, *Fats Waller And His Rhythm: The Middle Years, Part 1* 1936-1938 recordings (Bluebird)★★★★, *A Good Man Is Hard To Find: The Middle Years, Part 2* 1938-1940 recordings (Bluebird)★★★★, *The Last Years* 1940-1943 recordings (Bluebird)★★★★, *Last Testament: 1943* (Drive Archive)★★★, *The Definitive Fats Waller, Vol. 1: His Piano His Rhythm* 1935-1939 recordings (Stash)★★★★, *The Definitive Fats Waller, Vol. 2: Hallelujah* 1935-1939 recordings (Stash)★★★★.

● FURTHER READING: *The Music Of Fats Waller*, John R.T. Davies. *Fats Waller*, Charles Fox. *Fats Waller*, Maurice Waller and Anthony Calabrese. *Ain't Misbehavin': The Story Of Fats Waller*,

E.W Kirkeby, D.P. Schiedt and S. Traill. *Fats Waller: His Life And Times*, Joel Vance. *Stride: The Music Of Fats Waller*, Paul S. Machlin. *Fats Waller: His Life & Times*, Alyn Shipton. *Misbehavin' With Fats*, Harold D. Sill.
● FILMS: *Hooray For Love* (1935), *King Of Burlesque* (1936) *Stormy Weather* (1943).

WALTERS, CHARLES

b. 17 November 1911, Pasadena, California, USA, d. 13 August 1982, Malibu, California, USA. A distinguished choreographer and director for some of the classic film musicals from the 40s through to 60s; his work is well-known, but his name is not so familiar. Walters studied at the University of Southern California before joining the famous Fanchon and Marco road shows as a dancer in 1934. In the late 30s he danced in several Broadway shows including *Between The Devil* and *Du Barry Was A Lady* (1939), and subsequently worked as a stage director before moving to Hollywood and making his debut as a choreographer for the Lucille Ball-Victor Mature RKO movie *Seven Days Leave* (1942). He then switched to MGM, and continued to direct the dance routines in top musicals such as *Presenting Lily Mars*, *Du Barry Was A Lady*, *Girl Crazy*, *Best Foot Forward*, *Broadway Rhythm*, *Meet Me In St. Louis*, *The Harvey Girls*, *Ziegfeld Follies*, and *Summer Holiday* (1947). At that stage producer Arthur Freed assigned Walters as director for the 1947 remake of *Good News* with June Allyson and Peter Lawford, and his deft handling of this fairly complicated project led to him directing a variety of mostly entertaining musicals starring some of the Studio's major stars such as Fred Astaire, Judy Garland, Esther Williams, Leslie Caron, and Frank Sinatra. They included *Easter Parade*, *The Barkleys Of Broadway*, *Summer Stock*, *Texas Carnival*, *The Belle Of New York*, *Dangerous When Wet*, *Lili*, *Torch Song*, *Easy To Love*, *The Glass Slipper*, *The Tender Trap*, and *High Society* (1956). Actually, *The Tender Trap* was not really a musical - more a sophisticated comedy with music - and in the late 50s Walters directed other comedies such as *Don't Go Near The Water* and *Please Don't Eat The Daisies*. By then, of course, the sun had set on the big budget movie musical, and after directing *Billy Rose's Jumbo* (1962) and *The Unsinkable Molly Brown* (1964), Walters left MGM. He made just one more picture, *Walk, Don't Run*, for Columbia, which also happened to be Cary Grant's screen swansong. His best films - particularly *Lili*, *Easter Parade*, *High Society* and *Dangerous When Wet* - are notable for their charm and élan, and the way in which the director uses the camera to create a wonderful feeling of movement. In later years Walters emerged from retirement intermittently to direct a few television sitcoms and Lucille Ball specials, and to give the occasional lecture. He died at the age of 70 of lung cancer.

WARREN, HARRY

b. Salvatore Guaragna Warren, 24 December 1893, Brooklyn, New York, USA, d. 22 September 1981, Los Angeles, California, USA. One of the most important of all the popular film composers, Warren is probably best remembered for the innovative 30s film musicals he scored with lyricist Al Dubin. A son of Italian immigrants, from a family of 12, Warren taught himself to play accor-

dion and piano, and joined a touring carnival show in his teens. Later, he worked in a variety of jobs at the Vitagraph film studios, and played piano in silent-movie houses. After serving in the US Navy in World War I, he started writing songs. The first, 'I Learned To Love You When I Learned My ABCs', gained him a job as a song-plugger for publishers Stark and Cowan, and in 1922 they published his 'Rose Of The Rio Grande', written with Edgar Leslie and Ross Gorman, which became a hit for popular vocalist Marion Harris. During the remainder of the 20s, his most successful songs were 'I Love My Baby, My Baby Loves Me' (with Bud Green), '(Home In) Pasadena' (with Edgar Leslie and Grant Clarke) and 'Nagasaki' (with Al Dubin). In the early 30s Warren contributed songs to several Broadway shows including Billy Rose's revue *Sweet And Low* ('Cheerful Little Earful' and 'Would You Like To Take A Walk?'), *Crazy Quilt* ('I Found A Million Dollar Baby'), and Ed Wynn's 1931 hit, *The Laugh Parade*, ('Ooh! That Kiss', 'The Torch Song' and 'You're My Everything'). Another of his 1931 songs, 'By The River Saint Marie', was a number 1 hit for Guy Lombardo and his Royal Canadians. Between 1929 and 1932, Warren wrote for a few minor movies, but made Hollywood his permanent home in 1933, when hired by Darryl F. Zanuck to work with Al Dubin on Warner Brothers' first movie-musical, *42nd Street*. Starring Dick Powell, Ruby Keeler and Bebe Daniels, and choreographed by Busby Berkeley, the film included songs such as 'Shuffle Off To Buffalo', 'You're Getting To Be A Habit With Me' and 'Young And Healthy'. During the 30s, Warren and Dubin wrote songs for some 20 films, including several starring Dick Powell, such as *Gold Diggers Of 1933* (1933, 'We're In The Money', 'Pettin' In The Park', 'The Shadow Waltz', and the powerful plea on behalf of the ex-servicemen, victims of the Depression, 'My Forgotten Man'), *Footlight Parade* (1933, co-starring James Cagney, and featuring 'By A Waterfall' and 'Shanghai Lil'), *Dames* (1934, 'I Only Have Eyes For You'), *Twenty Million Sweethearts* (1934, I'll String Along With You'), *Gold Diggers Of 1935* (Warren's first Oscar-winner 'Lullaby Of Broadway', effectively sung by Winifred Shaw, and 'The Words Are In My Heart'), *Broadway Gondolier* (1935, 'Lulu's Back In Town'), and *Gold Diggers Of 1937* (1936, 'All's Fair In Love And War' and 'With Plenty Of Money And You'.

The team's other scores included the Eddie Cantor vehicle, *Roman Scandals* (1933, 'Keep Young And Beautiful'), *Go Into Your Dance* (1935, starring Al Jolson and his wife, Ruby Keeler, and featuring 'A Latin From Manhattan' and 'About A Quarter To Nine'), *Moulin Rouge* (1934, with Constance Bennett and Franchot Tone, and the song, 'The Boulevard Of Broken Dreams'). Warren and Dubin also contributed some numbers to *Melody For Two* (1937), including one of their evergreens, 'September In The Rain'. Shortly before taking his leave of Warners and Dubin in 1939, Warren teamed with Johnny Mercer to write songs for two more Dick Powell films, *Going Places* (1938) with Louis Armstrong and Maxine Sullivan singing the Academy Award nominee, 'Jeepers Creepers', and *Hard To Get* (1938, 'You Must Have Been A Beautiful Baby'). Warren's move to 20th Century-Fox led him to work with lyricist Mack Gordon, whose main collaborator was Harry Revel. During the 40s, Warren and Gordon wrote some of World War II's most evocative songs. They composed for films such as *Down Argentine Way* (1940, starring Betty Grable and Don Ameche), *Tin Pan Alley* (1940, 'You Say The Sweetest Things, Baby', *That Night In Rio* (1941, featuring Carmen Miranda singing 'I, Yi, Yi, Yi, Yi, [I Like You Very Much]'), two films starring Glenn Miller and his Orchestra, *Sun Valley Serenade* (1941, 'Chattanooga Choo Choo', 'I Know Why', 'It Happened In Sun Valley), and *Orchestra Wives* (1942, 'Serenade In Blue', 'At Last', I've Got A Gal In Kalamazoo'), *Springtime In The Rockies* (1942, 'I Had The Craziest Dream'), *Iceland* (1942, 'There Will Never Be Another You'), *Sweet Rosie O'Grady* (1943, 'My Heart Tells Me'), and *Hello, Frisco, Hello* (1943, starring Alice Faye singing Warren's second Oscar-winner, 'You'll Never Know'). While at Fox Warren also wrote the songs for another Alice Faye movie, in partnership with Leo Robin. In Busby Berkeley's *The Gang's All Here* (1943), Faye sang their ballad, 'No Love, No Nothin'', while Carmen Miranda was her usual flamboyant self as 'The Lady With The Tutti-Frutti Hat'. Warren wrote his last score at Fox, with Mack Gordon, for the lavish *Billy Rose's Diamond Horseshoe* (1945), starring Dick Haymes, Betty Grable, and Phil Silvers. Two songs from the film, 'I Wish I Knew' and 'The More I See You', are considered to be among their very best. From 1945-52 Warren worked for MGM Pictures, and won his third Oscar, in partnership with Johnny Mercer, for 'On The Atchison, Topeka And The Santa Fe', from the Judy Garland/Ray Bolger film, *The Harvey Girls* (1946). Warren and Mercer also provided songs for the Fred Astaire/Vera-Ellen movie *The Belle Of New York*, which included 'Baby Doll', 'Seeing's Believing', 'I Want To Be A Dancing Man' and 'Bachelor Dinner Song'. In 1949, after 10 years apart, MGM reunited Fred Astaire and Ginger Rogers, for their last musical together, *The Barkleys Of Broadway*. The musical score, by Warren and Ira Gershwin included the ballad, 'You'd Be Hard To Replace', the novelty, 'My One And Only Highland Fling' and the danceable 'Shoes With Wings On'.

Other Warren collaborators while he was at MGM included Dorothy Fields, Arthur Freed and Mack Gordon, the latter for some songs to the Judy Garland/Gene Kelly film *Summer Stock* (1950), including 'If You Feel Like Singing' and 'You, Wonderful You'. In 1952, Warren teamed with lyricist Leo Robin for Paramount's *Just For You*, starring Bing Crosby and Jane Wyman. The songs included 'A Flight Of Fancy', 'I'll Si Si Ya In Bahia' and 'Zing A Little Zong'. In the following year, together with Jack Brooks, he provided Dean Martin with one of his biggest hits, 'That's Amore', from the film *The Caddy* (1953), which sold over three million copies. Warren remained under contract to Paramount until 1961, writing mostly scores for dramatic films such as *The Rose Tattoo* (1955) and *An Affair To Remember* (1957). In the early 50s he went into semi-retirement. On his 80th birthday he was elected to the Songwriters Hall Of Fame. Warren was one of the most respected of the songwriters from the 30s, and a year before his death in 1981, many of those hits that he wrote with Al Dubin were celebrated again in Broadway and London stage versions of the movie *42nd Street*.

● COMPILATIONS: *The Songs Of Harry Warren* (1979)★★★, featuring various artists *Who's Harry Warren?, Volume One: Jeepers Creepers* (1982)★★★, featuring various artists *Who's Harry Warren?, Volume Two: 42nd Street* (1982)★★★.
● FURTHER READING: *Harry Warren And The Hollywood Musical*, Tony Thomas.

WASHINGTON, NED

b. 15 August 1901, Scranton, Pennsylvania, USA, d. 20 December 1976, Beverly Hills, California, USA. A prolific lyricist, especially for films, from the 20s through to the 60s. As a child Washington had some of his poetry published, and, later, in the 20s worked in a variety of jobs in New York and Hollywood while writing songs in his spare time. His chief collaborators included composers Victor Young, Dimitri Tiomkin, Lester Lee, Allie Wrubel, Michael Cleary, George Duning, Max Steiner, Bronislaw Kaper, Jimmy McHugh, Waler Jurman, Sammy Stept, and Leigh Harline. In the late 20s and early 30s Washington contributed songs to Broadway shows such as *Earl Carroll's Vanities, Vanderbilt Revue, Murder At The Vanities, Blackbirds Of 1934*, and *Hello, Paris*. He had his first major hit with 'Can't We Talk It Over?' in 1932, and it was followed by 'I'm Getting Sentimental Over You' which Tommy Dorsey adopted as his signature tune. Washington's other notable songs in the 30s included 'Got The South In My Soul', 'A Hundred Years From Today' (immortalised by Jack Teagarden), 'Smoke Rings', (Glen Gray's theme tune), 'Love Is The Thing', 'My Love', and '(I Don't Stand A) Ghost Of A Chance'. From 1935 onwards he wrote prolifically for films. In the late 30s and 40s these included *Here Comes The Band, A Night At The Opera, The Hit Parade, Tropic Holiday, A Night At Earl Carroll's, I Wanted Wings, For Whom The Bell Tolls*, and *Passage To Marseilles*. His most successful songs of that period were 'You're My Thrill', 'The Nearness Of You', 'When I See An Elephant Fly' (from *Dumbo*), and 'Stella By Starlight'. In 1940 he won an Academy Award for 'When You Wish Upon A Star' (with Leigh Harline) from the animated feature *Pinocchio*, and another Oscar for the original score (with Harline and Paul J. Smith). During his career he wrote the lyrics for some 40 movie titles songs. From 1950, through to the early 60s these included 'My Foolish Heart', 'High Noon (Do Not Forsake Me)' (for which he won his third Oscar in 1952), 'The Greatest Show On Earth', 'Take The High Ground', 'The High And The Mighty', 'The Man From Laramie', 'Land Of The Pharaohs', 'The Maverick Queen', 'Gunfight At The O.K. Corral', 'Wild Is The Wind', 'Search For Paradise', 'The Roots Of Heaven', 'These Thousand Hills', 'The Unforgiven', 'Town Without Pity', 'Advise And Consent', 'Circus World' (1964 Golden Globe Award), and 'Ship Of Fools' (1965). He also wrote the lyrics for the *Rawhide* television theme, and two memorable numbers, 'The Heat Is On' and 'Sadie Thompson's Song' for the Rita Hayworth picture *Miss Sadie Thompson* (1953). Washington was a member of ASCAP from 1930, and served as its director from 1957-76. He was also inducted into the National Academy of Popular Music Songwriters' Hall of Fame.

WATCH YOUR STEP

After interpolating songs into other people's shows for several years, this 'syncopated musical' containing Irving Berlin's first complete Broadway score, was presented at the New Amsterdam Theatre in New York on 8 December 1914. The slight book, by Harry B. Smith, was based on Augustin Daly's play *Round The Clock*, which is said to have been adapted from a French farce. Audiences probably believed that fact when faced with a story in which a character dies leaving a great deal of money to anyone who can claim they have never been in love. The stars were the world's premier ballroom dancers, Vernon And Irene Castle, who were making their final professional appearance together. Shortly after this show closed Vernon left to join the Canadian Air Force and was killed in an air crash in 1918. Berlin's delightful score for *Watch Your Step* introduced some of the elements and rhythms from Tin Pan Alley to the hallowed halls of the legitimate musical theatre, and the composer also included an operatic parody in which selections from *Rigoletto* and *Carmen*, amongst others, were given the ragtime treatment. The mostly happy and singable songs included 'Play A Simple Melody', 'They Always Follow Me Around', 'Show Us How To Do The Fox-Trot', 'The Minstrel Parade', 'When I Discovered You', 'Settle Down In A One-Horse Town', 'When It's Night Time In Dixieland', 'Lock Me In Your Harem And Throw Away The Key', and 'I've Got To Go Back To Texas'. The New York run of 175 performances was followed by a further 275 in London, where the cast included Joseph Coyne, Ethel Levey, and the versatile Lupino Lane in his first West End show. Over 80 years after it made its New York debut, *Watch Your Step* was presented in concert at Her Majesty's Theatre in London in 1995, with a cast headed by Henry Goodman and opera diva Lesley Garrett.

WATERS, ETHEL

b. 31 October 1896, Chester, Pennsylvania, USA, d. 1 September 1977. One of the most influential of popular singers, Waters' early career found her working in vaudeville. As a consequence, her repertoire was more widely based and popularly angled than those of many of her contemporaries. It is reputed that she was the first singer to perform W.C. Handy's 'St Louis Blues' in public, and she later popularized blues and jazz-influenced songs such as 'Stormy Weather' and 'Travellin' All Alone', also scoring a major success with 'Dinah'. She first recorded in 1921, and on her early dates she was accompanied by artists such as Fletcher Henderson, Coleman Hawkins, James P. Johnson and Duke Ellington. Significantly, for her acceptance in white circles, she also recorded with Jack Teagarden, Benny Goodman and Tommy Dorsey.

From the late 20s, Waters appeared in several Broadway musicals, including *Africana*, *Blackbirds Of 1930*, *Rhapsody In Black*, *As Thousands Cheer*, *At Home Abroad*, and *Cabin In The Sky*, in which she introduced several diverting songs such as 'I'm Coming Virginia', 'Baby Mine', 'My Handy Man Ain't Handy No More', 'Till The Real Thing Comes Along', 'Suppertime', 'Harlem On My Mind', 'Heat Wave', 'Got A Bran' New Suit' (with Eleanor Powell),

'Hottentot Potentate', and 'Cabin In The Sky'. In the 30s she stopped the show regularly at the Cotton Club in Harlem with 'Stormy Weather', and appeared at Carnegie Hall in 1938. She played a few dramatic roles in the theatre, and appeared in several films, including *On With The Show*, *Check And Double Check*, *Gift Of The Gab*, *Tales Of Manhattan*, *Cairo*, *Cabin In The Sky*, *Stage Door Canteen*, *Pinky*, *Member Of The Wedding*, and *The Sound And The Fury* (1959). In the 50s she was also in the US television series *Beulah* for a while, and had her own Broadway show, *An Evening With Ethel Waters* (1957).

Throughout the 60s and on into the mid-70s she sang as a member of the organization which accompanied evangelist Billy Graham. Although less highly regarded in blues and jazz circles than either Bessie Smith or Louis Armstrong, in the 30s Waters transcended the boundaries of these musical forms to far greater effect than either of these artists and spread her influence throughout popular music. Countless young hopefuls emulated her sophisticated, lilting vocal style and her legacy lived on in the work of outstanding and, ironically, frequently better-known successors, such as Connee Boswell, Ruth Etting, Adelaide Hall, Mildred Bailey, Lee Wiley, Lena Horne and Ella Fitzgerald. Even Billie Holiday (with whom Waters was less than impressed, commenting, 'She sings as though her shoes are too tight'), acknowledged her influence. A buoyant, high-spirited singer with a light, engaging voice that frequently sounds 'whiter' than most of her contemporaries, Waters' career was an object lesson in determination and inner drive. Her appalling childhood problems and troubled early life, recounted in the first part of her autobiography, *His Eye Is On The Sparrow*, were overcome through grit and the application of her great talent.

● ALBUMS: *His Eye Is On The Sparrow* (1963)★★★, *Ethel Waters Reminisces* (1963)★★★.

● COMPILATIONS: *Ethel Waters* (1979)★★★, *The Complete Bluebird Sessions (1938-39)* (1986)★★★★, *On The Air (1941-51)* (1986)★★★★, *Ethel Waters On Stage And Screen (1925-40)* (1989)★★★★, *Who Said Blackbirds Are Blue?* (1989)★★★, *Classics 1921-23*, (Classics 1993)★★★, *Classics 1923-25*, (Classics 1993)★★★, *Ethel Waters 1926-29* (Classics 1993)★★★.

● FURTHER READING: *His Eye Is On The Sparrow*, Ethel Waters. *To Me It's Wonderful*, Ethel Waters.

WATTSTAX

During the 60s, the Memphis-based Stax label established itself as a leading outlet for southern soul music. Otis Redding, Sam And Dave, Rufus Thomas and Booker T. And The MGs were among the successful acts of its early, halcyon era. By 1973 the company had severed its ties with Atlantic Records, opting instead for a liaison with Gulf-Western group, whose ties with the Paramount Film Studio gave rise to this feature. The black ghetto of Watts, a suburb of Los Angeles, had been the site of several riots and came to symbolise aspects of the African-American struggle. Yet crippling poverty remained, inspiring Stax to stage and film a concert there, celebrating the area's communal aspects while criticising social policies. Interviews and documentary-styled footage brought home the scandalous slum conditions while the sometimes emotional music offered a sense of hope. The entire contemporary Stax roster made contributions, including established stars Isaac Hayes, Eddie Floyd, Rufus Thomas, Carla Thomas, the Bar Kays and Johnnie Taylor. The label's new generation of acts - Luther Ingram, Mel And Tim, Frederick Knight and the Dramatics - was set beside veterans Albert King and Little Milton, celebrating the achievements Stax, although white-owned, had made. Compered by Richard Prior, punctuated by a speech by the Reverend Jesse Jackson and commemorated further by a double-album set, *Wattstax* glistens with justified pride. It also captures several leading soul acts at the height of their popularity.

WAXMAN, FRANZ

b. Franz Wachsmann, 24 December 1906, Koenigshuette, Germany, d. 24 February 1967, Los Angeles, California, USA. An important composer, arranger, and conductor of background film music from the middle 30s until the 60s. Waxman studied music in Berlin and Dresden, and earned his living as a nightclub pianist. After composing the music for Fritz Lang's film *Liliom* (1933), during the Austrian director's brief sojourn in France, on his way to the USA, Waxman, too, moved to Hollywood in 1934. Signed to Universal, his first music score, for the acclaimed *The Bride Of Frankenstein* (1935) ('a sophisticated masterpiece of black comedy'), was later reused in other movies. In a somewhat lighter vein, Waxman's next few projects included more conventional comedies such as *Diamond Jim* (co-composer Ferde Grofé); *Three Kids And A Queen*, and *Remember Last Night*. He also provided the music for the Robert Taylor-Irene Dunne sentimental film, *Magnificent Obsession*. In the late 30s, for MGM, Waxman's scores included *Captains Courageous*, *The Bride Wore Red*, *Test Pilot* (star combination: Clark Gable-Myrna Loy-Spencer Tracy), *The Young In Heart* (the first of Waxman's 11 Academy Award nominations), *A Christmas Carol* and *Huckleberry Finn*.

In 1941, Waxman composed the music for another highly-regarded horror film, the second re-make of *Dr Jekyll And Mr Hyde*, and for *On Borrowed Time*, a fantasy where death raised its ugly head. But, yet again, he contrasted those scores with music for two classic comedies starring Katharine Hepburn, *The Philadelphia Story*, and *Woman Of The Year* - the film in which Hepburn met Spencer Tracy for the first time. Waxman's other 40s scores, sometimes as many as seven or eight a year, included *On Borrowed Time*, *Rebecca*, *Suspicion*, *Strange Cargo*, *Boom Town*, *Tortilla Flat*, *Edge Of Darkness*, *Air Force*, *Old Acquaintance*, *Destination Tokyo*, *To Have And Have Not*, *Operation Burma!*, *The Horn Blows At Midnight*, *Mr Skeffington*, *Humoresque*, *Possessed*, *Dark Passage*, *Sorry, Wrong Number*, and *Johnny Holiday*. In 1947, Waxman founded the Los Angeles Music Festival, an organization which introduced many new works by classical composers, and was its musical director until 1966. In the early 50s he won two Academy Awards for his scores to *Sunset Boulevard* (1950) and *A Place In The Sun* (1951). Also in 1950, he composed the music for *Dark City*, the film in which Charlton Heston made his Hollywood debut. Throughout the rest of the 50s, and into the 60s Waxman wrote some other memorable scores for movies such as

The Blue Veil, *Phone Call From A Stranger*, *My Cousin Rachel*, *Come Back*, *Little Sheba*, *Prince Valiant*, *Rear Window*, *The Silver Chalice*, *Untamed*, *Mister Roberts*, *The Virgin Queen*, *Crime In The Streets*, *The Spirit Of St. Louis*, *Peyton Place*, *Sayonara* ('Katsumi Love Theme' and 'Mountains Beyond The Moon', lyric by Carl Sigman), *Run Silent, Run Deep*, *Home Before Dark*, *The Nun's Story*, *The Story Of Ruth*, *My Geisha*, *Hemingway's Adventures Of Young Man*, *Taras Bulba*, *Lost Command*, and *The Longest Hundred Miles* (television movie 1967). Waxman also composed several serious works, including 'Elegy For Strings'. A good deal of his soundtrack music has been made available on records.

● ALBUMS: *Sunset Boulevard-The Classic Film Scores Of Franz Waxman* (RCA 1974)★★★★.

WE'RE NOT DRESSING

Just one of the movies to be based (in this case very loosely) on Scottish author J.M. Barrie's play, *The Admirable Crichton*. This 1934 Paramount release had a screenplay by Horace Jackson, Francis Martin, and George Marion Jnr. which retained the desert island theme, while amending the characterization to suit the contracted stars. Carole Lombard plays the pampered rich girl whose yacht is shipwrecked on a Pacific island. Resourceful sailor Bing Crosby stops crooning long enough to build a shelter for the hardy cast, which included Ethel Merman, Leon Errol, George Burns and Gracie Allen. He also has lots of comfort and affection for Lombard. Harry Revel and Mack Gordon came up with a great bunch of songs, such as 'Love Thy Neighbour', 'May I?', 'Once In A Blue Moon', 'She Reminds Me Of You', 'I Positively Refuse To Sing', 'Goodnight Lovely Little Lady', and 'Let's Play House'. Man-hungry Merman duetted with Errol on the splendid 'It's Just An Old Spanish Custom'. Norman Taurog directed this frothy confection which proved yet again, that at this stage of his career Crosby could do no wrong.

WEBB, LIZBETH

b. 30 January 1926, Caversham, Oxfordshire, England. A much-admired ingénue in West End musicals during the late 40s and early 50s, Lizbeth Webb began her career as a singer with dance bands. Following a recommendation from an eminent leader of one of those popular ensembles, Geraldo, Charles B. Cochran chose her to understudy Carol Lynne in the Vivian Ellis/A.P. Herbert musical, *Big Ben* (1946). After Lynne, in Ellis's own words, 'retired from the cast to open her nursery', Webb took over the role of Grace Green in fine style, and was rewarded less than a year later, when Cochran, Ellis, and Herbert created *Bless The Bride* especially for her. As the young English girl, Lucy Veracity Willow, Webb captivated audiences with her delightful performance of one of Ellis's most exquisite ballads, 'The Silent Heart', and also shared two outstanding duets with Georges Guétary, 'I Was Never Kissed Before' and 'This Is My Lovely Day'. In the 50s she continued to shine in shows such as *Gay's The Word* ('On Such A Night As This', 'Sweet Thames'), in 1951, and *Guys And Dolls* (as Miss Sarah Brown, 1953). She also appeared in the 1953 *Royal Variety Performance*, and toured the UK provinces in *Jubilee Girl* (1956). In 1959, she appeared in the BBC

Television adaptation of Eric Maschwitz and Hans May's 1948 hit musical, *Carissima*, before retiring from the stage in order to marry and become Lady Campbell. However, she was seen again in the West End some 10 years later in a brief revival of *The Merry Widow* at the Cambridge Theatre. Sadly, an injury prevented her from singing hit numbers from *Bless The Bride* in *Spread A Little Happiness*, a joyful celebration of the life of Vivian Ellis, following the composer's death in June 1996.

WEBB, MARTI

b. 1944, Cricklewood, London, England. In 1963, at the age of 19, singer Marti Webb was 'plucked from the chorus' of the London production of Leslie Bricusse and Anthony Newley's hit musical *Stop the World - I Want To Get Off*, to star opposite Tommy Steele in the even more successful *Half A Sixpence*. Although she was not chosen to recreate her role in the subsequent 1967 film version, she did dub the singing voice of her replacement, actress Julia Foster. Webb played Nancy in a national tour of Lionel Bart's *Oliver!* in 1965, and again two years later in the major West End revival. In the early 70s she appeared in one of the in-vogue 'biblical' musicals, *Godspell*, with a superior cast which included Jeremy Irons, David Essex and Julie Covington. She also featured in a musical adaptation of J.B. Priestley's *The Good Companions*, which had a score by André Previn and Johnny Mercer. Much better all round, was *The Card*, with songs by Tony Hatch and Jackie Trent, in which Webb impressed with her duet with Jim Dale on 'Opposite Your Smile', and the solo 'I Could Be The One'. It was in the 80s, however, that she came to prominence after successfully replacing Elaine Page in *Evita*. In 1980 she appeared in an invited concert and a television broadcast of the 'song cycle' *Tell Me On A Sunday*, with a score by Andrew Lloyd Webber and lyricist Don Black. This spawned both a studio and television soundtrack album, and Webb took one of the show's songs, 'Take That Look Off Your Face', into the UK Top 10. Two years later, when an expanded version of *Tell Me On A Sunday* was joined with *Variations* to form the two-part 'theatrical concert', *Song And Dance*, Webb's 50 minute solo performance was hailed as a 'remarkable *tour de force*'. She also took over various roles in other Lloyd Webber productions, including his longest-running British musical, *Cats*. Webb's singles include 'Didn't Mean To Fall In Love', 'Ready For Roses Now', 'Ben' (UK Top 5), and three popular television themes: 'Always There' from *Howard's Way* (UK Top 20); 'Someday Soon' from *The Onedin Line* and a duet with Paul Jones on 'I Could Be So Good For You', from *Minder*. In the early 90s Webb toured the UK and the Channel Islands with *The Magic Of The Musicals*, co-starring with television's *Opportunity Knocks* winner, Mark Rattray. Since then, her various projects have included a season performing George Gershwin songs at London's Café Royal in the company of broadcaster David Jacobs, presenting *The Don Black Story* on BBC Radio 2, appearing in pantomime, a Summer Season in Blackpool with Michael Barrymore, and major UK tours of *Evita* and *The Goodbye Girl* (1997/8, with Gary Wilmot).

● ALBUMS: *Tell Me On A Sunday* (Polydor 1980)★★, *Won't*
Change Places* (Polydor 1981)★★, *I'm Not That Kind Of Girl* (Polydor 1983)★★, *Encore* (Starblend 1985)★★, *Always There* (BBC 1986)★★, *Sings Gershwin* (BBC 1987)★★, *Marti Webb - The Album* (1993)★★, *Performance* (Ronco 1993)★★, with Dave Willetts, Carl Wayne *Songs From Evita* (1994)★★.

WEBSTER, PAUL FRANCIS

b. 20 December 1907, New York City, New York, USA, d. 18 March 1984, Beverly Hills, California, USA. An important lyricist for movie songs from the 40s through to the 60s, Webster was educated at Cornell and New York Universities, but dropped out without graduating, to take a job first as a seaman, and then as a dancing instructor. He developed an interest in lyric writing, and in 1932 had a hit with 'Masquerade' (music by John Jacob Loeb). Among his other songs in the early 30s were 'My Moonlight Madonna' (music by William Scotti), 'Two Cigarettes In The Dark' (with Lew Pollack), and 'Got The Jitters' (Loeb). In 1934, Webster and Pollack were hired to write for films, and it was while he was in Hollywood that Webster collaborated with composer Duke Ellington on *Jump For Joy* ('I Got It Bad (And That Ain't Good)', 'Jump For Joy'), an all-black musical that opened in Los Angeles in 1941. He also had hits in the 40s with 'Lily Of Laguna' (music by Ted Fio Rito), and a succession of songs composed by Hoagy Carmichael, among them, 'Baltimore Oriole', 'The Lamplighter's Serenade', 'Doctor, Lawyer, Indian Chief' and 'Memphis In June'. Several of those numbers were introduced in minor films, but in the 50s and 60s Webster wrote the lyrics for numerous songs and themes that featured in some of the highest-grossing movies of the times. These included *The Great Caruso* (1951, 'The Loveliest Night Of The Year', with Irving Aaronson and Juventino Rosas), *Calamity Jane* (1953, 'Secret Love' (Oscar-winner), 'The Deadwood Stage', 'The Black Hills Of Dakota', with Sammy Fain), *Lucky Me* (1954, 'I Speak To The Stars', with Fain), *Battle Cry* (1955, 'Honey Babe', with Max Steiner), *Marjorie Morningstar* (1958, 'A Very Precious Love', with Fain), *The Alamo* (1960, 'The Green Leaves Of Summer', with Dimitri Tiomkin), *55 Days At Peking* (1963, 'So Little Time', with Tiomkin), *The Sandpiper* (1965, 'The Shadow Of Your Smile' (Oscar-winner), with Johnny Mandel) and *Doctor Zhivago* (1965, 'Somewhere My Love (Lara's Theme)', with Maurice Jarre). In addition, Webster collaborated on the immensely popular title themes for several other films, including 'Love Is A Many Splendored Thing' (1955, (Oscar-winner) with Fain), 'Friendly Persuasion (Thee I Love)' (1956, with Tiomkin), 'Anastasia' (1956, with Alfred Newman), 'Giant' (1956, with Tiomkin), 'April Love' (1957, with Fain), 'A Certain Smile' (1958, with Fain), 'Rio Bravo' (1950, with Tiomkin), 'The Guns Of Navarone' (1961, with Tiomkin), 'El Cid' (love theme, 1961, with Miklos Rozsa), and 'Tender Is The Night' (1962, with Fain). He also wrote the lyrics for 'Like Young' (music by André Previn), 'Black Coffee' (with Sonny Burke), which received a memorable rendering from Peggy Lee, and 'The Twelfth Of Never' (Jerry Livingston), a US Top 10 entry for both Johnny Mathis and Donny Osmond. His other collaborators included Henry Mancini, Frank Churchill, Walter Jurrman, and Louis Alter. Apart from his three Academy Awards, Webster was nominated on more than 10 other occasions. Among his honours were ASCAP, Dramatist's Guild, *Photoplay*, Limelight Film Critics, and Grammy Awards. He was elected to the Songwriters Hall of Fame in 1972.

WEDDING BELLS
(see *Royal Wedding*)

WEILL, KURT
b. 2 March 1900, Dessau, Germany, d. 3 April 1950, New York City, New York, USA. A distinguished composer, often for the musical theatre, Weill studied piano and composition as a child, and at the age of 20 was conducting opera with local companies. By the mid-20s he had established a reputation as a leading composer in the modern idiom. He was eager to make opera a popular form, accessible to the widest audience, and was also politically aware, wanting his work to have social significance. In collaboration with Bertolt Brecht he composed *Little Mahagonny* (later expanded to become *The Rise And Fall Of The City Of Mahagonny*) and then achieved success with *The Threepenny Opera* (1928). Although a massive hit in Germany, the show failed in the USA in 1933, but was well received when it was revived in 1954/5. It has since been continually re-staged all over the world. The show's best-known song, 'Mack The Knife', became a standard in the repertoires of numerous singers. Weill and his wife, singer Lotte Lenya, emigrated to the USA in 1935. En route, he spent some time in England, working with Desmond Carter and Reginald Arkell on the musical satire, *A Kingdom For A Cow*, which was presented at the Savoy Theatre. On arriving in the USA, he formed a working association with Group Theatre, the influential left-wing drama company which was home to such rising talents as Lee J. Cobb, John Garfield, Clifford Odet, Frances Farmer and Elia Kazan. He also wrote scores for the theatre, including *Johnny Johnson* (1936, with Paul Green), *The Eternal Road* (1937, Franz Werfel), and *Knickerbocker Holiday* (1938, with Maxwell Anderson). The last show starred the non-singing actor Walter Huston, but ironically his version of 'September Song' proved to one of the most memorable and enduring moments in popular music. In 1941 Weill collaborated with Ira Gershwin (lyrics) and Moss Hart (book) for *Lady In The Dark*, which starred Gertrude Lawrence, and featured 'My Ship', 'The Saga Of Jenny' and 'One Life To Live'. Two years later came *One Touch Of Venus* (Ogden Nash and S.J. Perelman), in which the lovely 'Speak Low' was introduced by Mary Martin and Kenny Baker. This was followed by The *Firebrand Of Florence* (1945, Ira Gershwin and Edwin Justus Mayer), *Street Scene* (1947, Langston Hughes and Elmer Rice), *Down In the Valley*, 1948, a 20-minute folk opera for radio), *Love Life* (1948, Alan Jay Lerner), and *Lost In The Stars* (1949, Anderson). Weill was working on *Huckleberry Finn*, an adaptation of Mark Twain's celebrated novel, when he died in 1950. In 1995, a new production of *The Rise And Fall Of The City Of Mahagonny* was presented by the English National Opera at the Coliseum in London, and three years later, *Propheten*, the re-discovered, previously suppressed final

act of Weill's 1937 production *Eternal Road*, received its world premiere as part of the 1998 Proms at London's Royal Albert Hall.

● FURTHER READING: *The Days Grow Short: The Life And Music Of Kurt Weill*, Ronald Saunders. *Kurt Weill: Composer In A Divided World*, Ronald Taylor. *Speak Low (When You Speak Love): The Letters Of Kurt Weill And Lotte Lenya*, Lys Symonette and Kim Kowalke (editors).

WELCH, ELISABETH
b. 27 February 1908, New York City, New York, USA. After working in obscurity as a singer and dancer in various New York nightspots, Welch attracted considerable attention with her appearance in the 1923 Broadway musical *Runnin' Wild*, in which she introduced a new dance to the tune of the 'Charleston'. She appeared in several all-black revues, on and Off Broadway, during the next few years, including *Chocolate Dandies* (1924) and Lew Leslie's *Blackbirds Of 1928*. It was with the latter show that she first visited Europe, appearing at the Moulin Rouge in Paris in 1929. She was a great success and returned to the city the following year. By 1933 she had decided that she preferred life away from the USA, and settled in London. During the 30s she established herself as a star of London's nightlife and continued to appear in revues, musicals and plays throughout the next few decades. These have included *Nymph Errant* (1933), *Glamorous Night* (1935, in which she introduced her signature song, 'Solomon'), *It's In The Bag* (1937), *Arc De Triomphe*, (1943), *Tuppence Coloured* (1947), *Penny Plain* (1951), *The Crooked Mile* (1959), *Cindy-Ella* or *I Gotta Shoe* (1962), *Pippin* (1973), and *Aladdin* (1979), as well as numerous regional productions. Several of the songs with which she is associated, such as 'As Time Goes By', 'Love for Sale', 'Stormy Weather', 'La Vie En Rose', have since become standards. A remarkable survivor, she continues to appear on radio and television and to make records. She also played a cameo role, singing 'Stormy Weather', in Derek Jarman's 1980 film *The Tempest*. In 1985, while returning home from the London theatre where she was appearing in *Jerome Kern Goes To Hollywood*, she was battered unconscious by a mugger, but was back on stage less than 24 hours later. A year after that she was in New York, performing her one-woman show, *Time To Start Living*, and in 1989 she starred in a one night concert revival of *Nymph Errant*, the show in which she had first appeared in 1933. Fifty years on, the cream of British showbusiness gathered at the Lyric Theatre in London to pay tribute to Elisabeth Welch, and give her an unprecedented (as far as anyone there could remember) five standing ovations.

● ALBUMS: *Elisabeth Welch Sings The Irving Berlin Songbook* (1958)★★★★, *Elisabeth Welch In Concert* (1986)★★, *Where Have You Been* (1987)★★★, *This Thing Called Love* (1989)★★★.

● COMPILATIONS: *Miss Elisabeth Welch (1933-40)* (1979)★★★, with Paul Robeson *Songs From Their Films 1933-1940* (Conifer 1994)★★★★.

WEST SIDE STORY (FILM MUSICAL)
So many film musicals have been adapted from stage successes, but it can never be easy to follow up a groundbreaking and highly praised production with a film that

keeps those same attractive qualities. *West Side Story*, released by United Artists in September 1961 (made for the Mirisch Company), did just that, and remains an historical musical movie. This contemporary interpretation of Shakespeare's *Romeo And Juliet* naturally benefited from the involvement of Jerome Robbins. He came up with the original idea, and is the film's choreographer and co-director with Robert Wise. The movie concentrates on the Sharks and Jets, two rival gangs who only mix when it is time to 'rumble' on the tough streets of New York. But life is never black and white, and complications are rife when the ex-leader of the Jets, Tony (Richard Beymer), falls in love with Maria (Natalie Wood), the sister of the Sharks' man-in-charge, Puerto Rican Bernardo (George Chakiris). The devoted couple do their best to isolate themselves from the action around them but it is almost impossible. Even when Bernardo's lover Anita (beautifully played by Rita Moreno) rushes to the drugstore in an attempt to warn the Jets of imminent trouble, she is almost raped by the gang who lose control. In the end everything goes tragically wrong. Tony tries to stop a fight between the gangs but ends up stabbing Bernardo, after the Sharks leader has himself killed the leader of the Jets (Russ Tamblyn). Desperate to see Maria, Tony almost goes on the run, knowing that the other Sharks will immediately be out for revenge. In a moving scene Tony is killed, and Maria weeps at his side. The final significant and poignant image is of both gangs joining together to carry Tony's body from the scene. *West Side Story*, with a screenplay by Ernest Lehman (Arthur Laurents wrote the original book for the 1957 show), is an extremely powerful piece. At some moments, its musical pace has an almost operatic feel about it. Individual performances are outstanding - Wood and Beymer make pleasant lovers, though they were not particularly known for their musical talent, and their voices had to be dubbed by Jim Bryant and Marni Nixon. Yet the love songs - 'Maria', 'Tonight', 'One Hand, One Heart', 'Somewhere' - and Wood's 'I Feel Pretty' - are all handled superbly. However, it is really the ensemble work, particularly the sequences that involve dance and concentrate on the gang mentality, that make *West Side Story* stand out from the crowd. The combination of Leonard Bernstein's music, the young Stephen Sondheim's lyrics, and Robbins' staggering choreography puts the film in a league of its own. The opening, with its rapid focus in on the Jets, is hard hitting and sharp, as is the gang's attempts to calm their anger and frustration in 'Cool'. Moreno (dubbed by Betty Wand) also finely handles 'A Boy Like That' and the irresistible 'America', mocking the attractions of New York living. In a lighter moment, with a slightly serious underside, the Jets make fun of their upbringing and present social situation in 'Gee, Officer Krupke!' It's a joy to see performed and an early reminder of how witty Sondheim's lyrics could be ('My daddy beats my mummy/My mummy clobbers me/My grandpa is a Commie/My grandma pushes tea'). With all these factors in its favour it is not surprising that *West Side Story* collected 10 Oscars (including best picture) and was one of the 60s biggest successes at the box office, grossing more than any musical in 1962. Years later, although it appears a little dated in some respects, it retains a cult status, and more than that, is respected and loved by critics and audiences alike.

WEST SIDE STORY (STAGE MUSICAL)

In 1949, when Jerome Robbins first shared his idea of updating William Shakespeare's love story *Romeo And Juliet* with Arthur Laurents and Leonard Bernstein, the trio agreed that it should be set in New York City's Lower East Side, and concentrate on a feud between Jews and Catholics. Six years later, however, when they eventually got around to developing the concept, the then-current well-publicised conflict between native New Yorkers and Mexican immigrants caused them to set this musical around the gang fights involving Puerto Ricans on the Upper West Side. When it opened on 26 September 1957 at Broadway's Winter Garden Theatre, audiences were initially stunned by the powerful blend of dynamic choreography and thrilling music - with its Latin, jazz, and rock influences - which complemented perfectly the contemporary theme of brooding urban discord and violence. It was like nothing that had gone before, Laurents' story of two gangs, the American Sharks and Puerto Rican Jets, during those last days of summer. Persuaded to attend a school dance by his friend Riff (Mickey Calin), the Jets leader, Tony (Larry Kert) meets and falls in love with Maria (Carol Lawrence), sister of Sharks boss Bernardo (Kenneth LeRoy). This means there is big trouble ahead, and in a knife fight - a rumble - the following day, Riff is killed by Bernardo. Incensed by the death of his friend, Tony slays Bernardo, and is then told (wrongly) that Maria is dead. While grieving and wandering aimlessly around, he sees her, but as they run joyfully towards each other, Bernardo's friend Chino (Jamie Sanchez) shoots Tony dead. As the curtain falls, the conscience-stricken Jets and Sharks come together to carry his body away. Advancing and enhancing this harrowing tale at every stage, was a magnificent score composed by Leonard Bernstein and lyricist Stephen Sondheim. The finger-clicking 'Prologue' and 'Jet Song', prefaced tender ballads such as 'Something's Coming' and 'Maria' (Tony), 'Tonight' and 'One Hand, One Heart' (Tony and Maria), and 'Somewhere', as well as the electrifying 'America', in which Bernardo's girl Anita (Chita Rivera) and some of the Shark girls, mock the Puerto Rican obsession with the USA, and cynically contrast the immigrants' expectations, with the reality of their new homeland. Even the innocent Maria's 'I Feel Pretty' is tempered by the jokey warning remarks of her friends, while the Jets lampoon their own anti-social behaviour - as well as various shrinks and social workers - in the hilarious 'Gee, Officer Krupke'. 'A Boy Like That', Anita's bitter question of Maria after she protects Tony, even though he murdered Bernardo, is answered simply with the poignant 'I Have A Love'. By the time lyricist Stephen Sondheim came on board, Bernstein had already written the words to some of those songs, but during the subsequent creative process, his lyrical contribution gradually became so minor that he gave Sondheim full credit. *West Side Story* received almost 100% favourable reviews, and ran for 732 performances on Broadway, before touring, and returning to New York in 1960 for a further 249 performances. The costumes for

Broadway were by Irene Sharaff, and there were Tony Awards for director/choreographer Jerome Robbins, and Oliver Smith's now-famous fire escape sets. Robbins' co-choreographer was Peter Gennaro. Robbins was in charge again when *West Side Story* made its London debut on 12 December 1958 at Her Majesty's Theatre. Chita Rivera and Ken LeRoy reprised their roles, along with Marlys Watters (Maria), Don McKay (Tony), and George Chakiris (Riff). There were major New York revivals in 1968 at the State (89 performances, with Kurt Peterson as Tony, Victoria Mallory as Maria, and Barbara Luna as Anita), and 1980, 333 performances, Ken Marshall, Jossie de Guzman, Debbie Allen). West End audiences saw the show again in 1974 (Lionel Morton, Petra Siniawski, Christina Matthews, Roger Finch, Paul Hart), 1984 (Richard A. Pettyfer (Riff), Steven Pacey (Tony), Sam Williams (Bernardo), Jan Hartley (Maria), Lee Robinson (Anita), and 1998 (David Habbin (Tony), Katie Knight-Adams (Maria), Anna-Jane Casey (Anita), Edward Baker-Duly (Riff), and Graham MacDuff (Bernardo). The latter production was supervised by Arthur Laurents, Jerome Robbins having died some three months before it opened. Leonard Bernstein conducted the original full-length score for the first time in 1984 in a recording with opera stars Kiri Te Kanawa and José Carreras. The event, which was filmed and televised, ensured the album's substantial sales. Numerous other cast albums have been issued, and in 1996 RCA Victor released *The Songs Of West Side Story*, which was inspired by a 1992 AIDS Project Los Angeles benefit concert. Produced by David Pack, leader of the rock group Ambrosia, it featured many pop and country recording artists such as Kenny Loggins, Wynonna, Trisha Yearwood, Aretha Franklin, Phil Collins, Natalie Cole, Selena, and Patti LaBelle. The show has also spawned many hit singles in radically different interpretations from artists such as P.J. Proby ('Somewhere' and 'Maria') and the Nice ('America'). In 1997 it became the first Western musical to be licensed to China.

WHAT A CRAZY WORLD

This 1963 feature was adapted from a stage production at the Stratford Theatre Royal, London. The film cast pop singer Joe Brown as a chirpy cockney who, having taken a job at a music publisher, writes a hit song. Actor Harry H. Corbett played Brown's father, vocalist Susan Maughan his sister, in an East End family sociologists might describe as dysfunctional. Although far from a milestone, *What A Crazy World* is saved from ignominy by Brown's perky performance and Marty Wilde's role as 'quick-to-fists' heavy. Freddie And The Dreamers were among the other pop acts on offer and Brown enjoyed a minor UK hit single with the title song. *What A Crazy World* also included 'Layabout's Lament', 'Bruvvers' and 'Wasn't That A Handsome Punch-Up', suggesting a somewhat one-dimensional view of life in London's tower blocks. Rather more Stanley Holloway than Lennon/McCartney, the film was eclipsed upon release by the changed face of British pop.

WHAT LOLA WANTS

(see *Damn Yankees*)

WHAT MAKES SAMMY RUN?

Many years before director Robert Altman took the lid off the Hollywood screenwriters' power game in his 1992 film *The Player*, this show, with its theme of greed and corruption in the movie business, opened at the 54th Street Theatre in New York on 27 February 1964. Budd and Stuart Schulberg's libretto was based on the former's novel, and told of the all-time, first class American heel - Sammy Glick (Steve Lawrence). By consistently stealing his colleagues' ideas and projects, (particularly those of his friend Al Manheim (Robert Alda), Glick graduates from his job as a copy boy on the New York *Record* to a position as a screenwriter at World Wide Pictures in Hollywood (he comes up with a vehicle for the studio's latest star, entitled *Monsoon*, having lifted the plot from the 1932 classic *Rain*!). Regarded as the studio's new genius, he becomes first a producer, and then, eventually, head of the studio. The price he has had to pay is the loss of a good woman, a fellow-writer from his early days, Kit Sargent (Sally Ann Howes), the burden of an unfaithful nympho-maniac wife, Laurette Harrington (Bernice Massi), and the suicide of Sidney Fineman (Arny Freeman), his mentor at the studio. Surely he must feel guilty about that? Not Sammy, he just keeps on running. Ervin Drake's score contained no hits for the popular singer Steve Lawrence to make his own, but 'A Room Without Windows' and 'My Home Town' did achieve some modest popularity. The rest of the numbers included 'The Friendliest Thing', 'A Tender Spot', 'Something To Live For', 'A New Pair Of Shoes', 'Lights! Camera! Platitude!', 'Maybe Some Other Time', 'You Can Trust Me', 'Kiss Me No Kisses', 'I Feel Humble', and 'Some Days Everything Goes Wrong'. Abe Burrows directed what became a popular attraction, with a run decent of 540 performances. Steve Lawrence made one other appearance in a Broadway book musical when he starred with his wife Eydie Gormé in *Golden Rainbow* (1968), which was based on Arnold Schulmans' play *A Hole In The Head*, and ran for nearly a year.

WHAT'S UP TIGER LILY

This 1966 curio was nominally directed by Woody Allen, at that point better known as a stand-up nightclub comedian and script writer for Sid Ceasar. Allen took and already-printed Japanese film *Kizino Mini* and overdubbed it with dialogue suggested by the scenes, rather than use a literal translation. The sub-James Bond plot inspired moments of mirth, but in truth the idea outstripped the final result which was not a box-office success. John Sebastian, leader of the Lovin' Spoonful was recruited to provide soundtrack music. At that point the group was one of the hottest US groups, scoring international success with 'Daydream' and 'Summer In The City'. The Spoonful not only completed a *What's Up Tiger Lily* album, but also appeared briefly in the film, playing. Sebastian quickly showed dis-satisfaction with the project - 'The best bits were left on the cutting room floor,' he ruefully recalled. Allen, of course, went on to become one of the world's most renowned film directors. *What's Up Tiger Lily* remains an unusual part of his métier and has become an often-forgotten portion of the Lovin' Spoonful's back catalogue. The experience, however, led to Sebastian's involvement in the much more worthwhile Francis Ford Coppola venture, *You're A Big Boy Now*.

WHERE THE BOYS ARE

This 1960 feature provided Connie Francis with her first film role. She played one of a group of boy and girl students on holiday in Fort Lauderdale, Texas. Neither a sex comedy nor a satisfying teen-orientated film, *Where The Boys Are* can be described, charitably, as naive. Its insouciant qualities have not worn well, although the portrayal of males and females in such close proximity did cause a minor furore upon release. Frank Gorshin, Paula Prentiss, George Hamilton and Yvette Mimieux co-starred alongside Francis, who scored an international hit with the Neil Sedaka-penned title song.

WHERE'S CHARLEY?

Frank Loesser's first Broadway book musical was based on the much-loved English farce, *Charley's Aunt*, by Brandon Thomas, which was first performed in London in 1892. *Where's Charley?* opened at the St. James Theatre in New York on 11 October 1948 with a book by George Abbott which was set at Oxford University in England. Undergraduates Jack Chesney (Byron Palmer) and Charley Wykeham (Ray Bolger) have invited two young ladies, Amy Spettigue (Allyn Ann McLerie) and Kitty Verdun (Doretta Morrow), to lunch, on the understanding that they are to be chaperoned by Charley's rich widowed Aunt Donna Lucia D'Alvadorez. Her train is late, so Charley, who is appearing in drag in the University show, substitutes for her, and sparks off a sequence of hilarious events which ends with Charley being found out when his skirt falls down, and the real Aunt Donna marrying Jack's impoverished father, Sir Francis Chesney (Paul England). Ray Bolger was outstanding, and his version of the show's hit song, 'Once In Love With Amy', is one of the golden moments in the history of the musical theatre. Loesser's score also contained another number which attained some popularity, 'My Darling, My Darling', along with other equally engaging items such as the rousing 'New Ashmolean Marching Society And Students' Conservatory Band', 'Make A Miracle', 'Lovelier Than Ever', 'The Woman In His Room', and 'At The Red Rose Cotillion'. *Where's Charley* was a charming, thoroughly likeable show, and audiences continued to flock to see it for 792 performances. After touring on the road in the USA, it was revived briefly on Broadway, with Bolger, in 1951. He also starred in the 1952 movie version. In 1991 Loesser's wife, Jo Sullivan, and their daughter Emily Loesser, were in an acclaimed production of the show which was presented at the North Shore Music Theatre in Massachusetts. Although Bolger's distinctive recording of 'Once In Love With Amy' has turned up on many records over the years, and was virtually copied word for word by Barry Manilow on his 1991 album *Showstoppers*, no full-length recording of the original Broadway cast of *Where's Charley?* was issued. However, an album was released from the 1958 London production, which starred Norman Wisdom, and ran for 380 performances. In 1993 it was reissued on CD - in stereo for the first time.

WHICH WITCH

Billed as the 'Norwegian Operamusical', *Which Witch* was originally commissioned as a concert piece for the Bergen International Festival in May 1987. While in that form it toured Scandinavia, North America, and Europe and was the subject of a best-selling album, before being transformed into the full-blown musical which opened at the Piccadilly Theatre in London on 22 October 1992. The show was the brainchild of Benedicte Adrian and Ingrid Bjornov, members of the highly successful Norwegian pop group, Dollie Deluxe. They composed the music together, and Adrian, a coloratura soprano, played the leading role while Bjornov served as musical director. The librettist and director was Piers Haggard, and the lyrics were written by Kit Hesketh-Harvey, one half of the satirical comedy team of Kit And The Widow. The 'historically authenticated' 16th century story concerns an Italian girl, Maria Vittoria (Adrian), who spurns an arranged marriage to the German banker Anton Fugger (Stig Rosen), and declares her love for the Catholic Bishop Daniel (Graham Bickley). However, his sister, Anna Regina (Vivien Parry), spreads the word that Maria is a witch and she is burned at the stake. Audiences were taken aback by some of the special effects - one scene included 'several male demons with flapping genitals exposed - rutting with witches'. The score, 'a pastiche of 19th century composers', contained in excess of 30 numbers, including items such as 'The Blessing', 'Bad Omens', 'Maria's Curse', 'Black Mass', 'The Exorcism', and 'Almighty God'. One song which caught the attention was entitled '2,665,866,746,664 Little Devils'. The show was savaged by the critics in 'some of the worst reviews since Pearl Harbour'. Scandinavian package tours supplemented the few local patrons for a time, and King Harald and Queen Sonja of Norway visited the 'most heavily-panned London stage musical in a generation', but, after a run of 10 weeks, *Which Witch* was withdrawn with losses estimated at around £2 million. Theatre watchers were quick to point out that other recent 'disasters' at the Piccadilly Theatre had included *Moby Dick*, *King*, and *Metropolis*.

WHISTLE DOWN THE WIND

Based on the original novel by Mary Hayley Bell, and the film starring Hayley Mills and Alan Bates, this musical was originally intended for the screen rather than the stage. The change followed an acclaimed preview performance in July 1995 at Andrew Lloyd Webber's annual Sydmonton summer festival. *Whistle Down The Wind* subsequently had its world premiere at the National Theatre, Washington, DC, on 12 December 1996. Patricia Knop's book shifted the location from England's Lancashire Dales to a small, late 50s Louisiana town deep in America's southern bible-belt, but retained the basic storyline of three children led by Swallow (Irene Molloy), who, with her brother Poor Baby (Cameron Bowen) and sister Brat (Abbi Hutcherson), discover an escaped killer in a barn, and presume he is Jesus Christ. Davis (*The Phantom Of The Opera*) Gaines played The Man/Jesus; also prominent were Steve Scott Springer (Amos), Lacey Hornkohl (Candy), Ray Walker (the Preacher), Mike Hartman

(Sheriff Cookridge) and Candy Buckley (Aunt Dot). Lloyd Webber's 'pleasing' score, with lyrics by Jim Steinman, included the opening 'Vaults Of Heaven', 'Safe Haven', 'Tire Tracks And Broken Hearts' (Candy, Amos), 'Wrestle With The Devil' (Preacher, Aunt Dot, Congregation), the ever-present 'When Children Rule The World', and the title song. Joey McKneely was responsible for the choreography, and director Harold Prince reunited with Lloyd Webber for the first time since *The Phantom Of The Opera*. Following a lukewarm critical reception ('a tuneless whistle') during the limited Washington run, Whistle *Down The Wind* was set for Broadway in April, then June, and eventually postponed indefinitely.

As is usual when a musical fails to achieve its potential, the book was blamed, so by the time this 'shaken, stirred, and refried - 80 per cent different' show arrived at London's Adelphi Theatre on 1 July 1998, original librettist Patricia Knop was credited with two collaborators - Gale Edwards and Lloyd Webber. Edwards also directed this £6 million production, which boasted five new songs. In addition to the aforementioned highlights, the refreshed score, which contained 'influences of hymns and emotive gospel, through rock 'n' roll and wistful ballads', now consisted of 'I Never Get What I Pray For', 'Home By Now', 'It Just Doesn't Get Any Better Than This', 'The Vow', 'Cold', 'Unsettled Scores', 'If Only', 'Long Overdue For A Miracle', 'Annie Christmas', 'No Matter What', 'Try Not To Be Afraid', 'A Kiss Is A Terrible Thing To Waste', 'Charlie Christmas', 'Off Ramp Exit To Paradise', 'The Hunt' and 'Nature Of The Beast'. Marcus Lovett (The Man) and Lottie Mayor (Swallow) led the cast, which also featured Dean Collinson (Arnos), Veronica Hart (Candy), James Graeme (Boone), John Turner (Sheriff), and Walter Reynolds (Edward). The 'lamentable' choreography was the work of Anthony Van Laast. This 'over-manipulative production, with its revivalist meeting live snakes, adventurous mix of Christian faith, mortality and racism', was played out on Peter J. Davison's 'striking two-tier set'. In particular, general opinion seemed to be that the tricky situation of Swallow's burgeoning sexuality in her relationship with The Man, was not satisfactorily handled by the authors. Reviews varied from 'an intensely strong evening of musical theatre', via 'so much piffle down the wind', to 'Lloyd Webber has mugged an innocent film'. Among the first recordings of the songs were 'When Children Rule The World' by the Red Hill Children, Tina Arena's version of the title song, and Boyzone's UK chart-topping 'No Matter What'.

Some years earlier, Lloyd Webber had been intrigued by a production of *Whistle Down The Wind* performed by the National Youth Theatre at the 1993 Edinburgh Festival, and later in the year at the Lilian Baylis Theatre in London. As the NYT's sponsor, he brought it to the attention of various producers, most of whom considered it 'too English'. The superb 1961 screenplay, with its 'touching evocation of childhood innocence and adult mendacity' was largely retained by composer Richard Taylor and his co-adaptor and lyricist Russell Labey. A well-regarded English professional production of their work subsequently took place at the Everyman Theatre, Cheltenham, in 1997.

WHITE CHRISTMAS

With this title, the score for this musical just had to be written by Irving Berlin, and a good score it was too. The problem with this film, which was released by Paramount in 1954, lay with the screenplay. It required three men, Norman Krasna, Norman Panama and Melvin Frank, to devise the story about Bob (Captain) Wallace (Bing Crosby) and Phil (Private First Class) Davis (Danny Kaye), who leave the US Army at the end of World War II and form a successful song-and-dance act, which eventually leads to them producing their own shows. After meeting with the Haynes Sisters singing duo (Rosemary Clooney and Vera-Ellen), the quartet end up at a Vermont holiday resort run by the ex-GIs' former (and much-respected) commanding officer (Dean Jagger). Business is bad owing to the lack of snow, but everything turns out fine when Wallace and Davis organize a benefit show, which - surprise, surprise - ends with the much-needed flakes drifting down while everyone sings 'White Christmas', and Crosby and Kaye are melting into the arms of Clooney and Vera-Ellen, respectively. Irving Berlin 'borrowed' the song from the 1942 Crosby-Fred Astaire film *Holiday Inn*, which was similar in many ways to *White Christmas*. The rest of the songs were a mixture of old and new. One of the most appealing was 'Sisters', in which Crosby and Kaye, waving feather boas and with their trousers rolled up to the knees, parody a typical Haynes Sisters routine. The remainder included 'The Best Things Happen While You're Dancing', 'The Old Man', 'Gee, I Wish I Was Back In The Army', 'Count Your Blessings Instead Of Sheep', 'Love, You Didn't Do Right By Me', 'Blue Skies', 'Choreography', 'Snow', 'What Can You Do With A General', 'I'd Rather See A Minstrel Show' and 'Mandy'. Also in the cast were Mary Wickes, John Brascia, Anne Whitfield, Grady Sutton, Sig Ruman, and the 21-year-old dancer George Chakiris. The dances and musical numbers were staged by Robert Alton and the film was nicely photographed in Technicolor and VistaVision by Loyal Griggs. The director was Michael Curtiz. *White Christmas* proved to be a tremendous box-office success, becoming one of the Top 20 films of the 50s in the USA, and the fifth highest-grossing musical.

WHITE, GEORGE

b. George Wietz, 1890, New York, USA, d. 11 October 1968, Hollywood, California, USA. A producer, director, author, dancer, and actor, White's first taste of show business came in his teens when he formed a burlesque dancing team with Ben (or Benny) Ryan. Later, he had generally modest solo roles in shows such as *The Echo* (1910), *Ziegfeld Follies*, *The Whirl Of Society*, *The Pleasure Seekers*, *The Midnight Girl*, and *Miss 1917* which had music mainly by the young Jerome Kern. In 1919, he produced and directed the first of a series of revues, *George White's Scandals*, which combined the best of America's own burgeoning popular music (as opposed to the imported European variety) with fast-moving sketches and glamorous women. The shows were similar to, although perhaps not quite so lavish, as the undisputed leader of the genre, the *Ziegfeld Follies*. The *Scandals* appeared annually until 1926, and that edition, the longest runner of them all with 424 performances, was particularly notable for its score by De Sylva, Brown And Henderson, which introduced several enduring numbers such as 'Lucky Day', 'Black Bottom', and 'Birth Of The Blues'. There was no *George White Scandals* in 1927, but there was a show *about* the *Scandals* entitled *Manhattan Mary*, which ran for a decent 264 peformances. White produced it and also co-write the book with Billy K. Wells. It too, had songs by De Sylva, Brown And Henderson, which included 'The Five-Step' and 'It Won't Be Long Now', and starred White himself and the highly popular zany comedian Ed Wynn. The *Scandals* proper resumed in 1928, and there were further editions in 1929 and 1931. In the latter show, the future movie star, Alice Faye, appeared in the chorus, and this time the songs were by Lew Brown and Ray Henderson (De Sylva had gone to work in Hollywood). Ethel Merman introduced the lovely 'Life Is Just A Bowl Of Cherries' and 'Ladies And Gentlemen, That's Love', as well as duetting with Rudy Vallee on 'My Song'. Vallee also sang 'The Thrill Is Gone' (with Everett Marshall) and 'This Is The Missus' (with Peggy Moseley). *George White's Music Hall Varieties* replaced the *Scandals* in 1932, and in the cast was another Hollywood star of the future, tap-dancer supreme Eleanor Powell, and the likeable song-and dance man (among other things) Harry Richman, who introduced Herman Hupfield's delightful ballad, 'Let's Put Out The Lights And Go To Sleep'. There were two more stage presentations of *George White's Scandals* - in 1936 and 1939 - but fashions had changed, and they only ran for just over 100 performances each. *George White's Scandals* of 1934, 1935, and 1945 were filmed, and the first two launched Alice Faye on her way to a glittering movie career. Over the years, the stage productions and the films showcased some of America's most talented artists, such as Bert Lahr, Gracie Barrie, Cliff Edwards, Willie and Eugene Howard, Ann Miller, Ray Middleton, Ella Logan, Ann Pennington, Lou Holtz, W.C Fields, Dolores Costello, Ray Bolger, and Ethel Barrymore. Other songwriters involved included Irving Caesar, George Gershwin (five scores), Jack Yellen, Harold Arlen, Sammy Stept, and Herb Magidson.

WHITING, RICHARD

b. 12 November 1891, Peoria, Illinois, USA, d. 19 February 1938, Beverly Hills, California, USA. A self-taught pianist with no formal tuition in composition, Whiting wrote his first songs in the years before World War I. Among them was 'It's Tulip Time In Holland', a very popular number which Whiting exchanged the rights to for a new piano. During the war years Whiting wrote several successful songs, some of which capitalized on the current vogue for minstrel-type music. These included 'Where The Black-Eyed Susans Grow' (lyric by David Darford), 'Mammy's Little Coal Black Rose' (Raymond Egan) and 'Where The Morning Glories Grow' (Gus Kahn). Whiting and Egan also collaborated on 'Till We Meet Again' which was an immensely popular hit, coming as it did in 1918, the final year of the war. In the post-war years, Whiting had further successes with 'The Japanese Sandman' (Egan), 'Ain't We Got Fun?' (Egan-Kahn), 'Sleepy Time Gal' (Egan-Joseph B. Alden), 'Ukelele Lady' (Kahn), 'Breezin' Along With The Breeze' and 'Honey' (both with Haven Gillespie-Seymour

Simons). He also collaborated on both the music and lyric, with Neil Moret, for the beautiful (and successful) 'She's Funny that Way' (1928). Towards the end of the 20s Whiting went to Hollywood, and for the next decade wrote for films such as *Close Harmony*, *The Dance Of Life*, *Innocents Of Paris*, *Monte Carlo*, *Paramount On Parade*, *Safety In Numbers*, *My Weakness*, *Bottoms Up*, *Bright Eyes*, *Transatlantic Merry-Go-Round*, *Big Broadcast Of 1936*, *Rhythm On The Range*, *Sing, Baby, Sing*, *Ready, Willing And Able*, *Hollywood Hotel*, and *Cowboy From Brooklyn* (1938). From these came numerous songs such as 'Louise', 'My Ideal', 'I Can't Escape From You' (all with Leo Robin), 'Too Marvellous For Words' (with Johnny Mercer), 'Beyond The Blue Horizon' (Robin-additional music W. Frank Harling), 'On The Good Ship Lollipop' (Sidney Clare), 'Miss Brown To You' (Robin-additional music Ralph Rainger) and 'Hooray For Hollywood' and 'Have You Got Any Castles, Baby?' (both Mercer). Prior to 1920, Whiting had dabbled unsuccessfully on Broadway with shows such as *Robinson Crusoe Jr.*, *Toot Sweet*, *A Lonely Romeo*, and *George White's Scandals Of 1919*. In 1931 he tried again with *Free For All*, which was another failure, but in the following year he was moderately successful with *Take A Chance* in which Ethel Merman introduced his 'Eadie Was A Lady' (lyrics Buddy De Sylva, additional music Nacio Herb Brown). Merman and Jack Haley also duetted on one of the songwriters' future standards, 'You're An Old Smoothie'. Since Whiting died in February 1938 at the age of only 46, his daughter, the classy singer Margaret Whiting, has continued to include some of the best of his work on her records, and in her concert and cabaret performances - even into the 90s. Whiting's younger daughter, Barbara, is a lively, vivacious actress and singer, who gave a particularly engaging performance in the Esther Williams film musical *Dangerous When Wet*.

WHO'S TOMMY, THE

The Who made rock 'n' roll history in 1969 when they released the album of *Tommy*, a rock opera containing a medley of songs telling the story of a young boy, who is struck deaf, dumb and blind when his war-hero father is murdered by his mother's lover, and then goes on to become a wizard of the pinball machines. It was filmed in 1975 by the flamboyant director Ken Russell, and several live concert versions were presented during the 70s. Pete Townshend, its principal composer, refused to participate in the 1979 West End stage production which ran at the Queen's Theatre for 118 performances. Fourteen years later, *The Who's Tommy* became the surprise hit of the Broadway season when it opened at the St. James Theatre in New York on 22 April 1993 to ecstatic reviews. Townshend collaborated with director Des McAnuff on a revised book, which up-dated the story to World War II, and the role of the grown Tommy, so often played by Roger Daltrey, was taken this time by Michael Cerveris, with Marcia Mitzman (Mrs. Walker), Jonathan Dokuchitz (Captain Walker), Paul Kandel (Uncle Ernie), and Anthony Barrile (Cousin Kevin) The by now familiar score was enhanced by a staggering array of psychedelic lighting and audio effects, kaleidoscopic projections, and banks of videos screens, with at one point, during 'Pinball

Wizard', the whole theatre itself being transformed into a huge, glittering pinball machine. One stunning scene, in which several paratroopers descend into an aircraft cockpit, equals the *Miss Saigon* helicopter sequence, and made sense of the US television ads for the show which claimed that it 'stimulates senses you never knew you had'. Naturally enough all this glitz was noted by the Tony Awards committee, and *The Who's Tommy* won outright for director, scenic design (John Arnone), choreography (Wayne Cilento), and lighting design (Chris Parry), and tied with *Kiss Of The Spider Woman* for best score. General opinion seemed to be that the show was 'going to pack them in for some time, as for sheer rock 'n' roll fun *Tommy* is hard to beat'. That sentiment was borne out when a scaled-down production 'broke all previous records' on the US national tour in late 1993/4, with former MTV DJ Steve Isaacs in the title role. However, the Broadway production closed on 17 June 1995 after 899 performances. The much-hyped London version burst into the Shaftesbury Theatre on 5 March 1996, with 19-year-old newcomer Paul Keating as Tommy, pop star Kim Wilde (Mrs. Walker), Alistair Robins (Captain Walker), Hal Fowler (Cousin Kevin), Ian Bartholomew (Uncle Ernie), and Nicola Hughes (the Acid Queen). Mixed reviews, ranging from 'Deaf, dumb and blind kid is a wizard' . . . to 'No sense, no feeling in this piece of Tommy-rot', boded ill, and the show, re-titled *Tommy* in London, failed to run for a year, closing on 8 February 1997. About a week later, it scored a hat trick at the Laurence Olivier Awards, winning for Outstanding Musical Production, best director (McAnuff) and lighting (Parry).

● FURTHER READING: *The Who's Tommy: The Musical*, Pete Townshend.

WHOOPEE! (FILM MUSICAL)

Eddie Cantor recreated his original role in this screen version of the Broadway hit, *Whoopee!* ('A Musical Comedy Of The Great Wide West'), when it was released by United Artists in 1930. In William Conselman's screenplay, which was adapted from a story by Anthony McGuire and Owen Davis' play, *The Nervous Wreck*, Cantor played a manic hypochondriac who lands up on an Arizona ranch where he reveals his depression via lines such as 'Last week I bought a suit with two pair of pants - and burned a hole in the coat!' Nothing depressing about the songs though, even if most of the Broadway originals were not retained. Among the survivors were Walter Donaldson and Gus Kahn's highly amusing title number and 'The Song Of The Setting Sun'. Donaldson and Kahn also wrote several songs especially for the film, including 'Stetson', the 'poignant' 'A Girl Friend Of A Boyfriend Of Mine', and the enduring 'My Baby Just Cares For Me'. Also in the cast were Eleanor Hunt, Ethel Shutta, Paul Gregory, John Rutherford, Spencer Charters, and Betty Grable in only her third film. The dances and ensembles were staged by Busby Berkeley, who was making his screen debut. His innovative style was immediately established in the opening number in which an overhead camera displayed more than 60 cowboys and girls weaving a series of intricate patterns. *Whoopee!*, which made Eddie Cantor a box-office star and proved to be one of his biggest hits, was pho-

tographed in 'All Technicolor' (two colour Technicolor, actually), produced by Samuel Goldwyn and Florenz Ziegfeld, and directed by Thorton Freeland.

WHOOPEE! (STAGE MUSICAL)

This lavish Florenz Ziegfeld production, which was a vehicle for the zany talents of the energetic 'eye-popping' comedian Eddie Cantor, opened at the New Amsterdam Theatre in New York on 4 December 1948. It had a score by Walter Donaldson (music) and Gus Kahn (lyrics), two writers who were more at home in Tin Pan Alley than on Broadway. True to form, two of the their songs for this show became huge all-time hits. William Anthony McGuire's book, which was based on Owen Davis' 1923 play, *The Nervous Wreck*, concerns Henry Williams (Cantor), a timid hypochondriac, who has been sent to a health farm in California. He helps the lovely Sally Morgan (Frances Upton) to escape from the amorous clutches of the local Sheriff Bob Wells (Jack Rutherford). They take refuge in the local Indian reservation, the home of Sally's heart's desire, Wanenis (Paul Gregory), who, in the end, turns out to be as milky-white as she is. The situation gave Cantor a good excuse to wear his trade-mark blackface for a time, and race around like a man possessed. He also introduced 'Makin' Whoopee', with its salutary lesson on life and love: 'Picture a little love nest, down where the roses cling/Picture that same sweet love nest, think what a year can bring/He's washing dishes, and baby clothes/He's so ambitious, he even sews/But don't forget folks, that's what you get folks/For makin' whoopee'. The other enduring number in the show, 'Love Me Or Leave Me', was sung by Ruth Etting. It became forever associated with her, and titled the 1955 film biography in which she was portrayed by Doris Day. The rest of the score included 'I'm Bringing You A Red, Red Rose', which also became popular through Etting's recording, and 'Come West, Little Girl, Come West', 'Until You Get Somebody Else', 'The Song Of The Setting Sun', 'Here's To The Girl Of My Heart!', and 'Gypsy Joe'. Buddy Ebsen, the lanky dancer who seemed able to twist his body into every conceivable shape, made his Broadway debut in this show, and George Olsen's Orchestra, purveyors of the sweetest sounds around, were also on board for most of the time, except for a couple of months when it was replaced by Paul Whiteman and his men. Ziegfeld's glamour and Cantor's antics ensured that *Whoopee* had a decent run of 379 performances, and the comedian also starred in the 1930 film version. The show was revived on Broadway in 1979 with Charles Repole, and stayed around for nearly six months.

WILCOX, HERBERT

b. Herbert Sydney Wilcox, 19 April 1892, Cork, Eire, d. 15 May 1977, London, England. A distinguished producer and director, who was one of the leading figures in the British film industry from the 20s through to the 50s. The date and place of birth given here are those usually accepted, but other sources have suggested that Wilcox was born in Norwood, South London, in 1890. However, it is generally agreed that he went to school in Brighton and appeared as a chorus boy in one of the local theatres.

Then he worked as a journalist for a time before serving as a pilot in the Royal Flying Corps during World War I. After becoming an invalid and leaving the forces, he entered the film business in 1919, and produced his first picture, *The Wonderful Story*, in 1922. He had a hit in the following year with a silent version of *Chu Chu Chow*, and from then on produced and/or directed (and occasionally wrote the screenplays) for a string of highly successful pictures. Among the comedies, dramas, and historical features, many of which starred his wife, Anna Neagle (they married in 1943), were several musicals. These included *Say It With Music* (1932), *Yes, Mr. Brown, Goodnight Vienna*, (USA: *Magic Night*), *Bitter Sweet, Limelight* (USA: *Backstage*), *This'll Make You Whistle*, and *London Melody* (USA: *Girls In The Street*) (1937). In 1939 Wilcox went to Hollywood to produce and direct several films. Included among them were the screen adaptations of three famous Broadway musicals: *Irene, No, No, Nanette*, and *Sunny*. Anna Neagle played the lead in each of the trio.

On returning to Britain, she co-starred with Michael Wilding in Wilcox's celebrated 'London' films: *Piccadilly Incident, The Courtneys Of Curzon Street* (USA: *The Courtney Affair*), *Spring In Park Lane*, and *Maytime In Mayfair* (1950). These were enormously popular romantic comedies, containing just the occasional song. During the rest of the 50s, as well as making other acclaimed dramatic movies such as *Odette*, Wilcox worked on British musicals such as *Lilacs In The Spring* (USA: *Let's Make Up*), *King's Rhapsody, The Lady Is A Square*, and *The Heart Of A Man*. The latter was his final film. Changes in public taste, several box office flops, unwise financial investments, and the advent of commercial television in Britain, are just some of the reasons given for Wilcox's subsequent financial decline which culminated in his much-publicized bankruptcy in 1964. He was discharged two years later, and, a year after that, his wife opened in the long-running musical comedy *Charlie Girl*, which was resident at the Adelphi Theatre in London for almost five and a half years. Wilcox is said to have suggested (uncredited) ideas for some of the songs, but otherwise he remained in retirement until his death in 1977. During his long career, he won numerous national and international awards, including the Gold Cup of All Nations at the Venice Film Festival in 1937. Although not considered an outstanding director, his flair and showmanship as a producer put him in the same league as the Hollywood greats.

● FURTHER READING: *Twenty-Five Thousand Sunsets* (his autobiography).

WILD ANGELS, THE

'The Most Terrifying Film Of Our Time . . . Their Credo Is Violence . . . Their God Is Hate. And They Call Themselves The Wild Angels.' These and other 'shocking' by-lines were employed to promote this 1966 feature, directed by low-budget cult figure, Roger Corman. Banned in the UK and subject to censorship in the USA, *The Wild Angels* is a genre classic, combining Corman's B-picture standards with Californian biker lore. Peter Fonda starred as the leader of a Hell's Angels-styled gang, organised on ritualistic, neo-Nazi lines. His character was called Heavenly Blues which inspired one of the film's musical interludes, 'Blues' Theme'. This piece was also recorded by garage band Chocolate Watchband under the pseudonym, the Hogs. Bruce Dern and Michael J. Pollard were among the supporting cast, alongside Nancy Sinatra, who expanded the tough image invoked by her concurrent hit single, 'These Boots Are Made For Walking'. Although Corman was essentially a moralist - the 'evil' in his films were generally punished - *The Wild Angels* brought to an end the style and content of a previous generation of exploitative movies. The frothy 'beach movies' of Annette (Funicello) were made passé thanks to this view of the darker side of Californian subculture. Instead a host of outlaw chic features followed, notably *Hell's Angels On Wheels* and *Born Losers*. Fonda himself used the outsider notion, but with more telling effect, on the innovative *Easy Rider. The Wild Angels* boasted an excellent soundtrack, written by Mike Curb, later president of MGM Records and a political figure with right-wing sympathies. Performed by protégés Davie Allen And The Arrows, the music combines Link Wray-influenced guitar work with emergent psychedelia, encapsulating perfectly the mood of this memorable film.

WILD IN THE COUNTRY

Although not on a par with *Jailhouse Rock* or *King Creole*, this 1961 feature is one of Elvis Presley's better films. He portrays an unsettled teenager, rescued from potential delinquency by the attentions of his social worker, his psychiatrist and his girl-friend, played respectively by Hope Lange, Millie Perkins and Tuesday Weld. Based on *The Lonely Country*, a novel by J.R. Salamanca, *Wild In The Country* was bolstered by an excellent screenplay by veteran Clifford Odet who provided worthwhile scenes in which the cast could flourish. Five songs were recorded for the soundtrack, two of which, 'Lonely Man' and the title song, were relegated to the respective b-sides of 'Surrender' and 'I Feel So Bad'. The remainder appeared on subsequent albums; the notion of issuing soundtracks as promotional items had not yet been established in Presley's career.

WILD PARTY, THE

Football players, drop-outs, petty criminals and jazz musicians team up in an unlikely Hollywood farrago made in 1956 and directed by Harry Horner and starring Anthony Quinn and Nehemiah Persoff. Jazz, on-screen and off, is provided by a host of talented studio-cum-jazz musicians. Amongst them are Georgie Auld, Teddy Buckner, Pete Candoli, Bob Cooper, Buddy De Franco, Maynard Ferguson, Frank Rosolino, Bud Shank and Alvin Stoller. Persoff's on-screen piano playing was dubbed by Pete Jolly.

WILD ROSE

(see *Sally*)

WILL ROGERS FOLLIES, THE

Broadway veterans Cy Coleman (music) and Betty Comden and Adolph Green (book and lyrics) created this big, glitzy show which was sub-titled 'A Life In Revue'. It was summed up neatly by one critic thus: 'The time is the present, and Gregory Peck's recorded voice as impresario Florenz Ziegfeld instructs the theatrically resurrected Rogers, 16 showgirls, 16 other actors, and six dogs, on how to stage the life story of America's favourite humorist in the style of the *Ziegfeld Follies*.' *The Will Rogers Follies* opened at the Palace Theatre in New York on 1 May 1991, with television and film actor Keith Carradine in the central role of the folksy philosopher Rogers. He was surrounded by a production which was guaranteed to dazzle due to the presence of the master of flash and panache, director and choreographer Tommy Tune. Just a few of the evening's highlights featured a chorus line of girls dressed as steers, a pink powder-puff ballet, and an amazing stagewide staircase which changed colours throughout. With appearances in the real *Ziegfeld Follies*, and his celebrated newspaper columns and radio programmes, Rogers is generally accepted as being America's first multimedia superstar, but one who despite his fame stayed in touch with the people until his death in an air crash in 1935. Comden and Green attempted to sum up this facet of his character in the lyric of 'Never Met A Man I Didn't Like', the only really memorable number in a score which also included 'Let's Go Flying', 'Will-A-Mania', 'Give A Man Enough Rope', 'My Big Mistake', 'No Man Left For Me', and 'Without You'. Singer-songwriter Mac Davies and Larry Gatlin were two of the replacements for Carradine during the show's highly successful run of 1,420 performances. Just before it closed in September 1993, old-stager Mickey Rooney played the role of Rogers' father, Clem, for a time. The show won a Grammy for best original cast album, along with Drama Desk and Drama Critics Awards, and Tonys for best musical, score, director, choreographer, lighting, and costumes. There was some unpleasantness when Tommy Tune was accused of sexism and racism with regard to one of the show's billboards, which displayed three half-naked women, and the fact that the large cast did not contain one non-white performer.

WILLETTS, DAVE

b. 24 June 1952, Birmingham, West Midlands, England. A singer and actor, with a reputation as 'one of the best singing voices in town', Willetts seemed to emerge from nowhere in the 80s to take over leading roles in two blockbusting West End musicals. He had no singing, dancing or acting lessons, and before he was 20, rarely went to the theatre. However, while working during the day as a quality control supervisor for a Midlands firm of engineers, he became involved in local amateur dramatics. His sensitive performance as Charlie in the Charles Strouse musical *Flowers For Algernon*, came to the notice of Bob Hamlyn, artistic director of the Belgrade Theatre, Coventry. Hamlyn cast him in his first professional part, as 'the third flunky from the left', in another Strouse show, *Annie*. By now in his thirties, Willetts began his incredible rise to the top. Director Trevor Nunn put him into the chorus of *Les Misérables* at London's Palace Theatre, and within a year he was understudy for the lead role of Jean Valjean, which he eventually took over in 1986 after Colm Wilkinson left to join the Broadway production. In the following year, when Michael Crawford also departed England for the US premiere of *The Phantom Of Opera*, Willetts succeeded

him at Her Majesty's in the West End's hottest ticket. He subsequently played the Phantom in Manchester, and won the *Evening News* Theatre Award. Since then, apart from his involvement as Major Lee in Petula Clark's ill-fated American Civil War musical, *Someone Like You* (1990), Willetts' career has prospered. Highlights have included appearances at London's premier cabaret space, Pizza On The Park (1991), a return to the London production of *Les Misérables* (1992), and the title role of Jesus in a concert version of *Jesus Christ Superstar* at the Barbican Centre and the subsequent 1993 European tour; he also co-starred with Lorna Luft in the touring concert staging of *The Magical World Of The Musicals* (1995), and took the leading role in an acclaimed Leicester Haymarket production of *Sweeney Todd* (1996). In the same year, Willetts created the title role in a new musical by Tony Rees and Gary Young, *Jekyll*, at the Churchill Theatre, Bromley. Willetts originated leading characters in the UK premieres of *Tycoon* and *Lonely Hearts*, and has also starred in his own UK and international concerts and one-man shows. In 1997, he and Bonnie Langford headed a small cast at London's Jermyn Theatre, in *A Lot Of Living!*, an intimate revue featuring the songs of Charles Strouse. Subsequently, he portrayed Jean Valjean once again, in the 10th Anniversary production of *Les Misérables* in Sydney, Australia. Early in 1999, Willetts was co-starred with Marti Webb in a UK tour of *The Magic Of The Musicals In Concert*.

● ALBUMS: *On And Off Stage* (1990)★★★, *Stages Of Love* (1992)★★, *Timeless* (1995)★★★, and various cast and concept albums.

WILLIAMS, BERT

b. 1877, New Providence, Nassau, Bahamas, d. 5 March 1922. After moving to the USA, Williams worked in vaudeville with moderate success. In 1898 he teamed up with George Walker, and the two song and dance men became a success in New York City in the show *In Dahomey*, and also toured overseas. When Walker died in 1907, Williams continued on his own. In 1913 he met impresario Florenz Ziegfeld, who saw his act at the Lafayette in Harlem and was so impressed that he brought Williams into his *Ziegfeld Follies*. Williams appeared in every *Follies* until 1920, featuring such songs as 'You Ain't So Warm!' and 'Nobody', a number with which he became indelibly identified. Despite his great popularity in these shows, Williams was still subjected to severe racial discrimination; on a mundane if wounding level, he could not buy a drink in the bar of the theatre he helped to fill every night. In March 1922, Williams was onstage at the Shubert-Garrick Theatre in Detroit, in a performance of *Under The Bamboo Tree*, when he collapsed and died as a result of pneumonia.

WILLIAMS, CHARLES

b. Isaac Cozerbreit, 8 May 1893, London, England, d. 7 September 1978, Findon Valley, Worthing, England. Williams was one of Britain's most prolific composers of light music, and he was also responsible for numerous film scores, often uncredited on screen. During his early career as a violinist he led for Sir Landon Ronald, Sir

Thomas Beecham and Sir Edward Elgar. Like many of his contemporaries, he accompanied silent films, and became conductor of the New Gallery Cinema in London's Regent Street. He worked on the first British all-sound movie, Alfred Hitchcock's *Blackmail*, from which followed many commissions as composer or conductor: *The Thirty Nine Steps* (1935), *Kipps* (1941), *The Night Has Eyes* (1942), *The Young Mr Pitt* (1942), *The Way To The Stars* (1945 - assisting Nicholas Brodszky who is reported to have written only four notes of the main theme, leaving the rest to Williams), *The Noose* (1946), *While I Live* (1947) from which came his famous 'Dream Of Olwen', *The Romantic Age* (1949), *Flesh And Blood* - from which came 'Throughout The Years' (1951) and the American film *The Apartment* (1960) which used Williams' 'Jealous Lover' (originally heard in the British film *The Romantic Age*) as the title theme, reaching number 1 in the US charts. In total Williams is reputed to have worked on at least 100 films. London publishers Chappells established their recorded music library in 1942, using Williams as composer and conductor of the Queen's Hall Light Orchestra. These 78s made exclusively for radio, television, newsreel and film use, contain many pieces that were to become familiar as themes, such as 'Devil's Galop' signature tune of *Dick Barton - Special Agent*, 'Girls In Grey' *BBC Television Newsreel*, 'High Adventure' *Friday Night Is Music Night*, 'Majestic Fanfare' *Australian Television News*. In his conducting capacity at Chappells he made the first recordings of works by several composers who were later to achieve fame in their own right, such as Robert Farnon, Sidney Torch, Clive Richardson and Peter Yorke. Williams' first recognition as a composer came in the early 30s for 'The Blue Devils' (which he had actually written in 1929 as 'The Kensington March'), followed in the 40s and 50s by 'Voice Of London', 'Rhythm On Rails', 'The Falcons', 'Heart O' London', 'Model Railway', 'The Music Lesson', 'Dream Of Olwen', 'The Old Clockmaker', 'The Starlings', 'A Quiet Stroll', 'Sleepy Marionette', 'Side Walk' and many more. For EMI's Columbia label, with his own Concert Orchestra (as well as the Queen's Hall Light Orchestra), from 1946 onwards he conducted over 30 78s of popular light and film music.

● ALBUMS: *Charles Williams* (EMI 1993)★★★★, with Tom Teasley *Poetry, Prose, Percussion And Song* (T&T 1998)★★★.

WILLIAMS, ESTHER

b. 8 August 1921 or 1923, Inglewood, Los Angeles, California, USA. One of MGM's top film musicals stars in the 40s and 50s, Esther Williams' mother boasted that her daughter (one of five children) swam before she walked. By the time she was 15, she had won every national swimming competition and was set to represent the USA in the Olympic Games in Finland, but they were cancelled following the outbreak of World War II. She studied for a time at the University of Southern California before joining Billy Rose's Aquacade in San Francisco, in which her co-star was Johnny Weissmuller. While in the show she was spotted by MGM talent scouts, and made her film debut in 1942 as one of Mickey Rooney's girlfriends in *Andy Hardy's Double Life*. She had some swimming scenes in that one, and in *Bathing Beauty* (1944). For *Zeigfeld Follies*

(1946), special water ballets were created for her. Her first starring role came in *Fiesta* (1947), with Richardo Montalban, and this was followed by a string of dazzling Technicolor movies in which her glamorous looks and pleasing personality were permanently on display. These included *This Time For Keeps, On An Island With You, Take Me Out To The Ball Game, Neptune's Daughter, The Duchess Of Idaho, Pagan Love Song, Texas Carnival, Skirts Ahoy!, Million Dollar Mermaid, Dangerous When Wet, Easy To Love,* and *Jupiter's Darling* (1955). With the demise of the big-budget Hollywood musicals she played several straight roles, but her appeal had diminished, and her last picture, *The Magic Fountain*, was released in 1961. While MGM went to great lengths to show-case her superb swimming ability in some of the most lavish and spectacular aqua-sequences ever seen on the screen, and co-starred her with several attractive leading men (including cartoon characters Tom and Jerry), her acting ability was not allowed to develop, and her quite pleasant singing voice was rather neglected. However, she did sing a lovely version of 'The Sea Of The Moon' (Harry Warren-Arthur Freed) in *The Pagan Love Song*, and handled some of Arthur Schwartz and Johnny Mercer's numbers extremely well in *Dangerous When Wet*. She also introduced Frank Loesser's Oscar-winning 'Baby, It's Cold Outside' with Ricardo Montalban in *Neptune's Daughter*. In 1962 she stopped making films, and went - as she herself put it - from 'show business into business business'. Initially this concerned commercial swimming pools, but two husbands later - actor Fernando Lamas, and Edward Bell, whom she met at the 1984 Olympics - it had evolved into swimsuits. In a big way.

● FILMS: *Andy Hardy's Double Life* (1942), *A Guy Named Joe* (1943), *Bathing Beauty* (1944), *Thrill Of Romance* (1945), *Till The Clouds Roll By* cameo (1946), *The Hoodlum Saint* (1946), *Ziegfeld Follies* (1946), *Easy To Wed* (1946), *Fiesta* (1947), *This Time For Keeps* (1947), *On An Island With You* (1948), *Take Me Out To The Ball Game* (1949), *Neptune's Daughter* (1949), *Pagan Love Song* (1949), *Duchess Of Idaho* (1950), *Texas Carnival* (1950), *Callaway Went Thataway* cameo (1951), *Skirts Ahoy!* (1952), *Million Dollar Mermaid* (1952), *Easy To Love* (1953), *Dangerous When Wet* (1953), *Jupiter's Darling* (1955), *The Unguarded Moment* (1956), *Raw Wind In Eden* (1958), *The Magic Fountain* (1961), *The Big Show* (1961), *That's Entertainment! III* co-host (1994).

WILLIAMS, JOHN

b. John Towner Williams, 8 February 1932, Flushing, Long Island, New York, USA. A composer, arranger, and conductor for film background music from the early 60s to the present. As a boy, Williams learned to play several instruments, and studied composition and arranging in Los Angeles after moving there with his family in 1948. Later, he studied piano at the Juilliard School Of Music, before composing his first score for the film *I Passed For White* in 1960. it was followed by others, such as *Because They're Young, The Secret Ways, Bachelor Flat, Diamond Head, Gidget Goes To Rome,* and *None But The Brave*, directed by, and starring Frank Sinatra. Williams scored Ronald Reagan's last film, *The Killers*, in 1964, and continued with *Please Come Home, How To Steal A Million, The Rare Breed* and *A Guide For Married Men*. In 1967 Williams gained the first of more than 25 Oscar nominations for his adaptation of the score to *Valley Of The Dolls*, and after writing original scores for other movies such as *Sergeant Ryker*, *Daddy's Gone A-Hunting*, and *The Reivers*, he won the Academy Award in 1971 for 'best adaptation' for *Fiddler On The Roof*. In the early 70s, Williams seemed to be primarily concerned with 'disaster' movies, such as *The Poseidon Adventure*, *The Towering Inferno*, *Earthquake* and *Jaws*, for which he won his second Oscar in 1975. He then proceeded to score some of the most commercially successful films in the history of the cinema, including the epic *Star Wars*, *Close Encounters Of The Third Kind*, *Superman*, *The Empire Strikes Back*, *Raiders Of The Lost Ark*, *E.T. The Extra Terrestrial* - still the highest-grossing film of all time more than 10 years later - and another Academy Award winner for Williams. On and on Williams marched with *The Return Of The Jedi*, *Indiana Jones And The Temple Of Doom*, *Indiana Jones And The Last Crusade*, *The River*, *The Accidental Tourist*, *Born On The Fourth Of July* and *Presumed Innocent* (1990). As for recordings, he had US singles hits with orchestral versions of several of his films' themes and main titles, and a number of his soundtracks entered the album charts. Real pop prestige came to Williams in 1977, when record producer Meco Monardo conceived a disco treatment of his themes for *Star Wars*, which included music played in the film by the Cantina Band. 'Star Wars/Cantina Band' by Meco, spent two weeks at number 1 in the USA. For his work in the early 90s, Williams received Oscar nominations for the highly successful *Home Alone* (the score, and 'Somewhere In My Memory', lyric by Leslie Bricusse), the score for Oliver Stone's highly controversial *JFK*, and 'When You're Alone' (again with Bricusse) for Steven Spielberg's *Hook*. After contributing the music to *Far And Away* and *Home Alone 2: Lost In New York* (1992), Williams returned to Spielberg in 1993 to score the director's dinosaur drama, *Jurassic Park*, and another multi Oscar winner, *Schindler's List*. Williams himself won an Academy Award for his sensitive music for the latter picture. As well as his highly impressive feature film credits, Williams has written for television productions such as *Heidi*, *Jane Eyre* and *The Screaming Woman*.

In 1985, he was commissioned by NBC Television to construct themes for news stories, which resulted in pieces such as 'The Sound Of The News', and featured a fanfare for the main bulletin, a scherzo for the breakfast show, and several others, including 'The Pulse Of Events', and 'Fugue For Changing Times'. Williams' impressive list of blockbuster movies is unlikely to ever be beaten.

WILLIAMS, PAUL

b 19 September 1940, Omaha, Nebraska, USA. Popular composer Paul Williams entered show business as a stunt man and film actor, appearing as a child in *The Loved One* (1964) and *The Chase* (1965). He turned to songwriting, and in the 70s composed many appealing and commercially successful numbers, such as We've Only Just Begun', 'Rainy Days And Mondays', and 'I Won't Last A Day Without You' (written with Roger Nichols), all three of which were popular for the Carpenters'; 'Out In The Country' (Nicholls), 'Cried Like A Baby' (with Craig

Doerge), 'Family Of Man' (Jack S. Conrad), 'Love Boat Theme' and 'My Fair Share' (both Charles Fox), 'You And Me Against The World', 'Inspiration', and 'Loneliness' (all with Ken Ascher), 'Nice To be Around' (with Johnny Williams), and 'An Old Fashioned Song', 'That's Enough For Me', and 'Waking Up Alone' (words and music by Paul Williams. Williams recorded his first solo album for Reprise in 1970 before moving to A&M Records the following year. None of these albums sold well, but Williams developed a highly praised night-club act in the early 70s. His first film score was for *Phantom Of The Paradise*, Brian de Palma's update of the *Phantom Of The Opera* story, in which Williams starred. This was followed by songs for *A Star Is Born* (1976), another modern version of an old movie, which starred Kris Kristofferson and Barbra Streisand, and included the Oscar-winning song 'Evergreen' (with Barbra Streisand). However, Williams' most impressive score was for the 30s pastiche *Bugsy Malone*, a gangster spoof with a cast consisting entirely of children. His later scores included *The End* (1977) and *The Muppet Movie* (1979), including 'Rainbow Connection', with Kenny Ascher). In 1988, Williams appeared at Michael's Pub in New York. His varied programme included some numbers intended for a future Broadway musical, as well as details of his recovery from the ravages of drugs and alcohol. In 1992, he contributed music and lyrics for the songs in the feature film *The Muppet Christmas Carol*, which starred Michael Caine, and continues to appear occasionally in movies and on television.

● ALBUMS: *Someday Man* (Reprise 1970)★★, *Just An Old Fashioned Love Song* (A&M 1971)★★, *Life Goes On* (A&M 1972)★★, *Here Comes Inspiration* (A&M 1974)★★, *A Little Bit Of Love* (A&M 1974)★★, *Phantom Of The Paradise* film soundtrack (A&M 1975)★★, *Ordinary Fool* (A&M 1975)★★, *Bugsy Malone* film soundtrack (A&M 1975)★★.

● COMPILATIONS: *Best Of* (A&M 1975)★★, *Classics* (A&M 1977)★★.

● FILMS: as an actor *The Loved One* (1965), *The Chase* (1966), *Watermelon Man* (1970), *Battle For The Planet Of The Apes*, *Phantom Of The Paradise* (1974), *Smokey And The Bandit* (1977), *The Muppet Movie* (1979), *The Lady Is A Tramp* (1980), *Smokey And The Bandit II* (1980), *Smokey And The Bandit III* (1983), *Twelfth Night* (1987), *Old Gringo* (1989), *Solar Crisis* (1990), *Chill Factor* (1990), *The Doors* (1991), *Police Rescue* (1994), *A Million To Juan* (1994), *Headless Body In Topless Bar* (1995), *Firestorm* (1995). As a composer: television *The Stranger Who Looks Like Me* (1974), *Phantom Of Paradise* (1974), additional music *Lifeguard* (1976), television *The Boy In The Plastic Bubble* (1976), *Bugsy Malone* (1976), television *Emmet Otter's Jug-Band Christmas* (1977), television theme song *The Love Boat* (1977), *The End* (1978), *The Muppet Christmas Carol* (1992).

WILLSON, MEREDITH

b. Robert Meredith Reiniger, 18 May 1902, Mason City, Iowa, USA, d. 15 June 1984, Santa Monica, California, USA. An instrumentalist and musical director - then a composer-lyricist-librettist - Willson was 55-years-old when he made his Broadway debut in 1957 with the hit musical *The Music Man*. Educated at the Damrosch Institute of Musical Art in New York, Willson was a flute and piccolo soloist with John Philip Sousa's concert band from 1921-23, and with the New York Philharmonic from 1924-29, playing under Arturo Toscanini. During the 30s and early 40s he worked extensively on radio as musical director on shows such as *Ship Of Joy*, *Carefree Carnival*, *Good News Of 1938*, *Maxwell House Coffee Time*, *Fanny Brice* and *John Nesbitt*. When he was in his late 30s, he composed a symphony, 'The Missions', and scored movies such as Charles Chaplin's *The Great Dictator* (1940) and Lillian Hellman's *The Little Foxes* (1941). He had composed the incidental music for Hellman's stage play of the same name, two years earlier. During World War II, Willson was a major in the Armed Forces Radio Service, and when he was released he had his own radio show from 1946 into the early 50s, and also hosted *The Big Show* with actress Tallulah Bankhead, and composed its closing theme, 'May The Good Lord Bless And Keep You'.

In December 1957, *The Music Man*, for which Willson wrote the book, music and lyrics, opened on Broadway to unanimously favourable reviews. It was set in Willson's home state of Iowa, c.1912, and starred Robert Preston, who was making his first appearance in a Broadway - in fact, any - musical. Preston triumphed in the role of the likeable conman, Professor Harold Hill, and Barbara Cook was splendid as librarian Marion Paroo. A wonderful set of songs, set in a variety of musical styles, included 'Rock Island', 'Goodnight My Someone', 'The Sadder-But-Wiser Girl', 'Marion The Librarian', 'My White Knight', 'Wells Fargo Wagon', 'Shi-poopi', 'Lida Rose', 'Will I Ever Tell You?', 'Gary, Indiana', 'Till There Was You', and the classics, 'Seventy-Six Trombones' and 'Trouble' ('Right here in River City/With a capital "T"/ That rhymes with "P"/That stands for pool!'). Willson won Tony and Drama Critics Circle Awards, and the show ran in New York for 1,375 performances. It was filmed in 1962 with Preston, and Shirley Jones who replaced Cook. Apart from the original cast and film soundtrack records, Willson and his wife Rini performed the score on an album, complete with their own individual comments.

Willson's next musical, *The Unsinkable Molly Brown* (1960), had Tammy Grimes in the title role, and ran for over a year. The appealing score included 'I Ain't Down Yet', 'Belly Up To The Bar Boys', 'Keep A-Hoppin'' and 'Are You Sure?'. Debbie Reynolds replaced Grimes in the 1964 film version. Willson's final Broadway score (he also wrote the book) was for *Here's Love* (1963). Adapted from George Seaton's 1947 comedy-fantasy movie about a department store's Santa Claus, it starred Janis Paige and Craig Stevens, and ran for 334 performances. The songs included 'The Big Clown Balloons', 'Arm In Arm', 'You Don't Know' and 'Pine Cones And Holly Berries'. Broadway legend Chita Rivera was in the cast of Willson's stage musical swansong, *1491*, which closed out of town in 1969.

● FURTHER READING: *And There I Stood With My Piccolo*, Meredith Willson. *But He Doesn't Know The Territory*, Meredith Willson.

WILSON, JULIE

b. Julia May Wilson, 21 October 1924, Omaha, Nebraska, USA. An actress and singer, Wilson is acknowledged as one of the greatest interpreters of standard popular songs in the world of cabaret. Her sophisticated image, with a figure-hugging gown, and a gardenia tucked into her swept-back gleaming black hair, is a reminder of a bygone era. She started young, being voted 'Miss Nebraska' when she was only 17. A year later, she joined the chorus of a touring edition of the *Earl Carroll's Vanities* which was passing through Omaha, and ended up in New York. From there, she moved to a Miami nightclub, doing a solo act five shows a night. It was in Miami that she believes she learnt how to control an audience with the occasional aggressive 'drop-dead bitchy' remark. Next stop was Los Angeles where she won a contest on Mickey Rooney's radio show. The prize was a two-week engagement at Hollywood's top nightclub, the Mocambo. Soon afterwards she was offered the part of Lois Lane in the touring version of the musical *Kiss Me, Kate*, and in 1951 recreated the role at the London Coliseum. She stayed in London for nearly four years, appearing in various shows, including *Bet Your Life* (1952), and undergoing voice training at RADA. Back in the USA, during the remainder of the 50s and throughout most of the 60s, Wilson took over roles on Broadway in *The Pajama Game* and *Kismet*, played in various regional productions, returned to London for *Bells Are Ringing*, and did some television work, including the soap opera *The Secret Storm*. In the 1969/70 Broadway season she appeared in two flop musicals, and subsequently played several cabaret engagements at New York's Brothers and Sisters club, as well as continuing to tour. In the mid-70s she went into semi-retirement in order to look after her ailing parents in Omaha. She returned to the New York cabaret scene with an evening of Cole Porter songs at Michael's Pub in 1984. Since then, she has attracted excellent reviews in two otherwise unsuccessful New York musicals, *Legs Diamond* (1988) and *Hannah ... 1939* (1990), recorded several superb albums, as well as, in critic Clive Barnes' words, 'putting over a torch song with the sultry heat of a flame thrower' in cabaret. There was great rejoicing at nightspots around the world, including London's Pizza On The Park, when in 1993, along with her long-time accompanist William Roy, she celebrated her 50 years in showbusiness.

● ALBUMS: *Love* (Dolphin 1956)★★★, *This Could Be The Night* film soundtrack (MGM 1957)★★, *My Old Flame* (Vik 1957)★★★, *Julie Wilson At The St. Regis* (Vik 1957)★★★, *Meet Julie Wilson* (Cameo 1960)★★★, with Kay Stevens, Connie Russell, Cara Williams *Playgirls* (Warners 1964)★★★, *Jimmy* Broadway Cast (RCA Victor 1969)★★, *Julie Wilson At Brothers And Sisters* (Arden 1974)★★★, *Bet Your Life* London Cast reissue (Blue Pear c.80s)★★★, *Sings The Kurt Weill Songbook* (DRG 1987)★★★★, *Sings The Stephen Sondheim Songbook* (DRG 1987)★★★★, *Legs Diamond* Broadway Cast (RCA Victor 1988)★★★, *Hannah...1939* off-Broadway Cast (1990)★★★, *Sings The Cole Porter Songbook* (DRG 1989)★★★★, *Sings The Harold Arlen Songbook* (DRG 1990)★★★★, *Live From The Russian Tea Room* (Cabaret Records 1993)★★★, and Ben Bagley recordings.

● FILMS: *The Strange One* (1957), *This Could Be The Night* (1957).

WILSON, SANDY

b. Alexander Galbraith Wilson, 19 May 1924, Sale, Cheshire, England. A composer, lyricist and author, Wilson studied at Harrow and Oxford University, where he wrote and appeared in many undergraduate productions. He began to make his mark in the West End by contributing songs to revues such as *Slings And Arrows* (1948) and *Oranges And Lemons* (1949). In 1950 he provided the lyrics for a provincial production of Michael Pertwee's musical play *Caprice*, and then was the author and composer of *See You Later* (1951) and *See You Again* (1952). His big break came in 1953 when he was asked to write the book, music and lyrics for *The Boy Friend*, a light-hearted spoof of the musical comedies of the 20s. The delightful score included 'I Could Be Happy With You', 'A Room In Bloomsbury', 'Won't You Charleston With Me?', 'It's Never Too Late To Fall In Love', 'Fancy Forgetting', and the lively title song. After starting its life as an hour-long entertainment at the tiny Player's Theatre, in London, *The Boy Friend* moved first to the Embassy Theatre, where it was expanded, before finally transferring to Wyndhams' Theatre in the West End on 14 January 1954. It ran for over five years, and Julie Andrews made her New York stage debut in the Broadway production, which lasted for over a year. The show has subsequently been produced in many countries throughout the world, and enjoyed revivals in New York (1958) and London (1967 and 1993). The 1971 film version was directed by Ken Russell, and starred Twiggy, Christopher Gable, Moyra Fraser and Tommy Tune. As well as *The Boy Friend*, Sandy Wilson has been the composer and/or author and lyricist of some of the most civilized and enjoyable shows (British or otherwise) ever to play the West End. They included *The Buccaneer* (1955), *Valmouth* (1958), *Pieces Of Eight* (1959), *Call It Love* (1960), *Divorce Me, Darling!* (1965), *As Dorothy Parker Once Said* (1966), *Sandy Wilson Thanks The Ladies* (in which he also appeared, 1971), *His Monkey Wife* (1971), *The Clapham Wonder* (1978) and *Aladdin* (1979).

● FURTHER READING: all by Sandy Wilson *This Is Sylvia. The Boy Friend. I Could Be Happy: His Autobiography. Ivor* (a biography of Ivor Novello). *The Roaring Twenties.*

WISDOM, NORMAN

b. 4 February 1915, Paddington, London, England. A slapstick comedian, singer and straight actor, Wisdom has been a much-loved entertainer for four decades in the UK, not to mention other such unlikely places as Russia, China, and - more recently - Albania. He broke into films in 1953 with *Trouble In Store*, and during the remainder of the 50s, had a string of box-office smashes with *One Good Turn, Man Of The Moment, Up In The World, Just My Luck, The Square Peg* and *Follow A Star*. Dressed in his famous tight-fitting Gump suit, he was usually accompanied by straight man Jerry Desmonde, and, more often than not, portrayed the little man battling against the odds, eventually overcoming prejudice and snobbery, to win justice and his inevitably pretty sweetheart. He nearly always sang in his films, and his theme song, 'Don't Laugh At Me', which he co-wrote with June Tremayne, was a number 3 hit in 1954 on EMI/Columbia. He also made the Top 20 in 1957 with a version of the Five Keys' 'Wisdom Of A Fool'. In 1958, Wisdom appeared in the London production of *Where's Charley?*, a musical based on Brandon Thomas's classic farce, *Charley's Aunt*. Frank Loesser's score included 'Once In Love With Amy' and 'My Darling, My Darling', and the show ran for 18 months. In 1965, he

played the lead in Leslie Bricusse and Anthony Newley's musical *The Roar Of The Greasepaint - The Smell Of The Crowd*, which toured UK provincial theatres. He was not considered sufficiently well-known in the USA to play the part on Broadway, but did make his New York debut in the following year, when he starred in *Walking Happy*, a musical version of *Hobson's Choice* with a score by Sammy Cahn and Jimmy Van Heusen. Wisdom also appeared on US television in the role of Androcles, with Noël Coward as Julius Caesar, in Richard Rodgers' musical adaptation of Bernard Shaw's *Androcles And The Lion*. His feature films during the 60s included *On the Beat, A Stitch In Time*, and *The Night They Raided Minsky's* with Jason Robards and Britt Ekland. Thanks to television re-runs of his films he is regarded with warm affection by many sections of the British public, and can still pack theatres, although, like many showbusiness veterans, he is not called on to appear much on television. In his heyday, he made two celebrated 'live' one-hour appearances on *Sunday Night At The London Palladium* in the company of Bruce Forsyth, which are considered to be classics of their kind. In 1992, with the UK rapidly running out of traditional funny men (Benny Hill and Frankie Howerd both died in that year), Wisdom experienced something of a renaissance when he played the role of a gangster in the movie *Double X*, starred in a radio series, *Robbing Hood*, released the album *A World Of Wisdom*, completed a sell-out tour of the UK, and published his autobiography. In the following year he celebrated 50 years in showbusiness, and was still performing regularly. In 1995, he was awarded the OBE, and toured Albania as a guest of the Minister of Culture. Apparently, whereas the country's state censors banned most American and British films with their 'Marxist messages', Wisdom, in his customary role as 'the plucky proletarian', was considered politically and morally inoffensive. He was given the freedom of the capital, Tirana, met President Sali Berisha, attended several rallies in his honour, and gave a 90-minute television performance.

In 1997 a plaque was unveiled in his honour at Pinewood Studios where he made some of his most successful films from 1953-56 (12 of them were released on video in 1994). In 1998, his long and successful career was celebrated on BBC Radio 2 with the documentary programme *Don't Laugh At Me: Norman Wisdom's 50 Years Of Laughter*, and a weekend retrospective of his films at the Barbican.

● ALBUMS: *I Would Like To Put On Record* (Wing 1956)★★★, *Where's Charley?* stage production (Columbia 1958)★★, *Walking Happy* Broadway Cast (Capitol 1966)★★★, *Androcles And The Lion* television soundtrack (RCA Victor 1967)★★, *The Night They Raided Minsky's* (United Artists 1969)★★★, with Des O'Connor, Beryl Reid, Mike Sammes Singers *One Man's Music: A Tribute To Noel Gay* (Columbia 1969)★★★, *Jingle Jangle* (Class Original Cast, 1982)★★★.

● COMPILATIONS: *A World Of Wisdom* (Decca 1992)★★★, *The Wisdom Of A Fool* (See For Miles 1997)★★★.

● VIDEOS: *Live On Stage* (1992).

● FURTHER READING: *Trouble In Store*, Richard Dacre. *Don't Laugh At Me*, Norman Wisdom. *'Cos I'm A Fool*, Norman Wisdom with Bernard Bale.

● FILMS: *A Date With A Dream* as a 'shadow boxer' (1948), *Trouble In Store* (1953), *One Good Turn* (1954), *Man Of The*

Moment (1955), As Long as They're Happy (1955), Up In The World (1956), Just My Luck (1957), The Square Peg (1958), Follow A Star (1959), The Bulldog Breed (1960), There Was A Crooked Man (1960), On The Beat (1962), The Girl On The Boat (1962), A Stitch In Time (1963), The Early Bird (1965), The Sandwich Man (1966), Press For Time (1966), The Night They Raided Minsky's (1968), What's Good For The Goose (1969), Double X (1992).

WISH YOU WERE HERE

In the early 50s, when Broadway audiences were enjoying such lavish musicals as Call Me Madam, The King And I, Can-Can and Kismet, Wish You Were Here went one better than all of them, and splashed out on a real swimming pool that was built into the stage. Perhaps the show's director, producer, choreographer, and co-librettist Joshua Logan still had fond watery memories of his association with the enormously successful South Pacific a few years earlier. In any event, the pool attracted a good deal of early publicity, as did a record of the title song by Eddie Fisher which soared to the top of the US chart just three weeks after the show opened at the Imperial Theatre on 25 June 1952. The story, which was adapted by Joshua Logan and Arthur Kober from Kober's 1937 play, Having A Wonderful Time, is set in Camp Karefree, a Jewish adult summer vacation resort in the Catskill Mountains. Teddy Stern (Patricia Marand) loses interest in her mature boyfriend, Herbert Fabricant (Harry Clark), when the young, suave and slinky waiter-cum-dancer Chick Miller (Jack Cassidy) sweeps her off her feet. It is all perfectly legal because, back home in New York, Chick is actually a law student. As well as the title number, which also became a hit for Jane Froman and Guy Lombardo, Harold Rome's amusing and tuneful score contained another appealing ballad, 'Where Did The Night Go', along with 'Tripping The Light Fantastic', 'Could Be', 'Ballad Of A Social Director', 'Mix And Mingle', 'Camp Kare-Free', 'Summer Afternoon', 'Shopping Around', 'Don José Of Far Rockaway' and 'Flattery'. Wish You Were Here was a warm and friendly show, so it was not surprising that it ran for nearly a year and a half, a total of 598 performances. The 1953 London production, with Bruce Trent, Shani Wallis, Elizabeth Larner and Dickie Henderson, stayed at the Casino Theatre (complete with swimming pool) for eight months. (The 1987 British film of the same name that starred Emily Lloyd and Tom Bell, is in no way related to this musical production.)

WITH A SONG IN MY HEART

Susan Hayward gave an outstanding performance in this 1952 20th Century-Fox film which was based on the life of the popular singer Jane Froman. There was hardly a dry eye in the house as producer Lamar Trotti's screenplay traced Froman's brave fight back to the top following a terrible air crash during World War II that left her confined to a wheelchair. David Wayne was fine as her mentor and husband, and so was Thelma Ritter, who played her hard-bitten nurse and companion. The 22-year-old Robert Wagner had a small but effective role as a shell-shocked young airman, and also in the strong supporting cast were Rory Calhoun, Richard Allan, Una Merkel, Helen Wescott, Leif Erikson, Max Showalter and Lyle Talbot. It was Jane

Froman's own voice that was heard on the soundtrack singing a marvellous selection of songs, many of which were particularly associated with her. There were especially endearing versions of 'With A Song In My Heart' (Richard Rodgers-Lorenz Hart), 'I'll Walk Alone' (Jule Styne-Sammy Cahn), 'I'm Through With Love' (Gus Kahn-Matty Malneck-Fud Livingstone) and 'They're Either Too Young Or Too Old' (Frank Loesser), along with excellent readings of 'Embraceable You' (George and Ira Gershwin), 'It's A Good Day' (Peggy Lee-Dave Barbour), 'Indiana' (James Hanley-Ballard MacDonald), 'Blue Moon' (Rodgers-Hart), 'Deep In The Heart Of Texas' (Don Swander-June Hershey), 'Tea For Two' (Vincent Youmans-Irving Caesar), 'That Old Feeling' (Lew Brown-Sammy Fain), and several more. Musical director Alfred Newman won an Oscar for his scoring. Billy Daniels staged the dance numbers and the impressive Technicolor photography was by Leon Shamroy. Walter Lang directed what was certainly one of the best films of its kind.

WIZ, THE (FILM MUSICAL)

Suspension of belief is a basic requirement for this kind of movie, but casting 34-year-old Diana Ross in a role that Judy Garland played when she was half her age, does stretch the imagination somewhat. Admittedly, Dorothy, the Harlem schoolteacher Ross portrays in Joel Schumacher's screenplay, is only 24 when she and smart dog Toto are whisked away from a snowy street in New York to Munchkinland. Her subsequent adventures still involve that trio of familiar characters, the Scarecrow (Michael Jackson), the Tin Man (Nipsey Russell), and the Lion (Ted Ross), while four Munchkins (the 1939 film had well over a hundred) also survive. As for the music, Charlie Smalls' original score for the 1975 Broadway musical, on which this film was based, is supplemented by material from Quincy Jones, Ashford And Simpson, Anthony Jackson, and Luther Vandross. Among the highlights are 'Don't Nobody Bring Me No Bad News', by Mabel King (Evilene) and her Sweatshop Flying Monkeys (aboard motor cycles), Ted Ross's 'I'm A Mean Ole' Lion', Diana Ross's 'Ease On Down The Road', Russell's 'Slide Some Oil On Me' and 'What Would I Do If I Could Feel?', along with 'Believe In Yourself', which was given an intensely emotional reading by Lena Horne (Glinda the Good) towards the end. Richard Pryor was The Wiz (actually a failed politician), Thelma Carpenter played Miss One, the Good Witch of the North, and the other songs included 'The Feeling That We Have', 'Can I Go On Not Knowing?', 'Glinda's Theme', 'He's The Wizard', 'Soon As I Get Home', 'You Can't Win', 'Poppy Girls', 'Be A Lion', 'Emerald City Ballet', 'Is This What Feeling Gets?', and 'Everybody Rejoice'. It was staged by Louis Johnson, with members of the Louis Johnson Dance Theatre, amid Tony Walton's terrific sets, and directed by Sidney Lumet. This generally disappointing film was photographed by Oswald Morris in Technicolor and Panavision, and produced by Motown for Universal in 1978.

WIZ, THE (STAGE MUSICAL)

Unlike the 1903 Broadway version of The Wizard Of Oz, this enjoyable reworking of L. Frank Baum's novel stayed closely to the original, much-loved story, and added an all-black cast and a high-level sound system that dispensed a brand new rock score. It opened at the Majestic Theater in New York on 5 January 1975, and in William F. Brown's book, Dorothy (Stephanie Mills), is once again whisked off to the Land Of Oz on a whirlwind so that she can skip along the Yellow Brick Road with familiar characters such as the Scarecrow (Hinton Battle), the Tinman (Tiger Haynes), the Lion (Ted Ross), the extremely wicked witch (Mabel King), and wonderful Wizard (Andre De Shields). Charlie Smalls' powerful score was skilfully integrated into the plot, and contained the insinuating 'Ease On Down The Road', which became a soul-music favourite, along with 'He's The Wizard', 'Slide Some Oil On Me', 'Be A Lion', 'Don't Nobody Bring Me No Bad News', and 'If You Believe'. After surviving some predictably poor reviews (this was not a typical Broadway show), enthusiastic word-of-mouth boosted the show's appeal, and resulted in a remarkable four-year run of 1,672 performances. Tony Awards went to Geoffrey Holder for his brilliant costumes and direction, and *The Wiz* also won for best musical, score, supporting actress (Dee Dee Bridgewater), supporting actor (Ted Ross), and choreographer (George Faison). The show toured the USA, and was briefly seen again on Broadway in 1984 when Stephanie Mills recreated her original role. She portrayed Dorothy yet again in 1993, when *The Wiz* played a limited engagement at the Beacon Theatre in New York. In 1984, a London (not West End) production starred Elaine Delmar, Celena Duncan, and Clarke Peters.

WIZARD OF OZ, THE (FILM MUSICAL)

It is not an easy task to conjure up a fairy tale that genuinely wins over both children and adults alike, but *The Wizard Of Oz*, released by MGM in August 1939, succeeded in every respect and became the third-highest-grossing film in the US during the 30s. To this day, this adaptation of L. Frank Baum's tale *The Wonderful Wizard Of Oz* remains a constant family favourite for new generations. Considering the many production problems that besieged the film behind the scenes, it is ironic that the film appears to have few obvious flaws and is very complete in structure. Not only did the film have three writers - Florence Ryerson, Noel Langley and Edgar Allan Woolf - but producer Mervyn LeRoy (assisted by a budding Arthur Freed), had numerous problems engaging an appropriate director. Having considered at least three others, Victor Fleming was assigned the prestigious job. However, even then, Fleming was not able to stay with the project until its conclusion. A few weeks before shooting was completed he was re-assigned to *Gone With The Wind*. It fell to King Vidor, Fleming's replacement, to direct the famous 'Over the Rainbow' scene, which was nearly cut at one point in the filming. Even the actors who eventually played several of the leading parts were not the director's first choice. Indeed it is only because 11 years-old Shirley Temple was unavailable that Judy Garland, who was six years older (and many felt, too old) won the role of Dorothy. Life for Dorothy on a farm in Kansas is miserable, and she muses 'if happy little bluebirds fly beyond the rainbow, why oh why can't I?' Suddenly a tornado

strikes, and before she knows what has happened, the strength of the winds have swept her up and taken her to another land far away. Up to this point in the film, Dorothy's world has been black and white, but the moment the door is opened to Oz, everything is more colourful (Technicolor photography by Harold Rasson and Allen Darby) than she and the audience could ever have imagined. Helped by Glinda the Good Witch (Billie Burke) and over a hundred midgets playing the Munchkins, Dorothy sets off down the yellow brick road to meet the Wizard in Emerald City, and eventually to find a way back home. During her journey, she meets the Scarecrow (Ray Bolger) who longs for a brain, the Tin Woodman (Jack Haley) anxious for a heart, and the Cowardly Lion (Bert Lahr) who strives to be brave. Together they defeat the Wicked Witch of the West (Margaret Hamilton), only to find the giant all-powerful Oz is simply Frank Morgan shouting into a loud microphone and pulling a few levers. However, Dorothy's friends are eventually convinced that they have gained the qualities they desire, and with the help of her magical ruby slippers, Dorothy is whisked back home, or rather, she wakes up, for it has all been a dream. Faced with all her family and friends, most of whom played leading roles in her dream of Oz, Dorothy famously declares that she will never run away again and 'there's no place like home'. This ending offended many fans of Baum's books because in his writings Oz is a real place, not just a figment of the imagination. Harold Arlen and E.Y. 'Yip' Harburg's charming score presented Garland with the immortal 'Over The Rainbow', which won an Oscar and proved to a be double-edged sword; in later years she would refuse to sing it for considerable periods of time. Other numbers included 'We're Off To See The Wizard', 'Follow The Yellow Brick Road', 'Ding-Dong! The Witch Is Dead', 'If I Were King Of The Forest', and 'The Merry Land Of Oz'. Ray Bolger gave a memorable comic performance in 'If I Only Had A Brain' (choreography was by Bobby Connolly). Two years later, a stage version of the original film, adapted by John Kane and complete with Arlen and Harburg's songs, was presented at the Barbican Theatre in London by the Royal Shakespeare Company. Heading the cast were Gillian Bevan (Dorothy), Billie Brown (Wicked Witch), Trevor Peacock (Cowardly Lion), Paul Greenwood (Scarecrow), and Simon Green (Tin Man). This Kane conception was subsequently seen at various centres in the USA, including the Muny Theatre, St. Louis, (starring comedienne Phyllis Diller as the Wicked Witch), and the Paper Mill Playhouse in New Jersey, before arriving at Madison Square Garden, New York, in 1997. Condensed to 90 minutes, one act, by director Robert Johnson, this limited-run production starred the popular television actress Roseanne as the Wicked Witch, along with Jessica Grove (Dorothy), Lara Teeter (Scarecrow), Michael Gruber (Tin Man), Gerry Vichi (Wizard), and Ken Page (Lion). It returned to the same venue in 1998, with Eartha Kitt (Wicked Witch) and Mickey Rooney as the Wizard. Kitt sang 'The Jitterbug', a song that was cut from the film. In 1996, in the televised *The Wizard Of Oz In Concert* benefit for the Children's Defence Fund, country/pop singer Jewel was Dorothy, with rock stars Jackson Browne (Scarecrow), Roger

Daltrey (Tin Man), Natalie Cole (Glinda), along with Broadway's Nathan Lane (Cowardly Lion) and Joel Grey (Wizard). The magic of The *Wizard Of Oz* still lingers in many forms, and this was emphasised in 1994 when a highly acclaimed documentary, *In Search Of Oz*, was screened by BBC Television. Almost 50 years after it made its historic debut, Warner Brothers announced the film would be re-released on Christmas Day 1998.

● FURTHER READING: *The Making Of 'The Wizard Of Oz'*, Al Jean Harmetz. *Who Put The Rainbow In The Wizard Of Oz? Yip Harburg, Lyricist*, Harold Meyerson and Ernie Harburg. *The Wizard Of Oz Collector's Treasury*, Jay Scarron William Stillman. *The Wizard Of Oz*, Salman Rushdie. *The Official 50th Anniversary Pictorial History*, John Fricke, Jay Scarfone, William Stillman. *Notes On A Cowardly Lion*, John Lahr.

WIZARD OF OZ, THE (STAGE MUSICAL)

Although it was adapted by L. Frank Baum from his own 1900 novel for children, *The Wonderful World Of Oz*, this stage show differed in several respects from the story that is so familiar to millions via the 1939 classic film which starred Judy Garland. It is probably true to say that it blew into the Majestic Theatre in New York on 20 January 1903, because the opening scene contains a spectacular hurricane effect which transports the young and shy Dorothy Gale (Anna Laughlin) and Imogene the Cow from their home in Kansas to the Land Of Oz. She becomes involved in some exciting adventures with most of the customary characters, including the Tin Woodman and the Scarecrow, who were played by two star comedians from vaudeville, David Montgomery and Fred Stone, and the Cowardly Lion (Arthur Hill), before eventually being confronted by the formidable Wizard (Bobby Gaylor) himself. Unlike the 1939 film of *The Wizard Of Oz*, with its wonderful score by Harold Arlen and E.Y. 'Yip' Harburg, the songs for this show were a kind of a hotch-potch cobbled together from a variety of composers and lyricists, mainly L. Frank Baum (lyrics) with Paul Tietjens and A. Baldwin Stone (music), along with others such as Theodore Morse, Vincent Bryan, Edward Hutchinson, James O'Dea, and Glen MacDonough. They included 'Hurrah For Baffins Bay', 'Sammy', 'In Michigan', 'Niccolo's Piccolo', 'Alas For A Man Without Brains', and 'When You Love Love Love'. *The Wizard Of Oz* ran for 293 performances, which meant that, in a Broadway season when 26 other musicals made their debut, it was a big hit.

WODEHOUSE, P.G.

b. Pelham Grenville Wodehouse, 15 October 1881, Guildford, Surrey, England, d. 14 February 1975, Southampton, Long Island, New York, USA. A lyricist and librettist, and the author of a series of more than 90 humorous novels, mostly dealing with an 'hilarious, light-hearted satire on life among the British gentry, notably the inane Bertie Wooster and his impeccable valet, Jeeves'. His father was a British judge, based in Hong Kong, and Wodehouse lived in the colony with his parents until he was four, and then, for the next four years, was entrusted to a family in London, along with his three brothers. After elementary education at various boarding schools, he attended Dulwich College in the outskirts of London, and excelled at Latin and Greek. He graduated in 1900, and worked for a time at the Hong Kong & Shanghai Bank in London. A year later, he joined *The Globe* newspaper, eventually becoming the editor of the humorous column, 'By The Way'.

In 1904, he wrote the lyric for 'Put Me In My Cell', for a new show, *Sergeant Brue*, which opened in December at the Strand Theatre. Two years later, the renowned actor-manager, Seymour Hicks, offered him the job of writing song lyrics for the Aldwych shows. It was at the Aldwych Theatre that Wodehouse met the young American composer Jerome Kern, who was just beginning to make a name for himself. Together, they wrote the song, 'Mr. Chamberlain', a satire on the British politician, Joseph Chamberlain, for *The Beauty Of Bath*. It stopped the show each night, and became a country-wide hit. During the next few years, in between his prolific literary output which involved several trips to the USA, Wodehouse contributed sketches and lyrics to three more London shows, *The Gay Gordons*, *The Bandit's Daughter*, and *Nuts And Wine*.

In September 1914, he married an English widow, Ethel Rowley, in New York, and finally settled in the USA. Three months later, in his capacity as the drama critic of *Vanity Fair*, he attended the first night of the musical comedy *Very Good Eddie*, which had music by Jerome Kern, and a libretto by Philip Bartholomae and Guy Bolton. When Kern introduced Wodehouse and Bolton, it marked the beginning of collaboration during which the trio (two Englishmen and one New Yorker), contributed books, music and lyrics to a number of witty, entertaining, and highly successful Broadway musicals. Firstly though, there were two false starts: Wodehouse was called in to assist the lyricist-librettist Anne Caldwell, on *Pom-Pom* (1916), and then the new team was asked to 'Americanize' and provide a new book and some additional songs for a Viennese operetta called *Miss Springtime*. The show was a hit, and contained some charming Wodehouse lyrics in numbers such as 'Throw Me A Rose', 'My Castle In The Air', and the risqué 'A Very Good Girl On Sunday'. The trio's first original musical comedy, *Have A Heart* (1917), had music by Kern, and lyrics by Wodehouse, who also collaborated with Bolton on the book. Although critically acclaimed, the show ran for less than a 100 performances, despite an outstanding score which included 'You Said Something', 'And I Am All Alone', 'They All Look Alike', 'Honeymoon Inn', 'I See You There', and 'Napoleon'.

The young team's initial impact was made in February 1917 with *Oh, Boy!*, the first, and the more successful of their two famous Princess Theatre Musicals. Kern and Bolton had already worked together at the Princess in 1915, with lyricist Schuyler Greene. The tiny theatre had a capacity of only 299, and so was not able to handle the large operetta-style productions that were currently in vogue, or afford to employ established performers and writers. Kern, Wodehouse, and Bolton were interested in writing more intimate shows anyway, with songs that were integrated into plots that sometimes bordered on farce with their tales of misidentity and suchlike, but came as a welcome relief from the stodginess of the

European imports. *Oh, Boy!* was a prime example of what they were aiming for, and proved to be a smash hit from the start, eventually running for over 450 performances. One of the show's stars, Anna Wheaton, helped to promote the production with her successful record of one of the hit numbers, 'Till The Clouds Roll By', and some of the other songs (nearly 20 of them) included 'Ain't It A Grand And Glorious Feeling', 'A Package Of Seeds', 'Flubby Dub', 'The Cave Man', 'Nesting Time In Flatbush', 'Words Are Not Needed', 'An Old Fashioned Waltz', and the delightfully rueful duet, 'You Never Knew About Me'. The production transferred to London two years later, where it was re-titled *Oh, Joy!*, and gave Beatrice Lillie her first role in a book musical.

While *Oh, Boy!* was resident at the Princess Theatre, Wodehouse was involved with four other New York shows in 1917. Firstly, he collaborated again with Kern and Bolton for *Leave It To Jane*, a musical adaptation of George Ade's comedy, *The College Widow*. This was similar in style to *Oh, Boy!*, and included The Siren's Song', 'The Crickets Are Calling', 'Leave It To Jane', 'The Sun Shines Brighter', 'Wait Till Tomorrow', 'Cleopatterer' (an amusing piece of Egyptian hokum), and several more. The show was revived off-Broadway more than 40 years later, in 1959, and ran for over two years. For Wodehouse, *Leave It To Jane* was followed by *Kitty Darlin'* (music by Rudolph Friml), *The Riviera Girl* (music by Emmerich Kalman and Kern), and *Miss 1917* (music by Victor Herbert and Kern). The young rehearsal pianist for *Miss 1917* was George Gershwin, in his first professional job in the theatre. In February 1918, Wodehouse, Bolton, and Kern completed *Oh, Lady!, Lady!!*, their final Princess Theatre show together. The all-star cast included Vivienne Segal, who sang 'Not Yet', 'Do Look At Him', 'It's A Hard, Hard World for A Man', and 'When The Ships Come Home', amongst others. It is sometimes said that disagreements over financial affairs between Kern and Wodehouse caused them to part, at least temporarily. In any event, although the three men were to work in pairs during the next few years, the brief spell when they combined to contribute to the dawn of a joyous revolution of the American musical theatre was over, except for *Sitting Pretty* (1924), which proved to be a 95 performance disappointment.

During the next two years Wodehouse contributed book and/or lyrics to productions such as *See You Later, The Girl Behind The Gun, The Canary, Oh, My Dear!, The Rose Of China*, and *The Golden Moth*, with a variety of composer, lyricists and librettists, such as Jean Schwartz, Joseph Szulc, Ivan Caryll, George Barr, Louis Verneuill, Anne Caldwell, Louis Hirsch, and Jerome Kern, with whom he wrote 'The Church Around The Corner' and 'You Can't Keep A Good Girl Down' for *Sally* (1920). In the early 20s, he collaborated with Kern again on two successful London shows, *The Cabaret Girl* and *The Beauty Prize*. Two years later, Bolton and Wodehouse wrote the book for George and Ira Gershwin's hit, *Oh, Kay!*, and they were both involved again in *The Nightingale* (1927) ('Breakfast In Bed', 'May Moon', 'Two Little Ships'), with music by Armand Vecsey. In 1927, Jerome Kern staged his masterpiece, *Show Boat*, with lyrics by Oscar Hammerstein. Interpolated into their score, was 'Bill', a song which was written by Kern and Wodehouse nearly 10 years previously, and cut from the original scores of *Oh, Lady! Lady!!* (1918) and *Zip Goes A Million* (1919). It was sung in *Show Boat* by Helen Morgan, and provided Wodehouse with the biggest song hit of his career. In the following year, he collaborated with lyricist Ira Gershwin, his brother George, and Sigmund Romberg, for the popular *Rosalie*, starring Marilyn Miller ('Hussars March', 'Oh Gee! Oh Joy!', 'Say So', 'West Point Song', 'Why Must We Always Be Dreaming?'). Ironically, for someone who had been at the forefront of the radical changes in American show music for the past 10 years, Wodehouse's final set of Broadway lyrics were for an operetta. With lyricist Clifford Grey and composer Rudolph Friml, he contributed numbers such as 'March Of The Musketeers' and 'Your Eyes' to Florenz Ziegfeld's music adaptation of Alexander Dumas' *The Three Musketeers* (1928), which starred Vivienne Segal and Dennis King, and ran for over 300 performances. With a final flourish, Wodehouse's Broadway career ended with a smash hit, when he and Bolton provided the book for Cole Porter's *Anything Goes* (1934). In that same year, Bertie Wooster and Jeeves appeared together in a novel for first time, and Wodehouse, who had been balancing several balls in the air for most of his working life, at last allowed the musical one to drop to earth. During the 30s he spent some time in Hollywood, adapting his novel, *A Damsel In Distress*, for the screen.

In July 1940, while at his villa in Le Touquet on the French Riviera, he was taken into custody by the German invading forces, charged with being an enemy alien, and interned in the local lunatic asylum at Tost in Upper Silesia. In June 1941, he was moved to Berlin, and subsequently broadcast a series of humorous talks about his experiences as a prisoner of war, which were transmitted to America. In Britain, where the population was constantly under siege from German aircraft, Wodehouse was reviled in the press and on radio, and there was talk of him being tried for treason - although most of the British population had not heard what turned out to be fairly innocuous broadcasts. Still in custody, he was transferred to Paris, and eventually liberated in August 1944. He returned to the USA in 1947, and became an American citizen in 1955.

He continued to write constantly, and in 1971, on his 90th birthday, his 93rd volume was published. Four years later, perhaps in a belated national gesture of reconciliation, Wodehouse, was created a Knight Commander of the British Empire in the UK New Year honours list, just two months before he had a heart attack, and died in a Long Island hospital in February 1975. As for the charges levelled at him during World War II, according to secret British government files released in 1996, Wodehouse was considered 'a vain and stupid ass' rather than a traitor. In June 1998, those infamous letters describing his life in wartime Berlin and Paris were part of 6,300 pieces of Wodehouse memorabilia which realised $351,900 (£211,140) at Sotheby's in New York, following the death of their owner, publisher James Heineman.

● FURTHER READING: *P.G. Wodehouse: Portrait Of A Master*, David A. Jasen. *From Wodehouse To Wittgenstein*, Anthony Quinton.

WOMAN OF THE YEAR

A vehicle for the celebrated film actress Lauren Bacall, who had enjoyed a great deal of success in the 1970 Broadway musical *Applause*. *Woman Of The Year* opened at the Palace Theatre in New York on 29 March 1981, with music and lyrics by John Kander and Fred Ebb, and a book by Peter Stone which was based on the 1942 film starring Spencer Tracy and Katharine Hepburn. Stone changed the characters of the two principals from a seen-it-all sportswriter (Tracy) who falls for a famous political commentator (Hepburn), to a satirical cartoonist, Sam Craig (Harry Guardino), who is permanently feuding with the high-powered, hard-bitten television personality, Tess Harding (Bacall). The arguments continue to rage (only more so) after they are married. According to the critics, it would have been nothing without Lauren Bacall, but the score was entertaining without being brilliant, and included 'Woman Of the Year', 'When You're Right, You're Right', 'So What Else Is New?', 'One Of The Boys', 'Sometimes A Day Goes By', and 'We're Gonna Work It Out'. The highlight of the show comes towards the end of the second act, when the super-successful Tess, and Marilyn Cooper as a down-trodden, disillusioned housewife, argue that 'The Grass Is Always Greener' (Tess: 'You can hold a husband, that's wonderful'/Cooper: 'What's so wonderful? There's more to life than husbands'/Tess: 'I could use a husband'/Cooper: 'You can have *my* husband'/Tess: 'I've already *had* your husband . . .'). During the show's run of 770 performances, two of the actresses who succeeded Lauren Bacall were also stars of the big screen - Raquel Welch and Debbie Reynolds. Ms. Bacall and Ms. Cooper won Tony Awards for their strong, amusing performances, and there were additional Tonys for the show's score and book.

WONDER MAN

This was the second of Danny Kaye's highly original and vastly entertaining films, and the first in which he played more than one role. It was produced by Sam Goldwyn for RKO, and released in 1945. Buzzy Bellew (Danny Kaye) is a loud and audacious nightclub performer who is all set to marry his dance partner (Vera-Ellen) when he is killed by a bunch of hoodlums. His spirit enters the body of his twin brother, the meek and mild Edwin Dingle (Danny Kaye), and insists that he take revenge for the murder. This situation was tailor-made for Kaye to display the full range of his highly individual manic talents, which were supplemented by the ingenious Oscar-winning special effects of John Fulton and A.W. Johns. The musical highlights included two hilarious spoofs, 'Opera Number' (written by Sylvia Fine) and the mangling of the Russian folk song 'Otchi Tchorniya', along with 'Bali Boogie' (Fine) and 'So-o-o-o-o In Love' (Leo Robin-David Rose). Virginia Mayo plays Edwin's librarian girlfriend, and also in the strong supporting cast were Steve Cochran, Allen Jenkins, S.Z. Sakall, Donald Woods, Edward S. Brophy, Otto Kruger, Natalie Schafer, and, of course, the stunning Goldwyn Girls. The screenplay was written by Don Hartman, Melville Shavelson and Philip Rapp, and was based on a story by Arthur Sheekam which was adapted by Jack Jevne and Eddie Moran. John Wray staged the dance numbers, and this popular film, which confirmed Kaye as a star of world class, was beautifully photographed in Technicolor by Victor Milner. The director who made sense out of all the confusion was Bruce Humberstone.

WONDERFUL LIFE

Cliff Richard followed-up his box-office successes *The Young Ones* and *Summer Holiday* with this 1964 offering. The Shadows, Melvin Hayes and Una Stubbs, each of whom also appeared in the latter film, co-starred alongside the singer and Susan Hampshire, later to find fame as Fleur in television's *The Forsyte Saga*. The plot revolved around a group of young actors who, frustrated with the outmoded ideas of a film director, attempt to complete their own version of the feature in secret. Although far from challenging, *Wonderful Life* (US title *Swinger's Paradise*) was a breezy, carefree exercise, buoyed by the undoubted enthusiasm of its participants. Indeed Richard took one of its most memorable songs, 'On The Beach', to number 7 in the UK charts while the soundtrack album peaked at number 2. Nevertheless, its wind kissed light-heartedness proved out-of-date when compared to the wry wit and documentary styled pop cinema pioneered by Dick Lester in the Beatles' *A Hard Day's Night*. However, *Wonderful Life* director Sidney Furie later reaped rewards for his work on *Lady Sings The Blues*.

WONDERFUL TOWN

Given that the score for this show was the work of the *On The Town* team of Leonard Bernstein (music) and Betty Comden and Adolph Green (lyrics), it does not take a great deal of imagination to realise that the wonderful, friendly, and generally too-good-to-be-true city in question is New York. This musical advertisement for the 'Big Apple' opened at the Winter Garden in New York on 25 February 1953. It had a book by Joseph Fields and Jerome Chodorov, based on their play *My Sister Eileen*, which was adapted from stories by Ruth McKinney. It concerns two young ladies, Ruth Sherwood (Rosalind Russell) and, of course, her sister, Eileen (Edie Adams), who have travelled from Ohio to the big city in an effort to find fame and fortune. Ruth is a writer who cannot seem to get a man, while Eileen the actress has difficulty holding them off. During their subsequent hilarious adventures, Eileen goes to jail for assaulting a policeman, and the editor of the classy *Manhattan* magazine, Robert Baker (George Gaynes), makes it clear that he hates Ruth's stories, but then falls in love with their writer. No big hits emerged from the effervescent, tuneful, and amusing score, which included 'Christopher Street', 'Ohio', 'One Hundred Easy Ways', 'What A Waste', 'A Little Bit In Love', 'Conga!', 'Swing!', 'It's Love', and 'Wrong Note Rag', although the lovely 'A Quiet Girl' is inclined to linger in the memory. Rosalind Russell, who had starred in the non-musical 1942 film of *My Sister Eileen*, was outstanding in this rare Broadway appearance. *Wonderful Town* ran for 559 performances in New York, and a further 207 in London with Pat Kirkwood and Shani Wallis. Over 30 years later, in 1986, a major West End revival starred one of Britain's favourite comedy actresses, Maureen Lipman, and in 1994 the New

York City Opera offered another, with Kay McClelland and Crista Moore. The 1955 musical film, with Betty Garrett, Janet Leigh, and Jack Lemmon, reverted to the original title of the play, *My Sister Eileen*.

WONDERWALL

This much-maligned film was released in 1968. Taking a highly-voyeuristic theme, it concerned the antics of an absent-minded scientist (Jack McGowran) who, having discovered a hole in a wall, peeps into another world; a flat occupied by a photographic model (Jane Birkin). He espies a peripheral world of sex and drugs and while hamstrung by the era's dalliance with triviality, *Wonderwall* does pose questions about perception. George Harrison contributed the atmospheric soundtrack, which became the first release on the Beatles' Apple label. Indian musicians provided accompaniment on the bulk of the score, but former Liverpool beat group the Remo Four are also featured. Eric Clapton contributed distinctive guitar lines, particularly on 'Microbes' and while as self-indulgent as the film inspiring it, the album does contain several notable moments. Although far from essential, *Wonderwall* is equally not as insignificant as many critics have described it.

WOOD, HAYDN

b. 25 March 1882, Slaithwaite, Yorkshire, England, d. 11 March 1959, London, England. Wood's 'Roses Of Picardy' (lyrics by Fred E. Weatherly, who collaborated with Eric Coates and many others) has ensured his place in 20th century popular music, although he also wrote other well-remembered melodies, such as 'The Horse Guards - Whitehall', used by BBC radio since the 40s to introduce *Down Your Way*. Many of his songs (as well as 'Picardy' he composed 'A Brown Bird Singing' and 'Love's Garden Of Roses') were written for his wife, the soprano Dorothy Court, and their success has tended to overshadow the sheer volume of his musical output: 15 suites, nine rhapsodies, eight overtures, six choral compositions, three large concertante pieces as well as over 60 assorted works. A childhood spent on the Isle of Man (in the Irish sea) inspired 'Mannin Veen' (1932/3) (the title of this Manx tone poem means 'Dear Isle of Man'), and 'Mylecharane' written just after the end of World War II. His major suites included 'Moods' (1932) from which comes the concert waltz 'Joyousness', 'Paris' (distinguished by the march 'Montmartre'), 'London Landmarks' (which includes the above-mentioned 'Horse Guards - Whitehall'), 'Snapshots Of London' and 'London Cameos'. Some other notable works: 'Virginia - A Southern Rhapsody', 'Sketch Of A Dandy', 'The Seafarer - A Nautical Rhapsody', 'Soliloquy' and 'Serenade To Youth'.
● ALBUMS: *British Light Music - Haydn Wood* (Marco Polo 1992)★★★★.

WOODS, HARRY

b. Henry MacGregor Woods, 4 November 1896, North Chelmsford, Massachusetts, USA, d. 14 January 1970, Phoenix, Arizona, USA. A popular songwriter during the 20s and 30s, Woods sometimes wrote both music and lyrics, but collaborated mostly with lyricist Mort Dixon.

Woods was physically handicapped, lacking three - some say all - of the fingers of his left hand, but he still managed to play the piano with the other one. He was educated at Harvard, and then served in the US Army in World War I. He started writing songs in the early 20s, and 'I'm Going' South' was interpolated into the Broadway show *Bombo*, which starred Al Jolson. During the late 20s Woods provided Jolson with some of his biggest hits, such as 'When The Red Red Robin Comes Bob-Bob-Bobbin' Along' and 'I'm Looking Over A Four-Leaf Clover' (with Dixon). His other 20s songs included 'Paddlin' Madelin' Home', (a hit in 1925 for Cliff Edwards, and still remembered over 60 years later by 'revival bands' such as the Pasadena Roof Orchestra), 'Me Too', 'Is It Possible?', 'Just Like A Butterfly', 'Side By Side', 'Where The Wild Flowers Grow', 'Since I Found You', 'In The Sing Song Sycamore Tree', 'She's A Great Great Girl', 'Riding To Glory' and 'Lonely Little Bluebird'.
In 1929, Woods wrote 'A Little Kiss Each Morning' and 'Heigh-Ho, Everybody, Heigh-Ho' for Rudy Vallee to sing in his debut movie *Vagabond Lover*. During the 30s he spent three years in England, writing songs for such movies as *Evergreen* ('When You've Got A Little Springtime In Your Heart' and 'Over My Shoulder'), *It's Love Again* ('I Nearly Let Love Go Slipping Through My Fingers', 'Gotta Dance My Way To Heaven'), *Jack Ahoy* ('My Hat's On The Side Of My Head'), *Aunt Sally* ('We'll All Go Riding On A Rainbow'), and *Road House* ('What A Little Moonlight Can Do', a song which helped to launch Billie Holiday's career). Wood also collaborated with British songwriters and music publishers Jimmy Campbell and Reg Connelly on 'Just An Echo In The Valley' and the all-time standard, 'Try A Little Tenderness'. Back in the USA in 1936, Woods wrote big hits for Fats Waller ('When Somebody Thinks You're Wonderful') and Arthur Tracy ('The Whistling Waltz'). His other songs included 'Here Comes The Sun', 'It Looks Like Love', 'River Stay 'Way From My Door', 'All Of A Sudden', 'A Little Street Where Old Friends Meet', 'Loveable', 'Pink Elephants', 'We Just Couldn't Say Goodbye', 'Oh, How She Can Love', 'You Ought To See Sally On Sunday', 'Dancing With My Shadow', 'I'll Never Say "Never" Again' and 'So Many Memories'. Among his other collaborators were Gus Kahn, Arthur Freed, Benny Davis, and Howard Johnson and Kate Smith, who worked with Woods on Smith's theme song 'When The Moon Comes Over The Mountain'. Woods retired from songwriting in the early 40s, and eventually went to live in Arizona where he died in 1970 following a car crash.

WOODSTOCK

The three-day music festival in Max Yasgur's Bethil farm has passed into legend, partly through the notion of survival in adversity, but largely because of the ensuing successful documentary film and album. *Woodstock* captures the spirit of those three-days in July 1969 - the haphazard organisation, the naive ideals, the storms - but most of all it showcases many of the era's finest acts. Several would later claim that their performance at *Woodstock* was poor, but there is no denying the excitement generated by Sly And The Family Stone and Santana, the sheer power of

Joe Cocker and the Grease Band and the allegorical anguish pouring out of 'The Star-Spangled Banner' when in the hands of Jimi Hendrix. Although several performers on the Woodstock bill were not featured on the film or album, enough remains in both to give the full flavour of this extraordinary event. A recent director's cut adds previously-unseen footage and a related Woodstock Diary largely comprised of 'new' performances. The legend refuses to die.

WORDS AND MUSIC (FILM MUSICAL)

Not the 1929 college musical of that name which starred the 22-year-old John (Duke) Wayne in his fifth film, but the lavish film biography of Richard Rodgers and Lorenz Hart, one of the most celebrated songwriting teams in the history of American popular music. It has been said many times that an authentic life story of Hart - a hard drinking, homosexual depressive - would make a fascinating movie, but in 1948 Hollywood obviously was not ready for that kind of reality, and so screenwriter Fred Finklehoffe turned in the usual fudged fairy tale which was typical of most bio-pics. Hart (Mickey Rooney) is portrayed as a cigar-smoking nice guy, whose first working meeting with Rodgers (Tom Drake) results in the assembly of the complicated lyric to 'Manhattan', which he has seemingly jotted down in various parts of a magazine on his way over. From then on, Rodgers, who in real life could be an extremely difficult man, is portrayed as having the patience of Job, even when Hart goes off on his binges for weeks at a time - erratic behaviour which led to his death at the age of only 44. So much for the plot - it was irrelevant anyhow, given the marvellous songs and the talented performers who were on hand to sing them. In a film full of musical highlights, perhaps the most memorable were Gene Kelly and Vera-Ellen's sizzling dance to 'Slaughter On Tenth Avenue', Lena Horne's sparkling 'Where Or When' and 'The Lady Is A Tramp', Mickey Rooney and Judy Garland reunited on film after a break of several years with 'I Wish I Were In Love Again', Judy going to town by herself on 'Johnny One Note', June Allyson and the Blackburn Twins with the delicious 'Thou Swell', Mel Tormé ('Blue Moon'), Perry Como ('Blue Room' and 'Mountain Greenery' [with Allyn McLerie]), and not forgetting Rooney's charming version of 'Manhattan'. Also contributing were Betty Garrett, Ann Sothern, Cyd Charisse, Janet Leigh, Marshall Thompson, Dee Turnell, Jeanette Nolan, Harry Antrim, and Clinton Sundberg. Robert Alton and Gene Kelly handled the choreography, and the director who put the whole complicated affair together was Norman Taurog. Words And Music was photographed in Technicolor and produced by Alan Freed's famous MGM unit. It grossed over $3.5 million in the USA and Canada alone, and was one of the leading musicals of the decade.

WORDS AND MUSIC (STAGE MUSICAL)

By the early 30s Noël Coward was at the peak of his creativity. This is clear from the material he wrote for this revue which opened at the Adelphi Theatre in London on 16 September 1932. There were normally at least one or two particularly memorable songs in any Coward show, but in Words And Music he really excelled himself. The score included the classic 'Mad About The Boy', 'Mad Dogs And Englishmen' (the author's most famous comedy number), and 'The Party's Over Now', which Coward subsequently used to close his cabaret act. In addition, there other, lesser-known items such as 'Let's Say Goodbye', 'Something To Do With Spring', and 'Three White Feathers'. Given the privilege and pleasure of introducing those songs were cast members John Mills, Romney Brent, Doris Hare, Norah Howard, Joyce Barbour, and Ivy St Helier. Ironically the show failed to last for more than five months, which meant that it was the first collaboration between Coward and impresario Charles B. Cochran to lose money. Much of the material formed the basis of Set To Music, a revue which starred Beatrice Lillie, and ran for 129 performances on Broadway early in 1939.

WRIGHT, ROBERT

b. 25 September 1914, Daytona Beach, Florida, USA. Together with George Forrest (b. 31 July 1915, Brooklyn, New York, USA), Wright has formed one of the longest partnerships in the American musical theatre. They first met in their teens at Miami High School, where they collaborated on the show Hail To Miami High! After writing numerous jazzy songs together in the early 30s, the team were hired to provide some fresh material - based on non-copyright music - for the film of Sigmund Romberg's stage operetta Maytime. So successful were they, that, during the remainder of their stay in Hollywood, the two men worked as co-lyricists for previously written stage and/or screen songs by Rudolph Friml, Victor Herbert, Richard Rodgers, George Posford, Edward Ward, and Herbert Stothart, amongst others. Two of their most popular film songs were 'The Donkey Serenade' (music: Friml-Stothart), which was introduced in The Firefly by Allan Jones; and the title number for one of the best of the Nelson Eddy and Jeanette MacDonald vehicles, Sweethearts. They also contributed to films such as Sinner Take All, Maytime ('Street Singer'), Saratoga, Mannequin ('Always And Always'), Three Comrades, Balalaika ('At The Balaika', 'The Volga Boatman', 'Ride, Cossak, Ride'), The Women, Music In My Heart ('It's A Blue World', 'Ho! Punchinello'), and Flying With Music ('Pennies For Peppino') (1942). In the early 40s Wright and Forrest turned to Broadway and began adapting the romantic music of classical and operetta composers - with new lyrics - for lavish stage musicals. One of their first efforts, Song Of Norway (Edvard Grieg, 1944), proved an enormous hit, and was followed by Gypsy Lady (Victor Herbert, 1946), Magdalena (Heitor Villa-Lobos, 1948), The Great Waltz (Johann Strouse (1949) and Kismet (Alexander Borodin, 1953). The latter contained several of their most memorable songs, including 'Stranger In Paradise', 'And This Is My Beloved', and 'Baubles, Bangles And Beads'. In 1961 Wright and Forrest wrote their first original Broadway score for Kean (they had written the words and music for a London production of The Love Doctor two years earlier), which, despite the presence of Alfred Drake and pleasant songs such as 'Elena' and 'Sweet Danger', folded after only three months. Four years later, Anya, an adaptation of Guy Bolton and Marcelle Maurette's play

Anastasia, signalled a return to their previous policy - this time using the music of Sergei Rachmaninov - but the critically acclaimed production lasted for only two weeks. *Anya* was later drastically revised and re-titled *The Anastasia Affaire*. The songwriters' latest stage musical (to date) is *Grand Hotel*, which opened on Broadway in 1989, and ran for almost three years. The score is mostly their own work, with some additional numbers by Maury Yeston. Throughout their long careers, Wright and Forrest are reputed to have contributed material to some 16 produced stage musicals, 18 stage revues, 58 motion pictures, and numerous cabaret acts. In 1994 - the year Wright celebrated his 80th birthday - they were reported to be working on three projects for the stage. In the same year they travelled from their Miami base to London, and were present at a BBC Radio 2 concert production of their best-known work, *Kismet*, which they had written over 40 years ago.

WRUBEL, ALLIE

b. 15 January 1905, Middletown, Connecticut, USA, d. 13 December 1973, Twenty-nine Palms, California, USA. A popular songwriter from the 30s through to the 50s, who frequently wrote both music and lyrics. After studying medicine at Columbia University, Wrubel played the saxophone with several dance bands, including a one-year stint with Paul Whiteman in the 20s, and toured England with his own band in 1924. He spent some time working as a theatre manager before having his first song published in 1931. 'Now You're In My Arms' (written with Morton Downey), was followed by 'As You Desire Me', 'I'll Be Faithful' (Jan Garber) and 'Farewell To Arms' (Paul Whiteman). In 1934, like many of his contemporaries, Wrubel began to write songs for films, often with lyricist Mort Dixon. Their 'Try To See It My Way' was interpolated into the Dubin-Warren score for *Dames*. During the 30s Wrubel also contributed to *Happiness Ahead* ('Pop! Goes Your Heart'), *Flirtation Walk* ('Mr And Mrs Is The Name'), *I Live For Love* ('Mine Alone'), *In Caliente* ('The Lady In Red'), *Sweet Music* ('Fare Thee Well, Annabelle' and 'I See Two Lovers'), *The Toast Of New York* ('The First Time I Saw You'), *Life Of The Party* ('Let's Have Another Cigarette'), and *Radio City Revels* ('Goodnight Angel' and 'There's A New Moon Over The Old Mill'). The films featured some of the biggest stars of the day, such as Dick Powell, Ruby Keeler, and Rudy Vallee. Around that time Wrubel also collaborated with Herb Magidson on 'Gone With The Wind' (an all-time standard), 'The Masquerade Is Over' (popularized by Dick Robertson, Sarah Vaughan and Patti Page), and 'Music Maestro Please', one of the most popular songs of the 30s in versions by Tommy Dorsey and Lew Stone. During the 40s and 50s Wrubel continued to write songs for movies such as *Sing Your Way Home*, in which Anne Jeffreys sang Wrubel and Madgison's Oscar-nominated 'I'll Buy That Dream' ('A honeymoon in Cairo, in a brand-new autogiro/Then, home by rocket in a wink'), *Song Of The South* (the Oscar-winning 'Zip-A-Dee-Doo-Dah', written with Ray Gilbert), *Duel In The Sun* ('Gotta Get Me Somebody To Love'), *The Fabulous Dorseys* ('To Me'), *I Walk Alone* ('Don't Call It Love'), and two full-length Walt Disney cartoons, *Make*

Mine Music , in which the Andrews Sisters sang his 'Johnny Fedora And Alice Blue Bonnet', and *Melody Time*, the Andrews Sisters again, with Wrubel's story about a tiny tugboat, 'Little Toot'.

During the 50s Wrubel's output declined, although he did contribute several numbers to *Never Steal Anything Small* (1959), which featured an ageing James Cagney duetting with Cara Williams on 'I'm Sorry, I Want A Ferrari'. He also wrote 'What Does A Woman Do?' for the thriller *Midnight Lace* (1960). During a career spanning nearly 30 years, his other songs included 'Gypsy Fiddler', 'The You And Me That Used To Be', 'I Can't Love You Anymore', 'I'm Home Again', 'I'm Stepping Out With A Memory Tonight' (a hit for Glenn Miller and Kate Smith), 'Where Do I Go From You?'), 'There Goes That Song Again' (revived by Gary Miller in the UK in 1961), 'The Lady From Twenty-nine Palms', '1400 Dream Street', 'Please, My Love' and 'Corabelle'. Among his collaborators were Walter Bullock, Nat Shilkret, Ned Washington, Abner Silver, and Charles Newman. Wrubel was a Charter member of the Composers Hall of Fame. He died from a heart attack in 1973 at the location mentioned in one of his popular songs - Twenty-nine Palms, in the state of California.

WUTHERING HEIGHTS
(see Taylor, Bernard J.)

WYNTER, MARK

b. Terence Lewis, 29 January 1943, Woking, Surrey, England. Wynter was one of several UK heart-throbs in the early 60s who took their cue from the USA. Once the extrovert champion of many a school sports day, he was serving in a general store by day, and sang with the Hank Fryer Band in Peckham Co-op Hall, London in the evening, when his well-scrubbed, good looks betrayed star potential to Ray Mackender, a Lloyds underwriter who dabbled in pop management. As 'Mark Wynter', the boy was readied for his new career with vocal exercises, tips on stage demeanour from a RADA coach, and advice about a middle-of-the-road repertoire from Lionel Bart. After exploratory intermission spots in metropolitan palais, he was signed to Decca Records, and had UK chart entries until 1964 - beginning with 'Image Of A Girl' (1960) at number 11. At the height of his fame two years later, he reached the Top 10 with covers of Jimmy Clanton's 'Venus In Blue Jeans' and Steve Lawrence's 'Go Away Little Girl'. From then on, he resorted to a-side revivals of such 50s chestnuts as 'It's Almost Tomorrow' and 'Only You', but was overcome, like so many others, by the burgeoning beat boom. Wynter turned his attention to the theatre, both straight and musical. He played the leading role in *Conduct Unbecoming* for more than a year at the Queen's Theatre in London, and for six months in Australia. He appeared with Evelyn Laye and Stanley Baxter in the musical *Phil The Fluter*, with Julia McKenzie in *On The Twentieth Century*, and in *Charley's Aunt*. He also starred in *Side By Side By Sondheim* in Toronto, Chichester, and on the UK tour. In the 1982 Chichester Festival season he acted in several plays including *On The Rocks* and *Henry V*, and also sang in *Valmouth*. Wynter played the male lead in Sheridan Morley's *Noël And Gertie* in London, Hong Kong, and New York. His other work in musicals during the 80s included the role of the King in a revival of *The King And I*, the title roles in *Hans Andersen* and *Barnum*, the 1986 revival of *Charlie Girl* with Cyd Charisse and Paul Nicholas in London, and the part of Robert Browning in *Robert And Elizabeth*. During the 90s Wynter spent two years on that famous rubbish dump in the New London Theatre which is inhabited by Andrew Lloyd Webber's *Cats*, and was also seen as the Phantom and M. Andre in *The Phantom Of The Opera*, and starred as Vittorio opposite Bonnie Langford in the 1998 West End revival of *Sweet Charity*. He has appeared frequently in the provinces and portrayed Emile de Becque in a national tour of *South Pacific*. For BBC Radio 2, Wynter narrated *The Danny Kaye Story*, and his television work has included a series with Dora Bryan-*According To Dora*, as well as *Tale Of Two Rivers* with Petula Clark, his own series *Call In On Wynter*, *A Tribute To Terence Rattigan*, *Cedar Tree*, *Sally Ann*, *Once Upon A Time*, *Sounds Like A Story*, *Just For Fun*, *The Haunted House Of Horrors*, *Red*, *The Jealous Mirror*, and *Superman*.

● ALBUMS: *The Warmth Of Wynter* (Decca 1961)★★, *Mark Wynter* (Golden Guinea 1964)★★★, *Mark Wynter* (Ace Of Clubs 1965)★★★, *Recollected* (Sequel 1991)★★★.

XANADU

Xanadu rivals *Sgt. Pepper's Lonely Hearts Club Band* as one of the greatest follies in pop/rock cinema history. Taking its cue from the Hollywood classic *The Lost Horizon*, this 1980 release attempted to weld the legend of a timeless place to a musical format. The presence of veteran dancer/choreographer Gene Kelly made the use of rock inappropriate, resulting in a *mélange* of anachronisms and pomposity. Singer Olivia Newton-John, excellent in *Grease*, is uncertain in her role, while the Electric Light Orchestra, their creative peak now past, play music with form but little substance. Nevertheless, the title track featuring both these acts reached the top of the UK chart when issued as a single and the soundtrack itself, a double set, peaked at number 2. This is probably a tribute to ELO and Ms Newton-John, rather than the cinematic charms of *Xanadu*.

YANA

b. Pamela Guard, 16 February 1932, Romford, Essex, England, d. 21 November 1989, London, England. A popular singer in the UK during the 50s and 60s, Yana became a model while still in her teens, before being 'discovered' when singing at a private party at London's Astor club. This led to engagements at several top nightspots, and a contract with Columbia Records. In the 50s her single releases included sultry renderings of 'Small Talk', 'Something Happened To My Heart', 'Climb Up The Wall', 'If You Don't Love Me', 'I Miss You, Mama', 'I Need You Now' and 'Mr Wonderful'. Her glamorous image made her a natural for television, and she was given her own BBC series in 1956. Later, following the advent of ITV, she appeared regularly on *Sunday Night At The London Palladium*. In 1958, Yana starred in Richard Rodgers and Oscar Hammerstein II's *Cinderella* at the London Coliseum: her solo numbers in the show and on the Original Cast album were 'In My Own Little Corner' and 'A Lovely Night', and she duetted with Tommy Steele ('When You're Driving Through The Moonlight'), Betty Marsden ('Impossible') and Bruce Trent ('Do I Love You?' and 'Ten Minutes Ago'). Two years later she was back in the West End with Norman Wisdom in the London Palladium's longest-running pantomime, *Turn Again Whittington*. She was something of a pantomime 'specialist', and throughout the 60s and into the 70s, was one of Britain's leading principal boys. It is probably not a coincidence that the second of her three marriages was to the actor Alan Curtis, who is renowned for his performances of the 'Demon King' and other 'nasty' pantomime characters, although he is probably better known in the 90s for his PA work at important cricket matches. In her heyday Yana toured abroad, including the Middle East, and she appeared on several US variety shows hosted by Bob Hope and Ed Sullivan. She also played small roles in the British films *Zarak*, with Victor Mature and Michael Wilding, and *Cockleshell Heroes*, an early Anthony Newley feature. Her last performance is said to have been as the 'Good Fairy' in *The Wizard Of Oz* at an English provincial theatre in 1983. She died of throat cancer six years later.

YANKEE DOODLE DANDY

James Cagney won the best actor Oscar for his magnificent portrayal of Broadway showman George M. Cohan in this film, which was one of the most enjoyable film biographies ever to come out of Hollywood. Everything was right about it, especially the screenplay by Robert Bruckner and Edmund Joseph. Beginning with Cohan being called to the White House to receive the Congressional Medal of Honour from President Roosevelt for his outstanding services to the American Musical Theatre, the veteran performer then relates his spectacular rise from young vaudevillian with the family act the Four Cohans, to his position as the legendary American theatrical actor, singer, songwriter, director and much else. The supporting cast was particularly fine, too, with Walter Huston as Cohan's father, Rosemary DeCamp as his mother, and Jeanne Cagney (the actor's own sister) in the role of his sister. Richard Whorf played Sam H. Harris, who co-produced many of Cohan's hits, and Joan Leslie was George's wife Mary. Also featured were Irene Manning, George Tobias, George Barbier, Frances Langford, S.Z. Sakall, Eddie Foy Jnr., Walter Catlett, and Odette Myril. However, there was no doubt that it was Cagney's film. He also started out as a song-and-dance man in vaudeville, and this early training served him well. The straight-legged strut, and ebullient, cocky style suited the character perfectly. It was all a joy to see, particularly the re-enactment of scenes from one of Cohan's most successful shows, *Little Johnny Jones* (1904), which involved two immortal numbers, 'The Yankee Doodle Boy' and 'Give My Regards To Broadway'. Many of his other songs - several of them unashamed flag-wavers - were represented in the film as well, including 'Mary's A Grand Old Name', 'Harrigan', 'You're A Grand Old Flag', 'Over There', 'I Was Born In Virginia', 'The Man Who Owns Broadway', 'So Long, Mary', 'Forty-Five Minutes From Broadway', 'Oh, You Wonderful Girl', and 'Off The Record'. Musical directors Ray Heindorf and Heinz Roemheld won Oscars for their 'scoring of a musical picture', and the superb dance sequences were staged by LeRoy Prinz, Seymour Felix, and John Boyle. The excellent black and white photography was by James Wong Howe, and the film was produced by Hal B. Wallis for Warner Brothers. The director of this classic all-time great musical was Michael Curtiz.

YELLEN, JACK

b. 6 July 1892, Razcki, Poland, d. 17 April 1991, Springfield, New York, USA. Growing up in the USA after his family emigrated there in 1897, Yellen began writing both words and music for songs while still at school in Buffalo. Eventually he decided to concentrate on just lyrics, and, after working as a reporter on the local newspaper for a time, he moved to New York to pursue a professional songwriting career. During World War I he served in the US Army, but still had some success with 'All Aboard For Dixie Land' (1913), 'Are You From Dixie?' (both with music by George L. Cobb), and 'How's Ev'ry Little Thing In Dixie?' and 'Peaches' (both with Albert Gumble). In 1920 he wrote 'Down By The O-H-I-O' with Abe Olman. Many of his songs of this period and in the 20s were used in Broadway revues and shows such as *What's In A Name?*, *Bombo*, *Rain Or Shine*, *John Murray Anderson's Almanac*, and *George White's Scandals*. After serving in the US Army during World War I, Yellen was introduced to composer Milton Ager, and they began a fruitful association that initially resulted in 'A Young Man's Fancy', 'Who Cares?', 'Hard-Hearted Hannah, The Vamp Of Savannah', 'Crazy Words, Crazy Tune', and 'Ain't She Sweet?'. The latter was

one of the smash hit songs that typified the 'Roaring Twenties.' In 1928, Yellen and Ager moved to Hollywood, where they collaborated on such songs as 'I'm The Last Of The Red Hot Mommas' (from the film *Honky Tonk*), 'Happy Feet', 'Glad Rag Doll' (with Dan Dougherty), 'A Bench In The Park', and 'Happy Days Are Here Again'. The latter became the theme song of the Democratic Party and President Franklin D. Roosevelt, and was synonymous with the promised emergence from the Depression and Roosevelt's 'New Deal'. Much later, it was the enduring income from Barbra Streisand's highly individual, ironic and anti-political slow version of the song, which she recorded on her first album in 1963, that helped to sustain Yellen in the last bed-ridden days of his life. In 1925 Yellen joined with Lew Pollack on both words and music for a single song, written to record his emotions on the death of his mother. When it was sung by Sophie Tucker, 'My Yiddishe Momme', one of the all-time great 'sob' songs, became a huge success with audiences of all races and creeds. In the 30s, Yellen also worked with Harold Arlen and Ray Henderson, and wrote lyrics and/or screenplays for several musical films, including the early Technicolor *King Of Jazz*, *Chasing Rainbows*, *George White's Scandals*, *George White's Scandals Of 1935*, *Sing, Baby, Sing*, *King Of Burlesque*, *Happy Landing*, and two Shirley Temple vehicles, *Captain January* and *Rebecca Of Sunnybrook Farm*. From 1939 onwards, Yellen concentrated once more on Broadway, writing with Sammy Fain, Henderson and others, for shows such as *George White's Scandals*, *Boys And Girls Together*, *Son O'Fun*, and *Ziegfeld Follies Of 1943*. Among his best songs from this period were 'Are You Havin' Any Fun?' and 'Something I Dreamed Last Night' (both Fain). Over the years, Yellen was particularly associated with Sophie Tucker for whom he wrote several amusing songs, including 'Stay At Home Papa' (with Dougherty), 'No One Man Is Ever Going To Worry Me' (Ted Shapiro), 'Life Begins At Forty' (Shapiro), and 'Is He My Boy Friend?' (Ager). Yellen retired in the late 40s to concentrate on his egg farm business, and was inducted into the Songwriters Hall Of Fame in 1976. He was one of the first members of ASCAP in 1917, and served on its board from 1951-69.

YELLOW SUBMARINE

Released in 1968, and named and inspired by one of the Beatles' most enduring pop songs, *Yellow Submarine* was a full-length animated feature that deftly combined comic-book imagery with psychedelia. Any lingering disappointment that the Beatles did not provide the voices for their characters vanished in a sea of colour and surrealism. Creations such as the anti-music Blue Meanies and their herald, Glove, were particularly memorable and if several songs were already established Beatles favourites, the quartet did contribute some excellent new compositions, including John Lennon's acerbic 'Hey Bulldog', George Harrison's anthemic 'It's All Too Much' and Paul McCartney's naggingly memorable 'All Together Now'. The group do briefly appear at the close singing the last-named song, but the film's strength lies in its brilliant combination of sound and visuals.

YENTL

With this 1984 release, which was filmed in the UK and Czechoslovakia, Barbra Streisand became the first woman to write, produce, direct, sing and star in a movie. Her screenplay, written in collaboration with Jack Rosenthal, was adapted from Isaac Bashevis Singer's short story, *Yentl, The Yeshiva Boy*, and set in Eastern Europe at the turn of the century. Streisand plays Yentl, the Jewish girl who disguises herself as a young man so that she can study the Torah and make her way in a male-dominated community. Complications arise when Yentl marries Hadass (Amy Irving), who just happens to be the fiancée of Avigdor (Mandy Patinkin), the man Yentl actually loves. Most observers noted that the scene in which Yentl, having walked away from the relationship, boards a ship bound for America, is very reminiscent of the famous 'Don't Rain On My Parade' sequence in Streisand's first picture, *Funny Girl*. The original song score, which won Academy Awards for composer Michel Legrand and lyricists Alan and Marilyn Bergman, was a Streisand *tour de force*, and consisted of mostly touching and emotional numbers such as 'Where Is It Written?', 'This Is One Of Those Moments', 'No Wonder', 'The Way He Makes Me Feel', 'Tomorrow Night', 'Will Someone Ever Look At Me That Way?', 'No Matter What Happens', and 'A Piece Of Sky'. An especially poignant song was 'Papa, Can You Hear Me' - the film is also a tribute from Streisand to the father she hardly knew. All in all, although far too long, *Yentl* is generally considered to be fine piece of work that certainly does not merit its sometime nickname, *Tootsie On The Roof*. Also among the cast were Steven Hill and Nehemiah Persoff, Bernard Spear, and David de Kyser. This MGM-United Artists picture was beautifully photographed in Metrocolor and Panavision by David Watkin.

YES MADAM?

Bobby Howes, Bertha Belmore, and Vera Pearce, three of the stars of the original stage show that had a good run at the London Hippodrome in 1934/5, recreated their roles for this popular film version which was released by the Associated British Picture Corporation in 1938. Binnie Hale, who played the heroine on stage, was not present, but her part as Howes' cousin was played by the delightful Diana Churchill. In the somewhat frivolous plot, they are both obliged to work as servants for a month in order to qualify for an inheritance of more that £100,000. Obviously there will be many complications, especially when the supporting cast contains names such as Fred Emney, Wylie Watson, and Billy Milton. The score, with music by Jack Waller, Joseph Tunbridge, and Harry Weston, and lyrics by R.P. Weston, Bert Lee, and Clifford Grey, contained some jolly and engaging numbers, including 'Czechoslovakian Love Song', 'Dreaming A Dream', 'The Girl The Soldier Always Leaves Behind', 'Sitting Beside O' You', 'Too Many Outdoor Sports', 'What Are You Going To Do?', and 'Zip-Tee-Tootle-Tee-Too-Pom-Pom'. Stalwarts Clifford Grey, Bert Lee, and William Freshman adapted their screenplay from the musical play, which itself was based on a novel by K.R.G. Browne. Norman Lee produced this popular slice of fun, and the producer was Walter C. Mycroft. An earlier, non-musical film treatment of Browne's book starred Frank Pettingell and Kay Hammond.

YES, MR BROWN

The celebrated stage duo of Jack Buchanan and Elsie Randolph came to the screen in this comedy-musical which was released by British & Dominion (Woolf & Freedom) Films in 1933. Set in Vienna (as per usual) Douglas Furber's screenplay was adapted from the German play *Business With America* by Paul Frank and Ludwig Hershfield. It concerns Nicholas Baumann (Buchanan), the manager of a factory who is expecting a visit from his important American boss (Hartley Power). Just before he arrives, Nicholas's glamorous wife, Clary (Margot Grahame), walks out on him because he cannot stand the sight (or the smell) of her pet dog. Complications arise when he persuades his secretary, Ann Webber (Randolph), to stand in for her. Buchanan's deft comic touch supplemented his already established romantic image, and Randolph was her usual amusing self. Also in the cast were Vera Pearce and Clifford Heatherley. The songs included 'Leave A Little Love For Me' and 'Yes, Mr. Brown' (both Paul Abraham-Robert Gilbert-Armin Robinson-Douglas Furber). Herbert Wilcox was the producer, and he co-directed this diverting little film with Jack Buchanan.

YOU ARE WHAT YOU EAT

This 1968 feature was directed by Barry Feinstein who co-produced it with Peter Yarrow of Peter, Paul And Mary. Described by its creators as an 'anti-documentary', *You Are What You Eat* featured hippies, love-ins, body painting, concerts and surfing without ever addressing the fulfilment participants felt in such counter-culture activities. Voyeuristic rather than participatory, the film is of interest for cameo appearances, rather than as a whole. Los Angeles scenemaker Vito, an ageing guru associated with the Mothers Of Invention and the Byrds, makes a rare on-screen appearance, as does San Franciscan drug supplier Super Spade, who was later murdered by less altruistic criminals. Musicians Barry McGuire and David Crosby make fleeting appearances, but the soundtrack is derived from performances by John Herald, formerly of the Greenbriar Boys, Tiny Tim (who duets memorably with Eleanor Goodman on 'I Got You Babe'), Paul Butterfield and the Electric Flag. The last-named's contribution, 'Freak Out', sounds like an out-take from their work on the previous year's exploitation film, *The Trip*. Future Band producer John Simon was musical director and among his solo performances was 'My Name Is Jack', later a hit for Manfred Mann. *You Are What You Eat* is not essential viewing, but has more value than its many denigrators would claim.

YOU WERE NEVER LOVELIER

After their compatibility and box-office appeal had been established in *You'll Never Get Rich* in 1941, Fred Astaire and Rita Hayworth were brought together again a year later for this Columbia release that was set in Buenos Aires. The screenplay, by Michael Fessier, Ernest Pagano, and Delmar Daves, cast Astaire as an American nightclub dancer and gambler who goes to Argentina for the sport, but ends up working in Adolph Menjou's ritzy hotel when his money runs out. Astaire's life becomes fraught with misunderstandings, when one of Menjou's daughters, played by Rita Hayworth, thinks he is wooing her with expensive flowers - in fact, they are being sent by her father in an attempt to 'get her off his hands'! Naturally, Fred gets the girl in the end, with the assistance of some of Jerome Kern's most endearing music and Johnny Mercer's lyrics. Hayworth, whose singing was dubbed by Nan Wynn, 'danced her socks off' in 'Shorty George' and 'I'm Old Fashioned', and blended blissfully with Astaire for the delightfully romantic 'You Were Never Lovelier' and 'Dearly Beloved'. Xavier Cugat and his Orchestra provided a few genuine Latin-American rhythms in 'Chiu Chiu (Niconar Molinare)' and 'Wedding In The Spring' (both with Lina Romay), and 'Audition Dance' (with Astaire). Also in the cast was Larry Parks, just a few years before he hit the big time in *The Jolson Story*. Val Raset conceived the imaginative dance sequences, and *You Were Never Lovelier* was directed by William A. Seiter. Rita Hayworth's association with Fred Astaire had been a joy, and two years later she was marvellous all over again when she joined that other great screen dancer, Gene Kelly, in *Cover Girl*.

YOU'LL NEVER GET RICH

Rita Hayworth fulfilled her promise as one of the screen's leading dancers, when she partnered Fred Astaire in this 1941 Columbia release. With America on the brink of entry into World War II, Michael Fessier and Ernest Pagano's screenplay cast Astaire as a Broadway dance director who is smitten by chorus girl Rita Hayworth. However, he is drafted into the US Army before he can consolidate his position. He turns out to be a rather perverse soldier, and spends a good deal of time in the guardhouse. While there, he performs an incredibly fast solo tap dance accompanied by a moody version of 'Since I Kissed My Baby Goodbye' by the Delta Rhythm Boys. That number was part of the superb Cole Porter score, which also included 'The Boogie Barcarolle', 'Dream Dancing' (a sadly underrated song), 'Shootin' The Works For Uncle Sam', and 'A-stairable Rag'. After Astaire has negotiated his release from detention in order to help to produce a musical entertainment for the troops, he serenades Hayworth (naturally, she is one of stars of the show) onstage with the lovely 'So Near And Yet So Far' ('I just start getting you keen on clinches galore with me/When fate steps in on the scene and mops up the floor with me'), before the exuberant finalé, 'Wedding Cake Walk'. Astaire and Hayworth were perfect together, and Robert Benchley, as the amorous producer who is responsible for their romantic involvement in the first place, was excellent too. Sidney Lanfield directed, and the choreographer was Robert Alton.

YOU'RE A BIG BOY NOW

Released in 1967, *You're A Big Boy Now* marked the directorial debut of Francis Ford Coppola, famed for later, award-winning films, *The Godfather* and *Apocalypse Now*. This rites-of-passage feature starred Peter Kastner as a teenage stacker at the New York Public Library. He tries to leave his home for the city's downtown attractions, bewitched by the elusive Miss Thing, only to encounter an often-confusing outside world. In one memorable scene he stands in an arcade, gazing at a pornographic film, unaware his tie is caught in the machinery. An excellent comedy about sexual awakening, *You're A Big Boy Now* is a quiet masterpiece, capturing the trauma and uncertainty of late puberty. John Sebastian of the Lovin' Spoonful, who had already scored Woody Allen's *What's Up Tiger Lily*, composed the entire soundtrack, later issued on the Kama Sutra label. One of its tracks, the haunting 'Darling Be Home Soon', reached number 15 in the US charts when issued as a single.

YOU'RE A GOOD MAN, CHARLIE BROWN

Sometimes known as the 'Peanuts' musical, this show, which was based on Charles Schultz's enormously successful American comic strip of that name, opened off-Broadway at Theatre 80 St. Marks, on 7 March 1967. Music, book and lyrics were by Clark Gesner, and told of a day in the life of the strip's familiar young characters. They include the sensitive, but bemused Charlie Brown (Gary Burghoff), Lucy (Reva Rose), Patty (Karen Johnson), Schroeder (Skip Hinnant), Linus (Bob Balaban), and, of course, the lovable pooch Snoopy (Bill Hinnant), who, in his imaginary persona as a World World I pilot, is in pursuit of his opposite number, the German flying ace, the Red Baron. They all get involved in numbers such as 'My Blanket And Me', 'Little Known Facts', 'T.E.A.M.' 'Suppertime', 'You're A Good Man, Charlie Brown', 'Book Report', 'Happiness', and 'Queen Lucy'. To the surprise of many, Charlie and his friends appealed for a total of 1,597 performances in New York, while road companies carried the message throughout the USA. The concept was unfamiliar to British audiences, and the London production folded after nearly three months. Early in 1999, a new production was on its way to Broadway, with regular characters Charlie (Anthony Rapp), Lucy (Ilana Levine), Schroeder (Stanley Wayne Mathis), Linus (B.D. Wong), and Snoopy (Roger Bart), being joined by Charlie's little sister Sally (Kristin Chenoweth).

YOUMANS, VINCENT

b. Vincent Miller (Millie) Youmans, 27 September 1898, New York, USA, d. 5 April 1946, Denver, Colorado, USA. An important composer and producer for the stage during the 20s and 30s, whose career was cut short by a long illness. He worked for a Wall Street finance company before enlisting in the US Navy during World War I, and co-producing musicals at Great Lakes Naval Training Station. On leaving the navy, he worked as a song-plugger for Harms Music, and as a rehearsal pianist for shows with music by the influential composer Victor Herbert. Youmans wrote his first Broadway score in 1921 for *Two Little Girls In Blue*, with lyrics by Ira Gershwin. One of the show's songs, 'Oh Me, Oh My, Oh You', was a hit for novelty singer Frank Crumit. Youmans' next show, *Wildflower* (1923), with book and lyrics by Otto Harbach and Oscar Hammerstein II, ran for a creditable 477 performances, and included 'April

Blossoms', and 'Bambalina', which was recorded by Paul Whiteman and Ray Miller. *Mary Jane McKane* ('Toodle-oo', 'You're Never Too Old To Learn') and *Lollipop* ('Take A Little One-Step') both reached the Broadway stage in 1924, and in the following year, Youmans collaborated with lyricist Irving Caesar on the quintessential 20s score for *No, No, Nanette*, one of the decade's most successful musicals. It contained several hits songs, including 'Too Many Rings Around Rosie', 'You Can Dance With Any Girl At All', and the much-recorded standards, 'I Want To Be Happy' and 'Tea For Two'. It was filmed, with modifications to its score, in 1930, 1940, and in 1950 as *Tea For Two*, starring Doris Day and Gordon MacRae.

In contrast, Youmans' 1926 show, *Oh, Please*, with numbers such as 'I Know That You Know', and 'Like He Loves Me' (lyrics by Anne Caldwell), was a relative failure, despite the presence of Beatrice Lillie in the cast. A year later, Youmans composed the music for *Hit The Deck*, which ran for 352 performances, and featured 'Sometimes I'm Happy' (lyric by Clifford Grey and Irving Caesar) and 'Halleluja' (lyric by Clifford Grey and Leo Robin). It was filmed in 1930, and again in 1955 with an all-star cast including Tony Martin, Vic Damone, Debbie Reynolds, Jane Powell, and Ann Miller. The latter release contained a new Youmans song, 'Keepin' Myself For You', with a lyric by Sidney Clare. Despite containing some of his best songs, Youmans' next few shows were flops. *Rainbow* ran for only 29 performances, *Great Day*, with the title song, 'More Than You Know' and 'Without A Song' (lyrics by Billy Rose and Edward Eliscu), lasted for 36 performances, *Smiles*, starring Marilyn Miller, and Adele and Fred Astaire, and featuring 'Time On My Hands' (lyric by Mack Gordon and Harold Adamson), just 63 performances, and *Through The Years*, with the title song, 'Kinda Like You', and 'Drums In My Heart' (lyrics by Edward Heyman), a mere 20 performances. Youmans' last Broadway show, *Take A Chance*, did much better. It starred Jack Haley and Ethel Merman, and ran for 243 performances. Youmans contributed three songs with lyrics by Buddy De Sylva: 'Should I Be Sweet?', 'Oh, How I Long To Belong To You', and Miss Merman's show-stopper, 'Rise 'N' Shine', which was also a hit for Paul Whiteman. Apparently disenchanted with Broadway, Youmans moved to Hollywood and wrote his only major original film score for *Flying Down To Rio* (1933). Celebrated as the film that brought Fred Astaire and Ginger Rogers together as a dance team, the musical numbers, with lyrics by Gus Kahn and Edward Eliscu, consisted of 'The Carioca', 'Orchids In the Moonlight', 'Music Makes Me', and the peppy title number. Youmans' previous flirtations with the big screen, *Song Of The West* and *What A Widow* (both 1930), produced nothing particularly memorable, and the film adaptation of his stage show *Take A Chance* (with Lilian Roth replacing Ethel Merman), dispensed with most of the songs. However, the aforementioned *Hit The Deck* was a box-office favourite, and *No, No, Nanette* was filmed twice - as an early talkie with Bernice Claire in 1930, and 10 years later with Anna Neagle in the starring role.

In the early 30s, Youmans contracted tuberculosis and spent much of the rest of his life in sanitoria. In 1934, his publishing firm collapsed, and a year later he was declared bankrupt for over half a million dollars. In 1943, he seemed well enough to return to New York to plan his most ambitious project, an extravaganza entitled *The Vincent Youmans Ballet Revue*. This was a combination of Latin-American and classical music, including Ravel's 'Daphnis And Chloe', with choreography by Leonide Massine. It was a critical and commercial disaster, losing over four million dollars. Youmans retired to New York, and then to Denver, Colorado, where he died in 1946. Despite his relatively small catalogue of songs and his penchant for rarely using the same collaborator, Youmans is rated among the élite composers of his generation, and was inducted into the Songwriters Hall of Fame. In 1971, an acclaimed revival of *No, No, Nanette* starring Ruby Keeler, began its run of 861 performances on Broadway.

● COMPILATIONS: *Through The Years With Vincent Youmans* (1972)★★★★, *Wildflower/Gershwin's Tiptoes'* (1979)★★★.

● FURTHER READING: *Days To Be Happy, Years To Be Sad, The Life And Music Of Vincent Youmans*, G. Bordman.

YOUNG AT HEART

Adapted by Julius J. Epstein and Lenore Coffee from Fannie Hurst's novel *Sister Act*, and the 1938 Claude Rains-John Garfield movie *The Four Daughters*, this 1954 Warner Brothers release provided a glimpse of the American suburban family viewed through the proverbial rose-coloured spectacles. The story concerns three sisters (one was dropped from the original), played by Doris Day, Dorothy Malone and Elizabeth Fraser, who live with their music teacher father (Robert Keith) and crusty aunt (Ethel Barrymore). Day is engaged to budding songwriter Gig Young, but one day, old chip-on-the-shoulder Frank Sinatra turns up on the doorstep and ruins the whole arrangement. Day marries Sinatra, but his career prospects remain at zero (the people 'upstairs' never give him a break), and one dark, snowy night he attempts to 'take the easy way out'. His will to live is rekindled when his wife tells him they are about to become a threesome. Perhaps because of the film's sentimental character, the Sinatra-Day combination failed to work as well as might have been expected, although, individually, they had some satisfying moments. At the time, both were probably at the peak of their vocal powers, and a collection of engaging songs gave them ample chance to shine - Day with such as 'Hold Me In Your Arms' (Ray Heindorf-Charles Henderson-Don Pippin) and the more upbeat 'Ready, Willing And Able' (Floyd Huddleston-Al Rinker-Dick Gleason), and Sinatra on 'Someone To Watch Over Me' (George and Ira Gershwin), 'Just One Of Those Things' (Cole Porter) and 'One For My Baby' (Harold Arlen-Johnny Mercer). Sinatra sings a number of these while working in a local 'joint' for what he calls 'tips on a plate'. Other numbers included 'You, My Love' (Mack Gordon-Jimmy Van Heusen), 'There's A Rising Moon (For Every Falling Star)' (Paul Francis Webster-Sammy Fain) and 'Young At Heart' (Carolyn Leigh-Johnny Richards). Photographed in Warnercolor and directed by Gordon Douglas, this was the kind of film that - at the time - made audiences feel warm all over.

YOUNG MAN WITH A HORN

Directed by Michael Curtiz, this film made in 1950 follows broadly upon Dorothy Baker's novel which was in its turn very loosely based on the life of Bix Beiderbecke. Any chance of reality went out the window with the casting of Kirk Douglas and the choice of Harry James to dub the character's trumpet playing. Hoagy Carmichael appears as a pianist but despite the fact that he actually did play piano with Bix he was ghosted by Buddy Cole. Amongst other musicians involved, mostly off-screen, are Babe Russin, Nick Fatool, Jack Jenney, Willie Smith, Stan Wrightsman and Jimmy Zito. Doris Day plays Douglas's long-suffering girlfriend and has a chance to sing between the melodramatics. (Alternative title: *Young Man Of Music*).

YOUNG ONES, THE

Cliff Richard had already appeared in two films, *Expresso Bongo* and *Serious Charge*, prior to starring in this unashamedly teen-orientated vehicle. It combined many of the genre's sub-plots - unsympathetic adults, romance and an inevitable, jejune show that is finally performed despite adversity. Unashamedly light and frothy, *The Young Ones* (titled *Wonderful To Be Young* in the USA) also boasted a highly popular soundtrack album. The memorable title track, a number 1 single in its own right, defines the innocence of Britain's pre-Beatles 60s, while 'When The Girl In Your Arms Is The Girl In Your Heart' remains one of the singer's most affecting ballads. *The Young Ones* confirmed Richard's status as one of the most popular entertainers of his era. The film was released in 1962 and was directed by Sidney J. Furie. The musical interludes other than those by Cliff and the Shadows were composed by Stanley Black.

YOUNG, VICTOR

b. 8 August 1900, Chicago, Illinois, USA, d. 11 November 1956, Palm Springs, California, USA. A violinist, conductor, bandleader, arranger and composer, Young is said to have been responsible for over 300 film scores and themes. He studied at the Warsaw Conservatory in 1910 before joining the Warsaw Philharmonic as a violinist, and touring Europe. He returned to the USA at the outbreak of World War I, and later, in the early 20s, toured as a concert violinist, and then became a concert master in theatre orchestras. On 'defecting' to popular music, he served for a while as violinist-arranger with the popular pianist-bandleader Ted Fio Rito. During the 30s, Young worked a great deal on radio, conducting for many artists including Al Jolson, Don Ameche and Smith Ballew. He also started recording with his own orchestra, and had a string of hits from 1931-54, including 'Gems From "The Band Wagon"', 'The Last Round-Up', 'Who's Afraid Of The Big Bad Wolf', 'The Old Spinning Wheel', 'This Little Piggie Went To Market' (featuring Jimmy Dorsey, Bunny Berigan and Joe Venuti), 'Flirtation Walk', 'Ev'ry Day', 'Way Back Home', 'About A Quarter To Nine' and 'She's A Latin From Manhattan' (both from the Jolson movie *Go Into Your Dance*), 'It's A Sin To Tell A Lie', 'Mona Lisa', 'The Third Man Theme', 'Ruby', 'Limelight Theme', and 'The High And The Mighty'. He also provided the orchestral accompaniments for other artists, such as Dick Powell, Eddie Cantor, Deanna Durbin, Helen Forrest, Frances Langford, trumpet virtuoso Rafael Mendez, Cliff Edwards, the Boswell Sisters, and western movies singer Rex Allen. Most notably, it was Young's orchestra that backed Judy Garland on her record of 'Over The Rainbow', the Oscar-winning song from the legendary 1939 film *The Wizard Of Oz*. He also backed Bing Crosby on two of his million-sellers: 'Too-Ra-Loo-Ra-Loo-Ral (That's An Irish Lullaby)', from *Going My Way* (the 'Best Picture' of 1944), and British doctor Arthur Colahan's somewhat unconventional song, 'Galway Bay' (1948).

Young's extremely successful and prolific career as a film composer, musical director, conductor, and arranger, began in the early 30s with Paramount. Some of his best-known film works included *Wells Fargo* (1937), *Swing High, Swing Low* (1937), *Breaking The Ice* (1938), *Golden Boy* (1939), *Man Of Conquest* (1939), *Arizona* (1940), *I Wanted Wings* (1941), *Hold Back The Dawn* (1941), *Flying Tigers* (1942), *Silver Queen* (1942), *The Glass Key* (1942), *Take A Letter, Darling* (1942), *For Whom The Bell Tolls* (1943), *The Uninvited* (1944), *Samson And Delilah* (1949), *Rio Grande* (1950), *Scaramouche* (1952), *The Greatest Show On Earth* (1952), *Shane* (1953) and *Three Coins In The Fountain* (1954). In 1956, Young was awarded a posthumous Academy Award for his score for Mike Todd's spectacular film *Around The World In Eighty Days*. His record of the title song made the US charts in 1957, and had a vocal version by Bing Crosby on the b-side. He also wrote some television themes, including 'Blue Star' for the US *Medic* series, and contributed music to two minor Broadway shows, *Pardon Our French* (1950) and *Seventh Heaven* (1955). Young's popular songs were written mostly with lyricist Ned Washington. These included 'Can't We Talk It Over?', 'A Hundred Years From Today' (from the revue *Blackbirds Of 1933/34*), and three beautiful and enduring ballads: 'A Ghost Of A Chance' (co-writer, Bing Crosby), 'Stella By Starlight' and 'My Foolish Heart' (film title song). Young's other lyricists included Will J. Harris ('Sweet Sue'), Wayne King, Haven Gillespie, and Egbert Van Alstyne ('Beautiful Love'), Sam M. Lewis ('Street Of Dreams'), Edward Heyman ('When I Fall In Love' and 'Love Letters') and Sammy Cahn (the film title song, 'Written On The Wind'). Young also wrote 'Golden Earrings' with the songwriting team of Jay Livingston and Ray Evans.

● ALBUMS: *April In Paris* (c.50s)★★★, *Cinema Rhapsodies* (c.50s)★★★, *Gypsy Magic* (c.50s)★★, *Imagination* (c.50s)★★★, *Night Music* (c.50s)★★★, *Pearls On Velvet* (c.50s)★★, *Themes From 'For Whom The Bell Tolls' And 'Golden Earrings'* (c.50s)★★★, *Valentino Tangos* (c.50s)★★, *Hollywood Rhapsodies* (c.50s)★★★, *Around The World In 80 Days* film soundtrack (1957)★★★★, *Forever Young* (1959)★★★, *Love Themes From Hollywood* (1959)★★★, *Wizard Of Oz/Pinocchio* (Ace Of Hearts/Decca 1966)★★, *The Quiet Man/Samson And Delilah* film soundtracks (Varese International 1979)★★★.

YOUR ARMS TOO SHORT TO BOX WITH GOD

(see *Dont Bother Me I Cant Cope*)

YOUR OWN THING

By the late 60s, rock music had become the dominant force in the world of popular entertainment generally, but its first big impact on Broadway was still to come in April 1968 with *Hair*. Some three months before that, on 13 January, this modern conception of William Shakespeare's *Twelfth Night*, complete with a rock score by Hal Hester and Danny Apolinar, arrived at the off-Broadway Orpheum Theatre. Donald Driver's book takes a sly dig at men's fashionably long hair in a story that involves brother and sister Viola (Leland Palmer) and Sebastian (Rusty Thatcher), who, unbeknown to each other, are chasing the same singing job with a rock group based at a fashionable discotheque operated by Olivia (Marian Mercer). Orson (Tom Ligon), the manager of The Four Apocalypse, needs a male vocalist, so Viola adopts an effective disguise. Too effective, as it turns out, because Olivia decides that she fancies him/her, and the complications begin. After some delicate negotiations, Olivia transfers her affections to the far more suitable (and manly) Sebastian, and Viola gets the job - and Orson too. The songs, some of which had fairly predictable titles, included 'The Now Generation', 'I'm On My Way To The Top', 'The Flowers', 'I'm Me!', 'Come Away Death' (lyric-Shakespeare), and 'The Middle Years'. None of them threatened to break into the US charts, which were being headed at the time by artists such as the Beatles, Aretha Franklin, and the Lemon Pipers. One innovation in *Your Own Thing* was the clever use of film and slide projectors to mix traditional aspects of the piece with this contemporary treatment. The show enjoyed an impressive run of 933 performances in New York, but failed to impress in London, and was withdrawn after six weeks.

ZABRISKIE POINT

Released in 1969 and directed by Michelangelo Antonioni, *Zabriskie Point* is a flawed, yet elegant, attempt at chronicling a malaise affecting the US counter-culture of the late 60s. In his previous feature, *Blow Up*, Antonioni had captured the spiritual ennui at the heart of 'Swinging London', but here the crux of his statement seems tantalizingly out of his grasp. The use of unknown actors, Mark Frechette and Daria Halprin, in the starring roles was ambitious, but neither acted convincingly and it was left to veteran Rod Taylor to bring cohesion to the plot. The script, in part written by Sam Shepard, carries little weight and it is for visuals and imagery that the film is best recalled. These memorable scenes include a Death Valley love-in and an apocalyptic finale, over which Pink Floyd contribute the eerie 'Come In Number 51, You're Time Is Up', otherwise known as 'Careful With That Axe, Eugene'. The group was initially commissioned to compose the entire score, but eventually Antonioni opted for a variety of artists, including Kaleidoscope, the Youngbloods, John Fahey, Jerry Garcia and Patti Page. His choices were astute and indeed the popularity of the attendant soundtrack album has outlasted that of the film generating it.

ZACHARIA

Billed as 'the first electric western', *Zacharia* was initially scripted by members of the Firesign Theatre, a radical comedy troupe blending elements of satire, 50s radio serials and counter-culture quirkiness. Their work for the film was radically altered during production, causing the group to disown the entire project. The notion of equating rock musicians with outlaws was already a cliché by the time *Zacharia* was first screened in 1971, and the final print did little to alter that notion. Coyly billed 'Ahead Of Its Time', the film boasts interesting musical cameos by the James Gang, Doug Kershaw and former John Coltrane drummer Elvin Jones, but the best moments are courtesy of Country Joe And The Fish who play a band of outlaws, the Crackers. This San Franciscan quintet capture the irreverence the Firesign Theatre first extolled, but the rest of the film is burdened by an aura of misplaced self-importance.

ZAKS, JERRY

b. 7 September 1946, Stuttgart, Germany. A director and actor, mainly for the theatre, Zaks was educated at Dartmouth College and Smith College in the USA, before training for the stage with Curt Dempster. He made his first principal stage appearance in 1974, playing the role of Kenickie in the Broadway revival of *Grease*. During the next six years, as well as performing in straight theatre in New York and various other US cities, he was seen in the Broadway musicals *The 1940s' Radio Hour* (as Neil Tilden, 1978) and the critically acclaimed *Tintypes* (as Charlie, 1980). Zaks began to direct in the early 80s, but, apart from working on a major US regional tour of *Tintypes*, and the 1987 Broadway revival of *Anything Goes*, most of his efforts during that decade were concerned with non-musical productions. He also served as resident director at Lincoln Centre Theatre from 1986-90. During the 90s, Zaks' reputation as an extremely inventive 'master comedy strategist' has been affirmed with his direction of the highly successful revivals of the musicals *Guys And Dolls* (1992) and *A Funny Thing Happened On The Way To The Forum* (1996) - both staring Nathan Lane. He also helmed the Leiber And Stoller revue *Smokey Joe's Café* (1995), Stephen Sondheim and John Weidman's *Assassins* (1991, off-Broadway), and pop legend Paul Simon's debut Broadway show, *The Capeman* (1998). Late in 1998, he took over as director of the Broadway-bound musical *The Civil War*, after its tryout at the Alley Theatre in Houston, Texas. Zaks won a Tony Award for *Guys And Dolls*, and three others for *The House Of Blue Leaves* (1986), *Lend Me A Tenor* (1989), and *Six Degrees Of Separation* (1991). His other honours have included Outer Circle, Obie, and Drama League awards. In addition, he was the 1994 recipient of the George Abbott Award for Lifetime Achievement in the Theatre, and in 1998 a concert tribute in his honour was presented at the Ensemble Theatre in New York. In 1996, he made his movie debut, directing Meryl Streep, Diane Keaton, Leonardo di Caprio, and Robert DeNiro in *Marvin's Room*.

ZIEGFELD

Hailed as the most expensive British musical ever when it opened at the London Palladium on 26 April 1988, *Ziegfeld* had a £3.2 million budget and a 60-strong cast. This 'opulent and gaudy' show was the brainchild of veteran impresario Harold Fielding and director and choreographer Joe Layton, and purported to be a celebration of the *Ziegfeld Follies*, while also telling the life story of master showman Florenz Ziegfeld himself. Ned Sherrin and Alistair Beaton wrote the book in which the legendary 'girl glorifier', played by Len Cariou, is portrayed as a shifty, egotistical manipulator, and an incorrigible womanizer. One critic pointed out that it was 'dedicated to a man with no heart', and that may well have been the reason why, in spite of some great old songs, 450 costumes, 27 sets, and plenty of girls sited on revolving staircases, roulette wheels, and most other places, by August the show was in trouble. Fielding brought in his old friend Tommy Steele to revamp the production, and Topol, who had enjoyed a personal triumph in London with *Fiddler On The Roof* in 1967, replaced Cariou. But it was all to no avail, and *Ziegfeld* crashed in October after a run of just over five months. It recouped hardly any of its original investment, and Harold Fielding faced reported personal losses of £2.5 million. Shortly after it closed, the elaborate costumes and scenery were bought by the producers of the 'vaudeville-burlesque revue' *Ziegfeld: A Night At The Follies*, which played regional cities in the USA in the early 90s.

ZIEGFELD FOLLIES (FILM MUSICAL)

William Powell, who had played the leading role in the 1936 screen biography, *The Great Ziegfeld*, portrayed the master showman again in this film which was released 10 years later. From his seat in that big theatre in the sky - heaven - Florenz Ziegfeld plans one final revue that will serve as his memorial. The resulting show, a collection of unconnected sketches and songs, was certainly spectacular, featuring as it did many of MGM's brightest stars of the day. Three of these, Fred Astaire, Cyd Charisse and Lucille Ball, accurately captured the Ziegfeld mood with 'Bring On The Beautiful Girls' (Earl Brent-Roger Edens) - followed closely by 'Bring On Those Beautiful Men', and from then on the lavish production numbers, interspersed with the laughs, followed thick and fast. The lovely Lena Horne, eyes ablaze, raised the temperature with 'Love' (Ralph Blane-Hugh Martin), Judy Garland sent up the much-loved Greer ('Mrs. Miniver') Garson in 'Madame Crematon', and two refugees from the world of opera, James Melton and Marion Bell, rendered 'The Drinking Song' from Verdi's *La Traviata*. However, most of the honours went to Fred Astaire who, with Lucille Bremer, provided two of the films outstanding moments, with the lovely ballad, 'This Heart Of Mine' (Arthur Freed-Harry Warren), and the exquisitely staged 'Limehouse Blues' (Philip Braham-Douglas Furber). Astaire also revived a number called 'The Babbitt And The Bromide' (George Gershwin-Ira Gershwin), which he had introduced with his sister Adele in the Broadway musical *Funny Face* (1927). In this film Astaire performed it with his main 'rival', Gene Kelly - it was the first time they had danced on the screen together. Kathryn Grayson, surrounded by a substance that looked remarkably like foam, brought the curtain down on Ziegfeld's final performance, confirming the impresario's lifelong creed with 'There's Beauty Everywhere', written by Earl Brent and Arthur Freed. Freed himself produced the whole stylish and extravagant affair, which was directed by Vincente Minnelli and choreographed by Robert Alton.

ZIEGFELD FOLLIES (STAGE MUSICAL)

This series of high-class, spectacular, and elaborate revues, each one containing a mixture of skits, dances, songs, variety acts, and at least 50 beautiful women, was inaugurated in 1907 by Florenz Ziegfeld, 'the greatest showman in theatrical history'. From 1907-10, the shows were known as the *Follies*, and presented at the Jardin de Paris in New York. One of the first of the stars to emerge from the *Follies* was Nora Bayes, who also wrote and introduced the enormously popular 'Shine On Harvest Moon' with her second husband Jack Norworth in the 1908 edition. Yet another 'moon' song, 'By The Light Of The Silvery Moon', written by Edward Madden and Gus Edwards, turned up in the *Follies* of 1909. Other artists making one or more appearances in that first quartet of shows included Grace La Rue, Bickell And Watson, Helen Broderick, Mae Murray, Sophie Tucker, Lillian Lorraine, the black comedian Bert Williams, and 'funny girl' Fanny Brice, who appeared in nine editions of the *Follies* through until 1936. Also featured were the Anna Held Girls, named after Ziegfeld's first 'wife'. From 1911 onwards, the name up in lights became the *Ziegfeld Follies* (one of Ziegfeld's signs, 'the largest electric light sign in American history', measured 80 feet long and 45 feet high, with 32,000 square feet of glass, and weighed eight tons), and was presented annually under that title until 1927, with the exception of 1926, when, owing to contractual wrangles, it was called *No Foolin'* and then *Ziegfeld's American Revue*. During those 17 years a host of the most beautiful showgirls, along with the cream of America's vaudeville performers and popular songwriters, contributed to what was billed as 'A National Institution Glorifying The American Girl'. Unlike a book show where the score is usually written mainly by one team of songwriters (with the odd interpolation), the musical items for each edition of the *Follies* were the work of several hands, including Dave Stamper, Gene Buck, Victor Herbert, Raymond Hubbell, Harry Smith, Gus Edwards, Joseph McCarthy, and Rudolph Friml. Some of the many enduring numbers that first saw the light of day in the *Ziegfeld Follies* include 'Woodman, Woodman, Spare That Tree' (1911, Irving Berlin), 'Row, Row, Row' (1912, James V. Monaco and William Jerome), 'The Darktown Poker Club' (1914, Jean Havaz, Will Vodery and Bert Williams), 'Hold Me In Your Loving Arms' and 'Hello, Frisco!' (1915, Louis A. Hirsch and Gene Buck), 'A Pretty Girl Is Like A Melody', 'Mandy' and 'You'd Be Surprised' (1919, Irving Berlin), 'Tell Me, Little Gypsy' and 'The Girls Of My Dreams' (1920, Irving Berlin), 'Second Hand Rose' (1921, Grant Clarke and James F. Hanley), 'My Man' (1921, Channing Pollock and Maurice Yvain), 'Mr. Gallagher And Mr. Sheen' (1922, Ed Gallagher and Al Shean), and 'Shaking The Blues Away' (1927, Irving Berlin). After a break, during which Ziegfeld lost a fortune in the Wall Street Crash, the impresario mounted the last *Follies* of his lifetime in 1931, but the score consisted mainly of old numbers, such as 'Half Caste Woman', 'You Made Me Love You', and the first *Ziegfeld Follies* hit, 'Shine On Harvest Moon'. After he died in July 1932, the rights to the shows' title was bought by the Shubert Brothers, who, in collaboration with Ziegfeld's widow, Billie Burke, presented further editions, notably in 1934 and 1936. Both starred the late producer's brightest star, Fanny Brice, and, somewhat ironically, introduced better songs than were in the last few 'genuine' editions, such as 'I Like The Likes Of You' and 'What Is There To Say?' (1934, Vernon Duke and E.Y. 'Yip' Harburg), and 'Island In The West Indies' and 'I Can't Get Started' (1936, Vernon Duke and Ira Gershwin). None of the last three *Follies*, in 1943, 1956, and 1957, were critically well received, although the 1943 show ran for 553 performances - more than any of the others in the long series. The 1957 Golden Jubilee edition was down to eight girls, but had a genuine star in Beatrice Lillie. She was the last in a glittering line of performers, most of whom owed their start to the *Ziegfeld Follies*, including Fanny Brice, Bert Williams, Ann Pennington, W.C. Fields, Eddie Cantor, Will Rogers, Lillian Lorraine, Leon Errol, Ray Dooley, Nora Bayes, Vivienne Segal, Helen Morgan, Marilyn Miller, Ed Wynn, Ruth Etting, and Eddie Dowling. The vast array of brilliant directors, choreographers, set and costume designers, who combined to create what are remembered as the most dazzling and extravagant shows ever seen on Broadway are too numerous to name; and the live elephants that appeared on stage in the 1914 edition were not credited individually. A live recording of a complete performance of *Ziegfeld Follies 1934* was discovered, and released on CD in 1997. Eve Arden made her Broadway debut in this *Follies*, and Fanny Brice is also supported by Everett Marshall, the Howard Brothers, Brice Hutchins, Judith Barron, Vivian Janis, and Buddy and Grace Ebsen. Although the transfer proved to be of poor quality, it is undoubtedly a historically valuable release.

● ALBUMS: *Ziegfeld Follies 1934* (AEI 1997)★★★★.

● FURTHER READING: *The Ziegfeld Follies*, M. Farnsworth. *Stars Of The Ziegfeld Follies*, J. Phillips.

ZIEGFELD GIRL

The trials and tribulations of a trio of showgirls in the most famous series of revues ever to grace Broadway - the *Ziegfeld Follies* - were discussed and dissected in this Pandro S. Berman MGM production that came to the screen in 1941. Judy Garland, Hedy Lamarr and Lana Turner were the three young hopefuls who were aiming for the top. Garland was the only one to make it in the end, with Lamarr and Turner swapping public acclaim for private happiness. The uneven, and sometimes maudlin screenplay was written by Marguerite Roberts and Sonia Levien. James Stewart, Tony Martin, Philip Dorn, and Jackie Cooper were prominent in a splendid cast that also included Ian Hunter, Edward Everett Horton, Eve Arden, Dan Dailey, Paul Kelly, Fay Holden, and Felix Bressart. Charles Winninger played Ed Gallagher, with Al Shean as himself, in a recreation of the question-and-answer song, 'Mr. Gallagher And Mr. Shean', which the famous vaudeville duo introduced in the *Ziegfeld Follies* of 1922. Garland was in fine form on a variety of numbers that included 'Minnie From Trinidad' (Roger Edens), 'You Never Looked So Beautiful' (Harold Adamson-Walter Donaldson), 'I'm Always Chasing Rainbows' (Joseph McCarthy-Harry Carroll), and, with Winninger, 'Laugh? I Thought I'd Split My Sides' (Edens), and Tony Martin gave a typically fine performance of 'You Stepped Out Of A Dream' (Nacio Herb Brown-Gus Kahn). Busby Berkeley's staging of the dance sequences was as brilliantly imaginative as always, and the lavish sets and costumes were created by Cedric Gibbons and Adrian, respectively; the latter was coming to the end of his long and distinguished stint at MGM. The film contained several reminders of the 1936 celluloid tribute to the master showman, *The Great Ziegfeld*, including that enormous fluted spiral structure which amazed audiences again as it did the first time round. Robert Z. Leonard directed this opulent production which will be best remembered for its music and production numbers.

ZIEGFELD, FLORENZ

b. 21 March 1867, Chicago, Illinois, USA, d. 22 July 1932, New York, USA. The most important and influential producer in the history of the Broadway musical. It is said that Ziegfeld was involved in his first real-life, but accidental, 'spectacular' at the age of four, when he and his family were forced to seek shelter under a bridge in Lake Park during the great Chicago fire of 1871. While in his teens, he was constantly running a variety of shows, and in 1893, his father, who was the founder of the Chicago Music College, sent him to Europe to find classical musicians and orchestras. Florenz returned with the Von Bulow Military Band - and Eugene Sandow, 'the world's strongest man'. The actress Anna Held, with whom Ziegfeld went through a form of marriage in 1897 (they were 'divorced' in 1913), also came from Europe, and she made her US stage debut in Ziegfeld's first Broadway production, *A Parlor Match*, in 1896. He followed that with *Papa's Wife*, *The Little Duchess*, *The Red Feather*, *Mam'selle Napoleon*, and *Higgledy Piggledy* (1904). Two years later, Held gave an appealing performance in Ziegfeld's *The Parisian Model*, and introduced two songs that are always identified with her, 'It's Delightful To Be Married' and 'I Just Can't Make My Eyes Behave'. Her success in this show, combined with her obvious star quality and potential, is said to have been one of the major factors in the impresario's decision to launch a series of lavish revues in 1907 which came to be known as the *Ziegfeld Follies*. These spectacular extravaganzas, full of beautiful women, talented performers, and the best popular songs of the time, continued annually for most of the 20s. In addition, Ziegfeld brought his talents as America's master showman to other (mostly) hit productions such as *The Soul Kiss* (1908), *Miss Innocence*, *Over The River*, *A Winsome Widow*, *The Century Girl*, *Miss 1917*, *Sally*, *Kid Boots*, *Annie Dear*, *Louie The 14th*, *Ziegfeld's American Revue* (later retitled *No Foolin'*), and *Betsy* (1926). After breaking up with Anna Held, Ziegfeld married the glamorous actress, Billie Burke. He opened his own newly built Ziegfeld Theatre in 1927 with *Rio Rita*, which ran for nearly 500 performances. The hits continued to flow with *Show Boat* (1927), *Rosalie*, *The Three Musketeers*, and *Whoopee!* (1928). In 1929, with the Depression beginning to bite, he was not so fortunate with *Show Girl*, which only managed 111 performances, and to compound the failure, he suffered massive losses in the Wall Street Crash of the same year. *Bitter Sweet* (1929) was a bitter disappointment, and potential hits such as *Simple Simon*, with a score by Richard Rodgers and Lorenz Hart, *Smiles* with Fred Astaire and his sister Adele, the last *Follies* of his lifetime (1931), and *Hot-Cha* (1932) with Bert Lahr, simply failed to take off. It is said that he would have been forced into bankruptcy if his revival of *Show Boat*, which opened at the Casino on 12 May 1932, had not been a substantial hit. Ironically, Ziegfeld, whose health had been failing for some time, died of pleurisy in July, two months into the run. His flamboyant career, coupled with a reputation as a notorious womanizer, has been the subject of at least three films: *The Great Ziegfeld* (1936) with William Powell which won two Oscars; *Ziegfeld Follies*, William Powell again, with Fred Astaire; and a television movie, *Ziegfeld: The Man And His Women* (1978).

● FURTHER READING: *Ziegfeld, The Great Glorifier*, E. Cantor and D Freedman. *Ziegfeld*, C. Higham. *The World Of Flo Ziegfeld*, R. Carter. *The Ziegfeld Touch*, Richard and Paulette Ziegfeld.

ZIEGLER, ANNE, AND WEBSTER BOOTH

Anne Ziegler (b. Irene Frances Eastwood, 1910, Liverpool, England), and Webster Booth (b. Leslie Webster Booth, 21 January 1902, Birmingham, England, d. 22 June 1984, Llandudno, Wales). From an early age Anne Ziegler trained as a classical pianist, and later became a skilled accompanist. After studying with voice trainer John Tobin, she moved to London in 1934 and played in the chorus of the operetta *By Appointment*, and sang in restaurants and hotels. In 1936, after being chosen from 250 applicants to play the leading soprano role of Marguerita in an early colour film of *Faust*, she met the tenor, Webster Booth. He attended choir school at Lincoln Cathedral, and sang solos there at the age of seven. After his voice had broken when he was 13, he worked in accountant's office before gaining a patron for his musical education. In 1924 he joined the D'Oyly Carte Opera Company, and stayed with them for three years. Subsequently, he sang oratorios in every concert hall in Britain. He made his first recordings for HMV Records in 1928, and in the early 30s, performed at Drury Lane and Covent Garden. He married Anne Ziegler in 1938, and, two years later, they formed a double act and toured UK variety theatres. During World War II and for some years afterwards, they were extremely popular on stage, radio and records. Like so many others, their appeal faded in the mid-50s and they emigrated to South Africa, where they lived and worked until 1978. Apart from their appearances there in concerts and operettas, Booth also played the part of comedian Tommy Handley for a year in a re-creation of the famous war-time radio series ITMA. On their return to the UK they settled in North Wales, where they taught music, and continued to appear together on stage, radio and television. They sang their last duet, 'I'll See You Again', at a concert in June 1983. Booth died a year later in Llandudno.

● ALBUMS: *Sweethearts In Song* (Encore 1979)★★★, *Music For Romance* (Encore 1980)★★★, *Golden Age Of Anne Ziegler And Webster Booth* (Golden Age 1983)★★★, *Love's Old Sweet Song* (EMI 1995)★★★★, *In Opera And Song* (Memoir 1997)★★★.

● FURTHER READING: *Duet*, Anne Ziegler and Webster Booth.

ZIMMER, HANS

b. 1957, Frankfurt, Germany. Apparently, from the age of six, Zimmer wanted to be a composer, although he had no formal musical education. When he was 16 he went to school in England, and, during the 70s, toured with bands throughout the UK. After spending some time at Air-Edel, writing jingles for television commercials, he collaborated with the established movie composer Stanley Myers, to write the score for Nicolas Roeg's *Eureka* (1981), and several other British films during the 80s, including *Moonlighting*, *Success Is The Best Revenge*, *Insignificance*, and *The Nature Of The Beast* (1988). His solo credits around that time included movies with such themes as apartheid (*A World Apart*), a psychological thriller (*Paperhouse*), a couple of eccentric comedies (*Twister* and *Driving Miss Daisy*), a tough Michael Douglas detective yarn (*Black Rain*), and a 'stiflingly old-fashioned' version of a Stefan Zweig short story, *Burning Secret* (1988). In that year Zimmer is said to have provided the music for 14 films in the UK and abroad, including the blockbuster, *Rain Man*, starring Dustin Hoffman and Tom Cruise. *Rain Man* earned Zimmer a nomination for an Academy Award ('When they found out that I was only 30, I didn't get it!').

He continued apace in the early 90s with scores for such as *Bird On A Wire*; *Chicago Joe And The Showgirl* (written with Shirley Walker), *Days Of Thunder*, *Green Card* (starring Gerard Depardieu in his English-language debut), *Pacific Heights*, *Backdraft*, *K2* (a crashing, electro-Mahlerian score), *Regarding Henry*, *Thelma And Louise* ('a twanging, shimmering score'), *Radio Flyer*, *Toys* (with Trevor Horn), *The Power Of One*, *A League Of Their Own*, *Point Of No Return*, *Where Sleeping Dogs Lie* (with Mark Mancina), *The Assassin*, *Cool Runnings*, *Calendar Girl*, *Point Of No Return*, *True Romance*, *The House Of The Spirits*, *Younger And Younger*, *The Lion King* (1994, Academy and Golden Globe Awards), *Africa: The Serengeti*, *I'll Do Anything*, *Renaissance Man*, *Drop Zone*, *Two Deaths*, *Crimson Tide*, *Beyond Rangoon*, *Nine Months*, *Something To Talk About*, *The Whole Wide World*, *Broken Arrow*, *Muppet Treasure Island*, *The Fan*, *The Preacher's Wife*, *Smilla's Sense Of Snow*, *The Peacemaker*, *Scream 2*, *As Good As It Gets*, *The Last Days*, *The Prince Of Egypt*, and *The Thin Red Line* (1998). In 1992 Zimmer composed the music for 'one of the most bizarre television re-creations to date', the 10-hour series, *Millennium*. His other work for the small screen includes the popular *First Born* (1988), *Space Rangers* (1992), *The Critic* (1994, series theme), and *High Incident* (1996, series theme). Zimmer is most certainly a major figure in music; his accomplishments in the film world for such a comparatively young man are already awesome.

ZORBA

Two years after their great success with *Cabaret*, composer John Kander and lyricist Fred Ebb reunited first for *The Happy Time*, and then for this musical, which, like *Cabaret*, had an unusual and sometimes sinister theme. *Zorba* opened at the Imperial theatre in New York on 17 November 1968, with a book by Joseph Stein that was set in Crete and based on the novel *Zorba The Greek* by Nikos Kazantzakis. It told of the earthy and larger-than-life Zorba (Herschel Bernardi) and his young friend Nikos (John Cunningham), who has inherited a disused mine on the island. In spite of financial failures, and tragedies involving the deaths of those close to him, including the French prostitute Hortense (Maria Karnilova), who was in love with him, Zorba rises above it all, secure in the passionate belief that life is for living - right to the very end. Kander and Ebbs' score caught the style and mood of the piece perfectly with songs such as 'Y'assou', 'The First Time', "Life Is', 'The Top Of The Hill', 'No Boom Boom', 'The Butterfly'. 'Only Love', 'Happy Birthday', and 'I Am Free'. Boris Aronson won a Tony Award for his imaginative and colourful sets, and *Zorba* ran for 305 performances. In October 1983 the show was revived on Broadway with Anthony Quinn and Lila Kedrova, both of whom had won such acclaim for their performances in the 1964 film *Zorba The Greek*. Kedrova won a Tony Award, and the production ran for longer than the original, a total of 362 performances.

INDEX

Schaffner, Franklin, 250
Schallert, William, 110
Scheff, Fritzi, 424
Scheff, Jerry, 185, 193
Scherer, John, 319
Schertzer, Hymie, 295
Schertzinger, Victor, 70, 180, 186, 202, 216, 263, 331, 347, 382, 386, 410, 461, 511, 536
Schiedt, D.P., 624
Schifrin, Lalo, 536-537
Schikel, Richard, 298
Schiner, Gink, 292
Schlemmer, Henry W., 136
Schlesinger, Helen, 63
Schmidt, Addie, 589
Schmidt, Harvey, 41, 201, 302, 462, 537, 582
Schoebel, Elmer, 331
Schoelen, Jill, 475
Schoen, Vic, 20, 500
Schoenbaum, Charles, 585
Schoenberg, Arnold, 371
Schofield, Paul, 429
Schofield, Phillip, 176, 506, 537
Scholfield, Andrew, 76
Scholl, Jack, 603
Schon, Bonnie, 354
Schönberg, Boublil, 84
Schrafft, Elizabeth Lambert, 390
Schroder, Helen, 332
Schroeder, Barbet, 352
Schubert, Franz, 77, 523
Schulman, Susan, 178, 501, 565
Schultz, Frank, 547
Schultz, Michael, 112
Schumacher, Joel, 112
Schuman, William, 382
Schuur, Diane, 265
Schwab, Lawrence, 402, 442
Schwaiger, Ernest, 174
Schwartz, Arthur, 34, 41, 47, 57, 104, 138, 140, 143, 147, 159, 170, 174, 190, 202, 207-208, 218, 241, 295, 309, 344, 378, 382, 410, 447, 481, 516, 538, 599, 638
Schwartz, Jean, 35, 555, 645
Schwartz, Stephen, 32, 43, 129, 246, 392, 478, 480, 491, 520, 538
Schweppe, Mazel, 462
Scola, Kathryn, 13
Scooler, Zvee, 204
Scorsese, Martin, 256, 360, 421
Scott, Allan, 113, 513, 542
Scott, Clarence, 481
Scott, Freddie, 464
Scott, George, 474, 505
Scott, Hazel, 505
Scott, Ivy, 290
Scott, Janette, 353
Scott, John, 159
Scott, Leslie, 481
Scott, Randolph, 513, 567
Scott, Raymond, 362
Scott, Robin, 531
Scott, Simon, 258
Scott, Steve, 632
Scott, Tom, 597
Scott, Tom Everett, 597
Scott, Val, 299
Scragg, Clem, 372
Seal, Elizabeth, 219, 285, 310, 417, 468, 539
Seamen, Phil, 249
Sears, 36, 171, 173, 475, 517
Sears, Fred, 517
Sears, Ted, 171, 173
Seaton, George, 428, 546, 596
Seaton, Horace, 210
Seaton, Lynn, 428
Seaton, Ray, 225
Sebastian, Alexandra, 5
Sebastian, John, 631, 653
Seberg, Jean, 271, 467
Sebesky, Don, 470
Secada, Jon, 258
Secombe, Harry, 88-89, 321, 349, 388, 430, 457, 463, 476, 539-540
Secunda, Sholem, 124
Sedaka, Neil, 301
Sedric, Gene, 622
Seeger, Pete, 13, 170, 204, 315
Seekers, 6, 77, 445, 496, 633
Seff, Manuel, 222, 248
Segal, Vivienne, 5, 79, 120, 142, 306, 469, 540, 645, 658
Seigel, Don, 213, 299
Seiter, William A., 513, 578, 653
Selby, Tony, 467
Selden, Albert, 545
Selden, Kathy, 556
Selena, 278, 447, 585, 631
Sellers, David, 512
Sellers, Peter, 206, 349, 443, 512, 539, 567
Selton, Morton, 452
Selvin, Ben, 235, 263, 292, 453
Sembello, Michael, 216
Sendin, Ashleigh, 534
Sennett, Mack, 389, 474
Seraphim, Michael, 560
Sergeievsky, Anatoly, 128
Seton, Joan, 375
Seurat, Georges, 586
Severinsen, Doc, 397
Seville, David, 6
Sewell, George, 210, 455
Sex Pistols, 6, 259, 471
Seyler, Athene, 77, 313, 531
Seymour, James, 225, 248
Seymour, Jane, 475
Seymour, Madelaine, 495
Shade, Lilian, 118
Shadwell, Charles, 509
Shaffer, Peter, 91, 148
Shakespeare, Robbie, 517
Shakespeare, William, 14, 85, 520, 594
Shale, Betty, 196
Shamroy, Leon, 341, 546, 566, 571, 598, 602, 642
Shank, Bud, 636
Shankar, Ravi, 203, 245-246, 496
Shankly, Jeff, 321
Shannon, Del, 17, 314
Shannon, Harry, 267
Shaper, Hal, 463
Shapiro, Dan, 124, 199, 221, 575
Shapiro, Debbie, 105
Shapiro, Helen, 314, 479, 493
Shapiro, Mel, 611
Shapiro, Mooney, 429
Shapiro, Ted, 220, 609-610
Sharaff, Irene, 232, 631
Sharif, Omar, 231-232
Sharon, Ula, 434
Sharp, Albert, 211
Sharp, Dee, 177
Sharp, Richard D., 560
Sharpsteen, Ben, 172-173
Shavelson, Melville, 212, 646
Shaw, Artie, 297, 328, 397
Shaw, Arvell, 581
Shaw, Bernard, 130, 334, 367, 436
Shaw, David, 501
Shaw, Dinah, 546
Shaw, Dorothy, 238-239
Shaw, George Bernard, 130, 334, 367, 436
Shaw, Mark, 40
Shaw, Martin, 27
Shaw, Oscar, 434, 619
Shaw, Reta, 405, 467
Shaw, Sebastian, 87
Shaw, Winifred, 624
Shawhan, April, 456
Shay, Dorothy, 414
Shayne, Tamara, 312, 323
Shean, Al, 435, 533, 658
Shearer, Douglas, 259
Shearer, Norma, 583
Shearing, George, 65, 202, 318
Sheehan, Gladys, 281
Sheekman, Arthur, 339, 521, 599
Sheldon, Gene, 177
Sheldon, Sydney, 501
Shell, Mark Jude, 43
Shelley, Carole, 313, 548
Shelley, Joshua, 394
Shelley, Pat, 158
Shelley, Paul, 353
Shelley, Rosamund, 456
Shelton, Anne, 423, 430, 578, 621
Shendar, Jacob E., 69
Shepard, Franklin, 415
Shepard, Sam, 454, 656
Shepard, Thomas Z., 81, 144, 561
Shepherd, Cybill, 35, 483
Sheppard, Chris, 54
Sheran, Paul, 563
Sheridan, Ann, 52, 450
Sheridan, Paul, 594
Sherkot, Leon, 158
Sherman Brothers, 558
Sherman, Al, 160, 604
Sherman, Allan, 267
Sherman, Hal, 284
Sherman, Hiram, 90
Sherman, Joe, 89
Sherman, Lowell, 543
Sherman, Richard, 130, 173, 223, 544, 576
Sherman, Richard M., And Robert B., 544
Sherrin, Ned, 206, 256, 409, 532, 559, 562, 657
Sherrin, Scott, 200
Sherry, Edward, 391
Sherwin, Manning, 307, 423
Sherwood, Bobby, 468
Sherwood, Ruth, 646
Sherwood, William, 117
Shevelove, Burt, 232, 238, 545, 611
Shields, Arthur, 546
Shields, Brooke, 258, 529
Shilkret, Jack, 166
Shilkret, Nat, 291, 649
Shimoda, Yukis, 465
Shiner, Ronald, 369
Shipley, Julie, 596
Shipman, David, 234
Shipman, Dee, 560
Shipp, Jesse A., 308
Shipton, Alyn, 624
Shire, David, 40, 48, 65, 447, 534, 545-546, 582
Shire, Talia, 546
Shirelles, 160, 171, 370
Shirley And Lee, 370
Shirley, Jack, 158, 533
Shivers, A.S., 20
Shoemaker, Ann, 38, 270
Shore, Dinah, 10, 42, 106, 111, 151, 199, 277, 363, 439, 546-547, 599, 601, 603, 613
Short, Bobby, 41, 412, 472
Short, Hassard, 47, 198, 298, 434
Short, John, 67
Short, Martin, 251, 377, 474
Shorter, Wayne, 529
Shrimpton, Jean, 493
Shubert Brothers, 658
Shubert, Lee, 422
Shulman, Arnold, 130, 231
Shuman, Mort, 97, 315, 487, 549
Shutta, Ethel, 635
Shy, Gus, 251
Siberry, Michael, 455, 565
Sibley, Brian, 174
Sibson, Bill, 154, 237
Sibtain, Chook, 467
Sidney, George, 18, 24, 269, 278, 346, 468, 547, 599, 620
Sidney, Robert, 598, 638
Sidran, Ben, 317
Siegel, Arthur, 41, 46
Siegel, Don, 419
Sigler, Maurice, 531, 599
Sigma, 400
Sigman, Carl, 359, 393, 417
Signorelli, Frank, 331
Sikes, Bill, 457
Silbar, Jeff, 419
Sillward, Edward, 31
Silva, Alan, 200
Silver Dream Racer, 194, 550
Silver, Abner, 160, 253, 649
Silver, Cliff, 509
Silver, Joe, 267
Silver, Johnny, 266
Silvers, Louis, 461
Silvers, Phil, 68, 104, 141, 147, 175, 232, 289, 299, 337, 401, 411, 438, 561, 584, 586, 616, 625
Silvers, Sid, 84, 92, 223, 593
Silvestri, Alan, 550
Silvestri, Martin, 206
Silvestri, Ruth, 396
Sim, Alastair, 262, 427, 531
Simard, Jennifer, 306
Simkins, Michael, 141
Simm, Ray, 558
Simmons, Anthony, 70
Simmons, Jean, 266, 364, 378, 383, 561
Simms, Ginny, 351, 447
Simon And Garfunkel, 256, 372, 429
Simon, Carly, 448, 553
Simon, John, 652
Simon, Lucy, 540
Simon, Nat, 603
Simon, Neil, 138, 251, 271, 342, 462, 493
Simon, Paul, 111, 265
Simon, Scott, 258
Simon, Vicki, 456
Simpson, Vera, 306, 468, 541
Sims, Zoot, 589
Sinatra, Frank, 42, 61-62, 81, 94, 104, 106, 109, 116, 138, 151-152, 154, 160, 165, 175, 196, 199, 202, 205, 236, 249, 257, 266, 275, 279-280, 289-290, 292, 296, 298, 300, 316, 322, 326, 332, 337, 347, 362, 366, 371, 377, 379, 383, 385, 400, 407, 411-412, 420-423, 427, 439, 459, 468-469, 485, 499, 503, 512, 545, 551, 553-554, 557, 575, 578, 581, 584, 593, 601, 606, 616, 620, 624, 638, 654
Sinatra, Nancy, 50, 89, 398, 552, 554, 636
Sinatra, Tina, 553
Sinclair, Arthur, 195, 555
Sinclair, Edward, 122
Sinclair, Gordon, 285
Sinclair, John, 122, 285
Sinclair, John Gordon, 285
Sinden, Donald, 581
Sing, Will, 169
Singer, Kurt, 335
Singleton, Zutty, 351, 442, 576
Siniawski, Petra, 631
Sinitta, 268
Sirmay, Albert, 47, 371
Sissle, Noble, 42, 74, 297, 549, 556, 622
Sistrom, Joesph, 570
Skall, William, 447
Skellern, Peter, 575
Skelton, Red, 16, 153, 181, 331, 382, 441, 527, 531, 599
Skinner, Randy, 571
Skinns, Caron, 206
Skip Bifferty, 559
Skipp, Nova, 532
Skipper, Susan, 159
Skolsky, Sidney, 325
Skutezky, Victor, 313
Slack, Freddie, 165, 500, 557
Slade, Julian, 220, 227, 532, 557
Slaughter, Walter, 79
Sleep, Wayne, 101, 150, 563
Slezak, Walter, 105, 200, 306, 435
Slick, Aaron, 379, 546-547
Sloan, Olive, 559
Sloan, P.F., 293
Sloane, A. Baldwin, 19, 261
Sloane, Nicola, 194
Sloane, Tod, 375
Sloman, John, 65, 571
Slutsker, Peter, 295
Sly And The Family Stone, 647
Slyter, Jilly, 131
Small Faces, 605
Small, Florrie, 533
Smalle, Ed, 175
Smart, Leroy, 517
Smart, Terry, 506
Smight, Jack, 564
Smith, Al, 307
Smith, Alexis, 441, 447, 505
Smith, Arthur, 426
Smith, Bessie, 70, 568, 622, 626
Smith, Betty, 607
Smith, Bilge, 221, 291
Smith, Brian, 313
Smith, Buster, 360
Smith, Carlton, 344
Smith, Connie, 349
Smith, Dorothy, 288
Smith, Edgar, 472
Smith, Fred, 591
Smith, Harry, 145, 244, 286, 591, 626, 658
Smith, Jack, 191
Smith, James, 27, 398
Smith, Jim, 155
Smith, Jimmy, 448, 537, 599
Smith, Joe, 360, 568, 588
Smith, John, 479
Smith, Kate, 59, 138, 175, 218, 349, 540, 647
Smith, Keely, 288
Smith, Ken, 288
Smith, Kent, 106
Smith, Lily, 210
Smith, Loring, 283
Smith, Maggie, 540
Smith, Martin, 70, 398
Smith, Muriel, 114, 342, 430, 566
Smith, Oliver, 43, 437
Smith, P.J., 172
Smith, Patricia, 279
Smith, Patti, 75, 596
Smith, Paul, 230
Smith, Paul Gerard, 230
Smith, Rex, 536, 588
Smith, Richard, 596
Smith, Robert, 286, 591
Smith, Robert B., 591
Smith, Roger, 614
Smith, Rufus, 24
Smith, Sally, 512
Smith, Sammi, 350
Smith, Sheridan, 97
Smith, Stanley, 251, 343
Smith, Stephen, 441, 566
Smith, Steve, 4
Smith, Steven C., 288
Smith, Sue, 449
Smith, Ursula, 16, 410
Smith, Webb, 172
Smith, Wendy, 279
Smith, Willie, 316, 655
Smith, Winchell, 87
Smithson, Florence, 27
Smuin, Michael, 26, 564
Snibson, Bill, 409
Snodgrass, Augustus, 476
Snook, Gareth, 141, 399, 415
Snooks, Baby, 88
Snow, Enoch, 116
Snow, Hank, 486
Snow, Phoebe, 265
Snow, Tom, 222-223
Snyder, Ted, 253
Soames, David, 601
Sobieski, Carol, 23
Soboloff, Arnold, 590
Soft Machine, 569
Soles, P.J., 516
Solms, Kenny, 239, 388
Solo, Robert, 539
Sommer, Elke, 473
Sondheim, Stephen, 21, 24, 46, 56, 62, 98, 110, 127, 141, 143, 156, 175, 223, 226, 228, 238, 267, 309, 318, 358, 361, 377, 400, 408, 413, 415, 474, 492, 520, 545, 560, 563-564, 584-586, 594, 605, 619, 630, 640, 657
Sonia, 200, 210, 258-259, 282, 415, 457, 558, 580, 583, 598, 658
Sonning, Jill, 321
Sonny And Cher, 251
Sonny Red, 490
Sony Broadway, 92, 372, 564
Soper, Gay, 110, 532, 594
Sorokin, Sid, 292, 467
Sorrentino, Rosanne, 23
Sothern, Ann, 219, 339, 354, 519, 599, 648
Soubrious, Bernadette, 60
Soul, David, 77, 131
Soules, Dale, 392
Sound Barrier, 29
Sousa, John Philip, 158
Sousa, Pamela, 522
Southern, Sheila, 202
Southlanders, 228
Spacek, Sissy, 117
Spacey, Kevin, 412
Spada, James, 234, 422, 580
Sparks, Billy, 494
Sparks, Ned, 225, 247-248, 461
Spear, Bernard, 130, 283, 376, 436, 652
Spear, David, 652
Spear, Eric, 216
Special EFX, 265
Spector, Phil, 67, 166, 185, 251, 308, 370, 378
Speight, Johnny, 493
Spence, Ralph, 66, 290
Spencer, David, 32
Spencer, Earle, 239
Spencer, Elizabeth, 477
Spencer, Frank, 148
Spencer, Grace, 217
Spencer, Herbert, 89, 239
Spencer, John, 635
Spencer, Marian, 216
Spencer, Ralph, 179
Spencer, Vicki, 611
Spenz, Liza, 608
Sperling, Milton, 586
Spettigue, Amy, 632
Spewack, Bella And Sam, 346, 567
Spewack, Sam, 346, 365, 479, 567
Spialek, Hans, 236
Spielberg, Steven, 329
Spigelgass, Leonard, 167
Spielman, Fred, 567
Spinella, Stephen, 328, 484
Spinetti, Victor, 275, 284, 455
Spiridoff, Major Alexius, 130
Spitzer, Marion, 176
Spivak, Charlie, 584
Spoliansky, Mischa, 195, 509
Spoto, Donald, 170, 426
Sprague, Jason, 16
Springer, Steve Scott, 632
Springfield, Dusty, 365, 462, 549, 591
Springfield, Rick, 340
Springfields, 312, 329, 617
Springsteen, Bruce, 448, 462
Squibb, Joe, 210
Squire, Graham, 132
Squires, Rosemary, 163
St Helier, Ivy, 70, 648
St. Helier, Ivy, 70, 648
Staccato, Johnny, 606
Stacey, John, 535
Stacy, Jess, 295, 569, 589
Staddon, James, 282, 594
Stafford Sisters, 165
Stafford, Jo, 6, 165, 309, 355-356, 390, 423
Stafford, Steve, 476
Staller, David, 101, 485
Stamford, Jack, 370
Stamp, Terence, 480
Stamp-Taylor, Enid, 410, 495
Stamper, Dave, 658
Standells, 511
Stanford, Jack, 26
Stanford, Stan, 214
Stanley, Dorothy, 210, 371, 548
Stanley, Gavin, 251
Stanley, George, 490
Stanton, Dorothy, 356
Stanton, Harry, 528
Stanwyck, Barbara, 44, 528-529, 563
Stapleton, Cyril, 382
Stapleton, Jean, 55, 156-157
Stapleton, Maureen, 99